MW01165652

StenEd® *Conflict Free*

REAL-TIME

MACHINE SHORTHAND
FOR
EXPANDING CAREERS

MEDICAL
DICTIONARY
FOR STENOTYPISTS

George Patrick Andrews

Stenotype Educational Products, Inc.
P.O. Box 959, Melrose, Florida 32666
Phone: 904/475-3332 • Fax: 904/475-2152

ISBN 0-938643-32-0
StenEd #555

PREFACE

With the growing number of medical cases in the courts, the growing number of court reporters who choose medical testimony as their specialty, and the growing number of stenotypists who choose medical transcription as a career, a comprehensive medical dictionary tailored to the needs of the stenotypist has become essential.

StenEd's **Medical Dictionary for Stenotypists** is that dictionary. This dictionary provides stenotype outlines for all words contained in Stedman's Medical Dictionary and Dorland's Illustrated Medical Dictionary that are not designated as "obsolete," as well as for all medications contained in the Physicians' Desk Reference (PDR). Because it is based on the conflict-free StenEd theory, the outlines given are the best for today's—and tomorrow's—CAT and text entry technology. Working reporters, captioners, real-time writers, and medical transcriptionists will find this text an indispensable reference.

If you learned StenEd theory, you will find that most of the writing techniques presented in this text are already familiar to you, but there are a few additional stroke-saving options because of their frequency in the medical literature (e.g., AOITS for -itis; -OS/KPI for -oscopy). By using principles taught in StenEd basic theory and those presented in this dictionary, you will remain conflict-free even though the medical literature contains a large number of homonyms and word-boundary problem situations. And, as is becoming more apparent every day, the need for conflict-free writing is growing in the transcription industry—whether for providing immediate copy following a hearing or deposition, for transcribing medical dictation for physicians and hospitals, or for captioning. Even with new translation technology that provides for on-line editing, dealing with conflicts is so time-consuming that little or no speed advantage is gained over traditional typing/scoping methods.

If you have not learned StenEd theory, you will still be able to use this dictionary. Because StenEd retains many traditional court reporting principles and is logical—using phonetic outlines when possible, using the spelling to differentiate when two or more words are pronounced the same, and using consistent principles to solve the remaining conflicts—most non-StenEd writers can read and use most of the stenotype outlines presented in this text. In fact, many non-StenEd writers today adopt various StenEd principles/outlines to their particular writing style to help eliminate their conflicts.

In addition to providing stenotype outlines for words contained in Stedman's, Dorland's, and the Physicians' Desk Reference (PDR), StenEd's **Medical Dictionary for Stenotypists** provides even more information. **Appendix 1** presents a comprehensive listing of medical acronyms and abbreviations. **Appendix 2** presents prefixes, suffixes, roots, and combining forms alphabetized by word part, with corresponding steno outlines and a brief definition. **Appendix 3** contains a listing of medical soundalikes, everyday English soundalikes that will be encountered in medical dictation, and some groups of words that are often confused. **Appendix 4** presents outlines for alphabetic letters used to write acronyms as well as outlines that may be used for text entry commands.

An attempt has been made to present a consistent pronunciation system. In many cases, words have been verified in four or five sources, and the pronunciation indicated in the majority of sources has been used. Keep in mind that there are regional variations in the way words are pronounced. By using principles learned in StenEd basic theory and those presented throughout this dictionary, you will be able to come up with an outline consistent with the way it is pronounced. Many pronunciation variations are already accounted for and will translate using the StenEd medical translating dictionary, even though they may not be shown in this dictionary.

For those with an interest in learning more about medical terminology, disease processes, diagnostic and therapeutic procedures, and anatomy and physiology, StenEd's **Medical Terminology for Stenotypists** is the best source for stenotypists. In addition to being one of the most comprehensive medical terminology texts on the market, **Medical Terminology for Stenotypists** provides stenotype outlines for all medical words defined and discussed. The book is divided into three parts. Part 1, Construction and Pronunciation of Medical Words, contains five chapters covering construction of medical words, stenotype considerations, pronunciation, prefixes, and suffixes. Part 2, General Medical Terminology, contains three chapters covering information necessary for the direct application of medical terminology (e.g., disease processes, diagnosis and diagnostic techniques, and therapeutic and surgical procedures). Part 3, Anatomy and Physiology, is the equivalent of a complete anatomy and physiology textbook. It covers the organs and functions of all body systems, and presents roots, words using each root, and stenotype outlines. The book also contains five appendices and a completely cross-referenced index.

It is hoped that this dictionary will help you identify and correctly spell any medical term you may encounter. By using StenEd's medical translating dictionary (available in DOS format), you will get a perfect translation of all words contained in this dictionary without having to look up the spelling. Because this dictionary was developed from many sources, it is the most complete and up-to-date listing of medical terms on the market.

George Patrick Andrews
Beverly Loeblein Ritter

CONTENTS

INTRODUCTION

The vast majority of medical word parts come from Greek and Latin. Most Greek words ultimately enter the English language through other languages—chiefly Latin, but also French. Most classical learning up to the twentieth century was accomplished in Latin and Greek, and by perpetuating the Greek and Latin terminology, it has been possible to maintain some form of unity throughout the centuries.

COMPONENTS OF MEDICAL WORDS

Most medical words were—and are—created by piecing together word roots, prefixes, suffixes, and combining forms.

The **root** is the **foundation** of the word, the part that **conveys the central meaning**. The root is the part to which prefixes and suffixes are attached to modify the meaning. A root may be combined with another root to form a compound word.

arteri-	=	artery	(from the Greek and Latin "arteria")
cardi-	=	heart	(from the Greek "kardia")
psych-	=	mind	(from the Greek "psyche")

A **prefix** is a word part **added before a root** to modify its meaning. Prefixes are often prepositions (i.e., often give a meaning related to space or time). Throughout this dictionary, prefixes (as well as combining forms of roots) are followed by a hyphen when they occur by themselves (e.g., pre-). Following are some examples of prefixes.

dis-	=	apart, away from
hypo-	=	under, below
peri-	=	around

A **suffix** is a word part **added at the end of a root** to further clarify or modify its meaning. Suffixes are preceded by a hyphen when they occur by themselves in this dictionary (e.g., -ectomy). Following are some examples of suffixes.

-ic	=	pertaining to, characterized by
-itis	=	inflammation
-ous	=	possessing, full of

Roots often end with a consonant, especially when the original word termination (ending) is dropped. For example, the Greek makros (large, long) is trimmed to macr- (note that the "k" is changed to a "c"); the Latin lactis (milk) is trimmed to lact-.

When a root ending with a consonant is combined with a word part beginning with a vowel, the root is not altered (remains pure); e.g., psych- + -osis = psychosis; lact- + -ic = lactic.

However, when a root ending with a consonant is combined with another word or word part (e.g., a suffix) beginning with a consonant, a **combining vowel** is inserted between the two to facilitate pronunciation (e.g., psych- + -pathic = psychopathic). This combining vowel is usually an "o," but sometimes "i" or "u." A **combining form** is created by the addition of the vowel to the root.

Occasionally, other letters of the root are changed to create the combining form (e.g., the root "cept-" is pure in "receptor," but a spelling change occurs in "recipient").

Throughout this dictionary, combining forms of roots are followed by a hyphen when they occur by themselves. Following are some examples of combining forms of roots.

Root	+	Combining Vowel	=	Combining Form
arteri-		o		arterio-
cardi-		o		cardio-
hepat-		o		hepato-

Appendix 2 contains a complete, alphabetized list of all prefixes, roots, combining forms, and suffixes presented in this dictionary, with corresponding outlines and brief definitions.

CONSTRUCTION OF MEDICAL WORDS

As mentioned in the previous section, most medical words are created by piecing together word roots, prefixes, suffixes, and combining forms.

Following are some examples of how medical words are constructed. Note that the root may be in the pure or combining form.

ROOT + SUFFIX

Root		Suffix		Word	Meaning
cardio-	+	-megaly	=	cardiomegaly	enlarged heart

PREFIX + ROOT + SUFFIX

Prefix		Root		Suffix		Word	Meaning
sub-	+	lingu-	+	-al	=	sublingual	under the tongue

MULTIPLE ROOTS + SUFFIX

Roots			Suffix		Word	Meaning
gastro-	+	enter-	+ -itis	=	gastroenteritis	inflammation of stomach and intestines

MULTIPLE PREFIXES + MULTIPLE ROOTS + SUFFIX

Prefix(es)			Roots			Suffix		Word
di-	+ chloro-	+ tetra-	+ fluoro-	+ eth-	+	-an	=	dichlorotetrafluoroethane

(a colorless gas with a faint ethereal odor used as an aerosol propellant)

PLURAL FORMS

When a singular form is changed to a plural form, a spelling change may be required. The pronunciation may also change (e.g., the hard "g" in the singular form alga is changed to a soft "g" ("j" sound) in the plural form algae.

ENGLISH PLURALS

Most English plurals are formed by adding -s or -es to the end of a word. There are exceptions, however. Examples:

SINGULAR		PLURAL	
cyst	S*IS	cysts	S*IS/-S
child	KHAOILD	children	KHIRN or KHIL/DREN
mouse	MOUS	mice	MAOIS
foot	FAOT	feet	FAOET
ox	OX	oxen	OX/-N
man	MAN	men	MEN
deer	DAOER	deer	DAOER

FOREIGN PLURALS

Certain words borrowed from other languages have retained their plural forms from the language of origin. Following are some examples of how Latin, Greek, and French plurals are formed:

SINGULAR		PLURAL	
crisis	KRAOI/SIS	crises	KRAOI/SAOEZ
appendix	AI/PEND/IX	appendices	AI/PEND/SAOEZ
bronchus	BRON/KUS	bronchi	BRON/KAOI
viscus	VIS/KUS	viscera	VIS/RA
bacterium	BAK/TAOERM	bacteria	BAK/TAOER/YA
ganglion	GANG/LON	ganglia	GANG/LA
vena	VAOE/NA	venae	VAOE/NAE
carcinoma	KARS/NOE/MA	carcinomata	KARS/NOEM/TA
fuseau	FU/ZOE	fuseaux	FU/ZOEZ

WRITING MEDICAL WORDS ON THE STENOTYPE MACHINE

Prefixes and combining forms of roots are generally written with a short combining vowel (except prefixes ending in the letter "u" (e.g., acu- = AK or AK/YAOU). Examples:

re-	=	RE
pre-	=	PRE
di-	=	DI
pro-	=	PRO
gastro-	=	GAS/TRO
micro-	=	MAOI/KRO
latero-	=	LAT/RO
cardio-	=	KARD/YO

An apparent exception occurs with the suffixes -oma and -osis. When a root is combined with these suffixes, the "o" is not a combining vowel attached to the root but an integral part of the suffix. Since the "o" is the accented part of the word, and since it is part of the suffix, it is written long, especially for readability. For example, psychosis is written SAOI/KOE/SIS; sarcoma is written SAR/KOE/MA (although SAOI/KO/SIS and SAR/KO/MA will translate correctly).

COMBINING FORMS MAY BE DIVIDED INTO FIVE DIFFERENT TYPES:

1. When all sounds except the combining vowel can be written in one stroke, the combining form may be written in one stroke and the combining vowel dropped; e.g., neuro- is written NAOUR; neo- is written NAOE; sclero- is written SKLAOER. (Note that these combining forms may also be written NAOU/RO; NAOE/YO, and SKLAOE/RO.)

2. When all sounds except the combining vowel cannot be written in one stroke, the combining form must be written in two strokes, and the combining vowel is written short; e.g., gastro- is written GAS/TRO; neutro- is written NAOU/TRO; nephro- is written NEF/RO.

3. When the combining form contains a medial vowel between two consonants, it generally must be written in two strokes; e.g., myelo- is written MAOI/LO; thanato- is written THAN/TO; palato- is written PAL/TO.

    There are a couple of exceptions, however, because of the frequency of their use. For example, hepato- may be written HEPT, HEP/TO, or HE/PAT.

4. Combining forms containing more than one consonant and that end with -io- or -eo- are written in two strokes, with YO being the second stroke to cover the vowel sounds; e.g., polio- is written POEL/YO; homeo- is written HOEM/YO; epithelio- is written EP/THAOEL/YO.

©1992 *StenEd*® Medical Dictionary

ix

Exception #1: When two consonants that cannot be written together precede the -io-, the combining form is written in two strokes, the second consonant begins the second stroke, and the "i" is dropped; e.g., ganglio- is written GANG/LO; neuroglio- is written NAOU/ROG/LO. (Note that these combining forms may also be written GANG/LAOE/YO and NAOU/ROG/LAOE/YO.)

Exception #2: When the "i" is pronounced long or when the "e" gets the accent, the accented vowel is written long and the "o" is dropped; e.g., glio- is written GLAOI ; bio- is written BAO*I; neo- is written NAOE. (Note that these combining forms may also be written GLAOI/YO, BAOI/YO, and NAOE/YO).

5. Combining forms containing two S's before the combining vowel are written with only one S and the combining vowel is dropped; e.g., glosso- is written GLOS. (Note that this combining form may also be written GLOS/SO.)

DEFINITIVE WRITING REVISITED

A few simple rules, taught in StenEd Basic Theory, will help in producing clear, distinctive, conflict-free outlines:

- Definitively outline the sounds in the word.

- Do not use the same outline for more than one word. **This is the most important aspect of conflict-free writing!**

- When the sound is the same but the spelling is different, **take advantage of the spelling** to show what the word is, following the StenEd Homonym Resolution guidelines (e.g., site = SAOIT, sight = SAOIGT; wrote = WROET, rote = ROET).

- When the sound is the same and the spelling is different, but the spelling can't be used to differentiate the outline on the stenotype machine, use an asterisk (*) in the outline for (1) the word not actually spelled on the stenotype machine, or, as a last resort, (2) the most infrequent of the two words.

  For example, **foul** = FOUL (note that this word is spelled out on the keyboard, so no asterisk is used); **fowl** = FO*UL (this word is not actually spelled out on the keyboard, so it would receive the asterisk; also, it is the more infrequent of the two—another reason it would get the asterisk).

- When the stenotype machine does not have the consonants you need, choose substitute letters wisely. For example, some short forms allow the final -G to stand for a "j" or "k" sound (e.g., change = KHAIN/ -J or KHAING; thank = THAN/-K or THANG), but do not assume you can always do this (e.g., bang = BANG; bank = BAN/-K).

- Do not use the same consonant group to stand for two different sounds. For example, since -FRP is used for -mp, do not use it for any other consonant group (e.g., -rch, -nch, etc.) as this practice will definitely result in conflicts (using the same outline for more than one word).

CREATING SHORT FORMS — *A Few Words of Caution*

StenEd has made an exhaustive attempt to include concise, accurate, and flexible outline options for all medical words included in this dictionary. Prefixes, suffixes, combining forms of roots, and all medical terms are presented in this dictionary with the shortest definitive outline. It is very important that you write the **prefixes and combining forms of roots** as they are presented in this text. It may sometimes appear that some of the outlines shown in this dictionary could be shortened, but keep in mind that there are many opportunities for mistranslations in medical writing. You will avoid them by using the outlines shown for the prefixes, combining forms, and suffixes as presented throughout this dictionary.

Short forms, briefs, and phrases have been included where possible and when appropriate (e.g., the common phrase "within normal limits" is written W*NL; b.i.d. = B*ID; hospital = HOPT; etc.). However, because many medical words are similar, shortening the steno outline too much may create many ambiguities, and you may find that you cannot identify the correct medical word from the notes you write. For this reason, it is better to try to cover all the sounds in the word, even if it means writing more strokes than you are used to. Also, you must be careful, when entering the outline and when proofing your transcriptions, that you have not entered a homonym incorrectly.

AVOIDING CONFLICTS WITH HIGH FREQUENCY WORDS AND DANGEROUS STAND-ALONE STROKES

Certain word endings must be written with an asterisk to differentiate the stroke from a frequently occurring word (e.g., whiny is written WHAOI/N*I, not WHAOI/NI). This avoids many mistranslations (e.g., WHAOI/N*I/O/POENT translates "whiny opponent"; WHAOI/NI/O/POENT = "why any opponent").

"AL" is dangerous because it both ends and begins words (e.g., suicidal; allergy). The easiest way to prevent mistranslations when a word ends in -al is to combine "AL" with the consonant immediately preceding it, even if it means doubling the consonant. Do not use "AL" as a separate stroke to end a word (e.g., suicidal should be written SAOU/SAOI/DAL, not SAOU/SAOID/AL). To further illustrate the opportunity for mistranslation, the word "costal" is presented as KOS/TAL in this dictionary, and this is the preferred outline for this word. While "costal" could also be written KO*S/AL, this presents the possibility for a mistranslation, as in the following sentence: "That will cost alcoholics their jobs." If you have included KO*S/AL as a dictionary entry, and if you write the word "alcoholics" as AL/KHOL/IK/-S, the sentence would translate "That will costal [KHOL]ics their jobs."

"ER" is dangerous because it is such a common word ending. Always use an asterisk when "er" begins a word. For example, "fender" may be written FEND/ER or FEN/DER, but "error" must be written *ER/ROR, "erythematous" must be written *ER/THEM/TOUS.

There are other "dangerous" strokes not discussed here. They will probably be obvious to you when you encounter them in this dictionary.

Regarding the asterisk: Don't assume that the asterisk is always used to differentiate homonyms. As a matter of fact, StenEd resolves most homonyms using the rules in Basic Theory. Homonyms are differentiated with an asterisk only when the outline cannot be varied on the stenotype machine. The asterisk is more often needed for prefixes and suffixes, especially when they may be used by themselves as words.

PRESENTATION OF MATERIAL

ACCEPTABLE OUTLINE OPTIONS

Because of the magnitude of this dictionary, it was impossible to show every acceptable steno option for every word. An example is the root "nucle(o)-." In order to save space, the acceptable optional outlines are presented under the root, but only the first choice appears throughout the dictionary. For example, under "nucle(o)-," four variations are given: NAOUK/L(O), NAOU/KL(O), NAOUK/LAOE/Y(O), and NAOU/KLAOE/Y(O). The only outline shown for the word "nuclear," however, is NAOUK/LAR, which is the first choice above, but it may also be written the other three ways. Similarly, the only choice shown for "antinuclear" is A*ENT/NAOUK/LAR, but the word may also be written using the other variations.

When looking up a word, keep in mind that there is flexibility with regard to syllabic breaks within each word. If VEN/TRAL is shown for ventral, you may also write the word VENT/RAL if this is the style you have developed. Similarly, words such as "plastic" may be written PLA*S/IK or PLAS/TIK, "cystic" may be written S*IS/IK or SIS/TIK. Let your theory training guide you in this regard.

Keep in mind that the preferred outlines shown have evolved from extensive computer translation testing and usage. If you adopt the writing style presented in this dictionary and in *Medical Terminology for Stenotypists*, you will benefit from sparkling computer translations and avoid many word boundary mistranslations. For instance, GAS/TRIK is shown as the outline for the word "gastric." This outline is shown instead of GA*S/RIK (which is also an acceptable way to write the word) because by writing it thus you will not have to modify your writing style when you encounter the combining form "gastro-," which should be written GAS/TRO.

HOMONYMS/CONFLICTS

Throughout this dictionary, different outlines have been assigned to each word in a homonym/conflict set. Those homonyms that otherwise would not be obvious have been cross-referenced with a note about the corresponding homonym. For example, the entry for "affusion" is as follows:

> affusion   AI/FAOUS
>   (*not* AF/FAOUGS; see after fusion)

In the above example, the homonym/conflict is not an actual dictionary entry (e.g., you could not look up "after fusion" as a separate entry), but you are directed to "see" that there is a conflict if the recommended outline is not used.

Again, the preferred outlines shown throughout this dictionary have evolved from extensive computer translation testing and usage. If you adopt the writing style presented in this dictionary, you will benefit from perfect computer translations and avoid many conflict/word boundary mistranslations.

Appendix 3 contains an extensive Conflict Resolution Summary, in which all cross-referenced words that appear throughout the dictionary are alphabetized and again cross-referenced within the appendix.

HYPHENATED WORDS

For compound adjectives (e.g., follicle-stimulating hormone), the hyphen must be included in the outline (FOL/K-L/H-F/STIM/LAIT/-G/HOR/MOEN).

For prefixes and combining forms ending in a vowel followed by a root word beginning with the same vowel, however, inclusion of a hyphen in the outline is not necessary, even though the word is spelled with one (although it is also correct to include the hyphen in these outlines). For example, **anti-immune** may be written A*ENT/IM/MAOUN or A*ENT/H-F/IM/MAOUN. The hyphen appears in this type of word for purposes of readability (i.e., to prevent two of the same vowel from appearing together).

Similarly, the hyphen is usually not required for medicines spelled with a hyphen (e.g., Theo-Dur may be written THAOE/DUR or THAOE/H-F/DUR).

The hyphen must be included when two proper names appear together (e.g., Ross-Jones test is written ROSZ/H-F/JOENZ/T*ES).

There is some variation in the hyphenation of words among the various medical dictionaries; e.g., cranioaural and cranio-aural. Both of these forms of the word may be considered correct. If a word is shown without a hyphen in this text (e.g., cranioaural), but your work environment dictates that a hyphen be placed between the two word parts (e.g., cranio-aural), simply replace the dictionary entry with the form you need.

SPELLING VARIATIONS

There are quite often two or more ways to spell a medical word (e.g., chamecephalic/chamaecephalic). This is sometimes due to misspellings that have appeared in the medical literature, and the misspellings have been perpetuated by medical dictionaries. Also, the spelling of some words has changed to reflect modern spelling rules and usage (e.g., hypophyseal is now usually spelled hypophysial). This dictionary generally presents only one way to spell words (particularly when a conflict would result), with the preferred spelling determined by comparing spellings in four medical dictionaries (Stedman's, Dorland's, Melloni's, and Taber's) and three English dictionaries (Random House, Webster's, and American Heritage). Some words appear with different spellings for different uses, in which case both spellings appear in this dictionary (e.g., calix, calyx). If your environment dictates the use of a spelling variation not adopted in this dictionary, simply edit the entry in the translating dictionary to reflect the different spelling.

MEDICAL ACRONYMS AND ABBREVIATIONS

Although the main body of this dictionary contains some acronyms and abbreviations, **Appendix 1**, "Medical Acronyms and Abbreviations," contains a complete listing of acronyms and abbreviations you will likely encounter in the field of medicine, with corresponding words for which the abbreviations stand.

Appendix 4, "Alphabetic Letters and Text Entry Commands," presents StenEd's method of writing individual letters — both upper- and lowercase. These recommended outlines facilitate spelling out acronyms and even an occasional word for which you cannot get a translation. Appendix 4 also contains StenEd's outlines for punctuation and special symbols (e.g., the degree symbol (°)) and recommended text entry commands for use with on-line editing software.

OUTLINE PRESENTATION

The outlines shown in this dictionary may reflect some theoretical principles that you may not currently use (e.g., *S for final -st; *F for -V; -FRP for -mp; -FRB for -rve; etc.). The principles shown below are recommended for writing medical terminology (and general steno writing) because they are more efficient, reducing the number of strokes in words that can be quite lengthy. If you did not learn these principles in Basic Theory and do not wish to use them, you may use the more written out forms (e.g., -M/-P for -mp, -R/-V for -rve, (c)AOI/TIS for -itis, etc.).

Following is a list, with examples, of the major theoretical principles used in this dictionary. (Note: Throughout this dictionary, (c) before an outline or stroke means a consonant; (v) means a vowel.)

*S for -st	digest	DI/J*ES
FRP for -mp	clamp	KLAFRP
FRB for -rve	nerve	NEFRB
-FM for -sm	spasm	SPAFM
AI for words beginning with a-	accuse	AI/KAOUZ
unless pronounced with consonant	active	AKT/IV or AK/TIV
-N/-FP or -FRPBLG for -nch	bench	BEN/-FP or BEFRPBLG
-R/-FP or *RPBLG for -rch	arch	AR/-FP or A*RPBLG
-RBS for "shus" sound	vicious	VIRBS
-RBL for "shal" sound	crucial	KRAOURBL
	partial	PAR/-RBL
GS for "shun" sound	palpation	PAL/PAIGS
	portion	PORGS
	deception	DE/SEPGS
*BGS for "kshun" sound	infarction	IN/FA*RBGS
	action	A*BGS
-K/S- for X in middle of word (when so pronounced)	toxin	TOK/SIN
-X for X in middle of word (when so pronounced)	anorexia	AN/REX/YA
-NG for ng and sometimes for NK and NJ	swing	SWING
	bronchial	BRONG/YAL
	change	KHAING

-(v)NL for (v)NAL	spinal	SPAOINL
	external	EX/TERNL
-(v)RL for -(v)RAL	oral	ORL
-AIRL for -arial	urticarial	URT/KAIRL
-AIRN for -arian	ovarian	O/VAIRN
-AOERL for -erial	bacterial	BAK/TAOERL
-AOERM for -erium	bacterium	BAK/TAOERM
-OIRL for -orial	sensorial	SEN/SOIRL
-OIRN for -orian	historian	HIS/TOIRN
(c)AOITS for -itis	bronchitis	BRON/KAOITS
OLG for -ology	psychology	SAOI/KOLG
OS/KPI for -oscopy	laparoscopy	LAP/ROS/KPI
OG/FI for -ography	arthrography	AR/THROG/FI

OMITTING "E" WHEN TWO CONSONANTS MAY BE WRITTEN ON THE INITIAL SIDE

A stroke may be saved when writing some words containing two or more syllables when two consonants are separated by an "e" (and occasionally an "a"). This principle may only be used when the second syllable is accented.

This principle cannot always be used. Thus, it is only recommended for advanced writers who understand how conflicts are avoided. Use caution if you use this principle and be sure that you do not create any conflicts. For example, "derive" must be written DE/RAOIV, because the outline for drive is "DRAOIV."

English	Advanced Outline	Optional Outline
believe	BLAOEV	BE/LAOEV
deliberate	DLIB/RAT	DE/LIB/RAT
dementia	DMEN/SHA	DE/MEN/SHA
depend	DPEND	DE/PEND
derivative	DRIV/TIV	DE/RIV/TIV
felonious	FLOEN/YOUS	FE/LOEN/YOUS
ferocious	FROERBS	FE/ROERBS
pharyngeal	FRIN/JAL	FA/RIN/JAL
semester	SM*ES/ER	SE/M*ES/ER
senility	SNIL/TI	SE/NIL/TI

INFLECTED ENDINGS AND PLURAL FORMS

Inflected endings (e.g., -s, -ed, and -ing) are generally written as a separate stroke (e.g., cysts is written S*IS/-S; inverted is written IN/VERT/-D; grinding is written GRAOIND/-G). However, when the final stroke of a multistroke word does not contain a vowel, the inflected ending may be added to that stroke (e.g., circles is written SIRK/-LS; girdled is written GIRD/-LD; strangling is written STRANG/-LG). Keep in mind that the plural forms of words in which the outline ends in D are generally written -DZ (e.g., grinds is written GRAOINDZ).

Note that words that are not plurals but that end in S are written with the S attached (e.g., biceps is written B*I/SEPS).

A

a-	AI
A and D Ointment	ARBGS/AND/D-RBGS/OINT/-MT
Aaron	AIR/RON
Aarskog	ARZ/KOG
	ARS/KOG
ab	AB
ab-	AB
abacterial	AI/BAK/TAOERL
Abadie	AB/DAOE
	AB/BA/DAOE
abampere	AB/AM/PAOER
abapical	AI/BAP/KAL
	AB/AP/KAL
abarognosis	AB/ROG/NOE/SIS
	AB/AR/OG/NOE/SIS
	AI/BAR/OG/NOE/SIS
abarticular	AB/AR/TIK/LAR
abarticulation	AB/AR/TIK/LAIGS
abasia	AI/BAIZ/YA
abasic	AI/BAIS/IK
abate	AI/BAIT
abatement	AI/BAIT/-MT
abatic	AI/BAT/IK
abaxial	AB/AX/YAL
abaxile	AB/AK/SIL
abbau	AB/BOU
Abbe	AB/BAO*E
	AB/BAI
Abbokinase	AB/KAOI/NAIS
Abbokinase Open-Cath	AB/KAOI/NAIS/OEP/KA*T
	AB/KAOI/NAIS/OEP/-N/KA*T
Abbo-Pac	AB/PAK
Abbott	AB/OT
Abderhalden	AB/DER/HAL/DEN
	AB/DER/HALD/-N
abdomen	ABD/MEN
	AB/DO/MEN
	AB/DOE/MEN
abdomin(o)-	AB/DOM/N(O)
abdominal	AB/DOM/NAL
abdominalis	AB/DOM/NAI/LIS
abdominis	AB/DOM/NIS
abdominocentesis	AB/DOM/NO/SEN/TAOE/SIS
abdominocyesis	AB/DOM/NO/SAOI/E/SIS
abdominocystic	AB/DOM/NO/S*IS/IK
abdominogenital	AB/DOM/NO/JEN/TAL
abdominohysterectomy	AB/DOM/NO/H*IS/REKT/M*I
abdominohysterotomy	AB/DOM/NO/H*IS/ROT/M*I
abdominopelvic	AB/DOM/NO/PEL/VIK
abdominoperineal	AB/DOM/NO/P*ER/NAOEL
abdominoplasty	AB/DOM/NO/PLAS/TI
abdominoscopy	AB/DOM/NOS/KPI
abdominoscrotal	AB/DOM/NO/SKROE/TAL
abdominothoracic	AB/DOM/NO/THRAS/IK
abdominouterotomy	AB/DOM/NO/YAOUT/ROT/M*I
abdominovaginal	AB/DOM/NO/VAJ/NAL
abdominovesical	AB/DOM/NO/VES/KAL
abduce	AB/DAOUS
abducens	AB/DAOUS/ENZ
	AB/DAOU/SENZ
abducent	AB/DAOUS/ENT
	AB/DAOU/SENT
abducentis	AB/DAOU/SEN/TIS
abduct	AB/DUKT
abduction	AB/D*UBGS
abductor	AB/DUK/TOR
Abegg	AB/EG
	AB/BEG
Abelin	AB/LIN
abembryonic	AB/EM/BRON/IK
abepithymia	AB/EP/THAOIM/YA
abequose	AB/KWOES
Abercrombie	AB/ER/KROM/BAOE
Abernethy	AB/ER/NAOE/TH*I
	AB/ER/N*ET/TH*I
aberrans	AB/ER/RANZ
aberrant	AB/ER/RANT
aberrantes	AB/RAN/TAOEZ
aberratio	AB/RAI/SHOE
	AB/RAIRB/YOE
aberration	AB/RAIGS
aberrometer	AB/ROM/TER
abesterase	AB/ES/TRAIS
	AB/ES/TER/AIS

abetalipoproteinemia	AI/BAIT/LIP/PROET/NAOEM/YA
ab extra	AB/EX/TRA
abeyance	AI/BAINS
abfarad	AB/FA/RAD
abhenry	AB/HEN/RI
abient	AB/YENT
abietate	AB/YE/TAIT
abietic	AB/YET/IK
abietinate	AB/YE/TIN/AIT
abietinic	AB/YE/TIN/IK
ab igne	AB/IG/NAOE
ability	ABLT
abiogenesis	AB/YO/JEN/SIS
abiogenetic	AB/YO/JE/NET/IK
abiogenous	AB/YOJ/NOUS
abionergy	AB/YON/ER/JI
abiophysiology	AB/YO/FIZ/YOLG
abiosis	AB/YOE/SIS
abiotic	AB/YOT/IK
abiotrophic	AB/YO/TROFK
abiotrophy	AB/YOT/RO/FI
abirritant	AB/IR/TANT
abirritation	AB/IR/TAIGS
abirritative	AB/IR/TAIT/IV
abiuret	AI/B*I/YAOU/RET
	AI/B*I/RET
abiuretic	AI/B*I/YAOU/RET/IK
	AI/B*I/RET/IK
ablactation	AB/LAK/TAIGS
ablactatorum	AB/LAKT/TOR/UM
ablastemic	AI/BLAS/TEM/IK
ablastin	AI/BLAS/TIN
ablate	AB/LAIT
ablatio placentae	AB/LAI/SHOE/PLA/SEN/TAE
ablation	AB/LAIGS
ablepharia	AI/BLE/FAIR/YA
ablepharon	AI/BLEF/RON
ablepharous	AI/BLEF/ROUS
ablephary	AI/BLEF/RI
ablepsia	AI/BLEPS/YA
ablepsy	AI/BLEP/SI
abluent	AB/LAOUNT
ablution	AB/LAOUGS
ablutomania	AB/LAOUT/MAIN/YA
abmortal	AB/MOR/TAL
abnerval	AB/NER/VAL
abneural	AB/NAOURL
abnormal	AB/NOR/MAL
abnormality	AB/NOR/MAL/TI
abnormally	AB/NORM/LI
abnormity	AB/NORM/TI
abohm	AB/OEM
abomasitis	AB/OEM/SAOITS
abomasum	AB/O/MAI/SUM
aborad	AB/OR/RAD
aboral	AB/ORL
aboriginal	AB/RIJ/NAL
abort	AI/BORT
abortient	AI/BOR/SHENT
abortifacient	AI/BORT/FAIRBT
abortigenic	AI/BORT/JEN/IK
abortin	AI/BOR/TIN
abortion	AI/BORGS
abortionist	AI/BORGS/*IS
abortive	AI/BORT/IV
abortivus	AI/BOR/TAOI/VUS
abortus	AI/BOR/TUS
abouchement	AI/BAOURB/-MT
abrachia	AI/BRAIK/YA
abrachiatism	AI/BRAIK/YA/TIFM
abrachiocephalia	AI/BRAIK/YO/SFAIL/YA
abrachiocephalus	AI/BRAIK/YO/SEF/LUS
abrachiocephaly	AI/BRAIK/YO/SEF/LI
abrachius	AI/BRAIK/YUS
abradant	AI/BRAI/DANT
abrade	AI/BRAID
Abrahams	AI/BRA/HAMZ
	AIB/RA/HAMZ
	AI/BRA/HAMS
	AIB/RA/HAMS
Abrams	AI/BRAMZ
	AI/BRAMS
abrasio	AI/BRAIS/YOE
	AI/BRAIZ/YOE
abrasion	AI/BRAIGS
abrasive	AI/BRAIS/IV
abrasiveness	AI/BRAIS/IV/*NS
	AI/BRAIS/IVNS
abrasor	AI/BRAI/ZOR

	AI/BRAI/SOR	acanthocyte	AI/KA*NT/SAO*IT
abreact	AB/RE/AKT	acanthocytosis	AI/KA*NT/SAOI/TOE/SIS
abreaction	AB/RE/A*BGS	acanthoid	AI/KAN/THOID
abrosia	AI/BROEZ/YA	acantholysis	AK/AN/THOL/SIS
abruptio placentae	AB/RUP/SHOE/PLA/SEN/TAE	acantholytic	AI/KA*NT/LIT/IK
abruption	AB/RUPGS	acanthoma	AK/AN/THOE/MA
Abrus	AI/BRUS	acanthopelvis	AI/KA*NT/PEL/VIS
abscess	AB/SESZ	acanthopodia	AI/KA*NT/POED/YA
abscessus	AB/SES/SUS	acanthor	AI/KAN/THOR
abscise	AB/SAOIZ	acanthorrhexis	AI/KA*NT/REK/SIS
abscissa	AB/SIS/SA	acanthosis	AK/AN/THOE/SIS
abscissic	AB/SISZ/IK	acanthotic	AK/AN/THOT/IK
abscission	AB/SIGS	acanthrocyte	AI/KAN/THRO/SAO*IT
absconsio	AB/SKON/SHOE	acanthrocytosis	AI/KAN/THRO/SAOI/TOE/SIS
	AB/SKONS/YOE	a capite ad calcem	A/KAP/TAOE/AD/KAL/SAOEM
abscopal	AB/SKOE/PAL		A/KAP/TAOE/AD/KAL/SEM
	AB/SKOP/PAL	acapnia	AI/KAP/NA
absence	AB/SENS		AI/KAP/NAOE/YA
absentia	AB/SEN/SHA	acapnial	AI/KAP/NAL
Absidia	AB/SID/YA		AI/KAP/NAOE/YAL
absinthe	AB/S*INT	acapnic	AI/KAP/NIK
absinthin	AB/SIN/THIN	Acarapis	AI/KARB/PIS
absinthium	AB/S*INT/YUM	acarbia	AI/KARB/YA
absinthol	AB/SIN/THOL	acardia	AI/KARD/YA
absolute	AB/SLAOUT	acardiac	AI/KARD/YAK
absorb	AB/SORB	acardiacus	AI/KAR/DAOI/KUS
absorbable	AB/SORB/-BL	acardiotrophia	AI/KARD/YO/TROEF/YA
absorbance	AB/SORB/BANS	acardius	AI/KARD/YUS
absorbefacient	AB/SORB/FAIRBT	acar(o)-	AK/KR(O)
absorben	AB/SOR/BEN		(not AK/RO; see acro-)
	AB/SORB/-N	acari	AK/KRAOI
absorbency	AB/SOR/BEN/SI		AK/RAOI
	AB/SORB/EN/SI	acarian	AI/KAIR/YAN
	AB/SORB/-N/SI	acariasis	AK/KRAOI/SIS
absorbent	AB/SORB/ENT		AK/RAOI/SIS
	AB/SOR/BENT	acaricide	AI/KAR/SAO*ID
absorptiometer	AB/SORP/SHOM/TER		AI/KAIR/SAO*ID
absorption	AB/SORPGS	acarid	AK/KRID
absorptive	AB/SORP/TIV		AK/R*ID
	AB/SORPT/IV		(not AK/RID; see acrid)
absorptivity	AB/SORP/TIV/TI	Acaridae	AI/KAR/DAE
abstergent	AB/STERJ/ENT		AI/KAR/DAOE
	AB/STER/JENT	acaridan	AI/KAR/DAN
abstinence	A*BS/NENS	acaridiasis	AI/KAR/DAOI/SIS
	AB/STI/NENS		AK/AR/DAOI/SIS
abstract	AB/STRAKT	Acarina	AK/RAOI/NA
abstraction	AB/STRA*BGS		AK/KRAOI/NA
abstriction	AB/STR*IBGS	acarine	AK/RAOIN
abterminal	AB/TERM/NAL		AK/KRAOIN
abtorsion	AB/TORGS	acarinosis	AI/KAR/NOE/SIS
abtropfung	AB/TROP/FAOUNG		AK/RI/NOE/SIS
abulia	AI/BAOUL/YA	acariosis	AI/KAR/YOE/SIS
abulic	AI/BAOUL/IK	acarodermatitis	AK/KRO/DERM/TAOITS
abulomania	AI/BAOUL/MAIN/YA	acaroid	AK/KROID
abuse	AI/BAOUS		AK/ROID
	AI/BAOUZ	acarologist	AK/KRO*LGS
abut	AI/BUT		AK/RO*LGS
abutment	AI/BUT/-MT	acarology	AK/KROLG
abvolt	AB/VOELT		AK/ROLG
	AB/VOLT	acarophobia	AK/KRO/FOEB/YA
acacia	AI/KAI/SHA		(not AK/RO/FOEB/YA; see
	AI/KAIS/YA		acrophobia)
Acacia	K-P/AI/KAI/SHA	acarotoxic	AK/KRO/TOX/IK
	K-P/AI/KAIS/YA		AK/RO/TOX/IK
acalcerosis	AI/KALS/ROE/SIS	Acartomyia	AI/KART/MAOI/YA
acalcicosis	AI/KALS/KOE/SIS	acarus	AK/KRUS
acalculia	AI/KAL/KAOUL/YA		AK/RUS
acampsia	AI/KAFRPS/YA	Acarus	K-P/AK/KA/RUS
	AI/KAMS/YA		K-P/AK/RUS
	AI/KAM/-PS/YA	acatalasemia	AI/KAT/LAI/SAOEM/YA
acanth(o)-	AI/KA*NT	acatalasia	AI/KAT/LAIZ/YA
	AI/KAN/TH(O)	acatalepsia	AI/KAT/LEPS/YA
	AK/AN/TH(O)	acatalepsy	AI/KAT/LEP/SI
acantha	AI/KAN/THA	acataleptic	AI/KAT/LEPT/IK
acanthaceous	AK/AN/THAIRBS	acatamathesia	AI/KAT/MA/THAOEZ/YA
acanthamebiasis	AI/KA*NT/MAOE/BAOI/SIS	acataphasia	AI/KAT/FAIZ/YA
Acanthamoeba	AI/KA*NT/MAOE/BA	acatastasia	AK/TAS/TAIZ/YA
acanthella	AI/KAN/THEL/LA	acatastatic	AK/TAS/TAT/IK
	AK/AN/THEL/LA	acathectic	AK/THEKT/IK
acanthesthesia	AI/KA*NT/ES/THAOEZ/YA		AI/KA/THEKT/IK
	AI/KAN/THES/THAOEZ/YA	acathexia	AK/THEX/YA
acanthion	AI/KA*NT/YON		AI/KA/THEX/YA
Acanthocephala	AI/KA*NT/SEF/LA	acathexis	AK/THEK/SIS
acanthocephalan	AI/KA*NT/SEF/LAN		AI/KA/THEK/SIS
acanthocephaliasis	AI/KA*NT/SEF/LAOI/SIS	acathisia	AK/THIZ/YA
acanthocephalous	AI/KA*NT/SEF/LOUS		AI/KA/THIZ/YA
Acanthocephalus	AI/KA*NT/SEF/LUS	acaudal	AI/KAU/DAL
Acanthocheilonema	AI/KA*NT/KAOIL/NAOE/MA	acaudate	AI/KAU/DAIT
acanthocheilonemiasis	AI/KA*NT/KAOIL/NAOE/MAOI/		

accelerans	AK/SEL/RANZ	acephalobrachia	AI/SEF/LO/BRAIK/YA
accelerant	AK/SEL/RANT	acephalobrachius	AI/SEF/LO/BRAIK/YUS
accelerating	AK/SEL/RAIT/-G	acephalocardia	AI/SEF/LO/KARD/YA
acceleration	AK/SEL/RAIGS	acephalocardius	AI/SEF/LO/KARD/YUS
accelerator	AK/SEL/RAI/TOR	acephalocheiria	AI/SEF/LO/KAOIR/YA
accelerin	AK/SEL/RIN	acephalocheirus	AI/SEF/LO/KAOI/RUS
accelerometer	AK/SEL/ROM/TER	acephalocyst	AI/SEF/LO/S*IS
accentuation	AK/SENT/YAIGS	acephalogaster	AI/SEF/LO/GAS/TER
	AK/SENT/WAIGS	acephalogasteria	AI/SEF/LO/GAS/TAOER/YA
accentuator	AK/SENT/YAI/TOR	acephalogastria	AI/SEF/LO/GAS/TRA
	AK/SENT/WAI/TOR		AI/SEF/LO/GAS/TRAOE/YA
acceptor	AK/SEP/TOR	acephalopodia	AI/SEF/LO/POED/YA
	(*not* SEP/TOR; see ceptor)	acephalopodius	AI/SEF/LO/POED/YUS
acces pernicieux	AK/SAI/PER/NIS/YU	acephalorhachia	AI/SEF/LO/RAIK/YA
	AK/SAI/PER/NIS/YAOU	acephalostomia	AI/SEF/LO/STOEM/YA
	AK/SAI/PERN/SU	acephalostomus	AI/SEF/LO*S/MUS
	AK/SAI/PERN/SAOU	acephalothoracia	AI/SEF/LO/THRAIS/YA
accessiflexor	AK/SES/FLEK/SOR	acephalothorus	AI/SEF/LO/THOR/RUS
	AK/SES/SI//FLEK/SOR	acephalous	AI/SEF/LOUS
accessoria	AK/SES/SOR/YA	acephalus	AI/SEF/LUS
	AK/SES/SOER/YA	acephaly	AI/SEF/LI
accessoriae	AK/SES/SOR/YAE	acepromazine	AS/PROEM/ZAOEN
	AK/SES/SOER/YAE	acerin	AS/RIN
accessorii	AK/SES/SOR/YAOI		AI/SER/RIN
	AK/SES/SOER/YAOI	acervul-	AI/SEFRB/L-
accessorius	AK/SES/SOR/YUS		AI/SEFRB/YAOU/L-
	AK/SES/SOER/YUS		AI/SEFRB/YU/L-
accessory	AK/SESZ/RI		AI/SER/VAOU/L-
	AK/SES/RI	acervuli	AI/SEFRB/LAOI
accident	AKS/DENT	acervuline	AI/SEFRB/LAOIN
	SDENT	acervulus	AI/SEFRB/LUS
accidental	AKS/DEN/TAL	acescence	AI/SES/ENS
	SDENT/TAL	acescent	AI/SES/ENT
accident-prone	AKS/DENT/H-F/PROEN	acesodyne	AI/SES/DAOIN
	SDENT/H-F/PROEN	acestoma	AI/SES/TOE/MA
accipiter	AK/SIP/TER	acet(o)-	AI/SAOET
acclimatation	AI/KLAOIM/TAIGS		AI/SAOE/TO
acclimation	AK/LI/MAIGS		AS/TO
	AK/KLI/MAIGS		AS/ET
acclimatization	AI/KLAOIM/TI/ZAIGS	aceta	AI/SAOE/TA
accole	AK/LAI	acetabul(o)-	AS/TAB/L(O)
	AK/KO/LAI		AS/TAB/YAOU/L(O)
accommodation	AI/KOM/DAIGS		AS/TAB/YU/L(O)
accommodative	AI/KOM/DAIT/IV	acetabula	AS/TAB/LA
accommodometer	AI/KOM/DOM/TER	acetabular	AS/TAB/LAR
accomplice	AI/KOM/PLIS	acetabulectomy	AS/TAB/LEKT/M*I
	AI/KOFRP/LIS	acetabuli	AS/TAB/LAOI
accouchement	AI/KAOURB/-MT	acetabuloplasty	AS/TAB/LO/PLAS/TI
accouchement forcé	AI/KAOURB/-MT/FOR/SAI	acetabulum	AS/TAB/LUM
accoucheur	AI/KAOU/SHER	Acetaco	AS/TA/KOE
	AI/KAOURB/ER		AS/TAI/KOE
accoucheuse	AI/KAOU/SHEZ	acetal	AS/TAL
	AI/KAOURB/EZ	acetaldehydase	AS/TALD/HAOI/DAIS
accrementition	AK/REMT/TIGS		AS/TALD/HAOI/DAIS
	AK/RE/MEN/TIGS		AS/ET/ALD/HAOI/DAIS
accreta	AI/KRAOE/TA		AS/ET/ALD/HAOID/AIS
accretio	AI/KRAOE/SHOE	acetaldehyde	AS/TALD/HAOID
	AI/KRAOERB/YOE		AS/ET/ALD/HAOID
accretion	AI/KRAOEGS	acetamide	AS/ET/AM/AOID
accrochage	AK/RO/SHAJ		AS/ET/AM/MAOID
	AK/KRO/SHAJ		AI/SET/MAOID
Accutane	AK/YAOU/TAIN	acetamidine	AS/TAM/DAOEN
	AK/YU/TAIN		AS/ET/AM/DAOEN
	AK/KAOU/TAIN	acetamidobenzene	AS/ET/AM/DO/BEN/ZAOEN
Ace	K-P/AIS	acetamidobenzoate	AS/ET/AM/DO/BENZ/WAIT
acebutolol	AS/BAOUT/LOL	accedamidofluorene	AS/ET/AM/DO/FLAOU/RAOEN
	AS/BAOUT/LOEL		AS/ET/AM/DO/FLAOUR/AOEN
acecarbromal	AS/KAR/BROE/MAL	acetaminophen	AS/ET/AM/NO/FEN
acecainide hydrochloride	AS/KAI/NAOID/HAOI/DRO/KLOR/		AS/ET/AI/MAOEN/FEN
	AOID	acetaminosalol	AS/TAM/NO/SAL/OL
aceclidine	AI/SEK/LI/DAOEN	acetanilid	AS/TAN/LID
acedapsone	AS/DAP/SOEN	acetannin	AS/TAN/NIN
acedia	AI/SAOED/YA	acetarsol	AS/TAR/SOL
acefylline piperazine	AI/SEF/LAOEN/PAOI/PER/ZAOEN		AS/ET/AR/SOL
acellular	AI/SEL/YAOU/LAR	acetarsone	AS/TAR/SOEN
acelom	AI/SE/LOM		AS/ET/AR/SOEN
	AI/SAOEL/OM	acetas	AI/SAOE/TAS
acelomate	AI/SAOEL/MAIT	acetate	AS/TAIT
acelomatous	AI/SE/LOEM/TOUS	acetazolamide	AS/TA/ZOL/MAOID
acelous	AI/SE/LOUS		AS/ET/ZOL/MAOID
	AI/SAOEL/OUS	acetenyl	AI/SAOET/NIL
acenesthesia	AI/SEN/ES/THAOEZ/YA		AI/SAOE/TIN/IL
acenocoumarin	AI/SAOEN/KAOUM/RIN	aceteugenol	AS/ET/YAOUJ/NOL
acenocoumarol	AI/SAOEN/KAOUM/ROL	aceti	AI/SAOE/TAOI
acentric	AI/SEN/TRIK	acetic	AI/SAOET/IK
acephal(o)-	AI/SEF/L(O)		AI/SET/IK
acephalia	AI/SFAIL/YA	aceticoceptor	AI/SAOET/KO/SEP/TOR
acephaline	AI/SEF/LAOIN		AI/SET/KO/SEP/TOR
acephalism	AI/SEF/LIFM	acetify	AI/SET/FI

acetimeter	AS/TIM/TER	acetylglutamate	AI/SAOE/TIL/GLAOUT/MAIT
acetin	AS/TIN	acetylization	AI/SET/LAOI/ZAIGS
acetoacetate	AS/TO/AS/TAIT		AI/SET/LI/ZAIGS
	AI/SAOET/AS/TAIT	acetylmethadol	AS/TIL/M*ET/DOL
acetoacetic	AS/TO/AI/SAOET/IK	acetylmethyl	AS/TIL/M*ET/IL
	AS/TO/AI/SET/IK	acetylornithinase	AS/TIL/ORN/THIN/AIS
acetoacetyl	AS/TO/AI/SAOE/TIL	asetylornithine	AS/TIL/ORN/THAOEN
	AS/TO/AI/SAOET/IL	acetylphenylhydrazine	AS/TIL/FENL/HAOI/DRA/ZAOEN
	AS/TO/AS/TIL	acetylphosphatase	AS/TIL/FOS/FA/TAIS
acetoacetylcoenzyme	AS/TO/AS/TIL/KO/EN/ZAOIM	acetylpropionic	AS/TIL/PROEP/YON/IK
acetoacetyl-succinic	AS/TO/AS/TIL/SUK/SIN/IK	acetylpyridine	AS/TIL/PIR/DAOEN
Acetobacter	AI/SAOET/BAK/TER	acetylsalicylic	AS/TIL/SAL/SIL/IK
acetobutylicum	AI/SAOET/BAOU/TIL/KUM	acetylstrophanthidin	AS/TIL/STROE/FA*NT/DIN
	AS/TO/BAOU/TIL/KUM	acetylsulfadiazine	AS/TIL/SUL/FA/DAOI/ZAOEN
acetoform	AI/SAOET/FORM	acetylsulfaguanidine	AS/TIL/SUL/FA/GAUN/DAOEN
acetohexamide	AS/TO/HEX/MAOID	acetylsulfanilamide	AS/TIL/SUL/FA/NIL/MAOID
acetohydroxamic	AS/TO/HAOI/DROX/MIK	acetylsulfathiazole	AS/TIL/SUL/FA/THAOI/ZOEL
	AS/TO/HAOI/DROK/SAM/IK	acetyltannic	AS/TIL/TAN/IK
acetoin	AI/SET/WIN	acetyltannin	AS/TIL/TAN/NIN
	AI/SET/OIN	acetyltransferase	AS/TIL/TRA*NS/FRAIS
	AS/ET/WIN	achalasia	AK/LAIZ/YA
acetokinase	AS/TO/KAOI/NAIS	Achard	ARB/AR
acetol	AS/TOL		ARB/SHAR
acetolactate	AS/TO/LAK/TAIT		AI/SHAR
	AI/SAOET/LAK/TAIT	Achatina	AK/TAOI/NA
acetolactic	AS/TO/LAKT/IK	ache	AIK
	AI/SAOET/LAKT/IK	acheilia	AI/KAOIL/YA
acetolysis	AS/TOL/SIS	acheilous	AI/KAOIL/OUS
acetomenaphthone	AS/TO/ME/NAF/THOEN		AI/KAOI/LOUS
acetomeroctol	AS/TO/MER/OK/TOL	acheiral	AI/KAOIRL
	AS/TO/ME/ROK/TOL	acheiria	AI/KAOIR/YA
acetometer	AS/TOM/TER	acheiropodia	AI/KAOIR/POED/YA
acetomorphine	AS/TO/MOR/FAOEN	acheiropody	AI/KAOI/ROP/DI
acetonaphthone	AS/TO/NAF/THOEN	acheirous	AI/KAOI/ROUS
acetonation	AS/TO/NAIGS	acheirus	AI/KAOI/RUS
acetone	AS/TOEN	achievement	AI/KHAOEVMT
acetonemia	AS/TO/NAOEM/YA		AI/KHAOEV/-MT
acetonemic	AS/TO/NAOEM/IK	achill(o)-	AI/KIL/L(O)
acetonglycosuria	AS/TOEN/GLAOIK/SAOUR/YA		AI/KIL
acetonitrile	AS/TO/NAOI/TRIL		AK/L(O)
acetonum	AS/TOEN/UM	Achilles	AI/KIL/LAOEZ
	AS/TOE/NUM	Achillis	AI/KIL/LIS
acetonumerator	AS/TO/NAOUM/RAI/TOR	achillobursitis	AI/KIL/BUR/SAOITS
acetonuria	AS/TO/NAOUR/YA		AI/KIL/LO/BUR/SAOITS
aceto-orcein	AS/TO/ORS/YIN	achillodynia	AI/KIL/DIN/YA
acetophenazine maleate	AS/TO/FEN/ZAOEN/MAL/YAIT		AI/KIL/LO/DIN/YA
acetophenetidin	AS/TO/FE/NET/DIN		AK/LO/DIN/YA
acetophenide	AS/TO/FEN/AOID	achillorrhaphy	AK/LOR/FI
	AS/TO/FAOE/NAOID		AI/KIL/LOR/FI
acetosal	AI/SAOET/SAL	achillotenotomy	AI/KIL/TE/NOT/M*I
acetosoluble	AS/TO/SOL/YAOUBL		AI/KIL/TEN/OT/M*I
	AS/TO/SOL/YUBL		AI/KIL/LO/TE/NOT/M*I
acetosulfone sodium	AS/TO/SUL/FOEN/SOED/YUM		AI/KIL/LO/TEN/OT/M*I
acetous	AS/TOUS	achillotomy	AK/LOT/M*I
acetphenarsine	AS/ET/FEN/AR/SAOEN		AI/KIL/LOT/M*I
acetphenetidin	AS/ET/FE/NET/DIN	achlorhydria	AI/KLOR/HAOI/DRAOE/YA
acetphenolisatin	AS/ET/FAOEN/LAOIS/TIN	achlorhydric	AI/KLOR/HAOI/DRIK
acetpyrogall	AS/ET/PAOIR/GAL	achloroblepsia	AI/KLOR/BLEPS/YA
acetrizoate sodium	AS/TR*I/ZOE/AIT/SOED/YUM	achlorophyllous	AI/KLOR/FAOI/LOUS
	AS/TR*I/ZOE/WAIT/SOED/YUM		AI/KLOR/FIL/LOUS
acetrizoic	AS/TR*I/ZOIK	achloropsia	AI/KLOR/ROPS/YA
	AS/TR*I/ZOE/IK	acholangic	AI/KOE/LAN/JIK
acetum	AI/SAOET/UM		AI/KLAN/JIK
	AI/SAOE/TUM	Acholeplasma	AI/KOEL/PLAZ/MA
aceturate	AI/SET/YAOU/RAIT	Acholeplasmata	AI/KOEL/PLAZ/MA/TA
	AI/SET/YU/RAIT	acholia	AI/KOEL/YA
acetyl	AS/TIL	acholic	AI/KOL/IK
acetyladenylate	AS/TIL/AI/DEN/LAIT	acholuria	AI/KOE/LAOUR/YA
acetylamin(o)-	AS/TIL/AM/NO	acholuric	AI/KOE/LAOUR/IK
acetylaminobenzene	AS/TIL/AM/NO/BEN/ZAOEN	achondrogenesis	AI/KON/DRO/JEN/SIS
acetylaminofluorene	AS/TIL/AM/NO/FLAOU/RAOEN	achondroplasia	AI/KON/DRO/PLAIZ/YA
	AS/TIL/AM/NO/FLAOUR/AOEN	achondroplastic	AI/KON/DRO/PLA*S/IK
acetylaniline	AS/TIL/AN/LAOIN	achondroplasty	AI/KON/DRO/PLAS/TI
	AS/TIL/AN/LIN	achordal	AI/KHOR/DAL
acetylase	AI/SET/LAIS		AI/KOER/DAL
acetylation	AI/SET/LAIGS	achordate	AI/KOER/DAIT
acetylator	AI/SET/LAI/TOR		AI/KHOR/DAIT
acetylcarbromal	AI/SAOE/TIL/KAR/BROE/MAL	achoresis	AI/KOE/RAOE/SIS
acetylcholine	AS/TIL/KOE/LAOEN	achrestic	AI/KR*ES/IK
acetylcholinesterase	AS/TIL/KOEL/N*ES/RAIS	achroacyte	AI/KROE/WA/SAO*IT
acetyl-CoA	AS/TIL/KO/ARBGS	achroacytosis	AI/KROE/WA/SAOI/TOE/SIS
acetylcoenzyme A	AS/TIL/KO/EN/ZAOIM/ARBGS	achromasia	AI/KROE/MAIZ/YA
acetylcysteine	AS/TIL/S*IS/YIN	achromat	AK/RO/MAT
acetyldigitoxin	AI/SAOE/TIL/DIJ/TOK/SIN		AI/KROE/MAT
	AS/TIL/DIJ/TOK/SIN		AI/KROE/MAIT
acetyldigoxin	AI/SAOE/TIL/DI/GOK/SIN	achromate	AI/KROE/MAIT
	AS/TIL/DI/GOK/SIN	achromatic	AI/KROE/MAT/IK
acetylene	AI/SET/LAOEN	achromatin	AI/KROEM/TIN
acetylenic	AI/SET/LEN/IK	achromatinic	AI/KROEM/TIN/IK
		achromatism	AI/KROEM/TIFM

achromatize	AI/KROEM/TAOIZ	acidyl	AS/DIL
achromatocyte	AI/KROE/MAT/SAO*IT		AS/ID/IL
achromatolysis	AI/KROEM/TOL/SIS	acidylation	AI/SID/LAIGS
achromatophil	AI/KROE/MAT/FIL	acies	AI/SAOEZ
achromatophilia	AI/KROE/MAT/FIL/YA		AIS/YAOEZ
	AI/KROEM/TO/FIL/YA	Aci-Jel	AS/JEL
achromatopia	AI/KROEM/TOEP/YA		AS/SI/JEL
achromatopic	AI/KROEM/TOP/IK		AS/H-F/JEL
achromatopsia	AI/KROEM/TOPS/YA		AS/SI/H-F/JEL
achromatopsy	AI/KROEM/TOP/SI	acinar	AS/NAR
achromatosis	AI/KROEM/TOE/SIS	acinesia	AS/NAOEZ/YA
achromatous	AI/KROEM/TOUS	acinetic	AS/NET/IK
achromaturia	AI/KROEM/TAOUR/YA	Acinetobacter	AS/NAOET/BAK/TER
achromia	AI/KROEM/YA	acini	AS/NAOI
achromic	AI/KROEM/IK	acinic	AI/SIN/IK
achromin	AI/KROE/MIN	aciniform	AI/SIN/FORM
achromocyte	AI/KROEM/SAO*IT	acinitis	AS/NAOITS
achromoderma	AI/KROEM/DER/MA	acinose	AS/NOES
achromophil	AI/KROEM/FIL	acinotubular	AS/NO/TAOUB/LAR
achromophilous	AI/KROE/MOF/LOUS	acinous	AS/NOUS
achromotrichia	AI/KROEM/TRIK/YA	acinus	AS/NUS
Achromycin	AK/RO/MAOI/SIN	acladiosis	AI/KLAD/YOE/SIS
	AI/KROE/MAOI/SIN		AK/LAD/YOE/SIS
	AK/KRO/MAOI/SIN	Acladium	AI/KLAID/YUM
achrooamyloid	AI/KROE/AM/LOID	aclasia	AK/KLAIZ/YA
	AK/RO/AM/LOID	aclasis	AK/LA/SIS
achroocytosis	AI/KROE/SAOI/TOE/SIS	aclastic	AI/KLA*S/IK
	AK/RO/SAOI/TOE/SIS	acleistocardia	AI/KLAO*IS/KARD/YA
achroodextrin	AI/KROE/DEX/TRIN	acme	AK/MAOE
	AK/RO/DEX/TRIN	acmesthesia	AK/MES/THAOEZ/YA
achylia	AI/KAO*IL/YA	acne	AK/NAOE
	(not AI/KAOIL/YA; see acheilia)	acneform	AK/NE/FORM
achylic	AI/KAO*IL/IK		(not AK/NAOE/FORM; see
	AI/KAOIL/IK (okay)		acneiform)
achylica	AI/KAO*IL/KA	Acnederm	AK/NAOE/DERM
	AI/KAOIL/KA (okay)	acnegen	AK/NAOE/JEN
achylous	AI/KAO*IL/OUS	acnegenic	AK/NAOE/JEN/IK
	AI/KAO*I/LOUS	acneiform	AK/NAOE/FORM
	(not AI/KAOIL/OUS, etc.; see	acnemia	AK/NAOEM/YA
	acheilous)	acnes	AK/NAOEZ
achymia	AI/KAOIM/YA	acnitis	AK/NAOITS
achymosis	AK/MOE/SIS	acnitrazole	AK/NAOI/TRA/ZOEL
acicul-	AI/SIK/L-	Acno Cleanser	AK/NOE/KLENZ/ER
	AI/SIK/YAOU/L-		AK/NO/KLENZ/ER
	AI/SIK/YU/L-	Acno Lotion	AK/NOE/LOEGS
acicular	AI/SIK/LAR		AK/NO/LOEGS
aciculum	AI/SIK/LUM	Acnomel Cream	AK/NO/MEL/KRAOEM
acid	AS/ID	acognosia	AK/OG/NOEZ/YA
	AS/SID		AI/KOG/NOEZ/YA
acid(o)-	AS/D(O)	acognosy	AI/KOG/NOE/SI
	AI/SID	acolasia	AK/LAIS/YA
acidalbumin	AS/ID/AL/BAOU/MIN	acology	AI/KOLG
	AS/DAL/BAOU/MIN	acolous	AK/LOUS
acidaminuria	AS/ID/AM/NAOUR/YA	acomia	AI/KOEM/YA
	AS/DAM/NAOUR/YA	aconative	AI/KON/TIV
acidemia	AS/DAOEM/YA	aconine	AK/NIN
acid-fast	AS/ID/H-F/FA*S	aconitase	AI/KON/TAIS
acidic	AI/SID/IK	aconitate	AI/KON/TAIT
acidifiable	AI/SID/FIBL	aconite	AK/NAOIT
acidifier	AI/SID/FI/ER	aconitine	AI/KON/TAOEN
acidify	AI/SID/FI		AI/KON/TIN
acidimeter	AS/DIM/TER	aconuresis	AK/ON/YAOU/RAOE/SIS
acidimetry	AS/DIM/TRI		AK/NAOU/RAOE/SIS
acidism	AS/DIFM	acoprosis	AK/PROE/SIS
acidity	AI/SID/TI		AI/KO/PROE/SIS
Acid Mantle	AS/ID/MANT/-L	acoprous	AI/KOP/ROUS
Acid Mantle Creme	AS/ID/MANT/-L/KRAO*EM	acor	AI/KOR
acidogenic	AS/DO/JEN/IK	acorea	AI/KO/RAOE/YA
acidology	AS/DOLG	acoria	AI/KOER/YA
acidopathy	AS/DOP/TH*I	acorin	AK/RIN
acidophil	AI/SID/FIL	acormus	AI/KOR/MUS
	AS/SID/FIL	acortan	AI/KOR/TAN
acidophile	AI/SID/FAOIL	Acosta	AI/KOS/TA
	AS/SID/FAOIL	acous-	AI/KAOUS
acidophilic	AS/DO/FIL/IK	-acousia	AI/KAOUZ/YA
acidophilism	AS/DOF/LIFM	acousmatamnesia	AI/KAOUS/MAT/AM/NAOEZ/YA
acidosic	AS/DOES/IK		AI/KAOUS/MA/TAM/NAOEZ/YA
acidosis	AS/DOE/SIS	acoustic	AI/KAO*US/IK
acidosteophyte	AS/DO*S/YO/FAOIT	acousticophobia	AI/KAO*US/KO/FOEB/YA
acidotic	AS/DOT/IK	acoustics	AI/KAO*US/IK/-S
acidul-	AI/SID/L-	acoustogram	AI/KAO*US/GRAM
	AI/SID/YAOU/L-		AI/KAOUS/TO/GRAM
	AI/SID/YU/L-	acquired	AI/KWAOIR/-D
acidulate	AI/SID/LAIT	acquisita	AI/KWIZ/TA
acidulated	AI/SID/LAIT/-D		AK/WI/SAOI/TA
acidulous	AI/SID/LOUS		AK/KWI/SAOI/TA
acidum	AS/DUM	acquisition	AK/WI/SIGS
aciduria	AS/DAOUR/YA		AK/KWI/SIGS
aciduric	AS/DAOUR/IK	acquisitus	AI/KWIZ/TUS

	AI/KWIS/TUS
acragnosis	AK/RAG/NOE/SIS
acral	AK/RAL
acrania	AI/KRAIN/YA
acranial	AI/KRAIN/YAL
acranius	AI/KRAIN/YUS
acraturesis	AI/KRAT/YAOU/RAOE/SIS
Acree-Rosenheim	AK/RAOE/H-F/ROEZ/EN/HAOIM
	AK/RAOE/H-F/ROES/EN/HAOIM
	AK/RAOE/H-F/ROEZ/-N/HAOIM
	AK/RAOE/H-F/ROES/-N/HAOIM
Acrel	AK/REL
Acremoniella	AK/RE/MOEN/YEL/LA
acremoniosis	AK/RE/MOEN/YOE/SIS
Acremonium	AK/RE/MOEN/YUM
acribometer	AK/RI/BOM/TER
acrid	AK/RID
acridine	AK/RI/DAOEN
	AK/RI/DIN
acriflavine	AK/RI/FLAIVN
	AK/RI/FLAI/VIN
acrimony	AK/RI/MOE/N*I
acrinol	AK/RI/NOL
acrinyl sulfocyanate	AK/RAOI/NIL/SUL/FO/SAOI/NAIT
acrisorcin	AK/RI/SOR/SIN
	AK/RI/SOER/SIN
acritical	AI/KRIT/KAL
acritochromacy	AI/KRIT/KROEM/SI
acro-	AK/RO
acroagnosis	AK/RO/AG/NOE/SIS
acroanesthesia	AK/RO/ANS/THAOEZ/YA
	AK/RO/AN/ES/THAOEZ/YA
acroarthritis	AK/RO/AR/THRAOITS
acroasphyxia	AK/RO/AS/FIX/YA
acroataxia	AK/RO/AI/TAX/YA
acroblast	AK/RO/BLA*S
acrobrachycephaly	AK/RO/BRAK/SEF/LI
acrobystitis	AK/RO/BIS/TAOITS
acrocentric	AK/RO/SEN/TRIK
acrocephalia	AK/RO/SFAIL/YA
acrocephalic	AK/RO/3FAL/IK
acrocephalopolysyndactyly	AK/RO/SEF/LO/POL/SIN/DAKT/LI
acrocephalosyndactylia	AK/RO/SEF/LO/SIN/DAK/TIL/YA
acrocephalosyndactylism	AK/RO/SEF/LO/SIN/DAKT/LIFM
acrocephalosyndactyly	AK/RO/SEF/LO/SIN/DAKT/LI
acrocephalous	AK/RO/SEF/LOUS
acrocephaly	AK/RO/SEF/LI
acrochordon	AK/RO/KOER/DON
	AK/RO/KHOR/DON
	AK/RO/KOR/DON
acrocinesia	AK/RO/SI/NAOEZ/YA
acrocinesis	AK/RO/SI/NAOE/SIS
acrocinetic	AK/RO/SI/NET/IK
acrocontracture	AK/RO/KON/TRAK/KHUR
acrocyanosis	AK/RO/SAOI/NOE/SIS
acrocyanotic	AK/RO/SAOI/NOT/IK
acrodermatitis	AK/RO/DERM/TAOITS
acrodermatosis	AK/RO/DERM/TOE/SIS
acrodolichomelia	AK/RO/DOL/KO/MAOEL/YA
acrodont	AK/RO/DONT
acrodynia	AK/RO/DIN/YA
acrodynic	AK/RO/DIN/IK
acrodysesthesia	AK/RO/DIS/ES/THAOEZ/YA
acrodysostosis	AK/RO/DIS/OS/TOE/SIS
acrodysplasia	AK/RO/DIS/PLAIZ/YA
acroedema	AK/RO/E/DAOE/MA
acroesthesia	AK/RO/ES/THAOEZ/YA
acrofacial	AK/RO/FAIRBL
acrogenous	AK/ROJ/NOUS
acrogeria	AK/RO/JAOER/YA
acrognosis	AK/ROG/NOE/SIS
acrohyperhidrosis	AK/RO/HAO*IP/HAOI/DROE/SIS
acrohypothermy	AK/RO/HO*IP/THER/M*I
acrohysterosalpingectomy	AK/RO/H*IS/RO/SAL/PIN/JEKT/M*I
acrokeratoelastoidosis	AK/RO/KER/TO/E/LAS/TOI/DOE/SIS
	AK/RO/KER/TO/LAS/TOI/DOE/SIS
acrokeratosis	AK/RO/KER/TOE/SIS
acrokinesia	AK/RO/KI/NAOEZ/YA
acroleic	AK/ROEL/YIK
acrolein	AK/ROEL/YIN
acroleukopathy	AK/RO/LAOU/KOP/TH*I
acromacria	AK/RO/MAK/RAOE/YA
	AK/RO/MAK/RA
acromania	AK/RO/MAIN/YA
acromastitis	AK/RO/MAS/TAOITS
acromegalia	AK/RO/ME/GAIL/YA
acromegalic	AK/RO/ME/GAL/IK
acromegalogigantism	AK/RO/MEG/LO/JAOI/GAN/TIFM
acromegaloidism	AK/RO/MEG/LOID/IFM
	AK/RO/MEG/LOI/DIFM
acromegaly	AK/RO/MEG/LI
acromelalgia	AK/RO/MEL/AL/JA
acromelia	AK/RO/MAOEL/YA
acromelic	AK/RO/MEL/IK
	AK/RO/MAOEL/IK
acrometagenesis	AK/RO/MET/JEN/SIS
acromi(o)-	AI/KROEM/Y(O)
acromial	AI/KROEM/YAL
acromialis	AI/KROEM/YAI/LIS
acromicria	AK/RO/MIK/RAOE/YA
	AK/RO/MIK/RA
	AK/RO/MAOI/KRAOE/YA
	AK/RO/MAOIK/RA
acromii	AI/KROEM/YAOI
acromioclavicular	AI/KROEM/YO/KLA/VIK/LAR
acromioclaviculares	AI/KROEM/YO/KLA/VIK/LAI/RAOEZ
acromioclavicularis	AI/KROEM/YO/KLA/VIK/LAI/RIS
acromiocoracoid	AI/KROEM/YO/KOR/KOID
acromiohumeral	AI/KROEM/YO/HAOUM/RAL
acromion	AI/KROEM/YON
acromionectomy	AI/KROEM/YON/EKT/M*I
	AI/KROEM/YO/NEKT/M*I
acromioscapular	AI/KROEM/YO/SKAP/LAR
acromiothoracic	AI/KROEM/YO/THRAS/IK
acromphalus	AI/KROM/FLUS
	AK/ROM/FLUS
acromyotonia	AK/RO/MAOI/TOEN/YA
acromyotonus	AK/RO/MAOI/OT/NUS
	AK/RO/MAOI/YOT/NUS
acronarcotic	AK/RO/NAR/KOT/IK
acroneurosis	AK/RO/NAOU/ROE/SIS
acronine	AK/RO/NAOEN
acronym	AK/RO/NIM
acronyx	AK/RO/NIX
acro-osteolysis	AK/RO/O*S/YOL/SIS
acropachy	AK/RO/PAK/KI
	AI/KROP/KI
acropachyderma	AK/RO/PAK/DER/MA
acroparalysis	AK/RO/PRAL/SIS
acroparesthesia	AK/RO/PAR/ES/THAOEZ/YA
acropathology	AK/RO/PA/THOLG
acropathy	AI/KROP/TH*I
acropeptide	AK/RO/PEP/TAOID
acropetal	AI/KROP/TAL
acrophobia	AK/RO/FOEB/YA
acropigmentation	AK/RO/PIG/MEN/TAIGS
acroposthitis	AK/RO/POS/THAOITS
acropurpura	AK/RO/PURP/RA
acroscleroderma	AK/RO/SKLAOER/DER/MA
acrosclerosis	AK/RO/SKLE/ROE/SIS
acrosin	AK/RO/SIN
acrosome	AK/RO/SOEM
acrosomal	AK/RO/SOE/MAL
acrosomin	AK/RO/SOE/MIN
acrosphenosyndactylia	AK/RO/SFAOEN/SIN/DAK/TIL/YA
acrospiroma	AK/RO/SPAOI/ROE/MA
acrostealgia	AK/RO*S/YAL/JA
acrosyndactyly	AK/RO/SIN/DAKT/LI
acroteric	AK/RO/TER/IK
acrotic	AI/KROT/IK
acrotism	AK/RO/TIFM
acrotrophodynia	AK/RO/TROF/DIN/YA
acrotrophoneurosis	AK/RO/TROF/NAOU/ROE/SIS
acrylaldehyde	AK/RIL/ALD/HAOID
acrylamide	AI/KRIL/MAOID
acrylate	AI/KRIL/AIT
	AI/KRIL/LAIT
acrylic	AI/KRIL/IK
acrylonitrile	AK/RI/LO/NAOI/TRIL
act	AKT
actaplanin	AK/TA/PLAI/NIN
Acthar	AK/THAR
Acthar Gel	AK/THAR/JEL
acthiazidum	AK/THAOI/ZAOI/DUM
	AK/THAOI/ZAOID/UM
Actidil	AKT/DIL
Actidose	AKT/DOES
Actidose-Aqua	AKT/DOES/AK/WA
Actifed	AKT/FED
actin	AK/TIN
acting-out	AKT/-G/H-F/OUT
actinic	AK/TIN/IK
actinica	AK/TIN/KA
actinicity	AKT/NIS/TI
actinides	AK/TIN/DAOEZ

actiniform	AK/TIN/FORM	acupoint	AK/POINT
actinism	AKT/NIFM		AK/YAOU/POINT
actinium	AK/TIN/YUM	acupressure	AK/PRES/SHUR
actin(o)-	AKT/N(O)		AK/YAOU/PRERB/SHUR
actinobacillosis	AKT/NO/BAS/LOE/SIS	acupuncture	AK/PUNG/KHUR
Actinobacillus	AKT/NO/BA/SIL/LUS		AK/YAOU/PUNG/KHUR
actinobolin	AKT/NOB/LIN	acupuncturist	AK/PUNG/KHUR/*IS
actinochemistry	AKT/NO/KEM/STRI		AK/YAOU/PUNG/KHUR/*IS
actinocongestin	AKT/NO/KON/JES/TIN	acus	AI/KUS
actinocutitis	AKT/NO/KAOU/TAOITS	acusection	AK/S*EBGS
actinodermatitis	AKT/NO/DERM/TAOITS		AK/YAOU/S*EBGS
actinogen	AK/TIN/JEN	acusector	AK/SEK/TOR
actinogenesis	AKT/NO/JEN/SIS		AK/YAOU/SEK/TOR
actinogenic	AKT/NO/JEN/IK	-acusia	AI/KAOUZ/YA
actinogram	AK/TIN/GRAM	acusis	AI/KAOU/SIS
actinograph	AK/TIN/GRAF	acustica	AI/KAO*US/KA
actinography	AKT/NOG/FI	acustici	AI/KAO*US/SAOI
actinohematin	AKT/NO/HEM/TIN	acusticofacial	AI/KAO*US/KO/FAIRBL
	AKT/NO/HAOEM/TIN	acusticus	AI/KAO*US/KUS
actinoides	AKT/NOI/DAOEZ	acuta	AI/KAOU/TA
actinolite	AK/TIN/LAOIT	acute	AI/KAOUT
actinology	AKT/NOLG	acuti	AI/KAOU/TAOI
Actinomadura	AKT/NO/MAD/YAOU/RA	acutorsion	AK/TORGS
	AKT/NO/MAD/YU/RA		AK/YAOU/TORGS
actinometer	AKT/NOM/TER	acutus	AI/KAOU/TUS
actinometry	AKT/NOM/TRI	acyanoblepsia	AI/SAOI/NO/BLEPS/YA
actinomycelial	AKT/NO/MAOI/SAOEL/YAL	acyanopsia	AI/SAOI/NOPS/YA
actinomyces	AKT/NO/MAOI/SAOEZ	acyanotic	AI/SAOI/NOT/IK
Actinomyces	K-P/AKT/NO/MAOI/SAOEZ	acyclia	AI/SAOIK/LA
Actinomycetaceae	AKT/NO/MAOIS/TAIS/YAE	acyclic	AI/SAOIK/LIK
Actinomycetales	AKT/NO/MAOIS/TAI/LAOEZ	acyclovir	AI/SAOI/KLO/VIR
actinomycete	AKT/NO/MAOI/SAOET	acyl	AS/IL
actinomycetemcomitans	AKT/NO/MAOI/SAOE/TEM/KOM/		AS/SIL
	TANZ	acyladenylate	AS/IL/AI/DEN/LAIT
	AKT/NO/MAOI/SAOET/EM/KOM/		AS/LA/DEN/LAIT
	TANZ	acylamidase	AS/IL/AM/DAIS
actinomycetes	AKT/NO/MAOI/SAOE/TAOEZ		AS/LAM/DAIS
actinomycetic	AKT/NO/MAOI/SET/IK	acylamino	AS/IL/AM/NOE
actinomycetin	AKT/NO/MAOI/SAOE/TIN		AS/LAM/NOE
actinomycin	AKT/NO/MAOI/SIN	acylase	AS/LAIS
	AK/TIN/MAOI/SIN	acylation	AS/LAIGS
actinomycoma	AKT/NO/MAOI/KOE/MA	acyl-CoA	AS/IL/KO/ARBGS
actinomycosis	AKT/NO/MAOI/KOE/SIS		AS/IL/H-F/KO/ARBGS
actinomycotic	AKT/NO/MAOI/KOT/IK	acylcoenzyme A	AS/IL/KO/EN/ZAOIM/ARBGS
actinomycotin	AKT/NO/MAOIK/TIN	acylmutase	AS/IL/MAOU/TAIS
actinoneuritis	AKT/NO/NAOU/RAOITS	acylphosphatase	AS/IL/FOS/FA/TAIS
actinophage	AK/TIN/FALJ	acylsphingosine	AS/IL/SFING/SAOEN
actinophytosis	AKT/NO/FAOI/TOE/SIS	acyltransferase	AS/IL/TRA*NS/FRAIS
Actinoplanaceae	AKT/NO/PLA/NAIS/YAE	acystia	AI/S*IS/YA
Actinoplanes	AKT/NO/PLAI/NAOEZ	acystinervia	AI/S*IS/NEFRB/YA
Actinopoda	AKT/NOP/DA	acystineuria	AI/S*IS/NAOUR/YA
actinoquinol	AK/TIN/KWIN/OL	ad	A*D
actinotherapeutics	AKT/NO/THER/PAOUT/IK/-S		(*not* AD; see add)
actinotherapy	AKT/NO/THER/PI	ad-	AD
actinotoxemia	AKT/NO/TOK/SAOEM/YA	adactylia	AI/DAK/TIL/YA
action	A*BGS	adactylism	AI/DAKT/LIFM
activate	AKT/VAIT	adactylous	AI/DAKT/LOUS
activating	AKT/VAIT/-G	adactyly	AI/DAKT/LI
activation	AKT/VAIGS	Adalat	AD/LAT
activator	AKT/VAI/TOR	Adam	AD/DAM
activatus	AKT/VAI/TUS	adamantine	AD/MAN/TAOEN
active	AKT/IV		AD/MAN/TAOIN
	AK/TIV		AD/MAN/TIN
activity	AK/TIV/TI	adamantinoma	AD/MANT/NOE/MA
actodigin	AK/TO/DIJ/JIN	adamantinum	AD/MAN/TAOIN/UM
actometer	AK/TOM/TER		AD/MAN/TAOI/NUM
actomyosin	AK/TO/MAOI/SIN		AD/MANT/NUM
actual	AK/KHUL	adamantoblast	AD/MAN/TO/BLA*S
actuary	AK/KHAOU/WAIR	adamantoblastoma	AD/MAN/TO/BLAS/TOE/MA
	AKT/WAIR	adamantoma	AD/MAN/TOE/MA
	AK/KHAOU/AIR	adamas	AD/MAS
acu-	AK	Adami	AI/DAM/MAOE
	AK/YAOU		AD/DAM/MAOE
	AK/YU	Adamkiewicz	AD/AM/KAOE/VIX
	AI/KAOU		AD/DAM/KAOE/VIX
Acuaria spiralis	AK/YAIR/YA/SPAOI/RAI/LIS	Adams	AD/AMZ
	AK/WAIR/YA/SPAOI/RAI/LIS		AD/AMS
	AK/YAOU/AIR/YA/SPAOI/RAI/LIS		AD/DAMZ
aculosure	AK/KLOE/SHUR		AD/DAMS
	AK/YAOU/KLOE/SHUR	Adam's apple	AD/DAM/AOES/AP/-L
acufilopressure	AK/FAOIL/PRERB/SHUR	Adams-Stokes	AD/AMZ/H-F/STOEKS
	AK/YAOU/FAOIL/PRERB/SHUR		AD/AMS/H-F/STOEKS
acuity	AI/KAOU/TI		AD/DAMZ/H-F/STOEKS
aculeate	AI/KAOUL/YAIT		AD/DAMS/H-F/STOEKS
acuminate	AI/KAOUM/NAIT	Adamson	AD/AM/SON
acuminatum	AI/KAOUM/NAI/TUM		AD/DAM/SON
	AI/KAOUM/NAIT/UM	adansonian	AD/AN/SOEN/YAN
acuology	AK/YOLG	ad antrum	AD/AN/TRUM
	AK/YAOU/OLG		A*D/AN/TRUM

Adapin	AD/PIN	adenochondroma	AD/NO/KON/DROE/MA
adaptation	AD/AP/TAIGS	adenocyst	AD/NO/S*IS
	AI/DAP/TAIGS	adenocystic	AD/NO/S*IS/IK
adapter	AI/DAPT/ER	adenocystoma	AD/NO/SIS/TOE/MA
	AI/DAP/TER	adenocyte	AD/NO/SAO*IT
adaptometer	AD/AP/TOM/TER	adenodiastasis	AD/NO/DI/A*S/SIS
	AI/DAP/TOM/TER	adenodynia	AD/NO/DIN/YA
adaptor	AI/DAP/TOR	adenoepithelioma	AD/NO/EP/THAOEL/YOE/MA
ad aquaeductum	AD/AK/WAE/DUK/TUM	adenofibroma	AD/NO/FAOI/BROE/MA
	AD/AK/WAOE/DUK/TUM	adenofibromyoma	AD/NO/FAOI/BRO/MAOI/YOE/MA
	AD/AK/WE/DUK/TUM	adenofibrosis	AD/NO/FAOI/BROE/SIS
	A*D/AK/WAE/DUK/TUM	adenogenesis	AD/NO/JEN/SIS
	A*D/AK/WAOE/DUK/TUM	adenogenous	AD/NOJ/NOUS
	A*D/AK/WE/DUK/TUM	adenographic	AD/NO/GRAFK
adaxial	AD/AX/YAL	adenography	AD/NOG/FI
add	AD	adenohypophysial	AD/NO/HO*IP/FIZ/YAL
addenda	AI/DEN/DA	adenohypophysectomy	AD/NO/HAOI/POF/SEKT/M*I
addendum	AI/DEN/DUM	adenohypophysis	AD/NO/HAOI/POF/SIS
adder	AD/ER	adenohypophysitis	AD/NO/HAOI/POF/SAOITS
addict	AD/IKT	adenoid	AD/NOID
	AD/DIKT	adenoidectomy	AD/NOI/DEKT/M*I
addiction	AI/D*IBGS		AD/NOID/EKT/M*I
addictive	AI/DIKT/IV	adenoides	AD/NOI/DAOEZ
addiment	AD/-MT	adenoidism	AD/NOI/DIFM
	AD/DIMT		AD/NOID/IFM
Addis	AD/DIS	adenoiditis	AD/NOI/DAOITS
addisin	AD/DI/SIN	adenoids	AD/NOIDZ
	(*not* AD/SIN)	adenoleiomyofibroma	AD/NO/LAOI/MAOI/FAOI/BROE/MA
Addison	AD/DI/SON	adenolipoma	AD/NO/LI/POE/MA
	(*not* AD/SON; see Adson)	adenolipomatosis	AD/NO/LIP/MA/TOE/SIS
addisoni	AD/SOE/NAOI		AD/NO/LI/POEM/TOE/SIS
addisonian	AD/SOEN/YAN	adenologaditis	AD/NO/LOG/DAOITS
addisonism	AD/SON/IFM	adenology	AD/NOLG
additive	AD/TIV	adenolymphitis	AD/NO/LIM/FAOITS
additivity	AD/TIV/TI	adenolymphocele	AD/NO/LIM/FO/SAO*EL
adducent	AI/DAOUS/ENT	adenolymphoma	AD/NO/LIM/FOE/MA
	AI/DAOU/SENT	adenoma	AD/NOE/MA
	AD/DAOUS/ENT	adenomalacia	AD/NO/MA/LAI/SHA
	AD/DAOU/SENT	adenomatoid	AD/NOEM/TOID
adduct	AD/DUKT	adenomatosis	AD/NOEM/TOE/SIS
	AI/DUKT	adenomatosum	AD/NOEM/TOE/SUM
adducta	AD/DUK/TA		AD/NOEM/TOES/UM
	AI/DUK/TA	adenomatous	AD/NOEM/TOUS
adduction	AD/D*UBGS	adenomegaly	AD/NO/MEG/LI
	AI/D*UBGS	adenomere	AD/NO/MAOER
adductor	AD/DUK/TOR	adenomyoepithelioma	AD/NO/MAOI/EP/THAOEL/YOE/MA
	AI/DUK/TOR		
adductoris	AD/DUK/TOR/RIS	adenomyofibroma	AD/NO/MAOI/FAOI/BROE/MA
	AD/DUK/TOER/RIS	adenomyoma	AD/NO/MAOI/YOE/MA
	AD/DUK/TOE/RIS	adenomyomatosis	AD/NO/MAOI/YOEM/TOE/SIS
	AI/DUK/TOR/RIS	adenomyomatous	AD/NO/MAOI/YOEM/TOUS
	AI/DUK/TOER/RIS	adenomyometritis	AD/NO/MAOI/ME/TRAOITS
	AI/DUK/TOE/RIS	adenomyosarcoma	AD/NO/MAOI/SAR/KOE/MA
adductorius	AD/DUK/TOR/YUS	adenomyosis	AD/NO/MAOI/YOE/SIS
	AD/DUK/TOER/YUS	adenoneural	AD/NO/NAOURL
	AI/DUK/TOR/YUS		AD/NO/NAOU/RAL
	AI/DUK/TOER/YUS	adenopathy	AD/NOP/TH*I
Adeflor	AD/FLOR	adenopharyngitis	AD/NO/FARN/JAOITS
	AD/FLOER	adenophlegmon	AD/NO/FLEG/MON
Adelmann	AD/EL/MAN	Adenophorasida	AD/NO/FOE/RAS/DA
adelomorphic	AI/DEL/MOR/FIK		AD/NO/FRAS/DA
adelomorphous	AI/DEL/MOR/FOUS	adenophthalmia	AD/NOF/THAL/MAOE/YA
aden(o)-	AD/N(O)		AD/NOF/THAL/MA
adenalgia	AD/NAL/JA	adenophyma	AD/NO/FAOI/MA
adenase	AD/NAIS	adenopituicyte	AD/NO/PI/TAOU/SAO*IT
adenasthenia	AD/EN/AS/THAOEN/YA	adenosalpingitis	AD/NO/SAL/PIN/JAOITS
	AD/NAS/THAOEN/YA	adenosarcoma	AD/NO/SAR/KOE/MA
adendric	AI/DEN/DRIK	adenosclerosis	AD/NO/SKLE/ROE/SIS
adendritic	AI/DEN/DRIT/IK	adenose	AD/NOES
adenectomy	AD/NEKT/M*I	adenosinase	AD/NOE/SIN/AIS
adenectopia	AD/NEK/TOEP/YA		AD/NOES/NAIS
adenemphraxis	AD/NEM/FRAK/SIS	adenosine	AI/DEN/SAOEN
	AD/EN/EM/FRAK/SIS	adenosinetriphosphatase	AI/DEN/SAOEN/TR*I/FOS/FA/TAIS
adenia	AI/DAOEN/YA		AI/DEN/SIN/TR*I/FOS/FA/TAIS
adenic	AI/DEN/IK	adenosis	AD/NOE/SIS
	AI/DAOEN/IK	adenosyl	AI/DEN/SIL
adeniform	AI/DEN/FORM	S-adenosylhomocystein	S-RBGS/AI/DEN/SIL/HOEM/S*IS/YIN
adenine	AD/NAOEN		S-RBGS/H-F/AI/DEN/SIL/HOEM/S*IS/YIN
adenitis	AD/NAOITS	S-adenosylmethionine	S-RBGS/AI/DEN/SIL/ME/THAOI/NAOEN
adenization	AD/NAOI/ZAIGS		S-RBGS/H-F/AI/DEN/SIL/ME/THAOI/NAOEN
	AD/NI/ZAIGS	adenotome	AD/NO/TOEM
adenoacanthoma	AD/NO/AK/AN/THOE/MA	adenotomy	AD/NOT/M*I
adenoameloblastoma	AD/NO/AI/MEL/BLAS/TOE/MA	adenotonsillectomy	AD/NO/TONS/LEKT/M*I
	AD/NO/AM/LO/BLAS/TOE/MA		
adenoblast	AD/NO/BLA*S		
adenocancroid	AD/NO/KAN/KROID		
adenocarcinoma	AD/NO/KARS/NOE/MA		
adenocele	AD/NO/SAO*EL		
adenocellulitis	AD/NO/SEL/YAOU/LAOITS		

adenous	AD/NOUS	adipolytic	AD/PO/LIT/IK
adenoviral	AD/NO/VAOIRL	adipometer	AD/POM/TER
Adenoviridae	AD/NO/VIR/DAE	adiponecrosis	AD/PO/NE/KROE/SIS
adenovirus	AD/NO/VAOI/RUS	adipopectic	AD/PO/PEKT/IK
adenyl	AD/NIL	adipopexia	AD/PO/PEX/YA
adenylate	AI/DEN/LAIT	adipopexic	AD/PO/PEX/IK
adenylic	AD/NIL/IK	adipopexis	AD/PO/PEK/SIS
adenylosuccinase	AD/NIL/SUKS/NAIS	adiposa	AD/POE/SA
adenylosuccinate	AD/NIL/SUKS/NAIT	adipose	ADPOE/SAE
adenylosuccinic	AD/NIL/SUK/SIN/IK	adiposalgia	AD/PO/SAL/JA
adenylpyrophosphatase	AD/NIL/PAOIR/FOS/FA/TAIS		AD/POES/AL/JA
adenylpyrophosphate	AD/NIL/PAOIR/FOS/FAIT	adipose	AD/POES
adenylyl	AI/DEN/LIL	adiposis	AD/POE/SIS
	AD/NI/LIL	adipositas	AD/POS/TAS
adeps	AD/EPS	adipositis	AD/PO/SAOITS
adequacy	AD/KWA/SI	adiposity	AD/POS/TI
adequal	AD/KWAL	adiposogenital	AD/POE/SO/JEN/TAL
adermia	AI/DERM/YA	adiposogenitalis	AD/POE/SO/JEN/TAI/LIS
adermogenesis	AI/DERM/JEN/SIS	Adipost	AD/PO*ES
adhere	AD/HAOER	adiposum	AD/POE/SUM
adherence	AD/HAOERNS		AD/POES/UM
adherent	AD/HAOERNT	adiposuria	AD/PO/SAOUR/YA
adhesin	AD/HAOE/ZIN	adiposus	AD/POE/SUS
	AD/HAOE/SIN	adipsa	AI/DIP/SA
adhesio	AD/HAOEZ/YOE	adipsia	AI/DIPS/YA
adhesion	AD/HAOEGS	adipsous	AI/DIP/SOUS
adhesiones	AD/HAOEZ/YOE/NAOEZ	adipsy	AI/DIP/SI
adhesiotomy	AD/HAOEZ/YOT/M*I	aditus	AD/TUS
adhesive	AD/HAOES/IV	adjection	AD/J*EBGS
adhesiveness	AD/HAOES/IV/*NS	adjunct	AD/JUNGT
	AD/HAOES/IVNS		AD/J*UNGT
adhibendus	AD/HI/BEN/DUS	adjunctive	AD/JUNGT/IV
adiabatic	AI/DAOI/BAT/IK		AD/JUNG/TIV
adiactinic	AI/DI/AK/TIN/IK	adjustable	AD/J*US/-BL
adiadoch(o)-	AI/DAOI/DOEK	adjustment	AD/J*US/-MT
	AI/DAOI/DOE/KO	adjuvant	AD/JAOU/VANT
	AI/DI/AD/KO		AD/JU/VANT
	AI/DAOI/AD/KO		AD/JAOUVNT
adiadochocinesia	AI/DAOI/DOEK/SI/NAOEZ/YA	adjuvanticity	AD/JAOU/VAN/TIS/TI
adiadochocinesis	AI/DAOI/DOEK/SI/NAOE/SIS		AD/JU/VAN/TIS/TI
adiadochokinesia	AI/DAOI/DOEK/KI/NAOEZ/YA		AD/JAOUVN/TIS/TI
adiadochokinesis	AI/DAOI/DOEK/KI/NAOE/SIS	Adler	AD/LER
adiadochokinetic	AI/DAOI/DOEK/KI/NET/IK	adlerian	AD/LER/YAN
adiaphoresis	AI/DAOI/FRAOE/SIS	ad lib	AD/LIB
	AI/DAOI/FOE/RAOE/SIS	ad lib.	AD/L*IB
adiaphoretic	AI/DAOI/FRET/IK		(not AD/LIB; see ad lib)
adiaphoria	AI/DAOI/FOER/YA	ad libitum	AD/LIB/TUM
adiaspiromycosis	AD/YA/SPAOIR/MAOI/KOE/SIS		A*D/LIB/TUM
	AID/YA/SPAOIR/MAOI/KOE/SIS	adlumidine	AD/LAOUM/DIN
adiaspore	AD/YA/SPOER	adlumine	AD/LAOU/MIN
	AID/YA/SPOER	admaxillary	AD/MAX/LAIR
adiathermance	AI/DAOI/THER/MANS	admedial	AD/MAOED/YAL
adiathermancy	AI/DAOI/THER/MAN/SI	admedian	AD/MAOED/YAN
adicillin	AD/SLIN	adminicula	AD/MI/NIK/LA
	AD/SIL/LIN	adminiculum	AD/MI/NIK/LUM
Adie	AI/DAOE	adnata	AD/NAI/TA
adiemorrhysis	AD/YEM/OER/SIS	adnatum	AD/NAI/TUM
	AD/YEM/OR/SIS		AD/NAIT/UM
	AD/YE/MOR/SIS	ad nauseam	AD/NAUZ/YAM
	AI/DAOI/MOR/SIS		A*D/NAUZ/YAM
	AI/DAOI/MOER/SIS	adnerval	AD/NER/VAL
adient	AD/YENT	adneural	AD/NAOURL
Adinida	AI/DIN/DA	adnex(o)-	AD/NEX
adip(o)-	AD/P(O)		AD/NEK/S(O)
adipectomy	AD/PEKT/M*I	adnexa	AD/NEK/SA
adipes	AD/PAOEZ	adnexal	AD/NEK/SAL
Adipex	AD/PEX	adnexectomy	AD/NEK/SEKT/M*I
Adipex-P	AD/PEX/P-RBGS		AD/NEX/EKT/M*I
	AD/PEX/H-F/P-RBGS	adnexitis	AD/NEK/SAOITS
adiphenine	AI/DIF/NAOEN		AD/NEX/AOITS
	AD/FEN/AOEN	adnexogenesis	AD/NEX/JEN/SIS
	AD/FEN/NAOEN	adnexopexy	AD/NEX/PEK/SI
adipic	AI/DIP/IK	adnexorganogenic	AD/NEX/ORG/NO/JEN/IK
adipis	AD/PIS	adnexum	AD/NEK/SUM
adipocele	AD/PO/SAO*EL		AD/NEX/UM
adipocellular	AD/PO/SEL/YAOU/LAR	adolescence	AD/LES/ENS
adipoceratous	AD/PO/SER/TOUS	adolescent	AD/LES/ENT
adipocere	AD/PO/SAOER	adolescentium	AD/LES/SEN/SHUM
adipocyte	AD/PO/SAO*IT		AD/LES/SENT/YUM
adipofibroma	AD/PO/FAOI/BROE/MA	adonidin	AI/DON/DIN
adipogenesis	AD/PO/JEN/SIS	adonin	AI/DOE/NIN
adipogenic	AD/PO/JEN/IK	adonite	AD/NAOIT
adipogenous	AD/POJ/NOUS	adonitol	AI/DON/TOL
adipohepatic	AD/PO/HE/PAT/IK	adoral	AD/ORL
adipoid	AD/POID	ad pelvis	AD/PEL/VIS
adipokinesis	AD/PO/KI/NAOE/SIS		A*D/PEL/VIS
adipokinetic	AD/PO/KI/NET/IK	ad pontem	AD/PON/TEM
adipokinin	AD/PO/KAOI/NIN		A*D/PON/TEM
adipolysis	AD/POL/SIS	adren(o)-	AI/DRAOEN

Term	Steno	Term	Steno
	AD/RAOEN	adrenostatic	AI/DRAOEN/STAT/IK
	AI/DRAOE/N(O)	adrenosterone	AI/DRAOE/NO*S/ROEN
	AD/RE/N(O)		AD/RE/NO*S/ROEN
	AD/RAOE/N(O)	adrenotoxin	AI/DRAOEN/TOK/SIN
adrenal	AI/DRAOENL	adrenotrophic	AI/DRAOEN/TROEFK
	AD/RAOENL		AI/DRAOEN/TROFK
adrenalectomize	AI/DRAOENL/EKT/MAOIZ	adrenotrophin	AI/DRAOEN/TROEFN
	AI/DRAOEN/LEKT/MAOIZ		AI/DRAOEN/TROFN
adrenalectomy	AI/DRAOENL/EKT/M*I	adrenotropic	AI/DRAOEN/TROEP/IK
	AI/DRAOEN/LEKT/M*I		AI/DRAOEN/TROP/IK
Adrenalin	AI/DREN/L*IN	adrenotropin	AI/DRAOEN/TROE/PIN
adrenaline	AI/DREN/LIN		AI/DRAOEN/TROP/PIN
	AI/DREN/LAOEN	adrenoxidase	AD/REN/OX/DAIS
adrenalinemia	AI/DREN/LIN/AOEM/YA		AD/RE/NOX/DAIS
adrenalinogenesis	AI/DREN/LIN/JEN/SIS	Adriamycin	AI/DRA/MAOI/SIN
adrenalinuria	AI/DREN/LIN/YAOUR/YA		AI/DRAOE/YA/MAOI/SIN
adrenalism	AI/DREN/LIFM	adromia	AI/DROEM/YA
adrenalitis	AI/DRAOENL/AOITS	ad saccum	AD/SAK/UM
	AI/DRAOEN/LAOITS		AD/SAK/KUM
adrenalone	AI/DREN/LOEN		A*D/SAK/UM
adrenalopathy	AI/DRAOENL/OP/TH*I		A*D/SAK/KUM
	AI/DRAOEN/LOP/TH*I	Adson	AD/SON
adrenalotropic	AI/DREN/LO/TROP/IK	adsorb	AD/SORB
adrenarche	AD/REN/AR/KAOE	adsorbate	AD/SOR/BAIT
	AD/RE/NAR/KAOE		AD/SORB/AIT
adrenergic	AD/RE/NERJ/IK	adsorbent	AD/SORB/ENT
	AD/REN/ERJ/IK		AD/SOR/BENT
	AI/DRE/NERJ/IK	adsorption	AD/SORPGS
	AI/DREN/ERJ/IK	adsternal	AD/STERNL
adrenic	AI/DREN/IK	adterminal	AD/TERM/NAL
	AI/DRAOEN/IK	adtorsion	AD/TORGS
adrenin	AI/DRAOE/NIN	adult	AI/DULT
adrenine	AI/DRAOE/NAOEN		DULT
adrenitis	AD/RE/NAOITS	adulterant	AI/DULT/RANT
adrenoceptive	AI/DRAOEN/SEPT/IV	adulteration	AI/DULT/RAIGS
	AI/DREN/SEPT/IV	adultomorphism	AI/DULT/MOR/FIFM
adrenoceptor	AI/DRAOEN/SEP/TOR		AI/DUL/TO/MOR/FIFM
	AI/DREN/SEP/TOR	adultorum	AI/DUL/TOR/UM
adrenochrome	AI/DRAOEN/KROEM		AI/DUL/TOER/UM
	AD/RAOEN/KROEM		AD/UL/TOR/UM
adrenocortic(o)-	AI/DRAOEN/KORT/K(O)		AD/UL/TOER/UM
	AD/RAOEN/KORT/K(O)	adumbration	AI/DUM/BRAIGS
adrenocortical	AD/RAOEN/KORT/KAL		AD/UM/BRAIGS
adrenocorticohyperplasia	AI/DRAOEN/KORT/KO/HAO*IP/ PLAIZ/YA	advance	AD/VANS
adrenocorticomimetic	AI/DRAOEN/KORT/KO/MAOI/ MET/IK	Advance	K-P/AD/VANS
		advancement	AD/VANS/-MT
	AI/DRAOEN/KORT/KO/MI/MET/IK	advehentes	AD/VAOE/HEN/TAOEZ
adrenocorticotrophic	AI/DRAOEN/KORT/KO/TROFK		AD/VE/HEN/TAOEZ
adrenocorticotrophin	AI/DRAOEN/KORT/KO/TROFN	adventitia	AD/VEN/TIRB/SHA
adrenocorticotropic	AI/DRAOEN/KORT/KO/TROP/IK		AD/VEN/TIRB/YA
	AI/DRAOEN/KORT/KO/TROEP/IK		AD/VEN/TI/SHA
adrenocorticotropin	AI/DRAOEN/KORT/KO/TROE/PIN	adventitial	AD/VEN/TIRBL
	AI/DRAOEN/KORT/KO/TROP/PIN	adventitious	AD/VEN/TIRBS
adrenodoxin	AI/DRAOEN/DOK/SIN	Advil	AD/VIL
adrenogenic	AI/DRAOEN/JEN/IK	adynamia	AI/DAOI/NAIM/YA
adrenogenous	AD/REN/OJ/NOUS		AD/NAIM/YA
	AD/RE/NOJ/NOUS	adynamic	AI/DAOI/NAM/IK
	AI/DRE/NOJ/NOUS		AD/NAM/IK
	AI/DREN/OJ/NOUS	Aeby	AI/BI
adrenoglomerulotropin	AI/DRAOEN/GLOE/MER/LO/ TROE/PIN	Aedes	AI/DAOEZ
		aegypti	AE/JIP/TAOI
adrenogram	AI/DRAOEN/GRAM		E/JIP/TAOI
	AI/DREN/GRAM	Aegyptianella pullorum	E/JIPGS/EL/LA/PUL/LOR/UM
	AD/REN/GRAM		E/JIPGS/EL/LA/PUL/LOER/UM
adrenokinetic	AI/DRAOEN/KI/NET/IK		E/JIPGS/EL/LA/PUL/LOE/RUM
adrenoleukodystrophy	AI/DRAOEN/LAOUK/DIS/TRO/FI		AE/JIPGS/EL/LA/PUL/LOR/UM
adrenolutin	AI/DRAOEN/LAOU/TIN		AE/JIPGS/EL/LA/PUL/LOER/UM
adrenolytic	AI/DRAOEN/LIT/IK		AE/JIPGS/EL/LA/PUL/LOE/RUM
	AI/DREN/LIT/IK	aegyptica	AE/JIPT/KA
	AD/REN/LIT/IK		E/JIPT/KA
adrenomedullotropic	AI/DRAOEN/ME/DUL/TROP/IK	aer(o)-	AER
	AI/DRAOEN/MED/LO/TROP/IK		AER/R(O)
adrenomegaly	AI/DRAOEN/MEG/LI	aerasthenia	AER/AS/THAOEN/YA
	AI/DREN/MEG/LI	aerate	AER/RAIT
	AD/REN/MEG/LI	aerated	AER/RAIT/-D
adrenomimetic	AI/DRAOEN/MAOI/MET/IK	aeration	AER/RAIGS
	AI/DRAOEN/MI/MET/IK	aeremia	AER/AOEM/YA
adrenomyeloneuropathy	AI/DRAOEN/MAOI/LO/NAOU/ ROP/TH*I		AER/RAOEM/YA
		aerendocardia	AER/*END/KARD/YA
adrenopathy	AI/DRAOE/NOP/TH*I		AER/EN/DO/KARD/YA
	AD/RE/NOP/TH*I	aerial	AER/YAL
	AD/RAOEN/OP/TH*I		(not AERL or AIRL)
adrenopause	AI/DRAOEN/PAUZ	aeriferous	AER/RIF/ROUS
	AI/DREN/PAUZ		AER/IF/ROUS
	AD/REN/PAUZ	aeriform	AER/FORM
adrenoprival	AI/DRAOEN/PRAOIVL		AER/RI/FORM
adrenoreactive	AI/DRAOEN/RE/AKT/IV	aeroatelectasis	AER/AT/LEKT/SIS
adrenoreactive	AI/DRAOEN/RE/AKT/IV	Aerobacter	AER/BAK/TER
adrenoreceptor	AI/DRAOEN/RE/SEP/TOR	aerobe	AER/ROEB

	AER/OEB		AES/KAOU/LAIP/YAN
aerobic	AER/ROEB/IK	aesculin	AES/KLIN
	AER/OEB/IK		AES/KAOU/LIN
AeroBid	AER/BID	afebrile	AI/FEB/RAOIL
aerobiology	AER/BAO*I/OLG		AI/FEB/RIL
aerobioscope	AER/BAO*I/SKOEP	afetal	AI/FAOE/TAL
aerobiosis	AER/BAO*I/YOE/SIS	affect	AFKT
aerobiotic	AER/BAO*I/OT/IK		AI/FEKT
aerobullosis	AER/BUL/LOE/SIS		AF/FEKT
aerocele	AER/SAO*EL	affection	AI/F*EBGS
Aerococcus	AER/KOK/KUS	affective	AFKT/IV
aerocolpos	AER/KOL/POS		AI/FEKT/IV
aerocystography	AER/SIS/TOG/FI		AF/FEKT/IV
aerocystoscope	AER/S*IS/SKOEP	affectivity	AFK/TIV/TI
aerocystoscopy	AER/SIS/TOS/KPI		AI/FEK/TIV/TI
aerodermectasia	AER/DER/MEK/TAIZ/YA		AF/FEK/TIV/TI
	AER/DERM/EK/TAIZ/YA	affectomotor	AFK/TO/MOE/TOR
aerodontalgia	AER/DON/TAL/JA		AI/FEK/TO/MOE/TOR
aerodontia	AER/DON/SHA	afferent	AFRNT
aerodontics	AER/DONT/IK/-S		AF/FRENT
aerodynamics	AER/DAOI/NAM/IK/-S		AF/FERNT
aeroembolism	AER/EM/BLIFM	afferentia	AFRN/SHA
aeroemphysema	AER/EFRP/SAOE/MA		AF/FREN/SHA
	AER/EM/FI/SAOE/MA		AF/REN/SHA
aerogastria	AER/GAS/TRA		AF/FER/EN/SHA
	AER/GAS/TRAOE/YA	affinity	AI/FIN/TI
aerogel	AER/JEL	affinous	AF/NOUS
aerogen	AER/JEN	affirm	AI/FIRM
aerogenes	AER/ROJ/NAOEZ	affirmation	AFR/MAIGS
aerogenesis	AER/JEN/SIS		AF/FIR/MAIGS
aerogenic	AER/JEN/IK	afflux	AF/LUX
aerogenous	AER/ROJ/NOUS		AF/FLUX
aerogram	AER/GRAM	affluxion	AI/FL*UBGS
aerohydrotherapy	AER/HAOI/DRO/THER/PI		AF/L*UBGS
aeroionotherapy	AER/AOI/NO/THER/PI	affusion	AI/FAOUGS
Aerolate Jr.	AER/LAIT/J-R		(not AF/FAOUGS; see after fusion)
Aerolate Liquid	AER/LAIT/LIK/WID	afibrillar	AI/FAOI/BRIL/LAR
Aerolate Sr.	AER/LAIT/S-R	afibrinogenemia	AI/FAOI/BRIN/JE/NAOEM/YA
aeromedicine	AER/MED/SIN		AI/FAOI/BRIN/JEN/AOEM/YA
aerometer	AER/ROM/TER	aflatoxicosis	AF/LA/TOX/KOE/SIS
aeromonad	AER/MOE/NAD	aflatoxin	AF/LA/TOK/SIN
Aeromonas	AER/MOE/NAS	africanus	AF/RI/KAI/NUS
aeroneurosis	AER/NAOU/ROE/SIS		AFR/KAI/NUS
aero-odontalgia	AER/O/DON/TAL/JA	Afrin	AF/RIN
aero-odontodynia	AER/O/DONT/DIN/YA	Afrinol	AF/RI/NOL
aero-otitis	AER/O/TAOITS		AF/RIN/OL
aeropathy	AER/ROP/TH*I	after-	AFR
aeropause	AER/PAUZ	afteraction	AFR/A*BGS
aeroperitoneum	AER/PERT/NAOEM	afterbirth	AFR/B*IRT
aeroperitonia	AER/P*ER/TOEN/YA	aftercare	AFR/KAIR
aerophagia	AER/FAI/JA	aftercataract	AFR/KAT/RAKT
aerophagy	AER/ROF/JI	afterchroming	AFR/KROEM/-G
aerophil	AER/FIL	aftercontraction	AFR/KON/TRA*BGS
aerophile	AER/FAOIL	aftercurrent	AFR/KURNT
aerophilic	AER/FIL/IK	afterdischarge	AFR/DIS/KHARJ
aerophilous	AER/ROF/LOUS		AFR/DARJ
aerophobia	AER/FOEB/YA	aftereffect	AFR/EFKT
aerophyte	AER/FAOIT		AFR/EF/FEKT
aeropiesotherapy	AER/PAOI/AOES/THER/PI		AFR/E/FEKT
	AER/PAOI/ES/THER/PI	aftergilding	AFR/GILD/-G
aeroplankton	AER/PLANG/TON	afterhearing	AFR/HAER/-G
aeroplethysmograph	AER/PLE/THIZ/MO/GRAF	afterimage	AFR/IM/AJ
aeroporotomy	AER/POE/ROT/M*I	afterimpression	AFR/IM/PREGS
	AER/PO/ROT/M*I	afterload	AFR/LOED
Aeroseb	AER/SEB	aftermovement	AFR/MOVMT
Aeroseb-Dex	AER/SEB/DEX		AFR/MAOUVMT
Aeroseb-HC	AER/SEB/H-RBGS/KR*RBGS	afterpains	AFR/PAIN/-S
aerosialophagy	AER/SAOI/LOF/JI	afterperception	AFR/PER/SEPGS
aerosinusitis	AER/SAOIN/SAOITS	afterpotential	AFR/POE/TEN/-RBL
aerosis	AER/ROE/SIS	aftersensation	AFR/SEN/SAIGS
aerosol	AER/SOL	aftersound	AFR/SOUND
aerosolization	AER/SOL/ZAIGS	aftertaste	AFR/TA*IS
aerosolology	AER/SOL/OLG	aftertouch	AFR/TUFP
aerostatics	AER/STAT/IK/-S		AFR/TOUFP
aerotaxis	AER/TAK/SIS	aftertreatment	AFR/TRAOEMT
aerotherapeutics	AER/THER/PAOUT/IK/-S		AFR/TRAOET/-MT
aerotherapy	AER/THER/PI	aftervision	AFR/VIGS
aerotitis	AER/TAOITS	aftosa	AF/TOE/SA
aerotolerant	AER/TOL/RANT	afunction	AI/FUNGS
aerotonometer	AER/TOE/NOM/TER	agalactia	AI/GLAK/SHA
aerotropism	AER/ROT/RO/PIFM	agalactorrhea	AI/GLAKT/RAOE/YA
	AER/OT/RO/PIFM	agalactosis	AI/GAL/AK/TOE/SIS
aerotympanal	AER/TIFRP/NAL		AI/GLAK/TOE/SIS
aerourethroscope	AER/YAOU/RAO*ET/RO/SKOEP	agalactosuria	AI/GLAKT/SAOUR/YA
aerourethroscopy	AER/YAOU/RAO*ET/ROS/KPI	agalactous	AI/GLAK/TOUS
	AER/YAOUR/THROS/KPI		AI/GLAKT/OUS
aeruginosum	AER/RAOUJ/NOE/SUM	agalorrhea	AI/GAL/RAOE/YA
	AER/RAOUJ/NOES/UM	agamete	AI/GAM/AOET
aesculapian	AES/KLAIP/YAN		AG/MAOET

agametic	AI/GA/MET/IK	agglutogenic	AI/GLAOU/TO/JEN/IK
	AG/MET/IK	agglutometer	AG/LAOU/TOM/TER
agamic	AI/GAM/IK		AG/GLAOU/TOM/TER
agammaglobulinemia	AI/GAM/GLOB/LI/NAOEM/YA	aggre-	AG/RE-
	AI/GAM/GLOB/LIN/AOEM/YA		AG/GRE-
agamocytogeny	AI/GAM/SAOI/TOJ/N*I	aggregate	AG/RE/GAIT
Agamofilaria	AI/GAM/FLAIR/YA		AG/RE/GAT
	AI/GAM/FAOI/LAIR/YA	aggregated	AG/RE/GAIT/-D
agamogenesis	AG/MO/JEN/SIS	aggregation	AG/RE/GAIGS
	AI/GAM/JEN/SIS	aggregen	AG/RE/JEN
agamogenetic	AG/MO/JE/NET/IK	aggregometer	AG/RE/GOM/TER
	AI/GAM/JE/NET/IK	aggregometry	AG/RE/GOM/TRI
agamogony	AG/MOG/N*I	aggressin	AI/GRES/SIN
Agamomermis culicis	AG/MO/MER/MIS/KAOUL/SIS	aggression	AI/GREGS
agamont	AG/MONT	aggressive	AI/GRESZ/IV
agamous	AG/MOUS		AI/GRES/SIV
aganglionic	AI/GANG/LON/IK	aging	ALJ/-G
aganglionosis	AI/GANG/LO/NOE/SIS	agitata	AJ/TAI/TA
agapism	AG/PIFM	agitate	AJ/TAIT
agar	AG/AR	agitated	AJ/TAIT/-D
	AG/GAR	agitation	AJ/TAIGS
	AI/GAR	agitographia	AJ/TO/GRAF/YA
agaric	AI/GAR/IK	agitolalia	AJ/TO/LAIL/YA
	AG/AR/IK	agitophasia	AJ/TO/FAIZ/YA
	AG/GAR/IK	aglaucopsia	AI/GLAU/KOPS/YA
Agaricales	AI/GAR/KAI/LAOEZ	aglomerular	AI/GLOE/MER/LAR
agaricic	AI/GAR/IK/IK	aglossia	AI/GLOS/YA
	AI/GAR/IS/IK	aglossostomia	AI/GLOS/STOEM/YA
	AG/RIK/IK	aglucon	AI/GLAOU/KON
	AG/RIS/IK	aglucone	AI/GLAOU/KOEN
agaricinic	AI/GAR/SIN/IK	aglutition	AI/GLAOU/TIGS
Agaricus	AI/GAR/KUS		AG/LAOU/TIGS
agarose	AG/ROES	aglycemia	AI/GLAOI/SAOEM/YA
agastria	AI/GAS/TRA	aglycon	AI/GLAOI/KON
	AI/GAS/TRAOE/YA	aglycone	AI/GLAOI/KOEN
agastric	AI/GAS/TRIK	aglycosuria	AI/GLAOIK/SAOUR/YA
agastroneuria	AI/GAS/TRO/NAOUR/YA	aglycosuric	AI/GLAOIK/SAOUR/IK
Agave	AI/GAU/VAI	agmatology	AG/MA/TOLG
	AI/GAU/VAOE	agmen	AG/M*EN
	AI/GA/VAI		(not AG/MEN; see ago men)
	AI/GA/VAOE	agmina	AG/MI/NA
age	ALJ		AG/MIN/NA
agenesia	AI/JE/NAOEZ/YA	agminata	AG/MI/NAI/TA
	AJ/NAOEZ/YA	agminate	AG/MI/NAIT
agenesis	AI/JEN/SIS	agminated	AG/MI/NAIT/-D
agenitalism	AI/JEN/TAL/IFM	agnail	AG/NAIL
agenized	AI/JAOEN/AOIZ/-D	agnathia	AG/NA*IT/YA
	AI/JEN/AOIZ/-D	agnathous	AG/NAI/THOUS
	ALJ/NAOIZ/-D		AG/NA*IT/OUS
agenosomia	AI/JEN/SOEM/YA	agnathus	AG/NAI/THUS
	AI/J*EN/SOEM/YA	agnea	AG/NAOE/YA
agenosomus	AI/JEN/SOE/MUS	Agnew	AG/NAOU
	AI/J*EN/SOE/MUS	agni	AG/NAOI
agent	AGT	agnogenic	AG/NO/JEN/IK
	AI/JENT	agnosia	AG/NOEZ/YA
	ALJ/ENT		AG/NOES/YA
Agent Orange	AGT/ORN/-J	agnosis	AG/NOE/SIS
	AI/JENT/ORN/-J	agnosterol	AG/NO*S/ROL
	ALJ/ENT/ORN/-J		AG/NOS/TROL
agerasia	AI/JER/AIZ/YA	agofollin	AI/GOF/LIN
	AJ/RAIZ/YA	agomphiasis	AG/OM/FAOI/SIS
ageusia	AI/GAOUZ/YA		AI/GOM/FAOI/SIS
	AI/GAOUS/YA	agomphious	AI/GOM/FOUS
ageusic	AI/GAOUZ/IK		AI/GOM/FAOE/OUS
	AI/GAOUS/IK		AI/GOM/FAOE/YOUS
ageustia	AI/GAO*US/YA	agomphosis	AG/OM/FOE/SIS
agger	AJ/ER		AI/GOM/FOE/SIS
	AG/ER	agonad	AI/GOE/NAD
aggeres	AJ/RAOEZ	agonadal	AI/GON/DAL
	AG/RAOEZ	agonadism	AI/GON/DIFM
agglomerate	AI/GLOM/RAIT		AI/GOE/NA/DIFM
agglomerated	AI/GLOM/RAIT/-D		AI/GOE/NAD/IFM
agglomeration	AI/GLOM/RAIGS	agonal	AG/NAL
agglutinable	AI/GLAOUT/NABL	agoniadin	AG/NAOI/DIN
agglutinant	AI/GLAOUT/NANT	agonist	AG/N*IS
agglutination	AI/GLAOUT/NAIGS	agony	AG/N*I
agglutinative	AI/GLAOUT/NA/TIV	agoraphilia	AG/RA/FIL/YA
	AI/GLAOUT/NAIT/IV	agoraphobia	AG/RA/FOEB/YA
agglutinator	AI/GLAOUT/NAI/TOR		AI/GOR/FOEB/YA
agglutinin	AI/GLAOUT/NIN	agoraphobic	AG/RA/FOEB/IK
agglutinogen	AI/GLAOU/TIN/JEN		AI/GOR/FOEB/IK
	AG/LAOU/TIN/JEN	Agostini	AG/STAOE/NAOE
agglutinogenic	AI/GLAOUT/NO/JEN/IK		AG/OS/TAOE/NAOE
	AI/GLAOU/TIN/JEN/IK	agouti	AI/GAOU/TAOE
agglutinophilic	AI/GLAOUT/NO/FIL/IK	-agra	AG/RA
	AI/GLAOU/TIN/FIL/IK	agraffe	AI/GRAF
agglutinoscope	AI/GLAOUT/NO/SKOEP	agrammatica	AG/RA/MAT/KA
	AI/GLAOU/TIN/SKOEP		AI/GRA/MAT/KA
agglutogen	AI/GLAOU/TO/JEN	agrammatism	AI/GRAM/TIFM

agrammatologia	AI/GRAM/TO/LOE/JA	alanosine	AI/LAN/SAOEN
agranulo-	AI/GRAN/LO	Alanson	AL/LAN/SON
	AI/GRAN/YAOU/LO		AL/AN/SON
	AI/GRAN/YU/LO	alantin	AI/LAN/TIN
agranulocyte	AI/GRAN/LO/SAO*IT	alantol	AI/LAN/TOL
agranulocytic	AI/GRAN/LO/SIT/IK	alanyl	AL/NIL
agranulocytosis	AI/GRAN/LO/SAOI/TOE/SIS	alanyl-leucine	AL/NIL/LAOU/SIN
agranuloplastic	AI/GRAN/LO/PLA*S/IK	alar	AI/LAR
agraphia	AI/GRAF/YA		AL/LAR
agraphic	AI/GRAFK	alares	AL/LAI/RAOEZ
agria	AG/RAOE/YA	alaria	AI/LAIR/YA
	AI/GRAOE/YA	alaris	AI/LAI/RIS
agrius	AI/GRAOE/YUS	alastrim	AI/LAS/TRIM
	AG/RAOE/YUS		AI/LA*S/RIM
agromania	AG/RO/MAIN/YA	alastrimic	AL/AS/TRIM/IK
agrypnia	AI/GRIP/NA		AI/LAS/TRIM/IK
	AI/GRIP/NAOE/YA	alastrinic	AL/AS/TRIN/IK
agrypnocoma	AI/GRIP/NO/KO/MA		AI/LAS/TRIN/IK
	AI/GRIP/NO/KOE/MA	alata	AI/LAI/TA
agrypnodal	AI/GRIP/NOE/DAL	alate	AI/LAIT
agrypnode	AI/GRIP/NOED	alba	AL/BA
agrypnotic	AI/GRIP/NOT/IK	albae	AL/BAE
ague	AI/GAOU	Albarran	AL/BAR/RAN
agyria	AI/JAOIR/YA		AL/BA/RAN
agyric	AI/JAOIR/IK	albedo	AL/BAOE/DOE
ahaptoglobinemia	AI/HAPT/GLOEB/NAOEM/YA	Albee	AL/BAOE
ahistidasia	AI/H*IS/DAIZ/YA		(not AUL/BAOE; see Allbee)
A-hydroCort	ARBGS/HAOI/DRO/KORT	albendazole	AL/BEND/ZOEL
ahylognosia	AI/HAOI/LOG/NOES/YA	Albers	AL/BERZ
aichmophobia	AOIK/MO/FOEB/YA		AL/BERS
	AIK/MO/FOEB/YA	Albers-Schonberg	AL/BERZ/H-F/SHAIN/BERG
aid	AID		AL/BERZ/H-F/SHERN/BERG
AIDS	A*IDZ		AL/BERS/H-F/SHAIN/BERG
ailantic	AI/LANT/IK		AL/BERS/H-F/SHERN/BERG
	AIL/ANT/IK	Albert	AL/BERT
aileron	AIL/RON	Albertini	AL/BER/TAOE/NAOE
ailment	AIL/-MT	albicans	AL/BI/KANZ
ailurophilia	AI/LAOUR/FIL/YA	albicantia	AL/BI/KANT/YA
	AI/LAOU/RO/FIL/YA		AL/BI/KAN/SHA
ailurophobia	AI/LAOUR/FOEB/YA	albiceps	AL/BI/SEPS
	AI/LAOU/RO/FOEB/YA	albida	AL/BI/DA
ainhum	AOIN/YAOUM	albiduria	AL/BI/DAOUR/YA
	AOIN/YUM	albidus	AL/BI/DUS
	AIN/HUM	Albini	AL/BAOE/NAOE
	AOIN/HUM	albinism	AL/BI/NIFM
air	AIR		AL/BIN/IFM
Aird	AIRD	albinismus	AL/BI/NIZ/MUS
air sickness	AIR/SIK/*NS		AL/BI/NIS/MUS
airway	AIR/WA*I	albino	AL/BAOI/NOE
Ajellomyces	AI/JEL/MAOI/SAOEZ	albinoidism	AL/BI/NOI/DIFM
ajmaline	AJ/MA/LAOEN		AL/BI/NOID/IFM
ajowan oil	AJ/WAN/OIL	albinotic	AL/BI/NOT/IK
akamushi	AK/MAOU/SHAOE	albinuria	AL/BI/NAOUR/YA
akari	AK/RAOI	Albinus	AL/BAOI/NUS
akaryocyte	AK/KAR/YO/SAO*IT	albocinereous	AL/BO/SI/NAOER/YOUS
akaryota	AK/KAR/YOE/TA	albopictus	AL/BO/PIK/TUS
akaryote	AI/KAR/YOET	Albrecht	AL/BREKT
	AI/KAIR/YOET	Albright	AL/BRAOIGT
akatama	AK/TA/MA		AL/BRAOIT
	AK/TAM/MA	albuginea	AL/BAOU/JIN/YA
akembe	AI/KEM/BAOE	albugineotomy	AL/BAOU/JIN/YOT/M*I
Akerlund	EK/ER/LAOUND	albugineous	AL/BAOU/JIN/YOUS
	EK/ER/LUND	albuginitis	AL/BAOUJ/NAOITS
	AK/ER/LAOUND		AL/BAOU/JI/NAOITS
	AK/ER/LUND	albugo	AL/BAOU/GOE
akidogalvanocautery	AK/DO/GAL/VAN/KAUT/RI	albukalin	AL/BAOU/KAI/LIN
akinesia	AI/KI/NAOEZ/YA	albumen	AL/BAOU/MEN
akinesic	AI/KI/NAOEZ/IK		AL/BAOUM/EN
akinesis	AI/KI/NAOE/SIS		AL/BAOUM/-N
akinesthesia	AI/KINS/THAOEZ/YA	albumin	AL/BAOU/MIN
	AI/KIN/ES/THAOEZ/YA		AL/BAOUM/MIN
akinetic	AI/KI/NET/IK	albumin(o)-	AL/BAOUM/N(O)
Akineton	AI/KIN/TON	Albuminar	AL/BAOUM/NAR
aklomide	AK/LO/MAOID	Albuminar-5	AL/BAOUM/NAR/5
aknephascopia	AK/NEF/SKOEP/YA		AL/BAOUM/NAR/H-F/5
ala	AI/LA	Albuminar-25	AL/BAOUM/NAR/25
	AL/LA		AL/BAOUM/NAR/H-F/25
alacrima	AI/LAK/RI/MA	albuminate	AL/BAOUM/NAIT
alactasia	AI/LAK/TAIZ/YA	albuminaturia	AL/BAOUM/NA/TAOUR/YA
alae	AI/LAE		AL/BAOUM/NA/KHUR/YA
	AL/LAE	albuminemia	AL/BAOUM/NAOEM/YA
alaeque	AI/LAOE/KWAOE	albuminiferous	AL/BAOUM/NIF/ROUS
	AI/LAE/KWAOE	albuminimeter	AL/BAOUM/NIM/TER
alalia	AI/LAIL/YA	albuminimetry	AL/BAOUM/NIM/TRI
alalic	AI/LAL/IK	albuminiparous	AL/BAOUM/NIP/ROUS
alamecin	AL/MAOE/SIN	albuminocholia	AL/BAOUM/NO/KOEL/YA
alangine	AI/LAN/JAOEN	albuminocytologic	AL/BAOUM/NO/SAOIT/LOJ/IK
	AI/LAN/JIN	albuminocytological	AL/BAOUM/NO/SAOIT/LOJ/KAL
alanine	AL/NAOEN	albuminogenous	AL/BAOUM/NOJ/NOUS
		albuminoid	AL/BAOUM/NOID

albuminolysin	AL/BAOUM/NOL/SIN	aldose	AL/DOES
albuminolysis	AL/BAOUM/NOL/SIS	aldoside	AL/DO/SAOID
albuminometer	AL/BAOUM/NOM/TER	aldosterone	AL/DO*S/ROEN
albuminoptysis	AL/BAOUM/NOPT/SIS		AL/DO/STER/OEN
albuminoreaction	AL/BAOUM/NO/RE/A*BGS		AL/DO/STAOER/OEN
albuminorrhea	AL/BAOUM/NO/RAOE/YA	aldosteronism	AL/DO*S/RON/IFM
albuminous	AL/BAOUM/NOUS		AL/DO*S/ROEN/IFM
albuminuretic	AL/BAOUM/NAOU/RET/IK		AL/DO/STER/NIFM
albuminuria	AL/BAOUM/NAOUR/YA		AL/DO/STAOER/NIFM
albuminuric	AL/BAOUM/NAOUR/IK	aldosteronogenesis	AL/DO/STER/NO/JEN/SIS
albuminurinicus	AL/BAOUM/NAOU/RIN/KUS	aldosteronoma	AL/DO/STER/NOE/MA
	AL/BAOU/MIN/YAOU/RIN/KUS	aldosteronopenia	AL/DO/STER/NO/PAOEN/YA
albumoid	AL/BAOU/MOID	aldosteronuria	AL/DO/STER/NAOUR/YA
albumoscope	AL/BAOUM/SKOEP	aldotetrose	AL/DO/TET/ROES
-albumose	AL/BAOU/MOES	aldoxime	AL/DOK/SAOEM
Albutein	AL/BAOUT/YIN		AL/DOX/AOEM
	AL/BAOU/TAOEN		AL/DOK/SAOIM
albuterol	AL/BAOUT/ROL	Aldrich	AL/DRIFP
alcaligenes	AL/KLIJ/NAOEZ	aldrin	AL/DRIN
	AL/KA/LLJ/NAOEZ	alecithal	AI/LES/THAL
Alcaligenes	K-P/AL/KLIJ/NAOEZ	alemmal	AI/LEM/MAL
	K-P/AL/KA/LLJ/NAOEZ	alepric	AI/LEP/RIK
alchemy	AL/KE/M*I	aleprylic	AL/PRIL/IK
	AL/KEM/M*I	alethia	AI/LAO*ET/YA
alcian	ALS/YAN	aletocyte	AI/LAOE/TO/SAO*IT
Alcian blue	K-P/ALS/YAN/BLU		AI/LAOET/SAO*IT
alclofenac	AL/KLOEF/NAK	aleukemia	AI/LAOU/KAOEM/YA
	AL/KLOE/FEN/AK	aleukemic	AI/LAOU/KAOEM/IK
alclometazone	AL/KLO/MET/ZOEN	aleukia	AI/LAOUK/YA
Alcock	AL/KOK	aleukocytic	AI/LAOUK/SIT/IK
alcogel	AL/KO/JEL	aleukocytosis	AI/LAOUK/SAOI/TOE/SIS
alcohol	KHOL	aleurioconidium	AI/LAOUR/YO/KO/NID/YUM
	AL/KHOL	aleuriospore	AI/LAOUR/YO/SPOER
	AL/KO/HOL	aleurone	AI/YAOU/ROEN
alcoholate	AL/KHOL/AIT		AL/YU/ROEN
	AL/KO/HOL/AIT	aleuronoid	AI/LAOUR/NOID
	KHOL/AIT	Aleutian	AI/LAOUGS
alcoholemia	AL/KHOL/AOEM/YA	Alexander	AL/KPAND/ER
	AL/KO/HOL/AOEM/YA		AL/KPAN/DER
	KHOL/AOEM/YA	alexeteric	AI/LEX/TER/IK
alcoholic	AL/KHOL/IK	alexia	AI/LEX/YA
	KHOL/IK	alexic	AL/LEX/IK
alcoholica	AL/KHOL/KA	alexidine	AI/LEX/DAOEN
	KHOL/KA	alexin	AI/LEK/SIN
alcoholicum	AL/KHOL/KUM	alexinic	AL/EK/SIN/IK
	KHOL/KUM		AL/KPIN/IK
alcoholism	AL/KHOL/IFM	alexipharmac	AI/LEX/FAR/MAK
	KHOL/IFM		AI/LEK/SI/FAR/MAK
alcoholization	AL/KHOL/ZAIGS	alexithymia	AI/LEX/THAOIM/YA
	KHOL/ZAIGS	aleydigism	AI/LAOID/GIFM
alcoholize	AL/KHOL/AOIZ		AI/LAOI/DIG/IFM
	KHOL/AOIZ	alfacalcidol	AL/FA/KALS/DOL
alcoholometer	AL/KHOL/OM/TER	alfadolone acetate	AL/FAD/LOEN/AS/TAIT
	KHOL/OM/TER	alfaxalone	AL/FAX/LOEN
alcoholuria	AL/KHOL/YAOUR/YA	alfentanil hydrochloride	AL/FENT/NIL/HAOI/DRO/KLOR/
	KHOL/YAOUR/YA		AOID
alcoholysis	AL/KHOL/SIS	alga	AL/GA
	KHOL/SIS	algae	AL/JAE
alcuronium chloride	AL/KAOUR/OEN/YUM/KLOR/	algal	AL/GAL
	AOID	alganesthesia	AL/GANS/THAOEZ/YA
	AL/KAOU/ROEN/YUM/KLOR/		AL/GAN/ES/THAOEZ/YA
	AOID	algaroba	AL/GA/ROE/BA
Aldactazide	AL/DAKT/ZAOID		ALG/ROE/BA
	AL/DAK/TA/ZAOID	alge-	AL/JAOE
Aldactone	AL/DAK/TOEN		AL/JE
aldadiene	AL/DA/DI/AOEN		AL/J-
	ALD/DI/AOEN	algedonic	AL/JAOE/DON/IK
aldaric	AL/DAR/IK		AL/JE/DON/IK
aldeh-	ALD/H-	algefacient	AL/JAOE/FAIRBT
	AL/DE/H-		AL/JE/FAIRBT
aldehol	ALD/HOL	algeldrate	AL/JEL/DRAIT
aldehydase	ALD/HAOI/DAIS	algeoscopy	AL/JOS/KPI
	ALD/HAOID/AIS		AL/JAOE/OS/KPI
aldehyde	ALD/HAOID	algera	AL/JAOE/RA
aldehyde-lyase	ALD/HAOID/LAOI/AIS		AL/JE/RA
	ALD/HAOID/LAOI/YAIS	algesi(o)-	AL/JAOEZ/Y(O)
Alder	ALD/ER	algesia	AL/JAOEZ/YA
	AL/DER	algesic	AL/JAOEZ/IK
aldin	AL/DIN	algesichronometer	AL/JAOEZ/KROE/NOM/TER
aldobiuronic	AL/DO/B*I/YAOU/RON/IK	algesidystrophy	AL/JAOEZ/DIS/TRO/FI
Aldoclor	AL/DO/KLOR	algesimeter	AL/JE/SIM/TER
aldocortin	AL/DO/KOR/TIN		AL/JAOE/SIM/TER
aldohexose	AL/DO/HEK/SOES	algesimetry	AL/JE/SIM/TRI
	AL/DO/HEX/OES		AL/JAOE/SIM/TRI
aldolase	AL/DO/LAIS	algesiogenic	AL/JAOEZ/YO/JEN/IK
Aldomet	AL/DO/MET	algesiometer	AL/JAOEZ/YOM/TER
aldonic	AL/DON/IK	algesthesia	AL/JES/THAOEZ/YA
aldopentose	AL/DO/PEN/TOES	algesthesis	AL/JES/THAOE/SIS
Aldoril	AL/DO/RIL	algestone acetophenide	AL/JES/TOEN/AS/TO/FAOE/

	NAOID	alkalemia	AL/KLAOEM/YA
algetic	AL/JET/IK	alkalescence	AL/KLES/ENS
-algia	AL/JA	alkalescent	AL/KLES/ENT
algicide	AL/JI/SAO*ID	alkali	AL/KLAOI
algid	AL/JID	alkalify	AL/KAL/FI
algin	AL/JIN	alkaligenous	AL/KLIJ/NOUS
alginate	AL/JI/NAIT	alkalimeter	AL/KLIM/TER
alginic	AL/JIN/IK	alkalimetry	AL/KLIM/TRI
Alginobacter	AL/JI/NO/BAK/TER	alkaline	AL/KLAOIN
Alginomonas	AL/JI/NO/MOE/NAS		AL/KLIN
alginuresis	AL/JIN/YAOU/RAOE/SIS	alkalinity	AL/KLIN/TI
algi(o)-	AL/J(O)	alkalinization	AL/KLIN/ZAIGS
algioglandular	AL/JO/GLAND/LAR	alkalinize	AL/KLIN/AOIZ
algiometabolic	AL/JO/MET/BOL/IK	alkalinuria	AL/KLIN/YAOUR/YA
algiomotor	AL/JO/MOE/TOR	alkalitherapy	AL/KLAOI/THER/PI
algiomuscular	AL/JO/MUS/KLAR	alkalization	AL/KAL/ZAIGS
algiovascular	AL/JO/VAS/KLAR		AL/KLAOI/ZAIGS
Algisin	AL/JI/SIN	alkalize	AL/KLAOIZ
algo-	AL/GO	alkalizer	AL/KLAOIZ/ER
algodystrophy	AL/GO/DIS/TRO/FI	alkalogenic	AL/KLO/JEN/IK
algogenesia	AL/GO/JE/NAOEZ/YA	alkaloid	AL/KLOID
algogenesis	AL/GO/JEN/SIS	alkalometry	AL/KLOM/TRI
algogenic	AL/GO/JEN/IK	alkalosis	AL/KLOE/SIS
algoid	AL/GOID	alkalotherapy	AL/KLO/THER/PI
algolagnia	AL/GO/LAG/NA	alkalotic	AL/KLOT/IK
	AL/GO/LAG/NAOE/YA	alkaluria	AL/KLAOUR/YA
algologist	AL/GO*LGS	alkamine	AL/KA/MAOEN
algology	AL/GOLG		AL/KA/MIN
algometer	AL/GOM/TER	alkane	AL/KAIN
algometry	AL/GOM/TRI	alkanet	AL/KA/NET
algophilia	AL/GO/FIL/YA	alkapton	AL/KAP/TON
algophobia	AL/GO/FOEB/YA	alkaptonuria	AL/KAP/TO/NAOUR/YA
algopsychalia	AL/GO/SAOI/KAIL/YA	alkaptonuric	AL/KAP/TO/NAOUR/IK
algor	AL/GOR	Alka-Seltzer	AL/KA/SELT/SER
algorithm	AL/GO/R*IT/-M		AL/KA/SELT/ZER
algoscopy	AL/GOS/KPI	Alka-Seltzer Plus	AL/KA/SELT/SER/PLUS
algosis	AL/GOE/SIS		AL/KA/SELT/ZER/PLUS
algospasm	AL/GO/SPAFM	alkatriene	AL/KA/TR*I/AOEN
algovascular	AL/GO/VAS/KLAR		AL/KA/TRAOI/AOEN
alible	AL/-BL	alkavervir	AL/KA/VER/VIR
	AL/LIBL	alkene	AL/KAOEN
alices	AL/SAOEZ	alkenyl	AL/KENL
	AL/LI/SAOEZ		AL/KEN/IL
alicyclic	AL/SIK/LIK	Alkeran	AL/KER/RAN
	AL/LI/SIK/LIK		AL/KE/RAN
alienation	AL/YE/NAIGS	alkide	AL/KAOID
	AIL/YEN/NAIGS	alkyl	AL/KIL
	AIL/YEN/AIGS	alkylamine	AL/KIL/MAOEN
alienia	AI/LAOI/AOEN/YA		AL/KIL/AM/MIN
alienism	AIL/YEN/IFM		AL/KIL/AM/MAOEN
alienist	AIL/YEN/*IS	alkylate	AL/KLAIT
aliflurane	AL/FLAOU/RAIN		AL/KI/LAIT
aliform	AL/FORM	alkylating	AL/KLAIT/-G
alifurane	AL/FAOU/RAIN		AL/KI/LAIT/-G
alignment	AI/LAOIN/-MT	alkylation	AL/KLAIGS
aliment	AL/-MT		AL/KI/LAIGS
	AL/LIMT	alkylogen	AL/KIL/JEN
alimentarius	AL/MEN/TAIR/YUS	alkyne	AL/KAOIN
alimentary	AL/-MT/RI	allachesthesia	AL/KES/THAOEZ/YA
	AL/LIMT/RI	allanic	AI/LAN/IK
	AL/MEN/TRI	allantiasis	AL/AN/TAOI/SIS
	AL/MEN/TAIR		AL/LAN/TAOI/SIS
	AL/LIMT/TAIR	allanto-	AI/LAN/TO
alimentation	AL/MEN/TAIGS		AL/LAN/TO
	AL/-MT/TAIGS	allantochorion	AI/LAN/TO/KOER/YON
	AL/LIMT/TAIGS	allantogenesis	AI/LAN/TO/JEN/SIS
alimentology	AL/MEN/TOLG	allantoic	AL/AN/TOIK
	AL/-MT/TOLG		AL/AN/TOE/IK
	AL/LIMT/TOLG		AL/LAN/TOIK
alimentotherapy	AL/MENT/THER/PI		AL/LAN/TOE/IK
	AL/MEN/TO/THER/PI	allantoicase	AL/AN/TOI/KAIS
	AL/-MT/TO/THER/PI		AL/LAN/TOI/KAIS
alinasal	AL/NAI/ZAL	allantoid	AI/LAN/TOID
	AL/LI/NAI/ZAL	allantoidean	AI/LAN/TOID/YAN
alinjection	AL/IN/J*EBGS		AL/LANT/OID/YAN
alipamide	AI/LIP/MAOID	allantoido-	AL/AN/TOID
aliphatic	AL/FAT/IK		AL/AN/TOID
alipogenic	AI/LIP/JEN/IK		AL/LAN/TOID
alipoid	AI/LIP/OID		AL/LAN/TOI/DO
alipoidic	AI/LIP/OID/IK		AI/LAN/TOI/DO
alipotropic	AI/LIP/TROP/IK		AI/LAN/TOI/DO
aliquant	AL/KWANT	allantoidoangiopagous	AL/AN/TOID/AN/JOP/GOUS
aliquot	AL/KWOT		AL/LAN/TOID/AN/JOP/GOUS
alisphenoid	AL/SFAOE/NOID	allantoidoangiopagus	AL/AN/TOID/AN/JOP/GUS
alizarin	AI/LIZ/RIN		AL/LAN/TOID/AN/JOP/GUS
alizarinopurpurin	AL/ZAR/NO/PURP/RIN	allantoin	AI/LANT/WIN
alkadiene	AL/KA/DI/AOEN		AL/LANT/WIN
alkal(o)-	AL/KL(O)	allantoinase	AL/LAN/TOE/NAIS
	AL/KA/L(O)		AL/LAN/TOI/NAIS

	AI/LAN/TOE/NAIS	allo-	AL/LO (for readability)
	AI/LAN/TOI/NAIS		AL
allantoinuria	AI/LANT/WIN/YAOUR/YA		AI/LO
	AI/LANT/WIN/YAOUR/YA	alloalbuminemia	AL/LO/AL/BAOUM/NAOEM/YA
allantois	AI/LAN/WIS		AL/AL/BAOUM/NAOEM/YA
allanturic	AL/AN/TAOUR/IK	alloantibody	AL/LO/A*ENT/BOD/DI
	AI/LAN/TAOUR/IK		AL/LO/ANT/BOD/DI
	AI/LAN/TAOUR/IK		AL/A*ENT/BOD/DI
allassotherapy	AI/LAS/THER/PI		AL/ANT/BOD/DI
	AI/LAS/SO/THER/PI	alloantigen	AL/LO/A*ENT/JEN
allaxis	AI/LAK/SIS		AL/LO/ANT/JEN
Allbee	AUL/BAOE		AL/A*ENT/JEN
	(not AL/BAOE; see Albee)		AL/ANT/JEN
allel(o)-	AI/LAOEL	alloantiserum	AL/LO/A*ENT/SAOERM
	AI/LAOE/L(O)		AL/LO/ANT/SAOERM
	AI/LAOEL		AL/A*ENT/SAOERM
	AI/LAOE/L(O)		AL/ANT/SAOERM
allele	AL/LAOEL	alloarthroplasty	AL/LO/AR/THRO/PLAS/TI
	AI/LAOEL		AL/AR/THRO/PLAS/TI
allelic	AI/LAOEL/IK	allobar	AL/LO/BAR
allelism	AL/LIFM		AL/BAR
allelocatalysis	AI/LAOEL/KA/TAL/SIS	allobarbital	AL/LO/BARB/TAL
allelocatalytic	AI/LAOEL/KAT/LIT/IK		AL/BARB/TAL
allelochemics	AI/LAOEL/KEM/IK/-S	allobiosis	AL/LO/BAO*I/YOE/SIS
allelomorph	AI/LAOEL/MOR-F		AL/BAO*I/YOE/SIS
allelomorphic	AI/LAOEL/MOR/FIK	allocentric	AL/LO/SEN/TRIK
allelomorphism	AI/LAOEL/MOR/FIFM		AL/SEN/TRIK
allelotaxis	AI/LAOEL/TAK/SIS	allocheiral	AL/LO/KAOIRL
allelotaxy	AI/LAOEL/TAK/SI		AL/LO/KAOI/RAL
Allen	AL/EN		AL/KAOIRL
	AL/LEN		AL/KAOI/RAL
	AL/-N	allocheiria	AL/LO/KAOIR/YA
Allerdryl	AL/ER/DRIL		AL/KAOIR/YA
	AL/LER/DRIL	allochesthesia	AL/LO/KES/THAOEZ/YA
Allerest	AL/R*ES		AL/KES/THAOEZ/YA
	AL/ER/R*ES	allochetia	AL/LO/KAOE/SHA
allerg(o)-	AI/LERG		AL/KAOE/SHA
	AL/ERG	allochezia	AL/LO/KAOEZ/YA
	AI/LERG		AL/KAOEZ/YA
	AI/LER/G(O)	allocholane	AL/LO/KOE/LAIN
	AL/LER/G(O)		AL/KOE/LAIN
allergen	AL/ER/JEN	allocholesterol	AL/LO/KL*ES/ROL
	AL/LER/JEN		AL/KL*ES/ROL
allergenic	AL/ER/JEN/IK	allochroic	AL/LO/KROIK
	AL/LER/JEN/IK		AL/LO/KROE/IK
allergic	AI/LERJ/IK		AL/KROIK
allergid	AL/ER/JID		AL/KROE/IK
	AL/LER/JID	allochroism	AL/LO/KROE/IFM
allergin	AL/ER/JIN		AL/KROE/IFM
	AL/LER/JIN	allochromacy	AL/LO/KROEM/SI
allergist	AL/ER/J*IS		AL/KROEM/SI
	AL/LER/J*IS	allochromasia	AL/LO/KROE/MAIZ/YA
allergization	AL/ERJ/ZAIGS		AL/KROE/MAIZ/YA
	AL/ERJ/JI/ZAIGS	allocinesia	AL/LO/SI/NAOEZ/YA
	AI/LERJ/ZAIGS		AL/SI/NAOEZ/YA
allergize	AL/ER/JAOIZ	allocolloid	AL/LO/KOL/OID
	AL/LER/JAOIZ		AL/LO/KLOID
allergodermia	AL/ERG/DERM/YA		AL/KOL/OID
	AL/LERG/DERM/YA		AL/KLOID
allergological	AL/ERG/LOJ/KAL	allocortex	AL/LO/KOR/TEX
	AL/LERG/LOJ/KAL		AL/KOR/TEX
allergologist	AL/ER/GO*LGS	allocortol	AL/LO/KOR/TOL
	AL/LER/GO*LGS		AL/KOR/TOL
allergology	AL/ER/GOLG	allocortolone	AL/LO/KORT/LOEN
	AL/LER/GOLG		AL/KORT/LOEN
allergosis	AL/ER/GOE/SIS	allocrine	AL/LO/KRIN
	AL/LER/GOE/SIS		AL/KRIN
allergy	AL/ER/JI	allocytophilic	AL/LO/SAOIT/FIL/IK
	AL/LER/JI		AL/SAOIT/FIL/IK
Allescheria	AL/ES/KAOER/YA	allodesmism	AL/LO/DES/MIFM
	AL/LES/KAOER/YA		AL/DES/MIFM
allesthesia	AL/ES/THAOEZ/YA	allodiploid	AL/LO/DIP/LOID
	AL/LES/THAOEZ/YA		AL/DIP/LOID
allethrin	AL/THRIN	allodiploidy	AL/LO/DIP/LOI/DI
	AI/LE/THRIN		AL/DIP/LOI/DI
allethrolone	AI/L*ET/RO/LOEN	allodynia	AL/LO/DIN/YA
alliaceous	AL/YAIRBS		AL/DIN/YA
alligation	AL/LI/GAIGS	alloerotic	AL/LO/E/ROT/IK
	A*L/GAIGS		AL/E/ROT/IK
	(not AL/GAIGS; see allegation)	alloeroticism	AL/LO/E/ROT/SIFM
alligator	AL/GAI/TOR		AL/E/ROT/SIFM
Allingham	AL/-G/HAM	alloerotism	AL/LO/ER/TIFM
	AL/LING/HAM		AL/LO/*ER/TIFM
Allis	AL/LIS		AL/ER/TIFM
alliteration	AI/LIT/RAIGS		AL/*ER/TIFM
allithiamine	AL/THAOI/MIN	allogamy	AL/OG/M*I
	AL/THAOI/MAOEN		AL/LOG/M*I
allium	AL/YUM		AI/LOG/M*I
Allium	K-P/AL/YUM	allogeneic	AL/LO/JE/NAOE/IK

	AL/LO/JE/NAI/IK	alloploidy	AL/LO/PLOI/DI
	AL/JE/NAOE/IK		AL/PLOI/DI
	AL/JE/NAI/IK	allopolyploid	AL/LO/POL/PLOID
allogenic	AL/LO/JEN/IK		AL/POL/PLOID
	AL/JEN/IK	allopolyploidy	AL/LO/POL/PLOI/DI
allogotrophia	AL/GO/TROEF/YA		AL/POL/PLOI/DI
allograft	AL/LO/GRAFT	allopregnane	AL/LO/PREG/NAIN
	AL/GRAFT		AL/PREG/NAIN
allogroup	AL/LO/GROUP	allopregnanediol	AL/LO/PREG/NAIN/DI/OL
	AL/LO/GRAOUP		AL/LO/PREG/NAIN/DI/YOL
	AL/GROUP		AL/PREG/NAIN/DI/OL
	AL/GRAOUP		AL/PREG/NAIN/DI/YOL
allohexaploid	AL/LO/HEX/PLOID	allopregnenolone	AL/LO/PREG/NEN/LOEN
	AL/HEX/PLOID		AL/PREG/NEN/LOEN
alloimmune	AL/LO/IM/MAOUN	allopsychic	AL/LO/SAOIK/IK
	AL/IM/MAOUN		AL/SAOIK/IK
alloimmunization	AL/LO/IM/NI/ZAIGS	allopsychosis	AL/LO/SAOI/KOE/SIS
	AL/IM/NI/ZAIGS		AL/SAOI/KOE/SIS
alloisomer	AL/LO/AOIS/MER	allopurinol	AL/LO/PAOUR/NOL
	AL/AOIS/MER		AL/PAOUR/NOL
alloisomerism	AL/LO/AOI/SOM/RIFM	allorhythmia	AL/LO/R*IT/MA
	AL/AOI/SOM/RIFM		AL/LO/R*IT/MAOE/YA
allokeratoplasty	AL/LO/KER/TO/PLAS/TI		AL/R*IT/MA
	AL/KER/TO/PLAS/TI		AL/R*IT/MAOE/YA
allokinesis	AL/LO/KI/NAOE/SIS	allorhythmic	AL/LO/R*IT/MIK
	AL/KI/NAOE/SIS		AL/R*IT/MIK
allokinetic	AL/LO/KI/NET/IK	allorphine	AL/LOR/FAOEN
	AL/KI/NET/IK	allose	AL/LOES
allolactose	AL/LO/LAK/TOES		AL/OES
	AL/LAK/TOES	allosensitization	AL/LO/SENS/TI/ZAIGS
allolalia	AL/LO/LAIL/YA		AL/SENS/TI/ZAIGS
	AL/LAIL/YA	allosome	AL/LO/SOEM
allomerism	AI/LOM/RIFM		AL/SOEM
	AL/LOM/RIFM	allosteric	AL/LO/STER/IK
allometric	AL/LO/MET/RIK		AL/STER/IK
	AL/MET/RIK	allotetraploid	AL/LO/TET/RA/PLOID
allometron	AL/LO/MET/RON		AL/TET/RA/PLOID
	AL/LO/ME/TRON	allotherm	AL/LO/THERM
	AL/MET/RON		AL/THERM
	AL/ME/TRON	allotope	AL/LO/TOEP
allometry	AI/LOM/TRI		AL/TOEP
	AL/LOM/TRI	allotopia	AL/LO/TOEP/YA
allomorphism	AL/LO/MOR/FIFM		AL/TOEP/YA
	AL/MOR/FIFM	allotopic	AL/LO/TOP/IK
allongement	AI/LON/-J/-MT		AL/TOP/IK
	AL/ON/-J/-MT	allotoxin	AL/LO/TOK/SIN
allonic	AI/LON/IK		AL/TOK/SIN
	AL/LON/IK	allotransplantation	AL/LO/TRA*NS/PLAN/TAIGS
allonomous	AI/LON/MOUS		AL/TRA*NS/PLAN/TAIGS
	AL/LON/MOUS	allotrichia circumscripta	AL/LO/TRIK/YA/SIR/KUM/SKRIP/
allopath	AL/LO/PA*T		TA
	AL/PA*T		AL/TRIK/YA/SIR/KUM/SKRIP/TA
allopathic	AL/LO/PA*T/IK	allotrio-	AI/LOT/RO
	AL/PA*T/IK		AI/LOT/RAOE/YO
allopathist	AL/LOP/TH*IS	allotriodontia	AI/LOT/RO/DON/SHA
	AL/LOP/TH*IS	allotriogeustia	AI/LOT/RO/GAO*US/YA
	AI/LOP/TH*IS	allotriolith	AI/LOT/RO/L*IT
allopathy	AL/LOP/TH*I	allotriophagia	AI/LOT/RO/FAI/JA
	AL/LOP/TH*I	allotriophagy	AI/LOT/ROF/JI
	AI/LOP/TH*I	allotriosmia	AI/LOT/ROZ/MAOE/YA
allopentaploid	AL/LO/PENT/PLOID	allotriploid	AL/LO/TRIP/LOID
	AL/PENT/PLOID		AL/TRIP/LOID
allophanamide	AL/LO/FAN/AM/ID	allotriuria	AI/LOT/RAOE/YAOUR/YA
	AL/FAN/AM/ID		AI/LOT/RAOUR/YA
allophanate	AL/LO/FAN/AIT	allotrope	AL/LO/TROEP
	AL/FAN/AIT		AL/TROEP
allophanic	AL/LO/FAN/IK	allotrophic	AL/LO/TROEFK
	AL/FAN/IK		AL/LO/TROFK
allophasis	AL/OF/SIS		AL/TROEFK
	AL/LOF/SIS		AL/TROFK
	AI/LOF/SIS	allotropic	AL/LO/TROP/IK
allophenic	AL/LO/FAOEN/IK		AL/TROP/IK
	AL/FAOEN/IK	allotropism	AI/LOT/RO/PIFM
allophore	AL/LO/FOER	allotropy	AI/LOT/RO/PI
	AL/FOER	allotrylic	AL/LO/TRIL/IK
allophthalmia	AL/OF/THAL/MA		AL/TRIL/IK
	AL/OF/THAL/MAOE/YA	allotype	AL/LO/TAOIP
alloplasia	AL/LO/PLAIZ/YA		AL/TAOIP
	AL/PLAIZ/YA	allotypic	AL/LO/TIP/IK
alloplasmatic	AL/LO/PLAZ/MAT/IK		AL/TIP/IK
	AL/PLAZ/MAT/IK	allotypy	AL/LO/TAOI/PI
alloplast	AL/LO/PLA*S		AL/TAOI/PI
	AL/PLA*S	alloxan	AL/LOK/SAN
alloplastic	AL/LO/PLA*S/IK		AI/LOK/SAN
	AL/PLA*S/IK	alloxanic	AL/LO/ZAN/IK
alloplasty	AL/LO/PLAS/TI	alloxantin	AL/LOK/SAN/TIN
	AL/PLAS/TI		AI/LOX/AN/TIN
alloploid	AL/LO/PLOID		AL/LOK/SAN/TIN
	AL/PLOID	alloxazine	AI/LOX/ZAOEN

alloxur	AL/OK/SAOUR	alpha1-antitrypsin	AL/FA/1/A*ENT/TRIP/SIN
	AL/LOK/SAOUR	alpha-blocker	AL/FA/BLOK/ER
	AI/LOK/SAOUR	alpha-dinitrophenol	AL/FA/DI/NAOI/TRO/FAOE/NOL
alloxuremia	AL/OK/SAOU/RAOEM/YA	alphadione	AL/FA/DI/OEN
	AL/OX/YAOU/RAOEM/YA	alphadolone acetate	AL/FAD/LOEN/AS/TAIT
	AI/LOK/SAOU/RAOEM/YA	alpha-estradiol	AL/FA/ES/TRA/DI/OL
	AI/LOX/YAOU/RAOEM/YA	alpha-fetoprotein	AL/FA/FAOET/PRO/TAOEN
alloxuria	AL/OX/YAOUR/YA	alpha-2 globulin	AL/FA/2/GLOB/LIN
	AL/OK/SAOUR/YA	alpha-hypophamine	AL/FA/HAOI/POF/MIN
	AL/LOK/SAOUR/YA	Alpha Keri	AL/FA/KER/RAOE
alloxuric	AL/OK/SAOUR/IK		AL/FA/KER/RI
	AL/OX/SAOUR/IK	Alphaketoglutaric Acid	AL/FA/KAOET/GLAOU/TAR/IK/AS/
	AL/LOK/SAOUR/IK		ID
	AI/LOK/SAOUR/IK	alphalipoproteinemia	AL/FA/LIP/PROET/NAOEM/YA
alloxyproteic	AL/OX/PRO/TAOE/IK		AL/FA/LIP/PRO/TAOEN/AOEM/YA
	AL/OX/PRO/TAI/IK	alpha-lobeline	AL/FA/LOEB/LAOEN
	AI/LOX/PRO/TAOE/IK		AL/FA/LOB/LAOEN
	AI/LOX/PRO/TAI/IK		AL/FA/LOEB/LIN
alloy	AL/LOI		AL/FA/LOB/LIN
alloyage	AL/LOIJ	alphalytic	AL/FA/LIT/IK
	AI/LOIJ	alphamimetic	AL/FA/MAOI/MET/IK
	AL/LOI/AJ	alphanaphthol	AL/FA/NAF/THOL
	AI/LOI/AJ	Alpha Plus	AL/FA/PLUS
allspice	AL/SPAOIS	alphaprodine	AL/FA/PRO/DAOEN
all-trans-retinal	AUL/TRA*NS/RET/NAL		AL/FA/PROE/DAOEN
	AUL/H-F/TRA*NS/H-F/RET/NAL	alpharsonic	AL/FAR/SON/IK
allulose	AL/YAOU/LOES	alphasone	AL/FA/SOEN
	AL/YU/LOES	alpha-tocopherol	AL/FA/TOE/KOF/ROL
alluranic	AL/YAOU/RAN/IK	alphatoluic	AL/FA/TOL/YAOU/IK
	AL/YU/RAN/IK		AL/FA/TOL/YIK
allyl	AL/IL	Alphatrex	AL/FA/TREX
	AL/LIL	alpha-tropeine	AL/FA/TROEP/YIN
allyl-	AL/IL	Alphavirus	AL/FA/VAOI/RUS
	AL/LIL	alphos	AL/FOS
allylamine	AL/IL/AM/AOEN	alprazolam	AL/PRAIZ/LAM
	AL/IL/AM/MIN		AL/PRAZ/LAM
allylbarbital	AL/IL/BARB/TAL	alprenolol	AL/PREN/LOL
allylestrenol	AL/IL/ES/TRE/NOL	alprostadil	AL/PRO*S/DIL
allylguaiacol	AL/IL/GAOI/KOL	alrestatin sodium	AL/RE/STAT/TIN/SOED/YUM
allylmercaptomethylpenicillin		Alsberg	ALS/BERG
	AL/IL/MER/KAPT/M*ET/IL/PEN/		ALZ/BERG
	SLIN	alseroxylon	AL/SER/OX/LON
	AL/IL/MER/KAPT/M*ET/IL/PEN/	Alstrom	AL/STROM
	SIL/LIN		AL/STRUM
allylnormorphine	AL/IL/NOR/MOR/FAOEN	alter	AL/TER
allysine	AL/LI/SAOEN		ALT/ER
	AL/SAOEN	alterant	ALT/RANT
almadrate sulfate	AL/MA/DRAIT/SUL/FAIT		AL/TER/ANT
Almeida	AL/MAI/DA		AL/TRANT
	AL/MAOE/DA	alterego	AL/TER/E/GOE
Almen	AL/MAIN	alteregoism	AL/TER/E/GO/IFM
almond	AL/MOND		AL/TER/E/GOE/IFM
	AU/MOND		AL/TER/AOEG/IFM
almoner	AL/MO/NER	ALternaGEL	AL/TER/NA/JEL
alochia	AI/LOEK/YA	alternans	AL/TER/NANZ
aloe	AL/LOE	Alternaria	AL/TER/NAIR/YA
	AI/LOE	alternariatoxicosis	AL/TER/NAIR/YA/TOX/KOE/SIS
Aloe	K-P/AL/LOE	alternating	AL/TER/NAIT/-G
	K-P/AI/LOE	alternation	AL/TER/NAIGS
aloe-emodin	AL/LOE/EM/DIN	alternocular	AL/TER/NOK/LAR
aloetic	AL/WET/IK	Althaea	AL/THAE/YA
	AL/LO/ET/IK	Althausen	ALT/HOUZ/EN
	AL/LOE/ET/IK		ALT/HOU/ZEN
alogia	AI/LOE/JA		ALT/HOUZ/-N
aloin	AL/WIN	althea	AL/THAOE/YA
	AL/LO/WIN	Althea	K-P/AL/THAOE/YA
	AL/LOE/WIN	althiazide	AL/THAOI/ZAOID
alonimid	AI/LON/MID	altitude	ALT/TAOUD
alopecia	AL/PAOE/SHA	altitudinal	ALT/TAOUD/NAL
	AL/PAOES/YA	Altmann	ALT/MAN
alopecic	AL/PAOES/IK	Altmann-Gersh	ALT/MAN/H-F/GER/-RB
Alouette	AL/LAOU/WET	altofrequent	AL/TO/FRAOE/KWENT
	AL/WET		AL/TO/FRAOEKT
aloxanthin	AL/OK/SAN/THIN	altricious	AL/TRIRBS
aloxiprin	AI/LOX/PRIN	altrigendrism	AL/TRI/JEN/DRIFM
Alper	AL/PER	altronic	AL/TRON/IK
Alpers	AL/PERZ	altrose	AL/TROES
	AL/PERS	Alu-Cap	AL/YAOU/KAP
alpertine	AL/PER/TAOEN		AL/YU/KAP
alpha	AL/FA	Aludrox	AL/YAOU/DROX
alpha-adrenergic	AL/FA/AD/RE/NERJ/IK		AL/YU/DROX
	AL/FA/AI/DRE/NERJ/IK	alum	AL/UM
	AL/FA/AD/REN/ERJ/IK		AL/LUM
alpha-allocortol	AL/FA/AL/LO/KOR/TOL	alumen	AI/LAOUM/-N
	AL/FA/AL/KOR/TOL		AI/LAOUM/EN
alpha-allocortolone	AL/FA/AL/LO/KORT/LOEN		AI/LAOU/MEN
	AL/FA/AL/KORT/LOEN	alum-hematoxylin	AL/UM/HAOEM/TOX/LIN
alpha amylase	AL/FA/AM/LAIS		AL/UM/HEM/TOX/LIN
alpha-amylose	AL/FA/AM/LOES	alumina	AI/LAOUM/NA

aluminated	AI/LAOUM/NAIT/-D		AM/RAN/THUM
aluminium	AL/YAOU/MIN/YUM	amarga	AI/MAR/GA
	AL/YU/MIN/YUM	amarine	AM/RIN
	AL/MIN/YUM	amaroid	AM/ROID
aluminon	AI/LAOUM/NON	amaroidal	AM/ROI/DAL
aluminosis	AI/LAOUM/NOE/SIS	amarthritis	AM/AR/THRAOITS
aluminum	AI/LAOUM/NUM	amarum	AI/MAR/UM
alundum	AI/LUN/DUM		AI/MA/RUM
Alupent	AL/YAOU/PENT	amasesis	AM/SAOE/SIS
	AL/YU/PENT		AI/MA/SAOE/SIS
Alurate	AL/YAOU/RAIT	amasthenic	AM/AS/THEN/IK
	AL/YU/RAIT	amastia	AI/MA*S/YA
Alu-Tab	AL/YAOU/TAB	amastigote	AI/MA*S/GOET
	AL/YU/TAB	amathophobia	AI/MA*T/FOEB/YA
alve(o)-	AL/VAOE	amativeness	AM/TIV/*NS
	AL/VAOE/Y(O)	Amato	AI/MA/TOE
	AL/VO		AI/MAT/TOE
alvei	AL/VAOE/YAOI	amatol	AM/TOL
	AL/VAOI	amaurosis	AM/AU/ROE/SIS
alveoalgia	AL/VAOE/AL/JA		AM/ROE/SIS
	AL/VO/AL/JA	amaurotic	AM/AU/ROT/IK
alveobronchiolitis	AL/VAOE/BRONG/YO/LAOITS		AM/ROT/IK
	AL/VO/BRONG/YO/LAOITS	amaxophobia	AI/MAK/SO/FOEB/YA
alveol(o)-	AL/VAOE/L(O)		AI/MAX/FOEB/YA
alveolalgia	AL/VAOE/LAL/JA	amazia	AI/MAIZ/YA
alveolar	AL/VAOE/LAR	ambageusia	AM/BA/GAOUS/YA
alveolare	AL/VAOE/LAI/RAOE	Ambard	AM/BARD
alveolares	AL/VAOE/LAI/RAOEZ		(not AM/BAR, regardless of
alveolaris	AL/VAOE/LAI/RIS		pronunciation)
alveolate	AL/VAOE/LAIT	ambenonium	AM/BAOE/NOEN/YUM
alveolectomy	AL/VAOE/LEKT/M*I		AM/BE/NOEN/YUM
alveoli	AL/VAOE/LAOI	amber	AM/BER
alveolingual	AL/VAOE/LING/WAL	Ambenyl	AM/BENL
	AL/VO/LING/WAL		AM/BEN/IL
alveolitis	AL/VAOE/LAOITS		AM/BE/NIL
alveolocapillary	AL/VAOE/LO/KAP/LAIR	Ambenyl-D	AM/BENL/D-RBGS
alveoloclasia	AL/VAOE/LO/KLAIZ/YA		AM/BEN/IL/D-RBGS
alveolodental	AL/VAOE/LO/DEN/TAL		AM/BE/NIL/D-RBGS
alveololabial	AL/VAOE/LO/LAIB/YAL	Amberg	AM/BERG
alveololabialis	AL/VAOE/LO/LAIB/YAI/LIS	ambergris	AM/BER/GRIS
alveolingual	AL/VAOE/LO/LING/WAL	ambi-	AM/BI
alveolomerotomy	AL/VAOE/LO/ME/ROT/M*I	ambidexterity	AM/BI/DEX/TER/TI
alveolonasal	AL/VAOE/LO/NAI/ZAL	ambidextrality	AM/BI/DEX/TRAL/TI
alveolopalatal	AL/VAOE/LO/PAL/TAL		AM/BI/D*EX/RAL/TI
alveoloplasty	AL/VAOE/LO/PLAS/TI	ambidextrism	AM/BI/DEX/TRIFM
alveoloschisis	AL/VAOE/LOS/KI/SIS		AM/BI/D*EX/RIFM
alveolotomy	AL/VAOE/LOT/M*I	ambidextrous	AM/BI/DEX/TROUS
alveolus	AL/VAOE/LUS	ambiens	AM/BAOE/YENZ
alveoplasty	AL/VAOE/PLAS/TI		AM/BI/YENZ
	AL/VO/PLAS/TI	ambient	AM/BAOENT
alverine	AL/VE/RAOEN		AM/BI/ENT
alveus	AL/VAOE/YUS		AM/BI/YENT
alvine	AL/VIN	ambiguous	AM/BIG/YOUS
alvus	AL/VUS	ambilateral	AM/BI/LAT/RAL
alymphia	AI/LIM/FAOE/YA	ambilevosity	AM/BI/LE/VOS/TI
	AI/LIM/FA	ambilevous	AM/BI/LAOE/VOUS
alymphocytosis	AI/LIM/FO/SAOI/TOE/SIS		AM/BI/LAOEV/OUS
alymphoplasia	AI/LIM/FO/PLAIZ/YA	ambiopia	AM/BI/OEP/YA
alymphopotent	AI/LIM/FO/POE/TENT	ambisexual	AM/BI/SEX/YAOUL
Alzheimer	ALZ/HAOIM/ER	ambisinister	AM/BI/SIN/STER
	ALS/HAOIM/ER		AM/BI/SINS/TER
	ALTS/HAOIM/ER	ambisinistrous	AM/BI/SI/NIS/TROUS
a.m.	A*M		AM/BI/SNIS/TROUS
ama	AI/MA	ambivalence	AM/BIV/LENS
amacratic	AM/KRAT/IK	ambivalent	AM/BIV/LENT
amacrinal	AM/KRAOINL	ambiversion	AM/BI/VERGS
	AM/KRINL	ambivert	AM/BI/VERT
amacrine	AM/KRIN	ambly-	AM/BLI
amadinone	AI/MAD/NOEN	amblyaphia	AM/BLI/AIF/YA
amae	AI/MAE	amblychromasia	AM/BLI/KROE/MAIZ/YA
amalgam	AI/MAL/GAM	amblychromatic	AM/BLI/KROE/MAT/IK
amalgam-	AI/MALG/M-	amblygeustia	AM/BLI/GAO*US/YA
	AI/MAL/GA/M-	Amblyomma	AM/BLI/OM/MA
amalgamable	AI/MALG/MABL	amblyope	AM/BLI/OEP
amalgamate	AI/MALG/MAIT	amblyopia	AM/BLI/OEP/YA
amalgamation	AI/MALG/MAIGS		AM/BLOEP/YA
amalgamator	AI/MALG/MAI/TOR	amblyopiatrics	AM/BLI/OEP/YAT/RIK/-S
amalic	AI/MAL/IK	amblyopic	AM/BLI/OEP/IK
Amanita	AM/NAOI/TA	amblyoscope	AM/BLI/YO/SKOEP
amanitine	AM/NAOI/TIN		AM/BLO/SKOEP
amanitotoxin	AI/MAN/TO/TOK/SIN		AM/BLI/SKOEP
Amann's test	AI/MAN/AOES/T*ES		AM/BLAOE/SKOEP
amantadine	AI/MANT/DAOEN	ambo	AM/BOE
	AI/MAN/TA/DAOEN	ambo-	AM/BO
amara	AI/MAR/RA	amboceptor	AM/BO/SEP/TOR
	AI/MA/RA	amboceptorgen	AM/BO/SEP/TOR/JEN
amaranth	AM/RA*NT	ambomalleal	AM/BO/MAL/YAL
Amaranth	K-P/AM/RA*NT	ambomycin	AM/BO/MAOI/SIN
amaranthum	AM/RA*NT/UM	ambon	AM/BON

ambos	AM/BOES	amelus	AM/LUS
ambrettolic	AM/BRET/TOL/IK	amenia	AI/MAOEN/YA
ambrin	AM/BRIN	amenorrhea	AI/MEN/RAOE/YA
ambrosin	AM/BROE/SIN	amenorrheal	AI/MEN/RAOE/YAL
ambruticin	AM/BRAOU/TAOI/SIN		AI/MEN/RAOEL
ambucetamide	AM/BAOU/SET/MAOID	amenorrheic	AI/MEN/RAOE/IK
ambulance	AM/BLANS	amensalism	AI/MENS/LIFM
	PWLANS		AI/MEN/SAL/IFM
ambulant	AM/BLANT	amentia	AI/MEN/SHA
	AM/BAOU/LANT	amential	AI/MEN/-RBL
ambulation	AM/BLAIGS	Americaine	AI/MER/KAIN
	AM/BAOU/LAIGS	americana	AI/MER/KAI/NA
ambulatory	AM/BLA/TOIR	americanum	AI/MER/KAI/NUM
ambuphylline	AM/BAOUF/LIN		AI/MER/KAIN/UM
	AM/BAOUF/LAOEN	americanus	AI/MER/KAI/NUS
ambustion	AM/BUGS	americium	AM/RIS/YUM
ambutoxate	AM/BAOU/TOK/SAIT	amerism	AM/RIFM
amcinafal	AM/SIN/FAL	ameristic	AM/R*IS/IK
amcinafide	AM/SIN/FAOID	Ames	AIMZ
amcinonide	AM/SIN/NAOID		AIMS
	AM/SIN/NID	ametabolon	AI/ME/TAB/LON
ameba	AI/MAOE/BA	ametabolous	AI/ME/TAB/LOUS
amebacidal	AI/MAOE/BA/SAOI/DAL	ametachromophil	AI/MET/KROEM/FIL
	(*not* AI/MAOEB/SAOI/DAL; see	amethocaine	AI/M*ET/KAIN
	amebicidal)	amethopterin	AI/M*ET/OPT/RIN
amebacide	AI/MAOE/BA/SAO*ID		AI/M*ET/TER/RIN
	(*not* AI/MAOEB/SAO*ID; see		AM/THOPT/RIN
	amebicide)	ametria	AI/MAOE/TRAOE/YA
amebadiastase	AI/MAOE/BA/DI/AS/TAIS		AI/MAOE/TRA
amebaism	AI/MAOE/BA/IFM	ametriodinic acid	AI/MAOE/TRO/DIN/IK/AS/ID
amebae	AI/MAOE/BAE		AI/MAOE/TRAOE/YO/DIN/IK/AS/
ameban	AI/MAOE/BAN		ID
amebiasis	AI/MAOE/BAOI/SIS	ametrometer	AM/TROM/TER
	AM/BAOI/SIS	ametropia	AM/TROEP/YA
amebic	AI/MAOEB/IK	ametropic	AM/TROEP/IK
amebicidal	AI/MAOEB/SAOI/DAL		AM/TROP/IK
amebicide	AI/MAOEB/SAO*ID	amfenac	AM/FE/NAK
amebiform	AI/MAOEB/FORM	amfonelic	AM/FO/NEL/IK
amebiosis	AI/MAOE/BAO*I/YOE/SIS	amiantaceous	AM/YAN/TAIRBS
	AM/BAO*I/YOE/SIS	amianthoid	AM/YAN/THOID
amebism	AI/MAOE/BIFM		AM/YA*NT/OID
	AI/MAOEB/IFM	amibiarson	AM/BI/AR/SOEN
	AM/BIFM		AM/BI/AR/SON
amebocyte	AI/MAOE/BO/SAO*IT	Amicar	A*M/KAR
	AI/MAOEB/SAO*IT		AM/MI/KAR
amebodiastase	AI/MAOE/BO/DI/AS/TAIS		(*not* AM/KAR)
ameboid	AI/MAOE/BOID	amichloral	AM/KLORL
ameboididity	AI/MAOE/BOI/DID/TI		AM/KLOR/RAL
ameboidism	AI/MAOE/BOI/DIFM	Amici	AI/MAOE/KHAOE
	AI/MAOE/BOID/IFM	amicine	AM/MI/SIN
ameboma	AM/BOE/MA		(*not* AM/SIN)
	A/MAOE/BOE/MA	amicrobic	AI/MAOI/KROEB/IK
amebosis	AM/BOE/SIS	amicroscopic	AI/MAOI/KRO/SKOP/IK
	AI/MAOE/BOE/SIS	amiculum	AI/MIK/LUM
amebula	AI/MAOEB/LA		AI/MIK/YAOU/LUM
	AI/MAOEB/YAOU/LA		AI/MIK/YU/LUM
	AI/MAOEB/YU/LA	Amida	AM/MI/DA
amebulae	AI/MAOEB/LAE		AM/DA
	AI/MAOEB/YAOU/LAE	amidapsone	AM/DAP/SOEN
	AI/MAOEB/YU/LAE	amidase	AM/DAIS
amebule	AI/MAOEB/BAOUL	amide	AM/AOID
	AI/MAOEB/YAOUL		AM/ID
ameburia	AM/BAOUR/YA	amidin	AM/DIN
	AI/MAOE/BAOUR/YA	amidine	AM/DAOEN
amedalin	AI/MAOED/LIN	amidine-lyase	AM/DAOEN/LAOI/AIS
	AI/MED/LIN		AM/DAOEN/LAOI/YAIS
ameiosis	AI/MAO*I/YOE/SIS	amidinohydrolase	AM/DIN/HAOI/DRO/LAIS
	(*not* AI/MAOI/YOE/SIS; see miosis)	amidinotransferase	AM/DIN/TRA*NS/FRAIS
amelanotic	AI/MEL/NOT/IK		AM/DIN/TRA*NS/FER/AIS
amelia	AI/MAOEL/YA	amido-	AM/DO
amelification	AI/MEL/FI/KAIGS	amidoazotoluene	AM/DO/A*Z/TOL/YAOEN
amelioration	AI/MAOEL/YO/RAIGS		AM/DO/A*Z/TOL/YAOU/AOEN
	AI/MAOEL/YOR/RAIGS	amidobenzene	AM/DO/BEN/ZAOEN
amelo-	AI/MEL	amidogen	AM/DO/JEN
	AM/LO*	amidohexose	AM/DO/HEX/OES
	AM/ME/LO		AM/DO/HEK/SOES
	(*not* AM/LO; see amylo-)	amidohydrolase	AM/DO/HAOI/DRO/LAIS
ameloblast	AI/MEL/BLA*S	amido-ligase	AM/DO/LAOI/GAIS
	AM/LO*/BLA*S	amidonaphthol	AM/DO/NAF/THOL
ameloblastoma	AI/MEL/BLAS/TOE/MA	amidopyrine	AM/DO/PAOI/RAOEN
	AM/LO*/BLAS/TOE/MA	Amidostomum anseris	AM/DO*S/MUM/ANS/RIS
amelodentinal	AM/LO*/DENT/NAL		AM/DO*S/MUM/AN/SER/RIS
	AI/MEL/DENT/NAL	amidoxime	AM/DOK/SAOIM
amelogenesis	AM/LO*/JEN/SIS		AM/DOK/SAOEM
	AI/MEL/JEN/SIS	amidulin	AI/MID/LIN
amelogenic	AM/LO*/JEN/IK		AI/MID/YAOU/LIN
	AI/MEL/JEN/IK		AI/MID/YU/LIN
amelogenin	AM/LO*/JEN/NIN	amikacin sulfate	AM/KAI/SIN/SUL/FAIT
	AI/MEL/JEN/NIN	Amikin	AM/MI/KIN

	(not AM/KIN)	aminoheterocyclic	AI/MAOEN/HET/RO/SAOIK/LIK
amiloride hydrochloride	AI/MIL/RAOID/HAOI/DRO/KLOR/		AI/MAOEN/HET/RO/SIK/LIK
	AOID		AM/NO/HET/RO/SAOIK/LIK
amimia	AI/MIM/YA		AM/NO/HET/RO/SIK/LIK
aminacrine	AM/NAK/RIN	aminohippurate	AI/MAOEN/HIP/RAIT
aminarsone	AM/NAR/SOEN		AM/NO/HIP/RAIT
aminate	AM/NAIT	aminohippuric	AI/MAOEN/HI/PAOUR/IK
amine	AI/MAOEN		AI/MAOEN/HIP/PAOUR/IK
	AM/MIN		AM/NO/HI/PAOUR/IK
	AM/AOEN		AM/NO/HIP/PAOUR/IK
-aminergic	AM/NERJ/IK	aminoimidazole	AI/MAOEN/IM/ID/A*Z/OEL
aminitrozole	AM/NAOI/TRO/ZOEL		AI/MAOEN/IM/MID/A*Z/OEL
amino acid	AI/MAOE/NOE/AS/ID		AM/NO/IM/DAZ/OEL
	AI/MAOEN/AS/ID	aminoisobutyric	AI/MAOEN/AOIS/BAOU/TIR/IK
amino-	AI/MAOEN		AM/NO/AOIS/BAOU/TIR/IK
	AI/MAOE/NO	aminoisometradine	AI/MAOEN/AOIS/MET/RA/DAOEN
	AM/NO		AM/NO/AOIS/MET/RA/DAOEN
aminoacetate	AI/MAOEN/AS/TAIT	Aminolete	AM/NO/LAOET
	AM/NO/AS/TAIT		AI/MAOEN/LAOET
aminoacetic	AI/MAOEN/AI/SAOET/IK	aminolevulinate	AI/MAOEN/LEV/LIN/AIT
	AI/MAOEN/AI/SET/IK		AI/MAOEN/LEV/LI/NAIT
	AM/NO/AI/SAOET/IK		AM/NO/LEV/LIN/AIT
	AM/NO/AI/SET/IK		AM/NO/LEV/LI/NAIT
aminoacidemia	AI/MAOEN/AS/DAOEM/YA	aminolevulinic	AI/MAOEN/LEV/LIN/IK
	AM/NO/AS/DAOEM/YA		AM/NO/LEV/LIN/IK
aminoacidopathy	AI/MAOEN/AS/DOP/TH*I	aminolipid	AI/MAOEN/LIP/ID
	AM/NO/AS/DOP/TH*I		AM/NO/LIP/ID
aminoaciduria	AI/MAOEN/AS/DAOUR/YA	aminolipin	AI/MAOEN/LIP/PIN
	AM/NO/AS/DAOUR/YA		AM/NO/LIP/PIN
aminoacridine	AI/MAOEN/AK/RI/DAOEN	aminolysis	AM/NOL/SIS
	AM/NO/AK/RI/DIN	aminometradine	AI/MAOEN/MET/RA/DAOEN
aminoacyl	AI/MAOEN/AS/IL		AM/NO/MET/RA/DAOEN
aminoacyladenylate	AI/MAOEN/AS/LA/DEN/LAIT	aminometramide	AI/MAOEN/MET/RA/MAOID
	AI/MAOEN/AS/IL/AI/DEN/LAIT		AM/NO/MET/RA/MAOID
aminoacylase	AI/MAOEN/AS/LAIS	Aminomine	AM/NO/MAOEN
	AM/NO/AS/LAIS		AI/MAOEN/MAOEN
aminoadipic	AI/MAOEN/AI/DIP/IK	aminonitrogen	AI/MAOEN/NAOI/TRO/JEN
aminoazotoluene	AI/MAOEN/A*Z/TOL/YAOEN		AM/NO/NAOI/TRO/JEN
	AI/MAOEN/A*Z/TOL/YAOU/AOEN	aminonitrothiazole	AI/MAOEN/NAOI/TRO/THAOI/
	AM/NO/A*Z/TOL/YAOEN		ZOEL
	AM/NO/A*Z/TOL/YAOU/AOEN		AM/NO/NAOI/TRO/THAOI/ZOEL
aminobenzene	AI/MAOEN/BEN/ZAOEN	aminopentamide	AI/MAOEN/PENT/MAOID
	AM/NO/BEN/ZAOEN		AM/NO/PENT/MAOID
aminobenzenesulfonamide	AI/MAOEN/BEN/ZAOEN/SUL/	aminopeptidase	AI/MAOEN/PEPT/DAIS
	FON/MAOID		AM/NO/PEPT/DAIS
	AM/NO/BEN/ZAOEN/SUL/FON/	aminophenazone	AI/MAOEN/FEN/ZOEN
	MAOID		AM/NO/FEN/ZOEN
aminobenzoate	AI/MAOEN/BENZ/WAIT	aminophenol	AI/MAOEN/FAOE/NOL
	AM/NO/BENZ/WAIT		AM/NO/FAOE/NOL
aminobenzoic	AM/NO/BEN/ZOIK	aminopherase	AI/MAOEN/FER/AIS
	AM/NO/BEN/ZOE/IK		AM/NOF/RAIS
aminobetahydroxypropionic		aminophylline	AI/MAOEN/FLIN
	AI/MAOEN/BAIT/HAOI/DROX/		AI/MAOEN/FIL/LIN
	PROEP/YON/IK		AM/NOF/LIN
	AM/NO/BAIT/HAOI/DROX/PROEP/	Aminoplex	AM/NO/PLEX
	YON/IK		AI/MAOEN/PLEX
aminobutyrate	AI/MAOEN/BAOUT/RAIT	aminopolypeptidase	AI/MAOEN/POL/PEPT/DAIS
	AM/NO/BAOUT/RAIT		AM/NO/POL/PEPT/DAIS
aminobutyric	AI/MAOEN/BAOU/TIR/IK	aminopromazine	AI/MAOEN/PROEM/ZAOEN
	AM/NO/BAOU/TIR/IK		AM/NO/PROEM/ZAOEN
aminocaproic	AI/MAOEN/KA/PROIK	aminopropionic	AI/MAOEN/PROEP/YON/IK
	AI/MAOEN/KA/PROE/IK		AM/NO/PROEP/YON/IK
	AM/NO/KA/PROIK	aminopropiophenone	AI/MAOEN/PROEP/YO/FAOE/
	AM/NO/KA/PROE/IK		NOEN
aminocarbonyl	AM/NO/KARB/NIL		AM/NO/PROEP/YO/FAOE/NOEN
	AM/NO/KAR/BO/NIL	aminopterin	AM/NOPT/RIN
Amino-Cerv	AM/NO/SEFRB	aminopteroylglutamic	AM/NOPT/ROIL/GLAOU/TAM/IK
	AI/MAOEN/SEFRB	aminopurine	AI/MAOEN/PAOU/RAOEN
aminodeltaguanidovaleric	AI/MAOEN/DELT/GAUN/DO/VA/		AI/MAOEN/PAOUR/AOEN
	LER/IK		AI/MAOEN/PAOU/RIN
	AM/NO/DELT/GAUN/DO/VA/LER/		AI/MAOEN/PAOUR/RIN
	IK		AM/NO/PAOU/RAOEN
aminodinitrophenol	AI/MAOEN/DI/NAOI/TRO/FAOE/		AM/NO/PAOUR/AOEN
	NOL		AM/NO/PAOU/RIN
	AM/NO/DI/NAOI/TRO/FAOE/NOL		AM/NO/PAOUR/RIN
aminoethanoic	AI/MAOEN/*ET/NOIK	aminopyridine	AM/NO/PIR/DAOEN
	AI/MAOEN/*ET/NOE/IK		AI/MAOEN/PIR/DAOEN
	AM/NO/*ET/NOIK	aminopyrine	AM/NO/PAOI/RAOEN
	AM/NO/*ET/NOE/IK		AI/MAOEN/PAOI/RAOEN
aminoethanol	AI/MAOEN/*ET/NOL		AM/NO/PAOI/RIN
	AM/NO/*ET/NOL		AI/MAOEN/PAOI/RIN
aminoform	AI/MIN/FORM	aminorex	AI/MIN/REX
	AI/MAOEN/FORM	aminosaccharide	AI/MAOEN/SAK/RAOID
aminoglutaric	AI/MAOEN/GLAOU/TAR/IK		AM/NO/SAK/RAOID
	AM/NO/GLAOU/TAR/IK	aminosalicylate	AI/MAOEN/SAL/SIL/AIT
aminoglutethimide	AI/MAOEN/GLAOU/T*ET/MAOID		AM/NO/SAL/SIL/AIT
	AM/NO/GLAOU/T*ET/MAOID	aminosalicylic	AM/NO/SAL/SIL/IK
aminoglycoside	AM/NO/GLAOIK/SAOID		AI/MAOEN/SAL/SIL/IK
aminogram	AI/MAOEN/GRAM	aminosidine	AI/MAOEN/SAOI/DIN

	AI/MAOEN/SAOI/DAOEN	amnion	AM/NAOE/YOE/MA
	AM/NO/SAOI/DIN		AM/NAOE/YON
	AM/NO/SAOI/DAOEN		(not AM/NON)
Aminosine	AM/NO/SAOEN	amnionic	AM/NAOE/YON/IK
	AI/MAOEN/SAOEN		AM/NON/IK
aminosis	AM/NOE/SIS	amnionitis	AM/NAOE/NAOITS
Aminostasis	AM/NO/STAI/SIS	amniorrhea	AM/NO/RAOE/YA
	AI/MAOEN/STAI/SIS	amniorrhexis	AM/NO/REK/SIS
aminostiburia	AI/MAOEN/STAOI/BAOUR/YA	amnios	AM/NAOE/YOS
	AM/NO/STAOI/BAOUR/YA		AM/NAOE/OS
aminosuccinic	AI/MAOEN/SUK/SIN/IK		(not AM/NOS)
	AM/NO/SUK/SIN/IK	amnioscope	AM/NO/SKOEP
aminosuria	AI/MAOEN/SAOUR/YA		AM/NAOE/SKOEP
	AM/NO/SAOUR/YA	amnioscopy	AM/NOS/KPI
Aminotate	AM/NO/TAIT		AM/NAOE/OS/KPI
amino-terminal	AI/MAOEN/TERM/NAL	Amniota	AM/NAOE/YOE/TA
aminothiazole	AI/MAOEN/THAOI/ZOEL		AM/NOE/TA
	AI/MAOEN/THAOI/ZOL	amniote	AM/NAOE/YOET
	AM/NO/THAOI/ZOEL		AM/NAOE/OET
	AM/NO/THAOI/ZOL	amniotic	AM/NAOE/YOT/IK
aminotransferase	AI/MAOEN/TRA*NS/FRAIS		AM/NOT/IK
	AM/NO/TRA*NS/FRAIS	amniotome	AM/NO/TOEM
aminotrate	AM/NO/TRAIT	amniotomy	AM/NAOE/YOT/M*I
	AI/MAOEN/TRAIT		AM/NOT/M*I
aminotriazole	AM/NO/TR*I/ZOL	amobarbital	AM/BARB/TAL
	AM/NO/TR*I/ZOEL		AM/MO/BARB/TAL
	AM/NO/TRAOI/ZOL	A-mode	ARBGS/MOED
	AM/NO/TRAOI/ZOEL		ARBGS/H-F/MOED
aminovaleric	AI/MAOEN/VA/LER/IK	amodiaquine	AM/DAOI/KWIN
	AM/NO/VA/LER/IK		AM/MO/DAOI/KWIN
Aminoxin	AM/NOK/SIN	amoeba	AI/MAO*E/BA
aminuria	AM/NAOUR/YA		(not AI/MAOE/BA; see ameba)
amiodarone	AI/MAOE/YO/DA/ROEN	Amoeba	K-P/AI/MAO*E/BA
	AI/MAOE/DA/ROEN	amoebae	AI/MAO*E/BAE
amiphenazole	AM/FEN/ZOEL		(not AI/MAOE/BAE; see amebae)
amiquinsin	AM/KWIN/SIN	amoebic	AI/MAO*EB/IK
amisometradine	AM/AOIS/MET/RA/DAOEN		(not AI/MAOEB/IK; see amebic)
	AM/SO/MET/RA/DAOEN	Amoebida	AI/MAOEB/DA
amithiozone	AM/THAOI/ZOEN		AI/MAO*EB/DA
amitosis	AM/TOE/SIS	Amoebobacter	AI/MAOEB/BAK/TER
	AI/MAOI/TOE/SIS		AI/MAOE/BO/BAK/TER
amitotic	AM/TOT/IK		AI/MAO*E/BO/BAK/TER
	AI/MAOI/TOT/IK	Amoebotaenia	AI/MAOE/BO/TAOEN/YA
amitriptyline	AM/TRIPT/LAOEN		AI/MAOE/BO/TAEN/YA
ammeter	AM/MAOET/ER		AI/MAO*E/BO/TAOEN/YA
	AM/MAOE/TER		AI/MAO*E/BO/TAEN/YA
Ammi	AM/MAOE	amok	AI/MOK
ammoaciduria	AM/MO/AS/DAOUR/YA	Amomum	AI/MOE/MUM
Ammon	AM/MON	amopyroquin	AM/PAOIR/KWIN
ammonemia	AM/NAOEM/YA	amor	AI/MOR
ammonia	AI/MOEN/YA	amorph	AI/MOR/-F
ammoniac	AI/MOEN/YAK	amorpha	AI/MOR/FA
ammoniacal	AM/NAOI/KAL	amorphagnosia	AI/MOR/FAG/NOES/YA
	AM/MO/NAOI/KAL		AI/MOR/FAG/NOEZ/YA
ammonia-lyase	AI/MOEN/YA/LAOI/AIS	amorphia	AI/MOR/FAOE/YA
	AI/MOEN/YA/LAOI/YAIS		(not AI/MOR/FA; see amorpha)
ammoniate	AI/MOEN/YAIT	amorphic	AI/MOR/FIK
ammoniated	AI/MOEN/YAIT/-D	amorphinism	AI/MOR/FI/NIFM
ammoniemia	AM/MOEN/YAOEM/YA		AI/MOR/FIN/IFM
ammonification	AI/MOEN/FI/KAIGS	amorphism	AI/MOR/FIFM
ammonioferric	AI/MOEN/YO/FER/IK	amorphosynthesis	AI/MOR/FO/S*INT/SIS
ammonirrhea	AI/MOEN/RAOE/YA		AI/MOR/FO/SIN/THE/SIS
ammonium	AI/MOEN/YUM	amorphous	AI/MOR/FOUS
ammoniuria	AI/MOEN/YAOUR/YA	amorphus	AI/MOR/FUS
ammonolysis	AM/MO/NOL/SIS	Amoss	AI/MOSZ
	AI/MOE/NOL/SIS	amotio	AI/MOE/SHOE
	(not AM/NOL/SIS; see aminolysis)		AI/MOERB/YOE
ammonotelic	AI/MOE/NO/TEL/IK	amoxapine	AI/MOX/PAOEN
	AI/MOEN/TEL/IK	amoxicillin	AI/MOX/SLIN
amnalgesia	AM/NAL/JAOEZ/YA		AI/MOX/SIL/LIN
amnemonic	AM/NE/MON/IK	Amoxil	AI/MOK/SIL
amnemonica	AM/NE/MON/KA		AI/MOX/IL
amnesia	AM/NAOEZ/YA	amperage	AFRP/RAJ
	AM/NAOE/SHA		AM/PER/AJ
amnesiac	AM/NAOEZ/YAK		AM/PRAJ
amnesic	AM/NAOEZ/IK		AM/PAOER/AJ
amnestic	AM/N*ES/IK	ampere	AM/PAOER
amni(o)-	AM/NO	Ampere	K-P/AM/PAOER
	AM/NAOE	ampereometry	AM/PAOER/OM/TRI
	AM/NAOE/Y(O)	amphamphoterodiplopia	AM/FAM/FOET/RO/DI/PLOEP/YA
	AM/NAOE/YAOI		AM/FAM/FOT/RO/DI/PLOEP/YA
amnii	AM/NO/SAO*EL	ampheclexis	AM/FE/KLEK/SIS
amniocele	AM/NO/SEN/TAOE/SIS	amphetamine	AM/FET/MAOEN
amniocentesis	AM/NO/KOER/YAL	amphi-	AM/FI
amniochorial	AM/NO/KOER/YON/IK	amphiarkyochrome	AM/FI/ARK/YO/KROEM
amniochorionic	AM/NO/JEN/SIS	amphiarthrodial	AM/FI/AR/THROED/YAL
amniogenesis	AM/NOG/FI	amphiarthroses	AM/FI/AR/THROE/SAOEZ
amniography	AM/NAOE/OG/FI	amphiarthrosis	AM/FI/AR/THROE/SIS
amnioma	AM/NOE/MA	amphiaster	AM/FI/A*S/ER

	AM/FI/AS/TER		AM/FO/TRIS/TI
amphibaric	AM/FI/BAR/IK	amphoterism	AM/FOET/RIFM
Amphibia	AM/FIB/YA		AM/FOT/RIFM
amphibious	AM/FIB/YOUS	amphoterodiplopia	AM/FOT/RO/DI/PLOEP/YA
amphiblastic	AM/FI/BLA*S/IK	amphoterous	AM/FOT/ROUS
amphiblastula	AM/FI/BLA*S/LA	amphotonia	AM/FO/TOEN/YA
amphiblestritis	AM/FI/BLES/TRAOITS	amphotony	AM/FOT/N*I
amphiblestrodes	AM/FI/BLES/TROE/DAOEZ	ampicillin	AFRP/SLIN
amphibolic	AM/FI/BOL/IK		AFRP/SIL/LIN
amphibolous	AM/FIB/LOUS	amplexation	AM/PLEK/SAIGS
amphicarcinogenic	AM/FI/KARS/NO/JEN/IK		AM/PLEX/AIGS
amphicelous	AM/FI/SE/LOUS	amplexus	AM/PLEK/SUS
	AM/FI/SAOEL/OUS	amplification	AM/PLIF/KAIGS
amphicentric	AM/FI/SEN/TRIK		AFRP/LIF/KAIG
amphichroic	AM/FI/KROIK		AFRP/FI/KAIGS
	AM/FI/KROE/IK	amplifier	AM/PLI/FI/ER
amphichromatic	AM/FI/KROE/MAT/IK		AFRP/LI/FI/ER
amphicrania	AM/FI/KRAIN/YA		AFRP/FI/ER
amphicreatine	AM/FI/KRAOE/TIN		AFRP/FI
	AM/FI/KRAOE/YA/TIN	amplitude	AM/PLI/TAOUD
amphicreatinine	AM/FI/KRAOE/YAT/NIN		AFRP/TAOUD
	AM/FI/KRAOE/YAT/NAOEN		AFRP/LI/TAOUT
	AM/FI/KRAOE/AT/NIN	amplum	AM/PLUM
	AM/FI/KRAOE/AT/NAOEN	amprotropine	AM/PRO/TROE/PAOEN
amphicyte	AM/FI/SAO*IT	ampule	AM/PAOUL
amphicytula	AM/FI/SIT/LA		AFRP/YAOUL
	AM/FI/SIT/YAOU/LA	ampulla	AM/PUL/LA
	AM/FI/SIT/YU/LA	ampullae	AM/PUL/LAE
amphidiarthrosis	AM/FI/DI/AR/THROE/SIS	ampullar	AM/PUL/LAR
amphidiploid	AM/FI/DIP/LOID	ampullaria	AFRP/LAIR/YA
amphigastrula	AM/FI/GAS/TRAOU/LA		AM/PUL/LAIR/YA
	AM/FI/GA*S/RAOU/LA	ampullaris	AFRP/LAI/RIS
amphigenetic	AM/FI/JE/NET/IK		AFRP/LAR/RIS
amphigonadism	AM/FI/GON/DIFM		AM/PUL/LAI/RIS
amphigonium	AM/FI/GOEN/YUM		AM/PUL/LAR/RIS
amphigony	AM/FIG/N*I	ampullary	AFRP/LAIR
amphikaryon	AM/FI/KAR/YON		AM/PUL/LAIR
Amphileptus	AM/FI/LEP/TUS	ampullate	AM/PUL/LAIT
amphileukemic	AM/FI/LAOU/KAOEM/IK		AM/PUL/AIT
Amphimerus	AM/FIM/RUS	ampullitis	AFRP/LAOITS
amphimicrobe	AM/FI/MAOI/KROEB		AM/PUL/LAOITS
amphimixis	AM/FI/MIK/SIS		AM/PUL/AOITS
amphimorula	AM/FI/MOR/LA	ampullula	AM/PUL/YAOU/LA
amphinucleolus	AM/FI/NAOU/KLAOE/LUS		AM/PUL/YU/LA
amphinucleus	AM/FI/NAOUK/LUS		(not AM/PUL/LA; see ampulla)
Amphioxus	AM/FI/OK/SUS	amputate	AFRP/TAIT
amphipath	AM/FI/PA*T		AM/PAOU/TAIT
amphipathic	AM/FI/PA*T/IK	amputation	AFRP/TAIGS
amphiphilic	AM/FI/FIL/IK		AM/PAOU/TAIGS
amphiphobic	AM/FI/FOEB/IK	amputee	AFRP/TAOE
amphipyrenin	AM/FI/PAOIR/NIN		AM/PAOU/TAOE
Amphistoma	AM/F*IS/MA	amrinone	AM/RI/NOEN
amphistome	AM/FIS/TOEM	Amsler	AM/SLER
amphistomiasis	AM/FI/STOE/MAOI/SIS		AMS/LER
Amphistomum	AM/F*IS/MUM	Amsterdam	AM/STER/DAM
amphitene	AM/FI/TAOEN		AMS/TER/DAM
amphitheater	AM/FI/THAOE/TER	amuck	AI/MUK
amphithymia	AM/FI/THAOIM/YA	amusia	AI/MAOUZ/YA
amphitrichate	AM/FIT/RI/KAIT	Amussat	AM/MAOU/SA
amphitrichous	AM/FIT/RI/KOUS		AI/MAOU/SA
amphitypy	AM/FIT/PI	amyasthenia	AI/MAOI/AS/THAOEN/YA
amphixenosis	AM/FIX/NOE/SIS	amyasthenic	AI/MAOI/AS/THEN/IK
ampho-	AM/FO	amychophobia	AM/KO/FOEB/YA
amphochromatophil	AM/FO/KROE/MAT/FIL		AI/MAOI/KO/FOEB/YA
amphochromatophile	AM/FO/KROE/MAT/FAOIL		AI/MAOIK/FOEB/YA
amphochromophil	AM/FO/KROEM/FIL	amyctic	AI/MIKT/IK
amphochromophile	AM/FO/KROEM/FAOIL	amyelencephalia	AI/MAOIL/EN/SFAIL/YA
amphocyte	AM/FO/SAO*IT		AI/MAOI/LEN/SFAIL/YA
amphodiplopia	AM/FO/DI/PLOEP/YA	amyelencephalic	AI/MAOIL/EN/SFAL/IK
amphogenetic	AM/FO/JE/NET/IK		AI/MAOI/LEN/SFAL/IK
amphogenic	AM/FO/JEN/IK	amyelencephalus	AI/MAOIL/EN/SEF/LUS
Amphojel	AM/FO/JEL		AI/MAOI/LEN/SEF/LUS
	AM/FO/J*EL	amyelia	AI/MAOI/AOEL/YA
ampholyte	AM/FO/LAOIT	amyelic	AI/MAOI/EL/IK
amphomycin	AM/FO/MAOI/SIN		AI/MAOI/AOEL/IK
amphophil	AM/FO/FIL	amyelinated	AI/MAOI/LI/NAIT/-D
amphophile	AM/FO/FAOIL		AI/MAOI/LIN/AIT/-D
amphophilic	AM/FO/FIL/IK	amyelination	AI/MAOI/LI/NAIGS
amphophilous	AM/FOF/LOUS		AI/MAOI/LIN/AIGS
amphoric	AM/FOER/IK	amyelinic	AI/MAOI/LIN/IK
amphoricity	AM/FO/RIS/TI	amyeloic	AI/MAOI/LOIK
	AM/FRIS/TI		AI/MAOI/LOE/IK
amphoriloquy	AM/FO/RIL/KWI	amyelonic	AI/MAOI/LON/IK
	AM/FRIL/KWI	amyelotrophy	AI/MAOI/LOT/RO/FI
amphorophony	AM/FO/ROF/N*I	amyelous	AI/MAOI/LOUS
	AM/FROF/N*I	amyelus	AI/MAOI/LUS
amphoteric	AM/FO/TER/IK	amygdal(o)-	AI/MIGD/L(O)
amphotericin	AM/FO/TER/SIN		AI/MIG/DL(O)
amphotericity	AM/FO/TER/IS/TI		AI/MIG/DA/L(O)

amygdala	AI/MIGD/LA	amyous	AM/YOUS
amygdalae	AI/MIGD/LAE	amyxia	AI/MIX/YA
amygdalase	AI/MIGD/LAIS	amyxorrhea	AI/MIX/RAOE/YA
amygdalic	AI/MIGD/LIK	an(o)-	AI/N(O)
amygdalin	AI/MIGD/LIN		AIN
amygdaline	AI/MIGD/LAOEN		AN/N(O)
	AI/MIGD/LAOIN	ana	AN/NA
amygdaloid	AI/MIGD/LOID	ana-	AN
amygdaloideum	AI/MIGD/LOID/YUM		AN/NA
amygdalophenin	AI/MIGD/LOF/NIN		AI/NA
amygdalose	AI/MIGD/LOES	Anabaena	AN/BAOE/NA
amygdaloside	AI/MIGD/LO/SAOID		AN/BAE/NA
amyl	AI/MIL	anabasia	AN/BAIZ/YA
	AM/MIL		AN/BAIS/YA
	(not AM/IL; see am ill)	anabasine	AI/NAB/SIN
amyl(o)-	AM/L(O)	anabasis	AI/NAB/SIS
amylacea	AM/LAIS/YA	anabatic	AN/BAT/IK
	AM/LAI/SHA	anabiosis	AN/BAO*I/YOE/SIS
	AM/LAIRB/YA	anabiotic	AN/BAO*I/OT/IK
amylaceous	AM/LAIRBS	anabolergy	AN/BOL/ER/JI
amylase	AM/LAIS	anabolic	AN/BOL/IK
amylasuria	AM/LAIS/YAOUR/YA	anabolin	AI/NAB/LIN
	AM/LAI/SAOUR/YA	anabolism	AI/NAB/LIFM
amylatic	AM/LAT/IK	anabolistic	AI/NAB/L*IS/IK
amylemia	AM/LAOEM/YA	anabolite	AI/NAB/LAOIT
amylene	AM/MI/LAOEN	anacamptic	AN/KAFRP/TIK
	(not AM/LAOEN; see am lean)		AN/KAFRPT/IK
amylenization	AM/LEN/ZAIGS		AN/KAM/TIK
amylic	AI/MIL/IK	anacamptometer	AN/KAFRP/TOM/TER
amylin	AM/LIN		AN/KAM/TOM/TER
amylism	AM/LIFM	anacardic	AN/KARD/IK
amylobarbitone	AM/LO/BARB/TOEN	Anacardium	AN/KARD/YUM
amylocaine hydrochloride	AM/LO/KAIN/HAOI/DRO/KLOR/	anacardiol	AN/KARD/YOL
	AOID	anacardol	AN/KAR/DOL
amylocellulose	AM/LO/SEL/YAOU/LOES	anacatadidymus	AN/KAT/DID/MUS
amyloclast	AM/LO/KLA*S	anacatesthesia	AN/KAT/ES/THAOEZ/YA
amyloclastic	AM/LO/KLA*S/IK	anachoresis	AN/KOE/RAOE/SIS
amylocoagulase	AM/LO/KO/AG/LAIS	anachoretic	AN/KOE/RET/IK
amylodextrin	AM/LO/DEX/TRIN	anachoric	AN/KOER/IK
amylodyspepsia	AM/LO/DIS/PEPS/YA		AN/KHOR/IK
amylogen	AM/LO/JEN	anacidity	AN/SID/TI
amylogenesis	AM/LO/JEN/SIS		AN/NA/SID/TI
amylogenic	AM/LO/JEN/IK		(not AN/AI/SID/TI)
amyloglucosidase	AM/LO/GLAOU/KOES/DAIS	Anacin	AN/SIN
amylo-1,6-glucosidase	AM/LO/16/GLAOU/KOES/DAIS		AN/NA/SIN
	AM/LO/1/6/GLAOU/KOES/DAIS	anaclasimeter	AN/KLA/SIM/TER
amylohemicellulose	AM/LO/HEM/SEL/YAOU/LOES	anaclasis	AI/NAK/LA/SIS
amylohydrolysis	AM/LO/HAOI/DROL/SIS	anaclisis	AN/KLAOI/SIS
amyloid	AM/LOID	anaclitic	AN/KLIT/IK
amyloidemia	AM/LOI/DAOEM/YA	anacrotic	AN/KROT/IK
amyloidosis	AM/LOI/DOE/SIS	anacrotism	AI/NAK/RO/TIFM
amylolysis	AM/LOL/SIS	anacusis	AN/KAOU/SIS
amylolytic	AM/LO/LIT/IK	anadenia	AN/DAOEN/YA
amylomaltase	AM/LO/MAL/TAIS	anadicrotic	AN/DI/KROT/IK
amylopectin	AM/LO/PEK/TIN	anadicrotism	AN/DIK/RO/TIFM
amylopectinosis	AM/LO/PEKT/NOE/SIS	anadidymus	AN/DID/MUS
amylophagia	AM/LO/FAI/JA	anadipsia	AN/DIPS/YA
amylophosphorylase	AM/LO/FOS/FOR/LAIS	anadrenalism	AN/DRAOENL/IFM
amyloplast	AM/LO/PLA*S		AN/DRAOEN/LIFM
amyloplastic	AM/LO/PLA*S/IK		AN/AI/DRAOENL/IFM
amylopsin	AM/LOP/SIN		AN/AI/DRAOEN/LIFM
amylorrhea	AM/LO/RAOE/YA	anadrenia	AN/DRAOEN/YA
amylorrhexis	AM/LO/REK/SIS		AN/AI/DRAOEN/YA
amylose	AM/LOES	Anadrol	AN/DROL
amylosis	AM/LOE/SIS	Anadrol-50	AN/DROL/50
amylosuria	AM/LO/SAOUR/YA		AN/DROL/H-F/50
amylosynthesis	AM/LO/S*INT/SIS	anaero-	AN/RO
amylum	AM/LUM		AN/NAER
amyluria	AM/LAOUR/YA		AN/NAER/RO
amyo-	AI/MAOI		(not AN/AER or AN/AER/RO; see an
	AI/MAOI/YO		aero-)
amyocardia	AI/MAOI/KARD/YA	anaerobe	AN/ROEB
amyoesthesia	AI/MAOI/ES/THAOEZ/YA		AN/NAER/ROEB
amyoesthesis	AI/MAOI/ES/THAOE/SIS		(not AN/AER/ROEB; see an aerobe)
amyoplasia	AI/MAOI/PLAIZ/YA	anaerobic	AN/ROEB/IK
amyostasia	AI/MAOI/STAIZ/YA		AN/NAER/ROEB/IK
amyostatic	AI/MAOI/STAT/IK		(not AN/AER/ROEB/IK; see an
amyosthenia	AI/MAOI/OS/THAOEN/YA		aerobic)
	AI/MAOI/YOS/THAOEN/YA	anaerobiosis	AN/NAER/BAO*I/YOE/SIS
amyosthenic	AI/MAOI/OS/THEN/IK	anaerogenic	AN/NAOER/JEN/IK
	AI/MAOI/YOS/THEN/IK	anaerophyte	AN/NAER/FAOIT
amyotaxia	AI/MAOI/TAX/YA	anaeroplasty	AN/NAER/PLAS/TI
amyotaxy	AI/MAOI/TAK/SI	anaerosis	AN/ROE/SIS
amyotonia	AI/MAOI/TOEN/YA		AN/NAER/ROE/SIS
amyotrophia	AI/MAOI/TROEF/YA		(not AN/AER/ROE/SIS; see an
amyotrophic	AI/MAOI/TROEFK		aerosis)
	AI/MAOI/TROFK	anagen	AN/JEN
amyotrophy	AI/MAOI/OT/RO/FI		AN/NA/JEN
	AI/MAOI/YOT/RO/FI	anagenesis	AN/JEN/SIS

anagenetic	AN/JE/NET/IK	ananaphylaxis	AN/AN/NA/BOL/IK
anagestone acetate	AN/JES/TOEN/AS/TAIT	ananaphylaxis	AN/AN/FLAK/SIS
Anagnostakis	AI/NAG/NOS/TAI/KIS	ananastasia	AN/AN/STAIZ/YA
	AI/NAG/NOS/TAK/KIS	anancasm	AN/AN/KAFM
anagocytic	AN/AG/SIT/IK		AN/NAN/KAFM
	AI/NAG/SIT/IK	anancastia	AN/AN/KA*S/YA
anagogic	AN/GOJ/IK		AN/NAN/KA*S/YA
anagogy	AN/GOE/JI	anancastic	AN/AN/KA*S/IK
anagotoxic	AN/AG/TOX/IK		AN/NAN/KA*S/IK
	AI/NAG/TOX/IK	anandia	AN/AND/YA
anahormone	AN/HOR/MOEN		AN/NAND/YA
	AN/NA/HOR/MOEN	anandria	AN/AN/DRAOE/YA
Ana-Kit	AN/KIT		AN/NAN/DRAOE/YA
	AN/NA/KIT	anangioid	AN/AN/JOID
anakmesis	AN/AK/MAOE/SIS		AI/NAN/JOID
anal	AINL	anangioplasia	AN/AN/JO/PLAIZ/YA
	AI/NAL		AN/NAN/JO/PLAIZ/YA
analbuminemia	ANL/BAOUM/NAOEM/YA	anangioplastic	AN/AN/JO/PLA*S/IK
	AN/NAL/BAOUM/NAOEM/YA		AN/NAN/JO/PLA*S/IK
	(not AN/AL/BAOUM/NAOEM/YA)	anapeiratic	AN/PAOI/RAT/IK
analeptic	AN/LEPT/IK	anapepsia	AN/PEPS/YA
anales	AI/NAI/LAOEZ	anaphalantiasis	AN/AF/LAN/TAOI/SIS
analgesia	ANL/JAOEZ/YA		AN/NAF/LAN/TAOI/SIS
	AN/AL/JAOEZ/YA	anaphase	AN/FAEZ
analgesic	ANL/JAOEZ/IK		AN/FAIZ
	AN/AL/JAOEZ/IK	anaphia	AN/AIF/YA
analgesimeter	ANL/JAOE/SIM/TER		AN/AF/YA
analgetic	ANL/JET/IK		AI/NAIF/YA
	AN/AL/JET/IK	anaphoresis	AN/FRAOE/SIS
analgia	AN/AL/JA		AN/FO/RAOE/SIS
analgic	AN/AL/JIK		AN/FOE/RAOE/SIS
analis	AI/NAI/LIS	anaphoretic	AN/FRET/IK
anality	AI/NAL/TI	anaphoria	AN/FOER/YA
anallergic	AN/LERJ/IK	anaphrodisia	AN/NAF/RO/DAOEZ/YA
	(not AN/AI/LERJ/IK; see an		AN/NAF/RO/DIZ/YA
	allergic)	anaphrodisiac	AN/NAF/RO/DAOEZ/YAK
analog	AN/LOG		AN/NAF/RO/DIZ/YAK
	AN/NA/LOG		(not AN/AF/RO/DAOEZ/YAK, etc.)
analogous	AI/NAL/GOUS	anaphylact(o)-	AN/FLAKT
	ANL/GOUS		AN/FLAK/T(O)
analogue	AN/LO*G		AN/FAOI/LAKT
	AN/NA/LO*G		AN/FAOI/LAK/T(O)
	(not AN/LOG or AN/NA/LOG; see	anaphylactic	AN/FLAKT/IK
	analog)	anaphylactin	AN/FLAK/TIN
analogy	AI/NAL/JI	anaphylactogen	AN/FLAKT/JEN
	AI/NALG	anaphylactogenesis	AN/FLAKT/JEN/SIS
analphalipoproteinemia	AN/AL/FA/LIP/PRO/TAOEN/	anaphylactogenic	AN/FLAKT/JEN/IK
	AOEM/YA	anaphylactoid	AN/FLAK/TOID
	AN/AL/FA/LIP/PROET/NAOEM/YA	anaphylactotoxin	AN/FLAKT/TOK/SIN
Analpram	AINL/PRAM	anaphylatoxin	AN/FIL/TOK/SIN
	AI/NAL/PRAM	anaphylaxin	AN/FLAK/SIN
Analpram-HC	AINL/PRAM/H-RBGS/KR*RBGS	anaphylaxis	AN/FLAK/SIS
	AI/NAL/PRAM/H-RBGS/KR*RBGS	anaphylodiagnosis	AN/FIL/DAOIG/NOE/SIS
	AINL/PRAM/H-F/H-RBGS/	anaplasia	AN/PLAIZ/YA
	KR*RBGS		AN/PLAIS/YA
	AI/NAL/PRAM/H-F/H-RBGS/	Anaplasma	AN/PLAZ/MA
	KR*RBGS		AN/PLAS/MA
analysand	AI/NAL/SAND	Anaplasmataceae	AN/PLAZ/MA/TAIS/YAE
analyses	AI/NAL/SAOEZ		AN/PLAS/MA/TAIS/YAE
	ANL/SAOEZ	anaplasmodastat	AN/PLAZ/MOED/STAT
analysis	AI/NAL/SIS		AN/PLAS/MOED/STAT
	ANL/SIS	anaplasmosis	AN/PLAZ/MOE/SIS
analysor	AN/LAOI/ZOR		AN/PLAS/MOE/SIS
	AN/LAOI/SOR	anaplastia	AN/PLA*S/YA
analyst	AN/L*IS	anaplastic	AN/PLA*S/IK
	ANL/*IS	anaplasty	AN/PLAS/TI
analyte	AN/LAOIT	anaplerotic	AN/PLE/ROT/IK
analytic	AN/LIT/IK	anapophysis	AN/POF/SIS
	ANL/LIT/IK	Anaprox	AN/NA/PROX
analyzer	AN/LAOIZ/ER		(not AN/PROX; see an approximate)
	ANL/AOIZ/ER	anaptic	AI/NAPT/IK
anamnesis	AN/NAM/NAOE/SIS		AN/APT/IK
	AN/AM/NAOE/SIS	anarchic	AN/ARK/IK
anamnestic	AN/NAM/N*ES/IK	anaric	AI/NAIR/IK
	(not AN/AM/N*ES/IK; see an	anarithmia	AN/R*IT/MAOE/YA
	amnestic)	anarrhexis	AN/REK/SIS
Anamniota	AN/NAM/NOE/TA	anarthria	AN/AR/THRAOE/YA
	AN/NAM/NAOE/YOE/TA	anasarca	AN/SAR/KA
anamniote	AN/NAM/NOET	anasarcous	AN/SARK/OUS
	AN/NAM/NAOE/YOET	anascitic	AN/SIT/IK
anamniotic	AN/NAM/NOT/IK	Anaspaz	AN/SPAIZ
	AN/NAM/NAOE/OT/IK		AN/SPAZ
anamorphosis	AN/MOR/FOE/SIS	anastalsis	AN/STAL/SIS
	AN/NA/MOR/FOE/SIS	anastaltic	AN/STALT/IK
ananabasia	AN/NAN/BAIZ/YA	anastate	AN/STAIT
	AN/NAN/BAIS/YA	anastigmatic	AN/STIG/MAT/IK
	AN/AN/NA/BAIZ/YA		AN/AS/TIG/MAT/IK
	AN/AN/NA/BAIS/YA	anastole	AI/NA*S/LAOE
ananabolic	AN/NAN/BOL/IK		AN/A*S/LAOE

anastomose	AI/NA*S/MOES	ancylostomiasis	ANS/LO*S/MAOI/SIS
anastomoses	AI/NA*S/MOE/SAOEZ		AN/SI/LO*S/MAOI/SIS
anastomosing	AI/NA*S/MOES/-G		AN/KLO*S/MAOI/SIS
anastomosis	AI/NA*S/MOE/SIS		AN/KI/LO*S/MAOI/SIS
anastomotic	AI/NA*S/MOT/IK	Ancylostomidae	ANS/LO/STOEM/DAE
anastomotica	AI/NA*S/MOT/KA		AN/SI/LO/STOEM/DAE
anastral	AN/NAS/TRAL		AN/KLO/STOEM/DAE
	(not AN/AS/TRAL; see an astral)		AN/KI/LO/STOEM/DAE
anastrophic	AN/STROFK	Ancylostomum	ANS/LO*S/MUM
anatherapeusis	AN/THER/PAOU/SIS		AN/SI/LO*S/MUM
anatomic	AN/TOM/IK		AN/KLO*S/MUM
anatomica	AN/TOM/KA		AN/KI/LO*S/MUM
Anatomica	K-P/AN/TOM/KA	ancyroid	ANS/ROID
anatomical	AN/TOM/KAL		AN/SI/ROID
anatomically	AN/TOM/KLI	Andernach	AND/ER/NAK
anatomico-	AN/TOM/KO		AN/DER/NAK
anatomicomedical	AN/TOM/KO/MED/KAL	Anders	AN/DERZ
anatomicopathological	AN/TOM/KO/PA*T/LOJ/KAL		AN/DERS
anatomicophysiological	AN/TOM/KO/FIZ/YO/LOJ/KAL		AND/ERZ
anatomicosurgical	AN/TOM/KO/SURJ/KAL		AND/ERS
anatomicum	AN/TOM/KUM	Andersch	AN/DER/-RB
anatomist	AI/NAT/M*IS	Andersen	AN/DER/SEN
anatomy	AI/NAT/M*I		AND/ER/SEN
anatopism	AI/NAT/PIFM	Anderson	AN/DER/SON
anatoxic	AN/TOX/IK		AND/ER/SON
anatoxin	AN/TOK/SIN	Andes	AN/DAOEZ
anatoxireaction	AN/TOX/RE/A*BGS	andirine	AN/DAOI/RIN
anatricrotic	AN/TR*I/KROT/IK	andr(o)-	AN/DR(O)
anatricrotism	AN/TRIK/RO/TIFM	Andrade	AN/DRA/DAOE
anatripsis	AN/TRIP/SIS	Andral	AN/DRAL
anatriptic	AN/TRIPT/IK	Andrews	AN/DRAOUZ
anatrophic	AN/TROEFK	andriatrics	AN/DRAOE/YAT/RIK/-S
	AN/TROFK		AN/DRAOE/AT/RIK/-S
anatropia	AN/TROEP/YA	andriatry	AN/DRAOI/TRI
anatropic	AN/TROP/IK	andrin	AN/DRIN
	AN/TROEP/IK	androblastoma	AN/DRO/BLAS/TOE/MA
anaudia	AN/AUD/YA	androcyte	AN/DRO/SAO*IT
anavenin	AN/VEN/NIN	androgalactozemia	AN/DRO/GLAKT/ZAOEM/YA
anaxon	AN/NAK/SON	androgamone	AN/DRO/GAM/MOEN
	(not AN/AK/SON; see an axon)		AN/DRO/GAM/OEN
anazolene	AN/A*Z/LAOEN	androgen	AN/DRO/JEN
anazoturia	AN/A*Z/TAOUR/YA	androgenesis	AN/DRO/JEN/SIS
Anbesol	AN/BE/SOL	androgenic	AN/DRO/JEN/IK
Ancef	AN/SEF	androgenicity	AN/DRO/JE/NIS/TI
anchone	AN/KOE/NAOE		AN/DRO/JEN/IS/TI
anchor	ANG/KOR	androgenization	AN/DRO/JEN/ZAIGS
	AIN/KOR		AN/DROJ/NI/ZAIGS
	AING/KOR	androgenize	AN/DROJ/NAOIZ
anchorage	AN/KRAJ	androgenized	AN/DROJ/NAOIZ/-D
	AIN/KRAJ	androgenous	AN/DROJ/NOUS
	ANG/RAJ	androglossia	AN/DRO/GLOS/YA
ancillary	AN/SIL/RI	androgone	AN/DRO/GOEN
	ANS/LAIR	androgyne	AN/DRO/JAOIN
	AN/SIL/LAIR		AN/DRO/GAOIN
ancipital	AN/SIP/TAL	androgyneity	AN/DRO/JI/NAOE/TI
ancipitate	AN/SIP/TAIT	androgynism	AN/DROJ/NIFM
ancipitous	AN/SIP/TOUS	androgynoid	AN/DROJ/NOID
ancistroid	AN/SIS/TROID	androgynous	AN/DROJ/NO*US
	AN/S*IS/ROID		(not AN/DROJ/NOUS; see
Ancobon	AN/KO/BON		androgenous)
	AN/KOE/BON	androgynus	AN/DROJ/NUS
ancon	AN/KON	androgyny	AN/DROJ/N*I
anconad	AN/KO/NAD	android	AN/DROID
	AN/KOE/NAD	Android-5	AN/DROID/5
anconagra	AN/KO/NAG/RA		AN/DROID/H-F/5
	AN/KON/AG/RA	Android-10	AN/DROID/10
anconal	AN/KO/NAL		AN/DROID/H-F/10
	AN/KOE/NAL	Android-25	AN/DROID/25
anconeal	AN/KOEN/YAL		AN/DROID/H-F/25
anconeus	AN/KOEN/YUS	Android-F	AN/DROID/F-RBGS
anconitis	AN/KO/NAOITS		AN/DROID/H-F/F-RBGS
	AN/KOE/NAOITS	androidal	AN/DROI/DAL
anconoid	AN/KO/NOID	andrology	AN/DROLG
	AN/KOE/NOID	andromedotoxin	AN/DROM/DO/TOK/SIN
ancrod	AN/KROD	andromerogon	AN/DRO/MER/GON
ancylo-	AN/SLO	andromerogony	AN/DRO/ME/ROG/N*I
	AN/SI/LO	andromimetic	AN/DRO/MAOI/MET/IK
	AN/KLO	andromorphous	AN/DRO/MOR/FOUS
	AN/KI/LO	andropathy	AN/DROP/TH*I
Ancylostoma	ANS/LO*S/MA	androphile	AN/DRO/FAOIL
	AN/SI/LO*S/MA	androphilous	AN/DROF/LOUS
	AN/KLO*S/MA	androphobia	AN/DRO/FOEB/YA
	AN/KI/LO*S/MA	androstane	AN/DRO/STAIN
ancylostomatic	ANS/LO/STOE/MAT/IK	androstanediol	AN/DRO/STAIN/DI/OL
	AN/SI/LO/STOE/MAT/IK		AN/DRO/STAIN/DI/YOL
	AN/KLO/STOE/MAT/IK	androstanedione	AN/DRO/STAIN/DI/YOEN
	AN/KI/LO/STOE/MAT/IK		AN/DRO/STAIN/DI/OEN
ancylostome	AN/KIL/STOEM	androstanolone	AN/DRO/STAN/LOEN
	AN/SIL/STOEM	androstene	AN/DRO/STAOEN

androstenediol	AN/DRO/STAOEN/DI/OL		AI/NES/THET/ZAIGS
	AN/DRO/STAOEN/DI/YOL	anesthetize	AI/NES/THE/TAOIZ
androstenedione	AN/DRO/STAOEN/DI/YOEN		AI/N*ES/TAOIZ
	AN/DRO/STAOEN/DI/OEN		AN/ES/THE/TAOIZ
androstenolone	AN/DRO/STAOEN/LOEN	anesthetometer	AI/NES/THE/TOM/TER
androsterone	AN/DRO*S/ROEN		AN/ES/THE/TOM/TER
	AN/DROS/TROEN		ANS/THE/TOM/TER
	AN/DROS/TER/OEN	anesthetospasm	ANS/THET/SPAFM
anecdotal	AN/EK/DOE/TAL		AN/ES/THET/SPAFM
anecdote	AN/EK/DOET	anestrous	AN/ES/TRUS
anechoic	AN/KOIK	anestrum	AN/ES/TRUM
	AN/KOE/IK	anestrus	AN/ES/TRUS
anectasis	AN/EKT/SIS	anethene	AN/THAOEN
Anectine	AI/NEK/TAOEN	anethole	AN/THOEL
	AN/EK/TIN	anethopath	AI/NAO*ET/PA*T
	AI/NEK/TIN	Anethum	AI/NAO*ET/UM
Anel	AI/NEL		AI/NAOE/THUM
	AN/NEL	anetic	AI/NET/IK
anelectrode	A*N/LEK/TROED	anetoderma	AN/TO/DER/MA
	(* required; see an electrode)	aneugamy	AN/YAOUG/M*I
anelectrotonic	A*N/LEK/TRO/TON/IK	aneuploid	AN/YAOU/PLOID
	(* required; see an electrotonic)		AN/YU/PLOID
anelectrotonus	A*N/LEK/TROT/NUS	aneuploidy	AN/YAOU/PLOI/DI
	(* required; see an electrotonus)		AN/YU/PLOI/DI
anemia	AI/NAOEM/YA	aneurin	AI/NAOU/RIN
anemic	AI/NAOEM/IK		AI/NAOUR/RIN
anemometer	AN/MOM/TER	aneurine	AN/YAOU/RAOEN
anemonol	AI/NEM/NOL		AN/YU/RAOEN
anemonin	AI/NEM/NIN		AN/YAOU/RIN
anemonism	AI/NEM/NIFM		AN/YU/RIN
anemophilous	AN/MOF/LOUS	aneurogenic	AI/NAOUR/JEN/IK
anemophobia	AN/MO/FOEB/YA	aneurolemmic	AI/NAOUR/LEM/IK
anemotaxis	AN/MO/TAK/SIS	aneurysm	AN/RIFM
anemotrophy	AN/MOT/RO/FI		AN/YAOU/RIFM
anemotropism	AN/MOT/RO/PIFM		AN/YU/RIFM
anencephalia	AN/EN/SFAIL/YA	aneurysm-	AN/RIZ/M-
	AN/EN/SE/FAIL/YA		AN/YAOU/RIZ/M-
anencephalic	AN/EN/SFAL/IK		AN/YU/RIZ/M-
anencephalous	AN/EN/SEF/LOUS	aneurysmal	AN/RIZ/MAL
anencephalus	AN/EN/SEF/LUS	aneurysmatic	AN/RIZ/MAT/IK
anencephaly	AN/EN/SEF/LI	aneurysmectomy	AN/RIZ/MEKT/M*I
anenterous	AN/SPWER/ROUS	aneurysmogram	AN/RIZ/MO/GRAM
	AN/SPWER/OUS	aneurysmoplasty	AN/RIZ/MO/PLAS/TI
	AN/ENT/ROUS	aneurysmorrhaphy	AN/RIZ/MOR/FI
anenzymia	AN/EN/ZAOIM/YA	aneurysmotomy	AN/RIZ/MOT/M*I
anephric	AI/NEF/RIK	angelic	AN/JEL/IK
anephrogenesis	AI/NEF/RO/JEN/SIS	Angelica	AN/JEL/KA
anepia	AI/NEP/YA	angeline	AN/JE/LAOEN
anepiploic	AN/EP/PLOIK		AN/JE/LIN
	AN/EP/PLOE/IK	Angelucci	AN/JE/LAOU/KHAOE
anerethisia	AN/ER/THIZ/YA	Anghelescu	AN/JE/LES/KAOU
aneretic	AN/E/RET/IK	angi-	AN/JI
	(not AN/RET/IK; see anoretic)	angialgia	AN/JAL/JA
anergasia	AN/ER/GAIZ/YA		AN/JI/AL/JA
anergastic	AN/ER/GA*S/IK	angiasthenia	AN/JAS/THAOEN/YA
anergia	AN/ER/JA		AN/JI/AS/THAOEN/YA
anergic	AN/ERJ/IK	angiectasia	AN/JEK/TAIZ/YA
anergy	AN/ER/JI		AN/JI/EK/TAIZ/YA
aneroid	AN/ROID	angiectasis	AN/JEKT/SIS
	AN/ER/OID		AN/JI/EKT/SIS
anerythroblepsia	AN/R*IT/RO/BLEPS/YA	angiectatic	AN/JEK/TAT/IK
anerythroplasia	AN/R*IT/RO/PLAIZ/YA		AN/JI/EK/TAT/IK
anerythroplastic	AN/R*IT/RO/PLA*S/IK	angiectomy	AN/JEKT/M*I
anerythropoiesis	AN/R*IT/RO/POI/SIS		AN/JI/EKT/M*I
anerythropsia	AN/*ER/THROPS/YA	angiectopia	AN/JEK/TOEP/YA
	AN/ER/THROPS/YA		AN/JI/EK/TOEP/YA
anerythroregenerative	AN/R*IT/RO/RE/JEN/RA/TIV	angiitis	AN/JAOITS
Anestacon	AI/N*ES/KON		AN/JI/AOITS
	AI/NES/TA/KON	angina	AN/JI/NA
anesthecinesia	AN/ES/THE/SI/NAOEZ/YA		AN/JAOI/NA
	AI/NES/THE/SI/NAOEZ/YA	anginal	AN/JINL
anesthekinesia	AN/ES/THE/KI/NAOEZ/YA		AN/JI/NAL
	AI/NES/THE/KI/NAOEZ/YA		AN/JAOINL
anesthesia	ANS/THAOEZ/YA		AN/JAOI/NAL
	AN/ES/THAOEZ/YA	anginiform	AN/JIN/FORM
anesthesimeter	AN/ES/THE/SIM/TER	anginoid	AN/JI/NOID
	AI/NES/THE/SIM/TER		AN/JIN/OID
anesthesiologist	ANS/THAOEZ/YO*LGS	anginophobia	AN/JI/NO/FOEB/YA
	AN/ES/THAOEZ/YO*LGS		AN/JIN/FOEB/YA
anesthesiology	ANS/THAOEZ/YOLG	anginose	AN/JI/NOES
	AN/ES/THAOEZ/YOLG	anginosis	AN/JI/NOE/SIS
anesthesiophore	ANS/THAOEZ/YO/FOER	anginous	AN/JI/NOUS
	AN/ES/THAOEZ/YO/FOER	angio-	AN/JO
anesthetic	ANS/THET/IK	angioarchitecture	AN/JO/ARK/TEK/KHUR
	AN/ES/THET/IK	angioasthenia	AN/JO/AS/THAOEN/YA
anesthetist	AI/NES/THE/T*IS	angioataxia	AN/JO/AI/TAX/YA
	AI/N*ES/T*IS	angioblast	AN/JO/BLA*S
anesthetization	AN/ES/THET/ZAIGS	angioblastic	AN/JO/BLA*S/IK
	ANS/THET/ZAIGS	angioblastoma	AN/JO/BLAS/TOE/MA

angiocardiocinetic	AN/JO/KARD/YO/SI/NET/IK	angioneuralgia	AN/JO/NAOU/RAL/JA
angiocardiogram	AN/JO/KARD/YO/GRAM	angioneurectomy	AN/JO/NAOU/REKT/M*I
angiocardiography	AN/JO/KARD/YOG/FI	angioneuredema	AN/JO/NAOUR/DAOE/MA
angiocardiokinetic	AN/JO/KARD/YO/KI/NET/IK		AN/JO/NAOUR/E/DAOE/MA
angiocardiopathy	AN/JO/KARD/YOP/TH*I	angioneuroma	AN/JO/NAOU/ROE/MA
angiocarditis	AN/JO/KAR/DAOITS	angioneuromyoma	AN/JO/NAOUR/MAOI/YOE/MA
angiocavernous	AN/JO/KAVR/NOUS	angioneuropathic	AN/JO/NAOUR/PA*T/IK
angioceratoma	AN/JO/SER/TOE/MA	angioneuropathy	AN/JO/NAOU/ROP/TH*I
angiocheiloscope	AN/JO/KAOIL/SKOEP	angioneurosis	AN/JO/NAOU/ROE/SIS
angiocholecystitis	AN/JO/KOEL/SIS/TAOITS	angioneurotic	AN/JO/NAOU/ROT/IK
angiocholitis	AN/JO/KOE/LAOITS	angioneurotomy	AN/JO/NAOU/ROT/M*I
angiochondroma	AN/JO/KON/DROE/MA	angionoma	AN/JO/NOE/MA
Angiococcus	AN/JO/KOK/KUS	angioparalysis	AN/JO/PRAL/SIS
angiocrine	AN/JO/KRIN	angioparesis	AN/JO/PAR/SIS
angiocrinosis	AN/JO/KRI/NOE/SIS		AN/JO/PRAOE/SIS
angiocyst	AN/JO/S*IS		AN/JO/PA/RAOE/SIS
angioderm	AN/JO/DERM	angiopathic	AN/JO/PA*T/IK
angiodermatitis	AN/JO/DERM/TAOITS	angiopathology	AN/JO/PA/THOLG
angiodiascopy	AN/JO/DI/AS/KPI	angiopathy	AN/JOP/TH*I
	AN/JO/DAOI/AS/KPI	angiophacomatosis	AN/JO/FAK/MA/TOE/SIS
angiodiathermy	AN/JO/DAOI/THER/M*I	angioplany	AN/JO/PLAI/N*I
angiodynia	AN/JO/DIN/YA	angioplasty	AN/JO/PLAS/TI
angiodysplasia	AN/JO/DIS/PLAIZ/YA	angiopoiesis	AN/JO/POI/SIS
angiodystrophia	AN/JO/DIS/TROEF/YA	angiopoietic	AN/JO/POIT/IK
angiodystrophy	AN/JO/DIS/TRO/FI	angiopressure	AN/JO/PRERB/SHUR
angioedema	AN/JO/DAOE/MA	angioreticuloma	AN/JO/RE/TIK/LOE/MA
	AN/JO/E/DAOE/MA	angiorrhaphy	AN/JOR/FI
angioelephantiasis	AN/JO/EL/FAN/TAOI/SIS	angiorrhexis	AN/JO/REK/SIS
angioendothelioma	AN/JO/*END/THAOEL/YOE/MA	angiosarcoma	AN/JO/SAR/KOE/MA
angioendotheliomatosis	AN/JO/*END/THAOEL/YOEM/	angiosclerosis	AN/JO/SKLE/ROE/SIS
	TOE/SIS	angiosclerotic	AN/JO/SKLE/ROT/IK
angiofibrolipoma	AN/JO/FAOI/BRO/LI/POE/MA	angiosclerotica	AN/JO/SKLE/ROT/KA
angiofibroma	AN/JO/FAOI/BROE/MA	angioscope	AN/JO/SKOEP
angiofibrosis	AN/JO/FAOI/BROE/SIS	angioscopy	AN/JOS/KPI
angiofollicular	AN/JO/FLIK/LAR	angioscotoma	AN/JO/SKOE/TOE/MA
angiogenesis	AN/JO/JEN/SIS	angioscotometry	AN/JO/SKOE/TOM/TRI
angiogenic	AN/JO/JEN/IK	angiosis	AN/JOE/SIS
angioglioma	AN/JO/GLAOI/YOE/MA	angiospasm	AN/JO/SPAFM
angiogliomatosis	AN/JO/GLAOI/YOEM/TOE/SIS	angiospasmodic	AN/JO/SPAZ/MOD/IK
angiogliosis	AN/JO/GLAOI/YOE/SIS	angiospastic	AN/JO/SPA*S/IK
angiogram	AN/JO/GRAM	angiospastica	AN/JO/SPA*S/KA
angiograph	AN/JO/GRAF	angiosperm	AN/JO/SPERM
angiographic	AN/JO/GRAFK	angiospermin	AN/JO/SPER/MIN
angiography	AN/JOG/FI	angiostaxis	AN/JO/STAK/SIS
angiohemophilia	AN/JO/HAOEM/FIL/YA	angiostenosis	AN/JO/STE/NOE/SIS
angiohyalinosis	AN/JO/HAOI/LI/NOE/SIS	angiosteosis	AN/JO/*S/YOE/SIS
	AN/JO/HAOIL/NOE/SIS	angiosthenia	AN/JOS/THAOEN/YA
angioid	AN/JOID	angiostomy	AN/JO/*S/M*I
angioinvasive	AN/JO/IN/VAIS/IV	angiostrongyliasis	AN/JO/STRONG/LAOI/SIS
angiokeratoma	AN/JO/KER/TOE/MA	angiostrongylosis	AN/JO/STRONG/LOE/SIS
angiokeratosis	AN/JO/KER/TOE/SIS	Angiostrongylus	AN/JO/STRONG/LUS
angiokinesis	AN/JO/KI/NAOE/SIS	angiostrophy	AN/JOS/TRO/FI
angiokinetic	AN/JO/KI/NET/IK	angiotelectasia	AN/JO/TEL/EK/TAIZ/YA
angioleiomyoma	AN/JO/LAOI/MAOI/YOE/MA	angiotelectasis	AN/JO/TE/LEKT/SIS
angioleucitis	AN/JO/LAOU/SAOITS	angiotensin	AN/JO/TEN/SIN
angioleukitis	AN/JO/LAOU/KAOITS	angiotensinase	AN/JO/TENS/NAIS
angiolipofibroma	AN/JO/LIP/MAOI/YOE/MA	angiotensinogen	AN/JO/TEN/SIN/JEN
angiolipoleiomyoma	AN/JO/LIP/LAOI/MAOI/YOE/MA	angiotensinogenase	AN/JO/TEN/SIN/JEN/AIS
angiolipoma	AN/JO/LI/POE/MA	angiotome	AN/JO/TOEM
angiolith	AN/JO/L*IT	angiotomy	AN/JOT/M*I
angiolithic	AN/JO/L*IT/IK	angiotonase	AN/JO/TOEN/AIS
angiologia	AN/JO/LOE/JA		AN/JO/TOE/NAIS
angiology	AN/JOLG	angiotonia	AN/JO/TOEN/YA
angiolupoid	AN/JO/LAOU/POID	angiotonic	AN/JO/TON/IK
	AN/JO/LAOUP/OID	angiotonin	AN/JO/TOE/NIN
angiolymphangioma	AN/JO/LIM/FAN/JOE/MA	angiotribe	AN/JO/TRAOIB
angiolysis	AN/JOL/SIS	angiotripsy	AN/JO/TRIP/SI
angiolymphitis	AN/JO/LIM/FAOITS	angiotrophic	AN/JO/TROFK
angioma	AN/JOE/MA		AN/JO/TROEFK
angiomatoid	AN/JOEM/TOID	angle	ANG/-L
	AN/JOE/MA/TOID	Angle	K-P/ANG/-L
angiomatosis	AN/JOEM/TOE/SIS	angophrasia	AN/GO/FRAIZ/YA
	AN/JO/MA/TOE/SIS	angor	AN/GOR
	AN/JOE/MA/TOE/SIS		ANG/GOR
angiomatous	AN/JOEM/TOUS	angstrom	ANG/STROM
	AN/JOE/MA/TOUS		ANG/STREM
angiomegaly	AN/JO/MEG/LI	Angstrom	K-P/ANG/STROM
angiometer	AN/JOM/TER		K-P/ANG/STREM
angiomyocardiac	AN/JO/MAOI/KARD/YAK	Anguillula	ANG/WIL/YAOU/LA
angiomyofibroma	AN/JO/MAOI/FAOI/BROE/MA		ANG/WIL/YU/LA
angiomyolipoma	AN/JO/MAOI/LI/POE/MA	angul-	ANG/L-
angiomyoma	AN/JO/MAOI/YOE/MA		ANG/YAOU/L-
angiomyoneuroma	AN/JO/MAOI/NAOU/ROE/MA		ANG/YU/L-
angiomyopathy	AN/JO/MAOI/OP/TH*I		AN/GAOU/L-
	AN/JO/MAOI/YOP/TH*I	angular	ANG/LAR
angiomyosarcoma	AN/JO/MAOI/SAR/KOE/MA	angulare	ANG/LAI/RAOE
angiomyxoma	AN/JO/MIK/SOE/MA	angularis	ANG/LAI/RIS
angionecrosis	AN/JO/NE/KROE/SIS		ANG/LAR/RIS
angioneoplasm	AN/JO/NAOE/PLAFM	angulation	ANG/LAIGS

anguli	ANG/LAOI
angulus	ANG/LUS
anhalamine	AN/HAL/MAOEN
	AN/HAL/MIN
anhalonidine	AN/HA/LON/DAOEN
anhalonine	AN/HAL/NAOEN
	AN/HA/LOE/NIN
anhaphia	AN/HAF/YA
	AN/HAIF/YA
anhedonia	AN/HAOE/DOEN/YA
	AN/HE/DOEN/YA
anhematopoietic	AN/HEM/TO/POIT/IK
	AN/HAOEM/TO/POIT/IK
anhemopoietic	AN/HAOEM/POIT/IK
anhidrosis	AN/HAOI/DROE/SIS
	AN/HI/DROE/SIS
anhidrotic	AN/HAOI/DROT/IK
	AN/HI/DROT/IK
anhistic	AN/H*IS/IK
anhistous	AN/HIS/TOUS
	AN/H*IS/OUS
anhydrase	AN/HAOI/DRAIS
anhydration	AN/HAOI/DRAIGS
anhydremia	AN/HAOI/DRAOEM/YA
anhydride	AN/HAOI/DRAOID
anhydrochloric	AN/HAOI/DRO/KLOR/IK
anhydrogitalin	AN/HAOI/DRO/JIT/LIN
anhydroleucovorin	AN/HAOI/DRO/LAOUK/VORN
anhydrohydroxyprogesterone	
	AN/HAOI/DRO/HAOI/DROX/PRO/
	J*ES/ROEN
anhydromuscarine	AN/HAOI/DRO/MUS/KRIN
anhydrosugar	AN/HAOI/DRO/SHUG/AR
anhydrous	AN/HAOI/DROUS
ani	AI/NAOI
aniacinamidosis	AI/NAOI/SIN/AM/DOE/SIS
aniacinosis	AI/NAOI/SI/NOE/SIS
	AI/NAOI/SIN/NOE/SIS
anianthinopsy	AN/YA*NT/NOP/SI
	AN/YAN/THI/NOP/SI
Anichkov	AI/NIFP/KOV
anicteric	AN/IK/TER/IK
anidean	AI/NID/YAN
	AN/ID/YAN
anideus	AI/NID/YUS
	AN/ID/YUS
anidous	AN/DOUS
anidoxime	AN/DOK/SAOEM
anidrosis	AN/DROE/SIS
anidrotic	AN/DROT/IK
anile	AI/NAOIL
	AN/NIL
	(not AN/IL; see an ill)
anileridine	AN/LER/DAOEN
anilide	AN/NI/LID
	(AN/L*ID
	(not AN/LID; see annelid)
anilinction	AIN/LINGS
	AN/LINGS
anilinctus	AIN/LING/TUS
	AN/LING/TUS
aniline	AN/LIN
	AN/LAOEN
anilingus	AIN/LIN/GUS
	AN/LIN/GUS
anilinism	AN/LIN/IFM
anilinophil	AN/LIN/FIL
anilinophile	AN/LIN/FAOIL
anilinophilous	AN/LI/NOF/LOUS
	AN/LIN/OF/LOUS
anilinparasulfonic	AN/LIN/PAR/SUL/FON/IK
anilism	AN/LIFM
anility	AI/NIL/TI
anilopam	AN/IL/PAM
	AI/NIL/PAM
anil-quinoline	AN/IL/KWIN/LIN
	AI/NIL/KWIN/LIN
anima	AN/MA
animal	AN/MAL
animalis	AN/MAI/LIS
animality	AN/MAL/TI
animation	AN/MAIGS
animi	AN/MAOI
animism	AN/MIFM
animus	AN/MUS
anion	A*N/AOIN
	(not AN/AOIN; see an ion)
anionic	A*N/AOIN/IK
	(not AN/AOIN/IK; see an ionic)

anionotropy	AN/AOIN/OT/RO/PI
	AN/AOI/NOT/RO/PI
	A*N/AOIN/OT/RO/PI
	A*N/AOI/NOT/RO/PI
	AN/YON/OT/RO/PI
aniridia	AN/RID/YA
	AN/IR/RID/YA
	AN/AOIR/RID/YA
anisakiasis	AN/SA/KAOI/SIS
	AN/SAI/KAOI/SIS
anisakid	AN/SAI/KID
Anisakidae	AN/SAIK/DAE
Anisakis	AN/SAI/KIS
anisate	AN/NI/SAIT
	(not AN/SAIT; see ansate)
anise	AN/NIS
aniseikonia	AN/SAOI/KOEN/YA
aniseikonic	AN/SAOI/KON/IK
anisi	AI/NAOI/SAOI
anisic	AI/NIS/IK
	AN/NIS/IK
	AN/IS/IK
anisindione	AN/SIN/DI/OEN
	AN/SIN/DI/YOEN
anisine	AN/NI/SIN
	AN/S*IN
	(not AN/SIN; see Anacin)
aniso-	AN/NAOIS
	AN/SO
	(not AN/AOIS; see an iso-)
anisoaccommodation	AN/NAOIS/AI/KOM/DAIGS
anisochromasia	AN/NAOIS/KROE/MAIZ/YA
anisochromatic	AN/NAOIS/KROE/MAT/IK
anisochromia	AN/NAOIS/KROEM/YA
	AN/SO/KROEM/YA
anisocoria	AN/NAOIS/KOER/YA
	AN/SO/KOER/YA
anisocytosis	AN/NAOIS/SAOI/TOE/SIS
anisodactylous	AN/NAOIS/DAKT/LOUS
anisodactyly	AN/NAOIS/DAKT/LI
anisodiametric	AN/NAOIS/DAOI/MET/RIK
anisodont	AN/NAOIS/DONT
anisogamete	AN/SO/GAM/AOET
	AN/NAOIS/GAM/AOET
anisogametic	AN/SO/GA/MET/IK
	AN/NAOIS/GA/MET/IK
anisogamous	AN/SOG/MOUS
anisogamy	AN/SOG/M*I
	AN/NAOI/SOG/M*I
	AN/AOI/SOG/M*I
anisognathous	AN/SOG/NA/THOUS
	AN/NAOI/SOG/NA/THOUS
	AN/AOI/SOG/NA/THOUS
anisoic	AN/SOIK
	AN/SOE/IK
anisokaryosis	AN/NAOIS/KAR/YOE/SIS
	AN/SO/KAR/YOE/SIS
anisole	AN/SOEL
Anisolobis	AN/NAOIS/LOE/BIS
anisomastia	AN/NAOIS/MA*S/YA
	AN/SO/MA*S/YA
anisomelia	AN/NAOIS/MAOEL/YA
	AN/SO/MAOEL/YA
anisomeric	AN/NAOIS/MER/IK
	AN/SO/MER/IK
anisometrope	AN/NAOIS/MET/ROEP
	AN/SO/MET/ROEP
anisometropia	AN/NAOIS/ME/TROEP/YA
	AN/SO/ME/TROEP/YA
anisometropic	AN/NAOIS/ME/TROP/IK
	AN/SO/ME/TROP/IK
Anisomorpha	AN/NAOIS/MOR/FA
anisophoria	AN/NAOIS/FOER/YA
	AN/SO/FOER/YA
anisopia	AN/SOEP/YA
anisopiesis	AN/NAOIS/PAOI/E/SIS
	AN/NAOIS/PAOI/SIS
	AN/SO/PAOI/E/SIS
	AN/SO/PAOI/SIS
anisopoikilocytosis	AN/NAOIS/POIK/LO/SAOI/TOE/
	SIS
anisorythmia	AN/NAOIS/R*IT/MAOE/YA
	AN/SO/R*IT/MAOE/YA
anisosmotic	AN/SOZ/MOT/IK
	AN/SOS/MOT/IK
anisosphygmia	AN/NAOIS/SFIG/MAOE/YA
	AN/SO/SFIG/MAOE/YA
anisospore	AN/NAOIS/SPOER
anisosporous	AN/NAOI/SOS/PROUS

	AN/AOI/SOS/PROUS
	AN/SOS/PROUS
anisosthenic	AN/SOS/THEN/IK
anisotonic	AN/NAOIS/TON/IK
	AN/SO/TON/IK
anisotropal	AN/SOT/RO/PAL
	AN/SOT/ROE/PAL
anisotropic	AN/NAOIS/TROP/IK
	AN/SO/TROP/IK
anisotropine	AN/SO/TROE/PAOEN
	AN/NAOIS/TROE/PAOEN
anisotropous	AN/SOT/RO/POUS
anisotropy	AN/SOT/RO/PI
anisum	AI/NAOI/SUM
	AI/NAOIS/UM
	AN/NAOI/SUM
	AN/NAOIS/UM
anisuria	AN/NAOI/SAOUR/YA
	AN/SAOUR/YA
anisuric	AN/NAOI/SAOUR/IK
	AN/SAOUR/IK
anisyl	AN/SIL
	AN/NI/SIL
anitratus	AN/TRAI/TUS
anitrogenous	AI/NAOI/TROJ/NOUS
ankle	AIN/K-L
	AN/K-L
	(not AING/-L or ANG/-L)
ankyl(o)-	AN/KLO
	ANG/LO
	AN/KI/LO
ankyloblepharon	AN/KLO/BLEF/RON
ankylocheilia	AN/KLO/KAOIL/YA
ankylocolpos	AN/KLO/KOL/POS
ankylodactylia	AN/KLO/DAK/TIL/YA
ankylodactyly	AN/KLO/DAKT/LI
ankyloglossia	AN/KLO/GLOS/YA
ankylomele	AN/KLO/MAOE/LAOE
ankylopoietic	AN/KLO/POIT/IK
ankyloproctia	AN/KLO/PROK/SHA
ankylosed	AN/KLOES/-D
ankyloses	AN/KLOE/SAOEZ
ankylosis	AN/KLOE/SIS
ankylotic	AN/KLOT/IK
ankylotomy	AN/KLOT/M*I
ankylurethria	AN/KIL/YAOU/RAO*ET/RAOE/YA
	AN/KLAOU/RAO*ET/RAOE/YA
ankyroid	AN/KROID
	AN/KI/ROID
anlage	AN/LA/GE
	AN/LAIJ
anlagen	AN/LAG/-N
	AN/LAG/EN
anneal	AI/NAOEL
	AN/NAOEL
annectent	AI/NEK/TENT
	AI/NEKT/ENT
annelid	AN/LID
	AN/NE/LID
Annelida	AN/LAOI/DA
	AI/NEL/DA
annellide	AN/LAOID
	AN/NE/LAOID
annoyer	AI/NOI/ER
	AI/NOI/YER
annul-	AN/L-
	AN/YAOU/L-
	AN/YU/L-
	(see anul-)
annular	AN/LAR
annulare	AN/LAI/RAOE
	(see anulare)
annulares	AN/LAI/RAOEZ
annularia	AN/LAIR/YA
	(see anularia)
annularis	AN/LAI/RIS
	(see anularis)
annulatus	AN/LAI/TUS
annuli	AN/LAOI
	(see anuli)
annuloaortic	AN/LO/AI/ORT/IK
	AN/LO/AI/YORT/IK
annuloplasty	AN/LO/PLAS/TI
annulorrhaphy	AN/LOR/FI
annulospiral	AN/LO/SPAOIRL
annulus	AN/LUS
	(see anulus)
anochlesia	AN/KLAOEZ/YA
anochromasia	AN/KRO/MAIZ/YA

	AN/KROE/MAIZ/YA
anoci-	AI/NOES
	AI/NOE/SI
	AI/NOERB
anociassociation	AI/NOES/SOERBGS
	AI/NOES/SOEGS
	AI/NOES/AI/SOERB/YAIGS
	AI/NOES/AI/SOES/YAIGS
anociated	AI/NOES/YAIT/-D
	AI/NOERB/YAIT/-D
anociation	AI/NOES/YAIGS
	AI/NOERB/YAIGS
anocithesia	AN/NOES/THAOEZ/YA
anococcygeal	AIN/KOK/SIJ/YAL
	AI/NO/KOK/SIJ/YAL
anococcygei	AIN/KOK/SIJ/YAOI
	AI/NO/KOK/SIJ/YAOI
anococcygeum	AIN/KOK/SIJ/UM
	AI/NO/KOK/SIJ/UM
anodal	AN/NOE/DAL
	AN/OED/DAL
anode	AN/NOED
	(not AN/OED)
anoderm	AIN/DERM
	AI/NO/DERM
anodic	AN/NOED/IK
anodontia	AN/DON/SHA
	AN/NO/DON/SHA
anodontism	AN/DON/TIFM
	AN/NO/DON/TIFM
anodyne	AN/DAOIN
	AN/NO/DAOIN
anodynia	AN/DIN/YA
	AN/NO/DIN/YA
anoetic	AN/WET/IK
	AN/NO/ET/IK
anogenital	AI/NO/JEN/TAL
anoia	AI/NOI/YA
anol	AI/NOL
anomal(o)-	AI/NOM/L(O)
anomalad	AI/NOM/LAD
anomalopia	AI/NOM/LOEP/YA
anomaloscope	AI/NOM/LO/SKOEP
anomalotrophy	AI/NOM/LOT/RO/FI
anomalous	AI/NOM/LOUS
anomaly	AI/NOM/LI
anomer	AN/MER
	AN/NO/MER
anomeric	AN/MER/IK
	AN/NO/MER/IK
anomia	AI/NOEM/YA
anomic	AI/NOM/IK
anomie	AN/MAOE
	AN/NO/MAOE
anonychia	AN/NIK/YA
	AN/OEN/NIK/YA
anonychosis	AN/OIN/KOE/SIS
	AN/NI/KOE/SIS
anonymous	AI/NON/MOUS
anonyma	AI/NON/MA
anonymae	AI/NON/MAE
anoperineal	AIN/P*ER/NAOEL
	AI/NO/P*ER/NAOEL
Anopheles	AI/NOF/LAOEZ
anophelicide	AI/NOF/LI/SAO*ID
anophelifuge	AI/NOF/LI/FAOUJ
Anophelinae	AI/NOF/LAOI/NAE
anopheline	AI/NOF/LAOIN
Anophelini	AI/NOF/LAOI/NAOI
anophelism	AI/NOF/LIFM
anophoria	AN/FOER/YA
	AN/FOR/YA
	AN/NO/FOER/YA
	AN/NO/FOR/YA
anophthalmia	AN/OF/THAL/MAOE/YA
	AN/OF/THAL/MI/YA
anophthalmos	AN/OF/THAL/MOS
anophthalmus	AN/OF/THAL/MUS
anopia	AN/OEP/YA
	AN/NOEP/YA
anoplasty	AIN/PLAS/TI
	AI/NO/PLAS/TI
Anoplocephala	AN/OP/LO/SEF/LA
Anoplocephalidae	AN/OP/LO/SE/FAL/DAE
	AN/PLO/SE/FAL/DAE
Anoplura	AN/PLAOU/RA
anopsia	AN/OPS/YA
anorchia	AN/ORK/YA
	AN/NORK/YA

©1992 StenEd® Medical Dictionary

anorchidic	AN/OR/KID/IK	anoxiate	AI/NOX/YAIT
	AN/NOR/KID/IK		AN/OX/YAIT
anorchidism	AN/ORK/DIFM	anoxic	AN/OX/IK
	AN/NORK/DIFM		AI/NOX/IK
anorchis	AN/OR/KIS	Anrep	AN/REP
	AN/NOR/KIS	ansa	AN/SA
anorchism	AN/OR/KIFM	ansae	AN/SAE
	AN/NOR/KIFM	ansate	AN/SAIT
anorectal	AIN/REK/TAL	Ansbacher	ANS/BAK/ER
	AI/NO/REK/TAL	Anschutz	AN/SHUTS
anorectic	AN/REKT/IK		AN/SHITS
anorectitis	AIN/REK/TAOITS	anserine	ANS/RAOIN
	AI/NO/REK/TAOITS		ANS/RIN
anorectocolonic	AIN/REKT/KO/LON/IK		AN/SE/RAOIN
	AI/NO/REKT/KO/LON/IK		AN/SE/RIN
anorectum	AIN/REK/TUM	anserinus	ANS/RAOI/NUS
	AI/NO/REK/TUM		AN/SE/RAOI/NUS
anoretic	AN/RET/IK	anseris	AN/SER/RIS
anorexia	AN/REX/YA	ansiform	AN/SI/FORM
anorexiant	AN/REX/YANT	ansotomy	AN/SOT/M*I
anorexic	AN/REX/IK	Anspor	AN/SPOR
anorexigenic	AN/REX/JEN/IK		AN/SPOER
anorganic	A*N/OR/GAN/IK	Antabuse	ANT/BAOUS
	AN/NOR/GAN/IK		AN/TA/BAOUS
	(not AN/OR/GAN/IK; see an	antacid	ANT/AS/ID
	organic)	antagonism	AN/TAG/NIFM
anorganology	AN/ORG/NOLG	antagonist	AN/TAG/N*IS
	AN/NORG/NOLG	antalgesia	ANT/AL/JAOEZ/YA
anorgasmia	AN/OR/GAZ/MAOE/YA	antalgesic	ANT/AL/JAOEZ/IK
	AN/NOR/GAZ/MAOE/YA	antalgic	ANT/AL/JIK
anorgasmy	AN/OR/GAZ/M*I	antalkaline	ANT/AL/KLAOIN
	AN/NOR/GAZ/M*I		ANT/AL/KLIN
anorthopia	AN/OR/THOEP/YA	antaphrodisiac	ANT/AF/RO/DIZ/YAK
anorthosis	AN/OR/THOE/SIS		ANT/AF/RO/DAOEZ/YAK
anoscope	AIN/SKOEP	antaphroditic	ANT/AF/RO/DIT/IK
	AI/NO/SKOEP	antapoplectic	ANT/AP/PLEKT/IK
anoscopy	AI/NOS/KPI	antarctica	A*NT/ART/KA
anosigmoidoscopic	AIN/SIG/MOID/SKOP/IK		A*NT/ARKT/KA
	AI/NO/SIG/MOID/SKOP/IK	Antarctica	ANT/ART/KA
anosigmoidoscopy	AIN/SIG/MOI/DOS/KPI		ANT/ARKT/KA
	AI/NO/SIG/MOI/DOS/KPI	antarthritic	ANT/AR/THRIT/IK
anosmatic	AN/OZ/MAT/IK	antasthenic	ANT/AS/THEN/IK
anosmia	AN/OZ/MAOE/YA	antasthmatic	ANT/AS/MAT/IK
anosmic	AN/OZ/MIK		ANT/AZ/MAT/IK
anosodiaphoria	AI/NOE/SO/DAOI/FOER/YA	antatrophic	ANT/TROFK
	AI/NOES/DAOI/FOER/YA		AN/TA/TROFK
anosognosia	AI/NOE/SO/NOEZ/YA	antazoline	AN/TAZ/LAOEN
	AI/NOES/NOEZ/YA	ante-	AENT
	AI/NOE/SOG/NOEZ/YA	antebrachial	AENT/BRAIK/YAL
anosognosic	AI/NOE/SO/NOES/IK	antebrachii	AENT/BRAIK/YAOI
	AI/NOES/NOES/IK	antebrachium	AENT/BRAIK/YUM
	AI/NOE/SOG/NOES/IK	antecardium	AENT/KARD/YUM
anosphrasia	AN/OS/FRAIZ/YA	antecedent	AENT/SAOED/ENT
anospinal	AIN/SPAOINL		AENT/SAOE/DENT
	AI/NO/SPAOINL	ante cibum	AN/TAOE/SAOI/BUM
anosteoplasia	AN/O*S/YO/PLAIZ/YA		AN/TAOE/SAOIB/UM
anostosis	AN/OS/TOE/SIS		AENT/SAOI/BUM
anotia	AN/O/SHA		AENT/SAOIB/UM
	AN/OERB/YA	antecubital	AENT/KAOUB/TAL
	AN/NOERB/YA	antecurvature	AENT/KUFRB/KHUR
anotropia	AN/TROEP/YA	antefebrile	AENT/FEB/RAOIL
	AN/NO/TROEP/YA		AENT/FEB/RIL
anotus	AN/O/TUS	anteflect	AENT/FLEKT
	AN/NOE/TUS	anteflex	AENT/FLEX
anovaginal	AIN/VAJ/NAL	anteflexio	AENT/FLEX/YOE
	AI/NO/VAJ/NAL	anteflexion	AENT/FL*EBGS
anovaria	AN/O/VAIR/YA	antegrade	AENT/GRAID
	AN/VAIR/YA	antelocation	AENT/LOE/KAIGS
	AN/NO/VAIR/YA	antemetic	ANT/E/MET/IK
anovarism	AN/OEV/RIFM		ANT/MET/IK
	AN/NOEV/RIFM	antemortem	AENT/MOR/TEM
anovesical	AIN/VES/KAL		AENT/MORT/EM
	AI/NO/VES/KAL	ante mortem	AN/TAOE/MOR/TEM
anovul-	A*N/OV/L-		AN/TAOE/MORT/EM
	A*N/OV/YAOU/L-	antenatal	AENT/NAI/TAL
	A*N/OV/YU/L-	antenna	AN/TEN/NA
	AN/NOV/L-	antennae	AN/TEN/NAE
	AN/NOV/YAOU/L-	antepartal	AENT/PAR/TAL
	AN/NOV/YU/L-	antepartum	AENT/PAR/TUM
	(not AN/OV/L-, etc.)		AENT/PART/UM
anovular	A*N/OV/LAR	antephase	AENT/FAIZ
anovulation	A*N/OV/LAIGS	antephialtic	ANT/EF/YALT/IK
anovulatory	A*N/OV/LA/TOIR	anteposition	AENT/POGS
anovulomenorrhea	AN/OV/LO/MEN/RAOE/YA	anteprostate	AENT/PROS/TAIT
	AN/NOV/LO/MEN/RAOE/YA	anteprostatitis	AENT/PRO*S/TAOITS
anoxemia	AN/OK/SAOEM/YA	antepyretic	AENT/PAOI/RET/IK
anoxemic	AN/OK/SAOEM/IK	antergia	ANT/ER/JA
anoxia	AN/OX/YA	antergic	ANT/ERJ/IK
	AI/NOX/YA	antergy	ANT/ER/JI

anteriad	AN/TAOER/YAD	anthramucin	AN/THRA/MAOU/SIN
anterior	AN/TAOER/YOR	anthramycin	AN/THRA/MAOI/SIN
anteriora	AN/TAOER/YOR/RA	anthranilate	AN/THRAN/LAIT
	AN/TAOER/YOER/RA	anthranilic	AN/THRA/NIL/IK
	AN/TAOER/YOE/RA	anthraniloyl	AN/THRA/NIL/OIL
anteriores	AN/TAOER/YOR/RAOEZ		AN/THRA/NIL/WIL
	AN/TAOER/YOER/RAOEZ	anthrapurpurin	AN/THRA/PURP/RIN
	AN/TAOER/YOE/RAOEZ	anthraquinol	AN/THRA/KWIN/OL
anterioris	AN/TAOER/YOR/RIS	anthraquinone	AN/THRA/KWIN/OEN
	AN/TAOER/YOER/RIS		AN/THRA/KWI/NOEN
	AN/TAOER/YOE/RIS	anthrarobin	AN/THRA/ROE/BIN
anterius	AN/TAOER/YUS	anthrax	AN/THRAX
antero-	ANT/RO	anthrone	AN/THROEN
	AENT/RO	anthropo-	AN/THRO/PO
anteroclusion	ANT/RO/KLAOUGS		AN/THROEP
anteroexternal	ANT/RO/EX/TERNL		AN/THROE/PO
anterograde	ANT/RO/GRAID	anthropobiology	AN/THRO/PO/BAO*I/OLG
anteroinferior	ANT/RO/IN/FAOER/YOR	anthropocentric	AN/THRO/PO/SEN/TRIK
anterointernal	ANT/RO/SPWERNL	anthropodeoxycholic	AN/THRO/PO/DE/OX/KOL/IK
anterolateral	ANT/RO/LAT/RAL		AN/THRO/PO/DE/OX/KOEL/IK
anterolateralis	ANT/RO/LAT/RAI/LIS	anthropogenesis	AN/THRO/PO/JEN/SIS
anteromedial	ANT/RO/MAOED/YAL	anthropogenetic	AN/THRO/PO/JE/NET/IK
anteromedian	ANT/RO/MAOED/YAN	anthropogenic	AN/THRO/PO/JEN/IK
anteroposterior	ANT/RO/POS/TAOER/YOR	anthropogeny	AN/THRO/POJ/N*I
anteroseptal	ANT/RO/SEP/TAL	anthropography	AN/THRO/POG/FI
anterosuperior	ANT/RO/SPAOER/YOR	anthropoid	AN/THRO/POID
	ANT/RO/SU/PAOER/YOR	Anthropoidea	AN/THRO/POID/YA
anterotransverse	ANT/RO/TRA*NS/VERS	anthropokinetics	AN/THRO/PO/KI/NET/IK/-S
anterotic	ANT/ROT/IK	anthropology	AN/THRO/POLG
	ANT/E/ROT/IK	anthropometer	AN/THRO/POM/TER
anteroventral	AN/TRO/VEN/TRAL	anthropometric	AN/THRO/PO/MET/RIK
antesystole	AENT/S*IS/LAOE	anthropometrist	AN/THRO/POM/TR*IS
anteversion	AENT/VERGS	anthropometry	AN/THRO/POM/TRI
anteverted	AENT/VERT/-D	anthropomorphism	AN/THRO/PO/MOR/FIFM
antexed	AN/TEX/-D	anthroponomy	AN/THRO/PON/M*I
antexion	AN/T*EBGS	anthropopathy	AN/THRO/POP/TH*I
anthelicus	ANT/HEL/KUS	anthropophaga	AN/THRO/POF/GA
	AN/THEL/KUS	anthropophagy	AN/THRO/POF/JI
	ANT/HAOEL/KUS	anthropophilic	AN/THRO/PO/FIL/IK
anthelix	ANT/HAOE/LIX	anthropophobia	AN/THRO/PO/FOEB/YA
	AN/THAOE/LIX	anthroposcopy	AN/THRO/POS/KPI
anthelminthic	ANT/HEL/M*INT/IK	anthroposomatology	AN/THRO/POE/SOEM/TLG
	AN/THEL/M*INT/IK		AN/THRO/PO/SOEM/TOLG
anthelmintic	ANT/HEL/MINT/IK	anthroposophy	AN/THRO/POS/FI
	AN/THEL/MINT/IK	anthropozoonosis	AN/THRO/PO/ZOE/NOE/SIS
anthelmycin	ANT/HEL/MAOI/SIN	anthropozoophilic	AN/THRO/PO/ZOE/FIL/IK
anthelone	ANT/HAOE/LOEN	anti-	A*ENT
	A*NT/LOEN		AN/TI
	AN/THE/LOEN	antiabortifacient	A*ENT/AI/BORT/FAIRBT
anthelotic	ANT/HAOE/LOT/IK	antiachromotrichia	A*ENT/AI/KROEM/TRIK/YA
anthema	AN/THAOE/MA	antiacrodynia	A*ENT/AK/RO/DIN/YA
	A*NT/MA	antiadrenergic	A*ENT/AD/RE/NERJ/IK
anthemorrhagic	ANT/HEM/RAJ/IK	antiagglutinate	A*ENT/AI/GLAOUT/NAIT
anther	AN/THER	antiagglutinating	A*ENT/AI/GLAOUT/NAIT/-G
	A*NT/ER	antiagglutinin	A*ENT/AI/GLAOUT/NIN
antherozoid	AN/THRO/ZOID	antiaggressin	A*ENT/AI/GRES/SIN
	A*NT/RO/ZOID	antialbumin	A*ENT/AL/BAOU/MIN
antherpetic	ANT/HER/PET/IK	antialexic	A*ENT/AI/LEX/IK
anthiolimine	AN/THAOI/YOEL/MIN	antialexin	A*ENT/AI/LEK/SIN
	AN/THAOI/OEL/MIN	antiallergic	A*ENT/AI/LERJ/IK
anthocyanidin	AN/THO/SAOI/AN/DIN	antialopecia	A*ENT/AL/PAOE/SHA
	AN/THO/SAOI/YAN/DIN		A*ENT/AL/PAOES/YA
anthocyanin	AN/THO/SAOI/NIN	antiamboceptor	A*ENT/AM/BO/SEP/TOR
anthocyaninemia	AN/THO/SAOI/NIN/AOEM/YA	antiamebic	A*ENT/AI/MAOEB/IK
anthocyaninuria	AN/THO/SAOI/NIN/YAOUR/YA	antiamylase	A*ENT/AM/LAIS
Anthomyia	AN/THO/MAOI/YA	antianaphylactin	A*ENT/AN/FLAK/TIN
Anthony	A*NT/N*I	antianaphylaxis	A*ENT/AN/FLAK/SIS
	AN/THO/N*I	antiandrogen	A*ENT/AN/DRO/JEN
anthoxanthin	AN/THO/ZAN/THIN	antianemia	A*ENT/AI/NAOEM/YA
anthracemia	AN/THRA/SAOEM/YA	antianemic	A*ENT/AI/NAOEM/IK
anthracene	AN/THRA/SAOEN	antianginal	A*ENT/AN/JI/NAL
anthracia	AN/THRAIS/YA	antianopheline	A*ENT/AI/NOF/LAOIN
anthracic	AN/THRAS/IK	antiantibody	A*ENT/A*ENT/BOD/DI
anthracin	AN/THRA/SIN	antiantidote	A*ENT/A*ENT/DOET
anthracis	AN/THRA/SIS	antiantitoxin	A*ENT/A*ENT/TOK/SIN
anthraco-	AN/THRA/KO	antianxiety	A*ENT/ANG/ZAOI/TI
anthracoid	AN/THRA/KOID	antiapoplectic	A*ENT/AP/PLEKT/IK
anthracometer	AN/THRA/KOM/TER	antiarachnolysin	A*ENT/AR/AK/NOL/SIN
anthracomucin	AN/THRA/KO/MAOU/SIN	antiarrhythmic	A*ENT/AI/R*IT/MIK
anthraconecrosis	AN/THRA/KO/NE/KROE/SIS	antiarsenin	A*ENT/ARS/NIN
anthracosilicosis	AN/THRA/KO/SIL/KOE/SIS	antiarthritic	A*ENT/AR/THRIT/IK
anthracosis	AN/THRA/KOE/SIS	antiasthmatic	A*ENT/AS/MAT/IK
anthracotherapy	AN/THRA/KO/THER/PI		A*ENT/AZ/MAT/IK
anthracotic	AN/THRA/KOT/IK	antiatherogenic	A*ENT/A*T/RO/JEN/IK
anthracycline	AN/THRA/SAOI/KLAOEN	antiautolysin	A*ENT/AU/TOL/SIN
	AN/THRA/SAOIK/LAOEN	antibacterial	A*ENT/BAK/TAOERL
Anthra-Derm	AN/THRA/DERM	antibechic	A*ENT/BEK/IK
anthragallol	AN/THRA/GAL/OL	antibiogram	A*ENT/BAO*I/GRAM
anthralin	AN/THRA/LIN	antibiont	A*ENT/BAO*I/YONT

	A*ENT/BAO*I/ONT
antibiosis	A*ENT/BAO*I/YOE/SIS
antibiotic	A*ENT/BAO*I/OT/IK
antibiotin	A*ENT/BAO*I/TIN
antiblastic	A*ENT/BLA*S/IK
antiblennorrhagic	A*ENT/BLEN/RAJ/IK
antibody	A*ENT/BOD/DI
antibromic	A*ENT/BROEM/IK
antibubonic	A*ENT/BAOU/BON/IK
anticachectic	A*ENT/KA/KEKT/IK
anticalculous	A*ENT/KAL/KLOUS
anticanities	A*ENT/KA/NIRB/SHAOEZ
	A*ENT/KA/NIRB/AOEZ
anticarcinogen	A*ENT/KAR/SIN/JEN
anticarcinogenic	A*ENT/KARS/NO/JEN/IK
	A*ENT/KAR/SIN/JEN/IK
anticariogenic	A*ENT/KAIR/YO/JEN/IK
anticarious	A*ENT/KAIR/YOUS
anticatalyst	A*ENT/KAT/L*IS
anticatalyzer	A*ENT/KAT/LAOIZ/ER
anticataphylactic	A*ENT/KAT/FLAKT/IK
anticataphylaxis	A*ENT/KAT/FLAK/SIS
anticathexis	A*ENT/KA/THEK/SIS
anticathode	A*ENT/KA*T/OED
anticephalalgic	A*ENT/SEF/LAL/JIK
	A*ENT/SEFL/AL/JIK
anticheirotonus	A*ENT/KAOI/ROT/NUS
antichlorotic	A*ENT/KLOR/ROT/IK
anticholagogue	A*ENT/KOL/GOG
	A*ENT/KOEL/GOG
anticholelithogenic	A*ENT/KOEL/L*IT/JEN/IK
anticholerin	A*ENT/KOL/RIN
anticholesteremic	A*ENT/KLE*S/RAOEM/IK
anticholesterolemic	A*ENT/KL*ES/ROL/AOEM/IK
anticholinergic	A*ENT/KOEL/NERJ/IK
anticholinesterase	A*ENT/KOEL/N*ES/RAIS
antichymosin	A*ENT/KAOIM/SIN
anticipate	AN/TIS/PAIT
anticipation	AN/TIS/PAIGS
anticlinal	A*ENT/KLAOINL
anticnemion	AN/TIK/NAOEM/YON
anticoagulant	A*ENT/KO/AG/LANT
anticoagulated	A*ENT/KO/AG/LAIT/-D
anticoagulative	A*ENT/KO/AG/LA/TIV
anticoagulin	A*ENT/KO/AG/LIN
anticodon	A*ENT/KO/DON
anticollagenase	A*ENT/KLAJ/NAIS
anticomplement	A*ENT/KOM/PLEMT
anticomplementary	A*ENT/KOM/PLEMT/RI
anticonceptive	A*ENT/KON/SEPT/IV
anticoncipiens	A*ENT/KON/SIP/YENZ
anticontagious	A*ENT/KON/TAIJ/OUS
	A*ENT/KON/TAI/JOUS
anticonvulsant	A*ENT/KON/VUL/SANT
anticonvulsive	A*ENT/KON/VULS/IV
anticrotin	A*ENT/KROE/TIN
anticurare	A*ENT/KAOU/RA/RAOE
	A*ENT/KAOU/RAR/RAOE
anticus	AN/TAOI/KUS
anticutin	AN/TI/KAOU/TIN
anticytolysin	A*ENT/SAOI/TOL/SIN
anticytotoxin	A*ENT/SAOIT/TOK/SIN
anti-D	A*ENT/D-RBGS
antidepressant	A*ENT/DPRES/SANT
	A*ENT/DE/PRES/SANT
antidermatitis	A*ENT/DERM/TAOITS
antidiabetic	A*ENT/DAOI/BET/IK
antidiabetogenic	A*ENT/DAOI/BET/JEN/IK
	A*ENT/DAOI/BAOE/TO/JEN/IK
antidiarrheal	A*ENT/DAOI/RAOEL
	A*ENT/DAOI/RAOE/YAL
antidiarrheic	A*ENT/DAOI/RAOE/IK
antidiastase	A*ENT/DI/AS/TAIS
antidinic	A*ENT/DIN/IK
antidipsetic	A*ENT/DIP/SET/IK
antidipsia	A*ENT/DIPS/YA
antidipticum	A*ENT/DIPT/KUM
antidiuresis	A*ENT/DI/YAOU/RAOE/SIS
	A*ENT/DAOI/RAOE/SIS
antidiuretic	A*ENT/DI/YAOU/RET/IK
	A*ENT/DAOI/RET/IK
	A*ENT/DI/YU/RET/IK
	A*ENT/DI/RET/IK
antidiuretin	A*ENT/DI/YAOU/RAOE/TIN
	A*ENT/DI/RAOE/TIN
antidotal	A*ENT/DOE/TAL
antidote	A*ENT/DOET
antidotic	A*ENT/DOT/IK
antidromic	A*ENT/DROM/IK

antidysenteric	A*ENT/DIS/SPWER/IK
antidysentericum	A*ENT/DIS/SPWER/KUM
antidysrhythmic	A*ENT/DIS/R*IT/MIK
antidysuric	A*ENT/DIS/YAOUR/IK
antieczematic	A*ENT/EX/MAT/IK
	A*ENT/EK/ZE/MAT/IK
antieczematous	A*ENT/EK/SEM/TOUS
antiedematous	A*ENT/E/DEM/TOUS
antiedemic	A*ENT/E/DEM/IK
antiemetic	A*ENT/E/MET/IK
antiemulsin	A*ENT/E/MUL/SIN
antiendotoxic	A*ENT/*END/TOX/IK
antiendotoxin	A*ENT/*END/TOK/SIN
antienergic	A*ENT/EN/ERJ/IK
antienzyme	A*ENT/EN/ZAOIM
antiepileptic	A*ENT/EP/LEPT/IK
antiepithelial	A*ENT/EP/THAOEL/YAL
antierotica	A*ENT/E/ROT/KA
antiesterase	A*ENT/ES/TRAIS
	(not *ES/RAIS)
antiestrogen	A*ENT/ES/TRO/JEN
antiestrogenic	A*ENT/ES/TRO/JEN/IK
antifebrile	A*ENT/FEB/RAOIL
	A*ENT/FEB/RIL
antifebrin	A*ENT/FEB/RIN
antifertilizin	A*ENT/FERT/LAOI/ZIN
antifibrillatory	A*ENT/FIB/RIL/TOIR
antifibrinolysin	A*ENT/FAOI/BRIN/OL/SIN
	A*ENT/FAOI/BRI/NOL/SIN
antifibrinolytic	A*ENT/FAOI/BRIN/LIT/IK
antifilarial	A*ENT/FI/LAIRL
	A*ENT/FLAIRL
antiflatulent	A*ENT/FLAFP/LENT
antiflux	A*ENT/FLUX
antifolic	A*ENT/FOEL/IK
antifungal	A*ENT/FUN/GAL
anti-G	A*ENT/H-F/G-RBGS
	A*ENT/G-RBGS
antigalactagogue	A*ENT/GLAKT/GOG
antigalactic	A*ENT/GLAKT/IK
antigametocyte	A*ENT/GA/MAOET/SAO*IT
antigelatinase	A*ENT/JE/LAT/NAIS
antigen	A*ENT/JEN
antigenemia	A*ENT/JE/NAOEM/YA
antigenemic	A*ENT/JE/NAOEM/IK
antigenic	A*ENT/JEN/IK
antigenicity	A*ENT/JE/NIS/TI
	A*ENT/JEN/IS/TI
antiglobulin	A*ENT/GLOB/LIN
antiglyoxalase	A*ENT/GLAOI/OX/LAIS
antigoitrogenic	A*ENT/GOI/TRO/JEN/IK
antigonadotropic	A*ENT/GOE/NAD/TROEP/IK
	A*ENT/GOE/NAD/TROP/IK
antigonorrheic	A*ENT/GON/RAOE/IK
antigravity	A*ENT/GRAV/TI
antigrowth	A*ENT/GRO*ET
antihallucinatory	A*ENT/HA/LAOUS/NA/TOIR
	A*ENT/HAL/LAOUS/NA/TOIR
antihelix	A*ENT/HAOE/LIX
	A*ENT/HAOEL/IX
antihelmintic	A*ENT/HEL/MINT/IK
antihemagglutinin	A*ENT/HAOEM/GLAOUT/NIN
	A*ENT/HEM/GLAOUT/NIN
antihemolysin	A*ENT/HAOE/MOL/SIN
	A*ENT/HE/MOL/SIN
antihemolytic	A*ENT/HAOEM/LIT/IK
	A*ENT/HEM/LIT/IK
antihemophilic	A*ENT/HAOEM/FIL/IK
antihemorrhagic	A*ENT/HEM/RAJ/IK
antiheterolysin	A*ENT/HET/ROL/SIN
antihidrotic	A*ENT/HAOI/DROT/IK
	A*ENT/HI/DROT/IK
antihistamine	A*ENT/H*IS/MAOEN
	A*ENT/H*IS/MIN
antihistaminic	A*ENT/H*IS/MIN/IK
antihormone	A*ENT/HOR/MOEN
antihyaluronidase	A*ENT/HAOI/LAOU/RON/DAIS
antihydrophobic	A*ENT/HAOI/DRO/FOEB/IK
antihydropic	A*ENT/HAOI/DROP/IK
antihypercholesterolemic	A*ENT/HAO*IP/KL*ES/ROL/ AOEM/IK
antihyperglycemic	A*ENT/HAO*IP/GLAOI/SAOEM/IK
antihyperlipoproteinemic	A*ENT/HAO*IP/LIP/PROET/ NAOEM/IK
antihypertensive	A*ENT/HAO*IP/TENS/IV
antihypnotic	A*ENT/HIP/NOT/IK
antihypotensive	A*ENT/HO*IP/TENS/IV
antihysteric	A*ENT/HIS/TER/IK
anti-icteric	A*ENT/IK/TER/IK

anti-immune	A*ENT/IM/MAOUN		SIS
anti-infectious	A*ENT/IN/FEK/-RBS	antinauseant	A*ENT/NAI/TRAOE/YU/RAOE/SIS
anti-infective	A*ENT/IN/FEKT/IV		A*ENT/NAI/TRI/YAOU/RAOE/SIS
anti-inflammatory	A*ENT/IN/FLAM/TOIR		A*ENT/NAI/TRI/YU/RAOE/SIS
anti-insulin	A*ENT/INS/LIN	antinauseant	A*ENT/NAUZ/YANT
anti-intermediary	A*ENT/SPWER/MAOED/YAIR	antineoplastic	A*ENT/NAOE/PLA*S/IK
anti-invasin	A*ENT/IN/VAI/SIN	antineoplaston	A*ENT/NAOE/PLAS/TON
anti-isolysin	A*ENT/AOI/SOL/SIN	antinephritic	A*ENT/NE/FRIT/IK
antikenotoxin	A*ENT/KAOEN/TOK/SIN		A*ENT/NEF/RIT/IK
antiketogen	A*ENT/KAOET/JEN	antineuralgic	A*ENT/NAOU/RAL/JIK
antiketogenesis	A*ENT/KAOET/JEN/SIS		A*ENT/NAOUR/AL/JIK
antiketogenetic	A*ENT/KAOET/JE/NET/IK	antineuritic	A*ENT/NAOU/RIT/IK
antiketogenic	A*ENT/KAOET/JEN/IK	antineurotoxin	A*ENT/NAOUR/TOK/SIN
antiketoplastic	A*ENT/KAOET/PLA*S/IK	antineutrino	A*ENT/NAOU/TRAOE/NOE
antikinase	A*ENT/KAOI/NAIS	antineutron	A*ENT/NAOU/TRON
antikinesis	A*ENT/KI/NAOE/SIS	antiniad	AN/TIN/YAD
antilactase	A*ENT/LAK/TAIS	antinial	AN/TIN/YAL
antilactoserum	A*ENT/LAKT/SAOERM	antinion	AN/TIN/YON
antileishmanial	A*ENT/LERB/MAIN/YAL	antinomy	AN/TIN/M*I
antileprotic	A*ENT/LEP/ROT/IK	antinuclear	A*ENT/NAOUK/LAR
	A*ENT/LE/PROT/IK	Antiochenus	AN/SHOK/NUS
antilethargic	A*ENT/LE/THARJ/IK		ANT/YOK/NUS
antileukocidin	A*ENT/LAOU/KOES/DIN	antiodontalgic	A*ENT/O/DON/TAL/JIK
	A*ENT/LAOU/KOS/DIN		ANT/YO/DON/TAL/JIK
	A*ENT/LAOUK/SAOI/DIN	antioncogene	A*ENT/ON/KO/JAOEN
antileukocytic	A*ENT/LAOUK/SIT/IK	antioncotic	A*ENT/ON/KOT/IK
antileukoprotease	A*ENT/LAOUK/PROET/YAIS	antiophthalmic	A*ENT/OF/THAL/MIK
antileukotoxin	A*ENT/LAOUK/TOK/SIN	antiopsonin	A*ENT/OPS/NIN
antilewisite	A*ENT/LAOU/WI/SAOIT		A*ENT/OP/SO/NIN
	A*ENT/LAO*U/SAOIT		A*ENT/OP/SOE/NIN
	A*ENT/LAOU/SAOIT (but see	antiovulatory	A*ENT/OV/LA/TOIR
	Lucite)	antioxidant	A*ENT/OX/DANT
antilipase	A*ENT/LIP/AIS	antioxidase	A*ENT/OX/DAIS
antilipemic	A*ENT/LI/PAOEM/IK	antioxidation	A*ENT/OX/DAIGS
	A*ENT/LAOI/PAOEM/IK	antioxygen	A*ENT/OX/JEN
antilipoid	A*ENT/LIP/OID	antipaludian	A*ENT/PA/LAOUD/YAN
antilipotropic	A*ENT/LIP/TROP/IK	antiparallel	A*ENT/PAR/LEL
antilipotropism	A*ENT/LIP/OT/RO/PIFM	antiparalytic	A*ENT/PAR/LIT/IK
	A*ENT/LI/POT/RO/PIFM	antiparasitic	A*ENT/PAR/SIT/IK
Antilirium	A*ENT/LIR/YUM	antiparastata	A*ENT/TA/RA*S/TA
antilithic	A*ENT/L*IT/IK		A*ENT/PA/RAS/TA/TA
antilobium	A*ENT/LOEB/YUM	antiparastatitis	A*ENT/PA/RA*S/TAOITS
antiluetic	A*ENT/LAOU/ET/IK		A*ENT/PA/RAS/TA/TAOITS
antiluteogenic	A*ENT/LAOUT/YO/JEN/IK	antiparasympathomimetic	A*ENT/PAR/SIFRP/THO/MAOI/
antilysin	A*ENT/LAOI/SIN		MET/IK
antilysis	A*ENT/LAOI/SIS	antiparkinsonian	A*ENT/PARK/SOEN/YAN
antilytic	A*ENT/LIT/IK		A*ENT/PAR/KIN/SOEN/YAN
antimalarial	A*ENT/MA/LAIRL	antiparticle	A*ENT/PART/K-L
antimaniacal	A*ENT/MA/NAOI/KAL	antipathic	A*ENT/PA*T/IK
antimanic	A*ENT/MAN/IK	antipathogen	A*ENT/PA*T/JEN
antimephitic	A*ENT/ME/FIT/IK	antipathy	AN/TIP/TH*I
antimer	A*ENT/MER	antipedicular	A*ENT/PE/DIK/LAR
antimere	A*ENT/MAOER	antipediculotic	A*ENT/PE/DIK/LOT/IK
antimeristem	A*ENT/ME/RIS/TEM	antipellagra	A*ENT/PEL/LAG/RA
antimesenteric	A*ENT/MES/SPWER/IK		A*ENT/PEL/AG/RA
	A*ENT/MES/EN/TER/IK	antipepsin	A*ENT/PEP/SIN
antimetabolite	A*ENT/ME/TAB/LAOIT	antiperiodic	A*ENT/PAOER/YOD/IK
antimethemoglobinemic	A*ENT/MET/HAOEM/GLOEB/	antiperistalsis	A*ENT/P*ER/STAL/SIS
	NAOEM/IK	antiperistaltic	A*ENT/P*ER/STALT/IK
antimetropia	A*ENT/ME/TROEP/YA	anti-pernicious	A*ENT/PER/NIRBS
antimiasmatic	A*ENT/MAOI/AZ/MAT/IK	antiperspirant	A*ENT/PERS/PRANT
antimicrobial	A*ENT/MAOI/KROEB/YAL	antiphagocytic	A*ENT/FAG/SIT/IK
antimineralocorticoid	A*ENT/MIN/RAL/KORT/KOID	antiphlogistic	A*ENT/FLOE/J*IS/IK
antimitotic	A*ENT/MAOI/TOT/IK	antiphobic	A*ENT/FOEB/IK
antimongoloid	A*ENT/MONG/LOID	antiphthiriac	A*ENT/THIR/YAK
antimongolism	A*ENT/MONG/LIFM	antiphthisic	A*ENT/TIZ/IK
antimonial	A*ENT/MOEN/YAL	antiplasmin	A*ENT/PLAZ/MIN
antimonic	A*ENT/MON/IK	antiplasmodial	A*ENT/PLAZ/MOED/YAL
antimonid	A*ENT/MOE/NID	antiplastic	A*ENT/PLA*S/IK
antimonious	A*ENT/MOEN/YOUS	antiplatelet	A*ENT/PLAET/LET
antimonium	A*ENT/MOEN/YUM		A*ENT/PLAIT/LET
antimonous	A*ENT/MOE/NOUS	antipneumococcic	A*ENT/NAOUM/KOK/SIK
anti-Monson	A*ENT/MON/SON		A*ENT/NAOUM/KOX/IK
	A*ENT/H-F/MON/SON	antipodagric	A*ENT/POE/DAG/RIK
antimony	A*ENT/MOE/N*I	antipodal	AN/TIP/DAL
antimonyl	AN/TIM/NIL	antipode	A*ENT/POED
antimorph	A*ENT/MOR/-F	antipolycythemic	A*ENT/POL/SAOI/THAOEM/IK
antimorphic	A*ENT/MOR/FIK	antiport	A*ENT/PORT
antimuscarinic	A*ENT/MUS/KRIN/IK	antiporter	A*ENT/PORT/ER
	A*ENT/MUS/KA/RIN/IK		A*ENT/POR/TER
antimutagen	A*ENT/MAOUT/JEN	antiposia	A*ENT/POEZ/YA
antimutagenic	A*ENT/MAOUT/JEN/IK	antiposic	A*ENT/POES/IK
antimyasthenic	A*ENT/MAOI/AS/THEN/IK	antiprecipitin	A*ENT/PRE/SIP/TIN
	A*ENT/MAOI/YAS/THEN/IK	antiprogestin	A*ENT/PRO/JES/TIN
antimycobacterial	A*ENT/MAOIK/BAK/TAOERL	antiprostate	A*ENT/PROS/TAIT
antimycotic	A*ENT/MAOI/KOT/IK	antiprostatitis	A*ENT/PRO*S/TAOITS
antinarcotic	A*ENT/NAR/KOT/IK		A*ENT/PROS/TA/TAOITS
antinatriferic	A*ENT/NAI/TRIF/RIK	antiprotease	A*ENT/PROET/YAIS
antinatriuresis	A*ENT/NAI/TRAOE/YAOU/RAOE/	antiprothrombin	A*ENT/PRO/THROM/BIN

antiprotozoal	A*ENT/PROET/ZOEL	antitoxic	A*ENT/TOX/IK
antiprotozoan	A*ENT/PROET/ZOE/WAN	antitoxigen	A*ENT/TOX/JEN
antipruritic	A*ENT/PRAOU/RIT/IK	antitoxin	A*ENT/TOK/SIN
antipsoriatic	A*ENT/SOER/YAT/IK	antitoxinogen	A*ENT/TOK/SIN/JEN
	A*ENT/SOR/YAT/IK	antitoxinum	A*ENT/TOK/SAOIN/UM
antipsoric	A*ENT/SOER/IK	antitragicus	A*ENT/TRAJ/KUS
antipsychomotor	A*ENT/SAOIK/MOE/TOR	antitragohelicine	A*ENT/TRAIG/HEL/SAOEN
antipsychotic	A*ENT/SAOI/KOT/IK	antitragus	A*ENT/TRAI/GUS
antiputrefactive	A*ENT/PAOU/TRE/FAKT/IV	antitreponemal	A*ENT/TREP/NAOE/MAL
antipyogenic	A*ENT/PAOI/JEN/IK	antitrichomonal	A*ENT/TRIK/MOENL
antipyresis	A*ENT/PAOI/RAOE/SIS	antitrismus	A*ENT/TRIZ/MUS
antipyretic	A*ENT/PAOI/RET/IK	antitrope	A*ENT/TROEP
antipyrine	A*ENT/PAOI/RIN	antitropic	A*ENT/TROEP/IK
	A*ENT/PAOI/RAOEN		A*ENT/TROP/IK
antipyrotic	A*ENT/PAOI/ROT/IK	antitropin	A*ENT/TROE/PIN
antirabic	A*ENT/RAIB/IK	antitrypanosomal	A*ENT/TRI/PAN/SOE/MAL
antirachitic	A*ENT/RA/KIT/IK		A*ENT/TRAOI/PAN/SOE/MAL
antiradiation	A*ENT/RAID/YAIGS	antitrypsic	A*ENT/TRIPS/IK
antirennin	A*ENT/REN/NIN		A*ENT/TRIP/SIK
anti-Rh	A*ENT/RAIFP	antitrypsin	A*ENT/TRIP/SIN
	A*ENT/R-RBGS/H*BGZ	antitryptase	A*ENT/TRIP/TAIS
	A*ENT/H-F/RAIFP	antitryptic	A*ENT/TRIPT/IK
	A*ENT/H-F/R-RBGS/H*BGZ	antituberculin	A*ENT/TAOU/BERK/LIN
antirheumatic	A*ENT/RAOU/MAT/IK	antituberculotic	A*ENT/TAOU/BERK/LOT/IK
antiricin	A*ENT/RAOI/SIN	antituberculous	A*ENT/TAOU/BERK/LOUS
antirickettsial	A*ENT/RI/KETS/YAL	antitubulin	A*ENT/TAOUB/LIN
antirobin	A*ENT/ROE/BIN	antitumorigenesis	A*ENT/TAOU/MOR/JEN/SIS
anti-S	A*ENT/H-F/S-RBGS	antitumorigenic	A*ENT/TAOU/MOR/JEN/IK
	A*ENT/S-RBGS	antitussive	A*ENT/TUS/SIV
antisaluresis	A*ENT/SAL/RAOE/SIS		A*ENT/TUSZ/IV
	A*ENT/SAL/YAOU/RAOE/SIS	antityphoid	A*ENT/TAOI/FOID
	A*ENT/SAL/YU/RAOE/SIS	antityrosinase	A*ENT/TAOI/ROES/NAIS
antiscabietic	A*ENT/SKAIB/YET/IK	antiulcerative	A*ENT/ULS/RA/TIV
antiscabious	A*ENT/SKAIB/YOUS	antiuratic	A*ENT/YAOU/RAT/IK
antiscarlatinal	A*ENT/SKARL/TAOINL	antiurease	A*ENT/YAOUR/YAIS
	A*ENT/SKAR/LA/TAOINL	antiurokinase	A*ENT/YAOUR/KAOI/NAIS
antischistosomal	A*ENT/SH*IS/SOE/MAL	antivaccinationist	A*ENT/VAX/NAIGS/*IS
antiscorbutic	A*ENT/SKOR/BAOUT/IK	antivenene	A*ENT/VEN/AOEN
antiseborrheic	A*ENT/SEB/RAOE/IK		A*ENT/VEN/NAOEN
antisecretory	A*ENT/SE/KRAOT/RI	antivenereal	A*ENT/VE/NAOERL
antisensitizer	A*ENT/SENS/TAOIZ/ER	antivenin	A*ENT/VEN/NIN
antisepsis	A*ENT/SEP/SIS		A*ENT/VE/NIN
antiseptic	A*ENT/SEPT/IK	antivenom	A*ENT/VEN/OM
antisepticism	A*ENT/SEPT/SIFM	antivenomous	A*ENT/VEN/MOUS
antisepticize	A*ENT/SEPT/SAOIZ	antiviral	A*ENT/VAOIRL
antiserum	A*ENT/SAOERM	Antivert	A*ENT/VERT
antisialagogue	A*ENT/SAOI/AL/GOG	antivirotic	A*ENT/VAOI/ROT/IK
	A*ENT/SAOI/YAL/GOG	antivirulin	A*ENT/VIR/LIN
antisialic	A*ENT/SAOI/AL/IK	antivirus	A*ENT/VAOI/RUS
	A*ENT/SAOI/YAL/IK	antivitamer	A*ENT/VAOIT/MER
antisideric	A*ENT/SID/RIK	antivitamin	A*ENT/VAOIT/MIN
	A*ENT/SI/DER/IK	antivivisection	A*ENT/VIV/S*EBGS
antisocial	A*ENT/SOERBL	antivivisectionist	A*ENT/VIV/S*EBGS/*IS
antisocialism	A*ENT/SOERBL/IFM	antixenic	A*ENT/ZAOEN/IK
antispasmodic	A*ENT/SPAZ/MOD/IK	antixerophthalmia	A*ENT/ZAOER/OF/THAL/MA
antispastic	A*ENT/SPA*S/IK		A*ENT/ZAOER/OF/THAL/MAOE/ YA
antispermotoxin	A*ENT/SPERM/TOK/SIN	antixerophthalmic	A*ENT/ZAOER/OF/THAL/MIK
antistaphylococcal	A*ENT/STAF/LO/KOK/KAL	antixerotic	A*ENT/ZE/ROT/IK
antistaphylococcic	A*ENT/STAF/LO/KOX/IK		A*ENT/ZAOE/ROT/IK
	A*ENT/STAF/LO/KOK/SIK	antizyme	A*ENT/ZAOIM
antistaphylohemolysin	A*ENT/STAF/LO/HAOE/MOL/SIN	antizymohexase	A*ENT/ZAOIM/HEX/AIS
antistaphylolysin	A*ENT/STAF/LOL/SIN		A*ENT/ZAOIM/HEK/SAIS
antisteapsin	A*ENT/STAOE/AP/SIN	antizymotic	A*ENT/ZAOI/MOT/IK
	A*ENT/STAOE/YAP/SIN	Anton	AN/TON
antisterility	A*ENT/STRIL/TI	antophthalmic	ANT/OF/THAL/MIK
	A*ENT/STER/IL/TI	antorphine	AN/TOR/FAOEN
antistiffness	A*ENT/STIF/*NS	antoxyproteic	AN/TOX/PRO/TAI/IK
antistreptococcic	A*ENT/STREPT/KOX/IK		AN/TOX/PRO/TAOE/IK
	A*ENT/STREPT/KOK/SIK	antr(o)-	AN/TR(O)
antistreptokinase	A*ENT/STREPT/KAOI/NAIS	antra	AN/TRA
antistreptolysin	A*ENT/STREP/TOL/SIN	antracele	AN/TRA/SAO*EL
antisubstance	A*ENT/SUB/STANS	antral	AN/TRAL
antisudoral	A*ENT/SAOUD/RAL	antrectomy	AN/TREKT/M*I
antisudorific	A*ENT/SAOUD/RIFK	antritis	AN/TRAOITS
antisympathetic	A*ENT/SIFRP/THET/IK	antroatticotomy	AN/TRO/AT/KOT/M*I
antisyphilitic	A*ENT/SIF/LIT/IK	antrobuccal	AN/TRO/BUK/KAL
antitemplate	A*ENT/TEM/PLAET	antrocele	AN/TRO/SAO*EL
	A*ENT/TEM/PLAIT	antroduodenectomy	AN/TRO/DAOU/DEN/EKT/M*I
antitetanic	A*ENT/TE/TAN/IK		AN/TRO/DAOU/DE/NEKT/M*I
antitetanolysin	A*ENT/TET/NOL/SIN		AN/TRO/DWOD/NEKT/M*I
antithenar	A*ENT/THAOE/NAR	antrodynia	AN/TRO/DIN/YA
antithermic	A*ENT/THERM/IK	Antrocol	AN/TRO/KOL
antithrombin	A*ENT/THROM/BIN	antronalgia	AN/TRO/NAL/JA
antithromboplastin	A*ENT/THROM/BO/PLAS/TIN	antronasal	AN/TRO/NAI/ZAL
antidthrombotic	A*ENT/THROM/BOT/IK	antroneurolysis	AN/TRO/NAOU/ROL/SIS
antithyroid	A*ENT/THAOI/ROID	antrophore	AN/TRO/FOER
antithyrotoxic	A*ENT/THAOIR/TOX/IK	antrophose	AN/TRO/FOEZ
antithyrotropic	A*ENT/THAOIR/TROP/IK	antrophose	AN/TRO/FOES
antitonic	A*ENT/TON/IK		

antropyloric	AN/TRO/PAOI/LOR/IK	apancrea	AI/PAN/KRA
antroscope	AN/TRO/SKOEP		AI/PAN/KRAOE/YA
antroscopy	AN/TROS/KPI	apancreatic	AI/PAN/KRAT/IK
antrostomy	AN/TRO*S/M*I		AI/PAN/KRAOE/AT/IK
antrotome	AN/TRO/TOEM	aparalytic	AI/PAR/LIT/IK
antrotomy	AN/TROT/M*I	aparathyreosis	AI/PAR/THAOIR/YOE/SIS
antrotonia	AN/TRO/TOEN/YA	aparathyroidism	AI/PAR/THAOI/ROID/IFM
antrotympanic	AN/TRO/TIM/PAN/IK		AI/PAR/THAOI/ROI/DIFM
antrotympanitis	AN/TRO/TIFRP/NAOITS	aparathyrosis	AI/PAR/THAOI/ROE/SIS
antrum	AN/TRUM	apareunia	AI/PAR/YAOUN/YA
Anturane	AN/TAOU/RAIN		AI/PA/RAOUN/YA
	AN/KHU/RAIN	aparthrosis	AP/AR/THROE/SIS
anuclear	AI/NAOUK/LAR	apastia	AI/PA*S/YA
anucleate	AI/NAOUK/LAIT	apastic	AI/PA*S/IK
anul-	A*N/L-	Apatate	AP/TAIT
	A*N/YAOU/L-	apathetic	AP/THET/IK
	A*N/YU/L-	apathic	AI/PA*T/IK
	(not AN/Y-, etc.; see annul-)	apathism	AP/THIFM
anulare	A*N/LAI/RAOE	apathy	AP/TH*I
	(see annulare)	apatite	A*P/TAOIT
anularia	A*N/LAIR/YA		AP/PA/TAOIT
anularis	A*N/LAI/RIS		(not AP/TAOIT; see appetite)
anuli	A*N/LAOI	apazone	AP/ZOEN
	(see annuli)	apeidosis	AP/AOID/DOE/SIS
anulus	A*N/LUS		AP/AOI/DOE/SIS
	(see annulus)	apellous	AI/PEL/OUS
anuresis	AN/YAOU/RAOE/SIS		AI/PEL/LOUS
	AN/YU/RAOE/SIS	Apelt	AI/PELT
anuretic	AN/YAOU/RET/IK	apenteric	AP/SPWER/IK
	AN/YU/RET/IK	apepsia	AI/PEPS/YA
anuria	AI/NAOUR/YA	apepsinia	AI/PEP/SIN/YA
	AN/YAOUR/YA	aperient	AI/PAOER/YENT
anuric	AN/YAOUR/IK	aperiodic	AI/PAOER/YOD/IK
	AI/NAOUR/IK	aperiosteal	AI/P*ER/O*S/YAL
anus	AI/NUS	aperistalsis	AI/P*ER/STAL/SIS
anusitis	AIN/SAOITS	aperitive	AI/PER/TIV
	AI/NUS/AOITS	Apert	AI/PAR
	AI/NUS/SAOITS	Apert-Crouzon	AI/PAR/H-F/KRAOU/ZON
Anusol	AN/YAOU/SOL	apertognathia	AI/PERT/NAT/YA
	AN/YU/SOL		AI/PERT/NA*IT/YA
Anusol-HC	AN/YAOU/SOL/H-RBGS/KR*RBGS		AI/PER/TOG/NAT/YA
	AN/YU/SOL/H-RBGS/KR*RBGS		AI/PER/TOG/NA*IT/YA
anvil	AN/VIL	apertometer	AP/ER/TOM/TER
anxietas	ANG/ZAOI/TAS	apertura	AP/ER/TAOU/RA
anxiety	ANG/ZAOI/TI		AP/ER/KHUR/RA
anxiolytic	ANGS/YO/LIT/IK	aperturae	AP/PER/TAOU/RAE
aort(o)-	AI/YOR/T(O)		AP/ER/KHUR/RAE
	AI/OR/T(O)	aperture	AP/ER/KHUR
aorta	AI/YOR/TA		AP/ER/TAOUR
aortae	AI/YOR/TAE	Apetil	AP/TIL
aortal	AI/YOR/TAL	apex	AI/PEX
aortalgia	AI/YOR/TAL/JA	apexcardiogram	AI/PEX/KARD/YO/GRAM
aortarctia	AI/YOR/TARK/SHA	apexcardiography	AI/PEX/KARD/YOG/FI
aortartia	AI/YOR/TAR/SHA	apexification	AI/PEX/FI/KAIGS
aortectasia	AI/YOR/TEK/TAIZ/YA	apexigraph	AI/PEX/GRAF
aortectasis	AI/YOR/TEKT/SIS	Apgar	AP/GAR
aortectomy	AI/YOR/TEKT/M*I	aphagia	AI/FAI/JA
aortic	AI/YORT/IK	aphagopraxia	AI/FAG/PRAX/YA
aortic(o)-	AI/YORT/K(O)	aphakia	AI/FAIK/YA
	AI/ORT/K(O)	aphakial	AI/FAIK/YAL
aorticopulmonary	AI/YORT/KO/PUL/MO/NAIR	aphakic	AI/FAIK/IK
	AI/YORT/KO/PUM/NAIR	aphalangia	AI/FLAN/JA
aorticorenal	AI/YORT/KO/RAOENL		AF/LAN/JA
aortismus abdominalis	AI/YOR/TIS/MUS/AB/DOM/NAI/LIS	aphanisis	AI/FAN/SIS
		aphasia	AI/FAIZ/YA
aortitis	AI/YOR/TAOITS	aphasiac	AI/FAIZ/YAK
aorto-	AI/YORT	aphasic	AI/FAIZ/IK
	AI/ORT	aphasiologist	AI/FAIZ/YO*LGS
	AI/YOR/TO	aphasiology	AI/FAIZ/YOLG
	AI/OR/TO	aphasmid	AI/FAZ/MID
aortocoronary	AI/YORT/KOR/NAIR	Aphasmidia	AI/FAZ/MID/YA
aortogram	AI/YORT/GRAM	apheliotropism	AP/HAOEL/YOT/RO/PIFM
aortography	AI/YOR/TOG/FI	aphemesthesia	AF/MES/THAOEZ/YA
aortoiliac	AI/YORT/IL/YAK		AI/FE/MES/THAOEZ/YA
aortopathy	AI/YOR/TOP/TH*I	aphemia	AI/FAOEM/YA
aortoplasty	AI/YORT/PLAS/TI	aphemic	AI/FAOEM/IK
aortoptosia	AI/YOR/TOP/TOEZ/YA		AI/FEM/IK
aortoptosis	AI/YOR/TOP/TOE/SIS	aphephobia	AF/FOEB/YA
aortorenal	AI/YORT/RAOENL	apheresis	AI/FER/SIS
aortorrhaphy	AI/YOR/TOR/FI	apheter	AF/TER
aortosclerosis	AI/YORT/SKLE/ROE/SIS	-aphia	AIF/YA
aortostenosis	AI/YOR/STE/NOE/SIS	aphonia	AI/FOEN/YA
aortotomy	AI/YOR/TOT/M*I	aphonic	AI/FON/IK
aosmic	AI/OZ/MIK	aphonogelia	AI/FON/JAOEL/YA
	AI/YOZ/MIK		AI/FOEN/JAOEL/YA
AP	A-RBGS/P*RBGS	aphonous	AF/NOUS
apallesthesia	AI/PAL/ES/THAOEZ/YA	aphose	AI/FOEZ
	AI/PAL/STHAOEZ/YA		AI/FOES
apallic	AI/PAL/IK	aphosphagenic	AI/FOS/FA/JEN/IK

aphosphorosis	AI/FOS/FROE/SIS	apodous	AP/DOUS
	AI/FOS/FO/ROE/SIS	apody	AP/DI
aphotesthesia	AI/FOET/ES/THAOEZ/YA	apoenzyme	AP/EN/ZAOIM
	AI/FOT/ES/THAOEZ/YA	apoferritin	AP/FER/TIN
aphotic	AI/FOT/IK	apogamia	AP/GAM/YA
aphrasia	AI/FRAIZ/YA	apogamy	AI/POG/M*I
aphrenia	AF/FRAOEN/YA	apogee	AP/JAOE
aphrodisia	AF/RO/DIZ/YA	apolar	AI/POE/LAR
	AF/RO/DAOEZ/YA	apolegamic	AP/LE/GAM/IK
aphrodisiac	AF/RO/DIZ/YAK	apolegamy	AP/LEG/M*I
	AF/RO/DAOEZ/YAK	apolepsis	AP/LEP/SIS
aphrodisiomania	AF/RO/DIZ/YO/MAIN/YA	apolipoprotein	AP/LIP/PRO/TAOEN
	AF/RO/DAOEZ/YO/MAIN/YA	apoamixia	AP/MIX/YA
aphtha	AF/THA*	apomorphine	AP/MOR/FAOEN
	AP/THA		AP/MOR/FIN
	(not AF/THA; see after that)	aponeurectomy	AP/NAOU/REKT/M*I
aphthae	AF/THAE	aponeurology	AP/NAOU/ROLG
aphthoid	AF/THOID	aponeurorrhaphy	AP/NAOU/ROR/FI
aphthongia	AF/THON/JA	aponeuroses	AP/NAOU/ROE/SAOEZ
aphthosis	AF/THOE/SIS	aponeurosis	AP/NAOU/ROE/SIS
aphthous	AF/THOUS	aponeurositis	AP/NAOUR/SAOITS
aphylactic	AI/FLAKT/IK	aponeurotic	AP/NAOU/ROT/IK
aphylaxis	AI/FLAK/SIS	aponeurotica	AP/NAOU/ROT/KA
apical	AP/KAL	aponeurotome	AP/NAOUR/TOEM
apicalis	AP/KAI/LIS	aponeurotomy	AP/NAOU/ROT/M*I
apicectomy	AP/SEKT/M*I	apopathetic	AP/PA/THET/IK
apiciotomy	AI/PIS/YOT/M*I	apophlegmatic	AP/FLEG/MAT/IK
apices	AP/SAOEZ	apophylactic	AP/FLAKT/IK
apicis	AP/SIS	apophylaxis	AP/FLAK/SIS
apicitis	AP/SAOITS	apophysary	AI/POF/SAIR
apicoectomy	AP/KO/EKT/M*I	apophyses	Ai/POF/SAOEZ
apicolocator	AP/KO/LOE/KAI/TOR	apophysial	AP/FIZ/YAL
apicolysis	AP/KOL/SIS	apophysiopathy	AP/FIZ/YOP/TH*I
Apicomplexa	AP/KOM/PLEK/SA	apophysis	AI/POF/SIS
	AP/KPLEK/SA	apophysitis	AI/POF/SAOITS
apicoposterior	AP/KO/POS/TAOER/YOR	apoplasmatic	AP/PLAZ/MAT/IK
apicostome	AP/KO/STOEM	apoplasmia	AP/PLAZ/MAOE/YA
apicostomy	AP/KO*S/M*I	apoplectic	AP/PLEKT/IK
apicotomy	AP/KOT/M*I	apoplectiform	AP/PLEKT/FORM
apiculate	AI/PIK/LAIT	apoplectoid	AP/PLEK/TOID
apiculus	AI/PIK/LUS	apoplexia	AP/PLEX/YA
apicurettage	AP/KAOUR/TAJ	apoplexy	AP/PLEK/SI
apinealism	AP/PIN/LIFM	apoprotein	AP/PRO/TAOEN
	AP/PIN/YAL/IFM	apoptosis	AP/TOE/SIS
apinoid	AP/NOID		AP/OP/TOE/SIS
apiphobia	AIP/FOEB/YA	aporepressor	AP/RE/PRES/SOR
	AI/PI/FOEB/YA	aporia	AI/POER/YA
apiotherapy	AIP/YO/THER/PI	aposome	AP/SOEM
apisination	AI/PIS/NAIGS	aposorbic	AP/SORB/IK
apitoxin	AIP/TOK/SIN	apostasis	AI/PO*S/SIS
	AI/PI/TOK/SIN	apostaxis	AP/STAK/SIS
apituitarism	AI/PI/TAOU/TRIFM	apostema	AP/STAOE/MA
	AI/PI/TAOU/TAR/IFM		AP/OS/TAOE/MA
aplacental	AI/PLA/SEN/TAL	apostematosa	AP/STEM/TOE/SA
aplanatic	AP/LA/NAT/IK	apostematous	AP/STEM/TOUS
aplanatism	AI/PLAN/TIFM	aposthia	AI/POS/THAOE/YA
aplasia	AI/PLAIZ/YA		AI/POS/THA
aplasmic	AP/PLAZ/MIK	apostilb	AP/STIL/-B
aplastic	AI/PLA*S/IK	apothanasia	AP/THA/NAIZ/YA
apleuria	AI/PLAOUR/YA	apothecary	AI/PO*T/KAIR
Aplisol	AP/LI/SOL	apothecium	AP/THAOES/YUM
Aplitest	AP/LI/T*ES	apothem	AP/THEM
apnea	AP/NA	apotheme	AP/THAOEM
	AP/NAOE/YA	apotrophic	AP/TROFK
apneic	AP/NIK	apoxemena	AP/OK/SEM/NA
	AP/NAOE/IK	apoxesis	AP/OK/SAOE/SIS
apneumatic	AP/NAOU/MAT/IK	apozem	AP/ZEM
apneumatosis	AP/NAOUM/TOE/SIS	apozema	AP/OZ/MA
apneumia	AP/NAOUM/YA	apozeme	AP/ZAOEM
apneusis	AP/NAOU/SIS	apozymase	AP/ZAOI/MAIS
apneustic	AP/NAO*US/IK		AP/ZAOIM/AIS
apo-	AP	apparatus	AP/RA/TUS
apoatropine	AP/AT/RO/PAOEN		AP/RAI/TUS
apobiosis	AP/BAO*I/YOE/SIS		AP/PRA/TUS
apocamnosis	AP/KAM/NOE/SIS	apparent	AI/PARNT
apocarteresis	AP/KART/RAOE/SIS	appearance	AI/PAOERNS
apocenosis	AP/SE/NOE/SIS	appendage	AI/PEND/AJ
apochromat	AP/KROE/MAT		AI/PEN/DAJ
apochromatic	AP/KROE/MAT/IK	appendagitis	AI/PEND/JAOITS
apocleisis	AP/KLAOI/SIS	appendalgia	AP/EN/DAL/JA
apocope	AI/POK/PAOE	appendectomy	AP/EN/DEKT/M*I
apocoptic	AP/KOPT/IK	appendic(o)-	AI/PEND/K(O)
apocrine	AP/KRIN		AI/PEND/S(O) (if sounded)
apocrinitis	AP/KRI/NAOITS	appendical	AI/PEND/KAL
	AP/KRIN/AOITS	appendiceal	AP/EN/DIS/YAL
apocrustic	AP/KR*US/IK		AI/PEND/SAOEL
apodal	AI/POE/DAL	appendicectasis	AI/PEND/SEKT/SIS
apodemialgia	AP/DAOEM/YAL/JA	appendicectomy	AI/PEND/SEKT/M*I
apodia	AI/POED/YA	appendices	AI/PEND/SAOEZ

appendicism	AI/PEND/SIFM	apus	AI/PUS
appendicitis	AI/PEND/SAOITS	apyetous	AI/PAOI/TOUS
appendicocecostomy	AI/PEND/KO/SE/KO*S/M*I	apyknomorphous	AI/PIK/NO/MOR/FOUS
appendicocele	AI/PEND/KO/SAO*EL	apyogenous	AI/PAOI/OJ/NOUS
appendicoenterostomy	AI/PEND/KO/SPWRO*S/M*I		AI/PAOI/YOJ/NOUS
appendicolithiasis	AI/PEND/KO/LI/THAOI/SIS	apyous	AI/PAOI/OUS
appendicolysis	AI/PEND/KOL/SIS		AI/PAOI/YOUS
	AI/PEND/KO/LAOI/SIS	apyrase	AI/PAOI/RAIS
appendicopathy	AI/PEND/KOP/TH*I	apyrene	AI/PAOI/RAOEN
appendicostomy	AI/PEND/KO*S/M*I	apyretic	AI/PAOI/RET/IK
appendicular	AP/EN/DIK/LAR	apyrexia	AI/PAOI/REX/YA
appendicularis	AP/EN/DIK/LAI/RIS	apyrexial	AI/PAOI/REX/YAL
appendix	AI/PEND/IX	apyrimidinic	AI/PAOI/RIM/DIN/IK
	AI/PEN/DIX	apyrogenic	AI/PAOIR/JEN/IK
apperception	AP/PER/SEPGS	aqua	AK/WA
	AP/ER/SEPGS		AK/KWA
apperceptive	AP/PER/SEPT/IV	aqua-	AK/WA
	AP/ER/SEPT/IV		AK/KWA
appersonification	AI/PER/SON/FI/KAIGS	Aqua Care	AK/WA/KAIR
	AP/ER/SON/FI/KAIGS	aquacobalamin	AK/WA/KO/BAL/MIN
	AP/PER/SON/FI/KAIGS	Aquaderm	AK/WA/DERM
appestat	AP/STAT	aquae	AK/WAE
appetite	AP/TAOIT	aquaeductum	AK/WAE/DUK/TUM
appetition	AP/TIGS		AK/WAE/DUKT/UM
appetitive	AI/PET/TIV	aquaeductus	AK/WAE/DUK/TUS
applanation	AP/LA/NAIGS	Aquamed	AK/WA/MED
applanometer	AP/LA/NOM/TER	AquaMEPHYTON	AK/WA/MEF/TON
	AP/LAN/OM/TER	Aquanil	AK/WA/NIL
applanometry	AP/LA/NOM/TRI	aquaphobia	AK/WA/FOEB/YA
	AP/LAN/OM/TRI	Aquaphor	AK/WA/FOER
apple	AP/-L	aquapuncture	AK/WA/PUNG/KHUR
appliance	AI/PLAOINS	Aquaspirillum	AK/WA/SPAOI/RIL/UM
applicator	AP/LI/KAI/TOR	AquaTar	AK/WA/TAR
	AP/PLI/KAI/TOR	Aquatensen	AK/WA/TEN/SEN
applied	AI/PLI/-D	aquatic	AI/KWAT/IK
applique	AP/LI/KAI		AI/KWAUT/IK
	AP/PLI/KAI	aquaticus	AI/KWAT/KUS
apply	AI/PLI		AI/KWAUT/KUS
apposition	AP/SIGS	aqueduct	AK/WE/DUKT
	AP/ZIGS	aqueductus	AK/WE/DUK/TUS
	AP/POGS	aqueous	AI/KWOUS
apprehension	AP/HENGS		AK/WOUS
	AP/RE/HENGS		AIK/WOUS
	AP/PRE/HENGS	aquiparous	AK/WIP/ROUS
approach	AI/PROEFP		AI/KWIP/ROUS
approximal	AP/PROX/MAL	aquo-ion	AK/WO/AOIN
approximate	AI/PROX/MAT	aquosity	AI/KWOS/TI
	AI/PROX/MAIT	araban	AR/BAN
approximation	AI/PROX/MAIGS	arabanase	AI/RAB/NAIS
apractagnosia	AI/PRAK/TAG/NOES/YA	arabate	AR/BAIT
	AI/PRAK/TAG/NOEZ/YA	arabicum	AI/RAB/KUM
apractic	AI/PRAKT/IK	arabin	AR/BIN
apragmatism	AI/PRAG/MA/TIFM	arabinoadenosine	AR/BIN/AI/DEN/SAOEN
apramycin	AP/RA/MAOI/SIN	arabinocytidine	AR/BIN/SAOIT/DAOEN
apraxia	AI/PRAX/YA	arabinofuranosylcytosine	AR/BIN/FAOUR/NO/SIL/SAOIT/
apraxic	AI/PRAX/IK		SAOEN
Apresazide	AI/PRES/ZAOID		AI/RAB/NO/FAOUR/NO/SIL/
Apresoline	AI/PRES/LAOEN		SAOIT/SAOEN
Apresoline-Esidrix	AI/PRES/LAOEN/ES/DRIX	arabinose	AI/RAB/NOES
aprindine	AI/PRIN/DAOEN		AR/BIN/OES
aprobarbital	AP/RO/BARB/TAL	arabinoside	AI/RAB/NO/SAOID
aproctia	AI/PROK/SHA		AR/BIN/SAOID
aprofen	AP/RO/FEN	arabinosis	AI/RAB/NOE/SIS
aprofene	AP/RO/FAOEN	arabinosuria	AI/RAB/NO/SAOUR/YA
apron	AIP/RON	arabinosylcytosine	AI/RAB/NO/SIL/SAOIT/SAOEN
	AI/PRON		AR/BIN/SIL/SAOIT/SAOEN
aprophoria	AP/RO/FOER/YA	arabinulose	AR/BIN/LOES
	AP/RO/FOR/YA		AR/BIN/YAOU/LOES
aprosexia	AP/RO/SEX/YA		AR/BIN/YU/LOES
aprosody	AI/PROS/DI	arabite	AR/BAOIT
aprosopia	AP/RO/SOEP/YA	arabitol	AI/RAB/TOL
aprosopus	AI/PROS/PUS	arabonic	AR/BON/IK
	AI/PROES/PUS	arabopyranose	AR/BO/PAOIR/NOES
	AI/PROE/SO/PUS	arachic	AI/RAK/IK
aprotic	AI/PROET/IK	arachidate	AI/RAK/DAIT
	AI/PRO/TIK	arachidic	AI/RA/KID/IK
aprotinin	AI/PROET/NIN		AR/KID/IK
apselaphesia	AP/SEL/FAOEZ/YA	arachidonic	AI/RAK/DON/IK
apsithyria	APS/THAOIR/YA	arachn-	AI/RAK/N-
	AP/SI/THAOIR/YA		AR/AK/N-
apsychia	AI/SAOIK/YA	arachnephobia	AI/RAK/NE/FOEB/YA
apsychical	AI/SAOIK/KAL		AI/RAK/NAOE/FOEB/YA
aptitude	APT/TAOUD	Arachnia	AI/RAK/NAOE/YA
aptyalia	AP/TAOI/AIL/YA	arachnid	AI/RAK/NID
aptyalism	AP/TAOI/LIFM	Arachnida	AI/RAK/NI/DA
apudoma	AI/PUD/OEM/MA	arachnidism	AI/RAK/NI/DIFM
	AP/DOE/MA	arachnitis	AR/AK/NAOITS
apulmonism	AI/PUL/MO/NIFM		AI/RAK/NAOITS
apurinic	AI/PAOU/RIN/IK	arachnodactylia	AI/RAK/NO/DAK/TIL/YA

arachnodactyly	AI/RAK/NO/DAKT/LI	archiblast	ARK/BLA*S
arachnogastria	AI/RAK/NO/GAS/TRAOE/YA	archiblastic	ARK/BLA*S/IK
	AI/RAK/NO/GAS/TRA	archicenter	ARK/SEN/TER
arachnoid	AI/RAK/NOID	archicentric	ARK/SEN/TRIK
arachnoidal	AR/AK/NOI/DAL	archicerebellum	ARK/SER/BEL/UM
	AI/RAK/NOI/DAL		AR/KI/SER/BEL/UM
arachnoidea	AR/AK/NOID/YA	archicortex	ARK/KOR/TEX
	AI/RAK/NOID/YA		AR/KI/KOR/TEX
arachnoideae	AR/AK/NOID/YAE	archicyte	ARK/SAO*IT
	AI/RAK/NOID/YAE	archicytula	ARK/SIT/LA
arachnoides	AI/RAK/NOI/DAOEZ		ARK/SIT/YAOU/LA
	AR/AK/NOI/DAOEZ		ARK/SIT/YU/LA
arachnoidism	AI/RAK/NOI/DIFM	archigastrula	ARK/GAS/TRAOU/LA
	AI/RAK/NOI/IFM	archikaryon	ARK/KAR/YON
arachnoiditis	AI/RAK/NOI/DAOITS	archil	AR/KIL
	AI/RAK/NOID/AOITS	archimorula	ARK/MOR/YAOU/LA
arachnolysin	AR/AK/NOL/SIN		ARK/MOR/YU/LA
	AI/RAK/NOL/SIN	archin	AR/KIN
arachnophobia	AI/RAK/NO/FOEB/YA	archinephric	ARK/NEF/RIK
Aralen	AIR/LEN	archinephron	ARK/NEF/RON
	AR/LEN	archineuron	ARK/NAOU/RON
	AIR/RA/LEN	archipallial	ARK/PAL/YAL
	AR/RA/LEN	archipallium	ARK/PAL/YUM
aralkyl	AI/RAL/KIL	archistome	ARK/STOEM
Aramine	AIR/MIN	archistriatum	ARK/STRAOI/YAI/TUM
	AR/MIN		ARK/STRAOI/YAIT/UM
	AIR/RA/MIN		ARK/STRAOI/AIT/UM
	AR/RA/MIN		ARK/STRAOI/AI/TUM
Aran	AI/RAN	architectonic	ARK/TEK/TON/IK
	AR/RAN	archwire	A*RPBLG/WAOIR
Aran-Duchenne	AI/RAN/H-F/DAOU/SHEN		AR/-FP/WAOIR
	AR/RAN/H-F/DAOU/SHEN	arciform	ARS/FORM
Araneae	AI/RAIN/YAE		AR/SI/FORM
araneism	AI/RAIN/YIFM		AR/KI/FORM
araneoides	AI/RAIN/YOI/DAOEZ	arciformes	ARS/FOR/MAOEZ
araneous	AI/RAIN/YOUS		AR/SI/FOR/MAOEZ
arantii	AI/RAN/SHAOI		AR/KI/FOR/MAOEZ
	AI/RANT/YAOI	Arco-Lase	AR/KO/LAIS
Arantii	K-P/AI/RAN/SHAOI	Arco-Lase Plus	AR/KO/LAIS/PLUS
	K-P/AI/RANT/YAOI	arctation	ARK/TAIGS
Arantius	AI/RAN/-RBS	arcual	AR/KAOUL
	AI/RANT/YUS		ARK/YAOUL
araphia	AI/RAIF/YA		ARK/YUL
arbaprostil	AR/BA/PROS/TIL	arcualia	AR/KAOU/AIL/YA
arbor	AR/BOR		ARK/YAIL/YA
arboreal	AR/BOER/YAL	arcuat-	ARK/YAI/T-
	AR/BOR/YAL		ARK/WAI/T-
arbores	AR/BOR/RAOEZ		AR/KAOU/AI/T-
	AR/BOER/RAOEZ		AR/KAOU/WAI/T-
	AR/BOE/RAOEZ		ARK/YAOU/AI/T-
arborescent	ARB/RES/ENT		ARK/YAOU/WAI/T-
	AR/BRES/ENT	arcuata	ARK/YAI/TA
	AR/BO/RES/ENT	arcuatae	ARK/YAI/TAE
arborization	AR/BOR/ZAIGS	arcuate	ARK/YAIT
arborize	AR/BOR/AOIZ	arcuation	ARK/YAIGS
	AR/BO/RAOIZ	arcuatum	ARK/YAI/TUM
	(not ARB/RAOIZ)		ARK/YAIT/UM
arboroid	AR/BOR/OID	arcuatus	ARK/YAI/TUS
	AR/BO/ROID	arcus	AR/KUS
	ARB/ROID	ardanesthesia	ARD/ANS/THAOEZ/YA
arborvirus	AR/BOR/VAOI/RUS		ARD/AN/ES/THAOEZ/YA
arboviral	AR/BO/VAOIRL		AR/DANS/THAOEZ/YA
arbovirus	AR/BO/VAOI/RUS		AR/DAN/ES/THAOEZ/YA
arbutin	AR/BAOU/TIN	ardent	AR/DENT
arc	A*RK		ARD/ENT
	(not ARK; see ark)	ardor	AR/DOR
arcade	AR/KAID	area	AIR/YA
arcanum	AR/KAIN/UM		AER/YA
	AR/KAI/NUM		(not AR/YA; see aria)
arcate	AR/KAIT	areae	AIR/YAE
arch	A*RPBLG		AER/YAE
	AR/-FP		AR/YAE
archaic	AR/KAI/IK	areata	AIR/YAI/TA
archencephalon	ARK/EN/SEF/LON		AER/YAI/TA
	AR/KEN/SEF/LON		AR/YAI/TA
archenteric	AR/KEN/TER/IK	areatus	AIR/YAI/TUS
	ARK/SPWER/IK		AER/YAI/TUS
archenteron	ARK/SPWRON		AR/YAI/TUS
	ARK/SPWER/RON	areca	AI/RAOE/KA
	AR/KENT/RON	Areca	K-P/AI/RAOE/KA
	ARK/ENT/RON	arecaidine	AI/REK/DAOEN
archeo-	ARK/YO		AI/REK/AI/DAOEN
archeocyte	ARK/YO/SAO*IT	arecaine	AI/REK/AIN
archeokinetic	ARK/YO/KI/NET/IK	arecoline	AI/REK/LAOEN
archetype	ARK/TAOIP		AI/REK/LIN
	AR/KE/TAOIP	areflexia	AI/RE/FLEX/YA
	AR/KAOE/TAOIP	aregenerative	AI/RE/JEN/RA/TIV
archi-	ARK	arenaceous	AR/NAIRBS
	AR/KI	arenae	AI/RAOE/NAE

	AI/RE/NAE	aridosiliquate	AR/DO/SIL/KWAIT
Arenaviridae	AR/NA/VIR/DAE	aril	AR/RIL
	AI/RAOEN/VIR/DAE		AR/IL
arenavirus	AR/NA/VAOI/RUS		AIR/RIL
	AI/RAOEN/VAOI/RUS	arildone	AR/IL/DOEN
Arenavirus	K-P/AR/NA/VAOI/RUS		AR/RIL/DOEN
	K-P/AI/RAOEN/VAOI/RUS	arillode	AR/LOED
arenoid	AR/NOID		AR/RI/LOED
areola	AI/RAOE/LA	aristin	AI/RIS/TIN
areolae	AI/RAOE/LAE	Aristocort	AI/R*IS/KORT
areolar	AI/RAOE/LAR	Aristocort Forte	AI/R*IS/KORT/FOR/TAI
areolitis	AI/RAOE/LAOITS	aristogenesis	AI/R*IS/JEN/SIS
	AR/YO/LAOITS	aristogenics	AI/R*IS/JEN/IK/-S
areometer	AR/YOM/TER	Aristolochia	AI/R*IS/LOEK/YA
areometric	AR/YO/MET/RIK	aristolochic	AI/R*IS/LOEK/IK
areometry	AR/YOM/TRI	Aristo-Pak	AI/R*IS/PAK
Arey	AIR/RAOE	Aristospan	AI/R*IS/SPAN
Arfonad	AR/FO/NAD	Aristotle	AR/STOT/-L
	AR/FON/AD		ARS/TOT/-L
argamblyopia	AR/GAM/BLOEP/YA	aristotelian	AR/STO/TAOEL/YAN
	ARG/AM/BLOEP/YA		ARS/TO/TAOEL/YAN
Argand burner	AR/GAN/BURN/ER	arithmomania	AI/R*IT/MO/MAIN/YA
	AR/GAND/BURN/ER	arkyochrome	ARK/YO/KROEM
Argas	AR/GAS	arkyostichochrome	ARK/YO/STIK/KROEM
argasid	AR/GAS/ID	Arlidin	AR/LI/DIN
Argasidae	AR/GAS/DAE		ARL/DIN
argema	ARJ/MA	Arlt	ARLT
	AR/JE/MA	arm	ARM
argent(o)-	AR/JENT	armadillo	ARM/DIL/LOE
	AR/JEN/T(O)	armamentarium	ARM/MEN/TAIRM
argentaffin	AR/JENT/FIN		ARM/-MT/TAIRM
argentaffine	AR/JENT/FAOEN		AR/MAMT/TAIRM
argentaffinoma	AR/JEN/TAF/NOE/MA		ARM/MEN/TAIR/YUM
	AR/JENT/FI/NOE/MA		ARM/-MT/TAIR/YUM
argentation	AR/JEN/TAIGS		AR/MAMT/TAIR/YUM
	ARJ/EN/TAIGS	Armanni	AR/MAN/NAOE
argenti	ARJ/EN/TAOI	Armanni-Ebstein	AR/MAN/NAOE/H-F/EB/STAOEN
argentic	AR/JENT/IK		AR/MAN/NAOE/H-F/EB/STAOIN
argentine	AR/JEN/TAOEN	Armanni-Ehrlich	AR/MAN/NAOE/H-F/*ER/LIK
	ARJ/EN/TAOEN	armarium	AR/MAIR/YUM
argentophil	AR/JENT/FIL		AR/MAIRM
argentophile	AR/JENT/FAOIL	armature	ARM/KHUR
argentophilic	AR/JENT/FIL/IK		ARM/TAOUR
argentoproteinum	AR/JENT/PROET/YAOIN/UM		AR/MA/KHUR
	AR/JENT/PROET/YAOI/NUM		AR/MA/TAOUR
	AR/JENT/PRO/TAOEN/UM	armillatus	ARM/LAI/TUS
argentous	AR/JEN/TOUS	Armillifer	AR/MIL/FER
	AR/JENT/OUS	armpit	ARM/PIT
argentum	AR/JEN/TUM	Armour	K-P/AR/MOUR
argilla	AR/JIL/LA	Armstrong	A*RM/STRONG
argillaceous	ARJ/LAIRBS		ARM/STRO*NG
argin-	ARJ/N-	Arndt	ARND/-T
	AR/JI/N-		ARNT
arginase	ARJ/NAIS	Arneth	AR/NAIT
arginine	ARJ/NAOEN	arnica	ARN/KA
	ARJ/NIN	Arnica	K-P/ARN/KA
arginino-	ARJ/NIN	Arnold	AR/NOLD
	ARJ/NI/NO	Arnold-Chiari	AR/NOLD/H-F/KAOE/AR/RAOE
	ARJ/NI/NO	Arnott	AR/NOT
argininosuccinase	ARJ/NIN/SUX/NAIS	aroma	AI/ROE/MA
argininosuccinate	ARJ/NIN/SUX/NAIT	aromatase	AI/ROEM/TAIS
argininosuccinic	ARJ/NIN/SUK/SIN/IK	aromatic	AR/MAT/IK
argininosuccinicacidemia	ARJ/NIN/SUK/SIN/IK/AS/DAOEM/YA		AIR/MAT/IK
argininosuccinicaciduria	ARJ/NIN/SUK/SIN/IK/AS/DAOUR/YA	aromatica	AR/MAT/KA
			AIR/MAT/KA
arginyl	ARJ/NIL	aromatization	AI/ROEM/TI/ZAIGS
argipressin	ARJ/PRES/SIN	aromine	AI/ROE/MIN
argon	AR/GON	Aronson	AR/RON/SON
Argyll Robertson	AR/GAOIL/ROB/ERT/SON	arousal	AI/ROU/ZAL
argyremia	ARJ/RAOEM/YA		AI/ROUZ/ZAL
argyria	AR/JIR/YA	arouse	AI/ROUZ
	AR/JAOIR/YA	aryol	AI/ROIL
argyriasis	ARJ/RAOI/SIS		AR/ROIL
argyric	AR/JIR/IK	arprinocid	AR/PRAOIN/SID
	AR/JAOIR/IK		AR/PRIN/SID
argyrism	ARJ/RIFM	arrack	AI/RAK
argyrophil	ARJ/JAOI/RO/FIL	arrangement	AI/RAING/-MT
argyrophile	AR/JAOI/RO/FAOIL		AI/RAIN/-J/-MT
argyrophilic	AR/JAOI/RO/FIL/IK		AI/RAIN/J-MT
argyrosis	ARJ/ROE/SIS		ARNG/-MT
arhinencephalia	AI/RIN/EN/SFAIL/YA	arrector	AI/REK/TOR
	AI/RAOIN/EN/SFAIL/YA	arrector pili	AI/REK/TOR/PAOI/LAOI
-arial	AIRL	arrectores	AI/REK/TOR/RAOEZ
	AIR/YAL		AI/REK/TOER/RAOEZ
Arias-Stella	AR/YAS/H-F/STEL/LA		AR/REK/TOR/RAOEZ
ariboflavinosis	AI/RAOIB/FLAIV/NOE/SIS		AR/REK/TOER/RAOEZ
aridosiliculose	AR/DO/SI/LIK/LOES	arrest	AI/R*ES
aridosiliquata	AR/DO/SIL/KWAI/TA	arrested	AI/R*ES/-D
		arrhaphia	AI/RAIF/YA

arrhenic	AI/REN/IK	arsinosalicylic	ARS/NO/SAL/SIL/IK
Arrhenius	AI/RAOEN/YUS	arsonic	AR/SON/IK
	AI/REN/YUS	arsonium	AR/SOEN/YUM
arrheno-	AI/RAOEN		AR/SON/YUM
	AI/RAOE/NO	arsonvalization	AR/SON/VAL/ZAIGS
	AR/NO	arsphenamine	ARS/FEN/MIN
arrhenoblastoma	AI/RAOEN/BLAS/TOE/MA		ARS/FEN/MAOEN
arrhenogenic	AR/NO/JEN/IK		AR/SFEN/MIN
	AI/RAOEN/JEN/IK		AR/SFEN/MAOEN
arrhenokaryon	AR/NO/KAR/YON	arsthinol	ARS/THI/NOL
	AI/RAOEN/KAR/YON		ARS/THAOI/NOL
arrhenoma	AR/NOE/MA	Artane	AR/TAIN
	AI/RAOE/NOE/MA	artarine	ART/RIN
arrhenoplasm	AI/RAOEN/PLAFM		AR/TA/RIN
arrhenotocia	AI/RAOEN/TOE/SHA	artefact	AR/TE/FAKT
	AI/RAOEN/TOES/YA		(not ART/FAKT)
	AR/NO/TOE/SHA	artefacta	AR/TE/FAK/TA
	AR/NO/TOES/YA		ART/FAK/TA
arrhenotoky	AR/NOT/KI	artefactum	AR/TE/FAK/TUM
arrhigosis	AI/RI/GOE/SIS		ART/FAK/TUM
	AR/GOE/SIS	artem	AR/TEM
arrhinencephalia	AI/RIN/EN/SFAIL/YA	arteralgia	ART/RAL/JA
	AI/RIN/EN/SE/FAIL/YA		AR/TER/AL/JA
arrhinencephaly	AI/RIN/EN/SEF/LI	arterectomy	ART/REKT/M*I
arrhinia	AI/RIN/YA	arterenol	ART/RAOE/NOL
arrhythmia	AI/R*IT/MAOE/YA	arteri(o)-	AR/TAOER/Y(O)
arrhythmic	AI/R*IT/MIK	arteria	AR/TAOER/YA
arrhythmogenic	AI/R*IT/MO/JEN/IK	arteriae	AR/TAOER/YAE
arrhythmokinesis	AI/R*IT/MO/KI/NAOE/SIS	arteriae peronea	AR/TAOER/YAE/PE/ROEN/YA
arrow	AR/ROE	(word grouped)	AR/TAOER/YAE/PAOE/ROEN/YA
arrowroot	AR/ROE/RAOT	arterial	AR/TAOERL
Arroyo	K-P/AI/ROE/YOE		AR/TAOER/YAL
	K-P/AI/ROI/YOE	arteriale	AR/TAOER/YAI/LAOE
Arruga	AI/RAOU/GA	arterialization	AR/TAOER/YAL/ZAIGS
arsambide	AR/SAM/BAOID	arteriectasia	AR/TAOER/YEK/TAIZ/YA
arsanilic	ARS/NIL/IK	arteriectasis	AR/TAOER/YEKT/SIS
arsenamide	AR/SEN/MAOID	arteriectomy	AR/TAOER/YEKT/M*I
arsenate	ARS/NAIT	arteriectopia	AR/TAOER/YEK/TOEP/YA
	AR/SE/NAIT	arterioatony	AR/TAOER/YO/AT/N*I
arseniasis	ARS/NAOI/SIS	arteriocapillary	AR/TAOER/YO/KAP/LAIR
	AR/SE/NAOI/SIS	arteriodilating	AR/TAOER/YO/DI/LAIT/-G
arsenic	ARS/NIK	arteriogenesis	AR/TAOER/YO/JEN/SIS
	AR/SEN/IK	arteriogram	AR/TAOER/YO/GRAM
arsenical	AR/SEN/KAL	arteriograph	AR/TAOER/YO/GRAF
arsenicalism	AR/SEN/KLIFM	arteriographic	AR/TAOER/YO/GRAFK
	AR/SEN/KAL/IFM	arteriography	AR/TAOER/YOG/FI
arsenicophagy	AR/SEN/KOF/JI	arteriol(o)-	AR/TAOER/YOE/L(O)
arsenicum	AR/SEN/KUM		ART/RAOE/L-
arsenide	ARS/NAOID	arteriola	AR/TAOER/YOE/LA
	AR/SE/NAOID	arteriolae	AR/TAOER/YOE/LAE
arsenious	AR/SEN/YOUS	arteriolar	ART/RAOE/LAR
arsenism	ARS/NIFM		AR/TAOER/YOE/LAR
	AR/SEN/IFM	arteriole	AR/TAOER/YOEL
arsenite	ARS/NAOIT	arteriolith	AR/TAOER/YO/L*IT
	AR/SE/NAOIT	arteriolitis	AR/TAOER/YO/LAOITS
arsenium	AR/SEN/YUM	arteriology	AR/TAOER/YOLG
	AR/SAOEN/YUM	arteriolonecrosis	AR/TAOER/YOE/LO/NE/KROE/SIS
arseniuret	AR/SAOEN/YAOU/RET	arteriolonephrosclerosis	AR/TAOER/YOE/LO/NEF/RO/
	AR/SAOEN/YU/RET		SKLE/ROE/SIS
	AR/SEN/YAOU/RET	arteriolosclerosis	AR/TAOER/YOE/LO/SKLE/ROE/
	AR/SEN/YU/RET		SIS
arseniureted	AR/SAOEN/YAOU/RET/-D	arteriolosclerotic	AR/TAOER/YOE/LO/SKLE/ROT/IK
	AR/SAOEN/YU/RET/-D	arteriolovenous	AR/TAOER/YOE/LO/VAOEN/OUS
	AR/SEN/YAOU/RET/-D	arteriolovenular	AR/TAOER/YOE/LO/VEN/LAR
	AR/SEN/YU/RET/-D	arteriomalacia	AR/TAOER/YO/MA/LAI/SHA
arsenization	AR/SEN/ZAIGS	arteriometer	AR/TAOER/YOM/TER
arseno-	ARS/NO	arteriomotor	AR/TAOER/YO/MOE/TOR
arsenoactivation	ARS/NO/AKT/VAIGS	arteriomyomatosis	AR/TAOER/YO/MAOI/YOEM/TOE/
arsenoautohemotherapy	ARS/NO/AUT/HAOEM/THER/PI		SIS
arsenobenzene	ARS/NO/BEN/ZAOEN	arterionecrosis	AR/TAOER/YO/NE/KROE/SIS
arsenoblast	ARS/NO/BLA*S	arterionephrosclerosis	AR/TAOER/YO/NEF/RO/SKLE/
arsenoceptor	ARS/NO/SEP/TOR		ROE/SIS
arsenolysis	ARS/NOL/SIS	arteriopalmus	AR/TAOER/YO/PAL/MUS
arsenophagy	ARS/NOF/JI	arteriopathy	AR/TAOER/YOP/TH*I
arsenorelapsing	ARS/NO/RE/LAPS/-G	arterioplania	AR/TAOER/YO/PLAIN/YA
arsenoresistant	ARS/NO/RE/S*IS/ANT	arterioplasty	AR/TAOER/YO/PLAS/TI
	ARS/NO/RE/SIS/TANT	arteriopressor	AR/TAOER/YO/PRES/SOR
arsenotherapy	ARS/NO/THER/PI	arteriorenal	AR/TAOER/YO/RAOENL
arsenous	ARS/NOUS	arteriorrhaphy	AR/TAOER/YOR/FI
	AR/SEN/OUS	arteriorrhexis	AR/TAOER/YO/REK/SIS
arsenoxide	ARS/NOK/SAOID	arteriosclerosis	AR/TAOER/YO/SKLE/ROE/SIS
	ARS/NOX/AOID	arteriosclerotic	AR/TAOER/YO/SKLE/ROT/IK
	AR/SEN/OK/SAOID	arteriosity	AR/TAOER/YOS/TI
	AR/SEN/OX/AOID	arteriospasm	AR/TAOER/YO/SPAFM
arsenum	AR/SAOEN/UM	arteriospastic	AR/TAOER/YO/SPA*S/IK
	AR/SAOE/NUM	arteriostenosis	AR/TAOER/YO/STE/NOE/SIS
arsine	AR/SAOEN	arteriosteogenesis	AR/TAOER/YO*S/YO/JEN/SIS
	AR/SIN	arteriostosis	AR/TAOER/YOS/TOE/SIS
arsinic	AR/SIN/IK	arteriostrepsis	AR/TAOER/YO/STREP/SIS

arteriosum	AR/TAOER/YOE/SUM	arthropodic	AR/THRO/POED/IK
arteriosus	AR/TAOER/YOE/SUS	arthropodous	AR/THROP/DOUS
arteriosympathectomy	AR/TAOER/YO/SIFRP/THEKT/M*I	arthropyosis	AR/THRO/PAOI/YOE/SIS
arteriotome	AR/TAOER/YO/TOEM	arthrorheumatism	AR/THRO/RAOUM/TIFM
arteriotomy	AR/TAOER/YOT/M*I	arthrorisis	AR/THRO/RAOI/SIS
arteriotony	AR/TAOER/YOT/N*I	arthroscintigram	AR/THRO/SINT/GRAM
arterious	AR/TAOER/YOUS	arthroscintigraphy	AR/THRO/SIN/TIG/FI
arteriovenosa	AR/TAOER/YO/VAOE/NOE/SA	arthrosclerosis	AR/THRO/SKLE/ROE/SIS
arteriovenous	AR/TAOER/YO/VAOEN/OUS	arthroscope	AR/THRO/SKOEP
arteritides	ART/RIT/DAOEZ	arthroscopy	AR/THROS/KPI
arteritis	ART/RAOITS	arthrosis	AR/THROE/SIS
artery	ART/RI	arthrospore	AR/THRO/SPOER
arthr(o)-	AR/THR(O)	arthrosteitis	AR/THRO*S/YAOITS
	A*RT/R(O)	arthrostomy	AR/THRO*S/M*I
arthral	AR/THRAL	arthrosynovitis	AR/THRO/SIN/VAOITS
arthralgia	AR/THRAL/JA	arthrotome	AR/THRO/TOEM
arthralgic	AR/THRAL/JIK	arthrotomy	AR/THROT/M*I
arthrectomy	AR/THREKT/M*I	arthrotropic	AR/THRO/TROP/IK
arthrempyesis	AR/THREM/PAOI/E/SIS	arthrotyphoid	AR/THRO/TAOI/FOID
	AR/THREM/PAOI/SIS	arthroxerosis	AR/THRO/ZAOE/ROE/SIS
arthresthesia	AR/THRES/THAOEZ/YA		AR/THRO/ZE/ROE/SIS
arthrifluent	AR/THRI/FLAOUNT	arthroxesis	AR/THROX/SIS
	AR/THRIF/LAOUNT		AR/THROK/SE/SIS
arthrifuge	AR/THRI/FAOUJ	Arthus	AR/THUS
arthritic	AR/THRIT/IK	article	ART/K-L
arthriticum	AR/THRIT/KUM		ARL
arthritide	AR/THRI/TAOED	articul-	AR/TIK/L-
	AR/THRI/TAOID		AR/TIK/YAOU/L-
arthritides	AR/THRIT/DAOEZ		AR/TIK/YU/L-
arthritis	AR/THRAOITS	articular	AR/TIK/LAR
Arthritis Pain Formula	AR/THRAOITS/PAIN/FORM/	articulare	AR/TIK/LAI/RAOE
	YAOU/LA	articulares	AR/TIK/LAI/RAOEZ
	AR/THRAOITS/PAIN/FORM/YU/	articularia	AR/TIK/LAIR/YA
	LA	articularis	AR/TIK/LAI/RIS
arthritism	AR/THRI/TIFM		AR/TIK/LAR/RIS
Arthrobacter	AR/THRO/BAK/TER	articulate	AR/TIK/LAIT
arthrobacterium	AR/THRO/BAK/TAOER/YUM		AR/TIK/LAT
arthrocele	AR/THRO/SAO*EL	articulatio	AR/TIK/LAI/SHOE
arthrocentesis	AR/THRO/SEN/TAOE/SIS		AR/TIK/LAIRB/YOE
arthrochalasis	AR/THRO/KAL/SIS	articulation	AR/TIK/LAIGS
arthrochondritis	AR/THRO/KON/DRAOITS	articulationes	AR/TIK/LAI/SHOE/NAOEZ
arthroclasia	AR/THRO/KLAIZ/YA		AR/TIK/LAIRB/YOE/NAOEZ
arthroconidium	AR/THRO/KO/NID/YUM	articulationis	AR/TIK/LAI/SHOE/NIS
arthrodesia	AR/THRO/DAOEZ/YA		AR/TIK/LAIRB/YOE/NIS
arthrodesis	AR/THRO/D/SIS	articulationum	AR/TIK/LAI/SHOE/NUM
	AR/THRO/DAOE/SIS		AR/TIK/LAIRB/YOE/NUM
arthrodia	AR/THROED/YA	articulator	AR/TIK/LAI/TOR
arthrodial	AR/THROED/YAL	articulatory	AR/TIK/LA/TOIR
arthrodynia	AR/THRO/DIN/YA	articulo	AR/TIK/LOE
arthrodynic	AR/THRO/DIN/IK	articulostat	AR/TIK/LO/STAT
arthrodysplasia	AR/THRO/DIS/PLAIZ/YA	articulus	AR/TIK/LUS
arthroempyesis	AR/THRO/EM/PAOI/E/SIS	artifact	AR/TI/FAKT
	AR/THRO/EM/PAOI/SIS		(not ART/FAKT)
arthroendoscopy	AR/THRO/EN/DOS/KPI	artifactitious	ART/FAK/TIRBS
arthroereisis	AR/THRO/E/RAOI/SIS		AR/TI/FAK/TIRBS
	AR/THRO/RAOI/SIS	artifactual	ART/FAK/KHUL
arthrogenous	AR/THROJ/NOUS		AR/TI/FAK/KHUL
arthrogram	AR/THRO/GRAM	artificial	ART/FIRBL
arthrography	AR/THROG/FI	Artiodactyla	ART/YO/DAKT/LA
arthrogryposis	AR/THRO/GRI/POE/SIS	artiodactylous	ART/YO/DAKT/LOUS
arthrokatadysis	AR/THRO/KA/TAD/SIS	artistic	AR/T*IS/IK
arthrolith	AR/THRO/L*IT	aryepiglottic	AR/YEP/GLOT/IK
arthrolithiasis	AR/THRO/LI/THAOI/SIS		AR/EP/GLOT/IK
arthrologia	AR/THRO/LOE/JA	aryepiglotticus	AR/YEP/GLOT/KUS
arthrology	AR/THROLG		AR/EP/GLOT/KUS
arthrolysis	AR/THROL/SIS	aryepiglottidean	AR/YEP/GLO/TID/YAN
arthromeningitis	AR/THRO/MEN/JAOITS		AR/YEP/GLOT/TID/YAN
arthrometer	AR/THROM/TER		AR/EP/GLO/TID/YAN
arthrometry	AR/THROM/TRI		AR/EP/GLOT/TID/YAN
arthroneuralgia	AR/THRO/NAOU/RAL/JA	arylamidase	AR/IL/AM/DAIS
arthronosos	AR/THRO/NOE/SOS	arylamine	AR/IL/MAOEN
arthro-onychodysplasia	AR/THRO/OIN/KO/DIS/PLAIZ/YA		AR/IL/AM/MIN
arthro-ophthalmopathy	AR/THRO/OF/THAL/MOP/TH*I	arylarsonic	AR/IL/AR/SON/IK
arthropathia	AR/THRO/PA*T/YA	arylcyclohexylamine	AR/IL/SAOI/KLO/HEX/IL/AM/
arthropathic	AR/THRO/PA*T/IK		MAOEN
arthropathology	AR/THRO/PA/THOLG		AR/IL/SAOI/KLO/HEK/SIL/AM/
arthropathy	AR/THROP/TH*I		MAOEN
arthrophlysis	AR/THROF/LI/SIS	arylsulfatase	AR/IL/SUL/FA/TAIS
arthrophyma	AR/THRO/FAOI/MA	arytaenoideus	AR/TAE/NOID/YUS
arthrophyte	AR/THRO/FAOIT	arytenoepiglottic	AI/RIT/NO/EP/GLOT/IK
arthroplastic	AR/THRO/PLA*S/IK	arytenoepiglottidean	AI/RIT/NO/EP/GLO/TID/YAN
arthroplasty	AR/THRO/PLAS/TI		AI/RIT/NO/EP/GLOT/TID/YAN
arthropneumoroentgenography		arytenoid	AR/TAOE/NOID
	AR/THRO/NAOUM/RENT/GEN/	arytenoidea	AR/TAOE/NOID/YA
	OG/FI	arytenoideae	AR/TAOE/NOID/YAE
arthropod	AR/THRO/POD	arytenoidectomy	AR/TAOE/NOI/DEKT/M*I
Arthropoda	AR/THROP/DA	arytenoideus	AR/TAOE/NOID/YUS
arthropodiasis	AR/THRO/POE/DAOI/SIS	arytenoidopexy	AR/TAOE/NOID/PEK/SI
	AR/THRO/PO/DAOI/SIS		AR/TAOE/NOI/DO/PEK/SI

asacria	AI/SAI/KRAOE/YA	asemantic	AI/SE/MANT/IK
	AI/SAIK/RAOE/YA	asemasia	AS/MAIZ/YA
asafetida	AS/FET/DA	asemia	AI/SAOEM/YA
asaphia	AI/SAF/YA	Asendin	AI/SEN/DIN
	AI/SAIF/YA	asepsis	AI/SEP/SIS
Asarum	AS/RUM	aseptate	AI/SEP/TAIT
	AS/SA/RUM	aseptic	AI/SEPT/IK
	AS/SAR/UM	asepticism	AI/SEPT/SIFM
asbestiform	AS/B*ES/FORM	asequence	AI/SE/KWENS
	AS/BES/TI/FORM	asexual	AI/SEX/YAOUL
asbestoid	AS/BES/TOID	asexuality	AI/SEX/YAL/TI
asbestos	AS/BES/TOS		AI/SEX/YAOUL/TI
asbestosis	AS/BES/TOE/SIS	asexualization	AI/SEX/YAOUL/ZAIGS
Asbron	AS/BRON	ash	ARB
	AZ/BRON	Ashby	ARB/BI
A-scan	ARBGS/SKAN	Asherman	ARB/ER/MAN
	ARBGS/H-F/SKAN	Ashhurst	ARB/H*URS
ascariasis	AS/KA/RAOI/SIS	Ashley	ARB/LAOE
	AS/KRAOI/SIS	Ashman	ARB/MAN
ascaricidal	AS/KAR/SAOI/DAL	ashy	ARB/SHI
ascaricide	AS/KAR/SAO*ID	asialia	AI/SAOI/AIL/YA
ascarid	AS/KA/RID	asialism	AI/SAOI/LIFM
	AS/KRID	Asiatic	AIZ/YAT/IK
ascarides	AS/KAR/DAOEZ		AIRB/YAT/IK
Ascaridia	AS/KA/RID/YA	asiaticoside	AIZ/YAT/KO/SAO*ID
ascaridiasis	AS/KAR/DAOI/SIS		AIRB/YAT/KO/SAO*ID
Ascaridida	AS/KA/RID/DA	asiderosis	AI/SID/ROE/SIS
	AS/KRID/DA	asitia	AI/SI/SHA
Ascarididae	AS/KA/RID/DAE		AI/SIRB/SHA
	AS/KRID/DAE		AI/SIRB/YA
Ascarididea	AS/KAR/DID/YA	Askanazy	AS/KA/NA/ZI
Ascaridoidea	AS/KAR/DOID/YA		AS/KA/NAZ/SAOE
ascaridole	AS/KAR/DOEL	Ask-Upmark	AS/-K/UP/MARK
Ascaridorida	AS/KAR/DOR/DA	asocial	AI/SOERBL
ascaris	AS/KA/RIS	asoma	AI/SOE/MA
	AS/KRIS	asomata	AI/SOEM/TA
Ascaris	K-P/AS/KA/RIS	asomatophyte	AI/SOEM/TO/FAOIT
	K-P/AS/KRIS	asparaginase	AS/PARJ/IN/AIS
ascaron	AS/KA/RON		AS/PARJ/NAIS
	AS/KRON	asparagine	AS/PAR/JIN
Ascarops	AS/KA/ROPS	asparaginic	AS/PAR/JIN/IK
	AS/KROPS	asparaginyl	AS/PAR/JIN/IL
ascendens	AI/SEN/DENZ	asparagus	AS/PAR/GUS
ascending	AI/SEND/-G		AI/SPAR/GAS
ascensus	AI/SEN/SUS	Asparagus	K-P/AS/PAR/GUS
ascertainment	AS/SER/TAIN/-MT		K-P/AI/SPAR/GAS
	AS/ER/TAIN/-MT	asparmide	AS/PAR/MAOID
aschelminth	AS/KEL/M*INT	aspartame	AI/SPAR/TAIM
	AS/-K/HEL/M*INT		AS/PAR/TAIM
Aschelminthes	AS/KEL/MIN/THAOEZ	aspartase	AS/PAR/TAIS
	AS/-K/HEL/MIN/THAOEZ	aspartate	AS/PAR/TAIT
Ascher	ARB/SHER	asparthione	AS/PAR/THAOI/YOEN
Ascherson	ARB/ER/SON		AS/PAR/THAOI/OEN
	ARB/SHER/SON	aspartic	AS/PART/IK
Aschheim	ARB/HAOIM	aspartoacylase	AI/SPAR/TO/AS/LAIS
Aschheim-Zondek	ARB/HAOIM/H-F/ZON/DEK		AS/PAR/TO/AS/LAIS
aschistodactylia	AI/SH*IS/DAK/TIL/YA	aspartocin	AI/SPAR/TO/SIN
	AI/SK*IS/DAK/TIL/YA		AI/SPART/SIN
Aschner	ARB/NER	aspartokinase	AI/SPAR/TO/KAOI/NAIS
Aschoff	ARB/SHOF		AS/PAR/TO/KAOI/NAIS
asci	AS/SAOI	aspartyl	AS/PAR/TIL
ascia	AS/YA	aspartylglycosamine	AS/PAR/TIL/GLAOI/KOES/
ascites	AI/SAOI/TAOEZ		MAOEN
ascitic	AI/SIT/IK	aspartylglycosaminuria	AS/PAR/TIL/GLAOI/KOES/AM/
ascitogenous	AS/TOJ/NOUS		NAOUR/YA
Asclepias	AS/KLAOEP/YAS		AS/PAR/TIL/GLAOIK/SAM/
	AS/KLEP/YAS		NAOUR/YA
ascocarp	AS/KO/KARP	aspecific	AI/SPEFK
ascogenous	AS/KOJ/NOUS		AI/SPE/SIFK
ascogonium	AS/KO/GOEN/YUM	aspect	AS/PEKT
Ascoli	AS/KOE/LAOE	Aspercreme	AS/PER/KRAOEM
	AS/KO/LAOE		AS/PER/KRAO*EM
ascomycete	AS/KO/MAOI/SAOET	aspergill(o)-	AS/PER/JIL
Ascomycetes	AS/KO/MAOI/SAOE/TAOEZ		AS/PER/JIL/L(O)
ascomycetous	AS/KO/MAOI/SAOE/TOUS		AS/PERJ/L(O)
	AS/KO/MAOI/SAOET/OUS	aspergillar	AS/PER/JIL/LAR
ascorbase	AS/KOR/BAIS	aspergilli	AS/PER/JIL/LAOI
ascorbate	AS/KOR/BAIT	aspergillic	AS/PER/JIL/IK
ascorbemia	AS/KOR/BAOEM/YA	aspergillin	AS/PER/JIL/LIN
ascorbic	AS/KORB/IK	aspergilloma	AS/PER/JIL/LOE/MA
ascorburia	AS/KOR/BAOUR/YA		AS/PERJ/LOE/MA
ascorbyl palmitate	AS/KOR/BIL/PAL/MI/TAIT	aspergillomycosis	AS/PER/JIL/MAOI/KOE/SIS
ascospore	AS/KO/SPOER		AS/PERJ/LO/MAOI/KOE/SIS
Ascriptin	AI/SKRIP/TIN	aspergillosis	AS/PER/JIL/LOE/SIS
	AS/KRIP/TIN		AS/PERJ/LOE/SIS
ascus	AS/KUS	aspergillotoxicosis	AS/PER/JIL/TOX/KOE/SIS
-ase	(c)AIS		AS/PERJ/LO/TOX/KOE/SIS
asecretory	AI/SE/KRAOET/RI	aspergillus	AS/PER/JIL/LUS
Aselli	AI/SEL/LAOE	Aspergillus	K-P/AS/PER/JIL/LUS

aspergillustoxicosis	AS/PER/JIL/LUS/TOX/KOE/SIS	assurin	AS/YAOU/RIN
asperkinase	AS/PER/KAOI/NAIS		AS/YU/RIN
	AI/SPER/KAOI/NAIS	astacin	AS/TA/SIN
aspermatism	AI/SPERM/TIFM	astasia	AI/STAIZ/YA
aspermatogenic	AI/SPERM/TO/JEN/IK		AS/TAIZ/YA
aspermatogenesis	AI/SPERM/TO/JEN/SIS	astasia-abasia	AI/STAIZ/YA/AI/BAIZ/YA
aspermia	AI/SPERM/YA		AI/STAIZ/YA/H-F/AI/BAIZ/YA
aspersion	AS/PERGS	astatic	AI/STAT/IK
	AI/SPERGS		AS/TAT/IK
asphalgesia	AS/FAL/JAOEZ/YA	astatine	AS/TA/TAOEN
aspheric	AI/SFER/IK		AS/TA/TIN
	AI/SFAOER/IK	astaxanthin	AS/TA/ZAN/THIN
asphyctic	AS/FIKT/IK	asteatodes	AI/STAOE/TOE/DAOEZ
asphyctous	AS/FIK/TOUS		A*S/YA/TOE/DAOEZ
	AS/FIKT/OUS	asteatosis	AI/STAOE/TOE/SIS
asphygmia	AS/FIG/MAOE/YA		A*S/YA/TOE/SIS
	AI/SFIG/MAOE/YA	aster	AS/TER
asphyxia	AS/FIX/YA		A*S/ER
asphyxial	AS/FIX/YAL	astereognosis	AI/STAOER/YOG/NOE/SIS
asphyxiant	AS/FIX/YANT		AI/STER/YOG/NOE/SIS
asphyxiate	AS/FIX/YAIT	asteria	AI/STAOER/YA
asphyxiating	AS/FIX/YAIT/-G		AS/TAOER/YA
asphyxiation	AS/FIX/YAIGS	asteric	AI/STAOER/IK
Aspiculuris tetraptera	AS/PIK/LAOU/RIS/TET/RAPT/RA		AS/TAOER/IK
	AS/PIK/LAOUR/RIS/TET/RAPT/RA	asterion	AI/STAOER/YON
aspidin	AS/PID/DIN		AS/TAOER/YON
	AS/PI/DIN		AS/TER/YON
aspidinol	AS/PID/NOL	asterixis	A*S/RIK/SIS
aspidium	AS/PID/YUM		AS/TRIK/SIS
Aspidium	K-P/AS/PID/YUM		AI/STER/IK/SIS
aspidosamine	AS/PI/DO/SAM/AOEN		AI/STRIK/SIS
	AS/PI/DO/SAM/MAOEN	asternal	AI/STERNL
aspidosperma	AS/PI/DO/SPER/MA	asternia	AI/STERN/YA
aspidospermine	AS/PI/DO/SPER/MAOEN	Asterococcus	A*S/RO/KOK/KUS
	AS/PI/DO/SPER/MIN		AS/TRO/KOK/KUS
aspirate	AS/PRAIT	asteroid	AS/TROID
	AS/PI/RAIT		A*S/ROID
aspiration	AS/PRAIGS	asterubin	A*S/RAOU/BIN
	AS/PI/RAIGS		AS/TE/RAOU/BIN
aspirator	AS/PRAI/TOR	asthen(o)-	AS/THAOEN
	AS/PI/RAI/TOR		AS/THAOE/N(O)
aspirin	AS/PRIN		AS/THE/N(O)
	AS/PI/RIN	asthenia	AS/THAOEN/YA
Aspirol	AS/PROL	asthenic	AS/THEN/IK
	AS/PI/ROL	asthenobiosis	AS/THAOEN/BAO*I/YOE/SIS
asplenia	AI/SPLAOEN/YA	asthenocoria	AS/THAOEN/KOER/YA
asplenic	AI/SPLEN/IK	asthenometer	AS/THE/NOM/TER
asporogenic	AS/POR/JEN/IK	asthenope	AS/THE/NOEP
	AI/SPOR/JEN/IK		AS/THEN/OEP
asporogenous	AS/PROJ/NOUS	asthenopia	AS/THE/NOEP/YA
	AS/PO/ROJ/NOUS	asthenopic	AS/THE/NOP/IK
	AI/SPO/ROJ/NOUS	asthenospermia	AS/THE/NO/SPERM/YA
asporous	AS/POER/OUS		AS/THAOEN/SPERM/YA
	AS/POR/OUS	asthenoxia	AS/THE/NOX/YA
	AI/SPOR/OUS		AS/THEN/OX/YA
	AS/PROUS	asthma	AS/MA
asporulate	AS/POR/LAIT		A*Z/MA
	AI/SPOR/LAIT		(*not* AZ/MA; see as ma-)
assanation	AS/SA/NAIGS	asthmatic	AS/MAT/IK
	AS/NAIGS		AZ/MAT/IK
	ASZ/NAIGS	asmatica	AS/MAT/KA
assassin	AI/SAS/SIN		AZ/MAT/KA
assay	AS/SAI	asthmatiform	AS/MAT/FORM
Assezat	AS/SE/ZAU		AZ/MAT/FORM
	AS/SAOE/ZAU	asthmogenic	AS/MO/JEN/IK
assident	AS/SI/DENT		AZ/MO/JEN/IK
	AS/DENT	astigmagraph	AI/STIG/MA/GRAF
	ASZ/DENT		AS/TIG/MA/GRAF
assimilable	AI/SIM/LABL	astigmatic	AS/TIG/MAT/IK
assimilation	AI/SIM/LAIGS		AI/STIG/MAT/IK
assistant	AI/SIS/TANT	astigmatism	AI/STIG/MA/TIFM
Assmann	ASZ/MAN	astigmatometer	AS/TIG/MA/TOM/TER
associate	SOERBT		AI/STIG/MA/TOM/TER
	AI/SOERB/YAT	astigmatometry	AS/TIG/MA/TOM/TRI
	AI/SOERB/YAIT		AI/STIG/MA/TOM/TRI
	AI/SOES/YAT	astigmatoscope	AS/TIG/MAT/SKOEP
	AI/SOES/YAIT		AI/STIG/MAT/SKOEP
association	SOERBGS	astigmatoscopy	AS/TIG/MA/TOS/KPI
	SOEGS		AI/STIG/MA/TOS/KPI
	AI/SOERB/YAIGS	astigmia	AI/STIG/MAOE/YA
	AI/SOES/YAIGS	astigmic	AI/STIG/MIK
associationism	SOERBGS/IFM	astigmometer	AS/TIG/MOM/TER
	SOEGS/IFM		AI/STIG/MOM/TER
	AI/SOERB/YAIGS/IFM	astigmometry	AS/TIG/MOM/TRI
	AI/SOES/YAIGS/IFM		AI/STIG/MOM/TRI
assonance	AS/SO/NANS	astigmoscope	AI/STIG/MO/SKOEP
	AS/NANS		AS/TIG/MO/SKOEP
	ASZ/NANS	astigmoscopy	AS/TIG/MOS/KPI
assortment	AI/SORT/-MT		AI/STIG/MOS/KPI

astomatous	AI/STOEM/TOUS	asynodia	AI/SNAOE/SIS
astomia	AI/STOEM/YA		AI/SI/NOED/YA
astomous	AI/STOEM/OUS		AI/SNOED/YA
astomus	AI/STOE/MUS	asynovia	AI/SI/NOEV/YA
astragal(o)-	AS/TRAG/L(O)		AI/SNOEV/YA
	AI/STRAG/L(O)		AS/NOEV/YA
astragalar	AS/TRAG/LAR	asyntaxia	AI/SIN/TAX/YA
astragalectomy	AS/TRAG/LEKT/M*I	asystematic	AI/S*IS/MAT/IK
astragalocalcanean	AS/TRAG/LO/KAL/KAIN/YAN		AI/S-M/AT/IK
astragalocrural	AS/TRAG/LO/KRAOURL		AI/S-M/MAT/IK
astragalofibular	AS/TRAG/LO/FIB/LAR	asystole	AI/S*IS/LAOE
astragaloscaphoid	AS/TRAG/LO/SKAF/OID	asystolia	AI/SIS/TOEL/YA
astragalotibial	AS/TRAG/LO/TIB/YAL	asystolic	AI/SIS/TOL/IK
astragalus	AS/TRAG/LUS	Atabrine	AT/BRAOEN
Astragalus	K-P/AS/TRAG/LUS		AT/BRIN
astral	AS/TRAL	atactic	AI/TAKT/IK
Astramorph	AS/TRA/MOR/-F	atactica	AI/TAKT/KA
astrapophobia	AS/TRA/PO/FOEB/YA	atactiform	AI/TAKT/FORM
astricta	AI/STRIK/TA	atactilia	AI/TAK/TIL/YA
	AS/TRIK/TA	ataractic	AT/RAKT/IK
astriction	AI/STR*IBGS	ataralgesia	AT/RAL/JAOEZ/YA
	AS/TR*IBGS	Atarax	AT/RAX
astringe	AI/STRIN/-J	ataraxia	AT/RAX/YA
astringent	AS/TRIN/JENT	ataraxic	AT/RAX/IK
	AI/STRIN/JENT	ataraxy	AT/RAK/SI
astro-	AS/TRO	atavic	AT/VIK
astroblast	AS/TRO/BLA*S		AI/TAV/IK
astroblastoma	AS/TRO/BLAS/TOE/MA		AI/TAVK
astrocele	AS/TRO/SAO*EL	atavism	AT/VIFM
astrocyte	AS/TRO/SAO*IT	atavistic	AT/V*IS/IK
astrocytin	AS/TRO/SAOI/TIN	atavus	AT/VUS
astrocytoma	AS/TRO/SAOI/TOE/MA	ataxia	AI/TAX/YA
astrocytosis	AS/TRO/SAOI/TOE/SIS	ataxiadynamia	AI/TAX/YA/DAOI/NAIM/YA
astroependymoma	AS/TRO/E/PEND/MOE/MA		AI/TAX/YA/DAOI/NAM/YA
	AS/TRO/PEND/MOE/MA	ataxiagram	AI/TAX/YA/GRAM
astroglia	AS/TROG/LA	ataxiagraph	AI/TAX/YA/GRAF
	AS/TROG/LAOE/YA	ataxiameter	AI/TAX/YA/MAOET/ER
astroid	AS/TRO*ID		AI/TAX/YA/MAOE/TER
	A*S/RO*ID		AI/TAX/YAM/TER
	(see asteroid)	ataxiamnesic	AI/TAX/YAM/NAOEZ/IK
astrokinetic	AS/TRO/KI/NET/IK		AI/TAX/AM/NAOEZ/IK
astrophorous	AS/TROF/ROUS	ataxiaphasia	AI/TAX/YA/FAIZ/YA
astrosphere	AS/TRO/SFAOER	ataxiaphasic	AI/TAX/YA/FAIZ/IK
astrostatic	AS/TRO/STAT/IK	ataxic	AI/TAX/IK
Astrup	AS/TRUP	ataxiophemia	AI/TAX/YO/FAOEM/YA
Astwood	A*S/WAOD	ataxiophobia	AI/TAX/YO/FOEB/YA
asulfurosis	AI/SUL/FAOU/ROE/SIS	ataxy	AI/TAK/SI
	AI/SUL/FROE/SIS	atelectasis	AT/LEKT/SIS
asverin	AS/VER/RIN	atelectatic	AT/LEK/TAT/IK
asyllabia	AI/SIL/LAIB/YA	atelencephalia	AI/TEL/EN/SFAIL/YA
	AI/SI/LAIB/YA		AI/TEL/EN/SE/FAIL/YA
asylum	AI/SAOIL/UM	atelia	AI/TAOEL/YA
	AI/SAOI/LUM	ateliosis	AI/TAOEL/YOE/SIS
asymbolia	AI/SIM/BOEL/YA	ateliotic	AI/TAOEL/YOT/IK
asymmetric	AI/SMET/RIK	atelo-	AT/LO
	AI/SIM/MET/RIK	atelocardia	AT/LO/KARD/YA
	AI/SI/MET/RIK	atelocephalous	AT/LO/SEF/LOUS
asymmetrical	AI/SMET/RI/KAL	atelocephaly	AT/LO/SEF/LI
	AI/SIM/MET/RI/KAL	atelocheilia	AT/LO/KAOIL/YA
	AI/SI/MET/RI/KAL	atelocheiria	AT/LO/KAOIR/YA
asymmetros	AI/SMET/ROS	ateloencephalia	AT/LO/EN/SFAIL/YA
	AI/SIM/MET/ROS		AT/LO/EN/SE/FAIL/YA
	AI/SI/MET/ROS	ateloglossia	AT/LO/GLOS/YA
	AI/SIM/TROS	atelognathia	AT/LOG/NA*IT/YA
asymmetry	AI/SIM/TRI	atelomyelia	AT/LO/MAOI/AOEL/YA
asymphytous	AI/SIM/FI/TOUS	atelopidtoxin	AI/TEL/OP/ID/TOK/SIN
asymptomatic	AI/SIMT/MAT/IK		AT/LOP/ID/TOK/SIN
	AI/SIFRPT/MAT/IK	atelopodia	AT/LO/POED/YA
	AI/SIM/TO/MAT/IK	ateloprosopia	AT/LO/PRO/SOEP/YA
	AI/SIFRP/TO/MAT/IK	atelorachidia	AT/LO/RA/KID/YA
asynapsis	AI/SNAP/SIS	atelostomia	AT/LO/STOEM/YA
	AI/SI/NAP/SIS	atenolol	AI/TEN/LOL
	AI/SIN/AP/SIS	athalposis	AI/THAL/POE/SIS
asynchronism	AI/SIN/KRO/NIFM		A*T/AL/POE/SIS
asynchrony	AI/SIN/KRO/N*I	athelia	AI/THAOEL/YA
asynclitism	AI/SIN/KLI/TIFM	athermal	AI/THER/MAL
asyndesis	AI/SIND/SIS	athermancy	AI/THER/MAN/SI
	AI/SIN/DE/SIS	athermanous	AI/THERM/NOUS
asynechia	AI/SI/NEK/YA	athermic	AI/THERM/IK
	AI/SNEK/YA	athermosystaltic	AI/THERM/SIS/TALT/IK
asynergia	AI/SIN/ER/JA	athero-	A*T/RO
	AI/SI/NER/JA	atheroembolism	A*T/RO/EM/BLIFM
asynergic	AI/SIN/ERJ/IK		A*T/RO/EM/BO/LIFM
	AI/SI/NERJ/IK	atheroembolus	A*T/RO/EM/BLUS
asynergy	AI/SIN/ER/JI		A*T/RO/EM/BO/LUS
asynesia	AI/SI/NAOEZ/YA	atherogenesis	A*T/RO/JEN/SIS
	AI/SNAOEZ/YA	atherogenic	A*T/RO/JEN/IK
	(not AS/NAOEZ/YA; see acinesia)	atheroma	A*T/ROE/MA
asynesis	AI/SI/NAOE/SIS	atheromatosis	A*T/ROEM/TOE/SIS

	A*T/ROE/MA/TOE/SIS
atheromatous	A*T/ROEM/TOUS
	A*T/ROE/MA/TOUS
atherosclerosis	A*T/RO/SKLE/ROE/SIS
atherosclerotic	A*T/RO/SKLE/ROT/IK
atherosis	A*T/ROE/SIS
atherothrombosis	A*T/RO/THROM/BOE/SIS
atherothrombotic	A*T/RO/THROM/BOT/IK
athetoid	A*T/TOID
athetosic	A*T/TOES/IK
athetosis	A*T/TOE/SIS
athetotic	A*T/TOT/IK
athiaminosis	AI/THAOI/MI/NOE/SIS
athomin	A*T/MIN
athrepsia	A*T/REPS/YA
	AI/THREPS/YA
athrepsy	A*T/REP/SI
	AI/THREP/SI
athreptic	A*T/REPT/IK
	AI/THREPT/IK
athrocytosis	A*T/RO/SAOI/TOE/SIS
athrombia	AI/THROM/BAOE/YA
athrophagocytosis	A*T/RO/FAG/SAOI/TOE/SIS
athymia	AI/THAOIM/YA
athymism	AI/THAOIM/IFM
	AI/THAOI/MIFM
athymismus	AI/THAOI/MIS/MUS
athyrea	AI/THAOIR/YA
athyreosis	AI/THAOIR/YOE/SIS
athyreotic	AI/THAOIR/YOT/IK
athyria	AI/THAO*IR/YA
athyroidation	AI/THAOI/ROI/DAIGS
athyroidemia	AI/THAOI/ROI/DAOEM/YA
athyroidism	AI/THAOI/ROID/IFM
	AI/THAOI/ROI/DIFM
athyroidosis	AI/THAOI/ROI/DOE/SIS
athyrosis	AI/THAOI/ROE/SIS
athyrotic	AI/THAOI/ROT/IK
atite	AT/AOIT
	AT/TAOIT
Ativan	AT/VAN
	AT/TI/VAN
atlant(o)-	AT/LANT
	AT/LAN/TO
atlantad	AT/LAN/TAD
atlantal	AT/LAN/TAL
atlantis	AT/LAN/TIS
Atlantis	K-P/AT/LAN/TIS
atlantoaxial	AT/LANT/AX/YAL
atlantoaxialis	AT/LANT/AX/YAI/LIS
atlantodidymus	AT/LANT/DID/MUS
atlantoepistrophic	AT/LANT/EP/STROFK
atlantoepistrophica	AT/LANT/EP/STROF/KA
atlantoepistrophicae	AT/LANT/EP/STROF/SAE
atlantomastoid	AT/LANT/MAS/TOID
atlanto-occipital	AT/LANT/OK/SIP/TAL
atlanto-occipitalis	AT/LANT/OK/SIP/TAI/LIS
atlanto-odontoid	AT/LANT/O/DON/TOID
atlas	AT/LAS
atloaxoid	AT/LO/AK/SOID
	AT/LO/AX/OID
atlodidymus	AT/LO/DID/MUS
atloido-occipital	AT/LOID/OK/SIP/TAL
	AT/LOI/DO/OK/SIP/TAL
atlo-occipital	AT/LO/OK/SIP/TAL
atmo-	AT/MO
atmograph	AT/MO/GRAF
atmolysis	AT/MOL/SIS
atmometer	AT/MOM/TER
atmos	AT/MOS
atmosphere	AT/MOS/FAOER
atmospheric	AT/MOS/FAOER/IK
atmospherization	AT/MOS/FAOER/ZAIGS
	AT/MO/SFAOER/ZAIGS
atmotherapy	AT/MO/THER/PI
Atmungsferment	AT/MUNGS/FERMT
	AT/MUNGS/FER/-MT
atocia	AI/TOE/SHA
	AI/TOES/YA
atolide	AT/LAOID
	AT/TO/LAOID
atom	AT/OM
atomic	AI/TOM/IK
atomism	AT/MIFM
	AT/OM/IFM
atomistic	AT/M*IS/IK
atomization	AT/OM/ZAIGS
	AT/MI/ZAIGS
atomize	AT/MAOIZ

	AT/OM/AOIZ
atomizer	AT/MAOIZ/ER
	AT/OM/AOIZ/ER
atonia	AI/TOEN/YA
atonic	AI/TON/IK
atonicity	AT/NIS/TI
atony	AT/N*I
atopen	AT/PEN
	AT/TO/PEN
atopic	AI/TOP/IK
atopognosia	AI/TOP/OG/NOEZ/YA
atopognosis	AI/TOP/OG/NOE/SIS
atopy	AT/PI
atoxic	AI/TOX/IK
atoxigenic	AI/TOX/JEN/IK
ATP	ARBGS/T*RBGS/P*RBGS
ATP-diphosphatase	ARBGS/T*RBGS/P*RBGS/DI/FOS/FA/TAIS
ATP-monophosphatase	ARBGS/T*RBGS/P*RBGS/MON/FOS/FA/TAIS
atractosylidic	AI/TRAK/TO/SI/LID/IK
	AI/TRAK/TO/SLID/IK
atractylic	AI/TRAK/TIL/IK
	AI/TRAKT/LIK
atractyligenin	AI/TRAK/TIL/JEN/NIN
atractylin	AI/TRAKT/LIN
	AI/TRAK/TIL/LIN
atracurium	AT/RA/KAOUR/YUM
	AI/TRA/KAOUR/YUM
atransferrinemia	AI/TRA*NS/FRI/NAOEM/YA
	AI/TRA*NS/FRIN/AOEM/YA
	AI/TRA*NS/FER/NAOEM/YA
atraumatic	AI/TRAU/MAT/IK
atremia	AI/TRAOEM/YA
atrepsy	AI/TREP/SI
atreptic	AI/TREPT/IK
atresia	AI/TRAOEZ/YA
atresic	AI/TRAOEZ/IK
atretic	AI/TRET/IK
atretica	AI/TRET/KA
	AI/TRAOET/KA
atreto-	AI/TRAOET
	AI/TRAOE/TO
atretoblepharia	AI/TRAOET/BLE/FAIR/YA
atretocephalus	AI/TRAOET/SEF/LUS
atretocormus	AI/TRAOET/KOR/MUS
atretocystia	AI/TRAOET/S*IS/YA
atretogastria	AI/TRAOET/GAS/TRA
	AI/TRAOET/GAS/TRAOE/YA
atretolemia	AI/TRAOET/LAOEM/YA
atretometria	AI/TRAOET/MAOE/TRA
	AI/TRAOET/MAOE/TRAOE/YA
atretopsia	AI/TRAOET/TOPS/YA
atretorrhinia	AI/TRAOET/RIN/YA
atretostomia	AI/TRAOET/STOEM/YA
atreturethria	AI/TRAOE/TAOU/RAO*ET/RAOE/YA
	AI/TRAOE/KHU/RAO*ET/RAOE/YA
atri(o)-	AI/TR(O)
	AIT/R(O)
	AI/TRAOE/Y(O)
atria	AI/TRA
atrial	AI/TRAL
atrichia	AI/TRIK/YA
atrichosis	AT/RI/KOE/SIS
	AI/TRI/KOE/SIS
atrichous	AT/RI/KOUS
	AI/TRIK/OUS
atrii	AI/TRAOE/YAOI
	AI/TRAOI
atriocommissuropexy	AI/TRO/KOM/SAOUR/PEK/SI
atriocommissurotomy	AI/TRO/KOM/SAOU/ROT/M*I
atriomegaly	AI/TRO/MEG/LI
atrionector	AI/TRO/NEK/TOR
atriopeptin	AI/TRO/PEP/TIN
atrioseptal	AI/TRO/SEP/TAL
atrioseptopexy	AI/TRO/SEPT/PEK/SI
atrioseptoplasty	AI/TRO/SEPT/PLAS/TI
atrioseptostomy	AI/TRO/SEP/TO*S/M*I
atrioseptotomy	AI/TRO/SEP/TOT/M*I
atriostomy	AI/TRO*S/M*I
atriotome	AI/TRO/TOEM
atriotomy	AI/TROT/M*I
atrioventricular	AI/TRO/YO/VEN/TRIK/LAR
atrioventricularis	AI/TRO/YO/VEN/TRIK/LAI/RIS
atriplicism	AI/TRIP/LI/SIFM
atrium	AI/TRUM
	AI/TRAOE/YUM

Atrohist	AT/RO/H*IS	auditopsychic	AUD/TO/SAOIK/IK
Atromid	AT/RO/MID	auditorii	AUD/TOR/YAOI
Atromid-S	AT/RO/MID/S-RBGS		AUD/TOER/YAOI
	AT/RO/MID/H-F/S-RBGS	auditory	AUD/TOIR
Atropa	AT/RO/PA	auditus	AU/DAOI/TUS
atrophedema	AI/TROF/DAOE/MA		AUD/TUS
atrophia	AI/TROEF/YA	Auenbrugger	OUN/BRAOUG/ER
atrophic	AI/TROFK		OU/EN/BRAOUG/ER
atrophica	AI/TROF/KA	Auer	OU/ER
atrophicans	AI/TROF/KANZ		AU/ER
atrophicum	AI/TROF/KUM	Auerbach	OU/ER/BAK
atrophoderma	AT/RO/FO/DER/MA		OU/ER/BAUK
	AI/TROE/FO/DER/MA		AUR/BAK
atrophodermatosis	AT/RO/FO/DERM/TOE/SIS		AUR/BAUK
	AI/TROE/FO/DERM/TOE/SIS	Aufrecht	OUF/REKT
atrophy	AT/RO/FI		OU/FREKT
atropine	AT/RO/PAOEN		AUF/REKT
atropinic	AT/RO/PIN/IK		AU/FREKT
atropinism	AT/RO/PIN/IFM	augmentation	AUG/MEN/TAIGS
atropinization	AT/RO/PIN/ZAIGS		AUG/-MT/TAIGS
atropism	AT/RO/PIFM	Augmentin	AUG/MEN/TIN
atrotoxin	AT/RO/TOK/SIN		AUG/-MT/TIN
attachment	AI/TAFP/-MT	augmentor	AUG/MEN/TOR
attack	AI/TAK		AUG/-MT/TOR
attar	AT/TAR	augnathus	AUG/NAI/THUS
attend	AI/TEND		AUG/NA/THUS
attention	AI/TENGS		AUG/NA*T/THUS
attenuant	AI/TEN/YAOUNT	Aujeszky	AU/JES/KI
	AI/TEN/YUNT	aur-	AUR
	AI/TEN/YANT		AU/R-
	AI/TEN/WANT	aura	AU/RA
attenuate	AI/TEN/YAIT	aurae	AU/RAE
	AI/TEN/WAIT	Aurafair	AUR/FAIR
attenuated	AI/TEN/YAIT/-D		AU/RA/FAIR
	AI/TEN/WAIT/-D	aural	AURL
attenuation	AI/TEN/YAIGS		AU/RAL
	AI/TEN/WAIGS	Auralgan	AURL/GAN
attenuator	AI/TEN/YAI/TOR		AU/RAL/GAN
	AI/TEN/WAI/TOR		AUR/RAL/GAN
Attenuvax	AI/TEN/YAOU/VAX	auramine	AUR/MAOEN
	AI/TEN/YU/VAX		AU/RA/MAOEN
attic	AT/IK	auranofin	AU/RAN/FIN
	AT/TIK	aurantia	AU/RAN/SHA
atticitis	AT/KAOITS		AU/RANT/YA
atticoantrotomy	AT/KO/AN/TROT/M*I	aurantiamarin	AU/RANT/YAM/RIN
atticomastoid	AT/KO/MAS/TOID	aurantiasis	AU/RAN/TAOI/SIS
atticotomy	AT/KOT/M*I	aurem	AUR/EM
attitude	AT/TAOUD		AU/REM
attitudinal	AT/TAOUD/NAL	aureolic	AU/RAOE/LIK
attollens	AI/TOL/ENZ		AUR/YOEL/IK
	AI/TOL/LENZ	aureolin	AU/RAOE/LIN
attonita	AI/TON/TA	Aureomycin	AUR/YO/MAOI/SIN
attractant	AI/TRAK/TANT	aureoviridis	AUR/YO/VIR/DIS
attraction	AI/TRA*BGS	aures	AU/RAOEZ
attrahens	AT/RA/HENZ		AUR/RAOEZ
	AT/TRA/HENZ	aurescens	AU/RES/ENZ
attrition	AI/TRIGS	auriasis	AU/RAOI/SIS
atypia	AI/TIP/YA	auric	AUR/IK
atypic	AI/TIP/IK	auricle	AUR/K-L
atypical	AI/TIP/KAL	auricul(o)-	AU/RIK/L(O)
atypism	AI/TIP/IFM		AU/RIK/YAOU/L(O)
Aub	AUB		AU/RIK/YU/L(O)
Auberger	AU/BERG/ER	auricula	AU/RIK/LA
	AU/BER/GER	auriculae	AU/RIK/LAE
Aubert	AU/BAIR	auricular	AU/RIK/LAR
	OEB/BAIR	auriculare	AU/RIK/LAI/RAOE
Auchmeromyia	AUK/MER/MAOI/YA	auriculares	AU/RIK/LAI/RAOEZ
aucubin	AU/KAOU/BIN	auricularia	AU/RIK/LAIR/YA
	AUK/YAOU/BIN	auricularis	AU/RIK/LAI/RIS
	AUK/YU/BIN	auriculocranial	AU/RIK/LO/KRAIN/YAL
audile	AU/DAOIL	auriculotemporal	AU/RIK/LO/TEFRP/RAL
	AU/DIL	auriculo-occipital	AU/RIK/LO/OK/SIP/TAL
audio	AUD/YOE	auriculoventricular	AU/RIK/LO/VEN/TRIK/LAR
audio-	AUD/YO	aurid	AUR/ID
audioanalgesia	AUD/YO/ANL/JAOEZ/YA	aurides	AUR/DAOEZ
audiogenic	AUD/YO/JEN/IK	auriform	AUR/FORM
audiogram	AUD/YO/GRAM	aurin	AU/RIN
audiologist	AUD/YO*LGS	aurinarium	AUR/NAIR/YUM
audiology	AUD/YOLG	aurinasal	AUR/NAI/ZAL
audiometer	AUD/YOM/TER	aurintricarboxylic	AU/RIN/TR*I/KAR/BOK/SIL/IK
audiometric	AUD/YO/MET/RIK		AU/RIN/TR*I/KAR/BOX/IL/IK
audiometrician	AUD/YO/ME/TRIGS	auriphone	AUR/FOEN
audiometry	AUD/YOM/TRI	auripigment	AUR/PIG/-MT
audiovisual	AUD/YO/VIRBL	auris	AU/RIS
audition	AU/DIGS		AUR/RIS
auditiva	AUD/TAOI/VA	auriscalpium	AUR/SKAL/PUM
auditivae	AUD/TAOI/VAE		AUR/SKAL/PAOE/UM
auditive	AUD/TIV		AUR/SKAL/PAOE/YUM
auditognosis	AUD/TOG/NOE/SIS	auriscope	AUR/SKOEP

aurist	AUR/*IS
	AU/R*IS
auristics	AU/R*IS/IK/-S
auro-	AUR
	AU/RO
aurochromoderma	AUR/KROEM/DER/MA
auromercaptoacetanilid	AUR/MER/KAPT/AS/TAN/LID
aurone	AU/ROEN
	AUR/ROEN
aurotherapy	AUR/THER/PI
aurothioglucose	AUR/THAOI/GLAOU/KOES
aurothioglycanide	AUR/THAOI/GLAOIK/NAOID
aurothiomalate	AUR/THAOI/MAI/LAIT
	AUR/THAOI/MAL/AIT
aurum	AUR/UM
	AUR/RUM
auscult	AUS/KULT
auscultate	AUS/KUL/TAIT
auscultation	AUS/KUL/TAIGS
auscultatory	AUS/KULT/TOIR
auscultoplectrum	AUS/KULT/PLEK/TRUM
auscultoscope	AUS/KULT/SKOEP
Austin Flint	AUS/TIN/FLINT
Australia	AUS/TRAIL/YA
Australian	AUS/TRAIL/YAN
australiensis	AUS/TRAIL/YEN/SIS
australis	AUS/TRAI/LIS
	AUS/TRA/LIS
aut(o)-	AUT
	AU/T(O)
autarcesiology	AUT/AR/SAOES/YOLG
autarcesis	AUT/AR/SAOE/SIS
autarcetic	AUT/AR/SET/IK
autechoscope	AU/TEK/SKOEP
autecic	AU/TAOES/IK
autecious	AU/TAOERBS
autecology	AUT/KOLG
autemesia	AUT/MAOEZ/YA
autesthetic	AUT/ES/THET/IK
authenticity	AU/THEN/TIS/TI
autism	AU/TIFM
autistic	AU/T*IS/IK
autoactivation	AUT/AKT/VAIGS
autoagglutination	AUT/AI/GLAOUT/NAIGS
autoagglutinin	AUT/AI/GLAOUT/NIN
autoallergic	AUT/AI/LERJ/IK
autoallergization	AUT/AI/LERJ/ZAIGS
autoallergy	AUT/AL/ER/JI
autoamputation	AUT/AFRP/TAIGS
	AUT/AM/PAOU/TAIGS
autoanalysis	AUT/ANL/SIS
autoanalyzer	AUT/AN/LAOIZ/ER
autoanamnesis	AUT/AN/AM/NAOE/SIS
autoanaphylaxis	AUT/AN/FLAK/SIS
autoantibody	AUT/A*ENT/BOD/DI
autoanticomplement	AUT/A*ENT/KOM/PLEMT
autoantigen	AUT/A*ENT/JEN
autoantisepsis	AUT/A*ENT/SEP/SIS
autoantitoxin	AUT/A*ENT/TOK/SIN
autoassay	AUT/AS/SAI
autoaudible	AUT/AUD/-BL
autobacteriophage	AUT/BAK/TAOER/YO/FAIJ
autobiotic	AUT/BAO*I/OT/IK
autoblast	AUT/BLA*S
autocatalysis	AUT/KA/TAL/SIS
autocatalyst	AUT/KAT/L*IS
autocatalytic	AUT/KAT/LIT/IK
autocatharsis	AUT/KA/THAR/SIS
autocatheterism	AUT/KA*T/TRIFM
	AUT/KA*T/TER/IFM
autocatheterization	AUT/KA*T/TER/ZAIGS
autocerebrospinal	AUT/SER/BRO/SPAOINL
autocholecystectomy	AUT/KOEL/SIS/TEKT/M*I
autochthonous	AU/TOK/THO/NOUS
	AU/TOK/THON/OUS
autoclasia	AUT/KLAIZ/YA
autoclasis	AU/TOK/LA/SIS
autoclave	AUT/KLAIV
autocoid	AUT/KOID
autoconduction	AUT/KON/D*UBGS
	AUT/K*UBGS
autocrine	AUT/KRIN
autocystoplasty	AUT/S*IS/PLAS/TI
autocytolysin	AUT/SAOI/TOL/SIN
autocytolysis	AUT/SAOI/TOL/SIS
autocytolytic	AUT/SAOIT/LIT/IK
autocytotoxin	AUT/SAOI/TOK/SIN
autodermic	AUT/DERM/IK
autodestruction	AUT/DE/STR*UBGS

	AUT/DR*UBGS
autodigestion	AUT/DI/JEGS
autodiploid	AUT/DIP/LOID
autodiploidy	AUT/DIP/LOI/DI
autodrainage	AUT/DRAIN/AJ
autoecholalia	AUT/EK/LAIL/YA
autoeczematization	AUT/EK/ZEM/TI/ZAIGS
autoerotic	AUT/E/ROT/IK
autoeroticism	AUT/E/ROT/SIFM
autoerotism	AUT/ER/TIFM
autoerythrophagocytosis	AUT/R*IT/RO/FAG/SAOI/TOE/SIS
autofluorescence	AUT/FLAOU/RES/ENS
autofluoroscope	AUT/FLAOUR/SKOEP
autofundoscope	AUT/FUND/SKOEP
autofundoscopy	AUT/FUN/DOS/KPI
autogamous	AU/TOG/MOUS
autogamy	AU/TOG/M*I
autogeneic	AUT/JE/NAOE/IK
	AUT/JE/NAI/IK
autogenesis	AUT/JEN/SIS
autogenetic	AUT/JE/NET/IK
autogenic	AUT/JEN/IK
autogenous	AU/TOJ/NOUS
autognosis	AU/TOG/NOE/SIS
autognostic	AU/TOG/NO*S/IK
autograft	AUT/GRAFT
autografting	AUT/GRAFT/-G
autogram	AUT/GRAM
autographism	AU/TOG/RA/FIFM
autohemagglutination	AUT/HEM/AI/GLAOUT/NAIGS
	AUT/HEM/GLAOUT/NAIGS
autohemagglutinin	AUT/HEM/AI/GLAOUT/NIN
	AUT/HEM/GLAOUT/NIN
autohemic	AUT/HAOEM/IK
autohemolysin	AUT/HAOE/MOL/SIN
autohemolysis	AUT/HAOE/MOL/SIS
autohemolytic	AUT/HAOEM/LIT/IK
autohemopsonin	AUT/HEM/OP/SOE/NIN
	AUT/HAOEM/OP/SOE/NIN
autohemotherapy	AUT/HAOEM/THER/PI
autohemotransfusion	AUT/HAOEM/TRA*NS/FAOUGS
autohexaploid	AUT/HEX/PLOID
autohistoradiograph	AUT/H*IS/RAID/YO/GRAF
autohormonoclasis	AUT/HOR/MOEN/OK/LA/SIS
	AUT/HORM/NOK/LA/SIS
autohypnosis	AUT/HIP/NOE/SIS
autohypnotic	AUT/HIP/NOT/IK
autohypnotism	AUT/HIP/NO/TIFM
autoimmune	AUT/IM/MAOUN
autoimmunity	AUT/IM/MAOUN/TI
autoimmunization	AUT/IM/NI/ZAIGS
autoimmunocytopenia	AUT/IM/NO/SAOIT/PAOEN/YA
autoinfection	AUT/IN/F*EBGS
autoinfusion	AUT/IN/FAOUGS
autoinoculable	AUT/IN/OK/LABL
autoinoculation	AUT/IN/OK/LAIGS
autointerference	AUT/SPWER/FAOERNS
autointoxicant	AUT/SPWOX/KANT
autointoxication	AUT/SPWOX/KAIGS
autoisolysin	AUT/AOI/SOL/SIN
autokeratoplasty	AUT/KER/TO/PLAS/TI
autokinesia	AUT/KI/NAOEZ/YA
autokinesis	AUT/KI/NAOE/SIS
autokinetic	AUT/KI/NET/IK
autolaryngoscopy	AUT/LARN/GOS/KPI
autolavage	AUT/LA/VAJ
autolesion	AUT/LAOEGS
autoleukoagglutinin	AUT/LAOUK/AI/GLAOUT/NIN
	AUT/LAOUK/GLAOUT/NIN
autoleukocytotherapy	AUT/LAOUK/SAOIT/THER/PI
autologous	AU/TOL/GOUS
autology	AU/TOLG
autolysate	AU/TOL/SAIT
autolysin	AU/TOL/SIN
autolysis	AU/TOL/SIS
autolysosome	AUT/LAOIS/SOEM
autolytic	AUT/LIT/IK
autolyze	AUT/LAOIZ
automata	AU/TOM/TA
automatic	AUT/MAT/IK
automatism	AU/TOM/TIFM
automatograph	AUT/MAT/GRAF
automaton	AU/TOM/TON
automixis	AUT/MIK/SIS
automnesia	AU/TOM/NAOEZ/YA
automysophobia	AUT/MIS/FOEB/YA
autonarcosis	AUT/NAR/KOE/SIS
autonephrectomy	AUT/NE/FREKT/M*I
	AUT/NEF/REKT/M*I

autonephrotoxin	AUT/NEF/RO/TOK/SIN	autospray	AUT/SPRAI
autonomic	AUT/NOM/IK	autostimulation	AUT/STIM/LAIGS
autonomotropic	AUT/NOM/TROP/IK	autosuggestibility	AUT/SUG/J*ES/-BLT
autonomous	AU/TON/MOUS		AUT/SUGT/-BLT
autonomy	AU/TON/M*I	autosuggestion	AUT/SUG/JEGS
auto-ophthalmoscope	AUT/OF/THAL/MO/SKOEP		AUT/SUGS
auto-ophthalmoscopy	AUT/OF/THAL/MOS/KPI	autosynnoia	AUT/SIN/NOI/YA
auto-oxidation	AUT/OX/DAIGS		AUT/SI/NOI/YA
auto-oxidizable	AUT/OX/DAOIZ/-BL	autosynthesis	AUT/S*INT/SIS
autopath	AUT/PA*T	autotelic	AUT/TEL/IK
autopathic	AUT/PA*T/IK	autotemnous	AUT/TEM/NOUS
autopathography	AUT/PA/THOG/FI	autotetraploid	AUT/TET/RA/PLOID
autopathy	AU/TOP/TH*I	autotherapy	AUT/THER/PI
autopentaploid	AUT/PENT/PLOID	autotomographic	AUT/TOEM/GRAFK
autopepsia	AUT/PEPS/YA	autotomography	AUT/TOE/MOG/FI
autophagia	AUT/FAI/JA	autotomy	AU/TOT/M*I
autophagic	AUT/FAIJ/IK	autotopagnosia	AUT/TOP/AG/NOEZ/YA
	AUT/FAJ/IK	autotoxemia	AUT/TOK/SAOEM/YA
autophagolysosome	AUT/FAG/LAOIS/SOEM	autotoxic	AUT/TOX/IK
	AUT/FAI/GO/LAOIS/SOEM	autotoxicosis	AUT/TOX/KOE/SIS
autophagosome	AUT/FAG/SOEM	autotoxin	AUT/TOK/SIN
autophagy	AU/TOF/JI	autotoxis	AUT/TOK/SIS
autopharmacologic	AUT/FARM/KO/LOJ/IK	autotransfusion	AUT/TRA*NS/FAOUGS
autopharmacology	AUT/FARM/KOLG	autotransplant	AUT/TRA*NS/PLANT
autophil	AUT/FIL	autotransplantation	AUT/TRA*NS/PLAN/TAIGS
autophilia	AUT/FIL/YA	autotrepanation	AUT/TREP/NAIGS
autophobia	AUT/FOEB/YA	autotriploid	AUT/TRIP/LOID
autophonometry	AUT/FOE/NOM/TRI	autotroph	AUT/TROF
autophony	AU/TOF/N*I		AUT/TROEF
autophthalmoscope	AU/TOF/THAL/MO/SKOEP	autotrophic	AUT/TROFK
autoplasmotherapy	AUT/PLAZ/MO/THER/PI	autotrophy	AU/TOT/RO/FI
autoplast	AUT/PLA*S	autotuberculin	AUT/TAOU/BERK/LIN
autoplastic	AUT/PLA*S/IK	autotuberculinization	AUT/TAOU/BERK/LIN/ZAIGS
autoplasty	AUT/PLAS/TI	autovaccination	AUT/VAX/NAIGS
Autoplex	AUT/PLEX	autovaccine	AUT/VAK/SAOEN
autoploid	AUT/PLOID	autovaccinotherapy	AUT/VAX/NO/THER/PI
autoploidy	AUT/PLOI/DI	autoxemia	AU/TOK/SAOEM/YA
autopod	AUT/POD	autoxidation	AU/TOX/DAIGS
autopodia	AUT/POED/YA	autoxidizable	AU/TOX/DAOIZ/-BL
autopodium	AUT/POED/YUM	autozygous	AUT/ZAOIG/OUS
autopoisonous	AUT/POIZ/NOUS	autumnal	AU/TUM/NAL
	AUT/POI/SON/OUS	auxano-	AUX/NO
autopolymer	AUT/POL/MER		AUK/SAN
autopolymerization	AUT/POL/MER/ZAIGS	auxanogram	AUK/SAN/GRAM
autopolyploid	AUT/POL/PLOID	auxanographic	AUK/SAN/GRAFK
autopolyploidy	AUT/POL/PLOI/DI	auxanography	AUX/NOG/FI
autoprecipitin	AUT/PRE/SIP/TIN	auxanology	AUX/NOLG
autoprotection	AUT/PRO/T*EBGS	auxesis	AUK/ZAOE/SIS
autoproteolysis	AUT/PROET/YOL/SIS		AUK/SAOE/SIS
autoprotolysis	AUT/PRO/TOL/SIS	auxetic	AUK/SET/IK
autopsy	AU/TOP/SI	auxiliary	AUK/SIL/RI
	AUPS		AUK/SIL/YAIR
autopsychic	AUT/SAOIK/IK		AUX/IL/RI
autopsychorhythmia	AUT/SAOIK/R*IT/MA		AUK/SIL/YA/RI
	AUT/SAOIK/R*IT/MAOE/YA	auxiliomotor	AUK/SIL/YO/MOE/TOR
autopsychotherapy	AUT/SAOIK/THER/PI	auxilytic	AUX/LIT/IK
autoradiogram	AUT/RAID/YO/GRAM	auxo-	AUX
autoradiograph	AUT/RAID/YO/GRAF		AUK/SO
autoradiography	AUT/RAID/YOG/FI	auxoaction	AUX/A*BGS
autoreactive	AUT/RE/AKT/IV	auxoamylase	AUX/AM/LAIS
autoregulation	AUT/REG/LAIGS	auxocardia	AUX/KARD/YA
autoreinfection	AUT/RE/IN/F*EBGS	auxochrome	AUX/KROEM
autoreinfusion	AUT/RE/IN/FAOUGS	auxochromous	AUX/KROEM/OUS
autoreproduction	AUT/RE/PRO/D*UBGS	auxocyte	AUX/SAO*IT
	AUT/RE/PR*UBGS	auxodrome	AUX/DROEM
autorrhaphy	AU/TOR/FI	auxoflore	AUX/FLOR
autosensitization	AUT/SENS/TI/ZAIGS		AUX/FLOER
	AUT/SENS/TAOI/ZAIGS	auxoflur	AUX/FLUR
autosensitize	AUT/SENS/TAOIZ	auxogluc	AUX/GLUK
autosensitized	AUT/SENS/TAOIZ/-D		AUX/GLAOUK
autosepticemia	AUT/SEPT/SAOEM/YA	auxohormone	AUX/HOR/MOEN
autoserodiagnosis	AUT/SAOER/DAOIG/NOE/SIS	auxometer	AUK/SOM/TER
autoserotherapy	AUT/SAOER/THER/PI		AUX/OM/TER
autoserous	AUT/SAOER/OUS	auxometric	AUX/MET/RIK
autoserum	AUT/SAOERM	auxometry	AUK/SOM/TRI
	AUT/SAOER/UM		AUX/OM/TRI
autosexing	AUT/SEX/-G	auxoneurotropic	AUX/NAOUR/TROP/IK
autosexualism	AUT/SEX/YAOUL/IFM	auxospireme	AUX/SPAOI/RAOEM
	AUT/SEX/YUL/IFM	auxospore	AUX/SPOER
autosite	AUT/SAOIT	auxotherapy	AUX/THER/PI
autositic	AUT/SIT/IK	auxotonic	AUX/TON/IK
autosmia	AU/TOZ/MAOE/YA	auxotox	AUX/TOX
autosomal	AUT/SOE/MAL	auxotroph	AUX/TROEF
autosomatognosis	AUT/SOEM/TOG/NOE/SIS		AUX/TROF
autosomatognostic	AUT/SOEM/TOG/NO*S/IK	auxotrophic	AUX/TROFK
autosome	AUT/SOEM	avalanche	AV/LAFRPBLG
autospermotoxin	AUT/SPERM/TOK/SIN		AV/LAN/-FP
autosplenectomy	AUT/SPLAOE/NEKT/M*I	avalvular	AI/VAL/VAOU/LAR
	AUT/SPLE/NEKT/M*I	avantin	AV/AN/TIN

avascular	AI/VAS/KLAR	axiomesio-occlusal	AX/YO/MAOEZ/YO/O/KLAOU/ZAL
avascularization	AI/VAS/KLAR/ZAIGS	axion	AX/YON
Avellis	AI/VEL/LIS	axio-occlusal	AX/YO/O/KLAOU/ZAL
	AV/EL/LIS	axioplasm	AX/YO/PLAFM
Avena	AI/VAOE/NA	axiopodia	AX/YO/POED/YA
avenin	AI/VAOE/NIN	axiopodium	AX/YO/POED/YUM
avenolith	AI/VAOEN/L*IT	axiopulpal	AX/YO/PUL/PAL
aversion	AI/VERGS	axioversion	AX/YO/VERGS
aversive	AI/VERS/IV	axipetal	AK/SIP/TAL
Aviadenovirus	AIV/YAD/NO/VAOI/RUS	axis	AK/SIS
	AI/VI/AD/NO/VAOI/RUS	axo-	AX
	AIV/AD/NO/VAOI/RUS		AK/SO
avian	AIV/YAN	axoaxonic	AX/AK/SON/IK
aviator	AIV/YAI/TOR	axodendritic	AX/DEN/DRIT/IK
avidin	AV/DIN	axofugal	AK/SOF/GAL
avidity	AI/VID/TI		AX/OF/GAL
avifauna	AIV/FAU/NA	axograph	AX/GRAF
	AIV/VI/FAU/NA	axoid	AK/SOID
Avipoxvirus	AIV/POX/VAOI/RUS		AX/OID
	AI/VI/POX/VAOI/RUS	axoidean	AK/SOID/YAN
	AI/VAOE/POX/VAOI/RUS		AX/OID/YAN
avirulence	AI/VIR/LENS	axolemma	AX/LEM/MA
avirulent	AI/VIR/LENT	axolysis	AK/SOL/SIS
avis	AI/VIS		AX/OL/SIS
avitaminosis	AI/VAOIT/MI/NOE/SIS	axometer	AK/SOM/TER
avitaminotic	AI/VAOIT/MI/NOT/IK		AX/OM/TER
	AI/VAOIT/MIN/OT/IK	axon	AK/SON
Avitene	AV/TAOEN	axonal	AX/NAL
avium	AIV/YUM		AK/SONL
avivement	AI/VIV/-MT	axoneme	AX/NAOEM
Avogadro	AV/GAD/ROE	axonography	AX/NOG/FI
avogram	AV/GRAM	axonometer	AX/NOM/TER
avoidance	AI/VOI/DANS	axonopathy	AX/NOP/TH*I
avoidant	AI/VOI/DANT	axonotmesis	AK/SON/OT/MAOE/SIS
avoirdupois	AVR/DAOU/POIZ		AX/NOT/MAOE/SIS
	AVR/DAOU/POIS	axopetal	AK/SOP/TAL
	AV/ER/DAOU/POIZ	axophage	AX/FALJ
	AV/ER/DAOU/POIS	axoplasm	AX/PLAFM
avoparcin	AV/PAR/SIN	axoplasmic	AX/PLAZ/MIK
avulsion	AI/VULGS	axopodia	AX/POED/YA
axanthopsia	AK/SAN/THOPS/YA	axopodium	AX/POED/YUM
	AX/AN/THOPS/YA	axosomatic	AX/SMAT/IK
Axenfeld	AX/EN/FELT		AX/SOE/MAT/IK
	AX/EN/FELD	axospongium	AX/SPON/JUM
	AX/-N/FELT	axostyle	AX/STAOIL
	AX/-N/FELD	Axotal	AX/TAL
axenic	AI/ZEN/IK	axotomy	AK/SOT/M*I
axes	AK/SAOEZ		AX/OT/M*I
axial	AX/YAL	Ayala	AI/YA/LA
axialis	AX/YAI/LIS		AI/YAL/LA
axiation	AX/YAIGS	Ayerst	AI/*ERS
Axid	AK/SID		AI/Y*ERS
	AX/ID	Ayerza	AI/YER/ZA
axifugal	AK/SIF/GAL		AI/YER/THA
axil	AK/SIL	Aygestin	AI/JES/TIN
axile	AK/SAOIL	Ayr	A*IR
axilla	AK/SIL/LA	az-	A*Z
axillae	AK/SIL/LAE		(not AZ; see as)
axillares	AX/LAI/RAOEZ	aza-	AIZ
	AX/LAR/RAOEZ		AI/ZA
axillaris	AX/LAI/RIS	azabon	AIZ/BON
	AX/LAR/RIS	azaclorzine	AIZ/KLOR/ZAOEN
axillary	AX/LAIR	azacosterol	AIZ/KO*S/ROL
axio-	AX/YO	azacrine	AIZ/KRIN
axiobuccal	AX/YO/BUK/KAL		AIZ/KRAOEN
axiobuccocervical	AX/YO/BUK/SEFRB/KAL	azacyclonol	AIZ/SAOI/KLO/NOL
axiobuccogingival	AX/YO/BUK/JING/VAL	azacytidine	AIZ/SAOIT/DAOEN
axiobuccolingual	AX/YO/BUK/LING/WAL	azafluorene	AIZ/FLAOUR/AOEN
axiocervical	AX/YO/SEFRB/KAL		AIZ/FLAOU/RAOEN
axiodistal	AX/YO/DIS/TAL	azaguanine	AIZ/GAU/NAOEN
axiodistocervical	AX/YO/D*IS/SEFRB/KAL	azamethonium	AIZ/ME/THOEN/YUM
axiodistogingival	AX/YO/D*IS/JING/VAL	azan	AI/ZAN
axiodistoincisal	AX/YO/D*IS/IN/SAOI/ZAL	azanator	AIZ/NAI/TOR
axiodisto-occlusal	AX/YO/D*IS/O/KLAOU/ZAL	azanidazole	AIZ/NID/ZOEL
axiogingival	AX/YO/JING/VAL	azaperone	AIZ/PER/OEN
axioincisal	AX/YO/IN/SAOI/ZAL	azapetine	AI/ZAP/TAOEN
axiolabial	AX/YO/LAIB/YAL	azapropazone	AIZ/PROEP/ZOEN
axiolabiogingival	AX/YO/LAIB/YO/JING/VAL	azaribine	AI/ZAR/BAOEN
axiolabiolingual	AX/YO/LAIB/YO/LING/WAL	azaserine	AIZ/SAOER/AOEN
axiolingual	AX/YO/LING/WAL		AIZ/SAOER/RAOEN
axiolinguocervical	AX/YO/LING/WO/SEFRB/KAL	azaspirodecanedione	AIZ/SPAOIR/DEK/AN/DI/OEN
axiolinguoclusal	AX/YO/LING/WO/KLAOU/ZAL	azastene	AIZ/STAOEN
axiolinguogingival	AX/YO/LING/WO/JING/VAL	azatadine	AI/ZAT/DAOEN
axiolinguo-occlusal	AX/YO/LING/WO/O/KLAOU/ZAL	azathioprine	AIZ/THAOI/PRAOEN
axiomesial	AX/YO/MAOEZ/YAL	azathymine	AIZ/THAOI/MAOEN
axiomesiocervical	AX/YO/MAOEZ/YO/SEFRB/KAL	azauridine	AIZ/YAOUR/DAOEN
axiomesiodistal	AX/YO/MAOEZ/YO/DIS/TAL		A*Z/AUR/DAOEN
axiomesiogingival	AX/YO/MAOEZ/YO/JING/VAL	azelaic	A*Z/LAI/IK
axiomesioincisal	AX/YO/MAOEZ/YO/IN/SAOI/ZAL	azeotrope	AIZ/YO/TROEP

azeotropic	AIZ/YO/TROP/IK
azeotropy	AIZ/YOT/RO/PI
azepindole	AIZ/PIN/DOEL
	AI/ZE/PIN/DOEL
azerin	A*Z/RIN
	AZ/ER/RIN
azide	AZ/SID
	AI/ZID
	A*Z/ID
	(*not* AZ/ID or AS/ID)
azidothymidine	A*Z/DO/THAOIM/DAOEN
azipramine	AI/ZIP/RA/MAOEN
Azlin	A*Z/LIN
azlocillin	A*Z/LO/SLIN
	A*Z/LO/SIL/LIN
Azmacort	AS/MA/KORT
	AZ/MA/KORT
azo-	A*Z
	AI/ZO
	AZ/ZO
	(*not* AZ; see as)
azoamyly	AI/ZOE/AM/LI
azobenzene	A*Z/BEN/ZAOEN
azobilirubin	A*Z/BIL/RAOU/BIN
azocarmine	A*Z/KAR/MIN
Azo Gantanol	AIZ/GANT/NOL
	A*Z/GANT/NOL
Azo Gantrisin	AIZ/GAN/TRI/SIN
	A*Z/GAN/TRI/SIN
azoic	AI/ZOIK
	AI/ZOE/IK
azoimide	A*Z/IM/AOID
azole	A*Z/OEL
azolimine	AI/ZOEL/MAOEN
azolitmin	A*Z/LIT/MIN
azomycin	AIZ/MAOI/SIN
	A*Z/MAOI/SIN
azoo-	AI/ZOE
	AI/ZAO
azoospermatism	AI/ZOE/SPERM/TIFM
azoospermia	AI/ZOE/SPERM/YA
azophloxin	A*Z/FLOK/SIN
azopigment	AIZ/PIG/-MT
	A*Z/PIG/-MT
azoprotein	A*Z/PRO/TAOEN
azosulfamide	A*Z/SUL/FA/MAOID
	AIZ/SUL/FA/MAOID
azote	A*Z/OET
	AI/ZOET
azotemia	A*Z/TAOEM/YA
azotemic	A*Z/TAOEM/IK
azotenesis	A*Z/TE/NAOE/SIS
azothermia	A*Z/THERM/YA
azotification	A*Z/OET/FI/KAIGS
azotize	A*Z/TAOIZ
Azotobacter	AI/ZOET/BAK/TER
	AI/ZOE/TO/BAK/TER
Azotobacteraceae	AI/ZOET/BAKT/RAIS/YAE
	AI/ZOE/TO/BAKT/RAIS/YAE
azotometer	A*Z/TOM/TER
Azotomonas	AI/ZOET/MOE/NAS
	AI/ZOE/TO/MOE/NAS
azotomycin	AI/ZOET/MAOI/SIN
	AI/ZOE/TO/MAOI/SIN
azotorrhea	A*Z/TO/RAOE/YA
azoturia	A*Z/TAOUR/YA
azoturic	A*Z/TAOUR/IK
azovan	A*Z/VAN
azoxybenzene	A*Z/OX/BEN/ZAOEN
AZT	A-RBGS/STK*RBGS/T*RBGS
Aztec	A*Z/TEK
	AS/TEK
	(*not* AZ/TEK)
aztreonam	A*Z/TRAOE/NAM
azul	AI/ZAOUL
	A*Z/YAOUL
azulene	A*Z/YAOU/LAOEN
	A*Z/YU/LAOEN
Azulfidine	AI/ZUL/FI/DAOEN
azure	A*Z/YUR
	AZ/YUR
	ARB/YUR
azuresin	A*Z/YAOU/RE/SIN
	A*Z/YU/RE/SIN
	A*Z/YAOU/REZ/SIN
	A*Z/YU/REZ/SIN
azurophil	A*Z/YUR/FIL
	A*Z/YAOUR/FIL
azurophile	A*Z/YUR/FAOIL

	A*Z/YAOUR/FAOIL
azurophilia	A*Z/YUR/FIL/YA
	A*Z/YAOUR/FIL/YA
azurophilic	A*Z/YUR/FIL/IK
	A*Z/YAOUR/FIL/IK
azygogram	A*Z/GO/GRAM
azygography	A*Z/GOG/FI
azygos	A*Z/GOS
azygosperm	AI/ZAOIG/SPERM
azygospore	AI/ZAOIG/SPOER
azygous	A*Z/GOUS
	AI/ZAOIG/OUS

B

Babbitt	BAB/BIT
Babcock	BAB/KOK
Babes	BA/BAIZ
Babes-Ernst	BA/BAIZ/H-F/*ERNS
Babesia	BA/BAOEZ/YA
Babesiella	BA/BAOEZ/YEL/LA
Babesiidae	BAB/ZAOI/DAE
	BAB/ZAOE/DAE
	BA/BAOE/ZAOI/DAE
	BA/BAOE/ZAOE/DAE
babesiosis	BA/BAOEZ/YOE/SIS
Babinski	BA/BIN/SKAOE
	BA/BIN/SKI
baby	BAI/BI
bacampicillin	BA/KAFRP/SLIN
	BAK/AFRP/SLIN
	BA/KAFRP/SIL/LIN
	BAK/AFRP/SIL/LIN
bacca	BAK/KA
baccate	BAK/AIT
	BAK/KAIT
Baccelli	BA/KHEL/LAOE
	BAK/KHEL/LAOE
bacciform	BAK/SI/FORM
	BAKS/FORM
Bachman	BAK/MAN
	BAUK/MAN
Bachmann	BAK/MA*N
	BAUK/MA*N
Baciguent	BAS/KWENT
	BAS/IG/WENT
bacill(o)-	BA/SIL
	BAS/L(O)
Bacillaceae	BAS/LAIS/YAE
	BAS/LAI/SAE
bacillar	BAS/LAR
bacillary	BAS/LAIR
bacillemia	BAS/LAOEM/YA
bacilli	BA/SIL/LAOI
bacilliculture	BA/SIL/KUL/KHUR
bacilliferous	BAS/LIF/ROUS
bacilliform	BA/SIL/FORM
bacilliformis	BA/SIL/FOR/MIS
bacillin	BA/SLIN
	BA/SIL/LIN
bacilliparous	BAS/LIP/ROUS
bacillogenic	BA/SIL/JEN/IK
bacillogenous	BAS/LOJ/NOUS
bacillomyxin	BA/SIL/MIK/SIN
bacillosis	BAS/LOE/SIS
bacilluria	BAS/LAOUR/YA
bacillus	BA/SIL/LUS
Bacillus	K-P/BA/SIL/LUS
bacitracin	BAS/TRAI/SIN
back	BAK
backache	BAK/A*IK
backbone	BAK/BOEN
backcross	BAK/KROSZ
backflow	BAK/FLOE
background	BAK/GRO*UND
	BAK/GROUND
backing	BAK/-G
backknee	BAK/NAOE
backscatter	BAK/SKAT/ER
baclofen	BAK/LO/FEN
	BAK/LOE/FEN
Bacon	K-P/BAI/KON
bacony	BAI/KON/N*I
bacoti	BA/KOE/TAOE
B-A-C Tablets	PW-RBGS/ARBGS/KR-RBGS/TAB/ LET/-S
	PW-RBGS/H-F/ARBGS/H-F/ KR-RBGS/TAB/LET/-S
bacter-	BAK/TER
	BAKT/R-
	BAK/TR-
-bacter	BAK/TER
bacteremia	BAK/TRAOEM/YA
	BAK/TER/AOEM/YA
	BAKT/RAOEM/YA
bacteri-	BAK/TAOER
bacteri(o)-	BAK/TAOER/Y(O)
bacteria	BAK/TAOER/YA
bacterial	BAK/TAOERL

	BAK/TAOER/YAL
bactericholia	BAK/TAOER/KOEL/YA
bactericidal	BAK/TAOER/SAOI/DAL
bactericide	BAK/TAOER/SAO*ID
bactericidin	BAK/TAOER/SAOI/DIN
bacterid	BAKT/RID
	BAK/TRID
	BAK/TER/ID
bacteriform	BAK/TAOER/FORM
bacterin	BAKT/RIN
	BAK/TRIN
	BAK/TER/RIN
bacterinia	BAKT/RIN/YA
	BAK/TRIN/YA
	BAK/TE/RIN/YA
bacterioagglutinin	BAK/TAOER/YO/AI/GLAOUT/NIN
bacteriochlorin	BAK/TAOER/YO/KLOR/RIN
bacteriochlorophyll	BAK/TAOER/YO/KLOR/FIL
bacteriocidal	BAK/TAOER/YO/SAOI/DAL
bacteriocide	BAK/TAOER/YO/SAO*ID
bacteriocidin	BAK/TAOER/YO/SAOI/DIN
bacteriocin	BAK/TAOER/YO/SIN
bacteriocinogenic	BAK/TAOER/YO/SIN/JEN/IK
bacterioclasis	BAK/TAOER/YOK/LA/SIS
bacterioerythrin	BAK/TAOER/YO/*ER/THRIN
	BAK/TAOER/YO/ER/THRIN
bacteriofluorescein	BAK/TAOER/YO/FLAOU/RES/YIN
bacteriofluorescin	BAK/TAOER/YO/FLAOU/RES/SIN
bacteriogenic	BAK/TAOER/YO/JEN/IK
bacteriogenous	BAK/TAOER/YOJ/NOUS
bacteriohemagglutinin	BAK/TAOER/YO/HEM/GLAOUT/ NIN
	BAK/TAOER/YO/HEM/AI/ GLAOUT/NIN
bacteriohemolysin	BAK/TAOER/YO/HAOE/MOL/SIN
bacterioid	BAK/TAOER/YOID
bacteriologic	BAK/TAOER/YO/LOJ/IK
bacteriological	BAK/TAOER/YO/LOJ/KAL
bacteriologist	BAK/TAOER/YO*LGS
bacteriology	BAK/TAOER/YOLG
bacteriolysant	BAK/TAOER/YOL/SANT
bacteriolysin	BAK/TAOER/YOL/SIN
bacteriolysis	BAK/TAOER/YOL/SIS
bacteriolytic	BAK/TAOER/YO/LIT/IK
bacteriolyze	BAK/TAOER/YO/LAOIZ
bacterio-opsonin	BAK/TAOER/YO/OP/SOE/NIN
bacteriopexy	BAK/TAOER/YO/PEK/SI
bacteriophage	BAK/TAOER/YO/FAIJ
bacteriophagia	BAK/TAOER/YO/FAI/JA
bacteriophagic	BAK/TAOER/YO/FAJ/IK
bacteriophagology	BAK/TAOER/YO/FA/GOLG
bacteriophagum	BAK/TAOER/YOF/GUM
bacteriopheophorbide	BAK/TAOER/YO/FAOE/FOR/ BAOID
	BAK/TAOER/YO/FAOE/FOER/ BAOID
bacteriopheophorbin	BAK/TAOER/YO/FAOE/FOR/BIN
	BAK/TAOER/YO/FAOE/FOER/BIN
bacteriopheophytin	BAK/TAOER/YO/FAOE/FAOI/TIN
bacteriophorbin	BAK/TAOER/YO/FOR/BIN
	BAK/TAOER/YO/FOER/BIN
bacteriophytoma	BAK/TAOER/YO/FAOI/TOE/MA
bacterioplasmin	BAK/TAOER/YO/PLAZ/MIN
bacterioprecipitin	BAK/TAOER/YO/PRE/SIP/TIN
bacterioprotein	BAK/TAOER/YO/PRO/TAOEN
bacteriopsonic	BAK/TAOER/YOP/SON/IK
bacteriopsonin	BAK/TAOER/YOP/SOE/NIN
bacteriopurpurin	BAK/TAOER/YO/PURP/RIN
bacteriorhodopsin	BAK/TAOER/YO/ROE/DOP/SIN
bacteriosis	BAK/TAOER/YOE/SIS
bacteriospermia	BAK/TAOER/YO/SPERM/YA
bacteriostasis	BAK/TAOER/YO/*S/SIS
bacteriostat	BAK/TAOER/YO/STAT
bacteriostatic	BAK/TAOER/YO/STAT/IK
bacteriotherapy	BAK/TAOER/YO/THER/PI
bacteriotoxemia	BAK/TAOER/YO/TOK/SAOEM/YA
bacteriotoxic	BAK/TAOER/YO/TOX/IK
bacteriotoxin	BAK/TAOER/YO/TOK/SIN
bacteriotropic	BAK/TAOER/YO/TROP/IK
bacteriotropin	BAK/TAOER/YOT/RO/PIN
	BAK/TAOER/YOT/ROE/PIN
bacteriotrypsin	BAK/TAOER/YO/TRIP/SIN
bacteritic	BAKT/RIT/IK
	BAK/TRIT/IK
	BAK/TER/IT/IK
bacterium	BAK/TAOERM
	BAK/TAOER/YUM
bacteriuria	BAK/TAOER/YAOUR/YA
bacteriuric	BAK/TAOER/YAOUR/IK

bacteroid	BAKT/ROID
	BAK/TROID
	BAK/TER/OID
Bacteroidaceae	BAKT/ROI/DAIS/YAE
	BAKT/ROI/DAI/SAE
	BAK/TROI/DAIS/YAE
	BAK/TROI/DAI/SAE
Bacteroides	BAKT/ROI/DAOEZ
	BAK/TROI/DAOEZ
bacteroidosis	BAKT/ROI/DOE/SIS
	BAK/TROI/DOE/SIS
Bactine	BAK/TAOEN
Bactocill	BAK/TO/SIL
Bactoscilla	BAK/TOS/SIL/LA
Bactrim	BAK/TRIM
baculiform	BA/KAOUL/FORM
bacul-	BAK/L-
	BAK/YAOU/L-
	BAK/YU/L-
Baculoviridae	BAK/LO/VIR/DAE
baculovirus	BAK/LO/VAOI/RUS
baculum	BAK/LUM
badge	BAJ
Baelz	BAILTS
	BAILZ
Baer	BA*ER
bag	BAG
bagassosis	BAG/SOE/SIS
bahnung	BA/NUNG
Bailey	BA*I/LAOE
	BAI/LAO*E
	(*not* BAI/LAOE or BAIL/LAOE; see bailee)
Baillarger	BAOI/YAR/JAI
Bainbridge	BAIN/BRIJ
bake	BAIK
Baker	K-P/BAIK/ER
Balamuth	BAL/MAOUT
	BAL/M*UT
	BAL/MAO*UT
balance	BAL/LANS
balanced	BAL/LANS/-D
balan(o)-	BAL/N(O)
	BA/LAN
balanic	BA/LAN/IK
balanitis	BAL/NAOITS
balanoplasty	BAL/NO/PLAS/TI
balanoposthitis	BAL/NO/POS/THAOITS
balanoposthomycosis	BAL/NO/POS/THO/MAOI/KOE/SIS
balanopreputial	BAL/NO/PRE/PAOURBL
balantidial	BAL/AN/TID/YAL
balantidiasis	BAL/ANT/DAOI/SIS
	BAL/AN/TI/DAOI/SIS
balantidicidal	BA/LAN/TID/SAOI/DAL
	BAL/AN/TID/SAOI/DAL
Balantidium	BAL/AN/TID/YUM
balantidosis	BA/LANT/DOE/SIS
	BAL/ANT/DOE/SIS
balanus	BAL/NUS
bald	BAULD
	BALD
baldness	BAULD/*NS
	BALD/*NS
Baldy	BAUL/DI
ball	BAL
Ball	K-P/BAL
Ballance	BA*L/LANS
	BAL/LA*NS
ball-and-socket	BAL/AND/SOK/ET
	BAL/AND/SOKT
	BAL/H-F/AND/H-F/SOK/ET
	BAL/H-F/AND/H-F/SOKT
Ballet	K-P/BAL/LAI
ballism	BAL/IFM
	BAL/LIFM
ballismus	BA/LIZ/MUS
	BAL/LIZ/MUS
	BAL/IZ/MUS
ballist(o)-	BL*IS
	BLIS/T(O)
	BA/L*IS
	BA/LIS/T(O)
	BAL/LIS/T(O)
	BAL/L*IS
ballistic	BL*IS/IK
ballistocardiogram	BLIS/TO/KARD/YO/GRAM
ballistocardiograph	BLIS/TO/KARD/YO/GRAF
ballistocardiography	BLIS/TO/KARD/YOG/FI
ballistophobia	BLIS/TO/FOEB/YA
balloon	BA/LAON
	BAL/LAON
ballooning	BA/LAON/-G
	BAL/LAON/-G
balloonseptostomy	BA/LAON/SEP/TO*S/M*I
	BAL/LAON/SEP/TO*S/M*I
ballotable	BA/LOT/-BL
	BAL/LOT/-BL
ballottement	BA/LOT/-MT
	BAL/LOT/-MT
ball-valve	BAL/H-F/VAL/-V
balm	BAUM
	BAL/-M
Balme	BA*UM
	BA*L/-M
Balmex	BAL/MEX
balne(o)-	BAL/NO
	BAL/NAOE
	BAL/NAOE/Y(O)
Balneol	BAL/NAOE/OL
	BAL/NAOE/YOL
balneology	BAL/NAOE/YOLG
	BAL/NAOE/OLG
balneotherapeutics	BAL/NO/THER/PAOUT/IK/-S
balneotherapy	BAL/NO/THER/PI
Balnetar	BAL/NE/TAR
balneum	BAL/NAOE/YUM
	BAL/NAOE/UM
balsam	BAL/SAM
	BAUL/SAM
balsamic	BAL/SAM/IK
	BAUL/SAM/IK
balteum	BALT/YUM
	BAL/TAOE/YUM
	BAL/TAOE/UM
Baltimore	BALT/MOR
	BALT/MOER
Bamberger	BAM/BERG/ER
	BAM/BER/GER
bamboo	BAM/BAO
bamethan sulfate	BAI/M*ET/THAN/SUL/FAIT
bamifylline	BA/MIF/LIN
bamipine	BAM/PAOEN
bamnidazole	BAM/NID/ZOEL
Bancap	BAN/KAP
Bancroft	BAN/KROFT
bancroftiasis	BAN/KROF/TAOI/SIS
bancroftosis	BAN/KROF/TOE/SIS
band	BAND
bandage	BAND/AJ
	BAN/DAJ
Band-Aid	BA*ND/H-F/AID
	BA*ND/AID
	(*not* BAND/H-F/AID, BAN/DAID; see band-aid)
	(*not* BAND/AID; see band aid)
Bandeloux	BAND/LAOU
	BAN/DE/LAOU
banding	BAND/-G
Bandl	BAND/-L
bands	BANDZ
bane	BAIN
bang	BANG
Bang	K-P/BANG
Bangkok	BANG/KOK
banisterine	BA/N*IS/RIN
	BA/N*IS/RAOEN
	BAN/*IS/RIN
	BAN/*IS/RAOEN
bank	BAN/-K
	BA*NG
Bannister	K-P/BAN/NIS/TER
Banti	BAN/TAOE
Banting	BANT/-G
bantingism	BANT/-G/IFM
bar	BAR
Bar	K-P/BAR
baragnosis	BAR/AG/NOE/SIS
Barany	BAR/N*I
	BA/RA/N*I
	BAR/RA/N*I
barba	BAR/BA
barbae	BAR/BAE
barbaloin	BARB/LOIN
	BAR/BA/LOIN
	BAR/BAL/WIN
barbed	BAR/-BD
	(*not* BARB/-D; see bashed)
barbital	BARB/TAL

barbiturate	BAR/BIFP/RAT
	BAR/BIT/RAT
barbituric	BARB/TAOUR/IK
	BAR/BI/TAOUR/IK
barbiturism	BAR/BIFP/RIFM
	BAR/BIT/RIFM
barbotage	BARB/TAJ
	BAR/BO/TAJ
	BAR/BOE/TAJ
barbula hirci	BAR/BAOU/LA/HIR/SAOI
Barcroft	BAR/KROFT
Bard	K-P/BARD
Bardenheuer	BARD/EN/HOIR
	BARD/-N/HOIR
	BAR/DEN/HOIR
Bardet	BAR/DAI
Bardinet	BARD/NAI
bare	BAIR
baresthesia	BAR/ES/THAOEZ/YA
baresthesiometer	BAR/ES/THAOEZ/YOM/TER
bari-	BAIR
	BAR
bariatric	BAR/YAT/RIK
	BAIR/YAT/RIK
baric	BAR/IK
baricity	BA/RIS/TI
barilla	BA/RIL/LA
baritosis	BAR/TOE/SIS
	BAIR/TOE/SIS
barium	BAIR/YUM
	BAR/YUM
bark	BARK
Barkan	BAR/KAN
barking cough	BARK/-G/KAUF
barley	BAR/LAOE
Barlow	BAR/LOE
barn	BARN
Barnes	BARNZ
	BARNS
bar(o)	BAR
	BAR/R(O)
baroceptor	BAR/SEP/TOR
barognosis	BAR/OG/NOE/SIS
barograph	BAR/GRAF
barometrograph	BAR/MET/RO/GRAF
barophilic	BAR/FIL/IK
baroreceptor	BAR/RE/SEP/TOR
baroreflex	BAR/RE/FLEX
baroscope	BAR/SKOEP
barosinusitis	BAR/SAOIN/SAOITS
barospirator	BAR/SPAOI/RAI/TOR
barostat	BAR/STAT
barotaxis	BAR/TAK/SIS
barotitis	BAR/O/TAOITS
	BAR/TAOITS
barotrauma	BAR/TRAU/MA
barotropism	BAR/OT/RO/PIFM
Barr	BA*R
Barraquer	BAR/RAK/ER
	BAR/RA/KER
Barre	BAR/RAI
barrel	BAIRL
	BARL
	BAIR/EL
	BAR/EL
barren	BAIRN
	BAIR/-N
	BAR/-N
	BAR/REN
	(*not* BARN; see barn)
Barrett	BAR/RET
	BAIR/RET
barrier	BAIR/YER
	BAR/YER
Bart	BART
Barth	BA*RT
Bartholin	BART/LIN
	BAR/TO/LIN
bartholinian	BART/LIN/YAN
	BAR/TO/LIN/YAN
bartholinitis	BART/LIN/AOITS
	BART/LI/NAOITS
Barton	BAR/TON
Bartonella	BART/NEL/LA
	BAR/TO/NEL/LA
Bartonellaceae	BART/NEL/LAIS/YAE
	BAR/TO/NEL/LAIS/YAE
bartonellemia	BART/NEL/AOEM/YA
	BART/NEL/LAOEM/YA

	BAR/TO/NEL/AOEM/YA
	BAR/TO/NEL/LAOEM/YA
bartonelliasis	BART/NEL/LAOI/SIS
	BAR/TO/NEL/LAOI/SIS
bartonellosis	BART/NEL/LOE/SIS
	BAR/TO/NEL/LOE/SIS
Bartonia	BAR/TOEN/YA
Baruch	BAR/RAOUK
	BAR/AOUK
baruria	BAR/YAOUR/YA
	BA/RAOUR/YA
bary-	BAR/RI
	(*not* BAR; see bari- and baro-)
barye	BAR/RAOE
baryglossia	BAR/RI/GLOS/YA
barylalia	BAR/RI/LAIL/YA
baryphonia	BAR/RI/FOEN/YA
baryta	BA/RAOI/TA
barytron	BAR/TRON
	BAR/RI/TRON
bas(o)-	BAI/S(O)
	(*not* BAIS; see base and basi-)
basad	BAI/SAD
basal	BAI/SAL
basalioma	BAI/SAL/YOE/MA
basalis	BAI/SAI/LIS
	BA/SAI/LIS
Basaljel	BAI/SAL/JEL
basaloid	BAIS/LOID
	BAI/SAL/OID
	BAI/SA/LOID
basaloma	BAIS/LOE/MA
	BAI/SA/LOE/MA
basculation	BAS/KLAIGS
	BAS/KAOU/LAIGS
base	BAIS
basedoid	BAS/DOID
Basedow	BAS/DOE
basedowian	BAS/DOE/YAN
basedowiform	BAS/DOE/FORM
basement	BAIS/-MT
baseline	BAIS/LAOIN
	BAIS/LAO*IN
baseplate	BAIS/PLAET
	BAIS/PLA*ET
bases	BAI/SAOEZ
	BAIS/-S
bas-fond	BAU/FON
	BAU/FOND
basi-	BAI/SI
	(*not* BAIS; see base and baso-)
-basia	BAIS/YA
	BAIZ/YA
basial	BAIS/YAL
basialis	BAIS/YAI/LIS
basialveolar	BAI/SI/AL/VAOE/LAR
basiarachnitis	BAI/SI/AR/AK/NAOITS
basiarachnoiditis	BAI/SI/AI/RAK/NOI/DAOITS
basibregmatic	BAI/SI/BREG/MAT/IK
basic	BAIS/IK
basichromatin	BAI/SI/KROEM/TIN
basichromiole	BAI/SI/KROEM/YOEL
basicity	BA/SIS/TI
basicranial	BAI/SI/KRAIN/YAL
basicytoparaplastin	BAI/SI/SAOIT/PAR/PLAS/TIN
basidia	BA/SID/YA
Basidiobolus	BA/SID/YO/BOE/LUS
	BA/SID/YOB/LUS
basidiocarp	BA/SID/YO/KARP
Basidiomycetes	BA/SID/YO/MAOI/SAOE/TAOEZ
basidiomycetous	BA/SID/YO/MAOI/SAOE/TOUS
	BA/SID/YO/MAOI/SAOET/OUS
basidiospore	BA/SID/YO/SPOER
basidium	BA/SID/YUM
basifacial	BAI/SI/FAIRBL
basigenous	BA/SIJ/NOUS
basihyal	BAI/SI/HAOIL
basihyoid	BAI/SI/HAOI/OID
basil	BAI/SIL
	BAS/IL
basilad	BAS/LAD
basilar	BAS/LAR
basilaris	BAS/LAI/RIS
	BAS/LAR/RIS
basilateral	BAI/SI/LAT/RAL
basilemma	BAI/SI/LEM/MA
basilic	BA/SIL/IK
basilicon	BA/SIL/KON
basilicus	BA/SIL/KUS

©1992 StenEd® Medical Dictionary

basiloma	BAS/LOE/MA	bathyhyperesthesia	BA*T/HAO*IP/ES/THAOEZ/YA
basilysis	BA/SIL/SIS	bathyhypesthesia	BA*T/HIP/ES/THAOEZ/YA
basin	BAI/SIN	bathypnea	BA*T/NAOE/YA
basinasal	BAI/SI/NAI/ZAL	-batia	BAI/SHA
basinasial	BAI/SI/NAIZ/YAL		BAIRB/YA
basio-	BAIS/YO	Batson	BAT/SON
basioccipital	BAI/SI/OK/SIP/TAL	battarism	BAT/RIFM
	BAIS/YOK/SIP/TAL	battarismus	BAT/RIZ/MUS
basioglossus	BAIS/YO/GLOS/SUS	Batten	K-P/BAT/-N
basion	BAIS/YON	battery	BAT/RI
basios	BAIS/YOES		BAT/TRI
	BAIS/YOS	Battey	BAT/TAOE
basiotic	BAIS/YOT/IK	Battle	K-P/BAT/-L
basipetal	BAI/SIP/TAL	batyl	BAT/IL
basipharyngeal	BAI/SI/FRIN/JAL		BAIT/IL
basipharyngeus	BAI/SI/FRIN/JUS	Baudelocque	BOED/LOK
basiphilic	BAI/SI/FIL/IK		BOE/DLOK
basiphobia	BAI/SI/FOEB/YA	baudetii	BOE/DET/YAOI
	BAIS/FOEB/YA		BAU/DET/YAOI
basirhinal	BAI/SI/RAOINL	Bauhin	BOE/HAN
	BAI/SI/RAOI/NAL	Baume	BOE/MA*I
basis	BAIS/SIS		BAU/MAI
basisphenoid	BAI/SI/SFAOE/NOID	Baumes	BOE/MEZ
basitemporal	BAI/SI/TEFRP/RAL	Baumgarten	BAUM/GART/-N
basium	BAIS/YUM		BAUM/GAR/TEN
basivertebral	BAI/SI/VERT/BRAL	bay	BAI
basivertebrales	BAI/SI/VERT/BRAI/LAOEZ	bayberry	BAI/BER/RI
basket	BAS/KET	Bayer	BA*IR
baso-	BAI/SO		BAI/YER
	(not BAIS; see base and basi-)	bayonet	BAI/NET
basocellulare	BAI/SO/SEL/YAOU/LAI/RAOE		BAI/YO/NET
basocyte	BAI/SO/SAO*IT	Bazin	BA/ZAN
basocytopenia	BAI/SO/SAOIT/PAOEN/YA	B-C-Bid	B-RBGS/KR-RBGS/BID
basocytosis	BAI/SO/SAOI/TOE/SIS		B-RBGS/H-F/KR-RBGS/H-F/BID
basoerythrocyte	BAI/SO/R*IT/RO/SAO*IT	Bdella	DEL/LA
basoerythrocytosis	BAI/SO/R*IT/RO/SAOI/TOE/SIS	bdellepithecium	DEL/EP/THAOES/YUM
basograph	BAI/SO/GRAF	bdellometer	DEL/LOM/TER
basolateral	BAI/SO/LAT/RAL	bdellotomy	DEL/LOT/M*I
basometachromophil	BAI/SO/MET/KROEM/FIL	bdellovibrio	DEL/VIB/RAOE/YOE
basometachromophile	BAI/SO/MET/KROEM/FAOIL	beach	BAEFP
basopenia	BAI/SO/PAOEN/YA	bead	BAOED
basophil	BAI/SO/FIL	beaded	BAOED/-D
basophile	BAI/SO/FAOIL	beading	BAOED/-G
basophilia	BAI/SO/FIL/YA	beaker	BAOEK/ER
basophilic	BAI/SO/FIL/IK	Beale	BAOEL
basophilism	BAI/SOF/LIFM	beam	BAOEM
basophilocyte	BAI/SO/FIL/SAO*IT	bean	BAOEN
basoplasm	BAI/SO/PLAFM	bear	BAER
basos	BAI/SOE/-S	beard	BAOERD
basosquamous	BAI/SO/SKWAIM/OUS	bearing	BAER/-G
bass	BASZ	bearing down	BAER/-G/DOUN
	BAISZ	beat	BAET
Bassen	BAS/SEN	Beau	K-P/BO*E
Basset	BAS/SAI	Beauvaria	BOE/VAIR/YA
bassiana	BAS/YAI/NA	Beauveria	BOE/VAOER/YA
	BASZ/YAI/NA	becanthone hydrochloride	BE/KAN/THOEN/HAOI/DRO/
Bassini	BA/SAOE/NAOE		KLOR/AOID
	BAS/SAOE/NAOE	bechic	BEK/IK
Bassler	BAS/LER	Beck	K-P/BEK
	BASZ/LER	Becker	BEK/ER
bassorin	BAS/SO/RIN	Beckmann	BEK/MAN
	BAS/SOR/RIN	Beclard	BAI/KLAR
	BASZ/RIN		BE/KLAR
bast	BA*S	beclomethasone	BEK/LO/M*ET/SOEN
bastard	BAS/TARD	Beclovent	BEK/LO/VENT
	BA*S/ARD	Beconase	BEK/NAIS
Bastedo	BAS/TAOE/DOE		BEK/NAIZ
basylous	BAS/LOUS	becquerel	BEK/REL
bat	BAT	Becquerel	K-P/BEK/REL
bath	BA*T	bed	BED
bathmic	BA*T/MIK	bedbug	BED/BUG
bathmotropic	BA*T/MO/TROP/IK	bedfast	BED/FA*S
	BA*T/MO/TROEP/IK	bedlam	BED/LAM
bathmotropism	BA*T/MOT/RO/PIFM	bedlamism	BED/LAM/IFM
batho-	BA*T	Bednar	BED/NAR
bathochrome	BA*T/KROEM	bedpan	BED/PAN
bathochromic	BA*T/KROEM/IK	bedsore	BED/SOER
bathochromy	BA*T/KROE/M*I	bed-wetting	BED/H-F/WET/-G
bathoflore	BA*T/FLOR	bee	BAOE
	BA*T/FLOER	beech	BAOEFP
bathomorphic	BA*T/MOR/FIK	beef	BAOEF
bathophobia	BA*T/FOEB/YA	Beelith	BAOE/L*IT
bathrocephaly	BA*T/RO/SEF/LI	beer	BAOER
bathy-	BA*T	Beer	K-P/BAOER
bathyanesthesia	BA*T/ANS/THAOEZ/YA	beeswax	BAOES/WAX
	BA*T/AN/ES/THAOEZ/YA		BAOEZ/WAX
bathycardia	BA*T/KARD/YA	beeturia	BAOE/TAOUR/YA
bathyesthesia	BA*T/ES/THAOEZ/YA		BAOET/YAOUR/YA
bathygastry	BA*T/GAS/TRI	Beevor	BAOE/VOR

Begbie	BEG/BAOE	benign	BE/NAOIN
Begg	B*EG	benignant	BE/NIG/NANT
begma	BEG/MA	benignum	BE/NIG/NUM
behavior	BE/HAIV/YOR	Benique	BEN/KAI
	BHAIV/YOR		BAIN/KAI
behavioral	BE/HAIV/YORL	Bennet	B*EN/ET
	BHAIV/YORL		B*EN/NET
behaviorism	BE/HAIV/YOR/IFM	Bennett	BEN/ET
	BHAIV/YOR/IFM		BEN/NET
behaviorist	BE/HAIV/YOR/*IS	bennetti	BEN/NET/TAOI
	BHAIV/YOR/*IS		BEN/ET/TAOI
Behcet	BAI/SET	Benoquin	BEN/KWIN
behenic	BE/HEN/IK	benorterone	BE/NORT/ROEN
Behla	BAI/LA		BE/NOR/TROEN
	BEL/LA	benoxaprofen	BEN/OX/PRO/FEN
Behring	BAI/RING	benoxinate	BEN/OX/NAIT
	(not BAIR/-G; see baring)	benperidol	BEN/PER/DOL
bejel	BEJ/EL		BEN/P*ER/DOL
Bekesy	BEK/SI	benserazide	BEN/SER/ZAOID
	BEK/KE/SI	Bensley	BENS/LAOE
Bekhterev	BEK/TER/YEV		BENZ/LAOE
	BEKT/REV	Benson	BEN/SON
bel	B*EL	Bensulfoid	BEN/SUL/FOID
	(not BEL; see bell)	bentazepam	BEN/TAZ/PAM
belch	BEL/-FP	bentiromide	BEN/TIR/MAOID
belching	BEL/-FPG	bentonite	BENT/NAOIT
belemnoid	BE/LEM/NOID		BEN/TON/AOIT
belfantii	BEL/FANT/YAOI	Bentyl	BEN/TIL
bell	BEL	benz(o)-	BENZ
Bell	K-P/BEL		BENZ(O)
Belladenal	BEL/AD/NAL	Benzac	BEN/ZAK
Belladenal-S	BEL/AD/NAL/S-RBGS	benzalacetophenone	BEN/ZAL/AS/TO/FAOE/NOEN
belladonna	BEL/DON/NA	benzaldehyde	BEN/ZALD/HAOID
belladonnine	BEL/DON/NAOEN		BENZ/ALD/HAOID
	BEL/DON/AOEN	benzalin	BENZ/LIN
bellaradine	BEL/AR/DIN	benzalkonium	BEN/ZAL/KOEN/YUM
	BEL/AR/DAOEN		BENZ/AL/KOEN/YUM
	BEL/LAR/DIN	benzamidase	BEN/ZAM/DAIS
	BEL/LAR/DAOEN		BENZ/AM/DAIS
bell-crowned	BEL/KROUN/-D	benzamidosalicylate	BEN/ZAM/DO/SAL/SIL/AIT
	BEL/H-F/KROUN/-D	benzamine	BENZ/MAOEN
Bell-Dally	K-P/BEL/H-F/DAL/LI		BEN/ZA/MAOEN
Bellergal	BEL/ER/GAL	Benzamycin	BENZ/MAOI/SIN
	BEL/LER/GAL		BEN/ZA/MAOI/SIN
Bellergal-S	BEL/ER/GAL/S-RBGS	benzanthracene	BEN/ZAN/THRA/SAOEN
	BEL/LER/GAL/S-RBGS		BENZ/AN/THRA/SAOEN
Bellini	BEL/LAOE/NAOE	benzanthrene	BEN/ZAN/THRAOEN
	BE/LAOE/NAOE		BENZ/AN/THRAOEN
Bellocq	BEL/LOK	benzazoline	BENZ/A*Z/LAOEN
	BEL/OK		BENZ/ZAZ/LAOEN
belly	BEL/LI	benzbromarone	BENZ/BROEM/ROEN
bellyache	BEL/LI/A*IK	benzcurine	BENZ/KAOU/RAOEN
belly button	BEL/LI/BUT/TON		BENZ/KAOUR/AOEN
belonephobia	BEL/NAOE/FOEB/YA	Benzedrex	BENZ/DREX
belonoid	BEL/NOID	benzene	BEN/ZAOEN
belonoskiascopy	BEL/NO/SKAOI/AS/KPI	benzeneamine	BEN/ZAOEN/MAOEN
beloxamide	BEL/OX/MAOID	benzenoid	BENZ/NOID
belt	BELT	benzestrofol	BEN/ZES/TRO/FOEL
bemegride	BEM/GRAOID		BEN/ZES/TRO/FOL
bemidone	BEM/DOEN	benzestrol	BEN/ZES/TROL
Beminal	BAOEM/NAL		BENZ/ES/TROL
Ben-Gay	BEN/GAI	benzethonium	BENZ/THOEN/YUM
	BEN/H-F/GAI		BEN/ZE/THOEN/YUM
benactyzine	BEN/AKT/ZAOEN	benzhexol	BENZ/HEK/SOL
	BEN/AK/TI/ZAOEN		BENZ/HEX/OL
Benadryl	BEN/DRIL	benzhydramine	BENZ/HAOI/DRA/MAOEN
benapryzine	BEN/PRAOI/ZAOEN	benzidine	BENZ/DAOEN
Bence Jones	BENS/JOENZ	benzilonium	BENZ/LOEN/YUM
	BENS/JOENS	benzimidazole	BEN/ZIM/DAI/ZOEL
bend	BEND		BENZ/IM/DAI/ZOEL
Benda	BEN/DA	benzin	BEN/ZIN
bendazac	BEND/ZAK	benzindamine	BEN/ZIND/MAOEN
Bender	K-P/BEND/ER		BENZ/IND/MAOEN
Bender Gestalt	BEND/ER/GES/TALT	benzine	B*EN/ZAOEN
	K-P/BEND/ER/GES/TALT	benziodarone	BEN/ZAOE/DA/ROEN
bendrofluazide	BEN/DRO/FLAOU/ZAOID		BEN/ZAOE/YO/DA/ROEN
bendroflumethiazide	BEN/DRO/FLAOUM/THAOI/ ZAOID	benzoate	BENZ/WAIT
		benzoated	BENZ/WAIT/-D
	BEN/DRO/FLAOU/ME/THAOI/ ZAOID	benzocaine	BENZ/KAIN
		benzoctamine	BEN/ZOKT/MAOEN
bends	BENDZ		BENZ/OKT/MAOEN
bene	BAOE/NAOE	benzodepa	BENZ/DEP/PA
	BE/NAOE	benzodiazepine	BENZ/DI/AZ/PAOEN
beneceptor	BEN/SEP/TOR	benzodioxan	BENZ/DI/OK/SAN
Benedek	BEN/DEK	benzogynestryl	BENZ/GAOI/NES/TRIL
Benedict	BEN/DIKT	benzoic	BEN/ZOIK
Benedikt	BEN/D*IKT		BEN/ZOE/IK
Benemid	BEN/MID	benzoin	BEN/ZOIN
benigma	BE/NIG/MA		BEN/ZO/WIN

benzoinatus	BEN/ZOI/NAI/TUS
	BEN/ZOIN/AI/TUS
	BENZ/WI/NAI/TUS
benzol	BEN/ZOL
benzolism	BENZ/LIFM
benzomethamine	BENZ/M*ET/MAOEN
benzomorphan	BENZ/MOR/FAN
benzonatate	BEN/ZOEN/TAIT
benzone	BEN/ZOEN
benzononatine	BEN/ZOEN/NAI/TIN
	BEN/ZOE/NO/NAI/TIN
benzopurpurin	BENZ/PURP/RIN
benzopurpurine	BENZ/PURP/RAOEN
benzopyran	BENZ/PIR/RAN
benzopyrronium	BENZ/PIR/ROEN/YUM
benzoquinone	BENZ/KWIN/OEN
	BENZ/KWI/NOEN
benzoquinonium	BENZ/KWI/NOEN/YUM
benzoresinol	BENZ/REZ/NOL
benzosulfimide	BENZ/SUL/FI/MAOID
benzotherapy	BENZ/THER/PI
benzothiadiazide	BENZ/THAOI/DAOI/ZAOID
benzothiadiazine	BENZ/THAOI/DAOI/ZAOEN
benzoxiquine	BEN/ZOX/KWIN
	BENZ/OX/KWIN
benzoxyline	BEN/ZOX/LAOEN
	BENZ/OX/LAOEN
benzoyl	BEN/ZOIL
	BENZ/OIL
benzoylaminoacetic	BEN/ZOIL/AM/NO/AI/SAOET/IK
	BEN/ZOIL/AM/NO/AI/SET/IK
benzoylcholinesterase	BEN/ZOIL/KOEL/N*ES/RAIS
benzoylglucuronic	BEN/ZOIL/GLAOUK/RON/IK
benzoylglycine	BEN/ZOIL/GLAOI/SIN
benzoylpas	BEN/ZOIL/PAS
Benzoyl Peroxide	BEN/ZOIL/PROK/SAOID
	BEN/ZOIL/PROX/AOID
benzoylphenylcarbinol	BEN/ZOIL/FENL/KARB/NOL
benzperidol	BENZ/PER/DOL
	BENZ/P*ER/DOL
benzphetamine	BENZ/FET/MAOEN
benzpiperylon	BENZ/PI/PER/LOEN
	BENZ/PI/PER/LON
benzpyrene	BENZ/PAOI/RAOEN
benzpyrinium	BENZ/PAOI/RIN/YUM
benzpyrrole	PENZ/PIR/ROEL
	BENZ/PIR/ROL
benzquinamide	BENZ/KWIN/MAOID
benzstigminum	BENZ/STIG/MI/NUM
	BENZ/STIG/MIN/UM
benzthiazide	BENZ/THAOI/ZAOID
benztropine	BENZ/TROE/PAOEN
benzurestat	BEN/ZUR/STAT
	BENZ/YAOUR/STAT
benzydamine	BEN/ZID/MAOEN
benzydroflumethiazide	BEN/ZID/RO/FLAOUM/THAOI/
	ZAOID
	BEN/ZID/RO/FLAOU/ME/THAOI/
	ZAOID
benzyl	BEN/ZIL
	BENZ/IL
benzylic	BEN/ZIL/IK
benzylidene	BEN/ZIL/DAOEN
benzyloxycarbonyl	BEN/ZIL/OX/KARB/NIL
benzyloxyphenol	BEN/ZIL/OX/FAOE/NOL
	BENZ/IL/OX/FAOE/NOL
benzylpenicillin	BEN/ZIL/PEN/SLIN
	BEN/ZIL/PEN/SIL/LIN
bephenium	BE/FEN/YUM
Berard	BAI/RAR
Beraud	BAI/ROE
berbera	BERB/RA
	BER/BRA
berberine	BERB/RAOEN
	BER/BE/RAOEN
	BER/BER/AOEN
Berg	BERG
Berger	BERG/ER
Bergeron	BERJ/RON
Bergmann	BERG/MAN
Bergonie	BAIR/GOEN/YAI
	BER/GOEN/YAI
	BER/GON/YAI
beriberi	BER/BER/RAOE
	BER/RI/BER/RI
	BER/RAOE/BER/RAOE
beriberic	BER/BER/IK
	BER/RAOE/BER/IK
	BER/RI/BER/IK

berkelium	BERK/LAOE/YUM
	BERK/LAOE/UM
Berlin	BER/LIN
berlock	BER/LOK
berloque	BER/LO*K
Bernard	BER/NAR
	BER/NARD
Bernays' sponge	BER/NAIZ/AOE/SPON/-J
	BER/NAIS/AOE/SPON/-J
Bernhardt	BERN/HART
Bernheim	BERN/HAOIM
Bernheimer	BERN/HAOIM/ER
	BERN/HAOI/MER
Bernouilli	BER/NAOU/LAOE
Bernstein	BERN/STAOIN
	BERN/STAOEN
Berocca	BE/ROE/KA
	BER/ROE/KA
berry	BER/RI
Berry	K-P/BER/RI
Bertiella	BERT/YEL/LA
bertielliasis	BERT/YE/LAOI/SIS
	BERT/YEL/LAOI/SIS
bertiellosis	BERT/YE/LOE/SIS
	BERT/YEL/LOE/SIS
Bertin	BER/TIN
Bertini	BER/TAOE/NAOI
	BER/TAOI/NAOI
berylliosis	BE/RIL/YOE/SIS
	BERL/YOE/SIS
beryllium	BE/RIL/YUM
	BER/IL/YUM
	BRIL/YUM
berythromycin	BE/R*IT/RO/MAOI/SIN
Besnier	BES/NAI
	BES/NAOE/YAI
	BES/NI/YAI
besnoiti	BES/NOI/TAOI
Besnoitia	BES/NOIT/YA
besnoitiasis	BES/NOI/TAOI/SIS
Besnoitiidae	BES/NOI/TAOE/DAE
besnoitiosis	BES/NOI/TYOE/SIS
Besredka	BES/RED/KA
Best	K-P/B*ES
bestiality	B*ES/YAL/TI
	BAO*ES/YAL/TI
besylate	BES/LAIT
beta (stand alone word)	BAI/TA
beta (as word part)	BAIT
	BAI/TA
beta-acetylpropionic	BAIT/AS/TIL/PROEP/YON/IK
beta-adrenergic	BAIT/AD/RE/NERJ/IK
	BAIT/AI/DRE/NERJ/IK
beta-allocortol	BAIT/AL/LO/KOR/TOL
	BAIT/AL/KOR/TOL
beta-allocortolone	BAIT/AL/LO/KORT/LOEN
	BAIT/AL/KORT/LOEN
beta-aminobutyric	BAIT/AM/NO/BAOU/TIR/IK
	BAIT/AI/MAOEN/BAOU/TIR/IK
beta-aminoisobutyric	BAIT/AM/NO/AOIS/BAOU/TIR/IK
	BAIT/AI/MAOEN/AOIS/BAOU/TIR/
	IK
Betabacterium	BAIT/BAK/TAOER/YUM
	BAIT/BAK/TAOERM
beta-blocker	BAIT/BLOK/ER
	BAIT/H-F/BLOK/ER
betacism	BAIT/SIFM
beta-cholestanol	BAIT/KL*ES/NOL
betacyaninuria	BAIT/SAOI/NIN/YAOUR/YA
Betadine	BAIT/DAOEN
	BAIT/DAOIN
beta-estradiol	BAIT/ES/TRA/DI/OL
betaglobulin	BAIT/GLOB/LIN
betahistine	BAIT/HIS/TAOEN
beta-hydroxybutyric	BAIT/HAOI/DROX/BAOU/TIR/IK
beta-hypophamine	BAIT/HAOI/POF/MIN
betaine	BAOET/AOEN
	BAOET/YAOEN
betaine-aldehyde	BAOET/AOEN/ALD/HAOID
	BAOET/YAOEN/ALD/HAOID
beta-ketobutyric	BAIT/KAOET/BAOU/TIR/IK
beta-ketopalmitic	BAIT/KAOET/PAL/MIT/IK
beta-lactose	BAIT/LAK/TOES
betalipoproteinemia	BAIT/LIP/PROET/NAOEM/YA
	BAIT/LIP/PRO/TAOEN/AOEM/YA
betalysin	BAI/TAL/SIN
betamethasone	BAIT/M*ET/SOEN
betamicin sulfate	BAIT/MAOI/SIN/SUL/FAIT
betanaphthol	BAIT/NAF/THOL

beta-naphtholsulfonic	BAIT/NAF/THOL/SUL/FON/IK
betanaphthyl	BAIT/NAF/THIL
betanidine	BE/TAN/DAOEN
beta-oxybutyria	BAIT/OX/BAOU/TIR/YA
beta-oxybutyric	BAIT/OX/BAOU/TIR/IK
Betapen	BAIT/PEN
Betapen-VK	BAIT/PEN/V-RBGS/K*RBGS
beta-phenylpropionic	BAIT/FENL/PROEP/YON/IK
betapropiolactone	BAIT/PROEP/YO/LAK/TOEN
betaquinine	BAIT/KWI/NIN
	BAIT/KWIN/NIN
Betatrex	BAIT/TREX
betatron	BAIT/TRON
Beta-Val	BAIT/VAL
betaxolol	BE/TAX/LOL
betazole	BAIT/ZOEL
bethanechol	BE/THAN/KOL
	BE/THAIN/KOL
bethanidine	BE/THAN/DAOEN
Betoptic	BET/OPT/IK
Bettendorff	BET/EN/DOR/-F
Betula	BEFP/LA
	BET/YAOU/LA
	BET/YU/LA
betweenbrain	BE/TWAOEN/BRAIN
	TWAOEN/BRAIN
Betz	BETS
Bevan Lewis	BEVN/LAO*U/WIS
	BEV/VAN/LAO*U/WIS
bevel	BEVL
bevonium	BE/VOEN/YUM
bezoar	BE/ZOER
	BAOE/ZOER
Bezold	BAI/ZOELT
	BAI/ZOELD
	BAI/ZOLT
	BAI/ZOLD
bezziana	BEZ/YAI/NA
bi-	B*I
bialamicol	BAOI/LAM/KOL
	B*I/LAM/KOL
Bianchi	BAOE/AN/KAOE
	BAOE/YAN/KAOE
biarticular	B*I/AR/TIK/LAR
biarticulate	B*I/AR/TIK/LAIT
	B*I/AR/TIK/LAT
biasteric	B*I/AS/TER/IK
biasterionic	B*I/AS/TER/YON/IK
biatriatum	B*I/AIT/RAI/TUM
	B*I/AIT/RAIT/UM
	B*I/AI/TRAI/TUM
	B*I/AI/TRAIT/UM
biauricular	B*I/AU/RIK/LAR
Biavax	B*I/YA/VAX
	BAOI/YA/VAX
	BAOI/VAX
bib	BIB
bibasic	B*I/BAIS/IK
bibenzonium	B*I/BEN/ZOEN/YUM
bibeveled	B*I/BEVL/-D
	B*I/BEV/EL/-D
bibliomania	BIB/LO/MAIN/YA
	BIB/LAOE/YO/MAIN/YA
bibliotherapy	BIB/LO/THER/PI
	BIB/LAOE/YO/THER/PI
Bibron	BIB/RON
bibulous	BIB/LOUS
	BIB/YAOU/LOUS
	BIB/YU/LOUS
bicameral	B*I/KAM/RAL
bicapsular	B*I/KAPS/LAR
	B*I/KAP/SLAR
bicarb	B*I/KARB
	B*I/KAR/-B
bicarbonate	B*I/KARB/NAIT
	B*I/KARB/NAT
bicarbonatemia	B*I/KARB/NAI/TAOEM/YA
	B*I/KARB/NAIT/AOEM/YA
bicardiogram	B*I/KARD/YO/GRAM
bicellular	B*I/SEL/YAOU/LAR
bicephalus	B*I/SEF/LUS
biceps	B*I/SEPS
Bichat	B*I/SHA
	B*I/SHAT
bichloride	B*I/KLOR/AOID
bichromate	B*I/KROE/MAIT
biciliate	B*I/SIL/YAIT
Bicillin	B*I/SLIN
	B*I/SIL/LIN

Bicillin C-R	B*I/SLIN/KR-RBGS/R-RBGS
	B*I/SIL/LIN/KR-RBGS/R-RBGS
Bicillin L-A	B*I/SLIN/L-RBGS/ARBGS
	B*I/SIL/LIN/L-RBGS/ARBGS
bicipital	B*I/SIP/TAL
bicipitis	B*I/SIP/TIS
bicipitofibular	B*I/SIP/TO/FIB/LAR
bicipitoradial	B*I/SIP/TO/RAID/YAL
bicipitoradialis	B*I/SIP/TO/RAID/YAI/LIS
Bicitra	B*I/SI/TRA
	B*I/SIT/RA
biclonal	B*I/KLOENL
	B*I/KLOE/NAL
biclonality	B*I/KLOE/NAL/TI
	B*I/KLOEN/AL/TI
BiCNU	BIK/NAOU
biconcave	B*I/KON/KAIV
bicondylaris	B*I/KOND/LAI/RIS
biconvex	B*I/KON/VEX
bicoudate	B*I/KAOU/DAIT
bicornate	B*I/KOR/NAIT
bicornous	B*I/KORN/OUS
	B*I/KOR/NOUS
bicornuate	B*I/KORN/YAIT
	B*I/KOR/NAOU/AIT
bicoronial	B*I/KO/ROEN/YAL
bicorporate	B*I/KORPT
	B*I/KORP/RAIT
	B*I/KORP/RAT
bicron	B*I/KRON
bicuspid	B*I/KUS/PID
bicuspidal	B*I/KUS/PI/DAL
bicuspidalis	B*I/KUS/PI/DAI/LIS
bicuspidate	B*I/KUS/PI/DAIT
bicuspidization	B*I/KUS/PID/ZAIGS
bicuspoid	B*I/KUS/POID
bid	BID
b.i.d.	B*ID
bidactyly	B*I/DAKT/LI
bidder	BID/ER
bidental	B*I/DEN/TAL
bidentate	B*I/DEN/TAIT
bidermoma	B*I/DER/MOE/MA
bidet	BI/DAI
	B*I/DAI
bidiscoidal	B*I/DIS/KOI/DAL
biduotertian	BID/YO/TERGS
	BID/WO/TERGS
biduous	BID/YOUS
	BID/YAOU/OUS
	BID/WOUS
Biederman	BAOED/ER/MAN
Biedert	BAOE/DERT
	BE/DERT
Biedl	BAOED/L
Bielschowsky	BAOEL/SHOU/SKI
	BAOEL/SHOUS/KI
Bier	BAO*ER
Biermer	BAOER/MER
	BAOERM/ER
Biett	BAOE/ET
	BAOE/YET
bifascicular	B*I/FA/SIK/LAR
	B*I/FAS/SIK/LAR
bifermentans	B*I/FER/MEN/TANZ
	B*I/FERMT/TANZ
bifid	B*I/FID
bifida	BIF/DA
Bifidobacterium	B*I/FI/DO/BAK/TAOERM
	B*I/FI/DO/BAK/TAOER/YUM
	BAOIF/DO/BAK/TAOERM
	BAOIF/DO/BAK/TAOER/YUM
bifidum	BIF/DUM
bifidus	BIF/DUS
bifocal	B*I/FOE/KAL
biforate	B*I/FOE/RAIT
	B*I/FOER/RAIT
biformyl	B*I/FOR/MIL
	B*I/FOER/MIL
bifurcate	B*I/FUR/KAIT
bifurcated	B*I/FUR/KAIT/-D
bifurcatio	B*I/FUR/KAI/SHOE
	B*I/FUR/KAIRB/YOE
bifurcation	B*I/FUR/KAIGS
bifurcationes	B*I/FUR/KAI/SHOE/NAOEZ
	B*I/FUR/KAIRB/YOE/NAOEZ
bifurcatum	B*I/FUR/KAI/TUM
	B*I/FUR/KAIT/UM
Bigelow	BIG/LOE

bigemina	B*I/JEM/NA		BIL/LO/PAIK
bigeminal	B*I/JEM/NAL		BIL/OEP/PAIK
bigemini	B*I/JEM/NAOI	bilophodont	B*I/LOF/DONT
bigeminum	B*I/JEM/NUM	Biltricide	BIL/TRI/SAO*ID
bigeminy	B*I/JEM/N*I	bimanual	B*I/MAN/YAOUL
bigerminal	B*I/JERM/NAL		B*I/MAN/YUL
bigitalin	B*I/JIT/LIN	bimastoid	B*I/MAS/TOID
Bignami	BAOEN/YA/MAOE	bimaxillary	B*I/MAX/LAIR
	BIN/YA/MAOE	bimeter	BIM/TER
bigonial	B*I/GOEN/YAL	bimethoxycaine	B*I/ME/THOX/KAIN
biischial	B*I/IS/KAL	Bimler	BIM/LER
	B*I/IS/KAOE/YAL	bimodal	B*I/MOE/DAL
bilabe	B*I/LAIB	bimolecular	B*I/MO/LEK/LAR
bilaminar	B*I/LAM/NAR	binangle	BIN/ANG/-L
bilateral	B*I/LAT/RAL		BIN/AING/-L
bilateralism	B*I/LAT/RAL/IFM	binary	B*I/NAIR
bile	BAOIL	binaural	BIN/AURL
Bilezyme	BAOIL/ZAOIM		BIN/AU/RAL
Bilharzia	BIL/HARZ/YA	binauralis	BIN/AU/RAI/LIS
bilharzial	BIL/HARZ/YAL	binauricular	BIN/AU/RIK/LAR
bilharziasis	BIL/HAR/ZAOI/SIS	bind	BAOIND
bilharzioma	BIL/HARZ/YOE/MA	binder	BAOIND/ER
bilharziosis	BIL/HARZ/YOE/SIS	binegative	B*I/NEG/TIV
bili-	BIL	Binet	B*I/NAI
	BAOI/LI		BI/NAI
	B*I/LI	binocle	BIN/OK/-L
bilianic	BIL/YAN/IK	binocular	BIN/OK/LAR
biliary	BIL/YAIR		B*I/NOK/LAR
biliation	BIL/YAIGS	binomial	B*I/NOEM/YAL
bilic	BAOIL/IK	binophthalmoscope	BIN/OF/THAL/MO/SKOEP
	BIL/IK	binoscope	BIN/SKOEP
bilicyanin	BIL/SAOI/NIN	binotic	BIN/OT/IK
bilidigestive	BIL/DI/J*ES/IV		B*I/NOT/IK
bilifaction	BIL/FA*BGS	binovular	BIN/OV/LAR
biliferi	B*I/LIF/RAOI	Binswanger	BIN/SWANG/ER
	BAOI/LIF/RAOI		BINS/WANG/ER
	BAOIL/IF/RAOI	binuclear	B*I/NAOUK/LAR
biliferous	BIL/IF/ROUS	binucleate	B*I/NAOUK/LAIT
	BAOIL/IF/ROUS	binucleation	B*I/NAOUK/LAIGS
bilification	BIL/FI/KAIGS	binucleolate	B*I/NAOU/KLAOE/LAIT
biliflavin	BIL/FLAIVN		B*I/NAOU/KLO/LAIT
	BIL/FLAI/VIN	Binz	BINZ
bilifulvin	BIL/FUL/VIN		BINTS
bilifuscin	BIL/FUS/SIN	bio-	BAO*I
biligenesis	BIL/JEN/SIS		BAOI/YO
biligenetic	BIL/JE/NET/IK	bioacoustics	BAO*I/AI/KAO*US/IK/-S
biligenic	BIL/JEN/IK	bioactive	BAO*I/AKT/IV
biligulate	B*I/LIG/LAIT	bioaeration	BAO*I/AER/RAIGS
bilihumin	BIL/HAOU/MIN	bioamine	BAO*I/AM/AOEN
bilin	B*I/LIN		BAO*I/AM/MAOEN
	BAOI/LIN	bioaminergic	BAO*I/AM/NERJ/IK
bilineata	B*I/LIN/YAI/TA	bioassay	BAO*I/AS/SAI
bilious	BIL/YOUS	bioastronautics	BAO*I/AS/TRO/NAUT/IK/-S
biliousness	BIL/YOUS/*NS	bioavailability	BAO*I/VAIBLT
biliprasin	BIL/PRAI/SIN		BAO*I/AI/VAIL/-BLT
biliptysis	BIL/IPT/SIS	bioblast	BAO*I/BLA*S
bilipurpurin	BIL/PURP/RIN	biocatalyst	BAO*I/KAT/L*IS
bilirachia	BIL/RAIK/YA	Biocal	BAO*I/KAL
bilirubin	BIL/RAOU/BIN	biocenosis	BAO*I/SE/NOE/SIS
bilirubinate	BIL/RAOUB/NAIT	biocenotic	BAO*I/SE/NOT/IK
bilirubinemia	BIL/RAOUB/NAOEM/YA	biochemical	BAO*I/KEM/KAL
bilirubinglobulin	BIL/RAOU/BIN/GLOB/LIN	biochemistry	BAO*I/KEM/STRI
bilirubin-glucuronoside	BIL/RAOU/BIN/GLAOUK/RON/	biochemorphic	BAO*I/KAOE/MOR/FIK
	SAOID		BAO*I/KEM/OR/FIK
bilirubinic	BIL/RAOU/BIN/IK	biochemorphology	BAO*I/KAOE/MOR/FOLG
bilirubinoid	BIL/RAOUB/NOID		BAO*I/KEM/OR/FOLG
bilirubinuria	BIL/RAOUB/NAOUR/YA	biocidal	BAO*I/SAOI/DAL
bilis	B*I/LIS	bioclimatics	BAO*I/KLAOI/MAT/IK/-S
	BAOI/LIS	bioclimatologist	BAO*I/KLAOIM/TO*LGS
bilitherapy	BIL/THER/PI	bioclimatology	BAO*I/KLAOIM/TOLG
biliuria	BIL/YAOUR/YA	biocolloid	BAO*I/KLOID
biliverdin	BIL/VER/DIN		BAO*I/KOL/OID
biliverdinate	BIL/VERD/NAIT	biocompatible	BAO*I/KPAT/-BL
biliverdinglobin	BIL/VER/DIN/GLOE/BIN		BAO*I/KOM/PAT/-BL
biliverdinic	BIL/VER/DIN/IK	biocompatibility	BAO*I/KPAT/-BLT
bilixanthin	BIL/ZAN/THIN		BAO*I/KOM/PAT/-BLT
bilixanthine	BIL/ZAN/THAOEN	biocybernetics	BAO*I/SAOIB/NET/IK/-S
Bill	B*IL		BAO*I/SAOI/BER/NET/IK/-S
Billroth	BIL/ROET	biocycle	BAO*I/SAOIK/-L
bilobate	B*I/LOE/BAIT	biocytin	BAO*I/SAOI/TIN
bilobed	B*I/LOEB/-D	biocytinase	BAO*I/SAOIT/NAIS
bilobular	B*I/LOB/LAR		BAO*I/SAOI/TIN/AIS
bilobulate	B*I/LOB/LAIT	biodegradable	BAO*I/DE/GRAID/-BL
bilocular	B*I/LOK/LAR	biodegradation	BAO*I/DEG/DAIGS
biloculare	B*I/LOK/LAI/RAOE		BAO*I/DEG/RA/DAIGS
	B*I/LOK/LAR/RAOE	biodetritus	BAO*I/DE/TRAOI/TUS
biloculate	B*I/LOK/LAIT	biodynamic	BAO*I/DAOI/NAM/IK
biloma	B*I/LOE/MA	bioecology	BAO*I/E/KOLG
Bilopaque	BIL/O/PAIK	bioelectricity	BAO*I/LEK/TRIS/TI

Term	Outline	Term	Outline
bioelectronics	BAO*I/LEK/TRON/IK/-S	biopsychic	BAO*I/SAOIK/IK
bioelement	BAO*I/EL/-MT	biopsychical	BAO*I/SAOIK/KAL
	BAO*I/EL/LEMT	biopsychology	BAO*I/SAOI/KOLG
bioenergetics	BAO*I/EN/ER/JET/IK/-S	biopsychosocial	BAO*I/SAOIK/SOERBL
bioengineering	BAO*I/ENG/NAOER/-G	biopterin	BAO*I/OPT/RIN
bioequivalence	BAO*I/E/KWIV/LENS		B*I/OPT/RIN
bioequivalent	BAO*I/E/KWIV/LENT	bioptic	BAO*I/OPT/IK
biofeedback	BAO*I/FAOED/BA*K		B*I/OPT/IK
	BAO*I/FAOED/BAK	bioptome	BAO*I/OP/TOEM
bioflavonoids	BAO*I/FLAIV/NOIDZ		B*I/OP/TOEM
biogen	BAO*I/JEN	biopyoculture	BAO*I/PAOI/KUL/KHUR
biogenesis	BAO*I/JEN/SIS	biorbital	B*I/ORB/TAL
biogenetic	BAO*I/JE/NET/IK	bioreversible	BAO*I/RE/VERS/-BL
biogenic	BAO*I/JEN/IK	biorheology	BAO*I/RAOE/YOLG
biogenous	BAO*I/OJ/NOUS		BAO*I/RAOE/OLG
biogeochemistry	BAO*I/JAOE/KEM/STRI	biorhythm	BAO*I/R*IT/-M
biogeography	BAO*I/JAOE/OG/FI	bioroentgenography	BAO*I/RENT/GEN/OG/FI
biograph	BAO*I/GRAF		BAO*I/RENT/JEN/OG/FI
biogravics	BAO*I/GRAVK/-S	bios	BAO*I/YOS
	BAO*I/GRAV/IK/-S		BAO*I/OS
biohydraulic	BAO*I/HAOI/DRAUL/IK	bioscience	BAO*I/SAOINS
bioimplant	BAO*I/IM/PLANT	bioscopy	BAO*I/OS/KPI
bioinstrument	BAO*I/STRUMT	biose	BAO*I/OES
	BAO*I/IN/STRUMT		BAO*I/YOES
biokinetics	BAO*I/KI/NET/IK/-S		BAOI/YOES
biologic	BAO*I/LOJ/IK	bioside	BAO*I/SAOID
biological	BAO*I/LOJ/KAL	biosis	BAO*I/YOE/SIS
biologist	BAO*I/O*LGS	biosmosis	BAO*I/OZ/MOE/SIS
biologos	BAO*I/OL/GOS		B*I/OZ/MOE/SIS
biology	BAO*I/OLG	biosocial	BAO*I/SOERBL
bioluminescence	BAO*I/LAOUM/NES/ENS	biospectrometry	BAO*I/SPEK/TROM/TRI
biolysis	BAO*I/OL/SIS	biospectroscopy	BAO*I/SPEK/TROS/KPI
biolytic	BAO*I/LIT/IK	biospeleology	BAO*I/SPAOEL/YOLG
biomass	BAO*I/MASZ	biosphere	BAO*I/SFAOER
biomaterial	BAO*I/MA/TAOERL	biostatics	BAO*I/STAT/IK/-S
	BAO*I/TERL	biostatistics	BAO*I/STA/T*IS/IK/-S
biomathematics	BAO*I/MA*T/MAT/IK/-S	biostereometrics	BAO*I/STER/YO/MET/RIK/-S
biome	BAO*I/OEM	biosynthesis	BAO*I/S*INT/SIS
biomechanics	BAO*I/ME/KAN/IK/-S	biosynthetic	BAO*I/SIN/THET/IK
	BAO*I/M-KS	biosystem	BAO*I/S-M
biomedical	BAO*I/MED/KAL		BAO*I/SIS/TEM
biomedicine	BAO*I/MED/SIN	Biot	BAOE/YOE
biomembrane	BAO*I/MEM/BRAIN	biota	BAO*I/YOE/TA
biomembranous	BAO*I/MEM/BRA/NOUS		BAO*I/O/TA
biometeorologist	BAO*I/MAOET/YO/RO*LGS	biotaxis	BAO*I/TAK/SIS
biometeorology	BAO*I/MAOET/YO/ROLG	biotaxy	BAO*I/TAK/SI
biometer	BAO*I/OM/TER	biotelemetry	BAO*I/TE/LEM/TRI
biometrician	BAO*I/ME/TRIGS		BAO*I/TLEM/TRI
biometrics	BAO*I/MET/RIK/-S	biothesiometer	BAO*I/THAOEZ/YOM/TER
biometry	BAO*I/OM/TRI	biotic	BAO*I/OT/IK
biomicroscope	BAO*I/MAOI/KRO/SKOEP		BAO*I/YOT/IK
biomicroscopy	BAO*I/MAOI/KROS/KPI	biotin	BAO*I/TIN
biomolecule	BAO*I/MOL/KAOUL	Biotin Forte	BAO*I/TIN/FOR/TAI
biomotor	BAO*I/MOE/TOR	biotinidase	BAO*I/TIN/DAIS
Biomphalaria	B*I/OM/FLAIR/YA	biotinide	BAO*I/OT/NAOID
bion	BAO*I/ON		BAO*I/YOT/NAOID
	B*I/ON	biotinyllysine	BAO*I/TIN/LAOI/SIN
bionecrosis	BAO*I/NE/KROE/SIS		BAO*I/TIN/IL/LAOI/SIN
bionergy	BAO*I/ON/ER/JI	biotomy	BAO*I/OT/M*I
	BAO*I/YON/ER/JI		BAO*I/YOT/M*I
bionic	BAO*I/ON/IK	biotope	BAO*I/TOEP
	BAO*I/YON/IK	biotoxication	BAO*I/TOX/KAIGS
bionomic	BAO*I/NOM/IK	biotoxicology	BAO*I/TOX/KOLG
bionomy	BAO*I/ON/M*I	biotoxin	BAO*I/TOK/SIN
	BAO*I/YON/M*I	biotransformation	BAO*I/TRA*NS/FOR/MAIGS
bionosis	BAO*I/NOE/SIS	biotrepy	BAO*I/OT/RE/PI
bionucleonics	BAO*I/NAOUK/LON/IK/-S		BAO*I/YOT/RE/PI
bio-osmotic	BAO*I/OZ/MOT/IK	biotripticum	BAO*I/TRIPT/KUM
biophage	BAO*I/FAIJ	biotropism	BAO*I/OT/RO/PIFM
biophagism	BAO*I/OF/JIFM		BAO*I/YOT/RO/PIFM
biophagous	BAO*I/OF/GOUS	biotype	BAO*I/TAOIP
biophagy	BAO*I/OF/JI	biotypology	BAO*I/TAOI/POLG
biopharmaceutics	BAO*I/FARM/SAOUT/IK/-S		BAO*I/TAOIP/OLG
biophilia	BAO*I/FIL/YA	biovar	BAO*I/VAR
biophotometer	BAO*I/FOE/TOM/TER	biovular	B*I/OV/LAR
biophylactic	BAO*I/FLAKT/IK	Biozyme	BAO*I/ZAOIM
biophylaxis	BAO*I/FLAK/SIS	Biozyme-C	BAO*I/ZAOIM/KR-RBGS
biophysical	BAO*I/FIZ/KAL	bipalatinoid	B*I/PAL/TIN/OID
biophysics	BAO*I/FIZ/IK/-S		B*I/PAL/TI/NOID
biophysiography	BAO*I/FIZ/YOG/FI	biparasitic	B*I/PAR/SIT/IK
biophysiology	BAO*I/FIZ/YOLG	biparasitism	B*I/PAR/SIT/IFM
bioplasia	BAO*I/PLAIZ/YA	biparental	B*I/PREN/TAL
bioplasm	BAO*I/PLAFM	biparietal	B*I/PRAOI/TAL
bioplasmic	BAO*I/PLAZ/MIK	biparous	BIP/ROUS
bioplast	BAO*I/PLA*S	bipartite	B*I/PAR/TAOIT
biopoiesis	BAO*I/POI/SIS	biped	B*I/PED
biopolymer	BAO*I/POL/MER	bipedal	BIP/DAL
biopsy	BAO*I/OP/SI		B*I/PED/DAL
	BAO*I/YOP/SI	bipennate	B*I/PEN/NAIT

©1992 StenEd® Medical Dictionary

bipennatus	B*I/PEN/NAI/TUS	bitewing	BAOIT/WING
bipenniform	B*I/PEN/FORM	bithionol	B*I/THAOI/NOL
biperforate	B*I/PER/FRAIT	bitolterol	B*I/TOL/TROL
biperiden	B*I/P*ER/DEN		B*I/TOLT/ROL
	B*I/PER/DEN	Bitot	BAOE/TOE
biphenamine	B*I/FEN/MAOEN	bitrochanteric	B*I/TROE/KAN/TER/IK
biphenotypic	B*I/FAOEN/TIP/IK	bitropic	B*I/TROP/IK
biphenotypy	B*I/FAOEN/TAOI/PAOE	bitten	BIT/-N
biphenyl	B*I/FENL	bitter	BIT/ER
biphosphate	B*I/FOS/FAIT	bitterling	BIT/ER/-LG
bipolar	B*I/POE/LAR		BIT/ER/LING
bipositive	B*I/POZ/TIV	bitters	BIT/ER/-S
bipotential	B*I/POE/TEN/-RBL	Bittner	BIT/NER
bipotentiality	B*I/POE/TEN/-RBL/TI	Bittorf	BIT/TOR/-F
biramous	B*I/RAIM/OUS	bitumen	B*I/TAOUM/-N
birch	B*IRPBLG		B*I/TAOU/MEN
	BIR/-FP	bituminosis	B*I/TAOUM/NOE/SIS
Bird	K-P/BIRD	biurate	B*I/YAOU/RAIT
birefractive	B*I/RE/FRAKT/IV	biuret	B*I/YAOU/RET
birefringence	B*I/RE/FRIN/JENS		B*I/YU/RET
birefringent	B*I/RE/FRIN/JENT	biuretic	B*I/YAOU/RET/IK
Birnberg	BIRN/BERG		B*I/YU/RET/IK
birotation	B*I/ROE/TAIGS		B*I/RET/IK
birth	B*IRT	bivalence	B*I/VAIL/ENS
birthmark	B*IRT/MARK		B*I/VAI/LENS
bisacodyl	BIS/AK/DIL		BIV/LENS
bisacromial	BIS/AI/KROEM/YAL	bivalency	B*I/VAIL/EN/SI
bisalbuminemia	BIS/AL/BAOUM/NAOEM/YA		B*I/VAI/LEN/SI
bisalt	B*I/SAULT	bivalent	B*I/VAIL/ENT
	B*I/SALT		B*I/VAI/LENT
bisaxillary	BIS/AX/LAIR		BIV/LENT
Bischoff	BIRB/AUF	bivalve	B*I/VAL/-V
	BIRB/KHOF	biventer	B*I/VEN/TER
biscoumacetate	BIS/KAOUM/AS/TAIT		B*I/VENT/ER
	BIS/KAOU/MAS/TAIT	biventral	B*I/VEN/TRAL
biscuit	BIS/KIT	biventricular	B*I/VEN/TRIK/LAR
biscuit-bake	BIS/KIT/H-F/BAIK	biventriculare	B*I/VEN/TRIK/LAI/RAOE
biscuit-firing	BIS/KIT/H-F/FAOIR/-G		B*I/VEN/TRIK/LAR/RAOE
biscuiting	BIS/KIT/-G	bivitelline	B*I/VAOI/TEL/LIN
bisdequalinium	BIS/DE/KWA/LIN/YUM	bixin	BIK/SIN
bisect	B*I/SEKT	bizygomatic	B*I/ZAOIG/MAT/IK
bisection	B*I/S*EBGS	Bjornstrom	BORN/STREM
biseptate	B*I/SEP/TAIT		BORN/STROM
bisexual	B*I/SEX/YAOUL	black	BLAK
	B*I/SEX/YUL	Black	K-P/BLAK
bisexuality	B*I/SEX/YAL/TI	Blackberg	BLAK/BERG
	B*I/SEX/YAOUL/TI	blackhead	BLAK/H*ED
	B*I/SEX/YUL/TI		BLAK/HED
bisferious	BIS/FAOER/YOUS	blackout	BLAK/O*UT
bishop	BIRB/OP	bladder	BLAD/ER
Bishop	K-P/BIRB/OP	blade	BLAID
bishydroxycoumarin	BIS/HAOI/DROX/KAOUM/RIN	bladevent	BLAID/VENT
bisiliac	BIS/IL/YAK	Blainville	BLAIN/VIL
bis in die	BIS/N-/DAOE/YAI	Blake	BLAIK
Biskra	BIS/KRA	Blakemore	BLAIK/MOER
Bismarck	BIZ/MA*RK		BLAIK/MOR
bismuth	BIZ/M*UT	Blalock	BLAI/LOK
bismuthia	BIZ/MAO*UT/YA	blanc	BLAN/*K
	BIZ/M*UT/YA	Blanchard	BLAN/KHARD
bismuthic	BIZ/M*UT/IK	bland	BLAND
bismuthism	BIZ/M*UT/IFM	Blasius	BLAS/YUS
	BIZ/MU/THIFM		BLAS/YAOUS
bismuthosis	BIZ/MU/THOE/SIS	blast	BLA*S
	BIZ/MAOU/THOE/SIS	-blast	BLA*S
bismuthyl	BIZ/MU/THIL	blast(o)-	BLA*S
bisobrin	BIS/BRIN		BLAS/T(O)
bisoxatin	BIS/OX/TIN	blastation	BLAS/TAIGS
bisphosphoglycerate	BIS/FOS/FO/GLIS/RAIT	blastema	BLAS/TAOE/MA
bispinous	B*I/SPAOIN/OUS	blastemia	BLAS/TAOEM/YA
bispore	B*I/SPOER	blastemic	BLAS/TEM/IK
bisque	BIS/-K	-blastic	BLA*S/IK
bistephanic	B*I/STE/FAN/IK	blastid	BLAS/TID
bisteroid	B*I/STAOER/OID	blastide	BLAS/TAOID
bistoury	BIS/TAOU/RI	blastin	BLAS/TIN
	BIS/KHAOU/RI	blastocele	BLA*S/SAO*EL
bistratal	B*I/STRAI/TAL	blastocelic	BLA*S/SAO*EL/IK
bisulfate	B*I/SUL/FAIT		BLA*S/SAOEL/IK
bisulfide	B*I/SUL/FAOID	blastochyle	BLA*S/KAOIL
bisulfite	B*I/SUL/FAOIT	Blastoconidium	BLA*S/KO/NID/YUM
bit	BIT	blastocyst	BLA*S/S*IS
bitartrate	B*I/TAR/TRAIT	Blastocystis	BLA*S/SIS/TIS
bite	BAOIT	blastocyte	BLA*S/SAO*IT
bite-block	BAOIT/H-F/BLOK	blastocytoma	BLA*S/SAOI/TOE/MA
bitegage	BAOIT/GAIJ	blastoderm	BLA*S/DERM
bitelock	BAOIT/LOK	blastoderma	BLA*S/DER/MA
bitemporal	B*I/TEFRP/RAL	blastodermal	BLA*S/DER/MAL
biteplate	BAOIT/PLAET	blastodermic	BLA*S/DERM/IK
biteplane	BAOIT/PLAEN	blastodisc	BLA*S/DIS/*K
biterminal	B*I/TERM/NAL	blastodisk	BLA*S/DIS/-K

blastogenesis	BLA*S/JEN/SIS	bleomycin sulfate	BLAOE/MAOI/SIN/SUL/FAIT
blastogenetic	BLA*S/JE/NET/IK		BLAOE/YO/MAOI/SIN/SUL/FAIT
blastogenic	BLA*S/JEN/IK	blephar(o)-	BLEF/R(O)
blastogeny	BLAS/TOJ/N*I	blepharadenitis	BLEF/AR/AD/NAOITS
blastokinin	BLA*S/KAOI/NIN		BLEF/RAD/NAOITS
blastolysis	BLAS/TOL/SIS	blepharal	BLEF/RAL
blastolytic	BLA*S/LIT/IK	blepharectomy	BLEF/REKT/M*I
blastoma	BLAS/TOE/MA	-blepharia	BLE/FAIR/YA
blastomata	BLAS/TOEM/TA		BLEF/AIR/YA
blastomatoid	BLAS/TOEM/TOID	blepharism	BLEF/RIFM
blastomatosis	BLAS/TOEM/TOE/SIS	blepharitis	BLEF/RAOITS
blastomatous	BLAS/TOEM/TOUS	blepharoadenitis	BLEF/RO/AD/NAOITS
blastomere	BLA*S/MAOER	blepharoadenoma	BLEF/RO/AD/NOE/MA
blastomerotomy	BLA*S/MAOER/OT/M*I	blepharoatheroma	BLEF/RO/A*T/ROE/MA
	BLA*S/MER/OT/M*I	blepharochalasis	BLEF/RO/KAL/SIS
blastomids	BLA*S/MIDZ	blepharochromidrosis	BLEF/RO/KROEM/DROE/SIS
blastomogenic	BLA*S/MO/JEN/IK	blepharoclonus	BLEF/ROK/LO/NUS
	BLA*S/MOE/JEN/IK	blepharocoloboma	BLEF/RO/KOL/BOE/MA
blastomogenous	BLA*S/MOJ/NOUS	blepharoconjunctivitis	BLEF/RO/KON/JUNGT/VAOITS
Blastomyces	BLA*S/MAOI/SAOEZ		BLEF/RO/KON/JUNG/VAOITS
blastomycete	BLA*S/MAOI/SAOET	blepharodiastasis	BLEF/RO/DI/A*S/SIS
blastomycetes	BLA*S/MAOI/SAOE/TAOEZ	blepharokeratoconjunctivitis	
blastomycetica	BLA*SO/MAOI/SET/KA		BLEF/RO/KER/TO/KON/JUNGT/
	BLA*S/MAOI/SAOET/KA		VAOITS
blastomycin	BLA*S/MAOI/SIN		BLEF/RO/KER/TO/KON/JUNG/
blastomycosis	BLA*S/MAOI/KOE/SIS		VAOITS
blastoneuropore	BLA*S/NAOUR/POER	blepharomelasma	BLEF/RO/ME/LAZ/MA
blastophore	BLA*S/FOER	blepharon	BLEF/RON
blastophthoria	BLAS/TOF/THOR/YA	blepharopachynsis	BLEF/RO/PA/KIN/SIS
blastophthoric	BLAS/TOF/THOR/IK	blepharophimosis	BLEF/RO/FAOI/MOE/SIS
blastophyllum	BLA*S/FIL/UM	blepharophyma	BLEF/RO/FAOI/MA
	BLA*S/FIL/LUM	blepharoplast	BLEF/RO/PLA*S
blastophyly	BLAS/TOF/LI	blepharoplastic	BLEF/RO/PLA*S/IK
blastopore	BLA*S/POER	blepharoplasty	BLEF/RO/PLAS/TI
blastoporic	BLA*S/POER/IK	blepharoplegia	BLEF/RO/PLAOE/JA
	BLA*S/POR/IK	blepharoptosia	BLEF/ROP/TOES/YA
blastosis	BLAS/TOE/SIS		BLEF/RO/TOES/YA
blastosphere	BLA*S/SFAOER	blepharoptosis	BLEF/RO/TOE/SIS
blastospore	BLA*S/SPOER		BLEF/ROP/TOE/SIS
blastostroma	BLA*S/STROE/MA	blepharopyorrhea	BLEF/RO/PAOI/RAOE/YA
blastotomy	BLAS/TOT/M*I	blepharorrhaphy	BLEF/ROR/FI
blastozooid	BLA*S/ZOE/OID	blepharosis	BLEF/ROE/SIS
blastul-	BLA*S/L-	blepharospasm	BLEF/RO/SPAFM
	BLAS/KHU/L-	blepharospasmus	BLEF/RO/SPAZ/MUS
	BLAS/TAOU/L-	blepharosphincterectomy	BLEF/RO/SFINGT/REKT/M*I
	BLAS/KHAOU/L-		BLEF/RO/SFING/TER/EKT/M*I
	BLA*S/YAOU/L-		BLEF/RO/SFING/TREKT/M*I
	BLA*S/YU/L-	blepharostat	BLEF/RO/STAT
blastula	BLA*S/LA	blepharostenosis	BLEF/RO/STE/NOE/SIS
blastulae	BLA*S/LAE	blepharosynechia	BLEF/RO/SIN/EK/YA
blastular	BLA*S/LAR		BLEF/RO/SI/NEK/YA
blastulation	BLA*S/LAIGS	blepharotomy	BLEF/ROT/M*I
Blatta	BLAT/TA	-blepharous	BLEF/ROUS
blattic	BLAT/IK	-blephary	BLEF/RI
blaze	BLAIZ	-blepsia	BLEPS/YA
bleach	BLAOEFP	Blessig	BLES/SIG
	BLAEFP		BLESZ/IG
bleached	BLAOEFP/-D	blight	BLAOIGT
	BLAEFP/-D	blind	BLAOIND
bleaching	BLAOEFP/-G	blindgut	BLAOIND/GUT
	BLAEFP/-G	blindness	BLAOIND/*NS
blear	BLAOER	blink	BLIN/-K
bleb	BLEB		BL*ING
bleed	BLAOED	Blinks	K-P/BLIN/-KS
bleeder	BLAOED/ER		BL*INGS
blemish	BLEM/IRB		K-P/BL*ING/-S
blenn(o)-	BLEN	blister	BL*IS/ER
	BLEN/N(O)		BLIS/TER
blennadenitis	BLEN/AD/NAOITS	bloat	BLOET
blennemesis	BLEN/EM/SIS	Blocadren	BLOK/DREN
blennogenic	BLEN/JEN/IK	block	BLOK
blennogenous	BLEN/OJ/NOUS	blockade	BLOK/KAID
	BLE/NOJ/NOUS	blockage	BLOK/AJ
blennoid	BLEN/OID	blocker	BLOK/ER
blenopthalmia	BLEN/OF/THAL/MA	blocking	BLOK/-G
	BLEN/OF/THAL/MAOE/YA	block-out	BLOK/H-F/OUT
blennorrhagia	BLEN/RAI/JA	blood	BLAOD
blennorrhagic	BLEN/RAJ/IK	blood bank	BLAOD/BAN/-K
blennorrhea	BLEN/RAOE/YA		BLAOD/BA*NG
blennorrheal	BLEN/RAOE/YAL	blood count	BLAOD/KOUNT
	BLEN/RAOEL	blood group	BLAOD/GROUP
blennostasis	BLEN/NO*S/SIS		BLAOD/GRAOUP
blennostatic	BLEN/STAT/IK	bloodless	BLAOD/LES
blennothorax	BLEN/THOR/AX	blood letting	BLAOD/LET/-G
blennuria	BLEN/NAOUR/YA	blood plasma	BLAOD/PLAZ/MA
	BLE/NAOUR/YA	blood puzzle	BLAOD/PUZ/-L
	BLEN/YAOUR/YA	blood pressure	BLAOD/PRERB/SHUR
Blenoxane	BLEN/OK/SAIN	blood serum	BLAOD/SAOERM
	BLEN/OX/AIN	bloodshot	BLAOD/SHOT

©1992 *StenEd*® Medical Dictionary

bloodstream	BLAOD/STRAO*EM	Bonnier	BOEN/YAI
blood type	BLAOD/TAOIP		BON/YAI
blood vessel	BLAOD/VES/EL	Bontril	BON/TRIL
	BLAOD/VES/SEL	Bontril Slow-Release	BON/TRIL/SLOE/RE/LAOES
blotch	BLOFP	Bonwill	BON/WIL
blowpipe	BLOE/PAOIP	Boophilus	BOE/OF/LUS
Bluboro	BLAOU/BOR/ROE	booster	BAO*S/ER
	BLU/BOR/ROE		BAOS/TER
blue	BLU	boot	BAOT
bluish	BLU/IRB	boracic	BOE/RAS/IK
Blum	BLUM		BO/RAS/IK
	BLAOUM		BOR/RAS/IK
Blumberg	BLUM/BERG		BOR/AS/IK
Blumenau	BLAOUM/NOU	borate	BOR/RAIT
Blumenbach	BLAOUM/EN/BAK		BOER/RAIT
	BLAOUM/-N/BAK	borated	BOR/RAIT/-D
	BLAOUM/EN/BAUK		BOER/RAIT/-D
	BLAOUM/-N/BAUK	borax	BOR/AX
blumenbachii	BLAOUM/EN/BAK/YAOI		BOER/AX
	BLAOU/MEN/BAK/YAOI	borborygmi	BOR/BRIG/MAOI
	BLAOUM/-N/BAK/YAOI		BOR/BO/RIG/MAOI
	BLAOUM/EN/BAUK/YAOI	borborygmus	BOR/BRIG/MUS
	BLAOU/MEN/BAUK/YAOI		BOR/BO/RIG/MUS
	BLAOUM/-N/BAUK/YAOI	border	BORD/ER
blunderbuss	BLUND/ER/BUSZ	borderline	BORD/ER/LAOIN
	BLUN/DER/BUSZ	Bordet	BOR/DAI
blush	BLURB	Bordet-Gengou	BOR/DAI/H-F/JAU/GAOU
board	BAORD	Bordetella	BORD/TEL/LA
Boari	BOER/RAOE	boric	BOR/IK
	BOE/AR/RAOE		BOER/IK
Boas	BOE/WAZ	boring	BOER/-G
	BOE/WAS	borism	BOR/IFM
	(not BOE/AZ)		BOER/IFM
Boas-Oppler	BOE/WAZ/H-F/OP/LER	bornane	BOR/NAIN
	BOE/WAS/H-F/OP/LER	borne	BOERN
bobbing	BOB/-G	Borneo	BORN/YOE
Bochdalek	BOK/DAL/EK	borneol	BORN/YOL
Bock	BOK	bornyl	BOR/NIL
Bockhart	BOK/HART	borocitrate	BOR/RO/SI/TRAIT
Bodansky	BOE/DAN/SKI		BOR/RO/SIT/TRAIT
	BOE/DAN/SKAOE		BOR/RO/SIT/RAIT
Bodian	BOED/YAN	borocitric	BOR/RO/SIT/RIK
Bodo	BOE/DOE	Borofair	BOR/RO/FAIR
Bodonidae	BOE/DON/DAE	boroglyceride	BOR/RO/GLIS/RAOID
body	BOD/DI	boroglycerin	BOR/RO/GLIS/RIN
Bohr	BO*R	boroglycerol	BOR/RO/GLIS/ROL
boil	BOIL	boron	BOR/RON
boilermaker	BOIL/ER/MAIK/ER	borophenylic	BOR/RO/FE/NIL/IK
bolasterone	BOEL/A*S/ROEN	borosalicylic	BOR/RO/SAL/SIL/IK
	BOEL/AS/TROEN	Borrel	BOR/REL
	BOE/LA*S/ROEN	Borrelia	BOR/REL/YA
	BOE/LAS/TROEN	borreliosis	BOR/REL/YOE/SIS
boldenone	BOELD/NOEN	Borsch	BOR/-RB
	BOEL/DE/NOEN	Borthen	BOR/TEN
boldin	BOL/DIN	boss	BOSZ
boldine	BOL/DAOEN	bosselated	BOS/LAIT/-D
boldo	BOL/DOE		BOSZ/LAIT/-D
boldoglucin	BOL/DO/GLAOU/SIN	bosselation	BOS/LAIGS
boldus	BOL/DUS		BOSZ/LAIGS
bolenol	BOEL/NOL	Bostock	BOS/TOK
	BOEL/NOEL	Boston	BOS/TON
boletic	BOL/ET/IK	bot	BOT
	BO/LET/IK	Botallo	BOE/TAL/LOE
Boley	BOE/LAOE	botanic	BO/TAN/IK
Bollinger	BOL/-G/ER		BOE/TAN/IK
	BOL/LIN/GER	botany	BOT/N*I
	BOL/LING/ER	botfly	BOT/FLAOI
bologram	BOE/LO/GRAM	bothria	BO*T/RAOE/YA
bolometer	BOE/LOM/TER	bothridium	BO*T/RID/YUM
bolometry	BOE/LOM/TRI	bothriocephaliasis	BO*T/RO/SEF/LAOI/SIS
boloscope	BOE/LO/SKOEP		BO*T/RAOE/YO/SEF/LAOI/SIS
bolus	BOE/LUS	Bothriocephalus	BO*T/RO/SEF/LUS
bomb	BOM		BO*T/RAOE/YO/SEF/LUS
bombard	BOM/BARD	bothrion	BO*T/RI/YON
bombesin	BOM/BE/SIN	bothritis	BO*T/RAOITS
bombicesterol	BOM/BI/S*ES/ROL	bothrium	BO*T/RAOE/YUM
	BOM/BI/SES/TROL		BO*T/RAOE/UM
bombykol	BOM/BI/KOL	bots	BOTS
Bombyx mori	BOM/BIX/MOR/RAOI		BOT/-S
Bonacal Plus	BON/KAL/PLUS	Bottcher	BET/SHER
bond	BOND	bottle	BOT/-L
bone	BOEN	botul-	BOFP/L-
bone ash	BOEN/ARB		BOFP/YAOU/L-
bonelet	BOEN/LET		BOFP/YU/L-
bone-salt	BOEN/H-F/SAULT		BOT/YAOU/L-
	BOEN/H-F/SALT		BOT/YU/L-
Bonine	BOE/NAOEN	botulin	BOFP/LIN
Bonnet	BOE/NAI	botulinal	BOFP/LAOINL
	BON/NAI	botulinic	BOFP/LIN/IK

botulinogenic	BOFP/LIN/JEN/IK	brachycephaly	BRAK/SEF/LI
botulinum	BOFP/LAOIN/UM	brachycheilia	BRAK/KAOIL/YA
	BOFP/LAOI/NUM	brachycnemic	BRAK/NAOEM/IK
botulinus	BOFP/LAOI/NUS	brachycranic	BRAK/KRAIN/IK
botulism	BOFP/LIFM	brachydactylia	BRAK/DAK/TIL/YA
botulismotoxin	BOFP/LIZ/MO/TOK/SIN	brachydactylic	BRAK/DAK/TIL/IK
botulogenic	BOFP/LO/JEN/IK	brachydactyly	BRAK/DAKT/LI
Bouchard	BAOU/SHAR	brachyesophagus	BRAK/E/SOF/GUS
bougie	BAOU/JAOE	brachyfacial	BRAK/FAIRBL
bougienage	BAOU/JAOE/NAJ	brachyglossal	BRAK/GLOS/SAL
bouillon	BAOUL/YON	brachygnathia	BRAK/IG/NA*IT/YA
	BAOU/YON		BRAK/NA*IT/YA
bound	BOUND	brachygnathous	BRAK/IG/NA/THOUS
bouquet	BAOU/KAI	brachykerkic	BRAK/KERK/IK
	BOE/KAI	brachymelia	BRAK/MAOEL/YA
bout	BOUT	brachymesophalangia	BRAK/MES/FLAN/JA
bouton	BAOU/TON	brachymetacarpalia	BRAK/MET/KAR/PAIL/YA
boutonniere	BAOUT/NAOER	brachymetacarpalism	BRAK/MET/KARP/LIFM
	BAOU/TON/NAOER	brachymetacarpia	BRAK/MET/KARP/YA
	BAOU/TON/YAIR	brachymetapody	BRAK/ME/TAP/DI
	BAOU/TON/NAIR	brachymetatarsia	BRAK/MET/TARS/YA
Bovie	BOE/VAOE	brachymetropia	BRAK/ME/TROEP/YA
bovina	BOE/VAOI/NA	brachymetropic	BRAK/ME/TROP/IK
bovine	BOE/VAOIN	brachymorphic	BRAK/MOR/FIK
bovinum	BOE/VAOIN/UM	brachyodont	BRAK/YO/DONT
	BOE/VAOI/NUM	brachypellic	BRAK/PEL/IK
bovis	BOE/VIS	brachypelvic	BRAK/PEL/VIK
bow	BOE	brachyphalangia	BRAK/FLAN/JA
	BOU	brachypodous	BRA/KIP/DOUS
bowel	BOU/EL	brachyprosopic	BRAK/PRO/SOP/IK
Bowen	BOE/-N	brachyrhinia	BRAK/RAOIN/YA
	BOE/WEN	brachyrhynchus	BRAK/RIN/KUS
bowenoid	BOE/EN/OID	brachyskelic	BRAK/SKEL/IK
	BOE/NOID	brachyskelous	BRAK/SKAOEL/OUS
	BOE/-N/OID		BRAK/SKAOE/LOUS
Bowie	BOE/WAOE	brachystaphyline	BRAK/STAF/LIN
bowleg	BOE/LEG	brachystasis	BRA/K*IS/SIS
Bowman	BOE/MAN	brachysyndactyly	BRAK/SIN/DAKT/LI
box	BOX	brachytelephalangia	BRAK/TEL/FLAN/JA
boxing	BOX/-G	brachytherapy	BRAK/THER/PI
box-note	BOX/H-F/NOET	brachytype	BRAK/TAOIP
boydii	BOID/YAOI	brachytypical	BRAK/TIP/KAL
Boyer	BOIR	brachyuranic	BRAK/YAOU/RAN/IK
	BOI/ER	bracing	BRAIS/-G
	BOI/YER	bracket	BRAK/ET
Bozeman	BOEZ/MAN	bract	BRAKT
Bozeman-Fritsch	BOEZ/MAN/H-F/FRIT/-RB	Bradford	BRAD/FORD
Braasch	BRAURB	brady-	BRAD
brace	BRAIS	bradyacusia	BRAD/AI/KAOUZ/YA
bracelet	BRAIS/LET		BRAD/YA/KAOUZ/YA
braces	BRAIS/-S	bradyarrhythmia	BRAD/AI/R*IT/MAOE/YA
brachi(o)-	BRAIK/Y(O)		BRAD/AI/R*IT/MA
brachia	BRAIK/YA		BRAD/YA/R*IT/MAOE/YA
brachial	BRAIK/YAL		BRAD/YA/R*IT/MA
brachiales	BRAIK/YAI/LAOEZ	bradyarthria	BRAD/AR/THRAOE/YA
brachialgia	BRAIK/YAL/JA	bradyauxesis	BRAD/AUK/SAOE/SIS
brachialis	BRAIK/YAI/LIS	bradycardia	BRAD/KARD/YA
brachiation	BRAIK/YAIGS	bradycardiac	BRAD/KARD/YAK
brachii	BRAIK/YAOI	bradycardic	BRAD/KARD/IK
brachiocarpal	BRAIK/YO/KAR/PAL	bradycinesia	BRAD/SI/NAOEZ/YA
brachiocephalic	BRAIK/YO/SFAL/IK	bradycinetic	BRAD/SI/NET/IK
brachiocephalica	BRAIK/YO/SFAL/KA	bradycrotic	BRAD/KROT/IK
brachiocephalicae	BRAIK/YO/SFAL/SAE	bradydiastole	BRAD/DI/A*S/LAOE
brachiocrural	BRAIK/YO/KRAOURL	bradyecoia	BRAD/E/KOI/YA
brachiocubital	BRAIK/YO/KAOUB/TAL		BRAD/KOI/YA
brachiocyllosis	BRAIK/YO/SIL/LOE/SIS	bradyesthesia	BRAD/ES/THAOEZ/YA
brachiocyrtosis	BRAIK/YO/SIR/TOE/SIS	bradygenesis	BRAD/JEN/SIS
brachiofaciolingual	BRAIK/YO/FAIRB/YO/LING/WAL	bradyglossia	BRAD/GLOS/YA
	BRAIK/YO/FAIS/YO/LING/WAL	bradykinesia	BRAD/KI/NAOEZ/YA
brachiogram	BRAIK/YO/GRAM	bradykinetic	BRAD/KI/NET/IK
brachioradial	BRAIK/YO/RAID/YAL	bradykinin	BRAD/KAOI/NIN
brachioradialis	BRAIK/YO/RAID/YAI/LIS	bradykininogen	BRAD/KAOI/NIN/JEN
brachioulnar	BRAIK/YO/UL/NAR		BRAD/KI/NIN/JEN
brachitol	BRAK/TOL	bradylalia	BRAD/LAIL/YA
brachium	BRAIK/YUM	bradylexia	BRAD/LEX/YA
brachius	BRAIK/YUS	bradylogia	BRAD/LOE/JA
Bracht-Wachter	BRAUKT/H-F/VAUK/TER	bradymenorrhea	BRAD/MEN/RAOE/YA
brachy-	BRAK	bradypepsia	BRAD/PEPS/YA
	BRA/KI	bradyphagia	BRAD/FAI/JA
brachybasia	BRAK/BAIS/YA	bradyphasia	BRAD/FAIZ/YA
brachybasocamptodactyly	BRAK/BAI/SO/KAFRP/TO/DAKT/	bradyphemia	BRAD/FAOEM/YA
	LI	bradyphrenia	BRAD/FRAOEN/YA
	BRAK/BAI/SO/KAM/TO/DAKT/LI		BRAD/FREN/YA
brachybasophalangia	BRAK/BAI/SO/FLAN/JA	bradypnea	BRAD/NAOE/YA
brachycardia	BRAK/KARD/YA		BRAD/IP/NAOE/YA
brachycephalia	BRAK/SFAIL/YA	bradypragia	BRAD/PRAI/JA
brachycephalic	BRAK/SFAL/IK	bradyrhythmia	BRAD/R*IT/MAOE/YA
brachycephalism	BRAK/SEF/LIFM		BRAD/R*IT/MA
brachycephalous	BRAK/SEF/LOUS	bradyspermatism	BRAD/SPERM/TIFM

bradysphygmia	BRAD/SFIG/MAOE/YA
bradystalsis	BRAD/STAL/SIS
bradytachycardia	BRAD/TAK/KARD/YA
bradyteleocinesia	BRAD/TEL/YO/SI/NAOEZ/YA
bradyteleokinesis	BRAD/TEL/YO/KI/NAOE/SIS
bradytocia	BRAD/TOE/SHA
bradytrophia	BRAD/TROEF/YA
bradytrophic	BRAD/TROFK
bradyuria	BRAD/YAOUR/YA
braid	BRAID
Braid	K-P/BRAID
braille	BRAIL
brain	BRAIN
Brain	K-P/BRAIN
braincase	BRAIN/KAIS
brain stem	BRAIN/STEM
brainwash	BRAIN/WARB
brainwashing	BRAIN/WARB/-G
brake	BRAIK
bran	BRAN
branch	BRAFRPBLG
	BRAN/-FP
brancher	BRAN/KHER
branchi(o)-	BRANG/YO
branchia	BRANG/YA
branchiae	BRANG/YAE
branchial	BRANG/YAL
branchiarum	BRANG/YAI/RUM
	BRANG/YAR/UM
	BRANG/YAIR/UM
branching	BRAN/-FPG
branchiogenetic	BRANG/YO/JE/NET/IK
branchiogenic	BRANG/YO/JEN/IK
branchiogenous	BRANG/YOJ/NOUS
branchioma	BRANG/YOE/MA
branchiomere	BRANG/YO/MAOER
branchiomeric	BRANG/YO/MER/IK
branchiomerism	BRANG/YOM/RIFM
branchiomotor	BRANG/YO/MOE/TOR
Brand	K-P/BRAND
brandy	BRAN/DI
Branham	BRAN/HAM
Branhamella	BRAN/HA/MEL/LA
branny	BRAN/N*I
brash	BRARB
brasiliensis	BRA/SIL/YEN/SIS
brassic	BRAS/IK
	BRASZ/IK
brassicae	BRAS/SAE
	BRAS/KAE
brassidic	BRA/SID/IK
brassilic	BRA/SIL/IK
brassy	BRAS/SI
Braun	BRA*UN
	(not BRAUN; see brawn)
brauni	BRAU/NAOI
brawn	BRAUN
brawny	BRAUN/N*I
Braxton Hicks	BRAX/TON/HIX
braze	BRAEZ
Brazilian	BRA/ZIL/YAN
braziliana	BRA/ZIL/YAI/NA
	BRA/ZIL/YA/NA
brazilein	BRA/ZIL/YIN
braziliense	BRA/ZIL/YEN/SAOE
braziliensis	BRA/ZIL/YEN/SIS
brazilin	BRA/ZIL/LIN
brazing	BRAEZ/-G
breadth	BRED/*T
break	BRAEK
breakoff	BRAEK/A*UF
breakthrough	BRAEK/THR*U
breast	BR*ES
breastbone	BR*ES/BOEN
breast-feed	BR*ES/FAOED
breath	BR*ET
breathe	BRAO*ET
breathing	BRAO*ET/-G
bredouillement	BRAID/WAOE/-MT
	BRAI/DWAOE/-MT
breech	BRAOEFP
breed	BRAOED
breeding	BRAOED/-G
Breezee Mist Foot Powder	BRAOE/ZAOE/M*IS/FAOT/POUD/ER
bregma	BREG/MA
bregmatic	BREG/MAT/IK
bregmatodymia	BREG/MA/TO/DIM/YA
brei	BRAOI

bremsstrahlung	BREMS/STRA/LUNG
	BREMZ/STRA/LUNG
Brenner	BREN/ER
brenz-catechin	BRENZ/KAT/KIN
Breonesin	BRAOE/NAOE/SIN
brephic	BREF/IK
	BREFK
brephoplastic	BREF/PLA*S/IK
brephotrophic	BREF/TROFK
Breschet	BRE/SHAI
Brethaire	BR*ET/AIR
Brethancer	BR*ET/AN/SER
Brethine	BR*ET/AOEN
	BRE/THAOEN
Bretonneau	BRET/NOE
	BRET/TON/NOE
bretylium	BRE/TIL/YUM
Bretylol	BRET/LOL
breve	BRAOE/VAOE
	BRE/VAOE
breves	BRAOE/VAOEZ
	BRAOE/VES
	BRE/VAOEZ
	BRE/VES
brevi-	BREV
Brevibacteriaceae	BREV/BAK/TAOER/YAIS/YAE
	BREV/BAK/TAOER/YAI/SAE
Brevibacterium	BREV/BAK/TAOERM
	BREV/BAK/TAOER/YUM
Brevibloc	BREV/BLOK
brevicollis	BREV/KOL/LIS
	BREV/KLIS
Brevicon	BREV/KON
breviflexor	BREV/FLEK/SOR
brevilineal	BREV/LIN/YAL
breviradiate	BREV/RAID/YAIT
	BREV/RAID/YAT
brevis	BRAOE/VIS
	BRE/VIS
Brevital	BREV/TAL
Brexin	BREK/SIN
	BREX/SIN
Bricanyl	BRIK/NIL
bridge	BRIJ
bridgework	BRIJ/WORK
bridle	BRAOID/-L
Bright	K-P/BRAOIGT
brightic	BRAOIGT/IK
brightism	BRAOIGT/IFM
Brill	BRIL
brim	BRIM
brimstone	BRIM/STOEN
brindle	BRIND/-L
Brinell	BRI/NEL
	BRIN/EL
	BRIN/NEL
Briquet	BRI/KAI
brisement	BRAOEZ/-MT
Brissaud	BRAOE/SOE
	BRAOES/SOE
	BRIS/SOE
bristle	BRIS/-L
brittle	BRIT/-L
broach	BROEFP
Broca	BROE/KA
Brocae	BROE/KAE
	BROE/SAE
brocresine	BROE/KRAOE/SAOEN
Broders	BROED/ERS
	BROE/DERS
Brodie	BROE/DAOE
Brodmann	BROD/MAN
brofoxine	BROE/FOK/SAOEN
	BROE/FOX/AOEN
broken	BROEK/-N
brom(o)-	BROEM
	BROE/MO
	BROM
broma	BROE/MA
Bromarest	BROEM/R*ES
Bromase	BROE/MAIS
bromate	BROE/MAIT
bromated	BROE/MAIT/-D
bromatherapy	BROEM/THER/PI
bromatology	BROEM/TOLG
bromatotherapy	BROEM/TO/THER/PI
bromatotoxin	BROEM/TO/TOK/SIN
bromatotoxismus	BROEM/TO/TOK/SIZ/MUS
bromatoxism	BROEM/TOK/SIFM

bromazepam	BROEM/TOX/IFM	bronchiogenic	BRONG/YO/JEN/IK
	BROE/MAIZ/PAM	bronchiol-	BRONG/YO/L-
	BROE/MAZ/PAM		BRON/KAOI/L-
bromazine	BROEM/ZAOEN	bronchiolar	BRON/KAOI/LAR
bromcresol	BROM/KRAOE/SOL		BRON/KAOE/LAR
bromelain	BROEM/LAIN	bronchiole	BRONG/YOEL
bromelin	BROEM/LIN	bronchiolectasia	BRONG/YO/LEK/TAIZ/YA
bromethol	BROE/M*ET/OL	bronchiolectasis	BRONG/YO/LEKT/SIS
Bromfed	BROEM/FED	bronchioli	BRON/KAOI/LAOI
	BROM/FED		BRON/KAOE/LAOI
bromhexine	BROM/HEK/SAOEN	bronchiolitis	BRONG/YO/LAOITS
bromhidrosis	BROM/HI/DROE/SIS	bronchiolopulmonary	BRON/KAOI/LO/PUL/MO/NAIR
	BROEM/HI/DROE/SIS		BRON/KAOE/LO/PUL/MO/NAIR
bromic	BROEM/IK		BRON/KAOI/LO/PUM/NAIR
bromide	BROE/MAOID		BRON/KAOE/LO/PUM/NAIR
bromidrosis	BROEM/DROE/SIS	bronchiolus	BRON/KAOI/LUS
brominated	BROEM/NAIT/-D		BRON/KAOE/LUS
bromindione	BROE/MIN/DI/OEN	bronchiospasm	BRONG/YO/SPAFM
bromine	BROE/MAOEN	bronchiostenosis	BRONG/YO/STE/NOE/SIS
	BROE/MIN	bronchiseptica	BRON/KI/SEPT/KA
brominism	BROEM/NIFM		BRONG/SEPT/KA
	BROE/MIN/IFM	bronchisepticin	BRON/KI/SEPT/SIN
brominized	BROE/MIN/AOIZ/-D		BRONG/SEPT/SIN
	BROEM/NAOIZ/-D	bronchisepticus	BRON/KI/SEPT/KUS
bromism	BROEM/IFM		BRONG/SEPT/KUS
	BROE/MIFM	bronchismus	BRON/KIZ/MUS
bromisovalum	BROEM/SO/VAL/UM	bronchitic	BRON/KIT/IK
bromization	BROEM/ZAIGS	bronchitis	BRON/KAOITS
bromized	BROE/MAOIZ/-D	bronchium	BRONG/YUM
bromobenzene	BROEM/BEN/ZAOEN	bronchoadenitis	BRONG/AD/NAOITS
bromochlorotrifluoroethane	BROEM/KLOR/TR*I/FLAOUR/*ET/	bronchoalveolar	BRONG/AL/VAOE/LAR
	AIN	bronchoalveolitis	BRONG/AL/VAOE/LAOITS
bromocresol	BROEM/KRAOE/SOL	bronchoaspergillosis	BRONG/AS/PERJ/LOE/SIS
bromocriptine	BROEM/KRIP/TAOEN		BRONG/AS/PER/JIL/LOE/SIS
bromodeoxyuridine	BROEM/DE/OX/YAOUR/DAOEN	bronchoblastomycosis	BRONG/BLA*S/MAOI/KOE/SIS
bromoderma	BROEM/DER/MA	bronchoblennorrhea	BRONG/BLEN/RAOE/YA
bromodiphenhydramine	BROEM/DI/FEN/HAOI/DRA/	bronchocandidiasis	BRONG/KAND/DAOI/SIS
	MAOEN	bronchocavernous	BRONG/KAVR/NOUS
bromohyperhidrosis	BROEM/HAO*IP/HI/DROE/SIS	bronchocele	BRONG/SAO*EL
bromohyperidrosis	BROEM/HAO*IP/DROE/SIS	bronchoconstriction	BRONG/KON/STR*IBGS
bromoiodism	BROEM/AOI/D1FM	bronchoconstrictor	BRONG/KON/STRIK/TOR
bromomania	BROEM/MAIN/YA	bronchodilatation	BRONG/DIL/TAIGS
bromomenorrhea	BROEM/MEN/RAOE/YA	bronchodilation	BRONG/DI/LAIGS
bromophenol	BROEM/FAOE/NOL	bronchodilator	BRONG/DI/LAI/TOR
bromopnea	BROE/MOP/NA	bronchoedema	BRONG/E/DAOE/MA
	BROE/MOP/NAOE/YA	bronchoegophony	BRONG/E/GOF/N*I
	BROEM/OP/NA	bronchoesophageal	BRONG/E/SOF/JAOEL
	BROEM/OP/NAOE/YA	bronchoesophagology	BRONG/E/SOF/GOLG
bromosulfophthalein	BROEM/SUL/FO/THAL/YIN	bronchoesophagoscopy	BRONG/E/SOF/GOS/KPI
bromouracil	BROEM/YAOUR/SIL	bronchofiberscope	BRONG/FAOI/BER/SKOEP
bromous	BROEM/OUS	bronchofibroscopy	BRONG/FAOI/BROS/KPI
bromoxanide	BROE/MOX/NAOID	bronchogenic	BRONG/JEN/IK
bromperidol	BROM/P*ER/DOL	bronchogram	BRONG/GRAM
	BROM/PER/DOL	bronchographic	BRONG/GRAFK
brompheniramine	BROEM/FEN/IR/MAOEN	bronchography	BRON/KOG/FI
bromphenol	BROM/FAOE/NOL	broncholith	BRONG/L*IT
bromphenylacetylcysteine	BROEM/FENL/AS/TIL/S*IS/YIN	broncholithiasis	BRONG/LI/THAOI/SIS
	BROM/FENL/AS/TIL/S*IS/YIN	bronchologic	BRONG/LOJ/IK
bromphenylmercapturic	BROEM/FENL/MER/KAP/TAOUR/	bronchology	BRON/KOLG
	IK	bronchomalacia	BRONG/MA/LAI/SHA
	BROM/FENL/MER/KAP/TAOUR/	bronchomoniliasis	BRONG/MON/LAOI/SIS
	IK	bronchomotor	BRONG/MOE/TOR
bromsulfophthalein	BROM/SUL/FO/THAL/YIN	bronchomucotropic	BRONG/MAOUK/TROP/IK
bromthymol	BROM/THAOI/MOL	bronchomycosis	BRONG/MAOI/KOE/SIS
bromum	BROE/MUM	bronchonocardiosis	BRONG/NOE/KARD/YOE/SIS
	BROEM/UM	broncho-oidiosis	BRONG/OID/YOE/SIS
bromurated	BROEM/YAOU/RAIT/-D		BRONG/O/ID/YOE/SIS
bromuret	BROEM/YAOU/RET	bronchopancreatic	BRONG/PAN/KRAT/IK
broncatar	BRON/KA/TAR	bronchopathy	BRON/KOP/TH*I
bronch(o)-	BRONG	bronchophony	BRON/KOF/N*I
	BRON/K(O)	bronchoplasty	BRONG/PLAS/TI
bronchadenitis	BRON/KAD/NAOITS	bronchoplegia	BRONG/PLAOE/JA
bronchi	BRON/KAOI	bronchopleural	BRONG/PLAOURL
bronchi(o)-	BRONG/Y(O)	bronchopleuropneumonia	BRONG/PLAOUR/NAOU/MOEN/
bronchia	BRONG/YA		YA
bronchial	BRONG/YAL	bronchopneumonia	BRONG/NAOU/MOEN/YA
bronchiales	BRONG/YAI/LAOEZ	bronchopneumonic	BRONG/NAOU/MON/IK
bronchiarctia	BRONG/YARK/SHA	bronchopneumonitis	BRONG/NAOUM/NAOITS
bronchic	BRONG/IK	bronchoneumopathy	BRONG/NAOU/MOP/TH*I
	BRON/KIK	bronchopulmonary	BRONG/PUL/MO/NAIR
bronchiectasia	BRONG/YEK/TAIZ/YA		BRONG/PUM/NAIR
bronchiectasic	BRONG/YEK/TAIZ/IK	bronchoradiography	BRONG/RAID/YOG/FI
bronchiectasis	BRONG/YEKT/SIS	bronchorrhagia	BRONG/RAI/JA
bronchiectatic	BRONG/YEK/TAT/IK	bronchorrhaphy	BRON/KOR/FI
bronchiloquy	BRON/KIL/KWAOE	bronchorrhea	BRONG/RAOE/YA
	BRON/KIL/KWI	bronchoscope	BRONG/SKOEP
bronchioalveolar	BRONG/YO/AL/VAOE/LAR	bronchoscopic	BRONG/SKOP/IK
bronchiocele	BRONG/YO/SAO*EL	bronchoscopy	BRON/KOS/KPI
bronchiocrisis	BRONG/YO/KRAOI/SIS	bronchosinusitis	BRONG/SAOIN/SAOITS

bronchospasm	BRONG/SPAFM	bubonulus	BAOU/BON/LUS
bronchospirochetosis	BRONG/SPAOIR/KAOE/TOE/SIS		BAOU/BON/YAOU/LUS
bronchospirography	BRONG/SPAOI/ROG/FI		BAOU/BON/YU/LUS
bronchospirometer	BRONG/SPAOI/ROM/TER	bucainide	BAOU/KAI/NAOID
bronchospirometry	BRONG/SPAOI/ROM/TRI		BAOU/KAIN/AOID
bronchostaxis	BRONG/STAK/SIS	bucardia	BAOU/KARD/YA
bronchostenosis	BRONG/STE*S/NOE/SIS	bucc(o)-	BUK
bronchostomy	BRON/KO*S/M*I		BUK/K(O)
bronchotome	BRONG/TOEM		BUX
bronchotomy	BRON/KOT/M*I		BUK/SI
bronchotracheal	BRONG/TRAIK/YAL	bucca	BUK/KA
bronchotyphoid	BRONG/TAOI/FOID	buccae	BUK/KAE
bronchotyphus	BRONG/TAOI/FUS	buccal	BUK/KAL
bronchovesicular	BRONG/VE/SIK/LAR	buccalis	BUK/KAI/LIS
bronchus	BRON/KUS	buccally	BUK/KAL/LI
Bronkaid	BRON/KAID	buccinator	BUX/NAI/TOR
	BRO*NG/AID	buccinatoria	BUK/SIN/TOER/YA
	BRON/-K/AID		BUX/NA/TOER/YA
Bronkaid Mist	BRON/KAID/M*IS	buccinatorius	BUK/SIN/TOER/YUS
	BRO*NG/AID/M*IS		BUX/NA/TOER/YUS
	BRON/-K/AID/M*IS	buccoaxial	BUK/AX/YAL
Bronkephrine	BRON/KEF/RIN	buccoaxiocervical	BUK/AX/YO/SEFRB/KAL
Bronkodyl	BRONG/DIL	buccoaxiogingival	BUK/AX/YO/JING/VAL
Bronkolixir	BRONG/LIK/SIR	buccocervical	BUK/SEFRB/KAL
	BRONG/LIX/SIR	buccoclusal	BUK/KLAOU/ZAL
Bronkometer	BRONG/MAOET/ER	buccoclusion	BUK/KLAOUGS
	BRONG/MAOE/TER	buccodistal	BUK/DIS/TAL
Bronkosol	BRONG/SOL	buccogingival	BUK/JING/VAL
Bronkotabs	BRONG/TAB/-S	buccoglossopharyngitis	BUK/GLOS/FARN/JAOITS
brontophobia	BRON/TO/FOEB/YA	buccolabial	BUK/LAIB/YAL
bronze	BRONZ	buccolingual	BUK/LING/WAL
bronzed	BRONZ/-D	buccolingually	BUK/LING/WAL/LI
brood	BRAOD	buccomaxillary	BUK/MAX/LAIR
broom	BRAOM	buccomesial	BUK/MAOEZ/YAL
broth	BRO*T	bucco-occlusal	BUK/O/KLAOU/ZAL
brow	BROU	buccopharyngeal	BUK/FRIN/JAL
browlift	BROU/LIFT	buccoplacement	BUK/PLAIS/-MT
brown	BROUN	buccopulpal	BUK/PUL/PAL
Brown	K-P/BROUN	buccostomy	BUK/KO*S/M*I
brownian	BROUN/YAN		BUK/O*S/M*I
Bruce	BRAOUS	buccoversion	BUK/VERGS
Brucella	BRAOU/SEL/LA	buccula	BUK/LA
Brucellaceae	BRAOUS/LAIS/YAE		BUK/YAOU/LA
	BRAOU/SEL/LAIS/YAE		BUK/YU/LA
brucellar	BRAOU/SEL/LAR	Bucet	BAOU/SET
brucellergin	BRAOU/SEL/ER/JIN	Buchner	BUK/NER
	BRAOU/SEL/LER/JIN	Buchwald	BUK/WALD
brucelliasis	BRAOUS/LAOI/SIS		BAOUK/WALD
	BRAOU/SEL/LAOI/SIS	buck	BUK
brucellin	BRAOUS/SEL/LIN	Buck	K-P/BUK
brucellosis	BRAOUS/LOE/SIS	buckle	BUK/-L
	BRAOU/SEL/LOE/SIS	buckling	BUK/-LG
Bruch	BR*UK	buckthorn	BUK/THORN
brucine	BRAOU/SAOEN	Bucky	BUK/KI
	BRAOU/SIN	Bucky-Potter	BUK/KI/H-F/K-P/POT/ER
Bruck	BRUK	Bucladin	BAOU/KLA/DIN
Brucke	BRAOE/KAOE		BAOUK/LA/DIN
Brugia	BRAOU/JA	Bucladin-S	BAOU/KLA/DIN/S-RBGS
	BRAOUJ/YA		BAOUK/LA/DIN/S-RBGS
bruise	BRAOUZ	buclizine	BAOU/KLI/ZAOEN
bruissement	BRAOU/WAOES/-MT		BAOUK/LI/ZAOEN
bruit	BRAOU/WAOE	buclosamide	BUK/LOES/MAOID
bruits (s not sounded)	BRAOU/WAOE/-S	bucnemia	BUK/NAOEM/YA
Brumpt	BRUFRPT	bucrylate	BAOU/KRI/LAIT
	BRUM/-PT		BAOUK/RI/LAIT
brumpti	BRUFRP/TAOI	bud	BUD
	BRUM/TAOI	Budd	B*UD
brunescens	BRAOU/NES/ENZ	budding	BUD/-G
	BRAOU/NES/ENS	Budge	K-P/BUJ
brunescent	BRAOU/NES/ENT	buetschlii	BAOURB/LAOE/YAOI
Brunner	BRAOUN/ER		BAOURB/LAOI
brunneroma	BRAOUN/ROE/MA		BAOUFP/LAOE/YAOI
brunnerosis	BRAOUN/ROE/SIS		BAOUFP/LAOI
Bruns	BRUNZ	bufadienolide	BAOUF/DI/EN/LAOID
Brunschwig	BRAOUN/SWIG		BAOUF/DAOI/EN/LAOID
	BRUN/SWIG	bufagenin	BAOUF/JEN/NIN
brush	BRURB	bufagin	BAOUF/JIN
brushite	BRURB/AOIT	bufanolide	BAOU/FAN/LAOID
bruxism	BRUK/SIFM	bufatrienolide	BAOUF/TR*I/EN/LAOID
	BRUX/IFM	bufenolide	BAOU/FEN/LAOID
bubata	BAOU/BAI/TA	buffalo	BUF/LOE
bubble	BUBL	buffer	BUFR
	BUB/-L		BUF/ER
bubo	BAOU/BOE	Bufferin	BUF/RIN
bubonalgia	BAOU/BON/AL/JA	buffering	BUFR/-G
	BAOU/BO/NAL/JA		BUF/ER/-G
bubonic	BAOU/BON/IK	buffy	BUF/FI
bubonicae	BAOU/BON/SAE	bufilcon	BAOU/FIL/KON
bubonocele	BAOU/BON/SAO*EL		

bufin	BAOU/FIN	bundle branch	BUND/-L/BRAFRPBLG
Bufo	BAOU/FOE		BUND/-L/BRAN/-FP
Bufonidae	BAOU/FON/DAE	bundle of His	BUND/-L/OF/HIS
buformin	BAOU/FOR/MIN	bungarotoxin	BUNG/RO/TOK/SIN
bufotalin	BAOUF/TAL/LIN	Bunge	BAOUN/GAOE
bufotenin	BAOU/FOET/NIN	Bungner	BING/NER
bufotenine	BAOUF/TEN/AOEN		BUNG/NER
	BAOUF/TEN/NAOEN	buninoid	BAOUN/NOID
bufotherapy	BAOUF/THER/PI	buniodyl	BAOU/NAOI/DIL
bufotoxin	BAOUF/TOK/SIN	bunion	BUN/YON
bug	BUG	bunionectomy	BUN/YON/EKT/M*I
buggery	BUG/RI	bunionette	BUN/YON/ET
	BUG/ER/RI		BUN/YON/NET
Bugs Bunny (vitamins)	BUGS/BUN/N*I	bunodont	BAOUN/DONT
	BUG/-S/BUN/N*I		BAOU/NO/DONT
Buisson	BAOU/SON	bunolol	BAOUN/LOL
	BAOUS/SON		BAOU/NO/LOL
Bulama	BAOU/LA/MA	bunolophodont	BAOUN/LOF/DONT
	BAOU/LAM/MA		BAOU/NO/LOF/DONT
bulb	BUL/-B	bunoselenodont	BAOUN/SE/LEN/DONT
bulb(o)-	BUL/B(O)		BAOUN/SLEN/DONT
bulbar	BUL/BAR		BAOU/NO/SE/LEN/DONT
bulbi	BUL/BAOI		BAOU/NO/SLEN/DONT
bulbiform	BUL/BI/FORM	Bunostomum	BAOUN/STOE/MUM
bulbiformia	BUL/BI/FORM/YA		BAOUN/STOEM/UM
bulbitis	BUL/BAOITS		BAOU/NO/STOE/MUM
bulboatrial	BUL/BO/AI/TRAL		BAOU/NO/STOEM/UM
	BUL/BO/AIT/RAL	Bunsen	BUN/SEN
	BUL/BO/AI/TRAOE/YAL		BUNS/-N
	BUL/BO/AIT/RAOE/YAL		BUNS/EN
bulbocapnine	BUL/BO/KAP/NAOEN	Bunyan	BUN/YAN
	BUL/BO/KAP/NIN	Bunyaviridae	BUN/YA/VIR/DAE
bulbocavernosus	BUL/BO/KAVR/NOE/SUS	Bunyavirus	BUN/YA/VAOI/RUS
bulbogastrone	BUL/BO/GAS/TROEN	buphthalmia	BAOUF/THAL/MAOE/YA
bulboid	BUL/BOID	buphthalmos	BAOUF/THAL/MOS
bulboidea	BUL/BOID/YA	buphthalmus	BAOUF/THAL/MUS
bulbonuclear	BUL/BO/NAOUK/LAR	bupicomide	BAOU/PIK/MAOID
bulbopontine	BUL/BO/PON/TAOEN	bupivacaine	BAOU/PIV/KAIN
	BUL/BO/PON/TAOIN	Buprenex	BAOUP/REN/EX
bulborum	BUL/BOR/UM		BAOUP/RE/NEX
	BUL/BOER/UM		BAOU/PRE/NEX
bulbosacral	BUL/BO/SAI/KRAL	buprenorphine	BAOU/PRE/NOR/FAOEN
bulbospinal	BUL/BO/SPAOINL	buprestoides	BAOU/PRES/TOI/DAOEZ
bulbospiral	BUL/BO/SPAOIRL	bupropion	BAOU/PROEP/YON
bulbospongiosus	BUL/BO/SPON/JOE/SUS	bur	B*UR
bulbourethral	BUL/BO/YAOU/RAO*ET/RAL	Burckhardt	BURK/HART
bulbourethrales	BUL/BO/YAOUR/THRAI/LAOEZ	Burdach	BAOUR/DAK
bulbourethralis	BUL/BO/YAOUR/THRAI/LIS		BUR/DAK
bulbous	BUL/BOUS	Burdachi	BURD/KAOI
bulbus	BUL/BUS		BUR/DA/KAOI
bulesis	BAOU/LAOE/SIS		BAOUR/DAK/KAOI
bulging	BUL/-J/-G		BUR/DAK/KAOI
bulimia	BAOU/LAOEM/YA	burden	BURD
	BAOU/LIM/YA		BURD/-N
bulimiac	BAOU/LAOEM/YAK	buret	BAOU/RET
	BAOU/LIM/YAK	burette	BAOU/R*ET
bulimic	BAOU/LAOEM/IK	burimamide	BAOU/RIM/MAOID
	BAOU/LIM/IK	burn	BURN
bulkage	BUL/KAJ	Burn	K-P/BURN
bulla	BUL/LA	burner	BURN/ER
bullae	BUL/LAE	Burnett	BUR/NET
bullate	BUL/LAIT	burnetii	BUR/NET/YAOI
	BUL/AIT	burnish	BURN/IRB
bullation	BUL/LAIGS	burnisher	BURN/SHER
	BUL/AIGS		BURN/IRB/ER
Buller	BUL/ER	burnishing	BURN/IRB/-G
	BUL/LER	burnout	BURN/O*UT
bulliens	BUL/YENZ	Burns	BURNZ
	BUL/YENS		BURNS
bullosa	BUL/LOE/SA	burnt	BURNT
bullosis	BUL/LOE/SIS	burr	BUR
bullosum	BUL/LOE/SUM	burrow	BUR/ROE
	BUL/LOES/UM	burs(o)-	BURS
bullous	BUL/OUS		BUR/S(O)
	BUL/LOUS	bursa	BUR/SA
bullular	BUL/YAOU/LAR	bursae	BUR/SAE
	BUL/YU/LAR	bursal	BUR/SAL
	BUL/LAR	bursalogy	BUR/SALG
bumetanide	BAOU/MET/NAOID		BUR/SAL/JI
Bumex	BAOU/MEX	bursata	BUR/SAI/TA
Buminate	BAOUM/NAIT	bursectomy	BUR/SEKT/M*I
bump	BUFRP	bursic	BURS/IK
	BUM/-P	bursinic	BUR/SIN/IK
BUN	B*UN	bursitis	BUR/SAOITS
	B-RBGS/*URBGS/N*RBGS	bursolith	BURS/L*IT
bunamidine	BUN/AM/DAOEN	bursopathy	BUR/SOP/TH*I
	BAOU/NAM/DAOEN	bursotomy	BUR/SOT/M*I
bunamiodyl	BAOUN/MAOI/DIL	burst	B*URS
bundle	BUND/-L	bursula	BUR/SAOU/LA

		butyryl	BAOUT/RIL
	BURS/YAOU/LA	butyrylcholine esterase	BAOUT/RIL/KOE/LAOEN/ES/
	BURS/YU/LA		TRAIS
Burton	BUR/TON	Buzzi	BUZ/ZAOE
Bury	K-P/BUR/RI		BUZ/SAOE
buski	BUS/KAOI	bypass	B*I/PASZ
BuSpar	BAOU/SPAR	by-product	B*I/PRUKT
buspirone	BAOU/SPAOI/ROEN		B*I/PROD/UKT
busulfan	BAOU/SUL/FAN		B*I/PRO/DUKT
butabarbital	BAOUT/BARB/TAL	byssaceous	BIS/SAIRBS
butacaine	BAOUT/KAIN	byssinosis	BIS/NOE/SIS
butaclamol	BAOUT/KLAI/MOL	byssinotic	BIS/NOT/IK
butadiazamide	BAOUT/DI/AZ/MAOID	byssocausis	BIS/KAU/SIS
butalbital	BAOU/TAL/BI/TAL	byssoid	BIS/OID
butallylonal	BAOUT/LIL/NAL		BIS/SOID
butamben	BAOU/TAM/BEN	byssus	BIS/SUS
butamirate	BAOUT/MAOI/RAIT		
	BAOUT/MIR/RAIT		
butamisole	BAOU/TAM/SOEL		
butamoxane	BAOUT/MOK/SAIN		
	BAOUT/MOX/AIN		
butane	BAOU/TAIN		
butanilicaine	BAOUT/NIL/KAIN		
butanoic	BAOUT/NOIK		
	BAOUT/NOE/IK		
butanol	BAOUT/NOL		
butanoyl	BAOUT/NOIL		
	BAOU/TAN/OIL		
butaperazine	BAOUT/PER/ZAOEN		
butaverine	BAOU/TAV/RAOEN		
Butazolidin	BAOUT/ZOL/DIN		
Butesin	BAOUT/SIN		
Butesin Picrate	BAOUT/SIN/PIK/RAIT		
butethal	BAOUT/THAL		
butethamate	BAOU/T*ET/MAIT		
butethamine	BAOU/T*ET/MAOEN		
buthalital	BAOU/THAL/TAL		
buthiazide	BAOU/THAOI/ZAOID		
butirosin	BAOU/TAOER/SIN		
Butisol	BAOUT/SOL		
Butisol Sodium	BAOUT/SOL/SOED/YUM		
butoconazole	BAOUT/KOEN/ZOEL		
	BAOUT/KON/ZOEL		
butonate	BAOUT/NAIT		
butoprozine	BAOUT/PRO/ZAOEN		
butopyronoxyl	BAOUT/PAOIR/NOK/SIL		
butorphanol	BAOU/TOR/FA/NOL		
	BAOU/TOR/FA/NOEL		
butoxamine	BAOU/TOX/MAOEN		
butoxycarbonyl	BAOU/TOX/KARB/NIL		
butriptyline	BAOU/TRIPT/LAOEN		
Butschli	BIFP/LAOE		
butt	BUT		
butter	BUT/ER		
Butter	K-P/BUT/ER		
butterfly	BUT/ER/FLAOI		
	BUT/ER/FLI		
buttock	BUT/TOK		
	BUT/OK		
button	BUT/TON		
buttonhole	BUT/TON/HOEL		
butyl	BAOU/TIL		
	BAOUT/IL		
butylcarboxylic	BAOU/TIL/KAR/BOK/SIL/IK		
butylene	BAOUT/LAOEN		
butylethyl	BAOU/TIL/*ET/IL		
butylic	BAOU/TIL/IK		
butylmercaptan	BAOU/TIL/MER/KAP/TAN		
butyloxycarbonyl	BAOU/TIL/OX/KARB/NIL		
butylparaben	BAOU/TIL/PAR/BEN		
butyr(o)-	BAOUT/R(O)		
	BAOU/TIR		
butyraceous	BAOUT/RAIRBS		
butyrase	BAOUT/RAIS		
butyrate	BAOUT/RAIT		
Butyribacterium	BAOU/TIR/BAK/TAOERM		
	BAOU/TIR/BAK/TAOER/YUM		
butyric	BAOU/TIR/IK		
butyricum	BAOU/TIR/KUM		
butyrin	BAOUT/RIN		
butyrinase	BAOU/TIR/NAIS		
butyrine	BAOU/TRAOEN		
butyrocholinesterase	BAOUT/RO/KOEL/N*ES/RAIS		
butyroid	BAOUT/ROID		
butyromel	BAOU/TIR/MEL		
butyrometer	BAOUT/ROM/TER		
butyrophenone	BAOUT/RO/FAOE/NOEN		
	BAOU/TIR/FAOE/NOEN		
butyroscope	BAOU/TIR/SKOEP		
butyrous	BAOUT/ROUS		

C

cabalii	KA/BAL/YAOI
cabinet	KAB/NET
Cabot	KAB/OT
cabufocon A	KAB/FOE/KON/ARBGS
cac(o)-	KAK
	KA/K(O)
cacao	KA/KOU
	KA/KAI/YOE
cacatory	KAK/TOIR
cacesthenic	KAK/ES/THEN/IK
cacesthesia	KAK/ES/THAOEZ/YA
cachectic	KA/KEKT/IK
cachecticorum	KA/KEKT/KOR/UM
cachectin	KA/KEK/TIN
cachet	KA/SHAI
cachexia	KA/KEX/YA
cachexial	KA/KEX/YAL
cachinnation	KAK/NAIGS
cacodemonomania	KAK/DE/MON/MAIN/YA
	KAK/DAOEM/NO/MAIN/YA
cacodontia	KAK/DON/SHA
cacodyl	KAK/DIL
cacodylate	KAK/DIL/AIT
	KAK/DIL/LAIT
cacodylic	KAK/DIL/IK
cacogenesis	KAK/JEN/SIS
cacogenic	KAK/JEN/IK
cacogeusia	KAK/GAOUS/YA
	KAK/GAOUZ/YA
cacomelia	KAK/MAOEL/YA
cacomorphosis	KAK/MOR/FOE/SIS
cacoplastic	KAK/PLA*S/IK
cacorhythmic	KAK/R*IT/MIK
cacosmia	KAK/OZ/MAOE/YA
	KA/KOZ/MAOE/YA
cactinomycin	KAK/TIN/MAOI/SIN
	KAKT/NO/MAOI/SIN
cacumen	KAK/YAOU/MEN
cacumina	KAK/YAOUM/NA
cacuminal	KAK/YAOUM/NAL
	KA/KAOUM/NAL
cadaver	KA/DAVR
	KA/DAV/ER
cadaveric	KA/DAV/RIK
	KA/DAVR/IK
	KA/DAVRK
cadaverine	KA/DAV/RIN
	KA/DAVR/RIN
cadaverous	KA/DAV/ROUS
	KA/DAVR/OUS
cadmiosis	KAD/MAOE/YOE/SIS
	KAD/MI/YOE/SIS
cadmium	KAD/MUM
	KAD/MAOE/UM
	KAD/MAOE/YUM
caduca	KA/DAOU/KA
caduceus	KA/DAOUS/YUS
caducous	KA/DAOUK/OUS
caerulea	SAE/RAOUL/YA
Cafergot	KAFR/GOT
	KAF/ER/GOT
caffearine	KAF/YA/RIN
	KAF/FAOE/RIN
caffeic	KAF/YIK
	KAF/FAOE/IK
caffeine	KAF/FAOEN
	KAF/AOEN
caffeinism	KAF/FAOEN/IFM
	KAF/AOEN/IFM
	KAF/YIN/IFM
caffetannic	KAF/TAN/IK
Caffey	KAF/FAOE
caffuric	KAF/YAOUR/IK
	KAF/FAOUR/IK
cage	KAIJ
Cain	KA*IN
Cajal	KA/HAL
cajennense	KAIJ/NEN/SAOE
	KAJ/NEN/SAOE
caked	KAIK/-D
Calabar	KAL/BAR
calage	KA/LAJ
	(not KLAJ; see collage)
calamine	KAL/MAOIN

calamus	KAL/MUS
Calan	KA/LAN
	KAL/LAN
Cal-Bid	KAL/BID
	KAL/H-F/BID
calcane(o)-	KAL/KAIN/Y(O)
calcanea	KAL/KAIN/YA
calcaneal	KAL/KAIN/YAL
calcanean	KAL/KAIN/YAN
calcanei	KAL/KAIN/YAOI
calcaneitis	KAL/KAIN/YAOITS
calcaneoapophysitis	KAL/KAIN/YO/AI/POF/SAOITS
calcaneoastragaloid	KAL/KAIN/YO/AI/STRAG/LOID
	KAL/KAIN/YO/AS/TRAG/LOID
calcaneocavus	KAL/KAIN/YO/KAI/VUS
calcaneocuboid	KAL/KAIN/YO/KAOU/BOID
	KAL/KAIN/YO/KAOUB/OID
calcaneocuboidea	KAL/KAIN/YO/KAOU/BOID/YA
calcaneodynia	KAL/KAIN/YO/DIN/YA
calcaneocuboideum	KAL/KAIN/YO/KAOU/BOID/YUM
calcaneofibular	KAL/KAIN/YO/FIB/LAR
calcaneonavicular	KAL/KAIN/YO/NA/VIK/LAR
calcaneoplantar	KAL/KAIN/YO/PLAN/TAR
calcaneoscaphoid	KAL/KAIN/YO/SKAF/OID
calcaneotibial	KAL/KAIN/YO/TIB/YAL
calcaneovalgocavus	KAL/KAIN/YO/VAL/GO/KAI/VUS
calcaneovalgus	KAL/KAIN/YO/VAL/GUS
calcaneovarus	KAL/KAIN/YO/VAI/RUS
calcaneum	KAL/KAIN/YUM
calcaneus	KAL/KAIN/YUS
calcar	KAL/KAR
calcarea	KAL/KAIR/YA
calcareous	KAL/KAIR/YOUS
calcarine	KAL/KRAOEN
	KAL/KRIN
	KAL/KA/RAOEN
	KAL/KA/RIN
calcariuria	KAL/KAIR/YAOUR/YA
	KAL/KAR/YAOUR/YA
calcaroid	KAL/KA/ROID
	KAL/KROID
calcemia	KAL/SAOEM/YA
calcemic	KAL/SAOEM/IK
calcergy	KAL/SER/JI
	KALS/ER/JI
calcerosis	KALS/ROE/SIS
Calcet	KAL/SET
Calcet Plus	KAL/SET/PLUS
calcibilia	KALS/BIL/YA
Calcibind	KALS/BAOIND
calcic	KALS/IK
calcicosilicosis	KALS/KO/SIL/KOE/SIS
calcicosis	KALS/KOE/SIS
calcidiol	KALS/DI/OL
Calcidrine	KALS/DRAOEN
Calcidrine Syrup	KALS/DRAOEN/SIR/RUP
calcifames	KAL/SIF/MAOEZ
calcifediol	KAL/SIF/DI/OL
calciferol	KAL/SIF/ROL
calciferous	KAL/SIF/ROUS
calcific	KAL/SIFK
calcificans	KAL/SIF/KANZ
calcification	KALS/FI/KAIGS
calcified	KALS/FI/-D
calcify	KALS/FI
calcifying	KALS/FI/-G
calcigerous	KAL/SIJ/ROUS
calcii	KALS/YAOI
Calcimar	KALS/MAR
calcimeter	KAL/SIM/TER
calcination	KALS/NAIGS
calcine	KAL/SAOEN
	KAL/SIN
calcinosis	KALS/NOE/SIS
calciokinesis	KALS/YO/KI/NAOE/SIS
calciokinetic	KALS/YO/KI/NET/IK
calciol	KALS/YOL
calciorrhachia	KALS/YO/RAIK/YA
calciostat	KALS/YO/STAT
calciotraumatic	KALS/YO/TRAU/MAT/IK
calciotropism	KALS/YOT/RO/PIFM
Calciparine	KAL/SIP/RIN
calcipectic	KALS/PEKT/IK
calcipenia	KALS/PAOEN/YA
calcipenic	KALS/PAOEN/IK
calcipexic	KALS/PEX/IK
calcipexis	KALS/PEK/SIS
calcipexy	KALS/PEK/SI
calciphilia	KALS/FIL/YA

calciphylactic	KALS/FLAKT/IK
calciphylaxis	KALS/FLAK/SIS
calciprivia	KALS/PRIV/YA
calciprivic	KALS/PRIVK
	KALS/PRIV/IK
calcipyelitis	KALS/PAOI/LAOITS
calcis	KAL/SIS
calcite	KAL/SAOIT
calcitetrol	KALS/TET/ROL
calcitonin	KALS/TOE/NIN
calcitriol	KALS/TR*I/OL
	KALS/TRAOI/OL
calcitroic	KALS/TROIK
	KALS/TROE/IK
calcium	KALS/YUM
calciumedetate	KALS/YUM/ED/TAIT
calciuria	KALS/YAOUR/YA
calcodynia	KAL/KO/DIN/YA
calcoglobule	KAL/KO/GLOB/YAOUL
calcoglobulin	KAL/KO/GLOB/LIN
calcophorous	KAL/KOF/ROUS
calcospherite	KAL/KO/SFAOER/AOIT
	KAL/KO/SFAOER/RAOIT
calcspar	KAL/-K/SPAR
calcul-	KAL/KL-
	KAL/KAOU/L-
calculary	KAL/KLAIR
calculi	KAL/KLAOI
calculia	KAL/KAOUL/YA
calculifragous	KAL/KLIF/RA/GOUS
calculogenesis	KAL/KLO/JEN/SIS
calculosis	KAL/KLOE/SIS
calculous	KAL/KLOUS
calculus	KAL/KLUS
Caldani	KAL/DA/NAOE
CaldeCORT	KALD/KORT
	KAL/DE/KORT
Calderol	KALD/ROL
	KAL/DE/ROL
Caldesene	KALD/SAOEN
	KAL/DE/SAOEN
Caldwell	KALD/WEL
Caldwell-Moloy	KALD/WEL/H-F/MO/LOI
calefacient	KAL/FAIRBT
Calel	KAL/LEL
	KA/LEL
Calel-D	KAL/LEL/D-RBGS
	KA/LEL/D-RBGS
calf	KAF
cali-	KAL
caliber	KAL/BER
calibrate	KAL/BRAIT
calibration	KAL/BRAIGS
calibrator	KAL/BRAI/TOR
calic-	KAL/S-
	KAL/K-
caliceal	KAL/SAOEL
calicectasis	KAL/SEKT/SIS
calicectomy	KAL/SEKT/M*I
calices	KAL/SAOEZ
caliciform	KA/LIS/FORM
	KLIS/FORM
calicine	KAL/SAOEN
Caliciviridae	KA/LIS/VIR/DAE
	KLIS/VIR/DAE
Calicivirus	KA/LIS/VAOI/RUS
	KLIS/VAOI/RUS
calico	KAL/KOE
calicoplasty	KAL/KO/PLAS/TI
calicotomy	KAL/KOT/M*I
calicul-	KLIK/L-
	KLIK/YAOU/L-
	KLIK/YU/L-
	KA/LIK/L-
	KA/LIK/YAOU/L-
	KA/LIK/YU/L-
caliculi	KLIK/LAOI
caliculus	KLIK/LUS
calidum	KAL/DUM
caliectasis	KAL/YEKT/SIS
caliectomy	KAL/YEKT/M*I
californium	KAL/FORN/YUM
caligation	KAL/GAIGS
caligo	KA/LAOI/GOE
calioplasty	KAL/YO/PLAS/TI
caliorrhaphy	KAL/YOR/FI
caliotomy	KAL/YOT/M*I
calipers	KAL/PER/-S
calisthenics	KAL/STHEN/IK/-S

	KALS/THEN/IK/-S
calix	KAI/LIX
	KAL/IX
Call	K-P/KAUL
Callander	KAL/LAN/DER
Callaway	KAL/LA/WAI
Calleja	KA/YAI/HA
	KAL/YAI/HA
Call-Exner	K-P/KAUL/H-F/EX/NER
Calliphora	KA/LIF/RA
	KAL/LIF/RA
Calliphoridae	KAL/FOR/DAE
	KAL/FOER/DAE
Callison	KAL/LI/SON
Callitroga	KAL/LI/TROE/GA
	KAL/TROE/GA
callosal	KAL/LOE/SAL
	KA/LOE/SAL
callositas	KA/LOS/TAS
	KAL/LOS/TAS
callosity	KA/LOS/TI
	KAL/LOS/TI
callosomarginal	KA/LOES/MARJ/NAL
	KAL/LOES/MARJ/NAL
callosum	KA/LOES/UM
	KAL/LOES/UM
callous	KAL/OUS
	KAL/LOUS
callus	KAL/LUS
calm	KAUM
calmative	KAUM/TIV
	KAL/MA/TIV
Calmette	KAL/MET
Calmette-Guerin	KAL/MET/H-F/GAI/RAN
calmodulin	KAL/MOD/LIN
calomel	KAL/MEL
calor	KAI/LOR
caloradiance	KAL/RAID/YANS
calorescence	KAL/RES/ENS
Calori	KA/LOR/RAOE
	KA/LOER/RAOE
	KA/LOE/RAOE
caloric	KA/LOR/IK
	KA/LOER/IK
calorica	KA/LOR/KA
	KA/LOER/KA
caloricity	KAL/RIS/TI
caloricum	KA/LOR/KUM
	KA/LOER/KUM
calorie	KAL/RAOE
calorifacient	KA/LOR/FAIRBT
calorific	KAL/RIFK
calorigenetic	KA/LOR/JE/NET/IK
calorigenic	KA/LOR/JEN/IK
	KA/LOER/JEN/IK
	KAL/RI/JEN/IK
calorimeter	KAL/RIM/TER
calorimetric	KA/LOR/MET/RIK
calorimetry	KAL/RIM/TRI
caloripuncture	KAL/RI/PUNG/KHUR
caloriscope	KA/LOR/SKOEP
calorism	KAL/RIFM
	KAIL/RIFM
caloritropic	KA/LOR/TROP/IK
calory	KAL/RI
Calot	KA/LOE
calotte	KA/LOT
Calphosan	KAL/FO/SAN
Cal-Plus	KAL/PLUS
calsequestrin	KAL/SE/KWES/TRIN
	KALS/KWES/TRIN
Caltrate	KAL/TRAIT
calusterone	KAL/YAO*US/ROEN
calutron	KAL/YAOU/TRON
	KAL/YU/TRON
calvacin	KAL/VA/SIN
calvaria	KAL/VAIR/YA
calvariae	KAL/VAIR/YAE
calvarial	KAL/VAIRL
calvarium	KAL/VAIRM
Calvatia	KAL/VAI/SHA
Calve	KAL/VAI
calves	KAV/-S
Calvert	KAL/VERT
Calvin	KAL/VIN
calvities	KAL/VIRB/AOEZ
	KAL/VIRB/SHAOEZ
calx	KAL/-X
calyces	KAL/SAO*EZ

	K*AL/SAOEZ
	(*not* KAL/SAOEZ or KAL/LI/
	SAOEZ; see calices)
calycine	KAL/SAO*EN
calycle	KAL/K-L
Calymmatobacterium	KA/LIM/TO/BAK/TAOERM
	KLIM/TO/BAK/TAOERM
calyx	KAI/L*IX
	KAL/*IX
	(*not* KAI/LIX or KAL/IX; see calix)
Camalox	KAM/LOX
cambendazole	KAM/BEND/ZOEL
cambium	KAM/BUM
	KAM/BAOE/UM
cameloid	KAM/LOID
camelpox	KAM/EL/POX
camera	KAM/RA
camerae	KAM/RAE
Camerer	KAM/RER
Cameroon	KAM/RAON
camerostome	KAM/RO/STOEM
camisole	KAM/SOEL
campanula	KAM/PAN/LA
Campbell	KAM/BEL
	KAFRP/BEL
campesterol	KAM/P*ES/ROL
	KAM/PES/TROL
campestris	KAM/PES/TRIS
camphane	KAM/FAIN
camphene	KAM/FAOEN
camphetamide	KAM/FET/MAOID
camphoglycuronic	KAM/FO/GLAOIK/RON/IK
camphol	KAM/FOL
campholic	KAM/FOL/IK
Campho-Phenique	KAM/FO/FE/NAOEK
camphor	KAM/FOR
camphora	KAM/FOR/RA
	KAM/FOER/RA
camphoraceous	KAM/FRAIRBS
	KAM/FO/RAIRBS
camphorae	KAM/FRAE
	KAM/FOR/RAE
camphorate	KAM/FRAIT
	KAM/FO/RAIT
camphorated	KAM/FRAIT/-D
	KAM/FO/RAIT/-D
camphoric	KAM/FOR/IK
	KAM/FOER/IK
camphorsulfonate	KAM/FOR/SUL/FO/NAIT
camphotamide	KAM/FOT/MAOID
camphramine	KAM/FRA/MAOEN
camphyl	KAM/FIL
campimeter	KAM/PIM/TER
campimetry	KAM/PIM/TRI
campospasm	KAM/PO/SPAFM
campotomy	KAM/POT/M*I
campto-	KAFRPT
	KAMT
	KAFRP/TO
	KAM/TO
camptocormia	KAFRPT/KORM/YA
camptocormy	KAFRPT/KOR/M*I
camptodactylia	KAFRPT/DAK/TIL/YA
camptodactylism	KAFRPT/DAKT/LIFM
camptodactyly	KAFRPT/DAKT/LI
camptomelia	KAFRP/TO/MAOEL/YA
camptomelic	KAFRP/TO/MEL/IK
	KAFRP/TO/MAOEL/IK
camptospasm	KAFRP/TO/SPAFM
Campylobacter	KAFRP/LO/BAK/TER
campylobacteriosis	KAFRP/LO/BAK/TAOER/YOE/SIS
campylodactyly	KAFRP/LO/DAKT/LI
campylognathia	KAFRP/LO/NA*IT/YA
camsylate	KAMS/LAIT
	KAM/SI/LAIT
	KAM/SLAIT
camylofine	KA/MIL/FIN
Canada	KAN/DA
Canada-Cronkhite	KAN/DA/H-F/KRON/KAOIT
Canadian	KA/NAID/YAN
canadine	KAN/DAOEN
canal	KA/NAL
canales	KA/NAI/LAOEZ
canalicul(o)-	KAN/LIK/L(O)
	KAN/LIK/YAOU/L(O)
	KAN/LIK/YU/L(O)
canalicular	KAN/LIK/LAR
canaliculi	KAN/LIK/LAOI
canaliculization	KAN/LIK/LI/ZAIGS

canaliculodacryocystostomy	KAN/LIK/LO/DAK/RO/SIS/TO*S/
	M*I
canaliculorhinostomy	KAN/LIK/LO/RAOI/N*OS/M*I
canaliculus	KAN/LIK/LUS
canaliform	KA/NAL/FORM
canaliformis	KA/NAL/FOR/MIS
canalis	KA/NAI/LIS
canalization	KAN/LI/ZAIGS
	KAN/LAOI/ZAIGS
canaloplasty	KAN/LO/PLAS/TI
Canavalia	KAN/VAIL/YA
canavalin	KAN/VAL/LIN
	KAN/VAI/LIN
canavanase	KAN/AV/NAIS
	KA/NAV/NAIS
canavanine	KAN/AV/NIN
	KA/NAV/NIN
cancell-	KANS/L-
	KANS/EL/L-
	KAN/SEL/L-
cancellated	KANS/LAIT/-D
cancelli	KANS/LAOI
cancellous	KANS/LOUS
cancellus	KANS/LUS
cancer	KANS/ER
	KAN/SER
cancer(o)-	KANS/R(O)
	KAN/SER/R(O)
	KANS/ER/R(O)
canceration	KANS/RAIGS
canceremia	KANS/RAOEM/YA
cancericidal	KANS/RI/SAOI/DAL
cancerigenic	KANS/RI/JEN/IK
cancerin	KANS/RIN
cancerism	KANS/RIFM
cancerocidal	KANS/RO/SAOI/DAL
cancerogenic	KANS/RO/JEN/IK
cancerophobia	KANS/RO/FOEB/YA
cancerous	KANS/ROUS
cancra	KAN/KRA
cancriform	KAN/KRI/FORM
cancroid	KAN/KROID
cancrum	KAN/KRUM
candela	KAND/LA
	KAN/DEL/LA
candi-	KAND/-
	KAN/DI/-
candicans	KAND/KANZ
candicidin	KAND/SAOI/DIN
Candida	KAND/DA
candidal	KAND/DAL
candidemia	KAND/DAOEM/YA
candidiasis	KAND/DAOI/SIS
candidid	KAND/DID
candidin	KAND/DIN
candidosis	KAND/DOE/SIS
candiduria	KAND/DAOUR/YA
candle	KAND/-L
cane	KAIN
canescent	KA/NES/ENT
canicola	KA/NIK/LA
canicularis	KA/NIK/LAI/RIS
Canidae	KAN/DAE
canine	KAI/NAOIN
canini	KAI/NAOI/NAOI
caniniform	KAI/NAOIN/FORM
caninorum	KAIN/NOR/UM
	KAIN/NOER/UM
caninum	KAI/NAOIN/UM
	KAI/NAOI/NUM
caninus	KAI/NAOI/NUS
canis	KAI/NIS
canister	KAN/STER
canities	KA/NIRB/AOEZ
	KA/NI/SHAOEZ
	KA/NIRB/SHAOEZ
canker	KAN/KER
canna	KAN/NA
cannabidiol	KAN/BI/DI/OL
cannabinoid	KA/NAB/NOID
cannabinol	KA/NAB/NOL
cannabis	KAN/BIS
cannabism	KAN/BIFM
cannibal	KAN/BAL
cannibalism	KAN/BAL/IFM
	KAN/BLIFM
Cannizzaro	KAN/ZAR/ROE
	KAN/ZA/ROE
cannon	KAN/NON

Cannon	K-P/KAN/NON	capitis	KAP/TEL/LUM
cannul-	KAN/L-		KAP/TIS
	KAN/YAOU/L-	capitonnage	KAP/TO/NAJ
	KAN/YU/L-		KAP/TON/NAJ
cannula	KAN/LA	capitopedal	KAP/TO/PED/DAL
cannulate	KAN/LAIT	Capitrol	KAP/TROL
cannulation	KAN/LAIGS	Capitrol Shampoo	KAP/TROL/SHAM/PAO
cannulization	KAN/LI/ZAIGS	capitul-	KPIFP/L-
Canomyces	KAIN/MAOI/SAOEZ		KPIFP/YAOU/L-
	KAI/NO/MAOI/SAOEZ		KPIFP/YU/L-
canon	KA/NON		KA/PIFP/L-
canrenoate	KAN/REN/WAIT		KA/PIFP/YAOU/L-
canrenone	KAN/REN/OEN		KA/PIFP/YU/L-
cant	KANT		KA/PIT/L-
Cantelli	KAN/TEL/LAOE		KA/PIT/YAOU/L-
canth(o)-	KA*NT		KA/PIT/YU/L-
	KAN/TH(O)		KA/PIT/KHU/L-
canthal	KAN/THAL	capitula	KPIFP/LA
canthariasis	KA*NT/RAOI/SIS	capitular	KPIFP/LAR
cantharic	KAN/THAR/IK	capituli	KPIFP/LAOI
cantharidal	KAN/THAR/DAL	capitulorum	KPIFP/LOR/UM
cantharidate	KAN/THAR/DAIT		KPIFP/LOER/UM
cantharides	KAN/THAR/DAOEZ	capitulum	KPIFP/LUM
cantharidic	KAN/THAR/DIK	Caplan	KA*P/LAN
cantharidin	KAN/THAR/DIN		(*not* KAP/LAN; see Kaplan)
cantharidis	KAN/THAR/DIS	Caplets	KAP/LET/-S
cantharidism	KAN/THAR/DIFM	-capnia	KAP/NA
Cantharis	KAN/THAR/RIS		KAP/NAOE/YA
Cantharone	KA*NT/ROEN	capno-	KAP/NO
Cantharone Plus	KA*NT/ROEN/PLUS	Capnocytophaga	KAP/NO/SAOI/TOF/GA
canthectomy	KAN/THEKT/M*I	capnogram	KAP/NO/GRAM
canthi	KAN/THAOI	capnograph	KAP/NO/GRAF
canthitis	KAN/THAOITS	capnohepatography	KAP/NO/HEP/TOG/FI
cantholysis	KAN/THOL/SIS	capnophilic	KAP/NO/FIL/IK
canthoplasty	KA*NT/PLAS/TI	capobenate	KAP/BEN/AIT
canthorrhaphy	KAN/THOR/FI	capobenic	KAP/BEN/IK
canthotomy	KAN/THOT/M*I	capon	KAI/PON
canthus	KAN/THUS	caponize	KAI/PON/AOIZ
Cantil	KAN/TIL	capotement	KA/POET/-MT
cantilever	KANT/LAOEVR	Capoten	KAP/TEN
Cantor	K-P/KAN/TOR	Capozide	KAP/ZAOID
cantonensis	KANT/NEN/SIS	capping	KAP/-G
cantus galli	KAN/TUS/GAL/LAOI	Capps	KAPS
cap	KAP	caprate	KAP/RAIT
capacit-	KPAS/T-	capreolary	KAP/RO/LAIR
	KA/PAS/T-		KAP/RAOE/LAIR
capacitance	KPAS/TANS	capreolate	KAP/RO/LAIT
capacitation	KPAS/TAIGS		KAP/RAOE/LAIT
capacitor	KPAS/TOR	capreomycin	KAP/RO/MAOI/SIN
capacity	KPAS/TI		KAP/RAOE/MAOI/SIN
capactin	KAP/AK/TIN	capric	KAP/RIK
Capastat Sulfate	KAP/STAT/SUL/FAIT	caprillic	KA/PRIL/IK
capeline	KAP/LIN	capriloquism	KA/PRIL/KWIFM
capillarectasia	KAP/LAR/EK/TAIZ/YA	caprin	KAP/RIN
	KAP/LAIR/EK/TAIZ/YA	caprine	KAP/RAOEN
Capillaria	KAP/LAIR/YA	caprizant	KAP/RI/ZANT
capillariasis	KAP/LA/RAOI/SIS	caproate	KAP/RO/AIT
capillariomotor	KAP/LAIR/YO/MOE/TOR		KAP/RO/WAIT
capillarioscopy	KAP/LAIR/YOS/KPI	caproic	KA/PROIK
capillaritis	KAP/LA/RAOITS		KA/PROE/IK
	KAP/LAR/AOITS		KAP/ROIK
	KAP/LAIR/AOITS		KAP/ROE/IK
capillarity	KAP/LAIR/TI	caproin	KA/PROIN
	KAP/LAR/TI		KA/PROE/WIN
capillaron	KAP/LA/RON	caproleic	KA/PROEL/YIK
capillaropathy	KAP/LA/ROP/TH*I	caprone	KAP/ROEN
	KAP/LAR/OP/TH*I	caproyl	KAP/ROIL
	KAP/LAIR/OP/TH*I		KAP/ROE/IL
capillaroscopy	KAP/LA/ROS/KPI	caproylamine	KAP/ROIL/AM/MIN
	KAP/LAR/OS/KPI		KAP/RO/IL/AM/MIN
	KAP/LAIR/OS/KPI	caproylate	KAP/ROIL/AIT
capillary	KAP/LAIR		KAP/ROI/LIAT
capilli	KA/PIL/LAOI	caprylate	KAP/RI/LAIT
capillitii	KAP/LIRB/YAOI	caprylic	KAP/RIL/IK
	KAP/LIT/YAOI	caprylin	KAP/RI/LIN
capillitium	KAP/LIRB/UM	capsaicin	KAP/SAI/SIN
	KAP/LIRB/YUM	Capseals	KAP/SAOEL/-S
	KAP/LIT/YUM	capsic	KAPS/IK
capillomotor	KAP/LO/MOE/TOR	capsicin	KAP/SAOI/SIN
capillus	KA/PIL/LUS	capsicum	KAPS/KUM
capistration	KAP/STRAIGS	capsid	KAP/SID
capita	KAP/TA	capsitis	KAP/SAOITS
capital	KAP/TAL	capsomer	KAP/SO/MER
capitata	KAP/TAI/TA	capsomere	KAP/SO/MAOER
capitate	KAP/TAIT	capsotomy	KAP/SOT/M*I
capitation	KAP/TAIGS	capsul(o)-	KAPS/L(O)
capitatum	KAP/TAI/TUM		KAP/SL(O)
	KAP/TAIT/UM		KAP/SAOU/L(O)
capitellum	KAP/TEL/UM	capsula	KAPS/LA

capsulae	KAPS/LAE
capsular	KAPS/LAR
capsulare	KAPS/LAI/RAOE
capsularia	KAPS/LAIR/YA
capsularis	KAPS/LAI/RIS
capsulation	KAPS/LAIGS
capsulatus	KAPS/LAI/TUS
capsule	KAP/SAOUL
capsulectomy	KAPS/LEKT/M*I
capsulitis	KAPS/LAOITS
capsulolenticular	KAPS/LO/LEN/TIK/LAR
capsuloma	KAPS/LOE/MA
capsuloplasty	KAPS/LO/PLAS/TI
capsulorrhaphy	KAPS/LOR/FI
capsulotome	KAPS/LO/TOEM
capsulotomy	KAPS/LOT/M*I
capt(o)-	KAPT
	KAP/TO
captamine	KAPT/MAOEN
captodiame	KAPT/DI/YAM
captodiamine	KAPT/DAOI/MAOEN
captodramin	KAPT/DRAM/AOEN
	KAPT/DRA/MAOEN
captopril	KAPT/PRIL
capture	KAP/KHUR
capuride	KAP/YAOU/RAOID
Capuron	KAP/YAOU/RON
caput	KAP/UT
	KA/PUT
Carabelli	KAR/BEL/LAOE
caramel	KAR/MEL
Carafate	KAR/FAIT
caramiphen	KA/RAM/FEN
Carassini	KAR/SAOE/NAOE
carat	KAR/RAT
caraway	KAIR/WAI
	KAR/RA/WAI
	(not KAR/WAI)
carb(o)-	KARB
	KAR/B(O)
carbachol	KARB/KOL
carbadox	KARB/DOX
carbamate	KARB/MAIT
carbamazepine	KARB/MAZ/PAOEN
	KAR/BAM/AZ/PAOEN
carbamic	KAR/BAM/IK
carbamide	KARB/MAOID
carbaminohemoglobin	KAR/BAM/NO/HAOEM/GLOE/BIN
carbamoate	KARB/MOE/AIT
	KARB/MOE/WAIT
carbamoyl	KARB/MOIL
carbamoylaspartate	KARB/MOIL/AS/PAR/TAIT
carbamoylaspartic	KARB/MOIL/AS/PART/IK
carbamoylation	KARB/MOIL/AIGS
	KARB/MOI/LAIGS
carbamoylcarbamic	KARB/MOIL/KAR/BAM/IK
carbamoylglutamic	KARB/MOIL/GLAOU/TAM/IK
carbamoyltransferase	KARB/MOIL/TRA*NS/FRAIS
carbamyl	KARB/MIL
carbamylcholine	KARB/MIL/KOE/LAOEN
carbamylation	KARB/MIL/AIGS
	KARB/MI/LAIGS
carbanion	KARB/AN/AOIN
	KARB/A*N/AOIN
carbantel	KAR/BAN/TEL
carbaril	KARB/RIL
carbarsone	KAR/BAR/SOEN
carbaspirin	KAR/BAS/PRIN
	KARB/AS/PRIN
carbate	KAR/BAIT
carbazide	KARB/ZAOID
carbazochrome	KAR/BAZ/KROEM
carbazocine	KAR/BAZ/SAOEN
carbazole	KARB/ZOEL
carbazotate	KAR/BAZ/TAIT
carbazotic	KARB/ZOT/IK
carbenicillin	KAR/BEN/SLIN
	KAR/BEN/SIL/LIN
carbenium	KAR/BEN/YUM
carbenoxolone	KAR/BEN/OX/LOEN
carbetapentane	KAR/BAIT/PEN/TAIN
	KAR/BET/PEN/TAIN
carbethyl	KAR/B*ET/IL
	KARB/*ET/IL
carbhemoglobin	KARB/HAOEM/GLOE/BIN
carbide	KAR/BAOID
carbidopa	KARB/DOE/PA
carbimazole	KAR/BAOIM/ZOEL
carbimide	KAR/BI/MAOID

	(not KARB/MAOID)
carbinol	KARB/NOL
carbinoxamine	KAR/BIN/OX/MAOEN
	KARB/NOX/MAOEN
carbo (word)	KAR/BOE
carbo- (prefix)	KARB
	KAR/BO
Carbocaine	KARB/KAIN
carbobenzoxy	KARB/BEN/ZOK/SI
	KARB/BENZ/OK/SI
carbocation	KARB/KAT/AOIN
carbocholine	KARB/KOE/LAOEN
carbochromene	KARB/KROE/MAOEN
carbocyclic	KARB/SAOIK/LIK
carbocysteine	KARB/SIS/TAOEN
	KARB/SIS/TAOE/YIN
	KARB/S*IS/YIN
carbodiimide	KARB/DI/IM/ID
carbogaseous	KARB/GAS/YOUS
carbogen	KARB/JEN
carbohemia	KARB/HAOEM/YA
carbohemoglobin	KAR/BO/HAOEM/GLOE/BIN
	(not KARB/HAOEM/GLOE/BIN; see
	carbhemoglobin)
carbohydrase	KARB/HAOI/DRAIS
carbohydrate	KARB/HAOI/DRAIT
carbohydraturia	KARB/HAOI/DRA/TAOUR/YA
carbohydrazide	KARB/HAOI/DRA/ZAOID
carbohydrogenic	KARB/HAOI/DRO/JEN/IK
carbolate	KARB/LAIT
carbolated	KARB/LAIT/-D
carbol-fuchsin	KAR/BOL/FUK/SIN
	KAR/BOL/FAOUK/SIN
carboligase	KARB/LAOI/GAIS
carbol-gentian	KAR/BOL/JENGS
carbolic	KAR/BOL/IK
carbolism	KARB/LIFM
carbolize	KARB/LAOIZ
carboluria	KARB/LAOUR/YA
carbolxylene	KAR/BOL/ZAOI/LAOEN
carbomer	KARB/MER
carbometry	KAR/BOM/TRI
carbomycin	KARB/MAOI/SIN
carbon	KAR/BON
carbonate	KARB/NAIT
	KARB/NAT
carbon dioxide	KAR/BON/DI/OK/SAOID
carbonemia	KARB/NAOEM/YA
carbonic	KAR/BON/IK
carbonium	KAR/BOEN/YUM
carbonize	KARB/NAOIZ
carbonometer	KARB/NOM/TER
carbonometry	KARB/NOM/TRI
carbonuria	KARB/NAOUR/YA
carbonyl	KARB/NIL
carbophilic	KARB/FIL/IK
carboprost	KARB/PRO*S
carborundum	KARB/RUN/DUM
carboxamide	KAR/BOX/MAOID
	KAR/BOX/AM/AOID
carboxy-	KAR/BOX
	KAR/BOK/SI
carboxyanhydride	KAR/BOX/AN/HAOI/DRAOID
carboxycathepsin	KAR/BOX/KA/THEP/SIN
carboxydismutase	KAR/BOX/DIS/MAOU/TAIS
Carboxydomonas	KAR/BOX/DO/MOE/NAS
carboxyglutamate	KAR/BOX/GLAOUT/MAIT
carboxyglutamic	KAR/BOX/GLAOU/TAM/IK
carboxyhemoglobin	KAR/BOX/HAOEM/GLOE/BIN
carboxyhemoglobinemia	KAR/BOX/HAOEM/GLOEB/
	NAOEM/YA
carboxyl	KAR/BOK/SIL
	KAR/BOX/IL
carboxylase	KAR/BOX/LAIS
carboxylation	KAR/BOX/LAIGS
carboxylesterase	KAR/BOK/SIL/ES/TRAIS
	KAR/BOK/SIL/*ES/RAIS
carboxylic	KAR/BOK/SIL/IK
carboxyltransferase	KAR/BOK/SIL/TRA*NS/FRAIS
	KAR/BOK/SIL/TRA*NS/FER/AIS
carboxy-lyase	KAR/BOX/LAOI/AIS
	KAR/BOX/LAOI/YAIS
carboxymethylcellulose	KAR/BOX/M*ET/IL/SEL/YAOU/
	LOES
carboxymyoglobin	KAR/BOX/MAOI/GLOE/BIN
carboxypeptidase	KAR/BOX/PEPT/DAIS
carboxypolypeptidase	KAR/BOX/POL/PEPT/DAIS
carboxyurea	KAR/BOX/YAOU/RAOE/YA
carbromal	KAR/BROE/MAL

carbuncle	KAR/BUN/K-L	cardiodilator	KARD/YO/DI/LAI/TOR
	KAR/BUNG/-L	cardiodiosis	KARD/YO/DAOI/SIS
carbuncul-	KAR/BUN/KL-		KARD/YO/DI/YOE/SIS
	KAR/BUNG/L-	cardiodynamics	KARD/YO/DAOI/NAM/IK/-S
	KAR/BUN/KAOU/L-	cardiodynia	KARD/YO/DIN/YA
	KAR/BUNG/YAOU/L-	cardioesophageal	KARD/YO/E/SOF/JAOEL
	KAR/BUN/YU/L-	cardiogenesis	KARD/YO/JEN/SIS
carbuncular	KAR/BUN/KLAR	cardiogenic	KARD/YO/JEN/IK
carbunculoid	KAR/BUN/KLOID	cardiogram	KARD/YO/GRAM
carbunculosis	KAR/BUN/KLOE/SIS	cardiograph	KARD/YO/GRAF
carbutamide	KAR/BAOUT/MAOID	cardiographic	KARD/YO/GRAFK
carbuterol	KAR/BAOUT/ROL	cardiography	KARD/YOG/FI
carcass	KAR/KASZ	cardiohemothrombus	KARD/YO/HAOEM/THROM/BUS
carcin(o)-	KARS/N(O)	cardiohepatic	KARD/YO/HE/PAT/IK
	KAR/SIN	cardiohepatomegaly	KARD/YO/HEPT/MEG/LI
carcinectomy	KARS/NEKT/M*I	cardioid	KARD/YOID
carcinemia	KARS/NAOEM/YA	cardioinhibitor	KARD/YO/IN/HIB/TOR
carcinoembryonic	KARS/NO/EM/BRON/IK	cardioinhibitory	KARD/YO/IN/HIB/TOIR
	KARS/NO/EM/BRAOE/YON/IK	cardiokinetic	KARD/YO/KI/NET/IK
carcinogen	KAR/SIN/JEN	cardiokymogram	KARD/YO/KAOIM/GRAM
	KARS/NO/JEN	cardiokymographic	KARD/YO/KAOIM/GRAFK
carcinogenesis	KARS/NO/JEN/SIS	cardiokymography	KARD/YO/KAOI/MOG/FI
carcinogenic	KARS/NO/JEN/IK	cardiolipin	KARD/YO/LIP/PIN
carcinogenicity	KARS/NO/JE/NIS/TI	cardiolith	KARD/YO/L*IT
carcinoid	KARS/NOID	cardiologist	KARD/YO*LGS
carcinolysis	KARS/NOL/SIS	cardiology	KARD/YOLG
carcinolytic	KARS/NO/LIT/IK	cardiolysin	KARD/YOL/SIN
carcinoma	KARS/NOE/MA	cardiolysis	KARD/YOL/SIS
carcinomata	KARS/NOEM/TA	cardiomalacia	KARD/YO/MA/LAI/SHA
carcinomatoid	KARS/NOEM/TOID	cardiomegalia	KARD/YO/ME/GAIL/YA
carcinomatophobia	KARS/NOEM/TO/FOEB/YA	cardiomegaly	KARD/YO/MEG/LI
carcinomatosis	KARS/NOEM/TOE/SIS	cardiomelanosis	KARD/YO/MEL/NOE/SIS
carcinomatous	KARS/NOEM/TOUS	cardiometer	KARD/YOM/TER
carcinomectomy	KARS/NO/MEKT/M*I	cardiometry	KARD/YOM/TRI
carcinophilia	KARS/NO/FIL/YA	cardiomotility	KARD/YO/MOE/TIL/TI
carcinophilic	KARS/NO/FIL/IK	cardiomotor	KARD/YO/MOE/TOR
carcinophobia	KARS/NO/FOEB/YA	cardiomuscular	KARD/YO/MUS/KLAR
	KAR/SIN/FOEB/YA	cardiomyoliposis	KARD/YO/MAOI/LI/POE/SIS
carcinosarcoma	KARS/NO/SAR/KOE/MA	cardiomyopathy	KARD/YO/MAOI/OP/TH*I
carcinosis	KARS/NOE/SIS		KARD/YOMAOI/YOP/TH*I
carcinostatic	KARS/NO/STAT/IK	cardiomyopexy	KARD/YO/MAOI/PEK/SI
carcinous	KARS/NOUS	cardiomyotomy	KARD/YO/MAOI/OT/M*I
Cardarelli	KARD/REL/LAOE		KARD/YO/MAOI/YOT/M*I
Carden	KARD/-N	cardionecrosis	KARD/YO/NE/KROE/SIS
	KAR/DEN	cardionector	KARD/YO/NEK/TOR
cardi(o)-	KARD/Y(O)	cardionephric	KARD/YO/NEF/RIK
cardia	KARD/YA	cardioneural	KARD/YO/NAOURL
cardiac	KARD/YAK	cardioneurosis	KARD/YO/NAOU/ROE/SIS
cardiac ballet	KARD/YAK/BAL/LAI	cardio-omentopexy	KARD/YO/OEMT/PEK/SI
cardiaci	KAR/DAOI/SAOI	cardiopaludism	KARD/YO/PAL/DIFM
	KAR/DAOI/KAOI	cardiopath	KARD/YO/PA*T
cardiacum	KAR/DAOI/KUM	cardiopathia	KARD/YO/PA*T/YA
cardiacus	KAR/DAOI/KUS	cardiopathia nigra	KARD/YO/PA*T/YA/NAOI/GRA
cardial	KARD/YAL	cardiopathic	KARD/YO/PA*T/IK
cardialgia	KARD/YAL/JA	cardiopathy	KARD/YOP/TH*I
	KARD/AL/JA	cardiopericardiopexy	KARD/YO/P*ER/KARD/YO/PEK/SI
cardiant	KARD/YANT	cardiopericarditis	KARD/YO/P*ER/KAR/DAOITS
cardiasthenia	KARD/YAS/THAOEN/YA	cardiophobia	KARD/YO/FOEB/YA
	KARD/AS/THAOEN/YA	cardiophone	KARD/YO/FOEN
cardiataxia	KARD/YA/TAX/YA	cardiophony	KARD/YOF/N*I
cardiatelia	KARD/YA/LAOEL/YA	cardiophrenia	KARD/YO/FRAOEN/YA
cardiectasia	KARD/YEK/TAIZ/YA	cardiophrenic	KARD/YO/FREN/IK
cardiectasis	KARD/YEKT/SIS	cardioplasty	KARD/YO/PLAS/TI
cardiectomized	KARD/YEKT/MAOIZ/-D	cardioplegia	KARD/YO/PLAOE/JA
cardiectomy	KARD/YEKT/M*I	cardioplegic	KARD/YO/PLAOEJ/IK
cardiectopia	KARD/YEK/TOEP/YA	cardiopneumatic	KARD/YO/NAOU/MAT/IK
Cardilate	KARD/LAIT	cardiopneumograph	KARD/YO/NAOUM/GRAF
Cardilate Tablets	KARD/LAIT/TAB/LET/-S	cardiopneumonopexy	KARD/YO/NAOUM/NO/PEK/SI
cardinal	KARD/NAL	cardioptosia	KARD/YO/TOEZ/YA
cardinalis	KARD/NAI/LIS		KARD/YOP/TOEZ/YA
carding	KARD/-G	cardioptosis	KARD/YOP/TOE/SIS
cardioaccelerating	KARD/YO/AK/SEL/RAIT/-G		KARD/YOP/TOE/SIS
cardioaccelerator	KARD/YO/AK/SEL/RAI/TOR	cardiopulmonary	KARD/YO/PUL/MO/NAIR
cardioactive	KARD/YO/AK/TIV		KARD/YO/PUM/NAIR
cardioangiography	KARD/YO/AN/JOG/FI	cardiopuncture	KARD/YO/PUNG/KHUR
cardioangiology	KARD/YO/AN/JOLG	cardiopyloric	KARD/YO/PAOI/LOR/IK
cardioaortic	KARD/YO/AI/ORT/IK	Cardioquin	KARD/YO/KWIN
	KARD/YO/AI/YORT/IK	cardiorenal	KARD/YO/RAOENL
cardioarterial	KARD/YO/AR/TAOERL	cardiorrhaphy	KARD/YOR/FI
	KARD/YO/AR/TAOER/YAL	cardiorrhexis	KARD/YO/REK/SIS
cardiocairograph	KARD/YO/KAOIR/GRAF	cardioschisis	KARD/YOS/KI/SIS
cardiocele	KARD/YO/SAO*EL	cardiosclerosis	KARD/YO/SKLE/ROE/SIS
cardiocentesis	KARD/YO/SEN/TAOE/SIS	cardioscope	KARD/YO/SKOEP
cardiochalasia	KARD/YO/KA/LAIS/YA	cardioselective	KARD/YO/SLEKT/IV
	KARD/YO/KA/LAIZ/YA	cardioselectivity	KARD/YO/SLEK/TIV/TI
cardiocirculatory	KARD/YO/SIRK/LA/TOIR	cardiospasm	KARD/YO/SPAFM
cardiocirrhosis	KARD/YO/SI/ROE/SIS	cardiosphygmogram	KARD/YO/SFIG/MO/GRAM
cardioclasia	KARD/YO/KLAIZ/YA	cardiosphygmograph	KARD/YO/SFIG/MO/GRAF
cardiodiaphragmatic	KARD/YO/DAOI/FRAG/MAT/IK	cardiosplenopexy	KARD/YO/SPLEN/PEK/SI

	KARD/YO/SPLAOEN/PEK/SI	Carnivora	KAR/NIV/RA
cardiotachometer	KARD/YO/TA/KOM/TER	carnivore	KARN/VOR
cardiotachometry	KARD/YO/TA/KOM/TRI		KARN/VOER
cardiotherapy	KARD/YO/THER/PI	carnivorous	KAR/NIV/ROUS
cardiothrombus	KARD/YO/THROM/BUS	carno-	KARN
cardiothyrotoxicosis	KARD/YO/THAOIR/TOX/KOE/SIS		KAR/NO
cardiotocograph	KARD/YO/TOEK/GRAF	carnosine	KARN/SAOEN
cardiotocography	KARD/YO/TOE/KOG/FI		KARN/SIN
cardiotomy	KARD/YOT/M*I	carnosinemia	KARN/SI/NAOEM/YA
cardiotonic	KARD/YO/TON/IK	carnosinuria	KARN/SI/NAOUR/YA
cardiotopometry	KARD/YO/TOE/POM/TRI	carnosity	KAR/NOS/TI
cardiotoxic	KARD/YO/TOX/IK	caro	KAI/ROE
cardiotuberculous	KARD/YO/TAOU/BERK/LOUS	carolinianus	KAR/LIN/YAI/NUS
cardiovalvotomy	KARD/YO/VAL/VOT/M*I		KAR/LAOIN/YAI/NUS
cardiovalvular	KARD/YO/VAL/VAOU/LAR	carotenase	KAR/TEN/AIS
cardiovalvulitis	KARD/YO/VAL/VAOU/LAOITS		KA/ROT/NAIS
cardiovalvulotome	KARD/YO/VAL/VAOUL/TOEM		KAR/OT/NAIS
	KARD/YO/VAL/VAOU/LO/TOEM	carotene	KAR/TAOEN
cardiovalvulotomy	KARD/YO/VAL/VAOU/LOT/M*I		KAIR/TAOEN
cardiovascular	KARD/YO/VAS/KLAR	carotenemia	KAR/TE/NAOEM/YA
cardiovasculorenal	KARD/YO/VAS/KLO/RAOENL		KAR/TEN/AOEM/YA
cardiovasology	KARD/YO/VAS/OLG		KAR/TAOE/NAOEM/YA
cardioversion	KARD/YO/VERGS	carotenodermia	KROT/NO/DERM/YA
cardioverter	KARD/YO/VERT/ER		KA/ROT/NO/DERM/YA
carditis	KAR/DAOITS	carotenoid	KA/ROT/NOID
cardium	KARD/YUM	carotenosis	KAR/TE/NOE/SIS
cardius	KARD/YUS		KAR/TAOE/NOE/SIS
Cardizem	KARD/ZEM	carotic	KA/ROT/IK
care	KAIR		(*not* KROT/IK; see -crotic)
carebaria	KAR/BAIR/YA	carotici	KA/ROT/SAOI
carfentanil	KAR/FENT/NIL	caroticotympanic	KA/ROT/KO/TIM/PAN/IK
caribi	KA/RAOE/BAOE		KROT/KO/TIM/PAN/IK
carica	KAR/KA	caroticotympanici	KA/ROT/KO/TIM/PAN/SAOI
caricous	KAR/KOUS		KROT/KO/TIM/PAN/SAOI
caries	KAIR/RAOEZ	caroticotympanicus	KA/ROT/KO/TIM/PAN/KUS
	(*not* KAIR/RI/-S; see carries)		KROT/KO/TIM/PAN/KUS
carina	KA/RAOI/NA	caroticus	KA/ROT/KUS
carinae	KA/RAOI/NAE		KROT/KUS
carinate	KAR/NAIT	carotid	KA/ROT/ID
	KAR/RI/NAIT		KROT/ID
carination	KAIR/NAIGS	carotin	KAR/TIN
	KAR/RI/NAIGS	carotis	KA/ROT/TIS
	(not KAR/NAIGS; see carnation)		KROT/TIS
cariniform	KA/RIN/FORM	carotodynia	KA/ROT/DIN/YA
carinii	KA/RIN/YAOI		KROT/DIN/YA
cario-	KAIR/YO	caroxazone	KA/ROX/ZOEN
cariogenesis	KAIR/YO/JEN/SIS	carp	KARP
cariogenic	KAIR/YO/JEN/IK	carp(o)-	KARP
cariogenicity	KAIR/YO/JE/NIS/TI		KAR/P(O)
cariology	KAIR/YOLG	carpal	KAR/PAL
	(not KAR/YOLG; see karyology)	carpale	KAR/PAI/LAOE
cariosity	KAIR/YOS/TI	carpea	KARP/YA
cariostatic	KAIR/YO/STAT/IK	carpectomy	KAR/PEKT/M*I
carious	KAIR/YOUS	Carpenter	K-P/KAR/PEN/TER
carisoprodate	KAR/SO/PRO/DAIT		K-P/KARP/EN/TER
carisoprodol	KAR/SO/PRO/DOL	carpeum	KARP/YUM
carissin	KA/RIS/SIN	carphenazine	KAR/FEN/ZAOEN
Carlen	KAR/LEN	carphologia	KAR/FO/LOE/JA
	KARL/-N	carphology	KAR/FOLG
Carlton	KARL/TON	carpi	KAR/PAOI
carmalum	KAR/MAL/UM	carpitis	KAR/PAOITS
carmantadine	KAR/MANT/DAOEN	carpocarpal	KARP/KAR/PAL
Carmichael	KAR/MAOI/KAL	Carpoglyphus	KARP/GLAOI/FUS
	KAR/MAOI/KEL	Carpoglyptus	KARP/GLIP/TUS
	KAR/MAOIK/EL	carpometacarpal	KARP/MET/KAR/PAL
carminate	KARM/NAIT	carpometacarpeae	KARP/MET/KARP/YAE
carminative	KAR/MIN/TIV	carpopedal	KARP/PAOE/DAL
carmine	KAR/MIN		KARP/PED/DAL
	KAR/MAOEN	carpophalangeal	KARP/FLAN/JAL
carminic	KAR/MIN/IK	carpoptosia	KAR/POP/TOEZ/YA
carminophil	KAR/MIN/FIL	carpoptosis	KAR/POP/TOE/SIS
carminophile	KAR/MIN/FAOIL	carprofen	KAR/PRO/FEN
carminophilous	KARM/NOF/LOUS	carpus	KAR/PUS
Carmody	KARM/DI	Carr	KA*R
Carmol	KAR/MOL	Carrel	KAR/REL
carmustine	KAR/MUS/TAOEN	carrier	KAIR/YER
carnassial	KAR/NAS/YAL	carrion	KAIR/YON
carnaubic	KAR/NAUB/IK	Carrion	K-P/KAIR/YON
carnaubyl	KAR/NAU/BIL	carrot	KAR/ROT
carneae	KARN/YAE	carrying	KAIR/RI/-G
carneous	KARN/YOUS	cart	KART
carnes	KAR/NAOEZ	cartazolate	KAR/TAZ/LAIT
carnidazole	KAR/NID/ZOEL	carteolol	KART/YO/LOEL
carnification	KARN/FI/KAIGS		KART/YO/LOL
carniform	KARN/FORM	Carter	KART/ER
carnis	KAR/NIS	carteri	KART/RAOI
carnitine	KARN/TAOEN		KAR/TER/RAOI
	KARN/TIN	cartesian	KAR/TAOEGS
Carnitor	KARN/TOR	carthamic	KAR/THAM/IK

carthamus	KA*RT/MUS	catabasial	KAT/BAIS/YAL
	KAR/THA/MUS		KAT/BAIZ/YAL
cartilage	KART/LAJ	catabasis	KA/TAB/SIS
cartilagin	KART/LA/JIN	catabatic	KAT/BAT/IK
cartilaginea	KART/LA/JIN/YA	catabiosis	KAT/BAO*I/YOE/SIS
cartilagines	KART/LAJ/NAOEZ	catabiotic	KAT/BAO*I/OT/IK
cartilaginification	KART/LA/JIN/FI/KAIGS	catabolergy	KAT/BOL/ER/JI
cartilaginiform	KART/LA/JIN/FORM	catabolic	KAT/BOL/IK
cartilaginis	KART/LAJ/NIS	catabolism	KA/TAB/LIFM
cartilaginoid	KART/LAJ/NOID	catabolite	KA/TAB/LAOIT
cartilaginous	KART/LAJ/NOUS	catabolize	KA/TAB/LAOIZ
cartilago	KART/LAI/GOE	catachronobiology	KAT/KROEN/BAO*I/OLG
cartilagotropic	KART/LAG/TROP/IK	catacrotic	KAT/KROT/IK
Cartwright	KART/RAOIGT	catacrotism	KA/TAK/RO/TIFM
	KART/WRAOIGT	catadicrotic	KAT/DI/KROT/IK
carubinose	KA/RAOUB/NOES	catadicrotism	KAT/DI/KRO/TIFM
caruncle	KAR/UN/K-L	catadidymus	KAT/DID/MUS
	KAR/UNG/-L	catadioptric	KAT/DI/OP/TRIK
caruncul-	KA/RUN/KL-		KAT/DI/OPT/RIK
	KA/RUNG/L-	catagen	KAT/JEN
	KA/RUN/KAOU/L-	catagenesis	KAT/JEN/SIS
	KA/RUNG/YAOU/L-	catagenetic	KAT/JE/NET/IK
	KA/RUNG/YU/L-	catagmatic	KAT/AG/MAT/IK
caruncula	KA/RUN/KLA	catalase	KAT/LAIS
carunculae	KA/RUN/KLAE	catalasea	KAT/LAIS/YA
Carus	KAR/RUS	catalatic	KAT/LAT/IK
	KA/RUS	catalepsy	KAT/LEP/SI
carvacrol	KAFRB/KROL	cataleptic	KAT/LEPT/IK
	KAR/VA/KROL	cataleptiform	KAT/LEPT/FORM
carver	KAFRB/ER	cataleptoid	KAT/LEP/TOID
	KAR/VER	catalogia	KAT/LOE/JA
carzenide	KARZ/NAOID	catalysis	KA/TAL/SIS
Casal	KA/SAL	catalyst	KAT/L*IS
casamino	KAS/MAOE/NOE	catalytic	KAT/LIT/IK
	KAS/AI/MAOE/NOE	catalyze	KAT/LAOIZ
cascade	KAS/KAID	catalyzer	KAT/LAOIZ/ER
cascara	KAS/KAR/RA	catamenia	KAT/MAOEN/YA
	KAS/KAI/RA	catamenial	KAT/MAOEN/YAL
case	KAIS	catamenogenic	KAT/MEN/JEN/IK
casease	KAIS/YAIS	catamite	KAT/MAOIT
caseation	KAIS/YAIGS	catamnesis	KAT/AM/NAOE/SIS
casebook	KAIS/BAOK	catamnestic	KAT/AM/N*ES/IK
casei	KAIS/YAOI	catapasm	KAT/PAFM
casein	KAIS/YIN	cataphasia	KAT/FAIZ/YA
	KAI/SAOEN	cataphora	KA/TAF/RA
caseinate	KAIS/YIN/AIT	cataphoresis	KAT/FRAOE/SIS
	KAIS/YI/NAIT	cataphoretic	KAT/FRET/IK
	KAI/SAOE/NAIT	cataphoria	KAT/FOER/YA
caseinogen	KAIS/YIN/JEN	cataphoric	KAT/FOER/IK
caseinogenate	KAIS/YIN/JE/NAIT	cataphrenia	KAT/FRAOEN/YA
caseogenous	KAIS/YOJ/NOUS	cataphylaxis	KAT/FLAK/SIS
caseo-iodine	KAIS/YO/AOI/DAOIN	cataplasia	KAT/PLAIZ/YA
caseose	KAIS/YOES	cataplasis	KA/TAP/LA/SIS
caseoserum	KAIS/YO/SAOERM		KAT/AP/LA/SIS
caseous	KAIS/YOUS		KAT/PLAI/SIS
caseum	KAIS/YUM	cataplasm	KAT/PLAFM
caseworm	KAIS/WORM	cataplasma	KAT/PLAZ/MA
Casoni	KA/SOE/NAOE	cataplectic	KAT/PLEKT/IK
Casselberry	KAS/EL/BER/RI	cataplexy	KAT/PLEK/SI
	KAS/SEL/BER/RI	catapophysis	KAT/POF/SIS
Casser	KAS/SER	Catapres	KAT/PRES
	KASZ/ER	Catapres-TTS	KAT/PRES/T-RBGS/T*RBGS/
casserian	KA/SAOERN		S*RBGS
	KAS/SAOERN	cataract	KAT/RAKT
cassette	KA/SET	cataracta	KAT/RAK/TA
	KAS/SET	cataractogenesis	KAT/RAKT/JEN/SIS
Cassia	KAS/YA	cataractogenic	KAT/RAKT/JEN/IK
	KASZ/YA	cataractopiesis	KAT/RAKT/PAOI/E/SIS
cast	KA*S		KAT/RAKT/PAOI/SIS
cast brace	KA*S/BRAIS	cataractous	KAT/RAK/TOUS
castellani	KA*S/LAI/NAOI		KAT/RAKT/OUS
	KA*S/LAN/NAOI	cataria	KA/TAIR/YA
	KAS/TEL/LAI/NAOI	catarrh	KA/TAR
	KAS/TEL/LAN/NAOI	catarrhal	KA/TARL
Castellani	KA*S/LAN/NAOE	catarrhalis	KAT/RAI/LIS
	KA*S/LA/NAOE	Catarrhina	KAT/RAOI/NA
casting	KA*S/-G	catarrhine	KAT/RAOIN
Castle	K-P/KAS/-L	catastalsis	KAT/STAL/SIS
castor	KAS/TOR	catastaltic	KAT/STALT/IK
castrate	KAS/TRAIT	catastasis	KA/TA*S/SIS
castration	KAS/TRAIGS	catastate	KAT/STAIT
castroid	KAS/TROID	catastatic	KAT/STAT/IK
Castroviejo	KAS/TRO/VAI/HOE	catastrophic	KAT/STROFK
	KAS/TRO/VAOE/YAI/HOE	catatasis	KA/TAT/SIS
casual	KARBL	catatonia	KAT/TOEN/YA
casualty	KARBL/TI	catatoniac	KAT/TOEN/YAK
cat	KAT	catatonic	KAT/TON/IK
cata-	KAT	catatrichy	KAT/TRI/KI
	KA/TA		KAT/TRIK/KI

catatricrotic	KAT/TR*I/KROT/IK	cauliflower	KAUL/FLOU/ER
catatricrotism	KAT/TR*I/KRO/TIFM	caumesthesia	KAU/MES/THAOEZ/YA
catatropia	KAT/TROEP/YA		KAUM/ES/THAOEZ/YA
catechase	KAT/KAIS	causal	KAU/ZAL
catechin	KAT/KIN		KAUZ/ZAL
catechinic	KAT/KIN/IK	causalgia	KAUZ/AL/JA
catechol	KAT/KOL		KAU/ZAL/JA
catecholamine	KAT/KOL/MAOEN	causative	KAUZ/TIV
	KAT/KOEL/MAOEN	cause	KAUZ
catecholaminergic	KAT/KOL/AM/NERJ/IK	caustic	KA*US/IK
catechu	KAT/KAOU	causticize	KA*US/SAOIZ
catechuic	KAT/KAOU/IK	cauterant	KAUT/RANT
catelectrotonus	KAT/LEK/TROT/NUS	cauterization	KAUT/RI/ZAIGS
Catenabacterium	KAT/NA/BAK/TAOERM		KAUT/RAOI/ZAIGS
	KAT/NA/BAK/TAOER/YUM	cauterize	KAUT/RAOIZ
catenate	KAT/NAIT	cautery	KAUT/RI
catenating	KAT/NAIT/-G	cava	KAI/VA
catenoid	KAT/NOID	cavae	KAI/VAE
catenulate	KA/TEN/LAIT	caval	KAIVL
	KA/TEN/YAOU/LAIT		KAI/VAL
	KA/TEN/YU/LAIT	cavalry	KAVL/RI
caterpillar	KAT/PIL/LAR	cavascope	KAV/SKOEP
	KAT/ER/PIL/LAR	cave	KAIV
catgut	KAT/GUT	caveola	KAIV/YOE/LA
catharsis	KA/THAR/SIS		KAV/YOE/LA
cathartic	KA/THART/IK	caveolae	KAIV/YOE/LAE
cathectic	KA/THEKT/IK		KAV/YOE/LAE
cathemoglobin	KA/THAOEM/GLOE/BIN	caveolated	KAV/YO/LAIT/-D
	KAT/HAOEM/GLOE/BIN		KAIV/YO/LAIT/-D
cathepsin	KA/THEP/SIN	cavern	KAVRN
catheptic	KA/THEPT/IK		KAV/ERN
catheresis	KA/THAOER/SIS	cavern-	KAVR/N-
catheretic	KA*T/RET/IK		KAV/ER/N-
catheter	KA*T/TER		KAI/VER/N-
catheterization	KA*T/TER/ZAIGS	caverna	KA/VER/NA
catheterize	KA*T/TRAOIZ		KAI/VER/NA
	KA*T/TER/AOIZ	cavernae	KA/VER/NAE
catheterism	KA*T/TRIFM		KAI/VER/NAE
	KA*T/TER/IFM	caverniloquy	KAVR/NIL/KWI
catheterostat	KA*T/TER/STAT	cavernitis	KAVR/NAOITS
cathetometer	KA*T/TOM/TER	cavernoma	KAVR/NOE/MA
cathexis	KA/THEK/SIS	cavernosa	KAVR/NOE/SA
cathodal	KA*T/DAL	cavernosae	KAVR/NOE/SAE
	KA/THOE/DAL	cavernoscope	KAVR/NO/SKOEP
	KA*T/OED/DAL	cavernoscopy	KAVR/NOS/KPI
cathode	KA*T/OED	cavernosi	KAVR/NOE/SAOI
	KA/THOED	cavernositis	KAVR/NO/SAOITS
cathodic	KA/THOD/IK	cavernosorum	KAVR/NO/SOR/UM
catholysis	KA/THOL/SIS		KAVR/NO/SOER/UM
	KA*T/OL/SIS	cavernostomy	KAVR/NO*S/M*I
catholyte	KA*T/LAOIT	cavernosum	KAVR/NOE/SUM
cati	KAI/TAOI		KAVR/NOES/UM
cation	KAT/AOIN	cavernosus	KAVR/NOE/SUS
cationic	KAT/AOIN/IK	cavernous	KAVR/NOUS
	KAT/AOI/ON/IK		KAVRN/OUS
	KAT/YON/IK	cavi	KAI/VAOI
cationogen	KAT/AOIN/JEN	caviae	KAIV/YAE
	KAT/YON/JEN	cavicola	KA/VIK/LA
	KAT/AOI/ON/JEN	cavilla	KA/VIL/LA
catlin	KAT/LIN	cavita	KAV/TA
catling	KAT/-LG	cavitary	KAV/TAIR
	KAT/LING	cavitas	KAV/TAS
catochus	KAT/KUS	cavitates	KAV/TAI/TAOEZ
catoptric	KA/TOPT/RIK	cavitation	KAV/TAIGS
	KA/TOP/TRIK	cavitis	KAI/VAOITS
catoptroscope	KA/TOP/TRO/SKOEP	cavity	KAV/TI
CAT scan	KAT/SKAN	cavogram	KAIV/GRAM
	KA*T/SKAN	cavography	KAI/VOG/FI
Caucasian	KAU/KAIGS	cavosurface	KAIV/SUR/FAS
caucasica	KAU/KAS/KA	cavovalgus	KAIV/VAL/GUS
cauda	KAU/DA	cavum	KAIV/UM
caudad	KAU/DAD		KAI/VUM
caudae	KAU/DAE	cavus	KAI/VUS
cauda equina	KAU/DA/E/KWAOI/NA		KA/VUS
caudal	KAU/DAL	Cazenave	KAZ/NAUV
caudale	KAU/DAI/LAOE	CBC	KR-RBGS/B*RBGS/KR*RBGS
caudalis	KAU/DAI/LIS	cc	KR*K
caudalizing	KAUD/LAOIZ/-G	ce- (long e)	SE-
caudalward	KAU/DAL/WARD		(not SAOE; see "see")
caudate	KAU/DAIT	ceasmic	SE/AS/MIK
caudati	KAU/DAI/TAOI	cebocephalus	SAOEB/SEF/LUS
caudatolenticular	KAU/DAI/TO/LEN/TIK/LAR		SE/BO/SEF/LUS
caudatum	KAU/TAI/TUM	cebocephaly	SAOEB/SEF/LI
caudatus	KAU/DAI/TUS		SE/BO/SEF/LI
caudectomy	KAU/DEKT/M*I	cec(o)-	SAOEK
caudocephalad	KAU/DO/SEF/LAD		SE/K(O)
caudolenticular	KAU/DO/LEN/TIK/LAR		SE/S(O)
caul	KA*UL	ceca	SE/KA
	(not KAUL; see call)	cecal	SE/KAL

cecalis	SE/KAI/LIS	cell(o)-	(*not* SEL or S*EL; see sell and cel)
cecectomy	SE/SEKT/M*I		SEL (except where noted)
cecitis	SE/SAOITS		SEL/L(O)
Ceclor	SE/KLOR		KREL/L(O)
cecocele	SAOEK/SAO*EL	cella	KREL/LA
cecocolic	SAOEK/KOL/IK		S*EL/LA
cecocolon	SAOEK/KO/LON		(*not* SEL/LA; see sella)
cecocolopexy	SAOEK/KOEL/PEK/SI	cellae	KREL/LAE
cecocolostomy	SAOEK/KO/LO*S/M*I		S*EL/LAE
cecofixation	SAOEK/FIK/SAIGS		(*not* SEL/LAE; see sellae)
cecoileostomy	SAOEK/*IL/YO*S/M*I	cellase	SEL/AIS
cecopexy	SAOEK/PEK/SI	cellicolous	SEL/LIK/LOUS
cecoplication	SAOEK/PLI/KAIGS	cellobiase	SEL/BAOI/AIS
	SAOEK/PLAOI/KAIGS		SEL/BAOI/YAIS
cecorrhaphy	SE/KOR/FI	cellobiose	SEL/BAO*I/OES
cecosigmoidostomy	SAOEK/SIG/MOI/DO*S/M*I		SEL/BAO*I/YOES
cecostomy	SE/KO*S/M*I	cellohexose	SEL/HEX/OES
cecotomy	SE/KOT/M*I		SEL/HEK/SOES
cecum	SE/KUM	celloidin	SEL/LOI/DIN
	SAOEK/UM	cellon	SEL/LON
cecutiens	SE/KAOUT/YENZ	cellona	SEL/LOE/NA
	SE/KAOURB/ENZ	cellophane	SEL/FAIN
	SE/KAOU/SHENZ	cellose	SEL/LOES
Cedilanid	SE/DI/LAN/ID/D-RBGS	cellotetrose	SEL/TET/ROES
	SAOED/LAN/ID/D-RBGS	cellotriose	SEL/TR*I/OES
CeeNU	SE/NAOU	cellul(o)-	SEL/YAOU/L(O)
cefaclor	SEF/KLOR		SEL/YU/L(O)
cefadroxil	SEF/DROK/SIL		KREL/YAOU/L(O)
	SEF/DROX/IL		KREL/YU/L(O)
Cefadyl	SEF/DIL		(*not* SEL/L(O); see cello-)
cefamandole nafate	SEF/MAN/DOEL/NAF/AIT	cellula	SEL/YAOU/LA
cefazolin	SE/FAZ/LIN	cellulae	SEL/YAOU/LAE
Cefizox	SEF/ZOX	cellular	SEL/YAOU/LAR
Cefobid	SEF/BID	cellularity	SEL/YAOU/LAIR/TI
Cefol	SE/FOL	cellulase	SEL/YAOU/LAIS
cefonicid	SE/FON/SID	cellule	SEL/YAOUL
cefoperazone	SEF/PER/ZOEN	cellulicidal	SEL/YAOU/LIS/DAL
ceforanide	SE/FOR/NAOID	cellulifugal	SEL/YAOU/LIF/GAL
	SE/FOER/NAOID	cellulin	SEL/YAOU/LIN
Cefotan	SEF/TAN	cellulipetal	SEL/YAOU/LIP/TAL
cefotaxime	SEF/TAK/SAOEM	cellulite	SEL/YAOU/LAOIT
cefotetan	SEF/TE/TAN	cellulitis	SEL/YAOU/LAOITS
	SEF/TAOE/TAN	cellulofibrous	SEL/YAOU/LO/FAOI/BROUS
cefoxitin	SE/FOX/TIN	celluloid	SEL/YAOU/LOID
ceftazidime	SEF/TAZ/DAOEM	Cellulomonas	SEL/YAOU/LO/MOE/NAS
ceftizoxome	SEFT/ZOK/SAOEM	celluloneuritis	SEL/YAOU/LO/NAOU/RAOITS
	SEF/TI/ZOK/SAOEM	cellulosae	SEL/YAOU/LOE/SAE
ceftriaxone	SEF/TR*I/AK/SOEN	cellulosan	SEL/YAOU/LOE/SAN
	SEF/TR*I/AX/OEN	cellulose	SEL/YAOU/LOES
cel	S*EL	cellulosic	SEL/YAOU/LOES/IK
	KR*EL		SEL/YAOU/LOS/IK
	(*not* SEL or KREL; see sell and cell)	cellulosity	SEL/YAOU/LOS/TI
celarium	SE/LAIRM	cellulotoxic	SEL/YAOU/LO/TOX/IK
	SE/LAIR/YUM	cellulous	SEL/YAOU/LOUS
-cele	SAO*EL	Cellvibrio	SEL/VIB/ROE
celectome	SE/LEK/TOEM		SEL/VIB/RAOE/YOE
celectomy	SE/LEKT/M*I		KREL/VIB/RAOE/YOE
celenteron	SE/LENT/RON	celo-	SE/LO
celestine	SE/LES/TAOEN		SAOEL
Celestone	SE/LES/TOEN	celom	SE/LOM
celi(o)-	SAOEL/Y(O)	celoma	SE/LOE/MA
celiac	SAOEL/YAK	celomate	SAOEL/MAIT
celiaca	SE/LAOI/KA	celomic	SE/LOM/IK
celiagra	SAOEL/YAG/RA	Celontin	SE/LON/TIN
celiectomy	SAOEL/YEKT/M*I	celonychia	SAOEL/NIK/YA
celiocentesis	SAOEL/YO/SEN/TAOE/SIS	celophlebitis	SAOEL/FLE/BAOITS
celiocolpotomy	SAOEL/YO/KOL/POT/M*I	celoschisis	SE/LOS/KI/SIS
celioenterotomy	SAOEL/YO/SPWROT/M*I	celoscope	SAOEL/SKOEP
	SAOEL/YO/SPWER/ROT/M*I	celoscopy	SE/LOS/KPI
celiogastrostomy	SAOEL/YO/GAS/TRO*S/M*I	celosomia	SAOEL/SOEM/YA
celiogastrotomy	SAOEL/YO/GAS/TROT/M*I	celosomy	SAOEL/SOE/M*I
celiohysterectomy	SAOEL/YO/H*IS/REKT/M*I	celosomus	SAOEL/SOE/MUS
celiohysterotomy	SAOEL/YO/H*IS/ROT/M*I	celothelium	SAOEL/THAOEL/YUM
celioma	SAOEL/YOE/MA	celotomy	SE/LOT/M*I
celiomyalgia	SAOEL/YO/MAOI/AL/JA	celozoic	SAOEL/ZOIK
	SAOEL/YO/MAOI/YAL/JA		SAOEL/ZOE/IK
celiomyomectomy	SAOEL/YO/MAOI/MEKT/M*I	celsi	SEL/SAOI
celiomyomotomy	SAOEL/YO/MAOI/MOT/M*I	Celsius	SELS/YUS
celiomyositis	SAOEL/YO/MAOI/SAOITS	cement	SEMT
celioparacentesis	SAOEL/YO/PAR/SEN/TAOE/SIS		SMENT
celiopathy	SAOEL/YOP/TH*I	cement(o)-	SEMT
celiorraphy	SAOEL/YOR/FI		SE/MENT
celiosalpingectomy	SAOEL/YO/SAL/PIN/JEKT/M*I		SEMT/TO
celiosalpingotomy	SAOEL/YO/SAL/PIN/GOT/M*I		SE/MEN/TO
celioscope	SAOEL/YO/SKOEP		SMENT
celioscopy	SAOEL/YOS/KPI		SMEN/TO
celiotomy	SAOEL/YOT/M*I	cemental	SEMT/TAL
celitis	SE/LAOITS		SE/MEN/TAL
cell	KREL	cementation	SEMT/TAIGS

cementicle	SE/MEN/TAIGS	centrifuge	SEN/TRI/FAOUJ
	SEMT/K-L	centrifugum	SEN/TRIF/GUM
	SE/MENT/K-L	centrilobular	SEN/TRI/LOB/LAR
cementification	SEMT/FI/KAIGS	centriole	SEN/TROEL
	SE/MENT/FI/KAIGS		SEN/TRAOE/OEL
cementin	SEMT/TIN		SEN/TRAOE/YOEL
	SE/MEN/TIN	centripetal	SEN/TRIP/TAL
cementitis	SEMT/AOITS	centroacinar	SEN/TRO/AS/NAR
	SEMT/TAOITS	centroblast	SEN/TRO/BLA*S
	SE/MEN/TAOITS	centrocecal	SEN/TRO/SE/KAL
cementoalveolar	SEMT/AL/VAOE/LAR	Centrocestus	SEN/TRO/SES/TUS
cementoblast	SEMT/BLA*S	centrocyte	SEN/TRO/SAO*IT
cementoblastoma	SEMT/BLAS/TOE/MA	centrodesmus	SEN/TRO/DES/MUS
cementoclasia	SEMT/KLAIZ/YA	centrokinesia	SEN/TRO/KI/NAOEZ/YA
cementoclast	SEMT/KLA*S	centrokinetic	SEN/TRO/KI/NET/IK
cementocyte	SEMT/SAO*IT	centrolecithal	SEN/TRO/LES/THAL
cementodentinal	SEMT/DENT/NAL	centrolobular	SEN/TRO/LOB/LAR
cementogenesis	SEMT/JEN/SIS	centromedianus	SEN/TRO/MAOED/YAI/NUS
cementoma	SEMT/TOE/MA	centromere	SEN/TRO/MAOER
	SE/MEN/TOE/MA	centromeric	SEN/TRO/MER/IK
cementopathia	SEMT/PA*T/YA	centrophose	SEN/TRO/FOEZ
cementoperiostitis	SEMT/P*ER/OS/TAOITS	centroplasm	SEN/TRO/PLAFM
cementosis	SEMT/TOE/SIS	centrosclerosis	SEN/TRO/SKLE/ROE/SIS
	SE/MEN/TOE/SIS	centrosome	SEN/TRO/SOEM
cementum	SEMT/UM	centrosphere	SEN/TRO/SFAOER
	SE/MEN/TUM	centrostaltic	SEN/TRO/STALT/IK
cenadelphus	SEN/DEL/FUS	centrotherapy	SEN/TRO/THER/PI
cenencephalocele	SEN/EN/SEF/LO/SAO*EL	centrum	SEN/TRUM
cenesthesia	SEN/ES/THAOEZ/YA	Centrum, Jr.	SEN/TRUM/J-R
cenesthesic	SEN/ES/THAOEZ/IK	Centruroides	SEN/TRAOU/ROI/DAOEZ
cenesthesiopathy	SEN/ES/THAOEZ/YOP/TH*I	cenuriasis	SEN/YAOU/RAOI/SIS
cenesthetic	SEN/ES/THET/IK		SEN/YU/RAOI/SIS
cenesthopathy	SEN/ES/THOP/TH*I	cenuris	SE/NAOU/RIS
ceno-	SE/NO		SE/NAOUR/RIS
	SAOEN (sometimes)	cenurosis	SEN/YAOU/ROE/SIS
cenobium	SE/NOEB/YUM		SEN/YU/ROE/SIS
cenocyte	SAOEN/SAO*IT	Ceo-Two	SE/YO/TWO
cenocytic	SAOEN/SIT/IK		SE/YO/H-F/TWO
cenogenesis	SAOEN/JEN/SIS	Cepacol	SAOEP/KOL
cenosis	SE/NOE/SIS		SEP/KOL
cenosite	SE/NO/SAOIT	CEPASTAT	SAOEP/STAT
	(*not* SAOEN/SAOIT; see seen site)		SEP/STAT
cenotic	SE/NOT/IK	cephal(o)-	SEF/L(O)
cenotrope	SAOEN/TROEP		SEF/AL
cenotype	SE/NO/TAOIP		SFAL
	(*not* SAOEN/TAOIP; see seen type)		SE/FAL
censor	KREN/SOR		(*not* SEFL; see self-)
	(not SEN/SOR; see sensor)	cephalad	SEF/LAD
censorship	KREN/SOR/SHIP	cephalalgia	SEF/LAL/JA
center	SEN/TER	cephaledema	SEF/LE/DAOE/MA
	SENT/ER		SEF/AL/DAOE/MA
centesimal	SEN/TES/MAL	cephalemia	SEF/LAOEM/YA
centesis	SEN/TAOE/SIS	cephalexin	SEF/LEK/SIN
centi-	SENT	cephalgia	SE/FAL/JA
	SEN/TI		SFAL/JA
centibar	SENT/BAR	cephalhematocele	SEF/AL/HAOE/MAT/SAO*EL
centigrade	SENT/GRAID	cephalhematoma	SEF/AL/HAOEM/TOE/MA
centigram	SENT/GRAM	cephalhydrocele	SEF/AL/HAOI/DRO/SAO*EL
centiliter	SENT/LAOET/ER	-cephalia	SFAIL/YA
centimeter	SENT/MAOET/ER		SE/FAIL/YA
centimorgan	SENT/MOR/GAN	cephalic	SFAL/IK
centinormal	SENT/NOR/MAL		SE/FAL/IK
centipede	SENT/PAOED	cephalica	SFAL/KA
centipoise	SENT/POIZ		SE/FAL/KA
	SENT/POIS	cephalic-medullary	SFAL/IK/MED/LAIR
centistoke	SENT/STOEK	cephalin	SEF/LIN
centiunit	SENT/YAOUNT	-cephalism	SEF/LIFM
centr(o)-	SEN/TR(O)	cephalitis	SEF/LAOITS
centra	SEN/TRA	cephalization	SEF/LI/ZAIGS
centrad	SEN/TRAD	cephalocaudad	SEF/LO/KAU/DAD
centrage	SEN/TRAIJ	cephalocaudal	SEF/LO/KAU/DAL
central	STRAL	cephalocele	SEF/LO/SAO*EL
	SEN/TRAL	cephalocentesis	SEF/LO/SEN/TAOE/SIS
centrales	SEN/TRAI/LAOEZ	cephalocercal	SEF/LO/SER/KAL
centralis	SEN/TRAI/LIS	cephalochord	SEF/LO/KHORD
centraphose	SEN/TRA/FOEZ	Cephalochordata	SEF/LO/KHOR/DAI/TA
centration	SEN/TRAIGS		SEF/LO/KOER/DAI/TA
Centrax	SEN/TRAX	cephalochordate	SEF/LO/KHOR/DAIT
centraxonial	SEN/TRAK/SOEN/YAL		SEF/LO/KOER/DAIT
centre	SEN/TRE	cephalocyst	SEF/LO/S*IS
centrencephalic	SEN/TREN/SFAL/IK	cephalodactyly	SEF/LO/DAKT/LI
centriacinar	SEN/TRI/AS/NAR	cephalodidymus	SEF/LO/DID/MUS
centric	SEN/TRIK	cephalodiprosopus	SEF/LO/DI/PROS/PUS
centriciput	SEN/TRIS/PUT		SEF/LO/DI/PRO/SOE/PUS
centrifugal	SEN/TRIF/GAL	cephalodymia	SEF/LO/DIM/YA
centrifugalization	SEN/TRIF/GAL/ZAIGS	cephalodymus	SEF/LO/DMUS
centrifugalize	SEN/TRIF/GAL/AOIZ	cephalodynia	SEF/LO/DIN/YA
centrifugate	SEN/TRIF/GAIT	cephalogenesis	SEF/LO/JEN/SIS
centrifugation	SEN/TRIF/GAIGS	cephaloglycin	SEF/LO/GLAOI/SIN

cephalogram	SEF/LO/GRAM
cephalogyric	SEF/LO/JAOIR/IK
cephalohematocele	SEF/LO/HAOE/MAT/SAO*EL
	SEF/LO/HE/MAT/SAO*EL
cephalohematoma	SEF/LO/HAOEM/TOE/MA
	SEF/LO/HEM/TOE/MA
cephalohemometer	SEF/LO/HAOE/MOM/TER
cephalomegaly	SEF/LO/MEG/LI
cephalomelus	SEF/LOM/LUS
cephalomeningitis	SEF/LO/MEN/JAOITS
cephalometer	SEF/LOM/TER
cephalometric	SEF/LOM/MET/RIK
cephalometry	SEF/LOM/TRI
cephalomotor	SEF/LO/MOE/TOR
cephalonia	SEF/LOEN/YA
cephalont	SEF/LONT
cephalopagus	SEF/LOP/GUS
cephalopathy	SEF/LOP/TH*I
cephalopelvic	SEF/LO/PEL/VIK
cephalopelvimetry	SEF/LO/PEL/VIM/TRI
cephalopharyngeus	SEF/LO/FRIN/JUS
cephaloplegia	SEF/LO/PLAOE/JA
cephaloridine	SEF/LOR/DAOEN
	SEF/LOER/DAOEN
cephalorrhachidian	SEF/LO/RA/KID/YAN
cephalosporanic	SEF/LO/SPRAN/IK
	SEF/LO/SPO/RAN/IK
cephalosporin	SEF/LO/SPORN
cephalosporinase	SEF/LO/SPOR/NAIS
cephalosporiosis	SEF/LO/SPOR/YOE/SIS
Cephalosporium	SEF/LO/SPOR/YUM
cephalostat	SEF/LO/STAT
cephalostyle	SEF/LO/STAOIL
cephalotetanus	SEF/LO/TET/NUS
cephalothin	SEF/LO/THIN
cephalothoracic	SEF/LO/THRAS/IK
cephalothoracoiliopagus	SEF/LO/THOR/KO/IL/YOP/GUS
cephalothoracopagus	SEF/LO/THOR/KOP/GUS
cephalotome	SEF/LO/TOEM
cephalotomy	SEF/LOT/M*I
cephalotoxin	SEF/LO/TOK/SIN
cephalotribe	SEF/LO/TRAOIB
cephalotropic	SEF/LO/TROP/IK
cephalous	SEF/LOUS
cephalus	SEF/LUS
-cephaly	SEF/LI
cephapirin	SEF/PAOI/RIN
cephradine	SEF/RA/DAOEN
Cephulac Syrup	SEF/YAOU/LAK
ceptor	SEP/TOR
-ceptor	SEP/TOR
cera	SE/RA
	(not SAOER/RA; see sera)
ceraceous	SE/RAIRBS
ceramic	SE/RAM/IK
ceramidase	SER/AM/DAIS
	SER/RAM/DAIS
ceramide	SER/MAOID
ceramodontics	SE/RAM/DONT/IK/-S
cerasin	SER/RA/SIN
	(not SER/SIN; see ceresin)
cerasine	SER/SAOEN
cerat(o)-	SER/T(O)
cerate	SE/RAIT
ceratin	SER/TIN
ceratocricoid	SER/TO/KRAOI/KOID
ceratocricoidea	SER/TO/KRAOI/KOID/YA
ceratocricoideum	SER/TO/KRAOI/KOID/YUM
ceratocricoideus	SER/TO/KRAOI/KOID/YUS
ceratoglossus	SER/TO/GLOS/SUS
ceratohyal	SER/TO/HAOIL
ceratonosus	SER/TON/SUS
ceratopharyngeus	SER/TO/FRIN/JUS
Ceratophyllidae	SER/TO/FIL/DAE
Ceratophyllus	SER/TOF/LUS
ceratum	SE/RAI/TUM
	SE/RAIT/UM
cerc(o)-	SERK
	SER/K(O)
cercaria	SER/KAIR/YA
cercariae	SER/KAIR/YAE
cercaricidal	SER/KAIR/SAOI/DAL
cerci	SER/SAOI
cerclage	SER/KLAJ
	SAIR/KLAJ
cercocystis	SERK/SIS/TIS
cercoid	SER/KOID
cercomer	SERK/MER
cercomonad	SERK/MOE/NAD

	SER/KOM/NAD
Cercomonas	SERK/MOE/NAS
	SER/KOM/NAS
cercopithecoid	SERK/P*IT/KOID
Cercopithecoidea	SERK/P*IT/KOID/YA
Cercopithecus	SERK/P*IT/KUS
cercus	SER/KUS
cerea flexibilitas	SAOER/YA/FLEX/BIL/TAS
cereal	KRAOER/YAL
	(not SAOER/YAL; see serial)
cerealin	SE/RAOE/LIN
cerealose	SE/RAOE/LOES
cerebell(o)-	SER/BEL
	SER/BEL/L(O)
cerebella	SER/BEL/LA
cerebellar	SER/BEL/LAR
cerebellaris	SER/BEL/LAI/RIS
	SER/BEL/LAR/RIS
cerebellarium	SER/BEL/LAIR/YUM
	SER/BEL/LAIRM
cerebelli	SER/BEL/LAOI
cerebellifugal	SER/BEL/LIF/GAL
cerebellin	SER/BEL/LIN
cerebellipetal	SER/BEL/LIP/TAL
cerebellitis	SER/BEL/LAOITS
cerebellofugal	SER/BEL/LOF/GAL
cerebellolental	SER/BEL/LEN/TAL
cerebello-medullaris	SER/BEL/MED/LAI/RIS
cerebellomedullary	SER/BEL/MED/LAIR
cerebello-olivares	SER/BEL/OL/VAI/RAOEZ
	SER/BEL/OL/VAIR/RAOEZ
cerebello-olivary	SER/BEL/OL/VAIR
cerebellopontile	SER/BEL/PON/TAOIL
	SER/BEL/PON/TAOEL
	SER/BEL/PON/TIL
cerebellopontine	SER/BEL/PON/TAOEN
	SER/BEL/PON/TAOIN
cerebellorubral	SER/BEL/RAOU/BRAL
	SER/BEL/RAOUB/RAL
cerebellorubrospinal	SER/BEL/RAOUB/RO/SPAOINL
cerebellospinal	SER/BEL/SPAOINL
cerebellospinalis	SER/BEL/SPAOI/NAI/LIS
cerebellum	SER/BEL/UM
	SER/BEL/LUM
cerebr(o)-	SER/BR(O)
	SE/RAOEB/R(O)
	SE/RAOE/BR(O)
cerebra	SE/RAOEB/RA
	SER/BRA
cerebral	SER/BRAL
	SE/RAOEB/RAL
cerebrale	SER/BRAI/LAOE
cerebrales	SER/BRAI/LAOEZ
cerebralgia	SER/BRAL/JA
cerebralis	SER/BRAI/LIS
cerebration	SER/BRAIGS
cerebri	SER/BRAOI
cerebriform	SE/RAOEB/RI/FORM
	SE/REB/RI/FORM
cerebrifugal	SER/BRIF/GAL
cerebripetal	SER/BRIP/TAL
cerebritis	SER/BRAOITS
cerebrocardiac	SER/BRO/KARD/YAK
cerebrocerebellar	SER/BRO/SER/BEL/LAR
cerebrocuprein	SER/BRO/KAOU/PRAOEN
	SER/BRO/KAOUP/RAOEN
	SER/BRO/KAOU/PRAOE/YIN
cerebrogalactose	SER/BRO/GLAK/TOES
cerebrogalactoside	SER/BRO/GLAKT/SAOID
cerebrohyphoid	SER/BRO/HAOI/FOID
cerebroid	SER/BROID
cerebrology	SER/BROLG
cerebroma	SER/BROE/MA
cerebromacular	SER/BRO/MAK/LAR
cerebromalacia	SER/BRO/MA/LAI/SHA
cerebromedullary	SER/BRO/MED/LAIR
cerebromeningeal	SER/BRO/ME/NIN/JAL
cerebromeningitis	SER/BRO/MEN/JAOITS
cerebron	SER/BRON
cerebronic	SER/BRON/IK
cerebro-ocular	SER/BRO/OK/LAR
cerebropathia	SER/BRO/PA*T/YA
cerebropathy	SER/BROP/TH*I
cerebrophysiology	SER/BRO/FIZ/YOLG
cerebropontile	SER/BRO/PON/TIL
cerebroretinal	SER/BRO/RET/NAL
cerebrosclerosis	SER/BRO/SKLE/ROE/SIS
cerebrose	SER/BROES
cerebroside	SER/BRO/SAOID

cerebrosidosis	SER/BRO/SAOI/DOE/SIS	ceryl	SER/IL
cerebrosis	SER/BROE/SIS		SAOER/IL
cerebrospinal	SER/BRO/SPAOINL	cesarean	SE/SAIRN
cerebrospinalis	SER/BRO/SPAOI/NAI/LIS		SE/ZAIRN
cerebrospinant	SER/BRO/SPAOI/NANT		SE/SAIR/YAN
cerebrospinase	SER/BRO/SPAOI/NAIS		SE/ZAIR/YAN
cerebrosterol	SER/BRO/STAOER/OL	cesium	SAOEZ/YUM
	SER/BRO/STAOER/ROL	cest(o)-	S*ES
cerebrostomy	SER/BRO*S/M*I		SES/T(O)
cerebrotomy	SER/BROT/M*I	Cestan	SES/TAN
cerebrotendinous	SER/BRO/TEND/NOUS	cesticidal	S*ES/SAOI/DAL
cerebrotomy	SER/BROT/M*I	Cestoda	SES/TOE/DA
cerebrotonia	SER/BRO/TOEN/YA	Cestodaria	S*ES/DAIR/YA
cerebrovascular	SER/BRO/VAS/KLAR	cestode	SES/TOED
cerebrum	SE/RAOEB/RUM	cestodiasis	S*ES/DAOI/SIS
	SE/RAOE/BRUM	cestodology	S*ES/DOLG
	SER/BRUM		SES/TO/DOLG
cerecloth	SAOER/KLO*T	cestoid	SES/TOID
Cerenkov	KAIRN/KOV	Cestoidea	SES/TOID/YA
	KAIR/EN/KOV	cetaben sodium	SAOET/BEN/SOED/YUM
	KAIR/-N/KOV	Cetacaine	SET/KAIN
ceresin	SER/SIN	cetaceum	SE/TAIS/YUM
cereus	SAOER/YUS		SE/TAIRB/UM
cerevisiae	SER/VIS/YAE	cetalkonium	SET/AL/KOEN/YUM
cerin	SE/RIN	Cetaphil Skin Cleanser	SAOET/FIL/SKIN/KLENZ/ER
	SER/RIN	cethexonium	SET/HEK/SOEN/YUM
Cerithidea	SER/THID/YA	cetostearyl	SE/TO/STAOER/RIL
cerium	SAOER/YUM		SE/TO/STAOE/RIL
	SER/YUM	Cetraria	SE/TRAIR/YA
	(not SAOERM; see serum)	cetrimonium	SE/TR*I/MOEN/YUM
ceroid	SE/ROID		SET/RI/MOEN/YUM
	SAOER/OID	cetyl	SE/TIL
	SAOER/ROID		SAOET/IL
ceroplasty	SE/RO/PLAS/TI	Cetylcide	SE/TIL/SAO*ID
Cerose-DM	SE/ROES/D-RBGS/M*RBGS	cetylpyridinium	SE/TIL/PAOIR/DIN/YUM
cerosin	SER/RO/SIN	cetyltrimethylammonium	SE/TIL/TR*I/M*ET/IL/MOEN/YUM
	(not SER/SIN; see ceresin)		SE/TIL/TR*I/M*ET/IL/AI/MOEN/
certifiable	SERT/FIBL		YUM
certification	SERT/FI/KAIGS	cevadine	SEV/DAOEN
certify	SERT/FI	Cevi-Bid	SE/VAOI/BID
Cerubidine	SE/RAOUB/DAOEN	Cevi-Fer	SE/VAOI/FER
cerulea	SE/RAOUL/YA	Ce-Vi-Sol	SE/VAOI/SOL
cerulein	SE/RAOUL/YIN	cevitamic	SEV/TAM/IK
ceruloplasmin	SE/RAOU/LO/PLAZ/MIN	ceylonicum	SAI/LON/KUM
cerumen	SE/RAOU/MEN	Chabertia	SHA/BERT/YA
	SE/RAOUM/-N		KHA/BERT/YA
Cerumenex	SE/RAOUM/NEX	Chaddock	KHAD/OK
ceruminal	SE/RAOUM/NAL		KHAD/DOK
ceruminolysis	SE/RAOUM/NOL/SIS	Chadwick	KHAD/WIK
ceruminolytic	SE/RAOUM/NO/LIT/IK	chafe	KHAIF
ceruminoma	SE/RAOUM/NOE/MA	Chagas	KHAG/GAS
ceruminosis	SE/RAOUM/NOE/SIS	chagoma	KHA/GOE/MA
ceruminous	SE/RAOUM/NOUS	chain	KHAIN
ceruse	SE/RAOUS	Chain	K-P/KHAIN
cervi	SER/VAOI	chaining	KHAIN/-G
cervic(o)-	SEFRB/K(O)	chalasia	KA/LAIS/YA
	SEFRB/S-		(not KA/LAIZ/YA; see chalazia)
	SER/VI/K(O)	chalasis	KA/LAI/SIS
	SER/VI/S-	chalaza	KA/LAI/ZA
cervical	SEFRB/KAL	chalazia	KA/LAIZ/YA
cervicales	SEFRB/KAI/LAOEZ	chalazion	KA/LAIZ/YON
cervicalis	SEFRB/KAI/LIS	chalcone	KAL/KOEN
cervicectomy	SEFRB/SEKT/M*I	chalcosis	KA*L/KOE/SIS
cervices	SEFRB/SAOEZ		(not KAL/KOE/SIS; see chalicosis)
cervicis	SEFRB/SIS	chalicosis	KAL/KOE/SIS
cervicitis	SEFRB/SAOITS	chalinoplasty	KAL/NO/PLAS/TI
cervicoaxillary	SEFRB/KO/AX/LAIR	chalice	KHAL/LIS
cervicobrachial	SEFRB/KO/BRAIK/YAL		KHAL/IS
cervicobrachialgia	SEFRB/KO/BRAIK/YAL/JA	chalk	KHAUK
cervicobregmatic	SEFRB/KO/BREG/MAT/IK	chalkitis	KAL/KAOITS
cervicobuccal	SEFRB/KO/BUK/KAL	chalky	KHAUK/KI
cervicocolpitis	SEFRB/KO/KOL/PAOITS	challenge	KHAJ
cervicodorsal	SEFRB/KO/DOR/SAL		KHAL/EN/-J
cervicodynia	SEFRB/KO/DIN/YA	chalone	KAI/LOEN
cervicofacial	SEFRB/KO/FAIRBL		KAL/OEN
cervicography	SEFRB/KOG/FI	chalonic	KA/LON/IK
cervicolabial	SEFRB/KO/LAIB/YAL	chalybeate	KA/LIB/YAIT
cervicolingual	SEFRB/KO/LING/WAL		KAL/IB/YAIT
cervicolinguoaxial	SEFRB/KO/LING/WO/AX/YAL	chamazulene	KA/MAZ/LAOEN
cervico-occipital	SEFRB/KO/OK/SIP/TAL		KA/MAZ/YAOU/LAOEN
cervicoplasty	SEFRB/KO/PLAS/TI		KA/MAZ/YU/LAOEN
cervicoscapular	SEFRB/KO/SKAP/LAR	chamber	KHAIM/BER
cervicothoracic	SEFRB/KO/THRAS/IK		KHAM/BER
cervicotomy	SEFRB/KOT/M*I	Chamberlain	KHAIM/BER/LIN
cervicovaginitis	SEFRB/KO/VAJ/NAOITS		KHAM/BER/LIN
cervicovesical	SEFRB/KO/VES/KAL	Chamberlen	KHAIM/BER/LEN
cervimeter	SER/VIM/TER		KHAM/BER/LEN
cervix	SER/VIX	chamecephalic	KAM/SFAL/IK
	SEFRB/IX	chamecephalous	KAM/SEF/LOUS

©1992 StenEd® Medical Dictionary

chamecephaly	KAM/SEF/LI	cheilosis	KAOI/LOE/SIS
chameprosopic	KAM/PRO/SOP/IK		(see chylosis)
chameprosopy	KAM/PROS/PI	cheilostomatoplasty	KAOIL/STOEM/TO/PLAS/TI
chamfer	KHAM/FER	cheilotomy	KAOI/LOT/M*I
Champetier de Ribes	SHAFRPT/YAI/DE/RAOEB	cheir(o)-	KAOIR
	SHAFRP/TAOE/YAI/DE/RAOEB		KAOI/R(O)
	SHAM/TAOE/YAI/DE/RAOEB	cheiragra	KAOI/RAG/RA
Chance	K-P/KHANS	cheiralgia	KAOI/RAL/JA
chancre	SHAN/KER		KAOIR/AL/JA
chancriform	SHAN/KRI/FORM	cheirarthritis	KAOI/RAR/THRAOITS
chancroid	SHAN/KROID		KAOIR/AR/THRAOITS
chancroidal	SHAN/KROI/DAL	-cheiria	KAOIR/YA
chancrous	SHAN/KROUS	cheirobrachialgia	KAOIR/BRAIK/YAL/JA
Chandler	K-P/KHAND/LER	cheirocinesthesia	KAOIR/SIN/ES/THAOEZ/YA
change	KHAING	cheirognomy	KAOI/ROG/NO/M*I
	KHAIN/-J	cheirognostic	KAOI/ROG/NO*S/IK
channel	KHAN/EL	cheirokinesthesia	KAOIR/KINS/THAOEZ/YA
chaotropic	KAI/TROEP/IK		KAOIR/KIN/ES/THAOEZ/YA
	KAI/YO/TROEP/IK	cheirokinesthetic	KAOIR/KINS/THET/IK
chaotropism	KAI/TROEP/IFM		KAOIR/KIN/ES/THET/IK
	KAI/YO/TROEP/IFM	cheirology	KAOI/ROLG
chap	KHAP	cheiromegaly	KAOIR/MEG/LI
Chapman	KHAP/MAN	cheiroplasty	KAOIR/PLAS/TI
chappa	KHAP/PA	cheiropodalgia	KAOIR/POE/DAL/JA
chapped	KHAP/-D		KAOIR/PO/DAL/JA
character	KARK/TER	cheiropompholyx	KAOIR/POM/FLIX
characteristic	KARK/TR*IS/IK		KAOIR/POM/FO/LIX
characterization	KARK/TER/ZAIGS	cheiroscope	KAOIR/SKOEP
	KARK/TER/SAIGS	cheirospasm	KAOIR/SPAFM
characterology	KARK/TER/OLG	chelate	KAOE/LAIT
	KARK/TROLG	chelating	KAOE/LAIT/-G
charcoal	KHAR/KOEL	chelation	KAOE/LAIGS
Charcot	SHAR/KOE	chelicera	KAOE/LIS/RA
charlatan	SHARL/TAN		KE/LIS/RA
charlatanism	SHARL/TAN/IFM	chelicerae	KAOE/LIS/RAE
charlatanry	SHARL/TAN/RI		KE/LIS/RAE
Charles	KHARLZ	chelidon	KEL/DON
	SHARLS	Chelonia	KAOE/LOEN/YA
charley horse	KHAR/LAOE/HORS	chelonian	KAOE/LOEN/YAN
charring	KHAR/-G	chem(o)-	KAOEM
chart	KHART		KAOE/MO
chasma	KAZ/MA		KEM
chasmus	KAZ/MUS	chemabrasion	KAOEM/BRAIGS
Chassaignac	SHAS/AIN/YAK	chemanesia	KAOEM/NAOEZ/YA
	SHAS/SAIN/YAK	chemasthenia	KEM/AS/THAOEN/YA
chaude-pisse	SHOED/PAOES	chemexfoliation	KEM/EX/FOEL/YAIGS
chauffage	SHOE/FAJ		KAOEM/EX/FOEL/YAIGS
	SHOE/FAUJ	chemiatric	KEM/YAT/RIK
Chauffard	SHOE/FAR		KAOEM/YAT/RIK
chaulmoogra	KHAUL/MAO/GRA	chemiatry	KEM/YA/TRI
	KHAUL/MAOG/RA		KAOEM/YA/TRI
chaulmoogric	KHAUL/MAO/GRIK	chemical	KEM/KAL
	KHAUL/MAOG/RIK	chemicobiological	KEM/KO/BAO*I/LOJ/KAL
Chaussier	SHOES/YAI	chemicobiologically	KEM/KO/BAO*I/LOJ/KLI
Chauveau	SHOE/VOE	chemicocautery	KEM/KO/KAUT/RI
chauvoei	SHOE/VOE/YAOI	chemicogenesis	KEM/KO/JEN/SIS
Cheadle	KHAOED/-L	chemicoluminescense	KEM/KO/LAOUM/NES/ENS
check	KHEK	chemicophysical	KEM/KO/FIZ/KAL
checkbite	KHEK/BAOIT	chemicophysiologic	KEM/KO/FIZ/YO/LOJ/IK
check-bite	KHEK/H-F/BAOIT	cheminosis	KEM/NOE/SIS
checkerboard	KHEK/ER/BAORD	chemiotaxis	KEM/YO/TAK/SIS
Chediak	KHED/YAK	chemiotherapy	KEM/YO/THER/PI
cheek	KHAOEK	chemise	SHEM/AOEZ
cheesy	KHAOEZ/SI	chemism	KEM/IFM
cheil(o)-	KAOIL	chemisorption	KEM/SORPGS
	KAOI/L(O)	chemist	KEM/*IS
cheilectomy	KAOI/LEKT/M*I	chemistry	KEM/STRI
cheilectropion	KAOI/LEK/TROEP/YON		KEMS/TRI
-cheilia	KAOIL/YA	chemistry-12	KEM/STRI/12
cheilion	KAOIL/YON	chemoattractant	KAOEM/AI/TRAK/TANT
cheilitis	KAOI/LAOITS	chemoautotroph	KAOEM/AUT/TROEF
cheiloalveoloschisis	KAOIL/AL/VAOE/LOS/KI/SIS	chemoautotrophic	KAOEM/AUT/TROFK
cheiloangioscopy	KAOIL/AN/JOS/KPI	chemobiodynamics	KAOEM/BAO*I/DAOI/NAM/IK/-S
cheilocarcinoma	KAOIL/KARS/NOE/MA	chemobiotic	KAOEM/BAO*I/OT/IK
cheilognathoglossoschisis	KAOIL/NA*T/GLOS/OS/KI/SIS	chemocautery	KAOEM/KAUT/RI
	KAOIL/NA*T/GLOS/SOS/KI/SIS	chemoceptor	KAOEM/SEP/TOR
cheilognathopalatoschisis	KAOIL/NA*T/PAL/TOS/KI/SIS	chemocoagulation	KAOEM/KO/AG/LAIGS
cheilognathoprosoposchisis	KAOIL/NA*T/PROS/POS/KI/SIS	chemodectoma	KAOEM/DEK/TOE/MA
cheilognathoschisis	KAOIL/NA/THOS/KI/SIS	chemodectomatosis	KAOEM/DEKT/MA/TOE/SIS
	KAOI/LOG/NA/THOS/KI/SIS		KAOEM/DEK/TOEM/TOE/SIS
cheilognathouranoschisis	KAOIL/NA*T/YAOUR/NOS/KI/SIS	chemodifferentiation	KAOEM/DIFRN/SHAIGS
	KAOI/LOG/NA/THO/YAOUR/NOS/	chemoheterotroph	KAOEM/HET/RO/TROEF
	KI/SIS	chemoheterotrophic	KAOEM/HET/RO/TROFK
cheilophagia	KAOIL/FAI/JA		KAOEM/HET/RO/TROEFK
cheiloplasty	KAOIL/PLAS/TI	chemohormonal	KAOEM/HOR/MOENL
cheilorrhaphy	KAOI/LOR/FI	chemoimmunology	KAOEM/IM/NOLG
cheiloschisis	KAOI/LOS/KI/SIS	chemokinesis	KAOEM/KI/NAOE/SIS
cheiloscope	KAOIL/SKOEP	chemokinetic	KAOEM/KI/NET/IK
cheiloscopy	KAOI/LOS/KPI	chemolithotroph	KAOEM/L*IT/TROEF

chemolithotrophic	KAOEM/L*IT/TROF	childbearing	KHAOILD/BAER/-G
chemoluminescence	KAOEM/L*IT/TROFK	childbirth	KHAOILD/B*IRT
chemolysis	KAOEM/LAOUM/NES/ENS	childhood	KHAOILD/HAOD
	KAOE/MOL/SIS	Children's Panadol	KHIRN/AOES/PAN/DOL
	KEM/OL/SIS		KHIL/DREN/AOES/PAN/DOL
chemomorphosis	KAOEM/MOR/FOE/SIS	chill	KHIL
chemonucleolysis	KAOEM/NAOUK/LOL/SIS	chilo-	see cheilo-
chemoorganotroph	KAOEM/ORG/NO/TROEF	chilomastigiasis	KAOIL/MA*S/GAOI/SIS
chemoorganotrophic	KAOEM/ORG/NO/TROFK	Chilomastix	KAOIL/MAS/TIX
chemopallidectomy	KAOEM/PAL/DEKT/M*I	chilomastosis	KAOIL/MAS/TOE/SIS
chemopallidothalamectomy	KAOEM/PAL/DO/THAL/MEKT/M*I	Chilopoda	KAOI/LOP/DA
chemopallidotomy	KAOEM/PAL/DOT/M*I	chilopodiasis	KAOIL/POE/DAOI/SIS
chemopharmacodynamic	KAOEM/FARM/KO/DAOI/NAM/IK	chimera	KAOI/MAOE/RA
chemophysiology	KAOEM/FIZ/YOLG		KAOI/MAOER/RA
chemoprophylaxis	KAOEM/PROEF/LAK/SIS	chimeric	KAOI/MAOER/IK
chemoreception	KAOEM/RE/SEPGS		KAOI/MER/IK
chemoreceptor	KAOEM/RE/SEP/TOR	chimerism	KAOI/MAOER/IFM
chemoreflex	KAOEM/RE/FLEX		KAOI/MER/IFM
chemoresistance	KAOEM/RE/SIS/TANS	chimpanzee	KHIM/PAN/ZAOE
chemosensitive	KAOEM/SENS/TIV	chin	KHIN
chemosensory	KAOEM/SENS/RI	China	KHAO*I/NA
chemoserotherapy	KAOEM/SAOER/THER/PI		K-P/KHAOI/NA
chemosis	KAOE/MOE/SIS	chincap	KHIN/KAP
chemosmosis	KEM/OZ/MOE/SIS	Chinese	KHAOI/NAOEZ
	KAOE/MOZ/MOE/SIS	chiniofon	KIN/YO/FON
chemosmotic	KEM/OZ/MOT/IK	chip	KHIP
	KAOE/MOZ/MOT/IK	chip-blower	KHIP/H-F/BLOE/ER
chemosphere	KAOEM/SFAOER	chir(o)-	KAOIR
chemostat	KAOEM/STAT		KAOI/R(O)
chemosterilant	KAOEM/STER/LANT		see cheiro-
chemosurgery	KAOEM/SURJ/RI	-chiria	KAOIR/YA
	KAOEM/S-RJ	chiropractic	KAOIR/PRAKT/IK
chemosynthesis	KAOEM/S*INT/SIS	chiropractor	KAOIR/PRAK/TOR
chemosynthetic	KAOEM/SIN/THET/IK	Chiroptera	KAOI/ROPT/RA
chemotactic	KAOEM/TAKT/IK		KAOI/ROP/TRA
chemotaxin	KAOEM/TAK/SIN	chirurgeon	KAOI/RUR/JON
chemotaxis	KAOEM/TAK/SIS	chirurgery	KAOI/RURJ/RI
chemothalamectomy	KAOEM/THAL/MEKT/M*I	-chirurgia	KAOI/RUR/JA
chemothalamotomy	KAOEM/THAL/MOT/M*I		KAOI/RURJ/YA
chemotherapeutic	KAOEM/THER/PAOUT/IK	chirurgica	KAOI/RURJ/KA
chemotherapeutics	KAOEM/THER/PAOUT/IK/-S	chirurgicum	KAOI/RURJ/KUM
chemotherapy	KAOEM/THER/PI	chisel	KHIZ/EL
chemotic	KAOE/MOT/IK	chi-square	KAOI/SKWAIR
chemotransmitter	KAOEM/TRA*NS/MIT/ER	chitin	KAOI/TIN
chemotrophic	KAOEM/TROFK	chitinase	KAOIT/NAIS
chemotropic	KAOEM/TROP/IK	chitinous	KAOIT/NOUS
chemotropism	KAOEM/TROEP/IFM	chitobiose	KAOIT/BAO*I/OES
	KAOE/MOT/RO/PIFM	chitodextrinase	KAOIT/DEX/TRI/NAIS
Chemstrip	KEM/STRIP	chitonic	KAOI/TON/IK
Chemstrip bG	KEM/STRIP/B-RBGS/G*RBGS	chitosamine	KAOI/TOES/MAOEN
chemurgy	KEM/UR/JI	chitosan	KAOI/SAN
Chenais	SHE/NAIZ	chitose	KAOI/TOES
chenic	KAOEN/IK	chitotriose	KAOIT/TR*I/OES
Chenix	KAOEN/IX	chlamydemia	KLAM/DAOEM/YA
cheno-	KAOEN	chlamydia	KLA/MID/YA
	KAOE/NO	Chlamydia	K-P/KLA/MID/YA
chenodeoxycholate	KAOEN/DE/OX/KOE/LAIT	Chlamydiaceae	KLA/MID/YAIS/YAE
chenodeoxycholic	KAOEN/DE/OX/KOEL/IK	chlamydiae	KLA/MID/YAE
chenodiol	KAOEN/DI/OL	chlamydial	KLA/MID/YAL
chenotherapy	KAOEN/THER/PI	Chlamydiales	KLA/MID/YAI/LAOEZ
Cheracol	KHER/KOL	chlamydiosis	KLA/MID/YOE/SIS
Cheracol Plus	KHER/KOL/PLUS	Chlamydoconidium	KLAM/DO/KO/NID/YUM
cherry	KHER/RI	Chlamydophrys	KLA/MID/FRIS
cherub	KHER/UB	Chlamydozoaceae	KLA/MID/ZOE/AIS/YAE
cherubism	KHER/BIFM		KLAM/DO/ZOE/AIS/YAE
	KHER/UB/IFM	Chlamydozoon	KLAM/DO/ZAON
Chervin	SHER/VAN	chloasma	KLOE/AZ/MA
chest	KH*ES	chlophedianol	KLOEF/DAOI/NOL
chestnut	KH*ES/NUT	chlor(o)-	KLOR
chevron	SHEV/RON		KLOER
chew	KHAOU		KLOR/R(O)
chewing	KHAOU/-G		KLOER/R(O)
chi	KAOI	chloracetization	KLOR/AS/TI/ZAIGS
chiasm	KAOI/AFM	chloracne	KLOR/AK/NAOE
chiasma	KAOI/AZ/MA	Chlorafed	KLOR/FED
chiasmal	KAOI/AZ/MAL	chloral	KLORL
chiasmapexy	KAOI/AZ/MA/PEK/SI		KLOR/RAL
chiasmata	KAOI/AZ/MA/TA	chloral hydrate	KLORL/HAOI/DRAIT
chiasmatic	KAOI/AZ/MAT/IK	chloralism	KLORL/IFM
chiasmatica	KAOI/AZ/MAT/KA	chloralization	KLORL/ZAIGS
chiasmatis	KAOI/AZ/MA/TIS	chloralose	KLOR/LOES
chiasmatypy	KAOI/AZ/MA/TAOI/PI	chlorambucil	KLOR/AM/BAOU/SIL
chiasmic	KAOI/AZ/MIK	chloramine	KLOR/MAOEN
chickenpox	KHIK/-N/POX	chloraminophene	KLOR/AM/NO/FAOEN
	KHIK/EN/POX	chloramiphene	KLOR/AM/FAOEN
chigger	KHIG/ER	chloramphenicol	KLOR/AM/FEN/KOL
chigoe	KHIG/GOE	chloranilic	KLOR/NIL/IK
chilblain	KHIL/BLAIN	Chloraseptic	KLOR/SEPT/IK
child	KHAOILD	chlorata	KLOE/RAI/TA

	KLOR/RAI/TA
chlorate	KLOR/AIT
	KLOR/RAIT
chlorazanil	KLOE/RAZ/NIL
	KLOR/AZ/NIL
chlorazene	KLOR/ZAOEN
chlorazol	KLOR/ZOL
chlorbenzoxamine	KLOR/BEN/ZOX/MAOEN
	KLOR/BENZ/OX/MAOEN
chlorbenzoxyethamine	KLOR/BEN/ZOX/*ET/MAOEN
	KLOR/BENZ/OX/*ET/MAOEN
chlorbetamide	KLOR/BET/MAOID
chlorbutol	KLOR/BAOU/TOL
chlorcyclizine	KLOR/SIK/LI/ZAOEN
	KLOR/SAOI/KLI/ZAOEN
chlordane	KLOR/DAIN
chlordantoin	KLOR/DAN/TOIN
	KLOR/DANT/WIN
chlordiazepoxide	KLOR/DI/AZ/POK/SAOID
chlordimorine	KLOR/DIM/RAOEN
chlorellin	KLOE/REL/LIN
chloremia	KLOE/RAOEM/YA
chlorenchyma	KLOR/ENG/MA
	KLOE/RENG/MA
Chloresium	KLOE/RAOEZ/YUM
chlorethene	KLOR/*ET/AOEN
chloretic	KLOE/RET/IK
chlorguanide	KLOR/GAU/NAOID
chlorhexadol	KLOR/HEX/DOL
chlorhexidine	KLOR/HEX/DAOEN
chlorhistechia	KLOR/HIS/TEK/YA
chlorhydrex	KLOR/HAOI/DREX
chlorhydria	KLOR/HAOI/DRA
	KLOR/HAOI/DRAOE/YA
chlorhydric	KLOR/HAOI/DRIK
chloric	KLOR/IK
chloridation	KLOR/DAIGS
chloride	KLOR/AOID
	KLOR/RAOID
chloridimeter	KLOR/DIM/TER
chloridimetry	KLOR/DIM/TRI
chloridion	KLOR/ID/AOIN
	KLOE/RID/AOIN
chloridometer	KLOR/DOM/TER
chloridorrhea	KLOR/ID/RAOE/YA
chloriduria	KLOR/DAOUR/YA
chlorin	KLOR/RIN
chlorinata	KLOR/NAI/TA
chlorinate	KLOR/NAIT
chlorindanol	KLOR/IND/NOL
chlorine	KLOR/AOEN
	KLOR/RAOEN
chloriodized	KLOR/AOI/DAOIZ/-D
chloriodoquin	KLOR/YO/DOE/KWIN
chlorisondamine	KLOR/AOI/SOND/MAOEN
	KLOR/SOND/MAOEN
chlorite	KLOR/AOIT
	KLOR/RAOIT
chlormadinone	KLOR/MAD/NOEN
chlormerodrin	KLOR/MER/DRIN
chlormethazanone	KLOR/ME/THAZ/NOEN
chlormethyl	KLOR/M*ET/IL
chlormezanone	KLOR/MEZ/NOEN
chloroacetic	KLOR/AI/SAOET/IK
chloroacetophenone	KLOR/AS/TO/FAOE/NOEN
chloroanemia	KLOR/AI/NAOEM/YA
chloroazodin	KLOR/A*Z/DIN
	KLOR/AZ/DIN
Chlorobacteriaceae	KLOR/BAK/TAOER/YAIS/YAE
Chlorobacterium	KLOR/BAK/TAOERM
Chlorobium	KLOR/ROEB/YUM
	KLOE/ROEB/YUM
chlorobrightism	KLOR/BRAOIGT/IFM
	KLOR/BRAOIT/IFM
chlorobutanol	KLOR/BAOUT/NOL
Chlorochromatium	KLOR/KROE/MAT/YUM
	KLOR/KROE/MAI/SHUM
	KLOR/KROE/MAIRB/UM
chlorocresol	KLOR/KRAOE/SOL
chlorocruorin	KLOR/KRAOU/RIN
chloroerythroblastoma	KLOR/R*IT/RO/BLAS/TOE/MA
chloroethane	KLOR/*ET/AIN
chloroethylene	KLOR/*ET/LAOEN
chloroform	KLOR/FORM
chloroformate	KLOR/FOR/MAIT
chloroformi	KLOR/FOR/MAOI
chloroformism	KLOR/FORM/IFM
	KLOR/FOR/MIFM
chloroformization	KLOR/FORM/ZAIGS

chlorogenic	KLOR/JEN/IK
chloroguanide	KLOR/GAU/NAOID
	KLOR/GAUN/AOID
chlorohemin	KLOR/HAOE/MIN
chloroleukemia	KLOR/LAOU/KAOEM/YA
chloroma	KLOE/ROE/MA
	KLOR/ROE/MA
chloromercuribenzoate	KLOR/MER/KAOUR/BENZ/WAIT
	KLOR/MERK/RI/BENZ/WAIT
chloromethane	KLOR/M*ET/AIN
chlorometry	KLOE/ROM/TRI
	KLOR/OM/TRI
Chloromycetin	KLOR/MAOI/SAOE/TIN
chloromyeloma	KLOR/MAOI/LOE/MA
chloronaphthalene	KLOR/NA*FT/LAOEN
	KLOR/NAF/THA/LAOEN
chloropenia	KLOR/PAOEN/YA
chloropenic	KLOR/PAOEN/IK
chloropercha	KLOR/PER/KHA
chloropexia	KLOR/PEX/YA
chlorophane	KLOR/FAIN
chlorophenol	KLOR/FAOE/NOL
chlorophenothane	KLOR/FEN/THAIN
	KLOR/FAOEN/THAIN
chlorophyl	KLOR/FIL
chlorophylase	KLOR/FIL/AIS
chloropicrin	KLOR/PIK/RIN
chloroplast	KLOR/PLA*S
chloroprivic	KLOR/PRAOIVK
chloroprednisone	KLOR/PRED/NI/SOEN
chloroprocaine	KLOR/PRO/KAIN
chloropsia	KLOE/ROPS/YA
	KLOR/OPS/YA
chloropyramine	KLOR/PIR/MAOEN
chloroquine	KLOR/KWAOIN
	KLOR/KWIN
chlorosis	KLOR/ROE/SIS
	KLOE/ROE/SIS
chlorothen	KLOR/THEN
chlorothiazide	KLOR/THAOI/ZAOID
chlorothymol	KLOR/THAOI/MOL
chlorotic	KLOE/ROT/IK
	KLOR/ROT/IK
chlorotrianisene	KLOR/TR*I/AN/SAOEN
chlorous	KLOR/OUS
chlorovinyldichloroarsine	KLOR/VAOINL/DI/KLOR/AR/SAOEN
	KLOR/VAOINL/DI/KLOR/AR/SIN
chloroxine	KLOE/ROK/SAOEN
	KLOR/OK/SAOEN
chloroxylenol	KLOR/ZAOIL/NOL
chlorphenesin	KLOR/FEN/SIN
chlorphenindione	KLOR/FEN/IN/DI/OEN
chlorpheniramine	KLOR/FEN/IR/MAOEN
chlorphenol red	KLOR/FAOE/NOL/RED
chlorphenoxamine	KLOR/FEN/OX/MAOEN
chlorphentermine	KLOR/FEN/TER/MAOEN
chlorproethazine	KLOR/PRO/*ET/ZAOEN
chlorproguanil	KLOR/PRO/GAU/NIL
chlorpromazine	KLOR/PROEM/ZAOEN
chlorpropamide	KLOR/PROEP/MAOID
chlorprothixene	KLOR/PRO/THIK/SAOEN
chlorquinaldol	KLOR/KWINL/DOL
	KLOR/KWIN/AL/DOL
chlortetracycline	KLOR/TET/RA/SAOI/KLAOEN
chlorthalidone	KLOR/THAL/DOEN
Chlorthalidone Tablets	KLOR/THAL/DOEN/TAB/LET/-S
chlorthenoxazin	KLOR/THEN/OX/ZIN
Chlor-Trimeton	KLOR/TRAOIM/TON
chloruresis	KLOR/YAOU/RAOE/SIS
chloruretic	KLOR/YAOU/RET/IK
chloruria	KLOR/YAOUR/YA
chlorzoxazone	KLOR/ZOX/ZOEN
Chlumsky	KLUM/SKI
cho-	KOE
	(not KO; see co-)
choana	KOE/NA
	KOE/AI/NA
choanae	KOE/AI/NAE
choanal	KOE/NAL
choanoid	KOE/NOID
choanomastigote	KOE/NO/MA*S/GOET
Choanotaenia	KOE/NO/TAOEN/YA
chocolate	KHOK/LAT
Chodzko	KHODZ/KOE
choke	KHOEK
chokes	KHOEK/-S
Cholac	KOE/LAK
cholagogic	KOEL/GOJ/IK

cholagogue	KOEL/GOG
cholaic	KOE/LAI/IK
cholalic	KOE/LAL/IK
cholane	KOE/LAIN
cholaneresis	KOEL/NER/SIS
cholangi(o)-	KLAN/J(O)
	KOE/LAN/J(O)
cholangiectasis	KLAN/JEKT/SIS
cholangioadenoma	KLAN/JO/AD/NOE/MA
cholangiocarcinoma	KLAN/JO/KARS/NOE/MA
cholangiocellular	KLAN/JO/SEL/YAOU/LAR
cholangiocholecystocholedochectomy	
	KLAN/JO/KOEL/S*IS/KLED/
	KEKT/M*I
	KLAN/JO/KOEL/S*IS/KOL/DO/
	KEKT/M*I
cholangioenterostomy	KLAN/JO/SPWRO*S/M*I
cholangiofibrosis	KLAN/JO/FAOI/BROE/SIS
cholangiogastrostomy	KLAN/JO/GAS/TRO*S/M*I
cholangiogram	KLAN/JO/GRAM
cholangiography	KLAN/JOG/FI
cholangiohepatitis	KLAN/JO/HEP/TAOITS
cholangiohepatoma	KLAN/JO/HEP/TOE/MA
cholangiojejunostomy	KLAN/JO/JEJ/NO*S/M*I
cholangiolar	KLAN/JAOE/LAR
	KOE/LAN/JAOE/LAR
cholangiole	KLAN/JOEL
cholangiolitis	KLAN/JO/LAOITS
cholangioma	KLAN/JOE/MA
cholangiopancreatography	KLAN/JO/PAN/KRA/TOG/FI
cholangioscopy	KLAN/JOS/KPI
cholangiostomy	KLAN/JO*S/M*I
cholangiotomy	KLAN/JOT/M*I
cholangitic	KLAN/JIT/IK
	KOE/LAN/JIT/IK
cholangitis	KLAN/JAOITS
	KOE/LAN/JAOITS
cholanic	KOE/LAN/IK
cholanopoiesis	KOE/LAN/POI/SIS
	KOEL/NO/POI/SIS
cholanopoietic	KOE/LAN/POIT/IK
	KOEL/NO/POIT/IK
cholanthrene	KOE/LAN/THRAOEN
cholate	KOE/LAIT
chole-	KOEL
	KOE/LE
cholebilirubin	KOEL/BIL/RAOU/BIN
cholecalciferol	KOEL/KAL/SIF/ROL
cholechromopoiesis	KOEL/KROEM/POI/SIS
cholecyanin	KOEL/SAOI/NIN
cholecyst(o)-	KOEL/S*IS
	KOEL/SIS/T(O)
cholecystagogic	KOEL/S*IS/GOJ/IK
cholecystagogue	KOEL/S*IS/GOG
cholecystalgia	KOEL/SIS/TAL/JA
cholecystatony	KOEL/SIS/TAT/N*I
cholecystectasia	KOEL/SIS/TEK/TAIZ/YA
	KOEL/S*IS/EK/TAIZ/YA
cholecystectomy	KOEL/SIS/TEKT/M*I
cholecystendysis	KOEL/SIS/TEND/SIS
cholecystenteric	KOEL/S*IS/SPWER/IK
	KOEL/SIS/TEN/TER/IK
cholecystenteroanastomosis	KOEL/S*IS/SPWER/RO/AI/NA*S/
	MOE/SIS
	KOEL/SIS/TENT/RO/AI/NA*S/
	MOE/SIS
cholecystenterorrhaphy	KOEL/S*IS/SPWROR/FI
	KOEL/S*IS/SPWER/ROR/FI
	KOEL/SIS/TENT/ROR/FI
cholecystenterostomy	KOEL/S*IS/SPWRO*S/M*I
cholecystenterotomy	KOEL/S*IS/SPWROT/M*I
cholecystic	KOEL/S*IS/IK
cholecystis	KOEL/SIS/TIS
cholecystitis	KOEL/SIS/TAOITS
cholecystocholangiogram	KOEL/S*IS/KLAN/JO/GRAM
cholecystocolonic	KOEL/S*IS/KO/LON/IK
cholecystocolostomy	KOEL/S*IS/KO/LO*S/M*I
cholecystocolotomy	KOEL/S*IS/KO/LOT/M*I
cholecystoduodenostomy	KOEL/S*IS/DAOU/DEN/O*S/M*I
	KOEL/S*IS/DAOU/DE/NO*S/M*I
	KOEL/S*IS/DAOU/DAOE/NO*S/
	M*I
	KOEL/S*IS/DWOD/NO*S/M*I
cholecystoenterostomy	KOEL/S*IS/SPWRO*S/M*I
cholecystogastric	KOEL/S*IS/GAS/TRIK
cholecystogastrostomy	KOEL/S*IS/GAS/TRO*S/M*I
cholecystogram	KOEL/S*IS/GRAM
cholecystography	KOEL/SIS/TOG/FI
cholecystoileostomy	KOEL/S*IS/*IL/YO*S/M*I

cholecystointestinal	KOEL/S*IS/SPW*ES/NAL
cholecystojejunostomy	KOEL/S*IS/JEJ/NO*S/M*I
cholecystokinase	KOEL/S*IS/KAOI/NAIS
cholecystokinetic	KOEL/S*IS/KI/NET/IK
cholecystokinin	KOEL/S*IS/KAOI/NIN
	KOEL/S*IS/KIN/NIN
cholecystolithiasis	KOEL/S*IS/LI/THAOI/SIS
cholecystolithotripsy	KOEL/S*IS/L*IT/TRIP/SI
cholecystonephrostomy	KOEL/S*IS/NE/FRO*S/M*I
cholecystopathy	KOEL/SIS/TOP/TH*I
cholecystopexy	KOEL/S*IS/PEK/SI
cholecystoptosis	KOEL/S*IS/TOE/SIS
cholecystopyelostomy	KOEL/S*IS/PAOI/LO*S/M*I
cholecystorrhaphy	KOEL/SIS/TOR/FI
cholecystosis	KOEL/SIS/TOE/SIS
cholecystosonography	KOEL/S*IS/SOE/NOG/FI
cholecystostomy	KOEL/SIS/TO*S/M*I
cholecystotomy	KOEL/SIS/TOT/M*I
choledoch	KOEL/DOK
choledoch(o)-	KLED/K(O)
	KOL/DO/K-
	KOE/LED/K(O)
choledocha	KLED/KA
	KOE/LED/KA
choledochal	KOL/DOK/KAL
	KLED/KAL
choledochectomy	KLED/KEKT/M*I
	KOL/DO/KEKT/M*I
choledochendysis	KLED/KEND/SIS
	KOL/DO/KEND/SIS
choledochi	KLED/KAOI
	KOE/LED/KAOI
choledochiarctia	KLED/KI/ARKT/YA
	KLED/KI/ARK/SHA
choledochitis	KLED/KAOITS
	KOL/DO/KAOITS
choledochocele	KLED/KO/SAO*EL
choledochocholedochostomy	KLED/KO/KLED/KO*S/M*I
	KLED/KO/KOL/DO/KO*S/M*I
choledochoduodenostomy	KLED/KO/DAOU/DAOE/NO*S/M*I
	KLED/KO/DAOU/DE/NO*S/M*I
	KLED/KO/DWOD/NO*S/M*I
choledochoenterostomy	KLED/KO/SPWRO*S/M*I
choledochogastrostomy	KLED/KO/GAS/TRO*S/M*I
choledochogram	KLED/KO/GRAM
choledochography	KLED/KOG/FI
choledochohepatostomy	KLED/KO/HEP/TO*S/M*I
choledochoileostomy	KLED/KO/*IL/YO*S/M*I
choledochojejunostomy	KLED/KO/JEJ/NO*S/M*I
choledocholith	KLED/KO/L*IT
choledocholithiasis	KLED/KO/LI/THAOI/SIS
choledocholithotomy	KLED/KO/LI/THOT/M*I
choledocholithotripsy	KLED/KO/L*IT/TRIP/SI
choledocholithotrity	KLED/KO/LI/THOT/RI/TI
choledochoplasty	KLED/KO/PLAS/TI
choledochorrhaphy	KLED/KOR/FI
choledochoscope	KLED/KO/SKOEP
choledochostomy	KLED/KO*S/M*I
choledochotomy	KLED/KOT/M*I
choledochous	KLED/KOUS
choledochus	KLED/KUS
Choledyl	KOEL/DIL
choleglobin	KOEL/GLOE/BIN
cholehematin	KOEL/HAOEM/TIN
	KOEL/HEM/TIN
cholehemia	KOEL/HAOEM/YA
choleic	KOE/LAOE/IK
cholelith	KOEL/L*IT
cholelithiasis	KOEL/LI/THAOI/SIS
cholelithic	KOEL/L*IT/IK
cholelithotomy	KOEL/LI/THOT/M*I
cholelithotripsy	KOEL/L*IT/TRIP/SI
cholelithotrity	KOEL/LI/THOT/RI/TI
cholelithogenic	KOEL/L*IT/JEN/IK
cholemesis	KOE/LEM/SIS
cholemia	KOE/LAOEM/YA
cholemic	KOE/LAOEM/IK
cholemimetry	KOEL/MIM/TRI
cholephosphatase	KOEL/FOS/FA/TAIS
cholepathia	KOEL/PA*T/YA
choleperitoneum	KOEL/PERT/NAOEM
choleperitonitis	KOEL/PERT/NAOITS
cholepoiesis	KOEL/POI/SIS
cholepoietic	KOEL/POIT/IK
choleprasin	KOEL/PRAI/SIN
cholera	KOL/RA
cholerae	KOL/RAE
choleragen	KOL/RA/JEN
choleraic	KOL/RAI/IK

choleraphage	KOL/RA/FAIJ
choleresis	KOE/LER/SIS
choleretic	KOEL/RET/IK
	KOL/RET/IK
cholerheic	KOL/RAOE/IK
choleria	KOE/LER/YA
choleric	KOL/RIK
choleriform	KOL/RI/FORM
	KOE/LER/FORM
cholerigenic	KOL/RI/JEN/IK
cholerigenous	KOL/RIJ/NOUS
cholerine	KOL/RAOEN
	KOL/RIN
cholerization	KOL/RI/ZAIGS
choleroid	KOL/ROID
choleromania	KOL/RO/MAIN/YA
cholerrhagia	KOEL/RAI/JA
cholerrhagic	KOEL/RAJ/IK
cholestane	KOE/LES/TAIN
cholestanol	KOE/L*ES/NOL
cholestanone	KOE/L*ES/NOEN
cholestasia	KOE/LES/TAIZ/YA
	KOEL/STAIZ/YA
cholestasis	KOE/L*ES/SIS
	KOEL/STAI/SIS
cholestatic	KOEL/STAT/IK
	KOE/LES/TAT/IK
cholesteatoma	KL*ES/YA/TOE/MA
	KOEL/STAOE/TOE/MA
cholesteatomatous	KL*ES/YA/TOEM/TOUS
	KOEL/STAOE/TOEM/TOUS
cholesteatosis	KOEL/STAOE/TOE/SIS
	KL*ES/YA/TOE/SIS
cholestene	KOE/LES/TAOEN
cholestenone	KL*ES/NOEN
	KOE/L*ES/NOEN
cholester-	KL*ES/R-
	KOE/L*ES/R-
	KOE/LES/TR-
cholesteremia	KL*ES/RAOEM/YA
cholesteremic	KL*ES/RAOEM/IK
cholesterin	KL*ES/RIN
cholesterinemia	KL*ES/RIN/AOEM/YA
cholesterinized	KL*ES/RIN/AOIZ/-D
cholesterinosis	KL*ES/RI/NOE/SIS
cholesterinuria	KL*ES/RI/NAOUR/YA
cholesteroderma	KL*ES/RO/DER/MA
cholesterogenesis	KL*ES/RO/JEN/SIS
cholesterohistechia	KL*ES/RO/HIS/TEK/YA
cholesterohydrothorax	KL*ES/RO/HAOI/DRO/THOR/AX
cholesterol	KL*ES/ROL
cholesterolemia	KL*ES/ROL/AOEM/YA
cholesterolemic	KL*ES/ROL/AOEM/IK
cholesteroleresis	KL*ES/ROL/ER/SIS
cholesterologenesis	KL*ES/ROL/JEN/SIS
cholesterolopoiesis	KL*ES/ROL/POI/SIS
cholesterolosis	KL*ES/RO/O/SIS
	KL*ES/RO/LOE/SIS
cholesteroluria	KL*ES/ROL/YAOUR/YA
cholesterosis	KL*ES/ROE/SIS
choletelin	KOE/LET/LIN
choletherapy	KOEL/THER/PI
choleuria	KOEL/YAOUR/YA
choleverdin	KOEL/VER/DIN
Cholewa	KOE/LAI/VA
cholic	KOEL/IK
cholicele	KOEL/SAO*EL
choline	KOE/LAOEN
	KOE/LIN
cholinephosphotransferase	KOE/LAOEN/FOS/FO/TRA*NS/FRAIS
cholinergic	KOEL/NERJ/IK
	KOL/NERJ/IK
cholinester	KOEL/NES/TER
	KOE/LIN/ES/TER
cholinesterase	KOEL/N*ES/RAIS
	KOEL/NES/TRAIS
cholinoceptive	KOEL/NO/SEPT/IV
cholinoceptor	KOEL/NO/SEP/TOR
cholinolytic	KOEL/NO/LIT/IK
cholinomimetic	KOEL/NO/MAOI/MET/IK
	KOEL/NO/MI/MET/IK
cholo-	KOL
cholochrome	KOL/KROEM
cholocyanin	KOL/SAOI/NIN
chologenetic	KOL/JE/NET/IK
cholohematin	KOL/HAOEM/TIN
	KOL/HEM/TIN
cholohemothorax	KOL/HAOEM/THOR/AX
chololith	KOL/L*IT
chololithiasis	KOL/LI/THAOI/SIS
chololithic	KOL/L*IT/IK
choloplania	KOL/PLAIN/YA
cholopoiesis	KOL/POI/SIS
cholorrhea	KOL/RAOE/YA
choloscopy	KOE/LOS/KPI
cholothorax	KOL/THOR/AX
	KOEL/THOR/AX
Choloxin	KOE/LOK/SIN
choloyl	KOE/LOIL
	KOE/LOE/IL
choluria	KOE/LAOUR/YA
choluric	KOE/LAOUR/IK
cholylcoenzyme A	KOE/LIL/KO/EN/ZAOIM/ARBGS
chondr(o)-	KON/DR(O)
chondral	KON/DRAL
chondralgia	KON/DRAL/JA
chondralloplasia	KON/DRAL/PLAIZ/YA
chondrectomy	KON/DREKT/M*I
chondric	KON/DRIK
Chondrichthyes	KON/DRIK/THAOEZ
chondrification	KON/DRIF/KAIGS
	KON/DRI/FI/KAIGS
chondrify	KON/DRI/FI
chondrigen	KON/DRI/JEN
chondrin	KON/DRIN
chondritis	KON/DRAOITS
chondroadenoma	KON/DRO/AD/NOE/MA
chondroangioma	KON/DRO/AN/JOE/MA
chondroblast	KON/DRO/BLA*S
chondroblastoma	KON/DRO/BLAS/TOE/MA
chondrocalcific	KON/DRO/KAL/SIFK
chondrocalcinosis	KON/DRO/KALS/NOE/SIS
chondrocarcinoma	KON/DRO/KARS/NOE/MA
chondroclast	KON/DRO/KLA*S
chondrocostal	KON/DRO/KOS/TAL
chondrocranium	KON/DRO/KRAIN/YUM
chondrocyte	KON/DRO/SAO*IT
chondrodermatitis	KON/DRO/DERM/TAOITS
chondrodynia	KON/DRO/DIN/YA
chondrodysplasia	KON/DRO/DIS/PLAIZ/YA
chondrodystrophia	KON/DRO/DIS/TROEF/YA
chondrodystrophy	KON/DRO/DIS/TRO/FI
chondroectodermal	KON/DRO/EKT/DER/MAL
chondroendothelioma	KON/DRO/*END/THAOEL/YOE/MA
chondroepiphysial	KON/DRO/EP/FIZ/YAL
chondroepiphysitis	KON/DRO/EP/FI/SAOITS
chondrofibroma	KON/DRO/FAOI/BROE/MA
chondrogen	KON/DRO/JEN
chondrogenesis	KON/DRO/JEN/SIS
chondrogenic	KON/DRO/JEN/IK
chondroglossus	KON/DRO/GLOS/SUS
chondroglucose	KON/DRO/GLAOU/KOES
chondrography	KON/DROG/FI
chondrohypoplasia	KON/DRO/HO*IP/PLAIZ/YA
chondroid	KON/DROID
chondroitic	KON/DROIT/IK
	KON/DRO/IT/IK
chondroitin	KON/DROI/TIN
chondroitinuria	KON/DROI/TIN/YAOUR/YA
chondrolipoma	KON/DRO/LI/POE/MA
chondrology	KON/DROLG
chondrolysis	KON/DROL/SIS
chondroma	KON/DROE/MA
chondromalacia	KON/DRO/MA/LAI/SHA
chondromatosis	KON/DRO/MA/TOE/SIS
	KON/DROEM/TOE/SIS
chondromatous	KON/DROEM/TOUS
chondromere	KON/DRO/MAOER
chondrometaplasia	KON/DRO/MET/PLAIZ/YA
chondromitome	KON/DRO/MAOI/TOEM
chondromucin	KON/DRO/MAOU/SIN
chondromucoid	KON/DRO/MAOU/KOID
chondromucoprotein	KON/DRO/MAOUK/PRO/TAOEN
chondromyoma	KON/DRO/MAOI/YOE/MA
chondromyxoma	KON/DRO/MIK/SOE/MA
chondromyxosarcoma	KON/DRO/MIX/SAR/KOE/MA
chondronecrosis	KON/DRO/NE/KROE/SIS
chondro-osseous	KON/DRO/OS/YOUS
chondro-osteodystrophy	KON/DRO/O*S/YO/DIS/TRO/FI
chondropathology	KON/DRO/PA/THOLG
chondropathy	KON/DROP/TH*I
chondropharyngeus	KON/DRO/FRIN/JUS
chondrophyte	KON/DRO/FAOIT
chondroplasia	KON/DRO/PLAIZ/YA
chondroplast	KON/DRO/PLA*S
chondroplastic	KON/DRO/PLA*S/IK

chondroplasty	KON/DRO/PLAS/TI	chorioma	KOER/YOE/MA
chondroporosis	KON/DRO/PROE/SIS	choriomammotropin	KOER/YO/MAM/TROE/PIN
	KON/DRO/PO/ROE/SIS	choriomeningitis	KOER/YO/MEN/JAOITS
chondroprotein	KON/DRO/PRO/TAOEN	chorion	KOER/YON
chondrosamine	KON/DROES/MAOEN	chorionepithelioma	KOER/YON/EP/THAOEL/YOE/MA
	KON/DROES/MIN	chorionic	KOER/YON/IK
chondrosaminic	KON/DROES/MIN/IK	chorioplacental	KOER/YO/PLA/SEN/TAL
	KON/DRO/SA/MIN/IK	Chorioptes	KOER/YOP/TAOEZ
chondrosarcoma	KON/DRO/SAR/KOE/MA	chorioptic	KOER/YOPT/IK
chondrosarcomatosis	KON/DRO/SAR/KOEM/TOE/SIS	chorioretinal	KOER/YO/RET/NAL
chondrosarcomatous	KON/DRO/SAR/KOEM/TOUS	chorioretinitis	KOER/YO/RET/NAOITS
chondroseptum	KON/DRO/SEP/TUM	chorioretinopathy	KOER/YO/RET/NOP/TH*I
chondrosin	KON/DRO/SIN	chorista	KOE/RIS/TA
chondrosis	KON/DROE/SIS	choristoblastoma	KOE/R*IS/BLAS/TOE/MA
chondroskeleton	KON/DRO/SKEL/TON		KOE/RIS/TO/BLAS/TOE/MA
chondrosome	KON/DRO/SOEM	choristoma	KOE/RIS/TOE/MA
chondrosteoma	KON/DRO*S/YOE/MA		KOER/STOE/MA
chondrosternal	KON/DRO/STERNL	choroid	KOE/ROID
chondrosternoplasty	KON/DRO/STERN/PLAS/TI		KOER/OID
chondrotome	KON/DRO/TOEM	choroid(o)-	KOE/ROID
chondrotomy	KON/DROT/M*I		KOE/ROI/D(O)
chondrotrophic	KON/DRO/TROFK	choroidal	KOE/ROI/DAL
chondroxiphoid	KON/DRO/ZIF/OID	choroidea	KOE/ROID/YA
chondrus	KON/DRUS	choroideae	KOE/ROID/YAE
chonechondrosternon	KOEN/KON/DRO/STER/NON	choroidectomy	KOE/ROI/DEKT/M*I
	KOE/NAOE/KON/DRO/STER/NON	choroideremia	KOE/ROID/RAOEM/YA
chop	KHOP		KOE/ROI/DER/AOEM/YA
chord	KHORD	choroiditis	KOE/ROI/DAOITS
	(not KORD; see cord)	choroidocyclitis	KOE/ROID/SIK/LAOITS
chord(o)-	KHORD	choroidoiritis	KOE/ROID/AOI/RAOITS
	KHOR/DO	choroidopathy	KOE/ROI/DOP/TH*I
	(not KOERD or KOER/DO; see	choroidoretinitis	KOE/ROID/RET/NAOITS
	cordo-)	choroidosis	KOE/ROI/DOE/SIS
chorda	KHOR/DA	chorology	KOE/ROLG
chordae	KHOR/DAE	Christchurch	KRAO*IS/KH*URPBLG
chordal	KHOR/DAL		KRAO*IS/KHUR/-FP
chordalis	KHOR/DAI/LIS	Christian	KRIS/KHAN
chorda-mesoderm	KHORD/MES/DERM		KR*IS/YAN
Chordata	KHOR/DAI/TA	Christison	KR*IS/SON
chordate	KHOR/DAIT	Christmas	KRIS/MAS
chordectomy	KHOR/DEKT/M*I		KR*IS/MAS
chordee	KHOR/DAOE	-chroic	KROIK
	KHOR/DAI		KROE/IK
chorditis	KHOR/DAOITS	-chroism	KROIFM
	(not KOR/DAOITS; see corditis)		KROE/IFM
chordoblastoma	KHORD/BLAS/TOE/MA	chrom(o)-	KROEM (in most cases)
chordocarcinoma	KHORD/KARS/NOE/MA		KROE/M(O)
chordoepithelioma	KHORD/EP/THAOEL/YOE/MA	chromaffin	KROE/MAFN
chordoid	KHOR/DOID		KROE/MAF/FIN
chordoma	KHOR/DOE/MA	chromaffinity	KROEM/FIN/TI
chordosarcoma	KHORD/SAR/KOE/MA	chromaffinoma	KROE/MAF/NOE/MA
chordoskeleton	KHORD/SKEL/TON	chromaffinopathy	KROE/MAF/NOP/TH*I
chordotomy	KHOR/DOT/M*I	Chromagen	KRO*EM/JEN
	(not KOR/DOT/M*I; see cordotomy)		(not KROEM/JEN; see chromogen)
chorea	KOE/RAOE/YA	chroman	KROE/MAN
chorea-acanthocytosis	KOE/RAOE/YA/AI/KA*NT/SAOI/	chromane	KROE/MAIN
	TOE/SIS	chromanol	KROEM/NOL
choreal	KOE/RAOEL		KROE/MAN/OL
	KOE/RAOE/YAL	chromaphil	KROE/MA/FIL
choreatic	KOER/YAT/IK		(not KROEM/FIL; see chromophil)
choreic	KOE/RAOE/IK	chromargentaffin	KROEM/AR/JENT/FIN
choreiform	KOE/RAOE/FORM	-chromasia	KROE/MAIZ/YA
choreoathetoid	KOER/YO/A*T/TOID	chromat(o)-	KROEM/T(O)
choreoathetosis	KOER/YO/A*T/TOE/SIS		KROE/MAT
choreoid	KOER/YOID	chromate	KROE/MAIT
choreophrasia	KOER/YO/FRAIZ/YA	chromatelopsia	KROE/MAT/LOPS/YA
chori(o)-	KOER/Y(O)		KROE/MAT/LOPS/YA
	KHOR/Y(O)	chromatic	KROE/MAT/IK
chorioadenoma	KOER/YO/AD/NOE/MA	chromatid	KROEM/TID
chorioallantoic	KOER/YO/AL/AN/TOIK	chromatin	KROEM/TIN
	KOER/YO/AL/LAN/TOIK	chromatinic	KROEM/TIN/IK
chorioallantois	KOER/YO/AI/LANT/WIS	chromatin-negative	KROEM/TIN/NEG/TIV
	KOER/YO/AL/LANT/WIS	chromatinolysis	KROEM/TI/NOL/SIS
chorioamnionitis	KOER/YO/AM/NAOE/NAOITS		KROEM/TIN/OL/SIS
	KOER/YO/AM/NO/NAOITS	chromatinorrhexis	KROE/MAT/NO/REK/SIS
chorioangiofibroma	KOER/YO/AN/JO/FAOI/BROE/MA	chromatin-positive	KROEM/TIN/POZ/TIV
chorioangioma	KOER/YO/AN/JOE/MA	chromatism	KROEM/TIFM
chorioangiomatosis	KOER/YO/AN/JOEM/TOE/SIS	Chromatium	KROE/MAI/SHUM
	KOER/YO/AN/JO/MA/TOE/SIS		KROE/MAIRB/YUM
chorioangiosis	KOER/YO/AN/JOE/SIS	chromatize	KROEM/TAOIZ
chorioblastoma	KOER/YO/BLAS/TOE/MA	chromatoblast	KROEM/TO/BLA*S
chorioblastosis	KOER/YO/BLAS/TOE/SIS	chromatodysopia	KROEM/TO/DIS/OEP/YA
choriocapillaris	KOER/YO/KAP/LAI/RIS	chromatogenous	KROEM/TOJ/NOUS
choriocarcinoma	KOER/YO/KARS/NOE/MA	chromatogram	KROE/MAT/GRAM
choriocele	KOER/YO/SAO*EL	chromatograph	KROE/MAT/GRAF
chorioepithelioma	KOER/YO/EP/THAOEL/YOE/MA	chromatographic	KROE/MAT/GRAFK
choriogenesis	KOER/YO/JEN/SIS		KROEM/TO/GRAFK
choriogonadotropin	KOER/YO/GON/DO/TROE/PIN	chromatography	KROEM/TOG/FI
chorioidea	KOER/YOID/YA	chromatoid	KROEM/TOID

chromatoidal	KROEM/TOI/DAL	chromopexis	KROEM/PEK/SIS
chromatokinesis	KROEM/TO/KI/NAOE/SIS	chromopexy	KROEM/PEK/SI
chromatology	KROEM/TOLG	chromophage	KROEM/FAIJ
chromatolysis	KROEM/TOL/SIS	chromophane	KROEM/FAIN
chromatolysm	KROE/MAT/LIFM	chromophil	KROEM/FIL
chromatolytic	KROEM/TO/LIT/IK	chromophile	KROEM/FAOIL
chromatometer	KROEM/TOM/TER	chromophilia	KROEM/FIL/YA
chromatopectic	KROEM/TO/PEKT/IK	chromophilic	KROEM/FIL/IK
chromatopexis	KROEM/TO/PEK/SIS	chromophilous	KROE/MOF/LOUS
chromatophagus	KROEM/TOF/GUS	chromophobe	KROEM/FOEB
chromatophil	KROE/MAT/FIL	chromophobia	KROEM/FOEB/YA
	KROEM/TO/FIL	chromophobic	KROEM/FOEB/IK
chromatophile	KROE/MAT/FAOIL	chromophore	KROEM/FOER
	KROEM/TO/FAOIL	chromophoric	KROEM/FOER/IK
chromatophilia	KROEM/TO/FIL/YA	chromophorous	KROE/MOF/ROUS
chromatophilic	KROEM/TO/FIL/IK	chromophose	KROEM/FOES
chromatophilous	KROEM/TOF/LOUS		KROEM/FOEZ
chromatophore	KROE/MAT/FOER	chromophototherapy	KROEM/FOET/THER/PI
	KROEM/TO/FOER	chromoplasm	KROEM/PLAFM
chromatophorotropic	KROEM/TO/FOER/TROP/IK	chromoplast	KROEM/PLA*S
chromatoplasm	KROEM/TO/PLAFM	chromoplastid	KROEM/PLAS/TID
chromatopseudopsis	KROEM/TO/SAOU/DOP/SIS	chromoprotein	KROEM/PRO/TAOEN
chromatopsia	KROEM/TOPS/YA	chromoretinography	KROEM/RET/NOG/FI
chromatoptometer	KROEM/TOP/TOM/TER	chromorhinorrhea	KROEM/RAOIN/RAOE/YA
chromatoptometry	KROEM/TOP/TOM/TRI	chromosantonin	KROEM/SANT/NIN
chromatoskiameter	KROEM/TO/SKAOI/AM/TER	chromoscope	KROEM/SKOEP
chromatosome	KROE/MAT/SOEM	chromoscopy	KROE/MOS/KPI
chromatotaxis	KROEM/TO/TAK/SIS	chromosomal	KROEM/SOE/MAL
chromatotropism	KROEM/TOT/RO/PIFM	chromosomal map	KROEM/SOE/MAL/MAP
chromaturia	KROEM/TAOUR/YA	chromosome	KROEM/SOEM
chrome	KROEM	chromosome map	KROEM/SOEM/MAP
-chromemia	KROE/MAOEM/YA	chromosome mapping	KROEM/SOEM/MAP/-G
chromene	KROE/MAOEN	chromosome pairing	KROEM/SOEM/PAIR/-G
chromenol	KROE/MEN/OL	chromospermism	KROEM/SPERM/IFM
	(not KROEM/NOL; see chromanol)		KROEM/SPER/MIFM
chromesthesia	KROE/MES/THAOEZ/YA	chromotherapy	KROEM/THER/PI
	KROEM/ES/THAOEZ/YA	chromotoxic	KROEM/TOX/IK
	KROEMS/THAOEZ/YA	chromotrichia	KROEM/TRIK/YA
chromhidrosis	KROEM/HAOI/DROE/SIS	chromotrichial	KROEM/TRIK/YAL
	KROEM/DROE/SIS	chromotrope	KROEM/TROEP
	KROEM/HID/ROE/SIS	chromotropic	KROEM/TROEP/IK
-chromia	KROEM/YA		KROEM/TROP/IK
chromic	KROEM/IK	chromoureteroscopy	KROEM/YAOU/RAOET/ROS/KPI
chromicize	KROEM/SAOIZ	chromourinography	KROEM/YAOUR/NOG/FI
chromicized	KROEM/SAOIZ/-D	chron(o)-	KROEN
chromidia	KROE/MID/YA		KRON
chromidial	KROE/MID/YAL		KROE/NO
chromidiation	KROE/MID/YAIGS	chronaxia	KROE/NAX/YA
chromidien	KROE/MID/YEN	chronaxie	KROE/NAK/SAOE
chromidiosis	KROE/MID/YOE/SIS	chronaximeter	KROE/NAK/SIM/TER
chromidium	KROE/MID/YUM		KRON/AK/SIM/TER
chromidrosis	KROE/MI/DROE/SIS	chronaximetric	KROE/NAX/MET/RIK
	KROE/MID/ROE/SIS		KRON/AX/MET/RIK
	(not KROEM/DROE/SIS; see	chronaximetry	KROE/NAK/SIM/TRI
	chromhidrosis)		KRON/AK/SIM/TRI
chromium	KROEM/YUM	chronaxy	KROE/NAK/SI
Chromobacterium	KROEM/BAK/TAOERM	chronic	KRON/IK
chromoblast	KROEM/BLA*S	chronica	KRON/KA
chromoblastomycosis	KROEM/BLA*S/MAOI/KOE/SIS	chronicity	KROE/NIS/TI
chromocenter	KROEM/SEN/TER		KRON/IS/TI
chromocholoscopy	KROEM/KOE/LOS/KPI	chronicum	KRON/KUM
chromoclastogenic	KROEM/KLA*S/JEN/IK	chroniosepsis	KRON/YO/SEP/SIS
chromocrinia	KROEM/KRIN/YA	chronobiologic	KRON/BAO*I/LOJ/IK
chromocystoscopy	KROEM/SIS/TOS/KPI		KROEN/BAO*I/LOJ/IK
chromocyte	KROEM/SAO*IT	chronobiological	KRON/BAO*I/LOJ/KAL
chromogen	KROEM/JEN		KROEN/BAO*I/LOJ/KAL
chromogene	KROEM/JAOEN	chronobiologically	KRON/BAO*I/LOJ/KLI
chromogenesis	KROEM/JEN/SIS		KROEN/BAO*I/LOJ/KLI
chromogenic	KROEM/JEN/IK	chronobiologist	KRON/BAO*I/O*LGS
chromogranin	KROEM/GRAN/NIN		KROEN/BAO*I/O*LGS
	KROEM/GRA/NIN	chronobiology	KRON/BAO*I/OLG
chromoisomerism	KROEM/AOI/SOM/RIFM		KROEN/BAO*I/OLG
chromolipoid	KROEM/LIP/OID	chronognosis	KRON/OG/NOE/SIS
chromolysis	KROE/MOL/SIS	chronograph	KRON/GRAF
chromomere	KROEM/MAOER		KROEN/GRAF
chromometer	KROE/MOM/TER	chronometer	KROE/NOM/TER
chromomycosis	KROEM/MAOI/KOE/SIS	chronometry	KROE/NOM/TRI
chromonar	KROEM/NAR		KRON/OM/TRI
chromone	KROE/MOEN	chronomyometer	KRON/MAOI/OM/TER
chromonema	KROEM/NAOE/MA		KRON/MAOI/YOM/TER
chromonemal	KROEM/NAOE/MAL	chronon	KROE/NON
chromonemata	KROEM/NAOEM/TA	chrono-oncology	KRON/ON/KOLG
	KROEM/NEM/TA	chronopharmacology	KRON/FARM/KOLG
chromoneme	KROEM/NAOEM	chronophobia	KRON/FOEB/YA
chromonychia	KROEM/NIK/YA	chronophotograph	KRON/FOET/GRAF
chromoparic	KROEM/PAR/IK		KRON/FRAF
chromopathy	KROE/MOP/TH*I	chronoscope	KRON/SKOEP
chromopectic	KROEM/PEKT/IK	chronotaraxis	KRON/TA/RAK/SIS
chromopexic	KROEM/PEX/IK		KROEN/TA/RAK/SIS

chronotropic	KRON/TROP/IK	chymorrhea	KAOIM/RAOE/YA
	KROEN/TROP/IK	chymosin	KAOIM/SIN
chronotropism	KRON/OT/RO/PIFM		KAOI/MOE/SIN
	KROE/NOT/RO/PIFM	chymosinogen	KAOIM/SIN/JEN
Chronulac	KRON/YAOU/LAK	chymotrypsin	KAOIM/TRIP/SIN
	KRON/YU/LAK	chymotrypsinogen	KAOIM/TRIP/SIN/JEN
chrotoplast	KROET/PLA*S	chymous	KAOIM/OUS
chrys(o)-	KRIS	chymus	KAOI/MUS
	KRI/S(O)	Ciaccio	KHA/KHOE
chrysarobin	KRIS/ROE/BIN	Ciarrocchi	KHAR/ROE/KAOE
chrysazin	KRIS/ZIN	Cibacalcin	SAOEB/KAL/SIN
chrysazine	KRIS/ZAOEN	Cibalith-S Syrup	SAOEB/L*IT/S-RBGS
chrysenic	KRI/SEN/IK	cibarian	SI/BAIRN
chrysiasis	KRI/SAOI/SIS		SI/BAIR/YAN
chrysocyanosis	KRIS/SAOI/NOE/SIS	cibisotome	SI/BIS/TOEM
chrysoderma	KRIS/DER/MA	cibophobia	SAOIB/FOEB/YA
chrysoidin	KRIS/OI/DIN		SIB/FOEB/YA
	KRI/SOI/DIN	cicatrectomy	SIK/TREKT/M*I
Chrysomyia	KRIS/MAOI/YA	cicatrices	SIK/TRI/SAOEZ
chrysophanic	KRIS/FAN/IK		SIK/TRAOI/SAOEZ
chrysophoresis	KRIS/FRAOE/SIS	cicatriceum	SIK/TRIRB/UM
Chrysops	KRIS/OPS		SIK/TRIRB/YUM
	KRI/SOPS		SIK/TRIS/YUM
chrysorrhoea	KRIS/RAOE/YA	cicatricial	SIK/TRIRBL
Chrysosporium	KRIS/SPOR/YUM	cicatricotomy	SIK/TRI/KOT/M*I
chrysotherapy	KRIS/THER/PI		SIK/TRAOI/KOT/M*I
chthonophagia	THON/FAI/JA	cicatrisata	SIK/TRI/SAI/TA
chthonophagy	THON/OF/JI		SIK/TRAOI/SAI/TA
chunk	KHUN/-K	cicatrisotomy	SIK/TRI/SOT/M*I
	KH*UNG		SIK/TRAOI/SOT/M*I
Churchill	KHUR/KHIL	cicatrix	SIK/TRIX
Chvostek	VOS/TEK		SI/KAI/TRIX
chyl(o)-	KAOIL	cicatrizant	SI/KAT/RI/ZANT
	KAOI/L(O)		SIK/AT/RI/ZANT
chylangioma	KAOI/LAN/JOE/MA	cicatrization	SIK/TRI/ZAIGS
chylaqueous	KAOI/LAIK/WOUS	cicatrize	SIK/TRAOIZ
chyle	KAOIL	cicatrizing	SIK/TRAOIZ/-G
chylectasia	KAOI/LEK/TAIZ/YA	ciclopirox olamine	SAOI/KLO/PIR/OX/OEL/MAOEN
chylemia	KAOI/LAOEM/YA	cicloprofen	SAOI/KLO/PRO/FEN
chyli	KAOI/LAOI	cicutoxin	SIK/TOK/SIN
chylic	KAOIL/IK		SIK/YAOU/TOK/SIN
chylica	KAOIL/KA	-cidal	SAOI/DAL
chylidrosis	KAOIL/DROE/SIS	-cide	SAO*ID
chylifacient	KAOIL/FAIRBT	cigarette	SIG/RET
chylifaction	KAOIL/FA*BGS	ciguatera	SIG/WA/TER/RA
chylifactive	KAOIL/FAKT/IV		SIG/WA/TAIR/RA
chyliferous	KAOI/LIF/ROUS	ciguatoxin	SIG/WA/TOK/SIN
chylification	KAOIL/FI/KAIGS	cilastatin sodium	SAOIL/STAT/TIN/SOED/YUM
	KAOI/LIF/KAIGS	cili(o)-	SIL/Y(O)
chyliform	KAOI/LI/FORM	cilia	SIL/YA
	KAO*IL/FORM	ciliare	SIL/YAI/RAOE
	(not KAOIL/FORM)	ciliares	SIL/YAI/RAOEZ
chylocele	KAOIL/SAO*EL	ciliaris	SIL/YAI/RIS
chylocyst	KAOIL/S*IS	ciliariscope	SIL/YAIR/SKOEP
chyloderma	KAOIL/DER/MA		SIL/YAR/SKOEP
chyloid	KAOI/LOID	ciliarotomy	SIL/YA/ROT/M*I
chylology	KAOI/LOLG	ciliary	SIL/YAIR
chylomediastinum	KAOIL/MAOED/YAS/TAOIN/UM	ciliastatic	SIL/YA/STAT/IK
chylomicrograph	KAOIL/MAOI/KRO/GRAF	Ciliata	SIL/YAI/TA
chylomicra	KAOIL/MAOI/KRA	ciliate	SIL/YAIT
chylomicron	KAOIL/MAOI/KRON	ciliated	SIL/YAIT/-D
chylomicronemia	KAOIL/MAOI/KRO/NAOEM/YA	ciliectomy	SIL/YEKT/M*I
chylopericarditis	KAOIL/P*ER/KAR/DAOITS	cilioequatorial	SIL/YO/EK/WA/TOIRL
chylopericardium	KAOIL/P*ER/KARD/YUM		SIL/YO/E/KWA/TOIRL
chyloperitoneum	KAOIL/PERT/NAOEM	ciliogenesis	SIL/YO/JEN/SIS
chylophoric	KAOIL/FOER/IK	Ciliophora	SIL/YOF/RA
chylopleura	KAOIL/PLAOUR/RA	ciliophoran	SIL/YOF/RAN
chylopneumothorax	KAOIL/NAOUM/THOR/AX	cilioposterocapsular	SIL/YO/PO*S/RO/KAPS/LAR
chylopoiesis	KAOIL/POI/SIS	cilioretinal	SIL/YO/RET/NAL
chylopoietic	KAOIL/POIT/IK	cilioscleral	SIL/YO/SKLAOERL
chylorrhea	KAOIL/RAOE/YA	ciliospinal	SIL/YO/SPAOINL
chylosa	KAOI/LOE/SA	ciliotomy	SIL/YOT/M*I
chylosis	KAO*I/LOE/SIS	ciliotoxicity	SIL/YO/TOK/SIS/TI
	(not KAOI/LOE/SIS; see cheilosis)	cilium	SIL/YUM
chylosus	KAOI/LOE/SUS	-cillin	SLIN
chylothorax	KAOIL/THOR/AX		SIL/LIN
chylous	KAOIL/OUS	cillo	SIL/LOE
	KAOI/LOUS	Cillobacterium	SIL/BAK/TAOERM
chyluria	KAOI/LAOUR/YA	cillosis	SIL/LOE/SIS
chylus	KAOI/LUS	cimbia	SIM/BAOE/YA
chym(o)-	KAOIM		(not SIM/BA; see cymba)
	KAOI/M(O)	cimetidine	SAOI/MET/DAOEN
chymase	KAOI/MAIS		SI/MET/DAOEN
chyme	KAOIM	Cimex	SAOI/MEX
chymification	KAOIM/FI/KAIGS	cimices	SIM/SAOEZ
chymodenin	KAOIM/DAOE/NIN	cimicid	SAOIM/SID
chymopapain	KAOIM/PAP/AIN	Cimicidae	SAOI/MIS/DAE
	KAOIM/PA/PAIN	cimicosis	SIM/KOE/SIS
chymopoiesis	KAOIM/POI/SIS	Cimino	SIM/NOE

Cinalone	SIN/LOEN	cinnamylic	SIN/MIL/IK
cinanesthesia	SIN/ANS/THAOEZ/YA	cinnarizine	SI/NAR/ZAOEN
cinanserin	SI/NANS/RIN		SIN/NAR/ZAOEN
	SIN/ANS/RIN	cinnipirine	SI/NIP/RAOEN
cinching	SIFRPBLG/-G		SIN/NIP/RAOEN
	SIN/-FPG	cinnopentazone	SIN/PENT/ZOEN
cinchol	SIN/KOL	Cinobac	SIN/BAK
cinchona	SIN/KOE/NA	cinocentrum	SIN/SEN/TRUM
cinchonic	SIN/KON/IK	cinology	SI/NOLG
cinchonidine	SIN/KOEN/DAOEN	cinometer	SI/NOM/TER
	SIN/KON/DAOEN	Cinonide	SIN/NAOID
cinchonine	SIN/KO/NAOEN	cinoplasm	SIN/PLAFM
	SIN/KO/NIN	cinoxacin	SI/NOX/SIN
cinchonism	SIN/KO/NIFM		SIN/OX/SIN
cinchophen	SIN/KO/FEN	cinoxate	SI/NOK/SAIT
cinclisis	SIN/KLI/SIS		SIN/OK/SAIT
cine-	SIN	cinromide	SIN/RO/MAOID
cineangiocardiography	SIN/AN/JO/KARD/YOG/FI	cintazone	SINT/ZOEN
cineangiograph	SIN/AN/JO/GRAF	cion	SAOI/YON
cineangiography	SIN/AN/JOG/FI	cionectomy	SAOI/NEKT/M*I
cinecienta	SIN/SAOE/YEN/TA	cionitis	SAOI/NAOITS
	SIN/SI/YEN/TA	cionoptosis	SAOI/NOP/TOE/SIS
	SIN/SEN/TA		SAOI/YON/OP/TOE/SIS
cinedensigraphy	SIN/DEN/SIG/FI	cionorrhaphy	SAOI/NOR/FI
cinefluorography	SIN/FLAOU/ROG/FI	cionotome	SAOI/YON/TOEM
cinegastroscopy	SIN/GAS/TROS/KPI		SAOI/ON/TOEM
cinemascopia	SIN/MA/SKOEP/YA	cionotomy	SAOI/NOT/M*I
cinemascopy	SIN/MAS/KPI	-cipient	SIP/YENT
cinematics	SIN/MAT/IK/-S	ciprocinonide	SIP/RO/SAOIN/NAOID
cinematization	SIN/MAT/ZAIGS	ciprofibrate	SIP/RO/FAOI/BRAIT
cinematography	SIN/MA/TOG/FI		SAOI/PRO/FAOI/BRAIT
cinematoradiography	SIN/MA/TO/RAID/YOG/FI	ciprofloxacin	SIP/RO/FLOX/SIN
cinemicrography	SIN/MAOI/KROG/FI	cirantin	SIR/AN/TIN
cineol	SIN/YOL		SI/RAN/TIN
cineole	SIN/YOEL	circadian	SIR/KAID/YAN
cinepazet maleate	SIN/PAZ/ET/MAL/YAIT	circellus	SIR/SEL/LUS
cinephlebography	SIN/FLE/BOG/FI	circhoral	SIR/KHORL
cinephotomicrography	SIN/FOET/MAOI/KROG/FI		SIR/KOR/RAL
cineplastics	SIN/PLA*S/IK/-S	circinata	SIRS/NAI/TA
cineplasty	SIN/PLAS/TI	circinate	SIRS/NAIT
cineradiography	SIN/RAID/YOG/FI	circinatus	SIRS/NAI/TUS
cinerea	SI/NAOER/YA	circle	SIRK/-L
cinereal	SI/NAOERL	circle of Willis	SIRK/-L/OF/WIL/LIS
	SI/NAOER/YAL	circlet	SIRK/LET
cinereus	SI/NAOER/YUS	circling	SIRK/-LG
cineritious	SIN/RIRBS	circuit	SIR/KIT
cineroentgenofluorography	SIN/RENT/GEN/FLAOU/ROG/FI	circul-	SIRK/L-
cineroentgenography	SIN/RENT/GEN/OG/FI		SIRK/YAOU/L-
cinesalgia	SIN/SAL/JA		SIRK/YU/L-
	SIN/ES/AL/JA	circular	SIRK/LAR
cineseismography	SIN/SAOIZ/MOG/FI	circulares	SIRK/LAI/RAOEZ
-cinesia	SI/NAOEZ/YA	circulate	SIRK/LAIT
	SAOI/NAOEZ/YA	circulating	SIRK/LAIT/-G
-cinesis	SI/NAOE/SIS	circulation	SIRK/LAIGS
	SAOI/NAOE/SIS	circulatory	SIRK/LA/TOIR
-cinetic	SI/NET/IK	circuli	SIRK/LAOI
	SAOI/NET/IK	circulus	SIRK/LUS
cinetoplasm	SIN/ET/PLAFM	circum-	SIR/KUM
	SI/NET/PLAFM		(*not* SIRK; see circumstance)
cinetoplasma	SIN/ET/PLAZ/MA	circumanal	SIR/KUM/AINL
	SI/NET/PLAZ/MA	circumarticular	SIR/KUM/AR/TIK/LAR
cineurography	SIN/YAOU/ROG/FI	circumaxillary	SIR/KUM/AX/LAIR
cingestol	SIN/JES/TOL	circumbulbar	SIR/KUM/BUL/BAR
cingul-	SIN/GL-	circumcallosal	SIR/KUM/KAL/LOE/SAL
	SING/L-	circumcize	SIR/KUM/SAOIZ
	SIN/GAOU/L	circumcision	SIR/KUM/SIGS
	SING/YAOU/L	circumclusion	SIR/KUM/KLAOUGS
	SING/YU/L	circumcornea	SIR/KUM/KORN/YA
cingula	SIN/GLA	circumcorneal	SIR/KUM/KORN/YAL
cingulate	SIN/GLAIT	circumcrescent	SIR/KUM/KRES/ENT
cingule	SIN/GAOUL	circumduction	SIR/KUM/D*UBGS
cingulectomy	SIN/GLEKT/M*I	circumference	SIR/KUM/FRENS
cinguli	SIN/GLAOI	circumferentia	SIR/KUM/FREN/SHA
cingulotomy	SIN/GLOT/M*I	circumferential	SIR/KUM/FREN/-RBL
cingulum	SIN/GLUM	circumflex	SIR/KUM/FLEX
cingulumotomy	SIN/GLUM/OT/M*I	circumflexa	SIR/KUM/FLEK/SA
cinnabar	SIN/BAR	circumflexae	SIR/KUM/FLEK/SAE
cinnamaldehyde	SIN/MALD/HAOID	circumflexus	SIR/KUM/FLEK/SUS
cinnamate	SIN/MAIT	circumgemmal	SIR/KUM/JEM/MAL
cinnamedrine	SIN/AM/DRAOEN	circuminsular	SIR/KUM/INS/LAR
cinnamein	SIN/AM/YIN	circumintestinal	SIR/KUM/SPW*ES/NAL
cinnamene	SIN/MAOEN	circumlental	SIR/KUM/LEN/TAL
	SIN/AM/MEN	circummandibular	SIR/KUM/MAN/DIB/LAR
cinnamic	SI/NAM/IK	circumnuclear	SIR/KUM/NAOUK/LAR
	SIN/AM/IK	circumocular	SIR/KUM/OK/LAR
cinnamol	SIN/MOL	circumoral	SIR/KUM/ORL
cinnamomi	SIN/MOE/MAOI	circumorbital	SIR/KUM/ORB/TAL
cinnamon	SIN/MON	circumpolarization	SIR/KUM/POE/LAR/ZAIGS
cinnamyl	SIN/MIL	circumpulpar	SIR/KUM/PUL/PAR

circumrenal	SIR/KUM/RAOENL	Cladosporium	KLAD/SPOR/YUM
circumscribe	SIR/KUM/SKRAOIB	Claforan	KLAF/RAN
circumscribed	SIR/KUM/SKRAOIB/-D	clairaudience	KLAIR/AUD/YENS
circumscripta	SIR/KUM/SKRIP/TA	clairsentience	KLAIR/SEN/SHENS
circumscriptum	SIR/KUM/SKRIP/TUM		KLAIR/SENT/YENS
circumscriptus	SIR/KUM/SKRIP/TUS	clairvoyance	KLAIR/VOINS
circumstantiality	SIRK/-RBL/TI	clairvoyant	KLAIR/VOINT
	SIR/KUM/STAN/-RBL/TI	clamoxyquin	KLAM/OX/KWIN
Circumstraint	SIR/KUM/STRAINT		KLA/MOX/KWIN
circumtonsillar	SIR/KUM/TONS/LAR	clamp	KLAFRP
circumtractor	SIR/KUM/TRAK/TOR	clang	KLANG
circumvallate	SIR/KUM/VAL/AIT	clap	KLAP
circumvascular	SIR/KUM/VAS/KLAR	clapotage	KLAP/TAJ
circumventricular	SIR/KUM/VEN/TRIK/LAR	clapotement	KLA/POET/-MT
circumvolute	SIR/KUM/VOL/YAOUT		KLA/POT/-MT
	SIR/KUM/VOE/LAOUT	Clapton	KLAP/TON
circumvolutio	SIR/KUM/VOE/LAOU/SHOE	Clara	KLAIR/RA
	SIR/KUM/VOE/LAOURB/YOE		KLAR/RA
cirrhogenous	SIR/ROJ/NOUS	clarificant	KLA/RIF/KANT
	SI/ROJ/NOUS		KLAIR/IF/KANT
cirrhonosus	SIR/RON/SUS		KLAR/IF/KANT
	SI/RON/SUS	clarification	KLAIR/FI/KAIGS
cirrhosis	SIR/ROE/SIS		KLAR/FI/KAIGS
	SI/ROE/SIS	clarify	KLAIR/FI
cirrhotic	SIR/ROT/IK		KLAR/FI
	SI/ROT/IK	Clark	KLARK
cirri	SIR/RAOI	Clarke	KLA*RK
cirrose	SIR/ROES	-clasia	KLAIZ/YA
cirrous	SIR/ROUS	-clasis	(v)K/LA/SIS
cirrus	SIR/RUS	clasmatocyte	KLAZ/MAT/SAO*IT
cirs(o)-	SIRS	clasmatocytosis	KLAZ/MAT/SAOI/TOE/SIS
	SIR/S(O)	clasmatodendrosis	KLAZ/MAT/DEN/DROE/SIS
cirsectomy	SIR/SEKT/M*I	clasmatosis	KLAZ/MA/TOE/SIS
cirsenchysis	SIR/SENG/SIS	clasmocytoma	KLAZ/MO/SAOI/TOE/MA
	SIR/SEN/KI/SIS	clasp	KLAS/-P
cirsocele	SIRS/SAO*EL	class	KLASZ
cirsodesis	SIR/SOD/SIS	classic	KLASZ/IK
cirsoid	SIR/SOID		KLAS/SIK
cirsomphalos	SIR/SOM/FLOS	classification	KLAS/FI/KAIGS
	SIR/SOM/FA/LOS		KLASZ/FI/KAIGS
cirsophthalmia	SIR/SOF/THAL/MA	-clast	KLA*S
	SIR/SOF/THAL/MAOE/YA	clastic	KLA*S/IK
cirsotome	SIRS/TOEM	clasto-	KLA*S
cirsotomy	SIR/SOT/M*I		KLAS/TO
cisplatin	SIS/PLA/TIN	clastogenic	KLA*S/JEN/IK
cissa	SIS/SA	clastothrix	KLA*S/THRIX
cistern	SIS/TERN	clathrate	KLA*T/RAIT
cisterna	SIS/TER/NA	clathrin	KLA*T/RIN
cisternae	SIS/TER/NAE	Clauberg	KLAU/BERG
cisternal	SIS/TERNL	Claude	KLAUD
cisternographic	SIS/TERN/GRAFK	claudicant	KLAUD/KANT
	SIS/TER/NO/GRAFK	claudication	KLAUD/KAIGS
cisternography	SIS/TERN/OG/FI	claudicatory	KLAUD/KA/TOIR
	SIS/TER/NOG/FI	Claudius	KLAUD/YUS
cisternostomy	SIS/TER/NO*S/M*I	claustra	KLAUS/TRA
cistron	SIS/TRON	claustral	KLAUS/TRAL
cistronic	SIS/TRON/IK	claustrophilia	KLAUS/TRO/FIL/YA
cisvestism	SIS/VES/TIFM	claustrophobia	KLAUS/TRO/FOEB/YA
cisvestitism	SIS/V*ES/TIFM		KLA*US/FOEB/YA
Citracal	SIT/RA/KAL	claustrophobic	KLAUS/TRO/FOEB/IK
citral	SIT/RAL		KLA*US/FOEB/IK
citrase	SIT/RAIS	claustrum	KLAUS/TRUM
citratase	SIT/RA/TAIS	clausura	KLAU/SAOU/RA
citrate	SIT/RAIT	clava	KLAI/VA
	SI/TRAIT	clavacin	KLAIV/SIN
citrated	SIT/RAIT/-D	claval	KLAIVL
	SI/TRAIT/-D	clavate	KLAI/VAIT
citric	SIT/RIK	clavatus	KLA/VAI/TUS
citridesmolase	SIT/RI/DES/MO/LAIS		KLAI/VAI/TUS
citrin	SIT/RIN	clavelization	KLAV/LI/ZAIGS
Citrobacter	SIT/RO/BAK/TER		KLAVL/ZAIGS
Citrocarbonate	SIT/RO/KARB/NAIT	clavi	KLAI/VAOI
citrogenase	SI/TROJ/NAIS	clavic(o)-	KLAV/K(O)
Citrolith	SIT/RO/L*IT		KLA/VIK
citronella	SIT/RO/NEL/LA	Claviceps	KLAV/SEPS
citrophosphate	SIT/RO/FOS/FAIT	Claviceps purpurea	KLAV/SEPS/PUR/PAOUR/YA
citrovorum	SIT/RO/VOR/UM	Clavicipitaceae	KLAV/SIP/TAIS/YAE
citrulline	SIT/RUL/LAOEN	Clavicipitales	KLAV/SIP/TAI/LAOEZ
	SIT/RUL/LIN	clavicle	KLAV/K-L
citrullinemia	SIT/RUL/NAOEM/YA	clavicoracoaxillary	KLAV/KOR/KO/AX/LAIR
citrullinuria	SIT/RUL/NAOUR/YA	clavicotomy	KLAV/KOT/M*I
citta	SIT/TA	clavicul-	KLA/VIK/L-
cittosis	SIT/TOE/SIS		KLA/VIK/YAOU/L-
Civatte	SI/VAT		KLA/VIK/YU/L-
Civinini	KHAOEV/NAOE/NAOE	clavicula	KLA/VIK/LA
	SIV/NAOE/NAOE	claviculae	KLA/VIK/LAE
cladiosis	KLAD/YOE/SIS	clavicular	KLA/VIK/LAR
Clado	KLA/DOE	claviculare	KLA/VIK/LAI/RAOE
cladosporiosis	KLAD/SPOR/YOE/SIS	claviculares	KLA/VIK/LAI/RAOEZ

clavicularis	KLA/VIK/LAI/RIS	clinocephalism	KLAOIN/SEF/LIFM
claviculi	KLA/VIK/LAOI	clinocephalous	KLAOIN/SEF/LOUS
claviculus	KLA/VIK/LUS	clinocephaly	KLAOIN/SEF/LI
claviformin	KLAV/FOR/MIN	clinodactylism	KLAOIN/DAKT/LIFM
clavipectoral	KLAV/PEKT/RAL	clinodactyly	KLAOIN/DAKT/LI
clavipectoralis	KLAV/PEKT/RAI/LIS	clinography	KLAOI/NOG/FI
clavulanic	KLAV/LAN/IK	clinoid	KLAOI/NOID
clavus	KLAI/VUS	clinology	KLAOI/NOLG
claw	KLAU	clinometer	KLAOI/NOM/TER
clawfoot	KLAU/FAOT	Clinoril	KLAOIN/RIL
clawhand	KLAU/HAND	clinoscope	KLAOIN/SKOEP
clay	KLAI	clinostatic	KLAOIN/STAT/IK
Claybrook	KLAI/BRAOK	clinostatism	KLAOIN/STAT/IFM
clazolam	KLAIZ/LAM	clinotherapy	KLAOIN/THER/PI
clazolimine	KLAI/ZOEL/MAOEN	clioquinol	KLAOI/KWIN/OL
clean	KLAOEN	clioxanide	KLAOI/OX/NAOID
cleaning	KLAOEN/-G	clip	KLIP
cleanse	KLENZ	cliprofen	KLI/PRO/FEN
cleansing	KLENZ/-G	cliseometer	KLIS/YOM/TER
clear	KLAOER	clithridium	KL*IT/RID/YUM
clearance	KLAOERNS	clithrophobia	KL*IT/RO/FOEB/YA
Clearasil	KLAOER/SIL	clition	KLIT/YON
clearer	KLAOER/ER	clitor-	KLIT/R-
clearing	KLAOER/-G		KLI/TOR
cleavage	KLAOEVJ		KLAOIT/R-
	KLAOEV/AJ	clitoral	KLIT/RAL
	KLAOE/VAJ		KLI/TORL
cleaver	KLAOEVR	clitorectomy	KLIT/REKT/M*I
cleft	KLEFT	clitoric	KLI/TOR/IK
cleid(o)-	KLAOID		KLIT/RIK
	KLAOI/D(O)	clitorid(o)-	KLI/TOR/D(O)
cleidagra	KLAOI/DAG/RA		KLAOI/TOR/D(O)
cleidal	KLAOI/DAL		KLIT/RID
cleidarthritis	KLAOI/DAR/THRAOITS	clitoridean	KLIT/RI/DAOEN
	KLAOID/AR/THRAOITS		KLIT/RI/DAOE/YAN
cleidocostal	KLAOID/KOS/TAL	clitoridectomy	KLIT/RI/DEKT/M*I
cleidocranial	KLAOID/KRAIN/YAL	clitorides	KLI/TOR/DAOEZ
cleidocranialis	KLAOID/KRAIN/YAI/LIS		KLAOI/TOR/DAOEZ
cleidoic	KLAOI/DOIK	clitoridis	KLI/TOR/DIS
	KLAOI/DOE/IK		KLAOI/TOR/DIS
cleidomastoid	KLAOID/MAS/TOID	clitoriditis	KLIT/RI/DAOITS
cleidotomy	KLAOI/DOT/M*I	clitoridotomy	KLIT/RI/DOT/M*I
cleidotripsy	KLAOID/TRIP/SI	clitorimegaly	KLIT/RI/MEG/LI
-cleisis	KLAOI/SIS	clitoris	KLIT/RIS
cleistothecium	KLAO*IS/THAOES/YUM		KLI/TOR/RIS
	KLAOIS/TO/THAOES/YUM		KLAOI/TOR/RIS
clemastine	KLEM/AS/TAOEN	clitorism	KLIT/RIFM
	KLEM/STAOEN	clitoritis	KLIT/RAOITS
clemizole	KLEM/ZOEL	clitoromegaly	KLI/TOR/MEG/LI
clenching	KLEFRPBLG/-G		KLIT/RO/MEG/LI
	KLEN/-FPG	clitoroplasty	KLIT/RO/PLAS/TI
Cleocin	KLAOE/SIN	clitorotomy	KLIT/ROT/M*I
	KLAOE/YO/SIN	clival	KLAOIVL
cleoid	KLAOE/OID		KLAOI/VAL
clericorum	KLER/KOR/UM	clivi	KLAOI/VAOI
click	KLIK	clivography	KLAOI/VOG/FI
clicking	KLIK/-G	clivus	KLAOI/VUS
clidinium	KLAOI/DIN/YUM	cloaca	KLOE/AI/KA
	KLI/DIN/YUM	cloacae	KLOE/AI/SAE
climacophobia	KLAOIM/KO/FOEB/YA	cloacal	KLOE/AI/KAL
climacteric	KLAOI/MAK/TER/IK	cloacitis	KLOE/SAOITS
	KLAOI/MAKT/RIK	cloacogenic	KLOE/KO/JEN/IK
	KLAOI/MAK/TRIK	clobazam	KLOEB/ZAM
climacterium	KLAOI/MAK/TAOERM	clobetasol	KLOE/BAIT/SOEL
climatic	KLAOI/MAT/IK		KLOE/BAIT/SOL
climatology	KLAOIM/TOLG	clock	KLOK
climatotherapeutics	KLAOIM/TO/THER/PAOUT/	clocortolone	KLOE/KORT/LOEN
	IK/-S	clodanolene	KLOE/DAN/LAOEN
climatotherapy	KLAOIM/TO/THER/PI	clodazon hydrochloride	KLOED/ZOEN/HAOI/BRO/KLOR/
climax	KLAOI/MAX		AOID
climb	KLAOIM	clofazimine	KLOE/FAZ/MAOEN
climbing	KLAOIM/-G	clofedanol	KLOE/FED/NOEL
climograph	KLAOIM/GRAF		KLOE/FED/NOL
clinarthrosis	KLIN/AR/THROE/SIS	clofenamide	KLOE/FEN/MAOID
clindamycin	KLIND/MAOI/SIN	clofibrate	KLOE/FAOI/BRAIT
	KLIN/DA/MAOI/SIN		KLOEF/BRAIT
cline	KLAOIN	clogestone	KLOE/JES/TOEN
cling	KLING	clomacran	KLOEM/KRAN
clinging	KLING/-G	clomegestone	KLOEM/JES/TOEN
clinic	KLIN/IK		KLOE/ME/JES/TOEN
clinica	KLIN/KA	Clomid	KLOE/MID
clinical	KLIN/KAL	clomiphene	KLOEM/FAOEN
clinician	KLI/NIGS	clomipramine	KLOE/MIP/RA/MAOEN
	KLIN/IGS	clonal	KLOENL
clinicogenetic	KLIN/KO/JE/NET/IK		KLOE/NAL
clinicopathologic	KLIN/KO/PA*T/LOJ/IK	clonality	KLOE/NAL/TI
clino-	KLAOIN	clonazepam	KLOE/NAZ/PAM
	KLAOI/NO		KLOE/NAIZ/PAM
clinocephalic	KLAOIN/SFAL/IK	clone	KLOEN

clonic	KLON/IK	cnemial	NAOEM/YAL
clonicity	KLON/IS/TI	cnemis	NAOE/MIS
clonicotonic	KLON/KO/TON/IK	cnemitis	NAOE/MAOITS
clonidine	KLOEN/DAOEN	cnemius	NAOEM/YUS
cloning	KLOEN/-G	cnemoscoliosis	NAOEM/SKOEL/YOE/SIS
clonism	KLON/IFM	cnida	NAOI/DA
	KLOEN/IFM	cnidae	NAOI/DAE
clonismus	KLOE/NIZ/MUS	Cnidaria	NAOI/DAR/YA
clonixeril	KLOE/NIX/RIL	cnidarian	NAOI/DAR/YAN
clonixin	KLOE/NIK/SIN	cnidoblast	NAOID/BLA*S
clonogenic	KLOEN/JEN/IK	cnidocil	NAOID/SIL
clonograph	KLON/GRAF	cnidocyst	NAOID/S*IS
	KLOEN/GRAF	cnidosis	NAOI/DOE/SIS
clonorchiasis	KLOE/NOR/KAOI/SIS	Cnidospora	NAOID/SPOR/RA
clonorchiosis	KLOE/NORK/YOE/SIS	Cnidosporidia	NAOID/SPRID/YA
Clonorchis sinensis	KLOE/NOR/KIS/SAOI/NEN/SIS	co-	KO
	KLOE/NOR/KIS/SI/NEN/SIS	CO₂	KR-RBGS/O*RBGS/2
clonospasm	KLON/SPAFM	coacervate	KO/AS/ER/VAIT
	KLOEN/SPAFM	coacervation	KO/AS/ER/VAIGS
Clonothrix	KLOEN/THRIX	coadaptation	KO/AD/AP/TAIGS
clonus	KLOE/NUS	coadun-	KO/AD/N-
clopamide	KLOE/PAM/AOID		KO/AD/YAOU/N-
clopenthixol	KLOE/PEN/THIX/OEL		KO/AD/YU/N-
	KLOE/PEN/THIX/OL	coadunation	KO/AD/NAIGS
	KLOE/PEN/THIK/SOEL	coadunition	KO/AD/NIGS
	KLOE/PEN/THIK/SOL	CoAdvil	KO/AD/VIL
clopidol	KLOEP/DOEL	coagglutination	KO/AI/GLAOUT/NAIGS
	KLOEP/DOL	coagglutinin	KO/AI/GLAOUT/NIN
clopimozide	KLOE/PIM/ZAOID	coagul-	KO/AG/L-
clopirac	KLOEP/RAK		KO/AG/YAOU/L-
cloprednol	KLOE/PRED/NOEL		KO/AG/YU/L-
	KLOE/PRED/NOL	coagula	KO/AG/LA
cloprostenol	KLOE/PRO*S/NOEL	coagulability	KO/AG/LABLT
	KLOE/PRO*S/NOL	coagulable	KO/AG/LABL
Cloquet	KLOE/KAI	coagulant	KO/AG/LANT
clorazepate	KLOR/AZ/PAIT	coagulase	KO/AG/LAIS
clorexolone	KLOE/REX/LOEN	coagulate	KO/AG/LAIT
cloroperone	KLOR/PER/OEN	coagulated	KO/AG/LAIT/-D
clorophene	KLOR/FAOEN	coagulation	KO/AG/LAIGS
Clorpactin	KLOR/PAK/TIN	coagulative	KO/AG/LA/TIV
clorprenaline	KLOR/PREN/LAOEN	coagulator	KO/AG/LAI/TOR
clortermine	KLOR/TER/MAOEN	coagulogram	KO/AG/LO/GRAM
closantel	KLOE/SAN/TEL	coagulopathy	KO/AG/LOP/TH*I
closiramine	KLOE/SIR/MAOEN	coagulum	KO/AG/LUM
clostridia	KLOS/TRID/YA	coal	KOEL
clostridial	KLOS/TRID/YAL	coalescence	KO/LES/ENS
clostridiopeptidase	KLOS/TRID/YO/PEPT/DAIS	coapt	KO/APT
clostridium	KLOS/TRID/YUM	coaptation	KO/AP/TAIGS
Clostridium	K-P/KLOS/TRID/YUM	coarct	KO/ARKT
clostripain	KLOS/TRI/PAIN	coarctate	KO/ARK/TAIT
clostrisel	KLOS/TRI/SEL	coarctation	KO/ARK/TAIGS
closure	KLOE/SHUR	coarctotomy	KO/ARK/TOT/M*I
	KLOEZ/SHUR	coarse	KAORS
	KLOEZ/YUR		(not KORS; see course)
closylate	KLOE/SI/LAIT	coarticulation	KO/AR/TIK/LAIGS
	(not KLOES/LAIT; see close late)	coat	KOET
clot	KLOT	coating	KOET/-G
cloth	KLO*T	Coats	KOETS
clothiapine	KLOE/THAOI/PAOEN	cobalamin	KO/BAL/MIN
clotrimazole	KLOE/TRIM/ZOEL	cobalt	KO/BALT
clottage	KLOT/AJ	cobaltosis	KO/BAL/TOE/SIS
clouding	KLOUD/-G	cobaltous	KO/BAL/TOUS
Cloudman	KLOUD/MAN	cobamic	KO/BAM/IK
clove	KLOEV	cobamide	KO/BAM/AOID
cloxacillin	KLOX/SLIN	cobaya	KO/BAI/YA
	KLOX/SIL/LIN	Cobb	KO*B
Cloxapen	KLOX/PEN		(not KOB; see cob)
cloxyquin	KLOX/KWIN	cobinamide	KO/BIN/MAOID
clozapine	KLOEZ/PAOEN	cobinic	KO/BIN/IK
clubbing	KLUB/-G	Cobolin-M	KO/BOL/LIN/M-RBGS
clubfoot	KLUB/FAOT		KO/BOE/LIN/M-RBGS
clubhand	KLUB/HAND	cobra	KO/BRA
clump	KLUFRP	cobralysin	KO/BRAL/SIN
clumping	KLUFRP/-G	cobrotoxin	KO/BRO/TOK/SIN
cluneal	KLAOUN/YAL	cobweb	KOB/WEB
clunes	KLAOU/NAOEZ	cobyric	KO/BIR/IK
clunis	KLAOU/NIS	cobyrinamide	KO/BRIN/MAOID
clunium	KLAOUN/YUM		KO/BIR/IN/MAOID
clupearum	KLAOUP/YAI/RUM	cobyrinic	KO/BRIN/IK
	KLAOUP/YAIR/UM		KO/BIR/IN/IK
clupeine	KLAOUP/YIN	coca	KO/KA
cluttering	KLUT/ER/-G	cocaine	KO/KAIN
Clutton	KLUT/TON	cocainism	KO/KAIN/IFM
clysis	KLAOI/SIS	cocainization	KO/KAIN/ZAIGS
clysma	KLIZ/MA	cocarboxylase	KO/KAR/BOX/LAIS
clysmata	KLIZ/MA/TA	cocarcinogen	KO/KARS/NO/JEN
clyster	KL*IS/ER	coccal	KOK/KAL
clysterize	KL*IS/RAOIZ	-coccemia	KOK/SAOEM/YA
cm	KR*M	cocci	KOK/SAOI

94

cocci (coccidioidomycosis) test	
	KOK/SAOE/T*ES
cocci-	KOX
	KOK/SI
coccidi(o)-	KOK/SID/Y(O)-
coccidia	KOK/SID/YA
Coccidia	K-P/KOK/SID/YA
coccidial	KOK/SID/YAL
coccidian	KOK/SID/YAN
Coccidiasina	KOK/SID/YA/SAOI/NA
coccidioidal	KOK/SID/YOI/DAL
coccidioides	KOK/SID/YOI/DAOEZ
Coccidioides	K-P/KOK/SID/YOI/DAOEZ
coccidioidin	KOK/SID/YOI/DIN
coccidioidoma	KOK/SID/YOI/DOE/MA
coccidioidomycosis	KOK/SID/YOID/MAOI/KOE/SIS
coccidiosis	KOK/SID/YOE/SIS
coccidiostat	KOK/SID/YO/STAT
coccidiostatic	KOK/SID/YO/STAT/IK
coccidium	KOK/SID/YUM
coccigenic	KOK/SI/JEN/IK
coccillana	KOX/YA/NA
	KOX/YAN/NA
coccinella	KOX/NEL/LA
coccinellin	KOX/NEL/LIN
cocco-	KOK
	KOK/KO
coccobacillary	KOK/BAS/LAIR
coccobacilli	KOK/BA/SIL/LAOI
coccobacillus	KOK/BA/SIL/LUS
coccobacteria	KOK/BAK/TAOER/YA
coccode	KOK/OED
	KOK/KOED
coccogenic	KOK/JEN/IK
coccogenous	KOK/OJ/NOUS
	KOK/KOJ/NOUS
coccoid	KOK/OID
	KOK/KOID
-coccosis	KOK/KOE/SIS
cocculin	KOK/LIN
cocculus	KOK/LUS
coccus	KOK/KUS
coccy-	KOX (in most cases)
	KOK/SI
coccyalgia	KOX/YAL/JA
coccycephalus	KOX/SEF/LUS
coccydynia	KOK/SI/DIN/YA
	(not KOX/DIN/YA; see coxodynia)
coccyg(o)-	KOX/G(O)
	KOK/SIJ
	KOX/J-
	KOK/SI/J-
coccygalgia	KOX/GAL/JA
coccygea	KOK/SIJ/YA
coccygeal	KOK/SIJ/YAL
coccygectomy	KOX/JEKT/M*I
coccygei	KOK/SIJ/YAOI
coccygeopubic	KOK/SIJ/YO/PAOUB/IK
	KOK/SIJ/PAOUB/IK
coccygerector	KOX/JE/REK/TOR
	KOK/SIJ/REK/TOR
coccyges	KOX/JAOEZ
coccygeum	KOK/SIJ/YUM
	KOK/SIJ/UM
coccygeus	KOK/SIJ/YUS
coccygis	KOX/JIS
coccygodynia	KOX/GO/DIN/YA
coccygotomy	KOX/GOT/M*I
coccyodynia	KOX/YO/DIN/YA
coccyx	KOK/SIX
	KOX/IX
cochineal	KOFP/NAOEL
cochle(o)-	KOK/L(O)
	KOK/LAOE/Y(O)
cochlea	KOK/LA
cochleae	KOK/LAE
cochlear	KOK/LAR
cochleare	KOK/LAI/RAOE
cochleariform	KOK/LAR/FORM
	KOK/LAIR/FORM
cochlearis	KOK/LAI/RIS
cochleate	KOK/LAIT
cochleitis	KOK/LAOE/AOITS
	(not KOK/LAOITS; see cochlitis)
cochleosacculotomy	KOK/LO/SAK/LOT/M*I
cochleotopic	KOK/LO/TOP/IK
cochleovestibular	KOK/LO/VES/TIB/LAR
Cochliomyia	KOK/LO/MAOI/YA
cochlitis	KOK/LAOITS

cocillana	KOES/LA/NA
	KOES/LAN/NA
cock	KOK
cockade	KOK/AID
	KOK/KAID
Cockayne	KOK/AIN
	KOK/KAIN
cocked	KOK/-D
cocktail	KOK/TAIL
cocks comb	KOK/S/KOEM
cocoa	KO/KOE
	KOE/KOE
coconscious	KO/KON/-RBS
coconsciousness	KO/KON/-RBS/*NS
cocontraction	KO/KON/TRA*BGS
	KO/KR*BGS
coconut	KOEK/NUT
cocoon	KO/KAON
coction	KO*BGS
cocto-	KOKT
	KOK/TO
cocto-immunogen	KOKT/IM/MAOUN/JEN
	KOKT/IM/NO/JEN
coctolabile	KOKT/LAI/BAOIL
	KOKT/LAI/BIL
coctoprecipitin	KOKT/PRE/SIP/TIN
coctoprotein	KOKT/PRO/TAOEN
coctostabile	KOKT/STAI/BAOIL
	KOKT/STAI/BIL
coctostable	KOKT/STAIBL
coculine	KOK/LAOEN
cocultivation	KO/KULT/VAIGS
cod	KOD
code	KOED
Codalan	KOED/LAN
codecarboxylase	KO/DE/KAR/BOX/LAIS
codehydrogenase	KO/DE/HAOI/DROJ/NAIS
codeine	KO/DAOEN
codex	KO/DEX
Codex medicamentarium	KO/DEX/MED/KA/MEN/TAIRM
Codex medicamentarius	KO/DEX/MED/KA/MEN/TAIR/YUS
Codiclear	KOED/KLAOER
Codimal	KOED/MAL
Codivilla	KOED/VIL/LA
Codman	KOD/MAN
codominance	KO/DOM/NANS
codominant	KO/DOM/NANT
codon	KO/DON
coefficient	KO/FIRBT
-coele	SAO*EL
Coelenterata	SE/LENT/RAI/TA
	SAOE/LENT/RAI/TA
coelenterate	SE/LENT/RAIT
	SAOE/LENT/RAIT
coelom	see celom
coeno-	see ceno-
coenzyme	KO/EN/ZAOIM
coenzymometer	KO/ENZ/MOM/TER
	KO/EN/ZAOI/MOM/TER
coetaneous	KO/TAIN/YOUS
	KO/E/TAIN/YOUS
coeur	KAO*UR
	KOUR
	(not KAOUR; see cure)
coexcitation	KO/KPAOI/TAIGS
cofactor	KO/FAK/TOR
coffee	KOF/FAOE
coffin	KOFN
	KOF/FIN
cogener	KOEJ/NER
	KO/JEN/ER
Cogentin	KO/JEN/TIN
cognition	KOG/NIGS
cognitive	KOG/NI/TIV
cohesion	KO/HAOEGS
cohesive	KO/HAOES/IV
Co-Gesic	KO/JAOEZ/IK
Cohnheim	KOEN/HAOIM
	KON/HAOIM
cohoba	KO/HOE/BA
cohobation	KO/HOE/BAIGS
cohort	KO/HORT
cohydrogenase	KO/HAOI/DROJ/NAIS
coil	KOIL
coin-counting	KOIN/H-F/KOUNT/-G
coinosite	KOIN/SAOIT
coisogeneic	KO/AOIS/JE/NAI/IK
coital	KOI/TAL
coition	KO/IGS

	KOIGS		KOL/JEN
coitophobia	KOIT/FOEB/YA	collagenase	KLAJ/NAIS
	KOI/TO/FOEB/YA		KOL/JE/NAIS
coitus	KOI/TUS	collagenation	KLAJ/NAIGS
col	KO*L		KOL/JE/NAIGS
	(*not* KOL; frequent prefix)	collagenic	KOL/JEN/IK
col(o)-	KO/L(O)	collagenitis	KLAJ/NAOITS
	KOL	collagenization	KLAJ/NI/ZAIGS
cola	KO/LA	collagenoblast	KLAJ/NO/BLA*S
Colace	KO/LAIS	collagenocyte	KLAJ/NO/SAO*IT
colamine	KOEL/MAOEN	collagenogenic	KOL/JEN/JEN/IK
	KOEL/MIN		KLAJ/NO/JEN/IK
colaspase	KO/LAS/PAIS	collagenolysis	KOL/JEN/OL/SIS
colation	KO/LAIGS		KLAJ/NOL/SIS
colatorium	KOL/TOIRM	collagenolytic	KLAJ/NO/LIT/IK
colature	KOEL/KHUR	collagenosis	KLAJ/NOE/SIS
	KOL/KHUR	collagenous	KLAJ/NOUS
ColBENEMID	KOL/BEN/MID	collapse	KLAPS
colchicine	KOL/KHI/SIN	collar	KLAR
colchicinic	KOL/KHI/SIN/IK	collarette	KOL/RET
cold	KOELD	collastin	KLAS/TIN
	KOLD	collateral	KLAT/RAL
cold-blooded	KOELD/BLAOD/-D	collaterale	KLAT/RAI/LAOE
	KOLD/BLAOD/-D	collateralia	KLAT/RAIL/YA
coldsore	KOELD/SOER	collateralis	KLAT/RAI/LIS
	KOLD/SOER	collecting	KLEKT/-G
Cole	KO*EL	collenchyma	KLENG/MA
	(*not* KOEL; see coal)		KOL/LENG/MA
colectasia	KO/LEK/TAIZ/YA	Colles	KOL/LAOEZ
colectomy	KO/LEKT/M*I		KOL/AOEZ
Coleman	KOEL/MAN	Collesi	KLAOE/SAOI
coles	KO/LAOEZ		KOL/LAOE/SAOI
Colestid	KO/LES/TID	colli	KOL/LAOI
colestipol	KO/L*ES/POL	collicul-	KLIK/L-
	KO/L*ES/POEL		KLIK/YAOU/L-
coli	KO/LAOI		KLIK/YU/L-
coli-	KOEL (in most cases)		KOL/LIK/L-
	KO/LI		KOL/LIK/YAOU/L-
	KOL		KOL/LIK/YU/L-
colibacillemia	KOEL/BAS/LAOEM/YA	colliculectomy	KLIK/LEKT/M*I
colibacilli	KOEL/BA/SIL/LAOI	colliculi	KLIK/LAOI
colibacillosis	KOEL/BAS/LOE/SIS	colliculitis	KLIK/LAOITS
colibacilluria	KOEL/BAS/LAOUR/YA	colliculus	KLIK/LUS
colibacillus	KOEL/BA/SIL/LUS	colligation	KOL/GAIGS
colic	KOL/IK	colligative	KLIG/TIV
colica	KOL/KA	collimation	KOL/MAIGS
colicin	KOL/SIN	collimator	KOL/MAI/TOR
colicino-	KOL/SIN	Collin	KOL/LIN
	KOL/SI/NO-	collinearity	KLIN/YAIR/TI
colicinogen	KOL/SIN/JEN	Collins	KOL/LINS
colicinogenic	KOL/SIN/JEN/IK		KOL/LINZ
colicinogeny	KOL/SIN/OJ/N*I		KOL/LIN/-S
	KOL/SI/NOJ/N*I	colliotomy	KOL/YOT/M*I
colicky	KOL/KI	collip	KOL/IP
	KOL/IK/KI		KOL/LIP
colicoplegia	KOL/KO/PLAOE/JA		KL*IP
colicystitis	KO/LI/SIS/TAOITS		(*not* KLIP; see clip)
	(*not* KOEL/SIS/TAOITS; see	Collip	K-P/KOL/IP
	cholecystitis)		K-P/KOL/LIP
coliform	KOL/FORM		K-P/KL*IP
	KO/LI/FORM	colliquation	KOL/KWAIGS
	(*not* KOEL/FORM)	colliquative	KLIK/WA/TIV
colinearity	KO/LIN/YAIR/TI	collision	KLIGS
colinephritis	KOEL/NE/FRAOITS	collochemistry	KOL/KEM/STRI
colipase	KO/LIP/AIS	collodiaphysial	KOL/DAOI/FIZ/YAL
coliphage	KOL/FAIJ	collodion	KLOED/YON
	KOEL/FAIJ	collodium	KLOED/YUM
colipuncture	KOEL/PUNG/KHUR	colloid	KLOID
colisepsis	KOEL/SEP/SIS		KOL/OID
colistimethate	KO/L*IS/M*ET/AIT	colloidal	KLOI/DAL
colistin	KO/LIS/TIN	colloidale	KLOI/DAI/LAOE
colitides	KO/LIT/DAOEZ		KOL/OI/DAI/LAOE
colitis	KO/LAOITS		KOL/LOI/DAI/LAOE
colitose	KOL/TOES	colloidin	KLOI/DIN
colitoxemia	KOEL/TOK/SAOEM/YA	colloido-	KLOID
colitoxicosis	KOEL/TOX/KOE/SIS		KLOI/DO-
colitoxin	KOEL/TOK/SIN	colloidoclasia	KLOID/KLAIZ/YA
coliuria	KO/LI/YAOUR/YA	colloidoclasis	KLOID/KLAI/SIS
	(*not* KOEL/YAOUR/YA; see	colloidoclastic	KLOID/KLA*S/IK
	choleuria)	colloidogen	KLOID/JEN
coll-	KL-	colloidophagy	KLOI/DOF/JI
	KOL		KOL/OI/DOF/JI
	KOL/L-		KOL/LOI/DOF/JI
colla	KOL/LA	colloxylin	KLOX/LIN
collacin	KOL/LA/SIN		KOL/LOX/LIN
	(*not* KOL/SIN; see colicin)	collum	KOL/LUM
collagen	KOL/JEN		KLUM
collagen(o)-	KLAJ/N-		(*not* KOL/UM; see column)
	KOL/JE/N-	collu-	KOL

©1992 *StenEd* Medical Dictionary

	KOL/YAOU		cholerrhagia)
	KOL/YU	colorrhaphy	KO/LOR/FI
collunaria	KOL/NAIR/YA	colorrhea	KOEL/RAOE/YA
collunarium	KOL/NAIRM	coloscope	KOL/SKOEP
collutoria	KOL/TOER/YA		KOEL/SKOEP
collutorium	KOL/TOIRM	coloscopy	KO/LOS/KPI
collutory	KOL/TOIR	ColoScreen	KOEL/SKRAOEN
collyria	KLIR/YA	ColoScreen Self-Test	KOEL/SKRAOEN/SEFL/T*ES
	KO/LIR/YA	colosigmoidostomy	KOEL/SIG/MOI/DO*S/M*I
collyrium	KLIR/YUM	colostomy	KO/LO*S/M*I
	KO/LIR/YUM		KLO*S/M*I
colo-	KOEL	colostration	KO/LOS/TRAIGS
	KO/LO	colostric	KO/LOS/TRIK
	KOL	colostrorrhea	KO/LOS/TRO/RAOE/YA
coloboma	KOL/BOE/MA		KLOS/TRO/RAOE/YA
colocecostomy	KOEL/SE/KO*S/M*I	colostrous	KO/LOS/TROUS
colocentesis	KOEL/SEN/TAOE/SIS		KLOS/TROUS
colocholecystostomy	KOEL/KOEL/SIS/TO*S/M*I	colostrum	KO/LOS/TRUM
coloclysis	KOEL/KLAOI/SIS		KLOS/TRUM
coloclyster	KOEL/KL*IS/ER	colotomy	KO/LOT/M*I
colocolic	KOEL/KOL/IK		KLOT/M*I
colocolostomy	KOEL/KLO*S/M*I	colotyphoid	KOEL/TAOI/FOID
	KOEL/KO/LO*S/M*I	colovaginal	KOEL/VAJ/NAL
colocutaneous	KOEL/KAOU/TAIN/YOUS	colovesical	KOEL/VES/KAL
colocynth	KOEL/S*INT	colp(o)-	KOL/P(O)
colocynthidism	KOEL/S*INT/DIFM	colpalgia	KOL/PAL/JA
colocynthin	KOEL/SIN/THIN	colpatresia	KOL/PA/TRAOEZ/YA
colocynthis	KOEL/SIN/THIS	colpectasia	KOL/PEK/TAIZ/YA
colocystoplasty	KOEL/S*IS/PLAS/TI	colpectasis	KOL/PEKT/SIS
colodyspepsia	KOEL/DIS/PEPS/YA	colpectomy	KOL/PEKT/M*I
coloenteritis	KOEL/SPWRAOITS	colpeurynter	KOL/PAOU/RINT/ER
colofixation	KOEL/FIK/SAIGS	colpeurysis	KOL/PAOUR/SIS
colohepatopexy	KOEL/HEPT/PEK/SI	colpismus	KOL/PIZ/MUS
coloileal	KOEL/*IL/YAL	colpitic	KOL/PIT/IK
cololysis	KO/LOL/SIS	colpitis	KOL/PAOITS
colometrometer	KOEL/ME/TROM/TER	colpium	KOL/PUM
colominic	KOL/MIN/IK		KOL/PAOE/UM
colon	KO/LON	colpocele	KOL/PO/SAO*EL
colonalgia	KOEL/NAL/JA	colpoceliocentesis	KOL/PO/SAOEL/YO/SEN/TAOE/
	KO/LON/AL/JA		SIS
colonic	KO/LON/IK	colpoceliotomy	KOL/PO/SAOEL/YOT/M*I
	(not KLON/IK; see clonic)	colpocleisis	KOL/PO/KLAOI/SIS
colonitis	KOEL/NAOITS	colpocystitis	KOL/PO/SIS/TAOITS
	KO/LON/AOITS	colpocystocele	KOL/PO/S*IS/SAO*EL
colonization	KOL/NI/ZAIGS	colpocystoplasty	KOL/PO/S*IS/PLAS/TI
	KOL/NAOI/ZAIGS	colpocystotomy	KOL/PO/SIS/TOT/M*I
colonogram	KO/LON/GRAM	colpocystoureterocystotomy	KOL/PO/S*IS/YAOU/RAOET/RO/
colonometer	KOL/NOM/TER		SIS/TOT/M*I
	KOEL/NOM/TER	colpocystoureterotomy	KOL/PO/S*IS/YAOU/RAOET/ROT/
colonopathy	KOEL/NOP/TH*I		M*I
	KO/LON/OP/TH*I	colpocytogram	KOL/PO/SAOIT/GRAM
colonorrhagia	KOEL/NO/RAI/JA	colpocytology	KOL/PO/SAOI/TOLG
	KO/LON/RAI/JA	colpodynia	KOL/PO/DIN/YA
colonorrhea	KOEL/NO/RAOE/YA	colpohyperplasia	KOL/PO/HAO*IP/PLAIZ/YA
	KO/LON/RAOE/YA	colpohysterectomy	KOL/PO/H*IS/REKT/M*I
colonoscope	KO/LON/SKOEP	colpohysteropexy	KOL/PO/H*IS/RO/PEK/SI
	KLON/SKOEP	colpohysterotomy	KOL/PO/H*IS/ROT/M*I
colonoscopy	KOEL/NOS/KPI	colpomicroscope	KOL/PO/MAOI/KRO/SKOEP
	KO/LON/OS/KPI	colpomicroscopic	KOL/PO/MAOI/KRO/SKOP/IK
colony	KOL/N*I	colpomicroscopy	KOL/PO/MAOI/KROS/KPI
colopathy	KO/LOP/TH*I	colpomycosis	KOL/PO/MAOI/KOE/SIS
colopexia	KOEL/PEX/YA	colpomyomectomy	KOL/PO/MAOI/MEKT/M*I
colopexostomy	KOEL/PEK/SO*S/M*I	colpopathy	KOL/POP/TH*I
	KOEL/PEX/O*S/M*I	colpoperineoplasty	KOL/PO/P*ER/NAOE/PLAS/TI
colopexotomy	KOEL/PEK/SOT/M*I	colpoperineorrhaphy	KOL/PO/P*ER/NAOE/YOR/FI
	KOEL/PEX/OT/M*I	colpopexy	KOL/PO/PEK/SI
colopexy	KOEL/PEK/SI	colpoplasty	KOL/PO/PLAS/TI
colophony	KO/LOF/N*I	colpopoiesis	KOL/PO/POI/SIS
coloplication	KOEL/PLI/KAIGS	colpoptosia	KOL/PO/TOES/YA
	KOEL/PLAOI/KAIGS		KOL/POP/TOES/YA
coloproctectomy	KOEL/PROK/TEKT/M*I	colpoptosis	KOL/PO/TOE/SIS
coloproctia	KOEL/PROK/SHA		KOL/POP/TOE/SIS
coloproctitis	KOEL/PROK/TAOITS	colporectopexy	KOL/PO/REKT/PEK/SI
coloproctostomy	KOEL/PROK/TO*S/M*I	colporrhagia	KOL/PO/RAI/JA
coloptosia	KO/LOP/TOES/YA	colporrhaphy	KOL/POR/FI
coloptosis	KO/LOP/TOE/SIS	colporrhexis	KOL/PO/REK/SIS
color	KO/LOR	-colpos	KOL/POS
coloration	KOL/RAIGS	colposcope	KOL/PO/SKOEP
colorectal	KOEL/REK/TAL	colposcopic	KOL/PO/SKOP/IK
	KOL/REK/TAL	colposcopy	KOL/POS/KPI
colorectitis	KOEL/REK/TAOITS	colpospasm	KOL/PO/SPAFM
colorectostomy	KOEL/REK/TO*S/M*I	colpostat	KOL/PO/STAT
colorectum	KOEL/REK/TUM	colpostenosis	KOL/PO/STE/NOE/SIS
colorimeter	KOL/RIM/TER	colpostenotomy	KOL/PO/STE/NOT/M*I
colorimetric	KO/LOR/MET/RIK	colpotherm	KOL/PO/THERM
	KOL/RI/MET/RIK	colpotomy	KOL/POT/M*I
colorimetry	KOL/RIM/TRI	colpoureterocystotomy	KOL/PO/YAOU/RAOET/RO/SIS/
colorrhagia	KO/LO/RAI/JA		TOT/M*I
	(not KOEL/RAI/JA; see	colpoureterotomy	KOL/PO/YAOU/RAOET/ROT/M*I

colpoxerosis	KOL/PO/ZAOE/ROE/SIS	commitment	KMIT/-MT
	KOL/PO/ZE/ROE/SIS	common	KMON
colterol mesylate	KOELT/ROEL/MES/LAIT	commotio	KMOE/SHOE
	KOELT/ROL/MES/LAIT		KMOERB/YOE
columella	KOL/MEL/LA	commune	KMAOU/NAOE
	KOL/YAOU/MEL/LA		KMAOUN/NAOE
columellae	KOL/MEL/LAE	communes	KMAOU/NAOEZ
	KOL/YAOU/MEL/LAE		KMAOUN/NAOEZ
column	KOL/UM	communicable	KMAOUN/KABL
columna	KO/LUM/NA	communicans	KMAOUN/KANS
	KLUM/NA	communicantes	KMAOUN/KAN/TAOEZ
columnae	KO/LUM/NAE	communication	KMAOUN/KAIGS
	KLUM/NAE	communis	KMAOU/NIS
columnar	KO/LUM/NAR		KMAOUN/NIS
	KLUM/NAR	community	KMUNT
columnella	KOL/UM/NEL/LA		KMAOUN/TI
	KO/LUM/NEL/LA	Comolli	KO/MOL/LAOE
columnellae	KOL/UM/NEL/LAE	comorbidity	KO/MOR/BID/TI
	KO/LUM/NEL/LAE	compact	KOM/PAKT
columning	KOL/UM/-G	compacta	KOM/PAK/TA
columnization	KOL/UM/ZAIGS	compaction	KOM/PA*BGS
	KOL/UM/NI/ZAIGS	compages thoracis	KOM/PAI/GAOEZ/THRAI/SIS
Coly-Mycin	KOEL/MAOI/SIN	comparascope	KOM/PAR/SKOEP
colypeptic	KOEL/PEPT/IK		KOM/PAIR/SKOEP
Colyte	KO/LAOIT	comparative	KOM/PAIR/TIV
coma	KO/MA		KPAIR/TIV
comatose	KOEM/TOES	comparator	KOFRP/RAI/TOR
	KOM/TOES		KOM/PRAI/TOR
combat	KOM/BAT	compartment	KOM/PART-MT
combination	KOM/BI/NAIGS		KPART/-MT
	KBINGS	compartmentalization	KOM/PART/MEN/TAL/ZAIGS
	KBIN/NAIGS		KPART/MEN/TAL/ZAIGS
combing	KOEM/-G	compartmentation	KOM/PART/MEN/TAIGS
combustible	KOM/B*US/-BL		KPART/MEN/TAIGS
	KB*US/-BL	compatibility	KOM/PAT/-BLT
combustion	KOM/BUGS		KPAT/-BLT
	KBUGS	compatible	KOM/PAT/-BL
Combipres	KOM/BI/PRES		KPAT/-BL
comedo	KOM/DOE	Compazine	KOFRP/ZAOEN
	KMAOE/DOE		KOM/PA/ZAOEN
	KO/MAOE/DOE	compensation	KOFRP/SAIGS
comedo-	KO/MAOED		KOM/PEN/SAIGS
	KMAOED	compensated	KOFRP/SAIT-D
	KOM/DO		KOM/PEN/SAIT/-D
	KO/MAOE/DO	compensatory	KOM/PENS/TOIR
comedocarcinoma	KO/MAOED/KARS/NOE/MA		KPENS/TOIR
	KMAOED/KARS/NOE/MA	Compete Multivitamins	KOM/PAOET/MULT/VAOIT/MIN/-S
comedogenic	KOM/DO/JEN/IK	competence	KOFRP/TENS
comedomastitis	KO/MAOED/MAS/TAOITS	competent	KOFRP/TENT
	KMAOED/MAS/TAOITS	competition	KOFRP/TIGS
comedones	KOM/DOE/NAOEZ	compimeter	KOM/PIM/TER
comenic	KO/MEN/IK	complaint	KOM/PLAINT
comes	KO/MAOEZ		KPLAINT
cometal	KOM/TAL	complement	KOM/PLEMT
comfortization	KOM/FORT/ZAIGS		KOFRP/LEMT
	K-FRT/ZAIGS	complement	KOM/PLEMT
Comhist	KOM/H*IS		KOFRP/LEMT
comitans	KOM/TANS		KOM/PLE/MEN/T-
comitantes	KOM/TAN/TAOEZ		KOFRP/LE/MEN/T-
comites	KOM/TAOEZ	complemental	KOM/PLEMT/TAL
comma	KOM/MA	complementarity	KOM/PLEMT/TAIR/TI
commensal	KMEN/SAL		KOM/PLE/MEN/TAIR/TI
commensalism	KMENS/LIFM	complementary	KOM/PLEMT/RI
commi-	KOM	complementation	KOM/PLEMT/TAIGS
	KMI	complemented	KOM/PLEMT/-D
comminute	KOM/NAOUT	completa	KOM/PLAOE/TA
comminuted	KOM/NAOUT/-D	complete	KOM/PLAOET
comminution	KOM/NAOUGS		KPLAOET
commissur(o)-	KOM/SAOUR	complex	KOM/PLEX
	KMIS/R(O)		KPLEX
	KMIRB/R(O)	complexing	KOM/PLEX/-G
	KOM/SAOUR/R(O)		KPLEX/-G
	KOM/SAOU/R(O)	Complex 15	KOM/PLEX/15
commissura	KOM/SAOU/RA	complexion	KOM/PL*EBGS
	KOM/SAOUR/RA	complexus	KOM/PLEK/SUS
commissurae	KOM/SAOU/RAE		KPLEK/SUS
	KOM/SAOUR/RAE	compliance	KOM/PLAOINS
commissural	KOM/SAOURL		KPLAOINS
	KMIS/RAL	complic-	KOFRP/K-
commissure	KOM/SAOUR		KOM/PLI/K-
	KOM/SHUR		KOFRP/LI/K-
commissuropexy	KOM/SAOUR/PEK/SI	complicata	KOFRP/KAI/TA
	KMIS/RO/PEK/SI	complicate	KOFRP/KAIT
commissurorrhaphy	KOM/SAOU/ROR/FI	complicated	KOFRP/KAIT/-D
	KOM/SAOUR/OR/FI	complication	KOFRP/KAIGS
	KMIS/ROR/FI	component	KOM/POENT
commissurotomy	KOM/SAOUR/OT/M*I	compos	KOM/POS
	KOM/SAOU/ROT/M*I	compos mentis	KOM/POS/MEN/TIS
	KMIS/ROT/M*I	compound	KOM/POUND

	KPOUND	concordant	KON/KOR/DANT
Compound W	KOM/POUND/W-RBGS	concrement	KON/KRAOEMT
	KPOUND/W-RBGS		KON/KREMT
comprehension	KOFRP/HENGS	concrescence	KON/KRES/ENS
	KOM/PRE/HENGS	concrete	KON/KRAOET
comprehensive	KOFRP/HENS/IV	concretio	KON/KRAOE/SHOE
	KOM/PRE/HENS/IV		KON/KRAOERB/YOE
compress	KOM/PRESZ	concretion	KON/KRAOEGS
	KPRESZ	concretism	KON/KRAOET/IFM
compressibility	KOM/PRESZ/-BLT		KON/KRAOE/TIFM
	KPRESZ/-BLT	concretization	KON/KRAOET/ZAIGS
compression	KOM/PREGS	concussion	KON/KUGS
	KPREGS	concussor	KON/KUS/SOR
compressor	KOM/PRES/SOR	condensation	KON/DEN/SAIGS
	KPRES/SOR	condense	KON/DENS
compressorium	KOM/PRES/SOER/YUM	condenser	KON/DENS/ER
	KOM/PRES/SOR/YUM	condition	KON/DIGS
	KPRES/SOER/YUM		K-N
	KPRES/SOR/YUM	conditioning	KON/DIGS/-G
compressum	KOM/PRES/SUM		K-NG
	KPRES/SUM	condom	KON/DOM
compressus	KOM/PRES/SUS	conduct	KON/DUKT
	KPRES/SUS		KUKT
compromised	KOFRP/MAOIZ/-D	conductance	KON/DUK/TANS
	KOM/PRO/MAOIZ/-D		KUK/TANS
Compton	KOFRP/TON	conduction	KON/D*UBGS
compulsion	KOM/PULGS		K*UBGS
	KPULGS	conductivity	KON/DUK/TIV/TI
compulsive	KOM/PULS/IV		KUK/TIV/TI
	KPULS/IV	conductor	KON/DUK/TOR
computed	KOM/PAOUT/-D		KUK/TOR
	KPAOUT/-D	conduit	KON/DAOUT
computerized	KOM/PAOUT/RAOIZ/-D	conduplicate	KON/DAOUP/KAIT
	KPAOUT/RAOIZ/-D		KON/DAOUP/LI/KAIT
con-	KON		KON/DAOU/PLI/KAIT
conalbumin	KON/AL/BAOU/MIN	conduplicato	KON/DAOUP/KAI/TOE
conanine	KON/NAOEN		KON/DAOUP/LI/KAI/TOE
conarial	KO/NAIRL		KON/DAOU/PLI/KAI/TOE
conarium	KO/NAIRM	condurango	KON/DRAN/GOE
conation	KO/NAIGS		KON/DAOU/RAN/GOE
conative	KON/TIV	condyl(o)-	KOND/L(O)
conatus	KO/NAI/TUS		KON/DI/L(O)
	KO/NA/TUS	condylar	KOND/LAR
conavanine	KON/VAN/NIN	condylare	KOND/LAI/RAOE
concameration	KON/KAM/RAIGS	condylaris	KOND/LAI/RIS
concanavalin	KON/KA/NAV/LIN	condylarthrosis	KOND/LAR/THROE/SIS
concatenate	KON/KAT/NAIT		KON/DIL/AR/THROE/SIS
concatenation	KON/KAT/NAIGS	condyle	KON/DAOIL
Concato	KON/KA/TOE	condylectomy	KOND/LEKT/M*I
concave	KON/KAIV	condyli	KOND/LAOI
concavity	KON/KAV/TI	condylicus	KON/DIL/KUS
concavoconcave	KON/KAIV/KON/KAIV	condylion	KON/DIL/YON
concavoconvex	KON/KAIV/KON/VEX	condyloid	KOND/LOID
concealed	KON/SAOEL/-D	condyloidei	KOND/LOID/YAOI
conceive	KON/SAOEV	condyloideum	KOND/LOID/YUM
concentrate	KONS/TRAIT	condyloideus	KOND/LOID/YUS
	KON/SEN/TRAIT	condyloma	KOND/LOE/MA
concentration	KONS/TRAIGS	condylomata	KOND/LOEM/TA
	KON/SEN/TRAIGS	condylomatoid	KOND/LOEM/TOID
concentric	KON/SEN/TRIK	condylomatosis	KOND/LOEM/TOE/SIS
concentrica	KON/SEN/TRI/KA	condylomatous	KOND/LOEM/TOUS
	KON/SENT/RI/KA	condylotomy	KOND/LOT/M*I
concentricus	KON/SEN/TRI/KUS	condylous	KOND/LOUS
	KON/SENT/RI/KUS	condylus	KOND/LUS
concept	KON/SEPT	cone	KOEN
consepti	KON/SEP/TAOI	conexus	KO/NEK/SUS
conception	KON/SEPGS	confabulation	KON/FAB/LAIGS
conceptive	KON/SEPT/IV	confectio	KON/FEK/SHOE
Conceptrol	KON/SEP/TROL	confection	KON/F*EBGS
conceptual	KON/SEP/KHUL	confectiones	KON/FEK/SHOE/NAOEZ
conceptus	KON/SEP/TUS	confectionis	KON/FEK/SHOE/NIS
concha	KON/KA	confertus	KON/FER/TUS
conchae	KON/KAE	confidentiality	K-FT/SHAL/TI
conchal	KON/KAL		KON/FI/DEN/SHAL/TI
conchalis	KON/KAI/LIS		K-FT/-RBL/TI
conchiform	KON/KI/FORM		KON/FI/DEN/-RBL/TI
conchiolin	KON/KAOI/LIN	configuration	KON/FIG/RAIGS
conchiolinosteomyelitis	KON/KAOI/LIN/O*S/YO/MAOI/ LAOITS	confinement	KON/FAOIN/-MT
		conflict	KON/FLIKT
conchitis	KON/KAOITS	confluence	KON/FLAOUNS
conchoidal	KON/KOI/DAL	confluens	KON/FLAOUNZ
conchoscope	KON/KO/SKOEP	confluent	KON/FLAOUNT
conchotome	KON/KO/TOEM	confocal	KON/FOE/KAL
conchotomy	KON/KOT/M*I	conformation	KON/FOR/MAIGS
conclination	KON/KLI/NAIGS	conformer	KON/FORM/ER
concoction	KON/KO*BGS	confrication	KON/FRI/KAIGS
concomitance	KON/KOM/TANS	confrontation	KON/FRON/TAIGS
concomitant	KON/KOM/TANT	confusion	KON/FAOUGS
concordance	KON/KOR/DANS	confusional	KON/FAOUGS/NAL

congelation	KON/JE/LAIGS
congeneic	KON/JE/NAI/IK
congener	KON/JE/NER
	KON/JAOEN/ER
congeneric	KON/JE/NER/IK
congenerous	KON/JEN/ROUS
congenic	KON/JEN/IK
congenita	KON/JEN/TA
congenital	KON/JEN/TAL
congenitalis	KON/JEN/TAI/LIS
congenitum	KON/JEN/TUM
congenitus	KON/JEN/TUS
Congespirin	KON/JES/PRIN
Congess	KON/JESZ
Congess Jr.	KON/JESZ/J-R
Congess Sr.	KON/JESZ/S-R
Congestac	KON/JES/TAK
congested	KON/J*ES/-D
congestin	KON/JEGS/TIN
congestion	KON/JEGS
congestive	KON/J*ES/IV
congius	KON/JUS
conglobata	KON/GLOE/BAI/TA
conglobate	KON/GLOE/BAIT
conglobation	KON/GLOE/BAIGS
conglomerate	KON/GLOM/RAIT
	KON/GLOM/RAT
conglutin	KON/GLAOU/TIN
conglutinant	KON/GLAOUT/NANT
conglutinatio	KON/GLAOUT/NAI/SHOE
	KON/GLAOUT/NAIRB/YOE
conglutination	KON/GLAOUT/NAIGS
conglutinin	KON/GLAOUT/NIN
Congo	KON/GOE
congolensis	KONG/LEN/SIS
	KON/GO/LEN/SIS
Congolian	KON/GOEL/YAN
congophilic	KONG/FIL/IK
	KON/GO/FIL/IK
congressus	KON/GRES/SUS
coni	KO/NAOI
-conia	KOEN/YA
conic	KON/IK
conical	KON/KAL
conicum	KON/KUM
-conid	KO/NID
	KON/ID
conidia	KO/NID/YA
conidial	KO/NID/YAL
conidiobolus	KO/NID/YO/BOE/LUS
conidiogenous	KO/NID/YOJ/NOUS
conidiophore	KO/NID/YO/FOER
conidium	KO/NID/YUM
coniine	KO/NAOEN
	KOEN/YAOEN
conio-	KOEN/YO
coniofibrosis	KOEN/YO/FAOI/BROE/SIS
coniology	KOEN/YOLG
coniolymphstasis	KOEN/YO/LIM/-F/STA/SIS
	KOEN/YO/LIM/STA/SIS
coniometer	KOEN/YOM/TER
coniophage	KOEN/YO/FAIJ
coniosis	KOEN/YOE/SIS
coniotomy	KOEN/YOT/M*I
coniotoxicosis	KOEN/YO/TOX/KOE/SIS
conium	KOEN/YUM
Conium	K-P/KOEN/YUM
conization	KOEN/ZAIGS
	KON/ZAIGS
conjug-	KON/JU/G-
	KON/JAOU/G-
conjugal	KON/JU/GAL
conjugant	KON/JU/GANT
conjugase	KON/JU/GAIS
conjugata	KON/JU/GAI/TA
conjugate	KON/JU/GAIT
conjugated	KON/JU/GAIT/-D
conjugation	KON/JU/GAIGS
conjugon	KON/JU/GON
conjunctiv(o)-	KON/JUNG/VO
	KON/JUNGT/V(O)
	KON/JUNG/TAOIV
	KON/JUNG/TAOI/V(O)
conjunctiva	KON/JUNG/TAOI/VA
	KON/JUNG/TAOE/VA
conjunctivae	KON/JUNG/TAOI/VAE
conjunctival	KON/JUNG/TAOIVL
	KON/JUNG/TAOI/VAL
	KON/JUNGT/VAL
conjunctivales	KON/JUNGT/VAI/LAOEZ
conjunctivi	KON/JUNG/TAOI/VAOI
	KON/JUNG/VAOI
	KON/JUNGT/VAOI
conjunctiviplasty	KON/JUNG/VI/PLAS/TI
	KON/JUNGT/VI/PLAS/TI
conjunctivitis	KON/JUNG/VAOITS
	KON/JUNGT/VAOITS
conjunctivodacryocystorhinostomy	
	KON/JUNG/VO/DAK/RO/S*IS/ RAOI/NO*S/M*I
	KON/JUNGT/VO/DAK/RO/S*IS/ RAOI/NO*S/M*I
	KON/JUNG/TAOIV/DAK/RO/S*IS/ RAOI/NO*S/M*I
conjunctivodacryocystostomy	
	KON/JUNG/VO/DAK/RO/SIS/TO*S/ M*I
	KON/JUNGT/VO/DAK/RO/SIS/ TO*S/M*I
	KON/JUNG/TAOIV/DAK/RO/SIS/ TO*S/M*I
conjunctivoma	KON/JUNG/VOE/MA
	KON/JUNGT/VOE/MA
conjunctivoplasty	KON/JUNG/VO/PLAS/TI
	KON/JUNGT/VO/PLAS/TI
	KON/JUNG/TAOIV/PLAS/TI
conjunctivorhinostomy	KON/JUNG/VO/RAOI/NO*S/M*I
	KON/JUNGT/VO/RAOI/NO*S/M*I
	KON/JUNG/TAOIV/RAOI/NO*S/ M*I
conjunctum	KON/JUNG/TUM
	KON/JUNGT/UM
Conn	KO*N
	(not KON; see con)
connatal	KON/NAI/TAL
connate	KON/NAIT
connect	KEKT
	KON/NEKT
connectin	KON/NEK/TIN
	KEKT/TIN
connecting	KEKT/-G
	KON/NEKT/-G
connection	K*EBGS
	KON/N*EBGS
connective	KEKT/IV
	KON/NEKT/IV
connector	KEKT/TOR
	KEK/TOR
	KON/NEK/TOR
Connell	KONL
	KON/EL
connexon	KON/NEK/SON
connexus	KON/NEK/SUS
conoid	KO/NOID
	KOEN/OID
conoideum	KO/NOID/YUM
conomyoidin	KOEN/MAOI/OI/DIN
	KOEN/MAOI/YOI/DIN
conori	KO/NOE/RAOI
	KO/NOR/RAOI
	KO/NOER/RAOI
conquinine	KON/KWI/NAOEN
	KON/KWIN/NIN
consanguineous	KON/SANG/WIN/YOUS
consanguinity	KON/SANG/WIN/TI
conscience	KON/SHENS
conscious	KON/-RBS
consciousness	KON/-RBS/*NS
conscious-sedation	KON/-RBS/SE/DAIGS
consensual	KON/SEN/SHAOUL
	KON/SEN/SHUL
conservation	KONS/VAIGS
	KON/SER/VAIGS
conservative	KON/SEFRB/TIV
conserve	KON/SEFRB
consolidant	KON/SOL/DANT
consolidation	KON/SOL/DAIGS
consolute	KONS/LAOUT
	KON/SLAOUT
	KON/SO/LAOUT
consonance	KONS/NANS
	KON/SO/NANS
consonant	KONS/NANT
	KON/SO/NANT
consonation	KONS/NAIGS
	KON/SO/NAIGS
conspecific	KON/SPE/SIFK
	KON/SPEFK

constancy	KON/STAN/SI	contractile	KON/TRAK/TAOIL
constant	KON/STANT		KR-T/TAOIL
Constant-T	KON/STANT/T-RBGS		KON/TRAK/TIL
const-	KO*NS		(*not* KR-T/TIL; see contract till)
	KON/ST-	contractility	KON/TRAK/TIL/TI
	KONS/T-		KR-T/TIL/TI
constellation	KO*NS/LAIGS	contraction	KON/TRA*BGS
constellatus	KO*NS/LAI/TUS		KR*BGS
constipate	KO*NS/PAIT	contractural	KON/TRAK/KHURL
constipated	KO*NS/PAIT/-D		KR-T/KHURL
constipation	KO*NS/PAIGS	contracture	KON/TRAK/KHUR
constitution	KO*NS/TAOUGS		KR-T/KHUR
constitutional	KO*NS/TAOUGS/NAL	contrafissura	KON/TRA/FIRB/SHUR/RA
constitutive	KO*NS/TAOUT/IV		KON/TRA/FIS/SAOU/RA
constriction	KON/STR*IBGS	contrafissure	KON/TRA/FIRB/SHUR
constrictive	KON/STRIKT/IV	contraindicant	KON/TRA/IND/KANT
constrictor	KON/STRIK/TOR	contraindication	KON/TRA/IND/KAIGS
constructive	KRUKT/IV	contrainsular	KON/TRA/INS/LAR
	KON/STRUKT/IV	contralateral	KON/TRA/LAT/RAL
construction	KR*UBGS	contraparetic	KON/TRA/PA/RET/IK
	KON/STR*UBGS	contrasexual	KON/TRA/SEX/YAOUL
constructional	KR*UBGS/NAL	contrast	KON/TRA*S
	KON/STR*UBGS/NAL	contrastimulant	KON/TRA/STIM/LANT
consult	KON/SULT	contrastimulism	KON/TRA/STIM/LIFM
consultand	KON/SUL/TAND	contrastimulus	KON/TRA/STIM/LUS
consultant	KON/SUL/TANT	contravolitional	KON/TRA/VO/LIGS/NAL
consultation	KON/SUL/TAIGS		KON/TRA/VOE/LIGS/NAL
	KONS/TAIGS	contrecoup	KON/TRA/KAOU
consumption	KON/SUMGS		KON/TRA/KOUP
	KON/SUFRPGS	contrectation	KON/TREK/TAIGS
consumptive	KON/SUMT/IV	control	KON/TROL
	KON/SUFRPT/IV		KROL
Contac	KON/TAK	contund	KON/TUND
contact	KON/TAKT	contuse	KON/TAOUZ
	KAKT		KON/TAOUS
contactant	KON/TAK/TANT	contusion	KON/TAOUGS
	KAKT/TANT	contusive	KON/TAOUS/IV
contactologist	KON/TAK/TO*LGS	conular	KON/LAR
	KAKT/O*LGS	conus	KO/NUS
contactology	KON/TAK/TOLG	Conus	K-P/KO/NUS
	KAKT/OLG	convalscence	KON/VA/LES/ENS
contactus	KON/TAK/TUS	convalescent	KON/VA/LES/ENT
contagion	KON/TAIJ/JON	convallaria	KON/VA/LAIR/YA
contagiosity	KON/TAIJ/YOS/TI	convection	KON/V*EBGS
contagious	KON/TAIJ/JOUS	convergence	KON/VERJ/ENS
	KON/TAI/JOUS	convergent	KON/VERJ/ENT
contagiousness	KON/TAIJ/JOUS/*NS	convergiometer	KON/VERJ/YOM/TER
	KON/TAI/JOUS/*NS	conversion	KON/VERGS
contagiosum	KON/TAIJ/YOE/SUM	convertase	KON/VER/TAIS
	KON/TAIJ/YOES/UM	convertin	KON/VER/TIN
	KON/TAI/JOE/SUM	convex	KON/VEX
	KON/TAI/JOES/UM	convex(o)-	KON/VEX
contagium	KON/TAI/JUM		KON/VEK/S(O)
	KON/TAIJ/UM	convexa	KON/VEK/SA
contaminant	KON/TAM/NANT	convexity	KON/VEX/TI
contaminate	KON/TAM/NAIT	convexobasia	KON/VEX/BAIS/YA
contamination	KON/TAM/NAIGS	convexoconcave	KON/VEX/KON/KAIV
content	KON/TENT	convexoconvex	KON/VEX/KON/VEX
contiguitatem	KONT/GAOU/TAIT/EM	convol-	KON/VO/L-
	KONT/GAOU/TAI/TEM		KON/VOE/L-
	KON/TIG/WI/TAIT/EM	convolute	KON/VO/LAOUT
	KON/TIG/WI/TAI/TEM	convoluted	KON/VO/LAOUT/-D
contiguity	KONT/GAOU/TI	convolution	KON/VO/LAOUGS
contigous	KON/TIG/YOUS	convolutional	KON/VO/LAOUGS/NAL
continence	KONT/NENS	convolutionary	KON/VO/LAOUGS/NAIR
continent	KONT/NENT		KON/VO/LAOUGS/AIR
continua	KON/TIN/YA	convulsant	KON/VUL/SANT
	KON/TIN/WA	convulsibility	KON/VULS/-BLT
continued	KONT/-D	convulsion	KON/VULGS
	KON/TIN/YAOU/-D	convulsivant	KON/VULS/VANT
continuitatem	KONT/NAOU/TAIT/EM	convulsive	KON/VULS/IV
	KONT/NAOU/TAI/TEM	convulsivum	KON/VUL/SAOI/VUM
	KON/TIN/WI/TAIT/EM		KON/VUL/SAOIV/UM
	KON/TIN/WI/TAI/TEM	cookei	KAOK/YAOI
continuity	KONT/NAOU/TI	Cooley	KAOL/LAOE
continuous	KONT/OUS		KAO/LAOE
	KON/TIN/YOUS	Coolidge	KAOL/IJ
contorta	KON/TOR/TA	cooling	KAOL/-G
contorted	KON/TORT/-D	Coombs	KAOMS
contour	KON/TAOUR		KAOMZ
contoured	KON/TAOUR/-D	Cooper	KAOP/ER
contra-	KON/TRA	cooperi	KAOP/RAOI
contra-angle	KON/TRA/ANG/-L	Cooperia	KAO/PAOER/YA
contra-aperture	KON/TRA/AP/ER/KHUR	cooperid	KAOP/RID
contrabevel	KON/TRA/BEVL	Coopernail	KAOP/ER/NAIL
contraception	KON/TRA/SEPGS	coordinate	KWORD/NAIT
contraceptive	KON/TRA/SEPT/IV		KORD/NAIT
contract	KON/TRAKT		KAORD/NAIT
	KR-T	coordination	KWORD/NAIGS

	KORD/NAIGS	coracoclaviculare	KOR/KO/KLA/VIK/LAI/RAOE
	KAORD/NAIGS	coracoclavicularis	KOR/KO/KLA/VIK/LAI/RIS
coossification	KO/OS/FI/KAIGS	coracocostal	KOR/KO/KOS/TAL
	KO/OSZ/FI/KAIGS	coracohumeral	KOR/KO/HAOUM/RAL
coossify	KO/OS/FI	coracohumerale	KOR/KO/HAOUM/RAI/LAOE
	KO/OSZ/FI	coracoid	KOR/KOID
copaiba	KO/PAOI/BA	coracoiditis	KOR/KOI/DAOITS
	KO/PAI/BA	coracoradialis	KOR/KO/RAID/YAI/LIS
copaibic	KO/PAOIB/IK	coracoulnaris	KOR/KO/UL/NAI/RIS
	KO/PAIB/IK	coralliform	KO/RAL/FORM
coparaffinate	KO/PAR/FIN/AIT	corallin	KOR/LIN
	KO/PAR/AF/NAIT	coralloid	KOR/LOID
cope	KOEP	corbantism	KOR/BAN/TIFM
copepod	KOEP/POD	cord	KORD
Copepoda	KO/PEP/DA	cord(o)-	KORD
coping	KOEP/-G		KOR/D(O)
cophica	KOF/KA		KOER/D(O)
copiopia	KOP/YOEP/YA	cordabrasion	KORD/BRAIGS
copolymer	KO/POL/MER	cordal	KOR/DAL
copper	KOP/ER	Cordarone	KORD/ROEN
copperas	KOP/RAS	cordate	KOR/DAIT
copperhead	KOP/ER/HED	cordatum	KOR/DAI/TUM
copracrasia	KOP/RA/KRAIZ/YA		KOR/DAIT/UM
copragogue	KOP/RA/GOG	cordectomy	KOR/DEKT/M*I
coprecipitation	KO/PRE/SIP/TAIGS	cordial	KORD/YAL
coprecipitin	KO/PRE/SIP/TIN	cordiale	KORD/YAI/LAOE
copremesis	KOP/REM/SIS	cordianine	KOR/DAOI/NAOEN
copro-	KOP/RO	cordiform	KORD/FORM
coproantibody	KOP/RO/A*ENT/BOD/DI	cordis	KOR/DIS
coprolagnia	KOP/RO/LAG/NAOE/YA	corditis	KOR/DAOITS
coprolalia	KOP/RO/LAIL/YA	cordopexy	KORD/PEK/SI
coprolith	KOP/RO/L*IT	cordotomy	KOR/DOT/M*I
coprology	KOP/ROLG	Cordran	KOR/DRAN
coproma	KOP/ROE/MA	Cordran-N	KOR/DRAN/N-RBGS
coprophagia	KOP/RO/FAI/JA	Cordylobia	KORD/LOEB/YA
coprophagous	KOP/ROF/GOUS	core	KOER
	KO/PROF/GOUS		(not KOR; see cor-)
coprophagy	KOP/ROF/JI	core(o)-	KOR/Y(O)
	KO/PROF/JI		KOER/Y(O)
coprophil	KOP/RO/FIL	corecleisis	KOER/KLAOI/SIS
coprophilia	KOP/RO/FIL/YA	corectasia	KOR/EK/TAIZ/YA
coprophiliac	KOP/RO/FIL/YAK	corectasis	KOR/EKT/SIS
coprophilic	KOP/RO/FIL/IK	corectome	KOR/EK/TOEM
coprophilous	KOP/ROF/LOUS	corectomedialysis	KOR/EKT/MAOE/DI/AL/SIS
coprophobia	KOP/RO/FOEB/YA		KOR/EKT/M*I/DI/AL/SIS
coprophrasia	KOP/RO/FRAIZ/YA		KOR/EKT/MAOED/YAL/SIS
coproplanesia	KOP/RO/PLA/NAOEZ/YA		KO/REKT/MAOED/YAL/SIS
	KOP/RO/PLAN/AOEZ/YA	corectomy	KOR/EKT/M*I
coproporphyria	KOP/RO/POR/FIR/YA		KOR/REKT/M*I
coproporphyrin	KOP/RO/POR/FRIN	corectopia	KOR/EK/TOEP/YA
coproporphyrinogen	KOP/RO/POR/FRIN/JEN	coredialysis	KOR/DI/AL/SIS
coproporphyrinuria	KOP/RO/POR/FRIN/YAOUR/YA	corediastasis	KOR/DI/A*S/SIS
coprostane	KOP/ROS/TAIN	coregonin	KO/REG/NIN
	KOP/RO/STAIN	corelysis	KO/REL/SIS
coprostanol	KOP/RO*S/NOL		KOR/EL/SIS
	KOP/RO/STAI/NOL	coremium	KO/RAOEM/YUM
	KOP/RO/STAIN/OL	coremorphosis	KOR/MOR/FOE/SIS
coprostanone	KOP/RO*S/NOEN	corenclisis	KOR/EN/KLI/SIS
coprostasis	KOP/RO*S/SIS	coreometer	KOR/YOM/TER
	KOP/RO/STAI/SIS	coreometry	KOR/YOM/TRI
coprostenol	KOP/ROS/TEN/OL	coreoplasty	KOR/YO/PLAS/TI
	(not KOP/RO*S/NOL; see	corepexy	KOR/PEK/SI
	coprostanol)	corepraxy	KOR/PRAK/SI
coprosterin	KOP/RO*S/RIN	corepressor	KO/RE/PRES/SOR
	KOP/RO/STAOER/RIN	corestenoma	KOR/STE/NOE/MA
coprosterol	KOP/RO*S/ROL	coretomedialysis	KOR/TO/MAOED/YAL/SIS
	KOP/RO/STAOER/OL		KO/RET/MAOE/DI/AL/SIS
coprostigmastane	KOP/RO/STIG/MAS/TAIN		KOR/RET/M*I/DI/AL/SIS
coprozoa	KOP/RO/ZOE/WA		KOR/ET/MAOE/DI/AL/SIS
coprozoic	KOP/RO/ZOIK		KOR/ET/M*I/DI/AL/SIS
	KOP/RO/ZOE/IK	coretomy	KO/RET/M*I
coptosis	KOP/TOE/SIS		KOR/ET/M*I
copul-	KOP/L-	Corgard	KOR/GARD
	KOP/YAOU/L-	Cori	KOR/RAOE
	KOP/YU/L-		KOER/RAOE
copula	KOP/LA		KO/RAOE
copulation	KOP/LAIGS	coria	KOR/YA
coquille	KO/KAOEL	coriaceous	KOR/YAIRBS
cor	KO*R	coriander	KOR/YAND/ER
	(not KOR; frequent prefix)	Coricidin	KOR/SAOE/DIN
corac(o)-	KOR/K(O)	corium	KOR/YUM
	KOER/K(O)	corm	KORM
coracidia	KOR/SID/YA	cormethasone	KOR/M*ET/SOEN
coracidium	KOR/SID/YUM	corn	KORN
coracoacromial	KOR/KO/AI/KROEM/YAL	corne(o)-	KORN/Y(O)
coracoacromiale	KOR/KO/AI/KROEM/YAI/LAOE	cornea	KORN/YA
coracobrachial	KOR/KO/BRAIK/YAL	corneae	KORN/YAE
coracobrachialis	KOR/KO/BRAIK/YAI/LIS	corneal	KORN/YAL
coracoclavicular	KOR/KO/KLA/VIK/LAR	cornealis	KORN/YAI/LIS

corneitis	KORN/YAOITS	corrector	KREK/TOR
corneoblepharon	KORN/YO/BLEF/RON		KREKT/TOR
corneocyte	KORN/YO/SAO*IT	correlation	KOR/LAIGS
corneoiritis	KORN/YO/AOI/RAOITS	correlative	KREL/TIV
corneosclera	KORN/YO/SKLAOER/RA	correspondence	KOR/SPOND/ENS
corneoscleral	KORN/YO/SKLAOERL	Corrigan	KOR/GAN
corneous	KORN/YOUS		KOR/RI/GAN
corner	KORN/ER	corrigent	KOR/JENT
corneum	KORN/YUM	corrin	KOR/RIN
corniculata	KOR/NIK/LAI/TA	corrode	KROED
corniculate	KOR/NIK/LAIT	corroid	KOR/OID
	KOR/NIK/LAT		KOR/ROID
corniculum	KOR/NIK/LUM		(not KOER/OID; see choroid)
Corning	KORN/-G	corrosion	KROEGS
cornoid	KORN/OID	corrosive	KROES/IV
	(not KOR/NOID; see coronoid)	corrugator	KOR/GAI/TOR
cornu	KOR/NAOU	corset	KORS/ET
cornua	KORN/YA		KOR/SET
	KORN/WA	Corsican	KORS/KAN
	KOR/NAOU/WA	cort-	KOR/T-
cornual	KOR/NAOUL		KORT
	KORN/WAL		

NOTE: *Because cort- begins so many words in the medical literature, it is most desirable that you write the word "court" with the outline KOURT.*

	(not KORN/YAL; see corneal)	Cortaid	KOR/TAID
cornuate	KORN/YAIT	Cortef	KOR/TEF
	KOR/NAOU/AIT	Cortenema	KOR/TEN/MA
cornucommissural	KOR/NAOU/KMIS/RAL	cortex	KOR/TEX
	KOR/NAOU/KOM/SAOURL	cortexone	KOR/TEK/SOEN
cornucopia	KORN/KOEP/YA	Corti	KOR/TAOE
cornus	KOR/NUS	cortic(o)-	KORT/K(O)
corolla	KO/ROE/LA	Corticaine	KORT/KAIN
	KO/ROEL/LA	cortical	KORT/KAL
corona	KO/ROE/NA	corticalis	KORT/KAI/LIS
coronad	KOR/NAD	-corticalism	KORT/KAL/IFM
coronae	KO/ROE/NAE		KORT/KLIFM
coronal	KOR/NAL	corticalization	KORT/KAL/ZAIGS
	KO/ROENL	corticalosteotomy	KORT/KAL/O*S/YOT/M*I
coronale	KOR/NAI/LAOE	corticate	KORT/KAIT
coronalis	KOR/NAI/LIS	corticectomy	KORT/SEKT/M*I
coronaria	KOR/NAIR/YA	cortices	KORT/SAOEZ
coronarism	KOR/NAIR/IFM	corticifugal	KORT/SIF/GAL
coronaritis	KOR/NA/RAOITS	corticipetal	KORT/SIP/TAL
coronary	KOR/NAIR	corticis	KORT/SIS
coronarium	KOR/NAIRM	corticoadrenal	KORT/KO/AD/RAOENL
coronata	KOR/NAI/TA		KORT/KO/AI/DRAOENL
Coronaviridae	KO/ROEN/VIR/DAE	corticoafferent	KORT/KO/AFRNT
coronavirus	KO/ROEN/VAOI/RUS	corticoautonomic	KORT/KO/AUT/NOM/IK
	KOR/NA/VAOI/RUS	corticobulbar	KORT/KO/BUL/BAR
corone	KO/ROE/NAOE	corticocerebellum	KORT/KO/SER/BEL/UM
coroner	KORN/NER	corticocerebral	KORT/KO/SER/BRAL
	(not KOR/NER; see corner)	corticodiencephalic	KORT/KO/DI/EN/SFAL/IK
coronet	KOR/NET	corticoefferent	KORT/KO/EFRNT
coronion	KO/ROEN/YON	corticofugal	KORT/KOF/GAL
coronitis	KOR/NAOITS	corticoid	KORT/KOID
coronoid	KOR/NOID	corticoliberin	KORT/KO/LIB/RIN
coronoidectomy	KOR/NOI/DEKT/M*I	corticomedial	KORT/KO/MAOED/YAL
coroparelcysis	KOR/PAR/ELS/SIS	corticomesencephalic	KORT/KO/MES/EN/SFAL/IK
	KOR/PRELS/SIS	corticonuclear	KORT/KO/NAOUK/LAR
	KOR/PAR/EL/SI/SIS	corticonucleares	KORT/KO/NAOUK/LAI/RAOEZ
	KOR/PREL/SI/SIS	corticopeduncular	KORT/KO/PE/DUNG/LAR
coroplasty	KOE/RO/PLAS/TI		KORT/KO/PE/DUN/KLAR
coroscopy	KO/ROS/KPI	corticopetal	KORT/KOP/TAL
corotomy	KO/ROT/M*I	corticopleuritis	KORT/KO/PLAOU/RAOITS
Corper	KORP/ER	corticopontinae	KORT/KO/PON/TAOI/NAE
corpora	KORP/RA	corticopontine	KORT/KO/PON/TAOIN
corporal	KORP/RAL		KORT/KO/PON/TAOEN
corporeal	KOR/POER/YAL	corticoreticulares	KORT/KO/RE/TIK/LAI/RAOEZ
	KOR/POR/YAL	corticospinal	KORT/KO/SPAOINL
	KOR/POIRL	corticospinales	KORT/KO/SPAOI/NAI/LAOEZ
corporic	KOR/POER/IK	corticosteroid	KORT/KO/STAOER/OID
	KOR/POR/IK	corticosterone	KORT/KO*S/ROEN
	KORP/RIK	corticostriatal	KORT/KO/STRAOI/AI/TAL
corporis	KORP/RIS	corticostriatal-spinal	KORT/KO/STRAOI/AI/TAL/ SPAOINL
corporum	KORP/RUM		
	KOR/POER/UM	corticostriatospinal	KORT/KO/STRAOI/AIT/SPAOINL
	KOR/POR/UM	corticotensin	KORT/KO/TEN/SIN
corps	KOERP	corticothalamic	KORT/KO/THA/LAM/IK
corpse	KORPS	corticotrope	KORT/KO/TROEP
corpulence	KORP/LENS	corticotroph	KORT/KO/TROF
corpulency	KORP/LEN/SI	corticotrophic	KORT/KO/TROFK
corpulent	KORP/LENT	corticotrophin	KORT/KO/TROEFN
corpus	KOR/PUS	corticotropic	KORT/KO/TROP/IK
corpuscle	KOR/PUS/-L	corticotropin	KORT/KO/TROE/PIN
corpuscul-	KOR/PUS/KL-	Corticoviridae	KORT/KO/VIR/DAE
	KOR/PUS/KAOU/L-	Cortifair	KORT/FAIR
corpuscula	KOR/PUS/KLA	Cortifoam	KORT/FOEM
corpuscular	KOR/PUS/KLAR	cortilymph	KORT/LIM/-F
corpusculum	KOR/PUS/KLUM	cortin	KOR/TIN
correction	KR*EBGS		
corrective	KREKT/IV		

cortisol	KORT/SOL	costovertebral	KO*S/VERT/BRAL
cortisone	KORT/SOEN	costovertebrales	KO*S/VERT/BRAI/LAOEZ
Cortisporin	KORT/SPORN	costoxiphoid	KO*S/ZIF/OID
cortivazol	KOR/TAOIV/ZOL		KO*S/ZAOI/FOID
cortol	KOR/TOL	costoxiphoidea	KO*S/ZI/FOID/YA
cortolone	KORT/LOEN		KO*S/ZAOI/FOID/YA
Cortone	KOR/TOEN	cosyntropin	KO/SIN/TROE/PIN
Cortril	KOR/TRIL	cot	KOT
Cortrophin	KOR/TROEFN	Cotard	KO/TAR
Cortrosyn	KOR/TRO/SIN	cotarnine	KO/TAR/NAOEN
corundum	KO/RUND/UM	Cotazym	KOET/ZAOIM
	KO/RUN/DUM	Cotazym-S	KOET/ZAOIM/S-RBGS
coruscation	KOR/SKAIGS	cothromboplastin	KO/THROM/BO/PLAS/TIN
	KOR/US/KAIGS	cotinine	KOET/NAOEN
Corvisart	KOFRB/SAR	cotransport	KO/TRA*NS/PORT
	KOR/VI/SAR		KO/TR-PT
corymbiform	KO/RIM/BI/FORM	Cotrim	KO/TRIM
	KO/RIM/FORM	co-trimoxazole	KO/TR*I/MOX/ZOEL
corymbose	KOR/RIM/BOES	cotton	KOT/TON
	KOR/IM/BOES	cottonpox	KOT/TON/POX
corynebacteria	KO/RAOI/NAOE/BAK/TAOER/YA	cotunnii	KO/TUN/YAOI
Corynebacteriaceae	KO/RAOI/NAOE/BAK/TAOER/ YAIS/YAE	Cotunnius	KO/TUN/YUS
		co-twin	KO/TWIN
corynebacteriophage	KO/RAOI/NAOE/BAK/TAOER/YO/ FAIJ	cotyle	KOT/LAOE
		cotyledon	KOT/LAOE/DON
corynebacterium	KO/RAOI/NAOE/BAK/TAOERM	cotyledontoxin	KOT/LAOE/DON/TOK/SIN
Corynebacterium	K-P/KO/RAOI/NAOE/BAK/ TAOERM	CoTylenol	KO/TAOIL/NOL
		cotylica	KO/TIL/KA
coryneform	KO/RAOIN/FORM	cotyloid	KOT/LOID
corytuberine	KOR/TAOUB/RAOEN	cotylopubic	KOT/LO/PAOUB/IK
coryza	KO/RAOI/ZA	cotylosacral	KOT/LO/SAI/KRAL
coryzavirus	KO/RAOIZ/VAOI/RUS	cotype	KO/TAOIP
	KO/RAOI/ZA/VAOI/RUS	couching	KOUFP/-G
Corzide	KOR/ZAOID	cough	KAUF
Coschwitz	KORB/VITS		KOF
cosensitize	KO/SENS/TAOIZ	coulomb	KAOU/LOM
Cosmegen	KOZ/ME/JEN	Coumadin	KOUM/DIN
cosmesis	KOZ/MAOE/SIS		KAO*UM/DIN
cosmetic	KOZ/MET/IK		(not KAOUM/DIN; see cumidine)
cosmetology	KOZ/ME/TOLG	coumaranone	KAOU/MAR/NOEN
cosmic	KOZ/MIK	coumaric	KAOU/MAIR/IK
cosmid	KOZ/MID		KAOU/MAR/IK
cosmopolitan	KOZ/MO/POL/TAN		KAOUM/RIK
cost(o)-	KO*S	coumarilic	KAOUM/RIL/IK
	KOS/T(O)	coumarin	KAOUM/RIN
costa	KOS/TA	coumarol	KAOUM/ROL
costae	KOS/TAE	coumetarol	KAOU/MET/ROL
costal	KOS/TAL	counseling	KOUNS/-LG
costale	KOS/TAI/LAOE		KOUN/SEL/-G
costales	KOS/TAI/LAOEZ	count	KOUNT
costalis	KOS/TAI/LIS	counter	KOUNT/ER
costalgia	KOS/TAL/JA	counter-	KO*UNT
costalia	KOS/TAIL/YA		KOUN/TER
costalis	KOS/TAI/LIS	counterbalance	KO*UNT/BAL/LANS
costarum	KOS/TAI/RUM	conterconditioning	KO*UNT/K-NG
	KOS/TAIR/UM		KO*UNT/KON/DIGS/-G
costatectomy	KO*S/TEKT/M*I	countercurrent	KO*UNT/KURNT
costectomy	KOS/TEKT/M*I	counterdepressant	KO*UNT/DPRES/SANT
Costen	KOS/TEN	counterdie	KO*UNT/DAOI
costicartilage	KO*S/KART/LAJ	counterelectrophoresis	KO*UNT/LEK/TRO/FRAOE/SIS
costicervical	KO*S/SEFRB/KAL	counterextension	KO*UNT/EX/TENGS
costiferous	KOS/TIF/ROUS	counterimmunoelectrophoresis	
costiform	KO*S/FORM		KO*UNT/IM/NO/LEK/TRO/ FRAOE/SIS
costispinal	KO*S/SPAOINL		
costive	KO*S/IV	counterincision	KO*UNT/IN/SIGS
costiveness	KO*S/IV/*NS	counterinvestment	KO*UNT/IN/V*ES/-MT
	KO*S/IVNS	counterirritant	KO*UNT/IR/TANT
costocentral	KO*S/SEN/TRAL	counterirritation	KO*UNT/IR/TAIGS
	KO*S/STRAL	counteropening	KO*UNT/OEP/-G
costocervicalis	KO*S/SEFRB/KAI/LIS		KO*UNT/OEP/-NG
costochondral	KO*S/KON/DRAL	counterphobia	KO*UNT/FOEB/YA
costochondritis	KO*S/KON/DRAOITS	counterphobic	KO*UNT/FOEB/IK
costoclavicular	KO*S/KLA/VIK/LAR	counterpoison	KO*UNT/POI/SON
costocoracoid	KO*S/KOR/KOID	counterpulsation	KO*UNT/PUL/SAIGS
costogenic	KO*S/JEN/IK	counterpuncture	KO*UNT/PUNG/KHUR
costoinferior	KO*S/IN/FAOER/YOR	countershock	KO*UNT/SHOK
costophrenic	KO*S/FREN/IK	counterstain	KO*UNT/STAIN
costopleural	KO*S/PLAOURL	countersuggestion	KO*UNT/SUG/JEGS
costopneumopexy	KO*S/NAOUM/PEK/SI		KO*UNT/SUGS
costoscapular	KO*S/SKAP/LAR	countertraction	KO*UNT/TRA*BGS
costoscapularis	KO*S/SKAP/LAI/RIS	countertransference	KO*UNT/TRA*NS/FRENS
costosternal	KO*S/STERNL		KO*UNT/TRA*NS/FERNS
costosternoplasty	KO*S/STERN/PLAS/TI	countertransport	KO*UNT/TRA*NS/PORT
costosuperior	KO*S/SPAOER/YOR		KO*UNT/TR-PT
costotome	KO*S/TOEM	counting	KOUNT/-G
costotomy	KOS/TOT/M*I	coup	KOUP
costotransversaria	KO*S/TRA*NS/VER/SAIR/YA	coup de sabre	KAOU/DE/SAUB
costotransverse	KO*S/TRA*NS/VERS		KOUP/DE/SAUB
costotransversectomy	KO*S/TRA*NS/VER/SEKT/M*I	couple	KUP/-L

coupling	KUP/-LG	craniomalacia	KRAIN/YO/MA/LAI/SHA
course	KOURS	craniomeningocele	KRAIN/YO/ME/NING/SAO*EL
court	KOURT	craniometaphysial	KRAIN/YO/MET/FIZ/YAL
	(not KORT; see corti-)	craniometer	KRAIN/YOM/TER
couvade	KAOU/VAUD	craniometric	KRAIN/YO/MET/RIK
couvercle	KAOU/VERK/-L	craniometry	KRAIN/YOM/TRI
	KAOU/VER/K-L	craniopagus	KRAIN/YOP/GUS
	KAOUVRK/-L	craniopathy	KRAIN/YOP/TH*I
	KAOUVR/K-L	craniopharyngeal	KRAIN/YO/FRIN/JAL
covalence	KO/VAIL/ENS	craniopharyngioma	KRAIN/YO/FRIN/JOE/MA
covalent	KO/VAIL/ENT	craniophore	KRAIN/YO/FOER
covariance	KO/VAIRNS	cranioplasty	KRAIN/YO/PLAS/TI
cover	KOVR	craniopuncture	KRAIN/YO/PUNG/KHUR
coverglass	KOVR/GLASZ	craniorhachidian	KRAIN/YO/RA/KID/YAN
coverslip	KOVR/SLIP	craniorachischisis	KRAIN/YO/RA/KIS/KI/SIS
cow	KOU	craniosacral	KRAIN/YO/SAI/KRAL
Cowper	KOUP/ER	cranioschisis	KRAIN/YOS/KI/SIS
	KOU/PER	craniosclerosis	KRAIN/YO/SKLE/ROE/SIS
Cowper's gland	KOUP/ER/AOES/GLAND	cranioscopy	KRAIN/YOS/KPI
	KOU/PER/AOES/GLAND	craniospinal	KRAIN/YO/SPAOINL
cowperi	KOUP/RAOI	craniostenosis	KRAIN/YO/STE/NOE/SIS
	KOU/PER/RAOI	craniostosis	KRAIN/YOS/TOE/SIS
cowperian	KOU/PAOERN	craniosynostosis	KRAIN/YO/SIN/OS/TOE/SIS
	KOU/PAOER/YAN	craniotabes	KRAIN/YO/TAI/BAOEZ
cowperitis	KOUP/RAOITS	craniotome	KRAIN/YO/TOEM
	KOU/PER/AOITS	craniotomy	KRAIN/YOT/M*I
cowpox	KOU/POX	craniotonoscopy	KRAIN/YO/TOE/NOS/KPI
cox	KOX	craniotopography	KRAIN/YO/TOE/POG/FI
Cox	K-P/KOX	craniotrypesis	KRAIN/YO/TRI/PAOE/SIS
cox(o)-	KOX	craniotympanic	KRAIN/YO/TIM/PAN/IK
	KOK/SO	craniovertebral	KRAIN/YO/VERT/BRAL
coxa	KOK/SA	cranitis	KRAI/NAOITS
coxae	KOK/SAE	cranium	KRAIN/YUM
coxal	KOK/SAL	crapul-	KRAP/L-
coxalgia	KOX/AL/JA		KRAP/YAOU/L-
	KOK/SAL/JA		KRAP/YU/L-
Coxiella	KOX/YEL/LA	crapulent	KRAP/LENT
coxitis	KOK/SAOITS	crapulosa	KRAP/LOE/SA
	KOX/AOITS	crapulous	KRAP/LOUS
coxodynia	KOX/DIN/YA	craquele	KRAK/LAI
coxofemoral	KOX/FEM/RAL	crash	KRARB
coxotomy	KOK/SOT/M*I	-crasia	KRAIZ/YA
	KOX/OT/M*I	crasis	KRAI/SIS
coxotuberculosis	KOX/TAOU/BERK/LOE/SIS	crassamentum	KRAS/MEN/TUM
coxsackievirus	KOK/SAK/VAOI/RUS	crassus	KRAS/SUS
	KOK/SAK/VAOI/RUS	crater	KRAIT/ER
cozymase	KO/ZAOI/MAIS	crateriform	KRAI/TER/FORM
	KO/ZAOIM/AIS	craterization	KRAI/TER/ZAIGS
crab	KRAB	cravat	KRA/VAT
Crabtree	KRAB/TRAOE	crave	KRAIZ
crack	KRAK	crazing	KRAIZ/-G
crackle	KRAK/-L	cream	KRAOEM
cradle	KRAID/-L	crease	KRAOES
Cramer	KRAIM/ER	creatinase	KRAOE/YAT/NAIS
cramp	KRAFRP		KRAOE/AT/NAIS
Crampton	KRAFRP/TON		KRAOE/TIN/AIS
Crandall	KRAN/DAL	creatine	KRAOE/TAOEN
crani(o)-	KRAIN/Y(O)		KRAOE/YA/TIN
crania	KRAIN/YA		(not KRAOE/TIN; see cretin)
craniad	KRAIN/YAD	creatinemia	KRAOE/TIN/AOEM/YA
cranial	KRAIN/YAL		KRAOE/TI/NAOEM/YA
craniales	KRAIN/YAI/LAOEZ	creatininase	KRAOE/AT/NIN/AIS
cranialis	KRAIN/YAI/LIS		KRAOE/TIN/NAIS
craniamphitomy	KRAIN/YAM/FIT/M*I	creatinine	KRAOE/AT/NIN
	KRAIN/AM/FIT/M*I		KRAOE/YAT/NIN
Craniata	KRAIN/YAI/TA		KRAOE/AT/NAOEN
craniectomy	KRAIN/YEKT/M*I		KRAOE/YAT/NAOEN
cranii	KRAIN/YAOI	creatinuria	KRAOE/AT/NAOUR/YA
cranioacromial	KRAIN/YO/AI/KROEM/YAL		KRAOE/TIN/YAOUR/YA
cranioaural	KRAIN/YO/AURL		KRAOE/TI/NAOUR/YA
craniobuccal	KRAIN/YO/BUK/KAL	Crede	KRAI/DAI
craniocarpotarsal	KRAIN/YO/KARP/TAR/SAL	creep	KRAOEP
craniocele	KRAIN/YO/SAO*EL	creeping	KRAOEP/-G
craniocerebral	KRAIN/YO/SER/BRAL	creme	KRAO*EM
cranioclasia	KRAIN/YO/KLAIZ/YA	cremaster	KRAOE/MA*S/ER
cranioclasis	KRAIN/YOK/LA/SIS		KRAOE/MAS/TER
cranioclast	KRAIN/YO/KLA*S	cremasteric	KRAOE/MAS/TER/IK
craniocleidodysostosis	KRAIN/YO/KLAOID/DIS/OS/TOE/	cremasterica	KRAOE/MAS/TER/KA
	SIS	cremate	KRAOE/MAIT
craniodiaphysial	KRAIN/YO/DAOI/FIZ/YAL	cremation	KRAOE/MAIGS
craniodidymus	KRAIN/YO/DID/MUS	crematorium	KRAOEM/TOIRM
craniofacial	KRAIN/YO/FAIRBL	cremnocele	KREM/NO/SAO*EL
craniofenestria	KRAIN/YO/FE/NES/TRA	crena	KRAOE/NA
	KRAIN/YO/FE/NES/TRAOE/YA	crenae	KRAOE/NAE
craniognomy	KRAIN/YOG/NO/M*I	crenate	KRAOE/NAIT
craniograph	KRAIN/YO/GRAF		KRE/NAIT
craniography	KRAIN/YOG/FI		KREN/NAIT
craniolacunia	KRAIN/YO/LA/KAOUN/YA	crenated	KRAOE/NAIT/-D
craniology	KRAIN/YOLG		KRE/NAIT/-D

crenation	KREN/NAIT/-D	cricothyroideus	KRAOIK/THAOI/ROID/YUS
	KRAOE/NAIGS	cricothyroidotomy	KRAOIK/THAOI/ROI/DOT/M*I
	KRE/NAIGS	cricothyrotomy	KRAOIK/THAOI/ROT/M*I
	KREN/NAIGS	cricotomy	KRAOI/KOT/M*I
crenilabrin	KRENL/AI/BRIN	cricotracheale	KRAOIK/TRAIK/YAI/LAOE
	KREN/LAI/BRIN	cricotracheotomy	KRAOIK/TRAIK/YOT/M*I
crenocyte	KRAOEN/SAO*IT	Crile	KRAOIL
crenocytosis	KRAOEN/SAOI/TOE/SIS	Crimean	KRAOI/MAOEN
Crenosoma vulpis	KRAOEN/SOE/MA/VUL/PIS		KRAOI/MAOE/YAN
crenotherapy	KREN/THER/PI	criminal	KRIM/NAL
crenulation	KREN/LAIGS		KR-L
Creon	KRAOE/YON	criminology	KRIM/NOLG
creophagism	KRAOE/OF/JIFM		KR-L/OLG
	KRAOE/YOF/JIFM		KR-L/NOLG
creophagy	KRAOE/OF/JI	crines	KRAOI/NAOEZ
	KRAOE/YOF/JI	-crinia	KRIN/YA
creosol	KRAO*E/SOL	crinin	KRIN/NIN
	KRAOE/YO/SOL		KRI/NIN
	(not KRAOE/SOL; see cresol)	crinis	KRAOI/NIS
creosote	KRAOE/SOET	crinogenic	KRIN/JEN/IK
	KRAOE/YO/SOET		KRAOIN/JEN/IK
crepitant	KREP/TANT	crinology	KRAOI/NOLG
crepitation	KREP/TAIGS		KRI/NOLG
crepitus	KREP/TUS	crinophagy	KRIN/OF/JI
crepuscular	KRE/PUS/KLAR		KRI/NOF/JI
	KRAOE/PUS/KLAR		KRAOI/NOF/JI
crescent	KRES/ENT	cripple	KRIP/-L
crescentic	KRE/SENT/IK	crippled	KRIP/-LD
	KRES/SENT/IK	crippling	KRIP/-LG
crescograph	KRES/KO/GRAF	crises	KRAOI/SAOEZ
cresol	KRAOE/SOL	crisis	KRAOI/SIS
cresolase	KRAOES/LAIS	crispation	KRIS/PAIGS
cresolphthalein	KRAOE/SOL/THAL/YIN	crista	KRIS/TA
cresorcin	KRE/SOR/SIN	crista ampullaris	KRIS/TA/AFRP/LAI/RIS
cresorcinol	KRE/SORS/NOL		KRIS/TA/AM/PAOU/LAI/RIS
cresoxydiol	KRES/OX/DI/OL		KRIS/TA/AFRP/LAR/RIS
cresoxypropanediol	KRES/OX/PRO/PAIN/DI/OL		KRIS/TA/AM/PAOU/LAR/RIS
crest	KR*ES	crista galli	KRIS/TA/GAL/LAOI
CREST	K-PS/KR*ES/K-PS		KRIS/TA/GAUL/LAOI
cresta	KRES/TA	cristae	KRIS/TAE
cresyl	KRES/IL	cristal	KR*IS/TAL
cresylate	KRES/LAIT		(not KRIS/TAL; see crystal)
creta	KRAOE/TA	cristata	KRIS/TAI/TA
cretin	KRAOE/TIN	criteria	KRAOI/TAOER/YA
cretinism	KRAOET/NIFM	criterion	KRAOI/TAOER/YON
cretinistic	KRAOET/N*IS/IK	Critchley	KRIFP/LAOE
cretinoid	KRAOET/NOID	crith	KR*IT
cretinous	KRAOET/NOUS	crithidia	KRI/THID/YA
Creutzfeldt	KROITS/FELT	Crithidia	K-P/KRI/THID/YA
crevice	KREV/IS	crithidial	KRI/THID/YAL
crevicular	KRE/VIK/LAR	critical	KRIT/KAL
crib	KRIB	Criticare	KRIT/KAIR
cribbing	KRIB/-G	crocein	KROE/SAOEN
cribra	KRAOI/BRA		KROES/YIN
	KRIB/RA	crocidismus	KROK/DIZ/MUS
cribral	KRAOI/BRAL		KROES/DIZ/MUS
	KRIB/RAL	crocus	KROE/KUS
cribrate	KRIB/RAIT	crofilicon	KROE/FIL/KON
cribration	KRAOI/BRAIGS	Crohn	KROEN
	KRIB/RAIGS	cromoglycate	KROEM/GLAOI/KAIT
cribriform	KRIB/RI/FORM	cromoglycic	KROEM/GLAOIS/IK
cribrosa	KRAOI/BROE/SA		KROEM/GLIS/IK
	KRIB/ROE/SA	cromolyn	KROEM/LIN
cribrum	KRAOI/BRUM	cromolyn sodium	KROEM/LIN/SOED/YUM
	KRIB/RUM	Crooke	KRAO*K
Cricetinae	KRAOI/SAOET/NAE	Crooke-Russell	KRAO*K/H-F/RUS/EL
Cricetus	KRAO/SAOE/TUS		KRAO*K/H-F/RUS/SEL
Crichton	KRAOI/TON	crop	KROP
crick	KRIK	cropropamide	KROE/PROEP/MAOID
crico-	KRAOIK	Crosby	KROZ/BI
	KRAOI/KO		KROS/BI
cricoarytaenoideus	KRAOIK/AR/TAE/NOID/YUS	cross	KROSZ
cricoarytenoid	KRAOIK/AR/TAOE/NOID	crossbar	KROSZ/BAR
cricoarytenoidea	KRAOIK/AR/TAOE/NOID/YA	crossbite	KROSZ/BAOIT
cricoarytenoideum	KRAOIK/AR/TAOE/NOID/YUM	crossbreed	KROSZ/BRAOED
cricoarytenoideus	KRAOIK/AR/TAOE/NOID/YUS	crossbreeding	KROSZ/BRAOED/-G
cricoid	KRAOI/KOID	cross-bridges	KROSZ/H-F/BRLJ/-S
cricoidea	KRAOI/KOID/YA	crossed	KROSZ/-D
cricoideae	KRAOI/KOID/YAE	cross-eye	KROSZ/H-F/YAOI
cricoidectomy	KRAOI/KOI/DEKT/M*I	crossfoot	KROSZ/FAOT
cricoidynia	KRAOI/KOI/DIN/YA	crossing-over	KROSZ/-G/H-F/OEFR
cricopharyngeal	KRAOIK/FRIN/JAL		KROSZ/-G/H-F/OEVR
cricopharyngeum	KRAOIK/FRIN/JUM	crossmatch	KROSZ/MAFP
cricopharyngeus	KRAOIK/FRIN/JUS	crossmatching	KROSZ/MAFP/-G
cricothyreoideus	KRAOIK/THAOIR/YOID/YUS	cross-over	KROSZ/H-F/OEFR
cricothyreotomy	KRAOIK/THAOIR/YOT/M*I		KROSZ/H-F/OEVR
cricothyroid	KRAOIK/THAOI/ROID	cross-reactivation	KROSZ/H-F/RE/AKT/VAIGS
cricothyroidea	KRAOIK/THAOI/ROID/YA	cross-reactivity	KROSZ/H-F/RE/AK/TIV/TI
cricothyroideum	KRAOIK/THAOI/ROID/YUM	cross-sensitization	KROSZ/H-F/SENS/TI/ZAIGS

crossway	KROSZ/WA*I	crymodynia	KRAOIM/DIN/YA
crotalid	KROET/LID	crymophilic	KRAOIM/FIL/IK
	KROT/LID	crymophylactic	KRAOIM/FLAKT/IK
crotalin	KROET/LIN	crymotherapeutic	KRAOIM/THER/PAOUT/IK
	KROT/LIN	crymotherapy	KRAOIM/THER/PI
crotaline	KROET/LAOEN	cryo-	KRAOI
	KROT/LAOEN		KRAOI/YO
crotalism	KROET/LIFM	cryoanesthesia	KRAOI/YO/ANS/THAOEZ/YA
crotalotoxin	KROET/LO/TOK/SIN		(not KRAOI/ANS/THAOEZ/YA; see
Crotalus	KROT/LUS		cryanesthesia)
crotamine	KROET/MAOEN	cryoanalgesia	KRAOI/ANL/JAOEZ/YA
crotamiton	KROET/MAOI/TON	cryobank	KRAOI/BA*NG
	KROE/TAM/TON		KRAOI/BAN/-K
crotaphion	KROE/TAF/YON	cryobiology	KRAOI/BAO*I/OLG
crotethamide	KROE/T*ET/MAOID	cryocardioplegia	KRAOI/KARD/YO/PLAOE/JA
-crotic	KROT/IK	cryocautery	KRAOI/KAUT/RI
Croton	KROE/TON	cryoconization	KRAOI/KON/ZAIGS
croton oil	KROE/TON/OIL	cryocrit	KRAOI/KRIT
Crotona	KROE/TOE/NA	cryoextraction	KRAOI/EX/TRA*BGS
crotonase	KROET/NAIS	cryoextractor	KRAOI/EX/TRAK/TOR
	KROE/TON/AIS	cryofibrinogen	KRAOI/FAOI/BRIN/JEN
crotonic	KROE/TON/IK	cryofibrinogenemia	KRAOI/FAOI/BRIN/JEN/AOEM/YA
crotonism	KROET/NIM		KRAOI/FAOI/BRIN/JE/NAOEM/YA
crotonyl	KROET/NIL	cryofluorane	KRAOI/FLAOU/RAIN
crotoxin	KROE/TOK/SIN	cryogammaglobulin	KRAOI/GAM/GLOB/LIN
croup	KRAOUP	cryogen	KRAOI/JEN
crouposa	KRAOU/POE/SA	cryogenic	KRAOI/JEN/IK
croupous	KRAOUP/OUS	cryogenics	KRAOI/JEN/IK/-S
croupy	KRAOU/PI	cryoglobulin	KRAOI/GLOB/LIN
	KRAOUP/PI	cryoglobulinemia	KRAOI/GLOB/LIN/AOEM/YA
Crouzon	KRAOU/ZON		KRAOI/GLOB/LI/NAOEM/YA
crowding	KROUD/-G	cryohydrate	KRAOI/HAOI/DRAIT
crowing	KROE/-G	cryohypophysectomy	KRAOI/HAOI/POF/SEKT/M*I
crown	KROUN		KRAOI/HO*IP/FI/SEKT/M*I
crowning	KROUN/-G	cryolysis	KRAOI/OL/SIS
cruces	KRAOU/SAOEZ	cryometer	KRAOI/OM/TER
crucial	KRAOURBL	cryopallidectomy	KRAOI/PAL/DEKT/M*I
cruciata	KRAOURB/YAI/TA	cryopathy	KRAOI/OP/TH*I
	KRAOU/SHAI/TA	cryopexy	KRAOI/PEK/SI
cruciate	KRAOURB/YAIT	cryophilic	KRAOI/FIL/IK
	KRAOU/SHAIT	cryophylactic	KRAOI/FLAKT/IK
cruciatum	KRAOURB/YAI/TUM	cryoprecipitability	KRAOI/PRE/SIPT/-BLT
	KRAOURB/YAIT/UM	cryoprecipitate	KRAOI/PRE/SIP/TAIT
	KRAOU/SHAI/TUM	cryoprecipitated	KRAOI/PRE/SIP/TAIT/-D
	KRAOU/SHAIT/UM	cryoprecipitation	KRAOI/PRE/SIP/TAIGS
crucible	KRAOUS/-BL	cryopreservation	KRAOI/PREZ/VAIGS
	KRAOURB/-BL	cryoprobe	KRAOI/PROEB
crucifixion	KRAOUS/F*IBGS	cryoprotective	KRAOI/PRO/TEKT/IV
cruciform	KRAOUS/FORM	cryoprotein	KRAOI/PRO/TAOEN
cruciforme	KRAOUS/FOR/MAOE	cryopulvinectomy	KRAOI/PUL/VI/NEKT/M*I
cruciformis	KRAOUS/FOR/MIS	cryoscope	KRAOI/SKOEP
crude	KRAOUD	cryoscopic	KRAOI/SKOP/IK
cruenta	KRAOUN/TA	cryoscopical	KRAOI/SKOP/KAL
	KRAOU/EN/TA	cryoscopy	KRAOI/OS/KPI
Cruex	KRAOU/EX	cryospasm	KRAOI/SPAFM
crufomate	KRAOUF/MAIT	cryospray	KRAOI/SPRAI
cruor	KRAOUR	cryostat	KRAOI/STAT
crura	KRAOU/RA	cryostylet	KRAOI/STAOI/LET
	KRUR/RA	cryosurgery	KRAOI/SURJ/RI
	KRAOUR/RA		KRAOI/S-RJ
crural	KRAOURL	cryothalamectomy	KRAOI/THAL/MEKT/M*I
	KRURL	cryotherapy	KRAOI/THER/PI
crureus	KRAOU/RAOE/YUS	cryotolerant	KRAOI/TOL/RANT
cruris	KRAOU/RIS	cryounit	KRAOI/YAOUNT
	KRUR/RIS	crypt	KRIPT
	KRAOUR/RIS	crypt(o)-	KRIPT
crus	KRAOUS		KRIP/T(O)
	KRUS	crypta	KRIP/TA
crush	KRURB	cryptae	KRIP/TAE
crusotomy	KRAOUS/OT/M*I	cryptanamnesia	KRIPT/AN/AM/NAOEZ/YA
	KRAOU/SOT/M*I		KRIPT/TAN/AM/NAOEZ/YA
crust	KR*US	cryptectomy	KRIPT/TEKT/M*I
crusta	KRUS/TA	cryptenamine	KRIP/TEN/MAOEN
Crustacea	KRUS/TAI/SHA		KRIP/TEN/MAOIN
	KRUS/TAIRB/YA	cryptesthesia	KRIP/TES/THAOEZ/YA
crustacean	KRUS/TAIGS		KRIP/ES/THAOEZ/YA
crustae	KRUS/TAE	cryptic	KRIPT/IK
crustal	KRUS/TAL	cryptitis	KRIP/TAOITS
crustosus	KRUS/TOE/SUS	cryptococcoma	KRIPT/KOK/KOE/MA
crutch	KRUFP	cryptococcosis	KRIPT/KOK/KOE/SIS
Cruveilhier	KRAOU/VAIL/YAI	Cryptococcus	KRIPT/KOK/KUS
crux	KRUX	cryptocrystalline	KRIPT/KR*IS/LAOEN
cry	KRAOI	cryptodeterminant	KRIPT/DE/TERM/NANT
cryalgesia	KRAOI/AL/JAOEZ/YA		KRIPT/DERM/NANT
cryanesthesia	KRAOI/ANS/THAOEZ/YA	cryptodidymus	KRIPT/DID/MUS
cryesthesia	KRAOI/ES/THAOEZ/YA	cryptoempyema	KRIPT/EM/PAOI/E/MA
crymo-	KRAOIM	cryptogenetic	KRIPT/JE/NET/IK
	KRAOI/MO	cryptogenic	KRIPT/JEN/IK
crymoanesthesia	KRAOIM/ANS/THAOEZ/YA	cryptoglioma	KRIPT/GLAOI/YOE/MA

cryptolith	KRIPT/L*IT	culdoplasty	KUL/DO/PLAS/TI
cryptomenorrhea	KRIPT/MEN/RAOE/YA	culdoscope	KUL/DO/SKOEP
cryptomere	KRIPT/MAOER	culdoscopy	KUL/DOS/KPI
cryptomerorachischisis	KRIPT/MAOER/RA/KIS/KI/SIS	culdotomy	KUL/DOT/M*I
cryptophthalmia	KRIP/TOF/THAL/MA	Culex	KAOU/LEX
	KRIP/TOF/THAL/MAOE/YA	Culicidae	KAOU/LIS/DAE
cryptophthalmos	KRIP/TOF/THAL/MOS	culicidal	KAOUL/SAOI/DAL
cryptophthalmus	KRIP/TOF/THAL/MUS	culicide	KAOUL/SAO*ID
cryptoplasmic	KRIPT/PLAZ/MIK	culicifuge	KAOU/LIS/FAOUJ
cryptopodia	KRIPT/POED/YA	culicis	KAOUL/SIS
cryptopyic	KRIPT/PAOI/IK	Culicoides	KAOUL/KOI/DAOEZ
cryptopyrrole	KRIPT/PIR/ROEL	culicosis	KAOUL/KOE/SIS
cryptoradiometer	KRIPT/RAID/YOM/TER	culinary	KAOUL/NAIR
cryptorchid	KRIP/TOR/KID		KUL/NAIR
cryptorchidectomy	KRIP/TORK/DEKT/M*I	Culiseta	KAOUL/SAOE/TA
cryptorchidism	KRIP/TORK/DIFM	Cullen	KUL/LEN
	KRIP/ORK/DIFM		KUL/-N
cryptorchidopexy	KRIP/TORK/DO/PEK/SI	culling	KUL/-G
cryptorchidy	KRIP/TORK/DI	culmen	KUL/MEN
cryptorchism	KRIP/TOR/KIFM	culmina	KUL/MI/NA
	KRIP/TORK/IFM	Culp	KUL/-P
cryptorrhea	KRIPT/RAOE/YA	cult	KULT
cryptorrheic	KRIPT/RAOE/IK	cultivation	KULT/VAIGS
cryptorrhetic	KRIPT/RET/IK	culturable	KUL/KHUR/-BL
cryptoscope	KRIPT/SKOEP		KUL/KHURBL
cryptoscopy	KRIP/TOS/KPI	cultural	KUL/KHURL
cryptosporidiosis	KRIPT/SPRID/YOE/SIS	culture	KUL/KHUR
Cryptosporidium	KRIPT/SPRID/YUM	cumetharol	KAOU/M*ET/ROL
cryptosterol	KRIP/TO*S/ROL	cumidine	KAOUM/DIN
Cryptostroma	KRIPT/STROE/MA		KAOUM/DAOEN
cryptotia	KRIP/TOE/SHA	cumul-	KAOUM/L-
cryptotoxic	KRIPT/TOX/IK		KAOUM/YAOU/L-
cryptoxanthin	KRIPT/ZAN/THIN		KAOUM/YU/L-
cryptozoite	KRIPT/ZOE/AOIT		KAOU/MAOU/L-
cryptozygous	KRIP/TOZ/GOUS	cumulative	KAOUM/LA/TIV
	KRIPT/ZAOIG/OUS	cumuli	KAOUM/LAOI
crystal	KRIS/TAL	cumulus	KAOUM/LUS
crystalbumin	KRIS/TAL/BAOU/MIN	cune(o)-	KAOUN/Y(O)
crystall(o)-	KR*IS/L(O)	cuneate	KAOUN/YAIT
	KRIS/TAL/L(O)	cuneatus	KAOUN/YAI/TUS
crystalli	KRIS/TAL/LAOE	cunei	KAOUN/YAOI
	KR*IS/LAOE	cuneiform	KAOU/NAOE/FORM
crystallin	KR*IS/LIN	cuneiformia	KAOU/NAOE/FORM/YA
	KRIS/TAL/LIN	cuneiformis	KAOU/NAOE/FOR/MIS
crystalline	KR*IS/LAOEN	cuneocuboid	KAOUN/YO/KAOU/BOID
	KRIS/LAOIN		KAOUN/YO/KAOUB/OID
crystallitis	KR*IS/LAOITS	cuneocuboideum	KAOUN/YO/KAOU/BOID/YUM
crystallization	KRIS/TAL/ZAIGS	cuneonavicular	KAOUN/YO/NA/VIK/LAR
	KR*IS/LI/ZAIGS	cuneonavicularis	KAOUN/YO/NA/VIK/LAI/RIS
crystallography	KR*IS/LOG/FI	cuneoscaphoid	KAOUN/YO/SKAF/OID
crystalloid	KR*IS/LOID	cuneus	KAOUN/YUS
crystalloiditis	KR*IS/LOI/DAOITS	cuniculi	KAOU/NIK/LAOI
crystalluria	KR*IS/LAOUR/YA	cuniculus	KAOU/NIK/LUS
Crysticillin	KR*IS/SLIN	cunnilinction	KUN/LINGS
	KR*IS/SIL/LIN	cunnilinctus	KUN/LING/TUS
Crystodigin	KRIS/TO/DII/JIN	cunnilinguism	KUN/LING/WIFM
	KRIS/TO/DI/JIN	cunnilingus	KUN/LIN/GUS
CT	KR-RBGS/T*RBGS		KUN/LING/GUS
Ctenocephalides	TAOEN/SFAL/DAOEZ	cunnus	KUN/NUS
ctetology	TAOE/TOLG	cuorin	KAOU/RIN
ctetosome	TET/SOEM	cup	KUP
CT scan	KR-RBGS/T*RBGS/SKAN	cupped	KUP/-D
cubeb	KAOU/BEB	cupping	KUP/-G
cubebic	KAOU/BEB/IK	cupremia	KAOU/PRAOEM/YA
cubic	KAOUB/IK	cupric	KAOU/PRIK
cubicle	KAOUB/K-L		KAOUP/RIK
cubit	KAOU/BIT	Cuprid	KAOU/PRID
cubit(o)-	KAOUB/T(O)	Cuprimine	KAOU/PRI/MAOEN
cubita	KAOUB/TA		KAOUP/RI/MAOEN
cubital	KAOUB/TAL	cupriuresis	KAOI/PRI/YAOU/RAOE/SIS
cubitalis	KAOUB/TAI/LIS	cupriuria	KAOU/PRI/YAOUR/YA
cubiti	KAOUB/TAOI	cuprous	KAOU/PROUS
cubitocarpal	KAOUB/TO/KAR/PAL		KAOUP/ROUS
cubitoradial	KAOUB/TO/RAID/YAL	cupruresis	KAOU/PRAOU/RAOE/SIS
cubitus	KAOUB/TUS	cupruretic	KAOU/PRAOU/RET/IK
cuboid	KAOU/BOID	cupul(o)-	KAOUP/L(O)-
	KAOUB/OID		KAOUP/YAOU/L(O)-
cuboidal	KAOU/BOI/DAL		KAOUP/YU/L(O)-
cuboideonaviculare	KAOU/BOID/YO/NA/VIK/LAI/		KAOU/PAOU/L(O)-
	RAOE	cupula	KAOUP/LA
cue	KAOU	cupulae	KAOUP/LAE
cuff	KUF	cupular	KAOUP/LAR
cuffing	KUF/-G	cupulare	KAOUP/LAI/RAOE
cuirass	KWAOE/RASZ	cupuliform	KAOUP/LI/FORM
	KWI/RASZ	cupulogram	KAOUP/LO/GRAM
cul-de-sac	KUL/DE/SAK	cupulolithiasis	KAOUP/LO/LI/THAOI/SIS
culdo-	KUL/DO	cupulometry	KAOUP/LOM/TRI
	KULD	curage	KAOU/RAJ
culdocentesis	KUL/DO/SEN/TAOE/SIS	curare	KAOU/RAR/RAOE

	KAOU/RA/RAOE
curariform	KAOU/RAR/FORM
curarimimetic	KAOU/RAR/MAOI/MET/IK
curarization	KAOU/RAR/ZAIGS
curativa	KAOUR/TAOI/VA
curative	KAOUR/TIV
curb	KURB
curcumin	KUR/KAOU/MIN
curd	KURD
curdling	KURD/-LG
curve	KUFRB
curet	KAOU/RET
curettage	KAOUR/TAJ
curette	KAOU/R*ET
	KAO*U/RET
	(not KAOU/RET; see curet)
curettement	KAOU/RET/-MT
curie	KAOUR/RAOE
	KAOU/RAOE
Curie	K-P/KAOUR/RAOE
	K-P/KAOU/RAOE
curiegram	KAOUR/RAOE/GRAM
	KAOU/RAOE/GRAM
curie-hour	KAOUR/RAOE/HOUR
	KAOU/RAOE/HOUR
curietherapy	KAOUR/RAOE/THER/PI
	KAOU/RAOE/THER/PI
curing	KAOUR/-G
curioscopy	KAOUR/YOS/KPI
curium	KAOUR/YUM
curling	KURL/-G
Curling	K-P/KURL/-G
current	KURNT
Curretab	KUR/TAB
curricula	KRIK/LA
	KUR/RIK/LA
curriculum	KRIK/LUM
	KUR/RIK/LUM
curse	KURS
cursive	KURS/IV
curvatura	KUFRB/TAOU/RA
	KUFRB/KHUR/RA
curvaturae	KUFRB/TAOU/RAE
	KUFRB/KHUR/RAE
curvature	KUFRB/KHUR
curve	KUFRB
curvus	KUR/VUS
Cushing's	KURB/-G/AOES
cushingoid	KURB/-G/OID
	KURB/GOID
cushion	KUGS
cusp	KUS/-P
cuspad	KUS/PAD
cuspal	KUS/PAL
cuspid	KUS/PID
cuspidate	KUS/PI/DAIT
cuspides	KUS/PI/DAOEZ
cuspidis	KUS/PI/DIS
cuspis	KUS/PIS
custodial	KUS/TOED/YAL
cut	KUT
cut-	KAOUT
	KAOU/T-
cutanea	KAOU/TAIN/YA
cutaneomucosal	KAOU/TAIN/YO/MAOU/KOE/SAL
-cutaneostomy	KAOU/TAIN/YO*S/M*I
cutaneous	KAOU/TAIN/YOUS
cutaneum	KAOU/TAIN/YUM
cutaneus	KAOU/TAIN/YUS
cutdown	KUT/DO*UN
Cuterebra	KAOUT/RAOE/BRA
Cuterebridae	KAOUT/REB/RI/DAE
cuticle	KAOUT/K-L
cuticul-	KAOU/TIK/L-
	KAOU/TIK/YAOU/L-
	KAOU/TIK/YU/L-
cuticula	KAOU/TIK/LA
cuticulae	KAOU/TIK/LAE
cuticular	KAOU/TIK/LAR
cuticularization	KAOU/TIK/LAR/ZAIGS
cuticulin	KAOU/TIK/LIN
cuticulum	KAOU/TIK/LUM
cutidure	KAOUT/DAOUR
cutiduris	KAOUT/DAOU/RIS
cutin	KAOU/TIN
cutinization	KAOU/TIN/ZAIGS
	KAOU/NI/ZAIGS
cutireaction	KAOU/TI/RE/A*BGS
	KAO*UT/RE/A*BGS

	(not KAOUT/RE/A*BGS; see cute reaction)
cutis	KAOU/TIS
cutisector	KAOUT/SEK/TOR
	KAOU/TI/SEK/TOR
cutization	KAOUT/ZAIGS
cuttlefish	KUT/-L/FIRB
cuvet	KAOU/VET
cuvette	KAO*U/VET
	KAOU/V*ET
	(not KAOU/VET; see cuvet)
Cuvier	KAOUV/YAI
cuvieri	KAOUV/YAI/RAOI
	KAOUV/YER/RAOI
	KAOU/VAOI/RAOI
	KAOU/VAOE/RAOI
cyamemazine	SAOI/MEM/ZAOEN
cyan(o)-	SAOI/N(O)
	SAOI/AN
	SAOI/YAN
cyanalcohol	SAOI/AN/KHOL
	SAOI/AN/AL/KHOL
cyanamide	SAOI/AN/MAOID
cyanate	SAOI/NAIT
cyanemia	SAOI/NAOEM/YA
cyanhematin	SAOI/AN/HEM/TIN
cyanhemoglobin	SAOI/AN/HAOEM/GLOE/BIN
cyanide	SAOI/NAOID
cyanin	SAOI/NIN
cyanidenon	SAOI/NID/NON
cyanidol	SAOI/AN/DOL
cyanmethemoglobin	SAOI/AN/MET/HAOEM/GLOE/BIN
cyanmetmyoglobin	SAOI/AN/MET/MAOI/GLOE/BIN
cyanoalcohol	SAOI/NO/KHOL
	SAOI/NO/AL/KHOL
Cyanobacteria	SAOI/NO/BAK/TAOER/YA
cyanocobalamin	SAOI/NO/KO/BAL/MIN
cyanocrystallin	SAOI/NO/KR*IS/LIN
cyanoform	SAOI/AN/FORM
cyanogen	SAOI/AN/JEN
cyanogenic	SAOI/AN/JEN/IK
	SAOI/NO/JEN/IK
cyanogenesis	SAOI/NO/JEN/SIS
cyanogenetic	SAOI/NO/JE/NET/IK
cyanohydrin	SAOI/NO/HAOI/DRIN
cyanophil	SAOI/AN/FIL
cyanophile	SAOI/AN/FAOIL
cyanophilous	SAOI/NOF/LOUS
cyanophoric	SAOI/NO/FOER/IK
cyanophose	SAOI/NO/FOEZ
Cyanophyceae	SAOI/NO/FAOIS/YAE
cyanopia	SAOI/NOEP/YA
cyanoplatinate	SAOI/NO/PLAT/NAIT
cyanopsia	SAOI/NOPS/YA
cyanopsin	SAOI/NOP/SIN
cyanose	SAOI/NOES
cyanosed	SAOI/NOES/-D
cyanosis	SAOI/NOE/SIS
cyanotic	SAOI/NOT/IK
cyanotica	SAOI/NOT/KA
cyanuria	SAOI/NAOUR/YA
cyanuric	SAOI/NAOUR/IK
cyanurin	SAOI/NAOU/RIN
	SAOI/NAOUR/RIN
Cyathostoma	SAOI/THO*S/MA
Cyathostomum	SAOI/THO*S/MUM
cybernetics	SAOIB/NET/IK/-S
	SAOI/BER/NET/IK/-S
	SAOIB/ER/NET/IK/-S
cybrid	SAOI/BRID
cycl(o)-	SAOI/KL(O)
	SAOIK/L(O)
cyclacillin	SAOI/KLA/SLIN
	SAOI/KLA/SIL/LIN
Cyclacillin Tablets	SAOI/KLA/SLIN/TAB/LET/-S
	SAOI/KLA/SIL/LIN/TAB/LET/-S
cyclamate	SAOI/KLA/MAIT
cyclamic	SAOI/KLAM/IK
cyclamide	SAOI/KLA/MAOID
cyclamin	SAOI/KLA/MIN
cyclandelate	SAOI/KLAND/LAIT
cyclarbamate	SAOI/KLARB/MAIT
	SAOI/KLAR/BA/MAIT
cyclarthrodial	SIK/LAR/THROED/YAL
cyclarthrosis	SIK/LAR/THROE/SIS
cyclase	SAOI/KLAIS
cyclazocine	SAOI/KLAIZ/SAOEN
	SAOI/KLAZ/SAOEN
	SAOI/KLA/ZOE/SIN

cycle	SAOIK/-L	cyclosis	SAOI/KLOE/SIS
cyclectomy	SAOI/KLEKT/M*I	cyclospasm	SAOI/KLO/SPAFM
	SIK/LEKT/M*I	cyclosporine	SAOI/KLO/SPORN
cyclencephalia	SAOI/KLEN/SFAIL/YA		SAOI/KLO/SPOR/AOEN
	SIK/LEN/SFAIL/YA		SAOI/KLO/SPOR/RAOEN
cyclencephalus	SAOI/KLEN/SEF/LUS	cyclostat	SAOI/KLO/STAT
	SIK/LEN/SEF/LUS	cyclotherapy	SAOI/KLO/THER/PI
cyclencephaly	SAOI/KLEN/SEF/LI	cyclothiazide	SAOI/KLO/THAOI/ZAOID
	SIK/LEN/SEF/LI	cyclothyme	SAOI/KLO/THAOIM
cyclic	SAOIK/LIK	cyclothymia	SAOI/KLO/THAOIM/YA
	SAOI/KLIK	cyclothymiac	SAOI/KLO/THAOIM/YAK
	SIK/LIK	cyclothymic	SAOI/KLO/THAOIM/IK
cyclicotomy	SAOI/KLI/KOT/M*I	cyclotol	SAOI/KLO/TOL
	SAOIK/LI/KOT/M*I	cyclotome	SAOI/KLO/TOEM
	SIK/LI/KOT/M*I	cyclotomy	SAOI/KLOT/M*I
cyclindole	SAOI/KLIN/DOEL	cyclotron	SAOI/KLO/TRON
-cycline	SAOI/KLAOEN	cyclotropia	SAOI/KLO/TROEP/YA
	SAOIK/LAOEN	cyclozoonosis	SAOI/KLO/ZOE/NOE/SIS
cyclitis	SIK/LAOITS	cycrimine	SAOI/KRI/MAOIN
	SAOI/KLAOITS	Cycrin	SAOI/KRIN
cyclizine	SAOI/KLI/ZAOEN	cyesis	SAOI/E/SIS
cyclobarbital	SAOI/KLO/BARB/TAL	cyheptamide	SAOI/HEPT/MAOID
cyclobendazole	SAOI/KLO/BEND/ZOEL	Cyklokapron	SAOI/KLO/KAP/RON
cyclobenzaprine	SAOI/KLO/BENZ/PRAOEN	Cylert	SAOI/LERT
cyclocephalia	SAOI/KLO/SFAIL/YA	cylicotomy	SIL/KOT/M*I
cyclocephaly	SAOI/KO/SEF/LI	cylinder	SIL/IN/DER
cyclochoroiditis	SAOI/KLO/KOE/ROI/DAOITS	cylindr(o)-	SLIN/DR(O)-
Cyclocort	SAOI/KLO/KORT		SI/LIN/DR(O)-
cyclocryotherapy	SAOI/KLO/KRAOI/THER/PI		SIL/IN/DR(O)-
cyclocumarol	SAOI/KLO/KAOUM/ROL	cylindrarthrosis	SIL/IN/DRAR/THROE/SIS
	SAOI/KLO/KAOUM/ROEL		SLIN/DRAR/THROE/SIS
cyclodamia	SAOI/KLO/DAIM/YA	cylindric	SLIN/DRIK
cyclodialysis	SAOI/KLO/DI/AL/SIS		SI/LIN/DRIK
cyclodiathermy	SAOI/KLO/DAOI/THER/M*I	cylindrical	SLIN/DRI/KAL
cycloduction	SAOI/KLO/D*UBGS		SI/LIN/DRI/KAL
cycloelectrolysis	SAOI/KLO/LEK/TROL/SIS	cylindriform	SLIN/DRI/FORM
cyclogeny	SAOI/KLOJ/N*I		SI/LIN/DRI/FORM
cyclogram	SAOI/KLO/GRAM	cylindroadenoma	SIL/IN/DRO/AD/NOE/MA
cycloguanide	SAOI/KLO/GAU/NAOID		SLIN/DRO/AD/NOE/MA
cycloguanil	SAOI/KLO/GAU/NIL	cylindrocellular	SIL/IN/DRO/SEL/YAOU/LAR
cyclohexanehexol	SAOI/KLO/HEX/AIN/HEX/OL		SLIN/DRO/SEL/YAOU/LAR
	SAOI/KLO/HEK/SAIN/HEK/SOL	cylindroid	SIL/IN/DROID
cyclohexanesulfamic	SAOI/KLO/HEX/AIN/SUL/FAM/IK		SLIN/DROID
	SAOI/KLO/HEK/SAIN/SUL/FAM/ IK	cylindroma	SIL/IN/DROE/MA
			SLIN/DROE/MA
cyclohexanol	SAOI/KLO/HEX/NOL	cylindromatous	SIL/IN/DROEM/TOUS
cyclohexatriene	SAOI/KLO/HEX/TR*I/AOEN		SIL/IN/DROM/TOUS
	SAOI/KLO/HEX/TRAOI/AOEN		SLIN/DROEM/TOUS
cycloheximide	SAOI/KLO/HEX/MAOID		SLIN/DROM/TOUS
cyclohexitol	SAOI/KLO/HEX/TOL	cylindrosarcoma	SIL/IN/DRO/SAR/KOE/MA
cyclohexylsulfamic	SAOI/KLO/HEK/SIL/SUL/FAM/IK		SLIN/DRO/SAR/KOE/MA
	SAOI/KLO/HEX/IL/SUL/FAM/IK	cylindruria	SIL/IN/DRAOUR/YA
cycloid	SAOI/KLOID		SLIN/DRAOUR/YA
cycloisomerase	SAOI/KLO/AOI/SOM/RAIS	cylite	SAOI/LAOIT
cyclokeratitis	SAOI/KLO/KER/TAOITS	cyllosis	SIL/LOE/SIS
cyclol	SAOI/KLOL	cyllosoma	SIL/SOE/MA
cyclo-ligase	SAOI/KLO/LAOI/GAIS	Cylomine	SAOIL/MAOEN
cyclomastopathy	SAOI/KLO/MAS/TOP/TH*I	cymarin	SAOIM/RIN
cyclomethycaine	SAOI/KLO/M*ET/KAIN	cymba	SIM/BA
cyclonamine	SAOI/KLO/NAI/MAOEN	cymba conchae	SIM/BA/KON/KAE
cyclopentamine	SAOI/KLO/PENT/MAOEN	cymbiform	SIM/BI/FORM
cyclopentane	SAOI/KLO/PEN/TAIN	cymbocephalia	SIM/BO/SFAIL/YA
cyclopentaphenanthrene	SAOI/KLO/PENT/FE/NAN/ THRAOEN	cymbocephalic	SIM/BO/SFAL/IK
		cymbocephalous	SIM/BO/SEF/LOUS
cyclopentaphene	SAOI/KLO/PENT/FAOEN	cymbocephaly	SIM/BO/SEF/LI
cyclopentenophenanthrene	SAOI/KLO/PEN/TAOEN/FE/NAN/ THRAOEN	cyme	SAOIM
		cymosa	SAOI/MOE/SA
cyclopenthiazide	SAOI/KLO/PEN/THAOI/ZAOID	cynanche	SIN/AN/KAOE
cyclopentolate	SAOI/KLO/PENT/LAIT		SI/NAN/KAOE
cyclopeptide	SAOI/KLO/PEP/TAOID	cynanthropy	SAOI/NAN/THRO/PI
cyclophenazine	SAOI/KLO/FEN/ZAOEN	cynic	SIN/IK
cyclophorase	SAOI/KLO/FOER/AIS	cynocephalic	SAOI/NO/SFAL/IK
cyclophoria	SAOI/KLO/FOER/YA	cynocephaly	SAOIN/SEF/LI
cyclophorometer	SAOI/KLO/FOE/ROM/TER	cynodont	SAOIN/DONT
cyclophosphamide	SAOI/KLO/FOS/FA/MAOID	cynophobia	SAOIN/FOEB/YA
cyclophotocoagulation	SAOI/KLO/FOET/KO/AG/LAIGS	cyo-	SAOI
Cyclophyllidae	SAOI/KLO/FIL/DAE		SAOI/YO
Cyclophyllidea	SAOI/KLO/FIL/LID/YA	cyogenic	SAOI/JEN/IK
cyclopia	SAOI/KLOEP/YA	Cyon	SE/YON
cyclopian	SAOI/KLOEP/YAN		SI/YON
cyclopin	SAOI/KLO/PIN	cyonin	SAOI/YO/NIN
cycloplegia	SAOI/KLO/PLAOE/JA		(*not* SAOI/NIN; see cyanin)
cycloplegic	SAOI/KLO/PLAOEJ/IK	cyophoria	SAOI/FOER/YA
cyclopropane	SAOI/KLO/PRO/PAIN	cyophoric	SAOI/FOER/IK
cyclops	SAOI/KLOPS	cyopin	SAOI/PIN
cycloscope	SAOI/KLO/SKOEP	cyotrophy	SAOI/OT/RO/FI
cyclose	SAOI/KLOES	-cyphosis	SAOI/FOE/SIS
cycloserine	SAOI/KLO/SER/AOEN	cypionate	SIP/YO/NAIT
	SAOI/KLO/SER/RAOEN	cypothrin	SAOIP/THRIN

cyprazepam	SAOI/PRAZ/PAM
cypridology	SAOI/PRI/DOLG
	SIP/RI/DOLG
cypridopathy	SAOI/PRI/DOP/TH*I
	SIP/RI/DOP/TH*I
cypridophobia	SAOI/PRI/DO/FOEB/YA
	SIP/RI/DO/FOEB/YA
Cyprinidae	SAOI/PRIN/DAE
cyprinin	SIP/RI/NIN
	SAOI/PRI/NIN
cyproheptadine	SAOI/PRO/HEPT/DAOEN
	SIP/RO/HEPT/DAOEN
cyproquinate	SAOI/PRO/KWI/NAIT
cyproterone	SAOI/PROET/ROEN
Cyprus	SAOI/PRUS
cyrtograph	SIRT/GRAF
	SIR/TO/GRAF
cyrtometer	SIR/TOM/TER
cyrtosis	SIR/TOE/SIS
cyst	S*IS
cyst(o)-	S*IS
	SIS/T(O)
cystadenocarcinoma	S*IS/AD/NO/KARS/NOE/MA
	SIS/TAD/NO/KARS/NOE/MA
cystadenoma	S*IS/AD/NOE/MA
	SIS/TAD/NOE/MA
cystalgia	S*IS/AL/JA
	SIS/TAL/JA
cystamine	S*IS/MAOEN
-cystanastomosis	S*IS/NA*S/MOE/SIS
cystathionase	S*IS/THAOI/NAIS
cystathionine	S*IS/THAOI/NAOEN
cystathioninuria	S*IS/THAOI/NIN/YAOUR/YA
cystatrophia	S*IS/TROEF/YA
cystauchenitis	SIS/TAUK/NAOITS
cystauchenotomy	SIS/TAUK/NOT/M*I
cystauxe	SIS/TAUK/SAOE
cystectasia	SIS/TEK/TAIZ/YA
	S*IS/EK/TAIZ/YA
cystectasy	SIS/TEKT/SI
	S*IS/EKT/SI
cystectomy	SIS/TEKT/M*I
cysteic	SIS/TAOE/IK
cysteine	SIS/TAOE/YIN
cysteinsulfinic	S*IS/YIN/SUL/FIN/IK
cysteinyl	SIS/TAOEN/IL
cystelcosis	SIS/TEL/KOE/SIS
cystencephalus	SIS/TEN/SEF/LUS
cystendesis	SIS/TEN/DAOE/SIS
cysterethism	SIS/TER/THIFM
cysthypersarcosis	S*IS/HAO*IP/SAR/KOE/SIS
-cystia	S*IS/YA
cystic	S*IS/IK
cystic(o)-	S*IS/K(O)
cystica	S*IS/KA
cysticerci	S*IS/SER/SAOI
cysticercoid	S*IS/SER/KOID
cysticercosis	S*IS/SER/KOE/SIS
cysticercus	S*IS/SER/KUS
Cysticercus	K-P/S*IS/SER/KUS
cysticolithectomy	S*IS/KO/LI/THEKT/M*I
cysticolithotripsy	S*IS/KO/L*IT/TRIP/SI
cysticorrhaphy	S*IS/KOR/FI
cysticotomy	S*IS/KOT/M*I
cysticum	S*IS/KUM
cysticus	S*IS/KUS
cystides	S*IS/DAOEZ
cystido-	S*IS/DO
cystidoceliotomy	S*IS/DO/SAOEL/YOT/M*I
	S*IS/DO/SAO*EL/YOT/M*I
cystidolaparotomy	S*IS/DO/LAP/ROT/M*I
cystidotrachelotomy	S*IS/DO/TRAIK/LOT/M*I
cystifelleotomy	S*IS/FEL/YOT/M*I
cystifellotomy	S*IS/FEL/LOT/M*I
cystiferous	SIS/TIF/ROUS
cystiform	SIS/TI/FORM
	(not S*IS/FORM; see cyst form)
cystigerous	SIS/TIJ/ROUS
cystine	SIS/TAOEN
	SIS/TIN
cystinemia	S*IS/NAOEM/YA
cystinosis	S*IS/NOE/SIS
cystinuria	S*IS/NAOUR/YA
cystinuric	S*IS/NAOUR/IK
cystinyl	S*IS/NIL
cystis	SIS/TIS
cystistaxis	S*IS/STAK/SIS
cystitis	SIS/TAOITS
cystitome	SIS/TI/TOEM

	(not S*IS/TOEM; see cystotome)
cystitomy	SIS/TIT/M*I
cystoblast	S*IS/BLA*S
cystocarcinoma	S*IS/KARS/NOE/MA
cystocele	S*IS/SAO*EL
cystochrome	S*IS/KROEM
cystochromoscopy	S*IS/KROE/MOS/KPI
cystocolostomy	S*IS/KO/LO*S/M*I
	S*IS/KLO*S/M*I
cystodiaphanoscopy	S*IS/DAOI/FAN/OS/KPI
cystodiverticulum	S*IS/DI/VER/TIK/LUM
cystoduodenostomy	S*IS/DAOU/DEN/O*S/M*I
	S*IS/DAOU/DE/NO*S/M*I
	S*IS/DWOD/NO*S/M*I
cystodynia	S*IS/DIN/YA
cystoelytroplasty	S*IS/LIT/RO/PLAS/TI
	S*IS/E/LIT/RO/PLAS/TI
cystoenterocele	S*IS/SPWER/RO/SAO*EL
cystoenterostomy	S*IS/SPWRO*S/M*I
	S*IS/SPWER/RO*S/M*I
cystoepiplocele	S*IS/PIP/LO/SAO*EL
	S*IS/E/PIP/LO/SAO*EL
cystoepithelioma	S*IS/EP/THAOEL/YOE/MA
cystofibroma	S*IS/FAOI/BROE/MA
cystogastrostomy	S*IS/GAS/TRO*S/M*I
cystogram	S*IS/GRAM
cystography	SIS/TOG/FI
cystoid	SIS/TOID
cystojejunostomy	S*IS/JEJ/NO*S/M*I
cystolith	S*IS/L*IT
cystolithectomy	S*IS/LI/THEKT/M*I
cystolithiasis	S*IS/LI/THAOI/SIS
cystolithic	S*IS/L*IT/IK
cystolithotomy	S*IS/LI/THOT/M*I
cystolutein	S*IS/LAOUT/YIN
cystoma	SIS/TOE/MA
cystomatitis	S*IS/MA/TAOITS
	SIS/TOEM/TAOITS
cystomatous	SIS/TOEM/TOUS
cystometer	SIS/TOM/TER
cystometrogram	S*IS/MET/RO/GRAM
	S*IS/MAOE/TRO/GRAM
cystometrography	S*IS/ME/TROG/FI
cystometry	SIS/TOM/TRI
cystomorphous	S*IS/MOR/FOUS
cystomyoma	S*IS/MAOI/YOE/MA
cystomyxoadenoma	S*IS/MIX/AD/NOE/MA
cystomyxoma	S*IS/MIK/SOE/MA
cystonephrosis	S*IS/NE/FROE/SIS
cystoneuralgia	S*IS/NAOU/RAL/JA
	S*IS/NAOUR/AL/JA
cystoparalysis	S*IS/PRAL/SIS
cystopexy	S*IS/PEK/SI
cystophorous	SIS/TOF/ROUS
cystophotography	S*IS/FOE/TOG/FI
	S*IS/FRAF/FI
cystophthisis	SIS/TOF/THI/SIS
cystoplasty	S*IS/PLAS/TI
cystoplegia	S*IS/PLAOE/JA
cystoproctostomy	S*IS/PROK/TO*S/M*I
cystoptosia	SIS/TOP/TOEZ/YA
	S*IS/TOEZ/YA
cystoptosis	SIS/TOP/TOE/SIS
	S*IS/TOE/SIS
cystopyelitis	S*IS/PAOI/LAOITS
cystopyelography	S*IS/PAOI/LOG/FI
cystopyelonephritis	S*IS/PAOI/LO/NEF/RAOITS
cystoradiography	S*IS/RAID/YOG/FI
cystorectostomy	S*IS/REK/TO*S/M*I
cystorrhagia	S*IS/RAI/JA
cystorrhaphy	SIS/TOR/FI
cystorrhea	S*IS/RAOE/YA
cystosarcoma	S*IS/SAR/KOE/MA
cystoschisis	SIS/TOS/KI/SIS
cystosclerosis	S*IS/SKLE/ROE/SIS
cystoscope	S*IS/SKOEP
cystoscopic	S*IS/SKOP/IK
cystoscopy	SIS/TOS/KPI
cystose	SIS/TOES
-cystosis	SIS/TOE/SIS
cystospasm	S*IS/SPAFM
Cystospaz	S*IS/SPAZ
Cystospaz-M	S*IS/SPAZ/M-RBGS
cystospermitis	S*IS/SPER/MAOITS
cystostomy	SIS/TO*S/M*I
cystotome	S*IS/TOEM
cystotomy	SIS/TOT/M*I
cystotrachelotomy	S*IS/TRAIK/LOT/M*I
cystoureteritis	S*IS/YAOU/RAOET/RAOITS

cystoureterogram	S*IS/YAOU/RAOET/RO/GRAM	cytokalipenia	SAOIT/KAL/PAOEN/YA
cystoureterography	S*IS/YAOU/RAOET/ROG/FI	cytokerastic	SAOIT/KE/RA*S/IK
cystoureteropyelitis	S*IS/YAOU/RAOET/RO/PAOI/ LAOITS	cytokine	SAOIT/KAOIN
		cytokinesis	SAOIT/KI/NAOE/SIS
cystoureteropyelonephritis	S*IS/YAOU/RAOET/RO/PAOI/LO/ NE/FRAOITS	cytokinin	SAOIT/KAOI/NIN
			SAOIT/KIN/NIN
cystourethritis	S*IS/YAOUR/THRAOITS	cytolemma	SAOIT/LEM/MA
	S*IS/YAOU/RAO*ET/RAOITS	cytolipin	SAOIT/LIP/PIN
cystourethrocele	S*IS/YAOU/RAO*ET/RO/SAO*EL	cytologic	SAOIT/LOJ/IK
cystourethrogram	S*IS/YAOU/RAO*ET/RO/GRAM	cytological	SAOIT/LOJ/KAL
cystourethrography	S*IS/YAOUR/THROG/FI	cytologist	SAOI/TO*LGS
	S*IS/YAOU/RAO*ET/ROG/FI	cytology	SAOI/TOLG
cystourethroscope	S*IS/YAOU/RAO*ET/RO/SKOEP	cytolymph	SAOIT/LIM/-F
cystous	SIS/TOUS	cytolysate	SAOI/TOL/SAIT
	S*IS/OUS	cytolysin	SAOI/TOL/SIN
cystyl-aminopeptidase	SIS/TIL/AM/NO/PEPT/DAIS	cytolysis	SAOI/TOL/SIS
cyt(o)-	SAOIT	cytolysosome	SAOIT/LAOIS/SOEM
	SAOI/T(O)	cytolytic	SAOIT/LIT/IK
Cytadren	SAOIT/DREN	cytoma	SAOI/TOE/MA
cytapheresis	SAOIT/FRAOE/SIS	cytomachia	SAOIT/MAK/YA
cytarabine	SAOI/TAR/BAOEN	cytomatosis	SAOI/TOEM/TOE/SIS
	SAOI/TAIR/BAOEN		SAOIT/MA/TOE/SIS
cytarme	SIT/AR/MAOE	cytomatrix	SAOIT/MAI/TRIX
	SAOI/TAR/MAOE	cytomegalic	SAOIT/MEG/LIK
cytase	SAOI/TAIS		SAOIT/ME/GAL/IK
-cyte	SAO*IT	cytomegaliviruria	SAOIT/MEG/LO/VAOI/RAOUR/YA
-cythemia	SAOI/THAOEM/YA	cytomegalovirus	SAOIT/MEG/LO/VAOI/RUS
-cytic	SIT/IK	Cytomel	SAOIT/MEL
cytidine	SAOIT/DAOEN	cytomembrane	SAOIT/MEM/BRAIN
	SAOIT/DIN	cytomere	SAOIT/MAOER
cytidylic	SAOIT/DIL/IK	cytometaplasia	SAOIT/MET/PLAIZ/YA
	SIT/DIL/IK	cytometer	SAOI/TOM/TER
cytoanalyzer	SAOIT/AN/LAOIZ/ER	cytometry	SAOI/TOM/TRI
	SAOIT/ANL/AOIZ/ER	cytomicrosome	SAOIT/MAOI/KRO/SOEM
cytoarchitectonic	SAOIT/ARK/TEK/TON/IK	cytomitome	SAOIT/MAOI/TOEM
cytoarchitectural	SAOIT/ARK/TEK/KHURL	cytomorphology	SAOIT/MOR/FOLG
cytoarchitecture	SAOIT/ARK/TEK/KHUR	cytomorphosis	SAOIT/MOR/FOE/SIS
cytobiology	SAOIT/BAO*I/OLG	cyton	SAOI/TON
cytobiotaxis	SAOIT/BAO*I/TAK/SIS	cytonecrosis	SAOIT/NE/KROE/SIS
-cytoblastoma	SAOIT/BLAS/TOE/MA	-cytopathia	SAOIT/PA*T/YA
cytocentrum	SAOIT/SEN/TRUM	cytopathic	SAOIT/PA*T/IK
cytochalasin	SAOIT/KAL/SIN	cytopathogenesis	SAOIT/PA*T/JEN/SIS
cytochemism	SAOIT/KEM/IFM	cytopathogenetic	SAOIT/PA*T/JE/NET/IK
cytochemistry	SAOIT/KEM/STRI	cytopathogenic	SAOIT/PA*T/JEN/IK
cytochrome	SAOIT/KROEM	cytopathogenicity	SAOIT/PA*T/JE/NIS/TI
cytochylema	SAOIT/KAOI/LAOE/MA	cytopathologic	SAOIT/PA*T/LOJ/IK
cytocidal	SAOIT/SAOI/DAL	cytopathological	SAOIT/PA*T/LOJ/KAL
cytocide	SAOIT/SAO*ID	cytopathologically	SAOIT/PA*T/LOJ/KLI
citocinesis	SAOIT/SI/NAOE/SIS	cytopathologist	SAOIT/PA/THO*LGS
cytoclasis	SAOI/TOK/LA/SIS	cytopathology	SAOIT/PA/THOLG
cytoclastic	SAOIT/KLA*S/IK	cytopathy	SAOI/TOP/TH*I
cytoclesis	SAOIT/KLAOE/SIS	cytopempsis	SAOIT/PEFRP/SIS
cytocletic	SAOIT/KLET/IK		SAOIT/PEM/SIS
cytocrit	SAOIT/KRIT	cytopenia	SAOIT/PAOEN/YA
cytoctony	SAOI/TOKT/N*I	cytophagous	SAOI/TOF/GOUS
cytocuprein	SAOIT/KAOUP/RIN	cytophagy	SAOI/TOF/JI
cytocyst	SAOIT/S*IS	cytophanere	SAOIT/FA/NAOER
cytode	SAOI/TOED	cytopharynx	SAOIT/FARNGS
cytodendrite	SAOIT/DEN/DRAOIT	cytopherometric	SAOIT/FER/MET/RIK
cytodesma	SAOIT/DEZ/MA	cytophil	SAOIT/FIL
cytodiagnosis	SAOIT/DAOIG/NOE/SIS	cytophilic	SAOIT/FIL/IK
cytodiagnostic	SAOIT/DAOIG/NO*S/IK	cytophotometer	SAOIT/FOE/TOM/TER
cytodieresis	SAOIT/DI/ER/SIS	cytophotometric	SAOIT/FOET/MET/RIK
cytodifferentiation	SAOIT/DIFRN/SHAIGS	cytophotometry	SAOIT/FOE/TOM/TRI
cytodistal	SAOIT/DIS/TAL	cytophylactic	SAOIT/FLAKT/IK
cytoflav	SAOIT/FLAV	cytophylaxis	SAOIT/FLAK/SIS
cytoflavin	SAOIT/FLAIVN	cytophyletic	SAOIT/FLET/IK
cytogene	SAOIT/JAOEN		SAOIT/FAOI/LET/IK
cytogenesis	SAOIT/JEN/SIS	cytophysics	SAOIT/FIZ/IK/-S
cytogenetic	SAOIT/JE/NET/IK	cytophysiology	SAOIT/FIZ/YOLG
cytogenetical	SAOIT/JE/NET/KAL	cytopigment	SAOIT/PIG/-MT
cytogeneticist	SAOIT/JE/NET/S*IS	cytopipette	SAOIT/PAOI/PET
cytogenetics	SAOIT/JE/NET/IK/-S	cytoplasm	SAOIT/PLAFM
cytogenic	SAOIT/JEN/IK	cytoplasmic	SAOIT/PLAZ/MIK
cytogenous	SAOI/TOJ/NOUS	cytoplast	SAOIT/PLA*S
cytogeny	SAOI/TOJ/N*I	cytopoiesis	SAOIT/POI/SIS
cytoglomerator	SAOIT/GLOM/RAI/TOR	cytopoietic	SAOIT/POIT/IK
cytoglucopenia	SAOIT/GLAOUK/PAOEN/YA	cytopreparation	SAOI/TO/PREP/RAIGS
cytoglycopenia	SAOIT/GLAOIK/PAOEN/YA		(*not* SAOIT/PREP/RAIGS; see site
cytogony	SAOI/TOG/N*I		preparation)
cytohet	SAOIT/HET	cytoproximal	SAOIT/PROX/MAL
cytohistogenesis	SAOIT/H*IS/JEN/SIS	cytopyge	SAOIT/PAOI/JAOE
cytohistologic	SAOIT/H*IS/LOJ/IK	cytoreticulum	SAOIT/RE/TIK/LUM
cytohistology	SAOIT/HIS/TOLG	cytorrhyctes	SAOIT/RIK/TAOEZ
cytohormone	SAOIT/HOR/MOEN	Cytosar	SAOIT/SAR
cytohyaloplasm	SAOIT/HAOI/LO/PLAFM	Cytosar-U	SAOIT/SAR/URBGS
cytohydrolist	SAOIT/HAOI/DRO/L*IS	cytoscopy	SAOI/TOS/KPI
cytoid	SAOI/TOID	cytoside	SAOIT/SAOID
cyto-inhibition	SAOIT/IN/BIGS	cytosiderin	SAOIT/SID/RIN

cytosine	SAOIT/SAOEN
cytosine arabinoside	SAOIT/SAOEN/AI/RAB/NO/SAOID
cytosis	SAOI/TOE/SIS
cytoskeletal	SAOIT/SKEL/TAL
cytoskeleton	SAOIT/SKEL/TON
cytosmear	SAOIT/SMAOER
cytosol	SAOIT/SOL
cytosolic	SAOIT/SOL/IK
cytosome	SAOIT/SOEM
cytospongium	SAOIT/SPON/JUM
cytost	SAOI/TO*S
cytostasis	SAOI/TO*S/SIS
cytostatic	SAOIT/STAT/IK
cytostome	SAOIT/STOEM
cytostromatic	SAOIT/STROE/MAT/IK
cytotactic	SAOIT/TAKT/IK
cytotaxia	SAOIT/TAX/YA
cytotaxigen	SAOIT/TAX/JEN
cytotaxin	SAOIT/TAK/SIN
cytotaxis	SAOIT/TAK/SIS
Cytotec	SAOIT/TEK
cytotherapy	SAOIT/THER/PI
cytothesis	SAOI/TO*T/SIS
cytotoxic	SAOIT/TOX/IK
cytotoxicity	SAOIT/TOK/SIS/TI
cytotoxicosis	SAOIT/TOX/KOE/SIS
cytotoxin	SAOIT/TOK/SIN
cytotrochin	SAOIT/TROE/KIN
cytotrophoblast	SAOIT/TROF/BLA*S
cytotropic	SAOIT/TROP/IK
cytotropism	SAOI/TOT/RO/PIFM
Cytovene	SAOIT/VAOEN
Cytoxan	SAOI/TOK/SAN
cytozoic	SAOIT/ZOIK
	SAOIT/ZOE/IK
cyttarrhagia	SIT/RAI/JA
cytul-	SIT/L-
	SIT/YAOU/L-
	SIT/YU/L-
cytula	SIT/LA
cytuloplasm	SIT/LO/PLAFM
cyturia	SAOI/TAOUR/YA
	SI/TAOUR/YA
Czapek	KHAI/PEK
Czermak	KHER/MAK
	KHAIR/MAK
Czerny	KHER/N*I
	KHAIR/N*I

D

dacarbazine	DA/KARB/ZAOEN
DaCosta	DA/KOS/TA
dacry-	DAK/RI
	DAK/RAOE
dacryadenalgia	DAK/RI/AD/NAL/JA
	DAK/RAD/NAL/JA
dacryadenitis	DAK/RI/AD/NAOITS
	DAK/RAD/NAOITS
dacryagogatresia	DAK/RI/GOG/TRAOEZ/YA
	DAK/RA/GOG/TRAOEZ/YA
dacryagogic	DAK/RI/GOJ/IK
	DAK/RA/GOJ/IK
dacryagogue	DAK/RI/GOG
	DAK/RA/GOG
dacrycystalgia	DAK/RI/SIS/TAL/JA
dacrycystitis	DAK/RI/SIS/TAOITS
dacryelcosis	DAK/RI/EL/KOE/SIS
	DAK/REL/KOE/SIS
dacryo-	DAK/RO
	DAK/RI/YO
	DAK/RAOE/YO
dacryoadenalgia	DAK/RO/AD/NAL/JA
dacryoadenectomy	DAK/RO/AD/NEKT/M*I
dacryoadenitis	DAK/RO/AD/NAOITS
dacryoblennorrhea	DAK/RO/BLEN/RAOE/YA
dacryocanaliculitis	DAK/RO/KAN/LIK/LAOITS
dacryocele	DAK/RO/SAO*EL
dacryocyst	DAK/RO/S*IS
dacryocystalgia	DAK/RO/SIS/TAL/JA
dacryocystectasia	DAK/RO/SIS/TEK/TAIZ/YA
dacryocystectomy	DAK/RO/SIS/TEKT/M*I
dacryocystis	DAK/RO/SIS/TIS
dacryocystitis	DAK/RO/SIS/TAOITS
dacryocystoblennorrhea	DAK/RO/S*IS/BLEN/RAOE/YA
dacryocystocele	DAK/RO/S*IS/SAO*EL
dacryocystoethmoidostomy	DAK/RO/S*IS/*ET/MOI/DO*S/M*I
dacryocystogram	DAK/RO/S*IS/GRAM
dacryocystoptosia	DAK/RO/SIS/TOP/TOEZ/YA
dacryocystoptosis	DAK/RO/SIS/TOP/TOE/SIS
dacryocystorhinostenosis	DAK/RO/S*IS/RAOIN/STE/NOE/SIS
dacryocystorhinostomy	DAK/RO/S*IS/RAOI/NO*S/M*I
dacryocystorhinotomy	DAK/RO/S*IS/RAOI/NOT/M*I
dacryocystostenosis	DAK/RO/S*IS/STE/NOE/SIS
dacryocystostomy	DAK/RO/SIS/TO*S/M*I
dacryocystosyringotomy	DAK/RO/S*IS/SIRN/GOT/M*I
dacryocystotome	DAK/RO/S*IS/TOEM
dacryocystotomy	DAK/RO/SIS/TOT/M*I
dacryogenic	DAK/RO/JEN/IK
dacryohelcosis	DAK/RO/HEL/KOE/SIS
dacryohemorrhea	DAK/RO/HEM/RAOE/YA
dacryolith	DAK/RO/L*IT
dacryolithiasis	DAK/RO/LI/THAOI/SIS
dacryoma	DAK/ROE/MA
dacryon	DAK/RON
dacryops	DAK/ROPS
dacryopyorrhea	DAK/RO/PAOI/RAOE/YA
dacryopyosis	DAK/RO/PAOI/YOE/SIS
dacryorhinocystotomy	DAK/RO/RAOIN/SIS/TOT/M*I
dacryorrhea	DAK/RO/RAOE/YA
dacryoscintigraphy	DAK/RO/SIN/TIG/FI
dacryosinusitis	DAK/RO/SAOIN/SAOITS
dacryosolenitis	DAK/RO/SOEL/NAOITS
dacryostenosis	DAK/RO/STE/NOE/SIS
dacryosyrinx	DAK/RO/SIRNGS
	DAK/RO/SIR/INGS
dactinomycin	DAKT/NO/MAOI/SIN
	DAK/TIN/MAOI/SIN
dactyl	DAK/TIL
dactyl(o)-	DAKT/L(O)
	DAK/TIL
dactylalgia	DAKT/LAL/JA
dactylate	DAKT/LAIT
dactyledema	DAK/TIL/DAOE/MA
	DAK/TIL/E/DAOE/MA
dactyli	DAKT/LAOI
dactylia	DAK/TIL/YA
-dactylism	DAKT/LIFM
dactylitis	DAKT/LAOITS
dactylium	DAK/TIL/YUM
dactylocampsis	DAKT/LO/KAFRP/SIS
dactylocampsodynia	DAKT/LO/KAFRPS/DIN/YA
	DAKT/LO/KAFRP/SO/DIN/YA
dactylodynia	DAKT/LO/DIN/YA

dactylogram	DAK/TIL/GRAM
dactylography	DAKT/LOG/FI
dactylogryposis	DAKT/LO/GRI/POE/SIS
dactylology	DAKT/LOLG
dactylolysis	DAKT/LOL/SIS
dactylomegaly	DAKT/LO/MEG/LI
dactylophasia	DAKT/LO/FAIZ/YA
dactyloscopy	DAKT/LOS/KPI
dactylospasm	DAKT/LO/SPAFM
-dactylous	DAKT/LOUS
dactylus	DAKT/LUS
-dactyly	DAKT/LI
dacuronium	DAK/ROEN/YUM
dahlin	DAU/LIN
dahllite	DAU/LAOIT
	DAUL/LAOIT
Daily Gold Pack	DAI/LI/GOELD/PAK
	DAI/LI/GOLD/PAK
Dakin	DAI/KIN
Dalalone	DAL/LOEN
Dale	K-P/DAIL
daledalin	DA/LED/LIN
Dallergy	DAL/ER/JI
Dallergy-Jr.	DAL/ER/JI/JR
Dalmane	DAL/MAIN
Dalrymple	DAL/RIFRP/-L
	DAL/RIM/P-L
dalton	DAL/TON
	DAUL/TON
Dalton	K-P/DAL/TON
	K-P/DAUL/TON
daltonian	DAL/TOEN/YAN
	DAUL/TOEN/YAN
daltonism	DAL/TON/IFM
	DAUL/TON/IFM
	DAULT/NIFM
	DALT/NIFM
dam	DAM
Dam	K-P/DAM
Damalinia	DAM/LIN/YA
Damason	DAI/MA/SON
Damason-P	DAI/MA/SON/P-RBGS
dammar	DAM/MAR
damp	DAFRP
damping	DAFRP/-G
Dana	DAI/NA
danazol	DAN/ZOEL
	DAN/ZOL
	DAIN/ZOL
dance	DANS
dancing	DANS/-G
D & C	D-RBGS/M-ND/KR-RBGS
D and C	D-RGBS/AND/KR-RBGS
D & E	D-RBGS/M-ND/ERBGS
D and E	D-RGBS/AND/ERBGS
dander	DAND/ER
dandruff	DAN/DRUF
dandy	DAN/DI
Dandy	K-P/DAN/DI
Dane	DAIN
Danex	DAN/EX
	DAI/NEX
Danforth	DAN/FO*RT
Danlos	DAN/LOS
Danocrine	DAN/KRIN
dansyl	DAN/SIL
danthron	DAN/THRON
Dantrium	DAN/TRUM
	DAN/TRAOE/UM
dantrolene	DAN/TRO/LAOEN
Danysz	DA/NAOEZ
	DAN/NAOEZ
daphnetin	DAF/NAOE/TIN
Daphnia	DAF/NA
	DAF/NAOE/YA
daphnin	DAF/NIN
dappen	DAP/-N
dapsone	DAP/SOEN
Dar es Salaam	DAR/ES/SA/LAM
	DAR/ES/SA/LAUM
Daranide	DAR/NAOID
Daraprim	DAR/PRIM
Darbid	DAR/BID
Darier	DAR/YAI
Darkshevich	DARK/SHAI/VIFP
	DARK/SHAIV/IFP
	DARK/SHEV/IRP
Darling	K-P/DARL/-G
darlingi	DAR/LIN/GAOI

	DARL/IN/GAOI	Deaver	DAOEVR
d'Arsonval	DAR/SON/VAL	debanding	DE/BAND/-G
dartoic	DAR/TOIK	debilitant	DE/BIL/TANT
	DAR/TOE/IK	debilitating	DE/BIL/TAIT/-G
dartoid	DAR/TOID	debility	DEBLT
dartos	DAR/TOES	debouch	DE/BAOURB
	DAR/TOS	debouchement	DAI/BAOURB/-MT
dartrous	DAR/TROUS		DAI/BAOURB/MAU
Darvocet	DAFRB/SET	debrancher	DE/BRAN/KHER
Darvocet-N	DAFRB/SET/N-RBGS		DE/BRAFRPBLG/ER
Darvon	DAR/VON	debranching	DE/BRAFRPBLG/-G
Darvon-N	DAR/VON/N-RBGS		DE/BRAN/-FPG
Darwin	DAR/WIN	debride	DE/BRAOED
darwinian	DAR/WIN/YAN		DAI/BRAOED
data	DAI/TA	debridement	DE/BRAOED/-MT
	DAT/TA		DAI/BRAOED/-MT
Datril	DAI/TRIL	debris	DE/BRAOE
datur-	DA/TAOUR/R-		DAI/BRAOE
	DA/TAOU/R-	Debrisan	DEB/RI/SAN
	DAI/TAOUR/R-	debrisoquin	DE/BRIS/KWIN
	DAI/TAOU/R-		DEB/RIS/KWIN
Datura	DA/TAOUR/RA	Debrox	DE/BROX
	DAI/TAOUR/RA	debt	DET
daturine	DA/TAOUR/RIN	deca-	DEK
	DAI/TAOUR/RIN	decacurie	DEK/KAOUR/RAOE
	DA/TAOUR/RAOEN	Decaderm	DEK/DERM
	DAI/TAOUR/RAOEN	Decadron	DEK/DRON
daturism	DA/TAOUR/IFM	Deca-Durabolin	DEK/DAOU/RAB/LIN
	DAI/TAOUR/IFM	decagram	DEK/GRAM
Daubenton	DOE/BEN/TON	decalcification	DE/KALS/FI/KAIGS
	DAU/BEN/TON	decalcify	DE/KALS/FI
daughter	DAUT/ER	decaliter	DEK/LAOET/ER
daunomycin	DAUN/MAOI/SIN	decalvant	DE/KAL/VANT
	DAU/NO/MAOI/SIN	decameter	DEK/MAOET/ER
daunorubicin	DAUN/RAOUB/SIN	decamethonium	DEK/ME/THOEN/YUM
	DAU/NO/RAOUB/SIN	decamine	DEK/MAOEN
Davidoff	DAIV/DOF	decane	DEK/AIN
	DAIV/DAUF	decanem	DEK/NEM
Davis	DAI/VIS	decannulation	DE/KAN/LAIGS
Dawson	DAU/SON	decanoic	DEK/NOIK
Day	K-P/DAI		DEK/NOE/IK
Dayalets	DAI/LET/-S	decanoin	DEK/NOE/WIN
	DAI/LETS	decanormal	DEK/NOR/MAL
Dayalets Filmtab	DAI/LET/-S/FIL/-M/TAB	decant	DE/KANT
	DAI/LETS/FIL/-M/TAB	decantation	DE/KAN/TAIGS
Dayalets Plus Iron	DAI/LET/-S/PLUS/AOIRN	decapacitation	DE/KPAS/TAIGS
	DAI/LETS/PLUS/AOIRN		DE/KA/PAS/TAIGS
dazadrol	DAIZ/DROEL	decapeptide	DEK/PEP/TAOID
	DAIZ/DROL	decapitate	DE/KAP/TAIT
	DAZ/DROEL	decapitation	DE/KAP/TAIGS
	DAZ/DROL	decapitator	DE/KAP/TAI/TOR
dazzling	DAZ/-LG	decapsulation	DE/KAPS/LAIGS
D.D.S.	D*DZ	decarbonization	DE/KAR/BON/ZAIGS
de-	DE		DE/KARB/NI/ZAIGS
deacidification	DE/AI/SID/FI/KAIGS	decarboxylase	DE/KAR/BOX/LAIS
deactivation	DE/AKT/VAIGS	decarboxylation	DE/KAR/BOX/LAIGS
deacylase	DE/AS/LAIS	Decaspray	DEK/SPRAI
dead	DED	decavitamin	DEK/VAOIT/MIN
deaf	DEF	decay	DE/KAI
deafferentate	DE/AFRN/TAIT	deceased	DE/SAOES/-D
deafferentation	DE/AFRN/TAIGS	deceit	DE/SAOET
deaf-mute	DEF/H-F/MAOUT	deceleration	DE/SEL/RAIGS
deafmutism	DEF/MAO/TIFM	decent	DE/SENT
	DEF/MAOUT/IFM	decentered	DE/SEN/TER/-D
deafness	DEF/*NS	decentration	DE/SEN/TRAIGS
dealbation	DE/AL/BAIGS	deceration	DE/SAOER/RAIGS
dealcoholization	DE/KHOL/ZAIGS		DE/SE/RAIGS
	DE/AL/KHOL/ZAIGS	decerebellation	DE/SER/BEL/LAIGS
deallergization	DE/AL/ERJ/ZAIGS	decerebrate	DE/SER/BRAIT
	DE/AL/ER/JI/ZAIGS	decerebration	DE/SER/BRAIGS
deallergize	DE/AL/ER/JAOIZ	decerebrize	DE/SER/BRAOIZ
deamidase	DE/AM/DAIS	dechloridation	DE/KLOR/DAIGS
deamidation	DE/AM/DAIGS	dechlorination	DE/KLOR/NAIGS
deamidization	DE/AM/DI/ZAIGS	dechlorurant	DE/KLOR/YAOU/RANT
	DE/AM/DAOI/ZAIGS	dechloruration	DE/KLOR/YAOU/RAIGS
deamidize	DE/AM/DAOIZ	decholesterinization	DE/KL*ES/RIN/ZAIGS
deaminase	DE/AM/NAIS	decholestrolization	DE/KL*ES/ROL/ZAIGS
deamination	DE/AM/NAIGS	Decholin	DE/KOE/LIN
deaminization	DE/AM/NI/ZAIGS		DEK/LIN
	DE/AM/NAOI/ZAIGS	deci-	DES
deaminize	DE/AM/NAOIZ	decibel	DES/BEL
Dean	K-P/DAOEN	decidu-	DE/SID/Y-
deanol	DAOE/NOL		DE/SID/W-
deaquation	DE/AI/KWAIGS	decidua	DE/SID/YA
	DE/KWAIGS	decidual	DE/SID/YAL
dearterialization	DE/AR/TAOERL/ZAIGS	deciduate	DE/SID/YAIT
dearticulation	DE/AR/TIK/LAIGS	deciduation	DE/SID/YAIGS
death	D*ET	decidui	DE/SID/YAOI
death-rattle	D*ET/RAT/-L	deciduitis	DE/SID/YAOITS

deciduoma	DE/SID/YOE/MA	deference	DEFRNS
deciduomatosis	DE/SID/YOEM/TOE/SIS		DEF/RENS
	DE/SID/YOE/MA/TOE/SIS	deferens	DEFRNZ
deciduosis	DE/SID/YOE/SIS		DEF/RENZ
deciduous	DE/SID/YOUS	deferent	DEFRNT
decigram	DES/GRAM		DEF/RENT
deciliter	DES/LAOET/ER	deferentectomy	DEFRN/TEKT/M*I
decima	DES/MA		DEF/REN/TEKT/M*I
decimeter	DES/MAOET/ER	deferential	DEFRN/-RBL
decimorgan	DES/MOR/GAN		DEF/REN/-RBL
decinormal	DES/NOR/MAL	deferentialis	DEFRN/SHAI/LIS
decipara	DES/PAR/RA		DEF/REN/SHAI/LIS
	DES/PA/RA	deferentis	DEFRN/TIS
decision	DE/SIGS		DEF/REN/TIS
deck	DEK	deferentitis	DEFRN/TAOITS
declination	DEK/LI/NAIGS		DEF/REN/TAOITS
declinator	DEK/LI/NAI/TOR	deferoxamine	DEF/ROX/MAOEN
decline	DE/KLAOIN		DE/FER/OX/MAOEN
declive	DE/KLAOIV	defervescence	DEFR/VES/ENS
declivis	DE/KLAOI/VIS		DEF/ER/VES/ENS
Declomycin	DEK/LO/MAOI/SIN	defervescent	DEFR/VES/ENT
decoagulant	DE/KO/AG/LANT		DEF/ER/VES/ENT
decoction	DE/KO*BGS	defibrillation	DE/FIB/RI/LAIGS
decollation	DE/KLAIGS		DE/FIB/RIL/LAIGS
	DE/KOL/LAIGS	defibrillator	DE/FIB/RI/LAI/TOR
decoloration	DE/KOL/RAIGS		DE/FIB/RIL/LAI/TOR
decoloratus	DE/KOL/RAI/TUS	defibrinate	DE/FAOI/BRI/NAIT
decolorize	DE/KOL/RAOIZ		DE/FAOI/BRIN/AIT
decompensation	DE/KOFRP/SAIGS	defibrinated	DE/FAOI/BRI/NAIT/-D
decomplementize	DE/KOM/PLEMT/AOIZ		DE/FAOI/BRIN/AIT/-D
	DE/KOM/PLEMT/TAOIZ	defibrination	DE/FAOI/BRI/NAIGS
decompose	DE/KPOEZ		DE/FAOI/BRIN/AIGS
	DE/KOM/POEZ	deficiency	DE/FIRBT/SI
decomposition	DE/KOFRP/SIGS		DE/FIRB/SI
decompression	DE/KPREGS		DE/FIRB/EN/SI
	DE/KOM/PREGS	deficiens	DE/FIRB/ENZ
Deconamine	DE/KON/MAOEN		DE/FIS/YENZ
deconditioning	DE/KON/DIGS/-G	deficit	DEF/SIT
	DE/K-N/-G	definition	DEF/NIGS
decongestant	DE/KON/JES/TANT	definitive	DE/FIN/TIV
decongestive	DE/KON/J*ES/IV	deflection	DE/FL*EBGS
Deconsal	DE/KON/SAL	deflective	DE/FLEKT/IV
decontamination	DE/KON/TAM/NAIGS	defloration	DE/FLOR/AIGS
decortication	DE/KORT/KAIGS		DE/FLOR/RAIGS
decortization	DE/KORT/ZAIGS		DEF/LO/RAIGS
decrement	DEK/REMT	deflorescence	DE/FLOR/ES/ENS
decremental	DEK/REMT/TAL		DE/FLOE/RES/ENS
decrepitate	DE/KREP/TAIT		DEF/LO/RES/ENS
decrepitation	DE/KREP/TAIGS	defluoridation	DE/FLAOUR/DAIGS
decrudescence	DE/KRAOU/DES/ENS		DE/FLOR/DAIGS
decrustation	DE/KRUS/TAIGS	defluvium	DE/FLAOUV/YUM
decubation	DE/KAOU/BAIGS	defluxio	DE/FLUX/YOE
decubital	DE/KAOUB/TAL		DE/FLUK/SHOE
decubitus	DE/KAOUB/TUS	defluxion	DE/FL*UBGS
decumbin	DE/KUM/BIN	deformability	DE/FORM/-BLT
decurrent	DE/KURNT	deformans	DE/FOR/MANZ
decussate	DE/KUS/SAIT	deformation	DE/FOR/MAIGS
decussatio	DE/KUS/SAI/SHOE	deforming	DE/FORM/-G
	DE/KUS/SAIRB/YOE	deformity	DE/FORM/TI
decussation	DE/KUS/SAIGS	defundation	DE/FUN/DAIGS
decussationes	DE/KUS/SAI/SHOE/NAOEZ	defundectomy	DE/FUN/DEKT/M*I
	DE/KUS/SAIRB/YOE/NAOEZ	defurfuration	DE/FUR/FRAIGS
decussorium	DE/KUS/SOER/YUM	deg150anglionate	DE/GANG/LO/NAIT
	DE/KUS/SOR/YUM		DE/GANG/LON/AIT
dedentition	DE/DEN/TIGS	degassing	DE/GAS/-G
dedifferentiation	DE/DIFRN/SHAIGS		DE/GASZ/-G
dedolation	DED/LAIGS	degeneracy	DE/JEN/RA/SI
	DAOED/LAIGS	degenerate	DE/JEN/RAIT
	DE/DOE/LAIGS		DE/JEN/RAT
de-efferentation	DE/EFRN/TAIGS	degeneratio	DE/JEN/RAI/SHOE
deem	DAOEM		DE/JEN/RAIRB/YOE
deemanate	DE/EM/NAIT	degeneration	DE/JEN/RAIGS
deep	DAOEP	degenerative	DE/JEN/RA/TIV
de-epicardialization	DE/EP/KARD/YAL/ZAIGS	degenitalize	DE/JEN/TAL/AOIZ
Deetjen	DAIT/YEN	degerm	DE/JERM
	DAOET/YEN	deglobulinization	DE/GLOB/LIN/ZAIGS
	DAOET/JEN	degloving	DE/GLOV/-G
defatigation	DE/FAT/GAIGS	deglutible	DE/GLAOUT/-BL
defatted	DE/FAT/-D	deglutition	DE/GLAOU/TIGS
defecate	DEF/KAIT	deglutitive	DE/GLAOUT/TIV
defecation	DEF/KAIGS	deglutitory	DE/GLAOUT/TOIR
defect	DE/FEKT	degradation	DEG/DAIGS
	DEFKT		DEG/RA/DAIGS
defective	DE/FEKT/IV	degranulation	DE/GRAN/LAIGS
	DEFKT/IV	degree	DE/GRAOE
defemination	DE/FEM/NAIGS	degrowth	DE/GRO*ET
defeminization	DE/FEM/NI/ZAIGS	degustation	DE/GUS/TAIGS
defense	DE/FENS	dehalogenase	DE/HAL/JEN/AIS
	DEFNS	dehematize	DE/HEM/TAOIZ

	DE/HAOEM/TAOIZ	delinquency	DLIN/KWEN/SI
dehemoglobinize	DE/HAOEM/GLOEB/NAOIZ		DE/LIN/KWEN/SI
	DE/HEM/GLOEB/NAOIZ	delinquent	DLIN/KWENT
dehepatized	DE/HEP/TAOIZ/-D		DE/LIN/KWENT
dehiscence	DE/HIS/ENS	deliquesce	DEL/KWES
dehumanization	DE/HAOU/MAN/ZAIGS	deliquescense	DEL/KWES/ENS
	DE/HAOUM/NI/ZAIGS	deliquescent	DEL/KWES/ENT
dehumidifier	DE/HAOU/MID/FI/ER	deliri-	DLIR/Y-
dehydrant	DE/HAOI/DRANT		DLAOER/Y-
dehydrase	DE/HAOI/DRAIS		DE/LIR/Y-
dehydratase	DE/HAOI/DRA/TAIS		DE/LAOER/Y-
dehydrate	DE/HAOI/DRAIT	deliria	DLIR/YA
dehydrated	DE/HAOI/DRAIT/-D	deliriant	DLIR/YANT
dehydration	DE/HAOI/DRAIGS	delirifacient	DLIR/FAIRBT
dehydroacetic	DE/HAOI/DRO/AI/SAOET/IK	delirious	DLIR/YOUS
dehydroascorbic	DE/HAOI/DRO/AS/KORB/IK	delirium	DLIR/YUM
dehydrobilirubin	DE/HAOI/DRO/BIL/RAOU/BIN	delitescence	DEL/TES/ENS
dehydrocholaneresis	DE/HAOI/DRO/KOEL/NER/SIS	deliver	DLIVR
dehydrocholate	DE/HAOI/DRO/KOE/LAIT		DE/LIVR
dehydrocholesterol	DE/HAOI/DRO/KL*ES/ROL	delivery	DLIV/RI
dehydrocholic	DE/HAOI/DRO/KOEL/IK		DE/LIV/RI
	DE/HAOI/DRO/KOL/IK	dell	DEL
dehydrocorticosterone	DE/HAOI/DRO/KORT/KO*S/ROEN	delle	DEL/LE
dehydrocorydaline	DE/HAOI/DRO/KO/RID/LAOEN		(not DEL/LA; see Bdella)
	DE/HAOI/DRO/KO/RID/LIN	dellen	DEL/-N
dehydroemetine	DE/HAOI/DRO/EM/TAOEN		DEL/LEN
dehydroepiandrosterone	DE/HAOI/DRO/EP/AN/DRO*S/ROEN	delling	DEL/-G
dehydrogenase	DE/HAOI/DRO/JEN/AIS	delmadinone	DEL/MAD/NOEN
	DE/HAOI/DROJ/NAIS	delomorphic	DEL/MOR/FIK
dehydrogenate	DE/HAOI/DRO/JEN/AIT	delomorphous	DEL/MOR/FOUS
	DE/HAOI/DROJ/NAIT	delouse	DE/LOUS
dehydrogenation	DE/HAOI/DRO/JEN/AIGS	delousing	DE/LOUS/-G
	DE/HAOI/DROJ/NAIGS	Delpech	DEL/PEK
dehydroisoandrosterone	DE/HAOI/DRO/AOIS/AN/DRO*S/ROEN	del Peru	DEL/PE/RAOU
		delphinine	DEL/FI/NAOEN
dehydromorphine	DE/HAOI/DRO/MOR/FAOEN		DEL/FIN/AOEN
	DE/HAOI/DRO/MOR/FIN	delphisine	DEL/FI/SAOEN
dehydropeptidase	DE/HAOI/DRO/PEPT/DAIS		DEL/FI/SIN
dehydroretinal	DE/HAOI/DRO/RET/NAL	Delsym	DEL/SIM
dehydroretinaldehyde	DE/HAOI/DRO/RET/NALD/HAOID	delta	DEL/TA
dehydroretinoic	DE/HAOI/DRO/RET/NOIK	delta-	DELT
	DE/HAOI/DRO/RET/NOE/IK		DEL/TA
dehydroretinol	DE/HAOI/DRO/RET/NOL	deltacortisone	DELT/KORT/SOEN
dehydrosugar	DE/HAOI/DRO/SHUG/AR	Deltasone	DELT/SOEN
dehydrotestosterone	DE/HAOI/DRO/TES/TO*S/ROEN	deltoid	DEL/TOID
dehypnotize	DE/HIP/NO/TAOIZ	deltoideum	DEL/TOID/YUM
deiminase	DE/IM/NAIS	deltoideus	DEL/TOID/YUS
deinstitutionalization	DE/INS/TAOUGS/NAL/ZAIGS	de lunatico inquirendo	DE/LAOU/NAT/KOE/IN/KWI/REN/DOE
deiodination	DE/AOI/DIN/AIGS		
deionization	DE/AOIN/ZAIGS	delusion	DLAOUGS
Deiters	DAOET/ERS		DE/LAOUGS
	DAOET/ERZ	delusional	DLAOUGS/NAL
deja entendu	DAI/JA/EN/TEN/DAOU		DE/LAOUGS/NAL
deja eprouve	DAI/JA/ON/TON/DAOU	demarcation	DE/MAR/KAIGS
	DAI/JA/AI/PRAOU/VAI	Demarquay	DEM/AR/KAI
	DAI/JA/EP/PRAOU/VAI	demasculinization	DE/MAS/KLIN/ZAIGS
deja fait	DAI/JA/FAI	demasculinizing	DE/MAS/KIN/AOIZ/-G
deja pense	DAI/JA/PON/SAI	Dematiaceae	DE/MAT/YAIS/YAE
	DAI/JA/PEN/SAI	dematiacious	DE/MAT/YAIRBS
deja raconte	DAI/JA/RA/KON/TAI	Demazin	DEM/ZIN
deja vecu	DAI/JA/VAI/KAOU	deme	DAEM
	DAI/JA/VE/KAOU		(not DAOEM; see deem)
deja voulu	DAI/JA/VAOU/LAOU	demecarium	DEM/KAIRM
deja vu	DAI/JA/VAOU		DEM/KAIR/YUM
dejecta	DE/JEK/TA	demeclocycline	DEM/KLO/SAOI/KLAOEN
dejection	DE/J*EBGS	demecolcine	DEM/KOL/SAOEN
Dejerine	DEJ/RAOEN	dement	DEMT
delacrimation	DE/LAK/RI/MAIGS		DMENT
delactation	DE/LAK/TAIGS		DE/MENT
Delafield	DEL/FAOELD	demented	DEMT/-D
delamination	DE/LAM/NAIGS		DMENT/-D
Delaney clause	DE/LAI/NAOE/KLAUZ		DE/MENT/-D
delay	DLAI	dementia	DMEN/SHA
	DE/LAI		DE/MEN/SHA
delayed	DLAI/-D	Demerol	DEM/ROL
	DE/LAI/-D	demethylase	DE/M*ET/LAIS
Delbet	DEL/BAI	demethylation	DE/M*ET/LAIGS
de-lead	DE/LAED	demethylchlortetracycline	DE/M*ET/IL/KLOR/TET/RA/SAOI/KLAOEN
deleterious	DEL/TAOER/YUS		
deletion	DLAOEGS	demi-	DEM
	DE/LAOEGS	demifacet	DEM/FAS/ET
Delfen	DEL/FEN		DEM/FA/SET
Delhi	DEL/LAOE	demigauntlet	DEM/GAUNT/LET
	DEL/HAOE	Demilets	DEM/LET/-S
delicate	DEL/KAT	demilune	DEM/LAOUN
delimit	DE/LIMT	demimonstrosity	DEM/MON/STROS/TI
delimitation	DE/LIM/TAIGS	demineralization	DE/MIN/RAL/ZAIGS
	DE/LIMT/TAIGS	demipenniform	DEM/PEN/FORM
		Demi-Regroton	DEM//REG/RO/TON

demodectic	DEM/DEKT/IK	dentales	DEN/TAI/LAOEZ
Demodex	DEM/DEX	dentalgia	DEN/TAL/JA
Demodicidae	DEM/DIS/DAE	dentalis	DEN/TAI/LIS
demodicidosis	DEM/DIS/DOE/SIS	dentary	DENT/RI
demodicosis	DEM/DI/KOE/SIS	dentata	DEN/TAI/TA
demogram	DEM/GRAM	dentate	DEN/TAIT
demography	DE/MOG/FI	dentatectomy	DENT/TEKT/M*I
demoniac	DE/MOEN/YAK	dentati	DEN/TAI/TAOI
	DE/MON/YAK	dentatothalamic	DEN/TAIT/THA/LAM/IK
demonomania	DE/MON/MAIN/YA		DEN/TAI/TO/THA/LAM/IK
	DAOEM/NO/MAIN/YA	dentatum	DEN/TAI/TUM
demonopathy	DE/MON/OP/TH*I		DEN/TAIT/UM
	DAOEM/NOP/TH*I	dente	DEN/TAOE
demonophobia	DE/MON/FOEB/YA	dentes	DEN/TAOEZ
	DAOEM/NO/FOEB/YA	dentia	DEN/SHA
demonstrator	DEM/STRAI/TOR	dentibuccal	DENT/BUK/KAL
	DMON/STRAI/TOR	denticle	DENT/K-L
	DEM/MON/STRAI/TOR	denticulate	DEN/TIK/LAIT
demorphinization	DE/MOR/FIN/ZAIGS	denticulated	DEN/TIK/LAIT/-D
demoxepam	DEM/OX/PAM	denticulatum	DEN/TIK/LAI/TUM
Demser	DEM/SER		DEN/TIK/LAIT/UM
demucosation	DE/MAOUK/SAIGS	dentification	DENT/FI/KAIGS
demulcent	DE/MULS/ENT		DEN/TIF/KAIGS
	DE/MUL/SENT	dentiform	DENT/FORM*
Demulen	DEM/YAOU/LEN	dentifrice	DENT/FRIS
	DEM/YU/LEN	dentigerous	DEN/TIJ/ROUS
demustardization	DE/MUS/TARD/ZAIGS	dentilabial	DENT/LAIB/YAL
demutization	DE/MAOUT/ZAIGS	dentilingual	DENT/LING/WAL
demyelinate	DE/MAOI/LI/NAIT	dentimeter	DEN/TIM/TER
	DE/MAOI/LIN/AIT	dentin	DEN/TIN
demyelinating	DE/MAOI/LI/NAIT/-G	dentin(o)-	DENT/N(O)
	DE/MAOI/LIN/AIT/-G		DEN/TI/N(O)
demyelination	DE/MAOI/LI/NAIGS	dentinal	DENT/NAL
	DE/MAOIL/NAIGS	dentinalgia	DENT/NAL/JA
demyelinization	DE/MAOI/LIN/ZAIGS	dentine	DEN/TAOEN
denarcotize	DE/NARK/TAOIZ	dentinoblast	DENT/NO/BLA*S
denasality	DE/NAI/ZAL/TI	dentinoblastoma	DENT/NO/BLAS/TOE/MA
denatality	DE/NAI/TAL/TI	dentinocemental	DENT/NO/SEMT/TAL
denatonium	DE/NA/TOEN/YUM	dentinoenamel	DENT/NO/E/NAM/EL
denaturant	DE/NAIFP/RANT	dentinogenesis	DENT/NO/JEN/SIS
denaturation	DE/NAIFP/RAIGS	dentinogenic	DENT/NO/JEN/IK
denature	DE/NAI/KHUR	dentinoid	DENT/NOID
denatured	DE/NAI/KHUR/-D	dentinoma	DENT/NOE/MA
dendr(o)-	DEN/DR(O)	dentinosteoid	DEN/TIN/O*S/YOID
dendraxon	DEN/DRAK/SON		DENT/NO*S/YOID
dendric	DEN/DRIK	dentinum	DENT/NUM
dendriceptor	DEN/DRI/SEP/TOR	dentiparous	DEN/TIP/ROUS
dendriform	DEN/DRI/FORM	dentis	DEN/TIS
dendrite	DEN/DRAOIT	dentist	DEN/T*IS
dendritic	DEN/DRIT/IK		DENT/*IS
dendriticum	DEN/DRIT/KUM	dentistry	DENT/STRI
dendrodendritic	DEN/DRO/DEN/DRIT/IK	dentition	DEN/TIGS
dendrogram	DEN/DRO/GRAM	-dentium	DEN/SHUM
dendroid	DEN/DROID	dentoalveolar	DENT/AL/VAOE/LAR
dendron	DEN/DRON	dentoalveolitis	DENT/AL/VAOE/LAOITS
dendrophagocytosis	DEN/DRO/FAG/SAOI/TOE/SIS	dentode	DEN/TOED
denervate	DE/NER/VAIT	dentofacial	DENT/FAIRBL
denervated	DE/NER/VAIT/-D	dentography	DEN/TOG/FI
denervation	DER/NER/VAIGS	dentoid	DEN/TOID
dengue	DEN/GAI	dentoidin	DEN/TOI/DIN
	DEN/GAOE	dentolegal	DENT/LAOEL
denial	DE/NAOIL		DENT/LAOE/GAL
denidation	DE/NAIGS	dentoliva	DENT/LAOI/VA
denitrification	DE/NAOI/TRIF/KAIGS	dentomechanical	DENT/ME/KAN/KAL
denitrifier	DE/NAOI/TRI/FI/ER		DENT/M-K/KAL
denitrify	DE/NAOI/TRI/FI	dentosurgical	DENT/SURJ/KAL
denitrifying	DE/NAOI/TRI/FI/-G	dentotropic	DENT/TROP/IK
denitrogenation	DE/NAOI/TRO/JE/NAIGS	dentulous	DENT/LOUS
	DE/NAOI/TRO/JEN/AIGS		DEN/KHU/LOUS
	DE/NAOI/TROJ/NAIGS		DEN/TAOU/LOUS
Denman	DEN/MAN	denture	DEN/KHUR
Denonvilliers	DEN/VAOEL/YAI		DEN/TAOUR
	DEN/NO/VAOEL/YAI	denturist	DEN/KHUR/*IS
	DEN/NON/VAOEL/YAI	denucleated	DE/NAOUK/LAIT/-D
Denorex	DEN/REX	denudation	DE/NAOU/DAIGS
dens	DENZ	denude	DE/NAOUD
	(not DENS; see dense)	denutrition	DE/NAOU/TRIGS
dense	DENS	Denver	DEN/VER
densimeter	DEN/SIM/TER	deodorant	DE/OED/RANT
densimetric	DENS/MET/RIK	deodorize	DE/OED/RAOIZ
densitometer	DENS/TOM/TER	deodorized	DE/OED/RAOIZ/-D
densitometry	DENS/TOM/TRI	deodorizer	DE/OED/RAOIZ/ER
density	DENS/TI	deontology	DE/ON/TOLG
densography	DEN/SOG/FI	deoppilant	DE/OP/LANT
dent(o)-	DENT	deoppilation	DE/OP/LAIGS
	DEN/T(O)	deoppilative	DE/OP/LAIT/IV
dentagra	DEN/TAG/RA	deorsumduction	DE/OR/SUM/D*UBGS
	DENT/GRA	deorsumvergence	DE/OR/SUM/VER/JENS
dental	DEN/TAL	deorsumversion	DE/OR/SUM/VERGS

deossification	DE/OS/FI/KAIGS	depraved	DPRAIV/-D
deoxidation	DE/OX/DAIGS		DE/PRAIV/-D
deoxidize	DE/OX/DAOIZ	depravity	DPRAV/TI
deoxy-	DE/OX		DE/PRAV/TI
deoxyadenosine	DE/OX/AI/DEN/SAOEN	depress	DPRESZ
deoxyadenylic	DE/OX/AD/NIL/IK		DE/PRESZ
deoxycholaneresis	DE/OX/KOEL/NER/SIS	depressant	DPRES/SANT
deoxycholate	DE/OX/KOE/LAIT		DE/PRES/SANT
deoxycholic	DE/OX/KOEL/IK	depressed	DPRESZ/-D
deoxycorticosterone	DE/OX/KORT/KO*S/ROEN		DE/PRESZ/-D
deoxycortone	DE/OX/KOR/TOEN	depression	DPREGS
deoxycytidine	DE/OX/SAOIT/DAOEN		DE/PREGS
deoxycytidylic	DE/OX/SAOIT/DIL/IK	depressive	DPRES/SIV
deoxyepinephrine	DE/OX/EP/NEF/RIN		DPRESZ/IV
deoxygenation	DE/OX/JE/NAIGS		DE/PRES/SIV
	DE/OX/JEN/AIGS		DE/PRESZ/IV
deoxyguanosine	DE/OX/GAUN/SAOEN	depressomotor	DPRES/SO/MOE/TOR
deoxyguanylic	DE/OX/GAU/NIL/IK		DE/PRES/SO/MOE/TOR
	DE/OX/GAUN/IL/IK	depressor	DPRES/SOR
deoxyhemoglobin	DE/OX/HAOEM/GLOE/BIN		DE/PRES/SOR
deoxyhexose	DE/OX/HEX/OES	deprimens	DEP/RI/MENZ
	DE/OX/HEK/SOES	deprimens oculi	DEP/RI/MENZ/OK/LAOI
deoxypentose	DE/OX/PEN/TOES	deprivation	DEP/RI/VAIGS
deoxyriboaldolase	DE/OX/RAOIB/ALD/LAIS	Deprol	DEP/ROL
deoxyribodipyrimidine	DE/OX/RAOIB/DI/PAOI/RIM/		DEP/ROEL
	DAOEN	deprostil	DE/PROS/TIL
deoxyribonuclease	DE/OX/RAOIB/NAOUK/LAIS	deproteinization	DE/PRO/TAOEN/ZAIGS
deoxyribonucleic	DE/OX/RAOIB/NAOU/KLAI/IK	depside	DEP/SAOID
	DE/OX/RAOIB/NAOU/KLAOE/IK	depth	D*EPT
deoxyribonucleoprotein	DE/OX/RAOIB/NAOUK/LO/PRO/	deptropine	DEP/TRO/PAOEN
	TAOEN		DEP/TROE/PAOEN
deoxyribonucleoside	DE/OX/RAOIB/NAOUK/LO/SAOID	depula	DEP/LA
deoxyribonucleotide	DE/OX/RAOIB/NAOUK/LO/TAOID		DEP/YAOU/LA
deoxyribose	DE/OX/RAOI/BOES		DEP/YU/LA
deoxyribosephosphate	DE/OX/RAOI/BOES/FOS/FAIT	depulization	DE/PAOUL/ZAIGS
deoxyriboside	DE/OX/RAOIB/SAOID	depur-	DEP/R-
deoxyribosyl	DE/OX/RAOIB/SIL		DEP/YAOU/R-
deoxyribotide	DE/OX/RAOIB/TAOID		DEP/YU/R-
deoxythymidylic	DE/OX/THAOIM/DIL/IK	depurant	DEP/RANT
deoxyvirus	DE/OX/VAOI/RUS	depurate	DEP/RAIT
deozonize	DE/OEZ/NAOIZ	depurative	DEP/RA/TIV
	DE/O/ZOEN/AOIZ		DEP/RAIT/IV
Depakene	DEP/KAOEN	depurator	DEP/RAI/TOR
Depakote	DEP/KOET	dequalinium	DE/KWA/LIN/YUM
depancreatize	DE/PAN/KRA/TAOIZ	deradelphus	DER/DEL/FUS
Depen	DE/PEN		DAIR/DEL/FUS
dependence	DPEND/ENS	derailment	DE/RAIL/-MT
	DE/PEND/ENS	deranencephalia	DER/AN/EN/SFAIL/YA
dependent	DPEND/ENT		DAIR/AN/EN/SFAIL/YA
	DE/PEND/ENT	deranencephalia	DER/AN/EN/SFAIL/YA
Dependovirus	DPEN/DO/VAOI/RUS		DAIR/AN/EN/SFAIL/YA
	DE/PEN/DO/VAOI/RUS	derangement	DE/RAING/-MT
depepsinized	DE/PEPS/NAOIZ/-D		DE/RAIN/-J/-MT
depersonalization	DE/PERNL/ZAIGS	derealization	DE/RAEL/ZAIGS
	DE/PERS/NAL/ZAIGS	dereism	DE/RE/IFM
dephosphorylation	DE/FOS/FOR/LAIGS	dereistic	DE/RE/*IS/IK
depigmentation	DE/PIG/MEN/TAIGS	derencephalia	DER/EN/SFAIL/YA
depilate	DEP/LAIT		DAIR/EN/SFAIL/YA
depilation	DEP/LAIGS	derencephalocele	DER/EN/SFAL/SAO*EL
depilatory	DPIL/TOIR		DER/EN/SEF/LO/SAO*EL
	DE/PIL/TOIR		DAIR/EN/SFAL/SAO*EL
deplasmolysis	DE/PLAZ/MOL/SIS		DAIR/EN/SEF/LO/SAO*EL
deplasmolyze	DE/PLAZ/MO/LAOIZ	derencephalus	DER/EN/SEF/LUS
deplete	DPLAOET		DAIR/EN/SEF/LUS
	DE/PLAOET	derencephaly	DER/EN/SEF/LI
depletion	DPLAOEGS		DAIR/EN/SEF/LI
	DE/PLAOEGS	derepression	DE/RE/PREGS
Depo-Cobolin	DEP/KO/BOL/LIN	de Ribes	DE/RAOEBS
	DEP/KO/BOE/LIN	deric	DER/IK
depolarization	DE/POE/LAR/ZAIGS		DAIR/IK
	DE/POEL/RI/ZAIGS	dericin	DER/SIN
depolarize	DE/POEL/RAOIZ	Derifil	DER/FIL
depolarizer	DE/POEL/RAOIZ/ER	derism	DE/RIFM
depolarizing	DE/POEL/RAOIZ/-G		DER/IFM
depolymerase	DE/POL/MER/AIS	derivant	DER/VANT
depolymerization	DE/POL/MER/ZAIGS	derivation	DER/VAIGS
depolymerize	DE/POL/MER/AOIZ	derivative	DRIV/TIV
Depo-Medrol	DEP/MED/ROL		DE/RIV/TIV
Deponit	DEP/NIT	derivatorius	DRIV/TOER/YUS
Depo-Predate	DEP/PRE/DAIT		DRIV/TOR/YUS
Depo-Provera	DEP/PRO/VER/RA		DE/RIV/TOER/YUS
depopulation	DEP/POP/LAIGS		DE/RIV/TOR/YUS
deposit	DPOZ/SIT	derived	DE/RAOIV/-D
	DE/POZ/SIT		(not DRAOIV/-D)
depot	DE/POE	derm(o)-	DERM
Depo-Testosterone	DEP/TES/TO*S/ROEN		DER/M(O)
depravation	DEP/RA/VAIGS	derma	DER/MA
deprave	DPRAIV	dermabrader	DERM/BRAID/ER
	DE/PRAIV	dermabrasion	DERM/BRAIGS

Dermacentor	DERM/SEN/TOR	dermatopolyneuritis	DERMT/POL/NAOU/RAOITS
dermad	DER/MAD	dermatorrhagia	DERMT/RAI/JA
dermagraphy	DER/MAG/FI	dermatorrhea	DERMT/RAOE/YA
dermahemia	DERM/HAOEM/YA	dermatorrhexis	DERMT/REK/SIS
Dermaide	DERM/AID	dermatosclerosis	DERMT/SKLE/ROE/SIS
dermal	DER/MAL	dermatoscopy	DERM/TOS/KPI
dermalaxia	DERM/LAX/YA	dermatoses	DERM/TOE/SAOEZ
dermametropathism	DERM/ME/TROP/THIFM	dermatosis	DERM/TOE/SIS
dermamyiasis	DERM/MAOI/AOI/SIS	dermatoskeleton	DERMT/SKEL/TON
	DERM/MAOI/YAOI/SIS	dermatotherapy	DERMT/THER/PI
Dermanyssidae	DERM/NIS/DAE	dermatothlasia	DERMT/THRAIZ/YA
Dermanyssus	DERM/NIS/SUS		DERMT/TH-/LAIZ/YA
dermat(o)-	DERM/T(O)	dermatotome	DERMT/TOEM
	DERMT	dermatotropic	DERMT/TROP/IK
dermatalgia	DERM/TAL/JA	-dermatous	DERM/TOUS
dermatan	DERM/TAN	dermatoxenoplasty	DERMT/ZAOEN/PLAS/TI
dermatic	DER/MAT/IK		DERMT/ZEN/PLAS/TI
dermatitides	DERM/TIT/DAOEZ	dermatozoiasis	DERMT/ZOE/AOI/SIS
dermatitidis	DERM/TIT/DIS	dermatozoon	DERMT/ZAON
dermatitis	DERM/TAOITS	dermatozoonosis	DERMT/ZOE/NOE/SIS
dermatoalloplasty	DERMT/AL/LO/PLAS/TI	dermatrophia	DERM/TROEF/YA
	DERMT/AL/PLAS/TI	dermatrophy	DER/MAT/RO/FI
dermatoarthritis	DERMT/AR/THRAOITS	dermenchysis	DER/MENG/SIS
dermatoautoplasty	DERMT/AUT/PLAS/TI		DER/MEN/KI/SIS
Dermatobia	DERM/TOEB/YA	-dermia	DERM/YA
dermatobiasis	DERMT/BAOI/SIS	dermic	DERM/IK
dermatocandidiasis	DERMT/KAND/DAOI/SIS	dermis	DER/MIS
dermatocele	DERMT/SAO*EL	dermo-	DERM
dermatocellulitis	DERMT/SEL/YAOU/LAOITS		DER/MO
dermatochalasis	DERMT/KA/LAI/SIS	dermoanergy	DERM/AN/ER/JI
	DERMT/KAL/SIS	dermoblast	DERM/BLA*S
dermatochalazia	DERMT/KA/LAIZ/YA	dermocyma	DERM/SAOI/MA
dermatoconiosis	DERMT/KOEN/YOE/SIS	dermocymus	DERM/SAOI/MUS
dermatoconjunctivitis	DERMT/KON/JUNG/VAOITS	dermographia	DERM/GRAF/YA
	DERMT/KON/JUNGT/VAOITS	dermographism	DER/MOG/FIFM
dermatocyst	DERMT/S*IS		DER/MOG/RA/FIFM
dermatodynia	DERMT/DIN/YA	dermography	DER/MOG/FI
dermatodysplasia	DERMT/DIS/PLAIZ/YA	dermohygrometer	DERM/HAOI/GROM/TER
dermatofibroma	DERMT/FAOI/BROE/MA	dermoid	DER/MOID
dermatofibrosarcoma	DERMT/FAOI/BRO/SAR/KOE/MA	dermoidectomy	DER/MOI/DEKT/M*I
dermatofibrosis	DERMT/FAOI/BROE/SIS	Dermolate	DERM/LAIT
dermatogen	DER/MAT/JEN	dermolipoma	DERM/LI/POE/MA
dermatoglyphics	DERMT/GLIFK/-S	dermolysin	DER/MOL/SIN
dermatograph	DER/MAT/GRAF	dermolysis	DER/MOL/SIS
dermatographia	DERMT/GRAF/YA	dermometer	DER/MOM/TER
dermatographic	DERMT/GRAFK	dermometry	DER/MOM/TRI
dermatographism	DERM/TOG/FIFM	dermomycosis	DERM/MAOI/KOE/SIS
dermatography	DERM/TOG/FI	dermomyotome	DERM/MAOI/TOEM
dermatoheteroplasty	DERMT/HET/RO/PLAS/TI	dermonecrotic	DERM/NE/KROT/IK
dermatoid	DERM/TOID	dermoneurosis	DERM/NAOU/ROE/SIS
dermatologic	DERMT/LOJ/IK	dermoneurotropic	DERM/NAOUR/TROP/IK
dermatological	DERMT/LOJ/KAL	dermonosology	DERM/NOE/SOLG
dermatologically	DERMT/LOJ/KLI	dermopathic	DERM/PA*T/IK
dermatologist	DERM/TO*LGS	dermopathy	DER/MOP/TH*I
dermatology	DERM/TOLG	dermophlebitis	DERM/FLE/BAOITS
dermatolysis	DERM/TOL/SIS	Dermoplast	DERM/PLA*S
dermatoma	DERM/TOE/MA	dermoplasty	DERM/PLAS/TI
dermatome	DERM/TOEM	dermoreaction	DERM/RE/A*BGS
dermatomegaly	DERMT/MEG/LI	dermoskeleton	DERM/SKEL/TON
dermatomere	DERMT/MAOER	dermostenosis	DERM/STE/NOE/SIS
dermatomic	DERM/TOM/IK	dermostosis	DER/MOS/TOE/SIS
dermatomyces	DERMT/MAOI/SAOEZ	dermosynovitis	DERM/SIN/VAOITS
dermatomycin	DERMT/MAOI/SIN	dermosyphilopathy	DERM/SIF/LOP/TH*I
dermatomycosis	DERMT/MAOI/KOE/SIS	dermotoxin	DERM/TOK/SIN
dermatomyiasis	DERMT/MAOI/AOI/SIS	dermotropic	DERM/TROP/IK
	DERMT/MAOI/YAOI/SIS	dermovaccine	DERM/VAK/SAOEN
dermatomyoma	DERMT/MAOI/YOE/MA	dermovascular	DERM/VAS/KLAR
dermatomyositis	DERMT/MAOI/SAOITS	dermovirus	DERM/VAOI/RUS
dermatoneurology	DERMT/NAOU/ROLG	derodidymus	DER/DID/MUS
dermatoneurosis	DERMT/NAOU/ROE/SIS		DAIR/DID/MUS
dermatonosology	DERMT/NOE/SOLG	derotation	DE/ROE/TAIGS
dermato-ophthalmitis	DERMT/OF/THAL/MAOITS	desalination	DE/SAL/NAIGS
dermatopathia	DERMT/PA*T/YA	desalivation	DE/SA*L/VAIGS
dermatopathic	DERMT/PA*T/IK	desamidize	DE/SAM/DAOIZ
dermatopathology	DERMT/PA/THOLG	desaturase	DE/SAFP/RAIS
dermatopathy	DERM/TOP/TH*I	desaturate	DE/SAFP/RAIT
Dermatophagoides	DERM/TOF/GOI/DAOEZ	desaturation	DE/SAFP/RAIGS
dermatopharmacology	DERMT/FARM/KOLG	Desault	DE/SOE
dermatophiliasis	DERMT/FI/LAOI/SIS	Descemet	DES/SE/MAI
dermatophilosis	DERMT/FI/LOE/SIS		(not DES/MAI; see December may)
Dermatophilus	DERM/TOF/LUS	descemetitis	DES/ME/TAOITS
dermatophobia	DERMT/FOEB/YA	descemetocele	DES/MET/SAO*EL
dermatophone	DERMT/FOEN	descend	DE/SEND
dermatophylaxis	DERMT/FLAK/SIS	descendens	DE/SEN/DENZ
dermatophyte	DERMT/FAOIT	descending	DE/SEND/-G
dermatophytid	DERM/TOF/TID	descensus	DE/SEN/SUS
dermatophytosis	DERMT/FAOI/TOE/SIS	descent	DE/SENT
dermatoplastic	DERMT/PLA*S/IK	Deschamps	DAI/SHAU
dermatoplasty	DERMT/PLAS/TI		DE/SHAU

descinolone	DES/IN/LOEN	desquamate	DES/KWA/MAIT
	DES/SIN/LOEN	desquamation	DES/KWA/MAIGS
descriptive	DE/SKRIPT/IV	desquamativa	DES/KWAM/TAOI/VA
Desenex	DES/NEX	desquamative	DES/KWAM/TIV
desensitization	DE/SENS/TI/ZAIGS	desquamativum	DES/KWAM/TAOI/VUM
	DE/SENS/TAOI/ZAIGS		DES/KWAM/TAOIV/UM
desensitize	DE/SENS/TAOIZ	desquamatory	DES/KWAM/TOIR
deserpidine	DE/SERP/DAOEN	desternalization	DE/STERNL/ZAIGS
desexualize	DE/SEX/YAOUL/AOIZ	desthiobiotin	DES/THAOI/BAO*I/TIN
Desferal	DES/FE/RAL	destillata	D*ES/LAI/TA
	DES/FERL		D*ES/LA/TA
	DES/FRAL	destruction	DE/STR*UBGS
desferrioxamine	DES/FER/YOX/MAOEN		DR*UBGS
deshydremia	DES/HAOI/DRAOEM/YA	destructive	DE/STRUK/TIV
-desia	DAOEZ/YA		DRUKT/IV
desiccant	DES/KANT	destrudo	DES/TRAOU/DOE
desiccate	DES/KAIT	destruens	DES/TRAOUNZ
desiccation	DES/KAIGS		DES/TRAOUNS
desiccative	DES/KAIT/IV		DES/TRAOU/ENZ
desiccator	DES/KAI/TOR	desulfhydrase	DE/SUL/-F/HAOI/DRAIS
desipramine	DES/IP/RA/MAOEN		DE/SUL/FAOI/DRAIS
-desis	(O)D/SIS	desulfinase	DE/SUL/FIN/AIS
	DAOE/SIS	desulfurase	DE/SUL/FRAIS
Desitin	DES/TIN		DE/SUL/FAOU/RAIS
deslanoside	DES/LAN/SAOID		DE/SUL/FUR/RAIS
desm(o)-	DEZ/M(O)	desynchronous	DE/SIN/KRON/OUS
	DES/M(O)		DE/SIN/KRO/NOUS
desmalgia	DEZ/MAL/JA	Desyrel	DES/REL
desmectasia	DEZ/MEK/TAIZ/YA	detachment	DE/TAFP/-MT
desmectasis	DEZ/MEKT/SIS	detector	DE/TEK/TOR
desmepithelium	DEZ/MEP/THAOEL/YUM	deterenol	DE/TER/NOL
desmin	DEZ/MIN		DE/TER/NOEL
desmitis	DEZ/MAOITS	detergent	DE/TERJ/ENT
desmocranium	DEZ/MO/KRAIN/YUM		DE/TER/JENT
desmocyte	DEZ/MO/SAO*IT	deterioration	DE/TAOER/RAIGS
desmocytoma	DEZ/MO/SAOI/TOE/MA		DE/TAOER/YO/RAIGS
desmodynia	DEZ/MO/DIN/YA	determinant	DE/TERM/NANT
desmogenous	DEZ/MOJ/NOUS		DERM/NANT
desmography	DEZ/MOG/FI	determinate	DE/TERM/NAT
desmohemoblast	DEZ/MO/HAOEM/BLA*S		DERM/NAT
	DEZ/MO/HEM/BLA*S	determination	DE/TERM/NAIGS
desmoid	DEZ/MOID		DERMGS
desmolase	DEZ/MO/LAIS		DERM/NAIGS
desmology	DEZ/MOLG	determine	DERM
desmoma	DEZ/MOE/MA		DE/TER/MIN
desmon	DEZ/MON	determiner	DE/TERM/NER
desmoneoplasm	DEZ/MO/NAOE/PLAFM		DERM/ER
desmopathy	DEZ/MOP/TH*I	determinism	DE/TERM/NIFM
desmoplasia	DEZ/MO/PLAIZ/YA		DERM/NIFM
desmoplastic	DEZ/MO/PLA*S/IK		DERM/IFM
desmopressin	DEZ/MO/PRES/SIN	detersive	DE/TERS/IV
desmorrhexis	DEZ/MO/REK/SIS	dethyroidism	DE/THAOI/ROID/IFM
desmosine	DEZ/MO/SAOEN		DE/THAOI/ROI/DIFM
	DEZ/MO/SIN	dethyroidize	DE/THAOI/ROI/DAOIZ
desmosis	DEZ/MOE/SIS		DE/THAOI/ROID/AOIZ
desmosome	DEZ/MO/SOEM	de tolu	DE/TOL/YAOU
desmosterol	DEZ/MO*S/ROL	detonating	DET/NAIT/-G
desmotomy	DEZ/MOT/M*I	detonation	DET/NAIGS
desmotropism	DEZ/MOT/RO/PIFM	detorsion	DE/TORGS
desoleolecithin	DES/OEL/YO/LES/THIN	detoxicate	DE/TOX/KAIT
desomorphine	DES/MOR/FAOEN	detoxication	DE/TOX/KAIGS
desonide	DES/NAOID	detoxification	DE/TOX/FI/KAIGS
desorb	DE/SORB	detoxify	DE/TOX/FI
desorption	DE/SORPGS	detrition	DE/TRIGS
DesOwen	DES/O/WEN	detritus	DE/TRAOI/TUS
desoximetasone	DES/OX/MET/SOEN	detruncation	DE/TRUN/KAIGS
desoxy-	DES/OX	detrusor	DE/TRAOU/SOR
desoxycorticosterone	DES/OX/KORT/KO*S/ROEN	detubation	DE/TAOU/BAIGS
desoxycortone	DES/OX/KOR/TOEN	detumescence	DE/TAOU/MES/ENS
desoxyephedrine	DES/OX/EF/DRAOEN	deturgescence	DE/TUR/JES/ENS
	DES/OX/EF/DRIN	deutencephalon	DAOU/TEN/SEF/LON
desoxymorphine	DES/OX/MOR/FAOEN	deuter(o)-	DAOU/R(O)
	DES/OX/MOR/FIN		DAOU/TER
desoxyphenobarbital	DES/OX/FAOEN/BARB/TAL	deuteranomalopia	DAOUT/RA/NOM/LOEP/YA
desoxyribonuclease	DES/OX/RAOIB/NAOUK/LAIS	deuteranomalopsia	DAOUT/RA/NOM/LOPS/YA
desoxyribose	DES/OX/RAOI/BOES	deuteranomalous	DAOUT/RA/NOM/LOUS
Desoxyn	DES/OK/SIN	deuteranomaly	DAOUT/RA/NOM/LI
desoxy-sugar	DES/OX/SHUG/AR	deuteranope	DAOUT/RA/NOEP
despeciate	DE/SPAOERB/YAIT	deuteranopia	DAOUT/RA/NOEP/YA
	DE/SPAOES/YAIT	deuteranopic	DAOUT/RA/NOP/IK
despeciated	DE/SPAOERB/YAIT/-D		DAOUT/RA/NOEP/IK
	DE/SPAOES/YAIT/-D	deuteranopsia	DAOUT/RA/NOPS/YA
despeciation	DE/SPAOERB/YAIGS	deuterate	DAOUT/RAIT
	DE/SPAOES/YAIGS	deuterion	DAOU/TAOERN
despecification	DE/SPES/FI/KAIGS		DAOU/TAOER/YON
despumation	DES/PAOU/MAIGS	deuterium	DAOU/TAOERM
Desquam	DES/KWAM		DAOU/TAOER/YUM
Desquam-E	DES/KWAM/ERBGS	deuteroconidium	DAOUT/RO/KO/NID/YUM
Desquam-X	DES/KWAM/KP-RBGS	deuterofat	DAOUT/RO/FAT

deuterohemin	DAOUT/RO/HEM/MIN	dextranomer	DEX/TRA/NAIS
	DAOUT/RO/HAOE/MIN	dextransucrase	DEX/TRAN/MER
deuterohemophilia	DAOUT/RO/HAOEM/FIL/YA	dextranucrase	DEX/TRAN/SAOU/KRAIS
Deuteromycetes	DAOUT/RO/MAOI/SAOE/TAOEZ	dextrase	DEX/TRAIS
deuteron	DAOUT/RON	dextrate	DEX/TRAIT
deuteropathic	DAOUT/RO/PA*T/IK	dextraural	DEX/TRAURL
deuteropathy	DAOUT/ROP/TH*I	dextri	DEX/TRAOI
deuteropine	DAOUT/RO/PAOEN	dextriferron	DEX/TRI/FER/RON
	DAOUT/RO/PIN	dextrin	DEX/TRIN
deuteroplasm	DAOUT/RO/PLAFM	dextrinase	DEX/TRI/NAIS
deuteroporphyrin	DAOUT/RO/POR/FRIN	dextrinate	DEX/TRI/AIT
deuterosome	DAOUT/RO/SOEM		DEX/TRI/NAIT
deuterotocia	DAOUT/RO/TOE/SHA	dextrinize	DEX/TRIN/AOIZ
	DAOUT/RO/TOES/YA		DEX/TRI/NAOIZ
deuterotoky	DAOUT/ROT/KI	dextrinogenic	DEX/TRIN/JEN/IK
deuthyalosome	DAOU/THAOI/AL/SOEM	dextrinose	DEX/TRIN/OES
deuto-	DAOUT		DEX/TRI/NOES
	DAOU/TO	dextrinosis	DEX/TRIN/NOE/SIS
deutogenic	DAOUT/JEN/IK		DEX/TRIN/O/SIS
deutomerite	DAOU/TOM/RAOIT	dextrinuria	DEX/TRIN/YAOUR/YA
	DAOUT/MAOER/AOIT		DEX/TRI/NAOUR/YA
deuton	DAOU/TON	dextroamphetamine	DEX/TRO/AM/FET/MAOEN
deutonephron	DAOUT/NEF/RON	dextrocardia	DEX/TRO/KARD/YA
deutoplasm	DAOUT/PLAFM	dextrocardiogram	DEX/TRO/KARD/YO/GRAM
deutoplasmic	DAOUT/PLAZ/MIK	dextrocerebral	DEX/TRO/SER/BRAL
deutoplasmigenon	DAOUT/PLAZ/MI/JEN/NON	dextroclination	DEX/TRO/KLI/NAIGS
deutoplasmolysis	DAOUT/PLAZ/MOL/SIS	dextrocompound	DEX/TRO/KOM/POUND
Deutschlander	DOIFP/LAND/ER	dextrocular	DEX/TROK/LAR
	DOIFP/LEND/ER	dextrocularity	DEX/TROK/LAIR/TI
devaluation	DE/VAL/YAIGS		DEX/TROK/LAR/TI
	DE/VAL/WAIGS	dextrocycloduction	DEX/TRO/SAOI/KLO/D*UBGS
devascularization	DE/VAS/KLAR/ZAIGS	dextroduction	DEX/TRO/D*UBGS
development	DWOP/-MT	dextrogastria	DEX/TRO/GAS/TRA
	DE/VEL/OP/-MT		DEX/TRO/GAS/TRAOE/YA
developmental	DWOP/-MT/TAL	dextroglucose	DEX/TRO/GLAOU/KOES
	DE/VEL/OP/-MT/TAL	dextrogram	DEX/TRO/GRAM
Devergie	DEVR/JAOE	dextrogyral	DEX/TRO/JAOIRL
	DEV/ER/JAOE	dextrogyration	DEX/TRO/JAOI/RAIGS
deviance	DAOEV/YANS	dextromanual	DEX/TRO/MAN/YAOUL
deviant	DAOEV/YANT	dextromenthol	DEX/TRO/MEN/THOL
deviation	DAOEV/YAIGS	dextromethorphan	DEX/TRO/ME/THOR/FAN
device	DE/VAOIS	dextromoramide	DEX/TRO/MOR/MAOID
deviometer	DAOEV/YOM/TER	dextropedal	DEX/TROP/DAL
devisceration	DE/VIS/RAIGS	dextroposition	DEX/TRO/POGS
devitalization	DE/VAOIT/LI/ZAIGS	dextropositioned	DEX/TRO/POGS/-D
	DE/VAOI/TAL/ZAIGS	dextropropoxyphene	DEX/TRO/PRO/POX/FAOEN
devitalize	DE/VAOIT/LAOIZ	dextrorotary	DEX/TRO/ROET/RI
devitalized	DE/VAOIT/LAOIZ/-D	dextrorotation	DEX/TRO/ROE/TAIGS
devolution	DEV/LAOUGS	dextrorotatory	DEX/TRO/ROET/TOIR
devolutive	DE/VOL/TIV	dextrose	DEX/TROES
	DEV/LAOUT/IV	dextrosinistral	DEX/TRO/SNIS/TRAL
Devonshire	DEVN/SHAOIR		DEX/TRO/SI/NIS/TRAL
	DEVN/SHIR	dextrosozone	DEX/TRO/SOE/ZOEN
devorative	DEV/RAIT/IV	dextrosuria	DEX/TRO/SAOUR/YA
	DEV/RA/TIV	dextrothyroxine	DEX/TRO/THAOI/ROK/SAOEN
	DEV/VOR/TIV	dextrotorsion	DEX/TRO/TORGS
De Watteville	DE/WAT/VIL	dextrotropic	DEX/TRO/TROP/IK
deworming	DE/WORM/-G	dextroversion	DEX/TRO/VERGS
dexamethasone	DEX/M*ET/SOEN	dextroverted	DEX/TRO/VERT/-D
dexamisole	DEX/AM/SOEL	dextrum	DEX/TRUM
dexamphetamine	DEX/AM/FET/MAOEN	dezocine	DEZ/SAOEN
Dexasone	DEX/SOEN	dhobie itch	DOE/BAOE
Dexatrim	DEX/TRIM	di-	DI
dexbrompheniramine	DEX/BROM/FEN/IR/MAOEN	di-	DI
	DEX/BROM/FE/NIR/MAOEN	dia-	DAOI
dexchlorpheniramine	DEX/KLOR/FEN/IR/MAOEN	DiaBeta	DAOI/BAI/TA
	DEX/KLOR/FE/NIR/MAOEN		DAOI/BAOE/TA
dexclamol	DEX/KLA/MOL	diabetes	DAOI/BAOE/TAOEZ
	DEX/KLA/MOEL	diabetic	DAOI/BET/IK
Dexedrine	DEX/DRAOEN	diabetica	DAOI/BET/KA
dexetimide	DEK/SET/MAOID	diabeticorum	DAOI/BET/KOR/UM
deximafen	DEK/SIM/FEN		DAOI/BET/KOER/UM
dexiocardia	DEX/YO/KARD/YA	diabetid	DAOI/BAOE/TID
dexiotropic	DEX/YO/TROP/IK	diabetogenic	DAOI/BET/JEN/IK
dexivacaine	DEK/SIV/KAIN	diabetogenous	DAOI/BE/TOJ/NOUS
Dexol	DEX/OL	diabetograph	DAOI/BET/GRAF
dexpanthenol	DEX/PA*NT/NOL		DAOI/BAOET/GRAF
dexpropranolol	DEX/PRO/PRAN/LOL	diabetology	DAOI/BE/TOLG
	DEX/PRO/PRAN/LOEL		DAOI/BAOE/TOLG
dexter	D*EX/ER	diabetometer	DAOI/BE/TOM/TER
	DEX/TER		DAOI/BAOE/TOM/TER
dextr(o)-	DEX/TR(O)	Diabinese	DI/AB/NAOES
dextra	DEX/TRA		DAOI/AB/NAOES
dextrad	DEX/TRAD	diabrosis	DAOI/BROE/SIS
dextrae	DEX/TRAE	diabrotic	DAOI/BROT/IK
dextral	DEX/TRAL	diacele	DAOI/SAO*EL
dextrality	DEX/TRAL/TI	diacetate	DI/AS/TAIT
dextran	DEX/TRAN	diacetemia	DI/AS/TAOEM/YA
dextranase	DEX/TRAN/AIS	diacetic	DI/SET/IK
			DI/SAOET/IK

diaceticaciduria	DI/SET/IK/AS/DAOUR/YA
diacetonuria	DI/AS/TO/NAOUR/YA
diaceturia	DI/AS/TAOUR/YA
diacetyl	DI/AS/TIL
diacetylcholine	DI/AS/TIL/KOE/LAOEN
diacetylmonoxime	DI/AS/TIL/MON/OK/SAOIM
diacetylmorphine	DI/AS/TIL/MOR/FAOEN
	DI/AI/SAOE/TIL/MOR/FAOEN
diacetyltannic	DI/AS/TIL/TAN/IK
diachorema	DAOI/KOE/RAOE/MA
diachoresis	DAOI/KOE/RAOE/SIS
diachronic	DAOI/KRON/IK
diachylon	DI/AK/LON
diacid	DI/AS/ID
diaclasia	DAOI/KLAIZ/YA
diaclasis	DI/AK/LA/SIS
diaclast	DAOI/KLA*S
diaclastic	DAOI/KLA*S/IK
diacrinous	DI/AK/RI/NOUS
diacrisis	DI/AK/RI/SIS
diacritic	DAOI/KRIT/IK
diacritical	DAOI/KRIT/KAL
diactinic	DI/AK/TIN/IK
diactinism	DI/AKT/NIFM
	DI/AK/TIN/IFM
diacylglycerol	DI/AS/IL/GLIS/ROL
diad	DI/AD
diaderm	DAOI/DERM
diadermic	DAOI/DERM/IK
diadocho-	DI/AD/KO
	DAOI/AD/KO
	DAOI/DOEK
	DAOI/DOE/KO
diadochocinesia	DI/AD/KO/SI/NAOEZ/YA
diadochocinetic	DI/AD/KO/SI/NET/IK
diadochokinesia	DI/AD/KO/KI/NAOEZ/YA
diadochokinesis	DI/AD/KO/KI/NAOE/SIS
diadochokinetic	DI/AD/KO/KI/NET/IK
diagnose	DAOIG/NOES
	DAOIG
diagnoses	DAOIG/NOE/SAOEZ
	DAOIGZ
diagnosis	DAOIG/NOE/SIS
	DAOIGS
diagnostic	DAOIG/N*OS/IK
diagnosticate	DAOIG/NO*S/KAIT
diagnostician	DAOIG/NOS/TIGS
diagnostics	DAOIG/N*OS/IK/-S
diagnosticum	DAOIG/NO*S/KUM
diagonal	DI/AG/NAL
diagonalis	DI/AG/NAI/LIS
diagram	DAOI/GRAM
diagrammatic	DAOI/GRA/MAT/IK
	DAOI/GRAM/MAT/IK
diagraph	DAOI/GRAF
diakinesis	DAOI/KI/NAOE/SIS
dial	DAOIL
diallyl	DI/AL/IL
	DI/AL/LIL
diallylbarbituric	DI/AL/IL/BARB/TAOUR/IK
	DI/AL/LIL/BARB/TAOUR/IK
diallylbisnortoxiferin	DI/AL/IL/BIS/NOR/TOX/FER/RIN
	DI/AL/LIL/BIS/NOR/TOX/FER/RIN
Dialose	DAOI/LOES
Dialose Plus	DAOI/LOES/PLUS
dialurate	DI/AL/RAIT
	DI/AL/YAOU/RAIT
	DI/AL/YU/RAIT
dialuric	DAOI/LAOUR/IK
dialysance	DI/LAOI/SANS
dialysate	DI/AL/SAIT
dialysis	DI/AL/SIS
dialyzable	DAOI/LAOIZ/-BL
dialize	DAOI/LAOIZ
dialyzed	DAOI/LAOIZ/-D
dialyzer	DAOI/LAOIZ/ER
diamagnetic	DAOI/MAG/NET/IK
di-amelia	DI/AI/MAOEL/YA
diameter	DI/AM/TER
diamide	DI/AM/ID
	DI/AM/AOID
diamidine	DI/AM/DAOEN
diamine	DAOI/MAOEN
	DAOI/MIN
diaminoacetic	DI/AM/NO/AI/SAOET/IK
	DI/AM/NO/AI/SET/IK
diaminoacridine	DI/AM/NO/AK/RI/DAOEN
	DI/AM/NO/AK/RI/DIN
diaminodiphenylsulfone	DI/AM/NO/DI/FENL/SUL/FOEN

diaminodiphosphatide	DI/AM/NO/DI/FOS/FA/TAOID
diaminomonophosphatide	DI/AM/NO/MON/FOS/FA/TAOID
diamino oxyhydrase	DI/AM/NOE/OX/HAOI/DRAIS
diaminopimelate	DI/AM/NO/PIM/LAIT
diaminuria	DI/AM/NAOUR/YA
diamniotic	DI/AM/NOT/IK
	DI/AM/NAOE/YOT/IK
diamocaine	DI/AM/KAIN
diamonds	DAOI/MONDZ
diamorphine	DAOI/MOR/FAOEN
Diamox	DAOI/MOX
diamthazole	DI/AM/THA/ZOEL
diandria	DI/AN/DRA
	DI/AN/DRAOE/YA
diandry	DI/AN/DRI
dianhydroantiarigenin	DI/AN/HAOI/DRO/A*ENT/AR/JEN/NIN
dianoetic	DAOI/NO/ET/IK
	DAOI/NOE/ET/IK
diantebrachia	DI/AENT/BRAIK/YA
diapamide	DI/AP/MAOID
Diaparene	DAOIP/RAOEN
	DAOI/PA/RAOEN
	DI/AP/RAOEN
diapause	DAOI/PAUZ
diapedesis	DAOI/PE/DAOE/SIS
diapedetic	DAOI/PE/DET/IK
diaper	DAOIP/ER
	DAOI/PER
diaphane	DAOI/FAIN
diaphaneity	DAOI/FA/NAOE/TI
diaphanometer	DI/AF/NOM/TER
diaphanometry	DI/AF/NOM/TRI
diaphanoscope	DI/AF/NO/SKOEP
diaphanoscopy	DI/AF/NOS/KPI
diaphemetric	DAOI/FE/MET/RIK
diaphen	DAOI/FEN
diaphorase	DI/AF/RAIS
diaphoresis	DAOI/FRAOE/SIS
diaphoretic	DAOI/FRET/IK
diaphragm	DAOI/FRAM
diaphragma	DAOI/FRAG/MA
diaphragmalgia	DAOI/FRAG/MAL/JA
diaphragmata	DAOI/FRAG/MA/TA
diaphragmatic	DAOI/FRAG/MAT/IK
diaphragmatica	DAOI/FRAG/MAT/KA
diaphragmatitis	DAOI/FRAG/MA/TAOITS
diaphragmatocele	DAOI/FRAG/MAT/SAO*EL
diaphragmatis	DAOI/FRAG/MA/TIS
diaphragmitis	DAOI/FRAG/MAOITS
diaphragmodynia	DAOI/FRAG/MO/DIN/YA
diaphysary	DI/AF/SAIR
diaphyseal	*see* diaphysial
diaphysectomy	DAOI/FI/SEKT/M*I
	DAOI/FIZ/EKT/M*I
diaphyses	DI/AF/SAOEZ
diaphysial	DAOI/FIZ/YAL
diaphysis	DI/AF/SIS
diaphysitis	DI/AF/SAOITS
	DAOI/FI/SAOITS
Diapid	DAOI/PID
diapiresis	DAOI/PAOI/RAOE/SIS
diaplacental	DAOI/PLA/SEN/TAL
diaplasis	DI/AP/LA/SIS
diaplastic	DAOI/PLA*S/IK
diaplexus	DAOI/PLEK/SUS
diapnoic	DI/AP/NOIK
	DI/AP/NOE/IK
diapnotic	DI/AP/NOT/IK
diapophysis	DAOI/POF/SIS
diapyesis	DAOI/PAOI/E/SIS
diapyetic	DAOI/PAOI/ET/IK
diarrhea	DAOI/RAOE/YA
diarrheal	DAOI/RAOEL
diarrheic	DAOI/RAOE/IK
diarrheogenic	DAOI/RAOE/YO/JEN/IK
diarthric	DI/AR/THRIK
diarthrodial	DI/AR/THROED/YAL
diarthroses	DI/AR/THROE/SAOEZ
diarthrosis	DI/AR/THROE/SIS
diarthrotic	DI/AR/THROT/IK
diarticular	DI/AR/TIK/LAR
diaschisis	DI/AS/KI/SIS
diascope	DAOI/SKOEP
diascopy	DI/AS/KPI
diaspironecrobiosis	DI/AS/PRO/NEK/RO/BAO*I/YOE/SIS
diaspironecrosis	DI/AS/PRO/NE/KROE/SIS
diastalsis	DAOI/STAL/SIS

diastaltic	DAOI/STALT/IK
diastase	DI/AS/TAIS
diastasic	DAOI/STAIZ/IK
	DAOI/STAIS/IK
diastasimetry	DI/A*S/SIM/TRI
diastasis	DI/A*S/SIS
diastasuria	DI/AS/TAIS/YAOUR/YA
diastatic	DAOI/STAT/IK
diastema	DAOI/STAOE/MA
diastemata	DAOI/STAOEM/TA
	DAOI/STEM/TA
diastematocrania	DAOI/STAOEM/TO/KRAIN/YA
	DAOI/STEM/TO/KRAIN/YA
diastematomyelia	DAOI/STAOEM/TO/MAOI/AOEL/
	YA
	DAOI/STEM/TO/MAOI/AOEL/YA
diastematopyelia	DAOI/STAOEM/TO/PAOI/AOEL/
	YA
	DAOI/STEM/TO/PAOI/AOEL/YA
diaster	DI/AS/TER
	DI/A*S/ER
diastereoisomer	DAOI/STER/YO/AOIS/MER
diastereoisomeric	DAOI/STER/YO/AOIS/MER/IK
diastereoisomerism	DAOI/STER/YO/AOI/SOM/RIFM
diastole	DI/A*S/LAOE
diastolic	DAOI/STOL/IK
diastomyelia	DI/AS/TO/MAOI/AOEL/YA
diastrophic	DAOI/STROFK
diastrophism	DI/AS/TRO/FIFM
diataxia	DAOI/TAX/YA
diatela	DAOI/TAOE/LA
diathermal	DAOI/THER/MAL
diathermancy	DAOI/THERM/SI
	DAOI/THER/MAN/SI
diathermanous	DAOI/THERM/NOUS
diathermic	DAOI/THERM/IK
diathermocoagulation	DAOI/THER/KO/AG/LAIGS
diathermy	DAOI/THER/M*I
diathesis	DI/A*T/SIS
diathetic	DAOI/THET/IK
diatom	DAOI/TOM
diatomaceous	DAOI/TO/MAIRBS
	DAOI/TOE/MAIRBS
	DAOI/TOM/AIRBS
diatomic	DAOI/TOM/IK
diatoric	DAOI/TOR/IK
	DAOI/TOER/IK
diatrizoate	DAOI/TR*I/ZOE/AIT
diatrizoic	DAOI/TR*I/ZOIK
	DAOI/TR*I/ZOE/IK
Di-Atro Tablets	DI/AT/RO/TAB/LET/-S
diauchenos	DI/AUK/NOS
diauxic	DI/AUX/IK
diauxie	DI/AUK/SAOE
diaveridine	DAOI/VER/DAOEN
diaxon	DI/AK/SON
diaxone	DI/AK/SOEN
diazepam	DI/AZ/PAM
diazine	DAOI/ZAOEN
	DI/AZ/ZIN
diazo-	DI/A*Z
	DI/AZ/ZO
diazobenzene	DI/A*Z/BEN/ZAOEN
diazobenzenesulfonic	DI/A*Z/BEN/ZAOEN/SUL/FON/IK
diazoma	DAOI/ZOE/MA
diazomethane	DI/A*Z/M*ET/AIN
diazonal	DAOI/ZOENL
diazone	DAOI/ZOEN
diazosulfobenzol	DI/A*Z/SUL/FO/BEN/ZOL
diazotization	DI/A*Z/TI/ZAIGS
	DI/A*Z/TAOI/ZAIGS
diazotize	DI/A*Z/TAOIZ
diazoxide	DAOI/ZOK/SAOID
	DI/A*Z/OK/SAOID
dibasic	DI/BAIS/IK
dibenzanthracene	DI/BENS/AN/THRA/SAOEN
dibenz-dibutyl anthraquinol	
	DI/BENZ/DI/BAOU/TIL/AN/THRA/
	KWIN/OL
dibenzepin	DI/BENZ/PIN
dibenzheptropine	DI/BENZ/HEP/TRO/PAOEN
dibenzopyridine	DI/BENZ/PIR/DAOEN
dibenzothiazine	DI/BENZ/THAOI/ZAOEN
dibenzthione	DI/BENZ/THAOI/OEN
dibenzylchlorethamine	DI/BEN/ZIL/KLOR/*ET/MAOEN
Dibenzyline	DI/BENZ/LAOEN
diblastula	DI/BLA*S/LA
dibrachia	DI/BRAIK/YA
dibrachius	DI/BRAIK/YUS

dibromide	DI/BROE/MAOID
dibromoketone	DI/BROEM/KAOE/TOEN
dibromomethyl	DI/BROEM/M*ET/IL
dibromopropamidine	DI/BROEM/PRO/PAM/DAOEN
dibromsalan	DI/BROM/SA/LAN
	DI/BROMS/LAN
dibucaine	DI/BAOU/KAIN
dibunate	DI/BAOU/NAIT
dibutoline	DI/BAOUT/LAOEN
dibutyl	DI/BAOU/TIL
	DI/BAOUT/IL
dicacodyl	DI/KAK/DIL
Dical	DI/KAL
Dical-D	DI/KAL/D-RBGS
Dical Gelcaps	DI/KAL/JEL/KAP/-S
dicalcic	DI/KALS/IK
dicalcium phosphate	DI/KALS/YUM/FOS/FAIT
dicamphendion	DI/KAM/FEND/YON
dicamphor	DI/KAM/FOR
dicarbonate	DI/KARB/NAIT
dicarboxylic	DI/KAR/BOK/SIL/IK
dicelous	DI/SE/LOUS
	DI/SAO*EL/OUS
	DI/SAOEL/OUS
dicentric	DI/SEN/TRIK
dicephalous	DI/SEF/LOUS
dicephalus	DI/SEF/LUS
dicephaly	DI/SEF/LI
dicheilia	DI/KAOIL/YA
dicheiria	DI/KAOIR/YA
dicheirus	DI/KAOI/RUS
dichlor(o)-	DI/KLOR
	DI/KLOR/RO
dichloralphenazone	DI/KLORL/FEN/ZOEN
	DI/KLORL/FEN/A*Z/OEN
dichloramine	DI/KLOR/MAOEN
dichlordioxydiamidoarsenobenzol	
	DI/KLOR/DI/OX/DI/AM/DO/ARS/
	NO/BEN/ZOL
dichlorhydrin	DI/KLOR/HAOI/DRIN
dichloride	DI/KLOR/AOID
dichlorisone	DI/KLOR/SOEN
dichloroacetic	DI/KLOR/AI/SAOET/IK
	DI/KLOR/AI/SET/IK
dichlorobenzene	DI/KLOR/BEN/ZAOEN
dichlorodiethyl sulfide	DI/KLOR/DI/*ET/IL/SUL/FAOID
dichlorodifluoromethane	DI/KLOR/DI/FLAOUR/M*ET/AIN
dichlorodiphenyl	DI/KLOR/DI/FENL
dichlorodiphenyltrichloroethane	
	DI/KLOR/DI/FENL/TR*I/KLOR/
	*ET/AIN
dichloroformoxime	DI/KLOR/FOR/MOK/SAOIM
	DI/KLOR/FOR/MOK/SIM
dichlorohydrin	DI/KLOR/HAOI/DRIN
dichloroindophenol	DI/KLOR/IND/FAOE/NOL
	DI/KLOR/IN/DO/FAOE/NOL
dichloroisopropyl	DI/KLOR/AOIS/PRO/PIL
dichloroisoproterenol	DI/KLOR/AOIS/PRO/TER/NOL
dichloromethyl	DI/KLOR/M*ET/IL
dichlorophenoxyacetic	DI/KLOR/FEN/OX/AI/SAOET/IK
	DI/KLOR/FEN/OX/AI/SET/IK
dichlorotetrafluoroethane	DI/KLOR/TET/RA/FLAOUR/*ET/
	AIN
dichlorophen	DI/KLOR/FEN
dichlorphenamide	DI/KLOR/FEN/MAOID
dichlorophenarsine	DI/KLOR/FEN/AR/SAOEN
dichlorvos	DI/KLOR/VOS
dichogeny	DI/KOJ/N*I
dichorial	DI/KOER/YAL
dichorionic	DI/KOER/YON/IK
dichotic	DI/KOT/IK
dichotomization	DI/KOT/MI/ZAIGS
dichotomous	DI/KOT/MOUS
dichotomy	DI/KOT/M*I
dichroic	DI/KROIK
	DI/KROE/IK
dichroine	DI/KROE/AOEN
dichroism	DI/KROE/IFM
dichromasy	DI/KROEM/SI
dichromat	DI/KROE/MAT
dichromate	DI/KROE/MAIT
dichromatic	DI/KROE/MAT/IK
dichromatism	DI/KROEM/TIFM
dichromatopsia	DI/KROEM/TOPS/YA
dichromic	DI/KROEM/IK
dichromophil	DI/KROEM/FIL
dichromophile	DI/KROEM/FAOIL
dichromophilism	DI/KROE/MOF/LIFM
dichronine	DI/KROE/NAOEN

dick	DIK	diethylamine	DI/*ET/IL/AM/AOEN
Dick	K-P/DIK		DI/*ET/IL/AM/MIN
dicliditis	DIK/LI/DAOITS	diethylbarbituric	DI/*ET/IL/BARB/TAOUR/IK
diclidostosis	DIK/LID/OS/TOE/SIS	diethylcarbamazine	DI/*ET/IL/KAR/BAM/ZAOEN
	DIK/LI/DOS/TOE/SIS	diethylene	DI/*ET/LAOEN
diclofenac	DI/KLOEF/NAK	diethylenediamine	DI/*ET/LAOEN/DAOI/MAOEN
	DI/KLOE/FEN/AK	diethylenetriamine	DI/*ET/LAOEN/TR*I/MAOEN
dicloralurea	DI/KLORL/YAOU/RAOE/YA	diethyl ether	DI/*ET/IL/AO*ET/ER
dicloxacillin	DI/KLOX/SLIN	diethylmalonylurea	DI/*ET/IL/MAL/NIL/YAOU/RAOE/
	DI/KLOX/SIL/LIN		YA
dicophane	DI/KO/FAIN	diethylolamine	DI/*ET/LOL/MAOEN
	DAOIK/FAIN	diethylpropion	DI/*ET/IL/PROEP/YON
dicoria	DI/KOER/YA	diethylstilbestrol	DI/*ET/IL/STIL/BES/TROL
dicotyledon	DI/KOT/LAOE/DON	diethyl-sulfone	DI/*ET/IL/SUL/FOEN
dicrotic	DI/KROT/IK		DI/*ET/IL/H-F/SUL/FOEN
dicrotism	DI/KRO/TIFM	diethyltoluamide	DI/*ET/IL/TOE/LAOU/MAOID
	DI/KROE/TIFM		DI/*ET/IL/TOL/YAOU/MAOID
diction	D*IBGS	diethyltryptamine	DI/*ET/IL/TRIPT/MAOEN
Dictyocaulus	DIKT/YO/KAU/LUS		DI/*ET/IL/TRIPT/MIN
dictyokinesis	DIKT/YO/KI/NAOE/SIS	dietitian	DAOI/TIGS
dictyoma	DIKT/YOE/MA		DAOIT/TIGS
dictyosome	DIKT/YO/SOEM	Dietl	DAOET/-L
dictyotene	DIKT/YO/TAOEN	dietotherapy	DAOI/TO/THER/PI
dicumarol	DI/KAOUM/ROL	dietotoxic	DAOI/TO/TOX/IK
dicyclic	DI/SAOIK/LIK	dietotoxicity	DAOI/TO/TOK/SIS/TI
dicyclomine	DI/SAOI/KLO/MAOEN	Dieudonne	DAOU/DON/NAI
dicysteine	DI/SIS/TAOEN		DAOU/DON/NAOE
	DI/S*IS/YIN	Dieulafoy	DAOUL/FOI
didactic	DI/DAKT/IK		DAOUL/FWAU
didactylism	DI/DAKT/LIFM		DAOU/LA/FOI
didactylous	DI/DAKT/LOUS		DAOU/LA/FWAU
didelphia	DI/DEL/FA	Dieutrim Capsules	DI/YAOU/TRIM/KAP/SAOUL/-S
	DI/DEL/FAOE/YA	difarnesyl	DI/FARN/SIL
didelphic	DI/DEL/FIK	difenoxamide	DI/FEN/OX/MAOID
Didelphis	DI/DEL/FIS	difenoxin	DI/FEN/OK/SIN
didermoma	DI/DER/MOE/MA	difenoxylic	DI/FEN/OX/LIK
Didrex	DI/DREX	differen-	DIFRN
Didronel	DI/DRO/NEL		DIF/FREN
	DI/DROE/NEL	difference	DIFRNS
didym(o)-	DID/M(O)	different	DIFRNT
didymalgia	DID/MAL/JA	differential	DIFRN/-RBL
didymitis	DID/MAOITS	differentiate	DIFRN/SHAIT
didymodynia	DID/MO/DIN/YA	differentiation	DIFRN/SHAIGS
didymous	DID/MOUS	difficile	DIF/SAOI/LAOE
didymus	DID/MUS		DIF/SIL/LAOE
die	DAOI	diffluence	DIF/FLAOUNS
diechoscope	DI/EK/SKOEP		DIF/LAOUNS
diecious	DI/AOERBS	diffluent	DIF/FLAOUNT
Dieffenbach	DAOEFN/BAUK		DIF/LAOUNT
	DAOEFN/BAK	diffraction	DIF/FRA*BGS
Diego	DAOE/YAI/GOE		DI/FRA*BGS
	DAOE/AI/GOE	diffu-	DIF/FAOU
diel	DI/EL		DI/FAOU
dieldrin	DI/EL/DRIN	diffusa	DIF/FAOU/SA
dielectric	DI/LEK/TRIK	diffusate	DIF/FAOU/ZAIT
dielectrography	DI/LEK/TROG/FI	diffuse	DIF/FAOUS
dielectrolysis	DI/LEK/TROL/SIS		DIF/FAOUZ
diembryony	DI/EM/BRON/N*I	diffusible	DIF/FAOUZ/-BL
	DI/EM/BRAOE/YON/N*I	diffusiometer	DIF/FAOUZ/YOM/TER
diencephala	DI/EN/SEF/LA	diffusion	DIF/FAOUGS
diencephalic	DI/EN/SFAL/IK	diffusum	DIF/FAOU/SUM
diencephalohypophysial	DI/EN/SEF/LO/HO*IP/FIZ/YAL		DIF/FAOUS/UM
diencephalon	DI/EN/SEF/LON	diflorasone	DI/FLOR/SOEN
diener	DAOEN/ER	difluanine	DI/FLAOU/NAOEN
dienestrol	DI/AOEN/ES/TROL	diflucortolone	DI/FLAOU/KORT/LOEN
	DI/NES/TROL	diflumidone	DI/FLAOUM/DOEN
	DAOI/NES/TROL	diflunisal	DI/FLAOUN/SAL
Dientamoeba fragilis	DI/ENT/MAOE/BA/FRAJ/LIS	difluprednate	DI/FLAOU/PRED/NAIT
	DI/SPWA/MAOE/BA/FRAJ/LIS	diftalone	DIFT/LOEN
dieresis	DI/ER/SIS	digametic	DI/GA/MET/IK
dieretic	DI/RET/IK	digastric	DI/GAS/TRIK
diesophagus	DI/E/SOF/GUS	digastricus	DI/GAS/TRI/KUS
diesterase	DI/ES/TRAIS	Digenea	DI/JAOEN/YA
diestrous	DI/ES/TROUS	digenesis	DI/JEN/SIS
diestrum	DI/ES/TRUM	digenetic	DI/JE/NET/IK
diestrus	DI/ES/TRUS	Digepepsin	DIJ/PEP/SIN
diethazine	DI/*ET/ZAOEN	digest	DI/J*ES
diet	DAOIT	digestant	DI/JES/TANT
	DAOI/ET	digestion	DI/JEGS
dietary	DAOI/TAIR	digestive	DI/J*ES/IV
	DAOIT/TAIR	digestorius	DI/JES/TOR/YUS
dietetic	DAOI/TET/IK		DI/JES/TOER/YUS
	DAOIT/TET/IK	Digibind	DIJ/BAOIND
dietetics	DAOI/TET/IK/-S	digin	DIJ/JIN
	DAOIT/TET/IK/-S	digit	DIJT
diethadione	DI/*ET/DI/OEN	digital	DIJ/TAL
diethanolamine	DI/*ET/NOL/MAOEN	digitales	DIJ/TAI/LAOEZ
diethazine	DI/*ET/ZAOEN	digitalgia paresthetica	DIJ/TAL/JA/PARS/THET/KA
diethyl-	DI/*ET/IL		DIJ/TAL/JA/PAR/ES/THET/KA

digitalin	DIJ/TAL/LIN	dihydrotachysterol	DI/HAOI/DRO/TA/K*IS/ROL
digitalis	DIJ/TAL/LIS	dihydrotestosterone	DI/HAOI/DRO/TES/TO*S/ROEN
	DIJ/TAI/LIS	dihydrotheelin	DI/HAOI/DRO/THAOE/LIN
digitalism	DIJ/TAL/IFM	dihydrouracil	DI/HAOI/DRO/YAOUR/SIL
	DIJT/LIFM	dihydrouridine	DI/HAOI/DRO/YAOUR/DAOEN
digitalization	DIJ/TAL/ZAIGS	dihydroxy-	DI/HAOI/DROX
digitaloid	DIJ/TAL/OID	dihydroxyacetone	DI/HAOI/DROX/AS/TOEN
digitalose	DIJ/TAL/OES	dihydroxyaluminum	DI/HAOI/DROX/AL/LAOUM/NUM
digitate	DIJ/TAIT		DI/HAOI/DROX/LAOUM/NUM
digitatio	DIJ/TAI/SHOE	dihydroxycholecalciferol	DI/HAOI/DROX/KOEL/KAL/SIF/
	DIJ/TAIRB/YOE		ROL
digitation	DIJ/TAIGS	dihydroxyestrin	DI/HAOI/DROX/ES/TRIN
digitationes	DIJ/TAI/SHOE/NAOEZ	dihydroxyfluorane	DI/HAOI/DROX/FLAOU/RAIN
	DIJ/TAIRB/YOE/NAOEZ	dihydroxyphenylalanine	DI/HAOI/DROX/FENL/AL/NAOEN
digiti	DIJ/TAOI	diiodide	DI/AOI/DAOID
digitiform	DIJ/TI/FORM	diiodohydroxyquin	DI/AOI/OED/HAOI/DROX/KWIN
digitigrade	DIJ/TI/GRAID	diiodopyramine	DI/AOI/DO/PIR/MAOEN
digitin	DIJ/TIN		DI/AOI/OED/PIR/MAOEN
digitogenin	DIJ/TOJ/NIN	diiodothyronine	DI/AOI/OED/THAOIR/NAOEN
digitonin	DIJ/TOE/NIN	diiodotyrosine	DI/AOI/OED/TAOIR/SAOEN
digitoplantar	DIJ/TO/PLAN/TAR	diisocyanate	DI/AOIS/SAOI/NAIT
digitorum	DIJ/TORM	diisopromine	DI/AOIS/PRO/MAOEN
	DIJ/TOR/UM	diisopropyl	DI/AOIS/PRO/PIL
	DIJ/TOR/RUM	dikaryon	DI/KAR/YON
digitorus	DIJ/TORS	dikaryote	DI/KAR/YOET
	DIJ/TOR/RUS	dikaryotic	DI/KAR/YOT/IK
	DIJ/TOER/RUS	diketohydrindylidene	DI/KAOET/HAOI/DRIN/DIL/
digitoxicity	DIJ/TOK/SIS/TI		DAOEN
digitoxin	DIJ/TOK/SIN	diketohydrindamine	DI/KAOET/HAOI/DRIND/MAOEN
digitoxose	DIJ/TOK/SOES	diketone	DI/KAOE/TOEN
	DIJ/TOX/OES	diketopiperazine	DI/KAOET/PAOI/PER/ZAOEN
digitus	DIJ/TUS	dilaceration	DI/LAS/RAIGS
diglossia	DI/GLOS/YA	Dilantin	DI/LAN/TIN
diglutathione	DI/GLAOUT/THAOI/OEN	dilatancy	DI/LAI/TAN/SI
diglyceride	DI/GLIS/RAOID	dilatant	DI/LAI/TANT
	DI/GLIS/RID	dilatation	DIL/TAIGS
diglycocoll	DI/GLAOIK/KOL	dilatator	DIL/TAI/TOR
dignathus	DIG/NAI/THUS	dilate	DI/LAIT
digoxin	DI/JOK/SIN	dilation	DI/LAIGS
	DI/GOK/SIN	dilation and curettage	DI/LAIGS/AND/KUR/TAJ
digynia	DI/JIN/YA	dilation and evacuation	DI/LAIGS/AND/E/VAK/YAIGS
digyny	DI/JIN/N*I	dilator	DI/LAI/TOR
	DI/JI/N*I	Dilatrate	DI/LA/TRAIT
diheterozygote	DI/HET/RO/ZAOI/GOET	Dilatrate-SR	DI/LA/TRAIT/S-RBGS/R*RBGS
dihexyverine	DI/HEX/VER/AOEN	Dilaudid	DI/LAU/DID
	DI/HEX/VER/RAOEN	Dilaudid-HP	DI/LAU/DID/H-RBGS/P*RBGS
dihomocinchonine	DI/HOEM/SIN/KO/NAOEN	dildo	DIL/DOE
	DI/HOEM/SIN/KO/NIN	dill	DIL
dihybrid	DI/HAOI/BRID	Dilor	DI/LOR
dihydr(o)-	DI/HAOI/DR(O)	Dilor-G	DI/LOR/G-RBGS
dihydralazine	DI/HAOI/DRAL/ZAOEN	diloxanide	DI/LOX/NAOID
dihydrate	DI/HAOI/DRAIT	diltiazem	DIL/TAOI/ZEM
dihydrated	DI/HAOI/DRAIT/-D	diluent	DIL/YAOUNT
dihydrazone	DI/HAOI/DRA/ZOEN	dilute	DI/LAOUT
dihydric	DI/HAOI/DRIK	dilution	DI/LAOUGS
dihydrocholesterol	DI/HAOI/DRO/KL*ES/ROL		(not DLAOUGS; see delusion)
dihydrocodeine	DI/HAOI/DRO/KO/DAOEN	Dimacol	DAOIM/KOL
dihydrocodeinone	DI/HAOI/DRO/KO/DAOE/NOEN	dimargarin	DI/MARG/RIN
	DI/HAOI/DRO/KO/DAOEN/OEN		DI/MARJ/RIN
dihydrocoenzyme	DI/HAOI/DRO/KO/EN/ZAOIM	dimazole	DAOIM/ZOEL
dihydrocortisol	DI/HAOI/DRO/KORT/SOL	dimazon	DI/MAI/ZON
dihydrocortisone	DI/HAOI/DRO/KORT/SOEN	dimefadane	DI/MEF/DAIN
dihydrodiethylstilbestrol	DI/HAOI/DRO/DI/*ET/IL/STIL/	dimefilcon	DI/ME/FIL/KON
	BES/TROL	dimefline	DI/MEF/LAOEN
dihydroergocornine	DI/HAOI/DRO/ERG/KOR/NAOEN	dimelia	DI/MAOEL/YA
	DI/HAOI/DRO/ERG/KOR/NAOIN	dimelus	DI/MAOE/LUS
dihydroergocristine	DI/HAOI/DRO/ERG/KRIS/TAOEN	dimenhydrinate	DI/MEN/HAOI/DRI/NAIT
dihydroergocryptine	DI/HAOI/DRO/ERG/KRIP/TAOEN	dimension	DI/MENGS
dihydroergotamine	DI/HAOI/DRO/*ER/GOT/MAOEN		DMENGS
	DI/HAOI/DRO/ER/GOT/MAOEN	dimer	DI/MER
dihydroergotoxine	DI/HAOI/DRO/ERG/TOK/SAOEN	dimercaprol	DI/MER/KAP/ROL
dihydrofolate	DI/HAOI/DRO/FOE/LAIT	dimercaptosuccinate	DI/MER/KAPT/SUX/NAIT
dihydrofolliculin	DI/HAOI/DRO/FLIK/LIN	dimercurion	DI/MER/KAOUR/YON
dihydrol	DI/HAOI/DROL	dimeric	DI/MER/IK
dihydrolipoamide	DI/HAOI/DRO/LIP/AM/ID	dimerous	DIM/ROUS
	DI/HAOI/DRO/LIP/AM/AOID	dimetacrine	DI/MET/KRAOEN
dihydrolipoic	DI/HAOI/DRO/LI/POIK	dimetallic	DI/ME/TAL/IK
	DI/HAOI/DRO/LI/POE/IK	Dimetane	DAOIM/TAIN
dihydrolutidine	DI/HAOI/DRO/LAOUT/DIN	Dimetane-DC	DAOIM/TAIN/D-RBGS/KR*RBGS
	DI/HAOI/DRO/LAOUT/DAOEN	Dimetane-DX	DAOIM/TAIN/D-RBGS/KP*RBGS
dihydromorphinone	DI/HAOI/DRO/MOR/FI/NOEN	Dimetapp	DAOIM/TAP
dihydro-orotase	DI/HAOI/DRO/OR/ROE/TAIS	dimethicone	DI/M*ET/KOEN
	DI/HAOI/DRO/O/ROE/TAIS	dimethindene	DI/M*ET/IN/DAOEN
dihydro-orotate	DI/HAOI/DRO/OR/ROE/TAIT		DI/ME/THIN/DAOEN
	DI/HAOI/DRO/O/ROE/TAIT	dimethisoquin	DI/ME/THAOIS/KWIN
dihydroporphyrin	DI/HAOI/DRO/POR/FRIN	dimethisterone	DI/ME/TH*IS/ROEN
dihydropteroic	DI/HAOI/DRO/TE/ROIK		DI/M*ET/*IS/ROEN
	DI/HAOI/DRO/TE/ROE/IK	dimethothiazine	DI/M*ET/THAOI/ZAOEN
dihydrostreptomycin	DI/HAOI/DRO/STREPT/MAOI/SIN	dimethoxanate	DI/ME/THOX/NAIT

dimethoxyphenylethylamine	
	DI/ME/THOX/FENL/*ET/IL/AM/
	MIN
dimethyl	DI/M*ET/IL
dimethylacetal	DI/M*ET/IL/AS/TAL
dimethylamine	DI/M*ET/IL/AM/MIN
dimethylaminoazobenzene	DI/M*ET/IL/MAOEN/A*Z/BEN/
	ZAOEN
	DI/M*ET/IL/AM/NO/A*Z/BEN/
	ZAOEN
	DI/M*ET/IL/A/MAOEN/A*Z/BEN/
	ZAOEN
dimethylarsine	DI/M*ET/IL/AR/SIN
dimethylarsinic	DI/M*ET/IL/AR/SIN/IK
dimethylbenzene	DI/M*ET/IL/BEN/ZAOEN
dimethyl carbate	DI/M*ET/IL/KAR/BAIT
dimethylcarbinol	DI/M*ET/IL/KARB/NOL
dimethylcysteine	DI/M*ET/IL/SIS/TAOEN
	DI/M*ET/IL/S*IS/YIN
dimethylethylcarbinol	DI/M*ET/IL/*ET/IL/KARB/NOL
dimethylethylcarbinolchloral	
	DI/M*ET/IL/*ET/IL/KARB/NOL/
	KLORL
dimethylethylpyrrole	DI/M*ET/IL/*ET/IL/PIR/ROEL
dimethylguanidine	DI/M*ET/IL/GAUN/DAOEN
	DI/M*ET/IL/GAUN/DIN
dimethylketone	DI/M*ET/IL/KAOE/TOEN
dimethylphenanthrene	DI/M*ET/IL/FE/NAN/THRAOEN
dimethylphenylpiperazinium	
	DI/M*ET/IL/FENL/PAOI/PER/ZIN/
	YUM
dimethylphosphine	DI/M*ET/IL/FOS/FAOEN
dimethyl phthalate	DI/M*ET/IL/THAL/AIT
dimethylpiperazine	DI/M*ET/IL/PAOI/PER/ZAOEN
dimethyl sulfate	DI/M*ET/IL/SUL/FAIT
dimethyl sulfoxide	DI/M*ET/IL/SUL/FOK/SAOID
	DI/M*ET/IL/SUL/FOX/AOID
dimethyltryptamine	DI/M*ET/IL/TRIPT/MAOEN
dimetria	DI/MAOE/TRAOE/YA
dimidiata	DI/MID/YAI/TA
dimidiate	DI/MID/YAIT
diminution	DIM/NAOUGS
Dimmer	K-P/DIM/ER
dimorphic	DI/MOR/FIK
dimorphism	DI/MOR/FIFM
dimorphobiotic	DI/MOR/FO/BAO*I/OT/IK
dimorpholamine	DI/MOR/FOL/MAOEN
dimorphous	DI/MOR/FOUS
dimoxamine	DI/MOX/MAOEN
dimoxyline	DI/MOX/LAOEN
dimple	DIFRP/-L
dimpling	DIFRP/-LG
dineric	DI/NER/IK
dineuric	DI/NAOUR/IK
dinical	DIN/KAL
dinitr(o)-	DI/NAOI/TR(O)
dinitrate	DI/NAOI/TRAIT
dinitrated	DI/NAOI/TRAIT/-D
dinitroaminophenol	DI/NAOI/TRO/AM/NO/FAOE/NOL
dinitrobenzene	DI/NAOI/TRO/BEN/ZAOEN
dinitrocellulose	DI/NAOI/TRO/SEL/YAOU/LOES
dinitrochlorobenzene	DI/NAOI/TRO/KLOR/BEN/ZAOEN
dinitrocresol	DI/NAOI/TRO/KRAOE/SOL
dinitrofluorobenzene	DI/NAOI/TRO/FLAOUR/BEN/
	ZAOEN
dinitrogen	DI/NAOI/TRO/JEN
dinitrophenol	DI/NAOI/TRO/FAOE/NOL
dinitroresorcinol	DI/NAOI/TRO/RE/SORS/NOL
Dinoflagellata	DAOIN/FLAJ/LAI/TA
dinoflagellate	DAOIN/FLAJ/LAIT
dinoprost	DAOIN/PRO*S
dinoprostone	DAOIN/PROS/TOEN
dinucleotide	DI/NAOUK/LO/TAOID
Dioctophyma	DI/OKT/FAOI/MA
dioctophymiasis	DI/OKT/FI/MAOI/SIS
Dioctophymoidea	DI/OKT/FAOI/MOID/YA
dioctyl	DI/OK/TIL
Diodon	DAOI/DON
	DI/YO/DON
diodone	DAOI/DOEN
	DI/YO/DOEN
Diogenes	DI/OJ/NAOEZ
diolamine	DI/OL/MAOEN
	DI/OEL/MAOEN
diopsimeter	DI/OP/SIM/TER
diopter	DI/OPT/ER
	DI/OP/TER
dioptometer	DI/OP/TOM/TER
dioptometry	DI/OP/TOM/TRI

dioptoscopy	DI/OP/TOS/KPI
dioptric	DI/OP/TRIK
	DI/OPT/RIK
dioptrics	DI/OP/TRIK/-S
	DI/OPT/RIK/-S
dioptrometer	DI/OP/TROM/TER
dioptrometry	DI/OP/TROM/TRI
dioptroscopy	DI/OP/TROS/KPI
dioptry	DI/OP/TRI
diorthosis	DI/OR/THOE/SIS
diose	DI/OES
	DI/YOES
diosgenin	DI/OS/JEN/NIN
diovular	DI/OV/LAR
diovulatory	DI/OV/LA/TOIR
dioxane	DI/OK/SAIN
dioxide	DI/OK/SAOID
dioxin	DI/OK/SIN
dioxybenzone	DI/OX/BEN/ZOEN
dioxygenase	DI/OX/JEN/AIS
dioxyline	DI/OX/LAOEN
dip	DIP
dipalmitin	DI/PAL/MI/TIN
dipentene	DI/PEN/TAOEN
dipeptidase	DI/PEPT/DAIS
dipeptide	DI/PEP/TAOID
dipeptidyl	DI/PEPT/DIL
diperodon	DI/PER/DON
Dipetalonema	DI/PET/LO/NAOE/MA
dipetalonemiasis	DI/PET/LO/NAOE/MAOI/SIS
diphallia	DI/FAL/YA
diphallus	DI/FAL/LUS
diphasic	DI/FAIZ/IK
diphebuzol	DI/FEB/ZOL
diphemanil	DI/FAOEM/NIL
diphemethoxidine	DI/FEM/THOX/DAOEN
diphenadione	DI/FEN/DI/OEN
diphenan	DI/FEN/NAN
diphenhydramine	DI/FEN/HAOI/DRA/MAOEN
diphenidol	DI/FEN/DOL
dephenol	DI/FAOE/NOL
	DI/FEN/OL
diphenolase	DI/FEN/LAIS
diphenoxylate	DI/FEN/OX/LAIT
diphenyl (word)	DI/FAOENL
	DI/FAOE/NIL
diphenyl-	DI/FENL
(combining form)	DI/FEN/IL
diphenylamine	DI/FENL/AM/MIN
diphenylaminearsine	DI/FENL/AM/MIN/AR/SIN
diphenylamino-azo-benzene	DI/FENL/AM/NO/A*Z/BEN/ZAOEN
diphenylchlorarsine	DI/FENL/KLOR/AR/SAOEN
	DI/FENL/KLOR/AR/SIN
diphenylcyanarsin	DI/FENL/SAOI/NAR/SIN
diphenylenimine	DI/FEN/LAOEN/MAOEN
	DI/FENL/AOEN/MAOEN
diphenylhydantoin	DI/FENL/HAOI/DANT/WIN
	DI/FENL/HAOI/DAN/TOIN
diphenyloxazole	DI/FENL/OX/ZOEL
	DI/FEN/LOX/ZOEL
diphenylpyraline	DI/FENL/PIR/LAOEN
diphonia	DI/FOEN/YA
diphosgene	DI/FOS/JAOEN
diphosphate	DI/FOS/FAIT
diphosphatide	DI/FOS/FA/TAOID
diphosphoglycerate	DI/FOS/FO/GLIS/RAIT
diphosphopyridine	DI/FOS/FO/PIR/DAOEN
diphosphothiamin	DI/FOS/FO/THAOI/MIN
diphtheria	DIF/THAOER/YA
diphtheriae	DIF/THAOER/YAE
diphtherial	DIF/THAOERL
diphtheric	DIF/THER/IK
	DIF/THAOER/IK
diphtherin	DIF/THRIN
	DIF/THE/RIN
diphtheritic	DIF/THRIT/IK
	DIF/THE/RIT/IK
diphtheritica	DIF/THRIT/KA
	DIF/THER/IT/KA
diphtheritis	DIF/THRAOITS
	DIF/THE/RAOITS
diphtheroid	DIF/THROID
	DIF/THE/ROID
diphtherotoxin	DIF/THAOER/TOK/SIN
	DIF/THRO/TOK/SIN
diphthongia	DIF/THON/JA
diphyllobothriasis	DI/FIL/BO*T/RAOI/SIS
Diphyllobothriidae	DI/FIL/BO*T/RAOE/DAE
Diphyllobothrium	DI/FIL/BO*T/RUM

	DI/FIL/BO*T/RAOE/UM	dipsotherapy	DIPS/THER/PI
diphyodont	DIF/YO/DONT	dipstick	DIP/STIK
dipipanone	DI/PIP/NOEN	Diptera	DIPT/RA
dipiproverine	DI/PAOI/PROEV/RAOEN	dipteran	DIPT/RAN
dipivefrin	DI/PIV/FRIN	dipterous	DIPT/ROUS
diplacusia	DIP/LA/KAOUZ/YA	dipus	DI/PUS
diplacusis	DIP/LA/KAOU/SIS	dipygus	DI/PAOI/GUS
diplasmatic	DI/PLAZ/MAT/IK		DIP/GUS
diplegia	DI/PLAOE/JA	dipylidiasis	DIP/LI/DAOI/SIS
diplegic	DI/PLAOEJ/IK	Dipylidium	DIP/LID/YUM
diplo-	DIP/LO		DI/PAOI/LID/YUM
diploalbuminuria	DIP/LO/AL/BAOUM/NAOUR/YA	dipyridamole	DI/PAOI/RID/MOEL
diplobacillary	DIP/LO/BAS/LAIR	dipyrimidine	DI/PAOI/RIM/DAOEN
diplobacilli	DIP/LO/BA/SIL/LAOI	dipyrene	DI/PAOI/RAOEN
diplobacillus	DIP/LO/BA/SIL/LUS	dipyrithione	DI/PIR/THAOI/OEN
diplobacteria	DIP/LO/BAK/TAOER/YA	dipyrone	DI/PAOI/ROEN
diplobacterium	DIP/LO/BAK/TAOERM	direct	DREKT
diploblastic	DIP/LO/BLA*S/IK		DI/REKT
diplocardia	DIP/LO/KARD/YA	director	DREK/TOR
diplocephalus	DIP/LO/SEF/LUS		DI/REK/TOR
diplocephaly	DIP/LO/SEF/LI	dirhinic	DI/RAOIN/IK
diplocheiria	DIP/LO/KAOIR/YA	dirigation	DIR/GAIGS
diplococcal	DIP/LO/KOK/KAL	dirigomotor	DIR/GO/MOE/TOR
diplococcemia	KIP/LO/KOK/SAOEM/YA	Dirofilaria	DAOIR/FLAIR/YA
diplococci	DIP/LO/KOK/SAOI		DI/RO/FLAIR/YA
diplococcin	DIP/LO/KOK/SIN	dirofilariasis	DAOIR/FIL/RAOI/SIS
diplococcoid	DIP/LO/KOK/KOID		DIR/FIL/RAOI/SIS
	DIP/LO/KOK/OID		DI/RO/FIL/RAOI/SIS
diplococcus	DIP/LO/KOK/KUS	dis-	DIS
Diplococcus	K-P/DIP/LO/KOK/KUS	disability	DIS/-BLT
diplocoria	DIP/LO/KOER/YA		DIS/ABLT
diploe	DIP/LOI	disaccharidase	DI/SAK/RI/DAIS
	DIP/LO/WAOE	disaccharide	DI/SAK/RAOID
diploetic	DIP/LO/ET/IK	disacchariduria	DI/SAK/RI/DAOUR/YA
diplogenesis	DIP/LO/JEN/SIS	disaccharose	DI/SAK/ROES
Diplogonoporus	DIP/LO/GO/NOP/RUS	disacidify	DIS/AI/SID/FI
diplogram	DIP/LO/GRAM	disaggregation	DIS/AG/RE/GAIGS
diploic	DIP/LOIK		DIS/AG/GAIGS
	DIP/LOE/IK	Disalcid	DI/SAL/SID
diploica	DIP/LOI/KA	disarticulation	DIS/AR/TIK/LAIGS
	DIP/LOE/KA	disassimilate	DIS/AI/SIM/LAIT
diploicae	DIP/LOI/SAE	disassimilation	DIS/AI/SIM/LAIGS
	DIP/LOE/SAE	disc	DIS/*K
diploici	DIP/LOI/SAOI	discectomy	DIS/SEKT/M*I
	DIP/LOE/SAOI		DIS/EKT/M*I
diploid	DIP/LOID	discharge	DIS/KHARJ
diploidy	DIP/LOI/DI	dischronation	DIS/KROE/NAIGS
	DI/PLOI/DI	dischronism	DIS/KROE/NIFM
diplokaryon	DIP/LO/KAR/YON	disci	DIS/KAOI
diplomate	DIP/LO/MAIT		DIS/SAOI
diplomelituria	DIP/LO/MEL/TAOUR/YA	disciform	DIS/FORM
diplomyelia	DIP/LO/MAOI/EL/YA		DIS/SI/FORM
diplon	DIP/LON	discission	DIS/SIGS
diplonema	DIP/LO/NAOE/MA	disclination	DIS/KLI/NAIGS
diploneural	DIP/LO/NAOURL	disco-	DIS/KO
diplont	DIP/LONT	discoblastic	DIS/KO/BLA*S/IK
diplopagus	DIP/LOP/GUS	discoblastula	DIS/KO/BLA*S/LA
diplophase	DIP/LO/FAIZ	discobolus	DIS/KO/BOE/LUS
diplophonia	DIP/LO/FOEN/YA	discogastrula	DIS/KO/GAS/TRAOU/LA
diplopia	DI/PLOEP/YA	discogenetic	DIS/KO/JE/NET/IK
diplopiometer	DI/PLOEP/YOM/TER	discogenic	DIS/KO/JEN/IK
diplopodia	DIP/LO/POED/YA	discogram	DIS/KO/GRAM
diploscope	DIP/LO/SKOEP	discography	DIS/KOG/FI
diplosomatia	DIP/LO/SOE/MAI/SHA	discoid	DIS/KOID
diplosome	DIP/LO/SOEM	discoidal	DIS/KOI/DAL
diplosomia	DIP/LO/SOEM/YA	discopathy	DIS/KOP/TH*I
diplotene	DIP/LO/TAOEN	discophorous	DIS/KOF/ROUS
diploteratology	DIP/LO/TER/TOLG	discoplacenta	DIS/KO/PLA/SEN/TA
dipodia	DI/POED/YA	discord	DIS/KORD
dipole	DI/POEL	discordance	DIS/KOR/DANS
dipotassium	DI/PO/TAS/YUM	discordant	DIS/KOR/DANT
dipping	DIP/-G	discoria	DIS/KOER/YA
Diprolene	DIP/RO/LAOEN	discotomy	DIS/KOT/M*I
	DI/PRO/LAOEN	discrepancy	DIS/KREP/SI
diproprionate	DI/PROEP/RO/NAIT		DIS/KREP/AN/SI
dipropyltryptamine	DI/PRO/PIL/TRIPT/MAOEN	discrete	DIS/KRAET
diprosopus	DI/PROS/PUS		(*not* DIS/KRAOET; see discreet)
	DI/PRO/SOE/PUS	discrimination	DIS/KRIM/NAIGS
diprotrizoate	DI/PRO/TR*I/ZOE/AIT	discus	DIS/KUS
dips(o)-	DIPS	discuss	DIS/KUSZ
	DIP/S(O)	discussive	DIS/KUS/SIV
dipsesis	DIP/SAOE/SIS		DIS/KUSZ/IV
dipsetic	DIP/SET/IK	discutient	DIS/KAOU/SHENT
dipsia	DIPS/YA		DIS/KAOURB/ENT
dipsogen	DIPS/JEN	disdiaclast	DIS/DAOI/KLA*S
dipsogenic	DIPS/JEN/IK	disease	DI/SAOEZ
dipsomania	DIPS/MAIN/YA		D-Z
dipsophobia	DIPS/FOEB/YA	disengagement	DIS/EN/GAIJ/-MT
dipsosis	DIP/SOE/SIS	disequilibrium	DIS/E/KWI/LIB/RUM

disgerminoma	DIS/JERM/NOE/MA		DI/S-
dish	DIRB		DIS
disharmonic	DIS/HAR/MON/IK	Disse	DIS/SAOE
disharmony	DIS/HARM/N*I	dissecans	DIS/KANZ
dishemopoietic	DIS/HAOEM/POIT/IK	dissect	DIS/SEKT
disillusion	DIS/IL/LAOUGS		DI/SEKT
disimmune	DIS/IM/MAOUN	dissection	DIS/S*EBGS
disimmunity	DIS/IM/MAOUN/TI		DI/S*EBGS
disimmunize	DIS/IM/NAOIZ	dissector	DIS/SEK/TOR
disimpaction	DIS/IM/PA*BGS		DI/SEK/TOR
disinfect	DIS/IN/FEKT	disseminata	DIS/SEM/NAI/TA
disinfectant	DIS/IN/FEK/TANT	disseminated	DIS/SEM/NAIT/-D
disinfection	DIS/IN/F*EBGS	dissepiment	DIS/SEP/-MT
disinfestation	DIS/IN/FES/TAIGS	dissimilate	DIS/SIM/LAIT
disinhibition	DIS/IN/BIGS	dissimilation	DIS/SIM/LAIGS
disinomenine	DI/SI/NOM/NIN	dissimilis	DIS/SIM/LIS
disinsected	DIS/IN/SEKT/-D	dissipation	DIS/PAIGS
disinsection	DIS/IN/S*EBGS	dissociable	DIS/SOERB/-BL
disinsectization	DIS/IN/SEKT/ZAIGS		DIS/SOES/-BL
disinsector	DIS/IN/SEK/TOR	dissociant	DIS/SOERB/YANT
disinsertion	DIS/IN/SERGS		DIS/SOES/YANT
disintegrant	DIS/SPWE/GRANT	dissociate	DIS/SOERB/YAIT
	DIS/INT/GRANT		DIS/SOES/YAIT
disintegration	DIS/SPWE/GRAIGS	dissociated	DIS/SOERB/YAIT/-D
	DIS/INT/GRAIGS		DIS/SOES/YAIT/-D
disinvagination	DIS/IN/VAJ/NAIGS	dissociation	DIS/SOERB/YAIGS
disjoint	DIS/JOINT		DIS/SOES/YAIGS
disjugate	DIS/JAOU/GAIT	dissociative	DIS/SOERB/TIV
disjunction	DIS/JUNGS	dissogeny	DIS/SOJ/N*I
disjunctive	DIS/JUNGT/IV	dissolution	DIS/SLAOUGS
	DIS/JUNG/TIV		DIS/SO/LAOUGS
disk	DIS/-K	dissolve	DIS/SOL/-V
disko-	see disco-	dissolvent	DIS/SOL/VENT
dislocatio	DIS/LOE/KAI/SHOE	dissonance	DIS/NANS
	DIS/LOE/KAIRB/YOE	dissonant	DIS/NANT
dislocation	DIS/LOE/KAIGS	dissymmetry	DIS/SIM/TRI
dismember	DIS/MEB	dist(o)-	D*IS
	DIS/MEM/BER		DIS/T(O)
dismemberment	DIS/MEB/-MT	distad	DIS/TAD
	DIS/MEM/BERMT	distal	DIS/TAL
dismutase	DIS/MAOU/TAIS	distales	DIS/TAI/LAOEZ
dismutation	DIS/MAOU/TAIGS	distalis	DIS/TAI/LIS
disocclude	DIS/O/KLAOUD	distally	DIS/TAL/LI
disodium	DI/SOED/YUM	distance	DIS/TANS
disome	DI/SOEM	distantial	DIS/TAN/-RBL
disomic	DI/SOEM/IK	distemper	DIS/TEFRP/ER
disomus	DI/SOE/MUS	distemperoid	DIS/TEFRP/ROID
disomy	DI/SOE/M*I	distend	DIS/TEND
Disonate	DI/SOE/NAIT	distensibility	DIS/TENS/-BLT
	DIS/NAIT	distention	DIS/TENGS
Disophrol	DI/SOF/ROL	distichia	DIS/TIK/YA
	DIS/FROL	distichiasis	D*IS/KAOI/SIS
disopromine	DI/SO/PRO/MAOEN	distichous	D*IS/KOUS
disopyramide	DI/SO/PIR/MAOID	distill	DIS/TIL
disorder	DIS/ORD/ER		DIS/STIL
disorganization	DIS/ORGS	distillate	DIS/TIL/LAIT
	DIS/ORG/ZAIGS		DIS/STIL/LAIT
disorientation	DIS/OR/YEN/TAIGS		DIS/TIL/LAT
	DIS/OER/YEN/TAIGS		DIS/STIL/LAT
dispar	DIS/PAR	distillation	D*IS/LAIGS
disparate	DIS/PRAT		DIS/TIL/LAIGS
	DIS/PA/RAT		DIS/STIL/LAIGS
disparity	DIS/PAIR/TI	distobuccal	D*IS/BUK/KAL
	DIS/PAR/TI	distobucco-occlusal	D*IS/BUK/O/KLAOU/ZAL
dispensary	DIS/PENS/RI	distobuccopulpal	D*IS/BUK/PUL/PAL
dispensatory	DIS/PENS/TOIR	distocervical	D*IS/SEFRB/KAL
dispense	DIS/PENS	distoclination	D*IS/KLI/NAIGS
dispermia	DI/SPERM/YA		D*IS/KLAOI/NAIGS
dispermine	DI/SPER/MIN	distoclusal	D*IS/KLAOU/ZAL
dispermy	DI/SPER/M*I	distoclusion	D*IS/KLAOUGS
dispersal	DIS/PER/SAL	distogingival	D*IS/JING/VAL
dispersate	DIS/PER/SAIT	distoincisal	D*IS/IN/SAOI/ZAL
disperse	DIS/PERS	distolabial	D*IS/LAIB/YAL
dispersible	DIS/PERS/-BL	distolabioincisal	D*IS/LAIB/YO/IN/SAOI/ZAL
dispersion	DIS/PERGS	distolabiopulpal	D*IS/LAIB/YO/PUL/PAL
dispersity	DIS/PERS/TI	distolingual	D*IS/LING/WAL
dispersoid	DIS/PER/SOID	distolinguoincisal	D*IS/LING/WO/IN/SAOI/ZAL
dispert	DIS/PERT	distolinguo-occlusal	D*IS/LING/WO/O/KLAOU/ZAL
dispira	DI/SPAOI/RA	distolinguopulpal	D*IS/LING/WO/PUL/PAL
dispireme	DI/SPAOI/RAOEM	distomia	DI/STOEM/YA
displaceability	DIS/PLAIS/-BLT	distomolar	D*IS/MOE/LAR
displacement	DIS/PLAIS/-MT	distomus	DI/STOE/MUS
dispore	DI/SPOER	disto-occlusal	D*IS/O/KLAOU/ZAL
disporous	DI/SPOR/OUS	disto-occlusion	D*IS/O/KLAOUGS
disposition	DIS/POGS	distoplacement	D*IS/PLAIS/-MT
disproportion	DIS/PRO/PORGS	distopulpal	D*IS/PUL/PAL
disruption	DIS/RUPGS	distopulpolabial	D*IS/PUL/PO/LAIB/YAL
disruptive	DIS/RUPT/IV	distopulpolingual	D*IS/PUL/PO/LING/WAL
diss-	DIS/S-	distortion	DIS/TORGS

distortor	DIS/TOR/TOR	dixyrazein	DI/ZIR/ZAOEN
distortum	DIS/TOR/TUM	dizygotic	DI/ZAOI/GOT/IK
	DIS/TORT/UM	dizygous	DI/ZAOIG/OUS
distoversion	D*IS/VERGS	dizziness	DIZ/*NS
distractibility	DIS/TRAKT/-BLT		DIZ/ZI/*NS
distraction	DIS/TRA*BGS	djenkolic	JEN/KOL/IK
distress	DIS/TRESZ	DNA	D-RBGS/N*RBGS/A*RBGS
distribution	DRIBGS	DOA	D-RBGS/O*RBGS/A*RBGS
	DIS/TRI/BAOUGS	D.O.A.	D-FPLT/O*FPLT/A*FPLT
distributive	DRIBT/IV	Doan's	DO*EN/AOES
	DIS/TRIB/TIV		DOEN/AOES
districhiasis	DIS/TRI/KAOI/SIS	Dobie	DOE/BAOE
distrix	DIS/TRIX	dobutamine	DOE/BAOUT/MAOEN
disturbance	DIS/TUR/BANS	Dobutrex	DOE/BAOU/TREX
disubstituted	DI/SUB/STAOUT/-D		DOEB/TREX
	DI/SUBS/TAOUT/-D	docimasia	DOES/MAIZ/YA
disulfamide	DI/SUL/FA/MAOID	docimastic	DOES/MA*S/IK
disulfate	DI/SUL/FAIT	dock	DOK
disulfide	DI/SUL/FAOID	doconazole	DOE/KOEN/ZOEL
disulfiram	DI/SUL/FI/RAM	docosanoic	DOE/KOES/NOIK
	DI/SUL/FRAM		DOE/KOES/NOE/IK
disymmetros	DI/SIM/TROS	doctor	DR-
diterpene	DI/TER/PAOEN		DOK/TOR
dithiazanine	DI/THAOI/AZ/NAOEN	doctrine	DOK/TRIN
dithiol	DI/THAOI/OL	docusate	DOK/YAOU/SAIT
dithranol	D*IT/RA/NOL		DOK/YU/SAIT
dithymol	DI/THAOI/MOL	dodecadactylitis	DOE/DEK/DAKT/LAOITS
Ditropan	DI/TROE/PAN	dodecadactylon	DOE/DEK/DAKT/LON
Dittrich	DIT/RIK	dodecane	DOED/KAIN
	DIT/TRIK	dodecanoic	DOE/DEK/NOIK
Diucardin	DI/YAOU/KAR/DIN		DOE/DEK/NOE/IK
Diulo	DI/YAOU/LOE	dodecarbonium	DOE/DE/KAR/BOEN/YUM
Diupres	DI/YAOU/PRES		DOED/KAR/BOEN/YUM
diurea	DI/YAOU/RAOE/YA	dodecyl	DOED/SIL
diureide	DI/YAOUR/YID	Doderlein	DED/ER/LAOIN
	DI/YAOUR/YAOID		DED/ER/LAOEN
diureses	DI/YAOU/RAOE/SAOEZ	Dogiel	DOEJ/YEL
diuresis	DI/YAOU/RAOE/SIS		DOE/JEL
	DAOI/RAOE/SIS	dogmatic	DOG/MAT/IK
diuretic	DI/YAOU/RET/IK	dogmatist	DOG/MA/T*IS
	DAOI/RET/IK	Dohle	DAOE/LAOE
	(not DI/RET/IK; see dieretic)	Doisy	DOI/SI
diuria	DI/YAOUR/YA	dol	DO*EL
Diuril	DI/YAOU/RIL		(not DOEL; see dole)
diurnal	DI/URNL	dolabrate	DOE/LAB/RAIT
diurnule	DI/UR/NAOUL	dolabriform	DOE/LAB/RI/FORM
	DI/URN/YAOUL	Dolacet	DOL/SET
Diutensen	DI/YAOU/TEN/SEN	Dolene	DOE/LAOEN
Diutensen-R	DI/YAOU/TEN/SEN/R-RBGS	dolich(o)-	DOL/K(O)
diutinum	DI/YAOUT/NUM	dolichocephalia	DOL/KO/SFAIL/YA
divagation	DI/VA/GAIGS	dolichocephalic	DOL/KO/SFAL/IK
divalence	DI/VAI/LENS	dolichocephalism	DOL/KO/SEF/LIFM
divalency	DI/VAI/LEN/SI	dolichocephalous	DOL/KO/SEF/LOUS
divalent	DI/VAI/LENT	dolichocephaly	DOL/KO/SEF/LI
	DIV/LENT	dolichocolon	DOL/KO/KO/LON
divalproex	DI/VAL/PRO/EX	dolichocranial	DOL/KO/KRAIN/YAL
	DI/VAL/PROEX	dolichofacial	DOL/KO/FAIRBL
divarication	DI/VAIR/KAIGS	dolichohieric	DOL/KO/HAOI/ER/IK
	DI/VAR/KAIGS	dolichokerkic	DOL/KO/KERK/IK
divergence	DI/VERJ/ENS	dolichoknemic	DOL/KO/NAOEM/IK
	DI/VER/JENS	dolichol	DOL/KOL
divergent	DI/VERJ/ENT	dolichomorphic	DOL/KO/MOR/FIK
	DI/VER/JENT	dolichopellic	DOL/KO/PEL/IK
diversion	DI/VERGS	dolichopelvic	DOL/KO/PEL/VIK
diverticul(o)-	DI/VER/TIK/L(O)	dolichoprosopic	DOL/KO/PRO/SOEP/IK
	DI/VER/TIK/YAOU/L(O)		DOL/KO/PRO/SOP/IK
	DI/VER/TIK/YU/L(O)	dolichoprosopous	DOL/KO/PROS/POUS
diverticula	DI/VER/TIK/LA	dolichostenomelia	DOL/KO/STEN/MAOEL/YA
diverticular	DI/VER/TIK/LAR	dolichouranic	DOL/KO/YAOU/RAN/IK
diverticularization	DI/VER/TIK/LAR/ZAIGS	dolichuranic	DOL/KAOU/RAN/IK
diverticulectomy	DI/VER/TIK/LEKT/M*I	Dolobid	DOEL/BID
diverticuleve	DI/VER/TIK/LAOEV		DOL/BID
diverticulitis	DI/VER/TIK/LAOITS	Dolophine	DOEL/FAOEN
diverticulogram	DI/VER/TIK/LO/GRAM		DOL/FAOEN
diverticuloma	DI/VER/TIK/LOE/MA	dolor	DOE/LOR
diverticulopexy	DI/VER/TIK/LO/PEK/SI	dolores	DOE/LOR/RAOEZ
diverticulosis	DI/VER/TIK/LOE/SIS		DOE/LOER/RAOEZ
diverticulum	DI/VER/TIK/LUM	dolorific	DOEL/RIFK
divicine	DAOIV/SAOEN	dolorimeter	DOEL/RIM/TER
	DI/VIS/AOEN	dolorimetry	DOEL/RIM/TRI
divide	DI/VAOID	dolorogenic	DOEL/RO/JEN/IK
	DWAOID		DOE/LOR/JEN/IK
dividens	DIV/DENZ	dolorology	DOEL/ROLG
divinyl	DI/VAOINL	dolorosa	DOEL/ROE/SA
division	DI/VIGS	Dolprn	DOL/PR*N
	DWIGS	Dolprn Tablets	DOL/DOL/PR*N/TAB/LET/-S
divulse	DI/VULS	Dolprn #3 Tablets	DOL/DOL/PR*N/N-B/3/TAB/LET/-S
divulsion	DI/VULGS	Domagk	DOE/MAK
divulsor	DI/VUL/SOR	domain	DOE/MAIN

130

Dombrock	DOM/BROK	dorsi	DOR/SAOI
Domeboro	DOEM/BOR/ROE	dorsiduct	DORS/DUKT
dome	DOEM	dorsiflexion	DORS/FL*EBGS
domiciliary	DOM/SIL/YAIR	dorsimesal	DORS/MES/SAL
	DOEM/SIL/YAIR	dorsispinal	DORS/SPAOINL
domiciliated	DOM/SIL/YAIT/-D	dorsoanterior	DORS/AN/TAOER/YOR
	DOEM/SIL/YAIT/-D	dorsocephalad	DORS/SEF/LAD
dominance	DOM/NANS	dorsodynia	DORS/DIN/YA
dominant	DOM/NANT	dorsointercostal	DORS/SPWER/KOS/TAL
domiphen	DOEM/FEN	dorsolateral	DORS/LAT/RAL
domperidone	DOM/P*ER/DOEN	dorsolateralis	DORS/LAT/RAI/LIS
	DOM/PER/DOEN	dorsolumbar	DORS/LUM/BAR
Donath	DOE/NA*T	dorsomedian	DORS/MAOED/YAN
Donatussin	DON/TUS/SIN	dorsomesial	DORS/MAOEZ/YAL
Donders	DON/DERS	dorsonasal	DORS/NAI/ZAL
	DON/DERZ	dorsonuchal	DORS/NAOU/KAL
donee	DOE/NAOE	dorsoposterior	DORS/POS/TAOER/YOR
Don Juan	DON/WHAN	dorsoradial	DORS/RAID/YAL
	DON/WHAUN	dorsoscapular	DORS/SKAP/LAR
Don Juanism	DON/WHAN/IFM	dorsoventrad	DORS/VEN/TRAD
	DON/WHAUN/IFM	dorsoventral	DORS/VEN/TRAL
Donnagel	DON/JEL	dorsum	DOR/SUM
Donnagel-PG	DON/JEL/P-RBGS/G*RBGS		DORS/UM
Donnan	DON/NAN	Doryx	DOR/IX
Donnatal	DON/TAL		DOER/IX
Donnazyme	DON/ZAOIM	dosage	DOES/AJ
Donne	DON/NAI	dose	DOES
donor	DOE/NOR	dosi	DOE/SAOI
Donovan	DON/VAN	dosimeter	DOE/SIM/TER
Donovania	DON/VAIN/YA	dosimetric	DOE/SI/MET/RIK
donovanosis	DON/VA/NOE/SIS	dosimetrist	DOE/SIM/TR*IS
-dont	DONT	dosimetry	DOE/SIM/TRI
-dontia	DON/SHA	dosis	DOE/SIS
-dontic	DONT/IK	dossier	DOS/YAI
-dontism	DON/TIFM	dot	DOT
	DONT/IFM	dotage	DOE/TAJ
-dontist	DON/T*IS		DOET/AJ
	DONT/*IS	dotard	DOE/TARD
-dontitis	DON/TAOITS	dotardness	DOE/TARD/*NS
-dontium	DON/SHUM	dothiepin	DOE/THAOI/PIN
-dontus	DON/TUS	double bind	DUBL/BAOIND
Doose	DAOS	double-blind	DUBL/H-F/BLAOIND
dopa	DOE/PA	doublet	DUB/LET
dopamantine	DOEP/MAN/TAOEN	doubling	DUBL/-G
dopamine	DOEP/MAOEN		DUB/-LG
dopaminergic	DOEP/MAOEN/ERJ/IK	douche	DAOURB
	DOEP/MIN/ERJ/IK	Douglas	DUG/LAS
dopa-oxidase	DOEP/OX/DAIS	douglascele	DUG/LA/SAO*EL
dopase	DOE/PAIS		DUG/LAS/SAO*EL
dope	DOEP	douglasi	DUG/LA/SAOI
Doppler	DOP/LER		DUG/LAS/SAOI
Dopram	DOE/PRAM	douglasitis	DUG/LA/SAOITS
Dopter	DOP/TER	douloureux	DAOUL/RAOU
	DOPT/ER		DAOU/LAOU/RAOU
Doral	DOE/RAL	dourine	DAOU/RAOEN
	DO/RAL	dowel	DOU/EL
doraphobia	DOER/FOEB/YA	down	DOUN
dorastine	DOR/AS/TAOEN	Down	K-P/DOUN
Dorcol	DOR/KOL	down-regulation	DOUN/H-F/REG/LAIGS
Dorello	DOE/REL/LOE	Down's syndrome	K-P/DOUN/AOES/SIN/DROEM
Dorendorf	DORN/DOR/-F		DOUN/AOES/SIN/DROEM
	DOR/EN/DOR/-F	Downey	DOU/NAOE
Dorfman	DOR/-F/MAN		DOUN/NAOE
Doriden	DOR/DEN	downgrowth	DOUN/GRO*ET
Dorland	DOR/LAND	Downs	DOUNZ
dormancy	DOR/MAN/SI		DOUNS
dormant	DOR/MANT	doxapram	DOX/PRAM
dormifacient	DORM/FAIRBT	doxaprost	DOX/PRO*S
Dorn	DORN	doxepin	DOX/PIN
dornase	DOR/NAIS	Doxidan	DOX/DAN
Dorner	DORN/ER	doxogenic	DOX/JEN/IK
Dorno	DOR/NOE	doxorubicin	DOX/RAOUB/SIN
Dorothy Reed	DOR/TH*I/RAOED	Doxy-Caps	DOX/KAP/-S
doromainia	DOR/MAIN/YA	doxycycline	DOX/SAOI/KLAOEN
	DOER/MAIN/YA	doxylamine	DOK/SIL/MAOEN
dors(o)-	DORS	Doxy-Tabs	DOX/TAB/-S
	DOR/S(O)	Doyen	DWA/YAN
dorsa	DOR/SA		DOI/YEN
dorsabdominal	DORS/AB/DOM/NAL		DOI/YAN
	DOR/SAB/DOM/NAL	Doyere	DWA/YAIR
dorsad	DOR/SAD		DOI/YAIR
dorsal	DOR/SAL		DOI/YER
dorsale	DOR/SAI/LAOE	Doyne	DOIN
dorsales	DOR/SAI/LAOEZ	Dr.	DR-FPLT
dorsalgia	DOR/SAL/JA	drachm	DRA*M
dorsalia	DOR/SAIL/YA		(not DRAM; see dram)
dorsalis	DOR/SAI/LIS	draconic	DRA/KON/IK
dorsalizing	DORS/LAOIZ/-G	dracontiasis	DRAK/ON/TAOI/SIS
Dorset	DOR/SET	dracuncul-	DRA/KUN/KL-

	DRA/KUN/KAOU/L-	drop	DROP
	DRA/KUNG/L-	dropacism	DROP/SIFM
	DRA/KUNG/YAOU/L-	droperidol	DROE/P*ER/DOL
	DRA/KUNG/YU/L-		DROE/PER/DOL
dracuncular	DRA/KUN/KLAR	droplet	DROP/LET
dracunculiasis	DRA/KUN/KLAOI/SIS	dropper	DROP/ER
Dracunculoidea	DRA/KUN/KLOID/YA	dropping	DROP/-G
dracunculosis	DRA/KUN/KLOE/SIS	dropsical	DROPS/KAL
Dracunculus	DRA/KUN/KLUS		DROP/SI/KAL
draft	DRAFT	dropsy	DROP/SI
drag	DRAG	Drosophila	DROE/SOF/LA
dragee	DRA/JAI	drosopterin	DROE/SOPT/RIN
	DRA/SHAI	drowsiness	DROUZ/*NS
Dragendorff	DRAG/EN/DOR/-F		DROU/SI/*NS
Drager	DRAIG/ER	droxacin	DROX/SIN
	DRAG/ER	droxifilcon A	DROX/FIL/KON/A-RBGS
drain	DRAIN	drug	DRUG
drainage	DRAIN/AJ	drug-fast	DRUG/H-F/FA*S
dram	DRAM	druggist	DRUG/*IS
Dramamine	DRAM/MAOEN	drug-resistant	DRUG/H-F/RE/SIS/TANT
dramatism	DRAM/TIFM	drum	DRUM
dramatization	DRAM/TI/S*AIGS	drumhead	DRUM/HED
drape	DRAIP	Drummond	DRUM/OND
Draper	DRAIP/ER		DRUM/MOND
drapetomania	DRAP/TO/MAIN/YA	drumstick	DRUM/STIK
drastic	DRA*S/IK	drunk	DR*UNG
draught	DRA*FT		DRUN/-K
	DRAUFT	drunkenness	DR*UNG/-N/*NS
	(not DRAFT; see draft)		DRUN/KEN/*NS
draw-sheet	DRAU/H-F/SHAOET	drupe	DRAOUP
dream	DRAOEM	drusen	DRAOU/SEN
Drechsel	DREK/SEL	dry ice	DRAOI/AOIS
	DREX/EL	Drysdale	DRAOIZ/DAIL
Drechslera	DRERB/LER/RA	Drysol	DRAOI/SOL
	DRERB/LE/RA	dual	DAOUL
drench	DREFRPBLG	dualism	DAOUL/IFM
	DREN/-FP	dualist	DAOUL/*IS
drepanidium	DREP/NID/YUM	dualistic	DAOUL/*IS/IK
drepanocyte	DREP/NO/SAO*IT	Duane	DWAIN
drepanocytemia	DREP/NO/SAOI/TAOEM/YA	duazomycin	DAOU/A*Z/MAOI/SIN
drepanocythemia	DREP/NO/SAOI/THAOEM/YA		DAOU/AZ/MAOI/SIN
drepanocytic	DREP/NO/SIT/IK	Dubini	DAOU/BAOE/NAOE
drepanocytosis	DREP/NO/SAOI/TOE/SIS	Dubois	DAOUB/WA
Dresbach	DRES/BAK		DAOUB/WAU
	DRES/BAUK		DAOU/BOIS
dresser	DRESZ/ER	duboisine	DAOU/BOI/SAOEN
dressing	DRESZ/-G	Dubos	DAOU/BOS
Dressler	DRES/LER		DAOU/BOES
	DRESZ/LER	Duboscq	DAOU/BOS/-K
Drew-Smythe	DRAO*U/SM*IT	Duchenne	DAOU/SHEN
	DRAO*U/SMAO*IT	Duckworth	DUK/WO*RT
	DRAO*U/H-F/SM*IT	Ducrey	DAOU/KRAI
	DRAO*U/H-F/SMAO*IT	duct	DUKT
dribble	DRIB/-L	ductal	DUK/TAL
drift	DRIFT	ductile	DUK/TAOIL
drifting	DRIFT/-G		DUK/TIL
drill	DRIL	duction	D*UBGS
drinidene	DRAOIN/DAOEN	ductless	DUKT/LES
drink	DR*ING	ductular	DUKT/LAR
	DRIN/-K	ductule	DUK/TAOUL
drip	DRIP		DUKT/YAOUL
Dristan	DRIS/TAN	ductuli	DUKT/LAOI
Drithocreme	DR*IT/KRAO*EM		DUK/TAOU/LAOI
	DR*IT/KRAOEM	ductulus	DUKT/LUS
Dritho-Scalp	DR*IT/SKAL/-P		DUK/TAOU/LUS
drive	DRAOIV	ductus	DUK/TUS
Drixoral	DRIX/ORL	Duddell	DUD/EL
	DRIK/SORL	Duffy	DUF/FI
Drize	DRIZ	Dugas	DAOU/GA
	DRAOIZ		DAOU/GAS
drobuline	DROEB/LAOEN	Duhot	DAOU/HOE
	DROE/BAOU/LAOEN	Duhring	DAOUR/-G
drocarbil	DROE/KAR/BIL		DAOU/RING
drocinonide	DROE/SIN/NAOID	Duhrssen	DAOER/SEN
drocode	DROE/KOED		DUR/SEN
dromedary	DROM/DAIR	Dujarier	DAOU/JAR/YAI
dromic	DROEM/IK	Duke	K-P/DAOUK
	DROM/IK	Dukes	DAOUKS
dromo-	DROM	Dulbecco	DAOUL/BEK/KOE
	DROEM		DUL/BEK/KOE
	DROE/MO	dulcin	DUL/SIN
dromograph	DROM/GRAF	dulcis	DUL/SIS
dromomania	DROM/MAIN/YA	dulcite	DUL/SAOIT
dromostanolone	DROEM/STAN/LOEN	dulcitol	DULS/TOL
	DROE/MOS/TAN/LOEN		DUL/SAOI/TOL
dromotropic	DROEM/TROP/IK	Dulcolax	DUL/KO/LAX
	DROM/TROP/IK	dulcose	DUL/KOES
dromotropism	DROE/MOT/RO/PIFM	dull	DUL
dronabinol	DROE/NAB/NOL	dullness	DUL/*NS

©1992 *StenEd*® **Medical Dictionary**

dulse	DULS	duplitized	DAOUP/LI/TAOIZ/-D
dumas	DAOU/MAS		DAOU/PLI/TAOIZ/-D
dumb	DUM	dupp	DUP
dumbbell	DUM/BEL	Dupre	DAOU/PRAI
dumbness	DUM/*NS	Dupuy	DAOUP/WAOE
dummy	DUM/M*I	Dupuytren	DAOUP/WAOE/TREN
Dumontpallier	DAOU/MON/PAL/YAI		DAOU/POI/TREN
	DAOU/MONT/PAL/YAI	dura	DAOU/RA
dumping	DUFRP/-G		DAOUR/RA
Dunbar	DUN/BAR	Durabolin	DAOU/RAB/LIN
Duncan	DUN/KAN	Dura-Gest	DAOUR/J*ES
Dunfermline	DUN/FERM/LIN	dural	DAOURL
Dunham	DUN/HAM	dura mater	DAOUR/MAI/TER
Dunn	D*UN		DAOU/RA/MAI/TER
	(not DUN; see dun)		DAOUR/RA/MAI/TER
DuoCet	DAOU/SET		DAOU/RA/MAT/ER
	DAOU/WO/SET		DAOUR/RA/MAT/ER
duocrinin	DAOU/KRIN/NIN	duramatral	DAOUR/MAI/TRAL
duoden(o)-	DAOU/DAOEN	Duramorph	DAOUR/MOR/-F
	DAOU/DAOE/N(O)	Duran	DAOU/RAN
	DWOD/N(O)	Duran-Reynals	DAOU/RAN/H-F/RAI/NALS
	DAOU/DEN	Durand	DAOU/RAND
	DAOU/DE/N(O)	Duranest	DAOUR/N*ES
duodena	DAOU/DAOE/NA	durapatite	DUR/AP/TAOIT
	DWOD/NA	Duraphyl	DAOUR/FIL
duodenal	DAOU/DAOENL	duraplasty	DAOUR/PLAS/TI
	DWOD/NAL	Duraquin	DAOUR/KWIN
duodenale	DWOD/NAI/LAOE	Dura-Tap	DAOUR/TAP
	DAOU/DAOE/NAI/LAOE	Dura-Tap/PD	DAOUR/TAP/P-RBGS/D*RBGS
duodenales	DWOD/NAI/LAOEZ	duration	DAOU/RAIGS
	DAOU/DAOE/NAI/LAOEZ	Dura-Vent	DAOUR/VENT
duodenalis	DWOD/NAI/LIS	Dura-Vent/A	DAOUR/VENT/ARBGS
	DAOU/DAOE/NAI/LIS	Dura-Vent/DA	DAOUR/VENT/D-RBGS/A*RBGS
duodenectomy	DAOU/DEN/EKT/M*I	Durck	DURK
	DAOU/DE/NEKT/M*I	Duret	DAOU/RAI
	DWOD/NEKT/M*I		DAOU/RET
duodeni	DAOU/DAOE/NAOI	Durham	DUR/HAM
	DWOD/NAOI	Duricef	DAOUR/SEF
duodenitis	DWOD/NAOITS		DUR/SEF
	DAOU/DAOE/NAOITS	duroarachnitis	DAOUR/AR/AK/NAOITS
duodenocholangeitis	DAOU/DAOEN/KOE/LAN/JAOITS		DAOU/RO/AR/AK/NAOITS
duodenocholecystostomy	DAOU/DAOEN/KOEL/SIS/TO*S/	Duroziez	DAOU/ROEZ/YEZ
	M*I		DAOU/ROEZ/YAOEZ
duodenocholedochotomy	DAOU/DAOEN/KLED/KOT/M*I	durum	DAOUR/UM
duodenocolic	DAOU/DAOEN/KOL/IK		DAOU/RUM
duodenocystostomy	DAOU/DAOEN/SIS/TO*S/M*I		(not DAOURM; see do you
duodenoduodenostomy	DAOU/DAOEN/DAOU/DAOE/		remember)
	NO*S/M*I	dust	D*US
	DAOU/DAOEN/DAOU/DEN/O*S/	Dutemps	DAOU/TAUM
	M*I		DAOU/TEM
duodenoenterostomy	DAOU/DAOEN/SPWRO*S/M*I	Dutton	DUT/TON
	DAOU/DAOEN/SPWER/RO*S/M*I	Duttonella	DUT/NEL/LA
duodenogram	DWOD/NO/GRAM	duttonii	DUT/TON/YAOI
duodenohepatic	DWOD/NO/HE/PAT/IK		DUT/TOEN/YAOI
	DAOU/DAOEN/HE/PAT/IK	Duval	DAOU/VAUL
duodenoileostomy	DAOU/DAOEN/*IL/YO*S/M*I		DU/VAL
duodenojejunostomy	DAOU/DAOEN/JEJ/NO*S/M*I		(not DAOU/VAL; due value)
duodenolysis	DAOU/DEN/OL/SIS	Duverney	DAOU/VER/NAI
	DAOU/DE/NOL/SIS		DAOU/VER/NAOE
	DWOD/NOL/SIS	dwarf	DWAR/-F
duodenopancreatectomy	DAOU/DAOEN/PAN/KRA/TEKT/	dwarfism	DWAR/FIFM
	M*I	dy-	DAOI
duodenopyloric	DAOU/DAOEN/PAOI/LOR/IK		DI (except dyad)
	DWOD/NO/PAOI/LOR/IK	dyad	DAOI/AD
duodenorrhaphy	DAOU/DEN/OR/FI		D*I/AD
	DAOU/DE/NOR/FI		(not DI/AD; see diad)
	DWOD/NOR/FI	dyaster	DAOI/AS/TER
duodenoscope	DAOU/DAOEN/SKOEP		DAOI/A*S/ER
duodenoscopy	DWOD/NOS/KPI	Dyazide	DAOI/ZAOID
	DAOU/DEN/OS/KPI	Dycill	DAOI/SIL
	DAOU/DE/NOS/KPI	Dyclone	DAOI/KLOEN
duodenostomy	DAOU/DEN/O*S/M*I	dyclonine	DAOI/KLOE/NAOEN
	DAOU/DE/NO*S/M*I	dydrogesterone	DAOI/DRO/J*ES/ROEN
	DWOD/NO*S/M*I	dye	DAO*I
duodenotomy	DWOD/NOT/M*I		(not DAOI; see die)
	DAOU/DEN/OT/M*I	-dymus	(o)D/MUS
	DAOU/DE/NOT/M*I	dynam(o)-	DAOIN/M(O)
duodenum	DAOU/DAOEN/UM		DAOI/NAM
	DWOD/NUM	dynamia	DAOI/NAIM/YA
Duofilm	DAOU/FIL/-M	dynamic	DAOI/NAM/IK
Duo-Medihaler	DAOU/MED/HAIL/ER	dynamogenesis	DAOIN/MO/JEN/SIS
duoparental	DAOU/PREN/TAL	dynamogenic	DAOIN/MO/JEN/IK
Duoplant	DAOU/PLANT	dynamogeny	DAOI/NAM/MOJ/N*I
duovirus	DAOU/VAOI/RUS	dynamograph	DAOI/NAM/GRAF
Duplay	DAOU/PLAI	dynamometer	DAOIN/MOM/TER
duplication	DAOUP/KAIGS	dynamometry	DAOIN/MOM/TRI
	DAOUP/LI/KAIGS	dynamoneure	DAOI/NAM/NAOUR
	DAOU/PLI/KAIGS	dynamopathic	DAOI/NAM/PA*T/IK
duplicitas	DAOU/PLIS/TAS		

dynamophore	DAOI/NAM/FOER	dysenteriae	DIS/SPWAOER/YAE
dynamoscope	DAOI/NAM/SKOEP		DIS/SPWER/YAE
dynamoscopy	DAOIN/MOS/KPI	dysenteric	DIS/SPWER/IK
Dynapen	DAOIN/PEN	dysenteriform	DIS/SPWER/FORM
dynatherm	DAOIN/THERM	dysentery	DIS/SPWER/RI
dyne	DAO*IN		DIS/SPWAIR
	(not DAOIN; see dine)	dysequilibrium	DIS/E/KWI/LIB/RUM
dynein	DAOIN/AOEN	dyserethesia	DIS/*ER/THAOEZ/YA
	DAOIN/YIN		DIS/ER/THAOEZ/YA
-dynia	DIN/YA	dyserethism	DIS/*ER/THIFM
dyphylline	DAOI/FLIN		DIS/ER/THIFM
	DAOI/FIL/LIN	dysergia	DIS/ER/JA
Dyrenium	DAOI/REN/YUM	dysesthesia	DIS/ES/THAOEZ/YA
dys-	DIS	dysesthetic	DIS/ES/THET/IK
dysacousia	DIS/KAOUZ/YA	dysfibrinogenemia	DIS/FAOI/BRIN/JEN/AOEM/YA
	DIS/AI/KAOUZ/YA		DIS/FAOI/BRIN/JE/NAOEM/YA
dysacusis	DIS/KAOU/SIS	dysfunction	DIS/FUNGS
	DIS/AI/KAOU/SIS	dysgalactia	DIS/GLAK/SHA
dysadaptation	DIS/AD/AP/TAIGS	dysgammaglobulinemia	DIS/GAM/GLOB/LI/NAOEM/YA
dysadrenalism	DIS/DRAOENL/IFM		DIS/GAM/GLOB/LIN/AOEM/YA
	DIS/AD/RAOENL/IFM	dysgenesia	DIS/JE/NAOEZ/YA
	DIS/AI/DRAOENL/IFM	dysgenesis	DIS/JEN/SIS
dysadrenia	DIS/DRAOEN/YA	dysgenic	DIS/JEN/IK
	DIS/AD/RAOEN/YA	dysgenics	DIS/JEN/IK/-S
	DIS/AI/DRAOEN/YA	dysgenitalism	DIS/JEN/TAL/IFM
dysallilognathia	DIS/AL/LO/NA*IT/YA	dysgenopathy	DIS/JEN/OP/TH*I
dysanagnosia	DIS/AN/AG/NOEZ/YA	dysgerminoma	DIS/JERM/NOE/MA
dysantigraphia	DIS/A*ENT/GRAF/YA	dysgeusia	DIS/GAOUS/YA
	DIS/A*ENT/GRAIF/YA		DIS/GAOUZ/YA
dysaphia	DIS/AIF/YA	dysglandular	DIS/GLAND/LAR
dysaphic	DIS/AIF/IK	dysglobulinemia	DIS/GLOB/LI/NAOEM/YA
dysaptation	DIS/AP/TAIGS		DIS/GLOB/LIN/AOEM/YA
dysarteriotony	DIS/AR/TAOER/YOT/N*I	dysglycemia	DIS/GLAOI/SAOEM/YA
dysarthria	DIS/AR/THRA	dysgnathia	DIS/NA*T/YA
	DIS/AR/THRAOE/YA		DIS/NA*IT/YA
dysarthric	DIS/AR/THRIK	dysgnathic	DIS/NA*T/IK
dysarthrosis	DIS/AR/THROE/SIS	dysgnosia	DIS/NOEZ/YA
dysautonomia	DIS/AUT/NOEM/YA	dysgonesis	DIS/GOE/NAOE/SIS
dysbarism	DIS/BAR/IFM	dysgonic	DIS/GON/IK
dysbasia	DIS/BAIZ/YA	dysgrammatism	DIS/GRAM/TIFM
dysbetalipoproteinemia	DIS/BAIT/LIP/PROET/NAOEM/YA	dysgraphia	DIS/GRAF/YA
	DIS/BAIT/LIP/PRO/TAOEN/AOEM/		DIS/GRAIF/YA
	YA	dysharmonica	DIS/HAR/MON/KA
dysbolism	DIS/BO/LIFM	dyshematopoiesis	DIS/HEM/TO/POI/SIS
	DIS/BOE/LIFM		DIS/HAOEM/TO/POI/SIS
dysbulia	DIS/BAOUL/YA	dyshematopoietic	DIS/HEM/TO/POIT/IK
dysbulic	DIS/BAOUL/IK		DIS/HAOEM/TO/POIT/IK
dyscalculia	DIS/KAL/KAOUL/YA	dyshemopoiesis	DIS/HAOEM/POI/SIS
dyscephalia	DIS/SFAIL/YA	dyshemopoietic	DIS/HAOEM/POIT/IK
dyscephaly	DIS/SEF/LI	dyshepatia	DIS/HE/PAI/SHA
dyscheiral	DIS/KAOIRL	dyshesion	DIS/HAOEGS
dyscheiria	DIS/KAOIR/YA	dyshidria	DIS/HID/RAOE/YA
dyschezia	DIS/KAOEZ/YA	dyshidrosis	DIS/HID/ROE/SIS
dyschiasia	DIS/KAOI/AIZ/YA		DIS/DROE/SIS
dyscholia	DIS/KOEL/YA	dyshormonal	DIS/HOR/MOENL
dyschondrogenesis	DIS/KON/DRO/JEN/SIS	dyshormonic	DIS/HOR/MON/IK
dyschondroplasia	DIS/KON/DRO/PLAIZ/YA	dyshormonism	DIS/HOR/MOEN/IFM
dyschondrosteosis	DIS/KON/DRO*S/YOE/SIS		DIS/HORM/NIFM
dyschroa	DIS/KROE/WA	dysidria	DIS/ID/RAOE/YA
dyschroia	DIS/KROI/YA	dysidrosis	DIS/ID/RO/SIS
dyschromasia	DIS/KROE/MAIZ/YA		DIS/ID/ROE/SIS
dyschromatopsia	DIS/KROEM/TOPS/YA	dysimmunity	DIS/IM/MAOUN/TI
dyschromatosis	DIS/KROEM/TOE/SIS	dyskaryosis	DIS/KAR/YOE/SIS
dyschromia	DIS/KROEM/YA	dyskaryotic	DIS/KAR/YOT/IK
dyschylia	DIS/KAOIL/YA	dyskeratoma	DIS/KER/TOE/MA
dyscinesia	DIS/SI/NAOEZ/YA	dyskeratosis	DIS/KER/TOE/SIS
dyscoimesis	DIS/KOI/MAOE/SIS	dyskeratotic	DIS/KER/TOT/IK
dyscontrol	DIS/KROL	dyskinesia	DIS/KI/NAOEZ/YA
	DIS/KON/TROL	dyskinetic	DIS/KI/NET/IK
dyscoria	DIS/KOER/YA	dyslalia	DIS/LAIL/YA
dyscorticism	DIS/KORT/SIFM	dyslexia	DIS/LEX/YA
dyscrasia	DIS/KRAIZ/YA	dyslexic	DIS/LEX/IK
dyscrasic	DIS/KRAIS/IK	dyslipidoses	DIS/LIP/DOE/SAOEZ
dyscratic	DIS/KRAT/IK	dyslipidosis	DIS/LIP/DOE/SIS
-dyscrinia	DIS/KRIN/YA	dyslipoproteinemia	DIS/LIP/PROET/AOEM/YA
dysdiadochocinesia	DIS/DI/AD/KO/SI/NAOEZ/YA	dyslochia	DIS/LOEK/YA
dysdiadochocinetic	DIS/DI/AD/KO/SI/NET/IK	dyslogia	DIS/LOE/JA
dysdiadochokinesia	DIS/DI/AD/KO/KI/NAOEZ/YA	dysmasesis	DIS/MA/SAOE/SIS
dysdiadochokinetic	DIS/DI/AD/KO/KI/NET/IK	dysmature	DIS/MA/KHUR
dysdipsia	DIS/DIPS/YA	dysmaturity	DIS/MA/KHUR/TI
dysecoia	DIS/KOI/YA	dysmegalopsia	DIS/MEG/LOPS/YA
dysembryoma	DIS/EM/BROE/MA	dysmelia	DIS/MAOEL/YA
dysembryoplasia	DIS/EM/BRO/PLAIZ/YA	dysmenorrhea	DIS/MEN/RAOE/YA
dysemia	DIS/AOEM/YA	dysmenorrhoeica	DIS/MEN/RAOE/KA
dysencephalia splanchnocystica		dysmetabolism	DIS/ME/TAB/LIFM
	DIS/EN/SFAIL/YA/SPLANG/NO/	dysmetria	DIS/MAOE/TRAOE/YA
	S*IS/KA		DIS/MAOE/TRA
dyseneia	DIS/E/NAOE/YA	dysmetropsia	DIS/ME/TROPS/YA
	(not DIS/NAOE/YA; see dyspnea)	dysmimia	DIS/MIM/YA

©1992 *StenEd*® Medical Dictionary

dysmnesia	DIS/NAOEZ/YA	dysstasia	DIS/STAIS/YA
dysmnesic	DIS/NAOEZ/IK		DIS/STAIZ/YA
dysmorphia	DIS/MOR/FA	dysstatic	DIS/STAT/IK
	DIS/MOR/FAOE/YA	dyssyllabia	DIS/SLAIB/YA
dysmorphic	DIS/MOR/FIK		DIS/SIL/LAIB/YA
dysmorphism	DIS/MOR/FIFM	dyssymbolia	DIS/SIM/BOEL/YA
dysmorphogenesis	DIS/MOR/FO/JEN/SIS	dyssymboly	DIS/SIM/BO/LI
dysmorphology	DIS/MOR/FOLG	dyssynergia	DIS/SIN/ER/JA
dysmorphophobia	DIS/MOR/FO/FOEB/YA		DIS/NER/JA
dysmorphopsia	DIS/MOR/FOPS/YA	dyssystole	DIS/S*IS/LAOE
dysmorphosis	DIS/MOR/FOE/SIS	dystaxia	DIS/TAX/YA
dysmyelination	DIS/MAOI/LI/NAIGS	dystectia	DIS/TEK/SHA
dysmyotonia	DIS/MAOI/TOEN/YA	dysteleology	DIS/TAOEL/YOLG
dysnomia	DIS/NOEM/YA	dystelephalangy	DIS/TEL/FLAN/JI
dysnystaxis	DIS/NIS/TAK/SIS	dysthymia	DIS/THAOIM/YA
dysodontiasis	DIS/O/DON/TAOI/SIS	dysthymic	DIS/THAOIM/IK
dysontogenesis	DIS/ONT/JEN/SIS	dysthyreosis	DIS/THAOIR/YOE/SIS
dysontogenetic	DIS/ONT/JE/NET/IK	dysthyroid	DIS/THAOI/ROID
dysopia	DIS/OEP/YA	dysthyroidal	DIS/THAOI/ROI/DAL
dysopsia	DIS/OPS/YA	dysthyroidea	DIS/THAOI/ROID/YA
dysorexia	DIS/REX/YA	dysthyroidism	DIS/THAOI/ROI/DIFM
dysorganoplasia	DIS/ORG/NO/PLAIZ/YA	dystimbria	DIS/TIM/BRA
dysoria	DIS/OER/YA		DIS/TIM/BRAOE/YA
dysoric	DIS/OER/IK	dystithia	DIS/T*IT/YA
dysosmia	DIS/OZ/MAOE/YA	dystocia	DIS/TOE/SHA
	DIS/OZ/MA		DIS/TOES/YA
dysosteogenesis	DIS/O*S/YO/JEN/SIS	dystonia	DIS/TOEN/YA
dysostosis	DIS/OS/TOE/SIS	dystonic	DIS/TON/IK
dysoxidative	DIS/OX/DAIT/IV	dystopia	DIS/TOEP/YA
dysoxidizable	DIS/OX/DAOIZ/-BL	dystopic	DIS/TOP/IK
dyspallia	DIS/PAL/YA	dystopy	DIS/TO/PI
dyspancreatism	DIS/PAN/KRA/TIFM	dystrophia	DIS/TROEF/YA
dyspareunia	DIS/PA/RAOUN/YA	dystrophic	DIS/TROFK
dyspepsia	DIS/PEPS/YA	dystrophica	DIS/TROF/KA
dyspeptic	DIS/PEPT/IK	dystrophodextrin	DIS/TROF/DEX/TRIN
dyspeptica	DIS/PEPT/KA	dystrophoneurosis	DIS/TROF/NAOU/ROE/SIS
dysperistalsis	DIS/P*ER/STAL/SIS	dystrophy	DIS/TRO/FI
dysphagia	DIS/FAI/JA	dystropic	DIS/TROE/PIK
dysphagy	DIS/FA/JI		DIS/TROP/IK
dysphagocytosis	DIS/FAG/SAOI/TOE/SIS	dystropy	DIS/TRO/PI
dysphasia	DIS/FAIZ/YA	dystrypsia	DIS/TRIPS/YA
dysphemia	DIS/FAOEM/YA	dysuresia	DIS/YAOU/RAOES/YA
dysphonia	DIS/FOEN/YA		DIS/YAOU/RAOEZ/YA
dysphonic	DIS/FON/IK	dysuria	DIS/YAOUR/YA
dysphoretic	DIS/FRET/IK	dysuriac	DIS/YAOUR/YAK
dysphoria	DIS/FOER/YA	dysuric	DIS/YAOURK
dysphoriant	DIS/FOER/YANT		DIS/YAOUR/IK
dysphoric	DIS/FOER/IK	dysury	DIS/YAOUR/RI
dysphrasia	DIS/FRAIZ/YA		DIS/YAOU/RI
dysphrenia	DIS/FRAOEN/YA	dysversion	DIS/VERGS
dysphylaxia	DIS/FLAX/YA	dysvitaminosis	DIS/VAOIT/MI/NOE/SIS
dyspigmentation	DIS/PIG/MEN/TAIGS	dyszoospermia	DIS/ZOE/SPERM/YA
dyspinealism	DIS/PIN/YAL/IFM	Dytuss	DAOI/TUSZ
dyspituitarism	DIS/PI/TAOU/TRIFM		
dysplasia	DIS/PLAIZ/YA		
dysplastic	DIS/PLA*S/IK		
dyspnea	DIS/NA		
	DIS/NAOE/YA		
	DIS/-P/NAOE/YA		
dyspneic	DIS/NIK		
	DIS/NAOE/IK		
	DIS/-P/NIK		
	DIS/-P/NAOE/IK		
dyspoiesis	DIS/POI/SIS		
dysponderal	DIS/POND/RAL		
	DIS/PON/DRAL		
dysponesis	DIS/PO/NAOE/SIS		
	DIS/POE/NAOE/SIS		
dyspragia	DIS/PRAI/JA		
	DIS/PRAIJ/YA		
dyspraxia	DIS/PRAX/YA		
dysprosium	DIS/PROES/YUM		
dysprosody	DIS/PROS/DI		
dysproteinemia	DIS/PROET/NAOEM/YA		
	DIS/PRO/TAOEN/AOEM/YA		
dysproteinemic	DIS/PROET/NAOEM/IK		
	DIS/PRO/TAOEN/AOEM/IK		
dysraphia	DIS/RAF/YA		
	DIS/RAIF/YA		
dysraphism	DIS/RA/FIFM		
dysrhythmia	DIS/R*IT/MA		
	DIS/R*IT/MAOE/YA		
dyssebacea	DIS/SE/BAI/SHA		
	DIS/SE/BAIRB/YA		
dyssocial	DIS/SOERBL		
dyssomnia	DIS/SOM/NA		
	DIS/SOM/NAOE/YA		
dysspermia	DIS/SPERM/YA		
dysspondylism	DIS/SPOND/LIFM		

E

e-	E
Eagle	K-P/AOEG/-L
Eales	AOELS
ear	AOER
earache	AOER/A*IK
eardrum	AOER/DRUM
early	*ER/LI
ear-minded	AOER/MAOIND/-D
earth	*ERT
earthy	*ER/TH*I
	*ERT/TH*I
earwax	AOER/WAX
Eaton	E/TON
Ebbinghaus	EB/-G/HAUS
	EB/-G/HOUS
Eberth	AI/BERT
	E/BERT
Ebner	EB/NER
ebonation	AOEB/NAIGS
	E/BOE/NAIGS
ebranlement	AI/BRAN/LA/MAU
	AI/BRAN/LA/MON
	E/BRAN/LA/MAU
	E/BRAN/LA/MON
ebrietas	E/BRAOI/TAS
ebriety	E/BRAOI/TI
Ebstein	EB/STAOIN
	EB/STAOEN
ebull-	EB/L-
	EB/YAOU/L-
	EB/YU/L-
ebullism	EB/LIFM
ebullition	EB/LIGS
ebur	E/BUR
eburnation	E/BUR/NAIGS
eburneous	E/BURN/YOUS
eburnitis	E/BUR/NAOITS
ec-	EK
ecarteur	AI/KAR/TER
	E/KAR/TER
ecaudate	E/KAU/DAIT
ecbolic	EK/BOL/IK
ecboline	EK/BO/LAOEN
eccentr(o)-	EK/SEN/TR(O)
	KPEN/TR(O)
eccentric	EK/SEN/TRIK
	KPEN/TRIK
eccentrochondroplasia	EK/SEN/TRO/KON/DRO/PLAIZ/YA
	KPEN/TRO/KON/DRO/PLAIZ/YA
eccentro-osteochondrodysplasia	
	EK/SEN/TRO/O*S/YO/KON/DRO/ DIS/PLAIZ/YA
	KPEN/TRO/O*S/YO/KON/DRO/ DIS/PLAIZ/YA
eccentropiesis	EK/SEN/TRO/PAOI/E/SIS
	KPEN/TRO/PAOI/E/SIS
eccephalosis	EK/SEF/LOE/SIS
ecchondroma	EK/KON/DROE/MA
ecchondrosis	EK/KON/DROE/SIS
ecchondrotome	EK/KON/DRO/TOEM
ecchordosis physaliphora	EK/KHOR/DOE/SIS/FIS/LIF/RA
ecchymoma	EK/MOE/MA
ecchymose	EK/MOES
ecchymosed	EK/MOES/-D
ecchymoses	EK/MOE/SAOEZ
ecchymosis	EK/MOE/SIS
ecchymotic	EK/MOT/IK
eccoprotic	EK/PROT/IK
	EK/KO/PROT/IK
eccrine	EK/RIN
eccrinology	EK/RI/NOLG
eccrisiology	EK/KRIS/YOLG
eccrisis	EK/RI/SIS
eccritic	E/KRIT/IK
	EK/KRIT/IK
eccyesis	EK/SAOI/E/SIS
ecdemic	EK/DEM/IK
ecdovirus	EK/DO/VAOI/RUS
ecdysiasm	EK/DIZ/YAFM
ecdysis	EKD/SIS
	EK/DI/SIS
ecgonine	EK/GO/NAOEN
	EK/GO/NIN
echeosis	EK/YOE/SIS

echidninus	EK/ID/NAOI/NUS
	E/KID/NAOI/NUS
Echidnophaga gallinacea	EK/ID/NOF/GA/GAL/NAIS/YA
	E/KID/NOF/GA/GAL/NAIS/YA
echinate	EK/NAIT
echino-	E/KAOIN
	E/KAOI/NO
Echinochasmus	E/KAOIN/KAZ/MUS
echinococciasis	E/KAOIN/KOK/KAOI/SIS
echinococcosis	E/KAOIN/KOK/KOE/SIS
echinococcotomy	E/KAOIN/KOK/KOT/M*I
echinococcus	E/KAOIN/KOK/KUS
Echinococcus	K-P/E/KAOIN/KOK/KUS
echinocyte	E/KAOIN/SAO*IT
echinoderm	E/KAOIN/DERM
Echinodermata	E/KAOIN/DERM/TA
Echinolaelaps	E/KAOIN/LAOE/LAPS
echinophthalmia	E/KIN/OF/THAL/MA
	E/KIN/OF/THAL/MAOE/YA
	E/KAOIN/OF/THAL/MA
	E/KAOIN/OF/THAL/MAOE/YA
Echinorhynchus	E/KAOIN/RIN/KUS
echinosis	EK/NOE/SIS
Echinostoma	E/KAOIN/STOE/MA
	EK/NO*S/MA
echinostomiasis	E/KAOIN/STOE/MAOI/SIS
	EK/NO/STOE/MAOI/SIS
echinulate	E/KIN/LAIT
	E/KIN/YAOU/LAIT
	E/KIN/YU/LAIT
Echis	E/KIS
	EK/KIS
echo	EK/KOE
echo-	EK
	EK/KO
echoacousia	EK/AI/KAOUZ/YA
	EK/KAOUZ/YA
echoaortography	EK/AI/YOR/TOG/FI
	EK/AI/OR/TOG/FI
echocardiogram	EK/KARD/YO/GRAM
echocardiography	EK/KARD/YOG/FI
echoencephalogram	EK/EN/SEF/LO/GRAM
echoencephalograph	EK/EN/SEF/LO/GRAF
echoencephalography	EK/EN/SEF/LOG/FI
echo-free	EK/KOE/H-F/FRAOE
echogenic	EK/JEN/IK
echogram	EK/GRAM
echograph	EK/GRAF
echographer	E/KOG/FER
echographia	EK/GRAF/YA
echography	E/KOG/FI
echoica	E/KOI/KA
echokinesia	EK/KI/NAOEZ/YA
echokinesis	EK/KI/NAOE/SIS
echolalia	EK/LAIL/YA
echolalus	EK/LAI/LUS
echolocation	EK/LOE/KAIGS
echolucent	EK/LAOUS/ENT
echomatism	E/KOEM/TIFM
echomimia	EK/MIM/YA
echomotism	EK/MOE/TIFM
echopathy	E/KOP/TH*I
echophonia	EK/FOEN/YA
echophonocardiography	EK/FOEN/KARD/YOG/FI
echophony	E/KOF/N*I
echophotony	EK/FOT/N*I
echophrasia	EK/FRAIZ/YA
echopraxia	EK/PRAX/YA
echopraxis	EK/PRAK/SIS
echo-ranging	EK/RAING/-G
	EK/RAIN/-J/-G
echoscope	EK/SKOEP
echothiophate	EK/THAOI/FAIT
echovirus	EK/VAOI/RUS
Eck's	EK/AOES
Ecker	EK/ER
eclabium	EK/LAIB/YUM
eclampsia	E/KLAFRPS/YA
	EK/LAFRPS/YA
eclampsism	E/KLAFRP/SIFM
	E/KLAM/-P/SIFM
eclamptic	E/KLAFRP/TIK
	EK/LAFRP/TIK
eclamptism	E/KLAFRP/TIFM
	EK/LAFRP/TIFM
eclamptogenic	E/KLAFRPT/JEN/IK
	EK/LAFRPT/JEN/IK
eclectic	E/KLEKT/IK
	EK/LEKT/IK

eclecticism	E/KLEKT/SIFM	ectocervical	EKT/SEFRB/KAL
	EK/LEKT/SIFM	ectocervix	EKT/SER/VIX
eclipse	E/KLIPS	ectochoroidea	EKT/KOE/ROID/YA
eclysis	EK/LI/SIS	ectocolon	EKT/KO/LON
ecmnesia	EK/NAOEZ/YA	ectocolostomy	EKT/KO/LO*S/M*I
ecmovirus	EK/MO/VAOI/RUS	ectocommensal	EKT/KMEN/SAL
eco-	E/KO	ectocondyle	EKT/KON/DAOIL
	AOEK	ectocornea	EKT/KORN/YA
	EK	ectocrine	EKT/KRIN
ecochleation	E/KOK/LAIGS	ectocuneiform	EKT/KAOU/NAOE/FORM
ecogenetic	E/KO/JE/NET/IK	ectocyst	EKT/S*IS
	AOEK/JE/NET/IK	ectocytic	EKT/SIT/IK
	EK/JE/NET/IK	ectoderm	EKT/DERM
ecoid	E/KOID	ectodermal	EKT/DER/MAL
E. coli	EFPLT/KO/LAOI	ectodermatosis	EKT/DERM/TOE/SIS
ecologist	E/KO*LGS	ectodermic	EKT/DERM/IK
ecology	E/KOLG	ectodermoidal	EKT/DER/MOI/DAL
ecomania	E/KO/MAIN/YA	ectodermosis	EKT/DER/MOE/SIS
	AOEK/MAIN/YA	ectoentad	EKT/SPWAD
econazole	E/KON/ZOEL		EKT/EN/TAD
Economo	E/KON/MOE	ectoental	EKT/SPWAL
economy	KMI		EKT/EN/TAL
	E/KON/M*I	ectoenzyme	EKT/EN/ZAOIM
ecoparasite	E/KO/PAR/SAOIT	ectoethmoid	EKT*ET/MOID
	AOEK/PAR/SAOIT	ectogenic	EKT/JEN/IK
ecophobia	E/KO/FOEB/YA	ectogenous	EK/TOJ/NOUS
	AOEK/FOEB/YA	ectoglia	EK/TOG/LA
ecospecies	E/KO/SPAOE/SHAOEZ		EK/TOG/LAOE/YA
	AOEK/SPAOE/SHAOEZ	ectoglobular	EKT/GLOB/LAR
ecostate	E/KOS/TAIT	ectogony	EK/TOG/N*I
ecosystem	E/KO/S-M	ectohormone	EKT/HOR/MOEN
	AOEK/S-M	ectolecithal	EKT/LES/THAL
	EK/S-M	ectolysis	EK/TOL/SIS
ecotaxis	E/KO/TAK/SIS	ectomeninx	EKT/MAOE/NINGS
	AOEK/TAK/SIS		EKT/MEN/INGS
	EK/TAK/SIS	ectomere	EKT/MAOER
ecotone	E/KO/TOEN	ectomerogony	EKT/ME/ROG/N*I
	AOEK/TOEN	ectomesenchyme	EKT/MES/EN/KAOIM
	EK/TOEN	ectomesoblast	EKT/MES/BLA*S
Ecotrin	EK/TRIN	-ectomize	EKT/MAOIZ
ecouteur	AI/KAOU/TER	ectomorph	EKT/MOR/-F
	E/KAOU/TER	ectomorphic	EKT/MOR/FIK
ecouvillon	AI/KAOUV/YON	ectomorphy	EKT/MOR/FI
	E/KAOUV/YON	-ectomy	EKT/M*I
ecouvillonage	AI/KAOUV/YO/NAJ	ectonuclear	EKT/NAOUK/LAR
	E/KAOUV/YO/NAJ	ectopagus	EK/TOP/GUS
ecphoria	EK/FOER/YA	ectoparasite	EKT/PAR/SAOIT
ecphorize	EK/FRAOIZ	ectoparasiticide	EKT/PAR/SIT/SAO*ID
	EK/FO/RAOIZ	ectoparasitism	EKT/PAR/SAOI/TIFM
	EK/FOE/RAOIZ	ectopectoralis	EKT/PEKT/RAI/LIS
ecphory	EK/FRI	ectoperitoneal	EKT/PERT/NAOEL
	EK/FO/RI	ectoperitonitis	EKT/PERT/NAOITS
	EK/FOE/RI	ectophyte	EKT/FAOIT
ecphylactic	EK/FLAKT/IK	ectopia	EK/TOEP/YA
ecphylaxis	EK/FLAK/SIS	ectopic	EK/TOP/IK
ecphyma	EK/FAOI/MA	ectopism	EKT/PIFM
ecsomatics	EK/SOE/MAT/IK/-S	ectoplacenta	EKT/PLA/SEN/TA
ecsovirus	EK/SO/VAOI/RUS	ectoplacental	EKT/PLA/SEN/TAL
ecstasy	EX/TA/SI	ectoplasm	EKT/PLAFM
	EK/STA/SI	ectoplasmatic	EKT/PLAZ/MAT/IK
ecstatic	EK/STAT/IK	ectoplasmic	EKT/PLAZ/MIK
	EX/TAT/IK	ectoplast	EKT/PLA*S
ect(o)-	EKT	ectoplastic	EKT/PLA*S/IK
	EK/T(O)	ectopotomy	EKT/POT/M*I
ectacolia	EKT/KOEL/YA	ectopterygoid	EKT/TER/GOID
	EK/TA/KOEL/YA	ectopy	EKT/PI
ectad	EK/TAD	ectoretina	EKT/RET/NA
ectal	EK/TAL	ectosarc	EKT/SARK
ectasia	EK/TAIZ/YA	ectoscopy	EK/TOS/KPI
ectasis	EKT/SIS	ectoskeleton	EKT/SKEL/TON
	EK/TA/SIS	ectosphere	EKT/SFAOER
ectasy	EKT/SI	ectosteal	EK/TO*S/YAL
	EK/TA/SI	ectostosis	EK/TOS/TOE/SIS
ectatic	EK/TAT/IK		EKT/STOE/SIS
ectental	EK/TEN/TAL	ectosuggestion	EKT/SUGS
ecterograph	EKT/RO/GRAF		EKT/SUG/JEGS
	EK/TER/GRAF	ectosymbiont	EKT/SIM/BONT
ectethmoid	EKT*ET/MOID		EKT/SIM/BAOE/ONT
ecthyma	EK/THAOI/MA		EKT/SIM/BAOE/YONT
ecthymatiform	EK/THAOI/MAT/FORM	ectothrix	EKT/THRIX
ecthymiform	EK/THAOIM/FORM	ectotoxin	EKT/TOK/SIN
ecthyreosis	EK/THAOIR/YOE/SIS	ectozoa	EKT/ZOE/WA
ectiris	EK/TAOI/RIS	ectozoal	EKT/ZOEL
ectantigen	EKT/A*ENT/JEN		EKT/ZOE/WAL
ectobiology	EKT/BAO*I/OLG	ectozoan	EKT/ZOE/WAN
ectoblast	EKT/BLA*S	ectozoon	EKT/ZAON
ectocardia	EKT/KARD/YA	ectr(o)-	EK/TR(O)
ectocardiac	EKT/KARD/YAK	ectrocheiry	EK/TRO/KAOI/RI
ectocardial	EKT/KARD/YAL	ectrodactylia	EK/TRO/DAK/TIL/YA

ectrodactylism	EK/TRO/DAKT/LIFM	effacement	E/FAIS/-MT
ectrodactyly	EK/TRO/DAKT/LI	effect	E/FEKT
ectrogenic	EK/TRO/JEN/IK		EFKT
ectrogeny	EK/TROJ/N*I	effectiveness	EFKT/IV/*NS
ectromelia	EK/TRO/MAOEL/YA		E/FEKT/IV/*NS
ectromelic	EK/TRO/MEL/IK		EFKT/IVNS
ectromelus	EK/TROM/LUS		E/FEKT/IVNS
ectrometacarpia	EK/TRO/MET/KARP/YA	effector	EFKT/TOR
ectrometatarsia	EK/TRO/MET/TARS/YA		E/FEK/TOR
ectrophalangia	EK/TRO/FLAN/JA	effeminate	E/FEM/NAT
ectropion	EK/TROEP/YON	effemination	E/FEM/NAIGS
ectropionize	EK/TROEP/YO/NAOIZ	efferent	EFRNT
ectropium	EK/TROEP/YUM		EF/FRENT
ectropody	EK/TROP/DI	efferentes	EFRN/TAOEZ
ectrosis	EK/TROE/SIS		EF/FREN/TAOEZ
ectrosyndactylia	EK/TRO/SIN/DAK/TIL/YA	efferential	EFRN/-RBL
ectrosyndactyly	EK/TRO/SIN/DAKT/LI		EF/FREN/-RBL
ectrotic	EK/TROT/IK	Effer-Syllium	EFR/SIL/YUM
ectylurea	EK/TIL/YAOU/RAOE/YA	effer-	EFR
ectype	EK/TAOIP		EF/FER
ectypia	EK/TAOIP/YA	effervesce	EFR/VES
	EK/TIP/YA	effervescent	EFR/VES/ENT
ecuresis	EK/YAOU/RAOE/SIS	effervescing	EFR/VES/-G
E-Cypionate	E/SIP/YO/NAIT	efficax	EF/KAX
	ERBGS/SIP/YO/NAIT	efficiency	FIRBT/SI
eczema	EX/MA		E/FIRB/EN/SI
	EK/ZE/MA	efficient	FIRBT
	KPAOE/MA		E/FIRBT
	EK/ZAOE/MA		E/FIRB/ENT
eczematization	KPEM/TI/ZAIGS	effleurage	EF/LAOU/RAJ
	EK/ZEM/TI/ZAIGS		EF/FLAOU/RAJ
eczematogenic	KPEM/TO/JEN/IK	effloresce	EF/LO/RES
	EK/ZEM/TO/JEN/IK		EF/FLO/RES
eczematoid	KPEM/TOID	efflorescence	EF/LO/RES/ENS
	EK/ZEM/TOID		EF/FLO/RES/ENS
eczematoides	KPEM/TOI/DAOEZ	efflorescent	EF/LO/RES/ENT
	EK/ZEM/TOI/DAOEZ		EF/FLO/RES/ENT
eczematous	KPEM/TOUS	effluve	E/FLAOUV
	EK/ZEM/TOUS		EF/LAOUV
edathamil	E/DA*T/MIL		EF/FLAOUV
Eddowes	ED/DOEZ	effluvia	E/FLAOUV/YA
Edebohls	ED/BOELZ		EF/FLAOUV/YA
	ED/BOELS	effluvium	E/FLAOUV/YUM
Edecrin	ED/KRIN		EF/FLAOUV/YUM
edema	E/DAOE/MA	effort	EFRT
edemagen	E/DAOEM/JEN	effraction	E/FRA*BGS
edematigenous	E/DEM/TIJ/NOUS		EF/FRA*BGS
edematization	E/DEM/TI/ZAIGS	effumability	E/FAOUM/-BLT
edematodes	E/DEM/TOE/DAOEZ		EF/FAOUM/-BLT
edematogenic	E/DEM/TO/JEN/IK	effuse	E/FAOUZ
edematosa	E/DEM/TOE/SA		E/FAOUS
edematous	E/DEM/TOUS		EF/FAOUZ
Edentata	E/DEN/TAI/TA		EF/FAOUS
edentate	E/DEN/TAIT	effusion	E/FAOUGS
edentia	E/DEN/SHA		EF/FAOUGS
edentulate	E/DENT/LAIT	eflornithine	E/FLORN/THAOEN
edentulous	E/DENT/LOUS	Efudex	EF/DEX
edestin	E/DES/TIN		EF/YAOU/DEX
edetate	ED/TAIT	egersimeter	E/GER/SIM/TER
edetic	E/DET/IK	egersis	E/GER/SIS
edge	EJ	egesta	E/JES/TA
edge-strength	EJ/H-F/STR*ENT	egestion	E/JEGS
Edinger	ED/IN/GER	egg	EG
	ED/-G/ER	egg cluster	EG/KL*US/ER
Edinger-Westphal	ED/IN/GER/H-F/V*ES/FAL	Eggleston	EG/-L/STON
	ED/IN/GER/H-F/V*ES/FAUL	egilops	AOEJ/LOPS
	ED/-G/ER/H-F/V*ES/FAL		E/JI/LOPS
	ED/-G/ER/H-F/V*ES/FAUL	eglandulous	E/GLAND/LOUS
edipism	ED/PIFM	ego	E/GOE
edisylate	E/DIS/LAIT	ego-	E/GO
Edlefsen	ED/LEF/SEN		AOEG
Edman	ED/MAN	ego-alien	E/GO/AIL/YEN
edrophonium	ED/RO/FOEN/YUM		AOEG/AIL/YEN
educable	EJ/KABL	egobronchophony	E/GO/BRON/KOF/N*I
	ED/KABL		AOEG/BRON/KOF/N*I
educt	E/DUKT	egocentric	E/GO/SEN/TRIK
eduction	E/D*UBGS		AOEG/SEN/TRIK
edulcorant	E/DUL/KO/RANT	egocentricity	E/GO/SEN/TRIS/TI
	E/DUL/KRANT		AOEG/SEN/TRIS/TI
edulcorate	E/DUL/KO/RAIT	ego-dystonic	E/GO/DIS/TON/IK
	E/DUL/KRAIT		AOEG/DIS/TON/IK
edulis	ED/LIS	egoism	E/GO/IFM
	ED/YAOU/LIS		AOEG/IFM
	ED/YU/LIS	egomania	E/GO/MAIN/YA
Edwards	ED/WARDZ		AOEG/MAIN/YA
Edwardsiella	ED/WARDZ/YEL/LA	egophonic	E/GO/FON/IK
EEG	ERBGS/*ERBGS/G*RBGS		AOEG/FON/IK
eff-	E/F-	egophony	E/GOF/N*I
	EF/F-	ego-syntonic	E/GO/SIN/TON/IK

	AOEG/SIN/TON/IK	elastogel	E/LA*S/JEL
egotism	E/GO/TIFM	elastoid	E/LAS/TOID
	AOEG/TIFM	elastoidin	E/LAS/TOI/DIN
egotropic	E/GO/TROP/IK	elastoidosis	E/LAS/TOI/DOE/SIS
	AOEG/TROP/IK	elastolysis	E/LAS/TOL/SIS
Egyptian	E/JIPGS	elastolytic	E/LA*S/LIT/IK
Ehlers	AI/LERZ	elastoma	E/LAS/TOE/MA
	AI/LERS	elastometer	E/LAS/TOM/TER
Ehrenritter	*ER/EN/RIT/ER	elastometry	E/LAS/TOM/TRI
Ehrlich	*ER/LIK	elastomucin	E/LA*S/MAOU/SIN
Ehrlichia	*ER/LIK/YA		E/LA*S/MAOU/KIN
Ehrlichieae	*ER/LIK/YAE	elastopathy	E/LAS/TOP/TH*I
ehrlichiosis	*ER/LIK/YOE/SIS	elastorrhexis	E/LA*S/REK/SIS
Eichhorst	AOIK/HO*RS	elastose	E/LAS/TOES
	IK/HO*RS	elastosis	E/LAS/TOE/SIS
Eichstedt	IK/STET	elastotic	E/LAS/TOT/IK
Eicken	AOI/KEN	elation	E/LAIGS
	AOIK/-N	Elavil	EL/VIL
eicosanoate	AOIK/KO/SA/NOE/AIT	elbow	EL/BOE
eicosanoic	AOIK/SA/NOIK	elbowed	EL/BOE/-D
	AOIK/SA/NOE/IK	Eldepryl	ELD/PRIL
eidetic	AOI/DET/IK		EL/DE/PRIL
eidogen	AOID/JEN	elder	ELD/ER
eidoptometry	AOI/DOP/TOM/TRI		EL/DER
Eijkman	AOIK/MAN	Eldercaps	ELD/ER/KAP/-S
	IK/MAN	Eldertonic	ELD/ER/TON/IK
Eikenella corrodens	AOIK/NEL/LA/KROE/DENZ	Eldopaque	ELD/PAIK
eikonometer	AOIK/NOM/TER		EL/DO/PAIK
eiloid	AOI/LOID	Eldoquin Forte	ELD/KWIN/FOR/TAI
Eimeria	AOI/MAOER/YA		EL/DO/KWIN/FOR/TAI
Einhorn	AOIN/HORN	eldrin	EL/DRIN
einstein	AOIN/STAOIN	elective	E/LEKT/IV
einsteinium	AOIN/STAOIN/YUM	electr(o)-	LEK/TR(O)
Einthoven	AOIN/TOE/VEN		E/LEK/TR(O)
	AOIN/TO/VEN	Electra	LEK/TRA
eisanthema	AOIS/A*NT/MA		E/LEK/TRA
	AOI/SA*NT/MA	electric	LEK/TRIK
Eisenmenger	AOI/SEN/MENG/ER	electroacupuncture	LEK/TRO/AK/PUNG/KHUR
	AOIS/EN/MENG/ER	electroaffinity	LEK/TRO/AI/FIN/TI
eisodic	AOI/SOD/IK	electroanalgesia	LEK/TRO/ANL/JAOEZ/YA
Eitelberg	AOIT/EL/BERG	electroanalysis	LEK/TRO/ANL/SIS
	AOI/TEL/BERG	electroanesthesia	LEK/TRO/ANS/THAOEZ/YA
ejacul-	E/JAK/L-	electroappendectomy	LEK/TRO/AP/EN/DEKT/M*I
	E/JAK/YAOU/L-	electroaugmentation	LEK/TRO/AUG/MEN/TAIGS
	E/JAK/YU/L-	electroaxonography	LEK/TRO/AX/NOG/FI
ejaculate	E/JAK/LAIT		LEK/TRO/AK/SON/OG/FI
ejaculatio	E/JAK/LAI/SHOE	electrobasograph	LEK/TRO/BAI/SO/GRAF
	E/JAK/LAIRB/YOE	electrobasography	LEK/TRO/BAI/SOG/FI
ejaculation	E/JAK/LAIGS	electrobiology	LEK/TRO/BAO*I/OLG
ejaculator	E/JAK/LAI/TOR	electrobioscopy	LEK/TRO/BAO*I/OS/KPI
ejaculatorius	E/JAK/LA/TOR/YUS	electrocardiogram	LEK/TRO/KARD/YO/GRAM
	E/JAK/TA/TOER/YUS	electrocardiograph	LEK/TRO/KARD/YO/GRAF
ejaculatory	E/JAK/LA/TOIR	electrocardiography	LEK/TRO/KARD/YOG/FI
ejaculum	E/JAK/LUM	electrocardiophonogram	LEK/TRO/KARD/YO/FOEN/GRAM
ejecta	E/JEK/TA	electrocardiophonograph	LEK/TRO/KARD/YO/FOEN/GRAF
ejection	E/J*EBGS	electrocardiophonography	LEK/TRO/KARD/YO/FOE/NOG/FI
ejector	E/JEK/TOR	electrocardioscopy	LEK/TRO/KARD/YOS/KPI
EKG	ERBGS/K*RBGS/G*RBGS	electrocatalysis	LEK/TRO/KA/TAL/SIS
ekiri	E/KAOI/RAOI	electrocauterization	LEK/TRO/KAUT/RI/ZAIGS
elaborate	E/LAB/RAT	electrocautery	LEK/TRO/KAUT/RI
	E/LAB/RAIT	electrocerebral	LEK/TRO/SER/BRAL
elaboration	E/LAB/RAIGS	electrochemical	LEK/TRO/KEM/KAL
elacin	EL/SIN	electrochemistry	LEK/TRO/KEM/STRI
elaidic	EL/LAI/ID/IK	electrocholecystectomy	LEK/TRO/KOEL/SIS/TEKT/M*I
	EL/YID/IK	electrocholecystocausis	LEK/TRO/KOEL/S*IS/KAU/SIS
elaiopathia	E/LAI/PA*T/YA	electrochromatography	LEK/TRO/KROEM/TOG/FI
elaiopathy	E/LAI/OP/TH*I	electrocision	LEK/TRO/SIGS
	E/LAI/YOP/TH*I	electrocoagulation	LEK/TRO/KO/AG/LAIGS
elaioplast	E/LAI/PLA*S	electrocochleogram	LEK/TRO/KOK/LO/GRAM
elantrine	EL/AN/TRAOEN	electrocochleograph	LEK/TRO/KOK/LO/GRAF
elapid	EL/PID	electrocochleographic	LEK/TRO/KOK/LO/GRAFK
Elapidae	E/LAP/DAE	electrocochleography	LEK/TRO/KOK/LOG/FI
Elase	E/LAIS	electrocontractility	LEK/TRO/KON/TRAK/TIL/TI
elasmobranch	E/LAS/MO/BRA*NG		LEK*/KR-T/TIL/TI
	E/LAS/MO/BRAN/-K	electroconvulsive	LEK/TRO/KON/VULS/IV
elassosis	EL/SOE/SIS	electrocorticogram	LEK/TRO/KORT/KO/GRAM
elast(o)-	E/LA*S	electrocorticography	LEK/TRO/KORT/KOG/FI
	E/LAS/T(O)	electrocryptectomy	LEK/TRO/KRIP/TEKT/M*I
elastance	E/LAS/TANS	electrocute	LEK/TRO/KAOUT
elastase	E/LAS/TAIS	electrocution	LEK/TRO/KAOUGS
elastic	E/LA*S/IK	electrocystography	LEK/TRO/SIS/TOG/FI
elastica	E/LA*S/KA	electrocystoscope	LEK/TRO/S*IS/SKOEP
elasticin	E/LA*S/SIN	electrode	LEK/TROED
elasticity	E/LAS/TIS/TI	electrodeposition	LEK/TRO/DEP/SIGS
elasticum	E/LA*S/KUM		LEK/TRO/DEPGS
elasticus	E/LA*S/KUS	electrodermal	LEK/TRO/DER/MAL
elastin	E/LAS/TIN	electrodermatome	LEK/TRO/DERM/TOEM
elastinase	E/LA*S/NAIS	electrodesiccation	LEK/TRO/DES/KAIGS
elastofibroma	E/LA*S/FAOI/BROE/MA	electrodiagnosis	LEK/TRO/DAOIG/NOE/SIS

electrodiagnostics	LEK/TRO/DAOIG/NO*S/IK/-S	electropathology	LEK/TRO/PA/THOLG
electrodialysis	LEK/TRO/DI/AL/SIS	electropherogram	LEK/TRO/FER/GRAM
electrodialyzer	LEK/TRO/DAOI/LAOIZ/ER	electrophil	LEK/TRO/FIL
electrodiaphake	LEK/TRO/DAOI/AF/KAOE	electrophile	LEK/TRO/FAOIL
electrodiaphane	LEK/TRO/DAOI/FAIN	electrophilic	LEK/TRO/FIL/IK
electrodiaphanoscope	LEK/TRO/DI/AF/NO/SKOEP	electrophobia	LEK/TRO/FOEB/YA
electrodiaphany	LEK/TRO/DI/AF/N*I	electrophoresis	LEK/TRO/FRAOE/SIS
electroencephalogram	LEK/TRO/EN/SEF/LO/GRAM	electrophoretic	LEK/TRO/FRET/IK
	LEK/TRO/SEF/GRAM	electrophoretogram	LEK/TRO/FRET/GRAM
electroencephalograph	LEK/TRO/EN/SEF/LO/GRAF	electrophorus	LEK/TROF/RUS
	LEK/TRO/SEF/GRAF	electrophotometer	LEK/TRO/FOE/TOM/TER
electroencephalographic	LEK/TRO/EN/SEF/LO/GRAFK	electrophototherapy	LEK/TRO/FOET/THER/PI
	LEK/TRO/SEF/GRAFK	electrophrenic	LEK/TRO/FREN/IK
electroencephalography	LEK/TRO/EN/SEF/LOG/FI	electrophysiologic	LEK/TRO/FIZ/YO/LOJ/IK
	LEK/TRO/SEF/LOG/FI	electrophysiology	LEK/TRO/FIZ/YOLG
electroencephaloscope	LEK/TRO/EN/SEF/LO/SKOEP	electropneumograph	LEK/TRO/NAOUM/GRAF
	LEK/TRO/SEF/SKOEP	electropositive	LEK/TRO/POZ/TIV
electroendosmosis	LEK/TRO/EN/DOS/MOE/SIS	electropuncture	LEK/TRO/PUNG/KHUR
	LEK/TRO/EN/DOZ/MOE/SIS	electroradiology	LEK/TRO/RAID/YOLG
electroenterostomy	LEK/TRO/SPWRO*S/M*I	electroradiometer	LEK/TRO/RAID/YOM/TER
electroexcision	LEK/TRO/KPIGS	electroresection	LEK/TRO/RE/S*EBGS
electrofocusing	LEK/TRO/FOE/KUS/-G	electroretinogram	LEK/TRO/RET/NO/GRAM
electrogastroenterostomy	LEK/TRO/GAS/TRO/SPWRO*S/M*I	electroretinograph	LEK/TRO/RET/NO/GRAF
electrogastrogram	LEK/TRO/GAS/TRO/GRAM	electroretinography	LEK/TRO/RET/NOG/FI
electrogastrograph	LEK/TRO/GAS/TRO/GRAF	electrosalivogram	LEK/TRO/SLAOIV/GRAM
electrogastrography	LEK/TRO/GAS/TROG/FI		LEK/TRO/SA/LAOIV/GRAM
electrogoniometer	LEK/TRO/GOEN/YOM/TER	electroscission	LEK/TRO/SIGS
electrogram	LEK/TRO/GRAM	electroscope	LEK/TRO/SKOEP
electrograph	LEK/TRO/GRAF	electrosection	LEK/TRO/S*EBGS
electrography	LEK/TROG/FI	electroselenium	LEK/TRO/SE/LAOEN/YUM
electrogustometry	LEK/TRO/GUS/TOM/TRI	electroshock	LEK/TRO/SHOK
electrohemostasis	LEK/TRO/HAOE/MO*S/SIS	electrosol	LEK/TRO/SOL
	LEK/TRO/HAOEM/STAI/SIS	electrospectrogram	LEK/TRO/SPEK/TRO/GRAM
electrohysterogram	LEK/TRO/H*IS/RO/GRAM	electrospectrography	LEK/TRO/SPEK/TROG/FI
electrohysterograph	LEK/TRO/H*IS/RO/GRAF	electrospinogram	LEK/TRO/SPAOIN/GRAM
electrohysterography	LEK/TRO/H*IS/ROG/FI	electrospinography	LEK/TRO/SPAOI/NOG/FI
electroimmunodiffusion	LEK/TRO/IM/NO/DIF/FAOUGS	electrostatic	LEK/TRO/STAT/IK
	LEK/TRO/IM/NO/DI/FAOUGS	electrostenolysis	LEK/TRO/STE/NOL/SIS
electrokinetic	LEK/TRO/KI/NET/IK	electrostethograph	LEK/TRO/ST*ET/GRAF
electrokymogram	LEK/TRO/KAOIM/GRAM	electrostimulation	LEK/TRO/STIM/LAIGS
electrokymograph	LEK/TRO/KAOIM/GRAF	electrostriatogram	LEK/TRO/STRAOI/AIT/GRAM
electrokymography	LEK/TRO/KAOI/MOG/FI		LEK/TRO/STRAOI/YAIT/GRAM
electrolepsy	LEK/TRO/LEP/SI	electrostriction	LEK/TRO/STR*IBGS
electrolithotrity	LEK/TRO/LI/THOT/RI/TI	electrosurgery	LEK/TRO/SURJ/RI
electrolysis	LEK/TROL/SIS		LEK/TRO/S-RJ
electrolyte	LEK/TRO/LAOIT	electrosynthesis	LEK/TRO/S*INT/SIS
electrolytic	LEK/TRO/LIT/IK	electrotaxis	LEK/TRO/TAK/SIS
electrolyzable	LEK/TRO/LAOIZ/-BL	electrothanasia	LEK/TRO/THA/NAIZ/YA
electrolyze	LEK/TRO/LAOIZ	electrotherapeutics	LEK/TRO/THER/PAOUT/IK/-S
electrolyzer	LEK/TRO/LAOIZ/ER	electrotherapeutist	LEK/TRO/THER/PAOUT/*IS
electromagnet	LEK/TRO/MAG/NET	electrotherapist	LEK/TRO/THER/P*IS
electromagnetic	LEK/TRO/MAG/NET/IK	electrotherapy	LEK/TRO/THER/PI
electromagnetism	LEK/TRO/MAG/NE/TIFM	electrotherm	LEK/TRO/THERM
electromanometer	LEK/TRO/MA/NOM/TER	electrotome	LEK/TRO/TOEM
electromassage	LEK/TRO/MA/SAJ	electrotomy	LEK/TROT/M*I
	LEK/TRO/MAS/SAJ	electrotonic	LEK/TRO/TON/IK
electrometer	LEK/TROM/TER	electrotonus	LEK/TROT/NUS
electrometrogram	LEK/TRO/MET/RO/GRAM	electrotropism	LEK/TROT/RO/PIFM
electromicturation	LEK/TRO/MIK/KHU/RAIGS	electroultrafiltration	LEK/TRO/UL/TRA/FIL/TRAIGS
	LEK/TRO/MIKT/RAIGS	electroureterogram	LEK/TRO/YAOU/RAOET/RO/
electromigratory	LEK/TRO/MAOI/GRA/TOIR		GRAM
electromorph	LEK/TRO/MOR/-F	electroureterography	LEK/TRO/YAOU/RAOET/ROG/FI
electromotive	LEK/TRO/MOET/IV	electrovagogram	LEK/TRO/VAIG/GRAM
electromyogram	LEK/TRO/MAOI/GRAM	electrovalence	LEK/TRO/VAIL/ENS
electromyograph	LEK/TRO/MAOI/GRAF	electrovalent	LEK/TRO/VAIL/ENT
electromyography	LEK/TRO/MAOI/OG/FI	electroversion	LEK/TRO/VERGS
	LEK/TRO/MAOI/YOG/FI	electrovert	LEK/TRO/VERT
electron	LEK/TRON	electuary	E/LEKT/WAIR
electronarcosis	LEK/TRO/NAR/KOE/SIS		E/LEK/KHAOU/AIR
electron-dense	LEK/TRON/-H-F/DENS		E/LEK/KHAOU/WAIR
electronegative	LEK/TRO/NEG/TIV	eledoisin	EL/DOI/SIN
electronegativity	LEK/TRO/NEG/TIV/TI	eleidin	E/LAOE/DIN
electroneurography	LEK/TRO/NAOU/ROG/FI	element	EL/-MT
electroneurolysis	LEK/TRO/NAOU/ROL/SIS		L-MT
electroneuromyography	LEK/TRO/NAOUR/MAOI/OG/FI	elemental	EL/MEN/TAL
	LEK/TRO/NAOUR/MAOI/YOG/FI		EL/-MT/TAL
electronic	LEK/TRON/IK		L-MT/TAL
electronics	LEK/TRON/IK/-S	elementary	EL/-MT/RI
electronograph	LEK/TRON/GRAF		L-MT/RI
electron-volt	LEK/TRON/VOELT	eleo-	EL/YO
	LEK/TRON/VOLT	eleoma	EL/YOE/MA
electronystagmogram	LEK/TRO/NIS/TAG/MO/GRAM	eleometer	EL/YOM/TER
electronystagmograph	LEK/TRO/NIS/TAG/MO/GRAF	eleopathy	EL/YOP/TH*I
electronystagmography	LEK/TRO/NIS/TAG/MOG/FI	eleoplast	EL/YO/PLA*S
electro-oculogram	LEK/TRO/OK/LO/GRAM	eleopten	EL/YOP/TEN
electro-oculography	LEK/TRO/OK/LOG/FI	eleosaccharum	EL/YO/SAK/RUM
electro-olfactogram	LEK/TRO/OL/FAKT/GRAM	eleostearic	EL/YO/STAOER/IK
electro-osmosis	LEK/TRO/OZ/MOE/SIS	eleotherapy	EL/YO/THER/PI
electroparacentesis	LEK/TRO/PAR/SEN/TAOE/SIS	eleothorax	EL/YO/THOR/AX

140

elephantiac	EL/FANT/YAK		EM/BE/LIN
elephantiasic	EL/FANT/YAS/IK	embol(o)-	EM/BL(O)
elephantiasis	EL/FAN/TAOI/SIS		EM/BO/L(O)
elephantoid	EL/FAN/TOID		EM/BOL
eleutheromania	E/LAO*UT/RO/MAIN/YA	embolalia	EM/BO/LAIL/YA
elevation	EL/VAIGS	embole	EM/BLAOE
elevator	EL/VAI/TOR	embolectomy	EM/BLEKT/M*I
elevatum	EL/VAI/TUM	embolemia	EM/BLAOEM/YA
	EL/VAIT/UM	emboli	EM/BLAOI
eliminant	E/LIM/NANT	embolia	EM/BOEL/YA
eliminate	E/LIM/NAIT	embolic	EM/BOL/IK
elimination	E/LIM/NAIGS	emboliform	EM/BOL/FORM
elinguation	E/LING/WAIGS	embolism	EM/BLIFM
elinin	EL/NIN	embolization	EM/BOL/ZAIGS
elixir	E/LIK/SIR	embololalia	EM/BLO/LAIL/YA
	E/LIX/IR	embolomycotic	EM/BLO/MAOI/KOT/IK
Elixophyllin	E/LIX/OF/LIN	embolophasia	EM/BLO/FAIZ/YA
	E/LIK/SOF/LIN	embolophrasia	EM/BLO/FRAIZ/YA
Elixophyllin-GG	E/LIX/OF/LIN/G-RBGS/G*RBGS	emboly	EM/BLI
	E/LIK/SOF/LIN/G-RBGS/G*RBGS	embolus	EM/BLUS
Elixophyllin-KI	E/LIX/OF/LIN/K-RBGS/*IRBGS	embouchment	EM/BAOURB/-MT
	E/LIK/SOF/LIN/K-RBGS/*IRBGS	embrasure	EM/BRAI/SHUR
Elixophyllin SR	E/LIX/OF/LIN/S-RBGS/R*RBGS	embrocation	EM/BROE/KAIGS
	E/LIK/SOF/LIN/S-RBGS/R*RBGS		EM/BRO/KAIGS
Ellermann	EL/ER/MAN	embry(o)-	EM/BR(O)
Elliot	EL/YOT		EM/BRAOE/Y(O)
ellipses	E/LIP/SAOEZ	embryectomy	EM/BREKT/M*I
ellipsin	E/LIP/SIN		EM/BRAOE/EKT/M*I
ellipsis	E/LIP/SIS	embryo	EM/BROE
ellipsoid	E/LIP/SOID	embryoblast	EM/BRO/BLA*S
ellipsoidal	E/LIP/SOI/DAL	embryocardia	EM/BRO/KARD/YA
ellipsoidea	E/LIP/SOID/YA	embryogenesis	EM/BRO/JEN/SIS
ellipto-	E/LIPT	embryogenetic	EM/BRO/JE/NET/IK
	E/LIP/TO	embryogenic	EM/BRO/JEN/IK
elliptocytary	E/LIPT/SAOIT/RI	embryogeny	EM/BROJ/N*I
elliptocyte	E/LIPT/SAO*IT	embryologist	EM/BRO*LGS
elliptocytosis	E/LIPT/SAOI/TOE/SIS	embryology	EM/BROLG
elliptocytotic	E/LIPT/SAOI/TOT/IK	embryoma	EM/BROE/MA
Ellis	EL/LIS	embryomorphous	EM/BRO/MOR/FOUS
Ellison	EL/SON	embryonal	EM/BRONL
Ellsworth	ELZ/WORTH	embryonate	EM/BRO/NAIT
Elocon	EL/KON	embryonic	EM/BRON/IK
Eloesser	EL/ES/SER	embryoniform	EM/BRON/FORM
elongation	E/LON/GAIGS	embryonism	EM/BRO/NIFM
Elschnig	EL/-RB/NIG	embryonization	EM/BRON/ZAIGS
	EL/SH-/NIG	embryonoid	EM/BRO/NOID
	(*not* ELS/NIG; see else anything)	embryony	EM/BRO/N*I
Elspar	EL/SPAR	embryopathia	EM/BRO/PA*T/YA
eluate	EL/YAIT	embryopathology	EM/BRO/PA/THOLG
	EL/YAOU/AIT	embryopathy	EM/BROP/TH*I
	EL/YAOU/WAIT	embryophore	EM/BRO/FOER
elucaine	E/LAOU/KAIN	embryoplastic	EM/BRO/PLA*S/IK
eluent	EL/YAOUNT	embryoscope	EM/BRO/SKOEP
	E/LAOUNT	embryoscopy	EM/BROS/KPI
elusion	E/LAOUGS	embryotome	EM/BRO/TOEM
elute	E/LAOUT	embryotomy	EM/BROT/M*I
elution	E/LAO*UGS	embryotoxicity	EM/BRO/TOK/SIS/TI
	(*not* E/LAOUGS; see elusion)	embryotoxon	EM/BRO/TOK/SON
elutriate	E/LAOU/TRAIT	embryotroph	EM/BRO/TROEF
	E/LAOUT/RAIT	embryotrophic	EM/BRO/TROFK
	E/LAOU/TRAOE/AIT	embryotrophy	EM/BROT/RO/FI
elutriation	E/LAOU/TRAIGS	Emcyt	EM/SIT
	E/LAOUT/RAIGS	emedullate	E/MED/LAIT
	E/LAOU/TRAOE/AIGS	emergence	E/MERJ/ENS
	E/LAOUT/TRAOE/YAIGS	emergency	M-RJ
Elzholz	ELZ/HOLZ		E/MERJ/EN/SI
	ELZ/HOELZ	emergent	E/MERJ/ENT
	ELTS/HOLTS	Emerson	EM/ER/SON
	ELTS/HOELTS	emery	EM/RI
emaciated	E/MAIS/YAIT/-D	-emesia	MAOEZ/YA
	E/MAIRB/YAIT/-D	emesis	EM/SIS
emaciation	E/MAIS/YAIGS	ematatrophia	EM/TA/TROEF/YA
	E/MAIRB/YAIGS	Emete-Con	E/MET/KON
emaculation	E/MAK/LAIGS	emetic	E/MET/IK
eman	EM/MAN	emeticology	E/MET/KOLG
emanation	EM/NAIGS	emetine	EM/TAOEN
emanator	EM/NAI/TOR		EM/TIN
emanatorium	EM/NAI/TOER/YUM	emetocathartic	EM/TO/KA/THART/IK
	EM/NA/TOER/YUM	emetology	EM/TOLG
emancipation	E/MANS/PAIGS	Emetrol	EM/TROL
emarginate	E/MARJ/NAIT		EM/TROEL
emargination	E/MARJ/NAIGS	-emia	AOEM/YA
emasculation	E/MAS/KLAIGS	emiction	E/M*IBGS
embalm	EM/BAUM	emigrated	EM/GRAIT/-D
embarrass	EM/BAR/RASZ	emigration	EM/GRAIGS
Embden	EM/DEN	emilium	E/MIL/YUM
embed	EM/BED	eminence	EM/NENS
embedding	EM/BED/-G	eminentia	EM/NEN/SHA
embelin	EM/BLIN	eminentiae	EM/NEN/SHAE

emiocytosis	AOEM/YO/SAOI/TOE/SIS	emulsion	E/MULGS
emissaria	EM/SAIR/YA	emulsive	E/MULS/IV
emissarium	EM/SAIRM	emulsoid	E/MUL/SOID
	EM/SAIR/YUM	Emulsoil	E/MUL/SOIL
emissary	EM/SAIR	emulsum	E/MUL/SUM
emission	E/MIGS	emunctory	E/MUNGT/RI
emissivity	E/MIS/SIV/TI		E/MUNG/TOIR
	AOEM/SIV/TI	emuresis	EM/YAOU/RAOE/SIS
Emko	EM/KOE	E-Mycin	E/MAOI/SIN
emmen-	E/MEN		ERBGS/MAOI/SIN
	EM/MEN	emylcamate	E/MIL/KA/MAIT
emmenagogic	E/MEN/GOJ/IK		EM/IL/KAM/AIT
emmenagogue	E/MEN/GOG	en-	EN
emmenia	E/MEN/YA	enalapril	E/NAL/PRIL
	E/MAOEN/YA	enamel	E/NAM/EL
emmenic	E/MEN/IK	enamelo-	E/NAM/LO
emmeniopathy	E/MEN/YOP/TH*I		EN/AM/LO
	E/MAOEN/YOP/TH*I	enameloblast	EN/AM/LO/BLA*S
emmenology	EM/NOLG	enameloblastoma	E/NAM/LO/BLAS/TOE/MA
Emmert	EM/ERT	enamelogenesis	E/NAM/LO/JEN/SIS
Emmet	EM/ET	enameloma	E/NAM/LOE/MA
emmetrope	EM/TROEP	enamelum	E/NAM/LUM
emmetropia	EM/TROEP/YA	enanthal	E/NAN/THAL
emmetropic	EM/TROP/IK	enanthate	E/NAN/THAIT
emmetropization	EM/TROEP/ZAIGS	enanthem	EN/AN/THEM
Emmonsiella	E/MONS/YEL/LA	enanthema	EN/AN/THAOE/MA
emodin	EM/DIN	enanthematous	EN/AN/THEM/TOUS
emollient	E/MOL/YENT	enanthesis	EN/AN/THAOE/SIS
emot-	E/MOE/T-	enanthic	EN/A*NT/IK
emote	E/MOET		E/NA*NT/IK
emoti(o)-	E/MOE/SH(O)	enanthrope	EN/AN/THROEP
	E/MOERB/Y(O)	enantio-	E/NANT/YO
emotiometabolic	E/MOE/SHO/MET/BOL/IK		EN/ANT/YO
emotiomotor	E/MOE/SHO/MOE/TOR	enantiobiosis	EN/ANT/YO/BAO*I/YOE/SIS
emotiomuscular	E/MOE/SHO/MUS/KLAR	enantiomer	E/NANT/YO/MER
emotion	E/MOEGS	enantiomeric	E/NANT/YO/MER/IK
emotional	E/MOEGS/NAL	enantiomerism	E/NANT/YOM/RIFM
emotionality	E/MOEGS/NAL/TI	enantiomorph	E/NANT/YO/MOR/-F
emotionalize	E/MOEGS/LAOIZ	enantiomorphic	E/NANT/YO/MOR/FIK
emotiovascular	E/MOE/SHO/VAS/KLAR	enantiomorphism	E/NANT/YO/MOR/FIFM
emotive	E/MOET/IV	enantiomorphous	E/NANT/YO/MOR/FOUS
emotivity	E/MOE/TIV/TI	enantiopathia	EN/ANT/YO/PA*T/YA
empasm	EM/PAFM	enantiopathic	EN/ANT/YO/PA*T/IK
empasma	EM/PAZ/MA	enantiopathy	EN/ANT/YOP/TH*I
empathic	EM/PA*T/IK	enarkyochrome	EN/ARK/YO/KROEM
empathize	EFRP/THAOIZ	enarthritis	EN/AR/THRAOITS
empathy	EFRP/TH*I	enarthrodial	EN/AR/THROED/YAL
emperipolesis	EM/P*ER/PLAOE/SIS	enarthrosis	EN/AR/THROE/SIS
	EM/P*ER/PO/LAOE/SIS	en bloc	EN/BLOK
	EM/P*ER/POE/LAOE/SIS	encainide	EN/KAI/NAOID
emphases	EFRP/SAOEZ	encanthis	EN/KAN/THIS
	EM/FA/SAOEZ	encapsulated	EN/KAPS/LAIT/-D
emphasis	EFRP/SIS	encapsulation	EN/KAPS/LAIGS
	EM/FA/SIS	encapsuled	EN/KAP/SAOUL/-D
emphlysis	EM/FLI/SIS	encarditis	EN/KAR/DAOITS
emphractic	EM/FRAKT/IK	encasing	EN/KAIS/-G
emphraxis	EM/FRAK/SIS	encatarrhaphy	EN/KA/TAR/FI
emphysatherapy	EM/FIZ/THER/PI	encelialgia	EN/SAOEL/YAL/JA
emphysema	EFRP/SAOE/MA	encelitis	EN/SE/LAOITS
	EM/FI/SAOE/MA	enceliitis	EN/SAOEL/YAOITS
emphysematosa	EFRP/SEM/TOE/SA	encephal(o)-	EN/SEF/L(O)
	EM/FI/SEM/TOE/SA		EN/SFAL
emphysematous	EFRP/SEM/TOUS	encephala	EN/SEF/LA
	EM/FI/SEM/TOUS	encephalalgia	EN/SEF/LAL/JA
empiric	EM/PIR/IK	encephalatrophic	EN/SEF/LA/TROFK
empirical	EM/PIR/KAL	encephalatrophy	EN/SEF/LAT/RO/FI
empiricism	EM/PIR/SIFM	encephalauxe	EN/SEF/LAUK/SAOE
Empirin	EM/PRIN	encephalemia	EN/SEF/LAOEM/YA
	EFRP/RIN	encephali	EN/SEF/LAOI
emprosthotonos	EM/PROS/THOT/NOS	encephalic	EN/SFAL/IK
emprosthotonus	EM/PROS/THOT/NUS	encephalitic	EN/SEF/LIT/IK
emptysis	EFRPT/SIS	encephalitides	EN/SEF/LIT/DAOEZ
	EFRP/TI/SIS	encephalitis	EN/SEF/LAOITS
	EM/TI/SIS	encephalitogen	EN/SEF/LAOIT/JEN
empyema	EM/PAOI/E/MA		EN/SEF/LIT/JEN
	EM/PAOI/YAOE/MA	encephalitogenic	EN/SEF/LAOIT/JEN/IK
empyemic	EM/PAOI/AOEM/IK		EN/SEF/LIT/JEN/IK
	EM/PAOI/YAOEM/IK	Encephalitozoon	EN/SEF/LAOIT/ZAON
empyesis	EM/PAOI/E/SIS		EN/SEF/LIT/ZAON
	EM/PAOI/SIS		EN/SFAL/TO/ZAON
	EM/PAOI/YAOE/SIS	encephalization	EN/SEF/LI/ZAIGS
empyocele	EM/PAOI/SAO*EL	encephalo-arteriography	EN/SEF/LO/AR/TAOER/YOG/FI
empyreuma	EM/PAOI/RAOU/MA	encephalocele	EN/SEF/LO/SAO*EL
empyreumatic	EM/PAOI/RAOU/MAT/IK	encephaloclastic	EN/SEF/LO/KLA*S/IK
emulgent	E/MUL/JENT	encephalocystocele	EN/SEF/LO/S*IS/SAO*EL
emulsification	E/MULS/FI/KAIGS	encephalodialysis	EN/SEF/LO/DI/AL/SIS
emulsifier	E/MULS/FI/ER	encephalodynia	EN/SEF/LO/DIN/YA
emulsify	E/MULS/FI	encephalodysplasia	EN/SEF/LO/DIS/PLAIZ/YA
emulsin	E/MUL/SIN	encephalofacial	EN/SEF/LO/FAIRBL

encephalogram	EN/SEF/LO/GRAM
encephalography	EN/SEF/LOG/FI
encephaloid	EN/SEF/LOID
encephalolith	EN/SEF/LO/L*IT
encephalology	EN/SEF/LOLG
encephaloma	EN/SEF/LOE/MA
encephalomalacia	EN/SEF/LO/MA/LAI/SHA
encephalomeningitis	EN/SEF/LO/MEN/JAOITS
encephalomeningocele	EN/SEF/LO/ME/NING/SAO*EL
encephalomeningopathy	EN/SEF/LO/MEN/GOP/TH*I
encephalomere	EN/SEF/LO/MAOER
encephalometer	EN/SEF/LOM/TER
encephalomyelitis	EN/SEF/LO/MAOI/LAOITS
encephalomyelocele	EN/SEF/LO/MAOI/LO/SAO*EL
encephalomyeloneuropathy	EN/SEF/LO/MAOI/LO/NAOU/ROP/TH*I
encephalomyelonic	EN/SEF/LO/MAOI/LON/IK
encephalomyelopathy	EN/SEF/LO/MAOI/LOP/TH*I
encephalomyeloradiculitis	EN/SEF/LO/MAOI/LO/RA/DIK/LAOITS
encephalomyeloradiculoneuritis	
	EN/SEF/LO/MAOI/LO/RA/DIK/LO/NAOU/RAOITS
encephalomyeloradiculopathy	
	EN/SEF/LO/MAOI/LO/RA/DIK/LOP/TH*I
encephalomyocarditis	EN/SEF/LO/MAOI/KAR/DAOITS
encephalon	EN/SEF/LON
encephalonarcosis	EN/SEF/LO/NAR/KOE/SIS
encephalo-ophthalmic	EN/SEF/LO/OF/THAL/MIK
encephalopathia	EN/SEF/LO/PA*T/YA
encephalopathic	EN/SEF/LO/PA*T/IK
encephalopathy	EN/SEF/LOP/TH*I
encephalopsy	EN/SEF/LOP/SI
encephalopuncture	EN/SEF/LO/PUNG/KHUR
encephalopyosis	EN/SEF/LO/PAOI/YOE/SIS
encephalorachidian	EN/SEF/LO/RA/KID/YAN
encephaloradiculitis	EN/SEF/LO/RA/DIK/LAOITS
encephalorrhachidian	*see* encephalorachidian
encephalorrhagia	EN/SEF/LO/RAI/JA
encephaloschisis	EN/SEF/LOS/KI/SIS
encephalosclerosis	EN/SEF/LO/SKLE/ROE/SIS
encephaloscope	EN/SEF/LO/SKOEP
encephaloscopy	EN/SEF/LOS/KPI
encephalosepsis	EN/SEF/LO/SEP/SIS
encephalosis	EN/SEF/LOE/SIS
encephalospinal	EN/SEF/LO/SPAOINL
encephalothlipsis	EN/SEF/LO/TLIP/SIS
	EN/SEF/LO/TH-/LIP/SIS
encephalotome	EN/SEF/LO/TOEM
encephalotomy	EN/SEF/LOT/M*I
encephalotrigeminal	EN/SEF/LO/TR*I/JEM/NAL
-encephaly	EN/SEF/LI
encheiresis	EN/KAOI/RAOE/SIS
enchondral	EN/KON/DRAL
enchondralis	EN/KON/DRAI/LIS
enchondroma	EN/KON/DROE/MA
enchondromatosis	EN/KON/DRO/MA/TOE/SIS
	EN/KON/DROEM/TOE/SIS
enchondromatous	EN/KON/DROEM/TOUS
enchondrosarcoma	EN/KON/DRO/SAR/KOE/MA
enchondrosis	EN/KON/DROE/SIS
enchylema	EN/KAOI/LAOE/MA
enchyma	ENG/MA
	EN/KI/MA
enclave	EN/KLAIV
enclitic	EN/KLIT/IK
enclomiphene	EN/KLOEM/FAOEN
encoding	EN/KOED/-G
encolpism	EN/KOL/PIFM
encopresis	EN/KO/PRAOE/SIS
encranial	EN/KRAIN/YAL
encranius	EN/KRAIN/YUS
encyesis	EN/SAOI/E/SIS
encyopyelitis	EN/SAOI/PAOI/LAOITS
encyst	EN/S*IS
encysted	EN/S*IS/-D
encystment	EN/S*IS/-MT
endadelphos	END/DEL/FOS
endamebic	END/MAOEB/IK
	EN/DA/MAOEB/IK
Endamoeba	END/MAOE/BA
	EN/DA/MAOE/BA
endangiitis	END/AN/JAOITS
	EN/DAN/JAOITS
endangium	END/AN/JUM
	EN/DAN/JUM
endaortic	END/AI/ORT/IK
endaortitis	END/AI/OR/TAOITS

endarterectomize	END/ART/REKT/MAOIZ
endarterectomy	END/ART/REKT/M*I
endarterial	END/AR/TAOERL
endarteritis	END/ART/RAOITS
endarterium	END/AR/TAOERM
endarteropathy	END/ART/ROP/TH*I
end-artery	END/H-F/ART/RI
endaural	END/AURL
endbrain	END/BRAIN
end-brush	END/H-F/BRURB
end-bud	END/H-F/BUD
end-bulb	END/H-F/BUL/-B
end-diastolic	END/H-F/DAOI/STOL/IK
endeictic	EN/DAOIK/TIK
endemia	EN/DAOEM/YA
endemial	EN/DAOEM/YAL
endemic	EN/DEM/IK
endemica	EN/DEM/KA
endemiology	EN/DAOEM/YOLG
endemoepidemic	EN/DEM/EP/DEM/IK
	END/MO/EP/DEM/IK
Endep	EN/DEP
endepidermis	END/EP/DER/MIS
endergic	EN/DERJ/IK
	END/ERJ/IK
endergonic	EN/DER/GON/IK
	END/ER/GON/IK
endermatic	EN/DER/MAT/IK
endermic	EN/DERM/IK
endermism	EN/DER/MIFM
endermosis	EN/DER/MOE/SIS
enderon	END/RON
enderonic	END/RON/IK
end-feet	END/H-F/FAOET
endgut	END/GUT
ending	END/-G
end-nuclei	END/H-F/NAOUK/LAOI
endo-	*END
	EN/DO
	(*not* END)
endoabdominal	*END/AB/DOM/NAL
endoaneurysmoplasty	*END/AN/RIZ/MO/PLAS/TI
endoaneurysmorrhaphy	*END/AN/RIZ/MOR/FI
endoangiitis	*END/AN/JAOITS
endoaortitis	*END/AI/OR/TAOITS
endoappendicitis	*END/AI/PEND/SAOITS
endoarteritis	*END/ART/RAOITS
endoauscultation	*END/AUS/KUL/TAIGS
endobacillary	*END/BAS/LAIR
endobasion	*END/BAIS/YON
endobiotic	*END/BAO*I/OT/IK
endoblast	*END/BLA*S
endoblastic	*END/BLA*S/IK
endobronchial	*END/BRONG/YAL
endobronchitis	*END/BRON/KAOITS
endocardia	*END/KARD/YA
endocardiac	*END/KARD/YAK
endocardial	*END/KARD/YAL
endocardiography	*END/KARD/YOG/FI
endocardiopathy	*END/KARD/YOP/TH*I
endocarditic	*END/KAR/DIT/IK
endocarditis	*END/KAR/DAOITS
endocardium	*END/KARD/YUM
endoceliac	*END/SAOEL/YAK
endocellular	*END/SEL/YAOU/LAR
endocervical	*END/SEFRB/KAL
endocervicitis	*END/SEFRB/SAOITS
endocervix	*END/SEFRB/IX
endochondral	*END/KON/DRAL
endochorion	*END/KOER/YON
endochrome	*END/KROEM
endocolitis	*END/KO/LAOITS
endocolpitis	*END/KOL/PAOITS
endocorpuscular	*END/KOR/PUS/KLAR
endocranial	*END/KRAIN/YAL
endocranitis	*END/KRAI/NAOITS
endocranium	*END/KRAIN/YUM
endocrin(o)-	*END/KRIN/(O)
	*END/KRI/N(O)
	EN/DOK/RI/N(O)
endocrinasthenia	*END/KRIN/AS/THAOEN/YA
endocrinasthenic	*END/KRIN/AS/THEN/IK
endocrine	*END/KRIN
	*END/KRAOIN
endocrinic	*END/KRIN/IK
endocrinism	EN/DOK/RI/NIFM
endocrinium	*END/KRIN/YUM
endocrinologist	*END/KRI/NO*LGS
endocrinology	*END/KRI/NOLG

endocrinoma	*END/KRI/NOE/MA	endometrium	*END/MAOE/TRUM
endocrinopathic	*END/KRIN/PA*T/IK		*END/MAOE/TRAOE/UM
endocrinopathy	*END/KRI/NOP/TH*I	endometropic	*END/ME/TROP/IK
endocrinosis	*END/KRI/NOE/SIS		*END/MAOE/TROP/IK
endocrinosity	*END/KRI/NOS/TI	endometry	EN/DOM/TRI
	*END/KRIN/OS/TI	endomitosis	*END/MAOI/TOE/SIS
endocrinotherapy	*END/KRIN/THER/PI	endomitotic	*END/MAOI/TOT/IK
endocrinotropic	*END/KRIN/TROP/IK	endomorph	*END/MOR/-F
endocrinous	EN/DOK/RI/NOUS	endomorphic	*END/MOR/FIK
endocyclic	*END/SAOIK/LIK	endomorphy	*END/MOR/FI
endocyma	*END/SAOI/MA	endomotorsonde	*END/MOE/TOR/SOND
endocyst	*END/S*IS	Endomyces	*END/MAOI/SAOEZ
endocystitis	*END/SAOIS/TAOITS	Endomycetales	*END/MAOIS/TAI/LAOEZ
endocyte	*END/SAO*IT	endomyocardial	*END/MAOI/KARD/YAL
endocytosis	*END/SAOI/TOE/SIS	endomyocarditis	*END/MAOI/KAR/DAOITS
endoderm	*END/DERM	endomyometritis	*END/MAOI/MAOE/TRAOITS
endodermal	*END/DER/MAL		*END/MAOI/ME/TRAOITS
endodiascope	*END/DAOI/SKOEP	endomysium	*END/MIS/YUM
endodiascopy	*END/DI/AS/KPI	endonasal	*END/NAI/ZAL
endodontia	*END/DON/SHA	endoneural	*END/NAOURL
endodontic	*END/DONT/IK	endoneurial	*END/NAOUR/YAL
endodontics	*END/DONT/IK/-S		(not *END/NAOURL; see
endodontist	*END/DONT/*IS		endoneural)
	*END/DON/T*IS	endoneuritis	*END/NAOU/RAOITS
endodontitis	*END/DON/TAOITS	endoneurium	*END/NAOURM
endodontium	*END/DON/SHUM		*END/NAOUR/YUM
endodontologist	*END/DON/TO*LGS	endonuclear	*END/NAOUK/LAR
endodontology	*END/DON/TOLG	endonuclease	*END/NAOUK/LAIS
endodyocyte	*END/DAOI/SAO*IT	endonucleolus	*END/NAOU/KLAOE/LUS
endodyogeny	*END/DAOI/OJ/N*I	endoparasite	*END/PAR/SAOIT
	*END/DI/OJ/N*I	endoparasitism	*END/PAR/SAOI/TIFM
endoenteritis	*END/SPWRAOITS	endopelvic	*END/PEL/VIK
endoenzyme	*END/EN/ZAOIM	endopelvina	*END/PEL/VAOI/NA
endoepidermal	*END/EP/DER/MAL	endopeptidase	*END/PEPT/DAIS
endoepithelial	*END/EP/THAOEL/YAL	endoperiarteritis	*END/P*ER/ART/RAOITS
endoergic	*END/ERJ/IK	endopericardiac	*END/P*ER/KARD/YAK
endoesophagitis	*END/E/SOF/JAOITS	endopericardial	*END/P*ER/KARD/YAL
endoexoteric	*END/KPO/TER/IK	endopericarditis	*END/P*ER/KAR/DAOITS
endofaradism	*END/FAR/DIFM	endoperimyocarditis	*END/P*ER/MAOI/KAR/DAOITS
endogalvanism	*END/GAL/VA/NIFM	endoperineuritis	*END/P*ER/NAOU/RAOITS
endogamous	EN/DOG/MOUS	endoperitoneal	*END/PERT/NAOEL
endogamy	EN/DOG/M*I	endoperitonitis	*END/PERT/NAOITS
endogastric	*END/GAS/TRIK	endoperoxide	*END/PROK/SAOID
endogastritis	*END/GAS/TRAOITS	endophasia	*END/FAIZ/YA
endogenetic	*END/JE/NET/IK	endophlebitis	*END/FLE/BAOITS
endogenic	*END/JEN/IK	endophthalmitis	EN/DOF/THAL/MAOITS
endogenote	*END/JAOE/NOET	endophylaxination	*END/FLAX/NAIGS
endogenous	EN/DOJ/NOUS	endophyte	*END/FAOIT
endoglobar	*END/GLOE/BAR	endophytic	*END/FIT/IK
endoglobular	*END/GLOB/LAR	endoplasm	*END/PLAFM
endognathion	EN/DOG/NA*T/YON	endoplasmic	*END/PLAZ/MIK
	EN/DOG/NA*IT/YON	endoplast	*END/PLA*S
	*END/NA*IT/YON	endoplastic	*END/PLA*S/IK
endoherniorrhaphy	*END/HERN/YOR/FI	endopolygeny	*END/PLIJ/N*I
endoherniotomy	*END/HERN/YOT/M*I	endopolyploid	*END/POL/PLOID
endointoxication	*END/SPWOX/KAIGS	endopolyploidy	*END/POL/PLOI/DI
endolabyrinthitis	*END/LAB/RIN/THAOITS	endoradiography	*END/RAID/YOG/FI
endolaryngeal	*END/LARN/JAL	endoradiosonde	*END/RAID/YO/SOND
endolarynx	*END/LARNGS	endoreduplication	*END/RE/DAOUP/KAIGS
Endolimax	*END/LAOI/MAX	end organ	END/OR/GAN
endolith	*END/L*IT	endorhinitis	*END/RAOI/NAOITS
endolymph	*END/LIM/-F	Endorphan	EN/DOR/FAN
endolympha	*END/LIM/FA	Endorphenyl	EN/DOR/FENL
endolymphatic	*END/LIM/FAT/IK	endorphin	EN/DOR/FIN
endolymphaticus	*END/LIM/FAT/KUS	endorphinergic	EN/DOR/FIN/ERJ/IK
endolymphic	*END/LIM/FIK		EN/DOR/FI/NERJ/IK
endolysin	EN/DOL/SIN	endorrhachis	*END/RAI/KIS
endolysis	EN/DOL/SIS	endosalpingiosis	*END/SAL/PIN/JOE/SIS
endomastoiditis	*END/MAS/TOI/DAOITS	endosalpingitis	*END/SAL/PIN/JAOITS
endomeninx	*END/MAOE/NINGS	endosalpingoma	*END/SAL/PIN/GOE/MA
	*END/MEN/INGS	endosalpingosis	*END/SAL/PIN/GOE/SIS
endomerogony	*END/ME/ROG/N*I	endosalpinx	*END/SAL/PINGS
endomesoderm	*END/MES/DERM	endosarc	*END/SARK
endometrectomy	*END/ME/TREKT/M*I	endoscope	*END/SKOEP
endometria	*END/MAOE/TRA	endoscopic	*END/SKOP/IK
	*END/MAOE/TRAOE/YA	endoscopist	EN/DOS/KP*IS
endometrial	*END/MAOE/TRAL	endoscopy	EN/DOS/KPI
endometrioid	*END/MAOE/TROID	endosecretory	*END/SE/KRAOET/RI
	*END/MAOE/TRAOE/OID		*END/SE/KRE/TOIR
endometrioides	*END/MAOE/TROI/DAOEZ	endosepsis	*END/SEP/SIS
	*END/MAOE/TRAOE/OI/DAOEZ	endoskeleton	*END/SKEL/TON
endometrioma	*END/MAOE/TROE/MA	endosmometer	EN/DOZ/MOM/TER
	*END/MAOE/TRAOE/YOE/MA	endosmosis	EN/DO/MOE/SIS
endometriosis	*END/MAOE/TROE/SIS		EN/DOZ/MOE/SIS
	*END/MAOE/TRAOE/YOE/SIS	endosmotic	EN/DOS/MOT/IK
endometriotic	*END/MAOE/TROT/IK		EN/DOZ/MOT/IK
	*END/MAOE/TRAOE/OT/IK	endosome	*END/SOEM
endometritis	*END/ME/TRAOITS	endospore	*END/SPOER
	*END/MAOE/TRAOITS	endosporium	*END/SPOR/YUM

endosteal	EN/DO*S/YAL	energometer	EN/ER/GOM/TER
endosteitis	EN/DO*S/YAOITS	energy	N-RJ
endosteoma	EN/DO*S/YOE/MA		EN/ER/JI
endostethoscope	*END/ST*ET/SKOEP	enervate	EN/ER/VAIT
endosteum	EN/DO*S/YUM	enervation	EN/ER/VAIGS
endostitis	EN/DOS/TAOITS	Enfamil	EN/FA/MIL
endostoma	EN/DOS/TOE/MA	Enfamil Nursette	EN/FA/MIL/NUR/SET
	*END/STOE/MA	enflagellation	EN/FLAJ/LAIGS
endosymbiont	*END/SIM/BONT	enflurane	EN/FLAOU/RAIN
	*END/SIM/BAOE/YONT	engagement	EN/GAIJ/-MT
endosymbiosis	*END/SIM/BOE/SIS	engastrius	EN/GAS/TRUS
	*END/SIM/BAOE/YOE/SIS		EN/GAS/TRAOE/YUS
	*END/SIM/BAO*I/YOE/SIS	Engel	ENG/EL
endotendineum	*END/TEN/DIN/YUM		EN/GEL
endotenon	*END/TEN/NON	Engelmann	ENG/EL/MAN
endotheli(o)-	*END/THAOEL/Y(O)		EN/GEL/MAN
endothelia	*END/THAOEL/YA	engine	EN/JIN
endothelial	*END/THAOEL/YAL	engineering	ENG/NAOER/-G
endothelialis	*END/THAOEL/YAI/LIS	English	ENG/LIRB
endothelialization	*END/THAOEL/YAL/ZAIGS	englobe	EN/GLOEB
endotheliitis	*END/THAOEL/YAOITS	englobement	EN/GLOEB/-MT
endothelioblastoma	*END/THAOEL/YO/BLAS/TOE/MA	Engman	ENG/MAN
endotheliochorial	*END/THAOEL/YO/KOER/YAL	engorge	EN/GORJ
endotheliocyte	*END/THAOEL/YO/SAO*IT	engorged	EN/GORJ/-D
endotheliocytosis	*END/THAOEL/YO/SAOI/TOE/SIS	engorgement	EN/GORJ/-MT
endothelioid	*END/THAOEL/YOID	engram	EN/GRAM
endotheliolysin	*END/THAOEL/YOL/SIN	engraphia	EN/GRAF/YA
endotheliolytic	*END/THAOEL/YO/LIT/IK	en grappe	EN/GRAP
endothelioma	*END/THAOEL/YOE/MA	enhancement	EN/HANS/-MT
endotheliomatosis	*END/THAOEL/YOEM/TOE/SIS	enhematospore	EN/HEM/TO/SPOER
	*END/THAOEL/YO/MA/TOE/SIS	enhemospore	EN/HAOEM/SPOER
endotheliosarcoma	*END/THAOEL/YO/SAR/KOE/MA		EN/HEM/SPOER
endotheliosis	*END/THAOEL/YOE/SIS	eniotypy	EN/YO/TAOI/PI
endotheliotoxin	*END/THAOEL/YO/TOK/SIN	Enkaid	EN/KAID
endothelium	*END/THAOEL/YUM	enkephalin	EN/KEF/LIN
endothermal	*END/THER/MAL	enkephalinergic	EN/KEF/LIN/ERJ/IK
endothermic	*END/THERM/IK		EN/KEF/LI/NERJ/IK
endothermy	*END/THER/M*I	enlargement	EN/LARJ/-MT
endothoracic	*END/THRAS/IK	Enlon	EN/LON
endothoracica	*END/THRAS/KA	enol	E/NOL
endothrix	*END/THRIX	enolase	E/NOL/AIS
endothyroidopexy	*END/THAOI/ROID/PEK/SI		E/NO/LAIS
endothyropexy	*END/THAOIR/PEK/SI	enolization	E/NOL/ZAIGS
endotoxemia	*END/TOK/SAOEM/YA	enol pyruvate	E/NOL/PAOI/RAOU/VAIT
endotoxic	*END/TOX/IK	enophthalmia	EN/OF/THAL/MA
endotoxicosis	*END/TOX/KOE/SIS		EN/OF/THAL/MAOE/YA
endotoxin	*END/TOK/SIN	enophthalmos	EN/OF/THAL/MOS
endotoxoid	*END/TOX/OID	enophthalmus	EN/OF/THAL/MUS
endotracheal	*END/TRAIK/YAL	enorganic	EN/OR/GAN/IK
endotracheitis	*END/TRAIK/YAOITS	enostosis	EN/OS/TOE/SIS
endotrachelitis	*END/TRAIK/LAOITS	Enovid	E/NOV/ID
	*END/TRAK/LAOITS	enoyl	AOEN/WIL
endotrypsin	*END/TRIP/SIN		E/NOIL
endourethral	*END/YAOU/RAO*ET/RAL	en plaque	EN/PLAK
endouterine	*END/YAOUT/RIN	enpromate	EN/PRO/MAIT
endovaccination	*END/VAX/NAIGS	Enrich	EN/R*IFP
endovasculitis	*END/VAS/KLAOITS		K-P/EN/RIFP
endovenitis	*END/VAOE/NAOITS	Enrich Liquid Nutrition	EN/R*IFP/LIK/WID/NAOU/TRIGS
endovenous	*END/VAOEN/OUS	enrichment	EN/RIFP/-MT
end piece	END/PAOES	ens	ENZ
endplate	END/PLAET	ensheathing	EN/SHAO*ET/-G
end point	END/POINT	ensiform	ENS/FORM
end product	END/PRUKT		EN/SI/FORM
	END/PRO/DUKT	ensiformis	ENS/FOR/MIS
	END/PROD/UKT		EN/SI/FOR/MIS
endrysone	EN/DRI/SOEN	ensisternum	EN/SIS/TER/NUM
end-tidal	END/H-F/TAOI/DAL	ensomphalus	EN/SOM/FLUS
Endurance Packs	EN/DAOURNS/PAK/-S		EN/SOM/FA/LUS
Enduron	EN/DAOU/RON	enstrophe	EN/STROE/FAOE
Enduronyl	EN/DAOUR/NIL	Ensure	EN/SH*UR
	EN/DUR/NIL		K-P/EN/SHUR
Enduronyl Forte	EN/DAOUR/NIL/FOR/TAI	Ensure HN	EN/SH*UR/H-RBGS/N*RBGS
	EN/DUR/NIL/FOR/TAI		K-P/EN/SHUR/H-RBGS/N*RBGS
endyma	END/MA	Ensure Plus	EN/SH*UR/PLUS
	EN/DI/MA		K-P/EN/SHUR/PLUS/H-RBGS/
endymal	END/MAL		N*RBGS
	EN/DI/MAL	Ensure Plus HN	EN/SH*UR/PLUS/H-RBGS/
-ene	AOEN		N*RBGS
enediol	AOEN/DI/OL		K-P/EN/SHUR/PLUS
enema	EN/MA	Ensure Pudding	EN/SH*UR/PUD/-G
enemata	EN/MA/TA		K-P/EN/SHUR/PUD/-G
enemator	EN/MAI/TOR	ent-	SPW-
enemiasis	EN/MAOI/SIS		ENT
Ener-B	EN/ER/B-RBGS		EN/T-
	EN/ER/BAOE	entad	SPWAD
energetic	EN/ER/JET/IK		EN/TAD
energetics	EN/ER/JET/IK/-S	ental	SPWAL
energid	EN/ER/JID		EN/TAL
energizer	EN/ER/JAOIZ/ER	entamebiasis	ENT/MAOE/BAOI/SIS

	SPWA/MAOE/BAOI/SIS
entamebic	ENT/MAOEB/IK
	SPWA/MAOEB/IK
Entamoeba	ENT/MAOE/BA
	SPWA/MAOE/BA
entasia	SPWAIZ/YA
	EN/TAIZ/YA
entasis	SPWA/SIS
	ENT/SIS
entatic	SPWAT/IK
	EN/TAT/IK
entelechy	SPWEL/KI
	EN/TEL/KI
entepicondyle	SPWEP/KON/DAOIL
	EN/TEP/KON/DAOIL
enter(o)-	SPWER/R(O)
	SPWR(v)- if part of stroke
	ENT/R-
enteraden	SPWER/DEN
enteradenitis	SPWER/AD/NAOITS
enteral	SPWERL
	SPWRAL
	ENT/RAL
enteralgia	SPWRAL/JA
	SPWER/RAL/JA
	ENT/RAL/JA
enteramine	SPWER/AM/MIN
	SPWER/AM/MAOEN
enterectasis	SPWREKT/SIS
	SPWER/REKT/SIS
enterectomy	SPWREKT/M*I
	SPWER/REKT/M*I
enterelcosis	SPWREL/KOE/SIS
	SPWER/REL/KOE/SIS
	SPWER/EL/KOE/SIS
enteric	SPWER/IK
entericoid	SPWER/KOID
entericoides	SPWER/KOI/DAOEZ
enteritidis	SPWRIT/DIS
	SPWER/RIT/DIS
enteritis	SPWRAOITS
	SPWER/RAOITS
enteroanastomosis	SPWER/RO/AI/NA*S/MOE/SIS
enteroanthelone	SPWER/RO/A*NT/LOEN
enteroantigen	SPWER/RO/A*ENT/JEN
enteroapocleisis	SPWER/RO/AP/KLAOI/SIS
Enterobacter	SPWER/RO/BAK/TER
enterobacteria	SPWER/RO/BAK/TAOER/YA
Enterobacteriaceae	SPWER/RO/BAK/TAOER/YAIS/YAE
enterobacteriotherapy	SPWER/RO/BAK/TAOER/YO/THER/PI
enterobacterium	SPWER/RO/BAK/TAOERM
enterobiasis	SPWER/RO/BAOI/SIS
enterobiliary	SPWER/RO/BIL/YAIR
Enterobius	SPWER/ROEB/YUS
enterobrosia	SPWER/RO/BROEZ/YA
enterobrosis	SPWER/RO/BROE/SIS
enterocele	SPWER/RO/SAO*EL
enterocentesis	SPWER/RO/SEN/TAOE/SIS
enterocholecystostomy	SPWER/RO/KOEL/SIS/TO*S/M*I
enterocholecystotomy	SPWER/RO/KOEL/SIS/TOT/M*I
enterochromaffin	SPWER/RO/KROE/MAFN
enterocleisis	SPWER/RO/KLAOI/SIS
enteroclysis	SPWER/ROK/LI/SIS
	SPWER/OK/LI/SIS
enteroclysm	SPWER/RO/KLIFM
enterococcemia	SPWER/RO/KOK/SAOEM/YA
enterococci	SPWER/RO/KOK/SAOI
enterococcus	SPWER/RO/KOK/KUS
enterocolectomy	SPWER/RO/KO/LEKT/M*I
enterocolitis	SPWER/RO/KO/LAOITS
enterocolostomy	SPWER/RO/KO/LO*S/M*I
enterocutaneous	SPWER/RO/KAOU/TAIN/YOUS
enterocyst	SPWER/RO/S*IS
enterocystocele	SPWER/RO/S*IS/SAO*EL
enterocystoma	SPWER/RO/SIS/TOE/MA
enterocyte	SPWER/RO/SAO*IT
enterodynia	SPWER/RO/DIN/YA
enteroenterostomy	SPWER/RO/SPWRO*S/M*I
enteroepiplocele	SPWER/RO/PIP/LO/SAO*EL
	SPWER/RO/E/PIP/LO/SAO*EL
enterogastric	SPWER/RO/GAS/TRIK
enterogastritis	SPWER/RO/GAS/TRAOITS
enterogastrone	SPWER/RO/GAS/TROEN
enterogenous	SPWROJ/NOUS
	SPWER/ROJ/NOUS
enteroglucagon	SPWER/RO/GLAOUK/GON
enterogram	SPWER/RO/GRAM
enterograph	SPWER/RO/GRAF
enterography	SPWER/ROG/FI
enterohepatic	SPWER/RO/HE/PAT/IK
enterohepatitis	SPWER/RO/HEP/TAOITS
enterohepatocele	SPWER/RO/HEPT/SAO*EL
enterohepatopexy	SPWER/RO/HEPT/PEK/SI
enterohydrocele	SPWER/RO/HAOI/DRO/SAO*EL
enteroidea	SPWROID/YA
	SPWER/ROID/YA
enterointestinal	SPWER/RO/SPW*ES/NAL
enterokinase	SPWER/RO/KAOI/NAIS
enterokinesia	SPWER/RO/KI/NAOEZ/YA
enterokinesis	SPWER/RO/KI/NAOE/SIS
enterokinetic	SPWER/RO/KI/NET/IK
enterolith	SPWER/RO/L*IT
enterolithiasis	SPWER/RO/LI/THAOI/SIS
enterologist	SPWRO*LGS
	SPWER/RO*LGS
enterology	SPWROLG
	SPWER/ROLG
enterolysis	SPWROL/SIS
	SPWER/ROL/SIS
enteromegalia	SPWER/RO/ME/GAIL/YA
enteromegaly	SPWER/RO/MEG/LI
enteromenia	SPWER/RO/MAOEN/YA
enteromere	SPWER/RO/MAOER
enteromerocele	SPWER/RO/MAOER/SAO*EL
enterometer	SPWER/ROM/TER
Enteromonas	SPWER/RO/MOE/NAS
	SPWER/ROM/NAS
enteromycosis	SPWER/RO/MAOI/KOE/SIS
enteron	SPWER/RON
enteroneuritis	SPWER/RO/NAOU/RAOITS
enteronitis	SPWER/RO/NAOITS
enteroparesis	SPWER/RO/PRAOE/SIS
	SPWER/RO/PAR/SIS
enteropathica	SPWER/RO/PA*T/KA
enteropathogen	SPWER/RO/PA*T/JEN
enteropathogenesis	SPWER/RO/PA*T/JEN/SIS
enteropathogenic	SPWER/RO/PA*T/JEN/IK
enteropathy	SPWROP/TH*I
	SPWER/ROP/TH*I
enteropeptidase	SPWER/RO/PEPT/DAIS
enteropexy	SPWER/RO/PEK/SI
enteroplasty	SPWER/RO/PLAS/TI
enteroplegia	SPWER/RO/PLAOE/JA
enteroplex	SPWER/RO/PLEX
enteroplexy	SPWER/RO/PLEK/SI
enteroproctia	SPWER/RO/PROK/SHA
enteroptosia	SPWER/RO/TOEZ/YA
	SPWER/ROP/TOEZ/YA
enteroptosis	SPWER/RO/TOE/SIS
	SPWER/ROP/TOE/SIS
enteroptotic	SPWER/RO/TOT/IK
	SPWER/ROP/TOT/IK
enterorenal	SPWER/RO/RAOENL
enterorrhagia	SPWER/RO/RAI/JA
enterorrhaphy	SPWROR/FI
	SPWER/ROR/FI
enterorrhexis	SPWER/RO/REK/SIS
enteroscope	SPWER/RO/SKOEP
enterosepsis	SPWER/RO/SEP/SIS
enterosorption	SPWER/RO/SORPGS
enterospasm	SPWER/RO/SPAFM
enterostasis	SPWRO*S/SIS
	SPWER/RO*S/SIS
enterostaxis	SPWER/RO/STAK/SIS
enterostenosis	SPWER/RO/STE/NOE/SIS
enterostomal	SPWER/RO/STOE/MAL
enterostomy	SPWRO*S/M*I
	SPWER/RO*S/M*I
enterotome	SPWER/RO/TOEM
enterotomy	SPWROT/M*I
	SPWER/ROT/M*I
enterotoxemia	SPWER/RO/TOK/SAOEM/YA
enterotoxication	SPWER/RO/TOX/KAIGS
enterotoxigenic	SPWER/RO/TOX/JEN/IK
enterotoxin	SPWER/RO/TOK/SIN
enterotoxism	SPWER/RO/TOK/SIFM
	SPWER/RO/TOX/IFM
enterotropic	SPWER/RO/TROP/IK
enterovaginal	SPWER/RO/VAJ/NAL
enterovenous	SPWER/RO/VAOEN/OUS
enterovesical	SPWER/RO/VES/KAL
enteroviral	SPWER/RO/VAOIRL
enterovirus	SPWER/RO/VAOI/RUS
Enterovirus	K-P/SPWER/RO/VAOI/RUS
enterozoic	SPWER/RO/ZOIK
	SPWER/RO/ZOE/IK

enterozoon	SPWER/RO/ZAON	entropion	EN/TRIP/SIS
-entery	SPWER/RI		SPWROEP/YON
Entex	EN/TEX		EN/TROEP/YON
	SPWEX	entropionize	SPWROEP/YON/AOIZ
enthalpy	EN/THAL/PI		EN/TROEP/YON/AOIZ
enthesis	*ENT/SIS	entropium	SPWROEP/YUM
	EN/THAOE/SIS		EN/TROEP/YUM
enthesitis	EN/THE/SAOITS	entropy	SPWRO/PI
enthesopathic	EN/THAOES/PA*T/IK		SPWROE/PI
enthesopathy	EN/THAOE/SOP/TH*I		EN/TRO/PI
enthetic	EN/THET/IK		EN/TROE/PI
enthetobiosis	EN/THET/BAO*I/YOE/SIS	Entuss	EN/TUSZ
enthlasis	*ENT/LA/SIS		SPWUSZ
	EN/TLA/SIS	Entuss-D	EN/TUSZ/D-RBGS
en thyrse	EN/TIRS		SPWUSZ/D-RBGS
entire	SPWAOIR	entypy	SPWI/PI
entiris	SPWAOI/RIS		ENT/PI
	EN/TAOI/RIS		SPWAOI/PI
entity	SPWI/TI		EN/TAOI/PI
	ENT/TI	enucleate	E/NAOUK/LAIT
ento-	SPWO	enucleated	E/NAOUK/LAIT/-D
	ENT	enucleation	E/NAOUK/LAIGS
	EN/TO	enuresis	EN/YAOU/RAOE/SIS
entoblast	SPWO/BLA*S	enuretic	EN/YAOU/RET/IK
entocele	SPWO/SAO*EL	envelop	EN/VEL/OP
entochondrostosis	SPWO/KON/DROS/TO/SIS	envelope	EN/VE/LOEP
	SPWO/KON/DROS/TOE/SIS	envenomation	EN/VEN/MAIGS
entochoroidea	SPWO/KOE/ROID/YA	Enviclusive	EN/VI/KLAOUS/IV
entocnemial	SPWOK/NAOEM/YAL	Envinet	EN/VI/NET
entocone	SPWO/KOEN	environment	VAOIRMT
entoconid	SPWO/KO/NID		EN/VAOIRMT
entocornea	SPWO/KORN/YA	Envisan	EN/VI/SAN
entocranial	SPWO/KRAIN/YAL	envy	EN/VI
entocranium	SPWO/KRAIN/YUM	enzootic	EN/ZOE/OT/IK
entocuneiform	SPWO/KAOU/NAOE/FORM	enzygotic	EN/ZAOI/GOT/IK
entocyte	SPWO/SAO*IT	enzymatic	ENZ/MAT/IK
entoderm	SPWO/DERM		EN/ZI/MAT/IK
entodermal	SPWO/DER/MAL	enzyme	EN/ZAOIM
entodermic	SPWO/DERM/IK	enzymic	EN/ZAOIM/IK
entoectad	SPWO/EK/TAD		EN/ZIM/IK
Entolase	SPWO/LAIS	enzymicum	EN/ZAOIM/KUM
Entoloma sinuatum	SPWO/LOE/MA/SAOIN/YAI/TUM	enzymoimmunoelectrophoresis	
entome´	SPWOEM		EN/ZAOIM/IM/NO/LEK/TRO/
entomere	SPWO/MAOER		FRAOE/SIS
entomesoderm	SPWO/MES/DERM	enzymologist	EN/ZAOI/MO*LGS
entomion	SPWOEM/YON	enzymology	EN/ZAOI/MOLG
entomogenous	SPWO/MOJ/NOUS	enzymolysis	EN/ZAOI/MOL/SIS
	ENT/MOJ/NOUS	enzymopathy	EN/ZAOI/MOP/TH*I
entomologist	SPWO/MO*LGS	enzymosis	EN/ZAOI/MOE/SIS
	ENT/MO*LGS	enzymuria	EN/ZAOIM/YAOUR/YA
entomology	SPWO/MOLG	eonism	E/NIFM
	ENT/MOLG		E/YO/NIFM
entomophobia	SPWO/MO/FOEB/YA	eopsia	E/OPS/YA
Entomophthora	SPWO/MOF/THRA	eos (eosinophils)	E/YOE/-S
	SPWO/MOF/THO/RA	eosin	E/SIN
Entomophthoraceae	SPWO/MOF/THRAIS/YAE		E/YO/SIN
Entomophthorales	SPWO/MOF/THRAI/LAOEZ	eosino-	E/SIN
entomophthoramycosis	SPWO/MOF/THRA/MAOI/KOE/SIS		E/YO/SIN
	SPWO/MOF/THO/RA/MAOI/KOE/	eosinocyte	E/SIN/SAO*IT
	SIS	eosinopenia	E/SIN/PAOEN/YA
Entomopoxvirus	SPWO/MO/POX/VAOI/RUS	eosinophil	E/SIN/FIL
entophthalmia	SPWOF/THAL/MA	eosinophile	E/SIN/FAOIL
	SPWOF/THAL/MAOE/YA	eosinophilia	E/SIN/FIL/YA
	EN/TOF/THAL/MA	eosinophilic	E/SIN/FIL/IK
	EN/TOF/THAL/MAOE/YA	eosinophilopoietin	E/SIN/FIL/POI/TIN
entopic	SPWOP/IK	eosinophilosis	E/SIN/FI/LOE/SIS
	EN/TOP/IK	eosinophilotactic	E/SIN/FIL/TAKT/IK
entoplasm	SPWO/PLAFM	eosinophilous	E/SIN/OF/LOUS
entoplastic	SPWO/PLA*S/IK	eosinophiluria	E/SIN/FIL/YAOUR/YA
entoptic	SPWOPT/IK	eosinotactic	E/SIN/TAKT/IK
	EN/TOPT/IK	eosinotaxis	E/SIN/TAK/SIS
entoptoscope	SPWOPT/SKOEP	eosolate	E/OES/LAIT
	EN/TOPT/SKOEP	eosophobia	E/SOE/FOEB/YA
entoptoscopy	SPWOP/TOS/KPI	epactal	E/PAK/TAL
	EN/TOP/TOS/KPI	epallobiosis	EP/AL/LO/BAO*I/YOE/SIS
entoretina	SPWO/RET/NA		EP/AL/BAO*I/YOE/SIS
entosarc	SPWO/SARK	epamniotic	EP/AM/NOT/IK
entostosis	SPWOS/TOE/SIS		EP/AM/NAOE/OT/IK
	EN/TOS/TOE/SIS	eparsalgia	EP/AR/SAL/JA
entotympanic	SPWO/TIM/PAN/IK	eparterial	EP/AR/TAOERL
entozoa	SPWO/ZOE/WA	epaxial	EP/AX/YAL
Entozoa	K-P/SPWO/ZOE/WA	epencephalic	EP/EN/SFAL/IK
entozoal	SPWO/ZOEL	epencephalon	EP/EN/SEF/LON
	SPWO/ZOE/WAL	ependopathy	EP/EN/DOP/TH*I
entozoon	SPWO/ZAON	ependym(o)-	EP/END/M(O)
Entozyme	SPWO/ZAOIM		E/PEND/M(O)
entrails	SPWRAIL/-S	ependyma	EP/END/MA
	EN/TRAIL/-S		E/PEND/MA
entripsis	SPWRIP/SIS		

ependymal	EP/END/MAL	epidemiologic	EP/DAOEM/YO/LOJ/IK
	E/PEND/MAL	epidemiologist	EP/DAOEM/YO*LGS
ependymitis	EP/END/MAOITS	epidemiology	EP/DAOEM/YOLG
	E/PEND/MAOITS	epiderm	EP/DERM
ependymoblast	EP/END/MO/BLA*S	epiderm(o)-	EP/DERM
ependymoblastoma	EP/END/MO/BLAS/TOE/MA		EP/DER/M(O)
ependymocyte	EP/END/MO/SAO*IT	epiderma	EP/DER/MA
ependymocytoma	EP/END/MO/SAOI/TOE/MA	epidermal	EP/DER/MAL
ependymoma	EP/END/MOE/MA	epidermalization	EP/DER/MAL/ZAIGS
ependymopathy	EP/END/MOP/TH*I	epidermat(o)-	EP/DERM/T(O)
epersalgia	EP/ER/SAL/JA		EP/DER/MAT
Eperythrozoon	EP/R*IT/RO/ZAON		EP/DERMT
eperythrozoonosis	EP/R*IT/RO/ZOE/NOE/SIS	epidermatic	EP/DER/MAT/IK
ephapse	EF/APS	epidermatidis	EP/DER/MAT/DIS
	E/FAPS	epidermatitis	EP/DERM/TAOITS
ephaptic	E/FAPT/IK	epidermatoplasty	EP/DERM/TO/PLAS/TI
ephebiatrics	E/FAOEB/YAT/RIK/-S	epidermic	EP/DERM/IK
ephebic	E/FAOEB/IK	epidermicula	EP/DER/MIK/LA
	E/FEB/IK	epidermidalization	EP/DER/MID/LI/ZAIGS
ephebogenesis	EF/BO/JEN/SIS	epidermides	EP/DERM/DAOEZ
ephebogenic	EF/BO/JEN/IK	epidermidis	EP/DERM/DIS
ephebology	EF/BOLG	epidermidosis	EP/DERM/DOE/SIS
ephedrine	E/FED/RIN	epidermis	EP/DER/MIS
	EF/DRIN	epidermitis	EP/DER/MAOITS
ephelides	E/FAOEL/DAOEZ	epidermization	EP/DERM/ZAIGS
	E/FEL/DAOEZ	epidermodysplasia	EP/DERM/DIS/PLAIZ/YA
	EF/AOEL/DAOEZ	epidermoid	EP/DER/MOID
ephelis	E/FAOE/LIS	epidermoidoma	EP/DER/MOI/DOE/MA
	EF/E/LIS	epidermolysis	EP/DER/MOL/SIS
ephemera	E/FEM/RA	epidermolytic	EP/DERM/LIT/IK
ephemeral	E/FEM/RAL	epidermomycosis	EP/DERM/MAOI/KOE/SIS
	E/FAOEM/RAL	epidermophytid	EP/DER/MOF/TID
epi-	EP	epidermophytin	EP/DER/MOF/TIN
epiallopregnanolone	EP/AL/PREG/NAN/LOEN	Epidermophyton	EP/DER/MOF/TON
	EP/AL/LO/PREG/NAN/LOEN	epidermophytosis	EP/DERM/FAOI/TOE/SIS
epiandrosterone	EP/AN/DRO*S/ROEN	epidermopoiesis	EP/DERM/POI/SIS
epiblast	EP/BLA*S	epidermosis	EP/DER/MOE/SIS
epiblastic	EP/BLA*S/IK	epidermotropic	EP/DERM/TROP/IK
epiblepharon	EP/BLEF/RON	epidermotropism	EP/DER/MOT/RO/PIFM
epibole	E/PIB/LAOE	epidialysis	EP/DI/AL/SIS
epiboly	E/PIB/LI	epidiascopy	EP/DI/AS/KPI
epibulbar	EP/BUL/BAR	epididym(o)-	EP/DID/M(O)
epicanthal	EP/KAN/THAL	epididymal	EP/DID/MAL
epicanthic	EP/KA*NT/IK	epididymectomy	EP/DID/MEKT/M*I
epicanthine	EP/KAN/THAOEN	epididymidectomy	EP/DID/MI/DEKT/M*I
epicanthus	EP/KAN/THUS	epididymides	EP/DI/DIM/DAOEZ
epicarcinogen	EP/KAR/SIN/JEN		EP/DID/MI/DAOEZ
epicardia	EP/KARD/YA	epididymidis	EP/DI/DIM/DIS
epicardial	EP/KARD/YAL		EP/DID/MI/DIS
epicardiectomy	EP/KARD/YEKT/M*I	epididymis	EP/DID/MIS
epicardiolysis	EP/KARD/YOL/SIS	epididymisoplasty	EP/DID/MIS/PLAS/TI
epicardium	EP/KARD/YUM	epididymitis	EP/DID/MAOITS
epicauma	EP/KAU/MA	epididymodeferentectomy	EP/DID/MO/DEFRN/TEKT/M*I
epicentral	EP/SEN/TRAL	epididymodeferential	EP/DID/MO/DEFRN/-RBL
	EP/STRAL	epididymo-orchitis	EP/DID/MO/OR/KAOITS
epichitosamine	EP/KAOE/TOES/MIN	epididymoplasty	EP/DID/MO/PLAS/TI
epichordal	EP/KHOR/DAL	epididymotomy	EP/DID/MOT/M*I
epichorion	EP/KOER/YON	epididymovasectomy	EP/DID/MO/VA/SEKT/M*I
epicillin	EP/SLIN	epididymovasostomy	EP/DID/MO/VA/SO*S/M*I
	EP/SIL/LIN	epidural	EP/DAOURL
epicladosporic	EP/KLAD/SPOR/IK	epidurale	EP/DAOU/RAI/LAOE
epicomus	EP/KO/MUS	epidurography	EP/DAOU/ROG/FI
	E/PIK/MUS	epiestriol	EP/ES/TROL
epicondylalgia	EP/KOND/LAL/JA		EP/ES/TRAOE/OL
epicondyle	EP/KON/DAOIL	epifascial	EP/FARBL
epicondyli	EP/KOND/LAOI	Epifoam	EP/FOEM
epicondylian	EP/KON/DIL/YAN	epigaster	EP/GAS/TER
epicondylic	EP/KON/DIL/IK	epigastralgia	EP/GAS/TRAL/JA
epicondylitis	EP/KOND/LAOITS	epigastric	EP/GAS/TRIK
epicondylus	EP/KOND/LUS	epigastrica	EP/GAS/TRI/KA
epicoracoid	EP/KOR/KOID	epigastricae	EP/GAS/TRI/SAE
epicorneascleritis	EP/KORN/YA/SKLE/RAOITS	epigastrium	EP/GAS/TRUM
epicostal	EP/KOS/TAL		EP/GAS/TRAOE/UM
epicranial	EP/KRAIN/YAL	epigastrius	EP/GAS/TRUS
epicranium	EP/KRAIN/YUM		EP/GAS/TRAOE/YUS
epicranius	EP/KRAIN/YUS	epigastrocele	EP/GAS/TRO/SAO*EL
epicrisis	EP/KRAOI/SIS	epigenesis	EP/JEN/SIS
epicritic	EP/KRIT/IK	epigenetic	EP/JE/NET/IK
epicuticle	EP/KAOUT/K-L	epigenetics	EP/JE/NET/IK/-S
epicystitis	EP/SIS/TAOITS	epiglottectomy	EP/GLOT/TEKT/M*I
epicystotomy	EP/SIS/TOT/M*I	epiglottic	EP/GLOT/IK
epicyte	EP/SAO*IT	epiglottica	EP/GLOT/KA
epidemic	EP/DEM/IK	epiglotticum	EP/GLOT/KUM
epidemica	EP/DEM/KA	epiglotticus	EP/GLOT/KUS
epidemicity	EP/DE/MIS/TI	epiglottidea	EP/GLO/TID/YA
	EP/DEM/IS/TI		EP/GLOT/TID/YA
epidemicum	EP/DEM/KUM	epiglottidean	EP/GLO/TID/YAN
epidemiogenesis	EP/DAOEM/YO/JEN/SIS		EP/GLOT/TID/YAN
epidemiography	EP/DAOEM/YOG/FI	epiglottidectomy	EP/GLOT/DEKT/M*I

epiglottidis	EP/GLOT/DIS	epiphysiopathy	EP/FIZ/YOP/TH*I
epiglottiditis	EP/GLOT/DAOITS	epiphysis	E/PIF/SIS
epiglottis	EP/GLOT/TIS	epiphysitis	E/PIF/SAOITS
epiglottitis	EP/GLOT/TAOITS	epiphyte	EP/FAOIT
epignathous	E/PIG/NA/THOUS	epiphytic	EP/FIT/IK
epignathus	E/PIG/NA/THUS	epipial	EP/PAOIL
epigonal	E/PIG/NAL		EP/PAOI/YAL
epihyal	EP/HAOIL	epiplastic	EP/PLA*S/IK
epihyoid	EP/HAOI/OID	epipleural	EP/PLAOURL
epikeratophakia	EP/KER/TO/FAK/YA	epiplo-	E/PIP/LO
	EP/KER/TO/FAIK/YA		PIP/LO
epikeratoprosthesis	EP/KER/TO/PROS/THAOE/SIS		EP/PLO
epilamellar	EP/LA/MEL/LAR	epiplocele	E/PIP/LO/SAO*EL
epilans	EP/LANZ		PIP/LO/SAO*EL
epilate	EP/LAIT	epiploectomy	EP/PLOE/EKT/M*I
epilating	EP/LAIT/-G		EP/PLO/EKT/M*I
epilation	EP/LAIGS	epiploenterocele	E/PIP/LO/SPWER/RO/SAO*EL
epilatory	E/PIL/TOIR		PIP/LO/SPWER/RO/SAO*EL
epilemma	EP/LEM/MA	epiploic	EP/PLOIK
epilemmal	EP/LEM/MAL		EP/PLOE/IK
epilepidoma	EP/LEP/DOE/MA	epiploicae	EP/PLOI/SAE
epilepsia	EP/LEPS/YA		EP/PLOE/SAE
epilepsy	EP/LEP/SI	epiploitis	E/PIP/LO/AOITS
epilept(o)-	EP/LEPT		PIP/LO/AOITS
	EP/LEP/T(O)	epiplomerocele	E/PIP/LO/MAOER/SAO*EL
epileptic	EP/LEPT/IK		PIP/LO/MAOER/SAO*EL
epileptica	EP/LEPT/KA	epiplomphalocele	EP/PLOM/FAL/SAO*EL
epileptiform	EP/LEPT/FORM	epiploon	E/PIP/LON
epileptogenic	EP/LEPT/JEN/IK		E/PIP/LO/WON
epileptogenous	EP/LEP/TOJ/NOUS		PIP/LON
epileptoid	EP/LEP/TOID		PIP/LO/WON
epileptologist	EP/LEP/TO*LGS	epiplopexy	E/PIP/LO/PEK/SI
epileptology	EP/LEP/TOLG		PIP/LO/PEK/SI
epilesional	EP/LAOEGS/NAL	epiploplasty	E/PIP/LO/PLAS/TI
epiloia	EP/LOI/YA		PIP/LO/PLAS/TI
epimandibular	EP/MAN/DIB/LAR	epiplorrhaphy	E/PIP/LOR/FI
epimastical	EP/MA*S/KAL		PIP/LOR/FI
epimastigote	EP/MA*S/GOET	epipteric	EP/TER/IK
epimenorrhagia	EP/MEN/RAI/JA	epipygus	EP/PAOI/GUS
epimenorrhea	EP/MEN/RAOE/YA	epipyramis	EP/PIR/MIS
epimer	EP/MER	epirhamnose	EP/RAM/NOEZ
epimerase	EP/MER/AIS		EP/RAM/NOES
	E/PIM/RAIS	epirotulian	EP/ROE/TAOUL/YAN
epimere	EP/MAOER	epirozole	E/PIR/ZOEL
epimerite	EP/MAOER/AOIT	episarkin	EP/SAR/KIN
	EP/MER/AOIT	episclera	EP/SKLAOER/RA
epimestrol	EP/MES/TROL	episcleral	EP/SKLAOERL
epimetrium	EP/MAOET/RUM	episclerales	EP/SKLE/RAI/LAOEZ
	EP/MAOE/TRAOE/YUM	episcleritis	EP/SKLE/RAOITS
epimicroscope	EP/MAOI/KRO/SKOEP	episi(o)-	E/PIZ/Y(O)
epimorphic	EP/MOR/FIK		E/PIS/Y(O)
epimorphosis	EP/MOR/FOE/SIS	episioperineoplasty	E/PIZ/YO/P*ER/NAOE/PLAS/TI
epimysiotomy	EP/MIS/YOT/M*I	episioperineorrhaphy	E/PIZ/YO/P*ER/NAOE/YOR/FI
epimysium	EP/MIS/YUM	episioplasty	E/PIZ/YO/PLAS/TI
epinephrine	EP/NEF/RIN	episiorrhaphy	E/PIZ/YOR/FI
epinephrinemia	EP/NEF/RI/NAOEM/YA	episiostenosis	E/PIZ/YO/STE/NOE/SIS
epinephros	EP/NEF/ROS	episiotomy	E/PIZ/YOT/M*I
epinephryl	EP/NEF/RIL	episode	EP/SOED
epineural	EP/NAOURL	episodic	EP/SOD/IK
epineurial	EP/NAOUR/YAL	episodica	EP/SOD/KA
	(not EP/NAOURL; see epineural)	episome	EP/SOEM
epineurium	EP/NAOURM	epispadia	EP/SPAID/YA
	EP/NAOUR/YUM	epispadiac	EP/SPAID/YAK
epinosic	EP/NOES/IK	epispadial	EP/SPAID/YAL
epinosis	EP/NOE/SIS	epispadias	EP/SPAID/YAS
epionychium	EP/YO/NIK/YUM	epispastic	EP/SPA*S/IK
epiorchium	EP/ORK/YUM	epispinal	EP/SPAOINL
epiotic	EP/OT/IK	episplenitis	EP/SPLAOE/NAOITS
	EP/OET/IK		EP/SPLE/NAOITS
epipastic	EP/PA*S/IK	epistasis	E/P*IS/SIS
EpiPen	EP/PEN	epistasy	E/P*IS/SI
EpiPen Jr.	EP/PEN/J-R	epistatic	EP/STAT/IK
epipericardial	EP/P*ER/KARD/YAL	epistaxis	EP/STAK/SIS
epipharyngeal	EP/FRIN/JAL	epistemophilia	E/P*IS/MO/FIL/YA
epipharyngitis	EP/FARN/JAOITS	episternal	EP/STERNL
epipharynx	EP/FARNGS	episternum	EP/STER/NUM
epiphenomenon	EP/FE/NOM/NON	episthotonos	E/PIS/THOT/NOS
epiphora	E/PIF/RA	epistrophei	EP/STROEF/YAOI
epiphrenal	EP/FRAOENL		EP/STROF/YAOI
epiphrenic	EP/FREN/IK	epistropheus	EP/STROEF/YUS
epiphysaria	EP/FI/SAIR/YA		EP/STROF/YUS
epiphyseal	see epiphysial	epitarsus	EP/TAR/SUS
epiphyses	E/PIF/SAOEZ	epitaxy	EP/TAK/SI
epiphysial	EP/FIZ/YAL	epitela	EP/TAOE/LA
epiphysialis	EP/FIZ/YAI/LIS	epitendineum	EP/TEN/DIN/YUM
epiphysiodesis	EP/FIZ/YOD/SIS	epitenon	E/PIT/NON
epiphysioid	EP/FIZ/YOID		EP/TAOE/NON
epiphysiolysis	EP/FIZ/YOL/SIS	epitestosterone	EP/TES/TO*S/ROEN
epiphysiometer	EP/FIZ/YOM/TER	epithalamic	EP/THA/LAM/IK

epithalamus	EP/THAL/MUS			EP/STAOIN
epithalaxia	EP/THA/LAX/YA	epul-		EP/L-
epitheli(o)-	EP/THAOEL/Y(O)			EP/YAOU/L-
epithelia	EP/THAOEL/YA			EP/YU/L-
epithelial	EP/THAOEL/YAL			EP/YAOUL
epitheliale	EP/THAOEL/YAI/LAOE	epulides		EP/YAOUL/DAOEZ
epithelialis	EP/THAOEL/YAI/LIS	epulis		EP/LIS
epithelialization	EP/THAOEL/YAL/ZAIGS			EP/YAOU/LIS
epithelialize	EP/THAOEL/YAL/AOIZ	epuloerectile		EP/LO/E/REK/TAOIL
epitheliitis	EP/THAOEL/YAOITS	epulofibroma		EP/LO/FAOI/BROE/MA
epithelioceptor	EP/THAOEL/YO/SEP/TOR	epuloid		EP/LOID
epitheliochorial	EP/THAOEL/YO/KOER/YAL	epulosis		EP/LOE/SIS
epitheliocyte	EP/THAOEL/YO/SAO*IT	epulotic		EP/LOT/IK
epitheliofibril	EP/THAOEL/YO/FAOI/BRIL	Equagesic		EK/WA/JAOEZ/IK
epitheliogenetic	EP/THAOEL/YO/JE/NET/IK	Equanil		EK/WA/NIL
epitheliogenic	EP/THAOEL/YO/JEN/IK	equate		E/KWAIT
epithelioglandular	EP/THAOEL/YO/GLAND/LAR	equation		E/KWAIGS
epithelioid	EP/THAOEL/YOID	equational		E/KWAIGS/NAL
epitheliolysin	EP/THAOEL/YOL/SIN	equator		E/KWAI/TOR
epitheliolysis	EP/THAOEL/YOL/SIS	equatorial		E/KWA/TOIRL
epitheliolytic	EP/THAOEL/YO/LIT/IK			EK/WA/TOIRL
epithelioma	EP/THAOEL/YOE/MA	equi (word)		E/KWAOI
epitheliomatosis	EP/THAOEL/YOEM/TOE/SIS	equi- (prefix)		E/KWI
	EP/THAOEL/YO/MA/TOE/SIS			EK/WI
epitheliomatous	EP/THAOEL/YO/MA/TOUS	equiaxial		E/KWI/AX/YAL
epitheliomuscular	EP/THAOEL/YO/MUS/KLAR	equicaloric		E/KWI/KA/LOR/IK
epitheliopathy	EP/THAOEL/YOP/TH*I			E/KWI/KA/LOER/IK
epitheliosis	EP/THAOEL/YOE/SIS	equidistant		E/KWI/DIS/TANT
epitheliotoxin	EP/THAOEL/YO/TOK/SIN	equilateral		E/KWI/LAT/RAL
epitheliotropic	EP/THAOEL/YO/TROP/IK	equilenin		EK/WI/LEN/NIN
epithelite	EP/THAOE/LAOIT	equilibration		E/KWIL/BRAIGS
epithelium	EP/THAOEL/YUM	equilibrator		E/KWIL/BRAI/TOR
epithelization	EP/THAOEL/ZAIGS	equilibrium		E/KWI/LIB/RUM
epithem	EP/THEM	equilin		EK/WI/LIN
epithesis	E/P*IT/SIS	equimolar		E/KWI/MOE/LAR
epithet	EP/THET	equimolecular		E/KWI/MOE/LEK/LAR
epithiazide	EP/THAOI/ZAOID	equination		EK/WI/NAIGS
Epitol	EP/TOL			EK/WI/NAIGS
epitonic	EP/TON/IK	equine		E/KWAOIN
epitope	EP/TOEP	equinophobia		E/KWAOIN/FOEB/YA
epitoxoid	EP/TOK/SOID			EK/WI/NO/FOEB/YA
	EP/TOX/OID	equinovalgus		E/KWAOIN/VAL/GUS
Epitrate	EP/TRAIT			EK/WI/NO/VAL/GUS
epitrichial	EP/TRIK/YAL	equinovarus		E/KWAOIN/VAI/RUS
epitrichium	EP/TRIK/YUM			EK/WI/NO/VAI/RUS
epitriquetrum	EP/TR*I/KWAOE/TRUM	equinus		E/KWAOI/NUS
epitrochlea	EP/TROK/LA	equipotential		E/KWI/POE/TEN/-RBL
	EP/TROK/LAOE/YA			EK/WI/POE/TEN/-RBL
epitrochlear	EP/TROK/LAR	equipotentiality		E/KWI/POE/TEN/-RBL/TI
epitrochleoanconaeus	EP/TROK/LO/AN/KO/NAOE/YUS			EK/WI/POE/TEN/-RBL/TI
epituberculosis	EP/TAOU/BERK/LOE/SIS	equisetosis		E/KWI/SE/TOE/SIS
epiturbinate	EP/TURB/NAIT			EK/WI/SE/TOE/SIS
epitympanic	EP/TIM/PAN/IK	equisetum		E/KWI/SE/TUM
epitympanum	EP/TIFRP/NUM			EK/WI/SE/TUM
epitype	EP/TAOIP	equitoxic		E/KWI/TOX/IK
epizoa	EP/ZOE/WA			EK/WI/TOX/IK
epizoic	EP/ZOIK	equivalence		E/KWIV/LENS
	EP/ZOE/IK	equivalency		E/KWIV/LEN/SI
epizoicide	EP/ZOI/SAO*ID	equivalent		E/KWIV/LENT
	EP/ZOE/SAO*ID	equorum		E/KWOR/UM
epizoology	EP/ZOE/OLG			E/KWOER/UM
epizoon	EP/ZAON	equuli		EK/YAOU/LAOI
epizootic	EP/ZOE/OT/IK			EK/WAOU/LAOI
epizootiology	EP/ZOE/OT/YOLG	equulosis		EK/YAOU/LOE/SIS
epluchage	AI/PLAOU/SHAJ			EK/WAOU/LOE/SIS
	AI/PLAOU/SHAUJ	Equus		EK/WUS
	E/PLAOU/SHAJ	er-		*ER
	E/PLAOU/SHAUJ	-er		ER
Epogen	EP/JEN	erasion		E/RAIGS
epontic	E/PONT/IK	Erb		*ERB
eponychia	EP/NIK/YA	erbium		ERB/YUM
eponychium	EP/NIK/YUM	ercalcidiol		*ER/KAL/SID/YOL
eponym	EP/NIM	ercalciol		*ER/KALS/YOL
eponymic	EP/NIM/IK	ercalcitriol		*ER/KAL/SIT/ROL
eponymous	E/PON/MOUS	Erdmann		ERD/MAN
epoophorectomy	EP/AOF/REKT/M*I	erect		E/REKT
	EP/OEF/REKT/M*I	erectile		E/REK/TAOIL
epoophori	EP/AOF/RAOI	erection		E/R*EBGS
	EP/OEF/RAOI	erector		E/REK/TOR
epoophoron	EP/AOF/RON	eremophilia		*ER/MO/FIL/YA
	EP/OEF/RON	eremophobia		*ER/MO/FOEB/YA
epoprostenol	EP/PRO*S/NOL	erethism		*ER/THIFM
	E/PO/PRO*S/NOL	erethismic		*ER/THIZ/MIK
epoxy	E/POK/SI			*ER/THIS/MIK
epoxytropine tropate	E/POX/TROE/PAOEN/TROE/PAIT	erethistic		*ER/TH*IS/IK
epsilon	EPS/LON	erethitic		*ER/THIT/IK
Epsom salt	EP/SOM/SALT	ereuthophobia		*ER/YAO*UT/FOEB/YA
	EP/SOM/SAULT	erg		ERG
Epstein	EP/STAOEN	ergasia		*ER/GAIZ/YA

ergasiology	*ER/GAIZ/YOLG	eroticism	E/ROT/SIFM
ergasiomania	*ER/GAIZ/YO/MAIN/YA	erotization	*ER/TI/ZAIGS
ergasiophobia	*ER/GAIZ/YO/FOEB/YA		E/ROT/ZAIGS
ergasthenia	*ER/GAS/THAOEN/YA	eroticize	E/ROT/SAOIZ
ergastic	*ER/GA*S/IK	eroticomania	E/ROT/KO/MAIN/YA
ergastoplasm	*ER/GA*S/PLAFM	erotism	*ER/TIFM
-ergia	ER/JA	erotize	*ER/TAOIZ
	ERJ/YA	erotogenesis	*ER/TO/JEN/SIS
ergin	*ER/JIN		E/ROE/TO/JEN/SIS
ergine	ERG/AOEN	erotogenic	*ER/TO/JEN/IK
	*ER/GAOEN		E/ROT/JEN/IK
ergo-	ERG	erotology	*ER/TOLG
	*ER/GO	erotomania	*ER/TO/MAIN/YA
ergobasine	ERG/BAI/SAOEN		E/ROT/MAIN/YA
	ERG/BAI/SIN	erotomaniac	*ER/TO/MAIN/YAK
ergocalciferol	ERG/KAL/SIF/ROL		E/ROT/MAIN/YAK
ergocardiogram	ERG/KARD/YO/GRAM	erotomanic	*ER/TO/MAN/IK
ergocardiography	ERG/KARD/YOG/FI		E/ROT/MAN/IK
ergocornine	ERG/KOR/NAOEN	erotopath	*ER/TO/PA*T
ergocristine	ERG/KRIS/TAOEN		E/ROT/PA*T
ergocryptine	ERG/KRIP/TAOEN	erotopathic	*ER/TO/PA*T/IK
ergodynamograph	ERG/DAOI/NAM/GRAF		E/ROT/PA*T/IK
ergoesthesiograph	ERG/ES/THAOEZ/YO/GRAF	erotopathy	*ER/TOP/TH*I
ergogenic	ERG/JEN/IK	erotophobia	*ER/TO/FOEB/YA
ergogram	ERG/GRAM		E/ROT/FOEB/YA
ergograph	ERG/GRAF	erotosexual	*ER/TO/SEX/YAOUL
ergographic	ERG/GRAFK		E/ROT/SEX/YAOUL
Ergoloid	ERG/LOID	erratic	E/RAT/IK
ergomaniac	ERG/MAIN/YAK	errhine	*ER/RAOIN
Ergomar	ERG/MAR	error	*ER/ROR
Ergomar Mesylates	ERG/MAR/MES/LAIT/-S	ertacalciol	ERT/KALS/YOL
ergometer	*ER/GOM/TER	erubescence	*ER/BES/ENS
ergometrine	ERG/MET/RAOEN		*ER/YAOU/BES/ENS
	ERG/MET/RIN	erubescent	*ER/BES/ENT
ergon	*ER/GON		*ER/YAOU/BES/ENT
ergonomic	ERG/NOM/IK	erucic	E/RAOUS/IK
ergonomics	ERG/NOM/IK/-S	eructatio	E/RUK/TAI/SHOE
ergonovine	ERG/NOE/VAOEN		E/RUK/TAIRB/YOE
	ERG/NOE/VIN	eructation	E/RUK/TAIGS
ergosine	ERG/SOAEN	erupt	E/RUPT
	ERG/SIN	eruption	E/RUPGS
ergostat	ERG/STAT	eruptive	E/RUPT/IV
Ergostat	K-P/ERG/STAT	Erycette	*ER/SET
ergosterin	*ER/GO*S/RIN		*ER/RI/SET
ergosterol	*ER/GO*S/ROL	EryDerm	*ER/DERM
ergostetrine	ERG/STET/RAOEN		*ER/RI/DERM
	ERG/STET/RIN	EryGel	*ER/JEL
ergot	*ER/GOT		*ER/RI/JEL
ergotamine	*ER/GOT/MAOEN	Erymax	*ER/MAX
	*ER/GOT/MIN		*ER/RI/MAX
ergotaminine	ERG/TAM/NAOEN	EryPed	*ER/PED
	*ER/GOT/AM/NAOEN		*ER/RI/PED
ergotherapy	ERG/THER/PI	erysipelas	*ER/SIP/LAS
ergothioneine	ERG/THAOI/NAOEN	erysipelatous	*ER/SI/PEL/TOUS
ergotinic	ERG/TIN/IK	erysipeloid	*ER/SIP/LOID
ergotism	ERG/TIFM	Erysipelothrix	*ER/SIP/LO/THRIX
ergotized	ERG/TAOIZ/-D		*ER/SI/PEL/THRIX
	*ER/GO/TAOIZ/-D	erysipelotoxin	*ER/SIP/LO/TOK/SIN
ergotocine	ERG/TOE/SAOEN	erysiphake	E/RIS/FAIK
ergotoxicosis	ERG/TOX/KOE/SIS	Ery-Tab	*ER/TAB
ergotoxine	ERG/TOK/SAOEN		*ER/RI/TAB
	ERG/TOK/SIN	eryth-	*ER/TH-
ergotropic	ERG/TROP/IK	erythema	*ER/THAOE/MA
Erichsen	*ER/IK/SEN	erythema a calore	*ER/THAOE/MA/A/KAL/RAOE
erigentes	*ER/JEN/TAOEZ	erythematopultaceous	*ER/THEM/TO/PUL/TAIRBS
eriksonii	*ER/IK/SOEN/YAOI	erythematosa	*ER/THEM/TOE/SA
	*ER/IK/SON/YAOI	erythematosus	*ER/THEM/TOE/SUS
	ERK/SOEN/YAOI	erythematous	*ER/THEM/TOUS
	ERK/SON/YAOI	erythematovesicular	*ER/THEM/TO/VE/SIK/LAR
erinacei	*ER/NAIS/YAOI	erythemogenic	*ER/THEM/JEN/IK
eriodictyon	*ER/YO/DIKT/YON		*ER/THAOEM/JEN/IK
Erlandsen	*ER/LAND/SEN	erythermalgia	*ER/THER/MAL/JA
Erlanger	*ER/LANG/ER	erythr(o)-	R*IT/R(O)
Erlenmeyer	*ER/LEN/MAOI/ER		E/R*IT/R(O)
Ernst	*ERNS		*ER/THR(O)-
	ERNS/-T	erythralgia	*ER/THRAL/JA
erode	E/ROED	erythrasma	*ER/THRAZ/MA
erogenous	E/ROJ/NOUS	erythredema	R*IT/RE/DAOE/MA
eros	E/ROS	erythremia	*ER/THRAOEM/YA
erose	E/ROES	erythrin	*ER/THRIN
erosio	E/ROES/YOE		R*IT/RIN
erosion	E/ROEGS		E/R*IT/RIN
erosiva	E/ROE/SAOI/VA	erythrism	*ER/THRIFM
	*ER/SAOI/VA		R*IT/RIFM
erosive	E/ROES/IV		E/R*IT/RIFM
erot(o)-	E/ROT	erythristic	*ER/THR*IS/IK
	E/ROET	erythrite	R*IT/RAOIT
	*ER/T(O)	erythritol	R*IT/RI/TOL
erotic	E/ROT/IK	erythrityl	R*IT/RI/TIL

erythroblast	R*IT/RO/BLA*S	erythroplasia	R*IT/RO/PLAIZ/YA
erythroblastemia	R*IT/RO/BLAS/TAOEM/YA	erythroplastid	R*IT/RO/PLAS/TID
erythroblastic	R*IT/RO/BLA*S/IK	erythropoiesis	R*IT/RO/POI/SIS
erythroblastoma	R*IT/RO/BLAS/TOE/MA	erythropoietic	R*IT/RO/POIT/IK
erythroblastomatosis	R*IT/RO/BLAS/TOEM/TOE/SIS	erythropoietin	R*IT/RO/POI/TIN
erythroblastopenia	R*IT/RO/BLA*S/PAOEN/YA	erythroprosopalgia	R*IT/RO/PROS/PAL/JA
erythroblastosis	R*IT/RO/BLAS/TOE/SIS	erythropsia	*ER/THROPS/YA
erythroblastotic	R*IT/RO/BLAS/TOT/IK		R*IT/ROPS/YA
erythrocatalysis	R*IT/RO/KA/TAL/SIS	erythropyknosis	R*IT/RO/PIK/NOE/SIS
erythrochloropia	R*IT/RO/KLOR/OEP/YA	erythrose	R*IT/ROES
erythrochloropsia	R*IT/RO/KLOR/OPS/YA		*ER/THROES
erythrochromia	R*IT/RO/KROEM/YA	erythrosedimentation	R*IT/RO/SED/MEN/TAIGS
Erythrocin	R*IT/RO/SIN	erythrosin	R*IT/RO/SIN
Erythrocin Lactobionate	R*IT/RO/SIN/LAKT/BAO*I/NAIT	erythrosine sodium	R*IT/RO/SAOEN/SOED/YUM
Erythrocin Piggyback	R*IT/RO/SIN/PIG/GI/BA*K	erythrosis	*ER/THROE/SIS
	R*IT/RO/SIN/PIG/GI/BAK	erythrostasis	R*IT/RO/STAI/SIS
Erythrocin Stearate	R*IT/RO/SIN/STAOER/AIT	erythroxyline	*ER/THROX/LAOEN
erythroclasis	*ER/THROK/LA/SIS	erythrulose	R*IT/RAOU/LOES
erythroclastic	R*IT/RO/KLA*S/IK	erythruria	*ER/THRAOUR/YA
erythrocuprein	R*IT/RO/KAOUP/RIN	Eryzole	*ER/ZOEL
erythrocyanosis	R*IT/RO/SAOI/NOE/SIS		*ER/RI/ZOEL
erythrocyt(o)-	R*IT/RO/SAOIT	Esbach	ES/BAUK
	E/R*IT/RO/SAOIT		ES/BAK
	R*IT/RO/SAOI/T(O)	escape	ES/KAIP
	E/R*IT/RO/SAOI/T(O)	-escense	ES/ENS
erythrocytapheresis	R*IT/RO/SAOIT/FER/SIS		ES/SENS
erythrocyte	R*IT/RO/SAO*IT	-escent	ES/ENT
erythrocythemia	R*IT/RO/SAOI/THAOEM/YA		ES/SENT
erythrocytic	R*IT/RO/SIT/IK	eschar	ES/KAR
erythrocytoblast	R*IT/RO/SAOIT/BLA*S	escharotic	ES/KA/ROT/IK
erythrocytolysin	R*IT/RO/SAOI/TOL/SIN		ES/KROT/IK
erythrocytolysis	R*IT/RO/SAOI/TOL/SIS	escharotica	ES/KA/ROT/KA
erythrocytometer	R*IT/RO/SAOI/TOM/TER		ES/KROT/KA
erythrocytometry	R*IT/RO/SAOI/TOM/TRI	escharotomy	ES/KA/ROT/M*I
erythrocytopenia	R*IT/RO/SAOIT/PAOEN/YA		ES/KROT/M*I
erythrocytophagous	R*IT/RO/SAOI/TOF/GOUS	Escherich	ERB/RIK
erythrocytophagy	R*IT/RO/SAOI/TOF/JI		ERB/RAOIK
erythrocytopoiesis	R*IT/RO/SAOIT/POI/SIS	Escherichia coli	ERB/RIK/YA/KO/LAOI
erythrocytorrhexis	R*IT/RO/SAOIT/REK/SIS		ERB/RAOIK/YA/KO/LAOI
erythrocytoschisis	R*IT/RO/SAOI/TOS/KI/SIS	Escherichieae	ERB/RIK/YAE
erythrocytosis	R*IT/RO/SAOI/TOE/SIS	escorcin	ES/KOR/SIN
erythrocyturia	R*IT/RO/SAOI/TAOUR/YA	escorcinol	ES/KORS/NOL
erythrodegenerative	R*IT/RO/DE/JEN/RA/TIV	esculapian	ES/KLAIP/YAN
erythroderma	R*IT/RO/DER/MA		ES/KAOU/LAIP/YAN
erythrodermatitis	R*IT/RO/DERM/TAOITS	esculent	ES/KLENT
erythrodermia	R*IT/RO/DERM/YA		ES/KAOU/LENT
erythrodextrin	R*IT/RO/DEX/TRIN	esculin	ES/KLIN
erythrodontia	R*IT/RO/DON/SHA		ES/KAOU/LIN
erythrogen	R*IT/RO/JEN	escutcheon	ES/KUFP/-N
erythrogenesis	R*IT/RO/JEN/SIS		ES/KUFP/YON
erythrogenic	R*IT/RO/JEN/IK	eseptate	E/SEP/TAIT
erythrogonia	R*IT/RO/GOEN/YA	eseridine	ES/ER/DAOEN
erythrogonium	R*IT/RO/GOEN/YUM	eserine	ES/RAOEN
erythrogranulose	R*IT/RO/GRAN/LOES		ES/RIN
erythroid	*ER/THROID	Esgic	ES/JIK
	R*IT/ROID	Esidrix	ES/DRIX
erythrokeratoderma	R*IT/RO/KER/TO/DER/MA	Esimil	ES/MIL
erythrokeratodermia	R*IT/RO/KER/TO/DERM/YA	-esis	(c)AOE/SIS
erythrokinetics	R*IT/RO/KI/NET/IK/-S	Eskalith	ES/KA/L*IT
erythrol	*ER/THROL	esmarch	ES/MARK
	R*IT/ROL	Esmarch	K-P/ES/MARK
erythroleukemia	R*IT/RO/LAOU/KAOEM/YA	esmolol	ES/MO/LOL
erythroleukoblastosis	R*IT/RO/LAOUK/BLAS/TOE/SIS	eso-	ES
erythroleukosis	R*IT/RO/LAOU/KOE/SIS		ES/SO
erythrolysin	*ER/THROL/SIN	esocataphoria	ES/KAT/FOER/YA
erythrolysis	*ER/THROL/SIS	esodeviation	ES/DAOEV/YAIGS
erythromelalgia	R*IT/RO/MEL/AL/JA	esodic	E/SOD/IK
erythromelia	R*IT/RO/MAOEL/YA	esoethmoiditis	ES/*ET/MOI/DAOITS
erythrometer	*ER/THROM/TER	esogastritis	ES/GAS/TRAOITS
erythrometry	*ER/THROM/TRI	esophag(o)-	E/SOF/G(O)
erythromycin	R*IT/RO/MAOI/SIN		E/SOF/J-
	R*IT/MAOI/SIN	esophagalgia	E/SOF/GAL/JA
Erythromycin Base Filmtab	R*IT/RO/MAOI/SIN/BAIS/FIL/-M/TAB	esophageae	E/SOF/JAE
	R*IT/MAOI/SIN/BAIS/FIL/-M/TAB		E/SOF/JAOE
erythron	*ER/THRON	esophageal	E/SOF/JAOEL
erythroneocytosis	R*IT/RO/NAOE/SAOI/TOE/SIS		E/SOF/JAL
erythronormoblastic	R*IT/RO/NORM/BLA*S/IK		ES/FAJ/YAL
erythropenia	R*IT/RO/PAOEN/YA		ES/FALJ/YAL
erythrophage	R*IT/RO/FALJ	esophagectasia	E/SOF/JEK/TAIZ/YA
erythrophagia	R*IT/RO/FAI/JA	esophagectasis	E/SOF/JEKT/SIS
erythrophagocytosis	R*IT/RO/FAG/SAOI/TOE/SIS	esophagectomy	E/SOF/JEKT/M*I
erythrophil	R*IT/RO/FIL	esophageus	ES/FAI/JUS
erythrophilic	R*IT/RO/FIL/IK		ES/FALJ/YUS
erythrophore	R*IT/RO/FOER	esophagi	E/SOF/JAOI
erythrophose	R*IT/RO/FOEZ		E/SOF/GAOI
	R*IT/RO/FOES	esophagism	E/SOF/JIFM
erythropia	*ER/THROEP/YA	esophagitis	E/SOF/JAOITS
erythroplakia	R*IT/RO/PLAIK/YA	esophagobronchial	E/SOF/GO/BRONG/YAL
		esophagocardiomyotomy	E/SOF/GO/KARD/YO/MAOI/OT/

	M*I
esophagocardioplasty	E/SOF/GO/KARD/YO/PLAS/TI
esophagocele	E/SOF/GO/SAO*EL
esophagocologastrostomy	E/SOF/GO/KOEL/GAS/TRO*S/M*I
esophagocoloplasty	E/SOF/GO/KOEL/PLAS/TI
esophagoduodenostomy	E/SOF/GO/DAOU/DEN/O*S/M*I
	E/SOF/GO/DAOU/DE/NO*S/M*I
	E/SOF/GO/DWOD/NO*S/M*I
esophagodynia	E/SOF/GO/DIN/YA
esophagoenterostomy	E/SOF/GO/SPWRO*S/M*I
esophagoesophagostomy	E/SOF/GO/E/SOF/GO*S/M*I
esophagofiberscope	E/SOF/GO/FAOI/BER/SKOEP
esophagofundopexy	E/SOF/GO/FUND/PEK/SI
esophagogastrectomy	E/SOF/GO/GAS/TREKT/M*I
esophagogastric	E/SOF/GO/GAS/TRIK
esophagogastroanastomosis	E/SOF/GO/GAS/TRO/AI/NA*S/
	MOE/SIS
esophagogastromyotomy	E/SOF/GO/GAS/TRO/MAOI/OT/M*I
esophagogastroplasty	E/SOF/GO/GAS/TRO/PLAS/TI
esophagogastroscopy	E/SOF/GO/GAS/TROS/KPI
esophagogastrostomy	E/SOF/GO/GAS/TRO*S/M*I
esophagogram	E/SOF/GO/GRAM
esophagography	E/SOF/GOG/FI
esophagojejunogastrostomosis	
	E/SOF/GO/JE/JAOUN/GAS/TRO*S/
	MOE/SIS
esophagojejunogastrostomy	E/SOF/GO/JE/JAOUN/GAS/TRO*S/
	M*I
esophagojejunostomy	E/SOF/GO/JEJ/NO*S/M*I
esophagolaryngectomy	E/SOF/GO/LARN/JEKT/M*I
esophagology	E/SOF/GOLG
esophagomalacia	E/SOF/GO/MA/LAI/SHA
esophagometer	E/SOF/GOM/TER
esophagomycosis	E/SOF/GO/MAOI/KOE/SIS
esophagomyotomy	E/SOF/GO/MAOI/OT/M*I
esophagopharynx	E/SOF/GO/FARNGS
esophagoplasty	E/SOF/GO/PLAS/TI
esophagoplication	E/SOF/GO/PLI/KAIGS
	E/SOF/GO/PLAOI/KAIGS
esophagoptosia	E/SOF/GO/TOES/YA
esophagoptosis	E/SOF/GO/TOE/SIS
	E/SOF/GOP/TOE/SIS
esophagorespiratory	E/SOF/GO/RES/PRA/TOIR
esophagoscope	E/SOF/GO/SKOEP
esophagoscopy	E/SOF/GOS/KPI
esophagospasm	E/SOF/GO/SPAFM
esophagostenosis	E/SOF/GO/STE/NOE/SIS
esophagostoma	E/SOF/GO*S/MA
esophagostomiasis	see oesophagostomiasis
esophagostomy	E/SOF/GO*S/M*I
esophagotome	E/SOF/GO/TOEM
esophagotomy	E/SOF/GOT/M*I
esophagotracheal	E/SOF/GO/TRAIK/YAL
esophagus	E/SOF/GUS
esophoria	ES/FOER/YA
esophoric	ES/FOER/IK
esophylaxis	ES/FLAK/SIS
esosphenoiditis	ES/SFAOE/NOI/DAOITS
Esoterica	ES/TER/KA
esotropia	ES/TROEP/YA
esotropic	ES/TROP/IK
espnoic	ES/-P/NOIK
	ES/-P/NOE/IK
esproquin	ES/PRO/KWIN
espundia	ES/PAOUND/YA
esquillectomy	ES/KWIL/EKT/M*I
	ES/KWI/LEKT/M*I
esquinancea	ES/KWI/NANS/YA
essence	ES/ENS
	ES/SENS
essentia	E/SEN/SHA
essential	E/SEN/-RBL
Esser	ES/ER
Essig	ES/SIG
est- (word beginning)	ES/T-
	(not *ES; see words ending in -est)
-est (word ending)	*ES
Estar	ES/TAR
ester	ES/TER
	(not *ES/ER)
esterapenia	ES/TER/PAOEN/YA
	ES/TRA/PAOEN/YA
esterase	ES/TRAIS
	ES/TER/AIS
	(not *ES/RAIS)
esterification	ES/TER/FI/KAIGS
esterified	ES/TER/FI/-D
esterify	ES/TER/FI
esterize	ES/TRAOIZ

	ES/TER/AOIZ
esterolysis	ES/TROL/SIS
	ES/TER/OL/SIS
esterolytic	ES/TRO/LIT/IK
	ES/TER/LIT/IK
Estes	ES/TAOES
	ES/TES
esthematology	ES/THAOEM/TOLG
	ES/THEM/TOLG
esthesi(o)-	ES/THAOEZ/Y(O)
	ES/THAOES/Y(O)
esthesia	ES/THAOEZ/YA
esthesic	ES/THAOEZ/IK
esthesioblast	ES/THAOEZ/YO/BLA*S
esthesiodic	ES/THAOEZ/YOD/IK
esthesiogenesis	ES/THAOEZ/YO/JEN/SIS
esthesiogenic	ES/THAOEZ/YO/JEN/IK
esthesiography	ES/THAOEZ/YOG/FI
esthesiology	ES/THAOEZ/YOLG
esthesiometer	ES/THAOEZ/YOM/TER
esthesiometry	ES/THAOEZ/YOM/TRI
esthesioneure	ES/THAOEZ/YO/NAOUR
esthesioneuroblastoma	ES/THAOEZ/YO/NAOUR/BLAS/
	TOE/MA
esthesioneurocytoma	ES/THAOEZ/YO/NAOUR/SAOI/
	TOE/MA
esthesioneurosis	ES/THAOEZ/YO/NAOU/ROE/SIS
esthesionosus	ES/THAOEZ/YON/SUS
esthesiophysiology	ES/THAOEZ/YO/FIZ/YOLG
esthesioscopy	ES/THAOEZ/YOS/KPI
esthesis	ES/THAOE/SIS
	ES/THE/SIS
esthesodic	ES/THAOE/SOD/IK
	ES/THE/SOD/IK
esthetic	ES/THET/IK
esthetics	ES/THET/IK/-S
esthiomene	ES/THOM/NAOE
	ES/THAOE/YOM/NAOE
	ES/THAOE/OM/NAOE
esthiomenous	ES/THOM/NOUS
	ES/THAOE/YOM/NOUS
	ES/THAOE/OM/NOUS
Estinyl	ES/TI/NIL
estival	ES/TI/VAL
	ES/TAOIVL
estivation	ES/TI/VAIGS
estivoautumnal	ES/TI/VO/AU/TUM/NAL
Estlander	*ES/LAND/ER
estolate	ES/TO/LAIT
Estrace	ES/TRA*IS
	(not ES/TRAIS; see esterase)
Estraderm	ES/TRA/DERM
estradiol	ES/TRA/DI/OL
	ES/TRA/DI/YOL
Estradurin	ES/TRA/DAOURN
estragon	ES/TRA/GON
estramustine	ES/TRA/MUS/TAOEN
estrane	ES/TRAIN
Estratab	ES/TRA/TAB
Estratest	ES/TRA/T*ES
estratriene	ES/TRA/TR*I/AOEN
estrazinol	ES/TRAZ/NOL
estrenol	ES/TRE/NOL
estrin	ES/TRIN
estrinization	ES/TRIN/ZAIGS
estriol	ES/TROL
	ES/TRAOE/OL
estrodienol	ES/TRO/DAOE/NOL
	ES/TRO/DAOEN/OL
estrofurate	ES/TRO/FAOUR/AIT
estrogen	ES/TRO/JEN
estrogenic	ES/TRO/JEN/IK
estrogenicity	ES/TRO/JE/NIS/TI
estrogenous	ES/TROJ/NOUS
estrone	ES/TROEN
estrophilin	ES/TRO/FLIN
	ES/TRO/FIL/LIN
estrous	ES/TROUS
Estrovis	ES/TRO/VIS
estrual	ES/TRAOUL
	ES/TRAL
estruation	ES/TRAOU/AIGS
estrum	ES/TRUM
estrus	ES/TRUS
esylate	ES/LAIT
et	ET
etafedrine	ET/FED/RAOEN
	ET/FED/RIN
etafenone	E/TAF/NOEN

etafilcon A	ET/FIL/KON/A-RBGS	ethmonasal	*ET/MO/NAI/ZAL
etamsylate	E/TAMS/LAIT	ethmopalatal	*ET/MO/PAL/TAL
	E/TAM/SLAIT	ethmosphenoid	*ET/MO/SFAOE/NOID
etat	AI/TAU	ethmoturbinal	*ET/MO/TURB/NAL
	E/TAU	ethmovomerine	*ET/MO/VOEM/RIN
etazolate	E/TAZ/LAIT	ethmyphitis	*ET/MI/FAOITS
Eternod	AI/TER/NOE	ethnic	*ET/NIK
	E/TER/NOE	ethnobiology	*ET/NO/BAO*I/OLG
ethacridine	*ET/AK/RI/DAOEN	ethnocentrism	*ET/NO/SEN/TRIFM
ethacrynate	*ET/KRAOI/NAIT	ethnography	*ET/NOG/FI
ethacrynic	*ET/KRIN/IK	ethnology	*ET/NOLG
ethadione	*ET/DI/OEN	ethoheptazine	*ET/HEPT/ZAOEN
ethal	*ET/THAL	ethohexadiol	*ET/HEX/DI/OL
ethaldehyde	*ET/ALD/HAOID		*ET/HEK/SAID/YOL
ethambutol	*ET/AM/BAOU/TOL	ethological	*ET/LOJ/KAL
ethamivan	*ET/AM/VAN	ethologist	E/THO*LGS
Ethamolin	E/THAM/LIN	ethology	E/THOLG
	*ET/MOL/LIN	ethomoxane	*ET/MOK/SAIN
ethamoxytriphetol	*ET/MOX/TR*I/FAOE/TOL	ethopharmacology	*ET/FARM/KOLG
ethamsylate	E/THAMS/LAIT	ethopropazine	*ET/PROEP/ZAOEN
	*ET/AMS/LAIT	ethosuximide	*ET/SUX/MAOID
	E/THAM/SLAIT	ethotoin	*ET/TOIN
	*ET/AM/SLAIT		*ET/TOE/WIN
ethanal	*ET/NAL	ethotrimeprazine	*ET/TR*I/MEP/RA/ZAOEN
ethane	*ET/AIN	ethoxazene	E/THOX/ZAOEN
	E/THAIN	ethoxy	E/THOK/SI
ethanedial	*ET/AIN/DAOIL	ethoxybutamoxane	*ET/OX/BAOUT/MOK/SAIN
	*ET/AIN/DI/YAL	ethoxyzolamide	*ET/OX/ZOL/MAOID
ethanediamine	*ET/AIN/DAOI/MAOEN	Ethrane	*ET/RAIN
ethanedinitril	*ET/AIN/DI/NAOI/TRIL	ethybenztropine	*ET/BENZ/TROE/PAOEN
ethanedisulfonate	*ET/AIN/DI/SUL/FO/NAIT	ethyl	*ET/IL
ethanoic	*ET/NOIK	ethylaldehyde	*ET/IL/ALD/HAOID
	*ET/NOE/IK	ethylamine	*ET/IL/AM/MIN
ethanol	*ET/NOL	ethylate	*ET/LAIT
ethanolamine	*ET/NOL/MAOEN	ethylation	*ET/IL/AIGS
ethanolaminephosphotransferase		ethylbenztropine	*ET/IL/BENZ/TROE/PAOEN
	*ET/NOL/MAOEN/FOS/FO/	ethylcarbonate	*ET/IL/KARB/NAIT
	TRA/NS/FRAIS	ethylcellulose	*ET/IL/SEL/YAOU/LOES
Ethatab	*ET/TAB	ethylene	*ET/LAOEN
ethaverine	*ET/AV/RAOEN	ethylenediamine	*ET/LAOEN/DAOI/MAOEN
	*ET/VER/AOEN	ethylenediaminetetraacetate	
	*ET/VER/RAOEN		*ET/LAOEN/DAOI/MAOEN/TET/
ethchlorvynol	*ET/KLOR/VAOI/NOL		RA/AS/TAIT
	*ET/KLOFRB/NOL	ethylenediaminetetraacetic	*ET/LAOEN/DAOI/MAOEN/TET/
ethene	*ET/AOEN		RA/AI/SAOET/IK
ethenoid	*ET/NOID	ethylestrenol	*ET/IL/ES/TRE/NOL
ethenyl	*ET/NIL	ethylhydrazide	*ET/IL/HAOI/DRA/ZAOID
ethenylbenzene	*ET/NIL/BEN/ZAOEN	ethylic	E/THIL/IK
ether	AO*ET/ER	ethylidene	*ET/IL/DAOEN
	(not E/THER)	ethylidyne	*ET/IL/DAOIN
ethereal	E/THAOERL	ethylisobutrazine	*ET/IL/AOIS/BAOU/TRA/ZAOEN
	E/THAOER/YAL	ethylmorphine	*ET/IL/MOR/FAOEN
etherification	E/THER/FI/KAIGS	ethylnoradrenaline	*ET/IL/NOR/DREN/LIN
etherism	AO*ET/RIFM	ethylnorepinephrine	*ET/IL/NOR/EP/NEF/RIN
	AO*ET/ER/IFM	ethylpapaverine	*ET/IL/PA/PAV/RAOEN
etherization	AO*ET/RI/ZAIGS	ethylparaben	*ET/IL/PAR/BEN
	E/THER/ZAIGS	ethylphenacemide	*ET/IL/FEN/AS/MAOID
etherize	*ET/RAOIZ	ethylphenylephrine	*ET/IL/FENL/EF/RAOEN
ethiazide	E/THAOI/ZAOID		*ET/IL/FENL/EF/RIN
ethical	*ET/KAL	ethylstibamine	*ET/IL/STIB/MAOEN
ethics	*ET/IK/-S	ethylsuccinate	*ET/IL/SUX/NAIT
ethidene	*ET/DAOEN	ethylvinyl	*ET/IL/VAOINL
ethidium	E/THID/YUM	ethynodiol	E/THAOIN/DI/OL
ethinamate	E/THIN/MAIT	ethynyl	*ET/NIL
ethindrone	E/THIN/DROEN	etiane	AOET/YAIN
ethinyl	E/THAOI/NIL	etianic	AOET/YAN/IK
ethinylestrenol	*ET/NIL/ES/TRE/NOL	etidocaine	E/TAOID/KAIN
ethiodized	*ET/AOI/DAOIZ/-D	etidronate	ET/DROE/NAIT
Ethiodol	E/THAOI/DOL	etidronic	ET/DRON/IK
ethionamide	E/THAOI/ON/MAOID	etilefrine	ET/LEF/RIN
	E/THAOI/YON/MAOID	etioallocholane	AOET/YO/AL/KOE/LAIN
ethionine	E/THAOI/NAOEN		AOET/YO/AL/LO/KOE/LAIN
	E/THAOI/NIN	etiocholane	AOET/YO/KOE/LAIN
ethisterone	E/TH*IS/ROEN	etiocholanolone	AOET/YO/KOE/LAN/LOEN
ethm(o)-	*ET/M(O)	etiogenic	AOET/YO/JEN/IK
ethmocarditis	*ET/MO/KAR/DAOITS	etiolated	AOET/YO/LAIT/-D
ethmocephalus	*ET/MO/SEF/LUS	etiolation	AOET/YO/LAIGS
ethmocranial	*ET/MO/KRAIN/YAL	etiologic	AOET/YO/LOJ/IK
ethmofrontal	*ET/MO/FRON/TAL	etiological	AOET/YO/LOJ/KAL
ethmoid	*ET/MOID	etiology	AOET/YOLG
ethmoidal	*ET/MOI/DAL	etiopathic	AOET/YO/PA*T/IK
ethmoidale	*ET/MOI/DAI/LAOE	etiopathology	AOET/YO/PA/THOLG
ethmoidales	*ET/MOI/DAI/LAOEZ	etioporphyrin	AOET/YO/POR/FRIN
ethmoidalis	*ET/MOI/DAI/LIS	etiotropic	AOET/YO/TROP/IK
ethmoidectomy	*ET/MOI/DEKT/M*I	etomidate	E/TOM/DAIT
ethmoiditis	*ET/MOI/DAOITS	etoposide	AOET/POE/SAOID
ethmoidotomy	*ET/MOI/DOT/M*I	etoprine	ET/PRAOEN
ethmolacrimal	*ET/MO/LAK/RI/MAL	etorphine	E/TOR/FAOEN
ethmomaxillary	*ET/MO/MAX/LAIR		ET/OR/FAOEN

etozolin	ET/ZOE/LIN	eumorphism	YAOU/MOR/FIFM
Etrafon-A	E/TRA/FON/A-RBGS	Eumycetes	YAOU/MAOI/SAOE/TAOEZ
	ET/RA/FON/A-RBGS	eunoia	YAOU/NOI/YA
Etrafon Forte	E/TRA/FON/FOR/TAI	eunuch	YAOU/NUK
	ET/RA/FON/FOR/TAI	eunuchism	YAOU/NUK/IFM
etretinate	E/TRET/NAIT		YAOUN/KIFM
ETS-2%	ERBGS/T*RBGS/S*RBGS/2/P*KT	eunuchoid	YAOU/NUK/OID
	ETS/2/P*KT		YAOUN/KOID
etymemazine	ET/MEM/ZAOEN	eunuchoidism	YAOU/NUK/OID/IFM
eu-	YAOU		YAOUN/KOID/IFM
euallele	YAOU/LAOEL	euosmia	YAOU/OZ/MA
	YAOU/AI/LAOEL		YAOU/OZ/MAOE/YA
euallelic	YAOU/LAOEL/IK	eupancreatism	YAOU/PAN/KRA/TIFM
	YAOU/AI/LAOEL/IK	euparal	YAOUP/RAL
euangiotic	YAOU/AN/JOT/IK	Euparyphium	YAOUP/RIF/YUM
Eubacteriales	YAOU/BAK/TAOER/YAI/LAOEZ		YAOU/PRIF/YUM
Eubacterium	YAOU/BAK/TAOERM	eupaverin	YAOU/PAV/RIN
eubiotics	YAOU/BAO*I/OT/IK/-S	eupepsia	YAOU/PEPS/YA
eubolism	YAOUB/LIFM	eupepsy	YAOU/PEP/SI
	YAOU/BOE/LIFM	eupeptic	YAOU/PEPT/IK
eucaine	YAOU/KAIN	euperistalsis	YAOU/P*ER/STAL/SIS
eucalyptol	YAOUK/LIP/TOL	euphenics	YAOU/FAOEN/IK/-S
Eucalyptus	YAOUK/LIP/TUS		YAOU/FEN/IK/-S
eucapnia	YAOU/KAP/NA	Euphorbia	YAOU/FORB/YA
	YAOU/KAP/NAOE/YA	euphoretic	YAOU/FRET/IK
eucasin	YAOU/KAI/SIN	euphoria	YAOU/FOER/YA
eucatropine	YAOU/KAT/RO/PAOEN	euphoriant	YAOU/FOER/YANT
Eucerin	YAOU/SER/RIN	euphoric	YAOU/FOER/IK
Eucestoda	YAOU/SES/TOE/DA	euphorigenic	YAOU/FOER/JEN/IK
euchlorhydria	YAOU/KLOR/HAOI/DRA	euphoristic	YAOU/FR*IS/IK
	YAOU/KLOR/HAOI/DRAOE/YA		YAOUF/R*IS/IK
eucholia	YAOU/KOEL/YA	euplasia	YAOU/PLAIZ/YA
euchromatic	YAOU/KROE/MAT/IK	euplastic	YAOU/PLA*S/IK
euchromatin	YAOU/KROEM/TIN	euploid	YAOU/PLOID
euchromatopsy	YAOU/KROEM/TOP/SI	euploidy	YAOU/PLOI/DI
euchromosome	YAOU/KROEM/SOEM	eupnea	YAOUP/NA
euchylia	YAOU/KIL/YA		YAOUP/NAOE/YA
eucolloid	YAOU/KLOID	eupneic	YAOUP/NIK
	YAOU/KOL/OID		YAOUP/NAOE/IK
eucorticalism	YAOU/KORT/KAL/IFM	eupractic	YAOU/PRAKT/IK
	YAOU/KORT/KLIFM	eupraxia	YAOU/PRAX/YA
eucrasia	YAOU/KRAIZ/YA	eupraxic	YAOU/PRAX/IK
eucupine	YAOU/KAOU/PAOEN	euprocin	YAOU/PRO/SIN
eudemonia	YAOUD/MOEN/YA	Euproctis	YAOU/PROK/TIS
	YAOU/DE/MOEN/YA	Eurax	YAOU/RAX
eudiaphoresis	YAOU/DAOI/FRAOE/SIS		YAOUR/AX
eudipsia	YAOU/DIPS/YA	eurhythmia	YAOU/R*IT/MA
euergasia	YAOU/ER/GAIZ/YA		YAOU/R*IT/MAOE/YA
euesthesia	YAOU/ES/THAOEZ/YA	European	YAOUR/PAOEN
eugamy	YAOUG/M*I		YAOURP/PAOEN
eugenic	YAOU/JEN/IK	europium	YAOU/ROEP/YUM
eugenicist	YAOU/JEN/S*IS	eury-	YAOUR
eugenics	YAOU/JEN/IK/-S		YAOU/RI
eugenism	YAOUJ/NIFM	eurycephalic	YAOUR/SFAL/IK
	YAOU/JEN/IFM	eurycephalous	YAOUR/SEF/LOUS
eugenist	YAOU/JEN/*IS	eurycranial	YAOUR/KRAIN/YAL
eugenol	YAOUJ/NOL	eurygnathic	YAOU/RIG/NA*T/IK
	YAOU/JE/NOL		YAOUR/NA*T/IK
Euglena	YAOU/GLAOE/NA	eurygnathism	YAOU/RIG/NA/THIFM
Euglenidae	YAOU/GLAOEN/DAE	eurygnathous	YAOU/RIG/NA/THOUS
euglobulin	YAOU/GLOB/LIN	euryon	YAOUR/YON
euglycemia	YAOU/GLAOI/SAOEM/YA	euryopia	YAOUR/YOEP/YA
euglycemic	YAOU/GLAOI/SAOEM/IK	euryphotic	YAOUR/FOET/YA
eugnathia	YAOU/NA*IT/YA		YAOUR/FOT/IK
	YAOU/NA*T/YA	eurysomatic	YAOUR/SOE/MAT/IK
eugnathic	YAOU/NA*T/IK	eurythermic	YAOUR/THERM/IK
eugnosia	YAOU/NOEZ/YA	euscope	YAOU/SKOEP
eugnostic	YAOU/NO*S/IK	Eusimulium	YAOUS/MAOUL/YUM
eugonic	YAOU/GON/IK		YAOU/SI/MAOUL/YUM
euhydration	YAOU/HAOI/DRAIGS	eusitia	YAOU/SIT/YA
eukaryon	YAOU/KAR/YON	eusplanchnia	YAOU/SPLANG/NA
eukaryosis	YAOU/KAR/YOE/SIS		YAOU/SPLANG/NAOE/YA
Eukaryotae	YAOU/KAR/YOE/TAE	eusplenia	YAOU/SPLAOEN/YA
eukaryote	YAOU/KAR/YOET	eustachian	YAOU/STAIK/YAN
eukaryotic	YAOU/KAR/YOT/IK		YAOU/STAIGS
eukeratin	YAOU/KER/TIN	eustachitis	YAOU/STAI/KAOITS
eukinesia	YAOU/KI/NAOEZ/YA	eustachium	YAOU/STAIK/YUM
eukinesis	YAOU/KI/NAOE/SIS	eusthenia	YAOU/STHAOEN/YA
eukinetic	YAOU/KI/NET/IK	eusthenuria	YAOU/STHEN/YAOUR/YA
eulaminate	YAOU/LAM/NAIT	Eustrongylus	YAOU/STRONG/LUS
Eulenburg	YAOU/LEN/BURG		YAOU/STRON/JI/LUS
	OIL/EN/BURG	eusystole	YAOU/S*IS/LAOE
Eulexin	YAOU/LEK/SIN	eusystolic	YAOU/SIS/TOL/IK
eumelanin	YAOU/MEL/NIN	eutectic	YAOU/TEKT/IK
eumelanosome	YAOU/MEL/NO/SOEM	eutelegenesis	YAOU/TEL/JEN/SIS
eumenorrhea	YAOU/MEN/RAOE/YA	euthanasia	YAO*UT/NAIZ/YA
eumetria	YAOU/MAOE/TRA	euthenic	YAOU/THEN/IK
	YAOU/MAOE/TRAOE/YA	euthenics	YAOU/THEN/IK/-S
eumorphic	YAOU/MOR/FIK	eutherapeutic	YAOU/THER/PAOUT/IK

Eutheria	YAOU/THAOER/YA	exarteritis	KPAN/THROP/IK
eutherian	YAOU/THAOERN		EX/ART/RAOITS
	YAOU/THAOER/YAN		KPART/RAOITS
euthermic	YAOU/THERM/IK	exarticulation	EX/AR/TIK/LAIGS
Euthroid	YAOU/THROID		KPAR/TIK/LAIGS
euthymic	YAOU/THAOIM/IK	excalation	EX/KLAIGS
euthymism	YAOU/THAOIM/MIFM		EX/KA/LAIGS
	YAOU/THAOIM/IFM	excarnation	EX/KAR/NAIGS
euthyphoria	YAO*UT/FOER/YA	excavatio	EX/KA/VAI*SHOE
euthyroid	YAOU/THAOI/ROID	excavation	EX/KA/VAIGS
euthyroidism	YAOU/THAOI/ROI/DIFM	excavationes	EX/KA/VAI/SHOE/NAOEZ
euthyscope	YAO*UT/SKOEP	excavator	EX/KA/VAI/TOR
euthyscopy	YAOU/THIS/KPI	Excedrin	KPED/RIN
eutocia	YAOU/TOE/SHA	excementosis	EX/SEMT/TOE/SIS
eutonic	YAOU/TON/IK		KPEMT/TOE/SIS
Eutonyl	YAOUT/NIL	excentric	KPEN/TRIK
eutopic	YAOU/TOP/IK	excerebration	EX/SER/BRAIGS
eutrichosis	YAOU/TRI/KOE/SIS		KPER/BRAIGS
Eutron	YAOU/TRON	excernent	EX/SER/NENT
eutrophia	YAOU/TROEF/YA		KPER/NENT
eutrophic	YAOU/TROFK	excess	KPESZ
eutrophy	YAOU/TRO/FI	excessive	KPESZ/IV
euvolia	YAOU/VOEL/YA		KPES/SIV
Evac-Q-Kit	E/VAK/YAOU/KIT	exchange	EX/KHAING
Evac-Q-Kwik	E/VAK/YAOU/KWIK		EX/KHAIN/-J
evacuant	E/VAK/YANT	exchanger	EX/KHAING/ER
evacuation	E/VAK/YAIGS		EX/KHAIN/JER
evacuator	E/VAK/YAI/TOR	excipient	KPIP/YENT
evagination	E/VAJ/NAIGS	excise	KPAOIZ
evanescent	EV/NES/ENT		KPAOIS
Evans	EVNS	excision	KPIGS
	EVNZ	excisional	KPIGS/NAL
evaporate	E/VAP/RAIT	excitable	KPAOIT/-BL
evaporation	E/VAP/RAIGS	excitability	KPAOIT/-BLT
evasion	E/VAIGS	excitant	KPAOI/TANT
eventration	E/VEN/TRAIGS		KPAOIT/TANT
eversion	E/VERGS	excitation	KPAOI/TAIGS
evert	E/VERT	excitatory	KPAOIT/TOIR
evertor	E/VER/TOR	excitement	KPAOIT/-MT
evidement	AI/VAOED/-MT	exciting	KPAOIT/-G
	E/VAOED/-MT	excito-	KPAOI/TO
evideur	AIV/DAOUR		EX/SAOI/TO
	EV/DAOUR		(not KPAOIT; see excite)
evil	AOEVL	excitoanabolic	KPAOI/TO/AN/BOL/IK
	E/VIL	excitocatabolic	KPAOI/TO/KAT/BOL/IK
eviration	EV/RAIGS	excitoglandular	KPAOI/TO/GLAND/LAR
	E/VAOI/RAIGS	excitometabolic	KPAOI/TO/MET/BOL/IK
evisceration	E/VIS/RAIGS	excitomotor	KPAOI/TO/MOE/TOR
evisceroneurotomy	E/VIS/RO/NAOU/ROT/M*I	excitomotory	KPAOI/TO/MOET/RI
evocation	EV/KAIGS	excitomuscular	KPAOI/TO/MUS/KLAR
	E/VOE/KAIGS	excitonutrient	KPAOI/TO/NAOU/TRENT
evocator	EV/KAI/TOR		KPAOI/TO/NAOU/TRAOENT
evolution	EV/LAOUGS	excitor	KPAOI/TOR
evolutive	E/VOL/TIV		KPAOIT/TOR
	EV/LAOUT/IV	excitosecretory	KPAOI/TO/SE/KRAOET/RI
evulsio	E/VULS/YOE	excitovascular	KPAOI/TO/VAS/KLAR
evulsion	E/VULGS	exclave	EX/KLAIV
Ewart	YAOU/ART	exclusion	EX/KLAOUGS
	YAOU/WART	excochleation	EX/KOK/LAIGS
Ewing	YAOU/-G	exconjugant	EX/KON/JAOU/GANT
ex-	EX		EX/KON/JU/GANT
	KP-	excoriate	EX/KOR/YAIT
exacerbate	KPAS/BAIT	excoriation	EX/KOR/YAIGS
	KPAS/ER/BAIT	excoriee des jeunes filles	EX/KOR/YAI/DE/JAOUN/FIL
exacerbation	KPAS/BAIGS	excrement	EX/KREMT
	KPAS/ER/BAIGS	excrementitial	EX/KREMT/TIRBL
exaltation	KPAL/TAIGS	excrementitious	EX/KREMT/TIRBS
examination	KPAM/NAIGS	excrescence	EX/KRES/ENS
examiner	KPAM/NER	excrescent	EX/KRES/ENT
exania	KPAIN/YA	excreta	EX/KRAOE/TA
	EX/AIN/YA	excrete	EX/KRAOET
exanimation	EX/AN/MAIGS	excretion	EX/KRAOEGS
	KPAN/MAIGS	excretorii	EX/KRE/TOR/YAOI
ex anopsia	EX/AI/NOPS/YA	excretorius	EX/KRE/TOR/YUS
exanthem	KPAN/THEM	excretory	EX/KRE/TOIR
	EX/AN/THEM		EX/KRAOET/RI
exanthema	KPAN/THAOE/MA	excursion	EX/KURGS
	EX/AN/THAOE/MA	excursive	EX/KURS/IV
exanthemata	KPAN/THEM/TA	excycloduction	EX/SAOI/KLO/D*UBGS
	EX/AN/THEM/TA	excyclophoria	EX/SAOI/KLO/FOER/YA
exanthematic	KPA*NT/MAT/IK	excyclotropia	EX/SAOI/KLO/TROEP/YA
	EX/A*NT/MAT/IK	excyclovergence	EX/SAOI/KLO/VERJ/ENS
exanthematous	KPAN/THEM/TOUS	excystation	EX/SIS/TAIGS
	EX/AN/THEM/TOUS	Exelderm	KPEL/DERM
exanthesis	KPAN/THAOE/SIS		EX/EL/DERM
	EX/AN/THAOE/SIS	exemia	KPAOEM/YA
exanthrope	EX/AN/THROEP	exencephalia	EX/EN/SFAIL/YA
	KPAN/THROEP		KPEN/SFAIL/YA
exanthropic	EX/AN/THROP/IK	exencephalic	EX/EN/SFAL/IK

	KPEN/SFAL/IK	exoenzyme	KPO/EN/ZAOIM
exencephalocele	EX/EN/SEF/LO/SAO*EL	exogamy	KPOG/M*I
	KPEN/SEF/LO/SAO*EL	exogastric	KPO/GAS/TRIK
exencephalon	EX/EN/SEF/LON	exogastritis	KPO/GAS/TRAOITS
	KPEN/SEF/LON	exogastrula	KPO/GAS/TRAOU/LA
exencephalous	EX/EN/SEF/LOUS	exogastrulation	KPO/GAS/TRAOU/LAIGS
	KPEN/SEF/LOUS		KPO/GAS/TRU/LAIGS
exencephalus	EX/EN/SEF/LUS	exogenetic	KPO/JE/NET/IK
	KPEN/SEF/LUS	exogenic	KPO/JEN/IK
exencephaly	EX/EN/SEF/LI	exogenote	KPO/JAOE/NOET
	KPEN/SEF/LI	exogenous	KPOJ/NOUS
exenteration	KPENT/RAIGS	exognathia	KPOG/NA*IT/YA
	EX/ENT/RAIGS	exognathion	KPOG/NA*IT/YON
	EX/SPWER/RAIGS		EK/SOG/NA*IT/YON
exenterative	KPENT/RA/TIV	exolever	KPO/LAOEVR
	EX/ENT/RA/TIV	exometer	KPOM/TER
	EX/SPWER/RA/TIV	exomphalos	KPOM/FLOS
exenteritis	KPENT/RAOITS		KPOM/FA/LOS
	EX/SPWRAOITS	exomysium	KPO/MIS/YUM
	EX/SPWER/RAOITS	exon	KPON
exercise	KPER/SAOIZ		EK/SON
	EX/ER/SAOIZ	exon shuffle	KPON/SHUF/-L
exeresis	KPER/SIS		EK/SON/SHUF/-L
	EX/ER/SIS	exonuclease	KPO/NAOUK/LAIS
exergonic	KPER/GON/IK	exopathic	KPO/PA*T/IK
	EX/ER/GON/IK	exopathy	KPOP/TH*I
exertion	KPERGS	exopeptidase	KPO/PEPT/DAIS
exertional	KPERGS/NAL	Exophiala	KPO/FAOI/LA
exesion	KPAOEGS	exophoria	KPO/FOER/YA
	EX/AOEGS	exophoric	KPO/FOER/IK
exfetation	EX/FAOE/TAIGS	exophthalmic	KPOF/THAL/MIK
exflagellation	EX/FLAJ/LAIGS		EX/OF/THAL/MIK
exfoliatio	EX/FOEL/YAI/SHOE	exophthalmica	KPOF/THAL/MI/KA
	EX/FOEL/YAIRB/YOE		EX/OF/THAL/MI/KA
exfoliation	EX/FOEL/YAIGS	exophthalmogenic	EX/OF/THAL/MO/JEN/IK
exfoliativa	EX/FOEL/YA/TAOI/VA		KPOF/THAL/MO/JEN/IK
exfoliative	EX/FOEL/YA/TIV	exophthalmometer	KPOF/THAL/MOM/TER
exhalation	EX/HA/LAIGS		EX/OF/THAL/MOM/TER
	KPHA/LAIGS	exophthalmometric	EX/OF/THAL/MO/MET/RIK
exhale	KPAIL		KPOF/THAL/MO/MET/RIK
	KPHAIL	exophthalmometry	EX/OF/THAL/MOM/TRI
	EX/HAIL		KPOF/THAL/MOM/TRI
exhaustion	KPAUGS	exophthalmos	KPOF/THAL/MOS
exhibit	KPIBT		EX/OF/THAL/MOS
exhibition	KPIBGS	exophthalmus	KPOF/THAL/MUS
	EX/BIGS		EX/OF/THAL/MUS
exhibitionism	KPIBGS/IFM	exophyte	KPO/FAOIT
	EX/BIGS/IFM	exophytic	KPO/FIT/IK
exhibitionist	KPIBGS/*IS	exoplasm	KPO/PLAFM
	EX/BIGS/*IS	ex ore	EX/OR/RAOE
exhilarant	KPIL/RANT	exosepsis	KPO/SEP/SIS
exhumation	KPAOU/MAIGS	exoserosis	KPO/SE/ROE/SIS
	KPAOUM/AIGS	exoskeleton	KPO/SKEL/TON
	KPAOUM/MAIGS	exosmose	KPOS/MOES
exhume	KPAOUM		KPOZ/MOES
exilis	KPAOI/LIS		EX/OS/MOES
	KPAOIL/LIS		EX/OZ/MOES
existential	KPIS/TEN/-RBL	exosmosis	KPOS/MOE/SIS
	EX/STEN/-RBL		KPOZ/MOE/SIS
exitus	EX/TUS		EX/OZ/MOE/SIS
	KPI/TUS		EX/OS/MOE/SIS
Exna	EX/NA	exospore	KPO/SPOER
Exner	EX/NER	exosporium	KPO/SPOR/YUM
exo-	KPO	exostectomy	KPOS/TEKT/M*I
	EK/SO		EX/OS/TEKT/M*I
	(not EX; see ex-)	exostosectomy	KPOS/TO/SEKT/M*I
exoantigen	KPO/A*ENT/JEN		EX/OS/TO/SEKT/M*I
exocardia	KPO/KARD/YA	exostoses	KPOS/TOE/SAOEZ
exocardial	KPO/KARD/YAL		EX/OS/TOE/SAOEZ
exocataphoria	KPO/KAT/FOER/YA	exostosis	KPOS/TOE/SIS
exoccipital	EX/OK/SIP/TAL		EX/OS/TOE/SIS
	KPOK/SIP/TAL	exostotic	KPOS/TOT/IK
exocele	KPO/SAO*EL		EX/OS/TOT/IK
exocervix	KPO/SER/VIX	exoteric	KPO/TER/IK
exochorion	KPO/KOER/YON		EX/TER/IK
exocolitis	KPO/KO/LAOITS	exothelioma	KPO/THAOEL/YOE/MA
exocrine	KPO/KRIN	exothermal	KPO/THER/MAL
exocrinology	KPO/KRI/NOLG	exothermic	KPO/THERM/IK
exocrinosity	KPO/KRI/NOS/TI	exotic	KPOT/IK
exocuticle	KPO/KAOUT/K-L	exotoxic	KPO/TOX/IK
exocyclic	KPO/SAOIK/LIK	exotoxin	KPO/TOK/SIN
	KPO/SIK/LIK	exotropia	KPO/TROEP/YA
exocytosis	KPO/SAOI/TOE/SIS	exotropic	KPO/TROP/IK
exodeviation	KPO/DAOEV/YAIGS	expander	EX/PAND/ER
exodic	KPOD/IK	expansion	EX/PANGS
exodontia	KPO/DON/SHA	expansiveness	EX/PANS/IV/*NS
exodontics	KPO/DONT/IK/-S		EX/PANS/IVNS
exodontist	KPO/DON/T*IS	expectancy	EX/PEK/TAN/SI
	KPO/DONT/*IS		KP-PT/AN/SI

expectation	EX/PEK/TAIGS	exteriorize	EX/TAOER/YOR/AOIZ
expectorant	EX/PEK/TRANT	extern	EX/TERN
	EX/PEKT/RANT	externa	EX/TER/NA
	KP-PT/RANT	externae	EX/TER/NAE
expectorate	EX/PEK/TRAIT (required)	external	EX/TERNL
	(not EX/PEKT/RAIT or KP-PT/	externalia	EX/TER/NAIL/YA
	RAIT; see expect rate)	externalize	EX/TERNL/AOIZ
expectoration	EX/PEK/TRAIGS		EX/TERN/LAOIZ
	EX/PEKT/RAIGS	externi	EX/TER/NAOI
	KP-PT/RAIGS	externus	EX/TER/NUS
experience	EX/PAOERNS	exteroceptive	EX/TRO/SEPT/IV
experiment	EX/PAOERMT	exteroceptor	EX/TRO/SEP/TOR
experimenter	EX/PAOERMT/ER	exterofection	EX/TRO/F*EBGS
expirate	EX/PRAIT	exterofective	EX/TRO/FEKT/IV
	EX/PI/RAIT	exterogestate	EX/TRO/JES/TAIT
expiration	EX/PRAIGS	extima	EX/TI/MA
	EX/PI/RAIGS		*EX/MA
expiratory	EX/PAOIR/TOIR	extinction	EX/TINGS
	EK/SPAOIR/TOIR	extinguish	EX/TING/WIRB
	EX/PRA/TOIR	extirpation	EX/TIR/PAIGS
expire	EX/PAOIR	Exton	EX/TON
explant	EX/PLANT	extorsion	EX/TO*RGS
explantation	EX/PLAN/TAIGS		(not EX/TORGS; see extortion)
explode	EX/PLOED	extortor	EX/TOR/TOR
exploration	EX/PLO/RAIGS	extra-	EX/TRA
	EX/PLOE/RAIGS	extra-adrenal	EX/TRA/AI/DRAOENL
exploratoria	EX/PLOR/TOR/YA	extra-alveolar	EX/TRA/AL/VAOE/LAR
	EX/PLOER/TOR/YA	extra-anthropic	EX/TRA/AN/THROP/IK
exploratory	EX/PLOR/TOIR	extra-articular	EX/TRA/AR/TIK/LAR
	EX/PLOER/TOIR	extrabronchial	EX/TRA/BRONG/YAL
explore	EX/PLOR	extrabuccal	EX/TRA/BUK/KAL
	EX/PLOER	extrabulbar	EX/TRA/BUL/BAR
explorer	EX/PLOR/ER	extracaliceal	EX/TRA/KAL/SAOEL
	EX/PLOER/ER		EX/TRA/KA/LIS/YAL
explosion	EX/PLOEGS	extracanthic	EX/TRA/KA*NT/IK
explosive	EX/PLOES/IV	extracapsular	EX/TRA/KAPS/LAR
exponent	EX/POENT	extracapsularia	EX/TRA/KAPS/LAIR/YA
expose	EX/POEZ	extracardial	EX/TRA/KARD/YAL
exposure	EX/POE/SHUR	extracarpal	EX/TRA/KAR/PAL
express	EX/PRESZ	extracellular	EX/TRA/SEL/YAOU/LAR
expressate	EX/PRES/SAIT	extracerebral	EX/TRA/SER/BRAL
expression	EX/PREGS	extrachromosomal	EX/TRA/KROEM/SOE/MAL
expressivity	EX/PRES/SIV/TI	extraciliary	EX/TRA/SIL/YAIR
expulsion	EX/PULGS	extracorporal	EX/TRA/KORP/RAL
expulsive	EX/PULS/IV	extracorporeal	EX/TRA/KOR/POR/YAL
exquisite	EX/KWI/SIT		EX/TRA/KOR/POER/YAL
	EX/KWIZ/SIT	extracorpuscular	EX/TRA/KOR/PUS/KLAR
exsanguinate	EX/SANG/WI/NAIT	extracorticalis	EX/TRA/KORT/KAI/LIS
exsanguination	EX/SANG/WI/NAIGS	extracorticospinal	EX/TRA/KORT/KO/SPAOINL
exsanguine	EX/SANG/WIN	extracranial	EX/TRA/KRAIN/YAL
exsanguinotransfusion	EX/SANG/WIN/TRA*NS/FAOUGS	extract	EX/TRAKT
exsect	EX/SEKT	extractant	EX/TRAK/TANT
	KPEKT	extraction	EX/TRA*BGS
exsection	EX/S*EBGS	extractive	EK/TRAKT/IV
	KP*EBGS	extractor	EX/TRAK/TOR
exsector	EX/SEK/TOR	extractum	EX/TRAK/TUM
	(not KPEK/TOR; see executor)	extracystic	EX/TRA/S*IS/IK
Exsel Shampoo	KP*EL/SHAM/PAO	extradural	EX/TRA/DAOURL
	EX/S*EL/SHAM/PAO	extraembryonic	EX/TRA/EM/BRON/IK
exsicc-	EX/K-	extraepiphysial	EX/TRA/EP/FIZ/YAL
	EX/SI/K-	extrafusal	EX/TRA/FAOU/SAL
	KPI/K-		EX/TRA/FAOU/ZAL
exsiccant	EX/SIK/KANT	extragenic	EX/TRA/JEN/IK
	EX/KANT	extragenital	EX/TRA/JEN/TAL
exsiccate	EX/KAIT	extrahepatic	EX/TRA/HE/PAT/IK
exsiccated	EX/KAIT/-D	extrajection	EX/TRA/J*EBGS
exsiccation	EX/KAIGS	extraligamentous	EX/TRA/LIG/MEN/TOUS
exsiccatum	EX/KAI/TUM	extramalleolus	EX/TRA/MAL/LAOE/LUS
	EX/KAIT/UM	extramarginal	EX/TRA/MARJ/NAL
exsomatize	EX/SOEM/TAOIZ	extramastoiditis	EX/TRA/MAS/TOI/DAOITS
	KPOEM/TAOIZ	extramedullary	EX/TRA/MED/LAIR
exsorption	KPORPGS	extrameningeal	EX/TRA/ME/NIN/JAL
	EX/SORPGS	extramural	EX/TRA/MAOURL
exstrophy	EK/STRO/FI	extraneous	EX/TRAIN/YOUS
	EX/TRO/FI	extranuclear	EX/TRA/NAOUK/LAR
	EX/STRO/FI	extraocular	EX/TRA/OK/LAR
exsufflation	EX/SUF/FLAIGS	extraoculogram	EX/TRA/OK/LO/GRAM
exsufflator	EX/SUF/FLAI/TOR	extraoral	EX/TRA/ORL
extend	EX/TEND	extraosseous	EX/TRA/OS/YOUS
extender	EX/TEND/ER	extraovular	EX/TRA/OV/LAR
Extendryl	EX/TEN/DRIL	extrapapillary	EX/TRA/PAP/LAIR
extensibility	EX/TENS/-BLT	extraparenchymal	EX/TRA/PRENG/MAL
extension	EX/TENGS		EX/TRA/PA/RENG/MAL
extensometer	EX/TEN/SOM/TER	extrapelvic	EX/TRA/PEL/VIK
extensor	EX/TEN/SOR	extrapericardial	EX/TRA/P*ER/KARD/YAL
extensoris	EX/TEN/SOR/RIS	extraperineal	EX/TRA/P*ER/NAOEL
	EX/TEN/SOER/RIS	extraperiosteal	EX/TRA/P*ER/O*S/YAL
Extentabs	EX/TEN/TAB/-S	extraperitoneal	EX/TRA/PERT/NAOEL
exterior	EX/TAOER/YOR	extraphysiologic	EX/TRA/FIZ/YO/LOJ/IK

158

extraplacental	EX/TRA/PLA/SEN/TAL	eyeteeth	YAOI/TAO*ET
extraplantar	EX/TRA/PLAN/TAR	eyewash	YAOI/WARB
extrapleural	EX/TRA/PLAOURL		
extrapolation	EX/TRAP/LAIGS		
extraprostatic	EX/TRA/PROS/TAT/IK		
extraprostatitis	EX/TRA/PRO*S/TAOITS		
extrapsychic	EX/TRA/SAOIK/IK		
extrapulmonary	EX/TRA/PUL/MO/NAIR		
	EX/TRA/PUM/NAIR		
extrapyramidal	EX/TRA/PI/RAM/DAL		
extrarectus	EX/TRA/REK/TUS		
extrarenal	EX/TRA/RAOENL		
extrasensory	EX/TRA/SENS/RI		
extraserous	EX/TRA/SAOER/OUS		
extrasomatic	EX/TRA/SOE/MAT/IK		
	EX/TRA/SMAT/IK		
extrasuprarenal	EX/TRA/SU/PRA/RAOENL		
extrasystole	EX/TRA/S*IS/LAOE		
extratarsal	EX/TRA/TAR/SAL		
extrathoracic	EX/TRA/THRAS/IK		
extratracheal	EX/TRA/TRAIK/YAL		
extratubal	EX/TRA/TAOU/BAL		
extratympanic	EX/TRA/TIM/PAN/IK		
extrauterine	EX/TRA/YAOUT/RIN		
extravaginal	EX/TRA/VAJ/NAL		
extravasate	EX/TRAV/SAIT		
extravasation	EX/TRAV/SAIGS		
extravascular	EX/TRA/VAS/KLAR		
extraventricular	EX/TRA/VEN/TRIK/LAR		
extraversion	EX/TRA/VERGS		
extravert	EX/TRA/VERT		
extravisual	EX/TRA/VIRBL		
extrema	EX/TRAOE/MA		
extreme	EX/TRAOEM		
extremita	EX/TREM/TA		
extremital	EX/TREM/TAL		
extremitas	EX/TREM/TAS		
extremitates	EX/TREM/TAI/TAOEZ		
extremitatis	EX/TREM/TAI/TIS		
extremity	EX/TREM/TI		
extrication	EX/TRI/KAIGS		
extrinsic	EX/TRINZ/IK		
	EX/TRINS/IK		
extro-	EX/TRO		
extrogastrulation	EX/TRO/GAS/TRAOU/LAIGS		
	EX/TRO/GAS/TRU/LAIGS		
extrospection	EX/TRO/SP*EBGS		
extroversion	EX/TRO/VERGS		
extrovert	EX/TRO/VERT		
extrude	EX/TRAOUD		
extrudoclusion	EX/TRAOUD/KLAOUGS		
extrusion	EX/TRAOUGS		
extubate	EX/TAOU/BAIT		
extubation	EX/TAOU/BAIGS		
exuberant	KPAOUB/RANT		
exudate	KPAOU/DAIT		
exudation	KPAOU/DAIGS		
exudativa	KPAOUD/TAOI/VA		
exudative	KPAOUD/TIV		
	KPAOU/DAIT/IV		
exudativum	KPAOUD/TAOI/VUM		
	KPAOUD/TAOIV/UM		
exude	KPAOUD		
exulcerans	EX/ULS/RANZ		
	KPULS/RANZ		
exulceratio	EX/ULS/RAI/SHOE		
	KPULS/RAI/SHOE		
exumbilication	EX/UM/BIL/KAIGS		
	KPUM/BIL/KAIGS		
exuviae	KPAOUV/YAE		
exuviation	KPAOUV/YAIGS		
ex vacuo	EX/VAK/YOE		
	EX/VAK/WOE		
ex vivo	EX/VAOE/VOE		
eye	YAOI		
eyeball	YAOI/BAL		
eyebrow	YAOI/BROU		
eyecup	YAOI/KUP		
eyeglasses	YAOI/GLASZ/S		
eyegrounds	YAOI/GROUNDZ		
eyelash	YAOI/LARB		
eyelet	YAOI/LET		
eyelid	YAOI/LID		
eye-minded	YAOI/H-F/MAOIND/-D		
eyepiece	YAOI/PAOES		
eyepoint	YAOI/POINT		
eyespot	YAOI/SPOT		
eyestone	YAOI/STOEN		
eyestrain	YAOI/STRAIN		

F

faba	FAI/BA
fabella	FA/BEL/LA
fabellae	FA/BEL/LAE
Faber	FAB/ER
fabism	FAI/BIFM
fabrication	FAB/KAIGS
	FAB/RI/KAIGS
Fabricius	FA/BRIS/YUS
	FA/BRIRBS
Fabry	FAB/RI
fabulation	FAB/LAIGS
face	FAIS
face-bow	FAIS/BOE
face-lift	FAIS/H-F/LIFT
facet	FAS/ET
	FA/SET
facetectomy	FAS/TEKT/M*I
facette	FA/S*ET
	(*not* FA/SET; see facet)
faci(o)-	FAI/SH(O)
	FAIRB/Y(O)
	FAIS/Y(O)
facial	FAIRBL
facialis	FAI/SHAI/LIS
	FAIRB/YAI/LIS
faciei	FAI/SHAOI
	FAIRB/YAOI
-facient	FAIRBT
	FAI/SHENT
	FAIRB/ENT
facies	FAI/SHAOEZ
	FARB/AOEZ
facilitated	FA/SIL/TAIT/-D
facilitation	FA/SIL/TAIGS
facilitative	FA/SIL/TAIT/IV
facilitory	FA/SIL/TOIR
facing	FAIS/-G
faciobrachial	FAI/SHO/BRAIK/YAL
faciocephalalgia	FAI/SHO/SEF/LAL/JA
faciocervical	FAI/SHO/SEFRB/KAL
faciogenital	FAI/SHO/JEN/TAL
faciolingual	FAI/SHO/LING/WAL
facioplasty	FAI/SHO/PLAS/TI
facioplegia	FAI/SHO/PLAOE/JA
facioscapulohumeral	FAI/SHO/SKAP/LO/HAOUM/RAL
faciostenosis	FAI/SHO/STE/NOE/SIS
F-actin	F-RBGS/AK/TIN
factitial	FAK/TIRBL
factitious	FAK/TIRBS
factor	FAK/TOR
factorial	FAK/TOIRL
Factor IX Complex	FAK/TOR/9/KOM/PLEX
Factrel	FAK/TREL
facultative	FAK/UL/TAIT/IV
faculty	FAK/UL/TI
fading	FAID/-G
faecalis	FAOE/KAI/LIS
	FAE/KAI/LIS
Faget	FA/JAI
fagicladosporic	FAJ/KLAD/SPOR/IK
fagopyrism	FAG/PAOI/RIFM
	FA/GOP/RIFM
Fahraeus	FA/RAOE/YUS
Fahrenheit	FARN/HAOIT
	FAIRN/HAOIT
failure	FAIL/YUR
faint	FAINT
faith	FA*IT
falcatae	FAL/KAI/TAE
falcate	FAL/KAIT
falces	FAL/SAOEZ
falcial	FAL/-RBL
	FALS/YAL
falciform	FALS/FORM
	FAL/SI/FORM
falciforme	FALS/FOR/MAOE
	FAL/SI/FOR/MAOE
falciformis	FALS/FOR/MIS
	FAL/SI/FOR/MIS
falcine	FAL/SAOEN
falcular	FAL/KLAR
fallopi-	FLOEP/Y-
	FA/LOEP/Y-
	FAL/LOEP/Y-

fallopian	FLOEP/YAN
fallopii	FLOEP/YAOI
Fallopius	FLOEP/YUS
Fallot	FA/LOE
	FAL/LOE
fallout	FAUL/O*UT
false	FAULS
	FALS
false-negative	FAULS/H-F/NEG/TIV
false-positive	FAULS/H-F/POZ/TIV
falsification	FAULS/FI/KAIGS
falsifying	FAULS/FI/-G
Falta	FAL/TA
falx	FAL/-X
fames	FAI/MAOEZ
familial	FA/MIL/YAL
familiaris	FA/MIL/YAI/RIS
family	FAM/LI
famine	FAM/MIN
famotidine	FA/MOET/DAOEN
famotine	FAM/TAOEN
fan	FAN
Fanconi	FAN/KOE/NAOE
fang	FANG
fango	FAN/GOE
fangotherapy	FANG/THER/PI
	FAN/GO/THER/PI
Fannia	FAN/YA
Fansidar	FANS/DAR
fantascope	FANT/SKOEP
fantast	FAN/TA*S
fantasy	FANT/SI
fantridone	FAN/TRI/DOEN
Fantus	FAN/TUS
Farabeuf	FAR/BUF
farad	FA/RAD
	FA*R/AD
	(not FAR/AD or FAR/RAD)
faradaic	FAR/DAI/IK
faraday	FAR/DAI
	FAR/RA/DAI
	FA/RA/DAI
Faraday	K-P/FAR/DAI
	K-P/FAR/RA/DAI
	K-P/FA/RA/DAI
faradic	FA/RAD/IK
faradimeter	FAR/DIM/TER
faradism	FAR/DIFM
faradization	FA/RAD/ZAIGS
	FAR/DI/ZAIGS
faradocontractility	FAR/DO/KON/TRAK/TIL/TI
	FAR/DO/KR-T/TIL/TI
faradomuscular	FAR/DO/MUS/KLAR
faradopalpation	FAR/DO/PAL/PAIGS
faradotherapy	FAR/DO/THER/PI
Farber	FARB/ER
	FAR/BER
farciminosus	FAR/SIM/NOE/SUS
farcy	FAR/SI
fardel	FAR/DEL
farina	FA/RAOE/NA
farinaceous	FAR/NAIRBS
farinata	FAR/NAI/TA
farinometer	FAR/NOM/TER
farinosa	FAR/NOE/SA
farnesene	FARN/SAOEN
farnesol	FARN/SOL
Farnsworth	FARNS/WO*RT
Farr	FA*R
farsighted	FAR/SAOIGT/-D
farsightedness	FAR/SAOIGT/D*NS
	FAR/SAOIGT/-D/*NS
fasci(o)-	FARB/Y(O)
	FAS/Y(O)
fascia	FARB/YA
	FAI/SHA
fasciae	FARB/YAE
fasciagram	FARB/YA/GRAM
fasciagraphy	FARB/YAG/FI
fascial	FARBL
fascialis	FARB/YAI/LIS
fasciaplasty	FARB/YA/PLAS/TI
fasciatus	FARB/YAI/TUS
fascicle	FAS/K-L
fascicul-	FA/SIK/L-
	FAS/SIK/L-
fascicular	FA/SIK/LAR
fasciculate	FA/SIK/LAIT
fasciculated	FA/SIK/LAIT/-D

fasciculation	FA/SIK/LAIGS		
fasciculi	FA/SIK/LAOI	febrilis	FE/BRAOI/LIS
fasciculus	FA/SIK/LUS	febris	FAOE/BRIS
fasciectomy	FARB/YEKT/M*I	fecal	FAOE/KAL
	FARB/EKT/M*I	fecalith	FAOEK/L*IT
fasciitis	FAS/YAOITS	fecaloid	FAOEK/LOID
	FARB/YAOITS	fecaloma	FAOEK/LOE/MA
fasciodesis	FARB/YOD/SIS	fecaluria	FAOEK/LAOUR/YA
	FAS/YOD/SIS	feces	FAOE/SAOEZ
fasciola	FA/SAOE/LA	Fechner	FEK/NER
	FA/SAOI/LA	fecula	FEK/LA
fasciolae	FA/SAOE/LAE	feculent	FEK/LENT
	FA/SAOI/LAE	fecund	FAOE/KUND
fasciolar	FA/SAOE/LAR		FEK/UND
	FA/SAOI/LAR	fecundate	FAOE/KUN/DAIT
fascioliasis	FARB/YO/LAOI/SIS	fecundatio	FAOE/KUN/DAI/SHOE
	FAS/YO/LAOI/SIS		FAOE/KUN/DAIRB/YOE
	FA/SAOI/LAOI/SIS	fecundation	FAOE/KUN/DAIGS
fasciolid	FA/SAOE/LID		FEK/UN/DAIGS
	FA/SAOI/LID	fecundity	FAOE/KUND/TI
Fascioloides	FARB/YO/LOI/DAOEZ		FE/KUND/TI
	FAS/YO/LOI/DAOEZ	Fedahist	FED/H*IS
	FA/SAOI/LOI/DAOEZ	Fede	FAI/DAI
fasciolopsiasis	FARB/YO/LOP/SAOI/SIS		FE/DAI
	FAS/YO/LOP/SAOI/SIS	fee	FAOE
	FA/SAOI/LOP/SAOI/SIS	feebleminded	FAOEBL/MAOIND/-D
Fasciolopsis	FARB/YO/LOP/SIS	feeblemindedness	FAOEBL/MAOIND/D*NS
	FAS/YO/LOP/SIS	feedback	FAOED/BA*K
	FA/SAOI/LOP/SIS	feed-forward	FAOED/H-F/FWARD
fascioplasty	FARB/YO/PLAS/TI		FAOED/H-F/FOR/WARD
fasciorrhaphy	FARB/YOR/FI	feeding	FAOED/-G
fasciotomy	FARB/YOT/M*I	feel	FAOEL
fascitis	FA/SAOITS	feeling	FAOEL/-G
	FAS/SAOITS	feet	FAOET
fast	FA*S	Fehling	FAI/LING
fastidious	FAS/TID/YOUS		FE/LING
fastidium	FAS/TID/YUM		(*not* FAIL/-G or FEL/-G; see failing
fastigatum	FA*S/GAI/TUM		and felling)
	FA*S/GAIT/UM	fel	F*EL
fastigial	FAS/TI/JAL		(not FEL; see fell)
	FAS/TIJ/YAL	Feldberg	FELD/BERG
fastigium	FAS/TIJ/JUM	Feldene	FEL/DAOEN
	FAS/TIJ/YUM	Feldman	FELD/MAN
	FAS/TIJ/UM	Felicola	FEL/KOE/LA
Fastin Capsules	FAS/TIN/KAP/SAOUL/-S	Felidae	FAOEL/DAE
fasting	FA*S/-G	feline	FAOE/LAOIN
fastness	FA*S/*NS	felineum	FAOE/LAOIN/YUM
fat	FAT		FE/LAOIN/YUM
fatal	FAI/TAL	Felix	FAI/LIX
fatality	FA/TAL/TI		FAOE/LIX
	FAI/TAL/TI	Fell	K-P/FEL
fate	FAIT		(*not* FEL or F*EL; see fell and fel)
fatigability	FAT/GABLT	fellatio	FLAI/SHOE
fatigable	FAT/GABL		FE/LAI/SHOE
fatigue	FA/TAOEG		FEL/LAI/SHOE
fat-pad	FAT/H-F/PAD	fellation	FLAIGS
fatty	FAT/TI		FE/LAIGS
fauces	FAU/SAOEZ		FEL/LAIGS
Fauchard	FOE/SHAR	fellatorism	FEL/TOR/IFM
faucial	FAURBL	fellatrix	FEL/TRIX
faucitis	FAU/SAOITS	felleae	FEL/YAE
faucium	FAUS/YUM	felon	FEL/LON
fauna	FAU/NA	feltwork	FELT/WORK
faveolar	FAI/VAOE/LAR	Felty	FEL/TI
faveolate	FAI/VAOE/LAIT	felypressin	FEL/PRES/SIN
faveoli	FAI/VAOE/LAOI	female	FAOE/MAEL
faveolus	FAI/VAOE/LUS	Femcet	FEM/SET
favid	FAIVD	feminarum	FEM/NAIR/UM
	FAI/VID		FEM/NAR/UM
favism	FAIV/IFM	femininae	FEM/NAOI/NAE
	FAI/VIFM	feminine	FEM/NIN
Favre	FAV/RAI	femininity	FEM/NIN/TI
	FAVR	femininus	FEM/NAOI/NUS
favus	FAI/VUS	feminism	FEM/NIFM
Fazio	FAZ/YOE	feminization	FEM/NI/ZAIGS
fear	FAOER	feminonucleus	FEM/NO/NAOUK/LUS
feature	FAOE/KHUR	femme	FAM
febricant	FEB/RI/KANT		FEM
febricide	FEB/RI/SAO*ID	femor(o)-	FEM/R(O)
febricity	FE/BRIS/TI	femora	FEM/RA
	FAOE/BRIS/TI	femoral	FEM/RAL
febricula	FE/BRIK/LA	femorale	FEM/RAI/LAOE
febrifacient	FEB/RI/FAIRBT	femoralis	FEM/RAI/LIS
febrific	FE/BRIFK	femoris	FEM/RIS
febrifuga	FE/BRIF/GA	femorocele	FEM/RO/SAO*EL
febrifugal	FE/BRIF/GAL	femoroiliac	FEM/RO/IL/YAK
febrifuge	FEB/RI/FAOUJ	femoropopliteal	FEM/RO/POP/LIT/YAL
febrile	FEB/RIL	femorotibial	FEM/RO/TIB/YAL
	FEB/RAOIL	Femstat	FEM/STAT

femur	FAOE/MUR	ferri-albuminic	FER/RI/AL/BAOU/MIN/IK
fenalamide	FEN/AL/MAOID	Ferribacterium	FER/RI/BAK/TAOERM
	FE/NAL/MAOID	ferric	FER/IK
fenbendazole	FEN/BEND/ZOEL	ferricyanide	FER/RI/SAOI/NAOID
fenbufen	FEN/BAOUFN	ferricytochrome	FER/RI/SAOIT/KROEM
fencamine	FEN/KA/MAOEN	Ferrier	FER/YER
fenclofenac	FEN/KLOEF/NAK		FER/YAI
fenclonine	FEN/KLO/NAOEN	feriheme	FER/RI/HAOEM
	FEN/KLOE/NAOEN	ferrihemochrome	FER/RI/HAOEM/KROEM
fenclorac	FEN/KLOR/AK	ferrihemoglobin	FER/RI/HAOEM/GLOE/BIN
fendosal	FEND/SAL	ferriporphyrin	FER/RI/POR/FRIN
Fenesin	FEN/SIN	ferriprotoporphyrin	FER/RI/PROET/POR/FRIN
fenestra	FE/NES/TRA	ferritin	FER/TIN
	FEN/ES/TRA		FER/RI/TIN
fenestrae	FE/NES/TRAE		FER/RAOI/TIN
	FEN/ES/TRAE	ferro-	FER
fenestrate	FEN/STRAIT		FER/RO
	FEN/ES/TRAIT	Ferrobacillus	FER/BA/SIL/LUS
fenestrated	FEN/STRAIT/-D	ferrochelatase	FER/KAOEL/TAIS
	FEN/ES/TRAIT/-D	ferrocholinate	FER/KOEL/NAIT
fenestration	FEN/STRAIGS	ferrocyanide	FER/SAOI/NAOID
	FEN/ES/TRAIGS	ferrocyanogen	FER/SAOI/AN/JEN
fenestrel	FEN/ES/TREL	ferrocytochrome	FER/SAOIT/KROEM
	FE/NES/TREL	ferroflocculation	FER/RO/FLOK/LAIGS
fenethylline	FEN/*ET/LAOEN	ferroheme	FER/HAOEM
	FEN/*ET/LIN	ferrohemochrome	FER/RO/HAOEM/KROEM
fenfluramine	FEN/FLAOUR/MAOEN	ferrokinetics	FER/KI/NET/IK/-S
fenisorex	FEN/AOIS/REX	ferroporphyrin	FER/POR/FRIN
fenmetozole	FEN/MET/ZOEL	ferroprotein	FER/PRO/TAOEN
fennel	FENL	ferroprotoporphyrin	FER//PROET/POR/FRIN
fenobam	FEN/BAM	Ferro-Sequels	FER/SE/KWEL/-S
fenoprofen	FEN/PRO/FEN	ferrosilicon	FER/RO/SIL/KON
fenoterol	FEN/TER/OEL	ferrosoferric	FER/ROES/FER/IK
	FEN/TER/OL		FER/ROE/SO/FER/IK
fenpipalone	FEN/PIP/LOEN	ferrotherapy	FER/THER/PI
fenpipramide	FEN/PIP/RA/MAOID	ferrous	FER/OUS
fenspiride	FEN/SPIR/AOID	ferrugination	FE/RAOUJ/NAIGS
fentanyl	FENT/NIL	ferruginea	FER/RAOU/JIN/YA
fenticlor	FENT/KLOR		FER/JIN/YA
fenugreek	FEN/YAOU/GRAOEK	ferruginous	FER/RAOUJ/NOUS
	FEN/YU/GRAOEK	ferrule	FER/YAOUL
Fenwick	FEN/WIK	ferrum	FER/UM
Feosol	FAOE/SOL		FER/RUM
Feostat	FAOE/STAT	Ferry	K-P/FER/RI
feral	FAOERL	fertile	FER/TIL
	FERL		FER/TAOIL
Ferancee	FER/AN/SAOE	fertility	FER/TIL/TI
Ferancee-HP	FER/AN/SAOE/H-RBGS/P*RBGS	fertilization	FERT/LI/ZAIGS
Fereol	FER/YOEL		FER/TIL/ZAIGS
Fergon	FER/GON		FERT/ZAIGS
Fergusson	FERG/SON	fertilizin	FER/TIL/ZIN
	FER/GUS/SON		FERT/LAOI/ZIN
ferment	FERMT	fervens	FER/VENZ
	FER/-MT		FEFRB/ENZ
fermentable	FERMT/-BL	fervescence	FER/VES/ENS
	FER/-MT/-BL	fescue	FES/KAOU
fermental	FERMT/TAL	feseri	FAOES/RAOI
	FER/MEN/TAL	Festal	FES/TAL
fermentation	FERMT/TAIGS	fester	F*ES/ER
	FER/MEN/TAIGS	festinans	F*ES/NANZ
fermentative	FERMT/TIV	festinant	F*ES/NANT
	FER/-MT/TIV	festination	F*ES/NAIGS
fermentemia	FERMT/TAOEM/YA	festoon	FES/TAON
	FER/MEN/TAOEM/YA	festooning	FES/TAON/-G
fermentogen	FERMT/JEN	fet(o)-	FAOET
	FER/MENT/JEN		FAOE/T(O)
fermentoid	FERMT/OID	fetal	FAOE/TAL
	FER/MEN/TOID	fetalis	FAOE/TAI/LIS
fermentum	FERMT/UM	fetalism	FAOET/LIFM
	FER/MEN/TUM		FAOE/TAL/IFM
fermium	FERM/YUM	fetalization	FAOE/TAL/ZAIGS
Fernandez	FER/NAN/DEZ		FAOET/LI/ZAIGS
ferning	FERN/-G	fetation	FAOE/TAIGS
Fero-Folic	FER/FOEL/IK	feticide	FAOET/SAO*ID
	FER/RO/FOEL/IK	fetid	FET/ID
Fero-Grad	FER/GRAD		FAOE/TID
	FER/RO/GRAD	fetish	FET/IRB
Fero-Grad-500	FER/GRAD/5/HUN		FAOE/TIRB
	FER/RO/GRAD/5/HUN	fetishism	FET/SHIFM
Fero-Gradumet	FER/GRAD/MET		FAOE/TIRB/IFM
	FER/RO/GRAD/MET	fetishist	FET/SH*IS
Ferralet	FER/LET		FAOET/SH*IS
	FER/RA/LET	fetlock	FET/LOK
ferrated	FER/RAIT/-D	fetochorionic	FAOET/KOER/YON/IK
ferratin	FER/TIN	fetoglobulin	FAOET/GLOB/LIN
ferredoxin	FER/DOK/SIN	fetography	FAOE/TOG/FI
Ferrein	FER/RIN	fetology	FAOE/TOLG
ferri-	FER/RI	fetometry	FAOE/TOM/TRI
	(not FER; see ferro-)	fetopathy	FAOE/TOP/TH*I

fetoplacental	FAOET/PLA/SEN/TAL	fibrinopenia	FAOI/BRIN/PAOEN/YA
fetoprotein	FAOET/PRO/TAOEN	fibrinopeptide	FAOI/BRIN/PEP/TAOID
fetor	FAOE/TOR	fibrinoplastic	FAOI/BRIN/PLA*S/IK
fetoscope	FAOET/SKOEP	fibrinoplastin	FAOI/BRIN/PLAS/TIN
fetoscopic	FAOET/SKOP/IK	fibrinoplatelet	FAOI/BRIN/PLAET/LET
fetoscopy	FAOE/TOS/KPI		FAOI/BRIN/PLAIT/LET
fetotoxicity	FAOET/TOK/SIS/TI	fibrinopurulent	FAOI/BRIN/PAOUR/LENT
fetoxylate	FE/TOX/LAIT	fibrinorrhea	FAOI/BRIN/RAOE/YA
Fetrin	FAOE/TRIN	fibrinosa	FAOI/BRI/NOE/SA
fetuin	FAOE/TAOU/WIN	fibrinoscopy	FAOI/BRI/NOS/KPI
fetus	FAOE/TUS		FAOI/BRIN/OS/KPI
Feulgen	FOIL/GEN	fibrinose	FAOI/BRI/NOES
FEV	F-RBGS/*ERBGS/V*RBGS	fibrinous	FAOI/BRIN/OUS
fever	FAOEVR		FAOI/BRI/NOUS
feverish	FAOEVR/RIRB	fibrinuria	FAOI/BRI/NAOUR/YA
	FAOEVR/IRB		FAOI/BRIN/YAOUR/YA
fiber	FAOI/BER	fibroadenia	FAOI/BRO/AI/DAOEN/YA
	FAOIB/ER	fibroadenoma	FAOI/BRO/AD/NOE/MA
Fiberall	FAOIB/RAUL	fibroadenosis	FAOI/BRO/AD/NOE/SIS
	(not FAOI/BER/AUL or FAOIB/ER/	fibroadipose	FAOI/BRO/AD/POES
	AUL)	fibroangioma	FAOI/BRO/AN/JOE/MA
fibercolonoscope	FAOI/BER/KO/LON/SKOEP	fibroareolar	FAOI/BRO/AI/RAOE/LAR
FiberCon	FAOI/BER/KON	fibroatrophy	FAOI/BRO/AT/RO/FI
fibergastroscope	FAOI/BER/GAS/TRO/SKOEP	fibroblast	FAOI/BRO/BLA*S
fiber-illuminated	FAOI/BER/IL/LAOUM/NAIT/-D	fibroblastic	FAOI/BRO/BLA*S/IK
Fibermed	FAOI/BER/MED	fibroblastoma	FAOI/BRO/BLAS/TOE/MA
fiberoptic	FAOI/BER/OPT/IK	fibrobronchitis	FAOI/BRO/BRON/KAOITS
fiberoptics	FAOI/BER/OPT/IK/-S	fibrocalcific	FAOI/BRO/KAL/SIFK
fiberscope	FAOI/BER/SKOEP	fibrocarcinoma	FAOI/BRO/KARS/NOE/MA
fibr(o)-	FAOI/BR(O)	fibrocartilage	FAOI/BRO/KART/LAJ
	FAOIB/R(O)	fibrocartilagines	FAOI/BRO/KART/LAJ/NAOEZ
fibra	FAOI/BRA	fibrocartilagineus	FAOI/BRO/KART/LA/JIN/YUS
fibrae	FAOI/BRAE	fibrocartilaginous	FAOI/BRO/KART/LAJ/NOUS
fibremia	FAOI/BRAOEM/YA	fibrocartilago	FAOI/BRO/KART/LAI/GOE
fibril	FAOI/BRIL		FAOI/BRO/KART/LA/GOE
fibrilla	FAOI/BRIL/LA	fibrocaseous	FAOI/BRO/KAIS/YOUS
fibrilla-	FIB/RI/LA-	fibrocellular	FAOI/BRO/SEL/YAOU/LAR
	FIB/RIL/LA-	fibrochondritis	FAOI/BRO/KON/DRAOITS
	FAOI/BRI/LA-	fibrochondroma	FAOI/BRO/KON/DROE/MA
	FAOI/BRIL/LA-	fibrocollagenous	FAOI/BRO/KLAJ/NOUS
fibrillae	FAOI/BRIL/LAE	fibrocongestive	FAOI/BRO/KON/J*ES/IV
fibrillar	FAOI/BRI/LAR	fibrocyst	FAOI/BRO/S*IS
	FAOI/BRIL/LAR	fibrocystic	FAOI/BRO/S*IS/IK
fibrillare	FAOI/BRI/LAI/RAOE	fibrocystoma	FAOI/BRO/SIS/TOE/MA
	FIB/RI/LAI/RAOE	fibrocyte	FAOI/BRO/SAO*IT
fibrillary	FIB/RI/LAIR	fibrocytogenesis	FAOI/BRO/SAOIT/JEN/SIS
	FAOI/BRI/LAIR	fibrodysplasia	FAOI/BRO/DIS/PLAIZ/YA
fibrilate	FIB/RI/LAIT	fibroelastic	FAOI/BRO/E/LA*S/IK
	FAOI/BRI/LAIT	fibroelastosis	FAOI/BRO/E/LAS/TOE/SIS
fibrillated	FIB/RI/LAIT/-D	fibroenchondroma	FAOI/BRO/EN/KON/DROE/MA
	FAOI/BRI/LAIT/-D	fibroepithelioma	FAOI/BRO/EP/THAOEL/YOE/MA
fibrillation	FIB/RI/LAIGS	fibrofascitis	FAOI/BRO/FA/SAOITS
	FAOI/BRI/LAIGS	fibrofatty	FAOI/BRO/FAT/TI
fibrillo-	FAOI/BRIL	fibrofibrous	FAOI/BRO/FAOI/BROUS
fibrilloblast	FAOI/BRIL/BLA*S	fibrofolliculoma	FAOI/BRO/FLIK/LOE/MA
fibrillogenesis	FAOI/BRIL/JEN/SIS	fibrogenesis	FAOI/BRO/JEN/SIS
fibrillolysis	FAOI/BRIL/LOL/SIS	fibrogenic	FAOI/BRO/JEN/IK
	FAOI/BRIL/OL/SIS	fibroglia	FAOI/BROG/LA
fibrillolytic	FAOI/BRIL/LIT/IK	fibroglioma	FAOI/BRO/GLAOI/YOE/MA
fibrin	FAOI/BRIN	fibrogliosis	FAOI/BRO/GLAOI/YOE/SIS
fibrinase	FAOI/BRI/NAIS	fibrohemorrhagic	FAOI/BRO/HEM/RAJ/IK
	FAOI/BRI/NAIS	fibrohistiocytic	FAOI/BRO/H*IS/YO/SIT/IK
fibrino-	FAOI/BRIN	fibroid	FAOI/BROID
	FAOI/BRI/NO	fibroidectomy	FAOI/BROI/DEKT/M*I
fibrinocellular	FAOI/BRIN/SEL/YAOU/LAR	fibroin	FAOI/BROIN
fibrinogen	FAOI/BRIN/JEN		FAOI/BROE/WIN
fibrinogenase	FAOI/BRIN/JEN/AIS	fibrokeratoma	FAOI/BRO/KER/TOE/MA
	FAOI/BRIN/OJ/NAIS	fibroleiomyoma	FAOI/BRO/LAOI/MAOI/YOE/MA
fibrinogenemia	FAOI/BRIN/JE/NAOEM/YA	fibrolipoma	FAOI/BRO/LI/POE/MA
	FAOI/BRIN/JEN/AOEM/YA	fibrolipomatous	FAOI/BRO/LI/POEM/TOUS
fibrinogenesis	FAOI/BRIN/JEN/SIS	fibroma	FAOI/BROE/MA
fibrinogenic	FAOI/BRIN/JEN/IK	fibromatogenic	FAOI/BROEM/TO/JEN/IK
fibrinogenolysis	FAOI/BRIN/JEN/OL/SIS	fibromatoid	FAOI/BROEM/TOID
	FAOI/BRIN/JE/NOL/SIS	fibromatosa	FAOI/BROEM/TOE/SA
fibrinogenolytic	FAOI/BRIN/JEN/LIT/IK	fibromatosis	FAOI/BROEM/TOE/SIS
fibrinogenopenia	FAOI/BRIN/JEN/PAOEN/YA	fibromatous	FAOI/BROEM/TOUS
fibrinogenopenic	FAOI/BRIN/JEN/PAOEN/IK	fibromectomy	FAOI/BRO/MEKT/M*I
fibrinogenous	FAOI/BRI/NOJ/NOUS	fibromembranous	FAOI/BRO/MEM/BRA/NOUS
	FAOI/BRIN/OJ/NOUS	fibromuscular	FAOI/BRO/MUS/KLAR
fibrinoid	FAOI/BRI/NOID	fibromyectomy	FAOI/BRO/MAOI/EKT/M*I
	FAOI/BRIN/OID	fibromyitis	FAOI/BRO/MAOI/AOITS
fibrinokinase	FAOI/BRIN/KAOI/NAIS		FAOI/BRO/MAOI/YAOITS
fibrinolysin	FAOI/BRI/NOL/SIN	fibromyoma	FAOI/BRO/MAOI/YOE/MA
	FAOI/BRIN/OL/SIN	fibromyomectomy	FAOI/BRO/MAOI/MEKT/M*I
	FAOI/BRIN/LAOI/SIN	fibromyositis	FAOI/BRO/MAOI/SAOITS
fibrinolysis	FAOI/BRI/NOL/SIS	fibromyotomy	FAOI/BRO/MAOI/OT/M*I
	FAOI/BRIN/OL/SIS		FAOI/BRO/MAOI/YOT/M*I
fibrinolysokinase	FAOI/BRIN/LAOIS/KAOI/NAIS	fibromyxoma	FAOI/BRO/MIK/SOE/MA
fibrinolytic	FAOI/BRIN/LIT/IK	fibromyxosarcoma	FAOI/BRO/MIX/SAR/KOE/MA

fibronectin	FAOI/BRO/NEK/TIN		
fibroneuroma	FAOI/BRO/NAOU/ROE/MA	filariform	FI/LAIR/FORM
fibronuclear	FAOI/BRO/NAOUK/LAR		FLAIR/FORM
fibro-osteoma	FAOI/BRO/O*S/YOE/MA	Filarioidea	FI/LAIR/YOID/YA
fibropapilloma	FAOI/BRO/PAP/LOE/MA		FLAIR/YOID/YA
fibropituicyte	FAOI/BRO/PI/TAOU/SAO*IT	Filatov	FI/LAT/OV
fibroplasia	FAOI/BRO/PLAIZ/YA	file	FAOIL
fibroplastic	FAOI/BRO/PLA*S/IK	filial	FIL/YAL
fibroplate	FAOI/BRO/PLAET	Filibon	FIL/BON
	FAOI/BRO/PLAIT	Filibon Forte	FIL/BON/FOR/TAI
fibropolypus	FAOI/BRO/POL/PUS	filicin	FIL/SIN
fibropsammoma	FAOI/BRO/SAM/MOE/MA	filiform	FIL/FORM
fibropurulent	FAOI/BRO/PAOUR/LENT	filiforme	FIL/FOR/MAOE
fibroreticulate	FAOI/BRO/RE/TIK/LAIT	filioparental	FIL/YO/PREN/TAL
fibrosa	FAOI/BROE/SA		FIL/YO/PA/REN/TAL
fibrosarcoma	FAOI/BRO/SAR/KOE/MA	filipin	FIL/PIN
fibrosclerosis	FAOI/BRO/SKLE/ROE/SIS	filipuncture	FIL/PUNG/KHUR
fibroscopy	FAOI/BROS/KPI	filix	FAOI/LIX
fibrose	FAOI/BROES	fillet	FIL/ET
fibroserous	FAOI/BRO/SAOER/OUS	filling	FIL/-G
fibrosi	FAOI/BROE/SAOI	film	FIL/-M
fibrosing	FAOI/BROES/-G	film badge	FIL/-M/BAJ
fibrosis	FAOI/BROE/SIS	filopod	FAOIL/POD
fibrositis	FAOI/BRO/SAOITS		FIL/POD
fibrothorax	FAOI/BRO/THOR/AX	filopodia	FAOIL/POED/YA
fibrosum	FAOI/BROES/UM	filopodium	FAOIL/POED/YUM
	FAOI/BROE/SUM	filopressure	FAOIL/PRERB/SHUR
fibrosus	FAOI/BROE/SUS	filovaricosis	FAOIL/VAIR/KOE/SIS
fibrotic	FAOI/BROT/IK	filter	FILT/ER
fibrotuberculosis	FAOI/BRO/TAOU/BERK/LOE/SIS		FIL/TER
fibrous	FAOI/BROUS	filterable	FILT/RABL
fibrovascular	FAOI/BRO/VAS/KLAR		FIL/TER/-BL
fibroxanthoma	FAOI/BRO/ZAN/THOE/MA		FIL/TERBL
fibul(o)-	FIB/L(O)	filtrate	FIL/TRAIT
	FIB/YAOU/L(O)	filtration	FIL/TRAIGS
	FIB/YU/L(O)	filtrum	FIL/TRUM
fibula	FIB/LA	filtrum ventriculi	FIL/TRUM/VEN/TRIK/LAOI
fibulae	FIB/LAE	filum	FAOI/LUM
fibular	FIB/LAR		FAOIL/UM
fibulare	FIB/LAI/RAOE	fimbri(o)-	FIM/BR-
fibulares	FIB/LAI/RAOEZ		FIM/BRAOE/Y-
fibularis	FIB/LAI/RIS	fimbria	FIM/BRA
fibulocalcaneal	FIB/LO/KAL/KAIN/YAL	fimbriae	FIM/BRAE
ficin	FAOI/SIN	fimbriate	FIM/BRAIT
Fick	F*IK	fimbriated	FIM/BRAIT/-D
	(*not* FIK; see "if I can")	fimbriation	FIM/BRAIGS
Ficker	FIK/ER	fimbriatum	FIM/BRAI/TUM
ficosis	FAOI/KOE/SIS	fimbriectomy	FIM/BREKT/M*I
fidicinales	FAOI/DIS/NAI/LAOEZ	fimbriocele	FIM/BRO/SAO*EL
Fiedler	FAOED/LER	fimbrioplasty	FIM/BRO/PLAS/TI
field	FAOELD	finder	FAOIND/ER
Field	K-P/FAOELD	finding	FAOIND/-G
Fielding	K-P/FAOELD/-G	fine	FAOIN
fig	FIG	fineness	FAOIN/*NS
figurata	FIG/RAI/TA	finger	FING/ER
figuration	FIG/RAIGS		FIN/GER
figuratum	FIG/RAI/TUM	fingeragnosia	FING/ER/AG/NOEZ/YA
	FIG/RAIT/UM	fingernail	FING/ER/NAIL
figuratus	FIG/RAI/TUS	fingerprint	FING/ER/PRINT
figure	FIG/YUR	fingerprinting	FING/ER/PRINT/-G
fila	FAOI/LA	finger-sucking	FING/ER/H-F/SUK/-G
filaceous	FAOI/LAIRBS	Finney	FIN/NAOE
	FI/LAIRBS	Finnish	FIN/NIRB
filaggrin	FIL/AG/RIN		(*not* FIN/IRB; see finish)
	FIL/AG/GRIN	Finsen	FIN/SEN
filamen	FIL/LA/MEN		FINS/-N
	F*IL/MEN	Fiogesic	FAOE/JAOEZ/IK
	(*not* FIL/MEN)	Fioricet	FAOE/YOR/SET
filament	FIL/-MT		FI/YOR/SET
filamenta	FIL/MEN/TA	Fiorinal	FAOE/YOR/NAL
filamentous	FIL/MEN/TOUS		FI/YOR/NAL
filamentum	FIL/MEN/TUM	fire	FAOIR
filar	FAOI/LAR	firedamp	FAOIR/DAFRP
filaria	FI/LAIR/YA	first aid	F*IRS/AID
	FLAIR/YA	Fischer	F*IRB/ER
	FAOI/LAIR/YA	Fishberg	FIRB/BERG
filariae	FI/LAIR/YAE	Fisher	K-P/FIRB/ER
	FLAIR/YAE	fisherii	FIRB/RAOI
	FAOI/LAIR/YAE		FIRB/ER/YAOI
filarial	FI/LAIRL	Fishman	FIRB/MAN
	FLAIRL	fissile	FIS/SIL
	FAOI/LAIRL	fission	FIGS
filariasis	FIL/RAOI/SIS	fissionable	FIGS/-BL
filaricidal	FI/LAIR/SAOI/DAL	fissiparity	FIS/PAIR/TI
	FLAIR/SAOI/DAL	fissiparous	FIS/SIP/ROUS
filaricide	FI/LAIR/SAO*ID		FIS/SIP/ROUS
	FLAIR/SAO*ID		FAOI/SIP/ROUS
filariensis	FI/LAIR/YEN/SIS	Fissipedia	FIS/PAOED/YA
	FLAIR/YEN/SIS	fissula	FIRB/LA

	FIS/LA	flatulence	FLAFP/LENS
fissura	FI/SAOU/RA	flatulent	FLAFP/LENT
	FIS/SAOU/RA	Flatulex	FLAFP/LEX
	FIRB/SHUR/RA	flatus	FLAI/TUS
fissurae	FI/SAOU/RAE	flatworm	FLAT/WORM
	FIS/SAOU/RAE	flaunt	FLAUNT
	FIRB/SHUR/RAE	flava	FLAI/VA
fissural	FIRB/RAL	flavanone	FLAIV/NOEN
fissurata	FIRB/RAI/TA	flavedo	FLA/VAOE/DOE
fissuration	FIRB/RAIGS	flavescens	FLA/VES/ENZ
fissure	FIRB/SHUR		FLAI/VES/ENZ
fist	F*IS	flavescent	FLA/VES/ENT
fistul(o)-	F*IS/L(O)		FLAI/VES/ENT
	FIS/KHU/L(O)	flavianic	FLAIV/YAN/IK
	F*IS/YAOU/L(O)	flavin	FLAIVN
	F*IS/YU/L(O)		FLAI/VIN
	FIS/TAOU/L(O)	flavine	FLAI/VAOEN
	FIS/KHAOU/L(O)	Flavivirus	FLAIV/VAOI/RUS
fistula	F*IS/LA	flavo-	FLAIV
fistulae	F*IS/LAE		FLAI/VO
fistular	F*IS/LAR	Flavobacterium	FLAIV/BAK/TAOERM
fistulation	F*IS/LAIGS	flavoenzyme	FLAIV/EN/ZAOIM
fistulatome	F*IS/LA/TOEM	flavokinase	FLAIV/KAOI/NAIS
fistulectomy	F*IS/LEKT/M*I	flavone	FLAI/VOEN
fistulization	F*IS/LI/ZAIGS	flavonoid	FLAIV/NOID
fistuloenterostomy	F*IS/LO/SPWRO*S/M*I	flavonol	FLAIV/NOL
fistulotomy	F*IS/LOT/M*I	flavoprotein	FLAIV/PRO/TAOEN
fistulous	F*IS/LOUS	flavor	FLAIVR
fit	FIT		FLAI/VOR
fitness	FIT/*NS	flavoxate	FLAI/VOK/SAIT
Fitz	FITS	flavum	FLAI/VUM
fix	FIX		FLAIV/UM
fixate	FIK/SAIT	flavus	FLAI/VUS
	FIX/AIT	flaxseed	FLAX/SAOED
fixation	FIK/SAIGS	flazalone	FLAIZ/LOEN
	FIX/AIGS	flea	FLAE
fixative	FIX/TIV		(not FLAOE; see flee)
fixator	FIK/SAI/TOR	flecainide	FLE/KAI/NAOID
fixe	FIK/SAI		FLE/KAIN/AOID
fixing	FIX/-G	Flechsig	FLEK/SIG
flabby	FLAB/BI	flechsigi	FLEX/GAOI
flabellum	FLA/BEL/UM		FLEK/SI/GAOI
	FLA/BEL/LUM	fleck	FLEK
flaccid	FLAK/SID	fleece	FLAOES
	FLAS/ID	Fleet	K-P/FLAOET
	FLAS/SID		FLAOET (in word groups)
flaccidity	FLA/SID/TI	Fleet Babylax	FLAOET/BAIB/LAX
	FLAK/SID/TI		FLAOET/BAI/BI/LAX
Flack	FLA*K	Fleet Bisacodyl Enema	FLAOET/BIS/KO/DIL/EN/MA
flagella	FLA/JEL/LA	Fleet Children's Enema	FLAOET/KHIRN/AOES/EN/MA
flagellar	FLA/JEL/LAR	Fleet Enema	FLAOET/EN/MA
Flagellata	FLAJ/LAI/TA	Fleet Mineral Oil Enema	FLAOET/MIN/RAL/OIL/EN/MA
flagellate	FLAJ/LAIT	Fleet Phospho-Soda	FLAOET/FOS/FO/SOE/DA
flagellated	FLAJ/LAIT/-D	Fleet Prep Kits	FLAOET/PREP/KIT/-S
flagellation	FLAJ/LAIGS	Fleet Relief	FLAOET/RE/LAOEF
flagelliform	FLA/JEL/FORM	Fleischer	FLAOIRB/ER
	FLAJ/LI/FORM	Fleischmann	FLAOIRB/MAN
flagellin	FLAJ/LIN	Fleitmann	FLAOIT/MAN
	FLA/JEL/LIN	Flemming	FLEM/-G
flagellosis	FLAJ/LOE/SIS	flesh	FLERB
flagellospore	FLA/JEL/SPOER	fleshfly	FLERB/FLAOI
flagellula	FLA/JEL/YAOU/LA	fletazepam	FLE/TAZ/PAM
	FLA/JEL/YU/LA	Fletcher	FLEFP/ER
	(not FLA/JEL/LA; see flagella)	fletcherism	FLEFP/RIFM
flagellum	FLA/JEL/UM	flex	FLEX
	FLA/JEL/LUM	flexa	FLEK/SA
Flagyl	FLAG/IL	Flexeril	FLEX/RIL
	FLA/GIL	flexibilitas	FLEX/BIL/TAS
flail	FLAIL	flexibilitas cerea	FLEX/BIL/TAS/SAOER/YA
flame	FLAIM	flexibility	FLEX/-BLT
flammable	FLAM/-BL	flexible	FLEX/-BL
flange	FLAN/-J	flexile	FLEK/SAOIL
flank	FLA*NG		FLEX/AOIL
	FLAN/-K	fleximeter	FLEK/SIM/TER
flap	FLAP	flexion	FL*EBGS
flare	FLAER	Flexner	FLEX/NER
	(not FLAIR; see flair)	flexor	FLEK/SOR
flash	FLARB	flexoris	FLEK/SOR/RIS
flashback	FLARB/BA*K	flexuose	FLEX/YOES
flask	FLAS/-K	flexura	FLEK/SHUR/RA
flasking	FLAS/-K/-G	flexurae	FLEK/SHUR/RAE
	FLAS/K-G	flexural	FLEX/RAL
flat	FLAT		FLEK/SHURL
Flatau	FLA/TOU		FLEX/YURL
flatfoot	FLAT/FAOT	flexure	FLEK/SHUR
flatness	FLAT/*NS		FLEX/YUR
flatul-	FLAFP/L-	flicker	FLIK/ER
	FLAT/YAOU/L-	flicks	FLIK/-S
	FLAT/YU/L-	flight into disease	FLAOIGT/SPWAO/DI/SAOEZ

flight into health	FLAOIGT/SPWAO/D-Z	fluctuating	FLUK/YAIT/-G
flight of ideas	FLAOIGT/SPWAO/H*ELT	fluctuation	FLUK/YAIGS
flint	FLAOIGT/OF/Y-DZ	flucytosine	FLAOU/SAOIT/SAOEN
Flint	FLINT	fludalanine	FLAOU/DAL/NAOEN
Flintstones	K-P/FLINT	fludazonium	FLAOUD/ZOEN/YUM
flip	FLINT/STOEN/-S	fludorex	FLAOUD/REX
floater	FLIP	fludrocortisone	FLAOU/DRO/KORT/SOEN
floating	FLOET/ER		FLAOU/DROE/KORT/SOEN
floc	FLOET/-G	fluent	FLAOUNT
	FLO*K	flufenamic	FLAOU/FE/NAM/IK
	(*not* FLOK; see flock)		FLAOU/FEN/AM/IK
floccilegium	FLOX/LAOE/JUM	flufenisal	FLAOU/FEN/SAL
	FLOX/LAOEJ/YUM	fluid	FLAOUD
floccillation	FLOX/LAIGS	fluidextract	FLAOUD/EX/TRAKT
	FLOK/SI/LAIGS	fluidextractum	FLAOUD/EX/TRAK/TUM
floccose	FLOK/OES	fluidglycerate	FLAOUD/GLIS/RAIT
	FLOK/KOES	fluidism	FLAOU/DIFM
floccosum	FLOK/KOES/UM		FLAOUD/IFM
	FLOK/KOE/SUM	fluidity	FLAOUD/TI
floccul-	FLOK/L-˙		FLAOU/ID/TI
	FLOK/YAOU/L-	fluidounce	FLAOUD/O*UNS
	FLOK/YU/L-		(*not* FLAOUD/OUNS; see fluid
	FLOK/KAOU/L-		ounce)
flocculable	FLOK/LABL	fluidrachm	FLAOU/DRA*M
floccular	FLOK/LAR	fluidram	FLAOU/DRAM
flocculate	FLOK/LAIT	Flu-Imune	FLU/IM/MAOUN
flocculation	FLOK/LAIGS		FLAOU/IM/MAOUN
floccule	FLOK/YAOUL	fluke	FLAOUK
flocculence	FLOK/LENS	flumen	FLAOUM/-N
flocculent	FLOK/LENT		FLAOU/MEN
flocculi	FLOK/LAOI	flumequine	FLAOUM/KWIN
flocculonodular	FLOK/LO/NOD/LAR	flumethasone	FLAOU/M*ET/SOEN
flocculoreaction	FLOK/LO/RE/A*BGS	flumethiazide	FLAOU/ME/THAOI/ZAOID
flocculus	FLOK/LUS		FLAOUM/THAOI/ZAOID
floctafenine	FLOKT/FEN/AOEN	flumina	FLAOUM/NA
flood	FLAOD	flumizole	FLAOUM/ZOEL
Flood	K-P/FLAOD	flumoxonide	FLAOU/MOX/NAOID
flooding	FLAOD/-G	flunarizine	FLAOU/NAR/ZAOEN
floor	FLAOR	flunidazole	FLAOU/NID/ZOEL
flor-	FLOR	flunisolide	FLAOU/NIS/LAOID
	FLOER		FLAOU/NIS/LID
	FLOE/R-	flunitrazepam	FLAOU/NAOI/TRAZ/PAM
flora	FLOR/RA	flunixin	FLAOU/NIK/SIN
florantyrone	FLOR/ANT/ROEN	fluocinolone	FLAOU/SIN/LOEN
Florence	FLORNS	fluocinonide	FLAOU/SIN/NAOID
	FLOR/ENS	fluocortin	FLAOU/KOR/TIN
flores	FLOR/RAOEZ	fluocortolone	FLAOU/KORT/LOEN
Florey	FLOR/RAOE	Fluogen	FLAOU/JEN
florid	FLOR/ID	fluohydrisone	FLAOU/HAOI/DRI/SOEN
floriform	FLOR/FORM	fluohydrocortisone	FLAOU/HAOI/DRO/KORT/SOEN
florizine	FLOR/ZAOEN	Fluonid	FLAOU/NID
Florone	FLOR/ROEN	fluor	FLAO*UR
	FLOR/OEN	fluor(o)-	FLAOUR
Floropryl	FLOR/PRIL		FLAOU/R(O)
Florschutz	FLOR/SHITS		FLOR
	FLOR/SHUTS		FLOR/R(O)
Florvite	FLOR/VAOIT	fluorane	FLAOU/RAIN
floss	FLOSZ		FLAOUR/AIN
flotation	FLOE/TAIGS	fluorapatite	FLAOUR/AP/TAOIT
Flourens	FLAOU/RENS	fluorescein	FLAOU/RES/YIN
	FLAOUR/ENS		FLAOUR/ES/YIN
flow	FLOE	fluoresceinurea	FLAOU/RES/YIN/YAOU/RAOE/YA
flower	FLOU/ER	fluorescence	FLAOU/RES/ENS
Flower	K-P/FLOU/ER		FLAOUR/ES/ENS
flowmeter	FLOE/MAOET/ER	fluorescent	FLAOU/RES/ENT
flow tract	FLOE/TRAKT		FLAOUR/ES/ENT
floxacillin	FLOX/SLIN	fluorescin	FLAOU/RES/SIN
	FLOX/SIL/LIN		FLAOUR/ES/SIN
floxuridine	FLOK/SAOUR/DAOEN	fluoric	FLAOUR/IK
	FLOX/YAOUR/DAOEN	fluoridation	FLAOUR/DAIGS
flu	FLU	fluoride	FLAOUR/AOID
	(not FLAOU or FLAO*U; see flew		FLAOUR/RAOID
	and flue)	fluoridization	FLAOUR/DI/ZAIGS
fluanisone	FLAOU/AN/SOEN	fluoridize	FLAOUR/DAOIZ
fluazacort	FLAOU/AZ/KORT	fluorimeter	FLAOU/RIM/TER
flubendazole	FLAOU/BEND/ZOEL	Fluori-Methane	FLAOUR/M*ET/AIN
flucindole	FLAOU/SIN/DOEL	fluorimetry	FLAOU/RIM/TRI
flucloronide	FLAOU/KLOR/NAOID	fluorine	FLAOU/RAOEN
flucloxacillin	FLAOU/KLOX/SLIN		FLAOUR/AOEN
	FLAOU/KLOX/SIL/LIN	Fluoritab	FLAOUR/TAB
flucrylate	FLAOU/KRI/LAIT	fluoroacetate	FLAOUR/AS/TAIT
	FLAOUK/RI/LAIT	fluorochrome	FLAOUR/KROEM
fluctu-	FLUK/Y-	fluorochroming	FLAOUR/KROEM/-G
	FLUK/W-	fluorocortisol	FLAOUR/KORT/SOL
	FLUK/KH-	fluorocyte	FLAOUR/SAO*IT
	FLUKT/Y-	fluorodinitrobenzene	FLAOUR/DI/NAOI/TRO/BEN/
	FLUKT/W-		ZAOEN
fluctuans	FLUK/YANZ	fluorography	FLAOU/ROG/FI
fluctuate	FLUK/YAIT		FLAOUR/OG/FI

fluorohydrocortisone	FLAOUR/HAOI/DRO/KORT/SOEN	follicul(o)-	FOL/KLIS
fluorometer	FLAOU/ROM/TER		FLIK/L(O)
	FLAOUR/OM/TER		FLIK/YAOU/L(O)
fluorometholone	FLAOUR/M*ET/LOEN		FLIK/YU/L(O)
fluorometry	FLAOU/ROM/TRI		FOL/LIK/L(O)
	FLAOUR/OM/TRI		FOL/LIK/YAOU/L(O)
fluoronephelometer	FLAOUR/NEF/LOM/TER		FOL/LIK/YU/L(O)
fluorophenylalanine	FLAOUR/FENL/AL/NAOEN		FO/LIK/L(O)
fluorophosphate	FLAOUR/FOS/FAIT		FO/LIK/YAOU/L(O)
fluorophotometry	FLAOUR/FOE/TOM/TRI		FO/LIK/YU/L(O)
fluororoentgenography	FLAOUR/RENT/GEN/OG/FI	follicular	FLIK/LAR
fluoroscope	FLAOUR/SKOEP	follicularis	FLIK/LAI/RIS
fluoroscopic	FLAOUR/SKOP/IK	folliculi	FLIK/LAOI
fluoroscopical	FLAOUR/SKOP/KAL	folliculin	FLIK/LIN
fluoroscopy	FLAOU/ROS/KPI	folliculitis	FLIK/LAOITS
	FLAOUR/OS/KPI	folliculoma	FLIK/LOE/MA
fluorosilicate	FLAOUR/SIL/KAIT	folliculorum	FLIK/LOR/UM
fluorosis	FLAOU/ROE/SIS		FLIK/LOER/UM
fluorouracil	FLAOUR/YAOUR/SIL	folliculosis	FLIK/LOE/SIS
Fluothane	FLAOU/THAIN	folliculus	FLIK/LUS
fluotracen	FLAOU/TRAI/SEN	follitropin	FOL/TROE/PIN
	FLAOU/TRAIS/-N	Follmann	FOEL/MAN
fluoxetine	FLAOU/OX/TAOEN		FOL/MAN
fluoxymesterone	FLAOU/OX/M*ES/ROEN	followup	FOL/LOE/*UP
flupentixol	FLAOU/PEN/TIK/SOL	follow-up	FOL/LOE/H-F/UP
fluperamide	FLAOU/PER/MAOID	Foltz	FOELTS
fluperolone	FLAOU/PER/LOEN		FOLTS
fluphenazine	FLAOU/FEN/ZAOEN	fomentation	FOEMT/TAIGS
fluprednisolone	FLAOU/PRED/NIS/LOEN		FOE/MEN/TAIGS
fluprostenol	FLAOU/PRO*S/NOEL	fomes	FOE/MAOEZ
	FLAOU/PRO*S/NOL	fomite	FOE/MAOIT
fluquazone	FLAOU/KWA/ZOEN	fomites	FOEM/TAOEZ
	FLAOUK/WA/ZOEN	fonazine	FOEN/ZAOEN
flurandrenolide	FLAOUR/AN/DREN/LAOID	Fonsecaea	FONS/SAOE/YA
	FLAOUR/RAN/DREN/LAOID		FONS/SAE/YA
flurazepam	FLAOU/AZ/PAM	fontactoscope	FON/TAKT/SKOEP
	FLAOU/RAZ/PAM	Fontan	FON/TAN
flurbiprofen	FLAOUR/BIP/RO/FEN	Fontana	FON/TAN/NA
flurocitabine	FLAOUR/SAOIT/BAOEN	fontanel	FONT/NEL
Fluro-Ethyl	FLAOUR/*ET/IL		FON/TA/NEL
flurogestone	FLAOUR/JES/TOEN	fontanelle	FONT/N*EL
flurothyl	FLAOUR/THIL		FON/TA/N*EL
fluroxene	FLAOUR/OX/SAOEN	fonticuli	FON/TIK/LAOI
	FLAOUR/ROK/SAOEN	fonticulus	FON/TIK/LUS
flush	FLURB	food	FAOD
fluspiperone	FLAOU/SPIP/ROEN	foot	FAOT
fluspirilene	FLAOU/SPIR/LAOEN	footcandle	FAOT/KAND/-L
flutamide	FLAOUT/MAOID	footdrop	FAOT/DROP
flutter	FLUT/ER	foot lambert	FAOT/LAM/BERT
flutter-fibrillation	FLUT/ER/FIB/RI/LAIGS	footplate	FAOT/PLAET
flux	FLUX		FAOT/PLAIT
fluxion	FL*UBGS	foot-pound	FAOT/POUND
fly	FLAOI	foot-poundal	FAOT/POUN/DAL
foam	FOEM	for-	FOR
focal	FOE/KAL	forage	FOR/AJ
Fochier	FORB/YAI		(*not* FORJ; **see** forge)
foci	FOE/SAOI	foramen	FRAI/MEN
focil	FOE/SIL		FO/RAI/MEN
focile	FOES/LAOE		FOE/RAI/MEN
focimeter	FOE/SIM/TER	foramin-	FRAM/N-
focus	FOE/KUS		FO/RAM/N-
foe	FOE		FOE/RAM/N-
foeniculi	FE/NIK/LAOI	foramina	FRAM/NA
foetida	FAOET/DA	foraminal	FRAM/NAL
	FET/DA	Foraminifera	FRAM/NIF/RA
fog	FOG	foraminiferous	FRAM/NIF/ROUS
Fogarty	FOE/GAR/TI	foraminotomy	FRAM/NOT/M*I
fogging	FOG/-G	foraminulum	FOR/MIN/LUM
foil	FOIL	Forane	FOR/AIN
folacin	FOEL/SIN	foration	FOE/RAIGS
folate	FOE/LAIT		FOR/RAIGS
fold	FOELD		FOER/RAIGS
	FOLD	Forbe	FORB
Foley	FOE/LAOE		FOERB
folia	FOEL/YA	Forbes	FORB
foliaceous	FOEL/YAIRBS		FOERB
folian	FOEL/YAN	force	FORS
foliar	FOEL/YAR	forceps	FOR/SEPS
foliate	FOEL/YAIT	forcipate	FORS/PAIT
folic	FOEL/IK		FOR/SI/PAIT
Folin	FOL/LIN	forcipressure	FOR/SI/PRERB/SHUR
folinate	FOEL/NAIT		(*not* FORS/PRERB/SHUR)
folinic	FOE/LIN/IK	Fordyce	FOR/DAOIS
folium	FOEL/YUM	fore-	FOER
Folius	FOEL/YUS	forearm	FOER/ARM
folliberin	FLIB/RIN	forebrain	FOER/BRAIN
	FOL/LIB/RIN	foreconscious	FOER/KON/-RBS
follicle	FOL/K-L	forefinger	FOER/FING/ER
folliclis	FOL/KLAOE	forefoot	FOER/FAOT

foregilding	FOER/GILD/-G	fortior	FORT/YOR
foregut	FOER/GUT	fortuitous	FOR/TAOU/TOUS
forehead	FOER/HED	For Two Capsules	F-R/TWO/KAP/SAOUL/-S
forehead-plasty	FOER/HED/PLAS/TI	foscarnet	FOS/KAR/NET
foreign	FORN	Fosfree	FOS/FRAOE
forekidney	FOER/KID/NAOE	Foshay	FOE/SHAI
Forel	FO/REL		FO/SHAI
	FOE/REL	fossa	FOS/SA
foremilk	FOER/MIL/-K	fossae	FOS/SAE
forensic	FRENZ/IK	fossette	FOE/SET
	FO/RENZ/IK		FOS/SET
	FOE/RENZ/IK	fossil	FOS/SIL
	FOR/ENZ/IK		FOS/IL
foreplay	FOER/PLAI	fossul-	FOS/L-
forepleasure	FOER/PLERB/SHUR		FOS/YAOU/L-
forequarter	FOER/KWART/ER		FOS/YU/L-
foreskin	FOER/SKIN	fossula	FOS/LA
forestomach	FOER/STOM/AK	fossulae	FOS/LAE
forewaters	FOER/WAT/ER/-S	fossulate	FOS/LAIT
fork	FORK	foster	FO*S/ER
forklike	FORK/LAO*IK	Foster	K-P/FO*S/ER
form	FORM	Fothergill	FO*T/ER/GIL
-form	FORM	Fototar	FOET/TAR
Formad	FOR/MAD	Fouchet	FAOU/SHAI
formaldehyde	FOR/MALD/HAOID	foudroyant	FAOU/DROINT
formaldehydogenic	FOR/MALD/HAOID/JEN/IK	foul	FOUL
formalin	FORM/LIN	foulage	FAOU/LAJ
formalize	FORM/LAOIZ	Foulis	FOU/LIS
	FOR/MAL/AOIZ	foundation	FOUN/DAIGS
formamidase	FOR/MAM/DAIS	founder	FOUND/ER
formant	FOR/MANT	fountain	FOUN/TAIN
formate	FOR/MAIT		FOUN/TIN
formatio	FOR/MAI/SHOE	fourchette	FAOUR/SHET
	FOR/MAIRB/YOE	Fourneau	FAOUR/NOE
formation	FOR/MAIGS	Fournier	FAOURN/YAI
formationes	FOR/MAI/SHOE/NAOEZ	fovea	FOEV/YA
	FOR/MAIRB/YOE/NAOEZ	foveae	FOEV/YAE
formative	FORM/TIV	foveate	FOEV/YAIT
formazan	FORM/ZAN	foveated	FOEV/YAIT/-D
formboard	FORM/DORD	foveation	FOEV/YAIGS
	FORM/BAORD	foveola	FOE/VAOE/LA
forme	FO*RM	foveolae	FOE/VAOE/LAE
	(not FORM; see form)	foveolar	FOE/VAOE/LAR
forme fruste	FORM/FRAO*US	foveolare	FOE/VAOE/LAI/RAOE
	FO*RM/FRAO*US		FOE/VO/LAI/RAOE
forme tardive	FORM/TAR/DAOEV	foveolate	FOEV/YO/LAIT
	FO*RM/TAR/DAOEV		FOE/VAOE/LAIT
formic	FORM/IK	Foville	FOE/VAOEL
formication	FORM/KAIGS		FOE/VIL
formiciasis	FORM/SAOI/SIS	fowl	FO*UL
Formicoidea	FORM/KOID/YA	Fowler	FO*UL/ER
formimino	FOR/MIM/NOE		FOUL/ER
formiminoglutamic	FOR/MIM/NO/GLAOU/TAM/IK	fowlpox	FO*UL/POX
formocresol	FORM/KRAOE/SOL	Fox	K-P/FOX
formocortal	FORM/KOR/TAL	foxglove	FOX/GLOV
formol	FOR/MOL	fraction	FRA*BGS
form-order	FORM/H-F/ORD/ER	fractional	FRA*BGS/NAL
formosulfathiazole	FORM/SUL/FA/THAOI/ZOL	fractionating	FRA*BGS/AIT/-G
	FORM/SUL/FA/THAOI/ZOEL		FRA*BGS/NAIT/-G
formul-	FORM/L-	fractionation	FRA*BGS/AIGS
	FOR/MAOU/L-		FRA*BGS/NAIGS
	FORM/YAOU/L-	fracture	FRAK/KHUR
	FORM/YU/L-	fractography	FRAK/TOG/FI
formula	FORM/LA	fracture-dislocation	FRAK/KHUR/DIS/LOE/KAIGS
formulae	FORM/LAE		FRAK/KHUR/H-F/DIS/LOE/KAIGS
Formula B-50	FORM/LA/B-RBGS/50	Fraenkel	FRAEN/KEL
formulary	FORM/LAIR	fragiform	FRAJ/FORM
formulate	FORM/LAIT	fragilis	FRAJ/LIS
formulation	FORM/LAIGS	fragilitas	FRA/JIL/TAS
Formula VM-75	FORM/LA/V-RBGS/M*RBGS/7/5	fragility	FRA/JIL/TI
formyl	FOR/MIL	fragilocyte	FRA/JIL/SAO*IT
formylase	FORM/LAIS	fragilocytosis	FRA/JIL/SAOI/TOE/SIS
formylkynurenine	FOR/MIL/KI/NAOUR/NAOEN	fragment	FRAG/-MT
formylmethionine	FOR/MIL/ME/THAOI/NAOEN	fragmentation	FRAG/MEN/TAIGS
formylporphyrin	FOR/MIL/POR/FRIN	fragmentography	FRAG/MEN/TOG/FI
formyltransferase	FOR/MIL/TRA*NS/FRAIS	fraise	FRA*IZ
fornicate	FORN/KAIT		FRAEZ
fornication	FORN/KAIGS		(not FRAIZ; see phrase)
fornices	FORN/SAOEZ	frambesia	FRAM/BAOEZ/YA
fornicis	FORN/SIS	frambesiform	FRAM/BAOEZ/FORM
fornix	FOR/NIX	frambesioma	FRAM/BAOEZ/YOE/MA
	FORN/IX	frame	FRAIM
Forrel	FOR/REL	framework	FRAIM/WORK
Forssman	FORSZ/MAN	Francis	FRAN/SIS
Forster	FERS/TER	Francisella	FRANS/SEL/LA
	F*ERS/ER	francium	FRANS/YUM
	FER/STER	frank	FRA*NG
Fortaz	FOR/TAZ		FRAN/-K
forte	FOR/TAI	Frank	K-P/FRA*NG

	K-P/FRAN/-K
Frankel	FRAN/KEL
Frankenhauser	FRAN/KEN/HOIZ/ER
	FRAN/KEN/HOUZ/ER
Frankfort	FRANG/FORT
Frankl	FRAN/K-L
	FRA*NG/-L
Franklin	FRAN/KLIN
	FRA*NG/LIN
	FRANG/LIN
franklinic	FRAN/KLIN/IK
	FRA*NG/LIN/IK
	FRANG/LIN/IK
franklinism	FRAN/KLIN/IFM
	FRA*NG/LIN/IFM
	FRANG/LIN/IFM
franklinization	FRAN/KLIN/ZAIGS
	FRA*NG/LIN/ZAIGS
	FRANG/LIN/ZAIGS
Fraser	FRAIZ/ER
	FRAIS/ER
fraternal	FRA/TERNL
Fraunhofer	FROUN/HOFR
	FRAUN/HOFR
	FROUN/HOF/ER
	FRAUN/HOF/ER
Frazier	FRAIZ/YER
freckle	FREK/-L
Fredet	FRE/DAI
free	FRAOE
Freeman	FRAO*E/MAN
	FRAOE/MA*N
freemartin	FRAOE/MAR/TIN
freeze-cleaving	FRAOEZ/KLAOEV/-G
freeze-drying	FRAOEZ/DRAOI/-G
freeze-etching	FRAOEZ/EFP/-G
freeze-fracturing	FRAOEZ/FRAK/KHUR/-G
freeze-substitution	FRAOEZ/SUB/STAOUGS
freezing	FRAOEZ/-G
Frei	FRAO*I
Freiberg	FRAOI/BERG
fremitus	FREM/TUS
frena	FRAOE/NA
frenal	FRAOENL
French	FREFRPBLG
	FREN/-FP
frenectomy	FRAOE/NEKT/M*I
	(not FRE/NEKT/M*I; see
	phrenectomy)
frenetic	FRE/NET/IK
Frenkel	FREN/KEL
	FRENG/EL
frenoplasty	FRAOEN/PLAS/TI
frenosecretory	FRAOEN/SE/KRAOET/RI
frenotomy	FRAOE/NOT/M*I
frentizole	FRENT/ZOEL
frenul-	FREN/L-
	FREN/YAOU/L-
	FREN/YU/L-
frenula	FREN/LA
frenuloplasty	FREN/LO/PLAS/TI
frenulum	FREN/LUM
frenum	FRAOEN/UM
	FRAOEN/NUM
frenzy	FREN/ZI
frequency	FRAOEKT/SI
	FRAOE/KWEN/SI
	FRAOEK/WEN/SI
Frerichs	FRAI/RIX
	FRAOE/RIX
freshening	FRERB/-NG
fressreflex	FRES/RE/FLEX
	FRESZ/RE/FLEX
fret	FRET
freta	FRAOE/TA
fretum	FRAOE/TUM
Freud, Sigmund	SIG/MUND/FROID
freudian	FROID/YAN
freudian slip	FROID/YAN/SLIP
Freund	FROIND
freundii	FROIND/YAOI
friable	FRAOIBL
friar	FRAOIR
fricative	FRIK/TIV
Fricke	FRIK/KAOE
friction	FR*IBGS
frictional	FR*IBGS/NAL
Friderichsen	FRID/RIK/SEN
Friedlander	FRAOED/LAND/ER

	FRAOED/LEND/ER
Friedman	FRAOED/MAN
Friedmann	FRAO*ED/MAN
	FRAOED/MA*N
	(not FRAOED/MAN; see Friedman)
Friedreich	FRAOED/RAOIK
friente	FRAOE/EN/TAOE
	FRAOE/YEN/TAOE
frigid	FRIJ/ID
frigidity	FRI/JID/TI
frigidum	FRIJ/DUM
frigolabile	FRIG/LAI/BAOIL
	FRIG/LAI/BIL
frigorific	FRIG/RIFK
frigorism	FRIG/RIFM
frigostabile	FRIG/STAI/BAOIL
	FRIG/STAI/BIL
frigostable	FRIG/STAIBL
frigotherapy	FRIG/THER/PI
fringe	FRIN/-J
frit	FRIT
Fritsch	FRIT/-RB
	FRIFP
frog	FROG
Frohlich	FRAI/LIK
Frohn	FRON
Froin	FROIN
frolement	FROEL/-MT
	FROL/-MT
Froment	FROE/MAU
	FROEMT
Frommel	FROM/EL
frondose	FRON/DOES
frondosum	FRON/DOES/UM
	FRON/DOE/SUM
frons	FRONZ
	FRONS
front(o)-	FRONT
	FRON/T(O)
frontad	FRON/TAD
frontal	FRON/TAL
frontales	FRON/TAI/LAOEZ
frontalis	FRON/TAI/LIS
frontipetal	FRON/TIP/TAL
frontis	FRON/TIS
frontocortical	FRONT/KORT/KAL
frontomalar	FRONT/MAI/LAR
frontomaxillary	FRONT/MAX/LAIR
frontomental	FRONT/MEN/TAL
frontonasal	FRONT/NAI/ZAL
fronto-occipital	FRONT/OK/SIP/TAL
frontoparietal	FRONT/PRAOI/TAL
frontotemporal	FRONT/TEFRP/RAL
frontotemporale	FRONT/TEFRP/RAI/LAOE
frontozygomatic	FRONT/ZAOIG/MAT/IK
Froriep	FROE/RAOEP
frost	FRO*S
Frost	K-P/FRO*S
frostbite	FRO*S/BAOIT
frottage	FROE/TAJ
frotteur	FROE/TUR
	FROE/TAOUR
frotteurism	FROE/TUR/IFM
	FROE/TAOUR/IFM
fruct(o)-	FRUKT
	FRUK/T(O)
fructification	FRUKT/FI/KAIGS
	FRUK/TIF/KAIGS
fructivorous	FRUK/TIV/ROUS
fructofuranose	FRUKT/FAOUR/NOES
fructofuranosidase	FRUK/TO/FAOUR/NOES/DAIS
	FRUKT/FAOUR/NO/SAO*ID/AIS
	FRUKT/FAOUR/NO/SAOI/DAIS
fructokinase	FRUKT/KAOI/NAIS
fructolysis	FRUK/TOL/SIS
fructosan	FRUKT/SAN
fructose	FRUK/TOES
fructose-biphosphate	FRUK/TOES/B*I/FOS/FAIT
fructosemia	FRUKT/SAOEM/YA
fructoside	FRUKT/SAO*ID
fructosuria	FRUKT/SAOUR/YA
fructosyl	FRUKT/SIL
fructosyltransferase	FRUKT/SIL/TRA*NS/FRAIS
fructus	FRUK/TUS
fructovegetative	FRUKT/VEJ/TAIT/IV
frugivorous	FRAOU/JIV/ROUS
fruit	FRAOUT
fruitarian	FRAOU/TAIRN
	FRAOUT/TAIRN

fruitarianism	FRAOU/TAIRN/IFM	fundiform	FUND/FORM
frusemide	FRAOUS/MAOID	fundiforme	FUND/FOR/MAOE
	FRUS/MAOID	fundoplication	FUND/PLAOI/KAIGS
frustration	FRUS/TRAIGS		FUND/PLI/KAIGS
Fuchs	FAOUKS	funduliformis	FUND/LI/FOR/MIS
fuchsin	FUK/SIN		FUN/DUL/FOR/MIS
	FAOUK/SIN		FUN/DAOUL/FOR/MIS
fuchsino-	FUK/SIN	Fundulus	FUND/LUS
	FUKS/NO	fundus	FUN/DUS
	FAOUK/SIN	funduscope	FUND/SKOEP
	FAOUKS/NO	funduscopy	FUN/DUS/KPI
fuchsinophil	FUK/SIN/FIL	fundusectomy	FUND/SEKT/M*I
	FUKS/NO/FIL	fungal	FUNG/GAL
fuchsinophilia	FUK/SIN/FIL/YA		F*UN/GAL
	FUKS/NO/FIL/YA		(not FUN/GAL)
fuchsinophilic	FUK/SIN/FIL/IK	fungate	FUNG/GAIT
	FUKS/NO/FIL/IK		FUNG/AIT
fuchsinophilous	FUKS/NOF/LOUS	fungating	FUNG/GAIT/-G
	FUK/SI/NOF/LOUS		FUNG/AIT/-G
	FUK/SIN/OF/LOUS	fungemia	FUN/JAOEM/YA
fucose	FAOU/KOES	fungi	FUN/JAOI
fucosidase	FAOU/KOES/DAIS	fungicidal	FUN/JI/SAOI/DAL
fucoside	FAOUK/SAOID	fungicide	FUN/JI/SAO*ID
fucosidosis	FAOUK/SAOI/DOE/SIS	fungicidin	FUN/JI/SAOI/DIN
fucoxanthin	FAOUK/ZAN/THIN	fungiform	FUN/JI/FORM
fugacity	FAOU/GAS/TI	Fungi Imperfecti	FUN/JAOI/IM/PER/FEK/TAOI
-fugal	(O)F/GAL	fungilliform	FUN/JIL/FORM
	(O)F/YAOU/GAL	Fungi-Nail	FUN/JI/NAIL
	(O)/YU/GAL	fungistasis	FUN/JI/STAI/SIS
fugax	FAOU/GAX	fungistat	FUN/JI/STAT
-fuge	FAOUJ	fungistatic	FUN/JI/STAT/IK
fugitive	FAOUJ/TIV	fungisterol	FUN/J*IS/ROL
fugue	FAOUG	fungitoxic	FUN/JI/TOX/IK
fugutoxin	FAOU/GAOU/TOK/SIN	fungitoxicity	FUN/JI/TOK/SIS/TI
	FAOUG/TOK/SIN	Fungizone	FUN/JI/ZOEN
fulcra	FUL/KRA	fungoid	FUN/GOID
fulcrum	FUL/KRUM		FUNG/OID
fulgur-	FULG/R-	Fungoid Creme	FUN/GOID/KRAO*EM
	FUL/GU/R-	Fungoid Solution	FUN/GOID/SLAOUGS
	FUL/GAOU/R-		FUN/GOID/SO/LAOUGS
	(not FUL/GR-)	Fungoid Tincture	FUN/GOID/TING/KHUR
fulgurant	FULG/RANT	fungosa	FUN/GOE/SA
	(not FUL/GRANT)	fungosity	FUN/GOS/TI
fulgurate	FULG/RAIT	fungous	FUNG/OUS
	(not FUL/GRAIT)		FUN/GOUS
fulgurating	FULG/RAIT/-G	fungus	FUN/GUS
	(not FUL/GRAIT/-G)	funic	FAOUN/IK
fulguration	FULG/RAIGS	funicle	FAOUN/K-L
	(not FUL/GRAIGS)	funicul(o)-	FAOU/NIK/L(O)
fuliginous	FAOU/LLJ/NOUS		FAOU/NIK/YAOU/L(O)
fulminans	FUL/MI/NANZ		FAOU/NIK/YU/L(O)
fulminant	FUL/MI/NANT	funicular	FAOU/NIK/LAR
fulminate	FUL/MI/NAIT	funiculi	FAOU/NIK/LAOI
fulminating	FUL/MI/NAIT/-G	funiculitis	FAOU/NIK/LAOITS
Fulvicin	FUL/VI/SIN	funiculoepididymitis	FAOU/NIK/LO/EP/DID/MAOITS
Fulvicin-P/G	FUL/VI/SIN/P-RBGS/G-RBGS	funiculopexy	FAOU/NIK/LO/PEK/SI
	FUL/VI/SIN/P-RBGS/OI/G-RBGS	funiculus	FAOU/NIK/LUS
Fulvicin-U/F	FUL/VI/SIN/URBGS/F-RBGS	funiform	FAOUN/FORM
	FUL/VI/SIN/URBGS/OI/F-RBGS	funis	FAOU/NIS
fulvius	FUL/VAOE/YUS	funnel	FUNL
fumagillin	FAOUM/JIL/LIN	funny	FUN/N*I
fumarase	FAOUM/RAIS	fur	FUR
fumarate	FAOUM/RAIT	Furacin	FAOUR/SIN
Fumarcee	FAOU/MAR/SAOE	furaltadone	FAOU/RALT/DOEN
fumaric	FAOU/MAR/IK	furan	FAOU/RAN
fume	FAOUM	furane	FAOU/RAIN
fumigant	FAOUM/GANT	furanose	FAOUR/NOES
fumigate	FAOUM/GAIT	furantoin	FAOU/RANT/WIN
fumigation	FAOUM/GAIGS	furazolidone	FAOUR/ZOL/DOEN
fumigatus	FAOUM/GAI/TUS	furazolium	FAOUR/ZOEL/YUM
fuming	FAOUM/-G	furcal	FUR/KAL
functio	FUNG/SHOE	furcation	FUR/KAIGS
functio laesa	FUNG/SHOE/LAOE/SA	furcocercous	FURK/SERK/OUS
function	FUNGS	furcula	FURK/LA
functional	FUNGS/NAL	furfur	FUR/FUR
functionalis	FUNGS/NAI/LIS	furfur-	FUR/FR-
	FUNGS/AI/LIS		FUR/FU/R-
functionalism	FUNGS/NAL/IFM		FUR/FAOU/R-
functionating	FUNGS/NAIT/-G	furfuraceous	FUR/FRAIRBS
	FUNGS/AIT/-G	furfural	FUR/FRAL
fund(o)-	FUND	furfures	FUR/FRAOEZ
	FUN/D(O)	furfurol	FUR/FROL
fundal	FUN/DAL	furfuryl	FUR/FRIL
fundament	FUND/-MT	furibund	FAOUR/BUND
fundamental	FUND/MEN/TAL	furnace	FUR/NAS
	FUND/-MT/TAL	Furonatal	FAOUR/NAI/TAL
fundectomy	FUN/DEKT/M*I	furor	FAOU/ROR
fundi	FUN/DAOI		FAOUR/ROR
fundic	FUND/IK	furosemide	FAOU/ROES/MAOID

	FAOU/ROES/MID
Furoxone	FAOU/ROK/SOEN
	FUR/OK/SOEN
furrow	FUR/ROE
furuncle	FAOU/RUN/K-L
	FAOU/RUNG/-L
	FU/RUN/K-L
	FU/RUNG/-L
furuncul-	FAOU/RUN/KL-
	FAOU/RUN/KAOU/L-
	FAOU/RUNG/L-
	FAOU/RUNG/YAOU/L-
	FAOU/RUNG/YU/L-
	FU/RUN/KL-
	FU/RUN/KAOU/L-
	FU/RUNG/L-
	FU/RUNG/YAOU/L-
	FU/RUNG/YU/L-
furuncular	FAOU/RUN/KLAR
furunculoid	FAOU/RUN/KLOID
furunculosis	FAOU/RUN/KLOE/SIS
furunculous	FAOU/RUN/KLOUS
furunculus	FAOU/RUN/KLUS
fusariotoxicosis	FAOU/SAIR/YO/TOX/KOE/SIS
	FAOU/SAR/YO/TOX/KOE/SIS
Fusarium	FAOU/SAIRM
	FAOU/ZAIRM
fuscin	FAOU/SIN
	FAOUS/SIN
fuse	FAOUZ
fuseau	FU/ZOE
fuseaux	FU/ZOEZ
fus(o)-	FAOUZ
	FAOUS
	FAOU/Z(O)
	FAOU/S(O)
fusi	FAOU/SAOI
fusible	FAOUZ/-BL
	FAOUS/-BL
fusidate	FAOUS/DAIT
fusidic	FAOU/SID/IK
fusiform	FAOUZ/FORM
	FAOUS/FORM
fusiformis	FAOUZ/FOR/MIS
	FAOUZ/FOR/MIS
fusimotor	FAOUZ/MOE/TOR
fusion	FAOUGS
fusional	FAOUGS/NAL
Fusobacterium	FAOUZ/BAK/TAOERM
fusocellular	FAOUZ/SEL/YAOU/LAR
fusospirillary	FAOUZ/SPAOIR/LAIR
fusospirillosis	FAOUZ/SPAOIR/LOE/SIS
fusospirochetal	FAOUZ/SPAOIR/KAOE/TAL
fusospirochetosis	FAOUZ/SPAOIR/KAOE/TOE/SIS
fusostreptococcicosis	FAOUZ/STREPT/KOX/KOE/SIS
fustic	F*US/IK
fustigation	F*US/GAIGS
fusus	FAOU/SUS
fututrix	FAOU/TAOU/TRIX
FVC	F-RBGS/SR*RBGS/KR*RBGS

G

G-actin	G-RBGS/AK/TIN
gadfly	GAD/FLAOI
gadoleic	GAD/LAOE/IK
gadolinium	GAD/LIN/YUM
Gadus	GAI/DUS
Gaenslen	GENZ/LEN
	GENS/LEN
Gaffky	GAF/KI
Gaffkya	GAF/KAOE/YA
Gafsa	GAF/SA
gag	GAG
gage	GAEJ
	(*not* GALJ; see gauge)
gain	GAIN
Gairdner	GAIRD/NER
Gaisbock	GAOIS/BEK
gait	GAIT
galact(o)-	GLAKT
	GLAK/T(O)
	GA/LAKT
	GA/LAK/T(O)
	GAL/AK/T(O)
galactacrasia	GLAKT/KRAIZ/YA
galactagogin	GLAKT/GOG/GIN
galactagogue	GLAKT/GOG
galactan	GLAK/TAN
galactemia	GAL/AK/TAOEM/YA
	GLAK/TAOEM/YA
galactia	GLAK/SHA
galactic	GLAKT/IK
galactidrosis	GLAKT/DROE/SIS
galactin	GLAK/TIN
galactischia	GAL/AK/TIS/KA
	GLAK/TIS/KA
	GAL/AK/TIS/KAOE/YA
	GLAK/TIS/KAOE/YA
galactitol	GLAKT/TOL
galactoblast	GLAKT/BLA*S
galactobolic	GLAKT/BOL/IK
galactocele	GLAKT/SAO*EL
galactocerebroside	GLAKT/SER/BRO/SAOID
galactochloral	GLAKT/KLORL
galactogen	GLAKT/JEN
galactogenous	GAL/AK/TOJ/NOUS
	GLAK/TOJ/NOUS
galactography	GAL/AK/TOG/FI
	GLAK/TOG/FI
galactokinase	GLAKT/KAOI/NAIS
galactolipid	GLAKT/LIP/ID
galactolipin	GLAKT/LIP/PIN
galactoma	GAL/AK/TOE/MA
	GLAK/TOE/MA
galactometastasis	GLAKT/ME/TA*S/SIS
galactometer	GAL/AK/TOM/TER
	GLAK/TOM/TER
galactonic	GAL/AK/TON/IK
	GLAK/TON/IK
galactopexic	GLAKT/PEX/IK
galactopexy	GLAKT/PEK/SI
galactophagous	GAL/AK/TOF/GOUS
	GLAK/TOF/GOUS
galactophlebitis	GLAKT/FLE/BAOITS
galactophlysis	GAL/AK/TOF/LI/SIS
	GLAK/TOF/LI/SIS
galactophore	GLAKT/FOER
galactophoritis	GLAKT/FOE/RAOITS
galactophorous	GAL/AK/TOF/ROUS
	GLAK/TOF/ROUS
galactophygous	GAL/AK/TOF/GO*US
	GLAK/TOF/GO*US
galactoplania	GLAKT/PLAIN/YA
galactopoiesis	GLAKT/POI/SIS
galactopoietic	GLAKT/POIT/IK
galactopyra	GLAKT/PAOI/RA
galactopyranose	GLAKT/PIR/NOES
galactorrhea	GLAKT/RAOE/YA
galactosamine	GLAKT/SAM/MIN
	GLAKT/SAM/AOEN
galactosaminoglycan	GLAKT/TOES/AM/NO/GLAOI/KAN
galactosan	GLAKT/SAN
galactosazone	GLAKT/SAI/ZOEN
galactoschesis	GAL/AK/TOS/KE/SIS
	GLAK/TOS/KE/SIS
galactoscope	GLAKT/SKOEP
galactose	GLAK/TOES
galactosemia	GLAKT/SAOEM/YA
galactosidase	GLAKT/SAOI/DAIS
	GLAKT/SAOID/AIS
galactoside	GLAKT/SAOID
galactosis	GAL/AK/TOE/SIS
	GLAK/TOE/SIS
galactostasia	GLAKT/STAIZ/YA
galactostasis	GAL/AK/TO*S/SIS
	GLAK/TO*S/SIS
galactosuria	GLAKT/SAOUR/YA
galactosyl	GLAKT/SIL
galactotherapy	GLAKT/THER/PI
galactotoxin	GLAKT/TOK/SIN
galactotoxismus	GLAKT/TOK/SIZ/MUS
galactotrophy	GAL/AK/TOT/RO/FI
	GLAK/TOT/RO/FI
galactous	GLAK/TOUS
	GLAKT/OUS
galactowaldenase	GLAKT/WALD/NAIS
galactozymase	GLAKT/ZAOI/MAIS
galacturia	GAL/AK/TAOUR/YA
	GLAK/TAOUR/YA
glacturonan	GLAK/TAOUR/NAN
galacturonic	GLAKT/RON/IK
	GLAK/TAOU/RON/IK
galacturonose	GLAK/TAOUR/NOES
galanga	GA/LAN/GA
galangal	GA/LAN/GAL
galaxioides	GLAX/YOI/DAOEZ
	GA/LAX/YOI/DAOEZ
gale	GAEL
	GAIL
galea	GAIL/YA
Galeati	GAL/YA/TAOE
galeatomy	GAIL/YAT/M*I
galeatus	GAL/YAI/TUS
Galeazzi	GAL/YAT/ZAOE
	GAL/YAZ/ZAOE
Galen	GAI/LEN
	GAIL/-N
galena	GAI/LAOE/NA
	GA/LAOE/NA
Galeni	GA/LAOE/NAOI
galenic	GA/LEN/IK
	GAI/LEN/IK
galenica	GA/LEN/KA
	GAI/LEN/KA
galenicals	GA/LEN/KAL/-S
	GAI/LEN/KAL/-S
galenism	GAIL/NIFM
	GAI/LEN/IFM
galeropia	GAL/ROEP/YA
galeropsia	GAL/ROPS/YA
gall	GAUL
Gall	K-P/GAUL
galla	GAL/LA
gallamine	GAL/MAOEN
gallbladder	GAUL/BLAD/ER
gallein	GAL/YIN
galli	GAL/LAOI
	GAUL/LAOI
Galliformes	GAL/FOR/MAOEZ
gallinacea	GAL/NAIS/YA
gallinaceous	GAL/NAIRBS
gallinae	GA/LAOI/NAE
	GAL/LAOI/NAE
gallinaginis	GAL/NAG/NIS
gallinarium	GAL/NAIRM
Gallionella	GAL/YO/NEL/LA
gallipot	GAL/POT
gallisin	GAL/SIN
gallium	GAL/YUM
gallnut	GAUL/NUT
gallocyanin	GAL/SAOI/NIN
gallocyanine	GAL/SAOI/NAOEN
gallon	GAL/LON
gallop	GAL/OP
galloping	GAL/OP/-G
gallsickness	GAUL/SIK/*NS
gallstone	GAUL/STOEN
Gallus	GAL/LUS
galoche	GA/LOERB
Galton	GAL/TON
	GAUL/TON
galtonian	GAL/TOEN/YAN
galvan(o)-	GAL/VAN
	GAL/VA/N(O)
galvanic	GAL/VAN/IK

galvanism	GAL/VA/NIFM	gamont	GAM/ONT
galvanization	GAL/VAN/ZAIGS	gamophagia	GAM/FAI/JA
galvanocaustic	GAL/VAN/KA*US/IK	gamophobia	GAM/FOEB/YA
galvanocautery	GAL/VAN/KAUT/RI	gampsodactyly	GAFRP/SO/DAKT/LI
galvanochemical	GAL/VAN/KEM/KAL		GAM/SO/DAKT/LI
galvanocontractility	GAL/VAN/KON/TRAK/TIL/TI	Gamulin	GAM/LIN
	GAL/VAN/KR-T/TIL/TI	Gamulin Rh	GAM/LIN/RAIFP
galvanofaradization	GAL/VAN/FAR/DI/ZAIGS		GAM/LIN/R-RBGS/H*BGZ
galvanogustometer	GAL/VAN/GUS/TOM/TER	ganciclovir	GANS/KLOEVR
galvanolysis	GAL/VA/NOL/SIS		GANS/KLOE/VIR
galvanometer	GAL/VA/NOM/TER	Gandy	GAN/DI
galvanomuscular	GAL/VAN/MUS/KLAR	gangli(o)-	GANG/L(O)
galvanonervous	GAL/VAN/NEFRB/OUS		GAN/GL(O)
galvanopalpation	GAL/VAN/PAL/PAIGS		GAN/GLAOE/Y(O)
galvanoscope	GAL/VAN/SKOEP	ganglia	GANG/LA
galvanosurgery	GAL/VAN/SURJ/RI	ganglial	GANG/LAL
	GAL/VAN/S-RJ	gangliate	GAN/GLAIT
galvanotaxis	GAL/VAN/TAK/SIS		GANG/LAOE/AIT
galvanotherapeutics	GAL/VAN/THER/PAOUT/IK/-S		GAN/GLAOE/AIT
galvanotherapy	GAL/VAN/THER/PI		(not GANG/LAIT; see gang late)
galvanotonic	GAL/VAN/TON/IK	gangliated	GAN/GLAIT/-D
galvanotonus	GAL/VA/NOT/NUS		GANG/LAOE/AIT/-D
galvanotropism	GAL/VAN/NOT/RO/PIFM		GAN/GLAOE/AIT/-D
gamabufagin	GAM/BAOUF/JIN	gangliectomy	GANG/LEKT/M*I
gamabufogenin	GAM/BAOUF/JEN/NIN	gangliform	GANG/LI/FORM
gamabufotalin	GAM/BAOUF/TAL/LIN	gangliitis	GANG/LAOITS
Gambian	GAM/BAOEN	ganglioblast	GANG/LO/BLA*S
	GAM/BAOE/YAN	gangliocyte	GANG/LO/SAO*IT
gambiense	GAM/BAOE/YEN/SAOE	gangliocytoma	GANG/LO/SAOI/TOE/MA
	GAM/BEN/SAOE	ganglioform	GANG/LO/FORM
gambir	GAM/BIR	ganglioglioma	GANG/LO/GLAOI/YOE/MA
game	GAIM	ganglioglioneuroma	GANG/LO/GLAOI/NAOU/ROE/MA
gamet(o)-	GA/MAOET	gangliolysis	GANG/LOL/SIS
	GAM/T(O)	gangliolytic	GANG/LO/LIT/IK
	GA/MAOE/T(O)	ganglioma	GANG/LOE/MA
gametangia	GAM/TAN/JA	ganglion	GANG/LON
gametangium	GAM/TAN/JUM	ganglionate	GANG/LO/NAIT
gamete	GAM/AOET	ganglionated	GANG/LO/NAIT/-D
	GAM/MAOET	ganglionectomy	GANG/LO/NEKT/M*I
	GA/MAOET	ganglioneure	GANG/LO/NAOUR
gametic	GA/MET/IK	ganglioneuroblastoma	GANG/LO/NAOUR/BLAS/TOE/MA
gametocidal	GA/MAOET/SAOI/DAL	ganglioneurofibroma	GANG/LO/NAOUR/FAOI/BROE/
	GAM/TO/SAOI/DAL		MA
gametocide	GA/MAOET/SAO*ID	ganglioneuroma	GANG/LO/NAOUR/ROE/MA
	GAM/TO/SAO*ID	ganglioneuromatosis	GANG/LO/NAOUR/MA/TOE/SIS
gametocyst	GA/MAOET/S*IS		GANG/LO/NAOUR/ROEM/TOE/SIS
	GA/MET/S*IS	ganglionic	GANG/LON/IK
gametocyte	GA/MAOET/SAO*IT	ganglionitis	GANG/LO/NAOITS
	GA/MET/SAO*IT	ganglionostomy	GANG/LO/NO*S/M*I
gametocytemia	GA/MAOET/SAOI/TAOEM/YA	ganglioplegic	GANG/LO/PLAOEJ/IK
gametogenesis	GAM/TO/JEN/SIS	ganglioside	GANG/LO/SAOID
gametogenic	GAM/TO/JEN/IK	gangliosidoses	GANG/LO/SAOI/DOE/SAOEZ
gametogony	GAM/TOG/N*I	gangliosidosis	GANG/LO/SAOI/DOE/SIS
gametoid	GAM/TOID	gangliospore	GANG/LO/SPOER
gametokinetic	GAM/TO/KI/NET/IK	gangliosympathectomy	GANG/LO/SIFRP/THEKT/M*I
gametologist	GAM/TO*LGS	gangosa	GAN/GOE/SA
gametology	GAM/TOLG	gangraenosa	GAN/GRAE/NOE/SA
gametophagia	GAM/TO/FAI/JA	gangrene	GAN/GRAOEN
gametophyte	GA/MAOET/FAOIT	gangrenosa	GAN/GRE/NOE/SA
gametotropic	GAM/TO/TROP/IK		GAN/GRAOE/NOE/SA
Gamgee	GAM/JAOE	gangrenosis	GAN/GRE/NOE/SIS
gamic	GAM/IK	gangrenous	GAN/GRE/NOUS
gamma	GAM/MA	ganja	GAN/JA
gamma	GAM	ganoblast	GAN/BLA*S
(compound word part)	GAM/MA	Ganser	GANS/ER
gamma benzene	GAM/BEN/ZAOEN/	Gant	GANT
hexachloride	HEX/KLOR/AOID	Gantanol	GANT/NOL
gammacism	GAM/SIFM	Gantrisin	GAN/TRI/SIN
gamma globulin	GAM/GLOB/LIN	gap	GAP
gammaglobulinemia	GAM/GLOB/LI/NAOEM/YA	gape	GAIP
	GAM/GLOB/LIN/AOEM/YA	gapes	GAIP/-S
gammaglobulinopathy	GAM/GLOB/LI/NOP/TH*I		GAIPS
	GAM/GLOB/LIN/OP/TH*I	Garamycin	GAR/MAOI/SIN
gamma-glutamyl	GAM/GLAOUT/MIL/	Garceau	GAR/SOE
transpeptidase	TRA*NS/PEPT/DAIS	Gardner	GA*RD/NER
gammagram	GAM/GRAM		GARD/N*ER
gammagraphic	GAM/GRAFK		(not GARD/NER; see gardener)
gamma-lactone	GAM/LAK/TOEN	gargalanesthesia	GAR/GAL/ANS/THAOEZ/YA
gammaloidosis	GAM/LOI/DOE/SIS	gargalesthesia	GAR/GAL/ES/THAOEZ/YA
gamma-pipradol	GAM/PIP/RA/DOL	gargalesthetic	GAR/GAL/ES/THET/IK
Gammar	GAM/MAR	gargarism	GARG/RIFM
gammopathy	GA/MOP/TH*I	gargle	GARG/-L
	GAM/OP/TH*I	gargoylism	GAR/GOIL/IFM
Gamna-Favre	GAM/NA/FAVR	Garland	K-P/GAR/LAND
gamobium	GA/MOEB/YUM	garlic	GAR/LIK
gamogenesis	GAM/JEN/SIS	garnet	GARN/ET
gamogenetic	GAM/JE/NET/IK		GAR/NET
gamogony	GA/MOG/N*I	Garre	GAR/RAI
	GAM/OG/N*I		GAR/RAOE

Garretson	GART/ET/SON	gastrodynia	GAS/TRO/DIN/YA
	GAR/RET/SON	gastroenteralgia	GAS/TRO/SPWRAL/JA
garrot	GAR/ROT		GAS/TRO/SPWER/AL/JA
Gartner	GAIRT/NER	gastroenteric	GAS/TRO/SPWER/IK
	GART/NER	gastroenteritis	GAS/TRO/SPWRAOITS
gartnerian	GART/NAOERN		GAS/TRO/SPWER/RAOITS
	GART/NAOER/YAN	gastroenteroanastomosis	GAS/TRO/SPWER/RO/AI/NA*S/
gas	GAS		MOE/SIS
gaseous	GAS/YOUS	gastroenterocolitis	GAS/TRO/SPWER/RO/KO/LAOITS
	GARBS	gastroenterocolostomy	GAS/TRO/SPWER/RO/KO/LO*S/
-gasia	GAIZ/YA		M*I
gasiform	GAS/FORM	gastroenterologist	GAS/TRO/SPWRO*LGS
Gaskell	GAS/KEL		GAS/TRO/SPWER/RO*LGS
gasogenic	GAS/JEN/IK	gastroenterology	GAS/TRO/SPWROLG
gasometer	GAS/OM/TER		GAS/TRO/SPWER/ROLG
gasometric	GAS/MET/RIK	gastroenteropathy	GAS/TRO/SPWER/ROP/TH*I
gasometry	GAS/OM/TRI	gastroenteroplasty	GAS/TRO/SPWER/RO/PLAS/TI
Gass	GASZ	gastroenteroptosis	GAS/TRO/SPWER/RO/TOE/SIS
Gasser	GAS/ER		GAS/TRO/SPWER/ROP/TOE/SIS
gasserectomy	GAS/REKT/M*I	gastroenterostomy	GAS/TRO/SPWRO*S/M*I
gasserian	GAS/SAOERN		GAS/TRO/SPWER/RO*S/M*I
	GA/SAOERN	gastroenterotomy	GAS/TRO/SPWROT/M*I
gassing	GAS/-G		GAS/TRO/SPWER/ROT/M*I
gaster	GA*S/ER	gastroepiploic	GAS/TRO/EP/PLOIK
	GAS/TER	gastroepiploica	GAS/TRO/EP/PLOI/KA
Gasterophilidae	GAS/TRO/FIL/DAE	gastroesophageal	GAS/TRO/E/SOF/JAOEL
Gasterophilus	GAS/TROF/LUS	gastroesophagitis	GAS/TRO/E/SOF/JAOITS
gastr(o)-	GAS/TR(O)	gastroesophagostomy	GAS/TRO/E/SOF/GO*S/M*I
gastradenitis	GAS/TRAD/NAOITS	gastrofiberscope	GAS/TRO/FAOI/BER/SKOEP
gastralgia	GAS/TRAL/JA	gastrogastrostomy	GAS/TRO/GAS/TRO*S/M*I
gastralgokenosis	GAS/TRAL/GO/KAOE/NOE/SIS	gastrogavage	GAS/TRO/GA/VAJ
gastramine	GAS/TRA/MIN	gastrogenic	GAS/TRO/JEN/IK
gastratrophia	GAS/TRA/TROEF/YA	gastrograph	GAS/TRO/GRAF
gastrectasia	GAS/TREK/TAIZ/YA	gastrohepatic	GAS/TRO/HE/PAT/IK
gastrectasis	GAS/TREKT/SIS	gastrohepatitis	GAS/TRO/HEP/TAOITS
gastrectomy	GAS/TREKT/M*I	gastrohydrorrhea	GAS/TRO/HAOI/DRO/RAOE/YA
gastric	GAS/TRIK	gastrohypertonic	GAS/TRO/HAO*IP/TON/IK
-gastria	GAS/TRA	gastroileac	GAS/TRO/*IL/YAK
	GAS/TRAOE/YA	gastroileitis	GAS/TRO/*IL/YAOITS
gastrica	GAS/TRI/KA	gastroileostomy	GAS/TRO/*IL/YO*S/M*I
gastricae	GAS/TRI/SAE	gastrointestinal	GAS/TRO/SPW*ES/NAL
gastricum	GAS/TRI/KUM	gastrojejunal	GAS/TRO/JE/JAOUNL
gastricus	GAS/TRI/KUS	gastrojejunocolic	GAS/TRO/JE/JAOUN/KOL/IK
gastrin	GAS/TRIN	gastrojejunoesophagostomy	GAS/TRO/JE/JAOUN/E/SOF/GO*S/
gastrinoma	GAS/TRI/NOE/MA		M*I
gastritic	GAS/TRIT/IK	gastrojejunostomy	GAS/TRO/JEJ/NO*S/M*I
gastritis	GAS/TRAOITS	gastrokinesograph	GAS/TRO/KI/NES/GRAF
gastroacephalus	GAS/TRO/AI/SEF/LUS		GAS/TRO/KI/NAOES/GRAF
gastroadenitis	GAS/TRO/AD/NAOITS	gastrolavage	GAS/TRO/LA/VAJ
gastroadynamic	GAS/TRO/AI/DAOI/NAM/IK	gastrolienal	GAS/TRO/LAOI/NAL
gastroalbumorrhea	GAS/TRO/AL/BAOUM/RAOE/YA	gastrolith	GAS/TRO/L*IT
gastroamorphus	GAS/TRO/AI/MOR/FUS	gastrolithiasis	GAS/TRO/LI/THAOI/SIS
gastroanastomosis	GAS/TRO/AI/NA*S/MOE/SIS	gastrologist	GAS/TRO*LGS
gastroatonia	GAS/TRO/AI/TOEN/YA	gastrology	GAS/TROLG
gastroblennorrhea	GAS/TRO/BLEN/RAOE/YA	gastrolysis	GAS/TROL/SIS
gastrocardiac	GAS/TRO/KARD/YAK	gastromalacia	GAS/TRO/MA/LAI/SHA
gastrocele	GAS/TRO/SAO*EL	gastromegaly	GAS/TRO/MEG/LI
gastrochronorrhea	GAS/TRO/KRON/RAOE/YA	gastromelus	GAS/TROM/LUS
	GAS/TRO/KROEN/RAOE/YA	gastromely	GAS/TROM/LI
gastrocnemii	GAS/TROK/NAOEM/YAOI	gastromycosis	GAS/TRO/MAOI/KOE/SIS
gastrocnemiosemimembranous		gastromyotomy	GAS/TRO/MAOI/OT/M*I
	GAS/TROK/NAOEM/YO/SEM/	gastromyxorrhea	GAS/TRO/MIX/RAOE/YA
	MEM/BRA/NOUS	gastronesteostomy	GAS/TRO/N*ES/YO*S/M*I
gastrocnemius	GAS/TROK/NAOEM/YUS	gastropancreatitis	GAS/TRO/PAN/KRA/TAOITS
gastrocolic	GAS/TRO/KOL/IK	gastropagus	GAS/TROP/GUS
gastrocolicum	GAS/TRO/KOL/KUM	gastroparalysis	GAS/TRO/PRAL/SIS
gastrocolitis	GAS/TRO/KO/LAOITS	gastroparasitus	GAS/TRO/PAR/SAOI/TUS
gastrocoloptosis	GAS/TRO/KOEL/TOE/SIS	gastroparesis	GAS/TRO/PRAOE/SIS
gastrocolostomy	GAS/TRO/KO/LO*S/M*I		GAS/TRO/PAR/SIS
gastrocolotomy	GAS/TRO/KO/LOT/M*I	gastroparietal	GAS/TRO/PRAOI/TAL
gastrocutaneous	GAS/TRO/KAOU/TAIN/YOUS	gastropathic	GAS/TRO/PA*T/IK
gastrodialysis	GAS/TRO/DI/AL/SIS	gastropathy	GAS/TROP/TH*I
gastrodidymus	GAS/TRO/DID/MUS	gastroperitonitis	GAS/TRO/PERT/NAOITS
gastrodisciasis	GAS/TRO/DIS/KAOI/SIS	gastropexy	GAS/TRO/PEK/SI
Gastrodiscoides hominis	GAS/TRO/DIS/KOI/DAOEZ/HOM/	gastrophrenic	GAS/TRO/FREN/IK
	NIS	gastroplasty	GAS/TRO/PLAS/TI
Gastrodiscus hominis	GAS/TRO/DIS/KUS/HOM/NIS	gastroplegia	GAS/TRO/PLAOE/JA
gastrodisk	GAS/TRO/DIS/-K	gastroplication	GAS/TRO/PLI/KAIGS
gastroduodenal	GAS/TRO/DAOU/DAOENL		GAS/TRO/PLAOI/KAIGS
	GAS/TRO/DWOD/NAL	gastropneumonic	GAS/TRO/NAOU/MON/IK
gastroduodenectomy	GAS/TRO/DAOU/DEN/EKT/M*I	gastropod	GAS/TRO/POD
	GAS/TRO/DAOU/DE/NEKT/M*I	Gastropoda	GAS/TROP/DA
gastroduodenitis	GAS/TRO/DWOD/NAOITS	gastroptosia	GAS/TRO/TOEZ/YA
	GAS/TRO/DAOU/DEN/AOITS		GAS/TRO/TOES/YA
gastroduodenoscopy	GAS/TRO/DAOU/DEN/NOS/KPI	gastroptosis	GAS/TRO/TOE/SIS
	GAS/TRO/DAOU/DEN/OS/KPI	gastroptyxis	GAS/TRO/TIK/SIS
gastroduodenostomy	GAS/TRO/DAOU/DE/NO*S/M*I	gastropulmonary	GAS/TRO/PUL/MO/NAIR
	GAS/TRO/DAOU/DEN/O*S/M*I		GAS/TRO/PUM/NAIR
	GAS/TRO/DWOD/NO*S/M*I	gastropylorectomy	GAS/TRO/PAOIL/REKT/M*I

gastropyloric	GAS/TRO/PAOI/LOR/IK	gelatinolytic	JEL/TIN/LIT/IK
gastroradiculitis	GAS/TRO/RA/DIK/LAOITS	gelatinosa	JEL/TI/NOE/SA
gastrorrhagia	GAS/TRO/RAI/JA	gelatinosum	JEL/TI/NOE/SUM
gastrorrhaphy	GAS/TROR/FI	gelatinous	JE/LAT/NOUS
gastrorrhea	GAS/TRO/RAOE/YA	gelatinum	JEL/TAOI/NUM
gastrorrhexis	GAS/TRO/REK/SIS	gelation	JE/LAIGS
gastroschisis	GAS/TROS/KI/SIS	gelatose	JEL/TOES
gastroscope	GAS/TRO/SKOEP	gelatum	JE/LAI/TUM
gastroscopic	GAS/TRO/SKOP/IK	geld	GELD
gastroscopy	GAS/TROS/KPI	gelding	GELD/-G
Gastrosed	GAS/TRO/SED	geleophysic	JEL/YO/FIZ/IK
gastroselective	GAS/TRO/SLEKT/IV		JAOEL/YO/FIZ/IK
gastrosia	GAS/TROEZ/YA	Gelfoam	JEL/FOEM
gastrosis	GAS/TROE/SIS	Gelineau	JEL/NOE
gastrospasm	GAS/TRO/SPAFM	Gelle	JEL/LAI
gastrosplenic	GAS/TRO/SPLEN/IK	Gellhorn	GEL/HORN
gastrostaxis	GAS/TRO/STAK/SIS	gelometer	JEL/OM/TER
gastrostenosis	GAS/TRO/STE/NOE/SIS	gelose	JEL/LOES
gastrostogavage	GAS/TRO*S/GA/VAJ	gelosis	JE/LOE/SIS
	GAS/TROS/TO/GA/VAJ	gelotherapy	JEL/THER/PI
gastrostolavage	GAS/TRO*S/LA/VAJ	gelototherapy	JEL/TO/THER/PI
	GAS/TROS/TO/LA/VAJ	gelotripsy	JEL/TRIP/SI
gastrostomy	GAS/TRO*S/M*I	Gelpirin	JEL/PRIN
gastrosuccorrhea	GAS/TRO/SUK/RAOE/YA	gelsemine	JELS/MAOEN
gastrothoracopagus	GAS/TRO/THOR/KOP/GUS	Gelusil	JEL/YAOU/SIL
gastrotome	GAS/TRO/TOEM		JEL/YU/SIL
gastrotomy	GAS/TROT/M*I	Gely	JAI/LI
gastrotonometer	GAS/TRO/TOE/NOM/TER	Gemella	JE/MEL/LA
gastrotoxic	GAS/TRO/TOX/IK	gemellary	JEM/LAIR
gastrotoxin	GAS/TRO/TOK/SIN	gemellipara	JEM/LIP/RA
gastrotropic	GAS/TRO/TROP/IK	gemellology	JEM/LOLG
gastrotympanites	GAS/TRO/TIFRP/NAOI/TAOEZ		JEM/EL/OLG
gastrovascular	GAS/TRO/VAS/KLAR	gemellus	JE/MEL/LUS
gastroxia	GAS/TROX/YA	gemfibrozil	JEM/FAOI/BRO/ZIL
gastroxynsis	GAS/TROK/SIN/SIS	geminate	JEM/NAIT
gastrula	GAS/TRAOU/LA	gemination	JEM/NAIGS
gastrulation	GAS/TRAOU/LAIGS	gemini	JEM/NAOI
Gatch	GAFP	geminous	JEM/NOUS
gate	GAET	geminus	JEM/NUS
	(*not* GAIT; see gait)	gemistocyte	JE/M*IS/SAO*IT
gatism	GAI/TIFM		JEM/*IS/SAO*IT
	GAIT/IFM	gemistocytic	JE/M*IS/SIT/IK
Gaucher	GOE/SHAI		JEM/*IS/SIT/IK
gauge	GAIJ	gemistocytoma	JE/M*IS/SAOI/TOE/MA
gaultheria	GAUL/THAOER/YA		JEM/*IS/SAOI/TOE/MA
Gaultheria	K-P/GAUL/THAOER/YA	gemma	JEM/MA
gauntlet	GAUNT/LET	gemmangioma	JEM/AN/JOE/MA
gauss	GOUSZ	gemmation	JEM/AIGS
Gauss	K-P/GOUSZ		JE/MAIGS
gaussian	GOUS/YAN		JEM/MAIGS
	GOUGS	gemmule	JEM/YAOUL
gaussing	GOUSZ/-G	-gen-	JEN
gauze	GAUZ	gena	JAOE/NA
gavage	GA/VAJ	genal	JAOENL
Gavard	GA/VAR	Genapax Tampons	JEN/PAX/TAM/PON/-S
	GA/VARD	gender	JEND/ER
Gaviscon	GAV/SKON	gene	JAOEN
	GAVS/KON	genealogy	JAOEN/YALG
	GAV/IS/KON	-geneic	JE/NAI/IK
gay	GAI		JE/NAOE/IK
Gay-Lussac	GAI/LAOU/SAK	geneogenous	JAOEN/YOJ/NOUS
gaze	GAIZ	genera	JEN/RA
gear	GAOER	general	JEN
Gegenbaur	GAIG/EN/BOUR		JEN/RAL
	GEG/EN/BOUR	generalisata	JEN/RAL/SAI/TA
Geigel	GAOIG/EL		JEN/SAI/TA
	GAOI/GEL	generalist	JEN/RAL/*IS
Geiger	GAOIG/ER	generalization	JEN/ZAIGS
	GAOI/GER		JEN/RAL/ZAIGS
Geiger counter	GAOIG/ER/KOUNT/ER	generalize	JEN/AOIZ
	GAOI/GER/KOUNT/ER		JEN/RAL/AOIZ
Geiger-Muller	GAOIG/ER/H-F/MIL/ER	generalized	JEN/AOIZ/-D
	GAOI/GER/H-F/MIL/ER		JEN/RAL/AOIZ/-D
gel	JEL	generate	JEN/RAIT
gelase	JEL/AIS	generation	JEN/RAIGS
gelasmus	JE/LAZ/MUS	generative	JEN/RA/TIV
	JE/LAS/MUS	generator	JEN/RAI/TOR
gelastic	JE/LA*S/IK	generic	JE/NER/IK
gelate	JEL/AIT		JE/NAIR/IK
gelatification	JE/LAT/FI/KAIGS	geneses	JEN/SAOEZ
gelatigenous	JEL/TIJ/NOUS	genesial	JE/NAOEZ/YAL
gelatin	JEL/TIN		JE/NAOES/YAL
gelatinase	JE/LAT/NAIS	genesic	JE/NES/IK
gelatiniferous	JE/LAT/NIF/ROUS		JE/NAOEZ/IK
	JEL/TIN/IF/ROUS	genesiology	JE/NAOEZ/YOLG
gelatiniform	JEL/TIN/FORM		JE/NAOES/YOLG
gelatinization	JE/LAT/NI/ZAIGS	genesis	JEN/SIS
gelatinize	JE/LAT/NAOIZ	genesistasis	JEN/S*IS/SIS
gelatinoid	JE/LAT/NOID	genestatic	JEN/STAT/IK

genetic	JE/NET/IK		JEN/SHO/B*I/AIS
geneticist	JE/NET/S*IS	genu	JAOE/NAOU
genetics	JE/NET/IK/-S	genua	JEN/YA
genetotrophic	JE/NET/TROFK		JEN/YAOU/WA
	JE/NET/TROEFK	genual	JEN/YAL
genetous	JE/NET/OUS		JEN/YAOUL
Geneva Convention	JE/NAOE/VA/KON/VENGS		JEN/YUL
Gengou	JAU/GAOU	genucubital	JEN/YAOU/KAOUB/TAL
	JEN/GAOU	genufacial	JEN/YAOU/FAIRBL
genial	JEN/YAL	genupectoral	JEN/YAOU/PEKT/RAL
	JAOEN/YAL	genus	JAOE/NUS
	JE/NAOI/YAL	Gen-XENE	JEN/ZAOEN
	JE/NAOIL	genyantrum	JEN/YAN/TRUM
genian	JE/NAOI/YAN	geo-	JAOE
	JE/NAOIN		JAOE/YO
genic	JEN/IK	geobiology	JAOE/BAO*I/OLG
-genicity	JE/NIS/TI	geochemistry	JAOE/KEM/STRI
genicul-	JE/NIK/L-	Geocillin	JAOE/SLIN
	JE/NIK/YAOU/L-		JAOE/SIL/LIN
	JE/NIK/YU/L-	geode	JAOE/OED
genicula	JE/NIK/LA	geogen	JAOE/JEN
genicular	JE/NIK/LAR	geomedicine	JAOE/MED/SIN
geniculate	JE/NIK/LAIT	geopathology	JAOE/PA/THOLG
geniculatum	JE/NIK/LAI/TUM	Geopen	JAOE/PEN
geniculum	JE/NIK/LUM	geophagia	JAOE/FAI/JA
-genin	JEN/NIN	geophagism	JAOE/OF/JIFM
	JE/NIN	geophagist	JAOE/OF/J*IS
genio-	JAOEN/YO	geophagy	JAOE/OF/JI
	JE/NAOI	geophilic	JAOE/FIL/IK
geniocheiloplasty	JAOEN/YO/KAOIL/PLAS/TI	Geophilus	JAOE/OF/LUS
genioglossus	JAOEN/YO/GLOS/SUS	Georgi	JOR/GAOE
	JE/NAOI/GLOS/SUS		JOER/GAOE
geniohyoglossus	JAOEN/YO/HAOI/GLOS/SUS		GAI/OR/GAOE
geniohyoid	JAOEN/YO/HAOI/OID	georginae	JOR/JAOI/NAE
	JE/NAOI/HAOI/OID		JOER/JAOI/NAE
geniohyoideus	JAOEN/YO/HAOI/OID/YUS	geotaxis	JAOE/TAK/SIS
	JE/NAOI/HAOI/OID/YUS	geotrichosis	JAOE/TRI/KOE/SIS
genion	JE/NAOI/YON	Geotrichum	JAOE/OT/RI/KUM
genioplasty	JAOEN/YO/PLAS/TI	geotropic	JAOE/TROP/IK
	JE/NAOI/PLAS/TI	geotropism	JAOE/OT/RO/PIFM
genit(o)-	JEN/T(O)	gephyrophobia	JE/FAOIR/FOEB/YA
genital	JEN/TAL	Geraghty	GER/RA/TI
genitalia	JEN/TAIL/YA		GER/TI
genitality	JEN/TAL/TI	geraniol	JE/RAIN/YOL
genitaloid	JEN/TAL/OID	geratic	JE/RAT/IK
genitocrural	JEN/TO/KRAOURL	geratology	JER/TOLG
genitofemoral	JEN/TO/FEM/RAL	gerbil	JER/BIL
genitofemoralis	JEN/TO/FEM/RAI/LIS	Gerdy	JER/DI
genitography	JEN/TOG/FI		GER/DI
genitoinfectious	JEN/TO/IN/FEK/-RBS	gereology	JER/YOLG
genitoinguinale	JEN/TO/ING/WI/NAI/LAOE	Gerhardt	GER/HART
genitoplasty	JEN/TO/PLAS/TI		GAOER/HART
genitospinal	JEN/TO/SPAOINL		JER/HART
genitourinary	JEN/TO/YAOUR/NAIR	geriatric	JER/YAT/RIK
genius	JAOEN/YUS	geriatrician	JER/YA/TRIGS
Gennari	JEN/NAR/RAOE	geriatrics	JER/YAT/RIK/-S
	JEN/NA/ROAE	Gerimed	JER/MED
geno-	J*EN	Geriplex-FS	JER/PLEX/F-RBGS/S*RBGS
	JEN/NO	Geritonic	JER/TON/IK
	(not JEN; see general)	Gerlach	GER/LAK
genoblast	J*EN/BLA*S	Gerlier	JERL/YAI
genocopy	J*EN/KOP/PI	germ	JERM
genodermatology	J*EN/DERM/TOLG	germanium	JER/MAIN/YUM
genodermatosis	J*EN/DERM/TOE/SIS	germicidal	JERM/SAOI/DAL
genome	JAOE/NOEM	germicide	JERM/SAO*ID
	JE/NOEM	germinal	JERM/NAL
genomic	JE/NOM/IK	germination	JERM/NAIGS
	JAOE/NOM/IK	germinativa	JERM/NA/TAOI/VA
genophobia	J*EN/FOEB/YA	germinative	JERM/NA/TIV
Genora	JEN/OR/RA		JERM/NAIT/IV
genospecies	JAOEN/SPAOE/SAOEZ	germinoma	JERM/NOE/MA
genote	JAOE/NOET	gero-	JER
genotoxic	JAOEN/TOX/IK		JER/RO
genotype	J*EN/TAOIP	geroderma	JER/DER/MA
genotypic	J*EN/TIP/IK	gerodermia	JER/DERM/YA
genotypical	J*EN/TIP/KAL	gerodontia	JER/DON/SHA
-genous	-J/NOUS	gerodontic	JER/DONT/IK
Gentafair	JENT/FAIR	gerodontics	JER/DONT/IK/-S
gentamicin	JENT/MAOI/SIN	gerodontist	JER/DONT/*IS
gentian	JENGS		JER/DON/T*IS
gentianophil	JENGS/FIL	gerodontology	JER/DON/TOLG
gentianophile	JENGS/FAOIL	geromarasmus	JER/MA/RAZ/MUS
gentianophilic	JENGS/FIL/IK	geromorphism	JER/MOR/FIFM
gentianophilous	JENGS/OF/LOUS	geront(o)-	JER/ONT
	JENGS/NOF/LOUS		JE/RONT
gentianophobic	JENGS/FOEB/IK		JERN/T(O)
gentianose	JENGS/OES		JER/ON/T(O)
gentian violet	JENGS/VAOI/LET		JE/RON/T(O)
gentiobiase	JEN/SHO/BAO*I/AIS	gerontal	JER/ON/TAL

	JE/RON/TAL	Gifford	GIF/FORD
gerontin	JER/ON/TIN	gigant(o)-	JAOI/GANT
	JE/RON/TIN		JAOI/GAN/T(O)
gerontine	JER/ON/TAOEN	gigantea	JAOI/GANT/YA
	JE/RON/TAOEN	giganteus	JAOI/GANT/YUS
gerontologist	JERN/TO*LGS	gigantica	JAOI/GANT/KA
gerontology	JERN/TOLG	gigantism	JAOI/GAN/TIFM
gerontophile	JER/ONT/FAOIL	gigantocellulare	JAOI/GANT/SEL/YAOU/LAI/RAOE
	JE/RONT/FAOIL	gigantocellularis	JAOI/GANT/SEL/YAOU/LAI/RIS
gerontophilia	JER/ONT/FIL/YA	gigantomastia	JAOI/GANT/MA*S/YA
	JE/RONT/FIL/YA	gigantosoma	JAOI/GANT/SOE/MA
gerontophobia	JER/ONT/FOEB/YA	gigas	JAOI/GAS
	JE/RONT/FOEB/YA	Gigli	JAOEL/YAOE
gerontopia	JERN/TOEP/YA		JAOE/LAOE
gerontotherapeutics	JER/ONT/THER/PAOUT/IK/-S	Gigli's saw	JAOEL/YAOE/AOES/SAU
	JE/RONT/THER/PAOUT/IK/-S		JAOE/LAOE/AOES/SAU
gerontotherapy	JER/ONT/THER/PI	Gila monster	HAOE/LA/MON/STER
	JE/RONT/THER/PI	gilbert	GIL/BERT
gerontotoxon	JER/ONT/TOK/SON	Gilbert	K-P/GIL/BERT
	JE/RONT/TOK/SON	Gilchrist	GIL/KR*IS
gerontoxon	JERN/TOK/SON	gilchristi	GIL/KRIS/TAOI
geropsychiatry	JER/SAOI/KAOI/TRI	gildable	GILD/-BL
Gerota	GAI/ROE/TA	Gilead	GIL/YAD
	GE/ROE/TA	Gilford	GIL/FORD
Geroton	JER/TON	gill	GIL
Geroton Forte	JER/TON/FOR/TAI	Gilles de la Tourette	JAOEL/DE/LA/TAOU/RET
Gersh	GER/-RB	Gillette	JI/LET
Gerson	GAIR/SON		JIL/LET
	GER/SON	Gilliam	GIL/YAM
Gerstmann	G*ERS/MAN	Gillies	GIL/LAOEZ
gestagen	J*ES/JEN		GIL/LAOES
gestagenic	J*ES/JEN/IK	Gillmore	GIL/MOR
gestalt	GE/STALT	Gilmer	GIL/MER
	GE/STAULT	Gimbernat	GIM/BER/NAT
gestaltism	GE/STALT/IFM	Gimbernati	GIM/BER/NAI/TAOI
	GE/STAULT/IFM		GIM/BER/NAT/TAOI
gestation	JES/TAIGS	ginger	JIN/JER
gestational	JES/TAIGS/NAL	gingiv(o)-	JING/JI/V(O)
gestationis	JES/TAI/SHOE/NIS		JIN/JAOI/V(O)
gestoses	JES/TOE/SAOEZ	gingiva	JING/VA
gestosis	JES/TOE/SIS		JIN/JI/VA
gesture	JES/KHUR		JIN/JAOI/VA
geus-	GAOUZ	gingivae	JING/VAE
	GAOUS		JIN/JI/VAE
-geusia	GAOUZ/YA		JIN/JAOI/VAE
Gevrabon	JEV/RA/BON	gingival	JING/VAL
Gevral	JEV/RAL		JIN/JIVL
Ghon	GO*N		JIN/JI/VAL
	GAUN		JIN/JAOIVL
Ghon-Sachs	GO*N/H-F/SA*KS		JIN/JAOI/VAL
	GAUN/H-F/SA*KS	gingivalgia	JING/VAL/JA
ghost	GO*ES	Gingival Index	JING/VAL/IN/DEX
GI	G-RBGS/*IRBGS	gingivalis	JING/VAI/LIS
Giacomini	JAK/MAOE/NAOE	gingivally	JING/VAL/LI
Giannuzzi	JA/NAOUT/SAOE	gingivectomy	JING/VEKT/M*I
	JA/NAOUT/ZAOE	gingivitis	JING/VAOITS
	JA/NAOU/ZAOE	gingivoaxial	JING/VO/AX/YAL
Gianotti	JAOE/NOT/TAOE	gingivobuccoaxial	JING/VO/BUK/AX/YAL
	JA/NOT/TAOE	gingivoglossitis	JING/VO/GLOS/SAOITS
giant	JAOINT	gingivolabial	JING/VO/LAIB/YAL
giantism	JAOIN/TIFM	gingivolinguoaxial	JING/VO/LING/WO/AX/YAL
	JAOINT/IFM	gingivo-osseous	JING/VO/OS/YOUS
Giardia	JARD/YA	gingivoplasty	JING/VO/PLAS/TI
	JAOE/ARD/YA	gingivostomatitis	JING/VO/STOEM/TAOITS
giardiasis	JAR/DAOI/SIS	gingivosis	JING/VOE/SIS
	JAOE/AR/DAOI/SIS	gingly-	JIN/GLI
	JAOI/AR/DAOI/SIS		GIN/GLI
gibberish	JIB/RIRB	ginglyform	JIN/GLI/FORM
gibbon	GIB/BON	ginglymoarthrodial	JIN/GLI/MO/AR/THROED/YAL
Gibbon	K-P/GIB/BON		JIN/GLIM/AR/THROED/YAL
gibbosity	GI/BOS/TI	ginglymoid	JIN/GLI/MOID
	GIB/BOS/TI	ginglymus	JIN/GLI/MUS
gibbous	GIB/OUS	ginseng	JIN/SENG
Gibbs	GIBS	Giordano	JOR/DAN/NOE
gibbus	GIB/BUS		JOR/DA/NOE
Gibert	JAOE/BAIR	Giordano-Giovannetti	JOR/DAN/NOE/H-F/JOEV/NET/
Gibney	GIB/NAOE		TAOE
Gibraltar	JI/BRAL/TAR		JOR/DA/NOE/H-F/JOEV/NET/
Gibson	GIB/SON		TAOE
gibsoni	GIB/SOE/NAOI	Girard	JI/RARD
	GIB/SON/NAOI	girdle	GIRD/-L
gid	GID	gitalin	JIT/LIN
giddiness	GID/DI/*NS	gitaloxin	JIT/LOK/SIN
	GID/*NS	githagism	G*IT/JIFM
Giemsa	JAOEM/SA	githago	GI/THAI/GOE
	GAOEM/SA	gitogenin	JIT/JEN/NIN
Gierke	GAOER/KAOE		JI/TOJ/NIN
	GIR/KAOE	gitonin	JIT/NIN
Gieson	GAOE/SON		

gitoxin	JI/TOK/SIN	glide	GLAOI/YAL
gitter	GIT/ER		GLAOID
gitterzelle	GIT/ER/ZEL/LE	gliobacteria	GLAOI/BAK/TAOER/YA
Giuffrida-Ruggieri	JAOUF/RAOE/DA/RAOU/JAOER/	glioblast	GLAOI/BLA*S
	RAOE	glioblastoma	GLAOI/BLAS/TOE/MA
	JAOU/FRAOE/DA/RAOU/JAOER/	glioblastosis cerebri	GLAOI/BLAS/TOE/SIS/SER/BRAOI
	RAOE	gliocladium	GLAOI/KLAID/YUM
gizzard	GIZ/ARD	gliococcus	GLAOI/KOK/KUS
glabella	GLA/BEL/LA	gliocytoma	GLAOI/SAOI/TOE/MA
glabellad	GLA/BEL/AD	gliofibrillary	GLAOI/FAOI/BRI/LAIR
	GLA/BEL/LAD	gliogenous	GLAOI/OJ/NOUS
glabellum	GLA/BEL/UM	glioma	GLAOI/YOE/MA
glabrate	GLAI/BRAIT	gliomatosis	GLAOI/YOEM/TOE/SIS
	GLAIB/RAIT		GLAOI/MA/TOE/SIS
glabrous	GLAI/BROUS	gliomatous	GLAOI/YOEM/TOUS
	GLAIB/ROUS	glioneuroma	GLAOI/NAOU/ROE/MA
glacial	GLAIRBL	gliophagia	GLAOI/FAI/JA
gladiate	GLAD/YAIT	gliopil	GLAOI/PIL
	GLAID/YAIT	gliosarcoma	GLAOI/SAR/KOE/MA
gladiolus	GLA/DAOI/LUS	gliosis	GLAOI/YOE/SIS
	GLAD/YOE/LUS	gliosome	GLAOI/SOEM
gladiomanubrial	GLAD/YO/MA/NAOUB/RAL	glipizide	GLIP/ZAOID
glairy	GLAI/RI	glischrin	GLIS/KRIN
	GLAIR/RI	glischruria	GLIS/KRAOUR/YA
glance	GLANS	glissade	GLIS/AID
gland	GLAND		GLIS/SAID
glanderous	GLAND/ROUS	glissadic	GLIS/SAD/IK
glanders	GLAND/ERZ	Glisson	GLIS/SON
	GLAN/DERZ	glissoni	GLIS/NAOI
	GLAND/ER/-S		GLIS/SOE/NAOI
	GLAN/DER/-S		GLIS/SON/NAOI
glandes	GLAN/DAOEZ	glissonitis	GLIS/NAOITS
glandilemma	GLAND/LEM/MA		GLISZ/NAOITS
glandis	GLAN/DIS	glistening	GLIS/-NG
glandul-	GLAND/L-	glitter	GLIT/ER
	GLAN/DAOU/L-	global	GLOE/BAL
	GLAND/YAOU/L-	globe	GLOEB
	GLAND/YU/L-	globi	GLOE/BAOI
glandula	GLAND/LA	globin	GLOE/BIN
glandulae	GLAND/LAE	globinometer	GLOEB/NOM/TER
glandular	GLAND/LAR	Globocephalus	GLOEB/SEF/LUS
glandulare	GLAND/LAI/RAOE	globoid	GLOE/BOID
glandularis	GLAND/LAI/RIS		GLOEB/OID
glandule	GLAN/DAOUL	globosa	GLOE/BOE/SA
	GLAND/YAOUL	globose	GLOE/BOES
glandulous	GLAND/LOUS	globoside	GLOEB/SAOID
glans	GLANZ	globul-	GLOB/L-
	(not GLANS; see glance)		GLOB/YAOU/L-
glans clitoridis	GLANZ/KLI/TOR/DIS		GLOB/YU/L-
glans penis	GLANZ/PAOE/NIS	globular	GLOB/LAR
Glanzmann	GLANZ/MAN	globule	GLOB/YAOUL
glaphenine	GLA/FEN/AOEN	globuli	GLOB/LAOI
glare	GLAIR	globuliferous	GLOB/LIF/ROUS
glarometer	GLAIR/OM/TER	globulin	GLOB/LIN
	GLA/ROM/TER	globulinemia	GLOB/LI/NAOEM/YA
glaserian	GLAI/SAOERN		GLOB/LIN/AOEM/YA
	GLA/SAOERN	globulinuria	GLOB/LI/NAOUR/YA
Glasgow	GLAS/GOE		GLOB/LIN/YAOUR/YA
glass	GLASZ	globulomaxillary	GLOB/LO/MAX/LAIR
glasses	GLASZ/-S	globulose	GLOB/LOES
glassy	GLAS/SI	globulus	GLOB/LUS
Glauber	GLOUB/ER	globus	GLOE/BUS
	GLOU/BER	glomal	GLOE/MAL
glaucoma	GLAU/KOE/MA	glomangioma	GLOE/MAN/JOE/MA
glaucomatocyclitic	GLAU/KOEM/TO/SIK/LIT/IK	glomangiosis	GLOE/MAN/JOE/SIS
	GLAU/KOEM/TO/SI/KLIT/IK	glome	GLOEM
glaucomatous	GLAU/KOEM/TOUS	glomectomy	GLOE/MEKT/M*I
glaucosis	GLAU/KOE/SIS	glomera	GLOM/RA
glaucosuria	GLAUK/SAOUR/YA	glomerate	GLOM/RAIT
glaucus	GLAU/KUS	glomerul(o)-	GLOE/MER/L(O)
glaze	GLAIZ		GLOE/MER/YAOU/L(O)
Gleason	GLAOE/SON		GLOE/MER/YU/L(O)
gleet	GLAOET	glomerular	GLOE/MER/LAR
gleety	GLAOE/TI	glomerule	GLOM/ER/YAOUL
	GLAOET/TI		GLOM/RAOUL
gleno-	GLAOEN	glomeruli	GLOE/MER/LAOI
	GLAOE/NO	glomerulitis	GLOE/MER/LAOITS
glenohumeral	GLAOEN/HAOUM/RAL	glomerulonephritis	GLOE/MER/LO/NE/FRAOITS
glenohumeralia	GLAOEN/HAOUM/RAIL/YA		GLOE/MER/LO/NEF/RAOITS
glenoid	GLAOE/NOID	glomerulonephropathy	GLOE/MER/LO/NEF/ROP/TH*I
	GLAOEN/OID		GLOE/MER/LO/NE/FROP/TH*I
glenoidalis	GLAOE/NOI/DAI/LIS	glomerulopathy	GLOE/MER/LOP/TH*I
Gley	GLAI	glomerulosclerosis	GLOE/MER/LO/SKLE/ROE/SIS
gli(o)-	GLAOI	glomerulose	GLOE/MER/LOES
	GLAOI/Y(O)	glomerulotropin	GLOE/MER/LO/TROE/PIN
glia	GLAOI/YA	glomerulus	GLOE/MER/LUS
gliacyte	GLAOI/SAO*IT	glomic	GLOEM/IK
gliadin	GLAOI/DIN	glomoid	GLOE/MOID
glial	GLAOIL	glomus	GLOE/MUS

glonoin	GLOE/NOIN
gloss(o)-	GLOS
	GLOS/S(O)
glossa	GLOS/SA
glossagra	GLOS/AG/RA
	GLOS/SAI/GRA
glossal	GLOS/SAL
glossalgia	GLOS/AL/JA
glossectomy	GLOS/EKT/M*I
	GLOS/SEKT/M*I
glossi	GLOS/SAOI
-glossia	GLOS/YA
	GLOSZ/YA
Glossina	GLOS/SAOI/NA
glossitis	GLOS/SAOITS
glossocele	GLOS/SAO*EL
glossocinesthetic	GLOS/SINS/THET/IK
	GLOS/SIN/ES/THET/IK
glossocoma	GLO/SOK/MA
	GLOS/SOK/MA
glossodontotropism	GLOS/DONT/TROEP/IFM
	GLOS/DONT/TROE/PIFM
glossodynamometer	GLOS/DAOIN/MOM/TER
glossodynia	GLOS/DIN/YA
glossodyniotropism	GLOS/DIN/YO/TROEP/IFM
	GLOS/DIN/YO/TROE/PIFM
glossoepiglottic	GLOS/EP/GLOT/IK
glossoepiglottidean	GLOS/EP/GLO/TID/YAN
	GLOS/EP/GLOT/TID/YAN
glossograph	GLOS/GRAF
glossohyal	GLOS/HAOIL
glossokinesthetic	GLOS/KINS/THET/IK
	GLOS/KIN/ES/THET/IK
glossolalia	GLOS/LAIL/YA
glossology	GLOS/OLG
glossolysis	GLOS/OL/SIS
glossomantia	GLOS/MAN/SHA
glossoncus	GLOS/ON/KUS
glossopalatinus	GLOS/PAL/TAOI/NUS
glossopathy	GLOS/OP/TH*I
glossopharyngeal	GLOS/FRIN/JAL
glossopharyngeum	GLOS/FRIN/JUM
glossopharyngeus	GLOS/FRIN/JUS
glossoplasty	GLOS/PLAS/TI
glossoplegia	GLOS/PLAOE/JA
glossoptosia	GLOS/OP/TOES/YA
glossoptosis	GLOS/OP/TOE/SIS
glossopyrosis	GLOS/PAOI/ROE/SIS
glossorrhaphy	GLOS/OR/FI
	GLOS/SOR/FI
glossoscopy	GLOS/OS/KPI
glossospasm	GLOS/SPAFM
glossosteresis	GLOS/STRAOE/SIS
	GLOS/STE/RAOE/SIS
glossotomy	GLOS/OT/M*I
	GLOS/SOT/M*I
glossotrichia	GLOS/TRIK/YA
glossus	GLOS/SUS
glottal	GLOT/TAL
glottic	GLOT/IK
glottides	GLOT/DAOEZ
glottidis	GLOT/DIS
glottidospasm	GLOT/DO/SPAFM
glottis	GLOT/TIS
glottitis	GLO/TAOITS
	GLOT/TAOITS
glottology	GLO/TOLG
	GLOT/TOLG
gloves	GLOV/-S
glow	GLOE
glubionate	GLAOUB/YO/NAIT
gluc(o)-	GLAOUK
	GLAOU/K(O)
glucagon	GLAOUK/GON
glucagonoma	GLAOUK/GON/O/MA
	GLAOUK/GO/NOE/MA
glucal	GLAOU/KAL
glucan	GLAOU/KAN
glucanotransferase	GLAOUK/NO/TRA*NS/FRAIS
glucase	GLAOU/KAIS
glucatonia	GLAOUK/TOEN/YA
glucemia	GLAOU/SAOEM/YA
gluceptate	GLAOU/SEP/TAIT
Glucerna	GLAOU/SER/NA
glucide	GLAOU/SAO*ID
glucinium	GLAOU/SIN/YUM
gluciphore	GLAOUS/FOER
glucoamylase	GLAOUK/AM/LAIS
glucoascorbic	GLAOUK/AS/KORB/IK

glucocerebroside	GLAOUK/SER/BRO/SAOID
glucocorticoid	GLAOUK/KORT/KOID
glucocorticotrophic	GLAOUK/KORT/KO/TROEFK
glucocyamine	GLAOUK/SAOI/MAOEN
glucofuranose	GLAOUK/FAOUR/NOES
glucogenesis	GLAOUK/JEN/SIS
glucogenic	GLAOUK/JEN/IK
glucohemia	GLAOUK/HAOEM/YA
glucoinvertase	GLAOUK/IN/VER/TAIS
glucokinase	GLAOUK/KAOI/NAIS
glucokinetic	GLAOUK/KI/NET/IK
glucolipid	GLAOUK/LIP/ID
glucolysis	GLAOU/KOL/SIS
glucolytic	GLAOUK/LIT/IK
gluconate	GLAOUK/NAIT
gluconeogenesis	GLAOUK/NAOE/JEN/SIS
gluconeogenetic	GLAOUK/NAOE/JE/NET/IK
gluconic	GLAOU/KON/IK
gluconolactonase	GLAOU/KON/LAKT/NAIS
glucopenia	GLAOUK/PAOEN/YA
glucophore	GLAOUK/FOER
glucoprotein	GLAOUK/PRO/TAOEN
glucoproteinase	GLAOUK/PRO/TAOEN/AIS
glucopyranose	GLAOUK/PIR/NOES
	GLAOUK/PAOIR/NOES
glucoregulation	GLAOUK/REG/LAIGS
glucosamine	GLAOUK/SA/MAOEN
	GLAOUK/SAM/AOEN
glucosan	GLAOUK/SAN
glucose	GLAOU/KOES
glucosephosphate	GLAOU/KOES/FOS/FAIT
glucosidase	GLAOU/KOES/DAIS
	GLAOUK/SAOID/AIS
glucoside	GLAOUK/SAOID
glucosidolytic	GLAOUK/SAOID/LIT/IK
glucosin	GLAOUK/SIN
glucosone	GLAOUK/SOEN
glucosulfone	GLAOUK/SUL/FOEN
glucosum	GLAOU/KOE/SUM
glucosuria	GLAOUK/SAOUR/YA
glucosyl	GLAOUK/SIL
glucosyltransferase	GLAOUK/SIL/TRA*NS/FRAIS
Glucotrol	GLAOUK/TROEL
	GLAOUK/TROL
glucur-	GLAOUK/R-
	GLAOU/KAOU/R-
	GLAOUK/YAOU/R-
	GLAOUK/YU/R-
glucuronate	GLAOU/KAOUR/NAIT
glucurone	GLAOUK/ROEN
glucuronic	GLAOUK/RON/IK
glucuronidase	GLAOUK/RON/DAIS
glucuronide	GLAOU/KAOUR/NAOID
glucuronolactone	GLAOUK/ROEN/LAK/TOEN
glucuronose	GLAOU/KAOUR/NOES
glucuronosyltransferase	GLAOUK/RON/SIL/TRA*NS/
	FRAIS
glue	GLAOU
glue-sniffing	GLAOU/H-F/SNIF/-G
Gluge	GLAOU/JAOE
	GLAOU/GE
	GLAOUG
glutaea	GLAOU/TAE/YA
	(not GLAOUT/YA; see glutea)
glutaeae	GLAOU/TAE/YAE
	(not GLAOUT/YAE; see gluteae)
glutaei	GLAOU/TAE/YAOI
	(not GLAOUT/YAOI; see glutei)
glutaeofemorales	GLAOUT/YO/FAOEM/RAI/LAOEZ
	GLAOUT/YO/FEM/RAI/LAOEZ
glutamate	GLAOUT/MAIT
glutamic	GLAOU/TAM/IK
glutamic-aspartic transaminase	GLAOU/TAM/IK/AS/PART/IK/ TRA*NS/AM/NAIS
glutamic-oxaloacetic transaminase	GLAOU/TAM/IK/OX/LO/AI/SET/ IK/TRA*NS/AM/NAIS
	GLAOU/TAM/IK/OX/LO/AI/SAOET/ IK/TRA*NS/AM/NAIS
glutamic-pyruvic transaminase	GLAOU/TAM/IK/PAOI/ RAOUVK/TRA*NS/AM/NAIS
glutaminase	GLAOU/TAM/NAIS
glutamine	GLAOUT/MAOEN
	GLAOU/TAM/MIN
	GLAOU/TAM/MIN
glutaminic	GLAOU/TAM/MIN/IK
glutaminyl	GLAOU/TAM/NIL
glutamoyl	GLAOUT/MOIL
glutamyl	GLAOUT/MIL
	GLAOU/TAM/IL

glutamyltransferase	GLAOUT/MIL/TRA*NS/FRAIS	glycocalyx	GLAOIK/KAL/IX
	GLAOU/TAM/IL/TRA*NS/FRAIS		GLAOIK/KAI/L*IX
glutaral	GLAOUT/RAL		GLAOIK/KAL/*IX
glutaraldehyde	GLAOUT/RALD/HAOID	glycocholate	GLAOIK/KOE/LAIT
glutathione	GLAOUT/THAOI/OEN		GLAOIK/KOL/AIT
	GLAOUT/THAOI/YOEN	glycocholic	GLAOIK/KOEL/IK
glutathionemia	GLAOUT/THAOI/NAOEM/YA		GLAOIK/KOL/IK
glutathionuria	GLAOUT/THAOI/NAOUR/YA	glycocin	GLAOIK/SIN
glute(o)-	GLAOUT/Y(O)	glycoclastic	GLAOIK/KLA*S/IK
glutea	GLAOUT/YA	glycocoll	GLAOIK/KOL
gluteae	GLAOUT/YAE	glycocorticoid	GLAOIK/KORT/KOID
gluteal	GLAOUT/YAL	glycocyaminase	GLAOIK/SAOI/AM/NAIS
glutei	GLAOUT/YAOI	glycocyamine	GLAOIK/SAOI/MAOEN
glutelin	GLAOUT/LIN		GLAOIK/SAOI/MIN
gluten	GLAOUT/-N	glycogelatin	GLAOIK/JEL/TIN
	GLAOU/TEN	glycogen	GLAOIK/JEN
glutenin	GLAOUT/NIN	glycogenase	GLAOIK/JEN/AIS
gluteofascial	GLAOUT/YO/FARBL		GLAOIK/JE/NAIS
gluteofemoral	GLAOUT/YO/FEM/RAL	glycogenesis	GLAOIK/JEN/SIS
gluteoinguinal	GLAOUT/YO/ING/WINL	glycogenetic	GLAOIK/JE/NET/IK
gluteorum	GLAOUT/YOR/UM	glycogenetica	GLAOIK/JE/NET/KA
	GLAOUT/YOER/UM	glycogenic	GLAOIK/JEN/IK
gluteotuberosal	GLAOUT/YO/TAOUB/ROE/SAL	glycogenica	GLAOIK/JEN/KA
glutethimide	GLAOU/T*ET/MAOID	glycogenolysis	GLAOIK/JEN/OL/SIS
gluteus	GLAOUT/YUS		GLAOIK/JE/NOL/SIS
glutin	GLAOU/TIN	glycogenolytic	GLAOIK/JEN/LIT/IK
glutinoid	GLAOUT/NOID	glycogenosis	GLAOIK/JE/NOE/SIS
glutinous	GLAOUT/NOUS	glycogenous	GLAOI/KOJ/NOUS
glutitis	GLAOU/TAOITS	glycogeusia	GLAOIK/GAOUZ/YA
Glutofac	GLAOUT/FAK		GLAOIK/GAOUS/YA
glutolin	GLAOUT/LIN	glycoglycinuria	GLAOIK/GLAOIS/NAOUR/YA
glutoscope	GLAOUT/SKOEP	glycohemia	GLAOIK/HAOEM/YA
glutose	GLAOU/TOES	glycohemoglobin	GLAOIK/HAOEM/GLOE/BIN
glyburide	GLAOI/BAOU/RAOID	glycohistechia	GLAOIK/HIS/TEK/YA
glyc(o)-	GLAOIK	glycoid	GLAOI/KOID
	GLAOI/K(O)	glycol	GLAOI/KOL
	GLAOI/S-	glycolaldehyde	GLAOI/KOL/ALD/HAOID
	GLIS	glycolaldehydetransferase	GLAOI/KOL/ALD/HAOID/TRA*NS/
glycal	GLAOI/KAL		FRAIS
glycan	GLAOI/KAN	glycolate	GLAOIK/LAIT
glycanohydrolase	GLAOI/KAN/HAOI/DRO/LAIS	glycoleucine	GLAOIK/LAOU/SIN
glycase	GLAOI/KAIS	glycolic	GLAOI/KOL/IK
glycate	GLAOI/KAIT	glycolipid	GLAOIK/LIP/ID
glycation	GLAOI/KAIGS	glycolyl	GLAOIK/LIL
glycemia	GLAOI/SAOEM/YA	glycolylurea	GLAOIK/LIL/YAOU/RAOE/YA
glycemic	GLAOI/SAOEM/IK	glycolysis	GLAOI/KOL/SIS
glycemin	GLAOIS/MIN	glycolytic	GLAOIK/LIT/IK
glycer(o)-	GLIS/R(O)-	glycometabolic	GLAOIK/MET/BOL/IK
glyceraldehyde	GLIS/RALD/HAOID	glycometabolism	GLAOIK/ME/TAB/LIFM
glycerate	GLIS/RAIT	glycone	GLAOI/KOEN
glyceric	GLAOI/SER/IK	glyconeogenesis	GLAOIK/NAOE/JEN/SIS
	GLI/SER/IK	glyconic	GLAOI/KON/IK
	GLIS/RIK	glyconucleoprotein	GLAOIK/NAOUK/LO/PRO/TAOEN
glyceridase	GLIS/RI/DAIS	glycopenia	GLAOIK/PAOEN/YA
	GLI/SER/DAIS	glycopeptide	GLAOIK/PEP/TAOID
glyceride	GLIS/RAOID	glycopexic	GLAOIK/PEX/IK
glycerin	GLIS/RIN	glycopexis	GLAOIK/PEK/SIS
glycerinated	GLIS/RI/NAIT/-D	Glycophagus	GLAOI/KOF/GUS
	GLIS/RIN/AIT/-D	glycophenol	GLAOIK/FAOE/NOL
glycerinum	GLIS/RAOI/NUM	glycophilia	GLAOIK/FIL/YA
glycerite	GLIS/RAOIT	glycophorin	GLAOIK/FOER/RIN
glyceritum	GLIS/RAOI/TUM	glycopolyuria	GLAOIK/POL/YAOUR/YA
glycerogel	GLIS/RO/JEL	glycoprival	GLAOIK/PRAOIVL
glycerogelatin	GLIS/RO/JEL/TIN	glycoprotein	GLAOIK/PRO/TAOEN
glyceroketone	GLIS/RO/KAOE/TOEN	glycoptyalism	GLAOIK/TAOI/LIFM
glycerokinase	GLIS/RO/KAOI/NAIS	glycopyrrolate	GLAOIK/PIR/LAIT
glycerol	GLIS/ROL	glycoregulation	GLAOIK/REG/LAIGS
glycerolize	GLIS/ROL/AOIZ	glycoregulatory	GLAOIK/PIR/ROEN/YUM
	GLIS/RO/LAOIZ	glycorrhachia	GLAOIK/RAIK/YA
glycerolphosphate	GLIS/ROL/FOS/FAIT	glycorrhea	GLAOIK/RAOE/YA
glycerone	GLIS/ROEN	glycosamine	GLAOIK/SAM/MIN
glycerophilic	GLIS/RO/FIL/IK	glycosaminoglycan	GLAOI/KOES/AM/NO/GLAOI/KAN
glycerophosphatase	GLIS/RO/FOS/FA/TAIS	glycosaminolipid	GLAOI/KOES/AM/NO/LIP/ID
glycerophosphate	GLIS/RO/FOS/FAIT	glycosecretory	GLAOIK/SE/KRAOET/RI
glycerophosphocholine	GLIS/RO/FOS/FO/KOE/LAOEN	glycosemia	GLAOIK/SAOEM/YA
glycerophosphoric	GLIS/RO/FOS/FOR/IK	glycosene	GLAOIK/SAOEN
glycerophosphorylcholine	GLIS/RO/FOS/FOR/IL/KOE/	glycosialia	GLAOIK/SAOI/AIL/YA
	LAOEN		GLAOIK/SAOI/AL/YA
glycerose	GLIS/ROES	glycosialorrhea	GLAOIK/SAOI/LO/RAOE/YA
glyceryl	GLIS/RIL	glycosidase	GLAOI/KOES/DAIS
glycidol	GLIS/DOL	glycoside	GLAOIK/SAOID
glycinate	GLIS/NAIT	glycosidic	GLAOIK/SID/IK
	GLAOIS/NAIT	glycosometer	GLAOIK/SOM/TER
glycine	GLAOI/SAOEN	glycosphingolipid	GLAOIK/SFING/LIP/ID
glycinemia	GLAOIS/NAOEM/YA	glycostatic	GLAOIK/STAT/IK
glycinin	GLIS/NIN	glycosuria	GLAOIK/SAOUR/YA
glycinuria	GLAOIS/NAOUR/YA	glycosuric	GLAOIK/SAOUR/IK
glycobiarsol	GLAOIK/B*I/AR/SOL	glycosyl	GLAOIK/SIL
glycocalix	GLAOIK/KAI/LIX	glycosylated	GLAOI/KOES/LAIT/-D

180

glycosylation	GLAOIK/SIL/AIT/-D	goitrogen	GOI/TRO/JEN
	GLAOIK/SIL/AIGS	goitrogenic	GOI/TRO/JEN/IK
	GLAOI/KOES/LAIGS	goitrogenicity	GOI/TRO/JE/NIS/TI
glycosyltransferase	GLAOIK/SIL/TRA*NS/FRAIS	goitrogenous	GOI/TROJ/NOUS
glycotaxis	GLAOIK/TAK/SIS	goitrous	GOI/TROUS
glycotrophic	GLAOIK/TROFK	gold	GOELD
glycotropic	GLAOIK/TROP/IK		GOLD
glycuresis	GLAOIK/RAOE/SIS		
	GLAOI/KAOU/RAOE/SIS	Goldberg	GOELD/BERG
glycuronate	GLAOI/KAOUR/NAIT	Goldberger	GOELD/BERG/ER
glycuronic	GLAOIK/RON/IK	Goldblatt	GOELD/BLAT
	GLAOI/KAOU/RON/IK	Goldflam	GOELD/FLAM
glycuronidase	GLAOIK/RON/DAIS	Goldman	GOELD/MAN
	GLAOI/KAOU/RON/DAIS	Goldmann	GOELD/MA*N
glycuronide	GLAOI/KAOUR/NAOID	Goldscheider	GOELD/SHAOID/ER
glycuronose	GLAOI/KAOUR/NOES	Goldstein	GOELD/STAOEN
glycuronuria	GLAOIK/RO/NAOUR/YA		GOELD/STAOIN
	GLAOI/KAOUR/NAOUR/YA	Goldthwait	GOELD/TH-/WAIT
glycyclamide	GLAOI/SAOI/KLA/MAOID		GOELD/TWAIT
glycyl	GLAOI/SIL		GOELD/THAIT
	GLIS/IL	golf	GOL/-F
	GLIS/SIL	Golgi	GOL/JAOE
Glycyphagus	GLAOI/SIF/GUS	Golgi-Mazzoni	GOL/JAOE/H-F/MA/ZOE/NAOE
glycyrrhiza	GLIS/RAOI/ZA		GOL/JAOE/H-F/MAT/ZOE/NAOE
glycyrrhizic	GLIS/RAOIZ/IK	Golgi-Rezzonico	GOL/JAOE/H-F/RE/ZON/KOE
glycyrrhizin	GLIS/RAOI/ZIN	golgiokinesis	GOL/JO/KI/NAOE/SIS
glyoxal	GLAOI/OK/SAL	golgiosome	GOL/JO/SOEM
glyoxalase	GLAOI/OX/LAIS	Goll	GOL
glyoxaline	GLAOI/OX/LIN	Goltz	GOELTS
	GLAOI/OX/LAOEN		GOLTS
Gly-Oxide	GLAOI/OK/SAOID	GoLYTELY	GOE/LAOIT/LI
	GLAOI/OX/AOID	Gombault	GOM/BOE
glyoxylate	GLAOI/OX/LAIT	gomenol	GOEM/NOL
glyoxylic	GLAOI/OK/SIL/IK	gomitoli	GOE/MIT/LAOI
glysobuzole	GLAOIS/BAOU/ZOEL		GOM/IT/LAOE
gm	G*M	Gomori	GOE/MOR/RAOE
Gmelin	MAI/LIN	gomphiasis	GOM/FAOI/SIS
	MAOE/LIN	gomphosis	GOM/FOE/SIS
G-myticin	G-RBGS/MAOIT/SIN	gonad	GOE/NAD
gnarled	NARL/-D	gonad(o)-	GON/D(O)
gnashing	NARB/-G		GOE/NAD
gnat	NAT		GOE/NA/D-
gnath(o)-	NA*T	gonadal	GOE/NAD/DAL
	NA*/TH(O)		GON/DAL
gnathalgia	NA*T/AL/JA	gonadectomize	GOE/NAD/EKT/MAOIZ
-gnathia	NA*IT/YA		GON/DEKT/MAOIZ
	NA*T/YA	gonadectomy	GOE/NAD/EKT/M*I
gnathic	NA*T/IK		GON/DEKT/M*I
gnathion	NA*T/YON	gonadial	GOE/NAD/YAL
gnathitis	NA*T/AOITS	gonadoblastoma	GON/DO/BLAS/TOE/MA
gnathocephalus	NA*T/SEF/LUS	gonadocrin	GOE/NAD/KRIN
gnathodynamics	NA*T/DAOI/NAM/IK/-S	gonadogenesis	GON/DO/JEN/SIS
gnathodynamometer	NA*T/DAOIN/MOM/TER	gonadoinhibitory	GON/DO/IN/HIB/TOIR
gnathodynia	NA*T/DIN/YA	gonadokinetic	GON/DO/KI/NET/IK
gnathography	NA*THOG/FI	gonadoliberin	GOE/NAD/LIB/RIN
gnathologic	NA*T/LOJ/IK	gonadopathy	GON/DOP/TH*I
gnathological	NA*T/LOJ/KAL	gonadopause	GOE/NAD/PAUZ
gnathology	NA*THOLG	gonadorelin	GOE/NAD/REL/LIN
	NA*T/OLG		GON/DO/REL/LIN
gnathopalatoschisis	NA*T/PAL/TOS/KI/SIS	gonadotherapy	GON/DO/THER/PI
gnathoplasty	NA*T/PLAS/TI	gonadotrope	GOE/NAD/TROEP
gnathoschisis	NA*THOS/KI/SIS		GON/DO/TROEP
	NA*T/OS/KI/SIS	gonadotroph	GOE/NAD/TROEF
gnathostatics	NA*T/STAT/IK/-S		GON/DO/TROEF
Gnathostoma	NA*THO*S/MA	gonadotrophic	GOE/NAD/TROEFK
	NA*T/O*S/MA		GON/DO/TROEFK
gnathostomatics	NA*T/STOE/MAT/IK/-S	gonadotrophin	GOE/NAD/TROEFN
gnathostomiasis	NA*T/STOE/MAOI/SIS		GON/DO/TROEFN
gnoscopine	NOS/KO/PAOEN	gonadotropic	GOE/NAD/TROEP/IK
gnosia	NOEZ/YA		GON/DO/TROEP/IK
	NOES/YA	gonadotropin	GOE/NAD/TROE/PIN
gnosis	NOE/SIS		GON/DO/TROE/PIN
gnotobiology	NOET/BAO*I/OLG	gonaduct	GON/DUKT
gnotobiota	NOET/BAO*I/YOE/TA	gonagra	GON/AG/RA
gnotobiote	NOET/BAO*I/YOET	gonalgia	GOE/NAL/JA
	NOET/BAO*I/OET	gonarthritis	GON/AR/THRAOITS
gnotobiotic	NOET/BAO*I/OT/IK	gonarthrocace	GON/AR/THROK/SAOE
gnotobiotics	NOET/BAO*I/OT/IK/-S	gonarthromeningitis	GON/AR/THRO/MEN/JAOITS
gnotophoresis	NOET/FRAOE/SIS	gonarthrosis	GON/AR/THROE/SIS
gnotophoric	NOET/FOER/IK	gonarthrotomy	GON/AR/THROT/M*I
goal	GOEL	gonatocele	GOE/NAT/SAO*EL
goblet	GOB/LET	gonecyst	GON/S*IS
Godelier	GOE/DAIL/YAI	gonecystic	GON/S*IS/IK
	GOE/DEL/YAI	gonecystis	GON/SIS/TIS
godovnik	GOE/DOV/NIK	gonecystitis	GON/SIS/TAOITS
	GO/DOV/NIK	gonecystolith	GON/S*IS/L*IT
goggle	GOG/-L	gonecystopyosis	GON/S*IS/PAOI/YOE/SIS
goiter	GOIT/ER	goneitis	GON/YAOITS
	GOI/TER	gonepoiesis	GON/POI/SIS
		gonepoietic	GON/POIT/IK

Gongylonema	GON/JIL/NAOE/MA	Gottron	GOT/TRON
	GON/JI/LO/NAOE/MA	Gottstein	GOT/STAOIN
gongylonemiasis	GON/JIL/NAOE/MAOI/SIS		GOT/STAOEN
	GON/JI/LO/NAOE/MAOI/SIS	gouge	GOUJ
goni(o)-	GOEN/Y(O)	Gould	GAOULD
gonia	GOEN/YA	Gouley	GAOU/LAOE
gonial	GOEN/YAL	gout	GOUT
goniocraniometry	GOEN/YO/KRAIN/YOM/TRI	gouty	GOUT/TI
goniodysgenesis	GOEN/YO/DIS/JEN/SIS		GOU/TI
gonioma	GOEN/YOE/MA		
goniometer	GOEN/YOM/TER	Gowers	GOU/ERS
gonion	GOEN/YON	gowersi	GOU/ER/SAOI
goniophotography	GOEN/YO/FOE/TOG/FI		GOU/ERS/SAOI
	GOEN/YO/FRAF/FI	Graaf	GRAF
goniopuncture	GOEN/YO/PUNG/KHUR	graafian	GRAF/YAN
gonioscope	GOEN/YO/SKOEP	gracile	GRAS/SIL
gonioscopy	GOEN/YOS/KPI	gracilis	GRAS/LIS
goniospasis	GOEN/YOS/PA/SIS		GRA/SIL/LIS
goniosynechia	GOEN/YO/SI/NEK/YA	gradatim	GRAI/DAI/TIM
goniotomy	GOEN/YOT/M*I	grade	GRAID
gonitis	GOE/NAOITS	Gradenigo	GRAD/NAOE/GOE
-gonium	GOEN/YUM	gradient	GRAID/YENT
gono-	GON	graduate	GRAJ/WAIT
gonoblennorrhea	GON/BLEN/RAOE/YA		GRAD/YAIT
gonocele	GON/SAO*EL	graduated	GRAJ/WAIT/-D
gonochorism	GON/OK/RIFM		GRAD/YAIT/-D
	GO/NOK/RIFM	Grafco	GRAF/KOE
gonochorismus	GON/OK/RIZ/MUS	Graefe	GRAI/FAOE
gonocide	GON/SAO*ID	Grafenberg	GRAFN/BERG
gonococcal	GON/KOK/KAL		GRAF/EN/BERG
gonococcemia	GON/KOK/SAOEM/YA	graft	GRAFT
gonococci	GON/KOK/SAOI	grafting	GRAFT/-G
gonococcic	GON/KOK/SIK	Graham	GRA/HAM
gonococcicide	GON/KOX/SAOID		GRAI/HAM
gonococcide	GON/KOK/SAO*ID	Grahamella	GRAI/MEL/LA
gonococcus	GON/KOK/KUS		GRAM/EL/LA
gonocyte	GON/SAO*IT		GRAM/MEL/LA
gonohemia	GON/HAOEM/YA	grahamellosis	GRAI/AM/LOE/SIS
gonomery	GON/OM/RI		GRAI/HAM/LOE/SIS
	GO/NOM/RI		GRAM/LOE/SIS
gononephrotome	GON/NEF/RO/TOEM	Graham Little	GRA/HAM/LIT/-L
gono-opsonin	GON/OPS/NIN		GRAI/HAM/LIT/-L
gonophage	GON/FAIJ	Graham Steell	GRA/HAM/STAOEL
gonophore	GON/FOER		GRAI/HAM/STAOEL
gonophorus	GOE/NOF/RUS	grain	GRAIN
gonorrhea	GON/RAOE/YA	grainage	GRAIN/AJ
gonorrheal	GON/RAOEL	gram	GRAM
	GON/RAOE/YAL	-gram	GRAM
gonosome	GON/SOEM	Gram's stain	GRA*M/AOES/STAIN
gonotome	GON/TOEM		K-P/GRAM/AOES/STAIN
gonotoxemia	GON/TOK/SAOEM/YA	gram-centimeter	GRAM/SENT/MAOET/ER
gonotoxin	GON/TOK/SIN	gram-equivalent	GRAM/E/KWIV/LENT
gonotrophic	GON/TROFK	gramicidin	GRAM/SAOI/DIN
	GON/TROEFK	gram-ion	GRAM/AOIN
Gonyaulax catanella	GON/YAU/LAX/KAT/NEL/LA	gram-meter	GRAM/MAOET/ER
gonycampsis	GON/KAFRP/SIS	gram-molecule	GRAM/MOL/KAOUL
	GON/KAM/SIS	Gram-negative	GRAM/NEG/TIV
gonycrotesis	GON/KROE/TAOE/SIS	Gram-positive	GRAM/POZ/TIV
gonyectyposis	GON/YEKT/POE/SIS	grana	GRAI/NA
gonyocele	GON/YO/SAO*EL	granatum	GRA/NAI/TUM
gonyoncus	GON/YON/KUS	granddaughter	GRAND/DAUT/ER
Goodell	GAOD/EL	grandiose	GRAND/YOES
	GAOD/DEL	grandiosity	GRAND/YOS/TI
Goodenough Draw-a-Person Test		grandis	GRAN/DIS
	GAOD/NUF/DRAU/A/PERN/T*ES	grand mal	GRAN/MAL
Goodpasture	GAOD/PAS/KHUR		GRAUN/MAL
Goormaghtigh	GAOR/MAG/TIG	Grandry	GRAN/DRI
	GAOR/MA/TIG		GRAUN/DRI
goose bumps	GAOS/BUFRP/-S	Granger	K-P/GRAIN/JER
goose flesh	GAOS/FLERB		K-P/GRAN/JER
Gordius	GORD/YUS	granoplasm	GRAN/PLAFM
Gordon	GOR/DON	granul-	GRAN/L-
gorge	GORJ		GRAN/YAOU/L-
gorget	GOR/JET		GRAN/YU/L-
Gorham	GOR/HAM	granula	GRAN/LA
Gorlin	GOR/LIN	granular	GRAN/LAR
Gorman	GOR/MAN	granulase	GRAN/LAIS
Gosselin	GOS/LA	granulata	GRAN/LAI/TA
	GOSZ/LA	granulate	GRAN/LAIT
	GOS/LIN	granulatio	GRAN/LAI/SHOE
	GOSZ/LIN		GRAN/LAIRB/YOE
gossypol	GOS/POL	granulation	GRAN/LAIGS
	GOSZ/POL	granulationes	GRAN/LAI/SHOE/NAOEZ
gossypose	GOS/POES		GRAN/LAIRB/YOE/NAOEZ
	GOSZ/POES	granule	GRAN/YAOUL
Gothic	GO*T/IK	Granulex	GRAN/LEX
Gothlin	G*ET/LIN	granuliform	GRAN/LI/FORM
	GET/LIN	granulo-	GRAN/LO
			GRAN/YAOU/LO
Gottlieb	GOT/LAOEB		GRAN/YU/LO

granuloadipose	GRAN/LO/AD/POES	gravidocardiac	GRAV/DO/KARD/YAK
granuloblast	GRAN/LO/BLA*S	gravidopuerperal	GRAV/DO/PAOURP/RAL
granuloblastosis	GRAN/LO/BLAS/TOE/SIS		GRAV/DO/PAOU/ERP/RAL
granulocorpuscle	GRAN/LO/KOR/PUS/-L	gravimeter	GRA/VIM/TER
granulocyte	GRAN/LO/SAO*IT	gravimetric	GRAV/MET/RIK
granulocytic	GRAN/LO/SIT/IK	gravior	GRAIV/YOR
granulocytopathy	GRAN/LO/SAOI/TOP/TH*I	gravireceptor	GRAV/RE/SEP/TOR
granulocytopenia	GRAN/LO/SAOIT/PAOEN/YA	gravis	GRAI/VIS
granulocytopoiesis	GRAN/LO/SAOIT/POI/SIS		GRAV/VIS
granulocytopoietic	GRAN/LO/SAOIT/POIT/IK	gravistatic	GRAV/STAT/IK
granulocytosis	GRAN/LO/SAOI/TOE/SIS	gravitation	GRAV/TAIGS
granulofatty	GRAN/LO/FAT/TI	gravitational	GRAV/TAIGS/NAL
granuloma	GRAN/LOE/MA	gravitometer	GRAV/TOM/TER
granulomata	GRAN/LOEM/TA	gravity	GRAV/TI
granulomatis	GRAN/LOEM/TIS	Grawitz	GRA/VITS
granulomatosa	GRAN/LOEM/TOE/SA		GRAU/VITS
granulomatosis	GRAN/LOEM/TOE/SIS	gray	GRAI
granulomatous	GRAN/LOEM/TOUS	grease	GRAES
granulomere	GRAN/LO/MAOER	great	GRAET
granulopenia	GRAN/LO/PAOEN/YA	Greeff	GRAIF
granuloplasm	GRAN/LO/PLAFM	green	GRAOEN
granuloplastic	GRAN/LO/PLA*S/IK	Greene	GRAO*EN
granulopoiesis	GRAN/LO/POI/SIS	Greenhow	GRAOEN/HOU
granulopoietic	GRAN/LO/POIT/IK	greenstick	GRAOEN/ST*IK
granulopotent	GRAN/LO/POE/TENT	greffotome	GREF/TOEM
granulosa	GRAN/LOE/SA	gregaloid	GREG/LOID
granulose	GRAN/LOES	Gregarina	GREG/RAOI/NA
granulosis	GRAN/LOE/SIS	gregarine	GREG/RAOEN
granulosity	GRAN/LOS/TI		GREG/RIN
granulosus	GRAN/LOE/SUS	Gregarinida	GREG/RAOIN/DA
granulovacuolar	GRAN/LO/VAK/YOE/LAR	gregarinosis	GREG/RI/NOE/SIS
granulovascular	GRAN/LO/VAS/KLAR	Gregory	GREG/RI
granum	GRAI/NUM	Grenet	GREN/ET
	GRAIN/UM	gression	GREGS
grape	GRAIP	Greville	GRE/VIL
graph	GRAF		GRAI/VIL
-graph	GRAF	grey	GRA*I
graph(o)-	GRAF		(not GRAI; see gray)
	GRA/F(O)	grid	GRID
graphanesthesia	GRAF/ANS/THAOEZ/YA	grief	GRAOEF
graphesthesia	GRAF/ES/THAOEZ/YA	Griesinger	GRAOE/ZING/ER
-graphia	GRAIF/YA		GRAOE/SING/ER
	GRAF/YA	Griffith	GRIF/F*IT
graphic	GRAFK	Grifulvin	GRAOI/FUL/VIN
graphica	GRAF/KA		GRI/FUL/VIN
graphite	GRAF/AOIT	Grignard	GRAOEN/YAR
graphitosis	GRAF/TOE/SIS		GRIN/YAR
graphocatharsis	GRAF/KA/THAR/SIS	Grindelia	GRIN/DAOEL/YA
graphokinesthesia	GRAF/KINS/THAOEZ/YA	grinding	GRAOIND/-G
graphokinesthetic	GRAF/KINS/THET/IK	grinding-in	GRAOIND/-G/H-F/N-
graphology	GRA/FOLG	grip	GRIP
graphomania	GRAF/MAIN/YA	grippal	GRIP/PAL
graphomotor	GRAF/MOE/TOR	grippe	GR*IP
graphopathology	GRAF/PA/THOLG		(not GRIP; see grip)
graphophobia	GRAF/FOEB/YA	Grisactin	GRIS/AK/TIN
graphorrhea	GRAF/RAOE/YA		GRIZ/AK/TIN
graphoscope	GRAF/SKOEP	Grisactin Ultra	GRIS/AK/TIN/UL/TRA
graphospasm	GRAF/SPAFM		GRIZ/AK/TIN/UL/TRA
-graphy	(v)G/FI	grisea	GRIS/YA
	(v)G/RA/FI	griseae	GRIS/YAE
Graser	GRAIS/ER	griseofulvin	GRIS/YO/FUL/VIN
Grashey	GRARB/SHAOE	griseomycin	GRIS/YO/MAOI/SIN
	GRA/SHAOE	griseus	GRIS/YUS
grasp	GRAS/-P	Grisolle	GRAOE/ZOL
grass	GRASZ		GRAOE/SOL
Grasset	GRA/SAI		GRI/SOL
	GRA/SET	Gris-PEG	GRIS/PEG
	GRAS/SET	gristle	GRIS/-L
gratification	GRAT/FI/KAIGS	Gritti	GRAOE/TAOE
grating	GRAIT/-G		GRAOET/TAOE
Gratiolet	GRA/TAOE/LAI	groan	GROEN
grattage	GRA/TAJ	Grocco	GROK/KOE
grave	GRAIV	grog	GROG
	GRA/VAOE	groin	GROIN
gravel	GRAVL	Gronblad	GREN/BLAD
Graves	GRAIVS		GRON/BLAD
	GRAIVZ	groove	GRAOV
gravid	GRAV/ID	gross	GROESZ
	GRA/VID	Gross	K-P/GROESZ
	GRAVD	group	GRAOUP
gravid-	GRAV/D-		GROUP
gravida	GRAV/DA	grouping	GRAOUP/-G
gravidarum	GRAV/DAIR/UM	group-specific	GRAOUP/H-F/SPEFK
	GRAV/DAR/UM	group-transfer	GRAOUP/H-F/TR-FR
	GRAV/DAI/RUM		GRAOUP/H-F/TRA*NS/FER
gravidic	GRA/VID/IK	Grove	K-P/GROEV
gravidism	GRAV/DIFM	Grover	GROEVR
graviditas	GRA/VID/TAS	grown	GROUN
gravidity	GRA/VID/TI	growth	GRO*ET

grub	GRO*UT	Gull	K-P/GUL
	GRUB	gullet	GUL/ET
Gruber	GRAOUB/ER	Gullstrand	GUL/STRAND
gruel	GRAOUL	gulonic	GAOU/LON/IK
gruff	GRUF	gulonolactone	GAOU/LON/LAK/TOEN
gruffs	GRUF/-S		GAOUL/NO/LAK/TOEN
	GRUFS	gulose	GAOU/LOES
grumose	GRAOU/MOES	gum	GUM
grumous	GRAOUM/OUS	gumboil	GUM/BOIL
	GRAOU/MOUS	gumma	GUM/MA
gryochrome	GRAOI/KROEM	gummata	GUM/TA
	GRAOI/YO/KROEM	gummate	GUM/AIT
gryphosis	GRI/FOE/SIS		GUM/MAIT
gryposis	GRI/POE/SIS	gummatous	GUM/TOUS
g-tolerance	G*/TOL/RANS	gummi	GUM/MAOI
g-tolerance	G*/H-F/TOL/RANS	gummy	GUM/M*I
gua-	GAU	Gumprecht	GUM/PREKT
	(because of machine limitation)	Gunn	G*UN
		Gunning	G*UN/-G
guaiac	GAOI/AK	Gunz	GINTS
guaiacin	GAOI/SIN		GINZ
guaiacol	GAOI/KOL	Gunzberg	GINTS/BERG
Guaifed	GAOI/FED	gurgulio	GUR/GAOUL/YOE
Guaifed-PD	GAOI/FED/P-RBGS/D*RBGS	gurjun	GUR/JUN
guaifenesin	GAOI/FEN/SIN	gurney	GUR/NAOE
Guiatussin	GAOI/TUS/SIN	Gussenbauer	GAOUS/EN/BOU/ER
guanabenz	GAUN/BENZ		GAOUS/EN/BOUR
guanacline	GAUN/KLAOEN	gust-	GUS/T-
guanadrel	GAUN/DREL		G*US
guanase	GAUN/AIS	Gustase	GUS/TAIS
	GAU/NAIS	Gustase Plus	GUS/TAIS/PLUS
guanethidine	GAUN/*ET/DAOEN	gustation	GUS/TAIGS
guanidine	GAUN/DAOEN	gustatism	G*US/TIFM
	GAUN/DIN	gustatoria	G*US/TOR/YA
guanidinemia	GAUN/DIN/AOEM/YA		G*US/TOER/YA
guanidinoacetate	GAUN/DIN/AS/TAIT	gustatorius	G*US/TOR/YUS
	GAUN/DAOEN/AS/TAIT		G*US/TOER/YUS
guanine	GAU/NAOEN	gustatory	G*US/TOIR
	GAU/NIN	gustin	GUS/TIN
guanochlor	GAUN/KLOR	gustometer	GUS/TOM/TER
guanophore	GAUN/FOER	gustometry	GUS/TOM/TRI
guanosine	GAUN/SAOEN	gut	GUT
	GAUN/SIN	Guthrie	G*UT/RAOE
guanoxan	GAUN/OK/SAN	gutta	GUT/TA
guanyl	GAU/NIL	gutta-percha	GUT/TA/PER/KHA
	GAUN/IL	guttae	GUT/TAE
guanylate	GAUN/LAIT	guttata	GUT/TAI/TA
guanylic	GAU/NIL/IK		GAOU/TAI/TA
	GAUN/IL/IK		GAOU/TA/TA
guanyloribonuclease	GAUN/LO/RAOIB/NAOUK/LAIS	guttate	GUT/TAIT
guanylyl	GAUN/LIL	guttatim	GUT/TAI/TIM
guard	GARD	guttation	GUT/TAIGS
guarding	GARD/-G	guttering	GUT/ER/-G
Guarnieri	GARN/YER/RAOE	guttoris	GUT/TOR/RIS
gubernacular	GAOUB/NAK/LAR		GUT/TOER/RIS
	GAOUB/ER/NAK/LAR	guttur	GUT/TUR
	GAOU/BER/NAK/LAR	guttural	GUT/RAL
gubernaculum	GAOUB/NAK/LUM	gutturophony	GUT/ROF/N*I
	GAOUB/ER/NAK/LUM	gutturotetany	GUT/RO/TET/N*I
	GAOU/BER/NAK/LUM	Gutzeit	GAOUT/ZAOET
Gubler	GAOUB/LER		GAOUT/ZAOIT
	GUB/LER		GUT/ZAOET
Gudden	GAOUD/-N		GUT/ZAOIT
	GAOU/DEN	Guyon	GAOE/YON
	GUD/-N	Gwathmey	GA*T/MAOE
guddeni	GAOUD/NAOI		G-/WA*T/MAOE
	GAOU/DEN/NAOI	gymn(o)-	JIM/N(O)
	GUD/NAOI	Gymnamoebida	JIM/NA/MAOEB/DA
Gueneau de Mussy	GAI/NOE/DE/MIS/SI	gymnastics	JIM/NA*S/IK/-S
	GAI/NOE/DE/MUS/SI	Gymnoascaceae	JIM/NO/AS/KAIS/YAE
Guerin	GAI/RAN	gymnobacteria	JIM/NO/BAK/TAOER/YA
Guibor	GAOE/BOR	gymnobacterium	JIM/NO/BAK/TAOERM
guidance	GAOI/DANS	gymnocyte	JIM/NO/SAO*IT
guide	GAOID	Gymnodinium	JIM/NO/DIN/YUM
guideline	GAOID/LAOIN	gymnophobia	JIM/NO/FOEB/YA
Guidi	G-/WAOE/DAOE	gymnoplast	JIM/NO/PLA*S
	GAOE/DAOE	gymnosperm	JIM/NO/SPERM
Guillain	GAOE/YAN	gymnospore	JIM/NO/SPOER
	GI/YAN	gyn(o)-	GAOIN
guillotine	GAOE/TAOEN		GAOI/N(O)
	GIL/TAOEN		JIN
Guinard	GAOE/NAR		JI/N(O)
	GAOE/NARD		JAOIN
Guinea	GIN/NAOE		JAOI/N(O)
guinea pig	GIN/NAOE/PIG	gynander	JI/NAND/ER
	GI/NAOE/PIG	gynandr(o)-	JI/NAN/DR(O)
Guinon	GAOE/NAU		GAOI/NAN/DR(O)
	GAOE/NON	gynandria	JI/NAN/DRA
Guiteras	GAOE/TAI/RAS		JI/NAN/DRAOE/YA
	GAOE/TER/RAS		

	GAOI/NAN/DRA	gypsum	JIP/SUM
	GAOI/NAN/DRAOE/YA	gyr(o)-	JAOIR
gynandrism	JI/NAN/DRIFM		JAOI/R(O)
	GAOI/NAN/DRIFM	gyral	JAOIRL
gynandroblastoma	JI/NAN/DRO/BLAS/TOE/MA		JAOI/RAL
	GAOI/NAN/DRO/BLAS/TOE/MA	gyrata	JAOI/RAI/TA
gynandroid	JI/NAN/DROID	gyrate	JAOI/RAIT
	GAOI/NAN/DROID	gyration	JAOI/RAIGS
gynandromorph	JI/NAN/DRO/MOR/-F	gyratum	JAOI/RAI/TUM
	GAOI/NAN/DRO/MOR/-F	gyre	JAOIR
gynandromorphism	JI/NAN/DRO/MOR/FIFM	gyrectomy	JAOI/REKT/M*I
	GAOI/NAN/DRO/MOR/FIFM	Gyrencephala	JAOI/REN/SEF/LA
gynandromorphous	JI/NAN/DRO/MOR/FOUS	gyrencephalic	JAOI/REN/SFAL/IK
	GAOI/NAN/DRO/MOR/FOUS	gyri	JAOI/RAOI
gynandry	JI/NAN/DRI	-gyria	JAOIR/YA
	GAOI/NAN/DRI	-gyric	JAOIR/IK
gynanthropia	JAOI/NAN/THROEP/YA	gyrochrome	JAOIR/KROEM
	GAOI/NAN/THROEP/YA	gyrometer	JAOI/ROM/TER
gynanthropism	JAOI/NAN/THRO/PIFM	Gyromitra esculenta	GAOIR/MAOE/TRA/ES/KAOU/
	GAOI/NAN/THRO/PIFM		LEN/TA
gynatresia	GAOIN/TRAOEZ/YA	gyrosa	JAOI/ROE/SA
	JIN/TRAOEZ/YA	gyrose	JAOI/ROES
Gyne-Lotrimin	GAOIN/LOE/TRI/MIN	gyrospasm	JAOIR/SPAFM
gynec(o)-	GAOIN/K(O)	gyrous	JAOI/ROUS
	JIN/K(O)		JAOIR/OUS
gynecic	GAOI/NAOES/IK	gyrus	JAOI/RUS
	GAOI/NES/IK		
	JI/NAOES/IK		
	JI/NES/IK		
gynecium	GAOI/NAOES/YUM		
	JI/NAOES/YUM		
gynecogen	GAOIN/KO/JEN		
	JIN/KO/JEN		
gynecogenic	GAOIN/KO/JEN/IK		
	JIN/KO/JEN/IK		
gynecography	GAOIN/KOG/FI		
	JIN/KOG/FI		
gynecoid	GAOIN/KOID		
	JIN/KOID		
gynecologic	GAOIN/KO/LOJ/IK		
	JIN/KO/LOJ/IK		
gynecological	GAOIN/KO/LOJ/KAL		
	JIN/KO/LOJ/KAL		
gynecologist	GAOIN/KO*LGS		
	JIN/KO*LGS		
gynecology	GAOIN/KOLG		
	JIN/KOLG		
gynecomania	GAOIN/KO/MAIN/YA		
	JIN/KO/MAIN/YA		
gynecomastia	GAOIN/KO/MA*S/YA		
	JIN/KO/MA*S/YA		
gynecomastism	GAOIN/KO/MAS/TIFM		
	JIN/KO/MAS/TIFM		
gynecomasty	GAOIN/KO/MAS/TI		
	JIN/KO/MAS/TI		
gynecomazia	GAOIN/KO/MAIZ/YA		
	JIN/KO/MAIZ/YA		
gynecopathy	GAOIN/KOP/TH*I		
	JIN/KOP/TH*I		
gynecophoral	GAOIN/KOF/RAL		
	JIN/KOF/RAL		
gynecophorous	GAOIN/KOF/ROUS		
	JIN/KOF/ROUS		
gyneduct	GAOIN/DUKT		
	JIN/DUKT		
gynephilia	GAOIN/FIL/YA		
	JIN/FIL/YA		
gynephobia	GAOIN/FOEB/YA		
	JIN/FOEB/YA		
gyniatrics	GAOIN/YAT/RIK/-S		
	JIN/YAT/RIK/-S		
gyniatry	GAOIN/YAT/RI		
	JIN/YAT/RI		
gynocardia	GAOIN/KARD/YA		
gynocardic	GAOIN/KARD/IK		
gynogenesis	GAOIN/JEN/SIS		
	JIN/JEN/SIS		
Gynol	GAOI/NOL		
gynopathic	GAOIN/PA*T/IK		
	JIN/PA*T/IK		
gynopathy	GAOI/NOP/TH*I		
	JI/NOP/TH*I		
	JIN/OP/TH*I		
gynoplastics	GAOIN/PLA*S/IK/-S		
	JAOIN/PLA*S/IK/-S		
	JIN/PLA*S/IK/-S		
gynoplasty	GAOIN/PLAS/TI		
	JAOIN/PLAS/TI		
	JIN/PLAS/TI		

H

Haab	HAUB
Haase	HAUS
habena	HA/BAOE/NA
habenae	HA/BAOE/NAE
habenal	HA/BAOENL
habenar	HA/BAOE/NAR
habenul-	HA/BEN/L-
	HA/BEN/YAOU/L-
	HA/BEN/YU/L-
habenula	HA/BEN/LA
habenulae	HA/BEN/LAE
habenular	HA/BEN/LAR
habenularum	HA/BEN/LAIR/UM
habit	HABT
habitat	HAB/TAT
habitual	HA/BIFP/YAL
	HA/BIFP/WAL
	HA/BIT/YAL
habituation	HA/BIFP/YAIGS
	HA/BIFP/WAIGS
	HA/BIT/YAIGS
habitus	HAB/TUS
habromania	HAB/RO/MAIN/YA
Habronema	HAB/RO/NAOE/MA
habronemiasis	HAB/RO/NAOE/MAOI/SIS
hachement	ARB/-MT
	ARB/MAU
hacking	HAK/-G
hacking cough	HAK/-G/KAUF
Haeckel	HEK/EL
	HAEK/EL
haem(o)-	HAOEM
	HAOE/M(O)
	HEM
	HAEM
	HAE/M(O)
Haemadipsa	HAOEM/DIP/SA
Haemaphysalis	HAOEM/FIS/LIS
Haematobia	HAOEM/TOEB/YA
Haematopinus	HAOEM/TO/PAOI/NUS
Haematosiphon	HAOEM/TO/SAOI/FON
Haemobartonella	HAOEM/BART/NEL/LA
Haemodipsus	HAOEM/DIP/SUS
Haemogregarina	HAOEM/GREG/RAOI/NA
Haemonchus	HAOE/MON/KUS
Haemoproteidae	HAOEM/PRO/TAOE/DAE
Haemoproteus	HAOEM/PROET/YUS
haemorrhagia	HAOEM/RAI/JA
haemorrhoidales	HEM/ROI/DAI/LAOEZ
haemorrhoidalis	HEM/ROI/DAI/LIS
haemosporidia	HAOEM/SPRID/YA
Haemosporidia	K-P/HAOEM/SPRID/YA
haemosporidium	HAOEM/SPRID/YUM
Haemosporina	HAOEM/SPOE/RAOI/NA
Haemostrongylus	HAOEM/STONG/LUS
	HAOEM/STRON/JI/LUS
Haenel	HAI/NEL
	HAINL
hafnium	HAF/NAOE/UM
	HAF/NAOE/YUM
	(not HAF/NUM; see half numb)
Hagedorn	HAG/DORN
	HAUG/DORN
Hageman	HAG/MAN
Hagenbach	HAG/EN/BAK
hagiotherapy	HAG/YO/THER/PI
Haglund	HAG/LAOUND
	HAG/LUND
Hagner	HAG/NER
hahnemannian	HAUN/MAUN/YAN
	HAN/MAN/YAN
hahnemannism	HAUN/MAUN/IFM
	HAUN/MAN/IFM
hahnium	HAUN/YUM
Haidinger	HAOI/DING/ER
	HAOID/IN/GER
	HAOID/-G/ER
Haines	HAINZ
	HAINS
hair	HAIR
hairball	HAIR/BAL
haircap	HAIR/KAP
haircast	HAIR/KA*S
hairy	HAIR/RI

halation	HA/LAIGS
	HAL/AIGS
halazepam	HAL/AZ/PAM
halazone	HAL/ZOEN
Halberstaedter	HAL/BER/STET/ER
Halberstaedter-Prowazek	HAL/BER/STET/ER/H-F/PRO/VAT/SEK
	HAL/BER/STET/ER/H-F/PRO/VAT/ZEK
halcinonide	HAL/SIN/NAOID
Halcion	HALS/YON
Haldane	HAL/DAIN
Haldol	HAL/DOL
Hale	K-P/HA*IL
	(not HAIL or HAEL; see hail and heal)
Hales	HAILS
halethazole	HA/L*ET/ZOEL
half-life	HAF/LAOIF
half-moon	HAF/MAON
half-retinal	HAF/RET/NAL
half-time	HAF/TAOIM
halfway house	HAF/WA*I/HOUS
Haley	HAI/LAOE
Haley's M-O	HAI/LAOE/AOES/M-RBGS/ORBGS
halide	HAL/AOID
haliphagia	HAL/FAI/JA
halisteresis	HA/L*IS/RAOE/SIS
halisteretic	HA/L*IS/RET/IK
halitosis	HAL/TOE/SIS
halituous	HA/LIT/YOUS
halitus	HAL/TUS
Hall	K-P/HAL
hallachrome	HAL/KROEM
Hall band	K-P/HAL/BAND
Hallberg	HAUL/BERG
	HAL/BERG
Halle	HAL/LAI
Haller	HAL/ER
halleri	HAL/RAOI
hallex	HAL/LEX
halli	HAL/LAOI
hallices	HAL/LI/SAOEZ
	(not HAL/SAOEZ; see halluces)
Hallion	HAL/YON
Hallopeau	HAL/POE
Hall-Stone	K-P/HAL/H-F/K-P/STOEN
hallucal	HAL/KAL
hallucalism	HAL/KLIFM
	HAL/KAL/IFM
halluces	HAL/SAOEZ
hallucin-	HA/LAOUS/N-
	HAL/LAOUS/N-
hallucination	HA/LAOUS/NAIGS
hallucinative	HA/LAOUS/NA/TIV
hallucinatory	HA/LAOUS/NA/TOIR
hallucinogen	HA/LAOUS/NO/JEN
hallucinogenesis	HA/LAOUS/NO/JEN/SIS
hallucinogenic	HA/LAOUS/NO/JEN/IK
hallucinosis	HA/LAOUS/NOE/SIS
hallucinotic	HA/LAOUS/NOT/IK
hallucis	HAL/SIS
hallucism	HAL/SIFM
hallus	HAL/LUS
hallux	HAL/UX
	HAL/LUX
Hallwachs	HAL/VAKS
halmatogenesis	HAL/MAT/JEN/SIS
	HAL/MA/TO/JEN/SIS
halo	HAI/LOE
halo-	HAL
haloanisone	HAL/AN/SOEN
halobacteria	HAL/BAK/TAOER/YA
halobacterium	HAL/BAK/TAOERM
Halobacterium	K-P/HAL/BAK/TAOERM
halodermia	HAL/DERM/YA
haloduric	HAL/DAOUR/IK
halofenate	HAL/FEN/AIT
Halog	HAL/OG
halogen	HAL/JEN
halogenation	HAL/JE/NAIGS
Halogeton	HAL/JAOE/TON
	HAL/GAOE/TON
haloid	HAL/OID
halometer	HAL/OM/TER
	HA/LOM/TER
halometry	HAL/OM/TRI
	HA/LOM/TRI
halopemide	HAL/PEM/AOID

haloperidol	HAL/P*ER/DOL	haploid	HAP/LOID
	HAL/PER/DOL	haploidentity	HAP/LO/AOID/TI
halophil	HAL/FIL		HAP/LO/AOI/DENT/TI
halophile	HAL/FAOIL	haploidy	HAP/LOI/DI
halophilic	HAL/FIL/IK	haplology	HAP/LOLG
halopredone	HAL/PRE/DOEN	haplomycosis	HAP/LO/MAOI/KOE/SIS
haloprogin	HAL/PRO/JIN	haplont	HAP/LONT
	HAL/PROE/JIN	haplopathy	HAP/LOP/TH*I
halosteresis	HA/LO*S/RAOE/SIS	haplophase	HAP/LO/FAEZ
Halotestin	HAL/TES/TIN	haplopia	HAP/LOEP/YA
Halotex	HAL/TEX	haploprotein	HAP/LO/PRO/TAOEN
halothane	HAL/THAIN	haploscope	HAP/LO/SKOEP
halowax	HAL/WAX	haploscopic	HAP/LO/SKOP/IK
halquinol	HAL/KWIN/OEL	Haplosporidia	HAP/LO/SPRID/YA
Halske	HAL/SKAOE	haplotype	HAP/LO/TAOIP
Halstead	HAL/STED	Hapsburg	HAPS/BURG
Halstead-Reitan	HAL/STED/H-F/RAOI/TAN	hapt(o)-	HAPT
Haltran	HAL/TRAN		HAP/T(O)
hamamelidis	HAM/MEL/DIS	hapten	HAPT/-N
hamamelis	HAM/MEL/LIS		HA*P/TEN
	HAM/MAOE/LIS		(*not* HAP/TEN; **see happen ten**)
Hamamelis	K-P/HAM/MEL/LIS	haptene	HAP/TAOEN
	K-P/HAM/MAOE/LIS	haptenic	HAP/TEN/IK
hamarthritis	HAM/AR/THRAOITS	haptic	HAPT/IK
hamartia	HAM/AR/SHA		HAP/TIK
	HA/MAR/SHA	haptics	HAPT/IK/-S
hamartial	HAM/AR/-RBL		HAP/TIK/-S
	HA/MAR/-RBL	haptin	HAP/TIN
hamarto-	HAM/ART	haptodysphoria	HAPT/DIS/FOER/YA
	HA/MART	haptoglobin	HAPT/GLOE/BIN
	HAM/AR/TO	haptometer	HAP/TOM/TER
	HA/MAR/TO	haptosporus	HAPT/SPOER/RUS
hamartoblastoma	HAM/ART/BLAS/TOE/MA	Harden	K-P/HARD/-N
hamartochondromatosis	HAM/ART/KON/DROEM/TOE/SIS	hardening	HARD/-NG
hamartoma	HAM/AR/TOE/MA	Harder	K-P/HARD/ER
hamartomatosis	HAM/AR/TOEM/TOE/SIS	harderian	HAR/DER/YAN
hamartomatous	HAM/AR/TOEM/TOUS	Harding	HARD/-G
hamartophobia	HAM/ART/FOEB/YA	hardness	HARD/*NS
hamartoplasia	HAM/ART/PLAIZ/YA	Hardy	K-P/HAR/DI/
hamate	HAM/AIT	Hardy-Weinberg	K-P/HAR/DI/H-F/VAOIN/BERG
hamatum	HA/MAI/TUM		K-P/HAR/DI/H-F/WAOIN/BERG
	HAM/AI/TUM	Hare	K-P/HA*ER
Hamberger	HAM/BERG/ER	harelip	HAIR/LIP
Hamburger	K-P/HAM/BURG/ER		HA*ER/LIP
Hamilton	HAM/IL/TON	harlequin	HARL/KWIN
Hamman	HAM/MAN	haricot	HAR/KOT
Hammar	HAM/MAR	harmaline	HARM/LAOIN
Hammarsten	HAM/MAR/STEN	harmidine	HARM/DAOEN
hammer	HAM/ER	harmine	HAR/MAOEN
Hammerschlag	HAM/ER/SH/LAUG	harmonia	HAR/MOEN/YA
	HAM/ER/SLAUG	harmonic	HAR/MON/IK
hammock	HAM/OK	harmonious	HAR/MOEN/YOUS
Hammond	HAM/OND	harmony	HARM/N*I
hamster	HAM/STER	Harmonyl	HARM/NIL
hamstring	HAM/STRING	harpaxophobia	HAR/PAX/FOEB/YA
hamul-	HAM/L-	harpoon	HAR/PAON
	HAM/YAOU/L-	Harrington	HAR/-G/TON
	HAM/YU/L-	Harris	HAR/RIS
hamular	HAM/LAR	Harrison	HAR/SON
hamuli	HAM/LAOI		HAR/RI/SON
hamulus	HAM/LUS	harrowing	HAR/ROE/-G
hamycin	HA/MAOI/SIN	Hartel	HAR/TEL
Hancock	HAN/KOK	Harting	HART/-G
hand	HAND	Hartley	HART/LAOE
Hand	K-P/HAND	Hartman	HART/MAN
handedness	HAND/D*NS	Hartmann	HA*RT/MAN
	HAND/-D/*NS	Hartmannella	HART/MA/NEL/LA
handicap	HAND/KAP		HART/MAN/EL/LA
Handley	HAND/LAOE	hartmanni	HART/MAN/NAOI
Handow	HAN/DOU	hartshorn	HARTS/HORN
handpiece	HAND/PAOES	harveian	HAFRB/YAN
hang	HANG	Harvey	HAR/VAOE
hangnail	HANG/NAIL	Haser	HAIS/ER
hannah	HAN/NA	Hashimoto	HARB/MOE/TOE
Hannover	HAN/NOEVR	hashish	HARB/IRB
Hanot	HAN/NOE		HA/SHAOERB
	AN/NOE	hashishism	HARB/SHIFM
Hansen	HAN/SEN		HA/SHAOERB/IFM
	HANS/-N	Haskins	HAS/KINS
hansenii	HAN/SEN/YAOI		HAZ/KINS
Hanson	HAN/SON	Hasner	HAS/NER
hapalonychia	HAP/LO/NIK/YA		HAUS/NER
haph-	HAF	Hassall	HAS/SAL
haphalgesia	HAF/AL/JAOEZ/YA	Hassall-Henle	HAS/SAL/H-F/HEN/LAOE
haphephobia	HAF/FOEB/YA	Hasselbalch	HAS/EL/BAL/-K
haplo-	HAP/LO		HAS/EL/BAUL/-K
haplobacteria	HAP/LO/BAK/TAOER/YA	hatchet	HAFP/ET
haplodiploidy	HAP/LO/DIP/LOI/DI	Hauch	HO*UK
haplodont	HAP/LO/DONT		(*not* HOUK; **see how can**)

Haudek	HAU/DEK		HEB/FRAOEN/YAK
haunch	HAUFRPBLG	hebephrenic	HAOEB/FREN/IK
	HAUN/-FP		HEB/FREN/IK
haupt	HAUPT	Heberden	HAOEB/ER/DEN
Hauser	HOUZ/ER		HEB/ER/DEN
	HOUS/ER	hebetic	HAOE/BET/IK
haustellum	HAU/STEL/UM		HE/BET/IK
	HAUS/TEL/UM	hebetude	HEB/TAOUD
haustoria	HAUS/TOER/YA	hebiatrics	HAOEB/YAT/RIK/-S
	HAU/STOER/YA	heboid	HAOE/BOID
haustorium	HAU/STOIRM		HEB/OID
	HAUS/TOIRM	heboidophrenia	HAOE/BOID/FRAOEN/YA
	HAU/STOER/YUM		HEB/OID/FRAOEN/YA
	HAUS/TOER/YUM	Hebra	HAOE/BRA
haustra	HAUS/TRA	hebraeum	HE/BRAOE/UM
	HAU/STRA		HAOE/BRAOE/UM
haustral	HAUS/TRAL	hecateromeric	HEK/TER/MER/IK
	HAU/STRAL	hecatomeral	HEK/TOM/RAL
haustration	HAUS/TRAIGS	hecatomeric	HEK/TO/MER/IK
	HAU/STRAIGS	Hecht	HEKT
haustrum	HAUS/TRUM	heckle	HEK/-L
	HAU/STRUM	hectic	HEKT/IK
haustus	HAUS/TUS	hecto-	HEKT
haut mal	HOE/MAL		HEK/TO
	HOET/MAL	hectogram	HEKT/GRAM
haut-mal	HOE/H-F/MAL	hectoliter	HEKT/LAOET/ER
	HOET/H-F/MAL	hectometer	HEK/TOM/TER
Haverhill fever	HAIV/RIL/FAOEVR	Hedera	HED/RA
	HAIVR/IL/FAOEVR	hederiform	HED/RI/FORM
	HAIVR/HIL/FAOEVR	hedgehog	HEJ/HOG
Haverhillia	HAIVR/HIL/YA/MULT/FOR/MIS	hedonia	HAOE/DOEN/YA
	HAIV/RIL/YA/MULT/FOR/MIS	hedonic	HAOE/DON/IK
	HAVR/HIL/YA/MULT/FOR/MIS	hedonism	HAOED/NIFM
Havers	HAVRS	hedonophobia	HAOED/NO/FOEB/YA
	HAIVRS	hedratresia	HED/RA/TRAOEZ/YA
haversian	HA/VERGS	hedrocele	HED/RO/SAO*EL
	HAI/VERGS	heel	HAOEL
hawkinsin	HAU/KIN/SIN	Heerfordt	HAIR/FORT
hawkinsinuria	HAU/KIN/SI/NAOUR/YA		HAOER/FORT
Hawley	HAU/LAOE	Hegar	HAI/GAR
Hay	K-P/HAI	Hegglin	HEG/LIN
Hayem	AI/YAU	Heidenhain	HAOID/EN/HAOIN
	AI/YAUM		HAOID/EN/HAIN
	HAI/YEM		HAOI/DEN/HAOIN
Hayem-Widal	AI/YAU/H-F/VAOE/DAL		HAOI/DEN/HAIN
	AI/YAUM/H-F/VAOE/DAL	height	HAOIGT
	HAI/YEM/H-F/VAOE/DAL	Heilbronner	HAOIL/BRON/ER
	(not VI/DAL; see Vidal)	Heim	HAOIM
hay fever	HAI/FAOEVR	Heim-Kreysig	HAOIM/H-F/KRAOI/ZIG
HCO₃	H-RBGS/KR*RBGS/O*RBGS/3		HAOIM/H-F/KRAOI/SIG
head¹	HED	Heimlich	HAOIM/LIK
Head	K-P/HED	Heimlich maneuver	HAOIM/LIK/MA/NAOUVR
headache	HAIK	Heine	HAOIN
	HED/A*IK		HAOI/NE
Head & Shoulders	HED/M-ND/SHOELD/ER/-S	Heineke	HAOIN/KAOE
	HED/M-ND/SHOULD/ER/-S	Heinz	HAOINZ
headcap	HED/KAP		HAOINTS
headgear	HED/GAOER	Heister	K-P/HAO*IS/ER
headgut	HED/GUT	HeLa	HAOE/LA
head-nodding	HED/H-F/NOD/-G	helcoid	HEL/KOID
head-tilt	HED/H-F/TILT	helcology	HEL/KOLG
heal	HAEL	helcoma	HEL/KOE/MA
	(not HAOEL; see heel)	helcomenia	HEL/KO/MAOEN/YA
healer	HAEL/ER	helcosis	HEL/KOE/SIS
healing	HAEL/-G	Held	K-P/HELD
health	H*ELT	helianthin	HAOEL/YAN/THIN
Health Maintenance Organization		heliation	HAOEL/YAIGS
	H*ELT/MAINT/NANS/ORGS	helic(o)-	HEL/KO, HEL/S(O)
healthy	HEL/TH*I	helical	HEL/KAL
hear	HAER	helices	HEL/SAOEZ
	(not HAOER; see here)	helicin	HEL/SIN
hearing	HAER/-G	helicinae	HEL/SAOI/NAE
hearing aid	HAER/-G/AID	helicine	HEL/SAOIN
heart	HART	helicis	HEL/SIS
heartbeat	HART/BA*ET	helicoid	HEL/KOID
	(not HART/BAET; see heart beat)	helicopod	HEL/KO/POD
heart block	HART/BLOK	helicopodia	HEL/KO/POED/YA
heartburn	HART/BURN	helicotrema	HEL/KO/TRAOE/MA
heart failure	HART/FAIL/YUR	heliencephalitis	HAOEL/YEN/SEF/LAOITS
heartworm	HART/WORM	helio-	HAOEL/YO
heat	HAOET	helioaerotherapy	HAOEL/YO/AER/THER/PI
heatstroke	HAOET/STROEK	Heliodorus	HAOEL/YO/DOR/RUS
heaves	HAOEVS	helion	HAOEL/YON
	HAOEV/-S	heliopathia	HAOEL/YO/PA*T/YA
hebdomadal	HEB/DOM/DAL	heliopathy	HAOEL/YOP/TH*I
Hebeloma	HEB/LOE/MA	heliophobia	HAOEL/YO/FOEB/YA
hebephrenia	HAOEB/FRAOEN/YA	heliosin	HAOEL/YOE/SIN
	HEB/FRAOEN/YA	heliosis	HAOEL/YOE/SIS
hebephreniac	HAOEB/FRAOEN/YAK	heliotaxis	HAOEL/YO/TAK/SIS

heliotherapy	HAOEL/YO/THER/PI	hemagogue	HAOEM/GOG
heliotrope	HAOEL/YO/TROEP		HEM/GOG
heliotropism	HAOEL/YOT/RO/PIFM	hemal	HAOE/MAL
helium	HAOEL/YUM	hemalum	HAOE/MAL/UM
helix	HAOE/LIX		HEM/AL/UM
	HAOEL/IX	hemamebiasis	HAOEM/MAOE/BAOI/SIS
hellebore	HEL/BOER		HEM/MAOE/BAOI/SIS
helleborin	HE/LEB/RIN	hemanalysis	HAOEM/NAL/SIS
	HEL/BOR/RIN		HEM/NAL/SIS
helleborism	HEL/BOR/IFM	hemangi(o)-	HE/MAN/J(O)
helleborus	HE/LEB/RUS		HAOE/MAN/J(O)
Hellebrand	HEL/BRAND	hemangiectasia	HAOE/MAN/JEK/TAIZ/YA
Heller	HEL/ER		HEM/AN/JEK/TAIZ/YA
Hellin	HEL/LIN	hemangiectasis	HAOE/MAN/JEKT/SIS
helmet	HEL/MET		HEM/AN/JEKT/SIS
Helmholtz	HEL/-M/HOELTS	hemangioameloblastoma	HE/MAN/JO/AI/MEL/BLAS/TOE/
	HEL/-M/HOLTS		MA
helminth	HEL/M*INT		HE/MAN/JO/AM/LO/BLAS/TOE/
helminth-	HEL/M*INT		MA
	HEL/MIN/TH-	hemangioblast	HE/MAN/JO/BLA*S
helminthagogue	HEL/M*INT/GOG	hemangioblastoma	HE/MAN/JO/BLAS/TOE//MA
helminthemesis	HEL/MIN/THEM/SIS	hemangioblastomatosis	HE/MAN/JO/BLA*S/MA/TOE/SIS
helminthiasis	HEL/MIN/THAOI/SIS		HE/MAN/JO/BLAS/TOEM/TOE/SIS
helminthic	HEL/M*INT/IK	hemangioendothelioblastoma	
helminthicide	HEL/M*INT/SAO*ID		HE/MAN/JO/*END/THAOEL/YO/
helminthism	HEL/MIN/THIFM		BLAS/TOE/MA
helminthoid	HEL/MIN/THOID	hemangioendothelioma	HE/MAN/JO/*END/THAOEL/YOE/
	HEL/M*INT/OID		MA
helminthology	HEL/MIN/THOLG	hemangioendotheliosarcoma	
	HEL/M*INT/OLG		HE/MAN/JO/*END/THAOEL/YO/
helminthoma	HEL/MIN/THOE/MA		SAR/KOE/MA
helminthophobia	HEL/M*INT/FOEB/YA	hemangiofibroma	HE/MAN/JO/FAOI/BROE/MA
helminthous	HEL/MIN/THOUS	hemangioma	HE/MAN/JOE/MA
	HEL/M*INT/OUS	hemangiomatosis	HE/MAN/JOEM/TOE/SIS
helmintic	HEL/MINT/IK		HE/MAN/JO/MA/TOE/SIS
Heloderma	HAOEL/DER/MA	hemangiopericyte	HE/MAN/JO/P*ER/SAO*IT
heloma	HAOE/LOE/MA	hemangiopericytoma	HE/MAN/JO/P*ER/SAOI/TOE/MA
Helophilus	HAOE/LOF/LUS	hemangiosarcoma	HE/MAN/JO/SAR/KOE/MA
helosis	HAOE/LOE/SIS	hemapheic	HAOEM/FAOE/IK
helotomy	HAOE/LOT/M*I		HEM/FAOE/IK
helper	HEL/PER	hemaphein	HAOEM/FAOE/YIN
Helvella	HEL/VEL/LA		HEM/FAOE/YIN
Helvellaceae	HEL/VE/LAIS/YAE	hemapheism	HAOEM/FAOE/IFM
	HEL/VEL/LAIS/YAE		HEM/FAOE/IFM
Helweg	HEL/VEG	hemapheresis	HAOEM/FER/SIS
Helweg-Larssen	HEL/VEG/LAR/SEN		HEM/FER/SIS
hema-	HAOE/MA	hemapoiesis	HAOE/MA/POI/SIS
	HEM		HEM/POI/SIS
	HAOEM (sometimes)	hemapoietic	HAOE/MA/POIT/IK
hemachromatosis	HAOE/MA/KROEM/TOE/SIS		HEM/POIT/IK
	HEM/KROEM/TOE/SIS	hemapophysis	HAOEM/POF/SIS
hemachrome	HAOE/MA/KROEM		HEM/POF/SIS
	HEM/KROEM	hemarthron	HEM/AR/THRON
hemachrosis	HAOE/MA/KROE/SIS		HE/MAR/THRON
	HEM/KROE/SIS	hemarthros	HEM/AR/THROS
hemacytometer	HAOE/MA/SAOI/TOM/TER		HEM/AR/THROES
	HEM/SAOI/TOM/TER		HE/MAR/THROES
hemacytometry	HAOE/MA/SAOI/TOM/TRI		HE/MAR/THROS
	HEM/SAOI/TOM/TRI	hemarthrosis	HAOE/MAR/THROE/SIS
hemacytozoon	HAOE/MA/SAOIT/ZAON		HEM/AR/THROE/SIS
	HEM/SAOIT/ZAON	hemartoma	HAOEM/AR/TOE/MA
hemadostenosis	HEM/AD/STE/NOE/SIS		HEM/AR/TOE/MA
	HAOEM/DO/STE/NOE/SIS	Hemaspan	HAOEM/SPAN
hemadrometer	HAOEM/DROM/TER	hemastrontium	HAOEM/STRON/SHUM
	HEM/DROM/TER		HEM/STRON/SHUM
hemadromograph	HAOE/MA/DROEM/GRAF		HEM/AS/TRON/SHUM
	HEM/DROEM/GRAF	hemat(o)-	HEM/T(O)
hemadromometer	HAOE/MA/DROE/MOM/TER		HAOEM/T(O)
	HEM/DROE/MOM/TER		HAOE/MAT
hemadsorbent	HAOEM/AD/SORB/ENT		HE/MAT
	HEM/AD/SORB/ENT	hematachometer	HAOE/MA/TA/KOM/TER
hemadsorption	HAOEM/AD/SORPGS		HEM/TA/KOM/TER
	HEM/AD/SORPGS	hematal	HEM/TAL
hemadynamometer	HAOE/MA/DAOIN/MOM/TER	hematapostema	HEM/TA/POS/TAOE/MA
	HEM/DAOIN/MOM/TER		HAOE/MAT/POS/TAOE/MA
hemadynamometry	HAOEM/DAOIN/MOM/TRI	hemate	HEM/AIT
	HEM/DAOIN/MOM/TRI	hematein	HAOEM/TAOEN
hemafacient	HAOEM/FAIRBT		HAOEM/TAOE/YIN
	HEM/FAIRBT		HEM/TAOEN
hemafecia	HAOEM/FAOES/YA		HEM/TAOE/YIN
	HEM/FAOES/YA	hematemesis	HEM/TEM/SIS
hemagglutination	HAOEM/GLAOUT/NAIGS		HAOEM/TEM/SIS
	HEM/GLAOUT/NAIGS	hematencephalon	HEM/AT/EN/SEF/LON
hemagglutinative	HAOEM/GLAOUT/NA/TIV		HAOE/MAT/EN/SEF/LON
	HEM/GLAOUT/NA/TIV	hematherapy	HAOE/MA/THER/PI
hemagglutinin	HAOEM/GLAOUT/NIN		HEM/THER/PI
	HEM/GLAOUT/NIN	hematherm	HAOEM/THERM
hemagogic	HAOEM/GOJ/IK		HEM/THERM
	HEM/GOJ/IK	hemathermal	HAOEM/THER/MAL

hemathermous	HEM/THER/MAL	hematohidrosis	HAOEM/TO/HID/ROE/SIS
	HAOEM/THERM/OUS		HEM/TO/HID/ROE/SIS
	HEM/THERM/OUS	hematohistioblast	HAOEM/TO/H*IS/YO/BLA*S
hemathidrosis	HAOE/MAT/HAOI/DROE/SIS		HEM/TO/H*IS/YO/BLA*S
	HEM/AT/HAOI/DROE/SIS	hematohiston	HAOEM/TO/HIS/TON
hemathorax	HAOE/MA/THOR/AX		HEM/TO/HIS/TON
	HEM/THOR/AX	hematohyaloid	HAOEM/TO/HAOI/LOID
hematic	HAOE/MAT/IK		HEM/TO/HAOI/LOID
hematid	HAOEM/TID	hematoid	HAOEM/TOID
	HEM/TID		HEM/TOID
hematidrosis	HAOE/MAT/DROE/SIS	hematoidin	HAOEM/TOI/DIN
	HEM/AT/DROE/SIS		HEM/TOI/DIN
hematimeter	HAOEM/TIM/TER	hematologist	HAOEM/TO*LGS
	HEM/TIM/TER		HEM/TO*LGS
hematimetry	HAOEM/TIM/TRI	hematology	HAOEM/TOLG
	HEM/TIM/TRI		HEM/TOLG
hematin	HAOEM/TIN	hematolin	HAOEM/TOE/LIN
	HEM/TIN		HEM/TOE/LIN
hematinemia	HAOEM/TI/NAOEM/YA	hematolymphangioma	HAOEM/TO/LIM/FAN/JOE/MA
	HEM/TI/NAOEM/YA		HEM/TO/LIM/FAN/JOE/MA
hematinic	HAOEM/TIN/IK	hematolysis	HAOEM/TOL/SIS
	HEM/TIN/IK		HEM/TOL/SIS
hematinuria	HAOEM/TIN/YAOUR/YA	hematolytic	HAOEM/TO/LIT/IK
	HEM/TIN/YAOUR/YA		HEM/TO/LIT/IK
hematobia	HEM/TOEB/YA	hematoma	HAOEM/TOE/MA
hematobilia	HAOEM/TO/BIL/YA		HEM/TOE/MA
	HEM/TO/BIL/YA	hematomancy	HAOEM/TO/MAN/SI
hematobium	HAOEM/TOEB/YUM		HEM/TO/MAN/SI
	HEM/TOEB/YUM	hematomanometer	HAOEM/TO/MA/NOM/TER
hematoblast	HAOEM/TO/BLA*S		HEM/TO/MA/NOM/TER
	HEM/TO/BLA*S	hematomediastinum	HAOEM/TO/MAOED/YAS/TAOIN/
hematocele	HAOEM/TO/SAOEL		UM
	HEM/TO/SAO*EL		HEM/TO/MAOED/YAS/TAOIN/UM
hematocelia	HAOEM/TO/SAOEL/YA	hematometakinesis	HAOEM/TO/MET/KI/NAOE/SIS
	HEM/TO/SAOEL/YA		HEM/TO/MET/KI/NAOE/SIS
hematocephalus	HAOEM/TO/SEF/LUS	hematometer	HAOEM/TOM/TER
	HEM/TO/SEF/LUS		HEM/TOM/TER
hematocephaly	HAOEM/TO/SEF/LI	hematometra	HAOEM/TO/MAOE/TRA
	HEM/TO/SEF/LI		HEM/TO/MAOE/TRA
hematochezia	HAOEM/TO/KAOEZ/YA	hematometry	HAOEM/TOM/TRI
	HEM/TO/KAOEZ/YA		HEM/TOM/TRI
hematochlorin	HAOEM/TO/KLOR/RIN	hematomphalocele	HAOE/MAT/OM/FAL/SAO*EL
	HEM/TO/KLOR/RIN		HEM/AT/OM/FAL/SAO*EL
hematochromatosis	HAOEM/TO/KROEM/TOE/SIS	hematomyelia	HAOEM/TO/MAOI/AOEL/YA
	HEM/TO/KROEM/TOE/SIS		HEM/TO/MAOI/AOEL/YA
hematochyluria	HAOEM/TO/KAOI/LAOUR/YA	hematomyelitis	HAOEM/TO/MAOI/LAOITS
	HEM/TO/KAOI/LAOUR/YA		HEM/TO/MAOI/LAOITS
hematocolpometra	HAOEM/TO/KOL/PO/MAOE/TRA	hematomyelopore	HAOEM/TO/MAOI/LO/POER
	HEM/TO/KOL/PO/MAOE/TRA		HEM/TO/MAOI/LO/POER
hematocolpos	HAOEM/TO/KOL/POS	hematonic	HAOEM/TON/IK
	HEM/TO/KOL/POS		HEM/TON/IK
hematocrit	HE/MAT/KRIT	hematopathology	HAOEM/TO/PA/THOLG
	HAOE/MAT/KRIT		HEM/TO/PA/THOLG
	HAOEM/TO/KRIT	hematopathy	HAOEM/TOP/TH*I
	HEM/TO/KRIT		HEM/TOP/TH*I
hematocryal	HAOEM/TOK/RAL	hematopenia	HAOEM/TO/PAOEN/YA
	HEM/TOK/RAL		HEM/TO/PAOEN/YA
hematocyst	HAOEM/TO/S*IS	hematopericardium	HAOEM/TO/P*ER/KARD/YUM
	HEM/TO/S*IS		HEM/TO/P*ER/KARD/YUM
hematocystis	HAOEM/TO/SIS/TIS	hematoperitoneum	HAOEM/TO/PERT/NAOEM
	HEM/TO/SIS/TIS		HEM/TO/PERT/NAOEM
hematocyte	HAOEM/TO/SAO*IT	hematophage	HAOEM/TO/FAIJ
	HEM/TO/SAO*IT		HEM/TO/FAIJ
hematocytoblast	HAOEM/TO/SAOIT/BLA*S	hematophagia	HAOEM/TO/FAI/JA
	HEM/TO/SAOIT/BLA*S		HEM/TO/FAI/JA
hematocytolysis	HAOEM/TO/SAOI/TOL/SIS	hematophagocyte	HAOEM/TO/FAG/SAO*IT
	HEM/TO/SAOI/TOL/SIS		HEM/TO/FAG/SAO*IT
hematocytometer	HAOEM/TO/SAOI/TOM/TER	hematophagous	HAOEM/TOF/GOUS
	HEM/TO/SAOI/TOM/TER		HEM/TOF/GOUS
hematocytopenia	HAOEM/TO/SAOIT/PAOEN/YA	hematophagus	HAOEM/TOF/GUS
	HEM/TO/SAOIT/PAOEN/YA		HEM/TOF/GUS
hematocytozoon	HAOEM/TO/SAOIT/ZAON	hematophagy	HAOEM/TOF/JI
	HEM/TO/SAOIT/ZAON		HEM/TOF/JI
hematocyturia	HAOEM/TO/SAOI/TAOUR/YA	hematophilia	HAOEM/TO/FIL/YA
	HEM/TO/SAOI/TAOUR/YA		HEM/TO/FIL/YA
hematodyscrasia	HAOEM/TO/DIS/KRAIZ/YA	hematoplastic	HAOEM/TO/PLA*S/IK
	HEM/TO/DIS/KRAIZ/YA		HEM/TO/PLA*S/IK
hematodystrophy	HAOEM/TO/DIS/TRO/FI	hematopoiesis	HAOEM/TO/POI/SIS
	HEM/TO/DIS/TRO/FI		HEM/TO/POI/SIS
hematoencephalic	HAOEM/TO/EN/SFAL/IK	hematopoietic	HAOEM/TO/POIT/IK
	HEM/TO/EN/SFAL/IK		HEM/TO/POIT/IK
hematogenesis	HAOEM/TO/JEN/SIS	hematopoietin	HAOEM/TO/POI/TIN
	HEM/TO/JEN/SIS		HEM/TO/POI/TIN
hematogenic	HAOEM/TO/JEN/IK	hematoporphyria	HAOEM/TO/POR/FIR/YA
	HEM/TO/JEN/IK		HEM/TO/POR/FIR/YA
hematogenous	HAOEM/TOJ/NOUS	hematoporphyrin	HAOEM/TO/POR/FRIN
	HEM/TOJ/NOUS		HEM/TO/POR/FRIN
hematogone	HAOEM/TO/GOEN	hematoporphyrinemia	HAOEM/TO/POR/FRI/NAOEM/YA
	HEM/TO/GOEN		HEM/TO/POR/FRI/NAOEM/YA

hematoporphyrinism	HAOEM/TO/POR/FRIN/IFM	hemiablepsia	HEM/AI/BLEPS/YA
	HEM/TO/POR/FRIN/IFM	hemiacardius	HEM/AI/KARD/YUS
hematoporphyrinuria	HAOEM/TO/POR/FRI/NAOUR/YA	hemiacephalus	HEM/AI/SEF/LUS
	HEM/TO/POR/FRI/NAOUR/YA	hemiacetal	HEM/AS/TAL
hematopsia	HAOEM/TOPS/YA	hemiachromatopsia	HEM/AI/KROEM/TOPS/YA
	HEM/TOPS/YA	hemiacrosomia	HEM/AK/RO/SOEM/YA
hematorrhachis	HAOEM/TO/TOR/KIS	hemiageusia	HEM/AI/GAOUZ/YA
	HEM/TOR/KIS	hemiageustia	HEM/AI/GAO*US/YA
hematorrhea	HAOEM/TO/RAOE/YA	hemialbumin	HEM/AL/BAOU/MIN
	HEM/TO/RAOE/YA	hemialbumose	HEM/AL/BAOU/MOES
hematosalpinx	HAOEM/TO/SAL/PINGS	hemialbumosuria	HEM/AL/BAOUM/SAOUR/YA
	HEM/TO/SAL/PINGS	hemialgia	HEM/AL/JA
hematoscheocele	HAOEM/TOS/KO/SAO*EL	hemiamblyopia	HEM/AM/BLI/OEP/YA
	HEM/TOS/KO/SAO*EL	hemiamyosthenia	HEM/AI/MAOI/OS/THAOEN/YA
hematoscope	HAOEM/TO/SKOEP	hemianacusia	HEM/AN/KAOUZ/YA
	HEM/TO/SKOEP	hemianalgesia	HEM/ANL/JAOEZ/YA
hematoscopy	HAOEM/TOS/KPI	hemianencephaly	HEM/AN/EN/SEF/LI
	HEM/TOS/KPI	hemianesthesia	HEM/ANS/THAOEZ/YA
hematosepsis	HAOEM/TO/SEP/SIS	hemianopia	HEM/AI/NOEP/YA
	HEM/TO/SEP/SIS	hemianopic	HEM/AI/NOEP/IK
hematoside	HAOEM/TO/SAOID	hemianopsia	HEM/AN/OPS/YA
	HEM/TO/SAOID	hemianoptic	HEM/AN/OPT/IK
hematosin	HAOEM/TOE/SIN	hemianosmia	HEM/AN/OZ/MA
	HEM/TOE/SIN		HEM/AN/OZ/MAOE/YA
hematosis	HAOEM/TOE/SIS	hemiaplasia	HEM/AI/PLAIZ/YA
	HEM/TOE/SIS	hemiapraxia	HEM/AI/PRAX/YA
hematospectrophotometer	HAOEM/TO/SPEK/TRO/FOE/TOM/	hemiarthroplasty	HEM/AR/THRO/PLAS/TI
	TER	hemiarthrosis	H*EM/AR/THROE/SIS
	HEM/TO/SPEK/TRO/FOE/TOM/		HEM/MI/AR/THROE/SIS
	TER		(*not* HEM/AR/THROE/SIS; see
hematospectroscope	HAOEM/TO/SPEK/TRO/SKOEP		hemarthrosis)
	HEM/TO/SPEK/TRO/SKOEP	hemiasynergia	HEM/AS/NER/JA
hematospectroscopy	HAOEM/TO/SPEK/TROS/KPI		HEM/AI/SI/NER/JA
	HEM/TO/SPEK/TROS/KPI	hemiataxia	HEM/AI/TAX/YA
hematospermatocele	HAOEM/TO/SPERM/TO/SAO*EL	hemiataxy	HEM/AI/TAK/SI
	HEM/TO/SPERM/TO/SAO*EL	hemiathetosis	HEM/A*T/TOE/SIS
hematospermia	HAOEM/TO/SPERM/YA	hemiatrophy	HEM/AT/RO/FI
	HEM/TO/SPERM/YA	hemiaxial	HEM/AX/YAL
hematostatic	HAOEM/TO/STAT/IK	hemiballism	HEM/BAL/IFM
	HEM/TO/STAT/IK	hemiballismus	HEM/BAL/IZ/MUS
hematosteon	HAOEM/TO*S/YON	hemibladder	HEM/BLAD/ER
	HEM/TO*S/YON	hemiblock	HEM/BLOK
hematotherapy	HAOEM/TO/THER/PI	hemic	HAOEM/IK
	HEM/TO/THER/PI		HEM/IK
hematothermal	HAOEM/TO/THER/MAL	hemicanities	HEM/KA/NIRB/AOEZ
	HEM/TO/THER/MAL	hemicardia	HEM/KARD/YA
hematothorax	HAOEM/TO/THOR/AX	hemicardius	HEM/KARD/YUS
	HEM/TO/THOE/RAX	hemicellulase	HEM/SEL/YAOU/LAIS
hematotoxic	HAOEM/TO/TOX/IK	hemicellulose	HEM/SEL/YAOU/LOES
	HEM/TO/TOX/IK	hemicentrum	HEM/SEN/TRUM
hematotoxicosis	HAOEM/TO/TOX/KOE/SIS	hemicephalalgia	HEM/SEF/LAL/JA
	HEM/TO/TOX/KOE/SIS	hemicephalia	HEM/SFAIL/YA
hematotoxin	HAOEM/TO/TOK/SIN	hemicephalus	HEM/SEF/LUS
	HEM/TO/TOK/SIN	hemicerebrum	HEM/SER/BRUM
hematotrachelos	HAOEM/TO/TRA/KAOE/LOS	hemichorea	HEM/KOE/RAOE/YA
	HEM/TO/TRA/KAOE/LOS	hemichromatopsia	HEM/KROEM/TOPS/YA
hematotropic	HAOEM/TO/TROP/IK	hemichromosome	HEM/KROEM/SOEM
	HEM/TO/TROP/IK	hemicolectomy	HEM/KO/LEKT/M*I
hematotympanum	HAOEM/TO/TIFRP/NUM	hemicorporectomy	HEM/KORP/REKT/M*I
	HEM/TO/TIFRP/NUM	hemicrania	HEM/KRAIN/YA
hematoxic	HAOE/MA/TOX/IK	hemicraniectomy	HEM/KRAIN/YEKT/M*I
	HEM/TOX/IK	hemicraniosis	HEM/KRAIN/YOE/SIS
hematoxin	HAOE/MA/TOK/SIN	hemicraniotomy	HEM/KRAIN/YOT/M*I
	HEM/TOK/SIN	hemidecortication	HEM/DE/KORT/KAIGS
hematoxylin	HAOEM/TOX/LIN	hemidesmosome	HEM/DES/MO/SOEM
	HEM/TOX/LIN	hemidiaphoresis	HEM/DAOI/FRAOE/SIS
hematozemia	HAOEM/TO/ZAOEM/YA	hemidiaphragm	HEM/DAOI/FRAM
	HEM/TO/ZAOEM/YA	hemidrosis	HEM/DROE/SIS
hematozoa	HAOEM/TO/ZOE/WA	hemidysergia	HEM/DIS/ER/JA
	HEM/TO/ZOE/WA	hemidysesthesia	HEM/DIS/ES/THAOEZ/YA
hematozoic	HAOEM/TO/ZOIK	hemidystrophy	HEM/DIS/TRO/FI
	HEM/TO/ZOIK	hemiectromelia	HEM/EK/TRO/MAOEL/YA
hematozoon	HAOEM/TO/ZAON	hemielastin	HEM/E/LAS/TIN
	HEM/TO/ZAON	hemiencephalus	HEM/EN/SEF/LUS
hematuresis	HAOEM/TAOU/RAOE/SIS	hemiepilepsy	HEM/EP/LEP/SI
	HEM/TAOU/RAOE/SIS	hemifacial	HEM/FAIRBL
hematuria	HAOEM/TAOUR/YA	hemigastrectomy	HEM/GAS/TREKT/M*I
	HEM/TAOUR/YA	hemigeusia	HEM/GAOUZ/YA
hematuric	HAOEM/TAOUR/IK	hemigigantism	HEM/JAOI/GAN/TIFM
	HEM/TAOUR/IK	hemiglossal	HEM/GLOS/SAL
heme	HAO*EM (*required*)	hemiglossectomy	HEM/GLOS/EKT/M*I
hemendothelioma	HAOEM/*END/THAOEL/YOE/MA		HEM/GLOS/SEKT/M*I
	HEM/*END/THAOEL/YOE/MA	hemiglossitis	HEM/GLOS/SAOITS
hemeralopia	HEM/RA/LOEP/YA	hemignathia	HEM/NA*T/YA
hemeranopia	HEM/RA/NOEP/YA	hemihepatectomy	HEM/HEP/TEKT/M*I
hemerythrin	HAOEM/R*IT/RIN	hemihidrosis	HEM/HI/DROE/SIS
	HEM/R*IT/RIN		HEM/HAOI/DROE/SIS
hemi-	HEM	hemihydranencephaly	HEM/HAOI/DRAN/EN/SEF/LI
-hemia	HAOEM/YA	hemihypalgesia	HEM/HAOI/PAL/JAOEZ/YA

hemihyperesthesia	HEM/HAO*IP/ES/THAOEZ/YA	hemispherium	HEM/SFAOERM
hemihyperhidrosis	HEM/HAO*IP/HI/DROE/SIS		HEM/SFAOER/YUM
	HEM/HAO*IP/HAOI/DROE/SIS	hemisphygmia	HEM/SFIG/MA
hemihyperidrosis	HEM/HAO*IP/DROE/SIS		HEM/SFIG/MAOE/YA
hemihypermetria	HEM/HAO*IP/MAOE/TRAOE/YA	Hemispora	HEM/SPOR/RA
hemihyperplasia	HEM/HAO*IP/PLAIZ/YA		HE/MIS/PRA
hemihypertonia	HEM/HAO*IP/TOEN/YA		HEM/IS/PRA
hemihypertrophy	HEM/HAOI/PERT/FI	hemispore	HEM/SPOER
hemihypesthesia	HEM/HAOI/PES/THAOEZ/YA	hemistrumectomy	HEM/STRAOU/MEKT/M*I
	HEM/HAOIP/ES/THAOEZ/YA	hemisyndrome	HEM/SIN/DROEM
hemihypoesthesia	HEM/HO*IP/ES/THAOEZ/YA	hemisystole	HEM/S*IS/LAOE
hemihypometria	HEM/HO*IP/MAOE/TRAOE/YA	hemiterata	HEM/TER/TA
hemihypoplasia	HEM/HO*IP/PLAIZ/YA	hemiteratic	HEM/TRAT/IK
hemihypotonia	HEM/HO*IP/TOEN/YA		HEM/TER/AT/IK
hemikaryon	HEM/KAR/YON	hemiterpene	HEM/TER/PAOEN
hemiketal	HEM/KAOE/TAL	hemitetany	HEM/TET/N*I
hemilaminectomy	HEM/LAM/NEKT/M*I	hemithermoanesthesia	HEM/THERM/ANS/THAOEZ/YA
hemilaryngectomy	HEM/LARN/JEKT/M*I	hemithorax	HEM/THOR/AX
hemilateral	HEM/LAT/RAL	hemithyroidectomy	HEM/THAOI/ROI/DEKT/M*I
hemilesion	HEM/LAOEGS	hemitomias	HEM/TOEM/YAS
hemilingual	HEM/LING/WAL	hemitonia	HEM/TOEN/YA
hemimacroglossia	HEM/MAK/RO/GLOS/YA	hemitoxin	HEM/TOK/SIN
hemimandibulectomy	HEM/MAN/DIB/LEKT/M*I	hemitremor	HEM/TREM/MOR
hemimelia	HEM/MAOEL/YA	hemivagotony	HEM/VAI/GOT/N*I
hemimelica	HEM/MEL/KA	hemivertebra	HEM/VERT/BRA
Hemimetabola	HEM/ME/TAB/LA	hemizygosity	HEM/ZAOI/GOS/TI
hemimetabolous	HEM/ME/TAB/LOUS	hemizygote	HEM/ZAOI/GOET
hemin	HAOE/MIN	hemizygotic	HEM/ZAOI/GOT/IK
	HEM/MIN	hemizygous	HEM/ZAOIG/OUS
heminephrectomy	HEM/NE/FREKT/M*I	hemlock	HEM/LOK
	HEM/NEF/REKT/M*I	hemo-	HAOEM
heminephroureterectomy	HEM/NEF/RO/YAOU/RAOET/		HAOE/MO
	REKT/M*I	hemoagglutination	HAOEM/AI/GLAOUT/NAIGS
hemineurasthenia	HEM/NAOUR/AS/THAOEN/YA	hemoagglutinin	HAOEM/AI/GLAOUT/NIN
hemiobesity	HEM/O/BAOEZ/TI	hemoalkalimeter	HAOEM/AL/KA/LIM/TER
hemiopalgia	HEM/O/PAL/JA		HAOEM/AL/KLIM/TER
	HEM/OP/AL/JA	hemoantitoxin	HAOEM/A*ENT/TOK/SIN
	HEM/YO/PAL/JA	hemobilia	HAOEM/BIL/YA
	HEM/YOP/AL/JA	hemobilinuria	HAOEM/BIL/NAOUR/YA
hemiopia	HEM/OEP/YA	hemoblast	HAOEM/BLA*S
hemiopic	HEM/OP/IK	hemoblastosis	HAOEM/BLAS/TOE/SIS
	HEM/OEP/IK	hemocatharsis	HAOEM/KA/THAR/SIS
hemipagus	HE/MIP/GUS	hemocatheresis	HAOEM/KA*T/RAOE/SIS
	HEM/IP/GUS	hemocatheretic	HAOEM/KA*T/RET/IK
hemiparalysis	HEM/PRAL/SIS	hemocele	HAOEM/SAO*EL
hemiparanesthesia	HEM/PAR/ANS/THAOEZ/YA	hemocelom	HAOEM/SE/LOM
hemiparaplegia	HEM/PAR/PLAOE/JA	hemocholecyst	HAOEM/KOEL/S*IS
hemiparesis	HEM/PRAOE/SIS	hemocholecystitis	HAOEM/KOEL/SIS/TAOITS
	HEM/PAR/SIS	hemochorial	HAOEM/KHOR/YAL
hemiparesthesia	HEM/PAR/ES/THAOEZ/YA	hemochromatosis	HAOEM/KROEM/TOE/SIS
hemiparetic	HEM/PA/RET/IK	hemochromatotic	HAOEM/KROEM/TOT/IK
hemiparkinsonism	HEM/PAR/SON/IFM	hemochrome	HAOEM/KROEM
	HEM/PAR/KIN/SON/IFM	hemochromogen	HAOEM/KROEM/JEN
hemipelvectomy	HEM/PEL/VEKT/M*I	hemochromometer	HAOEM/KROE/MOM/TER
hemipeptone	HEM/PEP/TOEN	hemochromometry	HAOEM/KROE/MOM/TRI
hemiphalangectomy	HEM/FAL/AN/JEKT/M*I		HAOEM/KROEM/OM/TRI
	HEM/FLAN/JEKT/M*I	hemoclasia	HAOEM/KLAIZ/YA
hemipinta	HEM/PIN/TA	hemoclasis	HAOE/MOK/LA/SIS
hemiplacenta	HEM/PLA/SEN/TA	hemoclastic	HAOEM/KLA*S/IK
hemiplegia	HEM/PLAOE/JA	hemoclip	HAOEM/KLIP
hemiplegic	HEM/PLAOEJ/IK	hemocoagulin	HAOEM/KO/AG/LIN
hemiprostatectomy	HEM/PRO*S/TEKT/M*I	hemoconcentration	HAOEM/KON/SEN/TRAIGS
Hemiptera	HAOE/MIPT/RA		HAOEM/KONS/TRAIGS
	HE/MIPT/RA	hemoconia	HAOEM/KOEN/YA
	HEM/IPT/RA	hemoconiosis	HAOEM/KOEN/YOE/SIS
hemipterous	HAOE/MIPT/ROUS	hemocrine	HAOEM/KRIN
	HE/MIPT/ROUS	hemocrinia	HAOEM/KRIN/YA
	HEM/IPT/ROUS	hemocrinotherapy	HAOEM/KRIN/THER/PI
hemipylorectomy	HEM/PAOIL/REKT/M*I	hemocryoscopy	HAOEM/KRAOI/OS/KPI
hemipyonephrosis	HEM/PAOI/NE/FROE/SIS	hemoculture	HAOEM/KUL/KHUR
	HEM/PAOI/NEF/ROE/SIS	hemocuprein	HAOEM/KAOUP/RIN
hemirachischisis	HEM/RA/KIS/KI/SIS		HAOEM/KAOU/PRIN
hemisacralization	HEM/SAI/KRAL/ZAIGS	hemocyanin	HAOEM/SAOI/NIN
hemiscotosis	HEM/SKOE/TOE/SIS	hemocyte	HAOEM/SAO*IT
hemisection	HEM/S*EBGS	Hemocyte-F	HAOEM/SAO*IT/F-RBGS
hemisensory	HEM/SENS/RI	Hemocyte Plus	HAOEM/SAO*IT/PLUS
hemiseptum	HEM/SEP/TUM	Hemocyte Tablets	HAOEM/SAO*IT/TAB/LET/-S
hemisoantibody	HAOEM/AOIS/A*ENT/BOD/DI	hemocytoblast	HAOEM/SAOIT/BLA*S
hemisomnambulism	HEM/SOM/NAM/BLIFM	hemocytoblastoma	HAOEM/SAOIT/BLAS/TOE/MA
hemisomus	HEM/SOE/MUS	hemocytocatheresis	HAOEM/SAOIT/KA/THER/SIS
hemisotonic	HEM/AOIS/TON/IK		HAOEM/SAOIT/KA*T/RAOE/SIS
hemispasm	HEM/SPAFM	hemocytoma	HAOEM/SAOI/TOE/MA
hemisphaeria	HEM/SFAER/YA	hemocytometer	HAOEM/SAOI/TOM/TER
hemisphaerium	HEM/SFAERM	hemocytometry	HAOEM/SAOI/TOM/TRI
	HEM/SFAER/YUM	hemocytophagia	HAOEM/SAOIT/FAI/JA
hemisphere	HEM/SFAER	hemocytophagic	HAOEM/SAOIT/FAJ/IK
hemispherectomy	HEM/SFAOER/EKT/M*I	hemocytopoiesis	HAOEM/SAOIT/POI/SIS
hemispheria	HEM/SFAOER/YA	hemocytotripsis	HAOEM/SAOIT/TRIP/SIS
hemispherii	HEM/SFAOER/YAOI	hemocytozoon	HAOEM/SAOIT/ZAON

hemodiagnosis	HAOEM/DAOIG/NOE/SIS		HE/MOF/LUS
hemodialysis	HAOEM/DI/AL/SIS	Hemophilus	K-P/HAOE/MOF/LUS
hemodialyzer	HAOEM/DAOI/LAOIZ/ER		K-P/HE/MOF/LUS
hemodiapedisis	HAOEM/DAOI/PE/DAOE/SIS	hemophobia	HAOEM/FOEB/YA
hemodiastase	HAOEM/DI/AS/TAIS	hemophoresis	HAOEM/FRAOE/SIS
hemodilution	HAOEM/DI/LAOUGS	hemophoric	HAOEM/FOER/IK
hemodromograph	HAOEM/DROEM/GRAF	hemophotograph	HAOEM/FOET/GRAF
	HAOEM/DROM/GRAF		HAOEM/FRAF
hemodromometer	HAOEM/DROE/MOM/TER	hemophotometer	HAOEM/FOE/TOM/TER
hemodynamic	HAOEM/DAOI/NAM/IK	hemophthalmia	HAOE/MOF/THAL/MA
hemodynamics	HAOEM/DAOI/NAM/IK/-S		HAOEM/OF/THAL/MA
hemodynamometer	HAOEM/DAOIN/MOM/TER	hemophthalmos	HAOE/MOF/THAL/MOS
hemodynamometry	HAOEM/DAOIN/MOM/TRI		HAOEM/OF/THAL/MOS
hemodyscrasia	HAOEM/DIS/KRAIZ/YA	hemophthalmus	HAOE/MOF/THAL/MUS
hemodystrophy	HAOEM/DIS/TRO/FI		HAOEM/OF/THAL/MUS
hemoendothelial	HAOEM/*END/THAOEL/YAL	hemophthisis	HAOE/MOF/THI/SIS
Hemofil	HAO*EM/FIL		HAOE/MOF/THAOI/SIS
	HAOEM/F*IL	hemopiesic	HAOEM/PAOI/AOES/IK
	(not HAOEM/FIL; see hemophil)		HAOEM/PAOI/AOEZ/IK
hemofiltration	HAOEM/FIL/TRAIGS	hemopiezometer	HAOEM/PAOI/ZOM/TER
hemoflagellate	HAOEM/FLAJ/LAIT	hemoplastic	HAOEM/PLA*S/IK
hemofuscin	HAOEM/FUS/SIN	hemoplasty	HAOEM/PLAS/TI
	HAOEM/FAOUS/SIN	hemopleura	HAOEM/PLAOU/RA
hemogenesis	HAOEM/JEN/SIS	hemopneumopericardium	HAOEM/NAOUM/P*ER/KARD/
hemogenic	HAOEM/JEN/IK		YUM
hemoglobin	HAOEM/GLOE/BIN	hemopneumothorax	HAOEM/NAOUM/THOR/AX
hemoglobinated	HAOEM/GLOEB/NAIT/-D	hemopoiesic	HAOEM/POIS/IK
hemoglobinemia	HAOEM/GLOEB/NAOEM/YA	hemopoiesis	HAOEM/POI/SIS
hemoglobinemic	HAOEM/GLOEB/NAOEM/IK	hemopoietic	HAOEM/POIT/IK
hemoglobiniferous	HAOEM/GLOEB/NIF/ROUS	hemopoietin	HAOEM/POI/TIN
hemoglobinocholia	HAOEM/GLOEB/NO/KOEL/YA	hemoporphyrin	HAOEM/POR/FRIN
hemoglobinolysis	HAOEM/GLOEB/NOL/SIS	hemoposia	HAOEM/POEZ/YA
hemoglobinometer	HAOEM/GLOEB/NOM/TER	hemoprecipitin	HAOEM/PRE/SIP/TIN
hemoglobinometry	HAOEM/GLOEB/NOM/TRI	hemoproctia	HAOEM/PROK/SHA
hemoglobinopathy	HAOEM/GLOEB/NOP/TH*I	hemoprotein	HAOEM/PRO/TAOEN
hemoglobinopepsia	HAOEM/GLOEB/NO/PEPS/YA	hemopsonin	HAOE/MOP/SOE/NIN
hemoglobinophilia	HAOEM/GLOEB/NO/FIL/YA	hemoptic	HAOE/MOPT/IK
hemoglobinophilic	HAOEM/GLOEB/NO/FIL/IK	hemoptoic	HAOE/MOP/TOIK
hemoglobinous	HAOEM/GLOEB/NOUS		HAOE/MOP/TOE/IK
hemoglobinuria	HAOEM/GLOEB/NAOUR/YA	hemoptysic	HAOE/MOP/TAOIS/IK
hemoglobinuric	HAOEM/GLOEB/NAOUR/IK		HE/MOP/TAOIS/IK
hemogram	HAOEM/GRAM	hemoptysis	HAOE/MOPT/SIS
hemohistioblast	HAOEM/H*IS/YO/BLA*S		HE/MOPT/SIS
hemohydraulics	HAOEM/HAOI/DRAUL/IK/-S	hemopyelectasia	HAOEM/PAOI/LEK/TAIZ/YA
hemokinesis	HAOEM/KI/NAOE/SIS	hemopyelectasis	HAOEM/PAOI/LEKT/SIS
hemokinetic	HAOEM/KI/NET/IK	hemorepellant	HAOEM/RE/PEL/LANT
hemolamella	HAOEM/LA/MEL/LA	hemorrhachis	HAOE/MOR/KIS
hemolipase	HAOEM/LIP/AIS	hemorrhage	HEM/RAJ
hemolith	HAOEM/L*IT	hemorrhagenic	HEM/RA/JEN/IK
hemology	HAOE/MOLG	hemorrhagic	HEM/RAJ/IK
hemolymph	HAOEM/LIM/-F	hemorrhagica	HEM/RAJ/KA
hemolymphangioma	HAOEM/LIM/FAN/JOE/MA	hemorrhagicum	HEM/RAJ/KUM
hemolysate	HAOE/MOL/SAIT	hemorrhagin	HEM/RAI/JIN
hemolysin	HAOE/MOL/SIN		HEM/RAJ/JIN
hemolysinogen	HAOE/MOL/SIN/JEN	hemorrhagiparous	HEM/RA/JIP/ROUS
hemolysis	HAOE/MOL/SIS		HEM/RAJ/IP/ROUS
hemolysoid	HAOE/MOL/SOID	hemorrhea	HEM/RAOE/YA
hemolysophilic	HAOEM/LAOIS/FIL/IK	hemorrheology	HAOEM/RAOE/OLG
hemolytic	HAOEM/LIT/IK	hemorrhoid	HEM/ROID
hemolyzable	HAOEM/LAOIZ/-BL	hemorrhoidal	HEM/ROI/DAL
hemolyzation	HAOE/MOL/ZAIGS	hemorrhoidectomy	HEM/ROI/DEKT/M*I
	HAOEM/LI/ZAIGS	hemorrhoidolysis	HEM/ROI/DOL/SIS
hemolyze	HAOEM/LAOIZ		HEM/ROID/OL/SIS
hemomanometer	HAOEM/MA/NOM/TER	hemosalpinx	HAOEM/SAL/PINGS
hemomediastinum	HAOEM/MAOED/YAS/TAOIN/UM	hemoscope	HAOEM/SKOEP
hemometer	HAOE/MOM/TER	hemosialemesis	HAOEM/SAOI/LEM/SIS
hemometra	HAOEM/MAOE/TRA		HAOEM/SAOIL/EM/SIS
hemometry	HAOE/MOM/TRI	hemosiderin	HAOEM/SID/RIN
hemonephrosis	HAOEM/NE/FROE/SIS	hemosiderinuria	HAOEM/SID/RIN/YAOUR/YA
hemo-opsonin	HAOEM/OP/SOE/NIN		HAOEM/SID/RI/NAOUR/YA
Hemopad	HAOEM/PAD	hemosiderosis	HAOEM/SID/ROE/SIS
hemopathic	HAOEM/PA*T/IK	hemospermia	HAOEM/SPERM/YA
hemopathology	HAOEM/PA/THOLG	hemosporine	HAOEM/SPORN
hemopathy	HAOE/MOP/TH*I	hemostasia	HAOEM/STAIZ/YA
hemoperfusion	HAOEM/PER/FAOUGS	hemostasis	HAOEM/STAI/SIS
hemopericardium	HAOEM/P*ER/KARD/YUM		HAOE/MO*S/SIS
hemoperitoneum	HAOEM/PERT/NAOEM	hemostat	HAOEM/STAT
hemopexin	HAOEM/PEK/SIN	hemostatic	HAOEM/STAT/IK
hemophage	HAOEM/FAIJ	hemostatica	HAOEM/STAT/KA
hemophagia	HAOEM/FAI/JA	hemostyptic	HAOEM/STIP/TIK
hemophagocyte	HAOEM/FAG/SAO*IT		HAOEM/STIPT/IK
hemophagocytosis	HAOEM/FAG/SAOI/TOE/SIS	hemotachometer	HAOEM/TA/KOM/TER
hemophil	HAOEM/FIL	hemotherapeutic	HAOEM/THER/PAOUT/IK
hemophile	HAOEM/FAOIL	hemotherapeutics	HAOEM/THER/PAOUT/IK/-S
hemophilia	HAOEM/FIL/YA	hemotherapy	HAOEM/THER/PI
hemophiliac	HAOEM/FIL/YAK	hemothorax	HAOEM/THOR/AX
hemophilic	HAOEM/FIL/IK	hemothymia	HAOEM/THAOIM/YA
hemophilioid	HAOEM/FIL/YOID	hemotoxic	HAOEM/TOX/IK
hemophilus	HAOE/MOF/LUS	hemotoxin	HAOEM/TOK/SIN

hemotoxism	HAOEM/TOK/SIFM
	HAOEM/TOX/IFM
hemotroph	HAOEM/TROF
	HAOEM/TROEF
hemotrophic	HAOEM/TROFK
	HAOEM/TROEFK
hemotropic	HAOEM/TROP/IK
hemotympanum	HAOEM/TIFRP/NUM
hemozoic	HAOEM/ZOIK
	HAOEM/ZOE/IK
hemozoon	HAOEM/ZAON
hemuresis	HEM/YAOU/RAOE/SIS
	HEM/YU/RAOE/SIS
henbane	HEN/BAIN
Henderson	HEND/ER/SON
	HEN/DER/SON
Henke	HEN/KAOE
Henle	HEN/LAOE
henna	HEN/NA
Henoch	HEN/OEK
	HEN/OK
henry	HEN/RI
Henry	K-P/HEN/RI
Hensen	HENS/-N
	HEN/SEN
Hensing	HENS/-G
	HEN/SING
hentzii	HENTS/YAOI
hepar	HAOE/PAR
heparan	HEP/RAN
heparin	HEP/RIN
Heparin Flush Kit	HEP/RIN/FLURB/KIT
Heparin Lock Flush	HEP/RIN/LOK/FLURB/
Solution	SLAOUGS
heparinase	HEP/RIN/AIS
heparinate	HEP/RIN/AIT
heparinemia	HEP/RI/NAOEM/YA
heparinic	HEP/RIN/IK
heparinize	HEP/RIN/AOIZ
heparitin	HEP/RI/TIN
hepat(o)-	HEPT
	HEP/T(O)
	HE/PAT
hepatalgia	HEP/TAL/JA
hepatatrophia	HEP/TA/TROEF/YA
hepatatrophy	HEP/TAT/RO/FI
hepatectomize	HEP/TEKT/MAOIZ
hepatectomy	HEP/TEKT/M*I
-hepatia	HE/PAI/SHA
	HE/PAIRB/YA
hepatic	HE/PAT/IK
hepatic(o)-	HE/PAT/K(O)
hepatica	HE/PAT/KA
hepaticae	HE/PAT/SAE
hepaticocholangiojejunostomy	
	HE/PAT/KO/KLAN/JO/JEJ/NO*S/
	M*I
hepaticocholedochostomy	HE/PAT/KO/KLED/KO*S/M*I
	HE/PAT/KO/KOL/DO/KO*S/M*I
hepaticodochotomy	HE/PAT/KO/DOE/KOT/M*I
hepaticoduodenostomy	HE/PAT/KO/DAOU/DEN/O*S/M*I
	HE/PAT/KO/DAOU/DE/NO*S/M*I
	HE/PAT/KO/DWOD/NO*S/M*I
hepaticoenterostomy	HE/PAT/KO/SPWRO*S/M*I
	HE/PAT/KO/SPWER/RO*S/M*I
hepaticogastrostomy	HE/PAT/KO/GAS/TRO*S/M*I
hepaticojejunostomy	HE/PAT/KO/JEJ/NO*S/M*I
hepaticolithotomy	HE/PAT/KO/LI/THOT/M*I
hepaticolithotripsy	HE/PAT/KO/L*IT/TRIP/SI
hepaticopancreatic	HE/PAT/KO/PAN/KRAT/IK
hepaticopancreatica	HE/PAT/KO/PAN/KRAT/KA
hepaticopulmonary	HE/PAT/KO/PUL/MO/NAIR
	HE/PAT/KO/PUM/NAIR
hepaticostomy	HE/PAT/KO*S/M*I
hepaticotomy	HE/PAT/KOT/M*I
hepaticum	HE/PAT/KUM
hepaticus	HE/PAT/KUS
hepatin	HEP/TIN
hepatis	HEP/TIS
	HAOEP/TIS
hepatism	HEP/TIFM
hepatitic	HEP/TIT/IK
hepatitides	HEP/TIT/DAOEZ
hepatitis	HEP/TAOITS
hepatization	HEP/TI/ZAIGS
hepatize	HEP/TAOIZ
hepatized	HEP/TAOIZ/-D
hepatobiliary	HEPT/BIL/YAIR
hepatoblastoma	HEPT/BLAS/TOE/MA

hepatobronchial	HEPT/BRONG/YAL
hepatocarcinogenesis	HEPT/KARS/NO/JEN/SIS
hepatocarcinogenic	HEPT/KARS/NO/JEN/IK
hepatocarcinoma	HEPT/KARS/NOE/MA
hepatocele	HE/PAT/SAO*EL
	HEPT/SAO*EL
hepatocellular	HEPT/SEL/YAOU/LAR
hepatocholangiocarcinoma	HEPT/KLAN/JO/KARS/NOE/MA
hepatocholangioduodenostomy	
	HEPT/KLAN/JO/DAOU/DEN/O*S/
	M*I
	HEPT/KLAN/JO/DAOU/DE/NO*S/
	M*I
	HEPT/KLAN/JO/DWOD/NO*S/M*I
hepatocholangioenterostomy	
	HEPT/KLAN/JO/SPWRO*S/M*I
	HEPT/KLAN/JO/SPWER/RO*S/M*I
hepatocholangiogastrostomy	
	HEPT/KLAN/JO/GAS/TRO*S/M*I
hepatocholangiojejunostomy	
	HEPT/KLAN/JO/JEJ/NO*S/M*I
hepatocholangiostomy	HEPT/KLAN/JO*S/M*I
hepatocholangitis	HEPT/KOE/LAN/JAOITS
	HEPT/KLAN/JAOITS
hepatocirrhosis	HEPT/SIR/ROE/SIS
hepatocolic	HEPT/KOL/IK
hepatocolicum	HEPT/KOL/KUM
hepatocuprein	HEPT/KAOU/PRIN
	HEPT/KAOUP/RIN
hepatocystic	HEPT/S*IS/IK
hepatocyte	HEPT/SAO*IT
hepatoduodenale	HEPT/DWOD/NAI/LAOE
	HEPT/DAOU/DE/NAI/LAOE
hepatoduodenostomy	HEPT/DAOU/DEN/O*S/M*I
	HEPT/DAOU/DE/NO*S/M*I
	HEPT/DWOD/NO*S/M*I
hepatodynia	HEPT/DIN/YA
hepatodysentery	HEPT/DIS/SPWAIR
	HEPT/DIS/EN/TAIR
	HEPT/DIS/SPWER/RI
hepatodystrophy	HEPT/DIS/TRO/FI
hepatoenteric	HEPT/SPWER/IK
hepatoenterostomy	HEPT/SPWRO*S/M*I
hepatoflavin	HEPT/FLAIVN
hepatofugal	HEP/TOF/GAL
	HEPT/FAOU/GAL
hepatogastric	HEPT/GAS/TRIK
hepatogastricum	HEPT/GAS/TRI/KUM
hepatogenic	HEPT/JEN/IK
hepatogenous	HEP/TOJ/NOUS
hepatoglycemia	HEPT/GLAOI/SAOEM/YA/
glycogenetica	GLAOIK/JE/NET/KA
hepatogram	HEPT/GRAM
hepatography	HEP/TOG/FI
hepatohemia	HEPT/HAOEM/YA
hepatoid	HEP/TOID
hepatojugular	HEPT/JUG/LAR
hepatojugularometer	HEPT/JUG/LA/ROM/TER
hepatolenticular	HEPT/LEN/TIK/LAR
hepatolienal	HEPT/LAOI/NAL
hepatolienography	HEPT/LAOI/NOG/FI
hepatolienomegaly	HEPT/LAOI/NO/MEG/LI
hepatolith	HEPT/L*IT
hepatolithectomy	HEPT/LI/THEKT/M*I
hepatolithiasis	HEPT/LI/THAOI/SIS
hepatologist	HEP/TO*LGS
hepatology	HEP/TOLG
hepatolysin	HEP/TOL/SIN
hepatolysis	HEP/TOL/SIS
hepatolytic	HEPT/LIT/IK
hepatoma	HEP/TOE/MA
hepatomalacia	HEPT/MA/LAI/SHA
hepatomegalia	HEPT/ME/GAIL/YA
hepatomegaly	HEPT/MEG/LI
hepatomelanosis	HEPT/MEL/NOE/SIS
hepatometry	HEP/TOM/TRI
hepatomphalocele	HEP/TOM/FAL/SAO*EL
	HEP/TOM/FLO/SAO*EL
hepatomphalos	HEP/TOM/FLOS
hepatonecrosis	HEPT/NE/KROE/SIS
hepatonephric	HEPT/NEF/RIK
hepatonephritic	HEPT/NE/FRIT/IK
hepatonephritis	HEPT/NE/FRAOITS
hepatonephromegaly	HEPT/NEF/RO/MEG/LI
hepatopancreatic	HEPT/PAN/KRAT/IK
hepatopancreatica	HEPT/PAN/KRAT/KA
hepatopancreaticae	HEPT/PAN/KRAT/SAE
hepatopath	HEPT/PA*T
hepatopathic	HEPT/PA*T/IK

hepatopathy	HEP/TOP/TH*I	hereditaria	HE/RED
hepatoperitonitis	HEPT/PERT/NAOITS	hereditary	HE/RED/TAIR/YA
hepatopetal	HEP/TOP/TAL	heredity	HE/RED/TAIR
hepatopexy	HEP/TOP/PEK/SI	heredoataxia	HE/RED/TI
hepatophlebitis	HEPT/FLE/BAOITS	heredobiologic	HER/DO/AI/TAX/YA
hepatophlebography	HEPT/FLE/BOG/FI	heredodegeneration	HER/DO/BAO*I/LOJ/IK
hepatophlebotomy	HEPT/FLE/BOT/M*I	heredodiathesis	HER/DO/DE/JEN/RAIGS
hepatophyma	HEPT/FAOI/MA	heredofamilial	HER/DO/DI/A*T/SIS
hepatopleural	HEPT/PLAOURL	heredoimmunity	HER/DO/FA/MIL/YAL
hepatopneumonic	HEPT/NAOU/MON/IK	heredoinfection	HER/DO/IM/MAOUN/TI
hepatoportal	HEPT/POR/TAL	heredolues	HER/DO/IN/F*EBGS
hepatoptosis	HEPT/TOE/SIS	heredoluetic	HER/DO/LAOU/AOEZ
	HEP/TOP/TOE/SIS	heredopathia	HER/DO/LAOU/ET/IK
hepatopulmonary	HEPT/PUL/MO/NAIR	heredosyphilis	HER/DO/PA*T/YA
	HEPT/PUM/NAIR	heredosyphilitic	HER/DO/SIF/LIS
hepatorenal	HEPT/RAOENL	heredosyphilology	HER/DO/SIF/LIT/IK
hepatorenale	HEPT/RE/NAI/LAOE		HER/DO/SIF/LOLG
hepatorrhagia	HEPT/RAI/JA	Herelle	HE/REL
hepatorrhaphy	HEP/TOR/FI	Herellea	HE/REL/YA
hepatorrhea	HEPT/RAOE/YA	Herff	HER/-F
hepatorrhexis	HEPT/REK/SIS	Hering	H*ER/-G
hepatoscan	HEPT/SKAN		(not HER/-G; see herring)
hepatoscopy	HEP/TOS/KPI	heritability	HERT/-BLT
hepatosis	HEP/TOE/SIS		HER/TABLT
hepatosplenitis	HEPT/SPLAOE/NAOITS	heritable	HERT/-BL
hepatosplenography	HEPT/SPLAOE/NOG/FI		HER/TABL
hepatosplenomegaly	HEPT/SPLAOEN/MEG/LI	heritage	HER/TAJ
	HEPT/SPLEN/MEG/LI	Herlitz	HER/LITS
hepatosplenometry	HEPT/SPLAOE/NOM/TRI	Hermann	H*ER/MAN
hepatosplenopathy	HEPT/SPLAOE/NOP/TH*I		HER/MA*N
hepatostomy	HEP/TO*S/M*I		(not HER/MAN; see her man)
hepatotherapy	HEPT/THER/PI	hermaphrodism	HER/MAF/RO/DIFM
hepatotomy	HEP/TOT/M*I	hermaphrodite	HER/MAF/RO/DAOIT
hepatotoxemia	HEPT/TOK/SAOEM/YA	hermaphroditism	HER/MAF/RO/DAOIT/IFM
hepatotoxic	HEPT/TOX/IK	hermaphroditismus	HER/MAF/RO/DAOI/TIZ/MUS
hepatotoxicity	HEPT/TOK/SIS/TI	Hermetia illucens	HER/MAOE/SHA/IL/LAOU/SENZ
hepatotoxin	HEPT/TOK/SIN	hermetic	HER/MET/IK
hepatotropic	HEPT/TROP/IK	hermetically	HER/MET/KLI
Hepatozoon	HEPT/ZAON	hermsii	HERMS/YAOI
Hep-B-Gammagee	HEP/B-RBGS/GAM/JAOE	herni(o)-	HERN/Y(O)
Hep-Forte	HEP/FOR/TAI	hernia	HERN/YA
Hep-Lock	HEP/LOK	hernial	HERN/YAL
hepta-	HEPT	herniary	HERN/YAIR
	HEP/TA	herniate	HERN/YAIT
heptabarbital	HEPT/BARB/TAL	herniated	HERN/YAIT/-D
heptachromic	HEPT/KROEM/IK	herniation	HERN/YAIGS
heptad	HEP/TAD	hernioappendectomy	HERN/YO/AP/EN/DEKT/M*I
heptadactylia	HEPT/DAK/TIL/YA	hernioenterotomy	HERN/YO/SPWROT/M*I
heptadactylism	HEPT/DAKT/LIFM	herniography	HERN/YOG/FI
heptadactyly	HEPT/DAKT/LI	hernioid	HERN/YOID
heptaminol	HEP/TAM/NOL	herniolaparotomy	HERN/YO/LAP/ROT/M*I
heptanal	HEPT/NAL	herniology	HERN/YOLG
heptapeptide	HEPT/PEP/TAOID	hernioplasty	HERN/YO/PLAS/TI
heptaploid	HEPT/PLOID	herniopuncture	HERN/YO/PUNG/KHUR
heptaploidy	HEPT/PLOI/DI	herniorrhaphy	HERN/YOR/FI
heptatomic	HEPT/TOM/IK	herniotome	HERN/YO/TOEM
heptavalent	HEPT/VAIL/ENT	herniotomy	HERN/YOT/M*I
Heptavax	HEPT/VAX	heroic	HAOE/ROIK
Heptavax-B	HEPT/VAX/B-RBGS		HAOE/ROE/IK
heptazone	HEPT/ZOEN	heroin	HER/ROIN
heptoglobin	HEPT/GLOE/BIN		HER/RO/WIN
heptoglobinemia	HEPT/GLOEB/NAOEM/YA		(not HER/WIN; see her win)
heptose	HEP/TOES	heroinism	HER/ROIN/IFM
heptosuria	HEPT/SAOUR/YA	herpangina	HER/PAN/JI/NA
heptulose	HEPT/LOES		HERP/AN/JI/NA
	HEP/TAOU/LOES		HER/PAN/JAOI/NA
Heptuna	HEP/TAOU/NA		HERP/AN/JAOI/NA
Heptuna Plus	HEP/TAOU/NA/PLUS	Herpecin-L	HERP/SIN/L-RBGS
herb	ERB	herpes	HER/PAOEZ
	HERB	herpesencephalitis	HER/PAOEZ/EN/SEF/LAOITS
herbaceous	*ER/BAIRBS	herpes simplex	HER/PAOEZ/SIM/PLEX
	HER/BAIRBS	Herpesviridae	HER/PAOEZ/VAOI/RI/DAE
herbal	ERBL	herpesvirus	HER/PAOEZ/VAOI/RUS
	HERBL	Herpesvirus	K-P/HER/PAOEZ/VAOI/RUS
	*ER/BAL	herpetic	HER/PET/IK
	HER/BAL	herpeticum	HER/PET/KUM
herbalist	ERB/L*IS	herpeticus	HER/PET/KUS
	HERB/L*IS	herpetiform	HER/PET/FORM
Herbert	HER/BERT	herpetiformis	HER/PET/FOR/MIS
herbicide	HERB/SAO*ID	herpetologist	HERP/TO*LGS
	ERB/SAO*ID	herpetology	HERP/TOLG
herbivore	HERB/VOER	Herpetomonas	HERP/TOM/NAS
	ERB/VOER	herpetophobia	HER/PET/FOEB/YA
herbivorous	HER/BIV/ROUS		HERP/TO/FOEB/YA
	*ER/BIV/ROUS	Herpetoviridae	HERP/TO/VIR/DAE
Herbst	H*ERBS	herpetovirus	HERP/TO/VAOI/RUS
	HERBS/-T	Herring	K-P/HER/-G
herd	HERD	Herrmannsdorfer	HER/MANS/DOR/FER
hered(o)-	HER/D(O)	hersage	AIR/SAJ

	*ER/SAJ
	HER/SAJ
Hertwig	HERT/VIG
	HERT/WIG
hertz	HERTS
Hertz	K-P/HERTS
hertzian	HERTS/YAN
Herxheimer	HERX/HAOIM/ER
herzstoss	HERZ/STOSZ
	HAIRZ/STOSZ
Heschl	HERB/-L
	(*not* HERBL; **see** herbal)
hesitancy	HEZ/TAN/SI
Hespan	HES/PAN
hesperanopia	HES/PRA/NOEP/YA
hesperetin	HES/PER/TIN
hesperidin	HES/PER/DIN
Hess	HESZ
Hesselbach	HES/EL/BAK
	HES/EL/BAUK
Hesselbachi	HES/EL/BAU/KAOI
	HES/EL/BAI/KAOI
hetacillin	HET/SLIN
	HET/SIL/LIN
hetaflur	HET/FLAOUR
	HET/FLUR
hetastarch	HET/STA*RPBLG
	HET/STAR/-FP
heter(o)-	HET/R(O)
heteradelphia	HET/RA/DEL/FA
	HET/RA/DEL/FAOE/YA
heteradelphus	HET/RA/DEL/FUS
heteradenia	HET/RA/DAOEN/YA
heteradenic	HET/RA/DEN/IK
heterakid	HET/RAI/KID
Heterakis	HET/RAI/KIS
heteralius	HET/RAIL/YUS
heterauxesis	HET/RAUK/ZAOE/SIS
heteraxial	HET/RAX/YAL
heterecious	HET/RAOERBS
heterecism	HET/RAOE/SIFM
heterergic	HET/RERJ/IK
heteresthesia	HET/RES/THAOEZ/YA
heteriform	HET/RI/FORM
heteroagglutination	HET/RO/AI/GLAOUT/NAIGS
heteroagglutinin	HET/RO/AI/GLAOUT/NIN
heteroalbumose	HET/RO/AL/BAOU/MOES
heteroalbumosuria	HET/RO/AL/BAOUM/SAOUR/YA
heteroallele	HET/RO/AI/LAOEL
	HET/RO/AL/LAOEL
heteroallelic	HET/RO/AI/LAOEL/IK
	HET/RO/AL/LAOEL/IK
heteroantibody	HET/RO/A*ENT/BOD/DI
heteroantigen	HET/RO/A*ENT/JEN
heteroantiserum	HET/RO/A*ENT/SAOERM
heteroatom	HET/RO/AT/OM
Heterobilharzia	HET/RO/BIL/HARZ/YA
heteroblastic	HET/RO/BLA*S/IK
heterocellular	HET/RO/SEL/YAOU/LAR
heterocentric	HET/RO/SEN/TRIK
heterocephalus	HET/RO/SEF/LUS
heterocheiral	HET/RO/KAOIRL
heterochromatic	HET/RO/KROE/MAT/IK
heterochromatin	HET/RO/KROEM/TIN
heterochromatinization	HET/RO/KROEM/TIN/ZAIGS
heterochromatosis	HET/RO/KROEM/TOE/SIS
heterochromia	HET/RO/KROEM/YA
heterochromic	HET/RO/KROEM/IK
heterochromosome	HET/RO/KROEM/SOEM
heterochromous	HET/RO/KROEM/OUS
heterochron	HET/RO/KRON
	HET/RO/KROEN
heterochronia	HET/RO/KROEN/YA
heterochronic	HET/RO/KRON/IK
heterochronous	HET/ROK/RO/NOUS
heterochthonous	HET/ROK/THO/NUS
heterochylia	HET/RO/KAOIL/YA
heterocinesia	HET/RO/SI/NAOEZ/YA
heterocladic	HET/RO/KLAD/IK
heterocomplement	HET/RO/KOM/PLEMT
heterocrine	HET/RO/KRIN
heterocrisis	HET/RO/KRAOI/SIS
	HET/ROK/RI/SIS
heterocyclic	HET/RO/SAOIK/LIK
heterocytolysin	HET/RO/SAOI/TOL/SIN
heterocytotoxin	HET/RO/SAOIT/TOK/SIN
heterocytotropic	HET/RO/SAOIT/TROP/IK
heterodermic	HET/RO/DERM/IK
heterodesmotic	HET/RO/DES/MOT/IK
	HET/RO/DEZ/MOT/IK
heterodidymus	HET/RO/DID/MUS
heterodisperse	HET/RO/DIS/PERS
heterodont	HET/RO/DONT
Heterodoxus spiniger	HET/RO/DOK/SUS/SPAOIN/GER
heterodromous	HET/ROD/RO/MOUS
	HET/ROED/RO/MOUS
heteroduplex	HET/RO/DAOU/PLEX
heterodymus	HET/ROD/MUS
heteroecious	HET/RO/AOERBS
heteroerotic	HET/RO/E/ROT/IK
heteroerotism	HET/RO/*ER/TIFM
heterofermenter	HET/RO/FERMT/ER
heterogamete	HET/RO/GAM/AOET
heterogametic	HET/RO/GA/MET/IK
heterogamety	HET/RO/GAM/TI
heterogamous	HET/ROG/MOUS
heterogamy	HET/ROG/M*I
heteroganglionic	HET/RO/GANG/LON/IK
heterogeneic	HET/RO/JE/NAOE/IK
	HET/RO/JE/NAI/IK
heterogeneity	HET/RO/JE/NAOE/TI
	HET/RO/JE/NAI/TI
heterogeneous	HET/RO/JAOEN/YOUS
heterogenesis	HET/RO/JEN/SIS
heterogenetic	HET/RO/JE/NET/IK
heterogenic	HET/RO/JEN/IK
heterogenicity	HET/RO/JE/NIS/TI
heterogenote	HET/RO/JAOE/NOET
heterogenous	HET/ROJ/NOUS
heteroglobulose	HET/RO/GLOB/LOES
heterogony	HET/ROG/N*I
heterograft	HET/RO/GRAFT
heterography	HET/ROG/FI
heterohemagglutination	HET/RO/HEM/AI/GLAOUT/NAIGS
heterohemagglutinin	HET/RO/HEM/AI/GLAOUT/NIN
heterohemolysin	HET/RO/HAOE/MOL/SIN
heterohexosan	HET/RO/HEX/SAN
heterohypnosis	HET/RO/HIP/NOE/SIS
heteroimmune	HET/RO/IM/MAOUN
heteroimmunity	HET/RO/IM/MAOUN/TI
heteroinfection	HET/RO/IN/F*EBGS
heteroinoculable	HET/RO/IN/OK/LABL
heteroinoculation	HET/RO/IN/OK/LAIGS
heterointoxication	HET/RO/SPWOX/KAIGS
heterokaryon	HET/RO/KAR/YON
heterokaryosis	HET/RO/KAR/YOE/SIS
heterokaryotic	HET/RO/KARYOT/IK
heterokeratoplasty	HET/RO/KER/TO/PLAS/TI
heterokinesia	HET/RO/KI/NAOEZ/YA
heterokinesis	HET/RO/KI/NAOE/SIS
heterolactic	HET/RO/LAKT/IK
heterolalia	HET/RO/LAIL/YA
heterolateral	HET/RO/LAT/RAL
heterolipid	HET/RO/LIP/ID
heteroliteral	HET/RO/LIT/RAL
heterolith	HET/RO/L*IT
heterologous	HET/ROL/GOUS
heterology	HET/ROLG
heterolysin	HET/ROL/SIN
heterolysis	HET/ROL/SIS
heterolysosome	HET/RO/LAOIS/SOEM
heterolytic	HET/RO/LIT/IK
heteromastigote	HET/RO/MA*S/GOET
heteromeral	HET/ROM/RAL
heteromeric	HET/RO/MER/IK
heteromerous	HET/ROM/ROUS
heterometabolous	HET/RO/ME/TAB/LOUS
heterometaplasia	HET/RO/MET/PLAIZ/YA
heterometric	HET/RO/MET/RIK
heterometropia	HET/RO/ME/TROEP/YA
heteromorphic	HET/RO/MOR/FIK
heteromorphism	HET/RO/MOR/FIFM
heteromorphosis	HET/RO/MOR/FOE/SIS
heteromorphous	HET/RO/MOR/FOUS
heteronomous	HET/RON/MOUS
heteronomy	HET/RON/M*I
heteronuclear	HET/RO/NAOUK/LAR
heteronymous	HET/RO*N/MOUS
	HET/RON/MO*US
	(*not* HET/RON/MOUS; **see** heteronomous)
hetero-osteoplasty	HET/RO/O*S/YO/PLAS/TI
hetero-ovular	HET/RO/OV/LAR
heteropagus	HET/ROP/GUS
heteropancreatism	HET/RO/PAN/KRA/TIFM
heteropathy	HET/ROP/TH*I
heteropentosan	HET/RO/PENT/SAN
heterophagosome	HET/RO/FAG/SOEM

heterophagy	HET/ROF/JI	heteroxenous	HET/ROX/NOUS
heterophany	HET/ROF/N*I	heteroxeny	HET/ROX/N*I
heterophasia	HET/RO/FAIZ/YA	heterozoic	HET/RO/ZOIK
heterophasis	HET/RO/FAI/SIS		HET/RO/ZOE/IK
heterophemia	HET/RO/FAOEM/YA	heterozygosis	HET/RO/ZAOI/GOE/SIS
heterophemy	HET/ROF/M*I	heterozygosity	HET/RO/ZAOI/GOS/TI
heterophil	HET/RO/FIL	heterozygote	HET/RO/ZAOI/GOET
heterophilic	HET/RO/FIL/IK	heterozygotic	HET/RO/ZAOI/GOT/IK
heterophile	HET/RO/FAOIL	heterozygous	HET/RO/ZAOIG/OUS
heterophonia	HET/RO/FOEN/YA	Heublein	HOIB/LAOIN
heterophoralgia	HET/RO/FOE/RAL/JA	Heubner	HOIB/NER
heterophoria	HET/RO/FOER/YA	heuristic	HAOU/R*IS/IK
heterophoric	HET/RO/FOER/IK	Heuser	HOIZ/ER
heterophthalmia	HET/ROF/THAL/MA	hexa-	HEX
	HET/ROF/THAL/MAOE/YA	hexabasic	HEX/BAIS/IK
heterophthalmos	HET/ROF/THAL/MOS	hexabione	HEX/BAO*I/OEN
heterophthalmus	HET/ROF/THAL/MUS	hexabiose	HEX/BAO*I/OES
heterophthongia	HET/ROF/THON/JA	hexacanth	HEX/KA*NT
heterophyes	HET/ROF/YAOEZ	hexacarbacholine	HEX/KARB/KOE/LAOEN
Heterophyes	K-P/HET/ROF/YAOEZ	hexachlorobenzene	HEX/KLOR//BEN/ZAOEN
heterophyiasis	HET/RO/FAOI/AOI/SIS	hexachlorocyclohexane	HEX/KLOR/SAOI/KLO/HEX/AIN
heterophyid	HET/RO/FAOI/ID		HEX/KLOR/SAOI/KLO/HEK/SAIN
Heterophyidae	HET/RO/FAOI/DAE	hexachlorophane	HEX/KLOR/FAIN
heterophyidiasis	HET/RO/FAOI/DAOI/SIS	hexachlorophene	HEX/KLOR/FAOEN
heteroplasia	HET/RO/PLAIZ/YA	hexachromic	HEX/KROEM/IK
heteroplasm	HET/RO/PLAFM	hexacosane	HEX/KO/SAIN
heteroplastic	HET/RO/PLA*S/IK		HEX/AK/SAIN
heteroplastid	HET/RO/PLAS/TID	hexacosanol	HEX/KOES/NOL
heteroplasty	HET/RO/PLAS/TI	hexacosyl	HEX/KO/SIL
heteroploid	HET/RO/PLOID	hexad	HEX/AD
heteroploidy	HET/RO/PLOI/DI		HEK/SAD
heteropodal	HET/ROP/DAL	hexadactylia	HEX/DAK/TIL/YA
heteropolymeric	HET/RO/POL/MER/IK	hexadactylism	HEX/DAKT/LIFM
heteropolysaccharide	HET/RO/POL/SAK/RAOID	hexadactyly	HEX/DAKT/LI
heteroproteose	HET/RO/PROET/YOES	hexadecanoate	HEX/DEK/NOE/AIT
heteropsia	HET/ROPS/YA	hexadecanoic	HEX/DEK/NOIK
Heteroptera	HET/ROPT/RA		HEX/DEK/NOE/IK
heteroptics	HET/ROPT/IK/-S	hexadecanol	HEX/DEK/NOL
heteropyknosis	HET/RO/PIK/NOE/SIS	hexadiphane	HEX/DI/FAIN
heteropyknotic	HET/RO/PIK/NOT/IK	Hexadrol	HEX/DROL
heterosaccharide	HET/RO/SAK/RAOID	hexafluorenium	HEX/FLAOU/REN/YUM
heteroscope	HET/RO/SKOEP		HEX/FLAOU/RAOEN/YUM
heteroscopy	HET/ROS/KPI	hexagon	HEX/GON
heteroserotherapy	HET/RO/SAOER/THER/PI	hexahydric	HEX/HAOI/DRIK
heterosexual	HET/RO/SEX/YAOUL	hexamer	HEX/MER
heterosexuality	HET/RO/SEX/YAL/TI	hexamethone	HEX/M*ET/OEN
heterosis	HET/ROE/SIS	hexamethonium	HEX/ME/THOEN/YUM
heterosmia	HET/ROZ/MAOE/YA	hexamethylated	HEX/M*ET/LAIT/-D
heterosomal	HET/RO/SOE/MAL	hexamidine	HEK/SAM/DAOEN
heterosome	HET/RO/SOEM		HEX/AM/DAOEN
heterospecific	HET/RO/SPEFK	hexamine	HEX/MAOEN
	HET/RO/SPE/SIFK		HEX/MIN
heterospore	HET/RO/SPOER	Hexamita	HEK/SAM/TA
heterosporous	HET/ROS/PROUS		HEX/AM/TA
heterostimulation	HET/RO/STIM/LAIGS	hexamitiasis	HEK/SAM/TAO/SIS
heterosuggestion	HET/RO/SUG/JEGS		HEX/AM/TAOI/SIS
	HET/RO/SUGS	hexamylose	HEX/AM/LOES
heterotaxia	HET/RO/TAX/YA	hexane	HEK/SAIN
heterotaxic	HET/RO/TAX/IK		HEX/AIN
heterotaxis	HET/RO/TAK/SIS	hexanoate	HEX/NOE/AIT
heterotaxy	HET/RO/TAK/SI	hexanoic	HEX/NOIK
heterothallic	HET/RO/THAL/IK		HEX/NOE/IK
heterothallism	HET/RO/THAL/IFM	hexanoyl	HEX/NOIL
heterotherapy	HET/RO/THER/PI		HEX/NOE/IL
heterotherm	HET/RO/THERM	hexaploid	HEX/PLOID
heterothermic	HET/RO/THERM/IK	hexaploidy	HEX/PLOI/DI
heterothermy	HET/RO/THER/M*I	Hexapoda	HEK/SAP/DA
heterotic	HET/ROT/IK		HEX/AP/DA
heterotonia	HET/RO/TOEN/YA	hexatomic	HEX/TOM/IK
heterotopia	HET/RO/TOEP/YA	hexavaccine	HEX/VAK/SAOEN
heterotopic	HET/RO/TOP/IK	hexavalent	HEX/VAI/LENT
heterotopous	HET/ROT/POUS	hexavitamin	HEX/VAOIT/MIN
heterotopy	HET/ROT/PI	hexedine	HEX/DAOEN
heterotransplant	HET/RO/TRA*NS/PLANT	hexestrol	HEK/SES/TROL
heterotransplantation	HET/RO/TRA*NS/PLAN/TAIGS		HEX/ES/TROL
heterotrichosis	HET/RO/TRI/KOE/SIS	hexethal	HEX/THAL
heterotrichous	HET/ROT/RI/KOUS	hexetidine	HEK/SET/DAOEN
heterotroph	HET/RO/TROF		HEX/ET/DAOEN
	HET/RO/TROEF	hexhydric	HEX/HAOI/DRIK
heterotrophia	HET/RO/TROEF/YA	hexitol	HEX/TOL
heterotrophic	HET/RO/TROFK	hexobarbital	HEX/BARB/TAL
heterotrophy	HET/ROT/RO/FI	hexobendine	HEX/BEN/DAOEN
heterotropia	HET/RO/TROEP/YA	hexocyclium	HEX/SIK/LUM
heterotropy	HET/ROT/RO/PI		HEX/SAOI/KLUM
heterotrypsin	HET/RO/TRIP/SIN		HEX/SAOIK/LUM
heterotypic	HET/RO/TIP/IK	hexokinase	HEX/KAOI/NAIS
heterotypical	HET/RO/TIP/KAL	hexonate	HEX/NAIT
heterovaccine	HET/RO/VAK/SAOEN	hexon	HEK/SON
heteroxanthine	HET/RO/ZAN/THIN	hexone	HEX/OEN

hexonic	HEK/SOEN	hidrosis	HI/DROE/SIS
hexosamine	HEK/SON/IK		HID/ROE/SIS
	HEX/SAM/AOEN		HAOI/DROE/SIS
	HEX/OES/AM/MIN	hidrotic	HI/DROT/IK
	HEK/SOES/AM/MIN		HID/ROT/IK
hexosaminidase	HEX/SA/MIN/DAIS		HAOI/DROT/IK
	HEX/OES/MIN/DAIS	hiemal	HAOI/MAL
	HEK/SOES/MIN/DAIS	hiemalis	HAOI/MAI/LIS
hexosan	HEX/SAN	hier(o)-	HAOI/R(O)
hexosazone	HEX/SAI/ZOEN		HAOIR
hexose	HEX/OES	hieralgia	HAOI/RAL/JA
	HEK/SOES		HAOIR/AL/JA
hexosebiphosphatase	HEX/OES/B*I/FOS/FA/TAIS	hierarchy	HAOIR/AR/KI
	HEK/SOES/B*I/FOS/FA/TAIS		HAOIR/RAR/KI
hexosediphosphatase	HEX/OES/DI/FOS/FA/TAIS	hierolisthesis	HAOIR/LIS/THE/SIS
	HEK/SOES/DI/FOS/FA/TAIS		HAOIR/LIS/THAOE/SIS
hexosephosphatase	HEX/OES/FOS/FA/TAIS	hierophobia	HAOIR/FOEB/YA
	HEK/SOES/FOS/FA/TAIS	hierotherapy	HAOIR/THER/PI
hexosephosphate	HEX/OES/FOS/FAIT	Higashi	HI/GA/SHAOE
	HEK/SOES/FOS/FAIT		HI/GARB/SHAOE
hexosephosphoric	HEX/OES/FOS/FOER/IK	Highmore	HAOI/MOR
	HEK/SOES/FOS/FOER/IK	highmori	HAOI/MOR/RAOI
hexosyltransferase	HEX/SIL/TRA*NS/FRAIS		HAOI/MOE/RAOI
hexoxidase	HEX/OX/DAIS	highmorianum	HAOI/MOR/YAIN/UM
hexu-	HEX		HAOI/MOER/YAIN/UM
	HEX/YAOU	Hikojima	HIK/JAOE/MA
	HEX/YU	hila	HAOI/LA
hexulose	HEX/LOES	hilar	HAOI/LAR
hexuronic	HEX/RON/IK	hili	HAOI/LAOI
hexyl	HEK/SIL	hilifuge	HAOI/LI/FAOUJ
	HEX/IL	hilitis	HAOI/LAOITS
hexylamine	HEK/SIL/AM/MAOEN	Hill	K-P/HIL
	HEX/IL/AM/MAOEN	Hillis	HIL/LIS
hexylcaine	HEK/SIL/KAIN	hillock	HIL/LOK
	HEX/IL/KAIN		HIL/OK
hexylresorcinol	HEK/SIL/RE/SORS/NOL	Hilton	HIL/TON
	HEX/IL/RE/SORS/NOL	hilum	HAOI/LUM
Hey	K-P/HA*I	hilus	HAOI/LUS
	(not HAI; see hay)	himantosis	HAOI/MAN/TOE/SIS
Heyns	HAO*INZ	hindbrain	HAOIND/BRAIN
	(not HAOINZ; see Heinz)	hindfoot	HAOIND/FAOT
hiat(o)-	HAOI/AI/T-	hindgut	HAOIND/GUT
	HAOI/AIT	hindquarter	HAOIND/KWART/ER
	HAOI/YAI/T-	hindwater	HAOIND/WAT/ER
	HAOI/YAIT	Hines	HAOINS
hiatal	HAOI/AI/TAL		(not HAOINZ or HAO*INZ; see
hiation	HAOI/AIGS		Heinz and Heyns)
hiatopexia	HAOI/AIT/PEX/YA	hinge	HIN/-J
hiatopexy	HAOI/AIT/PEK/SI	hinge-bow	HIN/-J/BOE
hiatus	HAOI/AI/TUS	Hinman	HIN/MAN
hibernate	HAOI/BER/NAIT	Hinton	HIN/TON
	HAOIB/NAIT	hip	HIP
hibernation	HAOI/BER/NAIGS	hipped	HIP/-D
	HAOIB/NAIGS	Hippel	HIP/EL
hibernoma	HAOI/BER/NOE/MA	Hippelates	HIP/LAI/TAOEZ
	HAOIB/NOE/MA	hippo	HIP/POE
Hibiclens	HIB/KLENZ	hippo-	HIP
Hibistat	HIB/STAT		HIP/PO
Hibistat Towelette	HIB/STAT/TOUL/ET	Hippobosca	HIP/BOS/KA
hiccough	HIK/KAUF	Hippoboscidae	HIP/BOS/KI/DAE
hiccup	HIK/*UP		HIP/BOS/DAE
	HIK/KUP	hippocampal	HIP/KAM/PAL
Hicks	HIX	hippocampi	HIP/KAM/PAOI
hidebound	HAOID/BOUND	hippocampus	HIP/KAM/PUS
hidden	HID/-N	Hippocrates	HI/POK/RA/TAOEZ
hidr(o)-	HID/R(O)-		HI/POK/TAOEZ
	HAOI/DR(O)-	hippocratic	HIP/KRAT/IK
hidradenitis	HAOI/DRAD/NAOITS	hippocratica	HIP/KRAT/KA
	HID/RAD/NAOITS	Hippocratic Oath	HIP/KRAT/IK/O*ET
hidradenoid	HAOI/DRAD/NOID	hippocraticus	HIP/KRAT/KUS
hidradenoides	HAOI/DRAD/NOI/DAOEZ	hippocratism	HI/POK/TIFM
hidradenoma	HAOI/DRAD/NOE/MA		HI/POK/RA/TIFM
hidroadenoma	HID/RO/AD/NOE/MA	hippocratist	HI/POK/T*IS
hidrocystoma	HID/RO/SIS/TOE/MA		HI/POK/RA/T*IS
hidrocystomatosis	HID/RO/SIS/TOEM/TOE/SIS	hippurase	HIP/RAIS
hidromeiosis	HID/RO/MAO*I/YOE/SIS		HIP/YAOU/RAIS
	HAOI/DRO/MAO*I/YOE/SIS		HIP/YU/RAIS
hidropoiesis	HID/RO/POI/SIS	hippurate	HIP/RAIT
	HAOI/DRO/POI/SIS		HIP/YAOU/RAIT
hidropoietic	HID/RO/POIT/IK		HIP/YU/RAIT
	HAOI/DRO/POIT/IK	hippuria	HI/PAOUR/YA
hidrorrhea	HID/RO/RAOE/YA		HIP/YAOUR/YA
	HAO*I/DRO/RAOE/YA	hippuric	HI/PAOUR/IK
	(not HAOI/DRO/RAOE/YA; see		HIP/YAOUR/IK
	hydrorrhea)	hippuricase	HI/PAOUR/KAIS
hidrosadenitis	HID/RO/SAD/NAOITS		HIP/YAOUR/KAIS
	HAOI/DRO/SAD/NAOITS	hippus	HIP/PUS
hidroschesis	HID/ROS/KE/SIS	Hiprex	HIP/REX
	HAOI/DROS/KE/SIS	hirci	HIR/SAOI

hircic	HIRS/IK	histo-	H*IS
hircismus	HIR/SIZ/MUS		HIS/TO
hircus	HIR/KUS	histoangic	H*IS/AN/JIK
Hirschberg	HIR/-RB/BERG	histoblast	H*IS/BLA*S
Hirschfeld	HIR/-RB/FELD	histochemical	H*IS/KEM/KAL
Hirschsprung	HIR/-RB/SPRAOUNG	histochemistry	H*IS/KEM/STRI
	HIR/-RB/SPRUNG	histochemotherapy	H*IS/KAOEM/THER/PI
hirsute	HIR/SAOUT	histochromatosis	H*IS/KROEM/TOE/SIS
hirsutic	HIR/SAOUT/IK	histoclastic	H*IS/KLA*S/IK
hirsuties	HIR/SAOUT/YAOEZ	histoclinical	H*IS/KLIN/KAL
	HIR/SAOU/SHAOEZ	histocompatibility	H*IS/KPAT/-BLT
hirsutism	HIR/SAOU/TIFM		H*IS/KOM/PAT/-BLT
	HIR/SAOUT/IFM	histocompatible	H*IS/KPAT/-BL
hirsutum	HIR/SAOUT/TUM		H*IS/KOM/PAT/-BL
	HIR/SAOUT/UM	histocyte	H*IS/SAO*IT
hirtellous	HIRT/LOUS	histocytosis	H*IS/SAOI/TOE/SIS
hirudicidal	HI/RAOUD/SAOI/DAL	histodiagnosis	H*IS/DAOIG/NOE/SIS
hirudicide	HI/RAOUD/SAO*ID	histodialysis	H*IS/DI/AL/SIS
hirudin	HIR/YAOU/DIN	histodifferentiation	H*IS/DIFRN/SHAIGS
	HIR/YU/DIN	histofluorescence	H*IS/FLAOU/RES/ENS
	HIR/DIN	histofluorescent	H*IS/FLAOU/RES/ENT
	HI/RAOU/DIN	histogenesis	H*IS/JEN/SIS
hirudin-	HIR/YAOU/DIN	histogenetic	H*IS/JE/NET/IK
	HIR/YU/DIN	histogenous	HIS/TOJ/NOUS
	HIR/DIN	histogeny	HIS/TOJ/N*I
Hirudinaria	HIR/YAOU/DI/NAIR/YA	histogram	H*IS/GRAM
Hirudinea	HIR/YAOU/DIN/YA	histography	HIS/TOG/FI
hirudiniasis	HI/RAOUD/NAOI/SIS	histohematic	H*IS/HAOE/MAT/IK
	HIR/YAOUD/NAOI/SIS		H*IS/HE/MAT/IK
hirudinization	HI/RAOUD/NI/ZAIGS	histohematin	H*IS/HAOEM/TIN
	HIR/YAOUD/NI/ZAIGS		H*IS/HEM/TIN
hirudinize	HI/RAOUD/NAOIZ	histohematogenous	H*IS/HAOEM/TOJ/NOUS
	HIR/YAOUD/NAOIZ		H*IS/HEM/TOJ/NOUS
Hirudo	HI/RAOU/DOE	histohydria	H*IS/HAOI/DRAOE/YA
His	HIS	histohypoxia	H*IS/HAOI/POX/YA
Hismanal	HIS/MA/NAL	histoid	HIS/TOID
hispanica	HIS/PAN/KA		H*IS/OID
Hiss	K-P/HISZ	histoincompatibility	H*IS/IN/KPAT/-BLT
hist(o)-	H*IS		H*IS/IN/KOM/PAT/-BLT
	HIS/T(O)	histoincompatible	H*IS/IN/KPAT/-BL
histadine	H*IS/DAOEN		H*IS/IN/KOM/PAT/-BL
histaffine	HIS/TAFN	histokinesis	H*IS/KI/NAOE/SIS
	HIS/TAF/FIN	histologic	H*IS/LOJ/IK
Histamic	HIS/TAM/IK	histological	H*IS/LOJ/KAL
histaminase	HIS/TAM/NAIS	histologist	HIS/TO*LGS
histamine	H*IS/MAOEN	histology	HIS/TOLG
	H*IS/MIN	histolysate	HIS/TOL/ZAIT
histamine-fast	H*IS/MAOEN/H-F/FA*S		HIS/TOL/SAIT
histaminemia	HIS/TAM/NAOEM/YA	histolysis	HIS/TOL/SIS
	H*IS/MI/NAOEM/YA	histolytic	H*IS/LIT/IK
	H*IS/MIN/AOEM/YA	histolytica	H*IS/LIT/KA
histaminergic	H*IS/MIN/ERJ/IK	histolyticum	H*IS/LIT/KUM
	H*IS/MI/NERJ/IK	histolyticus	H*IS/LIT/KUS
	HIS/TAM/NERJ/IK	histoma	HIS/TOE/MA
histaminia	H*IS/MIN/YA	histometaplastic	H*IS/MET/PLA*S/IK
histaminuria	H*IS/MI/NAOUR/YA	Histomonas	HIS/TOM/NAS
	H*IS/MIN/YAOUR/YA		HIS/TOEM/NAS
	HIS/TAM/NAOUR/YA	histomoniasis	HIS/TOM/NAOI/SIS
histangic	HIS/TAN/JIK		H*IS/MO/NAOI/SIS
histanoxia	H*IS/NOX/YA		H*IS/MOE/NAOI/SIS
Histaspan	H*IS/SPAN	histomorphology	H*IS/MOR/FOLG
Histaspan-D	H*IS/SPAN/D-RBGS	histomorphometry	H*IS/MOR/FOM/TRI
Histaspan-Plus	H*IS/SPAN/PLUS	histone	HIS/TOEN
histic	H*IS/IK	histonectomy	H*IS/NEKT/M*I
histidase	H*IS/DAIS	histoneurology	H*IS/NAOU/ROLG
histidinal	H*IS/DIN/NAL	histonomy	HIS/TON/M*I
histidinase	H*IS/DIN/AIS	histonuria	H*IS/NAOUR/YA
histidine	H*IS/DAOEN		HIS/TOEN/YAOUR/YA
	H*IS/DIN	histopathogenesis	H*IS/PA*T/JEN/SIS
histidinemia	H*IS/DI/NAOEM/YA	histopathology	H*IS/PA/THOLG
	H*IS/DIN/AOEM/YA	histophysiology	H*IS/FIZ/YOLG
histidinol	H*IS/DI/NOL	Histoplasma	H*IS/PLAZ/MA
	H*IS/DIN/OL	histoplasmin	H*IS/PLAZ/MIN
histidinuria	H*IS/DI/NAOUR/YA	histoplasmoma	H*IS/PLAZ/MOE/MA
	H*IS/DIN/YAOUR/YA	histoplasmosis	H*IS/PLAZ/MOE/SIS
histidyl	H*IS/DIL	historadiography	H*IS/RAID/YOG/FI
histio-	H*IS/YO	Histor-D	HIS/TOR/D-RBGS
histioblast	H*IS/YO/BLA*S	historetention	H*IS/RE/TENGS
histiocytary	H*IS/YO/SAOIT/RI	historian	HIS/TOIRN
histiocyte	H*IS/YO/SAO*IT	historrhexis	H*IS/REK/SIS
histiocytic	H*IS/YO/SIT/IK	histoteliosis	H*IS/TEL/YOE/SIS
histiocytoma	H*IS/YO/SAOI/TOE/MA	histotherapy	H*IS/THER/PI
histiocytomatosis	H*IS/YO/SAOI/TOEM/TOE/SIS	histothrombin	H*IS/THROM/BIN
histiocytosis	H*IS/YO/SAOI/TOE/SIS	histotome	H*IS/TOEM
histiogenic	H*IS/YO/JEN/IK	histotomy	HIS/TOT/M*I
histioid	H*IS/YOID	histotoxic	H*IS/TOX/IK
histio-irritative	H*IS/YO/IR/TAIT/IV	histotroph	H*IS/TROEF
histioma	H*IS/YOE/MA		H*IS/TROF
histionic	H*IS/YON/IK	histotrophic	H*IS/TROFK

histotropic	H*IS/TROP/IK	holorachischisis	HOL/RA/KIS/KI/SIS
histozoic	H*IS/ZOIK	holosaccharide	HOL/SAK/RAOID
	H*IS/ZOE/IK	holosystolic	HOL/SIS/TOL/IK
histozyme	H*IS/ZAOIM	holotelencephaly	HOL/TEL/EN/SEF/LI
histrionic	HIS/TRON/IK	holotonia	HOL/TOEN/YA
	HIS/TRAOE/ON/IK	holotonic	HOL/TON/IK
histrionism	HIS/TRO/NIFM	holotopy	HOE/LOT/PI
	HIS/TRAOE/NIFM	holotrichous	HOE/LOT/RI/KOUS
HisTussin	HIS/TUS/SIN		HO/LOT/RI/KOUS
Hitchens	HIFP/ENS	holotype	HOL/TAOIP
hitchhiker	HIFP/HAOIK/ER	holozoic	HOL/ZOIK
Hitzig	HIT/ZIG		HOL/ZOE/IK
hives	HAOIVS	Holt	HOELT
	HAOIV/-S	Holter	HOEL/TER
HMO	H-RBGS/M*RBGS/O*RBGS		HOELT/ER
hoarse	HAORS	Holth	HO*LT
	(not HORS or HOERS; see horse)	Holthouse	HOELT/HOUS
hoarseness	HAORS/*NS	Holzknecht	HOELTS/K-/NEKT
Hoboken	HOE/BOE/KEN		HOELTS/NEKT
	HOE/BOEK/-N	homalocephalus	HOM/LO/SEF/LUS
Hoche	HOEK	Homalomyia	HOM/LO/MAOI/YA
hock	HOK	homaluria	HOM/LAOUR/YA
hodegetics	HOD/JET/IK/-S	Homans	HOE/MANS
Hodge	HOJ	homatropine	HOE/MAT/RO/PAOEN
Hodgen	HOJ/-N	homaxial	HOE/MAX/YAL
Hodgkin	HOJ/KIN	Home	K-P/HOEM
Hodgson	HOJ/SON	homeo-	HOEM/YO
hodoneuromere	HOED/NAOUR/MAOER	homeochrome	HOEM/YO/KROEM
	HOE/DO/NAOUR/MAOER	homeocyte	HOEM/YO/SAO*IT
hodophobia	HOED/FOEB/YA	homeograft	HOEM/YO/GRAFT
	HOE/DO/FOEB/YA	homeokinesis	HOEM/YO/KI/NAOE/SIS
hof	HOEF	homeometric	HOEM/YO/MET/RIK
	HOF	homeomorphous	HOEM/YO/MOR/FOUS
Hofbauer	HOF/BOU/ER	homeo-osteoplasty	HOEM/YO/O*S/YO/PLAS/TI
Hoffa	HOF/FA	homeopath	HOEM/YO/PA*T
Hoffmann	HOF/MA*N	homeopathic	HOEM/YO/PA*T/IK
	(not HOF/MAN; see Hofmann)	homeopathist	HOEM/YOP/TH*IS
Hofmann	HOF/MAN	homeopathy	HOEM/YOP/TH*I
hofmannii	HOF/MAN/YAOI	homeoplasia	HOEM/YO/PLAIZ/YA
Hofmeister	HOF/MAO*IS/ER	homeoplastic	HOEM/YO/PLA*S/IK
hol(o)-	HOL	homeorrhesis	HOEM/YO/RAOE/SIS
	HOE/L(O)	homeosis	HOEM/YOE/SIS
holagogue	HOL/GOG	homeostasis	HOEM/YO/STAI/SIS
holandric	HOL/AN/DRIK		HOEM/YO*S/SIS
holarthritic	HOL/AR/THRIT/IK	homeostatic	HOEM/YO/STAT/IK
holarthritis	HOL/AR/THRAOITS	homeotherapeutics	HOEM/YO/THER/PAOUT/IK/-S
Holden	HOEL/DEN	homeotherapy	HOEM/YO/THER/PI
	K-P/HOELD/-N	homeotherm	HOEM/YO/THERM
Holder	K-P/HOELD/ER	homeothermal	HOEM/YO/THER/MAL
holism	HOE/LIFM	homeothermic	HOEM/YO/THERM/IK
	HOEL/IFM	homeotic	HOEM/YOT/IK
holistic	HOE/L*IS/IK	homeotransplant	HOEM/YO/TRA*NS/PLANT
	HOEL/*IS/IK	homeotransplantation	HOEM/YO/TRA*NS/PLAN/TAIGS
Holland	HOL/LAND	homeotypic	HOEM/YO/TIP/IK
Hollander	HOL/LAND/ER	homeotypical	HOEM/YO/TIP/KAL
Hollenhorst	HOL/EN/HO*RS	homergic	HOEM/ERJ/IK
hollow	HOL/LOE		HOM/ERJ/IK
hollow-back	HOL/LOE/BAK	homergy	HOM/ERJI
Holmes	HOEMS		HOEM/ERJI
	HOEMZ	homicidal	HOM/SAOI/DAL
	HOEL/-MS	homicide	HOM/SAO*ID
Holmgren	HOEM/GREN	homiculture	HOM/KUL/KHUR
	HOEL/-M/GREN	homidium	HOE/MID/YUM
holmium	HOL/MAOE/UM	hominal	HOM/NAL
	HOL/MAOE/YUM	hominid	HOM/NID
	HOL/MUM	Hominidae	HOE/MIN/DAE
holoacardius	HOL/AI/KARD/YUS	homininoxious	HOM/NAOE/NOK/-RBS
holoacrania	HOL/AI/KRAIN/YA	hominis	HOM/NIS
holoanencephaly	HOL/AN/EN/SEF/LI	hominivorax	HOM/NI/VOR/AX
holoantigen	HOL/ANT/JEN		HOEM/NI/VOR/AX
holoblastic	HOL/BLA*S/IK	hominoid	HOM/NOID
holocephalic	HOL/SFAL/IK	Hominoidea	HOM/NOID/YA
holocord	HOL/KORD	homme	HO*M
holocrine	HOL/KRIN	Homo sapiens	HOE/MOE/SAIP/YENZ
holodiastolic	HOL/DAOI/STOL/IK		HOEM/SAIP/YENZ
holoendemic	HOL/EN/DEM/IK	homo-	HOEM
holoenzyme	HOL/EN/ZAOIM		HOE/MO
hologamy	HOE/LOG/M*I	Homobasidiomycetidae	HOEM/BA/SID/YO/MAOI/SAOET/
hologastroschisis	HOL/GAS/TROS/KI/SIS		DAE
hologenesis	HOL/JEN/SIS	homobiotin	HOEM/BAO*I/TIN
hologram	HOL/GRAM	homoblastic	HOEM/BLA*S/IK
holography	HOL/OG/FI	homocarnosine	HOEM/KARN/SAOEN
	HO/LOG/FI	homocentric	HOEM/SEN/TRIK
hologynic	HOL/JIN/IK	homochlorcyclizine	HOEM/KLOR/SAOI/KLI/ZAOEN
holomastigote	HOL/MA*S/GOET	homochronous	HOE/MOK/RO/NOUS
holometabolous	HOL/ME/TAB/LOUS	homocinchonine	HOEM/SIN/KO/NAOEN
holomorphosis	HOL/MOR/FOE/SIS	homocladic	HOEM/KLAD/IK
holophytic	HOL/FIT/IK	homocyclic	HOEM/SIK/LIK
holoprosencephaly	HOL/PROS/EN/SEF/LI		HOEM/SAOIK/LIK

homocysteine	HOEM/S*IS/YIN		homosexuality	HOEM/SEX/YAL
homocystine	HOEM/SIS/TAOEN			HOEM/SEX/YAL/TI
homocystinemia	HOEM/S*IS/NAOEM/YA			HOEM/SEX/YAOUL/TI
homocystinuria	HOEM/S*IS/NAOUR/YA			HOEM/SEX/YUL/TI
homocytotropic	HOEM/SAOIT/TROP/IK		homosomal	HOEM/SOE/MAL
homodesmotic	HOEM/DEZ/MOT/IK		homospore	HOEM/SPOER
homodont	HOEM/DONT		homosporous	HOE/MOS/PROUS
homodromous	HOE/MOD/RO/MOUS		homosteroid	HOEM/STAOER/OID
homoerotic	HOEM/E/ROT/IK		homostimulant	HOEM/STIM/LANT
homoeroticism	HOEM/E/ROT/SIFM		homostimulation	HOEM/STIM/LAIGS
homoerotism	HOEM/*ER/TIFM		homosulfanilamide	HOEM/SUL/FA/NIL/MAOID
	HOEM/ER/TIFM		homothallic	HOM/THAL/IK
homofermenter	HOEM/FERMT/ER			HOEM/THAL/IK
homogamete	HOEM/GAM/AOET		homothalism	HOM/THAL/IFM
homogametic	HOEM/GA/MET/IK			HOEM/THAL/IFM
homogamous	HOE/MOG/MOUS		homotherm	HOEM/THERM
homogamy	HOE/MOG/M*I		homothermal	HOEM/THER/MAL
homogenate	HOE/MOJ/NAIT		homothermic	HOEM/THERM/IK
	HO/MOJ/NAIT		homotonia	HOEM/TOEN/YA
homogeneity	HOEM/JE/NAOE/TI		homotonic	HOEM/TON/IK
	HOEM/MOJ/NAOE/TI		homotopic	HOEM/TOP/IK
homogeneization	HOEM/JAOEN/YI/ZAIGS		homotransplant	HOEM/TRA*NS/PLANT
homogeneous	HOEM/JAOEN/YOUS		homotransplantation	HOEM/TRA*NS/PLAN/TAIGS
homogenesis	HOEM/JEN/SIS		homotropism	HOE/MOT/RO/PIFM
homogenetic	HOEM/JE/NET/IK		homotype	HOEM/TAOIP
homogenic	HOEM/JEN/IK		homotypic	HOEM/TIP/IK
homogenicity	HOEM/JE/NIS/TI		homotypical	HOEM/TIP/KAL
homogenization	HOE/MOJ/NI/ZAIGS		homovanillic	HOEM/VA/NIL/IK
	HO/MOJ/NI/ZAIGS		homozoic	HOEM/ZOIK
homogenize	HOE/MOJ/NAOIZ			HOEM/ZOE/IK
	HO/MOJ/NAOIZ		homozygosis	HOEM/ZAOI/GOE/SIS
homogenous	HOE/MOJ/NOUS		homozygosity	HOEM/ZAOI/GOS/TI
homogentisate	HOEM/JENT/SAIT		homozygote	HOEM/ZAOI/GOET
homogentisic	HOEM/JEN/TIS/IK		homozygous	HOEM/ZAOIG/OUS
homogentisicase	HOEM/JEN/TIS/KAIS		homunculus	HOE/MUN/KLUS
homogentisuria	HOEM/JENT/SAOUR/YA		honey	HON/NAOE
homogeny	HOE/MOJ/N*I		honeycombed	HON/NAOE/KOEM/-D
homoglandular	HOEM/GLAND/LAR		Hong Kong	HONG/KONG
homograft	HOEM/GRAFT		honk	HON/-K
homoio-	HOE/MOI		honorarium	HON/RAIRM
	HOE/MOI/YO			HON/RAIR/YUM
homoioplasia	HOE/MOI/PLAIZ/YA			
homoiopodal	HOE/MOI/OP/DAL		hood	HAOD
homoiostasis	HOE/MOI/O*S/SIS		hooded	HAOD/-D
homoiotherm	HOE/MOI/THERM		hoof	HAOF
homoiothermal	HOE/MOI/THER/MAL		hook	HAOK
homoiothermic	HOE/MOI/THERM/IK		Hooke	HAO*K
homoiothermism	HOE/MOI/THERM/IFM		Hooker	K-P/HAOK/ER
homoiothermy	HOE/MOI/THER/M*I		hooklet	HAOK/LET
homoiotoxin	HOE/MOI/TOK/SIN		hook-up	HAOK/H-F/UP
homokaryon	HOEM/KAR/YON		hookworm	HAOK/WORM
homokaryotic	HOEM/KAR/YOT/IK		hoose	HAOS
homokeratoplasty	HOEM/KER/TO/PLAS/TI		Hoover	HAOVR
homolateral	HOEM/LAT/RAL		Hope	K-P/HOEP
homolipid	HOEM/LIP/ID		Hopkins	HOP/KINS
homologen	HOE/MOL/JEN		Hoplopsyllus anomalus	HOP/LO/SIL/LUS/AI/NOM/LUS
homologic	HOEM/LOJ/IK		Hopmann	HOP/MAN
homologous	HOE/MOL/GOUS		Hoppe	HOP/PAOE
	HO/MOL/GOUS		hops	HOP/-S
homolography	HOM/LOG/FI		hordei	HORD/YAOI
homologue	HOEM/LOG		hordein	HORD/YIN
	HOM/LOG		hordeolaris	HORD/YO/LAI/RIS
homology	HOE/MOLG			HOR/DAOE/LAI/RIS
	HO/MOLG		hordeolum	HOR/DAOE/LUM
homolysin	HOE/MOL/SIN		hordeum	HORD/YUM
homolysis	HOE/MOL/SIS		horehound	HOER/HOUND
homomorphic	HOEM/MOR/FIK			HOR/HOUND
homomorphosis	HOEM/MOR/FOE/SIS		horizon	HO/RAOI/ZON
homonomous	HOE/MON/MOUS			HOE/RAOI/ZON
homonomy	HOE/MON/M*I		horizontal	HOR/ZON/TAL
homonuclear	HOEM/NAOUK/LAR		horizontalis	HOR/ZON/TAI/LIS
homonymous	HOE/MO*N/MOUS		hormesis	HOR/MAOE/SIS
	HOE/MON/MO*US		hormetic	HOR/MET/IK
	(not HOE/MON/MOUS; see		hormic	HORM/IK
	homonomous)		hormion	HORM/YON
homophene	HOEM/FAOEN		Hormodendrum	HORM/DEN/DRUM
homophil	HOEM/FIL		hormon(o)-	HORM/N(O)
homophilic	HOEM/FIL/IK			HOR/MOEN
homoplastic	HOEM/PLA*S/IK			HOR/MOE/N(O)
homoplasty	HOEM/PLAS/TI		hormonagogue	HOR/MOEN/GOG
homopolymer	HOEM/POL/MER		hormonal	HOR/MOENL
homopolysaccharide	HOEM/POL/SAK/RAOID		hormone	HOR/MOEN
homoproline	HOEM/PRO/LAOEN		hormonic	HOR/MON/IK
homoprotocatechuic	HOEM/PROET/KAT/KAOU/IK		hormonogen	HOR/MON/JEN
homorganic	HOM/OR/GAN/IK			HOR/MOEN/JEN
homosalate	HOEM/SAL/AIT		hormonogenesis	HORM/NO/JEN/SIS
homoserine	HOEM/SER/AOEN		hormonogenic	HORM/NO/JEN/IK
homosexual	HOEM/SEX/YAOUL		hormonology	HORM/NOLG
	HOEM/SEX/YUL		hormonopexic	HOR/MOEN/PEX/IK
			hormonopoiesis	HORM/NO/POI/SIS

hormonopoietic	HORM/NO/POIT/IK	humeroulnaris	HAOUM/RO/UL/NAI/RIS
hormonoprivia	HORM/NO/PRIV/YA	humerus	HAOUM/RUS
hormonosis	HORM/NOE/SIS	humidifier	HAOU/MID/FI/ER
hormonotherapy	HORM/NO/THER/PI	Humibid	HAOUM/BID
horn	HORN	humic	HAOUM/IK
Horn	K-P/HORN	humidify	HAOU/MID/FI
Horner	HORN/ER	humidity	HAOU/MID/TI
hornification	HORN/FI/KAIGS	humin	HAOU/MIN
horny	HOR/N*I	Hummelsheim	HUM/EL/SHAOIM
horopter	HOE/ROPT/ER	humor	HAOU/MOR
horopteric	HOR/OP/TER/IK	humoral	HAOU/MORL
	HOE/ROP/TER/IK		(not HAOUM/RAL; see humeral)
horripilation	HOR/PAOI/LAIGS	humoralism	HAOU/MORL/IFM
	HOR/RIP/LAIGS	humoris	HAOUM/RIS
horror	HOR/ROR	humorism	HAOUM/RIFM
horsefly	HORS/FLAOI	Humorsol	HAOU/MOR/SOL
horsepower	HORS/POU/ER	hump	HUFRP
horsepox	HORS/POX	humpback	HUFRP/BA*K
Horsley	HORS/LAOE	Humphry	HUM/FRI
Hortega	HOR/TAI/GA	humus	HAOU/MUS
hortobezoar	HORT/BE/ZOER	Humulin	HAOUM/LIN
Horton	HOR/TON	humulus	HAOUM/LUS
hospes	HOS/PAOEZ	hunchback	HUFRPBLG/BA*K
hospice	HOS/PIS		HUN/-FP/BA*K
hospital	HOPT	hunger	HUNG/ER
	HOS/PI/TAL	Hunner	HUN/ER
hospitalism	HOPT/IFM	Hunt	K-P/HUNT
	HOS/PIT/LIFM	Hunter	K-P/HUNT/ER
hospitalization	HOPT/ZAIGS	hunteri	HUNT/RAOI
	HOS/PIT/LI/ZAIGS		HUN/TER/RAOI
	HOS/PI/TAL/ZAIGS	hunterian	HUN/TAOERN
hospitalize	HOPT/AOIZ		HUN/TAOER/YAN
	HOPT/LAOIZ	hunting	HUNT/-G
	HOS/PIT/LAOIZ	Huntington	HUNT/-G/TON
host	HO*ES	Hurler	HUR/LER
hot	HOT		K-P/HURL/ER
hotfoot	HOT/FAO*T	Hurricaine	H*UR/KAIN
hot line	HOT/LAOIN		HUR/KA*IN
Hottentot	HOT/EN/TOT		(not HUR/KAIN; see hurricane)
hottentotism	HOT/EN/TOT/IFM	Hurst	H*URS
Hotz	HOTS	Hurthle	HUR/TEL
Hounsfield	HOUNS/FAOELD		HURT/EL
hourglass	HOUR/GLASZ		(not HURT/-L; see hurtle)
housefly	HOUS/FLAOI	Hurtley	HURT/LAOE
house officer	HOUS/AUF/SER	Huschke	HAOURB/KAOE
Houssay	HOUS/SAI		HURB/KAOE
Houston	HAOUS/TON	husk	HUS/-K
hoven	HOEVN	Hutchinson	HUFP/IN/SON
	HOE/VEN	Hutchinson-Gilford	HUFP/IN/SON/H-F/GIL/FORD
Hovius	HOEV/YUS	hutchinsonian	HUFP/IN/SOEN/YAN
Howard	HOU/ARD	Hutchison	HUFP/SON
Howell	HOU/EL	Huxley	HUX/LAOE
	(not HOUL; see howl)	huygenian	HAOI/JEN/YAN
Howell-Jolly	HOU/EL/H-F/JOE/LAOE	hy(o)-	HAOI
	HOU/EL/H-F/YOE/LI		HAOI/Y(O)
	HOU/EL/H-F/YOL/LI	hyacinthi	HAOI/SIN/THAOI
Hoyer	HOI/ER	hyal	HAOIL
	HOI/YAIR		HAOI/YAL
	HOI/YER	hyal(o)-	HAOI/L(O)
Hudson	HUD/SON	hyalin	HAOI/LIN
Hueck	H*EK	hyaline	HAOI/LAOIN
	(not HEK; see heck)		HAOI/LAOEN
Huet	HAOU/ET		HAO*I/LIN
Hueter	HAOE/TER		(not HAOI/LIN; see hyalin)
	(not HAOET/ER; see heater)	hyalinicum	HAOI/LIN/KUM
Huggins	HUG/GINS	hyalinization	HAOI/LIN/ZAIGS
Hughes	HAOUZ	hyalinosis	HAOI/LI/NOE/SIS
	HAOUS	hyalinuria	HAOI/LIN/YAOUR/YA
Huguenin	AOEG/NA	hyalitis	HAO*I/LAOITS
Huguier	AOEG/YAI		HAOI/YA/LAOITS
Huhner	HAOUN/ER		(not HAOI/LAOITS; see hilitis)
Hull	K-P/HUL	hyalobiuronic	HAOI/LO/B*I/YAOU/RON/IK
hum	HUM	hyalocyte	HAOI/LO/SAO*IT
human	HAOU/MAN	hyalogen	HAOI/AL/JEN
Humate-P	HAOU/MAIT/P-RBGS		HAOI/YAL/JEN
Humatrope	HAOUM/TROEP	hyalohyphomycosis	HAOI/LO/HAOIF/MAOI/KOE/SIS
humectant	HAOU/MEK/TANT	hyaloid	HAOI/LOID
humectation	HAOU/MEK/TAIGS	hyaloidea	HAOI/LOID/YA
humer(o)-	HAOUM/R(O)	hyaloideus	HAOI/LOID/YUS
humeral	HAOUM/RAL	hyaloidin	HAOI/LOI/DIN
humerale	HAOUM/RAI/LAOE	hyaloiditis	HAOI/LOI/DAOITS
humeralia	HAOUM/RAIL/YA	hyalomere	HAOI/LO/MAOER
humeralis	HAOUM/RAI/LIS	Hyalomma	HAOI/LOM/MA
humeri	HAOUM/RAOI	hyalomucoid	HAOI/LO/MAOU/KOID
humeroradial	HAOUM/RO/RAID/YAL	hyalonyxis	HAOI/LO/NIK/SIS
humeroradialis	HAOUM/RO/RAID/YAI/LIS	hyalophagia	HAOI/LO/FAI/JA
humeroscapular	HAOUM/RO/SKAP/LAR	hyalophagy	HAOI/LOF/JI
humeroulnar	HAOUM/RO/UL/NAR	hyaloplasm	HAOI/LO/PLAFM
humeroulnare	HAOUM/UL/NAI/RAOE	hyalophobia	HAOI/LO/FOEB/YA

hyaloplasm	HAOI/LO/PLASM	hydrastine	HAOI/DRAS/TAOEN
hyaloplasma	HAOI/LO/PLAZ/MA	hydrastinine	HAOI/DRA*S/NAOEN
hyaloserositis	HAOI/LO/SAOER/SAOITS	hydrastis	HAOI/DRAS/TIS
hyalosis	HAOI/LOE/SIS	hydratase	HAOI/DRA/TAIS
hyalosome	HAOI/AL/SOEM	hydrate	HAOI/DRAIT
	HAOI/YAL/SOEM	hydrated	HAOI/DRAIT/-D
	HAOI/LO/SOEM	hydration	HAOI/DRAIGS
hyalurate	HAOI/LAOU/RAIT	hydraulic	HAOI/DRAUL/IK
	HAOI/LAOUR/AIT	hydraulics	HAOI/DRAUL/IK/-S
hyaluronate	HAOI/LAOUR/NAIT	hydrazide	HAOI/DRA/ZAOID
hyaluronic	HAOI/LAOU/RON/IK	Hydra-Zide	HAOI/DRA/H-F/ZAOID
hyaluronidase	HAOI/LAOU/RON/DAIS	hydrazine	HAOI/DRA/ZAOEN
hyaluronoglucosaminidase	HAOI/LAOU/RON/GLAOUK/SA/		HAOI/DRA/ZIN
	MIN/DAIS	hydrazinolysis	HAOI/DRA/ZIN/OL/SIS
hyaluronoglucuronidase	HAOI/LAOU/RON/GLAOUK/RON/		HAOI/DRA/ZI/NOL/SIS
	DAIS	hydrazone	HAOI/DRA/ZOEN
hybaroxia	HAOIB/ROX/YA	Hydrea	HAOI/DRAOE/YA
	HAOI/BROX/YA	hydremia	HAOI/DRAOEM/YA
hybenzate	HAOI/BEN/ZAIT	hydremic	HAOI/DRAOEM/IK
hybrid	HAOI/BRID	hydrencephalocele	HAOI/DREN/SEF/LO/SAO*EL
hybridism	HAOI/BRID/IFM	hydrencephalomeningocele	HAOI/DREN/SEF/LO/ME/NING/
hybridity	HAOI/BRID/TI		SAO*EL
hybridization	HAOI/BRID/ZAIGS	hydrencephalus	HAOI/DREN/SEF/LUS
hybridoma	HAOI/BRI/DOE/MA	hydrencephaly	HAOI/DREN/SEF/LI
Hy-C	HAOI/KR-RBGS	hydrepigastrium	HAOI/DREP/GAS/TRUM
hycanthone	HAOI/KAN/THOEN		HAOI/DREP/GAS/TRAOE/UM
hyclate	HAOI/KLAIT	hydriatic	HAOI/DRAT/IK
Hycodan	HAOIK/DAN		HAOI/DRAOE/AT/IK
Hycomine	HAOIK/MAOEN	hydriatric	HAOI/DRAT/RIK
Hyco-Pap	HAOIK/PAP		HAOI/DRAOE/AT/RIK
Hycotuss	HAOIK/TUSZ	hydriatrics	HAOI/DRAT/RIK/-S
hydantoin	HAOI/DAN/TOIN		HAOI/DRAOE/AT/RIK/-S
hydantoinate	HAOI/DAN/TOI/NAIT	hydric	HAOI/DRIK
	HAOI/DAN/TOE/NAIT	hydride	HAOI/DRAOID
hydatid	HAOID/TID	hydrindicuria	HAOI/DRIND/KAOUR/YA
hydatidiform	HAOID/TID/FORM	Hydrisalic Gel	HAOI/DRI/SAL/IK/JEL
hydatidocele	HAOID/TID/SAO*EL	Hydrisinol	HAOI/DRIS/NOL
hydatidoma	HAOID/TI/DOE/MA	hydroa	HAOI/DROE/WA
hydatidosis	HAOID/TI/DOE/SIS		HID/ROE/WA
hydatidostomy	HAOID/TI/DO*S/M*I	hydroadipsia	HAOI/DRO/AI/DIPS/YA
hydatiduria	HAOID/TI/DAOUR/YA	hydroappendix	HAOI/DRO/AI/PEND/IX
Hydatigena	HAOID/TIJ/NA	hydrobilirubin	HAOI/DRO/BIL/RAOU/BIN
Hydatigera	HAOID/TIJ/RA	hydroblepharon	HAOI/DRO/BLEF/RON
hydatism	HAOID/TIFM	hydrobromate	HAOI/DRO/BROE/MAIT
hydatoid	HAOID/TOID	hydrobromic	HAOI/DRO/BROEM/IK
Hyde	HAO*ID	hydrobromide	HAOI/DRO/BROE/MAOID
	(not HAOID; see hide)		HAOI/DRO/BROEM/AOID
Hydeltra	HAOI/DEL/TRA	hydrocalix	HAOI/DRO/KAI/LIX
Hydeltrasol	HAOI/DEL/TRA/SOL		HAOI/DRO/KAL/IX
Hydeltra-T.B.A.	HAOI/DEL/TRA/T-FPLT/B*FPLT/	hydrocalycosis	HAOI/DRO/KAL/KOE/SIS
	A*FPLT	hydrocalyx	HAOI/DRO/KAI/L*IX
Hydergine	HAOID/ER/JAOEN		HAOI/DRO/KAL/*IX
	HAOID/ER/JAOEN	hydrocarbon	HAOI/DRO/KAR/BON
hydnocarpus	HID/NO/KAR/PUS	hydrocarbonism	HAOI/DRO/KARB/NIFM
hydr(o)-	HAOI/DR(O)	hydrocardia	HAOI/DRO/KARD/YA
hydracetin	HAOI/DRAS/TIN	hydrocele	HAOI/DRO/SAO*EL
hydracid	HAOI/DRAS/ID	hydrocelectomy	HAOI/DRO/SE/LEKT/M*I
hydradenitis	HAO*I/DRAD/NAOITS	hydrocephalic	HAOI/DRO/SFAL/IK
	(not HAOI/DRAD/NAOITS; see	hydrocephalocele	HAOI/DRO/SEF/LO/SAO*EL
	hidradenitis)	hydrocephaloid	HAOI/DRO/SEF/LOID
hydradenoma	HAO*I/DRAD/NOE/MA	hydrocephalus	HAOI/DRO/SEF/LUS
	(not HAOI/DRAD/NOE/MA; see	hydrocephaly	HAOI/DRO/SEF/LI
	hidradenoma)	Hydrocet	HAOI/DRO/SET
hydraeroperitoneum	HAOI/DRAER/PERT/NAOEM	Hydrochlor	HAOI/DRO/KLOR
hydragogue	HAOI/DRA/GOG	hydrochloric	HAOI/DRO/KLOR/IK
hydralazine	HAOI/DRAL/ZAOEN	hydrochloride	HAOI/DRO/KLOR/AOID
hydrallostane	HAOI/DRAL/STAIN	hydrochlorothiazide	HAOI/DRO/KLOR/THAOI/ZAOID
hydramine	HAOI/DRA/MAOEN	hydrocholecystis	HAOI/DRO/KOEL/SIS/TIS
	HAOI/DRA/MIN	hydrocholeresis	HAOI/DRO/KOE/LER/SIS
hydramitrazine	HAOI/DRA/MAOI/TRA/ZAOEN		HAOI/DRO/KOEL/RAOE/SIS
hydramnion	HAOI/DRAM/NON	hydrocholeretic	HAOI/DRO/KOEL/RET/IK
	HAOI/DRAM/NAOE/YON	hydrocholesterol	HAOI/DRO/KL*ES/ROL
hydramnios	HAOI/DRAM/NOS	hydrocinchonidine	HAOI/DRO/SIN/KON/DAOEN
	HAOI/DRAM/NAOE/YOS		HAOI/DRO/SIN/KON/DIN
hydranencephaly	HAOI/DRAN/EN/SEF/LI	hydrocirsocele	HAOI/DRO/SIRS/SAO*EL
Hydrangea	HAOI/DRAN/JA	hydrocodone	HAOI/DRO/KO/DOEN
hydrangiography	HAOI/DRAN/JOG/FI	Hydrocil	HAOI/DRO/SIL
hydrangiology	HAOI/DRAN/JOLG	Hydrocodone	HAOI/DRO/KO/DOEN
hydrangiotomy	HAOI/DRAN/JOT/M*I	hydrocolloid	HAOI/DRO/KLOID
hydrargyri	HAOI/DRARJ/RAOI		HAOI/DRO/KOL/OID
hydrargyria	HAOI/DRAR/JIR/YA	hydrocolpocele	HAOI/DRO/KOL/PO/SAO*EL
hydrargyrism	HAOI/DRARJ/RIFM	hydrocolpos	HAOI/DRO/KOL/POS
hydrargyrosis	HAOI/DRARJ/ROE/SIS	hydrocortamate	HAOI/DRO/KORT/MAIT
hydrargyrum	HAOI/DRARJ/RUM	hydrocortisone	HAOI/DRO/KORT/SOEN
hydrarthrodial	HAOI/DRAR/THROED/YAL	Hydrocortone	HAOI/DRO/KOR/TOEN
hydrarthron	HAOI/DRAR/THRON	hydrocotarnine	HAOI/DRO/KO/TAR/NAOEN
hydrarthrosis	HAOI/DRAR/THROE/SIS	hydrocupreine	HAOI/DRO/KAOU/PRAOEN
hydrarthrus	HAOI/DRAR/THRUS		HAOI/DRO/KAOUP/RAOEN
hydrase	HAOI/DRAIS	hydrocyanic	HAOI/DRO/SAOI/AN/IK

hydrocyanism	HAOI/DRO/SAOI/YAN/IK	hydropenic	HAOI/DRO/PAOEN/IK
hydrocyst	HAOI/DRO/SAOI/NIFM	hydropericarditis	HAOI/DRO/P*ER/KAR/DAOITS
hydrocyst	HAOI/DRO/S*IS	hydropericardium	HAOI/DRO/P*ER/KARD/YUM
hydrocystadenoma	HAOI/DRO/SIS/TAD/NOE/MA	hydroperinephrosis	HAOI/DRO/P*ER/NEF/ROE/SIS
hydrocystoma	HAOI/DRO/SIS/TOE/MA	hydroperion	HAOI/DRO/P*ER/YON
hydrodiascope	HAOI/DRO/DAOI/SKOEP	hydroperitoneum	HAOI/DRO/PERT/NAOEM
hydrodictiotomy	HAOI/DRO/DIKT/YOT/M*I	hydroperitonia	HAOI/DRO/P*ER/TOEN/YA
hydrodiffusion	HAOI/DRO/DIF/FAOUGS	hydroperoxidase	HAOI/DRO/PROX/DAIS
hydrodipsia	HAOI/DRO/DIPS/YA		HAOI/DRO/PER/OX/DAIS
hydrodipsomania	HAOI/DRO/DIPS/MAIN/YA	hydroperoxide	HAOI/DRO/PROK/SAOID
hydrodiuresis	HAOI/DRO/DI/YAOU/RAOE/SIS		HAOI/DRO/PER/OX/SAOID
Hydrodiuril	HAOI/DRO/DI/YAOU/RIL	hydropexia	HAOI/DRO/PEX/YA
	HAOI/DRO/DAOI/RIL	hydropexic	HAOI/DRO/PEX/IK
hydrodynamics	HAOI/DRO/DAOI/NAM/IK/-S	hydropexis	HAOI/DRO/PEK/SIS
hydroelectric	HAOI/DRO/LEK/TRIK	hydrophagocytosis	HAOI/DRO/FAG/SAOI/TOE/SIS
hydroencephalocele	HAOI/DRO/EN/SEF/LO/SAO*EL	hydrophil	HAOI/DRO/FIL
hydroflumethiazide	HAOI/DRO/FLAOUM/THAOI/ ZAOID	hydrophile	HAOI/DRO/FAOIL
		hydrophilia	HAOI/DRO/FIL/YA
hydrofluoric	HAOI/DRO/FLAOUR/IK	hydrophilic	HAOI/DRO/FIL/IK
hydrogel	HAOI/DRO/JEL	hydrophilism	HAOI/DROF/LIFM
hydrogen	HAOI/DRO/JEN	hydrophilous	HAOI/DROF/LOUS
hydrogenase	HAOI/DRO/JEN/AIS	hydrophobia	HAOI/DRO/FOEB/YA
	HAOI/DROJ/NAIS	hydrophobic	HAOI/DRO/FOEB/IK
hydrogenate	HAOI/DRO/JEN/AIT	hydrophobiae	HAOI/DRO/FOEB/YAE
	HAOI/DROJ/NAIT	hydrophorograph	HAOI/DRO/FOER/GRAF
hydrogenation	HAOI/DRO/JEN/AIGS	hydrophthalmia	HAOI/DROF/THAL/MA
	HAOI/DROJ/NAIGS		HAOI/DROF/THAL/MAOE/YA
hydrogenize	HAOI/DRO/JEN/AOIZ	hydrophthalmos	HAOI/DROF/THAL/MOS
	HAOI/DROJ/NAOIZ	hydrophthalmus	HAOI/DROF/THAL/MUS
hydrogenlyase	HAOI/DRO/JEN/LAOI/AIS	hydrophysometra	HAOI/DRO/FAOIS/MAOE/TRA
hydrogenoid	HAOI/DROJ/NOID	hydropic	HAOI/DROP/IK
	HAOI/DRO/JEN/OID	hydropigenous	HAOI/DRO/PIJ/NOUS
hydrogymnastic	HAOI/DRO/JIM/NA*S/IK	hydroplasma	HAOI/DRO/PLAZ/MA
hydrogymnastics	HAOI/DRO/JIM/NA*S/IK/-S	hydropneumatosis	HAOI/DRO/NAOUM/TOE/SIS
hydrohematonephrosis	HAOI/DRO/HEM/TO/NE/FROE/SIS	hydropneumogony	HAOI/DRO/NAOU/MOG/N*I
	HAOI/DRO/HAOEM/TO/NE/FROE/ SIS	hydropneumopericardium	HAOI/DRO/NAOUM/P*ER/KARD/ YUM
hydrohepatosis	HAOI/DRO/HEP/TOE/SIS	hydropneumoperitoneum	HAOI/DRO/NAOUM/PERT/ NAOEM
hydrohymenitis	HAOI/DRO/HAOIM/NAOITS		
hydrokinesitherapy	HAOI/DRO/KI/NAOEZ/THER/PI	hydropneumothorax	HAOI/DRO/NAOUM/THOR/AX
hydrokinetic	HAOI/DRO/KI/NET/IK	hydroponic	HAOI/DRO/PON/IK
hydrokinetics	HAOI/DRO/KI/NET/IK/-S	hydroponics	HAOI/DRO/PON/IK/-S
hydrol	HAOI/DROL	Hydropres	HAOI/DRO/PRES
hydrolabile	HAOI/DRO/LAI/BAOIL	hydrops	HAOI/DROPS
	HAOI/DRO/LAI/BIL	hydropyonephrosis	HAOI/DRO/PAOI/NE/FROE/SIS
hydrolability	HAOI/DRO/LABLT		HAOI/DRO/PAOI/NEF/ROE/SIS
hydrolabyrinth	HAOI/DRO/LAB/R*INT	hydroquinol	HAOI/DRO/KWIN/OL
hydrolase	HAOI/DRO/LAIS	hydroquinone	HAOI/DRO/KWIN/OEN
hydrology	HAOI/DROLG	hydrorachis	HAOI/DRO/RAI/KIS
hydro-lyase	HAOI/DRO/LAOI/AIS	hydrorachitis	HAOI/DRO/RAI/KAOITS
hydrolymph	HAOI/DROL/LIM/-F		HAOI/DRO/RA/KAOITS
hydrolysate	HAOI/DROL/SAIT	hydrorchis	HAOI/DROR/KIS
hydrolysis	HAOI/DROL/SIS	hydrorheostat	HAOI/DRO/RAOE/STAT
hydrolyst	HAOI/DRO/L*IS	hydrorrhea	HAOI/DRO/RAOE/YA
hydrolyte	HAOI/DRO/LAOIT	hydrosalpinx	HAOI/DRO/SAL/PINGS
hydrolytic	HAOI/DRO/LIT/IK	hydrosarca	HAOI/DRO/SAR/KA
hydrolyze	HAOI/DRO/LAOIZ	hydrosarcocele	HAOI/DRO/SARK/SAO*EL
hydroma	HAOI/DROE/MA	hydroscheocele	HAOI/DROS/KO/SAO*EL
hydromassage	HAOI/DRO/MA/SAJ		HAOI/DROS/KAOE/SAO*EL
	HAOI/DRO/MAS/SAJ	hydroscope	HAOI/DRO/SKOEP
hydromeningitis	HAOI/DRO/MEN/JAOITS	hydrosol	HAOI/DRO/SOL
hydromeningocele	HAOI/DRO/ME/NING/SAO*EL	hydrosoluble	HAOI/DRO/SOL/YUBL
hydrometer	HAOI/DROM/TER		HAOI/DRO/SOL/YAOUBL
hydrometra	HAOI/DRO/MAOE/TRA	hydrosphymograph	HAOI/DRO/SFIG/MO/GRAF
hydrometric	HAOI/DRO/MET/RIK	hydrospirometer	HAOI/DRO/SPAOI/ROM/TER
hydrometrocolpos	HAOI/DRO/MAOE/TRO/KOL/POS	hydrostabile	HAOI/DRO/STAI/BIL
hydrometry	HAOI/DROM/TRI		HAOI/DRO/STAI/BAOIL
hydromicrocephaly	HAOI/DRO/MAOI/KRO/SEF/LI	hydrostat	HAOI/DRO/STAT
Hydromine	HAOI/DRO/MAOEN	hydrostatic	HAOI/DRO/STAT/IK
hydromorphone	HAOI/DRO/MOR/FOEN	hydrostatics	HAOI/DRO/STAT/IK/-S
Hydromox	HAOI/DRO/MOX	hydrosudopathy	HAOI/DRO/SAOU/DOP/TH*I
hydromphalus	HAOI/DROM/FLUS	hydrosudotherapy	HAOI/DRO/SAOUD/THER/PI
hydromyelia	HAOI/DRO/MAOI/AOEL/YA	hydrosynthesis	HAOI/DRO/S*INT/SIS
hydromyelocele	HAOI/DRO/MAOI/LO/SAO*EL	hydrosyringomyelia	HAOI/DRO/SIRNG/MAOI/AOEL/ YA
hydromyelomeningocele	HAOI/DRO/MAOI/LO/ME/NING/ SAO*EL		
		hydrosus	HAOI/DROE/SUS
hydromyoma	HAOI/DRO/MAOI/YOE/MA	Hydrotaea	HAOI/DRO/TAOE/YA
hydronephrosis	HAOI/DRO/NE/FROE/SIS	hydrotaxis	HAOI/DRO/TAK/SIS
	HAOI/DRO/NEF/ROE/SIS	hydrotherapeutic	HAOI/DRO/THER/PAOUT/IK
hydronephrotic	HAOI/DRO/NE/FROT/IK	hydrotherapeutics	HAOI/DRO/THER/PAOUT/IK/-S
	HAOI/DRO/NEF/ROT/IK	hydrotherapy	HAOI/DRO/THER/PI
hydronium	HAOI/DROEN/YUM	hydrothermal	HAOI/DRO/THER/MAL
hydropancreatosis	HAOI/DRO/PAN/KRA/TOE/SIS	hydrothermic	HAOI/DRO/THERM/IK
hydroparasalpinx	HAOI/DRO/PAR/SAL/PINGS	hydrothionammonemia	HAOI/DRO/THAOI/NAM/NAOEM/ YA
hydroparotitis	HAOI/DRO/PAR/TAOITS		
	HAOI/DRO/PAR/O/TAOITS	hydrothionemia	HAOI/DRO/THAOI/NAOEM/YA
hydropathic	HAOI/DRO/PA*T/IK	hydrothionuria	HAOI/DRO/THAOI/NAOUR/YA
hydropathy	HAOI/DROP/TH*I	hydrothorax	HAOI/DRO/THOR/AX
hydropenia	HAOI/DRO/PAOEN/YA	hydrotomy	HAOI/DROT/M*I

hydrotropism	HAOI/DROT/RO/PIFM	hygiene	HAOI/JAOE/*IS
	HAOI/DRO/TROEP/IFM		HAOI/JAOEN
hydrotubation	HAOI/DRO/TAOU/BAIGS	hygienic	HAOI/JEN/IK
hydroureter	HAOI/DRO/YAOU/RAOET/ER		HAOI/JAOEN/IK
	HAOI/DRO/YAOUR/TER	hygienics	HAOI/JEN/IK/-S
hydroureterosis	HAOI/DRO/YAOU/RAOET/ROE/	hygienism	HAOI/JEN/IFM
	SIS		HAOI/JAOEN/IFM
hydrous	HAOI/DROUS	hygienist	HAOI/JAOEN/*IS
hydrovarium	HAOI/DRO/VAIRM		HAOI/JEN/*IS
hydroxamic	HAOI/DROK/SAM/IK	hygienization	HAOI/JEN/ZAIGS
hydroxide	HAOI/DROK/SAOID		HAOI/JAOEN/ZAIGS
	HAOI/DROX/AOID	hygr(o)-	HAOI/GR(O)
hydroxocobalamin	HAOI/DROX/KO/BAL/MIN	hygrechema	HAOI/GRE/KAOE/MA
hydroxocobemine	HAOI/DROX/KOEB/MAOEN	hygric	HAOI/GRIK
hydroxy-	HAOI/DROX	hygroblepharic	HAOI/GRO/BLE/FAR/IK
	HAOI/DROK/SI	hygroma	HAOI/GROE/MA
hydroxy acid	HAOI/DROX/AS/ID	hygromatous	HAOI/GROEM/TOUS
	HAOI/DROK/SI/AS/ID		HAOI/GROM/TOUS
hydroxyacylglutathione	HAOI/DROX/AS/IL/GLAOUT/	hygrometer	HAOI/GROM/TER
	THAOI/OEN	hygrometric	HAOI/GRO/MET/RIK
hydroxyamphetamine	HAOI/DROX/AM/FET/MAOEN	hygrometry	HAOI/GROM/TRI
hydroxyapatite	HAOI/DROX/AP/TAOIT	hygrophobia	HAOI/GRO/FOEB/YA
	HAOI/DROX/AP/PA/TAOIT	hygroscopic	HAOI/GRO/SKOP/IK
hydroxybenzene	HAOI/DROX/BEN/ZAOEN	hygrostomia	HAOI/GRO/STOEM/YA
hydroxybutyric	HAOI/DROX/BAOU/TIR/IK	Hygroton	HAOI/GRO/TON
hydroxycarbamide	HAOI/DROX/KARB/MAOID	hyla	HAO*I/LA
hydroxochloroquine	HAOI/DROX/KLOR/KWIN		(not HAOI/LA; see hila)
hydroxycholecalciferol	HAOI/DROX/KOEL/KAL/SIF/ROL	hylephobia	HAOIL/FOEB/YA
hydroxychroman	HAOI/DROX/KROE/MAN	hylic	HAOIL/IK
hydroxychromene	HAOI/DROX/KROE/MAOEN		HAOI/LIK
hydroxycorticosteroid	HAOI/DROX/KORT/KO/STAOER/	hyloma	HAOI/LOE/MA
	OID	Hylorel	HAOIL/REL
hydroxycorticosterone	HAOI/DROX/KORT/KO/STAOER/	hylotropic	HAOI/LO/TROP/IK
	OEN	hylotropy	HAOI/LOT/RO/PI
hydroxydione	HAOI/DROX/DI/OEN	hymen	HAOIM/-N
hydroxyephedrine	HAOI/DROX/EF/DRAOEN		HAO*I/MEN
	HAOI/DROX/FED/RAOEN		(not HAOI/MEN)
hydroxyergocalciferol	HAOI/DROX/ERG/KAL/SIF/ROL	hymen(o)-	HAOIM/N(O)
hydroxyestrin	HAOI/DROX/ES/TRIN	hymenal	HAOIM/NAL
hydroxyhemin	HAOI/DROX/HAOE/MIN	hymenales	HAOIM/NAI/LAOEZ
hydroxykynureninuria	HAOI/DROX/KAOI/NAOUR/NI/	hymenalis	HAOIM/NAI/LIS
	NAOUR/YA	hymenectomy	HAOIM/NEKT/M*I
	HAOI/DROX/KAOI/NAOUR/NIN/	hymenitis	HAOIM/NAOITS
	YAOUR/YA	hymenium	HAOI/MAOEN/YUM
hydroxyl	HAOI/DROK/SIL	hymenoid	HAOIM/NOID
hydroxylamine	HAOI/DROK/SIL/MAOEN	hymenolepiasis	HAOIM/NO/LE/PAOI/SIS
hydroxylamino	HAOI/DROK/SIL/AM/NOE	hymenolepidid	HAOIM/NO/LEP/DID
hydroxylase	HAOI/DROX/LAIS	Hymenolepididae	HAOIM/NO/LEP/DI/DAE
hydroxylation	HAOI/DROX/LAIGS		HAOIM/NO/LEP/DAOI/DAE
hydroxylysine	HAOI/DROK/SIL/SIN	Hymenolepis	HAOIM/NOL/PIS
hydroxymercuribenzoate	HAOI/DROX/MERK/RI/BENZ/	hymenology	HAOIM/NOLG
	WAIT	Hymenomycetes	HAOIM/NO/MAOI/SAOE/TAOEZ
	HAOI/DROX/MER/KAOUR/BENZ/	Hymenoptera	HAOIM/NOPT/RA
	WAIT		HAOIM/NOP/TRA
hydroxymethyltransferase	HAOI/DROX/M*ET/IL/TRA*NS/	hymenopteran	HAOIM/NOPT/RAN
	FRAIS	hymenopterism	HAOIM/NOPT/RIFM
hydroxynervone	HAOI/DROX/NER/VOEN	hymenorrhaphy	HAOIM/NOR/FI
hydroxyphenamate	HAOI/DROX/FEN/MAIT	hymenotomy	HAOIM/NOT/M*I
hydroxyphenylethylamine	HAOI/DROX/FENL/*ET/IL/AM/	hyo-	HAOI
	MIN		HAOI/YO
hydroxyphenyluria	HAOI/DROX/FENL/YAOUR/YA	hyobasioglossus	HAOI/BAIS/YO/GLOS/SUS
hydroxyprogesterone	HAOI/DROX/PRO/J*ES/ROEN	hyobranchial	HAOI/BRANG/YAL
hydroxyproline	HAOI/DROX/PRO/LAOEN	hyoepiglottic	HAOI/EP/GLOT/IK
	HAOI/DROX/PRO/LIN	hyoepiglottidean	HAOI/EP/GLO/TID/YAN
hydroxyprolinemia	HAOI/DROX/PROEL/NAOEM/YA		HAOI/EP/GLOT/TID/YAN
hydroxypropyl	HAOI/DROX/PRO/PIL	hyoglossal	HAOI/GLOS/SAL
hydroxyprostaglandin	HAOI/DROX/PRO*S/GLAN/DIN	hyoid	HAOI/OID
hydroxyquinoline	HAOI/DROX/KWIN/LAOEN	hyoidei	HAOI/OID/YAOI
hydroxysteroid	HAOI/DROX/STAOER/OID	hyoideum	HAOI/OID/YUM
hydroxystilbamidine	HAOI/DROX/STIL/BAM/DAOEN	hyoideus	HAOI/OID/YUS
hydroxytetracycline	HAOI/DROX/TET/RA/SAOI/	hyomandibular	HAOI/MAN/DIB/LAR
	KLAOEN	hyopharyngeus	HAOI/FRIN/JUS
hydroxytoluic	HAOI/DROX/TOE/LAOU/IK	hyoscine	HAOI/SAOEN
	HAOI/DROX/TOL/YAOU/IK		HAOI/SIN
hydroxytryptamine	HAOI/DROX/TRIPT/MAOEN	hyoscyamine	HAOI/SAOI/MAOEN
hydroxytryptophan	HAOI/DROX/TRIPT/FAN		HAOI/SAOI/MIN
hydroxytyramine	HAOI/DROX/TAOIR/MAOEN	hyoscyamus	HAOI/SAOI/MUS
hydroxyurea	HAOI/DROX/YAOU/RAOE/YA	Hyostrongylus rubidus	HAOI/STRONG/LUS/RAOUB/DUS
hydroxyvaline	HAOI/DROX/VAL/LIN	hyothyroid	HAOI/THAOI/ROID
hydroxyzine	HAOI/DROX/ZAOEN	hypacidemia	HAOI/PAS/DAOEM/YA
Hydrozoa	HAOI/DRO/ZOE/WA	hypacusia	HAOIP/KAOUZ/YA
hydrozoan	HAOI/DRO/ZOE/WAN	hypacusis	HAOIP/KAOU/SIS
hydruria	HAOI/DRAOUR/YA		HIP/KAOU/SIS
hydruric	HAOI/DRAOUR/IK	hypalbuminemia	HAOI/PAL/BAOUM/NAOEM/YA
hygieiolatry	HAOI/JOL/TRI		HIP/AL/BAOUM/NAOEM/YA
	HAOI/JAOE/OL/TRI	hypalgesia	HAOI/PAL/JAOEZ/YA
hygieiology	HAOI/JOLG	hypalgesic	HAOI/PAL/JAOEZ/IK
	HAOI/JAOE/OLG		HIP/AL/JAOEZ/IK
hygieist	HAOI/J*IS	hypalgetic	HAOI/PAL/JET/IK

hypalgia	HIP/AL/JET/IK	
	HAOI/PAL/JA	
	HIP/AL/JA	
hypamnion	HAOI/PAM/NON	
	HAOI/PAM/NAOE/YON	
hypamnios	HAOI/PAM/NOS	
	HAOI/PAM/NAOE/YOS	
hypanakinesia	HAOI/PAN/KI/NAOEZ/YA	
hypanakinesis	HAOI/PAN/KI/NAOE/SIS	
hyparterial	HAOI/PAR/TAOERL	
	HAOIP/AR/TAOERL	
	HIP/AR/TAOERL	
hypaxial	HAOI/PAX/YAL	
	HIP/AX/YAL	
hypazoturia	HAOI/PAZ/TAOUR/YA	
hypencephalon	HAOI/PEN/SEF/LON	
hypenchyme	HAOI/PEN/KAOIM	
hypengyophobia	HAOI/PENG/YO/FOEB/YA	
hyper-	HAO*IP	
	HAOI/PER (not in CAT)	
hyperabsorption	HAO*IP/AB/SORPGS	
hyperacanthosis	HAO*IP/AK/AN/THOE/SIS	
	HAO*IP/AI/KAN/THOE/SIS	
hyperacid	HAO*IP/AS/ID	
hyperacidaminuria	HAO*IP/AS/DAM/NAOUR/YA	
	HAO*IP/AS/ID/AM/NAOUR/YA	
hyperacidity	HAO*IP/AI/SID/TI	
hyperactive	HAO*IP/AKT/IV	
hyperactivity	HAO*IP/AK/TIV/TI	
hyperacusia	HAO*IP/AI/KAOUZ/YA	
hyperacusis	HAO*IP/AI/KAOU/SIS	
hyperacute	HAO*IP/AI/KAOUT	
hyperadenosis	HAO*IP/AD/NOE/SIS	
hyperadiposis	HAO*IP/AD/POE/SIS	
hyperadiposity	HAO*IP/AD/POS/TI	
hyperadrenalemia	HAO*IP/AI/DRAOENL/AOEM/YA	
	HAO*IP/AI/DRAOEN/LAOEM/YA	
hyperadrenalism	HAO*IP/AI/DRAOENL/IFM	
hyperadrenia	HAO*IP/AI/DRAOEN/YA	
hyperadrenocorticism	HAO*IP/AI/DRAOEN/KORT/SIFM	
hyperaffective	HAO*IP/AFKT/IV	
hyperaffectivity	HAO*IP/AFK/TIV/TI	
hyperalbuminemia	HAO*IP/AL/BAOUM/NAOEM/YA	
hyperalbuminosis	HAO*IP/AL/BAOUM/NOE/SIS	
hyperaldosteronemia	HAO*IP/AL/DO*S/ROEN/AOEM/YA	
	HAO*IP/AL/DO/STAOER/NAOEM/YA	
hyperaldosteronism	HAO*IP/AL/DO*S/RON/IFM	
	HAO*IP/AL/DO/STAOER/NIFM	
	HAO*IP/AL/DO/S/ROEN/IFM	
hyperaldosteronuria	HAO*IP/AL/DO/STAOER/NAOUR/YA	
hyperalert	HAO*IP/AI/LERT	
hyperalgesia	HAO*IP/AL/JAOEZ/YA	
hyperalgesic	HAO*IP/AL/JAOEZ/IK	
hyperalgetic	HAO*IP/AL/JET/IK	
hyperalimentation	HAO*IP/AL/MEN/TAIGS	
hyperalimentosis	HAO*IP/AL/MEN/TOE/SIS	
hyperalkalescence	HAO*IP/AL/KLES/ENS	
hyperalkalinity	HAO*IP/AL/KLIN/TI	
hyperallantoinuria	HAO*IP/AI/LANT/WI/NAOUR/YA	
	HAO*IP/AI/LANT/WIN/YAOUR/YA	
hyperalonemia	HAO*IP/AI/NAOEM/YA	
hyperalphalipoproteinemia	HAO*IP/AL/FA/LIP/PROET/NAOEM/YA	
hyperaminoacidemia	HAO*IP/AM/NO/AS/DAOEM/YA	
hyperaminoaciduria	HAO*IP/AM/NO/AS/DAOUR/YA	
hyperammonemia	HAO*IP/AM/NAOEM/YA	
hyperammonuria	HAO*IP/AM/NAOUR/YA	
hyperamylasemia	HAO*IP/AM/LAI/SAOEM/YA	
	HAO*IP/AM/LAIS/AOEM/YA	
hyperanacinesia	HAO*IP/AN/SI/NAOEZ/YA	
hyperanacinesis	HAO*IP/AN/IS/NAOE/SIS	
hyperanakinesia	HAO*IP/AN/KI/NAOEZ/YA	
hyperanakinesis	HAO*IP/AN/KI/NAOE/SIS	
hyperandrogenism	HAO*IP/AN/DRO/JEN/IFM	
hyperaphia	HAO*IP/AIF/YA	
hyperaphic	HAO*IP/AF/IK	
	HAO*IP/AFK	
hyperarousal	HAO*IP/AI/ROU/ZAL	
hyperazotemia	HAO*IP/A*Z/TAOEM/YA	
hyperazoturia	HAO*IP/A*Z/TAOUR/YA	
hyperbaric	HAO*IP/BAR/IK	
	HAO*IP/BAIR/IK	
hyperbarism	HAO*IP/BAR/IFM	
hyperbasophilic	HAO*IP/BAI/SO/FIL/IK	
	HAO*IP/BAS/FIL/IK	
hyperbetalipoproteinemia	HAO*IP/BAIT/LIP/PROET/	

	NAOEM/YA	
	HAO*IP/BAIT/LIP/PRO/TAOEN/AOEM/YA	
hyperbicarbonatemia	HAO*IP/KARB/NAIT/AOEM/YA	
	HAO*IP/KARB/NAI/TAOEM/YA	
hyperbilirubinemia	HAO*IP/BIL/RAOUB/NAOEM/YA	
hyperblastosis	HAO*IP/BLAS/TOE/SIS	
hyperbrachycephalic	HAO*IP/BRAK/SFAL/IK	
hyperbrachycephaly	HAO*IP/BRAK/SEF/LI	
hyperbradykininemia	HAO*IP/BRAD/KAOIN/NAOEM/YA	
	HAO*IP/BRAD/KAOI/NIN/AOEM/YA	
hyperbradykininism	HAO*IP/BRAD/KAOIN/NIFM	
	HAO*IP/BRAD/KAOI/NIN/IFM	
hyperbulia	HAO*IP/BAOUL/YA	
hypercalcemia	HAO*IP/KAL/SAOEM/YA	
hypercalcinemia	HAO*IP/KALS/NAOEM/YA	
hypercalcinuria	HAO*IP/KALS/NAOUR/YA	
hypercalciuria	HAO*IP/KALS/YAOUR/YA	
hypercalcuria	HAO*IP/KAL/KAOUR/YA	
hypercapnia	HAO*IP/KAP/NA	
	HAO*IP/KAP/NAOE/YA	
hypercapnic	HAO*IP/KAP/NIK	
hypercarbia	HAO*IP/KARB/YA	
hypercardia	HAO*IP/KARD/YA	
hypercarotenemia	HAO*IP/KAR/TAOEN/AOEM/YA	
hypercatabolic	HAO*IP/KAT/BOL/IK	
hypercatabolism	HAO*IP/KA/TAB/LIFM	
hypercatharsis	HAO*IP/KA/THAR/SIS	
hypercathartic	HAO*IP/KA/THART/IK	
hypercathexis	HAO*IP/KA/THEK/SIS	
hypercellular	HAO*IP/SEL/YAOU/LAR	
hypercellularity	HAO*IP/SEL/YAOU/LAIR/TI	
hypercementosis	HAO*IP/SEMT/TOE/SIS	
hyperchloremia	HAO*IP/KLO/RAOEM/YA	
	HAO*IP/KLOR/AOEM/YA	
hyperchloremic	HAO*IP/KLO/RAOEM/IK	
	HAO*IP/KLOR/AOEM/IK	
hyperchlorhydria	HAO*IP/KLOR/HAOI/DRA	
	HAO*IP/KLOR/HAOI/DRAOE/YA	
hyperchloridation	HAO*IP/KLOR/DAIGS	
hyperchloride	HAO*IP/KLOR/AOID	
hyperchloruration	HAL*IP/KLOR/RAIGS	
	HAO*IP/KLOR/YAOU/RAIGS	
	HAO*IP/KLOR/YU/RAIGS	
hyperchloruria	HAO*IP/KLOR/YAOUR/YA	
hypercholesteremia	HAO*IP/KL*ES/RAOEM/YA	
hypercholesteremic	HAO*IP/KL*ES/RAOEM/IK	
hypercholesterinemia	HAO*IP/KL*ES/RI/NAOEM/YA	
	HAO*IP/KL*ES/RIN/AOEM/YA	
hypercholesterolemia	HAO*IP/KL*ES/ROL/AOEM/YA	
hypercholesterolemic	HAO*IP/KLES/TROL/AOEM/IK	
hypercholesterolia	HAO*IP/KL*ES/ROL/YA	
	HAO*IP/KL*ES/ROEL/YA	
hypercholia	HAO*IP/KOEL/YA	
hyperchondroplasia	HAO*IP/KON/DRO/PLAIZ/YA	
hyperchromaffinism	HAO*IP/KROE/MAF/NIFM	
hyperchromasia	HAO*IP/KROE/MAIZ/YA	
hyperchromatic	HAO*IP/KROE/MAT/IK	
hyperchromatin	HAO*IP/KROEM/TIN	
hyperchromatism	HAO*IP/KROEM/TIFM	
hyperchromatopsia	HAO*IP/KROEM/TOPS/YA	
hyperchromatosis	HAO*IP/KROEM/TOE/SIS	
hyperchromemia	HAO*IP/KROE/MAOEM/YA	
hyperchromia	HAO*IP/KROEM/YA	
hyperchromic	HAO*IP/KROEM/IK	
hyperchylia	HAO*IP/KAOIL/YA	
hyperchylomicronemia	HAO*IP/KAOIL/MAOI/KRO/NAOEM/YA	
hypercinesia	HAO*IP/SI/NAOEZ/YA	
hypercinesis	HAO*IP/SI/NAOE/SIS	
hypercoagulability	HAO*IP/KO/AG/LABLT	
hypercoagulable	HAO*IP/KO/AG/LABL	
hypercorticism	HAO*IP/KORT/SIFM	
hypercorticoidism	HAO*IP/KORT/KOID/IFM	
hypercortisolism	HAO*IP/KORT/SOL/IFM	
	HAO*IP/KORT/SOEL/IFM	
hypercreatinemia	HAO*IP/KRAOE/YA/TIN/AOEM/YA	
hypercrine	HAO*IP/KRIN	
hypercrinemia	HAO*IP/KRI/NAOEM/YA	
	HAO*IP/KRIN/AOEM/YA	
hypercrinia	HAO*IP/KRIN/YA	
hypercrinism	HAO*IP/KRAOI/NIFM	
	HAO*IP/KRIN/IFM	
hypercrisia	HAO*IP/KRIS/YA	
hypercryalgesia	HAO*IP/KRAOI/AL/JAOEZ/YA	
hypercryesthesia	HAO*IP/KRAOI/ES/THAOEZ/YA	

hypercupremia	HAO*IP/KAOU/PRAOEM/YA	hyperfolliculoidism	HAO*IP/FLIK/LOI/DIFM
hypercupriuria	HAO*IP/KAOU/PRAOE/YAOUR/		HAL*IP/FLIK/LOID/IFM
	YA	hyperfunctioning	HAO*IP/FUNGS/-G
	HAO*IP/KAOU/PRI/YAOUR/YA	hypergalactia	HAO*IP/GLAK/SHA
hypercyanotic	HAO*IP/SAOI/NOT/IK	hypergalactosis	HAO*IP/GAL/AK/TOE/SIS
hypercyesia	HAO*IP/SAO/AOEZ/YA		HAO*IP/GLAK/TOE/SIS
hypercyesis	HAO*IP/SAOI/E/SIS	hypergalactous	HAO*IP/GLAK/TOUS
hypercythemia	HAO*IP/SAOI/THAOEM/YA	hypergammaglobulinemia	HAO*IP/GAM/GLOB/LI/NAOEM/
hypercytochromia	HAO*IP/SAOIT/KROEM/YA		YA
hypercytosis	HAO*IP/SAOI/TOE/SIS		HAO*IP/GAM/GLOG/LIN/AOEM/
hyperdactylia	HAO*IP/DAK/TIL/YA		YA
hyperdactylism	HAO*IP/DAKT/LIFM	hypergasia	HAO*IP/GAIZ/YA
hyperdactyly	HAO*IP/DAKT/LI	hypergastrinemia	HAO*IP/GAS/TRIN/AOEM/YA
hyperdiastole	HAO*IP/DI/A*S/LAOE		HAO*IP/GAS/TRI/NAOEM/YA
hyperdicrotic	HAO*IP/DI/KROT/IK	hypergenesis	HAO*IP/JEN/SIS
hyperdicrotism	HAO*IP/DIK/RO/TIFM	hypergenetic	HAO*IP/JE/NET/IK
	HAO*IP/DI/KROE/TIFM	hypergenitalism	HAO*IP/JEN/TAL/IFM
hyperdiploid	HAO*IP/DIP/LOID	hypergeusesthesia	HAO*IP/GAOUS/ES/THAOEZ/YA
hyperdiploidy	HAO*IP/DIP/LOI/DI	hypergeusia	HAO*IP/GAOUZ/YA
hyperdipsia	HAO*IP/DIPS/YA	hypergia	HAOI/PER/JA
hyperdistention	HAO*IP/DIS/TENGS	hypergic	HAOI/PERJ/IK
hyperdiuresis	HAO*IP/DI/YAOU/RAOE/SIS	hypergigantosoma	HAO*IP/JAOI/GANT/SOE/MA
hyperdontia	HAO*IP/DON/SHA	hyperglandular	HAO*IP/GLAND/LAR
hyperdynamia	HAO*IP/DAOI/NAIM/YA	hyperglobulia	HAO*IP/GLOB/YAOUL/YA
hyperdynamic	HAO*IP/DAOI/NAM/IK	hyperglobulinemia	HAO*IP/GLOB/LIN/AOEM/YA
hypereccrisia	HAO*IP/E/KRIS/YA		HAO*IP/GLOB/LI/NAOEM/YA
	HAO*IP/EK/KRIS/YA	hyperglobulism	HAO*IP/GLOB/LIFM
hypereccrisis	HAO*IP/EK/RI/SIS	hyperglucagonemia	HAO*IP/GLAOUK/GON/AOEM/YA
hypereccritic	HAO*IP/E/KRIT/IK	hyperglycemia	HAO*IP/GLAOI/SAOEM/YA
	HAO*IP/EK/KRIT/IK	hyperglycemic	HAO*IP/GLAOI/SAOEM/IK
hyperechema	HAO*IP/E/KAOE/MA	hyperglyceridemia	HAO*IP/GLIS/RI/DAOEM/YA
	HAO*IP/KAOE/MA	hyperglyceridemic	HAO*IP/GLIS/RI/DAOEM/IK
hyperelastica	HAO*IP/E/LA*S/KA	hyperglycinemia	HAO*IP/GLAOIS/NAOEM/YA
hyperelectrolytemia	HAO*IP/LEK/TRO/LAOI/TAOEM/	hyperglycinuria	HAO*IP/GLAOIS/NAOUR/YA
	YA	hyperglycistia	HAO*IP/GLAOI/S*IS/YA
hyperemesis	HAO*IP/EM/SIS	hyperglycodermia	HAO*IP/GLAOIK/DERM/YA
hyperemetic	HAO*IP/E/MET/IK	hyperglycogenolysis	HAO*IP/GLAOIK/JEN/OL/SIS
hyperemia	HAO*IP/AOEM/YA		HAO*IP/GLAOIK/JE/NOL/SIS
hyperemic	HAO*IP/AOEM/IK	hyperglycoplasmia	HAO*IP/GLAOIK/PLAZ/MAOE/YA
hyperemotivity	HAO*IP/E/MOE/TIV/TI	hyperglycorrhachia	HAO*IP/GLAOIK/RAIK/YA
hyperencephalus	HAO*IP/EN/SEF/LUS	hyperglycosemia	HAO*IP/GLAOIK/SAOEM/YA
hyperencephaly	HAO*IP/EN/SEF/LI	hyperglycosuria	HAO*IP/GLAOIK/SAOUR/YA
hyperendemic	HAO*IP/EN/DEM/IK	hyperglyoxylemia	HAO*IP/GLAOI/OX/LAOEM/YA
hyperendocrinia	HAO*IP/*END/KRIN/YA	hypergnosia	HAO*IP/NOEZ/YA
hyperendocrinism	HAO*IP/EN/DOK/RI/NIFM	hypergnosis	HAO*IP/NOE/SIS
hyperendocrisia	HAO*IP/*END/KRIS/YA	hypergonadism	HAO*IP/GOE/NAD/IFM
hyperenergia	HAO*IP/EN/ER/JA	hypergonadotropic	HAO*IP/GOE/NAD/TROP/IK
hypereosinophilia	HAO*IP/E/SIN/FIL/YA		HAO*IP/GON/DO/TROP/IK
hyperephidrosis	HAO*IP/EF/DROE/SIS	hypergranulosis	HAO*IP/GRAN/LOE/SIS
hyperepinephrinemia	HAO*IP/EP/NEF/RI/NAOEM/YA	hyperguanidinemia	HAO*IP/GAUN/DI/NAOEM/YA
hyperepinephry	HAO*IP/EP/NEF/RI		HAO*IP/GAUN/DIN/AOEM/YA
hyperepithymia	HAO*IP/EP/THAOIM/YA	hypergynecosmia	HAO*IP/GAOIN/KOZ/MA
hyperequilibrium	HAO*IP/E/KWI/LIB/RUM		HAO*IP/GAOIN/KOZ/MAOE/YA
hypererethism	HAO*IP/*ER/THIFM	hyperhedonia	HAO*IP/HAOE/DOEN/YA
hyperergasia	HAO*IP/ER/GAIZ/YA		HAO*IP/HE/DOEN/YA
hyperergia	HAO*IP/ER/JA	hyperhedonism	HAO*IP/HAOED/NIFM
hyperergic	HAO*IP/ERJ/IK	hyperhemoglobinemia	HAO*IP/HAOEM/GLOEB/NAOEM/
hyperergy	HAO*IP/ERJ/JI		YA
hypererythrocythemia	HAO*IP/R*IT/RO/SAOI/THAOEM/	hyperheparinemia	HAO*IP/HEP/RI/NAOEM/YA
	YA		HAO*IP/HEP/RIN/AOEM/YA
hyperesophoria	HAO*IP/ES/FOER/YA	hyperhepatia	HAO*IP/HE/PAT/YA
hyperesthesia	HAO*IP/ES/THAOEZ/YA		HAO*IP/HE/PAI/SHA
hyperesthetic	HAO*IP/ES/THET/IK	hyperhidrosis	HAO*IP/HAOI/DROE/SIS
hyperestrinemia	HAO*IP/ES/TRI/NAOEM/YA		HAO*IP/HI/DROE/SIS
hyperestrinism	HAO*IP/ES/TRIN/IFM	hyperhidrotic	HAO*IP/HAOI/DROT/IK
hyperestrogenemia	HAO*IP/ES/TRO/JEN/AOEM/YA		HAO*IP/HI/DROT/IK
hyperestrogenism	HAO*IP/ES/TRO/JEN/IFM	hyperhormonal	HAO*IP/HOR/MOENL
hyperestrogenosis	HAO*IP/ES/TRO/JE/NOE/SIS	hyperhormonic	HAO*IP/HOR/MON/IK
hypereuryopia	HAO*IP/YAOUR/OEP/YA	hyperhormonism	HAO*IP/HOR/MOEN/IFM
	HAO*IP/YAOUR/YOEP/YA	hyperhydration	HAO*IP/HAOI/DRAIGS
hypereuryprosopic	HAO*IP/YAOUR/PRO/SOP/IK	hyperhydrochloria	HAO*IP/HAOI/DRO/KLOR/YA
hyperevolutism	HAO*IP/E/VOL/TIFM	hyperhydropexy	HAO*IP/HAOI/DRO/PEK/SI
hyperexcretory	HAO*IP/EX/KRE/TOIR	hyperhydropexis	HAO*IP/HAOI/DRO/PEK/SIS
hyperexophoria	HAO*IP/KPO/FOER/YA	hyperhypophysism	HAO*IP/HAOI/POF/SIFM
hyperexplexia	HAO*IP/EX/PLEX/YA	hypericin	HAOI/PER/SIN
hyperextension	HAO*IP/EX/TENGS	hyperidrosis	HAO*IP/DROE/SIS
hyperferremia	HAO*IP/FER/RAOEM/YA	hyperidrotica	HAO*IP/DROT/KA
hyperferremic	HAO*IP/FER/RAOEM/IK	hyperimmune	HAO*IP/IM/MAOUN
hyperferricemia	HAO*IP/FER/SAOEM/YA	hyperimmunity	HAO*IP/IM/MAOUN/TI
hyperfibrinogenemia	HAO*IP/FAOI/BRIN/JE/NAOEM/	hyperimmunization	HAO*IP/IM/NI/ZAIGS
	YA	hyperimmunoglobulinemia	HAO*IP/IM/NO/GLOB/LIN/AOEM/
	HAO*IP/FAOI/BRIN/JEN/AOEM/		YA
	YA	hyperindicanemia	HAO*IP/IND/KAN/AOEM/YA
hyperfibrinolysis	HAO*IP/FAOI/BRIN/OL/SIS		HAO*IP/IND/KA/NAOEM/YA
	HAO*IP/FAOI/BRI/NOL/SIS	hyperinfection	HAO*IP/IN/F*EBGS
hyperflexion	HAO*IP/FL*EBGS	hyperinflation	HAO*IP/IN/FLAIGS
hyperfolliculinemia	HAO*IP/FLIK/LI/NAOEM/YA	hyperingestion	HAO*IP/IN/JEGS
hyperfolliculinism	HAO*IP/FLIK/LIN/IFM	hyperinosemia	HAO*IP/IN/SAOEM/YA
hyperfolliculinuria	HAO*IP/FLIK/LI/NAOUR/YA		HAO*IP/IN/NO/SAOEM/YA

hyperinosis	HAO*IP/IN/NOE/SIS	hypermyotonia	HAO*IP/MAOI/TOEN/YA
	(*not* HAO*IP/NOE/SIS; see	hypermyotrophy	HAO*IP/MAOI/OT/RO/FI
	hypergnosis)	hypernanosoma	HAO*IP/NAI/NO/SOE/MA
hyperinsulinar	HAO*IP/INS/LI/NAR	hypernasality	HAO*IP/NAI/ZAL/TI
	HAO*IP/INS/LIN/AR	hypernatremia	HAO*IP/NA/TRAOEM/YA
hyperinsulinemia	HAO*IP/INS/LIN/AOEM/YA	hypernatremic	HAO*IP/NA/TRAOEM/IK
hyperinsulinism	HAO*IP/INS/LIN/IFM	hyperneocytosis	HAO*IP/NAOE/SAOI/TOE/SIS
hyperinterrenal	HAO*IP/SPWER/RAOENL	hypernephritis	HAO*IP/NE/FRAOITS
hyperinterrenopathy	HAO*IP/SPWER/RE/NOP/TH*I	hypernephroid	HAO*IP/NEF/ROID
hyperinvolution	HAO*IP/IN/VO/LAOUGS	hypernephroma	HAO*IP/NE/FROE/MA
	HAO*IP/IN/VOE/LAOUGS		HAO*IP/NEF/ROE/MA
hyperiodemia	HAO*IP/AOI/DAOEM/YA	hyperneurotization	HAO*IP/NAOU/ROT/ZAIGS
hyperirritability	HAO*IP/IRT/-BLT	hypernitremia	HAO*IP/NAOI/TRAOEM/YA
hyperisotonia	HAO*IP/AOIS/TOEN/YA	hypernoia	HAO*IP/NOI/YA
hyperisotonic	HAO*IP/AOIS/TON/IK	hypernomic	HAO*IP/NOM/IK
hyperkalemia	HAO*IP/KLAOEM/YA	hypernormal	HAO*IP/NOR/MAL
	HAO*IP/KA/LAOEM/YA	hypernutrition	HAO*IP/NAOU/TRIGS
hyperkaliemia	HAO*IP/KAL/YAOEM/YA	hyperoncotic	HAO*IP/ON/KOT/IK
hyperkaluresis	HAO*IP/KAL/YAOU/RAOE/SIS	hyperonychia	HAO*IP/O/NIK/YA
hyperkeratinization	HAO*IP/KER/TIN/ZAIGS	hyperonychosis	HAO*IP/ON/KOE/SIS
hyperkeratomycosis	HAO*IP/KER/TO/MAOI/KOE/SIS		HAO*IP/OIN/KOE/SIS
hyperkeratosis	HAO*IP/KER/TOE/SIS	hyperope	HAO*IP/OEP
hyperketonemia	HAO*IP/KAOET/NAOEM/YA	hyperopia	HAO*IP/OEP/YA
hyperketonuria	HAO*IP/KAOET/NAOUR/YA	hyperopic	HAO*IP/OEP/IK
hyperketosis	HAO*IP/KAOE/TOE/SIS		HAO*IP/OP/IK
hyperkinemia	HAO*IP/KI/NAOEM/YA	hyperorality	HAO*IP/ORL/TI
hyperkinemic	HAO*IP/KI/NAOEM/IK		HAO*IP/O/RAL/TI
hyperkinesia	HAO*IP/KI/NAOEZ/YA	hyperorchidism	HAO*IP/ORK/DIFM
hyperkinesis	HAO*IP/KI/NAOE/SIS	hyperorexia	HAO*IP/O/REX/YA
hyperkinetic	HAO*IP/KI/NET/IK	hyperorthocytosis	HAO*IP/O*RT/SAOI/TOE/SIS
hyperkoria	HAO*IP/KOER/YA	hyperosmia	HAO*IP/OZ/MA
hyperlactacidemia	HAO*IP/LAK/TAS/DAOEM/YA		HAO*IP/OZ/MAOE/YA
hyperlactation	HAO*IP/LAK/TAIGS	hyperosmolality	HAO*IP/OZ/MO/LAL/TI
hyperlecithinemia	HAO*IP/LES/THIN/AOEM/YA	hyperosmolar	HAO*IP/OZ/MOE/LAR
hyperlethal	HAO*IP/LAOE/THAL	hyperosmolarity	HAO*IP/OZ/MO/LAIR/TI
hyperleukocytosis	HAO*IP/LAOUK/SAOI/TOE/SIS	hyperosmotic	HAO*IP/OZ/MOT/IK
hyperlexia	HAO*IP/LEX/YA	hyperosphresia	HAO*IP/OS/FRAOEZ/YA
hyperleydigism	HAO*IP/LAOI/DIG/IFM	hyperosphresis	HAO*IP/OS/FRAOE/SIS
hyperlipemia	HAO*IP/LI/PAOEM/YA	hyperosteogeny	HAO*IP/O*S/YOJ/N*I
hyperlipidemia	HAO*IP/LIP/DAOEM/YA	hyperosteoidosis	HAO*IP/O*S/YOI/DOE/SIS
hyperlipoidemia	HAO*IP/LIP/OI/DAOEM/YA	hyperostosis	HAO*IP/OS/TOE/SIS
	HAO*IP/LIP/OID/AOEM/YA	hyperostotic	HAO*IP/OS/TOT/IK
hyperlipoproteinemia	HAO*IP/LIP/PROET/NAOEM/YA	hyperovaria	HAO*IP/O/VAIR/YA
	HAO*IP/LIP/PRO/TAOEN/AOEM/	hyperovarianism	HAO*IP/O/VAIRN/IFM
	YA	hyperovarism	HAO*IP/OEV/RIFM
hyperliposis	HAO*IP/LI/POE/SIS	hyperoxaluria	HAO*IP/OX/LAOUR/YA
hyperlithemia	HAO*IP/LI/THAOEM/YA	hyperoxemia	HAO*IP/OK/SAOEM/YA
hyperlithic	HAO*IP/L*IT/IK	hyperoxia	HAO*IP/OX/YA
hyperlithuria	HAO*IP/LI/THAOUR/YA	hyperoxic	HAO*IP/OX/IK
hyperlogia	HAO*IP/LOE/JA	hyperoxidation	HAO*IP/OX/DAIGS
hyperlordosis	HAO*IP/LOR/DOE/SIS	hyperoxide	HAO*IP/OX/AOID
hyperlucency	HAO*IP/LAOU/SEN/SI	hyperpallesthesia	HAO*IP/PAL/ES/THAOEZ/YA
	HAO*IP/LAOUS/EN/SI	hyperpancreatism	HAO*IP/PAN/KRA/TIFM
hyperluteinization	HAO*IP/LAOU/TAOEN/ZAIGS	hyperpancreorrhea	HAO*IP/PAN/KRO/RAOE/YA
	HAO*IP/LAOUT/YIN/ZAIGS	hyperparasite	HAO*IP/PAR/SAOIT
hyperlutemia	HAO*IP/LAOU/TAOEM/YA	hyperparasitic	HAO*IP/PAR/SIT/IK
hyperlysinemia	HAO*IP/LAOIS/NAOEM/YA	hyperparasitism	HAO*IP/PAR/SAOIT/IFM
hyperlysinuria	HAO*IP/LAOIS/NAOUR/YA		HAO*IP/PAR/SAOI/TIFM
hypermagnesemia	HAO*IP/MAG/NE/SAOEM/YA	hyperparathyroidism	HAO*IP/PAR/THAOI/ROI/DIFM
hypermania	HAO*IP/MAIN/YA		HAO*IP/PAR/THAOI/ROID/IFM
hypermastia	HAO*IP/MA*S/YA	hyperparotidism	HAO*IP/PA/ROT/DIFM
hypermature	HAO*IP/MA/KHUR		HAO*IP/PROT/DIFM
hypermegasoma	HAO*IP/MEG/SOE/MA	hyperpathia	HAO*IP/PA*T/YA
hypermelanotic	HAO*IP/MEL/NOT/IK	hyperpepsia	HAO*IP/PEPS/YA
hypermenorrhea	HAO*IP/MEN/RAOE/YA	hyperpepsinemia	HAO*IP/PEPS/NAOEM/YA
hypermesosoma	HAO*IP/MES/SOE/MA	hyperpepsinia	HAO*IP/PEP/SIN/YA
hypermetabolic	HAO*IP/MET/BOL/IK	hyperpepsinuria	HAO*IP/PEPS/NAOUR/YA
hypermetabolism	HAO*IP/ME/TAB/LIFM	hyperperistalsis	HAO*IP/P*ER/STAL/SIS
hypermetamorphosis	HAO*IP/MET/MOR/FO/SIS	hyperpermeability	HAO*IP/PERM/YABLT
hypermetaplasia	HAO*IP/MET/PLAIZ/YA	hyperpexia	HAO*IP/PEX/YA
hypermetria	HAO*IP/MAOE/TRAOE/YA	hyperpexy	HAO*IP/PEK/SI
	HAO*IP/MAOE/TRA	hyperphagia	HAO*IP/FAI/JA
hypermetrope	HAO*IP/ME/TROEP	hyperphagic	HAO*IP/FALJ/IK
	HAO*IP/MET/ROEP		HAO*IP/FAJ/IK
hypermetropia	HAO*IP/ME/TROEP/YA	hyperphalangia	HAO*IP/FLAN/JA
hypermetropic	HAO*IP/ME/TROP/IK	hyperphalangism	HAO*IP/FLAN/JIFM
	HAO*IP/ME/TROEP/IK	hyperphasia	HAO*IP/FAIZ/YA
hypermicrosoma	HAO*IP/MAOI/KRO/SOE/MA	hyperphenylalaninemia	HAO*IP/FENL/AL/NIN/AOEM/YA
hypermimia	HAO*IP/MIM/YA		HAO*IP/FENL/AL/NI/NAOEM/YA
hypermineralization	HAO*IP/MIN/RAL/ZAIGS	hyperphonesis	HAO*IP/FOE/NAOE/SIS
hypermnesia	HAO*IP/NAOEZ/YA	hyperphonia	HAO*IP/FOEN/YA
	HAOI/PERM/NAOEZ/YA	hyperphoria	HAO*IP/FOER/YA
hypermnesic	HAO*IP/NAOEZ/IK	hyperphosphatasemia	HAO*IP/FOS/FA/TAI/SAOEM/YA
	HAOI/PERM/NAOEZ/IK		HAO*IP/FOS/FA/TAIS/AOEM/YA
hypermobility	HAO*IP/MOEBLT	hyperphosphatasia	HAO*IP/FOS/FA/TAIZ/YA
hypermodal	HAO*IP/MOE/DAL	hyperphosphatemia	HAO*IP/FOS/FA/TAOEM/YA
hypermorph	HAO*IP/MOR/-F	hyperphosphaturia	HAO*IP/FOS/FA/TAOUR/YA
hypermotility	HAO*IP/MOE/TIL/TI	hyperphosphoremia	HAO*IP/FOS/FRAOEM/YA
hypermyesthesia	HAO*IP/MAOI/ES/THAOEZ/YA	hyperphrenia	HAO*IP/FRAOEN/YA

hyperpiesia	HAO*IP/PAOI/AOEZ/YA
hyperpiesis	HAO*IP/PAOI/E/SIS
hyperpietic	HAO*IP/PAOI/ET/IK
hyperpigmentation	HAO*IP/PIG/MEN/TAIGS
hyperpinealism	HAO*IP/PIN/YAL/IFM
hyperpipecolatemia	HAO*IP/PIP/KOEL/TAOEM/YA
hyperpituitarism	HAO*IP/PI/TAOU/TRIFM
	HAO*IP/PI/TAOU/TAR/IFM
hyperplasia	HAO*IP/PLAIZ/YA
hyperplasmia	HAO*IP/PLAZ/MAOE/YA
hyperplastic	HAO*IP/PLA*S/IK
hyperplastica	HAO*IP/PLA*S/KA
hyperploid	HAO*IP/PLOID
hyperploidy	HAO*IP/PLOI/DI
hyperpnea	HAO*IP/NAOE/YA
	HAOI/PERP/NA
	HAOI/PERP/NAOE/YA
hyperpneic	HAO*IP/NAOE/IK
	HAOI/PERP/NIK
	HAOI/PERP/NAOE/IK
hyperpolarization	HAO*IP/POE/LAR/ZAIGS
	HAO*IP/POEL/RI/ZAIGS
hyperpolypeptidemia	HAO*IP/POL/PEPT/DAOEM/YA
hyperponesis	HAO*IP/PO/NAOE/SIS
	HAO*IP/POE/NAOE/SIS
hyperponetic	HAO*IP/PO/NET/IK
	HAO*IP/POE/NET/IK
hyperposia	HAO*IP/POEZ/YA
hyperpotassemia	HAO*IP/POT/SAOEM/YA
	HAO*IP/POET/SAOEM/YA
	HAO*IP/POE/TAS/SAOEM/YA
hyperpragia	HAO*IP/PRAI/JA
hyperpragic	HAO*IP/PRAJ/IK
hyperpraxia	HAO*IP/PRAX/YA
hyperprebetalipoproteinemia	
	HAO*IP/PRE/BAIT/LIP/PROET/ NAOEM/YA
	HAO*IP/PRE/BAIT/LIP/PRO/ TAOEN/AOEM/YA
hyperpresbyopia	HAO*IP/PRES/BI/OEP/YA
hyperproinsulinemia	HAO*IP/PRO/INS/LI/NAOEM/YA
	HAO*IP/PRO/INS/LIN/AOEM/YA
hyperprolactinemia	HAO*IP/PRO/LAKT/NAOEM/YA
hyperprolactinemic	HAO*IP/PRO/LAKT/NAOEM/IK
hyperprolinemia	HAO*IP/PROEL/NAOEM/YA
hyperprosexia	HAO*IP/PRO/SEX/YA
hyperproteinemia	HAL*IP/PROET/NAOEM/YA
	HAO*IP/PRO/TAOEN/AOEM/YA
hyperproteosis	HAO*IP/PROET/YOE/SIS
hyperpselaphesia	HAO*IP/SEL/FAOEZ/YA
hyperptyalism	HAO*IP/TAOI/LIFM
hyperpyremia	HAO*IP/PAOI/RAOEM/YA
hyperpyretic	HAO*IP/PAOI/RET/IK
hyperpyrexia	HAO*IP/PAOI/REX/YA
hyperpyrexial	HAO*IP/PAOI/REX/YAL
hyperreactive	HAO*IP/RE/AKT/IV
hyperreflexia	HAO*IP/RE/FLEX/YA
hyperreninemia	HAO*IP/RAOEN/NAOEM/YA
hyperreninemic	HAO*IP/RAOEN/NAOEM/IK
hyperresonance	HAO*IP/REZ/NANS
hypersalemia	HAO*IP/SA/LAOEM/YA
	HAO*IP/SAL/AOEM/YA
hypersaline	HAO*IP/SAI/LAOEN
	HAO*IP/SAI/LAOIN
hypersalivation	HAO*IP/S*AL/VAIGS
	HAO*IP/SAL/LI/VAIGS
	(not HAO*IP/SAL/VAIGS)
hypersarcosinemia	HAO*IP/SARK/SI/NAOEM/YA
	HAO*IP/SARK/SIN/AOEM/YA
hypersecretion	HAO*IP/SE/KRAOEGS
hypersegmentation	HAO*IP/SEG/MEN/TAIGS
hypersensibility	HAO*IP/SENS/-BLT
hypersensitive	HAO*IP/SENS/TIV
hypersensitiveness	HAO*IP/SENS/TIV/*NS
hypersensitivity	HAO*IP/SENS/TIV/TI
hypersensitization	HAO*IP/SENS/TI/ZAIGS
hyperserotonemia	HAO*IP/SAOER/TOE/NAOEM/YA
	HAO*IP/SAOER/TO/NAOEM/YA
hypersialosis	HAO*IP/SAOI/LOE/SIS
hyperskeocytosis	HAO*IP/SKAOE/SAOI/TOE/SIS
hypersomatatropism	HAO*IP/SOE/MAT/TROEP/IFM
	HAO*IP/SOEM/TO/TROEP/IFM
	HAO*IP/SOE/MAT/TROP/IFM
hypersomia	HAO*IP/SOEM/YA
hypersomnia	HAO*IP/SOM/NA
	HAO*IP/SOM/NAOE/YA
hypersonic	HAO*IP/SON/IK
hypersphyxia	HAO*IP/SFIX/YA
hypersplenia	HAO*IP/SPLAOEN/YA

hypersplenism	HAO*IP/SPLAOEN/IFM
	HAO*IP/SPLEN/IFM
hyperspongiosis	HAO*IP/SPON/JOE/SIS
Hyperstat	HAO*IP/STAT
hypersteatosis	HAO*IP/STAOE/TOE/SIS
hyperstereoroentgenegraphy	
	HAO*IP/STER/YO/RENT/GEN/OG/ FI
hypersthenia	HAO*IP/STHAOEN/YA
hypersthenic	HAO*IP/STHEN/IK
hypersthenuria	HAO*IP/STHEN/YAOUR/YA
	HAO*IP/STHE/NAOUR/YA
hypersusceptibility	HAO*IP/SUS/SEPT/-BLT
hypersympathicotonus	HAO*IP/SIM/PA*T/KO/TOE/NUS
hypersystole	HAO*IP/S*IS/LAOE
hypersystolic	HAO*IP/SIS/TOL/IK
hypertarachia	HAO*IP/TA/RAIK/YA
	HAO*IP/TA/RAK/YA
hypertelorism	HAO*IP/TEL/RIFM
	HAO*IP/TAOEL/RIFM
hypertension	HAO*IP/TENGS
hypertensive	HAO*IP/TENS/IV
hypertensor	HAO*IP/TEN/SOR
hypertestoidism	HAO*IP/TES/TOID/IFM
	HAO*IP/TES/TOI/DIFM
hypertetraploid	HAO*IP/TET/RA/PLOID
hyperthecosis	HAO*IP/THAOE/KOE/SIS
hyperthelia	HAO*IP/THAOEL/YA
hyperthermal	HAO*IP/THER/MAL
hyperthermalgesia	HAO*IP/THER/MAL/JAOEZ/YA
	HAO*IP/THERM/AL/JAOEZ/YA
hyperthermesthesia	HAO*IP/THER/MES/THAOEZ/YA
	(not HAO*IP/THERM/ES/THAOEZ/ YA)
hyperthermia	HAO*IP/THERM/YA
hyperthermoesthesia	HAO*IP/THERM/ES/THAOEZ/YA
hyperthermy	HAO*IP/THER/M*I
hyperthrombinemia	HAO*IP/THROM/BI/NAOEM/YA
	HAO*IP/THROM/BIN/AOEM/YA
hyperthymia	HAO*IP/THAOIM/YA
hyperthymic	HAO*IP/THAOIM/IK
hyperthymism	HAO*IP/THAOIM/IFM
	HAO*IP/THAOI/MIFM
hyperthymization	HAO*IP/THAOIM/ZAIGS
hyperthyrea	HAO*IP/THAOIR/YA
hyperthyreosis	HAO*IP/THAOIR/YOE/SIS
hyperthyroid	HAO*IP/THAOI/ROID
hyperthyroidism	HAO*IP/THAOI/ROI/DIFM
	HAO*IP/THAOI/ROID/IFM
hyperthyroidosis	HAO*IP/THAOI/ROI/DOE/SIS
hyperthyrosis	HAO*IP/THAOI/ROE/SIS
hyperthyroxinemia	HAO*IP/THAOI/ROX/NAOEM/YA
hypertonia	HAO*IP/TOEN/YA
hypertonic	HAO*IP/TON/IK
hypertonicity	HAO*IP/TOE/NIS/TI
hypertonus	HAO*IP/TOE/NUS
hypertoxic	HAO*IP/TOX/IK
hypertoxicity	HAO*IP/TOK/SIS/TI
hypertrichiasis	HAO*IP/TRI/KAOI/SIS
hypertrichophrydia	HAO*IP/TRIK/FRID/YA
hypertrichosis	HAO*IP/TRI/KOE/SIS
hypertriglyceridemia	HAO*IP/TR*I/GLIS/RI/DAOEM/YA
hypertriploid	HAO*IP/TRIP/LOID
hypertroph	HAO*IP/TROF
	HAO*IP/TROEF
hypertrophia	HAO*IP/TROEF/YA
hypertrophic	HAO*IP/TROFK
hypertrophy	HAOI/PERT/FI
	HAOI/PER/TRO/FI
hypertropia	HAO*IP/TROEP/YA
hypertyrosinemia	HAO*IP/TAOIR/SI/NAOEM/YA
	HAO*IP/TAOIR/SIN/AOEM/YA
hyperuresis	HAO*IP/YAOU/RAOE/SIS
hyperuricacidemia	HAO*IP/YAOURK/AS/DAOEM/YA
	HAO*IP/YAOUR/IK/AS/DAOEM/ YA
hyperuricaciduria	HAO*IP/YAOURK/AS/DAOUR/YA
	HAO*IP/YAOUR/IK/AS/DAOUR/ YA
hyperuricemia	HAO*IP/YAOUR/SAOEM/YA
hyperuricemic	HAO*IP/YAOUR/SAOEM/IK
hyperuricuria	HAO*IP/YAOUR/KAOUR/YA
hypervaccination	HAO*IP/VAX/NAIGS
hypervalinemia	HAO*IP/VAL/NAOEM/YA
hypervascular	HAO*IP/VAS/KLAR
hypervegetative	HAO*IP/VEJ/TAIT/IV
hyperventilation	HAO*IP/VENT/LAIGS
hyperviscosity	HAO*IP/VIS/KOS/TI
hypervitaminosis	HAO*IP/VAOIT/MI/NOE/SIS

hypervitaminotic	HAO*IP/VAOIT/MI/NOT/IK
hypervolemia	HAO*IP/VOE/LAOEM/YA
hypervolemic	HAO*IP/VOE/LAOEM/IK
hypervolia	HAO*IP/VOEL/YA
hypesthesia	HAOI/PES/THAOEZ/YA
	HIP/ES/THAOEZ/YA
hyph(o)-	HAOIF
	HAOI/F(O)
hypha	HAOI/FA
hyphae	HAOI/FAE
hyphal	HAOI/FAL
	HAOIFL
hyphedonia	HAOIP/HAOE/DOEN/YA
	HAOIP/HE/DOEN/YA
hyphema	HAOI/FAOE/MA
hyphemia	HAOI/FAOEM/YA
Hy-Phen	HAO*I/FEN
	(not HAOI/FEN; see hyphen)
Hy-Phen Tablets	HAO*I/FEN/TAB/LET/-S
hyphephilia	HIF/FIL/YA
hyphidrosis	HAOIP/HID/ROE/SIS
	HIP/HAOI/DROE/SIS
Hyphomyces destruens	HAOIF/MAOI/SAOEZ/DES/
	TRAOUNZ
hyphomycete	HAOIF/MAOI/SAOET
Hyphomycetes	HAOIF/MAOI/SAOE/TAOEZ
hyphomycetic	HAOIF/MAOI/SET/IK
hyphomycetoma	HAOIF/MAOIS/TOE/MA
hyphomycosis	HAOIF/MAOI/KOE/SIS
hypisotonic	HAOIP/AOIS/TON/IK
	HIP/AOIS/TON/IK
hypn(o)-	HIP/N/O
hypnagogic	HIP/NA/GOJ/IK
hypnagogue	HIP/NA/GOG
hypnalgia	HIP/NAL/JA
hypnapagogic	HIP/NAP/GOJ/IK
hypnesthesia	HIP/NES/THAOEZ/YA
hypnic	HIP/NIK
hypnoanalysis	HIP/NO/ANL/SIS
hypnoanalytic	HIP/NO/AN/LIT/IK
hypnoanesthesia	HIP/NO/ANS/THAOEZ/YA
hypnocatharsis	HIP/NO/KA/THAR/SIS
hypnocinematograph	HIP/NO/SIN/MAT/GRAF
hypnocyst	HIP/NO/S*IS
hypnodontia	HIP/NO/DON/SHA
hypnodontic	HIP/NO/DONT/IK
hypnodontics	HIP/NO/DONT/IK/-S
hypnogenesis	HIP/NO/JEN/SIS
hypnogenetic	HIP/NO/JE/NET/IK
hypnogenic	HIP/NO/JEN/IK
hypnogenous	HIP/NOJ/NOUS
hypnoid	HIP/NOID
hypnoidal	HIP/NOI/DAL
hypnoidization	HIP/NOID/ZAIGS
hypnolepsy	HIP/NO/LEP/SI
hypnologist	HIP/NO*LGS
hypnology	HIP/NOLG
hypnonarcoanalysis	HIP/NO/NARK/ANL/SIS
hypnonarcosis	HIP/NO/NAR/KOE/SIS
hypnopedia	HIP/NO/PAOED/YA
hypnophobia	HIP/NO/FOEB/YA
hypnopompic	HIP/NO/POFRP/IK
	HIP/NO/POM/PIK
hypnoses	HIP/NOE/SAOEZ
hypnosia	HIP/NOEZ/YA
hypnosis	HIP/NOE/SIS
hypnosophy	HIP/NOS/FI
hypnotherapy	HIP/NO/THER/PI
hypnotic	HIP/NOT/IK
hypnotism	HIP/NO/TIFM
hypnotist	HIP/NO/T*IS
hypnotization	HIP/NO/TAOI/ZAIGS
	HIP/NO/TI/ZAIGS
hypnotize	HIP/NO/TAOIZ
hypnotoid	HIP/NO/TOID
hypnozoite	HIP/NO/ZOE/AOIT
hypo (word)	HAOI/POE
hypo-	HO*IP
	HAOI/PO (not in CAT)
hypoacidity	HO*IP/AI/SID/TI
hypoactive	HO*IP/AKT/IV
hypoactivity	HO*IP/AK/TIV/TI
hypoacusis	HO*IP/AI/KAOU/SIS
hypoadenia	HO*IP/AI/DAOEN/YA
hypoadrenalemia	HO*IP/AI/DRAOENL/AOEM/YA
	HO*IP/AI/DRAOEN/LAOEM/YA
hypoadrenalism	HO*IP/AI/DRAOENL/IFM
	HO*IP/AI/DRAOEN/LIFM
hypoadrenia	HO*IP/AI/DRAOEN/YA

hypoadrenocorticism	HO*IP/AI/DRAOEN/KORT/SIFM
hypoaffective	HO*IP/AFKT/IV
hypoaffectivity	HO*IP/AFK/TIV/TI
hypoalbuminemia	HO*IP/AL/BAOUM/NAOEM/YA
hypoalbuminosis	HO*IP/AL/BAOUM/NOE/SIS
hypoaldosteronemia	HO*IP/AL/DO/STAOER/NAOEM/
	YA
hypoaldosteronism	HO*IP/AL/DO*S/RON/IFM
	HO*IP/AL/DO/STAOER/NIFM
hypoaldosteronuria	HO*IP/AL/DO*S/RO/NAOUR/YA
	HO*IP/AL/DO*S/RON/YAOUR/YA
	HO*IP/AL/DO/STAOER/NAOUR/
	YA
hypoalgesia	HO*IP/AL/JAOEZ/YA
hypoalimentation	HO*IP/AL/MEN/TAIGS
hypoalkaline	HO*IP/AL/KLIN
	HO*IP/AL/KLAOIN
hypoalkalinity	HO*IP/AL/KLIN/TI
hypoalonemia	HO*IP/AL/NAOEM/YA
hypoaminoacidemia	HO*IP/AM/NO/AS/DAOEM/YA
hypoandrogenism	HO*IP/AN/DRO/JEN/IFM
	HO*IP/AN/DROJ/NIFM
hypoazoturia	HO*IP/A*Z/TAOUR/YA
hypobaria	HO*IP/BAR/YA
	HO*IP/BAIR/YA
hypobaric	HO*IP/BAR/IK
	HO*IP/BAIR/IK
hypobarism	HO*IP/BAR/IFM
hypobaropathy	HO*IP/BA/ROP/TH*I
	HO*IP/BAR/OP/TH*I
hypobasophilism	HO*IP/BAI/SO/FIL/IFM
	HO*IP/BAS/FIL/IFM
	HO*IP/BA/SOF/LIFM
hypobetalipoproteinemia	HO*IP/BAIT/LIP/PROET/NAOEM/
	YA
hypobilirubinemia	HO*IP/BIL/RAOUB/NAOEM/YA
hypoblast	HO*IP/BLA*S
hypoblastic	HO*IP/BLA*S/IK
hypobranchial	HO*IP/BRANG/YAL
hypobromite	HO*IP/BROE/MAOIT
hypobromous	HO*IP/BROEM/OUS
hypobulia	HO*IP/BAOUL/YA
hypocalcemia	HO*IP/KAL/SAOEM/YA
hypocalcia	HO*IP/KALS/YA
hypocalcification	HO*IP/KALS/FI/KAIGS
hypocalcipectic	HO*IP/KALS/PEKT/IK
hypocalcipexy	HO*IP/KALS/PEK/SI
hypocalciuria	HO*IP/KALS/YAOUR/YA
hypocapnia	HO*IP/KAP/NA
	HO*IP/KAP/NAOE/YA
hypocapnic	HO*IP/KAP/NIK
hypocarbia	HO*IP/KARB/YA
hypocellular	HO*IP/SEL/YAOU/LAR
hypocellularity	HO*IP/SEL/YAOU/LAIR/TI
hypocoelom	HO*IP/SE/LOM
hypochloraemicum	HO*IP/KLOE/RAOEM/KUM
	HO*IP/KLOE/RAEM/KUM
hypochloremia	HO*IP/KLO/RAOEM/YA
	HO*IP/KLOE/RAOEM/YA
hypochloremic	HO*IP/KLO/RAOEM/IK
	HO*IP/KLOE/RAOEM/IK
hypochlorhydria	HO*IP/KLOR/HAOI/DRA
	HO*IP/KLOR/HAOI/DRAOE/YA
hypochloridation	HO*IP/KLOR/DAIGS
hypochloridemia	HO*IP/KLOR/DAOEM/YA
hypochlorite	HO*IP/KLOR/AOIT
hypochlorization	HO*IP/KLOR/ZAIGS
hypochlorous	HO*IP/KLOR/OUS
hypochloruria	HO*IP/KLOR/YAOUR/YA
	HO*IP/KLOE/RAOUR/YA
hypocholesteremia	HO*IP/KL*ES/RAOEM/YA
hypocholesteremic	HO*IP/KL*ES/RAOEM/IK
hypocholesterinemia	HO*IP/KL*ES/RI/NAOEM/YA
	HO*IP/KL*ES/RIN/AOEM/YA
hypocholesterolemia	HO*IP/KL*ES/ROL/AOEM/YA
	HO*IP/KL*ES/RO/LAOEM/YA
hypocholia	HO*IP/KOEL/YA
hypocholuria	HO*IP/KOE/LAOUR/YA
hypochondria	HO*IP/KON/DRA
	HO*IP/KON/DRAOE/YA
hypochondriac	HO*IP/KON/DRAOE/AK
hypochondriacal	HO*IP/KON/DRAOI/KAL
hypochondriasis	HO*IP/KON/DRAOI/SIS
hypochondrium	HO*IP/KON/DRUM
	HO*IP/KON/DRAOE/UM
hypochondroplasia	HO*IP/KON/DRO/PLAIZ/YA
hypochordal	HO*IP/KHOR/DAL
hypochromasia	HO*IP/KROE/MAIZ/YA

hypochromatic	HO*IP/KROE/MAT/IK	hypoexophoria	HO*IP/KPO/FOER/YA
hypochromatism	HO*IP/KROEM/TIFM	hypoferremia	HO*IP/FER/RAOEM/YA
hypochromatosis	HO*IP/KROE/TOE/SIS	hypoferric	HO*IP/FER/IK
hypochromemia	HO*IP/KROE/MAOEM/YA	hypoferrism	HO*IP/FER/IFM
hypochromia	HO*IP/KROEM/YA	hypofertile	HO*IP/FER/TIL
hypochromic	HO*IP/KROEM/IK		HO*IP/FER/TAOIL
hypochromica	HO*IP/KROEM/KA	hypofertility	HO*IP/FER/TIL/TI
hypochromotrichia	HO*IP/KROEM/TRIK/YA	hypofibrinogenemia	HO*IP/FAOI/BRIN/JE/NAOEM/YA
hypochrosis	HO*IP/KROE/SIS		HO*IP/FAOI/BRIN/JEN/AOEM/YA
hypochylia	HO*IP/KAOIL/YA	hypofunction	HO*IP/FUNGS
hypocinesia	HO*IP/SI/NAOEZ/YA	hypogalactia	HO*IP/GLAK/SHA
hypocinesis	HO*IP/SI/NAOE/SIS	hypogalactous	HO*IP/GLAK/TOUS
hypocitraturia	HO*IP/SI/TRAI/TAOUR/YA		HO*IP/GLAKT/OUS
	HO*IP/SIT/RAI/TAOUR/YA	hypogammaglobinemia	HO*IP/GAM/GLOEB/NAOEM/YA
hypocitremia	HO*IP/SI/TRAOEM/YA	hypogammaglobulinemia	HO*IP/GAM/GLOB/LI/NAOEM/YA
hypocitruria	HO*IP/SI/TRAOUR/YA		HO*IP/GAM/GLOB/LIN/AOEM/YA
hypocoagulability	HO*IP/KO/AG/LABLT	hypogangliognosis	HO*IP/GANG/LO/NOE/SIS
hypocoagulable	HO*IP/KO/AG/LABL	hypogastric	HO*IP/GAS/TRIK
hypocomplementemia	HO*IP/KOM/PLEMT/AOEM/YA	hypogastrium	HO*IP/GAS/TRUM
	HO*IP/KOM/PLEMT/TAOEM/YA	hypogastrocele	HO*IP/GAS/TRO/SAO*EL
hypocomplementemic	HO*IP/KOM/PLEMT/AOEM/IK	hypogastropagus	HO*IP/GAS/TROP/GUS
	HO*IP/KOM/PLEMT/TAOEM/IK	hypogastroschisis	HO*IP/GAS/TROS/KI/SIS
hypocondylar	HO*IP/KOND/LAR	hypogenesis	HO*IP/JEN/SIS
hypocone	HO*IP/KOEN	hypogenetic	HO*IP/JE/NET/IK
hypoconid	HO*IP/KO/NID	hypogeic	HO*IP/JAOE/IK
	HO*IP/KON/ID	hypogenitalism	HO*IP/JEN/TAL/IFM
hypoconule	HO*IP/KON/YAOUL	hypogeusesthesia	HO*IP/GAOUS/ES/THAOEZ/YA
hypoconulid	HO*IP/KON/LID	hypogeusia	HO*IP/GAOUZ/YA
	HO*IP/KON/YAOU/LID	hypoglandular	HO*IP/GLAND/LAR
	HO*IP/KON/YU/LID	hypoglobulia	HO*IP/GLOB/YAOUL/YA
hypocorticalism	HO*IP/KORT/KAL/IFM	hypoglossal	HO*IP/GLOS/SAL
	HO*IP/KORT/KLIFM	hypoglossi	HO*IP/GLOS/SAOI
hypocorticism	HO*IP/KORT/SIFM	hypoglossis	HO*IP/GLOS/SIS
hypocorticoidism	HO*IP/KORT/KOID/IFM	hypoglossus	HO*IP/GLOS/SUS
	HO*IP/KORT/KOI/DIFM	hypoglottis	HO*IP/GLOT/TIS
hypocrine	HO*IP/KRIN	hypoglucagonemia	HO*IP/GLAOUK/GON/AOEM/YA
hypocrinia	HO*IP/KRIN/YA	hypoglycemia	HO*IP/GLAOI/SAOEM/YA
hypocrinism	HO*IP/KRAOI/NIFM	hypoglycemic	HO*IP/GLAOI/SAOEM/IK
	HO*IP/KRIN/IFM	hypoglycemosis	HO*IP/GLAOIS/MOE/SIS
hypocupremia	HO*IP/KAOU/PRAOEM/YA	hypoglycogenolysis	HO*IP/GLAOIK/JE/NOL/SIS
hypocyclosis	HO*IP/SAOI/KLOE/SIS		HO*IP/GLAOIK/JEN/OL/SIS
hypocystotomy	HO*IP/SIS/TOT/M*I	hypoglycorrhachia	HO*IP/GLAOIK/RAIK/YA
hypocythemia	HO*IP/SAOI/THAOEM/YA		HO*IP/GLAOIK/RAK/YA
hypocytosis	HO*IP/SAOI/TOE/SIS	hypognathous	HAOI/POG/NA/THOUS
hypodactylia	HO*IP/DAK/TIL/YA		HO*IP/NA*T/OUS
hypodactylism	HO*IP/DAKT/LIFM	hypognathus	HAOI/POG/NA/THUS
hypodactyly	HO*IP/DAKT/LI		HO*IP/NA*T/THUS
hypoderm	HO*IP/DERM	hypogonadia	HO*IP/GOE/NAD/YA
Hypoderma	HO*IP/DER/MA	hypogonadism	HO*IP/GOE/NAD/IFM
hypodermatic	HO*IP/DER/MAT/IK		HO*IP/GON/DIFM
hypodermatoclysis	HO*IP/DERM/TOK/LI/SIS	hypogonadotropic	HO*IP/GOE/NAD/TROP/IK
hypodermatomy	HO*IP/DER/MAT/M*I		HO*IP/GON/DO/TROP/IK
hypodermatosis	HO*IP/DERM/TOE/SIS	hypogranulocytosis	HO*IP/GRAN/LO/SAOI/TOE/SIS
hypodermiasis	HO*IP/DER/MAOI/SIS	hypohepatia	HO*IP/HE/PAI/SHA
hypodermic	HO*IP/DERM/IK		HO*IP/HE/PAT/YA
hypodermis	HO*IP/DER/MIS	hypohidrosis	HO*IP/HAOI/DROE/SIS
hypodermoclysis	HO*IP/DER/MOK/LI/SIS		HO*IP/HID/ROE/SIS
hypodermolithiasis	HO*IP/DERM/LI/THAOI/SIS	hypohidrotic	HO*IP/HAOI/DROT/IK
hypodiaphragmatic	HO*IP/DAOI/FRAG/MAT/IK		HO*IP/HI/DROT/IK
hypodiploid	HO*IP/DIP/LOID	hypohormonal	HO*IP/HOR/MOENL
hypodiploidy	HO*IP/DIP/LOI/DI	hypohormonic	HO*IP/HOR/MON/IK
hypodipsia	HO*IP/DIPS/YA	hypohormonism	HO*IP/HOR/MOEN/IFM
hypodontia	HO*IP/DON/SHA	hypohydration	HO*IP/HAOI/DRAIGS
hypodynamia	HO*IP/DAOI/NAIM/YA	hypohydremia	HO*IP/HAOI/DRAOEM/YA
hypodynamic	HO*IP/DAOI/NAM/IK	hypohydrochloria	HO*IP/HAOI/DRO/KLOR/YA
hypoeccrisia	HO*IP/E/KRIS/YA	hypohyloma	HO*IP/HAOI/LOE/MA
hypoeccrisis	HO*IP/EK/RI/SIS	hypohypnotic	HO*IP/HIP/NOT/IK
hypoeccritic	HO*IP/E/KRIT/IK	hypohypophysism	HO*IP/HAOI/POF/SIFM
hypoechoic	HO*IP/E/KOIK	hypoidrosis	HO*IP/ID/ROE/SIS
	HO*IP/E/KOE/IK	hypoimmunity	HO*IP/IM/MAOUN/TI
hypoelectrolytemia	HO*IP/LEK/TRO/LAOI/TAOEM/YA	hypoinsulinemia	HO*IP/INS/LI/NAOEM/YA
hypoemotivity	HO*IP/E/MOE/TIV/TI		HO*IP/INS/LIN/AOEM/YA
hypoendocrinia	HO*IP/*END/KRIN/YA	hypoinsulinism	HO*IP/INS/LIN/IFM
hypoendocrinism	HO*IP/EN/DOK/RI/NIFM	hypoiodidism	HO*IP/AOI/OED/DIFM
hypoendocrisia	HO*IP/*END/KRIS/YA	hypoisotonic	HO*IP/AOIS/TON/IK
hypoeosinophilia	HO*IP/E/SIN/FIL/YA	hypokalemia	HO*IP/KLAOEM/YA
hypoepinephrinemia	HO*IP/EP/NEF/RIN/AOEM/YA		HO*IP/KA/LAOEM/YA
	HO*IP/EP/NEF/RI/NAOEM/YA	hypokalemic	HO*IP/KLAOEM/IK
hypoequilibrium	HO*IP/E/KWI/LIB/RUM		HO*IP/KA/LAOEM/IK
hypoergasia	HO*IP/ER/GAIZ/YA	hypokinemia	HO*IP/KI/NAOEM/YA
hypoergia	HO*IP/ER/JA	hypokinesia	HO*IP/KI/NAOEZ/YA
hypoergic	HO*IP/ERJ/IK	hypokinesis	HO*IP/KI/NAOE/SIS
hypoergy	HO*IP/ERJI	hypokinetic	HO*IP/KI/NET/IK
hypoesophoria	HO*IP/ES/FOER/YA	hypolactasia	HO*IP/LAK/TAIZ/YA
hypoesthesia	HO*IP/ES/THAOEZ/YA	hypolarynx	HO*IP/LARNGS
hypoesthetic	HO*IP/ES/THET/IK	hypolemmal	HO*IP/LEM/MAL
hypoestrinemia	HO*IP/ES/TRI/NAOEM/YA	hypolepidoma	HO*IP/LEP/DOE/MA
hypoestrogenemia	HO*IP/ES/TRO/JEN/AOEM/YA	hypolethal	HO*IP/LAOE/THAL
hypoevolutism	HO*IP/E/VOL/TIFM	hypoleukemia	HO*IP/LAOU/KAOEM/YA

hypoleydigism	HO*IP/LAOI/DIG/IFM	hypophosphaturia	HO*IP/FOS/FA/TAOUR/YA
hypolipemia	HO*IP/LI/PAOEM/YA	hypophosphite	HO*IP/FOS/FAOIT
hypolipidemic	HO*IP/LIP/DAOEM/IK	hypophosphoremia	HO*IP/FOS/FRAOEM/YA
hypolipoproteinemia	HO*IP/LIP/PROET/NAOEM/YA	hypophosphorous	HO*IP/FOS/FROUS
hypoliposis	HO*IP/LI/POE/SIS	hypophrasia	HO*IP/FRAIZ/YA
hypologia	HO*IP/LOE/JA	hypophrenia	HO*IP/FRAOEN/YA
hypolutemia	HO*IP/LAOU/TAOEM/YA	hypophrenic	HO*IP/FREN/IK
hypolymphemia	HO*IP/LIM/FAOEM/YA	hypophrenium	HO*IP/FRAOEN/YUM
hypomagnesemia	HO*IP/MAG/NE/SAOEM/YA		HO*IP/FREN/YUM
hypomania	HO*IP/MAIN/YA	hypophyseal	see hypophysial
hypomaniac	HO*IP/MAIN/YAK	hypophysectomize	HAOI/POF/SEKT/MAOIZ
hypomanic	HO*IP/MAN/IK	hypophysectomy	HAOI/POF/SEKT/M*I
hypomastia	HO*IP/MA*S/YA	hypophysial	HO*IP/FIZ/YAL
hypomazia	HO*IP/MAIZ/YA	hypophysin	HAOI/POF/SIN
hypomegasoma	HO*IP/MEG/SOE/MA	hypophysiogenea	HO*IP/FIZ/YO/JEN/YA
hypomelancholia	HO*IP/MEL/AN/KOEL/YA	hypophysioportal	HO*IP/FIZ/YO/POR/TAL
hypomelanism	HO*IP/MEL/NIFM	hypophysiopriva	HO*IP/FIZ/YO/PRAOI/VA
hypomelanosis	HO*IP/MEL/NOE/SIS	hypophysioprivic	HO*IP/FIZ/YO/PRIVK
hypomelia	HO*IP/MAOEL/YA	hypophysiotropic	HO*IP/FIZ/YO/TROP/IK
hypomenorrhea	HO*IP/MEN/RAOE/YA	hypophysis	HAOI/POF/SIS
hypomere	HO*IP/MAOER	hypophysitis	HAOI/POF/SAOITS
hypomesosoma	HO*IP/MES/SOE/MA	hypophysoma	HAOI/POF/SOE/MA
hypometabolic	HO*IP/MET/BOL/IK	hypophysopriva	HAOI/POF/SO/PRAOI/VA
hypometabolism	HO*IP/ME/TAB/LIFM	hypophysoprivic	HAOI/POF/SO/PRIVK
hypometria	HO*IP/MAOE/TRAOE/YA	hypopiesia	HO*IP/PAOI/AOEZ/YA
	HO*IP/MAOE/TRA	hypopiesis	HO*IP/PAOI/E/SIS
hypomicrosoma	HO*IP/MAOI/KRO/SOE/MA	hypopietic	HO*IP/PAOI/ET/IK
hypomineralization	HO*IP/MIN/RAL/ZAIGS	hypopigmentation	HO*IP/PIG/MEN/TAIGS
hypomnesia	HO*IP/NAOEZ/YA	hypopigmenter	HO*IP/PIG/-MT/ER
	HAOI/POM/NAOEZ/YA		HO*IP/PIG/MEN/TER
hypomnesis	HO*IP/NAOE/SIS	hypopinealism	HO*IP/PIN/YAL/IFM
	HAOI/POM/NAOE/SIS	hypopituitarism	HO*IP/PI/TAOU/TRIFM
hypomodal	HO*IP/MOE/DAL		HO*IP/PI/TAOU/TAR/IFM
hypomorph	HO*IP/MOR/-F	hypoplasia	HO*IP/PLAIZ/YA
hypomorphic	HO*IP/MOR/FIK	hypoplastic	HO*IP/PLA*S/IK
hypomotility	HO*IP/MOE/TIL/TI	hypoplasty	HO*IP/PLAS/TI
hypomyelination	HO*IP/MAOI/LI/NAIGS	hypoploid	HO*IP/PLOID
hypomyelinogenesis	HO*IP/MAOI/LIN/JEN/SIS	hypopnea	HO*IP/NAOE/YA
hypomyotonia	HO*IP/MAOI/TOEN/YA		HAOI/POP/NA
hypomyxia	HO*IP/MIX/YA		HAOI/POP/NAOE/YA
hyponanosoma	HO*IP/NAIN/SOE/MA	hypopneic	HO*IP/NAOE/IK
	HO*IP/NAI/NO/SOE/MA		HAOI/POP/NIK
hyponasality	HO*IP/NAI/ZAL/TI		HAOI/POP/NAOE/IK
hyponatremia	HO*IP/NA/TRAOEM/YA	hypoponesis	HO*IP/POE/NAOE/SIS
hyponatremic	HO*IP/NA/TRAOEM/IK	hypoporosis	HO*IP/POE/ROE/SIS
hyponatruria	HO*IP/NA/TRAOUR/YA	hypoposia	HO*IP/POEZ/YA
hyponeocytosis	HO*IP/NAOE/SAOI/TOE/SIS	hypopotassemia	HO*IP/POT/SAOEM/YA
hyponitremia	HO*IP/NAOI/TRAOEM/YA		HO*IP/POET/SAOEM/YA
hyponoia	HO*IP/NOI/YA		HO*IP/POE/TAS/SAOEM/YA
hyponoic	HO*IP/NOIK	hypopotassemic	HO*IP/POT/SAOEM/IK
	HO*IP/NOE/IK		HO*IP/POET/SAOM/IK
hyponychial	HO*IP/NIK/YAL		HO*IP/POE/TAS/SAOEM/IK
hyponychium	HO*IP/NIK/YUM	hypopotentia	HO*IP/POE/TEN/SHA
hyponychon	HAOI/PON/KON	hypopraxia	HO*IP/PRAX/YA
hypo-oncotic	HO*IP/ON/KOT/IK	hypoproaccelerinemia	HO*IP/PRO/AK/SEL/RI/NAOEM/YA
hypo-orchidia	HO*IP/OR/KID/YA		YA
hypo-orchidism	HO*IP/ORK/DIFM	hypoproconvertinemia	HO*IP/PRO/KON/VERT/NAOEM/YA
hypo-orthocytosis	HO*IP/O*RT/SAOI/TOE/SIS		YA
hypo-osmolality	HO*IP/OZ/MO/LAL/TI	hypoprosody	HO*IP/PROS/DI
hypo-ovaria	HO*IP/O/VAIR/YA	hypoproteinemia	HO*IP/PROET/NAOEM/YA
hypo-ovarianism	HO*IP/O/VAIRN/IFM		HO*IP/PRO/TAOEN/AOEM/YA
hypopallesthesia	HO*IP/PAL/ES/THAOEZ/YA	hypoproteinia	HO*IP/PRO/TAOEN/YA
hypopancreatism	HO*IP/PAN/KRA/TIFM	hypoproteinic	HO*IP/PRO/TAOEN/IK
hypopancreorrhea	HO*IP/PAN/KRO/RAOE/YA	hypoproteinosis	HO*IP/PROET/NOE/SIS
hypoparathyreosis	HO*IP/PAR/THAOIR/YOE/SIS		HO*IP/PRO/TAOE/NOE/SIS
hypoparathyroidism	HO*IP/PAR/THAOI/ROI/DIFM	hypoprothrombinemia	HO*IP/PRO/THROM/BI/NAOEM/YA
	HO*IP/PAR/THAOI/ROID/IFM		YA
hypopepsia	HO*IP/PEPS/YA		HO*IP/PRO/THROM/BIN/AOEM/YA
hypopepsinia	HO*IP/PEP/SIN/YA		YA
hypoperfusion	HO*IP/PER/FAOUGS	hypopselaphesia	HAOI/POP/SEL/FAOEZ/YA
hypoperistalsis	HO*IP/P*ER/STAL/SIS	hypoptyalism	HO*IP/TAOI/LIFM
hypopexia	HO*IP/PEX/YA		HAOI/POP/TAOI/LIFM
hypopexy	HO*IP/PEK/SI	hypopyon	HAOI/POEP/YON
hypophalangism	HO*IP/FLAN/JIFM	hyporeactive	HO*IP/RE/AKT/IV
hypophamine	HAOI/POF/MAOEN	hyporeflexia	HO*IP/RE/FLEX/YA
	HAOI/POF/MIN	hyporeninemia	HO*IP/RAOEN/NAOEM/YA
hypopharnyngeal	HO*IP/FRIN/JAL		HO*IP/REN/NAOEM/YA
hypopharyngoscope	HO*IP/FRING/SKOEP	hyporeninemic	HO*IP/RAOEN/NAOEM/IK
hypopharyngoscopy	HO*IP/FARN/GOS/KPI		HO*IP/REN/NAOEM/IK
hypopharynx	HO*IP/FARNGS	hyporiboflavinosis	HO*IP/RAOIB/FLAIV/NOE/SIS
hypophonesis	HO*IP/FOE/NAOE/SIS	hyporrhea	HO*IP/RAOE/YA
hypophonia	HO*IP/FOEN/YA	hyposalemia	HO*IP/SA/LAOEM/YA
hypophoria	HO*IP/FOER/YA	hyposalivation	HO*IP/SA/L/VAIGS
hypophosphatasemia	HO*IP/FOS/FA/TAI/SAOEM/YA		HO*IP/SAL/LI/VAIGS
	HO*IP/FOS/FA/TAIS/AOEM/YA		(not HO*IP/SAL/VAIGS)
hypophosphatasia	HO*IP/FOS/FA/TAIZ/YA	hyposarca	HO*IP/SAR/KA
hypophosphate	HO*IP/FOS/FAIT	hyposcheotomy	HAOI/POS/KOT/M*I
hypophosphatemia	HO*IP/FOS/FA/TAOEM/YA		HAOI/POS/KAOE/OT/M*I
hypophosphatemic	HO*IP/FOS/FA/TAOEM/IK		HAOI/POS/KAOE/YOT/M*I

hyposcleral	HO*IP/SKLAOERL	hypothyroxinemia	HO*IP/THAOI/ROX/NAOEM/YA
hyposecretion	HO*IP/SE/KRAOEGS	hypotonia	HO*IP/TOEN/YA
hyposensitive	HO*IP/SENS/TIV	hypotonic	HO*IP/TON/IK
hyposensitivity	HO*IP/SENS/TIV/TI	hypotonicity	HO*IP/TOE/NIS/TI
hyposensitization	HO*IP/SENS/TI/ZAIGS	hypotonus	HAOI/POT/NUS
hyposexuality	HO*IP/SEX/YAL/TI		HO*IP/TOE/NUS
hyposiagonarthritis	HO*IP/SAOI/AG/NAR/THRAOITS	hypotony	HAOI/POT/N*I
hyposialadenitis	HO*IP/SAOI/LAD/NAOITS	hypotoxicity	HO*IP/TOK/SIS/TI
hyposialosis	HO*IP/SAOI/LOE/SIS	hypotrichiasis	HO*IP/TRI/KAOI/SIS
hyposkeocytosis	HO*IP/SKAOE/SAOI/TOE/SIS	hypotrichosis	HO*IP/TRI/KOE/SIS
hyposmia	HAOI/POZ/MA	hypotriploid	HO*IP/TRIP/LOID
	HAOI/POZ/MAOE/YA	hypotrochanteric	HO*IP/TROE/KAN/TER/IK
hyposmolarity	HAOI/POZ/MO/LAIR/TI	hypotrophy	HAOI/POT/RO/FI
hyposmosis	HAOI/POZ/MOE/SIS	hypotropia	HO*IP/TROEP/YA
hyposmotic	HAOI/POZ/MOT/IK	hypotryptophanic	HO*IP/TRIPT/FAN/IK
hyposomatotropism	HO*IP/SOE/MAT/TROEP/IFM	hypotympanotomy	HO*IP/TIFRP/NOT/M*I
	HO*IP/SOEM/TO/TROEP/IFM	hypotympanum	HO*IP/TIFRP/NUM
hyposomia	HO*IP/SOEM/YA	hypouremia	HO*IP/YAOU/RAOEM/YA
hyposomnia	HO*IP/SOM/NA	hypouresis	HO*IP/YAOU/RAOE/SIS
	HO*IP/SOM/NAOE/YA	hypouricemia	HO*IP/YAOUR/SAOEM/YA
hyposomniac	HO*IP/SOM/NAK	hypouricuria	HO*IP/YAOUR/KAOUR/YA
	HO*IP/SOM/NAOE/AK	hypourocrinia	HO*IP/YAOUR/KRIN/YA
	HO*IP/SOM/NAOE/YAK	hypovaria	HO*IP/VAIR/YA
hypospadia	HO*IP/SPAID/YA	hypovarianism	HO*IP/VAIRN/IFM
hypospadiac	HO*IP/SPAID/YAK	hypovegetative	HO*IP/VEJ/TAIT/IV
hypospadias	HO*IP/SPAID/YAS	hypovenosity	HO*IP/VAOE/NOS/TI
hyposphresia	HAOI/POS/FRAOEZ/YA	hypoventilation	HO*IP/VENT/LAIGS
hyposphyxia	HO*IP/SFIX/YA	hypovitaminosis	HO*IP/VAOIT/MI/NOE/SIS
hyposplenism	HO*IP/SPLAOEN/IFM	hypovolemia	HO*IP/VOE/LAOEM/YA
	HO*IP/SPLEN/IFM	hypovolemic	HO*IP/VOE/LAOEM/IK
hypostasis	HAOI/PO*S/SIS	hypovolia	HO*IP/VOEL/YA
hypostatic	HO*IP/STAT/IK	hypoxanthine	HO*IP/ZAN/THAOEN
hypostatica	HO*IP/STAT/KA		HO*IP/ZAN/THIN
hyposteatolysis	HO*IP/STAOE/TOL/SIS	hypoxemia	HAOI/POK/SAOEM/YA
hyposteatosis	HO*IP/STAOE/TOE/SIS	hypoxia	HAOI/POX/YA
hyposthenia	HAOI/POS/THAOEN/YA	hypoxic	HAOI/POX/IK
	HO*IP/STHAOEN/YA	hypoxidosis	HAOI/POX/DOE/SIS
hypostheniant	HAOI/POS/THAOEN/YANT	hyps(o)-	HIPS
	HO*IP/STHAOEN/YANT		HIP/S(O)
hyposthenic	HAOI/POS/THEN/IK	hypsarrhythmia	HIPS/R*IT/MA
	HO*IP/STHEN/IK		HIPS/R*IT/MAOE/YA
hyposthenuria	HAOI/POS/THE/NAOUR/YA	hypsibrachycephalic	HIPS/BRAK/SFAL/IK
	HAOI/POS/THEN/YAOUR/YA	hypsicephalic	HIPS/SFAL/IK
hypostome	HO*IP/STOEM	hypsicephaly	HIPS/SEF/LI
hypostomia	HO*IP/STOEM/YA	hypsiconchous	HIPS/KON/KOUS
hypostosis	HAOIP/OS/TOE/SIS	hypsiloid	HIPS/LOID
	HIP/OS/TOE/SIS	hypsistaphylia	HIPS/STA/FIL/YA
hypostypsis	HO*IP/STIP/SIS	hypsistenocephalic	HIPS/STEN/SFAL/IK
hypostyptic	HO*IP/STIPT/IK	hypsocephalous	HIPS/SEF/LOUS
hyposympathicotonus	HO*IP/SIM/PA*T/KO/TOE/NUS	hypsochrome	HIPS/KROEM
hyposynergia	HO*IP/SI/NER/JA	hypsochromic	HIPS/KROEM/IK
	HO*IP/SIN/ER/JA	hypsochromy	HIPS/KROE/M*I
hyposystole	HO*IP/S*IS/LAOE	hypsodont	HIPS/DONT
hypotaxia	HO*IP/TAX/YA	hypsokinesis	HIPS/KI/NAOE/SIS
hypotelorism	HO*IP/TEL/RIFM	hypsonosus	HIPS/NOE/SUS
	HO*IP/TAOEL/RIFM		HIP/SOEN/SUS
hypotension	HO*IP/TENGS	hypsotherapy	HIPS/THER/PI
hypotensive	HO*IP/TENS/IV	hypurgia	HAOI/PUR/JA
hypotensor	HO*IP/TEN/SOR	Hyrtl	HIRT/-L
hypotetraploid	HO*IP/TET/RA/PLOID		HAOERT/-L
hypothalamic	HO*IP/THA/LAM/IK	Hyskon	HIS/KON
hypothalamicum	HO*IP/THA/LAM/KUM	hyster(o)-	H*IS/R(O)
hypothalamohypophysial	HO*IP/THAL/MO/HO*IP/FIZ/YAL		HIS/TR(O)
hypothalamotomy	HO*IP/THAL/MOT/M*I		HIS/TER
hypothalamus	HO*IP/THAL/MUS	hysteralgia	H*IS/RAL/JA
hypothenar	HAOI/PO*T/NAR	hysteratresia	H*IS/RA/TRAOEZ/YA
	HO*IP/THAOE/NAR	hysterectomy	H*IS/REKT/M*I
hypothermal	HO*IP/THER/MAL	hysteresis	H*IS/RAOE/SIS
hypothermia	HO*IP/THERM/YA	hystereurynter	H*IS/ER/YAOU/RINT/ER
hypothermic	HO*IP/THERM/IK		HIS/TER/YAOU/RINT/ER
hypothermy	HO*IP/THER/M*I		H*IS/RAOU/RINT/ER
hypotheses	HAOI/PO*T/SAOEZ	hystereurysis	H*IS/ER/YAOUR/SIS
hypothesis	HAOI/PO*T/SIS		HIS/TER/YAOUR/SIS
hypothrepsia	HO*IP/THREPS/YA		H*IS/RAOUR/SIS
hypothrombinemia	HO*IP/THROM/BI/NAOEM/YA	hysteria	HIS/TER/YA
	HO*IP/THROM/BIN/AOEM/YA	hysteriac	HIS/TER/YAK
hypothromboplastinemia	HO*IP/THROM/BO/PLA*S/ NAOEM/YA	hysteric	HIS/TER/IK
		hysterica	HIS/TER/KA
hypothymia	HO*IP/THAOIM/YA	hysterical	HIS/TER/KAL
hypothymic	HO*IP/THAOIM/IK	hysterically	HIS/TER/KLI
hypothymism	HO*IP/THAOIM/IFM	hystericism	HIS/TER/SIFM
	HO*IP/THAOI/MIFM	hystericoneuralgic	HIS/TER/KO/NAOU/RAL/JIK
hypothyrea	HO*IP/THAOIR/YA	hysterics	HIS/TER/IK/-S
hypothyreosis	HO*IP/THAOIR/YOE/SIS	hystericus	HIS/TER/KUS
hypothyroid	HO*IP/THAOI/ROID	hysteriform	HIS/TER/FORM
hypothyroidation	HO*IP/THAOI/ROI/DAIGS	hysterism	H*IS/RIFM
hypothyroidea	HO*IP/THAOI/ROID/YA	hysterobubonocele	H*IS/RO/BAOU/BON/SAO*EL
hypothyroidism	HO*IP/THAOI/ROI/DIFM	hysterocarcinoma	H*IS/RO/KARS/NOE/MA
hypothyrosis	HO*IP/THAOI/ROE/SIS	hysterocatalepsy	H*IS/RO/KAT/LEP/SI

hysterocele	H*IS/RO/SAO*EL
hysterocleisis	H*IS/RO/KLAOI/SIS
hysterocolpectomy	H*IS/RO/KOL/PEKT/M*I
hysterocolposcope	H*IS/RO/KOL/PO/SKOEP
hysterocystic	H*IS/RO/S*IS/IK
hysterocystocleisis	H*IS/RO/S*IS/KLAOI/SIS
hysterocystopexy	H*IS/RO/S*IS/PEK/SI
hysterodynia	H*IS/RO/DIN/YA
hysteroepilepsy	H*IS/RO/EP/LEP/SI
hysteroepileptogenic	H*IS/RO/EP/LEPT/JEN/IK
hysteroerotic	H*IS/RO/E/ROT/IK
hysterogenic	H*IS/RO/JEN/IK
histerogenous	H*IS/ROJ/NOUS
hysterogram	H*IS/RO/GRAM
hysterograph	H*IS/RO/GRAF
hysterography	H*IS/ROG/FI
hysteroid	H*IS/ROID
hysterolaparotomy	H*IS/RO/LAP/ROT/M*I
hysterolith	H*IS/RO/L*IT
hysterology	H*IS/ROLG
hysterolysis	H*IS/ROL/SIS
hysteromania	H*IS/RO/MAIN/YA
hysterometer	H*IS/ROM/TER
hysterometry	H*IS/ROM/TRI
hysteromyoma	H*IS/RO/MAOI/YOE/MA
hysteromyomectomy	H*IS/RO/MAOI/MEKT/M*I
hysteromyotomy	H*IS/RO/MAOI/OT/M*I
hysteronarcolepsy	H*IS/RO/NARK/LEP/SI
hysteroneurasthenia	H*IS/RO/NAOUR/AS/THAOEN/YA
hystero-oophorectomy	H*IS/RO/AOF/REKT/M*I
hysteropathy	H*IS/ROP/TH*I
hysteropexia	H*IS/RO/PEX/YA
hysteropexy	H*IS/RO/PEK/SI
hysterophore	H*IS/RO/FOER
hysteropia	H*IS/ROEP/YA
hysteroplasty	H*IS/RO/PLAS/TI
hysteroptosia	H*IS/ROP/TOEZ/YA
hysteroptosis	H*IS/ROP/TOE/SIS
hysterorrhaphy	H*IS/ROR/FI
hysterorrhexis	H*IS/RO/REK/SIS
hysterosalpingectomy	H*IS/RO/SAL/PIN/JEKT/M*I
hysterosalpingography	H*IS/RO/SAL/PIN/GOG/FI
hysterosalpingo-oophorectomy	
	H*IS/RO/SAL/PING/AOF/REKT/
	M*I
hysterosalpingostomy	H*IS/RO/SAL/PIN/GO*S/M*I
hysteroscope	H*IS/RO/SKOEP
hysteroscopy	H*IS/ROS/KPI
hysterospasm	H*IS/RO/SPAFM
hysterostat	H*IS/RO/STAT
hysterostomatocleisis	H*IS/RO/STOEM/TO/KLAOI/SIS
hysterostomatome	H*IS/RO/STOEM/TOEM
hysterostomatomy	H*IS/RO/STOE/MAT/M*I
hysterosystole	H*IS/RO/S*IS/LAOE
hysterotabetism	H*IS/RO/TAIB/TIFM
hysterothermometry	H*IS/RO/THER/MOM/TRI
hysterotome	H*IS/RO/TOEM
hysterotomy	H*IS/ROT/M*I
hysterotonin	H*IS/RO/TOE/NIN
hysterotrachelectasia	H*IS/RO/TRAIK/LEK/TAIZ/YA
	H*IS/RO/TRAK/LEK/TAIZ/YA
hysterotrachelectomy	H*IS/RO/TRAIK/LEKT/M*I
	H*IS/RO/TRAK/LEKT/M*I
hysterotracheloplasty	H*IS/RO/TRAIK/LO/PLAS/TI
	H*IS/RO/TRAK/LO/PLAS/TI
hysterotrachelorrhaphy	H*IS/RO/TRAIK/LOR/FI
	H*IS/RO/TRAK/LOR/FI
hysterotrachelotomy	H*IS/RO/TRAIK/LOT/M*I
	H*IS/RO/TRAK/LOT/M*I
hysterotraumatic	H*IS/RO/TRAU/MAT/IK
hysterotraumatism	H*IS/RO/TRAUM/TIFM
hysterotrismus	H*IS/RO/TRIS/MUS
	H*IS/RO/TRIZ/MUS
hysterotubography	H*IS/RO/TAOU/BOG/FI
hysterovagino-enterocele	H*IS/RO/VAJ/NO/SPWER/RO/
	SAO*EL
Hytone	HAOI/TOEN
Hytrin	HAOI/TRIN

I

-ia	YA
iamatology	AOI/MA/TOLG
ianthinopsia	AOI/A*NT/NOPS/YA
-iasis	(c)AOI/SIS
iathergy	AOI/A*T/ER/JI
iatr(o)-	AOI/AT/R(O)
	AOI/TR(O)
iatraliptic	AOI/TRA/LIPT/IK
iatraliptics	AOI/TRA/LIPT/IK/-S
iatreusiology	AOI/TRAOUS/YOLG
iatreusis	AOI/TRAOU/SIS
iatric	AOI/AT/RIK
iatrochemical	AOI/AT/RO/KEM/KAL
iatrochemist	AOI/AT/RO/KEM/*IS
iatrochemistry	AOI/AT/RO/KEM/STRI
iatrogenesis	AOI/AT/RO/JEN/SIS
iatrogenic	AOI/AT/RO/JEN/IK
iatrology	AOI/TROLG
iatromathematical	AOI/AT/RO/MA*T/MAT/KAL
iatromechanical	AOI/AT/RO/ME/KAN/KAL
	AOI/AT/RO/M-K/KAL
iatrophysical	AOI/AT/RO/FIZ/KAL
iatrophysicist	AOI/AT/RO/FIZ/S*IS
iatrophysics	AOI/AT/RO/FIZ/IK/-S
iatrotechnics	AOI/AT/RO/TEK/NIK/-S
iatrotechnique	AOI/AT/RO/TEK/NAOEK
Iberet	AOIB/RET
Iberet-500	AOIB/RET/5/HUN
Iberet-Folic	AOIB/RET/FOEL/IK
ibufenac	AOI/BAOUF/NAK
ibuprofen	AOIB/PRO/FEN
	AOI/BAOU/PRO/FEN
IBU-TAB	AOI/BAOU/TAB
-ic	IK
	(c)IK
ice	AOIS
Iceland	AOIS/LAND
ichnogram	IK/NO/GRAM
ichor	AOI/KOR
	AOI/KOER
ichoremia	AOIK/RAOEM/YA
	AOI/KOE/RAOEM/YA
ichoroid	AOIK/ROID
	AOI/KOE/ROID
ichorous	AOIK/ROUS
	AOI/KOR/OUS
	AOI/KOER/OUS
ichorrhea	AOIK/RAOE/YA
	AOI/KOE/RAOE/YA
ichorrhemia	AOIK/RAOEM/YA
	AOI/KOE/RAOEM/YA
ichthammol	IK/THAM/MOL
ichthyo-	IK/TH(O)
	IK/THAOE
	IK/THAOE/Y(O)
ichthyism	IK/THIFM
	IK/THAOE/IFM
ichthyismus	IK/THIZ/MUS
	IK/THAOE/IZ/MUS
ichthyoacanthotoxin	IK/THO/AI/KA*NT/TOK/SIN
	IK/THO/KA*NT/TOK/SIN
ichthyoacanthotoxism	IK/THO/AI/KA*NT/TOK/SIFK
	IK/THO/KA*NT/TOK/SIFM
ichthyocolla	IK/THO/KOL/LA
ichthyohemotoxin	IK/THO/HAOEM/TOK/SIN
ichthyohemotoxism	IK/THO/HAOEM/TOK/SIFM
ichthyoid	IK/THOID
	IK/THAOE/OID
ichthyolate	IK/THO/LAIT
ichthyology	IK/THOLG
ichthyolsulfonate	IK/THOL/SUL/FO/NAIT
ichthyolsulfonic	IK/THOL/SUL/FON/IK
ichthyootoxin	IK/THAOE/AO/TOK/SIN
	IK/THAO/TOK/SIN
ichthyootoxism	IK/THAOE/AO/TOK/SIFM
	IK/THAO/TOK/SIFM
ichthyophagia	IK/THO/FAI/JA
ichthyophagous	IK/THOF/GOUS
ichthyophobia	IK/THO/FOEB/YA
ichthyosarcotoxin	IK/THO/SARK/TOK/SIN
ichthyosarcotoxism	IK/THO/SARK/TOK/SIFM
ichthyosiform	IK/THOES/FORM
ichthyosiforme	IK/THOES/FOR/MAOE
ichthyosis	IK/THOE/SIS

ichthyosulfonate	IK/THO/SUL/FO/NAIT
ichthyotic	IK/THOT/IK
ichthyotoxic	IK/THO/TOX/IK
ichthyotoxicology	IK/THO/TOX/KOLG
ichthyotoxicon	IK/THO/TOX/KON
ichthyotoxicum	IK/THO/TOX/KUM
ichthyotoxin	IK/THO/TOK/SIN
ichthyotoxism	IK/THO/TOK/SIFM
iconomania	AOI/KON/MAIN/YA
icosahedral	AOIK/SA/HAOE/DRAL
icosanoic	AOIK/SA/NOIK
	AOIK/SA/NOE/IK
ictal	IK/TAL
icter(o)-	IKT/R(O)
	IK/TR(O)
	IK/TER
icteric	IK/TER/IK
icteritious	IKT/RIRBS
	IK/TRIRBS
icteroanemia	IKT/RO/AI/NAOEM/YA
icterogenic	IKT/RO/JEN/IK
icterogenicity	IKT/RO/JE/NIS/TI
icterohematuria	IKT/RO/HAOEM/TAOUR/YA
	IKT/RO/HEM/TAOUR/YA
icterohematuric	IKT/RO/HAOEM/TAOUR/IK
	IKT/RO/HEM/TAOUR/IK
icterohemoglobinuria	IKT/RO/HAOEM/GLOEB/NAOUR/ YA
icterohemolytic	IKT/RO/HAOEM/LIT/IK
icterohemorrhagic	IKT/RO/HEM/RAJ/IK
icterohepatitis	IKT/RO/HEP/TAOITS
icteroid	IKT/ROID
	IK/TROID
icterus	IKT/RUS
	IK/TRUS
ictometer	IK/TOM/TER
ictus	IK/TUS
ICU	IRBGS/KR-RBGS/URBGS
Icy Hot Balm	AOI/SI/HOT/BAUM
	AOIS/HOT/BAUM
Icy Hot Cream	AOI/SI/HOT/KRAOEM
	AOIS/HOT/KRAOEM
Icy Hot Stick	AOI/SI/HOT/STIK
	AOIS/HOT/STIK
idant	AOI/DANT
id	ID
idahoensis	AOID/HOE/EN/SIS
	AOID/HO/EN/SIS
-ide	AOID
idea	Y-D
	AOI/DAOE/YA
ideal	Y-L
	AOI/DAOEL
idealization	Y-L/ZAIGS
	AOI/DAOEL/ZAIGS
ideation	AOID/YAIGS
ideational	AOID/YAIGS/NAL
idee fixe	E/DAI/FAOEX
identical	AOID/KAL
	AOI/DENT/KAL
Identi-Dose	AOI/DENT/DOES
identification	AOID/FI/KAIGS
	AOI/DENT/FI/KAIGS
identify	AOID/FI
	AOI/DENT/FI
identity	AOID/TI
	AOI/DENT/TI
ideo-	AOID/YO
ideodynamism	AOID/YO/DAOIN/MIFM
ideogenetic	AOID/YO/JE/NET/IK
ideogenous	AOID/YOJ/NOUS
ideoglandular	AOID/YO/GLAND/LAR
ideokinetic	AOID/YO/KI/NET/IK
ideology	AOID/YOLG
ideometabolic	AOID/YO/MET/BOL/IK
ideometabolism	AOID/YO/ME/TAB/LIFM
ideomotion	AOID/YO/MOEGS
ideomotor	AOID/YO/MOE/TOR
ideomuscular	AOID/YO/MUS/KLAR
ideo-obsessional	AOID/YO/OB/SEGS/NAL
ideophobia	AOID/YO/FOEB/YA
ideophrenia	AOID/YO/FRAOEN/YA
ideophrenic	AOID/YO/FREN/IK
ideoplastia	AOID/YO/PLA*S/YA
ideovascular	ID/YO/VAS/KLAR
idi(o)-	ID/Y(O)
idioagglutinin	ID/YO/AI/GLAOUT/NIN
idiochromatin	ID/YO/KROEM/TIN
idiochromidia	ID/YO/KROE/MID/YA

idiochromosome	ID/YO/KROEM/SOEM
idiocrasy	ID/YOK/SI
	ID/YOK/RA/SI
idiocratic	ID/YO/KRAT/IK
idiocy	ID/YO/SI
idiodynamic	ID/YO/DAOI/NAM/IK
idiogamist	ID/YOG/M*IS
idiogenesis	ID/YO/JEN/SIS
idioglossia	ID/YO/GLOS/YA
idioglottic	ID/YO/GLOT/IK
idiogram	ID/YO/GRAM
idiographic	ID/YO/GRAFK
idioheteroagglutinin	ID/YO/HET/RO/AI/GLAOUT/NIN
idioheterolysin	ID/YO/HET/ROL/SIN
idiohypnotism	ID/YO/HIP/NO/TIFM
idio-imbecile	ID/YO/IM/BE/SIL
idioisoagglutinin	ID/YO/AOIS/AI/GLAOUT/NIN
idioisolysin	ID/YO/AOI/SOL/SIN
idiolalia	ID/YO/LAIL/YA
idiolog	ID/YO/LOG
idiologism	ID/YOL/JIFM
idiolysin	ID/YOL/SIN
idiomere	ID/YO/MAOER
idiomuscular	ID/YO/MUS/KLAR
idionodal	ID/YO/NOE/DAL
idiopathetic	ID/YO/PA/THET/IK
idiopathic	ID/YO/PA*T/IK
idiopathica	ID/YO/PA*T/KA
idiopathy	ID/YOP/TH*I
idiophore	ID/YO/FOER
idiophrenic	ID/YO/FREN/IK
idioplasm	ID/YO/PLAFM
idiopsychologic	ID/YO/SAOIK/LOJ/IK
idioreflex	ID/YO/RE/FLEX
idioretinal	ID/YO/RET/NAL
idiosome	ID/YO/SOEM
idiospasm	ID/YO/SPAFM
idiosyncrasy	ID/YO/SING/SI
	ID/YO/SIN/KRA/SI
idiosyncratic	ID/YO/SIN/KRAT/IK
idiot	ID/YOT
idiotope	ID/YO/TOEP
idiotopy	ID/YO/TOP/PI
idiotoxin	ID/YO/TOK/SIN
idiot-prodigy	ID/YOT/PROD/JI
idiotrophic	ID/YO/TROFK
idiotropic	ID/YO/TROP/IK
idiot-savant	ID/YOT/SA*VANT
idiotype	ID/YO/TAOIP
idiovariation	ID/YO/VAIR/YAIGS
idioventricular	ID/YO/VEN/TRIK/LAR
iditol	AOID/TOL
idonic	AOI/DON/IK
idose	AOI/DOES
idosis	AOI/DOE/SIS
idoxuridine	AOI/DOX/YAOUR/DAOEN
iduronic	AOI/DAOU/RON/IK
IFEX	AOI/FEX
ignatia	IG/NAI/SHA
igni-	IG/NI
	IG/NAOE
igniextirpation	IG/NI/EX/TIR/PAIGS
ignipedites	IG/NI/PE/DAOI/TAOEZ
ignioperation	IG/NI/OP/RAIGS
	IG/NI/OERPGS
ignipuncture	IG/NI/PUNG/KHUR
ignis	IG/NIS
ignisation	IG/NI/ZAIGS
ignotine	IG/NO/TAOEN
	IG/NO/TIN
ile(o)-	*IL/Y(O)
	(not IL/YO; see ilio-)
ileac	*IL/YAK
ileadelphus	*IL/YA/DEL/FUS
ileal	*IL/YAL
ileectomy	*IL/YEKT/M*I
ilei	*IL/YAOI
ileitis	*IL/YAOITS
ileocecal	*IL/YO/SE/KAL
ileocecostomy	*IL/YO/SE/KO*S/M*I
ileocecum	*IL/YO/SE/KUM
ileocolic	*IL/YO/KOL/IK
ileocolica	*IL/YO/KOL/KA
ileocolitis	*IL/YO/KO/LAOITS
ileocolonic	*IL/YO/KO/LON/IK
ileocolostomy	*IL/YO/KO/LO*S/M*I
ileocolotomy	*IL/YO/KO/LOT/M*I
ileocystoplasty	*IL/YO/S*IS/PLAS/TI
ileocystostomy	*IL/YO/SIS/TO*S/M*I

ileoentectropy	*IL/YO/SPWEK/TRO/PI
	*IL/YO/EN/TEK/TRO/PI
ileoileostomy	*IL/YO/*IL/YO*S/M*I
ileojejunitis	*IL/YO/JEJ/NAOITS
ileoneocystostomy	*IL/YO/NAOE/SIS/TO*S/M*I
ileopexy	*IL/YO/PEK/SI
ileoproctostomy	*IL/YO/PROK/TO*S/M*I
ileopubic	*IL/YO/PAOUB/IK
ileorectal	*IL/YO/REK/TAL
ileorectostomy	*IL/YO/REK/TO*S/M*I
ileorrhaphy	*IL/YOR/FI
ileosigmoid	*IL/YO/SIG/MOID
ileosigmoidostomy	*IL/YO/SIG/MOI/DO*S/M*I
ileostomy	*IL/YO*S/M*I
ileotomy	*IL/YOT/M*I
ileotransverse	*IL/YO/TRA*NS/VERS
ileotransversostomy	*IL/YO/TRA*NS/VER/SO*S/M*I
Iletin	IL/TIN
ileum	*IL/YUM
ileus	*IL/YUS
Ilex	AOI/LEX
Ilfeld	IL/FELD
ili(o)-	IL/Y(O)
ilia	IL/YA
iliac	IL/YAK
iliaca	IL/LAOI/KA
	IL/AOI/KA
iliacum	IL/LAOI/KUM
	IL/AOI/KUM
iliacus	IL/LAOI/KUS
	IL/AOI/KUS
iliadelphus	IL/YA/DEL/FUS
ilicin	IL/SIN
ilii	IL/YAOI
iliocana	IL/YO/KAI/NA
iliococcygeal	IL/YO/KOK/SLJ/YAL
iliocolotomy	IL/YO/KO/LOT/M*I
iliocostal	IL/YO/KOS/TAL
iliocostalis	IL/YO/KOS/TAI/LIS
iliofemoral	IL/YO/FEM/RAL
iliofemoroplasty	IL/YO/FEM/RO/PLAS/TI
iliohypogastric	IL/YO/HO*IP/GAS/TRIK
iliohypogastricus	IL/YO/HO*IP/GAS/TRI/KUS
ilioinguinal	IL/YO/ING/WINL
iliolumbar	IL/YO/LUM/BAR
iliolumbocostoabdominal	IL/YO/LUM/BO/KO*S/AB/DOM/ NAL
iliometer	IL/YOM/TER
iliopagus	IL/YOP/GUS
iliopectinea	IL/YO/PEK/TIN/YA
iliopectineal	IL/YO/PEK/TIN/YAL
iliopectineus	IL/YO/PEK/TIN/YUS
iliopelvic	IL/YO/PEL/VIK
iliopsoas	IL/YO/SOE/WAS
	IL/YOP/SOE/WAS
iliopubic	IL/YO/PAOUB/IK
iliopubica	IL/YO/PAOUB/KA
iliosacral	IL/YO/SAI/KRAL
iliosciatic	IL/YO/SAOI/AT/IK
iliospinal	IL/YO/SPAOINL
iliostomy	IL/YO*S/M*I
iliothoracopagus	IL/YO/THOR/KOP/GUS
iliotibial	IL/YO/TIB/YAL
iliotrochanteric	IL/YO/TROE/KAN/TER/IK
ilioxiphopagus	IL/YO/ZI/FOP/GUS
	IL/YO/ZAOI/FOP/GUS
ilium	IL/YUM
ill	IL
illacrimation	IL/AK/RI/MAIGS
	IL/LAK/RI/MAIGS
illaqueation	IL/AK/WAIGS
	IL/LAK/WAIGS
Illicium	IL/LIS/YUM
illinition	IL/IN/NIGS
	IL/LI/NIGS
	(not IL/NIGS; see ill in addition)
illness	IL/*NS
illucens	IL/LAOU/SENZ
illumination	IL/LAOUM/NAIGS
illuminator	IL/LAOUM/NAI/TOR
illuminism	IL/LAOUM/NIFM
illusion	IL/LAOUGS
illusional	IL/LAOUGS/NAL
illutation	IL/LAOU/TAIGS
	IL/YAOU/TAIGS
Ilopan	IL/PAN
Ilosone	IL/SOEN
Ilotycin	AOIL/LO/TAOI/SIN
Ilotycin Gluceptate	AOIL/LO/TAOI/SIN/GLAOU/SEP/

	TAIT	immunoadjuvant	IM/NO/AD/JAOU/VANT
im-	IM		IM/NO/AJ/VANT
ima	AOI/MA	immunoadsorbent	IM/NO/AD/SORB/ENT
imafen	IM/FEN	immunoassay	IM/NO/AS/SAI
image	IM/AJ	immunobiology	IM/NO/BAO*I/OLG
imagery	IM/AJ/RI	immunoblast	IM/NO/BLA*S
imaginal	IM/MAJ/NAL	immunoblastic	IM/NO/BLA*S/IK
imagines	IM/MAJ/NAOEZ	immunocatalysis	IM/NO/KA/TAL/SIS
imaging	IM/AJ/-G	immunochemistry	IM/NO/KEM/STRI
imago	IM/MAI/GOE	immunochemotherapy	IM/NO/KAOEM/THER/PI
imagocide	IM/MAIG/SAO*ID	immunocompetence	IM/NO/KOFRP/TENS
	IM/MAI/GO/SAO*ID	immunocompetent	IM/NO/KOFRP/TENT
imbalance	IM/BAL/LANS	immunocomplex	IM/NO/KOM/PLEX
imbecile	IM/BE/SIL		IM/NO/KPLEX
imbecility	IM/BE/SIL/TI	immunocompromised	IM/NO/KOM/PRO/MAOIZ/-D
imbed	IM/BED	immunoconglutinin	IM/NO/KON/GLAOUT/NIN
imbibition	IM/BI/BIGS	immunocyte	IM/NO/SAO*IT
imbibitional	IM/BI/BIGS/NAL	immunocytoadherence	IM/NO/SAOIT/AD/HAOERNS
imbricate	IM/BRI/KAIT	immunocytochemistry	IM/NO/SAOIT/KEM/STRI
imbricated	IM/BRI/KAIT/-D	immunodeficiency	IM/NO/DE/FIRBT/SI
imbrication	IM/BRI/KAIGS		IM/NO/DE/FIRB/EN/SI
Imferon	IM/FRON	immunodeficient	IM/NO/DE/FIRBT
	IM/FER/RON	immunodepressant	IM/NO/DPRES/SANT
imidamine	IM/ID/AM/MIN	immunodepression	IM/NO/DPREGS
imidazole	IM/ID/A*Z/OEL	immunodepressive	IM/NO/DPRES/SIV
imidazolyl	IM/ID/A*Z/LIL		IM/NO/DPRESZ/IV
imidazolylethylamine	IM/ID/A*Z/LIL/*ET/IL/AM/MIN	immunodepressor	IM/NO/DPRES/SOR
imide	IM/AOID	immunodermatology	IM/NO/DERM/TOLG
	IM/ID	immunodiagnosis	IM/NO/DAOIG/NOE/SIS
imido-	IM/DO	immunodiffusion	IM/NO/DIF/FAOUGS
	IM/MAOED	immunodominance	IM/NO/DOM/NANS
	IM/MAOE/DO	immunodominant	IM/NO/DOM/NANT
imidodipeptidase	IM/DO/DI/PEPT/DAIS	immunoelectrophoresis	IM/NO/LEK/TRO/FRAOE/SIS
imidogen	IM/MAOED/JEN	immunoenhancement	IM/NO/EN/HANS/-MT
	IM/MID/JEN	immunoenhancer	IM/NO/EN/HANS/ER
imidole	IM/DOEL	immunoferritin	IM/NO/FER/TIN
iminazole	IM/NAZ/OEL	immunofiltration	IM/NO/FIL/TRAIGS
	IM/IN/A*Z/OEL	immunofluorescence	IM/NO/FLAOU/RES/ENS
imino	IM/NOE	immunogen	IM/NO/JEN
	IM/MAOE/NOE		IM/MAOUN/JEN
imino-	IM/NO	immunogenetic	IM/NO/JE/NET/IK
	IM/MAOEN	immunogenetics	IM/NO/JE/NET/IK/-S
	IM/MAOE/NO	immunogenic	IM/NO/JEN/IK
iminocarbonyl	IM/NO/KARB/NIL	immunogenicity	IM/NO/JE/NIS/TI
iminodipeptidase	IM/NO/DI/PEPT/DAIS	immunoglobulin	IM/NO/GLOB/LIN
iminoglycinuria	IM/NO/GLAOIS/NAOUR/YA	immunoglobulinopathy	IM/NO/GLOB/LIN/OP/TH*I
	IM/MAOEN/GLAOIS/NAOUR/YA	immunohematology	IM/NO/HAOEM/TOLG
iminohydrolase	IM/NO/HAOI/DRO/LAIS		IM/NO/HEM/TOLG
iminourea	IM/MAOEN/YAOU/RAOE/YA	immunoheterogeneity	IM/NO/HET/RO/JE/NAOE/TI
imipenem	IM/PEN/EM		IM/NO/HET/RO/JE/NAI/TI
imipramine	IM/IP/RA/MAOEN	immunoheterogenous	IM/NO/HET/ROJ/NOUS
	IM/MIP/RA/MAOEN	immunohistochemical	IM/NO/H*IS/KEM/KAL
imitate	IM/TAIT	immunohistochemistry	IM/NO/H*IS/KEM/STRI
imitative	IM/TAIT/IV	immunohistofluorescence	IM/NO/H*IS/FLAOU/RES/ENS
Imlach	IM/LAK	immunoincompetent	IM/NO/IN/KOFRP/TENT
immature	IM/MA/KHUR	immunologic	IM/NO/LOJ/IK
immediate	MAOED	immunological	IM/NO/LOJ/KAL
	IM/MAOED/YAT	immunologically	IM/NO/LOJ/KLI
immedicable	IM/MED/KABL	immunologist	IM/NO*LGS
immersion	IM/MERGS	immunology	IM/NOLG
imminent	IM/NENT	immunomodulation	IM/NO/MOD/LAIGS
immiscible	IM/MIS/-BL	immunoparasitology	IM/NO/PAR/SAOI/TOLG
immittance	IM/MIT/TANS	immunoparesis	IM/NO/PAR/SIS
immitis	IM/MIT/TIS		IM/NO/PRAOE/SIS
immobile	IM/MOEBL	immunopathogenesis	IM/NO/PA*T/JEN/SIS
	IM/MOE/BIL	immunopathologic	IM/NO/PA*T/LOJ/IK
	IM/MAOI/BAOIL	immunopathology	IM/NO/PA/THOLG
immobility	IM/MOEBLT	immunophysiology	IM/NO/FIZ/YOLG
immobilization	IM/ MOEBL/ZAIGS	immunopotency	IM/NO/POET/EN/SI
	IM/MOEB/LI/ZAIGS		IM/NO/POE/TEN/SI
immobilize	IM/MOEBL/AOIZ	immunopotentiation	IM/NO/POE/TEN/SHAIGS
	IM/MOEB/LAOIZ	immunopotentiator	IM/NO/POE/TEN/SHAI/TOR
immortalization	IM/MOR/TAL/ZAIGS	immunoprecipitation	IM/NO/PRE/SIP/TAIGS
immun(o)-	IM/N(O)	immunoproliferative	IM/NO/PRO/LIFR/TIV
	IM/MAOU/N(O)	immunoprophylaxis	IM/NO/PROEF/LAK/SIS
	IM/YAOU/N(O)	immunoprotein	IM/NO/PRO/TAOEN
	IM/YU/N(O)	immunoradiometric	IM/NO/RAID/YO/MET/RIK
immune	IM/MAOUN	immunoradiometry	IM/NO/RAID/YOM/TRI
immunifacient	IM/MAOUN/FAIRBT	immunoreaction	IM/NO/RE/A*BGS
immunifaction	IM/MAOUN/FA*BGS	immunoreactive	IM/NO/RE/AKT/IV
immunisin	IM/MAOUN/SIN	immunoregulation	IM/NO/REG/LAIGS
	IM/MAOUN/ZIN	immunoresponsiveness	IM/NO/SPONS/IV/*NS
immunity	IM/MAOUN/TI		IM/NO/RE/SPONS/IV/*NS
immunization	IM/MAOUN/ZAIGS	immunoselection	IM/NO/SL*EBGS
	IM/NI/ZAIGS		IM/NO/SE/L*EBGS
immunizator	IM/NI/ZAI/TOR	immunosenescence	IM/NO/SE/NES/ENS
immunize	IM/MAOU/NAOIZ	immunosorbent	IM/NO/SORB/ENT
	IM/NAOIZ	immunostimulant	IM/NO/STIM/LANT
immunoabsorbent	IM/NO/AB/SORB/ENT	immunostimulating	IM/NO/STIM/LAIT/-G

immunostimulation	IM/NO/STIM/LAIGS	Imuran	IM/RAN
immunosuppressant	IM/NO/SPRES/SANT		IM/YAOU/RAN
	IM/NO/SUP/PRES/SANT		IM/YU/RAN
immunosuppression	IM/NO/SPREGS	imus	AOI/MUS
	IM/NO/SUP/PREGS	IMViC	IM/VIK
immunosuppressive	IM/NO/SPRES/SIV	in-	IN
	IM/NO/SUP/PRES/SIV	inacidity	IN/AI/SID/TI
immunosurgery	IM/NO/SURJ/RI	Inaba	IN/NAB/BA
	IM/NO/S-RJ		IN/NA/BA
immunosurveillance	IM/NO/SUR/VAI/LANS	inaction	IN/A*BGS
	IM/NO/SUR/VAIL/LANS	inactivate	IN/AKT/VAIT
immunosympathectomy	IM/NO/SIFRP/THEKT/M*I	inactivation	IN/AKT/VAIGS
immunotherapy	IM/NO/THER/PI	inactose	IN/AK/TOES
immunotolerance	IM/NO/TOL/RANS	inadequacy	IN/AD/KWA/SI
immunotoxin	IM/NO/TOK/SIN	inagglutinable	IN/AI/GLAOUT/NABL
immunotransfusion	IM/NO/TRA*NS/FAOUGS	inalimental	IN/AL/MEN/TAL
immunotropic	IM/NO/TROP/IK	inanimate	IN/AN/MAT
Imodium	IM/MOED/YUM	inanition	IN/NIGS
	IM/OED/YUM		IN/AI/NIGS
Imogam	IM/GAM	inapparent	IN/AI/PARNT
Imogam Rabies	IM/GAM/RAI/BAOEZ		IN/AI/PAIRNT
imolamine	IM/MOL/MAOEN	inappetence	IN/AP/TENS
Imovax	IM/VAX	Inapsine	IN/AP/SAOEN
Imovax Rabies	IM/VAX/RAI/BAOEZ	inarticulate	IN/AR/TIK/LAT
impact	IM/PAKT		IN/AR/TIK/LAIT
impacted	IM/PAKT/-D	in articulo mortis	N/AR/TIK/LOE/MOR/TIS
impaction	IM/PA*BGS	inassimilable	IN/AI/SIM/LABL
impairment	IM/PAIRMT	inattention	IN/AI/TENGS
impalpable	IM/PAL/PABL	inaxon	IN/AK/SON
impaludation	IM/PAL/DAIGS	inborn	IN/BORN
impar	IM/PAR	inbred	IN/BRED
imparidigitate	IM/PAR/DIJ/TAIT	inbreeding	IN/BRAOED/-G
impatency	IM/PAIT/EN/SI	incallosal	IN/KA/LOE/SAL
	IM/PAI/TEN/SI		IN/KAL/LOE/SAL
	IM/PAT/EN/SI	incandescent	IN/KAN/DES/ENT
impatent	IM/PAIT/ENT	incarcerate	IN/KARS/RAIT
	IM/PAI/TENT	incarcerated	IN/KARS/RAIT/-D
	IM/PAT/ENT	incarceration	IN/KARS/RAIGS
impedance	IM/PAOE/DANS	incarial	IN/KAIRL
impede	IM/PAOED	incarnant	IN/KAR/NANT
imperative	IM/PER/TIV	incarnatio	IN/KAR/NAI/SHOE
imperception	IM/PER/SEPGS		IN/KAR/NAIRB/YOE
imperfecta	IM/PER/FEK/TA	incarnative	IN/KARN/TIV
imperforate	IM/PER/FRAIT	incasement	IN/KAIS/-MT
	IM/PER/FRAT	incasing	IN/KAIS/-G
imperforation	IM/PER/FRAIGS	incendiarism	IN/SEND/RIFM
imperious	IM/PAOER/YOUS		IN/SEND/YA/RIFM
impermeable	IM/PERM/YABL	incertae sedis	IN/SER/TAOE/SE/DIS
impermeant	IM/PERM/YANT		IN/SER/TAE/SE/DIS
impersistence	IM/PER/SIS/TENS	incest	IN/S*ES
impervious	IM/PERB/YOUS	incestuous	IN/S*ES/YOUS
impetiginization	IM/PE/TIJ/NI/ZAIGS		IN/SES/KHOUS
	IFRP/TIJ/NI/ZAIGS	inch	IFRPBLG
impetiginous	IM/PE/TIJ/NOUS		IN/-FP
	IFRP/TIJ/NOUS	incidence	INS/DENS
impetigo	IM/PE/TAOI/GOE	incident	INS/DENT
	IFRP/TAOI/GOE	incineration	IN/SIN/RAIGS
impetus	IM/PE/TUS	incipient	IN/SIP/YENT
	IFRP/TUS	incis(o)-	IN/SAOIZ
impilation	IM/PAOI/LAIGS		IN/SAOI/Z(O)
	IM/PI/LAIGS		IN/SAOIS
implant	IM/PLANT		IN/SAOI/S(O)
implant(o)-	IM/PLANT	incisal	IN/SAOI/ZAL
	IM/PLAN/T(O)	incised	IN/SAOIZ/-D
implantation	IM/PLAN/TAIGS	incise	IN/SAOIZ
implantodontics	IM/PLANT/DONT/IK/-S	incision	IN/SIGS
implantodontist	IM/PLANT/DONT/*IS	incisional	IN/SIGS/NAL
	IM/PLANT/DON/T*IS	incisive	IN/SAOIS/IV
implantology	IM/PLAN/TOLG	incisivi	IN/SAOIS/VAOI
implosion	IM/PLOEGS		INS/SAOI/VAOI
impose	IM/POEZ	incisivorum	IN/SAOIS/VOR/UM
impotence	IFRP/TENS		IN/SAOIS/VOER/UM
impotency	IFRP/TEN/SI	incisivus	IN/SAOIS/VUS
impotentia	IFRP/TEN/SHA		INS/SAOI/VUS
	IM/POE/TEN/SHA	incisolabial	IN/SAOIZ/LAIB/YAL
impregnate	IM/PREG/NAIT	incisolingual	IN/SAOIZ/LING/WAL
impregnation	IM/PREG/NAIGS	incisoproximal	IN/SAOIZ/PROX/MAL
impressio	IM/PRES/YOE	incisor	IN/SAOI/ZOR
	IM/PRERB/YOE		IN/SAOI/SOR
impression	IM/PREGS	incisura	IN/SAOI/SAOU/RA
impressiones	IM/PRES/YOE/NAOEZ		IN/SAOI/SAOUR/RA
	IM/PRERB/YOE/NAOEZ		INS/SAOU/RA
imprint	IM/PRINT		INS/SAOUR/RA
imprinting	IM/PRINT/-G	incisurae	IN/SAOI/SAOU/RAE
improcreant	IM/PRO/KRAOENT		IN/SAOI/SAOUR/RAE
impuberal	IM/PAOUB/RAL		INS/SAOU/RAE
impuberism	IM/PAOUB/RIFM		INS/SAOUR/RAE
impulse	IM/PULS	incisure	IN/SAOI/SHUR
impulsion	IM/PULGS	incitant	IN/SAOI/TANT

incitogram	IN/SAOIT/GRAM	indeterminate	IN/DE/TERM/NAT
inclinatio	IN/KLI/NAI/SHOE		IN/DERM/NAT
	IN/KLI/NAIRB/YOE	index	IN/DEX
inclination	IN/KLI/NAIGS	Indian	IND/YAN
inclinationes	IN/KLI/NAI/SHOE/NAOEZ	Indiana	*IN/*IN
	IN/KLI/NAIRB/YOE/NAOEZ		IND/YA/NA
incline	IN/KLAOIN		IND/YAN/NA
inclinometer	IN/KLI/NOM/TER	indic-	IND/K-
inclusion	IN/KLAOUGS		IN/DI/K-
inco-	IN/KO	indican	IND/KAN
incoagulability	IN/KO/AG/LABLT	indicanemia	IND/KAN/AOEM/YA
incoagulable	IN/KO/AB/LABL	indicanidrosis	IND/KAN/DROE/SIS
incoercible	IN/KO/ERS/-BL	indicanmeter	IND/KAN/MAOET/ER
incoherent	IN/KO/HAOERNT	indicanorachia	IND/KAN/RAIK/YA
incompatibility	IN/KPAT/-BLT	indicant	IND/KANT
	IN/KOM/PAT/-BLT	indicanuria	IND/KAN/YAOUR/YA
incompatible	IN/KPAT/-BL	indicarmine	IND/KAR/MIN
	IN/KOM/PAT/-BL	indicatio	IND/KAI/SHOE
incompetence	IN/KOFRP/TENS		IND/KAIRB/YOE
incompetency	IN/KOFRP/TEN/SI	indication	IND/KAIGS
incompetent	IN/KOFRP/TENT	indicator	IND/KAI/TOR
incompleta	IN/KOM/PLAOE/TA	indices	IND/SAOEZ
incomplete	IN/KPLAOET	indicia	IN/DIRB/SHA
	IN/KOM/PLAOET		IN/DIRB/YA
incompletus	IN/KOM/PLAOE/TUS		IN/DI/SHA
incompressible	IN/KOM/PRESZ/-BL	indicis	IND/SIS
	IN/KOM/PRES/-BL	indicophose	IND/KO/FOEZ
inconstant	IN/KON/STANT	indifference	IN/DIFRNS
incontinence	IN/KONT/NENS	indifferent	IN/DIFRNT
incontinent	IN/KONT/NENT	indigenous	IN/DIJ/NOUS
incontinentia	IN/KONT/NEN/SHA	indigestible	IN/DI/J*ES/-BL
incoordination	IN/KWORD/NAIGS		IND/J*ES/-BL
	IN/KAORD/NAIGS	indigestion	IN/DI/JEGS
incorporation	IN/KORP/RAIGS		IND/JEGS
	IN/KORPGS	indigitation	IN/DIJ/TAIGS
incostapedial	IN/KO/STA/PAOED/YAL	indiglucin	IND/GLAOU/SIN
increase	IN/KRAOES	indigo	IND/GOE
increment	IN/KREMT	indigogen	IND/GO/JEN
Incremin	IN/KRE/MIN	indigopurpurine	IND/GO/PURP/RIN
incretion	IN/KRAOEGS	indigotin	IN/DIG/TIN
incretodiagnosis	IN/KRAOET/DAOIG/NOE/SIS		IND/GOE/TIN
incretogenous	IN/KRAOE/TOJ/NOUS	indigotindisulfonate	IND/GOE/TIN/DI/SUL/FO/NAIT
	IN/KRE/TOJ/NOUS	indigouria	IND/GO/YAOUR/YA
incretology	IN/KRAOE/TOLG	indiguria	IND/GAOUR/YA
	IN/KRE/TOLG	indirect	IN/DREKT
incretopathy	IN/KRAOE/TOP/TH*I		IN/DI/REKT
	IN/KRE/TOP/TH*I	indirubin	IND/RAOU/BIN
incretory	IN/KRAOE/TOIR	Indirubinuria	IND/RAOUB/NAOUR/YA
	IN/KRE/TOIR	indiscriminate	IN/DIS/KRIM/NAT
incretotherapy	IN/KRAOET/THER/PI		IN/DIS/KRIM/NAIT
incross	IN/KROSZ	indisposition	IN/DIS/POGS
incrustation	IN/KRUS/TAIGS		IN/DIS/PO/SIGS
incrusted	IN/KR*US/-D	indium	IND/YUM
incubate	IN/KAOU/BAIT	individuation	IND/VID/YAIGS
incubation	IN/KAOU/BAIGS		IND/VID/WAIGS
incubator	IN/KAOU/BAI/TOR	indo-	IND
incubus	IN/KAOU/BUS		IN/DO
incud(o)-	IN/KAOUD	Indocin	IND/SIN
	IN/KAOU/D(O)	indocyanine	IND/SAOI/NAOEN
incudal	IN/KAOU/DAL	indocybin	IND/SAOI/BIN
incudectomy	IN/KAOU/DEKT/M*I	indolacetic	IN/DOEL/AI/SAOET/IK
incudes	IN/KAOU/DAOEZ		IN/DOEL/AI/SET/IK
incudiform	IN/KAOUD/FORM	indolaceturia	IN/DOEL/AS/TAOUR/YA
incudis	IN/KAOU/DIS		IN/LAS/TAOUR/YA
incudomalleal	IN/KAOUD/MAL/YAL	indolamine	IN/DOL/MAOEN
incudomallearis	IN/KAOUD/MAL/YAI/RIS		IN/DOEL/MAOEN
incudostapedia	IN/KAOUD/STA/PAOED/YA	indole	IN/DOEL
incudostapedial	IN/KAOUD/STA/PAOED/YAL	indolent	IND/LENT
incuneatum	IN/KAOUN/YAI/TUM	indolic	IN/DOEL/IK
	IN/KAOUN/YAIT/UM		IN/DOL/IK
incurable	IN/KAOURBL	indologenous	IND/LOJ/NOUS
	IN/KAOUR/-BL	indoluria	IN/DOEL/YAOUR/YA
incurvation	IN/KUR/VAIGS	indolyl	IND/LIL
incus	IN/KUS	indomethacin	IND/M*ET/SIN
incycloduction	IN/SAOI/KLO/D*UBGS	indophenol	IND/FAOE/NOL
incyclophoria	IN/SAOI/KLO/FOER/YA	indophenol oxidase	IND/FAOE/NOL/OX/DAIS
incyclotropia	IN/SAOI/KLO/TROEP/YA	indophenolase	IND/FAOEN/LAIS
indanedione	IN/DAIN/DI/OEN		IN/FEN/LAIS
indanyl	IND/NIL	indoprofen	IND/PRO/FEN
	IN/DA/NIL	indoramin	IN/DOR/MIN
indapamide	IN/DAP/MAOID	indoxyl	IN/DOK/SIL
Indecidua	IN/DE/SID/YA	indoxylemia	IN/DOX/LAOEM/YA
indeciduate	IN/DE/SID/YAIT		IN/DOK/SIL/AOEM/YA
indenization	IN/DEN/ZAIGS	indoxyl-sulfate	IN/DOK/SIL/SUL/FAIT
indentation	IN/DEN/TAIGS	indoxyluria	IN/DOK/SIL/YAOUR/YA
Inderal	IN/DRAL		IN/DOX/LAOUR/YA
	IN/DER/RAL	indriline	IN/DRI/LAOEN
Inderide	IND/RAOID	induce	IN/DAOUS
	IN/DER/AOID	inducer	IN/DAOUS/ER

inducible	IN/DAOUS/-BL	inferius	IN/FAOER/YUS
inductance	IN/DUK/TANS	infero-	IN/FRO
induction	IN/D*UBGS	inferolateral	IN/FRO/LAT/RAL
inductor	IN/DUK/TOR	inferolateralis	IN/FRO/LAT/RAI/LIS
inductorium	IN/DUK/TOIRM	inferomedian	IN/FRO/MAOED/YAN
	IN/DUK/TOER/YUM	inferoposterior	IN/FRO/POS/TAOER/YOR
inductotherm	IN/DUKT/THERM	infertile	IN/FER/TIL
	IN/DUK/TO/THERM		IN/FER/TAOIL
inductothermy	IN/DUKT/THER/M*I	infertilitas	IN/FER/TIL/TAS
	IN/DUK/TO/THER/M*I	infertility	IN/FER/TIL/TI
indulin	IN/DAOU/LIN	infestation	IN/FES/TAIGS
	IND/LIN	in fetu	N-/FAOE/TAOU
indulinophil	IN/DAOU/LIN/FIL	infibulation	IN/FIB/LAIGS
	IND/LIN/FIL	infiltrate	IN/FIL/TRAIT
indulinophile	IN/DAOU/LIN/FAOIL	infiltration	IN/FIL/TRAIGS
	IND/LIN/FAOIL	infiltrative	IN/FIL/TRAIT/IV
indulinophilic	IN/DAOU/LIN/FIL/IK	infinity	IN/FIN/TI
	IND/LIN/FIL/IK	infirm	IN/FIRM
indur-	IN/DAOU/R-	infirmary	IN/FIRM/RI
	IND/R-	infirmity	IN/FIRM/TI
	IN/DR-	inflammable	IN/FLAM/-BL
indurata	IN/DAOU/RAI/TA	inflammagen	IN/FLAM/JEN
indurated	IN/DAOU/RAIT/-D	inflammation	IN/FLA/MAIGS
induration	IN/DAOU/RAIGS		IN/FLAM/MAIGS
indurative	IN/DAOUR/TIV	inflammatoria	IN/FLAM/TOR/YA
	IN/DAOU/RAIT/IV		IN/FLAM/TOER/YA
induratum	IN/DAOU/RAI/TUM	inflammatory	IN/FLAM/TOIR
	IN/DAOU/RAIT/UM	inflation	IN/FLAIGS
indusia	IN/DAOUZ/YA	inflator	IN/FLAI/TOR
indusium	IN/DAOUZ/YUM	inflection	IN/FL*EBGS
indusium griseum	IN/DAOUZ/YUM/GRIS/YUM	inflorescence	IN/FLO/RES/ENS
industrial	STRIL		IN/FLOR/ES/ENS
	IN/DUS/TRIL	influenza	IN/FLAOUN/ZA
	IN/DUS/TRAL		IN/FLAOU/EN/ZA
indux	IN/DUX	influenzal	IN/FLAOUN/ZAL
inebriant	IN/AOEB/RANT		IN/FLAOU/EN/ZAL
inebriation	IN/AOEB/RAIGS	Influenzavirus	IN/FLAOUN/ZA/VAOI/RUS
inebriety	IN/BRAOI/TI		IN/FLAOUNZ/VAOI/RUS
	IN/E/BRAOI/TI	infold	IN/FOELD
inelastic	IN/E/LA*S/IK		IN/FOLD
inert	IN/ERT	infolding	IN/FOELD/-G
inertia	IN/ER/SHA		IN/FOLD/-G
inevitable	IN/EVT/-BL	informed consent	IN/FORM/-D/KON/SENT
	IN/EV/TABL	informosome	IN/FORM/SOEM
in extremis	N/EX/TRAOE/MIS		IN/FOR/MO/SOEM
infancy	IN/FAN/SI	infra-	IN/FRA
infant	IN/FANT	infra-axillary	IN/FRA/AX/LAIR
infanti-	IN/FANT	infrabulge	IN/FRA/BUL/-J
	IN/FAN/TI	infracardiac	IN/FRA/KARD/YAK
	IN/FAN/TAOI	infracerebral	IN/FRA/SER/BRAL
infanticide	IN/FANT/SAO*ID	infraclass	IN/FRA/KLASZ
infanticulture	IN/FANT/KUL/KHUR	infraclavicular	IN/FRA/KLA/VIK/LAR
infantile	IN/FAN/TAOIL	infraclusion	IN/FRA/KLAOUGS
infantilis	IN/FAN/TAOI/LIS	infracondyloid	IN/FRA/KOND/LOID
	IN/FAN/TAOIL/LIS	infraconstrictor	IN/FRA/KON/STRIK/TOR
infantilism	IN/FANT/LIFM	infracortical	IN/FRA/KORT/KAL
infantisepticum	IN/FANT/SEPT/KUM	infracostal	IN/FRA/KOS/TAL
infantorium	IN/FAN/TOIRM	infracotyloid	IN/FRA/KOT/LOID
infantum	IN/FAN/TUM	infracristal	IN/FRA/KR*IS/TAL
infarct	IN/FARKT		IN/FRA/KRIS/TAL
infarctectomy	IN/FARK/TEKT/M*I	infraction	IN/FRA*BGS
infarction	IN/FA*RBGS	infracture	IN/FRAK/KHUR
Infatabs	IN/FA/TAB/-S	infradentale	IN/FRA/DEN/TAI/LAOE
infaust	IN/FO*US	infradian	IN/FRAID/YAN
	IN/FA*US	infradiaphragmatic	IN/FRA/DAOI/FRAG/MAT/IK
infect	IN/FEKT	infraduction	IN/FRA/D*UBGS
infected	IN/FEKT/-D	infraglenoid	IN/FRA/GLAOE/NAOID
infectible	IN/FEKT/-BL	infraglottic	IN/FRA/GLOT/IK
infection	IN/F*EBGS	infraglotticum	IN/FRA/GLOT/KUM
infectiosa	IN/FEK/SHOE/SA	infrahepatic	IN/FRA/HE/PAT/IK
infectiosity	IN/FEK/SHOS/TI	infrahyoid	IN/FRA/HAOI/OID
infectiosum	IN/FEK/SHOE/SUM	infrahyoidea	IN/FRA/HAOI/OID/YA
	IN/FEK/SHOES/UM	inframamillary	IN/FRA/MAM/LAIR
infectiosus	IN/FEK/SHOE/SUS	inframammary	IN/FRA/MAM/RI
infectious	IN/FEK/-RBS	inframandibular	IN/FRA/MAN/DIB/LAR
infectiousness	IN/FEK/-RBS/*NS	inframarginal	IN/FRA/MARJ/NAL
infective	IN/FEKT/IV	inframaxillary	IN/FRA/MAX/LAIR
infectivity	IN/FEKT/IV/TI	infranatant	IN/FRA/NAI/TANT
infecundity	IN/FAOE/KUND/TI	infranodal	IN/FRA/NOE/DAL
	IN/FE/KUND/TI	infranuclear	IN/FRA/NAOUK/LAR
inferent	IN/FERNT	infraocclusion	IN/FRA/O/KLAOUGS
	IN/FER/ENT	infraorbital	IN/FRA/ORB/TAL
	IN/FRENT	infraorbitale	IN/FRA/ORB/TAI/LAOE
inferior	IN/FAOER/YOR	infraorbitalis	IN/FRA/ORB/TAI/LIS
inferiores	IN/FAOER/YOR/RAOEZ	infrapatellar	IN/FRA/PA/TEL/LAR
inferioris	IN/FAOER/YOR/RIS	infrapatellare	IN/FRA/PAT/LAI/RAOE
inferiority	IN/FAOER/YOR/TI	infrapatellaris	IN/FRA/PAT/LAI/RIS
inferiorly	IN/FAOER/YOR/LI	infraplacement	IN/FRA/PLAIS/-MT
inferiorum	IN/FAOER/YOR/UM	infrapsychic	IN/FRA/SAOIK/IK

infrared	IN/FRA/RED	inhomogeneity	IN/HOEM/JE/NAOE/TI
infrascapular	IN/FRA/SKAP/LAR		IN/HOEM/JE/NAI/TI
infrasonic	IN/FRA/SON/IK	inhomogeneous	IN/HOEM/JAOEN/YOUS
infraspinati	IN/FRA/SPAOI/NAI/TAOI	ini(o)-	IN/Y(O)
infraspinatus	IN/FRA/SPAOI/NAI/TUS	iniac	IN/YAK
infraspinous	IN/FRA/SPAOIN/OUS	iniad	IN/YAD
infrasplenic	IN/FRA/SPLEN/IK	inial	IN/YAL
	IN/FRA/SPLAOEN/IK	iniencephalus	IN/YEN/SEF/LUS
infrasternal	IN/FRA/STERNL	iniencephaly	IN/YEN/SEF/LI
infrasternalis	IN/FRA/STER/NAI/LIS	iniodymus	IN/YOD/MUS
infrasubspecific	IN/FRA/SUB/SPEFK	inion	IN/YON
	IN/FRA/SUB/SPE/SIFK	iniopagus	IN/YOP/GUS
infratemporal	IN/FRA/TEFRP/RAL	iniops	IN/YOPS
infratemporalis	IN/FRA/TEFRP/RAI/LIS	initial	NIRBL
infratentorial	IN/FRA/TEN/TOIRL		IN/NIRBL
infrathoracic	IN/FRA/THRAS/IK	initiation	NIRB/YAIGS
infratonsillar	IN/FRA/TONS/LAR		IN/NIRB/YAIGS
infratracheal	IN/FRA/TRAIK/YAL	initis	IN/AOITS
infratrochlear	IN/FRA/TROK/LAR		IN/NAOITS
infratubal	IN/FRA/TAOU/BAL	inject	IN/JEKT
infraturbinal	IN/FRA/TURB/NAL	injectable	IN/JEKT/-BL
infraumbilical	IN/FRA/UM/BIL/KAL	injected	IN/JEKT/-D
infraversion	IN/FRA/VERGS	injectio	IN/JEK/SHOE
infriction	IN/FR*IBGS	injection	IN/J*EBGS
infundibul-	IN/FUN/DIB/L-	injector	IN/JEK/TOR
	IN/FUN/DIB/YAOU/L-	injure	JIR
	IN/FUN/DIB/YU/L-		IN/JUR
infundibula	IN/FUN/DIB/LA	injury	JIR/RI
infundibular	IN/FUN/DIB/LAR		IN/JUR/RI
infundibulectomy	IN/FUN/DIB/LEKT/M*I	inlay	IN/LAI
infundibuliform	IN/FUN/DIB/LI/FORM	inlet	IN/LET
infundibulin	IN/FUN/DIB/LIN	innate	IN/NAIT
infundibulofolloculitis	IN/FUN/DIB/LO/FLIK/LAOITS	innatus	IN/NAI/TUS
infundibuloma	IN/FUN/DIB/LOE/MA	innervate	IN/NER/VAIT
infundibulo-ovarian	IN/FUN/DIB/LO/O/VAIRN		IN/ER/VAIT
infundibulopelvic	IN/FUN/DIB/LO/PEL/VIK	innervation	IN/NER/VAIGS
infundibulum	IN/FUN/DIB/LUM		IN/ER/VAIGS
infusible	IN/FAOUZ/-BL	innidiation	IN/NID/YAIGS
infusion	IN/FAOUGS	innocens	IN/NO/SENZ
infusodecoction	IN/FAOUZ/DE/KO*BGS	innocent	IN/NO/SENT
Infusoria	IN/FAOU/SOER/YA		NENT
infusorial	IN/FAOU/SOIRL	innocuous	IN/NOK/YOUS
infusorian	IN/FAOU/SOIRN		IN/OK/YOUS
infusoriotoxin	IN/FAOU/SOER/YO/TOK/SIN	innominata	IN/NOM/NAI/TA
infusum	IN/FAOU/SUM	innominatal	IN/NOM/NAI/TAL
	IN/FAOUS/UM	innominate	IN/NOM/NAIT
ingest	IN/J*ES		IN/NOM/NAT
ingesta	IN/JES/TA	innominatus	IN/NOM/NAI/TUS
ingestant	IN/JES/TANT	Innovar	IN/NO/VAR
ingestion	IN/JEGS	innoxious	IN/NOK/-RBS
ingestive	IN/J*ES/IV	innutrition	IN/NAOU/TRIGS
ingrami	IN/GRAM/MAOI	ino-	IN
	IN/GRA/MAOI		IN/NO
Ingrassia	IN/GRAS/YA	inoblast	IN/BLA*S
	IN/GRASZ/YA	inoccipitia	IN/OX/PIT/YA
ingravescent	IN/GRA/VES/ENT	inochondritis	IN/KON/DRAOITS
ingrowth	IN/GRO*ET	Inocor	IN/NO/KOR
	IN/GRO*UT		IN/KOR
inguen	ING/WEN	inocula	IN/OK/LA
inguin(o)-	ING/WI/N(O)	inoculability	IN/OK/LABLT
	ING/WIN	inoculable	IN/OK/LABL
inguina	ING/WI/NA	inoculate	IN/OK/LAIT
inguinal	ING/WINL	inoculation	IN/OK/LAIGS
	ING/WI/NAL	inoculum	IN/OK/LUM
inguinale	ING/WI/NAI/LAOE	inocyte	IN/SAO*IT
inguinalis	ING/WI/NAI/LIS	inogen	IN/JEN
inguinoabdominal	ING/WIN/AB/DOM/NAL	inogenesis	IN/JEN/SIS
inguinocrural	ING/WIN/KRAOURL	inogenous	IN/OJ/NOUS
inguinodynia	ING/WIN/DIN/YA	inoglia	IN/OG/LA
inguinolabial	ING/WIN/LAIB/YAL		IN/OG/LAOE/YA
inguinoperitoneal	ING/WIN/PERT/NAOEL	inohymenitis	IN/HAOIM/NAOITS
inguinoscrotal	ING/WIN/SKROE/TAL	inolith	IN/L*IT
Inhal-Aid	IN/HAIL/AID	inomyositis	IN/MAOI/SAOITS
inhalant	IN/HAI/LANT	inopectic	IN/PEKT/IK
inhalation	IN/HA/LAIGS	inoperable	IN/OP/RABL
inhale	IN/HAIL	inophragma	IN/FRAG/MA
inhaler	IN/HAIL/ER	inorata	IN/OER/RAI/TA
inherent	IN/HERNT		IN/RAI/TA
inherit	IN/HERT		IN/NO/RAI/TA
inheritance	IN/HER/TANS	inorganic	IN/OR/GAN/IK
inhibin	IN/HIB/BIN	inosamine	IN/OES/MAOEN
inhibit	IN/HIBT	inosclerosis	IN/SKLE/ROE/SIS
inhibitine	IN/HIB/TAOEN	inoscopy	IN/OS/KPI
inhibition	IN/BIGS	inosculate	IN/OS/KLAIT
	IN/HI/BIGS	inosculation	IN/OS/KLAIGS
inhibitive	IN/HIB/TIV	inose	IN/OES
inhibitor	IN/HIB/TOR	inosemia	IN/SAOEM/YA
inhibitory	IN/HIB/TOIR	inosinate	IN/OES/NAIT
inhibitrope	IN/HIB/TROEP	inosine	IN/SAOEN

	IN/SIN		IN/SPI/ROM/TER
inosinic	IN/SIN/IK		IN/SPROM/TER
inosinyl	IN/OES/NIL	inspissate	IN/SPIS/SAIT
inosite	IN/NO/SAOIT (*required*)	inspissated	IN/SPIS/SAIT/-D
	(*not* IN/SAOIT; see incite)	inspissation	IN/SPIS/SAIGS
inositide	IN/OES/TAOID	inspissator	IN/SPIS/SAI/TOR
inositis	IN/SAOITS	instability	IN/STABLT
inositol	IN/OES/TOL	instar	IN/STAR
inositoluria	IN/SAOI/TOL/YAOUR/YA	instep	IN/STEP
inosituria	IN/SAOI/TAOUR/YA	Instat	IN/STAT
inositus	IN/SAOI/TUS	instillation	IN/STIL/LAIGS
inosose	IN/OES/OES	instillator	IN/STIL/LAI/TOR
inostosis	IN/OS/TOE/SIS	instinct	IN/STINGT
inosuria	IN/SAOUR/YA	instinctive	IN/STINGT/IV
inotagma	IN/TAG/MA		IN/STING/TIV
inotropic	IN/TROP/IK	instinctual	IN/STING/KHUL
inotropism	IN/OT/RO/PIFM	institute	STAOUT
in ovo	N-/O/VOE		*INS/TAOUT
in phase	N-/FAEZ		IN/STI/TAOUT
inquest	IN/KW*ES	instrument	STRUMT
inquiline	IN/KWI/LAOIN		IN/STRUMT
	IN/KWI/LIN	instrumental	STRUMT/TAL
inruction	IN/RUK/TAIGS		IN/STRUMT/TAL
insalivate	IN/SAL/VAIT	instrumentarium	STRUMT/TAIRM
insalivation	IN/SA*L/VAIGS		IN/STRUMT/TAIRM
	IN/SAL/LI/VAIGS	instrumentation	STRUMT/TAIGS
	(*not* IN/SAL/VAIGS)		IN/STRUMT/TAIGS
insalubrious	IN/SLAOUB/ROUS	insuccation	IN/SU/KAIGS
	IN/SA/LAOUB/ROUS		IN/SUK/KAIGS
insane	IN/SAIN	insudate	IN/SAOU/DAIT
insaniens	IN/SAIN/YENZ	insudation	IN/SAOU/DAIGS
insanitary	IN/SAN/TAIR	insufficiency	IN/SUF/SI
insanity	IN/SAN/TI		IN/SUF/FIRBT/SI
inscriptio	IN/SKRIP/SHOE		IN/SU/FIRBT/SI
inscription	IN/SKRIPGS	insufficientia	IN/SUF/FIRB/EN/SHA
inscriptiones	IN/SKRIP/SHOE/NAOEZ		IN/SU/FIRB/EN/SHA
insect	IN/SEKT	insufflate	IN/SUF/FLAIT
Insecta	IN/SEK/TA	insufflation	IN/SUF/FLAIGS
insectarium	IN/SEK/TAIRM	insufflator	IN/SUF/FLAI/TOR
insecticide	IN/SEKT/SAO*ID	insul-	INS/L-
insectifuge	IN/SEKT/FAOUJ		IN/SL-
Insectivora	IN/SEK/TIV/RA		IN/SAOU/L-
insectivore	IN/SEKT/VOER	insula	INS/LA
insectivorous	IN/SEK/TIV/ROUS	insulae	INS/LAE
insecurity	IN/SKURT	insular	INS/LAR
	IN/SE/KAOUR/TI	Insulatard	INS/LA/TARD
insemination	IN/SEM/NAIGS	insulate	INS/LAIT
insenescence	IN/SE/NES/ENS	insulation	INS/LAIGS
	INS/NES/ENS	insulator	INS/LAI/TOR
insensible	IN/SENS/-BL	insulin	INS/LIN
insert	IN/SERT	insulinemia	INS/LIN/AOEM/YA
insertio	IN/SER/SHOE		INS/LI/NAOEM/YA
insertion	IN/SERGS	insulinlipodystrophy	INS/LIN/LIP/DIS/TRO/FI
insheathed	IN/SHAO*ET/-D	insulinogenesis	INS/LIN/JEN/SIS
insidious	IN/SID/YOUS	insulinogenic	INS/LIN/JEN/IK
insight	IN/SAOIGT	insulinoid	INS/LIN/OID
insipid	IN/SIP/ID		INS/LI/NOID
insipidus	IN/SIP/DUS	insulinoma	INS/LI/NOE/MA
in situ	N-/SAOI/TAOU		INS/LIN/O/MA
	N-/SIT/TAOU	insulinopenia	INS/LIN/PAOEN/YA
insolation	IN/SOE/LAIGS	insulinopenic	INS/LIN/PAOEN/IK
	(*not* INS/LAIGS; see insulation)	insulism	INS/LIFM
insoluble	IN/SOL/YAOUBL	insulitis	INS/LAOITS
	IN/SOL/YUBL	insulogenic	INS/LO/JEN/IK
insomnia	IN/SOM/NA	insuloma	INS/LOE/MA
	IN/SOM/NAOE/YA	insulopathic	INS/LO/PA*T/IK
insomniac	IN/SOM/NAK	insult	IN/SULT
	IN/SOM/NAOE/AK	insultus	IN/SUL/TUS
	IN/SOM/NAOE/YAK	insusceptibility	IN/SUS/SEPT/-BLT
insomnic	IN/SOM/NIK	intake	SPWAIK
insonate	IN/SOE/NAIT		IN/TAIK
insorption	IN/SORPGS	Intal	SPWAL
inspection	IN/SP*EBGS		IN/TAL
inspectionism	IN/SP*EBGS/IFM	integration	SPWE/GRAIGS
inspersion	IN/SPERGS		INT/GRAIGS
inspirate	IN/SPRAIT	integrator	SPWE/GRAI/TOR
	IN/SPI/RAIT		INT/GRAI/TOR
inspiration	IN/SPRAIGS	integrity	SPWEG/TI
	IN/SPI/RAIGS		SPWEG/RI/TI
inspirator	IN/SPRAI/TOR	integument	SPWEG/YAOUMT
	IN/SPI/RAI/TOR		SPWEG/YUMT
inspiratory	IN/SPAOIR/TOIR		SPWEG/-MT
	IN/SPRA/TOIR	integumentary	SPWEG/YAOUMT/RI
	IN/SPIR/TOIR		SPWEG/YUMT/RI
inspire	IN/SPAOIR		SPWEG/-MT/RI
InspirEase	IN/SPI/RAOEZ	integumenti	SPWEG/MEN/TAOI
inspirium	IN/SPAOIR/YUM		SPWEG/YAOUMT/TAOI
	IN/SPIR/YUM		SPWEG/YUMT/TAOI
inspirometer	IN/SPAOI/ROM/TER	integumentum	SPWEG/MEN/TUM

	SPWEG/YAOUMT/UM	intercostohumeral	SPWER/KO*S/HAOUM/RAL
	SPWEG/YUMT/UM	intercostohumeralis	SPWER/KO*S/HAOUR/RAI/LIS
in tela	N-/TAOE/LA	intercourse	SPWER/KOURS
intellect	SPWLEKT	intercricothyrotomy	SPWER/KRAOIK/THAOI/ROT/M*I
	SPWEL/LEKT	intercristal	SPWER/KR*IS/TAL
intellection	SPWL*EBGS		SPWER/KRIS/TAL
	SPWEL/L*EBGS	intercritical	SPWER/KRIT/KAL
intellectualization	SPWLEK/KHUL/ZAIGS	intercross	SPWER/KROSZ
	SPWEL/LEK/KHUL/ZAIGS	intercrural	SPWER/KRAOURL
intelligence	SPWEL/JENS	intercrurales	SPWER/KRAOU/RAI/LAOEZ
intemperance	SPWEFRP/RANS	intercruralis	SPWER/KRAOU/RAI/LIS
	IN/TEFRP/RANS	intercurrent	SPWER/KURNT
intensification	SPWENS/FI/KAIGS	intercuspation	SPWER/KUS/PAIGS
intensimeter	SPWEN/SIM/TER	intercusping	SPWER/KUS/-PG
intensionometer	SPWENS/YO/NOM/TER	intercutaneomucous	SPWER/KAOU/TAIN/YO/MAOUK/
intensity	SPWENS/TI		OUS
intensive	SPWENS/IV		SPWER/KAOU/TAIN/YO/MAOU/
intensivist	SPWENS/V*IS		KOUS
intention	SPWENGS	interdeferential	SPWER/DEFRN/-RBL
inter-	SPWER		SPWER/DEF/REN/-RBL
interaccessory	SPWER/AK/SES/RI	interdental	SPWER/DEN/TAL
	SPWER/AK/SESZ/RI	interdentium	SPWER/DEN/SHUM
interacinar	SPWER/AS/NAR	interdigit	SPWER/DIJT
interacinous	SPWER/AS/NOUS	interdigital	SPWER/DIJ/TAL
interaction	SPWER/A*BGS	interdigitate	SPWER/DIJ/TAIT
interagglutination	SPWER/AI/GLAOUT/NAIGS	interdigitalis	SPWER/DIJ/TAI/LIS
interallelic	SPWER/AI/LAOEL/IK	interdigitation	SPWER/DIJ/TAIGS
	SPWER/AL/LAOEL/IK	interdisciplinary	SPWER/DIS/PLI/NAIR
interalveolar	SPWER/AL/VAOE/LAR	interface	SPWER/FAIS
interangular	SPWER/ANG/LAR	interfacial	SPWER/FAIRBL
interannular	SPWER/AN/LAR	interfascicular	SPWER/FA/SIK/LAR
interarch	SPWER/A*RPBLG	interfascicularis	SPWER/FA/SIK/LAI/RIS
	SPWER/AR/-FP	interfemoral	SPWER/FEM/RAL
interarticular	SPWER/AR/TIK/LAR	interference	SPWER/FAOERNS
interarytenoid	SPWER/AR/TAOE/NOID	interfering	SPWER/FAOER/-G
interasteric	SPWER/AI/STAOER/IK	interferometer	SPWER/FAOER/OM/TER
	SPWER/AS/TAOER/IK		SPWER/FE/ROM/TER
interatrial	SPWER/AI/TRAL	interferometry	SPWER/FAOER/OM/TRI
interauricular	SPWER/AU/RIK/LAR		SPWER/FE/ROM/TRI
interbody	SPWER/BOD/DI	interferon	SPWER/FAOER/RON
interbrain	SPWER/BRAIN		SPWER/FER/RON
intercadence	SPWER/KAI/DENS	interfibrillar	SPWER/FAOI/BRI/LAR
intercadent	SPWER/KAI/DENT	interfibrillary	SPWER/FAOI/BRI/LAIR
intercalary	SPWERK/LAIR	interfibrous	SPWER/FAOI/BROUS
	SPWER/KAL/RI	interfilamentous	SPWER/FIL/MEN/TOUS
intercalate	SPWERK/LAIT	interfilar	SPWER/FAOI/LAR
intercalated	SPWERK/LAIT/-D	interfollicular	SPWER/FLIK/LAR
intercalation	SPWERK/LAIGS	interfrontal	SPWER/FRON/TAL
intercalatum	SPWERK/LAI/TUM	interfurca	SPWER/FUR/KA
intercanalicular	SPWER/KAN/LIK/LAR	interfurcae	SPWER/FUR/SAE
intercanthic	SPWER/KA*NT/IK	interganglionic	SPWER/GANG/LON/IK
intercapillary	SPWER/KAP/LAIR	intergemmal	SPWER/JEM/MAL
intercapitales	SPWER/KAP/TAI/LAOEZ	intergenic	SPWER/JEN/IK
intercapitulares	SPWER/KA/PIFP/LAI/RAOEZ	interglobular	SPWER/GLOB/LAR
	SPWER/KA/PIT/LAI/RAOEZ	intergluteal	SPWER/GLAOUT/YAL
intercarotic	SPWER/KROT/IK	intergonial	SPWER/GOEN/YAL
	SPWER/KA/ROT/IK	intergrade	SPWER/GRAID
intercarotid	SPWER/KROT/ID	intergranular	SPWER/GRAN/LAR
	SPWER/KA/ROT/ID	intergyral	SPWER/JAOIRL
intercarpal	SPWER/KAR/PAL		SPWER/JAOI/RAL
intercarpeae	SPWER/KARP/YAE	interhemicerebral	SPWER/HEM/SER/BRAL
intercartilaginous	SPWER/KART/LAJ/NOUS	interhemispheric	SPWER/HEM/SFAOER/IK
intercavernous	SPWER/KAVR/NOUS	interictal	SPWER/IK/TAL
intercellular	SPWER/SEL/YAOU/LAR		SPWRIK/TAL
intercentra	SPWER/SEN/TRA	interilioabdominal	SPWER/IL/YO/AB/DOM/NAL
intercentral	SPWER/SEN/TRAL	interior	SPWAOER/YOR
	SPWER/STRAL	interinnominoabdominal	SPWER/IN/NOM/NO/AB/DOM/
intercentrum	SPWER/SEN/TRUM		NAL
intercept	SPWER/SEPT	interischiadic	SPWER/IS/KAD/IK
Intercept Contraceptive	SPWER/SEPT/KON/TRA/SEPT/IV	interkinesis	SPWER/KI/NAOE/SIS
interceptive	SPWER/SEPT/IV	interlabial	SPWER/LAIB/YAL
intercerebral	SPWER/SER/BRAL	interlamellar	SPWER/LA/MEL/LAR
interchondral	SPWER/KON/DRAL	interleukin-1	SPWER/LAOU/KIN/1
interchondrales	SPWER/KON/DRAI/LAOEZ	interleukin-2	SPWER/LAOU/KIN/2
interciliary	SPWER/SIL/YAIR	interligamentary	SPWER/LIG/-MT/RI
intercilium	SPWER/SIL/YUM	interligamentous	SPWER/LIG/MEN/TOUS
intercistronic	SPWER/SIS/TRON/IK	interlobar	SPWER/LOE/BAR
interclavicular	SPWER/KLA/VIK/LAR	interlobares	SPWER/LOE/BAI/RAOEZ
interclinoid	SPWER/KLAOI/NOID	interlobitis	SPWER/LOE/BAOITS
intercoccygeal	SPWER/KOK/SIJ/YAL	interlobular	SPWER/LOB/LAR
intercolumnar	SPWER/KLUM/NAR	interlobulares	SPWER/LOB/LAI/RAOEZ
	SPWER/KO/LUM/NAR	interlock	SPWER/LOK
intercondylar	SPWER/KOND/LAR	interlocking	SPWER/LOK/-G
intercondylaris	SPWER/KOND/LAI/RIS	intermalleolar	SPWER/MAL/LAOE/LAR
intercondylic	SPWER/KON/DIL/IK	intermamillary	SPWER/MAM/LAIR
intercondyloid	SPWER/KOND/LOID	intermammary	SPWER/MAM/RI
intercondyloidea	SPWER/KOND/LOID/YA	intermarriage	SPWER/MAIRJ
intercondylous	SPWER/KOND/LOUS	intermaxilla	SPWER/MAK/SIL/LA
intercostal	SPWER/KOS/TAL	intermaxillary	SPWER/MAX/LAIR

intermedia	SPWER/MAOED/YA
intermediary	SPWER/MAOED/YAIR
intermediate	SPWER/MAOED/YAT
intermedin	SPWER/MAOE/DIN
intermediolateral	SPWER/MAOED/YO/LAT/RAL
intermedius	SPWER/MAOED/YUS
intermembranous	SPWER/MEM/BRA/NOUS
intermeningeal	SPWER/ME/NIN/JAL
intermenstrual	SPWER/MEN/STRAL
	SPWER/MEN/STRAOUL
	SPWER/MEN/STRUL
intermenstrualis	SPWER/MENS/TRAI/LIS
	SPWER/MEN/STRAOU/AI/LIS
	SPWER/MEN/STRAOU/WAI/LIS
intermenstruum	SPWER/MEN/STRUM
	SPWER/MEN/STRAOUM
intermetacarpal	SPWER/MET/KAR/PAL
intermetacarpeae	SPWER/MET/KARP/YAE
intermetameric	SPWER/MET/MER/IK
intermetatarsal	SPWER/MET/TAR/SAL
intermetatarseae	SPWER/MET/TARS/YAE
intermetatarseum	SPWER/MET/TARS/YUM
intermission	SPWER/MIGS
intermitotic	SPWER/MAOI/TOT/IK
intermittence	SPWER/MIT/ENS
	SPWER/MIT/TENS
intermittency	SPWER/MIT/EN/SI
	SPWER/MIT/TEN/SI
intermittens	SPWER/MIT/ENZ
	SPWER/MIT/TENZ
intermittent	SPWER/MIT/ENT
	SPWER/MIT/TENT
intermolecular	SPWER/MO/LEK/LAR
intermural	SPWER/MAOURL
intermuscular	SPWER/MUS/KLAR
intermusculares	SPWER/MUS/KLAI/RAOEZ
intern	SPWERN
interna	SPWER/NA
internae	SPWER/NAE
internal	SPWERNL
internalization	SPWERNL/ZAIGS
internarial	SPWER/NAIRL
internasal	SPWER/NAI/ZAL
internatal	SPWER/NAI/TAL
internation	SPWER/NAIGS
interneuromeric	SPWER/NAOUR/MER/IK
interneuron	SPWER/NAOU/RON
internist	SPWERN/*IS
interni	SPWER/NAOI
internodal	SPWER/NOE/DAL
internode	SPWER/NOED
internodular	SPWER/NOD/LAR
internship	SPWERN/SHIP
internuclear	SPWERN/NAOUK/LAR
internum	SPWERN/UM
	SPWER/NUM
internuncial	SPWER/NUNS/YAL
	SPWER/NUN/-RBL
internus	SPWER/NUS
intero-	SPWER/RO
	(NOTE: this does not apply to word parts beginning with "o" that follow inter-)
interocclusal	SPWER/O/KLAOU/ZAL
interoceptive (intero-)	SPWER/RO/SEPT/IV
interoceptor (intero-)	SPWER/RO/SEP/TOR
interocular	SPWER/OK/LAR
interofection (intero-)	SPWER/RO/F*EBGS
interofective (intero-)	SPWER/RO/FEKT/IV
interogestate (intero-)	SPWER/RO/JES/TAIT
interoinferiorly (intero-)	SPWER/RO/IN/FAOER/YOR/LI
interolivary	SPWER/OL/VAIR
interorbital	SPWER/ORB/TAL
interossea	SPWER/OS/YA
interosseae	SPWER/OS/YAE
interosseal	SPWER/OS/YAL
interossei	SPWER/OS/YAOI
interosseous	SPWER/OS/YOUS
interosseus	SPWER/OS/YUS
interpalpebral	SPWER/PAL/PE/BRAL
interpandemic	SPWER/PAN/DEM/IK
interparietal	SPWER/PRAOI/TAL
interparoxysmal	SPWER/PAR/OK/SIZ/MAL
interpediculate	SPWER/PE/DIK/LAIT
interpeduncular	SPWER/PE/DUNG/LAR
interpedunculare	SPWER/PE/DUNG/LAI/RAOE
interpeduncularis	SPWER/PE/DUNG/LAI/RIS
interpelviabdominal	SPWER/PEL/VI/AB/DOM/NAL
interpersonal	SPWER/PERNL

	SPWER/PER/NAL
interphalangeae	SPWER/FLAN/JAE
interphalangeal	SPWER/FLAN/JAL
interphalangearum	SPWER/FLAN/JAI/RUM
interphase	SPWER/FAEZ
interphyletic	SPWER/FAOI/LET/IK
interpial	SPWER/PAOIL
	SPWER/PAOI/YAL
interplant	SPWER/PLANT
interplanting	SPWER/PLANT/-G
interpleural	SPWER/PLAOURL
interpolar	SPWER/POE/LAR
interpolated	SPWER/LAIT/-D
interpolation	SPWERP/LAIGS
interposition	SPWER/POGS
interpositum	SPWER/POZ/TUM
interpretation	SPWERP/TAIGS
	SPWER/PRE/TAIGS
interprismatic	SPWER/PRIZ/MAT/IK
interprotometamere	SPWER/PROET/MET/MAOER
interproximal	SPWER/PROX/MAL
interpubic	SPWER/PAOUB/IK
interpubicus	SPWER/PAOUB/KUS
interpupillary	SPWER/PAOUP/LAIR
interradial	SPWER/RAID/YAL
interradicular	SPWER/RA/DIK/LAR
interrenal	SPWER/RAOENL
interridge	SPWER/RIJ
interrupt	SPWER/RUPT
	SPWRUPT
interruptus	SPWER/RUP/TUS
	SPWRUP/TUS
intersacral	SPWER/SAI/KRAL
interscapilium	SPWER/SKA/PIL/YUM
interscapular	SPWER/SKAP/LAR
interscapulothoracic	SPWER/SKAP/LO/THRAS/IK
interscapulum	SPWER/SKAP/LUM
intersciatic	SPWER/SAOI/AT/IK
intersectio	SPWER/SEK/SHOE
intersection	SPWER/S*EBGS
intersectiones	SPWER/SEK/SHOE/NAOEZ
intersegment	SPWER/SEG/-MT
intersegmental	SPWER/SEG/MEN/TAL
interseptal	SPWER/SEP/TAL
interseptovalvular	SPWER/SEPT/VAL/VAOU/LAR
	SPWER/SEP/TO/VAL/VAOU/LAR
interseptum	SPWER/SEP/TUM
intersex	SPWER/SEX
intersexual	SPWER/SEX/YAOUL
intersexuality	SPWER/SEX/YAL/TI
interspace	SPWER/SPAIS
interspinal	SPWER/SPAOINL
interspinalis	SPWER/SPAOI/NAI/LIS
interspinous	SPWER/SPAOIN/OUS
intersternal	SPWER/STERNL
interstice	SPWER/STIS
interstices	SPWER/STI/SAOEZ
interstitial	SPWER/STIRBL
interstitialis	SPWER/STIRB/YAI/LIS
interstitium	SPWER/STIRB/UM
	SPWER/STIRB/YUM
intersystole	SPWER/*IS/LAOE
intertarsal	SPWER/TAR/SAL
intertarseae	SPWER/TARS/YAE
intertendineus	SPWER/TEN/DIN/YUS
interthalamic	SPWER/THA/LAM/IK
interthalamica	SPWER/THA/LAM/KA
interthalamicus	SPWER/THA/LAM/KUS
intertransversalis	SPWER/TRA*NS/VER/SAI/LIS
intertransverse	SPWER/TRA*NS/VERS
intertriginous	SPWER/TRIJ/NOUS
intertrigo	SPWER/TRAOI/GOE
	SPWER/TR*I/GOE
intertrochanteric	SPWER/TROE/KAN/TER/IK
intertrochanterica	SPWER/TROE/KAN/TER/KA
intertropical	SPWER/TROP/KAL
intertuberal	SPWER/TAOUB/RAL
intertubercular	SPWER/TAOU/BERK/LAR
intertubular	SPWER/TAOUB/LAR
interureteral	SPWER/YAOU/RAOET/RAL
interureteric	SPWER/YAOUR/TER/IK
intervaginal	SPWER/VAJ/NAL
interval	SPWER/VAL
intervalvular	SPWER/VAL/VAOU/LAR
intervascular	SPWER/VAS/KLAR
intervention	SPWER/VENGS
interventricular	SPWER/VEN/TRIK/LAR
intervertebral	SPWER/VERT/BRAL
intervertebrales	SPWER/VERT/BRAI/LAOEZ

intervertebralis	SPWER/VERT/BRAI/LIS	intradural	SPWRA/DAOURL
intervillous	SPWER/VIL/OUS	intraembryonic	SPWRA/EM/BRON/IK
interzonal	SPWER/ZOENL	intraepidermal	SPWRA/EP/DER/MAL
intestina	SPWES/TAOI/NA	intraepiphysial	SPWRA/EP/FIZ/YAL
intestinal	SPW*ES/NAL	intraepithelial	SPWRA/EP/THAOEL/YAL
intestine	SPWES/TIN	intraerythrocytic	SPWRA/R*IT/RO/SIT/IK
intestinale	SPW*ES/NAI/LAOE	intrafaradization	SPWRA/FAR/DI/ZAIGS
intestinales	SPW*ES/NAI/LAOEZ	intrafascicular	SPWRA/FA/SIK/LAR
intestinalis	SPW*ES/NAI/LIS	intrafat	SPWRA/FAT
intestino-intestinal	SPW*ES/NO/SPW*ES/NAL	intrafebrile	SPWRA/FEB/RAOIL
intestinotoxin	SPW*ES/NO/TOK/SIN		SPWRA/FEB/RIL
intestinum	SPWES/TAOIN/UM	intrafetation	SPWRA/FAOE/TAIGS
	SPWES/TAOI/NUM	intrafilar	SPWRA/FAOI/LAR
	SPW*ES/NUM	intrafissural	SPWRA/FIRB/RAL
intima	SPWI/MA		SPWRA/FIS/RAL
	INT/MA	intrafistular	SPWRA/F*IS/LAR
intimal	SPWI/MAL	intrafollicular	SPWRA/FLIK/LAR
	INT/MAL	intrafusal	SPWRA/FAOU/ZAL
intimi	SPWI/MAOI	intragalvanization	SPWRA/GAL/VAN/ZAIGS
	INT/MAOI	intragastric	SPWRA/GAS/TRIK
intimitis	SPWI/MAOITS	intragemmal	SPWRA/JEM/MAL
	INT/MAOITS	intragenic	SPWRA/JEN/IK
intoe	IN/TOE	intraglandular	SPWRA/GLAND/LAR
intolerance	SPWOL/RANS	intraglobular	SPWRA/GLOB/LAR
intorsion	SPWORGS	intragyral	SPWRA/JAOIRL
	IN/TORGS	intrahepatic	SPWRA/HE/PAT/IK
intorter	SPWORT/ER	intrahyoid	SPWRA/HAOI/OID
	IN/TORT/ER	intraictal	SPWRA/IK/TAL
intortor	SPWOR/TOR	intraintestinal	SPWRA/SPW*ES/NAL
	IN/TOR/TOR	intrajugular	SPWRA/JUG/LAR
intoxation	SPWOK/SAIGS	intralamellar	SPWRA/LA/MEL/LAR
intoxicant	SPWOX/KANT	intralaryngeal	SPWRA/LARN/JAL
intoxication	SPWOX/KAIGS	intralesional	SPWRA/LAOEGS/NAL
intra-	SPWRA	intraleukocytic	SPWRA/LAOUK/SIT/IK
intra-abdominal	SPWRA/AB/DOM/NAL	intraligamentous	SPWRA/LIG/MEN/TOUS
intra-acinous	SPWRA/AS/NOUS	intralingual	SPWRA/LING/WAL
intra-adenoidal	SPWRA/AD/NOI/DAL	Intralipid	SPWRA/LIP/ID
intra-appendicular	SPWRA/AP/EN/DIK/LAR	intralobar	SPWRA/LOE/BAR
intra-arachnoid	SPWRA/AI/RAK/NOID	intralobular	SPWRA/LOB/LAR
intra-arterial	SPWRA/AR/TAOERL	intralocular	SPWRA/LOK/LAR
intra-articular	SPWRA/AR/TIK/LAR	intraluminal	SPWRA/LAOUM/NAL
intra-atomic	SPWRA/AI/TOM/IK	intramammary	SPWRA/MAM/RI
intra-atrial	SPWRA/AI/TRAL	intramarginal	SPWRA/MARJ/NAL
intra-aural	SPWRA/AURL	intramastoid	SPWRA/MAS/TOID
intra-auricular	SPWRA/AU/RIK/LAR	intramastoiditis	SPWRA/MAS/TOI/DAOITS
intrabronchial	SPWRA/BRONG/YAL	intramatrical	SPWRA/MAI/TRI/KAL
intrabuccal	SPWRA/BUK/KAL		SPWRA/MAT/RI/KAL
intracanalicular	SPWRA/KAN/LIK/LAR	intramaxillary	SPWRA/MAX/LAIR
intracapsular	SPWRA/KAPS/LAR	intramedullary	SPWRA/MED/LAIR
intracardiac	SPWRA/KARD/YAK	intramembranous	SPWRA/MEM/BRA/NOUS
intracarpal	SPWRA/KAR/PAL	intrameningeal	SPWRA/ME/NIN/JAL
intracartilaginous	SPWRA/KART/LAJ/NOUS	intramolecular	SPWRA/MO/LEK/LAR
intracatheter	SPWRA/KA*T/TER	intramural	SPWRA/MAOURL
intracavitary	SPWRA/KAV/TAIR	intramuscular	SPWRA/MUS/KLAR
intracelial	SPWRA/SAOEL/YAL	intramyocardial	SPWRA/MAOI/KARD/YAL
intracellular	SPWRA/SEL/YAOU/LAR	intramyometrial	SPWRA/MAOI/MAOE/TRAL
intracephalic	SPWRA/SFAL/IK	intranarial	SPWRA/NAIR/YAL
intracerebellar	SPWRA/SER/BEL/LAR	intranasal	SPWRA/NAI/ZAL
intracerebral	SPWRA/SER/BRAL	intranatal	SPWRA/NAI/TAL
intracervical	SPWRA/SEFRB/KAL	intraneural	SPWRA/NAOURL
intrachondral	SPWRA/KON/DRAL	intranuclear	SPWRA/NAOUK/LAR
intrachondrial	SPWRA/KON/DRAOEL	intraocular	SPWRA/OK/LAR
	SPWRA/KON/DRAOE/YAL	intraoperative	SPWRA/OP/RA/TIV
	(not SPWRA/KON/DRAL; see		SPWRA/OERPT/IV
	intrachondral)	intraoral	SPWRA/ORL
intrachordal	SPWRA/KHOR/DAL	intraorbital	SPWRA/ORB/TAL
intracisternal	SPWRA/SIS/TERNL	intraosseous	SPWRA/OS/YOUS
intracistronic	SPWRA/SIS/TRON/IK	intraosteal	SPWRA/O*S/YAL
intracolic	SPWRA/KOL/IK	intraovarian	SPWRA/O/VAIRN
intracordal	SPWRA/KOR/DAL	intraovular	SPWRA/OV/LAR
intracoronal	SPWRA/KOR/NAL	intrapapillare	SPWRA/PAP/LAI/RAOE
intracorporal	SPWRA/KORP/RAL	intraparenchymatous	SPWRA/PARN/KIM/TOUS
intracorporeal	SPWRA/KOR/POER/YAL	intraparietal	SPWRA/PRAOI/TAL
intracorpuscular	SPWRA/KOR/PUS/KLAR	intrapartum	SPWRA/PAR/TUM
intracostal	SPWRA/KOS/TAL	intrapelvic	SPWRA/PEL/VIK
intracranial	SPWRA/KRAIN/YAL	intrapericardiac	SPWRA/P*ER/KARD/YAK
intracrureus	SPWRA/KRAOU/RAOE/YUS	intrapericardial	SPWRA/P*ER/KARD/YAL
intractable	SPWRAKT/-BL	intraperineal	SPWRA/P*ER/NAOEL
intracutaneous	SPWRA/KAOU/TAIN/YOUS	intraperitoneal	SPWRA/PERT/NAOEL
intracystic	SPWRA/S*IS/IK	intrapersonal	SPWRA/PERNL
intracytoplasmic	SPWRA/SAOIT/PLAZ/MIK		SPWRA/PERS/NAL
intrad	SPWRAD	intrapial	SPWRA/PAOIL
intradermal	SPWRA/DER/MAL		SPWRA/PAOI/YAL
intradermic	SPWRA/DERM/IK	intrapituitary	SPWRA/PI/TAOU/TAIR
intradermoreaction	SPWRA/DERM/RE/A*BGS	intraplacental	SPWRA/PLA/SEN/TAL
intraduct	SPWRA/DUKT	intrapleural	SPWRA/PLAOURL
intraductal	SPWRA/DUK/TAL	intrapontine	SPWRA/PON/TAOIN
intraduodenal	SPWRA/DAOU/DAOENL	intraprostatic	SPWRA/PROS/TAT/IK
	SPWRA/DWOD/NAL	intraprotoplasmic	SPWRA/PROET/PLAZ/MIK

intrapsychic	SPWRA/SAOIK/IK	intubator	IN/TAOU/BAIGS/*IS
intrapsychical	SPWRA/SAOIK/KAL		SPWAOU/BAI/TOR
intrapulmonary	SPWRA/PUL/MO/NAIR		IN/TAOU/BAI/TOR
	SPWRA/PUM/NAIR	intumesce	SPWAOU/MES
intrapulpal	SPWRA/PUL/PAL		IN/TAOU/MES
intrapyretic	SPWRA/PAOI/RET/IK	intumescence	SPWAOU/MES/ENS
intrarachidian	SPWRA/RA/KID/YAN		IN/TAOU/MES/ENS
	SPWRA/RAI/KID/YAN	intumescent	SPWAOU/MES/ENT
intrarectal	SPWRA/REK/TAL		IN/TAOU/MES/ENT
intrarenal	SPWRA/RAOENL	intumescentia	SPWAOUM/SEN/SHA
intraretinal	SPWRA/RET/NAL		SPWAOU/ME/SEN/SHA
intrascleral	SPWRA/SKLAOERL		SPWAOU/MES/SEN/SHA
intrascrotal	SPWRA/SKROE/TAL		IN/TAOUM/SEN/SHA
intrasellar	SPWRA/SEL/LAR		IN/TAOU/ME/SEN/SHA
intraseptal	SPWRA/SEP/TAL		IN/TAOU/MES/SEN/SHA
intraserous	SPWRA/SAOER/OUS	intussusc-	SPWUS/S-
intraspinal	SPWRA/SPAOINL		SPWUS/SUS/S-
intrasplenic	SPWRA/SPLEN/IK		IN/TUS/S-
intrasternal	SPWRA/STERNL		IN/TUS/SUS/S-
intrastitial	SPWRA/STIRBL	intussusception	SPWUS/SEPGS
intrastromal	SPWRA/STROE/MAL	intussusceptive	SPWUS/SEPT/IV
intrasynovial	SPWRA/SNOEV/YAL	intussusceptum	SPWUS/SEP/TUM
intratarsal	SPWRA/TAR/SAL	intussuscipiens	SPWUS/SIP/YENZ
intratendinous	SPWRA/TEND/NOUS	inu-	IN/L-
intratesticular	SPWRA/TES/TIK/LAR		IN/YAOU/L-
intrathecal	SPWRA/THAOE/KAL		IN/YU/L-
intrathenar	SPWRA/THAOE/NAR	Inula	IN/LA
intrathoracic	SPWRA/THRAS/IK	inulase	IN/LAIS
intrathyroid	SPWRA/THAOI/ROID	inulin	IN/LIN
intratonsillar	SPWRA/TONS/LAR	inulinase	IN/LIN/AIS
intratrabecular	SPWRA/TRA/BEK/LAR	inuloid	IN/LOID
intratracheal	SPWRA/TRAIK/YAL	inulol	IN/LOL
intratubal	SPWRA/TAOU/BAL	inunction	IN/UNGS
intratubular	SPWRA/TAOUB/LAR	inunctum	IN/UNG/TUM
intratympanic	SPWRA/TIM/PAN/IK	inundation	IN/UN/DAIGS
intraureteral	SPWRA/YAOU/RAOET/RAL	in utero	N-/YAOUT/ROE
intraurethral	SPWRA/YAOU/RAO*ET/RAL	invaccination	IN/VAX/NAIGS
intrauterine	SPWRA/YAOUT/RIN	in vacuo	N-/VAK/YOE
intravaginal	SPWRA/VAJ/NAL	invadens	IN/VAI/DENZ
intravasation	SPWRAV/ZAIGS		IN/VAID/ENZ
	IN/TRAV/ZAIGS	invaginate	IN/VAJ/NAIT
intravascular	SPWRA/VAS/KLAR	invagination	IN/VAJ/NAIGS
intravenation	SPWRA/VE/NAIGS	invaginator	IN/VAJ/NAI/TOR
	SPWRA/VAOE/NAIGS	invaginatus	IN/VAJ/NAI/TUS
intravenous	SPWRA/VAOEN/OUS	invalid	IN/VA/LID
intraventricular	SPWRA/VEN/TRIK/LAR		IN/VAL/ID
intraversion	SPWRA/VERGS	invalidism	IN/VA/LID/IFM
intravertebral	SPWRA/VERT/BRAL	invariable	IN/VAIRBL
intravesical	SPWRA/VES/KAL		IN/VAIR/YABL
intravillous	SPWRA/VIL/OUS	invasin	IN/VAI/ZIN
intravital	SPWRA/VAOI/TAL		IN/VAI/SIN
intra vitam	SPWRA/VAOI/TAM	invasion	IN/VAIGS
intravitelline	SPWRA/VAOI/TEL/LIN	invasive	IN/VAIS/IV
	SPWRA/VAOI/TEL/LAOEN	invasiveness	IN/VAIS/IV/*NS
	SPWRA/VI/TEL/LIN		IN/VAIS/IVNS
	SPWRA/VI/TEL/LAOEN	inventory	IN/VEN/TOIR
intravitreous	SPWRA/VIT/ROUS	invermination	IN/VERM/NAIGS
intrazole	SPWRA/ZOEL	inversa	IN/VER/SA
intrinsic	SPWRINZ/IK	inverse	IN/VERS
	SPWRINS/IK	Inversine	IN/VER/SAOEN
intro-	SPWRO	inversion	IN/VERGS
introducer	SPWRO/DAOUS/ER	inversus	IN/VER/SUS
introfier	SPWRO/FI/ER	invert	IN/VERT
introflexion	SPWRO/FL*EBGS	invertase	IN/VER/TAIS
introgastric	SPWRO/GAS/TRIK	Invertebrata	IN/VERT/BRAI/TA
introitus	SPWROI/TUS	invertebrate	IN/VERT/BRAIT
	IN/TROI/TUS		IN/VERT/BRAT
introjection	SPWRO/J*EBGS	invertin	IN/VER/TIN
intromission	SPWRO/MIGS	invertor	IN/VER/TOR
intromittent	SPWRO/MIT/ENT	invertose	IN/VER/TOES
	SPWRO/MIT/TENT	invest	IN/V*ES
intron	SPWRON	investing	IN/V*ES/-G
	IN/TRON	investment	IN/V*ES/-MT
Intron	K-P/SPWRON	inveterate	IN/VET/RAT
	K-P/IN/TRON	inviscation	IN/VIS/KAIGS
Intropin	SPWROE/PIN	invisible	IN/VIZ/-BL
	IN/TROE/PIN	in vitro	N-/VAOE/TROE
introrsus	SPWROR/SUS	in vivo	N-/VAOE/VOE
	IN/TROR/SUS	involucra	IN/VO/LAOU/KRA
introspection	SPWRO/SP*EBGS		IN/VOE/LAOU/KRA
introspective	SPWRO/SPEKT/IV	involucre	IN/VO/LAOUK/ER
introsusception	SPWRO/SUS/SEPGS		IN/VOE/LAOUK/ER
introversion	SPWRO/VERGS	involucrin	IN/VO/LAOU/KRIN
introvert	SPWRO/VERT		IN/VOE/LAOU/KRIN
intubate	SPWAOU/BAIT	involucrum	IN/VO/LAOU/KRUM
	IN/TAOU/BAIT		IN/VOE/LAOU/KRUM
intubation	SPWAOU/BAIGS	involuntary	IN/VOL/TAIR
	IN/TAOU/BAIGS		IN/VOL/UN/TAIR
intubationist	SPWAOU/BAIGS/*IS	involuntomotory	IN/VOL/UN/TO/MOET/RI

involute	IN/VO/LAOUT
	IN/VOE/LAOUT
involution	IN/VO/LAOUGS
	IN/VOE/LAOUGS
involutional	IN/VO/LAOUGS/NAL
	IN/VOE/LAOUGS/NAL
Io	AOI/YOE
io-	AOI
	AOI/YO
iobenzamic	AOI/BEN/ZAM/IK
iocarmate	AOI/KAR/MAIT
iocarmic	AOI/KARM/IK
iocetamic	AOI/SE/TAM/IK
iod(o)-	AOI/OED
	AOI/D-
	AOI/YOED
iodamide	AOI/OED/MAOID
Iodamoeba	AOI/OED/MAOE/BA
	AOI/OD/MAOE/BA
iodate	AOI/DAIT
iodatum	AOI/DAI/TUM
	AOI/DAIT/UM
iodemia	AOI/DAOEM/YA
ioderma	AOI/DER/MA
iodic	AOI/OD/IK
iodide	AOI/DAOID
iodidum	AOI/OED/DUM
iodimetry	AOI/DIM/TRI
iodinase	AOI/DIN/AIS
iodinate	AOI/DI/NAIT
	AOI/DIN/AIT
iodinated	AOI/DI/NAIT/-D
	AOI/DIN/AIT/-D
iodination	AOI/DI/NAIGS
	AOI/DIN/AIGS
iodine	AOI/DAOIN
iodinophil	AOI/DIN/FIL
iodinophile	AOI/DIN/FAOIL
iodinophilous	AOI/DIN/OF/LOUS
iodipamide	AOI/DIP/MAOID
iodism	AOI/DIFM
iodize	AOI/DAOIZ
iodized	AOI/DAOIZ/-D
iodoacetamide	AOI/OED/AI/SAOET/MAOID
iodoacetic	AOI/OED/AI/SAOET/IK
	AOI/OED/AI/SET/IK
iodoalphionic	AOI/OED/AL/FON/IK
	AOI/OED/AL/FAOE/ON/IK
iodobrassid	AOI/OED/BRAS/SID
	AOI/DO/BRAS/SID
iodocasein	AOI/DO/KAI/SAOEN
iodochlorhydroxyquin	AOI/DO/KLOR/HAOI/DROX/KWIN
	AOI/OED/KLOR/HAOI/DROX/
	KWIN
iodochlorhydroxyquinoline	AOI/DO/KLOR/HAOI/DROX/KWIN/
	LAOEN
	AOI/OED/KLOR/HAOI/DROX/
	KWIN/LAOEN
iodochlorol	AOI/DO/KLOR/OL
	AOI/DO/KLOR/ROL
iodocholesterol	AOI/OED/KL*ES/ROL
Iodo-Cortifair	AOI/DO/KORT/FAIR
	AOI/OED/KORT/FAIR
iododerma	AOI/OED/DER/MA
iodoform	AOI/OED/FORM
iodoformism	AOI/DO/FORM/IFM
	AOI/OED/FORM/IFM
iodoformum	AOI/DO/FOR/MUM
	AOI/OED/FOR/MUM
iodogenic	AOI/DO/JEN/IK
iodoglobulin	AOI/OED/GLOB/LIN
	AOI/DO/GLOB/LIN
iodogorgoic	AOI/OED/GOR/GOIK
	AOI/OED/GOR/GOE/IK
iodohippurate	AOI/OED/HIP/RAIT
iodolography	AOI/DO/LOG/FI
iodomethamate	AOI/OED/M*ET/MAIT
iodomethane	AOI/DO/M*ET/AIN
	AOI/OED/M*ET/AIN
iodometric	AOI/DO/MET/RIK
	AOI/OED/MET/RIK
iodometry	AOI/DOM/TRI
Iodo-Niacin	AOI/DO/NAOI/SIN
	AOI/OED/NAOI/SIN
iodopanoic	AOI/OED/PA/NOIK
	AOI/OED/PA/NOE/IK
iodophendylate	AOI/OED/FEND/LAIT
iodophenol	AOI/DO/FAOE/NOL
	AOI/OED/FAOE/NOL

iodophil	AOI/OED/FIL
	AOI/DO/FIL
iodophilia	AOI/OED/FIL/YA
	AOI/DO/FIL/YA
iodophor	AOI/OED/FOER
iodophthalein	AOI/OED/THAL/YIN
	AOI/OED/THAL/AOEN
iodoprotein	AOI/OED/PRO/TAOEN
iodopsin	AOI/DOP/SIN
iodopyracet	AOI/OED/PAOIR/SET
iodoquinol	AOI/OED/KWIN/OL
iodosalicylic	AOI/DO/SAL/SIL/IK
iodosobenzoic	AOI/DOE/SO/BEN/ZOIK
	AOI/DOE/SO/BEN/ZOE/IK
iodosulfate	AOI/DO/SUL/FAIT
iodotherapy	AOI/DO/THER/PI
iodothyroglobulin	AOI/OED/THAOIR/GLOB/LIN
	AOI/DO/THAOIR/GLOB/LIN
iodothyronine	AOI/OED/THAOIR/NAOEN
	AOI/DO/THAOIR/NAOEN
iodotyrosine	AOI/OED/TAOIR/SAOEN
	AOI/DO/TAOIR/SAOEN
iodoventriculography	AOI/DO/VEN/TRIK/LOG/FI
iodovolatilization	AOI/DO/VOL/TIL/ZAIGS
iodoxamate	AOI/DOX/MAIT
iodoxamic	AOI/DOK/SAM/IK
iodoxybenzoic	AOI/DOX/BEN/ZOIK
	AOI/DOX/BEN/ZOE/IK
iodum	AOI/DUM
	AOI/OED/UM
ioduria	AOI/DAOUR/YA
ioglycamic	AOI/GLAOI/KAM/IK
iohexol	AOI/HEX/OL
	AOI/HEK/SOL
iometer	AOI/OM/TER
ion	AOIN
	AOI/YON
Ionamin	AOI/YON/MIN
	AOI/YOEN/MIN
ionic	AOIN/IK
	AOI/YON/IK
Ionil	AOI/NIL
Ionil Plus	AOI/NIL/PLUS
Ionil Shampoo	AOI/NIL/SHAM/PAO
Ionil T Plus Shampoo	AOI/NIL/T-RBGS/PLUS
Ionil T Shampoo	AOI/NIL/T-RBGS/SHAM/PAO
ionium	AOI/OEN/YUM
ionization	AOIN/ZAIGS
ionize	AOIN/AOIZ
ionizing	AOIN/AOIZ/-G
iono-	AOIN
	AOI/NO
	AOI/YON
ionocolorimeter	AOI/NO/KOL/RIM/TER
ionogen	AOIN/JEN
ionogenic	AOIN/JEN/IK
ionogram	AOIN/GRAM
ionometer	AOI/NOM/TER
	AOIN/OM/TER
ionometry	AOIN/OM/TRI
	AOIN/OM/TRI
ionone	AOI/NOEN
ionopherogram	AOIN/FER/GRAM
ionophore	AOIN/FOER
	AOI/YON/FOER
ionophoresis	AOIN/FRAOE/SIS
	AOI/YON/FRAOE/SIS
ionophoretic	AOIN/FRET/IK
	AOI/YON/FRET/IK
ionophose	AOIN/FOEZ
ionoscope	AOIN/SKOEP
ionosphere	AOIN/SFAOER
ionotherapy	AOIN/THER/PI
ion-protein	AOIN/PRO/TAOEN
iontophoresis	AOI/ONT/FRAOE/SIS
	AOI/YONT/FRAOE/SIS
iontophoretic	AOI/ONT/FRET/IK
	AOI/YONT/FRET/IK
iontoquantimeter	AOI/ONT/KWAN/TIM/TER
	AOI/YONT/KWAN/TIM/TER
iontotherapy	AOI/ONT/THER/PI
	AOI/YONT/THER/PI
iopamidol	AOI/PAM/DOL
iopanoic	AOI/PA/NOIK
	AOI/PA/NOE/IK
iophendylate	AOI/FEND/LAIT
iophenoxic	AOI/FEN/OX/IK
iophobia	AOI/FOEB/YA
iopydol	AOI/PAOI/DOEL

iopydone	AOI/PAOI/DOEN	iridodonesis	IR/DO/DO/NAOE/SIS
iosefamic	AOI/SE/FAM/IK		IR/DO/DOE/NAOE/SIS
ioseric	AOI/SER/IK	iridokeratitis	IR/DO/KER/TAOITS
iosulamide	AOI/SUL/MAOID	iridokinesia	IR/DO/KI/NAOEZ/YA
iosumetic	AOI/SAOU/MET/IK	iridokinesis	IR/DO/KI/NAOE/SIS
iotacism	AOI/OET/SIFM	iridokinetic	IR/DO/KI/NET/IK
	AOI/YOET/SIFM	iridoleptynsis	IR/DO/LEP/TIN/SIS
iotetric	AOI/TET/RIK	iridology	IR/DOLG
iothalamate	AOI/THAL/MAIT	iridolysis	IR/DOL/SIS
iothalamic	AOI/THA/LAM/IK	iridomalacia	IR/DO/MA/LAI/SHA
iothiouracil	AOI/THAOI/YAOUR/SIL	iridomesodialysis	IR/DO/MES/DI/AL/SIS
iotroxic	AOI/YO/TROX/IK	iridomotor	IR/DO/MOE/TOR
Io-Tuss	AOI/YO/TUSZ	iridoncosis	IR/DON/KOE/SIS
ioxaglate	AOI/OX/AG/LAIT	iridoncus	IR/DON/KUS
ipecac	IP/KAK	iridoparalysis	IR/DO/PRAL/SIS
ipodate	AOIP/DAIT	iridopathy	IR/DOP/TH*I
Ipomoea	AOIP/MAOE/YA	iridoperiphakitis	IR/DO/P*ER/FAI/KAOITS
ipratropium	IP/RA/TROEP/YUM	iridoplegia	IR/DO/PLAOE/JA
iproniazid	AOI/PRO/NAOI/ZID	iridoptosis	IR/DOP/TOE/SIS
ipronidazole	AOI/PRO/NAOID/ZOEL	iridopupillary	IR/DO/PAOUP/LAIR
iproveratril	AOI/PRO/VER/TRIL	iridorrhexis	IR/DO/REK/SIS
ipsation	IP/SAIGS	iridoschisis	IR/DOS/KI/SIS
Ipsatol	IPS/TOL	iridosclerotomy	IR/DO/SKLE/ROT/M*I
	IP/SA/TOL	iridosteresis	IR/DO/STE/RAOE/SIS
ipsefact	IPS/FAKT	iridotasis	IR/DOT/SIS
	IP/SE/FAKT	iridotomy	IR/DOT/M*I
ipsilateral	IPS/LAT/RAL	Iridoviridae	IR/DO/VIR/DAE
	IP/SI/LAT/RAL	iridovirus	IR/DO/VAOI/RUS
ipsism	IP/SIFM	Iridovirus	K-P/IR/DO/VAOI/RUS
irascibility	IR/RAS/-BLT	irigenin	IR/JEN/NIN
Ircon	IR/KON	iris	AOI/RIS
Ircon-FA	IR/KON/F-RBGS/A*RBGS	Iris	K-P/AOI/RIS
irid(o)-	IR/D(O)	irisin	AOIR/SIN
iridal	AOIR/DAL	irisopsia	AOIR/SOPS/YA
	IR/DAL		AOI/RIS/OPS/YA
iridalgia	AOIR/RI/DAL/JA	iritic	AOI/RIT/IK
iridauxesis	IR/DAUK/ZAOE/SIS	iritides	AOI/RIT/DAOEZ
	IR/ID/AUK/ZAOE/SIS	iritis	AOI/RAOITS
iridectasis	IR/DEKT/SIS	iritoectomy	AOIR/TO/EKT/M*I
iridectome	IR/DEK/TOEM	iritomy	AOI/RIT/M*I
iridectomesodialysis	IR/DEKT/MES/DI/AL/SIS	irium	IR/YUM
iridectomize	IR/DEKT/MAOIZ	iron	AOIRN
iridectomy	IR/DEKT/M*I	Iromin	AOIR/MIN
iridectopia	IR/DEK/TOEP/YA		AOI/RO/MIN
iridectropium	IR/DEK/TROEP/YUM	Iromin-G	AOIR/MIN/G-RBGS
iridemia	IR/DAOEM/YA		AOI/RO/MIN/G-RBGS
iridencleisis	IR/DEN/KLAOI/SIS	Irospan	AOIR/SPAN
iridentropium	IR/DEN/TROEP/YUM		AOI/RO/SPAN
irideremia	IR/DER/AOEM/YA	irotomy	AOI/ROT/M*I
	AOIR/DAOEM/YA	irradiate	IR/RAID/YAIT
irides	IR/DAOEZ	irradiation	IR/RAID/YAIGS
iridescence	IR/DES/ENS	irrational	IR/RAGS/NAL
iridescent	IR/DES/ENT	irreducible	IR/RE/DAOUS/-BL
iridesis	AOIR/DAOE/SIS	irregular	IR/REG/LAR
	AOI/RID/SIS		IR/REG
	IR/DAOE/SIS	irregularity	IR/REG/LAR/TI
iridial	AOI/RID/YAL		IR/REG/TI
	IR/RID/YAL	irreinoculability	IR/RE/IN/OK/LABLT
iridian	AOI/RID/YAN	irrespirable	IR/RE/SPAOIRBL
	IR/RID/YAN		IR/RE/SPAOIR/-BL
iridic	AOI/RID/IK	irresponsibility	IR/SPONS/-BLT
	IR/RID/IK		IR/RE/SPONS/-BLT
iridin	IR/DIN	irresuscitable	IR/RE/SUS/TABL
	IR/RI/DIN	irreversibility	IR/VERS/-BLT
iridis	IR/DIS		IR/RE/VERS/-BLT
	AOIR/DIS	irreversible	IR/VERS/-BL
iridium	AOI/RID/YUM		IR/RE/VERS/-BL
	IR/RID/YUM	irrig-	IR/G-
iridization	IR/DI/ZAIGS		IR/RI/G-
irido-	IR/DO	irrigate	IR/GAIT
iridoavulsion	IR/DO/AI/VULGS	irrigation	IR/GAIGS
iridocapsulitis	IR/DO/KAPS/LAOITS	irrigator	IR/GAI/TOR
iridocele	IR/DO/SAO*EL	irrigoradioscopy	IR/GO/RAID/YOS/KPI
iridochoroiditis	IR/DO/KOE/ROI/DAOITS	irrigoscopy	IR/GOS/KPI
iridocoloboma	IR/DO/KOL/BOE/MA	irrit-	IRT
iridoconstrictor	IR/DO/KON/STRIK/TOR		IR/RIT
iridocorneal	IR/DO/KORN/YAL	irritability	IRT/-BLT
iridocornealis	IR/DO/KORN/YAI/LIS	irritable	IRT/-BL
iridocorneosclerectomy	IR/DO/KORN/YO/SKLE/REKT/M*I	irritant	IR/TANT
iridocyclectomy	IR/DO/SAOI/KLEKT/M*I	irritation	IR/TAIGS
iridocyclitis	IR/DO/SAOI/KLAOITS	irritans	IR/TANZ
iridocyclochoroiditis	IR/DO/SAOI/KLO/KOE/ROI/ DAOITS	irritative	IR/TAIT/IV
		irrumation	IR/RAOU/MAIGS
iridocystectomy	IR/DO/SIS/TEKT/M*I	irruption	IR/RUPGS
iridodesis	IR/DOD/SIS	irruptive	IR/RUPT/IV
iridodiagnosis	IR/DO/DAOIG/NOE/SIS	Isaacs	AOI/ZAKS
iridodialysis	IR/DO/DI/AL/SIS		AOI/SAKS
iridodiastasis	IR/DO/DI/A*S/SIS	Isambert	E/ZAUM/BAIR
iridodilator	IR/DO/DI/LAI/TOR		E/SAM/BAIR

isauxesis	AOI/SAUK/ZAOE/SIS	Ismelin	IS/-M (*not in* CAT)
	IS/AUK/ZAOE/SIS		IZ/ME/LIN
ische-	IS/KAOE		IS/ME/LIN
-ischemia	IS/KAOEM/YA	-ismus	IZ/MUS
ischemic	IS/KAOEM/IK	iso-	AOIS
	IS/KEM/IK		AOI/SO
ischesis	IS/KAOE/SIS	isoadrenocorticism	AOIS/AI/DRAOEN/KORT/SIFM
	IS/KE/SIS	isoagglutination	AOIS/AI/GLAOUT/NAIGS
ischi(o)-	IS/K(O)	isoagglutinin	AOIS/AI/GLAOUT/NIN
	IS/KAOE	isoagglutinogen	AOIS/AG/LAOU/TIN/JEN
	IS/KAOE/Y(O)		AOIS/AI/GLAOU/TIN/JEN
ischia	IS/KAOE/YA	isoallele	AOIS/AI/LAOEL
	IS/KA		AOIS/AL/LAOEL
ischiac	IS/KAOE/AK	isoalloxazine	AOIS/AI/LOX/ZAOEN
	IS/KAK		AOIS/AL/LOX/ZAOEN
ischiadic	IS/KAD/IK	isoamidone	AOIS/AM/DOEN
	IS/KAOE/AD/IK	isoaminile	AOIS/AM/NAOIL
ischiadica	IS/KAD/KA	isoamyl-	AOIS/AM/IL
	IS/KAOE/AD/KA		AOIS/AM/L-
ischiadici	IS/KAD/SAOI	isoamylamine	AOIS/AM/IL/AM/MIN
	IS/KAOE/AD/SAOI		AOIS/AM/LAM/MIN
ischiadicus	IS/KAD/KUS	isoamylase	AOIS/AM/LAIS
	IS/KAOE/AD/KUS	isoamylbarbituric	AOIS/AM/IL/BARB/TAOUR/IK
ischial	IS/KAL	isoamylhydrocupreine	AOIS/AM/IL/HAOI/DRO/KAOU/
	IS/KAOE/YAL		PRAOEN
ischialgia	IS/KAL/JA		AOIS/AM/IL/HAOI/DRO/KAOUP/
	IS/KAOE/AL/JA		RAOEN
ischias	IS/KAOE/YAS	isoamyl nitrate	AOIS/AM/IL/NAOI/TRAIT
	IS/KAS	isoanaphylaxis	AOIS/AN/FLAK/SIS
ischiatic	IS/KAT/IK	isoandrosterone	AOIS/AN/DRO*S/ROEN
	IS/KAOE/YAT/IK		AOIS/AN/DRO/STAOER/OEN
ischidrosis	IS/KI/DROE/SIS	isoantibody	AOIS/A*ENT/BOD/DI
	IS/KID/ROE/SIS	isoantigen	AOIS/A*ENT/JEN
ischiectomy	IS/KEKT/M*I	Iso-B	AOIS/B-RBGS
	IS/KAOE/EKT/M*I		AOI/SO/B-RBGS
ischii	IS/KAOI	isobar	AOIS/BAR
	IS/KAOE/YAOI	isobaric	AOIS/BAR/IK
ischio-	IS/KO	Iso-Bid	AOIS/BID
	IS/KAOE/YO	isobody	AOIS/BOD/DI
ischioanal	IS/KO/AINL	isobolism	AOI/SOB/LIFM
ischiobulbar	IS/KO/BUL/BAR	isobornyl	AOIS/BOR/NIL
ischiocapsular	IS/KO/KAPS/LAR		AOIS/BORNL
ischiocavernosus	IS/KO/KAVR/NOE/SUS	isobornyl thiocyanoacetate	AOIS/BOR/NIL/THAOI/SAOI/NO/
ischiocavernous	IS/KO/KAVR/NOUS		AS/TAIT
ischiocele	IS/KO/SAO*EL		AOIS/BORNL/THAOI/SAOI/NO/AS/
ischiococcygeal	IS/KO/KOK/SIJ/YAL		TAIT
ischiococcygeus	IS/KO/KOK/SIJ/YUS	isobucaine	AOIS/BAOU/KAIN
ischiodidymus	IS/KO/DID/MUS	isobutamben	AOIS/BAOU/TAM/BEN
ischiodymia	IS/KO/DIM/YA	isobutanol	AOIS/BAOUT/NOL
ischiodynia	IS/KO/DIN/YA	isobuteine	AOIS/BAOU/TAOEN
ischiofemoral	IS/KO/FEM/RAL		AOIS/BAOUT/YAOEN
ischiofibular	IS/KO/FIB/LAR	isobutyl	AOIS/BAOU/TIL
ischiogluteal	IS/KO/GLAOUT/YAL	isobutyric	AOIS/BAOU/TIR/IK
ischiohebotomy	IS/KO/HAOE/BOT/M*I	isobuzole	AOIS/BAOU/ZOEL
ischiomelus	IS/KOM/LUS	Isocal	AOIS/KAL
ischioneuralgia	IS/KO/NAOU/RAL/JA	isocaloric	AOIS/KA/LOR/IK
ischionitis	IS/KO/NAOITS	isocapnia	AOIS/KAP/NA
	IS/KAOE/NAOITS		AOIS/KAP/NAOE/YA
ischiopagia	IS/KO/PAI/JA	isocarboxazid	AOIS/KAR/BOX/ZID
ischiopagus	IS/KOP/GUS	isocarveol	AOIS/KAFRB/YOL
ischiopagy	IS/KOP/JI	isocellobiose	AOIS/SEL/BAO*I/OES
ischioperineal	IS/KO/P*ER/NAOEL	isocellular	AOIS/SEL/YAOU/LAR
ischioprostatic	IS/KO/PROS/TAT/IK	isocholesterin	AOIS/KL*ES/RIN
ischiopubic	IS/KO/PAOUB/IK	isocholesterol	AOIS/KL*ES/ROL
ischiorectal	IS/KO/REK/TAL	isochromatic	AOIS/KROE/MAT/IK
ischiorectalis	IS/KO/REK/TAI/LIS	isochromatophil	AOIS/KROE/MAT/FIL
ischiosacral	IS/KO/SAI/KRAL	isochromatophile	AOIS/KROE/MAT/FAOIL
ischiothoracopagus	IS/KO/THOR/KOP/GUS	isochromosome	AOIS/KROEM/SOEM
ischiotibial	IS/KO/TIB/YAL	isochron	AOIS/KRON
ischiovaginal	IS/KO/VAJ/NAL	isochronal	AOI/SOK/RO/NAL
ischiovertebral	IS/KO/VERT/BRAL	isochronia	AOIS/KROEN/YA
ischium	IS/KUM	isochronic	AOIS/KRON/IK
	IS/KAOE/UM	isochronism	AOI/SOK/RO/NIFM
ischochymia	IS/KO/KAOIM/YA	isochronous	AOI/SOK/RO/NOUS
ischogyria	IS/KO/JAOIR/YA	isochroous	AOI/SOK/ROUS
ischuretic	IS/KAOU/RET/IK	isocitrase	AOIS/SIT/RAIS
ischuria	IS/KAOUR/YA	isocitratase	AOIS/SIT/RA/TAIS
isethionate	AOIS/THAOI/NAIT	isocitrate	AOIS/SIT/RAIT
	IS/*ET/AOI/NAIT	isocitric	AOIS/SIT/RIK
isethionic	AOIS/THAOI/YON/IK	isocitritase	AOIS/SIT/RI/TAIS
	AOIS/THAOI/ON/IK	isocline	AOIS/KLAOIN
Ishihara	IRB/HA/RA	isocoagulase	AOIS/KO/AG/LAIS
isinglass	AOI/SIN/GLASZ	isocolloid	AOIS/KLOID
island	AOI/LAND		AOIS/KOL/OID
islet	AOI/LET	isocomplement	AOIS/KOM/PLEMT
	AOIL/ET	isocomplementophilic	AOIS/KOM/PLEMT/FIL/IK
islets of Langerhans	AOI/LET/-S/OF/LANG/ER/HANZ	isoconazole	AOIS/KON/ZOEL
	AOI/LET/-S/OF/LANG/ER/HANZ		AOIS/KOEN/ZOEL
-ism	IFM	isocoria	AOIS/KOER/YA

isocortex	AOIS/KOR/TEX	isomethadone	AOIS/M*ET/DOEN
isocyanate	AOIS/SAOI/NAIT	isometheptene	AOIS/M*ET/EP/TAOEN
isocyanic	AOIS/SAOI/NIK	isometric	AOIS/MET/RIK
	AOIS/SAOI/YAN/IK	isometropia	AOIS/ME/TROEP/YA
isocyanide	AOIS/SAOI/NAOID	isometry	AOI/SOM/TRI
isocyanin	AOIS/SAOI/NIN	isomicrogamete	AOIS/MAOI/KRO/GAM/AOET
isocyclic	AOIS/SAOIK/LIK	Isomil	AOIS/MIL
isocytolysin	AOIS/SAOI/TOL/SIN	isomorphic	AOIS/MOR/FIK
isocytosis	AOIS/SAOI/TOE/SIS	isomorphism	AOIS/MOR/FIFM
isocytotoxin	AOIS/SAOIT/TOK/SIN	isomorphous	AOIS/MOR/FOUS
isodactylism	AOIS/DAKT/LIFM	isomuscarine	AOIS/MUS/KRIN
isodense	AOIS/DENS	isomylamine	AOIS/MIL/MAOEN
isodesmosine	AOIS/DEZ/MO/SAOEN	isonaphthol	AOIS/NAF/THOL
isodiagnosis	AOIS/DAOIG/NOE/SIS	isoncotic	AOI/SON/KOT/IK
isodiametric	AOIS/DAOI/MET/RIK	isonephrotoxin	AOIS/NEF/RO/TOK/SIN
isodispersoid	AOIS/DIS/PER/SOID	isoniazid	AOIS/NAOI/ZID
	AOIS/DIS/PERS/OID	isonicotinic	AOIS/NIK/TIN/IK
isodontic	AOIS/DONT/IK	isonipecaine	AOIS/NIP/KAIN
isodose	AOIS/DOES	isonitrile	AOIS/NAOI/TRIL
isodulcit	AOIS/DUL/SIT	isonitrosoacetone	AOIS/NAOI/TROES/AS/TOEN
isodulcite	AOIS/DUL/SAOIT	isonormocytosis	AOIS/NORM/SAOI/TOE/SIS
isodynamic	AOIS/DAOI/NAM/IK		AOIS/NOR/MO/SAOI/TOE/SIS
isodynamogenic	AOIS/DAOIN/MO/JEN/IK	iso-oncotic	AOIS/ON/KOT/IK
	AOIS/DAOI/NAM/JEN/IK	iso-osmotic	AOIS/OZ/MOT/IK
isoeffect	AOIS/EFKT	isopathy	AOI/SOP/TH*I
isoelectric	AOIS/LEK/TRIK	isopentyl	AOIS/PEN/TIL
isoenergetic	AOIS/EN/ER/JET/IK	isoperistaltic	AOIS/P*ER/STALT/IK
isoenzyme	AOIS/EN/ZAOIM	isophagy	AOI/SOF/JI
isoerythrolysis	AOIS/R*IT/ROL/SIS	isophan	AOIS/FAN
	AOIS/E/R*IT/ROL/SIS	isophenolization	AOIS/FAOE/NOL/ZAIGS
	AOIS/*ER/THROL/SIS	isophoria	AOIS/FOER/YA
isoetharine	AOIS/*ET/RAOEN	isophotometer	AOIS/FOE/TOM/TER
isofluorphate	AOIS/FLAOUR/FAIT	isopia	AOI/SOEP/YA
isoflupredone	AOIS/FLAOU/PRE/DOEN	isoplassont	AOIS/PLAS/SONT
isoflurane	AOIS/FLAOU/RAIN	isoplastic	AOIS/PLA*S/IK
isogamete	AOIS/GAM/AOET	isopleth	AOIS/PL*ET
isogametic	AOIS/GA/MET/IK	isopotential	AOIS/POE/TEN/-RBL
isogamety	AOIS/GAM/TI	isoprecipitin	AOIS/PRE/SIP/TIN
isogamous	AOI/SOG/MOUS	isoprenaline	AOIS/PREN/LAOEN
isogamy	AOI/SOG/M*I	isoprene	AOIS/PRAOEN
isogeneic	AOIS/JE/NAOE/IK	isoprenoid	AOIS/PRAOEN/OID
	AOIS/JE/NAI/IK	isopropamide	AOIS/PROEP/MAOID
isogeneric	AOIS/JE/NER/IK	isopropanol	AOIS/PROEP/NOL
isogenesis	AOIS/JEN/SIS	isoprophenamine	AOIS/PRO/FEN/MAOEN
isogenic	AOIS/JEN/IK	isopropyl	AOIS/PRO/PIL
isogenous	AOI/SOJ/NOUS	isopropylarterenol	AOIS/PRO/PIL/AR/TAOER/NOL
isogentiobiose	AOIS/JEN/SHO/BAO*I/OES		AOIS/PRO/PIL/AR/TER/NOL
isoglutamine	AOIS/GLAOUT/MAOEN	isopropyl-benzanthracene	AOIS/PRO/PIL/BENZ/AN/THRA/
isoglyceryl	AOIS/GLIS/RIL		SAOEN
isognathous	AOI/SOG/NA/THOUS	isopropylcarbinol	AOIS/PRO/PIL/KARB/NOL
isograft	AOIS/GRAFT	isopropyl myristate	AOIS/PRO/PIL/MIR/IS/TAIT
isohemagglutination	AOIS/HAOEM/GLAOUT/NAIGS	isopropylthiogalactoside	AOIS/PRO/PIL/THAOI/GLAKT/
	AOIS/HEM/GLAOUT/NAIGS		SAOID
isohemagglutinin	AOIS/HAOEM/GLAOUT/NIN	isoproterenol	AOIS/PRO/TER/NOL
	AOIS/HEM/GLAOUT/NIN	isopter	AOI/SOPT/ER
isohemolysin	AOIS/HAOE/MOL/SIN		AOI/SOP/TER
isohemolysis	AOIS/HAOE/MOL/SIS	Isoptin	AOI/SOP/TIN
isohemolytic	AOIS/HAOEM/LIT/IK	isopyknic	AOIS/P*IK/NIK
isohydric	AOIS/HAOI/DRIK		AOIS/PIK/NIK
isohydruria	AOIS/HAOI/DRAOUR/YA	isopyknosis	AOIS/PIK/NOE/SIS
isohypercytosis	AOIS/HAO*IP/SAOI/TOE/SIS		AOIS/P*IK/NOE/SIS
isohypocytosis	AOIS/HO*IP/SAOI/TOE/SIS	isopyknotic	AOIS/PIK/NOT/IK
isoiconia	AOIS/AOI/KOEN/YA		AOIS/P*IK/NOT/IK
isoiconic	AOIS/AOI/KON/IK	isopyrocalciferol	AOIS/PAOIR/KAL/SIF/ROL
isoimmunization	AOIS/IM/NI/ZAIGS	isoquinoline	AOIS/KWIN/LAOEN
isolactose	AOIS/LAK/TOES	Isordil	AOI/SOR/DIL
isolate	AOIS/LAIT	isoriboflavin	AOIS/RAOIB/FLAIVN
isolation	AOIS/LAIGS	isorrhea	AOIS/RAOE/YA
isolator	AOIS/LAI/TOR	isorrheic	AOIS/RAOE/IK
isolecithal	AOIS/LES/THAL	isorrhopic	AOIS/ROP/IK
isoleucine	AOIS/LAOU/SIN	isorubin	AOIS/RAOU/BIN
isoleucyl	AOIS/LAOU/SIL	isosbestic	AOI/SOS/B*ES/IK
isoleukoagglutinin	AOIS/LAOUK/AI/GLAOUT/NIN	isoscope	AOIS/SKOEP
	AOIS/LAOUK/GLAOUT/NIN	isosensitization	AOIS/SENS/TI/ZAIGS
isologous	AOI/SOL/GOUS	isosensitize	AOIS/SENS/TAOIZ
isolysin	AOI/SOL/SIN	isoserotherapy	AOIS/SAOER/THER/PI
isolysis	AOI/SOL/SIS	isoserum	AOIS/SAOERM
isolytic	AOI/SLIT/IK	isosexual	AOIS/SEX/YAOUL
isomaltase	AOIS/MAL/TAIS	isosmotic	AOI/SOZ/MOT/IK
isomaltose	AOIS/MAL/TOES		AOI/SOS/MOT/IK
isomastigote	AOIS/MA*S/GOET	isosmoticity	AOI/SOZ/MO/TIS/TI
isomer	AOIS/MER		AOI/SOS/MO/TIS/TI
isomerase	AOI/SOM/RAIS	isosorbide	AOIS/SOR/BAOID
isomeric	AOIS/MER/IK	isospermotoxin	AOIS/SPERM/TOK/SIN
isomeride	AOI/SOM/RAOID	Isospora	AOI/SOS/PRA
isomerism	AOI/SOM/RIFM	isospore	AOIS/SPOER
isomerization	AOI/SOM/RAOI/ZAIGS	isosporiasis	AOI/SOS/PRAOI/SIS
	AOI/SOM/RI/ZAIGS	isosporous	AOI/SOS/PROUS
isomerous	AOI/SOM/ROUS	isostere	AOIS/STAOER

isosthenuria	AOI/SOS/THAOE/NAOUR/YA	ivory	AOI/VER/MEK/TIN
	AOI/SOS/THE/NAOUR/YA	ivory	AOIV/RI
	AOIS/STHAOE/NAOUR/YA	ivy	AOI/VI
isostimulation	AOIS/STIM/LAIGS	Ivy	K-P/AOI/VI
isosuccinic	AOIS/SUK/SIN/IK	Ixodes	IK/SOE/DAOEZ
isosulfamerazine	AOIS/SUL/FA/MER/ZAOEN	ixodiasis	IX/DAOI/SIS
isosulfan	AOIS/SUL/FAN	ixodic	IK/SOD/IK
isotherapy	AOIS/THER/PI	ixodid	IX/DID
isotherm	AOIS/THERM	Ixodidae	IK/SOD/DAE
isothermal	AOIS/THER/MAL	Ixodides	IK/SOD/DAOEZ
isothermic	AOIS/THERM/IK	Ixodiphagus	IX/DIF/GUS
isothermognosis	AOIS/THERM/NOE/SIS	ixodism	IX/DIFM
isothiocyanate	AOIS/THAOI/SAOI/NAIT	Ixodoidea	IX/DO/ID/YA
isothipendyl	AOIS/THAOI/PEN/DIL	ixomyelitis	IX/MAOI/LAOITS
isotone	AOIS/TOEN	Izar	AOI/ZAR
isotonia	AOIS/TOEN/YA	-ize	AOIZ
isotonic	AOIS/TON/IK		
isotonicity	AOIS/TOE/NIS/TI		
isotope	AOIS/TOEP		
isotopic	AOIS/TOP/IK		
isotopology	AOIS/TOE/POLG		
isotoxic	AOIS/TOX/IK		
isotoxin	AOIS/TOK/SIN		
isotransplant	AOIS/TRA*NS/PLANT		
isotransplantation	AOIS/TRA*NS/PLAN/TAIGS		
isotretinoin	AOIS/TRET/NOIN		
isotrimorphism	AOIS/TR*I/MOR/FIFM		
isotrimorphous	AOIS/TR*I/MOR/FOUS		
isotron	AOIS/TRON		
isotropic	AOIS/TROP/IK		
isotropous	AOI/SOT/RO/POUS		
isotropy	AOI/SOT/RO/PI		
isotype	AOIS/TAOIP		
isotypic	AOIS/TIP/IK		
isotypical	AOIS/TIP/KAL		
isouretin	AOIS/YAOU/RAOE/TIN		
isovaleric	AOIS/VA/LER/IK		
isovalericacidemia	AOIS/VA/LER/IK/AS/DAOEM/YA		
isovalthine	AOIS/VAL/THAOEN		
Isovex	AOIS/VEX		
isovolume	AOIS/VOL/YAOUM		
isovolumetric	AOIS/VOL/MET/RIK		
	AOIS/VOL/YAOU/MET/RIK		
isovolumic	AOIS/VOL/YAOUM/IK		
isoxsuprine	AOI/SOX/SAOU/PRAOEN		
isozyme	AOIS/ZAOIM		
issue	IRB/SHAOU		
israelii	IZ/RAIL/YAOI		
	IS/RAIL/YAOI		
isthmectomy	IS/MEKT/M*I		
isthmi	IS/MAOI		
isthmian	IS/MAOE/YAN		
isthmic	IS/MIK		
isthmitis	IS/MAOITS		
isthmoparalysis	IS/MO/PRAL/SIS		
isthmoplegia	IS/MO/PLAOE/JA		
isthmospasm	IS/MO/SPAFM		
isthmus	IS/MUS		
Isuprel	AOIS/PREL		
	AOI/SAOU/PREL		
	AOI/SU/PREL		
isuria	AOI/SAOUR/YA		
itaconic	IT/KON/IK		
italicus	AOI/TAL/KUS		
	IT/TAL/KUS		
Itard	E/TAR		
itate	AOI/TAIT		
itch	IFP		
itching	IFP/-G		
-ite	(C)AOIT		
iter	AOIT/ER		
	AOI/TER		
iteral	AOIT/RAL		
iteroparity	IT/RO/PAIR/TI		
iteroparous	IT/ROP/ROUS		
-ites	(c)AOI/TAOEZ		
ithycyphosis	*IT/SAOI/FOE/SIS		
ithykyphosis	*IT/KAOI/FOE/SIS		
ithylordosis	*IT/LOR/DOE/SIS		
ithyokyphosis	*IT/YO/KAOI/FOE/SIS		
-itides	(c)IT/DAOEZ		
-itis	(c)AOITS		
	(c)AOI/TIS		
Ito	E/TOE		
itramin	AOI/TRA/MIN		
IUD	IRBGS/*URBGS/D*RBGS		
IV	IRBGS/V*RBGS		
I.V.	IFPLT;V*FPLT		
ivermectin	AOIVR/MEK/TIN		

J

Jaboulay	JAB/LAI
	JA/BAOU/LAI
Jaccoud	JA/KAOU
	JA/KAOUD
jacket	JAKT
	JAK/ET
jackscrew	JAK/SKRAOU
Jackson	JAK/SON
jacksonian	JAK/SOEN/YAN
Jacob	JA/KOB
	JAI/KOB
	JAIK/OB
Jacobaeus	YAK/BAI/YUS
	JAK/BAI/YUS
jacobine	JAIK/BIN
Jacobson	JAI/KOB/SON
	JAIK/OB/SON
jacobsoni	JAI/KOB/SOE/NAOI
	JAIK/OB/SOE/NAOI
Jacquart	JA/KART
	JAK/KART
Jacquet	JA/KAI
	JAK/KAI
jactatio	JAK/TAI/SHOE
	JAK/TAIRB/YOE
jactation	JAK/TAIGS
jactitation	JAKT/TAIGS
	JAK/TI/TAIGS
jaculiferous	JAK/LIF/ROUS
Jadassohn	YAD/SOEN
	YA/DAS/SOEN
Jaeger	YAIG/ER
	YAI/GER
Jaffe	JA/FAI
	JAF/FAI
Jakob	YAK/OB
Jaksch	YAK/-RB
jalap	JAL/AP
James	JAIMZ
	JAIMS
Janet	JA/NAI
	JAN/ET
Janeway	JAIN/WAI
janiceps	JAN/SEPS
Janimine	JAN/MAOIN
	JAN/MAOEN
Janosik	YAN/SIK
Jansen	YAN/SEN
	JAN/SEN
Jansky	YAN/SKI
	JAN/SKI
Janus	JAN/NUS
	JAI/NUS
Japanese	JAP/NAOEZ
jar	JAR
jargon	JAR/GON
jargonaphasia	JAR/GON/FAIZ/YA
Jarisch	YA/RIRB
Jarjavay	JAR/JA/VAI
	JARJ/VAI
Jarvis	JAR/VIS
jasmine	JAZ/MIN
Jatropha	JAT/RO/FA
	JA/TROE/FA
jaundice	JAUN/DIS
jaw	JAU
jawbone	JAU/BOEN
Jaworski	YA/WOR/SKAOE
	JA/WOR/SKAOE
jealous	JEL/OUS
Jeanselme	JAN/SEL/-M
	JA/SEL/-M
jecoris	JEK/RIS
jecorize	JEK/RAOIZ
jecur	JEK/UR
	JAOE/KUR
Jeddah	JED/DA
jejun(o)-	JEJ/N(O)
	JE/JAOUN
	JE/JAOU/N(O)
jejunal	JE/JAOUNL
jejunales	JEJ/NAI/LAOEZ
jejunectomy	JEJ/NEKT/M*I
jejunitis	JEJ/NAOITS

jejunocecostomy	JE/JAOUN/SE/KO*S/M*I
jejunocolostomy	JE/JAOUN/KO/LO*S/M*I
jejunoileal	JE/JAOUN/*IL/YAL
jejunoileitis	JE/JAOUN/*IL/YAOITS
jejunoileostomy	JE/JAOUN/*IL/YO*S/M*I
jejunojejunostomy	JE/JAOUN/JEJ/NO*S/M*I
jejunoplasty	JE/JAOUN/PLAS/TI
jejunorrhaphy	JEJ/NOR/FI
jejunostomy	JEJ/NO*S/M*I
jejunotomy	JEJ/NOT/M*I
jejunum	JE/JAOUN/UM
	JE/JAOU/NUM
jell	J*EL
	(not JEL; see gel)
Jellinek	YEL/NEK
jellisoni	JEL/SOE/NAOI
jelly	JEL/LI
Jendrassik	YEN/DRAS/IK
	YEN/DRAS/SIK
Jenner	JEN/ER
jennerian	JEN/NAOERN
	JEN/NAOER/YAN
	JEN/NER/YAN
jennerization	JEN/RI/ZAIGS
Jensen	YEN/SEN
	JEN/SEN
Jericho	JER/KOE
jerk	JERK
Jevity	JEV/TI
Jewett	JAOU/ET
	JAOU/WET
jigger	JIG/ER
jimson weed	JIM/SON/WAOED
Jobert	JOE/BAIR
Jocasta	JOE/KAS/TA
Jochmann	YOEK/MAN
jodbasedow	YOD/BAS/DOE
Jod-Basedow	YOD/H-F/BAS/DOE
Joffroy	JOF/ROI
Johansson	YOE/HAN/3ON
	JOE/HAN/SON
Johne	YOE/NAOE
johnin	YOE/NIN
Johnson	JON/SON
Johnson-Stevens	JON/SON/H-F/STAOEVNS
joint	JOINT
joint mice	JOINT/MAOIS
Jolles	YOL/LES
Jolly	YOE/LI
	YOE/LAOE
Jonas	YOE/NAS
	JOE/NAS
Jones	JOENZ
	JOENS
Jonnesco	YOE/NES/KOE
	JOE/NES/KOE
Jonston	JON/STON
Joseph	YOE/SEF
	YOES/EF
	JOE/SEF
	JOES/EF
joule	JAO*UL
	(not JAOUL; see jewel)
Joule	K-P/JAO*UL
juccuya	YAOU/KAOU/YA
juga	JAOU/GA
jugal	JAOU/GAL
jugale	JAOU/GAI/LAOE
jugate	JAOU/GAIT
jugomaxillary	JAOU/GO/MAX/LAIR
jugul-	JUG/L-
	JUG/YAOU/L-
	JUG/YU/L-
jugular	JUG/LAR
jugularis	JUG/LAI/RIS
jugulation	JUG/LAIGS
juguli	JUG/LAOI
jugulum	JUG/LUM
jugum	JAOU/GUM
juice	JAOUS
Jukes	JAOUKS
julep	JAOUL/EP
	JAOU/LEP
jumentous	JAOU/MEN/TOUS
	JAOUMT/OUS
jump	JUFRP
jumping	JUFRP/-G
jumpy	JUM/PI
junction	JUNGS

junctional	JUNGS/NAL
junctura	JUNG/KHUR/RA
	JUNG/TAOU/RA
	JUNG/TUR/RA
juncturae	JUNG/KHUR/RAE
	JUNG/TAOU/RAE
	JUNG/TU/RAE
juncture	JUNG/KHUR
Jung	YAOUNG
	Y*UNG
	JUNG
	(not YUNG; see young)
Jungbluth	YAOUNG/BLAOUT
jungian	YAOUNG/YAN
	Y*UNG/YAN
jungle	JUNG/-L
Jungling	YENG/LING
	YENG/-LG
juniper	JAOUN/PER
Juniperus	JAOU/NIP/RUS
junk	JUN/-K
Junker	K-P/JUN/KER
Junod	JAOU/NOED
	(not JAOU/NOE; see Juneau)
jurisprudence	JURS/PRAOUD/ENS
	JURS/PRAOU/DENS
	JAOURS/PRAOUD/ENS
	JAOURS/PRAOU/DENS
jusculum	JUS/KLUM
justifiable	J*US/FIBL
justo major	JUS/TOE/MAI/JOR
justo minor	JUS/TOE/MAOI/NOR
jute	JAOUT
juvantia	JAOU/VAN/SHA
juvantibus	JAOU/VANT/BUS
juvenile	JAOUV/NAOIL
	JAOUV/NIL
juvenilis	JAOUV/NAOI/LIS
juxta-	J*UX
	JUX/TA
juxta-articular	J*UX/AR/TIK/LAR
juxtaepiphysial	J*UX/EP/FIZ/YAL
juxtaglomerular	J*UX/GLOE/MER/LAR
juxtallocortex	JUX/TAL/KOR/TEX
	JUS/TAL/LO/KOR/TEX
juxtangina	JUX/TAN/JI/NA
	JUX/TAN/JAOI/NA
juxtaposition	J*UX/POGS
juxtapyloric	J*UX/PAOI/LOR/IK
juxtarestiform	J*UX/R*ES/FORM
juxtaspinal	J*UX/SPAOINL
juxtavesical	J*UX/VES/KAL

K

Kabikinase	KAB/KAOI/NAIS
Kabolin	KAB/LIN
kabure	KA/BAOU/RAOE
	KA/BAOUR/RAOE
Kaes	KIZ
Kagami	KA/GAM/MAOE
	KA/GA/MAOE
kaiserling	KAOIZ/ER/-LG
	KAOIZ/ER/LING
Kaiserling	K-P/KAOIZ/ER/-LG
	K-P/KAOIZ/ER/LING
kakidrosis	KAK/DROE/SIS
kalemia	KLAOEM/YA
	KA/LAOEM/YA
kalemic	KLAOEM/IK
	KA/LAOEM/IK
kali	KAI/LAOI
	KAL/LAOE
kaliemia	KAIL/YAOEM/YA
	KAIL/AOEM/YA
kaligenous	KAI/LIJ/NOUS
	KA/LIJ/NOUS
kalimeter	KA/LIM/TER
kaliopenia	KAIL/YO/PAOEN/YA
kaliopenic	KAIL/YO/PAOEN/IK
kalium	KAIL/YUM
kaliuresis	KAIL/YAOU/RAOE/SIS
kaliuretic	KAIL/YAOU/RET/IK
kallidin	KAL/DIN
Kallikak	KAL/KAK
kallikrein	KAL/KRAOE/YIN
Kallmann	KAL/MAN
Kalmia	KAL/MAOE/YA
Kalmuk	KAL/MAOUK
	KAL/MUK
kaluresis	KAL/YAOU/RAOE/SIS
kaluretic	KAL/YAOU/RET/IK
Kaminer	KAM/NER
kanamycin	KAN/MAOI/SIN
Kandinsky	KAN/DIN/SKI
kangaroo	KANG/RAO
kansasiin	KAN/SAS/YIN
Kantrex	KAN/TREX
Kantrex Capsules	KAN/TREX/KAP/SAOUL/-S
Kantrex Injection	KAN/TREX/IN/J*EBGS
kao-	KAI
	KAI/YO
Kaochlor	KAI/KLOR
Kaochlor S-F	KAI/KLOR/S-RBGS/F-RBGS
kaolin	KAI/LIN
kaolinosis	KAI/LI/NOE/SIS
	KAI/LIN/O/SIS
Kaolin-Pectin Suspension	KAI/LIN/PEK/TIN/SUS/PENGS
Kaon	KAI/YON
Kaon Cl	KAI/YON/KR-RBGS/L*
Kaon Cl-10	KAI/YON/KR-RBGS/L*/10
Kaon Cl-20	KAI/YON/KR-RBGS/L*/20
Kaopectate	KAI/PEK/TAIT
Kaplan	KAP/LAN
Kaposi	KA/POE/SAOE
	KAP/SAOE
kappa	KAP/PA
kappacism	KAP/SIFM
	KAP/PA/SIFM
Karell	KA/REL
	KAR/EL
Karmen	KAR/MEN
	KARM/-N
Karnofsky	KAR/NOF/SKI
Kartagener	KAR/TAG/NER
	KAR/TAJ/NER
kary(o)-	KAR/Y(O)
karyapsis	KAR/YAP/SIS
	KAR/AP/SIS
karyenchyma	KAR/YENG/MA
	KAR/ENG/MA
karyochromatophil	KAR/YO/KROE/MAT/FIL
karyochrome	KAR/YO/KROEM
karyochylema	KAR/YO/KAOI/LAOE/MA
karyoclasis	KAR/YOK/LA/SIS
karyoclastic	KAR/YO/KLA*S/IK
karyocyte	KAR/YO/SAO*IT
karyogamic	KAR/YO/GAM/IK
karyogamy	KAR/YOG/M*I

karyogen	KAR/YO/JEN
karyogenesis	KAR/YO/JEN/SIS
karyogenic	KAR/YO/JEN/IK
karyogonad	KAR/YO/GOE/NAD
karyogram	KAR/YO/GRAM
karyokinesis	KAR/YO/KI/NAOE/SIS
karyokinetic	KAR/YO/KI/NET/IK
karyolobic	KAR/YO/LOEB/IK
karyology	KAR/YOLG
karyolymph	KAR/YO/LIM/-F
karyolysis	KAR/YOL/SIS
karyolytic	KAR/YO/LIT/IK
karyomegaly	KAR/YO/MEG/LI
karyomere	KAR/YO/MAOER
karyometry	KAR/YOM/TRI
karyomicrosome	KAR/YO/MAOI/KRO/SOEM
karyomit	KAR/YO/MIT
karyomitome	KAR/YOM/TOEM
karyomitosis	KAR/YO/MAOI/TOE/SIS
karyomitotic	KAR/YO/MAOI/TOT/IK
karyomorphism	KAR/YO/MOR/FIFM
karyon	KAR/YON
	(*not* KAIR/YON; see carrion)
karyophage	KAR/YO/FALJ
karyoplasm	KAR/YO/PLAFM
karyoplasmic	KAR/YO/PLAZ/MIK
karyoplasmolysis	KAR/YO/PLAZ/MOL/SIS
karyoplast	KAR/YO/PLA*S
karyoplastin	KAR/YO/PLAS/TIN
karyopyknosis	KAR/YO/PIK/NOE/SIS
karyopyknotic	KAR/YO/PIK/NOT/IK
karyoreticulum	KAR/YO/RE/TIK/LUM
karyorrhectic	KAR/YO/REKT/IK
karyorrhexis	KAR/YO/REK/SIS
-karyosis	KAR/YOE/SIS
karyosome	KAR/YO/SOEM
karyospherical	KAR/YO/SFAOER/KAL
karyostasis	KAR/YO*S/SIS
karyota	KAR/YOE/TA
-karyote	KAR/YOET
karyotheca	KAR/YO/THAOE/KA
karyotin	KAR/YO/TIN
karyotype	KAR/YO/TAOIP
karyotypic	KAR/YO/TIP/IK
karyozoic	KAR/YO/ZOIK
	KAR/YO/ZOE/IK
kasai	KA/SAOI
kasal	KAI/SAL
Kasof	KAI/SOF
katachromasis	KAT/KROEM/SIS
katal	KAT/TAL
	KA/TAL
katathermometer	KAT/THER/MOM/TER
Katayama	KAT/YA/MA
katine	KAI/TIN
Kato	KAI/TOE
katolysis	KA/TOL/SIS
Katz	KATS
katzenjammer	KAT/SEN/JAM/ER
	KATS/EN/JAM/ER
	KATS/JAM/ER
Kawasaki	KA/WA/SA/KAOE
Kay	KAI
Kay Ciel	KAI/SAOE/EL
Kayexalate	KAI/EX/LAIT
Kayser	KAOIZ/ER
Kazanjian	KA/ZAN/JAN
K-Dur	K-RBGS/DUR
Keating-Hart	KAOET/-G/HART
kebocephaly	KEB/SEF/LI
keel	KAOEL
Keeley	KAOE/LAOE
Keen	K-P/KAOEN
	KAO*EN
Keflet	KEF/LET
Keflex	KEF/LEX
Keflin	KEF/LIN
Keftab	KEF/TAB
Kefurox	KEF/ROX
	KEF/YAOU/ROX
Kefzol	KEF/ZOL
keirospasm	KAO*IR/SPAFM
	(not KAOIR/SPAFM; see cheirospasm)
Keith	KAO*ET
kelectome	KAOE/LEK/TOEM
Kell	KEL
Keller	KEL/ER
Kelling	KEL/-G

234   ©1992 *StenEd* **Medical Dictionary**

Kelly	KEL/LI	keratoiritis	KER/TO/AOI/RAOITS
keloid	KAOE/LOID		KER/TO/IR/RAOITS
keloidal	KAOE/LOI/DAL	keratoleptynsis	KER/TO/LEP/TIN/SIS
keloidosis	KAOE/LOI/DOE/SIS	keratoleukoma	KER/TO/LAOU/KOE/MA
keloplasty	KAOEL/PLAS/TI	keratolysis	KER/TOL/SIS
kelosomia	KAOEL/SOEM/YA	keratolytic	KER/TO/LIT/IK
kelosomus	KAOEL/SOE/MUS	keratoma	KER/TOE/MA
kelotomy	KAOE/LOT/M*I	keratomalacia	KER/TO/MA/LAI/SHA
kelp	KEL/-P	keratomata	KER/TOEM/TA
kelvin	KEL/VIN	keratome	KER/TOEM
Kelvin	K-P/KEL/VIN	keratometer	KER/TOM/TER
Kemadrin	KEM/DRIN	keratometric	KER/TO/MET/RIK
Kempner	KEFRP/NER	keratometry	KER/TOM/TRI
Kenalog	KEN/LOG	keratomileusis	KER/TO/MAOI/LAOU/SIS
Kenalog-10	KEN/LOG/10		KER/TO/MI/LAOU/SIS
Kenalog-40	KEN/LOG/40	keratomycosis	KER/TO/MAOI/KOE/SIS
Kenalog in Orabase	KEN/LOG/N-/OR/RA/BAIS	keratonosis	KER/TO/NOE/SIS
Kenalog Spray	KEN/LOG/SPRAI	keratonosus	KER/TON/SUS
Kendall	KEN/DAL	keratonyxis	KER/TO/NIK/SIS
Kennedy	KEN/DI	keratopachyderma	KER/TO/PAK/DER/MA
kennel	KEN/EL	keratopathy	KER/TOP/TH*I
Kenny	KEN/N*I	keratophakia	KER/TO/FAIK/YA
kenotoxin	KAOEN/TOK/SIN	keratoplasty	KER/TO/PLAS/TI
Kent	KENT	keratoprosthesis	KER/TO/PROS/THAOE/SIS
Kent-His	KENT/H-F/HIS	keratoprotein	KER/TO/PRO/TAOEN
Kenwood	KEN/WAOD	keratorrhexis	KER/TO/REK/SIS
Kenya	KEN/YA	keratorus	KER/TOR/RUS
kephalin	KEF/LIN		KER/TOE/RUS
Keralyt	KER/LAOIT	keratosa	KER/TOE/SA
	KER/LIT	keratoscleritis	KER/TO/SKLE/RAOITS
Kerandel	KER/AN/DEL	keratoscope	KER/TO/SKOEP
keraphyllocele	KER/FIL/SAO*EL	keratoscopy	KER/TOS/KPI
kerasin	KER/SIN	keratose	KER/TOES
kerat(o)-	KER/T(O)	keratoses	KER/TOE/SAOEZ
keratalgia	KER/TAL/JA	keratosis	KER/TOE/SIS
keratan	KER/TAN	keratosulfate	KER/TO/SUL/FAIT
keratectasia	KER/TEK/TAIZ/YA	keratotic	KER/TOT/IK
keratectomy	KER/TEKT/M*I	keratotome	KER/TO/TOEM
keratein	KER/TAOEN		KE/RAT/TOEM
	KER/TAOE/YIN	keratotomy	KER/TOT/M*I
keratiasis	KER/TAOI/SIS	keratotorus	KER/TO/TOR/RUS
keratic	KE/RAT/IK		KER/TO/TOE/RUS
	KER/AT/IK	keraunoneurosis	KE/RAUN/NAOU/ROE/SIS
keratin	KER/TIN	keraunophobia	KE/RAUN/FOEB/YA
keratinase	KER/TIN/AIS	Kerckring	KERK/RING
keratinization	KER/TIN/ZAIGS	kerectasis	KAOE/REKT/SIS
keratinize	KER/TIN/AOIZ	kerectomy	KAOE/REKT/M*I
keratinized	KER/TIN/AOIZ/-D	kerion	KAOER/YON
keratinocyte	KER/TIN/SAO*IT	keritherapy	KER/THER/PI
keratinoid	KER/TIN/OID	Kerley	KER/LAOE
	KE/RAT/NOID	Kerlone	KER/LOEN
keratinosome	KE/RAT/NO/SOEM	kerma	KER/MA
keratinous	KE/RAT/NOUS	kernel	KERN/EL
keratitis	KER/TAOITS	kernicterus	KER/NIKT/RUS
keratoacanthoma	KER/TO/AK/AN/THOE/MA	Kernig	KERN/IG
keratoangioma	KER/TO/AN/JOE/MA	keroid	KER/OID
keratoatrophoderma	KER/TO/AI/TROEF/DER/MA	kerosene	KER/SAOEN
	KER/TO/AT/ROEF/DER/MA	kerotherapy	KER/THER/PI
keratocele	KER/TO/SAO*EL	ket(o)-	KAOET
keratocentesis	KER/TO/SEN/TAOE/SIS		KAOE/T(O)
keratoconjunctivitis	KER/TO/KON/JUNGT/VAOITS	ketal	KAOE/TAL
	KER/TO/KON/JUNG/VAOITS	Ketalar	KAOET/LAR
keratoconus	KER/TO/KO/NUS		KET/LAR
	KER/TO/KOE/NUS	ketamine	KAOET/MAOEN
keratocricoid	KER/TO/KRAOI/KOID	Ketamine	K-P/KAOET/MAOEN
keratocyst	KER/TO/S*IS	keten	KAOE/TEN
keratocyte	KER/TO/SAO*IT	ketene	KAOE/TAOEN
keratoderma	KER/TO/DER/MA	kethoxal	KAOE/THOK/SAL
keratodermatitis	KER/TO/DERM/TAOITS	ketimine	KAOET/MIN
keratodermatocele	KER/TO/DERM/TO/SAO*EL	keto acid	KAOET/AS/ID
keratodermia	KER/TO/DERM/YA		KAOE/TOE/AS/ID
keratoectasia	KER/TO/EK/TAIZ/YA	ketoacid-lyase	KAOET/AS/ID/LAOI/AIS
keratoepithelioplasty	KER/TO/EP/THAOEL/YO/PLAS/TI	ketoacidosis	KAOET/AS/DOE/SIS
keratogenesis	KER/TO/JEN/SIS	ketoaciduria	KAOET/AS/DAOUR/YA
keratogenetic	KER/TO/JE/NET/IK	keto-aldehyde	KAOET/ALD/HAOID
keratogenous	KER/TOJ/NOUS	ketoaminoacidemia	KAOET/AI/MAOEN/AS/DAOEM/
keratoglobus	KER/TO/GLOE/BUS		YA
keratoglossus	KER/TO/GLOS/SUS	ketobemidone	KAOET/BEM/DOEN
keratohelcosis	KER/TO/HEL/KOE/SIS	ketoconazole	KAOET/KON/ZOEL
keratohemia	KER/TO/HAOEM/YA		KAOET/KOEN/ZOEL
keratohyal	KER/TO/HAOIL	ketodecarboxylase	KAOET/DE/KAR/BOX/LAIS
	KER/TO/HAOI/YAL	ketogenesis	KAOET/JEN/SIS
keratohyalin	KER/TO/HAOI/LIN	ketogenetic	KAOET/JE/NET/IK
keratohyaline	KER/TO/HAOI/LAOIN	ketogenic	KAOET/JEN/IK
keratoid	KER/TOID	ketoglutarate	KAOET/GLAOUT/RAIT
keratoiditis	KER/TOI/DAOITS	ketoglutaric	KAOET/GLAOU/TAR/IK
keratoiridocyclitis	KER/TO/IR/DO/SIK/LAOITS	ketoheptose	KAOET/HEP/TOES
keratoiridoscope	KER/TO/AOI/RID/SKOEP	ketohexose	KAOET/HEX/OES
	KER/TO/IR/DO/SKOEP		KAOET/HEK/SOES

ketohydrogenase	KAOET/HAOI/DRO/JEN/AIS	kine-	KIN
ketohydroxyestrin	KAOET/HAOI/DROX/ES/TRIN	kinematic	KIN/MAT/IK
ketol	KAOE/TOL	kinematics	KIN/MAT/IK/-S
ketole	KAOE/TOEL	kinematograph	KIN/MAT/GRAF
ketolysis	KAOE/TOL/SIS	kinemia	KI/NAOEM/YA
ketolytic	KAOET/LIT/IK	kinemic	KI/NAOEM/IK
ketone	KAOE/TOEN	kinemometer	KIN/MOM/TER
ketone-aldehyde	KAOE/TOEN/ALD/HAOID	kineplastic	KIN/PLA*S/IK
ketonemia	KAOET/NAOEM/YA	kineplastics	KIN/PLA*S/IK/-S
ketonic	KAOE/TON/IK	kineplasty	KIN/PLAS/TI
ketonization	KAOE/TOEN/ZAIGS	kinesalgia	KIN/SAL/JA
	KAOE/TON/ZAIGS	kinescope	KIN/SKOEP
ketonuria	KAOET/NAOUR/YA	Kinesed	KIN/SED
ketonurine	KAOE/TOEN/YAOURN	kinesia	KI/NAOEZ/YA
ketopantoic	KAOET/PAN/TOIK	kinesi-esthesiometer	KI/NAOEZ/ES/THAOEZ/YOM/TER
	KAOET/PAN/TOE/IK	kinesialgia	KI/NAOEZ/YAL/JA
ketopentose	KAOET/PEN/TOES	kinesiatric	KI/NAOEZ/YAT/RIK
ketoplasia	KAOET/PLAIZ/YA	kinesiatrics	KI/NAOEZ/YAT/RIK/-S
ketoplastic	KAOET/PLA*S/IK	kinesic	KI/NAOEZ/IK
ketopregnene	KAOET/PREG/NAOEN	kinesimeter	KIN/SIM/TER
ketoprofen	KAOET/PRO/FEN	kinesio-	KI/NAOEZ/YO
ketoreductase	KAOET/RE/DUK/TAIS		KI/NAOES/YO
ketose	KAOE/TOES	kinesiodic	KI/NAOEZ/YOD/IK
ketoside	KAOET/SAOID	kinesiology	KI/NAOEZ/YOLG
ketosis	KAOE/TOE/SIS	kinesiometer	KI/NAOEZ/YOM/TER
ketosteroid	KAOET/STAOER/OID	kinesioneurosis	KI/NAOEZ/YO/NAOU/ROE/SIS
ketosuccinamic	KAOET/SUX/NAM/IK	kinesiotherapy	KI/NAOEZ/YO/THER/PI
ketosuccinic	KAOET/SUK/SIN/IK	kinesipathist	KIN/SIP/TH*IS
ketosuria	KAOET/SAOUR/YA	kinesipathy	KIN/SIP/TH*I
keto-tetrahydrophenanthrene		kinesis	KI/NAOE/SIS
	KAOET/TET/RA/HAOI/DRO/FE/	kinesitherapy	KI/NAOEZ/THER/PI
	NAN/THRAOEN	kinesodic	KIN/SOD/IK
ketotetrose	KAOET/TET/ROES	kinesophobia	KI/NAOES/FOEB/YA
ketothiolase	KAOET/THAOI/LAIS		KI/NAOEZ/FOEB/YA
ketotic	KAOE/TOT/IK	kinesthesia	KINS/THAOEZ/YA
ketourine	KAOET/YAOURN		KIN/ES/THAOEZ/YA
ketoxime	KAOE/TOK/SAOIM	kinesthesiometer	KINS/THAOEZ/YOM/TER
key	KAOE		KIN/ES/THAOEZ/YOM/TER
Key	K-P/KAOE	kinesthesis	KINS/THAOE/SIS
keynote	KAOE/NOET		KIN/ES/THAOE/SIS
keyway	KAOE/WA*I	kinesthetic	KINS/THET/IK
kg	K*G		KIN/ES/THET/IK
khellin	KEL/LIN	kinetia	KI/NAOET/YA
kibisitome	KAOI/BIS/TOEM		KI/NAOE/SHA
kick	KIK	kinetic	KI/NET/IK
Kidd	K*ID	kineticist	KI/NET/S*IS
kidney	KID/NAOE	kinetics	KI/NET/IK/-S
Kiel	KAO*EL	kinetin	KAOI/NAOE/TIN
	(not KAOEL; see keel)		KI/NAOE/TIN
Kienbock	KAOEN/BEK	kinetism	KIN/TIFM
	KAOEN/BOK	kineto-	KI/NAOET
Kiernan	KAOER/NAN		KI/NET
Kiesselbach	KAOES/EL/BAK		KI/NAOE/TO
	KAOES/EL/BAUK	kinetocardiogram	KI/NAOET/KARD/YO/GRAM
Kilian	K*IL/YAN	kinetocardiograph	KI/NAOET/KARD/YO/GRAF
	(not KIL/YAN; see Killian)	kinetocardiography	KI/NAOET/KARD/YOG/FI
kiliense	KIL/YEN/SAOE	kinetochore	KI/NAOET/KOER
killeen	KIL/LAOEN	kinetogenic	KI/NAOET/JEN/IK
killer	KIL/ER	kinetographic	KI/NAOET/GRAFK
Killian	KIL/YAN	kinetonucleus	KI/NAOET/NAOUK/LUS
kilo-	KIL	kinetoplasm	KI/NAOET/PLAFM
	KIL/LO	kinetoplast	KI/NAOET/PLA*S
	KI/LO	kinetoscope	KI/NAOET/SKOEP
kilobase	KIL/BAIS	kinetoscopy	KIN/TOS/KPI
kilocalorie	KIL/KAL/RAOE	kinetoses	KIN/TOE/SAOEZ
kilocycle	KIL/SAOIK/-L	kinetosis	KIN/TOE/SIS
kilogram	KIL/GRAM	kinetosome	KI/NAOET/SOEM
kilogram-meter	KIL/GRAM/MAOET/ER	kinetotherapeutic	KI/NAOET/THER/PAOUT/IK
kilohertz	KIL/HERTS	kinetotherapy	KI/NAOET/THER/PI
kiloliter	KIL/LAOET/ER	king	KING
kilomegacycle	KIL/MEG/SAOIK/-L	King	K-P/KING
kilohm	KIL/OEM	kingdom	KING/DOM
kilometer	KIL/MAOET/ER	kinic	KIN/IK
	KLOM/TER		KAOIN/IK
	KI/LOM/TER	kinin	KAOI/NIN
kilonem	KIL/NEM	kininase	KAOI/NIN/AIS
kiloroentgen	KIL/RENT/GEN		KAOI/NIN/AIS
kilounit	KIL/YAOUNT	kininogen	KAOI/NIN/JEN
kilovolt	KIL/VOELT		KI/NIN/JEN
	KIL/VOLT	kininogenin	KAOI/NIN/JEN/NIN
kilovoltmeter	KIL/VOELT/MAOET/ER		KI/NIN/JEN/NIN
	KIL/VOLT/MAOET/ER	kink	KIN/-K
kilurane	KIL/YAOU/RAIN	kino-	KAOIN
	KIL/YU/RAIN		KIN
Kimmelstiel	KIM/EL/STAOEL		KAOI/NO
kinanesthesia	KIN/ANS/THAOEZ/YA	kinocentrum	KAOIN/SEN/TRUM
kinase	KAOI/NAIS		KIN/SEN/TRUM
kindling	KIND/-LG	kinocilia	KAOIN/SIL/YA
kindred	KIN/DRED	kinocilium	KAOIN/SIL/YUM

kinohapt	KAOIN/HAPT		*(not* NOT; see not)
	KIN/HAPT	knuckle	NUK/-L
kinology	KAOI/NOLG	knuckling	NUK/-LG
kinomometer	KAOIN/MOM/TER	Kobelt	KOE/BELT
kinoplasm	KAOIN/PLAFM		KO/BELT
	KIN/PLAFM	Kober	KOEB/ER
kinoplasmic	KAOIN/PLAZ/MIK		KOE/BER
	KIN/PLAZ/MIK		KO/BER
kinoplastic	KAOIN/PLA*S/IK	Kobert	KOE/BAIRT
kinosphere	KAOIN/SFAOER		KO/BAIRT
kinotoxin	KAOIN/TOK/SIN	Koch	KO*EK
kinovin	KI/NOE/VIN		*(not* KOEK; see coke)
kinship	KIN/SHIP	Kocher	KOEK/ER
kiotome	KAOI/TOEM	kocherization	KOEK/RI/ZAIGS
kiotomy	KAOI/OT/M*I		KOE/KER/ZAIGS
Kirchner	KAOERK/NER		KO/KER/ZAIGS
	KIRK/NER	kochii	KOEK/YAOI
Kirk	K*IRK	Kocks	KO*EX
	(not KIRK; see "can I recollect")		*(not* KOEX; see coax)
Kirkland	KIRK/LAND	Koenen	KAOE/NEN
Kirschner	KAOER/-RB/NER		KAOEN/-N
	KIR/-RB/NER	Kogoj	KOE/GOI
Kisch	KIRB		KO/GOI
kissing	KISZ/-G	Kohler	KAI/LER
Kitasato	KAOET/SA/TOE		KOE/LER
	KIT/SA/TOE		KOEL/ER
Kjeldahl	KEL/DAL	Kohlrausch	KOEL/RAUFP
Klapp	KLA*P		KOEL/RAURB
Klebs	KLEBS	Kohn	KO*EN
	KLEBZ	Kohnstamm	KOEN/STAM
Klebsiella	KLEBS/YEL/LA	koilo-	KOIL
	KLEB/SAOEL/LA		KOI/LO
	KLEB/SI/EL/LA	koilocyte	KOIL/SAO*IT
Kleffner	KLEF/NER	koilocytosis	KOIL/SAOI/TOE/SIS
Klein	KLAO*IN	koilonychia	KOIL/NIK/YA
	(not KLAOIN; see cline)	koilorrhachic	KOIL/RAK/IK
klepto-	KLEPT	koilosternia	KOIL/STERN/YA
	KLEPT/TO	koinonia	KOI/NOEN/YA
kleptolagnia	KLEPT/LAG/NAOE/YA	koinotropy	KOI/NOT/RO/PI
kleptomania	KLEPT/MAIN/YA	kojic	KOEJ/IK
kleptomaniac	KLEPT/MAIN/YAK	Kolliker	KEL/KER
kleptophobia	KLEPT/FOEB/YA	Kollmann	KOL/MAN
Klieg	KLAO*EG	Kolmer	KOEL/MER
	(not KLAOEG; see colleague)		KOL/MER
Klinefelter	KLAOIN/FELT/ER	kolytic	KOE/LIT/IK
	KLAOIN/FEL/TER		KOL/LIT/IK
Klinger	KL*ING/ER	Kolyum	KOL/YUM
	(not KLING/ER; see clinger)	Konakion	KOE/NAK/YON
Klippel	KLIP/EL		KO/NAK/YON
klismaphilia	KLIZ/MA/FIL/YA	Kondoleon	KON/DOEL/YON
	KLIS/MA/FIL/YA		KON/DOL/YON
Klondike	KLON/DAOIK	Konig	KEN/IG
Klonopin	KLON/PIN	konimeter	KOE/NIM/TER
K-Lor	K-RBGS/LOR		KO/NIM/TER
Klor-Con	KLOR/KON	koniocortex	KOEN/YO/KOR/TEX
Klorvess	KLOR/VESZ	kophemia	KOE/FAOEM/YA
Klotrix	KLOE/TRIX		KO/FAOEM/YA
Klumpke	KLAOUFRP/KAOE	Koplik	KOP/LIK
	KLAOUM/KAOE	kopophobia	KOP/FOEB/YA
	KLUFRP/KAOE	Kopp	KO*P
	KLUM/KAOE		*(not* KOP; see cop)
Kluver	KLAOUVR	kopratin	KOP/RA/TIN
Kluveri	KLAOUV/RAOI	koprosterin	KOP/RO/STAOER/RIN
K-Lyte	K-RBGS/LAOIT	Koranyi	KOE/RAN/YAOE
km	K*M		KO/RAN/YAOE
Knapp	NA*P	Korff	KOR/-F
	(not NAP; see nap)	koro	KOE/ROE
knead	NAED		KOR/ROE
	(not NAOED; see need)	Koro-Flex	KOR/FLEX
kneading	NAED/-G		KOR/RO/FLEX
knee	NAOE	Koromex	KOR/MEX
kneecap	NAOE/KAP		KOR/RO/MEX
Knemidokoptes	NAOEM/DO/KOP/TAOEZ	koronion	*see* coronion
	NEM/DO/KOP/TAOEZ	Korotkoff	KOE/ROT/KOF
knife	NAOIF		KOE/ROT/KAUF
knives	NAOIV/-S		KO/ROT/KOF
knismogenic	NIS/MO/JEN/IK		KO/ROT/KAUF
knismolagnia	NIS/MO/LAG/NA	Korsakoff	KORS/KOF
	NIS/MO/LAG/NAOE/YA		KORS/KAUF
knit	N*IT	Koshevnikoff	KOE/SHEV/NI/KOF
	(not NIT; see nit)		KO/SHEV/NI/KOF
knitting	N*IT/-G	Kovalevsky	KOV/LEV/SKI
knob	NOB		KOEV/LEV/SKI
knock	NOK	Kowarsky	KOE/VAR/SKI
knock-knee	NOK/NAOE		KO/VAR/SKI
Knoll	K-P/NOEL	Koyter	KOIT/ER
Knoop	NAOP		KOI/TER
K-Norm	K-RBGS/NORM	K-Phos	K-RBGS/FOS
knot	NO*T	Krabbe	KRA/BAOE

	KRAB/BAOE
Kraepelin	KRAIP/LIN
	KRAEP/LIN
Kraske	KRAS/KAOE
kratometer	KRA/TOM/TER
	KRAI/TOM/TER
krauomania	KRAU/MAIN/YA
kraurosis	KRAU/ROE/SIS
Krause	KROUS
Krebs	KREBS
	KREBZ
Kretschmann	KREFP/MAN
Kretschmer	KREFP/MER
Kretz	KRETS
Kreysig	KRAI/ZIG
	KRAI/SIG
	KRAOI/ZIG
	KRAOI/SIG
Krogh	KROEG
Kromayer	KROE/MAI/ER
	KROE/MAOI/ER
Krompecher	KROEM/PEK/ER
	KROM/PEK/ER
Kronecker	KROE/NEK/ER
Kronig	KRAI/NIG
Kronlein	KRAIN/LIN
	KRAIN/LAOIN
Kronofed-A	KRON/FED/ARBGS
	KROEN/FED/ARBGS
Kronofed-A-Jr.	KRON/FED/ARBGS/J-R
	KROEN/FED/ARBGS/J-R
Krueger	KRAOUG/ER
Krukenberg	KRAOUK/EN/BERG
Kruse	KRAO*UZ
	KRAO*US
	(not KRAOUZ or KRAOUS; see cruise and crus)
krypton	KRIP/TON
K-Tab	K-RBGS/TAB
KUB	K*UB
	K-RBGS/*URBGS/B*RBGS
Kugel	KAOUG/EL
Kugelberg	KAOUG/EL/BERG
Kuhne	KAOE/NAOE
	KAOE/NE
Kuhnt	KAOUNT
Kulchitzky	KAOUL/KIT/SKI
	KUL/KIT/SKI
Kulenkampff	KAOUL/EN/KAFRP/-F
	KAOUL/EN/KAM/-F
	KAOUL/EN/KAFRP
Kulp	K*UL/-P
	(not KUL/-P; see Culp)
Kulz	KILTS
	KULZ
Kummell	KIM/EL
Kuntscher	KINT/SHER
Kupffer	KAOUP/FER
	KUP/FER
kupramite	KAOU/PRA/MAOIT
	KAOUP/RA/MAOIT
Kupressoff	KAOU/PRES/SOF
	KAOU/PRES/SAUF
Kurloff	KUR/LOF
	KUR/LAUF
Kurzrok-Ratner	KURZ/ROK/RAT/NER
Kuss	KESZ
Kussmaul	KAOUS/MOUL
	KAOUS/MAUL
	KUS/MOUL
	KUS/MAUL
Kuster	K*IS/ER
Kustner	K*IS/NER
Kutrase	KAOU/TRAIS
kuttarosome	KUT/TAR/SOEM
Ku-Zyme	KAOU/ZAOIM
Kveim	K-/VAOEM
	VAOEM
Kwelcof	KWEL/KOF
Kwell	KW*EL
	(not KWEL; see quell)
Kwell Cream	KW*EL/KRAOEM
Kwell Lotion	KW*EL/LOEGS
Kwell Shampoo	KW*EL/SHAM/PAO
kyestein	KAOI/*ES/YIN
kyllosis	KIL/LOE/SIS
kym(o)-	KAOIM
	KAOI/M(O)
kymatism	KAOIM/TIFM

kymocyclograph	KAOIM/SAOI/KLO/GRAF
kymogram	KAOIM/GRAM
kymograph	KAOIM/GRAF
kymography	KAOI/MOG/FI
kymoscope	KAOIM/SKOEP
kymotrichous	KAOIM/TRIK/OUS
kynocephalus	KAOIN/SEF/LUS
kynurenic	KIN/YAOU/RAOEN/IK
	KIN/YAOU/REN/IK
kynureninase	KAOI/NAOU/REN/NAIS
	KIN/YAOU/REN/NAIS
	KIN/YAOU/RAOEN/NAIS
kynurenine	KAOI/NAOUR/NIN
	KAOI/NAOUR/NAOEN
	KAOI/NAOU/REN/NIN
kyogenic	KAOI/JEN/IK
kyph(o)-	KAOIF
	KAOI/F(O)
kyphos	KAOI/FOS
kyphoscoliosis	KAOIF/SKOEL/YOE/SIS
kyphosis	KAOI/FOE/SIS
kyphotic	KAOI/FOT/IK
kyphotone	KAOIF/TOEN
kyrtorrhachic	KIRT/RAK/IK

L

lab	LAB
Laband	LA/BAND
Labarraque	LAB/RAK
Labbe	LA/BAI
label	LAI/BEL
	LAIB/EL
la belle indifference	LA/BEL/IN/DIFRNS
	LA/BEL/IN/DIF/RANS
labetalol	LA/BET/LOL
labi(o)-	LAIB/Y(O)
labia	LAIB/YA
labial	LAIB/YAL
labiales	LAIB/YAI/LAOEZ
labialis	LAIB/YAI/LIS
labialism	LAIB/YAL/IFM
labially	LAIB/YAL/LI
labichorea	LAIB/KOE/RAOE/YA
Labidognatha	LAB/DOG/NA/THA
labii	LAIB/YAOI
labile	LAI/BAOIL
	LAI/BIL
lability	LABLT
labioalveolar	LAIB/YO/AL/VAOE/LAR
labiocervical	LAIB/YO/SEFRB/KAL
labiochorea	LAIB/YO/KOE/RAOE/YA
labioclination	LAIB/YO/KLI/NAIGS
labiodental	LAIB/YO/DEN/TAL
labiogingival	LAIB/YO/JING/VAL
labioglossolaryngeal	LAIB/YO/GLOS/LARN/JAL
labioglossopharyngeal	LAIB/YO/GLOS/FRIN/JAL
labiograph	LAIB/YO/GRAF
labioincisal	LAIB/YO/IN/SAOI/ZAL
labiolingual	LAIB/YO/LING/WAL
labiologic	LAIB/YO/LOJ/IK
labiology	LAIB/YOLG
labiomental	LAIB/YO/MEN/TAL
labiomycosis	LAIB/YO/MAOI/KOE/SIS
labionasal	LAIB/YO/NAI/ZAL
labiopalatine	LAIB/YO/PAL/TAOIN
labioplacement	LAIB/YO/PLAIS/-MT
labioplasty	LAIB/YO/PLAS/TI
labiorum	LAIB/YOR/UM
	LAIB/YOER/UM
labiotenaculum	LAIB/YO/TEN/AK/LUM
	LAIB/YO/TE/NAK/LUM
labioversion	LAIB/YO/VERGS
labium	LAIB/YUM
labor	LAI/BOR
laboratorian	LAB/TOIRN
	LAB/RA/TOIRN
laboratory	LAB/TOIR
	LAB/RA/TOIR
Laborde	LA/BORD
labra	LAI/BRA
labrale	LA/BRAI/LAOE
labrale inferius	LA/BRAI/LAOE/IN/FAOER/YUS
labrale superius	LA/BRAI/LAOE/SU/PAOER/YUS
labrocyte	LAB/RO/SAO*IT
labrum	LAI/BRUM
laburinine	LA/BAOUR/NAOEN
labyrinth	LAB/R*INT
labyrinthectomy	LAB/RIN/THEKT/M*I
labyrinthi	LAB/RIN/THAOI
labyrinthic	LAB/R*INT/IK
labyrinthine	LAB/RIN/THAOEN
	LAB/RIN/THAOIN
	LAB/RIN/THIN
labyrinthitis	LAB/RIN/THAOITS
labyrinthopexy	LAB/R*INT/PEK/SI
labyrinthotomy	LAB/RIN/THOT/M*I
labyrinthus	LAB/RIN/THUS
lac	LA*K
	(not LAK; see lack)
lacca	LAK/KA
laccase	LAK/AIS
lacerable	LAS/RABL
	LAS/ERBL
lacerate	LAS/RAIT
lacerated	LAS/RAIT/-D
laceration	LAS/RAIGS
lacertus	LA/SER/TUS
Lac-Hydrin	LAK/HAOI/DRIN
lacinia	LA/SIN/YA
laciniae tubae	LA/SIN/YAE/TAOU/BAE

laciniatum	LA/SIN/YAI/TUM
	LA/SIN/YAIT/UM
Lacril	LAK/RIL
Lacri-Lube	LAK/RI/LAOUB
lacrim(o)-	LAK/RI/M(O)
	LAK/RIM
lacrima	LAK/RI/MA
lacrimae	LAK/RI/MAE
lacrimal	LAK/RI/MAL
lacrimales	LAK/RI/MAI/LAOEZ
lacrimalis	LAK/RI/MAI/LIS
lacrimation	LAK/RI/MAIGS
lacrimator	LAK/RI/MAI/TOR
lacrimatory	LAK/RIM/TOIR
	LAK/RI/MA/TOIR
lacrimoethmoid	LAK/RIM/*ET/MOID
	LAK/RI/MO/*ET/MOID
lacrimonasal	LAK/RIM/NAI/ZAL
	LAK/RI/MO/NAI/ZAL
lacrimotome	LAK/RIM/TOEM
	LAK/RI/MO/TOEM
lacrimotomy	LAK/RI/MOT/M*I
Lacrisert	LAK/RI/SERT
lact(o)-	LAKT
	LAK/T(O)
lactacidemia	LAK/TAS/DAOEM/YA
lactacidin	LAK/TAS/DIN
lactacidosis	LAK/TAS/DOE/SIS
lactaciduria	LAK/TAS/DAOUR/YA
lactagogue	LAKT/GOG
Lactaid	LAK/TAID
lactalbumin	LAK/TAL/BAOU/MIN
lactam	LAK/TAM
lactamase	LAKT/MAIS
lactamide	LAK/TAM/ID
lactase	LAK/TAIS
lactate	LAK/TAIT
lactation	LAK/TAIGS
lactational	LAK/TAIGS/NAL
lactea	LAKT/YA
lacteal	LAKT/YAL
	LAK/TAOEL
lactenin	LAKT/NIN
lactescence	LAK/TES/ENS
lactescent	LAK/TES/ENT
lacteum	LAKT/YUM
lactic	LAKT/IK
lacticacidemia	LAK/TIK/AS/DAOEM/YA
	LAKT/IK/AS/DAOEM/YA
LactiCare	LAKT/KAIR
LactiCare-HC	LAKT/KAIR/H-RBGS/KR*RBGS
lacticemia	LAKT/SAOEM/YA
lactiferae	LAK/TIF/RAE
lactiferi	LAK/TIF/RAOI
lactiferous	LAK/TIF/ROUS
lactifugal	LAK/TIF/GAL
lactifuge	LAKT/FAOUJ
lactigenous	LAK/TIJ/NOUS
lactigerous	LAK/TIJ/ROUS
lactim	LAK/TIM
lactimorbus	LAKT/MOR/BUS
lactin	LAK/TIN
lactinate	LAKT/NAIT
lactinated	LAKT/NAIT/-D
Lactinex	LAKT/NEX
lactis	LAK/TIS
Lactisol	LAKT/SOL
lactivorous	LAK/TIV/ROUS
Lactobacillaceae	LAKT/BAS/LAIS/YAE
Lactobacilleae	LAKT/BA/SIL/LAE
lactobacilli	LAKT/BA/SIL/LAOI
lactobacillic	LAKT/BA/SIL/IK
lactobacillin	LAKT/BA/SIL/LIN
lactobacillus	LAKT/BA/SIL/LUS
Lactobacillus	K-P/LAKT/BA/SIL/LUS
lactobionate	LAKT/BAO*I/NAIT
lactobutyrometer	LAKT/BAOUT/ROM/TER
Lactocal	LAKT/KAL
Lactocal-F	LAKT/KAL/F-RBGS
lactocele	LAKT/SAO*EL
lactochrome	LAKT/KROEM
lactocrit	LAKT/KRIT
lactodensimeter	LAKT/DEN/SIM/TER
lactofarinaceous	LAKT/FAR/NAIRBS
lactoferrin	LAKT/FER/RIN
lactoflavin	LAKT/FLAIVN
lactogen	LAKT/JEN
lactogenesis	LAKT/JEN/SIS
lactogenic	LAKT/JEN/IK

lactoglobulin	LAKT/GLOB/LIN	laliatry	LA/LAOI/TRI
lactometer	LAK/TOM/TER	laliophobia	LAIL/YO/FOEB/YA
lactonase	LAKT/NAIS	lallation	LAL/LAIGS
lactone	LAK/TOEN	Lallemand	LAL/MAND
lacto-ovovegetarian	LAKT/OEV/VEJ/TAIRN		LAL/MAUN
lactoperoxidase	LAKT/PROX/DAIS	lalling	LAL/-G
lactophosphate	LAKT/FOS/FAIT	lalo-	LAL
lactoprecipitin	LAKT/PRE/SIP/TIN	lalochezia	LAL/KAOEZ/YA
lactoprotein	LAKT/PRO/TAOEN	lalognosis	LAL/OG/NOE/SIS
lactorrhea	LAKT/RAOE/YA	lalopathology	LAL/PA/THOLG
lactosazone	LAKT/SAI/ZOEN	lalopathy	LA/LOP/TH*I
lactoscope	LAKT/SKOEP		LAL/OP/TH*I
lactose	LAK/TOES	laloplegia	LAL/PLAOE/JA
lactoserum	LAKT/SAOERM	lalorrhea	LAL/RAOE/YA
lactoside	LAKT/SAOID	Lamarck	LA/MARK
lactosidosis	LAKT/SAOI/DOE/SIS	lamarckii	LA/MARK/YAOI
lactosum	LAK/TOE/SUM	Lamaze	LA/MAUZ
	LAK/TOES/UM	lambda	LAM/DA
lactosuria	LAKT/SAOUR/YA	lambdacism	LAM/DA/SIFM
lactotherapy	LAKT/THER/PI	lambdacismus	LAM/DA/SIZ/MUS
lactotoxin	LAKT/TOK/SIN	lambdoid	LAM/DOID
lactotrope	LAKT/TROEP	lambdoidal	LAM/DOI/DAL
lactotroph	LAKT/TROEF	lambert	LAM/BERT
lactotrophin	LAKT/TROEFN	Lambert	K-P/LAM/BERT
lactotropic	LAKT/TROP/IK	Lamblia intestinalis	LAM/BLAOE/YA/SPW*ES/NAI/LIS
lactotropin	LAKT/TROE/PIN	lambliasis	LAM/BLAOI/SIS
lactovegetarian	LAKT/VEJ/TAIRN	lame	LAIM
lactoylglutathione	LAK/TOIL/GLAOUT/THAOI/OEN	lame foliacee	LAM/FOL/YA/SAI
Lactrase	LAK/TRAIS	lamel	LAM/EL
lactulose	LAK/TAOU/LOES	lamella	LA/MEL/LA
	LAKT/LOES	lamellae	LA/MEL/LAE
	LAK/KHU/LOES	lamellar	LA/MEL/LAR
lacuna	LA/KAOU/NA		LAM/LAR
lacunae	LA/KAOU/NAE	lamellasome	LA/MEL/SOEM
lacunar	LA/KAOU/NAR	lamellate	LAM/LAIT
lacunare	LA/KAOU/NAI/RAOE	lamellated	LAM/LAIT/-D
	LAK/NAI/RAOE	lamelliform	LA/MEL/FORM
	LAK/YAOU/NAI/RAOE	lamellipodia	LA/MEL/POED/YA
	LAK/YU/NAI/RAOE	lamellipodium	LA/MEL/POED/YUM
lacune	LA/KAOUN	lamellosa	LAM/LOE/SA
lacunule	LA/KAOUN/YAOUL	lamin	LAM/MIN
lacus	LAI/KUS	lamin(o)-	LAM/N(O)
lacustris	LA/KUS/TRIS	lamina	LAM/NA
	LAI/KUS/TRIS	lamina propria	LAM/NA/PROEP/RA
Ladd	LA*D		LAM/NA/PRO/PRAOE/YA
	(not LAD; see lad)	laminae	LAM/NAE
Ladd-Franklin	LA*D/H-F/FRA*NG/LIN	laminagram	LAM/NA/GRAM
	LA*D/H-F/FRAN/-K/LIN	laminagraph	LAM/NA/GRAF
Laelaps	LAOE/LAPS	laminagraphy	LAM/NAG/FI
	LAE/LAPS	laminar	LAM/NAR
Laelaps echidninus	LAOE/LAPS/E/KID/NAOI/NUS	laminaria	LAM/NAIR/YA
	LAE/LAPS/E/KID/NAOI/NUS	Laminaria	K-P/LAM/NAIR/YA
Laennec	LAI/NEK	laminarin	LAM/NAR/RIN
	LAI/EN/EK		LAM/NAI/RIN
Laetrile	LAI/TRIL	laminarinase	LAM/NAR/NAIS
	LAE/TRIL		LAM/NAIR/NAIS
laeve	LAOE/VAOE	laminate	LAM/NAIT
	LAOE/VE	laminated	LAM/NAIT/-D
	LAE/VAOE	lamination	LAM/NAIGS
	LAE/VE	laminectomy	LAM/NEKT/M*I
laevis	LAOE/VIS	laminin	LAM/NIN
	LAE/VIS	laminitis	LAM/NAOITS
lafleuri	LA/FLAOU/RAOI	laminotomy	LAM/NOT/M*I
	LA/FLAOUR/RAOI	lamp	LAFRP
Lafora	LA/FOR/RA	lampbrush	LAFRP/BRURB
lag	LAG	Lamprene	LAM/PRAOEN
lagena	LA/JAOE/NA	lamprophonia	LAM/PRO/FOEN/YA
lagenae	LA/JAOE/NAE	lamprophonic	LAM/PRO/FON/IK
lageniform	LA/JEN/FORM	lana	LAN/NA
lagging	LAG/-G		LAI/NA
-lagnia	LAG/NA	lanae	LAN/NAE
	LAG/NAOE/YA		LAI/NAE
lagophthalmia	LAG/OF/THAL/MA	lanatoside	LA/NAT/SAOID
	LAG/OF/THAL/MAOE/YA	lance	LANS
lagophthalmos	LAG/OF/THAL/MOS	Lancefield	LANS/FAOELD
Lagrange	LA/GRA	lanceolate	LANS/YO/LAIT
	LA/GRAIN/-J	lanceolatum	LANS/YO/LAI/TUM
	LA/GRAING		LANS/YO/LAIT/UM
la grippe	LA/GR*IP	Lancereaux	LANS/ROE
	LA/GRIP	lancet	LANS/ET
laiose	LAOI/OES		LAN/SET
	LAOI/YOES	Lancet	K-P/LANS/ET
lake	LAIK		K-P/LAN/SET
Lake	K-P/LAIK	lancinating	LANS/NAIT/-G
laky	LAI/KI	Lancisi	LAN/KHAOE/SAOE
	LAIK/KI		LAN/SAOE/SAOE
lal(o)-	LAL	Landau	LAN/DOU
	LA/L(O)		LAN/DAU
-lalia	LAIL/YA	landmark	LAND/MARK

Landolfi	LAN/DOL/FAOE	laparosplenectomy	LAP/RO/SPLAOE/NEKT/M*I
Landolt	LAN/DOELT	laparosplenotomy	LAP/RO/SPLAOE/NOT/M*I
	LAN/DOLT	laparotome	LAP/RO/TOEM
Landouzy	LAN/DAOU/ZI	laparotomy	LAP/ROT/M*I
Landry	LAN/DRI	laparotrachelotomy	LAP/RO/TRAIK/LOT/M*I
Landsteiner	LAND/STAOIN/ER		LAP/RO/TRAK/LOT/M*I
Landstrom	LAND/STREM	laparotyphlotomy	LAP/RO/TIF/LOT/M*I
lane	LAEN	laparouterotomy	LAP/RO/YAOUT/ROT/M*I
Lane	K-P/LAEN	Lapicque	LA/PAOEK
	(not LAIN; see lain)	lapinization	LAP/NI/ZAIGS
Langdon	LANG/DON	lapinize	LAP/NAOIZ
Lange	LANG	lapinized	LAP/NAOIZ/ED
	LAING	lapis	LAP/IS
Langenbeck	LANG/EN/BEK		LAP/PIS
Langendorff	LANG/EN/DOR/-F		LAI/PIS
Langer	LANG/ER	lapsus	LAP/SUS
Langerhans	LANG/ER/HANZ	laqueiformis	LAK/WE/FOR/MIS
	LANG/ER/HANS		LAK/WAOE/FOR/MIS
langerhansian	LANG/ER/HANZ/YAN	larch	LA*RPBLG
	LANG/ER/HANS/YAN		LAR/-FP
langeroni	LANG/ROE/NAOI	lard	LARD
Langhans	LANG/HANZ	lardacein	LAR/DAIS/YIN
	LANG/HANS	lardaceous	LAR/DAIRBS
Langley	LANG/LAOE	large	LARJ
language	LANG/WAJ	larithmics	LA/R*IT/MIK/-S
laniary	LAN/YAIR	larixin	LA/RIK/SIN
Laniazid	LA/NAOI/ZID	larkspur	LARK/SPUR
lanolin	LAN/LIN	Larobec	LAR/BEK
lanosterol	LA/NO*S/ROL	Larodopa	LAR/DOE/PA
Lanoxicaps	LA/NOX/KAP/-S	Larrey	LAR/RAI
Lanoxin	LA/NOK/SIN		LAR/RAOE
Lantermann	LAN/TER/MAN	Larsen	LAR/SEN
	LANT/ER/MAN		LARS/-N
lanthanic	LA*NT/NIK	Larsson	LAR/SON
	LAN/THA/NIK	larva	LAR/VA
	LAN/THAN/IK	larvaceous	LAR/VAIRBS
lanthanide	LA*NT/NAOID	larvae	LAR/VAE
	LAN/THA/NAOID	larval	LAR/VAL
lanthanin	LA*NT/NIN	larvate	LAR/VAIT
	LAN/THA/NIN	larvi-	LAFRB
lanthanum	LA*NT/NUM		LAR/VI
	LAN/THA/NUM	larvicidal	LAFRB/SAOI/DAL
lanthionine	LAN/THAOI/NAOEN	larvicide	LAFRB/SAO*ID
lanuginous	LA/NAOUJ/NOUS	larviparous	LAR/VIP/ROUS
lanugo	LA/NAOU/GOE	larviphagic	LAFRB/FAIJ/IK
lanum	LAN/UM		LAFRB/FAJ/IK
	LAIN/UM	larviposition	LAFRB/POGS
	LAI/NUM	larvivorous	LAR/VIV/ROUS
Lanz	LANZ	laryng(o)-	LARNG
lapactic	LA/PAKT/IK		LARN/G(O)
lapar(o)-	LAP/R(O)		LA/RING
laparectomy	LAP/REKT/M*I		LA/RIN/G(O)
laparocele	LAP/RO/SAO*EL		LARN/J(O)
laparocholecystotomy	LAP/RO/KOEL/SIS/TOT/M*I	laryngalgia	LARN/GAL/JA
laparocolectomy	LAP/RO/KO/LEKT/M*I	laryngea	LARN/JA
laparocolostomy	LAP/RO/KO/LO*S/M*I		LA/RIN/JA
laparocolotomy	LAP/RO/KO/LOT/M*I	laryngeae	LARN/JAE
laparocystectomy	LAP/RO/SIS/TEKT/M*I		LA/RIN/JAE
laparocystidotomy	LAP/RO/S*IS/DOT/M*I	laryngeal	LARN/JAL
laparocystotomy	LAP/RO/SIS/TOT/M*I		LA/RIN/JAL
laparoenterostomy	LAP/RO/SPWRO*S/M*I	laryngectomy	LARN/JEKT/M*I
	LAP/RO/SPWER/RO*S/M*I	laryngemphraxis	LARN/JEM/FRAK/SIS
laparoenterotomy	LAP/RO/SPWROT/M*I	laryngendoscope	LARN/JEND/SKOEP
	LAP/RO/SPWER/ROT/M*I	larynges	LARN/JAOEZ
laparogastroscopy	LAP/RO/GAS/TROS/KPI		LA/RIN/JAOEZ
laparogastrostomy	LAP/RO/GAS/TRO*S/M*I	laryngeus	LARN/JUS
laparogastrotomy	LAP/RO/GAS/TROT/M*I		LA/RIN/JUS
laparohepatotomy	LAP/RO/HEP/TOT/M*I	laryngeus recurrens	LARN/JUS/RE/KURNZ
laparohysterectomy	LAP/RO/H*IS/REKT/M*I		LA/RIN/JUS/RE/KURNZ
laparohystero-oophorectomy		laryngis	LARN/JIS
	LAP/RO/H*IS/RO/AOF/REKT/M*I		LA/RIN/JIS
laparohysteropexy	LAP/RO/H*IS/RO/PEK/SI	laryngismal	LARN/JIZ/MAL
laparohysterosalpingo-oophorectomy		laryngismus	LARN/JIZ/MUS
	LAP/RO/H*IS/RO/SAL/PING/AOF/	laryngitic	LARN/JIT/IK
	REKT/M*I	laryngitis	LARN/JAOITS
laparohysterotomy	LAP/RO/H*IS/ROT/M*I	laryngocele	LARNG/SAO*EL
laparoileotomy	LAP/RO/*IL/YOT/M*I	laryngocentesis	LARNG/SEN/TAOE/SIS
laparomyitis	LAP/RO/MAOI/AOITS	laryngofission	LARNG/FIGS
laparomyomectomy	LAP/RO/MAOI/MEKT/M*I	laryngofissure	LARNG/FIRB/SHUR
laparomyositis	LAP/RO/MAOI/SAOITS	laryngogram	LARNG/GRAM
laparonephrectomy	LAP/RO/NE/FREKT/M*I	laryngograph	LARNG/GRAF
laparorrhaphy	LAP/ROR/FI	laryngography	LARN/GOG/FI
laparosalpingectomy	LAP/RO/SAL/PIN/JEKT/M*I	laryngohypopharynx	LARNG/HO*IP/FARNGS
laparosalpingo-oophorectomy		laryngology	LARN/GOLG
	LAP/RO/SAL/PING/AOF/REKT/	laryngomalacia	LARNG/MA/LAI/SHA
	M*I	laryngometry	LARN/GOM/TRI
laparosalpingotomy	LAP/RO/SAL/PIN/GOT/M*I	laryngoparalysis	LARNG/PRAL/SIS
laparoscope	LAP/RO/SKOEP	laryngopathy	LARN/GOP/TH*I
laparoscopy	LAP/ROS/KPI	laryngophantom	LARNG/FAN/TOM

laryngopharyngeal	LARNG/FRIN/JAL	lateroflexion	LAT/RO/FL*EBGS
laryngopharyngectomy	LARNG/FARN/JEKT/M*I	lateroposition	LAT/RO/POGS
laryngopharyngeus	LARNG/FRIN/JUS		LAT/RO/PO/SIGS
laryngopharyngitis	LARNG/FARN/JAOITS	lateropulsion	LAT/RO/PULGS
laryngopharynx	LARNG/FARNGS	laterotorsion	LAT/RO/TORGS
laryngophony	LARN/GOF/N*I	laterotrusion	LAT/RO/TRAOUGS
laryngophthisis	LARNG/THAOI/SIS	lateroversion	LAT/RO/VERGS
	LARN/GOF/THI/SIS	latex	LAI/TEX
laryngoplasty	LARNG/PLAS/TI	latexed	LAI/TEX/-D
laryngoplegia	LARNG/PLAOE/JA	Latham	LAI/THAM
laryngoptosis	LARNG/TOE/SIS	lathe	LA*IT
laryngopyocele	LARNG/PAOI/SAO*EL	lathyrism	LA*T/RIFM
laryngorhinology	LARNG/RAOI/NOLG	lathyritic	LA*T/RIT/IK
laryngorrhagia	LARNG/RAI/JA	lathyrogen	LA*T/RO/JEN
laryngorrhaphy	LARN/GOR/FI	lathyrogenic	LA*T/RO/JEN/IK
laryngorrhea	LARNG/RAOE/YA	latissimi	LA/TIS/MAOI
laryngoscleroma	LARNG/SKLE/ROE/MA		LA/TISZ/MAOI
laryngoscope	LARNG/SKOEP	latissimus	LA/TIS/MUS
laryngoscopic	LARNG/SKOP/IK		LA/TISZ/MUS
laryngoscopist	LARN/GOS/KP*IS	latitude	LAT/TAOUD
	LARN/GOS/KO/P*IS	latitudinal	LAT/TAOUD/NAL
laryngoscopy	LARN/GOS/KPI	latrodectism	LAT/RO/DEK/TIFM
laryngospasm	LARNG/SPAFM	Latrodectus	LAT/RO/DEK/TUS
laryngostasis	LARN/GO*S/SIS	lattice	LAT/TIS
laryngostat	LARNG/STAT	latum	LAI/TUM
laryngostenosis	LARNG/STE/NOE/SIS		LAIT/UM
laryngostomy	LARN/GO*S/M*I	latus	LAI/TUS
laryngostroboscope	LARNG/STROEB/SKOEP	laudable	LAUD/-BL
laryngotome	LARNG/TOEM	laudanine	LAUD/NAOEN
laryngotomy	LARN/GOT/M*I	laudanosine	LAUD/NO/SAOEN
laryngotracheal	LARNG/TRAIK/YAL	laudanum	LAUD/NUM
laryngotracheitis	LARNG/TRAIK/YAOITS	laugh	LAF
laryngotracheobronchitis	LARNG/TRAIK/YO/BRON/KAOITS	laughter	LAF/TER
laryngotracheobronchoscopy			LAFT/ER
	LARNG/TRAIK/YO/BRON/KOS/ KPI	Laugier	LAU/JAI
			LOE/JAI
laryngotracheoscopy	LARNG/TRAIK/YOS/KPI	Laumonier	LAU/MOEN/YAI
laryngotracheotomy	LARNG/TRAIK/YOT/M*I		LAU/MON/YAI
laryngovestibulitis	LARNG/VES/TIB/LAOITS		LOE/MOEN/YAI
laryngoxerosis	LARNG/ZE/ROE/SIS		LOE/MON/YAI
	LARNG/ZAOE/ROE/SIS	Launois	LAU/NOI
larynx	LARNGS		LOEN/WA
	LAR/INGS	laurel	LAURL
lasanum	LAS/NUM		LAUR/EL
lase	LA*IZ	Laurence	LA*URNS
	LAEZ		LA*UR/ENS
	(not LAIZ or LAIS; see laze and lace)		(not LAURNS or LAUR/ENS; see Lawrence)
Lasegue	LA/SAIG	lauric	LAUR/IK
	LA/SAOEG	Lauth	LA*UT
laser	LA*IZ/ER	lavage	LA/VAJ
	LAEZ/ER	lavation	LAI/VAIGS
	LAIZ/ER	Lavdovski	LAV/DOV/SKAOE
lash	LARB	lavement	LAIVMT
Lash	K-P/LARB		LAIV/-MT
lasing	LA*IZ/-G	Laveran	LAV/RAN
	LAEZ/-G	Laverania	LAV/RAIN/YA
Lasiohelea	LAS/YO/HAOEL/YA	laveur	LA/VAOUR
Lasix	LAI/SIX		LA/VUR
	LAIS/IX	law	LAU
lassitude	LAS/TAOUD	Lawford	LAU/FORD
	LASZ/TAOUD	Lawrence	LAURNS
lata	LAI/TA		LAUR/ENS
latae	LAI/TAE	lawrencium	LAU/RENS/YUM
latah	LA/TA	Lawson	LAU/SON
latebra	LAT/BRA	lawsone	LAU/SOEN
latency	LAIT/EN/SI	Lawsonia	LAU/SOEN/YA
	LAI/TEN/SI	laxa	LAK/SA
latent	LAIT/ENT	laxation	LAK/SAIGS
	LAI/TENT	laxative	LAX/TIV
	LAT/ENT	laxator	LAK/SAI/TOR
latentiation	LAI/TEN/SHAIGS	laxator tympani	LAK/SAI/TOR/TIFRP/NAOI
	LAI/TENS/YAIGS	layer	LAI/ER
later(o)-	LAT/R(O)		LAI/YER
latera	LAT/RA		(not LAIR; see lair)
laterad	LAT/RAD	lazaret	LAZ/RET
lateral	LAT/RAL	lazaretto	LAZ/RET/TOE
laterale	LAT/RAI/LAOE	Lazer Creme	LAIZ/ER/KRAO*EM
laterales	LAT/RAI/LAOEZ	LazerFormalyde	LAIZ/ER/FORM/LAOID
laterales et septi	LAT/RAI/LAOEZ/ET/SEP/TAOI	LazerSporin	LAIZ/ER/SPORN
lateralia	LAT/RAIL/YA	LazerSporin-C	LAIZ/ER/SPORN/KR-RBGS
lateralis	LAT/RAI/LIS	lb.	L*B
laterality	LAT/RAL/TI	LDH	L-RBGS/D*RBGS/H*RBGS
lateriflexion	LAT/RI/FL*EBGS	LDL	L-RBGS/D*RBGS/L*RBGS
lateris	LAT/RIS	leachii	LAEFP/YAOI
lateritious	LAT/RIRBS	leaching	LAEFP/-G
lateroabdominal	LAT/RO/AB/DOM/NAL		(not LAOEFP/-G; see leeching)
laterodeviation	LAT/RO/DAOEV/YAIGS	lead	LAED
lateroduction	LAT/RO/D*UBGS		LAOED

	(not LED; see led)
leaflet	LAOEF/LET
leak	LAEK
	(not LAOEK; see leek)
leakage	LAEK/AJ
leaping	LAOEP/-G
learning	LEARN/-G
leash	LAOERB
Leber	LAI/BER
	LAIB/ER
	LEB/ER
lecanopagus	LEK/NOP/GUS
lechopyra	LEK/PAOI/RA
lecith(o)-	LES/TH(O)
lecithal	LES/THAL
lecithalbumin	LES/THAL/BAOU/MIN
lecithid	LES/THID
lecithin	LES/THIN
lecithinase	LES/THIN/AIS
	LES/THI/NAIS
lecithinemia	LES/THIN/AOEM/YA
	LES/THI/NAOEM/YA
lecithoblast	LES/THO/BLA*S
lecithoprotein	LES/THO/PRO/TAOEN
lecithovitellin	LES/THO/VAOI/TEL/LIN
	LES/THO/VI/TEL/LIN
Leclanche	LE/KLAN/SHAI
lectin	LEK/TIN
lectotype	LEKT/TAOIP
lectularia	LEKT/LAIR/YA
	LEK/TAOU/LAIR/YA
lectularius	LEKT/LAIR/YUS
	LEK/TAOU/LAIR/YUS
Ledercillin	LED/ER/SLIN
	LED/ER/SIL/LIN
Lederer	LED/RER
Lederplex	LED/ER/PLEX
ledge	LEJ
Leduc	LE/DAOUK
lee	LAOE
Lee	K-P/LAOE
	LAO*E
leech	LAOEFP
leeching	LAOEFP/-G
Leeuwenhoek	LAOE/WEN/HOEK
	LAOU/EN/HOEK
	LAOU/WEN/HOEK
Le Fort	LE/FORT
left-eyed	LEFT/YAOI/-D
left-footed	LEFT/FAOT/-D
left-handed	LEFT/HAND/-D
left-sidedness	LEFT/SAOID/D*NS
leg	LEG
Legal	LAI/GAL
Legg	L*EG
Legionella	LAOEJ/NEL/LA
Legionella pneumophila	LAOEJ/NEL/LA/NAOU/MOF/LA
legionellosis	LAOEJ/NEL/LOE/SIS
Legionnaire's disease	LAOEJ/NAIR/AOES/DI/SAOEZ
legume	LE/GAOUM
	LEG/YAOUM
legumin	LE/GAOU/MIN
	LEG/MIN
leguminivorous	LE/GAOUM/NIV/ROUS
leiasthenia	LAOI/AS/THAOEN/YA
Leichtenstern	LAOIK/TEN/STERN
	LAOIKT/EN/STERN
	LIK/TEN/STERN
	LIKT/EN/STERN
leio-	LAOI
	LAOI/YO
leiodermia	LAOI/DERM/YA
leiodystonia	LAOI/DIS/TOEN/YA
leiomyoblastoma	LAOI/MAOI/BLAS/TOE/MA
leiomyofibroma	LAOI/MAOI/FAOI/BROE/MA
leiomyoma	LAOI/MAOI/YOE/MA
leiomyomatosis	LAOI/MAOI/MA/TOE/SIS
	LAOI/MAOI/YOEM/TOE/SIS
leiomyosarcoma	LAOI/MAOI/SAR/KOE/MA
leiotrichous	LAOI/OT/RI/KOUS
	LAOI/YOT/RI/KOUS
Leishman	LAOERB/MAN
Leishman-Donovan	LAOERB/MAN/H-F/DON/VAN
leishmania	LAOERB/MAIN/YA
Leishmania	K-P/LAOERB/MAIN/YA
leishmanial	LAOERB/MAIN/YAL
leishmaniana	LAOERB/MAN/YAI/NA
leishmaniasis	LAOERB/MA/NAOI/SIS
leishmanicidal	LAOERB/MAN/SAOI/DAL

leishmanid	LAOERB/MAN/ID
	LAOERB/MA/NID
leishmaniosis	LAOERB/MAN/YOE/SIS
leishmanoid	LAOERB/MA/NOID
	LAOERB/MAN/OID
Leloir	LAOEL/WAR
lema	LAO*E/MA
	(not LAOE/MA; see Lima)
Lembert	LA/BAIR
	LEM/BAIR
lemic	LAOEM/IK
-lemma	LEM/MA
lemmo-	LEM
	LEM/MO
lemmoblast	LEM/BLA*S
lemmoblastic	LEM/BLA*S/IK
lemmocyte	LEM/SAO*IT
lemnisci	LEM/NIS/SAOI
	LEM/NIS/KAOI
lemniscorum	LEM/NIS/KOR/UM
	LEM/NIS/KOER/UM
lemniscus	LEM/NIS/KUS
lemography	LAOE/MOG/FI
lemology	LAOE/MOLG
lemon	LEM/MON
lemoparalysis	LAOEM/PRAL/SIS
	LEM/PRAL/SIS
lemostenosis	LAOEM/STE/NOE/SIS
	LEM/STE/NOE/SIS
length	L*ENT
	L*ENGT
leniceps	LEN/SEPS
lenitive	LEN/TIV
Lennert	LEN/ERT
Lennox	LEN/OX
	LEN/NOX
Lenoir	LEN/WAU
	LEN/WOIR
lens	LENZ
lensectomy	LEN/SEKT/M*I
	LENZ/EKT/M*I
lensometer	LEN/ZOM/TER
	LENZ/OM/TER
lensopathy	LENZ/OP/TH*I
lent(o)-	LEN/T(O)
lenta	LEN/TA
Lente	LEN/TAI
Lente Insulin	LEN/TAI/INS/LIN
lentectomize	LEN/TEKT/MAOIZ
lentectomy	LEN/TEKT/M*I
lenti-	LENT (in most cases)
	LEN/TI
lenticel	LENT/SEL
lenticonus	LENT/KO/NUS
	LENT/KOE/NUS
lenticul(o)-	LEN/TIK/L(O)
	LEN/TIK/YAOU/L(O)
	LEN/TIK/YU/L(O)
lenticula	LEN/TIK/LA
lenticular	LEN/TIK/LAR
lenticulare	LEN/TIK/LAI/RAOE
lenticularis	LEN/TIK/LAI/RIS
lenticuli	LEN/TIK/LAOI
lenticulo-optic	LEN/TIK/LO/OPT/IK
lenticulopapular	LEN/TIK/LO/PAP/LAR
lenticulostriate	LEN/TIK/LO/STRAOI/AIT
	LEN/TIK/LO/STRAOI/YAIT
lenticulothalamic	LEN/TIK/LO/THA/LAM/IK
lenticulus	LEN/TIK/LUS
lentiform	LEN/TI/FORM
	(not LENT/FORM; lent form)
lentiformis	LENT/FOR/MIS
	LEN/TI/FOR/MIS
lentigenes	LEN/TIJ/NAOEZ
lentiginosis	LEN/TIJ/NOE/SIS
lentiginous	LEN/TIJ/NOUS
lentiglobus	LENT/GLOE/BUS
lentigo	LEN/TAOI/GOE
lentigomelanosis	LEN/TAOIG/MEL/NOE/SIS
	LEN/TAOI/GO/MEL/NOE/SIS
lentis	LEN/TIS
lentitis	LEN/TAOITS
Lentivirinae	LENT/VIR/NAE
lentivirus	LENT/VAOI/RUS
lentogenic	LENT/JEN/IK
lentula	LEN/TAOU/LA
	LEN/KHU/LA
Leo	LAOE/YOE
Leonardo	LAOE/NAR/DOE

leonine	LAOE/NAOEN	leptosomic	LEPT/SOEM/IK
leontiasis	LAOE/YON/TAOI/SIS	leptospira	LEPT/SPAOI/RA
	LAOE/ON/TAOI/SIS	Leptospira	K-P/LEPT/SPAOI/RA
leontina	LAOE/YON/TAOI/NA	leptospiral	LEPT/SPAOIRL
	LAOE/ON/TAOI/NA	leptospire	LEPT/SPAOIR
Leopold	LAI/POELD	leptospirosis	LEPT/SPAOI/ROE/SIS
	LAOE/POELD	leptospiruria	LEPT/SPAOI/RAOUR/YA
leotropic	LAOE/TROP/IK	leptostaphyline	LEPT/STAF/LAOIN
lep-	LEP	leptotene	LEPT/TAOEN
leper	LEP/ER	leptothricosis	LEPT/THRI/KOE/SIS
lepidic	LE/PID/IK		LEPT/THRAOI/KOE/SIS
lepido-	LEP/DO	leptothrix	LEPT/THRIX
Lepidoptera	LEP/DOPT/RA	Leptothrix	K-P/LEPT/THRIX
	LEP/DOP/TRA	Leptotrichia	LEPT/TRIK/YA
lepidosis	LEP/DOE/SIS	leptotrichosis	LEPT/TRI/KOE/SIS
lepocyte	LEP/SAO*IT	Leptotrombidium	LEPT/TROM/BID/YUM
lepothrix	LEP/THRIX	Lerch	L*ERPBLG
lepra	LEP/RA		LER/-FP
leprae	LEP/RAE	leresis	LE/RAOE/SIS
leprechaunism	LEP/RE/KAUN/IFM	Leri	LAI/RAI
	LEP/RE/KON/IFM		LAI/RAOE
leprid	LEP/RID		LE/RAOE
leprologist	LE/PRO*LGS	Leriche	LE/RAOEFP
	LEP/RO*LGS		LE/RAOERB
leprology	LE/PROLG	Lermoyez	LER/MO/YAI
	LEP/ROLG		LER/MOE/YAI
leproma	LE/PROE/MA		LER/MOI/YAI
	LEP/ROE/MA	lesbian	LEZ/BAN
lepromatous	LEP/ROEM/TOUS	lesbianism	LEZ/BAOE/YAN
	LE/PROEM/TOUS		LEZ/BAN/IFM
lepromin	LEP/RO/MIN		LEZ/BAOE/YAN/IFM
leprosarium	LEP/RO/SAIRM	lesbicus	LEZ/BI/KUS
leprosary	LEP/RO/SAIR		LES/BI/KUS
leprose	LEP/ROES	Lesch	LERB
leprosery	LEP/RO/SER/RI	lesion	LAOEGS
leprostatic	LEP/RO/STAT/IK	lesional	LAOEGS/NAL
leprosum	LE/PROE/SUM	Lesser	K-P/LES/SER
	LE/PROES/UM		K-P/LESZ/ER
	LEP/ROE/SUM	letalis	LAOE/TAI/LIS
	LEP/ROES/UM	let-down	LET/II-F/DOUN
leprosy	LEP/RO/SI	lethal	LAOE/THAL
leprotic	LEP/ROT/IK	lethality	LAOE/THAL/TI
	LE/PROT/IK	lethargy	L*ET/AR/JI
leprous	LEP/ROUS	lethe	LAOE/THAOE
-lepsis	LEP/SIS	letheral	LAO*ET/RAL
-lepsy	LEP/SI	lethica	L*ET/KA
lept(o)-	LEPT		LAO*ET/KA
	LEP/T(O)	Letter	K-P/LET/ER
-leptic	LEPT/IK	Letterer	LET/RER
leptocephalic	LEPT/SFAL/IK	leucantha	LAOU/KAN/THA
leptocephalous	LEPT/SEF/LOUS	leucemia	LAOU/SAOEM/YA
leptocephalus	LEPT/SEF/LUS	leucin	LAOU/SIN
leptocephaly	LEPT/SEF/LI	leucine	LAOU/SAOEN
leptochroa	LEPT/KROE/WA	leucinosis	LAOUS/NOE/SIS
leptochromatic	LEPT/KROE/MAT/IK	leucinuria	LAOUS/NAOUR/YA
leptocyte	LEPT/SAO*IT	leucismus	LAOU/SIZ/MUS
leptocytosis	LEPT/SAOI/TOE/SIS	leucitis	LAOU/SAOITS
leptodactylous	LEPT/DAKT/LOUS	leuco-	LAOUK
leptodactyly	LEPT/DAKT/LI		LAOU/KO
leptodermic	LEPT/DERM/IK	leucocelaenus	LAOUK/SE/LAOE/NUS
leptodontous	LEPT/DON/TOUS		LAOUK/SE/LAE/NUS
leptomeningeal	LEPT/ME/NIN/JAL	Leucocytozoon	LAOUK/SAOIT/ZAON
leptomeninges	LEPT/ME/NIN/JAOEZ	leucocytozoonosis	LAOUK/SAOIT/ZOE/NOE/SIS
leptomeningoma	LEPT/MEN/NIN/JOE/MA	leucoharmine	LAOUK/HAR/MAOEN
leptomeningitis	LEPT/MEN/JAOITS	leucoline	LAOUK/LAOEN
leptomeningopathy	LEPT/MEN/GOP/TH*I	leucomethylene	LAOUK/M*ET/LAOEN
leptomeninx	LEPT/MEN/INGS	Leuconostoc	LAOUK/NOS/TOK
	LEPT/MAOE/NINGS	leucosin	LAOUK/SIN
leptomere	LEPT/MAOER	leucovorin	LAOUK/VORN
leptomonad	LEPT/MOE/NAD	Leudet	LAOU/DAI
	LEPT/TOM/NAD		LAOU/DET
leptomonas	LEPT/MOE/NAS	leuk(o)-	LAOUK
	LEPT/TOM/NAS		LAOU/K(O)
Leptomonas	K-P/LEPT/MOE/NAS	leukanemia	LAOUK/NAOEM/YA
	K-P/LEPT/TOM/NAS	leukapheresis	LAOUK/FRAOE/SIS
leptonema	LEPT/NAOE/MA		LAOUK/FE/RAOE/SIS
leptonomorphology	LEPT/NO/MOR/FOLG	leukasmus	LAOU/KAZ/MUS
leptopellic	LEPT/PEL/IK	leukemia	LAOU/KAOEM/YA
leptophonia	LEPT/FOEN/YA	leukemic	LAOU/KAOEM/IK
leptophonic	LEPT/FON/IK	leukemid	LAOU/KAOEM/ID
leptopodia	LEPT/POED/YA		LAOU/KAOE/MID
leptoprosope	LEP/TOP/RO/SOEP	leukemogen	LAOU/KAOEM/JEN
leptoprosopia	LEPT/PRO/SOEP/YA	leukemogenesis	LAOU/KAOEM/JEN/SIS
leptoprosopic	LEPT/PRO/SOEP/IK	leukemogenic	LAOU/KAOEM/JEN/IK
leptorrhine	LEPT/RAOIN	leukemoid	LAOU/KAOE/MOID
leptoscope	LEPT/SKOEP		LAOU/KAOEM/OID
leptosomatic	LEPT/SMAT/IK	Leukeran	LAOUK/RAN
	LEPT/SOE/MAT/IK	leukexosis	LAOU/KEK/SOE/SIS
leptosome	LEPT/SOEM	leukin	LAOU/KIN

leukoagglutinin	LAOUK/AI/GLAOUT/NIN	leukopsin	LAOU/KOP/SIN
leukobilin	LAOUK/BIL/LIN	leukoriboflavin	LAOUK/RAOIB/FLAIVN
leukoblast	LAOUK/BLA*S		LAOUK/RAOIB/FLAI/VIN
leukoblastosis	LAOUK/BLAS/TOE/SIS	leukorrhagia	LAOUK/RAI/JA
leukochloroma	LAOUK/KLOE/ROE/MA	leukorrhea	LAOUK/RAOE/YA
leukocidin	LAOUK/SAOI/DIN	leukorrheal	LAOUK/RAOEL
	LAOU/KOS/DIN		LAOUK/RAOE/YAL
leukocoria	LAOUK/KOER/YA	leukosarcoma	LAOUK/SAR/KOE/MA
leukocrit	LAOUK/KRIT	leukosarcomatosis	LAOUK/SAR/KOEM/TOE/SIS
leukocyt(o)-	LAOUK/SAOIT	leukoscope	LAOUK/SKOEP
	LAOUK/SAOI/T(O)	leukosis	LAOU/KOE/SIS
leukocytactic	LAOUK/SAOI/TAKT/IK	leukotactic	LAOUK/TAKT/IK
leukocytal	LAOUK/SAOI/TAL	leukotaxia	LAOUK/TAX/YA
leukocytaxia	LAOUK/SAOI/TAX/YA	leukotaxine	LAOUK/TAK/SAOEN
leukocytaxis	LAOUK/SAOI/TAK/SIS		LAOUK/TAK/SIN
leukocyte	LAOUK/SAO*IT	leukotaxis	LAOUK/TAK/SIS
leukocythemia	LAOUK/SAOI/THAOEM/YA	leukotherapy	LAOUK/THER/PI
leukocytic	LAOUK/SIT/IK	leukothrombin	LAOUK/THROM/BIN
leukocytoblast	LAOUK/SAOIT/BLA*S	leukotic	LAOU/KOT/IK
leukocytoclasis	LAOUK/SAOI/TOK/LA/SIS	leukotome	LAOUK/TOEM
leukocytogenesis	LAOUK/SAOIT/JEN/SIS	leukotomy	LAOU/KOT/M*I
leukocytoid	LAOUK/SAOI/TOID	leukotoxic	LAOUK/TOX/IK
leukocytology	LAOUK/SAOI/TOLG	leukotoxicity	LAOUK/TOK/SIS/TI
leukocytolysin	LAOUK/SAOI/TOL/SIN	leukotoxin	LAOUK/TOK/SIN
leukocytolysis	LAOUK/SAOI/TOL/SIS	leukotrichia	LAOUK/TRIK/YA
leukocytolytic	LAOUK/SAOIT/LIT/IK	leukotrichous	LAOU/KOT/RI/KOUS
leukocytoma	LAOUK/SAOI/TOE/MA	leukotriene	LAOUK/TR*I/AOEN
leukocytometer	LAOUK/SAOI/TOM/TER	leukourobilin	LAOUK/YAOUR/BIL/LIN
leukocytopenia	LAOUK/SAOIT/PAOEN/YA	leukovirus	LAOUK/VAOI/RUS
leukocytophagy	LAOUK/SAOI/TOF/JI	leuprolide	LAOU/PRO/LAOID
leukocytoplania	LAOUK/SAOIT/PLAIN/YA	Levaditi	LEV/DAOE/TAOE
leukocytopoiesis	LAOUK/SAOIT/POI/SIS	levallorphan	LEV/LOR/FAN
leukocytosis	LAOUK/SAOI/TOE/SIS		LEV/LOER/FAN
leukocytotactic	LAOUK/SAOIT/TAKT/IK	levamfetamine	LAOE/VAM/FET/MAOEN
leukocytotaxia	LAOUK/SAOIT/TAX/YA	levamisole	LAOE/VAM/SOEL
leukocytotaxis	LAOUK/SAOIT/TAK/SIS	levan	LEV/VAN
leukocytotherapy	LAOUK/SAOIT/THER/PI		(not LEVN; see eleven)
leukocytotoxicity	LAOUK/SAOIT/TOK/SIS/TI	levansucrase	LEV/AN/SAOU/KRAIS
leukocytotoxin	LAOUK/SAOIT/TOK/SIN		LEV/AN/SU/KRAIS
leukocytotropic	LAOUK/SAOIT/TROP/IK	levarterenol	LEV/AR/TAOER/NOL
leukocyturia	LAOUK/SAOI/TAOUR/YA		LEV/ART/RAOE/NOL
leukoderivative	LAOUK/DRIV/TIV	Levatol	LEV/TOL
leukoderma	LAOUK/DER/MA	levator	LAOE/VAI/TOR
leukodermatous	LAOUK/DERM/TOUS		LE/VAI/TOR
leukodermia	LAOUK/DERM/YA	levatores	LAOEV/TOR/RAOEZ
leukodermic	LAOUK/DERM/IK		LEV/TOR/RAOEZ
leukodextrin	LAOUK/DEX/TRIN	levatoris	LAOEV/TOR/RIS
leukodontia	LAOUK/DON/SHA		LEV/TOR/RIS
leukodystrophia	LAOUK/DIS/TROEF/YA	level	LEVL
leukodystrophy	LAOUK/DIS/TRO/FI	Leventhal	LEVN/THAL
leukoedema	LAOUK/E/DAOE/MA		LEV/EN/THAL
	LAOUK/DAOE/MA	lever	LEVR
leukoencephalitis	LAOUK/EN/SEF/LAOITS		LAOEVR
leukoencephalopathy	LAOUK/EN/SEF/LOP/TH*I	leverage	LEV/RAJ
leukoencephaly	LAOUK/EN/SEF/LI		LEVR/AJ
leukoerythroblastic	LAOUK/R*IT/RO/BLA*S/IK		LAOEV/RAJ
leukoerythroblastosis	LAOUK/R*IT/RO/BLAS/TOE/SIS		LAOEVR/AJ
leukogram	LAOUK/GRAM	Levi	LAI/VAOE
leukokeratosis	LAOUK/KER/TOE/SIS	levicellular	LEV/SEL/YAOU/LAR
leukokinesis	LAOUK/KI/NAOE/SIS	levigating	LEV/GAIT/-G
leukokinetic	LAOUK/KI/NET/IK	levigation	LEV/GAIGS
leukokinetics	LAOUK/KI/NET/IK/-S	Levin	LEV/VIN
leukokraurosis	LAOUK/KRAU/ROE/SIS		(not LEVN; see eleven)
leukolymphosarcoma	LAOUK/LIM/FO/SAR/KOE/MA	Levine	LE/VAOEN
leukolysin	LAOU/KOL/SIN		LE/VAOIN
leukolysis	LAOU/KOL/SIS	levitation	LEV/TAIGS
leukolytic	LAOUK/LIT/IK	Leviviridae	LEV/VIR/DAE
leukoma	LAOU/KOE/MA	Levlen	LEV/LEN
leukomatous	LAOUK/KOEM/TOUS	levo-	LAOEV
leukomonocyte	LAOUK/MON/SAO*IT		LAOE/VO
leukomyelitis	LAOUK/MAOI/LAOITS	levobunolol	LAOEV/BAOUN/LOL
leukomyelopathy	LAOUK/MAOI/LOP/TH*I	levocardia	LAOEV/KARD/YA
leukomyoma	LAOUK/MAOI/YOE/MA	levocardiogram	LAOEV/KARD/YO/GRAM
leukon	LAOU/KON	levoclination	LAOEV/KLI/NAIGS
leukonecrosis	LAOUK/NE/KROE/SIS		LAOEV/KLAOI/NAIGS
leukonychia	LAOUK/NIK/YA	levocycloduction	LAOEV/SAOI/KLO/D*UBGS
leukopathia	LAOUK/PA*T/YA	levodopa	LAOEV/DOE/PA
leukopathy	LAOU/KOP/TH*I	Levo-Dromoran	LAOEV/DROEM/RAN
leukopedesis	LAOUK/PE/DAOE/SIS	levoduction	LAOEV/D*UBGS
leukopenia	LAOUK/PAOEN/YA	levoglucose	LAOEV/GLAOU/KOES
leukopenic	LAOUK/PAOEN/IK	levogram	LAOEV/GRAM
leukophagocytosis	LAOUK/FAG/SAOI/TOE/SIS	levogyral	LAOEV/JAOIRL
leukophlegmasia	LAOUK/FLEG/MAIZ/YA	levogyrate	LAOEV/JAOI/RAIT
leukoplakia	LAOUK/PLAIK/YA	levogyration	LAOEV/JAOI/RAIGS
leukopoiesis	LAOUK/POI/SIS	levogyrous	LAOEV/JAOI/ROUS
leukopoietic	LAOUK/POIT/IK		LAOEV/JAOIR/OUS
leukoprecipitin	LAOUK/PRE/SIP/TIN	levomethadyl acetate	LAOEV/M*ET/DIL/AS/TAIT
leukoprophylaxis	LAOUK/PROEF/LAK/SIS	levonordefrin	LAOEV/NOR/DEF/RIN
leukoprotease	LAOUK/PROET/YAIS		LAOEV/NORD/FRIN

levophaaacetoperane	LAOEV/FAS/TOP/RAIN	lichenoides	LAOI/KEN/OI/DAOEZ
Levophed	LAOEV/FED		LAOIK/NOI/DAOEZ
levophobia	LAOEV/FOEB/YA	Lichtheim	LIKT/THAOIM
levopropoxyphene	LAOEV/PRO/POX/FAOEN		LIK/THAOIM
levopropylcillin	LAOEV/PRO/PIL/SLIN	licorice	LIK/RIRB
	LAOEV/PRO/PIL/SIL/LIN		LIK/RIS
levorotary	LAOEV/ROET/RI	lid	LID
levorotation	LAOEV/ROE/TAIGS	Liddel	LID/EL
levorotatory	LAOEV/ROET/TOIR		LID/DEL
levorphanol	LAOE/VOR/FA/NOL	Lidex	LAOI/DEX
	LEV/OR/FA/NOL	Lidex-E	LAOI/DEX/ERBGS
levosin	LAOEV/SIN	lido-	LAOID
Levothroid	LAOEV/THROID		LAOI/DO
levothyroxine	LAOEV/THAOI/ROK/SAOEN	lidocaine	LAOID/KAIN
levotorsion	LAOEV/TORGS	lidofenin	LAOID/FEN/NIN
levoversion	LAOEV/VERGS	lidofilcon	LAOID/FIL/KON
levoxadrol	LAOE/VOX/DROL	lidoflazine	LAOID/FLAI/ZAOEN
Levoxine	LAOE/VOK/SAOEN	lie	LAOI
Levret	LEV/RAI	lieberkuhn	LAOEB/ER/KAOUN
	LEV/RET		LAOEB/ER/KAOEN
Levsin	LEV/SIN	Lieberkuhn	K-P/LAOEB/ER/KAOUN
Levsinex	LEV/SI/NEX		K-P/LAOEB/ER/KAOEN
levul-	LEV/L-	Liebermann	LAOEB/ER/MAN
	LEV/YAOU/L-	Liebermeister	LAOEB/ER/MAO*IS/ER
	LEV/YU/L-	Liebig	LAOE/BIG
levulan	LEV/LAN		LAOEB/IG
levulic	LEV/LIK	lien	LAOI/-N
levulin	LEV/LIN		(not LAOIN; see line)
levulinate	LEV/LI/NAIT	lien(o)-	LAOI/N(O)
	LEV/LIN/AIT		LAOE/AOEN
levulinic	LEV/LIN/IK		LAOI/E/N(O)
levulosan	LEV/LOE/SAN	lienal	LAOI/NAL
levulosazone	LEV/LOES/ZOEN	lienale	LAOI/NAI/LAOE
levulose	LEV/LOES	lienalis	LAOI/NAI/LIS
levulosemia	LEV/LO/SAOEM/YA	lienculus	LAOI/EN/KLUS
levulosuria	LEV/LO/SAOUR/YA	lienectomy	LAOI/NEKT/M*I
lewinii	LAOU/WIN/YAOI	lienis	LAOI/E/NIS
	LAOU/WIN/YAOE		LAOI/NIS
Lewis	LAO*U/WIS	lienitis	LAOI/NAOITS
	(not LAOU/WIS; see Louis)	lienocele	LAOI/NO/SAO*EL
lewisite	LAOU/WI/SAOIT		LAOI/AOEN/SAO*EL
	LAO*U/SAOIT	lienography	LAOI/NOG/FI
	(not LAOU/SAOIT; see Lucite)	lienomalacia	LAOI/NO/MA/LAI/SHA
-lexia	LEX/YA		LAOI/AOEN/MA/LAI/SHA
-lexic	LEX/IK	lienomedullary	LAOI/NO/MED/LAIR
-lexis	LEK/SIS		LAOI/AOEN/MED/LAIR
-lexy	LEK/SI	lienomyelogenous	LAOI/NO/MAOI/LOJ/NOUS
Leyden	LAOID/-N		LAOI/AOEN/MAOI/LOJ/NOUS
	LAOI/DEN	lienomyelomalacia	LAOI/NO/MAOI/LO/MA/LAI/SHA
Leyden-Moebius	LAOID/-N/H-F/MAOEB/YUS		LAOI/AOEN/MAOI/LO/MA/LAI/
	LAOI/DEN/H-F/MAOEB/YUS		SHA
Leydig	LAOI/DIG	lienopancreatic	LAOI/NO/PAN/KRAT/IK
leydigarche	LAOI/DIG/AR/KAOE		LAOI/AOEN/PAN/KRAT/IK
	LAOID/GAR/KAOE	lienopathy	LAOI/NOP/TH*I
Lhermitte	LAIR/MIT	lienorenal	LAOI/NO/RAOENL
	LER/MIT		LAOI/AOEN/RAOENL
liberate	LIB/RAIT	lienorenale	LAOI/NO/RE/NAI/LAOE
liberation	LIB/RAIGS		LAOI/AOEN/RE/NAI/LAOE
liberator	LIB/RAI/TOR	lienotoxin	LAOI/NO/TOK/SIN
liberomotor	LIB/RO/MOE/TOR		LAOI/AOEN/TOK/SIN
libidinal	LI/BID/NAL	lienteric	LAOI/SPWER/IK
libidinization	LI/BID/NI/ZAIGS		LAOI/EN/TER/IK
libidinous	LI/BID/NOUS		LAOIN/TER/IK
libido	LI/BAOE/DOE	lientery	LAOI/SPWAIR
	LI/BAOI/DOE		LAOI/EN/TAIR
Libman	LIB/MAN		LAOI/SPWER/RI
Libman-Sacks	LIB/MAN/H-F/SA*X		LAOIN/TAIR
libra	LAOI/BRA	lienunculus	LAOI/NUN/KLUS
	LAOIB/RA	Liepmann	LAOEP/MAN
	LAOE/BRA	Liesegang	LAOES/GANG
	LAOEB/RA		LAOEZ/GANG
Librax	LIB/RAX	Lieutaud	LAOU/TOE
Libritabs	LIB/RI/TAB/-S	life	LAOIF
Librium	LIB/RUM	ligament	LIG/-MT
	LIB/RAOE/UM	ligamenta	LIG/MEN/TA
	LIB/RAOE/YUM	ligamentae	LIG/MEN/TAE
lice	LAOIS	ligamenti	LIG/MEN/TAOI
license	LAOIS/ENS	ligamentopexis	LIG/-MT/PEK/SIS
	LAOI/SENS		LIG/MENT/PEK/SIS
licentiate	LAOI/SEN/SHAIT		LIG/MEN/TO/PEK/SIS
lichen	LAOI/KEN	ligamentopexy	LIG/-MT/PEK/SI
	(not LAOIK/-N; see liken)		LIG/MENT/PEK/SI
lichenification	LAOI/KEN/FI/KAIGS		LIG/MEN/TO/PEK/SI
lichenin	LAOI/KEN/NIN	ligamentosa	LIG/MEN/TOE/SA
	LAOI/KE/NIN	ligamentosus	LIG/MEN/TOE/SUS
	(not LAOIK/NIN; see like anyone)	ligamentous	LIG/MEN/TOUS
lichenization	LAOI/KEN/ZAIGS		LIG/-MT/OUS
lichenoid	LAOI/KEN/OID	ligamentum	LIG/MEN/TUM
	LAOIK/NOID		LIG/-MT/UM

ligand	LAOI/GAND		LING/WAFP/YAOU/L-
	LIG/GAND		LING/WAFP/YU/L-
	LI/GAND	Linguatula	LING/WAT/LA
ligase	LAOI/GAIS	linguatuliasis	LING/WAT/LAOI/SIS
	LIG/AIS	linguatulid	LING/WAT/LID
ligate	LAOI/GAIT	Linguatulidae	LING/WA/TAOUL/DAE
ligation	LAOI/GAIGS	linguatulosis	LING/WAT/LOE/SIS
ligator	LAOI/GAI/TOR	linguiform	LING/WI/FORM
ligature	LIG/KHUR	linguistic	LING/W*IS/IK
light	LAOIGT	lingul-	LING/L-
lightening	LAOIGT/-NG		LING/YAOU/L-
ligneous	LIG/NOUS		LING/YU/L-
	LIG/NAOE/OUS		LIN/GAOU/L-
ligni	LIG/NAOI	lingula	LING/LA
Lignieres	LAOEN/YAIRS	lingulae	LING/LAE
	LIN/YAIRS	lingular	LING/LAR
lignieresii	LAOEN/YAIRS/YAOI	lingularis	LING/LAI/RIS
	LIN/YAIRS/YAOI	lingulectomy	LING/LEKT/M*I
lignin	LIG/NIN	linguoaxial	LING/WO/AX/YAL
lignoceric	LIG/NO/SAOER/IK	linguocervical	LING/WO/SEFRB/KAL
	LIG/NO/SER/IK	linguoclination	LING/WO/KLI/NAIGS
lignum	LIG/NUM	linguoclusion	LING/WO/KLAOUGS
ligroin	LIG/ROIN	linguodental	LING/WO/DEN/TAL
limax	LAOI/MAX	linguodistal	LING/WO/DIS/TAL
limb	LIM	linguofacialis	LING/WO/FAIRB/YAI/LIS
limbal	LIM/BAL		LING/WO/FAI/SHAI/LIS
limbi	LIM/BAOI		LING/WO/FAIS/YAI/LIS
limbic	LIM/BIK	linguogingival	LING/WO/JING/VAL
Limbitrol	LIM/BI/TROL	linguoincisal	LING/WO/IN/SAOI/ZAL
limb-kinetic	LIM/H-F/KI/NET/IK	linguomesial	LING/WO/MAOEZ/YAL
limbus	LIM/BUS	linguo-occlusal	LING/WO/O/KLAOU/ZAL
lime	LAOIM	linguopapillitis	LING/WO/PAP/LAOITS
limen	LAOI/MEN	linguoplacement	LING/WO/PLAIS/-MT
limes	LAOI/MAOEZ	linguoplate	LING/WO/PLAET
limina	LIM/NA		LING/WO/PLAIT
liminal	LIM/NAL	linguopulpal	LING/WO/PUL/PAL
liminaris	LIM/NAI/RIS	linguoversion	LING/WO/VERGS
liminometer	LIM/NOM/TER	liniment	LIN/-MT
limit	LIMT	linimentum	LIN/MEN/TUM
limitans	LIM/TANZ		LIN/-MT/UM
	LIMT/TANZ	linin	LAOI/NIN
limitation	LIM/TAIGS	linitis	LI/NAOITS
	LIMT/TAIGS		LAOI/NAOITS
limitrophic	LIM/TROFK	link	LIN/-K
	LIM/TROEFK		L*ING
Limnatis nilotica	LIM/NAI/TIS/NAOI/LOT/KA	linkage	LIN/KAJ
limnemia	LIM/NAOEM/YA		L*ING/AJ
limnemic	LIM/NAOEM/IK	linker	LIN/KER
limnology	LIM/NOLG		L*ING/ER
limo	LAOI/MOE	Linognathus	LI/NOG/NA/THUS
limon	LAOI/MON		LIN/OG/NA/THUS
limonene	LIM/NAOEN	linoleate	LI/NOEL/YAIT
limonis	LAOI/MOE/NIS		LIN/OEL/YAIT
limophoitas	LAOIM/FOI/TAS	linoleic	LIN/LAOE/IK
limophthisis	LAOI/MOF/THI/SIS	linolein	LIN/OEL/YIN
limosis	LAOI/MOE/SIS		LI/NOEL/YIN
limotherapy	LAOIM/THER/PI	linolenic	LIN/LEN/IK
limp	LIFRP	linolic	LI/NOEL/IK
Lincocin	LIN/KO/SIN		LIN/OEL/IK
lincomycin	LIN/KO/MAOI/SIN	linseed	LIN/SAOED
lincture	LING/KHUR	lint	LINT
linctus	LING/TUS	lintin	LIN/TIN
lindane	LIN/DAIN	lintine	LIN/TAOEN
Lindau	LIN/DAU	linum	LAOI/NUM
	LIN/DOU		LAOIN/UM
Lindbergh	LIND/BERG	Lioresal	LAOI/YOR/SAL
Lindemann	LIND/MAN		LAOI/OER/SAL
	LIN/DE/MAN	liothyronine	LAOI/THAOIR/NAOEN
Lindner	LIND/NER	liotrix	LAOI/TRIX
line	LAOIN	lip	LIP
linea	LIN/YA	lip(o)-	LIP
lineae	LIN/YAE		LI/P(O)
lineage	LIN/YAJ		LAOIP (not in CAT)
	LIN/AJ		LAOI/P(O) (not in CAT)
lineal	LIN/YAL	lipacidemia	LIP/AS/DAOEM/YA
linear	LIN/YAR	lipaciduria	LIP/AS/DAOUR/YA
lineata	LIN/YAI/TA	lipancreatin	LI/PAN/KRA/TIN
liner	LAOIN/ER		LI/PAN/KRAOE/TIN
lingu(o)-	LING/W(O)	liparocele	LIP/RO/SAO*EL
lingua	LING/WA	liparodyspnea	LIP/RO/DIS/NAOE/YA
linguae	LING/WAE		LIP/RO/DIS/-P/NAOE/YA
lingual	LING/WAL	liparoid	LIP/ROID
linguale	LING/WAI/LAOE	lipase	LIP/AIS
lingualis	LING/WAI/LIS		LAOI/PAIS
lingually	LING/WAL/LI	lipasic	LI/PAIS/IK
linguatul-	LING/WAT/L-	lipasuria	LIP/AIS/YAOUR/YA
	LING/WAT/YAOU/L-	lipectomy	LIP/EKT/M*I
	LING/WAT/YU/L-		LI/PEKT/M*I
	LING/WAFP/L-	lipedema	LIP/DAOE/MA

lipemia	LI/PAOEM/YA	lipoma	LI/POE/MA
	LIP/AOEM/YA	lipomatoid	LI/POEM/TOID
lipemic	LI/PAOEM/IK	lipomatosa	LIP/MA/TOE/SA
lipid	LIP/ID		LI/POEM/TOE/SA
lipidase	LIP/DAIS	lipomatosis	LIP/MA/TOE/SIS
lipidemia	LIP/DAOEM/YA		LI/POEM/TOE/SIS
lipidic	LI/PID/IK	lipomatous	LI/POEM/TOUS
	LIP/ID/IK	lipomeningocele	LIP/ME/NING/SAO*EL
lipidol	LIP/DOL	lipometabolic	LIP/MET/BOL/IK
lipidolysis	LIP/DOL/SIS	lipometabolism	LIP/ME/TAB/LIFM
lipidolytic	LIP/DO/LIT/IK	lipomicron	LIP/MAOI/KRON
lipidoses	LIP/DOE/SAOEZ	lipomucopolysaccharidosis	LIP/MAOUK/POL/SAK/RI/DOE/SIS
lipidosis	LIP/DOE/SIS	lipomyohemangioma	LIP/MAOI/HE/MAN/JOE/MA
lipidtemns	LIP/ID/TEM/-S	lipomyoma	LIP/MAOI/YOE/MA
lipiduria	LIP/DAOUR/YA	lipomyxoma	LIP/MIK/SOE/MA
lipin	LIP/PIN	liponephrosis	LIP/NE/FROE/SIS
Lipmann	LIP/MAN	Lipo-Nicin	LIP/NAOI/SIN
lipoadenoma	LIP/AD/NOE/MA	liponucleoprotein	LIP/NAOUK/LO/PRO/TAOEN
lipoamide	LIP/AM/AOID	Liponyssus	LIP/NIS/SUS
	LIP/AM/ID	lipopectic	LIP/PEKT/IK
lipoarthritis	LIP/AR/THRAOITS	lipopenia	LIP/PAOEN/YA
lipoate	LIP/AIT	lipopenic	LIP/PAOEN/IK
	LIP/PO/AIT	lipopeptid	LIP/PEP/TID
lipoatrophia	LIP/AI/TROEF/YA	lipopexia	LIP/PEX/YA
lipoatrophic	LIP/AI/TROFK	lipopexic	LIP/PEX/IK
lipoatrophy	LIP/AT/RO/FI	lipophage	LIP/FALJ
Lipo-B-C	LAOI/PO/B-RBGS/KR*RBGS	lipophagia	LIP/FAI/JA
lipoblast	LIP/BLA*S	lipophagic	LIP/FALJ/IK
lipoblastoma	LIP/BLAS/TOE/MA		LIP/FAJ/IK
lipoblastomatosis	LIP/BLAS/TOEM/TOE/SIS	lipophagy	LI/POF/JI
lipocardiac	LIP/KARD/YAK		LIP/OF/JI
lipocatabolic	LIP/KAT/BOL/IK	lipophanerosis	LIP/FAN/ROE/SIS
lipocele	LIP/SAO*EL	lipophil	LIP/FIL
lipocellulose	LIP/SEL/YAOU/LOES	lipophilia	LIP/FIL/YA
lipoceratous	LIP/SER/TOUS	lipophilic	LIP/FIL/IK
lipocere	LIP/SAOER	lipophore	LIP/FOER
lipochondrodystrophy	LIP/KON/DRO/DIS/TRO/FI	lipophosphodiesterase	LIP/FOS/FO/DI/ES/TRAIS
lipochondroma	LIP/KON/DROE/MA	lipoplethoric	LIP/PLE/THOR/IK
lipochrome	LIP/KROEM	lipopolysaccharide	LIP/POL/SAK/RAOID
lipochromemia	LIP/KROE/MAOEM/YA	lipoprotein	LIP/PRO/TAOEN
lipochromogen	LIP/KROEM/JEN	lipoproteinemia	LIP/PROET/NAOEM/YA
lipoclasis	LI/POK/LA/SIS	lipoproteinemic	LIP/PROET/NAOEM/IK
lipoclastic	LIP/KLA*S/IK	lipoproteinosis	LIP/PROET/NOE/SIS
lipocorticoid	LIP/KORT/KOID	liporhodin	LIP/ROE/DIN
lipocrit	LIP/KRIT	liposarcoma	LIP/SAR/KOE/MA
lipocyanine	LIP/SAOI/NIN	liposis	LI/POE/SIS
lipocyte	LIP/SAO*IT	lipositol	LIP/OS/TOL
lipodermoid	LIP/DER/MOID		LI/POS/TOL
lipodieresis	LIP/DI/ER/SIS	liposoluble	LIP/SOL/YAOUBL
lipodieretic	LIP/DI/RET/IK	liposome	LIP/SOEM
lipodystrophia	LIP/DIS/TROEF/YA	liposuction	LIP/S*UBGS
lipodystrophy	LIP/DIS/TRO/FI	liposuctioning	LIP/S*UBGS/-G
lipoedema	LIP/E/DAOE/MA	lipothiamide	LIP/THAOI/MAOID
	(*not* LIP/DAOE/MA; see lipedema)	lipotrophic	LIP/TROFK
lipoferous	LIP/OF/ROUS	lipotrophy	LI/POT/RO/FI
	LI/POF/ROUS	lipotropic	LIP/TROP/IK
lipofibroma	LIP/FAOI/BROE/MA		LIP/TROEP/IK
lipofuscin	LIP/FAOU/SIN	lipotropin	LIP/TROE/PIN
	LIP/FUS/SIN	lipotropism	LIP/TROEP/IFM
lipofuscinosis	LIP/FAOUS/NOE/SIS		LI/POT/RO/PIFM
	LIP/FUS/NOE/SIS	lipotropy	LI/POT/RO/PI
lipogenesis	LIP/JEN/SIS	lipovaccine	LIP/VAK/SAOEN
lipogenetic	LIP/JE/NET/IK	lipovitellin	LIP/VAOI/TEL/LIN
lipogenic	LIP/JEN/IK		LIP/VI/TEL/LIN
lipogenous	LI/POJ/NOUS	lipoxanthine	LIP/ZAN/THIN
lipogranuloma	LIP/GRAN/LOE/MA		LIP/ZAN/THAOEN
lipogranulomatosis	LIP/GRAN/LOEM/TOE/SIS	lipoxenous	LIP/POX/NOUS
lipohemarthrosis	LIP/HEM/AR/THROE/SIS	lipoxeny	LI/POX/N*I
	LIP/HAOEM/AR/THROE/SIS	lipoxidase	LI/POX/DAIS
lipohemia	LIP/HAOEM/YA	lipoxygenase	LI/POX/JE/NAIS
lipohistiodieresis	LIP/H*IS/YO/DI/ER/SIS		LI/POX/JEN/AIS
lipohyalin	LIP/HAOI/LIN	lipoyl	LIP/OIL
lipoic	LI/POIK	lippa	LIP/PA
	LI/POE/IK	lipping	LIP/-G
lipoid	LIP/OID	Lippes Loop	LIP/-S/LAOP
lipoidal	LI/POI/DAL		LIPS/LAOP
	LIP/OI/DAL	lippitude	LIP/TAOUD
lipoidemia	LIP/OI/DAOEM/YA	lippitudo	LIP/TAOU/DOE
lipoides	LI/POI/DAOEZ	Lipschutz	LIP/SHITS
lipoidic	LI/POID/IK		LIP/SHUTS
lipoidolytic	LI/POID/LIT/IK	lipsotrichia	LIP/SO/TRIK/YA
lipoidosis	LIP/OI/DOE/SIS		LIPS/TRIK/YA
lipoidotropic	LI/POID/TROP/IK	lipuria	LI/PAOUR/YA
lipoidproteinosis	LIP/OID/PROET/NOE/SIS	lipuric	LI/PAOUR/IK
lipoidsiderosis	LIP/OID/SID/ROE/SIS	Liquaemin	LIK/WA/E/MIN
lipoiduria	LIP/OI/DAOUR/YA		LIK/WA/MIN
lipolipoidosis	LIP/LIP/OI/DOE/SIS	liquefacient	LIK/WE/FAIRBT
lipolysis	LI/POL/SIS	liquefaction	LIK/WE/FA*BGS
lipolytic	LIP/LIT/IK	liquefactive	LIK/WE/FAKT/IV

liquefy	LIK/WE/FI	lithodialysis	L*IT/DI/AL/SIS
liquefying	LIK/WE/FI/-G	lithogenesis	L*IT/JEN/SIS
liquescent	LI/KWES/ENT	lithogenic	L*IT/JEN/IK
liqueur	LIK/KUR	lithogenous	LI/THOJ/NOUS
	LIK/KER		L*IT/OJ/NOUS
Liqui-Cal	LIK/WI/KAL	lithogeny	LI/THOJ/N*I
Liqui-Char	LIK/WI/KHAR		L*IT/OJ/N*I
liquid	LIK/WID	lithoid	L*IT/OID
Liquid Pred	LIK/WID/PRED	lithokelyphopedion	L*IT/KEL/FO/PAOED/YON
Liquifilm	LIK/WI/FIL/-M	lithokelyphopedium	L*IT/KEL/FO/PAOED/YUM
Liquifilm Forte	LIK/WI/FIL/-M/FOR/TAI	lithokelyphos	L*IT/KEL/FOS
liquiform	LIK/WI/FORM	litholabe	L*IT/LAIB
Liquiprin	LIK/WI/PRIN	litholapaxy	LI/THOL/PAK/SI
liquogel	LIK/WO/JEL	lithology	LI/THOLG
liquor	LIK/KOR	litholysis	LI/THOL/SIS
liquores	LIK/WOR/RAOEZ	litholyte	L*IT/LAOIT
liquorice	L*IK/RIS	litholytic	L*IT/LIT/IK
	L*IK/RIRB	lithometer	LI/THOM/TER
	(*not* LIK/RIS or LIK/RIRB; see	lithomyl	L*IT/MIL
	licorice)	lithonephria	L*IT/NEF/RAOE/YA
liquoris	LIK/WOR/RIS		L*IT/NEF/RA
liquorrhea	LIK/RAOE/YA	lithonephritis	L*IT/NE/FRAOITS
Lisfranc	LIS/FRAN/-K	lithonephrotomy	L*IT/NE/FROT/M*I
	LIS/FRA*NG	lithopedion	L*IT/PAOED/YON
lisinopril	LAOI/SIN/PRIL	lithopedium	L*IT/PAOED/YUM
lisp	LIS/-P	lithophone	L*IT/FOEN
Lissauer	LIS/SOUR	lithoscope	L*IT/SKOEP
	LIS/SAUR	Lithostat	L*IT/STAT
Lissencephala	LIS/EN/SEF/LA	lithotome	L*IT/TOEM
	LIS/SEN/SEF/LA	lithotomist	LI/THOT/M*IS
lissencephalia	LIS/EN/SFAIL/YA	lithotomy	LI/THOT/M*I
	LIS/SEN/SFAIL/YA	lithotony	LI/THOT/N*I
lissencephalic	LIS/EN/SFAL/IK	lithotresis	L*IT/TRAOE/SIS
	LIS/SEN/SFAL/IK	lithotripsy	L*IT/TRIP/SI
lissencephaly	LIS/EN/SEF/LI	lithotripter	L*IT/TRIP/TER
	LIS/SEN/SEF/LI	lithotriptic	L*IT/TRIPT/IK
lissive	LIS/IV	lithotriptor	L*IT/TRIP/TOR
	LIS/SIV	lithotriptoscope	L*IT/TRIPT/SKOEP
	LISZ/IV	lithotriptoscopy	L*IT/TRIP/TOS/KPI
lissosphincter	LIS/SFINGT/ER	lithotrite	L*IT/TRAOIT
	LIS/SFING/TER	lithotrity	LI/THOT/RI/TI
lissotrichic	LIS/TRIK/IK	lithotroph	L*IT/TROEF
lissotrichous	LIS/TRIK/OUS		L*IT/TROF
	LI/SOT/RI/KOUS	lithotrophic	L*IT/TROFK
	LIS/SOT/RI/KOUS	lithous	L*IT/OUS
Lister	LIS/TER	lithoxiduria	L*IT/OX/DAOUR/YA
	K-P/L*IS/ER	lithuresis	L*IT/YAOU/RAOE/SIS
Listerella	L*IS/REL/LA		L*IT/RAOE/SIS
listerellosis	L*IS/REL/LOE/SIS	lithureteria	L*IT/YAOUR/TAOER/YA
Listeria	LIS/TAOER/YA	lithuria	LI/THAOUR/YA
listerial	LIS/TAOERL	litmus	LIT/MUS
listeriosis	LIS/TAOER/YOE/SIS	Litten	LIT/-N
listerism	L*IS/RIFM	litter	LIT/ER
Listing	K-P/L*IS/-G	Little	K-P/LIT/-L
Liston	LIS/TON	littoral	LIT/TRAL
lisuride	LAOI/SAOUR/AOID		LIT/TORL
	LAOI/SAOU/RAOID		(*not* LIT/RAL; see literal)
	LAOIS/RAOID	Littre	LAOET/TER
liter	LAOET/ER		(*not* LAOET/ER or LAOE/TER; see
literal	LIT/RAL		liter)
literalis	LIT/RAI/LIS	littritis	LI/TRAOITS
-lith	L*IT		LIT/TRAOITS
lith(o)-	L*IT	Litzmann	LITS/MAN
	LI/TH(O)	livedo	LI/VAOE/DOE
lithagogue	L*IT/GOG	livedoid	LIV/DOID
Lithane	L*IT/AIN	liver	LIVR
	LI/THAIN	livetin	LIV/TIN
litharge	L*IT/ARJ		LAOIV/TIN
lithate	L*IT/AIT	livid	LIVD
lithecbole	LI/THEK/BLAOE		LIV/ID
	LI/THEK/BO/LAOE	livida	LIV/DA
lithectasy	LI/THEKT/SI	lividity	LI/VID/TI
lithectomy	LI/THEKT/M*I	Livingston	LIV/-G/STON
lithemia	LI/THAOEM/YA		LIVG/STON
lithemic	LI/THAOEM/IK	Livolex	LIV/LEX
lithia	L*IT/YA	livor	LAOI/VOR
lithiasic	L*IT/YAS/IK	lixiviation	LIK/SIV/YAIGS
lithiasis	LI/THAOI/SIS	lixivium	LIK/SIV/YUM
lithic	L*IT/IK	LL	L-RBGS/L*RBGS
lithium	L*IT/YUM	L-Leucine	L-RBGS/LAOU/SAOEN
litho-	L*IT	L-Lysine	L-RBGS/LAOI/SAOEN
Lithobid	L*IT/BID	Loa loa	LOE/WA/LOE/WA
Lithobius	LI/THOEB/YUS	load	LOED
lithocenosis	L*IT/SE/NOE/SIS	loading	LOED/-G
lithocholic	L*IT/KOEL/IK	lobar	LOE/BAR
lithoclast	L*IT/KLA*S	lobares	LOE/BAI/RAOEZ
lithoclysmia	L*IT/KLIZ/MAOE/YA	lobate	LOE/BAIT
	L*IT/KLIZ/MA	lobation	LOE/BAIGS
lithocystotomy	L*IT/SIS/TOT/M*I	lobe	LOEB

lobectomy	LOE/BEKT/M*I		(*not* LEF/LER; see Loffler)
lobelia	LOE/BAOEL/YA	Loestrin	LO/ES/TRIN
lobeline	LOEB/LAOEN		(*not* LOE/ES/TRIN; see low estrin)
	LOEB/LIN	Loevit	LAOE/FIT
	LOB/LAOEN		LAOE/VIT
	LOB/LIN	Loewenthal	*see* Lowenthal
lobi	LOE/BAOI	Loewi	LA*I/VAOE
lobite	LOE/BAOIT		(*not* LAI/VAOE; see Levy)
lobitis	LOE/BAOITS	lofentanil	LOE/FENT/NIL
Loboa loboi	LOE/BOE/WA/LOE/BOI	Loffler	LEF/LER
lobo-	LOEB		LOF/LER
	LOE/BO	loffleria	LEF/LAOER/YA
lobomycosis	LOEB/MAOI/KOE/SIS	log(o)-	LOG
lobopod	LOEB/POD		LOE/G(O)
lobopodia	LOEBO/POED/YA	logadectomy	LOG/DEKT/M*I
lobopodium	LOEB/POED/YUM	logaditis	LOG/DAOITS
loborum	LOE/BOR/UM	logagnosia	LOG/AG/NOEZ/YA
	LOE/BOER/UM	logagraphia	LOG/GRAF/YA
lobose	LOE/BOES	logamnesia	LOG/AM/NAOEZ/YA
lobotomy	LOE/BOT/M*I	Logan	LOE/GAN
lobous	LOEB/OUS	logaphasia	LOG/FAIZ/YA
	LOE/BOUS	logasthenia	LOG/AS/THAOEN/YA
Lobstein	LOEB/STAOIN	logetronography	LOE/JET/RO/NOG/FI
	LOB/STAOIN		LOE/JET/RON/OG/FI
lobul-	LOB/L-	-logia	LOE/JA
	LOB/YAOU/L-		LOEJ/YA
	LOB/YU/L-	logic	LOJ/IK
lobular	LOB/LAR	logistic	LO/J*IS/IK
lobulate	LOB/LAIT		LOEJ/J*IS/IK
lobulated	LOB/LAIT/-D	logoclonia	LOG/KLON/YA
lobulation	LOB/LAIGS	logopathy	LOG/OP/TH*I
lobule	LOB/YAOUL	logopedia	LOG/PAOED/YA
lobulet	LOB/LET	logopedic	LOG/PAOED/IK
lobulette	LOB/L*ET	logopedics	LOG/PAOED/IK/-S
lobuli	LOB/LAOI	logoplegia	LOG/PLAOE/JA
lobulose	LOB/LOES	logorrhea	LOG/RAOE/YA
lobulous	LOB/LOUS	logospasm	LOG/SPAFM
lobulus	LOB/LUS	logotherapy	LOG/THER/PI
lobus	LOE/BUS	-logy	(V)LG
local	LOE/KAL	Lohlein	LAI/LIN
localization	LOE/KAL/ZAIGS		LAI/LAOEN
	LOEK/LI/ZAIGS		LAI/LAOIN
localized	LOEK/LAOIZ/-D	Lohnstein	LOEN/STAOIN
	LOE/KAL/AOIZ/-D	loiasis	LOE/AOI/SIS
localizer	LOEK/LAOIZ/ER	loin	LOIN
	LOE/KAL/AOIZ/ER	loliism	LOE/LI/IFM
localizing	LOEK/LAOIZ/-G		LOEL/YIFM
	LOE/KAL/AOIZ/-G	Lombard	LOM/BARD
locant	LOE/KANT	Lombardi	LOM/BAR/DAOE
locator	LOE/KAI/TOR	Lomotil	LOE/MOE/TIL
lochi(o)-	LOEK/Y(O)	lomustine	LOE/MUS/TAOEN
lochia	LOEK/YA	Lonalac	LOEN/LAK
lochial	LOEK/YAL	London	LON/DON
lochiocolpos	LOEK/YO/KOL/POS	long	LONG
lochiocyte	LOEK/YO/SAO*IT	Long	K-P/LONG
lochiometra	LOEK/YO/MAOE/TRA	longae	LON/GAE
lochiometritis	LOEK/YO/MAOE/TRAOITS		LON/JAE
	LOEK/YO/ME/TRAOITS	longevity	LON/JEV/TI
lochioperitonitis	LOEK/YO/PERT/NAOITS	longi	LON/GAOI
lochiorrhagia	LOEK/YO/RAI/JA		LON/JAOI
lochiorrhea	LOEK/YO/RAOE/YA	longicauda	LON/JI/KAU/DA
lochioschesis	LOEK/YOS/KE/SIS	longilineal	LON/JI/LIN/YAL
lochiostasis	LOEK/YO*S/SIS	longimanous	LON/JI/MAN/OUS
loci	LOE/SAOI	longipedate	LON/JI/PAOE/DAIT
	LOE/KAOI	longiradiate	LON/JI/RAID/YAIT
Locke	LO*K	longissimus	LON/JIS/MUS
	(*not* LOK; see lock)	longitudinal	LON/JI/TAOUD/NAL
lockjaw	LOK/JAU		LONG/TAOUD/NAL
Lockwood	LOK/WAOD	longitudinale	LON/JI/TAOUD/NAI/LAOE
loco	LOE/KOE	longitudinales	LON/JI/TAOUD/NAI/LAOEZ
loco-	LOEK	longitudinalis	LON/JI/TAOUD/NAI/LIS
	LOE/KO	longitype	LON/JI/TAOIP
Locoid	LOE/KOID	longitypical	LON/JI/TIP/KAL
locomotion	LOEK/MOEGS	longum	LON/GUM
locomotive	LOEK/MOET/IV		LONG/UM
locomotor	LOEK/MOE/TOR	longus	LON/GUS
locomotorial	LOEK/MOE/TOIRL	Loniten	LON/TEN
locomotorium	LOEK/MOE/TOIRM	loop	LAOP
locomotory	LOEK/MOET/RI	loop of Henle	LAOP/OF/HEN/LAOE
locular	LOK/LAR	loopful	LAOP/-FL
loculate	LOK/LAIT	loosening	LAOS/-NG
loculated	LOK/LAIT/-D	Lo/Ovral	LOE/OEV/RAL
loculi	LOK/LAOI	Lo-Ovral-28	LOE/OEV/RAL/28
loculus	LOK/LUS	lop-ear	LOP/AOER
locum	LOE/KUM	loperamide	LOE/PER/MAOID
	LOEK/UM	lophodont	LOF/DONT
locus	LOE/KUS	Lophophora williamsii	LOE/FOF/RA/WIL/YAMS/YAOI
Loeb	LAOEB		LOE/FOF/RA/WIL/YAMZ/YAOI
Loeffler	LE*F/LER	lophotrichate	LOE/FOT/RI/KAIT

lophotrichous	LOE/FOT/RI/KOUS	Lubrin	LAOU/BRIN
Lopid	LOE/PID	Luc	L*UK
lopremone	LOE/PRE/MOEN	lucanthone	LAOU/KAN/THOEN
Lopressor	LOE/PRES/SOR	Lucas	LAOU/KAS
Loprox	LOE/PROX	lucensomycin	LAOU/SENS/MAOI/SIN
Lorain	LO/RAIN		LAOU/SEN/SO/MAOI/SIN
lorajmine	LOR/AJ/MAOEN	lucency	LAOUS/EN/SI
lorazepam	LOR/AZ/PAM		LAOU/SEN/SI
	LOE/RAIZ/PAM	lucent	LAOUS/ENT
Lorcet	LOR/SET	lucid	LAOUS/ID
Lorcet-HD	LOR/SET/H-RBGS/D*RBGS		LAOU/SID
Lorcet Plus	LOR/SET/PLUS	lucida	LAOUS/DA
lordoscoliosis	LORD/SKOEL/YOE/SIS	lucidification	LAOU/SID/FI/KAIGS
	LOR/DO/SKOEL/YOE/SIS	lucidity	LAOU/SID/TI
lordosis	LOR/DOE/SIS	luciferase	LAOU/SIF/RAIS
lordotic	LOR/DOT/IK	luciferin	LAOU/SIF/RIN
lordotica	LOR/DOT/KA	lucifugal	LAOU/SIF/GAL
Lorelco	LO/REL/KOE	Lucilia	LAOU/SIL/YA
	LOE/REL/KOE	lucimycin	LAOUS/MAOI/SIN
Lorenz	LOE/RENZ	lucipetal	LAOU/SIP/TAL
	LOR/ENZ	Lucite	LAOU/SAOIT
Loroxide	LOR/OX/AOID	lucium	LAOUS/YUM
	LOR/OK/SAOID	Lucke	LUK/KAOE
Lortab	LOR/TAB		LIK/KAOE
Losec	LOE/SEK	luckenschadel	LUK/EN/SHAID/EL
Lostorfer	LOS/TOR/FER		LIK/EN/SHAID/EL
lotio	LOE/SHOE	lucotherapy	LAO*UK/THER/PI
	LOERB/YOE		(not LAOUK/THER/PI; see
lotion	LOEGS		leukotherapy)
Lotrimin	LOE/TRI/MIN	ludic	LAOUD/IK
Lotrisone	LOE/TRI/SOEN	Ludiomil	LAOUD/YO/MIL
Lotusate	LOE/TUS/AIT	Ludloff	LAOUD/LOF
	LOE/TUS/SAIT		LAOUD/LAUF
Lou Gehrig's disease	LOU/GER/IG/AOES/DI/SAOEZ		LUD/LOF
	LAOU/GER/IG/AOES/DI/SAOEZ		LUD/LAUF
Louis	LAOU/WIS	ludovici	LAOUD/VAOE/KHAOE
	LAOU/WAOE		LAOUD/VAOE/SAOE
loupe	LAOUP		LAOUD/VAOI/SAOE
louse	LOUS		LAOUD/VAOI/SAOI
lousicide	LOUS/SAO*ID	Ludwig	LAOUD/VIG
lousiness	LOUZ/*NS		LAOUD/WIG
	LOU/ZI/*NS		LUD/VIG
lousy	LOU/ZI		LUD/WIG
	LOU/SI	ludwigii	LAOUD/VIG/YAOI
lovastatin	LOEV/STAT/TIN		LAOUD/WIG/YAOI
	LOE/VA/STAT/TIN		LUD/VIG/YAOI
Low	K-P/LOE		LUD/WIG/YAOI
low-density	LOE/H-F/DENS/TI	Luer	LAOU/ER
Lowe	LO*E	lues	LAOU/AOEZ
	LAI/VE		LAOU/WAOEZ
	(not LOE or LAI/VAOE; see low and	luetic	LAOU/ET/IK
	Levi)	luetin	LAOU/TIN
Lowenberg	LAIVN/BERG	luette	LAOU/ET
	LAI/VEN/BERG	Luft	LUFT
Lowenstein	LAIVN/STAOIN	Lufyllin	LAOU/FLIN
	LAI/VEN/STAOIN		LAOU/FIL/LIN
Lowenthal	LAI/VEN/TAL	Lufyllin-400	LAOU/FLIN/4/HUN
	LAI/VEN/THAL		LAOU/FIL/LIN/4/HUN
Lower	K-P/LOE/ER	Lufyllin-GG	LAOU/FLIN/G-RBGS/G*RBGS
Lowila	LOE/LA		LAOU/FIL/LIN/G-RBGS/G*RBGS
	LOE/WI/LA	lug	LUG
loxapine	LOX/PAOEN	Lugol	LAOU/GOL
loxarthron	LOX/AR/THRON	lukewarm	LAOUK/WARM
loxarthrosis	LOX/AR/THROE/SIS	luliberin	LAOU/LIB/RIN
loxia	LOX/YA	lumb(o)-	LUM/B(O)
Loxitane	LOX/TAIN	lumbago	LUM/BAI/GOE
loxophthalmus	LOX/OF/THAL/MUS	lumbale	LUM/BAI/LAOE
Loxosceles	LOK/SOS/LAOEZ	lumbales	LUM/BAI/LAOEZ
	LOX/OS/LAOEZ	lumbalis	LUM/BAI/LIS
Loxoscelidae	LOX/OS/SEL/DAE	lumbar	LUM/BAR
	LOK/SOS/SEL/DAE	lumbarization	LUM/BAR/ZAIGS
loxoscelism	LOK/SOS/LIFM	lumbi	LUM/BAOI
	LOX/OS/LIFM	lumboabdominal	LUM/BO/AB/DOM/NAL
loxotomy	LOK/SOT/M*I	lumbocolostomy	LUM/BO/KO/LO*S/M*I
	LOX/OT/M*I	lumbocolotomy	LUM/BO/KO/LOT/M*I
Loxotrema ovatum	LOX/TRAOE/MA/O/VAI/TUM	lumbocostal	LUM/BO/KOS/TAL
	LOX/TRAOE/MA/O/VAIT/UM	lumbocostalis	LUM/BO/KOS/TAI/LIS
lozenge	LOZ/EN/-J	lumbocrural	LUM/BO/KRAOURL
Lozol	LOE/ZOL	lumbodorsal	LUM/BO/DOR/SAL
Lubarsch	LAOU/BAR/-RB	lumbodorsalis	LUM/BO/DOR/SAI/LIS
lubb	LUB	lumbodynia	LUM/BO/DIN/YA
lubb-dupp	LUB/DUP	lumboiliac	LUM/BO/IL/YAK
Lubraseptic	LAOU/BRA/SEPT/IK	lumboinguinal	LUM/BO/ING/WINL
	LAOUB/RA/SEPT/IK	lumbo-ovarian	LUM/BO/O/VAIRN
lubricant	LAOU/BRI/KANT	lumbosacral	LUM/BO/SAI/KRAL
	LAOUB/RI/KANT	lumborum	LUM/BOR/UM
lubricate	LAOU/BRI/KAIT		LUM/BOER/UM
	LAOUB/RI/KAIT	lumbrical	LUM/BRI/KAL
lubrication	LAOU/BRI/KAIGS		

lumbricales	LUM/BRI/KAI/LAOEZ		LAOU/TAOERB/UM
lumbricalis	LUM/BRI/KAI/LIS	luteectomy	LAOUT/YEKT/M*I
lumbrici	LUM/BRI/SAOI	luteic	LAOU/TAOE/IK
	LUM/BRAOI/SAOI		LAOUT/TAI/IK
lumbricidal	LUM/BRI/SAOI/DAL		LAOUT/YIK
lumbricide	LUM/BRI/SAO*ID	lutein	LAOUT/YIN
lumbricoid	LUM/BRI/KOID	luteinic	LAOUT/YIN/IK
lumbricoides	LUM/BRI/KOI/DAOEZ	luteinization	LAOUT/YIN/ZAIGS
lumbricosis	LUM/BRI/KOE/SIS	luteinize	LAOUT/NAOIZ
lumbricus	LUM/BRI/KUS		LAOUT/YIN/AOIZ
	LUM/BRAOI/KUS	luteinizing	LAOUT/NAOIZ/-G
lumbus	LUM/BUS		LAOUT/YIN/AOIZ/-G
lumen	LAOUM/-N	luteinoma	LAOUT/NOE/MA
	LAOU/MEN		LAOUT/YI/NOE/MA
lumichrome	LAOUM/KROEM	Lutembacher	LAOUT/EM/BAK/ER
lumiflavin	LAOUM/FLAIVN		LAOU/TEM/BAK/ER
	LAOUM/FLAI/VIN	luteogenic	LAOUT/YO/JEN/IK
lumina	LAOUM/NA	luteohormone	LAOUT/YO/HOR/MOEN
luminal	LAOUM/NAL	luteoid	LAOUT/YOID
luminescence	LAOUM/NES/ENS	luteola	LAOUT/YOE/LA
luminescent	LAOUM/NES/ENT	luteolin	LAOUT/YOE/LIN
luminiferous	LAOUM/NIF/ROUS	luteolysin	LAOUT/YOL/SIN
luminophore	LAOUM/NO/FOER	luteolysis	LAOUT/YOL/SIS
luminous	LAOUM/NOUS	luteoma	LAOUT/YOE/MA
lumirhodopsin	LAOUM/ROE/DOP/SIN	luteose	LAOUT/YOES
lump	LUFRP	luteotrope	LAOUT/YO/TROEP
lumpectomy	LUM/PEKT/M*I	luteotrophic	LAOUT/YO/TROFK
	LUFRP/EKT/M*I	luteotrophin	LAOUT/YO/TROEFN
Lumsden	LUMZ/DEN	luteotropic	LAOUT/YO/TROP/IK
	LUMS/DEN		LAOUT/YO/TROEP/IK
Luna	LAOU/NA	luteotropin	LAOUT/YO/TROE/PIN
lunacy	LAOUN/SI	lutetium	LAOU/TAOE/SHUM
lunar	LAOU/NAR		LAOU/TAOERB/UM
lunare	LAOU/NAI/RAOE	luteum	LAOUT/YUM
lunata	LAOU/NAI/TA	luteus	LAOU/TAOE/YUS
lunate	LAOU/NAIT		LAOUT/YUS
lunatic	LAOUN/TIK	Lutheran	LAO*UT/RAN
lunatomalacia	LAOU/NAI/TO/MA/LAI/SHA	lutropin	LAOU/TRO/PIN
lunatum	LAOU/NAI/TUM	lututrin	LAOU/TAOU/TRIN
	LAOU/NAIT/UM	Lutz	LUTS
Lundvall	LAOUND/VAL		LAOUTS
	LAOUND/VAUL	Lutzomyia	LAOUTS/MAOI/YA
	LUND/VAL	lux	LUX
	LUND/VAUL	luxans	LUK/SANZ
lung	LUNG		LUX/ANZ
lungmotor	LUNG/MOE/TOR	luxatio	LUK/SAI/SHOE
lungworm	LUNG/WORM		LUK/SAIRB/YOE
lunul-	LAOUN/L-	luxation	LUK/SAIGS
	LAOUN/YAOU/L-		LUX/AIGS
	LAOUN/YU/L-	luxurians	LUK/SHUR/YANZ
lunula	LAOUN/LA		LUX/YUR/YANZ
lunulae	LAOUN/LAE		LUX/YAOUR/YANZ
lupeose	LAOUP/YOES	luxuriant	LUK/SHUR/YANT
lupia	LAOUP/YA		LUX/YUR/YANT
lupiform	LAOUP/FORM		LUX/YAOUR/YANT
lupinidine	LAOU/PIN/DAOEN	luxus	LUK/SUS
lupinosis	LAOUP/NOE/SIS		LUX/SUS
lupoid	LAOU/POID	Luys	LAO*U/WAOEZ
	LAOUP/OID		(not LAOU/WAOEZ; see lues)
Lupron Depot	LAOU/PRON	Lwoff	LA/WOF
lupus	LAOU/PUS	lwoffi	LA/WOF/FAOI
lura	LAOU/RA	lyase	LAOI/AIS
	LAOUR/RA		LAOI/YAIS
lural	LAOURL	lycanthropy	LAOI/KAN/THRO/PI
	LAOU/RAL	lycine	LAO*I/SIN
	LAOUR/RAL		(not LAOI/SIN; see lysin)
Luria	LAOUR/YA	lycoctonine	LAOI/KOKT/NAOEN
	LUR/YA	lycopene	LAOIK/PAOEN
Luria-Nebraska	LAOUR/YA/NE/BRAS/KA	lycopenemia	LAOIK/PE/NAOEM/YA
	LAOUR/YA/N*E/N*E		LAOIK/PEN/AOEM/YA
	LUR/YA/NE/BRAS/KA	Lycoperdales	LAOIK/PER/DAI/LAOEZ
	LUR/YA/N*E/N*E	Lycoperdon	LAOIK/PER/DON
Luride	LAOUR/RAOID	lycoperdonosis	LAOIK/PERD/NOE/SIS
	LUR/RAOID	lycophora	LAOI/KOF/RA
	LAOU/RAOID	lycopodium	LAOIK/POED/YUM
Lurline PMS	LUR/LAOEN/P-RBGS/M*RBGS/	lycorexia	LAOIK/REX/YA
	S*RBGS	lye	LAO*I
Luroscrub	LUR/SKRUB		(not LAOI; see lie)
Luschka	LURB/KA	lygophilia	LAOIG/FIL/YA
Luse	LAOUS	lying-in	LAOI/-G/H-F/N-
lusoria	LAOU/SOER/YA	Lyme	LAO*IM
	LAOU/SOR/YA		(not LAOIM; see lime)
lusus	LAOU/SUS	lymecycline	LAOIM/SAOI/KLAOEN
lusus naturae	LAOU/SUS/NA/TAOU/RAE	Lymnaea	LIM/NAOE/YA
lute	LAOUT		LIM/NAE/YA
lute(o)-	LAOUT/Y(O)	lymph	LIM/-F
lutea	LAOUT/YA		(not LIFRP; see limp)
luteal	LAOUT/YAL	lymph(o)-	LIM/F(O)
lutecium	LAOU/TAOES/YUM	lympha	LIM/FA

lymphaden	LIM/FA/DEN	lymphocytomatosis	LIM/FO/SAOI/TOEM/TOE/SIS
lymphaden(o)-	LIM/FAD/N(O)	lymphocytomatous	LIM/FO/SAOI/TOEM/TOUS
lymphadenectasis	LIM/FAD/NEKT/SIS	lymphocytopenia	LIM/FO/SAOIT/PAOEN/YA
lymphadenectomy	LIM/FAD/NEKT/M*I	lymphocytopoiesis	LIM/FO/SAOIT/POI/SIS
lymphadenia	LIM/FA/DAOEN/YA	lymphocytopoietic	LIM/FO/SAOIT/POIT/IK
lymphadenitis	LIM/FAD/NAOITS	lymphocytorrhexis	LIM/FO/SAOIT/REK/SIS
lymphadenocele	LIM/FAD/NO/SAO*EL	lymphocytosis	LIM/FO/SAOI/TOE/SIS
lymphadenocyst	LIM/FAD/NO/S*IS	lymphocytotic	LIM/FO/SAOI/TOT/IK
lymphadenogram	LIM/FAD/NO/GRAM	lymphocytotoxicity	LIM/FO/SAOIT/TOK/SIS/TI
lymphadenography	LIM/FAD/NOG/FI	lymphocytotoxin	LIM/FO/SAOIT/TOK/SIN
lymphadenoid	LIM/FAD/NOID	lymphoderma	LIM/FO/DER/MA
lymphadenoleukopoiesis	LIM/FAD/NO/LAOUK/POI/SIS	lymphodermia	LIM/FO/DERM/YA
lymphadenoma	LIM/FAD/NOE/MA	lymphoduct	LIM/FO/DUKT
lymphadenomatosis	LIM/FAD/NOEM/TOE/SIS	lymphoepithelial	LIM/FO/EP/THAOEL/YAL
lymphadenopathy	LIM/FAD/NOP/TH*I	lymphoepithelioma	LIM/FO/EP/THAOEL/YOE/MA
lymphadenosis	LIM/FAD/NOE/SIS	lymphogenesis	LIM/FO/JEN/SIS
lymphadenotomy	LIM/FAD/NOT/M*I	lymphogenic	LIM/FO/JEN/IK
lymphadenovarix	LIM/FAD/NO/VAIR/IX	lymphogenous	LIM/FOJ/NOUS
lymphagogue	LIM/FA/GOG	lymphoglandula	LIM/FO/GLAND/LA
lymphageitis	*see* lymphangitis	lymphogram	LIM/FO/GRAM
lymphangi(o)-	LIM/FAN/J(O)	lymphogranuloma	LIM/FO/GRAN/LOE/MA
lymphangial	LIM/FAN/JAL	lymphogranulomatosis	LIM/FO/GRAN/LOEM/TOE/SIS
lymphangiectasia	LIM/FAN/JEK/TAIZ/YA	lymphography	LIM/FOG/FI
lymphangiectasis	LIM/FAN/JEKT/SIS	lymphohistiocytic	LIM/FO/H*IS/YO/SIT/IK
lymphangiectatic	LIM/FAN/JEK/TAT/IK	lymphohistiocytosis	LIM/FO/H*IS/YO/SAOI/TOE/SIS
lymphangiectodes	LIM/FAN/JEK/TOE/DAOEZ	lymphohistioplasmacytic	LIM/FO/H*IS/YO/PLAZ/MA/SIT/IK
lymphangiectomy	LIM/FAN/JEKT/M*I	lymphoid	LIM/FOID
lymphangiitis	*see* lymphangitis	lymphoidectomy	LIM/FOI/DEKT/M*I
lymphangioendothelioma	LIM/FAN/JO/*END/THAOEL/YOE/ MA	lymphoidocyte	LIM/FOID/SAO*IT
		lymphoidotoxemia	LIM/FOID/TOK/SAOEM/YA
lymphangiofibroma	LIM/FAN/JO/FAOI/BROE/MA	lymphokentric	LIM/FO/KEN/TRIK
lymphangiogram	LIM/FAN/JO/GRAM	lymphokine	LIM/FO/KAOIN
lymphangiography	LIM/FAN/JOG/FI	lymphokinesis	LIM/FO/KI/NAOE/SIS
lymphangiology	LIM/FAN/JOLG	lymphology	LIM/FOLG
lymphangioma	LIM/FAN/JOE/MA	lympholytic	LIM/FO/LIT/IK
lymphangiomatous	LIM/FAN/JOEM/TOUS	lymphoma	LIM/FOE/MA
lymphangiomyomatosis	LIM/FAN/JO/MAOI/MA/TOE/SIS	lymphomatoid	LIM/FOEM/TOID
	LIM/FAN/JO/MAOI/YOEM/TOE/ SIS	lymphomatosis	LIM/FOEM/TOE/SIS
		lymphomatosum	LIM/FOEM/TOE/SUM
lymphangion	LIM/FAN/JON		LIM/FOEM/TOES/UM
lymphangiophlebitis	LIM/FAN/JO/FLE/BAOITS	lymphomatous	LIM/FOEM/TOUS
lymphangioplasty	LIM/FAN/JO/PLAS/TI	lymphomyeloma	LIM/FO/MAOI/LOE/MA
lymphangiosarcoma	LIM/FAN/JO/SAR/KOE/MA	lymphomyxoma	LIM/FO/MIK/SOE/MA
lymphangiotomy	LIM/FAN/JOT/M*I	lymphonodi	LIM/FO/NOE/DAOI
lymphangitis	LIM/FAN/JAOITS	lymphonodus	LIM/FO/NOE/DUS
lymphapheresis	LIM/FA/FRAOE/SIS	lymphopathia	LIM/FO/PA*T/YA
	LIM/FA/FE/RAOE/SIS	lymphopathy	LIM/FOP/TH*I
lymphatic	LIM/FAT/IK	lymphopenia	LIM/FO/PAOEN/YA
lymphatici	LIM/FAT/SAOI	lymphoplasm	LIM/FO/PLAFM
lymphaticostomy	LIM/FAT/KO*S/M*I	lymphoplasmapheresis	LIM/FO/PLAZ/MA/FRAOE/SIS
lymphaticum	LIM/FAT/KUM	lymphoplasty	LIM/FO/PLAS/TI
lymphaticus	LIM/FAT/KUS	lymphopoiesis	LIM/FO/POI/SIS
lymphatism	LIM/FA/TIFM	lymphopoietic	LIM/FO/POIT/IK
lymphatitis	LIM/FA/TAOITS	lymphoproliferative	LIM/FO/PRO/LIFR/TIV
lymphatogenous	LIM/FA/TOJ/NOUS	lymphoreticular	LIM/FO/RE/TIK/LAR
lymphatology	LIM/FA/TOLG	lymphoreticulosis	LIM/FO/RE/TIK/LOE/SIS
lymphatolysin	LIM/FA/TOL/SIN	lymphorrhage	LIM/FO/RAJ
lymphatolysis	LIM/FA/TOL/SIS	lymphorrhagia	LIM/FO/RAI/JA
lymphatolytic	LIM/FA/TO/LIT/IK	lymphorrhea	LIM/FO/RAOE/YA
	LIM/FAT/LIT/IK	lymphorrhoid	LIM/FO/ROID
lymphectasia	LIM/FEK/TAIZ/YA	lymphosarcoma	LIM/FO/SAR/KOE/MA
lymphedema	LIM/FE/DAOE/MA	lymphosarcomatosis	LIM/FO/SAR/KOEM/TOE/SIS
lymphemia	LIM/FAOEM/YA	lymphosis	LIM/FOE/SIS
lymphenteritis	LIM/FENT/RAOITS	lymphosporidiosis	LIM/FO/SPRID/YOE/SIS
lymphepithelioma	LIM/FEP/THAOEL/YOE/MA	lymphostasis	LIM/FO*S/SIS
lymphization	LIM/FI/ZAIGS	lymphotaxis	LIM/FO/TAK/SIS
lymphnoditis	LIM/-F/NOE/DAOITS	lymphotism	LIM/FO/TIFM
	LIM/-F/NO/DAOITS	lymphotome	LIM/FO/TOEM
lymphoadenoma	LIM/FO/AD/NOE/MA	lymphotoxemia	LIM/FO/TOK/SAOEM/YA
lymphoblast	LIM/FO/BLA*S	lymphotoxicity	LIM/FO/TOK/SIS/TI
lymphoblastic	LIM/FO/BLA*S/IK	lymphotoxin	LIM/FO/TOK/SIN
lymphoblastoma	LIM/FO/BLAS/TOE/MA	lymphotrophy	LIM/FOT/RO/FI
lymphoblastomatous	LIM/FO/BLAS/TOEM/TOUS	lymphous	LIM/FOUS
lymphoblastomid	LIM/FO/BLAS/TOE/MID	lymphs	LIM/-FS
lymphoblastomosis	LIM/FO/BLA*S/MOE/SIS	lymphuria	LIM/FAOUR/YA
lymphoblastosis	LIM/FO/BLAS/TOE/SIS	lymph-vascular	LIM/-F/VAS/KLAR
lymphocele	LIM/FO/SAO*EL	lynestrenol	LIN/ES/TRE/NOL
lymphocerastism	LIM/FO/SER/AS/TIFM		LI/NES/TRE/NOL
	LIM/FO/SE/RAS/TIFM	lyo-	LAOI
lymphocinesia	LIM/FO/SI/NAOEZ/YA		LAOI/YO
lymphocinesis	LIM/FO/SI/NAOE/SIS	lyochrome	LAOI/KROEM
lymphocyst	LIM/FO/S*IS	lyoenzyme	LAOI/EN/ZAOIM
lymphocytapheresis	LIM/FO/SAOIT/FRAOE/SIS	lyogel	LAOI/JEL
	LIM/FO/SAOIT/FER/SIS	lyolysis	LAOI/OL/SIS
lymphocyte	LIM/FO/SAO*IT	Lyon	LAO*I/YON
lymphocythemia	LIM/FO/SAOI/THAOEM/YA		(*not* LAOI/YON; **see** lion)
lymphocytic	LIM/FO/SIT/IK	lyonization	LAOI/YON/ZAIGS
lymphocytoblast	LIM/FO/SAOIT/BLA*S		LAOIN/ZAIGS
lymphocytoma	LIM/FO/SAOI/TOE/MA	lyonized	LAOI/YON/AOIZ/-D

	LAOIN/AOIZ/-D	
lyophil	LAOI/FIL	
lyophile	LAOI/FAOIL	
lyophilic	LAOI/FIL/IK	
lyophilization	LAOI/OF/LI/ZAIGS	
	LAOI/FIL/ZAIGS	
lyophilize	LAOI/OF/LAOIZ	
lyophilizer	LAOI/OF/LAOIZ/ER	
lyophobe	LAOI/FOEB	
lyophobic	LAOI/FOEB/IK	
lyosol	LAOI/SOL	
lyosorption	LAOI/SORPGS	
lyotropic	LAOI/TROP/IK	
	LAOI/TROEP/IK	
lypressin	LAOI/PRES/SIN	
lyra	LAOI/RA	
lyre	LAOIR	
lys(o)-	LAOIS	
	LAOI/S(O)	
lysate	LAOI/SAIT	
lyse	LAOIZ	
lysemia	LAOI/SAOEM/YA	
lysergamide	LAOI/SERJ/MAOID	
lysergic	LAOI/SERJ/IK	
lysergide	LAOI/SER/JAOID	
lysidin	LIS/DIN	
lysimeter	LAOI/SIM/TER	
lysin	LAOI/SIN	
lysine	LAOI/SAOEN	
lysinemia	LAOIS/NAOEM/YA	
lysinogen	LAOI/SIN/JEN	
lysinogenesis	LAOI/SIN/JEN/SIS	
	LAOIS/NO/JEN/SIS	
lysinogenic	LAOI/SIN/JEN/IK	
	LAOIS/NO/JEN/IK	
lysinosis	LIS/NOE/SIS	
lysinuria	LAOIS/NAOUR/YA	
lysis	LAOI/SIS	
-lysis	(v)L/SIS	
	LAOI/SIS	
lysocephalin	LAOIS/SEF/LIN	
Lysodren	LAOIS/DREN	
lysogen	LAOIS/JEN	
lysogenesis	LAOIS/JEN/SIS	
lysogenic	LAOIS/JEN/IK	
lysogenicity	LAOIS/JE/NIS/TI	
lysogenization	LAOIS/JEN/ZAIGS	
lysogeny	LAOI/SOJ/N*I	
lysokinase	LAOIS/KAOI/NAIS	
lysolecithin	LAOIS/LES/THIN	
lysolecithinase	LAOIS/LES/THIN/AIS	
lysophosphatide	LAOIS/FOS/FA/TAOID	
lysophosphatidic	LAOIS/FOS/FA/TID/IK	
lysophosphatidylcholine	LAOIS/FOS/FA/TAOI/DIL/KOE/	
	LAOEN	
lysophosphatidylserine	LAOIS/FOS/FA/TAOI/DIL/SER/	
	AOEN	
lysophospholipase	LAOIS/FOS/FO/LIP/AIS	
lysosomal	LAOIS/SOE/MAL	
lysosome	LAOIS/SOEM	
lysostaphin	LAOIS/STAFN	
	LAOIS/STAF/FIN	
lysostripping	LAOIS/STRIP/-G	
lysotype	LAOIS/TAOIP	
lysozyme	LAOIS/ZAOIM	
lysozymuria	LAOIS/ZAOI/MAOUR/YA	
lyss(o)-	LIS	
	LIS/S(O)	
lyssa	LIS/SA	
Lyssavirus	LIS/VAOI/RUS	
	LIS/SA/VAOI/RUS	
lyssic	LIS/IK	
	LIS/SIK	
lyssodexis	LIS/DEK/SIS	
lyssoid	LIS/OID	
lyssophobia	LIS/FOEB/YA	
lysyl	LAOI/SIL	
lysyl-bradykinin	LAOI/SL/BRAD/KAOI/NIN	
lyterian	LAOI/TAOERN	
lytic	LIT/IK	
Lytren	LAOI/TREN	
lytta	LIT/TA	
Lytta	K-P/LIT/TA	
lyxitol	LIX/TOL	
lyxoflavin	LIX/FLAIVN	
	LIX/FLAI/VIN	
lyxose	LIK/SOES	
	LIX/OES	
lyxulose	LIX/LOES	

	LIX/YAOU/LOES	
	LIX/YU/LOES	
lyze	LAO*IZ	
	(not LAOIZ; see lyse)	

M

Maalox	MAI/LOX
Maalox Plus	MAI/LOX/PLUS
Maalox TC	MAI/LOX/T-RBGS/KR*RBGS
Macaca	MA/KA/KA
	MA/KAK/KA
Macchiavello	MAK/YA/VEL/LOE
	MAFP/YA/VEL/LOE
MacConkey	MAK/KON/KAOE
	M-K/KON/KAOE
mace	MAIS
Mace	K-P/MAIS
macellaria	MAS/LAIR/YA
macerate	MAS/RAIT
maceration	MAS/RAIGS
macerative	MAS/RA/TIV
Macewen	MAK/YAOUN
	MAK/YAOU/-N
Mach	MAUK
Mache	MAK/KE
	MA/KE
machine	MA/SHAOEN
Macht	MAKT
macies	MAI/SHAOEZ
	MAIRB/YAOEZ
macintosh	MAK/IN/TORB
Macintosh	K-P/MAK/IN/TORB
macis	MAI/SIS
Mackenrodt	MAK/EN/ROET
Mackenzie	MA/KEN/ZAOE
	MAK/KEN/ZAOE
Macleod	MA/KLOUD
	MAK/LOUD
maclurin	MA/KLAOUR/RIN
	MA/KLAOU/RIN
macr(o)-	MAK/R(O)
Macracanthorhynchus	MAK/RA/KA*NT/RIN/KUS
macradenous	MAK/RAD/NOUS
	MA/KRAD/NOUS
macrencephalia	MAK/REN/SFAIL/YA
macrencephaly	MAK/REN/SEF/LI
macroadenoma	MAK/RO/AD/NOE/MA
macroaggregate	MAK/RO/AG/RE/GAIT
	MAK/RO/AG/RE/GAT
macroaleuriospore	MAK*RO/AI/LAOUR/YO/SPOER
macroamylase	MAK*RO/AM/LAIS
macroamylasemia	MAK/RO/AM/LAI/SAOEM/YA
macroamylasemic	MAK/RO/AM/LAI/SAOEM/IK
macroanalysis	MAK/RO/ANL/SIS
macrobacterium	MAK/RO/BAK/TAOERM
Macrobdella	MAK/RO/DEL/LA
macrobiosis	MAK/RO/BAO*I/YOE/SIS
macrobiota	MAK/RO/BAO*I/YOE/TA
macrobiote	MAK/RO/BAO*I/OET
macrobiotic	MAK/RO/BAO*I/OT/IK
macrobiotics	MAK/RO/BAO*I/OT/IK/-S
macroblast	MAK/RO/BLA*S
macroblepharia	MAK/RO/BLE/FAIR/YA
macrobrachia	MAK/RO/BRAIK/YA
macrocardia	MAK/RO/KARD/YA
macrocardius	MAK/RO/KARD/YUS
macrocephalia	MAK/RO/SFAIL/YA
macrocephalic	MAK/RO/SFAL/IK
macrocephalous	MAK/RO/SEF/LOUS
macrocephalus	MAK/RO/SEF/LUS
macrocephaly	MAK/RO/SEF/LI
macrocheilia	MAK/RO/KAOIL/YA
macrocheiria	MAK/RO/KAOIR/YA
macrochemical	MAK/RO/KEM/KAL
macrochemistry	MAK/RO/KEM/STRI
macrochylomicron	MAK/RO/KAOIL/MAOI/KRON
macroclitoris	MAK/RO/KLI/TOR/RIS
	MAK/RO/KLIT/RIS
	MAK/RO/KLAOI/TOR/RIS
macrocnemia	MAK/RO/NAOEM/YA
	MAK/ROK/NAOEM/YA
macrococcus	MAK/RO/KOK/KUS
macrocolon	MAK/RO/KO/LON
macroconidia	MAK/RO/KO/NID/YA
macroconidium	MAK/RO/KO/NID/YUM
macrocornea	MAK/RO/KORN/YA
macrocrania	MAK/RO/KRAIN/YA
macrocranium	MAK/RO/KRAIN/YUM
macrocryoglobulin	MAK/RO/KRAOI/GLOB/LIN
macrocryoglobulinemia	MAK/RO/KRAOI/GLOB/LI/

	NAOEM/YA
	MAK/RO/KRAOI/GLOB/LIN/
	AOEM/YA
macrocyst	MAK/RO/S*IS
macrocytase	MAK/RO/SAOI/TAIS
macrocyte	MAK/RO/SAO*IT
macrocytic	MAK/RO/SIT/IK
macrocythemia	MAK/RO/SAOI/THAOEM/YA
macrocytosis	MAK/RO/SAOI/TOE/SIS
macrodactylia	MAK/RO/DAK/TIL/YA
macrodactylism	MAK/RO/DAKT/LIFM
macrodactyly	MAK/RO/DAKT/LI
Macrodantin	MAK/RO/DAN/TIN
Macrodex	MAK/RO/DEX
macrodont	MAK/RO/DONT
macrodontia	MAK/RO/DON/SHA
macrodontic	MAK/RO/DONT/IK
macrodontism	MAK/RO/DON/TIFM
macrodystrophia	MAK/RO/DIS/TROEF/YA
macrodystrophia	MAK/RO/DIS/TROEF/YA/
lipomatosa	LIP/MA/TOE/SA
macroelement	MAK/RO/EL/-MT
macroencephalon	MAK/RO/EN/SEF/LON
macroencephaly	MAK/RO/EN/SEF/LI
macroerythroblast	MAK/RO/R*IT/RO/BLA*S
macroerythrocyte	MAK/RO/R*IT/RO/SAO*IT
macroesthesia	MAK/RO/ES/THAOEZ/YA
macrofauna	MAK/RO/FAU/NA
macroflora	MAK/RO/FLOR/RA
macrogamete	MAK/RO/GAM/AOET
macrogametocyte	MAK/RO/GA/MAOET/SAO*IT
macrogamont	MAK/RO/GAM/ONT
macrogamy	MA/KROG/M*I
macrogastria	MAK/RO/GAS/TRA
	MAK/RO/GAS/TRAOE/YA
macrogenesy	MAK/RO/JEN/SI
macrogenia	MAK/RO/JAOEN/YA
	MAK/RO/JEN/YA
macrogenitosomia	MAK/RO/JEN/TO/SOEM/YA
macrogingivae	MAK/RO/JING/VAE
macroglia	MA/KROG/LA
	MA/KROG/LAOE/YA
	MAK/ROG/LA
	MAK/ROG/LAOE/YA
macroglobulin	MAK/RO/GLOB/LIN
macroglobulinemia	MAK/RO/GLOB/LI/NAOEM/YA
	MAK/RO/GLOB/LIN/AOEM/YA
macroglossia	MAK/RO/GLOS/YA
macrognathia	MAK/RO/NA*IT/YA
	MAK/RO/NA*T/YA
macrogol	MAK/RO/GOL
macrographia	MAK/RO/GRAF/YA
macrography	MA/KROG/FI
	MAK/ROG/FI
macrogyria	MAK/RO/JAOIR/YA
macrolabia	MAK/RO/LAIB/YA
macrolecithal	MAK/RO/LES/THAL
macroleukoblast	MAK/RO/LAOUK/BLA*S
macrolide	MAK/RO/LAOID
macrolymphocyte	MAK/RO/LIM/FO/SAO*IT
macrolymphocytosis	MAK/RO/LIM/FO/SAOI/TOE/SIS
macromania	MAK/RO/MAIN/YA
macromaniacal	MAK/RO/MA/NAOI/KAL
macromastia	MAK/RO/MA*S/YA
macromazia	MAK/RO/MAIZ/YA
macromelanosome	MAK/RO/MEL/NO/SOEM
macromelia	MAK/RO/MAOEL/YA
macromelus	MA/KROM/LUS
	MAK/ROM/LUS
macromere	MAK/RO/MAOER
macromerozoite	MAK/RO/MER/ZOE/AOIT
macromethod	MAK/RO/M*ET/OD
macromimia	MAK/RO/MIM/YA
macromolecular	MAK/RO/MO/LEK/LAR
macromolecule	MAK/RO/MOL/KAOUL
macromonocyte	MAK/RO/MON/SAO*IT
macromyeloblast	MAK/RO/MAOI/LO/BLA*S
macronodular	MAK/RO/NOD/LAR
macronormoblast	MAK/RO/NORM/BLA*S
macronormochromoblast	MAK/RO/NORM/KROEM/BLA*S
macronucleus	MAK/RO/NAOUK/LUS
macronutrient	MAK/RO/NAOU/TRENT
macronychia	MAK/RO/NIK/YA
macroparasite	MAK/RO/PAR/SAOIT
macropathology	MAK/RO/PA/THOLG
macropenis	MAK/RO/PAOE/NIS
macrophage	MAK/RO/FAIJ
macrophagocyte	MAK/RO/FAG/SAO*IT
macrophallus	MAK/RO/FAL/LUS

macrophthalmia	MAK/ROF/THAL/MA	Magan	MAI/GAN
	MAK/ROF/THAL/MAOE/YA	mageiric	MA/JAOI/RIK
macrophthalmous	MAK/ROF/THAL/MOUS		MA/JAOIR/IK
macropia	MA/KROEP/YA	Magendie	MA/JEN/DAOE
	MAK/ROEP/YA	magenstrasse	MA/GEN/STRAS/SE
macroplasia	MAK/RO/PLAIZ/YA		MA/GEN/STRASZ
macroplastia	MAK/RO/PLA*S/YA	magenta	MA/JEN/TA
macropodia	MAK/RO/POED/YA	maggot	MAG/OT
macropolycyte	MAK/RO/POL/SAO*IT		MAG/GOT
macropromyelocyte	MAK/RO/PRO/MAOI/LO/SAO*IT	magistery	MAJ/STAIR
macroprosopia	MAK/RO/PRO/SOEP/YA		MAJ/STER/RI
macroprosopous	MAK/RO/PROS/POUS	magistral	MAJ/STRAL
	MAK/RO/PROES/POUS	Magitot	MAJ/TOE
	MAK/RO/PRO/SOE/POUS	Mag-L	MAG/L-RBGS
macropsia	MA/KROPS/YA	magma	MAG/MA
	MAK/ROPS/YA	magna	MAG/NA
macroptic	MA/KROPT/IK	magnae	MAG/NAE
macrorhinia	MAK/RO/RIN/YA	Magnan	MAG/NAN
macroscelia	MAK/RO/SAOEL/YA	Magnatril	MAG/NA/TRIL
macroscopic	MAK/RO/SKOP/IK	magnesemia	MAG/NE/SAOEM/YA
macroscopical	MAK/RO/SKOP/KAL	magnesia	MAG/NAOEZ/YA
macroscopy	MA/KROS/KPI	magnesium	MAG/NAOEZ/YUM
macrosigmoid	MAK/RO/SIG/MOID	magnet	MAG/NET
macrosis	MA/KROE/SIS	magnetic	MAG/NET/IK
macrosmatic	MAK/ROZ/MAT/IK	magnetism	MAG/NE/TIFM
macrosomatia	MAK/RO/SO/MAI/SHA	magnetization	MAG/NET/ZAIGS
macrosomia	MAK/RO/SOEM/YA		MAG/NE/TAOI/ZAIGS
macrosplanchnic	MAK/RO/SPLANG/NIK	magnetize	MAG/NE/TAOIZ
macrospore	MAK/RO/SPOER	magneto-	MAG/NAOET
macrostereognosia	MAK/RO/STER/YO/NOEZ/YA		MAG/NAOE/TO
	MAK/RO/STER/YOG/NOEZ/YA	magnetocardiograph	MAG/NAOET/KARD/YO/GRAF
macrostereognosis	MAK/RO/STER/YO/NOE/SIS	magnetocardiography	MAG/NAOET/KARD/YOG/FI
	MAK/RO/STER/YOG/NOE/SIS	magnetoconstriction	MAG/NAOET/KON/STR*IBGS
macrostomia	MAK/RO/STOEM/YA	magnetoelectricity	MAG/NAOET/LEK/TRIS/TI
macrostomum	MAK/RO/STOE/MUM	magnetoencephalogram	MAG/NAOET/EN/SEF/LO/GRAM
	MAK/RO/STOEM/UM		MAG/NAOET/EN/SEF/GRAM
macrostructural	MAK/RO/STRUK/KHURL	magnetoencephalograph	MAG/NAOET/EN/SEF/LO/GRAF
macrotia	MA/KROE/SHA		MAG/NAOET/EN/SEF/GRAF
	MAK/ROE/SHA	magnetoencephalography	MAG/NAOET/EN/SEF/LOG/FI
macrotome	MAK/RO/TOEM	magnetoinduction	MAG/NAOET/IN/D*UBGS
macrotooth	MAK/RO/TAO*T	magnetology	MAG/NE/TOLG
mactans	MAK/TANZ	magnetometer	MAG/NE/TOM/TER
macul(o)-	MAK/L(O)	magneton	MAG/NE/TON
	MAK/YAOU/L(O)	magnetotherapy	MAG/NAOET/THER/PI
	MAK/YU/L(O)	magnetron	MAG/NE/TRON
macula	MAK/LA	magnetropism	MAG/NET/RO/PIFM
maculae	MAK/LAE	magnicellular	MAG/NI/SEL/YAOU/LAR
macular	MAK/LAR	magnification	MAG/NIF/KAIGS
macularis	MAK/LAI/RIS	magnify	MAG/NI/FI
maculary	MAK/LAIR	magnitude	MAG/NI/TAOUD
maculata	MAK/LAI/TA	magnocellular	MAG/NO/SEL/YAOU/LAR
maculate	MAK/LAIT	Magnolia	MAG/NOEL/YA
maculation	MAK/LAIGS	magnum	MAG/NUM
maculatum	MAK/LAI/TUM	magnus	MAG/NUS
	MAK/LAIT/UM	Magonate	MA*G/NAIT
maculatus	MAK/LAI/TUS		(not MAG/NAIT; see magnate)
macule	MAK/YAOUL	Mag-Ox	MAG/OX
maculocerebral	MAK/LO/SER/BRAL	Magsal	MAG/SAL
maculoerythematous	MAK/LO/*ER/THEM/TOUS	maidenhead	MAID/EN/HED
maculopapular	MAK/LO/PAP/LAR	maidism	MAI/DIFM
maculopapule	MAK/LO/PAP/YAOUL	Maier	MA*I/ER
maculopathy	MAK/LOP/TH*I		(not MAI/ER; see mayer)
maculosa	MAK/LOE/SA	maim	MAIM
maculovesicular	MAK/LO/VE/SIK/LAR	main	MAIN
MacWilliam	MAK/WIL/YAM	mainstreaming	MAIN/STRAOEM/-G
mad	MAD	maintain	MAIN/TAIN
madarosis	MAD/ROE/SIS	maintainer	MAIN/TAIN/ER
madder	MAD/ER	maise	MA*IZ
Maddox	MAD/DOX		(not MAIZ or MAEZ; see maize and
Madelung	MAD/LAOUNG		maze)
	MAD/LUNG	maintenance	MAINT/NANS
madescent	MA/DES/ENT	maisonneuve	MAIZ/NEV
madidanz	MAD/DANZ		MAI/ZO/NEV
madness	MAD/*NS	Maisonneuve	K-P/MAIZ/NEV
madurae	MA/DAOU/RAE		K-P/MAI/ZO/NEV
	MA/DAOUR/RAE	Maissiat	MAIS/YA
Madurella	MAD/REL/LA		MAIS/YAU
	MAD/YAOU/REL/LA	maize	MAIZ
	MAD/YU/REL/LA	Majocchi	MA/YOK/KAOE
maduromycosis	MA/DAOUR/MAOI/KOE/SIS		MA/YOE/KAOE
	MAD/RO/MAOI/KOE/SIS	major	MAI/JOR
mafenide	MAIF/NAOID	majora	MA/JOR/RA
	MAF/NAOID		MA/JOER/RA
Maffucci	MA/FAOU/KAOE	majores	MA/JOR/RAOEZ
	MA/FAOU/KHAOE		MA/JOER/RAOEZ
mafilcon	MA/FIL/KON	majoris	MA/JOR/RIS
magaldrate	MAG/AL/DRAIT		MA/JOER/RIS
magalhaesi	MAG/AL/HAOE/SAOI	majus	MAI/JUS
	MAG/AL/HAE/SAOI	mal	MA*L

	(*not* MAL or MAUL; see mall and maul)	mallein	MAL/YIN
mal-	MAL	malleinization	MAL/YIN/ZAIGS
	MAI/L-	malleoincudal	MAL/YO/IN/KAOU/DAL
mala	MAI/LA	malleolar	MAL/LAOE/LAR
malabsorption	MAL/AB/SORPGS		MA/LAOE/LAR
Malacarne	MAL/KAR/NAI	malleolaris	MAL/LAOE/LAI/RIS
malachite	MAL/KAOIT		MA/LAOE/LAI/RIS
malacia	MA/LAI/SHA	malleoli	MAL/LAOE/LAOI
	MA/LAIRB/YA		MA/LAOE/LAOI
malacic	MA/LAIS/IK	malleolus	MAL/LAOE/LUS
malaco-	MAL/KO		MA/LAOE/LUS
malacoma	MAL/KOE/MA	malleotomy	MAL/YOT/M*I
malacoplakia	MAL/KO/PLAIK/YA	malleus	MAL/YUS
malacosarcosis	MAL/KO/SAR/KOE/SIS	mallochorion	MAL/KOER/YON
malacosis	MAL/KOE/SIS	Mallophaga	MAL/LOF/GA
malacotic	MAL/KOT/IK		MA/LOF/GA
malactic	MA/LAKT/IK		MAL/OF/GA
maladie	MAL/DAOE	Mallory	MAL/RI
maladjustment	MAL/AD/J*US/-MT	mallow	MAL/LOE
malady	MAL/DI	malnutrition	MAL/NAOU/TRIGS
malagma	MA/LAG/MA	malocclusion	MAL/KLAOUGS
malaise	MA/LAIZ		MAL/O/KLAOUGS
malalignment	MAL/AI/LAOIN/-MT	Maloney	MA/LOE/NAOE
malar	MAI/LAR	malonic	MA/LON/IK
malari(o)-	MA/LAIR/Y(O)	malonyl	MAL/NIL
malaria	MA/LAIR/YA	malonylcoenzyme A	MAL/NIL/KO/EN/ZAOIM/
malariacidal	MA/LAIR/YA/SAOI/DAL		A-RBGS
malarial	MA/LAIRL	malonylurea	MAL/NIL/YAOU/RAOE/YA
malariologist	MA/LAIR/YO*LGS	Malpighi	MAL/PAOE/GAOE
malariology	MA/LAIR/YOLG		MAL/PIG/GAOE
malariotherapy	MA/LAIR/YO/THER/PI	malpighian	MAL/PIG/YAN
malarious	MA/LAIR/YOUS	malpighii	MAL/PIG/YAOI
malaris	MA/LAI/RIS	malposed	MAL/POEZ/-D
Malassez	MAL/SAI	malposition	MAL/POGS
Malassezia	MAL/SAOEZ/YA	malpractice	MAL/PRAK/TIS
malassimilation	MAL/AI/SIM/LAIGS	malpresentation	MAL/PREGS
	MAL/SIM/LAIGS		MAL/PRENT/TAIGS
malate	MAI/LAIT	malrotation	MAL/ROE/TAIGS
	MAL/AIT	malt	MALT
malathion	MAL/THAOI/YON		MAULT
	MA/LA*IT/YON	malt(o)-	MALT
malaxate	MAL/AK/SAIT		MAULT
	MAL/AX/AIT	maltase	MAL/TAIS
	MA/LAK/SAIT		MAUL/TAIS
	MA/LAX/AIT	maltobiose	MALT/BAO*I/OES
malaxation	MAL/AK/SAIGS	maltodextrin	MALT/DEX/TRIN
Malay	MAL/LAI	maltoflavin	MALT/FLAIVN
maldevelopment	MA*L/DWOP/-MT	maltol	MAL/TOL
	MA*L/DE/VEL/OP/-MT	maltosazone	MALT/SAI/ZOEN
	(*not* MAL/DWOP/-MT, etc.; see mall development)	maltose	MAL/TOES
		maltoside	MALT/SAO*ID
maldigestion	MAL/DI/JEGS	maltosuria	MALT/SAOUR/YA
male	MAEL	maltotetrose	MALT/TET/ROES
	(*not* MAIL; see mail)	maltotriose	MALT/TR*I/OES
maleate	MAL/YAIT	Maltsupex	MALT/SAOU/PEX
Malecot	MAL/KOE		MALT/SU/PEX
	MAL/KOT	maltum	MAL/TUM
maleic	MA/LAOE/IK		MALT/UM
	MA/LAI/IK	malturned	MAL/TURN/-D
malemission	MAL/E/MIGS	malum	MAI/LUM
	MAL/MIGS	malunion	MAL/YAOUN/YON
maleruption	MAL/E/RUPGS	Malva	MAL/VA
	MAL/RUPGS	Maly	MAL/LI
malformation	MAL/FOR/MAIGS	mamanpian	MA/MAN/PAOE/YAN
malfunction	MAL/FUNGS	mamelon	MAM/LON
Malgaigne	MAL/GAIN	mamelonated	MAM/LON/AIT/-D
maliasmus	MAL/YAS/MUS		MAM/LO/NAIT/-D
malic	MAL/IK	mamelonation	MAM/LO/NAIGS
	MAIL/IK		MAM/LON/AIGS
maligna	MA/LIG/NA	mamill-	MAM/L-
malignancy	MA/LIG/NAN/SI		MA/MIL
malignant	MA/LIG/NANT	mamilla	MA/MIL/LA
malignin	MA/LIG/NIN	mamillae	MA/MIL/LAE
malignogram	MA/LIG/NO/GRAM	mamillare	MAM/LAI/RAOE
malignum	MA/LIG/NUM	mamillaria	MAM/LAIR/YA
malinger	MA/LING/ER	mamillaris	MAM/LAI/RIS
malingerer	MA/LING/RER	mamillary	MAM/LAIR
malingering	MA/LING/ER/-G	mamillate	MAM/LAIT
malinterdigitation	MAL/SPWER/DIJ/TAIGS	mamillated	MAM/LAIT/-D
Mall	K-P/MAL	mamillation	MAM/LAIGS
malle(o)-	MAL/Y(O)	mamilliform	MA/MIL/FORM
malleability	MAL/YABLT	mamilliplasty	MA/MIL/PLAS/TI
malleable	MAL/YABL	mamillitis	MAM/LAOITS
malleal	MAL/YAL	mamillothalamic	MAM/LO/THA/LAM/IK
mallear	MAL/YAR	mamillothalamicus	MAM/LO/THA/LAM/KUS
malleation	MAL/YAIGS	mamm(o)-	MAM
mallebrin	MAL/BRIN		MAM/M(O)
mallei	MAL/YAOI		MA/M(O)
		mamma	MAM/MA

mammae	MAM/MAE	mania	MAIN/YA
mammal	MAM/MAL	maniac	MAIN/YAK
mammalgia	MA/MAL/JA	maniacal	MA/NAOI/KAL
	MAM/AL/JA	manic	MAN/IK
Mammalia	MA/MAIL/YA		MAIN/IK
	MAM/MAIL/YA	manic-depressive	MAN/IK/DPRES/SIV
mammalogy	MA/MALG		MAN/IK/DPRESZ/IV
	MAM/MALG	manicy	MAN/SI
mammaplasty	MAM/MA/PLAS/TI	manifest	MAN/F*ES
	(not MAM/PLAS/TI; see	manifestation	MAN/FES/TAIGS
	mammoplasty)	manikin	MA*N/KIN
mammaria	MA/MAIR/YA		MAN/K*IN
	MAM/MAIR/YA		(not MAN/KIN; see mannequin)
mammary	MAM/RI	maniloquism	MA/NIL/KWIFM
mammectomy	MA/MEKT/M*I	maniluvium	MAN/LAOUV/YUM
	MAM/EKT/M*I	maniphalanx	MAN/FAI/LANGS
	MAM/MEKT/M*I	manipulate	MA/NIP/LAIT
mammiform	MAM/FORM	manipulation	MA/NIP/LAIGS
mammilliform	see mamilliform	manipulus	MA/NIP/LUS
mammilliplasty	see mamilliplasty	manna	MAN/NA
mammillitis	see mamillitis	mannan	MAN/NAN
mammitis	MA/MAOITS	mannans	MAN/NANZ
	MAM/MAOITS	mannequin	MAN/KIN
mammogen	MAM/JEN	mannerism	MAN/RIFM
mammogenesis	MAM/JEN/SIS	mannite	MAN/AOIT
mammogram	MAM/GRAM		MAN/NAOIT
mammography	MA/MOG/FI	mannitol	MAN/TOL
	MAM/OG/FI	Mannkopf	MAN/KOF
	MAM/MOG/FI		MAN/KOP/-F
mammoplasia	MAM/PLAIZ/YA	manno-	MAN
mammoplasty	MAM/PLAS/TI		MAN/NO
mammose	MAM/MOES	mannosan	MAN/SAN
mammosomatotroph	MAM/SMAT/TROEF	mannose	MAN/OES
	MAM/SOE/MAT/TROEF		MAN/NOES
mammotomy	MA/MOT/M*I	mannoside	MAN/NO/SAOID
	MAM/MOT/M*I		(not MAN/SAOID; see man side)
mammotrope	MAM/TROEP	mannosidosis	MAN/SI/DOE/SIS
mammotroph	MAM/TROF		MAN/SAOI/DOE/SIS
	MAM/TROEF	mannuronic	MAN/RON/IK
mammotrophic	MAM/TROFK		MAN/YAOU/RON/IK
mammotrophin	MAM/TROEFN	manometer	MA/NOM/TER
mammotropic	MAM/TROP/IK		MAN/OM/TER
mammotropin	MAM/TROE/PIN	manometric	MAN/MET/RIK
	MA/MOT/RO/PIN	manometry	MA/NOM/TRI
Manchester	MAN/KH*ES/ER	manoptoscope	MAN/OPT/SKOEP
manchette	MAN/SHET		MA/NOPT/SKOEP
	MAN/KHET	manoscopy	MA/NOS/KPI
mancinism	MANS/NIFM	mansa	MAN/SA
	MAN/SI/NIFM	Manson	MAN/SON
mandarin	MAND/RIN	Mansonella	MANS/NEL/LA
Mandelamine	MAN/DEL/MIN		MAN/SO/NEL/LA
	MAN/DEL/MAOEN	mansonelliasis	MANS/NEL/LAOI/SIS
Mandelamine	MAN/DEL/MIN/SUS/PENGS/		MAN/SO/NEL/LAOI/SIS
Suspension Forte	FOR/TAI	mansoni	MAN/SOE/NAOI
	MAN/DEL/MAOEN/SUS/PENGS/		MAN/SON/NAOI
	FOR/TAI	Mansonia	MAN/SOEN/YA
mandelate	MAND/LAIT	Mansonioides	MAN/SOEN/YOI/DAOEZ
	MAN/DE/LAIT	mansonoides	MANS/NOI/DAOEZ
mandelic	MAN/DEL/IK		MAN/SO/NOI/DAOEZ
mandible	MAND/-BL	Mansonoides	K-P/MANS/NOI/DAOEZ
	MAN/DIBL		K-P/MAN/SO/NOI/DAOEZ
mandibul(o)-	MAN/DIB/L(O)	Mantadil	MANT/DIL
	MAN/DIB/YAOU/L(O)	Mantadil Cream	MANT/DIL/KRAOEM
	MAN/DIB/YU/L(O)	mantle	MANT/-L
mandibula	MAN/DIB/LA	Mantoux	MAN/TAOU
mandibulae	MAN/DIB/LAE	mantra	MAN/TRA
mandibular	MAN/DIB/LAR	manual	MAN/YAOUL
mandibulare	MAN/DIB/LAI/RAOE		MAN/YUL
mandibulares	MAN/DIB/LAI/RAOEZ		MAN/YAL
mandibularis	MAN/DIB/LAI/RIS	manubri-	MA/NAOUB/R-
mandibulectomy	MAN/DIB/LEKT/M*I		MA/NAOU/BR-
mandibulofacial	MAN/DIB/LO/FAIRBL		MA/NAOUB/RAOE/Y-
mandibulo-oculofacial	MAN/DIB/LO/OK/LO/FAIRBL		MA/NAOU/BRAOE/Y-
mandibulopharyngeal	MAN/DIB/LO/FRIN/JAL	manubria	MA/NAOUB/RA
mandibulum	MAN/DIB/LUM	manubrium	MA/NAOUB/RUM
Mandol	MAN/DOL	manudynamometer	MAN/YAOU/DAOIN/MOM/TER
	MAN/DOEL		MAN/YU/DAOIN/MOM/TER
Mandragora	MAN/DRAG/RA	manus	MAI/NUS
mandrake	MAN/DRAIK		MAN/NUS
mandrel	MAN/DREL	manzanita	MANZ/NAOE/TA
mandril	MAN/DRIL		MAN/SA/NAOE/TA
mandrin	MAN/DRIN		MAN/ZA/NAOE/TA
maneuver	MA/NAOUVR	Maolate	MAI/YO/LAIT
manganese	MANG/NAOEZ		(not MAI/LAIT; see malate)
manganic	MAN/GAN/IK	map	MAP
manganism	MANG/NIFM	mapping	MAP/-G
manganous	MANG/NOUS	maprotiline	MA/PROET/LAOEN
manganum	MANG/NUM	Maranon	MA/RAN/YON
mange	MAIN/-J	Maranta	MA/RAN/TA

258

marantic	MA/RANT/IK	marmorata	MARM/RAI/TA
marasmic	MA/RAZ/MIK	marmorated	MARM/RAIT/-D
marasmoid	MA/RAZ/MOID	marmoration	MARM/RAIGS
marasmus	MA/RAZ/MUS	marmoreal	MARM/MOER/YAL
Marax	MAI/RAX		MARM/MOR/YAL
marble	MARBL	marmot	MAR/MOT
marbleization	MARBL/ZAIGS	Marochetti	MAR/KET/TAOE
	MARB/LI/ZAIGS		MAR/KHET/TAOE
Marblen	MAR/BLEN	Marplan	MAR/PLAN
marc	MAR/*K	Marquis	K-P/MAR/KWIS
	(not MARK or MA*RK; see mark and Mark)	Marriott	MAIR/YOT
		marrow	MAR/ROE
Marcaine	MAR/KAIN	mars	MARZ
march	MA*RPBLG	Marseille	MAR/SAI
	MAR/-FP	Marsh	K-P/MAR/-RB
Marchand	MAR/SHAND	Marshall	MA*R/-RBL
	MAR/SHAUND		MAR/*RBL
marche a petits pas	MAR/-RB/A/PE/TAOE/PAU		(not MAR/-RBL; see marshal)
	MAR/-RB/A/PE/TAOE/PA	marshalli	MA*R/-RBL/LAOI
Marchi	MAR/KAO*E		MAR/*RBL/LAOI
	MA*R/KAOE	marsupia	MAR/SAOUP/YA
	(not MAR/KAOE; see marquee)	marsupial	MAR/SAOUP/YAL
Marchiafava	MARK/YA/FA/VA	Marsupialia	MAR/SAOUP/YAIL/YA
marcid	MAR/SID	marsupialization	MAR/SAOUP/YAL/ZAIGS
	MARS/ID	marsupium	MAR/SAOUP/YUM
marcov	MAR/KOV	martial	MART/-RBL
marcy	MAR/SI	Martin	K-P/MAR/TIN
Marcy	K-P/MAR/SI		MA*R/TIN
Marezine	MAIR/ZAOEN	Martinotti	MART/NOT/TAOE
	MAR/ZAOEN	maschaladenitis	MAS/KAL/AD/NAOITS
Marfan	MAR/FAN	maschale	MAS/KAL/LAOE
marfanoid	MAR/FAN/OID	maschalephidrosis	MAS/KAL/EF/DROE/SIS
	MAR/FA/NOID	maschaloncus	MAS/KAL/ON/KUS
margarid	MARG/RID	maschalyperidrosis	MAS/KAL/PER/DROE/SIS
	MAR/GA/RID		MAS/KAL/P*ER/DROE/SIS
margarine	MARJ/RIN	mascul-	MAS/KL-
	MARJ/RAOEN		MAS/KAOU/L-
Margaropus	MAR/GAR/PUS	masculation	MAS/KLAIGS
margin	MAR/JIN	masculinae	MAS/KLAOI/NAE
marginal	MARJ/NAL	masculine	MAS/KLIN
marginale traumatique	MARJ/NAL/TRAUM/TAOEK	masculinity	MAS/KLIN/TI
	MARJ/NAL/TRAU/MA/TAOEK	masculinization	MAS/KLIN/ZAIGS
marginalis	MARJ/NAI/LIS	masculinize	MAS/KLIN/AOIZ
marginata	MARJ/NAI/TA	masculinizing	MAS/KLIN/AOIZ/-G
	MARJ/NA/TA	masculinovoblastoma	MAS/KLIN/OEV/BLAS/TOE/MA
margination	MARJ/NAIGS	masculinus	MAS/KLAOI/NUS
marginatum	MARJ/NAI/TUM	maser	MAIZ/ER
	MARJ/NAIT/UM	mask	MAS/-K
marginatus	MARJ/NAI/TUS	masked	MAS/-KD
margines	MARJ/NAOEZ	masking	MAS/-K/-G
marginis	MARJ/NIS	Maslow	MAS/LOE
marginoplasty	MARJ/NO/PLAS/TI		MAZ/LOE
margo	MAR/GOE	masochism	MAS/KIFM
Marie	MA/RAOE	masochist	MAS/K*IS
marihuana	see marijuana	Mason	K-P/MAI/SON
marijuana	MAR/WA/NA	masque biliaire	MAS/-K/BIL/YAIR
	MAR/WAN/NA		MAS/*K/BIL/YAIR
	MAIR/WA/NA	mass	MASZ
	MAIR/WAN/NA	massa	MAS/SA
marina	MA/RAOI/NA	massae	MAS/SAE
	MA/RAOE/NA	massage	MA/SAJ
	MAIR/NA		MAS/SAJ
marine	MA/RAOEN	Masse	MA*SZ
Marinesco	MAR/NES/KOE	Masse Breast Cream	MA*SZ/BR*ES/KRAOEM
marinobufagin	MAR/NO/BAOUF/JIN	Masselon	MAS/LON
marinobufotoxin	MAR/NO/BAOUF/TOK/SIN		MAS/SE/LON
Marinol	MAIR/NOL	Massengill	MAS/EN/GIL
	MAR/NOL		MAS/SEN/GIL
Marion	MAIR/YON	masseter	MA/SAOET/ER
	MAR/YON		MAS/SAOET/ER
Mariotte	MAR/YOT	masseteric	MAS/TER/IK
	(not MAIR/YOT; see Marriott)		MASZ/TER/IK
mariposia	MAR/POEZ/YA	masseterica	MAS/TER/KA
marisca	MA/RIS/KA		MASZ/TER/KA
mariscal	MA/RIS/KAL	massetericae	MAS/TER/SAE
marital	MAIR/TAL		MASZ/TER/SAE
	MAR/TAL	massetericus	MAS/TER/KUS
maritonucleus	MAR/TO/NAOUK/LUS		MASZ/TER/KUS
	MAIR/TO/NAOUK/LUS	masseur	MA/SAOUR
Marjolin	MAR/JOE/LAN		MA/SUR
	MAR/JOE/LIN		MAS/SAOUR
marjoram	MARJ/RAM		MAS/SUR
mark	MARK	masseuse	MA/SAOUS
marker	MARK/ER		MAS/SAOUS
marking	MARK/-G	massicot	MAS/SI/KOT
Marlow	MAR/LOE		MAS/KO*T
MARLYN	MAR/LIN		MASZ/KOT
MARLYN Formula 50	MAR/LIN/FORM/LA/50		(not MAS/KOT; see mascot)
marma	MAR/MA	massive	MAS/SIV

	MASZ/IV
Masson	MAS/SON
massotherapy	MAS/THER/PI
mast	MA*S
mast(o)-	MA*S
	MAS/T(O)
mastadenitis	MA*S/AD/NAOITS
	MAS/TAD/NAOITS
mastadenoma	MA*S/AD/NOE/MA
	MAS/TAD/NOE/MA
Mastadenovirus	MA*S/AD/NO/VAOI/RUS
	MAS/TAD/NO/VAOI/RUS
mastalgia	MAS/TAL/JA
mastatrophia	MA*S/TROEF/YA
mastatrophy	MAS/TAT/RO/FI
mastauxe	MAS/TAUK/SAOE
mastectomy	MAS/TEKT/M*I
Master	K-P/MA*S/ER
Masters	MAS/TERZ
	MA*S/ERZ
-mastia	MA*S/YA
mastic	MA*S/IK
mastic-	MA*S/K
	MAS/TI/K-
masticate	MA*S/KAIT
mastication	MA*S/KAIGS
masticatoria	MA*S/KA/TOR/YA
	MA*S/KA/TOER/YA
masticatorius	MA*S/KA/TOR/YUS
	MA*S/KA/TOER/YUS
masticatory	MA*S/KA/TOIR
mastiche	MA*S/KAOE
Mastigophora	MA*S/GOF/RA
mastigophoran	MA*S/GOF/RAN
mastigophorous	MA*S/GOF/ROUS
mastigote	MA*S/GOET
mastitis	MAS/TAOITS
mastitoides	MA*S/TOI/DAOEZ
mastocarcinoma	MA*S/KARS/NOE/MA
mastoccipital	MAS/TOK/SIP/TAL
	(not MA*S/OK/SIP/TAL; see masto-occipital)
mastochondroma	MA*S/KON/DROE/MA
mastochondrosis	MA*S/KON/DROE/SIS
mastocyte	MA*S/SAO*IT
mastocytogenesis	MA*S/SAOIT/JEN/SIS
mastocytoma	MA*S/SAOI/TOE/MA
mastocytosis	MA*S/SAOI/TOE/SIS
mastodynia	MA*S/DIN/YA
mastogram	MA*S/GRAM
mastography	MAS/TOG/FI
mastoid	MAS/TOID
mastoidal	MAS/TOI/DAL
mastoidale	MAS/TOI/DAI/LAOE
mastoidalgia	MAS/TOI/DAL/JA
mastoidea	MAS/TOID/YA
mastoideae	MAS/TOID/YAE
mastoidectomy	MAS/TOI/DEKT/M*I
mastoideocentesis	MAS/TOID/YO/SEN/TAOE/SIS
mastoideum	MAS/TOID/YUM
mastoideus	MAS/TOID/YUS
mastoiditis	MAS/TOI/DAOITS
mastoidotomy	MAS/TOI/DOT/M*I
mastoidotympanectomy	MAS/TOID/TIFRP/NEKT/M*I
	MAS/TOI/DO/TIFRP/NEKT/M*I
mastoncus	MAS/TON/KUS
masto-occipital	MA*S/OK/SIP/TAL
mastoparietal	MA*S/PRAOI/TAL
mastopathia	MA*S/PA*T/YA
mastopathy	MAS/TOP/TH*I
mastopexy	MA*S/PEK/SI
mastoplasia	MA*S/PLAIZ/YA
mastoplastia	MA*S/PLA*S/YA
mastoplasty	MA*S/PLAS/TI
mastoptosis	MAS/TOP/TOE/SIS
mastorrhagia	MA*S/RAI/JA
mastoscirrhus	MA*S/SKIR/RUS
mastosis	MAS/TOE/SIS
mastosquamous	MA*S/SKWAIM/OUS
mastostomy	MAS/TO*S/M*I
mastosyrinx	MA*S/SIR/INGS
mastotic	MAS/TOT/IK
mastotomy	MAS/TOT/M*I
masturbate	MA*S/BAIT
	MAS/TUR/BAIT
	MA*S/UR/BAIT
masturbation	MA*S/BAIGS
	MAS/TUR/BAIGS
	MA*S/UR/BAIGS

Matas	MAT/TAS
matching	MAFP/-G
mate	MA/TAI
	MAIT
mater	MAI/TER
	MAIT/ER
	MAU/TER
	MAUT/ER
	(not MAT/ER; see matter)
materia	MA/TAOER/YA
material	MA/TAOERL
	TERL
materies	MA/TAOER/YAOEZ
materies morbi	MA/TAOER/YAOEZ/MOR/BAOI
materies peccans	MA/TAOER/YAOEZ/PEK/KANZ
Materna	MA/TER/NA
maternal	MA/TERNL
maternity	MA/TERN/TI
mating	MAIT/-G
-matic	MAT/IK
mating	MAIT/-G
-matosis	(v)M/TOE/SIS
	MA/TOE/SIS
-matous	(v)M/TOUS
	MA/TOUS
matrass	MAT/RASZ
matrical	MAT/RI/KAL
matricaria	MAT/RI/KAIR/YA
Matricaria	K-P/MAT/RI/KAIR/YA
matrices	MAI/TRI/SAOEZ
	MAT/RI/SAOEZ
matricial	MA/TRIRBL
	MAI/TRIRBL
matricide	MAT/RI/SAO*ID
matriclinous	MAT/RI/KLAOIN/OUS
matrilineal	MAT/RI/LIN/YAL
matrix	MAI/TRIX
	MAT/RIX
matroclinous	MAT/RO/KLAOI/NOUS
matrocliny	MAT/RO/KLAOI/N*I
matter	MAT/ER
Matulane	MAT/YAOU/LAIN
	MAT/YU/LAIN
matura-	MAFP/RA-
	MAFP/YAOU/RA-
	MAFP/YU/RA-
	MAT/YAOU/R-
	MAT/YU/R-
	MA/KHUR/RA-
maturant	MAFP/RANT
maturate	MAF/RAIT
maturation	MAFP/RAIGS
mature	MA/KHUR
	MA/TAOUR
maturity	MA/KHUR/TI
	MA/TAOUR/TI
matutinal	MA/TAOUT/NAL
Mauchart	MOE/KART
Maurer	MOU/RER
	MOUR/ER
Mauriac	MOER/YAK
Mauriceau	MOER/SOE
Mauthner	MOUT/NER
mauve	MAUV
	MOEV
Maxair Inhaler	MAX/AIR/IN/HAIL/ER
MaxEPA	MAX/ERBGS/P*RBGS/A*RBGS
Maxiflor	MAX/FLOR
maxill(o)-	MAK/SIL
	MAK/SIL/L(O)
	MAX/L(O)
maxilla	MAK/SIL/LA
maxillae	MAK/SIL/LAE
maxillare	MAX/LAI/RAOE
maxillares	MAX/LAI/RAOEZ
maxillaris	MAX/LAI/RIS
maxillary	MAX/LAIR
maxillectomy	MAX/LEKT/M*I
maxillitis	MAX/LAOITS
maxillodental	MAK/SIL/DEN/TAL
maxilloethmoidectomy	MAK/SIL/*ET/MOI/DEKT/M*I
maxillofacial	MAK/SIL/FAIRBL
maxillojugal	MAK/SIL/JAOU/GAL
maxillolabial	MAK/SIL/LAIB/YAL
maxillomandibular	MAK/SIL/MAN/DIB/LAR
maxillopalatine	MAK/SIL/PAL/TAOIN
maxillopharyngeal	MAK/SIL/FRIN/JAL
maxillotomy	MAX/LOT/M*I
maxilloturbinal	MAK/SIL/TURB/NAL

maxima	MAX/MA
maximal	MAX/MAL
maximi	MAX/MAOI
Maximow	MAX/MOV
maximum	MAX/MUM
maximus	MAX/MUS
Maxivate	MAX/VAIT
Maxovite	MAX/VAOIT
maxwell	MAX/WEL
Maxwell	K-P/MAX/WEL
Maxzide	MAX/ZAOID
May	MA*I
	K-P/MAI
mayer	MAI/ER
Mayer	K-P/MAI/ER
mayidism	MAI/DIFM
	MAI/ID/IFM
May-Vita	MA*I/H-F/VAOI/TA
	MAI/H-F/VAOI/TA
Mayo	MAI/YOE
Mayor	K-P/MAI/YOR
maza	MAZ/ZA
	MAZ/SA
Mazanor	MAZ/NOR
maze	MAEZ
	(not MAIZ; see maize)
mazic	MAIZ/IK
mazindol	MAI/ZIN/DOL
	MAIZ/IN/DOL
mazo-	MAIZ
	MAI/ZO
mazodynia	MAIZ/DIN/YA
mazolysis	MAI/ZOL/SIS
mazopathia	MAIZ/PA*T/YA
mazopathy	MAI/ZOP/TH*I
mazopexy	MAIZ/PEK/SI
mazoplasia	MAIZ/PLAIZ/YA
Mazzini	MA/ZAOE/NAOE
	MAZ/ZAOE/NAOE
Mazzoni	MA/ZOE/NAOE
	MAD/ZOE/NAOE
	MAZ/ZOE/NAOE
MB bands	M-RBGS/B*RBGS/BANDZ
McBurney	M-K/BUR/NAOE
McCarthy	M-K/KAR/TH*I
McClure	M-K/KLAOUR
McCrea	M-K/KRAI
McCune	M-K/KAOUN
McDonald	M-K/DON/ALD
McGinn	M-K/GIN
McGoon	M-K/GAON
McKee	M-K/KAOE
McLean	M-K/LAIN
	M-K/LAOEN
McMurray	M-K/MUR/RAOE
McPhail	M-K/FAIL
McPheeters	M-K/FAOET/ERS
McReynolds	M-K/REN/OLDZ
McVay	M-K/VAI
MCT Oil	M-RBGS/KR*RBGS/T*RBGS/OIL
M.D.	M*D
	M-FPLT/D*FPLT
meadow	MED/DOE
meal	MAOEL
mean	MAOEN
measle	MAOEZ/-L
measles	MAOEZ/-LS
measly	MAOEZ/LI
measure	MERB/SHUR
measuring tape	MERB/SHUR/-G/TAIP
measurement	MERB/SHURMT
	MERB/SHUR/-MT
meat(o)-	MAOE/YAI/T(O)
	MAOE/AI/T(O)
	MAOE/T(O)
meatal	MAOE/YAI/TAL
	MAOE/AI/TAL
meatomastoidectomy	MAOE/TO/MAS/TOI/DEKT/M*I
meatometer	MAOE/TO/TOM/TER
meatoplasty	MAOE/TO/PLAS/TI
meatorrhaphy	MAOE/TOR/FI
meatoscope	MAOE/AT/SKOEP
	MAOE/YAT/SKOEP
meatoscopy	MAOE/TOS/KPI
meatotome	MAOE/AT/TOEM
	MAOE/YAT/TOEM
meatotomy	MAOE/TOT/M*I
meatus	MAOE/YAI/TUS
	MAOE/AI/TUS

Mebaral	MEB/RAL
mebenazine	ME/BEN/ZAOEN
	MAOE/BEN/ZAOEN
mebendazole	ME/BEND/ZOEL
	MAOE/BEND/ZOEL
mebeverine	ME/BEV/RAOEN
	MAOE/BEV/RAOEN
mebhydroline	MEB/HAOI/DRO/LAOEN
mebrophenhydramine	MEB/RO/FEN/HAOI/DRA/MAOEN
mebutamate	ME/BAOUT/MAIT
mecamylamine	MEK/MIL/MIN
Mecca	MEK/KA
mechanic	ME/KAN/IK
	M-K
mechanical	ME/KAN/KAL
	M-K/KAL
mechanico-	ME/KAN/KO
mechanicoreceptor	ME/KAN/KO/RE/SEP/TOR
mechanicotherapeutics	ME/KAN/KO/THER/PAOUT/IK/-S
mechanicotherapy	ME/KAN/KO/THER/PI
mechanics	ME/KAN/IK/-S
	M-K/-S
mechanism	MEK/NIFM
mechanist	MEK/N*IS
	ME/KAN/*IS
mechano-	MEK/NO
mechanocardiography	MEK/NO/KARD/YOG/FI
mechanocyte	MEK/NO/SAO*IT
mechanogymnastics	MEK/NO/JIM/NA*S/IK/-S
mechanology	MEK/NOLG
mechanophobia	MEK/NO/FOEB/YA
mechanoreceptor	MEK/NO/RE/SEP/TOR
mechanoreflex	MEK/NO/RE/FLEX
mechanotherapy	MEK/NO/THER/PI
mechanothermy	MEK/NO/THER/M*I
meche	MAIRB
mechlorethamine	MEK/LOR/*ET/MAOEN
mecillinam	ME/SIL/NAM
mecism	MAOE/SIFM
Mecistocirrhus	MAOE/S*IS/SIR/RUS
	ME/S*IS/SIR/RUS
Meckel	MEK/EL
meckelectomy	MEK/LEKT/M*I
	MEK/EL/EKT/M*I
meckelii	MEK/EL/YAOI
Meclan	MEK/LAN
meclastine	ME/KLAS/TAOEN
meclizine	MEK/LI/ZAOEN
meclofenamate	MEK/LO/FEN/MAIT
meclofenoxate	MEK/LO/FEN/OK/SAIT
Meclomen	MEK/LO/MEN
mecloqualone	MEK/LO/KWA/LOEN
meclozine	MEK/LO/ZAOEN
mecometer	MAOE/KOM/TER
meconate	MEK/NAIT
meconic	ME/KON/IK
meconin	MEK/NIN
meconiorrhea	ME/KOEN/YO/RAOE/YA
meconism	MAOEK/NIFM
meconium	ME/KOEN/YUM
	MAOE/KOEN/YUM
mecrylate	ME/KRIL/AIT
mecystasis	ME/S*IS/SIS
medazepam	ME/DAZ/PAM
medi(o)-	MAOED/Y(O)
media	MAOED/YA
mediad	MAOED/YAD
mediae	MAOED/YAE
medial	MAOED/YAL
mediale	MAOED/YAI/LAOE
medialecithal	MAOED/YA/LES/THAL
mediales	MAOED/YAI/LAOEZ
medialis	MAOED/YAI/LIS
median	MAOED/YAN
mediana	MAOED/YAI/NA
mediani	MAOED/YAI/NAOI
medianum	MAOED/YAI/NUM
	MAOED/YAIN/UM
medianus	MAOED/YAI/NUS
mediastina	MAOED/YAS/TAOI/NA
mediastinal	MAOED/YAS/TAOINL
mediastinales	MAOED/YA*S/NAI/LAOEZ
mediastinalis	MAOED/YA*S/NAI/LIS
mediastinitis	MAOED/YA*S/NAOITS
mediastinogram	MAOED/YAS/TAOIN/GRAM
mediastinography	MAOED/YA*S/NOG/FI
mediastinopericarditis	MAOED/YA*S/NO/P*ER/KAR/DAOITS
mediastinoscope	MAOED/YAS/TAOIN/SKOEP

	MAOED/YAS/TIN/SKOEP	medphalan	MED/FA/LAN
mediastinoscopic	MAOED/YA*S/NO/SKOP/IK		MED/FLAN
mediastinoscopy	MAOED/YA*S/NOS/KPI	medrogestone	MED/RO/JES/TOEN
mediastinotomy	MAOED/YA*S/NOT/M*I	Medrol	MED/ROL
mediastinum	MAOED/YAS/TAOIN/UM	medroxyprogestrone	ME/DROX/PRO/J*ES/ROEN
	MAOED/YAS/TAOI/NUM		MED/ROX/PRO/J*ES/ROEN
mediastinus	MAOED/YAS/TAOI/NUS	medrylamine	MED/RIL/MAOEN
mediate	MAOED/YAT		ME/DRIL/MAOEN
	MAOED/YAIT	medrysone	MED/RI/SOEN
mediation	MAOED/YAIGS	medull(o)-	ME/DUL
mediator	MAOED/YAI/TOR		ME/DUL/L(O)
Mediatric	MAOED/YAT/RIK		MED/L(O)
	MED/YAT/RIK		MED/YAOU/L(O)
medic(o)-	MED/K(O)		MED/YU/L(O)
medicable	MED/KABL		ME/DAOU/L(O)
	MED/IK/-BL	medulla	ME/DUL/LA
Medicaid	MED/KAID		ME/DAOU/LA
medical	MED/KAL	medullae	ME/DUL/LAE
medicament	ME/DIK/-MT		ME/DAOU/LAE
	MED/KAMT	medulla oblongata	ME/DUL/LA/OB/LON/GA/TA
medicamentosa	MED/KA/MEN/TOE/SA		ME/DAOU/LA/OB/LON/GA/TA
medicamentosus	MED/KA/MEN/TOE/SUS		ME/DUL/LA/OB/LON/GAI/TA
medicamentous	MED/KA/MEN/TOUS		ME/DAOU/LA/OB/LON/GAI/TA
Medicare	MED/KAIR	medulla ossium	ME/DUL/LA/OS/YUM
medicaster	MED/KA*S/ER		ME/DAOU/LA/OS/YUM
medicate	MED/KAIT	medullar	MED/LAR
medicated	MED/KAIT/-D	medullare	MED/LAI/RAOE
medication	MED/KAIGS	medullary	MED/LAIR
medicator	MED/KAI/TOR	medullated	MED/LAIT/-D
medicephalic	MAOED/SFAL/IK	medullation	MED/LAIGS
medicinal	ME/DIS/NAL	medullectomy	MED/LEKT/M*I
medicine	MED/SIN	medullitis	MED/LAOITS
medicobiologic	MED/KO/BAO*I/LOJ/IK	medullization	MED/LI/ZAIGS
medicobiological	MED/KO/BAO*I/LOJ/KAL	medulloadrenal	ME/DUL/AI/DRAOENL
medicochirurgic	MED/KO/KAOI/RURJ/IK		ME/LO/AI/DRAOENL
medicochirurgical	MED/KO/KAOI/RURJ/KAL	medulloarthritis	ME/DUL/AR/THRAOITS
medicodental	MED/KO/DEN/TAL		ME/LO/AR/THRAOITS
medicolegal	MED/KO/LAOE/GAL	medulloblast	ME/DUL/BLA*S
	MED/LO/LAOEL		ME/LO/BLA*S
medicomechanical	MED/KO/ME/KAN/KAL	medulloblastoma	ME/DUL/BLAS/TOE/MA
	MED/KO/M-K/KAL		ME/LO/BLAS/TOE/MA
medicophysical	MED/KO/FIZ/KAL	medullocell	ME/DUL/KREL
medicophysics	MED/KO/FIZ/IK/-S		ME/LO/KREL
medicopsychological	MED/KO/SAOIK/LOJ/KAL	medulloencephalic	ME/DUL/EN/SFAL/IK
medicopsychology	MED/KO/SAOI/KOLG		ME/LO/EN/SFAL/IK
medicosocial	MED/KO/SOERBL	medulloepithelioma	ME/DUL/EP/THAOEL/YOE/MA
medicotopographical	MED/KO/TOP/GRAF/KAL		ME/LO/EP/THAOEL/YOE/MA
medicozoological	MED/KO/ZOE/LOJ/KAL	medulloid	MED/LOID
Medicone	MED/KOEN	medullomyoblastoma	ME/DUL/MAOI/BLAS/TOE/MA
Medicone Derma	MED/KOEN/DER/MA		ME/LO/MAOI/BLAS/TOE/MA
Medicone Derma-HC	MED/KOEN/DER/MA/H-RBGS/	medullosuprarenoma	ME/DUL/SU/PRA/RE/NOE/MA
	KR*RBGS		ME/LO/SU/PRA/RE/NOE/MA
Mediconet	MED/KO/NET	medullotherapy	ME/DUL/THER/PI
Medicopaste Bandage	MED/KO/PA*IS/BAND/AJ		ME/LO/THER/PI
medicus	MED/KUS	medullovasculosa	ME/DUL/VAS/KLOE/SA
medifrontal	MAOED/FRON/TAL		ME/LO/VAS/KLOE/SA
Medigesic	MED/JAOEZ/IK	medusa	ME/DAOU/SA
Medihaler	MED/HAIL/ER	medusae	ME/DAOU/SAE
Medihaler-Epi	MED/HAIL/ER/EP/PI	mefenamic	MEF/NAM/IK
Medihaler-Iso	MED/HAIL/ER/AOI/SOE	mefenorex	ME/FEN/REX
medii	MAOED/YAOI	mefexamide	ME/FEX/MAOID
Medilax	MED/LAX	Mefoxin	ME/FOK/SIN
medinensis	MED/NEN/SIS		MEF/OK/SIN
medio-	MAOED/YO	mega-	MEG
mediocarpal	MAOED/YO/KAR/PAL	Mega-B	MEG/B-RBGS
mediocarpea	MAOED/YO/KARP/YA	megabacterium	MEG/BAK/TAOERM
medioccipital	MAOED/YOK/SIP/TAL	megabladder	MEG/BLAD/ER
	MAOED/OK/SIP/TAL	megacalycosis	MEG/KAL/KOE/SIS
mediodens	MAOED/YO/DENZ	megacardia	MEG/KARD/YA
mediodorsal	MAOED/YO/DOR/SAL	Megace	MEG/AIS
mediolateral	MAOED/YO/LAT/RAL	megacecum	MEG/SE/KUM
medionecrosis	MAOED/YO/NE/KROE/SIS	megacephalia	MEG/SFAIL/YA
mediotarsal	MAOED/YO/TAR/SAL	megacephalic	MEG/SFAL/IK
mediotrusion	MAOED/YO/TRAOUGS	megacephalous	MEG/SEF/LOUS
mediotype	MAOED/YO/TAOIP	megacephaly	MEG/SEF/LI
Medipren	MED/PREN	megacholedochus	MEG/KOE/LED/KUS
mediscalenus	MAOED/SKA/LAOE/NUS	megacin	MEG/SIN
medisect	MAOED/SEKT	megacocci	MEG/KOK/SAOI
meditation	MED/TAIGS	megacoccus	MEG/KOK/KUS
Mediterranean	MED/TRAIN/YAN	megacolon	MEG/KO/LON
	MED/TER/RAIN/YAN	megacurie	MEG/KAOUR/RAOE
Medi-Tuss	MED/TUSZ	megacycle	MEG/SAOIK/-L
medium	MAOED/YUM	megacystis	MEG/SIS/TIS
medius	MAOED/YUS	megadactylia	MEG/DAK/TIL/YA
MEDLARS	MED/LARZ	megadactylism	MEG/DAKT/LIFM
	MED/LARS	megadactyly	MEG/DAKT/LI
MEDLINE	MED/LAOIN	megadolichocolon	MEG/DOL/KO/KO/LON
medorrhea	MAOED/RAOE/YA	megadont	MEG/DONT
	MED/RAOE/YA	megadontia	MEG/DON/SHA

megadontic	MEG/DONT/IK	megaprosopia	MEG/PRO/SOEP/YA
megadontism	MEG/DON/TIFM	megaprosopous	MEG/PROS/POUS
megadose	MEG/DOES	megarectum	MEG/REK/TUM
Megadose	K-P/MEG/DOES	megaseme	MEG/SAOEM
megaduodenum	MEG/DAOU/DAOEN/UM	megasigmoid	MEG/SIG/MOID
megadyne	MEG/DAOIN	megasoma	MEG/SOE/MA
megaesophagus	MEG/E/SOF/GUS	megasomia	MEG/SOEM/YA
megagamete	MEG/GAM/AOET	megaspore	MEG/SPOER
megagnathia	MEG/NA*IT/YA	megatherium	MEG/THAOER/YUM
megahertz	MEG/HERTS	megathrombocyte	MEG/THROM/BO/SAO*IT
megakaryoblast	MEG/KAR/YO/BLA*S	megaunit	MEG/YAOUNT
megakaryocyte	MEG/KAR/YO/SAO*IT	megaureter	MEG/YAOU/RAOET/ER
megakaryocytopoiesis	MEG/KAR/YO/SAOIT/POI/SIS	megaurethra	MEG/YAOU/RAO*ET/RA
megakaryocytosis	MEG/KAR/YO/SAOI/TOE/SIS	megavitamin	MEG/VAOIT/MIN
megal(o)-	MEG/L(O)	megavolt	MEG/VOELT
megalakria	MEG/LAK/RAOE/YA		MEG/VOLT
megalecithal	MEG/LES/THAL	megavoltage	MEG/VOELT/AJ
megalencephalon	MEG/LEN/SEF/LON		MEG/VOLT/AJ
megalencephaly	MEG/LEN/SEF/LI	megestrol	ME/JES/TROL
megalgia	ME/GAL/JA		ME/JES/TROEL
	MEG/AL/JA	Meglin	MAI/GLAN
-megalia	ME/GAIL/YA	meglumine	MEG/LAOU/MAOEN
megaloblast	MEG/LO/BLA*S		MEG/LU/MAOEN
megaloblastic	MEG/LO/BLA*S/IK	megohm	MEG/OEM
megaloblastoid	MEG/LO/BLAS/TOID	megophthalmos	MEG/OF/THAL/MOS
megalobulbus	MEG/LO/BUL/BUS	megoxycyte	MEG/OX/SAO*IT
megalocardia	MEG/LO/KARD/YA	megoxyphil	MEG/OX/FIL
megalocephala	MEG/LO/SEF/LA	megoxyphile	MEG/OX/FAOIL
megalocephalia	MEG/LO/SFAIL/YA	megrim	MAOE/GRIM
megalocephalic	MEG/LO/SFAL/IK	Meibom	MAOI/BOEM
megalocephaly	MEG/LO/SEF/LI	meibomian	MAOI/BOEM/YAN
megalocheiria	MEG/LO/KAOIR/YA	meibomianitis	MAOI/BOEM/YA/NAOITS
megaloclitoris	MEG/LO/KLI/TOR/RIS	meibomitis	MAOIB/MAOITS
	MEG/LO/KLIT/RIS	Meige's disease	MEJ/AOES/DI/SAOEZ
	MEG/LO/KLAOI/TOR/RIS		MEJ/AOES/D-Z
megalocornea	MEG/LO/KORN/YA	Meigs	MEGS
megalocystis	MEG/LO/SIS/TIS		MAOEGS
megalocyte	MEG/LO/SAO*IT	Meinicke	MAOIN/KAOE
megalocythemia	MEG/LO/SAOI/THAOEM/YA	meio-	MAO*I
megalocytic	MEG/LO/SIT/IK		MAO*I/YO
megalocytosis	MEG/LO/SAOI/TOE/SIS	meiogenic	MAO*I/JEN/IK
megalodactylia	MEG/LO/DAK/TIL/YA		(not MAOI/JEN/IK; see myogenic)
megalodactylism	MEG/LO/DAKT/LIFM	meiosis	MAO*I/YOE/SIS
megalodactylous	MEG/LO/DAKT/LOUS		(not MAOI/YOE/SIS; see miosis)
megalodactyly	MEG/LO/DAKT/LI	meiotic	MAO*I/OT/IK
megalodont	MEG/LO/DONT		MAO*I/YOT/IK
megalodontia	MEG/LO/DON/SHA		(not MAOI/OT/IK or MAOI/YOT/IK;
megaloencephalic	MEG/LO/EN/SFAL/IK		see miotic)
megaloencephalon	MEG/LO/EN/SEF/LON	Meissner	MAOIS/NER
megaloencephaly	MEG/LO/EN/SEF/LI	mel	MEL
megaloenteron	MEG/LO/SPWER/RON	mel(o)-	MEL
	MEG/LO/SPWRON		MAOE/L(O)
megaloesophagus	MEG/LO/E/SOF/GUS	melagra	ME/LAG/RA
megalogastria	MEG/LO/GAS/TRA		MEL/AG/RA
	MEG/LO/GAS/TRAOE/YA	melalgia	ME/LAL/JA
megaloglossia	MEG/LO/GLOS/YA		MEL/AL/JA
megalographia	MEG/LO/GRAF/YA	melamine	MEL/MAOEN
megalography	MEG/LOG/FI	melancholia	MEL/AN/KOEL/YA
megalohepatia	MEG/LO/HE/PAI/SHA	melancholiac	MEL/AN/KOEL/YAK
	MEG/LO/HE/PAT/YA	melancholic	MEL/AN/KOL/IK
megalokaryocyte	MEG/LO/KAR/YO/SAO*IT	melancholy	MEL/AN/KOL/LI
megalomania	MEG/LO/MAIN/YA	melan(o)-	MEL/N(O)
megalomaniac	MEG/LO/MAIN/YAK	melanedema	MEL/AN/DAOE/MA
megalomelia	MEG/LO/MAOEL/YA		MEL/AN/E/DAOE/MA
megalonychia	MEG/LO/NIK/YA	melanemesis	MEL/NEM/SIS
megalonychosis	MEG/LON/KOE/SIS	melanemia	MEL/NAOEM/YA
megalopenis	MEG/LO/PAOE/NIS	melanidrosis	MEL/AN/DROE/SIS
megalophallus	MEG/LO/FAL/LUS	melaniferous	MEL/NIF/ROUS
megalophthalmos	MEG/LOF/THAL/MOS	melanin	MEL/NIN
megalophthalmus	MEG/LOF/THAL/MUS	melaninogenica	MEL/NIN/JEN/KA
megalopia	MEG/LOEP/YA	melaninogenicus	MEL/NIN/JEN/KUS
megalopodia	MEG/LO/POED/YA	melanism	MEL/NIFM
megalopsia	MEG/LOPS/YA	melanistic	MEL/N*IS/IK
megaloscope	MEG/LO/SKOEP	melanoacanthoma	MEL/NO/AK/AN/THOE/MA
megalosplanchnic	MEG/LO/SPLANG/NIK	melanoameloblastoma	MEL/NO/AM/LO/BLAS/TOE/MA
megalosplenia	MEG/LO/SPLAOEN/YA	melanoblast	MEL/NO/BLA*S
megalosplenica	MEG/LO/SPLEN/KA	melanoblastoma	MEL/NO/BLAS/TOE/MA
megalospore	MEG/LO/SPOER	melanoblastosis	MEL/NO/BLAS/TOE/SIS
megalosyndactylia	MEG/LO/SIN/DAK/TIL/YA	melanocarcinoma	MEL/NO/KARS/NOE/MA
megalosyndactyly	MEG/LO/SIN/DAKT/LI	melanocyte	MEL/NO/SAO*IT
megalothymus	MEG/LO/THAOI/MUS	melanocytic	MEL/NO/SIT/IK
megaloureter	MEG/LO/YAOU/RAOET/ER	melanocytoma	MEL/NO/SAOI/TOE/MA
megalourethra	MEG/LO/YAOU/RAO*ET/RA	melanoderm	MEL/NO/DERM
-megaly	MEG/LI	melanoderma	MEL/NO/DER/MA
Mega-MaxEPA	MEG/MAX/ERBGS/P*RBGS/	melanodermatitis	MEL/NO/DERM/TAOITS
	A*RBGS	melanodermic	MEL/NO/DERM/IK
megamerozoite	MEG/MER/ZOE/AOIT	melanodes	MEL/NOE/DAOEZ
meganucleus	MEG/NAOUK/LUS	melanoepithelioma	MEL/NO/EP/THAOEL/YOE/MA
Megaplex	MEG/PLEX	melanoflocculation	MEL/NO/FLOK/LAIGS

melanogaster	MEL/NO/GAS/TER
melanogen	ME/LAN/JEN
	MEL/NO/JEN
melanogenemia	MEL/NO/JE/NAOEM/YA
melanogenesis	MEL/NO/JEN/SIS
melanogenic	MEL/NO/JEN/IK
melanoglossia	MEL/NO/GLOS/YA
melanoid	MEL/NOID
melanokeratosis	MEL/NO/KER/TOE/SIS
melanoleukoderma	MEL/NO/LAOUK/DER/MA
melanoma	MEL/NOE/MA
melanomatosis	MEL/NOEM/TOE/SIS
melanomatous	MEL/NOEM/TOUS
melanonychia	MEL/NO/NIK/YA
melanopathy	MEL/NOP/TH*I
melanophage	MEL/NO/FAIJ
melanophore	MEL/NO/FOER
melanophorin	MEL/NO/F/RIN
melanoplakia	MEL/NO/PLAIK/YA
melanoprecipitation	MEL/NO/PRE/SIP/TAIGS
melanoprotein	MEL/NO/PRO/TAOEN
melanoptysis	MEL/NOPT/SIS
melanorrhagia	MEL/NO/RAI/JA
melanorrhea	MEL/NO/RAOE/YA
melanosarcoma	MEL/NO/SAR/KOE/MA
melanosarcomatosis	MEL/NO/SAR/KOEM/TOE/SIS
melanoscirrhus	MEL/NO/SKIR/RUS
melanosis	MEL/NOE/SIS
melanosome	MEL/NO/SOEM
melanosity	MEL/NOS/TI
melanosome	MEL/NO/SOEM
melanotic	MEL/NOT/IK
melanotrichia	MEL/NO/TRIK/YA
melanotrichous	MEL/NOT/RI/KOUS
melanotroph	MEL/NO/TROEF
melanotropic	MEL/NO/TROP/IK
melanotropin	MEL/NO/TROE/PIN
melanura	MEL/NAOU/RA
melanuria	MEL/NAOUR/YA
melanuric	MEL/NAOUR/IK
melarsoprol	ME/LARS/PROL
	MEL/ARS/PROL
melasma	ME/LAZ/MA
melatonin	MEL/TOE/NIN
meleagridis	MEL/YAG/RI/DIS
	MAOEL/YAG/RI/DIS
melena	ME/LAOE/NA
melenemesis	MEL/NEM/SIS
melengestrol	MEL/EN/JES/TROEL
	MEL/EN/JES/TROL
melenic	ME/LAOEN/IK
meletin	MEL/TIN
-melia	MAOEL/YA
Melfiat	MEL/FAOE/YAT
	MEL/FAOE/YAUT
-melia	MAOEL/YA
melibiase	MEL/BAO*I/AIS
	MEL/B*I/AIS
melibiose	MEL/BAO*I/OES
	MEL/B*I/OES
melicera	MEL/SAOER/RA
	MEL/SE/RA
meliceris	MEL/SAOER/RIS
	MEL/SE/RIS
melioidosis	MEL/YOI/DOE/SIS
Melissa	ME/LIS/SA
melissophobia	ME/LIS/FOEB/YA
melissotherapy	ME/LIS/THER/PI
melitensis	MEL/TEN/SIS
melitin	M*EL/TIN
	MEL/LI/TIN
	(*not* MEL/TIN; see meletin)
melitis	MAOE/LAOITS
	ME/LAOITS
melitose	MEL/TOES
melitracen	MEL/TRAI/SEN
melitriose	MEL/TR*I/OES
	ME/LIT/ROES
	ME/LIT/RAOE/OES
melituria	MEL/TAOUR/YA
melituric	MEL/TAOUR/IK
Mellaril	MEL/RIL
Mellaril-S	MEL/RIL/S-RBGS
mellita	ME/LAOI/TA
	MEL/LAOI/TA
melliti	ME/LAOI/TAOI
	MEL/LAOI/TAOI
mellitic	ME/LIT/IK
	MEL/LIT/IK
mellitum	ME/LAOI/TUM
	MEL/LAOI/TUM
mellitus	ME/LAOI/TUS
	MEL/LAOI/TUS
Melnick	MEL/NIK
melocervicoplasty	MEL/SEFRB/KO/PLAS/TI
melodidymus	MEL/DID/MUS
melomania	MEL/MAIN/YA
melomelia	MEL/MAOEL/YA
melomelus	ME/LOM/LUS
melonoplasty	ME/LON/PLAS/TI
	MAOE/LON/PLAS/TI
Melophagus	ME/LOF/GUS
	MAOE/LOF/GUS
meloplasty	MEL/PLAS/TI
	MAOEL/PLAS/TI
melorheostosis	MEL/RAOE/OS/TOE/SIS
	MEL/RE/OS/TOE/SIS
melosalgia	MEL/SAL/JA
meloschisis	ME/LOS/KI/SIS
melotia	ME/LOE/SHA
melotus	ME/LOE/TUS
melphalan	MEL/FA/LAN
	MEL/FLAN
Meltzer	MELT/ZER
	MELT/SER
member	MEM/BER
	MEB
memberment	MEM/BERMT
	MEB/-MT
	MEM/BER/-MT
membra	MEM/BRA
membrana	MEM/BRAI/NA
	MEM/BRA/NA
membranacea	MEM/BRA/NAIS/YA
membranaceae	MEM/BRA/NAIS/YAE
membranacei	MEM/BRA/NAIS/YAOI
membranaceous	MEM/BRA/NAIRBS
membranaceum	MEM/BRA/NAIS/YUM
membranae	MEM/BRAI/NAE
	MEM/BRA/NAE
membranate	MEM/BRA/NAIT
membrane	MEM/BRAIN
membranectomy	MEM/BRA/NEKT/M*I
membranelle	MEM/BRA/NEL
membraniform	MEM/BRAIN/FORM
membranocartilaginous	MEM/BRA/NO/KART/LAJ/NOUS
membranoid	MEM/BRA/NOID
membranolysis	MEM/BRA/NOL/SIS
membranosus	MEM/BRA/NOE/SUS
membranous	MEM/BRA/NOUS
membri	MEM/BRAOI
membrum	MEM/BRUM
memoration	MEM/RAIGS
memory	MEM/RI
memotine	MEM/TAOEN
men(o)-	MEN (most of the time)
	MEN/N(O)
menacme	ME/NAK/MAOE
	MEN/AK/MAOE
menadiol	MEN/DI/OL
menadione	MEN/DI/OEN
menalgia	MEN/AL/JA
menaphthone	ME/NAF/THOEN
	MEN/AF/THOEN
menaquinone	MEN/KWIN/OEN
	MEN/KWAOI/NOEN
menarchal	ME/NAR/KAL
	MEN/AR/KAL
menarche	ME/NAR/KAOE
	MEN/AR/KAOE
menarcheal	ME/NARK/YAL
	MEN/ARK/YAL
menarchial	*see* menarcheal
Menaval	M*EN/VAL
	(*not* MEN/VAL; see men value)
Mendel	MEN/DEL
	MEND/EL
Mendeleeff	MEND/LAI/EF
	MEND/LAI/YEF
mendelevium	MEND/LAOEV/YUM
mendelian	MEN/DAOEL/YAN
	MEN/DEL/YAN
mendelism	MEND/LIFM
	MEN/DEL/IFM
mendelizing	MEND/LAOIZ/-G
	MEN/DEL/AOIZ/-G
Mendelsohn	MEN/DEL/SOEN
	MEN/DEL/SON

	MEND/EL/SOEN	meniscus	ME/NIS/KUS
	MEND/EL/SON	menocelis	MEN/SE/LIS
Menetrier	MAIN/TRAOE/YAIR	menolipsis	MEN/LIP/SIS
	MEN/TRAOE/YAIR	menometrorrhagia	MEN/MAOE/TRO/RAI/JA
Menge	MENG		MEN/MET/RO/RAI/JA
	MEN/GAOE	menopausal	MEN/PAU/ZAL
-menia	MAOEN/YA		MEN/NO/PAU/ZAL
Meniere	MEN/YAIR	menopause	M*EN/PAUZ
mening(o)-	ME/NING		MEN/NO/PAUZ
	ME/NIN/G(O)		(not MEN/PAUZ)
	MEN/J(O)	menophania	MEN/FAIN/YA
	MEN/IN/J(O)	menoplania	MEN/PLAIN/YA
meningea	ME/NIN/JA	menorrhagia	MEN/RAI/JA
meningeae	ME/NIN/JAE	menorrhalgia	MEN/RAL/JA
meningeal	ME/NIN/JAL	menorrhea	MEN/RAOE/YA
meningeocortical	ME/NIN/JO/KORT/KAL	menorrheal	MEN/RAOEL
meningeorrhaphy	ME/NIN/JOR/FI		MEN/RAOE/YAL
meninges	ME/NIN/JAOEZ	menoschesis	ME/NOS/KE/SIS
meningeus	ME/NIN/JUS		MEN/OS/KE/SIS
meningioma	ME/NIN/JOE/MA		MEN/SKAOE/SIS
meningiomatosis	ME/NIN/JOEM/TOE/SIS	menostasia	MEN/STAIZ/YA
meningis	ME/NIN/JIS	menostasis	ME/NO*S/SIS
meningism	MEN/IN/JIFM		MEN/O*S/SIS
	MEN/JIFM	menostaxis	MEN/STAK/SIS
	ME/NIN/JIFM	menotropin	MEN/TROE/PIN
meningismus	MEN/JIZ/MUS	menouria	MEN/YAOUR/YA
	MEN/IN/JIZ/MUS	menoxenia	MEN/ZAOEN/YA
meningitic	MEN/JIT/IK		MEN/OK/SAOEN/YA
	MEN/IN/JIT/IK	Menrium	MEN/RUM
meningitides	MEN/JIT/DAOEZ		MEN/RAOE/UM
	MEN/IN/JIT/DAOEZ	menses	M*EN/SAOEZ
meningitis	MEN/JAOITS		MEN/SAO*EZ
	MEN/IN/JAOITS		MENS/AOEZ
meningoarteritis	ME/NING/ART/RAOITS		(not MEN/SAOEZ; see men seize)
meningoblastoma	ME/NING/BLAS/TOE/MA	menstrua	MEN/STRA
meningocele	ME/NING/SAO*EL		MEN/STRAOU/WA
meningocephalitis	ME/NING/SEF/LAOITS	menstrual	MEN/STRAOUL
meningocerebritis	ME/NING/SER/BRAOITS		MEN/STRUL
meningococcemia	ME/NING/KOK/SAOEM/YA		MEN/STRAL
meningococci	ME/NING/KOK/SAOI	menstrualis	MEN/STRAI/LIS
meningococcidal	ME/NING/KOK/SAOI/DAL		MEN/STRAOU/AI/LIS
meningococcosis	ME/NING/KOK/KOE/SIS		MEN/STRAOU/WAI/LIS
meningococcus	ME/NING/KOK/KUS	menstruant	MEN/STRAOUNT
meningocortical	ME/NING/KORT/KAL		MEN/STRUNT
meningocyte	ME/NING/SAO*IT		MEN/STRANT
meningoencephalitis	ME/NING/EN/SEF/LAOITS	menstruate	MEN/STRAIT
meningoencephalocele	ME/NING/EN/SEF/LO/SAO*EL		MEN/STRAOU/AIT
meningoencephalomyelitis	ME/NING/EN/SEF/LO/MAOI/	menstruation	MEN/STRAIGS
	LAOITS		MEN/STRAOU/AIGS
meningoencephalomyelopathy		menstruous	MEN/STROUS
	ME/NING/EN/SEF/LO/MAOI/LOP/		MEN/STRAOU/OUS
	TH*I	menstruum	MEN/STRUM
meningoencephalopathy	ME/NING/EN/SEF/LOP/TH*I		MEN/STRAOUM
meningogenic	ME/NING/JEN/IK	mensual	MENS/YAL
meningomalacia	ME/NING/MA/LAI/SHA		MENS/YAOUL
meningomyelitis	ME/NING/MAOI/LAOITS		MENS/YUL
meningomyelocele	ME/NING/MAOI/LO/SAO*EL		MEN/SAOUL
meningomyeloencephalitis	ME/NING/MAOI/LO/EN/SEF/	mensuration	MENS/RAIGS
	LAOITS		MEN/SAOU/RAIGS
meningomyeloradiculitis	ME/NING/MAOI/LO/RA/DIK/		MEN/SHU/RAIGS
	LAOITS		MEN/SHUR/AIGS
meningo-osteophlebitis	ME/NING/O*S/YO/FLE/BAOITS	ment(o)-	MENT
meningopathy	MEN/GOP/TH*I		MEN/T(O)
	MEN/IN/GOP/TH*I	mentagra	MEN/TAG/RA
meningorachidian	ME/NING/RA/KID/YAN	mental	MEN/TAL
	ME/NING/RAI/KID/YAN	mentalis	MEN/TAI/LIS
meningoradicular	ME/NING/RA/DIK/LAR	mentality	MEN/TAL/TI
meningoradiculitis	ME/NING/RA/DIK/LAOITS	mentation	MEN/TAIGS
meningorrhagia	ME/NING/RAI/JA	Mentha	MEN/THA
meningorrhea	ME/NING/RAOE/YA	menthae	MEN/THAE
meningosis	MEN/GOE/SIS	menthane	MEN/THAIN
	MEN/IN/GOE/SIS	menthol	MEN/THOL
meningovascular	ME/NING/VAS/KLAR	menthyl	MEN/THIL
meninguria	MEN/GAOUR/YA	menti	MEN/TAOI
	MEN/IN/GAOUR/YA	mentoanterior	MENT/AN/TAOER/YOR
meninx	MAOE/NINGS	mentolabial	MENT/LAIB/YAL
	MEN/INGS	mentolabialis	MENT/LAIB/YAI/LIS
meniscal	ME/NIS/KAL	menton	MEN/TON
meniscectomy	MEN/SEKT/M*I	mento-occipital	MENT/OK/SIP/TAL
menisci	ME/NIS/SAOI	mentoparietal	MENT/PRAOI/TAL
meniscitis	MEN/SAOITS	mentoplasty	MENT/PLAS/TI
menisco-	ME/NIS/KO	mentoposterior	MENT/POS/TAOER/YOR
meniscocyte	ME/NIS/KO/SAO*IT	mentotransverse	MENT/TRA*NS/VERS
meniscocytosis	ME/NIS/KO/SAOI/TOE/SIS	mentula	MEN/TAOU/LA
meniscopexy	ME/NIS/KO/PEK/SI		MEN/KHU/LA
meniscorrhaphy	MEN/IS/KOR/FI	mentulagra	MEN/TAOU/LAG/RA
	MEN/SKOR/FI		MEN/KHU/LAG/RA
meniscosynovial	ME/NIS/KO/SNOEV/YAL	mentulate	MEN/TAOU/LAIT
meniscotome	ME/NIS/KO/TOEM		MEN/KHU/LAIT

mentum	MEN/TUM	meristem	MER/STEM
Menyanthes	MEN/YAN/THAOEZ	meristematic	MER/STE/MAT/IK
mepacrine	MEP/KRAOEN		MER/STEM/AT/IK
	MEP/KRIN	meristic	ME/R*IS/IK
meparfynol	ME/PAR/FI/NOL	meristosporus	ME/R*IS/SPOR/RUS
mepazine	MEP/ZAOEN	Merkel	MERK/EL
mepenzolate	ME/PENZ/LAIT		MERK/KEL
Mepergan	MEP/ER/GAN	meroacrania	MER/AI/KRAIN/YA
meperidine	ME/PER/DAOEN	meroanencephaly	MER/AN/EN/SEF/LI
mephenesin	ME/FEN/SIN	meroblastic	MER/BLA*S/IK
mephenoxalone	MEF/NOX/LOEN	merocele	MER/SAO*EL
mephentermine	ME/FEN/TER/MAOEN	merocoxalgia	MAOER/KOK/SAL/JA
	ME/FENT/ER/MAOEN		MER/KOX/AL/JA
mephenytoin	ME/FEN/TOIN	merocyte	MER/SAO*IT
	ME/FENT/WIN	merodiastolic	MER/DAOI/STOL/IK
mephitic	ME/FIT/IK	merogenesis	MER/JEN/SIS
mephobarbital	MEF/BARB/TAL	merogenetic	MER/JE/NET/IK
Mephyton	MEF/TON	merogenic	MER/JEN/IK
mepivacaine	ME/PIV/KAIN	merogonic	MER/GON/IK
meprednisone	ME/PRED/NI/SOEN	merogony	ME/ROG/N*I
	ME/PRED/NI/ZOEN	merology	ME/ROLG
meprobamate	ME/PROEB/MAIT	meromelia	MER/MAOEL/YA
Meprospan	MEP/RO/SPAN	meromicrosomia	MER/MAOI/KRO/SOEM/YA
meprylcaine	MEP/RIL/KAIN	meromyosin	MER/MAOI/SIN
mepyramine	ME/PIR/MAOEN	meronecrosis	MER/NE/KROE/SIS
mepyrapone	ME/PIR/POEN	meropia	ME/ROEP/YA
mEq	M*EK	merorachischisis	MER/RA/KIS/KI/SIS
mEq/L	M*EK/SL-RB/L-RBGS	merosmia	ME/ROZ/MAOE/YA
-mer	MER		ME/ROZ/MA
mer(o)-	MER	merostotic	MER/OS/TOT/IK
	ME/R-	merosystolic	MER/SIS/TOL/IK
	MAOER	merotomy	ME/ROT/M*I
	MAOE/R(O)	merozoite	MER/ZOE/AOIT
meralgia	ME/RAL/JA	merozygote	MER/ZAOI/GOET
meralluride	MER/AL/YAOU/RAOID	merphalan	MER/FA/LAN
	MER/AL/YU/RAOID		MER/FLAN
merbromin	MER/BROE/MIN	Merrifield knife	MER/FAOELD/NAOIF
mercapt(o)-	MER/KAPT		MER/RI/FAOELD/NAOIF
	MER/KAP/T(O)	Merritt	M*ER/RIT
mercaptal	MER/KAP/TAL		(not MER/RIT; see merit)
mercaptan	MER/KAP/TAN	mersalyl	MERS/LIL
mercaptoacetic	MER/KAPT/AI/SAOET/IK		MER/SA/LIL
mercaptol	MER/KAP/TOL	Merseburg	MAIRZ/BURG
mercaptomerin	MER/KAP/TOM/RIN	Merulius	ME/RAOUL/YUS
	MER/KAPT/MER/RIN	Meruvax	MER/YAOU/VAX
mercaptopurine	MER/KAPT/PAOUR/RAOEN		MER/YU/VAX
	MER/KAPT/PAOUR/RIN	merycism	MER/SIFM
mercapturic	MER/KAP/TAOUR/IK	merycismus	MER/SIZ/MUS
	MER/KAP/KHUR/IK	Merzbacher	MERTS/BAK/ER
Mercier	MERS/YAI		MERZ/BAK/ER
mercumatilin	MER/KAOUM/TIL/LIN	mes(o)-	MES
	MER/KAOU/MAT/LIN		MEZ
	MERK/MAT/LIN	mesad	MAOE/ZAD
mercuramide	MER/KAOUR/MAOID		MAOE/SAD
mercurammonium	MER/KAOUR/MOEN/YUM	mesal	MAOE/ZAL
mercurial	MER/KAOURL		MAOE/SAL
	MER/KAOUR/YAL	mesalamine	ME/SAL/MAOEN
mercurialentis	MER/KAOUR/YA/LEN/TIS	mesameboid	MES/AI/MAOE/BOID
mercurialis	MER/KAOUR/YAI/LIS		MES/MAOE/BOID
mercurialism	MER/KAOURL/IFM	mesangial	MES/AN/JAL
	MER/KAOUR/YAL/IFM	mesangiocapillary	MES/AN/JO/KAP/LAIR
mercurialization	MER/KAOURL/ZAIGS	mesangium	MES/AN/JUM
	MER/KAOUR/YAL/ZAIGS	Mesantoin	ME/SAN/TOIN
mercurialized	MER/KAOURL/AOIZ/-D		ME/SANT/WIN
	MER/KAOUR/YAL/AOIZ/-D	mesaortitis	MES/AI/YOR/TAOITS
mercuribenzoate	MER/KAOUR/BENZ/WAIT		MES/AI/OR/TAOITS
mercuric	MER/KAOUR/IK	mesaraic	MES/RAI/IK
mercurochrome	MER/KAOUR/KROEM	mesareic	MES/RAOE/IK
mercurophen	MER/KAOUR/FEN	mesarteritis	MES/ART/RAOITS
mercurophylline	MERK/RO/FLIN	mesaticephalic	ME/SAT/SFAL/IK
	MERK/RO/FIL/LIN	mesatikerkic	ME/SAT/KERK/IK
	MERK/ROF/LIN	mesatipellic	ME/SAT/PEL/IK
	MER/KAOUR/FLIN	mesatipelvic	ME/SAT/PEL/VIK
	MER/KAOUR/FIL/LIN	mesaxon	MES/AK/SON
mercurous	MERK/ROUS	mescal	MES/KAL
	MER/KAOU/ROUS	mescaline	MES/KLAOEN
mercury	MERK/RI		MES/KLIN
	MER/KAOU/RI		MES/KA/LAOEN
mereprine	MER/PRAOEN		MES/KA/LIN
merethoxylline	MER/THOX/LAOEN	mescalism	MES/KLIFM
meridian	ME/RID/YAN		MES/KA/LIFM
meridiani	ME/RID/YAI/NAOI	mesectic	ME/SEKT/IK
meridianus	ME/RID/YAI/NUS	mesectoblast	MES/EKT/BLA*S
meridional	ME/RID/YO/NAL	mesectoderm	MES/EKT/DERM
	ME/RID/YONL	mesencephal	MES/EN/SFAL
meridionales	ME/RID/YO/NAI/LAOEZ		MES/EN/SE/FAL
merisis	MER/SIS	mesencephalic	MES/EN/SFAL/IK
merism	MER/IFM	mesencephalitis	MES/EN/SEF/LAOITS
merispore	MER/SPOER	mesencephalohypophysial	MES/EN/SEF/LO/HO*IP/FIZ/YAL

mesencephalon	MES/EN/SEF/LON	mesobilin	MES/BIL/LIN
mesencephalotomy	MES/EN/SEF/LOT/M*I		MES/B*I/LIN
mesenchyma	ME/SENG/MA		MES/BAOI/LIN
	ME/SEN/KI/MA	mesobilene	MES/B*I/LAOEN
mesenchymal	ME/SENG/MAL		MES/BAOI/LAOEN
	ME/SEN/KI/MAL	mesobilirubin	MES/BIL/RAOU/BIN
mesenchyme	MES/EN/KAOIM	mesobilirubinogen	MES/BIL/RAOU/BIN/JEN
mesenchymoma	MES/EN/KAOI/MOE/MA	mesobiliviolin	MES/BIL/VAOI/LIN
	MES/ENG/MOE/MA	mesoblast	MES/BLA*S
	MES/EN/KI/MOE/MA	mesoblastema	MES/BLAS/TAOE/MA
mesenterectomy	MES/SPWREKT/M*I	mesoblastemic	MES/BLAS/TAOEM/IK
	MES/SPWER/REKT/M*I	mesoblastic	MES/BLA*S/IK
mesenteric	MES/SPWER/IK	mesobranchial	MES/BRANG/YAL
	MES/EN/TER/IK	mesobronchitis	MES/BRON/KAOITS
mesenterica	MES/SPWER/KA	mesocardia	MES/KARD/YA
	MES/EN/TER/KA	mesocardium	MES/KARD/YUM
mesenteriolum	MES/SPWER/RAOE/LUM	mesocarpal	MES/KAR/PAL
mesenteriopexy	MES/SPWER/YO/PEK/SI	mesocecal	MES/SE/KAL
mesenteriorrhaphy	MES/SPWER/YOR/FI	mesocecum	MES/SE/KUM
mesenteriplication	MES/SPWER/PLI/KAIGS	mesocephalic	MES/SFAL/IK
	MES/EN/TER/PLI/KAIGS	mesocephalon	MES/SEF/LON
mesenteritis	MES/SPWRAOITS	mesocephalous	MES/SEF/LOUS
	MES/SPWER/RAOITS	mesochondrium	MES/KON/DRUM
mesenterium	MES/SPWER/YUM		MES/KON/DRAOE/UM
mesenteron	MES/SPWER/RON	mesochoroidea	MES/KOE/ROID/YA
	MES/SPWRON	mesococci	MES/KOK/SAOI
	MES/ENT/RON	mesococcus	MES/KOK/KUS
mesentery	MES/SPWER/RI	mesocolic	MES/KOL/IK
mesentorrhaphy	MES/SPWOR/FI	mesocolon	MES/KO/LON
	MES/EN/TOR/FI	mesocolopexy	MES/KOEL/PEK/SI
mesi(o)-	MAOEZ/Y(O)	mesocoloplication	MES/KOEL/PLI/KAIGS
mesiad	MAOEZ/YAD	mesocord	MES/KORD
mesial	MAOEZ/YAL	mesocornea	MES/KORN/YA
mesialis	MAOEZ/YAI/LIS	mesocranic	MES/KRAIN/IK
mesially	MAOEZ/YAL/LI	mesocuneiform	MES/KAOU/NAOE/FORM
mesien	MAOEZ/YEN	mesocyst	MES/S*IS
mesiobuccal	MAOEZ/YO/BUK/KAL	mesocytoma	MES/SAOI/TOE/MA
mesiobucco-occlusal	MAOEZ/YO/BUK/O/KLAOU/ZAL	mesoderm	MES/DERM
mesiobuccopulpal	MAOEZ/YO/BUK/PUL/PAL	mesodermal	MES/DER/MAL
mesiocervical	MAOEZ/YO/SEFRB/KAL	mesodermalis	MES/DER/MAI/LIS
mesioclination	MAOEZ/YO/KLI/NAIGS	mesodermalizing	MES/DERM/LAOIZ/-G
mesioclusion	MAOEZ/YO/KLAOUGS	mesodermic	MES/DERM/IK
mesiodens	MAOEZ/YO/DENZ	mesodiastolic	MES/DAOI/STOL/IK
mesiodentes	MAOEZ/YO/DEN/TAOEZ	mesodont	MES/DONT
mesiodistal	MAOEZ/YO/DIS/TAL	mesodontic	MES/DONT/IK
mesiodistocclusal	MAOEZ/YO/D*IS/KLAOU/ZAL	mesodontism	MES/DON/TIFM
mesiogingival	MAOEZ/YO/JING/VAL	mesoduodenal	MES/DAOU/DAOENL
mesiognathic	MAOEZ/YO/NA*T/IK	mesoduodenum	MES/DAOU/DAOEN/UM
mesioincisal	MAOEZ/YO/IN/SAOI/ZAL	mesoenteriolum	MES/SPWER/RAOE/LUM
mesioincisodistal	MAOEZ/YO/IN/SAOIZ/DIS/TAL		MES/ENT/RAOE/LUM
mesiolabial	MAOEZ/YO/LAIB/YAL	mesoepididymis	MES/EP/DID/MIS
mesiolabioincisal	MAOEZ/YO/LAIB/YO/IN/SAOI/ZAL	mesoesophagus	MES/E/SOF/GUS
mesiolingual	MAOEZ/YO/LING/WAL	mesogaster	MES/GAS/TER
mesiolinguoincisal	MAOEZ/YO/LING/WO/IN/SAOI/ZAL	mesogastric	MES/GAS/TRIK
		mesogastrium	MES/GAS/TRUM
mesiolinguo-occlusal	MAOEZ/YO/LING/WO/O/KLAOU/ZAL	mesogenic	MES/JEN/IK
		mesogenitale	MES/JEN/TAI/LAOE
mesiolinguopulpal	MAOEZ/YO/LING/WO/PUL/PAL	mesoglea	MES/GLAOE/YA
mesion	MAOEZ/YON	mesoglia	ME/SOG/LA
mesio-occlusal	MAOEZ/YO/O/KLAOU/ZAL		ME/SOG/LAOE/YA
mesio-occlusion	MAOEZ/YO/O/KLAOUGS	mesoglioma	MES/GLAOI/YOE/MA
mesio-occlusodistal	MAOEZ/YO/O/KLAOUZ/DIS/TAL	mesogluteal	MES/GLAOUT/YAL
mesioplacement	MAOEZ/YO/PLAIS/-MT	mesogluteus	MES/GLAOUT/YUS
mesiopulpal	MAOEZ/YO/PUL/PAL	mesognathic	MES/NA*T/IK
mesiopulpolabial	MAOEZ/YO/PUL/PO/LAIB/YAL		MES/OG/NA*T/IK
mesiopulpolingual	MAOEZ/YO/PUL/PO/LING/WAL		MES/OG/NA*IT/IK
mesioversion	MAOEZ/YO/VERGS	mesognathion	MES/NA*IT/YON
mesiris	MES/AOI/RIS		MES/OG/NA*IT/YON
Mesmer	MES/MER	mesognathous	ME/SOG/NA/THOUS
	MEZ/MER	mesoileum	MES/*IL/YUM
mesmerism	MES/MER/IFM	meso-inositol	MES/IN/OES/TOL
	MEZ/MER/IFM	mesojejunum	MES/JE/JAOUN/UM
mesmerize	MES/MER/AOIZ	mesolecithal	MES/LES/THAL
	MEZ/MER/AOIZ	mesolepidoma	MES/LEP/DOE/MA
Mesnex	MES/NEX	mesolymphocyte	MES/LIM/FO/SAO*IT
mesnili	MES/NIL/LAOI	mesomelia	MES/MAOEL/YA
	MES/NI/LAOI	mesomelic	MES/MEL/IK
meso-	MES		MES/MAOEL/IK
	MEZ	mesomere	MES/MAOER
meso-aortitis	MES/AI/YOR/TAOITS	mesomeric	MES/MER/IK
	MES/AI/OR/TAOITS	mesomerism	ME/SOM/RIFM
mesoappendicitis	MES/AI/PEND/SAOITS		MES/MER/IFM
mesoappendix	MES/AI/PEND/IX	mesometritis	MES/MAOE/TRAOITS
mesoarial	MES/AIRL		MES/ME/TRAOITS
mesoarium	MES/AIRM	mesometrium	MES/MAOE/TRUM
mesobacteria	MES/BAK/TAOER/YA		MES/MAOE/TRAOE/UM
mesobacterium	MES/BAK/TAOERM	mesomorph	MES/MOR/-F
mesobilane	MES/B*I/LAIN	mesomorphic	MES/MOR/FIK
	MES/BAOI/LAOIN	mesomorphy	MES/MOR/FI

mesomucinase	MES/MAOUS/NAIS	mesuranic	MES/YAOU/RAN/IK
mesomula	ME/SOM/LA	met	MET
meson	MAOE/ZON	meta-	MET
	MAOE/SON		ME/TA
	MES/SON	meta-arthritic	MET/AR/THRIT/IK
mesonasal	MES/NAI/ZAL	metabasis	ME/TAB/SIS
mesonephric	MES/NEF/RIK	metabiosis	MET/BAO*I/YOE/SIS
mesonephricus	MES/NEF/RI/KUS	metabolic	MET/BOL/IK
mesonephroi	MES/NEF/ROI	metabolimeter	MET/BO/LIM/TER
mesonephroma	MES/NE/FROE/MA	metabolimetry	MET/BO/LIM/TRI
mesonephron	MES/NEF/RON	metabolin	ME/TAB/LIN
mesonephros	MES/NEF/ROS	metabolism	ME/TAB/LIFM
mesoneuritis	MES/NAOU/RAOITS	metabolite	ME/TAB/LAOIT
meso-omentum	MES/OEMT/UM	metabolizable	ME/TAB/LAOIZ/-BL
meso-ontomorph	MES/ONT/MOR/-F	metabolize	ME/TAB/LAOIZ
mesopexy	MES/PEK/SI	metabolous	ME/TAB/LOUS
mesophil	MES/FIL	metabutethamine	MET/BAOU/T*ET/MAOEN
mesophile	MES/FAOIL		MET/BAOU/T*ET/MIN
mesophilic	MES/FIL/IK	metabutoxycaine	MET/BAOU/TOX/KAIN
mesophlebitis	MES/FLE/BAOITS	metacarp(o)-	MET/KARP
mesophragma	MES/FRAG/MA		MET/KAR/P(O)
mesophryon	MES/OF/RON	metacarpal	MET/KAR/PAL
	ME/SOF/RON	metacarpalis	MET/KAR/PAI/LIS
mesopia	MES/OEP/YA	metacarpalium	MET/KAR/PAIL/YUM
mesopic	MES/OP/IK	metacarpea	MET/KARP/YA
	MES/OEP/IK	metacarpeae	MET/KARP/YAE
mesopneumon	MES/NAOU/MON	metacarpectomy	MET/KAR/PEKT/M*I
mesoporphyrin	MES/POR/FRIN	metacarpeum	MET/KARP/YUM
mesoprosopic	MES/PRO/SOP/IK	metacarpi	MET/KAR/PAOI
mesopulmonum	MES/PUL/MOEN/UM	metacarpocarpal	MET/KARP/KAR/PAL
	MES/PUL/MON/UM	metacarpophalangeae	MET/KARP/FLAN/JAE
mesorachischisis	MES/RA/KIS/KI/SIS	metacarpophalangeal	MET/KARP/FLAN/JAL
mesorchial	MES/ORK/YAL	metacarpus	MET/KAR/PUS
mesorchium	MES/ORK/YUM	metacentric	MET/SEN/TRIK
mesorectum	MES/REK/TUM	metacercaria	MET/SER/KAIR/YA
mesoretina	MES/RET/NA	metacercariae	MET/SER/KAIR/YAE
mesoridazine	MES/RID/ZAOEN	metacestode	MET/SES/TOED
mesoropter	MES/ROPT/ER	metachemical	MET/KEM/KAL
mesorrhaphy	MES/OR/FI	metachloral	MET/KLORL
	ME/SOR/FI	metachromasia	MET/KROE/MAIZ/YA
mesorrhine	MES/RAOIN	metachromatic	MET/KROE/MAT/IK
	MES/RIN	metachromatin	MET/KROEM/TIN
mesosalpinx	MES/SAL/PINGS	metachromatism	MET/KROEM/TIFM
mesoscapula	MES/SKAP/LA	metachromatophil	MET/KROE/MAT/FIL
mesoscapulae	MES/SKAP/LAE	metachromia	MET/KROEM/YA
mesoscope	MES/SKOEP	metachromic	MET/KROEM/IK
mesoseme	MES/SAOEM	metachroming	MET/KROEM/-G
mesosigmoid	MES/SIG/MOID	metachromophil	MET/KROEM/FIL
mesosigmoiditis	MES/SIG/MOI/DAOITS	metachromophile	MET/KROEM/FAOIL
mesosigmoidopexy	MES/SIG/MOID/PEK/SI	metachromosome	MET/KROEM/SOEM
mesoskelic	MES/SKEL/IK	metachronous	ME/TAK/RO/NOUS
mesosoma	MES/SOE/MA	metachrosis	MET/KROE/SIS
mesosomatous	MES/SOEM/TOUS	metacinesis	MET/SI/NAOE/SIS
mesosome	MES/SOEM	metacone	MET/KOEN
mesosomia	MES/SOEM/YA	metaconid	MET/KO/NID
mesostaphyline	MES/STAF/LAOIN		MET/KON/ID
	MES/STAF/LIN	metacontrast	MET/KON/TRA*S
mesostenium	MES/STAOEN/YUM	metaconule	MET/KON/YAOUL
mesosternum	MES/STER/NUM	metacresol	MET/KRAOE/SOL
mesostroma	MES/STROE/MA	metacryptozoite	MET/KRIPT/ZOE/AOIT
mesosyphilis	MES/SIF/LIS	metacyesis	MET/SAOI/E/SIS
mesosystolic	MES/SIS/TOL/IK	metaduodenum	MET/DAOU/DAOEN/UM
mesotarsal	MES/TAR/SAL		MET/DWOD/NUM
mesotendineum	MES/TEN/DIN/YUM	metadysentery	MET/DIS/SPWAIR
mesotendon	MES/TEN/DON	metafacial	MET/FAIRBL
mesothelia	MES/THAOEL/YA	metagaster	MET/GAS/TER
mesothelial	MES/THAOEL/YAL	metagastrula	MET/GAS/TRAOU/LA
mesothelioma	MES/THAOEL/YOE/MA	metagenesis	MET/JEN/SIS
mesothelium	MES/THAOEL/YUM	metagglutinin	MET/GLAOUT/NIN
mesothenar	MES/O*T/NAR	metaglobulin	MET/GLOB/LIN
mesothorium	MES/THOR/YUM	metagonimiasis	MET/GOEN/MAOI/SIS
	MES/THOER/YUM		MET/GON/MAOI/SIS
mesotropic	MES/TROP/IK	Metagonimus	MET/GON/MUS
mesotympanum	MES/TIFRP/NUM	metaicteric	MET/IK/TER/IK
mesouranic	MES/YAOU/RAN/IK	metainfective	MET/IN/FEKT/IV
mesovaria	MES/VAIR/YA	metakinesia	MET/KI/NAOEZ/YA
	MES/O/VAIR/YA	metakinesis	MET/KI/NAOE/SIS
mesovarium	MES/VAIRM	metal	MET/TAL
	MES/O/VAIRM	metaldehyde	MET/ALD/HAOID
Mesozoa	MES/ZOE/WA	metallic	ME/TAL/IK
messenger	MES/EN/JER	metallization	MET/LI/ZAIGS
	MES/SEN/JER	metallized	MET/LAOIZ/-D
mestanolone	MES/TAN/LOEN	metallo-	ME/TAL
mestenediol	MES/TAOEN/DI/OL		ME/TAL/LO
Mestinon	M*ES/NON	metallocyanide	ME/TAL/SAOI/NAOID
Mestinon Timespan	M*ES/NON/TAOIM/SPAN	metalloenzyme	ME/TAL/EN/ZAOIM
mestranol	MES/TRA/NOL	metalloflavodehydrogenase	ME/TAL/FLAIV/DE/HAOI/DRO/
	MES/TRA/NOEL		JEN/AIS
mesulphen	ME/SUL/FEN	metalloflavoprotein	ME/TAL/FLAIV/PRO/TAOEN

metalloid	MET/LOID	metatarsectomy	MET/TAR/SEKT/M*I
metallophil	ME/TAL/FIL	metatarseum	MET/TARS/YUM
metallophilia	ME/TAL/FIL/YA	metatarsi	MET/TAR/SAOI
metallophilic	ME/TAL/FIL/IK	metatarsophalangeae	MET/TARS/FLAN/JAE
metallophobia	ME/TAL/FOEB/YA	metatarsophalangeal	MET/TARS/FLAN/JAL
metalloporphyrin	ME/TAL/POR/FRIN	metatarsus	MET/TAR/SUS
metalloprotein	ME/TAL/PRO/TAOEN	metathalamus	MET/THAL/MUS
metalloscopy	MET/LOS/KPI	metathesis	ME/TA*T/SIS
metallothionein	ME/TAL/THAOI/NAOEN	metathetic	MET/THET/IK
metallurgy	MET/LUR/JI	metatroph	MET/TROF
metaluetic	MET/LAOU/ET/IK		MET/TROEF
metamer	MET/MER	metatrophia	MET/TROEF/YA
metamere	MET/MAOER	metatrophic	MET/TROFK
metameric	MET/MER/IK	metatrophy	MET/AT/RO/FI
metamerism	ME/TAM/RIFM		ME/TAT/RO/FI
metamorphopsia	MET/MOR/FOPS/YA	metatropic	MET/TROP/IK
metamorphosis	MET/MOR/FOE/SIS	metatypic	MET/TIP/IK
metamorphotic	MET/MOR/FOT/IK	metatypical	MET/TIP/KAL
Metamucil	MET/MAOU/SIL	metaxalone	ME/TAX/LOEN
metamyelocyte	MET/MAOI/EL/SAO*IT	metazoa	MET/ZOE/WA
	MET/MAOI/LO/SAO*IT	Metazoa	K-P/MET/ZOE/WA
Metandren	ME/TAN/DREN	metazoal	MET/ZOE/WAL
metanephric	MET/NEF/RIK		MET/ZOEL
metanephrine	MET/NEF/RIN	metazoan	MET/ZOE/WAN
metanephrogenic	MET/NEF/RO/JEN/IK		MET/ZOEN
metanephrogenous	MET/NE/FROJ/NOUS	metazonal	MET/ZOENL
metanephroi	MET/NEF/ROI	metazoon	MET/ZAON
metanephron	MET/NEF/RON	metazoonosis	MET/ZOE/NOE/SIS
metanephros	MET/NEF/ROS	Metchnikoff	MEFP/NI/KOF
metaneutrophil	MET/NAOU/TRO/FIL	metecious	ME/TAOERBS
metaneutrophile	MET/NAOU/TRO/FAOIL		MAOE/TAOERBS
metanil	MET/NIL	metencephalic	MET/EN/SFAL/IK
metanucleus	MET/NAOUK/LUS	metencephalon	MET/EN/SEF/LON
metapeptone	MET/PEP/TOEN	metencephalospinal	MET/EN/SEF/LO/SPAOINL
metaphase	MET/FAEZ	metenkephalin	MET/EN/KEF/LIN
metaphosphoric	MET/FOS/FOER/IK	meteoro-	MAOET/YOR
metaphyseal	*see* metaphysial		MAOET/YO/RO
metaphyses	ME/TAF/SAOEZ	meteorism	MAOET/YOR/IFM
metaphysial	MET/FIZ/YAL		MAOET/YO/RIFM
metaphysics	MET/FIZ/IK/-S	meteorology	MAOET/YOR/OLG
metaphysis	ME/TAF/SIS		MAOET/YO/ROLG
metaphysitis	ME/TAF/SAOITS	meteoropathy	MAOET/YOR/OP/TH*I
	MET/FI/SAOITS		MAOET/YO/ROP/TH*I
metaplasia	MET/PLAIZ/YA	meteorotropic	MAOET/YOR/TROP/IK
metaplasis	ME/TAP/LA/SIS	meter	MAOET/ER
metaplasm	MET/PLAFM	-meter	-M/TER
metaplastic	MET/PLA*S/IK	metergasia	MET/ER/GAIZ/YA
metaplexus	MET/PLEK/SUS	metergasis	MET/ER/GAI/SIS
metapneumonic	MET/NAOU/MON/IK	metestrum	MET/ES/TRUM
metapodialia	MET/POED/YAIL/YA		ME/TES/TRUM
	MET/POED/AIL/YA	metestrus	MET/ES/TRUS
metapophysis	MET/POF/SIS		ME/TES/TRUS
metapore	MET/POER	metformin	MET/FOR/MIN
Metaprel	MET/PREL	methacholine	M*ET/KOE/LAOEN
metaprotein	MET/PRO/TAOEN	methacrylate	M*ET/AK/RI/LAIT
metaproterenol	MET/PRO/TER/NOL	methacrylic	M*ET/KRIL/IK
metapsychology	MET/SAOI/KOLG	methacycline	M*ET/SAOI/KLAOEN
metapyretic	MET/PAOI/RET/IK	methadone	M*ET/DOEN
metapyrocatechase	MET/PAOIR/KAT/KAIS	Methalgen	ME/THAL/JEN
	MET/PAOI/RO/KAT/KAIS		M*ET/AL/JEN
metaraminol	MET/RAM/NOL	methallenestril	M*ET/LEN/ES/TRIL
metarteriole	MET/AR/TAOER/YOEL		M*ET/AL/NES/TRIL
metarubricyte	MET/RAOU/BRI/SAO*IT	methamphetamine	M*ET/AM/FET/MAOEN
	MET/RAOUB/RI/SAO*IT	methampyrone	M*ET/AM/PAOI/ROEN
metasomatome	MET/SOEM/TOEM	methandienone	M*ET/AN/DAOI/NOEN
metastable	MET/STAIBL		M*ET/AN/DI/NOEN
metastasectomy	ME/TA*S/SEKT/M*I	methandriol	M*ET/AN/DROL
metastases	ME/TA*S/SAOEZ		M*ET/AN/DRAOE/OL
metastasis	ME/TA*S/SIS	methandrostenolone	M*ET/AN/DRO/STEN/LOEN
metastasize	ME/TA*S/SAOIZ	methane	ME/T/AIN
metastatic	MET/STAT/IK	Methanobacteriaceae	M*ET/NO/BAK/TAOER/YAIS/YAE
metasternum	MET/STER/NUM	Methanobacterium	M*ET/NO/BAK/TAOERM
metastrongyle	MET/STRON/JAOIL	methanogen	M*ET/AN/JEN
Metastrongylidae	MET/STRON/JIL/DAE		M*ET/NO/JEN
Metastrongylus	MET/STRONG/LUS	methanogenic	M*ET/NO/JEN/IK
	MET/STRON/JI/LUS	methanol	M*ET/NOL
metasynapsis	MET/SNAP/SIS	methantheline	M*ET/A/NT/LAOEN
	MET/SI/NAP/SIS	methapyrilene	M*ET/PIR/LAOEN
metasyncrisis	MET/SIN/KRI/SIS	methaqualone	M*ET/KWAI/LOEN
metasyndesis	MET/SIN/DAOE/SIS	metharbital	M*ET/ARB/TAL
metasyphilis	MET/SIF/LIS	methargen	M*ET/AR/JEN
metasyphilitic	MET/SIF/LIT/IK	methazolamide	M*ET/ZOL/MAOID
metatars(o)-	MET/TARS		M*ET/ZOEL/MAOID
	MET/TAR/S(O)	methdilazine	M*ET/DIL/ZAOEN
metatarsal	MET/TAR/SAL	methectic	ME/THEKT/IK
metatarsalgia	MET/TAR/SAL/JA	methemalbumin	MET/HAOEM/AL/BAOU/MIN
metatarsalis	MET/TAR/SAI/LIS		MET/HEM/AL/BAOU/MIN
metatarsea	MET/TARS/YA	methemalbuminemia	MET/HAOEM/AL/BAOUM/
metatarseae	MET/TARS/YAE		NAOEM/YA

	MET/HEM/AL/BAOUM/NAOEM/YA	methylenophilous	M*ET/LE/NOF/LOUS
metheme	MET/HAOEM		M*ET/LEN/OF/LOUS
	MET/HAO*EM		M*ET/LAOEN/OF/LOUS
methemoglobin	MET/HAOEM/GLOE/BIN	methylergometrine	M*ET/IL/ERG/MET/RAOEN
methemoglobinemia	MET/HAOEM/GLOEB/NAOEM/YA	methylergonovine	M*ET/IL/ERG/NOE/VAOEN
methemoglobinemic	MET/HAOEM/GLOEB/NAOEM/IK	methylglucamine	M*ET/IL/GLAOUK/MAOEN
methemoglobinuria	MET/HAOEM/GLOEB/NAOUR/YA	methylglyoxal	M*ET/IL/GLAOI/OK/SAL
methenamine	ME/THEN/MAOEN	methylglyoxalase	M*ET/IL/GLAOI/OX/LAIS
	M*ET/EN/MAOEN	methylhexaneamine	M*ET/IL/HEK/SAIN/MAOEN
methene	M*ET/AOEN		M*ET/IL/HEK/SAIN/MIN
Methergine	M*ET/ER/JIN	methylic	ME/THIL/IK
methicillin	M*ET/SLIN	methylkinase	M*ET/IL/KAOI/NAIS
	M*ET/SIL/LIN	methylmalonic	M*ET/IL/MA/LON/IK
methimazole	ME/THIM/ZOEL	methylmalonyl	M*ET/IL/MAL/NIL
methiodal	M*ET/AOI/DAL	methylmercaptan	M*ET/IL/MER/KAP/TAN
	ME/THAOI/DAL	methylmorphine	M*ET/IL/MOR/FAOEN
methionine	ME/THAOI/NIN	methylnitrate	M*ET/IL/NAOI/TRAIT
	METHAOI/NAOEN	methylnortestosterone	MUET/IL/NOR/TES/TO*S/ROEN
methisazone	ME/THIS/ZOEN	methylol	M*ET/LOL
methixene	ME/THIK/SAOEN	methylose	M*ET/LOES
	ME/THIX/AOEN	methylparaben	M*ET/IL/PAR/BEN
methocarbamol	M*ET/KARB/MOL	methylpentose	M*ET/IL/PEN/TOES
method	M*ET/OD	methylphenidate	M*ET/IL/FEN/DAIT
	M*ETD	methylprednisolone	M*ET/IL/PRED/NIS/LOEN
methodic	ME/THOD/IK	methylresorcinol	M*ET/IL/RE/SORS/NOL
methodical	METHOD/KAL	methylrosaniline	M*ET/IL/ROE/ZAN/LAOEN
methodism	M*ET/DIFM		M*ET/IL/ROE/ZAN/LIN
	M*ETD/IFM		M*ET/IL/ROE/SAN/LAOEN
methodist	M*ET/D*IS		M*ET/IL/ROE/SAN/LIN
	M*ETD/*IS	methyltestosterone	M*ET/IL/TES/TO*S/ROEN
methodology	M*ET/DOLG	methylthioadenosine	M*ET/IL/THAOI/AI/DEN/SAOEN
	M*ETD/OLG	methylthiouracil	M*ET/IL/THAOI/YAOUR/SIL
methohexital	M*ET/HEX/TAL	methyltocol	M*ET/IL/TOE/KOL
methoin	M*ET/OIN	methyltransferase	M*ET/IL/TRA*NS/FRAIS
	M*ET/WIN	methyprylon	M*ET/PRAOI/LON
methomania	M*ET/MAIN/YA	methyprylone	M*ET/PRAOI/LOEN
methonitrite	M*ET/NAOI/TRAOIT	methysergide	M*ET/SER/JAOID
methonium	ME/THOEN/YUM	methysticum	ME/TH*IS/KUM
methophenazine	M*ET/FEN/ZAOEN	metmyoglobin	MET/MAOI/GLOE/BIN
methopholine	M*ET/FOE/LAOEN	metoclopramide	MET/KLOE/PRA/MAOID
methopterin	M*ET/OPT/RIN		MET/KLOEP/RA/MAOID
	M*ET/OP/TRIN		MET/KLOE/PRAM/AOID
methorphinan	M*ET/OR/FI/NAN	metocurine	MET/KAOUR/AOEN
methotrexate	M*ET/TREK/SAIT		MET/KAOUR/RAOEN
	M*ET/TREX/AIT		MET/KAOU/RAOEN
methotrimeprazine	M*ET/TR*I/MEP/RA/ZAOEN	metolazone	ME/TOL/ZOEN
methoxamine	ME/THOX/MAOEN		ME/TOEL/ZOEN
methoxsalen	ME/THOX/LEN	metonymy	ME/TON/MI
methoxy-	ME/THOX	metopagus	ME/TOP/GUS
methoxybenzoic	ME/THOX/BEN/ZOIK	metopic	ME/TOEP/IK
	ME/THOX/BEN/ZOE/IK		ME/TOP/IK
methoxyflurane	ME/THOX/FLAOU/RAIN	metopion	ME/TOEP/YON
	ME/THOX/FLAOUR/AIN	Metopirone	MET/PAOI/ROEN
methoxyl	ME/THOK/SIL	metopism	MET/PIFM
	ME/THOX/IL	metopodynia	MET/PO/DIN/YA
methoxyphenamine	ME/THOX/FEN/MAOEN	metopon hydrochloride	MET/PON/HAOI/DRO/KLOR/AOID
methscopolamine	M*ET/SKOE/POL/MAOEN		ME/TOE/PON/HAOI/DRO/KLOR/
methsuximide	M*ET/SUX/MAOID		AOID
methyclothiazide	M*ET/KLOE/THAOI/ZAOID	metopoplasty	MET/PO/PLAS/TI
methyl	M*ET/IL	metoposcopy	MET/POS/KPI
methylacrylic	M*ET/IL/AI/KRIL/IK	metoprine	MET/PRAOEN
methylamphetamine	M*ET/IL/AM/FET/MAOEN	metoprolol	ME/TOE/PRO/LOL
methylaspartate	M*ET/IL/AS/PAR/TAIT		ME/TOE/PRO/LOEL
methylate	M*ET/LAIT	Metorchis	MET/OR/KIS
methylated	M*ET/LAIT/-D	metoxenous	ME/TOX/NOUS
methylation	M*ET/LAIGS	metoxeny	ME/TOX/N*I
methylatropine	M*ET/IL/AT/RO/PAOEN	metr(o)-	MAOE/TR(O)
methylbenzene	M*ET/IL/BEN/ZAOEN		ME/TR-
methylbenzethonium	M*ET/IL/BENZ/THOEN/YUM		MET/RO
methylbromide	M*IT/IL/BROE/MAOID	metra	MAOE/TRA
methylcarnosine	M*ET/IL/KARN/SAOEN	metralgia	MAOE/TRAL/JA
methylcellulose	M*ET/IL/SEL/YAOU/LOES		ME/TRAL/JA
methylchloroform	M*ET/IL/KLOR/FORM	metratonia	MAOE/TRA/TOEN/YA
methylcholanthrene	M*ET/IL/KOE/LAN/THRAOEN	metratrophia	MAOE/TRA/TROEF/YA
methylcreosol	M*ET/IL/KRAOE/SOL	metratrophy	MAOE/TRAT/RO/FI
methylcrotonoyl	M*ET/IL/KROET/NOIL	metrectasia	MAOE/TREK/TAIZ/YA
methylcysteine	M*ET/IL/SIS/TAOEN	metrectopia	MAOE/TREK/TOEP/YA
methylcytosine	M*ET/IL/SAOIT/SAOEN	metreurynter	MAOE/TRAOU/RIN/TER
methyldichlorarsin	M*ET/IL/DI/KLOR/AR/SIN		MAOE/TRAOU/RINT/ER
methyldihydromorphinon	M*ET/IL/DI/HAOI/DRO/MOR/FI/	metreurysis	MAOE/TRAOUR/SIS
	NOEN	metria	MAOE/TRAOE/YA
methyldopa	M*ET/IL/DOE/PA	metric	MET/RIK
methyldopate	M*ET/IL/DOE/PAIT	Metric 21 Tablets	MET/RIK/2/1/TAB/LET/-S
methylene	M*ET/LAOEN	-metrician	ME/TRIGS
methylenesuccinic	M*ET/LAOEN/SUK/SIN/IK	metriocephalic	MET/RO/SFAL/IK
methylenophil	M*ET/LAOEN/FIL		MAOE/TRO/SFAL/IK
methylenophile	M*ET/LAOEN/FAOIL	metritis	MAOE/TRAOITS
methylenophilic	M*ET/LAOEN/FIL/IK		ME/TRAOITS
		-metrium	MAOE/TRUM

	MAOE/TRAOE/UM	mica	MI/BEL/LAOE
	MAOE/TRAOE/YUM		MAOI/KA
metrizamide	ME/TRIZ/MAOID	micaceous	MAOI/KAIRBS
metrizoate	MET/RI/ZOE/AIT	Micatin	MAOIK/TIN
metrocarcinoma	MAOE/TRO/KARS/NOE/MA	mication	MAOI/KAIGS
metrocele	MAOE/TRO/SAO*EL	micatosis	MAOIK/TOE/SIS
metrocolpocele	MAOE/TRO/KOL/PO/SAO*EL	micella	MAOI/SEL/LA
metrocystosis	MAOE/TRO/SIS/TOE/SIS		MI/SEL/LA
metrocyte	MAOE/TRO/SAO*IT	micellar	MAOI/SEL/LAR
Metrodin	MAOE/TRO/DIN		MI/SEL/LAR
	MET/RO/DIN	micelle	MAOI/SEL
metrodynamometer	MAOE/TRO/DAOIN/MOM/TER		MI/SEL
metrodynia	MAOE/TRO/DIN/YA	Michaelis	MAOE/KAI/LAOEZ
metroendometritis	MAOE/TRO/*END/ME/TRAOITS		MI/KAI/LAOEZ
metrofibroma	MAOE/TRO/FAOI/BROE/MA		MAOE/KAI/LIS
metrogel	MAOE/TRO/JEL		MI/KAI/LIS
	MET/RO/JEL	Micheli	MAOE/KAI/LAOE
metrogenous	ME/TROJ/NOUS		MI/KAI/LAOE
metrography	ME/TROG/FI		MI/SHEL/LAOE
metrology	ME/TROLG	miconazole	MAOI/KON/ZOEL
metrolymphangitis	MAOE/TRO/LIM/FAN/JAOITS	micr(o)-	MAOI/KR(O)
metromalacia	MAOE/TRO/MA/LAI/SHA	micra	MAOI/KRA
metromalacoma	MAOE/TRO/MAL/KOE/MA	micracoustic	MAOI/KRA/KAO*US/IK
metromalacosis	MAOE/TRO/MAL/KOE/SIS	micranatomy	MAOI/KRA/NAT/M*I
metromania	MET/RO/MAIN/YA	micrencephalia	MAOI/KREN/SFAIL/YA
metromenorrhagia	MAOE/TRO/MEN/RAI/JA	micrencephalon	MAOI/KREN/SEF/LON
metronidazole	MET/RO/NAOID/ZOEL	micrencephalous	MAOI/KREN/SEF/LOUS
	MAOE/TRO/NAOID/ZOEL	micrencephaly	MAOI/KREN/SEF/LI
metronoscope	ME/TRON/SKOEP	MICRhoGAM	MAOI/KRO/GAM
	MAOE/TRON/SKOEP	microabscess	MAOI/KRO/AB/SESZ
metroparalysis	MAOE/TRO/PRAL/SIS	microadenoma	MAOI/KRO/AD/NOE/MA
metropathia	MAOE/TRO/PA*T/YA	microadenopathy	MAOI/KRO/AD/NOP/TH*I
metropathic	MAOE/TRO/PA*T/IK	microaerobion	MAOI/KRO/AER/ROEB/YON
metropathy	ME/TROP/TH*I	microaerophil	MAOI/KRO/AER/FIL
	MAOE/TROP/TH*I	microaerophile	MAOI/KRO/AER/FAOIL
metroperitoneal	MAOE/TRO/PERT/NAOEL	microaerophilic	MAOI/KRO/AER/FIL/IK
metroperitonitis	MAOE/TRO/PERT/NAOITS	microaerophilous	MAOI/KRO/AER/OF/LOUS
metrophlebitis	MAOE/TRO/FLE/BAOITS		MAOI/KRO/AER/ROF/LOUS
-metropia	ME/TROEP/YA	microaerosol	MAOI/KRO/AER/SOL
metroplasty	MAOE/TRO/PLAS/TI	microaerotonometer	MAOI/KRO/AER/TOE/NOM/TER
	MET/RO/PLAS/TI	microaggregate	MAOI/KRO/AG/RE/GAT
metropolis	ME/TROP/LIS	microaleuriospore	MAOI/KRO/AI/LAOUR/YO/SPOER
metroptosis	MAOE/TRO/TOE/SIS	microammeter	MAOI/KRO/AM/TER
metrorrhagia	MAOE/TRO/RAI/JA	microanalysis	MAOI/KRO/ANL/SIS
metrorrhea	MAOE/TRO/RAOE/YA	microanastomosis	MAOI/KRO/AI/NA*S/MOE/SIS
metrorrhexis	MAOE/TRO/REK/SIS	microanatomist	MAOI/KRO/AI/NAT/M*IS
metrosalpingitis	MAOE/TRO/SAL/PIN/JAOITS	microanatomy	MAOI/KRO/AI/NAT/M*I
metrosalpingography	MAOE/TRO/SAL/PIN/GOG/FI	microaneurysm	MAOI/KRO/AN/RIFM
metroscope	MET/RO/SKOEP	microangiography	MAOI/KRO/AN/JOG/FI
metrostasis	ME/TRO*S/SIS	microangiopathic	MAOI/KRO/AN/JO/PA*T/IK
metrostaxis	MAOE/TRO/STAK/SIS	microangiopathy	MAOI/KRO/AN/JOP/TH*I
metrostenosis	MAOE/TRO/STE/NOE/SIS	microangioscopy	MAOI/KRO/AN/JOS/KPI
metrotherapy	MAOE/TRO/THER/PI	microarteriography	MAOI/KRO/AR/TAOER/YOG/FI
metrotomy	MAOE/TROT/M*I	microbacteria	MAOI/KRO/BAK/TAOER/YA
	ME/TROT/M*I	microbacterium	MAOI/KRO/BAK/TAOERM
metrotubography	MAOE/TRO/TAOU/BOG/FI	Microbacterium	K-P/MAOI/KRO/BAK/TAOERM
-metry	(v)M/TRI	microbalance	MAOI/KRO/BAL/LANS
Metubine	ME/TAOU/BAOEN	microbar	MAOI/KRO/BAR
metyrapone	ME/TIR/POEN	microbe	MAOI/KROEB
metyrosine	ME/TAOIR/SAOEN	microbial	MAOI/KROEB/YAL
	ME/TAOIR/SIN	microbian	MAOI/KROEB/YAN
Meulengracht	MOIL/EN/GRAKT	microbic	MAOI/KROEB/IK
	MOI/LEN/GRAKT	microbicidal	MAOI/KROEB/SAOI/DAL
mevalonic	MEV/LON/IK	microbicide	MAOI/KROEB/SAO*ID
Mevanin	MEV/NIN	microbid	MAOI/KRO/BID
Mevanin-C	MEV/NIN/KR-RBGS	microbioassay	MAOI/KRO/BAO*I/AS/SAI
mevinolin	ME/VIN/LIN	microbiologic	MAOI/KRO/BAO*I/LOJ/IK
mexenone	MEX/NOEN	microbiological	MAOI/KRO/BAO*I/LOJ/KAL
Mexican	MEX/KAN	microbiologist	MAOI/KRO/BAO*I/O*LGS
mexicana	MEX/KAI/NA	microbiology	MAOI/KRO/BAO*I/OLG
mexiletin	MEX/IL/TAOEN	microbiophotometer	MAOI/KRO/BAO*I/FOE/TOM/TER
	MEX/SIL/TAOEN	microbiota	MAOI/KRO/BAO*I/YOE/TA
Mexitil	MEX/TIL	microbiotic	MAOI/KRO/BAO*I/OT/IK
Meyenburg	MAOI/EN/BURG	microbism	MAOI/KRO/BIFM
	MAOI/YEN/BURG	microblast	MAOI/KRO/BLA*S
Meyer	MAOI/ER	microblepharia	MAOI/KRO/BLE/FAIR/YA
	MAOI/YER	microblepharism	MAOI/KRO/BLEF/RIFM
Meyerhof	MAOI/ER/HOF	microblepharon	MAOI/KRO/BLEF/RON
	MAOI/YER/HOF	microblephary	MAOI/KRO/BLEF/RI
Meynert	MAOI/NERT	microbody	MAOI/KRO/BOD/DI
meynerti	MAOI/NER/TAOI	microbrachia	MAOI/KRO/BRAIK/YA
Mezlin	MEZ/LIN	microbrachius	MAOI/KRO/BRAIK/YUS
mezlocillin	MEZ/LO/SLIN	microbrenner	MAOI/KRO/BREN/ER
	MEZ/LO/SIL/LIN	microburet	MAOI/KRO/BAOU/RET
mg	M*G	microcalix	MAOI/KRO/KAI/LIX
miana	MAOI/YAN/NA		MAOI/KRO/KAL/IX
	MAOI/YA/NA	microcalorie	MAOI/KRO/KAL/RAOE
mianserin	MAOE/ANS/RIN	microcalyx	MAOI/KRO/KAI/L*IX
Mibelli	MAOE/BEL/LAOE		MAOI/KRO/KAL/*IX

microcardia	MAOI/KRO/KARD/YA	microfilariae	MAOI/KRO/FLAIR/YAE
microcaulia	MAOI/KRO/KAUL/YA		MAOI/KRO/FI/LAIR/YAE
microcentrum	MAOI/KRO/SEN/TRUM		MAOI/KRO/FAOI/LAIR/YAE
microcephalia	MAOI/KRO/SFAIL/YA	microfilm	MAOI/KRO/FIL/-M
microcephalic	MAOI/KRO/SFAL/IK	microflora	MAOI/KRO/FLOR/RA
microcephalism	MAOI/KRO/SEF/LIFM	microgamete	MAOI/KRO/GAM/AOET
microcephalous	MAOI/KRO/SEF/LOUS	microgametocyte	MAOI/KRO/GA/MAOET/SAO*IT
microcephalus	MAOI/KRO/SEF/LUS		MAOI/KRO/GAM/TO/SAO*IT
microcephaly	MAOI/KRO/SEF/LI	microgamont	MAOI/KRO/GAM/ONT
microcheilia	MAOI/KRO/KAOIL/YA	microgamy	MAOI/KROG/M*I
microcheiria	MAOI/KRO/KAOIR/YA	microgastria	MAOI/KRO/GAS/TRA
microchemical	MAOI/KRO/KEM/KAL		MAOI/KRO/GAS/TRAOE/YA
microchemistry	MAOI/KRO/KEM/STRI	microgenesis	MAOI/KRO/JEN/SIS
microcide	MAOI/KRO/SAO*ID	microgenia	MAOI/KRO/JAOEN/YA
microcinematography	MAOI/KRO/SIN/MA/TOG/FI		MAOI/KRO/JEN/YA
microcirculation	MAOI/KRO/SIRK/LAIGS	microgenitalism	MAOI/KRO/JEN/TAL/IFM
microclimate	MAOI/KRO/KLAOI/MAT	microgli(o)-	MAOI/KROG/L(O)
microclyster	MAOI/KRO/KL*IS/ER		MAOI/KRO/LAOE/Y(O)
microcnemia	MAOI/KRO/NAOEM/YA	microglia	MAOI/KROG/LA
Micrococcaceae	MAOI/KRO/KOK/KAIS/YAE	microgliacyte	MAOI/KROG/LA/SAO*IT
micrococci	MAOI/KRO/KOK/SAOI	microglial	MAOI/KROG/LAL
micrococcus	MAOI/KRO/KOK/KUS	microgliocyte	MAOI/KROG/LO/SAO*IT
Micrococcus	K-P/MAOI/KRO/KOK/KUS	microglioma	MAOI/KROG/LOE/MA
microcolitis	MAOI/KRO/KO/LAOITS	microgliomatosis	MAOI/KROG/LOEM/TOE/SIS
microcolon	MAOI/KRO/KO/LON		MAOI/KRO/GLAOE/YOEM/TOE/SIS
microcolony	MAOI/KRO/KOL/N*I		MAOI/KRO/GLAOI/YOEM/TOE/SIS
microconcentration	MAOI/KRO/KON/SEN/TRAIGS	microgliosis	MAOI/KROG/LOE/SIS
microconidia	MAOI/KRO/KO/NID/YA	microglobulin	MAOI/KRO/GLOB/LIN
microconidium	MAOI/KRO/KO/NID/YUM	microglossia	MAOI/KRO/GLOS/YA
microcoria	MAOI/KRO/KOR/YA	micrognathia	MAOI/KRO/NA*IT/YA
	MAOI/KRO/KOER/YA		MAOI/KRO/NA*T/YA
microcornea	MAOI/KRO/KORN/YA	microgonioscope	MAOI/KRO/GOEN/YO/SKOEP
microcoulomb	MAOI/KRO/KAOU/LOM	microgram	MAOI/KRO/GRAM
microcoustic	MAOI/KRO/KAO*US/IK	micrograph	MAOI/KRO/GRAF
microcrania	MAOI/KRO/KRAIN/YA	micrography	MAOI/KROG/FI
microcrystal	MAOI/KRO/KRIS/TAL	Micro-Guard	MAOI/KRO/GARD
microcrystalline	MAOI/KRO/KR*IS/LAOEN	microgyri	MAOI/KRO/JAOI/RAOI
	MAOI/KRO/KR*IS/LIN	microgyria	MAOI/KRO/JAOIR/YA
microcurie	MAOI/KRO/KAOUR/RAOE		MAOI/KRO/JIR/YA
microcurie-hour	MAOI/KRO/KAOUR/RAOE/H-F/	microgyrus	MAOI/KRO/JAOI/RUS
	HOUR	microhematocrit	MAOI/KRO/HAOE/MAT/KRIT
microcyst	MAOI/KRO/S*IS	microhepatia	MAOI/KRO/HE/PAI/SHA
microcystometer	MAOI/KRO/SIS/TOM/TER		MAOI/KRO/HE/PAT/YA
microcytase	MAOI/KRO/SAOI/TAIS	microhistology	MAOI/KRO/HIS/TOLG
microcyte	MAOI/KRO/SAO*IT	microhm	MAOI/KROEM
microcythemia	MAOI/KRO/SAOI/THAOEM/YA	microincineration	MAOI/KRO/IN/SIN/RAIGS
microcytic	MAOI/KRO/SIT/IK	microincision	MAOI/KRO/IN/SIGS
microcytosis	MAOI/KRO/SAOI/TOE/SIS	microinfarct	MAOI/KRO/IN/FARKT
microcytotoxicity	MAOI/KRO/SAOIT/TOK/SIS/TI	microinjector	MAOI/KRO/IN/JEK/TOR
microdactylia	MAOI/KRO/DAK/TIL/YA	microinvasion	MAOI/KRO/IN/VAIGS
microdactylous	MAOI/KRO/DAKT/LOUS	Micro-K	MAOI/KRO/K-RBGS
microdactyly	MAOI/KRO/DAKT/LI	microkinematography	MAOI/KRO/KIN/MA/TOG/FI
microdensitometer	MAOI/KRO/DENS/TOM/TER	microkymatotherapy	MAOI/KRO/KAOI/MAT/THER/PI
microdentism	MAOI/KRO/DEN/TIFM	microlecithal	MAOI/KRO/LES/THAL
microdermatome	MAOI/KRO/DERM/TOEM	microlentia	MAOI/KRO/LEN/SHA
microdetermination	MAOI/KRO/DERM/NAIGS	microlesion	MAOI/KRO/LAOEGS
	MAOI/KRO/DERMGS	microleukoblast	MAOI/KRO/LAOUK/BLA*S
microdissection	MAOI/KRO/DI/S*EBGS	microliter	MAOI/KRO/LAOET/ER
	MAOI/KRO/DIS/S*EBGS	microlith	MAOI/KRO/L*IT
microdont	MAOI/KRO/DONT	microlithiasis	MAOI/KROL/THAOI/SIS
microdontia	MAOI/KRO/DON/SHA	micrology	MAOI/KROLG
microdontic	MAOI/KRO/DONT/IK	microlymphoidocyte	MAOI/KRO/LIM/FOI/DO/SAO*IT
microdontism	MAOI/KRO/DON/TIFM	micromandible	MAOI/KRO/MAND/-BL
microdosage	MAOI/KRO/DOES/AJ	micromania	MAOI/KRO/MAIN/YA
microdose	MAOI/KRO/DOES	micromaniacal	MAOI/KRO/MA/NAOI/KAL
microdrepanocytic	MAOI/KRO/DREP/NO/SIT/IK	micromanipulation	MAOI/KRO/MA/NIP/LAIGS
microdrepanocytosis	MAOI/KRO/DREP/NO/SAOI/TOE/	micromanipulator	MAOI/KRO/MA/NIP/LAI/TOR
	SIS	micromanometer	MAOI/KRO/MA/NOM/TER
microdysgenesia	MAOI/KRO/DIS/JE/NAOEZ/YA	micromanometric	MAOI/KRO/MAN/MET/RIK
microecology	MAOI/KRO/E/KOLG	micromastia	MAOI/KRO/MA*S/YA
microecosystem	MAOI/KRO/E/KO/S-M	micromaxilla	MAOI/KRO/MAK/SIL/LA
	MAOI/KRO/AOEK/S-M	micromazia	MAOI/KRO/MAIZ/YA
microelectrode	MAOI/KRO/LEK/TROED	micromelia	MAOI/KRO/MAOEL/YA
microelectrophoresis	MAOI/KRO/LEK/TRO/FRAOE/SIS	micromelic	MAOI/KRO/MEL/IK
microelectrophoretic	MAOI/KRO/LEK/TRO/FRET/IK		MAOI/KRO/MAOEL/IK
microembolus	MAOI/KRO/EM/BLUS	micromelus	MAOI/KROM/LUS
microencephaly	MAOI/KRO/EN/SEF/LI	micromere	MAOI/KRO/MAOER
microenvironment	MAOI/KRO/VAOIRMT	micromerozoite	MAOI/KRO/MER/ZOE/AOIT
microerythrocyte	MAOI/KRO/R*IT/RO/SAO*IT	micrometabolism	MAOI/KRO/ME/TAB/LIFM
microestimation	MAOI/KRO/*ES/MAIGS	micrometastasis	MAOI/KRO/ME/TA*S/SIS
microevolution	MAOI/KRO/EV/LAOUGS	micrometastatic	MAOI/KRO/MET/STAT/IK
microfarad	MAOI/KRO/FA/RAD	micrometeorology	MAOI/KRO/MAOET/YO/ROLG
microfauna	MAOI/KRO/FAU/NA	micrometer	MAOI/KROM/TER
microfibril	MAOI/KRO/FAOI/BRIL		MAOI/KRO/MAOET/ER
microfilament	MAOI/KRO/FIL/-MT	micromethod	MAOI/KRO/M*ET/OD
microfilaremia	MAOI/KRO/FIL/RAOEM/YA	micrometry	MAOI/KROM/TRI
microfilaria	MAOI/KRO/FLAIR/YA	micromicrocurie	MAOI/KRO/MAOI/KRO/KAOUR/
	MAOI/KRO/FI/LAIR/YA		RAOE
	MAOI/KRO/FAOI/LAIR/YA	micromicrogram	MAOI/KRO/MAOI/KRO/GRAM

micromicron	MAOI/KRO/MAOI/KRON
micromilligram	MAOI/KRO/MIL/GRAM
micromillimeter	MAOI/KRO/MIL/MAOET/ER
micromolar	MAOI/KRO/MOE/LAR
micromole	MAOI/KRO/MOEL
micromolecular	MAOI/KRO/MO/LEK/LAR
micromotoscope	MAOI/KRO/MOET/SKOEP
micromyelia	MAOI/KRO/MAOI/AOEL/YA
micromyeloblast	MAOI/KRO/MAOI/LO/BLA*S
Micronase	MAOI/KRO/NAIZ
	MAOI/KRO/NAIS
micromyelolymphocyte	MAOI/KRO/MAOI/LO/LIM/FO/SAO*IT
micron	MAOI/KRON
microneedle	MAOI/KRO/NAOED/-L
microneme	MAOI/KRO/NAOEM
microneurosurgery	MAOI/KRO/NAOUR/SURJ/RI
	MAOI/KRO/NAOUR/S-RJ
micronic	MAOI/KRON/IK
micronize	MAOI/KRO/NAOIZ
micronodular	MAOI/KRO/NOD/LAR
Micronor	MAOI/KRO/NOR
micronormoblast	MAOI/KRO/NORM/BLA*S
micronucleus	MAOI/KRO/NAOUK/LUS
micronutrient	MAOI/KRO/NAOU/TRENT
micronychia	MAOI/KRO/NIK/YA
micronychosis	MAOI/KRO/NI/KOE/SIS
micronystagmus	MAOI/KRO/NIS/TAG/MUS
micro-ohm	MAOI/KRO/OEM
microorganic	MAOI/KRO/OR/GAN/IK
microorganism	MAOI/KRO/ORG/NIFM
microorganismal	MAOI/KRO/ORG/NIZ/MAL
micropapulosa	MAOI/KRO/PAP/LOE/SA
microparasite	MAOI/KRO/PAR/SAOIT
micropathology	MAOI/KRO/PA/THOLG
micropenis	MAOI/KRO/PAOE/NIS
microperfusion	MAOI/KRO/PER/FAOUGS
microphage	MAOI/KRO/FAIJ
microphagocyte	MAOI/KRO/FAG/SAO*IT
microphakia	MAOI/KRO/FAIK/YA
microphallus	MAOI/KRO/FAL/LUS
microphobia	MAOI/KRO/FOEB/YA
microphone	MAOI/KRO/FOEN
microphonia	MAOI/KRO/FOEN/YA
microphonic	MAOI/KRO/FON/IK
microphonoscope	MAOI/KRO/FOEN/SKOEP
microphotograph	MAOI/KRO/FOET/GRAF
	MAOI/KRO/FRAF
microphthalmia	MAOI/KROF/THAL/MA
	MAOI/KROF/THAL/MAOE/YA
microphthalmos	MAOI/KROF/THAL/MOS
microphthalmoscope	MAOI/KROF/THAL/MO/SKOEP
microphthalmus	MAOI/KROF/THAL/MUS
microphysics	MAOI/KRO/FIZ/IK/-S
micropia	MAOI/KROEP/YA
micropinocytosis	MAOI/KRO/PAOIN/SAOI/TOE/SIS
	MAOI/KRO/PIN/SAOI/TOE/SIS
micropipet	*see* micropipette
micropipette	MAOI/KRO/PAOI/PET
	MAOI/KRO/PI/PET
micropituicyte	MAOI/KRO/PI/TAOU/SAO*IT
microplania	MAOI/KRO/PLAIN/YA
microplasia	MAOI/KRO/PLAIZ/YA
microplating	MAOI/KRO/PLAET/-G
	MAOI/KRO/PLAIT/-G
microplethysmography	MAOI/KRO/PL*ETS/MOG/FI
	MAOI/KRO/PL*ET/SMOG/FI
	MAOI/KRO/PL*ET/IZ/MOG/FI
microplus	MAOI/KRO/PLUS
micropodia	MAOI/KRO/POED/YA
micropolariscope	MAOI/KRO/POE/LAIR/SKOEP
	MAOI/KRO/PO/LAIR/SKOEP
micropolygyria	MAOI/KRO/POL/JAOIR/YA
micropore	MAOI/KRO/POER
microprecipitation	MAOI/KRO/PRE/SIP/TAIGS
micropredation	MAOI/KRO/PRE/DAIGS
micropredator	MAOI/KRO/PRED/TOR
microprobe	MAOI/KRO/PROEB
microprojection	MAOI/KRO/PRO/J*EBGS
microprojector	MAOI/KRO/PRO/JEK/TOR
micropromyelocyte	MAOI/KRO/PRO/MAOI/LO/SAO*IT
microprosopia	MAOI/KRO/PRO/SOEP/YA
microprosopus	MAOI/KRO/PRO/SOE/PUS
	MAOI/KRO/PROS/PUS
micropsia	MAOI/KROPS/YA
microptic	MAOI/KROPT/IK
micropuncture	MAOI/KRO/PUNG/KHUR
micropus	MAOI/KROE/PUS
micropyle	MAOI/KRO/PAOIL
microradiogram	MAOI/KRO/RAID/YO/GRAM
microradiography	MAOI/KRO/RAID/YOG/FI
microrchidia	MAOI/KROR/KID/YA
microrefractometer	MAOI/KRO/RE/FRAK/TOM/TER
microrespirometer	MAOI/KRO/RES/PROM/TER
microrhinia	MAOI/KRO/RIN/YA
microroentgen	MAOI/KRO/RENT/GEN
microsaccade	MAOI/KRO/SA/KAID
	MAOI/KRO/SAK/KAID
microscelous	MAOI/KROS/KE/LOUS
	MAOI/KRO/SKEL/OUS
microscintigraphy	MAOI/KRO/SIN/TIG/FI
microscope	MAOI/KRO/SKOEP
microscopic	MAOI/KRO/SKOP/IK
microscopical	MAOI/KRO/SKOP/KAL
microscopist	MAOI/KROS/KP*IS
	MAOI/KROS/KO/P*IS
microscopy	MAOI/KROS/KPI
microsecond	MAOI/KRO/SEKD
microsection	MAOI/KRO/S*EBGS
microseme	MAOI/KRO/SAOEM
microside	MAOI/KRO/SAOID
microslide	MAOI/KRO/SLAOID
microsmatic	MAOI/KROZ/MAT/IK
microsoma	MAOI/KRO/SOE/MA
microsomal	MAOI/KRO/SOE/MAL
microsomatia	MAOI/KRO/SOE/MAI/SHA
microsome	MAOI/KRO/SOEM
microsomia	MAOI/KRO/SOEM/YA
microspectrophotometer	MAOI/KRO/SPEK/TRO/FOE/TOM/TER
microspectrophotometry	MAOI/KRO/SPEK/TRO/FOE/TOM/TRI
microspectroscope	MAOI/KRO/SPEK/TRO/SKOEP
microsphere	MAOI/KRO/SFAOER
microspherocyte	MAOI/KRO/SFAOER/SAO*IT
microspherocytosis	MAOI/KRO/SFAOER/SAOI/TOE/SIS
microspherolith	MAOI/KRO/SFAOER/L*IT
microsphygmia	MAOI/KRO/SFIG/MA
	MAOI/KRO/SFIG/MAOE/YA
microsphygmy	MAOI/KRO/SFIG/M*I
microsphyxia	MAOI/KRO/SFIX/YA
microsplanchnic	MAOI/KRO/SPLANG/NIK
microsplanchnous	MAOI/KRO/SPLANG/NOUS
microsplenia	MAOI/KRO/SPLAOEN/YA
microsplenic	MAOI/KRO/SPLEN/IK
Microspora	MAOI/KRO/SPOR/RA
Microsporasida	MAOI/KRO/SPOR/AS/DA
microspore	MAOI/KRO/SPOER
microsporid	MAOI/KROS/PRID
Microsporidia	MAOI/KRO/SPRID/YA
microsporidian	MAOI/KRO/SPRID/YAN
microsporosis	MAOI/KRO/SPROE/SIS
Microsporum	MAOI/KROS/PRUM
	MAOI/KRO/SPOR/UM
microstat	MAOI/KRO/STAT
microsthenic	MAOI/KROS/THEN/IK
microstethophone	MAOI/KRO/ST*ET/FOEN
microstethoscope	MAOI/KRO/ST*ET/SKOEP
microstomia	MAOI/KRO/STOEM/YA
microstrabismus	MAOI/KRO/STRA/BIZ/MUS
microsurgery	MAOI/KRO/SURJ/RI
	MAOI/KRO/S-RJ
microsuture	MAOI/KRO/SAOU/KHUR
microsyringe	MAOI/KRO/SI/RIN/-J
	MAOI/KRO/SIRN/-J
microthelia	MAOI/KRO/THAOEL/YA
microthrombosis	MAOI/KRO/THROM/BOE/SIS
microthrombus	MAOI/KRO/THROM/BUS
microtia	MAOI/KROE/SHA
microtiter	MAOI/KRO/TAOIT/ER
microtome	MAOI/KRO/TOEM
microtomy	MAOI/KROT/M*I
microtonometer	MAOI/KRO/TOE/NOM/TER
microtransfusion	MAOI/KRO/TRA*NS/FAOUGS
microtrauma	MAOI/KRO/TRAU/MA
Microtrombidium	MAOI/KRO/TROM/BID/YUM
microtropia	MAOI/KRO/TROEP/YA
microtubule	MAOI/KRO/TAOUB/YAOUL
microunit	MAOI/KRO/YAOUNT
microvascular	MAOI/KRO/VAS/KLAR
microvasculature	MAOI/KRO/VAS/KLA/KHUR
microvesicle	MAOI/KRO/VES/K-L
microvilli	MAOI/KRO/VIL/LAOI
microvillus	MAOI/KRO/VIL/LUS
Microviridae	MAOI/KRO/VIR/DAE
microviscosimeter	MAOI/KRO/VIS/KO/SIM/TER
microvivisection	MAOI/KRO/VIV/S*EBGS

microvolt	MAOI/KRO/VOELT	milium	MIL/YUM
	MAOI/KRO/VOLT	milk	MIL/-K
microvoltometer	MAOI/KRO/VOEL/TOM/TER	milking	MIL/-K/-G
	MAOI/KRO/VOL/TOM/TER		MIL/K-G
microwatt	MAOI/KRO/WAT	Milkman	K-P/MIL/-K/MA*N
microwave	MAOI/KRO/WAEV		K-P/MIL/-K/MAN
microwelding	MAOI/KRO/WELD/-G	milk of magnesia	MIL/-K/OF/MAG/NAOEZ/YA
microxycyte	MAOI/KROX/SAO*IT	milkpox	MIL/-K/POX
microxyphil	MAOI/KROX/FIL	Millar	MIL/LAR
microzoa	MAOI/KRO/ZOE/WA	Millard	MAOE/YAR
microzoaria	MAOI/KRO/ZOE/AIR/YA		MIL/LARD
microzoon	MAOI/KRO/ZAON	Miller	K-P/MIL/ER
micrurgic	MAOI/KRURJ/IK	millet	MIL/ET
micrurgical	MAOI/KRURJ/KAL		MIL/LET
micrurgy	MAOI/KRUR/JI	milli-	MIL
miction	M*IBGS	milliammeter	MIL/AM/TER
micturate	MIK/KHU/RAIT	milliampere	MIL/AM/PAOER
	MIK/TAOU/RAIT	milliampere-minute	MIL/AM/PAOER/MIN/UT
micturition	MIK/KHU/RIGS	millibar	MIL/BAR
	MIK/TAOU/RIGS	millicoulomb	MIL/KAOU/LOM
mid-	MID	millicurie	MIL/KAOUR/RAOE
midaxilla	MID/AK/SIL/LA	millicurie-hour	MIL/KAOUR/RAOE/HOUR
midazolam	MI/DAZ/LAM	milliequivalent	MIL/KWIV/LENT
midbody	MID/BOD/DI		MIL/E/KWIV/LENT
midbrain	MID/BRAIN	Milligan	MIL/GAN
midcarpal	MID/KAR/PAL	milligram	MIL/GRAM
Middeldorpf	MID/EL/DORP/-F	milligramage	MIL/GRAM/AIJ
midfoot	MID/FAOT	milligram-hour	MIL/GRAM/HOUR
midforceps	MID/FOR/SEPS	Millikan	MIL/KAN
midfrontal	MID/FRON/TAL	millilambert	MIL/LAM/BERT
midge	MIJ	milliliter	MIL/LAOET/ER
midget	MIJ/ET	millimeter	MIL/MAOET/ER
	MIJT	millimicrocurie	MIL/MAOI/KRO/KAOUR/RAOE
midgetism	MIJ/TIFM	millimicrogram	MIL/MAOI/KRO/GRAM
	MIJT/IFM	millimicrometer	MIL/MAOI/KROM/TER
midgracile	MID/GRAS/IL	millimicron	MIL/MAOI/KRON
	MID/GRAS/SIL	millimole	MIL/MOEL
midgut	MID/GUT	millimu	MIL/MAOU
midline	MID/LAOIN	milling-in	MIL/-G/H-F/N-
midmenstrual	MID/MEN/STRAOUL	millinormal	MIL/NOR/MAL
midoccipital	MID/OK/SIP/TAL	milliosmol	MIL/OZ/MOL
Midol	MAOI/DOL	milliosmole	MIL/OZ/MOEL
midpain	MID/PAIN	millipede	MIL/PAOED
midperiphery	MID/PRIF/RI	milliphot	MIL/FOT
	MID/PE/RIF/RI	millirad	MIL/RAD
midplane	MID/PLAEN	milliroentgen	MIL/RENT/GEN
midportion	MID/PORGS	millisecond	MIL/SEKD
midriff	MID/RIF		MIL/SEK/OND
Midrin	MID/RIN	milliunit	MIL/YAOUNT
midsagittal plane	MID/SAJ/TAL/PLAEN	millivolt	MIL/VOELT
midsection	MID/S*EBGS		MIL/VOLT
midsternum	MID/STER/NUM	Millon	MIL/LON
midtarsal	MID/TAR/SAL	Mills	MILS
midtegmentum	MID/TEG/MEN/TUM		MILZ
midwife	MID/WAOIF	Milontin	MAOI/LON/TIN
midwifery	MID/WAOIF/RI		MI/LON/TIN
	MID/WIF/RI	milphae	MIL/FAE
Mierzejewski	MAOERZ/YEF/SKAOE	milphosis	MIL/FOE/SIS
	MAOERS/YEF/SKAOE	Milroy	MIL/ROI
Miescher	MAOERB/ER	Milton	MIL/TON
	MAOE/SHER	Miltown	MIL/TOUN
mieschulzi	MAOES/KUL/ZAOI	mimesis	MAOI/MAOE/SIS
migraine	MAOI/GRAIN		MI/MAOE/SIS
migrainoid	MAOI/GRA/NOID	mimetic	MAOI/MET/IK
	MAOI/GRAIN/OID		MI/MET/IK
migrainous	MAOI/GRA/NOUS	-mimia	MIM/YA
	MAOI/GRAIN/OUS	mimic	MIM/IK
migrans	MAOI/GRANZ	mimica	MIM/KA
migration	MAOI/GRAIGS	mimicry	MIM/KRI
migratory	MAOI/GRA/TOIR		MIM/IK/RI
	MAOIG/TOIR	mimmation	MAOI/MAIGS
Mikulicz	MIK/LIFP		MI/MAIGS
mil	M*IL	mimosis	MAOI/MOE/SIS
	(not MIL; see mill)		MI/MOE/SIS
mildew	MIL/DAOU	mind	MAOIND
Miles	MAOILS	mind-reading	MAOIND/H-F/RAED/-G
	MAOILZ	mineral	MIN/RAL
Miles Nervine	MAOILS/NER/VAOEN	mineralocoid	MIN/RAL/KOID
	MAOILZ/NER/VAOEN	mineralocorticoid	MIN/RAL/KORT/KOID
milia	MIL/YA	mingin	MIN/JIN
Milian	MIL/YAU	mini-	MIN
	MAOEL/YA	miniatus	MIN/YAI/TUS
	MIL/YAN	minify	MIN/FI
	MAOEL/YAN	Mini-Gamulin Rh	MIN/GAM/LIN/RAIFP
miliaria	MIL/YAIR/YA		MIN/GAM/LIN/R-RBGS/H*
miliaris	MIL/YAI/RIS	minilaparotomy	MIN/LAP/ROT/M*I
miliary	MIL/YAIR	minim	MIN/IM
milieu	MIL/YAOU		MIN/NIM
	MAOEL/YAOU	minima	MIN/MA

minimal	MIN/MAL	misopedy	MIS/OP/DI
minimae	MIN/MAE	missed	MISZ/-D
minimi	MIN/MAOI	Mission Prenatal	MIGS/PRE/NAI/TAL
minimum	MIN/MUM	Mission Surgical	MIGS/SURJ/KAL/
minimus	MIN/MUS	Supplement	SUP/PLEMT
Minipress	MIN/PRESZ	mistletoe	MIS/-L/TOE
minium	MIN/YUM	mistura	MIS/TAOU/RA
Minizide	MIN/ZAOID		MIS/KHUR/RA
mink	MIN/-K	mitapsis	MIT/AP/SIS
	M*ING	Mitchell	MIFP/EL
Minkowski	MIN/KOV/SKAOE	mite	MAOIT
	MIN/KOU/SKAOE	mitella	MAOI/TEL/LA
Minocin	MAOIN/SIN	Mithracin	M*IT/RA/SIN
minocycline	MIN/SAOI/KLAOEN	mithramycin	M*IT/RA/MAOI/SIN
minor	MAOI/NOR	mithridatism	M*IT/RI/DAI/TIFM
Minor	K-P/MAOI/NOR		M*IT/RI/DAIT/IFM
minora	MAOI/NOR/RA		M*IT/RID/TIFM
	MAOI/NOER/RA	miticidal	MAOIT/SAOI/DAL
	MI/NOR/RA	miticide	MAOIT/SAO*ID
	MI/NOER/RA	mitigate	MIT/GAIT
minorem	MAOI/NOR/EM	mitior	MIT/YOR
	MI/NOR/EM	mitis	MAOI/TIS
minores	MAOI/NOR/RAOEZ		(not MAOITS)
	MAOI/NOER/RAOEZ	mito-	MAOIT
	MI/NOR/RAOEZ		MAOI/TO
	MI/NOER/RAOEZ	mitochondria	MAOIT/KON/DRA
minoris	MAOI/NOR/RIS		MAOIT/KON/DRAOE/YA
	MAOI/NOER/RIS	mitochondrial	MAOIT/KON/DRAL
	MI/NOR/RIS		MAOIT/KON/DRAOE/YAL
	MI/NOER/RIS	mitochondriales	MAOIT/KON/DRAI/LAOEZ
Minot	MAOI/NOT		MAOIT/KON/DRAOE/YAI/LAOEZ
minoxidil	MI/NOX/DIL	mitochondrion	MAOIT/KON/DRON
	MIN/OX/DIL		MAOIT/KON/DRAOE/YON
Minsky	MIN/SKI	mitogen	MAOIT/JEN
	MINS/KI	mitogenesia	MAOIT/JE/NAOEZ/YA
mint	MINT	mitogenesis	MAOIT/JEN/SIS
Mintezol	MINT/ZOL	mitogenetic	MAOIT/JE/NET/IK
	MINT/ZOEL	mitogenic	MAOIT/JEN/IK
minus	MAOI/NUS	mitokinetic	MAOIT/KI/NET/IK
minute	MAOI/NAOUT	mitome	MAOI/TOEM
	MIN/UT	mitomycin	MAOIT/MAOI/SIN
minutissimum	MAOI/NAOU/TIS/MUM	mitoplasm	MAOIT/PLAFM
	MAOI/NAOU/TISZ/MUM	mitoses	MAOI/TOE/SAOEZ
minuthesis	MIN/YAO*UT/SIS	mitosin	MIT/SIN
mio-	MAOI	mitosis	MAOI/TOE/SIS
	MAOI/YO	mitosome	MIT/SOEM
miocardia	MAO*I/KARD/YA	mitospore	MAOIT/SPOER
	(not MAOI/KARD/YA; see myocardia)	mitotane	MAOIT/TAIN
miodidymus	MAOI/DID/MUS	mitotic	MAOI/TOT/IK
miodymus	MAOI/OD/MUS	mitoxantrone	MAOIT/ZAN/TROEN
miolecithal	MAOI/LES/THAL	mitral	MAOI/TRAL
mionectic	MAOI/NEKT/IK	mitralism	MAOI/TRAL/IFM
miopragia	MAOI/PRAI/JA	mitralization	MAOI/TRAL/ZAIGS
miopus	MAOI/YOE/PUS	mitramycin	MIT/RA/MAOI/SIN
miosis	MAOI/YOE/SIS	Mitrolan	MAOI/TRO/LAN
miosphygmia	MAOI/SFIG/MA	mitrotricuspid	MAOI/TRO/TR*I/KUS/PID
	MAOI/SFIG/MAOE/YA	Mitsuda	MIT/SAOU/DA
miotic	MAOI/OT/IK	mittelschmerz	MIT/EL/SH-/MAIRTS
	MAOI/YOT/IK		MIT/EL/SMAIRTS
miracidia	MAOIR/SID/YA		MIT/EL/SH-/MERTS
	MAOI/RA/SID/YA		MIT/EL/SMERTS
miracidium	MAOIR/SID/YUM	Mittendorf	MIT/EN/DOR/-F
	MAOI/RA/SID/YUM	mittor	MIT/TOR
mire	MAOIR	mixed	MIX/-D
mirror	MIR/ROR	mixoscopia	MIX/SKOEP/YA
miryachit	see myriachit	mixotrophic	MIX/TROFK
mis-action	MIS/A*BGS	Mixtard	MIX/TARD
misandry	MIS/AN/DRI	mixture	MIX/KHUR
misanthropia	MIS/AN/THROEP/YA	ml	M*L
misanthropy	MIS/AN/THRO/PI	mm	M*M
miscarriage	MIS/KAIRJ	M-mode	M-RBGS/MOED
	MIS/KAIR/AJ	M'Naghten	M-K/NAUT/-N
miscarry	MIS/KAR/RI		M-K/NAU/TEN
	MIS/KAIR/RI		MAK/NAUT/-N
misce	MIS/SAOE		MAK/NAU/TEN
miscegenation	MIS/SEJ/NAIGS	mneme	NAOE/MAOE
	MIS/JE/NAIGS	mnemenic	NAOE/MEN/IK
miscible	MIS/-BL	mnemic	NAOEM/IK
	MIS/SIBL	mnemism	NAOEM/IFM
misdiagnosis	MIS/DAOIG/NOE/SIS		NAOE/MIFM
miserere mei	MIZ/RAI/RAOE/MAI/YAOE	mnemonic	NAOE/MON/IK
miserotia	MIS/ROE/SHA		NE/MON/IK
	MIS/E/ROE/SHA	mnemonics	NAOE/MON/IK/-S
misfit	MIS/FIT		NE/MON/IK/-S
misogamy	MI/SOG/M*I	mnemotechnics	NAOEM/TEK/NIK/-S
misogyny	MI/SOJ/N*I	-mnesia	-M/NAOEZ/YA
misologia	MIS/LOE/JA		NAOEZ/YA
misoneism	MIS/NAOE/IFM	-mnesis	-M/NAOE/SIS
misopedia	MIS/PAOED/YA	Moban	MOE/BAN

Moberg	MOE/BERG
Mobigesic	MOEB/JAOEZ/IK
mobile	MOEBL
	MOE/BIL
	MOE/BAOIL
	MOEB/LAOE
mobility	MOEBLT
mobilization	MOEBL/ZAIGS
mobilize	MOEBL/AOIZ
	MOEB/LAOIZ
mobilometer	MOEB/LOM/TER
Mobisyl	MOEB/SIL
Mobitz	MOE/BITS
Mobius	MAOEB/YUS
moccasin	MOK/SIN
mockup	MOK/*UP
modality	MOE/DAL/TI
Modane	MOE/DAIN
mode	MOED
model	MOD/EL
moderator	MOD/RAI/TOR
Moderil	MOED/RIL
Modicon	MOD/KON
modification	MOD/FI/KAIGS
modifier	MOD/FI/ER
modioli	MOE/DAOI/LAOI
modioliform	MOED/YOEL/FORM
modiolus	MOE/DAOI/LUS
Modrastane	MOD/RA/STAIN
	MOED/RA/STAIN
modul-	MOD/L-
	MOJ/L-
	MOD/YAOU/L-
	MOD/YU/L-
modulating	MOD/LAIT/-G
modulation	MOD/LAIGS
modulator	MOD/LAI/TOR
modulus	MOD/LUS
Moduretic	MOD/YAOU/RET/IK
Moeller	MAOEL/ER
	MOEL/ER
Moerner	MERN/ER
mofebutazone	MOF/BAOUT/ZOEN
mogiarthria	MOJ/AR/THRAOE/YA
	MOJ/YAR/THRAOE/YA
mogigraphia	MOJ/GRAF/YA
mogilalia	MOJ/LAIL/YA
mogiphonia	MOJ/FOEN/YA
Mohrenheim	MORN/HAOIM
	MOR/EN/HAOIM
moiety	MOI/TI
moist	MO*IS
moisture	MOIS/KHUR
Moisturel	MOIS/KHUR/EL
	MOIS/KHU/REL
mol	MO*L
	(not MOL; see moll)
molal	MOE/LAL
molality	MOE/LAL/TI
molar	MOE/LAR
molares	MOE/LAI/RAOEZ
molariform	MOE/LAIR/FORM
	MOE/LAR/FORM
molarity	MOE/LAIR/TI
	MOE/LAR/TI
molarium	MOE/LAIRM
	MOE/LAIR/YUM
molasses	MO/LAS/SES
	MO/LASZ-S
mold	MOELD
	MOLD
molding	MOELD/-G
	MOLD/-G
mole	MOEL
molecular	MO/LEK/LAR
	MOE/LEK/LAR
molecule	MOL/KAOUL
molilalia	MOL/LAIL/YA
molimen	MOE/LAOI/MEN
molimina	MOE/LIM/NA
molindone	MOE/LIN/DOEN
Mol-Iron	MOEL/AOIRN
	MOL/AOIRN
Molisch	MOL/IRB
Moll	K-P/MOL
molle	MOL/LAOE
mollescuse	MOL/LES/KAOUS
	MO/LES/KAOUS
	MOL/ES/KAOUS
mollis	MOL/LIS
mollities	MOE/LIRB/AOEZ
	MOE/LIRB/SHAOEZ
mollusc	MOL/US/*K
	MOL/LUS/*K
Mollusca	MOL/LUS/KA
	MO/LUS/KA
molluscous	MOL/LUS/KOUS
	MO/LUS/KOUS
molluscum	MOL/LUS/KUM
	MO/LUS/KUM
mollusk	MOL/US/-K
	MOL/LUS/-K
Moloney	MO/LOE/NAOE
	MOE/LOE/NAOE
molt	MOELT
molting	MOELT/-G
molybdate	MOE/LIB/DAIT
	MO/LIB/DAIT
molybdenic	MOE/LIBD/NIK
	MOE/LIB/DE/NIK
	MO/LIBD/NIK
	MO/LIB/DE/NIK
molybdenosis	MOE/LIBD/NOE/SIS
	MOE/LIB/DE/NOE/SIS
	MO/LIBD/NOE/SIS
	MO/LIB/DE/NOE/SIS
molybdenous	MOE/LIBD/NOUS
	MOE/LIB/DE/NOUS
	MO/LIBD/NOUS
	MO/LIB/DE/NOUS
molybdenum	MOE/LIBD/NUM
	MOE/LIB/DE/NUM
	MO/LIBD/NUM
	MO/LIB/DE/NUM
molybdic	MOE/LIB/DIK
	MO/LIB/DIK
molybdous	MOE/LIB/DOUS
	MO/LIB/DOUS
molysmophobia	MO/LIZ/MO/FOEB/YA
	MOE/LIZ/MO/FOEB/YA
momentum	MOEMT/UM
	MOE/MEN/TUM
momism	MOM/IFM
monacid	MON/AS/ID
monad	MOE/NAD
	MON/AD
Monadidae	MON/AD/DAE
monadin	MON/DIN
Monakow	MOE/NAK/OV
	MOE/NAK/KOV
Monaldi	MOE/NAL/DAOE
	MO/NAL/DAOE
monamide	MON/AM/ID
	MON/AM/AOID
monamine	MON/AM/MIN
	MON/AM/AOID
monaminuria	MON/AM/NAOUR/YA
monangle	MON/ANG/-L
Monarda	MON/AR/DA
	MOE/NAR/DA
monarthric	MON/AR/THRIK
monarthritis	MON/AR/THRAOITS
monarticular	MON/AR/TIK/LAR
monaster	MON/AS/TER
	MON/A*S/ER
monathetosis	MON/A*T/TOE/SIS
monatomic	MON/TOM/IK
monaural	MON/AURL
monauralis	MON/AU/RAI/LIS
monaxon	MON/AK/SON
monaxonic	MON/AK/SON/IK
	MON/AX/ON/IK
Monckeberg	M*ENG/BERG
	MEN/KE/BERG
	MEN/KAOE/BERG
Mondini	MON/DAOE/NAOE
Mondonesi	MOND/NAI/ZAOE
	MOND/NAI/SAOE
	MON/DO/NAI/ZAOE
	MON/DO/NAI/SAOE
Mondor	MON/DOR
monecious	see monoecious
moner	MOE/NER
	(not MOEN/ER; see moaner)
Monera	MOE/NAOE/RA
moneran	MOE/NAOE/RAN
monerula	MOE/NER/LA
monesthetic	MON/ES/THET/IK
monestrous	MON/ES/TROUS

mongolian	MON/GOEL/YAN	Monoclate	MON/KLAIT
mongolism	MONG/LIFM	monocranius	MON/KRAIN/YUS
mongoloid	MONG/LOID	monocrotaline	MON/KROET/LIN
Moniezia expansa	MON/YAOEZ/YA/EX/PAN/SA	monocrotic	MON/KROT/IK
monilated	MON/LAIT/-D	monocrotism	MO/NOK/RO/TIFM
monilethrix	MOE/NIL/THRIX		MON/OK/RO/TIFM
	MO/NIL/THRIX	monocular	MON/OK/LAR
Monilia	MOE/NIL/YA		MO/NOK/LAR
	MO/NIL/YA	monoculus	MON/OK/LUS
Moniliaceae	MOE/NIL/YAIS/YAE		MO/NOK/LUS
	MO/NIL/YAIS/YAE	monocyclic	MON/SAOIK/LIK
moniliad	MOE/NIL/YID	monocyesis	MON/SAOI/E/SIS
	MO/NIL/YID	monocyte	MON/SAO*IT
monilial	MOE/NIL/YAL	monocytic	MON/SIT/IK
	MO/NIL/YAL	monocytoid	MON/SAOI/TOID
Moniliales	MOE/NIL/YAI/LAOEZ	monocytopenia	MON/SAOIT/PAOEN/YA
	MO/NIL/YAI/LAOEZ	monocytopoiesis	MON/SAOIT/POI/SIS
moniliasis	MOEN/LAOI/SIS	monocytosis	MON/SAOI/TOE/SIS
	MON/LAOI/SIS	monodactylia	MON/DAK/TIL/YA
moniliform	MOE/NIL/FORM	monodactylism	MON/DAKT/LIFM
	MO/NIL/FORM	monodactyly	MON/DAKT/LI
Moniliformis	MOE/NIL/FOR/MIS	monodal	MON/NOE/DAL
	MO/NIL/FOR/MIS		MO/NOE/DAL
moniliid	MOE/NIL/YID		MON/OE/DAL
	MO/NIL/YID	monodermoma	MON/DER/MOE/MA
moniliosis	MOE/NIL/YOE/SIS	monodiplopia	MON/DI/PLOEP/YA
	MO/NIL/YOE/SIS	monodisperse	MON/DIS/PERS
monism	MOE/NIFM	monoecious	MON/AOERBS
Monistat	MON/STAT		MO/NAOERBS
Monistat-Derm	MON/STAT/DERM	monoethanolamine	MON/*ET/NOL/MAOEN
monistic	MOE/N*IS/IK		MON/*ET/NOEL/MAOEN
	MO/N*IS/IK	monogametic	MON/GA/MET/IK
monitor	MON/TOR	monogamy	MON/OG/M*I
monkey paw	MON/KAOE/PAU		MO/NOG/M*I
monkeypox	MON/KAOE/POX	monoganglial	MON/GANG/LAL
mono-	MON	monogenesis	MON/JEN/SIS
	MON/NO	monogenetic	MON/JE/NET/IK
	MO/NO	monogenic	MON/JEN/IK
mono-amelia	MON/AI/MAOEL/YA	monogenous	MO/NOJ/NOUS
monoamide	*see* monamide	monogerminal	MON/JERM/NAL
monoamine	*see* monamine	Mono-Gesic	MON/JAOEZ/IK
monoaminergic	MON/AM/NERJ/IK	monograph	MON/GRAF
monoaminuria	*see* monaminuria	monohybrid	MON/HAOI/BRID
monoamniotic	MON/AM/NOT/IK	monohydrated	MON/HAOI/DRAIT/-D
	MON/AM/NAOE/YOT/IK	monohydric	MON/HAOI/DRIK
monoarticular	*see* monarticular	monohydrochloride	MON/HAOI/DRO/KLOR/AOID
monoassociated	MON/SOERB/-D	monoideism	MON/AOI/DAOE/YIFM
	MON/AI/SOERB/YAIT/-D	monoinfection	MON/IN/F*EBGS
monobacillary	MON/BAS/LAIR	monoiodotyrosine	MON/AOI/OED/TAOIR/SAOEN
monobactam	MON/BAK/TAM	monoisonitrosoacetone	MON/AOIS/NAOI/TROES/AS/
monobacterial	MON/BAK/TAOERL		TOEN
monobasic	MON/BAIS/IK		MON/AOIS/NAOI/TROE/SO/AS/
monobenzone	MON/BEN/ZOEN		TOEN
monoblast	MON/BLA*S	monokaryote	MON/KAR/YOET
monoblastoma	MON/BLAS/TOE/MA	monokaryotic	MON/KAR/YOT/IK
monoblepsia	MON/BLEPS/YA	monoketoheptose	MON/KAOET/HEP/TOES
monobrachia	MON/BRAIK/YA	monokine	MON/KAOIN
monobrachius	MON/BRAIK/YUS	monolayer	MON/LAI/ER
monobromated	MON/BROE/MAIT/-D	monolene	MON/LAOEN
monobrominated	MON/BROEM/NAIT/-D	monolepsis	MON/LEP/SIS
monocalcic	MON/KALS/IK	monolocular	MON/LOK/LAR
monocardian	MON/KARD/YAN	monomania	MON/MAIN/YA
monocellular	MON/SEL/YAOU/LAR	monomaniac	MON/MAIN/YAK
monocephalus	MON/SEF/LUS	monomastigote	MON/MA*S/GOET
monochlorphenamide	MON/KLOR/FEN/MAOID	monomaxillary	MON/MAX/LAIR
monochord	MON/KHORD	monomelic	MON/MEL/IK
monochorea	MON/KOE/RAOE/YA	monomer	MON/MER
monochorial	MON/KOER/YAL	monomeric	MON/MER/IK
monochorionic	MON/KOER/YON/IK	monometallic	MON/ME/TAL/IK
monochroic	MON/KROIK	monomicrobic	MON/MAOI/KROEB/IK
	MON/KROE/IK	monomolecular	MON/MOE/LEK/LAR
monochromasia	MON/KROE/MAIZ/YA		MON/MO/LEK/LAR
monochromasy	MON/KROEM/SI	monomorphic	MON/MOR/FIK
monochromatic	MON/KROE/MAT/IK	monomorphism	MON/MOR/FIFM
monochromatism	MON/KROEM/TIFM	monomorphous	MON/MOR/FOUS
monochromatophil	MON/KROE/MAT/FIL	monomphalus	MON/OM/FLUS
monochromatophile	MON/KROE/MAT/FAOIL	monomyoplegia	MON/MAOI/PLAOE/JA
monochromator	MON/KROE/MAI/TOR	monomyositis	MON/MAOI/SAOITS
monochromic	MON/KROEM/IK	mononeme	MON/NAOEM
monochromophil	MON/KROEM/FIL	mononephrous	MON/NEF/ROUS
monochromophile	MON/KROEM/FAOIL	mononeural	MON/NAOURL
monochromophilic	MON/KROEM/FIL/IK	mononeuralgia	MON/NAOU/RAL/JA
monocle	MON/K-L	mononeuric	MON/NAOUR/IK
monoclinic	MON/KLIN/IK	mononeuritis	MON/NAOU/RAOITS
monoclonal	MON/KLOENL	mononeuropathy	MON/NAOU/ROP/TH*I
monocontaminated	MON/KON/TAM/NAIT/-D	mononoea	MON/NAOE/YA
monocontamination	MON/KON/TAM/NAIGS	mononuclear	MON/NAOUK/LAR
monocorditis	MON/KOR/DAOITS	mononucleate	MON/NAOUK/LAIT
Monocid	MON/SID	mononucleosis	MON/NAOUK/LOE/SIS

mononucleotide	MON/NAOUK/LO/TAOID	monosulfonate	MON/SUL/FO/NAIT
monooctanoin	MON/OK/TAN/WIN	monosymmetros	MON/SIM/TROS
mono-osteitic	MON/O*S/YIT/IK	monosymptom	MON/SIFRP/TOM
monooxygenase	MON/OX/JEN/AIS		MON/SIM/TOM
	MON/OX/JE/NAIS	monosymptomatic	MON/SIFRPT/MAT/IK
monoparesis	MON/PRAOE/SIS		MON/SIMT/MAT/IK
	MON/PAR/SIS	monosynaptic	MON/SNAPT/IK
monoparesthesia	MON/PAR/ES/THAOEZ/YA		MON/SIN/APT/IK
monopatic	MON/PA*T/IK	monosyphilid	MON/SIF/LID
monopathy	MON/OP/TH*I	monosyphilide	MON/SIF/LAOID
	MO/NOP/TH*I	monoterminal	MON/TERM/NAL
monopenia	MON/PAOEN/YA	monoterpene	MON/TER/PAOEN
monophagia	MON/FAI/JA	monothermia	MON/THERM/YA
monophagism	MO/NOF/JIFM	monothetic	MON/THET/IK
monophasia	MON/FAIZ/YA	monothioglycerol	MON/THAOI/GLIS/ROL
monophasic	MON/FAEZ/IK	monotocous	MO/NOT/KOUS
	MON/FAIZ/IK	Monotremata	MON/TRAOEM/TA
monophenol	MON/FAOE/NOL	monotreme	MON/TRAOEM
monophobia	MON/FOEB/YA	Monotricha	MO/NOT/RI/KA
monophosphate	MON/FOS/FAIT		MON/OT/RI/KA
monophthalmos	MON/OF/THAL/MOS	monotrichate	MO/NOT/RI/KAIT
monophthalmus	MON/OF/THAL/MUS	monotrichic	MON/TRIK/IK
monophyletic	MON/FAOI/LET/IK	monotrichous	MO/NOT/RI/KOUS
monophyletism	MON/FAOIL/TIFM	monotropic	MON/TROP/IK
monophyletist	MON/FAOIL/T*IS	Mono-Vacc Test	MON/VAK/T*ES
monophyodont	MON/FAOI/DONT	monovalence	MON/VAI/LENS
monopia	MON/OEP/YA		MON/VAIL/ENS
monoplasmatic	MON/PLAZ/MAT/IK	monovalency	MON/VAI/LEN/SI
monoplast	MON/PLA*S		MON/VAIL/EN/SI
monoplastic	MON/PLA*S/IK	monovalent	MON/VAI/LENT
monoplegia	MON/PLAOE/JA		MON/VAIL/ENT
monoplegic	MON/PLAOEJ/IK	monovular	MON/OV/LAR
monoploid	MON/PLOID	monovulatory	MON/OV/LA/TOIR
monopodia	MON/POED/YA	monoxenic	MON/ZEN/IK
monopodial	MON/POED/YAL	monoxenous	MON/OX/NOUS
monopoiesis	MON/POI/SIS		MO/NOX/NOUS
monopotassium	MON/PO/TAS/YUM	monoxeny	MON/OX/N*I
	MON/POE/TAS/YUM		MO/NOX/N*I
monops	MON/OPS	monoxide	MON/OK/SAOID
monoptychial	MON/TAOIK/YAL		MO/NOK/SAOID
monopus	MON/PUS		MON/OX/AOID
monorchia	MON/ORK/YA		MO/NOX/AOID
monorchid	MON/ORK/ID	monozoic	MON/ZOIK
	MON/OR/KID		MON/ZOE/IK
monorchidic	MON/OR/KID/IK	monozygosity	MON/ZAOI/GOS/TI
monorchidism	MON/ORK/DIFM	monozygotic	MON/ZAOI/GOT/IK
monorchis	MON/OR/KIS	monozygous	MON/ZAOIG/OUS
monorchism	MON/OR/KIFM	Monro	MON/ROE
	MON/ORK/IFM	mons	MONZ
monorecidive	MON/RES/DAOEV	mons pubis	MONZ/PAOU/BIS
monorhinic	MON/RIN/IK	Monson	MON/SON
monos	MON/NOE/-S	monster	MON/STER
monosaccharide	MON/SAK/RAOID		MONS/TER
monosaccharose	MON/SAK/ROES	monstra	MON/STRA
monoscelous	MON/SEL/OUS	monstrosity	MON/STROS/TI
	MON/SKEL/OUS	monstrum	MON/STRUM
monoscenism	MON/SE/NIFM	montanus	MON/TAI/NUS
	MON/SAOEN/IFM		MON/TAN/NUS
monose	MON/OES	Monteggia	MON/TEJ/YA
monosemicarbazone	MON/SEM/KARB/ZOEN	montes	MON/TAOEZ
monosexual	MON/SEX/YAOUL	Montgomery	MONT/GOM/RI
monosodium	MON/SOED/YUM	monticuli	MON/TIK/LAOI
monosodium glutamate	MON/SOED/YUM/GLAOUT/MAIT	monticulus	MON/TIK/LUS
monosome	MON/SOEM	montis	MON/TIS
monosomia	MON/SOEM/YA	mood	MAOD
monosomic	MON/SOEM/IK	mood swing	MAOD/SWING
monosomous	MON/SOEM/OUS	moon	MAON
monosomy	MON/SOE/M*I	Moon	K-P/MAON
monospasm	MON/SPAFM	moor	MAOR
monospecific	MON/SPEFK	Moore	MAO*R
	MON/SPE/SIFK	Mooren	MAOR/-N
monospermy	MON/SPER/M*I	Mooser	MAOS/ER
Monosporium	MON/SPOER/YUM	Morand	MOR/RAN
	MON/SPOR/YUM		MOR/RAND
Monosporium apiospermum	MON/SPOER/YUM/AP/YO/SPER/MUM	morantel	MOE/RAN/TEL
	MON/SPOR/YUM/AP/YO/SPER/MUM		MO/RAN/TEL
		Morax	MOR/AX
			MOER/AX
monostearate	MON/STAOER/AIT	Moraxella	MOR/AK/SEL/LA
Monostoma	MOE/NO*S/MA		MOER/AK/SEL/LA
	MON/STOE/MA	morbi	MOR/BAOI
monostome	MON/STOEM	morbid	MORB/ID
Monostomum	MOE/NO*S/MUM		MOR/BID
	MON/STOE/MUM	morbidity	MOR/BID/TI
monostotic	MON/OS/TOT/IK		MORB/ID/TI
monostratal	MON/STRAI/TAL	morbidostatic	MORB/DO/STAT/IK
monostratified	MON/STRAT/FI/-D	morbific	MOR/BIFK
monosubstituted	MON/SUB/STAOUT/-D		MOR/BIF/IK
	MON/SUBS/TAOUT/-D	morbigenous	MOR/BLJ/NOUS

morbility	MOR/BIL/TI	morsus	MOR/SUS
morbilli	MOR/BIL/LAOI	mortal	MOR/TAL
morbilliform	MOR/BIL/FORM	mortality	MOR/TAL/TI
morbillorum	MORB/LOR/UM	mortar	MOR/TAR
	MORB/LOER/UM	Mortierella	MOR/TAOE/REL/LA
Morvillivirus	MOR/BIL/VAOI/RUS	mortician	MOR/TIGS
morbillous	MOR/BIL/OUS	mortification	MORT/FI/KAIGS
morbus	MOR/BUS	mortified	MORT/FI/-D
morcel	MOR/SEL	mortis	MOR/TIS
morcellation	MORS/LAIGS	mortise	MOR/TAOES
	MOR/SE/LAIGS	Morton	MOR/TON
	MOR/SEL/LAIGS	mortuary	MORT/YAIR
morcellement	MOR/SEL/-MT		MOR/KHAOU/AIR
mordant	MOR/DANT		MOR/TAOU/AIR
mordax	MOR/DAX		MORT/WAIR
mordicans	MORD/KANZ	mortuus	MORT/YUS
Morel	MOER/EL		MORT/WUS
	MOR/EL		MOR/KHUS
mores	MOR/AIZ	morul-	MOR/L-
	MOER/AIZ		MOR/YAOU/L-
Moreschi	MOE/RES/KAOE		MOR/YU/L-
Morestin	MOR/ES/TIN	morula	MOR/LA
	MOER/ES/TIN	morular	MOR/LAR
Moretti	MOE/RET/TAOE	morulation	MOR/LAIGS
	MO/RET/TAOE	Morulavirus	MOR/LA/VAOI/RUS
Morgagni	MOR/GAN/YAOE	moruloid	MOR/LOID
morgagnian	MOR/GAN/YAN	Morvan	MOR/VAN
morgagnii	MOR/GAN/YAOI	mosaic	MOE/ZAIK
morgan	MOR/GAN		MOE/ZAI/IK
Morgan	K-P/MOR/GAN	mosaicism	MOE/ZAI/SIFM
morgue	MORG	Moschcowitz	MOS/KO/WITS
	MOERG		MOS/KOE/WITS
moria	MOER/YA	moschus	MOS/KUS
	MOR/YA	Mosher	MOERB/ER
moribund	MOER/BUND		MORB/ER
	MOR/BUND	Mosler	MOS/LER
morin	MOR/RIN	mosquito	MOS/KAOE/TOE
	MOER/RIN		MO/SKAOE/TOE
Morison	MOR/SON	mosquitocidal	MOS/KAOET/SAOI/DAL
Morner	M*ERN/ER		MO/SKAOET/SAOI/DAL
	(*not* MERN/ER; see Moerner)	mosquitocide	MOS/KAOET/SAO*ID
morning glory	MORN/-G/GLOR/RI		MO/SKAOET/SAO*ID
Moro	MOR/ROE	moss	MOSZ
	MOER/ROE	Moss	K-P/MOSZ
moron	MOR/RON	Mosse	MOS/SAOE
	MOER/RON	Mosso	MOS/SOE
moroxydine	MO/ROX/DAOEN	mossy	MOS/SI
-morph	MOR/-F	Motais	MOE/TAIZ
morph(o)-	MOR/F(O)	mote	MOET
morphazinamide	MOR/FA/ZIN/MAOID	moth	MO*T
morphea	MOR/FAOE/YA	mother	MO*T/ER
morpheme	MOR/FAOEM		MO/THER
morphine	MOR/FAOEN	motile	MOE/TIL
morphinic	MOR/FIN/IK		MOE/TAOIL
morphinism	MOR/FI/NIFM	motilin	MOE/TIL/LIN
	MOR/FIN/IFM	motility	MOE/TIL/TI
morphinistic	MOR/FI/N*IS/IK	motion	MOEGS
	MOR/FIN/*IS/IK	motivation	MOET/VAIGS
morphinium	MOR/FIN/YUM	motive	MOET/IV
-morphism	MOR/FIFM	motoceptor	MOET/SEP/TOR
morphodifferentiation	MOR/FO/DIFRN/SHAIGS	motofacient	MOET/FAIRBT
morphogenesis	MOR/FO/JEN/SIS	Motofen	MOET/FEN
morphogenetic	MOR/FO/JE/NET/IK	motoneuron	MOET/NAOU/RON
morphologic	MOR/FO/LOJ/IK	motor	MOE/TOR
morphological	MOR/FO/LOJ/KAL	motoria	MOE/TOER/YA
morphology	MOR/FOLG		MOE/TOR/YA
morpholysis	MOR/FOL/SIS	motorial	MOE/TOIRL
morphometric	MOR/FO/MET/RIK	motoricity	MOET/RIS/TI
morphometry	MOR/FOM/TRI	motorium	MOE/TOIRM
morphon	MOR/FON	motorius	MOE/TOER/YUS
morphophysics	MOR/FO/FIZ/IK/-S		MOE/TOR/YUS
morphoplasm	MOR/FO/PLAFM	motorogerminative	MOET/RO/JERM/NA/TIV
morphosis	MOR/FOE/SIS	motormeter	MOE/TOR/MAOET/ER
morphosynthesis	MOR/FO/S*INT/SIS	Motrin	MOE/TRIN
morphotic	MOR/FOT/IK	Mott	MOT
morphotype	MOR/FO/TAOIP	mottled	MOT/-LD
-morphous	MOR/FOUS	mottling	MOT/-LG
Morquio	MOR/KAOE/YOE	mouche	MAOURB
morrhuate	MOR/YAIT	mouche volantes	MAOURB/VOE/LANT
	MOR/YAOU/AIT	moulage	MAOU/LAJ
	MOR/RAOU/AIT	mould	MO*ELD
morrhuic	MOR/RAOU/IK		MOULD
	MOR/YAOU/IK		(*not* MOELD; see mold)
Morris	MOR/RIS	moulding	MO*ELD/-G
Morrison	MOR/RI/SON		MOULD/-G
	(*not* MOR/SON; see Morison)	moult	MO*ELT
mors	MORZ		MOULT
morsal	MOR/SAL		(not MOELT; see molt)
morsulus	MOR/SAOU/LUS	mounding	MOUND/-G

mount	MOUNT	mucolysis	MAOU/KOL/SIS
mountant	MOUN/TANT	mucolytic	MAOUK/LIT/IK
mounting	MOUNT/-G	mucomembranous	MAOUK/MEM/BRA/NOUS
mourn	MOURN	Mucomyst	MAOUK/M*IS
	(*not* MORN; see morn)	mucopeptide	MAOUK/PEP/TAOID
mouse	MOUS	mucoperichondrial	MAOUK/P*ER/KON/DRAL
mousepox	MOUS/POX	mucoperichondrium	MAOUK/P*ER/KON/DRUM
mouth	MO*UT	mucoperiosteal	MAOUK/P*ER/O*S/YAL
mouth guard	MO*UT/GARD	mucoperiosteum	MAOUK/P*ER/O*S/YUM
mouth stick	MO*UT/STIK	mucopolysaccharidase	MAOUK/POL/SAK/RI/DAIS
mouthwash	MO*UT/WARB	mucopolysaccharide	MAOUK/POL/SAK/RAOID
movement	MAOUVMT	mucopolysaccharidoses	MAOUK/POL/SAK/RI/DOE/SAOEZ
	MOVMT	mucopolysaccharidosis	MAOUK/POL/SAK/RI/DOE/SIS
moxa	MOK/SA	mucopolysacchariduria	MAOUK/POL/SAK/RI/DAOUR/YA
moxalaxtam	MOX/LAK/TAM	mucoprotein	MAOUK/PRO/TAOEN
moxibustion	MOX/BUGS	mucopurulent	MAOUK/PAOUR/LENT
moxisylyte	MOK/SIS/LAOIT	mucopus	MAOUK/PUS
moxnidazole	MOX/NID/ZOEL	Mucor	MAOU/KOR
Moynihan	MOIN/HAN	Mucoraceae	MAOUK/RAIS/YAE
Mozart	MOET/SART	mucoraceous	MAOUK/RAIRBS
	MOE/ZART	Mucorales	MAOUK/RAI/LAOEZ
MRI	M-RBGS/R*RBGS/*IRBGS	mucorin	MAOUK/RIN
M-R-VAX	M-RBGS/R-RBGS/VAX	mucormycosis	MAOU/KOR/MAOI/KOE/SIS
MS Contin Tablets	M-RBGS/S*RBGS/KON/TIN/TAB/	mucoroides	MAOUK/ROI/DAOEZ
	LET/-S	mucosa	MAOU/KOE/SA
MSIR Oral Solution	M-RBGS/S*RBGS/*IRBGS/	mucosae	MAOU/KOE/SAE
	R*RBGS/ORL/SLAOUGS	mucosal	MAOU/KOE/SAL
MSIR Tablets	M-RBGS/S*RBGS/*IRBGS/	mucosanguineous	MAOUK/SANG/WIN/YOUS
	R*RBGS/TAB/LET/-S	mucosanguinolent	MAOUK/SANG/WIN/LENT
mu	MAOU	mucosectomy	MAOUK/SEKT/M*I
muc(o)-	MAOUK	mucosedative	MAOUK/SED/TIV
	MAOU/K(O)	mucoserous	MAOUK/SAOER/OUS
	MAOUS	mucosin	MAOU/KOE/SIN
	MAOU/S(O)	mucositis	MAOUK/SAOITS
mucase	MAOU/KAIS	mucosocutaneous	MAOU/KOES/KAOU/TAIN/YOUS
Much	MAO*UK		MAOU/KOE/SO/KAOU/TAIN/
	(*not* MAOUK; see muco-)		YOUS
mucicarmine	MAOUS/KAR/MAOIN	mucostatic	MAOUK/STAT/IK
	MAOUS/KAR/MIN	mucosulfatidosis	MAOUK/SUL/FAT/DOE/SIS
mucid	MAOUS/ID		MAOUK/SUL/FA/TI/DOE/SIS
muciferous	MAOU/SIF/ROUS	mucosum	MAOU/KOE/SUM
mucification	MAOUS/FI/KAIGS		MAOU/KOES/UM
muciform	MAOUS/FORM	mucosus	MAOU/KOE/SUS
mucigen	MAOUS/JEN	mucous	MAOU/KOUS
mucigenous	MAOU/SIJ/NOUS		MAOUK/OUS
mucigogue	MAOUS/GOG	mucoviscidosis	MAOUK/VIS/DOE/SIS
mucihematein	MAOUS/HAOEM/TAOEN	mucro	MAOU/KROE
mucilage	MAOUS/LAJ	mucron	MAOU/KRON
mucilaginous	MAOUS/LAJ/NOUS	mucronate	MAOU/KRO/NAIT
mucilago	MAOUS/LA/GOE	mucrones	MAOU/KROE/NAOEZ
	MAOUS/LAI/GOE	mucroniform	MAOU/KRON/FORM
mucilloid	MAOUS/LOID	mucus	MAOU/KUS
mucin	MAOU/SIN	Mudrane	MAOU/DRAIN
mucin(o)-	MAOUS/N(O)	Mudrane-2	MAOU/DRAIN/2
mucinase	MAOU/SI/NAIS	Mudrane GG	MAOU/DRAIN/G-RBGS/G*RBGS
mucinemia	MAOUS/NAOEM/YA	Mudrane GG-2	MAOU/DRAIN/G-RBGS/G*RBGS/2
mucinoblast	MAOUS/NO/BLA*S	Mueller	MAOUL/ER
mucinogen	MAOUS/NO/JEN	muelleri	MAOUL/RAOI
	MAOU/SIN/JEN	muffle	MUFL
mucinoid	MAOUS/NOID	mulberry	MUL/BER/RI
mucinolytic	MAOUS/NO/LIT/IK	Mulder	MUL/DER
mucinosa	MAOUS/NOE/SA	muliebria	MAOUL/YEB/RA
mucinosis	MAOUS/NOE/SIS		MAOUL/YEB/RAOE/YA
mucinous	MAOUS/NOUS		MAOUL/YAOEB/RA
mucinuria	MAOUS/NAOUR/YA		MAOUL/YAOEB/RAOE/YA
muciparous	MAOU/SIP/ROUS	muliebris	MAOUL/YEB/RIS
muciparum	MAOU/SIP/RUM		MAOUL/YAOEB/RIS
mucitis	MAOU/SAOITS	muliebrity	MAOUL/YEB/RI/TI
mucoalbuminous	MAOUK/AL/BAOUM/NOUS	mull	MUL
mucocele	MAOUK/SAO*EL	Muller	MUL/ER
mucocellulare	MAOU/SEL/YAOU/LAI/RAOE	Muller	K-P/MUL/ER
mucoclasis	MAOU/KOK/LA/SIS	Muller	MAOUL/ER
mucocolitis	MAOUK/KO/LAOITS		(*not* MIL/ER; see Miller)
mucocolpos	MAOUK/KOL/POS	mullerian	MAOU/LER/YAN
mucocyte	MAOUK/SAO*IT		MAOU/LAOER/YAN
mucocutaneous	MAOUK/KAOU/TAIN/YOUS		MIL/LER/YAN
mucoderm	MAOUK/DERM		MIL/LAOER/YAN
mucodermal	MAOUK/DER/MAL	mullerianoma	MIL/LAOER/YA/NOE/MA
mucoenteritis	MAOUK/SPWRAOITS		MAOU/LAOER/YA/NOE/MA
	MAOUK/SPWER/RAOITS	multangular	MUL/TANG/LAR
mucoepidermoid	MAOUK/EP/DER/MOID		(*not* MULT/ANG/LAR)
mucofibrous	MAOUK/FAOI/BROUS	multi-	MULT
mucoflocculent	MAOUK/FLOK/LENT	multiallelic	MULT/AI/LAOEL/IK
mucoglobulin	MAOUK/GLOB/LIN		MULT/AI/LEL/IK
mucoid	MAOU/KOID	multiarticular	MULT/AR/TIK/LAR
	MAOUK/OID	multiaxial	MULT/AX/YAL
mucolipid	MAOUK/LIP/ID	multibacillary	MULT/BAS/LAIR
mucolipidoses	MAOUK/LIP/DOE/SAOEZ	multicapsular	MULT/KAPS/LAR
mucolipidosis	MAOUK/LIP/DOE/SIS	multicellular	MULT/SEL/YAOU/LAR

Multiceps	MULT/SEPS	mural	MAOURL
multicuspid	MULT/KUS/PID	muramic	MAOU/RAM/IK
multicuspidate	MULT/KUS/PI/DAIT	muramidase	MAOU/RAM/DAIS
multicystic	MULT/S*IS/IK	murein	MAOUR/AOEN
multidentate	MULT/DEN/TAIT		MAOUR/RAOEN
multifactorial	MULT/FAK/TOIRL		*see* Murine and murine
multifamilial	MULT/FA/MIL/YAL	Muret	MU/RAI
multifarious	MULT/FAIR/YOUS		MU/RET
multifetation	MULT/FAOE/TAIGS	murexide	MAOU/REK/SAOID
	MULT/FE/TAIGS		MAOU/REK/SID
multifid	MULT/FID	muriate	MAOUR/YAIT
multifidi	MUL/TIF/DAOI	muriatic	MAOUR/YAT/IK
multifidus	MUL/TIF/DUS	Muridae	MAOUR/DAE
multifiliis	MULT/FIL/YIS	muriform	MAOUR/FORM
multifocal	MULT/FOE/KAL	murine	MAOU/RAOIN
multiform	MULT/FORM		MAOU/RIN
multiforme	MULT/FOR/MAOE		*see* murein
multiformis	MULT/FOR/MIS	Murine	MAOU/RAOEN
multiganglionic	MULT/GANG/LON/IK		*see* murein and murine
multigesta	MULT/JES/TA	muris	MUR/RIS
multiglandular	MULT/GLAND/LAR		MAOU/RIS
multigravida	MULT/GRAV/DA		MAOUR/RIS
multi-infection	MULT/IN/F*EBGS	murisepticum	MAOUR/SEPT/KUM
multilamellar	MULT/LA/MEL/LAR	muris-ratti	MUR/RIS/RAT/TAOI
multilobar	MULT/LOE/BAR		MAOU/RIS/RAT/TAOI
multilobate	MULT/LOE/BAIT		MAOUR/RIS/RAT/TAOI
multilobed	MULT/LOEB/-D	murium	MAOUR/YUM
multilobular	MULT/LOB/LAR	murmur	MUR/MUR
multilocal	MULT/LOE/KAL	muromonab	MAOUR/MOE/NAB
multilocular	MULT/LOK/LAR	Murphy	MUR/FI
multilocularis	MULT/LOK/LAI/RIS	murrina	MAOU/RAOE/NA
multimammae	MULT/MAM/MAE	Mus	MUS
multinodal	MULT/NOE/DAL	musca	MUS/KA
multinodular	MULT/NOD/LAR	Musca	K-P/MUS/KA
multinodulate	MULT/NOD/LAIT	muscacide	MUS/KA/SAO*ID
multinuclear	MULT/NAOUK/LAR	muscae	MUS/SAE
multinucleate	MULT/NAOUK/LAIT		MUS/KAE
multinucleosis	MULT/NAOUK/LOE/SIS	muscae volitantes	MUS/SAE/VOL/TAN/TAOEZ
multipapillosa	MULT/PAP/LOE/SA		MUS/KAE/VOL/TAN/TAOEZ
multipara	MUL/TIP/RA	muscarine	MUS/KRAOEN
multiparity	MULT/PAIR/TI		MUS/KRIN
	(*not* MULT/PAR/TI; see multiparty)		MUS/KA/RAOEN
			MUS/KA/RIN
multiparous	MUL/TIP/ROUS	muscarinic	MUS/KRIN/IK
multipartial	MULT/PAR/-RBL		MUS/KA/RIN/IK
multiphasic	MULT/FAEZ/IK	muscarinism	MUS/KRIN/IFM
multiple	MULT/P-L		MUS/KA/RIN/IFM
multiplex	MULT/PLEX	muscarius	MUS/KAIR/YUS
multiplicitas	MULT/PLIS/TAS	muscegenetic	MUS/JE/NET/IK
multipolar	MULT/POE/LAR	Musci	MUS/SAOI
multirooted	MULT/RAOT/-D	muscicide	MUS/SAO*ID
multirotation	MULT/ROE/TAIGS	Muscidae	MUS/DAE
multisensitivity	MULT/SENS/TIV/TI	Muscina	MUS/SAOI/NA
multisynaptic	MULT/SNAPT/IK		MU/SAOI/NA
	MULT/SI/NAPT/IK	muscle	MUS/-L
multiterminal	MULT/TERM/NAL	muscle-bound	MUS/-L/BOUND
Multitest CMI	MULT/T*ES/KR-RBGS/M*RBGS/	muscle-trimming	MUS/-L/H-F/TRIM/-G
	*IRBGS	muscul(o)-	MUS/KL(O)
multituberculate	MULT/TAOU/BERK/LAIT		MUS/KAOU/L(O)
multivalence	MULT/VAIL/ENS	musculamine	MUS/KAOUL/MAOEN
	MULT/VAI/LENS		MUS/KAOU/LAM/MIN
multivalency	MULT/VAI/LEN/SI		MUS/KLAM/MIN
	MULT/VAIL/EN/SI	muscular	MUS/KLAR
multivalent	MULT/VAIL/ENT	musculares	MUS/KLAI/RAOEZ
	MULT/VAI/LENT	muscularis	MUS/KLAI/RIS
multivesicular	MULT/VE/SIK/LAR	muscularity	MUS/KLAIR/TI
Mulvidren-F	MUL/VI/DREN/F-RBGS	muscularize	MUS/KLA/RAOIZ
mummification	MUM/FI/KAIGS		MUS/KLAR/AOIZ
mummified	MUM/FI/-D	musculation	MUS/KLAIGS
mummify	MUM/FI	musculature	MUS/KLA/KHUR
mummy	MUM/M*I	musculi	MUS/KLAOI
mummying	MUM/M*I/-G	musculoaponeurotic	MUS/KLO/AP/NAOU/ROT/IK
mumps	MUFRPS	musculocutaneous	MUS/KLO/KAOU/TAIN/YOUS
	MUFRP/-S	musculodermic	MUS/KLO/DERM/IK
Mumpsvax	MUFRPS/VAX	musculoelastic	MUS/KLO/E/LA*S/IK
	MUM/-PS/VAX	musculofascial	MUS/KLO/FARBL
mumu	MAOU/MAOU	musculointestinal	MUS/KLO/SPW*ES/NAL
Munchausen	MEN/KHOUZ/-N	musculomembranous	MUS/KLO/MEM/BRA/NOUS
	MEN/KHOU/ZEN	musculophrenic	MUS/KLO/FREN/IK
	MUN/KHOUZ/-N	musculorum	MUS/KLOR/UM
	MUN/KHOU/ZEN		MUS/KLOER/UM
Munchmeyer	MEFRPBLG/MAOI/ER	musculoskeletal	MUS/KLO/SKEL/TAL
	MEN/-FP/MAOI/ER	musculospiral	MUS/KLO/SPAOIRL
	MIFRPBLG/MAOI/ER	musculospiralis	MUS/KLO/SPAOI/RAI/LIS
	MIN/-FP/MAOI/ER	musculotendinous	MUS/KLO/TEND/NOUS
	MUFRPBLG/MAOI/ER	musculotonic	MUS/KLO/TON/IK
	MUN/-FP/MAOI/ER	musculotropic	MUS/KLO/TROP/IK
munity	MAOU/NI/TI	musculotubal	MUS/KLO/TAOU/BAL
	MAOUN/TI	musculotubarius	MUS/KLO/TAOU/BAIR/YUS
Munro	MUN/ROE		

musculus	MUS/KLUS	-mycetic	MAOI/SET/IK
mushbite	MURB/BAOIT	mycetism	MAOIS/TIFM
mushroom	MURB/RAOM	mycetismus	MAOIS/TIZ/MUS
musical	MAOUZ/KAL	myceto-	MAOI/SAOET
musicogenic	MAOUZ/KO/JEN/IK		MAOIS/TO
musicotherapy	MAOUZ/KO/THER/PI	mycetogenetic	MAOI/SAOET/JE/NET/IK
Musset	MAOU/SAI		MAOIS/TO/JE/NET/IK
mussitation	MUS/TAIGS	mycetogenic	MAOI/SAOET/JEN/IK
	MUSZ/TAIGS		MAOIS/TO/JEN/IK
Mussy	MAOUS/SI	mycetogenous	MAOIS/TOJ/NOUS
	MUS/SI	mycetoma	MAOIS/TOE/MA
must	M*US	Mycetozoa	MAOI/SAOET/ZOE/WA
mustard	MUS/TARD	Mycetozoida	MAOIS/TO/ZOI/DA
Mustargen	MUS/TAR/JEN		MAOI/SAOET/ZOI/DA
mustine	MUS/TAOEN	mycid	MAOI/SID
muta-	MAOUT	Myciguent	MAOIS/KWENT
	MAOU/TA		MAOI/SIG/WENT
mutacism	MAOUT/SIFM	-mycin	MAOI/SIN
mutafacient	MAOUT/FAIRBT	Mycitracin	MAOIS/TRAI/SIN
mutagen	MAOUT/JEN	myco-	MAOIK
mutagenesis	MAOUT/JEN/SIS		MAOI/K(O)
mutagenic	MAOUT/JEN/IK	mycobacteria	MAOIK/BAK/TAOER/YA
mutagenicity	MAOUT/JE/NIS/TI	mycobacterial	MAOIK/BAK/TAOERL
Mutamycin	MAOUT/MAOI/SIN	Mycobacteriaceae	MAOIK/BAK/TAOER/YAIS/YAE
mutant	MAOU/TANT	mycobacteriosis	MAOIK/BAK/TAOER/YOE/SIS
mutarotase	MAOUT/ROE/TAIS	mycobacterium	MAOIK/BAK/TAOERM
mutarotation	MAOUT/ROE/TAIGS	Mycobacterium	K-P/MAOIK/BAK/TAOERM
mutase	MAOU/TAIS	mycobactin	MAOIK/BAK/TIN
mutation	MAOU/TAIGS	mycocide	MAOIK/SAO*ID
mutational	MAOU/TAIGS/NAL	mycoderma	MAOIK/DER/MA
mute	MAOUT	Mycoderma	K-P/MAOIK/DER/MA
mutein	MAOU/TAOEN	mycodermatitis	MAOIK/DERM/TAOITS
	MAOUT/YIN	mycogastritis	MAOIK/GAS/TRAOITS
mutilans	MAOUT/LANZ	mycohemia	MAOIK/HAOEM/YA
mutilation	MAOUT/LAIGS	mycoides	MAOI/KOI/DAOEZ
mutism	MAOU/TIFM	mycolic	MAOI/KOL/IK
	MAOUT/IFM	Mycolog	MAOIK/LOG
muton	MAOU/TON	Mycolog-II	MAOIK/LOG/2
mutual	MAOU/KHUL		MAOIK/LOG/IRBGS/*IRBGS
	MAOU/KHAL	mycologist	MAOI/KO*LGS
mutualism	MAOU/KHUL/IFM	mycology	MAOI/KOLG
	MAOU/KHAL/IFM	mycomyringitis	MAOIK/MIRN/JAOITS
mutualist	MAOU/KHUL/*IS	mycopathology	MAOIK/PA/THOLG
	MAOU/KHAL/*IS	mycophage	MAOIK/FALJ
muzolimine	MAOU/ZOEL/MAOEN	mycoplasma	MAOIK/PLAZ/MA
muzzle	MUZ/-L	Mycoplasma	K-P/MAOIK/PLAZ/MA
M.V.I.-12	M-FPLT/V*FPLT/*IFPLT/12	mycoplasmal	MAOIK/PLAZ/MAL
M.V.I.-12 Multi-Dose	M-FPLT/V*FPLT/*IFPLT/12/	Mycoplasmataceae	MAOIK/PLAZ/MA/TAIS/YAE
	MULT/DOES	Mycoplasmatales	MAOIK/PLAZ/MA/TAI/LAOEZ
M.V.I.-12 Unit Vial	M-FPLT/V*FPLT/*IFPLT/12/	mycoplasmosis	MAOIK/PLAZ/MOE/SIS
	YAOUNT/VAOI/YAL	mycopus	MAOIK/PUS
MVM Capsules	M-RBGS/V*RBGS/M*RBGS/KAP/	mycorrhiza	MAOIK/RAOI/ZA
	SAOUL/-S	mycose	MAOI/KOES
my(o)-	MAOI	mycoses	MAOI/KOE/SAOEZ
	MAOI/Y(O)	mycosis	MAOI/KOE/SIS
myalgia	MAOI/AL/JA	mycostasis	MAOI/KO*S/SIS
	MAOI/YAL/JA	mycostat	MAOIK/STAT
myalgic	MAOI/AL/JIK	mycostatic	MAOIK/STAT/IK
	MAOI/YAL/JIK	Mycostatin	MAOIK/STAT/TIN
Myambutol	MAOI/AM/BAOU/TOL	mycosterol	MAOI/KO*S/ROL
-myarial	MAOI/AIRL	mycotic	MAOI/KOT/IK
	MAOI/YAIRL	mycotica	MAOI/KOT/KA
-myarian	MAOI/AIRN	mycotoxicosis	MAOIK/TOX/KOE/SIS
	MAOI/YAIRN	mycotoxin	MAOIK/TOK/SIN
myasis	MAOI/AI/SIS	Myco-Triacet	MAOIK/TR*I/SET
	MAOI/YAI/SIS		MAOIK/TRAOI/SET
myasthenia	MAOI/AS/THAOEN/YA	Myco-Triacet	MAOIK/TR*I/SET/2
myasthenic	MAOI/AS/THEN/IK		MAOIK/TRAOI/SET/IRBGS/
myatonia	MAOI/YA/TOEN/YA		*IRBGS
	MAOI/AI/TOEN/YA	mycovirus	MAOIK/VAOI/RUS
	(not MAOI/TOEN/YA; see	mycter(o)-	MIK/TR(O)
	myotonia)		MIKT/R(O)
myatony	MAOI/AT/N*I	mycteric	MIK/TER/IK
	MAOI/YAT/N*I	mycterophonia	MIK/TRO/FOEN/YA
myatrophy	MAOI/AT/RO/FI	mycteroxerosis	MIK/TRO/ZAOE/ROE/SIS
myautonomy	MAOI/AU/TON/M*I		MIK/TRO/ZE/ROE/SIS
myce-	MAOIS	mydaleine	MAOI/DAIL/YAOEN
	MAOI/SAOE		MAOI/DAI/LAOEN
Mycelex	MAOIS/LEX	mydatoxin	MAOID/TOK/SIN
Mycelex-G	MAOIS/LEX/G-RBGS	mydriasis	MI/DRAOI/SIS
mycelia	MAOI/SAOEL/YA	mydriatic	MID/RAT/IK
mycelial	MAOI/SAOEL/YAL		MID/RAOE/AT/IK
mycelian	MAOI/SAOEL/YAN	myectomy	MAOI/EKT/M*I
mycelioid	MAOI/SAOEL/YOID	myectopia	MAOI/EK/TOEP/YA
mycelium	MAOI/SAOEL/YUM	myectopy	MAOI/EKT/PI
-myces	MAOI/SAOEZ	myel(o)-	MAOI/L(O)
mycete	MAOI/SAOET	myelalgia	MAOI/LAL/JA
-mycete	MAOI/SAOET	myelapoplexy	MAOI/LAP/PLEK/SI
-mycetes	MAOI/SAOE/TAOEZ		MAOI/EL/AP/PLEK/SI

myelasthenia	MAOI/LAS/THAOEN/YA	myelolymphocyte	MAOI/LO/LIM/FO/SAO*IT
	MAOI/EL/AS/THAOEN/YA	myelolysis	MAOI/LOL/SIS
myelatelia	MAOI/LA/TAOEL/YA	myelolytic	MAOI/LO/LIT/IK
	MAOI/EL/TAOEL/YA	myeloma	MAOI/LOE/MA
	MAOI/EL/AI/TAOEL/YA	myelomalacia	MAOI/LO/MA/LAI/SHA
myelatrophy	MAOI/LAT/RO/FI	myelomatoid	MAOI/LOEM/TOID
	MAOI/EL/AT/RO/FI	myelomatosis	MAOI/LOEM/TOE/SIS
myelauxe	MAOI/LAUK/SAOE		MAOI/LO/MA/TOE/SIS
	MAOI/EL/AUK/SAOE	myelomeningitis	MAOI/LO/MEN/JAOITS
myelemia	MAOI/LAOEM/YA	myelomeningocele	MAOI/LO/ME/NING/SAO*EL
	MAOI/EL/AOEM/YA	myelomere	MAOI/LO/MAOER
myelencephalitis	MAOI/LEN/SEF/LAOITS	myelomonocyte	MAOI/LO/MON/SAO*IT
	MAOI/EL/EN/SEF/LAOITS	myeloneuritis	MAOI/LO/NAOU/RAOITS
myelencephalon	MAOI/LEN/SEF/LON	myelonic	MAOI/LON/IK
	MAOI/EL/EN/SEF/LON	myelo-opticoneuropathy	MAOI/LO/OPT/KO/NAOU/ROP/TH*I
myelencephalospinal	MAOI/LEN/SEF/LO/SPAOINL	myeloparalysis	MAOI/LO/PRAL/SIS
	MAOI/EL/EN/SEF/LO/SPAOINL	myelopathic	MAOI/LO/PA*T/IK
myelic	MAOI/EL/IK	myelopathy	MAOI/LOP/TH*I
myelin	MAOI/LIN	myeloperoxidase	MAOI/LO/PROX/DAIS
myelin(o)-	MAOI/LI/N(O)	myelopetal	MAOI/LOP/TAL
	MAOI/LIN	myelophage	MAOI/LO/FAIJ
myelinated	MAOI/LI/NAIT/-D	myelophthisic	MAOI/LO/TIZ/IK
	MAOI/LIN/AIT/-D	myelophthisis	MAOI/LOF/THI/SIS
myelination	MAOI/LI/NAIGS		MAOI/LO/TAOI/SIS
	MAOI/LIN/AIGS	myeloplast	MAOI/LO/PLA*S
myelinic	MAOI/LIN/IK	myeloplegia	MAOI/LO/PLAOE/JA
myelinization	MAOI/LIN/ZAIGS	myelopoiesis	MAOI/LO/POI/SIS
myelinoclasis	MAOI/LI/NOK/LA/SIS	myelopoietic	MAOI/LO/POIT/IK
	MAOI/LIN/OK/LA/SIS	myeloproliferative	MAOI/LO/PRO/LIFR/TIV
myelinogenesis	MAOI/LIN/JEN/SIS	myeloradiculitis	MAOI/LO/RA/DIK/LAOITS
myelinogenetic	MAOI/LIN/JE/NET/IK	myeloradiculodysplasia	MAOI/LO/RA/DIK/LO/DIS/PLAIZ/YA
myelinogeny	MAOI/LI/NOJ/N*I	myeloradiculopathy	MAOI/LO/RA/DIK/LOP/TH*I
	MAOI/LIN/OJ/N*I	myeloradiculopolyneuronitis	
myelinolysin	MAOI/LI/NOL/SIN		MAOI/LO/RA/DIK/LO/POL/NAOUR/
	MAOI/LIN/OL/SIN		NAOITS
myelinolysis	MAOI/LI/NOL/SIS	myelorrhagia	MAOI/LO/RAI/JA
	MAOI/LIN/OL/SIS	myelorrhaphy	MAOI/LOR/FI
myelinopathy	MAOI/LI/NOP/TH*I	myelosarcoma	MAOI/LO/SAR/KOE/MA
	MAOI/LIN/OP/TH*I	myelosarcomatosis	MAOI/LO/SAR/KOEM/TOE/SIS
myelinosis	MAOI/LI/NOE/SIS	myeloschisis	MAOI/LOS/KI/SIS
	MAOI/LIN/O/SIS	myelosclerosis	MAOI/LO/SKLE/ROE/SIS
myelinotoxic	MAOI/LIN/TOX/IK	myelosis	MAOI/LOE/SIS
myelinotoxicity	MAOI/LIN/TOK/SIS/TI	myelospongium	MAOI/LO/SPON/JUM
myelitic	MAOI/LIT/IK	myelosuppressive	MAOI/LO/SUP/PRES/SIV
myelitis	MAOI/LAOITS		MAOI/LO/SUP/PRESZ/IV
myeloarchitectonics	MAOI/LO/ARK/TEK/TON/IK/-S	myelosyphilis	MAOI/LO/SIF/LIS
myeloarchitecture	MAOI/LO/ARK/TEK/KHUR	myelosyphilosis	MAOI/LO/SIF/LOE/SIS
myeloblast	MAOI/LO/BLA*S	myelosyringosis	MAOI/LO/SIRN/GOE/SIS
myeloblastemia	MAOI/LO/BLAS/TAOEM/YA	myelotherapy	MAOI/LO/THER/PI
myeloblastoma	MAOI/LO/BLAS/TOE/MA	myelotome	MAOI/LO/TOEM
myeloblastomatosis	MAOI/LO/BLAS/TOEM/TOE/SIS	myelotomography	MAOI/LO/TOE/MOG/FI
	MAOI/LO/BLA*S/MA/TOE/SIS	myelotomy	MAOI/LOT/M*I
myeloblastosis	MAOI/LO/BLAS/TOE/SIS	myelotoxic	MAOI/LO/TOX/IK
myelocele	MAOI/LO/SAO*EL	myelotoxicity	MAOI/LO/TOK/SIS/TI
myeloclast	MAOI/LO/KLA*S	myelotoxin	MAOI/LO/TOK/SIN
myelocyst	MAOI/LO/S*IS	myenteric	MAOI/SPWER/IK
myelocystic	MAOI/LO/S*IS/IK		MAOI/EN/TER/IK
myelocystocele	MAOI/LO/S*IS/SAO*EL	myenteron	MAOI/SPWRON
myelocystomeningocele	MAOI/LO/S*IS/ME/NING/SAO*EL		MAOI/SPWER/RON
myelocyte	MAOI/LO/SAO*IT		MAOI/ENT/RON
myelocythemia	MAOI/LO/SAOI/THAOEM/YA	myesthesia	MAOI/ES/THAOEZ/YA
myelocytic	MAOI/LO/SIT/IK	myiasis	MAOI/AOI/SIS
myelocytoma	MAOI/LO/SAOI/TOE/MA		MAOI/YAOI/SIS
myelocytomatosis	MAOI/LO/SAOI/TOEM/TOE/SIS	myiocephalon	MAOI/YO/SEF/LON
myelocytosis	MAOI/LO/SAOI/TOE/SIS	myiocephalum	MAOI/YO/SEF/LUM
myelodiastasis	MAOI/LO/DI/A*S/SIS	myiodesopsia	MAOI/YO/DES/OPS/YA
myelodysplasia	MAOI/LO/DIS/PLAIZ/YA	myitis	MAOI/AOITS
myeloencephalic	MAOI/LO/EN/SFAL/IK		MAOI/YAOITS
myeloencephalitis	MAOI/LO/EN/SEF/LAOITS	Mykrox	MAOI/KROX
myelofibrosis	MAOI/LO/FAOI/BROE/SIS	Mylanta	MAOI/LAN/TA
myelogenesis	MAOI/LO/JEN/SIS	Mylanta-II	MAOI/LAN/TA/2
myelogenetic	MAOI/LO/JE/NET/IK		MAOI/LAN/TA/IRBGS/*IRBGS
myelogenic	MAOI/LO/JEN/IK	Mylicon	MAOIL/KON
myelogenous	MAOI/LOJ/NOUS	Mylicon-80	MAOIL/KON/8/0
myelogeny	MAOI/LOJ/N*I	Mylicon-125	MAOIL/KON/125
myelogone	MAOI/LO/GOEN	mylohyoid	MAOI/LO/HAOI/OID
myelogonic	MAOI/LO/GOEN/IK	mylohyoideus	MAOIL/HAOI/OID/YUS
myelogonium	MAOI/LO/GON/YUM	mylopharyngeus	MAOIL/FRIN/JUS
myelogram	MAOI/LO/GRAM	myo-	MAOI
	MAOI/EL/GRAM		MAOI/YO
myelography	MAOI/LOG/FI	myoalbumin	MAOI/AL/BAOU/MIN
myeloic	MAOI/LOIK	myoarchitectonic	MAOI/ARK/TEK/TON/IK
	MAOI/LOE/IK	myoatrophy	see myatrophy
myeloid	MAOI/LOID	myoblast	MAOI/BLA*S
myeloidin	MAOI/LOI/DIN	myoblastic	MAOI/BLA*S/IK
myeloidosis	MAOI/LO/DOE/SIS	myoblastoma	MAOI/BLAS/TOE/MA
myelokentric	MAOI/LO/KEN/TRIK	myobradia	MAOI/BRAID/YA
myeloleukemia	MAOI/LO/LAOU/KAOEM/YA	myocardi(o)-	MAOI/KARD/Y(O)
myelolipoma	MAOI/LO/LI/POE/MA	myocardia	MAOI/KARD/YA

myocardiac	MAOI/KARD/YAK	myograph	MAOI/GRAF
myocardial	MAOI/KARD/YAL	myographic	MAOI/GRAFK
myocardiogram	MAOI/KARD/YO/GRAM	myography	MAOI/OG/FI
myocardiograph	MAOI/KARD/YO/GRAF	myohemoglobin	MAOI/HAOEM/GLOE/BIN
myocardiolysis	MAOI/KARD/YOL/SIS	myohypertrophia	MAOI/HAO*IP/TROEF/YA
myocardiopathy	MAOI/KARD/YOP/TH*I	myoid	MAOI/OID
myocardiorrhaphy	MAOI/KARD/YOR/FI	myoidema	MAOI/OI/DAOE/MA
myocardiosis	MAOI/KARD/YOE/SIS	myoideum	MAOI/OID/YUM
myocarditic	MAOI/KAR/DIT/IK	myo-inositol	MAOI/IN/OES/TOL
myocarditis	MAOI/KAR/DAOITS	myointimal	MAOI/SPWI/MAL
myocardium	MAOI/KARD/YUM		MAOI/INT/MAL
myocardosis	MAOI/KAR/DOE/SIS	myoischemia	MAOI/IS/KAOEM/YA
myocele	MAOI/SAO*EL	myokerosis	MAOI/KAOE/ROE/SIS
myocelialgia	MAOI/SAOEL/YAL/JA		MAOI/KE/ROE/SIS
myocelitis	MAOI/SE/LAOITS	myokinase	MAOI/KAOI/NAIS
myocellulitis	MAOI/SEL/YAOU/LAOITS	myokinesimeter	MAOI/KIN/SIM/TER
myocerosis	MAOI/SE/ROE/SIS	myokinesis	MAOI/KI/NAOE/SIS
myochorditis	MAOI/KHOR/DAOITS	myokinetic	MAOI/KI/NET/IK
	MAOI/KOER/DAOITS	myokinin	MAOI/KAOI/NIN
myochrome	MAOI/KROEM		MAOI/KIN/NIN
myochronoscope	MAOI/KRON/SKOEP	myokymia	MAOI/KIM/YA
Myochrysine	MAOI/KRAOI/SIN	myolemma	MAOI/LEM/MA
	MAOI/KRAOI/SAOEN	myolipoma	MAOI/LI/POE/MA
myocinesimeter	MAOI/SIN/SIM/TER	myologia	MAOI/LOE/JA
myoclonia	MAOI/KLOEN/YA	myologist	MAOI/O*LGS
myoclonic	MAOI/KLON/IK	myology	MAOI/OLG
myoclonica	MAOI/KLON/KA	myolysis	MAOI/OL/SIS
myoclonus	MAOI/OK/LO/NUS	myoma	MAOI/YOE/MA
	MAOI/KLOE/NUS	myomagenesis	MAOI/YOEM/JEN/SIS
myocolpitis	MAOI/KOL/PAOITS	myomalacia	MAOI/MA/LAI/SHA
myocomma	MAOI/KOM/MA	myomata	MAOI/YOEM/TA
myocommata	MAOI/KOM/TA	myomatosis	MAOI/YOEM/TOE/SIS
myocrismus	MAOI/KRIS/MUS	myomatous	MAOI/YOEM/TOUS
myocutaneous	MAOI/KAOU/TAIN/YOUS		MAOI/OEM/TOUS
myocyte	MAOI/SAO*IT	myomectomy	MAOI/MEKT/M*I
myocytolysis	MAOI/SAOI/TOL/SIS	myomelanosis	MAOI/MEL/NOE/SIS
myocytoma	MAOI/SAOI/TOE/MA	myomere	MAOI/MAOER
myodegeneration	MAOI/DE/JEN/RAIGS	myometer	MAOI/OM/TER
myodemia	MAOI/DAOEM/YA	myometrial	MAOI/MAOE/TRAL
myodermal	MAOI/DER/MAL		MAOI/MAOE/TRAOE/YAL
myodiastasis	MAOI/DI/A*S/SIS	myometritis	MAOI/MAOE/TRAOITS
myodiopter	MAOI/DI/OPT/ER		MAOI/ME/TRAOITS
myodynamia	MAOI/DAOI/NAIM/YA	myometrium	MAOI/MAOET/RUM
myodynamic	MAOI/DAOI/NAM/IK		MAOI/MAOE/TRAOE/UM
myodynamics	MAOI/DAOI/NAM/IK/-S	myomitochondria	MAOI/MAOIT/KON/DRA
myodynamometer	MAOI/DAOIN/MOM/TER		MAOI/MAOIT/KON/DRAOE/YA
myodynia	MAOI/DIN/YA	myomitochondrion	MAOI/MAOIT/KON/DRON
myodystonia	MAOI/DIS/TOEN/YA		MAOI/MAOIT/KON/DRAOE/YON
myodystony	MAOI/D*IS/N*I	myomotomy	MAOI/MOT/M*I
myodystrophia	MAOI/DIS/TROEF/YA	myon	MAOI/YON
myodystrophy	MAOI/DIS/TRO/FI	myonecrosis	MAOI/NE/KROE/SIS
myoedema	MAOI/DAOE/MA	myoneme	MAOI/NAOEM
	MAOI/E/DAOE/MA	myonephropexy	MAOI/NEF/RO/PEK/SI
myoelastic	MAOI/E/LA*S/IK	myoneural	MAOI/NAOURL
myoelectric	MAOI/LEK/TRIK	myoneuralgia	MAOI/NAOU/RAL/JA
myoelectrical	MAOI/LEK/TRI/KAL	myoneurasthenia	MAOI/NAOU/RAS/THAOEN/YA
myoendocarditis	MAOI/*END/KAR/DAOITS		MAOI/NAOUR/AS/THAOEN/YA
myoepithelial	MAOI/EP/THAOEL/YAL	myoneure	MAOI/NAOUR
myoepithelioid	MAOI/EP/THAOEL/YOID	myoneuroma	MAOI/NAOU/ROE/MA
myoepithelioma	MAOI/EP/THAOEL/YOE/MA	myonosus	MAOI/ON/SUS
myoepithelium	MAOI/EP/THAOEL/YUM		MAOI/YON/SUS
myofascial	MAOI/FARBL	myonymy	MAOI/ON/M*I
myofascitis	MAOI/FA/SAOITS		MAOI/YON/M*I
	MAOI/FAS/SAOITS	myopachynsis	MAOI/PA/KIN/SIS
myofibril	MAOI/FAOI/BRIL	myopalmus	MAOI/PAL/MUS
myofibrilla	MAOI/FAOI/BRIL/LA	myoparalysis	MAOI/PRAL/SIS
myofibrillae	MAOI/FAOI/BRIL/LAE	myoparesis	MAOI/PRAOE/SIS
myofibrillar	MAOI/FAOI/BRIL/LAR		MAOI/PAR/SIS
myofibroblast	MAOI/FAOI/BRO/BLA*S	myopathia	MAOI/PA*T/YA
myofibroma	MAOI/FAOI/BROE/MA	myopathic	MAOI/PA*T/IK
myofibrosis	MAOI/FAOI/BROE/SIS	myopathy	MAOI/OP/TH*I
myofibrositis	MAOI/FAOI/BRO/SAOITS	myopericarditis	MAOI/P*ER/KAR/DAOITS
myofilament	MAOI/FIL/-MT	myoperitonitis	MAOI/PERT/NAOITS
Myoflex	MAOI/FLEX	myophage	MAOI/FAIJ
myofunctional	MAOI/FUNGS/NAL	myophagism	MAOI/OF/JIFM
myogelosis	MAOI/JE/LOE/SIS	myophone	MAOI/FOEN
myogen	MAOI/JEN	myophosphorylase	MAOI/FOS/FOER/LAIS
myogenesis	MAOI/JEN/SIS	myopia	MAOI/OEP/YA
myogenetic	MAOI/JE/NET/IK	myopic	MAOI/OP/IK
myogenic	MAOI/JEN/IK		MAOI/OEP/IK
myogenous	MAOI/OJ/NOUS	myoplasm	MAOI/PLAFM
myoglia	MAOI/OG/LA	myoplastic	MAOI/PLA*S/IK
	MAOI/OG/LAOE/YA	myoplasty	MAOI/PLAS/TI
myoglobin	MAOI/GLOE/BIN	myopolar	MAOI/POE/LAR
myoglobinuria	MAOI/GLOEB/NAOUR/YA	myoprotein	MAOI/PRO/TAOEN
myoglobulin	MAOI/GLOB/LIN	myopsis	MAOI/OP/SIS
myoglobulinuria	MAOI/GLOB/LI/NAOUR/YA	myopsychic	MAOI/SAOIK/IK
myognathus	MAOI/OG/NA/THUS	myoreceptor	MAOI/RE/SEP/TOR
myogram	MAOI/GRAM	myorhythmia	MAOI/R*IT/MA

	MAOI/R*IT/MAOE/YA	myrinx	MIRNGS
myorrhaphy	MAOI/OR/FI		MIR/INGS
	MAOI/YOR/FI		MAOI/RINGS
myorrhexis	MAOI/REK/SIS	myristic	MI/R*IS/IK
myosalgia	MAOI/SAL/JA	myristica	MI/R*IS/KA
myosalpingitis	MAOI/SAL/PIN/JAOITS	myristicin	MI/R*IS/SIN
myosalpinx	MAOI/SAL/PINGS	myristoleic	MI/R*IS/LAOE/IK
myosarcoma	MAOI/SAR/KOE/MA	myrmecia	MIR/MAOES/YA
myosclerosis	MAOI/SKLE/ROE/SIS		MIR/MAOE/SHA
myoscope	MAOI/SKOEP	myrosinase	MAOI/ROES/NAIS
myoseism	MAOI/SAOIFM	myrrh	MIR
myoseptum	MAOI/SEP/TUM	Myrtus	MIR/TUS
myosin	MAOI/SIN	Mysoline	MAOIS/LAOEN
myosinogen	MAOI/SIN/JEN	mysophilia	MAOIS/FIL/YA
myosinose	MAOI/SI/NOES	mysophobia	MAOIS/FOEB/YA
	MAOI/SIN/OES	mysophobiac	MAOIS/FOEB/YAK
myosinuria	MAOI/SIN/YAOUR/YA	mysophobic	MAOIS/FOEB/IK
	MAOI/SI/NAOUR/YA	mystax	M*IS/TAX
myositic	MAOI/SIT/IK		(*not* MIS/TAX; see mistax)
myositis	MAOI/SAOITS	mystin	MIS/TIN
myospasia	MAOI/SPAIZ/YA	mytacism	MAOIT/SIFM
myospasm	MAOI/SPAFM	mythomania	M*IT/MAIN/YA
myospasmia	MAOI/SPAZ/MA	mythophobia	M*IT/FOEB/YA
	MAOI/SPAZ/MAOE/YA	Mytrex	MAOI/TREX
myospasmus	MAOI/SPAZ/MUS	myurous	MAOI/YAOUR/OUS
myospherulosis	MAOI/SFAOER/LOE/SIS	myx(o)-	MIX
	MAOI/SFAOER/YAOU/LOE/SIS		MIK/S(O)
myosthenic	MAOI/OS/THEN/IK	myxadenitis	MIK/SAD/NAOITS
myosthenometer	MAOI/STHE/NOM/TER		MIX/AD/NAOITS
	MAOI/STHEN/OM/TER	myxadenoma	MIK/SAD/NOE/MA
myostroma	MAOI/STROE/MA		MIX/AD/NOE/MA
myostromin	MAOI/STROE/MIN	myxangitis	MIK/SAN/JAOITS
myosuria	MAOI/SAOUR/YA		MIX/AN/JAOITS
myosuture	MAOI/SAOU/KHUR	myxasthenia	MIK/SAS/THAOEN/YA
myosynizesis	MAOI/SIN/ZAOE/SIS		MIX/AS/THAOEN/YA
myotactic	MAOI/TAKT/IK	myxedema	MIX/DAOE/MA
myotasis	MAOI/OT/SIS		MIX/E/DAOE/MA
	MAOI/YOT/SIS		MIK/SE/DAOE/MA
myotatic	MAOI/TAT/IK	myxedematoid	MIX/DEM/TOID
myotenositis	MAOI/TEN/SAOITS	myxedematous	MIX/DEM/TOUS
myotenotomy	MAOI/TE/NOT/M*I	myxemia	MIK/SAOEM/YA
myothermic	MAOI/THERM/IK	myxiosis	MIX/YOE/SIS
myotility	MAOI/TIL/TI	Myxobacterales	MIX/BAKT/RAI/LAOEZ
myotome	MAOI/TOEM	myxochondrofibrosarcoma	MIX/KON/DRO/FAOI/BRO/SAR/
myotomic	MAOI/TOM/IK		KOE/MA
myotomy	MAOI/OT/M*I	myxochondroma	MIX/KON/DROE/MA
myotone	MAOI/TOEN	myxochondrosarcoma	MIX/KON/DRO/SAR/KOE/MA
myotonia	MAOI/TOEN/YA	Myxococcaceae	MIX/KOK/KAIS/YAE
myotonic	MAOI/TON/IK	Myxococcidium	MIX/KOK/SID/YUM
Myotonachol	MAOI/TON/KOL	Myxococcus	MIX/KOK/KUS
myotonoid	MAOI/OT/NOID	myxocystitis	MIX/SIS/TAOITS
myotonometer	MAOI/TOE/NOM/TER	myxocystoma	MIX/SIS/TOE/MA
myotonus	MAOI/OT/NUS	myxocyte	MIX/SAO*IT
myotony	MAOI/OT/N*I	myxoenchondroma	MIX/EN/KON/DROE/MA
myotrophic	MAOI/TROFK	myxoendothelioma	MIX/*END/THAOEL/YOE/MA
Myotrol	MAOI/TROL	myxofibroma	MIX/FAOI/BROE/MA
myotrophy	MAOI/OT/RO/FI	myxofibrosarcoma	MIX/FAOI/BRO/SAR/KOE/MA
myotropic	MAOI/TROP/IK	myxoglioma	MIX/GLAOI/YOE/MA
myotube	MAOI/TAOUB	myxoglobulosis	MIX/GLOB/LOE/SIS
myotubular	MAOI/TAOUB/LAR	myxoid	MIK/SOID
myotubule	MAOI/TAOUB/YAOUL		MIX/OID
myovascular	MAOI/VAS/KLAR	myxolipoma	MIX/LI/POE/MA
Myoviridae	MAOI/VIR/DAE	myxoma	MIK/SOE/MA
myriachit	MIR/YAFP/IT	myxomatodes	MIK/SOEM/TOE/DAOEZ
	MIR/YAFP/KHIT	myxomatosis	MIK/SOEM/TOE/SIS
	MIR/YA/KHIT	myxomatous	MIK/SOEM/TOUS
myrica	MIR/KA	myxomembranous	MIX/MEM/BRA/NOUS
	MI/RAOI/KA	myxomycte	MIX/MAOI/SAOET
myricin	MIR/SIN	Myxomycetes	MIX/MAOI/SAOE/TAOEZ
myring(o)-	MIRNG	myxomyoma	MIX/MAOI/YOE/MA
	MIRN/G(O)	myxoneurosis	MIX/NAOU/ROE/SIS
	MI/RING	myxopapilloma	MIX/PAP/LOE/MA
	MI/RIN/G(O)	myxopoiesis	MIX/POI/SIS
	MIRN/J-	myxorrhea	MIX/RAOE/YA
myringa	MIRN/GA	myxosarcoma	MIX/SAR/KOE/MA
	MI/RIN/GA	myxosarcomatous	MIX/SAR/KOEM/TOUS
myringectomy	MIRN/JEKT/M*I	Myxospora	MIX/SPOR/RA
myringis	MIRN/JIS	myxospore	MIX/SPOER
	MI/RIN/JIS	Myxosporea	MIX/SPO/RAOE/YA
myringitis	MIRN/JAOITS		MIX/SPOE/RAOE/YA
myringodectomy	MIRNG/DEKT/M*I	Myxosporidia	MIX/SPRID/YA
myringodermatitis	MIRNG/DERM/TAOITS	myxovirus	MIX/VAOI/RUS
myringomycosis	MIRNG/MAOI/KOE/SIS	Myxozoa	MIX/ZOE/WA
myringoplasty	MIRNG/PLAS/TI	myzesis	MAOI/ZAOE/SIS
myringorupture	MIRNG/RUP/KHUR	Myzomyia	MAOIZ/MAOI/YA
myringostapediopexy	MIRNG/STA/PAOED/YO/PEK/SI	Myzorhynchus	MAOIZ/RIN/KUS
	MIRNG/STAI/PAOED/YO/PEK/SI		
myringotome	MIRNG/TOEM		
myringotomy	MIRN/GOT/M*I		

Na	N-RBGS/A*BGZ
nabidrox	NAB/DROX
nabilone	NAB/LOEN
Naboth	NAI/BO*ET
nabothian	NA/BO*ET/YAN
nacreous	NAI/KROUS
	NAIK/ROUS
nadide	NAI/DAOID
nadolol	NAID/LOL
Naegeli	NAEG/LAOE
	(*not* NAIG/LAOE; see Nagele)
Naegleria	NAI/GLAOER/YA
	NAE/GLAOER/YA
Nafcil	NAF/SIL
nafcillin	NAF/SLIN
	NAF/SIL/LIN
nafenopin	NA/FEN/PIN
Naffziger	NAF/ZIG/ER
nafomine	NAF/MAOEN
nafoxidine	NAF/OX/DAOEN
nafronyl	NAF/RO/NIL
naftifine	NAF/TI/FAOEN
	NAFT/FAOEN
Naftin Cream	NAF/TIN/KRAOEM
Nagel	NAG/EL
	NA/GEL
Nagele	NAIG/LAOE
Nageotte	NAJ/YOT
Nagler	NAG/LER
nail	NAIL
nailing	NAIL/-G
Nairobi	NAOI/ROE/BAOE
	NAOI/ROE/BI
naked	NAIK/-D
nalbuphine	NAL/BAOU/FAOEN
Naldecon	NALD/KON
	NAL/DE/KON
Naldecon CX	NALD/KON/KR-RBGS/KP*RBGS
Naldecon DX	NALD/KON/D-RBGS/KP*RBGS
Naldecon EX	NALD/KON/ERBGS/KP*RBGS
Naldecon Senior	NALD/KON/SAOEN/YOR
Nalfon	NAL/FON
nalidixate	NAL/DIK/SAIT
	NAL/DIX/AIT
nalidixic	NAL/DIX/IK
nalmexone	NAL/MEK/SOEN
	NAL/MEX/OEN
nalorphine	NAL/OR/FAOEN
naloxone	NAL/OK/SOEN
	NAL/OX/OEN
naltrexone	NAL/TREK/SOEN
	NAL/TREX/OEN
nana	NAI/NA
nandrolone	NAN/DRO/LOEN
nanism	NAN/IFM
	NAI/NIFM
Nannizzia	NA/NIZ/YA
nano-	NAN
	NAI/NO
nanocephalia	NAN/SFAIL/YA
nanocephalic	NAN/SFAL/IK
nanocephalous	NAN/SEF/LOUS
nanocephaly	NAN/SEF/LI
nanocormia	NAN/KORM/YA
nanocurie	NAN/KAOUR/RAOE
nanogram	NAN/GRAM
nanoid	NAN/OID
nanoliter	NAN/LAOET/ER
nanomelia	NAN/MAOEL/YA
nanomelous	NA/NOM/LOUS
	NAI/NOM/LOUS
nanomelus	NA/NOM/LUS
	NAI/NOM/LUS
nanometer	NAN/OM/TER
	NAN/MAOET/ER
	NAI/NO/MAOET/ER
nanophthalmia	NAN/OF/THAL/MA
	NAN/OF/THAL/MAOE/YA
nanophthalmos	NAN/OF/THAL/MOS
nanophthalmus	NAN/OF/THAL/MUS
nanoplankton	NAN/PLA*NG/TON
	NAN/PLANG/TON
nanosecond	NAN/SEKD
nanosoma	NAN/SOE/MA
nanosomia	NAN/SOEM/YA
nanosomus	NAN/SOE/MUS
nanounit	NAN/YAOUNT
nanous	NAI/NOUS
	NAIN/OUS
nanus	NAI/NUS
nape	NAIP
napex	NAI/PEX
naphazoline	NA/FAZ/LAOEN
	NAF/A*Z/LAOEN
	NAF/AZ/LAOEN
naphtalin	NAF/TA/LIN
naphtalinum	NAF/TA/LAOI/NUM
	NAF/TA/LAOIN/UM
naphtha	NAF/THA
naphthalene	NAF/THA/LAOEN
naphthalenol	NAF/THAL/NOL
naphthalin	NAF/THA/LIN
naphthalinic	NAF/THA/LIN/IK
naphthalinum	NAF/THA/LAOIN/UM
	NAF/THA/LAOI/NUM
naphthamine	NAF/THA/MAOEN
naphthazoline	NAF/THAZ/LAOEN
naphthol	NAF/THOL
naphtholate	NAF/THO/LAIT
naphtholism	NAF/THO/LIFM
naphtholum	NAF/THOE/LUM
naphthoquinone	NAF/THO/KWIN/OEN
naphthoresorcine	NAF/THO/RE/SOR/SIN
naphthyl	NAF/THIL
naphthylpararosaniline	NAF/THIL/PAR/ROE/SAN/LIN
naphthylthiouruea	NAF/THIL/THAOI/YAOU/RAOE/YA
naphtol	NAF/TOL
napier	NAIP/YER
napiform	NAIP/FORM
napkin	NAP/KIN
naprapathy	NA/PRAP/TH*I
Naprosyn	NAP/RO/SIN
naproxen	NA/PROK/SEN
	NA/PROK/SAOEN
naproxol	NA/PROK/SOL
	NA/PROX/OL
napsylate	NAPS/LAIT
	NAP/SI/LAIT
naranol	NAR/NOEL
	NAR/NOL
narasin	NAR/SIN
Narath	NA/RAT
	NA/RA*T
narc(o)-	NARK
	NAR/K(O)
Narcan	NAR/KAN
narceine	NARS/YAOEN
	NAR/SAOEN
narcissism	NARS/SIFM
narcissistic	NARS/S*IS/IK
narcoanalysis	NARK/ANL/SIS
narcodiagnosis	NARK/DAOIG/NOE/SIS
narcohypnia	NARK/HIP/NA
	NARK/HIP/NAOE/YA
narcohypnosis	NARK/HIP/NOE/SIS
narcolepsy	NARK/LEP/SI
narcoleptic	NARK/LEPT/IK
narcolocal	NARK/LOE/KAL
narcoma	NAR/KOE/MA
narcose	NAR/KOES
narcosi	NAR/KOE/SAOI
narcosine	NARK/SAOEN
narcosis	NAR/KOE/SIS
narcostimulant	NARK/STIM/LANT
narcosynthesis	NARK/S*INT/SIS
narcotherapy	NARK/THER/PI
narcotic	NAR/KOT/IK
narcotico-acrid	NAR/KOT/KO/AK/RID
narcotico-irritant	NAR/KOT/KO/IR/TANT
narcotine	NARK/TAOEN
narcotism	NARK/TIFM
narcotize	NARK/TAOIZ
narcous	NARK/OUS
Nardil	NAR/DIL
nares	NAIR/RAOEZ
	NAI/RAOEZ
naris	NAIR/RIS
	NAI/RIS
nas(o)-	NAIZ
	NAI/Z(O)
nasal	NAI/ZAL

	(not NAI/SAL; see NaSal)	naturopathic	NAIFP/RO/PA*T/IK
NaSal	NAI/SAL		NAI/KHUR/PA*T/IK
Nasalcrom	NAI/ZAL/KROEM	naturopathy	NAIFP/ROP/TH*I
nasales	NAI/ZAI/LAOEZ		NAI/KHUR/OP/TH*I
Nasalide	NAIZ/LAOID	Nauheim	NOU/HAOIM
nasalis	NAI/ZAI/LIS		NAU/HAOIM
nascent	NAS/ENT	naupathia	NAU/PA*T/YA
	NAI/SENT	nause-	NAUZ/Y-
	NAIS/ENT		NAUS/Y-
nasi	NAI/ZAOI		NAU/SH-
nasioiniac	NAIZ/YO/IN/YAK	nausea	NAUZ/YA
nasion	NAIZ/YON	nauseant	NAUZ/YANT
nasitis	NAI/ZAOITS	nauseate	NAUZ/YAIT
Nasmyth	NAS/M*IT	nauseated	NAUZ/YAIT/-D
nasoalveolar	NAIZ/AL/VAOE/LAR	nauseating	NAUZ/YAIT/-G
nasoantral	NAIZ/AN/TRAL	nauseous	NAUZ/YOUS
nasoantritis	NAIZ/AN/TRAOITS		NAURBS
nasoantrostomy	NAIZ/AN/TRO*S/M*I	Navane	NAV/AIN
nasobregmatic	NAIZ/BREG/MAT/IK	navel	NAI/VEL
nasobronchial	NAIZ/BRONG/YAL		NAIV/EL
nasociliary	NAIZ/SIL/YAIR		*(not* NAIVL; see naval)
nasofrontal	NAIZ/FRON/TAL	navicul-	NA/VIK/L-
nasogastric	NAIZ/GAS/TRIK		NA/VIK/YAOU/L-
nasograph	NAIZ/GRAF		NA/VIK/YU/L-
nasolabial	NAIZ/LAIB/YAL	navicula	NA/VIK/LA
nasolacrimal	NAIZ/LAK/RI/MAL	navicular	NA/VIK/LAR
nasolacrimalis	NAIZ/LAK/RI/MAI/LIS	naviculare	NA/VIK/LAI/RAOE
nasomanometer	NAIZ/MA/NOM/TER	navicularia	NA/VIK/LAIR/YA
naso-occipital	NAIZ/OK/SIP/TAL	navicularicuneiformia	NA/VIK/LAIR/KAOU/NAOE/
naso-oral	NAIZ/ORL		FORM/YA
nasopalatine	NAIZ/PAL/TAOIN		NA/VIK/LAI/RAOE/KAOU/NAOE/
	NAIZ/PAL/TAOEN		FORM/YA
nasopharyngeal	NAIZ/FRIN/JAL	navicularis	NA/VIK/LAI/RIS
nasopharyngitis	NAIZ/FARN/JAOITS	navicularthritis	NA/VIK/LAR/THRAOITS
nasopharyngolaryngoscope	NAIZ/FRING/LARNG/SKOEP	nealbarbital	NAOE/AL/BARB/TAL
nasopharyngoscope	NAIZ/FRING/SKOEP	Neapolitan	NAOE/POL/TAN
nasopharngoscopy	NAIZ/FARN/GOS/KPI	nearsighted	NAOER/SAOIGT/-D
nasopharynx	NAIZ/FARNGS	nearsightedness	NAOER/SAOIGT/D*NS
nasorostral	NAIZ/ROS/TRAL	nearthrosis	NAOE/AR/THROE/SIS
nasoscope	NAIZ/SKOEP	Nebcin	NEB/SIN
nasoseptal	NAIZ/SEP/TAL	Nebenthau	NAIB/EN/THAU
nasoseptitis	NAIZ/SEP/TAOITS		NEB/EN/THAU
nasosinusitis	NAIZ/SAOIN/SAOITS	nebramycin	NEB/RA/MAOI/SIN
nasospinale	NAIZ/SPAOI/NAI/LAOE	nebul-	NEB/L-
nasoturbinal	NAIZ/TURB/NAL		NEB/YAOU/L-
nasus	NAI/ZUS		NEB/YU/L-
nat-	NAI/T-	nebula	NEB/LA
	NAIT	nebulae	NEB/LAE
Natabec Kapseals	NAIT/BEK/KAP/SAOEL/-S	nebularine	NEB/LAI/RIN
	NAT/BEK/KAP/SAOEL/-S		NEB/LAIR/RIN
natal	NAI/TAL	nebulization	NEB/LI/ZAIGS
Natal	NA/TAL	nebulize	NEB/LAOIZ
Natalins	NAIT/LINZ	nebulizer	NEB/LAOIZ/ER
	NAIT/LIN/-S	nebulous	NEB/LOUS
natality	NAI/TAL/TI	NebuPent	NEB/PENT
natamycin	NAIT/MAOI/SIN		NEB/YAOU/PENT
	NAT/MAOI/SIN	Necator	NAOE/KAI/TOR
nates	NAI/TAOEZ	necatoriasis	NAOE/KAIT/RAOI/SIS
natiforme	NAIT/FOR/MAOE	necatrix	NAOEK/TRIX
	NAT/FOR/MAOE		NEK/TRIX
natimortality	NAIT/MOR/TAL/TI	necessitatis	NE/SES/TAI/TIS
National Formulary	NAGS/NAL/FORM/LAIR	necessity	NES/TI
natis	NAI/TIS		NE/SES/TI
native	NAIT/IV		NE/SESZ/TI
-natologist	NAI/TO*LGS	neck	NEK
-natology	NAI/TOLG	necklace	NEK/LAS
natremia	NAI/TRAOEM/YA	necr(o)-	NEK/R(O)
	NA/TRAOEM/YA	necrectomy	NE/KREKT/M*I
natrexone	NA/TREK/SOEN		NEK/REKT/M*I
	NA/TREX/OEN	necrencephalus	NEK/REN/SEF/LUS
natriemia	NAI/TRAOE/AOEM/YA	necrobiosis	NEK/RO/BAO*I/YOE/SIS
natriferic	NAI/TRIF/RIK	necrobiotic	NEK/RO/BAO*I/OT/IK
natrium	NAI/TRUM		NEK/RO/BAO*I/YOT/IK
	NAI/TRAOE/UM	necrocytosis	NEK/RO/SAOI/TOE/SIS
natriuresis	NAI/TRAOE/YAOU/RAOE/SIS	necrocytotoxin	NEK/RO/SAOIT/TOK/SIN
natriuretic	NAI/TRAOE/YAOU/RET/IK	necrogenic	NEK/RO/JEN/IK
natron	NAI/TRON	necrogenous	NE/KROJ/NOUS
natrum	NAI/TRUM	necrogranulomatous	NEK/RO/GRAN/LOEM/TOUS
natruresis	NAI/TRAOU/RAOE/SIS	necrologist	NE/KRO*LGS
	NAT/RAOU/RAOE/SIS	necrology	NE/KROLG
natruretic	NAI/TRAOU/RET/IK	necrolysis	NE/KROL/SIS
	NAT/RAOU/RET/IK	necromania	NEK/RO/MAIN/YA
natural	NAFP/RAL	necrometer	NE/KROM/TER
	NAFP	necromimesis	NEK/RO/MAOI/MAOE/SIS
Nature's Remedy	NAI/KHUR/AOES/REM/DI		NEK/RO/MI/MAOE/SIS
Naturetin Tablets	NAIFP/RAOE/TIN/TAB/LET/-S	necronectomy	NEK/RO/NEKT/M*I
	NAFP/RAOE/TIN/TAB/LET/-S	necronodular	NEK/RO/NOD/LAR
naturopath	NAI/KHUR/PA*T	necroparasite	NEK/RO/PAR/SAOIT
	NAIFP/RO/PA*T	necropathy	NE/KROP/TH*I

necrophagous	NE/KROF/GOUS	Nembutal	NEM/BAOU/TAL
necrophilia	NEK/RO/FIL/YA	nemeses	NEM/SAOEZ
necrophilic	NEK/RO/FIL/IK	nemesis	NEM/SIS
necrophilism	NE/KROF/LIFM	nemic	NEM/IK
necrophilous	NE/KROF/LOUS	neo-	NAOE
necrophobia	NEK/RO/FOEB/YA		NAOE/YO
necrophorum	NE/KROF/RUM	neoantigen	NAOE/A*ENT/JEN
necrophorus	NE/KROF/RUS	neoarsphenamine	NAOE/AR/SFEN/MAOEN
necropsy	NEK/ROP/SI	neobiogenesis	NAOE/BAO*I.JEN/SIS
necrosadism	NEK/RO/SAI/DIFM	neoblastic	NAOE/BLA*S/IK
	NEK/RO/SAID/IFM	Neo-Calglucon	NAOE/KAL/GLAOU/KON
necroscopy	NE/KROS/KPI	neocerebellum	NAOE/SER/BEL/UM
necrose	NE/KROES	neochymotrypsinogen	NAOE/KAOIM/TRIP/SIN/JEN
	NE/KROEZ	neocinchophen	NAOE/SIN/KO/FEN
	NEK/ROES	neocinetic	NAOE/SI/NET/IK
necroses	NE/KROE/SAOEZ	neocortex	NAOE/KOR/TEX
necrosin	NEK/RO/SIN	neocystostomy	NAOE/SIS/TO*S/M*I
necrosis	NE/KROE/SIS	neocytosis	NAOE/SAOI/TOE/SIS
necrospermia	NEK/RO/SPERM/YA	neodarwinism	NAOE/DAR/WIN/IFM
necrospermic	NEK/RO/SPERM/IK	Neodecadron	NAOE/DEK/DRON
necrosteon	NE/KRO*S/YON	neodiathermy	NAOE/DAOI/THER/M*I
necrosteosis	NE/KRO*S/YOE/SIS	neodymium	NAOE/DIM/YUM
necrotic	NE/KROT/IK	neoencephalon	*see* neencephalon
necrotica	NE/KROT/KA	neofetal	NAOE/FAOE/TAL
necroticans	NE/KROT/KANZ	neofetus	NAOE/FAOE/TUS
necrotizing	NEK/RO/TAOIZ/-G	neoformans	NAOE/FOR/MANZ
necrotomy	NE/KROT/M*I	neoformation	NAOE/FOR/MAIGS
necrotoxin	NEK/RO/TOK/SIN	neoformative	NAOE/FORM/TIV
needle	NAOED/-L	neogala	NAOE/OG/LA
needless	NAOED/LES	neogenesis	NAOE/JEN/SIS
needling	NAOED/-LG	neogenetic	NAOE/JE/NET/IK
Neelsen	NAOEL/SEN	neoglottic	NAOE/GLOT/IK
neencephalon	NAOE/EN/SEF/LON	neoglottis	NAOE/GLOT/TIS
nefopam	NEF/PAM	neoglycogenesis	NAOE/GLAOIK/JEN/SIS
negation	NE/GAIGS	neohymen	NAOE/HAOIM/-N
negative	NEG/TIV	neokinetic	NAOE/KI/NET/IK
negative G	NEG/TIV/G-RBGS	neolalia	NAOE/LAIL/YA
negative S	NEG/TIVS-RBGS	neolalism	NAOE/LAL/IFM
negativism	NEG/TIV/IFM	neologism	NAOE/OL/JIFM
negativistic	NEG/TIV/*IS/IK		NAOE/LOE/JIFM
negatron	NEG/TRON	Neoloid	NAOE/LOID
NegGram	NEG/GRAM	neomembrane	NAOE/MEM/BRAIN
Negre	NAI/GRAI	neomorph	NAOE/MOR/-F
Negri	NAI/GRAOE	neomorphism	NAOE/MOR/FIFM
Negro	NAI/GROE	neomycin	NAOE/MAOI/SIN
	NAOE/GROE	neon	NAOE/YON
neighborwise	NAIB/WAO*IZ	neonatal	NAOE/NAI/TAL
	NAI/BOR/WAO*IZ	neonate	NAOE/NAIT
Neisser	NAOI/SER	neonatologist	NAOE/NAI/TO*LGS
	NAOIS/SER	neonatology	NAOE/NAI/TOLG
	(*not* NAOIS/ER; **see** nicer)	neonatorum	NAOE/NAI/TOR/UM
neisseria	NAOI/SAOER/YA		NAOE/NAI/TOER/UM
Neisseria	K-P/NAOI/SAOER/YA	neopallium	NAOE/PAL/YUM
neisseriae	NAOI/SAOER/YAE	neopathy	NAOE/OP/TH*I
Neisseriaceae	NAOI/SAOER/YAIS/YAE	neophobia	NAOE/FOEB/YA
neisserial	NAOI/SAOERL	neophrenia	NAOE/FREN/YA
	NAOI/SAOER/YAL	neoplasia	NAOE/PLAIZ/YA
neisseriology	NAOI/SAOER/YOLG	neoplasm	NAOE/PLAFM
nekton	NEK/TON	neoplastic	NAOE/PLA*S/IK
Nelaton	NAI/LA/TAU	neoplastigenic	NAOE/PLA*S/JEN/IK
	NAI/LA/TON	Neopsylla	NAOE/OPS/LA
	NAIL/TAU		NAOE/OP/SIL/LA
	NEL/TAU	neoptrin	NAOE/OP/TRIN
Nelson	NEL/SON	neopyrithiamin	NAOE/PIR/THAOI/MIN
nem	NEM	neoquassin	NAOE/KWAS/SIN
nema	NAOE/MA	neoretinene B	NAOE/RET/NAOEN/B-RBGS
nemathelminth	NEM/THEL/M*INT	Neorickettsia	NAOE/RI/KETS/YA
Nemathelminthes	NEM/THEL/MIN/THAOEZ	Neosar	NAOE/SAR
nemathelminthiasis	NEM/THEL/MIN/THAOI/SIS	Neosporin	NAOE/SPORN
nematization	NEM/TI/ZAIGS	Neosporin Cream	NAOE/SPORN/KRAOEM
nemato-	NEM/TO	Neosporin Ointment	NAOE/SPORN/OINT/-MT
nematoblast	NEM/TO/BLA*S	Neosporin Ophthalmic	NAOE/SPORN/OF/THAL/MIK/
Nematocera	NEM/TOS/RA	Ointment	OINT/-MT
nematocidal	NEM/TO/SAOI/DAL	Neosporin Ophthalmic	NAOE/SPORN/OF/THAL/MIK/
nematocide	NEM/TO/SAO*ID	Solution	SLAOUGS
	NE/MAT/SAO*ID	neostibosan	NAOE/STAOIB/SAN
nematocyst	NEM/TO/S*IS	neostigmine	NAOE/STIG/MAOEN
Nematoda	NEM/TOE/DA		NAOE/STIG/MIN
nematode	NEM/TOED	neostomy	NAOE/O*S/M*I
nematodiasis	NEM/TO/DAOI/SIS	neostriatum	NAOE/STRAOI/AI/TUM
Nematodirella	NEM/TO/DI/REL/LA		NAOE/STRAOI/YAI/TUM
	NAOEM/TO/DI/REL/LA	neostrophingic	NAOE/STROE/FIN/JIK
Nematodirus	NEM/TOED/RUS	Neo-Synalar Cream	NAOE/SIN/LAR/KRAOEM
nematoid	NEM/TOID	Neo-Synephrine	NAOE/SNEF/RIN
nematologist	NEM/TO*LGS		NAOE/SI/NEF/RIN
nematology	NEM/TOLG	neoteny	NAOE/OT/N*I
Nematomorpha	NEM/TO/MOR/FA	neothalamus	NAOE/THAL/MUS
nematosis	NEM/TOE/SIS	Neothylline	NAOE/THIL/LIN
nematospermia	NEM/TO/SPERM/YA	Neotoma	NAOE/OT/MA

neotropicalis	NAOE/TROP/KAI/LIS	nephropyeloplasty	NEF/RO/PAOI/LO/PLAS/TI
neotype	NAOE/TAOIP	nephropyosis	NEF/RO/PAOI/YOE/SIS
neotyrosine	NAOE/TAOIR/SAOEN	nephrorrhagia	NEF/RO/RAI/JA
neovascularization	NAOE/VAS/KLAR/ZAIGS	nephrorrhaphy	NEF/ROR/FI
nepenthic	NAOE/P*ENT/IK	nephrosclerosis	NEF/RO/SKLE/ROE/SIS
	NE/P*ENT/IK	nephrosclerotic	NEF/RO/SKLE/ROT/IK
neper	NEP/ER	nephroscope	NEF/RO/SKOEP
nephelo-	NEF/LO	nephroscopy	NE/FROS/KPI
nephelometer	NEF/LOM/TER	nephroses	NE/FROE/SAOEZ
nephelometry	NEF/LOM/TRI	nephrosis	NE/FROE/SIS
nephelopia	NEF/LOEP/YA	nephrosonephritis	NE/FROES/NE/FRAOITS
nephr(o)-	NEF/R(O)	nephrosonography	NEF/RO/SOE/NOG/FI
	NE/FR(O)	nephrospasia	NEF/RO/SPAIZ/YA
nephradenoma	NEF/RAD/NOE/MA	nephrosplenopexy	NEF/RO/SPLAOEN/PEK/SI
nephralgia	NE/FRAL/JA		NEF/RO/SPLEN/PEK/SI
	NEF/RAL/JA	nephrostoma	NE/FRO*S/MA
nephralgic	NE/FRAL/JIK	nephrostome	NEF/RO/STOEM
	NEF/RAL/JIK	nephrostomy	NE/FRO*S/M*I
nephrapostasis	NEF/RA/PO*S/SIS	nephrotic	NEF/ROT/IK
nephratonia	NEF/RA/TOEN/YA		NE/FROT/IK
nephrectasia	NEF/REK/TAIZ/YA	nephrotome	NEF/RO/TOEM
nephrectasis	NE/FREKT/SIS	nephrotomogram	NEF/RO/TOEM/GRAM
nephrectomize	NE/FREKT/MAOIZ	nephrotomography	NEF/RO/TOE/MOG/FI
nephrectomized	NE/FREKT/MAOIZ/-D	nephrotomy	NE/FROT/M*I
nephrectomy	NE/FREKT/M*I	nephrotoxic	NEF/RO/TOX/IK
nephredema	NEF/RE/DAOE/MA	nephrotoxicity	NEF/RO/TOK/SIS/TI
nephrelcosis	NEF/REL/KOE/SIS	nephrotoxin	NEF/RO/TOK/SIN
nephremia	NE/FRAOEM/YA	nephrotresis	NEF/RO/TRAOE/SIS
nephric	NEF/RIK	nephrotrophic	NEF/RO/TROFK
nephridia	NE/FRID/YA	nephrotropic	NEF/RO/TROP/IK
nephridium	NE/FRID/YUM	nephrotuberculosis	NEF/RO/TAOU/BERK/LOE/SIS
nephritic	NE/FRIT/IK	nephroureterectomy	NEF/RO/YAOU/RAOET/REKT/M*I
nephritides	NE/FRIT/DAOEZ		NEF/RO/YAOUR/TER/EKT/M*I
nephritis	NE/FRAOITS	nephroureterocystectomy	NEF/RO/YAOU/RAOET/RO/SIS/
nephritogenic	NE/FRIT/JEN/IK		TEKT/M*I
	NEF/RI/TO/JEN/IK	nephrozymase	NEF/RO/ZAOI/MAIS
nephroabdominal	NEF/RO/AB/DOM/NAL	nephrozymosis	NEF/RO/ZAOI/MOE/SIS
nephroangiosclerosis	NEF/RO/AN/JO/SKLE/ROE/SIS	Nephrox Suspension	NEF/ROX/SUS/PENGS
nephroblastema	NEF/RO/BLAS/TAOE/MA	nepiology	NEP/YOLG
nephroblastoma	NEF/RO/BLAS/TOE/MA	Neptazane	NAPT/ZAIN
nephrocalcinosis	NEF/RO/KALS/NOE/SIS		NEP/TA/ZAIN
Nephrocaps	NEF/RO/KAP/-S	neptunium	NEP/TAOUN/YUM
nephrocapsectomy	NEF/RO/KAP/SEKT/M*I	Nerium oleander	NAOER/YUM/OEL/YAND/ER
nephrocardiac	NEF/RO/KARD/YAK	neriine	NAOER/YAOEN
nephrocele	NEF/RO/SAO*EL	nerval	NER/VAL
nephrocolic	NEF/RO/KOL/IK	nerve	NEFRB
nephrocolopexy	NEF/RO/KOEL/PEK/SI	nervi	NER/VAOI
nephrocoloptosis	NEF/RO/KO/LOP/TOE/SIS	nervi-	NEFRB
nephrocystanastomosis	NEF/RO/S*IS/NA*S/MOE/SIS		NER/VI
nephrocystitis	NEF/RO/SIS/TAOITS	nervimotility	NEFRB/MOE/TIL/TI
nephrocystosis	NEF/RO/SIS/TOE/SIS	nervimotion	NEFRB/MOEGS
nephroerysipelas	NEF/RO/*ER/SIP/LAS	nervimotor	NEFRB/MOE/TOR
nephrogastric	NEF/RO/GAS/TRIK	nervimuscular	NEFRB/MUS/KLAR
nephrogenetic	NEF/RO/JE/NET/IK	nervine	NER/VAOIN
nephrogenic	NEF/RO/JEN/IK	nervi recurrens	NER/VAOI/RE/KURNZ
nephrogenous	NE/FROJ/NOUS	nervone	NER/VOEN
nephrogram	NEF/RO/GRAM	nervonic	NER/VON/IK
nephrography	NE/FROG/FI	nervorum	NER/VOR/UM
nephrohemia	NEF/RO/HAOEM/YA		NER/VOER/UM
nephrohydrosis	NEF/RO/HAOI/DROE/SIS	nervosa	NER/VOE/SA
nephrohypertrophy	NEF/RO/HAOI/PERT/FI	nervosism	NEFRB/SIFM
nephroid	NEF/ROID	nervous	NEFRB/OUS
nephrolith	NEF/RO/L*IT		NER/VOUS
nephrolithiasis	NEF/RO/LI/THAOI/SIS	nervous breakdown	NEFRB/OUS/BRAEK/DO*UN
nephrolithotomy	NEF/RO/LI/THOT/M*I		NER/VOUS/BRAEK/DO*UN
nephrologist	NE/FRO*LGS	nervousness	NEFRB/OUS/*NS
nephrology	NE/FROLG		NER/VOUS/*NS
nephrolysin	NE/FROL/SIN	nervus	NER/VUS
nephrolysis	NE/FROL/SIS	Nesacaine	NES/KAIN
nephrolytic	NEF/RO/LIT/IK	nesidi(o)-	NE/SID/Y(O)
nephroma	NE/FROE/MA	nesidiectomy	NE/SID/YEKT/M*I
nephromalacia	NEF/RO/MA/LAI/SHA	nesidioblast	NE/SID/YO/BLA*S
nephromegaly	NEF/RO/MEG/LI	nesidioblastoma	NE/SID/YO/BLAS/TOE/MA
nephromere	NEF/RO/MAOER	nesidioblastosis	NE/SID/YO/BLAS/TOE/SIS
nephron	NEF/RON	Nessler	NES/LER
nephronophthisis	NEF/RON/OF/THI/SIS	nesslerization	NES/LER/ZAIGS
nephroparalysis	NEF/RO/PRAL/SIS	nesslerize	NES/LER/AOIZ
nephropathia	NEF/RO/PA*T/YA	nest	N*ES
nephropathic	NEF/RO/PA*T/IK	Nestabs	NES/TAB/-S
nephropathy	NE/FROP/TH*I	nesteostomy	N*ES/YO*S/M*I
nephropexy	NEF/RO/PEK/SI	nestotherapy	N*ES/THER/PI
nephrophthisis	NEF/ROF/THI/SIS		NES/TO/THER/PI
	NE/FROF/THI/SIS	net	NET
nephropoietic	NEF/RO/POIT/IK	nethalide	N*ET/LAOID
nephroptosia	NEF/ROP/TOEZ/YA	netilmicin	NET/IL/MAOI/SIN
nephroptosis	NEF/ROP/TOE/SIS	Netromycin	NET/RO/MAOI/SIN
nephropyelitis	NEF/RO/PAOI/LAOITS	nettle	NET/-L
nephropyelography	NEF/RO/PAOI/LOG/FI	network	NET/WORK
nephropyelolithotomy	NEF/RO/PAOI/LO/LI/THOT/M*I	Neubauer	NOI/BOU/ER

	NAOU/BOU/ER	neuroamebiasis	NAOUR/AM/BAOI/SIS
Neuber	NOI/BER	neuroanastomosis	NAOUR/AI/NA*S/MOE/SIS
	NAOU/BER	neuroanatomy	NAOUR/AI/NAT/M*I
Neuberg	NOI/BERG	neuroarthropathy	NAOUR/AR/THROP/TH*I
	NAOU/BERG	neuroastrocytoma	NAOUR/AS/TRO/SAOI/TOE/MA
Neucalm	NAOU/KAUM	neuroaugmentation	NAOUR/AUG/MEN/TAIGS
Neufeld	NAOU/FELD	neuroaugmentive	NAOUR/AUG/-MT/IV
	NOI/FELD		NAOUR/AUG/MEN/TIV
Neumann	NOI/MAN	neurobehavioral	NAOUR/BE/HAIV/YORL
	NAO*U/MAN		NAOUR/BHAIV/YORL
	(not NAOU/MAN; see knew man)	neurobiologist	NAOUR/BAO*I/O*LGS
neur(o)-	NAOUR	neurobiology	NAOUR/BAOI/OLG
	NAOU/R(O)	neurobiotaxis	NAOUR/BAO*I/TAK/SIS
neurad	NAOU/AD	neuroblast	NAOUR/BLA*S
neuragmia	NAOU/RAG/MA	neuroblastoma	NAOUR/BLAS/TOE/MA
	NAOU/RAG/MAOE/YA	neurocanal	NAOUR/KA/NAL
neural	NAOURL	neurocardiac	NAOUR/KARD/YAK
neuralgia	NAOU/RAL/JA	neurocele	NAOUR/SAO*EL
	NAOUR/AL/JA	neurocentral	NAOUR/SEN/TRAL
neuralgic	NAOU/RAL/JIK		NAOUR/STRAL
	NAOUR/AL/JIK	neurocentrum	NAOUR/SEN/TRUM
neuralgiform	NAOU/RAL/JI/FORM	neuroceptor	NAOUR/SEP/TOR
	NAOUR/AL/JI/FORM	neurochemistry	NAOUR/KEM/STRI
neuramebimeter	NAOUR/AM/BIM/TER	neurochitin	NAOUR/KAOI/TIN
neuraminic	NAOUR/MIN/IK	Neurochol	NAOUR/KOL
neuraminidase	NAOUR/MIN/DAIS	neurochondrite	NAOUR/KON/DRAOIT
neuranagenesis	NAOUR/AN/JEN/SIS	neurochorioretinitis	NAOUR/KOER/YO/RET/NAOITS
neurapophysis	NAOUR/POF/SIS	neurochoroiditis	NAOUR/KOE/ROI/DAOITS
neurapraxia	NAOUR/PRAX/YA	neurocirculatory	NAOUR/SIRK/LA/TOIR
neurarchy	NAOUR/AR/KI	neurocladism	NAOU/ROK/LA/DIFM
neurasthenia	NAOUR/AS/THAOEN/YA	neuroclonic	NAOUR/KLON/IK
neurastheniac	NAOUR/AS/THAOEN/YAK	neurocommunications	NAOUR/KMAOUN/KAIGS/-S
neurasthenic	NAOUR/AS/THEN/IK	neurocranial	NAOUR/KRAIN/YAL
neurasthenica	NAOUR/AS/THEN/KA	neurocranium	NAOUR/KRAIN/YUM
neuratrophia	NAOUR/TROEF/YA	neurocrine	NAOUR/KRIN
neuratrophic	NAOUR/TROFK	neurocrinia	NAOUR/KRIN/YA
neuratrophy	NAOU/RAT/RO/FI	neurocristopathy	NAOUR/KRIS/TOP/TH*I
	NAOU/AT/RO/FI	neurocutaneous	NAOUR/KAOU/TAIN/YOUS
neuraxial	NAOUR/AX/YAL	neurocyte	NAOUR/SAO*IT
	NAOU/RAX/YAL	neurocytology	NAOUR/SAOI/TOLG
neuraxis	NAOU/RAK/SIS	neurocytolysin	NAOUR/SAOI/TOL/SIN
	NAOUR/AK/SIS	neurocytolysis	NAOUR/SAOI/TOL/SIS
neuraxon	NAOU/RAK/SON	neurocytoma	NAOUR/SAOI/TOE/MA
	NAOUR/AK/SON	neurodealgia	NAOU/ROED/YAL/JA
neuraxonal	NAOUR/AK/SONL	neurodeatrophia	NAOU/ROED/YA/TROEF/YA
	NAOUR/AK/SON/NAL	neurodegenerative	NAOUR/DE/JEN/RA/TIV
neuraxone	NAOU/RAK/SOEN	neurodendrite	NAOUR/DEN/DRAOIT
	NAOUR/AK/SOEN	neurodendron	NAOUR/DEN/DRON
neure	NAO*UR	neuroderm	NAOUR/DERM
neurectasia	NAOU/REK/TAIZ/YA	neurodermatica	NAOUR/DER/MAT/KA
	NAOUR/EK/TAIZ/YA	neurodermatitis	NAOUR/DERM/TAOITS
neurectasis	NAOU/REKT/SIS	neurodermatosis	NAOUR/DERM/TOE/SIS
	NAOUR/EKT/SIS	neurodiagnosis	NAOUR/DAOIG/NOE/SIS
neurectomy	NAOU/REKT/M*I	neurodynamic	NAOUR/DAOI/NAM/IK
	NAOUR/EKT/M*I	neurodynia	NAOUR/DIN/YA
neurectopia	NAOUR/EK/TOEP/YA	neuroectoderm	NAOUR/EKT/DERM
	NAOU/REK/TOEP/YA	neuroectodermal	NAOUR/EKT/DER/MAL
neurectopy	NAOUR/EKT/PI	neuroeffector	NAOUR/E/FEK/TOR
	NAOU/REKT/PI	neuroelectricity	NAOUR/LEK/TRIS/TI
neurenteric	NAOUR/SPWER/IK	neuroelectrotherapeutics	NAOUR/LEK/TRO/THER/PAOUT/IK/-S
neurepithelial	NAOUR/EP/THAOEL/YAL		
neurepithelium	NAOUR/EP/THAOEL/YUM	neuroencephalomyelopathy	NAOUR/EN/SEF/LO/MAOI/LOP/TH*I
neurergic	NAOU/RERJ/IK		
	NAOUR/ERJ/IK	neuroendocrine	NAOUR/*END/KRIN
neurexeresis	NAOUR/EK/SER/SIS	neuroendocrinology	NAOUR/*END/KRI/NOLG
neuriatria	NAOUR/YAT/RA	neuroepidermal	NAOUR/EP/DER/MAL
	NAOUR/YAT/RAOE/YA	neuroepithelial	NAOUR/EP/THAOEL/YAL
neuriatry	NAOU/RAOI/TRI	neuroepithelioma	NAOUR/EP/THAOEL/YOE/MA
neuridine	NAOUR/DAOEN	neuroepithelium	NAOUR/EP/THAOEL/YUM
neurilemma	NAOUR/LEM/MA	neurofibril	NAOUR/FAOI/BRIL
neurilemmal	NAOUR/LEM/MAL	neurofibrilla	NAOUR/FAOI/BRIL/LA
neurilemmitis	NAOUR/LEM/MAOITS	neurofibrillae	NAOUR/FAOI/BRIL/LAE
neurilemoma	NAOUR/LAOE/MOE/MA	neurofibrillar	NAOUR/FAOI/BRIL/LAR
	NAOUR/LE/MOE/MA	neurofibroma	NAOUR/FAOI/BROE/MA
neurility	NAOU/RIL/TI	neurofibromatosis	NAOUR/FAOI/BROEM/TOE/SIS
neurimotility	NAOUR/MOE/TIL/TI	neurofilament	NAOUR/FIL/-MT
neurimotor	NAOUR/MOE/TOR	neurogangliitis	NAOUR/GANG/LAOITS
neurine	NAOUR/AOEN	neuroganglion	NAOUR/GANG/LON
	NAOUR/RIN	neurogastric	NAOUR/GAS/TRIK
neurinoma	NAOUR/NOE/MA	neurogen	NAOUR/JEN
neurit	NAOUR/RIT	neurogenesis	NAOUR/JEN/SIS
neurite	NAOUR/AOIT	neurogenetic	NAOUR/JE/NET/IK
neuritic	NAOU/RIT/IK	neurogenic	NAOUR/JEN/IK
neuritides	NAOU/RIT/DAOEZ	neurogenous	NAOU/ROJ/NOUS
neuritis	NAOU/RAOITS	neurogli(o)-	NAOU/ROG/L(O)
neuriticum	NAOU/RIT/KUM		NAOU/ROG/LAOE/Y(O)
neuro-	NAOUR		NAOUR/GLAOI
	NAOU/RO		NAOUR/GLAOI/Y(O)
neuroallergy	NAOUR/AL/ER/JI	neuroglia	NAOU/ROG/LA

neurogliacyte	NAOU/ROG/LA/SAO*IT	neuronevus	NAOUR/NAOE/VUS
neuroglial	NAOU/ROG/LAL	neuronic	NAOUR/RON/IK
neurogliar	NAOU/ROG/LAR	neuronin	NAOUR/NIN
neurogliocyte	NAOU/ROG/LO/SAO*IT	neuronitis	NAOUR/NAOITS
neurogliocytoma	NAOU/ROG/LO/SAOI/TOE/MA	neuronopathy	NAOUR/NOP/TH*I
neuroglioma	NAOU/ROG/LOE/MA	neuronophage	NAOU/RON/FAIJ
	NAOUR/GLAOI/YOE/MA	neuronophagia	NAOU/RON/FAI/JA
neurogliomatosis	NAOU/ROG/LOEM/TOE/SIS	neuronophagy	NAOUR/NOF/JI
	NAOUR/GLAOI/YOEM/TOE/SIS	neuronosis	NAOUR/NOE/SIS
neurogliosis	NAOU/ROG/LOE/SIS	neuronotropic	NAOU/RON/TROP/IK
neuroglycopenia	NAOUR/GLAOIK/PAOEN/YA		NAOU/RON/TROEP/IK
neurogram	NAOUR/GRAM	neuronyxis	NAOUR/NIK/SIS
neurography	NAOU/ROG/FI	neuronymy	NAOU/RON/M*I
neurohemal	NAOUR/HAOE/MAL	neuro-oncology	NAOUR/ON/KOLG
neurohistology	NAOUR/HIS/TOLG	neuro-ophthalmology	NAOUR/OF/THAL/MOLG
neurohormonal	NAOUR/HOR/MOENL	neuro-otology	NAOUR/O/TOLG
neurohormone	NAOUR/HOR/MOEN	neuropacemaker	NAOUR/PAIS/MAIK/ER
neurohumor	NAOUR/HAOU/MOR	neuropapillitis	NAOUR/PAP/LAOITS
neurohumoral	NAOUR/HAOUM/RAL	neuroparalysis	NAOUR/PRAL/SIS
neurohypnologist	NAOUR/HIP/NO*LGS	neuroparalytic	NAOUR/PAR/LIT/IK
neurohypnology	NAOUR/HIP/NOLG	neuropath	NAOUR/PA*T
neurohypophysectomy	NAOUR/HAOI/POF/SEKT/M*I	neuropathic	NAOUR/PA*T/IK
neurohypophysial	NAOUR/HO*IP/FIZ/YAL	neuropathogenesis	NAOUR/PA*T/JEN/SIS
neurohypophysis	NAOUR/HAOI/POF/SIS	neuropathogenicity	NAOUR/PA*T/JE/NIS/TI
neuroid	NAOUR/OID	neuropathology	NAOUR/PA/THOLG
	NAOU/ROID	neuropathy	NAOU/ROP/TH*I
neuroimmunologic	NAOUR/IM/NO/LOJ/IK	neuropeptide	NAOUR/PEP/TAOID
neuroimmunology	NAOUR/IM/NOLG	neuropharmacological	NAOUR/FARM/KO/LOJ/KAL
neuroinduction	NAOUR/IN/D*UBGS	neuropharmacology	NAOUR/FARM/KOLG
neuroinidia	NAOUR/IN/ID/YA	neurophilic	NAOUR/FIL/IK
	NAOUR/NID/YA	neurophonia	NAOUR/FOEN/YA
neurokeratin	NAOUR/KER/TIN	neurophthisis	NAOU/ROF/THI/SIS
neurolabyrinthitis	NAOUR/LAB/RIN/THAOITS	neurophysin	NAOUR/FAOI/SIN
neuroleptanalgesia	NAOUR/LEP/TANL/JAOEZ/YA	neurophysiology	NAOUR/FIZ/YOLG
	NAOUR/LEPT/ANL/JAOEZ/YA	neuropil	NAOUR/PIL
neuroleptanalgesic	NAOUR/LEP/TANL/JAOEZ/IK	neuropile	NAOUR/PAOIL
	NAOUR/LEPT/ANL/JAOEZ/IK	neuropilem	NAOUR/PAOIL/EM
neuroleptanesthesia	NAOUR/LEP/TANS/THAOEZ/YA		NAOUR/PAOI/LEM
	NAOUR/LEPT/ANS/THAOEZ/YA	neuroplasm	NAOUR/PLAFM
neuroleptanesthetic	NAOUR/LEP/TANS/THET/IK	neuroplasmic	NAOUR/PLAZ/MIK
	NAOUR/LEPT/ANS/THET/IK	neuroplasty	NAOUR/PLAS/TI
neuroleptic	NAOUR/LEPT/IK	neuroplegic	NAOUR/PLAOEJ/IK
neurolinguistics	NAOUR/LING/W*IS/IK/-S	neuroplexus	NAOUR/PLEK/SUS
neurolipomatosis	NAOUR/LI/POEM/TOE/SIS	neuropodia	NAOUR/POED/YA
neurologic	NAOUR/LOJ/IK	neuropodion	NAOUR/POED/YON
neurological	NAOUR/LOJ/KAL	neuropodium	NAOUR/POED/YUM
neurologically	NAOUR/LOJ/KLI	neuropore	NAOUR/POER
neurologist	NAOU/RO*LGS	neuropotential	NAOUR/POE/TEN/-RBL
	NAOUR/O*LGS	neuroprobasia	NAOUR/PRO/BAIS/YA
neurology	NAOU/ROLG	neuropsychiatrist	NAOUR/SAOI/KAOI/TR*IS
	NAOUR/OLG	neuropsychiatry	NAOUR/SAOI/KAOI/TRI
neurolymph	NAOUR/LIM/-F	neuropsychic	NAOUR/SAOIK/IK
neurolymphomatosis	NAOUR/LIM/FOEM/TOE/SIS	neuropsychologic	NAOUR/SAOIK/LOJ/IK
neurolysin	NAOU/ROL/SIN	neuropsychological	NAOUR/SAOIK/LOJ/KAL
neurolysis	NAOU/ROL/SIS	neuropsychology	NAOUR/SAOI/KOLG
neurolytic	NAOUR/LIT/IK	neuropsychopathic	NAOUR/SAOIK/PA*T/IK
neuroma	NAOU/ROE/MA	neuropsychopathy	NAOUR/SAOI/KOP/TH*I
neuromalacia	NAOUR/MA/LAI/SHA	neuropsychopharmacology	NAOUR/SAOIK/FARM/KOLG
neuromast	NAOUR/MA*S	neuroradiology	NAOUR/RAID/YOLG
neuromatosa	NAOU/ROEM/TOE/SA	neurorecidive	NAOUR/RES/DAOEV
	NAOU/ROE/MA/TOE/SA	neurorecurrence	NAOUR/RE/KURNS
neuromatosis	NAOU/ROEM/TOE/SIS	neurorelapse	NAOUR/RE/LAPS
	NAOUR/MA/TOE/SIS	neuroretinitis	NAOUR/RET/NAOITS
neuromatous	NAOU/ROEM/TOUS	neuroretinopathy	NAOUR/RET/NOP/TH*I
neuromechanism	NAOUR/MEK/NIFM	neuroentgenography	NAOUR/RENT/GEN/OG/FI
neuromelanin	NAOUR/MEL/NIN	neurorrhaphy	NAOU/ROR/FI
neuromeningeal	NAOUR/ME/NIN/JAL		NAOUR/OR/FI
neuromere	NAOUR/MAOER	Neurorrhyctes	NAOUR/RIK/TAOEZ/
neuromimesis	NAOUR/MI/MAOE/SIS	hydrophobiae	HAOI/DRO/FOEB/YAE
	NAOUR/MAOI/MAOE/SIS	neurosarcocleisis	NAOUR/SARK/KLAOI/SIS
neuromimetic	NAOUR/MI/MET/IK	neurosarcoidosis	NAOUR/SAR/KOI/DOE/SIS
	NAOUR/MAOI/MET/IK	neurosarcoma	NAOUR/SAR/KOE/MA
neuromittor	NAOUR/MIT/TOR	neuroschwannoma	NAOUR/SWAN/NOE/MA
neuromuscular	NAOUR/MUS/KLAR		NAOUR/SH-/WAN/NOE/MA
neuromyasthenia	NAOUR/MAOI/AS/THAOEN/YA	neuroscience	NAOUR/SAOINS
neuromyelitis	NAOUR/MAOI/LAOITS	neuroscientist	NAOUR/SAOIN/T*IS
neuromyopathic	NAOUR/MAOI/PA*T/IK	neurosclerosis	NAOUR/SKLE/ROE/SIS
neuromyopathy	NAOUR/MAOI/OP/TH*I	neurosecretion	NAOUR/SE/KRAOEGS
neuromyositis	NAOUR/MAOI/SAOITS	neurosecretory	NAOUR/SE/KRAOET/RI
neuron	NAOU/RON	neurosegmental	NAOUR/SEG/MEN/TAL
neuronagenesis	NAOU/RON/JEN/SIS	neurosensory	NAOUR/SENS/RI
	NAOU/ROEN/JEN/SIS	neuroses	NAOU/ROE/SAOEZ
neuronal	NAOUR/NAL	neurosis	NAOU/ROE/SIS
	NAOU/RONL	neuroskeletal	NAOUR/SKEL/TAL
	NAOU/ROENL	neurosome	NAOUR/SOEM
neuronatrophy	NAOU/RON/AT/RO/FI	neurospasm	NAOUR/SPAFM
neurone	NAOUR/OEN	neurosplanchnic	NAOUR/SPLANG/NIK
	NAOU/ROEN	neurospongioma	NAOUR/SPON/JOE/MA
neuronephric	NAOUR/NEF/RIK	neurospongium	NAOUR/SPON/JUM

Neurospora	NAOU/ROS/PRA	neutrino	NAOU/TRAOE/NOE
neurostatus	NAOUR/STAT/TUS	neutroclusion	NAOU/TRO/KLAOUGS
neurosthenia	NAOUR/STHAOEN/YA	neutrocyte	NAOU/TRO/SAO*IT
neurostimulator	NAOUR/STIM/LAI/TOR	neutrocytopenia	NAOU/TRO/SAOIT/PAOEN/YA
neurosurgeon	NAOUR/SUR/JON	neutrocytosis	NAOU/TRO/SAOI/TOE/SIS
neurosurgery	NAOUR/SURJ/RI	neutroflavine	NAOU/TRO/FLAIVN
	NAOUR/S-RJ	neutron	NAOU/TRON
neurosuture	NAOUR/SAOU/KHUR	neutropenia	NAOU/TRO/PAOEN/YA
neurosyphilis	NAOUR/SIF/LIS	neutropenic	NAOU/TRO/PAOEN/IK
neurotabes	NAOUR/TAI/BAOEZ	neutrophil	NAOU/TRO/FIL
neurotagma	NAOUR/TAG/MA	neutrophile	NAOU/TRO/FAOIL
neurotendinous	NAOUR/TEND/NOUS	neutrophilia	NAOU/TRO/FIL/YA
neurotensin	NAOUR/TEN/SIN	neutrophilic	NAOU/TRO/FIL/IK
neurotension	NAOUR/TENGS	neutrophilopenia	NAOUR/TRO/FIL/PAOEN/YA
neuroterminal	NAOUR/TERM/NAL	neutrophilous	NAOU/TROF/LOUS
neurothekeoma	NAOUR/THAOEK/YOE/MA	neutrotaxis	NAOU/TRO/TAK/SIS
neurothele	NAOUR/THAOEL	nev(o)-	NAOEV
	NAOUR/THAOE/LAOE		NAOE/V(O)
neurotherapeutics	NAOUR/THER/PAOUT/IK/-S	nevi	NAOE/VAOI
neurotherapy	NAOUR/THER/PI	nevocarcinoma	NAOEV/KARS/NOE/MA
neurothlipsia	NAOUR/TLIPS/YA	nevocyte	NAOEV/SAO*IT
	NAOUR/TH/-LIPS/YA	nevocytic	NAOEV/SIT/IK
neurothlipsis	NAOUR/TLIP/SIS	nevoid	NAOE/VOID
	NAOUR/TH/-LIP/SIS	nevolipoma	NAOEV/LI/POE/MA
neurotic	NAOU/ROT/IK	nevose	NAOE/VOES
neurotica	NAOU/ROT/KA	nevous	NAOEV/OUS
neuroticism	NAOU/ROT/SIFM		NAOE/VOUS
neurotigenic	NAOU/ROT/JEN/IK	nevoxanthoendothelioma	NAOEV/ZANT/*END/THAOEL/
neurotization	NAOU/ROT/ZAIGS		YOE/MA
	NAOUR/TI/ZAIGS		NAOEV/ZAN/THO/*END/THAOEL/
neurotize	NAOUR/TAOIZ		YOE/MA
neurotmesis	NAOUR/OT/MAOE/SIS	nevus	NAOE/VUS
	NAOU/ROT/MAOE/SIS	newborn	NU/BORN
neurotome	NAOUR/TOEM		NAOU/BORN
neurotomography	NAOUR/TOE/MOG/FI	Newcastle	NAOU/KAS/-L
neurotomy	NAOU/ROT/M*I		NAOU/KA*S/-L
neurotonia	NAOUR/TOEN/YA		(not NU/KAS/-L)
neurotonic	NAOUR/TON/IK	newton	NAOU/TON
neurotonometer	NAOUR/TOE/NOM/TER	Newton	K-P/NAOU/TON
neurotony	NAOU/ROT/N*I	newtonian	NAOU/TOEN/YAN
neurotoxia	NAOUR/TOX/YA	newton-meter	NAOU/TON/MAOET/ER
neurotoxic	NAOUR/TOX/IK	nexin	NEK/SIN
neurotoxicity	NAOUR/TOK/SIS/TI	nexus	NEK/SUS
neurotoxin	NAOUR/TOK/SIN	Nia-Bid	NAOI/BID
neurotransducer	NAOUR/TRA*NS/DAOUS/ER	Niacels	NAO/SELS
neurotransmission	NAOUR/TRA*NS/MIGS		NAOI/SEL/-S
neurotransmitter	NAOUR/TRA*NS/MIT/ER	niacin	NAOI/SIN
neurotrauma	NAOUR/TRAU/MA	niacinamide	NAOI/SIN/AM/AOID
neurotripsy	NAOUR/TRIP/SI	Niagra	NAOI/AG/RA
neurotrophasthenia	NAOUR/TROEF/AS/THAOEN/YA	nialamide	NAOI/AL/MAOID
	NAOUR/TROE/FAS/THAOEN/YA	Niaplus	NAOI/PLUS
neurotrophic	NAOUR/TROFK	nib	N*IB
neurotrophy	NAOU/ROT/RO/FI		(not NIB; see anybody)
neurotropic	NAOUR/TROP/IK	nibble	NIBL
neurotropism	NAOU/ROT/RO/PIFM	niccolum	NIK/LUM
neurotropy	NAOU/ROT/RO/PI	niche	NIFP
neurotrosis	NAOUR/TROE/SIS		NIRB
neurotubule	NAOUR/TAOUB/YAOUL	nick	NIK
neurovaccine	NAOUR/VAK/SAOEN	nickel	NIK/EL
neurovaricosis	NAOUR/VAIR/KOE/SIS	nicking	NIK/-G
	NAOUR/VAR/KOE/SIS	Niclocide	NIK/LO/SAO*ID
neurovaricosity	NAOUR/VAIR/KOS/TI	Nicobid	NIK/BID
	NAOUR/VAR/KOS/TI	Nicol	NIK/OL
neurovariola	NAOUR/VA/RAOI/LA	Nicolar	NIK/LAR
neurovascular	NAOUR/VAS/KLAR	Nicolas	NIK/LAS
neurovegetative	NAOUR/VEJ/TAIT/IV	Nicolle	NI/KOL
neurovirulence	NAOUR/VIR/LENS	Nicorette	NIK/RET
neurovirulent	NAOUR/VIR/LENT	Nicotiana	NI/KOERB/YA/NA
neurovirus	NAOUR/VAOI/RUS		NI/KOERB/YAN/NA
neurovisceral	NAOUR/VIS/RAL	nicotinamide	NIK/TIN/MAOID
neurul-	NAOUR/L-	nicotinamidemia	NIK/TIN/AM/DAOEM/YA
	NAOUR/YAOU/L-	nicotinate	NIK/TIN/AIT
	NAOUR/YU/L-		NIK/TAOEN/AIT
neurula	NAOUR/LA	nicotine	NIK/TAOEN
neurulae	NAOUR/LAE	nicotinehydroxamic	NIK/TAOEN/HAOI/DROK/SAM/IK
neurulation	NAOUR/LAIGS	Nicotinex	NIK/TIN/EX
neururgic	NAOU/RURJ/IK	nicotinic	NIK/TIN/IK
Neusser	NOI/SER	nicotinism	NIK/TIN/IFM
	NAOU/SER	nicotinolytic	NIK/TIN/LIT/IK
	NAOUS/SER	nicotinomimetic	NIK/TIN/MI/MET/IK
neutr(o)-	NAOU/TR(O)		NIK/TIN/MAOI/MET/IK
neutral	NAOU/TRAL	nicotinyl	NIK/TIN/IL
neutralism	NAOU/TRAL/IFM	nicoumalone	NI/KAOUM/LOEN
neutrality	NAOU/TRAL/TI	nictation	NIK/TAIGS
neutralization	NAOU/TRAL/ZAIGS	nictitate	NIKT/TAIT
neutralize	NAOU/TRAL/AOIZ		NIK/TI/TAIT
Neutra-Phos	NAOU/TRA/FOS	nictitation	NIKT/TAIGS
Neutra-Phos-K	NAOU/TRA/FOS/K-RBGS		NIK/TI/TAIGS
neutretto	NAOU/TRET/TOE	nidal	NAOI/DAL

nidation	NAOI/DAIGS	nitrite	NAOI/TRAOIT
nidi	NAOI/DAOI	nitritoid	NAOI/TRI/TOID
nidulans	NID/YAOU/LANZ	nitrituria	NAOI/TRI/TAOUR/YA
	NID/YU/LANZ	nitro-anisol	NAOI/TRO/AN/SOL
nidus	NAOI/DUS	Nitrobacter	NAOI/TRO/BAK/TER
Niemann	NAOE/MAN	Nitrobacteraceae	NAOI/TRO/BAKT/RAIS/YAE
Niewenglowski	NAI/VEN/GLOV/SKAOE	nitrobacteria	NAOI/TRO/BAK/TAOER/YA
nifedipine	NI/FED/PAOEN	nitrobacterium	NAOI/TRO/BAK/TAOERM
	NAOI/FED/PAOEN	nitrobenzene	NAOI/TRO/BEN/ZAOEN
nifenazone	NI/FEN/ZOEN	nitrobenzol	NAOI/TRO/BEN/ZOL
Niferex	NAOIF/REX	Nitro-Bid	NAOI/TRO/BID
nifuradene	NAOI/FAOUR/DAOEN	nitrocellulose	NAOI/TRO/SEL/YAOU/LOES
nifuraldezone	NAOI/FAOUR/ALD/ZOEN	nitrochloroform	NAOI/TRO/KLOR/FORM
	NAOI/FAOU/RALD/ZOEN	nitrocycline	NAOI/TRO/SAOI/KLAOEN
nifuratel	NAOI/FAOUR/TEL	Nitrocystis	NAOI/TRO/SIS/TIS
nifuratrone	NAOI/FAOUR/TROEN	Nitrodisc	NAOI/TRO/DIS/-K
nifurdazil	NAOI/FAOURD/ZIL	Nitro-Dur	NAOI/TRO/DUR
nifurimide	NAOI/FAOUR/MAOID	nitrofuran	NAOI/TRO/FAOU/RAN
nifuroxime	NAOI/FAOU/ROK/SAOEM	nitrofurantoin	NAOU/TRO/FAOU/RAN/TOIN
	NAOI/FAOUR/OK/SAOEM		NAOU/TRO/FAOU/RANT/WIN
niger	NAOI/GER	nitrofurazone	NAOU/TRO/FAOUR/ZOEN
nigerose	NAOIJ/ROES	Nitrogard Buccal Tablets	NAOI/TRO/GARD/BUK/KAL/TAB/
	NAOI/JER/OES		LET/-S
Night Cast Regular	NAOIGT/KA*S/REG	nitrogen	NAOI/TRO/JEN
	NAOIGT/KA*S/REG/LAR	nitrogenase	NAOI/TRO/JEN/AIS
nightguard	NAOIGT/GARD		NAOI/TRO/JE/NAIS
nightmare	NAOIGT/MAIR		NAOI/TROJ/NAIS
nightshade	NAOIGT/SHAID	nitrogenization	NAOI/TRO/JEN/ZAIGS
night-terrors	NAOIGT/TER/ROR/-S	nitrogenous	NAOI/TROJ/NOUS
nigra	NAOI/GRA	nitroglycerin	NAOI/TRO/GLIS/RIN
nigral	NAOI/GRAL	Nitroglyn	NAOI/TRO/GLIN
nigricans	NAOI/GRI/KANZ	nitrohydrochloric	NAOI/TRO/HAOI/DRO/KLOR/IK
nigrities	NAOI/GRIRB/AOEZ	Nitrol Ointment	NAOI/TROL/OINT/-MT
nigroid	NAOI/GROID	Nitrolingual	NAOI/TRO/LING/WAL
nigrosin	NAOI/GRO/SIN	nitromannitol	NAOI/TRO/MAN/TOL
nigrosine	NAOI/GRO/SAOEN	nitromersol	NAOI/TRO/MER/SOL
Nigrospora	NAOI/GROS/PRA	nitrometer	NAOI/TROM/TER
nigrostriatal	NAOI/GRO/STRAOI/AI/TAL	nitromethane	NAOI/TRO/M*ET/AIN
	NAOI/GRO/STRAOI/YAI/TAL	nitromifene	NAOI/TROEM/FAOEN
nigrum	NAOI/GRUM	nitron	NAOI/TRON
nihilism	NAOI/LIFM	nitrophenylsulfenyl	NAOI/TRO/FENL/SUL/FENL
nihilistic	NAOI/L*IS/IK		NAOI/TRO/FENL/SUL/FEN/IL
nikethamide	NI/K*ET/MAOID	nitronaphthalene	NAOI/TRO/NAF/THA/LAOEN
Nikiforoff	NIK/FOR/AUF	Nitrong	NAOI/TRONG
Nikolsky	NI/KOL/SKI	nitrophenol	NAOI/TRO/FAOE/NOL
Nile	NAOIL	Nitropress	NAOI/TRO/PRESZ
Nilstat	NIL/STAT	nitropropiol	NAOI/TRO/PROEP/YOL
Nimotop Capsules	NIM/TOP/KAP/SAOUL/-S	nitroprotein	NAOI/TRO/PRO/TAOEN
ninhydrin	NIN/HAOI/DRIN	nitroprusside	NAOI/TRO/PRUS/AOID
niobium	NAOI/OEB/YUM		NAOI/TRO/PRUS/SAOID
	NAOI/YOEB/YUM	nitrosaccharose	NAOI/TRO/SAK/ROES
niphablepsia	NIF/BLEPS/YA	nitrosamine	NAOI/TROES/AM/AOEN
niphotyphlosis	NIF/TIF/LOE/SIS		NAOI/TROES/AM/MAOEN
nipple	NIP/-L		NAOI/TROES/AM/MIN
Nipride	NAOI/PRAOID	nitrosate	NAOI/TRO/SAIT
	NIP/RID	nitrosation	NAOI/TRO/SAIGS
niridazole	NAOI/RID/ZOEL	nitrose	NAOI/TROES
	NI/RID/ZOEL	nitrosification	NAOI/TROES/FI/KAIGS
nisin	NAO*I/SIN	nitrosifying	NAOI/TROES/FI/-G
nisobamate	NAOIS/BAM/AIT	nitroso-	NAOI/TROES
nisoxetine	NAOI/SOX/TAOEN		NAOI/TROE/SO
	NI/SOX/TAOEN	nitrosobacteria	NAOI/TROES/BAK/TAOER/YA
Nissl	NIS/-L	nitrosobacterium	NAOI/TROES/BAK/TAOERM
nisterime	NAOI/STAOER/AOEM	Nitrosococcus	NAOI/TROES/KOK/KUS
nisus	NAOI/SUS	Nitrosocystis	NAOI/TROES/SIS/TIS
nit	NIT	Nitrosogloea	NAOI/TROES/GLAOE/YA
Nitabuch	NAOET/BAOUK	nitroso-indol	NAOI/TROES/IN/DOL
	NIT/BAOUK	Nitrosomonas	NAOI/TROES/MOE/NAS
nitans	NAOI/TANZ	Nitrosospira	NAOI/TROES/SPAOI/RA
nitens	NAOI/TENZ	Nitrospan	NAOI/TRO/SPAN
niter	NAOI/TER	nitrososubstitution	NAOI/TROES/SUB/STAOUGS
	NAOIT/ER		NAOI/TROES/STUGS
niton	NAOI/TON	nitrosourea	NAOI/TROES/YAOU/RAOE/YA
nitr(o)-	NAOI/TR(O)	Nitrostat	NAOI/TRO/STAT
nitramine	NAOI/TRAM/MIN	nitrosugar	NAOI/TRO/SHUG/AR
nitras	NAOI/TRAS	nitrosyl	NAOI/TRO/SIL
nitratase	NAOI/TRA/TAIS	nitrous	NAOI/TROUS
nitrate	NAOI/TRAIT	nitrous oxide	NAOI/TROUS/OK/SAOID
nitrazepam	NAOI/TRAZ/PAM		NAOI/TROUS/OX/AOID
nitremia	NAOI/TRAOEM/YA	nitroxanthic	NAOI/TRO/ZAN/THIK
nitric	NAOI/TRIK		NAOI/TRO/ZANT/IK
nitridation	NAOI/TRI/DAIGS	nitroxoline	NAOI/TROX/LAOEN
nitride	NAOI/TRAOID	nitroxyl	NAOI/TROK/SIL
nitrification	NAOI/TRIF/KAIGS	nitryl	NAOI/TR*IL
nitrifier	NAOI/TRI/FI/ER	niveau	NAOE/VOE
nitrilase	NAOI/TRIL/AIS	Nix 1% Creme Rinse	NIX/1/P-KT/KRAO*EM/RINS
	NAOI/TRI/LAIS	nizatidine	NI/ZAT/DAOEN
nitrile	NAOI/TRIL	Nizoral	NAOI/ZORL
nitrimuriatic	NAOI/TRI/MAOUR/YAT/IK	Nobel	NOE/BEL

nobelium	NOE/BEL/YUM
	NOE/BAOEL/YUM
noble	NOEBL
Noble	K-P/NOEBL
Nocard	NOE/KARD
nocardia	NOE/KARD/YA
Nocardia	K-P/NOE/KARD/YA
Nocardiaceae	NOE/KARD/YAIS/YAE
nocardiae	NOE/KARD/YAE
nocardial	NOE/KARD/YAL
nocardiasis	NOE/KAR/DAOI/SIS
nocardin	NOE/KAR/DIN
nocardioform	NOE/KARD/YO/FORM
nocardiosis	NOE/KARD/YOE/SIS
noci-	NOES
	NOE/SI
nociassociation	NOES/SOERBGS
	NOES/AI/SOERB/YAIGS
nociceptive	NOES/SEPT/IV
nociceptor	NOES/SEP/TOR
nocifensor	NOES/FEN/SOR
noci-influence	NOES/IN/FLAOUNS
nociperception	NOES/PER/SEPGS
nocodazole	NOE/KOED/ZOEL
noctalbuminuria	NOK/TAL/BAOUM/NAOUR/YA
	NOKT/AL/BAOUM/NAOUR/YA
noctambulation	NOK/TAM/BLAIGS
	NOKT/AM/BLAIGS
noctambulic	NOK/TAM/BAOUL/IK
	NOKT/AM/BAOUL/IK
noctiphobia	NOKT/FOEB/YA
nocturia	NOK/TAOUR/YA
nocturna	NOK/TUR/NA
nocturnal	NOK/TURNL
nocturnus	NOK/TUR/NUS
nodal	NOE/DAL
node	NOED
nodi	NOE/DAOI
nodosa	NOE/DOE/SA
nodose	NOE/DOES
nodositas	NOE/DOS/TAS
nodosity	NOE/DOS/TI
nodosum	NOE/DOE/SUM
	NOE/DOES/UM
nodosus	NOE/DOE/SUS
nodous	NOED/OUS
	NOE/DOUS
No Doz	NO/DOEZ
	NOE/DOEZ
nodul-	NOD/L-
	NOD/YAOU/L-
	NOD/YU/L-
	NOJ/L-
nodular	NOD/LAR
nodularis	NOD/LAI/RIS
nodulate	NOD/LAIT
nodulated	NOD/LAIT/-D
nodulation	NOD/LAIGS
nodule	NOD/YAOUL
noduli	NOD/LAOI
nodulous	NOD/LOUS
nodulus	NOD/LUS
nodus	NOE/DUS
noematic	NOE/MAT/IK
	NOI/MAT/IK
	NOE/E/MAT/IK
noesis	NOE/E/SIS
	NOI/SIS
noetic	NOE/ET/IK
noeud vital	NAOU/VAOE/TAL
nogalamycin	NOE/GAL/MAOI/SIN
Noguchi	NOE/GAOU/KHAOE
Noguchia	NOE/GAOUFP/YA
noise	NOIZ
Nolahist	NOEL/H*IS
	NOE/LA/H*IS
Nolamine	NOEL/MAOEN
	NOE/LA/MAOEN
Nolex	NOE/LEX
noli-me-tangere	NOE/LAOI/MAOE/TAN/JE/RAOE
	NOE/LAOI/MAOE/TANG/RAOE
nolinium	NOE/LIN/YUM
Noludar	NOL/YAOU/DAR
	NOL/YU/DAR
Nolvadex	NOL/VA/DEX
noma	NOEM/MA
nomadic	NOE/MAD/IK
nomatophobia	NOEM/TO/FOEB/YA
nomenclature	NOEM/KLAI/KHUR

	NOE/MEN/KLAI/KHUR
	NOEM/EN/KLAI/KHUR
	NOE/MEN/KLA/KHUR
nomifensine	NOEM/FEN/SAOEN
Nomina Anatomica	NOM/NA/AN/TOM/KA
	NOEM/NA/AN/TOM/KA
nominal	NOM/NAL
nomogenesis	NOEM/JEN/SIS
nomogram	NOM/GRAM
	NOEM/GRAM
nomograph	NOM/GRAF
	NOEM/GRAF
nomography	NOE/MOG/FI
nomothetic	NOM/THET/IK
	NOEM/THET/IK
nomotopic	NOEM/TOP/IK
non-	NON
nona-	NOE/NA
	(not NOEN; see known)
nonadherent	NON/AD/HAOERNT
nonan	NOE/NAN
nonanedioic	NOE/NAIN/DI/OIK
nonanoic	NON/NOIK
	NON/NOE/IK
nonantigenic	NON/A*ENT/JEN/IK
nonapeptide	NOE/NA/PEP/TAOID
nonatopic	NON/AI/TOP/IK
nonbacterial	NON/BAK/TAOERL
nonbursate	NON/BUR/SAIT
noncariogenic	NON/KAIR/YO/JEN/IK
noncellular	NON/SEL/YAOU/LAR
non compos mentis	NON/KOM/POS/MEN/TIS
nonconductor	NON/KON/DUK/TOR
	NON/KUKT/TOR
nondepolarizer	NON/DE/POEL/RAOIZ/ER
nondisease	NON/DI/SAOEZ
	NON/D-Z
nondisjunction	NON/DIS/JUNGS
nonelectrolyte	NON/LEK/TRO/LAOIT
nonexpansional	NON/EX/PANGS/NAL
nonfluent	NON/FLAOUNT
nonheme	NON/HAOEM
nonhomogeneity	NON/HOEM/JE/NAOE/TI
	NON/HOEM/JE/NAI/TI
nongoitrous	NON/GOI/TROUS
noni-	NOE/NI
nonigravida	NOE/NI/GRAV/DA
nonimmune	NON/IM/MAOUN
noninfectious	NON/IN/FEK/-RBS
noninflammatory	NON/IN/FLAM/TOIR
noninvasive	NON/IN/VAIS/IV
noninvolution	NON/IN/VO/LAOUGS
	NON/IN/VOE/LAOUGS
nonipara	NOE/NIP/RA
nonketotic	NON/KAOE/TOT/IK
nonlamellated	NON/LAM/LAIT/-D
nonmedullated	NON/MED/LAIT/-D
nonmetal	NON/MET/TAL
nonmyelinated	NON/MAOI/LIN/AIT/-D
	NON/MAOI/LI/NAIT/-D
Nonne	NON/NAOE
non-neoplastic	NON/NAOE/PLA*S/IK
non-neuronal	NON/NAOU/RONL
	NON/NAOU/ROENL
	NON/NAOUR/NAL
non-nucleated	NON/NAOUK/LAIT/-D
nonocclusion	NON/O/KLAOUGS
	NON/KLAOUGS
nonolfactory	NON/OL/FAKT/RI
nonoliguric	NON/OL/GAOUR/IK
nononcogenic	NON/ON/KO/JEN/IK
nonopaque	NON/O/PAIK
nonose	NON/OES
nonparous	NON/PAR/OUS
nonpenetrance	NON/PEN/TRANS
nonphotochromogen	NON/FOET/KROEM/JEN
nonpitting	NON/PIT/-G
nonpolar	NON/POE/LAR
nonproprietary	NON/PRO/PRAOI/TAIR
nonrachitic	NON/RA/KIT/IK
nonradiable	NON/RAID/YABL
nonreflex	NON/RE/FLEX
nonreset	NON/RE/SET

nonreset nodus
  sinuatrialis
	NON/RE/SET/NOE/DUS/SAOIN/
	  AI/TRAI/LIS

nonrespiratory	NON/RES/PRA/TOIR
nonrotation	NON/ROE/TAIGS
nonsecretor	NON/SE/KRAOE/TOR
nonseptate	NON/SEP/TAIT

nonsister	NON/S*IS/ER	normokalemic	NORM/KA/LAOEM/IK
	NON/SIS/TER		NORM/KLAOEM/IK
nonspecific	NON/SPEFK	normokaliemia	NORM/KAL/YAOEM/YA
	NON/SPE/SIFK	normolineal	NORM/LIN/YAL
nonspherocytic	NON/SFAOER/SIT/IK	normo-orthocytosis	NORM/O*RT/SAOI/TOE/SIS
nontaster	NON/TA*IS/ER	normoplasia	NORM/PLAIZ/YA
nonulcerative	NON/ULS/RA/TIV	normosexual	NORM/SEX/YAOUL
nonunion	NON/YAOUN/YON	normoskeocytosis	NORM/SKAOE/SAOI/TOE/SIS
nonvalent	NON/VAIL/ENT	normospermic	NORM/SPERM/IK
	NON/VAI/LENT	normosthenuria	NORM/STHEN/YAOUR/YA
nonvascular	NON/VAS/KLAR		NORM/STHE/NAOUR/YA
nonvenereal	NON/VE/NAOERL	normotension	NORM/TENGS
nonverbal	NON/VER/BAL	normotensive	NORM/TENS/IV
nonviable	NON/VAOIBL	normothermia	NORM/THERM/YA
nonyl	NOE/NIL	normothermic	NORM/THERM/IK
nor	N-R	normotonia	NORM/TOEN/YA
nor-	NOR	normotonic	NORM/TON/IK
noradrenaline	NOR/DREN/LIN	normotopia	NORM/TOEP/YA
	NOR/AI/DREN/LIN	normotopic	NORM/TOP/IK
noradrenergic	NOR/AD/RE/NERJ/RIK	normotrophic	NORM/TROFK
	NOR/DREN/ERJ/RIK	normouricemia	NORM/YAOUR/SAOEM/YA
noramidopyrine	NOR/AM/DO/PAOI/RAOEN	normouricemic	NORM/YAOUR/SAOEM/IK
norandrostenolone	NOR/AN/DRO/STEN/LOEN	normouricuria	NORM/YAOUR/KAOUR/YA
Norcept-E	NOR/SEPT/E-RBGS	normouricuric	NORM/YAOUR/KAOUR/IK
Norcuron	NOR/KAOU/RON	normovolemia	NORM/VOE/LAOEM/YA
nordefrin	NOR/DEF/RIN		NORM/VOL/AOEM/YA
Nordette	NOR/DET	normovolemic	NORM/VOE/LAOEM/IK
Nordette-21	NOR/DET/2/1		NORM/VOL/AOEM/IK
Nordette-28	NOR/DET/28	normoxia	NOR/MOX/YA
norepinephrine	NOR/EP/NEF/RIN	Normozide	NORM/ZAOID
norethandrolone	NOR/*ET/AN/DRO/LOEN	norophthalmic	NOR/OF/THAL/MIK
Norethin	NOR/THIN	Noroxin	NOR/OK/SIN
norethindrone	NOR/*ET/IN/DROEN	Norpace	NOR/PAIS
norethisterone	NOR/*ET/*IS/ROEN	norpipanone	NOR/PIP/NOEN
norethynodrel	NOR/THAOIN/DREL	Norpramin	NOR/PRA/MIN
Norflex	NOR/FLEX		NOR/PRAM/MIN
norfloxacin	NOR/FLOX/SIN	Nor-QD	NOR/KW-RBGS/D*RBGS
Norgesic	NOR/JAOEZ/IK	Norris	NOR/RIS
Norgesic Forte	NOR/JAOEZ/IK/FOR/TAI	norsteroid	NOR/STAOER/OID
norgestrel	NOR/JES/TREL	norsympatol	NOR/SIFRP/TOEL
Norinyl	NOR/NIL		NOR/SIFRP/TOL
Norisodrine	NOR/AOIS/DRAOEN	norsynephrine	NOR/SNEF/RIN
	NOR/AOIS/DRIN		NOR/SI/NEF/RIN
Norlestrin	NOR/LES/TRIN	North American	NO*RT/MERN
norleucine	NOR/LAOU/SIN		NO*RT/AI/MER/KAN
	NOR/LAOU/SAOEN	Northrop	NO*RT/ROP
Norlutate	NOR/LAOU/TAIT		NOR/THROP
Norlutin	NOR/LAOU/TIN	Norton	NOR/TON
norm	NORM	nortriptyline	NOR/TRIPT/LAOEN
norm(o)-	NORM	norvaline	NOR/VAL/AOEN
	NOR/M(O)		NOR/VAI/LAOEN
norma	NOR/MA	Norwalk	NOR/WAUK
normae	NOR/MAE	NoSalt	NO*/SAULT
normal	NOR/MAL		NO*E/SAULT
normality	NOR/MAL/TI		NO*/SALT
normalization	NOR/MAL/ZAIGS		NO*E/SALT
normalize	NORM/LAOIZ	noscapine	NOS/KA/PAOEN
normergic	NORM/ERJ/IK	nose	NOEZ
	NOR/MERJ/IK	nosebleed	NOEZ/BLAO*ED
normetanephrine	NOR/MET/NEF/RIN	nosegay	NOEZ/GAI
normethadone	NOR/M*ET/DOEN	Nosema	NOE/SAOE/MA
normethandrone	NOR/M*ET/AN/DROEN	Nosematidae	NOE/SE/MAT/DAE
normobaric	NORM/BAR/IK		NOES/MAT/DAE
normoblast	NORM/BLA*S	nosematosis	NOE/SAOEM/TOE/SIS
normoblastic	NORM/BLA*S/IK	nosepiece	NOEZ/PAOES
normoblastosis	NORM/BLAS/TOE/SIS	nosetiology	NOES/AOET/YOLG
normocalcemia	NORM/KAL/SAOEM/YA	noso-	NOS
normocalcemic	NORM/KAL/SAOEM/IK		NOES
normocapnia	NORM/KAP/NA		NOE/SO
	NORM/KAP/NAOE/YA	nosochthonography	NOS/OK/THO/NOG/FI
normocapnic	NORM/KAP/NIK	nosocomial	NOS/KOEM/YAL
normocephalic	NORM/SFAL/IK	nosocomii	NOS/KOEM/YAOI
normocholesterolemia	NORM/KL*ES/ROL/AOEM/YA	nosocomium	NOS/KOEM/YUM
	NORM/KL*ES/RO/LAOEM/YA	nosode	NOS/OED
normocholesterolemic	NORM/KL*ES/ROL/AOEM/IK	nosogenesis	NOS/JEN/SIS
	NORM/KL*ES/RO/LAOEM/IK	nosogenic	NOS/JEN/IK
normochromasia	NORM/KROE/MAIZ/YA	nosogeny	NOE/SOJ/N*I
normochromia	NORM/KROEM/YA	nosogeography	NOS/JAOE/OG/FI
normochromic	NORM/KROEM/IK	nosographer	NOE/SOG/FER
normocrinic	NORM/KRIN/IK	nosographic	NOS/GRAFK
normocyte	NORM/SAO*IT	nosography	NOE/SOG/FI
normocytic	NORM/SIT/IK	nosointoxication	NOS/SPWOX/KAIGS
normocytosis	NORM/SAOI/TOE/SIS	nosologic	NOS/LOJ/IK
normoerythrocyte	NORM/R*IT/RO/SAO*IT	nosological	NOS/LOJ/KAL
Normodyne	NORM/DAOIN	nosologically	NOS/LOJ/KLI
normoglycemia	NORM/GLAOI/SAOEM/YA	nosology	NOE/SOLG
normoglycemic	NORM/GLAOI/SAOEM/IK	nosomania	NOS/MAIN/YA
normokalemia	NORM/KA/LAOEM/YA	nosometry	NOE/SOM/TRI
	NORM/KLAOEM/YA	nosomycosis	NOS/MAOI/KOE/SIS

nosonomy	NOE/SON/M*I	nucleation	NAOUK/LAIGS
nosoparasite	NOS/PAR/SAOIT	nuclei	NAOUK/LAOI
nosophilia	NOS/FIL/YA	nucleic	NAOU/KLAI/IK
nosophobe	NOS/FOEB		NAOU/KLAOE/IK
nosophobia	NOS/FOEB/YA	nucleide	NAOUK/LAOID
nosophyte	NOS/FAOIT		(not NAOU/KLAOID; see nuclide)
nosopoietic	NOS/POIT/IK	nucleiform	NAOU/KLAOE/FORM
Nosopsyllus	NOS/SIL/LUS	nuclein	NAOUK/LIN
nosotaxy	NOS/TAK/SI	nucleinase	NAOUK/LIN/AIS
nosotherapy	NOS/THER/PI	nucleinic	NAOUK/LIN/IK
nosotoxic	NOS/TOX/IK	nucleocapsid	NAOUK/LO/KAP/SID
nosotoxicity	NOS/TOK/SIS/TI	nucleochylema	NAOUK/LO/KAOI/LAOE/MA
nosotoxicosis	NOS/TOX/KOE/SIS	nucleochyme	NAOUK/LO/KAOIM
nosotoxin	NOS/TOK/SIN	nucleocytoplasmic	NAOUK/LO/SAOIT/PLAZ/MIK
nosotrophy	NOS/OT/RO/FI	nucleofugal	NAOUK/LOF/GAL
	NOE/SOT/RO/FI	nucleoglucoprotein	NAOUK/LO/GLAOUK/PRO/
nosotropic	NOS/TROP/IK		TAOEN
nostalgia	NOS/TAL/JA	nucleohistone	NAOUK/LO/HIS/TOEN
nostomania	NO*S/MAIN/YA	nucleoid	NAOUK/LOID
nostophobia	NO*S/FOEB/YA	nucleokeratin	NAOUK/LO/KER/TIN
nostras	NOS/TRAS	nucleolar	NAOU/KLAOE/LAR
nostril	NOS/TRIL	nucleoli	NAOU/KLAOE/LAOI
nostrum	NOS/TRUM	nucleoliform	NAOUK/LOL/FORM
notal	NOE/TAL		NAOU/KLAOE/LI/FORM
notalgia	NOE/TAL/JA		NAOU/KLAOE/OL/FORM
notancephalia	NOE/TAN/SFAIL/YA	nucleolin	NAOU/KLAOE/LIN
notanencephalia	NOE/TAN/EN/SFAIL/YA	nucleolinus	NAOU/KLAOE/LAOI/NUS
notatin	NOE/TAI/TIN		NAOUK/LO/LAOI/NUS
notch	NOFP	nucleoloid	NAOU/KLAOE/LOID
notched	NOFP/-D	nucleololus	NAOUK/LOL/LUS
notencephalocele	NOE/TEN/SEF/LO/SAO*EL	nucleolonema	NAOUK/LOE/LO/NAOE/MA
notencephalus	NOE/TEN/SEF/LUS	nucleolus	NAOU/KLAOE/LUS
Nothnagel	NOET/NA/GEL	nucleomicrosome	NAOUK/LO/MAOI/KRO/SOEM
notifiable	NOET/FIBL	nucleon	NAOUK/LON
	NOET/FI/-BL	nucleonic	NAOUK/LON/IK
noto-	NOET	nucleopetal	NAOUK/LOP/TAL
	NOE/TO	Nucleophaga	NAOUK/LOF/GA
notochord	NOET/KHORD	nucleophagocytosis	NAOUK/LO/FAG/SAOI/TOE/SIS
notochordal	NOET/KHOR/DAL	nucleophil	NAOUK/LO/FIL
Notoedres	NOET/ED/RAOEZ	nucleophile	NAOUK/LO/FAOIL
notogenesis	NOET/JEN/SIS	nucleophilic	NAOUK/LO/FIL/IK
notomelus	NOE/TOM/LUS	nucleophosphatase	NAOUK/LO/FOS/FA/TAIS
notum	NOE/TUM	nucleoplasm	NAOUK/LO/PLAFM
noumenal	NAOUM/NAL	nucleoprotein	NAOUK/LO/PRO/TAOEN
noumenon	NAOUM/NON	nucleoreticulum	NAOUK/LO/RE/TIK/LUM
nourish	NAOUR/IRB	nucleorrhexis	NAOUK/LO/REK/SIS
nourishment	NAOUR/SH-MT	nucleosidase	NAOUK/LO/SAOI/DAIS
nousic	NAOUS/IK	nucleoside	NAOUK/LO/SAOID
nov(o)-	NOEV	nucleosidediphosphatase	NAOUK/LO/SAOID/DI/FOS/FA/
	NOE/V(O)		TAIS
Novafed	NOEV/FED	nucleosidediphosphate	NAOUK/LO/SAOID/DI/FOS/FAIT
Novahistine	NOEV/HIS/TAOEN	nucleosin	NAOUK/LO/SIN
Novamine	NOEV/MAOEN	nucleosis	NAOUK/LOE/SIS
Novantrone	NOE/VAN/TROEN	nucleosome	NAOUK/LO/SOEM
novobiocin	NOEV/BAO*I/SIN	nucleospindle	NAOUK/LO/SPIND/-L
Novocain	NOEV/KAIN	nucleotherapy	NAOUK/LO/THER/PI
Novolin	NOEV/LIN	nucleotidase	NAOUK/LO/TAOID/AIS
NovolinPen	NOEV/LIN/PEN		NAOUK/LO/TAOI/DAIS
NovoPen	NOEV/PEN		NAOUK/LOT/DAIS
nov-ovalis	NOV/O/VAI/LIS	nucleotide	NAOUK/LO/TAOID
	NOEV/O/VAI/LIS	nucleotidyl	NAOUK/LO/TAOI/DIL
Novy	NOE/VI		NAOUK/LO/TAOID/IL
novyi	NOEV/YAOI	nucleotidyltransferase	NAOUK/LO/TAOI/DIL/TRA*NS/
noxa	NOK/SA		FRAIS
noxious	NO*BGS		NAOUK/LO/TAOID/IL/TRA*NS/
noxythiolin	NOX/THAOI/LIN		FRAIS
NPH Iletin	N-RBGS/P*RBGS/H*RBGS/INS/	nucleotoxin	NAOUK/LO/TOK/SIN
	LIN	nucleus	NAOUK/LUS
NPH Insulin	N-RBGS/P*RBGS/H*RBGS/INS/	nuclide	NAOU/KLAOID
	LIN		(not NAOUK/LAOID; see nucleide)
N-terminal	N-RBGS/TERM/NAL	Nucofed	NAOUK/FED
NTZ Long Acting	N-RBGS/T*RBGS/STK*RBGS/	Nucofed Expectorant	NAOUK/FED/EX/PEKT/RANT
Nasal Spray	LONG/AKT/-G/NAI/ZAL/SPRAI		NAOUK/FED/KP-PT/RANT
nu	NAO*U	Nucofed Pediatric	NAOUK/FED/PAOED/YAT/RIK/
Nubain	NAOU/BAIN	Expectorant	EX/PEKT/RANT
nubecula	NAOU/BEK/LA		NAOUK/FED/PAOED/YAT/RIK/
nubility	NAOUBLT		KP-PT/RANT
nucha	NAOU/KA	Nucofed Syrup	NAOUK/FED/SIR/RUP
nuchae	NAOU/KAE	nuda	NAOU/DA
nuchal	NAOU/KAL	nudophobia	NAOUD/FOEB/YA
Nuck	NUK	nugatory	NAOUG/TOIR
nucle(o)-	NAOUK/L(O)	Nu-Iron	NU/H-F/AOIRN
	NAOU/KL(O)	nulligravida	NUL/GRAV/DA
	NAOUK/LAOE/Y(O)	nullipara	NUL/LIP/RA
	NAOU/KLAOE/Y(O)	nulliparity	NUL/PAIR/TI
nuclear	NAOUK/LAR	nulliparous	NUL/LIP/ROUS
nuclease	NAOUK/LAIS	nullisomatic	NUL/SMAT/IK
nucleate	NAOUK/LAIT		NUL/SOE/MAT/IK
nucleated	NAOUK/LAIT/-D	numb	NUM

number	NUM/BER	nymphectomy	NIM/FEKT/M*I
numbness	NUM/*NS	nymphitis	NIM/FAOITS
numeric	NAOU/MER/IK	nymphocaruncular	NIM/FO/KA/RUN/KLAR
nummiform	NUM/FORM		NIM/FO/KA/RUNG/LAR
nummular	NUM/LAR	nymphohymeneal	NIM/FO/HAOIM/NAOEL
nummulare	NUM/LAI/RAOE	nympholabial	NIM/FO/LAIB/YAL
nummulation	NUM/LAIGS	nympholepsy	NIM/FO/LEP/SI
Numorphan	NAOU/MOR/FAN	nymphomania	NIM/FO/MAIN/YA
nunnation	NUN/NAIGS	nymphomaniac	NIM/FO/MAIN/YAK
Nupercainal	NAOUP/KAINL	nymphomaniacal	NIM/FO/MA/NAOI/KAL
	NAOUP/ER/KAINL	nymphoncus	NIM/FON/KUS
Nuprin	NAOU/PRIN	nymphotomy	NIM/FOT/M*I
nuptiality	NUP/-RBL/TI	Nyquil	NAOI/KWIL
	NUP/-RBL/TI	nystagmic	NIS/TAG/MIK
	NUP/SHAL/TI	nystagmiform	NIS/TAG/MI/FORM
nurse	NURS	nystagmogram	NIS/TAG/MO/GRAM
nurse anesthetist	NURS/AI/NES/THE/T*IS	nystagmograph	NIS/TAG/MO/GRAF
nurse-midwife	NURS/MID/WAOIF	nystagmography	NIS/TAG/MOG/FI
nurse-midwifery	NURS/MID/WAOIF/RI	nystagmoid	NIS/TAG/MOID
	NURS/MID/WIF/RI	nystagmus	NIS/TAG/MUS
nurse practitioner	NURS/PRAK/TIGS/ER	nystatin	NAOI/STAT/TIN
nursery	NURS/RI		N*IS/TIN
nursing	NURS/-G		NIS/TA/TIN
Nursoy	NUR/SOI	nystaxis	NIS/TAK/SIS
Nussbaum	NAOUS/BOUM	Nysten	NAOE/STEN
	NAOUS/BAUM		NIS/TEN
nut	NUT	Nystex	NIS/TEX
nutans	NAOU/TANZ	nyxis	NIK/SIS
nutation	NAOU/TAIGS		
nutatory	NAOUT/TOIR		
nutgall	NUT/GAUL		
	NUT/GAL		
nutmeg	NUT/MEG		
Nutracort	NAOU/TRA/KORT		
Nutraderm	NAOU/TRA/DERM		
Nutramigen	NAOU/TRAM/JEN		
nutriciae	NAOU/TRIS/YAE		
nutricius	NAOU/TRIS/YUS		
	(not NAOU/TRIRBS; see nutritious)		
nutrient	NAOU/TRENT		
	NAOU/TRAOENT		
nutrilite	NAOU/TRI/LAOIT		
nutriment	NAOU/TRIMT		
nutriology	NAOU/TROLG		
	NAOU/TRAOE/OLG		
nutrite	NAOU/TRAOIT		
nutrition	NAOU/TRIGS		
nutritional	NAOU/TRIGS/NAL		
nutritionist	NAOU/TRIGS/*IS		
nutritious	NAOU/TRIRBS		
nutritive	NAOU/TRI/TIV		
nutriture	NAOU/TRI/KHUR		
nutrose	NAOU/TROES		
Nutrox	NAOU/TROX		
Nuttallia	NUT/TAL/YA		
nuttallii	NUT/TAL/YAOI		
nux	NUX		
-nychia	NIK/YA		
nyct(o)-	NIKT		
	NIK/T(O)		
nyctalgia	NIK/TAL/JA		
nyctalope	NIKT/LOEP		
nyctalopia	NIKT/LOEP/YA		
nyctanopia	NIKT/NOEP/YA		
nyctaphonia	NIKT/FOEN/YA		
nycterine	NIKT/RAOIN		
	NIKT/RIN		
nycterohemeral	NIKT/RO/HAOEM/RAL		
	NIKT/RO/HEM/RAL		
nyctohemeral	NIKT/HAOEM/RAL		
	NIKT/HEM/RAL		
nyctophilia	NIKT/FIL/YA		
nyctophobia	NIKT/FOEB/YA		
nyctophonia	NIKT/FOEN/YA		
Nyctotherus	NIKT/THAOE/RUS		
	NIK/TO*T/RUS		
nyctotyphlosis	NIKT/TIF/LOE/SIS		
nycturia	NIK/TAOUR/YA		
nylidrin	NAOIL/DRIN		
	NIL/DRIN		
nylon	NAOI/LON		
nymph	NIM/-F		
nymph(o)-	NIM/F(O)		
nympha	NIM/FA		
nymphae	NIM/FAE		
nymphaeoides	NIM/FOI/DAOEZ		
	NIM/FAOE/OI/DAOEZ		
	NIM/FAOE/YOI/DAOEZ		
nymphal	NIM/FAL		

O

oak	OEK
oakum	OEK/UM
oasis	O/WAI/SIS
	O/AI/SIS
oat	OET
oath	O*ET
ob-	OB
obcecation	OB/SE/KAIGS
obdormition	OB/DOR/MIGS
obducent	OB/DAOUS/ENT
	OB/DAOU/SENT
obduction	OB/D*UBGS
O'Beirne	O/BIRN
obeliac	O/BAOEL/YAK
obeliad	O/BAOEL/YAD
obelion	O/BAOEL/YON
Ober	OEB/ER
	O/BER
Obermayer	OEB/ER/MAOI/ER
	O/BER/MAOI/ER
Obersteiner	OEB/ER/STAOIN/ER
	O/BER/STAOIN/ER
obese	O/BAOES
obesitas	O/BAOES/TAS
obesity	O/BAOES/TI
obex	O/BEX
obfuscation	OB/FUS/KAIGS
object	OB/JEKT
	OBT
objective	OB/JEKT/IV
	OBT/IV
obligate	OBL/GAIT
	OB/LI/GAIT
obligation	OBL/GAIGS
	OB/LI/GAIGS
obliqua	OB/LAOI/KWA
	OB/LAOIK/WA
obliquae	OB/LAOI/KWAE
	OB/LAOIK/WAE
oblique	OB/LAOEK
obliquity	OB/LIK/WI/TI
obliquum	OB/LAOI/KWUM
	OB/LAOIK/WUM
obliquus	OB/LAOI/KWUS
	OB/LAOIK/WUS
obliterans	OB/LIT/RANZ
obliteration	OB/LIT/RAIGS
oblongata	OB/LON/GA/TA
	OB/LON/GAI/TA
oblongatae	OB/LON/GAI/TAE
oblongatal	OB/LON/GAI/TAL
obnubilation	OB/NAOUB/LAIGS
O'Brien	O/BRAOIN
	O/BRAOI/-N
obscura	OB/SKAOU/RA
	OB/SKAOUR/RA
observe	OB/SEFRB
observer	OB/SEFRB/ER
obsession	OB/SEGS
obsessive	OB/SES/SIV
	OB/SESZ/IV
obsessive-compulsive	OB/SES/SIV/KPULS/IV
	OB/SESZ/IV/KPULS/IV
	OB/SES/SIV/KOM/PULS/IV
	OB/SESZ/IV/KOM/PULS/IV
obsolescence	OB/SLES/ENS
	OBS/LES/ENS
	OB/SO/LES/ENS
obsolete	OB/SLAOET
	OBS/LAOET
	OB/SO/LAOET
obstetric	OB/STET/RIK
obstetrica	OB/STET/RI/KA
obstetrical	OB/STET/RI/KAL
obstetrician	OB/STE/TRIGS
	O*BS/TRIGS
obstetrics	OB/STET/RIK/-S
obstinate	OB/STI/NAT
	O*BS/NAT
obstipation	OB/STI/PAIGS
	O*BS/PAIGS
obstipum	OB/STAOI/PUM
	OB/STAOIP/UM
obstruction	OB/STR*UBGS

obstruent	OB/STRAOUNT
obtund	OB/TUND
obtundent	OB/TUN/DENT
	OB/TUND/ENT
obturating	OB/TAOU/RAIT/-G
	OB/KHU/RAIT/-G
obturation	OB/TAOU/RAIGS
	OB/KHU/RAIGS
obturator	OB/TAOU/RAI/TOR
	OB/KHU/RAI/TOR
obturatori-	OB/TAOUR/TOR/Y-
	OB/TAOUR/TOER/Y-
	OB/TUR/TOR/Y-
	OB/TUR/TOER/Y-
	OB/KHUR/TOR/Y-
	OB/KHUR/TOER/Y-
obturatoria	OB/TAOUR/TOR/YA
obturatoriae	OB/TAOUR/TOER/YAE
obturatorii	OB/TAOUR/TOER/YAOI
obturatoris	OB/TAOUR/TOR/RIS
obturatorius	OB/TAOUR/TOR/YUS
obturbans	OB/TUR/BANZ
obtuse	OB/TAOUS
obtusion	OB/TAOUGS
occidentalis	OX/DEN/TAI/LIS
occipit(o)-	OK/SIPT
	OK/SIP/T(O)
occipital	OK/SIP/TAL
occipitale	OK/SIP/TAI/LAOE
occipitalis	OK/SIP/TAI/LIS
occipitalization	OK/SIP/TAL/ZAIGS
occipitis	OK/SIP/TIS
occipitoanterior	OK/SIPT/AN/TAOER/YOR
occipitoatlantal	OK/SIPT/AT/LAN/TAL
occipitoatloid	OK/SIPT/AT/LOID
occipitoaxial	OK/SIPT/AX/YAL
occipitoaxoid	OK/SIPT/AK/SOID
	OK/SIPT/AX/OID
occipitobasilar	OK/SIPT/BAS/LAR
occipitobregmatic	OK/SIPT/BREG/MAT/IK
occipitocalcarine	OK/SIP/TO/KAL/KRAOIN
	OK/SIP/TO/KAL/KA/RAOIN
	OK/SIPT/KAL/KAR/RIN
occipitocervical	OK/SIPT/SEFRB/KAL
occipitofacial	OK/SIPT/FAIRBL
occipitofrontal	OK/SIPT/FRON/TAL
occipitofrontalis	OK/SIPT/FRON/TAI/LIS
occipitomastoid	OK/SIPT/MAS/TOID
occipitomental	OK/SIPT/MEN/TAL
occipitoparietal	OK/SIPT/PRAOI/TAL
occipitoposterior	OK/SIPT/POS/TAOER/YOR
occipitotemporal	OK/SIPT/TEFRP/RAL
occipitothalamic	OK/SIPT/THA/LAM/IK
occiput	OX/PUT
	OK/SI/PUT
oc-	O/K-
	OK/K-
occlude	O/KLAOUD
occluder	O/KLAOUD/ER
occlus(o)-	O/KLAOUZ
	O/KLAOUS
	O/KLAOU/Z(O)
	O/KLAOU/S(O)
	OK/LAOUZ
	OK/LAOUS
	OK/LAOU/Z(O)
	OK/LAOU/S(O)
	OK/KLAOUZ
	OK/KLAOUS
	OK/KLAOU/Z(O)
	OK/KLAOU/S(O)
occlusal	O/KLAOU/ZAL
Occlusal	K-P/O/KLAOU/ZAL
occlusalis	OK/LAOU/SAI/LIS
occlusion	O/KLAOUGS
occlusive	O/KLAOUS/IV
occlusocervical	O/KLAOUZ/SEFRB/KAL
occlusodistal	O/KLAOUZ/DIS/TAL
occlusometer	OK/LAOU/SOM/TER
occlusorehabilitation	O/KLAOUZ/RE/BIL/TAIGS
Occucoat	OK/YAOU/KOET
occult	O/KULT
occulta	O/KUL/TA
occultum	O/KUL/TUM
occupancy	OK/PAN/SI
occupational	OK/PAIGS/NAL
Ocean Nasal Mist	OEGS/NAI/ZAL/M*IS
Ocean-A/S Nasal Spray	OEGS/ARBGS/S*RBGS/NAI/ZAL/
	SPRAI

©1992 StenEd® Medical Dictionary

	OEGS/ARBGS/SL-RB/S*RBGS/	oculography	OK/LOG/FI
	NAI/ZAL/SPRAI	oculogyration	OK/LO/JAOI/RAIGS
ocelli	O/SEL/LAOI	oculogyria	OK/LO/JAOIR/YA
ocellus	O/SEL/LUS	oculogyric	OK/LO/JAOIR/IK
ochlesis	OK/LAOE/SIS	oculomandibulodyscephaly	OK/LO/MAN/DIB/LO/DIS/SEF/LI
ochlophobia	OK/LO/FOEB/YA	oculometroscope	OK/LO/MET/RO/SKOEP
Ochoa	O/KHOE/WA	oculomotor	OK/LO/MOE/TOR
ochraceus	O/KRAIRBS	oculomotorius	OK/LO/MOE/TOER/YOUS
Ochrobium	O/KROEB/YUM	oculomycosis	OK/LO/MAOI/KOE/SIS
ochrodermia	O/KRO/DERM/YA	oculonasal	OK/LO/NAI/ZAL
ochrometer	O/KROM/TER	oculopathy	OK/LOP/TH*I
Ochromonadidae	O/KRO/MOE/NAD/DAE	oculoplastic	OK/LO/PLA*S/IK
ochronosis	O/KRO/NOE/SIS	oculoplethysmography	OK/LO/PL*ETS/MOG/FI
	O/KRON/O/SIS		OK/LO/PL*ET/SMOG/FI
ochronotic	O/KRO/NOT/IK		OK/LO/PL*ET/IZ/MOG/FI
	O/KRON/OT/IK	oculopneumoplethysmography	
Ochsner	OX/NER		OK/LO/NAOUM/PL*ETS/MOG/FI
	OK/SNER		OK/LO/NAOUM/PL*ET/SMOG/FI
ocrylate	OK/RI/LAIT		OK/LO/NAOUM/PL*ET/IZ/MOG/FI
octa-	OKT	oculopupillary	OK/LO/PAOUP/LAIR
	OK/TA	oculoreaction	OK/LO/RE/A*BGS
octabenzone	OKT/BEN/ZOEN	oculospinal	OK/LO/SPAOINL
octad	OK/TAD	oculovertebral	OK/LO/VERT/BRAL
octadecanoate	OKT/DEK/NOE/AIT	oculozygomatic	OK/LO/ZAOIG/MAT/IK
octagon	OKT/GON	oculus	OK/LUS
octamethyl	OKT/M*ET/IL/	ocytocin	OES/TOE/SIN
pyrophosphoramide	PAOIR/FOS/FOER/MAOID	odaxesmus	O/DAK/SEZ/MUS
Octamide	OKT/MAOID	odaxetic	O/DAK/SET/IK
octamylamine	OKT/MIL/MAOEN	odd	OD
octamylose	OK/TAM/LOES	Oddi	OD/DAOE
octan	OK/TAN	odditis	OD/DAOITS
octane	OK/TAIN		OD/DAOITS
octanoate	OKT/NOE/AIT	odogenesis	OED/JEN/SIS
octanoic	OKT/NOIK	odont(o)-	O/DONT
	OKT/NOE/IK		O/DON/T(O)
octapeptide	OKT/PEP/TAOID	odontagra	O/DON/TAG/RA
octaploid	OKT/PLOID	odontalgia	O/DON/TAL/JA
octaploidy	OKT/PLOI/DI	odontalgic	O/DON/TAL/JIK
octapressin	OKT/PRES/SIN	odontectomy	O/DON/TEKT/M*I
octarius	OK/TAIR/YUS	odonterism	O/DONT/RIFM
octavalent	OKT/VAIL/ENT	-odontia	(c)O/DON/SHA
	OKT/VAI/LENT	odontiasis	O/DON/TAOI/SIS
	OK/TAV/LENT	odontic	O/DONT/IK
octavus	OK/TAI/VUS	odontinoid	O/DONT/NOID
octet	OK/TET	odontitis	O/DON/TAOITS
octi-	OKT	odontoameloblastoma	O/DONT/AM/LO/BLAS/TOE/MA
	OK/TI	odontoblast	O/DONT/BLA*S
Octicair	OKT/KAIR	odontoblastoma	O/DONT/BLAS/TOE/MA
octigravida	OKT/GRAV/DA	odontobothrion	O/DONT/BO*T/RON
octipara	OK/TIP/RA		O/DONT/BO*T/RAOE/YON
octodrine	OKT/DRAOEN	odontobothritis	O/DONT/BO*T/RAOITS
octofollin	OKT/FOL/LIN	odontoclamis	O/DONT/KLAI/MIS
Octomitidae	OKT/MIT/DAE	odontoclast	O/DONT/KLA*S
Octomitus	OK/TOM/TUS	odontodynia	O/DONT/DIN/YA
octopamine	OK/TOEP/MAOEN	odontodysplasia	O/DONT/DIS/PLAIZ/YA
	OKT/PAM/AOEN	odontogen	O/DONT/JEN
octose	OK/TOES	odontogenesis	O/DONT/JEN/SIS
octoxynol	OK/TOX/NOL	odontogenetic	O/DONT/JE/NET/IK
octriptyline	OK/TRIPT/LAOEN	odontogenic	O/DONT/JEN/IK
octulose	OKT/LOES	odontogenous	O/DON/TOJ/NOUS
	OK/TAOU/LOES	odontogeny	O/DON/TOJ/N*I
	OK/KHU/LOES	odontogram	O/DONT/GRAM
octulosonic	OKT/LO/SON/IK	odontograph	O/DONT/GRAF
	OK/TAOU/LO/SON/IK	odontography	O/DON/TOG/FI
	OK/KHU/LO/SON/IK	odontoiatria	O/DONT/AOI/AT/RA
octyl gallate	OK/TIL/GAL/AIT		O/DONT/AOI/AT/RAOE/YA
	OK/TIL/GAL/LAIT	odontoid	O/DON/TOID
octylphenoxy	OK/TIL/FAOE/NOX/	odontolith	O/DONT/L*IT
polyethoxyethanol	POL/*ET/OX/*ET/NOL	odontolithiasis	O/DONT/LI/THAOI/SIS
ocufilcon	OK/FIL/KON	odontologist	O/DON/TO*LGS
ocul(o)-	OK/L(O)	odontology	O/DON/TOLG
	OK/YAOU/L(O)	odontoloxia	O/DONT/LOX/YA
	OK/YU/L(O)	odontoloxy	O/DONT/LOK/SI
ocular	OK/LAR		O/DON/TOL/OK/SI
ocularis	OK/LAI/RIS	odontolysis	O/DONT/TOL/SIS
ocularist	OK/LAR/*IS	odontoma	O/DON/TOE/MA
oculentum	OK/LEN/TUM	odontoneuralgia	O/DONT/NAOU/RAL/JA
oculi	OK/LAOI	odontonomy	O/DON/TON/M*I
oculist	OK/L*IS	odontonosology	O/DONT/NOE/SOLG
oculistics	OK/L*IS/IK/-S	odontoparallaxis	O/DONT/PAR/LAK/SIS
oculoauricular	OK/LO/AU/RIK/LAR	odontopathic	O/DONT/PA*T/IK
oculoauriculovertebral	OK/LO/AU/RIK/LO/VERT/BRAL	odontopathy	O/DON/TOP/TH*I
oculocardiac	OK/LO/KARD/YAK	odontoperiosteum	O/DONT/P*ER/O*S/YUM
oculocephalogyric	OK/LO/SEF/LO/JAOIR/IK	odontophobia	O/DONT/FOEB/YA
oculocerebrorenal	OK/LO/SER/BRO/RAOENL	odontoplast	O/DONT/PLA*S
oculocutaneous	OK/LO/KAOU/TAIN/YOUS	odontoplasty	O/DONT/PLAS/TI
oculodentodigital	OK/LO/DENT/DIJ/TAL	odontoprisis	O/DONT/TOP/RI/SIS
oculodermal	OK/LO/DER/MAL		O/DONT/PRAOI/SIS
oculofacial	OK/LO/FAIRBL	odontoptosis	O/DON/TOP/TOE/SIS

odontoradiograph	O/DONT/TOE/SIS	ole(o)-	OEL/Y(O)
odontorrhagia	O/DONT/RAID/YO/GRAF	olea	OEL/YA
odontorthosis	O/DONT/RAI/JA	Olea	K-P/OEL/YA
	O/DONT/OR/THOE/SIS	oleaginous	OEL/YAJ/NOUS
	O/DON/TOR/THOE/SIS	oleander	OEL/YAND/ER
odontoschism	O/DONT/SKIFM		OEL/YAN/DER
	O/DONT/SIFM	oleandomycin	OEL/YAND/MAOI/SIN
odontoscope	O/DONT/SKOEP		OEL/YAN/DO/MAOI/SIN
odontoscopy	O/DON/TOS/KPI	oleate	OEL/YAIT
odontoseisis	O/DONT/SAOI/SIS	olecranal	O/LEK/RA/NAL
odontosis	O/DON/TOE/SIS		O/LEK/RANL
odontotechny	O/DONT/TEK/N*I		OEL/KRAINL
odontotheca	O/DONT/THAOE/KA	olecranarthritis	O/LEK/RAN/AR/THRAOITS
odontotherapy	O/DONT/THER/PI	olecranarthrocace	O/LEK/RAN/AR/THROK/SAOE
odontotomy	O/DON/TOT/M*I	olecranarthropathy	O/LEK/RAN/AR/THROP/TH*I
odontotripsis	O/DONT/TRIP/SIS	olecrani	O/LEK/RA/NAOI
odor	O/DOR		OEL/KRAI/NAOI
odorant	OED/RANT	olecranoid	O/LEK/RA/NOID
odorata	OED/RAI/TA		OEL/KRAI/NOID
odoratism	OED/RA/TIFM	olecranon	O/LEK/RA/NON
	O/DOR/TIFM		OEL/KRAI/NON
odoriferae	OED/RIF/RAE	olefin	OEL/FIN
odoriferous	OED/RIF/ROUS	olei	OEL/YAOI
odorimeter	OED/RIM/TER	oleic	O/LAOE/IK
odorimetry	OED/RIM/TRI	olein	OEL/YIN
odoriphore	O/DOR/FOER	olenitis	OEL/NAOITS
odorivection	O/DOR/V*EBGS	oleoarthrosis	OEL/YO/AR/THROE/SIS
odorivector	O/DOR/VEK/TOR	oleochrysotherapy	OEL/YO/KRIS/THER/PI
odorography	OED/ROG/FI	oleocreosote	OEL/YO/KRAOE/SOET
odorous	OED/ROUS	oleodipalmitin	OEL/YO/DI/PAL/MI/TIN
O'Dwyer	O/DWAOI/ER	oleogomenol	OEL/YO/GOEM/NOL
odynacusis	O/DIN/KAOU/SIS	oleogranuloma	OEL/YO/GRAN/LOE/MA
-odynia	(c)O/DIN/YA	oleoinfusion	OEL/YO/IN/FAOUGS
odynometer	OED/NOM/TER	oleoma	OEL/YOE/MA
odynophagia	O/DIN/FAI/JA	oleomargarine	OEL/YO/MARJ/RIN
odynophobia	O/DIN/FOEB/YA	oleometer	OEL/YOM/TER
odynophonia	O/DIN/FOEN/YA	oleonucleoprotein	OEL/YO/NAOUK/LO/PRO/TAOEN
oedipal	ED/PAL	oleopalmitate	OEL/YO/PAL/MI/TAIT
oedipism	ED/PIFM	oleoresin	OEL/YO/REZ/SIN
Oedipus	ED/PUS	oleoresina	OEL/YO/RE/ZAOI/NA
Oehler	E/LER		OEL/YO/REZ/NA
oenanthal	E/NAN/THAL	oleoresinae	OEL/YO/RE/ZAOI/NAE
oenanthol	E/NAN/THOL		OEL/YO/REZ/NAE
oersted	*ER/STED	oleosacchara	OEL/YO/SAK/RA
oesophagostomiasis	E/SOF/GO/STOE/MAOI/SIS	oleosaccharum	OEL/YO/SAK/RUM
Oesophagostomum	E/SOF/GO*S/MUM	oleostearate	OEL/YO/STAOE/RAIT
official	FIRBL		OEL/YO/STAOER/AIT
	O/FIRBL	oleosus	OEL/YOE/SUS
officinal	O/FIS/NAL	oleotherapy	OEL/YO/THER/PI
officinalis	O/FIS/NAI/LIS	oleothorax	OEL/YO/THOR/AX
Ogawa	O/GA/WA	oleovitamin	OEL/YO/VAOIT/MIN
Ogen Tablets	O/JEN/TAB/LET/-S	oleum	OEL/YUM
Ogen Vaginal Cream	O/JEN/VAJ/NAL/KRAOEM	oleyl	O/LAOE/IL
-ogenous	OJ/NOUS	olfact	OL/FAKT
ogive	O/JAOIV	olfact(o)-	OL/FAK/T-
ogo	O/GOE	olfactie	OL/FAK/TAOE
Ogston	OG/STON	olfaction	OL/FA*BGS
Oguchi	O/GAOU/KHAOE	olfactism	OL/FAK/TIFM
O'Hara	O/HAR/RA	olfactive	OL/FAKT/IV
ohm	OEM	olfactology	OL/FAK/TOLG
Ohm	K-P/OEM	olfactometer	OL/FAK/TOM/TER
ohmammeter	OEM/AM/TER	olfactometry	OL/FAK/TOM/TRI
	OEM/AM/MAOET/ER	olphactophobia	OL/FAKT/FOEB/YA
ohmmeter	OEM/MAOET/ER	olfactorii	OL/FAK/TOR/YAOI
	OEM/TER		OL/FAK/TOER/YAOI
ohne Hauch	O/NAI/HOUK	olfactorius	OL/FAK/TOR/YUS
	O/NAI/HOUFP		OL/FAK/TOER/YUS
-oic	OIK	olfactory	OL/FAKT/RI
	(c)OE/IK		OL/FAK/TRI
-oid	OID	olfactus	OL/FAK/TUS
oidia	O/ID/YA	olfacty	OL/FAK/TI
oidio-	O/ID/YO	olibanum	O/LIB/NUM
	OID/YO	olig(o)-	OL/G(O)
Oidiomycetes	O/ID/YO/MAOI/SAOE/TAOEZ	oligakisuria	OL/GAK/SAOUR/YA
oidiomycin	O/ID/YO/MAOI/SIN	oligamnios	OL/GAM/NOS
oidiomycosis	O/ID/YO/MAOI/KOE/SIS		OL/GAM/NAOE/YOS
oidiomycotic	O/ID/YO/MAOI/KOT/IK	oligemia	OL/GAOEM/YA
-oidiosis	O/ID/YOE/SIS	oligemic	OL/GAOEM/IK
	OID/YOE/SIS	olighemia	OL/IG/HAOEM/YA
oidium	O/ID/YUM	olighidria	OL/IG/HID/RA
oil	OIL		OL/IG/HID/RAOE/YA
ointment	OINT/-MT	oligidria	OL/IG/ID/RA
Oken	O/KEN		OL/IG/ID/RAOE/YA
	(*not* OEK/-N; see oaken)	oligoamnios	OL/GO/AM/NOS
-ol	OL		OL/GO/AM/NAOE/YOS
	(c)OL	oligoblast	OL/GO/BLA*S
olaflur	OEL/FLUR	oligocardia	OL/GO/KARD/YA
olamine	OEL/MAOEN	oligocholia	OL/GO/KOEL/YA
	OL/MAOEN	oligochromasia	OL/GO/KROE/MAIZ/YA

oligochromemia	OL/GO/KROE/MAOEM/YA	Oliver	OL/VER
oligochylia	OL/GO/KAOIL/YA	olivifugal	OL/VIF/GAL
oligochymia	OL/GO/KAOIM/YA	olivipetal	OL/VIP/TAL
oligocystic	OL/GO/S*IS/IK	olivocerebellar	OL/VO/SER/BEL/LAR
oligocythemia	OL/GO/SAOI/THAOEM/YA	olivocochlear	OL/VO/KOK/LAR
oligocythemic	OL/GO/SAOI/THEM/IK	olivopontocerebellar	OL/VO/PON/TO/SER/BEL/LAR
oligocytosis	OL/GO/SAOI/TOE/SIS	Ollendorf	OL/EN/DOR/-F
oligodactylia	OL/GO/DAK/TIL/YA	Ollier	OL/YAI
oligodactyly	OL/GO/DAKT/LI	-ologist	O*LGS
oligodendria	OL/GO/DEN/DRA		OL/J*IS
	OL/GO/DEN/DRAOE/YA	-ology	OLG
oligodendroblast	OL/GO/DEN/DRO/BLA*S	olophonia	OL/FOEN/YA
oligodendroblastoma	OL/GO/DEN/DRO/BLAS/TOE/MA	Olshevsky	OL/SHEV/SKI
oligodendrocyte	OL/GO/DEN/DRO/SAO*IT	om(o)-	OEM
oligodendroglia	OL/GO/DEN/DROG/LA		O/M(O)
	OL/GO/DEN/DROG/LAOE/YA	-oma	(c)OE/MA
oligodendroglioma	OL/GO/DEN/DROG/LOE/MA		O/MA
	OL/GO/DEN/DROG/LAOE/YOE/MA	omacephalus	OEM/SEF/LUS
oligodipsia	OL/GO/DIPS/YA	omagra	O/MAI/GRA
oligodontia	OL/GO/DON/SHA	omalgia	OEM/AL/JA
oligodynamic	OL/GO/DAOI/NAM/IK		O/MAL/JA
oligogalactia	OL/GO/GLAK/SHA	omarthritis	OEM/AR/THRAOITS
	OL/GO/GLAKT/YA		O/MAR/THRAOITS
oligogenic	OL/GO/JEN/IK	omasitis	OEM/SAOITS
oligogenics	OL/GO/JEN/IK/-S	omasum	O/MAI/SUM
oligoglia	OL/GOG/LA		O/MAIS/UM
	OL/GO/GLAOE/YA	-omata	(c)OEM/TA
oligoglucan	OL/GO/GLAOU/KAN		(c)OE/MA/TA
oligohemia	OL/GO/HAOEM/YA		(c)O/MA/TA
oligohydramnios	OL/GO/HAOI/DRAM/NOS	Ombredanne	OM/BRAI/DAN
	OL/GO/HAOI/DRAM/NAOE/YOS		OM/BRE/DAN
oligohydruria	OL/GO/HAOI/DRAOUR/YA	ombrophobia	OM/BRO/FOEB/YA
oligohypermenorrhea	OL/GO/HAO*IP/MEN/RAOE/YA	ombrophore	OM/BRO/FOER
oligohypomenorrhea	OL/GO/HO*IP/MEN/RAOE/YA	omega	O/MAI/GA
oligolecithal	OL/GO/LES/THAL		O/MAOE/GA
oligomeganephronia	OL/GO/MEG/NE/FROEN/YA	oment(o)-	OEMT
oligomeganephronic	OL/GO/MEG/NE/FRON/IK		OEMT/T(O)
	OL/GO/MEG/NEF/RON/IK		O/MENT
oligomenorrhea	OL/GO/MEN/RAOE/YA		O/MEN/T(O)
oligomer	OL/GO/MER	omenta	O/MEN/TA
oligometallic	OL/GO/ME/TAL/IK		OEMT/TA
oligomorphic	OL/GO/MOR/FIK	omental	O/MEN/TAL
oligonatality	OL/GO/NAI/TAL/TI		OEMT/TAL
oligonecrospermia	OL/GO/NEK/RO/SPERM/YA	omentalis	O/MEN/TAI/LIS
oligonephronic	OL/GO/NEF/RON/IK		OEMT/TAI/LIS
oligonitrophilic	OL/GO/NAOI/TRO/FIL/IK	omentectomy	O/MEN/TEKT/M*I
oligonucleotide	OL/GO/NAOUK/LO/TAOID		OEMT/TEKT/M*I
oligo-ovulation	OL/GO/OV/LAIGS	omentitis	O/MEN/TAOITS
oligopepsia	OL/GO/PEPS/YA		OEMT/TAOITS
oligopeptide	OL/GO/PEP/TAOID	omentofixation	OEMT/FIK/SAIGS
oligophosphaturia	OL/GO/FOS/FA/TAOUR/YA		O/MENT/FIK/SAIGS
oligophrenia	OL/GO/FRAOEN/YA	omentopexy	OEMT/PEK/SI
oligophrenic	OL/GO/FREN/IK		O/MENT/PEK/SI
oligoplastic	OL/GO/PLA*S/IK	omentoplasty	OEMT/PLAS/TI
oligopnea	OL/GOP/NAOE/YA		O/MENT/PLAS/TI
	OL/GOP/NA	omentoportography	OEMT/POR/TOG/FI
oligoposia	OL/GO/POEZ/YA		O/MENT/POR/TOG/FI
oligoptyalism	OL/GO/TAOI/LIFM	omentorrhaphy	OEMT/TOR/FI
oligopyrene	OL/GO/PAOI/RAOEN		O/MEN/TOR/FI
oligopyrous	OL/GO/PAOI/ROUS	omentosplenopexy	OEMT/SPLAOEN/PEK/SI
oligoria	OL/GOR/YA		O/MENT/SPLAOEN/PEK/SI
	OL/GOER/YA	omentotomy	OEMT/TOT/M*I
oligosaccharide	OL/GO/SAK/RAOID		O/MEN/TOT/M*I
oligosialia	OL/GO/SAOI/AIL/YA	omentovolvulus	OEMT/VOL/VAOU/LUS
oligospermatism	OL/GO/SPERM/TIFM		O/MENT/VOL/VAOU/LUS
oligospermia	OL/GO/SPERM/YA	omentulum	OEMT/LUM
oligosymptomatic	OL/GO/SIFRPT/MAT/IK		O/MENT/LUM
	OL/GO/SIMT/MAT/IK	omentum	OEMT/UM
oligosynaptic	OL/GO/SNAPT/IK		O/MEN/TUM
	OL/GO/SI/NAPT/IK	omentumectomy	OEMT/TAOU/MEKT/M*I
oligothymia	OL/GO/THAOIM/YA		O/MEN/TAOU/MEKT/M*I
oligotrichia	OL/GO/TRIK/YA	omitis	O/MAOITS
oligotrichosis	OL/GO/TRI/KOE/SIS		OEM/AOITS
oligotrophia	OL/GO/TROEF/YA	ommatidium	OM/TID/YUM
oligotrophic	OL/GO/TROFK	ommochrome	OM/KROEM
oligotrophy	OL/GOT/RO/FI	Omnipaque	OM/NI/PAIK
oligozoospermatism	OL/GO/ZOE/SPERM/TIFM	Omnipen	OM/NI/PEN
oligozoospermia	OL/GO/ZOE/SPERM/YA	Omnipen-N	OM/NI/PEN/N-RBGS
oliguresia	OL/GAOU/RAOES/YA	omnipotence	OM/NIP/TENS
oliguresis	OL/GAOU/RAOE/SIS	omnivorous	OM/NIV/ROUS
oliguria	OL/GAOUR/YA	omocephalus	OEM/SEF/LUS
oliguric	OL/GAOUR/IK	omoclavicular	OEM/KLA/VIK/LAR
olisthy	O/LIS/TH*I	omodynia	OEM/DIN/YA
oliva	O/LAOI/VA	omohyoid	OEM/HAOI/OID
olivae	O/LAOI/VAE	omophagia	OEM/FAI/JA
olivarum	OL/VAIR/UM	omoplata	OEM/PLAT/TA
	OL/VAI/RUM	omosternum	OEM/STER/NUM
olivary	OL/VAIR	omothyroid	OEM/THAOI/ROID
olive	OL/IV	omphal(o)-	OM/FL(O)

	OM/FA/L(O)	oneir(o)-	O/NAOIR
	OM/FAL		O/NAOI/R(O)
omphalectomy	OM/FLEKT/M*I	oneiric	O/NAOIR/IK
	OM/FA/LEKT/M*I	oneirism	O/NAOI/RIFM
omphalelcosis	OM/FAL/EL/KOE/SIS	oneiroanalysis	O/NAOIR/ANL/SIS
omphalic	OM/FAL/IK	oneirocritical	O/NAOIR/KRIT/KAL
omphalitis	OM/FLAOITS	oncirodynia	O/NAOIR/DIN/YA
	OM/FA/LAOITS	oneirogenic	O/NAOIR/JEN/IK
omphaloangiopagous	OM/FLO/AN/JOP/GOUS	oneirogmus	O/NAOI/ROG/MUS
omphaloangiopagus	OM/FLO/AN/JOP/GUS	oneiroid	O/NAOI/ROID
omphalocele	OM/FLO/SAO*EL	oneirology	O/NAOI/ROLG
	OM/FAL/SAO*EL	oneirophrenia	O/NAOIR/FRAOEN/YA
omphalochorion	OM/FLO/KOER/YON	oneiroscopy	O/NAOI/ROS/KPI
omphaloenteric	OM/FLO/SPWER/IK	oniomania	OEN/YO/MAIN/YA
	OM/FLO/EN/TER/IK	onion	UN/YON
omphalogenesis	OM/FLO/JEN/SIS	onium	OEN/YUM
omphaloma	OM/FLOE/MA	onkinocele	ON/KIN/SAO*EL
omphalomesaraic	OM/FLO/MES/RAI/IK	onlay	ON/LA*I
omphalomesenteric	OM/FLO/MES/SPWER/IK	onomatology	ON/MA/TOLG
	OM/FLO/MES/EN/TER/IK	onomatomania	ON/MAT/MAIN/YA
omphaloncus	OM/FLON/KUS	onomatophobia	ON/MAT/FOEB/YA
omphalopagus	OM/FLOP/GUS	onomatopoiesis	ON/MAT/POI/SIS
omphalophlebitis	OM/FLO/FLE/BAOITS	onto-	ONT
omphalorrhagia	OM/FLO/RAI/JA		ON/TO
omphalorrhea	OM/FLO/RAOE/YA	ontogenesis	ONT/JEN/SIS
omphalorrhexis	OM/FLO/REK/SIS	ontogenetic	ONT/JE/NET/IK
omphalos	OM/FLOS	ontogenic	ONT/JEN/IK
omphalosite	OM/FLO/SAOIT	ontogeny	ON/TOJ/N*I
omphalospinous	OM/FLO/SPAOIN/OUS	onych(o)-	OIN/K(O)
omphalotomy	OM/FLOT/M*I		O/NIK
omphalotripsy	OM/FLO/TRIP/SI		ON/NI/K(O)
omphalovesical	OM/FLO/VES/KAL		(not ON/KO; see onco-)
omphalus	OM/FLUS	onychalgia	OIN/KAL/JA
	OM/FA/LUS	onychatrophia	OIN/KA/TROEF/YA
onanism	OEN/NIFM		O/NIK/TROEF/YA
	O/NA/NIFM	onychatrophy	OIN/KAT/RO/FI
	O/NAN/IFM		ON/IK/AT/RO/FI
Onchocerca	ON/KO/SER/KA	onychauxis	OIN/KAUK/SIS
onchocerciasis	ON/KO/SER/KAOI/SIS	onychectomy	OIN/KEKT/M*I
onchocercid	ON/KO/SER/KID	-onychia	(c)O/NIK/YA
	ON/KO/SERK/ID	onychitis	OIN/KAOITS
Onchocercidae	ON/KO/SERK/DAE	onychoclasis	OIN/KOK/LA/SIS
onchocercosis	ON/KO/SER/KOE/SIS	onychocryptosis	OIN/KO/KRIP/TOE/SIS
onco-	ON/KO	onychodystrophy	OIN/KO/DIS/TRO/FI
oncocyte	ON/KO/SAO*IT	onychogenic	OIN/KO/JEN/IK
oncocytic	ON/KO/SIT/IK	onychogram	O/NIK/GRAM
oncocytoma	ON/KO/SAOI/TOE/MA		OIN/KO/GRAM
oncodnavirus	ON/KOD/NA/VAOI/RUS	onychograph	O/NIK/GRAF
oncofetal	ON/KO/FAOE/TAL		OIN/KO/GRAF
oncogene	ON/KO/JAOEN	onychogryphosis	OIN/KO/GRI/FOE/SIS
oncogenesis	ON/KO/JEN/SIS	onychogryposis	OIN/KO/GRI/POE/SIS
oncogenetic	ON/KO/JE/NET/IK	onychoheterotopia	OIN/KO/HET/RO/TOEP/YA
oncogenic	ON/KO/JEN/IK	onychoid	OIN/KOID
oncogenicity	ON/KO/JE/NIS/TI	onychology	OIN/KOLG
oncogenous	ON/KOJ/NOUS	onycholysis	OIN/KOL/SIS
oncograph	ON/KO/GRAF	onychoma	OIN/KOE/MA
oncography	ON/KOG/FI	onychomadesis	OIN/KO/MA/DAOE/SIS
oncoides	ON/KOI/DAOEZ	onychomalacia	OIN/KO/MA/LAI/SHA
oncologist	ON/KO*LGS	onychomycosis	OIN/KO/MAOI/KOE/SIS
oncology	ON/KOLG	onychonosus	OIN/KON/SUS
oncolysate	ON/KOL/SAIT	onycho-osteodysplasia	OIN/KO/O*S/YO/DIS/PLAIZ/YA
oncolysis	ON/KOL/SIS	onychopathic	OIN/KO/PA*T/IK
oncolytic	ON/KO/LIT/IK	onychopathology	OIN/KO/PA/THOLG
oncoma	ON/KOE/MA	onychopathy	OIN/KOP/TH*I
Oncomelania	ON/KO/ME/LAIN/YA	onychophagia	OIN/KO/FAI/JA
oncometer	ON/KOM/TER	onychophagist	OIN/KOF/J*IS
oncometric	ON/KO/MET/RIK	onychophagy	OIN/KOF/JI
oncometry	ON/KOM/TRI	onychophosis	OIN/KO/FOE/SIS
oncophora	ON/KOF/RA	onychophyma	OIN/KO/FAOI/MA
oncornavirus	ON/KORN/VAOI/RUS	onychoplasty	OIN/KO/PLAS/TI
	ON/KOR/NA/VAOI/RUS	onychoptosis	OIN/KO/TOE/SIS
oncosis	ON/KOE/SIS	onychorrhexis	OIN/KO/REK/SIS
oncosphere	ON/KO/SFAOER	onychoschizia	OIN/KO/SKIZ/YA
oncotherapy	ON/KO/THER/PI	onychosis	OIN/KOE/SIS
oncothlipsis	ON/KO/TLIP/SIS	onychostroma	OIN/KO/STROE/MA
	ON/KO/TH-/LIP/SIS	onychotillomania	OIN/KO/TIL/MAIN/YA
oncotic	ON/KOT/IK		OIN/KOT/LO/MAIN/YA
oncotomy	ON/KOT/M*I	onychotomy	OIN/KOT/M*I
oncotropic	ON/KO/TROP/IK	onychotrophy	OIN/KOT/RO/FI
Oncovin	ON/KO/VIN	onyx	ON/IX
Oncovirinae	ON/KO/VIR/NAE	onyxis	ON/IK/SIS
oncovirus	ON/KO/VAOI/RUS		O/NIK/SIS
ondometer	ON/DOM/TER	oo-	AO
-one	(c)OEN	ooblast	AO/BLA*S
	OEN	oocenter	AO/SEN/TER
One-A-Day	WUN/A/DAI/MULT/	oocephalus	AO/SEF/LUS
Multivitamins	VAOIT/MIN/-S	oocinesia	AO/SI/NAOEZ/YA
One-A-Day Vitamins	WUN/A/DAI/VAOIT/MIN/-S	oocyesis	AO/SAOI/E/SIS
One-A-Day Stressgard	WUN/A/DAI/STRESZ/GARD	oocyst	AO/S*IS

oocytase	AO/SAOI/TAIS
oocyte	AO/SAO*IT
oocytin	AO/SAOI/TIN
oogamous	AOG/MOUS
oogamy	AOG/M*I
oogenesis	AO/JEN/SIS
oogenetic	AO/JE/NET/IK
oogenic	AO/JEN/IK
oogenous	O/OJ/NOUS
oogonia	AO/GOEN/YA
oogonium	AO/GOEN/YUM
ookinesia	AO/KI/NAOEZ/YA
ookinesis	AO/KI/NAOE/SIS
ookinete	AO/KI/NAOET
	AO/KAOI/NAOET
oolemma	AO/LEM/MA
Oomycetes	AO/MAOI/SAOE/TAOEZ
oomycosis	AO/MAOI/KOE/SIS
oophagia	AO/FAI/JA
oophagy	O/OF/JI
	AOF/JI
oophor(o)-	AOF/R(O)
	O/OF/RO
	OEF/R(O)
oophoralgia	AOF/FAL/JA
oophorectomize	AOF/REKT/MAOIZ]
oophorectomy	AOF/REKT/M*I
oophoritic	AOF/RIT/IK
oophoritis	AOF/RAOITS
oophorocystectomy	AOF/RO/SIS/TEKT/M*I
oophorocystosis	AOF/RO/SIS/TOE/SIS
oophorogenous	AOF/ROJ/NOUS
oophorohysterectomy	AOF/RO/H*IS/REKT/M*I
oophoroma	AOF/ROE/MA
oophoron	AOF/RON
oophoropathy	AOF/ROP/TH*I
oophoropeliopexy	AOF/RO/PEL/YO/PEK/SI
oophoropexy	AOF/RO/PEK/SI
oophoroplasty	AOF/RO/PLAS/TI
oophororrhaphy	AOF/ROR/FI
oophorosalpingectomy	AOF/RO/SAL/PIN/JEKT/M*I
oophorosalpingitis	AOF/RO/SAL/PIN/JAOITS
oophorostomy	AOF/RO*S/M*I
oophorotomy	AOF/ROT/M*I
oophorrhagia	AOF/RAI/JA
oophorus	AOF/RUS
oophyte	AO/FAOIT
ooplasm	AO/PLAFM
Oort	AORT
oosperm	AO/SPERM
oosphere	AO/SFAOER
Oospora	AOS/PRA
	O/OS/PRA
oosporangium	AO/SPRAN/JUM
oospore	AO/SPOER
ootheca	AO/THAOE/KA
ootherapy	AO/THER/PI
ootid	AO/TID
ootype	AO/TAOIP
oozooid	AO/ZOE/OID
opaca	O/PAI/KA
opacification	O/PAS/FI/KAIGS
opacity	O/PAS/TI
opalescent	OEP/LES/ENT
opalescin	OEP/LES/SIN
opalgia	O/PAL/JA
opaline	OEP/LAOEN
opalisin	O/PAL/SIN
opaque	O/PAIK
opeidoscope	OP/AOID/SKOEP
	O/PAOID/SKOEP
open	OEP
	OEP/-N
opening	OEP/-G
	OEP/-NG
operable	OP/RABL
operant	OP/RANT
operate	OP/RAIT
	OERPT
operation	OP/RAIGS
	OERPGS
operative	OP/RA/TIV
	OERPT/IV
operator	OP/RAI/TOR
	OERPT/TOR
opercul-	O/PERK/L-
	O/PER/KL-
	O/PER/KAOU/L-
	O/PERK/YAOU/L-

	O/PERK/YU/L-
opercula	O/PERK/LA
opercular	O/PERK/LAR
operculated	O/PERK/LAIT/-D
operculectomy	O/PERK/LEKT/M*I
operculi	O/PERK/LAOI
operculitis	O/PERK/LAOITS
operculum	O/PERK/LUM
operon	OP/RON
ophiasis	O/FAOI/SIS
Ophidia	O/FID/YA
ophidiasis	OEF/DAOI/SIS
	O/FI/DAOI/SIS
ophidic	O/FID/IK
ophidiophobia	O/FID/YO/FOEB/YA
ophidism	OEF/DIFM
	O/FID/IFM
ophritis	OF/RAOITS
ophryitis	OF/RAOE/YAOITS
ophryon	OF/RAOE/YON
Ophryoscolecidae	OF/RAOE/YO/SKOE/LES/DAE
ophryosis	OF/RAOE/YOE/SIS
ophryospinal	OF/RAOE/YO/SPAOINL
ophthalm(o)-	OF/THAL/M(O)
ophthalmagra	OF/THAL/MAG/RA
ophthalmalgia	OF/THAL/MAL/JA
ophthalmatrophia	OF/THAL/MA/TROEF/YA
ophthalmectomy	OF/THAL/MEKT/M*I
ophthalmencephalon	OF/THAL/MEN/SEF/LON
ophthalmia	OF/THAL/MA
	OF/THAL/MAOE/YA
ophthalmiatrics	OF/THAL/MAT/RIK-S
	OF/THAL/MAOE/AT/RIK/-S
ophthalmic	OF/THAL/MIK
ophthalmica	OF/THAL/MI/KA
ophthalmicus	OF/THAL/MI/KUS
ophthalmitic	OF/THAL/MIT/IK
ophthalmitis	OF/THAL/MAOITS
ophthalmobium	OF/THAL/MOEB/YUM
ophthalmoblennorrhea	OF/THAL/MO/BLEN/RAOE/YA
ophthalmocele	OF/THAL/MO/SAO*EL
ophthalmocopia	OF/THAL/MO/KOEP/YA
ophthalmodesmitis	OF/THAL/MO/DES/MAOITS
ophthalmodiaphanoscope	OF/THAL/MO/DAOI/FAN/SKOEP
ophthalmodiastimeter	OF/THAL/MO/DI/AS/TIM/TER
ophthalmodonesis	OF/THAL/MO/DOE/NAOE/SIS
ophthalmodynamometer	OF/THAL/MO/DAOIN/MOM/TER
ophthalmodynamometry	OF/THAL/MO/DAOIN/MOM/TRI
ophthalmodynia	OF/THAL/MO/DIN/YA
ophthalmoeikonometer	OF/THAL/MO/AOIK/NOM/TER
ophthalmogram	OF/THAL/MO/GRAM
ophthalmograph	OF/THAL/MO/GRAF
ophthalmography	OF/THAL/MO/G/FI
ophthalmogyric	OF/THAL/MO/JAOIR/IK
ophthalmoleukoscope	OF/THAL/MO/LAOUK/SKOEP
ophthalmolith	OF/THAL/MO/L*IT
ophthalmologic	OF/THAL/MO/LOJ/IK
ophthalmologist	OF/THAL/MO*LGS
ophthalmology	OF/THAL/MOLG
ophthalmomalacia	OF/THAL/MO/MA/LAI/SHA
ophthalmomandibulomeli	OF/THAL/MO/MAN/DIB/LO/MEL/IK
ophthalmomelanosis	OF/THAL/MO/MEL/NOE/SIS
ophthalmometer	OF/THAL/MOM/TER
ophthalmometroscope	OF/THAL/MO/MET/RO/SKOEP
ophthalmometry	OF/THAL/MOM/TRI
ophthalmomycosis	OF/THAL/MO/MAOI/KOE/SIS
ophthalmomyiasis	OF/THAL/MO/MAOI/AOI/SIS
ophthalmomyitis	OF/THAL/MO/MAOI/AOITS
ophthalmomyositis	OF/THAL/MO/MAOI/SAOITS
ophthalmomyotomy	OF/THAL/MO/MAOI/OT/M*I
ophthalmoneuritis	OF/THAL/MO/NAOU/RAOITS
ophthalmoneuromyelitis	OF/THAL/MO/NAOUR/MAOI/LAOITS
ophthalmopathy	OF/THAL/MOP/TH*I
ophthalmophacometer	OF/THAL/MO/FAI/KOM/TER
ophthalmophantom	OF/THAL/MO/FAN/TOM
ophthalmophlebotomy	OF/THAL/MO/FLE/BOT/M*I
ophthalmophthisis	OF/THAL/MOF/THI/SIS
ophthalmoplasty	OF/THAL/MO/PLAS/TI
ophthalmoplegia	OF/THAL/MO/PLAOE/JA
ophthalmoplegic	OF/THAL/MO/PLAOEJ/IK
ophthalmoptosis	OF/THAL/MOP/TOE/SIS
ophthalmoreaction	OF/THAL/MO/RE/A*BGS
ophthalmorrhagia	OF/THAL/MO/RAI/JA
ophthalmorrhea	OF/THAL/MO/RAOE/YA
ophthalmorrhexis	OF/THAL/MO/REK/SIS
ophthalmoscope	OF/THAL/MO/SKOEP
ophthalmoscopic	OF/THAL/MO/SKOP/IK

ophthalmoscopy	OF/THAL/MOS/KPI	opsinogen	OP/SIN/JEN
ophthalmostasis	OF/THAL/MO*S/SIS	opsinogenous	OPS/NOJ/NOUS
ophthalmostat	OF/THAL/MO/STAT	opsiometer	OPS/YOM/TER
ophthalmostatometer	OF/THAL/MO/STA/TOM/TER	-opsis	OP/SIS
ophthalmosteresis	OF/THAL/MO/STE/RAOE/SIS	opsiuria	OPS/YAOUR/YA
	OF/THAL/MO/STRAOE/SIS	opso-	OPS
ophthalmosynchysis	OF/THAL/MO/SIN/KI/SIS		OP/SO
ophthalmothermometer	OF/THAL/MO/THER/MOM/TER	opsoclonia	OPS/KLOEN/YA
ophthalmotomy	OF/THAL/MOT/M*I	opsoclonus	OPS/KLOE/NUS
ophthalmotonometer	OF/THAL/MO/TOE/NOM/TER	opsogen	OPS/JEN
ophthalmotonometry	OF/THAL/MO/TOE/NOM/TRI	opsomania	OPS/MAIN/YA
ophthalmotrope	OF/THAL/MO/TROEP	opsone	OP/SOEN
ophthalmotropometer	OF/THAL/MO/TROE/POM/TER	opsonic	OP/SON/IK
ophthalmovascular	OF/THAL/MO/VAS/KLAR	opsoniferous	OPS/NIF/ROUS
ophthalmoxerosis	OF/THAL/MO/ZAOE/ROE/SIS	opsonification	OP/SON/FI/KAIGS
	OF/THAL/MO/ZE/ROE/SIS	opsonify	OP/SON/FI
-opia	OEP/YA	opsonin	OPS/NIN
opian	OEP/YAN	opsoninopathy	OP/SOE/NIN/OP/TH*I
opianine	O/PAOI/NAOEN	opsonist	OPS/N*IS
	O/PAOI/NIN	opsonization	OPS/NAOI/ZAIGS
opianyl	O/PAOI/NIL		OPS/NI/ZAIGS
opiate	OEP/YAIT	opsonize	OPS/NAOIZ
	OEP/YAT	opsono-	OPS/NO
opilation	OEP/LAIGS	opsonocytophagic	OPS/NO/SAOIT/FAIJ/IK
opine	O/PAOEN		OPS/NO/SAOIT/FAJ/IK
opioid	OEP/YOID	opsonogen	OP/SON/JEN
opiomelanocortin	OEP/YO/MEL/NO/KOR/TIN	opsonology	OPS/NOLG
opipramol	O/PIP/RA/MOEL	opsonometry	OPS/NOM/TRI
	O/PIP/RA/MOL	opsonophilia	OPS/NO/FIL/YA
opisthe	O/PIS/THAOE	opsonophilic	OPS/NO/FIL/IK
opisthenar	O/PIS/THAOE/NAR	opsonophoric	OPS/NO/FOER/IK
	O/PIS/THE/NAR	opsonotherapy	OPS/NO/THER/PI
opisthencephalon	O/PIS/THEN/SEF/LON	opt-	OPT
opisthiobasial	O/PIS/THO/BAIS/YAL		OP/T-
	O/PIS/THAOE/YO/BAIS/YAL	optesthesia	OP/TES/THAOEZ/YA
opisthion	O/PIS/THON	optic	OPT/IK
	O/PIS/THAOE/YON	optic(o)-	OPT/K(O)
opisthionasial	O/PIS/THO/NAIZ/YAL	optica	OPT/KA
	O/PIS/THAOE/YO/NAIZ/YAL	optical	OPT/KAL
opisthocheilia	O/PIS/THO/KAOIL/YA	optically	OPT/KLI
	O/PIS/THO/KAOIL/YA	optici	OPT/SAOI
opisthogenia	O/PIS/THO/JAOEN/YA	optician	OP/TIGS
opisthognathism	O/PIS/THOG/NA/THIFM	opticianry	OP/TIGS/RI
opisthomastigote	O/PIS/THO/MA*S/GOET	opticist	OPT/S*IS
opisthoporeia	O/PIS/THO/POE/RAOI/YA	optiochiasmatic	OPT/KO/KAOI/AZ/MAT/IK
	O/PIS/THO/POE/RAOE/YA	opticociliary	OPT/KO/SIL/YAIR
opisthorchiasis	O/PIS/THOR/KAOI/SIS	opticokinetic	OPT/KO/KI/NET/IK
	OP/IS/THOR/KAOI/SIS	opticonasion	OPT/KO/NAIZ/YON
opisthorchid	O/PIS/THOR/KID	opticopupillary	OPT/KO/PAOUP/LAIR
	OP/IS/THOR/KID	Opticrom	OPT/KROEM
Opisthorchiidae	O/PIS/THOR/KAOE/DAE	optics	OPT/IK/-S
	OP/IS/THOR/KAOE/DAE	opticum	OPT/KUM
Opisthorchis	O/PIS/THOR/KIS	opticus	OPT/KUS
	OP/IS/THOR/KIS	Optilets	OPT/LET/-S
opisthorchosis	O/PIS/THOR/KOE/SIS	Optilets-500	OPT/LET/-S/5/HUN
opisthotic	O/PIS/THOT/IK	Optilets-M-500	OPT/LET/-S/M-RBGS/5/HUN
	OP/IS/THOT/IK	optimal	OPT/MAL
opisthotonic	O/PIS/THOT/NIK	optimeter	OP/TIM/TER
	OP/IS/THOT/NIK	Optimine	OPT/MAOEN
	O/PIS/THO/TON/IK	optimism	OPT/MIFM
opisthotonoid	O/PIS/THOT/NOID	optimum	OPT/MUM
	OP/IS/THOT/NOID	optist	OP/T*IS
opisthotonos	O/PIS/THOT/NOS	optoblast	OPT/BLA*S
	OP/IS/THOT/NOS	optochiasmic	OPT/KAOI/AZ/MIK
opisthotonus	O/PIS/THOT/NUS	optogram	OPT/GRAM
	OP/IS/THOT/NUS	optokinetic	OPT/KI/NET/IK
Opitz	O/PITS	optomeninx	OPT/MAOE/NINGS
opium	OEP/YUM		OPT/MEN/INGS
opobalsamum	OEP/BALS/MUM	optometer	OP/TOM/TER
	OP/BALS/MUM	optometrist	OP/TOM/TR*IS
opodidymus	OP/DID/MUS	optometry	OP/TOM/TRI
	OEP/DID/MUS	optomyometer	OPT/MAOI/OM/TER
opossum	O/POS/UM	optophone	OPT/FOEN
	O/POS/SUM	optotype	OPT/TAOIP
Oppenheim	OP/EN/HAOIM	Opuntia	O/PUN/SHA
oppilation	OP/LAIGS	or(o)-	OR/R(O)
oppilative	OP/LAIT/IV		OER/R(O)
Oppler	OP/LER		O/R(O)
opponens	O/POE/NENZ		O*R/R(O)
	O/POE/NENS	ora	OR/RA
	OP/POE/NENZ		O/RA
	OP/POE/NENS	Orabase	OR/RA/BAIS
opportunistic	TUNT/*IS/IK	orad	OR/RAD
	OP/TAOUN/*IS/IK		O/RAD
oppositipolar	O/POZ/TI/POE/LAR	orae	OR/RAE
	OP/POZ/TI/POE/LAR		O/RAE
opsialgia	OPS/YAL/JA	oral	ORL (required)
opsigenes	OP/SIJ/NAOEZ	orale	OR/RAI/LAOE
opsin	OP/SIN		O/RAI/LAOE

orality	OR/RAL/TI	orchiopathy	ORK/YOP/TH*I
	O/RAL/TI	orchiopexy	ORK/YO/PEK/SI
	ORL/TI	orchioplasty	ORK/YO/PLAS/TI
oralogy	OR/RALG	orchiorrhaphy	ORK/YOR/FI
	O/RALG	orchioscirrhus	ORK/YO/SKIR/RUS
orange	ORN/-J	orchiotherapy	ORK/YO/THER/PI
	OR/RAN/-J	orchiotomy	ORK/YOT/M*I
Orap Tablets	OR/RAP/TAB/LET/-S	orchis	OR/KIS
Ora-Testryl	OR/RA/TES/TRIL		ORK/IS
Orazinc	OR/RA/ZIN/-K	orchises	ORK/SAOEZ
orb	ORB	-orchism	ORK/IFM
Orbeli	OR/BAI/LAOE		OR/KIFM
	OR/BEL/LAOE	orchitic	OR/KIT/IK
orbicul-	OR/BIK/L-	orchitis	OR/KAOITS
	OR/BIK/YAOU/L-	orchitolytic	ORK/TO/LIT/IK
	OR/BIK/YU/L-	-orchium	ORK/YUM
orbicular	OR/BIK/LAR	orchotomy	OR/KOT/M*I
orbiculare	OR/BIK/LAI/RAOE	orcinol	ORS/NOL
orbicularis	OR/BIK/LAI/RIS	orciprenaline	ORS/PREN/LAOEN
orbicularis oris	OR/BIK/LAI/RIS/OR/RIS	order	ORD/ER
orbiculi	OR/BIK/LAOI	orderly	ORD/ER/LI
orbiculoanterocapsular	OR/BIK/LO/AENT/RO/KAPS/LAR	ordinate	ORD/NAT
orbiculociliary	OR/BIK/LO/SIL/YAIR		ORD/NAIT
orbiculoposterocapsular	OR/BIK/LO/PO*S/RO/KAPS/LAR	ordure	OR/DAOUR
orbiculus	OR/BIK/LUS	orectic	O/REKT/IK
orbit	ORBT	Oretic	O/RET/IK
	ORB/BIT	Oreticyl	O/RET/SIL
orbit(o)-	ORB/T(O)	orexia	O/REX/YA
orbita	ORB/TA	orexigenic	O/REX/JEN/IK
orbitae	ORB/TAE	oreximania	O/REX/MAIN/YA
orbital	ORB/TAL	Orexin	O/REK/SIN
orbitale	ORB/TAI/LAOE	orf	OR/-F
orbitales	ORB/TAI/LAOEZ	organ	OR/GAN
orbitalia	ORB/TAIL/YA	organ(o)-	ORG/N(O)
orbitalis	ORB/TAI/LIS		OR/GAN
orbitography	ORB/TOG/FI	organa	ORG/NA
orbitonasal	ORB/TO/NAI/ZAL	organacidia	ORG/NA/SID/YA
orbitonometer	ORB/TO/NOM/TER		OR/GAN/SID/YA
	ORB/TOE/NOM/TER	organella	ORG/NEL/LA
orbitonometry	ORB/TO/NOM/TRI	organellae	ORG/NEL/LAE
	ORB/TOE/NOM/TRI	organelle	ORG/NEL
orbitopagus	ORB/TOP/GUS	organic	OR/GAN/IK
orbitosphenoid	ORB/TO/SFAOE/NOID	organica	OR/GAN/KA
orbitosphenoidal	ORB/TO/SFAOE/NOI/DAL	organicism	OR/GAN/SIFM
orbitostat	ORB/TO/STAT	organicist	OR/GAN/S*IS
orbitotemporal	ORB/TO/TEFRP/RAL	Organidin	OR/GAN/DIN
orbitotomy	ORB/TOT/M*I	organism	ORG/NIFM
orbivirus	ORB/VAOI/RUS	organization	ORG/ZAIGS
orcein	ORS/YIN		ORGS
	OR/SAOE/YIN	organize	ORG/NAOIZ
orchectomy	OR/KEKT/M*I		ORG
orchella	OR/SHEL/LA	organizer	ORG/NAOIZ/ER
orchestra	ORK/STRA		ORG/ER
orchi(o)-	ORK/Y(O)	organochlorine	ORG/NO/KLOR/AOEN
	OR/K-	organofaction	ORG/NO/FA*BGS
orchialgia	ORK/YAL/JA	organoferric	ORG/NO/FER/IK
orchiatrophy	ORK/YAT/RO/FI	organogel	OR/GAN/JEL
orchic	ORK/IK		ORG/NO/JEL
	(not OR/KIK; see or kick)	organogenesis	ORG/NO/JEN/SIS
orchichorea	ORK/KOE/RAOE/YA	organogenetic	ORG/NO/JE/NET/IK
orchid	ORK/ID	organogenic	ORG/NO/JEN/IK
	(not OR/KID; see or kid)	organogeny	ORG/NOJ/N*I
orchid(o)-	ORK/D(O)	organography	ORG/NOG/FI
orchidalgia	ORK/DAL/JA	organoid	ORG/NOID
orchidectomy	ORK/DEKT/M*I	organoleptic	ORG/NO/LEPT/IK
orchidic	OR/KID/IK	organology	ORG/NOLG
-orchidism	ORK/DIFM	organoma	ORG/NOE/MA
orchiditis	ORK/DAOITS	organomegaly	ORG/NO/MEG/LI
orchidocelioplasty	ORK/DO/SAOEL/YO/PLAS/TI	organomercurial	ORG/NO/MER/KAOURL
orchidoepididymectomy	ORK/DO/EP/DID/MEKT/M*I		ORG/NO/MER/KAOUR/YAL
orchidometer	ORK/DOM/TER	organometallic	ORG/NO/ME/TAL/IK
orchidoncus	ORK/DON/KUS	organon	ORG/NON
orchidopathy	ORK/DOP/TH*I	organonomy	ORG/NON/M*I
orchidopexy	ORK/DO/PEK/SI	organopathy	ORG/NOP/TH*I
orchidoplasty	ORK/DO/PLAS/TI	organopexia	ORG/NO/PEX/YA
orchidoptosis	ORK/DOP/TOE/SIS	organopexy	ORG/NO/PEK/SI
orchidorrhaphy	ORK/DOR/FI	organophilic	ORG/NO/NIL/IK
orchidotomy	ORK/DOT/M*I	organophilicity	ORG/NO/FLIS/TI
orchiectomy	ORK/YEKT/M*I		ORG/NO/FI/LIS/TI
orchiepididymitis	ORK/EP/DID/MAOITS	organophilism	ORG/NO/FLIFM
	ORK/YEP/DID/MAOITS	organoscopy	ORG/NOS/KPI
orchilytic	ORK/LIT/IK	organosol	OR/GAN/SOL
orchiocatabasis	ORK/YO/KA/TAB/SIS	organotaxis	ORG/NO/TAK/SIS
orchiocele	ORK/YO/SAO*EL	organotherapy	ORG/NO/THER/PI
orchiococcus	ORK/YO/KOK/KUS	organotrophic	ORG/NO/TROFK
orchiodynia	ORK/YO/DIN/YA	organotropic	ORG/NO/TROP/IK
orchiomyeloma	ORK/YO/MAOI/LOE/MA	organotropism	ORG/NOT/RO/PIFM
orchioncus	ORK/YON/KUS	organotropy	ORG/NOT/RO/PI
orchioneuralgia	ORK/YO/NAOU/RAL/JA	organ-specific	OR/GAN/H-F/SPEFK

	OR/GAN/H-F/SPE/SIFK	orthocaine	O*RT/KAIN
organule	OR/GAN/YAOUL	orthocephalic	O*RT/SFAL/IK
organum	ORG/NUM	orthocephalous	O*RT/SEF/LOUS
orgasm	OR/GAFM	orthochorea	O*RT/KOE/RAOE/YA
orgasmic	OR/GAZ/MIK	orthochromatic	O*RT/KROE/MAT/IK
orgastic	OR/GA*S/IK	orthochromia	O*RT/KROEM/YA
-orial	OIRL	orthochromophil	O*RT/KROEM/FIL
	OER/YAL	orthochromophile	O*RT/KROEM/FAOIL
	OR/YAL	Orthoclone	O*RT/KLOEN
orientalis	OR/YEN/TAI/LIS	orthocrasia	O*RT/KRAIZ/YA
	OER/YEN/TAI/LIS	orthocresol	O*RT/KRAOE/SOL
orientation	OR/YEN/TAIGS	Ortho-Creme	O*RT/KRAO*EM
	OER/YEN/TAIGS	orthocytosis	O*RT/SAOI/TOE/SIS
orifacial	OR/RI/FAIRBL	orthodactylous	O*RT/DAKT/LOUS
orifice	OR/RI/FIS	orthodentin	O*RT/DEN/TIN
	O*R/FIS	orthodeoxia	O*RT/DE/OX/YA
	(*not* OR/FIS; see or fis-)	Ortho Diaphragm Kit	OR/THOE/DAO/FRAM/KIT
orificia	OR/RI/FIRB/SHA	orthodichlorobenzene	O*RT/DI/KLOR/BEN/ZAOEN
	OR/RI/FIRB/YA	Ortho Dienestrol	OR/THOE/DI/NES/TROL
	OR/RI/FI/SHA		OR/THOE/DI/EN/ES/TROL
orificial	OR/RI/FIRBL	orthodigita	O*RT/DIJ/TA
	(*not* OR/FIRBL; see or official)	orthodontia	O*RT/DON/SHA
orificialist	OR/RI/FIRBL/*IS	orthodontic	O*RT/DONT/IK
orificii	OR/RI/FIRB/YAOI	orthodontics	O*RT/DONT/IK/-S
	OR/RI/FIS/YAOI	orthodontist	O*RT/DON/T*IS
orificium	OR/RI/FIRB/UM	orthodontology	O*RT/DON/TOLG
origanum	O/RIG/NUM	orthodromic	O*RT/DROEM/IK
origin	ORJ		O*RT/DROM/IK
	O*R/JIN	orthogenesis	O*RT/JEN/SIS
	ORJ/JIN	orthogenic	O*RT/JEN/IK
	(*not* OR/JIN; see or gin)	orthogenics	O*RT/JEN/IK/-S
Orimune	OR/MAOUN	orthoglycemic	O*RT/GLAOI/SAOEM/IK
	OR/RI/MAOUN	orthognathia	OR/THOG/NA*T/YA
Orinase	OR/NAIS		OR/THOG/NA-IT/YA
	OR/RI/NAIS	orthognathic	OR/THOG/NA-T/IK
oris	OR/RIS		OR/THOG/NA-IT/IK
	(*not* OER/RIS; see orris)	orthognathics	OR/THOG/NA-T/IK/-S
Ornade	OR/NAID		OR/THOG/NA-IT/IK/-S
ornate	OR/NAIT	orthognathous	OR/THOG/NA/THOUS
Ornex	OR/NEX	orthograde	O*RT/GRAID
ornidazole	OR/NID/ZOEL	orthography	OR/THOG/FI
ornithine	ORN/THAOEN	Ortho-Gynol	O*RT/GAOI/NOL
	ORN/THIN		O*RT/GAOIN/OL
ornithinemia	ORN/THI/NAOEM/YA	orthokeratology	O*RT/KER/TOLG
ornithinuria	ORN/THI/NAOUR/YA	orthokeratosis	O*RT/KER/TOE/SIS
Ornithodoros	ORN/THOD/ROS	orthokinetics	O*RT/KI/NET/IK/-S
Ornithonyssus	ORN/THON/SUS	orthomechanical	O*RT/ME/KAN/KAL
	ORN/THO/NIS/SUS		O*RT/M-K/KAL
ornithosis	ORN/THOE/SIS	orthomechanotherapy	O*RT/MEK/NO/THER/PI
oro-	OR/RO		O*RT/ME/KAN/THER/PI
orodigitofacial	OR/RO/DIJ/TO/FAIRBL	orthomelic	O*RT/MAOEL/IK
orofacial	OR/RO/FAIRBL		O*RT/MEL/IK
orogranulocyte	OR/RO/GRAN/LO/SAO*IT	orthometer	OR/THOM/TER
orogranulocytic	OR/RO/GRAN/LO/SIT/IK	orthomolecular	O*RT/MO/LEK/LAR
orolingual	OR/RO/LING/WAL	orthomorphia	O*RT/MOR/FAOE/YA
oromaxillary	OR/RO/MAX/LAIR	Orthomyxoviridae	O*RT/MIX/VIR/DAE
oronasal	OR/RO/NAI/ZAL	orthomyxovirus	O*RT/MIX/VAOI/RUS
oropharyngeal	OR/RO/FRIN/JAL	Ortho-Novum	O*RT/NOE/VUM
oropharyngolaryngitis	OR/RO/FRING/LARN/JAOITS		O*RT/NOEV/UM
oropharynx	OR/RO/FARNGS	orthopaedic	O*RT/PAED/IK/
Oropsylla	O/ROP/SIL/LA	orthopaedics	O*RT/PAED/IK/-S
orosomucoid	OR/RO/SO/MAOU/KOID	orthopaedist	O*RT/PAED/*IS
	OR/RO/SO/MAOUK/OID	orthopedic	O*RT/PAOED/IK
orotate	OR/RO/TAIT	orthopedics	O*RT/PAOED/IK/-S
orotic	OR/ROT/IK	orthopedist	O*RT/PAOED/*IS
	O/ROT/IK	orthopercussion	O*RT/PER/KUGS
oroticaciduria	OR/ROT/IK/AS/DAOUR/YA	Ortho Personal	OR/THOE/PERNL/
	O/ROT/IK/AS/DAOUR/YA	Lubricant	LAOUB/KANT
orotidine	O/ROT/DAOEN	orthophony	OR/THOF/N*I
orotidylate	O/ROT/DIL/AIT	orthophoria	O*RT/FOER/YA
orotidylic	O/ROT/DIL/IK	orthophoric	O*RT/FOER/IK
orpanoxin	ORP/NOK/SIN	orthophosphate	O*RT/FOS/FAIT
orphan	O*R/FAN	orthophosphoric	O*RT/FOS/FOER/IK
orphenadrine	OR/FEN/DRAOEN	orthophrenia	O*RT/FRAOEN/YA
Orphengesic	OR/FEN/JAOEZ/IK	orthopia	OR/THOEP/YA
orris	OER/RIS	orthoplessimeter	O*RT/PLES/SIM/TER
	(*not* OR/RIS; see oris)	orthopnea	OR/THOP/NA
orseillin	OR/SAOI/LIN		OR/THOP/NAOE/YA
	OR/SAOIL/LIN	orthopneic	OR/THOP/NIK
orth(o)-	O*RT		OR/THOP/NAOE/IK
	OR/TH(O)	orthopod	O*RT/POD
orthergasia	O*RT/ER/GAIZ/YA	Orthopoxvirus	O*RT/POX/VAOI/RUS
orthesis	OR/THAOE/SIS	orthopraxis	O*RT/PRAK/SIS
orthetic	OR/THET/IK	orthopraxy	O*RT/PRAK/SI
orthetics	OR/THET/IK/-S	orthoprosthesis	O*RT/PROS/THAOE/SIS
Ortho	OR/THOE		O*RT/PROS/THE/SIS
orthoacid	OR/THO/AS/ID	orthopsychiatry	O*RT/SAOI/KAOI/TRI
orthoarteriotony	O*RT/AR/TAOER/YOT/N*I	Orthoptera	OR/THOPT/RA
orthobiosis	O*RT/BAO*I/YOE/SIS	orthoptic	OR/THOPT/IK

orthoptics	OR/THOPT/IK/-S	oscine	OS/SIN
orthoptist	OR/THOP/T*IS	oscitate	OS/TAIT
orthoptoscope	OR/THOPT/SKOEP	oscitation	OS/TAIGS
orthorhombic	O*RT/ROM/BIK	oscula	OS/KLA
orthorrhachic	O*RT/RAK/IK		OS/KAOU/LA
orthoscope	O*RT/SKOEP	osculum	OS/KLUM
orthoscopic	O*RT/SKOP/IK		OS/KAOU/LUM
orthoscopy	OR/THOS/KPI	-ose	OES
orthoses	OR/THOE/SAOEZ		(c)OES
orthosis	OR/THOE/SIS	-oses	(c)OE/SAOEZ
orthostatic	O*RT/STAT/IK		O/SAOEZ
orthostatism	O*RT/STAT/IFM	Osgood	OZ/GAOD
orthostereoscope	O*RT/STER/YO/SKOEP	OSHA	O/SHA
orthosympathetic	O*RT/SIFRP/THET/IK	-osis	(c)OE/SIS
orthotast	O*RT/TA*S		O/SIS
orthoterion	O*RT/TAOER/YON	Osler	OES/LER
	O*RT/TER/YON	osm(o)-	OZ/M(O)
orthothanasia	O*RT/THA/NAIZ/YA		OS/M(O)
orthotherapy	O*RT/THER/PI	osmate	OZ/MAIT
orthotic	OR/THOT/IK	osmatic	OZ/MAT/IK
orthotics	OR/THOT/IK/-S	osmazome	OZ/MA/ZOEM
orthotist	O*RT/T*IS	osmesis	OZ/MAOE/SIS
orthotolidine	O*RT/TOEL/DAOEN	osmesthesia	OZ/MES/THAOEZ/YA
	O*RT/TOL/DAOEN	-osmia	OZ/MAOE/YA
orthotonos	OR/THOT/NOS	osmic	OZ/MIK
orthotonus	OR/THOT/NUS	osmicate	OZ/MI/KAIT
orthotopic	O*RT/TOP/IK	osmication	OZ/MI/KAIGS
orthotropic	O*RT/TROP/IK	osmics	OZ/MIK/-S
orthovoltage	O*RT/VOELT/AJ	osmidrosis	OZ/MI/DROE/SIS
	O*RT/VOEL/TAJ	osmification	OZ/MIF/KAIGS
Ortho-White	O*RT/WHAOIT		OZ/MI/FI/KAIGS
orthropsia	OR/THROPS/YA	osmio-	OZ/MAOE
orthuria	OR/THAOUR/YA		OZ/MAOE/YO
Orudis	O/RAOU/DIS		OS/MAOE
Oryza	O/RAOI/ZA		OS/MAOE/YO
oryzenin	O/RAOIZ/NIN		(not OZ/MO; see osmo-)
oryzoid	OR/ZOID	osmiophilic	OZ/MAOE/FIL/IK
	OR/RI/ZOID		OZ/MAOE/YO/FIL/IK
	O/RAOI/ZOID	osmiophobic	OZ/MAOE/FOEB/IK
oryzoidea	OR/ZOID/YA		OZ/MAOE/YO/FOEB/IK
	OR/RI/ZOID/YA	osmium	OZ/MAOE/UM
oryzoideum	OR/ZOID/YUM		OZ/MUM
	OR/RI/ZOID/YUM	osmoceptor	OZ/MO/SEP/TOR
os	OS	osmodysphoria	OZ/MO/DIS/FOER/YA
osamine	OES/MAOEN	osmogram	OZ/MO/GRAM
osazone	OES/ZOEN	osmol	OZ/MOL
Os-Cal	O*S/KAL		(not OZ/MOEL; see osmole)
	OS/H-F/KAL	osmolality	OZ/MO/LAL/TI
	(not OS/KAL; see oscheal)	osmolar	OZ/MOE/LAR
Os-Cal Fortified	O*S/KAL/FORT/FI/-D	osmolarity	OZ/MO/LAIR/TI
	OS/H-F/KAL/FORT/FI/-D	osmole	OZ/MOEL
Os-Cal Plus	O*S/KAL/PLUS	Osmolite	OZ/MO/LAOIT
	OS/H-F/KAL/PLUS	osmology	OZ/MOLG
oscedo	OS/SAOE/DOE	osmometer	OZ/MOM/TER
osche(o)-	OS/K(O)	osmometry	OZ/MOM/TRI
	OS/KAOE/Y(O)	osmonosology	OZ/MO/NOE/SOLG
oscheal	OS/KAL	osmophil	OZ/MO/FIL
	OS/KAOE/YAL	osmophilic	OZ/MO/FIL/IK
oscheitis	OS/KAOITS	osmophobia	OZ/MO/FOEB/YA
	OS/KAOE/YAOITS	osmophore	OZ/MO/FOER
oschelephantiasis	OS/KEL/FAN/TAOI/SIS	osmoreceptor	OZ/MO/RE/SEP/TOR
	OS/-K/EL/FAN/TAOI/SIS	osmoregulation	OZ/MO/REG/LAIGS
oscheocele	OS/KO/SAO*EL	osmoregulatory	OZ/MO/REG/LA/TOIR
	OS/KAOE/YO/SAO*EL	osmoscope	OZ/MO/SKOEP
oscheohydrocele	OS/KO/HAOI/DRO/SAO*EL	osmose	OZ/MOES
	OS/KAOE/YO/HAOI/DRO/SAO*EL	osmosis	OZ/MOE/SIS
oscheolith	OS/KO/L*IT	osmosity	OZ/MOS/TI
	OS/KAOE/YO/L*IT	osmosology	OZ/MO/SOLG
oscheoma	OS/KOE/MA	osmostat	OZ/MO/STAT
	OS/KAOE/YOE/MA	osmotaxis	OZ/MO/TAK/SIS
oscheoplasty	OS/KO/PLAS/TI	osmotherapy	OZ/MO/THER/PI
	OS/KAOE/YO/PLAS/TI	osmotic	OZ/MOT/IK
oscill(o)-	OS/L(O)	osmyl	OZ/MIL
	O/SIL	osone	O/SOEN
	OS/SIL		(not O/ZOEN; see ozone)
oscillate	OS/LAIT	osphresi(o)-	OS/FRAOEZ/Y(O)
oscillation	OS/SLAIGS	osphresiolagnia	OS/FRAOEZ/YO/LAG/NA
oscillator	OS/LAI/TOR		OS/FRAOEZ/YO/LAG/NAOE/YA
oscillogram	O/SIL/GRAM	osphresiologic	OS/FRAOEZ/YO/LOJ/IK
	OS/SIL/GRAM	osphresiology	OS/FRAOEZ/YOLG
oscillograph	O/SIL/GRAF	osphresiometer	OS/FRAOEZ/YOM/TER
	OS/SIL/GRAF	osphresiophilia	OS/FRAOEZ/YO/FIL/YA
oscillography	OS/LOG/FI	osphresiophobia	OS/FRAOEZ/YO/FOEB/YA
oscillometer	OS/LOM/TER	osphresis	OS/FRAOE/SIS
oscillometric	OS/LO/MET/RIK	osphretic	OS/FRET/IK
oscillometry	OS/LOM/TRI	osphyarthrosis	OS/FAOE/AR/THROE/SIS
oscillopsia	OS/LOPS/YA	osphyomyelitis	OS/FAOE/YO/MAOI/LAOITS
oscilloscope	O/SIL/SKOEP		OS/FO/MAOI/LAOITS
	OS/SIL/SKOEP	osphyotomy	OS/FAOE/OT/M*I

	OS/FOT/M*I
ossa	OS/SA
ossature	OS/KHUR
	OSZ/KHUR
osse(o)-	OS/Y(O)
	OSZ/Y(O)
ossea	OS/YA
osseae	OS/YAE
ossei	OS/YAOI
ossein	OS/YIN
osselet	OS/LET
osseoalbumoid	OS/YO/AL/BAOU/MOID
osseoaponeurotic	OS/YO/AP/NAOU/ROT/IK
osseocartilaginous	OS/YO/KART/LAJ/NOUS
osseofibrous	OS/YO/FAOI/BROUS
osseomucin	OS/YO/MAOU/SIN
osseomucoid	OS/YO/MAOU/KOID
osseosonometer	OS/YO/SOE/NOM/TER
osseosonometry	OS/YO/SOE/NOM/TRI
osseous	OS/YOUS
osseus	OS/YUS
ossi-	OS
	OS/SI
	OSZ
ossicle	OS/K-L
	OS/SIK/-L
	OSZ/K-L
ossicul-	OS/SIK/L-
	OS/SIK/YAOU/L-
	OS/SIK/YU/L-
ossicula	OS/SIK/LA-
ossicular	OS/SIK/LAR
ossiculectomy	OS/SIK/LEKT/M*I
ossiculorum	OS/SIK/LOR/UM
	OS/SIK/LOER/UM
ossiculotomy	OS/SIK/LOT/M*I
ossiculum	OS/SIK/LUM
ossiferous	OS/SIF/ROUS
ossific	OS/SIFK
	OS/SIF/IK
ossificans	OS/SIF/KANZ
ossification	OS/FI/KAIGS
ossified	OS/FI/-D
ossifluence	OS/SIF/LAOUNS
ossifluent	OS/SIF/LAOUNT
ossiform	OS/FORM
ossify	OS/FI
ossifying	OS/FI/-G
ossiphone	OS/FOEN
ossis	OS/SIS
ossium	OS/YUM
ostalgia	OS/TAL/JA
oste(o)-	O*S/Y(O)
	OS/TAOE/Y(O)
osteal	O*S/YA*L
	OS/TAOE/YAL
	(not O*S/YAL; see ostial)
ostealgia	O*S/YAL/JA
ostealgic	O*S/YAL/JIK
osteanagenesis	O*S/YAN/JEN/SIS
osteanaphysis	O*S/YA/NAF/SIS
ostearthrotomy	O*S/YAR/THROT/M*I
ostectomy	OS/TEKT/M*I
osteectopia	O*S/YEK/TOEP/YA
ostein	O*S/YIN
osteite	O*S/YAOIT
osteitic	O*S/YIT/IK
osteitis	O*S/YAOITS
ostembryon	OS/TEM/BRON
	OS/TEM/BRAOE/YON
ostemia	OS/TAOEM/YA
ostempyesis	OS/TEM/PAOI/E/SIS
osteoacusis	O*S/YO/AI/KAOU/SIS
osteoanagenesis	O*S/YO/AN/JEN/SIS
osteoanesthesia	O*S/YO/ANS/THAOEZ/YA
osteoaneurysm	O*S/YO/AN/RIFM
osteoarthritis	O*S/YO/AR/THRAOITS
osteoarthropathy	O*S/YO/AR/THROP/TH*I
osteoarthrosis	O*S/YO/AR/THROE/SIS
osteoarthrotomy	O*S/YO/AR/THROT/M*I
osteoarticular	O*S/YO/AR/TIK/LAR
osteoblast	O*S/YO/BLA*S
osteoblastic	O*S/YO/BLA*S/IK
osteoblastoma	O*S/YO/BLAS/TOE/MA
osteocachectic	O*S/YO/KA/KEKT/IK
osteocachexia	O*S/YO/KA/KEX/YA
osteocamp	O*S/YO/KAFRP
osteocampsia	O*S/YO/KAFRPS/YA
osteocampsis	O*S/YO/KAFRP/SIS

osteocarcinoma	O*S/YO/KARS/NOE/MA
osteocartilaginous	O*S/YO/KART/LAJ/NOUS
osteocele	O*S/YO/SAO*EL
osteocementum	O*S/YO/SEMT/UM
	O*S/YO/SE/MEN/TUM
osteochondral	O*S/YO/KON/DRAL
osteochondritis	O*S/YO/KON/DRAOITS
osteochondrodysplasia	O*S/YO/KON/DRO/DIS/PLAIZ/YA
osteochondrodystrophia	O*S/YO/KON/DRO/DIS/TROEF/YA
osteochondrodystrophy	O*S/YO/KON/DRO/DIS/TRO/FI
osteochondrofibroma	O*S/YO/KON/DRO/FAOI/BROE/
	MA
osteochondrolysis	O*S/YO/KON/DROL/SIS
osteochondroma	O*S/YO/KON/DROE/MA
osteochondromatosis	O*S/YO/KON/DROEM/TOE/SIS
osteochondromyxoma	O*S/YO/KON/DRO/MIK/SOE/MA
osteochondropathia	O*S/YO/KON/DRO/PA*T/YA
osteochondropathy	O*S/YO/KON/DROP/TH*I
osteochondrosarcoma	O*S/YO/KON/DRO/SAR/KOE/MA
osteochondrosis	O*S/YO/KON/DROE/SIS
osteochondrous	O*S/YO/KON/DROUS
osteoclasia	O*S/YO/KLAIZ/YA
osteoclasis	O*S/YOK/LA/SIS
osteoclast	O*S/YO/KLA*S
osteoclastic	O*S/YO/KLA*S/IK
osteoclastoma	O*S/YO/KLAS/TOE/MA
osteoclasty	O*S/YO/KLAS/TI
osteocollagenous	O*S/YO/KLAJ/NOUS
osteocomma	O*S/YO/KOM/MA
osteocope	O*S/YO/KOEP
osteocopic	O*S/YO/KOP/IK
osteocranium	O*S/YO/KRAIN/YUM
osteocystoma	O*S/YO/SIS/TOE/MA
osteocyte	O*S/YO/SAO*IT
osteodentin	O*S/YO/DEN/TIN
osteodentinoma	O*S/YO/DENT/NOE/MA
osteodermatopoikilosis	O*S/YO/DERM/TO/POIK/LOE/SIS
osteodermatous	O*S/YO/DERM/TOUS
osteodermia	O*S/YO/DERM/YA
osteodesmosis	O*S/YO/DEZ/MOE/SIS
osteodiastasis	O*S/YO/DI/A*S/SIS
osteodynia	O*S/YO/DIN/YA
osteodysplasty	O*S/YO/DIS/PLAS/TI
osteodystrophia	O*S/YO/DIS/TROEF/YA
osteodystrophy	O*S/YO/DIS/TRO/FI
osteoectasia	O*S/YO/EK/TAIZ/YA
osteoectomy	O*S/YO/EKT/M*I
osteoenchondroma	O*S/YO/EN/KON/DROE/MA
osteoepiphysis	O*S/YO/E/PIF/SIS
osteofibrochondrosarcoma	O*S/YO/FAOI/BRO/KON/DRO/
	SAR/KOE/MA
osteofibroma	O*S/YO/FAOI/BROE/MA
osteofibromatosis	O*S/YO/FAOI/BROEM/TOE/SIS
osteofibrosis	O*S/YO/FAOI/BROE/SIS
osteofluorosis	O*S/YO/FLAOU/ROE/SIS
osteogen	O*S/YO/JEN
osteogenesis	O*S/YO/JEN/SIS
osteogenetic	O*S/YO/JE/NET/IK
osteogenic	O*S/YO/JEN/IK
osteogenous	O*S/YOJ/NOUS
osteogeny	O*S/YOJ/N*I
osteogram	O*S/YO/GRAM
osteography	O*S/YOG/FI
osteohalisteresis	O*S/YO/HA/L*IS/RAOE/SIS
	O*S/YO/HAL/STER/E/SIS
osteohydatidosis	O*S/YO/HAOID/TI/DOE/SIS
osteohypertrophy	O*S/YO/HAOI/PERT/FI
osteoid	O*S/YOID
osteolathyrism	O*S/YO/LA*T/RIFM
osteolipochondroma	O*S/YO/LIP/KON/DROE/MA
osteolipoma	O*S/YO/LI/POE/MA
osteologia	O*S/YO/LOE/JA
osteologist	O*S/YO*LGS
osteology	O*S/YOLG
osteolysis	O*S/YOL/SIS
osteolytic	O*S/YO/LIT/IK
osteoma	O*S/YOE/MA
osteomalacia	O*S/YO/MA/LAI/SHA
osteomalacic	O*S/YO/MA/LAIS/IK
osteomalacosis	O*S/YO/MAL/KOE/SIS
osteomatoid	O*S/YOEM/TOID
osteomatosis	O*S/YOEM/TOE/SIS
osteomere	O*S/YO/MAOER
osteometry	O*S/YOM/TRI
osteomiosis	O*S/YO/MAOI/YOE/SIS
osteomyelitic	O*S/YO/MAOI/LIT/IK
osteomyelitis	O*S/YO/MAOI/LAOITS
osteomyelodysplasia	O*S/YO/MAOI/LO/DIS/PLAIZ/YA
osteomyelography	O*S/YO/MAOI/LOG/FI

osteomyxochondroma	O*S/YO/MIX/KON/DROE/MA	ostracize	OS/TRA/SAOIZ
osteon	O*S/YON	ostracosis	OS/TRA/KOE/SIS
osteoncus	O*S/YON/KUS	ostreotoxism	OS/TRO/TOK/SIFM
osteone	O*S/YOEN		OS/TRAOE/YO/TOK/SIFM
osteonecrosis	O*S/YO/NE/KROE/SIS	ostreotoxismus	OS/TRO/TOK/SIZ/MUS
osteoneuralgia	O*S/YO/NAOU/RAL/JA		OS/TRAOE/YO/TOK/SIZ/MUS
osteonosus	O*S/YON/SUS	ot(o)-	OET
osteo-odontoma	O*S/YO/O/DON/TOE/MA		O/T(O)
osteopath	O*S/YO/PA*T	otalgia	O/TAL/JA
osteopathia	O*S/YO/PA*T/YA	otalgic	O/TAL/JIK
osteopathic	O*S/YO/PA*T/IK	othematoma	OET/HAOEM/TOE/MA
osteopathology	O*S/YO/PA/THOLG		O/THAOEM/TOE/MA
osteopathy	O*S/YOP/TH*I	othemorrhagia	OET/HEM/RAI/JA
osteopecilia	O*S/YO/PE/SIL/YA		O/THEM/RAI/JA
osteopedion	O*S/YO/PAOED/YON	-otia	(c)OE/SHA
osteopenia	O*S/YO/PAOEN/YA	otiatria	OET/YAT/RA
osteopenic	O*S/YO/PEN/IK		OET/YAT/RAOE/YA
osteoperiosteal	O*S/YO/P*ER/O*S/YAL	otiatrics	OET/YAT/RIK/-S
osteoperiostitis	O*S/YO/P*ER/OS/TAOITS	otic	OET/IK
osteopetrosis	O*S/YO/PE/TROE/SIS		O/TIK
osteopetrotic	O*S/YO/PE/TROT/IK		OT/IK
osteophage	O*S/YO/FAIJ	Otic Domeboro Solution	OT/IK/DOEM/BOR/ROE/SLAOUGS
osteophagia	O*S/YO/FAI/JA	Otic Tridesilon Solution	OT/IK/TR*I/DES/LON/SLAOUGS
osteophlebitis	O*S/YO/FLE/BAOITS	Otisan Drops	OT/SAN/DROP/-S
osteophone	O*S/YO/FOEN	otitic	O/TIT/IK
osteophony	O*S/YOF/N*I	otitis	O/TAOITS
osteophore	O*S/YO/FOER	otoacariasis	OET/AK/RAOI/SIS
osteophyma	O*S/YO/FAOI/MA	otoantritis	OET/AN/TRAOITS
osteophyte	O*S/YO/FAOIT	otobiosis	OET/BAO*I/YOE/SIS
osteophytosis	O*S/YO/FAOI/TOE/SIS	Otobius	O/TOEB/YUS
osteoplaque	O*S/YO/PLAK	otoblennorrhea	OET/BLEN/RAOE/YA
osteoplast	O*S/YO/PLA*S	otocephalus	OET/SEF/LUS
osteoplastic	O*S/YO/PLA*S/IK	otocephaly	OET/SEF/LI
osteoplastica	O*S/YO/PLA*S/KA	otocerebritis	OET/SER/BRAOITS
osteoplasty	O*S/YO/PLAS/TI	otocleisis	OET/KLAOI/SIS
osteopoikilosis	O*S/YO/POIK/LOE/SIS	otoconia	OET/KOEN/YA
osteopoikilotic	O*S/YO/POIK/LOT/IK	otoconite	O/TOK/NAOIT
osteoporosis	O*S/YO/PROE/SIS	otoconium	OET/KOEN/YUM
	O*S/YO/PO/ROE/SIS	Otocort	OET/KORT
osteoporotic	O*S/YO/PROT/IK		OT/KORT
	O*S/YO/PO/ROT/IK	otocranial	OET/KRAIN/YAL
osteoprogenitor	O*S/YO/PRO/JEN/TOR	otocranium	OET/KRAIN/YUM
osteopsathyrosis	O*S/YOP/SA*T/ROE/SIS	otocyst	OET/S*IS
osteopulmonary	O*S/YO/PUL/MO/NAIR	Otodectes	OET/DEK/TAOEZ
	O*S/YO/PUM/NAIR	otodynia	OET/DIN/YA
osteoradionecrosis	O*S/YO/RAID/YO/NE/KROE/SIS	otoencephalitis	OET/EN/SEF/LAOITS
osteorrhagia	O*S/YO/RAI/JA	otoganglion	OET/GANG/LON
osteorrhaphy	O*S/YOR/FI	otogenic	OET/JEN/IK
osteosarcoma	O*S/YO/SAR/KOE/MA	otogenous	O/TOJ/NOUS
osteosarcomatous	O*S/YO/SAR/KOEM/TOUS	otography	O/TOG/FI
osteosclerosis	O*S/YO/SKLE/ROE/SIS	otohemineurasthenia	OET/HEM/NAOUR/AS/THAOEN/
osteosclerotic	O*S/YO/SKLE/ROT/IK		YA
osteoseptum	O*S/YO/SEP/TUM		OET/HEM/NAOU/RAS/THAOEN/
osteosis	O*S/YOE/SIS		YA
osteospongioma	O*S/YO/SPON/JOE/MA	otolaryngologist	OET/LARN/GO*LGS
osteosteatoma	O*S/YO/STAOE/TOE/MA	otolaryngology	OET/LARN/GOLG
osteostixis	O*S/YO/STIK/SIS	otolite	OET/LAOIT
osteosuture	O*S/YO/SAOU/KHUR	otolith	OET/L*IT
osteosynovitis	O*S/YO/SIN/VAOITS	otolithiasis	OET/LI/THAOI/SIS
osteosynthesis	O*S/YO/S*INT/SIS	otologic	OET/LOJ/IK
osteotabes	O*S/YO/TAI/BAOEZ	otologist	O/TO*LGS
osteotelangiectasia	O*S/YO/TEL/AN/JEK/TAIZ/YA	otology	O/TOLG
osteothrombophlebitis	O*S/YO/THROM/BO/FLE/BAOITS	otomassage	OET/MA/SAJ
osteothrombosis	O*S/YO/THROM/BOE/SIS		OET/MAS/SAJ
osteotome	O*S/YO/TOEM	otomastoiditis	OET/MAS/TOI/DAOITS
osteotomoclasia	O*S/YO/TOEM/KLAIZ/YA	otomucormycosis	OET/MAOU/KOR/MAOI/KOE/SIS
osteotomoclasis	O*S/YO/TOE/MOK/LA/SIS	-otomy	(c)OT/M*I
osteotomy	O*S/YOT/M*I	otomyasthenia	OET/MAOI/AS/THAOEN/YA
osteotribe	O*S/YO/TRAOIB	otomycosis	OET/MAOI/KOE/SIS
osteotrite	O*S/YO/TRAOIT	otomyiasis	OET/MAOI/AOI/SIS
osteotrophy	O*S/YOT/RO/FI	otoneuralgia	OET/NAOU/RAL/JA
osteotylus	O*S/YOT/LUS	otoneurasthenia	OET/NAOUR/AS/THAOEN/YA
osteotympanic	O*S/YO/TIM/PAN/IK		OET/NAOU/RAS/THAOEN/YA
osthexia	OS/THEX/YA	otoneurologic	OET/NAOUR/LOJ/IK
osthexy	OS/THEK/SI	otoneurology	OET/NAOU/ROLG
ostia	O*S/YA	osopalatodigital	OET/PAL/TO/DIJ/TAL
ostial	O*S/YAL	otopathy	O/TOP/TH*I
	(*not* OS/TAOE/YAL; see osteal)	otopharyngeal	OET/FRIN/JAL
Osti-Derm	O*S/DERM	otophone	OET/FOEN
ostitic	OS/TIT/IK	otoplasty	OET/PLAS/TI
ostitis	OS/TAOITS	otopolypus	OET/POL/PUS
ostium	O*S/YUM	otopyorrhea	OET/PAOI/RAOE/YA
ostomate	O*S/MAIT	otopyosis	OET/PAOI/YOE/SIS
-ostomy	O*S/M*I	otor	O/TOR
ostosis	OS/TOE/SIS	otorhinolaryngologist	OET/RAOIN/LARN/GO*LGS
ostraceous	OS/TRAIRBS	otorhinolaryngology	OET/RAOIN/LARN/GOLG
ostrac-	OS/TRA/S-	otorhinology	OET/RAOI/NOLG
	O*S/RA/S-	otorrhagia	OET/RAI/JA
ostracism	OS/TRA/SIFM	otorrhea	OET/RAOE/YA

otosalpinx	OET/SAL/PINGS	overdose	OVR/DOES
otosclerosis	OET/SKLE/ROE/SIS	overdosage	OVR/DOES/AJ
otosclerotic	OET/SKLE/ROT/IK	overdrive	OVR/DRAOIV
otoscope	OET/SKOEP	overeruption	OVR/E/RUPGS
otoscopy	O/TOS/KPI	overextension	OVR/EX/TENGS
otosis	O/TOE/SIS	overflow	OVR/FLOE
otospongiosis	OET/SPON/JOE/SIS	overgrafting	OVR/GRAFT/-G
otosteal	O/TO*S/YAL	overgrowth	OVR/GRO*ET
otosteon	O/TO*S/YON		OVR/GRO*UT
ototomy	O/TOT/M*I	overhang	OVR/HANG
ototoxic	OET/TOX/IK	overhydration	OVR/HAOI/DRAIGS
ototoxicity	OET/TOK/SIS/TI	overinflation	OVR/IN/FLAIGS
Otrivin	O/TRI/VIN	overjet	OVR/JET
Otto	OT/TOE	overlap	OVR/LAP
ouabain	WAU/BAIN	overlay	OVR/LAI
Oudin	AOU/DAN	overlearning	OVR/LERN/-G
	YAOU/DAN	overproductivity	OVR/PRUK/TIV/TI
oul(o)-	see ulo-		OVR/PRO/DUK/TIV/TI
ounce	OUNS	overreaching	OVR/RAOEFP/-G
-ous	(c)OUS	overresponse	OVR/SPONS
	OUS		OVR/RE/SPONS
out	OUT	overriding	OVR/RAOID/-G
out-	O*UT	overripe	OVR/RAOIP
-out	O*UT	overshoot	OVR/SHAOT
outbreeding	O*UT/BRAOED/-G	overstain	OVR/STAIN
outlet	O*UT/LET	overstrain	OVR/STRAIN
outline	O*UT/LAOIN	overstress	OVR/STRESZ
outpatient	O*UT/PAIRBT	overt	OEVRT
outpocketing	O*UT/POKT/-G		OVRT
outpouching	O*UT/POUFP/-G		O/VERT
output	O*UT/PUT	overtoe	OVR/TOE
ov(o)-	OEV	Overton	OVR/TON
	O/V(O)	overtone	OVR/TOEN
ova	O/VA	overtransfusion	OVR/TRA*NS/FAOUGS
oval	OEVL	overventilation	OVR/VENT/LAIGS
ovalbumin	O/VAL/BAOU/MIN	overweight	OVR/WAIGT
	OEV/AL/BAOU/MIN	overwintering	OVR/WINT/ER/-G
ovale	O/VAI/LAOE	ovi	O/VAOI
ovalis	O/VAI/LIS	ovi-	OEV
ovalocytary	OEV/LO/SAOIT/RI	ovicidal	OEV/SAOI/DAL
ovalocyte	OEV/LO/SAO*IT	ovicide	OEV/SAO*ID
ovalocytosis	OEV/LO/SAOI/TOE/SIS	Ovide	O/VAOID
ovari(o)-	O/VAIR/Y(O)	oviducal	OEV/DAOU/KAL
ovaria	O/VAIR/YA	oviduct	OEV/DUKT
ovarialgia	O/VAIR/YAL/JA	oviductal	OEV/DUK/TAL
ovarian	O/VAIRN	oviferous	O/VIF/ROUS
	O/VAIR/YAN	oviform	OEV/FORM
ovarica	O/VAIR/KA	oviforme	OEV/FOR/MAOE
ovariectomy	O/VAIR/YEKT/M*I	ovigenesis	OEV/JEN/SIS
ovarii	O/VAIR/YAOI	ovigenetic	OEV/JE/NET/IK
ovariocele	O/VAIR/YO/SAO*EL	ovigenic	OEV/JEN/IK
ovariocentesis	O/VAIR/YO/SEN/TAOE/SIS	ovigenous	O/VIJ/NOUS
ovariocyesis	O/VAIR/YO/SAOI/E/SIS	ovigerm	OEV/JERM
ovariodysneuria	O/VAIR/YO/DIS/NAOUR/YA	ovigerous	O/VIJ/ROUS
ovariogenic	O/VAIR/YO/JEN/IK	ovigerus	O/VIJ/RUS
ovariohysterectomy	O/VAIR/YO/H*IS/REKT/M*I	ovillus	O/VIL/LUS
ovariolytic	O/VAIR/YO/LIT/IK	ovination	OEV/NAIGS
ovarioncus	O/VAIR/YON/KUS	ovine	O/VAOIN
ovariopathy	O/VAIR/YOP/TH*I	ovinia	O/VIN/YA
ovariopexy	O/VAIR/YO/PEK/SI	oviparity	OEV/PAIR/TI
ovariorrhexis	O/VAIR/YO/REK/SIS	oviparous	O/VIP/ROUS
ovariosalpingectomy	O/VAIR/YO/SAL/PIN/JEKT/M*I	oviposit	OEV/POZ/SIT
ovariosalpingitis	O/VAIR/YO/SAL/PIN/JAOITS	oviposition	OEV/POGS
ovariosteresis	O/VAIR/YO/STE/RAOE/SIS		OEV/PO/SIGS
ovariostomy	O/VAIR/YO*S/M*I	ovipositor	OEV/POZ/TOR
ovariotomy	O/VAIR/YOT/M*I	ovis	O/VIS
ovariotubal	O/VAIR/YO/TAOU/BAL	ovisac	OEV/SAK
ovaripriva	OEV/RI/PRAOI/VA	ovist	O/V*IS
	O/VAIR/PRAOI/VA		OEV/*IS
ovaritis	OEV/RAOITS	ovium	OEV/YUM
ovarium	O/VAIRM	ovo-	OEV
	O/VAIR/YUM		O/VO
ovary	OEV/RI	ovocenter	OEV/SEN/TER
Ovcon	OV/KON	ovocyte	OEV/SAO*IT
Ovcon-35	OV/KON/35	ovoflavin	OEV/FLAIVN
Ovcon-50	OV/KON/50	ovoglobulin	OEV/GLOB/LIN
over	OEVF	ovogonium	OEV/GOEN/YUM
	OEFR	ovoid	O/VOID
over-	OVR		OEV/OID
-over	OFR	ovolarviparous	OEV/LAR/VIP/ROUS
overbite	OVR/BAOIT	ovolysin	O/VOL/SIN
overclosure	OVR/KLOE/SHUR	ovolytic	OEV/LIT/IK
overcompensation	OVR/KOFRP/SAIGS	ovomucin	OEV/MAOU/SIN
overcorrection	OVR/KR*EBGS	ovomucoid	OEV/MAOU/KOID
overdenture	OVR/DEN/KHUR		OEV/MAOUK/OID
overdetermination	OVR/DERMGS	ovoplasm	OEV/VO/PLAFM
	OVR/DERM/NAIGS	ovoprecipitin	OEV/VO/PRE/SIP/TIN
overdominance	OVR/DOM/NANS	ovoprotogen	OEV/PROET/JEN
overdominant	OVR/DOM/NANT	ovotestis	OEV/TES/TIS

ovotherapy	OEV/THER/PI	oxilorphan	OX/LOR/FAN
ovotransferrin	OEV/TRA*NS/FER/RIN	oxim	OK/SIM
	OEV/TRA*NS/FRIN	oxime	OK/SAOEM
ovovitellin	OEV/VAOI/TEL/LIN		OK/SAOIM
ovoviviparity	OEV/VIV/PAIR/TI	oximeter	OK/SIM/TER
ovoviviparous	OEV/VAOI/VIP/ROUS		OX/IM/TER
Ovral	OEV/RAL	oximetry	OK/SIM/TRI
	OV/RAL		OX/IM/TRI
Ovral-28	OEV/RAL/28	oximinotransferase	OK/SIM/NO/TRA*NS/FRAIS
	OV/RAL/28	oxiperomide	OX/PER/MAOID
Ovrette	OEV/RET	oxiramide	OK/SIR/MAOID
	OV/RET	Oxistat	OX/STAT
ovu-	OV	oxisuran	OX/SAOU/RAN
	OV/YAOU		OX/SAOUR/RAN
	OV/YU	oxogestone	OX/JES/TOEN
ovula	OV/LA	oxolamine	OK/SOL/MAOEN
ovular	OV/LAR	oxolinic	OX/LIN/IK
ovulation	OV/LAIGS	oxonium	OK/SOEN/YUM
ovulatory	OV/LA/TOIR	oxophenarsine	OX/FEN/AR/SAOEN
ovule	OV/YAOUL		OX/FEN/AR/SIN
	OEV/YAOUL	oxoproline	OX/PRO/LAOEN
	O/VAOUL	oxoprolinuria	OX/PROEL/NAOUR/YA
ovulocyclic	OV/LO/SAOIK/LIK	oxosuccinic	OX/SUK/SIN/IK
ovulogenous	OV/LOJ/NOUS	oxprenolol	OX/PREN/LOL
ovulum	OV/LUM		OX/PREN/LOEL
ovum	O/VUM	Oxsoralen	OX/SOR/LEN
	OEV/VUM		OX/SOER/LEN
Owen	O/WEN		OK/SOR/LEN
owl	OUL	Oxsoralen-Ultra	OX/SOR/LEN/UL/TRA
oxacillin	OX/SLIN		OX/SOER/LEN/UL/TRA
	OX/SIL/LIN		OK/SOR/LEN/UL/TRA
oxalaldehyde	OK/SAL/ALD/HAOID	oxtriphylline	OX/TRIF/LAOEN
	OX/ALD/HAOID		OX/TR*I/FLIN
oxalate	OX/LAIT		OX/TR*I/FIL/LIN
oxalated	OX/LAIT/-D	oxy-	OX
oxalation	OX/LAIGS	Oxy-5	OX/5
oxalemia	OX/LAOEM/YA	Oxy-10	OX/10
oxalic	OK/SAL/IK	oxyachrestia	OX/AI/KR*ES/YA
	OX/AL/IK	oxyacoia	OX/AI/KOI/YA
oxalism	OX/LIFM	oxyaphia	OX/AIF/YA
oxalo	OX/LOE	oxybarbiturate	OX/BAR/BIFP/RAIT
oxalo-	OX/LO		OX/BAR/BIFP/RAT
oxaloacetate	OX/LO/AS/TAIT	oxybenzene	OX/BEN/ZAOEN
oxaloacetic	OX/LO/AI/SAOET/IK	oxybenzone	OX/BEN/ZOEN
	OX/LO/AI/SET/IK	oxybiotin	OX/BAO*I/TIN
oxalosis	OX/LOE/SIS	oxyblepsia	OX/BLEPS/YA
oxalosuccinic	OX/LO/SUK/SIN/IK	oxybutynin	OX/BAOUT/NIN
oxalourea	OX/LO/YAOU/RAOE/YA	oxybutyria	OX/BAOU/TIR/YA
oxaluria	OX/LAOUR/YA	oxybutyricacidemia	OX/BAOU/TIR/IK/AS/DAOEM/YA
oxaluric	OX/LAOUR/IK	oxycalorimeter	OX/KAL/RIM/TER
oxalyl	OX/LIL	oxycellulose	OX/SEL/YAOU/LOES
oxalylurea	OX/LIL/YAOU/RAOE/YA	oxycephalia	OX/SFAIL/YA
oxamic	OK/SAM/IK	oxycephalic	OX/SFAL/IK
oxamide	OK/SAM/AOID	oxycephalous	OX/SEF/LOUS
	OK/SAM/ID	oxycephaly	OX/SEF/LI
oxammonium	OX/MOEN/YUM	oxychloride	OX/KLOR/AOID
oxamniquine	OK/SAM/NI/KWIN	oxychlorosene	OX/KLOR/SAOEN
	OX/AM/NI/KWIN	oxycholine	OX/KOE/LAOEN
oxanamide	OK/SAN/MAOID		OK/KOE/LIN
oxandrolone	OK/SAN/DRO/LOEN	oxychromatic	OX/KROE/MAT/IK
	OX/AN/DRO/LOEN	oxychromatin	OX/KROEM/TIN
oxaphenamide	OX/FEN/MAOID	oxycinesia	OX/SI/NAOEZ/YA
oxaprozin	OX/PRO/ZIN	Oxy Clean	OX/KLAOEN
oxarbazole	OK/SARB/ZOEL	oxycodone	OX/KO/DOEN
	OX/ARB/ZOEL		OX/KOE/DOEN
oxatomide	OK/SAIT/MAOID	oxycorticoid	OX/KORT/KOID
oxazepam	OX/AZ/PAM	oxycyanide	OX/SAOI/NAOID
	OK/SAZ/PAM	oxydase	OX/DAIS
	OK/SAIZ/PAM	oxyecoia	OX/E/KOI/YA
oxazin	OX/ZIN	oxyesthesia	OX/ES/THAOEZ/YA
oxazole	OX/ZOEL	oxygen	OX/JEN
oxeladin	OK/SEL/DIN	oxygenase	OX/JEN/AIS
oxethazaine	OK/S*ET/ZAIN		OX/JE/NAIS
oxetorone	OK/SET/ROEN	oxygenate	OX/JEN/AIT
oxfendazole	OX/FEND/ZOEL		OX/JE/NAIT
-oxia	OX/YA	oxygenation	OX/JEN/AIGS
oxidant	OX/DANT		OX/JE/NAIGS
oxidase	OX/DAIS	oxygenator	OX/JEN/AI/TOR
oxidasis	OX/DAI/SIS		OX/JE/NAI/TOR
oxidation	OX/DAIGS	oxygenic	OX/JEN/IK
oxidation-reduction	OX/DAIGS/H-F/RE/D*UBGS	oxygenize	OX/JEN/AOIZ
oxidative	OX/DAIT/IV	oxygeusia	OX/GAOUS/YA
oxide	OK/SAOID	oxyhematoporphyrin	OX/HAOEM/TO/POR/FRIN
	OX/AOID		OX/HEM/TO/POR/FRIN
oxidize	OX/DAOIZ	oxyheme	OX/HAOEM
oxidopamine	OX/DOEP/MAOEN	oxyhemochromogen	OX/HAOEM/KROEM/JEN
oxidoreductase	OX/DO/RE/DUK/TAIS	oxyhemocyanine	OX/HAOEM/SAOI/NIN
oxidosis	OX/DOE/SIS	oxyhemoglobin	OX/HAOEM/GLOE/BIN
oxifungin	OX/FUN/GIN	oxyhydrocephalus	OX/HAOI/DRO/SEF/LUS

oxyhyperglycemia	OX/HAO*IP/GLAOI/SAOEM/YA
oxyiodide	OX/AOI/DAOID
oxykrinin	OX/KRIN/NIN
oxylalia	OX/LAIL/YA
oxylonprocaine	OX/LON/PRO/KAIN
oxyluciferin	OX/LAOU/SIF/RIN
oxymesterone	OX/M*ES/ROEN
oxymetazoline	OX/ME/TAZ/LAOEN
oxymetholone	OX/M*ET/LOEN
oxymorphone	OX/MOR/FOEN
oxymyoglobin	OX/MAOI/GLOE/BIN
oxymyohematin	OX/MAOI/HAOEM/TIN
	OX/MAOI/HEM/TIN
oxynervon	OX/NER/VON
oxynervone	OX/NER/VOEN
oxyneurine	OX/NAOU/RAOEN
Oxy Night Watch	OX/NAOIGT/WAFP
oxynitrilase	OX/NAOI/TRIL/AIS
oxyntic	OK/SINT/IK
oxyopia	OX/OEP/YA
oxyopter	OX/OPT/ER
oxyosis	OX/YOE/SIS
	OX/O/SIS
oxyosmia	OX/OZ/MA
	OX/OZ/MAOE/YA
oxyosphresia	OX/OS/FRAOEZ/YA
oxyparaplastin	OX/PAR/PLAS/TIN
oxypathia	OX/PA*T/YA
oxyperitoneum	OX/PERT/NAOEM
oxypertine	OX/PER/TAOEN
oxyphenbutazone	OX/FEN/BAOUT/ZOEN
oxyphencyclimine	OX/FEN/SAOI/KLI/MAOEN
oxyphenisatin	OX/FE/NAOIS/TIN
oxyphenonium	OX/FE/NOEN/YUM
oxyphenylethylamine	OX/FENL/*ET/IL/AM/MIN
oxyphil	OX/FIL
oxyphile	OX/FAOIL
oxyphilic	OX/FIL/IK
oxyphilous	OK/SIF/LOUS
oxyphonia	OX/FOEN/YA
oxyphorase	OX/FOER/AIS
oxyphosphate	OX/FOS/FAIT
oxyplasm	OX/PLAFM
oxypolygelatin	OX/POL/JEL/TIN
oxypurinase	OX/PAOUR/NAIS
oxypurine	OX/PAOUR/AOEN
	OX/PAOU/RAOEN
oxypurinol	OX/PAOUR/NOL
oxyrhine	OX/RAOIN
oxyrygmia	OX/RIG/MA
	OX/RIG/MAOE/YA
oxysalt	OX/SAULT
	OX/SALT
oxysantonin	OX/SANT/NIN
Oxyspirura	OX/SPAOI/RAOU/RA
oxytalan	OK/SIT/LAN
oxytalanolysis	OK/SIT/LAN/OL/SIS
	OK/SIT/LA/NOL/SIS
oxytetracycline	OX/TET/RA/SAOI/KLAOEN
oxythiamin	OX/THAOI/MIN
oxytocia	OX/TOE/SHA
oxytocic	OX/TOES/IK
oxytocin	OX/TOE/SIN
oxytropism	OK/SIT/RO/PIFM
oxytuberculin	OX/TAOU/BERK/LIN
oxyuria	OX/YAOUR/YA
oxyuriasis	OX/YAOU/RAOI/SIS
oxyuricide	OX/YAOUR/SAO*ID
oxyurid	OX/YAOUR/ID
Oxyuridae	OX/YAOUR/DAE
oxyurifuge	OX/YAOUR/FAOUJ
oxyuriosis	OX/YAOUR/YOE/SIS
Oxyuris	OX/YAOU/RIS
	OX/YAOUR/RIS
oz.	O*Z
ozena	O/ZAOE/NA
ozenous	OEZ/NOUS
	O/ZAOEN/OUS
ozo-	OEZ
	O/ZO
ozocerite	OEZ/SE/RAOIT
ozochrotia	OEZ/KROE/SHA
ozokerite	OEZ/KAOER/AOIT
	OEZ/KAOE/RAOIT
ozonator	OEZ/NAI/TOR
ozone	O/ZOEN
ozonide	OEZ/NAOID
ozonize	OEZ/NAOIZ
ozonizer	OEZ/NAOIZ/ER

ozonolysis	OEZ/NOL/SIS
ozonometer	OEZ/NOM/TER
ozonophore	O/ZOEN/FOER
ozonoscope	O/ZOEN/SKOEP
ozostomia	OEZ/STOEM/YA

P

PA	P-RBGS/A*RBGS
Pabalate	PAB/LAIT
Pabalate-SF	PAB/LAIT/S-RBGS/F*RBGS
Pablum	PA*B/LUM
pabul-	PAB/L-
	PAB/YAOU/L-
	PAB/YU/L-
pabular	PAB/LAR
pabulin	PAB/LIN
pabulum	PAB/LUM
Pacaps	PA/KAP/-S
	PAI/KAP/-S
Pacchioni	PAK/YOE/NAOE
pacchionian	PAK/YOEN/YAN
pacefollower	PAIS/FOL/LOE/ER
pacemaker	PAIS/MAIK/ER
pachismus	PA/KIZ/MUS
pachometer	PA/KOM/TER
pachy-	PAK
	PA/KI
pachyacria	PAK/AI/KRAOE/YA
	PAK/AI/KRA
pachyblepharon	PAK/BLEF/RON
pachycephalia	PAK/SFAIL/YA
pachycephalic	PAK/SFAL/IK
pachycephalous	PAK/SEF/LOUS
pachycephaly	PAK/SEF/LI
pachycheilia	PAK/KAOIL/YA
pachycholia	PAK/KOEL/YA
pachychromatic	PAK/KROE/MAT/IK
pachychymia	PAK/KAOIM/YA
pachycolpismus	PAK/KOL/PIZ/MUS
pachydactylia	PAK/DAK/TIL/YA
pachydactylous	PAK/DAKT/LOUS
pachydactyly	PAK/DAKT/LI
pachyderma	PAK/DER/MA
pachydermatocele	PAK/DER/MAT/SAO*EL
pachydermatosis	PAK/DERM/TOE/SIS
pachydermatous	PAK/DERM/TOUS
packydermia	PAK/DERM/YA
pachydermic	PAK/DERM/IK
pachydermoperiostosis	PAK/DERM/P*ER/OS/TOE/SIS
pachyglossia	PAK/GLOS/YA
pachygnathous	PA/KIG/NA/THOUS
pachygyria	PAK/JAOIR/YA
pachyhymenia	PAK/HAOI/MEN/YA
pachyhymenic	PAK/HAOI/MEN/IK
pachyleptomeningitis	PAK/LEPT/MEN/JAOITS
pachylosis	PAK/LOE/SIS
pachymenia	PAK/MAOEN/YA
pachymenic	PAK/MEN/IK
pachymeninges	PAK/ME/NIN/JAOEZ
pachymeningitis	PAK/MEN/JAOITS
pachymeningopathy	PAK/MEN/GOP/TH*I
pachymeninx	PAK/MAOE/NINGS
	PAK/MEN/INGS
pachymeter	PA/KIM/TER
pachymucosa	PAK/MAOU/KOE/SA
pachynema	PAK/NAOE/MA
pachynesis	PAK/NAOE/SIS
pachynsis	PA/KIN/SIS
pachyntic	PA/KINT/IK
pachyonychia	PAK/O/NIK/YA
	PAK/YO/NIK/YA
pachyostosis	PAK/OS/TOE/SIS
pachyotia	PAK/YOE/SHA
	PAK/O/SHA
pachypelviperitonitis	PAK/PEL/VI/PERT/NAOITS
pachyperiosteoderma	PAK/P*ER/O*S/YO/DER/MA
pachyperiostitis	PAK/P*ER/OS/TAOITS
pachyperitonitis	PAK/PERT/NAOITS
pachypleuritis	PAK/PLAOU/RAOITS
pachypodous	PA/KIP/DOUS
pachysalpingitis	PAK/SAL/PIN/JAOITS
pachysalpingo-ovaritis	PAK/SAL/PING/OEV/RAOITS
pachysomia	PAK/SOEM/YA
pachytene	PAK/TAOEN
pachyvaginalitis	PAK/VAJ/NAL/AOITS
	PAK/VAJ/NA/LAOITS
pachyvaginitis	PAK/VAJ/NAOITS
pacing	PAIS/-G
Pacini	PA/KHAOE/NAOE
	(*not* PA/SAOE/NAOE; see Pasini)
pacinian	PA/SIN/YAN

	PA/KHIN/YAN
pacinitis	PAS/NAOITS
	PAFP/NAOITS
pack	PAK
packed	PAK/-D
packer	PAK/ER
packing	PAK/-G
pad	PAD
padimate A	PAD/MAIT/ARBGS
padimate O	PAD/MAIT/ORBGS
Paecilomyces	PAOE/SIL/MAOI/SAOEZ
	PAE/SIL/MAOI/SAOEZ
Pagenstecher	PAG/EN/STEK/ER
Paget	PAJ/ET
pagetic	PA/JET/IK
pagetoid	PAJ/TOID
-pagia	PAI/JA
	PAIJ/YA
pagophagia	PAIG/FAI/JA
pagoplexia	PAIG/PLEX/YA
-pagus	-P/GUS
pain	PAIN
paint	PAINT
pair	PAIR
pairing	PAIR/-G
Pajot	PA/JOE
Pal	K-P/PAL
Palade	PAL/LAID
	PA/LAID
	(*not* PAL/AID; see pal aid)
palat(o)-	PAL/T(O)
palata	PA/LAI/TA
palatal	PAL/TAL
palate	PAL/LAT
palati	PA/LAOI/TAOI
palatiform	PA/LAT/FORM
palatina	PAL/TAOI/NA
palatinae	PAL/TAOI/NAE
palatinase	PA/LAT/NAIS
palatine	PAL/TAOIN
palatini	PAL/TAOI/NAOI
palatinose	PA/LAT/NOES
palatinus	PAL/TAOI/NUS
palatitis	PAL/TAOITS
palatoglossal	PAL/TO/GLOS/SAL
palatoglossus	PAL/TO/GLOS/SUS
palatognathous	PAL/TOG/NA/THOUS
palatogram	PAL/TO/GRAM
palatograph	PAL/TO/GRAF
palatography	PAL/TOG/FI
palatomaxillary	PAL/TO/MAX/LAIR
palatomyograph	PAL/TO/MAOI/GRAF
palatonasal	PAL/TO/NAI/ZAL
palatopharyngeal	PAL/TO/FRIN/JAL
palatopharyngeus	PAL/TO/FRIN/JUS
palatopharyngoplasty	PAL/TO/FRING/PLAS/TI
palatopharyngorrhaphy	PAL/TO/FARN/GOR/FI
palatoplasty	PAL/TO/PLAS/TI
palatoplegia	PAL/TO/PLAOE/JA
palatoproximal	PAL/TO/PROX/MAL
palatorrhaphy	PAL/TOR/FI
palatosalpingeus	PAL/TO/SAL/PIN/JUS
palatoschisis	PAL/TOS/KI/SIS
palatostaphylinus	PAL/TO/STAF/LAOI/NUS
palatouvularis	PAL/TO/YAOUV/LAI/RIS
palatovaginal	PAL/TO/VAJ/NAL
palatovaginalis	PAL/TO/VAJ/NAI/LIS
palatum	PA/LAI/TUM
	PA/LAIT/UM
pale	PA*IL
	(*not* PAIL or PAEL; see pail and peal)
paleencephalon	PAIL/YEN/SEF/LON
	PAI/LAOE/EN/SEF/LON
paleo-	PAIL/YO
paleocerebellar	PAIL/YO/SER/BEL/LAR
paleocerebellum	PAIL/YO/SER/BEL/UM
paleocinetic	PAIL/YO/SI/NET/IK
paleocortex	PAIL/YO/KOR/TEX
paleoencephalon	PAIL/YO/EN/SEF/LON
paleogenesis	PAIL/YO/JEN/SIS
paleogenetic	PAIL/YO/JE/NET/IK
paleokinetic	PAIL/YO/KI/NET/IK
paleologic	PAIL/YO/LOJ/IK
paleoneurology	PAIL/YO/NAOU/ROLG
paleontology	PAIL/YON/TOLG
paleopallium	PAIL/YO/PAL/YUM
paleopathology	PAIL/YO/PA/THOLG
paleopneumoniae	PAIL/YO/NAOU/MOEN/YAE

paleopsychology	PAIL/YO/SAOI/KOLG	palpebr-	PAL/PE/BR-
paleosensation	PAIL/YO/SEN/SAIGS		PAL/PAOE/BR-
paleostriatal	PAIL/YO/STRAOI/AI/TAL	palpebra	PAL/PE/BRA
	PAIL/YO/STRAOI/YAI/TAL		PAL/PAOE/BRA
paleostriatum	PAIL/YO/STRAOI/AI/TUM	palpebrae	PAL/PE/BRAE
	PAIL/YO/STRAOI/AIT/UM		PAL/PAOE/BRAE
	PAIL/YO/STRAOI/YAI/TUM	palpebral	PAL/PE/BRAL
	PAIL/YO/STRAOI/YAIT/UM	palpebrale	PAL/PE/BRAI/LAOE
paleothalamus	PAIL/YO/THAL/MUS	palpebrales	PAL/PE/BRAI/LAOEZ
palicinesia	PAL/SI/NAOEZ/YA	palpebralis	PAL/PE/BRAI/LIS
palikinesia	PAL/KI/NAOEZ/YA	palpebrarum	PAL/PE/BRAI/RUM
palilalia	PAL/LAIL/YA		PAL/PE/BRAIR/UM
palinal	PAL/NAL	palpebrate	PAL/PE/BRAIT
palindrome	PAL/IN/DROEM	palpebration	PAL/PE/BRAIGS
palindromia	PAL/IN/DROEM/YA	palpebritis	PAL/PE/BRAOITS
palindromic	PAL/IN/DROEM/IK	palpitate	PAL/PI/TAIT
	PAL/IN/DROM/IK	palpitatio cordis	PAL/PI/TAI/SHOE/KOR/DIS
palinesthesia	PAL/IN/ES/THAOEZ/YA	palpitation	PAL/PI/TAIGS
palingenesis	PAL/IN/JEN/SIS	palsy	PAL/ZI
palingraphia	PAL/IN/GRAF/YA		PAL/SI
	PAL/IN/GRAIF/YA	Paltauf	PAL/TOUF
palinmnesis	PAL/IN/NAOE/SIS		PAL/TAUF
palinopsia	PAL/NOPS/YA	palud-	PAL/D-
palinphrasia	PAL/IN/FRAIZ/YA		PAL/YAOU/D-
paliphrasia	PAL/FRAIZ/YA		PAL/YU/D-
palisade	PA*L/SAID	paludal	PAL/DAL
	PAL/SAED	paludism	PAL/DIFM
	PAL/LI/SAID	palustral	PA/LUS/TRAL
	(not PAL/SAID; see pal said)	pamabrom	PAM/BROM
pall-	PA/L-	pamaquine	PAM/KWAOEN
	PAL/L-		PAM/KWIN
palladium	PA/LAID/YUM	pamatolol	PAM/TOE/LOL
pallanesthesia	PAL/ANS/THAOEZ/YA		PAM/TOE/LOEL
pallescense	PAL/ES/ENS	Pamelor	PAM/LOR
pallesthesia	PAL/ES/THAOEZ/YA	Pamine	PAM/AOEN
pallesthetic	PAL/ES/THET/IK	pamoate	PAM/WAIT
pallhypesthesia	PAL/HAOI/PES/THAOEZ/YA		PAM/MO/AIT
pallial	PAL/YAL		PAM/MO/WAIT
palliate	PAL/YAIT	pampiniform	PAM/PIN/FORM
palliative	PAL/YA/TIV	pampiniforme	PAM/PIN/FOR/MAOE
pallid(o)-	PAL/D(O)	pampinocele	PAM/PIN/SAO*EL
pallida	PAL/DA	Pan	K-P/PAN
pallidal	PAL/DAL	pan-	PAN
pallidectomy	PAL/DEKT/M*I	panacea	PAN/SAOE/YA
pallidoamygdalotomy	PAL/DO/AI/MIGD/LOT/M*I	panacinar	PAN/AS/NAR
pallidoansection	PAL/DO/AN/S*EBGS	Panadol	PAN/DOL
pallidoansotomy	PAL/DO/AN/SOT/M*I	Panafil Ointment	PAN/FIL
pallidofugal	PAL/DOF/GAL	Panafil-White Ointment	PAN/FIL/WHAOIT/OINT/-MT
pallidotomy	PAL/DOT/M*I	panagglutinable	PAN/GLAOUT/NABL
pallidum	PAL/DUM		PAN/AI/GLAOUT/NABL
pallium	PAL/YUM	panagglutination	PAN/GLAOUT/NAIGS
pallor	PAL/LOR		PAN/AI/GLAOUT/NAIGS
palm	PAUM	panagglutinin	PAN/GLAOUT/NIN
	PAL/-M		PAN/AI/GLAOUT/NIN
palma	PAL/MA	panangiitis	PAN/AN/JAOITS
palmae	PAL/MAE	panarteritis	PAN/ART/RAOITS
palmanesthesia	PAL/MAN/ES/THAOEZ/YA	panarthritis	PAN/AR/THRAOITS
	PAL/MANS/THAOEZ/YA	panatrophy	PAN/AT/RO/FI
palmar	PAL/MAR	panautonomic	PAN/AUT/NOM/IK
palmare	PAL/MAI/RAOE	panblastic	PAN/BLA*S/IK
palmares	PAL/MAI/RAOEZ	pancarditis	PAN/KAR/DAOITS
palmaria	PAL/MAIR/YA	panchrest	PAN/KR*ES
palmaris	PAL/MAI/RIS	panchromatic	PAN/KROE/MAT/IK
	PAL/MAIR/RIS	panchromia	PAN/KROEM/YA
palmature	PAUM/KHUR	Pancoast	PAN/KO*ES
	PAL/MA/KHUR	pancolectomy	PAN/KO/LEKT/M*I
palmellin	PAL/MEL/LIN	pancre(o)-	PAN/KR(O)
Palmer	PAL/MER		PAN/KRAOE/Y(O)
palmesthesia	PAL/MES/THAOEZ/YA	pancrealgia	PAN/KRAL/JA
palmesthetic	PAL/MES/THET/IK	pancreas	PAN/KRAS
palmi	PAL/MAOI	Pancrease	PAN/KRAIS
palmic	PAL/MIK	pancreat(o)-	PAN/KRA/T(O)
palmital	PAL/MI/TAL		PAN/KRAOE/T(O)
palmitaldehyde	PAL/MI/TALD/HAOID	pancreata	PAN/KRAOE/TA
palmitate	PAL/MI/TAIT		PAN/KRAOE/TA
palmitic	PAL/MIT/IK	pancreatalgia	PAN/KRA/TAL/JA
palmitin	PAL/MI/TIN	pancreatectomy	PAN/KRA/TEKT/M*I
palmitoleic	PAL/MI/TO/LAOE/IK	pancreatemphraxis	PAN/KRAT/EM/FRAK/SIS
	PAUM/TO/LAOE/IK	pancreatic	PAN/KRAT/IK
palmityl	PAL/MI/TIL	pancreatica	PAN/KRAT/KA
palmodic	PAL/MOD/IK	pancreaticae	PAN/KRAT/SAE
palmoscopy	PAL/MOS/KPI	pancreatico-	PAN/KRAT/KO
palmus	PAL/MUS		PAN/KRAOE/AT/KO
palp	PAL/-P		PAN/KRAOE/YAT/KO
palpable	PAL/PABL	pancreaticoduodenal	PAN/KRAT/KO/DAOU/DAOENL
palpate	PAL/PAIT		PAN/KRAT/KO/DWOD/NAL
palpation	PAL/PAIGS	pancreaticoduodenostomy	PAN/KRAT/KO/DAOU/DE/NO*S/
palpatometry	PAL/PA/TOM/TRI		M*I
palpatopercussion	PAL/PA/TO/PER/KUGS		PAN/KRAT/KO/DWOD/NO*S/M*I

pancreaticoenterostomy	PAN/KRAT/KO/SPWRO*S/M*I
	PAN/KRAT/KO/SPWER/RO*S/M*I
pancreaticogastrostomy	PAN/KRAT/KO/GAS/TRO*S/M*I
pancreaticojejunostomy	PAN/KRAT/KO/JEJ/NO*S/M*I
pancreaticosplenic	PAN/KRAT/KO/SPLEN/IK
pancreaticus	PAN/KRAT/KUS
pancreatin	PAN/KRA/TIN
Pancreatin	K-P/PAN/KRA/TIN
pancreatis	PAN/KRA/TIS
pancreatism	PAN/KRA/TIFM
pancreatitis	PAN/KRA/TAOITS
pancreatocholecystostomy	PAN/KRAT/KOEL/SIS/TO*S/M*I
	PAN/KRA/TO/KOEL/SIS/TO*S/M*I
pancreatoduodenectomy	PAN/KRAT/DAOU/DEN/EKT/M*I
	PAN/KRAT/DAOU/DE/NEKT/M*I
	PAN/KRA/TO/DAOU/DEN/EKT/M*I
	PAN/KRA/TO/DAOU/DE/NEKT/M*I
pancreatoduodenostomy	PAN/KRAT/DAOU/DEN/O*S/M*I
	PAN/KRAT/DAOU/DE/NO*S/M*I
	PAN/KRA/TO/DAOU/DEN/O*S/M*I
	PAN/KRA/TO/DAOU/DE/NO*S/M*I
pancreatoenterostomy	PAN/KRAT/SPWRO*S/M*I
	PAN/KRAT/SPWER/RO*S/M*I
	PAN/KRA/TO/SPWRO*S/M*I
	PAN/KRA/TO/SPWER/RO*S/M*I
pancreatogastrostomy	PAN/KRAT/GAS/TRO*S/M*I
	PAN/KRA/TO/GAS/TRO*S/M*I
pancreatogenic	PAN/KRA/TO/JEN/IK
pancreatogenous	PAN/KRA/TOJ/NOUS
pancreatogram	PAN/KRAT/GRAM
pancreatography	PAN/KRA/TOG/FI
pancreatoid	PAN/KRA/TOID
pancreatojejunostomy	PAN/KRAT/JEJ/NO*S/M*I
	PAN/KRA/TO/JEJ/NO*S/M*I
pancreatolipase	PAN/KRAT/LIP/AIS
	PAN/KRA/TO/LIP/AIS
pancreatolith	PAN/KRAT/L*IT
pancreatolithectomy	PAN/KRAT/LI/THEKT/M*I
	PAN/KRA/TO/LI/THEKT/M*I
pancreatolithiasis	PAN/KRAT/LI/THAOI/SIS
	PAN/KRA/TO/LI/THAOI/SIS
pancreatolithotomy	PAN/KRAT/LI/THOT/M*I
	PAN/KRA/TO/LI/THOT/M*I
pancreatolysis	PAN/KRA/TOL/SIS
pancreatolytic	PAN/KRA/TO/LIT/IK
pancreatomegaly	PAN/KRA/TO/MEG/LI
pancreatomy	PAN/KRAT/M*I
pancreatoncus	PAN/KRA/TON/KUS
pancreatopathy	PAN/KRA/TOP/TH*I
pancreatopeptidase	PAN/KRA/TO/PEPT/DAIS
pancreatosis	PAN/KRA/TOE/SIS
pancreatotomy	PAN/KRA/TOT/M*I
pancreatotropic	PAN/KRA/TO/TROP/IK
pancreatropic	PAN/KRA/TROP/IK
pancreectomy	PAN/KREKT/M*I
	PAN/KRAOE/EKT/M*I
pancrelipase	PAN/KRAOE/LIP/AIS
	PAN/KRAOE/LAOI/PAIS
pancreolith	PAN/KRO/L*IT
pancreolithotomy	PAN/KRO/LI/THOT/M*I
pancreolysis	PAN/KROL/SIS
pancreolytic	PAN/KRO/LIT/IK
pancreopathy	PAN/KROP/TH*I
pancreoprivic	PAN/KRO/PRIVK
pancreotherapy	PAN/KRO/THER/PI
pancreotropic	PAN/KRO/TROP/IK
pancreozymin	PAN/KRO/ZAOI/MIN
pancuronium	PAN/KAOU/ROEN/YUM
pancystitis	PAN/SIS/TAOITS
pancytopenia	PAN/SAOIT/PAOEN/YA
pandemic	PAN/DEM/IK
pandemicity	PAND/MIS/TI
	PAN/DE/MIS/TI
pandiculation	PAN/DIK/LAIGS
Pandy	PAN/DI
panel	PANL
panelectroscope	PAN/LEK/TRO/SKOEP
panencephalitis	PAN/EN/SEF/LAOITS
panendography	PAN/EN/DOG/FI
panendoscope	PAN/*END/SKOEP
panendoscopy	PAN/EN/DOS/KPI
panepizootic	PAN/EP/ZOE/OT/IK
panesthesia	PAN/ES/THAOEZ/YA
panesthetic	PAN/ES/THET/IK
Paneth	PA/NAIT
pang	PANG
pangamic	PAN/GAM/IK

pangenesis	PAN/JEN/SIS
panglossia	PAN/GLOS/YA
Panhematin	PAN/HAOEM/TIN
panhematopenia	PAN/HAOEM/TO/PAOEN/YA
	PAN/HEM/TO/PAOEN/YA
panhidrosis	PAN/HI/DROE/SIS
	PAN/HID/ROE/SIS
panhydrometer	PAN/HAOI/DROM/TER
panhyperemia	PAN/HAO*IP/AOEM/YA
	PAN/HAOIP/RAOEM/YA
panhypogonadism	PAN/HO*IP/GOE/NAD/IFM
panhypopituitarism	PAN/HO*IP/PI/TAOU/TRIFM
panhysterectomy	PAN/H*IS/REKT/M*I
panhystero-oophorectomy	PAN/H*IS/RO/AOF/REKT/M*I
panhysterosalpingectomy	PAN/H*IS/RO/SAL/PIN/JEKT/M*I
panhysterosalpingo-oophorectomy	
	PAN/H*IS/RO/SAL/PING/AOF/REKT/M*I
panic	PAN/IK
panidrosis	PAN/DROE/SIS
panimmunity	PAN/IM/MAOUN/TI
	PAN/MAOUN/TI
panis	PAI/NIS
panleukopenia	PAN/LAOUK/PAOEN/YA
panlobular	PAN/LOB/LAR
panmeristic	PAN/MER/*IS/IK
panmixia	PAN/MIX/YA
panmixis	PAN/MIK/SIS
panmural	PAN/MAOURL
panmyeloid	PAN/MAOI/LOID
panmyelopathia	PAN/MAOI/LO/PA*T/YA
panmyelopathy	PAN/MAOI/LOP/TH*I
panmyelophthisis	PAN/MAOI/LOF/THI/SIS
panmyelosis	PAN/MAOI/LOE/SIS
panneuritis	PAN/NAOU/RAOITS
panni	PAN/NAOI
pannicul-	PA/NIK/L-
	PA/NIK/YAOU/L-
	PA/NIK/YU/L-
	PAN/NIK/L-
	PAN/NIK/YAOU/L-
	PAN/NIK/YU/L-
	PAN/IK/L-
	PAN/IK/YAOU/L-
	PAN/IK/YU/L-
panniculalgia	PA/NIK/LAL/JA
panniculectomy	PA/NIK/LEKT/M*I
panniculi	PA/NIK/LAOI
panniculitis	PA/NIK/LAOITS
panniculus	PA/NIK/LUS
pannus	PAN/NUS
panodic	PAN/OD/IK
	PA/NOD/IK
panophthalmia	PAN/OF/THAL/MA
	PAN/OF/THAL/MAOE/YA
panophthalmitis	PAN/OF/THAL/MAOITS
panoptic	PAN/OPT/IK
panosteitis	PAN/O*S/YAOITS
panostitis	PAN/OS/TAOITS
panotitis	PAN/O/TAOITS
	PAN/TAOITS
PanOxyl	PAN/OK/SIL
	PAN/OX/IL
panphobia	PAN/FOEB/YA
panplegia	PAN/PLAOE/JA
panproctocolectomy	PAN/PROKT/KO/LEKT/M*I
Pansch	PAN/-RB
pansclerosis	PAN/SKLE/ROE/SIS
Panscol	PAN/SKOL
panseptum	PAN/SEP/TUM
pansinuitis	PAN/SAOIN/YAOITS
pansinusectomy	PAN/SAOIN/SEKT/M*I
pansinusitis	PAN/SAOIN/SAOITS
panspermatism	PAN/SPERM/TIFM
panspermia	PAN/SPERM/YA
pansphygmograph	PAN/SFIG/MO/GRAF
pansporoblast	PAN/SPOR/BLA*S
pansporoblastic	PAN/SPOR/BLA*S/IK
Panstrongylus	PAN/STRONG/LUS
	PAN/STRON/JI/LUS
pansystolic	PAN/SIS/TOL/IK
pant	PANT
pant(o)-	PANT
	PAN/T(O)
pantachromatic	PANT/KROE/MAT/IK
pantalgia	PAN/TAL/JA
pantaloon	PANT/LAON
pantamorphia	PAN/TA/MOR/FAOE/YA
	PAN/TA/MOR/FA

	(not PANT/MOR/FAOE/YA; see pantomorphia)
pantamorphic	PAN/TA/MOR/FIK
	(not PANT/MOR/FIK; see pantomorphic)
pantanencephalia	PAN/TAN/EN/SFAIL/YA
pantanencephaly	PAN/TAN/EN/SEF/LI
pantankyloblepharon	PAN/TAN/KLO/BLEF/RON
	PAN/TANG/LO/BLEF/RON
	PAN/TAN/KAOIL/BLEF/RON
pantaphobia	PAN/TA/FOEB/YA
	(not PANT/FOEB/YA; see pantophobia)
pantatrophia	PANT/TROEF/YA
pantatrophy	PAN/TAT/RO/FI
pantetheine	PANT/THAOE/YIN
	PANT/THAOEN
pantethine	PANT/THIN
panthenol	PA*NT/NOL
	PAN/THE/NOL
pantherapist	PAN/THER/P*IS
panthodic	PAN/THOD/IK
panting	PANT/-G
pantoate	PAN/TO/AIT
pantogamy	PAN/TOG/M*I
pantograph	PANT/GRAF
pantoic	PAN/TOIK
	PAN/TOE/IK
pantomogram	PAN/TOEM/GRAM
pantomograph	PAN/TOEM/GRAF
pantomographic	PAN/TOEM/GRAFK
pantomography	PAN/TOE/MOG/FI
pantomorphia	PANT/MOR/FAOE/YA
	PANT/MOR/FA
pantomorphic	PANT/MOR/FIK
pantonine	PANT/NAOEN
pantophobia	PANT/FOEB/YA
pantophobic	PANT/FOEB/IK
Pantopon	PANT/PON
pantoscopic	PANT/SKOP/IK
pantothenate	PANT/THEN/AIT
	PAN/TO*ET/NAIT
pantothenic	PANT/THEN/IK
pantothenyl	PANT/THENL
pantoyl	PAN/TOIL
pantoyltaurine	PAN/TOIL/TAU/RAOEN
	PAN/TOIL/TAU/RIN
pantropic	PAN/TROP/IK
panturbinate	PAN/TURB/NAIT
Panum	PA/NAOUM
	PAN/UM
panus	PAI/NUS
panuveitis	PAN/YAOUV/YAOITS
Panwarfin	PAN/WAR/FIN
panzerherz	PAN/ZER/HERZ
panzootic	PAN/ZOE/OT/IK
pap	PAP
papain	PA/PAIN
papainase	PA/PAIN/AIS
Papanicolaou	PAP/NIK/LAI/YAOU
Papaver	PA/PAVR
	PA/PAIVR
papaveretum	PA/PAV/RAOE/TUM
papaverine	PA/PAV/RAOEN
	PA/PAV/RIN
papaya	PA/PAOI/YA
	PA/PAI/YA
	PA/PA/YA
papayotin	PA/PAI/TIN
paper	PAIP/ER
papescent	PA/PES/ENT
papill(o)-	PAP/L(O)
	PA/PIL
papilla	PA/PIL/LA
papillae	PA/PIL/LAE
papillares	PAP/LAI/RAOEZ
papillaris	PAP/LAI/RIS
papillary	PAP/LAIR
papillate	PAP/LAIT
papillectomy	PAP/LEKT/M*I
papilledema	PA/PIL/DAOE/MA
	PAP/LE/DAOE/MA
papilliferous	PAP/LIF/ROUS
papilliferum	PAP/LIF/RUM
papilliform	PA/PIL/FORM
papillitis	PAP/LAOITS
papilloadenocystoma	PAP/LO/AD/NO/SIS/TOE/MA
papillocarcinoma	PAP/LO/KARS/NOE/MA
papilloma	PAP/LOE/MA
papillomatosa	PAP/LOEM/TOE/SA
papillomatosis	PAP/LOEM/TOE/SIS
papillomatous	PAP/LOEM/TOUS
papillomavirus	PAP/LOEM/VAOI/RUS
papilloretinitis	PAP/LO/RET/NAOITS
papillosphincterotomy	PAP/LO/SFINGT/ROT/M*I
	PAP/LO/SFING/TER/OT/M*I
papillotome	PAP/LO/TOEM
papillotomy	PAP/LOT/M*I
papillula	PA/PIL/YAOU/LA
	PA/PIL/YU/LA
	(not PA/PIL/LA; see papilla)
papillulae	PA/PIL/YAOU/LAE
	PA/PIL/YU/LAE
	(not PA/PIL/LAE; see papillae)
Papin	PA/PAN
papoid	PAP/OID
Papovaviridae	PA/POEV/VIR/DAE
papovavirus	PA/POEV/VAOI/RUS
Pappenheim	PAP/EN/HAOIM
Pappenheimer	PAP/EN/HAOIM/ER
pappose	PAP/POES
pappous	PAP/POUS
	PAP/OUS
pappus	PAP/PUS
paprika	PAP/RAOE/KA
	PA/PRAOE/KA
Pap smear	PAP/SMAOER
Pap test	PAP/T*ES
papul(o)-	PAP/L(O)
	PAP/YAOU/L(O)
	PAP/YU/L(O)
papular	PAP/LAR
papulation	PAP/LAIGS
papule	PAP/YAOUL
papuliferous	PAP/YAOU/LIF/ROUS
	PAP/YU/LIF/ROUS
	PA*P/LIF/ROUS
	(not PAP/LIF/ROUS; see papilliferous)
papuloerythematous	PAP/LO/*ER/THEM/TOUS
papuloid	PAP/LOID
papulopustular	PAP/LO/P*US/LAR
	PAP/LO/PUS/KHU/LAR
	PAP/LO/PUS/TAOU/LAR
papulopustule	PAP/LO/PUS/TAOUL
	PAP/LO/P*US/YAOUL
	PAP/LO/PUS/KHAOUL
	PAP/LO/PUS/KHUL
papulosa	PAP/LOE/SA
papulosis	PAP/LOE/SIS
papulosquamous	PAP/LO/SKWAIM/OUS
papulosum	PAP/LOE/SUM
	PAP/LOES/UM
papulovesicle	PAP/LO/VES/K-L
papulovesicular	PAP/LO/VE/SIK/LAR
papyraceous	PAP/RAIRBS
papyraceus	PAP/RAIS/YUS
	(not PAP/RAIRBS; see papyraceous)
Paquelin	PAK/LAN
par (word)	PAR
par- (prefix)	PAR
	PA/R-
para (word)	PAR/RA
para- (prefix)	PAR
	PA/RA
-para (suffix)	-P/RA
para-aortic	PAR/AI/ORT/IK
paraaortica	PAR/AI/ORT/KA
para-appendicitis	PAR/AI/PEND/SAOITS
paraballism	PAR/BAL/IFM
parabanic	PAR/BAN/IK
parabasal	PAR/BAI/SAL
parabion	PAR/AB/YON
parabiont	PAR/AB/YONT
parabiosis	PAR/BAO*I/YOE/SIS
parabiotic	PAR/BAO*I/OT/IK
	PAR/BAO*I/YOT/IK
parablast	PAR/BLA*S
parablastic	PAR/BLA*S/IK
parablepsia	PAR/BLEPS/YA
paraboloid	PA/RAB/LOID
parabolus	PA/RAB/LUS
parabotulinum	PAR/BOFP/LAOIN/UM
	PAR/BOFP/LAOI/NUM
	PAR/BOT/LAOIN/UM
	PAR/BOT/LAOI/NUM
parabotulinus	PAR/BOFP/LAOI/NUS
	PAR/BOT/LAOI/NUS

316

parabulia	PAR/BAOUL/YA
paracanthoma	PAR/AK/AN/THOE/MA
paracanthosis	PAR/AK/AN/THOE/SIS
paracarbinoxamine	PAR/KARB/NOX/MAOEN
	PAR/KAR/BIN/OX/MAOEN
paracardiac	PAR/KARD/YAK
paracarmine	PAR/KAR/MIN
	PAR/KAR/MAOEN
paracasein	PAR/KAIS/YIN
paracele	PAR/SAO*EL
paracellulose	PAR/SEL/YAOU/LOES
paracelsian	PAR/SELS/YAN
Paracelsus	PAR/SEL/SUS
paracenesthesia	PAR/SE/NES/THAOEZ/YA
	PAR/SEN/ES/THAOEZ/YA
paracentesis	PAR/SEN/TAOE/SIS
paracentetic	PAR/SEN/TET/IK
paracentral	PAR/SEN/TRAL
	PAR/STRAL
paracephalus	PAR/SEF/LUS
paracerebellar	PAR/SER/BEL/LAR
paracervical	PAR/SEFRB/KAL
partacervix	PAR/SER/VIX
paracetaldehyde	PAR/AS/TALD/HAOID
paracetamol	PAR/AI/SET/MOL
	PAR/AS/ET/AM/OL
parachloralose	PAR/KLOR/LOES
parachloramine	PAR/KLOR/MIN
parachlorophenol	PAR/KLOR/FAOE/NOL
paracholera	PAR/KOL/RA
parachordal	PAR/KHOR/DAL
parachroia	PAR/KROI/YA
parachroma	PAR/KROE/MA
parachromatin	PAR/KROEM/TIN
parachromatism	PAR/KROEM/TIFM
parachromatopsia	PAR/KROEM/TOPS/YA
parachromatosis	PAR/KROEM/TOE/SIS
parachymosin	PAR/KAOIM/SIN
paracicatricial	PAR/SIK/TRIRBL
paracinesia	PAR/SI/NAOEZ/YA
paracinesis	PAR/SI/NAOE/SIS
paraclinical	PAR/KLIN/KAL
paracmasis	PAR/AK/MA/SIS
paracmastic	PAR/AK/MA*S/IK
paracme	PAR/AK/MAOE
paracnemidion	PAR/AK/NAOE/MID/YON
paracnemis	PAR/AK/NAOE/MIS
Paracoccidioides	PAR/KOK/SID/YOI/DAOEZ
Paracoccidioides brasiliensis	PAR/KOK/SID/YOI/DAOEZ/ BRA/SIL/YEN/SIS
	PAR/KOK/SID/YOI/DAOEZ/BRA/ ZIL/YEN/SIS
paracoccidiodin	PAR/KOK/SID/YOI/DIN
paracoccidioidomycosis	PAR/KOK/SID/YOID/MAOI/KOE/ SIS
	PAR/KOK/SID/YOI/DO/MAOI/KOE/ SIS
paracolitis	PAR/KO/LAOITS
paracolon	PAR/KO/LON
paracolpitis	PAR/KOL/PAOITS
paracolpium	PAR/KOL/PUM
	PAR/KOL/PAOE/YUM
paracone	PAR/KOEN
paraconid	PAR/KO/NID
	PAR/KON/ID
paracortex	PAR/KOR/TEX
paracoxalgia	PAR/KOX/AL/JA
	PAR/KOK/SAL/JA
paracresol	PAR/KRAOE/SOL
paracrine	PAR/KRIN
paracusia	PAR/KAOUZ/YA
paracusis	PAR/KAOU/SIS
paracyesis	PAR/SAOI/E/SIS
paracystic	PAR/S*IS/IK
paracystitis	PAR/SIS/TAOITS
paracystium	PAR/S*IS/YUM
paracytic	PAR/SAO*IT/IK
	PAR/SAOI/TIK
	PAR/S*IT/IK
	(not PAR/SIT/IK; see parasitic)
paradenitis	PAR/AD/NAOITS
paradental	PAR/DEN/TAL
paradentitis	PAR/DEN/TAOITS
paradentium	PAR/DEN/SHUM
paradentosis	PAR/DEN/TOE/SIS
paraderm	PAR/DERM
paradidymal	PAR/DID/MAL
paradidymides	PAR/DI/DIM/DAOEZ
paradidymis	PAR/DID/MIS

paradimethylaminobenzaldehyde	
	PAR/DI/M*ET/IL/AM/NO/BENZ/ ALD/HAOID
Paradione	PAR/DI/OEN
paradipsia	PAR/DIPS/YA
paradox	PAR/DOX
paradoxic	PAR/DOX/IK
paradoxical	PAR/DOX/KAL
paradysentery	PAR/DIS/SPWER/RI
	PAR/DIS/EN/TER/RI
paraeccrisis	PAR/EK/RI/SIS
paraepilepsy	PAR/EP/LEP/SI
paraequilibrium	PAR/E/KWI/LIB/RUM
paraesophageal	PAR/E/SOF/JAOEL
parafalx	PAR/FAL/-X
paraffin	PAR/FIN
paraffinoma	PAR/FI/NOE/MA
Parafilaria multipapillosa	PAR/FLAIR/YA/MULT/PAP/LOE/ SA
	PAR/FI/LAIR/YA/MULT/PAP/LOE/ SA
paraflagella	PAR/FLA/JEL/LA
paraflagellate	PAR/FLAJ/LAIT
paraflagellum	PAR/FLA/JEL/UM
Paraflex	PAR/FLEX
paraflocculus	PAR/FLOK/LUS
parafollicular	PAR/FLIK/LAR
paraformaldehyde	PAR/FOR/MALD/HAOID
Parafon	PAR/FON
Parafon Forte	PAR/FON/FOR/TAI
parafrenal	PAR/FRAOENL
parafuchsin	PAR/FUK/SIN
	PAR/FAOUK/SIN
parafunction	PAR/FUNGS
parafunctional	PAR/FUNGS/NAL
paragammacism	PAR/GAM/SIFM
paraganglia	PAR/GANG/LA
paraganglioma	PAR/GANG/LOE/MA
paraganglion	PAR/GANG/LON
ParaGard	PAR/GARD
paragelatose	PAR/JEL/TOES
paragene	PAR/JAOEN
paragenital	PAR/JEN/TAL
paragenitalis	PAR/JEN/TAI/LIS
parageusia	PAR/GAOUS/YA
	PAR/GAOUZ/YA
parageusic	PAR/GAOUS/IK
	PAR/GAOUZ/IK
paragglutination	PAR/GLAOUT/NAIGS
paraglobulin	PAR/GLOB/LIN
paraglobulinuria	PAR/GLOB/LI/NAOUR/YA
paraglossia	PAR/GLOS/YA
paraglossitis	PAR/GLOS/SAOITS
paragnathus	PA/RAG/NA/THUS
	PAR/AG/NA/THUS
paragnomen	PAR/AG/NOE/MEN
paragnosis	PAR/AG/NOE/SIS
paragonimiasis	PAR/GON/MAOI/SIS
paragonimosis	PAR/GON/MOE/SIS
Paragonimus	PAR/GON/MUS
paragonorrheal	PAR/GON/RAOEL
	PAR/GON/RAOE/YAL
paragrammatism	PAR/GRAM/TIFM
paragranuloma	PAR/GRAN/LOE/MA
paragraphia	PAR/GRAF/YA
parahemophilia	PAR/HAOEM/FIL/YA
parahepatic	PAR/HE/PAT/IK
paraheredity	PAR/HE/RED/TI
parahidrosis	PAR/HI/DROE/SIS
	PAR/HID/ROE/SIS
parahormome	PAR/HOR/MOEN
parahypnosis	PAR/HIP/NOE/SIS
parahypophysis	PAR/HAOI/POF/SIS
parakappacism	PAR/KAP/SIFM
parakeratosis	PAR/KER/TOE/SIS
parakinesia	PAR/KI/NAOEZ/YA
parakinesis	PAR/KI/NAOE/SIS
parakinetic	PAR/KI/NET/IK
paralalia	PAR/LAIL/YA
paralambdacism	PAR/LAMD/SIFM
	PAR/LAM/DA/SIFM
paralbumin	PAR/AL/BAOU/MIN
paraldehyde	PAR/ALD/HAOID
paraldehydism	PAR/ALD/HAOID/IFM
paraleprosis	PAR/LE/PROE/SIS
paralepsy	PAR/LEP/SI
paralexia	PAR/LEX/YA
paralexic	PAR/LEX/IK
paralgesia	PAR/AL/JAOEZ/YA

paralgesic	PAR/AL/JAOEZ/IK	paramutagenic	PAR/MAOUT/JEN/IK
paralgia	PAR/AL/JA	paramutation	PAR/MAOU/TAIGS
paralipophobia	LAR/LIP/FOEB/YA	paramyelin	PAR/MAOI/LIN
parallactic	PAR/LAKT/IK	paramyloidosis	PA/RAM/LOI/DOE/SIS
parallagma	PAR/LAG/MA		PAR/AM/LOI/DOE/SIS
parallax	PAR/LAX	paramylum	PA/RAM/LUM
parallela	PAR/LAOE/LA	paramyoclonus	PAR/MAOI/OK/LO/NUS
parallelism	PAR/LEL/IFM	paramyosinogen	PAR/MAOI/SIN/JEN
parallelogram	PAR/LEL/GRAM	paramyotone	PAR/MAOI/TOEN
parallelometer	PAR/LEL/OM/TER	paramyotonia	PAR/MAOI/TOEN/YA
parallergia	PAR/LER/JA	paramyotonus	PAR/MAOI/OT/NUS
parallergic	PAR/LERJ/IK	Paramyxoviridae	PAR/MIX/VIR/DAE
parallergin	PAR/AL/ER/JIN	paramyxovirus	PAR/MIX/VAOI/RUS
parallergy	PAR/AL/ER/JI	paranalgesia	PAR/ANL/JAOEZ/YA
paralogia	PAR/LOE/JA	paranasal	PAR/NAI/ZAL
paralogism	PA/RAL/JIFM	paranemic	PAR/NAOEM/IK
paralogy	PA/RAL/JI	paraneoplasia	PAR/NAOE/PLAIZ/YA
	PA/RALG	paraneoplastic	PAR/NAOE/PLA*S/IK
paraluteal	PAR/LAOUT/YAL	paranephric	PAR/NEF/RIK
paralutein	PAR/LAOUT/YIN	paranephritis	PAR/NE/FRAOITS
paralyses	PA/RAL/SAOEZ	paranephroi	PAR/NEF/ROI
	PRAL/SAOEZ	paranephroma	PAR/NE/FROE/MA
paralysis	PA/RAL/SIS	paranephros	PAR/NEF/ROS
	PRAL/SIS	paranesthesia	PAR/ANS/THAOEZ/YA
paralyssa	PAR/LIS/SA	paraneural	PAR/NAOURL
paralytic	PAR/LIT/IK	paraneurone	PAR/NAOU/ROEN
paralytica	PAR/LIT/KA		PAR/NAOUR/OEN
paralyticum	PAR/LIT/KUM	para-nitrosulfathiazole	PAR/NAOI/TRO/SUL/FA/THAOI/
paralytogenic	PAR/LIT/JEN/IK		ZOEL
paralyzant	PA/RAL/ZANT	paranoia	PAR/NOI/YA
	PAR/LAOI/ZANT	paranoiac	PAR/NOI/AK
paralyze	PAR/LAOIZ		PAR/NOI/YAK
paralyzer	PAR/LAOIZ/ER	paranoic	PAR/NOIK
paramagnetic	PAR/MAG/NET/IK		PAR/NOE/IK
paramagnetism	PAR/MAG/NE/TIFM	paranoica	PAR/NOI/KA
paramania	PAR/MAIN/YA	paranoid	PAR/NOID
paramastigote	PAR/MA*S/GOET	paranoides	PAR/NOI/DAOEZ
paramastitis	PAR/MAS/TAOITS	paranoidism	PAR/NOID/IFM
paramastoid	PAR/MAS/TOID	paranomia	PAR/NOEM/YA
paramastoiditis	PAR/MAS/TOI/DAOITS	paranormal	PAR/NOR/MAL
parameatal	PAR/MAOE/AI/TAL	paranosic	PAR/NOES/IK
	PAR/MAOE/YAI/TAL	paranosis	PAR/NOE/SIS
paramecia	PAR/MAOE/SHA	paranuclear	PAR/NAOUK/LAR
	PAR/MAOES/YA	paranucleate	PAR/NAOUK/LAIT
paramecium	PAR/MAOERB/YUM	paranucleolus	PAR/NAOU/KLAOE/LUS
	PAR/MAOES/YUM	paranucleus	PAR/NAOUK/LUS
Paramecium	PAR/MAOERB/YUM	paraomphalic	PAR/OM/FAL/IK
	PAR/MAOES/YUM	paraoperative	PAR/OP/RA/TIV
paramedian	PAR/MAOED/YAN		PAR/OERPT/IV
paramedic	PAR/MED/IK	paraoral	PAR/ORL
paramedical	PAR/MED/KAL	paraoxon	PAR/OK/SON
paramenia	PAR/MAOEN/YA	parapancreatic	PAR/PAN/KRAT/IK
parameningococcus	PAR/ME/NING/KOK/KUS	paraparesis	PAR/PAR/SIS
parameniscitis	PAR/MEN/SAOITS		PAR/PRAOE/SIS
parameniscus	PAR/ME/NIS/KUS	paraparetic	PAR/PA/RET/IK
paramesial	PAR/MAOEZ/YAL		PAR/PRET/IK
paramesonephric	PAR/MES/NEF/RIK	parapedesis	PAR/PE/DAOE/SIS
paramesonephricus	PAR/MES/NEF/RI/KUS	paraperitoneal	PAR/PERT/NAOEL
parameter	PA/RAM/TER	parapertussis	PAR/PER/TUS/SIS
	PRAM/TER	parapestis	PAR/PES/TIS
paramethadione	PAR/M*ET/DI/OEN	paraphasia	PAR/FAIZ/YA
paramethasone	PAR/M*ET/SOEN	paraphasic	PAR/FAIZ/IK
parametrial	PAR/MAOE/TRAL	paraphemia	PAR/FAOEM/YA
	PAR/MAOE/TRAOE/YAL	paraphernalia	PAR/FER/NAIL/YA
parametric	PAR/MET/RIK		PAR/FE/NAIL/YA
parametrismus	PAR/ME/TRIZ/MUS	paraphia	PA/RAIF/YA
parametritic	PAR/ME/TRIT/IK		PA/RAF/YA
parametritis	PAR/ME/TRAOITS	paraphilia	PAR/FIL/YA
parametria	PAR/MAOE/TRA	paraphiliac	PAR/FIL/YAK
	PAR/MAOE/TRAOE/YA	paraphimosis	PAR/FAOI/MOE/SIS
parametrium	PAR/MAOE/TRUM	paraphobia	PAR/FOEB/YA
	PAR/MAOE/TRAOE/UM	paraphonia	PAR/FOEN/YA
	PAR/MAOE/TRAOE/YUM	paraphora	PA/RAF/RA
paramimia	PAR/MIM/YA	paraphrasia	PAR/FRAIZ/YA
paramitome	PAR/MAOI/TOEM	paraphrenia	PAR/FRAOEN/YA
paramnesia	PAR/AM/NAOEZ/YA	paraphrenic	PAR/FREN/IK
Paramoeba	PAR/MAOE/BA	paraphrenitis	PAR/FRAOE/NAOITS
	PAR/MAO*E/BA	paraphronia	PAR/FROEN/YA
paramolar	PAR/MOE/LAR	paraphyseal	*see* paraphysial
paramorphia	PAR/MOR/FAOE/YA	paraphyses	PA/RAF/SAOEZ
	PAR/MOR/FA	paraphysial	PAR/FIZ/YAL
paramorphic	PAR/MOR/FIK	paraphysis	PA/RAF/SIS
paramorphine	PAR/MOR/FAOEN	parapineal	PAR/PIN/YAL
Paramphistomatidae	PAR/AM/F*IS/MAT/DAE	paraplasm	PAR/PLAFM
paramphistomiasis	PAR/AM/F*IS/MAOI/SIS	paraplasmic	PAR/PLAZ/MIK
Paramphistomum	PAR/AM/F*IS/MUM	paraplastic	PAR/PLA*S/IK
paramucin	PAR/MAOU/SIN	Paraplatin	PAR/PLAT/TIN
paramusia	PAR/MAOUZ/YA	paraplectic	PAR/PLEKT/IK
paramutable	PAR/MAOUT/-BL	paraplegia	PAR/PLAOE/JA

paraplegic	PAR/PLAOEJ/IK
paraplegiform	PAR/PLAOEJ/FORM
	PAR/PLEJ/FORM
parapleuritis	PAR/PLAOU/RAOITS
parapneumonia	PAR/NAOU/MOEN/YA
parapophysis	PAR/POF/SIS
parapoplexy	PAR/AP/PLEK/SI
Parapoxvirus	PAR/POX/VAOI/RUS
parapraxia	PAR/PRAX/YA
parapraxis	PAR/PRAK/SIS
paraproctia	PAR/PROK/SHA
paraproctitis	PAR/PROK/TAOITS
paraproctium	PAR/PROK/SHUM
paraprofessional	PAR/PRO/FEGS/NAL
paraprostatitis	PAR/PRO*S/TAOITS
paraprotein	PAR/PRO/TAOEN
paraproteinemia	PAR/PROET/NAOEM/YA
parapsia	PA/RAPS/YA
	PAR/APS/YA
parapsilosis	PAR/SAOI/LOE/SIS
parapsis	PAR/AP/SIS
parapsoriasis	PAR/SOE/RAOI/SIS
parapsychology	PAR/SAOI/KOLG
parapyelitic	PAR/PAOI/LIT/IK
parapyknomorphous	PAR/PIK/NO/MOR/FOUS
parapyramidal	PAR/PI/RAM/DAL
paraquat	PAR/KWAT
pararama	PAR/RAI/MA
pararectal	PAR/REK/TAL
parareducine	PAR/RE/DAOU/SIN
parareflexia	PAR/RE/FLEX/YA
pararenal	PAR/RAOENL
pararhizoclasia	PAR/RAOIZ/KLAIZ/YA
pararhotacism	PAR/ROET/SIFM
pararosanilin	PAR/ROE/SAN/LIN
	PAR/ROE/ZAN/LIN
pararrhythmia	PAR/R*IT/MA
	PAR/R*IT/MAOE/YA
pararthria	PAR/AR/THRAOE/YA
parasacral	PAR/SAI/KRAL
parasalpingeal	PAR/SAL/PIN/JAL
parasalpingitis	PAR/SAL/PIN/JAOITS
parascapular	PAR/SKAP/LAR
Parascaris	PA/RAS/KRIS
	PA/RAS/KA/RIS
	PAR/AS/KRIS
	PAR/AS/KA/RIS
parascarlatina	PAR/SKARL/TAOI/NA
	PAR/SKARL/TAOE/NA
parasecretion	PAR/SE/KRAOEGS
parasellar	PAR/SEL/LAR
paraseptal	PAR/SEP/TAL
parasexual	PAR/SEX/YAOUL
parasexuality	PAR/SEX/YAL/TI
parasigmatism	PAR/SIG/MA/TIFM
parasinoidal	PAR/SAOI/NOI/DAL
parasite	PAR/SAOIT
parasitemia	PAR/SAOI/TAOEM/YA
parasitic	PAR/SIT/IK
parasitica	PAR/SIT/KA
parasiticidal	PAR/SIT/SAOI/DAL
parasiticide	PAR/SIT/SAO*ID
parasiticus	PAR/SIT/KUS
parasitifer	PAR/SIT/FER
parasitism	PAR/SAOI/TIFM
	PAR/SI/TIFM
parasitization	PAR/SAOIT/ZAIGS
parasitize	PAR/SI/TAOIZ
	PAR/SAOI/TAOIZ
parasitogenesis	PAR/SAOIT/JEN/SIS
parasitogenic	PAR/SAOIT/JEN/IK
parasitoid	PAR/SAOI/TOID
parasitologist	PAR/SAOI/TO*LGS
parasitology	PAR/SAOI/TOLG
parasitome	PAR/SAOI/TOEM
parasitophobia	PAR/SAOI/TOEB/YA
parasitosis	PAR/SAOI/TOE/SIS
parasitotrope	PAR/SAOIT/TROEP
parasitotropic	PAR/SAOI/TROP/IK
parasitotropism	PAR/SAOI/TOT/RO/PIFM
parasitotropy	PAR/SAOI/TOT/RO/PI
parasitovorax	PAR/SAOI/TOV/RAX
parasomnia	PAR/SOM/NA
	PAR/SOM/NAOE/YA
paraspadia	PAR/SPAID/YA
paraspadias	PAR/SPAID/YAS
paraspasm	PAR/SPAFM
paraspasmus	PAR/SPAZ/MUS
paraspecific	PAR/SPEFK

	PAR/SPE/SIFK
Paraspirillum	PAR/SPAOI/RIL/UM
parasplenic	PAR/SPLEN/IK
parastasis	PAR/STAI/SIS
parasternal	PAR/STERNL
parasthenia	PAR/AS/THAOEN/YA
parastruma	PAR/STRAOU/MA
parasympathetic	PAR/SIFRP/THET/IK
parasympathicotonia	PAR/SIM/PA*T/KO/TOEN/YA
parasympatholytic	PAR/SIFRP/THO/LIT/IK
parasympathomimetic	PAR/SIFRP/THO/MI/MET/IK
	PAR/SIFRP/THO/MAOI/MET/IK
parasympathoparalytic	PAR/SIFRP/THO/PAR/LIT/IK
parasympathotonia	PAR/SIFRP/THO/TOEN/YA
parasynanche	PAR/SIN/AN/KAOE
	PAR/SI/NAN/KAOE
parasynapsis	PAR/SNAP/SIS
	PAR/SI/NAP/SIS
parasyndesis	PAR/SIN/DAOE/SIS
parasynovitis	PAR/SIN/VAOITS
parasyphilis	PAR/SIF/LIS
parasyphilitic	PAR/SIF/LIT/IK
parasyphilosis	PAR/SIF/LOE/SIS
parasystole	PAR/S*IS/LAOE
paratarsium	PAR/TARS/YUM
parataxia	PAR/TAX/YA
parataxic	PAR/TAX/IK
parataxis	PAR/TAK/SIS
paratenesis	PAR/TE/NAOE/SIS
paratenic	PAR/TEN/IK
paratenon	PAR/TEN/NON
paraterminal	PAR/TERM/NAL
Parathar	PAR/THAR
parathion	PAR/THAOI/YON
parathormone	PAR/THOR/MOEN
	PAR/THOER/MOEN
parathymia	PAR/THAOIM/YA
parathyr(o)-	PAR/THAOIR
	PAR/THAOI/R(O)
parathyrin	PAR/THAOI/RIN
parathyroid	PAR/THAOI/ROID
parathyroidal	PAR/THAOI/ROI/DAL
parathyroidectomize	PAR/THAOI/ROI/DEKT/MAOIZ
parathyroidectomy	PAR/THAOI/ROI/DEKT/M*I
parathyroidin	PAR/THAOI/ROI/DIN
parathyroidoma	PAR/THAOI/ROI/DOE/MA
parathyropathy	PAR/THAOI/ROP/TH*I
parathyroprival	PAR/THAOIR/PRAOIVL
parathyroprivia	PAR/THAOIR/PRIV/YA
parathyroprivic	PAR/THAOIR/PRIVK
parathyrotoxicosis	PAR/THAOIR/TOX/KOE/SIS
parathyrotrophic	PAR/THAOIR/TROFK
parathyrotropic	PAR/THAOIR/TROP/IK
paratonia	PAR/TOEN/YA
paratope	PAR/TOEP
paratrachoma	PAR/TRA/KOE/MA
	PAR/TRAI/KOE/MA
paratrichosis	PAR/TRI/KOE/SIS
paratrimma	PAR/TRIM/MA
paratripsis	PAR/TRIP/SIS
paratriptic	PAR/TRIPT/IK
paratrophic	PAR/TROFK
paratrophy	PAR/AT/RO/FI
paratuberculosis	PAR/TAOU/BERK/LOE/SIS
paratuberculous	PAR/TAOU/BERK/LOUS
paratype	PAR/TAOIP
paratyphlitis	PAR/TIF/LAOITS
paratyphoid	PAR/TAOI/FOID
paratyphosa	PAR/TAOI/FOE/SA
paratypic	PAR/TIP/IK
paratypical	PAR/TIP/KAL
paraumbilical	PAR/UM/BIL/KAL
paraumbilicales	PAR/UM/BIL/KAI/LAOEZ
paraungual	PAR/UNG/WAL
paraurethra	PAR/YAOU/RAO*ET/RA
paraurethral	PAR/YAOU/RAO*ET/RAL
paraurethrales	PAR/YAOUR/THRAI/LAOEZ
paraurethritis	PAR/YAOUR/THRAOITS
parauterine	PAR/YAOUT/RIN
paravaccinia	PAR/VAK/SIN/YA
paravaginal	PAR/VAJ/NAL
paravaginitis	PAR/VAJ/NAOITS
paravalvular	PAR/VAL/VAOU/LAR
paravenous	PAR/VAOEN/OUS
paravertebral	PAR/VERT/BRAL
paravitaminosis	PAR/VAOIT/MI/NOE/SIS
paraxial	PAR/AX/YAL
paraxon	PAR/AK/SON
Parazoa	PAR/ZOE/WA

parazone	PAR/ZOEN		(*not* PAR/TI; see party)
parazoon	PAR/ZAON	Park	K-P/PARK
Par-Decon	PAR/DE/KON	Parker	PARK/ER
parectasia	PAR/EK/TAIZ/YA	parkeri	PARK/RAOI
parectasis	PAR/EKT/SIS		PARK/ER/RAOI
parectropia	PAR/EK/TROEP/YA	Parkinson	PARK/SON
paregoric	PAR/GOR/IK		PAR/KIN/SON
	PAR/GOER/IK		PAR/IN/SON
paregorism	PAR/GOR/IFM	parkinsonian	PARK/SOEN/YAN
pareidolia	PAR/AOI/DOEL/YA		PAR/KIN/SOEN/YAN
pareira	PA/RAI/RA		PARK/IN/SOEN/YAN
parelectronomic	PAR/LEK/TRO/NOM/IK	parkinsonism	PARK/SON/IFM
parelectronomy	PAR/LEK/TRON/M*I		PAR/KIN/SON/IFM
parencephalia	PAR/EN/SFAIL/YA		PARK/IN/SON/IFM
parencephalitis	PAR/EN/SEF/LAOITS	Parlodel	PAR/LO/DEL
parencephalocele	PAR/EN/SEF/LO/SAO*EL		PARL/DEL
parencephalon	PAR/EN/SEF/LON	Parnate	PAR/NAIT
parencephalous	PAR/EN/SEF/LOUS	paroccipital	PAR/OK/SIP/TAL
parenchym(o)-	PRENG/M(O)	parodontal	PAR/DON/TAL
	PA/RENG/M(O)		PAR/O/DON/TAL
	PA/REN/KI/M(O)	parodontid	PAR/DON/TID
	PARN/KIM		PAR/O/DON/TID
	PAR/EN/KIM	parodontitis	PAR/DON/TAOITS
parenchyma	PRENG/MA		PAR/O/DON/TAOITS
parenchymal	PRENG/MAL	parodontium	PAR/DON/SHUM
parenchymatitis	PRENG/MA/TAOITS		PAR/O/DON/SHUM
	PAR/EN/KIM/TAOITS	parodontopathy	PAR/DON/TOP/TH*I
	PARN/KIM/TAOITS		PAR/O/DON/TOP/TH*I
parenchymatous	PARN/KIM/TOUS	parodontosis	PAR/DON/TOE/SIS
	PAR/EN/KIM/TOUS		PAR/O/DON/TOE/SIS
parenchymula	PARN/KIM/LA	parodynia	PAR/DIN/YA
	PAR/EN/KIM/LA		PAR/O/DIN/YA
parental	PA/REN/TAL	parole	PA/ROEL
	PREN/TAL	parolfactoria	PAR/OL/FAK/TOER/YA
parenteral	PA/RENT/RAL		PAR/OL/FAK/TOR/YA
	PRENT/RAL	parolfactory	PAR/OL/FAKT/RI
parentheses	PR*ENT/SAOEZ	parolivary	PAR/OL/VAIR
	PA/R*ENT/SAOEZ	paromomycin	PAR/MO/MAOI/SIN
Parepectolin	PAR/PEKT/LIN		PAR/MOE/MAOI/SIN
parepicele	PAR/EP/SAO*EL	paromphalocele	PAR/OM/FLO/SAO*EL
parepididymis	PAR/EP/DID/MUS		PAR/OM/FAL/SAO*EL
parepigastric	PAR/EP/GAS/TRIK	paroneiria	PAR/NAOIR/YA
parepithymia	PAR/EP/THAOIM/YA		PAR/O/NAOIR/YA
parerethisis	PAR/RAO*ET/SIS	paroniria	*see* paroneiria
	PAR/E/RAO*ET/SIS	paronychia	PAR/NIK/YA
parergasia	PAR/ER/GAIZ/YA		PAR/O/NIK/YA
parergastic	PAR/ER/GA*S/IK	paronychial	PAR/NIK/YAL
paresis	PAR/SIS		PAR/O/NIK/YAL
	PRAOE/SIS	paroophoric	PAR/AO/FOER/IK
	PA/RAOE/SIS	paroophoritis	PAR/AOF/RAOITS
paresthesia	PAR/ES/THAOEZ/YA		PAR/O/OF/RAOITS
paresthetic	PAR/ES/THET/IK	paroophoron	PAR/AOF/RON
paresthetica	PAR/ES/THET/KA		PAR/O/OF/RON
paretic	PA/RET/IK	parophthalmia	PAR/OF/THAL/MA
	PRET/IK		PAR/OF/THAL/MAOE/YA
pareunia	PAR/YAOUN/YA	parophthalmoncus	PAR/OF/THAL/MON/KUS
	PA/RAOUN/YA	paropsia	PAR/OPS/YA
parfocal	PAR/FOE/KAL	paropsis	PAR/OP/SIS
pargyline	PARJ/LAOEN	parorchidism	PAR/ORK/DIFM
	PARG/LAOEN	parorchidium	PAR/OR/KID/YUM
Parham	PAR/HAM	parorchis	PAR/OR/KIS
parhedonia	PAR/HAOE/DOEN/YA	parorexia	PAR/REX/YA
paridrosis	PAR/DROE/SIS		PAR/O/REX/YA
paries	PAI/RAOEZ	parosmia	PAR/OZ/MA
	PAIR/RAOEZ		PAR/OZ/MAOE/YA
	PAR/AOEZ	parosphresia	PAR/OS/FRAOEZ/YA
pariet(o)-	PRAOI/T(O)	parosphresis	PAR/OS/FRAOE/SIS
	PA/RAOI/T(O)	parosteal	PAR/O*S/YAL
parietal	PRAOI/TAL	parosteitis	PAR/O*S/YAOITS
parietales	PRAOI/TAI/LAOEZ	parosteosis	PAR/O*S/YOE/SIS
parietalis	PRAOI/TAI/LIS	parostitis	PAR/OS/TAOITS
parietes	PRAOI/TAOEZ	parostosis	PAR/OS/TOE/SIS
parietis	PRAOI/TIS	parotic	PA/ROT/IK
parietitis	PRAOI/TAOITS		PROT/IK
parietofrontal	PRAOI/TO/FRON/TAL	parotid	PA/ROT/ID
parietography	PRAOI/TOG/FI		PROT/ID
parietomastoid	PRAOI/TO/MAS/TOID	parotidea	PA/ROT/DAE/YA
parieto-occipital	PRAOI/TO/OK/SIP/TAL		PROT/DAOE/YA
parieto-occipitalis	PRAOI/TO/OK/SIP/TAI/LIS	parotideae	PA/ROT/DAOE/YAE
parietosphenoid	PRAOI/TO/SFAOE/NOID		PROT/DAOE/YAE
parietosplanchnic	PRAOI/TO/SPLANG/NIK	parotidean	PA/ROT/DAOE/YAN
parietosquamosal	PRAOI/TO/SKWAI/MOE/SAL		PROT/DAOE/YAN
parietotemporal	PRAOI/TO/TEFRP/RAL	parotidectomy	PA/ROT/DEKT/M*I
parietovisceral	PRAOI/TO/VIS/RAL		PROT/DEKT/M*I
Parinaud	PAR/NOE	parotideomasseterica	PA/ROT/DAOE/YO/MAS/TER/KA
	PAR/RI/NOE		PROT/DAOE/YO/MAS/TER/KA
Paris	PAR/RIS	parotideus	PA/ROT/DAOE/YUS
parity	PAIR/TI		PROT/DAOE/YUS
	PAR/RI/TI	parotiditis	PA/ROT/DAOITS

	PROT/DAOITS	passage	PAS/SAJ
parotidoauricularis	PA/ROT/DO/AU/RIK/LAI/RIS		PASZ/AJ
	PROT/DO/AU/RIK/LAI/RUS	Passavant	PAS/VANT
parotidoscirrhus	PA/ROT/DO/SKIR/RUS		PAS/SA/VANT
	PROT/DO/SKIR/RUS	passenger	PAS/SEN/JER
parotidosclerosis	PA/ROT/DO/SKLE/ROE/SIS		PAS/EN/JER
	PROT/DO/SKLE/ROE/SIS	Passiflora	PAS/FLOR/RA
parotin	PAR/TIN	passion	PAGS
	PA/ROE/TIN	passionate	PAGS/NAT
	PAR/O/TIN	passionnelle	PAS/YO/NEL
parotitic	PAR/O/TIT/IK		PARB/YO/NEL
parotitis	PAR/O/TAOITS		PAGS/NEL
parous	PAR/OUS	passive	PAS/SIV
	PAI/ROUS		PASZ/IV
-parous	-P/ROUS	passivism	PAS/VIFM
parovarian	PAR/O/VAIRN		PASZ/VIFM
parovariotomy	PAR/O/VAIR/YOT/M*I		PAS/SIV/IFM
parovaritis	PAR/OEV/RAOITS	passivity	PAS/SIV/TI
parovarium	PAR/O/VAIRM		PA/SIV/TI
paroxypropione	PAR/OX/PROEP/YOEN	passularum	PAS/LAIR/UM
paroxysm	PA/ROK/SIFM		PAS/YAOU/LAIR/UM
	PROK/SIFM		PAS/YU/LAIR/UM
	PAR/OK/SIFM	pasta	PAS/TA
paroxysmal	PAR/OK/SIZ/MAL	pastae	PAS/TAE
	PROK/SIZ/MAL	paste	PA*IS
parricide	PAR/SAO*ID	paster	PA*IS/ER
	PAR/RI/SAO*ID	pastern	PAS/TERN
Parrot	PAR/ROE	Pasteur	PAS/TAOUR
Parry	K-P/PAR/RI		PAS/TUR
	PAIR/RI	Pasteurella	PA*S/REL/LA
pars	PARZ		PAS/TAOU/REL/LA
pars planitis	PARZ/PLAI/NAOITS		PAS/TUR/REL/LA
pars tensa	PARZ/TEN/SA	Pasteurelleae	PA*S/REL/YAE
part	PART		PAS/TAOU/REL/YAE
partal	PAR/TAL		PAS/TUR/REL/YAE
partes	PAR/TAOEZ	pasteurellosis	PAS/TAOUR/LOE/SIS
parthenogenesis	PA*RT/NO/JEN/SIS		PAS/TUR/LOE/SIS
parthenophobia	PA*RT/NO/FOEB/YA		PA*S/REL/LOE/SIS
partial	PAR/-RBL	Pasteuria	PAS/TAOUR/YA
partialis	PAR/SHAI/LIS	Pasteuriaceae	PAS/TAOUR/YAIS/YAE
partialism	PAR/-RBL/IFM	pasteurianum	PAS/TAOUR/YAIN/UM
particle	PART/K-L		PAS/TAOUR/YAI/NUM
particulate	PAR/TIK/LAIT		PAS/TUR/YAIN/UM
	PAR/TIK/LAT		PAS/TUR/YAI/NUM
partim	PAR/TIM	pasteurization	PAS/KHUR/ZAIGS
partinium	PAR/TIN/YUM		PAS/TAOUR/ZAIGS
partis	PAR/TIS	pasteurizer	PAS/KHUR/AOIZ
partition	PAR/TIGS		PAS/TAOUR/AOIZ
partum	PART/UM	pasteurizer	PAS/KHUR/AOIZ/ER
	PAR/TUM		PAS/TAOUR/AOIZ/ER
parturient	PAR/TAOUR/YENT	Pastia	PA*S/YA
	PAR/KHUR/YENT	pastil	PAS/TIL
parturifacient	PAR/TAOUR/FAIRBT	pastille	PAS/TAOEL
	PAR/KHUR/FAIRBT	past-pointing	PA*S/H-F/POINT/-G
parturiometer	PAR/TAOUR/YOM/TER	pasty	PAIS/TI
	PAR/KHUR/YOM/TER	patagium	PA/TAI/JUM
parturition	PAR/TAOU/RIGS	patagia	PA/TAI/JA
	PAR/KHU/RIGS	patch	PAFP
parulides	PA/RAOUL/DAOEZ	patchouli	PA/KHAOU/LAOE
parulis	PA/RAOU/LIS		PAT/KHAOU/LAOE
parumapertus	PA/RAOUM/PER/TUS	patchy	PAFP/KHI
paruresis	PAR/YAOU/RAOE/SIS	patefaction	PAT/FA*BGS
paruria	PAR/YAOUR/YA	patell(o)-	PA/TEL
parv(o)-	PAFRB		PA/TEL/L(O)
	PAR/V(O)		PAT/L(O)
parva	PAR/VA	patella	PA/TEL/LA
parvalbumin	PAR/VAL/BAOU/MIN	patellae	PA/TEL/LAE
parvenu	PAFRB/NAOU	patellalgia	PAT/LAL/JA
parvicellular	PAFRB/SEL/YAOU/LAR	patellapexy	PA/TEL/PEK/SI
Parvobacteriaceae	PAFRB/BAK/TAOER/YAIS/YAE	patellar	PA/TEL/LAR
parvoline	PAFRB/LAOEN	patellectomy	PAT/LEKT/M*I
	PAFRB/LIN	patelliform	PA/TEL/FORM
Parvoviridae	PAFRB/VIR/DAE	patellofemoral	PA/TEL/FEM/RAL
parvovirus	PAFRB/VAOI/RUS	patellometer	PAT/LOM/TER
parvule	PAR/VAOUL	patency	PAIT/EN/SI
parvulum	PAFRB/LUM		PAI/TEN/SI
parvum	PAFRB/UM		PAIT/-N/SI
parvus	PAR/VUS	patent	PAI/TENT
pascal	PAS/KAL		PAIT/ENT
Pascal	K-P/PAS/KAL		PAT/ENT
Pascheff	PAS/KEF	Paterson	PAT/ER/SON
Paschen	PAS/KEN	path	PA*T
Paschutin	PAS/KAOU/TIN	path(o)-	PA*T
Pasini	PA/SAOE/NAOE		PA/TH(O)
pasiniazide	PAS/NAOI/ZAOID	pathema	PA/THAOE/MA
Pasmol	PAS/MOL	pathematic	PA*T/MAT/IK
	PAZ/MOL	pathergasia	PA*T/ER/GAIZ/YA
paspalism	PAS/PAL/IFM	pathergia	PA/THER/JA
	PAS/PA/LIFM	pathergia	PA*T/ER/JA

pathergic	PA*T/ERJ/IK	patten	PAT/-N
	PA*T/ER/JIK	pattern	PAT/ERN
pathergization	PA*T/ERJ/ZAIGS	patulin	PAT/YAOU/LIN
pathergy	PA*T/ERJI		PAT/YU/LIN
pathetic	PA/THET/IK	patulous	PAT/YAOU/LOUS
pathfinder	PA*T/FAOIND/ER		PAT/YU/LOUS
-pathia	PA*T/YA	paucibacillary	PAUS/BAS/LAIR
pathic	PA*T/IK	paucisynaptic	PAUS/SNAPT/IK
pathoamine	PA*T/AM/AOEN		PAUS/SI/NAPT/IK
	PA*T/AM/MIN	Paul	PA*UL
pathoanatomical	PA*T/AN/TOM/KAL		(not PAUL; see pall)
pathoanatomy	PA*T/AI/NAT/M*I	Pauling	PA*UL/-G
pathobiology	PA*T/BAO*I/OLG	paunch	PAUFRPBLG
pathobolism	PA/THOB/LIFM		PAUN/-FP
Pathocil	PA*T/SIL	pauperum	PAUP/RUM
pathoclisis	PA*T/KLIS/SIS	pause	PAUZ
pathocrine	PA*T/KRIN	pavement	PAIVMT
pathocrinia	PA*T/KRIN/YA	pavementing	PAIVMT/-G
pathodixia	PA*T/DIX/YA	Pautrier	PAU/TRAI
pathodontia	PA*T/DON/SHA		PAU/TRAOE/YAI
pathoformic	PA*T/FORM/IK		PAU/TRAOE/YER
pathogen	PA*T/JEN	Pavabid	PAV/BID
pathogenesis	PA*T/JEN/SIS	pavex	PAI/VEX
pathogenesy	PA*T/JEN/SI	pavilion	PA/VIL/YON
pathogenetic	PA*T/JE/NET/IK	Pavlov	PAV/LOV
pathogenic	PA*T/JEN/IK	pavor	PAI/VOR
pathogenicity	PA*T/JE/NIS/TI		(not PAIVR; see paver)
pathogeny	PA/THOJ/N*I	pavor diurnus	PAI/VOR/DI/UR/NUS
pathoglycemia	PA*T/GLAOI/SAOEM/YA	pavor nocturnus	PAI/VOR/NOK/TUR/NUS
pathognomonic	PA*T/OG/NO/MON/IK	Pavulon	PAV/LON
pathognomy	PA/THOG/NO/M*I		PAIV/LON
	PA*T/OG/NO/M*I	Pavy	PAI/VI
pathognostic	PA*T/OG/NO*S/IK	pawpaw	PAU/PAU
pathography	PA/THOG/FI	Paxton	PAX/TON
patholesia	PA*T/LAOES/YA	Payne	PA*IN
pathologic	PA*T/LOJ/IK		(not PAIN; see pain)
pathological	PA*T/LOJ/KAL	Payr	PAO*IR
pathologically	PA*T/LOJ/KLI		(not PAOIR; see pyre)
pathologicoanatomic	PA*T/LOJ/KO/AN/TOM/IK	Pazo Hemorrhoid	PA/ZOE/HEM/ROID/OINT/-MT
pathologist	PA/THO*LGS	Ointment	PAI/ZOE/HEM/ROID/OINT/-MT
	PA*T/O*LGS	Pazo Hemorrhoid	PA/ZOE/HEM/ROID/
pathology	PA/THOLG	Suppositories	SPOZ/TOIR/-S
	PA*T/OLG		PAI/ZOE/HEM/ROID/SPOZ/TOIR/-S
patholysis	PA/THOL/SIS	pazoxide	PA/ZOK/SAOID
pathomaine	PA*T/MAIN	PBC Tablets	P-RBGS/B*RBGS/KR*RBGS/TAB/
pathomania	PA*T/MAIN/YA		LET/-S
pathometabolism	PA*T/ME/TAB/LIFM	PBZ-SR Tablets	P-RBGS/B*RBGS/KR*RBGS/S-RBGS/
pathometer	PA/THOM/TER		R*RBGS/TAB/LET/-S
pathometric	PA*T/MET/RIK	PCE Dispertab	P-RBGS/KR*RBGS/*ERBGS/DIS/
pathometry	PA/THOM/TRI		PER/TAB
pathomimesis	PA*T/MI/MAOE/SIS	pCO₂	PAOE/SAOE/2
	PA*T/MAOI/MAOE/SIS		P*/KR*RBGS/O*RBGS/2
pathomimia	PA*T/MIM/YA	P-congenitale	P-RBGS/KON/JEN/TAI/LAOE
pathomimicry	PA*T/MIM/KRI	P-dextrocardiale	P-RBGS/DEX/TRO/KARD/YAI/LAOE
pathomiosis	PA*T/MAOI/YOE/SIS	peak	PAEK
pathomorphism	PA*T/MOR/FIFM	pearl	PERL
pathomorphology	PA*T/MOR/FOLG	pearlash	PERL/ARB
pathoneurosis	PA*T/NAOU/ROE/SIS	pearly	PER/LI
pathonomia	PA*T/NOEM/YA		PERL/LI
pathonomy	PA/THON/M*I	Pearson	PAOER/SON
pathophilia	PA*T/FIL/YA	peat	PAET
pathophobia	PA*T/FOEB/YA	peau d'orange	POE/DO/RAN/-J
pathophoresis	PA*T/FRAOE/SIS		POE/DOE/RAN/-J
	PA*T/FOE/RAOE/SIS	pebble	PEBL
pathophoric	PA*T/FOER/IK	peccant	PEK/KANT
pathophorous	PA*T/OF/ROUS	peccatiphobia	PEK/TI/FOEB/YA
	PA/THOF/ROUS		PEKT/FOEB/YA
pathophysiologic	PA*T/FIZ/YO/LOJ/IK	pechyagra	PEK/YAG/RA
pathophysiology	PA*T/FIZ/YOLG		PEK/YAI/GRA
pathopoiesis	PA*T/POI/SIS	pecilocin	PE/SIL/SIN
pathopsychology	PA*T/SAOI/KOLG	Pecquet	PEK/KAI
pathopsychosis	PA*T/SAOI/KOE/SIS		PE/KAI
pathoradiography	PA*T/RAID/YOG/FI	pectase	PEK/TAIS
pathoroentgenography	PA*T/RENT/GEN/OG/FI	pecten	PEK/TEN
pathosis	PA/THOE/SIS	pectenitis	PEKT/NAOITS
pathotropism	PA/THOT/RO/PIFM	pectenosis	PEKT/NOE/SIS
pathway	PA*T/WA*I	pectenotomy	PEKT/NOT/M*I
-pathy	(O)P/TH*I	pectic	PEKT/IK
patience	PAIRBS	pectin	PEK/TIN
	PAI/SHENS	pectin-	PEKT/N
	PAIRB/ENS		PEK/TI/N
patient	PAIRBT		PEK/TIN
	PAI/SHENT	pectinase	PEKT/NAIS
	PAIRB/ENT	pectinate	PEKT/NAIT
patricide	PAT/RI/SAO*ID	pectinata	PEKT/NAI/TA
Patrick	PAT/RIK	pectinati	PEKT/NAI/TAOI
patrilineal	PAT/RI/LIN/YAL	pectinatum	PEKT/NAI/TUM
patroclinous	PAT/RO/KLAOIN/OUS	pectinea	PEK/TIN/YA
patrogenesis	PAT/RO/JEN/SIS	pectineal	PEK/TIN/YAL

pectineale	PEK/TIN/YAI/LAOE
pectinesterase	PEK/TIN/ES/TRAIS
pectineus	PEK/TIN/YUS
pectiniform	PEK/TIN/FORM
pectization	PEKT/ZAIGS
pectolytic	PEKT/LIT/IK
pectora	PEK/TOR/RA
	PEK/TOER/RA
pectoral	PEKT/RAL
	PEK/TRAL
	PEK/TORL
pectorales	PEKT/RAI/LAOEZ
pectoralgia	PEKT/RAL/JA
pectoralis	PEKT/RAI/LIS
pectoriloquous	PEKT/RIL/KWOUS
pectoriloquy	PEKT/RIL/KWAOE
	PEKT/RIL/KWI
pectoris	PEK/TOR/RIS
	PEK/TOER/RIS
pectorophony	PEKT/ROF/N*I
pectose	PEK/TOES
pectous	PEK/TOUS
pectunculus	PEK/TUN/KLUS
	PEK/TUNG/LUS
pectunulus	PEK/TUN/LUS
	PEK/TUN/YAOU/LUS
	PEK/TUN/YU/LUS
pectus	PEK/TUS
ped(o)-	PAOE/D(O)
	PAOED
pedal	PED/DAL
	PAOE/DAL
Pedameth	PED/M*ET
pedarthrocace	PAOE/DAR/THROK/SAOE
	PAOED/AR/THROK/SAOE
pedatrophia	PED/TROEF/YA
pedatrophy	PED/AT/RO/FI
pederast	PED/RA*S
pederasty	PED/RAS/TI
pederosis	PAOED/ROE/SIS
pedes	PAOE/DAOEZ
pedesis	PE/DAOE/SIS
	PAOE/DAOE/SIS
pedi-	PED
	PAOED/Y-
PediaCare	PAOED/YA/KAIR
Pediacof	PAOED/YA/KOF
	PAOED/YA/KAUF
pediadontia	PAOED/YA/DON/SHA
pediadontist	PAOED/YA/DON/T*IS
pediadontology	PAOED/YA/DON/TOLG
Pediaflor	PAOED/YA/FLOR
pedialgia	PED/YAL/JA
Pedialyte	PAOED/YA/LAOIT
Pediapred	PAOED/YA/PRED
Pediasure	PAOED/YA/SHAOUR
pediatric	PAOED/YAT/RIK
pediatrician	PAOED/YA/TRIGS
	PAOED/TRIGS
pediatrics	PAOED/YAT/RIK/-S
pediatrist	PAOED/YAT/R*IS
pediatry	PAOED/YAT/RI
	PE/DAO/TRI
Pediazole	PAOED/YA/ZOEL
Pedi-Boro	PED/BOR/ROE
pedication	PED/KAIGS
pedicel	PED/SEL
pedicellate	PE/DIS/LAIT
	PED/SEL/LAIT
pedicellated	PE/DIS/LAIT/-D
	PED/SEL/LAIT/-D
pedicellation	PE/DIS/LAIGS
	PED/SEL/LAIGS
pedicle	PED/K-L
pedicled	PED/K-LD
pedicterus	PAOE/DIKT/RUS
	PE/DIKT/RUS
pedicul-	PE/DIK/L-
	PE/DIK/YAOU/L-
	PE/DIK/YU/L-
pedicular	PE/DIK/LAR
pediculate	PE/DIK/LAIT
pediculated	PE/DIK/LAIT/-D
pediculation	PE/DIK/LAIGS
pediculi	PE/DIK/LAOI
pediculicide	PE/DIK/LI/SAO*ID
Pediculidae	PED/KAOUL/DAE
pediculoides	PE/DIK/LOI/DAOEZ
Pediculoides	K-P/PE/DIK/LOI/DAOEZ

pediculophobia	PAOE/DIK/LO/FOEB/YA
	PE/DIK/LO/FOEB/YA
pediculosis	PE/DIK/LOE/SIS
pediculous	PE/DIK/LOUS
pediculus	PE/DIK/LUS
Pediculus	K-P/PE/DIK/LUS
pedicure	PED/KAOUR
Pedi-Dri	PED/DRAOI
pedigree	PED/GRAOE
pediluvium	PED/LAOUV/YUM
pediodontia	PAOED/YO/DON/SHA
pedionalgia	PED/YO/NAL/JA
	PAOED/YO/NAL/JA
pedioneuralgia	PED/YO/NAOU/RAL/JA
	PAOED/YO/NAOU/RAL/JA
pediophobia	PAOED/YO/FOEB/YA
PediOtic	PAOED/OET/IK
pediphalanx	PED/FAI/LANGS
Pedi-Pro	PED/PROE
pedis	PAOE/DIS
pedistibulum	PED/STIB/LUM
peditis	PAOE/DAOITS
	PE/DAOITS
Pedi-Vit	PED/VIT
pedodontia	PAOED/DON/SHA
pedodontic	PAOED/DONT/IK
pedodontics	PAOED/DONT/IK/-S
pedodontist	PAOED/DON/T*IS
pedodynamometer	PED/DAOIN/MOM/TER
pedogamy	PAOE/DOG/M*I
pedogenesis	PAOED/JEN/SIS
pedogram	PED/GRAM
pedograph	PED/GRAF
pedography	PE/DOG/FI
pedologist	PAOE/DO*LGS
	PE/DO*LGS
pedology	PAOE/DOLG
	PE/DOLG
pedometer	PAOE/DOM/TER
	PE/DOM/TER
pedomorphic	PAOED/MOR/FIK
pedomorphism	PAOED/MOR/FIFM
pedopathy	PAOE/DOP/TH*I
	PE/DOP/TH*I
pedophilia	PAOED/FIL/YA
pedophilic	PAOED/FIL/IK
pedophobia	PAOED/FOEB/YA
pedorthic	PE/DO*RT/IK
pedorthics	PE/DO*RT/IK/-S
pedorthist	PE/DOR/TH*IS
	PE/DO*RT/*IS
Pedoviridae	PED/VIR/DAE
peduncle	PE/DUN/K-L
	PE/DUNG/-L
peduncul(o)-	PE/DUN/KL(O)
	PE/DUNG/L(O)
	PE/DUN/KAOU/L(O)
	PE/DUNG/YAOU/L(O)
	PE/DUNG/YU/L(O)
peduncular	PE/DUN/KLAR
	PE/DUNG/LAR
peduncularis	PE/DUN/KLAI/RIS
	PE/DUNG/LAI/RIS
pedunculate	PE/DUN/KLAIT
	PE/DUNG/LAIT
pedunculated	PE/DUN/KLAIT/-D
	PE/DUNG/LAIT/-D
pedunculi	PE/DUN/KLAOI
	PE/DUNG/LAOI
pedunculorum	PE/DUN/KLOR/UM
	PE/DUN/KLOER/UM
	PE/DUNG/LOR/UM
	PE/DUNG/LOER/UM
pedunculotomy	PE/DUN/KLOT/M*I
	PE/DUNG/LOT/M*I
pedunculus	PE/DUN/KLUS
	PE/DUNG/LUS
peel	PAOEL
peeling	PAOEL/-G
peenash	PAOE/NARB
peg	PEG
Peganone	PEG/NOEN
pegology	PAOE/GOLG
pegoterate	PEG/TER/AIT
pegoxol	PEG/OK/SOL
pejorism	PAOEJ/RIFM
	PAOE/JOR/IFM
Pel	P*EL
Pel-Ebstein	P*EL/H-F/EB/STAOEN

pelade	PE/LAD	pelvina	PEL/VAOI/NA
	PE/LAUD	pelvini	PEL/VAOI/NAOI
pelage	PEL/AJ	pelvio-	PEL/VO
	PE/LAJ		PEL/VAOE/YO
pelagic	PE/LAJ/IK		PEL/VI/YO
pelagism	PEL/JIFM	pelviography	PEL/VOG/FI
pelargonate	PEL/ARG/NAIT		PEL/VAOE/OG/FI
pelargonic	PEL/AR/GON/IK	pelvioileoneocystostomy	PEL/VO/*IL/YO/NAOE/SIS/TO*S/M*I
Pelecypoda	PEL/SIP/DA		
Pelger	PEL/GER		PEL/VAOE/YO/*IL/YO/NAOE/SIS/TO*S/M*I
pelidisi	PEL/DAOE/SAOE		
pelidnoma	PAOE/LID/NOE/MA	pelviolithotomy	PEL/VO/LI/THOT/M*I
pelioma	PAOEL/YOE/MA		PEL/VAOE/YO/LI/THOT/M*I
	PEL/YOE/MA	pelvioneostomy	PEL/VO/NAOE/O*S/M*I
peliosis	PAOEL/YOE/SIS		PEL/VAOE/YO/NAOE/O*S/M*I
	PEL/YOE/SIS	pelvioperitonitis	PEL/VO/PERT/NAOITS
Pelizaeus	PAIL/ZAI/YUS		PEL/VAOE/YO/PERT/NAOITS
	PAIL/ZAOI/YUS	pelvioplasty	PEL/VO/PLAS/TI
	PEL/ZAI/YUS		PEL/VAOE/YO/PLAS/TI
	PEL/ZAOI/YUS	pelvioprostatic	PEL/VO/PROS/TAT/IK
pellagr-	PE/LAG/R-		PEL/VAOE/YO/PROS/TAT/IK
	PE/LAI/GR-	pelvioradiography	PEL/VO/RAID/YOG/FI
	PEL/GR-		PEL/VAOE/YO/RAID/YOG/FI
	PEL/LAG/R-	pelvioscopy	PEL/VOS/KPI
	PEL/LAI/GR-		PEL/VAOE/OS/KPI
pellagra	PE/LAG/RA	pelviostomy	PEL/VO*S/M*I
	PE/LAI/GRA		PEL/VAOE/O*S/M*I
pellagragenic	PE/LAG/RA/JEN/IK	pelviotomy	PEL/VOT/M*I
pellagral	PE/LAG/RAL		PEL/VAOE/YOT/M*I
pellagramin	PE/LAG/RA/MIN	pelviperitonitis	PEL/VI/PERT/NAOITS
pellagrin	PE/LAG/RIN	pelviprostatic	PEL/VI/PROS/TAT/IK
	PE/LAI/GRIN	pelviradiography	PEL/VI/RAID/YOG/FI
pellagroid	PE/LAG/ROID	pelvirectal	PEL/VI/REK/TAL
pellagrologist	PEL/GRO*LGS	pelviroentgenography	PEL/VI/RENT/GEN/OG/FI
pellagrology	PEL/GROLG	pelvis	PEL/VIS
pellagrose	PE/LAG/ROES	pelvisacral	PEL/VI/SAI/KRAL
pellagrosis	PEL/GROE/SIS	pelvisacrum	PEL/VI/SAI/KRUM
pellagrous	PE/LAG/ROUS	pelviscope	PEL/VI/SKOEP
pellant	PEL/LANT	pelvisection	PEL/VI/S*EBGS
pellate	PEL/LAIT	pelvisternum	PEL/VI/STER/NUM
Pellegrini	PEL/GRAOE/NAOE	pelvitherm	PEL/VI/THERM
pellet	PEL/ET	pelvitomy	PEL/VIT/M*I
pelletierii	PEL/TAOER/YAOI	pelvitrochanterian	PEL/VI/TROE/KAN/TAOERN
pellicle	PEL/K-L	pelviureteral	PEL/VI/YAOU/RAOET/RAL
pellicul-	PE/LIK/L-	pelviureterography	PEL/VI/YAOU/RAOET/ROG/FI
	PE/LIK/YAOU/L-	pelviureteroradiography	PEL/VI/YAOU/RAOET/RO/RAID/YOG/FI
	PE/LIK/YU/L-		
	PEL/LIK/L-	pelvivertebral	PEL/VI/VERT/BRAL
	PEL/LIK/YAOU/L-	pelvocephalography	PEL/VO/SEF/LOG/FI
	PEL/LIK/YUL-	pelvoscopy	see pelvioscopy
pellicular	PE/LIK/LAR	pelvospondylitis	PEL/VO/SPOND/LAOITS
pelliculous	PE/LIK/LOUS	pemoline	PEM/LAOEN
Pellizzi	PEL/LAOE/ZAOE		PEM/LIN
pelluc-	PE/LAOU/S-	pemphigoid	PEM/FI/GOID
	PE/LAOUS	pemphigus	PEM/FI/GUS
	PEL/LAOU/S-	pempidine	PEFRP/DAOEN
	PEL/LAOUS		PEM/PI/DAOEN
pellucid	PE/LAOUS/ID	pen-	PAOE/N(v)
	PE/LAOUS/SID		PAOEN
pellucida	PE/LAOUS/DA		PEN
pellucidi	PE/LAOUS/DAOI	pencil	PEN/SIL
pellucidum	PE/LAOUS/DUM	pendelluft	PEN/DEL/LUFT
pelma	PEL/MA	pendula	PEND/LA
pelmatic	PEL/MAT/IK	pendular	PEND/LAR
pelmatogram	PEL/MAT/GRAM	pendulous	PEND/LOUS
peloid	PAOE/LOID	pendulum	PEND/LUM
pelology	PE/LOLG	Penecort	PEN/KORT
	PAOE/LOLG	penectomy	PAOE/NEKT/M*I
pelopathy	PAOE/LOP/TH*I	penetrance	PEN/TRANS
pelotherapy	PAOEL/THER/PI	penetrans	PEN/TRANZ
pelta	PEL/TA	penetrate	PEN/TRAIT
peltate	PEL/TAIT	penetration	PEN/TRAIGS
peltation	PEL/TAIGS	penetrology	PEN/TROLG
pelves	PEL/VAOEZ	penetrometer	PEN/TROM/TER
pelvi-	PEL/VI	-penia	PAOEN/YA
	PEL/VAOE	penial	PAOEN/YAL
pelviabdominal	PEL/VI/AB/DOM/NAL	peniaphobia	PAOEN/YA/FOEB/YA
pelvic	PEL/VIK	penic	PAOEN/IK
pelvicaliceal	PEL/VI/KAL/SAOEL	penicillamine	PEN/SIL/MAOEN
pelvicalyceal	PEL/VI/KA*L/SAOEL	penicillanic	PEN/SIL/LAN/IK
pelvicellulitis	PEL/VI/SEL/YAOU/LAOITS	penicillary	PEN/SIL/RI
pelvicephalography	PEL/VI/SEF/LOG/FI	penicillate	PEN/SIL/LAIT
pelvicephalometry	PEL/VI/SEF/LOM/TRI		PEN/SIL/AIT
pelvifemoral	PEL/VI/FEM/RAL	penicilli	PEN/SIL/LAOI
pelvifixation	PEL/VI/FIK/SAIGS	penicilliary	PEN/SIL/LAIR
pelvigraph	PEL/VI/GRAF	penicillic	PEN/SIL/IK
pelvilithotomy	PEL/VI/LI/THOT/M*I	penicillin	PEN/SLIN
pelvimeter	PEL/VIM/TER		PEN/SIL/LIN
pelvimetry	PEL/VIM/TRI	penicillinase	PEN/SIL/NAIS

penicillinate	PEN/SIL/NAIT
penicillin-fast	PEN/SLIN/H-F/FA*S
	PEN/SIL/LIN/H-F/FA*S
penicilliosis	PEN/SIL/YOE/SIS
Penicillium	PEN/SIL/YUM
penicilloic	PEN/SIL/LOIK
	PEN/SIL/LOE/IK
penicilloyl	PEN/SIL/OIL
penicilloyl polylysine	PEN/SIL/OIL/POL/LAOI/SAOEN
penicillus	PEN/SIL/LUS
penile	PAOE/NAOIL
penillic	PE/NIL/IK
penin	PEN/NIN
penis	PAOE/NIS
penischisis	PAOE/NIS/KI/SIS
penitis	PAOE/NAOITS
Pen-Kera	PEN/KER/RA
pen light	PEN/LAOIGT
Penn	P*EN
pennate	PEN/NAIT
	PEN/AIT
PenNeedle	PEN/NAOED/-L
penniform	PEN/FORM
Penntuss	PEN/TUSZ
pennyroyal	PEN/ROIL
pennyweight	PEN/WAIGT
peno-	PAOEN
	PAOE/NO
penology	PAOE/NOLG
penopubic	PAOEN/PAOUB/IK
penoscrotal	PAOEN/SKROE/TAL
penotomy	PAOE/NOT/M*I
Penrose	PEN/ROEZ
penta-	PENT
	PEN/TA
pentabasic	PENT/BAIS/IK
pentachromic	PENT/KROEM/IK
pentacyclic	PENT/SIK/LIK
	PENT/SAOIK/LIK
pentad	PEN/TAD
pentadactyl	PENT/DAK/TIL
pentaerythritol	PENT/R*IT/RI/TOL
pentaerythrityl	PENT/R*IT/RI/TIL
pentagastrin	PENT/GAS/TRIN
pentagon	PENT/GON
pentalogy	PEN/TALG
	PEN/TAL/JI
Pentam	PEN/TAM
pentamer	PENT/MER
pentamethazene	PENT/M*ET/ZAOEN
pentamethonium	PENT/ME/THOEN/YUM
pentamide	PENT/MAOID
pentamidine	PEN/TAM/DAOEN
pentane	PEN/TAIN
pentanoic	PENT/NOIK
	PENT/NOE/IK
pentapeptide	PENT/PEP/TAOID
pentapiperide	PENT/PIP/RAOID
	PENT/PAOIP/RAOID
pentapiperium	PENT/PAOI/PER/YUM
pentaploid	PENT/PLOID
pentaploidy	PENT/PLOI/DI
pentaquine	PENT/KWAOIN
pentasomy	PENT/SOE/M*I
Pentaspan	PENT/SPAN
Pentastoma	PEN/TA*S/MA
pentastomiasis	PENT/STOE/MAOI/SIS
pentastomid	PENT/STOE/MID
	PENT/STOEM/ID
Pentastomida	PENT/STOEM/DA
	PENT/STOM/DA
pentatomic	PENT/TOM/IK
Pentatrichomonas	PENT/TRIK/MOE/NAS
	PENT/TRI/KOM/NAS
pentavaccine	PENT/VAK/SAOEN
pentavalent	PENT/VAI/LENT
	PENT/VAIL/ENT
	PEN/TAV/LENT
pentazocine	PEN/TAZ/SAOEN
pentdyopent	PENT/DAOI/PENT
pentene	PEN/TAOEN
pentetate	PENT/TAIT
	PEN/TE/TAIT
pentetic	PEN/TET/IK
penthienate	PEN/THAOI/NAIT
Penthrane	PEN/THRAIN
Pentids	PEN/TIDZ
pentifylline	PEN/TIF/LAOEN
pentitol	PENT/TOL

	PEN/TI/TOL
pentobarbital	PENT/BARB/TAL
pentolinium	PENT/LIN/YUM
penton	PEN/TON
pentone	PEN/TOEN
pentosan	PENT/SAN
pentose	PEN/TOES
pentosemia	PENT/SAOEM/YA
pentosidase	PEN/TOES/DAIS
pentoside	PENT/SAOID
pentosuria	PENT/SAOUR/YA
pentosuric	PENT/SAOUR/IK
pentosyl	PENT/SIL
pentosyltransferase	PENT/SIL/TRA*NS/FRAIS
Pentothal	PENT/THAL
pentoxide	PEN/TOK/SAOID
	PEN/TOX/AOID
pentoxifylline	PEN/TOK/SIF/LIN
	PEN/TOX/IF/LIN
Pentrax	PEN/TRAX
pentrinitrol	PEN/TR*I/NAOI/TROL
	PEN/TR*I/NAOI/TROEL
pentulose	PENT/LOES
	PEN/TAOU/LOES
	PEN/KHU/LOES
pentyl	PEN/TIL
pentylenetetrazol	PENT/LAOEN/TET/RA/ZOL
Pen-Vee K	PEN/VAOE/KAI
	PEN/VAOE/K-RBGS
Penzoldt	PEN/ZOELD
peotillomania	PAOE/TIL/MAIN/YA
peotomy	PAOE/OT/M*I
Pepcid	PEP/SID
peplomer	PEP/LO/MER
peplos	PEP/LOES
	PEP/LOS
pepo	.PAOE/POE
pepper	PEP/ER
Pepper	K-P/PEP/ER
peppermint	PEP/ER/MINT
peps-	PEP/S-
	PEPS
-pepsia	PEPS/YA
pepsic	PEPS/IK
	PEP/SIK
pepsin	PEP/SIN
pepsinate	PEPS/NAIT
pepsinia	PEP/SIN/YA
pepsiniferous	PEPS/NIF/ROUS
pepsinogen	PEP/SIN/JEN
pepsinogenous	PEPS/NOJ/NOUS
pepsinum	PEP/SAOI/NUM
	PEP/SAOIN/UM
	PEPS/NUM
pepsinuria	PEPS/NAOUR/YA
pept-	PEP/T-
	PEPT
peptase	PEP/TAIS
Peptavlon	PEP/TAV/LON
peptic	PEPT/IK
	PEP/TIK
peptid	PEP/TID
peptidase	PEPT/DAIS
peptide	PEPT/TAOID
peptidergic	PEPT/DERJ/IK
peptidoglycan	PEPT/DO/GLAOI/KAN
peptidoid	PEPT/DOID
peptidolytic	PEPT/DO/LIT/IK
pepdidyl	PEPT/DIL
peptinotoxin	PEPT/NO/TOK/SIN
peptization	PEPT/ZAIGS
Pepto-Bismol	PEPT/BIZ/MOL
Peptococcaceae	PEPT/KOK/KAIS/YAE
Peptococcus	PEPT/KOK/KUS
peptocrinine	PEPT/KRIN/AOEN
	PEPT/KRI/NAOEN
peptogenic	PEPT/JEN/IK
peptogenous	PEP/TOJ/NOUS
peptolysis	PEP/TOL/SIS
peptolytic	PEPT/LIT/IK
peptone	PEP/TOEN
peptonic	PEP/TON/IK
peptonization	PEP/TON/ZAIGS
peptonize	PEPT/NAOIZ
peptonoid	PEPT/NOID
peptonuria	PEPT/NAOUR/YA
Peptostreptococcus	PEPT/STREPT/KOK/KUS
peptotoxin	PEPT/TOK/SIN
per	PER

per-	PER	perfusion	PER/FAOUGS
	PE/R-	pergolide mesylate	PERG/LAOID/MES/LAIT
peracephalus	PER/SEF/LUS	Pergonal	PERG/NAL
	PER/AI/SEF/LUS	perhexiline maleate	PER/HEX/LAOEN/MAL/YAIT
peracetate	PER/AS/TAIT	peri-	P*ER
peracetic	PER/AI/SAOET/IK		PER/RI
	PER/AI/SET/IK		(*not* PER; see per, per-, and pero-)
peracid	PER/AS/ID	periacinal	P*ER/AS/NAL
peracidity	PER/SID/TI	periacinous	P*ER/AS/NOUS
	PER/AI/SID/TI	Periactin	P*ER/AK/TIN
peracute	PER/AI/KAOUT	periadenitis	P*ER/AD/NAOITS
per anum	PER/AI/NUM	periadventitial	P*ER/AD/VEN/TIRBL
	PER/AIN/UM	perialienitis	P*ER/AIL/YEN/AOITS
	(*not* PER/AN/UM; see per annum)		P*ER/AIL/YE/NAOITS
perarticulation	PER/AR/TIK/LAIGS	periampullary	P*ER/AFRP/LAIR
peraxillary	PER/AX/LAIR	perianal	P*ER/AINL
perazine	PER/ZAOEN	periangiocholitis	P*ER/AN/JO/KOE/LAOITS
perboric	PER/BOR/IK	periangioma	P*ER/AN/JOE/MA
	PER/BOER/IK	periangitis	P*ER/AN/JAOITS
percentile	PER/SEN/TAOIL	periaortic	P*ER/AI/ORT/IK
percentual	PER/SEN/KHUL		P*ER/AI/YORT/IK
percept	PER/SEPT	periaortitis	P*ER/AI/OR/TAOITS
perception	PER/SEPGS		P*ER/AI/YOR/TAOITS
perceptive	PER/SEPT/IV	periapex	P*ER/AI/PEX
perceptivity	PER/SEP/TIV/TI	periapical	P*ER/AP/KAL
perceptorium	PER/SEP/TOIRM	periappendicitis	P*ER/AI/PEND/SAOITS
perchloric	PER/KLOR/IK	periappendicular	P*ER/AP/EN/DIK/LAR
perchloride	PER/KLOR/AOID	periapt	P*ER/APT
percipient	PER/SIP/YENT	periaqueductal	P*ER/AK/WE/DUK/TAL
perco-	PERK	periarterial	P*ER/AR/TAOERL
	PER/KO	periarteritis	P*ER/ART/RAOITS
Percocet	PERK/SET	periarthric	P*ER/AR/THRIK
Percodan	PERK/DAN	periarthritis	P*ER/AR/THRAOITS
Percodan-Demi	PERK/DAN/DEM/M*I	periarticular	P*ER/AR/TIK/LAR
Percogesic	PERK/JAOEZ/IK	periatrial	P*ER/AI/TRAL
percolate	PERK/LAIT	periauricular	P*ER/AU/RIK/LAR
percolation	PERK/LAIGS	periaxial	P*ER/AX/YAL
percolator	PERK/LAI/TOR	periaxialis	P*ER/AX/YAI/LIS
percomorph	PERK/MOR/-F	periaxillary	P*ER/AX/LAIR
per contiguum	PER/KON/TIG/YUM	periaxonal	P*ER/AX/NAL
	PER/KON/TIG/YAOUM	periblast	P*ER/BLA*S
per continuum	PER/KON/TIN/YUM	peribronchial	P*ER/BRONG/YAL
	PER/KON/TIN/YAOUM	peribronchiolar	P*ER/BRON/KAOI/LAR
percuss	PER/KUSZ		P*ER/BRONG/YOE/LAR
percussible	PER/KUS/-BL	peribronchiolitis	P*ER/BRONG/YO/LAOITS
	PER/KUSZ/-BL	peribronchitis	P*ER/BRON/KAOITS
percussion	PER/KUGS	peribuccal	P*ER/BUK/KAL
percussive	PER/KUS/SIV	peribulbar	P*ER/BUL/BAR
	PER/KUSZ/IV	peribursal	P*ER/BUR/SAL
percussopunctator	PER/KUS/PUNG/TAI/TOR	pericaliceal	P*ER/KAL/SAOEL
	PER/KUS/P*UNG/TAI/TOR	pericallosal	P*ER/KAL/LOE/SAL
percussor	PER/KUS/SOR	pericalyceal	P*ER/KA*L/SAOEL
percutaneous	PER/KAOU/TAIN/YOUS	pericanalicular	P*ER/KAN/LIK/LAR
per cutem	PER/KAOU/TEM	pericapillary	P*ER/KAP/LAIR
percuteur	PER/KAOU/TAOUR	pericapsular	P*ER/KAPS/LAR
Perdiem Fiber Granules	PER/DAOEM/FAOI/BER/GRAN/	pericardectomy	PER/RI/KAR/DEKT/M*I
	YAOUL/-S	pericardi(o)-	P*ER/KARD/Y(O)
Perdiem Granules	PER/DAOEM/GRAN/YAOUL/-S		PER/RI/KARD/Y(O)
perencephaly	PER/EN/SEF/LI	pericardia	P*ER/KARD/YA
perennial	PREN/YAL	pericardiac	P*ER/KARD/YAK
	PER/EN/YAL	pericardiaca	P*ER/KAR/DAOI/KA
	PE/REN/YAL	pericardiacae	P*ER/KAR/DAOI/SAE
Perez	PER/REZ	pericardiacophrenica	P*ER/KAR/DAOI/KO/FREN/KA
	PE/REZ	pericardiacophrenicae	P*ER/KAR/DAOI/KO/FREN/SAE
perfection	PER/F*EBGS	pericardial	P*ER/KARD/YAL
perfectionism	PER/F*EBGS/IFM	pericardicentesis	P*ER/KARD/SEN/TAOE/SIS
perfilcon A	PER/FIL/KON/ARBGS	pericardiectomy	P*ER/KARD/YEKT/M*I
perflation	PER/FLAIGS	pericardiolysis	P*ER/KARD/YOL/SIS
perfoliatus	PER/FOEL/YAI/TUS	pericardii	P*ER/KARD/YAOI
perfor-	PER/FR-	pericardiocentesis	P*ER/KARD/YO/SEN/TAOE/SIS
	PER/FO/R-	pericardiomediastinitis	P*ER/KARD/YO/MAOED/YA*S/
	PER/FOE/R-		NAOITS
perforans	PER/FRANZ	pericardioperitoneal	P*ER/KARD/YO/PERT/NAOEL
perforantes	PER/FRAN/TAOEZ	pericardiophrenic	P*ER/KARD/YO/FREN/IK
perforated	PER/FRAIT/-D	pericardiopleural	P*ER/KARD/YO/PLAOURL
perforation	PER/FRAIGS	pericardiorrhaphy	P*ER/KARD/YOR/FI
perforative	PER/FRA/TIV	pericardiostomy	P*ER/KARD/YO*S/M*I
	PER/FRAIT/IV	pericardiotomy	P*ER/KARD/YOT/M*I
perforator	PER/FRAI/TOR	pericarditic	P*ER/KAR/DIT/IK
perforatorium	PER/FRA/TOIRM	pericarditis	P*ER/KAR/DAOITS
performic	PER/FORM/IK	pericardium	P*ER/KARD/YUM
perfrication	PER/FRI/KAIGS	pericardotomy	P*ER/KAR/DOT/M*I
perfrigeration	PER/FRIJ/RAIGS	pericecal	P*ER/SE/KAL
perfringens	PER/FRIN/JENZ	pericecitis	P*ER/SE/SAOITS
perfume	PER/FAOUM	pericellular	P*ER/SEL/YAOU/LAR
perfusate	PER/FAOU/SAIT	pericemental	P*ER/SEMT/TAL
	PER/FAOU/ZAIT	pericementitis	P*ER/SEMT/TAOITS
perfuse	PER/FAOUS		P*ER/SE/MEN/TAOTS
	PER/FAOUZ	pericementoclasia	P*ER/SEMT/KLAIZ/YA

pericementum	P*ER/SEMT/UM	perifascicular	P*ER/FA/SIK/LAR
	P*ER/SE/MEN/TUM	perifistular	P*ER/F*IS/LAR
pericentral	P*ER/SEN/TRAL		P*ER/FIS/KHU/LAR
	P*ER/STRAL	perifocal	P*ER/FOE/KAL
pericentriolar	P*ER/SEN/TROE/LAR	perifollicular	P*ER/FLIK/LAR
pericephalic	P*ER/SFAL/IK	perifolliculitis	P*ER/FLIK/LAOITS
perichareia	P*ER/KA/RAOI/YA	perifuse	P*ER/FAOUS
pericholangitis	P*ER/KOE/LAN/JAOITS	perifusion	P*ER/FAOUGS
pericholecystitis	P*ER/KOEL/SIS/TAOITS	perigangliitis	P*ER/GANG/LAOITS
perichondral	P*ER/KON/DRAL	periganglionic	P*ER/GANG/LON/IK
perichondrial	see perichondral	perigastric	P*ER/GAS/TRIK
perichondritis	P*ER/KON/DRAOITS	perigastritis	P*ER/GAS/TRAOITS
perichondrium	P*ER/KON/DRUM	perigemmal	P*ER/JEM/MAL
	P*ER/KON/DRAOE/UM	periglandular	P*ER/GLAND/LAR
perichondroma	P*ER/KON/DROE/MA	periglandulitis	P*ER/GLAND/LAOITS
perichord	P*ER/KHORD	periglial	P*ER/GLAOIL
perichordal	P*ER/KHOR/DAL	periglossitis	P*ER/GLOS/SAOITS
perichoroidal	P*ER/KOE/ROI/DAL	periglottic	P*ER/GLOT/IK
perichrome	P*ER/KROEM	periglottis	P*ER/GLOT/TIS
periclasia	P*ER/KLAIZ/YA	perihepatic	P*ER/HE/PAT/IK
Peri-Colace	P*ER/KO/LAIS	perihepatitis	P*ER/HEP/TAOITS
pericolic	P*ER/KOL/IK	perihernial	P*ER/HERN/YAL
pericolitis	P*ER/KO/LAOITS	perihilar	P*ER/HAOI/LAR
pericollagen	P*ER/KOL/JEN	peri-implantoclasia	P*ER/IM/PLANT/KLAIZ/YA
pericolonitis	P*ER/KOEL/NAOITS	peri-infarction	P*ER/IN/FA*RBGS
pericolpitis	P*ER/KOL/PAOITS	peri-insular	P*ER/INS/LAR
periconchal	P*ER/KON/KAL	peri-islet	P*ER/AOIL/ET
periconchitis	P*ER/KON/KAOITS	perijejunitis	P*ER/JEJ/NAOITS
pericorneal	P*ER/KORN/YAL	perikarya	P*ER/KAR/YA
pericoronal	P*ER/KOR/NAL	perikaryon	P*ER/KAR/YON
pericoronitis	P*ER/KOR/NAOITS	perikeratic	P*ER/KE/RAT/IK
pericoxitis	P*ER/KOK/SAOITS	perikyma	P*ER/KAOI/MA
	P*ER/KOX/AOITS	perikymata	P*ER/KAOIM/TA
pericranial	P*ER/KRAIN/YAL	perilabyrinth	P*ER/LAB/R*INT
pericranitis	P*ER/KRAI/NAOITS	perilabyrinthitis	P*ER/LAB/RIN/THAOITS
pericranium	P*ER/KRAIN/YUM	perilaryngeal	P*ER/LARN/JAL
pericryptal	P*ER/KRIP/TAL	perilaryngitis	P*ER/LARN/JAOITS
pericyazine	P*ER/SAOI/ZAOEN	perilenticular	P*ER/LEN/TIK/LAR
pericycle	P*ER/SAOIK/-L	perilesional	P*ER/LAOEGS/NAL
pericystic	P*ER/S*IS/IK	periligamentous	P*ER/LIG/MEN/TOUS
pericystitis	P*ER/SIS/TAOITS	perilobar	P*ER/LOE/BAR
pericystium	P*ER/S*IS/YUM	perilobulitis	P*ER/LOB/LAOITS
pericyte	P*ER/SAO*IT	perilymph-	P*ER/LIM/-F
pericytial	P*ER/SIRBL	perilympha	P*ER/LIM/FA
	P*ER/SIT/YAL	perilymphadenitis	P*ER/LIM/FAD/NAOITS
pericytoma	P*ER/SAOI/TOE/MA	perilymphangeal	P*ER/LIM/FAN/JAL
peridectomy	P*ER/DEKT/M*I	perilymphangitis	P*ER/LIM/FAN/JAOITS
perideferentitis	P*ER/DEFRN/TAOITS	perilymphatic	P*ER/LIM/FAT/IK
	P*ER/DEF/REN/TAOITS	perilymphatici	P*ER/LIM/FAT/SAOI
peridendritic	P*ER/DEN/DRIT/IK	perimastitis	P*ER/MAS/TAOITS
peridens	P*ER/DENZ	perimedullary	P*ER/MED/LAIR
peridental	P*ER/DEN/TAL	perimeningitis	P*ER/MEN/JAOITS
peridentitis	P*ER/DEN/TAOITS	perimeter	PRIM/TER
peridentium	P*ER/DEN/SHUM		PE/RIM/TER
periderm	P*ER/DERM	perimetric	P*ER/MET/RIK
periderma	P*ER/DER/MA	perimetritic	P*ER/ME/TRIT/IK
peridermal	P*ER/DER/MAL	perimetritis	P*ER/ME/TRAOITS
peridermic	P*ER/DERM/IK	perimetria	P*ER/MAOE/TRA
peridesmic	P*ER/DEZ/MIK	perimetrium	P*ER/MAOE/TRUM
peridesmitis	P*ER/DEZ/MAOITS	perimetrosalpingitis	P*ER/MAOE/TRO/SAL/PIN/
peridesmium	P*ER/DEZ/MUM		JAOITS
	P*ER/DEZ/MAOE/UM		P*ER/MET/RO/SAL/PIN/JAOITS
Peridex	P*ER/DEX	perimetry	PRIM/TRI
perididymis	P*ER/DID/MIS		PE/RIM/TRI
perididymitis	P*ER/DID/MAOITS	perimyelis	P*ER/MAOI/LIS
Peridin	P*ER/DIN	perimyelitis	P*ER/MAOI/LAOITS
Peridin-C	P*ER/DIN/KR-RBGS	perimyelography	P*ER/MAOI/LOG/FI
peridium	PE/RID/YUM	perimyocarditis	P*ER/MAOI/KAR/DAOITS
peridiverticulitis	P*ER/DI/VER/TIK/LAOITS	perimyoendocarditis	P*ER/MAOI/*END/KAR/DAOITS
periductal	P*ER/DUK/TAL	perimyositis	P*ER/MAOI/SAOITS
periductile	P*ER/DUK/TAOIL	perimysia	P*ER/MIS/YA
	P*ER/DUK/TIL	perimysial	P*ER/MIS/YAL
periduodenitis	P*ER/DAOU/DEN/AOITS	perimysiitis	P*ER/MIS/YAOITS
	P*ER/DAOU/DE/NAOITS	perimysitis	P*ER/MIS/AOITS
	P*ER/DWOD/NAOITS	perimysium	P*ER/MIS/YUM
peridural	P*ER/DAOURL	perinatal	P*ER/NAI/TAL
peridurogram	P*ER/DAOUR/GRAM	perinate	P*ER/NAIT
peridurography	P*ER/DAOU/ROG/FI	perinatologist	P*ER/NAI/TO*LGS
periencephalitis	P*ER/EN/SEF/LAOITS	perinatology	P*ER/NAI/TOLG
periencephalography	P*ER/EN/SEF/LOG/FI	perine(o)-	P*ER/NAOE
periencephalomeningitis	P*ER/EN/SEF/LO/MEN/JAOITS		P*ER/NAOE/Y(O)
perienteric	P*ER/SPWER/IK	perinea	P*ER/NAOE/YA
perienteritis	P*ER/SPWRAOITS	perineal	P*ER/NAOEL
perienteron	P*ER/SPWRON	perineales	P*ER/NAOE/YAI/LAOEZ
	P*ER/ENT/RON	perinealis	P*ER/NAOE/YAI/LIS
periependymal	P*ER/E/PEND/MAL	perinei	P*ER/NAOE/YAOI
periepithelioma	P*ER/EP/THAOEL/YOE/MA	perineocele	P*ER/NAOE/SAO*EL
periesophageal	P*ER/E/SOF/JAOEL	perineometer	P*ER/NAOE/OM/TER
periesophagitis	P*ER/E/SOF/JAOITS		P*ER/NAOE/YOM/TER

perineoplasty	P*ER/NAOE/PLAS/TI
perineorrhaphy	P*ER/NAOE/YOR/FI
perineoscrotal	P*ER/NAOE/SKROE/TAL
perineostomy	P*ER/NAOE/O*S/M*I
	P*ER/NAOE/YO*S/M*I
perineosynthesis	P*ER/NAOE/S*INT/SIS
perineotomy	P*ER/NAOE/OT/M*I
	P*ER/NAOE/YOT/M*I
perineovaginal	P*ER/NAOE/VAJ/NAL
perineovaginorectal	P*ER/NAOE/VAJ/NO/REK/TAL
perineovulvar	P*ER/NAOE/VUL/VAR
perinephria	P*ER/NEF/RA
	P*ER/NEF/RAOE/YA
perinephrial	P*ER/NEF/RAL
	P*ER/NEF/RAOEL
perinephric	P*ER/NEF/RIK
perinephritic	P*ER/NE/FRIT/IK
perinephritis	P*ER/NE/FRAOITS
perinephrium	P*ER/NEF/RUM
	P*ER/NEF/RAOE/UM
perineum	P*ER/NAOEM
perineural	P*ER/NAOURL
perineuria	P*ER/NAOUR/YA
perineurial	P*ER/NAOUR/YAL
	(not P*ER/NAOURL; see
	perineural)
perineuritic	P*ER/NAOU/RIT/IK
perineuritis	P*ER/NAOU/RAOITS
perineurium	P*ER/NAOUR/YUM
perinuclear	P*ER/NAOUK/LAR
periocular	P*ER/OK/LAR
period	PAOER/YOD
periodate	PER/AOI/DAIT
	PE/RAOI/DAIT
periodic	PAOER/YOD/IK
periodicity	PAOER/YO/DIS/TI
periodism	PAOER/YO/DIFM
	PAOER/YOD/IFM
periodontal	P*ER/O/DON/TAL
periodontia	P*ER/O/DON/SHA
periodontics	P*ER/O/DONT/IK/-S
periodontist	P*ER/O/DON/T*IS
periodontitis	P*ER/O/DON/TAOITS
periodontium	P*ER/O/DON/SHUM
periodontoclasia	P*ER/O/DONT/KLAIZ/YA
periodontology	P*ER/O/DON/TOLG
periodontolysis	P*ER/O/DON/TOL/SIS
periodontopathy	P*ER/O/DON/TOP/TH*I
periodontosis	P*ER/O/DON/TOE/SIS
periomphalic	P*ER/OM/FAL/IK
perionychia	P*ER/O/NIK/YA
perionychium	P*ER/O/NIK/YUM
perionyx	P*ER/ON/IX
perionyxis	P*ER/O/NIK/SIS
perioophoritis	P*ER/AOF/RAOITS
	P*ER/O/OF/RAOITS
perioophorosalpingitis	P*ER/AOF/RO/SAL/PIN/JAOITS
	P*ER/O/OF/RO/SAL/PIN/JAOITS
perioothecitis	P*ER/O/THAOE/SAOITS
perioperative	P*ER/OP/RA/TIV
	P*ER/OERPT/IV
periophthalmia	P*ER/OF/THAL/MA
	P*ER/OF/THAL/MAOE/YA
periophthalmic	P*ER/OF/THAL/MIK
periophthalmitis	P*ER/OF/THAL/MAOITS
periople	P*ER/OEP/-L
perioplic	P*ER/OP/LIK
perioptometry	P*ER/OP/TOM/TRI
perioral	P*ER/ORL
periorale	P*ER/O/RAI/LAOE
periorata	P*ER/O/RAI/TA
periorbit	P*ER/ORBT
periorbita	P*ER/ORB/TA
periorbital	P*ER/ORB/TAL
periorbititis	P*ER/ORB/TAOITS
periorchitis	P*ER/OR/KAOITS
periorchium	P*ER/ORK/YUM
periost	P*ER/O*S
periostalis	P*ER/OS/TAI/LIS
perioste(o)-	P*ER/O*S/Y(O)
periostea	P*ER/O*S/YA
periosteal	P*ER/O*S/YAL
periosteitis	P*ER/O*S/YAOITS
periosteoedema	P*ER/O*S/YO/E/DAOE/MA
	P*ER/O*S/YO/DAOE/MA
periosteoma	P*ER/O*S/YOE/MA
periosteomedullitis	P*ER/O*S/YO/MED/LAOITS
periosteomyelitis	P*ER/O*S/YO/MAOI/LAOITS
periosteopathy	P*ER/O*S/YOP/TH*I

periosteophyte	P*ER/O*S/YO/FAOIT
periosteoplastic	P*ER/O*S/YO/PLA*S/IK
periosteorrhaphy	P*ER/O*S/YO/YOR/FI
periosteosis	P*ER/O*S/YOE/SIS
periosteotome	P*ER/O*S/YO/TOEM
periosteotomy	P*ER/O*S/YOT/M*I
periosteous	P*ER/O*S/YOUS
periosteum	P*ER/O*S/YUM
periostitis	P*ER/OS/TAOITS
periostoma	P*ER/OS/TOE/MA
perostoses	P*ER/OS/TOE/SAOEZ
periostosis	P*ER/OS/TOE/SIS
periostosteitis	P*ER/OS/TO*S/YAOITS
periostotome	P*ER/O*S/TOEM
periostotomy	P*ER/OS/TOT/M*I
periotic	P*ER/OET/IK
	P*ER/OT/IK
periovaritis	P*ER/OEV/RAOITS
periovular	P*ER/OV/LAR
peripachymeningitis	P*ER/PAK/MEN/JAOITS
peripancreatic	P*ER/PAN/KRAT/IK
peripancreatitis	P*ER/PAN/KRA/TAOITS
peripapillary	P*ER/PAP/LAIR
peripartum	P*ER/PAR/TUM
	P*ER/PART/UM
peripatellar	P*ER/PA/TEL/LAR
peripatetic	P*ER/PA/TET/IK
peripenial	P*ER/PAOEN/YAL
peripericarditis	P*ER/P*ER/KAR/DAOITS
periphacitis	P*ER/FA/SAOITS
periphakitis	P*ER/FAI/KAOITS
	P*ER/FA/KAOITS
peripharyngeal	P*ER/FRIN/JAL
peripher(o)-	PRIF/R(O)
	PE/RIF/R(O)
peripherad	PRIF/RAD
peripheral	PRIF/RAL
peripheralis	PRIF/RAI/LIS
peripheraphose	PRIF/RA/FOES
peripheric	P*ER/FER/IK
peripherocentral	PRIF/RO/SEN/TRAL
	PRIF/RO/STRAL
peripheroceptor	PRIF/RO/SEP/TOR
peripheromittor	PRIF/RO/MIT/TOR
peripherophose	PRIF/RO/FOES
periphery	PRIF/RI
periphlebitic	P*ER/FLE/BIT/IK
periphlebitis	P*ER/FLE/BAOITS
periphoria	P*ER/FOER/YA
periphrastic	P*ER/FRA*S/IK
periphrenitis	P*ER/FRAOE/NAOITS
peripilar	P*ER/PAOI/LAR
Periplaneta	P*ER/PLA/NAOE/TA
periplasmic	P*ER/PLAZ/MIK
peripleural	P*ER/PLAOURL
peripleuritic	P*ER/PLAOU/RIT/IK
peripleuritis	P*ER/PLAOU/RAOITS
periplocin	PE/RIP/LOE/SIN
	P*ER/PLOE/SIN
peripneumonia	P*ER/NAOU/MOEN/YA
peripneumonitis	P*ER/NAOUM/NAOITS
peripolar	P*ER/POE/LAR
peripolesis	P*ER/POE/LAOE/SIS
periporitis	P*ER/PO/RAOITS
	P*ER/POE/RAOITS
periportal	P*ER/POR/TAL
periproctic	P*ER/PROKT/IK
periproctitis	P*ER/PROK/TAOITS
periprostatic	P*ER/PROS/TAT/IK
periprostatitis	P*ER/PRO*S/TAOITS
peripyema	P*ER/PAOI/E/MA
peripylephlebitis	P*ER/PAOIL/FLE/BAOITS
peripylic	P*ER/PAOIL/IK
peripyloric	P*ER/PAOI/LOR/IK
	P*ER/PAOI/LOER/IK
periradicular	P*ER/RA/DIK/LAR
perirectal	P*ER/REK/TAL
perirectitis	P*ER/REK/TAOITS
perirenal	P*ER/RAOENL
perireticulin	P*ER/RE/TIK/LIN
periretinal	P*ER/RET/NAL
perirhinal	P*ER/RAOINL
perirhizoclasia	P*ER/RAOIZ/KLAIZ/YA
perisalpingitis	P*ER/SAL/PIN/JAOITS
perisalpingo-ovaritis	P*ER/SAL/PING/OEV/RAOITS
perisalpinx	P*ER/SAL/PINGS
perisclerium	P*ER/SKLAOERM
	P*ER/SKLAOER/YUM
periscopic	P*ER/SKOP/IK

perisigmoiditis	P*ER/SIG/MOI/DAOITS	peritoneum	PERT/NAOEM
perisinuitis	P*ER/SAOIN/YAOITS	peritonism	PERT/NIFM
perisinuous	P*ER/SIN/YOUS	peritonitis	PERT/NAOITS
perisinus	P*ER/SAOI/NUS	peritonization	P*ER/TOEN/ZAIGS
perisinusitis	P*ER/SAOIN/SAOITS	peritonize	PERT/NAOIZ
perispermatitis	P*ER/SPERM/TAOITS	peritonsillar	P*ER/TONS/LAR
perisplanchnic	P*ER/SPLANG/NIK	peritonsillitis	P*ER/TONS/LAOITS
perisplanchnitis	P*ER/SPLANG/NAOITS	peritracheal	P*ER/TRAIK/YAL
perisplenic	P*ER/SPLEN/IK	Peritrate	P*ER/TRAIT
perisplenitis	P*ER/SPLAOE/NAOITS	peritrichal	PE/RIT/RI/KAL
perispondylic	P*ER/SPON/DIL/IK	peritrichate	PE/RIT/RI/KAIT
perispondylitis	P*ER/SPOND/LAOITS	peritrichic	P*ER/TRIK/IK
perissodactyl	PRIS/DAK/TIL	Peritrichida	P*ER/TRIK/DA
	PE/RIS/DAK/TIL	peritrichous	PE/RIT/RI/KOUS
Perissodactyla	PE/RIS/DAKT/LA	peritrochanteric	P*ER/TROE/KAN/TER/IK
	PRIS/DAKT/LA	peritubular	P*ER/TAOUB/LAR
perissodactylous	PE/RIS/DAKT/LOUS	perityphlic	P*ER/TIF/LIK
	PRIS/DAKT/LOUS	perityphlitis	P*ER/TIF/LAOITS
peristalsis	P*ER/STAL/SIS	periumbilical	P*ER/UM/BIL/KAL
peristaltic	P*ER/STALT/IK	periungual	P*ER/UNG/WAL
peristaphyline	P*ER/STAF/LAOIN	periureteral	P*ER/YAOU/RAOET/RAL
	P*ER/STAF/LIN	periureteric	P*ER/YAOUR/TER/IK
peristaphylitis	P*ER/STAF/LAOITS	periureteritis	P*ER/YAOU/RAOET/RAOITS
peristasis	PE/R*IS/SIS	periurethral	P*ER/YAOU/RAO*ET/RAL
peristole	PE/R*IS/LAOE	periurethritis	P*ER/YAOUR/THRAOITS
peristolic	P*ER/STOL/IK	periuterine	P*ER/YAOUT/RIN
peristoma	PE/R*IS/MA	periuvular	P*ER/YAOUV/LAR
	P*ER/STOE/MA	perivaginal	P*ER/VAJ/NAL
peristomal	P*ER/STOE/MAL	perivaginitis	P*ER/VAJ/NAOITS
peristomatous	P*ER/STOEM/TOUS	perivascular	P*ER/VAS/KLAR
peristome	P*ER/STOEM	perivascularis	P*ER/VAS/KLAI/RIS
periston	P*ER/STON	perivascularity	P*ER/VAS/KLAIR/TI
peristriate	P*ER/STRAOI/AIT	perivasculitis	P*ER/VAS/KLAOITS
	P*ER/STRAOI/YAIT	perivenous	P*ER/VAOEN/OUS
peristrumitis	P*ER/STRAOU/MAOITS	periventricular	P*ER/VEN/TRIK/LAR
peristrumous	P*ER/STRAOUM/OUS	periventriculares	P*ER/VEN/TRIK/LAI/RAOEZ
perisynovial	P*ER/SNOEV/YAL	perivertebral	P*ER/VERT/BRAL
perisyringitis	P*ER/SIRN/JAOITS	perivesical	P*ER/VES/KAL
perisystole	P*ER/S*IS/LAOE	perivesicular	P*ER/VE/SIK/LAR
perisystolic	P*ER/SIS/TOL/IK	perivesiculitis	P*ER/VE/SIK/LAOITS
peritectomy	P*ER/TEKT/M*I	perivisceral	P*ER/VIS/RAL
peritendinea	P*ER/TEN/DIN/YA	perivisceritis	P*ER/VIS/RAOITS
peritendineum	P*ER/TEN/DIN/YUM	perivitelline	P*ER/VAOI/TEL/LIN
peritendinitis	P*ER/TEND/NAOITS		P*ER/VI/TEL/LIN
peritendinous	P*ER/TEND/NOUS	perixenitis	P*ER/ZE/NAOITS
peritenon	P*ER/TEN/NON	perkeratosis	PER/KER/TOE/SIS
peritenoneum	P*ER/TEN/OEN/YUM	perkinism	PERK/NIFM
	P*ER/TE/NOEN/YUM		PER/KIN/IFM
peritenonitis	P*ER/TEN/NAOITS	perleche	PER/LERB
peritenontitis	P*ER/TEN/ON/TAOITS	Perlia	PERL/YA
perithecia	P*ER/THAOES/YA	perlingual	PER/LING/WAL
perithecium	P*ER/THAOES/YUM	Perls	PERLS
perithelia	P*ER/THAOEL/YA	permanent	PERM/NENT
perithelial	P*ER/THAOEL/YAL	permanentes	PERM/NEN/TAOEZ
perithelioma	P*ER/THAOEL/YOE/MA	permanganate	PER/MANG/NAIT
perithelium	P*ER/THAOEL/YUM	permanganic	PER/MAN/GAN/IK
perithoracic	P*ER/THRAS/IK	Permax	PER/MAX
perithyreoiditis	P*ER/THAOIR/YOI/DAOITS	permeability	PERM/YABLT
perithyroiditis	P*ER/THAOI/ROI/DAOITS	permeable	PERM/YABL
Peritinic	P*ER/TIN/IK	permeant	PERM/YANT
peritomist	PE/RIT/M*IS	permease	PERM/YAIS
peritomize	PE/RIT/MAOIZ	permeate	PERM/YAIT
peritomy	PE/RIT/M*I	permeation	PERM/YAIGS
peritonaei	PERT/NAE/YAOI	permissible	PER/MISZ/-BL
	P*ER/TO/NAE/YAOI		PER/MIS/-BL
peritone(o)-	PERT/NAOE	Permitil	PERM/TIL
	PERT/NAOE/Y(O)	pernasal	PER/NAI/ZAL
	P*ER/TO/NAOE	perniciosiform	PER/NIRB/YOES/FORM
	P*ER/TO/NAOE/Y(O)		PER/NIS/YOES/FORM
peritonea	PERT/NAOE/YA	pernicious	PER/NIRBS
peritoneal	PERT/NAOEL	pernio	PERN/YO*E
peritonealgia	PERT/NAOE/AL/JA		P*ERN/YOE
peritonealize	PERT/NAOEL/AOIZ		(not PERN/YOE; person owe)
peritonei	PERT/NAOE/YAOI	perniosis	PERN/YOE/SIS
peritoneocentesis	PERT/NAOE/SEN/TAOE/SIS	pero-	PER
peritoneoclysis	PERT/NAOE/OK/LI/SIS		PER/RO
	PERT/NAOE/KLAOI/SIS		PAOER
peritoneography	PERT/NAOE/OG/FI		PAOE/RO
peritoneomuscular	PERT/NAOE/MUS/KLAR	perobrachius	PAOER/BRAIK/YUS
peritoneopathy	PERT/NAOE/OP/TH*I	perocephalus	PAOER/SEF/LUS
peritoneopericardial	PERT/NAOE/P*ER/KARD/YAL	perochirus	PAOER/KAOI/RUS
peritoneopexy	PERT/NAOE/PEK/SI	perocormus	PAOER/KOR/MUS
peritoneoplasty	PERT/NAOE/PLAS/TI	perodactylia	PAOER/DAK/TIL/YA
peritoneoscope	PERT/NAOE/SKOEP	perodactylus	PAOER/DAKT/LUS
peritoneoscopy	PERT/NAOE/OS/KPI	perodactyly	PAOER/DAKT/LI
peritoneotome	PERT/NAOE/TOEM	peromelia	PAOER/MAOEL/YA
peritoneotomy	PERT/NAOE/OT/M*I	peromelus	PAOER/MAOEL/YA
	PERT/NAOE/YOT/M*I		PAOE/ROM/LUS
peritoneovenous	PERT/NAOE/VAOEN/OUS	peromely	PE/ROM/LI

peronarthrosis	PER/NAR/THROE/SIS	persulfuric	PER/SUL/FAOUR/IK
perone	PE/ROE/NAOE	per tertiam	PER/TER/SHAM
	PER/ROE/NAOE		PER/TERB/YAM
peronea	PER/NAOE/YA	Perthes	PER/TAOEZ
peroneae	PER/NAOE/YAE		PER/THAOEZ
	PE/ROEN/YAE	Pertik	PER/TIK
peroneal	PER/NAOEL	per tubam	PER/TAOU/BAM
	(not P*ER/NAOEL; see perineal)	pertubation	PER/TAOU/BAIGS
peroneotibial	PER/NAOE/TIB/YAL	pertussis	PER/TUS/SIS
peroneus	PER/NAOE/YUS	pertussoid	PER/TUS/OID
peronia	PE/ROEN/YA		PER/TUS/SOID
	PAOE/ROEN/YA	Peruvian	PRAOUV/YAN
peropus	PAOER/PUS		PE/RAOUV/YAN
peroral	PER/OR/RAL	peruvianum	PRAOUV/YAI/NUM
	PER/O*RL		PRAOUV/YAIN/UM
	(not PER/ORL; see per oral)		PE/RAOUV/YAI/NUM
per os	PER/OS		PE/RAOUV/YAIN/UM
perosmic	PER/OZ/MIK	per vaginam	PER/VA/JAOI/NAM
perosomus	PAOER/SOE/MUS		PER/VAJ/NAM
perosplanchnia	PAOER/SPLANG/NA	pervaporation	PER/VAP/RAIGS
	PAOER/SPLANG/NAOE/YA	perversion	PER/VERGS
perosseous	PER/OS/YOUS	pervert	PER/VERT
perox-	PER/OX	per vias naturales	PER/VAOI/YAS/NAFP/RAI/LAOEZ
	PROX		PER/VAOIS/NAFP/RAI/LAOEZ
	PE/ROX	pervigilium	PEFRB/JIL/YUM
peroxidase	PER/OX/DAIS		PER/VI/JIL/YUM
	PROX/DAIS	pervious	PEFRB/YOUS
peroxide	PER/OK/SAOID	pes	PES
	PROK/SAOID	pessary	PES/RI
peroxisome	PER/OX/SOEM		PESZ/RI
	PROX/SOEM	pessimism	PES/MIFM
peroxyacetic	PER/OX/AI/SAOET/IK		PESZ/MIFM
	PROX/AI/SAOET/IK	pessimistic	PES/M*IS/IK
peroxyacetyl	PER/OX/AI/SAOE/TIL		PESZ/M*IS/IK
	PROX/AI/SAOE/TIL	pessimum	PES/MUM
peroxy acid	PER/OX/AS/ID		PESZ/MUM
	PER/OK/SI/AS/ID	pest	P*ES
peroxydol	PE/ROX/DOL	pesticemia	P*ES/SAOEM/YA
peroxyformic	PER/OX/FORM/IK	pesticide	P*ES/SAO*ID
peroxyl	PER/OK/SIL	pestiferous	PES/TIF/ROUS
perpendicular	PERP/DIK/LAR	pestilence	P*ES/LENS
	PER/PEN/DIK/LAR	pestilential	P*ES/LEN/-RBL
perpendicularis	PERP/DIK/LAI/RIS	pestis	PES/TIS
	PER/PEN/DIK/LAI/RIS	pestle	PES/-L
perphenazine	PER/FEN/ZAOEN	pestology	PES/TOLG
per primam	PER/PRAOI/MAM	-petal	(v)P/TAL
per primam intentionem	PER/PRAOI/MAM/SPWEN/SHOE/	petalobacteria	PET/LO/BAK/TAOER/YA
	NEM	petechia	PE/TAOEK/YA
	PER/PRAOI/MAM/SPWEN/		PE/TEK/YA
	SHOEN/EM	petechiae	PE/TAOEK/YAE
per rectum	PER/REK/TUM		PE/TEK/YAE
Perroncito	PER/RON/SAOE/TOE	petechial	PE/TAOEK/YAL
	PERN/SAOE/TOE		PE/TEK/YAL
Persa-Gel	PERS/JEL	Peterman	PAOET/ER/MAN
	PER/SA/JEL	Peters	PAI/TERS
persalt	PER/SAULT		PAI/TERZ
	PER/SALT		PAOET/ERS
per saltum	PER/SAUL/TUM		PAOET/ERZ
	PER/SAULT/UM	Petersen	PAIT/ER/SEN
	PER/SAL/TUM		PAOET/ER/SEN
	PER/SALT/UM	petiolate	PET/YO/LAIT
Persantine	PER/SAN/TAOEN	petiolated	PET/YO/LAIT/-D
	PER/SAN/TIN	petiole	PET/YOEL
per secundam	PER/SE/KUN/DAM	petioled	PET/YOEL/-D
per secundam	PER/SE/KUN/DAM/	petiolus	PE/TAOI/LUS
intentionem	SPWEN/SHOE/NEM		PET/YOE/LUS
	PER/SE/KUN/DAM/SPWEN/	Petit	PE/TAOE
	SHOEN/EM	petit mal	PET/TAOE/MAL
persecutory	PERS/KAOUT/RI		PE/TAOE/MAL
perseveration	PER/SEV/RAIGS	petr(o)-	PET/R(O)
persic	PERS/IK	Petren	PAI/TREN
persica	PERS/KA	Petri	PAI/TRAOE
persicus	PERS/KUS	petrifaction	PET/RI/FA*BGS
persistence	PER/SIS/TENS	petrificans	PE/TRIF/KANZ
persister	PER/S*IS/ER		PET/RIF/KANZ
	PER/SIS/TER	petrissage	PAI/TRI/SAJ
persona	PER/SOE/NA		PAI/TRIS/SAJ
personalistic	PERNL/*IS/IK		PET/RI/SAJ
	PERS/NAL/*IS/IK		PET/RIS/SAJ
personality	PERNL/TI	petroccipital	PET/ROK/SIP/TAL
	PERS/NAL/TI	Petroff	PET/ROF
perspiratio	PERS/PRAI/SHOE	petrolate	PET/RO/LAIT
	PERS/PRAIRB/YOE	petrolatum	PET/RO/LAI/TUM
perspiration	PERS/PRAIGS		PET/RO/LAIT/UM
perstans	PER/STANZ	petroleum	PE/TROEL/YUM
perstillation	PER/STIL/LAIGS	petrolization	PET/ROL/ZAIGS
persuasion	PER/SWAIGS	petromastoid	PET/RO/MAS/TOID
persulfate	PER/SUL/FAIT	petro-occipital	PET/RO/OK/SIP/TAL
persulfide	PER/SUL/FAOID	petropharyngeus	PET/RO/FRIN/JUS

petrosa	PE/TROE/SA	phacozymase	FAK/ZAOI/MAIS
petrosae	PE/TROE/SAE	Phaenicia	FEN/SHAOE/YA
petrosal	PE/TROE/SAL		FEN/AOIS/YA
pertrosalpingostaphylinus	PET/RO/SAL/PING/STAF/LAOI/	phaeohyphomycosis	FAOE/HAOIF/MAOI/KOE/SIS
	NUS	phag(o)-	FAG
petrosectomy	PET/RO/SEKT/M*I		FA/G(O)
petrositis	PET/RO/SAOITS		FAJ
petrosomastoid	PE/TROES/MAS/TOID		FA/J(O)
	PET/ROES/MAS/TOID	phage	FAIJ
petrosphenoid	PET/RO/SFAOE/NOID	-phage	FAIJ
petrosphere	PET/RO/SFAOER	phagedena	FAJ/DAOE/NA
petrosquamosal	PET/RO/SKWA/MOE/SAL	phagedenic	FAJ/DAOEN/IK
	PET/RO/SKWAI/MOE/SAL		FAJ/DEN/IK
petrosquamous	PET/RO/SKWAIM/OUS	phagelysis	FAIJ/LAOI/SIS
petrostaphylinus	PET/RO/STAF/LAOI/NUS	-phagia	FAI/JA
petrosus	PE/TROE/SUS		FAIJ/YA
petrous	PET/ROUS	phagocytable	FAG/SAO*IT/-BL
	PAOE/TROUS	phagocyte	FAG/SAO*IT
petrousitis	PET/RAOU/SAOITS	phagocytic	FAG/SIT/IK
-pexia	PEX/YA	phagocytin	FAG/SAOI/TIN
pexic	PEX/IK	phagocytize	FAG/SAOI/TAOIZ
pexin	PEK/SIN		FAG/SAO*IT/AOIZ
pexinogen	PEK/SIN/JEN	phagocytoblast	FAG/SAOIT/BLA*S
pexis	PEK/SIS	phagocytolysis	FAG/SAOI/TOL/SIS
-pexy	PEK/SI	phagocytolytic	FAG/SAOIT/LIT/IK
Peyer	PAOI/ER	phagocytose	FAG/SAOI/TOES
	PAOI/YER	phagocytosis	FAG/SAOI/TOE/SIS
peyote	PAI/YOE/TAOE	phagocytotic	FAG/SAOI/TOT/IK
	PAI/YOE/TAI	phagodynamometer	FAG/DAOIN/MOM/TER
peyotl	PAI/YOET/-L	phagological	FAG/LOJ/KAL
Peyronie	PAI/RO/NAOE	phagology	FA/GOLG
Peyrot	PAI/ROE	phagolysis	FA/GOL/SIS
Pezzer	PAI/ZER	phagolysosome	FAG/LAOIS/SOEM
	PEZ/ER	phagolytic	FAG/LIT/IK
Pfannenstiel	FAN/EN/STAOEL	phagomania	FAG/MAIN/YA
Pfeiffer	FAOIFR	phagophobia	FAG/FOEB/YA
Pfeifferella	FAOIF/REL/LA	phagosome	FAG/SOEM
Pfizerpen	FAOI/ZER/PEN	phagotrophy	FA/GOT/RO/FI
	FIT/SER/PEN	phagotype	FAG/TAOIP
Pfizerpen-AS	FAOI/ZER/PEN/A-RBGS/S*RBGS	-phagy	(v)F/JI
	FIT/SER/PEN/A-RBGS/S*RBGS	phako-	see phaco-
Pfluger	FLAOUG/ER	-phakia	FAIK/YA
pfropfhebephrenia	FROF/HAOEB/FRAOEN/YA	phakitis	FA/KAOITS
	FROP/-F/HAOEB/FRAOEN/YA		FAI/KAOITS
pfropfschizophrenia	FROF/SKIZ/FRAOEN/YA	phakoma	see phacoma
	FROP/-F/SKIZ/FRAOEN/YA	phakomatosis	see phacomatosis
pH	PAIFP	phalacrosis	FAL/KROE/SIS
	P*/H*RBGS	phalang(o)-	FLANG
phacitis	FA/SAOITS		FLAN/G(O)
phaco-	FAK		FA/LANG
	FA/KO		FA/LAN/G(O)
phaco-allergica	FAK/AI/LERJ/KA		FLAN/J(O)
phacoanaphylactica	FAK/AN/FLAKT/KA		FAL/AN/J(O)
phacoanaphylaxis	FAK/AN/FLAK/SIS	phalangeal	FLAN/JAL
phacocele	FAK/SAO*EL	phalangearum	FLAN/JAI/RUM
phacocyst	FAK/S*IS		FLAN/JAIR/UM
phacocystectomy	FAK/SIS/TEKT/M*I	phalangectomy	FAL/AN/JEKT/M*I
phacocystitis	FAK/SIS/TAOITS		FLAN/JEKT/M*I
phacodonesis	FAK/DOE/NAOE/SIS	phalanges	FLAN/JAOEZ
	FAK/DON/E/SIS	phalangette	FAL/AN/JET
phacoemulsification	FAK/E/MULS/FI/KAIGS		FLAN/JET
phacoerysis	FAK/ER/SIS	-phalangia	FLAN/JA
	FAK/ER/RAOE/SIS	phalangis	FLAN/JIS
	FAK/ER/E/SIS	-phalangism	FLAN/JIFM
phacofragmentation	FAK/FRAG/MEN/TAIGS		FAL/AN/JIFM
phacogenetica	FAK/JE/NET/KA	phalangitis	FAL/AN/JAOITS
phacoglaucoma	FAK/GLAU/KOE/MA		FLAN/JAOITS
phacohymenitis	FAK/HAOIM/NAOITS	phalangization	FLAN/JI/ZAIGS
phacoid	FAK/OID	phalangophalangeal	FLANG/FLAN/JAL
phacoiditis	FAK/OI/DAOITS	phalangosis	FAL/AN/GOE/SIS
phacoidoscope	FA/KOID/SKOEP		FLAN/GOE/SIS
	FA/KOI/DO/SKOEP	phalanx	FAI/LANGS
phacolysin	FA/KOL/SIN		FA/LANGS
phacolysis	FA/KOL/SIS	phall(o)-	FAL
phacolytic	FAK/LIT/IK		FAL/L(O)
phacoma	FA/KOE/MA	phallalgia	FAL/AL/JA
phacomalacia	FAK/MA/LAI/SHA	phallanastrophe	FAL/AN/AS/TRO/FAOE
phacomatosis	FAK/MA/TOE/SIS		FAL/AI/NAS/TRO/FAOE
phacometachoresis	FAK/MET/KOE/RAOE/SIS	phallaneurysm	FAL/AN/RIFM
phacometecesis	FAK/MET/SAOE/SIS	phallectomy	FAL/EKT/M*I
phacometer	FA/KOM/TER	phalli	FAL/LAOI
phacopalingenesis	FAK/PAL/IN/JEN/SIS	phallic	FAL/IK
phacoplanesis	FAK/PLA/NAOE/SIS	phallicism	FAL/SIFM
phacosclerosis	FAK/SKLE/ROE/SIS	phalliform	FAL/FORM
phacoscope	FAK/SKOEP	phallism	FAL/IFM
phacoscopy	FA/KOS/KPI	phallitis	FAL/LAOITS
phacoscotasmus	FAK/SKOE/TAZ/MUS		FAL/AOITS
phacotherapy	FAK/THER/PI	phallocampsis	FAL/KAFRP/SIS
phacotoxic	FAK/TOX/IK		FAL/KAM/SIS

phallocrypsis	FAL/KRIP/SIS		FA/RIN/G(O)
phallodynia	FAL/DIN/YA		FRIN/J(O)
phalloid	FAL/OID		FARN/J(O)
phalloidin	FA/LOI/DIN	pharyngalgia	FARN/GAL/JA
	FAL/LOI/DIN	pharyngea	FRIN/JA
phalloncus	FAL/ON/KUS	pharyngeae	FRIN/JAE
	FAL/LON/KUS	pharyngeal	FRIN/JAL
phalloplasty	FAL/PLAS/TI	pharyngectasia	FARN/JEK/TAIZ/YA
phallorrhagia	FAL/RAI/JA	pharyngectomy	FARN/JEKT/M*I
phallorrhea	FAL/RAOE/YA	pharyngemphraxis	FARN/JEM/FRAK/SIS
phallotomy	FAL/LOT/M*I	pharynges	FRIN/JAOEZ
	FAL/OT/M*I	pharyngeum	FRIN/JUM
phallus	FAL/LUS	pharyngeus	FRIN/JUS
phanero-	FAN/RO	pharyngis	FRIN/JIS
phanerogam	FAN/RO/GAM	pharyngism	FARN/JIFM
phanerogenetic	FAN/RO/JE/NET/IK	pharyngismus	FARN/JIZ/MUS
phanerogenic	FAN/RO/JEN/IK	pharyngitic	FARN/JIT/IK
phaneromania	FAN/RO/MAIN/YA	pharyngitid	FRIN/JI/TID
phaneroplasm	FAN/RO/PLAFM	pharyngitis	FARN/JAOITS
phaneroscope	FAN/RO/SKOEP	pharyngobasilar	FRING/BAS/LAR
phanerosis	FAN/ROE/SIS	pharyngobasilaris	FRING/BAS/LAI/RIS
phanerosterol	FAN/RO*S/ROL	pharyngocele	FRING/SAO*EL
phanerozoite	FAN/RO/ZOE/AOIT	pharyngoceratosis	FRING/SER/TOE/SIS
phanquone	FAN/KWOEN	pharyngoconjunctival	FRING/KON/JUNGT/VAL
phantasia	FAN/TAIZ/YA		FRING/KON/JUNG/VAL
phantasm	FAN/TAFM		FRING/KON/JUNG/TAOIVL
phantasmagoria	FAN/TAZ/MA/GOER/YA	pharyngoconjunctivitis	FRING/KON/JUNGT/VAOITS
	FAN/TAZ/MA/GOR/YA		FRING/KON/JUNG/VAOITS
phantasmatology	FAN/TAZ/MA/TOLG	pharyngodynia	FRING/DIN/YA
phantasmatomoria	FAN/TAZ/MA/TO/MOER/YA	pharyngoepiglottic	FRING/EP/GLOT/IK
	FAN/TAZ/MA/TO/MOR/YA	pharyngoepiglottidean	FRING/EP/GLO/TID/YAN
phantasmology	FAN/TAZ/MOLG		FRING/EP/GLOT/TID/YAN
phantasmoscopia	FAN/TAZ/MA/SKOEP/YA	pharyngoesophageal	FRING/E/SOF/JAOEL
phantasmoscopy	FAN/TAZ/MOS/KPI	pharyngoesophagoplasty	FRING/E/SOF/GO/PLAS/TI
phantasy	FA*NT/SI	pharyngoglossal	FRING/GLOS/SAL
	(*not* FANT/SI; see fantasy)	pharyngoglossus	FRING/GLOS/SUS
phantom	FAN/TOM	pharyngokeratosis	FRING/KER/TOE/SIS
phantomize	FANT/MAOIZ	pharyngolaryngeal	FRING/LARN/JAL
	FAN/TOM/AOIZ	pharyngolaryngitis	FRING/LARN/JAOITS
pharcidous	FARS/DOUS	pharyngolith	FRING/L*IT
pharmacal	FARM/KAL	pharyngology	FARN/GOLG
pharmaceutic	FARM/SAOUT/IK	pharyngolysis	FARN/GOL/SIS
pharmaceutical	FARM/SAOUT/KAL	pharyngomaxillary	FRING/MAX/LAIR
pharmaceutics	FARM/SAOUT/IK/-S	pharyngomycosis	FRING/MAOI/KOE/SIS
pharmaceutist	FARM/SAOU/T*IS	pharyngonasal	FRING/NAI/ZAL
pharmacist	FARM/S*IS	pharyngo-oral	FRING/ORL
pharmaco-	FARM/KO	pharyngopalatine	FRING/PAL/TAOIN
pharmacochemistry	FARM/KO/KEM/STRI	pharngopalatinus	FRING/PAL/TAOI/NUS
pharmacodiagnosis	FARM/KO/DAOIG/NOE/SIS	pharyngoparalysis	FRING/PRAL/SIS
pharmacodynamic	FARM/KO/DAOI/NAM/IK	pharyngopathia	FRING/PA*T/YA
pharmacodynamics	FARM/KO/DAOI/NAM/IK/-S	pharyngopathy	FARN/GOP/TH*I
pharmacoendocrinology	FARM/KO/*END/KRI/NOLG	pharyngoperistole	FRING/PE/R*IS/LAOE
	FARM/KO/*END/KRIN/OLG	pharyngoplasty	FRING/PLAS/TI
pharmacogenetics	FARM/KO/JE/NET/IK/-S	pharyngoplegia	FRING/PLAOE/JA
pharmacognosist	FARM/KOG/NO/S*IS	pharyngorhinitis	FRING/RAOI/NAOITS
pharmacognostics	FARM/KOG/NO*S/IK/-S	pharyngorhinoscopy	FRING/RAOI/NOS/KPI
pharmacognosy	FARM/KOG/NO/SI	pharyngorrhagia	FRING/RAI/JA
pharmacography	FARM/KOG/FI	pharyngorrhea	FRING/RAOE/YA
pharmacokinetic	FARM/KO/KI/NET/IK	pharyngosalpingitis	FRING/SAL/PIN/JAOITS
pharmacokinetics	FARM/KO/KI/NET/IK/-S	pharyngoscleroma	FRING/SKLE/ROE/MA
pharmacologic	FARM/KO/LOJ/IK	pharyngoscope	FRING/SKOEP
pharmacological	FARM/KO/LOJ/KAL	pharyngoscopy	FARN/GOS/KPI
pharmacologist	FARM/KO*LGS	pharyngospasm	FRING/SPAFM
pharmacology	FARM/KOLG	pharyngostaphylinus	FRING/STAF/LAOI/NUS
pharmacomania	FARM/KO/MAIN/YA	pharyngostenosis	FRING/STE/NOE/SIS
pharmacometrics	FARM/KO/MET/RIK/-S	pharyngostoma	FARN/GO*S/MA
pharmacon	FARM/KON	pharyngostomy	FARN/GO*S/M*I
pharmaco-oryctology	FARM/KO/ORK/TOLG	pharyngotherapy	FRING/THER/PI
	FARM/KO/OR/IK/TOLG	pharyngotome	FRING/TOEM
pharmacopedia	FARM/KO/PAOED/YA	pharyngotomy	FARN/GOT/M*I
pharmacopedics	FARM/KO/PAOED/IK/-S	pharyngotonsillitis	FRING/TONS/LAOITS
pharmacopeia	FARM/KO/PAOE/YA	pharngotympanic	FRING/TIM/PAN/IK
pharmacopeial	FARM/KO/PAOEL	pharyngotyphoid	FRING/TAOI/FOID
	FARM/KO/PAOE/YAL	pharyngoxerosis	FRING/ZAOE/ROE/SIS
pharmacophilia	FARM/KO/FIL/YA		FRING/ZE/ROE/SIS
pharmacophobia	FARM/KO/FOEB/YA	pharynx	FARNGS
pharmacophore	FARM/KO/FOER		FAR/INGS
pharmacopsychosis	FARM/KO/SAOI/KOE/SIS	phase	FAEZ
pharmacocardiography	FARM/KO/KARD/YOG/FI		(*not* FAIZ; see faze)
pharmacoroentgenography	FARM/KO/RENT/GEN/OG/FI	-phasia	FAIZ/YA
pharmacotherapeutics	FARM/KO/THER/PAOUT/IK/-S	-phasic	FAIZ/IK
pharmacotherapy	FARM/KO/THER/PI	phasin	FAI/SIN
PharmaCreme	FARM/KRAOEM	phasein	FAI/SAOEN
pharmacy	FARM/SI		FAIS/YIN
Pharm.D.	FARM/D-FPLT	phasmid	FAZ/MID
	FARM/D-RBGS	Phasmidia	FAZ/MID/YA
pharyng(o)-	FRING	phasmophobia	FAZ/MO/FOEB/YA
	FRIN/G(O)	phatnoma	FAT/NOE/MA
	FARN/G(O)	phatnorrhagia	FAT/NO/RAI/JA

Phazyme	FAI/ZAOIM	phenodin	FAOEN/DIN
Phazyme-95	FAI/ZAOIM/9/5	phenogenetics	FAOEN/JE/NET/IK/-S
Phazyme-125	FAI/ZAOIM/125	phenol	FAOE/NOL
Ph.D.	P-RBGS/H*D		FAOEN/OL
	PAIFP/D-FPLT	phenolase	FAOEN/LAIS
	PAIFP/D-RBGS	phenolate	FAOEN/LAIT
phemfilcon	FEM/FIL/KON	phenolated	FAOEN/LAIT/-D
-phemia	FAOEM/YA	phenolemia	FAOE/NOL/AOEM/YA
phemitone	FEM/TOEN		FAOEN/LAOEM/YA
phen-	FEN	phenolic	FAOE/NOL/IK
	FE/N-	phenolization	FAOE/NOL/ZAIGS
	FAOEN	phenologist	FAOE/NO*LGS
	FAOE/N-		FE/NO*LGS
phenacaine	FEN/KAIN	phenology	FAOE/NOLG
phenacemide	FE/NAS/MAOID		FE/NOLG
phenacetamide	FEN/SET/MAOID	phenolphthalein	FAOE/NO/THAL/AOEN
phenacetin	FE/NAS/TIN		FAOE/NOL/THAL/YIN
phenacetolin	FEN/SET/LIN	phenolsulfonate	FAOE/NOL/SUL/FO/NAIT
phenaceturic	FE/NAS/TAOUR/IK	phenolsulfonphthalein	FAOE/NOL/SUL/FOEN/THAL/
	FEN/AS/TAOUR/IK		AOEN
phenacetylurea	FEN/AS/TIL/YAOU/RAOE/YA		FAOE/NOL/SUL/FOEN/THAL/YIN
Phena-Chlor	FEN/KLOR	phenoltetrachlorophthalein	FAOE/NOL/TET/RA/KLOR/THAL/
phenacridane	FE/NAS/RI/DAIN		YIN
	FE/NAK/RI/DAIN	phenoltetraiodophthalein	FAOE/NOL/TET/RA/AOI/DO/
phenacyclamine	FEN/SAOI/KLA/MAOEN		THAL/YIN
phenadoxone	FEN/DOK/SOEN	phenoluria	FAOEN/LAOUR/YA
phenaglycodol	FEN/GLAOIK/DOL		FAOE/NOL/YAOUR/YA
-phenamine	FEN/MAOEN	phenom	FAOE/NOM
phenanthrene	FE/NAN/THRAOEN	phenomena	FE/NOM/NA
phenanthrolene	FE/NAN/THRO/LAOEN	phenomenology	FE/NOM/NOLG
Phenaphen	FEN/FEN	phenomenon	FE/NOM/NON
Phenaphen-650	FEN/FEN/6/50	phenon	FAOE/NON
phenarsenamine	FEN/AR/SEN/AM/AOEN	phenoperidine	FAOEN/PER/DAOEN
	FEN/AR/SEN/MAOEN		FAOEN/P*ER/DAOEN
phenarsone	FEN/AR/SOEN	phenopropazine	FAOEN/PROEP/ZAOEN
phenate	FAOE/NAIT	phenothiazine	FAOEN/THAOI/ZAOEN
phenazacillin	FEN/AZ/SLIN	phenotype	FAOEN/TAOIP
	FEN/AZ/SIL/LIN	phenotypic	FAOEN/TIP/IK
Phenazine	FEN/ZAOEN	phenoxazine	FE/NOX/ZAOEN
phenazocine	FE/NAZ/SAOEN	phenoxazone	FE/NOX/ZOEN
	FEN/A*Z/SAOEN	phenoxide	FEN/OK/SAOID
	FEN/AIZ/SAOEN		FEN/OX/AOID
	FEN/AZ/SAOEN	phenoxybenzamine	FE/NOX/BENZ/MAOEN
phenazoline	FEN/A*Z/LAOEN	phenoxyethane	FE/NOX/*ET/AIN
	FEN/AZ/LAOEN	phenoxyethanol	FE/NOX/*ET/NOL
phenazone	FEN/ZOEN	phenoxyethylpenicillin	FE/NOX/*ET/IL/PEN/SLIN
phenazopyridine	FEN/A*Z/PIR/DAOEN		FE/NOX/*ET/IL/PEN/SIL/LIN
	FEN/AIZ/PIR/DAOEN	phenoxyethylpenicillin	FE/NOX/M*ET/IL/PEN/SLIN
	FEN/AZ/PIR/DAOEN		FE/NOX/M*ET/IL/PEN/SIL/LIN
phenbutazone	FEN/BAOUT/ZOEN	phenoxypropylpenicillin	FE/NOX/PRO/PIL/PEN/SLIN
phencyclidine	FEN/SAOI/KLI/DAOEN		FE/NOX/PRO/PIL/PEN/SIL/LIN
	FEN/SAOIK/LI/DAOEN	phenozygous	FAOEN/ZAOIG/OUS
phendimetrazine	FEN/DI/MET/RA/ZAOEN		FE/NOZ/GOUS
phene	FAOEN	phenpentermine	FEN/PEN/TER/MAOEN
phenelzine	FEN/EL/ZAOEN	phenbrobamate	FEN/PROEB/MAIT
Phenergan	FEN/ER/GAN	phenprocoumon	FEN/PRO/KAOU/MON
Phenergan-D	FEN/ER/GAN/D-RBGS	phenpromethamine	FEN/PRO/M*ET/MAOEN
Phenergan VC	FEN/ER/GAN/V-RBGS/KR*RBGS	phenpropionate	FEN/PROEP/YO/NAIT
phenetamine	FE/NET/MAOEN	phensuximide	FEN/SUX/MAOID
phenetharbital	FEN/THARB/TAL	phentermine	FEN/TER/MAOEN
phenethicillin	FE/N*ET/SLIN	phentolamine	FEN/TOL/MAOEN
	FE/N*ET/SIL/LIN	Phenurone	FEN/YAOU/ROEN
phenethyl	FE/N*ET/IL		FEN/YU/ROEN
	FEN/*ET/IL	phenyl	FENL
phenetsal	FE/NET/SAL		FEN/IL
pheneturide	FE/NET/RAOID		FAOE/NIL
	FE/NET/YAOU/RAOID	phenyl-	FENL
	FE/NET/YU/RAOID		FEN/IL
phenformin	FEN/FOR/MIN	phenylacetic	FENL/AI/SAOET/IK
phenglutarimide	FEN/GLAOU/TAR/MAOID	phenylaceturic	FENL/AS/TAOUR/IK
phengophobia	FENG/FOEB/YA	phenylacetylurea	FENL/AS/TIL/YAOU/RAOE/YA
	FEN/GO/FOEB/YA	phenylacrylic	FENL/AI/KRIL/IK
phenic	FAOEN/IK	phenylalaninase	FENL/AL/NIN/AIS
	FEN/IK	phenylalanine	FENL/AL/NAOEN
phenicarbazide	FEN/KARB/ZAOID	phenylamine	FE/NIL/MAOEN
phenindamine	FE/NIND/MAOEN	phenylbenzene	FENL/BEN/ZAOEN
	FE/NIN/DA/MAOEN	phenylbutazone	FENL/BAOUT/ZOEN
phenindione	FEN/IN/DI/OEN	phenylcarbinol	FENL/KARB/NOL
pheniramine	FE/NIR/MAOEN	phenylcinchoninate	FENL/SIN/KOEN/NAIT
	FEN/IR/MAOEN		FENL/SIN/KON/NAIT
phenmethylol	FEN/M*ET/LOL	phenylcinchoninic	FENL/SIN/KO/NIN/IK
phenmetrazine	FEN/MET/RA/ZAOEN	phenylene	FEN/LAOEN
pheno-	FAOEN		FENL/AOEN
	FAOE/NO	phenylephrine	FENL/EF/RIN
phenobarbital	FAOEN/BARB/TAL		FEN/LEF/RIN
phenobutiodil	FAOEN/BAOU/TAOI/DIL	phenylethyl	FENL/*ET/IL
	FEN/BAOU/TAOI/DIL	phenylethylbarbituric	FENL/*ET/IL/BARB/TAOUR/IK
phenocopy	FAOEN/KOP/PI	phenylethylmalonylurea	FENL/*ET/IL/MAL/NIL/YAOU/
phenodeviant	FAOEN/DAOEV/YANT		RAOE/YA

phenylglycolic	FENL/GLAOI/KOL/IK	Phillips' LaxCaps	(*not* FIL/IPS; see Philips) FIL/LIPS/AOE/LAX/KAP/-S
phenylhydrazine	FENL/HAOI/DRA/ZAOEN	Phillips' Milk of	FIL/LIPS/AOE/MIL/-K/OF/
phenylic	FE/NIL/IK	Magnesia	MAG/NAOEZ/YA
	FEN/IL/IK	philomimesia	FIL/MI/MAOES/YA
phenylindanedione	FENL/IN/DAIN/DI/OEN		FIL/MAOI/MAOES/YA
phenylisothiocyanate	FENL/AOIS/THAOI/SAOI/NAIT	Philopia casei	FIL/OEP/YA/KAIS/YAOI
phenylketone	FENL/KAOE/TOEN	philoprogenitive	FIL/PRO/JEN/TIV
phenylketonuria	FENL/KAOET/NAOUR/YA	philothion	FAOIL/THAOI/YON
phenyllactic	FENL/LAKT/IK		FIL/THAOI/YON
	FEN/LAKT/IK	philter	F*IL/TER
phenylmercuric	FENL/MER/KAOUR/IK		(*not* FIL/TER; see filter)
phenylmethanol	FENL/M*ET/NOL	philtra	F*IL/TRA
phenylpiperone	FENL/PIP/ROEN	philtrum	F*IL/TRUM
phenylpropanolamine	FENL/PROEP/NOL/MAOEN		(*not* FIL/TRUM; see filtrum)
phenylpropionic	FENL/PROEP/YON/IK	phimoses	FAOI/MOE/SAOEZ
phenylpropyl	FENL/PRO/PIL	phimosiectomy	FAOI/MOES/YEKT/M*I
phenylpropylmethylamine	FENL/PRO/PIL/M*ET/IL/AM/	phimosis	FAOI/MOE/SIS
	AOEN	phimotic	FAOI/MOT/IK
	FENL/PRO/PIL/M*ET/IL/AM/	pHisoDerm	FAOIS/DERM
	MAOEN	pHisoHex	FAOIS/HEX
	FENL/PRO/PIL/M*ET/IL/AM/MIN	phleb(o)-	FLEB
phenylpyruvic	FENL/PAOI/RAOUVK		FLE/B(O)
phenylpyruvicaciduria	FENL/PAOI/RAOUVK/AS/DAOUR/	phlebalgia	FLE/BAL/JA
	YA	phlebanesthesia	FLEB/ANS/THAOEZ/YA
phenylsalicylic	FENL/SAL/SIL/IK	phlebangioma	FLEB/AN/JOE/MA
phenylthiocarbamide	FENL/THAOI/KARB/MAOID	phlebarteriectasia	FLEB/AR/TAOER/YEK/TAIZ/YA
	FENL/THAOI/KAR/BAM/ID	phlebasthenia	FLEB/AS/THAOEN/YA
phenylthiocarbamoil	FENL/THAOI/KAR/BAM/OIL	phlebectasia	FLEB/EK/TAIZ/YA
	FENL/THAOI/KARB/MOIL	phlebectasis	FLE/BEKT/SIS
phenylthiohydantoin	FENL/THAOI/HAOI/DANT/WIN	phlebectomy	FLE/BEKT/M*I
	FENL/THAOI/HAOI/DAN/TOIN	phlebectopia	FLEB/EK/TOEP/YA
phenylthiourea	FENL/THAOI/YAOU/RAOE/YA	phlebectopi	FLE/BEKT/PI
phenyltoloxamine	FENL/TOL/OX/MAOEN	phlebemphraxis	FLEB/EM/FRAK/SIS
	FENL/TO/LOX/MAOEN	phlebeurysm	FLEB/RIFM
phenyltrimethylammonium	FENL/TR*I/M*ET/IL/AI/MOEN/		FLEB/YAOU/RIFM
	YUM		FLEB/YU/RIFM
phenyramidol	FEN/RAM/DOL	phlebexairesis	FLEB/KPAOIR/SIS
phenytoin	FEN/TOIN		FLEB/EK/SAOIR/SIS
pheo-	FAOE		FLEB/EX/SAOIR/SIS
	FAOE/YO	phlebismus	FLE/BIZ/MUS
pheochrome	FAOE/KROEM	phlebitic	FLE/BIT/IK
pheochromoblast	FAOE/KROEM/BLA*S	phlebitis	FLE/BAOITS
pheochromoblastoma	FAOE/KROEM/BLAS/TOE/MA	phleboclysis	FLE/BOK/LI/SIS
pheochromocyte	FAOE/KROEM/SAO*IT	phlebodynamics	FLEB/DAOI/NAM/IK/-S
pheochromocytoma	FAOE/KROEM/SAOI/TOE/MA	phlebofibrosis	FLEB/FAOI/BROE/SIS
pheomelanin	FAOE/MEL/NIN	phlebogenous	FLE/BOJ/NOUS
pheomelanogenesis	FAOE/MEL/NO/JEN/SIS	phlebogram	FLEB/GRAM
pheomelanosome	FAOE/MEL/NO/SOEM	phlebograph	FLEB/GRAF
pheophorbide	FAOE/FOER/BAOID	phlebography	FLE/BOG/FI
	FAOE/FOR/BAOID	phleboid	FLEB/OID
pheophorbin	FAOE/FOER/BIN	phlebolite	FLEB/LAOIT
	FAOE/FOR/BIN	phlebolith	FLEB/L*IT
pheophytin	FAOE/FAOI/TIN	phlebolithiasis	FLEB/LI/THAOI/SIS
pheresis	FE/RAOE/SIS	phlebology	FLE/BOLG
	(*not* FRAOE/SIS)	phlebomanometer	FLEB/MA/NOM/TER
-pheresis	FE/RAOE/SIS		FLEB/MAN/OM/TER
	FER/SIS	phlebometritis	FLEB/MAOE/TRAOITS
	FRAOE/SIS		FLEB/ME/TRAOITS
pheromone	FER/MOEN	phlebomyomatosis	FLEB/MAOI/MA/TOE/SIS
phetharbital	F*ET/ARB/TAL		FLEB/MAO/YOEM/TOE/SIS
phial	FAOI/YAL	phlebopexy	FLEB/PEK/SI
	FAO*IL	phlebophlebostomy	FLEB/FLE/BO*S/M*I
	(*not* FAOIL; see file)	phlebophthalmotomy	FLEB/OF/THAL/MOT/M*I
phialide	FAOI/LAOID	phlebopiezometry	FLEB/PAOI/ZOM/TRI
phialoconidia	FAOI/LO/KO/NID/YA	phleboplasty	FLEB/PLAS/TI
phialoconidium	FAOI/LO/KO/NID/YUM	phleborrhagia	FLEB/RAI/JA
	FAOI/LO/KON/ID/YUM	phleborrhaphy	FLE/BOR/FI
Phialophora	FAOI/LOF/RA	phleborrhexis	FLEB/REK/SIS
phialophore	FAOI/LO/FOER	phlebosclerosis	FLEB/SKLE/ROE/SIS
phialospore	FAOI/LO/SPOER	phlebosis	FLE/BOE/SIS
-phil	FIL	phlebostasia	FLEB/OS/TAIZ/YA
Philadelphia	FIL/DEL/FA	phlebostasis	FLE/BO*S/SIS
	FIL/DEL/FAOE/YA	phlebostenosis	FLEB/STE/NOE/SIS
philagrypnia	FAOIL/GRIP/NA	phlebostrepsis	FLEB/STREP/SIS
	FAOIL/GRIP/NAOE/YA	phlebothrombosis	FLEB/THROM/BOE/SIS
-phile	FAOIL	phlebotome	FLEB/TOEM
-philia	FIL/YA	phlebotomine	FLE/BOT/MAOEN
-philiac	FIL/YAK	phlebotomist	FLE/BOT/M*IS
philiater	FIL/YAIT/ER	phlebotomize	FLE/BOT/MAOIZ
	FIL/YAI/TER	phlebotomus	FLE/BOT/MUS
	FI/LAOI/TER	Phlebotomus	K-P/FLE/BOT/MUS
-philic	FIL/IK	phlebotomy	FLE/BOT/M*I
philippensis	FIL/PEN/SIS	Phlebovirus	FLEB/VAOI/RUS
Philippine	FIL/PAOEN	phlegm	FLEM
Philippe	FAOE/LAOEP	phlegmasia	FLEG/MAIZ/YA
	FI/LAOEP	phlegmatic	FLEG/MAT/IK
Philips	FIL/IPS	phlegmon	FLEG/MON
	(*not* FIL/LIPS; see Phillips)	phlegmona	FLEG/MOE/NA
Phillips	FIL/LIPS		

phlegmonosa	FLEG/MO/NOE/SA	phonocardiograph	FOEN/KARD/YO/GRAF
phlegmonosis	FLEG/MO/NOE/SIS	phonocardiographic	FOEN/KARD/YO/GRAFK
phlegmonous	FLEG/MO/NOUS	phonocardiography	FOEN/KARD/YOG/FI
	FLEG/MON/OUS	phonocatheter	FOEN/KA*T/TER
phlegmy	FLEM/M*I	phonocatheterization	FOEN/KA*T/TER/ZAIGS
phloem	FLOEM	phonoelectrocardioscope	FOEN/LEK/TRO/KARD/YO/SKOEP
	FLOE/EM	phonogram	FOEN/GRAM
phlogistic	FLOE/J*IS/IK	phonologist	FOE/NO*LGS
phlogiston	FLOE/JIS/TON	phonology	FOE/NOLG
phlogo-	FLOEG	phonomania	FOEN/MAIN/YA
	FLOE/GO	phonometer	FOE/NOM/TER
phlogocyte	FLOEG/SAO*IT	phonomyoclonus	FOEN/MAOI/OK/LO/NUS
phlogocytosis	FLOEG/SAOI/TOE/SIS	phonomyogram	FOEN/MAOI/GRAM
phlogogen	FLOEG/JEN	phonomyography	FOEN/MAOI/OG/FI
phlogogenic	FLOEG/JEN/IK	phonopathy	FOE/NOP/TH*I
phlogogenous	FLOE/GOJ/NOUS	phonophobia	FOEN/FOEB/YA
phlogosin	FLOEG/SIN	phonophore	FOEN/FOER
phlogotherapy	FLOEG/THER/PI	phonophotography	FOEN/FOE/TOG/FI
phlogotic	FLOE/GOT/IK		FOEN/FRAF/FI
phloretic	FLOE/RET/IK	phonopsia	FOE/NOPS/YA
phlorhizin	FLOE/RAOI/ZIN	phonoreceptor	FOEN/RE/SEP/TOR
phlorhizinize	FLOE/RAOIZ/NAOIZ	phonorenogram	FOEN/RAOEN/GRAM
phloroglucin	FLOR/GLAOU/SIN	phonoscope	FOEN/SKOEP
phloroglucinol	FLOR/GLAOUS/NOL	phonoscopy	FOE/NOS/KPI
phloroglucol	FLOR/GLAOU/KOL	phonoselectoscope	FOEN/SLEKT/SKOEP
phloxine	FLOK/SAOEN		FOEN/SE/LEKT/SKOEP
	FLOK/SIN		FOEN/SLEK/TO/SKOEP
phlycten	FLIK/TEN	phonostethograph	FOEN/ST*ET/GRAF
phlyctena	FLIK/TAOE/NA	phorbide	FOR/BAOID
phlyctenae	FLIK/TAOE/NAE		FOER/BAOID
phlyctenar	FLIKT/NAR	phorbin	FOR/BIN
phlyctenoid	FLIKT/NOID		FOER/BIN
phlyctenosis	FLIKT/NOE/SIS	phorbol	FOR/BOL
phlyctenotherapy	FLIKT/NO/THER/PI		FOER/BOL
phlyctenous	FLIKT/NOUS	-phore	FOER
phlyctenul-	FLIK/TEN/L-	-phoresis	FRAOE/SIS
	FLIK/TEN/YAOU/L-		FOE/RAOE/SIS
	FLIK/TEN/YU/L-		FO/RAOE/SIS
phlyctenula	FLIK/TEN/LA	phoresy	FOER/SI
phlyctenulae	FLIK/TEN/LAE		FOR/SI
phlyctenular	FLIK/TEN/LAR	-phoria	FOER/YA
phlyctenule	FLIK/TEN/YAOUL	phoriascope	FOER/YA/SKOEP
phlyctenulosis	FLIK/TEN/LOE/SIS	-phoric	FOER/IK
phobanthropy	FOE/BAN/THRO/PI	Phormia regina	FORM/YA/RE/JAOI/NA
phobia	FOEB/YA	phoro-	FOE/RO
phobic	FOEB/IK		FO/RO
phobophobia	FOEB/FOEB/YA		FOER
phocomelia	FOEK/MAOEL/YA		FOER/RO (not in CAT)
phocomelic	FOEK/MEL/IK		FO/RO (not in CAT)
phocomelus	FOE/KOM/LUS	phoroblast	FOER/BLA*S
phocomely	FOE/KOM/LI	phorocyte	FOER/SAO*IT
pholcodine	FOL/KO/DAOEN	phorocytosis	FOER/SAOI/TOE/SIS
pholedrine	FOL/DRAOEN	phorologist	FOE/RO*LGS
Phoma	FOE/MA		FO/RO*LGS
phon	FO*EN	phorology	FOE/ROLG
	(not FOEN; see phone)		FO/ROLG
phon(o)-	FOEN	phorometer	FOE/ROM/TER
	FOE/N(O)		FO/ROM/TER
phonacoscope	FOE/NAK/SKOEP	phorometry	FOE/ROM/TRI
phonacoscopy	FOEN/KOS/KPI		FO/ROM/TRI
phonal	FOENL	phoro-optometer	FOER/OP/TOM/TER
phonarteriogram	FOEN/AR/TAOER/YO/GRAM	phoroplast	FOER/PLA*S
phonarteriographic	FOEN/AR/TAOER/YO/GRAFK	phoropter	FOE/ROPT/ER
phonarteriography	FOEN/AR/TAOER/YOG/FI		FO/ROPT/ER
phonasthenia	FOE/NAS/THAOEN/YA	phoroscope	FOER/SKOEP
	FOEN/AS/THAOEN/YA	phorotone	FOER/TOEN
phonation	FOE/NAIGS	phorozoon	FOER/ZAON
phonatory	FOEN/TOIR	PhosChol	FOS/KOL
phonautograph	FOEN/AUT/GRAF	phose	FOEZ
phoneme	FOE/NAOEM		FOES
phonemic	FOE/NAOEM/IK	Phos-Flur	FOS/FLUR
phonendoscope	FOE/NEND/SKOEP	phosgene	FOS/JAOEN
	FOEN/*END/SKOEP	phosgenic	FOS/JEN/IK
phonendoskiascope	FOE/NEND/SKAOI/SKOEP	phosis	FOE/SIS
	FOEN/*END/SKAOI/SKOEP	phosph(o)-	FOS/F(O)
phonetic	FOE/NET/IK	phosphagen	FOS/FA/JEN
	FO/NET/IK	phosphagenic	FOS/FA/JEN/IK
phonetics	FOE/NET/IK/-S	pHos-pHaid	FOS/FAID
	FO/NET/IK/-S	phosphamic	FOS/FAM/IK
-phonia	FOEN/YA	phosphamidase	FOS/FAM/DAIS
phoniatrician	FOEN/YA/TRIGS	phosphaminase	FOS/FAM/NAIS
phoniatrics	FOEN/YAT/RIK/-S	phosphastat	FOS/FA/STAT
phonic	FON/IK	phosphatase	FOS/FA/TAIS
	FOEN/IK	phosphate	FOS/FAIT
phonism	FOE/NIFM	phosphated	FOS/FAIT/-D
	FOEN/IFM	phosphatemia	FOS/FA/TAOEM/YA
phonoangiography	FOEN/AN/JOG/FI	phosphatic	FOS/FAT/IK
phonoauscultation	FOEN/AUS/KUL/TAIGS	phosphatidal	FOS/FA/TAOI/DAL
phonocardiogram	FOEN/KARD/YO/GRAM	phosphatidase	FOS/FA/TAOI/DAIS

phosphatidate	FOS/FA/TAOID/AIS
	FOS/FA/TAOI/DAIT
	FOS/FA/TAOID/AIT
phosphatide	FOS/FA/TAOID
phosphatidic	FOS/FA/TID/IK
phosphatidosis	FOS/FA/TAOI/DOE/SIS
	FOS/FA/TI/DOE/SIS
phosphatidolipase	FOS/FA/TAOID/LIP/AIS
	FAS/FA/TAOI/DO/LIP/AIS
phosphatidyl	FOS/FA/TAOI/DIL
	FOS/FAT/DIL
phosphatidylcholine	FOS/FA/TAOI/DIL/KOE/LAOEN
	FOS/FAT/DIL/KOE/LAOEN
phosphatidylethanolamine	FOS/FA/TAOI/DIL/*ET/NOL/
	MAOEN
	FOS/FAT/DIL/*ET/NOL/MAOEN
phosphatidylglycerol	FOS/FA/TAOI/DIL/GLIS/ROL
	FOS/FAT/DIL/GLIS/ROL
phosphatidylinositide	FOS/FA/TAOI/DIL/IN/OES/TAOID
	FOS/FAT/DIL/IN/OES/TAOID
phosphatidylinositol	FOS/FA/TAOI/DIL/IN/OES/TOL
	FOS/FAT/DIL/IN/OES/TOL
phosphatidylserine	FOS/FA/TAOI/DIL/SER/AOEN
	FOS/FA/TAOI/DIL/SAOER/RIN
	FOS/FAT/DIL/SAOER/RIN
	FOS/FAT/DIL/SER/AOEN
phosphaturia	FOS/FA/TAOUR/YA
phosphene	FOS/FAOEN
phosphide	FOS/FAOID
phosphine	FOS/FAO*EN
	FOS/FIN
	(not FOS/FAOEN; see phosphene)
phosphite	FOS/FAOIT
phosphoacylase	FOS/FO/AS/LAIS
phosphoamidase	FOS/FO/AM/DAIS
phosphoamide	FOS/FO/AM/AOID
phosphoarginine	FOS/FO/ARJ/NAOEN
	FOS/FO/ARG/NAOEN
phosphocholine	FOS/FO/KOE/LAOEN
phosphocozymase	FOS/FO/KO/ZAOI/MAIS
	FOS/FO/KO/ZAOIM/AIS
phosphocreatine	FOS/FO/KRAOE/TAOEN
	FOS/FO/KRAOE/TIN
phosphodiester	FOS/FO/DI/ES/TER
phosphodiesterase	FOS/FO/DI/ES/TRAIS
	FOS/FO/DI/*ES/RAIS
phosphodismutase	FOS/FO/DIS/MAOU/TAIS
phosphoenolpyruvic	FOS/FO/E/NOL/PAOI/RAOUVK
	FOS/FO/E/NOL/PAOU/RAOUV/IK
phosphofructaldolase	FOS/FO/FRUK/TALD/LAIS
	FOS/FO/FRUK/TAL/DO/LAIS
	FOS/FO/FRUKT/ALD/LAIS
	FOS/FO/FRUKT/AL/DO/LAIS
phosphofructokinase	FOS/FO/FRUKT/KAOI/NAIS
	FOS/FO/FRUK/TO/KAOI/NAIS
phosphogalactoisomerase	FOS/FO/GLAKT/AOI/SOM/RAIS
	FOS/FO/GLAK/TO/AOI/SOM/RAIS
phosphoglobulin	FOS/FO/GLOB/LIN
phosphoglucokinase	FOS/FO/GLAOUK/KAOI/NAIS
phosphoglucomutase	FOS/FO/GLAOUK/MAOU/TAIS
phosphogluconate	FOS/FO/GLAOUK/NAIT
phosphogluconolactonase	FOS/FO/GLAOUK/NO/LAKT/NAIS
phosphoglucoprotein	FOS/FO/GLAOUK/PRO/TAOEN
phosphoglyceracetal	FOS/FO/GLIS/RAS/TAL
phosphoglyceraldehyde	FOS/FO/GLIS/RALD/HAOID
phosphoglycerate	FOS/FO/GLIS/RAIT
phosphoglyceric	FOS/FO/GLI/SER/IK
	FOS/FO/GLIS/RIK
phosphoglyceride	FOS/FO/GLIS/RAOID
phosphoglyceromutase	FOS/FO/GLIS/RO/MAOU/TAIS
phosphoguanidine	FOS/FO/GAUN/DAOEN
phosphohexoisomerase	FOS/FO/HEX/AOI/SOM/RAIS
phosphohexokinase	FOS/FO/HEX/KAOI/NAIS
phosphohexomutase	FOS/FO/HEX/MAOU/TAIS
phosphohexose	FOS/FO/HEK/SOES
	FOS/FO/HEX/OES
phosphohydrolase	FOS/FO/HAO/DRO/LAIS
phosphoinositide	FOS/FO/IN/OES/TAOID
phosphoketolase	FOS/FO/KAOET/LAIS
phosphokinase	FOS/FO/KAOI/NAIS
phospholecithinase	FOS/FO/LES/THIN/AIS
Phospholine	FOS/FO/LAOEN
Phospholine Iodide	FOS/FO/LIN/AOI/DAOID
phospholipase	FOS/FO/LIP/AIS
phospholipid	FOS/FO/LIP/ID
phospholipidemia	FOS/FO/LIP/DAOEM/YA
phospholipin	FOS/FO/LIP/PIN
phosphomonoesterase	FOS/FO/MON/ES/TRAIS
phosphomutase	FOS/FO/MAOU/TAIS

phosphonate	FOS/FO/NAIT
phosphonecrosis	FOS/FO/NE/KROE/SIS
phosphonium	FOEN/YUM
phosphonuclease	FOS/FO/NAOUK/LAIS
phosphopenia	FOS/FO/PAOEN/YA
phosphopentose	FOS/FO/PEN/TOES
phosphoprotein	FOS/FO/PRO/TAOEN
phosphoptomaine	FOS/FO/TOE/MAIN
phosphopyruvate	FOS/FO/PAOIR/VAIT
	FOS/FO/PAOI/RAOU/VAIT
phosphor	FOS/FOR
phosphorated	FOS/FRAIT/-D
	FOS/FO/RAIT/-D
	FOS/FO/AIT/-D
phosphorescence	FOS/FRES/ENS
	FOS/FO/RES/ENS
phosphorescent	FOS/FRES/ENT
	FOS/FO/RES/ENT
phosphoretted	FOS/FRET/-D
	FOS/FO/RET/-D
phosphorhidrosis	FOS/FOR/HAOI/DROE/SIS
	FOS/FOR/HI/DROE/SIS
	FOS/FOR/HID/ROE/SIS
phosphoriboisomerase	FOS/FO/RAOIB/AOI/SOM/RAIS
phosphoribokinase	FOS/FO/RAOIB/KAOI/NAIS
phosphoribosylamine	FOS/FO/RAOIB/SIL/MAOEN
phosphoribosylglycineamide	
	FOS/FO/RAOIB/SIL/GLAOI/SIN/
	MAOID
	FOS/FO/RAOIB/SIL/GLI/SIN/
	MAOID
phosphoribosylpyrophosphate	
	FOS/FO/RAOIB/SIL/PAOIR/FOS/
	FAIT
phosphoribosyltransferase	FOS/FO/RAOIB/SIL/TRA*NS/
	FRAIS
phosphoribulokinase	FOS/FO/RAOIB/LO/KAOI/NAIS
phosphoribulose	FOS/FO/RAOIB/LOES
phosphoric	FOS/FOER/IK
phosphorica	FOS/FOER/KA
phosphoridrosis	FOS/FOR/DROE/SIS
phosphorism	FOS/FRIFM
	FOS/FO/RIFM
	FOS/FOR/IFM
phosphorized	FOS/FRAOIZ/-D
	FOS/FO/RAOIZ/-D
	FOS/FOR/AOIZ/-D
phosphorolysis	FOS/FROL/SIS
	FOS/FO/ROL/SIS
phosphoroscope	FOS/FOER/SKOEP
phosphorous	FOS/FROUS
	FOS/FO/ROUS
	FOS/FOR/OUS
phosphorpenia	FOS/FOR/PAOEN/YA
phosphoruria	FOS/FO/RAOUR/YA
	FOS/FOR/YAOUR/YA
phosphorus	FOS/FRUS
	FOS/FO/RUS
	FOS/FOE/RUS
	FOS/FOR/RUS
phosphoryl	FOS/FRIL
	FOS/FO/RIL
phosphorylase	FOS/FOER/LAIS
	FOS/FOR/LAIS
phosphorylation	FOS/FOER/LAIGS
	FOS/FOR/LAIGS
phosphorylcholine	FOS/FRIL/KOE/LAOEN
	FOS/FO/RIL/KOE/LAOEN
phosphorylethanolamine	FOS/FRIL/*ET/NOL/MAOEN
	FOS/FO/RIL/*ET/NOL/MAOEN
phosphoserine	FOS/FO/SER/AOEN
	FOS/FO/SAOER/RAOEN
phosphosphingoside	FOS/FO/SFING/SAOID
phosphosugar	FOS/FO/SHUG/AR
phosphotransacetylase	FOS/FO/TRA*NS/SET/LAIS
	FOS/FO/TRA*NS/AI/SET/LAIS
phosphotransferase	FOS/FO/TRA*NS/FRAIS
phosphotriose	FOS/FO/TR*I/OES
phosphotungstate	FOS/FO/TUNG/STAIT
phosphotungstic	FOS/FO/TUNG/STIK
phosphovitellin	FOS/FO/VAOI/TEL/LIN
	FOS/FO/VI/TEL/LIN
phosphuresis	FOS/FAOU/RAOE/SIS
phosphuret	FOS/FAOU/RET
phosphuretic	FOS/FAOU/RET/IK
phosphuretted	FOS/FAOU/RET/-D
phosphuria	FOS/FAOUR/YA
phosvitin	FOS/VAOI/TIN
phot	FO*ET

photalgia	FOE/TAL/JA	photokinesis	FOET/KI/NAOE/SIS
photallochromy	FOE/TAL/KROE/M*I	photokinetic	FOET/KI/NET/IK
	FOE/TAL/LO/KROE/M*I	photokymograph	FOET/KAOIM/GRAF
photaugiaphobia	FOE/TAUJ/FOEB/YA	photolethal	FOET/LAOE/THAL
	FOE/TAU/JA/FOEB/YA	photology	FOE/TOLG
photechic	FOE/TEK/IK	photoluminescence	FOET/LAOUM/NES/ENS
photechy	FOE/TEK/KI	photoluminescent	FOET/LAOUM/NES/ENT
photerythrous	FOET/R*IT/ROUS	photolyase	FOET/LAOI/AIS
photesthesia	FOE/TES/THAOEZ/YA	photolysis	FOE/TOL/SIS
photesthesis	FOE/TES/THAOE/SIS	photolyte	FOET/LAOIT
	FOE/TES/THE/SIS	photolytic	FOET/LIT/IK
photic	FOE/TIK	photoma	FOE/TOE/MA
	FOET/IK	photomacrography	FOET/MA/KROG/FI
	FOT/IK	photomagnetism	FOET/MAG/NE/TIFM
photism	FOE/TIFM	photomania	FOET/MAIN/YA
	FOET/IFM	photometer	FOE/TOM/TER
photo-	FOET	photomethemoglobin	FOET/MET/HAOEM/GLOE/BIN
photoactinic	FOET/AK/TIN/IK	photometry	FOE/TOM/TRI
photoactive	FOET/AKT/IV	photomicrograph	FOET/MAOI/KRO/GRAF
photoallergic	FOET/AL/LERJ/IK	photomicrography	FOET/MAOI/KROG/FI
photoallergy	FOET/AL/ER/JI	photomicroscope	FOET/MAOI/KRO/SKOEP
photoautotroph	FOET/AUT/TROEF	photomicroscopy	FOET/MAOI/KROS/KPI
photoautotrophic	FOET/AUT/TROFK	photomorphogenesis	FOET/MOR/FO/JEN/SIS
photobacteria	FOET/BAK/TAOER/YA	photomyoclonic	FOET/MAOI/KLON/IK
photobacterium	FOET/BAK/TAOERM	photomyoclonus	FOET/MAOI/OK/LO/NUS
Photobacterium	K-P/FOET/BAK/TAOERM	photomyogenic	FOET/MAOI/JEN/IK
photobiologic	FOET/BAO*I/LOJ/IK	photon	FOE/TON
photobiological	FOET/BAO*I/LOJ/KAL	photoncia	FOE/TONS/YA
photobiology	FOET/BAO*I/OLG	photone	FOE/TOEN
photobiotic	FOET/BAO*I/OT/IK	photonosus	FOE/TON/SUS
photocatalysis	FOET/KA/TAL/SIS	photo-onycholysis	FOET/OIN/KOL/SIS
photocatalyst	FOET/KAT/L*IS	photo-ophthalmia	FOET/OF/THAL/MAOE/YA
photocatalytic	FOET/KAT/LIT/IK	photoparoxysmal	FOET/PROK/SIZ/MAL
photocatalyzer	FOET/KAT/LAOIZ/ER		FOET/PAR/OK/SIZ/MAL
photoceptor	FOET/SEP/TOR	photopathy	FOE/TOP/TH*I
photochemical	FOET/KEM/KAL	photoperceptive	FOET/PER/SEPT/IV
photochemistry	FOET/KEM/STRI	photoperiod	FOET/PAOER/YOD
photochemotherapy	FOET/KAOEM/THER/PI	photoperiodic	FOET/PAOER/YOD/IK
photochromogen	FOET/KROEM/JEN	photoperiodicity	FOET/PAOER/YO/DIS/TI
photochromogenic	FOET/KROEM/JEN/IK	photoperiodism	FOET/PAOER/YO/DIFM
photochromogenicity	FOET/KROEM/JE/NIS/TI		FOET/PAOER/YOD/IFM
photocoagulation	FOET/KO/AG/LAIGS	photopharmacology	FOET/FARM/KOLG
photocoagulator	FOET/KO/AG/LAI/TOR	photophilic	FOET/FIL/IK
photocontact	FOET/KON/TAKT	photophobia	FOET/FOEB/YA
	FOET/KAKT	photophobic	FOET/FOEB/IK
photoconvulsive	FOET/KON/VULS/IV	photophore	FOET/FOER
photocutaneous	FOET/KAOU/TAIN/YOUS	photophosphorylation	FOET/FOS/FOR/LAIGS
photodermatitis	FOET/DERM/TAOITS	photophthalmia	FOE/TOF/THAL/MA
photodermatosis	FOET/DERM/TOE/SIS		FOE/TOF/THAL/MAOE/YA
photodistribution	FOET/DRIBGS	photopia	FOE/TOEP/YA
	FOET/DIS/TRI/BAOUGS	photopic	FOE/TOP/IK
photodromy	FOE/TOD/RO/M*I	Photoplex	FOET/PLEX
photodynamic	FOET/DAOI/NAM/IK	photopsia	FOE/TOPS/YA
photodynesis	FOET/DAOI/NAOE/SIS	photoproduct	FOET/PRUKT
photodynia	FOET/DIN/YA		FOET/PROD/UKT
photodysphoria	FOET/DIS/FOER/YA		FOET/PRO/DUKT
	FOET/DIS/FOR/YA	photoprotection	FOET/PRO/T*EBGS
photoelectric	FOET/LEK/TRIK	photopsin	FOE/TOP/SIN
photoelectrical	FOET/LEK/TRI/KAL	photopsy	FOE/TOP/SI
photoelectrometer	FOET/LEK/TROM/TER	photoptarmosis	FOET/TAR/MOE/SIS
photoelectron	FOET/LEK/TRON	photoptometer	FOE/TOP/TOM/TER
photoelement	FOET/EL/-MT	photoptometry	FOE/TOP/TOM/TRI
photoerythema	FOET/*ER/THAOE/MA	photopupillary	FOET/PAOUP/LAIR
	FOET/ER/THAOE/MA	photoradiation	FOET/RAID/YAIGS
photoesthetic	FOET/ES/THET/IK	photoradiometer	FOET/RAID/YOM/TER
photofluorogram	FOET/FLAOUR/GRAM	photoreaction	FOET/RE/A*BGS
photofluorography	FOET/FLAOU/ROG/FI	photoreactivation	FOET/RE/AKT/VAIGS
photofluoroscope	FOET/FLAOUR/SKOEP	photoreception	FOET/RE/SEPGS
photogastroscope	FOET/GAS/TRO/SKOEP	photoreceptive	FOET/RE/SEPT/IV
photogen	FOET/JEN	photoreceptor	FOET/RE/SEP/TOR
photogene	FOET/JAOEN	photorespiration	FOET/RES/PRAIGS
photogenesis	FOET/JEN/SIS	photoretinitis	FOET/RET/NAOITS
photogenic	FOET/JEN/IK	photoretinopathy	FOET/RET/NOP/TH*I
photogenous	FOE/TOJ/NOUS	photoreversal	FOET/RE/VER/SAL
photogram	FOET/GRAM	photoscan	FOET/SKAN
photograph	FOET/GRAF	photoscanner	FOET/SKAN/ER
	FRAF	photoscope	FOET/SKOEP
photography	FOE/TOG/FI	photoscopy	FOE/TOS/KPI
	FRAF/FI	photosensitive	FOET/SENS/TIV
photohalide	FOET/HAL/AOID	photosensitivity	FOET/SENS/TIV/TI
photohematachometer	FOET/HAOEM/TA/KOM/TER	photosensitization	FOET/SENS/TI/ZAIGS
	FOET/HEM/TA/KOM/TER	photosensitize	FOET/SENS/TAOIZ
photohenric	FOET/HEN/RIK	photosensor	FOET/SEN/SOR
photoheterotroph	FOET/HET/RO/TROF	photostable	FOET/STAIBL
	FOET/HET/RO/TROEF	photostethoscope	FOET/ST*ET/SKOEP
photoheterotrophic	FOET/HET/RO/TROFK	photostress	FOET/STRESZ
photohmic	FOE/TOEM/IK	photosynthesis	FOET/S*INT/SIS
	FOE/TOE/MIK	photosynthetic	FOET/SIN/THET/IK
photoinactivation	FOET/IN/AKT/VAIGS	phototaxis	FOET/TAK/SIS

phototherapy	FOET/THER/PI	phthinoid	THIN/OID
photothermal	FOET/THER/MAL		THAOI/NOID
photothermy	FOET/THER/M*I	phthiriophobia	*see* pthiriophobia
phototimer	FOET/TAOIM/ER	Phthirus	*see* Pthirus
phototonus	FOE/TOT/NUS	phthisic	TIZ/IK
phototoxic	FOET/TOX/IK	phthisical	TIZ/KAL
phototoxicity	FOET/TOK/SIS/TI	phthisicky	TIZ/KI
phototoxis	FOET/TOK/SIS	phthisis	TAOI/SIS
phototrophic	FOET/TROFK		THAOI/SIS
phototropic	FOET/TROP/IK	phyco-	FAOIK
phototropism	FOE/TOT/RO/PIFM		FAOI/KO
phototurbidometric	FOET/TUR/BID/MET/RIK	phycobilin	FAOIK/BIL/LIN
	FOET/TURB/DO/MET/RIK		FAOIK/BAOI/LIN
photoxylin	FOE/TOX/LIN		FAOIK/B*I/LIN
photronreflectometer	FOE/TRON/RE/FLEK/TOM/TER	phycochrome	FAOIK/KROEM
photuria	FOE/TAOUR/YA	phycochromoprotein	FAOIK/KROEM/PRO/TAOEN
phragmoplast	FRAG/MO/PLA*S	phycocyanin	FAOIK/SAOI/NIN
-phrasia	FRAIZ/YA	phycoerythrin	FAOIK/R*IT/RIN
-phraxis	FRAK/SIS		FAOIK/*ER/THRIN
phren	FREN	phycologist	FAOI/KO*LGS
phren(o)-	FREN	phycology	FAOI/KOLG
	FRE/N(O)	Phycomycetes	FAOIK/MAOI/SAOE/TAOEZ
phrenalgia	FRE/NAL/JA	phycomycetosis	FAOIK/MAOIS/TOE/SIS
	FREN/AL/JA	phycomycetous	FAOIK/MAOI/SAOE/TOUS
phrenectomy	FR*E/NEKT/M*I	phycomycosis	FAOIK/MAOI/KOE/SIS
	(*not* FRE/NEKT/M*I; see	phygogalactic	FAOIG/GLAKT/IK
	frenectomy)		FAOI/GO/GLAKT/IK
phrenemphraxis	FREN/EM/FRAK/SIS	phyla	FAO*I/LA
phrenetic	FR*E/NET/IK		(*not* FAOI/LA; see fila)
	(*not* FRE/NET/IK; see frenetic)	phylacagogic	FAOI/LAK/GOJ/IK
-phrenia	FRAOEN/YA	phylactic	FAOI/LAKT/IK
phrenic	FREN/IK		FLAKT/IK
phrenicae	FREN/SAE	phylactotransfusion	FAOI/LAKT/TRA*NS/FAOUGS
phrenicectomized	FREN/SEKT/MAOIZ/-D		FLAKT/TRA*NS/FAOUGS
phrenicectomy	FREN/SEKT/M*I	phylaxiology	FAOI/LAX/YOLG
phrenici	FREN/SAOI		FLAX/YOLG
phreniclasia	FREN/KLAIZ/YA	phylaxis	FAOI/LAK/SIS
phreniclasis	FREN/KLAI/SIS		FLAK/SIS
phrenico-	FREN/KO	phyletic	FAOI/LET/IK
phrenicocolicum	FREN/KO/KOL/KUM	phyllidea	FIL/ID/YA
phrenicoexeresis	FREN/KO/KPER/SIS		FIL/LID/YA
	FREN/KO/EK/SER/SIS	-phyllin(e)	FLIN
	FREN/KO/EX/ER/SIS		FIL/LIN
phreniconeurectomy	FREN/KO/NAOU/REKT/M*I	phyllo-	FIL
phrenicopleural	FREN/KO/PLAOURL		FIL/LO
phrenicopleuralis	FREN/KO/PLAOU/RAI/LIS	phyllochlorin	FIL/KLOR/RIN
phrenicotomy	FREN/KOT/M*I	phyllochromanol	FIL/KROEM/NOL
phrenicotripsy	FREN/KO/TRIP/SI	phyllode	FIL/OED
phrenicum	FREN/KUM		FIL/LOED
phrenicus	FREN/KUS	phylloerythrin	FIL/R*IT/RIN
Phrenilin	FREN/LIN		FIL/*ER/THRIN
Phrenilin Forte	FREN/LIN/FOR/TAI	phyllolith	FIL/L*IT
phrenitis	FRE/NAOITS	phylloporphyrin	FIL/POR/FRIN
phrenocardia	FREN/KARD/YA	phyllopyrrole	FIL/PIR/ROEL
phrenocolic	FREN/KOL/IK		FIL/PIR/ROL
phrenocolopexy	FREN/KOEL/PEK/SI	phylloquinone	FIL/KWI/NOEN
phrenodynia	FREN/DIN/YA		FIL/KWIN/OEN
phrenogastric	FREN/GAS/TRIK		FIL/KWAOI/NOEN
phrenoglottic	FREN/GLOT/IK	phylloxanthine	FIL/ZAN/THAOEN
phrenograph	FREN/GRAF		FIL/ZAN/THIN
phrenohepatic	FREN/HE/PAT/IK	phylo-	FAOIL
phrenologist	FRE/NO*LGS		FAOI/LO
phrenology	FRE/NOLG	phyloanalysis	FAOI/LO/AI/NAL/SIS
phrenopathy	FRE/NOP/TH*I		FAOI/LO/ANL/SIS
phrenopericardial	FREN/P*ER/KARD/YAL		(*not* FAOIL, etc.; see file analysis)
phrenopericarditis	FREN/P*ER/KAR/DAOITS	phylobiology	FAOIL/BAO*I/OLG
phrenoplegia	FREN/PLAOE/JA	phylogenesis	FAOIL/JEN/SIS
phrenoptosia	FREN/OP/TOES/YA	phylogenetic	FAOIL/JE/NET/IK
phrenoptosis	FREN/OP/TOE/SIS	phylogenic	FAOIL/JEN/IK
phrenosin	FREN/SIN	phylogeny	FAOI/LOJ/N*I
phrenosinic	FREN/SIN/IK	phylum	FAO*I/LUM
phrenospasm	FREN/SPAFM		FAO*IL/UM
phrenosplenic	FREN/SPLEN/IK		(*not* FAOI/LUM or FAOIL/UM; see
phrenotropic	FREN/TROP/IK		filum)
phrictopathic	FRIKT/PA*T/IK	phyma	FAOI/MA
	FRIK/TO/PA*T/IK	phymata	FAOIM/TA
phronema	FROE/NAOE/MA	phymatoid	FAOIM/TOID
phrygian	FRIJ/YAN	phymatology	FAOIM/TOLG
phrynoderma	FRIN/DER/MA	phymatorhusin	FAOIM/TO/RAOU/SIN
phrynolysin	FRI/NOL/SIN	phymatorrhysin	FAOIM/TOR/SIN
pH-stat	PAIFP/STAT		FAOIM/TO/RIS/SIN
phthalate	THAL/AIT	phymatosis	FAOIM/TOE/SIS
phthalein	THAL/YIN	Physa	FAOI/SA
phthalic	THAL/IK	Physalia	FAOI/SAIL/YA
phthaloyl	THAL/OIL	physalides	FI/SAL/DAOEZ
phthalyl	THAL/IL		FAOI/SAL/DAOEZ
phthalylsulfacetamide	THAL/IL/SUL/FA/SET/MAOID	physaliform	FI/SAL/FORM
phthalylsulfathiazole	THAL/IL/SUL/FA/THAOI/ZOEL		FAOI/SAL/FORM
phthalylsulfonazole	THAL/IL/SUL/FON/ZOEL	physaliphora	FIS/LIF/RA

physaliphore	FI/SAL/FOER		FAOIT/GLAOUT/NIN
	FAOI/SAL/FOER	phytobezoar	FAOIT/BE/ZOER
physaliphorous	FIS/LIF/ROUS		FAOIT/BAOE/ZOER
physalis	FIS/LIS	phytochemistry	FAOIT/KEM/STRI
physallization	FIS/LI/ZAIGS	phytocholesterol	FAOIT/KL*ES/ROL
Physaloptera	FIS/LOPT/RA	phytochrome	FAOIT/KROEM
physalopteriasis	FIS/LOPT/RAOI/SIS	phytodemic	FAOIT/DEM/IK
physeal	*see* physial	phytodermatitis	FAOIT/DERM/TAOITS
physial	FIZ/YAL	phytodetritus	FAOIT/DE/TRAOI/TUS
physiatrician	FIZ/YA/TRIGS	phytofluene	FAOIT/FLAOU/AOEN
physiatrics	FIZ/YAT/RIK/-S	phytogenesis	FAOIT/JEN/SIS
physiatrist	FI/ZAOI/TR*IS	phytogenetic	FAOIT/JE/NET/IK
	FIZ/YAT/R*IS	phytogenic	FAOIT/JEN/IK
physiatry	FI/ZAOI/TRI	phytogenous	FAOI/TOJ/NOUS
	FIZ/YAT/RI	phytohemagglutinin	FAOIT/HAOEM/GLAOUT/NIN
physic	FIZ/IK		FAOIT/HEM/GLAOUT/NIN
physical	FIZ/KAL	phytohormone	FAOIT/HOR/MOEN
physician	FI/SIGS	phytoid	FAOI/TOID
physico-	FIZ/KO	phytol	FAOI/TOL
physicochemical	FIZ/KO/KEM/KAL	phytolectin	FAOIT/LEK/TIN
physicogenic	FIZ/KO/JEN/IK	Phytomastigophora	FAOIT/MA*S/GOF/RA
physicotherapeutics	FIZ/KO/THER/PAOUT/IK/-S	Phytomastigophorea	FAOIT/MA*S/GOF/RAOE/YA
physicotherapy	FIZ/KO/THER/PI	phytomenadione	FAOIT/MEN/DI/OEN
physics	FIZ/IK/-S	phytomitogen	FAOIT/MAOIT/JEN
physio-	FIZ/YO	phytonadione	FAOIT/NAI/DI/OEN
physiochemical	FIZ/YO/KEM/KAL	phytone	FAOI/TOEN
physiochemistry	FIZ/YO/KEM/STRI	phytonosis	FAOI/TON/SIS
physiocracy	FIZ/YOK/RA/SI	phytoparasite	FAOIT/PAR/SAOIT
physiogenesis	FIZ/YO/JEN/SIS	phytopathogenic	FAOIT/PA*T/JEN/IK
physiogenic	FIZ/YO/JEN/IK	phytopathology	FAOIT/PA/THOLG
physiognomonic	FIZ/YOG/NO/MON/IK	phytopathy	FAOI/TOP/TH*I
physiognomy	FIZ/YOG/NO/M*I	phytophagous	FAOI/TOF/GOUS
physiognosis	FIZ/YOG/NOE/SIS	phytopharmacology	FAOIT/FARM/KOLG
physiologic	FIZ/YO/LOJ/IK	phytophlyctodermatitis	FAOIT/FLIKT/DERM/TAOITS
physiologica	FIZ/YO/LOJ/KA	phytophotodermatitis	FAOIT/FOET/DERM/TAOITS
physiological	FIZ/YO/LOJ/KAL	phytoplankton	FAOIT/PLANG/TON
physiologically	FIZ/YO/LOJ/KLI	phytoplasm	FAOIT/PLAFM
physiologicoanatomical	FIZ/YO/LOJ/KO/AN/TOM/KAL	phytopneumoconiosis	FAOIT/NAOUM/KOEN/YOE/SIS
physiologist	FIZ/YO*LGS	phytoporphyrin	FAOIT/POR/FRIN
physiology	FIZ/YOLG	phytoprecipitin	FAOIT/PRE/SIP/TIN
physiolysis	FIZ/YOL/SIS	phytosensitinogen	FAOIT/SENS/TIN/JEN
physiomedical	FIZ/YO/MED/KAL	phytosis	FAOI/TOE/SIS
physiomedicalism	FIZ/YO/MED/KLIFM	phytosphingosine	FAOIT/SFING/SAOEN
	FIZ/YO/MED/KAL/IFM		FAOIT/SFING/SIN
physiometry	FIZ/YOM/TRI	phytostearin	FAOIT/STAOE/RIN
physioneurosis	FIZ/YO/NAOU/ROE/SIS		(*not* FAOIT/STAOER/RIN; see
physionomy	FIZ/YON/M*I		phytosterin)
physiopathic	FIZ/YO/PA*T/IK	phytosterin	FAOIT/STAOER/RIN
physiopathologic	FIZ/YO/PA*T/LOJ/IK		FAOI/TO*S/RIN
physiopathology	FIZ/YO/PA/THOLG	phytosterol	FAOIT/STAOER/OL
physiophyly	FIZ/YOF/LI		FAOIT/STAOER/ROL
physiopsychic	FIZ/YO/SAOIK/IK	phytosterolin	FAOIT/STAOER/LIN
physiopyrexia	FIZ/YO/PAOI/REX/YA	phytotherapy	FAOIT/THER/PI
physiotherapeutic	FIZ/YO/THER/PAOUT/IK	phytotoxic	FAOIT/TOX/IK
physiotherapeutist	FIZ/YO/THER/PAOUT/*IS	phytotoxin	FAOIT/TOK/SIN
	FIZ/YO/THER/PAOU/T*IS	phytotrichobezoar	FAOIT/TRIK/BE/ZOER
physiotherapist	FIZ/YO/THER/P*IS		FAOIT/TRIK/BAOE/ZOER
physiotherapy	FIZ/YO/THER/PI	phytovitellin	FAOIT/VAOI/TEL/LIN
physique	FI/ZAOEK		FAOIT/VI/TEL/LIN
	FIZ/AOEK	phytoxylin	FAOI/TOX/LIN
physis	FAOI/SIS	phytyl	FAOI/TIL
physo-	FAOIS	pia	PAOI/YA
	FAOI/SO		PAOE/YA
physocele	FAOIS/SAO*EL	pia-arachnitis	PAOI/YA/AR/AK/NAOITS
Physocephalus	FAOIS/SEF/LUS		PAOI/YA/AI/RAK/NAOITS
Physocephalus sexalatus	FAOIS/SEF/LUS/SEX/LAI/TUS	pia-arachnoid	PAOI/YA/AI/RAK/NOID
physocephaly	FAOIS/SEF/LI		PAOI/YA/AR/AK/NOID
physohematometra	FAOIS/HAOEM/TO/MAOE/TRA	pia-glia	PAOI/YA/GLAOI/YA
	FAOIS/HEM/TO/MAOE/TRA	pial	PAOI/YAL
physohydrometra	FAOIS/HAOI/DRO/MAOE/TRA		PAO*IL
physometra	FAOIS/MAOE/TRA		PAOE/YAL
Physopsis	FAOI/SOP/SIS	pia mater	PAOI/YA/MAI/TER
physopyosalpinx	FAOIS/PAOI/SAL/PINGS		PAOI/YA/MAIT/ER
Physostigma	FAOIS/STIG/MA		PAOE/YA/MAU/TER
physostigmine	FAOIS/STIG/MAOEN		PAOE/YA/MAUT/ER
	FAOIS/STIG/MIN	piamatral	PAOI/MAI/TRAL
physostigminism	FAOIS/STIG/MI/NIFM		PAOI/YA/MAI/TRAL
	FAOIS/STIG/MIN/IFM	piarachnitis	PAOI/AR/AK/NAOITS
phytanate	FAOI/TAN/AIT		PAOI/RAK/NAOITS
	FAOIT/NAIT	piarachnoid	PAOI/RAK/NOID
phytanic	FAOI/TAN/IK		PAOI/AI/AK/NOID
phytase	FAOI/TAIS	piarhemia	PAOI/AR/HAOEM/YA
phytate	FAOI/TAIT	piastrinemia	PAOI/AS/TRI/NAOEM/YA
phytic	FAOIT/IK	piblokto	PIB/LOK/TOE
	FIT/IK	pica	PAOI/KA
phytin	FAOI/TIN		PAOE/KA
phyto-	FAOIT	picealis	PAOIS/YAI/LIS
	FAOI/TO		PIS/YAI/LIS
phytoagglutinin	FAOIT/AI/GLAOUT/NIN	piceous	PAOIS/YOUS

	PIS/YOUS	pigmentata	PIG/MEN/TAI/TA
picis	PAOI/SIS	pigmentation	PIG/MEN/TAIGS
Pick	K-P/PIK	pigmented	PIG/-MT/-D
pickling	PIK/-LG	pigmentogenesis	PIG/MENT/JEN/SIS
Pickrell	PIK/REL	pigmentogenic	PIG/MENT/JEN/IK
pickwickian	PIK/WIK/YAN	pigmentolysin	PIG/MEN/TOL/SIN
pico-	PAOIK	pigmentolysis	PIG/MEN/TOL/SIS
	PAOI/KO	pigmentophage	PIG/MENT/FAIJ
picocurie	PAOIK/KAOUR/RAOE	pigmentophore	PIG/MENT/FOER
picodnavirus	PAOI/KOD/NA/VAOI/RUS	pigmentosa	PIG/MEN/TOE/SA
picogram	PAOIK/GRAM	pigmentosum	PIG/MEN/TOE/SUM
picolinic	PIK/LIN/IK		PIG/MEN/TOES/UM
picolinuric	PIK/LI/NAOUR/IK	pigmentum	PIG/MEN/TUM
picometer	PAOIK/MAOET/ER	pigmentum nigrum	PIG/MEN/TUM/NAOI/GRUM
picopicogram	PAOIK/PAOIK/GRAM	Pignet	PAOEN/YAI
Picornaviridae	PI/KORN/VIR/DAE	piitis	PAOI/AOITS
	PI/KOR/NA/VIR/DAE		PAOI/YAOITS
picornavirus	PI/KORN/VAOI/RUS	Pike	K-P/PAOIK
	PI/KOR/NA/VAOI/RUS	pil(o)-	PAOIL
	PAOI/KORN/VAOI/RUS		PAOI/L(O)
	PAOI/KOR/NA/VAOI/RUS	pila	PAOI/LA
picounit	PAOIK/YAOUNT	pilae	PAOI/LAE
picr(o)-	PIK/R(O)	pilar	PAOI/LAR
picramic	PIK/RAM/IK	pilary	PIL/RI
	PAOI/KRAM/IK	pilaster	PAOI/LA*S/ER
picrate	PIK/RAIT	Pilcher	PIL/KHER
picric	PIK/RIK	pile	PAOIL
picrocarmine	PIK/RO/KAR/MIN	pileous	PAOIL/YOUS
	PIK/RO/KAR/MAOEN	piles	PAOIL/-S
picroformol	PIK/RO/FOR/MOL	pileus	PAOIL/YUS
	PIK/RO/FOER/MOL	pili	PAOI/LAOI
picrogeusia	PIK/RO/GAOUZ/YA	pilial	PAOIL/YAL
	PIK/RO/GAOUS/YA		PIL/YAL
picrol	PIK/ROL	piliate	PAOIL/YAIT
picronigrosin	PIK/RO/NAOI/GRO/SIN		PIL/YAIT
	PIK/RO/NAO/GROE/SIN	Pilidae	PIL/DAE
picrosaccharometer	PIK/RO/SAK/ROM/TER	piliferous	PAOI/LIF/ROUS
picrotoxin	PIK/RO/TOK/SIN	piliform	PAOIL/FORM
picrotoxinin	PIK/RO/TOX/NIN	pilimictio	PAOIL/MIK/SHOE
picrotoxinism	PIK/RO/TOX/NIFM	pilimiction	PAOIL/M*IBGS
picryl	PIK/RIL	pilin	PAOI/LIN
Pictet	PIK/TET	pill	PIL
pictograph	PIKT/GRAF	pillar	PIL/LAR
	PIK/TO/GRAF	pillet	PIL/ET
pictor	PIK/TOR	pillion	PIL/YON
pictorial	PIK/TOIRL	pill-rolling	PIL/ROL/-G
piebald	PAOI/BAULD	pilobezoar	PAOIL/BE/ZOER
	PAOI/BALD		PAOIL/BAOE/ZOER
piebaldism	PAOI/BAULD/IFM	pilocarpine	PAOIL/KAR/PAOEN
	PAOI/BALD/IFM		PAOIL/KAR/PIN
piebaldness	PAOI/BAULD/*NS	Pilocarpus	PAOIL/KAR/PUS
	PAOI/BALD/*NS	pilocystic	PAOIL/S*IS/IK
piece	PAOES	pilocytic	PAOIL/SIT/IK
piedra	PAOE/AI/DRA	piloerection	PAOIL/E/R*EBGS
	PAOE/YAI/DRA	piloid	PAOI/LOID
Piedraia	PAOI/DRAOI/YA	pilojection	PAOIL/J*EBGS
Piedraiaceae	PAOI/DRAOI/AIS/YAE	pilology	PAOI/LOLG
pier	PAO*ER	pilomatricoma	PAOIL/MAI/TRI/KOE/MA
	(not PAOER; see peer)		PAOIL/MAT/RI/KOE/MA
Pierini	PAOE/RAOE/NAOE	pilomatrixoma	PAOIL/MAI/TRIK/SOE/MA
	PAOER/RAOE/NAOE	pilomotor	PAOIL/MOE/TOR
Pierre Robin	PAOE/YAIR/ROE/BAN	pilonidal	PAOIL/NAOI/DAL
Piersol	PAOER/SOL	pilorum	PAOI/LOR/UM
piesesthesia	PAOI/E/SES/THAOEZ/YA		PAOI/LOER/UM
	PAOI/SES/THAOEZ/YA	pilose	PAOI/LOES
	PAOIS/ES/THAOEZ/YA	pilosebaceous	PAOIL/SE/BAIRBS
piesimeter	PAOI/SIM/TER	pilosellus	PAOIL/SEL/LUS
piesometer	PAOI/SOM/TER	pilosis	PAOI/LOE/SIS
piesis	PAOI/SIS	Piltz	PILTS
-piesis	PAOI/SIS	pilul-	PIL/YAOU/L-
	PAOI/E/SIS		PIL/YU/L-
piezallochromy	PAOI/ZAL/KROE/M*I		(not PIL/L-)
piezo-	PAOI/ZO	pilula	PIL/YAOU/LA
	PAOI/AOEZ		(not PIL/LA)
	PAOI/E/ZO	pilulae	PIL/YAOU/LAE
piezocardiogram	PAOI/ZO/KARD/YO/GRAM		(not PIL/LAE)
	PAOI/AOEZ/KARD/YO/GRAM	pilular	PIL/YAOU/LAR
piezochemistry	PAOI/ZO/KEM/STRI		(not PIL/LAR; see pillar)
	PAOI/AOEZ/KEM/STRI	pilule	PIL/YAOUL
piezoelectric	PAOI/ZO/LEK/TRIK	pilus	PAOI/LUS
piezoelectricity	PAOI/ZO/LEK/TRIS/TI	Pima Syrup	PAOE/MA/SIR/RUP
piezogenic	PAOI/ZO/JEN/IK		PIM/MA/SIR/RUP
piezometer	PAOI/ZOM/TER	pimaricin	PI/MAR/SIN
pigeon	PIJ/JON	pimelic	PI/MEL/IK
pigment	PIG/-MT	pimelitis	PIM/LAOITS
pigment(o)-	PIG/MENT	pimelo-	PIM/LO
	PIG/MEN/T(O)	pimeloma	PIM/LOE/MA
pigmental	PIG/MEN/TAL	pimelopterygium	PIM/LO/TRIJ/YUM
pigmentary	PIG/MEN/TAIR		PIM/LO/TE/RIJ/YUM

pimelorrhea	PIM/LO/RAOE/YA	piorthopnea	PAOI/YOF/LA
pimelorthopnea	PIM/LOR/THOP/NA		PAOI/OR/THOP/NA
	PIM/LOR/THOP/NAOE/YA		PAOI/OR/THOP/NAOE/YA
pimelosis	PIM/LOE/SIS	pioscope	PAOI/SKOEP
pimeluria	PIM/LAOUR/YA	pipamazine	PI/PAM/ZAOEN
pimenta	PI/MEN/TA		PAOI/PAM/ZAOEN
Pimenta	K-P/PI/MEN/TA	pipamperone	PI/PAFRP/ROEN
pimento	PI/MEN/TOE		PAOI/PAFRP/ROEN
piminodine	PI/MIN/DAOEN	pipazethate	PI/PAZ/THAIT
pimozide	PIM/ZAOID	pipe	PAOIP
pimple	PIFRP/-L	pipecolic	PIP/KOL/IK
	PIM/P-L		PIP/KOEL/IK
pin	PIN	pipecolinic	PIP/KO/LIN/IK
pinacyanol	PIN/SAOI/NOL		PIP/KOL/NIK
pinacyanole	PIN/SAOI/NOEL	pipenzolate	PI/PENZ/LAIT
Pinard	PAOE/NAR		PAOI/PENZ/LAIT
	PAOE/NARD	piper	PAOIP/ER
	PI/NAR	Piper	K-P/PAOIP/ER
	PI/NARD	piperacetazine	PIP/ER/SET/ZAOEN
pince-ciseaux	PANS/SI/ZOE		PI/PER/SET/ZAOEN
	PANS/SAOE/ZOE		PAOI/PER/SET/ZAOEN
pincement	PANS/-MT	piperacillin	PAOI/PER/SLIN
	PINS/-MT		PAOI/PER/SIL/LIN
pincers	PINS/ER/-S	piperazine	PAOI/PER/ZAOEN
	PIN/SER/-S	piperidine	PAOI/PER/DAOEN
pindolol	PIND/LOL	piperidolate	PAOI/PER/DO/LAIT
	PIN/DO/LOL		PAOIP/RID/LAIT
pine	PAOIN		PAOI/PER/ID/LAIT
pineal	PIN/YAL	piperocaine	PAOI/PER/KAIN
pineal(o)-	PIN/YA/L(O)		PIP/RO/KAIN
	PIN/YAL		PAOIP/RO/KAIN
pineale	PIN/YAI/LAOE	piperoxan	PIP/ROK/SAN
pinealectomy	PIN/YAL/EKT/M*I		PAOIP/ROK/SAN
	PIN/YA/LEKT/M*I	pipet	*see* pipette
pinealism	PIN/YAL/IFM	pipette	PAOI/PET
pinealoblastoma	PIN/YAL/BLAS/TOE/MA		PI/PET
	PIN/YA/LO/BLAS/TOE/MA	pipobroman	PIP/BROE/MAN
pinealocyte	PIN/YAL/SAO*IT		PAOIP/BROE/MAN
	PIN/YA/LO/SAO*IT	piposulfan	PIP/SUL/FAN
pinealocytoma	PIN/YAL/SAOI/TOE/MA	pipotiazine	PIP/TAOI/ZAOEN
	PIN/YA/LO/SAOI/TOE/MA	pipoxolan	PI/POX/LAN
pinealoma	PIN/YA/LOE/MA	Pipracil	PIP/RA/SIL
pinealopathy	PIN/YA/LOP/TH*I	pipradrol	PIP/RA/DROL
pineapple	PAOIN/AP/-L		PAOI/PRA/DROL
Pinel	PAOE/NEL	piprinhydrinate	PIP/RIN/HAOI/DRI/NAIT
	PI/NEL	piprozolin	PIP/RO/ZOE/LIN
pinene	PAOI/NAOEN	pipsyl	PIP/SIL
pineoblastoma	PIN/YO/BLAS/TOE/MA	Piptocephalus	PIPT/SEF/LUS
pineocytoma	PIN/YO/SAOI/TOE/MA		PIP/TO/SEF/LUS
pinguecula	PING/WEK/LA	pique	PAO*EK
pinguicula	PING/WIK/LA		(*not* PAOEK or PAEK; see peek and
piniform	PIN/FORM		peak)
	PAOIN/FORM	piquizil	PIK/WI/ZIL
pinkeye	P*ING/YAOI	pirbuterol	PIR/BAOUT/ROL
	PIN/-K/YAOI		PIR/BAOUT/ROEL
pinledge	PIN/LEJ	Pirenella	PIR/NEL/LA
pinna	PIN/NA		PAOIR/NEL/LA
pinnae	PIN/NAE	piriform	PIR/FORM
pinnal	PIN/NAL		PAOIR/FORM
pinniped	PIN/PED	piriformis	PIR/FOR/MIS
pino-	PIN		PAOIR/FOR/MIS
	PAOIN	pirinitramide	PIR/NAOI/TRA/MAOID
pinocyte	PIN/SAO*IT	Pirogoff	PIR/GOF
	PAOIN/SAO*IT	pirolate	PIR/LAIT
pinocytic	PIN/SIT/IK	pirolazamide	PIR/LAIZ/MAOID
	PAOIN/SIT/IK	piromen	PIR/MEN
pinocytosis	PIN/SAOI/TOE/SIS		PAOIR/MEN
	PAOIN/SAOI/TOE/SIS	Piroplasma	PIR/PLAZ/MA
pinocytotic	PIN/SAOI/TOT/IK		PAOIR/PLAZ/MA
	PAOIN/SAOI/TOT/IK	Piroplasmida	PIR/PLAZ/MI/DA
pinosome	PIN/SOEM		PAOIR/PLAZ/MI/DA
	PAOIN/SOEM	piroplasmosis	PIR/PLAZ/MOE/SIS
Pins	PINZ		PAOIR/PLAZ/MOE/SIS
	PINS	piroxicam	PIR/OX/KAM
pint	PAOINT		PI/ROX/KAM
pinta	PIN/TA	pirprofen	PIR/PRO/FEN
pintado	PIN/TA/DOE	Pirquet	PIR/KAI
	PIN/TAD/DOE		PIR/KET
pintid	PIN/TID	pis	PAO*E
pinto	PIN/TOE		(*not* PAOE; see pee)
pintoid	PIN/TOID	Pisces	PAOI/SAOEZ
pinus	PAOI/NUS		PIS/AOEZ
pinworm	PIN/WORM	piscicide	PIS/SAO*ID
pio-	PAOI	pisiform	PIS/FORM
	PAOI/YO		PAOIS/FORM
pioepithelium	PAOI/EP/THAOEL/YUM	pisiformis	PIS/FOR/MIS
pion	PAOI/YON		PAOIS/FOR/MIS
pionemia	PAOI/NAOEM/YA	Piskacek	PIS/KAFP/EK
Piophila	PAOI/OF/LA		PIS/KA/KHEK

pisocuneiform	PAOIS/KAOU/NAOE/FORM	plagiocephalism	PLAI/JO/SEF/LIFM
pisohamatum	PAOIS/HA/MAI/TUM	plagiocephalous	PLAI/JO/SEF/LOUS
	PAOIS/HAM/AI/TUM	plagiocephaly	PLAI/JO/SEF/LI
pisometacarpeum	PAOIS/MET/KARP/YUM	plague	PLAIG
pistil	PIS/TIL	plakalbumin	PLAK/AL/BAOU/MIN
pit	PIT	plakin	PLAI/KIN
pita	PAOE/TA	plan(o)-	PLAIN
pitch	PIFP		PLAI/N(O)
pitchblende	PIFP/BLEND	plana	PLAI/NA
pith	P*IT	planarian	PLA/NAIRN
pithecoid	P*IT/KOID	planchet	PLAN/SHET
pithiatic	P*IT/YAT/IK		PLAN/KHET
pithiatism	PI/THAOI/TIFM	Planck	PLA*N/-K
	P*IT/AOI/TIFM		(not PLAN/-K or PLA*NG; see
pithiatric	P*IT/YAT/RIK		plank)
pithiatry	P*IT/AOI/TRI	plane	PLAEN
	PI/THAOI/TRI		(not PLAIN; see plain)
pithing	P*IT/-G	plania	PLAIN/YA
pithode	P*IT/OED	planigram	PLAIN/GRAM
Pithomyces	P*IT/MAOI/SAOEZ		PLAI/NI/GRAM
Pitkin	PIT/KIN	planigraphy	PLA/NIG/FI
Pitocin	PIT/SIN	planimeter	PLA/NIM/TER
Pitressin	PI/TRES/SIN		PLAI/NIM/TER
pitting	PIT/-G	planing	PLAEN/-G
pituicyte	PI/TAOU/SAO*IT	planithorax	PLAN/THOR/AX
pituicytoma	PI/TAOU/SAOI/TOE/MA	plank	PLAN/-K
pituit-	PI/TAOU/T-		PLA*NG
pituita	PI/TAOU/TA	plankter	PLA*NG/TER
pituitarigenic	PI/TAOU/TAIR/JEN/IK		PLANG/TER
pituitarism	PI/TAOU/TRIFM		PLAN/-K/TER
	PI/TAOU/TAR/IFM	plankton	PLA*NG/TON
pituitarium	PI/TAOU/TAIRM		PLANG/TON
pituitary	PI/TAOU/TAIR		PLAN/-K/TON
pituitectomy	PI/TAOU/TEKT/M*I	planktonic	PLA*NG/TON/IK
pituitous	PI/TAOU/TOUS		PLANG/TON/IK
pityriasis	PIT/RAOI/SIS		PLAN/-K/TON/IK
pityroid	PIT/ROID	planocellular	PLAIN/SEL/YAOU/LAR
pityroides	PIT/ROI/DAOEZ	planoconcave	PLAIN/KON/KAIV
Pityrosporon	PIT/ROS/PRON	planoconvex	PLAIN/KON/VEX
	PIT/RO/SPORN	planography	PLA/NOG/FI
Pityrosporum	PIT/ROS/PRUM	planomania	PLAN/MAIN/YA
	PIT/RO/SPOR/UM	planorbid	PLAN/ORB/ID
pivalate	PIV/LAIT		PLA/NOR/BID
pivampicillin	PIV/AFRP/SLIN	Planorbidae	PLAN/ORB/DAE
	PIV/AFRP/SIL/LIN		PLA/NORB/DAE
pivot	PIV/OT	Planorbis	PLAN/OR/BIS
pix	PIX		PLA/NOR/BIS
pixel	PIX/EL	planotopokinesia	PLAN/TOP/KI/NAOEZ/YA
	PIK/SEL		PLAIN/TOP/KI/NAOEZ/YA
pizotyline	PI/ZOET/LAOEN	planovalgus	PLAIN/VAL/GUS
placebo	PLA/SAOE/BOE	planta	PLAN/TA
placement	PLAIS/-MT	planta pedis	PLAN/TA/PAOE/DIS
placent(o)-	PLA/SENT	plantae	PLAN/TAE
	PLA/SEN/T(O)	Plantago	PLAN/TAI/GOE
	PLAS/EN/T-	plantalgia	PLAN/TAL/JA
	PLAS/SPWO	plantar	PLAN/TAR
placenta	PLA/SEN/TA	plantare	PLAN/TAI/RAOE
placentae	PLA/SEN/TAE	plantares	PLAN/TAI/RAOEZ
placental	PLA/SEN/TAL	plantaria	PLAN/TAIR/YA
Placentalia	PLAS/EN/TAIL/YA	plantaris	PLAN/TAI/RIS
placentation	PLAS/EN/TAIGS	plantation	PLAN/TAIGS
placentin	PLA/SEN/TIN	plantigrade	PLANT/GRAID
placentitis	PLAS/EN/TAOITS		PLAN/TI/GRAID
placentogenesis	PLA/SENT/JEN/SIS	planula	PLAN/YAOU/LA
placentogram	PLA/SENT/GRAM		PLAN/YU/LA
placentography	PLAS/EN/TOG/FI		(not PLAN/LA)
placentoid	PLA/SEN/TOID	planulae	PLAN/YAOU/LAE
placentologist	PLAS/EN/TO*LGS		PLAN/YU/LAE
placentology	PLAS/EN/TOLG		(not PLAN/LAE)
placentolysin	PLAS/EN/TOL/SIN	planum	PLAIN/UM
placentoma	PLAS/EN/TOE/MA		PLAI/NUM
placentopathy	PLAS/EN/TOP/TH*I	planuria	PLA/NAOUR/YA
placentotherapy	PLA/SENT/THER/PI	plaque	PLAK
Placido	PLA/SAOE/DOE	Plaquenil	PLAK/NIL
	PLAS/DOE	-plasia	PLAIZ/YA
	PLA/SAOI/DOE	plasm	PLAFM
Placidyl	PLAS/DIL	-plasm	PLAFM
placode	PLAK/OED	plasm(o)-	PLAZ/M(O)
placoid	PLAK/OID	plasma	PLAZ/MA
pladaroma	PLAD/ROE/MA	plasmablast	PLAZ/MA/BLA*S
pladarosis	PLAD/ROE/SIS	plasmacrit	PLAZ/MA/KRIT
plafond	PLA/FON	plasmacyte	PLAZ/MA/SAO*IT
	PLA/FOND	plasmacytic	PLAZ/MA/SIT/IK
plagarumbelli	PLAIJ/RUM/BEL/LAOI	plasmacytoblast	PLAZ/MA/SAOIT/BLA*S
	PLAJ/RUM/BEL/LAOI	plasmacytoma	PLAZ/MA/SAOI/TOE/MA
	PLAG/RUM/BEL/LAOI	plasmacytosis	PLAZ/MA/SAOI/TOE/SIS
plagio-	PLAI/JO	plasmagel	PLAZ/MA/JEL
	PLAIJ/YO	plasmagene	PLAZ/MA/JAOEN
plagiocephalic	PLAI/JO/SFAL/IK	plasmahaut	PLAZ/MA/HOUT

plasmal	PLAZ/MAL		PLA*S/KWAOI/NOEN
plasmalemma	PLAZ/MA/LEM/MA	plastosome	PLA*S/SOEM
plasmalogen	PLAZ/MAL/JEN	plastron	PLAS/TRON
plasmapheresis	PLAZ/MA/FRAOE/SIS	-plasty	PLAS/TI
	PLAZ/MA/FE/RAOE/SIS	plate	PLAET
plasmapheretic	PLAZ/MA/FRET/IK	plateau	PLA/TOE
	PLAZ/MA/FE/RET/IK		PLAT/TOE
Plasma-Plex	PLAZ/MA/PLEX	platelet	PLAET/LET
plasmarrhexis	PLAZ/MA/REK/SIS		PLAIT/LET
Plasmatein	PLAZ/MA/TAOEN	plateletpheresis	PLAET/LET/FRAOE/SIS
plasmatherapy	PLAZ/MA/THER/PI		PLAIT/LET/FRAOE/SIS
plasmatic	PLAZ/MAT/IK	platinectomy	PLAT/NEKT/M*I
plasmatofibrous	PLAZ/MA/TO/FAOI/BROUS	plating	PLAET/-G
plasmatogamy	PLAZ/MA/TOG/M*I	platinic	PLA/TIN/IK
plasmatorrhexis	PLAZ/MA/TO/REK/SIS	platinocyanide	PLAT/NO/SAOI/NAOID
plasmatosis	PLAZ/MA/TOE/SIS	platinode	PLAT/NOED
plasmenic	PLAZ/MEN/IK	Platinol	PLAT/NOL
plasmia	PLAZ/MAOE/YA	Platinol-AQ	PLAT/NOL/A-RBGS/KW*RBGS
	(*not* PLAZ/MA; see plasma)	platinosis	PLAT/NOE/SIS
plasmic	PLAZ/MIK	platinous	PLAT/NOUS
plasmid	PLAZ/MID	platinum	PLAT/NUM
plasmin	PLAZ/MIN	platy-	PLAT
plasminic	PLAZ/MIN/IK	platybasia	PLAT/BAIS/YA
plasminogen	PLAZ/MIN/JEN	platycelous	PLAT/SAOEL/OUS
plasminokinase	PLAZ/MIN/KAOI/NAIS		PLAT/SE/LOUS
plasminoplastin	PLAZ/MIN/PLAS/TIN	platycephalic	PLAT/SFAL/IK
plasmocellulare	PLAZ/MO/SEL/YAOU/LAI/RAOE	platycephalous	PLAT/SEF/LOUS
plasmocyte	PLAZ/MO/SAO*IT	platycephaly	PLAT/SEF/LI
plasmocytoma	PLAZ/MO/SAOI/TOE/MA	platycnemia	PLAT/IK/NAOEM/YA
plasmodia	PLAZ/MOED/YA	platycnemic	PLAT/IK/NAOEM/IK
plasmodial	PLAZ/MOED/YAL	platycnemism	PLAT/IK/NAOEM/IFM
plasmodiblast	PLAZ/MOED/BLA*S	platycoria	PLAT/KOER/YA
plasmodicidal	PLAZ/MOED/SAOI/DAL		PLAT/KOR/YA
plasmodicide	PLAZ/MOED/SAO*ID	platycrania	PLAT/KRAIN/YA
Plasmodiidae	PLAZ/MO/DAOI/DAE	platycyte	PLAT/SAO*IT
plasmodiotrophoblast	PLAZ/MOED/YO/TROF/BLA*S	platyglossal	PLAT/GLOS/SAL
plasmodium	PLAZ/MOED/YUM	platyhelminth	PLAT/HEL/M*INT
Plasmodium	K-P/PLAZ/MOED/YUM	Platyhelminthes	PLAT/HEL/MIN/THAOEZ
Plasmodroma	PLAZ/MO/DROE/MA	platyhieric	PLAT/HAOI/ER/IK
Plasmodromata	PLAZ/MO/DROEM/TA	platymeria	PLAT/MAOER/YA
plasmogamy	PLAZ/MOG/M*I	platymeric	PLAT/MAOER/IK
plasmogen	PLAZ/MO/JEN		PLAT/MER/IK
plasmoid	PLAZ/MOID	platymorphia	PLAT/MOR/FAOE/YA
plasmokinin	PLAZ/MO/KAOI/NIN	platymorphic	PLAT/MOR/FIK
plasmolemma	PLAZ/MO/LEM/MA	platymyarial	PLAT/MAOI/AIRL
plasmology	PLAZ/MOLG	platymyarian	PLAT/MAOI/AIRN
plasmolysis	PLAZ/MOL/SIS	platymyoid	PLAT/MAOI/OID
plasmolytic	PLAZ/MO/LIT/IK	platyopia	PLAT/OEP/YA
plasmolyzability	PLAZ/MO/LAOIZ/-BLT	platyopic	PLAT/OP/IK
plasmolyzable	PLAZ/MO/LAOIZ/-BL		PLAT/OEP/IK
plasmolyze	PLAZ/MO/LAOIZ	platypellic	PLAT/PEL/IK
plasmoma	PLAZ/MOE/MA	platypelloid	PLAT/PEL/OID
plasmon	PLAZ/MON	platypnea	PLA/TIP/NA
plasmoptysis	PLAZ/MOPT/SIS		PLA/TIP/NAOE/YA
plasmorrhexis	PLAZ/MO/REK/SIS	platypodia	PLAT/POED/YA
plasmoschisis	PLAZ/MOS/KI/SIS	Platyrrhina	PLAT/RAOI/NA
plasmosin	PLAZ/MO/SIN	platyrrhine	PLAT/RAOIN
plasmosome	PLAZ/MO/SOEM	platyrrhiny	PLAT/RAOI/NI
plasmotomy	PLAZ/MOT/M*I	platysma	PLA/TIZ/MA
plasmotrophoblast	PLAZ/MO/TROF/BLA*S	platysmal	PLA/TIZ/MAL
plasmotropic	PLAZ/MO/TROP/IK	platysmata	PLA/TIZ/MA/TA
plasmotropism	PLAZ/MOT/RO/PIFM	platyspondylia	PLAT/SPON/DIL/YA
plasmotype	PLAZ/MO/TAOIP	platyspondylisis	PLAT/SPON/DIL/SIS
plasmozyme	PLAZ/MO/ZAOIM	platystaphyline	PLAT/STAF/LAOIN
plasson	PLAS/SON	platystencephalia	PLAT/STEN/SFAIL/YA
-plast	PLA*S		PLA/TIS/TEN/SFAIL/YA
plastein	PLA*S/YIN	platystencephalic	PLAT/STEN/SFAL/IK
	PLAS/TAOEN		PLA/TIS/TEN/SFAL/IK
	PLAS/TAOE/YIN	platystencephalism	PLAT/STEN/SEF/LIFM
plaster	PLA*S/ER		PLA/TIS/TEN/SEF/LIFM
-plastia	PLA*S/YA	platystencephaly	PLAT/STEN/SEF/LI
plastic	PLA*S/IK		PLA/TIS/TEN/SEF/LI
plasticity	PLAS/TIS/TI	platytrope	PLAT/TROEP
plasticizer	PLA*S/SAOIZ/ER	Plaut	PLAUT
plastid	PLAS/TID	pleasure	PLERB/SHUR
	PLA*S/ID	plectonemic	PLEKT/NAOEM/IK
plastidogenetic	PLA*S/DO/JE/NET/IK		PLEK/TO/NAOEM/IK
plastin	PLAS/TIN	plectridium	PLEK/TRID/YUM
plastiosome	PLA*S/YO/SOEM	plectron	PLEK/TRON
plasto-	PLA*S	plectrum	PLEK/TRUM
	PLAS/TO	pledge	PLEJ
plastochondria	PLA*S/KON/DRA	pledget	PLEJ/ET
	PLA*S/KON/DRAOE/YA	plegaphonia	PLEG/FOEN/YA
plastochromanol	PLA*S/KROEM/NOL	-plegia	PLAOE/JA
plastodynamia	PLA*S/DAOI/NAIM/YA		PLAOEJ/YA
plastogamy	PLAS/TOG/M*I	-plegic	PLAOEJ/IK
plastogel	PLA*S/JEL		PLAOE/JIK
plastomere	PLA*S/MAOER	Plegine	PLEJ/AOEN
plastoquinone	PLA*S/KWIN/OEN	pleiades	PLAOE/DAOEZ

	PLAOI/DAOEZ	pleurodesis	PLAOU/ROD/SIS
pleio-	PLAOI		PLAOUR/OD/SIS
	PLAOI/YO	pleurodynia	PLAOUR/DIN/YA
pleiochloruria	PLAOI/KLOR/YAOUR/YA	pleuroesophageus	PLAOUR/ES/FAI/JUS
pleiotropia	PLAOI/TROEP/YA		PLAOUR/ES/FAIJ/YUS
pleiotropic	PLAOI/TROP/IK	pleurogenic	PLAOUR/JEN/IK
pleiotropism	PLAOI/OT/RO/PIFM	pleurogenous	PLAOUR/ROJ/NOUS
pleiotropy	PLAOI/OT/RO/PI		PLAOUR/OJ/NOUS
pleo-	PLAOE	pleurography	PLAOUR/OG/FI
	PLAOE/YO		PLAOU/ROG/FI
pleochroic	PLAOE/KROIK	pleurohepatitis	PLAOUR/HEP/TAOITS
	PLAOE/KROE/IK	pleurolith	PLAOUR/L*IT
pleochroism	PLAOE/OK/RO/IFM	pleurolysis	PLAOU/ROL/SIS
pleochromatic	PLAOE/KROE/MAT/IK		PLAOU/ROL/SIS
pleochromatism	PLAOE/KROEM/TIFM	pleuromelus	PLAOUR/MAOE/LUS
pleocytosis	PLAOE/SAOI/TOE/SIS	Pleuromonas	PLAOUR/MOE/NAS
pleokaryocyte	PLAOE/KAR/YO/SAO*IT	pleuroparietopexy	PLAOUR/PRAOI/TO/PEK/SI
pleomastia	PLAOE/MA*S/YA	pleuropericardial	PLAOUR/P*ER/KARD/YAL
pleomastic	PLAOE/MA*S/IK	pleuropericarditis	PLAOUR/P*ER/KAR/DAOITS
pleomazia	PLAOE/MAIZ/YA	pleuroperitoneal	PLAOUR/PERT/NAOEL
pleomorphic	PLAOE/MOR/FIK	pleuropneumonia	PLAOUR/NAOU/MOEN/YA
pleomorphism	PLAOE/MOR/FIFM	pleuropneumoniae	PLAOUR/NAOU/MOEN/YAE
pleomorphous	PLAOE/MOR/FOUS	pleuropneumonia-like	PLAOUR/NAOU/MOEN/YA/
pleonasm	PLAOE/NAFM		LAO*IK
pleonectic	PLAOE/NEKT/IK		PLAOUR/NAOU/MOEN/YA/H-F/
pleonexia	PLAOE/NEX/YA		LAOIK
pleonexy	PLAOE/NEK/SI	pleuropneumonolysis	PLAOUR/NAOUM/NOL/SIS
pleonosteosis	PLAOE/NO*S/YOE/SIS	pleuropulmonary	PLAOUR/PUL/MO/NAIR
	PLAOE/ON/O*S/YOE/SIS		PLAOUR/PUM/NAIR
	PLAOE/YON/O*S/YOE/SIS	pleurorrhea	PLAOUR/RAOE/YA
pleonotia	PLAOE/NOE/SHA	pleuroscopy	PLAOUR/ROS/KPI
pleoptics	PLAOE/OPT/IK/-S		PLAOUR/OS/KPI
pleoptophor	PLAOE/OPT/FOER	pleurosoma	PLAOUR/SOE/MA
plerocercoid	PLAOER/SER/KOID	pleurosomus	PLAOUR/SOE/MUS
	PLAOER/SERK/OID	pleurothotonos	PLAOUR/THOT/NOS
plerosis	PLAOE/ROE/SIS	pleurothotonus	PLAOUR/THOT/NUS
	PLE/ROE/SIS	pleurotome	PLAOUR/TOEM
Plesch	PLERB	pleurotomy	PLAOU/ROT/M*I
plesiomorphic	PLAOES/YO/MOR/FIK		PLAOUR/OT/M*I
plesiomorphism	PLAOES/YO/MOR/FIFM	pleurotyphoid	PLAOUR/TAOI/FOID
plesiomorphous	PLAOES/YO/MOR/FOUS	pleurovisceral	PLAOUR/VIS/RAL
plessesthesia	PLES/ES/THAOEZ/YA	plexal	PLEK/SAL
plessigraph	PLES/GRAF		PLEX/SAL
	PLESZ/GRAF	plexalgia	PLEK/SAL/JA
plessimeter	PLE/SIM/TER		PLEX/AL/JA
	PLES/SIM/TER	plexectomy	PLEK/SEKT/M*I
plessimetric	PLES/MET/RIK		PLEX/EKT/M*I
plessor	PLES/SOR	-plexia	PLEX/YA
plethora	PL*ET/RA	plexiform	PLEX/FORM
plethoric	PLE/THOR/IK	pleximeter	PLEK/SIM/TER
	PL*ET/RIK		PLEX/SIM/TER
plethysmo-	PLE/THIZ/MO	pleximetric	PLEX/MET/RIK
plethysmogram	PLE/THIZ/MO/GRAM	pleximetry	PLEK/SIM/TRI
plethysmograph	PLE/THIZ/MO/GRAF		PLEX/SIM/TRI
plethysmography	PL*ET/IS/MOG/FI	plexitis	PLEK/SAOITS
	PL*ET/IZ/MOG/FI		PLEX/AOITS
	PL*ET/SMOG/FI		PLEX/SAOITS
plethysmometry	PL*ET/IS/MOM/TRI	plexogenic	PLEX/JEN/IK
	PL*ET/IZ/MOM/TRI	plexometer	PLEK/SOM/TER
	PL*ET/SMOM/TRI		PLEX/OM/TER
pleur(o)-	PLAOUR		PLEX/SOM/TER
	PLAOU/R(O)	plexopathy	PLEK/SOP/TH*I
	PLAOUR/R(O)		PLEX/OP/TH*I
pleura	PLAOU/RA		PLEX/SOP/TH*I
	PLAOUR/RA	plexor	PLEK/SOR
pleuracentesis	PLAOUR/SEN/TAOE/SIS		PLEX/SOR
pleuracotomy	PLAOUR/KOT/M*I	plexus	PLEK/SUS
pleurae	PLAOU/RAE		PLEX/SUS
	PLAOUR/RAE	-plexy	PLEK/SI
pleural	PLAOURL	pliant	PLAOINT
	PLAOU/RAL	plica	PLAOI/KA
pleuralgia	PLAOU/RAL/JA	plicadentin	PLAOIK/DEN/TIN
	PLAOUR/AL/JA		PLAOI/KA/DEN/TIN
pleuralgic	PLAOU/RAL/JIK	plicae	PLAOI/SAE
	PLAOUR/AL/JIK	plicate	PLAOI/KAIT
pleurapophysis	PLAOUR/POF/SIS	plication	PLAOI/KAIGS
pleurectomy	PLAOU/REKT/M*I		PLI/KAIGS
	PLAOUR/EKT/M*I	plicotomy	PLAOI/KOT/M*I
pleurisy	PLAOUR/SI	pliers	PLAOI/ER/-S
pleuritic	PLAOU/RIT/IK		PLAOIR/-S
pleuritis	PLAOU/RAOITS		PLAOI/ERS
pleuritogenous	PLAOUR/TOJ/NOUS		PLAOIRS
pleurobronchitis	PLAOUR/BRON/KAOITS	Plimmer	PLIM/ER
pleurocele	PLAOUR/SAO*EL	plint	PLINT
pleurocentrum	PLAOUR/SEN/TRUM	plinth	PL*INT
pleurocholecystitis	PLAOUR/KOEL/SIS/TAOITS	-ploid	PLOID
pleuroclysis	PLAOUR/ROK/LI/SIS	ploidy	PLOI/DI
	PLAOUR/OK/LI/SIS	plombage	PLOM/BAJ
pleurocutaneous	PLAOUR/KAOU/TAIN/YOUS		PLOM/BAUJ

plosive	PLOES/IV	pneumatocardia	NAOUM/TO/KARD/YA
plug	PLUG	pneumatocele	NAOUM/TO/SAO*EL
plugger	PLUG/ER	pneumatocephalus	NAOUM/TO/SEF/LUS
plumbago	PLUM/BAI/GOE	pneumatodyspena	NAOUM/TO/DIS/NA
plumbi	PLUM/BAOI		NAOUM/TO/DIS/NAOE/YA
plumbic	PLUM/BIK	pneumatogram	NAOUM/TO/GRAM
plumbism	PLUM/BIFM	pneumatograph	NAOUM/TO/GRAF
plumbotherapy	PLUM/BO/THER/PI	pneumatohemia	NAOUM/TO/HAOEM/YA
plumbum	PLUM/BUM	pneumatology	NAOUM/TOLG
Plummer	PL*UM/ER	pneumatometer	NAOUM/TOM/TER
	PLUM/MER	pneumatometry	NAOUM/TOM/TRI
	(not PLUM/ER; see plumber)	pneumatophore	NAOUM/TO/FOER
plumose	PLAOU/MOES	pneumatorrhachis	NAOUM/TOR/KIS
plumula	PLUM/LA	pneumatoscope	NAOUM/TO/SKOEP
	PLUM/YAOU/LA		NAOU/MAT/SKOEP
	PLUM/YU/LA	pneumatosis	NAOUM/TOE/SIS
Plunket	PLUN/KET	pneumatotherapy	NAOUM/TO/THER/PI
plural	PLURL	pneumatothorax	NAOUM/TO/THOR/AX
pluri-	PLUR	pneumaturia	NAOUM/TAOUR/YA
	PLAOUR	pneumatype	NAOUM/TAOIP
pluricaussal	PLUR/KAU/ZAL	pneumectomy	NAOU/MEKT/M*I
	PLUR/KAU/SAL	pneumencephalography	NAOU/MEN/SEF/LOG/FI
pluricentric	PLUR/SEN/TRIK	pneumoalveolography	NAOUM/AL/VAOE/LOG/FI
pluriceptor	PLUR/SEP/TOR	pneumoamnios	NAOUM/AM/NOS
pluridyscrinia	PLUR/DIS/KRIN/YA		NAOUM/AM/NAOE/YOS
pluriglandular	PLUR/GLAND/LAR	pneumoangiogram	NAOUM/AN/JO/GRAM
plurigravida	PLUR/GRAV/DA	pneumoangiography	NAOUM/AN/JOG/FI
plurilocular	PLUR/LOK/LAR	pneumoarthrography	NAOUM/AR/THROG/FI
plurimenorrhea	PLUR/MEN/RAOE/YA	pneumobacillus	NAOUM/BA/SIL/LUS
plurinatality	PLUR/NAI/TAL/TI	pneumobulbar	NAOUM/BUL/BAR
plurinuclear	PLUR/NAOUK/LAR	pneumobulbous	NAOUM/BUL/BOUS
pluriorificial	PLUR/OR/RI/FIRBL	pneumocardial	NAOUM/KARD/YAL
pluriorificialis	PLUR/OR/FIS/YAI/LIS	pneumocardiograph	NAOUM/KARD/YO/GRAF
	PLUR/OR/FIRB/YAI/LIS	pneumocardiography	NAOUM/KARD/YOG/FI
pluripara	PLAOU/RIP/RA	pneumocele	NAOUM/SAO*EL
pluriparity	PLUR/PAIR/TI	pneumocentesis	NAOUM/SEN/TAOE/SIS
pluripolar	PLUR/POE/LAR	pneumocephalon	NAOUM/SEF/LON
pluripotent	PLAOU/RIP/TENT	pneumocephalus	NAOUM/SEF/LUS
pluripotential	PLUR/POE/TEN/-RBL	pneumocholecystitis	NAOUM/KOEL/SIS/TAOITS
pluripotentiality	PLUR/POE/TEN/SHAL/TI	pneumochysis	NAOU/MOK/SIS
	PLUR/POE/TEN/-RBL/TI	pneumococcal	NAOUM/KOK/KAL
pluriresistant	PLUR/RE/SIS/TANT	pneumococcemia	NAOUM/KOK/SAOEM/YA
pluritissular	PLUR/TIS/LAR	pneumococci	NAOUM/KOK/SAOI
	PLUR/TIRB/LAR	pneumococcic	NAOUM/KOK/SIK
plurivisceral	PLUR/VIS/RAL		NAOUM/KOX/IK
plus	PLUS	pneumococcidal	NAOUM/KOK/SAOI/DAL
plutomania	PLAOU/TO/MAIN/YA	pneumococcolysis	NAOUM/KOK/KOL/SIS
	PLAOUT/MAIN/YA		NAOUM/KOK/OL/SIS
plutonism	PLAOU/TON/IFM	pneumococcosis	NAOUM/KOK/KOE/SIS
	PLAOUT/NIFM	pneumococcosuria	NAOUM/KOK/SAOUR/YA
plutonium	PLAOU/TOEN/YUM	pneumococcus	NAOUM/KOK/KUS
P-mitrale	P-RBGS/MAOI/TRAI/LAOE	pneumocolon	NAOUM/KO/LON
PMS	P-RBGS/M*RBGS/S*RBGS	pneumoconioses	NAOUM/KOEN/YOE/SAOEZ
-pnea	-P/NA	pneumoconiosis	NAOUM/KOEN/YOE/SIS
	-P/NAOE/YA	pneumocrania	NAOUM/KRAIN/YA
	NAOE/YA	pneumocranium	NAOUM/KRAIN/YUM
pneo-	NAOE	pneumocyst	NAOUM/S*IS
	NAOE/YO	pneumocystiasis	NAOUM/SIS/TAOI/SIS
pneodynamics	NAOE/DAOI/NAM/IKS	pneumocystic	NAOUM/S*IS/IK
pneogaster	NAOE/GAS/TER	Pneumocystis	NAOUM/SIS/TIS
	NAOE/GA*S/ER	Pneumocystis carinii	NAOUM/SIS/TIS/KA/RAOIN/YAOI
pneogram	NAOE/GRAM	pneumocystography	NAOUM/SIS/TOG/FI
pneograph	NAOE/GRAF	pneumocystosis	NAOUM/SIS/TOE/SIS
pneometer	NAOE/OM/TER	pneumocystotomography	NAOUM/S*IS/TOE/MOG/FI
	NAOE/YOM/TER	pneumocyte	NAOUM/SAO*IT
pneometry	NAOE/OM/TRI	pneumoderma	NAOUM/DER/MA
	NAOE/YOM/TRI	pneumodograph	NAOU/MOD/GRAF
pneoscope	NAOE/SKOEP	pneumodynamics	NAOUM/DAOI/NAM/IK/-S
pneum(o)-	NAOUM	pneumoempyema	NAOUM/EM/PAOI/E/MA
	NAOU/M(O)	pneumoencephalitis	NAOUM/EN/SEF/LAOITS
pneuma	NAOU/MA	pneumoencephalogram	NAOUM/EN/SEF/LO/GRAM
pneumal	NAOU/MAL	pneumoencephalography	NAOUM/EN/SEF/LOG/FI
pneumarthrogram	NAOU/MAR/THRO/GRAM	pneumoencephalomyelogram	
pneumarthrography	NAOU/MAR/THROG/FI		NAOUM/EN/SEF/LO/MAOI/LO/GRAM
pneumarthrosis	NAOU/MAR/THROE/SIS	pneumoencephalomyelography	
pneumathemia	NAOUM/THAOEM/YA		NAOUM/EN/SEF/LO/MAOI/LOG/FI
pneumat(o)-	NAOUM/T(O)	pneumoencephalos	NAOUM/EN/SEF/LOS
	NAOU/MAT	pneumofasciogram	NAOUM/FAS/YO/GRAM
pneumatic	NAOU/MAT/IK	pneumogalactocele	NAOUM/GLAKT/SAO*EL
pneumaticae	NAOU/MAT/SAE	pneumogastric	NAOUM/GAS/TRIK
pneumatics	NAOU/MAT/IK/-S	pneumogastrography	NAOUM/GAS/TROG/FI
pneumaticum	NAOU/MAT/KUM	pneumogastroscopy	NAOUM/GAS/TROS/KPI
pneumatinuria	NAOU/MAT/NAOUR/YA	pneumogram	NAOUM/GRAM
	NAOUM/TI/NAOUR/YA	pneumograph	NAOUM/GRAF
pneumatism	NAOUM/TIFM	pneumography	NAOU/MOG/FI
pneumatist	NAOUM/T*IS	pneumogynogram	NAOUM/GAOIN/GRAM
pneumatization	NAOUM/TI/ZAIGS	pneumohemia	NAOUM/HAOEM/YA
	NAOU/MAT/ZAIGS		
pneumatized	NAOUM/TAOIZ/-D		

pneumohemopericardium	NAOUM/HAOEM/P*ER/KARD/ YUM	pneumopyothorax	NAOUM/PAOI/THOR/AX
pneumohemothorax	NAOUM/HAOEM/THOR/AX	pneumorachicentesis	NAOUM/RAIK/SEN/TAOE/SIS
pneumohydrometra	NAOUM/HAOI/DRO/MAOE/TRA	pneumorachis	NAOUM/RAI/KIS
pneumohydropericardium	NAOUM/HAOI/DRO/P*ER/KARD/ YUM	pneumoradiography	NAOUM/RAID/YOG/FI
		pneumoresection	NAOUM/RE/S*EBGS
pneumohydroperitoneum	NAOUM/HAOI/DRO/PERT/ NAOEM	pneumoretroperitoneum	NAOUM/RET/RO/PERT/NAOEM
		pneumoroentgenogram	NAOUM/RENT/GEN/GRAM
pneumohydrothorax	NAOUM/HAOI/DRO/THOR/AX	pneumoroentgenography	NAOUM/RENT/GE/NOG/FI
pneumohypoderma	NAOUM/HO*IP/DER/MA		NAOUM/RENT/GEN/OG/FI
pneumokidney	NAOUM/KID/NAOE	pneumorrhachis	NAOUM/RAI/KIS
pneumolith	NAOUM/L*IT		NAOU/MOR/KIS
pneumolithiasis	NAOUM/LI/THAOI/SIS	pneumorrhagia	NAOUM/RAI/JA
pneumology	NAOU/MOLG	pneumoscope	NAOUM/SKOEP
pneumolysis	NAOU/MOL/SIS	pneumosepticemia	NAOUM/SEPT/SAOEM/YA
pneumomalacia	NAOUM/MA/LAI/SHA	pneumoserosa	NAOUM/SE/ROE/SA
pneumomassage	NAOUM/MA/SAJ	pneumoserothorax	NAOUM/SAOER/THOR/AX
	NAOUM/MAS/SAJ	pneumosilicosis	NAOUM/SIL/KOE/SIS
pneumomediastinogram	NAOUM/MAOED/YAS/TAOIN/ GRAM	pneumosintes	NAOUM/SIN/TAOEZ
		pneumotachogram	NAOUM/TAK/GRAM
pneumomediastinography	NAOUM/MAOED/YA*S/NOG/FI	pneumotachograph	NAOUM/TAK/GRAF
pneumomediastinum	NAOUM/MAOED/YAS/TAOIN/UM	pneumotachometer	NAOUM/TA/KOM/TER
	NAOUM/MAOED/YAS/TAOI/NUM		NAOUM/TAK/OM/TER
pneumomelanosis	NAOUM/MEL/NOE/SIS	pneumotaxic	NAOUM/TAX/IK
pneumomometer	NAOU/MOM/TER	pneumotherapy	NAOUM/THER/PI
pneumometry	NAOU/MOM/TRI	pneumothermomassage	NAOUM/THERM/MA/SAJ
pneumomycosis	NAOUM/MAOI/KOE/SIS	pneumothorax	NAOUM/THOR/AX
pneumomyelography	NAOUM/MAOI/LOG/FI	pneumotomography	NAOUM/TOE/MOG/FI
pneumon-	NAOUM/N-	pneumotomy	NAOU/MOT/M*I
	NAOU/MOEN	pneumotropic	NAOUM/TROP/IK
	NAOU/MOE/N-	pneumotropism	NAOU/MOT/RO/PIFM
pneumonectasia	NAOUM/NEK/TAIZ/YA	pneumotympanum	NAOUM/TIFRP/NUM
pneumonectasis	NAOUM/NEKT/SIS	pneumotyphoid	NAOUM/TAOI/FOID
pneumonectomy	NAOUM/NEKT/M*I	pneumotyphus	NAOUM/TAOI/FUS
pneumonedema	NAOU/MOEN/DAOE/MA	Pneumovax	NAOUM/VAX
	NAOU/MON/E/DAOE/MA	pneumoventricle	NAOUM/VEN/TRI/K-L
	NAOU/MON/DAOE/MA		NAOUM/VEN/TRIK/-L
pneumonemia	NAOUM/NAOEM/YA	pneumoventriculi	NAOUM/VEN/TRIK/LAOI
pneumonere	NAOUM/NAOER	pneumoventriculography	NAOUM/VEN/TRIK/LOG/FI
pneumonia	NAOU/MOEN/YA	Pneumovirus	NAOUM/VAOI/RUS
pneumoniae	NAOU/MOEN/YAE	pneusis	NAO*U/SIS
pneumonic	NAOU/MON/IK		(not NAOU/SIS; see knew sis)
pneumonitis	NAOUM/NAOITS	pnigophobia	NAOIG/FOEB/YA
pneumonium	NAOU/MON/YUM		NAOI/GO/FOEB/YA
pneumonocele	NAOU/MON/SAO*EL	Pnu-Imune	NAO*U/IM/MAOUN
pneumonocentesis	NAOUM/NO/SEN/TAOE/SIS		NAOU/H-F/IM/MAOUN
pneumonocirrhosis	NAOUM/NO/SIR/ROE/SIS	p.o.	PO*
pneumonococcal	NAOUM/NO/KOK/KAL	pO2	POE/2
pneumonococcus	NAOUM/NO/KOK/KUS		P*/O*RBGS/2
pneumonoconiosis	NAOUM/NO/KOEN/YOE/SIS	pock	POK
pneumonocyte	NAOU/MON/SAO*IT	pocket	POKT
	NAOUM/NO/SAO*IT		POK/ET
pneumonograph	NAOU/MON/GRAF	pocketed	POKT/-D
pneumonography	NAOUM/NOG/FI		POK/ET/-D
pneumonolysis	NAOUM/NOL/SIS	pockmark	POK/MARK
pneumonomelanosis	NAOUM/NO/MEL/NOE/SIS	poculum	POK/LUM
pneumonometer	NAOUM/NOM/TER	Pod-Ben-25	POD/BEN/25
pneumonomoniliasis	NAOUM/NO/MON/LAOI/SIS	podagra	POE/DAG/RA
pneumonomycosis	NAOUM/NO/MAOI/KOE/SIS	podagral	POE/DAG/RAL
pneumonopathy	NAOUM/NOP/TH*I	podagric	POE/DAG/RIK
pneumonopexy	NAOUM/NO/PEK/SI	podagrous	POE/DAG/ROUS
pneumonophthisis	NAOUM/NOF/THAOI/SIS	podalgia	POE/DAL/JA
pneumonoresection	NAOUM/NO/RE/S*EBGS	podalic	POE/DAL/IK
	NAOU/MOEN/RE/S*EBGS	podarthritis	POD/AR/THRAOITS
pneumonorrhaphy	NAOUM/NOR/FI	podedema	POD/E/DAOE/MA
pneumonosis	NAOUM/NOE/SIS		POD/DAOE/MA
pneumonotherapy	NAOUM/NO/THER/PI	podia	POED/YA
	NAOU/MOEN/THER/PI	podiatric	POE/DAOI/TRIK
pneumonotomy	NAOUM/NOT/M*I	podiatrist	POE/DAOI/TR*IS
Pneumonyssoides	NAOUM/NIS/SOI/DAOEZ	podiatry	POE/DAOI/TRI
Pneumonyssus	NAOUM/NIS/SUS	podismus	POE/DIZ/MUS
pneumo-orbitography	NAOUM/ORB/TOG/FI	poditis	POE/DAOITS
pneumopaludism	NAOUM/PAL/DIFM	podium	POED/YUM
pneumopathy	NAOU/MOP/TH*I	podobromidrosis	POD/BROEM/DROE/SIS
pneumopericardium	NAOUM/P*ER/KARD/YUM	podocyte	POD/SAO*IT
pneumoperitoneal	NAOUM/PERT/NAOEL	pododerm	POD/DERM
pneumoperitoneum	NAOUM/PERT/NAOEM	pododermatitis	POD/DERM/TAOITS
pneumoperitonitis	NAOUM/PERT/NAOITS	pododynamometer	POD/DAOIN/MOM/TER
pneumopexy	NAOUM/PEK/SI	pododynia	POD/DIN/YA
pneumophagia	NAOUM/FAI/JA	podogram	POD/GRAM
pneumophila	NAOU/MOF/LA	podograph	POD/GRAF
pneumophonia	NAOUM/FOEN/YA	podolite	POD/LAOIT
pneumopleuritis	NAOUM/PLAOU/RAOITS	podologist	POE/DO*LGS
pneumopleuroparietopexy	NAOUM/PLAOUR/PRAOI/TO/PEK/ SI	podology	POE/DOLG
		podomechanotherapy	POD/MEK/NO/THER/PI
pneumoprecordium	NAOUM/PRE/KORD/YUM	podometer	POE/DOM/TER
pneumopreperitoneum	NAOUM/PRE/PERT/NAOEM	podophyllin	POD/FLIN
pneumopyelography	NAOUM/PAOI/LOG/FI		POD/FIL/LIN
pneumopyopericardium	NAOUM/PAOI/P*ER/KARD/YUM	podophyllotoxin	POD/FIL/TOK/SIN
		podophyllous	POE/DOF/LOUS

podophyllum	POD/FIL/UM	polarographic	POEL/RO/GRAFK
	POD/FIL/LUM	polarography	POEL/ROG/FI
Podophyllum	K-P/POD/FIL/UM	Polaroid	POEL/ROID
	K-P/POD/FIL/LUM	poldine	POEL/DAOEN
podopompholyx	POED/POM/FLIX		POL/DAOEN
	POED/POM/FO/LIX	pole	POEL
	POE/DO/POM/FLIX	polecki	POE/LEK/KAOI
	POE/DO/POM/FO/LIX		POL/EK/KAOI
podospasm	POD/SPAFM	poli	POE/LAOI
podospasmus	POD/SPAZ/MUS	policapram	POL/KAI/PRAM
podotrochilitis	POD/TROEK/LAOITS	policeman	POE/LAOES/MAN
Poecilia	PAOE/SIL/YA		PO/LAOES/MAN
pogoniasis	POEG/NAOI/SIS		PLIS/MAN
	POE/GO/NAOI/SIS	polio	POEL/YOE
pogonion	POE/GOEN/YON	polio-	POEL/YO
poi	POI	poliocidal	POEL/YO/SAOI/DAL
-poiesis	POI/SIS	polioclastic	POEL/YO/KLA*S/IK
	POI/E/SIS	poliodystrophia	POEL/YO/DIS/TROEF/YA
-poietic	POIT/IK	poliodystrophy	POEL/YO/DIS/TRO/FI
	POI/ET/IK	polioencephalitis	POEL/YO/EN/SEF/LAOTIS
poietin	POI/TIN	polioencephalomeningomyelitis	
	POI/E/TIN		POEL/YO/EN/SEF/LO/ME/NING/
poikilo-	POIK/LO		MAOI/LAOITS
poikiloblast	POIK/LO/BLA*S	polioencephalomyelitis	POEL/YO/EN/SEF/LO/MAOI/
poikilocyte	POIK/LO/SAO*IT		LAOITS
poikilocythemia	POIK/LO/SAOI/THAOEM/YA	polioencephalopathy	POEL/YO/EN/SEF/LOP/TH*I
poikilocytosis	POIK/LO/SAOI/TOE/SIS	polioencephalotropic	POEL/YO/EN/SEF/LO/TROP/IK
poikilodentosis	POIK/LO/DEN/TOE/SIS	poliomyelencephalitis	POEL/YO/MAOI/LEN/SEF/LAOITS
poikiloderma	POIK/LO/DER/MA	poliomyeliticidal	POEL/YO/MAOI/LIT/SAOI/DAL
poikilodermatomyositis	POIK/LO/DERM/TO/MAOI/SAOITS		POEL/YO/MAOI/LAOIT/SAOI/DAL
poikilonymy	POIK/LON/M*I	poliomyelitis	POEL/YO/MAOI/LAOITS
poikiloploid	POIK/LO/PLOID	poliomyeloencephalitis	POEL/YO/MAOI/LO/EN/SEF/
poikiloploidy	POIK/LO/PLOI/DI		LAOITS
poikilosmosis	POIK/LOZ/MOE/SIS	poliomyelopathy	POEL/YO/MAOI/LOP/TH*I
poikilosmotic	POIK/LOZ/MOT/IK	polioneuromere	POEL/YO/NAOUR/MAOER
poikilostasis	POIK/LO/STAI/SIS	polioplasm	POEL/YO/PLAFM
	POIK/LO*S/SIS	poliosis	POEL/YOE/SIS
poikilotherm	POIK/LO/THERM	poliothrix	POEL/YO/THRIX
poikilothermal	POIK/LO/THER/MAL	poliovirus	POEL/YO/VAOI/RUS
poikilothermic	POIK/LO/THERM/IK	poliovirus hominis	POEL/YO/VAOI/RUS/HOM/NIS
poikilothermism	POIK/LO/THERM/IFM	polipropene	POL/PRO/PAOEN
poikilothermous	POIK/LO/THERM/OUS	polish	POL/IRB
poikilothermy	POIK/LO/THER/M*I	polishing	POL/IRB/-G
poikilothrombocyte	POIK/LO/THROM/BO/SAO*IT	polisography	POL/SOG/FI
poikilothymia	POIK/LO/THAOIM/YA	Politzer	POL/IT/ZER
point	POINT		POLT/ZER
pointer	POINT/ER	politzerization	POL/IT/ZER/ZAIGS
pointillage	POINT/YAJ		POLT/ZER/ZAIGS
	POINT/LAJ	polkissen	POEL/KIS/-N
Point-Two Dental Rinse	POINT/TWO/DEN/TAL/RINS		POL/KIS/-N
Poirier	POIR/YAI	poll	POL
	POIR/YAIR	pollakidipsia	POL/KI/DIPS/YA
poise	POIZ		POL/KAOE/DIPS/YA
Poiseuille	POIZ/YAOE	pollakisuria	POL/KI/SAOUR/YA
	POIS/YAOE		POL/KAOE/SAOUR/YA
	POI/ZU/YAOE	pollakiuria	POL/KI/YAOUR/YA
poison	POI/SON		POL/KI/YAOUR/YA
poison ivy	POI/SON/AOIV/VI	polled	POL/-D
poison oak	POI/SON/OEK	pollen	POL/-N
poison sumac	POI/SON/SAOU/MAK	pollenarium	POL/NAIRM
poisoning	POI/SON/-G		POL/NAIR/YUM
poisonous	POIZ/NOUS	pollenogenic	POL/NO/JEN/IK
	POI/SON/OUS	pollex	POL/LEX
poker	POEK/ER		POL/EX
pokeroot	POEK/RAOT	pollices	POL/SAOEZ
pokeweed	POEK/WAOED	pollicis	POL/SIS
polacrilin	POL/KRIL/LIN	pollicization	POL/SI/ZAIGS
Poland	POE/LAND	pollinate	POL/NAIT
polar	POE/LAR	pollination	POL/NAIGS
Polaramine	POE/LAR/MAOEN	pollinium	PO/LIN/YUM
polarimeter	POEL/RIM/TER		POL/LIN/YUM
polarimetry	POEL/RIM/TRI	pollinosis	POL/NOE/SIS
polariscope	POE/LAIR/SKOEP	pollodic	PO/LOED/IK
	POE/LAR/SKOEP		POL/LOED/IK
polariscopic	POE/LAIR/SKOP/IK	pollution	PO/LAOUGS
	POE/LAR/SKOP/IK		PLAOUGS
polariscopy	POEL/RIS/KPI	Polocaine	POEL/KAIN
polaristrobometer	POE/LAIR/STROE/BOM/TER		POE/LO/KAIN
	POE/LAR/STROE/BOM/TER	polocyte	POEL/SAO*IT
polarity	POE/LAIR/TI		POE/LO/SAO*IT
	POE/LAR/TI	polonium	POE/LOEN/YUM
polarization	POE/LAR/ZAIGS	poloxalene	POL/OX/LAOEN
	POEL/RI/ZAIGS	poloxalkol	POL/OK/SAL/KOL
polarize	POEL/RAOIZ		POL/OX/AL/KOL
	POE/LAR/AOIZ	poloxamer	POL/OX/MER
polarizer	POEL/RAOIZ/ER	polster	POL/STER
	POE/LAR/AOIZ/ER		(not POEL/STER; see pollster)
polarogram	POE/LAR/GRAM	poltophagy	POL/TOF/JI
	POE/LAIR/GRAM	polus	POE/LUS

poly	POL/LI	polyclonal	POL/KLOENL
poly-	POL	polyclonia	POL/KLOEN/YA
Polya	POEL/YA	polycoria	POL/KOR/YA
polyacid	POL/AS/ID		POL/KOER/YA
polyacrylamide	POL/AI/KRIL/MAOID	Polycose	POL/KOES
polyadenia	POL/AI/DAOEN/YA	polycrotic	POL/KROT/IK
polyadenitis	POL/AD/NAOITS	polycrotism	PO/LIK/RO/TIFM
polyadenoma	POL/AD/NOE/MA		POL/IK/RO/TIFM
polyadenomatosis	POL/AD/NOEM/TOE/SIS		PLIK/RO/TIFM
polyadenopathy	POL/AD/NOP/TH*I	polycyclic	POL/SAOIK/LIK
polyadenosis	POL/AD/NOE/SIS	polycyesis	POL/SAOI/E/SIS
polyadenous	POL/AD/NOUS	polycystic	POL/S*IS/IK
polyagglutinability	POL/AI/GLAOUT/NABLT	polycysticum	POL/S*IS/KUM
polyalcohol	POL/KHOL	polycystoma	POL/SIS/TOE/MA
	POL/AL/KHOL	polycyte	POL/SAO*IT
polyalcoholism	POL/KHOL/IFM	polycythemia	POL/SAOI/THAOEM/YA
	POL/AL/KHOL/IFM	polydactylia	POL/DAK/TIL/YA
polyalgesia	POL/AI/JAOEZ/YA	polydactylism	POL/DAKT/LIFM
polyallelism	POL/AI/LAOEL/IFM	polydactylous	POL/DAKT/LOUS
polyamine	POL/AM/MIN	polydactyly	POL/DAKT/LI
	POL/AM/AOEN	polydentia	POL/DEN/SHA
	POL/AM/MAOEN	polydipsia	POL/DIPS/YA
polyandry	POL/AN/DRI	polydispersoid	POL/DIS/PER/SOID
Polyangiaceae	POL/AN/JAIS/YAE		POL/DIS/PERS/OID
polyangiitis	POL/AN/JAOITS	polydyscrinia	POL/DIS/KRIN/YA
Polyangium	POL/AN/JUM	polydysplasia	POL/DIS/PLAIZ/YA
polyanion	POL/AN/AOIN	polydysplastic	POL/DIS/PLA*S/IK
	POL/A*N/AOIN	polydysspondylism	POL/DIS/SPOND/LIFM
polyarteritis	POL/ART/RAOITS	polydystrophia	POL/DIS/TROEF/YA
polyarthric	POL/AR/THRIK	polydystrophic	POL/DIS/TROFK
polyarthritis	POL/AR/THRAOITS	polydystrophy	POL/DIS/TRO/FI
polyarticular	POL/AR/TIK/LAR	polyelectrolyte	POL/LEK/TRO/LAOIT
polyatomic	POL/AI/TOM/IK	polyembryony	POL/EM/BRAOE/N*I
polyavitaminosis	POL/AI/VAOIT/MI/NOE/SIS	polyendocrine	POL/*END/KRIN
polyaxon	POL/AK/SON	polyendocrinoma	POL/*END/KRI/NOE/MA
polyaxonic	POL/AK/SON/IK	polyene	POL/AOEN
polybasic	POL/BAIS/IK		POL/YAOEN
polyblast	POL/BLA*S	polyenic	POL/AOEN/IK
polyblennia	POL/BLEN/YA		POL/YAOEN/IK
polybutilate	POL/BAOUT/LAIT	polyerg	POL/ERG
polycarbophil	POL/KARB/FIL	polyergic	POL/ERJ/IK
polycardia	POL/KARD/YA	polyesthesia	POL/ES/THAOEZ/YA
polycellular	POL/SEL/YAOU/LAR	polyesthetic	POL/ES/THET/IK
polycentric	POL/SEN/TRIK	polyestradiol phosphate	POL/ES/TRA/DI/OL/FOS/FAIT
polycentricity	POL/SEN/TRIS/TI	polyestrous	POL/ES/TROUS
polycheiria	POL/KAOIR/YA	polyethadene	POL/*ET/DAOEN
polychemotherapy	POL/KAOEM/THER/PI	polyethylene	POL/*ET/LAOEN
polychlorinated	POL/KLOR/NAIT/-D	polyethylene glycol	POL/*ET/LAOEN/GLAOI/KOL
polychloruria	POL/KLOR/YAOUR/YA	polyferose	POL/FER/OES
polycholia	POL/KOEL/YA	polyfolliculinic	POL/FLIK/LIN/IK
polychondritis	POL/KON/DRAOITS	polyfructose	POL/FRUK/TOES
polychondropathia	POL/KON/DRO/PA*T/YA	polygalactia	POL/GLAK/SHA
polychondropathy	POL/KON/DROP/TH*I	polygalacturonase	POL/GLAK/TAOUR/NAIS
polychrest	POL/KR*ES	polygalacturonic	POL/GLAK/TAOU/RON/IK
polychromasia	POL/KROE/MAIZ/YA		POL/GLAKT/RON/IK
polychromatia	POL/KROE/MAI/SHA	polygamy	PLIG/M*I
polychromatic	POL/KROE/MAT/IK		PO/LIG/M*I
polychromatocyte	POL/KROE/MAT/SAO*IT		POE/LIG/M*I
polychromatocytosis	POL/KROEM/TO/SAOI/TOE/SIS	polyganglionic	POL/GANG/LON/IK
polychromatophil	POL/KROE/MAT/FIL	polygen	POL/JEN
	POL/KROEM/TO/FIL	polygene	POL/JAOEN
polychromatophile	POL/KROE/MAT/FAOIL	polygenic	POL/JEN/IK
	POL/KROEM/TO/FAOIL	polyglactin	POL/GLAK/TIN
polychromatophilia	POL/KROEM/TO/FIL/YA	polyglandular	POL/GLAND/LAR
polychromatophilic	POL/KROEM/TO/FIL/IK	polyglucosic	POL/GLAOU/KOES/IK
polychromatosis	POL/KROEM/TOE/SIS	polyglutamate	POL/GLAOUT/MAIT
polychrome	POL/KROEM	polyglutamic	POL/GLAOU/TAM/IK
polychromemia	POL/KROE/MAOEM/YA	polyglycolic	POL/GLAOI/KOL/IK
polychromia	POL/KROEM/YA	polygnathus	POL/NA*T/OUS
polychromic	POL/KROEM/IK		PO/LIG/NA/THUS
polychromophil	POL/KROEM/FIL		PLIG/NA/THUS
polychromophilia	POL/KROEM/FIL/YA	polygram	POL/GRAM
polychylia	POL/KAOIL/YA	polygraph	POL/GRAF
Polycillin	POL/SLIN	polygyny	PLIJ/N*I
	POL/SIL/LIN		PO/LIJ/N*I
Polycillin-N	POL/SLIN/N-RBGS		POE/LIJ/N*I
	POL/SIL/LIN/N-RBGS	polygyria	POL/JAOIR/YA
Polycillin-PRB	POL/SLIN/P-RBGS/R*RBGS/	polyhedral	POL/HAOE/DRAL
	B*RBGS	polyhedron	POL/HAOE/DRON
	POL/SIL/LIN/P-RBGS/R*RBGS/	polyhexose	POL/HEX/OES
	B*RBGS		POL/HEK/SOES
polycinematosomnography	POL/SIN/MA/TO/SOM/NOG/FI	polyhidrosis	POL/HAOI/DROE/SIS
Polycitra	POL/SIT/RA		POL/HID/ROE/SIS
	POL/SI/TRA		POL/HI/DROE/SIS
Polycitra-K	POL/SIT/RA/K-RBGS	Poly-Histine	POL/HIS/TAOEN
	POL/SI/TRA/K-RBGS	Poly-Histine CS	POL/HIS/TAOEN/KR-RBGS/
Polycitra-LC	POL/SIT/RA/L-RBGS/KR*RBGS		S*RBGS
	POL/SI/TRA/L-RBGS/KR*RBGS	Poly-Histine-D	POL/HIS/TAOEN/D-RBGS
polyclinic	POL/KLIN/IK	Poly-Histine DM	POL/HIS/TAOEN/D-RBGS/

	M*RBGS
polyhybrid	POL/HAOI/BRID
polyhydramnios	POL/HAOI/DRAM/NOS
	POL/HAOI/DRAM/NAOE/OS
polyhydric	POL/HAOI/DRIK
polyhydruria	POL/HAOI/DRAOUR/YA
polyhypermenorrhea	POL/HAO*IP/MEN/RAOE/YA
polyhypomenorrhea	POL/HO*IP/MEN/RAOE/YA
polyidrosis	POL/YI/DROE/SIS
	POL/ID/ROE/SIS
polyinfection	POL/IN/F*EBGS
polyionic	POL/AOIN/IK
	POL/AOI/ON/IK
polykaryocyte	POL/KAR/YO/SAO*IT
polylecithal	POL/LES/THAL
polyleptic	POL/LEPT/IK
polylogia	POL/LOE/JA
polylysine	POL/LAOI/SAOEN
polymacon	POL/MAI/KON
polymastia	POL/MA*S/YA
Polymastigida	POL/MAS/TIJ/DA
	POL/MA*S/GAOI/DA
polymastigote	POL/MA*S/GOET
polymazia	POL/MAIZ/YA
polymelia	POL/MAOEL/YA
polymelus	POE/LIM/LUS
	PLIM/LUS
polymenia	POL/MAOEN/YA
polymenorrhea	POL/MEN/RAOE/YA
polymer	POL/MER
polymerase	PO/LIM/RAIS
	POE/LIM/RAIS
	PLIM/RAIS
polymeria	POL/MAOER/YA
polymeric	POL/MER/IK
polymerid	PO/LIM/RID
	POE/LIM/RID
	POL/MER/ID
polymerism	PO/LIM/RIFM
	POE/LIM/RIFM
	POL/MER/IFM
polymerization	POL/MER/ZAIGS
	PO/LIM/RI/ZAIGS
	POE/LIM/RI/ZAIGS
polymerize	POL/MER/AOIZ
	PO/LIM/RAOIZ
	POE/LIM/RAOIZ
polymetacarpalia	POL/MET/KAR/PAIL/YA
polymetacarpalism	POL/MET/KARP/LIFM
	POL/MET/KAR/PAL/IFM
polymetacarpia	POL/MET/KARP/YA
polymetatarsalia	POL/MET/TAR/SAIL/YA
polymetatarsalism	POL/MET/TARS/LIFM
	POL/MET/TAR/SAL/IFM
polymetatarsia	POL/MET/TARS/YA
polymicrobial	POL/MAOI/KROEB/YAL
polymicrobic	POL/MAOI/KROEB/IK
polymicrogyria	POL/MAOI/KRO/JAOIR/YA
polymicrolipomatosis	POL/MAOI/KRO/LIP/MA/TOE/SIS
	POL/MAOI/KRO/LI/POEM/TOE/SIS
polymicrotome	POL/MAOI/KRO/TOEM
polymitus	PO/LIM/TUS
	PLIM/TUS
polymorph	POL/MOR/-F
polymorphic	POL/MOR/FIK
polymorphism	POL/MOR/FIFM
polymorphocellular	POL/MOR/FO/SEL/YAOU/LAR
polymorphocyte	POL/MOR/FO/SAO*IT
polymorphonuclear	POL/MOR/FO/NAOUK/LAR
polymorphous	POL/MOR/FOUS
Polymox	POL/MOX
polymyalgia	POL/MAOI/AL/JA
polymyarian	POL/MAOI/AIRN
polymyoclonus	POL/MAOI/OK/LO/NUS
polymyopathy	POL/MAOI/OP/TH*I
polymyositis	POL/MAOI/SAOITS
polymyxa	POL/MIK/SA
polymyxin	POL/MIK/SIN
polynesic	POL/NAOES/IK
	POL/NAOEZ/IK
polynesiensis	POL/NAOEZ/YEN/SIS
	POL/NAOES/YEN/SIS
polyneural	POL/NAOURL
polyneuralgia	POL/NAOU/RAL/JA
	POL/NAOUR/AL/JA
polyneuric	POL/NAOUR/IK
polyneuritic	POL/NAOU/RIT/IK
polyneuritis	POL/NAOU/RAOITS

polyneuromyositis	POL/NAOUR/MAOI/SAOITS
polyneuronitis	POL/NAOUR/NAOITS
polyneuropathy	POL/NAOU/ROP/TH*I
polyneuroradiculitis	POL/NAOUR/RA/DIK/LAOITS
polynoxylin	POL/NOX/LIN
polynuclear	POL/NAOUK/LAR
polynucleate	POL/NAOUK/LAIT
polynucleated	POL/NAOUK/LAIT/-D
polynucleosis	POL/NAOUK/LOE/SIS
polynucleotidase	POL/NAOUK/LO/TAOI/DAIS
	POL/NAOUK/LO/TAOID/AIS
polynucleotide	POL/NAOUK/LO/TAOID
polyodontia	POL/O/DON/SHA
polyol	POL/OL
	POL/YOL
polyomavirus	POL/OEM/VAOI/RUS
polyoncosis	POL/ON/KOE/SIS
polyonychia	POL/O/NIK/YA
polyopia	POL/OEP/YA
polyopsia	POL/OPS/YA
polyorchidism	POL/ORK/DIFM
polyorchis	POL/OR/KIS
polyorchism	POL/OR/KIFM
polyostotic	POL/OS/TOT/IK
polyotia	POL/O/SHA
	POL/YOE/SHA
polyovular	POL/OV/LAR
polyovulatory	POL/OV/LA/TOIR
polyoxyethylene	POL/OX/*ET/LAOEN
polyoxyl	POL/OK/SIL
	POL/OX/IL
polyp	POL/IP
polypapilloma	POL/PAP/LOE/MA
polypapilloma tropicum	POL/PAP/LOE/MA/TROP/KUM
polyparasitism	POL/PAR/SAOIT/IFM
polyparesis	POL/PA/RAOE/SIS
	POL/PAR/SIS
polypathia	POL/PA*T/YA
polypectomy	PO/LIP/EKT/M*I
	POL/PEKT/M*I
polypeptidase	POL/PEPT/DAIS
polypeptide	POL/PEP/TAOID
polypeptidemia	POL/PEPT/DAOEM/YA
polypeptidorrhachia	POL/PEPT/DO/RAIK/YA
polyperiostitis	POL/P*ER/OS/TAOITS
polyphagia	POL/FAI/JA
polyphalangia	POL/FLAN/JA
polyphalangism	POL/FLAN/JIFM
polyphallic	POL/FAL/IK
polypharmaceutic	POL/FARM/SAOUT/IK
polypharmacy	POL/FARM/SI
polyphase	POL/FAEZ
	POL/FAIZ
polyphasic	POL/FAEZ/IK
	POL/FAIZ/IK
polyphenic	POL/FAOEN/IK
	POL/FEN/IK
polyphenol	POL/FAOE/NOL
polyphenol oxidase	POL/FAOE/NOL/OX/DAIS
polyphobia	POL/FOEB/YA
polyphosphorylase	POL/FOS/FOER/LAIS
polyphrasia	POL/FRAIZ/YA
polyphyletic	POL/FAOI/LET/IK
polyphyletism	POL/FAOIL/TIFM
polyphyletist	POL/FAOIL/T*IS
polyphyodont	POL/FAOI/DONT
polypi	POL/PAOI
polypiform	POL/IP/FORM
	PO/LIP/FORM
polypionia	POL/PAOI/OEN/YA
polyplasmia	POL/PLAZ/MAOE/YA
polyplast	POL/PLA*S
polyplastic	POL/PLA*S/IK
Polyplax	POL/PLAX
polyplegia	POL/PLAOE/JA
polypleurodiaphragmotomy	POL/PLAOUR/DAOI/FRAM/OT/M*I
polyploid	POL/PLOID
polyploidy	POL/PLOI/DI
polypnea	POL/IP/NAOE/YA
polypneic	POL/IP/NAOE/IK
	POL/IP/NIK
polypodia	POL/POED/YA
polypoid	POL/IP/OID
	POL/POID
polypoidosis	POL/POI/DOE/SIS
polyporin	PO/LIP/RIN
	POL/IP/RIN
polyporous	PO/LIP/ROUS

	POL/IP/ROUS	polytrophic	POL/TROFK
Polyporus	PO/LIP/RUS		POL/TROEFK
	POL/IP/RUS	polytrophy	PO/LIT/RO/FI
polyposa	POL/POE/SA		POE/LIT/RO/FI
polyposia	POL/POEZ/YA	polytropic	POL/TROP/IK
polyposis	POL/POE/SIS	polytropous	PO/LIT/RO/POUS
polypotome	PO/LIP/TOEM		POE/LIT/RO/POUS
	POL/IP/TOEM	polyunguia	POL/UNG/WA
polypotrite	PO/LIP/TRAOIT		POL/UNG/WAOE/YA
	POL/IP/TRAOIT	polyunsaturated	POL/UN/SAFP/RAIT/-D
polypous	POL/POUS	polyuria	POL/YAOUR/YA
	POL/IP/OUS	polyvalent	POL/VAIL/ENT
polypragmasy	POL/PRAG/MA/SI		POL/VAI/LENT
polyptychial	POL/TIK/YAL		PO/LIV/LENT
	POL/TAOIK/YAL		POE/LIV/LENT
polypus	POL/PUS		PLIV/LENT
polyradiculitis	POL/RA/DIK/LAOITS	Poly-Vi-Flor	POL/VAOI/FLOR
polyradiculomyopathy	POL/RA/DIK/LO/MAOI/OP/TH*I	polyvinyl	POL/VAOINL
polyradiculoneuritis	POL/RA/DIK/LO/NAOU/RAOITS		POL/VAOI/NIL
polyradiculoneuropathy	POL/RA/DIK/LO/NAOU/ROP/TH*I	polyvinylacetate	POL/VAOINL/AS/TAIT
polyradiculopathy	POL/RA/DIK/LOP/TH*I	polyvinylbenzene	POL/VAOINL/BEN/ZAOEN
polyribonucleotide	POL/RAOIB/NAOUK/LO/TAOID	polyvinyl chloride	POL/VAOINL/KLOR/AOID
polyribosome	POL/RAOIB/SOEM	polyvinylpyrrolidone	POL/VAOINL/PIR/ROL/DOEN
polyrrhea	POL/RAOE/YA		POL/VAOINL/PI/ROL/DOEN
polys	POL/LI/-S	Poly-Vi-Sol	POL/VAOI/SOL
polysaccharide	POL/SAK/RAOID	Poly-Vitamin Fluoride	POL/VAOIT/MIN/FLAOUR/
polysarcia	POL/SARS/YA	Tablets	AOID/TAB/LET/-S
polysarcous	POL/SARK/OUS	polyzoic	POL/ZOIK
polyscelia	POL/SAOEL/YA		POL/ZOE/IK
polyscelus	PO/LIS/LUS	polyzygotic	POL/ZAOI/GOT/IK
	POE/LIS/LUS	polyzygous	POL/ZAOIG/OUS
polyscope	POL/SKOEP	pomade	POE/MAID
polysensitivity	POL/SENS/TIV/TI		POE/MAUD
polysensory	POL/SENS/RI	pomatum	POE/MAI/TUM
polyserositis	POL/SAOER/SAOITS	pomegranate	POM/GRAN/NAT
polysialia	POL/SAOI/AIL/YA		POM/GRA/NAT
polysinuitis	POL/SAOIN/YAOITS	pompholyhemia	POM/FLI/HAOEM/YA
polysinusectomy	POL/SAOIN/SEKT/M*I		POM/FO/LI/HAOEM/YA
polysinusitis	POL/SAOIN/SAOITS	pompholyx	POM/FLIX
polysomatic	POL/SMAT/IK		POM/FO/LIX
	POL/SOE/MAT/IK		POM/FOE/LIX
polysomaty	POL/SOEM/TI	pomphus	POM/FUS
polysome	POL/SOEM	pomum	POE/MUM
polysomia	POL/SOEM/YA	Ponaris	POE/NAIR/RIS
polysomic	POL/SOEM/IK		POE/NAR/RIS
polysomnogram	POL/SOM/NO/GRAM	ponceau	PON/SOE
polysomnography	POL/SOM/NOG/FI	ponderable	POND/RABL
polysomus	POL/SOE/MUS		POND/DERBL
polysomy	POL/SOE/M*I	ponderal	POND/RAL
polysorbate	POL/SOR/BAIT	Pondimin	POND/MIN
polyspermia	POL/SPERM/YA		POND/MAOEN
polyspermism	POL/SPERM/IFM	pondostatural	POND/STAFP/RAL
polyspermy	POL/SPER/M*I		PON/DO/STAFP/RAL
polysplenia	POL/SPLAOEN/YA	ponesiatrics	PO/NAOEZ/YAT/RIK/-S
Polysporin	POL/SPORN		POE/NAOEZ/YAT/RIK/-S
polysteraxic	POL/STER/AX/IK	Ponfick	PON/FIK
	POL/STRAX/IK	Pongidae	PON/JI/DAE
polystichia	POL/STIK/YA	pono-	POEN
polysulfide rubber	POL/SUL/FAOID/RUB/ER		POE/NO
polysurgical	POL/SURJ/KAL	ponograph	POEN/GRAF
polysuspensoid	POL/SUS/PEN/SOID	ponopalmosis	POEN/PAL/MOE/SIS
polysymbrachydactyly	POL/SIM/BRAK/DAKT/LI	ponophobia	POEN/FOEB/YA
polysynaptic	POL/SNAPT/IK	ponos	POE/NOS
	POL/SIN/APT/IK	pons	PONZ
polysyndactyly	POL/SIN/DAKT/LI	pons-oblongata	PONZ/OB/LON/GAI/TA
polytef	POL/TEF		PONZ/OB/LON/GA/TA
polytendinitis	POL/TEND/NAOITS	Ponstel	PON/STEL
polytendinobursitis	POL/TEND/NO/BUR/SAOITS	pont(o)-	PONT
polytene	POL/TAOEN		PON/T(O)
polyteny	POL/TAOE/N*I	pontes	PON/TAOEZ
polytetrafluoroethylene	POL/TET/RA/FLAOUR/*ET/	pontibrachium	PONT/BRAIK/YUM
	LAOEN		PONT/BRAK/YUM
polythelia	POL/THAOEL/YA	pontic	PONT/IK
polythelism	POL/THAOEL/IFM		PON/TIK
	POL/THAOE/LIFM	ponticular	PON/TIK/LAR
polythene	POL/THAOEN	ponticulus	PON/TIK/LUS
polythetic	POL/THET/IK	pontil	PON/TIL
polythiazide	POL/THAOI/ZAOID	pontile	PON/TAOIL
polytocous	PO/LIT/KOUS		PON/TAOEL
	POE/LIT/KOUS	pontine	PON/TAOIN
polytomogram	POL/TOEM/GRAM		PON/TAOEN
polytomographic	POL/TOEM/GRAFK	pontis	PON/TIS
polytomography	POL/TOE/MOG/FI	pontobulbar	PONT/BUL/BAR
polytrichia	POL/TRIK/YA	pontobulbare	PONT/BUL/BAI/RAOE
polytrichosis	POL/TRI/KOE/SIS	pontobulbia	PONT/BUL/BAOE/YA
Polytrichum	PO/LIT/RI/KUM		PONT/BUL/-B/YA
	POE/LIT/RI/KUM	Pontocaine	PONT/KAIN
	PLIT/RI/KUM	pontocerebellar	PONT/SER/BEL/LAR
polytrophia	POL/TROEF/YA	pontomedullary	PONT/MED/LAIR

pontomesencephalic	PONT/MES/EN/SFAL/IK
pontoon	PON/TAON
pontopeduncular	PONT/PE/DUN/KLAR
	PONT/PE/DUNG/LAR
pool	PAOL
Pool	K-P/PAOL
poor	PAOR
poples	POP/LAOEZ
poplitea	POP/LIT/YA
	POP/LI/TAOE/YA
popliteal	POP/LIT/YAL
	POP/LI/TAOEL
poplitei	POP/LIT/YAOI
	POP/LI/TAOE/YAOI
popliteum	POP/LIT/YUM
	POP/LI/TAOE/YUM
popliteus	POP/LIT/YUS
	POP/LI/TAOE/YUS
poppet	POP/ET
poppy	POP/PI
population	POP/LAIGS
por-	POR
	POER
	PO/R-
	POE/R-
poradenia	POR/DAOEN/YA
poradenitis	POR/AD/NAOITS
poradenolymphitis	POR/AD/NO/LIM/FAOITS
poral	POERL
	PORL
	POER/RAL
	POR/RAL
porcelain	PORS/LIN
	PORS/LAIN
porcelaneous	PORS/LAIN/YOUS
porci	POR/SAOI
porcine	POR/SAOIN
	POR/SAOEN
pore	POER
	(not POR; frequent word beginning)
porencephalia	POR/EN/SFAIL/YA
porencephalic	POR/EN/SFAL/IK
porencephalitis	POR/EN/SEF/LAOITS
porencephalous	POR/EN/SEF/LOUS
porencephaly	POR/EN/SEF/LI
Porges	POR/GES
pori	POR/RAOI
	POE/RAOI
poria	POR/YA
Porifera	POE/RIF/RA
	POR/RIF/RA
poriomania	POR/YO/MAIN/YA
porion	POR/YON
porocele	POR/SAO*EL
porocephaliasis	POR/SEF/LAOI/SIS
Porocephalida	POR/SFAL/DA
Porocephalidae	POR/SFAL/DAE
porocephalosis	POR/SEF/LOE/SIS
Porocephalus	POR/SEF/LUS
poroconidium	POR/KO/NID/YUM
porofocon	POR/FOE/KON
porokeratosis	POR/KER/TOE/SIS
porokeratotic	POR/KER/TOT/IK
poroma	POR/ROE/MA
	POR/O/MA
poroplastic	POR/PLA*S/IK
porosis	POR/ROE/SIS
	POR/O/SIS
	POE/ROE/SIS
porosity	POR/ROS/TI
	POR/OS/TI
	POE/ROS/TI
porospore	POR/SPOER
porotic	POR/ROT/IK
	POR/OT/IK
	POE/ROT/IK
porotomy	POR/OT/M*I
	POE/ROT/M*I
porous	POER/OUS
	POR/OUS
porphin	POR/FIN
porphobilin	POR/FO/BAOI/LIN
	POR/FO/B*I/LIN
	POR/FO/BIL/LIN
porphobilinogen	POR/FO/BAOI/LIN/JEN
	POR/FO/B*I/LIN/JEN
	POR/FO/BIL/LIN/JEN
porphobilinogenuria	POR/FO/BAOI/LIN/JEN/YAOUR/YA

	POR/FO/B*I/LIN/JEN/YAOUR/YA
	POR/FO/BIL/LIN/JEN/YAOUR/YA
porphyr(o)-	POR/FR(O)
	POR/FI/R(O)
	POR/FIR
porphyria	POR/FIR/YA
porphyrin	POR/FRIN
porphyrinemia	POR/FIR/NAOEM/YA
	POR/FRI/NAOEM/YA
	POR/FRIN/AOEM/YA
porphyrinogen	POR/FRIN/JEN
porphyrinopathy	POR/FIR/NOP/TH*I
	POR/FRO/NOP/TH*I
	POR/FRIN/OP/TH*I
porphyrinuria	POR/FIR/NAOUR/YA
	POR/FRI/NAOUR/YA
	POR/FRIN/YAOUR/YA
porphyrism	POR/FRIFM
porphyrismus	POR/FRIZ/MUS
porphyrization	POR/FRI/ZAIGS
	POR/FIR/ZAIGS
porphyruria	POR/FRAOUR/YA
	POR/FI/RAOUR/YA
	POR/FIR/YAOUR/YA
Porro	POR/ROE
porta	POR/TA
port(o)-	PORT
	POR/T(O)
portacaval	PORT/KAIVL
portacid	POR/TAS/ID
	PORT/AS/ID
portae	POR/TAE
Portagen	POR/TA/JEN
	PO*RT/JEN
	(not PORT/JEN; see port general(ly))
portal	POR/TAL
portcaustic	PORT/KA*US/IK
porter	PORT/ER
Porter	K-P/PORT/ER
Porteus	PORT/YUS
portio	POR/SHOE
portiones	POR/SHOE/NAOEZ
portiplexus	PORT/PLEK/SUS
portligature	PORT/LIG/KHUR
portobilioarterial	PORT/BIL/YO/AR/TAOERL
portoenterostomy	PORT/SPWRO*S/M*I
portogram	PORT/GRAM
portography	POR/TOG/FI
portosystemic	PORT/SIS/TEM/IK
	PORT/S-M/IK
portoumbilical	PORT/UM/BIL/KAL
portovenogram	PORT/VAOEN/GRAM
portovenography	PORT/VAOE/NOG/FI
Portuguese	POR/KHU/GAOEZ
	POR/TAOU/GAOEZ
porus	POR/RUS
	POE/RUS
posed	POEZ/-D
-posia	POEZ/YA
position	POGS
	PO/SIGS
positioner	POGS/ER
	PO/SIGS/ER
positive	POZ/TIV
positivity	POZ/TIV/TI
positrocephalogram	POZ/TRO/SEF/LO/GRAM
positron	POZ/TRON
Posner	POES/NER
posologic	POES/LOJ/IK
	POE/SO/LOJ/IK
posology	POE/SOLG
possum	POS/UM
	POS/SUM
post	PO*ES
post-	PO*S
postabortal	PO*S/AI/BOR/TAL
postaccessual	PO*S/AK/SERBL
	PO*S/AK/SES/YAOUL
	PO*S/AK/SES/YUL
postacetabular	PO*S/AS/TAB/LAR
postacidotic	PO*S/AS/DOT/IK
postadolescence	PO*S/AD/LES/ENS
postadolescent	PO*S/AD/LES/ENT
postalbumin	PO*S/AL/BAOU/MIN
postanal	PO*S/AINL
postanesthesia	PO*S/ANS/THAOEZ/YA
postanesthetic	PO*S/ANS/THET/IK
postapoplectic	PO*S/AP/PLEKT/IK

postaural	PO*S/AURL	posterotemporal	PO*S/RO/TEFRP/RAL
postaurale	PO*S/AU/RAI/LAOE	posterotransverse	PO*S/RO/TRA*NS/VERS
postauricular	PO*S/AU/RIK/LAR	posterula	POS/TER/LA
postaxial	PO*S/AX/YAL		POS/TER/YAOU/LA
postbrachial	PO*S/BRAIK/YAL		POS/TER/YU/LA
postbrachium	PO*S/BRAIK/YUM	postesophageal	PO*S/E/SOF/JAOEL
postbranchial	PO*S/BRANG/YAL	postestrus	PO*S/ES/TRUS
postbuccal	PO*S/BUK/KAL	postestrum	PO*S/ES/TRUM
postbulbar	PO*S/BUL/BAR	postethmoid	PO*S/*ET/MOID
postcalcaneal	PO*S/KAL/KAIN/YAL	postexed	POES/TEX/-D
postcapillary	PO*S/KAP/LAIR		POS/TEX/-D
postcardial	PO*S/KARD/YAL	postexion	POES/T*EBGS
postcardinal	PO*S/KARD/NAL		POS/T*EBGS
postcardiotomy	PO*S/KARD/YOT/M*I	postfebrile	PO*S/FEB/RAOIL
postcava	PO*S/KAI/VA		PO*S/FEB/RIL
postcaval	PO*S/KAIVL		PO*S/FAOE/BRIL
postcecal	PO*S/SE/KAL	postfundibular	PO*S/FUN/DIB/LAR
postcentral	PO*S/SEN/TRAL	postganglionic	PO*S/GANG/LON/IK
	PO*S/STRAL	postgenual	PO*S/JEN/YAL
postcentralis	PO*S/SEN/TRAI/LIS		PO*S/JEN/YAOUL
postcesarean	PO*S/SE/SAIRN		PO*S/JEN/YUL
postchiasmatic	PO*S/KAOI/AZ/MAT/IK	postglenoid	PO*S/GLAOE/NOID
	PO*S/KAOIS/MAT/IK	postglomerular	PO*S/GLOE/MER/LAR
postchroming	PO*S/KROEM/-G	postgrippal	PO*S/GRIP/PAL
postcibal	PO*S/SAOI/BAL	posthemiplegic	PO*S/HEM/PLAOEJ/IK
post cibum	PO*S/SAOI/BUM	posthemorrhage	PO*S/HEM/RAJ
	PO*ES/SAOI/BUM	posthemorrhagic	PO*S/HEM/RAJ/IK
postcisterna	PO*S/SIS/TER/NA	posthepatic	PO*S/HE/PAT/IK
postclavicular	PO*S/KLA/VIK/LAR	posthepatitic	PO*S/HEP/TIT/IK
postclimacteric	PO*S/KLAOI/MAKT/RIK	postherpetic	PO*S/HER/PET/IK
	PO*S/KLAOI/MAK/TER/IK	posthetomy	POS/THET/M*I
postcoital	PO*S/KOI/TAL	posthioplasty	POS/THO/PLAS/TI
post coitum	PO*S/KOI/TUM		POS/THAOE/YO/PLAS/TI
	PO*S/KOIT/UM	posthitis	POS/THAOITS
	PO*ES/KOIT/UM	postholith	POS/THO/L*IT
	PO*ES/KOIT/UM	posthumous	PO*S/HAOU/MOUS
postcoitus	PO*S/KOI/TUS		PO*S/HAOUM/OUS
postcommisural	PO*S/KMIS/RAL		POS/KHAOU/MOUS
	PO*S/KOM/SAOURL		POS/KHAOUM/OUS
	PO*S/KOM/SAOU/RAL	posthyoid	PO*S/HAOI/OID
postcondylar	PO*S/KOND/LAR	posthyoidean	PO*S/HAOI/OID/YAN
postcondylare	PO*S/KOND/LAI/RAOE	posthypnotic	PO*S/HIP/NOT/IK
postconnubial	PO*S/KO/NAOUB/YAL	posthypoglycemic	PO*S/HO*IP/GLAOI/SAOEM/IK
	PO*S/KON/NAOUB/YAL	posthypophysis	PO*S/HAOI/POF/SIS
postconvulsive	PO*S/KON/VULS/IV	posthypoxic	PO*S/HAOI/POX/IK
postcordial	PO*S/KORD/YAL	postictal	PO*S/IK/TAL
postcornu	PO*S/KOR/NAOU	posticus	POS/TAOI/KUS
postcostal	PO*S/KOS/TAL	postinfection	PO*S/IN/F*EBGS
postcranial	PO*S/KRAIN/YAL	postinfective	PO*S/IN/FEKT/IV
post crown	PO*ES/KROUN	postinfluenzal	PO*S/IN/FLAOUN/ZAL
postcubital	PO*S/KAOUB/TAL	postischial	PO*S/IS/KAL
postcyclodialysis	PO*S/SAOI/KLO/DI/AL/SIS		PO*S/IS/KAOE/YAL
post dam	PO*ES/DAM	postligation	PO*S/LAOI/GAIGS
postdevelopmental	PO*S/DWOP/-MT/TAL	postlingual	PO*S/LING/WAL
postdiastolic	PO*S/DAOI/STOL/IK	postlunar	PO*S/LAOU/NAR
postdicrotic	PO*S/DI/KROT/IK	postmalarial	PO*S/MA/LAIRL
postdigestive	PO*S/DI/J*ES/IV	postmastectomy	PO*S/MAS/TEKT/M*I
postdiphtheritic	PO*S/DIF/THRIT/IK	postmastoid	PO*S/MAS/TOID
postdormital	PO*S/DORM/TAL	postmature	PO*S/MA/KHUR
postdormitum	PO*S/DORM/TUM	postmaturity	PO*S/MA/KHUR/TI
postductal	PO*S/DUK/TAL	postmaximal	PO*S/MAX/MAL
postembryonic	PO*S/EM/BRON/IK	postmeatal	PO*S/MAOE/YAI/TAL
postencephalitic	PO*S/EN/SEF/LIT/IK		PO*S/MAOE/AI/TAL
postepileptic	PO*S/EP/LEPT/IK	postmedian	PO*S/MAOED/YAN
posteriad	POS/TAOER/YAD	postmediastinal	PO*S/MAOED/YAS/TAOINL
posterior	POS/TAOER/YOR		PO*S/MAOED/YA*S/NAL
posteriora	POS/TAOER/YOR/RA	postmediastinum	PO*S/MAOED/YAS/TAOIN/UM
	POS/TAOER/YOER/RA	postmeiotic	PO*S/MAO*I/OT/IK
	POS/TAOER/YOE/RA	postmenopausal	PO*S/MEN/NO/PAU/ZAL
posterioris	POS/TAOER/YOR/RIS	postmenstrua	PO*S/MEN/STRAOU/WA
	POS/TAOER/YOER/RIS	postmenstrual	PO*S/MEN/STRAOUL
	POS/TAOER/YOE/RIS	postmesenteric	PO*S/MES/SPWER/IK
posteriorum	POS/TAOER/YOR/UM	postminimus	PO*S/MIN/MUS
	POS/TAOER/YOER/UM	postmiotic	PO*S/MAOI/OT/IK
	POS/TAOER/YOE/RUM	postmitotic	PO*S/MAOI/TOT/IK
Posterisan	POS/TER/SAN	postmortal	PO*S/MOR/TAL
posterius	POS/TAOER/YUS	postmortem	PO*S/MOR/TEM
postero-	PO*S/RO		PO*S/MORT/EM
	POS/TRO	post-mortem	PO*S/H-F/MOR/TEM
posteroanterior	PO*S/RO/AN/TAOER/YOR		PO*S/H-F/MORT/EM
posteroclusion	PO*S/RO/KLAOUGS	postnares	PO*S/NAIR/RAOEZ
posteroexternal	PO*S/RO/EX/TERNL		PO*S/NAI/RAOEZ
posteroinferior	PO*S/RO/IN/FAOER/YOR	postnarial	PO*S/NAIRL
posterointernal	PO*S/RO/SPWERNL		PO*S/NAIR/YAL
posterolateral	PO*S/RO/LAT/RAL	postnaris	PO*S/NAIR/RIS
posteromedial	PO*S/RO/MAOED/YAL		PO*S/NAI/RIS
posteromedian	PO*S/RO/MAOED/YAN	postnasal	PO*S/NAI/ZAL
posteroparietal	PO*S/RO/PRAOI/TAL	postnatal	PO*S/NAI/TAL
posterosuperior	PO*S/RO/SPAOER/YOR	postnecrotic	PO*S/NE/KROT/IK

postneuritic	PO*S/NAOU/RIT/IK		POE/TAS/YUM
postnuclear	PO*S/NAOUK/LAR	potato	PO/TAI/TOE
postocular	PO*S/OK/LAR		POE/TAI/TOE
postop	PO*S/OP	potentia	POE/TEN/SHA
postoperative	PO*S/OP/RA/TIV	potential	POE/TEN/-RBL
	PO*S/OERPT/IV	potency	POET/EN/SI
postoperatively	PO*S/OP/RA/TIV/LI		POE/TEN/SI
	PO*S/OERPT/IV/LI	potentiality	POE/TEN/SHAL/TI
postoral	PO*S/ORL		POE/TEN/-RBL/TI
	POS/TORL	potentialization	POE/TEN/-RBL/ZAIGS
postorbital	PO*S/ORB/TAL	potentially	POE/TEN/-RBL/LI
postovulatory	PO*S/OV/LA/TOIR	potentiation	POE/TEN/SHAIGS
postpalatine	PO*S/PAL/TAOIN	potentiator	POE/TEN/SHAI/TOR
postpaludal	PO*S/PAL/DAL	potentiometer	POE/TEN/SHOM/TER
postparalytic	PO*S/PAR/LIT/IK	potification	POET/FI/KAIGS
postpartum	PO*S/PART/UM	potion	POEGS
post partum	PO*ES/PART/UM	potomania	POET/MAIN/YA
postpharyngeal	PO*S/FRIN/JAL	Pott	PO*T
postpituitary	PO*S/PI/TAOU/TAIR		(not POT; see pot)
postpneumonic	PO*S/NAOU/MON/IK	Potter	K-P/POT/ER
postpoliomyelitic	PO*S/POEL/YO/MAOI/LIT/IK		PO*T/ER
postponent	PO*S/POENT	Potts	POTS
postprandial	PO*S/PRAND/YAL	potus	POE/TUS
postpterygoidea	PO*S/TER/GOID/YA	pouch	POUFP
postpuberal	PO*S/PAOUB/RAL	poudrage	PAOU/DRAJ
postpubertal	PO*S/PAOUB/ER/TAL	poultice	POEL/TIS
postpuberty	PO*S/PAOUB/ER/TI	pound	POUND
postpubescence	PO*S/PAOU/BES/ENS	poundal	POUN/DAL
postpubescent	PO*S/PAOU/BES/ENT	Poupart	PAOU/PART
postpyknotic	PO*S/PIK/NOT/IK	Pouparti	PAOU/PAR/TAOI
postradiation	PO*S/RAID/YAIGS	pour	POUR
postrolandic	PO*S/ROE/LAND/IK		(not POER; see pore)
postrecovery	PO*S/RE/KOV/RI	poverty	POVR/TI
postsacral	PO*S/SAI/KRAL	povidone	POEV/DOEN
postscapular	PO*S/SKAP/LAR	povidone-iodine	POEV/DOEN/AOI/DAOIN
postscarlatinal	PO*S/SKARL/TAOINL	powder	POUD/ER
	PO*S/SKARL/TAOENL	powdery	POUD/RI
postsphenoid	PO*S/SFAOE/NOID	power	POU/ER
postsphenoidal	PO*S/SFAOE/NOI/DAL	pox	POX
postsphygmic	PO*S/SFIG/MIK	Poxviridae	POX/VIR/DAE
postsplenectomy	PO*S/SPLAOE/NEKT/M*I	poxvirus	POX/VAOI/RUS
postsplenic	PO*S/SPLEN/IK	P-pulmonale	P-RBGS/PUL/MO/NAI/LAOE
poststenotic	PO*S/STE/NOT/IK	practice	PRAK/TIS
poststertorous	PO*S/STERT/ROUS	practitioner	PRAK/TIGS/ER
postsylvian	PO*S/SIL/VAOE/YAN	practolol	PRAKT/LOEL
	PO*S/SIL/VAN		PRAK/TO/LOL
postsynaptic	PO*S/SNAPT/IK	prae-	PRAE
posttarsal	PO*S/TAR/SAL	praecox	PRAE/KOX
posttecta	PO*S/TEK/TA	praeputiales	PRAE/PAOU/SHAI/LAOEZ
posttibial	PO*S/TIB/YAL		PRAE/PAOURB/YAI/LAOEZ
posttransverse	PO*S/TRA*NS/VERS	praeputium	PRAE/PAOU/SHUM
posttraumatic	PO*S/TRAU/MAT/IK		PRAE/PAOURB/YUM
posttrematic	PO*S/TRAOE/MAT/IK	praesagientes	PRAE/SAJ/YEN/TAOEZ
posttussis	PO*S/TUS/SIS	praesenilis	PRAE/SE/NAOI/LIS
posttyphoid	PO*S/TAOI/FOID		PRAE/SE/NIL/LIS
postulate	POS/KHU/LAIT	praetiosa	PRAET/YOE/SA
	POS/TAOU/LAIT		PRAOET/YOE/SA
	PO*S/LAIT	praevia	PRAEV/YA
postural	POS/KHURL	praevius	PRAEV/YUS
posture	POS/KHUR	-pragia	PRAI/JA
Posture	K-P/POS/KHUR		PRAIJ/YA
Posture-D	POS/KHUR/D-RBGS	pragmatagnosia	PRAG/MAT/AG/NOEZ/YA
	K-P/POS/KHUR/D-RBGS	pragmatamnesia	PRAG/MAT/AM/NAOEZ/YA
postuterine	PO*S/YAOUT/RIN	pragmatic	PRAG/MAT/IK
postvaccinal	PO*S/VAX/NAL	pragmatics	PRAG/MAT/IK/-S
postvaccinial	PO*S/VAK/SIN/YAL	pragmatism	PRAG/MA/TIFM
postvalvar	PO*S/VAL/VAR	prairie	PRAIR/RAOE
postvalvular	PO*S/VAL/VAOU/LAR	pralidoxime	PRAL/DOK/SAOEM
postvital	PO*S/VAOI/TAL		PRAL/DOK/SAOIM
postzoster	PO*S/ZOS/TER	PrameGel	PRAM/JEL
postzygotic	PO*S/ZAOI/GOT/IK	Pramet	PRAM/ET
Potaba	POE/TAB/BA	Pramilet	PRAM/LET
	POE/TA/BA	Pramosone	PRAM/SOEN
potable	POET/-BL	pramoxine	PRA/MOK/SAOEM
Potain	POE/TAIN		PRA/MOK/SIN
potamophobia	POT/MO/FOEB/YA		PRAM/OK/SAOEN
potash	POT/ARB		PRAM/OK/SIN
potassa	PO/TAS/SA	prandial	PRAND/YAL
	POE/TAS/SA	pranolium	PRA/NOEL/YUM
potassemia	POT/SAOEM/YA		PRAI/NOEL/YUM
potassi-	PO/TAS	praseodymium	PRAIS/YO/DIM/YUM
	PO/TAS/SI-		PRAIZ/YO/DIM/YUM
	POE/TAS	pratensis	PRA/TEN/SIS
	POE/TAS/SI-	pratique	PRA/TAOEK
potassic	PO/TAS/IK	Pratt	PRAT
	PO/TAS/SIK	Prausnitz	PROUS/NITS
potassiocupric	PO/TAS/YO/KAOUP/RIK	Prax	PRAX
potassiomercuric	PO/TAS/YO/MER/KAOUR/IK	-praxia	PRAX/YA
potassium	PO/TAS/YUM	praxiology	PRAX/YOLG

praxis	PRAK/SIS	predator	PRED/TOR
prazepam	PRAZ/PAM	predecidual	PRE/DE/SID/YAL
praziquantel	PRAIZ/KWAN/TEL	predeciduous	PRE/DE/SID/YOUS
prazosin	PRAZ/SIN	predentin	PRE/DEN/TIN
pre-	PRE	prediabetes	PRE/DAOI/BAOE/TAOEZ
preadult	PRE/AI/DULT	prediastole	PRE/DI/A*S/LAOE
	PRE/AD/ULT	prediastolic	PRE/DAOI/STOL/IK
	PRE/DULT	predicrotic	PRE/DI/KROT/IK
preagonal	PRE/AG/NAL	predigestion	PRE/DI/JEGS
preagonic	PRE/AI/GON/IK	predispose	PRE/DIS/POES
	PRE/GON/IK	predisposing	PRE/DIS/POEZ/-G
prealbumin	PRE/AL/BAOU/MIN	predisposition	PRE/DIS/POGS
prealbuminuric	PRE/AL/BAOUM/NAOUR/IK	prediverticular	PRE/DI/VER/TIK/LAR
preanal	PRE/AINL	Prednicen	PRED/NI/SEN
preanesthesia	PRE/ANS/THAOEZ/YA	Prednicen-M	PRED/NI/SEN/M-RBGS
preanesthetic	PRE/ANS/THET/IK	prednisolone	PRED/NIS/LOEN
preantiseptic	PRE/A*ENT/SEPT/IK	prednisone	PRED/NI/SOEN
preaortic	PRE/AI/ORT/IK	prednylidene	PRED/NIL/DAOEN
preaseptic	PRE/AI/SEPT/IK	predormital	PRE/DORM/TAL
preataxic	PRE/AI/TAX/IK	predormitium	PRE/DOR/MIRB/UM
preaurale	PRE/AU/RAI/LAOE	predormitum	PRE/DORM/TUM
preauricular	PRE/AU/RIK/LAR	preeclampsia	PRE/E/KLAFRPS/YA
preaxial	PRE/AX/YAL		PRE/E/KLAMS/YA
prebacillary	PRE/BAS/LAIR	preelacin	PRE/EL/SIN
prebase	PRE/BAIS	preenzyme	PRE/EN/ZAOIM
prebetalipoprotein	PRE/BAIT/LIP/PRO/TAOEN	preepiglottic	PRE/EP/GLOT/IK
prebetalipoproteinemia	PRE/BAIT/LIP/PROET/NAOEM/YA	preeruptive	PRE/E/RUPT/IV
prebiotic	PRE/BAO*I/OT/IK	preexcitation	PRE/KPAOI/TAIGS
prebladder	PRE/BLAD/ER	preextraction	PRE/EX/TRA*BGS
prebrachium	PRE/BRAIK/YUM	preferential	PREFRN/-RBL
precancer	PRE/KANS/ER		PREF/REN/-RBL
precancerous	PRE/KANS/ROUS	preflagellate	PRE/FLAJ/LAIT
precapillary	PRE/KAP/LAIR	prefollicle	PRE/FOL/K-L
precarcinomatous	PRE/KARS/NOEM/TOUS		PRE/FOL/LIK/-L
precardiac	PRE/KARD/YAK	preformation	PRE/FOR/MAIGS
precardinal	PRE/KARD/NAL	preformationist	PRE/FOR/MAIGS/*IS
precardium	PRE/KARD/YUM	prefrontal	PRE/FRON/TAL
precartilage	PRE/KART/LAJ	prefunctional	PRE/FUNGS/NAL
precava	PRE/KAI/VA	Prefrin	PREF/RIN
precatorius	PREK/TOER/YUS	preganglionic	PRE/GANG/LON/IK
	PREK/TOR/YUS	pregenital	PRE/JEN/TAL
Precef	PRE/SEF	Pregestimil	PRE/J*ES/MIL
precentral	PRE/SEN/TRAL	preglomerular	PRE/GLOE/MER/LAR
	PRE/STRAL	pregnancy	PREG/NAN/SI
prechordal	PRE/KHOR/DAL	pregnane	PREG/NAIN
prechroming	PRE/KROEM/-G	pregnanediol	PREG/NAIN/DI/OL
precipitable	PRE/SIPT/-BL	pregnanetriol	PREG/NAIN/TR*I/OL
	PRE/SIP/TABL	pregnant	PREG/NANT
precipitant	PRE/SIP/TANT	pregnene	PREG/NAOEN
precipitate	PRE/SIP/TAIT	pregneninolone	PREG/NAOEN/IN/LOEN
precipitation	PRE/SIP/TAIGS	pregnenolone	PREG/NAOEN/LOEN
precipitin	PRE/SIP/TIN	Pregnyl	PREG/NIL
precipitinogen	PRE/SIP/TIN/JEN	pregonium	PRE/GOEN/YUM
precipitinogenoid	PRE/SIP/TIN/JEN/OID	pregranular	PRE/GRAN/LAR
	PRE/SIP/TIN/JE/NOID	pregravidic	PRE/GRA/VID/IK
precipitogen	PRE/SIP/TO/JEN	prehallux	PRE/HAL/UX
precipitoid	PRE/SIP/TOID		PRE/HAL/LUX
precipitophore	PRE/SIP/TO/FOER	prehelicine	PRE/HEL/SAOEN
precipitum	PRE/SIP/TUM	prehematinic	PRE/HAOEM/TIN/IK
precirrhosis	PRE/SIR/ROE/SIS	prehemiplegic	PRE/HEM/PLAOEJ/IK
preclavicular	PRE/KLA/VIK/LAR	prehensile	PRE/HEN/SIL
preclinical	PRE/KLIN/KAL		PRE/HEN/SAOIL
preclival	PRE/KLAOIVL	prehension	PRE/HENGS
precocious	PRE/KOERBS	prehepaticus	PRE/HE/PAT/KUS
precocity	PRE/KOS/TI	prehormone	PRE/HOR/MOEN
precognition	PRE/KOG/NIGS	prehyoid	PRE/HAOI/OID
precoid	PRE/KOID	prehypophysial	PRE/HO*IP/FIZ/YAL
precollagenous	PRE/KLAJ/NOUS	prehypophysis	PRE/HAOI/POF/SIS
precoma	PRE/KO/MA	preictal	PRE/IK/TAL
precommissural	PRE/KMIS/RAL	preicteric	PRE/IK/TER/IK
	PRE/KOM/SAOURL	preimmunization	PRE/IM/NI/ZAIGS
	PRE/KOM/SAOU/RAL	preinduction	PRE/IN/D*UBGS
preconscious	PRE/KON/-RBS	preinfarction	PRE/IN/FA*RBGS
preconvulsant	PRE/KON/VUL/SANT	preinterparietal	PRE/SPWER/PRAOI/TAL
preconvulsive	PRE/KON/VULS/IV		PRE/SPWER/PA/RAOI/TAL
Precorsin	PRE/KOR/SIN	preinvasive	PRE/IN/VAIS/IV
precordia	PRE/KORD/YA	preiotation	PRE/AOI/TAIGS
precordial	PRE/KORD/YAL	Preisz	PRAOISZ
precordialgia	PRE/KORD/YAL/JA	prelacrimal	PRE/LAK/RI/MAL
precordium	PRE/KORD/YUM	prelacteal	PRE/LAKT/YAL
precornu	PRE/KOR/NAOU	prelaryngeal	PRE/LARN/JAL
precostal	PRE/KOS/TAL	preleptotene	PRE/LEPT/TAOEN
precritical	PRE/KRIT/KAL	preleukemia	PRE/LAOU/KAOEM/YA
precuneal	PRE/KAOUN/YAL	preleukemic	PRE/LAOU/KAOEM/IK
precuneate	PRE/KAOUN/YAIT	prelimbic	PRE/LIM/BIK
precuneus	PRE/KAOUN/YUS	prelingual	PRE/LING/WAL
precursor	PRE/KUR/SOR	prelipoid	PRE/LIP/OID
precursory	PRE/KURS/RI	preload	PRE/LOED
predation	PRE/DAIGS	prelocalization	PRE/LOE/KAL/ZAIGS

prelocomotion	PRE/LOEK/MOEGS	preperception	PRE/PER/SEPGS
Prelone	PRE/LO*EN	preperforative	PRE/PER/FRA/TIV
Prelu-2	PRAI/LAOU/2	preperitoneal	PRE/PERT/NAOEL
	PRE/LAOU/2	prephenic	PRE/FEN/IK
Preludin	PRAI/LAOU/DIN		PRE/FAOEN/IK
	PRE/LAOU/DIN	preplacental	PRE/PLA/SEN/TAL
prelum	PRE/LUM	preponderance	PRE/POND/RANS
premalignant	PRE/MA/LIG/NANT		PRE/PON/DRANS
premammary	PRE/MAM/RI		P-P
premaniacal	PRE/MA/NAOI/KAL	prepotency	PRE/POE/TEN/SI
Premarin	PREM/RIN		PRE/POET/EN/SI
prematura	PRE/MA/KHUR/RA	prepotent	PRE/POE/TENT
	PRE/MA/TAOU/RA		PRE/POET/ENT
	PRE/MA/TAOUR/RA	prepotential	PRE/POE/TEN/-RBL
premature	PRE/MA/KHUR	preprandial	PRE/PRAND/YAL
	PRE/MA/TAOUR	preproinsulin	PRE/PRO/INS/LIN
prematurely	PRE/MA/KHUR/LI	preprophage	PRE/PRO/FAIJ
	PRE/MA/TAOUR/LI	preproprotein	PRE/PRO/PRO/TAOEN
prematurity	PRE/MA/KHUR/TI	preprosthetic	PRE/PROS/THET/IK
	PRE/MA/TAOUR/TI	prepsychotic	PRE/SAOI/KOT/IK
premaxilla	PRE/MAK/SIL/LA	prepuberal	PRE/PAOUB/RAL
premaxillary	PRE/MAX/LAIR	prepubertal	PRE/PAOUB/ER/TAL
premed	PRE/MED	prepuberty	PRE/PAOUB/ER/TI
premedical	PRE/MED/KAL	prepubescence	PRE/PAOU/BES/ENS
premedicant	PRE/MED/KANT	prepubescent	PRE/PAOU/BES/ENT
premedication	PRE/MED/KAIGS	prepuce	PRE/PAOUS
premeiotic	PRE/MAO*I/OT/IK	preputia	PRE/PAOU/SHA
premelanosome	PRE/MEL/NO/SOEM		PRE/PAOURB/YA
premenarchal	PRE/ME/NAR/KAL	preputial	PRE/PAOURBL
premenarche	PRE/ME/NAR/KAOE	preputiales	PRE/PAOU/SHAI/LAOEZ
	PRE/MEN/AR/KAOE		PRE/PAOURB/YAI/LAOEZ
premenarcheal	PRE/ME/NARK/YAL	preputiotomy	PRE/PAOU/SHOT/M*I
premenopausal	PRE/MEN/PAU/ZAL		PRE/PAOURB/YOT/M*I
premenstrua	PRE/MEN/STRAOU/WA	preputium	PRE/PAOU/SHUM
premenstrual	PRE/MEN/STRAOUL		PRE/PAOURB/UM
	PRE/MEN/STRAL	prepyloric	PRE/PAOI/LOR/IK
premenstruum	PRE/MEN/STRAOUM	prepylorica	PRE/PAOI/LOR/KA
	PRE/MEN/STRUM	prerectal	PRE/REK/TAL
premitotic	PRE/MAOI/TOT/IK	prereduced	PRE/RE/DAOUS/-D
premolar	PRE/MOE/LAR	prerenal	PRE/RAOENL
premolares	PRE/MOE/LAI/RAOEZ	prerennin	PRE/REN/NIN
premolarium	PRE/MOE/LAIRM	prereproductive	PRE/RE/PRUKT/IV
	PRE/MOE/LAIR/YUM		PRE/RE/PRO/DUKT/IV
premonition	PREM/NIGS	preretinal	PRE/RET/NAL
premonitory	PRE/MON/TOIR	presacral	PRE/SAI/KRAL
premonocyte	PRE/MON/SAO*IT	presby-	PRES/BI
premorbid	PRE/MOR/BID		PREBS
premortal	PRE/MOR/TAL	presbyacusia	PRES/BI/AI/KAOUZ/YA
premotor	PRE/MOE/TOR		PREBS/AI/KAOUZ/YA
premunition	PRE/MAOU/NIGS	presbyacusis	PRES/BI/AI/KAOU/SIS
premunitive	PRE/MAOUN/TIV		PREBS/AI/KAOU/SIS
premyeloblast	PRE/MAOI/LO/BLA*S	presbyatrics	PRES/BI/AT/RIK/-S
premyelocyte	PRE/MAOI/LO/SAO*IT		PREBS/AT/RIK/-S
prenarcosis	PRE/NAR/KOE/SIS	presbycardia	PRES/BI/KARD/YA
prenarcotic	PRE/NAR/KOT/IK		PREBS/KARD/YA
prenares	PRE/NAIR/RAOEZ	presbycusis	PRES/BI/KAOU/SIS
	PRE/NAI/RAOEZ		PREBS/KAOU/SIS
prenaris	PRE/NAIR/RIS	presbyesophagus	PRES/BI/E/SOF/GUS
	PRE/NAI/RIS		PREBS/E/SOF/GUS
prenasale	PRE/NAI/ZAI/LAOE	presbyope	PRES/BI/OEP
prenatal	PRE/NAI/TAL		PREBS/OEP
Prenate	PRE/NAIT	presbyophrenia	PRES/BI/FRAOEN/YA
preneoplastic	PRE/NAOE/PLA*S/IK		PRES/BO/FRAOEN/YA
Prentice	PREN/TIS		PREBS/FRAOEN/YA
prenyl	PREN/IL	presbyopia	PRES/BI/OEP/YA
prenylamine	PRE/NIL/MAOEN		PREBS/OEP/YA
preop	PRE/OP	presbyopic	PRES/BI/OP/IK
preoperative	PRE/OP/RA/TIV		PRES/BI/OEP/IK
	PRE/OERPT/IV		PREBS/OP/IK
preoptic	PRE/OPT/IK		PREBS/OEP/IK
preoral	PRE/ORL	presbytism	PRES/BI/TIFM
preosteoblast	PRE/O*S/YO/BLA*S	prescapula	PRE/SKAP/LA
preoxygenation	PRE/OX/JEN/AIGS	prescapular	PRE/SKAP/LAR
	PRE/OX/JE/NAIGS	presclerotic	PRE/SKLE/ROT/IK
prep	PREP	prescribe	PRE/SKRAOIB
prepalatal	PRE/PAL/TAL		PRAOIB
preparalytic	PRE/PAR/LIT/IK	prescription	PRE/SKRIPGS
preparation	PREP/RAIGS		PRIPGS
Preparation H	PREP/RAIGS/H-RBGS	presegmenter	PRE/SEG/-MT/ER
preparative	PRE/PAIR/TIV		PRE/SEG/MEN/TER
	PRE/PAR/TIV	presegmenting	PRE/SEG/-MT/-G
preparator	PREP/RAI/TOR	presenile	PRE/SE/NAOIL
prepartal	PRE/PAR/TAL	presenilis	PRE/SE/NAOI/LIS
prepatellar	PRE/PA/TEL/LAR		PRE/SE/NIL/LIS
prepatellares	PRE/PAT/LAI/RAOEZ	presenility	PRE/SNIL/TI
prepatellaris	PRE/PAT/LAI/RIS		PRE/SE/NIL/TI
prepatent	PRE/PAI/TENT	presenium	PRE/SAOEN/YUM
	PRE/PAIT/ENT	present	PRENT
Pre-Pen	PRE/PEN		PRE/SENT

	PRE/ZENT	priapism	PRAOI/PIFM
	PREZ/ENT	priapitis	PRAOI/PAOITS
	PRES/ENT	priapus	PRAOI/PUS
presentation	PRENT/TAIGS		PRAOI/AI/PUS
	PREZ/EN/TAIGS	Price	K-P/PRAOIS
	PRES/EN/TAIGS	Price-Jones	PRAOIS/JOENZ
preservative	PRE/SEFRB/TIV		PRAOIS/JOENS
presomite	PRE/SOE/MAOIT		K-P/PRAOIS/H-F/JOENZ
presphenoid	PRE/SFAOE/NOID		K-P/PRAOIS/H-F/JOENS
presphenoidal	PRE/SFAOE/NOI/DAL	prick	PRIK
presphygmic	PRE/SFIG/MIK	prickle	PRIK/-L
prespinal	PRE/SPAOINL	Priessnitz	PRAOES/NITS
prespinous	PRE/SPAOIN/OUS	Priestley	PRAO*ES/LAOE
prespondylolisthesis	PRE/SPOND/LO/LIS/THE/SIS	prilocaine	PRIL/KAIN
pressometer	PRES/SOM/TER	prima	PRAOI/MA
pressor	PRES/SOR	primaclone	PRAOIM/KLOEN
pressoreceptive	PRES/RE/SEPT/IV	primacy	PRAOIM/SI
	PRES/SO/RE/SEPT/IV	primal	PRAOI/MAL
pressoreceptor	PRES/RE/SEP/TOR	primaquine	PRAOIM/KWIN
	PRES/SO/RE/SEP/TOR		PRIM/KWIN
pressosensitive	PRES/SENS/TIV	primary	PRAOI/MAIR
	PRES/SO/SENS/TIV	primate	PRAOI/MAIT
pressosensitivity	PRES/SENS/TIV/TI	Primatene	PRAOIM/TAOEN
	PRES/SO/SENS/TIV/TI	Primatene Mist	PRAOIM/TAOEN/M*IS
pressure	PRERB/SHUR	Primates	PRAOI/MAI/TAOEZ
presternum	PRE/STER/NUM	Primaxin	PRAOI/MAK/SIN
presubiculum	PRE/SAOU/BIK/LUM	primed	PRAOIM/-D
presumptive	PRE/SUFRPT/IV	prime mover	PRAOIM/MAOUVR
	PRE/SUMT/IV		PRAOIM/MOVR
presuppurative	PRE/SUP/RA/TIV	primer	PRAOIM/ER
	PRE/SUP/YAOUR/TIV	Primer	K-P/PRAOIM/ER
	PRE/SUP/PAOUR/TIV	primerite	PRAOIM/RAOIT
presylvian	PRE/SIL/VAOE/YAN	primeverose	PRAOI/MEV/ROES
	PRE/SIL/VAN	primi-	PRAOIM
presymptom	PRE/SIM/TOM		PRAOI/MI
	PRE/SIFRP/TOM	primidone	PRIM/DOEN
presymptomatic	PRE/SIMT/MAT/IK	primigravid	PRAOIM/GRAVD
	PRE/SIFRPT/MAT/IK		PRAOIM/GRAV/ID
presynaptic	PRE/SNAPT/IK	primigravida	PRAOIM/GRAV/DA
	PRE/SI/NAPT/IK	primipara	PRAOI/MIP/RA
presystole	PRES/S*IS/TAOE	primiparity	PRAOIM/PAIR/TI
presystolic	PRE/SIS/TOL/IK	primiparous	PRAOI/MIP/ROUS
PreSun	PRE/SUN	primite	PRAOI/MAOIT
PreSun 4	PRE/SUN/4	primitiae	PRAOI/MIRB/YAE
PreSun 8	PRE/SUN/8		PRAOI/MIT/YAE
PreSun 15	PRE/SUN/15	primitive	PRIM/TIV
PreSun 29	PRE/SUN/29	primordia	PRAOI/MORD/YA
PreSun 39	PRE/SUN/39	primordial	PRAOI/MORD/YAL
PreSun for Kids	PRE/SUN/F-R/KIDZ	primordium	PRAOI/MORD/YUM
pretarsal	PRE/TAR/SAL	primum	PRAOI/MUM
pretecta	PRE/TEK/TA	primus	PRAOI/MUS
pretectal	PRE/TEK/TAL	primverose	PRIM/VER/OES
pretectum	PRE/TEK/TUM	princeps	PRIN/SEPS
preternatural	PRET/ER/NAFP/RAL	principal	PRINS/PAL
	PRET/ER/NAFP	principalis	PRINS/PAI/LIS
prethcamide	PR*ET/KA/MAOID	Principen	PRINS/PEN
prethyroid	PRE/THAOI/ROID	principes	PRINS/PAOEZ
prethyroideal	PRE/THAOI/ROID/YAL	principle	PRINS/P-L
prethyroidean	PRE/THAOI/ROID/YAN	Pringle	PRING/-L
pretibial	PRE/TIB/YAL	Prinivil	PRIN/VIL
pretracheal	PRE/TRAIK/YAL		PRAOIN/VIL
pretragal	PRE/TRAI/GAL	Prinzide	PRIN/ZAOID
pretrematic	PRE/TRAOE/MAT/IK	Prinzmetal	PRINZ/MET/TAL
pretuberculosis	PRE/TAOU/BERK/LOE/SIS		PRINS/MET/TAL
pretuberculous	PRE/TAOU/BERK/LOUS	prion	PRAOI/YON
pretympanic	PRE/TIM/PAN/IK	Priscoline	PRIS/KO/LAOEN
preurethritis	PRE/YAOUR/THRAOITS	prism	PRIFM
prevalence	PREV/LENS	prisma	PRIZ/MA
prevalent	PREV/LENT	prismata	PRIZ/MA/TA
preventive	PRE/VENT/IV	prismatic	PRIZ/MAT/IK
	PREVNT/IV	prismoid	PRIZ/MOID
preventorium	PRE/VEN/TOIRM	prismoptometer	PRIZ/MOP/TOM/TER
	PRE/VEN/TOER/YUM	prismosphere	PRIZ/MO/SFAOER
	PRE/VEN/TOR/YUM	privacy	PRAOIV/SI
preventriculus	PRE/VEN/TRIK/LUS	-prival	PRAOIVL
Prevenzyme	PRE/VEN/ZAOIM		PRAOI/VAL
prevertebral	PRE/VERT/BRAL		(v)P/RI/VAL
prevertebralis	PRE/VERT/BRAI/LIS	privet	PRIVT
prevesical	PRE/VES/KAL		PRIV/ET
previable	PRE/VAOIBL	-privic	PRIVK
previllous	PRE/VIL/OUS		PRIV/IK
previtamin	PRE/VAOIT/MIN		PRAOIVK
PreviDent	PREV/DENT		PRAOI/VIK
previous	PRAOEV/YOUS	Privine	PRAOI/VAOEN
previus	PRAOEV/YUS	p.r.n.	P*RN
prezone	PRE/ZOEN	pro	PROE
prezygapophysis	PRE/ZAOIG/POF/SIS	pro-	PRO
prezygotic	PRE/ZAOI/GOT/IK	proaccelerin	PRO/AK/SEL/RIN
prezymogen	PRE/ZAOIM/JEN	proacrosomal	PRO/AK/RO/SOE/MAL

proactinium	PRO/AK/TIN/YUM	procteurysis	PROK/TAOUR/SIS
proactinomycin	PRO/AKT/NO/MAOI/SIN	proctitis	PROK/TAOITS
proactivator	PRO/AKT/VAI/TOR	proctocele	PROKT/SAO*EL
proal	PROEL	proctoclysis	PROK/TOK/LI/SIS
	PRO/WAL	proctococcypexy	PROKT/KOX/PEK/SI
proamnion	PRO/AM/NON	proctocolectomy	PROKT/KO/LEKT/M*I
	PRO/AM/NAOE/YON	proctocolitis	PROKT/KO/LAOITS
proatlas	PRO/AT/LAS	proctocolonoscopy	PROKT/KOEL/NOS/KPI
probacteriophage	PRO/BAK/TAOER/YO/FALJ	proctocolpoplasty	PROKT/KOL/PO/PLAS/TI
proband	PRO/BAND	Proctocort	PROKT/KORT
probang	PRO/BANG	ProctoCream	PROKT/KRAOEM
Probahist	PROEB/H*IS	ProctoCream-HC	PROKT/KRAOEM/H-RBGS/
Pro-Banthine	PRO/BAN/THAOEN		KR*RBGS
probarbital	PRO/BARB/TAL	proctocystocele	PROKT/S*IS/SAO*EL
probe	PROEB	proctocystoplasty	PROKT/S*IS/PLAS/TI
Probec	PRO/BEK	proctocystotomy	PROKT/SIS/TOT/M*I
Probec-T	PRO/BEK/T-RBGS	proctodea	PROKT/DAOE/YA
probenecid	PRO/BEN/SID	proctodeal	PROKT/DAOEL
probilifuscin	PRO/BIL/FUS/SIN		PROKT/DAOE/YAL
probiosis	PRO/BAO*I/YOE/SIS	proctodeum	PROKT/DAOE/UM
probiotic	PRO/BAO*I/OT/IK	proctodynia	PROKT/DIN/YA
probit	PRO/BIT	proctoelytroplasty	PROKT/EL/TRO/PLAS/TI
problem	PROB	Proctofoam	PROKT/FOEM
	PROB/LEM	Proctofoam-HC	PROKT/FOEM/H-RBGS/KR*RBGS
proboscides	PRO/BOS/DAOEZ	proctogenic	PROKT/JEN/IK
proboscis	PRO/BOS/SIS	proctogenous	PROK/TOJ/NOUS
	PRO/BOS/KIS	proctologic	PROKT/LOJ/IK
proboscises	PRO/BOS/SAOEZ	proctologist	PROK/TO*LGS
probucol	PRO/BAOU/KOEL	proctology	PROK/TOLG
procainamide	PRO/KAIN/MAOID	proctoparalysis	PROKT/PRAL/SIS
procaine	PRO/KAIN	proctoperineoplasty	PROKT/P*ER/NAOE/PLAS/TI
procallus	PRO/KAL/LUS	proctoperineorrhaphy	PROKT/P*ER/NAOE/YOR/FI
Procan	PRO/KAN	proctopexy	PROKT/PEK/SI
procapsid	PRO/KAP/SID	proctophobia	PROKT/FOEB/YA
procarbazine	PRO/KARB/ZAOEN	proctoplasty	PROKT/PLAS/TI
procarboxypeptidase	PRO/KAR/BOX/PEPT/DAIS	proctoplegia	PROKT/PLAOE/JA
procarcinogen	PRO/KAR/SIN/JEN	proctopolypus	PROKT/POL/PUS
Procardia	PRO/KARD/YA	proctoptosia	PROK/TOP/TOES/YA
Procaryotae	see Prokaryotae	proctoptosis	PROK/TOP/TOE/SIS
procatarctic	PRO/KA/TARK/TIK	proctorrhagia	PROKT/RAI/JA
	PRO/KA/TARKT/IK	proctorrhaphy	PROK/TOR/FI
procatarxis	PRO/KA/TARK/SIS	proctorrhea	PROKT/RAOE/YA
procedure	PRO/SAOED/YUR	proctoscope	PROKT/SKOEP
procelia	PRO/SAOEL/YA	proctoscopy	PROK/TOS/KPI
procelous	PRO/SAOEL/OUS	proctosigmoid	PROKT/SIG/MOID
	PRO/SE/LOUS	proctosigmoidectomy	PROKT/SIG/MOI/DEKT/M*I
procentriole	PRO/SEN/TROEL	proctosigmoiditis	PROKT/SIG/MOI/DAOITS
procephalic	PRO/SFAL/IK	proctosigmoidopexy	PROKT/SIG/MOID/PEK/SI
Pro-Ception	PRO/SEPGS	proctosigmoidoscope	PROKT/SIG/MOID/SKOEP
procercoid	PRO/SER/KOID	proctosigmoidoscopy	PROKT/SIG/MOI/DOS/KPI
	PRO/SERK/OID	proctospasm	PROKT/SPAFM
procerus	PRO/SE/RUS	proctostasis	PROK/TO*S/SIS
	PRO/SAOER/RUS	proctostat	PROKT/STAT
process	PRO/SESZ	proctostenosis	PROKT/STE/NOE/SIS
processus	PRO/SES/SUS	proctostomy	PROK/TO*S/M*I
procheilia	PRO/KAOIL/YA	proctotome	PROKT/TOEM
procheilion	PRO/KAOIL/YON	proctotomy	PROK/TOT/M*I
procheilon	PRO/KAOI/LON	proctotoreusis	PROKT/TOE/RAOU/SIS
pro-choice	PRO/KHOIS	proctotresia	PROKT/TRAOEZ/YA
prochlorperazine	PRO/KLOR/PER/ZAOEN	proctovalvotomy	PROKT/VAL/VOT/M*I
prochondral	PRO/KON/DRAL	procumbent	PRO/KUM/BENT
prochordal	PRO/KHOR/DAL	procursiva	PRO/KUR/SAOI/VA
prochorion	PRO/KOER/YON	procursive	PRO/KURS/IV
prochromatin	PRO/KROEM/TIN	procurvation	PRO/KUR/VAIGS
prochromosome	PRO/KROEM/SOEM	procuticle	PRO/KAOUT/K-L
prochymosin	PRO/KAOIM/SIN	procyclidine	PRO/SAOI/KLI/DAOEN
procidentia	PROS/DEN/SHA	prodroma	PRO/DROE/MA
procinonide	PRO/SIN/NAOID	prodromal	PRO/DROE/MAL
procoagulant	PRO/KO/AG/LANT	prodromata	PRO/DROEM/TA
procollagen	PRO/KOL/JEN	prodrome	PRO/DROEM
procollagenase	PRO/KLAJ/NAIS	prodromi	PRO/DROE/MAOI
proconceptive	PRO/KON/SEPT/IV	prodromic	PRO/DROEM/IK
proconvertin	PRO/KON/VER/TIN	prodromous	PRO/DROEM/OUS
procreate	PRO/KRAOE/AIT	prodromus	PRO/DROE/MUS
	PRO/KRAOE/YAIT	prodrug	PRO/DRUG
procreation	PRO/KRAOE/AIGS	Prodrox	PRO/DROX
	PRO/KRAOE/YAIGS	product	PRUKT
	PRO/KRAIGS		PRO/DUKT
procreative	PRO/KRAOE/AIT/IV		PROD/UKT
	PRO/KRAOE/YAIT/IV	productive	PRUKT/IV
proct(o)-	PROKT		PRO/DUKT/IV
	PROK/T(O)	proecdysis	PRO/EK/DI/SIS
proctagra	PROK/TAG/RA	proelastase	PRO/E/LAS/TAIS
proctalgia	PROK/TAL/JA	proemial	PRO/AOEM/YAL
proctatresia	PROKT/TRAOEZ/YA	proencephalon	PRO/EN/SEF/LON
proctectasia	PROK/TEK/TAIZ/YA	proencephalus	PRO/EN/SEF/LUS
proctectomy	PROK/TEKT/M*I	proenzyme	PRO/EN/ZAOIM
proctencleisis	PROK/TEN/KLAOI/SIS	proerythroblast	PRO/R*IT/RO/BLA*S
procteurynter	PROK/TAOU/RINT/ER	proerythrocyte	PRO/R*IT/RO/SAO*IT

proesterase	PRO/ES/TRAIS		PROG/IV
	PRO/ES/TER/AIS	proguanil	PRO/GAUN/IL
proestrogen	PRO/ES/TRO/JEN		PRO/GAU/NIL
proestrum	PRO/ES/TRUM	Pro-Hepatone	PRO/HEP/TOEN
proestrus	PRO/ES/TRUS	ProHIBIT	PRO*/HIBT
Proetz	PRETS		(*not* PRO/HIBT; **see** prohibit)
Profasi	PROF/SAOE	prohormone	PRO/HOR/MOEN
	PRO/FA/SAOE	pro injectione	PROE/IN/JEK/SHOE/NAOE
profenamine	PRO/FEN/MAOEN		PRO/IN/JEK/SHOE/NAOE
proferment	PRO/FERMT	proinsulin	PRO/INS/LIN
professional	PRO/FEGS/NAL	pro-invasin	PRO/IN/VAI/SIN
Profeta	PRO/FAI/TA	proiosystole	PROI/YO/S*IS/LAOE
	PRO/FAOE/TA		PRO/YO/S*IS/LAOE
profibrinolysin	PRO/FAOI/BRI/NOL/SIN	proiosystolia	PROI/YO/SIS/TOL/YA
Profichet	PROEF/SHAI		PRO/YO/SIS/TOL/YA
	PRO/FI/SHAI	projection	PRO/J*EBGS
Profilate	PROEF/LAIT	prokaryon	PRO/KAR/YON
	PRO/FI/LAIT	prokaryosis	PRO/KAR/YOE/SIS
profile	PRO/FAOIL	Prokaryotae	PRO/KAR/YOE/TAE
profile-1	PRO/FAOIL/H-F/1	prokaryote	PRO/KAR/YOET
Profilnine	PRO/FIL/NAOEN	prokaryotic	PRO/KAR/YOT/IK
profilometer	PRO/FI/LOM/TER	prolabial	PRO/LAIB/YAL
proflavine	PRO/FLAIVN	prolabium	PRO/LAIB/YUM
	PRO/FLAI/VIN	prolactin	PRO/LAK/TIN
profluvium	PRO/FLAOUV/YUM	prolactinoma	PRO/LAKT/NOE/MA
profondometer	PRO/FON/DOM/TER	prolactoliberin	PRO/LAKT/LIB/RIN
proformiphen	PRO/FORM/FEN	prolactostatin	PRO/LAKT/STAT/TIN
profunda	PRO/FUN/DA	prolamin	PROEL/MIN
profundae	PRO/FUN/DAE		PRO/LAM/MIN
profundaplasty	PRO/FUND/PLAS/TI	prolamine	PROEL/MAOEN
	PRO/FUN/DA/PLAS/TI		PRO/LAM/AOEN
profundus	PRO/FUN/DUS		PRO/LAM/MAOEN
profundum	PRO/FUN/DUM	prolan	PRO/LAN
progamous	PROG/MOUS	prolapse	PRO/LAPS
	PRO/GAM/OUS	prolapsus	PRO/LAP/SUS
progaster	PRO/GAS/TER	prolepsis	PRO/LEP/SIS
	PRO/GA*S/ER	proleptic	PRO/LEPT/IK
progastrin	PRO/GAS/TRIN	proleukocyte	PRO/LAOUK/SAO*IT
progeneum	PRO/JAOEN/YUM	prolidase	PROEL/DAIS
progenia	PRO/JAOEN/YA	proliferans	PRO/LIF/RANZ
progenital	PRO/JEN/TAL		PRO/LIFRNZ
progenitalis	PRO/JEN/TAI/LIS	proliferate	PRO/LIF/RAIT
progenitor	PRO/JEN/TOR	proliferation	PRO/LIF/RAIGS
progeny	PROJ/N*I	proliferative	PRO/LIFR/TIV
progeria	PRO/JAOER/YA		PRO/LIF/RA/TIV
progeroid	PRO/JER/OID	proliferous	PRO/LIF/ROUS
	PRO/JAOER/OID	prolific	PRO/LIFK
Progestasert	PRO/J*ES/SERT		PRO/LIF/IK
progestational	PRO/JES/TAIGS/NAL	proligerous	PRO/LIJ/ROUS
progesteroid	PRO/J*ES/ROID	proligerus	PRO/LIJ/RUS
progesterone	PRO/J*ES/ROEN	prolinase	PROEL/NAIS
Progestimil	PRE/J*ES/MIL	proline	PRO/LAOEN
progestin	PRO/JES/TIN		PRO/LIN
progestogen	PRO/J*ES/JEN	prolinemia	PROEL/NAOEM/YA
progestomimetic	PRO/J*ES/MAOI/MET/IK	prolintane	PRO/LIN/TAIN
	PRO/J*ES/MI/MET/IK	Prolixin	PRO/LIK/SIN
proglossis	PRO/GLOS/SIS	Proloid	PRO/LOID
proglottid	PRO/GLOT/ID	prolongata	PRO/LON/GAI/TA
	PRO/GLOT/TID	prolonged	PRO/LONG/-D
proglottides	PRO/GLOT/DAOEZ	Proloprim	PROEL/PRIM
proglottis	PRO/GLOT/TIS		PRO/LO/PRIM
proglumide	PRO/GLAOU/MAOID	prolyl	PRO/LIL
Proglycem	PRO/GLAOI/SEM	prolylglycine	PRO/LIL/GLAOI/SAOEN
prognathic	PROG/NA*T/IK	prolymphocyte	PRO/LIM/FO/SAO*IT
	PROG/NA*IT/IK	promastigote	PRO/MA*S/GOET
prognathion	PROG/NA*IT/YON	promazine	PROEM/ZAOEN
prognathism	PROG/NA/THIFM	promegakaryocyte	PRO/MEG/KAR/YO/SAO*IT
prognathometer	PROG/NA/THOM/TER	promegaloblast	PRO/MEG/LO/BLA*S
prognathous	PROG/NA/THOUS	Promet	PRO/MET
prognose	PROG/NOES	prometaphase	PRO/MET/FAEZ
prognoses	PROG/NOE/SAOEZ		PRO/MET/FAIZ
prognosis	PROG/NOE/SIS	promethazine	PRO/M*ET/ZAOEN
prognostic	PROG/NO*S/IK	promethestrol	PRO/M*ET/ES/TROL
prognosticate	PROG/NO*S/KAIT		PRO/M*ET/STROL
prognosticator	PROG/NO*S/KAI/TOR	promethium	PRO/MAO*ET/YUM
prognostician	PROG/NOS/TIGS	promine	PRO/MAOEN
progonoma	PRO/GOE/NOE/MA	prominence	PROM/NENS
	PRO/GON/O/MA	prominens	PROM/NENZ
	PRO/GON/NOE/MA	prominent	PROM/NENT
progranulocyte	PRO/GRAN/LO/SAO*IT	prominentia	PROM/NEN/SHA
progravid	PRO/GRAVD	prominentiae	PROM/NEN/SHAE
	PRO/GRAV/ID	promitosis	PRO/MAOI/TOE/SIS
progress	PROG	promonocyte	PRO/MON/SAO*IT
	PROG/RESZ	ProMod	PRO/MOD
progression	PRO/GREGS	promontoria	PROM/ON/TOER/YA
progressiva	PRO/GRES/SAOI/VA		PROM/ON/TOR/YA
	PRO/GRES/SAOE/VA	promontorium	PROM/ON/TOIRM
progressive	PRO/GRES/SIV		PROM/ON/TOER/YUM
	PRO/GRESZ/IV		PROM/ON/TOR/YUM

promontory	PROM/ON/TOIR	propionate	PROEP/YO/NAIT
promoter	PRO/MOET/ER	Propionibacteriaceae	PROEP/YON/BAK/TAOER/YAIS/
promotion	PRO/MOEGS		YAE
promoxolane	PRO/MOX/LAIN	Propionibacterium	PROEP/YON/BAK/TAOERM
promyelocyte	PRO/MAOI/LO/SAO*IT	propionic	PROEP/YON/IK
pronasion	PRO/NAIZ/YON	propionicacidemia	PROEP/YON/IK/AS/DAOEM/YA
pronate	PRO/NAIT	propionyl	PROEP/YO/NIL
pronation	PRO/NAIGS	propitocaine	PRO/PIT/KAIN
pronatis	PRO/NAI/TIS	proplasia	PRO/PLAIZ/YA
pronatoflexor	PRO/NAIT/FLEK/SOR	proplasmacyte	PRO/PLAZ/MA/SAO*IT
	PRO/NAI/TO/FLEK/SOR	proplasmin	PRO/PLAZ/MIN
pronator	PRO/NAI/TOR	proplastid	PRO/PLAS/TID
pronatoris	PRO/NAI/TOR/RIS	proplex	PRO/PLEX
	PRO/NAI/TOER/RIS	proplexus	PRO/PLEK/SUS
prone	PROEN	propons	PRO/PONS
pronephric	PRO/NEF/RIK	propositi	PRO/POZ/TAOI
pronephroi	PRO/NEF/ROI	propositus	PRO/POZ/TUS
pronephron	PRO/NEF/RON	propoxycaine	PRO/POX/KAIN
pronephros	PRO/NEF/ROS	propoxyphene	PRO/POX/FAOEN
Pronestyl	PRO/NES/TIL	propranolol	PRO/PRAN/LOL
Pronestyl-SR	PRO/NES/TIL/S-RBGS/R*RBGS	propri(o)-	PROEP/R(O)
pronetalol	PRO/NET/LOL		PRO/PRAOE/Y(O)
pronethalol	PRO/N*ET/LOL	propria	PROEP/RA
prong	PRONG		PRO/PRAOE/YA
pronograde	PROEN/GRAID	propriae	PROEP/RAE
pronometer	PRO/NOM/TER		PRO/PRAOE/YAE
pronormoblast	PRO/NORM/BLA*S	proprietary	PRO/PRAOI/TAIR
pronuclei	PRO/NAOUK/LAOI	proprii	PROEP/RAOI
pronucleus	PRO/NAOUK/LUS		PRO/PRAOE/YAOI
prootic	PRO/OET/IK	proprioception	PROEP/RO/SEPGS
	PRO/OT/IK	proprioceptive	PROEP/RO/SEPT/IV
prop	PROP	proprioceptor	PROEP/RO/SEP/TOR
Propacet	PROP/SET	propriodentium	PROEP/RO/DEN/SHUM
	PROEP/SET	propriospinal	PROEP/RO/SPAOINL
propadiene	PROEP/DI/AOEN	proprotein	PRO/PRO/TAOEN
propagate	PROP/GAIT	proprium	PROEP/RUM
propagation	PROP/GAIGS		PRO/PRAOE/UM
propagative	PROP/GAIT/IV		PRO/PRAOE/YUM
Propagest	PROP/J*ES	proprius	PROEP/RUS
propagule	PROP/GAOUL		PRO/PRAOE/YUS
propalinal	PRO/PAL/NAL	proptometer	PROP/TOM/TER
propamidine	PRO/PAM/DAOEN	proptosis	PROP/TOE/SIS
propane	PRO/PAIN	proptotic	PROP/TOT/IK
	PRO/PAEN	propulsion	PRO/PULGS
propanedioic	PRO/PAIN/DI/OIK	propyl	PRO/PIL
propanetriol	PRO/PAIN/TR*I/OL	propylcarbinol	PRO/PIL/KARB/NOL
propanidid	PRO/PAN/DID	propylene	PROEP/LAOEN
propanoic	PROEP/NOIK		PRO/LAOEN
	PROEP/NOE/IK	propylhexedrine	PRO/PIL/HEX/DRAOEN
propanol	PROEP/NOL	propyliodone	PRO/PIL/AOI/DOEN
propanolol	PRO/PAN/LOL	propylparaben	PRO/PIL/PAR/BEN
propanoyl	PROEP/NOIL	propylthiouracil	PRO/PIL/THAOI/YAOUR/SIL
	PROEP/NOE/IL	propyromazine	PRO/PI/ROEM/ZAOEN
propantheline	PRO/PA*NT/LAOEN		PRO/PAOI/ROEM/ZAOEN
proparacaine	PRO/PAR/KAIN	proquazone	PRO/KWA/ZOEN
propatyl	PROEP/TIL	pro re nata	PROE/RAOE/NAI/TA
propedeutic	PRO/PE/DAOUT/IK		PROE/RE/NAI/TA
propene	PRO/PAOEN	prorennin	PRO/REN/NIN
propentdyopent	PRO/PENT/DAOI/PENT	prorrhaphy	PROR/FI
propenyl	PROEP/NIL	prorsad	PROR/SAD
propepsin	PRO/PEP/SIN	prorubricyte	PRO/RAOUB/RI/SAO*IT
propeptone	PRO/PEP/TOEN	proscillaridin	PRO/SI/LAR/DIN
properdin	PRO/PER/DIN		PRO/SIL/LAR/DIN
properitoneal	PRO/PERT/NAOEL	proscolex	PRO/SKOE/LEX
prophage	PRO/FAIJ	prosecretin	PRO/SE/KRAOE/TIN
prophase	PRO/FAEZ	prosect	PRO/SEKT
	PRO/FAIZ	prosection	PRO/S*EBGS
prophenpyridamine	PRO/FEN/PI/RID/MAOEN	prosector	PRO/SEK/TOR
	PRO/FEN/PAOI/RID/MAOEN	prosectorium	PRO/SEK/TOIRM
prophlogistic	PRO/FLOE/J*IS/IK		PRO/SEK/TOER/YUM
prophylactic	PROEF/LAKT/IK		PRO/SEK/TOR/YUM
	PRO/FLAKT/IK	prosencephalon	PROS/EN/SEF/LON
	PRO/FI/LAKT/IK	prosimian	PRO/SIM/YAN
	PRO/FAOI/LAKT/IK	Proskauer	PROS/KOU/ER
prophylaxes	PROEF/LAK/SAOEZ		PROS/KOUR
	PRO/FLAK/SAOEZ	proso-	PROS
	PRO/FI/LAK/SAOEZ	ProSobee	PRO/SOE/BAOE
	PRO/FAOI/LAK/SAOEZ	prosocele	PROS/SAO*EL
prophylaxis	PROEF/LAK/SIS	prosodemic	PROS/DEM/IK
	PRO/FLAK/SIS	prosody	PROS/DI
	PRO/FI/LAK/SIS	prosogaster	PROS/GAS/TER
	PRO/FAOI/LAK/SIS	prosop(o)-	PROS/P(O)
Prophyllin	PRO/FLIN	prosopagnosia	PROS/PAG/NOEZ/YA
	PRO/FIL/LIN	prosopagus	PRO/SOP/GUS
propicillin	PROEP/SLIN	prosopalgia	PROS/PAL/JA
	PROEP/SIL/LIN	prosopalgic	PROS/PAL/JIK
propiolactone	PROEP/YO/LAK/TOEN	prosopantritis	PROS/PAN/TRAOITS
propiomazine	PROEP/YOEM/ZAOEN	prosopectasia	PROS/PEK/TAIZ/YA
	PROEP/YO/MAI/ZAOEN	-prosopia	PRO/SOEP/YA

prosoplasia	PROS/PLAIZ/YA	prosthodontics	PROS/THO/DONT/IK/-S
prosopoanoschisis	PROS/PO/AI/NOS/KI/SIS	prosthodontist	PROS/THO/DON/T*IS
prosopodiplegia	PROS/PO/DI/PLAOE/JA	Prosthogonimus	PROS/THO/GON/MUS
prosopodysmorphia	PROS/PO/DIS/MOR/FA	prosthokeratoplasty	PROS/THO/KER/TO/PLAS/TI
	PROS/PO/DIS/MOR/FAOE/YA	Prostigmin	PRO/STIG/MIN
prosoponeuralgia	PROS/PO/NAOU/RAL/JA	Prostin	PROS/TIN
prosopopagus	PROS/PO/PGUS	Prostin VR Pediatric	PROS/TIN/V-RBGS/R*RBGS/
prosopoplegia	PROS/PO/PLAOE/JA		PAOED/YAT/RIK
prosopoplegic	PROS/PO/PLAOEJ/IK	prostrate	PROS/TRAIT
prosoposchisis	PROS/POS/KI/SIS	prostration	PROS/TRAIGS
prosopospasm	PROS/PO/SPAFM	protactinium	PRO/TAK/TIN/YUM
prosoposternodymus	PROS/PO/STER/NOD/MUS	protal	PRO/TAL
prosopothoracopagus	PROS/PO/THOR/KOP/GUS	protalbumose	PRO/TAL/BAOU/MOES
-prosopus	PRO/SOE/PUS	protaminase	PRO/TAM/NAIS
	PROS/PUS	protamine	PROET/MAOEN
prospective	PRO/SPEKT/IV		PROET/MIN
	PROS/PEKT/IV	protan	PRO/TAN
prospermia	PRO/SPERM/YA	protandrous	PRO/TAN/DROUS
prosta-	PRO*S	protandry	PRO/TAN/DRI
	PROS/TA	protanomalopia	PROET/NOM/LOEP/YA
prostacyclin	PRO*S/SAOI/KLIN	protanomalopsia	PROET/NOM/LOPS/YA
	PRO*S/SAOIK/LIN	protanomalous	PROET/NOM/LOUS
prostaglandin	PRO*S/GLAN/DIN	protanomaly	PROET/NOM/LI
prostalene	PRO*S/LAOEN	protanope	PROET/NOEP
prostanoic	PRO*S/NOIK	protanopia	PROET/NOEP/YA
	PRO*S/NOE/IK	protanopic	PROET/NOP/IK
Prostaphlin	PRO/STAF/LIN	protanopsia	PROET/NOPS/YA
prostat(o)-	PRO*S/T(O)	prote(o)-	PROET/Y(O)
	PROS/TA/T(O)	Protea	PROET/YA
	PROS/TAIT	protean	PROET/YAN
	PROS/TAI/T(O)	proteantigen	PRO/TAOE/A*ENT/JEN
prostata	PRO*S/TA		PROET/YANT/JEN
	PROS/TA/TA	protease	PROET/YAIS
	PROS/TAI/TA	protectant	PRO/TEK/TANT
prostatae	PRO*S/TAE	protectin	PRO/TEK/TIN
	PROS/TA/TAE	protection	PRO/T*EBGS
	PROS/TAI/TAE	protective	PRO/TEKT/IV
prostatalgia	PRO*S/TAL/JA	protector	PRO/TEK/TOR
prostatauxe	PRO*S/TAUK/SAOE	proteid	PROET/YID
prostate	PROS/TAIT	proteidic	PROET/YID/IK
prostatectomy	PRO*S/TEKT/M*I	protein	PRO/TAOEN
prostatelcosis	PROS/TAT/EL/KOE/SIS		PROET/YIN
prostateria	PRO*S/TAOER/YA	protein(o)-	PRO/TAOEN
prostatic	PROS/TAT/IK		PROET/N(O)-
prostatici	PROS/TAT/SAOI		PRO/TAOE/N(O)-
prostatico-	PROS/TAT/KO	proteinaceous	PROET/NAIRBS
prostaticovesical	PROS/TAT/KO/VES/KAL		PRO/TAOE/NAIRBS
prostaticovesiculectomy	PROS/TAT/KO/VE/SIK/LEKT/M*I		PRO/TAOEN/AIRBS
prostaticum	PROS/TAT/KUM	proteinase	PRO/TAOEN/AIS
prostaticus	PROS/TAT/KUS		PROET/YIN/AIS
prostatism	PRO*S/TIFM	proteinemia	PROET/NAOEM/YA
prostatitic	PRO*S/TIT/IK		PRO/TAOEN/AOEM/YA
prostatitis	PRO*S/TAOITS	proteinic	PRO/TAOEN/IK
prostatocystitis	PRO*S/TO/SIS/TAOITS		PROET/YIN/IK
	PROS/TAIT/SIS/TAOITS	proteinicum	PROET/YIN/KUM
prostatocystotomy	PRO*S/TO/SIS/TOT/M*I		PRO/TAOEN/KUM
	PROS/TAIT/SIS/TOT/M*I	proteinogenous	PRO/TAOEN/OJ/NOUS
prostatodynia	PRO*S/TO/DIN/YA		PROET/YIN/OJ/NOUS
prostatography	PRO*S/TOG/FI	proteinogram	PRO/TAOEN/GRAM
prostatolith	PROS/TAT/L*IT		PROET/YIN/GRAM
prostatolithotomy	PRO*S/TO/LI/THOT/M*I	proteinology	PRO/TAOEN/OLG
	PROS/TAT/LI/THOT/M*I		PROET/YI/NOLG
prostatomegaly	PRO*S/TO/MEG/LI		PROET/YIN/OLG
prostatometer	PRO*S/TOM/TER	proteinosis	PRO/TAOEN/O/SIS
prostatomy	PROS/TAT/M*I		PRO/TAOE/NOE/SIS
prostatomyomectomy	PRO*S/TO/MAOI/MEKT/M*I		PROET/YI/NOE/SIS
	PROS/TAIT/MAOI/MEKT/M*I	proteinotherapy	PRO/TAOEN/THER/PI
prostatorrhea	PRO*S/TO/RAOE/YA	proteinuria	PROET/NAOUR/YA
prostatoseminalvesiculectomy			PRO/TAOE/NAOUR/YA
	PRO*S/TO/SEM/NAL/VE/SIK/		PRO/TAOEN/YAOUR/YA
	LEKT/M*I		PROET/YI/NAOUR/YA
prostatotomy	PRO*S/TOT/M*I	proteinuric	PROET/NAOUR/IK
prostatotoxin	PRO*S/TO/TOK/SIN		PRO/TAOE/NAOUR/IK
prostatovesiculectomy	PRO*S/TO/VE/SIK/LEKT/M*I		PRO/TAOEN/YAOUR/IK
prostatovesiculitis	PRO*S/TO/VE/SIK/LAOITS		PROET/YI/NAOUR/IK
prostaxia	PRO/STAX/YA	Protenate	PROET/NAIT
Pros-Tech	PROS/TEK	protensity	PRO/TENS/TI
prosternation	PROS/TER/NAIGS	proteoclastic	PROET/YO/KLA*S/IK
	PRO/STER/NAIGS	proteoglycan	PROET/YO/GLAOI/KAN
prosth(o)-	PROS/TH(O)	proteohormone	PROET/YO/HOR/MOEN
prostheses	PROS/THAOE/SAOEZ	proteolipid	PROET/YO/LIP/ID
prosthesis	PROS/THAOE/SIS	proteolysin	PROET/YOL/SIN
prosthetic	PROS/THET/IK	proteolysis	PROET/YOL/SIS
prosthetics	PROS/THET/IK/-S	proteolytic	PROET/YO/LIT/IK
prosthetist	PROS/THE/T*IS	proteometabolic	PROET/YO/MET/BOL/IK
prosthetophacos	PROS/THE/TO/FAK/OES	proteometabolism	PROET/YO/ME/TAB/LIFM
prosthion	PROS/THAOE/YON	proteopectic	PROET/YO/PEKT/IK
	PROS/THON	proteopepsis	PROET/YO/PEP/SIS
prosthodontia	PROS/THO/DON/SHA	proteopeptic	PROET/YO/PEPT/IK

proteopexic	PROET/YO/PEX/IK	proton	PRO/TON
proteopexy	PROET/YO/PEK/SI	protoneuron	PROET/NAOU/RON
proteophilic	PROET/YO/FIL/IK	proto-oncogene	PROET/ON/KO/JAOEN
proteose	PROET/YOES	Protopam	PROET/PAM
proteosotherapy	PROET/YOES/THER/PI	protopathic	PROET/PA*T/IK
	PROET/YOE/SO/THER/PI	protopecten	PROET/PEK/TIN
proteosuria	PROET/YO/SAOUR/YA	Protophyta	PROET/FAOI/TA
proteotherapy	PROET/YO/THER/PI	protophyte	PROET/FAOIT
proteotoxin	PROET/YO/TOK/SIN	protophytology	PROET/FAOI/TOLG
proter	PRO/TER	protopianoma	PROET/PAOE/NOE/MA
proteuria	PROET/YAOUR/YA	protoplasia	PROET/PLAIZ/YA
	PRO/TAOE/YAOUR/YA	protoplasm	PROET/PLAFM
proteuric	PROET/YAOUR/IK	protoplasmatic	PROET/PLAS/MAT/IK
	PRO/TAOE/YAOUR/IK	protoplasmaticum	PROET/PLAZ/MAT/KUM
Proteus	PROET/YUS	protoplasmic	PROET/PLAZ/MIK
prothipendyl	PRO/THAOI/PEN/DIL	protoplasmolysis	PROET/PLAZ/MOL/SIS
prothrombase	PRO/THROM/BAIS	protoplast	PROET/PLA*S
prothrombin	PRO/THROM/BIN	protoporphyria	PROET/POR/FIR/YA
prothrombinase	PRO/THROM/BI/NAIS	protoporphyrin	PROET/POR/FRIN
	PRO/THROM/BIN/AIS	protoporphyrinuria	PROET/POR/FRIN/YAOUR/YA
prothrombinojen	PRO/THROM/BIN/JEN	protoproteose	PROET/PROET/YOES
	PRO/THROM/BIN/BI/NO/JEN	protopsis	PRO/TOP/SIS
prothrombinogenic	PRO/THROM/BIN/JEN/IK	protosalt	PROET/SAULT
	PRO/THROM/BI/NO/JEN/IK		PROET/SALT
prothrombinopenia	PRO/THROM/BIN/PAOEN/YA	protospasm	PROET/SPAFM
	PRO/THROM/BI/NO/PAOEN/YA	protospore	PROET/SPOER
prothrombokinase	PRO/THROM/BO/KAOI/NAIS	Protostat	PROET/STAT
prothymia	PRO/THAOIM/YA	Protostrongylus	PROET/STRONG/LUS
Protid	PRO/TID		PROET/STRON/JI/LUS
protide	PRO/TAOID	Protostrongylus rufescens	PROET/STRONG/LUS/RAOU/FES/
protinium	PRO/TIN/YUM		ENZ
protiodide	PRO/TAOI/DAOID		PROET/STRON/JI/LUS/RAOU/
protirelin	PRO/TAOIR/LIN		FES/ENZ
protist	PRO/T*IS	protosulfate	PROET/SUL/FAIT
Protista	PRO/TIS/TA	protosyphilis	PROET/SIF/LIS
protistologist	PRO/TIS/TO*LGS	prototaxic	PROET/TAX/IK
protistology	PRO/TIS/TOLG	Prototheca	PROET/THAOE/KA
protium	PROET/YUM	protothecosis	PROET/THAOE/KOE/SIS
proto-	PROET	prototoxin	PROET/TOK/SIN
protoactinium	PROET/AK/TIN/YUM	prototoxoid	PROET/TOK/SOID
protoalbumose	PROET/AL/BAOU/MOES		PROET/TOX/OID
protobe	PRO/TOEB	prototroph	PROET/TROF
protobiology	PROET/BAO*I/OLG		PROET/TROEF
protoblast	PROET/BLA*S	prototrophic	PROET/TROFK
protoblastic	PROET/BLA*S/IK	Protropin	PRO/TROE/PIN
protobrochal	PROET/BROE/KAL	prototropy	PRO/TOT/RO/PI
protocatechuic	PROET/KAT/KAOU/IK	prototype	PROET/TAOIP
protochloride	PROET/KLOR/AOID	protoveratrine	PROET/VER/TRAOEN
protochlorophyll	PROET/KLOR/FIL	protovertebra	PROET/VERT/BRA
protochondral	PROET/KON/DRAL	protovertebral	PROET/VERT/BRAL
protochondrium	PROET/KON/DRUM	protoxide	PRO/TOK/SAOID
	PROET/KON/DRAOE/UM		PRO/TOX/AOID
protocol	PROET/KOL	protozoa	PROET/ZOE/WA
protocone	PROET/KOEN	Protozoa	K-P/PROET/ZOE/WA
protoconid	PROET/KO/NID	protozoacide	PROET/ZOE/WA/SAO*ID
	PROET/KON/ID	protozoagglutinin	PROET/ZOE/GLAOUT/NIN
protocooperation	PROET/KAOPGS		PROET/ZOE/AI/GLAOUT/NIN
	PROET/KAOP/RAIGS	protozoal	PROET/ZOEL
protocoproporphyria	PROET/KOP/RO/POR/FIR/YA		PROET/ZOE/WAL
Protoctista	PRO/TOK/TIS/TA	protozoan	PROET/ZOEN
protoderm	PROET/DERM		PROET/ZOE/WAN
protodiastolic	PROET/DAOI/STOL/IK	protozoiasis	PROET/ZOE/AOI/SIS
protoduodenum	PROET/DAOU/DAOEN/UM	protozoicide	PROET/ZOE/SAO*ID
	PROET/DWOD/NUM		PROET/ZOI/SAO*ID
protoelastose	PROET/E/LAS/TOES	protozoology	PROET/ZOE/OLG
protoerythrocyte	PROET/R*IT/RO/SAO*IT	protozoon	PROET/ZAON
protofibril	PROET/FAOI/BRIL	protozoophage	PROET/ZOE/FAIJ
protofilament	PROET/FIL/-MT	protozootherapy	PROET/ZOE/THER/PI
protogaster	PROET/GAS/TER	protraction	PRO/TRA*BGS
protogen	PROET/JEN	protractor	PRO/TRAK/TOR
protoglobulose	PROET/GLOB/LOES	protransglutaminase	PRO/TRA*NS/GLAOU/TAM/NAIS
protogonocyte	PROET/GON/SAO*IT	protriptyline	PRO/TRIPT/LAOEN
protogonoplasm	PROET/GON/PLAFM	protrude	PRO/TRAOUD
protogynous	PRO/TOJ/NOUS	protrusio	PRO/TRAOUZ/YOE
protogyny	PRO/TOJ/N*I		PRO/TRAOUS/YOE
protoheme	PROET/HAOEM	protrusio acetabuli	PRO/TRAOUZ/YOE/AS/TAB/LAOI
	PROET/HAO*EM		PRO/TRAOUS/YOE/AS/TAB/LAOI
protoiodide	PROET/AOI/DAOID	protrusion	PRO/TRAOUGS
protokaryon	PROET/KAR/YON	protrusive	PRO/TRAOUS/IV
protokylol	PROET/KAOI/LOL	protrypsin	PRO/TRIP/SIN
	PROET/KAOI/LOEL	protuberance	PRO/TAOUB/RANS
protoleukocyte	PROET/LAOUK/SAO*IT	protuberans	PRO/TAOUB/RANZ
protolysate	PRO/TOL/SAIT	protuberant	PRO/TAOUB/RANT
Protomastigida	PROET/MAS/TIJ/DA	protuberantia	PRO/TAOUB/RAN/SHA
protomerite	PRO/TOM/RAOIT	proud	PROUD
	PROET/MER/AOIT	Proventil	PRO/VEN/TIL
protometer	PRO/TOM/TER	Proventil Inhaler	PRO/VEN/TIL/IN/HAIL/ER
protometrocyte	PROET/MAOE/TRO/SAO*IT	proventriculus	PRO/VEN/TRIK/LUS
Protomonadina	PROET/MON/DAOI/NA	Provera	PRO/VER/RA

provertebra	PRO/VERT/BRA	Pseudamphistomum	SAOU/DAM/F*IS/MUM
Providencia	PROV/DENS/YA		SAOUD/AM/F*IS/MUM
provirus	PRO/VAOI/RUS	pseudangina	SAOU/DAN/JAOI/NA
provisional	PRO/VIGS/NAL		SAOU/DAN/JI/NA
provitamin	PRO/VAOIT/MIN	pseudankylosis	SAOU/DAN/KLOE/SIS
provocative	PRO/VOK/TIV		SAOU/DANG/LOE/SIS
Provocholine	PROEV/KOE/LAOEN	pseudaphia	SAOU/DAIF/YA
	PROEV/KOL/AOEN		SAOU/DAF/YA
Prowazek	PRO/VAT/SEK	pseudarrhenia	SAOUD/RAOEN/YA
Prowazekella	PRO/VAZ/KEL/LA	pseudarthritis	SAOU/DAR/THRAOITS
	PRO/VATS/KEL/LA	pseudarthrosis	SAOU/DAR/THROE/SIS
prowazeki	PRO/VAT/SEK/KAOI	pseudelminth	SAOU/DEL/M*INT
	PROEV/ZAOE/KAOI	pseudencephalus	SAOU/DEN/SEF/LUS
Prowazekia	PROEV/ZAOEK/YA	pseudesthesia	SAOU/DES/THAOEZ/YA
	PRO/VAT/SEK/YA	pseudinoma	SAOUD/NOE/MA
Prower	PROU/ER	pseudoacanthosis	SAOUD/AK/AN/THOE/SIS
proxazole	PROX/ZOEL	pseudoacephalus	SAOUD/AI/SEF/LUS
proxemics	PROK/SEM/IK/-S	pseudoachondroplasia	SAOUD/AI/KON/DRO/PLAIZ/YA
	PROK/SAOEM/IK/-S	pseudoactinomycosis	SAOUD/AKT/NO/MAOI/KOE/SIS
proxim(o)-	PROX/M(O)	pseudoagglutination	SAOUD/AI/GLAOUT/NAIGS
proximad	PROX/MAD	pseudoagrammatism	SAOUD/AI/GRAM/TIFM
proximal	PROX/MAL	pseudoagraphia	SAOUD/AI/GRAF/YA
proximalis	PROX/MAI/LIS	pseudoalbuminuria	SAOUD/AL/BAOUM/NAOUR/YA
proximate	PROX/MAIT	pseudoallele	SAOUD/AI/LAOEL
	PROX/MAT		SAOUD/AL/LAOEL
proximoataxia	PROX/MO/AI/TAX/YA	pseudoallelic	SAOUD/AI/LAOEL/IK
proximobuccal	PROX/MO/BUK/KAL		SAOUD/AL/LAOEL/IK
proximoceptor	PROX/MO/SEP/TOR	pseudoallelism	SAOUD/AI/LAOEL/IFM
proximolabial	PROX/MO/LAIB/YAL		SAOUD/AL/LAOEL/IFM
proximolingual	PROX/MO/LING/WAL		SAOUD/AL/LIFM
proxymetacaine	PROX/MET/KAIN	pseudo-alopecia areata	SAOUD/AL/PAOE/SHA/AR/YAI/TA
Prozac	PRO/ZAK	pseudoalveolar	SAOUD/AL/VAOE/LAR
prozapine	PROEZ/PAOEN	pseudoanaphylactic	SAOUD/AN/FLAKT/IK
prozonal	PRO/ZOENL	pseudoanaphylaxis	SAOUD/AN/FLAK/SIS
prozone	PRO/ZOEN	pseudoanemia	SAOUD/AI/NAOEM/YA
prozygosis	PRO/ZAOI/GOE/SIS	pseudoaneurysm	SAOUD/AN/RIFM
prozymogen	PRO/ZAOIM/JEN	pseudoangina	SAOUD/AN/JAOI/NA
Prulet	PRAOU/LET		SAOUD/AN/JI/NA
prune	PRAOUN	pseudoangiosarcoma	SAOUD/AN/JO/SAR/KOE/MA
Prunus	PRAOU/NUS	pseudoankylosis	SAOUD/AN/KLOE/SIS
pruriginous	PRAOU/RIJ/NOUS		SAOUD/ANG/LOE/SIS
prurigo	PRAOU/RAOI/GOE	pseudoanodontia	SAOUD/AN/DON/SHA
pruritic	PRAOU/RIT/IK		SAOUD/AN/O/DON/SHA
pruritogenic	PRAOU/RIT/JEN/IK	pseudoantagonist	SAOUD/AN/TAG/N*IS
pruritus	PRAOU/RAOI/TUS	pseudoapoplexy	SAOUD/AP/PLEK/SI
Prussak	PRAOU/SAK	pseudoappendicitis	SAOUD/AI/PEND/SAOITS
	PRAOUS/SAK	pseudoapraxia	SAOUD/AI/PRAX/YA
	PRUS/SAK	pseudoarthrosis	SAOUD/AR/THROE/SIS
Prussian	PRUGS	pseudoasthma	SAOUD/AS/MA
prussiate	PRURB/YAIT	pseudoataxia	SAOUD/AI/TAX/YA
	PRUS/YAIT	pseudoathetosis	SAOUD/A*T/TOE/SIS
prussic	PRUS/IK	pseudoauthenticity	SAOUD/AU/THEN/TIS/TI
	PRUS/SIK	pseudobacillus	SAOUD/BA/SIL/LUS
psalis	SAI/LIS	pseudobacterium	SAOUD/BAK/TAOERM
psalterial	SAL/TAOER/YA	pseudobasedow	SAOUD/BAS/DOU
	SAL/TER/YA	pseudobile	SAOUD/BAOIL
psalterial	SAL/TAOERL	pseudoblepsia	SAOUD/BLEPS/YA
	SAL/TAOER/YAL	pseudoblepsis	SAOUD/BLEP/SIS
	SAL/TER/YAL	pseudobronchiectasis	SAOUD/BRONG/YEKT/SIS
psalterium	SAL/TAOERM	pseudobulbar	SAOUD/BUL/BAR
	SAL/TAOER/YUM	pseudocartilage	SAOUD/KART/LAJ
	SAL/TER/YUM	pseudocartilaginous	SAOUD/KART/LAJ/NOUS
psammo-	SAM	pseudocast	SAOUD/KA*S
	SAM/MO	pseudocele	SAOUD/SAO*EL
psammocarcinoma	SAM/KARS/NOE/MA	pseudoselom	SAOUD/SE/LOM
psammoma	SAM/MOE/MA	pseudocephalocele	SAOUD/SEF/LO/SAO*EL
	SA/MOE/MA	pseudochancre	SAOUD/SHAN/KER
psammomatous	SAM/MOEM/TOUS	pseudocholecystitis	SAOUD/KOEL/SIS/TAOITS
	SA/MOEM/TOUS	pseudocholesteatoma	SAOUD/KL*ES/YA/TOE/MA
psammopapillare	SAM/PAP/LAI/RAOE		SAOUD/KOEL/STAOE/TOE/MA
psammosarcoma	SAM/SAR/KOE/MA	pseudocholinesterase	SAOUD/KOEL/N*ES/RAIS
psammotherapy	SAM/THER/PI	pseudochorea	SAOUD/KOE/RAOE/YA
psammous	SAM/OUS	pseudochromesthesia	SAOUD/KROEM/ES/THAOEZ/YA
psauoscopy	SAU/OS/KPI		SAOUD/KROE/MES/THAOEZ/YA
pselaphesia	SEL/FAOEZ/YA	pseudochromhidrosis	SAOUD/KROEM/HI/DROE/SIS
pselaphesis	SE/LAF/SIS	pseudochromidrosis	SAOUD/KROEM/DROE/SIS
	SEL/FAOE/SIS	pseudochromosome	SAOUD/KROEM/SOEM
psellism	SEL/IFM	pseudochylous	SAOUD/KAOIL/OUS
pseud(o)-	SAOUD	pseudocirrhosis	SAOUD/SIR/ROE/SIS
	SAOU/D(O)	pseudoclaudication	SAOUD/KLAUD/KAIGS
pseudacousis	SAOUD/KAOU/SIS	pseudoclonus	SAOUD/KLOE/NUS
pseudacousma	SAOUD/KAOUZ/MA	pseudocoarctation	SAOUD/KO/ARK/TAIGS
pseudacromegaly	SAOU/DAK/RO/MEG/LI	pseudocolloid	SAOUD/KLOID
pseudactinomycosis	SAOU/DAKT/NO/MAOI/KOE/SIS		SAOUD/KOL/OID
pseudagraphia	SAOUD/GRAF/YA	pseudocollusion	SAOUD/KLAOUGS
pseudalbuminuria	SAOU/DAL/BAOUM/NAOUR/YA	pseudocoloboma	SAOUD/KOL/BOE/MA
Pseudallescheria boydii	SAOUD/AL/ES/KAOER/YA/BOID/ YAOI	pseudocolony	SAOUD/KOL/N*I
		pseudocoma	SAOUD/KO/MA
pseudallescheriasis	SAOUD/AL/ES/KAOER/YA/SIS	pseudocopulation	SAOUD/KOP/LAIGS

pseudo-corpus luteum	SAOUD/KOR/PUS/LAOUT/YUM
pseudocowpox	SAOUD/KOU/POX
pseudocoxalgia	SAOUD/KOX/AL/JA
	SAOUD/KOK/SAL/JA
pseudocrisis	SAOUD/KRAOI/SIS
	SAOU/DOK/RI/SIS
pseudocroup	SAOUD/KRAOUP
pseudocryptorchism	SAOUD/KRIP/TOR/KIFM
pseudocumene	SAOUD/KAOU/MAOEN
pseudocumol	SAOUD/KAOU/MOL
pseudocyesis	SAOUD/SAOI/E/SIS
pseudocylindroid	SAOUD/SLIN/DROID
	SAOUD/SIL/IN/DROID
	SAOUD/SI/LIN/DROID
pseudocyst	SAOUD/S*IS
pseudodeciduosis	SAOUD/DE/SID/YOE/SIS
pseudodementia	SAOUD/DMEN/SHA
	SAOUD/DE/MEN/SHA
pseudodextrocardia	SAOUD/DEX/TRO/KARD/YA
pseudodiabetes	SAOUD/DAOI/BAOE/TAOEZ
pseudodiastolic	SAOUD/DAOI/STOL/IK
pseudodigitoxin	SAOUD/DIJ/TOK/SIN
pseudodiphtheria	SAOUD/DIF/THAOER/YA
pseudodiphtheriticum	SAOUD/DIF/THRIT/KUM
	SAOUD/DIF/THE/RIT/KUM
pseudodipsia	SAOUD/DIPS/YA
pseudodiverticulum	SAOUD/DI/VER/TIK/LUM
pseudodominant	SAOUD/DOM/NANT
pseudodysentery	SAOUD/DIS/SPWER/RI
pseudoedema	SAOUD/E/DAOE/MA
	SAOUD/DAOE/MA
pseudoembryonic	SAOUD/EM/BRON/IK
pseudoemphysema	SAOUD/EFRP/SAOE/MA
	SAOUD/EM/FI/SAOE/MA
pseudoendometritis	SAOUD/*END/ME/TRAOITS
pseudoeosinophil	SAOUD/E/SIN/FIL
pseudoephedrine	SAOUD/EF/DRAOEN
	SAOUD/E/FED/RIN
pseudoepiphysis	SAOUD/E/PIF/SIS
pseudoerysipelas	SAOUD/*ER/SIP/LAS
pseudoesthesia	SAOUD/ES/THAOEZ/YA
pseudoexfoliation	SAOUD/EX/FOEL/YAIGS
pseudoexophoria	SAOUD/KPO/FOER/YA
pseudoexophthalmos	SAOUD/KPOF/THAL/MOS
	SAOUD/EX/OF/THAL/MOS
pseudoexstrophy	SAOUD/EX/STRO/FI
pseudoexstrophy	SAOUD/EK/STRO/FI
pseudofarcy	SAOUD/FAR/SI
pseudofluctuation	SAOUD/FLUK/YAIGS
	SAOUD/FLUK/KHAIGS
pseudofolliculitis	SAOUD/FLIK/LAOITS
pseudofracture	SAOUD/FRAK/KHUR
pseudofructose	SAOUD/FRUK/TOES
pseudoganglion	SAOUD/GANG/LON
pseudogene	SAOUD/JAOEN
pseudogestation	SAOUD/JES/TAIGS
pseudogeusesthesia	SAOUD/GAOUS/ES/THAOEZ/YA
pseudogeusia	SAOUD/GAOUS/YA
	SAOUD/GAOUZ/YA
pseudoglanders	SAOUD/GLAND/ER/-S
	SAOUD/GLAN/DER/-S
pseudoglaucoma	SAOUD/GLAU/KOE/MA
pseudoglioma	SAOUD/GLAOI/YOE/MA
pseudoglobulin	SAOUD/GLOB/LIN
pseudoglomerulus	SAOUD/GLOE/MER/LUS
pseudoglottic	SAOUD/GLOT/IK
pseudoglottis	SAOUD/GLOT/TIS
pseudoglucosazone	SAOUD/GLAOU/KOES/ZOEN
	SAOUD/GLAOUK/SAI/ZOEN
pseudogonorrhea	SAOUD/GON/RAOE/YA
pseudogout	SAOUD/GAOUT
pseudogynecomastia	SAOUD/GAOIN/KO/MA*S/YA
	SAOUD/JIN/KO/MA*S/YA
pseudohallucination	SAOUD/HA/LAOUS/NAIGS
	SAOUD/HAL/LAOUS/NAIGS
pseudohaustration	SAOUD/HAUS/TRAIGS
pseudohelminth	SAOUD/HEL/M*INT
pseudohemagglutination	SAOUD/HEM/AI/GLAOUT/NAIGS
pseudohematuria	SAOUD/HAOEM/TAOUR/YA
	SAOUD/HEM/TAOUR/YA
pseudohemophilia	SAOUD/HAOEM/FIL/YA
pseudohemoptysis	SAOUD/HAOE/MOPT/SIS
	SAOUD/HE/MOPT/SIS
pseudohereditary	SAOUD/HE/RED/TAIR
pseudohermaphrodism	SAOUD/HER/MAF/RO/DIFM
pseudohermaphrodite	SAOUD/HER/MAF/RO/DAOIT
pseudohermaphroditism	SAOUD/HER/MAF/RO/DAOIT/IFM
	SAOUD/HER/MAF/RO/DAOI/TIFM
pseudohernia	SAOUD/HERN/YA

pseudoheterotopia	SAOUD/HET/RO/TOEP/YA
pseudohydrocephalus	SAOUD/HAOI/DRO/SEF/LUS
pseudohydrocephaly	SAOUD/HAOI/DRO/SEF/LI
pseudohydronephrosis	SAOUD/HAOI/DRO/NE/FROE/SIS
pseudohyoscyamine	SAOUD/HAOI/SAOI/MIN
pseudohyperkalemia	SAOUD/HAO*IP/KLAOEM/YA
	SAOUD/HAO*IP/KA/LAOEM/YA
pseudohyperparathyroidism	SAOUD/HAO*IP/PAR/THAOI/ROI/DIFM
pseudohypertelorism	SAOUD/HAO*IP/TEL/RIFM
pseudohypertrichosis	SAOUD/HAO*IP/TRI/KOE/SIS
pseudohypertrophic	SAOUD/HAO*IP/TROFK
pseudohypertrophy	SAOUD/HAOI/PERT/FI
pseudohypha	SAOUD/HAOI/FA
pseudohypoaldosteronism	SAOUD/HO*IP/AL/DOS/TROEN/IFM
pseudohyponatremia	SAOUD/HO*IP/NA/TRAOEM/YA
pseudohypoparathyroidism	SAOUD/HO*IP/PAR/THAOI/ROI/DIFM
pseudohypophosphatasia	SAOUD/HO*IP/FOS/FA/TAIZ/YA
pseudohypothyroidism	SAOUD/HO*IP/THAOI/ROI/DIFM
pseudoicterus	SAOUD/IKT/RUS
pseudoileus	SAOUD/*IL/YUS
pseudoinfarction	SAOUD/IN/FA*RBGS
pseudoinfluenza	SAOUD/IN/FLAOUN/ZA
pseudointraligamentous	SAOUD/SPWRA/LIG/MEN/TOUS
pseudoion	SAOUD/AOIN
pseudoisochromatic	SAOUD/AOIS/KROE/MAT/IK
pseudoisocyanin	SAOUD/AOIS/SAOI/NIN
pseudojaundice	SAOUD/JAUN/DIS
pseudokeratin	SAOUD/KER/TIN
pseudolamellar	SAOUD/LA/MEL/LAR
pseudoleukemia	SAOUD/LAOU/KAOEM/YA
pseudoleukemica	SAOUD/LAOU/KAOEM/KA
	SAOUD/LAOU/KEM/KA
pseudoleukocythemia	SAOUD/LAOUK/SAOI/THAOEM/YA
pseudolipoma	SAOUD/LI/POE/MA
pseudolithiasis	SAOUD/LI/THAOI/SIS
pseudologia	SAOUD/LOE/JA
pseudoluxation	SAOUD/LUK/SAIGS
	SAOUD/LUX/AIGS
pseudoleukemica	SAOUD/LAOU/KAOEM/KA
pseudolutein	SAOUD/LAOUT/YIN
pseudolymphocyte	SAOUD/LIM/FO/SAO*IT
pseudolymphoma	SAOUD/LIM/FOE/MA
pseudolysogenic	SAOUD/LAOIS/JEN/IK
pseudolysogeny	SAOUD/LAOI/SOJ/N*I
pseudomalignancy	SAOUD/MA/LIG/NAN/SI
pseudomallei	SAOUD/MAL/YAOI
pseudomamma	SAOUD/MAM/MA
pseudomania	SAOUD/MAIN/YA
pseudomasturbation	SAOUD/MA*S/BAIGS
pseudomegacolon	SAOUD/MEG/KO/LON
pseudomelanosis	SAOUD/MEL/NOE/SIS
pseudomelia	SAOUD/MAOEL/YA
pseudomembrane	SAOUD/MEM/BRAIN
pseudomembranous	SAOUD/MEM/BRA/NOUS
pseudomeningitis	SAOUD/MEN/JAOITS
pseudomenstruation	SAOUD/MEN/STRAIGS
pseudometaplasia	SAOUD/MET/PLAIZ/YA
pseudomethemoglobin	SAOUD/MET/HAOEM/GLOE/BIN
pseudomicrocephalus	SAOUD/MAOI/KRO/SEF/LUS
pseudomilium	SAOUD/MIL/YUM
pseudomnesia	SAOU/DOM/NAOEZ/YA
pseudomonad	SAOUD/MOE/NAD
Pseudomonadaceae	SAOUD/MOEN/DAIS/YAE
Pseudomonadales	SAOUD/MOEN/DAI/LAOEZ
Pseudomonadineae	SAOUD/MOEN/DAOIN/YAE
Pseudomonas	SAOUD/MOEN/NAS
pseudomorph	SAOUD/MOR/-F
pseudomorphine	SAOUD/MOR/FAOEN
pseudomotor	SAOUD/MOE/TOR
pseudomucin	SAOUD/MAOU/SIN
pseudomucinous	SAOUD/MAOUS/NOUS
pseudomycelium	SAOUD/MAOI/SAOEL/YUM
pseudomyiasis	SAOUD/MAOI/AOI/SIS
pseudomyopia	SAOUD/MAOI/OEP/YA
pseudomyxoma	SAOUD/MIK/SOE/MA
pseudonarcotic	SAOUD/NAR/KOT/IK
pseudonarcotism	SAOUD/NARK/TIFM
pseudoneoplasm	SAOUD/NAOE/PLAFM
pseudoneuritis	SAOUD/NAOU/RAOITS
pseudoneuroma	SAOUD/NAOU/ROE/MA
pseudonit	SAOUD/NIT
pseudonystagmus	SAOUD/NIS/TAG/MUS
pseudo-osteomalacia	SAOUD/O*S/YO/MA/LAI/SHA
pseudo-osteomalacic	SAOUD/O*S/YO/MA/LAIS/IK

pseudo-ovum	SAOUD/O/VUM
	SAOUD/OEV/UM
pseudopannus	SAOUD/PAN/NUS
pseudopapilla	SAOUD/PA/PIL/LA
pseudopapilledema	SAOUD/PAP/LE/DAOE/MA
pseudoparalysis	SAOUD/PRAL/SIS
pseudoparaphrasia	SAOUD/PAR/FRAIZ/YA
pseudoparaplegia	SAOUD/PAR/PLAOE/JA
pseudoparasite	SAOUD/PAR/SAOIT
pseudoparenchyma	SAOUD/PRENG/MA
	SAOUD/PA/RENG/MA
pseudoparesis	SAOUD/PA/RAOE/SIS
	SAOUD/PAR/SIS
pseudopelade	SAOUD/PE/LAUD
	SAOUD/PAOE/LAID
pseudopellagra	SAOUD/PE/LAG/RA
	SAOUD/PEL/LAG/RA
pseudopericardial	SAOUD/P*ER/KARD/YAL
pseudopericarditis	SAOUD/P*ER/KAR/DAOITS
pseudoperitonitis	SAOUD/PERT/NAOITS
pseudophacos	SAOUD/FAK/OES
pseudophakia	SAOUD/FAIK/YA
	SAOUD/FAK/YA
pseudophakodonesis	SAOUD/FAIK/DOE/NAOE/SIS
	SAOUD/FAK/DOE/NAOE/SIS
pseudophlegmon	SAOUD/FLEG/MON
pseudophotesthesia	SAOUD/FOE/TES/THAOEZ/YA
	SAOUD/FOET/ES/THAOEZ/YA
pseudophthisis	SAOU/DOF/THI/SIS
pseudophyllid	SAOUD/FAOI/LID
	SAOUD/FIL/LID
Pseudophyllidea	SAOUD/FLID/YA
	SAOUD/FI/LID/YA
	SAOUD/FIL/LID/YA
pseudophyllidean	SAOUD/FLID/YAN
	SAOUD/FI/LID/YAN
	SAOUD/FIL/LID/YAN
pseudoplasm	SAOUD/PLAFM
pseudoplatelet	SAOUD/PLAET/LET
	SAOUD/PLAIT/LET
pseudoplegia	SAOUD/PLAOE/JA
pseudopneumonia	SAOUD/NAOU/MOEN/YA
pseudopocket	SAOUD/POKT
	SAOUD/POK/ET
pseudopod	SAOUD/POD
pseudopodia	SAOUD/POED/YA
pseudopodiospore	SAOUD/POED/YO/SPOER
pseudopodium	SAOUD/POED/YUM
pseudopoliomyelitis	SAOUD/POEL/YO/MAOI/LAOITS
pseudopolycythemia	SAOUD/POL/SAOI/THAOEM/YA
pseudopolydystrophy	SAOUD/POL/DIS/TRO/FI
pseudopolymelia	SAOUD/POL/MAOEL/YA
pseudopolyp	SAOUD/POL/IP
pseudopolyposis	SAOUD/POL/POE/SIS
pseudoporphyria	SAOUD/POR/FIR/YA
pseudopregnancy	SAOUD/PREG/NAN/SI
pseudoprimary	SAOUD/PRAOI/MAIR
pseudoprognathism	SAOUD/PROG/NA/THIFM
pseudoproteinuria	SAOUD/PROET/NAOUR/YA
pseudopseudohypoparathyroidism	
	SAOUD/SAOUD/HO*IP/PAR/ THAOI/ROI/DIFM
pseudopsia	SAOU/DOPS/YA
pseudopterygium	SAOUD/TRIJ/YUM
	SAOUD/TE/RIJ/YUM
pseudoptosis	SAOUD/TOE/SIS
	SAOU/DOP/TOE/SIS
pseudoptyalism	SAOUD/TAOI/LIFM
pseudopuberty	SAOUD/PAOUB/ER/TI
	SAOUD/PAOU/BER/TI
pseudorabies	SAOUD/RAI/BAOEZ
pseudoreaction	SAOUD/RE/A*BGS
pseudoreduction	SAOUD/RE/D*UBGS
pseudoreminiscence	SAOUD/REM/NIS/ENS
pseudoreplica	SAOUD/REP/LI/KA
pseudoretinitis pigmentosa	SAOUD/RET/NAOITS/PIG/MEN/ TOE/SA
pseudorheumatism	SAOUD/HAOUM/TIFM
pseudorickets	SAOUD/RIK/ET/-S
pseudorosette	SAOUD/ROE/ZET
pseudorubella	SAOUD/RAOU/BEL/LA
pseudosarcoma	SAOUD/SAR/KOE/MA
pseudosarcomatous	SAOUD/SAR/KOEM/TOUS
pseudoscarlatina	SAOUD/SKARL/TAOI/NA
	SAOUD/SKARL/TAOE/NA
pseudosclerema	SAOUD/SKLE/RAOE/MA
pseudosclerosis	SAOUD/SKLE/ROE/SIS
pseudoscrotum	SAOUD/SKROE/TUM
	SAOUD/SKROET/UM

pseudosmallpox	SAOUD/SMAUL/POX
	SAOUD/SMAL/POX
pseudoscutellaris	SAOUD/SKAOUT/LAI/RIS
	SAOUD/SKUT/LAI/RIS
pseudosmia	SAOU/DOZ/MA
	SAOU/DOZ/MAOE/YA
pseudostoma	SAOU/DO*S/MA
pseudostrabismus	SAOUD/STRA/BIZ/MUS
pseudostratified	SAOUD/STRAT/FI/-D
pseudostructure	SAOUD/STRUK/KHUR
pseudotabes	SAOUD/TAI/BAOEZ
pseudotetanus	SAOUD/TET/NUS
pseudothrill	SAOUD/THRIL
pseudotrachoma	SAOUD/TRA/KOE/MA
	SAOUD/TRAI/KOE/MA
pseudotrichiniasis	SAOUD/TRIK/NAOI/SIS
pseudotrichinosis	SAOUD/TRIK/NOE/SIS
pseudotriloculare	SAOUD/TR*I/LOK/LAI/RAOE
pseudotrismus	SAOUD/TRIZ/MUS
pseudotruncus arteriosus	SAOUD/TRUN/KUS/AR/TAOER/ YOE/SUS
pseudotubercle	SAOUD/TAOU/BER/K-L
	SAOUD/TAOUB/ER/K-L
pseudotuberculoma	SAOUD/TAOU/BERK/LOE/MA
pseudotuberculosis	SAOUD/TAOU/BERK/LOE/SIS
pseudotuberculosis-ovis	SAOUD/TAOU/BERK/LOE/SIS/O/ VIS
pseudotumor	SAOUD/TAOU/MOR
pseudouremia	SAOUD/YAOU/RAOEM/YA
pseudouridine	SAOUD/YAOUR/DAOEN
pseudovacuole	SAOUD/VAK/YOEL
pseudovalve	SAOUD/VAL/-V
pseudovariola	SAOUD/VA/RAOI/LA
pseudoventricle	SAOUD/VEN/TRI/K-L
	SAOUD/VEN/TRIK/-L
pseudovermicule	SAOUD/VERM/KAOUL
pseudovermiculus	SAOUD/VER/MIK/LUS
pseudovitamin	SAOUD/VAOIT/MIN
pseudovoice	SAOUD/VOIS
pseudovomiting	SAOUD/VOMT/-G
pseudoxanthine	SAOUD/ZAN/THAOEN
	SAOUD/ZAN/THIN
pseudoxanthoma elasticum	SAOUD/ZAN/THOE/MA/ E/LA*S/KUM
psi	SAO*I
	(*not* SAOI; see sigh)
psicose	SAOI/KOES
psilocin	SAOIL/SIN
	SIL/SIN
Psilocybe	SAOIL/SAOI/BAOE
	SIL/SAOI/BAOE
psilocybin	SAOIL/SAOI/BIN
	SIL/SAOI/BIN
psilosis	SAO*I/LOE/SIS
	(*not* SAOI/LOE/SIS; see sialosis)
psilothin	SIL/THIN
psilotic	SAO*I/LOT/IK
	(*not* SAOI/LOT/IK; see sialotic)
P-sinistrocardiale	P-RBGS/SNIS/TRO/KARD/YAI/ LAOE
	P-RBGS/SIN/IS/TRO/KARD/YAI/ LAOE
psittaci	SIT/SAOI
	SI/TAI/SAOI
	SIT/TAI/SAOI
psittacine	SIT/SAOIN
psittacosis	SIT/KOE/SIS
psoas	SOE/WAS
psoitis	SOE/AOITS
psomophagia	SOEM/FAI/JA
psomophagy	SOE/MOF/JI
psora	SOR/RA
	SOE/RA
psoralen	SOR/LEN
Psorcon	SOR/KON
psorelcosis	SOR/EL/KOE/SIS
	SOE/REL/KOE/SIS
psorenteritis	SOR/ENT/RAOITS
	SOR/SPWRAOITS
	SOR/SPWER/RAOITS
Psorergates	SOE/RERG/TAOEZ
	SOE/RER/GA/TAOEZ
psoriasic	SOE/RAOI/SIK
psoriasiform	SOE/RAOI/SI/FORM
	SOR/YAS/FORM
psoriasis	SOE/RAOI/SIS
psoriatic	SOR/YAT/IK
	SOER/YAT/IK
psoriatica	SOR/YAT/KA

psoriaticum	SOER/YAT/KA	psychogogic	SAOIK/GOJ/IK
	SOR/YAT/KUM	psychographic	SAOIK/GRAFK
	SOER/YAT/KUM	psychography	SAOI/KOG/FI
psoric	SOR/IK	psychohistory	SAOIK/H*IS/RI
	SOE/RIK		SAOIK/HIS/TRI
psoroid	SOR/OID	psychokinesia	SAOIK/KI/NAOEZ/YA
	SOE/ROID	psychokinesis	SAOIK/KI/NAOE/SIS
Psorophora	SOR/ROF/RA	psychokym	SAOIK/KAOIM
	SOE/ROF/RA		SAOIK/KIM
psorophthalmia	SORROF/THAL/MA	psycholagny	SAOIK/LAG/N*I
	SORROF/THAL/MAOE/YA	psycholepsy	SAOIK/LEP/SI
	SOE/ROF/THAL/MA	psycholeptic	SAOIK/LEPT/IK
	SOE/ROF/THAL/MAOE/YA	psycholinguistics	SAOIK/LING/W*IS/IK/-S
Psoroptes	SOR/ROP/TAOEZ	psychologic	SAOIK/LOJ/IK
	SOE/ROP/TAOEZ	psychological	SAOIK/LOJ/KAL
psoroptic	SOR/OPT/IK	psychologically	SAOIK/LOJ/KLI
	SOE/ROPT/IK	psychologist	SAOI/KO*LGS
psorosperm	SOR/SPERM	psychology	SAOI/KOLG
psorospermal	SOR/SPER/MAL	psychomathematics	SAOIK/MA*T/MAT/IK/-S
psorous	SOR/OUS	psychometer	SAOIK/KOM/TER
	SOER/OUS	psychometric	SAOIK/MET/RIK
psych(o)-	SAOIK	psychometrician	SAOIK/ME/TRIGS
	SAOI/K(O)	psychometrics	SAOIK/MET/RIK/-S
psychagogy	SAOIK/GOJ/JI	psychometry	SAOI/KOM/TRI
	SAOIK/GOE/JI	psychomotor	SAOIK/MOE/TOR
psychalgalia	SAOI/KAL/GAIL/YA	psychoneural	SAOIK/NAOURL
psychalgia	SAOI/KAL/JA	psychoneuroses	SAOIK/NAOU/ROE/SAOEZ
psychalgic	SAOI/KAL/JIK	psychoneurosis	SAOIK/NAOU/ROE/SIS
psychalia	SAOI/KAIL/YA	psychoneurotic	SAOIK/NAOU/ROT/IK
psychanalysis	SAOIK/NAL/SIS	psychonomic	SAOIK/NOM/IK
psychanopsia	SAOIK/NOPS/YA	psychonomy	SAOI/KON/M*I
psychataxia	SAOIK/TAX/YA	psychonosology	SAOIK/NOE/SOLG
psyche	SAOI/KAOE	psychonoxious	SAOIK/NOK/-RBS
psychedelic	SAOIK/DEL/IK	psychopath	SAOIK/PA*T
psychentonia	SAOI/KEN/TOEN/YA	psychopathia	SAOIK/PA*T/YA
	SAOIK/EN/TOEN/YA	psychopathic	SAOIK/PA*T/IK
	SAOIK/SPWOEN/YA	psychopathologist	SAOIK/PA/THO*LGS
psychiatric	SAOIK/YAT/RIK	psychopathology	SAOIK/PA/THOLG
psychiatrics	SAOIK/YAT/RIK/-S	psychopathy	SAOI/KOP/TH*I
psychiatrist	SAOI/KAOI/TR*IS	psychopharmaceutical	SAOIK/FARM/SAOUT/KAL
psychiatry	SAOI/KAOI/TRI	psychopharmacology	SAOIK/FARM/KOLG
psychic	SAOIK/IK	psychopharmacotherapy	SAOIK/FARM/KO/THER/PI
psychical	SAOIK/KAL	psychophylaxis	SAOIK/FLAK/SIS
psychism	SAOIK/IFM	psychophysical	SAOIK/FIZ/KAL
	SAOI/KIFM	psychophysics	SAOIK/FIZ/IK/-S
psycho (word)	SAOI/KOE	psychophysiologic	SAOIK/FIZ/YO/LOJ/IK
psychoacoustics	SAOIK/AI/KAO*US/IK/-S	psychophysiology	SAOIK/FIZ/YOLG
psychoactive	SAOIK/AKT/IV	psychoprophylactic	SAOIK/PROEF/LAKT/IK
psychoallergy	SAOIK/AL/ER/JI		SAOIK/PRO/FLAKT/IK
psychoanaleptic	SAOIK/AN/LEPT/IK	psychoprophylaxis	SAOIK/PROEF/LAK/SIS
psychoanalysis	SAOIK/ANL/SIS		SAOIK/PRO/FLAK/SIS
psychoanalyst	SAOIK/ANL/*IS	psychorelaxation	SAOIK/RE/LAK/SAIGS
	SAOIK/AN/L*IS	psychormic	SAOI/KOR/MIK
psychoanalytic	SAOIK/AN/LIT/IK	psychorrhea	SAOI/KRAOE/YA
psychoanalyze	SAOIK/ANL/AOIZ	psychorrhythmia	SAOIK/R*IT/MA
	SAOIK/AN/LAOIZ		SAOIK/R*IT/MAOE/YA
psychoauditory	SAOIK/AUD/TOIR	psychosensorial	SAOIK/SEN/SOIRL
psychobiological	SAOIK/BAO*I/LOJ/KAL	psychosensory	SAOIK/SENS/RI
psychobiology	SAOIK/BAO*I/OLG	psychoses	SAOI/KOE/SAOEZ
psychocatharsis	SAOIK/KA/THAR/SIS	psychosexual	SAOIK/SEX/YAOUL
psychocentric	SAOIK/SEN/TRIK	psychosin	SAOIK/SIN
psychochemistry	SAOIK/KEM/STRI	psychosine	SAOIK/SAOEN
psychochrome	SAOIK/KROEM	psychosis	SAOI/KOE/SIS
psychochromesthesia	SAOIK/KROE/MES/THAOEZ/YA	psychosocial	SAOIK/SOERBL
	SAOIK/KROEM/ES/THAOEZ/YA	psychosomatic	SAOIK/SMAT/IK
psychocortical	SAOIK/KORT/KAL		SAOIK/SOE/MAT/IK
psychocutaneous	SAOIK/KAOU/TAIN/YOUS	psychosomimetic	SAOI/KOES/MAOI/MET/IK
psychodiagnosis	SAOIK/DAOIG/NOE/SIS		SAOI/KOES/MI/MET/IK
psychodiagnostics	SAOIK/DAOIG/NO*S/IK/-S	psychostimulant	SAOIK/STIM/LANT
Psychodidae	SAOI/KOD/DAE	psychosurgery	SAOIK/SURJ/RI
	SAOI/KOED/DAE		SAOIK/S-RJ
psychodometer	SAOIK/DOM/TER	psychosynthesis	SAOIK/S*INT/SIS
psychodometry	SAOIK/DOM/TRI	psychotechnics	SAOIK/TEK/NIK/-S
psychodrama	SAOIK/DRA/MA	psychotherapeutic	SAOIK/THER/PAOUT/IK
psychodynamics	SAOIK/DAOI/NAM/IK/-S	psychotherapeutics	SAOIK/THER/PAOUT/IK/-S
psychodysleptic	SAOIK/DIS/LEPT/IK	psychotherapist	SAOIK/THER/P*IS
psychoendocrinology	SAOIK/*END/KRI/NOLG	psychotherapy	SAOIK/THER/PI
psychoexploration	SAOIK/EX/PLO/RAIGS	psychotic	SAOI/KOT/IK
psychogalvanic	SAOIK/GAL/VAN/IK	psychotogen	SAOI/KOT/JEN
psychogalvanometer	SAOIK/GAL/VA/NOM/TER	psychotogenic	SAOI/KOT/JEN/IK
psychogender	SAOIK/JEND/ER	psychotomimetic	SAOI/KOT/MAOI/MET/IK
psychogenic	SAOIK/JEN/IK		SAOI/KOT/MI/MET/IK
psychogenesis	SAOIK/JEN/SIS	psychotonic	SAOIK/TON/IK
psychogenetic	SAOIK/JE/NET/IK	psychotropic	SAOIK/TROP/IK
psychogenic	SAOIK/JEN/IK	psychro-	SAOI/KRO
psychogenous	SAOI/KOJ/NOUS	psychroalgia	SAOI/KRO/AL/JA
psychogeny	SAOI/KOJ/N*I	psychroesthesia	SAOI/KRO/ES/THAOEZ/YA
psychogeriatrics	SAOIK/JER/YAT/RIK/-S	psychrometer	SAOI/KROM/TER
psychogeusic	SAOIK/GAOUS/IK	psychrometry	SAOI/KROM/TRI

psychrophile	SAOI/KRO/FAOIL
psychrophilic	SAOI/KRO/FIL/IK
psychrophobia	SAOI/KRO/FOEB/YA
psychrophore	SAOI/KRO/FOER
psychrotherapy	SAOI/KRO/THER/PI
psyllium	S*IL/YUM
	(*not* SIL/YUM; see cilium)
PT 105 Capsules	P-RBGS/T*RBGS/10/5/KAP/
	SAOUL/-S
ptarmic	TARM/IK
	TAR/MIK
ptarmus	TAR/MUS
pteridine	TER/DAOEN
Pteridophyta	TER/DOF/TA
pteridophyte	TER/DO/FAOIT
pterin	TER/RIN
pterion	TAOER/YON
	TER/YON
pteriotic	TAOER/YOT/IK
	TER/YOT/IK
pternalgia	TER/NAL/JA
pteroic	TE/ROIK
	TE/ROE/IK
pteropterin	TER/OPT/RIN
pteroyldiglutamic	TER/OIL/DI/GLAOU/TAM/IK
pteroylglutamate	TER/OIL/GLAOUT/MAIT
pteroylglutamic	TER/OIL/GLAOU/TAM/IK
pteroylmonoglutamic	TER/OIL/MON/GLAOU/TAM/IK
pteroyltriglutamic	TER/OIL/TR*I/GLAOU/TAM/IK
pteryg(o)-	TER/G(O)
pterygium	TE/RIJ/YUM
	TRIJ/YUM
	TE/RIJ/UM
	TRIJ/UM
pterygoid	TER/GOID
pterygoidea	TER/GOID/YA
pterygoidei	TER/GOID/YAOI
pterygoideus	TER/GOID/YUS
pterygomandibular	TER/GO/MAN/DIB/LAR
pterygomaxillare	TER/GO/MAX/LAI/RAOE
pterygomaxillary	TER/GO/MAX/LAIR
pterygopalatine	TER/GO/PAL/TAOIN
pterygopalatini	TER/GO/PAL/TAOI/NAOI
pterygopalatinus	TER/GO/PAL/TAOI/NUS
pterygopharyngeus	TER/GO/FRIN/JUS
pterygoquadrate	TER/GO/KWAD/RAIT
	TER/GO/KWAUD/RAIT
pterygospinale	TER/GO/SPAOI/NAI/LAOE
pterygospinosum	TER/GO/SPAOI/NOE/SUM
	TER/GO/SPAOI/NOES/UM
pthiriasis	THAOI/RAOI/SIS
phthiriophobia	THAOIR/YO/FOEB/YA
Pthirus	THAOI/RUS
ptilosis	TAO*I/LOE/SIS
	(*not* TAOI/LOE/SIS; see tylosis)
ptomaine	TOE/MAIN
ptomainemia	TOE/MAI/NAOEM/YA
	TOE/MAIN/AOEM/YA
ptomainotoxism	TOE/MAIN/TOK/SIFM
ptomatine	TOEM/TAOEN
ptomatropine	TOE/MAT/RO/PAOEN
ptosed	TOEZ/-D
	TOES/-D
ptoses	TOE/SAOEZ
ptosis	TOE/SIS
-ptosis	TOE/SIS
	-P/TOE/SIS
ptotic	TOT/IK
ptyal(o)-	TAOI/L(O)
ptyalagogue	TAOI/AL/GOG
ptyalectasis	TAOI/LEKT/SIS
ptyalin	TAOI/LIN
ptyalinogen	TAOI/LIN/JEN
ptyalism	TAOI/LIFM
ptyalith	TAOI/L*IT
ptyalize	TAOI/LAOIZ
ptyalocele	TAOI/LO/SAO*EL
	TAOI/AL/SAO*EL
ptyalogenic	TAOI/LO/JEN/IK
ptyalography	TAOI/LOG/FI
ptyalolith	TAOI/LO/L*IT
ptyalolithiasis	TAOI/LO/LI/THAOI/SIS
ptyalolithotomy	TAOI/LO/LI/THOT/M*I
ptyaloreaction	TAOI/LO/RE/A*BGS
ptyalorrhea	TAOI/LO/RAOE/YA
ptyalose	TAOI/LOES
ptyocrinous	TAOI/OK/RI/NOUS
-ptysis	-PT/SIS
pub(o)-	PAOUB

	PAOU/B(O)
pubarche	PAOU/BAR/KAOE
puber	PAOU/BER
	PAOUB/ER
puberal	PAOUB/RAL
puberphonia	PAOU/BER/FOEN/YA
	PAOUB/ER/FOEN/YA
pubertal	PAOU/BER/TAL
	PAOUB/ER/TAL
pubertas	PAOU/BER/TAS
	PAOUB/ER/TAS
pubertas praecox	PAOU/BER/TAS/PRAE/KOX
	PAOUB/ER/TAS/PRAE/KOX
pubertas precox	PAOU/BER/TAS/PRE/KOX
	PAOUB/ER/TAS/PRE/KOX
puberty	PAOU/BER/TI
	PAOUB/ER/TI
puberum	PAOUB/RUM
pubes	PAOU/BAOEZ
pubescence	PAOU/BES/ENS
pubescent	PAOU/BES/ENT
pubic	PAOUB/IK
pubica	PAOUB/KA
pubicum	PAOUB/KUM
pubicus	PAOUB/KUS
pubioplasty	PAOUB/YO/PLAS/TI
pubiotomy	PAOUB/YOT/M*I
pubis	PAOU/BIS
pubisure	PAOUB/SAOUR
	PAOUB/SHUR
pubocapsular	PAOUB/KAPS/LAR
pubococcygeal	PAOUB/KOK/SLJ/YAL
pubofemoral	PAOUB/FEM/RAL
pubomadesis	PAOUB/MA/DAOE/SIS
puboprostatic	PAOUB/PROS/TAT/IK
puborectal	PAOUB/REK/TAL
pubosacral	PAOUB/SAI/KRAL
pubotibial	PAOUB/TIB/YAL
pubotuberous	PAOUB/TAOUB/ROUS
pubovesical	PAOUB/VES/KAL
pudenda	PAOU/DEN/DA
pudendae	PAOU/DEN/DAE
pudendal	PAOU/DEN/DAL
pudendalis	PAOU/DEN/DAI/LIS
pudendi	PAOU/DEN/DAOI
pudendum	PAOU/DEN/DUM
pudendus	PAOU/DEN/DUS
pudic	PAOUD/IK
puericulture	PAOU/ER/KUL/KHUR
	PAOU/RI/KUL/KHUR
puericulturist	PAOU/ER/KUL/KHUR/*IS
	PAOU/RI/KUL/KHUR/*IS
puerile	PAOU/ER/IL
	PAOU/RIL
puerpera	PAOU/ERP/RA
	PAOURP/RA
puerperae	PAOU/ERP/RAE
	PAOURP/RAE
puerperal	PAOU/ERP/RAL
	PAOURP/RAL
puerperalism	PAOU/ERP/RAL/IFM
	PAOURP/RAL/IFM
puerperant	PAOU/ERP/RANT
	PAOURP/RANT
puerperarum	PAOU/ERP/RAIR/UM
	PAOURP/RAIR/UM
puerperia	PAOU/ER/PAOER/YA
	PAOU/ER/PAOER/YA
puerperium	PAOU/ER/PAOER/YUM
	PAOU/ER/PAOER/YUM
	PAOU/PAOERM
puff	PUF
puffing	PUF/-G
pugil	PAOU/JIL
pugilistica	PAOUJ/L*IS/KA
pugillus	PAOU/JIL/LUS
pulex	PAOU/LEX
Pulex	K-P/PAOU/LEX
pulicicide	PAOU/LIS/SAO*ID
Pulicidae	PAOU/LIS/DAE
pulicide	PAOUL/SAO*ID
pull	PUL
pulley	PUL/LAOE
pullorum	PUL/LOR/UM
	PUL/LOER/UM
pullulanase	PUL/YUL/NAIS
	PUL/YAOUL/NAIS
pullulans	PUL/YAOU/LANZ
	PUL/YU/LANZ

pullulate	PUL/YAOU/LAIT	pump-oxygenator	PUFRP/OX/JE/NAI/TOR
	PUL/YU/LAIT		PUFRP/OX/JEN/NAI/TOR
	(not PUL/LAIT)	puna	PAOU/NA
pullulation	PUL/YAOU/LAIGS	punch	PUFRPBLG
	PUL/YU/LAIGS		PUN/-FP
pulmo	PUL/MOE	punchdrunk	PUFRPBLG/DR*UNG
pulm(o)-	PUL/M(O)		PUFRPBLG/DRUN-K
pulmoaortic	PUL/MO/AI/ORT/IK		PUN/-FP/DR*UNG
Pulmocare	PUL/MO/KAIR		PUN/-FP/DRUN-K
pulmogram	PUL/MO/GRAM	punched-out	PUFRPBLG/-D/H-F/OUT
pulmolith	PUL/MO/L*IT		PUN/-FPD/H-F/OUT
pulmometer	PUL/MOM/TER	puncta	PUNG/TA
pulmometry	PUL/MOM/TRI	punctata	PUNG/TAI/TA
pulmon-	PUL/MO/N-	punctate	PUNG/TAIT
pulmonal	PUL/MO/NAL	puncti	PUNG/TAOI
	PUL/MONL	punctiform	PUNGT/FORM
pulmonale	PUL/MO/NAI/LAOE		PUNG/TI/FORM
pulmonales	PUL/MO/NAI/LAOEZ	punctio	PUNG/SHOE
pulmonalis	PUL/MO/NAI/LIS	punctum	PUNG/TUM
pulmonary	PUL/MO/NAIR	punctumeter	PUNG/TUM/TER
	PUM/NAIR (short form)	punctura	PUNG/TAOU/RA
pulmonectomy	PUL/MO/NEKT/M*I		PUN/KHUR/RA
pulmones	PUL/MOE/NAOEZ	puncturatio	PUNG/TAOU/RAI/SHOE
pulmonic	PUL/MON/IK		PUNG/TAOU/RAIRB/YOE
pulmonis	PUL/MOE/NIS		PUN/KHU/RAI/SHOE
	PUL/MON/NIS		PUN/KHU/RAIRB/YOE
pulmonitis	PUL/MO/NAOITS	puncture	PUNG/KHUR
pulmonohepatic	PUL/MON/HE/PAT/IK	pungent	PUN/JENT
pulmonologist	PUL/MO/NO*LGS	punjabensis	PUN/JA/BEN/SIS
pulmonology	PUL/MO/NOLG	Puntius	PUNT/YUS
pulmonoperitoneal	PUL/MON/PERT/NAOEL	pupa	PAOU/PA
pulmonum	PUL/MOE/NUM	pupal	PAOU/PAL
	PUL/MOEN/UM	pupil	PAOU/PIL
pulmotor	PUL/MOE/TOR	pupill(o)-	PAOUP/L(O)
pulp	PUL/-P		PAOU/PIL
pulp(o)-	PUL/P(O)	pupilla	PAOU/PIL/LA
pulpa	PUL/PA	pupillae	PAOU/PIL/LAE
pulpae	PUL/PAE	pupillary	PAOUP/LAIR
pulpal	PUL/PAL	pupillograph	PAOU/PIL/GRAF
pulpalgia	PUL/PAL/JA	pupillography	PAOUP/LOG/FI
pulpar	PUL/PAR	pupillometer	PAOUP/LOM/TER
pulpation	PUL/PAIGS	pupillometry	PAOUP/LOM/TRI
pulpectomy	PUL/PEKT/M*I	pupillomotor	PAOUP/LO/MOE/TOR
pulpefaction	PUL/PE/FA*BGS	pupilloplegia	PAOUP/LO/PLAOE/JA
pulpi	PUL/PAOI	pupilloscope	PAOU/PIL/SKOEP
pulpifaction	PUL/PI/FA*BGS		PAOUP/LO/SKOEP
pulpiform	PUL/PI/FORM	pupilloscopy	PAOUP/LOS/KPI
pulpify	PUL/PI/FI	pupillostatometer	PAOU/PIL/STA/TOM/TER
pulpitides	PUL/PIT/DAOEZ	pupillotonia	PAOUP/LO/TOEN/YA
pulpitis	PUL/PAOITS	pupiparous	PAOU/PIP/ROUS
pulpless	PUL/-P/LES	pura	PAOU/RA
pulpoaxial	PUL/PO/AX/YAL		PAOUR/RA
pulpobuccoaxial	PUL/PO/BUK/AX/YAL	pure	PAOUR
pulpodistal	PUL/PO/DIS/TAL	purebred	PAOUR/BRED
pulpodontia	PUL/PO/DON/SHA	purgation	PUR/GAIGS
pulpodontics	PUL/PO/DONT/IK/-S	purgative	PURG/TIV
pulpolabial	PUL/PO/LAIB/YAL	purge	PURJ
pulpolingual	PUL/PO/LING/WAL	puric	PAOUR/IK
pulpolinguoaxial	PUL/PO/LING/WO/AX/YAL	purificatum	PAOUR/FI/KAI/TUM
pulpomesial	PUL/PO/MAOEZ/YAL	purificatus	PAOUR/FI/KAI/TUS
pulposus	PUL/POE/SUS	puriform	PAOUR/RI/FORM
pulpotomy	PUL/POT/M*I		PAOU/RI/FORM
pulpy	PUL/PI		(not PAOUR/FORM; see pure form)
pulsate	PUL/SAIT	purinase	PAOUR/NAIS
pulsatile	PULS/TAOIL	purine	PAOUR/AOEN
	PUL/SA/TAOIL		PAOUR/RAOEN
pulsation	PUL/SAIGS		PAOUR/RIN
pulsator	PUL/SAI/TOR	purinemia	PAOUR/NAOEM/YA
pulse	PULS	purinemic	PAOUR/NAOEM/IK
pulsellum	PUL/SEL/UM	Purinethol	PAOU/RAOEN/THOL
pulsimeter	PUL/SIM/TER		PAOU/RIN/THOL
pulsion	PULGS	purinolytic	PAOUR/NO/LIT/IK
pulsometer	PUL/SOM/TER	purinometer	PAOUR/NOM/TER
pulsus	PUL/SUS	purity	PAOUR/TI
pultaceous	PUL/TAIRBS	Purkinje	PUR/KIN/JAOE
pulverization	PUL/VER/ZAIGS	Purmann	PUR/MAN
pulverize	PUL/VER/AOIZ	puro-	PAOU/RO
pulverulent	PUL/VER/LENT		PAOUR/RO
	PUL/VER/YAOU/LENT		(not PAOUR; see pure)
	PUL/VER/YU/LENT	puromucous	PAOU/RO/MAOUK/OUS
pulvinar	PUL/VAOI/NAR	puromycin	PAOU/RO/MAOI/SIN
pulvinate	PUL/VI/NAIT	purple	PURP/-L
pulvis	PUL/VIS	purpur-	PURP/R-
pumex	PAOU/MEX		PUR/PAOU/R-
pumice	PUM/IS		PURP/YAOU/R-
	PUM/MIS		PURP/YU/R-
pump	PUFRP	purpura	PURP/RA
pumpkin	PUFRP/KIN	purpurea	PURP/RAOE/YA
	PUM/KIN	purpureaglycoside	PURP/RAOE/YA/GLAOIK/SAOID

purpuric	PUR/PAOUR/IK		
purpuriferous	PURP/RIF/ROUS	pyeloscopy	PAOI/LOS/KPI
purpurigenous	PURP/RIJ/NOUS	pyelostomy	PAOI/LO*S/M*I
purpurin	PURP/RIN	pyelotomy	PAOI/LOT/M*I
purpurine	PURP/RAOEN	pyeloureterectasis	PAOI/LO/YAOU/RAOET/REKT/SIS
purpurinuria	PURP/RI/NAOUR/YA	pyeloureterography	PAOI/LO/YAOU/RAOET/ROG/FI
	PURP/RIN/YAOUR/YA	pyeloureterolysis	PAOI/LO/YAOU/RAOET/ROL/SIS
purpuriparous	PURP/RIP/ROUS	pyeloureteroplasty	PAOI/LO/YAOU/RAOET/RO/PLAS/
purpurogenous	PURP/ROJ/NOUS		TI
purr	PUR	pyelovenous	PAOI/LO/VAOEN/OUS
purring	PUR/-G	pyemesis	PAOI/EM/SIS
Purtscher	PURT/KHER	pyemia	PAOI/AOEM/YA
	PAOURT/KHER	pyemic	PAOI/AOEM/IK
purul-	PAOUR/L-	Pyemotes	PAOI/MOE/TAOEZ
	PAOUR/YAOU/L-	pyencephalus	PAOI/EN/SEF/LUS
	PAOUR/YU/L-	pyesis	PAOI/E/SIS
purulence	PAOUR/LENS	pygal	PAOI/GAL
purulency	PAOUR/LEN/SI	pygalgia	PAOI/GAL/JA
purulent	PAOUR/LENT	pygist	PAOI/J*IS
puruloid	PAOUR/LOID	pygmalion	PIG/MAIL/YON
pus	PUS	pygmalionism	PIG/MAIL/YON/IFM
Pusey	PAOU/SAOE	pygmy	PIG/M*I
pustul-	P*US/L-	pygo-	PAOIG
	P*US/YAOU/L-		PAOI/GO
	P*US/YU/L-	pygoamorphus	PAOIG/AI/MOR/FUS
	PUS/KHU/L-	pygodidymus	PAOIG/DID/MUS
	PUS/TAOU/L-	pygomelus	PAOI/GOM/LUS
pustula	P*US/LA	pygopagus	PAOI/GOP/GUS
pustulant	P*US/LANT	pygopagy	PAOI/GOP/JI
pustular	P*US/LAR	pyic	PAOI/IK
pustulation	P*US/LAIGS	pyin	PAOI/YIN
pustule	PUS/KHAOUL	pykno-	PIK/NO
	P*US/YAOUL	pyknic	P*IK/NIK
	PUS/TAOUL		(not PIK/NIK; see picnic)
pustuliform	PUS/KHAOUL/FORM	pyknocyte	PIK/NO/SAO*IT
	PUS/TAOUL/FORM	pyknocytoma	PIK/NO/SAOI/TOE/MA
pustulocrustaceous	P*US/LO/KRUS/TAIRBS	pyknocytosis	PIK/NO/SAOI/TOE/SIS
pustulosa	P*US/LOE/SA	pyknodysostosis	PIK/NO/DIS/OS/TOE/SIS
pustulosis	P*US/LOE/SIS	pyknoepilepsy	PIK/NO/EP/LEP/SI
putamen	PAOU/TAI/MEN	pyknolepsy	PIK/NO/LEP/SI
	PAOU/TAIM/-N	pyknometer	PIK/NOM/TER
Putnam	PUT/NAM	pyknometry	PIK/NOM/TRI
putrefaciens	PAOU/TRE/FAI/SHENZ	pyknomorphic	PIK/NO/MOR/FIK
	PAOU/TRE/FAIRB/ENZ	pyknomorphous	PIK/NO/MOR/FOUS
putrefaction	PAOU/TRE/FA*BGS	pyknophrasia	PIK/NO/FRAIZ/YA
putrefactive	PAOU/TRE/FAKT/IV	pyknoplasson	PIK/NO/PLAS/SON
putrefy	PAOU/TRE/FI	pyknosis	PIK/NOE/SIS
putrescence	PAOU/TRES/ENS	pyknotic	PIK/NOT/IK
putrescent	PAOU/TRES/ENT	pyla	PAO*I/LA
putrescine	PAOU/TRES/SAOEN		(not PAOI/LA; see pila)
	PAOU/TRES/SIN	pylar	PAO*I/LAR
putrid	PAOU/TRID		(not PAOI/LAR; see pilar)
putrilage	PAOU/TRI/LAJ	pyle-	PAOIL
putromaine	PAOU/TROE/MAIN		PAOI/LAOE
	PAOU/TRO/MAIN		PAOI/LE
putty	PUT/TI	pylemphraxis	PAOI/LEM/FRAK/SIS
P-V-Tussin	P-RBGS/V-RBGS/TUS/SIN	pylephlebectasia	PAOIL/FLEB/EK/TAIZ/YA
pyarthrosis	PAOI/AR/THROE/SIS	pylephlebectasis	PAOIL/FLE/BEKT/SIS
pyecchysis	PAOI/EK/SIS	pylephlebitis	PAOIL/FLE/BAOITS
pyel(o)-	PAOI/L(O)	pylethrombophlebitis	PAOIL/THROM/BO/FLE/BAOITS
pyelectasia	PAOI/LEK/TAIZ/YA	pylethrombosis	PAOIL/THROM/BOE/SIS
pyelectasis	PAOI/LEKT/SIS	pylic	PAOI/LIK
pyelic	PAOI/EL/IK		PAOIL/IK
pyelitic	PAOI/LIT/IK	pylometer	PAOI/LOM/TER
pyelitis	PAOI/LAOITS	pylon	PAOI/LON
pyelocaliceal	PAOI/LO/KAL/SAOEL	pylor(o)-	PAOIL/R(O)
pyelocaliectasis	PAOI/LO/KAL/YEKT/SIS		PAOI/LOR
pyelocystanastomosis	PAOI/LO/S*IS/NA*S/MOE/SIS		PAOI/LOER
pyelocystitis	PAOI/LO/SIS/TAOITS	pyloralgia	PAOIL/RAL/JA
pyelocystostomosis	PAOI/LO/S*IS/STOE/MOE/SIS	pylorectomy	PAOIL/REKT/M*I
pyelofluoroscopy	PAOI/LO/FLAOU/ROS/KPI	pylori	PAOI/LOR/RAOI
pyelogram	PAOI/LO/GRAM	pyloric	PAOI/LOR/IK
pyelograph	PAOI/LO/GRAF	pyloricum	PAOI/LOR/KUM
	PAOI/EL/GRAF	pyloricus	PAOI/LOR/KUS
pyelography	PAOI/LOG/FI	pyloristenosis	PAOI/LOR/STE/NOE/SIS
pyeloileocutaneous	PAOI/LO/*IL/YO/KAOU/TAIN/	pyloritis	PAOIL/RAOITS
	YOUS	pylorodiosis	PAOI/LOR/DI/YOE/SIS
pyelointerstitial	PAOI/LO/SPWER/STIRBL		PAOI/LOR/DI/O/SIS
pyelolithotomy	PAOI/LO/LI/THOT/M*I	pyloroduodenitis	PAOI/LOR/DWOD/NAOITS
pyelolymphatic	PAOI/LO/LIM/FAT/IK		PAOI/LOR/DAOU/DAOE/NAOITS
pyelometry	PAOI/LOM/TRI		PAOI/LOR/DAOU/DE/NAOITS
pyeloneostomy	PAOI/LO/NAOE/O*S/M*I	pylorogastrectomy	PAOI/LOR/GAS/TREKT/M*I
pyelonephritis	PAOI/LO/NE/FRAOITS	pylloromyotomy	PAOI/LOR/MAOI/OT/M*I
pyelonephrosis	PAOI/LO/NE/FROE/SIS	pyloroplasty	PAOI/LOR/PLAS/TI
pyelonephrostomy	PAOI/LO/NE/FRO*S/M*I	pyloroptosia	PAOI/LOR/TOES/YA
pyelopathy	PAOI/LOP/TH*I	pyloroptosis	PAOI/LOR/TOE/SIS
pyelophlebitis	PAOI/LO/FLE/BAOITS	pyloroscopy	PAOIL/ROS/KPI
pyeloplasty	PAOI/LO/PLAS/TI	pylorospasm	PAOI/LOR/SPAFM
pyeloplication	PAOI/LO/PLI/KAIGS	pylorostomy	PAOIL/RO*S/M*I

pylorotomy	PAOIL/ROT/M*I	pyosalpinx	PAOI/SAL/PINGS
pylorus	PAOI/LOR/RUS	pyosapremia	PAOI/SAP/RAOEM/YA
pyo-	PAOI	pyosclerosis	PAOI/SKLE/ROE/SIS
	PAOI/YO	pyosemia	PAOI/SAOEM/YA
pyoblennorrhea	PAOI/BLEN/RAOE/YA	pyosepticemia	PAOI/SEPT/SAOEM/YA
pyocalix	PAOI/KAI/LIX	pyosin	PAOI/SIN
	PAOI/KAL/IX	pyosis	PAOI/YOE/SIS
pyocele	PAOI/SAO*EL		PAOI/O/SIS
pyocelia	PAOI/SAOEL/YA	pyospermia	PAOI/SPERM/YA
pyocephalus	PAOI/SEF/LUS	pyostatic	PAOI/STAT/IK
pyochezia	PAOI/KAOEZ/YA	pyostomatitis	PAOI/STOEM/TAOITS
Pyocidin	PAOI/SAOI/DIN	pyotherapy	PAOI/THER/PI
Pyocidin-Otic	PAOI/SAOI/DIN/OET/IK	pyothorax	PAOI/THOR/AX
	PAOI/SAOI/DIN/OT/IK	pyotoxinemia	PAOI/TOX/NAOEM/YA
pyococcic	PAOI/KOX/IK	pyoumbilicus	PAOI/UM/BIL/KUS
	PAOI/KOK/SIK	pyourachus	PAOI/YAOUR/KUS
pyococcus	PAOI/KOK/KUS	pyoureter	PAOI/YAOU/RAOET/ER
pyocolpocele	PAOI/KOL/PO/SAO*EL	pyovesiculosis	PAOI/VE/SIK/LOE/SIS
pyocolpos	PAOI/KOL/POS	pyoxanthine	PAOI/ZAN/THIN
pyoculture	PAOI/KUL/KHUR	pyoxanthose	PAOI/ZAN/THOES
pyocyanase	PAOI/SAOI/NAIS	PYP	P-RBGS/Y*RBGS/P*RBGS
pyocyanic	PAOI/SAOI/AN/IK	pyr-	PIR
	PAOI/SAOI/YAN/IK		PI/R(O)
pyocyanin	PAOI/SAOI/NIN		PAOIR
pyocyanogenic	PAOI/SAOI/NO/JEN/IK		PAOI/R(O)
pyocyanolysin	PAOI/SAOI/NOL/SIN	pyrabrom	PIR/BROM
pyocyanosis	PAOI/SAOI/NOE/SIS	pyracin	PIR/SIN
pyocyst	PAOI/S*IS		PAOIR/SIN
pyocystis	PAOI/SIS/TIS	pyramid	PIR/MID
pyocyte	PAOI/SAO*IT	pyramidal	PI/RAM/DAL
pyoderma	PAOI/DER/MA	pyramidale	PI/RAM/DAI/LAOE
pyodermatitis	PAOI/DERM/TAOITS	pyramidales	PI/RAM/DAI/LAOEZ
pyodermatosis	PAOI/DERM/TOE/SIS	pyramidalis	PI/RAM/DAI/LIS
pyodermia	PAOI/DERM/YA	pyramides	PI/RAM/DAOEZ
pyodermitis	PAOI/DER/MAOITS	pyramidis	PI/RAM/DIS
pyofecia	PAOI/FAOES/YA	pyramidotomy	PI/RAM/DOT/M*I
pyogen	PAOI/JEN	pyramidum	PI/RAM/DUM
pyogenes	PAOI/OJ/NAOEZ	pyramin	PIR/MIN
pyogenesis	PAOI/JEN/SIS	pyramine	PIR/MAOEN
pyogenetic	PAOI/JE/NET/IK	pyramis	PIR/MIS
pyogenic	PAOI/JEN/IK	pyran	PAOI/RAN
pyogenin	PAOI/OJ/NIN	pyranisamine	PIR/NIS/MAOEN
pyogenous	PAOI/OJ/NOUS		PAOIR/NIS/MAOEN
pyohemia	PAOI/HAOEM/YA	pyranone	PIR/NOEN
pyohemothorax	PAOI/HAOEM/THOR/AX		PAOIR/NOEN
pyohydronephrosis	PAOI/HAOI/DRO/NE/FROE/SIS	pyranose	PIR/NOES
pyoid	PAOI/OID		PAOIR/NOES
pyolabyrinthitis	PAOI/LAB/RIN/THAOITS	pyrantel	PI/RAN/TEL
pyolipic	PAOI/LIP/IK	pyranyl	PAOIR/NIL
pyometra	PAOI/MAOE/TRA		PIR/NIL
pyometritis	PAOI/ME/TRAOITS	pyrathiazine	PIR/THAOI/ZAOEN
pyometrium	PAOI/MAOE/TRUM	pyrazinamide	PIR/ZIN/MAOID
pyomyositis	PAOI/MAOI/SAOITS		PAOIR/ZIN/MAOID
pyonephritis	PAOI/NE/FRAOITS	pyrazine	PIR/ZAOEN
pyonephrolithiasis	PAOI/NEF/RO/LI/THAOI/SIS		PAOIR/ZAOEN
pyonephrosis	PAOI/NE/FROE/SIS	pyrazofurin	PIR/ZO/FAOUR/RIN
pyonephrotic	PAOI/NE/FROT/IK		PIR/ZO/FAOU/RIN
pyonychia	PAOI/NIK/YA	pyrazolone	PIR/ZOE/LOEN
pyo-ovarium	PAOI/O/VAIRM	pyrectic	PAOI/REKT/IK
pyopericarditis	PAOI/P*ER/KAR/DAOITS	pyrene	PAOI/REN
pyopericardium	PAOI/P*ER/KARD/YUM		PAOI/RAOEN
pyoperitoneum	PAOI/PERT/NAOEM	pyrenemia	PAOIR/NAOEM/YA
pyoperitonitis	PAOI/PERT/NAOITS	Pyrenochaeta romeroi	PAOIR/NO/KAOE/TA/ROEM/ROI
pyophagia	PAOI/FAI/JA	pyrenoid	PAOIR/NOID
pyophthalmia	PAOI/OF/THAL/MA	pyrenolysis	PAOIR/NOL/SIS
	PAOI/OF/THAL/MAOE/YA	Pyrenomycetes	PAOI/RAOEN/MAOI/SAOE/TAOEZ
pyophthalmitis	PAOI/OF/THAL/MAOITS	pyrethrin	PAOI/R*ET/RIN
pyophylactic	PAOI/FLAKT/IK		PAOI/RAO*ET/RIN
pyophysometra	PAOI/FAOIS/MAOE/TRA	pyrethrolone	PAOI/R*ET/RO/LOEN
pyoplania	PAOI/PLAIN/YA	pyrethron	PAOIR/THRON
pyopneumocholecystitis	PAOI/NAOUM/KOEL/SIS/TAOITS	pyrethrum	PAOI/RAO*ET/RUM
pyopneumocyst	PAOI/NAOUM/S*IS	pyretic	PAOI/RET/IK
pyopneumohepatitis	PAOI/NAOUM/HEP/TAOITS	pyreticosis	PAOI/RET/KOE/SIS
pyopneumopericardium	PAOI/NAOUM/P*ER/KARD/YUM	pyreto-	PAOI/RET
pyopneumoperitoneum	PAOI/NAOUM/PERT/NAOEM		PAOI/RAOET
pyopneumoperitonitis	PAOI/NAOUM/PERT/NAOITS		PIR/TO
pyopneumothorax	PAOI/NAOUM/THOR/AX		PAOIR/TO
pyopoiesis	PAOI/POI/SIS	pyretogen	PAOI/RET/JEN
pyopoietic	PAOI/POIT/IK	pyretogenesis	PAOIR/TO/JEN/SIS
pyoptysis	PAOI/OPT/SIS	pyretogenetic	PAOIR/TO/JE/NET/IK
pyopyelectasis	PAOI/PAOI/LEKT/SIS	pyretogenic	PAOIR/TO/JEN/IK
pyorrhea	PAOI/RAOE/YA	pyretogenous	PAOIR/TOJ/NOUS
pyorrheal	PAOI/RAOEL	pyretography	PAOIR/TOG/FI
	PAOI/RAOE/YAL	pyretology	PAOIR/TOLG
pyosalpingitis	PAOI/SAL/PIN/JAOITS	pyretolysis	PAOIR/TOL/SIS
pyosalpingo-oophoritis	PAOI/SAL/PING/AOF/RAOITS	pyretotherapy	PAOIR/TO/THER/PI
pyosalpingo-oothecitis	PAOI/SAL/PING/AO*T/SAOITS	pyretotyphosis	PAOIR/TO/TAOI/FOE/SIS
	PAOI/SAL/PING/AO/THAOE/	pyrexia	PAOI/REX/YA
	SAOITS	pyrexial	PAOI/REX/YAL

pyrexiogenic	PAOI/REX/YO/JEN/IK
pyrexiophobia	PAOI/REX/YO/FOEB/YA
pyrexy	PAOI/REK/SI
pyribenzyl	PIR/BEN/ZIL
pyridine	PIR/DAOEN
Pyridium	PI/RID/YUM
Pyridium Plus	PI/RID/YUM/PLUS
pyridofylline	PIR/DOF/LIN
pyridostigmine	PIR/DO/STIG/MAOEN
pyridoxal	PIR/DOK/SAL
pyridoxamine	PIR/DOX/MAOEN
pyridoxic	PIR/DOX/IK
pyridoxine	PIR/DOK/SAOEN
pyridoxol	PIR/DOK/SOL
pyridoxonium	PIR/DOK/SOEN/YUM
pyriform	P*IR/FORM
	(*not* PIR/FORM; see piriform)
pyrilamine	PAOI/RIL/MAOEN
	PIR/IL/MAOEN
pyrimethamine	PIR/M*ET/MAOEN
pyrimidine	PAOI/RIM/DAOEN
pyrinoline	PI/RIN/LAOEN
	PIR/IN/LAOEN
pyrithiamine	PIR/THAOI/MIN
pyro-	PAOIR
	PAOI/RO
pyroarsenic	PAOIR/AR/SEN/IK
pyroborate	PAOIR/BOR/AIT
pyroboric	PAOIR/BOR/IK
pyrocalciferol	PAOIR/KAL/SIF/ROL
pyrocatechase	PAOIR/KAT/KAIS
pyrocatechin	PAOIR/KAT/KIN
pyrocatechol	PAOIR/KAT/KOL
pyrocechatuic	PAOIR/SEK/TAOU/IK
pyrocinchonic	PAOIR/SIN/KON/IK
pyrocitric	PAOIR/SIT/RIK
pyrodextrin	PAOIR/DEX/TRIN
pyrogallic	PAOIR/GAL/IK
pyrogallol	PAOIR/GAL/OL
	PAOIR/GAL/LOL
pyrogallolphthalein	PAOIR/GAL/THAL/YIN
	PAOIR/GAL/OL/THAL/YIN
pyrogen	PAOIR/JEN
pyrogenetic	PAOIR/JE/NET/IK
pyrogenic	PAOIR/JEN/IK
pyrogenous	PAOI/ROJ/NOUS
pyroglobulin	PAOIR/GLOB/LIN
pyroglobulinemia	PAOIR/GLOB/LIN/AOEM/YA
	PAOIR/GLOB/LI/NAOEM/YA
pyroglutamate	PAOIR/GLAOUT/MAIT
pyroglutamic	PAOIR/GLAOU/TAM/IK
pyrolagnia	PAOIR/LAG/NA
	PAOIR/LAG/NAOE/YA
pyroligneous	PAOIR/LIG/NOUS
	PAOIR/LIG/NAOE/OUS
pyrolysis	PAOI/ROL/SIS
pyromania	PAOIR/MAIN/YA
pyromaniac	PAOIR/MAIN/YAK
pyrometer	PAOI/ROM/TER
pyrone	PAOI/ROEN
pyronin	PAOIR/NIN
pyronine	PAOIR/NAOEN
pyroninophilia	PAOIR/NIN/FIL/YA
pyronyxis	PAOIR/NIK/SIS
pyrophobia	PAOIR/FOEB/YA
pyrophosphatase	PAOIR/FOS/FA/TAIS
pyrophosphate	PAOIR/FOS/FAIT
pyrophosphokinase	PAOIR/FOS/FO/KAOI/NAIS
pyrophosphoramide	PAOIR/FOS/FOER/MAOID
pyrophosphoric	PAOIR/FOS/FOER/IK
pyrophosphorylase	PAOIR/FOS/FOER/LAIS
pyrophosphotransferase	PAOIR/FOS/FO/TRA*NS/FRAIS
pyroptothymia	PAOI/ROPT/THAOIM/YA
pyropuncture	PAOIR/PUNG/KHUR
pyroracemic	PAOIR/RA/SAOEM/IK
	PAOIR/RAI/SAOEM/IK
pyroscope	PAOIR/SKOEP
pyrosis	PAOI/ROE/SIS
pyrosulfuric	PAOIR/SUL/FAOUR/IK
pyrotartaric	PAOIR/TAR/TAR/IK
pyrotherapy	PAOIR/THER/PI
pyrotic	PAOI/ROT/IK
pyrotoxin	PAOIR/TOK/SIN
pyrovalerone	PIR/VAL/ROEN
pyroxamine	PI/ROX/MAOEN
	PIR/OX/MAOEN
pyroxylin	PAOI/ROX/LIN
pyrrobutamine	PIR/BAOUT/MAOEN
pyrrocaine	PIR/KAIN

pyrroetioporphyrin	PIR/AOET/YO/POR/FRIN
pyrrolase	PIR/LAIS
pyrrol	PIR/ROL
	PIR/OL
pyrrole	PIR/ROEL
	PIR/OEL
pyrrolidine	PI/ROL/DAOEN
	PIR/ROL/DAOEN
pyrrolidone	PI/ROL/DOEN
	PIR/ROL/DOEN
pyrroline	PIR/LAOEN
	PIR/LIN
pyrrolnitrin	PIR/OL/NAOI/TRIN
	PIR/ROL/NAOI/TRIN
pyrroloporphyria	PIR/LO/POR/FIR/YA
pyrroporphyrin	PIR/POR/FRIN
Pyrroxate	PAOI/ROK/SAIT
	PIR/ROK/SAIT
pyruvaldoxine	PAOIR/VAL/DOK/SAOEN
	PAOI/RAOU/VAL/DOK/SAOEN
pyruvate	PAOIR/VAIT
	PAOI/RAOU/VAIT
pyruvemia	PAOIR/VAOEM/YA
	PAOI/RAOU/VAOEM/YA
pyruvic	PAOI/RAOUVK
	PAOI/RAOUV/IK
pyrvinium	PIR/VIN/YUM
Pythagoras	PI/THAG/RAS
pythagorean	PI/THAG/RAOE/YAN
Pythium insidiosum	P*IT/YUM/IN/SID/YOE/SUM
	P*IT/YUM/IN/SID/YOES/UM
pythogenesis	PAO*IT/JEN/SIS
	PAOI/THO/JEN/SIS
pythogenic	PAO*IT/JEN/IK
	PAOI/THO/JEN/IK
pythogenous	PAOI/THOJ/NOUS
pyuria	PAOI/YAOUR/YA

Q

q.#h. (e.g., q.6h.)   KW#/H*PD (e.g., KW6/H*PD)
q.a.m.   KWA*M
q.d.   KW*D
q.i.d.   KW*ID
q.o.d.   KWO*D
Quaalude   KWAU/LAOUD
     KWAI/LAOUD
quack   KWAK
quackery   KWAK/RI
quader   KWAUD/ER
quadr-   KWAUD/R-
     KWAD/R-
quadrangle   KWAUD/RANG/-L
quadrangular   KWAUD/RANG/LAR
quadrant   KWAUD/RANT
quadrantal   KWAUD/RAN/TAL
quadrantanopia   KWAUD/RANT/NOEP/YA
quadrantanopsia   KWAUD/RANT/NOPS/YA
quadrat   KWAUD/RAT
quadrata   KWAUD/RAI/TA
quadrate   KWAUD/RAIT
quadrati   KWAUD/RAI/TAOI
quadratipronator   KWAUD/RAIT/PRO/NAI/TOR
     KWAUD/RAI/TI/PRO/NAI/TOR
quadratum   KWAUD/RAI/TUM
     KWAUD/RAIT/UM
quadratus   KWAUD/RAI/TUS
quadribasic   KWAUD/RI/BAIS/IK
quadriceps   KWAUD/RI/SEPS
quadricepsplasty   KWAUD/RI/SEPS/PLAS/TI
quadriceptor   KWAUD/RI/SEP/TOR
quadricuspid   KWAUD/RI/KUS/PID
quadridigitate   KWAUD/RI/DIJ/TAIT
quadrigemina   KWAUD/RI/JEM/NA
quadrigeminae   KWAUD/RI/JEM/NAE
quadrigeminal   KWAUD/RI/JEM/NAL
quadrigeminum   KWAUD/RI/JEM/NUM
quadrigeminus   KWAUD/RI/JEM/NUS
quadrigeminy   KWAUD/RI/JEM/N*I
quadrilateral   KWAUD/RI/LAT/RAL
quadrilocular   KWAUD/RI/LOK/LAR
Quadrinal   KWAUD/RI/NAL
quadripara   KWAUD/RIP/RA
quadriparesis   KWAUD/RI/PA/RAOE/SIS
     KWAUD/RI/PAR/SIS
quadripartite   KWAUD/RI/PAR/TAOIT
quadriplegia   KWAUD/RI/PLAOE/JA
quadriplegic   KWAUD/RI/PLAOEJ/IK
quadripod   KWAUD/RI/POD
quadripolar   KWAUD/RI/POE/LAR
quadrisect   KWAUD/RI/SEKT
quadrisection   KWAUD/RI/S*EBGS
quadritubercular   KWAUD/RI/TAOU/BERK/LAR
quadrivalent   KWAUD/RI/VAIL/ENT
     KWAUD/RI/VAI/LENT
quadruped   KWAUD/RU/PED
quadruplet   KWAUD/RUP/LET
     KWA/DRAOUP/LET
     KWAUD/RAOUP/LET
Quain   KWAIN
quaker   KWAIK/ER
quale   KWAI/LAOE
qualifying   KWAL/FI/-G
qualimeter   KWA/LIM/TER
     KWAU/LIM/TER
qualitative   KWAL/TAIT/IV
qualitive   KWAL/TIV
quality   KWAL/TI
     KWALT
quanta   KWAN/TA
quantasome   KWAN/TA/SOEM
quantatrope   KWAN/TA/TROEP
quantimeter   KWAN/TIM/TER
quantitative   KWANT/TAIT/IV
quantitive   KWANT/TIV
quantity   KWANT/TI
     KWANT
quantum   KWAN/TUM
     KWAUN/TUM
quantum libet   KWAN/TUM/LAOI/BET
     KWAUN/TUM/LAOI/BET
quantum satis   KWAN/TUM/SAI/TIS
     KWAN/TUM/SAT/TIS
     KWAUN/TUM/SAI/TIS

quantum sufficit   KWAUN/TUM/SAT/TIS
     KWAN/TUM/SUF/SIT
     KWAUN/TUM/SUF/SIT
quarantine   KWARN/TAOEN
quart   KWART
quartan   KWAR/TAN
quarter   KWART/ER
quarti   KWAR/TAOI
quartile   KWAR/TAOIL
quartipara   KWAR/TIP/RA
quartisect   KWART/SEKT
     KWAR/TI/SEKT
quartisternal   KWART/STERNL
     KWAR/TI/STERNL
quartz   KWARTS
Quarzan   KWAR/ZAN
quasi   KWAI/ZI
     KWAI/SI
     KWA/ZI
quasidominance   KWAI/ZAOI/DOM/NANS
quasidominant   KWAI/ZAOI/DOM/NANT
quassation   KWA/SAIGS
     KWAS/SAIGS
quater in die   KWAT/ER/N-/DAOE/YA
     KWAT/ER/N-/DAOE/YAI
quaternary   KWAT/ER/NAIR
     KWAUT/ER/NAIR
     KWA/TERN/RI
Quatrefages   KAT/ER/FAJ/EZ
     KAT/ER/FAUJ/EZ
quazepam   KWAZ/PAM
quazodine   KWAZ/DAOEN
     KWAIZ/DAOEN
Quebec   KE/BEK
     KWE/BEK
quebrachitol   KAI/BRAFP/TOL
Queckenstedt   KWEK/EN/STET
     KWEK/-N/STET
Quelidrine   KWEL/DRAOEN
quench   KWEFRPBLG
     KWEN/-FP
quenching   KWEFRPBLG/-G
     KWEN/-FPG
Quenu   KAI/NU
     KAI/NAOU
quenuthoracoplasty   KWAOE/NAOU/THOR/KO/PLAS/TI
     KAI/NU/THOR/KO/PLAS/TI
     KAI/NAOU/THOR/KO/PLAS/TI
quercetin   KWERS/TIN
     KWER/SE/TIN
quercitannic   KWERS/TAN/IK
Quercus   KWER/KUS
querulent   KWER/LENT
     KWER/YAOU/LENT
     KWER/YU/LENT
Quervain   KER/VAN
questionnaire   KWEGS/NAIR
Questran   KWES/TRAN
Questran Light   KWES/TRAN/LAOIGT
Questran Powder   KWES/TRAN/POUD/ER
Quetelet   KET/LAI
Queyrat   KAI/RAU
     KAI/RA
Quibron   KWIB/RON
Quibron-T   KWIB/RON/T-RBGS
quick   KWIK
Quick test   K-P/KWIK/T*ES
quickening   KWIK/-NG
quicklime   KWIK/LAOIM
quicksilver   KWIK/SIL/VER
quidding   KWID/-G
quiescent   KWAOI/ES/ENT
     KWAOE/ES/ENT
quillaia   KWIL/LAI/YA
quillaic   KWIL/LAI/IK
quinacrine   KWIN/KRIN
     KWIN/KRAOEN
Quinaglute   KWIN/GLAOUT
Quinalan   KWIN/LAN
quinaldic   KWIN/ALD/IK
quinaldine   KWIN/AL/DAOEN
quinaldinic   KWIN/AL/DIN/IK
Quinamm   KWIN/AM
     KWIN/NAM
quinate   KWAOI/NAIT
     KWIN/AIT
quince   KWINS
Quincke   KWIN/KAOE

quinestradiol	KWIN/ES/TRA/DI/OL
quinestradol	KWIN/ES/TRA/DOL
quinestrol	KWIN/ES/TROL
quinethazone	KWIN/*ET/ZOEN
quinfamide	KWIN/FA/MAOID
quingestanol	KWIN/J*ES/NOL
quingestrone	KWIN/JES/TROEN
quinhydrone	KWIN/HAOI/DROEN
quinic	KWIN/IK
Quinidex	KWIN/DEX
quinidine	KWIN/DAOEN
	KWIN/DIN
quinine	KWAOI/NAOIN
	KWAOI/NAOEN
	KWIN/AOIN
	KWIN/AOEN
	KWIN/NIN
quininic	KWAOI/NIN/IK
	KWI/NIN/IK
quininism	KWAOIN/NIFM
	KWIN/NIFM
Quinlan	KWIN/LAN
quinocide	KWIN/SAO*ID
quinoid	KWIN/OID
quinol	KWIN/OL
quinoline	KWIN/LAOEN
	KWIN/LIN
quinolinic	KWIN/LIN/IK
quinology	KWIN/OLG
	KWI/NOLG
quinolone	KWIN/LOEN
quinometry	KWI/NOM/TRI
	KWIN/OM/TRI
quinone	KWAOI/NOEN
	KWIN/OEN
	KWI/NOEN
Quinora	KWIN/RA
quinovin	KWIN/VIN
quinovose	KWIN/VOES
quinoxin	KWIN/OK/SIN
	KWI/NOK/SIN
Quinquaud	KAN/KOE
	KWIN/KOE
quinque-	KWIN/KWAOE
	KWIN/KWE
quinquecuspid	KWIN/KWAOE/KUS/PID
quinquedigitate	KWIN/KWAOE/DIJ/TAIT
quinquestriatus	KWIN/KWAOE/STRAOI/AI/TUS
	KWIN/KWAOE/STRAOI/YAI/TUS
quinquetubercular	KWIN/KWAOE/TAOU/BERK/LAR
quinquevalent	KWIN/KWAOE/VAIL/ENT
	KWIN/KWAOE/VAI/LENT
quinquina	KIN/KAOE/NA
	KWIN/KWI/NA
quinsy	KWIN/ZI
quintan	KWIN/TAN
quintana	KWIN/TAI/NA
	KWIN/TAN/NA
quintessence	KWIN/TES/ENS
quinti	KWIN/TAOI
quintipara	KWIN/TIP/RA
quintisternal	KWINT/STERNL
	KWIN/TI/STERNL
quintuplet	KWIN/TUP/LET
quittor	KWIT/TOR
quoad vitam	KWOE/AD/VAOI/TAM
quotidian	KWOE/TID/YAN
quotient	KWOE/SHENT
	KWOERB/ENT

R

rabbetting	RAB/ET/-G
	RAB/BET/-G
rabbia	RAB/YA
rabbitpox	RAB/BIT/POX
rabelaisin	RAB/LAI/SIN
rabic	RAIB/IK
rabicidal	RAIB/SAOI/DAL
rabid	RAB/ID
rabiei	RAIB/YAOI
rabies	RAI/BAOEZ
Rabies Immune Globulin	RAI/BAOEZ/IM/MAOUN/GLOB/
	LIN
rabiform	RAIB/FORM
race	RAIS
racefemine	RAIS/FEM/AOEN
racemase	RAIS/MAIS
	RAS/MAIS
racemate	RAIS/MAIT
	RAS/MAIT
raceme	RAI/SAOEM
	RAS/SAOEM
racemethionine	RAIS/ME/THAOI/NAOEN
racemic	RAI/SAOEM/IK
	RAI/SEM/IK
	RA/SAOEM/IK
	RA/SEM/IK
racemization	RAI/SAOEM/ZAIGS
	RAS/MI/ZAIGS
racemosa	RAS/MOE/SA
	RAIS/MOE/SA
racemose	RAS/MOES
	RAIS/MOES
racemosum	RAS/MOE/SUM
	RAS/MOES/UM
	RAIS/MOE/SUM
	RAIS/MOES/UM
racephedrine	RAIS/FED/RIN
	RAI/SEF/DRIN
racephenicol	RAIS/FEN/KOL
Racet Cream	RA/SET/KRAOEM
	RAI/SET/KRAOEM
rachi(o)-	RAIK/Y(O)
	RAIK
	RAI/KI
	RA/KI
rachial	RAIK/YAL
rachialbuminimeter	RAIK/AL/BAOUM/NIM/TER
	RAIK/YAL/BAOUM/NIM/TER
rachialbuminimetry	RAIK/AL/BAOUM/NIM/TRI
	RAIK/YAL/BAOUM/NIM/TRI
rachialbuminometer	RAIK/AL/BAOUM/NOM/TER
	RAIK/YAL/BAOUM/NOM/TER
rachialgia	RAIK/AL/JA
	RAIK/YAL/JA
rachianalgesia	RAIK/ANL/JAOEZ/YA
rachianesthesia	RAIK/ANS/THAOEZ/YA
rachicentesis	RAIK/SEN/TAOE/SIS
rachides	RAIK/DAOEZ
	RAK/DAOEZ
rachidial	RA/KID/YAL
	RAI/KID/YAL
rachidian	RA/KID/YAN
	RAI/KID/YAN
rachigraph	RAIK/GRAF
rachilysis	RA/KIL/SIS
	RAI/KIL/SIS
rachiocampsis	RAIK/YO/KAFRP/SIS
rachiocentesis	RAIK/YO/SEN/TAOE/SIS
rachiochysis	RAIK/YO/KIS/SIS
rachiodynia	RAIK/YO/DIN/YA
rachiokyphosis	RAIK/YO/KAOI/FOE/SIS
rachiometer	RAIK/YOM/TER
rachiomyelitis	RAIK/YO/MAOI/LAOITS
rachiopagus	RAIK/YOP/GUS
rachiopathy	RAIK/YOP/TH*I
rachioplegia	RAIK/YO/PLAOE/JA
rachioscoliosis	RAIK/YO/SKOEL/YOE/SIS
rachiotome	RAIK/YO/TOEM
rachiotomy	RAIK/YOT/M*I
rachipagus	RA/KIP/GUS
	RAI/KIP/GUS
rachiresistance	RAIK/RE/SIS/TANS
rachiresistant	RAIK/RE/SIS/TANT
rachis	RAI/KIS

rachisagra	RAI/KIS/AG/RA
rachischisis	RA/KIS/KI/SIS
	RAI/KIS/KI/SIS
rachisensibility	RAIK/SENS/-BLT
rachisensible	RAIK/SENS/-BL
rachises	RAIK/SAOEZ
rachitic	RA/KIT/IK
	RAI/KIT/IK
rachitis	RA/KAOITS
	RAI/KAOITS
rachitism	RAK/TIFM
	RAIK/TIFM
rachitogenic	RA/KIT/JEN/IK
rachitome	RAK/TOEM
rachitomy	RA/KIT/M*I
racial	RAIRBL
racket	RAK/ET
racoma	RAI/KOE/MA
rad	RAD
radarkymography	RAI/DAR/KAOI/MOG/FI
radectomy	RAI/DEKT/M*I
Radford	RAD/FORD
radi(o)-	RAID/Y(O)
radiability	RAID/YABLT
radiable	RAID/YABL
radiad	RAID/YAD
radial	RAID/YAL
radiale	RAID/YAI/LAOE
radiales	RAID/YAI/LAOEZ
radialis	RAID/YAI/LIS
radian	RAID/YAN
radiant	RAID/YANT
radiata	RAID/YAI/TA
radiate	RAID/YAIT
radiatio	RAID/YAI/SHOE
	RAID/YAIRB/YOE
radiation	RAID/YAIGS
radiationes	RAID/YAI/SHOE/NAOEZ
	RAID/YAIRB/YOE/NAOEZ
radiatum	RAID/YAI/TUM
	RAID/YAIT/UM
radical	RAD/KAL
radices	RAI/DI/SAOEZ
	RAD/SAOEZ
	(not RAID/SAOEZ; see raid seize)
radicicola	RAD/SIK/LA
radiciform	RAI/DIS/FORM
radicis	RAD/SIS
	RAI/DI/SIS
radicle	RAD/K-L
radicotomy	RAD/KOT/M*I
radicul(o)-	RA/DIK/L(O)
	RA/DIK/YAOU/L(O)
	RA/DIK/YU/L(O)
radicula	RA/DIK/LA
radiculalgia	RA/DIK/LAL/JA
radicular	RA/DIK/LAR
radiculectomy	RA/DIK/LEKT/M*I
radiculitis	RA/DIK/LAOITS
radiculodental	RA/DIK/LO/DEN/TAL
radiculoganglionitis	RA/DIK/LO/GANG/LO/NAOITS
radiculomedullary	RA/DIK/LO/MED/LAIR
radiculomeningomyelitis	RA/DIK/LO/ME/NING/MAOI/
	LAOITS
radiculomyelopathy	RA/DIK/LO/MAOI/LOP/TH*I
radiculoneuritis	RA/DIK/LO/NAOU/RAOITS
radiculoneuropathy	RA/DIK/LO/NAOU/ROP/TH*I
radiculopathy	RA/DIK/LOP/TH*I
radiectomy	RAID/YEKT/M*I
radiferous	RAI/DIF/ROUS
radii	RAID/YAOI
radio	RAID/YOE
radio-	RAID/YO
radioactinium	RAID/YO/AK/TIN/YUM
radioaction	RAID/YO/A*BGS
radioactive	RAID/YO/AKT/IV
radioactivity	RAID/YO/AK/TIV/TI
radioactor	RAID/YO/AK/TOR
radioallergosorbent	RAID/YO/AL/ER/GO/SORB/ENT
	RAID/YO/AI/LERG/SORB/ENT
radioanaphylaxis	RAID/YO/AN/FLAK/SIS
radioautogram	RAID/YO/AUT/GRAM
radioautograph	RAID/YO/AUT/GRAF
radioautography	RAID/YO/AU/TOG/FI
radiobe	RAID/YOEB
radiobicipital	RAID/YO/B*I/SIP/TAL
radiobiological	RAID/YO/BAO*I/LOJ/KAL
radiobiologist	RAID/YO/BAO*I/O*LGS
radiobiology	RAID/YO/BAO*I/OLG

radiocalcium	RAID/YO/KALS/YUM
radiocarbon	RAID/YO/KAR/BON
radiocarcinogenesis	RAID/YO/KARS/NO/JEN/SIS
radiocardiogram	RAID/YO/KARD/YO/GRAM
radiocardiography	RAID/YO/KARD/YOG/FI
radiocarpal	RAID/YO/KAR/PAL
radiocarpea	RAID/YO/KARP/YA
radiocarpeum	RAID/YO/KARP/YUM
radiocarpus	RAID/YO/KAR/PUS
radiochemical	RAID/YO/KEM/KAL
radiochemistry	RAID/YO/KEM/STRI
radiochemy	RAID/YO/KEM/M*I
radiochlorine	RAID/YO/KLOR/AOEN
radiochroism	RAID/YO/KROE/IFM
radiocinematograph	RAID/YO/SIN/MAT/GRAF
radiocinematography	RAID/YO/SIN/MA/TOG/FI
radiocobalt	RAID/YO/KO/BALT
radiocolloid	RAID/YO/KLOID
	RAID/YO/KOL/OID
radiocurable	RAID/YO/KAOURBL
	RAID/YO/KAOUR/-BL
radiocystitis	RAID/YO/SIS/TAOITS
radiode	RAID/YOED
radiodense	RAID/YO/DENS
radiodensity	RAID/YO/DENS/TI
radiodermatitis	RAID/YO/DERM/TAOITS
radiodiagnosis	RAID/YO/DAOIG/NOE/SIS
radiodiagnostics	RAID/YO/DAOIG/NO*S/IK/-S
radiodiaphane	RAID/YO/DAOI/FAIN
radiodigital	RAID/YO/DIJ/TAL
radiodontics	RAID/YO/DONT/IK/-S
radiodontist	RAID/YO/DON/T*IS
radioecology	RAID/YO/E/KOLG
radioelectrocardiogram	RAID/YO/LEK/TRO/KARD/YO/ GRAM
radioelectrocardiograph	RAID/YO/LEK/TRO/KARD/YO/ GRAF
radioelectrocardiography	RAID/YO/LEK/TRO/KARD/YOG/FI
radioelectrophysiologram	RAID/YO/LEK/TRO/FIZ/YOL/ GRAM
radioelectrophysiolograph	RAID/YO/LEK/TRO/FIZ/YOL/ GRAF
radioelectrophysiolography	RAID/YO/LEK/TRO/FIZ/YO/LOG/ FI
radioelement	RAID/YO/EL/-MT
radioencephalogram	RAID/YO/EN/SEF/LO/GRAM
radioencephalography	RAID/YO/EN/SEF/LOG/FI
radioepidermitis	RAID/YO/EP/DER/MAOITS
radioepithelitis	RAID/YO/EP/THAOE/LAOITS
radiofrequency	RAID/YO/FRAOEKT/SI
	RAID/YO/FRAOE/KWEN/SI
radiogallium	RAID/YO/GAL/YUM
radiogen	RAID/YO/JEN
radiogenesis	RAID/YO/JEN/SIS
radiogenic	RAID/YO/JEN/IK
radiogenics	RAID/YO/JEN/IK/-S
radiogold	RAID/YO/GOELD
radiogold colloid	RAID/YO/GOELD/KLOID
	RAID/YO/GOELD/KOL/OID
radiogram	RAID/YO/GRAM
radiograph	RAID/YO/GRAF
radiographic	RAID/YO/GRAFK
radiography	RAID/YOG/FI
radiohumeral	RAID/YO/HAOUM/RAL
radioimmunity	RAID/YO/IM/MAOUN/TI
radioimmunoassay	RAID/YO/IM/NO/AS/SAI
radioimmunodiffusion	RAID/YO/IM/NO/DIF/FAOUGS
	RAID/YO/IM/NO/DI/FAOUGS
radioimmunoelectrophoresis	
	RAID/YO/IM/NO/LEK/TRO/ FRAOE/SIS
radioimmunoprecipitatio	RAID/YO/IM/NO/PRE/SIP/TAIGS
radioimmunosorbent	RAID/YO/IM/NO/SORB/ENT
radioiodinated	RAID/YO/AOI/DIN/AIT/-D
radioiodine	RAID/YO/AOI/DAOIN
radioiron	RAID/YO/AOIRN
radioisotope	RAID/YO/AOIS/TOEP
radiokymography	RAID/YO/KAOI/MOG/FI
radiolabeled	RAID/YO/LAI/BEL/-D
radiolead	RAID/YO/LAED
radiolesion	RAID/YO/LAOEGS
radioligand	RAID/YO/LAOI/GAND
	RAID/YO/LIG/GAND
radiologic	RAID/YO/LOJ/IK
radiological	RAID/YO/LOJ/KAL
radiologist	RAID/YO*LGS
radiology	RAID/YOLG
radiolucency	RAID/YO/LAOUS/EN/SI
	RAID/YO/LAOU/SEN/SI
radiolucent	RAID/YO/LAOUS/ENT
	RAID/YO/LAOU/SENT
radiolus	RAI/DAOE/LUS
radiometallography	RAID/YO/MET/LOG/FI
radiometer	RAID/YOM/TER
radiomicrometer	RAID/YO/MAOI/KROM/TER
radiomimetic	RAID/YO/MAOI/MET/IK
	RAID/YO/MI/MET/IK
radiomuscular	RAID/YO/MUS/KLAR
radiomutation	RAID/YO/MAOU/TAIGS
radion	RAID/YON
radionecrosis	RAID/YON/NE/KROE/SIS
radioneuritis	RAID/YO/NAOU/RAOITS
radionitrogen	RAID/YO/NAOI/TRO/JEN
radionuclide	RAID/YO/NAOU/KLAOID
radiopacity	RAID/YO/PAS/TI
radiopalmar	RAID/YO/PAL/MAR
radiopaque	RAID/YO/PAIK
radioparency	RAID/YO/PARN/SI
radioparent	RAID/YO/PARNT
radiopathology	RAID/YO/PA/THOLG
radiopelvimetry	RAID/YO/PEL/VIM/TRI
radiopharmaceutical	RAID/YO/FARM/SAOUT/KAL
radiopharmacy	RAID/YO/FARM/SI
radiophobia	RAID/YO/FOEB/YA
radiophosphorus	RAID/YO/FOS/FRUS
radiophotography	RAID/YO/FOE/TOG/FI
	RAID/YO/FRAF/FI
radiophylaxis	RAID/YO/FLAK/SIS
radiophysics	RAID/YO/FIZ/IK/-S
radiopill	RAID/YO/PIL
radioplastic	RAID/YO/PLA*S/IK
radiopotassium	RAID/YO/POE/TAS/YUM
radiopotentiation	RAID/YO/POE/TEN/SHAIGS
radiopraxis	RAID/YO/PRAK/SIS
radiopulmonography	RAID/YO/PUL/MO/NOG/FI
radioreaction	RAID/YO/RE/A*BGS
radioreceptor	RAID/YO/RE/SEP/TOR
radioresistance	RAID/YO/RE/SIS/TANS
radioresistant	RAID/YO/RE/SIS/TANT
radioresponsive	RAID/YO/SPONS/IV
	RAID/YO/RE/SPONS/IV
radiosclerometer	RAID/YO/SKLE/ROM/TER
radioscope	RAID/YO/SKOEP
radioscopy	RAID/YOS/KPI
radiosensibility	RAID/YO/SENS/-BLT
radiosensitive	RAID/YO/SENS/TIV
radiosensitiveness	RAID/YO/SENS/TIV/*NS
	RAID/YO/SENS/TIVNS
radiosensitivity	RAID/YO/SENS/TIV/TI
radiosodium	RAID/YO/SOED/YUM
radiostereoscopy	RAID/YO/STER/YOS/KPI
radiostrontium	RAID/YO/STRON/SHUM
radiosulfur	RAID/YO/SUL/FUR
radiotelemetering	RAID/YO/TEL/MAOET/ER/-G
radiotelemetry	RAID/YO/TE/LEM/TRI
radiotellurium	RAID/YO/TEL/LAOUR/YUM
radiothanatology	RAID/YO/THAN/TOLG
radiotherapeutic	RAID/YO/THER/PAOUT/IK
radiotherapeutics	RAID/YO/THER/PAOUT/IK/-S
radiotherapist	RAID/YO/THER/P*IS
radiotherapy	RAID/YO/THER/PI
radiothermy	RAID/YO/THER/M*I
radiothorium	RAID/YO/THOR/YUM
	RAID/YO/THOER/YUM
	RAID/YO/THOIRM
radiothyroidectomy	RAID/YO/THAOI/ROI/DEKT/M*I
radiothyroxin	RAID/YO/THAOI/ROK/SIN
radiotomy	RAID/YOT/M*I
radiotoxemia	RAID/YO/TOK/SAOEM/YA
radiotracer	RAID/YO/TRAIS/ER
radiotransparency	RAID/YO/TRA*NS/PARN/SI
radiotransparent	RAID/YO/TRA*NS/PARNT
radiotropic	RAID/YO/TROP/IK
radiotropism	RAID/YOT/RO/PIFM
radioulnar	RAID/YO/UL/NAR
radioulnares	RAID/YO/UL/NAI/RAOEZ
radioulnaris	RAID/YO/UL/NAI/RIS
radisectomy	RAID/SEKT/M*I
radium	RAID/YUM
radius	RAID/YUS
radix	RAI/DIX
radon	RAI/DON
rads	RADZ
raffinase	RAF/NAIS
raffinose	RAF/NOES
rafoxanide	RA/FOX/NAOID
rage	RAIJ
ragocyte	RAG/SAO*IT

Raillietina	RAOIL/YE/TAOI/NA		RAZ/MUS/SEN
	RAOIL/YE/TAOE/NA	rasp	RAS/-P
raillietiniasis	RAOIL/YE/TI/NAOI/SIS	raspatory	RAS/PA/TOIR
	RAOIL/YET/NAOI/SIS	rasura	RA/SAOU/RA
Rainey	RAI/NAOE	rat	RAT
rale	RAL	rate	RAIT
ramal	RAI/MAL	Rathke	RA*T/KAOE
Raman	RAM/MAN	raticide	RAT/SAO*ID
ramex	RAI/MEX	ratio	RAI/SHOE
rami	RAI/MAOI		RAIRB/YOE
Ramibacterium	RAI/MAOI/BAK/TAOERM	ration	RAGS
	RAI/MAOE/BAK/TAOERM		RAIGS
ramicotomy	RAM/KOT/M*I	rational	RAGS/NAL
ramification	RAM/FI/KAIGS	rationale	RAGS/NAEL
ramify	RAM/FI	rationalization	RAGS/NAL/ZAIGS
Ramirez	RA/MIR/EZ	ratsbane	RATS/BAIN
	RA/MAOE/REZ	rat-tails	RAT/H-F/TAIL/-S
ramisection	RAM/S*EBGS	rattlesnake	RAT/-L/SNAIK
ramisectomy	RAM/SEKT/M*I	Rattus	RAT/TUS
ramitis	RA/MAOITS	Rau	RO*U
	RAM/AOITS		(*not* ROU or RAU; see row and raw)
Ramon	RA/MOEN	Rauber	ROU/BER
Ramon y Cajal	RA/MOEN/E/KA/HAL		ROUB/ER
ramose	RAI/MOES	Raudixin	RAU/DIK/SIN
ramosus	RAI/MOE/SUS	rausch	ROURB
	RA/MOE/SUS	Rauscher	ROURB/ER
ramous	RAI/MOUS	rauschbrand	ROURB/BRANT
	RAIM/OUS		ROURB/BRAND
ramp	RAFRP	Rauwolfia	ROU/WOL/FA
rampart	RAM/PART		ROU/WOL/FAOE/YA
Ramsay Hunt	RAM/SAOE/HUNT		RAU/WOL/FA
Ramsden	RAMS/DEN		RAU/WOL/FAOE/YA
	RAMZ/DEN	Rauzide	RAU/ZAOID
Ramstedt	RAM/STET	raviana	RAIV/YAI/NA
ramul-	RAM/L-	Ravius	RAIV/YUS
	RAM/YAOU/L-	rawii	ROU/YAOI
	RAM/YU/L-	ray	RAI
ramuli	RAM/LAOI	rayage	RAI/AJ
ramulus	RAM/LUS	Raymond	RAI/MON
ramus	RAI/MUS		RAI/MOND
ramycin	RA/MAOI/SIN		RAI/MAU
ranarum	RA/NAIR/UM	Raynaud	RAI/NOE
	RA/NAI/RUM	R-banding	R-RBGS/BAND/-G
rancid	RAN/SID	re (word)	R*E
	RANS/ID	re-	RE
rancidify	RAN/SID/FI	reablement	RE/AIBL/-MT
rancidity	RAN/SID/TI	reabsorb	RE/AB/SORB
R&C Lice Treatment Kit	R-RBGS/M-ND/KR-RBGS/LAOIS/	reabsorption	RE/AB/SORPGS
	TRAOEMT/KIT	react	RE/AKT
R&C Shampoo	R-RBGS/M-ND/KR-RBGS/SHAM/	reactance	RE/AK/TANS
	PAO	reactant	RE/AK/TANT
R&C Spray	R-RBGS/M-ND/KR-RBGS/SPRAI	reaction	RE/A*BGS
Randall	RAN/DAL	reaction-formation	RE/A*BGS/H-F/FOR/MAIGS
range	RAING	reactivate	RE/AKT/VAIT
	RAIN/-J	reactivation	RE/AKT/VAIGS
rangiferi	RAN/JIF/RAOI	reactivity	RE/AK/TIV/TI
ranimycin	RAN/MAOI/SIN	reactor	RE/AK/TOR
ranine	RAI/NAOIN	Read	K-P/RAED
ranitidine	RA/NAOIT/DAOEN	reading	RAED/-G
Ranke	RAN/KAOE	readthrough	RAED/THR*U
Rankin	RAN/KIN	reagent	RE/AI/JENT
ransom	RANS/OM		RE/AIJ/ENT
ranul-	RAN/L-		RE/AGT
	RAN/YAOU/L-	reagin	RE/AI/JIN
	RAN/YU/L-		RE/JIN
ranula	RAN/LA		RE/YA/JIN
ranular	RAN/LAR	reaginic	RE/JIN/IK
Ranunculus	RA/NUN/KLUS		RE/YA/JIN/IK
	RA/NUNG/LUS		RE/AI/JIN/IK
Ranvier	RAN/VAI	realgar	RE/AL/GAR
	RAN/VAOE/YAI	realistic	RAEL/*IS/IK
Raoult	RA/OEL	reality	RE/AL/TI
	RAU/OEL	reality awareness	RE/AL/TI/AI/WAIR/*NS
rape	RAIP	reality testing	RE/AL/TI/T*ES/-G
rapeseed oil	RAIP/SAOED/OIL	reamer	RAOEM/ER
raphania	RA/FAIN/YA		RAEM/ER
raphe	RAI/FAOE	reamputation	RE/AFRP/TAIGS
rapport	RA/POR	reattachment	RE/AI/TAFP/-MT
raptus	RAP/TUS	Reaumur	RAI/MUR
rarefaction	RAIR/FA*BGS		RAI/YU/MUR
rarefy	RAIR/FI	rebase	RE/BAIS
rasceta	RA/SAOE/TA	rebound	RE/BOUND
rash	RARB	rebreathing	RE/BRAO*ET/-G
rasion	RA*IGS	recalcification	RE/KALS/FI/KAIGS
	RAIZ/YON	recall	RE/KAUL
	(*not* RAIGS; see ration)		RAUL
Rasmussen	RAS/MUS/-N	recanalization	RE/KANL/ZAIGS
	RAZ/MUS/-N		RE/KAN/AL/ZAIGS
	RAS/MUS/SEN	recapitulation	RE/KPIFP/LAIGS

	RE/KA/PIFP/LAIGS	rectoabdominal	REKT/AB/DOM/NAL
receiver	RE/SAOEVR	rectocele	REKT/SAO*EL
	SEFR	rectoclysis	REK/TOK/LI/SIS
recellens	RE/SEL/ENZ	rectococcygeal	REKT/KOK/SIJ/YAL
	RE/SEL/LENZ	rectococcypexy	REKT/KOX/PEK/SI
receptacula	RE/SEP/TAK/LA	rectocolitis	REKT/KO/LAOITS
receptaculum	RE/SEP/TAK/LUM	rectocutaneous	REKT/KAOU/TAIN/YOUS
receptive	RE/SEPT/IV	rectocystotomy	REKT/SIS/TOT/M*I
receptolysin	RE/SEP/TOL/SIN	rectoischiadic	REKT/IS/KAD/IK
receptoma	RE/SEP/TOE/MA		REKT/IS/KAOE/AD/IK
receptor	RE/SEP/TOR	rectoischiadicum	REKT/IS/KAD/KUM
receptoric	RE/SEP/TOR/IK		REKT/IS/KAOE/AD/KUM
recess	RE/SESZ	rectolabial	REKT/LAIB/YAL
recession	RE/SEGS	rectoperineal	REKT/P*ER/NAOEL
recessitivity	RE/SIS/TIV/TI	rectoperineorrhaphy	REKT/P*ER/NAOE/YOR/FI
recessive	RE/SES/SIV	rectopexy	REKT/PEK/SI
	RE/SESZ/IV	rectophobia	REKT/FOEB/YA
recessus	RE/SES/SUS	rectoplasty	REKT/PLAS/TI
recidivation	RE/SID/VAIGS	rectoromanoscopy	REKT/ROEM/NOS/KPI
recidivism	RE/SID/VIFM	rectorrhaphy	REK/TOR/FI
recidivist	RE/SID/V*IS	rectoscope	REKT/SKOEP
recipe	RES/PAOE	rectoscopy	REK/TOS/KPI
recipient	RE/SIP/YENT	rectosigmoid	REKT/SIG/MOID
recipiomotor	RE/SIP/YO/MOE/TOR	rectosigmoidectomy	REKT/SIG/MOI/DEKT/M*I
reciprocal	RE/SIP/KAL	rectostenosis	REKT/STE/NOE/SIS
	RE/SIP/RO/KAL	rectostomy	REK/TO*S/M*I
reciprocation	RE/SIP/KAIGS	rectotome	REKT/TOEM
	RE/SIP/RO/KAIGS	rectotomy	REK/TOT/M*I
Recklinghausen	REK/LING/HOUZ/-N	rectourethral	REKT/YAOU/RAO*ET/RAL
	REK/-LG/HOUZ/-N	rectouterina	REKT/YAOUT/RAOI/NA
	REK/LING/HOU/ZEN	rectouterine	REKT/YAOUT/RIN
	REK/-LG/HOU/ZEN	rectovaginal	REKT/VAJ/NAL
reclination	REK/LI/NAIGS	rectovesical	REKT/VES/KAL
recognin	RE/KOG/NIN	rectovesicalis	REKT/VES/KAI/LIS
recognition	REK/NIGS	rectovestibular	REKT/VES/TIB/LAR
recollection	REK/L*EBGS	rectovulvar	REKT/VUL/VAR
recombinant	RE/KOM/BI/NANT	rectum	REK/TUM
	RE/KBIN/NANT	rectus	REK/TUS
recombinant DNA	RE/KOM/BI/NANT/D-RBGS/	recumbency	RE/KUM/BEN/SI
	N*RBGS/A*RBGS	recumbent	RE/KUM/BENT
	RE/KBIN/NANT/D-RBGS/N*RBGS/	recuperate	RE/KAOUP/RAIT
	A*RBGS	recuperation	RE/KAOUP/RAIGS
recombination	RE/KOM/BI/NAIGS	recuperative	RE/KAOUP/RA/TIV
	RE/KBIN/NAIGS		RE/KAOUP/TIV
Recombivax	RE/KOM/BI/VAX	recurrence	RE/KURNS
recompression	RE/KOM/PREGS	recurrens	RE/KURNZ
	RE/KPREGS	recurrent	RE/KURNT
recon	RE/KON	recurrentes	RE/KUR/REN/TAOEZ
reconditum	RE/KON/DAOI/TUM		RE/KURN/TAOEZ
	RE/KON/DAOIT/UM	recurrentis	RE/KUR/REN/TIS
reconstitution	RE/KONS/TAOUGS		RE/KURN/TIS
	RE/KON/STAOUGS	recurvation	RE/KUR/VAIGS
	RE/KO*NS/TAOUGS	recurvatum	RE/KUR/VAI/TUM
reconstruction	RE/KON/STR*UBGS		RE/KUR/VAIT/UM
	RE/KR*UBGS	red	RED
reconstructive	RE/KON/STRUKT/IV	redecussate	RE/DE/KUS/SAIT
	RE/KRUKT/IV	redfoot	RED/FAOT
recontour	RE/KON/TAOUR	redia	RAOED/YA
	RE/KON/TOUR	rediae	RAOED/YAE
record	REK/ORD	redifferentiation	RE/DIFRN/SHAIGS
	RE/KORD	redintegration	RE/DINT/GRAIGS
	RORD		RED/INT/GRAIGS
recording	RE/KORD/-G		RED/SPWE/GRAIGS
	RORD/-G	redislocation	RE/DIS/LOE/KAIGS
recovery	RE/KOV/RI	Redlich	RED/LIK
recrement	REK/REMT	redness	RED/*NS
recrementitious	REK/REMT/TIRBS	redox	RE/DOX
	REK/RE/MEN/TIRBS		RED/OX
recrudescence	RE/KRAOU/DES/ENS	redressement	RE/DRES/MON
recrudescent	RE/KRAOU/DES/ENT	redressement force	RE/DRES/MON/FOR/SAI
recruitment	RE/KRAOUT/-MT	redressment	RE/DRES/-MT
rect(o)-	REKT		RE/DRESZ/-MT
	REK/T(O)	red tide	RED/TAOID
recta	REK/TA	reduce	RE/DAOUS
rectae	REK/TAE	reduced	RE/DAOUS/-D
rectal	REK/TAL	reducible	RE/DAOUS/-BL
rectales	REK/TAI/LAOEZ	reductant	RE/DUK/TANT
rectalgia	REK/TAL/JA	reductase	RE/DUK/TAIS
rectalis	REK/TAI/LIS	reductic	RE/DUKT/IK
rectangular	REK/TANG/LAR	reduction	RE/D*UBGS
rectectomy	REK/TEKT/M*I	reductone	RE/DUK/TOEN
recti	REK/TAOI	redundant	RE/DUN/DANT
rectification	REKT/FI/KAIGS	reduplication	RE/DAOUP/KAIGS
rectified	REKT/FI/-D		RE/DAOUP/LI/KAIGS
rectifier	REKT/FI/ER		RE/DAOU/PLI/KAIGS
rectify	REKT/FI	reduviid	RE/DAOUV/YID
rectischiac	REK/TIS/KAK		RE/DAOU/VID
	REK/TIS/KAOE/AK	Reduviidae	RE/DAOU/VAOI/DAE
rectitis	REK/TAOITS	Reduvius	RE/DAOUV/YUS

Reed	K-P/RAOED	registrar	REJ/STRAR
re-education	RE/EJ/KAIGS	registration	REJ/STRAIGS
reef	RAOEF	registry	REJ/STRI
reenactment	RE/EN/AKT/-MT	Regitine	REJ/TAOEN
Reenstierna	RAOEN/STAOER/NA	Reglan	REG/LAN
reentry	RE/EN/TRI	regnancy	REG/NAN/SI
Rees	RAO*ES	Regnaud	REN/YOE
Reese	RAOES		RAIN/YOE
re-examine	RE/KPAM/MIN	Regonol	REG/NOL
	RE/KP-M	regress	RE/GRESZ
refect	RE/FEKT	regression	RE/GREGS
refection	RE/F*EBGS	regressive	RE/GRES/SIV
refectious	RE/FEK/-RBS		RE/GRESZ/IV
referral	RE/FERL	Regroton	REG/RO/TON
refine	RE/FAOIN		RE/GRO/TON
reflect	RE/FLEKT	regular	REG/LAR
reflected	RE/FLEKT/-D		REG
reflection	RE/FL*EBGS	regularity	REG/LAIR/TI
reflector	RE/FLEK/TOR		REG/TI
reflex	RE/FLEX	regulation	REG/LAIGS
reflexa	RE/FLEK/SA	regulative	REG/LA/TIV
reflexia	RE/FLEX/YA		REG/LAIT/IV
reflexo-	RE/FLEX	regurgitant	RE/GURJ/TANT
	RE/FLEK/SO	regurgitate	RE/GURJ/TAIT
reflexogenic	RE/FLEX/JEN/IK	regurgitation	RE/GURJ/TAIGS
reflexogenous	RE/FLEK/SOJ/NOUS	rehab	RE/HAB
	RE/FLEX/OJ/NOUS	rehabilitate	RE/BIL/TAIT
reflexograph	RE/FLEX/GRAF		RE/HABL/TAIT
reflexology	RE/FLEK/SOLG	rehabilitation	RE/BIL/TAIGS
	RE/FLEX/OLG		RE/HABL/TAIGS
reflexometer	RE/FLEK/SOM/TER	rehabilitative	RE/BIL/TAIT/IV
	RE/FLEX/OM/TER		RE/HABL/TAIT/IV
reflexophil	RE/FLEX/FIL	rehabilitee	RE/BIL/TAOE
reflexophile	RE/FLEX/FAOIL		RE/HABL/TAOE
reflexotherapy	RE/FLEX/THER/PI	rehalation	RE/HA/LAIGS
reflexum	RE/FLEX/UM	rehearsal	RE/HER/SAL
	RE/FLEK/SUM	Rehfuss	RAI/FUS
reflexus	RE/FLEK/SUS		RAI/FUSZ
	RE/FLEX/SUS		RE/FUS
reflux	RE/FLUX		RE/FUSZ
refract	RE/FRAKT	Rehydralyte	RE/HAOI/DRA/LAOIT
refracta	RE/FRAK/TA	rehydrate	RE/HAOI/DRAIT
refracted	RE/FRAKT/-D	rehydration	RE/HAOI/DRAIGS
refractile	RE/FRAK/TAOIL	Reichel	RAOIK/EL
	RE/FRAK/TIL		RAOI/KEL
refraction	RE/FRA*BGS	Reichert	RAOIK/ERT
refractionist	RE/FRA*BGS/*IS		RAOI/KERT
refractive	RE/FRAKT/IV	Reichmann	RAOIK/MAN
refractivity	RE/FRAK/TIV/TI	Reichstein	RAOIK/STAOIN
refractometer	RE/FRAK/TOM/TER	Reid	RAO*ED
refractometry	RE/FRAK/TOM/TRI		(not RAOED or RAED; see reed and
refractor	RE/FRAK/TOR		read)
refractoria	RE/FRAK/TOR/YA	Reil	RAO*IL
	RE/FRAK/TOER/YA		(not RAOIL; see rile)
refractory	RE/FRAKT/RI	Reilly	RAOIL/LI
refracture	RE/FRAK/KHUR		RAOI/LI
refrangibility	RE/FRAN/JIBLT	reimplantation	RE/IM/PLAN/TAIGS
	RE/FRANG/-BLT	reinfection	RE/IN/F*EBGS
refrangible	RE/FRAN/JIBL	reinforce	RE/IN/FORS
	RE/FRANG/-BL	reinforcement	RE/IN/FORS/-MT
refresh	RE/FRERB	reinforcer	RE/IN/FORS/ER
Refresh Lubricant	RE/FRERB/LAOUB/KANT	reinfusate	RE/IN/FAOU/SAIT
refrigerant	RE/FRIJ/RANT	reinfusion	RE/IN/FAOUGS
refrigeration	RE/FRIJ/RAIGS	reinjure	RE/IN/JUR
refringence	RE/FRIN/JENS		RE/JIR
refringent	RE/FRIN/JENT	Reinke	RAOIN/KAOE
Refsum	REF/SAOUM	reinnervation	RE/IN/ER/VAIGS
	REF/SUM		RE/IN/NER/VAIGS
refusion	RE/FAOUGS	reinoculation	RE/IN/OK/LAIGS
regainer	RE/GAIN/ER	reintegration	RE/SPWE/GRAIGS
regel	RAI/GEL		RE/INT/GRAIGS
	RE/GEL	reintubation	RE/SPWAOU/BAIGS
regenerate	RE/JEN/RAIT		RE/IN/TAOU/BAIGS
regeneration	RE/JEN/RAIGS	reinversion	RE/IN/VERGS
regia	RE/JA	reinvocation	RE/IN/VOE/KAIGS
	RAOEJ/YA		RE/IN/VO/KAIGS
	REJ/YA	Reisseisen	RAOIS/SEN
regimen	REJ/MEN	Reissner	RAOIS/NER
regio	RE/JOE	Reitan	RAOI/TAN
	RAOEJ/YOE	Reiter	RAOI/TER
	REJ/YOE		RAOIT/ER
region	REJ/JON	reiterature	RE/IT/RA/TAOU/RAOE
regional	RAOEJ/NAL		RE/IT/RA/KHUR/RAOE
	REJ/JONL	rejection	REJ/J*EBGS
regiones	RE/JOE/NAOEZ	rejuvenate	RE/JAOUV/NAIT
	RAOEJ/YOE/NAOEZ	rejuvenescence	RE/JAOUV/NES/ENS
regionis	RE/JOE/NIS	Rekoss	RAI/KOSZ
	RAOEJ/YOE/NIS		RE/KOSZ
registrant	REJ/STRANT	relapse	RE/LAPS

relation	RE/LAIGS	renogastric	RAOEN/GAS/TRIK
	RELGS	renogenic	RAOEN/JEN/IK
relationship	RE/LAIGS/SHIP	renogram	RAOEN/GRAM
	RELGS/SHIP	renography	RE/NOG/FI
relative	REL/TIV	renointestinal	RAOEN/SPW*ES/NAL
relax	RE/LAX	renomegaly	RAOEN/MEG/LI
relaxant	RE/LAK/SANT	renopathy	RE/NOP/TH*I
	RE/LAX/ANT	renopexy	RAOEN/PEK/SI
relaxation	RE/LAK/SAIGS	renoprival	RAOEN/PRAOIVL
	RE/LAX/SAIGS	renopulmonary	RAOEN/PUL/MO/NAIR
relaxer	RE/LAX/ER		RAOEN/PUM/NAIR
relaxin	RE/LAK/SIN	renotrophic	RAOEN/TROFK
relearning	RE/LERN/-G	renotrophin	RAOEN/TROEFN
Relefact TRH	REL/FAKT/T-RBGS/R*RBGS/		RAOEN/TROE/FIN
	H*RBGS	renotropic	RAOEN/TROP/IK
reliability	RE/LAOIBLT	renotropin	RAOEN/TROE/PIN
relief	RE/LAOEF	renovascular	RAOEN/VAS/KLAR
Relief Vasoconstrictor	RE/LAOEF/VAIS/KON/STRIK/TOR	Renpenning	REN/PEN/-G
relieve	RE/LAOEV	Renshaw	REN/SHAU
reline	RE/LAOIN	renule	REN/YAOUL
reluxation	RE/LUK/SAIGS	renunculus	RE/NUN/KLUS
	RE/LUX/AIGS		RE/NUN/KAOU/LUS
rem	R*EM	Reoviridae	RE/YO/VIR/DAE
REM	K-PS/R*EM	reovirus	RE/YO/VAOI/RUS
	R-RBGS/*ERBGS/M*RBGS	reoxidation	RE/OX/DAIGS
Remak	RAI/MAK	reoxygenation	RE/OX/JEN/AIGS
	RE/MAK	rep	REP
remediable	RE/MAOED/YABL	repaid	RE/PAID
remedial	RE/MAOED/YAL	repair	RE/PAIR
remedy	REM/DI	Repan	RE/PAN
remineralization	RE/MIN/RAL/ZAIGS	repand	RE/PAND
reminiscent	REM/NIS/ENT	reparative	RE/PAIR/TIV
remission	RE/MIGS		RE/PAR/TIV
remittence	RE/MIT/ENS	repatency	RE/PAIT/EN/SI
	REMT/ENS		RE/PAI/TEN/SI
	RE/MIT/TENS	repellent	RE/PEL/ENT
	REMT/TENS		RE/PEL/LENT
remittent	RE/MIT/ENT	repeller	RE/PEL/ER
	REMT/ENT	repens	RE/PENZ
	RE/MIT/TENT		REP/ENZ
	REMT/TENT	repercolation	RE/PERK/LAIGS
remnant	REM/NANT	repercussion	RE/PER/KUGS
remodeling	RE/MOD/EL/-G	repercussive	RE/PER/KUS/SIV
remotivation	RE/MOET/VAIGS		RE/PER/KUSZ/IV
ren	REN	repetatur	RAOEP/TAI/TAOUR
ren(o)-	RAOEN		REP/TAI/TAOUR
	RE/N(O)	repetition	REP/TIGS
renacidin	RE/NAS/DIN	repetition-compulsion	REP/TIGS/KPULGS
Renacidin	REN/SAOE/DIN		REP/TIGS/KOM/PULGS
renal	RAOENL	replant	RE/PLANT
renale	RE/NAI/LAOE	replantation	RE/PLAN/TAIGS
renales	RE/NAI/LAOEZ	replenisher	RE/PLEN/SHER
renalis	RE/NAI/LIS		RE/PLEN/IRB/ER
Renaut	RE/NOE	repletion	RE/PLAOEGS
renculi	REN/KLAOI	replica	REP/LI/KA
	REN/KAOU/LAOI	replicase	REP/LI/KAIS
renculus	REN/KLUS	replicate	REP/LI/KAIT
	REN/KAOU/LUS	replication	REP/LI/KAIGS
Rendu	RON/DAOU	replicator	REP/LI/KAI/TOR
	REN/DAOU	replicon	REP/LI/KON
renes	RE/NAOEZ	replisome	REP/LI/SOEM
Renese	RE/NAOES	repolarization	RE/POE/LAR/ZAIGS
	(not RE/NAOEZ; see renes)		RE/POEL/RI/ZAIGS
Renese-R	RE/NAOES/R-RBGS	reposition	RE/POGS
renicapsule	REN/KAP/SAOUL		RE/PO/SIGS
renicardiac	REN/KARD/YAK	repositioning	RE/POGS/-G
reniculi	RE/NIK/LAOI		RE/PO/SIGS/-G
reniculus	RE/NIK/LUS	repositor	RE/POZ/TOR
renifleur	REN/FLAOUR	repository	RE/POZ/TOIR
	REN/FLER	repress	RE/PRESZ
reniform	REN/FORM	repressible	RE/PRESZ/-BL
renin	RE/NIN	repression	RE/PREGS
reninism	RAOEN/NIFM	repressor	RE/PRES/SOR
	REN/NIFM	reproduction	RE/PRO/D*UBGS
renipelvic	REN/PEL/VIK		RE/PR*UBGS
reniportal	REN/POR/TAL	reproductive	RE/PRO/DUKT/IV
renipuncture	REN/PUNG/KHUR		RE/PRUKT/IV
renis	RE/NIS	reptile	REP/TAOIL
rennase	REN/AIS	Reptilia	REP/TIL/YA
	REN/NAIS	repullulation	RE/PUL/LAIGS
rennet	REN/ET		RE/PUL/YAOU/LAIGS
rennin	REN/NIN		RE/PUL/YU/LAIGS
renninogen	RE/NIN/JEN	repulsion	RE/PULGS
	REN/NIN/JEN	resanguinate	RE/SANG/WI/NAIT
rennogen	REN/JEN	resazurin	RE/SAZ/YAOU/RIN
	REN/NO/JEN		RE/SAZ/YU/RIN
renocortical	RAOEN/KORT/KAL	rescinnamine	RE/SIN/MAOEN
renocutaneous	RAOEN/KAOU/TAIN/YOUS		RE/SIN/MIN
renocystogram	RAOEN/S*IS/GRAM	resect	RE/SEKT

resectable	RE/SEKT/-BL	respond	RE/SPOND
resection	RE/S*EBGS		SPOND
resectoscope	RE/SEKT/SKOEP	respondent	RE/SPOND/ENT
	RE/SEK/TO/SKOEP		RE/SPON/DENT
resectoscopy	RE/SEK/TOS/KPI		SPOND/ENT
resene	RES/AOEN	response	RE/SPONS
reserpine	RE/SER/PAOEN		SPONS
	RE/SER/PIN	rest	R*ES
	RES/ER/PAOEN	restbite	R*ES/BAOIT
reservatus	RE/SER/VAI/TUS	restenosis	RE/STE/NOE/SIS
reserve	RE/SEFRB	restiform	R*ES/FORM
reservoir	REZ/VOIR	restiformia	R*ES/FORM/YA
reset nodus sinuatrialis	RE/SET/NOE/DUS/SAOIN/AI/	resting	RES/T-G
	TRAI/LIS	restis	RES/TIS
	RE/SET/NOE/DUS/SAOI/NAOU/AI/	restitutio	R*ES/TAOU/SHOE
	TRAI/LIS		R*ES/TAOURB/YOE
reshaping	RE/SHAIP/-G	restitution	R*ES/TAOUGS
resident	REZ/DENT	restoration	R*ES/RAIGS
residua	RE/ZID/YA		RES/TO/RAIGS
	RE/ZID/WA	restorative	RE/STOR/TIV
	RE/SID/YA		RE/STOER/TIV
	RE/SID/WA	Restoril	R*ES/RIL
residual	RE/ZID/YAL	restrain	RE/STRAIN
	RE/ZID/WAL	restraint	RE/STRAINT
	RE/SID/YAL	resublimed	RE/SU/BLAOIM/-D
	RE/SID/WAL		RE/SUB/LAOIM/-D
residue	REZ/DAOU	resultant	RE/SUL/TANT
residuum	RE/ZID/YUM		RULT/TANT
	RE/ZID/WUM	resupination	RE/SAOUP/NAIGS
	RE/SID/YUM	resurrection	REZ/R*EBGS
	RE/SID/WUM	resuscitate	RE/SUS/TAIT
resilience	RE/ZIL/YENS	resuscitation	RE/SUS/TAIGS
	RE/SIL/YENS	resuscitator	RE/SUS/TAI/TOR
resiliency	RE/ZIL/YEN/SI	resuture	RE/SAOU/KHUR
	RE/SIL/YEN/SI	retainer	RE/TAIN/ER
resilient	RE/ZIL/YENT	retardata	RE/TAR/DAI/TA
	RE/SIL/YENT	retardate	RE/TAR/DAIT
resin	REZ/SIN	retardation	RE/TAR/DAIGS
resina	REZ/NA	retarded	RE/TARD/-D
resinoid	REZ/NOID	retarder	RE/TARD/ER
resinol	REZ/NOL	retch	REFP
resinotannol	REZ/NO/TAN/OL	retching	REFP/-G
resinous	REZ/NOUS	rete	RE/TAOE
resistance	RE/SIS/TANS	rete testis	RE/TAOE/TES/TIS
resistentiae	RE/SIS/TEN/SHAE	retention	RE/TENGS
resistor	RE/SIS/TOR	retentive	RE/TENT/IV
resite	RES/AOIT	retethelioma	RAOET/THAOEL/YOE/MA
Resol	RE/SOL		RE/TAOE/THAOEL/YOE/MA
resole	RES/OEL	retia	RE/SHA
resolution	REZ/LAOUGS		RAOERB/YA
resolve	RE/SOL/-V		RAOET/YA
resolvent	RE/SOL/VENT	retial	RAOERBL
resonance	REZ/NANS		RAOET/YAL
resonant	REZ/NANT	reticul(o)-	RE/TIK/L(O)
resonator	REZ/NAI/TOR		RE/TIK/YAOU/L(O)
resorb	RE/SORB		RE/TIK/YU/L(O)
resorcin	RE/SOR/SIN	reticula	RE/TIK/LA
resorcinism	RE/SORS/NIFM	reticular	RE/TIK/LAR
resorcinol	RE/SORS/NOL	reticularis	RE/TIK/LAI/RIS
resorcinolphthalein	RE/SORS/NOL/THAL/YIN	reticulate	RE/TIK/LAIT
resorcinum	RE/SORS/NUM		RE/TIK/LAT
resorption	RE/SORPGS	reticulated	RE/TIK/LAIT/-D
Respaire	RES/PAIR	reticulating	RE/TIK/LAIT/-G
Respaire-SR	RES/PAIR/S-RBGS/R*RBGS	reticulation	RE/TIK/LAIGS
Respbid	RES/-P/BID	reticulatum	RE/TIK/LAI/TUM
	RES/BID		RE/TIK/LAIT/UM
respir-	RES/PR-	reticulatus	RE/TIK/LAI/TUS
	RES/PI/R-	reticulin	RE/TIK/LIN
	RES/PIR-	reticulitis	RE/TIK/LAOITS
	RES/PAOIR-	reticulocyte	RE/TIK/LO/SAO*IT
	RE/SPAOIR-	reticulocytogenic	RE/TIK/LO/SAOIT/JEN/IK
respirable	RE/SPAOIRBL	reticulocytopenia	RE/TIK/LO/SAOIT/PAOEN/YA
	RE/SPAOIR/-BL	reticulocytosis	RE/TIK/LO/SAOI/TOE/SIS
	RES/PAOIRBL	reticuloendothelial	RE/TIK/LO/*END/THAOEL/YAL
	RES/PAOIR/-BL	reticuloendothelioma	RE/TIK/LO/*END/THAOEL/YOE/
	RES/PIRBL		MA
	RES/PRABL	reticuloendotheliosis	RE/TIK/LO/*END/THAOEL/YOE/
respiration	RES/PRAIGS		SIS
respirator	RES/PRAI/TOR	reticuloendothelium	RE/TIK/LO/*END/THAOEL/YUM
respiratoria	RES/PRA/TOR/YA	reticulohistiocytary	RE/TIK/LO/H*IS/YO/SAOIT/RI
	RE/SPAOIR/TOR/YA	reticulohistiocytoma	RE/TIK/LO/H*IS/YO/SAOI/TOE/
respiratorii	RES/PRA/TOR/YAOI		MA
	RE/SPAOIR/TOR/YAOI	reticulohistiocytosis	RE/TIK/LO/H*IS/YO/SAOI/TOE/
respiratorius	RES/PRA/TOR/YUS		SIS
	RE/SPAOIR/TOR/YUS	reticuloid	RE/TIK/LOID
respiratory	RES/PRA/TOIR	reticuloma	RE/TIK/LOE/MA
	RE/SPAOIR/TOIR	reticulopenia	RE/TIK/LO/PAOEN/YA
respirometer	RES/PROM/TER	reticuloperithelium	RE/TIK/LO/P*ER/THAOEL/YUM
	RES/PI/ROM/TER	reticulopituicyte	RE/TIK/LO/PI/TAOU/SAO*IT

reticulopod	RE/TIK/LO/POD	retroclavicular	RET/RO/KLA/VIK/LAR
reticulopodium	RE/TIK/LO/POED/YUM	retroclusion	RET/RO/KLAOUGS
reticulosarcoma	RE/TIK/LO/SAR/KOE/MA	retrocochlear	RET/RO/KOK/LAR
reticulosis	RE/TIK/LOE/SIS	retrocolic	RET/RO/KOL/IK
reticulospinal	RE/TIK/LO/SPAOINL	retrocollic	RET/RO/KOL/LIK
reticulothelium	RE/TIK/LO/THAOEL/YUM		(*not* RET/RO/KOL/IK; see
reticulotomy	RE/TIK/LOT/M*I		retrocolic)
reticulum	RE/TIK/LUM	retrocollis	RET/RO/KOL/LIS
retiform	RET/FORM	retroconduction	RET/RO/K*UBGS
Retin-A	RET/TIN/ARBGS		RET/RO/KON/D*UBGS
retin(o)-	RET/N(O)	retrocondyloid	RET/RO/KOND/LOID
retina	RET/NA	retrocrural	RET/RO/KRAOURL
retinacul-	RET/NAK/L-	retrocursive	RET/RO/KURS/IV
	RET/NAK/YAOU/L-	retrodeviation	RET/RO/DAOEV/YAIGS
	RET/NAK/YU/L-	retrodisplacement	RET/RO/DIS/PLAIS/-MT
retinacula	RET/NAK/LA	retroepicondyloid	RET/RO/EP/KOND/LOID
retinaculi	RET/NAK/LAOI	retroesophageal	RET/RO/E/SOF/JAOEL
retinaculum	RET/NAK/LUM	retrofilling	RET/RO/FIL/-G
retinae	RET/NAE	retroflected	RET/RO/FLEKT/-D
retinal	RET/NAL	retroflexed	RET/RO/FLEX/-D
retinaldehyde	RET/NALD/HAOID	retroflexion	RET/RO/FL*EBGS
retinascope	RET/NA/SKOEP	retroflexus	RET/RO/FLEK/SUS
retinene	RET/NAOEN	retrogasserian	RET/RO/GAS/SAOERN
retinitis	RET/NAOITS		RET/RO/GAS/SAOER/YAN
retinoblastoma	RET/NO/BLAS/TOE/MA	retrognathia	RET/RO/NA*T/YA
retinocerebral	RET/NO/SER/BRAL	retrognathic	RET/RO/NA*T/IK
retinochoroid	RET/NO/KOE/ROID	retrognathism	RET/RO/NA*T/IFM
retinochoroiditis	RET/NO/KOE/ROI/DAOITS	retrograde	RET/RO/GRAID
retinodialysis	RET/NO/DI/AL/SI	retrography	RE/TROG/FI
retinograph	RET/NO/GRAF		RET/ROG/FI
retinography	RET/NOG/FI	retrogression	RET/RO/GREGS
retinoic	RET/NOIK	retrohyoid	RET/RO/HAOI/OID
	RET/NOE/IK	retrohyoidea	RET/RO/HAOI/OID/YA
retinoid	RET/NOID	retroinfection	RET/RO/IN/F*EBGS
retinol	RET/NOL	retroinsular	RET/RO/INS/LAR
retinomalacia	RET/NO/MA/LAI/SHA	retroiridian	RET/RO/AOI/RID/YAN
retinopapillitis	RET/NO/PAP/LAOITS		RET/RO/IR/RID/YAN
retinopathy	RET/NOP/TH*I	retrojection	RET/RO/J*EBGS
retinopexy	RET/NO/PEK/SI	retrojector	RET/RO/JEK/TOR
retinopiesis	RET/NO/PAOI/E/SIS	retrolabyrinthine	RET/RO/LAB/RIN/THAOEN
retinoschisis	RET/NOS/KI/SIS	retrolental	RET/RO/LEN/TAL
retinoscope	RET/NO/SKOEP	retrolenticular	RET/RO/LEN/TIK/LAR
retinoscopy	RET/NOS/KPI	retrolingual	RET/RO/LING/WAL
retinosis	RET/NOE/SIS	retromammary	RET/RO/MAM/RI
retinotopic	RET/NO/TOP/IK	retromandibular	RET/RO/MAN/DIB/LAR
retinotoxic	RET/NO/TOX/IK	retromastoid	RET/RO/MAS/TOID
retisolution	RET/SLAOUGS	retromesenteric	RET/RO/MES/SPWER/IK
retispersion	RET/SPERGS		RET/RO/MES/EN/TER/IK
retoperithelium	RAOET/P*ER/THAOEL/YUM	retromolar	RET/RO/MOE/LAR
	RE/TO/P*ER/THAOEL/YUM	retromorphosis	RET/RO/MOR/FOE/SIS
retort	RE/TORT		RET/RO/MOR/FO/SIS
Retortamonas	RE/TOR/TAM/NAS	retronasal	RET/RO/NAI/ZAL
retothelial	RAOET/THAOEL/YAL	retro-ocular	RET/RO/OK/LAR
	RE/TO/THAOEL/YAL	retroparotid	RET/RO/PROT/ID
retothelioma	RAOET/THAOEL/YOE/MA	retropatellar	RET/RO/PA/TEL/LAR
	RE/TO/THAOEL/YOE/MA	retroperitoneal	RET/RO/PERT/NAOEL
retothelium	RAOET/THAOEL/YUM	retroperitoneum	RET/RO/PERT/NAOEM
	RE/TO/THAOEL/YUM	retroperitonitis	RET/RO/PERT/NAOITS
retract	RE/TRAKT	retropharyngeal	RET/RO/FRIN/JAL
retractile	RE/TRAK/TAOIL	retropharyngitis	RET/RO/FARN/JAOITS
	RE/TRAK/TIL	retropharynx	RET/RO/FARNGS
retraction	RE/TRA*BGS	retroplacental	RET/RO/PLA/SEN/TAL
retractor	RE/TRAK/TOR	retroplasia	RET/RO/PLAIZ/YA
retrad	RE/TRAD	retropleural	RET/RO/PLAOURL
retrahens auriculam	RE/TRA/HENZ/AU/RIK/LAM	retroposed	RET/RO/POEZ/-D
	RAOET/RA/HENZ/AU/RIK/LAM	retroposition	RET/RO/POGS
retrahens aurem	RE/TRA/HENZ/AUR/EM	retroposon	RET/RO/POE/SON
	RAOET/RA/HENZ/AUR/EM	retropubic	RET/RO/PAOUB/IK
retrenchment	RE/TREFRPBLG/-MT	retropulsion	RET/RO/PULGS
	RE/TREN/-FP/-MT	retrorectal	RET/RO/REK/TAL
retrievable	RE/TRAOEVBL	retrosinus	RET/RO/SAOI/NUS
	RE/TRAOEV/-BL	retrospection	RET/RO/SP*EBGS
retrieval	RE/TRAOEVL	retrospective	RET/RO/SPEKT/IV
retro-	RET/RO	retrospondylolisthesis	RET/RO/SPOND/LO/LIS/THE/SIS
retroaction	RET/RO/A*BGS		RET/RO/SPOND/LO/LIS/THAOE/
retroactive	RET/RO/AKT/IV		SIS
retroauricular	RET/RO/AU/RIK/LAR	retrostalsis	RET/RO/STAL/SIS
retrobronchial	RET/RO/BRONG/YAL	retrosternal	RET/RO/STERNL
retrobuccal	RET/RO/BUK/KAL	retrosteroid	RET/RO/STAOER/OID
retrobulbar	RET/RO/BUL/BAR	retrosymphysial	RET/RO/SIM/FIZ/YAL
retrocalcaneal	RET/RO/KAL/KAIN/YAL	retrotarsal	RET/RO/TAR/SAL
retrocalcaneobursitis	RET/RO/KAL/KAIN/YO/BUR/	retrotonsillar	RET/RO/TONS/LAR
	SAOITS	retrourethral	RET/RO/YAOU/RAO*ET/RAL
retrocardiac	RET/RO/KARD/YAK	retrouterine	RET/RO/YAOUT/RIN
retrocatheterism	RET/RO/KA*T/TER/IFM	retrovaccination	RET/RO/VAX/NAIGS
	RET/RO/KA*T/TRIFM	retroversioflexion	RET/RO/VERS/YO/FL*EBGS
retrocecal	RET/RO/SE/KAL	retroversion	RET/RO/VERGS
retrocervical	RET/RO/SEFRB/KAL	retroverted	RET/RO/VERT/-D
retrocession	RET/RO/SEGS	retrovesical	RET/RO/VES/KAL

Retrovir	RET/RO/VIR	rhagadiform	RA/GAD/FORM
	RET/RO/VAOIR	-rhage	RAJ
Retroviridae	RET/RO/VIR/DAE	-rhagia	RAI/JA
retrovirus	RET/RO/VAOI/RUS		RAIJ/YA
retrusion	RE/TRAOUGS	rhagiocrine	RAJ/YO/KRIN
retrusive	RE/TRAOUS/IV		RAJ/YO/KRAOIN
return	RURN	rhagionid	RAJ/YON/ID
	RE/TURN	Rhagionidae	RAJ/YON/DAE
retzii	RETS/YAOI	rhamninose	RAM/NI/NOES
Retzius	RETS/YUS	rhamnose	RAM/NOES
reuniens	RE/YAOUN/YENZ	rhamnoside	RAM/NO/SAOID
reunient	RE/YAOUN/YENT	Rhamnus	RAM/NUS
Reuss	ROIS	-rhaphia	RAIF/YA
	ROISZ	-rhaphy	(O)R/FI
revaccination	RE/VAX/NAIGS	rhathymia	RA/THAOIM/YA
revascularization	RE/VAS/KLAR/ZAIGS	rhe	RAO*E
revehentes	REV/HEN/TAOEZ	-rhea	RAOE/YA
	RAOEV/HEN/TAOEZ	Rheaban	RAOE/BAN
revellent	RE/VEL/ENT	rhegma	REG/MA
Reverdin	RAI/VER/DAN	rhegmatogenous	REG/MA/TOJ/NOUS
reversal	RE/VER/SAL	rheic	RAOE/IK
reversible	RE/VERS/-BL	Rhein	RAO*IN
reversion	RE/VERGS	Rheinberg	RAOIN/BERG
reversionary	RE/VERGS/NAIR	rhenium	RAOEN/YUM
Reversol	REVR/SOL	rheo-	RAOE/YO
	RE/VER/SOL		RAOE/O(c)
revertant	RE/VER/TANT	rheobase	RAOE/YO/BAIS
Revilliod	RAIV/YOE	rheobasic	RAOE/YO/BAIS/IK
	RAI/VAOE/YOE	rheocardiography	RAOE/YO/KARD/YOG/FI
revivescence	RE/VAOI/VES/ENS	rheochrysidin	RAOE/YO/KRIS/DIN
	RE/VI/VES/ENS	rheoencephalogram	RAOE/YO/EN/SEF/LO/GRAM
revivification	RE/VIV/FI/KAIGS	rheoencephalography	RAOE/YO/EN/SEF/LOG/FI
revolute	REV/LAOUT	rheogram	RAOE/YO/GRAM
revulsant	RE/VUL/SANT	rheologist	RAOE/O*LGS
revulseur	RE/VUL/SER		RAOE/YO*LGS
	RE/VUL/SAOUR	rheology	RAOE/OLG
	RE/VUL/SUR		RAOE/YOLG
revulsion	RE/VULGS	Rheomacrodex	RAOE/YO/MAK/RO/DEX
revulsive	RE/VULS/IV	rheometer	RAOE/OM/TER
reward	RE/WARD		RAOE/YOM/TER
rewarm	RE/WARM	rheometry	RAOE/OM/TRI
rexia	REX/YA		RAOE/YOM/TRI
Reymond	RAOI/MOND	rheonome	RAOE/YO/NOEM
Reynals	RAI/NALS	rheopexy	RAOE/YO/PEK/SI
Reynold	REN/OLD	rheophore	RAOE/YO/FOER
Rezzonico	RE/ZON/KOE	rheoscope	RAOE/YO/SKOEP
	REZ/ZON/KOE	rheostat	RAOE/YO/STAT
R-Gene 10 Injection	R-RBGS/JAOEN/10/IN/J*EBGS	rheostosis	RAOE/OS/TOE/SIS
Rh	RAIFP		RAOE/YOS/TOE/SIS
	R-RBGS/H*BGZ	rheotachygraphy	RAOE/YO/TA/KIG/FI
rhabarberone	RA/BARB/ROEN	rheotaxis	RAOE/YO/TAK/SIS
rhabd(o)-	RABD	rheotome	RAOE/YO/TOEM
	RAB/D(O)	rheotrope	RAOE/YO/TROEP
Rhabdiasoidea	RABD/YA/SOED/YA	rheotropism	RAOE/OT/RO/PIFM
rhabditic	RAB/DIT/IK		RAOE/YOT/RO/PIFM
Rhabditida	RAB/DIT/DA	rhestocythemia	R*ES/SAOI/THAOEM/YA
Rhabditidae	RAB/DIT/DAE		RES/TO/SAOI/THAOEM/YA
rhabditiform	RAB/DIT/FORM	Rhesus	RAOE/SUS
Rhabditis	RAB/DAOITS		RE/SUS
rhabditoid	RAB/DI/TOID	rheum	RAOUM
	RABD/TOID	rheuma	RAOU/MA
Rhabditoidea	RAB/DI/TOID/YA	rheuma-	RAOUM
	RABD/TOID/YA		RAOU/MA
rhabdium	RABD/YUM	rheumapyra	RAOUM/PAOI/RA
	RAB/DUM	rheumarthritis	RAOU/MAR/THRAOITS
	RAB/DAOE/UM	rheumatalgia	RAOUM/TAL/JA
	RAB/DAOE/YUM	rheumatic	RAOU/MAT/IK
rhabdocyte	RABD/SAO*IT	rheumatica	RAOU/MAT/KA
rhabdoid	RAB/DOID	rheumaticosis	RAOU/MAT/KOE/SIS
Rhabdomonas	RABD/MOE/NAS	rheumaticum	RAOU/MAT/KUM
rhabdomyoblast	RABD/MAOI/BLA*S	rheumatid	RAOUM/TID
rhabdomyoblastoma	RABD/MAOI/BLAS/TOE/MA	rheumatism	RAOUM/TIFM
rhabdomyochondroma	RABD/MAOI/KON/DROE/MA	rheumatismal	RAOUM/TIZ/MAL
rhabdomyolysis	RABD/MAOI/OL/SIS	rheumatocelis	RAOUM/TO/SE/LIS
rhabdomyoma	RABD/MAOI/YOE/MA	rheumatogenic	RAOUM/TO/JEN/IK
rhabdomyomyxoma	RABD/MAOI/MIK/SOE/MA	rheumatoid	RAOUM/TOID
rhabdomyosarcoma	RABD/MAOI/SAR/KOE/MA	rheumatologist	RAOUM/TO*LGS
rhabdophobia	RABD/FOEB/YA	rheumatology	RAOUM/TOLG
rhabdosarcoma	RABD/SAR/KOE/MA	rheumatopyra	RAOUM/TO/PAOI/RA
rhabdosphincter	RABD/SFING/TER	rheumatosis	RAOUM/TOE/SIS
	RABD/SFINGT/ER	Rheumatrex	RAOUM/TREX
Rhabdoviridae	RABD/VIR/DAE	rheumic	RAOUM/IK
rhabdovirus	RABD/VAOI/RUS	rhexis	REK/SIS
rhacoma	see racoma	Rh factor	RAIFP/FAK/TOR
rhaebocrania	RAOEB/KRAIN/YA		R-RBGS/H*BGZ/FAK/TOR
rhaeboscelia	RAOEB/SAOEL/YA	rhigosis	RI/GOE/SIS
rhaebosis	RAOE/BOE/SIS	rhigotic	RI/GOT/IK
	RE/BOE/SIS	rhin(o)-	RAOIN
rhagades	RAG/DAOEZ		RAOI/N(O)

rhinal	RAOINL	rhinoplastic	RAOIN/PLA*S/IK
rhinalgia	RAOI/NAL/JA	rhinoplasty	RAOIN/PLAS/TI
	RAOIN/AL/JA	rhinopneumonitis	RAOIN/NAOUM/NAOITS
rhinallergosis	RAOI/NAL/ER/GOE/SIS	rhinopolypus	RAOIN/POL/PUS
	RAOIN/AL/ER/GOE/SIS	rhinoptia	RAOI/NOP/SHA
rhinaria	RAOI/NAIR/YA	rhinoreaction	RAOIN/RE/A*BGS
rhinarium	RAOI/NAIRM	rhinorrhagia	RAOIN/RAI/JA
	RAOI/NAIR/YUM	rhinorrhaphy	RAOI/NOR/FI
Rhindecon	RAOIN/DE/KON	rhinorrhea	RAOIN/RAOE/YA
	RIN/DE/KON	rhinosalpingitis	RAOIN/SAL/PIN/JAOITS
rhinedema	RAOIN/DAOE/MA	rhinoscleroma	RAOIN/SKLE/ROE/MA
	RAOIN/E/DAOE/MA	rhinoscope	RAOIN/SKOEP
rhinencephalia	RAOI/NEN/SFAIL/YA	rhinoscopic	RAOIN/SKOP/IK
	RAOIN/EN/SFAIL/YA	rhinoscopy	RAOI/NOS/KPI
rhinencephalic	RAOI/NEN/SFAL/IK	rhinosporidiosis	RAOIN/SPRID/YOE/SIS
	RAOIN/EN/SFAL/IK	Rhinosporidium	RAOIN/SPRID/YUM
rhinencephalon	RAOI/NEN/SEF/LON	Rhinosporidium seeberi	RAOIN/SPRID/YUM/SAOEB/RAOI
	RAOIN/EN/SEF/LON	rhinostegnosis	RAOIN/STEG/NOE/SIS
rhinencephalus	RAOI/NEN/SEF/LUS	rhinostenosis	RAOIN/STE/NOE/SIS
	RAOIN/EN/SEF/LUS	rhinostomy	RAOI/NO*S/M*I
rhinenchysis	RAOI/NENG/SIS	rhinotomy	RAOI/NOT/M*I
	RAOI/NEN/KI/SIS	rhinotracheitis	RAOIN/TRAIK/YAOITS
rhinesthesia	RAOI/NES/THAOEZ/YA	rhinovaccination	RAOIN/VAX/NAIGS
	RAOIN/ES/THAOEZ/YA	rhinoviral	RAOIN/VAOIRL
rhineurynter	RAOI/NAOU/RINT/ER	rhinovirus	RAOIN/VAOI/RUS
	RAOIN/YAOU/RINT/ER	Rhipicephalus	RAOIP/SEF/LUS
Rhinex	RAOI/NEX	rhizanesthesia	RAOI/ZANS/THAOEZ/YA
	RAOIN/EX		RAOI/ZAN/ES/THAOEZ/YA
rhinion	RIN/YON	rhizo-	RAOIZ
rhinism	RAOI/NIFM		RAOI/ZO
	RAOIN/IFM	Rhizobiaceae	RAOI/ZOEB/YAIS/YAE
rhinitis	RAOI/NAOITS	Rhizobium	RAOI/ZOEB/YUM
rhinoanemometer	RAOIN/AN/MOM/TER	rhizoblast	RAOIZ/BLA*S
rhinoantritis	RAOIN/AN/TRAOITS	rhizodontropy	RAOIZ/DON/TRO/PI
rhinobyon	RAOI/NOEB/YON	rhizodontrypy	RAOIZ/DON/TRI/PI
	RAOIN/BAOI/YON	rhizoid	RAOI/ZOID
rhinocanthectomy	RAOIN/KAN/THEKT/M*I	rhizoidal	RAOI/ZOI/DAL
rhinocele	RAOIN/SAO*EL	rhizolysis	RAOI/ZOL/SIS
rhinocephalia	RAOIN/SFAIL/YA	Rhizomastigida	RAOIZ/MAS/TIJ/DA
rhinocephalus	RAOIN/SEF/LUS	rhizome	RAOI/ZOEM
Rhinocephalus annulatus	RAOIN/SEF/LUS/AN/LAI/TUS	rhizomelia	RAOIZ/MAOEL/YA
rhinocephaly	RAOIN/SEF/LI	rhizomelic	RAOIZ/MEL/IK
rhinocheiloplasty	RAOIN/KAOIL/PLAS/TI		RAOIZ/MAOEL/IK
Rhinocladiella	RAOIN/KLAD/YEL/LA	rhizomeningomyelitis	RAOIZ/ME/NING/MAOI/LAOITS
rhinocleisis	RAOIN/KLAOI/SIS	rhizoneure	RAOIZ/NAOUR
rhinodacryolith	RAOIN/DAK/RO/L*IT	rhizoplast	RAOIZ/PLA*S
rhinodymia	RAOIN/DIM/YA	Rhizopoda	RAOIZ/POE/DA
rhinodynia	RAOIN/DIN/YA		RAOI/ZOP/DA
rhinoestrosis	RAOIN/ES/TROE/SIS	Rhizopodasida	RAOIZ/POE/DAS/DA
Rhinoestrus purpureus	RAOIN/ES/TRUS/PUR/PAOUR/ YUS	rhizopodium	RAOIZ/POED/YUM
		rhizopterin	RAOI/ZOPT/RIN
	RAOI/NES/TRUS/PUR/PAOUR/ YUS	Rhizopus	RAOI/ZOE/PUS
		rhizotomist	RAOI/ZOT/M*IS
rhinogenous	RAOI/NOJ/NOUS	rhizotomy	RAOI/ZOT/M*I
rhinokyphectomy	RAOIN/KAOI/FEKT/M*I	Rho-D	ROE/D-RBGS
rhinokyphosis	RAOIN/KAOI/FOE/SIS	rhod(o)-	ROED
rhinolalia	RAOIN/LAIL/YA		ROE/D(O)
Rhinolar	RAOIN/LAR	rhodamine	ROED/MAOEN
Rhinolar-EX	RAOIN/LAR/ERBGS/KP*RBGS		ROED/MIN
rhinolaryngitis	RAOIN/LARN/JAOITS	rhodanate	ROED/NAIT
rhinolaryngology	RAOIN/LARN/GOLG	rhodanese	ROED/NAOEZ
rhinolite	RAOIN/LAOIT		ROED/NAOES
rhinolith	RAOIN/L*IT	rhodanic	ROE/DAN/IK
rhinolithiasis	RAOIN/LI/THAOI/SIS	rhodanilate	ROE/DAN/LAIT
rhinologic	RAOIN/LOJ/IK	rhodanile	ROED/NAOIL
rhinologist	RAOI/NO*LGS	rhodeose	ROED/YOES
rhinology	RAOI/NOLG	rhodin	ROE/DIN
rhinomanometer	RAOIN/MA/NOM/TER	rhodium	ROED/YUM
rhinomanometry	RAOIN/MA/NOM/TRI	Rhodnius prolixus	ROD/NUS/PRO/LIK/SUS
rhinometer	RAOI/NOM/TER		ROD/NAOE/YUS/PRO/LIK/SUS
rhinommectomy	RAOIN/MEKT/M*I	rhodogenesis	ROED/JEN/SIS
	RAOI/NOM/MEKT/M*I	rhodophylactic	ROED/FLAKT/IK
rhinomucormycosis	RAOIN/MAOU/KOR/MAOI/KOE/ SIS	rhodophylaxis	ROED/FLAK/SIS
		rhodopsin	ROE/DOP/SIN
rhinomycosis	RAOIN/MAOI/KOE/SIS	Rhodotorula	ROED/TOR/LA
rhinonecrosis	RAOIN/NE/KROE/SIS		ROED/TOR/YAOU/LA
rhinonemmeter	RAOIN/NEM/TER	RhoGAM	ROE/GAM
rhinoneurosis	RAOIN/NAOU/ROE/SIS	rhombencephalon	ROM/BEN/SEF/LON
rhinopathia	RAOIN/PA*T/YA	rhombic	ROM/BIK
rhinopathy	RAOI/NOP/TH*I	rhomboatloideus	ROM/BO/AT/LOID/YUS
rhinopharyngeal	RAOIN/FRIN/JAL	rhombocele	ROM/BO/SAO*EL
rhinopharyngitis	RAOIN/FARN/JAOITS	rhomboid	ROM/BOID
rhinopharyngocele	RAOIN/FRING/SAO*EL	rhomboidal	ROM/BOI/DAL
rhinopharyngolith	RAOIN/FRING/L*IT	rhomboidale	ROM/BOI/DAI/LAOE
rhinopharynx	RAOIN/FARNGS	rhomboidalis	ROM/BOI/DAI/LIS
rhinophonia	RAOIN/FOEN/YA	rhomboideae	ROM/BOID/YAE
rhinophore	RAOIN/FOER	rhomboideus	ROM/BOID/YUS
rhinophycomycosis	RAOIN/FAOIK/MAOI/KOE/SIS	rhombomere	ROM/BO/MAOER
rhinophyma	RAOIN/FAOI/MA	rhonchal	RON/KAL

rhonchi	RON/KAOI	ribosylorotate	RAOIB/SIL/OR/TAIT
rhonchial	RONG/YAL		RAOIB/SIL/OR/RO/TAIT
	RON/KAOE/YAL	ribosylpurine	RAOIB/SIL/PAOUR/AOEN
rhonchus	RON/KUS	ribosyluridine	RAOIB/SIL/YAOUR/DAOEN
rhopheocytosis	ROEF/YO/SAOI/TOE/SIS	ribothymidine	RAOIB/THAOIM/DAOEN
rhoptry	ROP/TRI	ribothymidylic	RAOIB/THAOIM/DIL/IK
rhotacism	ROET/SIFM	ribotide	RAOIB/TAOID
rhubarb	RAOU/BARB	ribovirus	RAOIB/VAOI/RUS
rhus	RUS	ribulose	RAOIB/LOES
	RAOUS		RAOI/BAOU/LOES
Rhus	K-P/RUS		RAOIB/YAOU/LOES
	K-P/RAOUS	ribulosephosphate	RAOIB/LOES/FOS/FAIT
Rhus Tox Antigen	RUS/TOX/A*ENT/JEN		RAOI/BAOU/LOES/FOS/FAIT
rhusiopathiae	RUS/YO/PA*T/YAE		RAOIB/YAOU/LOES/FOS/FAIT
	RAOUS/YO/PA*T/YAE	Ricard	RI/KAR
rhyparia	RAOI/PAIR/YA		RAOE/KAR
rhypophagy	RAOI/POF/JI	rice	RAOIS
rhypophobia	RAOIP/FOEB/YA	Rich	K-P/RIFP
	RAOI/PO/FOEB/YA	Richard	RIFP/ARD
rhythm	R*IT/-M	Richards	RIFP/ARDZ
rhythmeur	R*IT/MER	Richardson	RIFP/ARD/SON
	R*IT/MUR	richardsoni	RIFP/ARD/SOE/NAOI
	R*IT/MAOUR	Richet	RI/SHAI
-rhythmia	R*IT/MA	Richmond	RIFP/MOND
	R*IT/MAOE/YA	Richter	RIK/TER
rhythmic	R*IT/MIK	ricin	RAOI/SIN
rhythmical	R*IT/MI/KAL		RIS/SIN
rhythmicity	R*IT/MIS/TI	ricinism	RIS/NIFM
rhythmotherapy	R*IT/MO/THER/PI		RAOIS/NIFM
rhytidectomy	RIT/DEKT/M*I	ricinoleate	RIS/NOEL/YAIT
rhytidoplasty	RIT/DO/PLAS/TI		RAOIS/NOEL/YAIT
rhytidosis	RIT/DOE/SIS	ricinoleic	RIS/NO/LAOE/IK
rhyzoglypticus	RAOIZ/GLIPT/KUS		RAOIS/NO/LAOE/IK
rib	RIB	Ricinus	RIS/NUS
ribaminol	RAOI/BAM/NOL	rickets	RIK/ET/-S
ribavirin	RAOIB/VAOI/RIN	rickettsemia	RIK/ET/SAOEM/YA
ribazole	RAOIB/ZOEL	rickettsia	RI/KETS/YA
Ribbert	RIB/ERT	Rickettsia	K-P/RI/KETS/YA
	RIB/BERT	Rickettsiaceae	RI/KETS/YAIS/YAE
Ribble	RIB/-L	rickettsiae	RI/KETS/YAE
ribbon	RIB/BON	rickettsial	RI/KETS/YAL
ribes	RAOI/BAOEZ	Rickettsiales	RI/KETS/YAI/LAOEZ
Ribes	RAOEBS	rickettsialpox	RI/KETS/YAL/POX
ribitol	RAOIB/TOL	rickettsicidal	RI/KETS/SAOI/DAL
ribityl	RAOIB/TIL	Rickettsieae	RI/KETS/SAOI/YAE
Ribo-2	RAOI/BOE/2		RIK/ET/SAOI/YAE
ribo-	RAOIB	rickettsiosis	RI/KETS/YOE/SIS
	RAOI/BO	rickettsiostatic	RI/KETS/YO/STAT/IK
riboflavin	RAOIB/FLAIVN	rickety	RIK/TI
ribofuranose	RAOIB/FAOUR/NOES	Rickles	RIK/-LS
ribofuranosyladenine	RAOIB/FAOU/RAN/SIL/AD/	rictal	RIK/TAL
	NAOEN	rictus	RIK/TUS
	RAOIB/FAOUR/AN/SIL/AD/	RID Lice Control Spray	R*ID/LAOIS/KROL/SPRAI
	NAOEN	RID Lice Treatment Kit	R*ID/LAOIS/TRAOEMT/KIT
ribofuranosylcytosine	RAOIB/FAOU/RAN/SIL/SAOIT/	Ridaura	RI/DAU/RA
	SAOEN		RI/DAUR/RA
	RAOIB/FAOUR/AN/SIL/SAOIT/	Rideal	RID/YAL
	SAOEN	Ridell	RAOI/DEL
ribofuranosylguanine	RAOIB/FAOU/RAN/SIL/GAU/		RI/DEL
	NAOEN	rider	RAOID/ER
	RAOIB/FAOU/RAN/SIL/GAUN/	ridge	RIJ
	AOEN	ridgel	RIJ/EL
	RAOIB/FAOUR/AN/SIL/GAU/		RID/JEL
	NAOEN	ridging	RIJ/-G
	RAOIB/FAOUR/AN/SIL/GAUN/	ridgling	RIJ/-LG
	AOEN		RIJ/LING
ribofuranosylthymine	RAOIB/FAOU/RAN/SIL/THAOI/	Ridley	RID/LAOE
	MAOEN	ridleyi	RID/LAOE/YAOI
	RAOIB/FAOUR/AN/SIL/THAOI/	Riedel	RAOE/DEL
	MAOEN	Rieder	RAOED/ER
ribofuranosyluracil	RAOIB/FAOU/RAN/SIL/YAOUR/		RAOE/DER
	SIL	Riegel	RAOE/GEL
	RAOIB/FAOUR/AN/SIL/YAOUR/	Rieger	RAOEG/ER
	SIL		RAOE/GER
ribonuclease	RAOIB/NAOUK/LAIS	Riegler	RAOEG/LER
ribonucleic	RAOIB/NAOU/KLAOE/IK	Riehl	RAO*EL
	RAOIB/NAOU/KLAI/IK	Riesman	RAOES/MAN
ribonucleinase	RAOIB/NAOU/KLAOE/NAIS	Rifadin	RIF/DIN
	RAOUB/NAOUK/LI/NAIS	Rifamate	RIF/MAIT
ribonucleoprotein	RAOIB/NAOUK/LO/PRO/TAOEN	rifamide	RIF/MAOID
ribonucleoside	RAOIB/NAOUK/LO/SAOID	rifampicin	RIF/AFRP/SIN
ribonucleotide	RAOIB/NAOUK/LO/TAOID	rifampin	RIF/AM/PIN
riboprine	RAOIB/PRAOEN	rifamycin	RIF/MAOI/SIN
ribopyranose	RAOIB/PIR/NOES	Riga	RAOE/GA
ribose	RAOI/BOES		RIG/GA
riboside	RAOIB/SAOID	right-eyed	RAOIGT/YAOI/-D
ribosome	RAOIB/SOEM	right-footed	RAOIGT/FAOT/-D
ribosuria	RAOIB/SAOUR/YA	right-handed	RAOIGT/HAND/-D
ribosyl	RAOIB/SIL	rigidity	RI/JID/TI

rigor	RIG/GOR	Robaxisal	ROE/BAX/SAL
	RAOI/GOR	Robbins	ROB/BINS
	RI/GOR		ROB/BINZ
rigor mortis	RIG/GOR/MOR/TIS	Robert	ROE/BAIR
	RAOI/GOR/MOR/TIS		ROB/ERT
	RI/GOR/MOR/TIS	Roberts	ROB/ERTS
Riley	RAOI/LAOE	Robertson	ROB/ERT/SON
rim	RIM	robin	ROE/BIN
rima	RAOI/MA	Robin	ROE/BAI
Rimactane	RI/MAK/TAIN		ROE/BAN
	RIM/AK/TAIN	Robinson	ROB/IN/SON
rimae	RAOI/MAE	Robinul	ROEB/NUL
rimal	RAOI/MAL	Robinul Forte	ROEB/NUL/FOR/TAI
rimose	RAOI/MOES	Robison	ROEB/SON
Rimso-50	RIM/SOE/50	Robitussin	ROEB/TUS/SIN
rimula	RIM/LA	Robitussin-CF	ROEB/TUS/SIN/KR-RBGS/F*RBGS
	RIM/YAOU/LA	Robitussin-DAC	ROEB/TUS/SIN/D-RBGS/A*RBGS/
	RIM/YU/LA		KR*RBGS
rinderpest	RIND/ER/P*ES	Robitussin-DM	ROEB/TUS/SIN/D-RBGS/M*RBGS
	RIN/DER/P*ES	Robitussin-PE	ROEB/TUS/SIN/P-RBGS/*ERBGS
Rindfleisch	RIND/FLAOIRB	Robles	ROEB/-LS
	RINT/FLAOIRB	roborant	ROB/RANT
ring	RING	robotic	ROE/BOT/IK
ringbone	RING/BOEN	Robson	ROB/SON
Ringer	K-P/RING/ER	robusta	ROE/BUS/TA
ringeri	RING/RAOI	Rocaltrol	ROE/KAL/TROL
	RING/ER/RAOI	roccellin	ROK/SEL/LIN
ring-knife	RING/H-F/NAOIF	Rocephin	ROE/SEFN
ringworm	RING/WORM		ROE/SEF/FIN
Rinne	RIN/NAOE	Rochalimaea	ROEK/LAOIM/YA
Riolan	RAOE/LAN	rod	ROD
	RAOE/YO/LAN	Rodentia	ROE/DEN/SHA
Riopan	RAOI/PAN	rodenticide	ROE/DENT/SAO*ID
Riopan Plus	RAOI/PAN/PLUS	rodentine	ROE/DEN/TAOEN
riparian	RI/PAIRN		ROE/DEN/TAOIN
	RI/PAIR/YAN	Rodex	ROE/DEX
	RAOI/PAIRN	rodocaine	ROED/KAIN
	RAOI/PAIR/YAN	rodonalgia	ROE/DON/AL/JA
Ripault	RI/POE	Rodrigues	ROD/RAOE/GES
	RI/PAULT		ROD/RI/GES
ripening	RAOIP/-NG	roentgen	RENT/GEN
Risdon	RIZ/DON	Roentgen	K-P/RENT/GEN
	RIS/DON	roentgenkymogram	RENT/GEN/KAOIM/GRAM
risk	RIS/-K	roentgenkymograph	RENT/GEN/KAOIM/GRAF
Risley	RIS/LAOE	roentgenkymography	RENT/GEN/KAOI/MOG/FI
	RIZ/LAOE	roentgeno-	RENT/GEN
risocaine	RAOIZ/KAIN		RENT/GE/NO
risorius	RI/SOER/YUS	roentgenocardiogram	RENT/GEN/KARD/YO/GRAM
	RI/SOR/YUS	roentgenocinematography	RENT/GEN/SIN/MA/TOG/FI
	RAOI/SOER/YUS	roentgenogram	RENT/GEN/GRAM
	RAOI/SOR/YUS	roentgenograph	RENT/GEN/GRAF
ristocetin	R*IS/SAOE/TIN	roentgenographic	RENT/GEN/GRAFK
	RIS/TO/SAOE/TIN	roentgenography	RENT/GEN/OG/FI
risus	RAOI/SUS	roentgenologist	RENT/GEN/O*LGS
risus caninus	RAOI/SUS/KAI/NAOI/NUS	roentgenology	RENT/GEN/OLG
risus sardonicus	RAOI/SUS/SAR/DON/KUS	roentgenolucent	RENT/GEN/LAOUS/ENT
Ritalin	RIT/LIN	roentgenometer	RENT/GEN/OM/TER
Ritalin-SR	RIT/LIN/S-RBGS/R*RBGS	roentgenometry	RENT/GEN/OM/TRI
Ritgen	RIT/GEN	roentgenopaque	RENT/GEN/PAIK
ritodrine	RIT/DRAOEN	roentgenoparent	RENT/GEN/PARNT
Ritter	RIT/ER	roentgenoscope	RENT/GEN/SKOEP
ritual	RIFP/YAL	roentgenoscopy	RENT/GEN/OS/KPI
	RIFP/WAL	roentgenotherapy	RENT/GEN/THER/PI
	RIFP/KHUL	Roferon-A	ROE/FAOER/RON/ARBGS
	RIT/KHUL	Rogaine	ROE/GAIN
rivalry	RAOIVL/RI	Roger	ROE/JAI
Riverius	RI/VAOER/YUS		ROJ/ER
	RI/VER/YUS	rogosa	ROE/GOE/SA
Rivers	RIVRS	Rohl	RA*IL
	RIV/ERS	Rokitansky	ROEK/TAN/SKI
	K-P/RIVR/-S		ROK/TAN/SKI
	K-P/RIV/ER/-S	rolandic	ROE/LAND/IK
Riviere	RIV/YAIR	Rolando	ROE/LAN/DOE
	RAOEV/YAIR	rolandometer	ROE/LAN/DOM/TER
Rivinus	RI/VAOE/NUS	role	ROEL
rivus	RAOI/VUS	role-playing	ROEL/PLAI/-G
rivus lacrimalis	RAOI/VUS/LAK/RI/MAI/LIS	roletamide	ROE/LET/MAOID
riziform	RIZ/FORM	rolitetracycline	ROEL/TET/RA/SAOI/KLAOEN
RL	R-RBGS/L*RBGS	roll	ROL
RMS Suppositories	R-RBGS/M*RBGS/S*RBGS/SPOZ/	roller	ROL/ER
	TOIR/-S	Roller	K-P/ROL/ER
R.N.	R*N	Rolleston	ROL/ES/TON
RNA	R-RBGS/N*RBGS/A*RBGS		ROL/LES/TON
roach	ROEFP	Rollet	ROE/LAI
Roach	K-P/ROEFP	Rollier	ROL/YAI
Roaf	ROEF	Romana	ROE/MAN/YA
roaring	ROER/-G	Romano	ROE/MAN/NOE
Robaxin	ROE/BAK/SIN		ROE/MA/NOE
Robaxin-750	ROE/BAK/SIN/7/50	Romanowsky	ROEM/NOV/SKI

Romberg	ROM/BERG	rototome	ROET/TOEM
rombergism	ROM/BERG/IFM	rotoxamine	ROE/TOX/MAOEN
Romer	RE/MER	Rotter	K-P/ROT/ER
Rondec	RON/DEK	rotula	ROT/YAOU/LA
Rondec-DM	RON/DEK/D-RBGS/M*RBGS		ROT/YU/LA
Rondec-TR	RON/DEK/T-RBGS/R*RBGS	rotulad	ROT/YAOU/LAD
Rondomycin	ROND/MAOI/SIN		ROT/YU/LAD
	RON/DO/MAOI/SIN	rotular	ROT/YAOU/LAR
rongeur	RON/JUR		ROT/YU/LAR
	RON/JAOUR	rotund	ROE/TUND
Ronne	REN/NAOE	rotundatus	ROE/TUN/DAI/TUS
ronnel	RON/EL	rotundus	ROE/TUN/DUS
	RON/NEL	rouge	RAOUJ
roof	RAOF		RAOURB
roofplate	RAOF/PLAET	Rouget	RAOU/JAI
room	RAOM	rough	RUF
root	RAOT	roughage	RUF/AJ
rootlet	RAOT/LET	Rougnon	RAOUN/YAU
root planing	RAOT/PLAEN/-G		RAOUN/YON
ropalocytosis	ROE/PAL/SAOI/TOE/SIS	rouleau	RAOU/LOE
ropizine	ROEP/ZAOEN	rouleaux	RAOU/LOEZ
Rorschach	ROR/SHAK	round	ROUND
rosacea	ROE/ZAI/SHA	roundworm	ROUND/WORM
	ROE/SAI/SHA	Rous	RO*US
	ROE/ZAIS/YA	Roussel	RAOU/SEL
	ROE/SAIS/YA	Rousselot	RAOUS/LOT
rosae	ROE/SAE		RAOUS/LOE
	ROE/ZAE	Roussy	RAOU/SI
rosaniline	ROE/ZAN/LIN		RAOUS/SI
	ROE/SAN/LIN	Roux	RAO*U
rosary	ROEZ/RI		(not RAOU; see rue)
Roscoe	ROS/KOE	Rovighi	ROE/VIG/GAOE
rose	ROEZ		ROE/VI/GAOE
Rose	K-P/ROEZ	Rowasa	ROE/WA/SA
rosein	ROEZ/YIN		ROE/WAS/SA
rosemary	ROEZ/MAIR	Rowntree	ROUN/TRAOE
Rosenbach	ROEZ/EN/BAK	Roxanol	ROX/NOL
	ROEZ/EN/BAUK	Roxicet	ROX/SET
Rosenmuller	ROEZ/EN/MIL/ER	Roxicodone	ROX/KO/DOEN
	ROEZ/EN/MUL/ER	Roxiprin	ROX/PRIN
Rosenthal	ROEZ/EN/TAUL	rpm	R*P/M*
	ROEZ/EN/TAL		ARP/YEM
	ROEZ/EN/THAL	-rrhage	RAJ
rosenthali	ROEZ/EN/THAL/LAOI	-rrhagia	RAI/JA
	ROEZ/EN/TAUL/LAOI		RAIJ/YA
	ROEZ/EN/TAL/LAOI	-rrhaphia	RAIF/YA
roseola	ROE/ZAOE/LA	-rrhaphy	(O)R/FI
	ROE/SAOE/LA	-rrhea	RAOE/YA
roseolous	ROE/ZAOE/LOUS	-rrheal	RAOEL
	ROE/SAOE/LOUS		RAOE/YAL
Roser	ROEZ/ER	-rrhexis	REK/SIS
rosette	ROE/ZET	R-Tannate	R-RBGS/TAN/AIT
rosin	ROZ/SIN		R-RBGS/TAN/NAIT
Ross	ROSZ	rub	RUB
Rossolimo	ROS/LAOE/MOE	rubber	RUB/ER
	ROS/SO/LAOE/MOE	rubber-dam	RUB/ER/H-F/DAM
Rostan	ROS/TAN	rubber policeman	RUB/ER/PLIS/MAN
rostellum	ROS/TEL/UM	rubeanic	RAOUB/YAN/IK
rostra	ROS/TRA	rubedo	RAOU/BAOE/DOE
rostrad	ROS/TRAD	rubefacient	RAOUB/FAIRBT
rostral	ROS/TRAL	rubefaction	RAOUB/FA*BGS
rostralis	ROS/TRAI/LIS	rubella	RAOU/BEL/LA
rostrate	ROS/TRAIT	rubellin	RAOU/BEL/LIN
rostriform	ROS/TRI/FORM	rubeola	RAOU/BAOE/LA
rostrum	ROS/TRUM		RAOUB/YOE/LA
rot	ROT	rubeosis	RAOUB/YOE/SIS
Rot	K-P/ROT	ruber	RAOUB/ER
rotameter	ROE/TAM/TER		RAOU/BER
rotary	ROET/RI	rubescent	RAOU/BES/ENT
rotate	ROE/TAIT	Rubex	RAOU/BEX
rotation	ROE/TAIGS	rubidiol	RAOU/BID/YOL
rotator	ROE/TAI/TOR	rubidium	RAOU/BID/YUM
rotatores	ROET/TOR/RAOEZ	rubidomycin	RAOU/BID/MAOI/SIN
	ROET/ROER/RAOEZ	rubidus	RAOUB/DUS
rotatoria	ROET/TOER/YA	rubiginose	RAOU/BIJ/NOES
	ROET/TOR/YA	rubiginous	RAOU/BIJ/NOUS
rotatory	ROET/TOIR	rubin	RAOU/BIN
rotavirus	ROET/VAOI/RUS	Rubin	K-P/RAOU/BIN
Rotch	ROFP	rubine	RAOU/BAOEN
rotenone	ROET/NOEN	Rubinstein	RAOU/BIN/STAOIN
rotexed	ROE/TEX/-D	Rubivirus	RAOUB/VAOI/RUS
rotexion	ROET/T*EBGS	Rubner	RAOUB/NER
Roth	RO*ET	rubor	RAOU/BOR
	RO*T	rubr(o)-	RAOUB/R(O)
Rothia	RO*T/YA		RAOU/BR(O)
Rothmund	RO*T/MUND	rubra	RAOUB/RA
rotifer	ROET/FER	rubratoxin	RAOUB/RA/TOK/SIN
Rotifera	ROE/TIF/RA	rubredoxin	RAOUB/RE/DOK/SIN
rotoscoliosis	ROET/SKOEL/YOE/SIS	rubriblast	RAOUB/RI/BLA*S

rubric	RAOUB/RIK
rubricyte	RAOUB/RI/SAO*IT
rubrospinal	RAOUB/RO/SPAOINL
rubrothalamic	RAOUB/RO/THA/LAM/IK
rubrum	RAOUB/RUM
ructus	RUK/TUS
Rudbeckia	RUD/BEK/YA
rudiment	RAOUD/-MT
	RAOU/DIMT
rudimenta	RAOUD/MEN/TA
rudimentary	RAOUD/-MT/RI
rudimentation	RAOUD/MEN/TAIGS
	RAOUD/-MT/TAIGS
rudimentum	RAOUD/MEN/TUM
	RAOUD/-MT/UM
rue	RAOU
Rufen	RAOU/FEN
Ruffini	RAOU/FAOE/NAOE
	RAOUF/FAOE/NAOE
rufous	RAOU/FOUS
	RAOUF/OUS
Rufus	RAOU/FUS
ruga	RAOU/GA
rugae	RAOU/JAE
	RAOU/GAE
rugarum	RAOU/GAIR/UM
	RAOU/GAI/RUM
rugine	RAOU/JAOEN
rugitus	RAOUJ/TUS
rugoscopy	RAOU/GOS/KPI
rugose	RAOU/GOES
rugosity	RAOU/GOS/TI
rugous	RAOU/GOUS
	RAOUG/OUS
rule	RAOUL
ruler	RAOUL/ER
rum	RUM
Rum-K	RUM/K-RBGS
rumbatron	RUM/BA/TRON
rumen	RAOUM/-N
	RAOU/MEN
rumenitis	RAOUM/NAOITS
rumenotomy	RAOUM/NOT/M*I
rumina	RAOUM/NA
ruminant	RAOUM/NANT
ruminantium	RAOUM/NAN/SHUM
rumination	RAOUM/NAIGS
	RAOU/MI/NAIGS
ruminative	RAOUM/NA/TIV
	RAOUM/NAIT/IV
ruminoreticulum	RAOUM/NO/RE/TIK/LUM
rump	RUFRP
Rumpel	RAOUM/PEL
Rumpf	RAOUM/-F
	RAOUFRP/-F
runaround	RUN/A*RND
Runeberg	RAOUN/BERG
runt	RUNT
rupia	RAOUP/YA
rupial	RAOUP/YAL
rupioid	RAOUP/YOID
rupture	RUP/KHUR
Rusconi	RAOUS/KOE/NAOE
	RUS/KOE/NAOE
rush	RURB
Russell	RUS/EL
	RUS/SEL
russelli	RUS/EL/LAOI
	RUS/SEL/LAOI
Russian	RUGS
rust	R*US
Rust	K-P/R*US
rut	RUT
ruthenium	RAOU/THAOEN/YUM
	RAOU/THEN/YUM
rutherford	R*UT/ER/FORD
Rutherford	K-P/R*UT/ER/FORD
rutherfordium	R*UT/ER/FORD/YUM
rutidosis	RAOUT/DOE/SIS
rutilism	RAOUT/LIFM
rutin	RAOU/TIN
rutinose	RAOUT/NOES
rutoside	RAOUT/SAOID
Ru-Tuss	RAOU/TUSZ
Ru-Tuss II	RAOU/TUSZ/2
Ruysch	RAOIRB
	ROIRB
Rx	R*X
rye	RAOI

Ryle tube (word grouped)	RAOIL/TAOUB
Ryle's tube (word grouped)	RAOIL/AOES/TAOUB
Ryna	RAOI/NA
Ryna-C	RAOI/NA/KR-RBGS
Ryna-CX	RAOI/NA/KR-RBGS/KP°RBGS
Rynatan	RAOIN/TAN
	RAOI/NA/TAN
Rynatuss	RAOIN/TUSZ
	RAOI/NA/TUSZ

S

S1	S-RBGS/1
S2	S-RBGS/2
S3	S-RBGS/3
S4	S-RBGS/4
Sabin	SAI/BIN
sabinism	SAB/NIFM
sabinol	SAB/NOL
Sabouraud	SAB/ROE
Sabouraudia	SAB/ROED/YA
Sabouraudites	SAB/ROE/DAOI/TAOEZ
sabra	SAB/RA
sabulous	SAB/LOUS
	SAB/YAOU/LOUS
	SAB/YU/LOUS
saburra	SA/BUR/RA
saburral	SA/BURL
	SA/BUR/RAL
sac	SA*K
	(*not* SAK; see sack)
sacbrood	SAK/BRAOD
saccade	SA/KAID
saccadic	SA/KAD/IK
saccate	SAK/AIT
	SAK/KAIT
sacchar(o)-	SAK/R(O)
saccharascope	SAK/RA/SKOEP
saccharase	SAK/RAIS
saccharate	SAK/RAIT
saccharated	SAK/RAIT/-D
saccharephidrosis	SAK/REF/DROE/SIS
saccharic	SA/KAR/IK
	SAK/RIK
saccharide	SAK/RAOID
	SAK/RID
sacchariferous	SAK/RIF/ROUS
saccharification	SA/KAR/FI/KAIGS
	SAK/RIF/KAIGS
saccharify	SA/KAR/FI
saccharimeter	SAK/RIM/TER
saccharin	SAK/RIN
saccharine	SAK/RAOIN
	SAK/RAOEN
saccharinol	SA/KAR/NOL
saccharinum	SAK/RAOIN/UM
	SAK/RAOI/NUM
saccharobiose	SAK/RO/BAO*I/OES
saccharocoria	SAK/RO/KOR/YA
	SAK/RO/KOER/YA
saccharogen	SAK/RO/JEN
saccharoglactorrhea	SAK/RO/GLAKT/RAOE/YA
saccharolytic	SAK/RO/LIT/IK
saccharometabolic	SAK/RO/MET/BOL/IK
saccharometabolism	SAK/RO/ME/TAB/LIFM
saccharometer	SAK/ROM/TER
Saccharomyces	SAK/RO/MAOI/SAOEZ
Saccharomycetaceae	SAK/RO/MAOIS/TAIS/YAE
Saccharomycetales	SAK/RO/MAOIS/TAI/LAOEZ
saccharomycetes	SAK/RO/MAOI/SAOE/TAOEZ
saccharomycetic	SAK/RO/MAOI/SET/IK
saccharomycetica	SAK/RO/MAOI/SET/KA
saccharomycetolysis	SAK/RO/MAOIS/TOL/SIS
Saccharomycopsis	SAK/RO/MAOI/KOP/SIS
saccharopine	SAK/RO/PAOEN
saccharorrhea	SAK/RO/RAOE/YA
saccharosan	SAK/RO/SAN
saccharose	SAK/ROES
saccharosuria	SAK/RO/SAOUR/YA
saccharum	SAK/RUM
saccharuria	SAK/RAOUR/YA
sacci	SAK/SAOI
sacciform	SAX/FORM
	SAK/SI/FORM
saccul-	SAK/L-
	SAK/YAOU/L-
	SAK/YU/L-
saccular	SAK/LAR
saccularis	SAK/LAI/RIS
sacculated	SAK/LAIT/-D
sacculation	SAK/LAIGS
saccule	SAK/YAOUL
sacculi	SAK/LAOI
sacculocochlear	SAK/LO/KOK/LAR
sacculoutricular	SAK/LO/YAOU/TRIK/LAR
sacculus	SAK/LUS
saccum	SAK/KUM
	SAK/UM
saccus	SAK/KUS
Sachs	SA*KS
	(*not* SAKS; see sax)
Sachsse	ZAK/SAOE
sacr(o)-	SAI/KR(O)
	SAIK/R(O)
sacra	SAI/KRA
sacrad	SAI/KRAD
sacral	SAI/KRAL
sacrale	SAI/KRAI/LAOE
sacrales	SAI/KRAI/LAOEZ
sacralgia	SAI/KRAL/JA
sacralis	SAI/KRAI/LIS
sacralization	SAI/KRAL/ZAIGS
sacrarthrogenic	SAI/KRAR/THRO/JEN/IK
sacrectomy	SAI/KREKT/M*I
sacri	SAI/KRAOI
sacroanterior	SAI/KRO/AN/TAOER/YOR
sacrococcygea	SAI/KRO/KOK/SIJ/YA
sacrococcygeal	SAI/KRO/KOK/SIJ/YAL
sacrococcygeum	SAI/KRO/KOK/SIJ/YUM
sacrococcygeus	SAI/KRO/KOK/SIJ/YUS
sacrococcyx	SAI/KRO/KOX/IX
	SAI/KRO/KOK/SIX
sacrocoxalgia	SAI/KRO/KOX/AL/JA
	SAI/KRO/KOK/SAL/JA
sacrocoxitis	SAI/KRO/KOK/SAOITS
	SAI/KRO/KOX/AOITS
sacrodynia	SAI/KRO/DIN/YA
sacroiliac	SAI/KRO/IL/YAK
sacroiliaca	SAI/KRO/IL/LAOI/KA
sacroiliitis	SAI/KRO/IL/YAOITS
sacrolisthesis	SAI/KRO/LIS/THE/SIS
	SAI/KRO/LIS/THAOE/SIS
sacrolumbalis	SAI/KRO/LUM/BAI/LIS
sacrolumbar	SAI/KRO/LUM/BAR
sacropelvina	SAI/KRO/PEL/VAOI/NA
sacroperineal	SAI/KRO/P*ER/NAOEL
sacroposterior	SAI/KRO/POS/TAOER/YOR
sacropromontory	SAI/KRO/PROM/ON/TOIR
sacropubic	SAI/KRO/PAOUB/IK
sacrosciatic	SAI/KRO/SAOI/AT/IK
	SAI/KRO/SAOI/YAT/IK
sacrospinal	SAI/KRO/SPAOINL
sacrotomy	SAI/KROT/M*I
sacrotransverse	SAI/KRO/TRA*NS/VERS
sacrouterine	SAI/KRO/YAOUT/RIN
sacrovertebral	SAI/KRO/VERT/BRAL
sacrum	SAI/KRUM
sactosalpinx	SAK/TO/SAL/PINGS
saddle	SAD/-L
S-adenosylhomocystein	S-RBGS/AI/DEN/SIL/HOEM/S*IS/YIN
	S-RBGS/H-F/AI/DEN/SIL/HOEM/S*IS/YIN
S-adenosylmethionine	S-RBGS/AI/DEN/SIL/ME/THAOI/NAOEN
	S-RBGS/H-F/AI/DEN/SIL/ME/THAOI/NAOEN
sadism	SAI/DIFM
	SAD/IFM
sadist	SAI/D*IS
	SAD/*IS
sadistic	SA/D*IS/IK
sadomasochism	SAI/DO/MAS/KIFM
	SAD/MAS/KIFM
sadomasochist	SAI/DO/MAS/K*IS
	SAD/MAS/K*IS
sadomasochistic	SAI/DO/MAS/K*IS/IK
	SAD/MAS/K*IS/IK
Saemisch	SAI/MIRB
Saenger	ZENG/ER
safety pin	SAIF/TI/PIN
safflower	SAF/LOU/ER
	SAF/FLOU/ER
saffron	SAF/RON
safranin	SAF/RA/NIN
safranophil	SAF/RA/NO/FIL
safranophile	SAF/RA/NO/FAOIL
safrol	SAF/ROL
safrole	SAF/ROEL
sage	SAIJ
sagitta	SAJ/TA
sagittal	SAJ/TAL
sagittalis	SAJ/TAI/LIS
sago	SAI/GOE
sagrada	SAI/GRAI/DA

	SA/GRAI/DA	salpingolysis	SAL/PIN/GOL/SIS
Saint	K-P/SAINT	salpingo-oophorectomy	SAL/PING/AOF/REKT/M*I
sal	SAL	salpingo-oophoritis	SAL/PING/AOF/RAOITS
salaam	SA/LAUM	salpingo-oophorocele	SAL/PING/AOF/RO/SAO*EL
SalAc	SAL/AK	salpingo-oothecitis	SAL/PING/AO/THAOE/SAOITS
Sal-Acid	SAL/AS/ID	salpingo-oothecocele	SAL/PING/AO/THAOEK/SAO*EL
Salactic	SA/LAKT/IK	salpingo-ovariectomy	SAL/PING/O/VAIR/YEKT/M*I
salamander	SAL/MAND/ER	salpingo-ovariotomy	SAL/PING/O/VAIR/YOT/M*I
salamanderin	SAL/MAND/RIN	salpingoperitonitis	SAL/PING/PERT/NAOITS
salbutamol	SAL/BAOUT/MOL	salpingopexy	SAL/PING/PEK/SI
salcolex	SAL/KO/LEX	salpingopharyngeal	SAL/PING/FRIN/JAL
sales	SAL/AOEZ	salpingoplasty	SAL/PING/PLAS/TI
salethamide	SAL/*ET/MAOID	salpingorrhagia	SAL/PING/RAI/JA
Salflex	SAL/FLEX	salpingorrhaphy	SAL/PIN/GOR/FI
salicin	SAL/SIN	salpingoscopy	SAL/PIN/GOS/KPI
salicyl	SAL/SIL	salpingostaphyline	SAL/PING/STAF/LAOIN
salicylaldehyde	SAL/SIL/ALD/HAOID	salpingostomatomy	SAL/PING/STOE/MAT/M*I
salicylamide	SAL/SIL/MAOID	salpingostomatoplasty	SAL/PING/STOE/MAT/PLAS/TI
	SAL/SIL/AM/ID		SAL/PING/STOEM/TO/PLAS/TI
salicylanilide	SAL/SIL/AN/LAOID	salpingostomy	SAL/PIN/GO*S/M*I
	SAL/SIL/AN/LID	salpingotomy	SAL/PIN/GOT/M*I
salicylase	SA/LIS/LAIS	salpinx	SAL/PINGS
	SAL/SIL/AIS	salsalate	SALS/LAIT
salicylate	SAL/SIL/AIT		SAL/SA/LAIT
	SA/LIS/LAIT	Salsitab	SALS/TAB
salicylated	SAL/SIL/AIT/-D		SAL/SI/TAB
	SA/LIS/LAIT/-D	salt	SALT
salicylazosulfapyridine	SAL/SIL/A*Z/SUL/FA/PIR/DAOEN		SAULT
	SAL/SIL/A*Z/SUL/FA/PIR/DIN	saltam	SAL/TAM
salicylemia	SAL/SIL/AOEM/YA	saltans	SAL/TANZ
salicylic	SAL/SIL/IK	saltation	SAL/TAIGS
salicylism	SAL/SIL/IFM	saltatorial	SALT/TOIRL
salicylize	SAL/SIL/AOIZ		SALT/TOR/YAL
salicylsalicylic	SAL/SIL/SAL/SIL/IK		SALT/TOER/YAL
salicylsulfonic	SAL/SIL/SUL/FON/IK	saltatoric	SALT/TOR/IK
salicyltherapy	SAL/SIL/THER/PI		SALT/TOER/IK
salicyluric	SAL/SIL/YAOUR/IK	saltatory	SALT/TOIR
salient	SAIL/YENT	Salter	SAULT/ER
salifiable	SAL/FIBL		SALT/ER
salify	SAL/FI	salting out	SAULT/-G/OUT
saligenin	SAL/JEN/NIN		SALT/-G/OUT
saligenol	SAL/JEN/OL	saltpeter	SALT/PAOET/ER
salimeter	SA/LIM/TER		SAULT/PAOET/ER
saline	SAI/LAOEN	salu-	SA/LAOU
	SAI/LAOIN		SLAOU
Salinex	SAL/NEX		SAL/YAOU
salinometer	SAL/NOM/TER		SAL/YU
salipyrine	SAL/PAOI/RAOEN	salubrious	SA/LAOUB/ROUS
saliva	SA/LAOI/VA		SLAOUB/ROUS
	SLAOI/VA	saluresis	SAL/YAOU/RAOE/SIS
salivant	SAL/VANT	saluretic	SAL/YAOU/RET/IK
salivaris	SAL/VAI/RIS	Saluron	SAL/YAOU/RON
salivary	SAL/VAIR	salutarium	SAL/YAOU/TAIRM
salivate	SAL/VAIT	salutary	SAL/YAOU/TAIR
salivation	SA*L/VAIGS	salutation	SAL/YAOU/TAIGS
	SAL/VA*IGS	Salutensin	SAL/YAOU/TEN/SIN
	(not SAL/VAIGS; see salvation)	Salutensin-Demi	SAL/YAOU/TEN/SIN/DEM/MAOE
salivator	SAL/VAI/TOR	salvarsan	SAL/VAR/SAN
salivatory	SAL/VA/TOER	salvation	SAL/VAIGS
salivin	SAL/VIN	salve	SAV
salivolithiasis	SA/LAOIV/LI/THAOI/SIS	Salvia	SAL/VAOE/YA
	SLAOIV/LI/THAOI/SIS		SAL/VA
Salk	SAUK	Salzmann	SALS/MAN
	SAUL/-K		SALZ/MAN
salmonella	SAL/MO/NEL/LA	samarium	SA/MAIRM
Salmonella	K-P/SAL/MO/NEL/LA		SA/MAIR/YUM
salmonellae	SAL/MO/NEL/LAE	Sambucus	SAM/BAOU/KUS
salmonellal	SAL/MO/NEL/LAL	sample	SAFRP/-L
Salmonelleae	SAL/MO/NEL/YAE		SAM/P-L
salmonellosis	SAL/MO/NEL/LOE/SIS	sampler	SAFRP/LER
salocoll	SAL/KOL		SAM/PLER
salol	SAL/OL	sampling	SAFRP/-LG
	SAI/LOL		SAM/P-LG
salping(o)-	SAL/PING	Sampson	SAFRP/SON
	SAL/PIN/G(O)		SAM/SON
	SAL/PIN/J(O)	Sanarelli	SAN/REL/LAOE
salpingectomy	SAL/PIN/JEKT/M*I	sanative	SAN/TIV
salpingemphraxis	SAL/PIN/JEM/FRAK/SIS	sanatorium	SAN/TOIRM
salpinges	SAL/PIN/JAOEZ	sanatory	SAN/TOIR
salpingian	SAL/PIN/JAN	Sanchez	SAN/KHEZ
salpingioma	SAL/PIN/JOE/MA	sand	SAND
salpingion	SAL/PIN/JON	sandalwood	SAN/DAL/WAOD
salpingitic	SAL/PIN/JIT/IK		SAND/AL/WAOD
salpingitis	SAL/PIN/JAOITS	sand crack	SAND/KRAK
salpingocatheterism	SAL/PING/KA*T/TRIFM	Sander	K-P/SAND/ER
salpingocele	SAL/PING/SAO*EL		K-P/SAN/DER
salpingocyesis	SAL/PING/SAOI/E/SIS	Sanders	SAND/ERS
salpingography	SAL/PIN/GOG/FI		SAN/DERS
salpingolithiasis	SAL/PING/LI/THAOI/SIS	sandfly	SAND/FLAOI

Sandimmune	SAN/DI/MAOUN	sapremia	SA/PRAOEM/YA
	SAND/IM/MAOUN	sapro-	SAP/RO
Sandoglobulin	SAND/GLOB/LIN		SA/PRO
	SAND/DO/GLOB/LIN	saprobe	SAP/ROEB
Sandostatin	SAND/STAT/TIN		SA/PROEB
	SAN/DO/STAT/TIN	saprobic	SAP/ROEB/IK
sandpaper	SAND/PAIP/ER		SA/PROEB/IK
Sandstrom	SAND/STREM	saprodontia	SAP/RO/DON/SHA
sane	SAIN	saprogen	SAP/RO/JEN
Sanger	SANG/ER	saprogenic	SAP/RO/JEN/IK
sangui-	SANG/WI	saprogenous	SA/PROJ/NOUS
sanguicolous	SANG/WIK/LOUS	saprophilous	SA/PROF/LOUS
sanguifacient	SANG/WI/FAIRBT	saprophyte	SAP/RO/FAOIT
sanguiferous	SANG/WIF/ROUS	saprophytic	SAP/RO/FIT/IK
sanguification	SANG/WIF/KAIGS	saprozoic	SAP/RO/ZOIK
	SANG/WI/FI/KAIGS		SAP/RO/ZOI/IK
sanguimotor	SANG/WI/MOE/TOR	saprozoite	SAP/RO/ZOE/AOIT
sanguimotory	SANG/WI/MOET/RI	saprozoonosis	SAP/RO/ZOE/NOE/SIS
sanguinaria	SANG/WI/NAIR/YA	saralasin	SA/RAL/SIN
sanguinarine	SANG/WI/NAI/RAOEN		SAR/AL/SIN
sanguine	SANG/WIN	Sarapin	SAR/PIN
sanguineous	SANG/WIN/YOUS	sarcina	SARS/NA
sanguineus	SANG/WIN/YUS		SAR/SAOI/NA
sanguino-	SANG/WIN	Sarcina	K-P/SARS/NA
	SANG/WI/NO		K-P/SAR/SAOI/NA
sanguinolent	SANG/WIN/LENT	sarcinae	SARS/NAE
sanguinolenta	SANG/WIN/LEN/TA		SAR/SAOI/NAE
sanguinolentis	SANG/WIN/LEN/TIS	sarcine	SAR/SAOEN
sanguinopoietic	SANG/WIN/POIT/IK	sarcitis	SAR/SAOITS
sanguinopurulent	SANG/WIN/PAOUR/LENT	sarc(o)-	SARK
sanguinous	SANG/WI/NOUS		SAR/K(O)
sanguirenal	SANG/WI/RAOENL	Sarcobiot	SARK/BAO*I/OT
sanguis	SANG/WIS		SARK/B*I/OT
sanguivorous	SANG/WIV/ROUS	sarcoblast	SARK/BLA*S
sanies	SAI/NAOEZ	sarcocarcinoma	SARK/KARS/NOE/MA
	SAIN/YAOEZ	sarcocele	SARK/SAO*EL
sanio-	SAIN/YO	sarcocyst	SARK/S*IS
saniopurulent	SAIN/YO/PAOUR/LENT	Sarcocystis	SARK/SIS/TIS
sanioserous	SAIN/YO/SAOER/OUS	sarcocystosis	SARK/SIS/TOE/SIS
sanious	SAIN/YOUS	sarcocyte	SARK/SAO*IT
sanipractic	SAN/PRAKT/IK	sarcode	SAR/KOED
sanitarian	SAN/TAIRN	Sarcodina	SARK/DAOI/NA
sanitarium	SAN/TAIRM		SARK/DAOE/NA
sanitary	SAN/TAIR	sarcoenchondroma	SARK/EN/KON/DROE/MA
sanitation	SAN/TAIGS	sarcogenic	SARK/JEN/IK
sanitization	SAN/TI/ZAIGS	sarcoglia	SAR/KOG/LA
	SAN/TAOI/ZAIGS		SAR/KOG/LAOE/YA
sanitize	SAN/TAOIZ	sarcohydrocele	SARK/HAOI/DRO/SAO*EL
sanitizer	SAN/TAOIZ/ER	sarcoid	SAR/KOID
sanity	SAN/TI	sarcoidosis	SAR/KOI/DOE/SIS
Sanorex	SAN/REX	sarcolemma	SARK/LEM/MA
Sansert	SAN/SERT	sarcolemmal	SARK/LEM/MAL
Sansom	SAN/SOM	sarcolemmic	SARK/LEM/IK
Sanson	SAN/SON	sarcolemmous	SARK/LEM/OUS
santal	SAN/TAL	sarcology	SAR/KOLG
santalum	SANT/LUM	sarcolysine	SARK/LAOI/SAOEN
Santini	SAN/TAOE/NAOE	sarcolysis	SARK/KOL/SIS
santonic	SAN/TON/IK	sarcolyte	SARK/LAOIT
santonica	SAN/TON/KA	sarcolytic	SARK/LIT/IK
santonin	SANT/NIN	sarcoma	SAR/KOE/MA
santoriana	SAN/TOR/YAI/NA	sarcomagenesis	SAR/KOEM/JEN/SIS
santorini	SANT/RAOI/NAOI	sarcomagenic	SAR/KOEM/JEN/IK
Santorini	SANT/RAOE/NAOE	Sarcomastigophora	SAR/MA*S/GOF/RA
sap	SAP	sarcomata	SAR/KOEM/TA
saphena	SA/FAOE/NA	sarcomatodes	SAR/KOEM/TOE/DAOEZ
saphenectomy	SAF/NEKT/M*I	sarcomatoid	SAR/KOEM/TOID
saphenous	SA/FAOEN/OUS	sarcomatosis	SAR/KOEM/TOE/SIS
saphenus	SA/FAOE/NUS		SARK/MA/TOE/SIS
sapid	SAP/ID	sarcomatosum	SAR/KOEM/TOE/SUM
sapiens	SAIP/YENZ		SAR/KOEM/TOES/UM
	SAIP/YENS		SARK/MA/TOE/SUM
sapientiae	SAIP/YEN/SHAE		SAR/MA/TOES/UM
sapo	SAI/POE	sarcomatous	SAR/KOEM/TOUS
sapo-	SAIP	sarcomere	SARK/MAOER
	SAP	sarcomphalocele	SAR/KOM/FAL/SAO*EL
	SAI/PO	sarconeme	SARK/NAOEM
	SA/PO	Sarcophaga	SAR/KOF/GA
sapogenin	SA/POJ/NIN	Sarcophagidae	SARK/FAJ/DAE
saponaceous	SAP/NAIRBS	sarcoplasm	SARK/PLAFM
	SAIP/NAIRBS	sarcoplasmic	SARK/PLAZ/MIK
saponatus	SAP/NAI/TUS	sarcoplast	SARK/PLA*S
	SAIP/NAI/TUS	sarcopoietic	SARK/POIT/IK
saponification	SA/PON/FI/KAIGS	Sarcopsylla penetrans	SARK/SIL/LA/PEN/TRANZ
saponify	SA/PON/FI		SAR/KOP/SIL/LA/PEN/TRANZ
saponin	SAP/NIN	Sarcoptes	SAR/KOP/TAOEZ
sapophore	SAP/FOER	Sarcoptes scabiei	SAR/KOP/TAOEZ/SKAIB/YAOI
Sappey	SAP/PAI	sarcoptic	SAR/KOPT/IK
	SAP/PAOE	sarcoptid	SAR/KOP/TID
sapphism	SAF/IFM	sarcoptidosis	SAR/KOPT/DOE/SIS

sarcosine	SARK/SAOEN		SKAULD
sarcosinemia	SARK/SI/NAOEM/YA	scale	SKAIL
sarcosis	SAR/KOE/SIS	scalene	SKAI/LAOEN
sarcosome	SARK/SOEM	scalenectomy	SKAIL/NEKT/M*I
sarcosporidia	SARK/SPRID/YA	scalenotomy	SKAIL/NOT/M*I
Sarcosporidia	K-P/SARK/SPRID/YA	scalenus	SKAI/LAOE/NUS
sarcosporidian	SARK/SPRID/YAN	scaler	SKAIL/ER
sarcosporidiasis	SARK/SPOR/DAOI/SIS	scaling	SKAIL/-G
sarcosporidiosis	SARK/SPRID/YOE/SIS	scall	SKAUL
sarcosporidium	SARK/SPRID/YUM	scalloping	SKAL/OP/-G
sarcostosis	SAR/KOS/TOE/SIS	scalp	SKAL/-P
sarcostyle	SARK/STAOIL	scalpel	SKAL/PEL
sarcotherapeutics	SARK/THER/PAOUT/IK/-S	scalpriform	SKAL/PRI/FORM
sarcotherapy	SARK/THER/PI	scalprum	SKAL/PRUM
sarcotic	SAR/KOT/IK	scaly	SKAIL/LI
sarcotripsy	SARK/TRIP/SI		SKAI/LI
sarcotubule	SARK/TAOUB/YAOUL	scammony	SKAM/N*I
sarcous	SARK/OUS	scan	SKAN
sardinae	SAR/DAOI/NAE	scandium	SKAND/YUM
sardonic	SAR/DON/IK	scanner	SKAN/ER
sarmassation	SARM/SAIGS	scanning	SKAN/-G
sarsa	SAR/SA	scanography	SKAN/OG/FI
sarsaparilla	SARS/PRIL/LA	scansion	SKANGS
	SARS/PA/RIL/LA	scansorius	SKAN/SOR/YUS
sarsasapogenin	SARS/SAP/JEN/NIN		SKAN/SOER/YUS
sartorii	SAR/TOR/YAOI	Scanzoni	SKAN/ZOE/NAOE
	SAR/TOER/YAOI	scapha	SKAF/FA
sartorius	SAR/TOR/YUS		SKAI/FA
	SAR/TOER/YUS	scaphae	SKAF/FAE
Sassafras	SAS/FRAS		SKAI/FAE
satellite	SAT/LAOIT	scaphion	SKAF/YON
satellitism	SAT/LAOI/TIFM		SKAIF/YON
	SAT/LAOIT/IFM	scapho-	SKAF
satellitosis	SAT/LAOI/TOE/SIS		SKA/FO
satiation	SAIRB/YAIGS	scaphocephalia	SKAF/SFAIL/YA
satiety	SA/TAOI/TI	scaphocephalic	SKAF/SFAL/IK
	SAIRB/YE/TI	scaphocephalism	SKAF/SEF/LIFM
Sattler	SAT/LER	scaphocephalous	SKAF/SEF/LOUS
saturate	SAFP/RAIT	scaphocephaly	SKAF/SEF/LI
saturation	SAFP/RAIGS	scaphohydrocephalus	SKAF/HAOI/DRO/SEF/LUS
saturni	SA/TUR/NAOI	scaphohydrocephaly	SKAF/HAOI/DRO/SEF/LI
	SAT/UR/NAOI	scaphoid	SKAF/OID
saturnine	SAT/UR/NAOIN	scaphoidea	SKAF/OID/YA
	SAT/UR/NAOEN		SKA/FOID/YA
saturnism	SAT/UR/NIFM	scaphoiditis	SKAF/OI/DAOITS
	SAT/URN/IFM	scapi	SKAI/PAOI
satyr	SAT/TIR	scapul(o)-	SKAP/L(O)
satyri	SAT/RAOI		SKAP/YAOU/L(O)
satyriasis	SAT/RAOI/SIS		SKAP/YU/L(O)
satyromania	SAT/RO/MAIN/YA	scapula	SKAP/LA
saucer	SAUS/ER	scapulae	SKAP/LAE
	(not SAU/SER; see saw ser-)	scapulalgia	SKAP/LAL/JA
saucerization	SAUS/ER/ZAIGS	scapular	SKAP/LAR
	SAUS/RI/ZAIGS	scapularis	SKAP/LAI/RIS
Sauer	SOU/ER	scapulary	SKAP/LAIR
Sauerbruch	SOU/ER/BRUK	scapulectomy	SKAP/LEKT/M*I
	SOUR/BRUK	scapuloanterior	SKAP/LO/AN/TAOER/YOR
sauna	SAUN/NA	scapuloclavicular	SKAP/LO/KLA/VIK/LAR
	SAU/NA	scapulodynia	SKAP/LO/DIN/YA
Saundby	SAUND/BI	scapulohumeral	SKAP/LO/HAOUM/RAL
Saunders	SAUN/DERS	scapulopexy	SKAP/LO/PEK/SI
	SAUND/ERS	scapuloposterior	SKAP/LO/POS/TAOER/YOR
sauriasis	SAU/RAOI/SIS	scapus	SKAI/PUS
sauriderma	SAUR/DER/MA	scar	SKAR
sauriosis	SAUR/YOE/SIS	scarf	SKAR/-F
sauroid	SAUR/OID	scarification	SKAR/FI/KAIGS
	SAU/ROID	scarificator	SKAR/FI/KAI/TOR
Saussure	SOE/SAOUR	scarifier	SKAR/FI/ER
Savage	K-P/SAV/AJ	scarify	SKAR/FI
saw	SAU	scarlatina	SKARL/TAOE/NA
sawdust	SA*U/D*US		SKARL/TAOI/NA
saxitoxin	SAX/TOK/SIN		SKAR/LA/TAOE/NA
Sayre	SAIR		SKAR/LA/TAOI/NA
scab	SKAB	scarlatinal	SKAR/LAT/NAL
scabetic	SKA/BET/IK		SKARL/TAOENL
scabicidal	SKAIB/SAOI/DAL		SKAR/LA/TAOENL
scabicide	SKAIB/SAO*ID		SKARL/TAOINL
scabiei	SKAIB/YAOI		SKAR/LA/TAOINL
scabies	SKAI/BAOEZ	scarlatinella	SKAR/LAT/NEL/LA
scabietic	SKAIB/YET/IK	scarlatiniform	SKARL/TAOEN/FORM
scabious	SKAIB/YOUS		SKARL/TIN/FORM
scabrities	SKAI/BRIRB/AOEZ		SKAR/LA/TAOEN/FORM
scala	SKAI/LA		SKAR/LA/TIN/FORM
scalae	SKAI/LAE	scarlatinoid	SKAR/LAT/NOID
scalariform	SKA/LAR/FORM		SKARL/TAOE/NOID
	SKA/LAIR/FORM		SKAR/LA/TAOE/NOID
scalaris	SKA/LAI/RIS	scarlatinosa	SKAR/LAT/NOE/SA
	SKA/LAIR/RIS		SKARL/TAOE/NOE/SA
scald	SKALD		SKAR/LA/TAOE/NOE/SA

scarlet	SKAR/LET		SHIS/TOR/KIS
	SKARL/ET	schistosis	SHIS/TOE/SIS
Scarpa	SKAR/PA	schistosoma	SH*IS/SOE/MA
scatemia	SKA/TAOEM/YA	schistosomal	SH*IS/SOE/MAL
scato-	SKAT	schistosome	SH*IS/SOEM
	SKA/TO	schistosomia	SH*IS/SOEM/YA
scatologia	SKAT/LOE/JA	schistosomiasis	SH*IS/SOE/MAOI/SIS
scatologic	SKAT/LOJ/IK	schistosomicidal	SH*IS/SOEM/SAOI/DAL
scatology	SKA/TOLG	schistosomicide	SH*IS/SOEM/SAO*ID
scatoma	SKA/TOE/MA	schistosomulum	SH*IS/SOEM/LUM
scatophagy	SKA/TOF/JI		SH*IS/SOEM/YAOU/LUM
scatophilia	SKAT/FIL/YA		SH*IS/SOEM/YU/LUM
scatoscopy	SKA/TOS/KPI	schistosomula	SH*IS/SOEM/LA
scatter	SKAT/ER		SH*IS/SOEM/YAOU/LA
scattergram	SKAT/ER/GRAM		SH*IS/SOEM/YU/LA
scattering	SKAT/ER/-G	Schistosomum	SH*IS/SOE/MUM
scatula	SKAFP/LA	schistosomus	SH*IS/SOE/MUS
	SKAT/YAOU/LA	schistosternia	SH*IS/STERN/YA
	SKAT/YU/LA	schistothorax	SH*IS/THOR/AX
scavenger	SKAVN/JER	schiz(o)-	SKIZ
	SKAV/EN/JER		SKITS
Scedosporium	SAOED/SPOR/YUM		SKIT/S(O)
scelalgia	SKAOE/LAL/JA	schizamnion	SKIZ/AM/NON
	SE/LAL/JA		SKIZ/AM/NAOE/YON
scelotyrbe	SEL/TIR/BAOE	schizaxon	SKIZ/AK/SON
	SEL/TER/BAOE	schizencephalic	SKIZ/EN/SFAL/IK
scent	SKRENT	schizencephaly	SKIZ/EN/SEF/LI
Schafer	SHAIFR	schizoaffective	SKIZ/AI/FEKT/IV
Schaffer	SHAFR		SKIZ/AFKT/IV
Schamberg	SHAM/BERG	schizocephalia	SKIZ/SFAIL/YA
Schanz	SHANTS	schizocyte	SKIZ/SAO*IT
	SHANZ	schizocytosis	SKIZ/SAOI/TOE/SIS
Schardinger	SHAR/DING/ER	schizogenesis	SKIZ/JEN/SIS
scharlach	SHAR/LAK	schizogenous	SKI/ZOJ/NOUS
Schaudinn	SHAU/DIN		SKIZ/OJ/NOUS
Schaumann	SHAU/MAN	schizogony	SKI/ZOG/N*I
Schauta	SHAU/TA		SKIZ/OG/N*I
Schede	SHAI/DAOE	schizogyria	SKIZ/JAOIR/YA
schedule	SKED/YAOUL	schizoid	SKIZ/OID
Scheele	SHAOEL	schizoidism	SKIZ/OI/DIFM
Scheibe	SHAOI/BAOE		SKIZ/OID/IFM
Scheiner	SHAO*IN/ER	schizokinesis	SKIZ/KI/NAOE/SIS
	SHAOI/NER	schizomycete	SKIZ/MAOI/SAOET
	(not SHAOIN/ER; see shiner)	Schizomycetes	SKIZ/MAOI/SAOE/TAOEZ
schema	SKAOE/MA	schizomycetic	SKIZ/MAO/SET/IK
schemata	SKAOE/MA/TA	schizomycosis	SKIZ/MAOI/KOE/SIS
	SKAOE/MAT/TA	schizont	SKI/ZONT
schematic	SKAOE/MAT/IK		SKIZ/ONT
	SKE/MAT/IK	schizonticide	SKI/ZONT/SAO*ID
schematograph	SKAOE/MAT/GRAF		SKIZ/ONT/SAO*ID
	SKE/MAT/GRAF	schizonychia	SKIZ/NIK/YA
scheme	SKAOEM	schizophasia	SKIZ/FAIZ/YA
-schesis	(v)S/KE/SIS	schizophrenia	SKIZ/FRAOEN/YA
Schick	SHIK	schizophreniac	SKIZ/FRAOEN/YAK
Schiefferdecker	SHAOEFR/DEK/ER	schizophrenic	SKIZ/FREN/IK
	SHAOEF/ER/DEK/ER		SKIZ/FRAOEN/IK
Schiff	SHIF	schizophreniform	SKIZ/FREN/FORM
Schilder	SHILD/ER	schizophrenoides	SKIZ/FRAOE/NOI/DAOEZ
	SHIL/DER	schizophrenosis	SKIZ/FRAOE/NOE/SIS
Schiller	SHIL/ER		SKIZ/FRE/NOE/SIS
Schilling	K-P/SH*IL/-G	schizoprosopia	SKIZ/PRO/SOEP/YA
schindylesis	SKIN/DI/LAOE/SIS	schizothemia	SKIZ/THAOEM/YA
	SKIND/LAOE/SIS	schizothorax	SKIZ/THOR/AX
	SKIN/DAOI/LAOE/SIS	schizotonia	SKIZ/TOEN/YA
Schiotz	SHAOE/ETS	schizotrichia	SKIZ/TRIK/YA
	SHAOE/OTS	schizotropic	SKIZ/TROP/IK
Schirmer	SHIRM/ER	schizotrypanosis	SKIZ/TRIP/NOE/SIS
	SHIR/MER	Schizotrypanum cruzi	SKIZ/TRIP/NUM/KRAOU/ZAOI
-schisis	(v)S/KI/SIS		SKIZ/TRAOIP/NUM/KRAOU/ZAOI
schistasis	SK*IS/SIS	schizotypal	SKIZ/TAOI/PAL
	SH*IS/SIS	schizozoite	SKIZ/ZOE/AOIT
schisto-	SH*IS	Schlatter	SH-/LAT/ER
	SK*IS	Schlemm	SH-/LEM
	SHIS/TO	Schlepper	SH-/LEP/ER
	SKIS/TO	Schlesinger	SH-/LAI/ZING/ER
schistocele	SH*IS/SAO*EL	Schlosser	SH-/LES/ER
schistocelia	SH*IS/SAOEL/YA		SH-/LOS/ER
schistocephalus	SH*IS/SEF/LUS	schlusskoagulum	SH-/LUS/KO/AG/LUM
schistocormia	SH*IS/KORM/YA	Schmidel	SH-/MAOE/DEL
schistocormus	SH*IS/KOR/MUS	Schmidt	SH-/MIT
schistocystis	SH*IS/SIS/TIS	Schmitz	SH-/MITS
schistocyte	SH*IS/SAO*IT	Schmorl	SH-/MORL
schistocytosis	SH*IS/SAOI/TOE/SIS	Schnabel	SH-/NAB/EL
schistoglossia	SH*IS/GLOS/YA		SH-/NABL
schistomelia	SH*IS/MAOEL/YA	Schneider	SH-/NAOID/ER
schistomelus	SHIS/TOM/LUS		SH-/NAOI/DER
schistoprosopia	SH*IS/PRO/SOEP/YA	schneiderian	SH-/NAOI/DAOER/YAN
schistoprosopus	SH*IS/PROS/PUS		SH-/NAOI/DER/YAN
schistorachis	SHIS/TOER/KIS	Schneidersitz	SH-/NAOI/DER/ZITS

	SH-/NAOI/DER/SITS	scintigram	SINT/SIS/TERN/OG/FI
Scholz	SHOELTS	scintigram	SINT/GRAM
	SHOLTS	scintigraphic	SINT/GRAFK
Schon	SHAIN	scintigraphy	SIN/TIG/FI
Schonbein	SHAIN/BAOIN	scintillascope	SIN/TIL/SKOEP
Schonberg	SHON/BERG	scintillation	SINT/LAIGS
	SHERN/BERG	scintillator	SINT/LAI/TOR
	SHAIN/BERG	scintillometer	SINT/LOM/TER
Schonlein	SHAIN/LAOIN	scintiphotograph	SINT/FOET/GRAF
school	SKAOL		SINT/FRAF
Schott	SHO*T	scintiphotography	SINT/FOE/TOG/FI
Schottmuller	SHOT/MIL/ER		SINT/FRAF/FI
Schreger	SH-/RAIG/ER	scintiscan	SINT/SKAN
	SH-/RAI/GER	scintiscanner	SINT/SKAN/ER
Schreiber	SH-/RAOIB/ER	scion	SAOI/YON
	SH-/RAOI/BER	sciopody	SKAOI/OP/DI
Schreiner	SH-/RAOIN/ER	sciosophy	SAOI/OS/FI
Schridde	SH-/RID/DAOE		SAOI/YOS/FI
	SH-/RID/DE	schirrhencanthis	SKIR/EN/KAN/THIS
Schroeder	SH-/RAID/ER		SIR/EN/KAN/THIS
	SH-/RAI/DER	scirrhoid	SKIR/OID
	SH-/ROED/ER		SIR/OID
	SH-/ROE/DER	scirrhoma	SKIR/ROE/MA
Schron	SH-/RAIN		SIR/ROE/MA
Schroth	SH-/ROET	scirrhosity	SKIR/OS/TI
Schrotter	SH-/RET/ER		SIR/OS/TI
Schuchardt	SHAOU/KART	scirrhous	SKIR/OUS
Schuffner	SHIF/NER		SKIR/ROUS
Schule	SHAOE/LAOE		SIR/OUS
	SHAOE/LE		SIR/ROUS
Schuller	SH*IL/ER	scirrhus	SKIR/RUS
	SHUL/ER		SIR/RUS
	(*not* SHIL/ER; see Schiller)	scirrophthalmia	SKIR/OF/THAL/MA
Schultz	SHAOULTS		SKIR/OF/THAL/MAOE/YA
	SHULTS	scission	S*IGS
Schultze	SHAOULT/SAOE		SIZ/YON
	SHAOULT/ZAOE		(*not* SIGS; see situation)
	SHULT/SAOE	scissiparity	SIS/PAIR/TI
	SHULT/ZAOE	scissors	SIZ/SORS
Schumm	SHAOUM		SIZ/SOR/-S
	SHUM	scissors-bite	SIZ/SORS/H-F/BAOIT
Schurmann	SH*UR/MAN		SIZ/SOR/-S/H-F/BAOIT
	(*not* SHUR/MAN or SHER/MAN)	scissors-shadow	SIZ/SORS/H-F/SHA/DOE
Schutz	SHITS		SIZ/SOR/-S/H-F/SHA/DOE
	SHUTS	scissura	SI/SAOU/RA
Schwabach	SH-/VA/BAK		SIS/SAOU/RA
	SH-/VAU/BAUK	scissurae	SI/SAOU/RAE
Schwalbe	SH-/VAL/BAOE		SIS/SAOU/RAE
	SH-/VAUL/BAOE	scissure	SIRB/SHUR
Schwann	SH-/VAN	scissure	SIRB/YUR
Schwann cell	SWAN/KREL	Sclavo-PPD	SKLA/VOE/P-RBGS/P*RBGS/
	SH-/VAN/KREL		D*RBGS
	SH-/WAN/KREL		SKLAI/VOE/P-RBGS/P*RBGS/
schwann-	SWAN/N- (short form)		D*RBGS
	SH-/WAN/N-	SclavoTest-PPD	SKLA/VOE/T*ES/P-RBGS/P*RBGS/
	SH-/VAN/N-		D*RBGS
schwannitis	SWAN/NAOITS		SKLAI/VOE/T*ES/P-RBGS/
schwannoglioma	SWAN/GLAOI/YOE/MA		P*RBGS/D*RBGS
schwannoma	SWAN/NOE/MA	scler(o)-	SKLAOER
schwannosis	SWAN/NOE/SIS		SKLE/R(O)-
Schwartz	SH-/WARTS		SKLER
	SWARTS	sclera	SKLAOER/RA
	SH-/VARTS		SKLER/RA
Schwarz	SH-/VARZ	scleradenitis	SKLAOER/AD/NAOITS
Schwediauer	SH-/VAID/YOU/ER	sclerae	SKLAOER/RAE
Schweigger-Seidel	SH-/VAOIG/ER/H-F/SAOI/DEL		SKLER/RAE
	SH-/VAOI/GER/H-F/SAOI/DEL	scleral	SKLAOERL
Schweitzer	SH-/VAOITS/ER		SKLERL
	SH-/VAOIT/SER	scleratitis	SKLAOER/TAOITS
	SH-/VAOIT/ZER	scleratogenous	SKLAOER/TOJ/NOUS
Schweninger	SH-/VEN/IN/GER	sclerectasia	SKLAOER/EK/TAIZ/YA
	SH-/VEN/-G/ER	sclerectasis	SKLE/REKT/SIS
sciage	SE/YAJ	sclerectoiridectomy	SKLE/REKT/IR/DEKT/M*I
	SE/AJ		SKLE/REK/TO/IR/DEKT/M*I
scialyscope	SAOI/AL/SKOEP	sclerectoiridodialysis	SKLE/REKT/IR/DO/DI/AL/SIS
	SAOI/YAL/SKOEP		SKLE/REK/TO/IR/DO/DI/AL/SIS
sciatic	SAOI/AT/IK	sclerectome	SKLE/REK/TOEM
	SAOI/YAT/IK	sclerectomy	SKLE/REKT/M*I
sciatica	SAOI/AT/KA	scleredema	SKLAOER/DAOE/MA
	SAOI/YAT/KA	sclerema	SKLE/RAOE/MA
science	SAOINS	sclerencephalia	SKLAOER/EN/SFAIL/YA
scientifically	SAOIN/TIF/KLI	sclerencephaly	SKLAOER/EN/SEF/LI
	SAOIN/TIFK/LI	sclerenchyma	SKLE/RENG/MA
scientist	SAOIN/T*IS	sclerenchymatous	SKLAOER/EN/KIM/TOUS
scieropia	SAOI/ROEP/YA		SKLAOERN/KIM/TOUS
	SAOIR/OEP/YA	scleriasis	SKLE/RAOI/SIS
scilla	SIL/LA	scleriritomy	SKLAOER/IR/RIT/M*I
scillaren	SIL/REN		SKLAOER/RIT/M*I
scinticisternography	SINT/SIS/TER/NOG/FI	scleritis	SKLE/RAOITS

scleroadipose	SKLAOER/AD/POES	scleciform	SKOE/LAOES/FORM
scleroatrophy	SKLAOER/AT/RO/FI		SKOE/LES/FORM
scleroblastema	SKLAOER/BLAS/TAOE/MA	scolecoid	SKOEL/KOID
scleroblastemic	SKLAOER/BLAS/TEM/IK	scolecology	SKOEL/KOLG
sclerocataracta	SKLAOER/KAT/RAK/TA	scolex	SKOE/LEX
sclerochoroidal	SKLAOER/KOE/ROI/DAL	scoli(o)-	SKOEL/Y(O)
sclerochoroiditis	SKLAOER/KOE/ROI/DAOITS	scoliokyphosis	SKOEL/YO/KAOI/FOE/SIS
scleroconjunctival	SKLAOER/KON/JUNG/TAOIVL	scoliometer	SKOEL/YOM/TER
	SKLAOER/KON/JUNGT/VAL	scoliorachitic	SKOEL/YO/RA/KIT/IK
	SKLAOER/KON/JUNG/VAL	scoliosiometry	SKOEL/YO/SAOE/OM/TRI
scleroconjunctivitis	SKLAOER/KON/JUNGT/VAOITS	scoliosis	SKOEL/YOE/SIS
	SKLAOER/KON/JUNG/VAOITS	scoliosometer	SKOEL/YO/SOM/TER
sclerocornea	SKLAOER/KORN/YA	scoliotic	SKOEL/YOT/IK
sclerocorneal	SKLAOER/KORN/YAL	scoliotone	SKOEL/YO/TOEN
sclerodactylia	SKLAOER/DAK/TIL/YA	Scolopendra	SKOEL/PEN/DRA
sclerodactyly	SKLAOER/DAKT/LI	scolopsia	SKOE/LOPS/YA
scleroderma	SKLAOER/DER/MA	scoop	SKAOP
	SKLER/DER/MA	scope	SKOEP
sclerodermatitis	SKLAOER/DERM/TAOITS	-scope	SKOEP
sclerodermatous	SKLAOER/DERM/TOUS	-scopic	SKOP/IK
sclerodesmia	SKLAOER/DEZ/MA	scopin	SKOE/PIN
	SKLAOER/DEZ/MAOE/YA	scopine	SKOE/PAOEN
sclerogenic	SKLAOER/JEN/IK	-scopist	-S/KP*IS
sclerogenous	SKLE/ROJ/NOUS		-S/KO/P*IS
sclerogummatous	SKLAOER/GUM/TOUS	scopo-	SKOEP
scleroid	SKLAOER/OID		SKOE/PO
scleroiritis	SKLAOER/AOI/RAOITS	scopolagnia	SKOEP/LAG/NA
	SKLAOER/IR/RAOITS		SKOEP/LAG/NAOE/YA
sclerokeratitis	SKLAOER/KER/TAOITS	scopolamine	SKOE/POL/MAOEN
sclerokeratoiritis	SKLAOER/KER/TO/AOI/RAOITS		SKOE/POL/MIN
	SKLAOER/KER/TO/IR/RAOITS	Scopolia	SKOE/POEL/YA
sclerokeratosis	SKLAOER/KER/TOE/SIS	scopoline	SKOEP/LAOEN
scleroma	SKLE/ROE/MA	scopometer	SKOE/POM/TER
scleromalacia	SKLAOER/MA/LAI/SHA	scopometry	SKOE/POM/TRI
Scleromate	SKLAOER/MAIT	scopomorphinism	SKOEP/MOR/FIN/IFM
scleromeninx	SKLAOER/MEN/INGS		SKOEP/MOR/FI/NIFM
	SKLAOER/MAOE/NINGS	scopophilia	SKOEP/FIL/YA
scleromere	SKLAOER/MAOER	scopophobia	SKOEP/FOEB/YA
sclerometer	SKLAOE/ROM/TER	scopto-	SKOPT
	SKLE/ROM/TER		SKOP/TO
scleromyxedema	SKLAOER/MIX/DAOE/MA	scoptolagnia	SKOPT/LAG/NA
scleronychia	SKLAOER/NIK/YA		SKOPT/LAG/NAOE/YA
scleronyxis	SKLAOER/NIK/SIS	scoptophilia	SKOPT/FIL/YA
sclero-oophoritis	SKLAOER/AOF/RAOITS	scoptophobia	SKOPT/FOEB/YA
	SKLAOER/OEF/RAOITS	Scopulariopsis	SKOP/LAIR/YOP/SIS
sclero-oothecitis	SKLAOER/AO/THAOE/SAOITS	scopulariopsosis	SKOP/LAIR/YOP/SOE/SIS
sclerophthalmia	SKLAOER/OF/THAL/MA	-scopy	(O)S/KPI
	SKLAOER/OF/THAL/MAOE/YA		(O)S/KO/PI (not in CAT)
scleroplasty	SKLAOER/PLAS/TI	scorbutic	SKOR/BAOUT/IK
scleroprotein	SKLAOER/PRO/TAOEN	scorbutica	SKOR/BAOUT/KA
sclerosal	SKLE/ROE/SAL	scorbutigenic	SKOR/BAOUT/JEN/IK
sclerosant	SKLAOER/SANT	scorbutus	SKOR/BAOU/TUS
sclerosarcoma	SKLAOER/SAR/KOE/MA	scordinema	SKORD/NAOE/MA
sclerose	SKLE/ROEZ	score	SKOER
	SKLE/ROES		SKOR
sclerosed	SKLE/ROEZ/-D	scoreboard	SKOER/BAORD
	SKLE/ROES/-D		SKOR/BAORD
scleroses	SKLE/ROE/SAOEZ	scored	SKOER/-D
sclerosing	SKLE/ROES/-G		SKOR/-D
sclerosis	SKLE/ROE/SIS	scorekeeper	SKOER/KAOEP/ER
scleroskeleton	SKLAOER/SKEL/TON		SKOR/KAOEP/ER
sclerostenosis	SKLAOER/STE/NOE/SIS	scorer	SKOER/ER
Sclerostoma	SKLE/RO*S/MA		SKOR/ER
sclerostomy	SKLE/RO*S/M*I	scoring	SKOER/-G
sclerotherapy	SKLAOER/THER/PI		SKOR/-G
sclerothrix	SKLAOER/THRIX	scorpion	SKORP/YON
sclerotia	SKLE/ROE/SHA		SKOERP/YON
	SKLE/ROERB/YA	Scorpionida	SKORP/YON/DA
sclerotic	SKLE/ROT/IK		SKOERP/YON/DA
sclerotica	SKLE/ROT/KA	scorpionism	SKORP/YON/IFM
scleroticectomy	SKLE/ROT/SEKT/M*I		SKOERP/YON/IFM
sclerotico-	SKLE/ROT/KO	Scotch	K-P/SKOFP
scleroticochoroidal	SKLE/ROT/KO/KOE/ROI/DAL		SKO*FP
scleroticochoroiditis	SKLE/ROT/KO/KOE/ROI/DAOITS	scoto-	SKOET
scleroticonyxis	SKLE/ROT/KO/NIK/SIS		SKOE/TO
scleroticopuncture	SKLE/ROT/KO/PUNG/KHUR	scotochromogen	SKOET/KROEM/JEN
scleroticotomy	SKLE/ROT/KOT/M*I	scotochromogenic	SKOET/KROEM/JEN/IK
sclerotium	SKLE/ROE/SHUM	scotochromogenicity	SKOET/KROEM/JE/NIS/TI
	SKLE/ROERB/UM	scotodinia	SKOET/DIN/YA
	SKLE/ROERB/YUM	scotogram	SKOET/GRAM
sclerotome	SKLAOER/TOEM	scotograph	SKOET/GRAF
sclerotomy	SKLE/ROT/M*I	scotographic	SKOET/GRAFK
sclerotrichia	SKLAOER/TRIK/YA	scotography	SKOE/TOG/FI
sclerotylosis	SKLAOER/TAOI/LOE/SIS	scotoma	SKOE/TOE/MA
sclerous	SKLAOER/OUS	scotomagraph	SKOE/TOEM/GRAF
sclerozone	SKLAOER/ZOEN	scotomata	SKOE/TOEM/TA
scoff	SKOF	scotomatous	SKOE/TOEM/TOUS
scoleces	SKOEL/SAOEZ	scotometer	SKOE/TOM/TER
scoleciasis	SKOEL/SAOI/SIS	scotometry	SKOE/TOM/TRI

scotomization	SKOE/TOM/ZAIGS	sea	SAE
	SKOET/MI/ZAIGS		(*not* SAOE; see "see")
	SKOE/TOEM/ZAIGS	seal	SAOEL
scotophilia	SKOET/FIL/YA	sealant	SAOEL/ANT
scotophobia	SKOET/FOEB/YA		SAOE/LANT
scotopia	SKOE/TOEP/YA	seam	SAEM
scotopic	SKOE/TOP/IK		(*not* SAOEM; see seem)
scotopsin	SKOE/TOP/SIN	searcher	S*ERPBLG/ER
scotoscopy	SKOE/TOS/KPI		SER/KHER
scototherapy	SKOET/THER/PI	seasick	SAE/SIK
Scott	SKO*T	seasickness	SAE/SIK/*NS
Scot-Tussin	SKOT/TUS/SIN	season	SE/SON
scour	SKOUR	seat	SAOET
scrape	SKRAIP	seaweed	SAE/WAOED
scrapie	SKRAP/PAOE	seatworm	SAOET/WORM
	SKRAI/PAOE	seb(o)-	SEB
scratch	SKRAFP		SE/B(O)
screatus	SKRAOE/AI/TUS	sebaceous	SE/BAIRBS
	SKRAOE/YAI/TUS	sebaceum	SE/BAI/SHUM
screen	SKRAOEN		SE/BAIRB/UM
screw	SKRAOU		SE/BAIRB/YUM
screwworm	SKRAOU/WORM	sebacic	SE/BAIS/IK
scribe	SKRAOIB	sebiagogic	SEB/YA/GOJ/IK
Scribner	SKRIB/NER	sebiferous	SE/BIF/ROUS
scribomania	SKRIB/MAIN/YA	Sebileau	SEB/LOE
scriptorius	SKRIP/TOER/YUS	sebiparous	SE/BIP/ROUS
	SKRIP/TOR/YUS	sebolith	SEB/L*IT
scrobiculate	SKROE/BIK/LAIT	seborrhea	SEB/RAOE/YA
scrobiculus	SKROE/BIK/LUS	seborrheal	SEB/RAOEL
scrobiculus cordis	SKROE/BIK/LUS/KOR/DIS		SEB/RAOE/YAL
scroful-	SKROF/L-	seborrheic	SEB/RAOE/IK
	SKROF/YAOU/L-	seborrheica	SEB/RAOE/KA
	SKROF/YU/L-	seborrheicum	SEB/RAOE/KUM
scrofula	SKROF/LA	seborrheid	SEB/RAOE/ID
scrofuloderma	SKROF/LO/DER/MA	seborrhoeicum	SEB/RAO*E/KUM
scrofulosorum	SKROF/LO/SOR/UM	seborrhoic	SEB/ROIK
	SKROF/LO/SOER/UM		SEB/ROE/IK
	SKROF/LOS/RUM	sebotropic	SEB/TROP/IK
scrofulotuberculosis	SKROF/LO/TAOU/BERK/LOE/SIS	Sebulex	SEB/YAOU/LEX
scrofulous	SKROF/LOUS		SEB/YU/LEX
scroll	SKROEL	sebum	SE/BUM
scrota	SKROE/TA	Sebutone	SEB/YAOU/TOEN
scrotal	SKROE/TAL		SEB/YU/TOEN
scrotales	SKROE/TAI/LAOEZ	Secernentasida	SE/SER/NEN/TAS/DA
scrotectomy	SKROE/TEKT/M*I	Seckel	SEK/EL
scroti	SKROE/TAOI	seclazone	SEK/LA/ZOEN
scrotiform	SKROET/FORM	seclusion	SE/KLAOUGS
scrotitis	SKROE/TAOITS	seco-	SAOEK
scrotocele	SKROE/TO/SAO*EL		SE/KO
scrotoplasty	SKROE/TO/PLAS/TI	secobarbital	SAOEK/BARB/TAL
scrotum	SKROET/UM	secodont	SAOEK/DONT
	SKROE/TUM	Seconal	SEK/NAL
scruple	SKRAOUP/-L		SEK/NOL
scrupulosity	SKRAOUP/LOS/TI	second	SEKD
scrupulous	SKRAOUP/LOUS	secondaries	SEK/DAIR/-S
scum	SKUM		SEK/ON/DAIR/-S
scurf	SKUR/-F	secondarily	SEK/DAIR/LI
scurvy	SKUR/VI		SEK/ON/DAIR/LI
scultetus	SKUL/TAOE/TUS	secondary	SEK/DAIR
scuta	SKAOU/TA		SEK/ON/DAIR
scutate	SKAOU/TAIT	secret(o)-	SE/KRAOET
scute	SKAOUT		SE/KRAOE/T(O)
scutiform	SKAOUT/FORM	secreta	SE/KRAOE/TA
Scutigera	SKAOU/TIJ/RA	secretagogue	SE/KRAOET/GOG
scutul-	SKAOUT/L-	secrete	SE/KRAOET
	SKAOUT/YAOU/L-	secretin	SE/KRAOE/TIN
	SKAOUT/YU/L-	secretinase	SE/KRAOET/NAIS
	SKAOUFP/L-	secretion	SE/KRAOEGS
	SKAOUFP/YAOU/L-	secretoinhibitory	SE/KRAOET/IN/HIB/TOIR
	SKAOUFP/YU/L-	secretomotor	SE/KRAOET/MOE/TOR
scutula	SKAOUT/LA	secretomotory	SE/KRAOET/MOET/RI
	SKAOUFP/LA	secretor	SE/KRAOE/TOR
scutular	SKAOUT/LAR	secretory	SE/KRAOET/RI
	SKAOUFP/LAR		SE/KRE/TOIR
scutulum	SKAOUT/LUM		SAOEK/RE/TOIR
	SKAOUFP/LUM	sectarian	SEK/TAIRN
scutum	SKAOUT/UM	sectile	SEK/TAOIL
	SKAOU/TUM		SEK/TIL
scybala	SIB/LA	sectio	SEK/SHOE
scybalous	SIB/LOUS	section	S*EBGS
scybalum	SIB/LUM	sectiones	SEK/SHOE/NAOEZ
scyphiform	SAOIF/FORM	sector	SEK/TOR
scyphoid	SAOI/FOID	sectoranopia	SEK/TOR/AN/OEP/YA
	SAOIF/OID		SEK/TOR/AI/NOEP/YA
scythropasmus	SAOI/THRO/PAZ/MUS	sectorial	SEK/TOIRL
scytoblastema	SAOIT/BLAS/TAOE/MA	Sectral	SEK/TRAL
se(v)-	SE (unless combined with a	secular	SEK/KLAR
	consonant)	secunda	SE/KUN/DA
	(*not* SAOE; see "see")		

secundi	SE/KUN/DAOI	sejunction	SE/JUNGS
secundi-	SE/KUND	selachian	SE/LAIK/YAN
	SE/KUN/DI	selaphobia	SAOEL/FOEB/YA
secundigravida	SE/KUND/GRAV/DA		SE/LA/FOEB/YA
secundina	SEK/UN/DAOI/NA	Seldane	SEL/DAIN
	SE/KUN/DAOI/NA	seldom	SEL/DOM
secundinae	SEK/UN/DAOI/NAE		SELD/OM
	SE/KUN/DAOI/NAE	selection	SL*EBGS
secundines	SEK/UN/DAOEN/-S		SE/L*EBGS
	SE/KUN/DAOEN/-S	selective	SLEKT/IV
	SEK/UN/DAOIN/-S		SE/LEKT/IV
	SE/KUN/DAOIN/-S	selectivity	SLEK/TIV/TI
secundipara	SEK/UN/DIP/RA		SE/LEK/TIV/TI
	SE/KUN/DIP/RA	selene	SE/LAOE/NAOE
secundiparity	SE/KUND/PAIR/TI		SLAOE/NAOE
secundiparous	SEK/UN/DIP/ROUS	selenium	SE/LAOEN/YUM
	SE/KUN/DIP/ROUS		SLAOEN/YUM
secundum	SE/KUND/UM		SE/LEN/YUM
	SE/KUN/DUM		SLEN/YUM
sed (sedimentation) rate	SED/RAIT	selenocysteine	SE/LAOEN/SIS/TAOEN
Sedapap	SED/PAP		SLAOEN/SIS/TAOEN
sedate	SE/DAIT	selenodont	SE/LAOEN/DONT
sedation	SE/DAIGS		SLAOEN/DONT
sedative	SED/TIV	selenomethionine	SE/LAOEN/ME/THAOI/NAOEN
sedentary	SED/EN/TAIR		SLAOEN/ME/THAOI/NAOEN
	SED/SPWAIR		SEL/NO/ME/THAOI/NAOEN
sedigitate	SE/DIJ/TAIT	Selenomonas	SE/LAOEN/MOE/NAS
sediment	SED/-MT		SLAOEN/MOE/NAS
sedimentable	SED/-MT/-BL		SAOEL/NO/MOE/NAS
sedimentate	SED/MEN/TAIT	selenous	SE/LAOEN/OUS
	SED/-MT/TAIT	self	SEL/-F
sedimentation	SED/MEN/TAIGS	self-	SEFL
	SED/-MT/TAIGS	-self	*S (attached to stroke)
sedimentator	SED/MEN/TAI/TOR	self-abasement	SEFL/AI/BAIS/-MT
	SED/-MT/TAI/TOR	self-absorbed	SEFL/AB/SORB/-D
sedimentometer	SED/MEN/TOM/TER	self-accusation	SEFL/AK/YAOU/SAIGS
sedimentum	SED/MEN/TUM	self-analysis	SEFL/ANL/SIS
	SED/-MT/UM		SEFL/AI/NAL/SIS
sedoheptulose	SAOED/HEPT/LOES	self-awareness	SEFL/AI/WAIR/*NS
	SAOED/HEP/TAOU/LOES	self-centeredness	SEFL/SEN/TER/D*NS
	SE/DO/HEPT/LOES		SEFL/SENT/ER/D*NS
	SE/DO/HEP/TAOU/LOES	self-commitment	SEFL/KMIT/-MT
sedopeptose	SAOED/PEP/TOES	self-conscious	SEFL/KON/-RBS
	SE/DO/PEP/TOES	self-control	SEFL/KROL
seeberi	SAOEB/RAOI		SEFL/KON/TROL
	SAOE/BER/RAOI	self-differentiation	SEFL/DIFRN/SHAIGS
seed	SAOED	self-digestion	SEFL/DI/JEGS
Seeligmuller	ZAI/LIG/MIL/ER	self-discovery	SEFL/DIS/KOV/RI
	ZAI/LIK/MIL/ER	self-fermentation	SEFL/FER/MEN/TAIGS
Seessel	ZAI/SEL		SEFL/FERMT/TAIGS
seg (segmented neutrophil)	SEG	self-fertilization	SEFL/FERT/LI/ZAIGS
segment	SEG/-MT		SEFL/FER/TIL/ZAIGS
segmenta	SEG/MEN/TA	self-hypnosis	SEFL/HIP/NOE/SIS
segmental	SEG/MEN/TAL	self-image	SEFL/IM/AJ
segmentales	SEG/MEN/TAI/LAOEZ	self-inductance	SEFL/IN/DUK/TANS
segmentalis	SEG/MEN/TAI/LIS	self-infection	SEFL/IN/F*EBGS
segmentation	SEG/MEN/TAIGS	self-inflicted	SEFL/IN/FLIKT/-D
segmentectomy	SEG/MEN/TEKT/M*I	selfing	SEL/-FG
segmented	SEG/-MTD	self-knowledge	SEFL/NOJ
	SEG/-MT/-D		SEFL/NOL/EJ
segmenter	SEG/-MT/ER	self-limited	SEFL/LIMT/-D
	SEG/MEN/TER	self-love	SEFL/LOV
segmenti	SEG/MEN/TAOI	self-poisoning	SEFL/POI/SON/-G
Segmentina	SEG/MEN/TAOI/NA	self-stimulation	SEFL/STIM/LAIGS
segmentum	SEG/MEN/TUM	self-suspension	SEFL/SUS/PENGS
segnis	SEG/NIS	self-tolerance	SEFL/TOL/RANS
segregation	SEG/GAIGS	selfwise	SEFL/WAO*IZ
	SEG/RE/GAIGS		SEL/-F/WAO*IZ
segregator	SEG/GAI/TOR	Selivanoff	SE/LIV/NOF
	SEG/RE/GAI/TOR	sella	SEL/LA
segs (segmented neutrophils)		sella turcica	SEL/LA/TURS/KA
	SEG/-S	sellae	SEL/LAE
Sehrt	SAIRT	sellar	SEL/LAR
Seidel	SAOI/DEL	sellaris	SEL/LAI/RIS
Seidelin	SAOID/LIN	Seller	K-P/SEL/ER
Seidlitz	SAOID/LITS	Sellick	SEL/IK
Seignette	SAO*IN/YET	Selsun Blue	SEL/SUN/BLU
	SAOIN/Y*ET	Selsun Lotion	SEL/SUN/LOEGS
	(not SAOIN/YET; see sign yet)	Selter	SEL/TER
Seiler	SAOIL/ER		SELT/ER
	SAOI/LER	semantic	SE/MANT/IK
seism(o)-	SAOIZ/M(O)	semantics	SE/MANT/IK/-S
	SAOIS/M(O)	semasiology	SE/MAIS/YOLG
seismesthesia	SAOIZ/MES/THAOEZ/YA	semelincident	SEM/EL/INS/DINT
seismocardiogram	SAOIZ/MO/KARD/YO/GRAM	semelparity	SEM/EL/PAIR/TI
seismocardiography	SAOIZ/MO/KARD/YOG/FI	semelparous	SEM/EL/PROUS
seismotherapy	SAOIZ/MO/THER/PI		SEM/EL/PA/ROUS
seizure	SAOEZ/YUR	semen	SE/MEN
	SAOEZ/SHUR	semenologist	see seminologist

semenology	*see* seminology	semiprone	SEM/PROEN
semenuria	*see* seminuria	semiquantitative	SEM/KWANT/TAIT/IV
semi-	SEM	semiquinone	SEM/KWIN/OEN
semialdehyde	SEM/ALD/HAOID		SEM/KWI/NOEN
semiantigen	SEM/A*ENT/JEN	semirecumbent	SEM/RE/KUM/BENT
semiapochromat	SEM/AP/KROE/MAT	semiprivate	SEM/PRAOIVT
semiapochromatic	SEM/AP/KROE/MAT/IK		SEM/PRAOI/VAT
semicanal	SEM/KA/NAL	semis	SE/MIS
semicanales	SEM/KA/NAI/LAOEZ	semisideratio	SEM/SID/RAI/SHOE
semicanalis	SEM/KA/NAI/LIS		SEM/SID/RAIRB/YOE
semicartilaginous	SEM/KART/LAJ/NOUS	semisomnus	SEM/SOM/NUS
Semicid	SEM/SID	semisopor	SEM/SOE/POER
semicircular	SEM/SIRK/LAR	semispeculum	SEM/SPEK/LUM
semicirculares	SEM/SIRK/LAI/RAOEZ	semispinal	SEM/SPAOINL
semicircularis	SEM/SIRK/LAI/RIS	semistarvation	SEM/STAR/VAIGS
semiclosed	SEM/KLOEZ/-D	Semisulcospina	SEM/SUL/KO/SPAOI/NA
semicoma	SEM/KO/MA	semisulcus	SEM/SUL/KUS
semicomatose	SEM/KOEM/TOES	semisupination	SEM/SAOUP/NAIGS
	SEM/KOM/TOES	semisupine	SEM/SAOU/PAOIN
semiconscious	SEM/KON/-RBS	semisynthetic	SEM/SIN/THET/IK
semicrista	SEM/KRIS/TA	semisystematic	SEM/S-M/MAT/IK
semidecussation	SEM/DE/KUS/SAIGS		SEM/S*IS/MAT/IK
semidiagrammatic	SEM/DAOI/GRA/MAT/IK	semitendinosus	SEM/TEND/NOE/SUS
semiflexion	SEM/FL*EBGS	semitendinous	SEM/TEND/NOUS
semifluctuating	SEM/FLUK/YAIT/-G	semitertian	SEM/TERGS
	SEM/FLUK/KHAIT/-G	semitrivial	SEM/TRIV/YAL
semiglutin	SEM/GLAOU/TIN	semivalent	SEM/VAIL/ENT
Semilente	SEM/LEN/TAI		SEM/VAI/LENT
Semilente Insulin	SEM/LEN/TAI/INS/LIN		SE/MIV/LENT
semilunar	SEM/LAOU/NAR		SEM/IV/LENT
semilunare	SEM/LAOU/NAI/RAOE	Semon	SE/MON
semiluxation	SEM/LUK/SAIGS	Semple'	SEFRP/-L
	SEM/LUX/AIGS		SEM/P-L
semimembranosi	SEM/MEM/BRA/NOE/SAOI	semustine	SE/MUS/TAOEN
semimembranosogastrocnemial		Senear	SE/NAOER
	SEM/MEM/BRA/NOES/GAS/TROK/	Senecio	SE/NAOES/YOE
	NAOEM/YAL		SE/NAOERB/YOE
	SEM/MEM/BRA/NOE/SO/GAS/		SE/NAOE/SHOE
	TROK/NAOEM/YAL	senecioic	SE/NAOES/YOIK
semimembranosus	SEM/MEM/BRA/NOE/SUS		SE/NAOES/YOE/IK
semimembranous	SEM/MEM/BRA/NOUS	seneciosis	SE/NAOES/YOE/SIS
semin(o)-	SEM/N(O)	senega	SEN/GA
	SAOEM/N(O)	senescence	SE/NES/ENS
semina	SAOEM/NA	senescent	SE/NES/ENT
seminal	SEM/NAL	Sengstaken	SENGS/TAIK/-N
seminalis	SEM/NAI/LIS		SENGS/TAI/KEN
	SAOEM/NAI/LIS	senile	SE/NAOIL
seminarcosis	SEM/NAR/KOE/SIS	senilis	SE/NAOI/LIS
semination	SEM/NAIGS		SE/NIL/LIS
seminiferous	SEM/NIF/ROUS	senilism	SE/NAOIL/IFM
	SAOEM/NIF/ROUS		SE/NIL/IFM
seminin	SAOEM/NIN	senility	SE/NIL/TI
	SEM/NIN		SNIL/TI
seminis	SEM/NIS	Seniors Chewable	SAOEN/YOR/-S/KHAOUBL/
seminologist	SAOEM/NO*LGS	Tablets	TAB/LET/-S
	SE/MEN/O*LGS	senium	SAOEN/YUM
	SEM/NO*LGS		SEN/YUM
seminology	SAOEM/NOLG	senna	SEN/NA
	SE/MIN/OLG	sennoside	SEN/SAOID
	SEM/NOLG		SEN/NO/SAOID
seminoma	SEM/NOE/MA	Senokot	SEN/KOT
	SAOEM/NOE/MA	Senokot-S	SEN/KOT/S-RBGS
seminomatous	SEM/NOEM/TOUS	SenokotXTRA	SEN/KOT/EX/TRA
	SAOEM/NOEM/TOUS	senopia	SE/NOEP/YA
seminormal	SEM/NOR/MAL	sensate	SEN/SAIT
seminose	SEM/NOES	sensation	SEN/SAIGS
seminuria	SAOEM/NAOUR/YA	sense	SENS
	SEM/NAOUR/YA	sensibiligen	SENS/BIL/JEN
semiography	SAOEM/YOG/FI	sensibilin	SENS/BIL/LIN
semiologic	SAOEM/YO/LOJ/IK	sensibilisin	SENS/BIL/SIN
semiology	SAOEM/YOLG	sensibilisinogen	SENS/BIL/SIN/JEN
semiopathic	SAOEM/YO/PA*T/IK	sensibilities	SENS/-BLTS
semiopen	SEM/OEP	sensibility	SENS/-BLT
	SEM/OEP/-N	sensibilization	SENS/BIL/ZAIGS
semiorbicular	SEM/OR/BIK/LAR		SENS/-BL/ZAIGS
semiosis	SAOEM/YOE/SIS	sensible	SENS/-BL
semiotic	SAOEM/YOT/IK	sensiferous	SEN/SIF/ROUS
	SEM/YOT/IK	sensigenous	SEN/SIJ/NOUS
semiotics	SAOEM/YOT/IK/-S	sensimeter	SEN/SIM/TER
	SEM/YOT/IK/-S	sensitive	SENS/TIV
semioval	SEM/OEVL	sensitivity	SENS/TIV/TI
	SEM/O/VAL	sensitization	SENS/TI/ZAIGS
semiovale	SEM/O/VAI/LAOE		SENS/TAOI/ZAIGS
semiparasite	SEM/PAR/SAOIT	sensitize	SENS/TAOIZ
semipenniform	SEM/PEN/FORM	sensitizer	SENS/TAOIZ/ER
semipermeable	SEM/PERM/YABL	sensitogen	SENS/TO/JEN
semiplacenta	SEM/PLA/SEN/TA	sensitometer	SENS/TOM/TER
semiplegia	SEM/PLAOE/JA	senso-	SENS
semipronation	SEM/PRO/NAIGS		SEN/SO

sensomobile	SENS/MOE/BAOIL	septipara	SEP/TIP/RA
	SENS/MOE/BAOEL	septivalent	SEPT/VAIL/ENT
	SENS/MOEBL		SEP/TIV/LENT
sensomobility	SENS/MOEBLT	septodermoplasty	SEPT/DERM/PLAS/TI
sensomotor	SENS/MOE/TOR	septomarginal	SEPT/MARJ/NAL
sensor	SEN/SOR	septonasal	SEPT/NAI/ZAL
Sensorcaine	SEN/SOR/KAIN	septoplasty	SEPT/PLAS/TI
sensori-	SENS/RI	septorhinoplasty	SEPT/RAOIN/PLAS/TI
sensoria	SEN/SOER/YA	septostomy	SEP/TO*S/M*I
	SEN/SOR/YA	septotome	SEPT/TOEM
sensorial	SEN/SOIRL	septotomy	SEP/TOT/M*I
	SEN/SOER/YAL	Septra	SEP/TRA
	SEN/SOR/YAL	Septra DS	SEP/TRA/D-RBGS/S*RBGS
sensoriglandular	SENS/RI/GLAND/LAR	Septra Tablets	SEP/TRA/TAB/LET/-S
sensorimetabolism	SENS/RI/ME/TAB/LIFM	septuagenarian	SEPT/JE/NAIRN
sensorimotor	SENS/RI/MOE/TOR	septula	SEPT/LU
sensorimuscular	SENS/RI/MUS/KLAR		SEP/TAOU/LA
sensorineural	SENS/RI/NAOURL		SEP/KHU/LA
sensorium	SEN/SOIRM	septulum	SEPT/LUM
	SEN/SOER/YUM		SEP/TAOU/LUM
	SEN/SOR/YUM		SEP/KHU/LUM
sensorivascular	SENS/RI/VAS/KLAR	septum	SEP/TUM
sensorivasomotor	SENS/RI/VAIS/MOE/TOR		SEPT/UM
	SENS/RI/VAS/MOE/TOR	septuplet	SEP/TUP/LET
sensory	SENS/RI		SEP/TAOUP/LET
sensual	SENS/YAOUL	sequel	SE/KWEL
	SENS/YUL	sequela	SE/KWEL/LA
sensualism	SENS/YAOUL/IFM		SE/KWAOE/LA
	SENS/YUL/IFM	sequelae	SE/KWEL/LAE
sensuality	SENS/YAL/TI		SE/KWAOE/LAE
	SENS/YAOUL/TI	sequence	SE/KWENS
	SENS/YUL/TI	sequence ladder	SE/KWENS/LAD/ER
sensuous	SENS/YOUS	sequential	SE/KWEN/-RBL
	SEN/SHOUS	sequester	SE/KW*ES/ER
sentic	SENT/IK	sequestra	SE/KWES/TRA
sentics	SENT/IK/-S	sequestral	SE/KWES/TRAL
sentient	SEN/SHENT	sequestrant	SE/KWES/TRANT
	SENT/YENT	sequestration	SE/KWES/TRAIGS
sentiment	SENT/-MT	sequestrectomy	SE/KWES/TREKT/M*I
sentinel	SENT/NEL	sequestrotomy	SE/KWES/TROT/M*I
sentisection	SENT/S*EBGS	sequestrum	SE/KWES/TRUM
	SEN/TI/S*EBGS	sequoiosis	SE/KOI/YOE/SIS
sepal	SE/PAL		SE/KWOI/YOE/SIS
sepaloid	SAOEP/LOID	ser(o)-	SAOER
	SEP/LOID		SAOER/R(O)
separation	SEP/RAIGS		SE/R(O)
	SPRAIGS	sera	SAOER/RA
separator	SEP/RAI/TOR	seral	SAOERL
	SPRAIT/TOR		SAOER/RAL
separatorium	SEP/RA/TOIRM	seralbumin	SAOER/AL/BAOU/MIN
	SEP/RA/TOER/YUM	serapheresis	SAOER/FRAOE/SIS
	SEP/RA/TOR/YUM	Ser-Ap-Es	SER/AP/ES
sepazonium	SEP/ZOEN/YUM	Serax	SER/AX
sepedogenesis	SEP/DO/JEN/SIS	sere	SAOER
sepedon	SEP/DON	serendipity	SERN/DIP/TI
sepedonogenesis	SEP/DOEN/JEN/SIS		SER/EN/DIP/TI
seperidol	SE/PER/DOL	serene	SE/RAOEN
sepia	SAOEP/YA	Serenoa	SER/NOE/WA
sepium	SAOEP/YUM	Serentil	SE/REN/TIL
-seps-	SEP/S-		SER/EN/TIL
sepses	SEP/SAOEZ	Sergent	SAIR/JAU
sepsis	SEP/SIS		SER/JAU
Sepsis violacea	SEP/SIS/VAOI/LAIS/YA	serial	SAOER/YAL
sept(o)-	SEPT	series	SAOER/RAOEZ
	SEP/T(O)		SAOER/AOEZ
septa	SEP/TA	seriflux	SER/FLUX
septal	SEP/TAL	serifuge	SER/FAOUJ
septales	SEP/TAI/LAOEZ	serine	SAOER/AOEN
septalis	SEP/TAI/LIS		(*not* SE/RAOEN; see serene)
septan	SEP/TAN	seriograph	SAOER/YO/GRAF
septate	SEP/TAIT	seriography	SAOER/YOG/FI
septation	SEP/TAIGS	serioscopy	SAOER/YOS/KPI
septectomy	SEP/TEKT/M*I	serious	SAOER/YOUS
septemia	SEP/TAOEM/YA	seriscission	SER/SIGS
septi	SEP/TAOI	seroalbuminous	SAOER/AL/BAOUM/NOUS
septic	SEPT/TIK	seroalbuminuria	SAOER/AL/BAOUM/NAOUR/YA
	SEPT/IK	seroanaphylaxis	SAOER/AN/FLAK/SIS
septicemia	SEPT/SAOEM/YA	serochrome	SAOER/KROEM
septicemic	SEPT/SAOEM/IK	serocolitis	SAOER/KO/LAOITS
septico-	SEPT/KO	seroconversion	SAOER/KON/VERGS
septicophlebitis	SEPT/KO/FLE/BAOITS	seroconvert	SAOER/KON/VERT
septicopyemia	SEPT/KO/PAOI/AOEM/YA	seroculture	SAOER/KUL/KHUR
septicopyemic	SEPT/KO/PAOI/AOEM/IK	serocystic	SAOER/S*IS/IK
septicozymoid	SEPT/KO/ZAOI/MOID	serodiagnosis	SAOER/DAOIG/NOE/SIS
septicum	SEPT/KUM	serodiagnostic	SAOER/DAOIG/NO*S/IK
septigravida	SEPT/GRAV/DA	seroenteritis	SAOER/SPWRAOITS
septile	SEPT/TAOIL	seroenzyme	SAOER/EN/ZAOIM
septimetritis	SEPT/ME/TRAOITS	seroepidemiologic	SAOER/EP/DAOEM/YO/LOJ/IK
septineuritis	SEPT/NAOU/RAOITS	seroepidemiology	SAOER/EP/DAOEM/YOLG

sero-fast	SAOER/H-F/FA*S	serovaccination	SAOER/VAX/NAIGS
	(*not* SAOER/FA*S; see sere fast)	serovar	SAOER/VAR
serofibrinous	SAOER/FAOI/BRI/NOUS	serozyme	SAOER/ZAOIM
	SAOER/FAOI/BRIN/OUS	Serpasil	SERP/SIL
serofibrous	SAOER/FAOI/BROUS	Serpasil-Apresoline	SERP/SIL/AI/PRES/LAOEN
seroflocculation	SAOER/FLOK/LAIGS	Serpasil-Esidrix	SERP/SIL/ES/DRIX
serofluid	SAOUR/FLAOUD	serpentaria	SER/PEN/TAIR/YA
serogastria	SAOER/GAS/TRAOE/YA	serpentine	SER/PEN/TAOEN
	SAOER/GAS/TRA		SER/PEN/TAOIN
serogenesis	SAOER/JEN/SIS	serpiginosa	SER/PIJ/NOE/SA
seroglobulin	SAOER/GLOB/LIN	serpiginosum	SER/PIJ/NOE/SUM
seroglycoid	SAOER/GLAOI/KOID		SER/PIG/NOES/UM
serohemorrhagic	SAOER/HEM/RAJ/IK	serpiginous	SER/PIJ/NOUS
serohepatitis	SAOER/HEP/TAOITS	serpigo	SER/PAOI/GOE
seroimmunity	SAOER/IM/MAOUN/TI	serrate	SER/RAIT
serolactescent	SAOER/LAK/TES/ENT	serrated	SER/RAIT/-D
serolemma	SAOER/LEM/MA	Serratia	SE/RAI/SHA
serolipase	SAOER/LIP/AIS		SE/RAIRB/YA
	SAOER/LAOI/PAIS		SER/RAI/SHA
serologic	SAOER/LOJ/IK		SER/RAIRB/YA
serological	SAOER/LOJ/KAL	Serratieae	SER/TAOI/YAE
serologist	SAOER/O*LGS	serration	SER/RAIGS
serology	SAOER/OLG	serratus	SER/RAI/TUS
	SE/ROLG	serrefine	SER/FAOEN
serolysin	SE/ROL/SIN		SAIR/FAOEN
seroma	SE/ROE/MA	Serres	SAIRS
seromembranous	SAOER/MEM/BRA/NOUS		SAIRZ
seromucoid	SAOER/MAOU/KOID	serrul-	SER/L-
	SAOER/MAOUK/OID		SER/YAOU/L-
seromucous	SAOER/MAOU/KOUS		SER/YU/L-
	SAOER/MAOUK/OUS	serrulate	SER/LAIT
seromucus	SAOER/MAOU/KUS	serrulated	SER/LAIT/-D
seromuscular	SAOUR/MUS/KLAR	Sertoli	SER/TOE/LAOE
Seromycin	SAOER/MAOI/SIN	serum	SAOERM
seronegative	SAOER/NEG/TIV		SAOER/UM
seronegativity	SAOER/NEG/TIV/TI	serumal	SE/RAOU/MAL
seroneutralization	SAOUR/NAOU/TRAL/ZAIGS	serum-fast	SAOERM/H-F/FA*S
seroperitoneum	SAOER/PERT/NAOEM	serumuria	SAOERM/YAOUR/YA
Serophene	SAOER/FAOEN		SAOER/UM/YAOUR/YA
serophysiology	SAOER/FIZ/YOLG	servation	SER/VAIGS
seroplastic	SAOER/PLA*S/IK	serve	SEFRB
seropneumothorax	SAOER/NAOUM/THOR/AX	Servetus	SER/VAOE/TUS
seropositive	SAOER/POZ/TIV	servomechanism	SEFRB/MEK/NIFM
seropositivity	SAOER/POZ/TIV/TI		SER/VO/MEK/NIFM
seroprevention	SAOER/PRE/VENGS	sesame	SES/MAOE
seroprognosis	SAOER/PROG/NOE/SIS	sesamoid	SES/MOID
seroprophylaxis	SAOER/PROEF/LAK/SIS	sesamoidea	SES/MOID/YA
seropurulent	SAOER/PAOUR/LENT	sesamoideae	SES/MOID/YAE
seropus	SAOER/PUS	sesamoiditis	SES/MOI/DAOITS
seroreaction	SAOER/RE/A*BGS	sesqui-	SES/KWI
serorelapse	SAOER/RE/LAPS	sesquihora	SES/KWI/HOR/RA
seroresistant	SAOER/RE/SIS/TANT	sesquihydrate	SES/KWI/HAOI/DRAIT
seroresistance	SAOER/RE/SIS/TANS	sesquioxide	SES/KWI/OK/SAOID
seroreversal	SAOER/RE/VER/SAL		SES/KWI/OX/AOID
serosa	SE/ROE/SA	sesquisulfate	SES/KWI/SUL/FAIT
serosae	SE/ROE/SAE	sesquisulfide	SES/KWI/SUL/FAOID
serosal	SE/ROE/SAL	sessile	SES/SIL
serosamucin	SE/ROES/MAOU/SIN		SES/SAOIL
	SE/ROE/SA/MAOU/SIN	set	SET
serosanguineous	SAOER/SANG/WIN/YOUS	seta	SE/TA
seroscopy	SAOER/OS/KPI	setaceous	SE/TAIRBS
	SE/ROS/KPI	setae	SE/TAE
serose	SAOER/OES	Setaria	SE/TAIR/YA
seroserous	SAOER/SAOER/OUS	setariasis	SAOET/RAOI/SIS
serositides	SAOER/SAOIT/DAOEZ		SAOET/RAOE/AI/SIS
	SAOER/SIT/DAOEZ	setback	SET/BA*K
serositis	SAOER/SAOITS	Setchenow	SEFP/NOF
serosity	SE/ROS/TI		SEFP/NOV
	SAOER/OS/TI	setiferous	SE/TIF/ROUS
serosum	SE/ROE/SUM	setigerous	SE/TIJ/ROUS
	SE/ROES/UM	seton	SE/TON
serosurvey	SAOER/SUR/VAI	setup	SET/*UP
serosynovial	SAOER/SNOEV/YAL	Seutin	SAOU/TAN
serosynovitis	SAOER/SIN/VAOITS	Sever	SAOEVR
serotaxis	SAOER/TAK/SIS		SAOEV/ER
serotherapeutical	SAOER/THER/PAOUT/KAL	sevoflurane	SEV/FLAOU/RAIN
serotherapist	SAOER/THER/P*IS		SAOEV/FLAOU/RAIN
serotherapy	SAOER/THER/PI	sevum	SE/VUM
serothorax	SAOER/THOR/AX		SAOEV/UM
serotina	SAOER/TAOI/NA	sew	SOE
serotinus	SAOER/TAOI/NUS	sewage	SAOUJ
serotonergic	SAOER/TO/NERJ/IK		SAOU/AJ
	SAOER/TOE/NERJ/IK	sewerge	SAORJ
serotonin	SAOER/TOE/NIN		SAOUR/AJ
serotoninergic	SAOER/TOEN/NERJ/IK	sex	SEX
	SAOER/TOE/NIN/ERJ/IK	sex-	SEX
serotoxin	SAOER/TOK/SIN		SEK/S-
serotype	SAOER/TAOIP	sex-conditioned	SEX/H-F/K-ND
serous	SAOER/OUS		SEX/H-F/KON/DIGS/-D

sexdigitate	SEX/DIJ/TAIT	Shiga	SHAOE/GA
sexduction	SEX/D*UBGS		SHI/GA
sex-influenced	SEX/H-F/IN/FLAOUNS/-D	shigella	SHI/GEL/LA
sexivalent	SEK/SIV/LENT	Shigella	K-P/SHI/GEL/LA
	SEX/VAIL/ENT	shigellae	SHI/GEL/LAE
sex-limited	SEX/H-F/LIMT/-D	shigellosis	SHIG/LOE/SIS
sex-linked	SEX/H-F/LIN/-KD	shikimate	SHI/KIM/AIT
	SEX/H-F/L*ING/-D	shikimic	SHI/KIM/IK
sexology	SEK/SOLG	shin	SHIN
	SEX/OLG	shingles	SHING/-LS
sexopathy	SEK/SOP/TH*I	ship	SHIP
	SEX/OP/TH*I	Shipley	SHIP/LAOE
sextan	SEX/TAN	shiver	SHIVR
sextigravida	S*EX/GRAV/DA	shoat	SHOET
	SEX/TI/GRAV/DA	shock	SHOK
sextipara	SEX/TIP/RA	shoddy	SHOD/DI
sextuplet	SEX/TUP/LET	shoe	SHAOU
	SEX/TAOUP/LET	Shope	SHOEP
sexual	SEX/YAOUL	shortsighted	SHORT/SAOIGT/-D
	SEX/YUL	shortsightedness	SHORT/SAOIGT/D*NS
	SEX/YAL	shot-compressor	SHOT/H-F/KPRES/SOR
sexuality	SEX/YAL/TI		SHOT/H-F/KOM/PRES/SOR
	SEX/YAOUL/TI	shot-feel	SHOT/H-F/FAOEL
	SEX/YUL/TI	shot-silk	SHOT/H-F/SIL/-K
sexualization	SEX/YAOUL/ZAIGS	shotty	SHOT/TI
	SEX/YUL/ZAIGS	shoulder	SHOELD/ER
	SEX/YAL/ZAIGS		SHOULD/ER
Seyler	SE/LER	shoulder-blade	SHOELD/ER/BLAID
shadow	SHAD/DOE		SHOULD/ER/BLAID
	SHA/DOE	shoulder slip	SHOELD/ER/SLIP
shadow-casting	SHAD/DOE/KA*S/-G		SHOULD/ER/SLIP
	SHA/DOE/KA*S/-G	show	SHOE
shadowgram	SHAD/DOE/GRAM	shower	SHOU/ER
	SHA/DOE/GRAM	Shrapnell	SHRAP/N*EL
shadowgraph	SHAD/DOE/GRAF		SHRA*P/NEL
	SHA/DOE/GRAF		SH-/RAP/N*EL
shadowgraphy	SHAD/DOE/GRAF/FI		SH-/RA*P/NEL
	SHA/DOE/GRAF/FI		(not SHRAP/NEL or SH-/RAP/NEL;
Shaeffer	SHAEFR		see shrapnel)
	SHAEF/ER	shudder	SHUD/ER
	(not SHAIFR or SHAIF/ER; see	Shulman	SHUL/MAN
	Schafer)	shunt	SHUNT
Shaffer	SHAIF/FER	Shwartzman	SWARTS/MAN
	(not SHAIFR or SHAIF/ER; see		SH-/WARTS/MAN
	Schafer)	Shy	K-P/SHAOI
shaft	SHAFT	siagantritis	SAOI/AG/AN/TRAOITS
shaggy	SHAG/GI	siagonantritis	SAOI/GON/AN/TRAOITS
shake	SHAIK	sial(o)-	SAOI/L(O)
shallow	SHAL/LOE		SAOIL
sham	SHAM		SAOI/AL
shamanism	SHAM/NIFM	sialaden	SAOI/AL/DEN
shamanismus	SHAM/NIZ/MUS	sialadenectomy	SAOI/LAD/NEKT/M*I
sham feeding	SHAM/FAOED/-G		SAOIL/AD/NEKT/M*I
shank	SHAN/-K	sialadenitis	SAOI/LAD/NAOITS
	SHA*NG		SAOIL/AD/NAOITS
shape	SHAIP	sialadenography	SAOI/LAD/NOG/FI
Sharpey	SHAR/PAOE		SAOIL/AD/NOG/FI
Shea	SHAI	sialadenosis	SAOI/LAD/NOE/SIS
shear	SHAER		SAOIL/AD/NOE/SIS
	(not SHAOER; see sheer)	sialadenotomy	SAOI/LAD/NOT/M*I
Shear	K-P/SHAER		SAOIL/AD/NOT/M*I
shears	SHAER/-S	sialadenotropic	SAOI/LAD/NO/TROP/IK
	SHAERS		SAOIL/AD/NO/TROP/IK
sheath	SHA*ET	sialagogic	SAOI/LA/GOJ/IK
	(not SHAO*ET; see sheathe)		SAOIL/GOJ/IK
sheathe	SHAO*ET	sialagogue	SAOI/AL/GOG
sheathing	SHAO*ET/-G	sialaporia	SAOI/LA/POER/YA
	SHA*ET/-G		SAOIL/POER/YA
Sheehan	SHAOE/HAN	sialectasia	SAOI/LEK/TAIZ/YA
	SHAOE/YAN		SAOIL/EK/TAIZ/YA
sheep-pox	SHAOEP/POX	sialectasis	SAOI/LEKT/SIS
sheet	SHAOET		SAOIL/EKT/SIS
Shekelton	SHEK/EL/TON	sialemesis	SAOI/LEM/SIS
Sheldon	SHEL/DON		SAOIL/EM/SIS
shelf	SHEL/-F	sialic	SAOI/AL/IK
shell	SHEL	sialidase	SAOI/AL/DAIS
shellac	SHEL/LAK	sialidosis	SAOI/AL/DOE/SIS
	(not SHE/LAK; see she lack)	sialine	SAOI/LAOEN
Shenton	SHEN/TON		SAOI/LAOIN
Shepard's Cream	SHEP/ARD/AOES/KRAOEM	sialism	SAOI/LIFM
Shepard's Skin Cream	SHEP/ARD/AOES/SKIN/KRAOEM	sialismus	SAOI/LIZ/MUS
Shepard's Soap	SHEP/ARD/AOES/SOEP	sialitis	SAOI/LAOITS
Shepherd	K-P/SHEP/ERD	sialoadenectomy	SAOI/LO/AD/NEKT/M*I
	K-P/SHEP/HERD	sialoadenitis	SAOI/LO/AD/NAOITS
Sherman	SHER/MAN	sialoadenotomy	SAOI/LO/AD/NOT/M*I
Sherrington	SHER/-G/TON	sialoaerophagia	SAOI/LO/AER/FAI/JA
	SHER/RING/TON	sialoaerophagy	SAOI/LO/AER/OF/JI
shield	SHAOELD	sialoangiectasis	SAOI/LO/AN/JEKT/SIS
shift	SHIFT	sialoangiography	SAOI/LO/AN/JOG/FI

sialoangiitis	SAOI/LO/AN/JAOITS	siderophile	SID/RO/FAOIL
sialocele	SAOI/LO/SAO*EL	siderophilin	SID/ROF/LIN
sialodochitis	SAOI/LO/DOE/KAOITS		SID/RO/FLIN
sialodochoplasty	SAOI/LO/DOEK/PLAS/TI		SID/RO/FIL/LIN
	SAOI/LO/DOE/KO/PLAS/TI	siderophilous	SID/ROF/LOUS
sialoductitis	SAOI/LO/DUK/TAOITS	siderophone	SID/RO/FOEN
sialogen	SAOI/LO/JEN		SI/DER/FOEN
sialogenous	SAOI/LOJ/NOUS	siderophore	SID/RO/FOER
sialogogic	SAOI/LO/GOJ/IK	sideroscope	SID/RO/SKOEP
sialogogue	SAOI/LO/GOG	siderosilicosis	SID/RO/SIL/KOE/SIS
sialogram	SAOI/LO/GRAM	siderosis	SID/ROE/SIS
sialograph	SAOI/LO/GRAF	Siderosphaera	SID/RO/SFAOER/RA
	SAOI/AL/GRAF		SID/RO/SFAOE/RA
sialography	SAOI/LOG/FI	siderotic	SID/ROT/IK
sialolith	SAOI/AL/L*IT	siderous	SID/ROUS
sialolithiasis	SAOI/LO/LI/THAOI/SIS	SIDS	SIDZ
sialolithotomy	SAOI/LO/LI/THOT/M*I	Siebold	SE/BOLT
sialology	SAOI/LOLG		SE/BOLD
sialoma	SAOI/LOE/MA	Siegert	SE/GERT
sialometaplasia	SAOI/LO/MET/PLAIZ/YA		SAOEG/ERT
sialometry	SAOI/LOM/TRI	Siegle	ZAOEG/-L
sialomucin	SAOI/LO/MAOU/SIN		SAOEG/-L
sialophagia	SAOI/LO/FAI/JA		SIG/-L
sialorrhea	SAOI/LO/RAOE/YA	siemens	SE/MENZ
sialoschesis	SAOI/LOS/KE/SIS		SE/MENS
sialosemiology	SAOI/LO/SAOEM/YOLG	Siemens	K-P/SE/MENZ
sialosis	SAOI/LOE/SIS		K-P/SE/MENS
sialostenosis	SAOI/LO/STE/NOE/SIS	Siemerling	SAOEM/ER/-LG
sialosyrinx	SAOI/LO/SIRNGS		SAOEM/ER/LING
	SAOI/LO/SIR/INGS	Sieur	SE/YUR
sialotic	SAOI/LOT/IK	sieve	SIV
sib	SIB	sievert	SE/VERT
sibericus	SAOI/BER/KUS	sigh	SAOI
sibilant	SIB/LANT	sight	SAOIGT
sibilus	SIB/LUS	sigma	SIG/MA
sibling	SIB/-LG	sigmasism	SIG/MA/SIFM
	SIB/LING	sigmatism	SIG/MA/TIFM
sibship	SIB/SHIP	sigmoid	SIG/MOID
Sibson	SIB/SON	sigmoid(o)-	SIG/MOID
sic	S*IK		SIG/MOI/D(O)
	(*not* SIK; see sick)	sigmoideae	SIG/MOID/YAE
sicca	SIK/KA	sigmoidectomy	SIG/MOI/DEKT/M*I
siccant	SIK/KANT	sigmoideum	SIG/MOID/YUM
siccative	SIK/TIV	sigmoiditis	SIG/MOI/DAOITS
sicchasia	SI/KAIZ/YA	sigmoidopexy	SIG/MOID/PEK/SI
	SIK/KAIZ/YA	sigmoidoproctostomy	SIG/MOID/PROK/TO*S/M*I
siccolabile	SIK/LAI/BIL	sigmoidorectostomy	SIG/MOID/REK/TO*S/M*I
	SIK/LAI/BAOIL	sigmoidoscope	SIG/MOID/SKOEP
siccostabile	SIK/STAI/BIL	sigmoidoscopy	SIG/MOI/DOS/KPI
	SIK/STAI/BAOIL	sigmoidosigmoidostomy	SIG/MOID/SIG/MOI/DO*S/M*I
siccus	SIK/KUS	sigmoidostomy	SIG/MOI/DO*S/M*I
sick	SIK	sigmoidotomy	SIG/MOI/DOT/M*I
sick bay	SIK/BAI	sigmoscope	SIG/MO/SKOEP
sickle	SIK/-L	Sigmund	ZIG/MAOUNT
sickle cell	SIK/-L/KREL		ZIG/MAOUND
sicklemia	SIK/LAOEM/YA		SIG/MUND
sicklemic	SIK/LAOEM/IK	sign	SAOIN
sickling	SIK/-LG	signa	SIG/NA
	SIK/LING	signature	SIG/NA/KHUR
sickness	SIK/*NS		SIGT
side	SAOID	signaturist	SIG/NA/KHUR/*IS
side effect	SAOID/EFKT		SIGT/*IS
	SAOID/E/FEKT	signe	SAO*EN
sider(o)-	SID/R(O)	significant	SIG/NIF/KANT
sideratio	SID/RAI/SHOE		SIG/KANT
	SID/RAIRB/YOE	significantly	SIG/NIF/KANT/LI
sideration	SID/RAIGS		SIG/KANT/LI
siderinuria	SID/RI/NAOUR/YA	Signorelli	SAOEN/YO/REL/LAOE
siderism	SID/RIFM		SIN/YO/REL/LAOE
sideroachrestic	SID/RO/AI/KR*ES/IK	Sigtab	SIG/TAB
Siderobacter	SID/RO/BAK/TER	silacea	SAOI/LAIS/YA
sideroblast	SID/RO/BLA*S		SI/LAIS/YA
sideroblastic	SID/RO/BLA*S/IK	silafocon	SIL/FOE/KON
sideroblastica	SID/RO/BLA*S/KA	silandrone	SI/LAN/DROEN
siderochrestic	SID/RO/KR*ES/IK	silane	SAOI/LAIN
siderochrestica	SID/RO/KR*ES/KA	silantiewi	SAOI/LAN/TAOU/WAOI
Siderococcus	SID/RO/KOK/KUS		SAOI/LANT/YAOU/WAOI
siderocyte	SID/RO/SAO*IT	Silber	SIL/BER
sideroderma	SID/RO/DER/MA	silence	SAOI/LENS
siderofibrosis	SID/RO/FAOI/BROE/SIS		SAOIL/ENS
siderogenous	SID/ROJ/NOUS	silent	SAOI/LENT
Sideromonas	SID/RO/MOE/NAS		SAOIL/ENT
sideronema	SID/RO/NAOE/MA	silex	SAOI/LEX
sideropenia	SID/RO/PAOEN/YA	Silex	K-P/SAOI/LEX
sideropenic	SID/RO/PAOEN/IK	silica	SIL/KA
Siderophacus	SID/ROEF/KUS	silicate	SIL/KAIT
	SID/ROE/FA/KUS	silicatosis	SIL/KA/TOE/SIS
siderophage	SID/RO/FAIJ	silicea	SI/LIS/YA
siderophil	SID/RO/FIL	siliceous	SI/LIRBS

400

silicic	SI/LIS/IK	sinal	SAOINL
	SLIS/IK	Sinarest	SAOIN/R*ES
silico-	SIL/KO	sincalide	SIN/KA/LAOID
silicoanthracosis	SIL/KO/AN/THRA/KOE/SIS		SIN/KLAOID
silicofluoride	SIL/KO/FLAOUR/AOID	sincipita	SIN/SIP/TA
	SIL/KO/FLAOU/RAOID	sincipital	SIN/SIP/TAL
silicol	SIL/KOL	sinciput	SIN/SI/PUT
silicon	SIL/KON		(not SINS/PUT; see since put(ting))
silicone	SIL/KOEN	Sine-Aid	SAOIN/AID
silicophosphate	SIL/KO/FOS/FAIT	sine delirio	SAOI/NAOE/DLIR/YOE
silicoproteinosis	SIL/KO/PROET/NOE/SIS		SAOI/NAOE/DE/LIR/YOE
silicosiderosis	SIL/KO/SID/ROE/SIS	sine dolore	SAOI/NAOE/DO/LOR/RAOE
silicosis	SIL/KOE/SIS		SAOI/NAOE/DO/LOER/RAOE
silicotic	SIL/KOT/IK	Sinemet	SAOIN/MET
silicotuberculosis	SIL/KO/TAOU/BERK/LOE/SIS	sinensis	SAOI/NEN/SIS
siliculose	SI/LIK/LOES		SI/NEN/SIS
	SLIK/LOES	Sine-Off	SAO*IN/AUF
siliqua	SIL/KWA		(not SAOIN/AUF; see sign off)
siliqua olivae	SIL/KWA/O/LAOI/VAE	Sinequan	SIN/KWAUN
siliquose	SIL/KWOES		SIN/KWAN
silk	SIL/-K	sinew	SIN/YAOU
Silvadene	SIL/VA/DAOEN	Sinex	SAOI/NEX
silvatic	SIL/VAT/IK	sing	SING
silver	SIL/VER	Singapore	SIN/GA/POER
Silver	K-P/SIL/VER		SING/POER
silverized	SIL/VER/AOIZ/-D	singe	SIN/-J
Silverman	SIL/VER/MAN	Singlet	SING/LET
silverskin	SIL/VER/SKIN	singultation	SIN/GUL/TAIGS
Silvester	SIL/V*ES/ER	singultous	SIN/GUL/TOUS
	SIL/VES/TER	singultus	SIN/GUL/TUS
Silvius	S*IL/VAOE/YUS	sinigrase	SIN/GRAIS
	S*IL/VUS	sinigrin	SIN/GRIN
	(not SIL/VAOE/YUS or SIL/VUS;	sinigrinase	SIN/GRIN/AIS
	see Sylvius)	sinister	SIN/STER
Simaruba	SIM/RAOU/BA	sinistr(o)-	SIN/STR(O)
simarubidin	SIM/RAOUB/DIN		SI/NIS/TR(O)
simesthesia	SIM/ES/THAOEZ/YA		SNIS/TR(O)
simethicone	SI/M*ET/KOEN	sinistra	SIN/STRA
	SAOI/M*ET/KOEN		SI/NIS/TRA
simian	SIM/YAN		SNIS/TRA
Similac	S*IM/LAK	sinistrad	SIN/STRAD
	SIM/LA*K		SI/NIS/TRAD
	SIM/MI/LAK		SINS/TRAD
	(not SIM/LAK; see similar lack)	sinistrae	SIN/STRAE
similia similibus	SI/MIL/YA/SI/MIL/BUS/		SI/NIS/TRAE
curantur	KAOU/RAN/TUR		SNIS/TRAE
	SMIL/YA/SMIL/BUS/KAOU/RAN/	sinistral	SIN/STRAL
	TUR		SI/NIS/TRAL
similimum	SI/MIL/MUM		SNIS/TRAL
	SMIL/MUM	sinistrality	SIN/STRAL/TI
Simmerlin	SIM/ER/LIN	sinistraural	SIN/STRAURL
Simmonds	SIM/ONDZ	sinistri	SIN/STRAOI
	SIM/MONDZ		SI/NIS/TRAOI
Simmons	SIM/MONS		SNIS/TRAOI
Simon	SAOI/MON	sinistrocardia	SIN/STRO/KARD/YA
	SI/MOEN	sinistrocerebral	SIN/STRO/SER/BRAL
Simonart	SI/MO/NAR	sinistrocular	SIN/STROK/LAR
	SIM/MO/NAR	sinistrocularity	SIN/STROK/LAIR/TI
Simonea folliculorum	SI/MOEN/YA/FLIK/LOR/UM	sinistrogyration	SIN/STRO/JAOI/RAIGS
Simonelli	SAOIM/NEL/LAOE	sinistromanual	SIN/STRO/MAN/YAOUL
Simons	SAOI/MONZ		SIN/STRO/MAN/YUL
	SAOI/MONS		SIN/STRO/MAN/YAL
Simonsiella	SAOI/MONS/YEL/LA	sinistropedal	SIN/STROP/DAL
simple	SIFRP/-L	sinistrorse	SIN/STRORS
	SIM/P-L	sinistrose	SIN/STROES
simpler	SIFRP/LER	sinistrotorsion	SIN/STRO/TORGS
	SIM/PLER	sinistrous	SIN/STROUS
simplex	SIM/PLEX		SI/NIS/TROUS
Simpson	SIFRP/SON		SNIS/TROUS
	SIM/-P/SON	sinistrum	SIN/STRUM
simpsoni	SIFRP/SO/NAOI		SI/NIS/TRUM
	SIFRP/SON/NAOI		SNIS/TRUM
	SIM/SO/NAOI	sink	SIN/-K
	SIM/SON/NAOI		S*ING
Sims	SIMZ	Sinkler	SIN/KLER
	SIMS	sino-	SAOIN
simul	SIM/UL		SAOI/NO
simulation	SIM/LAIGS	sinoatrial	SAOIN/AI/TRAL
simulator	SIM/LAI/TOR	sinoauricular	SAOIN/AU/RIK/LAR
Simuliidae	SAOIM/LAOE/DAE	sinobronchitis	SAOIN/BRON/KAOITS
	SIM/LAOE/DAE	sinography	SAOI/NOG/FI
Simulium	SI/MAOUL/YUM	sinopulmonary	SAOIN/PUL/MO/NAIR
	SAOI/MAOUL/YUM		SAOIN/PUM/NAIR
simultanagnosia	SAOI/MUL/TAN/AG/NOEZ/YA	sinospiral	SAOIN/SPAOIRL
	SAOIM/UL/TAN/AG/NOEZ/YA	sinovaginal	SAOIN/VAJ/NAL
	SAOI/MUL/TAIN/AG/NOEZ/YA	sinoventricular	SAOIN/VEN/TRIK/LAR
	SAOIM/UL/TAIN/AG/NOEZ/YA	sinter	SIN/TER
sin(o)-	SAOIN		SINT/ER
	SAOI/N(O)	sinu-	SIN/YAOU

	SIN/Y-	Sjogren	SHOE/GREN
	SAOIN/YAOU	Sjoqvist	SHOE/KW*IS
	SAOIN/Y-	skatol	SKAT/OL
sinuate	SIN/YAOU/AIT	skatole	SKAT/OEL
	SIN/YAIT	skatoxyl	SKA/TOK/SIL
sinuatrial	SIN/YAOU/AI/TRAL	skein	SKAIN
sinuauricular	SIN/YAOU/AU/RIK/LAR	skelasthenia	SKAOE/LAS/THAOEN/YA
Sinu-Clear	SAOIN/YAOU/KLAOER	Skelaxin	SKAOE/LAK/SIN
Sinufed	SAOIN/FED		SKE/LAK/SIN
	SAOIN/YAOU/FED	skeletal	SKEL/TAL
	SAOIN/YU/FED	skeleti	SKEL/TAOI
sinuitis	SAOIN/YAOITS	skeletin	SKEL/TIN
	SIN/YAOITS	skeletization	SKEL/TI/ZAIGS
Sinulin	SAOIN/YAOU/LIN	skeletodental	SKEL/TO/DEN/TAL
	SAOIN/YU/LIN	skeletogenous	SKEL/TOJ/NOUS
	SIN/YAOU/LIN	skeletogeny	SKEL/TOJ/N*I
	SIN/YU/LIN	skeletography	SKEL/TOG/FI
Sinumist	SAOIN/YAOU/M*IS	skeletology	SKEL/TOLG
	SAOIN/YU/M*IS	skeleton	SKEL/TON
sinuotomy	SAOIN/YOT/M*I	skeletopia	SKEL/TOEP/YA
	SAOIN/YAOU/OT/M*I	skeletopy	SKEL/TOE/PI
	SIN/YOT/M*I	Skene	SKAOEN
	SIN/YAOU/OT/M*I	skenitis	SKAOE/NAOITS
sinuous	SIN/YOUS	skenoscope	SKAOEN/SKOEP
sinus	SAOI/NUS	skeptophylaxis	SKEPT/FLAK/SIS
sinus-	SAOIN/S-		SKEP/TO/FLAK/SIS
sinusal	SAOIN/SAL	skew	SKAOU
	SAOI/NUS/SAL	skewfoot	SKAOU/FAOT
sinusitis	SAOIN/SAOITS	skia-	SKAOI
sinusoid	SAOIN/SOID		SKAOI/YA
sinusoidal	SAOIN/SOI/DAL	skiagram	SKAOI/GRAM
sinusoidalization	SAOIN/SOI/DAL/ZAIGS	skiagraph	SKAOI/GRAF
sinusotomy	SAOIN/SOT/M*I	skiagraphica	SKAOI/GRAF/KA
sinuum	SIN/YUM	skiagraphy	SKAOI/AG/FI
	SIN/YAOUM	skiameter	SKAOI/AM/TER
sinuventricular	SAOI/NAOU/VEN/TRIK/LAR	skiametry	SKAOI/AM/TRI
siphon	SAOI/FON	skiascope	SKAOI/SKOEP
siphonage	SAOIF/NAJ	skiascopy	SKAOI/AS/KPI
	SAOI/FON/AJ	skiascotometry	SKAOI/SKOE/TOM/TRI
Siphona irritans	SAOI/FOE/NA/IR/TANS	Skillern	SKIL/LERN
	SAOI/FON/NA/IR/TANS	skimming	SKIM/-G
Siphonaptera	SAOIF/NAPT/RA	skin	SKIN
	SAOI/FO/NAPT/RA	Skinner	SKIN/ER
Siphunculata	SAOI/FUN/KLAI/TA	Sklowsky	SKLOU/SKI
	SAOI/FUN/KAOU/LAI/TA	Skoda	SKOE/DA
Siphunculina	SAOI/FUN/KLAOI/NA	skodaic	SKOE/DAI/IK
	SAOI/FUN/KAOU/LAOI/NA	skull	SKUL
Sipple	SIP/-L	skullcap	SKUL/KAP
Sippy	SIP/PI	slab-off	SLAB/H-F/AUF
siqua	SAOI/KWA	slant	SLANT
sireniform	SAOI/REN/FORM	slaty	SLAI/TI
sirenomelia	SAOIR/NO/MAOEL/YA		SLAIT/TI
sirenomelus	SAOIR/NOM/LUS	SLE	S-RBGS/L*RBGS/*ERBGS
siriasis	SI/RAOI/SIS	sleep	SLAOEP
-sis	SIS	sleepiness	SLAOE/PI/*NS
siro	SAOI/ROE		SLAOEP/PI/*NS
sirup	*see* syrup	sleeplessness	SLAOEP/LES/*NS
sismotherapy	SIS/MO/THER/PI	sleep talking	SLAOEP/TAUK/-G
sisomicin	SIS/MAOI/SIN	sleep walker	SLAOEP/WAUK/ER
sissorexia	SIS/REX/YA	sleep walking	SLAOEP/WAUK/-G
sister	S*IS/ER	slide	SLAOID
	SIS/TER	slime	SLAOIM
Sistrurus	SIS/TRAOU/RUS	sling	SLING
site	SAOIT	slit	SLIT
siti(o)-	SIT/Y(O)	Slo-bid Gyrocaps	SLOE/BID/JAOIR/KAP/-S
sitiology	SIT/YOLG	Slo-Niacin Tablets	SLOE/NAOI/SIN/TAB/LET/-S
sitiomania	SIT/YO/MAIN/YA	slope	SLOEP
sito-	SAO*IT	Slo-Phyllin	SLOE/FLIN
	SAO*I/TO		SLOE/FIL/LIN
	(*not* SAOIT or SAOI/TO; see cyto-)	Slo-Phyllin GG	SLOE/FLIN/G-RBGS/G*RBGS
sitology	SAO*I/TOLG		SLOE/FIL/LIN/G-RBGS/G*RBGS
sitomania	SAO*IT/MAIN/YA	Slo-Phyllin Gyrocaps	SLOE/FLIN/JAOIR/KAP/-S
sitostane	SAO*IT/STAIN		SLOE/FIL/LIN/JAOIR/KAP/-S
sitosterol	SAO*I/TO*S/ROL	slotted	SLOT/-D
	SAO*IT/STAOER/OL	slough	SLUF
sitosterolemia	SAO*I/TO*S/ROL/AOEM/YA		SLOF
	SAO*IT/STAOER/LAOEM/YA	sloughing	SLUF/-G
sitotaxis	SAO*IT/TAK/SIS		SLOF/-G
sitotherapy	SAO*IT/THER/PI	slovenly	SLOVN/LI
sitotoxin	SAO*IT/TOK/SIN		SLOV/-N/LI
sitotoxism	SAO*IT/TOK/SIFM	Slow Fe	SLOE/FAOE
	SAO*IT/TOX/IFM	Slow-K	SLOE/K-RBGS
sitotropism	SAO*I/TOT/RO/PIFM		SLOE/KAI
situation	SIFP/WAIGS	slows	SLOE/-S
situational	SIFP/WAIGS/NAL		SLOEZ
situs	SAOI/TUS	Sluder	SLAOUD/ER
sitz	SITS	sludge	SLUJ
size	SAOIZ	sludging	SLUJ/-G
sizer	SAOIZ/ER	slug	SLUG

sluice	SLAOUS	sodic	SOED/IK
sluiceway	SLAOUS/WA*I	sodii	SOED/YAOI
slur	SLUR	sodiocitrate	SOED/YO/SI/TRAIT
slurry	SLUR/RI		SOED/YO/SIT/RAIT
slyke	SLAOIK	sodiotartrate	SOED/YO/TAR/TRAIT
SMA Infant Formula	S-RBGS/M*RBGS/A*RBGS/IN/	sodium	SOED/YUM
	FANT/FORM/LA	sodium bicarbonate	SOED/YUM/B*I/KARB/NAIT
small	SMAUL		SOED/YUM/B*I/KARB/NAT
	SMAL	sodium chloride	SOED/YUM/KLOR/AOID
smallpox	SMAUL/POX	sodium fluoride	SOED/YUM/FLAOUR/AOID
	SMAL/POX	sodium iodide	SOED/YUM/AOI/DAOID
smear	SMAOER	sodium phosphate	SOED/YUM/FOS/FAIT
Smee cell	SMAOE/KREL	Sodium Sulamyd	SOED/YUM/SAOUL/MID
smegma	SMEG/MA		SOED/YUM/SUL/MID
smegmalith	SMEG/MA/L*IT	sodoku	SOE/DOE/KAOU
smegmatic	SMEG/MAT/IK	sodomist	SOD/M*IS
smegmolith	SMEG/MO/L*IT	sodomite	SOD/MAOIT
smell	SMEL	sodomy	SOD/M*I
smell-brain	SMEL/BRAIN	Soemmering	SEM/RING
Smellie	SMEL/LAOE		SEM/ER/-G
smelly	SMEL/LI	Sofarin	SOEF/RIN
Smilax	SMAOI/LAX		SOE/FA/RIN
Smith	SM*IT	softening	SOF/-NG
Smith-Petersen	SM*IT/H-F/PAOET/ER/SEN		SOFT/-NG
smog	SMOG	soja	*see* soya
smoke	SMOEK	sokosha	SOE/KOE/SHA
smudge	SMUJ	sokosho	SOE/KOE//SHOE
Smurf Vitamins	SMUR/-F/VAOIT/MIN/-S	sol	SOL
smut	SMUT	Solanaceae	SOEL/NAIS/YAE
snail	SNAIL	solanaceous	SOEL/NAIRBS
snake	SNAIK	solandrine	SOE/LAN/DRIN
snakebite	SNAIK/BAOIT	solanine	SOEL/NAOEN
snap	SNAP	solanochromene	SOL/NO/KROE/MAOEN
snare	SNAIR		SOEL/NO/KROE/MAOEN
sneeze	SNAOEZ	solanocyte	SOE/LAN/SAO*IT
Snell	SNEL	solanoid	SOE/LA/NOID
Snellen	SNEL/-N		(*not* SOEL/NOID; see solenoid)
Snider	SNAOID/ER	Solanum	SOE/LAI/NUM
sniffle	SNIFL		SOE/LAIN/UM
	SNIF/-L		SOE/LAN/UM
snore	SNOER	solapsone	SOE/LAP/SOEN
	SNOR	Solaquin	SOEL/KWIN
snout	SNOUT	Solaquin Forte	SOEL/KWIN/FOR/TAI
snow	SNOE	solar	SOE/LAR
snowblindness	SNOE/BLAOIND/*NS	solare	SOE/LAI/RAOE
snuff	SNUF		SOE/LAR/RAOE
snuffles	SNUF/-LS	solarium	SOE/LAIRM
Snyder	SNAO*ID/ER		SOE/LAIR/YUM
	SNAO*I/DER	solasulfone	SOL/SUL/FOEN
	(*not* SNAOID/ER or SNAOI/DER;		SOEL/SUL/FOEN
	see Snider)	Solatene	SOL/TAOEN
soap	SOEP	solation	SOL/AIGS
soapstone	SOEP/STOEN		SOL/LAIGS
soar	SAOR	Solbar	SOL/BAR
socaloin	SOE/KAL/WIN	Solbar Plus	SOL/BAR/PLUS
socia	SOERB/YA	solder	SOD/ER
	SOE/SHA	sole	SOEL
socia parotidis	SOERB/YA/PROT/DIS	solei	SOEL/YAOI
	SOERB/YA/PA/ROT/DIS	Solenoglypha	SOEL/NOG/LI/FA
	SOE/SHA/PROT/DIS	solenoid	SOEL/NOID
	SOE/SHA/PA/ROT/DIS		SOL/NOID
social	SOERBL	solenonychia	SOEL/NO/NIK/YA
socialization	SOERBL/ZAIGS	Solenopotes capillatus	SOEL/NO/POE/TAOEZ/KAP/LAI/
socio-	SOES/YO		TUS
	SOERB/YO	solenopsin	SOEL/NOP/SIN
socioacusis	SOES/YO/AI/KAOU/SIS	Solenopsis	SOEL/NOP/SIS
sociobiologic	SOES/YO/BAO*I/LOJ/IK	soleus	SOEL/YUS
sociobiological	SOES/YO/BAO*I/LOJ/KAL		SOE/LAOE/YUS
sociobiologist	SOES/YO/BAO*I/O*LGS	Solfoton	SOL/FO/TON
sociobiology	SOES/YO/BAO*I/OLG	Solganal	SOL/GA/NAL
sociocentric	SOES/YO/SEN/TRIK		SOLG/NAL
sociocentrism	SOES/YO/SEN/TRIFM	solid	SOL/ID
sociocosm	SOES/YO/KOFM	Solidago	SOL/DAI/GOE
socioeconomic	SOES/YO/EK/NOM/IK	solidism	SOL/DIFM
	SOES/YO/KMIK	solidist	SOL/D*IS
sociogenesis	SOES/YO/JEN/SIS	solidistic	SOL/D*IS/IK
sociogenic	SOES/YO/JEN/IK	solidus	SOL/DUS
sociogram	SOES/YO/GRAM	soliped	SOL/PED
sociologist	SOES/YO*LGS	solipsism	SOE/LIP/SIFM
sociology	SOES/YOLG		SOL/IP/SIFM
sociomedical	SOES/YO/MED/KAL	solipsistic	SOE/LIP/S*IS/IK
sociometry	SOES/YOM/TRI		SOL/IP/S*IS/IK
sociopath	SOES/YO/PA*T	solitary	SOL/TAIR
sociopathic	SOES/YO/PA*T/IK	sollicitans	SLIS/TANZ
sociopathy	SOES/YOP/TH*I		SO/LIS/TANZ
sociotherapy	SOES/YO/THER/PI		SOL/LIS/TANZ
socket	SOKT	sol-lunar	SOL/LAOU/NAR
	SOK/ET	solubility	SOL/YAOUBLT
soda	SOE/DA		SOL/YUBLT

	SOL/-BLT
soluble	SOL/YAOUBL
	SOL/YUBL
	SOL/-BL
Solu-Cortef	SOL/KOR/TEF
	SOL/YAOU/KOR/TEF
	SOL/YU/KOR/TEF
solum	SOE/LUM
	SOEL/UM
Solu-Medrol	SOL/MED/ROL
	SOL/YAOU/MED/ROL
	SOL/YU/MED/ROL
solute	SOL/YAOUT
	SOE/LAOUT
solutio	SOE/LAOU/SHOE
	SOE/LAOURB/YOE
	SLAOU/SHOE
	SLAOURB/YOE
solution	SOE/LAOUGS
	SLAOUGS
	SO/LAOUGS
solvable	SOL/VABL
	SOL/-V/-BL
solvate	SOL/VAIT
solvation	SOL/VAIGS
solvent	SOL/VENT
Solvet	SOL/VET
solvolysis	SOL/VOL/SIS
soma	SOE/MA
Soma Compound	SOE/MA/KOM/POUND
Soma Tablets	SOE/MA/TAB/LET/-S
somal	SOE/MAL
soman	SOE/MAN
somasthenia	SOE/MAS/THAOEN/YA
	SOEM/AS/THAOEN/YA
somat(o)-	SOEM/T(O)
	SOE/MAT
	SMAT
somatagnosia	SOEM/TAG/NOES/YA
	SOEM/TAG/NOEZ/YA
somatalgia	SOEM/TAL/JA
somatasthenia	SOEM/TAS/THAOEN/YA
	SOE/MAT/AS/THAOEN/YA
somatesthesia	SOEM/TES/THAOEZ/YA
	SOEM/MAT/ES/THAOEZ/YA
somatesthetic	SOEM/TES/THET/IK
	SOE/MAT/ES/THET/IK
-somatia	SOE/MAI/SHA
	SOE/MAIRB/YA
	SMAI/SHA
	SMAIRB/YA
somatic	SOE/MAT/IK
	SMAT/IK
somatic(o)-	SOE/MAT/K(O)
	SMAT/KO
somaticosplanchnic	SOE/MAT/KO/SPLANG/NIK
somaticovisceral	SOE/MAT/KO/VIS/RAL
somatist	SOEM/T*IS
somatization	SOE/MAT/ZAIGS
	SMAT/ZAIGS
	SOEM/TI/ZAIGS
somatoceptor	SOEM/TO/SEP/TOR
	SOE/MAT/SEP/TOR
somatochrome	SOEM/TO/KROEM
	SOE/MAT/KROEM
somatoderm	SOEM/TO/DERM
	SOE/MAT/DERM
somatodidymus	SOEM/TO/DID/MUS
somatodymia	SOEM/TO/DIM/YA
somatoform	SOE/MAT/FORM
somatogenesis	SOEM/TO/JEN/SIS
somatogenetic	SOEM/TO/JE/NET/IK
	SOE/MAT/JE/NET/IK
somatogenic	SOEM/TO/JEN/IK
somatogram	SOE/MAT/GRAM
	SOEM/TO/GRAM
somatoliberin	SOEM/TO/LIB/RIN
somatology	SOEM/TOLG
somatomammotropin	SOEM/TO/MAM/TROE/PIN
somatome	SOEM/TOEM
somatomegaly	SOEM/TO/MEG/LI
somatomedin	SOEM/TO/MAOE/DIN
somatometry	SOEM/TOM/TRI
somatomic	SOEM/TOM/IK
somatopagus	SOEM/TOP/GUS
somatopathic	SOEM/TO/PA*T/IK
somatopathy	SOEM/TOP/TH*I
somatophrenia	SOEM/TO/FRAOEN/YA
somatophyte	SOEM/TO/FAOIT

	SOE/MAT/FAOIT
somatoplasm	SOEM/TO/PLAFM
	SOE/MAT/PLAFM
somatopleural	SOEM/TO/PLAOURL
somatopleure	SOEM/TO/PLAOUR
	SOE/MAT/PLAOUR
somatoprosthetics	SOEM/TO/PROS/THET/IK/-S
somatopsychic	SOEM/TO/SAOIK/IK
somatopsychosis	SOEM/TO/SAOI/KOE/SIS
somatoschisis	SOEM/TOS/KI/SIS
somatoscopy	SOEM/TOS/KPI
somatosensory	SOEM/TO/SENS/RI
somatosexual	SOEM/TO/SEX/YAOUL
somatosplanchnic	SOEM/TO/SPLANG/NIK
somatosplanchnopleuric	SOEM/TO/SPLANG/NO/PLAOUR/ IK
somatostatin	SOEM/TO/STAT/TIN
somatostatinoma	SOEM/TO/STAT/NOE/MA
somatotherapy	SOEM/TO/THER/PI
somatotonia	SOEM/TO/TOEN/YA
somatotopagnosis	SOEM/TO/TOP/AG/NOE/SIS
somatotopic	SOEM/TO/TOP/IK
somatotopy	SOEM/TOT/PI
somatotridymus	SOEM/TO/TRID/MUS
somatotrope	SOEM/TO/TROEP
	SOE/MAT/TROEP
somatotroph	SOEM/TO/TROEF
	SOE/MAT/TROEF
somatotrophic	SOEM/TO/TROFK
	SOEM/TO/TROEFK
somatotrophin	SOEM/TO/TROEFN
somatotropic	SOEM/TO/TROP/IK
somatropin	SOEM/TO/TROE/PIN
somatotropism	SOEM/TO/TROEP/IFM
somatotype	SOEM/TO/TAOIP
	SOE/MAT/TAOIP
somatotyping	SOEM/TO/TAOIP/-G
	SOE/MAT/TAOIP/-G
somatotypology	SOEM/TO/TAOI/POLG
somatotypy	SOEM/TO/TAOI/PI
	SOE/MAT/TAOI/PI
somatrem	SOEM/TREM
some-	SM-
-some	SOEM (long o)
	SM- (short o)
somesthesia	SOE/MES/THAOEZ/YA
	SOEM/ES/THAOEZ/YA
somesthetic	SOE/MES/THET/IK
	SOEM/ES/THET/IK
-somia	SOEM/YA
-somiasis	SOE/MAOI/SIS
-somic	SOEM/IK
somite	SOE/MAOIT
somn(o)-	SOM/N(O)
somnambulance	SOM/NAM/BLANS
	SOM/NAM/BAOU/LANS
somnambulation	SOM/NAM/BLAIGS
	SOM/NAM/BAOU/LAIGS
somnambulism	SOM/NAM/BLIFM
	SOM/NAM/BAOU/LIFM
somnambulist	SOM/NAM/BL*IS
	SOM/NAM/BAOU/L*IS
-somnia	SOM/NA
	SOM/NAOE/YA
somnifacient	SOM/NI/FAIRBT
somniferous	SOM/NIF/ROUS
somnific	SOM/NIFK
somnifugous	SOM/NIF/GOUS
somniloquence	SOM/NIL/KWENS
somniloquism	SOM/NIL/KWIFM
somniloquist	SOM/NIL/KW*IS
somniloquy	SOM/NIL/KWAOE
somnipathist	SOM/NIP/TH*IS
somnipathy	SOM/NIP/TH*I
somnocinematograph	SOM/NO/SIN/MAT/GRAF
somnocinematography	SOM/NO/SIN/MA/TOG/FI
somnolence	SOM/NO/LENS
somnolency	SOM/NO/LEN/SI
somnolent	SOM/NO/LENT
somnolentia	SOM/NO/LEN/SHA
somnolentium	SOM/NO/LEN/SHUM
somnolescence	SOM/NO/LES/ENS
somnolescent	SOM/NO/LES/ENT
somnolism	SOM/NO/LIFM
somnus	SOM/NUS
Somophyllin	SOE/MOF/LIN
	SOM/FLIN
	SOM/FIL/LIN
Somophyllin CRT	SOE/MOF/LIN/KR-RBGS/R*RBGS/

	T*RBGS	sotalol	SOET/LOL
	SOM/FLIN/KR-RBGS/R*RBGS/	Sotradecol	SOE/TRA/DE/KOL
	T*RBGS	Sottas	SOT/TAS
	SOM/FIL/LIN/KR-RBGS/R*RBGS/	Sotteau	SOE/TOE
	T*RBGS		SOT/TOE
Somophyllin DF	SOE/MOF/LIN/D-RBGS/F*RBGS	souffle	SAOUFL
	SOM/FLIN/D-RBGS/F*RBGS		SAOUF/-L
	SOM/FIL/LIN/D-RBGS/F*RBGS		(SAOU/FLAI)
Somophyllin-T	SOE/MOF/LIN/T-RBGS	soul	SOUL
	SOM/FLIN/T-RBGS		(*not* SOEL; see sole)
	SOM/FIL/LIN/T-RBGS	sound	SOUND
somosphere	SOEM/SFAOER	South American	SO*UT/MERN
sonarography	SOE/NAR/OG/FI	sow	SOU
soncogene	SON/KO/JAOEN		SO*E
sone	SOEN		(*not* SOE; see sew)
sonic	SON/IK	soya	SOE/YA
sonicate	SON/KAIT		SOI/YA
sonication	SON/KAIGS	Soyacal	SOI/KAL
sonifer	SON/FER		SOI/YA/KAL
sonification	SON/FI/KAIGS	soybean	SOI/BAOEN
sonifier	SON/FI/ER	spa	SPA
sonify	SON/FI		SPAU
sonitus	SON/TUS	space	SPAIS
Sonne	SON/NAOE	spadic	SPAID/IK
sonnei	SON/YAOI	spagyric	SPA/JIR/IK
sonochemistry	SON/KEM/STRI	spagyrist	SPAJ/R*IS
sonogram	SON/GRAM	spall	SPAUL
sonograph	SON/GRAF	Spallanzani	SPAL/AN/ZA/NAOE
sonographer	SOE/NOG/FER		SPAL/LAN/ZA/NAOE
	SO/NOG/FER	spallation	SPAUL/LAIGS
sonographic	SON/GRAFK		SPAL/LAIGS
sonography	SOE/NOG/FI	span	SPAN
	SO/NOG/FI	Span FF	SPAN/F-RBGS/F*RBGS
sonolucency	SON/LAOUS/EN/SI	Spanish	SPAN/IRB
sonolucent	SON/LAOUS/ENT	spannungs-P	SPAN/NUNGS/P-RBGS
sonomotor	SON/MOE/TOR		SPAN/NUNG/-S/P-RBGS
sonorous	SO/NOER/OUS	spanopnea	SPAN/OP/NA
	SO/NOR/OUS		SPAN/OP/NAOE/YA
	SOE/NOER/OUS	spar	SPAR
	SOE/NOR/OUS	sparganoma	SPARG/NOE/MA
soot	SAOT	sparganosis	SPARG/NOE/SIS
sophisticate	SF*IS/KAIT	sparganum	SPARG/NUM
	SOE/F*IS/KAIT	Sparine	SPA/RAOEN
	SO/F*IS/KAIT		SPAI/RAOEN
sophistication	SF*IS/KAIGS		SPAR/AOEN
	SOE/F*IS/KAIGS	spark	SPARK
	SO/F*IS/KAIGS	Sparta	SPAR/TA
sophomania	SOF/MAIN/YA	sparteine	SPAR/TAOEN
Sophora	SOE/FOR/RA		SPART/YAOEN
	SOE/FOER/RA		SPART/YIN
	SOF/RA	spartium	SPAR/SHUM
sophoretin	SOF/RAOE/TIN		SPART/YUM
sopor	SOE/POR	Spartus	SPAR/TUS
soporiferous	SOEP/RIF/ROUS	Spasgesic	SPAZ/JAOEZ/IK
	SOP/RIF/ROUS	spasm	SPAFM
soporific	SOEF/RIFK	spasm(o)-	SPAZ/M(O)
	SOP/RIFK	spasmodic	SPAZ/MOD/IK
soporose	SOEP/ROES	spasmodica	SPAZ/MOD/KA
	SOP/ROES	spasmodically	SPAZ/MOD/KLI
soporous	SOEP/ROUS	spasmogen	SPAZ/MO/JEN
	SOP/ROUS	spasmogenic	SPAZ/MO/JEN/IK
sorb	SORB	spasmology	SPAZ/MOLG
sorbefacient	SORB/FAIRBT	spasmolygmus	SPAZ/MO/LIG/MUS
sorbent	SORB/ENT	spasmolysant	SPAZ/MOL/ZANT
	SOR/BENT		SPAZ/MOL/SANT
sorbic	SORB/IK	spasmolysis	SPAZ/MOL/SIS
sorbin	SORB/IN	spasmolytic	SPAZ/MO/LIT/IK
sorbinose	SORB/NOES	spasmophile	SPAZ/MO/FAOIL
sorbitan	SORB/TAN	spasmophilia	SPAZ/MO/FIL/YA
sorbite	SOR/BAOIT	spasmophilic	SPAZ/MO/FIL/IK
sorbitol	SORB/TOL	spasmus	SPAZ/MUS
sorbitose	SORB/TOES	spastic	SPA*S/IK
Sorbitrate	SORB/TRAIT		SPAZ/TIK
sorbose	SOR/BOES	spastica	SPA*S/KA
Sordariaceae	SORD/RAOE/AIS/YAE	spastically	SPA*S/KLI
	SORD/RI/AIS/YAE		SPAZ/TIK/LI
sordellii	SOR/DEL/YAOI	spasticity	SPAS/TIS/TI
sordes	SOR/DAOEZ		SPAZ/TIS/TI
sore	SOER	spasticum	SPA*S/KUM
soreness	SOER/*NS		SPAS/TI/KUM
Sorensen	SORN/SEN	spatia	SPAI/SHA
	SOR/EN/SEN		SPAIRB/YA
Soret	SOE/RAI	spatial	SPAIRBL
soroche	SOE/ROE/KHAOE	spatic	SPAIT/IK
sororiation	SOE/ROR/YAIGS	spatium	SPAI/SHUM
	SOE/ROER/YAIGS		SPAIRB/UM
sorption	SORPGS		SPAIRB/YUM
Sorsby	SORS/BI	spatul-	SPAFP/L-
	SORZ/BI		SPAFP/YAOU/L-

	SPAFP/YU/L-	spermalist	SPERM/AI/GLAOUT/NAIGS
	SPAT/YAOU/L-		SPERM/L*IS
	SPAT/YU/L-	sperm-aster	SPERM/AS/TER
spatula	SPAFP/LA		SPERM/A*S/ER
spatular	SPAFP/LAR	spermat(o)-	SPERM/T(O)
spatulate	SPAFP/LAIT		SPER/MAT
spatulation	SPAFP/LAIGS	spermateliosis	SPERM/TAOEL/YOE/SIS
Spatz	SPATS	spermatemphraxis	SPER/MAT/EM/FRAK/SIS
spavin	SPAVN	spermatic	SPER/MAT/IK
	SPAI/VIN	spermatica	SPER/MAT/KA
spavined	SPAVN/-D	spermaticide	SPER/MAT/SAO*ID
	SPAI/VIN/-D	spermaticus	SPER/MAT/KUS
spay	SPAI	spermatid	SPERM/TID
spearmint	SPAOER/MINT	spermatin	SPERM/TIN
special	SPERBL	spermatism	SPERM/TIFM
specialism	SPERBL/IFM	spermatitis	SPERM/TAOITS
specialist	SPERBL/*IS	spermatoblast	SPERM/TO/BLA*S
specialization	SPERBL/ZAIGS	spermatocele	SPERM/TO/SAO*EL
specialize	SPERBL/AOIZ	spermatocelectomy	SPER/MAT/SE/LEKT/M*I
specialty	SPERBL/TI		SPERM/TO/SE/LEKT/M*I
speciation	SPAOERB/YAIGS	spermatocidal	SPERM/TO/SAOI/DAL
	SPAOES/YAIGS	spermatocide	SPERM/TO/SAO*ID
species	SPAOE/SHAOEZ	spermatocyst	SPERM/TO/S*IS
	SPAOE/SAOEZ	spermatocystectomy	SPERM/TO/SIS/TEKT/M*I
specific	SPEFK	spermatocystitis	SPERM/TO/SIS/TAOITS
	SPE/SIFK	spermatocystotomy	SPERM/TO/SIS/TOT/M*I
specificity	SPES/FIS/TI	spermatocytal	SPERM/TO/SAOI/TAL
specificness	SPEFK/*NS	spermatocyte	SPERM/TO/SAO*IT
	SPE/SIFK/*NS	spermatocytogenesis	SPERM/TO/SAOIT/JEN/SIS
specilla	SPE/CIL/LA	spermatocytoma	SPERM/TO/SAOI/TOE/MA
specillum	SPE/SIL/UM	spermatogenesis	SPERM/TO/JEN/SIS
specimen	SPES/MEN	spermatogenetic	SPERM/TO/JE/NET/IK
spectacle	SPEKT/K-L	spermatogenic	SPERM/TO/JEN/IK
spectacles	SPEKT/K-LS	spermatogenous	SPERM/TOJ/NOUS
Spectazole	SPEKT/ZOEL	spermatogeny	SPERM/TOJ/N*I
spectinomycin	SPEKT/NO/MAOI/SIN	spermatogone	SPERM/TO/GOEN
	SPEK/TIN/MAOI/SIN	spermatogonia	SPERM/TO/GOEN/YA
spectr(o)-	SPEK/TR(O)	spermatogonial	SPERM/TO/GOEN/YAL
spectra	SPEK/TRA	spermatogonium	SPERM/TO/GOEN/YUM
spectral	SPEK/TRAL	spermatoid	SPERM/TOID
spectrin	SPEK/TRIN	spermatology	SPERM/TOLG
Spectrobid	SPEK/TRO/BID	spermatolysin	SPERM/TOL/SIN
spectrochemistry	SPEK/TRO/KEM/STRI	spermatolysis	SPERM/TOL/SIS
spectrochrome	SPEK/TRO/KROEM	spermatolytic	SPERM/TO/LIT/IK
spectrocolorimeter	SPEK/TRO/KOL/RIM/TER	spermatomere	SPERM/TO/MAOER
spectrofluorometer	SPEK/TRO/FLAOU/ROM/TER	spermatomerite	SPERM/TO/MAOER/AOIT
spectrogram	SPEK/TRO/GRAM		SPERM/TO/MAOE/RAOIT
spectrograph	SPEK/TRO/GRAF	spermatopathia	SPERM/TO/PA*T/YA
spectrography	SPEK/TROG/FI	spermatopathy	SPERM/TOP/TH*I
spectrometer	SPEK/TROM/TER	spermatophobia	SPERM/TO/FOEB/YA
spectrometry	SPEK/TROM/TRI	spermatophore	SPERM/TO/FOER
spectrophobia	SPEK/TRO/FOEB/YA	spermatopoietic	SPERM/TO/POIT/IK
spectrophotofluorimetry	SPEK/TRO/FOET/FLAOU/RIM/TRI	spermatorrhea	SPERM/TO/RAOE/YA
spectrophotofluorometer	SPEK/TRO/FOET/FLAOU/ROM/	spermatoschesis	SPERM/TOS/KE/SIS
	TER	spermatosome	SPER/MAT/SOEM
spectrophotometer	SPEK/TRO/FOE/TOM/TER		SPERM/TO/SOEM
spectrophotometry	SPEK/TRO/FOE/TOM/TRI	spermatospore	SPER/MAT/SPOER
spectropolarimeter	SPEK/TRO/POEL/RIM/TER		SPERM/TO/SPOER
spectropyrheliometer	SPEK/TRO/PIR/HAOEL/YOM/TER	spermatotoxin	SPERM/TO/TOK/SIN
spectroscope	SPEK/TRO/SKOEP	spermatovum	SPER/MAT/OEV/UM
spectroscopic	SPEK/TRO/SKOP/IK		SPER/MAT/O/VUM
spectroscopy	SPEK/TROS/KPI	spermatoxin	SPERM/MA/TOK/SIN
spectrum	SPEK/TRUM		(not SPERM/TOK/SIN; see
specul-	SPEK/L-		spermotoxin)
	SPEK/YAOU/L-	spermatozoa	SPERM/TO/ZOE/WA
	SPEK/YU/L-	spermatozoal	SPERM/TO/ZOEL
specula	SPEK/LA		SPERM/TO/ZOE/WAL
speculum	SPEK/LUM	spermatozoan	SPERM/TO/ZOE/WAN
Spee	SPA*I	spermatozoicide	SPERM/TO/ZOI/SAO*ID
	(not SPAI; see spay)	spermatozoid	SPERM/TO/ZOID
speech	SPAOEFP	spermatozoon	SPERM/TO/ZAON
spelencephaly	SPAOE/LEN/SEF/LI	spermaturia	SPERM/TAOUR/YA
speleostomy	SPAOEL/YO*S/M*I	spermectomy	SPER/MEKT/M*I
spelter	SPELT/ER	spermi(o)-	SPERM/Y(O)
Spemann	SPAOE/MAN	spermia	SPERM/YA
Spencer	SPENS/ER	spermiation	SPERM/YAIGS
spencerii	SPENS/RAOI	spermicidal	SPERM/SAOI/DAL
	SPENS/ER/YAOI	spermicide	SPERM/SAO*ID
	SPEN/SER/YAOI	spermid	SPER/MID
Spengler	SPENG/LER		SPERM/ID
Spens	SPENZ	spermidine	SPERM/DAOEN
sperm	SPERM		SPERM/DIN
sperm(o)-	SPERM	spermiduct	SPERM/DUKT
	SPER/M(O)	spermin	SPER/MIN
sperma	SPER/MA	spermine	SPER/MAOEN
spermaceti	SPERM/SET/TAOE	spermiocyte	SPERM/YO/SAO*IT
spermacrasia	SPERM/KRAIZ/YA	spermiogenesis	SPERM/YO/GEN/SIS
spermagglutination	SPERM/GLAOUT/NAIGS	spermiogonium	SPERM/YO/GOEN/YUM
	SPER/MA/GLAOUT/NAIGS	spermiogram	SPERM/YO/GRAM

spermioteleosis	SPERM/YO/TAOEL/YOE/SIS		SFAOE/RO
spermioteleotic	SPERM/YO/TAOEL/YOT/IK	spherocylinder	SFAOER/SIL/IN/DER
	SPERM/YO/TEL/YOT/IK	spherocyte	SFAOER/SAO*IT
spermism	SPER/MIFM	spherocytic	SFAOER/SIT/IK
	SPERM/IFM	spherocytosis	SFAOER/SAOI/TOE/SIS
spermist	SPER/M*IS	spheroid	SFAOER/OID
	SPERM/*IS	spheroidal	SFE/ROI/DAL
spermium	SPERM/YUM		SFAOE/ROI/DAL
spermoblast	SPERM/BLA*S		SFAOER/OI/DAL
spermocytoma	SPERM/SAOI/TOE/MA	spheroidia	SFE/ROID/YA
spermolith	SPERM/L*IT		SFAOE/ROID/YA
spermoloropexis	SPERM/LOR/PEK/SIS		SFAOER/OID/YA
	SPERM/LOER/PEK/SIS	spherolith	SFAOER/L*IT
spermoloropexy	SPERM/LOR/PEK/SI	spheroma	SFAOE/ROE/MA
	SPERM/LOER/PEK/SI		SFAOER/ROE/MA
spermolysin	SPER/MOL/SIN		SFAOER/O/MA
spermolysis	SPER/MOL/SIS	spherometer	SFAOER/OM/TER
spermolytic	SPERM/LIT/IK		SFAOE/ROM/TER
spermoneuralgia	SPERM/NAOU/RAL/JA	spherophakia	SFAOER/FAIK/YA
spermophlebectasia	SPERM/FLEB/EK/TAIZ/YA	Spherophorous	SFAOE/ROF/ROUS
spermoplasm	SPERM/PLAFM		SFAOER/OF/ROUS
spermosphere	SPERM/SFAOER	spheroplast	SFAOER/PLA*S
spermospore	SPERM/SPOER	spheroprism	SFAOER/PRIFM
spermotoxic	SPERM/TOX/IK	spherospermia	SFAOER/SPERM/YA
spermotoxin	SPERM/TOK/SIN	spherule	SFAOER/YAOUL
spes	SPAOES	sphincter	SFING/TER
sphacelate	SFAS/LAIT		SFINGT/ER
sphacelation	SFAS/LAIGS	sphincter(o)-	SFINGT/RO
sphacelism	SFAS/LIFM		SFING/TRO
sphaceloderma	SFAS/LO/DER/MA	sphincteral	SFINGT/RAL
sphacelotoxin	SFAS/LO/TOK/SIN		SFING/TRAL
sphacelous	SFAS/LOUS	sphincteralgia	SFINGT/RAL/JA
sphacelus	SFAS/LUS		SFING/TRAL/JA
Sphaerophorus	SFAOE/ROF/RUS		SFING/TER/AL/JA
	SFAE/ROF/RUS	sphincterectomy	SFINGT/REKT/M*I
sphagiasmus	SFAIJ/YAZ/MUS		SFING/TREKT/M*I
	SFAIJ/AZ/MUS		SFING/TER/EKT/M*I
sphagitides	SFA/JIT/DAOEZ	sphincterial	SFING/TAOERL
sphagitis	SFA/JAOITS		SFING/TAOER/YAL
	SFAI/JAOITS	sphincteric	SFING/TER/IK
sphen(o)-	SFAOEN	sphincterismus	SFINGT/RIZ/MUS
	SFAOE/N(O)		SFING/TRIZ/MUS
sphenethmoid	SFAOE/N*ET/MOID		SFING/TER/IZ/MUS
	SFEN/*ET/MOID	sphincteritis	SFINGT/RAOITS
sphenion	SFAOEN/YON		SFING/TRAOITS
sphenobasilar	SFAOEN/BAS/LAR		SFING/TER/AOITS
sphenoccipital	SFAOE/NOK/SIP/TAL	sphincteroid	SFINGT/ROID
	(*not* SFAOEN/OK/SIP/TAL; see		SFING/TROID
	spheno-occipital)		SFING/TER/OID
sphenocephalus	SFAOEN/SEF/LUS	sphincterolysis	SFINGT/ROL/SIS
sphenocephaly	SFAOEN/SEF/LI		SFING/TROL/SIS
sphenoethmoid	SFAOEN/*ET/MOID		SFING/TER/OL/SIS
sphenofrontal	SFAOEN/FRON/TAL	sphincteroplasty	SFINGT/RO/PLAS/TI
sphenoid	SFAOE/NOID		SFING/TRO/PLAS/TI
sphenoidal	SFAOE/NOI/DAL	sphincteroscope	SFINGT/RO/SKOEP
sphenoidale	SFAOE/NOI/DAI/LAOE		SFING/TRO/SKOEP
sphenoidalis	SFAOE/NOI/DAI/LIS	sphincteroscopy	SFINGT/ROS/KPI
sphenoiditis	SFAOE/NOI/DAOITS		SFING/TROS/KPI
sphenoidostomy	SFAOE/NOI/DO*S/M*I		SFING/TER/OS/KPI
sphenoidotomy	SFAOE/NOI/DOT/M*I	sphincterotome	SFINGT/RO/TOEM
sphenomalar	SFAOEN/MAI/LAR		SFING/TRO/TOEM
sphenomaxillaris	SFAOEN/MAX/LAI/RIS		SFING/TER/TOEM
sphenomaxillary	SFAOEN/MAX/LAIR	sphincterotomy	SFINGT/ROT/M*I
sphenometer	SFAOE/NOM/TER		SFING/TROT/M*I
spheno-occipital	SFAOEN/OK/SIP/TAL		SFING/TER/OT/M*I
sphenopagus	SFAOE/NOP/GUS	sphing(o)-	SFING
sphenopalatine	SFAOEN/PAL/TAOIN		SFIN/G(O)
sphenoparietal	SFAOEN/PRAOI/TAL	sphinganine	SFING/NAOEN
sphenopetrosal	SFAOEN/PE/TROE/SAL		SFIN/GA/NAOEN
sphenopharyngeal	SFAOEN/FRIN/JAL	sphingogalactoside	SFING/GLAKT/SAOID
sphenorbital	SFAOE/NORB/TAL	sphingoglycolipid	SFING/GLAOIK/LIP/ID
sphenosalpingostaphylinus	SFAOEN/SAL/PING/STAF/LAOI/	sphingol	SFIN/GOL
	NUS	sphingolipid	SFING/LIP/ID
sphenosquamosal	SFAOEN/SKWAI/MOE/SAL	sphingolipidoses	SFING/LIP/DOE/SAOEZ
	SFAOEN/SKWA/MOE/SAL	sphingolipidosis	SFING/LIP/DOE/SIS
sphenotemporal	SFAOEN/TEFRP/RAL	sphingolipodystrophy	SFING/LIP/DIS/TRO/FI
sphenotic	SFAOE/NOT/IK	sphingomyelin	SFING/MAOI/LIN
sphenotresia	SFAOEN/TRAOEZ/YA	sphingomyelinosis	SFING/MAOIL/NOE/SIS
sphenotribe	SFAOEN/TRAOIB		SFING/MAOI/LI/NOE/SIS
sphenotripsy	SFAOEN/TRIP/SI	sphingophospholipid	SFING/FOS/FO/LIP/ID
sphenoturbinal	SFAOEN/TURB/NAL	sphingosine	SFING/SAOEN
sphenovomerine	SFAOEN/VOEM/RIN		SFING/SIN
	SFAOEN/VOEM/RAOEN	sphygm(o)-	SFIG/M(O)
	SFAOEN/VOEM/RAOIN	sphygmic	SFIG/MIK
sphenozygomatic	SFAOEN/ZAOIG/MAT/IK	sphygmobologram	SFIG/MO/BOEL/GRAM
sphere	SFAOER	sphygmobolometer	SFIG/MO/BOE/LOM/TER
spheresthesia	SFAOER/ES/THAOEZ/YA	sphygmobolometry	SFIG/MO/BOE/LOM/TRI
spherical	SFAOER/KAL	sphygmocardiogram	SFIG/MO/KARD/YO/GRAM
sphero-	SFAOER	sphygmocardiograph	SFIG/MO/KARD/YO/GRAF

sphygmocardioscope	SFIG/MO/KARD/YO/SKOEP	spinocostalis	SPAOIN/KOS/TAI/LIS
sphygmochronograph	SFIG/MO/KROEN/GRAF	spinogalvanization	SPAOIN/GAL/VAN/ZAIGS
	SFIG/MO/KRON/GRAF	spinoglenoid	SPAOIN/GLAOE/NOID
sphygomodynamometer	SFIG/MO/DAOIN/MOM/TER	spinogram	SPAOIN/GRAM
sphygmogram	SFIG/MO/GRAM	spinomuscular	SPAOIN/MUS/KLAR
sphygmograph	SFIG/MO/GRAF	spinoneural	SPAOIN/NAOURL
sphygmographic	SFIG/MO/GRAFK	spinopetal	SPAOI/NOP/TAL
sphygmography	SFIG/MOG/FI	spinose	SPAOI/NOES
sphygmoid	SFIG/MOID	spinosum	SPAOI/NOE/SUM
sphygmology	SFIG/MOLG		SPAOI/NOES/UM
sphygmomanometer	SFIG/MO/MA/NOM/TER	spinotectal	SPAOIN/TEK/TAL
sphygmomanometry	SFIG/MO/MA/NOM/TRI	spinotransversarius	SPAOIN/TRA*NS/VER/SAIR/YUS
sphygmometer	SFIG/MOM/TER	spinous	SPAOIN/OUS
sphygmometrograph	SFIG/MO/MET/RO/GRAF	spintharicon	SPIN/THAR/KON
sphygmometroscope	SFIG/MO/MET/RO/SKOEP	spinthariscope	SPIN/THAR/SKOEP
sphygmo-oscillometer	SFIG/MO/OS/LOM/TER	spintherism	SP*INT/RIFM
sphygmopalpation	SFIG/MO/PAL/PAIGS	spintherometer	SP*INT/ROM/TER
sphygmophone	SFIG/MO/FOEN	spintheropia	SP*INT/ROEP/YA
sphygmoplethysmograph	SFIG/MO/PLE/THIZ/MO/GRAF	spinulosa	SPIN/LOE/SA
sphygmoscope	SFIG/MO/SKOEP		SPAOIN/LOE/SA
sphygmoscopy	SFIG/MOS/KPI	spiperone	SPIP/ROEN
sphygmosystole	SFIG/MO/S*IS/LAOE	spir(o)-	SPAOIR
sphygmotonogram	SFIG/MO/TOEN/GRAM		SPAOI/R(O)
sphygmotonograph	SFIG/MO/TOEN/GRAF		SPIR
sphygmotonometer	SFIG/MO/TOE/NOM/TER	spiracle	SPIR/K-L
sphygmoviscosimetry	SFIG/MO/VIS/KO/SIM/TRI		SPAOIR/K-L
sphyrectomy	SFAOI/REKT/M*I	spiradenitis	SPAOI/RAD/NAOITS
sphyrotomy	SFAOI/ROT/M*I	spiradenoma	SPAOI/RAD/NOE/MA
spica	SPAOI/KA	spiral	SPAOIRL
spicae	SPAOI/KAE		SPAOI/RAL
spicata	SPI/KAI/TA	spirale	SPAOI/RAI/LAOE
spicul-	SPIK/L-	spirales	SPAOI/RAI/LAOEZ
	SPIK/YAOU/L-	spiralis	SPAOI/RAI/LIS
	SPIK/YU/L-	spiramycin	SPIR/MAOI/SIN
spicula	SPIK/LA	Spiranthes	SPAOI/RAN/THAOEZ
spicular	SPIK/LAR	spirem	SPAOI/REM
spicule	SPIK/YAOUL	spireme	SPAOI/RAOEM
spiculum	SPIK/LUM	spirilla	SPAOI/RIL/LA
spider	SPAOID/ER	Spirillaceae	SPAOIR/LAIS/YAE
	SPAOI/DER		SPAOI/RI/LAIS/YAE
spider burst	SPAOID/ER/B*URS	spirillar	SPAOI/RIL/LAR
Spiegelberg	SPAOEG/EL/BERG	spirillemia	SPAOIR/LAOEM/YA
Spieghel	SPAOEG/EL		SPAOI/RI/LAOEM/YA
	SPAOE/GEL		SPAOI/RIL/AOEM/YA
Spiegler	SPAOEG/LER	spirillicidal	SPAOI/RIL/SAOI/DAL
Spielmeyer	SPAOEL/MAOI/ER	spirillicide	SPAOI/RIL/SAO*ID
Spigelia	SPAOI/JAOEL/YA	spirillicidin	SPAOI/RIL/SAOI/DIN
spigelian	SPAOI/JAOEL/YAN	spirillolysis	SPAOIR/LOL/SIS
spigeline	SPAOI/JAOE/LAOEN		SPAOI/RI/LOL/SIS
Spigelius	SPAOI/JAOEL/YUS	spirillosis	SPAOIR/LOE/SIS
spignet	SPIG/NET		SPAOI/RI/LOE/SIS
spike	SPAOIK	spirillotropic	SPAOIR/LO/TROP/IK
spikenard	SPAOIK/NARD		SPAOI/RIL/TROP/IK
Spilanthes	SPAOI/LAN/THAOEZ	spirillotropism	SPAOIR/LOT/RO/PIFM
spill	SPIL		SPAOI/RI/LOT/RO/PIFM
Spiller	SPIL/ER	spirillum	SPAOI/RIL/UM
spillway	SPIL/WA*I	Spirillum	K-P/SPAOI/RIL/UM
spiloma	SPAOI/LOE/MA	spirit	SPIRT
spiloplaxia	SPAOIL/PLAX/YA		SPIR/RIT
	SPAOI/LO/PLAX/YA	spirituous	SPIRT/YOUS
spilus	SPAOI/LUS		SPIRT/KHOUS
spin	SPIN		SPIR/KHOUS
spin(o)-	SPAOIN	spiritus	SPIR/TUS
	SPAOI/N(O)	Spiro	SPAOI/ROE
spina	SPAOI/NA	Spirocerca	SPAOIR/SER/KA
spinacene	SPIN/SAOEN	Spirocerca lupi	SPAOIR/SER/KA/LAOU/PAOI
spinae	SPAOI/NAE	Spirocerca sanguinolenta	SPAOIR/SER/KA/SANG/WIN/LEN/
spinal	SPAOINL		TA
spinale	SPAOI/NAI/LAOE	Spirochaeta	SPAOIR/KAOE/TA
spinales	SPAOI/NAI/LAOEZ		SPAOIR/KAE/TA
spinalgia	SPAOI/NAL/JA	Spirochaetaceae	SPAOIR/KAOE/TAIS/YAE
	SPAOIN/AL/JA		SPAOIR/KAE/TAIS/YAE
spinalia	SPAOI/NAIL/YA	Spirochaetales	SPAOIR/KAOE/TAI/LAOEZ
spinalis	SPAOI/NAI/LIS		SPAOIR/KAE/TAI/LAOEZ
spinalium	SPAOI/NAIL/YUM	spirochetal	SPAOIR/KAOE/TAL
spinant	SPAOI/NANT	spirochete	SPAOIR/KAOET
spinate	SPAOI/NAIT	spirochetemia	SPAOIR/KAOE/TAOEM/YA
spinatus	SPAOI/NAI/TUS	spirocheticidal	SPAOIR/KAOET/SAOI/DAL
spindle	SPIND/-L	spirocheticide	SPAOIR/KAOET/SAO*ID
spine	SPAOIN	spirochetogenous	SPAOIR/KAOE/TOJ/NOUS
Spinelli	SPI/NEL/LAOE	spirochetolysin	SPAOIR/KAOE/TOL/SIN
spinifugal	SPAOI/NIF/GAL	spirochetolysis	SPAOIR/KAOE/TOL/SIS
spinipetal	SPAOI/NIP/TAL	spirochetolytic	SPAOIR/KAOET/LIT/IK
spinnbarkeit	SPIN/BAR/KAOIT	spirochetosis	SPAOIR/KAOE/TOE/SIS
spinobulbar	SPAOIN/BUL/BAR	spirochetotic	SPAOIR/KAOE/TOT/IK
spinocellular	SPAOIN/SEL/YAOU/LAR	spirocheturia	SPAOIR/KAOE/TAOUR/YA
spinocerebellar	SPAOIN/SER/BEL/LAR	spirogram	SPAOIR/GRAM
spinocollicular	SPAOIN/KLIK/LAR	spirograph	SPAOIR/GRAF
spinocortical	SPAOIN/KORT/KAL	spirographic	SPAOIR/GRAFK

spirography	SPAOI/ROG/FI	splenectopia	SPLAOE/NEK/TOEP/YA
Spirogyra	SPAOIR/JAOI/RA		SPLAOEN/EK/TOEP/YA
spiroid	SPAOI/ROID		SPLEN/EK/TOEP/YA
spiro-index	SPAOIR/IN/DEX	splenectopy	SPLAOE/NEKT/PI
spiroma	SPAOI/ROE/MA		SPLAOEN/EKT/PI
spirometer	SPAOI/ROM/TER	splenelcosis	SPLEN/EL/KOE/SIS
Spirometra	SPAOIR/MAOE/TRA		SPLAOEN/EL/KOE/SIS
spirometric	SPAOIR/MET/RIK	splenemphraxis	SPLEN/EM/FRAK/SIS
spirometry	SPAOI/ROM/TRI		SPLAOEN/EM/FRAK/SIS
Spironema	SPAOIR/NAOE/MA	spleneolus	SPLAOE/NAOE/LUS
spironolactone	SPAOIR/NO/LAK/TOEN	splenetic	SPLAOE/NET/IK
spirophore	SPAOIR/FOER		SPLE/NET/IK
spiroscope	SPAOIR/SKOEP	splenetica	SPLAOE/NET/KA
spiroscopy	SPAOI/ROS/KPI		SPLE/NET/KA
spirostan	SPAOIR/STAN	splenia	SPLAOEN/YA
Spirotricha	SPAOIR/TRIK/KA	splenial	SPLAOEN/YAL
	SPAOIR/TRI/KA	splenic	SPLEN/IK
spiruroid	SPAOI/RAOU/ROID	splenicterus	SPLEN/IKT/RUS
Spiruroidea	SPAOI/RAOU/ROID/YA		SPLEN/IK/TRUS
spissated	SPIS/SAIT/-D	spleniculus	SPLEN/IK/LUS
spissitude	SPIS/TAOUD		SPLAOEN/IK/LUS
	SPIS/SI/TAOUD	spleniform	SPLEN/FORM
spitting	SPIT/-G		SPLAOEN/FORM
spittle	SPIT/-L	spleniserrate	SPLEN/SER/RAIT
Spitzer	SPIT/SER		SPLEN/SER/AIT
	SPIT/ZER	splenitis	SPLAOE/NAOITS
Spitzka	SPITS/KA	splenium	SPLAOEN/YUM
splanchn(o)-	SPLANG/N(O)	splenius	SPLAOEN/YUS
splanchnapophysial	SPLANG/NAP/FIZ/YAL	splenoblast	SPLAOEN/BLA*S
splanchnapophysis	SPLANG/NA/POF/SIS	splenocele	SPLAOEN/SAO*EL
splanchnectopia	SPLANG/NEK/TOEP/YA	splenocleisis	SPLAOEN/KLAOI/SIS
splanchnesthesia	SPLANG/NES/THAOEZ/YA	splenocolic	SPLAOEN/KOL/IK
splanchnesthetic	SPLANG/NES/THET/IK	splenocyte	SPLAOEN/SAO*IT
splanchnic	SPLANG/NIK	splenodynia	SPLAOEN/DIN/YA
splanchnicectomy	SPLANG/NI/SEKT/M*I	splenogenous	SPLAOE/NOJ/NOUS
splanchnici	SPLANG/NI/SAOI	splenogram	SPLAOEN/GRAM
splanchnicotomy	SPLANG/NI/KOT/M*I	splenography	SPLAOE/NOG/FI
splanchnicus	SPLANG/NI/KUS	splenohepatomegalia	SPLAOEN/HEPT/ME/GAIL/YA
splanchnoblast	SPLANG/NO/BLA*S	splenohepatomegaly	SPLAOEN/HEPT/MEG/LI
splanchnocele	SPLANG/NO/SAO*EL	splenoid	SPLAOE/NOID
splanchnocranium	SPLANG/NO/KRAIN/YUM		SPLAOEN/OID
splanchnocystica	SPLANG/NO/S*IS/KA	splenokeratosis	SPLAOEN/KER/TOE/SIS
splanchnoderm	SPLANG/NO/DERM	splenolaparotomy	SPLAOEN/LAP/ROT/M*I
splanchnodiastasis	SPLANG/NO/DI/A*S/SIS	splenology	SPLAOE/NOLG
splanchnography	SPLANG/NOG/FI	splenolymphatic	SPLAOEN/LIM/FAT/IK
splanchnolith	SPLANG/NO/L*IT	splenolysin	SPLAOE/NOL/SIN
splanchnologia	SPLANG/NO/LOE/JA	splenolysis	SPLAOE/NOL/SIS
splanchnology	SPLANG/NOLG	splenoma	SPLAOE/NOE/MA
splanchnomegalia	SPLANG/NO/ME/GAIL/YA	splenomalacia	SPLAOEN/MA/LAI/SHA
splanchnomegaly	SPLANG/NO/MEG/LI	splenomedullary	SPLAOEN/MED/LAIR
splanchnomicria	SPLANG/NO/MIK/RAOE/YA	splenomegalia	SPLAOEN/ME/GAIL/YA
	SPLANG/NO/MAOI/KRAOE/YA	splenomegaly	SPLAOEN/MEG/LI
splanchnopathy	SPLANG/NOP/TH*I		SPLEN/MEG/LI
splanchnopleural	SPLANG/NO/PLAOURL	splenometry	SPLAOE/NOM/TRI
splanchnopleure	SPLANG/NO/PLAOUR	splenomyelogenous	SPLAOEN/MAOI/LOJ/NOUS
splanchnopleuric	SPLANG/NO/PLAOUR/IK	splenomyelomalacia	SPLAOEN/MAOI/LO/MA/LAI/SHA
splanchnoptosia	SPLANG/NO/TOES/YA	splenoncus	SPLAOE/NON/KUS
splanchnoptosis	SPLANG/NO/TOE/SIS	splenonephric	SPLAOEN/NEF/RIK
splanchnosclerosis	SPLANG/NO/SKLE/ROE/SIS	splenonephroptosis	SPLAOEN/NEF/ROP/TOE/SIS
splanchnoscopy	SPLANG/NOS/KPI	splenopancreatic	SPLAOEN/PAN/KRAT/IK
splanchnoskeleton	SPLANG/NO/SKEL/TON	splenoparectasis	SPLAOEN/PA/REKT/SIS
splanchnosomatic	SPLANG/NO/SOE/MAT/IK	splenopathy	SPLAOE/NOP/TH*I
	SPLANG/NO/SMAT/IK	splenopexia	SPLAOEN/PEX/YA
splanchnotomy	SPLANG/NOT/M*I	splenopexy	SPLAOEN/PEK/SI
splanchnotribe	SPLANG/NO/TRAOIB	splenophrenic	SPLAOEN/FREN/IK
splash	SPLARB	splenoportogram	SPLAOEN/PORT/GRAM
splay	SPLAI	splenoportography	SPLAOEN/POR/TOG/FI
splayfoot	SPLAI/FAOT	splenoptosia	SPLAOE/NOP/TOEZ/YA
spleen	SPLAOEN	splenoptosis	SPLAOE/NOP/TOE/SIS
splen	SPLEN	splenorenal	SPLAOEN/RAOENL
splen(o)-	SPLAOEN	splenorenopexy	SPLAOEN/RAOEN/PEK/SI
	SPLAOE/N(O)	splenorrhagia	SPLAOEN/RAI/JA
	SPLEN	splenorrhaphy	SPLAOEN/NOR/FI
	SPLE/N(O)	splenosis	SPLAOE/NOE/SIS
splenadenoma	SPLAOEN/AD/NOE/MA	splenotomy	SPLAOE/NOT/M*I
splenalgia	SPLAOE/NAL/JA	splenotoxin	SPLAOEN/TOK/SIN
	SPLAOEN/AL/JA	splenule	SPLEN/YAOUL
splenatrophy	SPLEN/AT/RO/FI	splenul	SPLEN/L-
splenauxe	SPLAOE/NAUK/SAOE		SPLEN/YAOU/L-
	SPLAOEN/AUK/SAOE		SPLEN/YU/L-
splenculus	SPLEN/KLUS	splenuli	SPLEN/LAOI
	SPLEN/KAOU/LUS	splenulus	SPLEN/LUS
splendens	SPLEN/DENZ	splenuncul-	SPLAOE/NUN/KL-
splenectasis	SPLAOE/NEKT/SIS		SPLAOE/NUNG/L-
	SPLAOEN/EKT/SIS		SPLAOE/NUN/KAOU/L-
splenectomize	SPLAOE/NEKT/MAOIZ		SPLAOE/NUNG/YAOU/L-
	SPLAOEN/EKT/MAOIZ		SPLAOE/NUNG/YU/L-
splenectomy	SPLAOE/NEKT/M*I	splenunculi	SPLAOE/NUN/KLAOI
	SPLAOEN/EKT/M*I		SPLAOE/NUNG/LAOI

splenunculus	SPLAOE/NUN/KLUS	spoon	SPAON
	SPLAOE/NUNG/LUS	spor(o)-	SPOR
splice	SPLAOIS		SPOER
splint	SPLINT		SPR(O)
splinter	SPLINT/ER		SPOR/R(O)
splinting	SPLINT/-G		SPOER/R(O)
splitting	SPLIT/-G		SPO/R(O)
spodiomyelitis	SPOED/YO/MAOI/LAOITS		SPOE/R(O)
spodo-	SPOD	sporadic	SPRAD/IK
	SPO/DO		SPO/RAD/IK
	SPOED	sporadin	SPOR/DIN
	SPOE/DO	sporadoneure	SPOE/RAD/NAOUR
spodogenous	SPO/DOJ/NOUS	sporangi(o)-	SPRAN/J(O)
	SPOE/DOJ/NOUS		SPOE/RAN/J(O)
spodogram	SPOD/GRAM		SPO/RAN/J(O)
	SPOED/GRAM	sporangia	SPRAN/JA
spodography	SPO/DOG/FI	sporangial	SPRAN/JAL
	SPOE/DOG/FI	sporangiophore	SPRAN/JO/FOER
spodophorous	SPO/DOF/ROUS	sporangiospore	SPRAN/JO/SPOER
	SPOE/DOF/ROUS	sporangium	SPRAN/JUM
spoke	SPOEK	sporation	SPOR/AIGS
spondaic	SPON/DAI/IK	spore	SPOER
spondee	SPON/DAOE		SPOR
spondyl(o)-	SPOND/L(O)	sporenrest	SPORN/R*ES
	SPON/DIL		SPOR/EN/R*ES
spondylalgia	SPOND/LAL/JA	sporetia	SPO/RAOE/SHA
spondylarthritis	SPON/DIL/AR/THRAOITS		SPO/RAOERB/YA
	SPOND/LAR/THRAOITS	sporicidal	SPOR/SAOI/DAL
spondylarthrocace	SPON/DIL/AR/THROK/SAOE		SPOER/SAOI/DAL
	SPOND/LAR/THROK/SAOE	sporicide	SPOR/SAO*ID
spondylarthropathy	SPON/DIL/AR/THROP/TH*I		SPOER/SAO*ID
	SPOND/LAR/THROP/TH*I	-sporidiosis	SPRID/YOE/SIS
spondylexarthrosis	SPON/DIL/EX/AR/THROE/SIS		SPO/RID/YOE/SIS
	SPOND/LEX/AR/THROE/SIS		SPOE/RID/YOE/SIS
spondylitic	SPOND/LIT/IK	sporidium	SPRID/YUM
spondylitis	SPOND/LAOITS		SPO/RID/YUM
spondylizema	SPOND/LAOI/ZAOE/MA		SPOE/RID/YUM
spondylocace	SPOND/LOK/SAOE	sporiferous	SPOR/IF/ROUS
spondylodesis	SPOND/LOD/SIS		SPOE/RIF/ROUS
spondylodidymia	SPOND/LO/DI/DIM/YA	-sporin	SPORN
spondylodymus	SPOND/LOD/MUS		SPOR/RIN
spondylodynia	SPOND/LO/DIN/YA	sporiparous	SPOR/IP/ROUS
spondyloepiphysial	SPOND/LO/EP/FIZ/YAL		SPOE/RIP/ROUS
spondylolisthesis	SPOND/LO/LIS/THE/SIS	sporoagglutination	SPOR/AI/GLAOUT/NAIGS
	SPOND/LO/LIS/THAOE/SIS	sporoblast	SPOR/BLA*S
spondylolisthetic	SPOND/LO/LIS/THET/IK	sporocyst	SPOR/S*IS
spondylolysis	SPOND/LOL/SIS	Sporocystinea	SPOR/SIS/TIN/YA
spondylomalacia	SPOND/LO/MA/LAI/SHA	sporodochium	SPOR/DOEK/YUM
spondylopathy	SPOND/LOP/TH*I	sporoduct	SPOR/DUKT
spondyloptosis	SPOND/LO/TOE/SIS	sporogenes	SPROJ/NAOEZ
	SPOND/LOP/TOE/SIS		SPO/ROJ/NAOEZ
spondylopyosis	SPOND/LO/PAOI/YOE/SIS	sporogenesis	SPOR/JEN/SIS
spondyloschisis	SPOND/LOS/KI/SIS	sporogenic	SPOR/JEN/IK
spondylosis	SPOND/LOE/SIS	sporogenous	SPROJ/NOUS
spondylosyndesis	SPOND/LO/SIN/DAOE/SIS		SPO/ROJ/NOUS
spondylotherapy	SPOND/LO/THER/PI		SPOE/ROJ/NOUS
spondylothoracic	SPOND/LO/THRAS/IK	sporogeny	SPROJ/N*I
spondylotic	SPOND/LOT/IK		SPO/ROJ/N*I
spondylotomy	SPOND/LOT/M*I		SPOE/ROJ/N*I
spondylous	SPOND/LOUS	sporogony	SPROG/N*I
sponge	SPON/-J		SPO/ROG/N*I
spongi(o)-	SPON/J(O)		SPOE/ROG/N*I
spongia	SPON/JA	sporont	SPOR/RONT
spongiform	SPON/JI/FORM		(not SPOR/ONT; see spore on the)
spongiitis	SPON/JAOITS	sporophore	SPOR/FOER
spongin	SPON/JIN	sporophyte	SPOR/FAOIT
spongioblast	SPON/JO/BLA*S	sporoplasm	SPOR/PLAFM
spongioblastoma	SPON/JO/BLAS/TOE/MA	sporoplasmic	SPOR/PLAZ/MIK
spongiocyte	SPON/JO/SAO*IT	sporotheca	SPOR/THAOE/KA
spongiocytoma	SPON/JO/SAOI/TOE/MA	Sporothrix	SPOR/THRIX
spongioid	SPON/JOID	sporotrichosis	SPOR/TRI/KOE/SIS
spongioma	SPON/JOE/MA	sporotrichotic	SPOR/TRI/KOT/IK
spongioplasm	SPON/JO/PLAFM	Sporotrichum	SPROT/RI/KUM
spongiosaplasty	SPON/JOES/PLAS/TI		SPO/ROT/RI/KUM
	SPON/JOE/SA/PLAS/TI		SPOE/ROT/RI/KUM
spongiosa	SPON/JOE/SA	sporozoa	SPOR/ZOE/WA
spongiose	SPON/JOES	sporozoan	SPOR/ZOE/WAN
spongiosi	SPON/JOE/SAOI	Sporozoasida	SPOR/ZOE/AS/DA
spongiosis	SPON/JOE/SIS		SPOR/ZO/AS/DA
spongiositis	SPON/JO/SAOITS	sporozoite	SPOR/ZOE/AOIT
spongiosum	SPON/JOE/SUM	sporozooid	SPOR/ZOE/OID
	SPON/JOES/UM	sporozoon	SPOR/ZAON
spongiosus	SPON/JOE/SUS		SPOR/ZOE/WON
spongiotic	SPON/JOT/IK	sporozoosis	SPOR/ZOE/O/SIS
spongium	SPON/JUM		SPOR/ZOE/YOE/SIS
spongy	SPON/JI	sport	SPORT
spontanea	SPON/TAIN/YA	sporul-	SPOR/L-
spontaneous	SPON/TAIN/YOUS		SPOR/YAOU/L-
spool	SPAOL		SPOR/YU/L-

sporular	SPOR/LAR		SIS
sporulation	SPOR/LAIGS	stachydrine	STAK/DRAOEN
sporule	SPOR/YAOUL		STAK/DRIN
spot	SPOT		STA/KID/RIN
sprain	SPRAIN	stachyose	STAK/YOES
spray	SPRAI	stactometer	STAK/TOM/TER
spreader	SPRED/ER	Stader	STAID/ER
Sprengel	SPRENG/EL		STAI/DER
	SPREN/GEL	Staderini	STAD/RAOE/NAOE
spring	SPRING	stadia	STAID/YA
Spritz	K-P/SPRITS	stadiometer	STAID/YOM/TER
sprout	SPROUT	stadium	STAID/YUM
spruce	SPRAOUS	Stadol	STAI/DOL
sprue	SPRAOU	staff	STAF
sprue-former	SPRAOU/FORM/ER	stage	STAIJ
S-P-T	S-RBGS/H-F/P-RBGS/H-F/T-RBGS	stagger	STAG/ER
spud	SPUD	staggers	STAG/ER/-S
Spumavirinae	SPAOUM/VIR/NAE	staghorn	STAG/HORN
Spumavirus	SPAOUM/VAOI/RUS	staging	STAIJ/-G
spur	SPUR	stagnation	STAG/NAIGS
spuriae	SPUR/YAE	Stahl	STA*UL
	SPAOUR/YAE		(*not* STAUL; see stall)
spurious	SPUR/YOUS	Stahr	STA*R
	SPAOUR/YOUS		(*not* STAR; see star)
sputa	SPAOU/TA	stain	STAIN
sputamentum	SPAOUT/MEN/TUM	staining	STAIN/-G
	SPAOUT/-MT/UM	stair	STAIR
sputum	SPAOUT/UM	staircase	STAIR/KAIS
	SPAOU/TUM	stalactite	STA/LAK/TAOIT
sputum Gram stain	SPAOUT/UM/GRA*M/STAIN	stalagmite	STA/LAG/MAOIT
	SPAOU/TUM/GRA*M/STAIN	stalagmometer	STAL/AG/MOM/TER
sputum smear	SPAOUT/UM/SMAOER	stalagmon	STA/LAG/MON
	SPAOU/TUM/SMAOER		STAL/AG/MON
squalene	SKWAI/LAOEN	staling	STAIL/-G
	SKWAL/AOEN	stalk	STAUK
squam(o)-	SKWAIM	-stalsis	STAL/SIS
	SKWAI/M(O)	staltic	STALT/IK
squama	SKWAI/MA	stamen	STAIM/-N
squamae	SKWAI/MAE	stamina	STAM/NA
squamate	SKWAI/MAIT	stammer	STAM/ER
squamatization	SKWAIM/TI/ZAIGS	stammering	STAM/ER/-G
squame	SKWAIM	Stammler	STAM/LER
squamocellular	SKWAIM/SEL/YAOU/LAR	Stamnosoma	STAM/NO/SOE/MA
squamocolumnar	SKWAIM/KLUM/NAR	stand	STAND
	SKWAIM/KO/LUM/NAR	standard	STAND/ARD
	SKWAIM/KOL/UM/NAR		STAN/DARD
squamofrontal	SKWAIM/FRON/TAL	standardization	STAND/ARD/ZAIGS
squamomastoid	SKWAIM/MAS/TOID		STAN/DARD/ZAIGS
squamo-occipital	SKWAIM/OK/SIP/TAL	standardize	STAN/DAR/DAOIZ
squamoparietal	SKWAIM/PRAOI/TAL		STAND/ARD/AOIZ
squamopetrosal	SKWAIM/PE/TROE/SAL		STAN/AR/DAOIZ
squamosa	SKWAI/MOE/SA		STAN/DARD/AOIZ
squamosae	SKWAI/MOE/SAE	standstill	STAND/ST*IL
squamosal	SKWAI/MOE/SAL	Stanford-Binet	STAN/FORD/BI/NAI
	SKWA/MOE/SAL		STAN/FORD/H-F/BI/NAI
squamosoparietal	SKWAI/MOES/PRAOI/TAL	Stanley	STAN/LAOE
squamosphenoid	SKWAIM/SFAOE/NOID	stannate	STAN/AIT
squamotemporal	SKWAIM/TEFRP/RAL		STAN/NAIT
squamous	SKWAIM/OUS	stannic	STAN/IK
	SKWAI/MOUS	stanniferous	STAN/IF/ROUS
squamozygomatic	SKWAIM/ZAOIG/MAT/IK		STAN/NIF/ROUS
squarrose	SKWAR/OES	stannosis	STAN/NOE/SIS
squarrous	SKWAR/OUS		STAN/O/SIS
squatting	SKWAUT/-G	stannous	STAN/OUS
	SKWAT/-G	stannum	STAN/UM
squeeze	SKWAOEZ	stanolone	STAN/LOEN
squill	SKWIL	stanozolol	STANOEZ/LOL
squillitic	SKWIL/LIT/IK		STAN/OEZ/LOEL
squint	SKWINT		STAN/ZOE/LOL
SSKI Solution	S-RBGS/S*RBGS/K*RBGS/*IRBGS/	stapedectomy	STAIP/DEKT/M*I
	SLAOUGS	stapedes	STAIP/DAOEZ
stab	STAB	stapedi(o)-	STA/PAOED/Y(O)
stabilate	STAIB/LAIT		STAI/PAOED/Y(O)
stabile	STAI/BAOIL	stapedial	STA/PAOED/YAL
	STAI/BIL		STAI/PAOED/YAL
	(*not* STAIBL; see stable)	stapedii	STA/PAOED/YAOI
stabilimeter	STAIB/LIM/TER		STAI/PAOED/YAOI
stability	STABLT	stapediolysis	STA/PAOED/YOL/SIS
stabilization	STAIB/LI/ZAIGS		STAI/PAOED/YOL/SIS
	STAIBL/ZAIGS	stapedioplasty	STA/PAOED/YO/PLAS/TI
stabilize	STAIB/LAOIZ		STAI/PAOED/YO/PLAS/TI
	STAIBL/AOIZ	stapediotenotomy	STA/PAOED/YO/TE/NOT/M*I
stabilizer	STAIB/LAOIZ/ER		STAI/PAOED/YO/TE/NOT/M*I
	STAIBL/AOIZ/ER	stapediovestibular	STA/PAOED/YO/VES/TIB/LAR
stable	STAIBL		STAI/PAOED/YO/VES/TIB/LAR
staccato	STA/KA/TOE	stapedis	STAI/PAOE/DIS
	STA/KAT/TOE		STA/PAOE/DIS
stachbotryotoxicosis	STAK/BOT/RO/TOX/KOE/SIS		STAIP/DIS
	STAK/BOT/RAOE/YO/TOX/KOE/	stapedius	STAI/PAOED/YUS

	STA/PAOED/YUS	statics	STAT/IK/-S
stapes	STAI/PAOEZ	statim	STAI/TIM
staph	STA*F	station	STAIGS
	(*not* STAF; see staff)	stationary	STAIGS/NAIR
Staphage Lysate	STAF/AJ/LAOI/SAIT		STAIGS/AIR
Staphcillin	STAF/SLIN	statistic	STA/T*IS/IK
	STAF/SIL/LIN	statistics	STA/T*IS/IK/-S
staphyl(o)-	STAF/L(O)	statoacoustic	STAT/AI/KAO*US/IK
staphylagra	STAF/LAG/RA	Statobex	STAT/BEX
staphylectomy	STAF/LEKT/M*I	statoconia	STAT/KOEN/YA
staphyledema	STAF/LE/DAOE/MA	statoconium	STAT/KOEN/YUM
staphylematoma	STAF/LEM/TOE/MA	statocyst	STAT/S*IS
staphyline	STAF/LAOIN	statokinetic	STAT/KI/NET/IK
	STAF/LAOEN	statokinetics	STAT/KI/NET/IK/-S
staphylinus	STAF/LAOI/NUS	statolith	STAT/L*IT
staphylion	STA/FIL/YON	statometer	STA/TOM/TER
staphylitis	STAF/LAOITS	statosphere	STAT/SFAOER
staphyloangina	STAF/LO/AN/JI/NA	statural	STAT/KHURL
	STAF/LO/AN/JAOI/NA		STAFP/RAL
staphylobacterin	STAF/LO/BAKT/RIN	stature	STAT/KHUR
staphylocide	STAF/LO/SAO*ID		STA/KHUR
staphylococcal	STAF/LO/KOK/KAL	status	STAI/TUS
staphylococcemia	STAF/LO/KOK/SAOEM/YA		STAT/TUS
staphylococci	STAF/LO/KOK/SAOI	statuvolence	STAFP/VOE/LENS
staphylococcia	STAF/LO/KOX/YA		STAT/YAOU/VOE/LENS
staphylococcic	STAF/LO/KOX/IK		STA/TAOUV/LENS
	STAF/LO/KOK/SIK	statuvolent	STAFP/VOE/LENT
staphylococcide	STAF/LO/KOK/SAO*ID		STAT/YAOU/VOE/LENT
staphylococcolysin	STAF/LO/KOK/KOL/SIN		STA/TAOUV/LENT
staphylococcolysis	STAF/LO/KOK/KOL/SIS	statuvolic	STAFP/VOL/IK
staphylococcoses	STAF/LO/KOK/KOE/SAOEZ		STAT/YAOU/VOL/IK
staphylococcosis	STAF/LO/KOK/KOE/SIS	statuvolism	STAFP/VOE/LIFM
staphylococcus	STAF/LO/KOK/KUS		STAT/YAOU/VOE/LIFM
Staphylococcus	K-P/STAF/LO/KOK/KUS		STA/TAOUV/LIFM
staphyloderma	STAF/LO/DER/MA	Staub	STAUB
staphylodermatitis	STAF/LO/DERM/TAOITS	Staub-Traugott	STAUB/H-F/TRAU/GOT
staphylodialysis	STAF/LO/DI/AL/SIS	staurion	STAUR/YON
staphylohemia	STAF/LO/HAOEM/YA	stauroplegia	STAUR/PLAOE/JA
staphylohemolysin	STAF/LO/HAOE/MOL/SIN		STAU/RO/PLAOE/JA
staphylokinase	STAF/LO/KAOI/NAIS	stave	STAIV
staphylolysin	STAF/LOL/SIN	stavesacre	STAIVS/AIK/ER
staphyloma	STAF/LOE/MA		STAIVS/AI/KER
staphylomatous	STAF/LOEM/TOUS	staxis	STAK/SIS
staphyloncus	STAF/LON/KUS	stay	STAI
staphylopharyngorrhaphy	STAF/LO/FARN/GOR/FI	steadiness	STED/DI/*NS
staphyloplasty	STAF/LO/PLAS/TI	steal	STAEL
staphyloplegia	STAF/LO/PLAOE/JA		(*not* STAOEL; see steel)
staphyloptosia	STAF/LOP/TOEZ/YA	steapsin	STAOE/AP/SIN
staphyloptosis	STAF/LOP/TOE/SIS	steapsinogen	STAOE/AP/SIN/JEN
staphylorrhaphy	STAF/LOR/FI	stear(o)-	STAOER
staphyloschisis	STAF/LOS/KI/SIS		STAOER/R(O)
staphylotome	STAF/LO/TOEM		STAOE/R(O)
staphylotomy	STAF/LOT/M*I	stearal	STAOERL
staphylotoxin	STAF/LO/TOK/SIN		STAOER/RAL
staphylotropic	STAF/LO/TROP/IK		STAOE/RAL
stapling	STAIP/-LG	stearaldehyde	STAOE/RALD/HAOID
star	STAR		STAOER/ALD/HAOID
starch	STA*RPBLG	stearate	STAOER/RAIT
	STAR/-FP		STAOE/RAIT
stare	STAER	stearic	STAOER/IK
	(*not* STAIR; see stair)		STAOE/RIK
starling	STARL/-G	steariform	STAOE/AR/FORM
	STAR/LING		STAOE/YAR/FORM
	STAR/-LG		STAOER/FORM
Starling	K-P/STARL/-G	stearin	STAOER/RIN
	K-P/STAR/LING		STAOE/RIN
	K-P/STAR/-LG	Stearns	STERNZ
Star-Otic Ear Solution	STAR/OT/IK/AOER/SLAOUGS		STERNS
starter	START/ER	stearrhea	STAOE/RAOE/YA
starvation	STAR/VAIGS	stearyl	STAOE/RIL
starve	STAFRB		STAOER/RIL
stases	STAI/SAOEZ	steat(o)-	STAOE/T(O)
-stasia	STAIZ/YA	steatite	STAOE/TAOIT
stasimorphia	STAS/MOR/FAOE/YA	steatitis	STAOE/TAOITS
	STAS/MOR/FA	steatocystoma	STAOE/TO/SIS/TOE/MA
stasimorphy	STAS/MOR/FI	steatocele	STAOE/AT/SAO*EL
stasis	STAI/SIS		STAOE/TO/SAO*EL
-stasis	(v)*S/SIS	steatogenesis	STAOE/TO/JEN/SIS
	STAI/SIS	steatogenous	STAOE/TOJ/NOUS
stat	STAT	steatolysis	STAOE/TOL/SIS
-stat	STAT	steatolytic	STAOE/TO/LIT/IK
statampere	STAT/AM/PAOER	steatoma	STAOE/TOE/MA
statcoulomb	STAT/KAOU/LOM	steatomery	STAOE/TOM/RI
state	STAIT	steatonecrosis	STAOE/TO/NE/KROE/SIS
statfarad	STAT/FA/RAD	steatopyga	STAOE/TO/PAOI/GA
stathenry	STAT/HEN/RI	steatopygia	STAOE/TO/PIJ/YA
stathmokinesis	STA*T/MO/KI/NAOE/SIS	steatopygous	STAOE/TOP/GOUS
static	STAT/IK	steatorrhea	STAOE/TO/RAOE/YA
statica	STAT/KA	steatosis	STAOE/TOE/SIS

steatozoon	STAOE/TO/ZAON	steradian	STE/RAID/YAN
Steenbock	STAOEN/BOK	sterane	STER/AIN
stege	STAOE/GAOE		STAOER/AIN
	STAOE/JAOE	Sterapred DS	STER/PRED/D-RBGS/S*RBGS
stegnosis	STEG/NOE/SIS	sterco-	STERK
stegnotic	STEG/NOT/IK		STER/KO
Stein	STAOIN	stercobilin	STERK/BAOI/LIN
Steinberg	STAOIN/BERG		STERK/B*I/LIN
Steinbrinck	STAOIN/BRIN/-K		STERK/BIL/LIN
	STAOIN/BR*ING	stercobilinogen	STERK/BAOI/LIN/JEN
Steiner	STAOIN/ER		STERK/B*I/LIN/JEN
Steinert	STAOIN/ERT		STERK/BIL/LIN/JEN
Steinmann	STAOIN/MAN	stercolith	STERK/L*IT
Stelazine	STEL/ZAOEN	stercoporphyrin	STERK/POR/FRIN
stele	STAO*EL	stercoraceous	STERK/RAIRBS
stella	STEL/LA	stercoral	STERK/RAL
stellae	STEL/LAE	stercoralis	STERK/RAI/LIS
stellata	STEL/LAI/TA	stercorin	STERK/RIN
	STEL/LA/TA	stercorolith	STERK/RO/L*IT
stellatae	STEL/LAI/TAE	stercoroma	STERK/ROE/MA
stellate	STEL/LAIT	stercorous	STERK/ROUS
	STEL/AIT	stercus	STER/KUS
stellectomy	STEL/EKT/M*I	stere	STAO*ER
	STEL/LEKT/M*I		(*not* STAOER; see steer)
stellite	STEL/LAOIT	stereo-	STER/YO
	STEL/AOIT		STAOER/YO
stellreflexe	STEL/RE/FLEX	stereoagnosis	STER/YO/AG/NOE/SIS
stellula	STEL/YAOU/LA	stereoanesthesia	STER/YO/ANS/THAOEZ/YA
	STEL/YU/LA	stereoarthrolysis	STER/YO/AR/THROL/SIS
	(*not* STEL/LA; see stella)	stereoauscultation	STER/YO/AUS/KUL/TAIGS
stellulae	STEL/YAOU/LAE	stereoblastula	STER/YO/BLA*S/LA
	STEL/YU/LAE	stereocampimeter	STER/YO/KAM/PIM/TER
	(*not* STEL/LAE; see stellae)	stereochemical	STER/YO/KEM/KAL
Stellwag	STEL/VAG	stereochemistry	STER/YO/KEM/STRI
	STEL/WAG	stereocilia	STER/YO/SIL/YA
stem	STEM	stereocilium	STER/YO/SIL/YUM
Stemetic	STE/MET/IK	stereocinefluorography	STER/YO/SIN/FLAOU/ROG/FI
sten	STEN	stereocolpogram	STER/YO/KOL/PO/GRAM
Stender	STEND/ER	stereocolposcope	STER/YO/KOL/PO/SKOEP
Stenger	STENG/ER	stereoelectroencephalography	
stenion	STEN/YON		STER/YO/LEK/TRO/EN/SEF/LOG/
steno	STEN/NOE		FI
Steno	K-P/STEN/NOE	stereoencephalometry	STER/YO/EN/SEF/LOM/TRI
steno-	STEN	stereoencephalotome	STER/YO/EN/SEF/LO/TOEM
	STEN/NO	stereoencephalotomy	STER/YO/EN/SEF/LOT/M*I
stenobregmatic	STEN/BREG/MAT/IK	stereofluoroscopy	STER/YO/FLAOU/ROS/KPI
stenocardia	STEN/KARD/YA	stereognosis	STER/YOG/NOE/SIS
stenocephalia	STEN/SFAIL/YA	stereognostic	STER/YOG/NO*S/IK
stenocephalic	STEN/SFAL/IK	stereogram	STER/YO/GRAM
stenocephalous	STEN/SEF/LOUS	stereograph	STER/YO/GRAF
stenocephaly	STEN/SEF/LI	stereography	STER/YOG/FI
stenochoria	STEN/KOER/YA	stereoisomer	STER/YO/AOIS/MER
stenocompressor	STEN/KPRES/SOR	stereoisomeric	STER/YO/AOIS/MER/IK
	STEN/KOM/PRES/SOR	stereoisomerism	STER/YO/AOI/SOM/RIFM
stenocoriasis	STEN/KO/RAOI/SIS	stereology	STER/YOLG
	STEN/KOE/RAOI/SIS	stereometer	STER/YOM/TER
stenocrotaphia	STEN/KROE/TAIF/YA	stereometry	STER/YOM/TRI
stenocrotaphy	STE/NO/KROT/FI	stereo-ophthalmoscope	STER/YO/OF/THAL/MO/SKOEP
-stenoma	STE/NOE/MA	stereo-orthopter	STER/YO/OR/THOPT/ER
	STAOE/NOE/MA	stereopathy	STER/YOP/TH*I
stenopaic	STEN/PAI/IK	stereophantoscope	STER/YO/FANT/SKOEP
stenopeic	STEN/PAOE/IK	stereophorometer	STER/YO/FOE/ROM/TER
stenophotic	STEN/FOET/IK	stereophoroscope	STER/YO/FOER/SKOEP
stenosal	STE/NOE/SAL	stereophotography	STER/YO/FOE/TOG/FI
stenosed	STEN/OES/-D		STER/YO/FRAF/FI
	STE/NOES/-D	stereophotomicrograph	STER/YO/FOET/MAOI/KRO/GRAF
stenoses	STE/NOE/SAOEZ	stereoplasm	STER/YO/PLAFM
stenosis	STE/NOE/SIS	stereopsis	STER/YOP/SIS
stenostomia	STEN/STOEM/YA	stereoradiography	STER/YO/RAID/YOG/FI
stenothermal	STEN/THER/MAL	stereoroentgenography	STER/YO/RENT/GEN/OG/FI
stenothermic	STEN/THERM/IK	stereoroentgenometry	STER/YO/RENT/GEN/OM/TRI
stenothorax	STEN/THOR/AX	stereosalpingography	STER/YO/SAL/PIN/GOG/FI
stenotic	STE/NOT/IK	stereoscope	STER/YO/SKOEP
stenoxenous	STEN/OX/NOUS	stereoscopic	STER/YO/SKOP/IK
Stensen	STEN/SEN	stereoscopy	STER/YOS/KPI
	STENS/-N	stereoselective	STER/YO/SLEKT/IV
stent	STENT	stereoskiagraphy	STER/YO/SKAOI/AG/FI
Stent	K-P/STENT	stereospecific	STER/YO/SPEFK
Stenvers	STEN/VERZ	stereotactic	STER/YO/TAKT/IK
step	STEP	stereotaxic	STER/YO/TAX/IK
stephanial	STE/FAIN/YAL	stereotaxis	STER/YO/TAK/SIS
stephanion	STE/FAIN/YON	stereotaxy	STER/YO/TAK/SI
Stephanofilaria	STEF/NO/FLAIR/YA	stereotropic	STER/YO/TROP/IK
Stephanofilaria stilesi	STEF/NO/FLAIR/YA/STAOI/LAOE/	stereotropism	STER/YOT/RO/PIFM
	SAOI	stereotype	STER/YO/TAOIP
stephanofilariasis	STEF/NO/FIL/RAOI/SIS	stereotypy	STER/YO/TAOI/PI
Stephanurus	STEF/NAOU/RUS	-steresis	STE/RAOE/SIS
Stephanurus dentatus	STEF/NAOU/RUS/DEN/TAI/TUS		STRAOE/SIS
steppage	STEP/AJ		*S/RAOE/SIS (if sounded)

	-S/TRAOE/SIS (if sounded)	steroid-	STAOER/OID
steric	STER/IK		STAOER/ROID
	(*not* STAOER/IK; see stearic)		STER/OID
sterid	STER/ID		STER/ROID
sterigma	STE/RIG/MA	steroidal	STAOER/OI/DAL
	STAOE/RIG/MA		STAOER/ROI/DAL
sterigmata	STE/RIG/MA/TA	steroidogenesis	STAOER/OID/JEN/SIS
	STAOE/RIG/MA/TA		STAOER/ROID/JEN/SIS
sterilant	STER/LANT	steroidogenic	STAOER/OID/JEN/IK
sterile	STERL		STAOER/ROID/JEN/IK
	STER/RIL	sterol	STAOER/OL
	STER/IL	-sterol	*S/ROL
	STER/RAOIL		*S/ROEL
sterilis	STE/RIL/LIS	stertor	STER/TOR
	STER/RIL/LIS	stertorous	STERT/ROUS
sterilisata	STE/RIL/SAI/TA	steth(o)-	ST*ET
	STER/RIL/SAI/TA		STE/TH(O)
	STER/IL/SAI/TA	stethacoustic	ST*ET/KAO*US/IK
	STERL/SAI/TA		ST*ET/AI/KAO*US/IK
sterility	STE/RIL/TI	stethalgia	ST*ET/AL/JA
	STRIL/TI		STE/THAL/JA
	STER/RIL/TI	stetharteritis	ST*ET/ART/RAOITS
	STER/IL/TI	stethemia	ST*ET/AOEM/YA
sterilization	STERL/ZAIGS		STE/THAOEM/YA
	STER/RIL/ZAIGS	stethendoscope	ST*ET/*END/SKOEP
	STER/LI/ZAIGS	stethocyrtograph	ST*ET/SIRT/GRAF
sterilize	STER/LAOIZ	stethocyrtometer	ST*ET/SIR/TOM/TER
	STERL/AOIZ	stethogoniometer	ST*ET/GOEN/YOM/TER
sterilizer	STER/LAOIZ/ER	stethograph	ST*ET/GRAF
	STERL/AOIZ/ER	stethography	STE/THOG/FI
Stern	K-P/STERN		ST*ET/OG/FI
stern(o)-	STERN	stethokyrtograph	ST*ET/KIRT/GRAF
	STER/N(O)	stethometer	ST*ET/OM/TER
sterna	STER/NA		STE/THOM/TER
sternad	STER/NAD	Stethomyia	ST*ET/MAOI/YA
sternal	STERNL	stethomyitis	ST*ET/MAOI/AOITS
sternalgia	STER/NAL/JA	stethomyositis	ST*ET/MAOI/SAOITS
sternalis	STER/NAI/LIS	stethoparalysis	ST*ET/PRAL/SIS
Sternberg	STERN/BERG	stethophone	ST*ET/FOEN
sternebra	STER/NAOE/BRA	stethophonometer	ST*ET/FOE/NOM/TER
sternebrae	STER/NAOE/BRAE	stethopolyscope	ST*ET/POL/SKOEP
sternen	STER/NEN	stethoscope	ST*ET/SKOEP
sterni	STER/NAOI	stethoscopic	ST*ET/SKOP/IK
sternochondroscapularis	STERN/KON/DRO/SKAP/LAI/RIS	stethoscopy	STE/THOS/KPI
sternoclavicular	STERN/KLA/VIK/LAR		ST*ET/OS/KPI
sternoclavicularis	STERN/KLA/VIK/LAI/RIS	stethospasm	ST*ET/SPAFM
sternocleidal	STERN/KLAOI/DAL	Stevens	STAOEVNZ
sternocleidomastoid	STERN/KLAOID/MAS/TOID		STAOEVNS
sternocleidomastoideus	STERN/KLAOID/MAS/TOID/YUS		STAOEV/ENZ
sternocostal	STERN/KOS/TAL		STAOE/VENZ
sternocostales	STERN/KOS/TAI/LAOEZ	Stewart	STAOU/WART
sternocostalis	STERN/KOS/TAI/LIS		STAO*URT
sternodymia	STERN/DIM/YA		(*not* STAOU/ART or STAOURT; see
sternodymus	STER/NOD/MUS		Stuart)
sternodynia	STERN/DIN/YA	S-T Forte	S-RBGS/T-RBGS/FOR/TAI
sternofascialis	STERN/FARB/YAI/LIS	sthen(o)-	STHEN
sternoglossal	STERN/GLOS/SAL		STHE/N(O)
sternogoniometer	STERN/GOEN/YOM/TER	sthenia	STHAOEN/YA
sternohyoid	STERN/HAOI/OID	sthenic	STHEN/IK
sternohyoidea	STERN/HAOI/OID/YA	sthenometer	STHE/NOM/TER
sternohyoidei	STERN/HAOI/OID/YAOI		STHEN/OM/TER
sternohyoideus	STERN/HAOI/OID/YUS	sthenometry	STHE/NOM/TRI
sternoid	STER/NOID		STHEN/OM/TRI
sternomastoid	STERN/MAS/TOID	sthenophotic	STHEN/FOET/IK
sternopagia	STERN/PAI/JA	sthenoplastic	STHEN/PLA*S/IK
sternopagus	STER/NOP/GUS	stibamine	STIB/MAOEN
sternopericardial	STERN/P*ER/KARD/YAL		STIB/MIN
sternoscapular	STERN/SKAP/LAR	stibenyl	STIB/NIL
sternoschisis	STER/NOS/KI/SIS	stibialism	STIB/YA/LIFM
sternothyreoideus	STERN/THAOIR/YOID/YUS		STIB/YAL/IFM
sternothyroid	STERN/THAOI/ROID	stibiated	STIB/YAIT/-D
sternothyroideus	STERN/THAOI/ROID/YUS	stibiation	STIB/YAIGS
sternotomy	STER/NOT/M*I	stibium	STIB/YUM
sternotracheal	STERN/TRAIK/YAL	stibocaptate	STIB/KAP/TAIT
sternotrypesis	STERN/TRAOI/PAOE/SIS	stibogluconate	STIB/GLAOUK/NAIT
sternovertebral	STERN/VERT/BRAL	stibonium	STI/BOEN/YUM
sternoxiphopagus	STERN/ZAOI/FOP/GUS	stibophen	STIB/FEN
	STERN/ZI/FOP/GUS	stichochrome	STIK/KROEM
sternum	STER/NUM	Sticker	K-P/STIK/ER
	STERN/UM	Sticta	STIK/TA
sternutatio	STER/NAOU/TAI/SHOE	Stieda	STAOE/DA
	STER/NAOU/TAIRB/YOE	stiedae	STAOE/DAE
sternutation	STER/NAOU/TAIGS	Stierlin	STAOER/LIN
sternutator	STER/NAOU/TAI/TOR		STIR/LIN
sternutatory	STER/NAOUT/TOIR	stifle	STAOIFL
steroid	STAOER/OID		STAOIF/-L
	STAOER/ROID	stigma	STIG/MA
	STER/OID	stigmal	STIG/MAL
	STER/ROID	stigmastane	STIG/MAS/TAIN

stigmasterol	STIG/MA*S/ROL		SOEM/TO/DIS/OED/YA
stigmata	STIG/MA/TA	stomatogastric	STOEM/TO/GAS/TRIK
stigmatic	STIG/MAT/IK	stomatoglossitis	STOEM/TO/GLOS/SAOITS
stigmatism	STIG/MA/TIFM	stomatognathic	STOEM/TO/NA*T/IK
stigmatization	STIG/MA/TI/ZAIGS		STOEM/TOG/NA*T/IK
	STIG/MAT/ZAIGS	stomatography	STOEM/TOG/FI
stigmatometer	STIG/MA/TOM/TER	stomatolalia	STOEM/TO/LAIL/YA
stigmatoscope	STIG/MAT/SKOEP	stomatologic	STOEM/TO/LOJ/IK
stigmatoscopy	STIG/MA/TOS/KPI	stomatological	STOEM/TO/LOJ/KAL
Stilbaceae	STIL/BAIS/YAE	stomatologist	STOEM/TO*LGS
stilbamidine	STIL/BAM/DAOEN	stomatology	STOEM/TOLG
stilbazium	STIL/BAZ/YUM	stomatomalacia	STOEM/TO/MA/LAI/SHA
stilbene	STIL/BAOEN	stomatomenia	STOEM/TO/MAOEN/YA
stilbestrol	STIL/BES/TROL	stomatomy	STOE/MAT/M*I
Stiles	STAOILZ	stomatomycosis	STOEM/TO/MAOI/KOE/SIS
	STAOILS	stomatonecrosis	STOEM/TO/NE/KROE/SIS
stilet	see stylet	stomatonoma	STOEM/TO/NOE/MA
stili	see styli	stomatopathy	STOEM/TOP/TH*I
stillbirth	STIL/B*IRT	stomatoplastic	STOEM/TO/PLA*S/IK
stillborn	STIL/BO*RN	stomatoplasty	STOEM/TO/PLAS/TI
Still	K-P/STIL	stomatorrhagia	STOEM/TO/RAI/JA
Stiller	K-P/STIL/ER	stomatoschisis	STOEM/TOS/KI/SIS
stillicidium	STIL/SID/YUM	stomatoscope	STOEM/TO/SKOEP
Stilling	STIL/-G		STOE/MAT/SKOEP
	STIL/LING	stomatosis	STOEM/TOE/SIS
Stilphostrol	STIL/FOS/TROEL	stomatotomy	STOEM/TOT/M*I
	STIL/FOS/TROL	-stomia	STOEM/YA
stilus	see stylus	-stomiasis	STOE/MAOI/SIS
stimul-	STIM/L-	stomion	STOEM/YON
	STIM/YAOU/L-	stomocephalus	STOEM/SEF/LUS
	STIM/YU/L-	stomodeal	STOEM/DAOEL
stimulant	STIM/LANT		STOEM/DAOE/YAL
stimulate	STIM/LAIT	stomodeum	STOEM/DAOEM
stimulation	STIM/LAIGS		STOEM/DAOE/UM
stimulator	STIM/LAI/TOR		STOEM/DAOE/YUM
stimuli	STIM/LAOI	stomoschisis	STOE/MOS/KI/SIS
stimulus	STIM/LUS	-stomosis	*S/MOE/SIS
sting	STING	Stomoxys	STOE/MOK/SIS
stipple	STIP/-L	-stomy	*S/M*I
stippling	STIP/-LG	stone	STOEN
stirpicultural	STIRP/KUL/KHURL	Stookey	STAO/KAOE
stirpiculture	STIRP/KUL/KHUR		STAOK/KAOE
stirrup	STIR/RUP	stool	STAOL
	(not STIR/UP; see stir up)	storage	STORJ
stitch	STIFP		STOR/AJ
stithe	STAO*IT	storax	STOR/AX
stochastic	STOE/KA*S/IK		STOER/AX
stock	STOK	storiform	STOR/FORM
Stock	K-P/STOK		STOER/FORM
Stocker	K-P/STOK/ER	stork	STORK
stocking	STOK/-G	storm	STORM
Stoerk	STERK	Storm van Leeuwen	STORM/VAN/LAOU/-N
stoichiology	STOIK/YOLG		STORM/VAN/LAOU/WEN
stoichiometry	STOIK/YOM/TRI		K-P/STORM/VAN/LAOU/-N
stoke	STOEK		K-P/STORM/VAN/LAOU/WEN
stoker	STOEK/ER	stosstherapy	STOS/THER/PI
Stokes	STOEKS		STOSZ/THER/PI
stolon	STOE/LON	strabism-	STRA/BIZ/M-
stoma	STOE/MA		STRA/BIS/M-
stomacace	STOE/MAK/SAOE	strabismal	STRA/BIZ/MAL
stomach	STOM/AK	strabismic	STRA/BIZ/MIK
stomach ache	STOM/AK/AIK	strabismology	STRA/BIZ/MOLG
stomachal	STOM/KAL	strabismometer	STRA/BIZ/MOM/TER
stomachalgia	STOM/KAL/JA	strabismus	STRA/BIZ/MUS
	STOM/AK/AL/JA	strabometer	STRA/BOM/TER
stomachic	STOE/MAK/IK	strabometry	STRA/BOM/TRI
	STOM/AK/IK	strabotome	STRAB/TOEM
stomachodynia	STOM/KO/DIN/YA	strabotomy	STRA/BOT/M*I
stomachoscopy	STOM/KOS/KPI	straddling	STRAD/-LG
	STOEM/KOS/KPI	strain	STRAIN
stomal	STOE/MAL	strainer	STRAIN/ER
stomalgia	STOE/MAL/JA	strait	STRAIT
stomat(o)-	STOEM/T(O)	straitjacket	STRAIT/JAK/ET
stomata	STOEM/TA	stramonium	STRA/MOEN/YUM
	STOE/MA/TA	strand	STRAND
	STOE/MAT/TA	Strandberg	STRAND/BERG
stomatal	STOEM/TAL	strangalesthesia	STRAN/GAL/ES/THAOEZ/YA
stomatalgia	STOEM/TAL/JA	strangle	STRANG/-L
stomatic	STOE/MAT/IK		STRAING/-L
stomatitides	STOEM/TIT/DAOEZ	strangulated	STRANG/LAIT/-D
stomatitis	STOEM/TAOITS	strangulation	STRANG/LAIGS
stomatocace	STOEM/TOK/SAOE	stranguria	STRAN/GAOUR/YA
stomatocatharsis	STOEM/TO/KA/THAR/SIS	strangury	STRANG/RI
stomatocyte	STOEM/TO/SAO*IT		STRAN/GAOU/RI
stomatocytosis	STOEM/TO/SAOI/TOE/SIS	strap	STRAP
stomatodeum	STOEM/TO/DAOE/UM	strapping	STRAP/-G
	STOEM/TO/DAOE/YUM	Strassburg	STRAS/BURG
stomatodynia	STOEM/TO/DIN/YA		STRAUS/BURG
stomatodysodia	SOEM/TO/DI/SOED/YA		STRASZ/BURG

Strasburger	STRAUSZ/BURG
	STRAS/BURG/ER
	STRAUS/BURG/ER
strata	STRAI/TA
	STRAT/TA
strati	STRAI/TAOI
	STRAT/TAOI
stratification	STRAT/FI/KAIGS
stratified	STRAT/FI/-D
stratiform	STRAT/FORM
stratigram	STRAT/GRAM
stratigraphy	STRA/TIG/FI
stratum	STRAI/TUM
	STRAT/UM
stratum basale	STRAI/TUM/BA/SAI/LAOE
stratum corneum	STRAI/TUM/KORN/YUM
stratum germinativum	STRAI/TUM/JERM/NA/TAOI/VUM
	STRAI/TUM/JERM/NA/TAOIV/UM
Straus	STROUS
Strauss	STROUSZ
strawberry	STRAU/BER/RI
streak	STRAOEK
stream	STRAOEM
streaming	STRAOEM/-G
streblodactyly	STREB/LO/DAKT/LI
streblomicrodactyly	STREB/LO/MAOI/KRO/DAKT/LI
stremma	STREM/MA
strength	STR*ENT
	STR*ENGT
strephenopodia	STREF/NO/POED/YA
strephexopodia	STREF/EX/POED/YA
	STREF/KPO/POED/YA
strephopodia	STREF/POED/YA
strephosymbolia	STREF/SIM/BOEL/YA
strepitus	STREP/TUS
strepogenin	STREP/JEN/NIN
strepsinema	STREPS/NAOE/MA
strepsitene	STREPS/TAOEN
	STREP/SI/TAOE
strept(o)-	STREPT
	STREP/T(O)
Streptase	STREP/TAIS
strepticemia	STREPT/SAOEM/YA
streptoangina	STREPT/AN/JI/NA
	STREPT/AN/JAOI/NA
streptobacilli	STREPT/BA/SIL/LAOI
streptobacillus	STREPT/BA/SIL/LUS
Streptobacillus	K-P/STREPT/BA/SIL/LUS
streptobacteria	STREPT/BAK/TAOER/YA
streptobacterin	STREPT/BAKT/RIN
streptobiosamine	STREPT/BAO*I/OES/MAOEN
streptobiose	STREPT/BAO*I/OES
streptocerca	STREPT/SER/KA
streptocerciasis	STREPT/SER/KAOI/SIS
Streptococcaceae	STREPT/KOK/KAIS/YAE
streptococcal	STREPT/KOK/KAL
streptococcemia	STREPT/KOK/SAOEM/YA
streptococci	STREPT/KOK/SAOI
streptococcic	STREPT/KOX/IK
	STREPT/KOK/SIK
streptococcicide	STREPT/KOX/SAO*ID
streptococcosis	STREPT/KOK/KOE/SIS
streptococcus	STREPT/KOK/KUS
Streptococcus	K-P/STREPT/KOK/KUS
streptoderma	STREPT/DER/MA
streptodermatitis	STREPT/DERM/TAOITS
streptodornase	STREPT/DOR/NAIS
streptofuranose	STREPT/FAOUR/NOES
streptogenes	STREP/TOJ/NAOEZ
streptokinase	STREPT/KAOI/NAIS
streptolysin	STREPT/TOL/SIN
streptomicrodactyly	STREPT/MAOI/KRO/DAKT/LI
Streptomyces	STREPT/MAOI/SAOEZ
Streptomycetaceae	STREPT/MAOIS/TAIS/YAE
streptomycete	STREPT/MAOI/SAOET
streptomycin	STREPT/MAOI/SIN
streptomycosis	STREPT/MAOI/KOE/SIS
streptonivicin	STREPT/NI/VAOI/SIN
	STREPT/NAOIV/SIN
streptose	STREP/TOES
streptosepticemia	STREPT/SEPT/SAOEM/YA
streptothricosis	STREPT/THRI/KOE/SIS
Streptothrix	STREPT/THRIX
streptotrichal	STREP/TOT/RI/KAL
streptotrichiasis	STREPT/TRI/KAOI/SIS
streptotrichosis	STREPT/TRI/KOE/SIS
streptozocin	STREPT/ZOE/SIN
stress	STRESZ
stress breaker	STRESZ/BRAEK/ER

Stresscaps	STRESZ/KAP/-S
Stress Formula B-Complex	STRESZ/FORM/LA/B-RBGS/KOM/PLEX
stress riser	STRESZ/RAOIZ/ER
stress shielding	STRESZ/SHAOELD/-G
Stresstabs	STRESZ/TAB/-S
stretcher	STREFP/ER
stri(o)-	STRAOI
	STRAOI/Y(O)
stria	STRAOI/YA
striae	STRAOI/YAE
striascope	STRAOI/SKOEP
striat-	STRAOI/AI/T-
	STRAOI/AIT/-
	STRAOI/YAI/T-
	STRAOI/YAIT/-
striata	STRAOI/AI/TA
striatal	STRAOI/AI/TAL
striate	STRAOI/AIT
striated	STRAOI/AIT/-D
striati	STRAOI/AI/TAOI
striation	STRAOI/AIGS
striatonigral	STRAOI/TO/NAOI/GRAL
	STRAOI/AIT/NAOI/GRAL
striatum	STRAOI/AI/TUM
	STRAOI/AIT/UM
stricture	STRIK/KHUR
stricturization	STRIK/KHUR/ZAIGS
stricturotome	STRIK/KHUR/TOEM
stricturotomy	STRIK/KHUR/OT/M*I
strident	STRAOID/ENT
	STRAOI/DENT
Stri-Dex	STRAOI/DEX
stridor	STRAOI/DOR
stridulous	STRID/LOUS
string	STRING
striocellular	STRAOI/SEL/YAOU/LAR
striocerebellar	STRAOI/SER/BEL/LAR
striomotor	STRAOI/MOE/TOR
striomuscular	STRAOI/MUS/KLAR
strionigral	STRAOI/NAOI/GRAL
strip	STRIP
stripe	STRAOIP
stripper	STRIP/ER
strobila	STROE/BAOI/LA
strobilae	STROE/BAOI/LAE
strobile	STROE/BAOIL
	STROE/BIL
strobilocercus	STROEB/LO/SER/KUS
strobiloid	STROEB/LOID
strobilus	STROE/BAOI/LUS
stroboscope	STROEB/SKOEP
stroboscopic	STROEB/SKOP/IK
Stroganoff	STROEG/NOF
stroke	STROEK
stroma	STROE/MA
stromal	STROE/MAL
stromata	STROEM/TA
stromatic	STROE/MAT/IK
stromatin	STROEM/TIN
stromatogenous	STROEM/TOJ/NOUS
stromatolysis	STROEM/TOL/SIS
stromatosis	STROEM/TOE/SIS
Stromeyer	STROE/MAOI/ER
	STROE/MAOI/YER
stromic	STROEM/IK
stromuhr	STROEM/YAOUR
	STROEM/YUR
	STROE/MAOUR
Strong	K-P/STRONG
strongyl-	STRONG/L- (where G stands for J)
	STRON/JI/L-
strongyle	STRON/JIL
strongyli	STRON/JI/LAOI
strongyliasis	STRON/JI/LAOI/SIS
strongylid	STRON/JI/LID
Strongylidae	STRON/JIL/DAE
strongylina	STRONG/LAOI/NA
Strongyloidea	STRONG/LOID/YA
Strongyloides	STRONG/LOI/DAOEZ
strongyloidiasis	STRONG/LOI/DAOI/SIS
strongyloidosis	STRONG/LOI/DOE/SIS
strongylosis	STRONG/LOE/SIS
strongylus	STRONG/LUS
Strongylus	K-P/STRONG/LUS
strontia	STRON/SHA
strontium	STRON/SHUM
strontiuresis	STRON/SHAOU/RAOE/SIS
	STRON/SHAOE/YAOU/RAOE/SIS

416   ©1992 *StenEd®* Medical Dictionary

strontiuretic	STRON/SHAOU/RET/IK	stylet	STAOI/LET
	STRON/SHAOE/YAOU/RET/IK	stylette	STAO*I/LET
strophanthin	STROE/FAN/THIN		STAOI/L*ET
Strophanthus	STROE/FAN/THUS		see stylet
stropho-	STROF	styli	STAOI/LAOI
strophocephalus	STROF/SEF/LUS	styliform	STAOIL/FORM
strophocephaly	STROF/SEF/LI	styliscus	STAOI/LIS/KUS
strophosomia	STROF/SOEM/YA	styloauricularis	STAOIL/AU/RIK/LAI/RIS
strophosomus	STROF/SOE/MUS	styloglossus	STAOIL/GLOS/SUS
strophulus	STROF/LUS	stylohyal	STAOIL/HAOIL
	STROF/YAOU/LUS	stylohyoid	STAOIL/HAOI/OID
	STROF/YU/LUS	styloid	STAOI/LOID
-strophy	-S/TRO/FI	styloidea	STAOI/LOID/YA
Stroud	STROUD	styloiditis	STAOI/LOI/DAOITS
Strovite	STROE/VAOIT	stylomandibular	STAOIL/MAN/DIB/LAR
Strovite Plus	STROE/VAOIT/PLUS	stylomastoid	STAOIL/MAS/TOID
struck	STRUK	stylomaxillary	STAOIL/MAX/LAIR
structural	STRUK/KHURL	stylomyloid	STAOIL/MAOI/LOID
	STRUK/KHUR/RAL	stylopharyngeus	STAOIL/FRIN/JUS
structuralism	STRUK/KHURL/IFM	stylopodium	STAOIL/POED/YUM
	STRUK/KHUR/RAL/IFM	stylostaphyline	STAOIL/STAF/LAOIN
structure	STRUK/KHUR	stylosteophyte	STAOI/LO*S/YO/FAOIT
struma	STRAOU/MA	stylostixis	STAOIL/STIK/SIS
strumae	STRAOU/MAE	Styloviridae	STAOIL/VIR/DAE
strumal	STRAOU/MAL	stylus	STAOI/LUS
strumectomy	STRAOU/MEKT/M*I	stymatosis	STAOIM/TOE/SIS
strumiform	STRAOUM/FORM	stypage	STAOIP/AJ
strumipriva	STRAOUM/PRAOI/VA		STAOE/PAJ
strumiprival	STRAOU/MIP/RI/VAL	stype	STAOIP
	STRAOUM/PRAOIVL	stypsis	STIP/SIS
strumiprivic	STRAOUM/PRIVK	styptic	STIPT/IK
strumiprivous	STRAOUM/MI/PRAOIV/OUS	styramate	STAOIR/MAIT
	STRAOU/MIP/RI/VOUS		STIR/MAIT
strumitis	STRAOU/MAOITS	styrax	STAOI/RAX
strumosa	STRAOU/MOE/SA	Styrax	K-P/STAOI/RAX
strumous	STRAOUM/OUS	styrene	STAOI/RAOEN
	STRAOU/MOUS	styrol	STAOI/ROL
Strumpell	STRIFRP/EL	styrolene	STAOIR/LAOEN
	STRIM/PEL	styrone	STAOI/ROEN
	STRUFRP/EL	sub-	SUB
	STRUM/PEL	subabdominal	SUB/AB/DOM/NAL
struvite	STRAOU/VAOIT	subabdominoperitoneal	SUB/AB/DOM/NO/PERT/NAOEL
strychnine	STRIK/NIN	subacetabular	SUB/AS/TAB/LAR
	STRIK/NAOIN	subacetate	SUB/AS/TAIT
	STRIK/NAOEN	subachilleal	SUB/AI/KIL/YAL
strychninism	STRIK/NIN/IFM	subacid	SUB/AS/ID
strychninization	STRIK/NIN/ZAIGS	subacidity	SUB/AI/SID/TI
strychninomania	STRIK/NIN/MAIN/YA	subacromial	SUB/AI/KROEM/YAL
strychnism	STRIK/NIFM	subacromialis	SUB/AI/KROEM/YAI/LIS
strychnize	STRIK/NAOIZ	subacute	SUB/AI/KAOUT
Strychnos	STRIK/NOS	subalimentation	SUB/AL/MEN/TAIGS
Stryker	STRAO*IK/ER	subanal	SUB/AINL
	(not STRAOIK/ER; see striker)	subaortic	SUB/AI/ORT/IK
Stuart	STAOURT	subapical	SUB/AP/KAL
	STAOU/ART	subaponeurotic	SUB/AP/NAOU/ROT/IK
	(not STAOU/WART; see Stewart)	subaponeurotica	SUB/AP/NAOU/ROT/KA
Stuart Formula	STAOURT/FORM/LA	subarachnoid	SUB/AI/RAK/NOID
	STAOU/ART/FORM/LA	subarachnoidal	SUB/AI/RAK/NOI/DAL
Stuartinic	STAOUR/TIN/IK	subarachnoidales	SUB/AI/RAK/NOI/DAI/LAOEZ
	STAOU/AR/TIN/IK	subarachnoideale	SUB/AI/RAK/NOID/YAI/LAOE
Stuartnatal	STAOURT/NAI/TAL	subarachnoideales	SUB/AI/RAK/NOID/YAI/LAOEZ
	STAOU/ART/NAI/TAL	subarcuate	SUB/ARK/YAIT
Stuart Prenatal	STAOURT/PRE/NAI/TAL		SUB/AI/KAOU/AIT
	STAOU/ART/PRE/NAI/TAL	subareolar	SUB/AI/RAOE/LAR
studeri	STAOUD/RAOI	subastragalar	SUB/AS/TRAG/LAR
study	STUD/DI		SUB/AI/STRAG/LAR
	STU/DI	subastringent	SUB/AI/STRIN/JENT
stump	STUFRP		SUB/AS/TRIN/JENT
stun	STUN	subatloidean	SUB/AT/LOID/YAN
stunt	STUNT	subatomic	SUB/AI/TOM/IK
stupe	STAOUP	subaural	SUB/AURL
stupefacient	STAOUP/FAIRBT	subaurale	SUB/AU/RAI/LAOE
stupefactive	STAOUP/FAKT/IV	subauricular	SUB/AU/RIK/LAR
stupor	STAOU/POR	subaxial	SUB/AX/YAL
stuporose	STAOUP/ROES	subaxillary	SUB/AX/LAIR
stuporous	STAOUP/ROUS	subbasal	SUB/BAI/SAL
stupp	STUP	subbasalis	SUB/BAI/SAI/LIS
sturdy	STUR/DI		SUB/BA/SAI/LIS
Sturge	STURJ	subbrachial	SUB/BRAIK/YAL
Sturm	STURM	subbrachycephalic	SUB/BRAK/SFAL/IK
stutter	STUT/ER	subcalcaneal	SUB/KAL/KAIN/YAL
stuttering	STUT/ER/-G	subcalcareous	SUB/KAL/KAIR/YOUS
sty	STAOI	subcalcarine	SUB/KAL/KRAOIN
stycosis	STAOI/KOE/SIS		SUB/KAL/KA/RAOIN
stye	STAO*I	subcallosa	SUB/KAL/LOE/SA
	see sty	subcallosal	SUB/KAL/LOE/SAL
styl(o)-	STAOIL		SUB/KA/LOE/SAL
	STAOI/L(O)	subcallosus	SUB/KAL/LOE/SUS
style	STAOIL	subcalorism	SUB/KAL/RIFM

subcapsular	SUB/KAIL/RIFM	subexcite	SAOUB/RIL
subcapsuloperiosteal	SUB/KAPS/LAR	subextensibility	SUB/KPAOIT
subcarbonate	SUB/KAPS/LO/P*ER/O*S/YAL	subfamily	SUB/EX/TENS/-BLT
subcardinal	SUB/KARB/NAIT	subfascial	SUB/FAM/LI
subcartilaginous	SUB/KARD/NAL	subfascialis	SUB/FARBL
subcecal	SUB/KART/LAJ/NOUS	subfertile	SUB/FARB/YAI/LIS
subcellular	SUB/SE/KAL		SUB/FER/TAOIL
subcentral	SUB/SEL/YAOU/LAR		SUB/FER/TIL
	SUB/SEN/TRAL	subfertility	SUB/FER/TIL/TI
	SUB/STRAL	subfissure	SUB/FIRB/SHUR
subception	SUB/SEPGS	subflavous	SUB/FLAIV/OUS
subchloride	SUB/KLOR/AOID	subfoliar	SUB/FOEL/YAR
subchondral	SUB/KON/DRAL	subfolium	SUB/FOEL/YUM
subchordal	SUB/KHOR/DAL	subgaleal	SUB/GAIL/YAL
subchorialis	SUB/KOER/YAI/LIS		SUB/GAL/YAL
subchorionic	SUB/KOER/YON/IK	subgallate	SUB/GAL/AIT
subchoroidal	SUB/KOE/ROI/DAL		SUB/GAL/LAIT
subchronic	SUB/KRON/IK	subgemmal	SUB/JEM/MAL
subclass	SUB/KLASZ	subgenus	SUB/JAOE/NUS
subclavia	SUB/KLAIV/YA	subgerminal	SUB/JERM/NAL
subclavian	SUB/KLAIV/YAN	subgingival	SUB/JING/VAL
subclavicular	SUB/KLA/VIK/LAR	subglenoid	SUB/GLAOE/NOID
subclavius	SUB/KLAIV/YUS	subglossal	SUB/GLOS/SAL
subclinical	SUB/KLIN/KAL	subglossitis	SUB/GLOS/SAOITS
subclone	SUB/KLOEN	subglottic	SUB/GLOT/IK
subcollateral	SUB/KLAT/RAL	subgranular	SUB/GRAN/LAR
subconjunctival	SUB/KON/JUNG/TAOIVL	subgrondation	SUB/GRON/DAIGS
	SUB/KON/JUNGT/VAL	subgrundation	SUB/GRUN/DAIGS
	SUB/KON/JUNG/VAL	subgyrus	SUB/JAOI/RUS
subconjunctivitis	SUB/KON/JUNGT/VAOITS	subhepatic	SUB/HE/PAT/IK
	SUB/KON/JUNG/VAOITS	subhumeral	SUB/HAOUM/RAL
subconscious	SUB/KON/-RBS	subhyaloid	SUB/HAOI/LOID
subconsciousness	SUB/KON/-RBS/*NS	subhyoid	SUB/HAOI/OID
subcontinuous	SUB/KONT/OUS	subhyoidean	SUB/HAOI/OID/YAN
	SUB/KON/TIN/YOUS	subicteric	SUB/IK/TER/IK
subcoracoid	SUB/KOR/KOID		SUB/IKT/RIK
subcortex	SUB/KOR/TEX	subicul-	SAOU/BIK/L-
subcortical	SUB/KORT/KAL		SAOU/BIK/YAOU/L-
subcostal	SUB/KOS/TAL		SAOU/BIK/YU/L-
subcostales	SUB/KOS/TAI/LAOEZ		SU/BIK/L-
subcostalgia	SUB/KOS/TAL/JA		SU/BIK/YAOU/L-
subcostalis	SUB/KOS/TAI/LIS		SU/BIK/YU/L-
subcostosternal	SUB/KO*S/STERNL	subicula	SAOU/BIK/LA
	SUB/KOS/TO/STERNL	subicular	SAOU/BIK/LAR
subcranial	SUB/KRAIN/YAL	subiculum	SAOU/BIK/LUM
subcrepitant	SUB/KREP/TANT	subiliac	SUB/IL/YAK
subcrepitation	SUB/KREP/TAIGS	subilium	SUB/IL/YUM
subcrural	SUB/KRAOURL	subimbibitional	SUB/IM/BI/BIGS/NAL
subcruralis	SUB/KRAOU/RAI/LIS	subinfection	SUB/IN/F*EBGS
subcrureus	SUB/KRAOUR/YUS	subinflammation	SUB/IN/FLA/MAIGS
subcu.	SUB/KAOU	subinflammatory	SUB/IN/FLAM/TOIR
	SUB/KAO*U	subintegumental	SUB/SPWEG/YAOUMT/TAL
subculture	SUB/KUL/KHUR		SUB/SPWEG/YUMT/TAL
subcurative	SUB/KAOUR/TIV		SUB/SPWEG/-MT/TAL
subcutanea	SUB/KAOU/TAIN/YA	subintimal	SUB/SPWI/MAL
subcutaneae	SUB/KAOU/TAIN/YAE		SUB/INT/MAL
subcutanei	SUB/KAOU/TAIN/YAOI	subintrance	SUB/SPWRANS
subcutaneous	SUB/KAOU/TAIN/YOUS		SUB/IN/TRANS
subcutaneus	SUB/KAOU/TAIN/YUS	subintrant	SUB/SPWRANT
subcuticular	SUB/KAOU/TIK/LAR		SUB/IN/TRANT
subcutis	SUB/KAOU/TIS	subinvolution	SUB/IN/VOE/LAOUGS
subdelirium	SUB/DLIR/YUM	subiodide	SUB/AOI/DAOID
	SUB/DE/LIR/YUM	subitum	SAOUB/TUM
subdeltoid	SUB/DEL/TOID		SAOU/BAOI/TUM
subdeltoidea	SUB/DEL/TOID/YA	subjacent	SUB/JAIS/ENT
subdental	SUB/DEN/TAL		SUB/JAI/SENT
subdermic	SUB/DERM/IK	subject	SUB/JEKT
subdiaphragmatic	SUB/DAOI/FRAG/MAT/IK		SUJT
subdorsal	SUB/DOR/SAL		SUBT
subduce	SUB/DAOUS	subjective	SUB/JEKT/IV
subduct	SUB/DUKT		SUJT/IV
subduction	SUB/D*UBGS		SUBT/IV
subdural	SUB/DAOURL	subjectivity	SUB/JEK/TIV/TI
subdurale	SUB/DAOU/RAI/LAOE		SUJT/TIV/TI
subendocardial	SUB/*END/KARD/YAL		SUBT/TIV/TI
subendothelial	SUB/*END/THAOEL/YAL	subjectoscope	SUB/JEKT/SKOEP
subendothelium	SUB/*END/THAOEL/YUM		SUB/JEK/TO/SKOEP
subendymal	SUB/END/MAL	subjugal	SUB/JAOU/GAL
subependymal	SUB/EP/END/MAL	subkingdom	SUB/KING/DOM
	SUB/E/PEND/MAL	sublabial	SUB/LAIB/YAL
subependymoma	SUB/EP/END/MOE/MA	sublatio	SUB/LAI/SHOE
	SUB/E/PEND/MOE/MA		SUB/LAIRB/YOE
subepidermal	SUB/EP/DER/MAL	sublation	SUB/LAIGS
subepidermic	SUB/EP/DERM/IK	sublesional	SUB/LAOEGS/NAL
subepiglottic	SUB/EP/GLOT/IK	sublethal	SUB/LAOE/THAL
subepithelial	SUB/EP/THAOEL/YAL	subleukemia	SUB/LAOU/KAOEM/YA
subepithelium	SUB/EP/THAOEL/YUM	subligamentous	SUB/LIG/MEN/TOUS
suberosis	SAOUB/ROE/SIS	sublimate	SUB/LI/MAIT
suberyl	SAOU/BERL		SUBL/MAIT

sublimation	SUB/LI/MAIGS	subpharyngeal	SUB/FRIN/JAL
	SUBL/MAIGS	subphrenic	SUB/FREN/IK
Sublimaze	SUB/LI/MAIZ	subphyla	SUB/FAO*I/LA
sublime	SUB/LAOIM		(*not* SUB/FAOI/LA)
	SU/BLAOIM	subphylum	SUB/FAO*I/LUM
subliminal	SUB/LIM/NAL		SUB/FAO*IL/UM
sublimis	SUB/LAOI/MIS		(*not* SUB/FAOI/LUM or SUB/
	SU/BLAOI/MIS		FAOIL/UM)
sublingual	SUB/LING/WAL	subpial	SUB/PAOI/YAL
sublinguales	SUB/LING/WAI/LAOEZ		SUB/PAOIL
sublingualis	SUB/LING/WAI/LIS	subpituitarism	SUB/PI/TAOU/TRIFM
sublinguitis	SUB/LING/WAOITS		SUB/PI/TAOU/TAR/IFM
sublobe	SUB/LOEB	subplacenta	SUB/PLA/SEN/TA
sublobular	SUB/LOB/LAR	subplacental	SUB/PLA/SEN/TAL
sublumbar	SUB/LUM/BAR	subpleural	SUB/PLAOURL
subluminal	SUB/LAOUM/NAL	subplexal	SUB/PLEK/SAL
subluxate	SUB/LUK/SAIT	subpreputial	SUB/PRE/PAOURBL
	SUB/LUX/AIT	subpubic	SUB/PAOUB/IK
subluxation	SUB/LUK/SAIGS	subpubicus	SUB/PAOUB/KUS
	SUB/LUX/AIGS	subpulmonary	SUB/PUL/MO/NAIR
sublymphemia	SUB/LIM/FAOEM/YA		SUB/PUM/NAIR
submammary	SUB/MAM/RI	subpulpal	SUB/PUL/PAL
submandibular	SUB/MAN/DIB/LAR	subpyramidal	SUB/PI/RAM/DAL
submandibularis	SUB/MAN/DIB/LAI/RIS	subrectal	SUB/REK/TAL
submania	SUB/MAIN/YA	subretinal	SUB/RET/NAL
submarginal	SUB/MARJ/NAL	subsalt	SUB/SALT
submaxilla	SUB/MAK/SIL/LA		SUB/SAULT
submaxillaris	SUB/MAX/LAI/RIS	subsartorial	SUB/SAR/TOIRL
submaxillaritis	SUB/MAK/SIL/RAOITS	subsartorialis	SUB/SAR/TOR/YAI/LIS
	SUB/MAX/IL/RAOITS		SUB/SAR/TOER/YAI/LIS
submaxillary	SUB/MAX/LAIR	subscaphocephaly	SUB/SKAF/SEF/LI
submaxillitis	SUB/MAX/LAOITS	subscapular	SUB/SKAP/LAR
submedial	SUB/MAOED/YAL	subscapularis	SUB/SKAP/LAI/RIS
submedian	SUB/MAOED/YAN	subscleral	SUB/SKLAOERL
submembranous	SUB/MEM/BRA/NOUS	subsclerotic	SUB/SKLE/ROT/IK
submental	SUB/MEN/TAL	subscription	SUB/SKRIPGS
submentalis	SUB/MEN/TAI/LIS	subserosa	SUB/SE/ROE/SA
submerged	SUB/MERJ/-D	subserosal	SUB/SE/ROE/SAL
submersion	SUB/MERGS	subserous	SUB/SAOER/OUS
submetacentric	SUB/MET/SEN/TRIK	subsibilant	SUB/SIB/LANT
submicronic	SUB/MAOI/KRON/IK	subsidence	SUB/SAOI/DENS
submicroscopic	SUB/MAOI/KRO/SKOP/IK		SUB/SAOID/ENS
submicroscopical	SUB/MAOI/KRO/SKOP/KAL	subsistence	SUB/S*IS/ENS
submorphous	SUB/MOR/FOUS	subsonic	SUB/SON/IK
submucosa	SUB/MAOU/KOE/SA	subspecialty	SUB/SPERBL/TI
submucosal	SUB/MAOU/KOE/SAL	subspecies	SUB/SPAOE/SHAOEZ
submucous	SUB/MAOUK/OUS		SUB/SPAOE/SAOEZ
	SUB/MAOU/KOUS	subspinale	SUB/SPAOI/NAI/LAOE
submuscularis	SUB/MUS/KLAI/RIS	subspinous	SUB/SPAOIN/OUS
subnarcotic	SUB/NAR/KOT/IK	subsplenial	SUB/SPLAOEN/YAL
subnasal	SUB/NAI/ZAL	substage	SUB/STAIJ
subnasale	SUB/NAI/ZAI/LAOE	substance	SUB/STANS
subnasion	SUB/NAIZ/YON	substandard	SUB/STAND/ARD
	SUB/NAIS/YON		SUB/STAN/DARD
	(*not* SUB/NAIGS; see subnation)	substantia	SUB/STAN/SHA
subnatant	SUB/NAI/TANT	substantiae	SUB/STAN/SHAE
subneural	SUB/NAOURL	substantiation	SUB/STAN/SHAIGS
subnitrate	SUB/NAOI/TRAIT	substernal	SUB/STERNL
subnormal	SUB/NOR/MAL	substernomastoid	SUB/STERN/MAS/TOID
subnormality	SUB/NOR/MAL/TI	substituent	SUB/STIFP/YENT
subnotochordal	SUB/NOET/KHOR/DAL		SUB/STIFP/WENT
	SUB/NOET/KOER/DAL	substitute	SUB/STAOUT
subnucleus	SUB/NAOUK/LUS		SUBS/TAOUT
subnutrition	SUB/NAOU/TRIGS		STUT
suboccipital	SUB/OK/SIP/TAL	substitution	SUB/STAOUGS
suboccipitalis	SUB/OK/SIP/TAI/LIS		SUBS/TAOUGS
suboccipitobregmatic	SUB/OK/SIPT/BREG/MAT/IK		STUGS
suboptimal	SUB/OPT/MAL	substitutive	SUB/STAOUT/IV
suboptimum	SUB/OPT/MUM		SUBS/TAOUT/IV
suborbital	SUB/ORB/TAL		STUT/IV
suborder	SUB/ORD/ER	substrate	SUB/STRAIT
suboxidation	SUB/OX/DAIGS	substratum	SUB/STRAIT/UM
suboxide	SUB/OK/SAOID		SUB/STRAI/TUM
	SUB/OX/AOID	substructure	SUB/STRUK/KHUR
subpapillary	SUB/PAP/LAIR	subsulcus	SUB/SUL/KUS
subpapular	SUB/PAP/LAR	subsulfate	SUB/SUL/FAIT
subparalytic	SUB/PAR/LIT/IK	subsultus	SUB/SUL/TUS
subparietal	SUB/PRAOI/TAL	subsylvian	SUB/SIL/VAOE/YAN
subpatellar	SUB/PA/TEL/LAR		SUB/SIL/VAN
subpectoral	SUB/PEKT/RAL	subsymphysial	SUB/SIM/FIZ/YAL
subpelviperitoneal	SUB/PEL/VI/PERT/NAOEL	subtalar	SUB/TAI/LAR
subpericardial	SUB/P*ER/KARD/YAL	subtalaris	SUB/TAI/LAI/RIS
subperiosteal	SUB/P*ER/O*S/YAL		SUB/TA/LAI/RIS
subperiosteocapsular	SUB/P*ER/O*S/YO/KAPS/LAR	subtarsal	SUB/TAR/SAL
subperitoneal	SUB/PERT/NAOEL	subtegumental	SUB/TEG/YAOUMT/TAL
subperitonealis	SUB/P*ER/TOEN/YAI/LIS		SUB/TEG/YUMT/TAL
subperitoneoabdominal	SUB/PERT/NAOE/AB/DOM/NAL		SUB/TEG/-MT/TAL
subperitoneopelvic	SUB/PERT/NAOE/PEL/VIK	subtelocentric	SUB/TEL/SEN/TRIK
subpetrosal	SUB/PE/TROE/SAL	subtemporal	SUB/TEFRP/RAL

subtendinea	SUB/TEN/DIN/YA	sucrase	SAOU/KRAIS
subtendinous	SUB/TEND/NOUS	sucrate	SAOU/KRAIT
subtenial	SUB/TAOEN/YAL	sucre	SAOU/KER
subtentorial	SUB/TEN/TOIRL		SAOUK/ER
subterminal	SUB/TERM/NAL	sucroclastic	SAOU/KRO/KLA*S/IK
subtetanic	SUB/TE/TAN/IK	sucrose	SAOU/KROES
subthalamic	SUB/THA/LAM/IK	sucrosemia	SAOU/KRO/SAOEM/YA
subthalamicum	SUB/THA/LAM/KUM	sucrosum	SAOU/KROE/SUM
subthalamus	SUB/THAL/MUS		SAOU/KROES/UM
subthyroideus	SUB/THAOI/ROID/YUS	sucrosuria	SAOU/KRO/SAOUR/YA
subthyroidism	SUB/THAOI/ROI/DIFM	suction	S*UBGS
	SUB/THAOI/ROID/IFM	suctorial	SUK/TOIRL
subtilis	SUB/TAOI/LIS	suctorian	SUK/TOIRN
	SUB/TIL/LIS	Sudafed	SAOUD/FED
subtilisin	SUB/TI/LAOI/SIN	Sudafed Plus	SAOUD/FED/PLUS
	SUB/TIL/SIN	Sudafed Sinus	SAOUD/FED/SAOI/NUS
subtilopeptidase	SUB/TIL/PEPT/DAIS	sudamen	SAOU/DAI/MEN
subtle	SUT/-L	sudamina	SAOU/DAM/NA
subtotal	SUB/TOE/TAL	sudaminal	SAOU/DAM/NAL
subtraction	SUB/TRA*BGS	Sudan	SAOU/DAN
subtrapezial	SUB/TRA/PAOEZ/YAL	sudano-	SAOU/DAN
subtribe	SUB/TRAOIB		SAOUD/NO
subtrochanteric	SUB/TROE/KAN/TER/IK	sudanophil	SAOU/DAN/FIL
subtrochlear	SUB/TROK/LAR	sudanophilia	SAOU/DAN/FIL/YA
subtuberal	SUB/TAOUB/RAL	sudanophilic	SAOU/DAN/FIL/IK
subtympanic	SUB/TIM/PAN/IK	sudanophilous	SAOU/DAN/OF/LOUS
subtypical	SUB/TIP/KAL	sudanophobic	SAOU/DAN/FOEB/IK
subumbilical	SUB/UM/BIL/KAL	sudarium	SAOU/DAIRM
subungual	SUB/UNG/WAL		SAOU/DAIR/YUM
suburethral	SUB/YAOU/RAO*ET/RAL	sudation	SAOU/DAIGS
subvaginal	SUB/VAJ/NAL	sudatoria	SAOUD/TOER/YA
subvalvar	SUB/VAL/VAR		SAOUD/TOR/YA
subvalvular	SUB/VAL/VAOU/LAR	sudatorium	SAOUD/TOIRM
subvertebral	SUB/VERT/BRAL	Sudeck	SAOU/DEK
subvirile	SUB/VIR/RIL	sudo-	SAOUD
	SUB/VIR/RAOIL		SAOU/DO
subvitaminosis	SUB/VAOIT/MI/NOE/SIS	sudor	SAOU/DOR
subvitrinal	SUB/VIT/RI/NAL	sudoral	SAOU/DORL
subvolution	SUB/VOE/LAOUGS		SAOU/DOR/RAL
subvomerine	SUB/VOEM/RAOIN	sudoralis	SAOUD/RAI/LIS
	SUB/VOEM/RAOEN	sudoresis	SAOUD/RAOE/SIS
	SUB/VOEM/RIN	sudoriferae	SAOUD/RIF/RAE
subwaking	SUB/WAIK/-G	sudoriferous	SAOUD/RIF/ROUS
subzonal	SUB/ZOENL	sudoriferus	SAOUD/RIF/RUS
subzygomatic	SUB/ZAOIG/MAT/IK	sudorific	SAOUD/RIFK
succagogue	SUK/GOG	sudorikeratosis	SAOU/DOR/KER/TOE/SIS
succedaneous	SUX/DAIN/YOUS	sudoriparous	SAOUD/RIP/ROUS
	SUK/SE/DAIN/YOUS	sudoriparum	SAOUD/RIP/RUM
succedaneum	SUX/DAIN/YUM	sudorometer	SAOUD/ROM/TER
	SUK/SE/DAIN/YUM	sudorrhea	SAOUD/RAOE/YA
succenturiate	SUK/SEN/KHUR/YAIT	sudoxicam	SAOU/DOX/KAM
	SUK/SEN/TAOUR/YAIT	suet	SAOU/ET
successive	SUK/SES/SIV		(not SAOUT; see suit)
	SUK/SESZ/IV	Sufenta	SAOU/FEN/TA
succi	SUK/SAOI	sufentanil	SAOU/FENT/NIL
succin(o)-	SUX/N(O)	suffocant	SUF/KANT
	SUK/SI/N(O)	suffocate	SUF/KAIT
succinate	SUX/NAIT	suffocation	SUF/KAIGS
succinic	SUK/SIN/IK	suffocative	SUF/KAIT/IV
succinodehydrogenase	SUX/NO/DE/HAOI/DRO/JEN/AIS	suffraginis	SUF/FRAJ/NIS
succinoresinol	SUX/NO/REZ/NOL	suffusion	SU/FAOUGS
succinous	SUX/NOUS		SUF/FAOUGS
succinum	SUX/NUM	sugar	SHUG/AR
succinyl	SUX/NIL	suggestibility	SUG/J*ES/-BLT
succinylcholine	SUX/NIL/KOE/LAOEN		SUGT/-BLT
succinyl-CoA	SUX/NIL/KO/A*RBGS	suggestible	SUG/J*ES/-BL
succinylcoenzyme	SUX/NIL/KO/EN/ZAOIM		SUGT/-BL
succinyldicholine	SUX/NIL/DI/KOE/LAOEN	suggestion	SUG/JEGS
succinylhomoserine	SUX/NIL/HOEM/SER/AOEN		SUGS
succinylsulfathiazole	SUX/NIL/SUL/FA/THAOI/ZOEL	suggestive	SUG/J*ES/IV
succisulfone	SUX/SUL/FOEN/		SUGT/IV
iminodiethanol	IM/NO/DI/*ET/NOL	suggillation	SUG/JI/LAIGS
succorrhea	SUK/RAOE/YA		SUG/JIL/LAIGS
succuba	SUK/YAOU/BA		SUJ/LAIGS
	SUK/YU/BA	suicidal	SAOU/SAOI/DAL
succubus	SUK/YAOU/BUS	suicide	SAOU/SAOID
	SUK/YU/BUS		SAOU/SAO*ID
succus	SUK/KUS	suicidology	SAOU/SAOI/DOLG
succussion	SU/KUGS	suillus	SAOU/IL/LUS
	SUK/KUGS	suint	SWINT
suck	SUK	suis	SAOU/WIS
sucker	SUK/ER	suit	SAOUT
suckle	SUK/-L	sulbentine	SUL/BEN/TAOEN
Sucquet	SIK/KAI	sulcal	SUL/KAL
	SI/KAI	sulcate	SUL/KAIT
	SUK/KAI	sulcated	SUL/KAIT/-D
	SU/KAI	sulcation	SUL/KAIGS
sucr(o)-	SAOU/KR(O)	sulci	SUL/SAOI
sucralfate	SAOU/KRAL/FAIT	sulciform	SULS/FORM

	SUL/SI/FORM
sulcomarginal	SUL/KO/MARJ/NAL
sulcomarginalis	SUL/KO/MARJ/NAI/LIS
sulcular	SUL/KLAR
	SUL/KAOU/LAR
sulculi	SUL/KLAOI
	SUL/KAOU/LAOI
sulculus	SUL/KLUS
	SUL/KAOU/LUS
sulcus	SUL/KUS
sulfa	SUL/FA
sulfa-	SUL/FA
sulfabenzamide	SUL/FA/BENZ/MAOID
Sulfacet	SUL/FA/SET
Sulfacet-R	SUL/FA/SET/R-RBGS
sulfacetamide	SUL/FA/SET/MAOID
sulfacetic	SUL/FA/SET/IK
sulfacid	SUL/FAS/ID
	SUL/-F/AS/ID
sulfactam	SUL/FAK/TAM
sulfacytine	SUL/FA/SAOI/TAOEN
sulfadiazine	SUL/FA/DAOI/ZAOEN
sulfadimethoxine	SUL/FA/DI/ME/THOK/SAOEN
sulfadimidine	SUL/FA/DIM/DAOEN
sulfadoxine	SUL/FA/DOK/SAOEN
sulfaethidole	SUL/FA/*ET/DOEL
sulfafurazole	SUL/FA/FAOUR/ZOEL
sulfaguanidine	SUL/FA/GAUN/DAOEN
sulfalene	SUL/FA/LAOEN
sulfamerazine	SUL/FA/MER/ZAOEN
sulfameter	SUL/FA/MAOET/ER
sulfamethazine	SUL/FA/M*ET/ZAOEN
sulfamethizole	SUL/FA/M*ET/ZOEL
sulfamethoxazole	SUL/FA/ME/THOX/ZOEL
	SUL/FA/M*ET/OX/ZOEL
sulfamethoxydiazine	SUL/FA/ME/THOX/DAOI/ZAOEN
sulfamethoxypyridazine	SUL/FA/ME/THOX/PI/RID/ZAOEN
	SUL/FA/ME/THOX/PAOI/RID/ZAOEN
sulfamoxole	SUL/FA/MOK/SOEL
	SUL/FA/MOX/OEL
sulfamylacetanilide	SUL/FA/MIL/AS/TAN/LAOID
Sulfamylon	SUL/FA/MAOI/LON
	SUL/FAM/LON
sulfanilamide	SUL/FA/NIL/MAOID
sulfanilylacetamide	SUL/FAN/LIL/SET/MAOID
	SUL/FAN/LIL/AI/SET/MAOID
sulfanilylbenzamide	SUL/FAN/LIL/BENZ/MAOID
sulfanitran	SUL/FA/NAOI/TRAN
sulfanuria	SUL/FA/NAOUR/YA
sulfaperin	SUL/FA/PER/RIN
sulfaphenazole	SUL/FA/FEN/ZOEL
sylfapyrazine	SUL/FA/PIR/ZAOEN
sulfapyridine	SUL/FA/PIR/DAOEN
sulfasalazine	SUL/FA/SAL/ZAOEN
sulfatase	SUL/FA/TAIS
sulfate	SUL/FAIT
sulfatemia	SUL/FAIT/AOEM/YA
	SUL/FA/TAOEM/YA
sulfathiazole	SUL/FA/THAOI/ZOEL
sulfatidate	SUL/FA/TAOI/DAIT
sulfatide	SUL/FA/TAOID
sulfatidosis	SUL/FA/TAOI/DOE/SIS
	SUL/FA/TI/DOE/SIS
sulfation	SUL/FAIGS
sulfhemoglobin	SUL/-F/HAOEM/GLOE/BIN
	SUL/FAOEM/GLOE/BIN
sulfhemoglobinemia	SUL/-F/HAOEM/GLOEB/NAOEM/YA
	SUL/FAOEM/GLOEB/NAOEM/YA
sulfhydrate	SUL/-F/HAOI/DRAIT
	SUL/FAOI/DRAIT
sulfhydryl	SUL/-F/HAOI/DRIL
	SUL/FAOI/DRIL
sulfide	SUL/FAOID
sulfindigotate	SUL/FIND/GO/TAIT
sulfindigotic	SUL/FIN/DI/GOT/IK
sulfinpyrazone	SUL/FIN/PIR/ZOEN
	SUL/FIN/PAOIR/ZOEN
sulfinpyruvic	SUL/FIN/PAOI/RAOUVK
	SUL/FIN/PAOI/RAOUV/IK
sulfisomidine	SUL/FI/SOEM/DAOEN
	SUL/FI/SOM/DAOEN
sulfisoxazole	SUL/FI/SOX/ZOEL
sulfite	SUL/FAOIT
sulfmethemoglobin	SUL/-F/MET/HAOEM/GLOE/BIN
sulfo-	SUL/FO
sulfoacid	SUL/FO/AS/ID
sulfoalanine	SUL/FO/AL/NAOEN
sulfobromophthalein	SUL/FO/BROEM/THAL/YIN
sulfocarbamide	SUL/FO/KARB/MAOID
sulfocarbolate	SUL/FO/KARB/LAIT
sulfoconjugation	SUL/FO/KON/JU/GAIGS
sulfocyanate	SUL/FO/SAOI/NAIT
sulfocyanic	SUL/FO/SAOI/AN/IK
sulfogel	SUL/FO/JEL
sulfohydrate	SUL/FO/HAOI/DRAIT
sulfolipid	SUL/FO/LIP/ID
sulfolysis	SUL/FOL/SIS
sulfomucin	SUL/FO/MAOU/SIN
sulfomyxin	SUL/FO/MIK/SIN
sulfonamide	SUL/FON/MAOID
sulfonamidemia	SUL/FOEN/AM/DAOEM/YA
sulfonamidocholia	SUL/FOEN/AM/DO/KOEL/YA
sulfonamidotherapy	SUL/FOEN/AM/DO/THER/PI
sulfonamiduria	SUL/FOEN/AM/DAOUR/YA
sulfonate	SUL/FO/NAIT
sulfonated	SUL/FO/NAIT/-D
sulfone	SUL/FOEN
sulfonic	SUL/FON/IK
sulfonylurea	SUL/FO/NIL/YAOU/RAOE/YA
sulfoprotein	SUL/FO/PRO/TAOEN
sulfoquinovosyl	SUL/FO/KWAOIN/VOE/SIL
	SUL/FO/KWIN/VOE/SIL
sulforhodamine	SUL/FO/ROED/MAOEN
sulformethoxine	SUL/FOR/ME/THOK/SAOEN
sulfosalicylic	SUL/FO/SAL/SIL/IK
sulfosalt	SUL/FO/SALT
	SUL/FO/SAULT
sulfosol	SUL/FO/SOL
sulfotransferase	SUL/FO/TRA*NS/FRAIS
sulfoxide	SUL/FOK/SAOID
	SUL/FOX/AOID
sulfoxone	SUL/FOK/SOEN
Sulfoxyl	SUL/FOK/SIL
	SUL/FOX/IL
sulfur	SUL/FUR
sulfurata	SUL/FRAI/TA
	SUL/FAOU/RAI/TA
	SUL/FUR/RAI/TA
sulfurated	.SUL/FRAIT/-D
	SUL/FAOU/RAIT/-D
	SUL/FUR/AIT/-D
sulfurator	SUL/FRAI/TOR
	SUL/FAOU/RAI/TOR
	SUL/FUR/AI/TOR
sulfuret	SUL/FUR/ET
	SUL/FAOU/RET
sulfureted	SUL/FUR/ET/-D
	SUL/FAOU/RET/-D
sulfuric	SUL/FAOUR/IK
sulfurize	SUL/FUR/AOIZ
sulfurous	SUL/FROUS
	SUL/FUR/OUS
	SUL/FAOUR/OUS
sulfurtransferase	SUL/FUR/TRA*NS/FRAIS
sulfuryl	SUL/FUR/IL
	SUL/FAOU/RIL
sulfydrate	SUL/FAOI/DRAIT
	SUL/FAOI/DRAT
sulindac	SUL/IN/DAK
sulisobenzone	SUL/SO/BEN/ZOEN
	SAOU/LAOIS/BEN/ZOEN
Sulkowitch	SUL/KO/WIFP
sullage	SUL/AJ
	SUL/LAJ
sulnidazole	SUL/NID/ZOEL
suloctidil	SUL/OKT/DIL
suloxifen	SUL/OX/FEN
sulpiride	SUL/PI/RAOID
	SUL/PIR/AOID
sulprostone	SUL/PROS/TOEN
sulthiame	SUL/THAOI/AIM
	SUL/THAOI/YAIM
Sultrin	SUL/TRIN
Sulzberger	SULZ/BERG/ER
sumac	SAOU/MAK
	SAOUM/AK
summation	SUM/MAIGS
summer	SUM/ER
Summer's Eve Medicated Douche	SUM/ER/AOES/AOEV/MED/KAIT/-D/DAOURB
summit	SUM/MIT
Sumner	SUM/NER
Sumycin	SAOU/MAOI/SIN
sun	SUN
sunburn	SUN/B*URN
sunflower	SUN/FLOU/ER

sunken	SUN/KEN	supernormal	SAO*UP/NOR/MAL
Sunkist	SUN/K*IS	supernumerary	SAO*UP/NAOUM/RAIR
sunscreen	SUN/SKRAOEN	supernutrition	SAO*UP/NAOU/TRIGS
sunstroke	SUN/STROEK	superoccipital	SAO*UP/OK/SIP/TAL
Supac	SAOU/PAK	superolateral	SAO*UP/RO/LAT/RAL
super	SAOUP/ER		SAOUP/RO/LAT/RAL
super-	SAO*UP	superolateralis	SAO*UP/RO/LAT/RAI/LIS
	SU/PER		SAOUP/RO/LAT/RAI/LIS
superabduction	SAO*UP/AB/D*UBGS	superovulation	SAO*UP/OV/LAIGS
superacid	SAO*UP/AS/ID	superoxide	SAO*UP/OK/SAOID
superacidity	SAO*UP/AI/SID/TI		SAO*UP/OX/AOID
superacromial	SAO*UP/AI/KROEM/YAL	superparasite	SAO*UP/PAR/SAOIT
superactivity	SAO*UP/AK/TIV/TI	superparasitism	SAO*UP/PAR/SAOI/TIFM
superacute	SAO*UP/AI/KAOUT		SAO*UP/PAR/SAOIT/IFM
superalimentation	SAO*UP/AL/MEN/TAIGS	superpetrosal	SAO*UP/PE/TROE/SAL
superalkalinity	SAO*UP/AL/KLIN/TI	superphosphate	SAO*UP/FOS/FAIT
superanal	SAO*UP/AINL	superpigmentation	SAO*UP/PIG/MEN/TAIGS
superaurale	SAO*UP/AU/RAI/LAOE	super-regeneration	SAO*UP/RE/JEN/RAIGS
supercarbonate	SAO*UP/KARB/NAIT	supersalt	SAO*UP/SALT
supercentral	SAO*UP/SEN/TRAL		SAO*UP/SAULT
	SAO*UP/STRAL	supersaturate	SAO*UP/SAFP/RAIT
supercilia	SAO*UP/SIL/YA	superscription	SAO*UP/SKRIPGS
superciliaris	SAO*UP/SIL/YAI/RIS	supersecretion	SAO*UP/SE/KRAOEGS
superciliary	SAO*UP/SIL/YAIR	supersedent	SAO*UP/SAOED/ENT
supercilii	SAO*UP/SIL/YAOI		SAO*UP/SAOE/DENT
supercilium	SAO*UP/SIL/YUM	supersensitization	SAO*UP/SENS/TI/ZAIGS
superclass	SAO*UP/KLASZ	supersoft	SAO*UP/SOFT
supercoil	SAO*UP/KOIL	supersonic	SAO*UP/SON/IK
superdicrotic	SAO*UP/DI/KROT/IK	supersphenoid	SAO*UP/SFAOE/NOID
superdistention	SAO*UP/DIS/TENGS	superstructure	SAO*UP/STRUK/KHUR
Superdophilus	SU/PER/DOF/LUS	supertension	SAO*UP/TENGS
superduct	SAO*UP/DUKT	supertraction	SAO*UP/TRA*BGS
superego	SAO*UP/E/GOE	supervascularization	SAO*UP/VAS/KLAR/ZAIGS
SuperEPA	SU/PER/ERBGS/P*RBGS/A*RBGS	supervenosity	SAO*UP/VAOE/NOS/TI
superexcitation	SAO*UP/KPAOI/TAIGS		SAO*UP/VE/NOS/TI
	SAO*UP/KPAOIT/TAIGS	supervention	SAO*UP/VENGS
superextended	SAO*UP/EX/TEND/-D	supervirulent	SAO*UP/VIR/LENT
superextension	SAO*UP/EX/TENGS	supervisor	SAO*UP/VAOI/SOR
superfamily	SAO*UP/FAM/LI		SAO*UP/VAOI/ZOR
superfatted	SAO*UP/FAT/-D	supervitaminosis	SAO*UP/VAOIT/MI/NOE/SIS
superfetation	SAO*UP/FAOE/TAIGS	supervoltage	SAO*UP/VOELT/AJ
	SAO*UP/FE/TAIGS		SAO*UP/VOLT/AJ
superficial	SAO*UP/FIRBL	supinate	SAOUP/NAIT
superficiale	SAO*UP/FIRB/YAI/LAOE	supination	SAOUP/NAIGS
	SAO*UP/FIS/YAI/LAOE	supinator	SAOUP/NAI/TOR
superficiales	SAO*UP/FIRB/YAI/LAOEZ	supinatoris	SAOUP/NA/TOR/RIS
	SAO*UP/FIS/YAI/LAOEZ		SAOU/PAOIN/TOR/RIS
superficialis	SAO*UP/FIRB/YAI/LIS	supine	SAOU/PAOIN
	SAO*UP/FIS/YAI/LIS	suppedania	SUP/DAIN/YA
superficies	SAO*UP/FIRB/AOEZ	suppedanium	SUP/DAIN/YUM
	SAO*UP/FI/SHAOEZ	supplemental	SUP/LEMT/TAL
superflexion	SAO*UP/FL*EBGS	supplementary	SUP/LEMT/RI
superfunction	SAO*UP/FUNGS	support	SUP/PORT
superfuse	SAO*UP/FAOUS	suppositoria	SPOZ/TOER/YA
	SAO*UP/FAOUZ		SUP/POZ/TOER/YA
superfusion	SAO*UP/FAOUGS	suppositorium	SPOZ/TOIRM
supergenual	SAO*UP/JEN/YAL		SUP/POZ/TOIRM
	SAO*UP/JEN/YAOUL	suppository	SPOZ/TOIR
	SAO*UP/JEN/YUL		SU/POZ/TOIR
superimpose	SAO*UP/IM/POEZ		SUP/POZ/TOIR
superimpregnation	SAO*UP/IM/PREG/NAIGS	suppressant	SU/PRES/SANT
superinduce	SAO*UP/IN/DAOUS		SUP/PRES/SANT
superinfection	SAO*UP/IN/F*EBGS	suppression	SU/PREGS
superinvolution	SAO*UP/IN/VOE/LAOUGS		SUP/PREGS
superior	SPAOER/YOR	suppressive	SU/PRES/SIV
	SU/PAOER/YOR		SUP/PRES/SIV
superiores	SPAOER/YOR/RAOEZ		SU/PRESZ/IV
	SU/PAOER/YOR/RAOEZ		SUP/PRESZ/IV
superioris	SPAOER/YOR/RIS	suppressor	SU/PRES/SOR
	SU/PAOER/YOR/RIS		SUP/PRES/SOR
superiority	SPAOER/YOR/TI	suppur-	SUP/R-
	SU/PAOER/YOR/TI		SUP/YAOU/R-
superiorum	SPAOER/YOR/UM		SUP/YU/R-
	SU/PAOER/YOR/UM	suppurant	SUP/RANT
superius	SPAOER/YUS	suppurantia	SUP/RAN/SHA
	SU/PAOER/YUS	suppurate	SUP/RAIT
superjacent	SAO*UP/JAIS/ENT	suppuration	SUP/RAIGS
	SAO*UP/JAI/SENT	suppurative	SUP/RA/TIV
Superkids Chewable Tablets	SU/PER/KIDZ/KHAOUBL/ TAB/LET/-S		SUP/RAIT/IV
			SUP/YUR/TIV
superlactation	SAO*UP/LAK/TAIGS	supra-	SU/PRA
superlethal	SAO*UP/LAOE/THAL	supra-acromial	SU/PRA/AI/KROEM/YAL
superligamen	SAO*UP/LIG/MEN	supra-anal	SU/PRA/AINL
supermaxilla	SAO*UP/MAK/SIL/LA	supra-anconeal	SU/PRA/AN/KOEN/YAL
supermedial	SAO*UP/MAOED/YAL	supra-arytenoid	SU/PRA/AR/TAOE/NOID
supermoron	SAO*UP/MOR/RON	supra-auricular	SU/PRA/AU/RIK/LAR
supermotility	SAO*UP/MOE/TIL/TI	supra-axillary	SU/PRA/AX/LAIR
supernatant	SAO*UP/NAI/TANT	suprabuccal	SU/PRA/BUK/KAL
supernate	SAO*UP/NAIT	suprabulge	SU/PRA/BUL/-J

supracardial	SU/PRA/KARD/YAL	supraspinal	SU/PRA/SPAOINL
supracardinal	SU/PRA/KARD/NAL	supraspinalis	SU/PRA/SPAOI/NAI/LIS
supracerebellar	SU/PRA/SER/BEL/LAR	supraspinatus	SU/PRA/SPAOI/NAI/TUS
supracerebral	SU/PRA/SER/BRAL	supraspinous	SU/PRA/SPAOIN/OUS
suprachoroid	SU/PRA/KOE/ROID	suprastapedial	SU/PRA/STA/PAOED/YAL
suprachoroidea	SU/PRA/KOE/ROID/YA		SU/PRA/STAI/PAOED/YAL
supraciliary	SU/PRA/SIL/YAIR	suprasternal	SU/PRA/STERNL
supraclavicular	SU/PRA/KLA/VIK/LAR	suprasylvian	SU/PRA/SIL/VAOE/YAN
supraclavicularis	SU/PRA/KLA/VIK/LAI/RIS		SU/PRA/SIL/VAN
supraclusion	SU/PRA/KLAOUGS	suprasymphysary	SU/PRA/SIM/FIZ/RI
supracondylar	SU/PRA/KOND/LAR	supratemporal	SU/PRA/TEFRP/RAL
supracondyloid	SU/PRA/KOND/LOID	supratentorial	SU/PRA/TEN/TOIRL
supracostal	SU/PRA/KOS/TAL	suprathoracic	SU/PRA/THRAS/IK
supracotyloid	SU/PRA/KOT/LOID	supratip	SU/PRA/TIP
supracranial	SU/PRA/KRAIN/YAL	supratonsillar	SU/PRA/TONS/LAR
supracristal	SU/PRA/KR*IS/TAL	supratrochlear	SU/PRA/TROK/LAR
	SU/PRA/KRIS/TAL	supraturbinal	SU/PRA/TURB/NAL
supradiaphragmatic	SU/PRA/DAOI/FRAG/MAT/IK	supratympanic	SU/PRA/TIM/PAN/IK
supraduction	SU/PRA/D*UBGS	supraumbilical	SU/PRA/UM/BIL/KAL
supraepicondylar	SU/PRA/EP/KOND/LAR	supravaginal	SU/PRA/VAJ/NAL
supraepitrochlear	SU/PRA/EP/TROK/LAR	supravalvar	SU/PRA/VAL/VAR
supragenual	SU/PRA/JEN/YAL	supravalvular	SU/PRA/VAL/VAOU/LAR
	SU/PRA/JEN/YAOUL	supraventricular	SU/PRA/VEN/TRIK/LAR
	SU/PRA/JEN/YUL	supraventricularis	SU/PRA/VEN/TRIK/LAI/RIS
supragingival	SU/PRA/JING/VAL	supravergence	SU/PRA/VERJ/ENS
supraglenoid	SU/PRA/GLAOE/NOID	supraversion	SU/PRA/VERGS
supraglottic	SU/PRA/GLOT/IK	supravital	SU/PRA/VAOI/TAL
suprahepatic	SU/PRA/HE/PAT/IK	Suprax	SU/PRAX
suprahyoid	SU/PRA/HAOI/OID	supraxiphoid	SU/PRA/ZIF/OID
suprainguinal	SU/PRA/ING/WINL		SU/PRA/ZAOI/FOID
suprainterparietal	SU/PRA/SPWER/PRAOI/TAL	suprema	SU/PRAOE/MA
supraintestinal	SU/PRA/SPW*ES/NAL	supreme	SU/PRAOEM
supraliminal	SU/PRA/LIM/NAL	suprofen	SAOU/PRO/FEN
supralumbar	SU/PRA/LUM/BAR	sura	SAOU/RA
supramalleolar	SU/PRA/MAL/LAOE/LAR		(*not* SAOUR/RA; see surra)
supramammary	SU/PRA/MAM/RI	surae	SAOU/RAE
supramandibular	SU/PRA/MAN/DIB/LAR	sural	SAOURL
supramarginal	SU/PRA/MARJ/NAL		SAOU/RAL
supramastoid	SU/PRA/MAS/TOID	surales	SAOU/RAI/LAOEZ
supramaxilla	SU/PRA/MAK/SIL/LA	suralimentation	SUR/AL/MEN/TAIGS
supramaxillary	SU/PRA/MAX/LAIR	suralis	SAOU/RAI/LIS
supramaximal	SU/PRA/MAX/MAL	suramin	SAOUR/MIN
suprameatal	SU/PRA/MAOE/AI/TAL	Surbex	SUR/BEX
	SU/PRA/MAOE/YAI/TAL	Surbex-750	SUR/BEX/7/50
supramental	SU/PRA/MEN/TAL	Surbex-T	SUR/BEX/T-RBGS
supramentale	SU/PRA/MEN/TAI/LAOE	surdimute	SURD/MAOUT
supranasal	SU/PRA/NAI/ZAL	surdimutism	SURD/MAOU/TIFM
supraneural	SU/PRA/NAOURL		SURD/MAOUT/IFM
supranormal	SU/PRA/NOR/MAL	surdimutitas	SURD/MAOUT/TAS
supranuclear	SU/PRA/NAOUK/LAR	surditas	SURD/TAS
supraoccipital	SU/PRA/OK/SIP/TAL	surdity	SURD/TI
supraocclusion	SU/PRA/O/KLAOUGS	surexcitation	SUR/KPAOI/TAIGS
supraocular	SU/PRA/OK/LAR		SUR/KPAOIT/TAIGS
supraoptic	SU/PRA/OPT/IK	surface	SUR/FAS
supraopticae	SU/PRA/OPT/SAE	surfactant	SUR/FAK/TANT
supraoptimal	SU/PRA/OPT/MAL	surge	SURJ
supraoptimum	SU/PRA/OPT/MUM	surgeon	SUR/JON
supraorbital	SU/PRA/ORB/TAL	surgery	SURJ/RI
suprapatellar	SU/PRA/PA/TEL/LAR		S-RJ
suprapatellaris	SU/PRA/PAT/LAI/RIS	surgical	SURJ/KAL
suprapelvic	SU/PRA/PEL/VIK	surgically	SURJ/KLI
suprapharmacologic	SU/PRA/FARM/KO/LOJ/IK	Surgicel Absorbable	SURJ/SEL/AB/SORB/-BL/
suprapharyngeal	SU/PRA/FRIN/JAL	Hemostat	HAOEM/STAT
supraphysiologic	SU/PRA/FIZ/YO/LOJ/IK	-suria	SAOUR/YA
supraphysiological	SU/PRA/FIZ/YO/LOJ/KAL	Surital	SAOUR/TAL
suprapontine	SU/PRA/PON/TAOIN		SUR/TAL
	SU/PRA/PON/TAOEN	Surmontil	SUR/MON/TIL
suprapubic	SU/PRA/PAOUB/IK	surra	SUR/RA
suprarenal	SU/PRA/RAOENL		SAOUR/RA
suprarenalectomy	SU/PRA/RAOENL/EKT/M*I	surrenal	SUR/RAOENL
	SU/PRA/RAOEN/LEKT/M*I	surrogate	SUR/GAT
suprarenalemia	SU/PRA/RAOENL/AOEM/YA		SUR/GAIT
	SU/PRA/RAOEN/LAOEM/YA	sursanure	SUR/SAI/NAOUR
suprarenalis	SU/PRA/RE/NAI/LIS		SUR/SAIN/YAOUR
suprarenalism	SU/PRA/RAOENL/IFM	sursumduction	SUR/SUM/D*UBGS
	SU/PRA/RAOEN/LIFM	sursumvergence	SUR/SUM/VERJ/ENS
suprarenalopathy	SU/PRA/RAOENL/OP/THI	sursumversion	SUR/SUM/VERGS
	SU/PRA/RAOEN/LOP/THI	surveillance	SUR/VAI/LANS
suprarene	SU/PRA/RAOEN		SUR/VAIL/LANS
suprarenogenic	SU/PRA/RAOEN/JEN/IK	survey	SUR/VAI
suprarenoma	SU/PRA/RE/NOE/MA	surveying	SUR/VAI/-G
suprarenopathy	SU/PRA/RE/NOP/TH*I	surveyor	SUR/VAI/YOR
suprarenotropic	SU/PRA/RAOEN/TROP/IK	survival	SUR/VAOIVL
suprarenotropism	SU/PRA/RE/NOT/RO/PIFM	susceptibility	SUS/SEPT/-BLT
suprascapular	SU/PRA/SKAP/LAR	susceptible	SUS/SEPT/-BL
suprascleral	SU/PRA/SKLAOERL	suscitate	SUS/TAIT
suprasellar	SU/PRA/SEL/LAR	suscitation	SUS/TAIGS
supraseptal	SU/PRA/SEP/TAL	suscitator	SUS/TAI/TOR
suprasonic	SU/PRA/SON/IK	suspenopsia	SUS/PEN/OPS/YA

suspensiometer	SUS/PENS/YOM/TER	sylvatic	SIL/VAI/RUM
suspension	SUS/PENGS	sylvatic	SIL/VAT/IK
suspensoid	SUS/PEN/SOID	Sylvest	SIL/V*ES
	SUS/PENS/OID	sylvian	SIL/VAOE/YAN
suspensoria	SUS/PEN/SOER/YA		SIL/VAN
	SUS/PEN/SOR/YA	sylvii	SIL/VAOE/YAOI
suspensorium	SUS/PEN/SOER/YUM		SIL/VAOI
	SUS/PEN/SOR/YUM	Sylvius	SIL/VAOE/YUS
suspensorius	SUS/PEN/SOER/YUS	symballophone	SIM/BAL/FOEN
	SUS/PEN/SOR/YUS	symbio-	SIM/BO-
suspensory	SUS/PENS/RI		SIM/BAOE/O-
Sus-Phrine	SUS/FRIN		SIM/BAOE/YO-
suspirious	SUS/PAOIR/YOUS		SIM/BAO*I/O-
Sustacal	S*US/KAL		SIM/BAO*I/YO-
Sustagen	S*US/JEN	symbiology	SIM/BOLG
sustentacula	SUS/TEN/TAK/LA	symbion	SIM/BON
sustentacular	SUS/TEN/TAK/LAR	symbionic	SIM/BON/IK
sustentaculum	SUS/TEN/TAK/LUM	symbiont	SIM/BONT
susurrus	SU/SUR/RUS	symbiosis	SIM/BOE/SIS
	SAOU/SUR/RUS	symbiote	SIM/BOET
Sutter	SUT/ER		SIM/BAOE/OET
Sutton	SUT/TON	symbiotic	SIM/BOT/IK
sutura	SAOU/TAOU/RA	symblepharon	SIM/BLEF/RON
	SAOU/KHUR/RA	symblepharopterygium	SIM/BLEF/RO/TRIJ/YUM
	SAOUFP/RA		SIM/BLEF/RO/TER/IJ/YUM
suturae	SAOU/TAOU/RAE	symbol	SIM/BOL
	SAOU/KHUR/RAE	symbolia	SIM/BOEL/YA
	SAOUFP/RAE	symbolism	SIM/BOL/IFM
sutural	SAOUFP/RAL		SIM/BO/LIFM
	SAOU/KHURL	symbolization	SIM/BOL/ZAIGS
	SAOU/KHUR/RAL	symboly	SIM/BO/LI
suturation	SAOUFP/RAIGS	symbrachydactylia	SIM/BRAK/DAK/TIL/YA
	SAOU/KHUR/RAIGS	symbrachydactylism	SIM/BRAK/DAKT/LIFM
	SAOU/KHUR/AIGS	symbrachydactyly	SIM/BRAK/DAKT/LI
suture	SAOU/KHUR	Syme	SAOIM
suum	SAOU/UM	Symington	SAOIM/-G/TON
suturectomy	SAOU/KHUR/EKT/M*I		SAOI/MING/TON
Suzanne	SAOU/ZAN	symmelia	SIM/MAOEL/YA
swab	SWAB	symmelus	SIM/LUS
	SWAUB		SIM/MAOE/LUS
swaddler	SWAD/LER	Symmers	SIM/ERZ
swage	SWAIJ		SIM/MERZ
swager	SWAIJ/ER	Symmetrel	SIM/TREL
swallow	SWAL/LOE	symmetrical	SMET/RI/KAL
swamp	SWAFRP		SIM/MET/RI/KAL
Swan	K-P/SWAN		SI/MET/RI/KAL
swarm	SWARM	symmetricum	SMET/RI/KUM
swarming	SWARM/-G		SIM/MET/RI/KUM
swayback	SWAI/BA*K		SI/MET/RI/KUM
sweat	SWET	symmetros	SIM/MET/ROS
Swediaur	SWAID/YAUR	symmetry	SIM/TRI
	SWED/YAUR	sympath(o)-	SIFRP/TH(O)
Swedish	SWAOED/IRB		SIM/PA/TH(O)
Sween Cream	SWAOEN/KRAOEM	sympathectomize	SIFRP/THEKT/MAOIZ
Sween Prep	SWAOEN/PREP	sympathectomy	SIFRP/THEKT/M*I
Sween-A-Peel	SWAOEN/A/PAOEL	sympathetectomy	SIFRP/THE/TEKT/M*I
	SWAOEN/AI/PAOEL		SIM/P*AT/TEKT/M*I
sweeny	SWAOE/N*I	sympathetic	SIFRP/THET/IK
	SWAOEN/N*I	sympathetic(o)-	SIFRP/THET/K(O)
sweep	SWAOEP		SIM/PA/THET/K(O)
Sweet	K-P/SWAOET	sympatheticomimetic	SIFRP/THET/KO/MAOI/MET/IK
swell	SWEL		SIFRP/THET/KO/MI/MET/IK
swellhead	SWEL/HED	sympatheticoparalytic	SIFRP/THET/KO/PAR/LIT/IK
Swift	K-P/SWIFT	sympatheticotonia	SIFRP/THET/KO/TOEN/YA
swimmer	SWIM/ER	sympatheticotonic	SIFRP/THET/KO/TON/IK
swine	SWAOIN	sympathetoblast	SIFRP/THET/BLA*S
swinepox	SWAOIN/POX	sympathic	SIM/PA*T/IK
swing	SWING	sympathicectomy	SIM/PA*T/SEKT/M*I
Swiss	SWISZ	sympathic(o)-	SIM/PA*T/K(O)
swoon	SWAON	sympathicoblast	SIM/PA*T/KO/BLA*S
sychnuria	SIK/NAOUR/YA	sympathicoblastoma	SIM/PA*T/KO/BLAS/TOE/MA
sycoma	SAO*I/KOE/MA	sympathicodiaphtheresis	SIM/PA*T/KO/DI/AF/THRAOE/SIS
	SAOI/KOE/MA		SIM/PA*T/KO/DI/AF/THE/RAOE/
sycosiform	SAO*I/KOES/FORM		SIS
	SAOI/KOES/FORM	sympathicogonioma	SIM/PA*T/KO/GOEN/YOE/MA
sycosis	SAO*I/KOE/SIS	sympathicolytic	SIM/PA*T/KO/LIT/IK
	(*not* SAOI/KOE/SIS; see psychosis)	sympathicomimetic	SIM/PA*T/KO/MAOI/MET/IK
			SIM/PA*T/KO/MI/MET/IK
Sydenham	SID/EN/HAM	sympathiconeuritis	SIM/PA*T/KO/NAOU/RAOITS
Sydney	SID/NAOE	sympathicopathy	SIM/PA*T/KOP/TH*I
syllabaris	SIL/BAI/RIS	sympathicotherapy	SIM/PA*T/KO/THER/PI
syllabize	SIL/BAOIZ	sympathicotonia	SIM/PA*T/KO/TOEN/YA
syllable-stumbling	SIL/-BL/STUM/-BLG	sympathicotonic	SIM/PA*T/KO/TON/IK
syllabus	SIL/BUS	sympathicotripsy	SIM/PA*T/KO/TRIP/SI
Syllact Powder	SIL/LAKT/POUD/ER	sympathicotonus	SIM/PA*T/KO/TOE/NUS
syllepsiology	SI/LEPS/YOLG	sympathicotrope	SIM/PA*T/KO/TROEP
	SIL/LEPS/YOLG	sympathicotrophic	SIM/PA*T/KO/TROFK
syllepsis	SI/LEP/SIS	sympathicotropic	SIM/PA*T/KO/TROP/IK
	SIL/LEP/SIS	sympathicus	SIM/PA*T/KUS
sylvarum	SIL/VAIR/UM		

sympathin	SIFRP/THIN	Synalar-HP	SIN/LAR/H-RBGS/P*RBGS
sympathism	SIFRP/THIFM	synalbumin	SIN/AL/BAOU/MIN
sympathist	SIFRP/TH*IS	synalgia	SIN/AL/JA
sympathizer	SIFRP/THAOIZ/ER		SI/NAL/JA
sympathoadrenal	SIFRP/THO/AI/DRAOENL	synalgic	SIN/AL/JIK
	SIFRP/THO/AD/RAOENL	Synalgos	SI/NAL/GOES
sympathoblast	SIFRP/THO/BLA*S		SIN/AL/GOES
sympathoblastoma	SIFRP/THO/BLAS/TOE/MA	Synalgos-DC	SI/NAL/GOES/D-RBGS/KR*RBGS
sympathochromaffin	SIFRP/THO/KROE/MAFN		SIN/AL/GOES/D-RBGS/KR*RBGS
	SIFRP/THO/KROE/MAF/FIN	synanastomosis	SIN/AI/NA*S/MOE/SIS
sympathogone	SIFRP/THO/GOEN		SIN/AN/A*S/MOE/SIS
sympathogonia	SIFRP/THO/GOEN/YA	synanche	see cynanche
sympathogonioma	SIFRP/THO/GOEN/YOE/MA	synandrogenic	SIN/AN/DRO/JEN/IK
sympathogonium	SIFRP/THO/GOEN/YUM	synanthem	SIN/AN/THEM
sympatholytic	SIFRP/THO/LIT/IK		SI/NAN/THEM
sympathomimetic	SIFRP/THO/MAOI/MET/IK	synanthema	SIN/AN/THAOE/MA
	SIFRP/THO/MI/MET/IK	synaphoceptor	SI/NAF/SEP/TOR
sympathoparalytic	SIFRP/THO/PAR/LIT/IK		SNAF/SEP/TOR
sympathy	SIFRP/TH*I	synapse	SIN/APS
symperitoneal	SIM/PERT/NAOEL		SI/NAPS
sympexion	SIM/PEX/YON	synapses	SI/NAP/SAOEZ
sympexis	SIM/PEK/SIS		SIN/AP/SAOEZ
symphalangia	SIM/FLAN/JA		SNAP/SAOEZ
symphalangism	SIM/FAL/AN/JIFM	synapsis	SI/NAP/SIS
	SIM/FLAN/JIFM		SIN/AP/SIS
symphalangy	SIM/FLAN/JI		SNAP/SIS
	SIM/FAL/AN/JI	synapt(o)-	SI/NAPT
symphony	SIM/FO/N*I		SI/NAP/T(O)
symphyogenetic	SIM/FO/JE/NET/IK		SIN/APT
	SIM/FAOE/YO/JE/NET/IK		SIN/AP/T(O)
symphyseal	see symphysial		SNAPT
symphyseos	SIM/FIZ/YOS		SNAP/T(O)
	SIM/FIS/YOS	synaptase	SI/NAP/TAIS
symphyses	SIM/FI/SAOEZ		SNAP/TAIS
symphysial	SIM/FIZ/YAL	synaptene	SI/NAP/TAOEN
symphysialis	SIM/FIZ/YAI/LIS		SNAP/TAOEN
symphysic	SIM/FIZ/IK	synaptic	SI/NAPT/IK
symphysiectomy	SIM/FIZ/YEKT/M*I		SNAPT/IK
symphysiolysis	SIM/FIZ/YOL/SIS	synaptology	SIN/AP/TOLG
symphysion	SIM/FIZ/YON	synaptonemal	SI.NAPT/NAOE/MAL
symphysiorrhaphy	SIM/FIZ/YOR/FI		SNAPT/NAOE/MAL
symphysiotome	SIM/FIZ/YO/TOEM	synaptosome	SI/NAPT/SOEM
symphysiotomy	SIM/FIZ/YOT/M*I		SNAPT/SOEM
symphysis	SIM/FI/SIS	synarthrodia	SIN/AR/THROED/YA
symphysodactyly	SIM/FI/SO/DAKT/LI	synarthrodial	SIN/AR/THROED/YAL
symplasm	SIM/PLAFM	synarthrophysis	SIN/AR/THRO/FAOI/SIS
symplasmatic	SIM/PLAZ/MAT/IK	synarthroses	SIN/AR/THROE/SAOEZ
symplast	SIM/PLA*S	synarthrosis	SIN/AR/THROE/SIS
symplex	S*IM/PLEX	synathresis	SIN/A*T/RAOE/SIS
	(not SIM/PLEX; see simplex)	synathroisis	SIN/A*T/ROI/SIS
sympodia	SIM/POED/YA	sync	SIN/*K
symport	SIM/PORT	syncanthus	SIN/KAN/THUS
symporter	SIM/PORT/ER	syncelom	SIN/SE/LOM
symptom	SIFRP/TOM		SIN/SAOEL/OM
	SIM/TOM	syncephalus	SIN/SEF/LUS
symptomatic	SIFRPT/MAT/IK	syncephaly	SIN/SEF/LI
	SIMT/MAT/IK	syncheilia	SIN/KAOIL/YA
	SIFRP/TO/MAT/IK	syncheiria	SIN/KAOIR/YA
	SIM/TO/MAT/IK	syncholia	SIN/KOEL/YA
symptomatica	SIFRPT/MAT/KA	synchondrectomy	SIN/KON/DREKT/M*I
	SIMT/MAT/KA	synchondroseotomy	SIN/KON/DROES/YOT/M*I
	SIFRP/TO/MAT/KA	synchondroses	SIN/KON/DROE/SAOEZ
	SIM/TO/MAT/KA	synchondrosis	SIN/KON/DROE/SIS
symptomatology	SIFRP/TOM/TOLG	synchondrotomy	SIN/KON/DROT/M*I
	SIM/TOM/TOLG	synchorial	SIN/KOER/YAL
	SIFRPT/MA/TOLG	synchronia	SIN/KROEN/YA
	SIMT/MA/TOLG	synchronism	SIN/KRO/NIFM
symptomatolytic	SIFRPT/MAT/LIT/IK	synchronous	SIN/KRO/NOUS
	SIMT/MAT/LIT/IK	synchrony	SIN/KRO/N*I
	SIFRP/TO/MAT/LIT/IK	synchrotron	SIN/KRO/TRON
	SIM/TO/MAT/LIT/IK	synchysis	SIN/KI/SIS
symptome	SIFRP/TOEM	syncinesis	SIN/SI/NAOE/SIS
	SIM/TOEM	synclinal	SIN/KLI/NAL
symptomolytic	SIFRPT/MO/LIT/IK		SIN/KLAOINL
	SIMT/MO/LIT/IK	synclitic	SIN/KLIT/IK
	SIFRP/TOM/LIT/IK	syncliticism	SIN/KLIT/SIFM
	SIM/TOM/LIT/IK	synclitism	SIN/KLI/TIFM
symptosis	SIFRP/TOE/SIS	synclonus	SIN/KLO/NUS
	SIM/TOE/SIS		SIN/KLOE/NUS
sympus	SIM/PUS	syncopal	SIN/KO/PAL
Syms	S*IMZ	syncope	SIN/KO/PAOE
	S*IMS	syncopic	SIN/KOP/IK
	(not SIMZ or SIMS; see Sims)	syncretio	SIN/KRAOE/SHOE
syn-	SIN		SIN/KRAOERB/YOE
Synacort	SIN/KORT	syncyanin	SIN/SAOI/NIN
synadelphus	SIN/DEL/FUS	syncyti(o)-	SIN/SIRB/Y(O)
	SIN/AI/DEL/FUS		SIN/SIT/Y(O)
synaetion	SIN/AOET/YON	syncytia	SIN/SIRB/YA
Synalar	SIN/LAR	syncytial	SIN/SIRBL

syncytioma	SIN/SIRB/YOE/MA	syngenetic	SIN/JE/NET/IK
syncytiotoxin	SIN/SIRB/YO/TOK/SIN	syngenic	SIN/JEN/IK
syncytiotrophoblast	SIN/SIRB/YO/TROEF/BLA*S	syngnathia	SIN/NA*T/YA
	SIN/SIRB/YO/TROF/BLA*S		SIN/NA*IT/YA
syncytium	SIN/SIRB/UM	syngonic	SIN/GON/IK
	SIN/SIRB/YUM	syngraft	SIN/GRAFT
syncytoid	SIN/SI/TOID	synidrosis	SIN/DROE/SIS
	SINS/TOID	synizesis	SIN/ZAOE/SIS
syndactyl	SIN/DAK/TIL	synkaryon	SIN/KAR/YON
syndactyle	SIN/DAK/TAOIL	Synkayvite	SIN/KAI/VAOIT
syndactylia	SIN/DAK/TIL/YA	synkinesia	SIN/KI/NAOEZ/YA
syndactylism	SIN/DAKT/LIFM	synkinesis	SIN/KI/NAOE/SIS
syndactylous	SIN/DAKT/LOUS	synkinetic	SIN/KI/NET/IK
syndactylus	SIN/DAKT/LUS	synnematin	SIN/MAI/TIN
syndactyly	SIN/DAKT/LI		SI/NAOEM/TIN
syndectomy	SIN/DEKT/M*I	synonychia	SIN/NIK/YA
syndermotica	SIN/DER/MOT/KA		SIN/O/NIK/YA
syndesis	SIN/DAOE/SIS	synonym	SIN/NIM
	SIN/DE/SIS	synophrys	SIN/OF/RIS
	SIND/SIS	synophthalmia	SIN/OF/THAL/MA
syndesm(o)-	SIN/DEZ/M(O)		SIN/OF/THAL/MAOE/YA
	SIN/DES/M(O)	synophthalmus	SIN/OF/THAL/MUS
syndesmectomy	SIN/DEZ/MEKT/M*I	synopses	SI/NOP/SAOEZ
syndesmectopia	SIN/DEZ/MEK/TOEP/YA		SNOP/SAOEZ
syndesmitis	SIN/DEZ/MAOITS	synopsis	SI/NOP/SIS
syndesmochorial	SIN/DEZ/MO/KOER/YAL		SNOP/SIS
syndesmodial	SIN/DEZ/MOED/YAL	synopsy	SIN/OP/SI
syndesmography	SIN/DEZ/MOG/FI	synoptophore	SIN/OPT/FOER
syndesmologia	SIN/DEZ/MO/LOE/JA	synoptoscope	SIN/OPT/SKOEP
syndesmology	SIN/DEZ/MOLG	synorchidism	SIN/ORK/DIFM
syndesmoma	SIN/DEZ/MOE/MA	synorchism	SIN/OR/KIFM
syndesmo-odontoid	SIN/DEZ/MO/O/DON/TOID		SIN/ORK/IFM
syndesmopexy	SIN/DEZ/MO/PEK/SI	synoscheos	SIN/OS/KOS
syndesmophyte	SIN/DEZ/MO/FAOIT		SIN/OS/KAOE/OS
syndesmoplasty	SIN/DEZ/MO/PLAS/TI	synosteology	SIN/O*S/YOLG
syndesmorrhaphy	SIN/DEZ/MOR/FI	synosteosis	SIN/O*S/YOE/SIS
syndesmoses	SIN/DEZ/MOE/SAOEZ	synosteotic	SIN/O*S/YOT/IK
syndesmosis	SIN/DEZ/MOE/SIS	synosteotomy	SIN/O*S/YOT/M*I
syndesmotic	SIN/DEZ/MOT/IK	synostosis	SIN/OS/TOE/SIS
syndesmotomy	SIN/DEZ/MOT/M*I	synostotic	SIN/OS/TOT/IK
syndrome	SIN/DROEM	synotia	SI/NOE/SHA
syndromic	SIN/DROM/IK		SI/NOERB/YA
	SIN/DROEM/IK	synotus	SI/NOE/TUS
syndromology	SIN/DRO/MOLG	synov-	SIN/V-
	SIN/DROM/OLG	synovectomy	SIN/VEKT/M*I
synechia	SI/NEK/YA	synovi(o)-	SNOEV/Y(O)
	SI/NAOEK/YA		SI/NOEV/Y(O)
synechiae	SI/NEK/YAE	synovia	SNOEV/YA
	SI/NAOEK/YAE	synovial	SNOEV/YAL
synechiotomy	SI/NEK/YOT/M*I	synovialis	SNOEV/YAI/LIS
synechotome	SI/NEK/TOEM	synovioblast	SNOEV/YO/BLA*S
synechotomy	SIN/KOT/M*I	synoviocyte	SNOEV/YO/SAO*IT
synechtenterotomy	SI/NEK/TENT/ROT/M*I	synovioma	SNOEV/YOE/MA
	SIN/EK/TENT/ROT/M*I	synoviosarcoma	SNOEV/YO/SAR/KOE/MA
synecology	SIN/E/KOLG	synoviparous	SIN/VIP/ROUS
	SIN/KOLG	synovitis	SIN/VAOITS
Synemol Cream	S*IN/MOL/KRAOEM	synovium	SNOEV/YUM
	SIN/MOL/KRAOEM	synpneumonic	SIN/NAOU/MON/IK
synencephalocele	SIN/EN/SEF/LO/SAO*EL	synpolydactyly	SIN/POL/DAKT/LI
synencephalus	SIN/EN/SEF/LUS	synreflexia	SIN/RE/FLEX/YA
synencephaly	SIN/EN/SEF/LI	syntactic	SIN/TAKT/IK
syneresis	SI/NER/SIS	syntactical	SIN/TAKT/KAL
synergenesis	SIN/ER/JEN/SIS	syntactics	SIN/TAKT/IK/-S
synergetic	SIN/ER/JET/IK	syntality	SIN/TAL/TI
synergia	SI/NER/JA	syntaxis	SIN/TAK/SIS
	SI/NERJ/YA	syntectic	SIN/TEKT/IK
	SIN/ER/JA	syntenic	SIN/TEN/IK
	SIN/ERJ/YA	syntenosis	SIN/TE/NOE/SIS
synergic	SI/NERJ/IK		SINT/NOE/SIS
	SIN/ERJ/IK	synteny	SINT/N*I
synergism	SIN/ERJ/IFM		SIN/TE/N*I
synergist	SIN/ERJ/*IS	synteresis	SINT/RAOE/SIS
synergistic	SIN/ERJ/*IS/IK		SIN/TRAOE/SIS
synergy	SIN/ERJI	synteretic	SIN/TRET/IK
synesthesia	SIN/ES/THAOEZ/YA		SIN/TER/ET/IK
synesthesialgia	SIN/ES/THAOEZ/YAL/JA		SINT/RET/IK
Syngamidae	SIN/GAM/DAE	syntexis	SIN/TEK/SIS
syngamous	SIN/GA/MOUS	synthase	SIN/THAIS
Syngamus	SIN/GA/MUS	synthermal	SIN/THER/MAL
syngamy	SIN/GA/M*I	synthescope	S*INT/SKOEP
syngeneic	SIN/JE/NAOE/IK	syntheses	S*INT/SAOEZ
	SIN/JE/NAI/IK	synthesis	S*INT/SIS
syngenesio-	SIN/JE/NAOEZ/YO	synthesize	S*INT/SAOIZ
	SIN/JE/NAOES/YO	synthetase	S*INT/TAIS
syngenesioplastic	SIN/JE/NAOEZ/YO/PLA*S/IK	synthetic	SIN/THET/IK
syngenesioplasty	SIN/JE/NAOEZ/YO/PLAS/TI	synthetism	S*INT/TIFM
syngenesiotransplantation	SIN/JE/NAOEZ/YO/TRA*NS/	synthorax	SIN/THOR/AX
	PLAN/TAIGS	Synthroid	SIN/THROID
syngenesis	SIN/JEN/SIS	Syntocinon	SIN/TOES/NON

syntonic	SIN/TON/IK
syntopie	SIN/TO/PAOE
syntopy	SIN/TO/PI
syntripsis	SIN/TRIP/SIS
syntrophism	SIN/TROEF/IFM
	SIN/TROE/FIFM
	SIN/TRO/FIFM
syntrophoblast	SIN/TROEF/BLA*S
	SIN/TROF/BLA*S
syntrophus	SIN/TRO/FUS
syntropic	SIN/TROP/IK
syntropy	SIN/TRO/PI
	SIN/TROE/PI
synul-	SIN/L-
	SIN/YAOU/L-
	SIN/YU/L-
synulosis	SIN/LOE/SIS
synulotic	SIN/LOT/IK
Syphacia	SAOI/FAI/SHA
	SAOI/FAIRB/YA
	SAOI/FAIS/YA
	SI/FAI/SHA
	SI/FAIRB/YA
	SI/FAIS/YA
syphil(o)-	SIF/L(O)
syphilemia	SIF/LAOEM/YA
syphilid	SIF/LID
syphilide	SIF/LAOID
syphilimetry	SIF/LIM/TRI
siphilionthus	SIF/LI/ON/THUS
syphiliphobia	SIF/LI/FOEB/YA
syphilis	SIF/LIS
syphilitic	SIF/LIT/IK
syphilitica	SIF/LIT/KA
syphiliticum	SIF/LIT/KUM
syphiloderm	SIF/LO/DERM
syphiloderma	SIF/LO/DER/MA
syphiloid	SIF/LOID
syphilologist	SIF/LO*LGS
syphilology	SIF/LOLG
syphiloma	SIF/LOE/MA
syphilomatous	SIF/LOEM/TOUS
syphilomania	SIF/LO/MAIN/YA
syphilophobia	SIF/LO/FOEB/YA
syphilophobic	SIF/LO/FOEB/IK
syphilophyma	SIF/LO/FAOI/MA
syphilopsychosis	SIF/LO/SAOI/KOE/SIS
syphilosis	SIF/LOE/SIS
syphilous	SIF/LOUS
syphitoxin	SIF/TOK/SIN
syrigmophonia	SI/RIG/MO/FOEN/YA
	SIR/IG/MO/FOEN/YA
syrigmus	SI/RIG/MUS
syring(o)-	SIRNG
	SIRN/G(O)
	SIRN/J-
	SI/RIN/G(O)
syringadenoma	SIRNG/AD/NOE/MA
syringadenosus	SIRNG/AD/NOE/SUS
syringe	SIRN/-J
	SI/RIN/-J
syringeal	SIRN/JAL
	SI/RIN/JAL
syringectomy	SIRN/JEKT/M*I
syringes	SIRN/JAOEZ
	SI/RIN/JAOEZ
syringitis	SIRN/JAOITS
syringoadenoma	*see* syringadenoma
syringobulbia	SIRNG/BUL/BAOE/YA
	SIRNG/BUL/BA
syringocarcinoma	SIRNG/KARS/NOE/MA
syringocele	SIRNG/SAO*EL
syringocystadenoma	SIRNG/SIS/TAD/NOE/MA
	SIRNG/S*IS/AD/NOE/MA
syringocystoma	SIRNG/SIS/TOE/MA
syringoencephalia	SIRNG/EN/SFAIL/YA
syringoencephalomyelia	SIRNG/EN/SEF/LO/MAOI/AOEL/ YA
syringoid	SIRN/GOID
	SI/RIN/GOID
syringoma	SIRN/GOE/MA
syringomeningocele	SIRNG/ME/NING/SAO*EL
syringomyelia	SIRNG/MAOI/AOEL/YA
syringomyelic	SIRNG/MAOI/EL/IK
syringomyelitis	SIRNG/MAOI/LAOITS
syringomyelocele	SIRNG/MAOI/LO/SAO*EL
syringomyelus	SIRNG/MAOI/LUS
syringopontia	SIRNG/PON/SHA
syringorrhaphy	SIRN/GOR/FI

syringotome	SIRNG/TOEM
syringotomy	SIRN/GOT/M*I
syrinx	SIRNGS
	SIR/INGS
syrosingopine	SIR/SING/PAOEN
	SAOIR/SING/PAOEN
Syrphidae	SIR/FI/DAE
syrup	SIR/RUP
syrupus	SIR/PUS
syssarcosic	SIS/AR/KOES/IK
	SIS/SAR/KOES/IK
syssarcosis	SIS/AR/KOE/SIS
	SIS/SAR/KOE/SIS
syssarcotic	SIS/AR/KOT/IK
	SIS/SAR/KOT/IK
syssomus	SIS/SOE/MUS
systaltic	SIS/TALT/IK
systaltism	SIS/TALT/IFM
	SIS/TAL/TIFM
systatic	SIS/TAT/IK
system	S-M
	SIS/TEM
	S*IS/EM
systema	SIS/TAOE/MA
systematic	S*IS/MAT/IK
	S-M/MAT/IK
systematization	S*IS/MAT/ZAIGS
	S-M/MAT/ZAIGS
systemic	SIS/TEM/IK
	S-M/IK
systematize	S*IS/MA/TAOIZ
	S-M/TAOIZ
	SIS/TEM/TAOIZ
systematology	S*IS/MA/TOLG
	S-M/TOLG
	SIS/TEM/TOLG
systemoid	S*IS/MOID
	S-M/OID
systogene	S*IS/JAOEN
systole	S*IS/LAOE
systolic	SIS/TOL/IK
systolometer	S*IS/LOM/TER
systremma	SIS/TREM/MA
syzygial	SI/ZIJ/YAL
syzygiology	SI/ZIJ/YOLG
	SI/ZIJ/OLG
syzygium	SI/ZIJ/YUM
	SI/ZIJ/UM
syzygy	SIZ/JI

T

tabacin	TAB/SIN
tabacism	TAB/SIFM
tabacosis	TAB/KOE/SIS
tabacum	TAB/KUM
tabagism	TAB/JIFM
tabanid	TAB/NID
Tabanidae	TA/BAN/DAE
Tabanus	TA/BAI/NUS
tabardillo	TAB/AR/DAOE/YOE
	TAB/DAOE/YOE
tabatiere anatomique	TAB/TAIR/AN/TO/MAOEK
tabella	TA/BEL/LA
tabellae	TA/BEL/LAE
tabes	TAI/BAOEZ
tabescence	TA/BES/ENS
tabescent	TA/BES/ENT
tabetic	TA/BET/IK
tabetiform	TA/BET/FORM
tabic	TAB/IK
tabid	TAB/ID
tabification	TAB/FI/KAIGS
tablature	TAB/LA/KHUR
table	TAIBL
tableau	TAB/LOE
tableaux	TAB/LOEZ
tablespoon	TAIBL/SPAON
tablet	TAB/LET
tabo-	TAIB
	TAI/BO
taboo	TA/BAO
taboparalysis	TAIB/PRAL/SIS
taboparesis	TAIB/PA/RAOE/SIS
	TAIB/PAR/SIS
tabul-	TAB/L-
	TAB/YAOU/L-
	TAB/YU/L-
tabula	TAB/LA
tabular	TAB/LAR
tabule	TAB/YAOUL
Tac-3	TA*K/3
Tacaryl	TAK/RIL
TACE Capsules	TAIS/KAP/SAOUL/-S
tache	TARB
tachetic	TA/KET/IK
tachistesthesia	TA/KIS/TES/THAOEZ/YA
tachistoscope	TA/K*IS/SKOEP
	TA/KIS/TO/SKOEP
tachogram	TAK/GRAM
tachograph	TAK/GRAF
tachography	TA/KOG/FI
tachometer	TA/KOM/TER
tachy-	TAK
	TA/KI
tachyalimentation	TAK/AL/MEN/TAIGS
tachyarrhythmia	TAK/AI/R*IT/MAOE/YA
	TAK/AI/R*IT/MA
tachyauxesis	TAK/AUK/ZAOE/SIS
tachycardia	TAK/KARD/YA
tachycardiac	TAK/KARD/YAK
tachycardic	TAK/KARD/IK
tachygastria	TAK/GAS/TRAOE/YA
	TAK/GAS/TRA
tachygenesis	TAK/JEN/SIS
tachykinin	TAK/KAOI/NIN
tachylalia	TAK/LAIL/YA
tachylogia	TAK/LOE/JA
tachymeter	TA/KIM/TER
tachypacing	TAK/PAIS/-G
tachyphagia	TAK/FAI/JA
tachyphasia	TAK/FAIZ/YA
tachyphemia	TAK/FAOEM/YA
tachyphrasia	TAK/FRAIZ/YA
tachyphrenia	TAK/FRAOEN/YA
tachyphylaxis	TAK/FLAK/SIS
tachypnea	TA/KIP/NA
	TA/KIP/NAOE/YA
tachypneic	TA/KIP/NIK
	TA/KIP/NAOE/IK
tachypragia	TAK/PRAG/YA
tachyrhythmia	TAK/R*IT/MA
	TAK/R*IT/MAOE/YA
tachysterol	TA/K*IS/ROL
	TA/K*IS/ROEL
tachysynthesis	TAK/S*INT/SIS

tachysystole	TAK/S*IS/LAOE
tachytrophism	TAK/TROEF/IFM
tachyzoite	TAK/ZOE/AOIT
tacrine	TAK/RAOEN
tactic	TAKT/IK
tacticity	TAK/TIS/TI
tactile	TAK/TIL
	TAK/TAOIL
tactilogical	TAKT/LOJ/KAL
tactilogically	TAKT/LOJ/KLI
taction	TA*BGS
tactometer	TAK/TOM/TER
tactor	TAK/TOR
tactual	TAK/KHUL
tactus	TAK/TUS
tad	TAD
tadpole	TAD/POEL
taedium	TAED/YUM
	(*not* TAOED/YUM; see tedium)
taeni-	TAEN/Y-
	(*not* TAOEN/Y-; see teni-)
taenia	TAEN/YA
Taenia	K-P/TAEN/YA
taeniacide	TAEN/YA/SAO*ID
taeniae	TAEN/YAE
taeniafugal	TAEN/YA/FAOU/GAL
taeniafuge	TAEN/YA/FAOUJ
taenial	TAEN/YAL
Taeniarhynchus	TAEN/YA/RIN/KUS
taeniasis	TAE/NAOI/SIS
taeniform	TAEN/FORM
taeniid	TAE/NAOE/ID
Taeniidae	TAE/NAOE/DAE
	TAE/NAOI/DAE
taenioid	TAEN/YOID
taenioides	TAEN/YOI/DAOEZ
taeniola	TAE/NAOI/LA
taeniorhynchus	TAEN/YO/RIN/KUS
tag	TAG
Tagamet	TAG/MET
tagatose	TAG/TOES
tagesrest	TAG/EZ/R*ES
tagliacotian	TAL/YA/KOEGS
taiga	TAOI/GA
tail	TAIL
tailbone	TAIL/BOEN
tailgut	TAIL/GUT
taka	TAK/KA
	TA/KA
Takayasu	TAK/YA/SAOU
take	TAIK
tal(o)-	TAI/L(O)
	TAIL
Talacen	TAL/SEN
talaje	TA/LA/HAI
	TA/LA/JAOE
talalgia	TA/LAL/JA
	TAL/AL/JA
talantropia	TAL/AN/TROEP/YA
talar	TAI/LAR
talaris	TAI/LAI/RIS
	TA/LAI/RIS
Talbot	TAL/BOT
talbutal	TAL/BAOU/TAL
talc	TAL-K
talcosis	TAL/KOE/SIS
talcum	TAL/KUM
tali	TAI/LAOI
talion	TAL/YON
talion dread	TAL/YON/DRED
taliped	TAL/PED
talipedic	TAL/PAOED/IK
talipes	TAL/PAOEZ
talipomanus	TAL/POM/NUS
	TAL/PO/MAI/NUS
tallow	TAL/LOE
Talma	TAL/MA
talocalcanea	TAIL/KAL/KAIN/YA
talocalcaneal	TAIL/KAL/KAIN/YAL
talocalcanean	TAIL/KAL/KAIN/YAN
talocalcaneonavicular	TAIL/KAL/KAIN/YO/NA/VIK/LAR
talocalcaneonavicularis	TAIL/KAL/KAIN/YO/NA/VIK/LAI/RIS
talocrural	TAIL/KRAOURL
talocruralis	TAIL/KRAOU/RAI/LIS
talofibular	TAIL/FIB/LAR
talon	TAL/LON
talonavicular	TAIL/NA/VIK/LAR
talonavicularis	TAIL/NA/VIK/LAI/RIS

talonid	TAL/NID	Tarinus	TA/RAOI/NUS
taloscaphoid	TAIL/SKAF/OID	tariric	TA/RAOI/RIK
talose	TAL/OES		TA/RIR/IK
	TAI/LOES	Tarlov	TAR/LOV
talotibial	TAIL/TIB/YAL	Tarnier	TARN/YAI
talus	TAI/LUS	tarragon	TAR/RA/GON
Talwin	TAL/WIN	tarry	TAR/RI
Talwin Nx	TAL/WIN/N-RBGS/KP*	tars(o)-	TARS
tama	TAI/MA		TAR/S(O)
tamarind	TAM/RIND	tarsadenitis	TAR/SAD/NAOITS
Tambocor	TAM/BO/KOR		TARS/AD/NAOITS
tambour	TAM/BUR	tarsal	TAR/SAL
	TAM/BAOUR	tarsale	TAR/SAI/LAOE
tamoxifen	TA/MOX/FEN	tarsalgia	TAR/SAL/JA
tampon	TAM/PON	tarsalia	TAR/SAIL/YA
tamponade	TAFRP/NAID	tarsalis	TAR/SAI/LIS
	TAM/PO/NAID	tarsea	TARS/YA
tamponage	TAFRP/NAJ	tarseae	TARS/YAE
	TAM/PO/NAJ	tarsectomy	TAR/SEKT/M*I
tamponing	TAM/PON/-G		TARS/EKT/M*I
tamponment	TAM/PON/-MT	tarsectopia	TAR/SEK/TOEP/YA
tan	TAN		TARS/EK/TOEP/YA
tandamine	TAND/MAOEN	tarsectopy	TAR/SEKT/PI
	TAN/DA/MAOEN		TARS/EKP/PI
tangentiality	TAN/JEN/SHAL/TI	tarsen	TAR/SEN
	TAN/JEN/-RBL/TI	tarseus	TARS/YUS
Tangier	TAN/JAOER	tarsi	TAR/SAOI
tangoreceptor	TANG/RE/SEP/TOR	tarsitis	TAR/SAOITS
	TAN/GO/RE/SEP/TOR	tarsocheiloplasty	TARS/KAOIL/PLAS/TI
tank	TAN/-K	tarsoclasia	TARS/KLAIZ/YA
	TA*NG	tarsoclasis	TAR/SOK/LA/SIS
tannase	TAN/AIS	tarsoepiphysial	TARS/EP/FIZ/YAL
	TAN/NAIS	tarsomalacia	TARS/MA/LAI/SHA
tannate	TAN/AIT	tarsomegaly	TARS/MEG/LI
	TAN/NAIT	tarsometatarsal	TARS/MET/TAR/SAL
tannex	TAN/NEX	tarsometatarsea	TARS/MET/TARS/YA
tannic	TAN/IK	tarsometatarseae	TARS/MET/TARS/YAE
tannin	TAN/NIN	tarsometatarsus	TARS/MET/TAR/SUS
tanning	TAN/-G	tarso-orbital	TARS/ORB/TAL
tannylacetate	TAN/IL/AS/TAIT	tarsophalangeal	TARS/FLAN/JAL
	TAN/RET	tarsophyma	TARS/FAOI/MA
tantalum	TANT/LUM	tarsoplasia	TARS/PLAIZ/YA
tantrum	TAN/TRUM	tarsoplasty	TARS/PLAS/TI
tanycyte	TAN/SAO*IT	tarsoptosis	TAR/SOP/TOE/SIS
tanyphonia	TAN/FOEN/YA	tarsorrhaphy	TAR/SOR/FI
TAO Capsules	TAI/YOE/KAP/SAOUL/-S	tarsotarsal	TARS/TAR/SAL
tap	TAP	tarsotibial	TARS/TIB/YAL
tape	TAIP	tarsotomy	TAR/SOT/M*I
tapet(o)-	TA/PAOET	tarsus	TARS/SUS
	TA/PAOE/T(O)	tart	TART
tapeta	TA/PAOE/TA	tartar	TAR/TAR
tapetal	TA/PAOE/TAL	tartarated	TART/RAIT/-D
tapetochoroidal	TA/PAOET/KOE/ROI/DAL		TAR/TAR/AIT/-D
tapetoretinal	TA/PAOET/RET/NAL	tartari	TART/RAOI
tapetoretinopathy	TA/PAOET/RET/NOP/TH*I	tartaric	TAR/TAR/IK
tapetum	TA/PAOE/TUM	tartarized	TART/RAOIZ/-D
	TA/PAOET/UM		TAR/TAR/AOIZ/-D
tapeworm	TAIP/WORM	tartrate	TAR/TRAIT
taphophilia	TAF/FIL/YA	tartrated	TAR/TRAIT/-D
taphophobia	TAF/FOEB/YA	tartrazine	TAR/TRA/ZAOEN
Tapia	TAP/YA	tasikinesia	TAS/KI/NAOEZ/YA
tapinocephalic	TAP/NO/SFAL/IK	tastant	TAIS/TANT
tapinocephaly	TAP/NO/SEF/LI	taste	TA*IS
tapioca	TAP/YOE/KA	taste bud	TA*IS/BUD
tapiroid	TAIP/ROID	taster	TA*IS/ER
	TAI/PIR/OID	tattoo	TAT/TAO
tapotage	TAP/TAJ	taur(o)-	TAUR
tapotement	TA/POET/-MT		TAU/R(O)
tar	TAR	tauri	TAU/RAOI
Taractan	TA/RAK/TAN	taurine	TAU/RAOEN
	TAR/AK/TAN		TAU/RIN
tarandi	TA/RAN/DAOI	taurocholaneresis	TAUR/KOEL/NER/SIS
tarantism	TARN/TIFM	taurocholanopoiesis	TAUR/KOE/LAN/POI/SIS
	TAR/AN/TIFM	taurocholate	TAUR/KOE/LAIT
tarantula	TA/RAN/KHU/LA	taurocholemia	TAUR/KOE/LAOEM/YA
	TA/RANT/LA	taurocholic	TAUR/KOEL/IK
taraxacum	TA/RAX/KUM	taurodontism	TAUR/DON/TIFM
tarda	TAR/DA	Taussig	TAUS/IG
Tardieu	TAR/DAOU		TAUS/SIG
	TARD/YAOU	taut	TAUT
tardive	TAR/DIV	tauto-	TAUT
	TARD/IV		TAU/TO
	TAR/DAOEV	tautomenial	TAUT/MAOEN/YAL
tardy	TAR/DI	tautomeral	TAU/TOM/RAL
tare	TA*ER	tautomerase	TAU/TOM/RAIS
target	TARGT	tautomeric	TAUT/MER/IK
	TARG/ET	tautomerism	TAU/TOM/RIFM
Tarin	TA/RIN	Tavist	TAV/*IS
Tarini	TA/RAOI/NAOI	Tavist-1	TAV/*IS/1

Tavist-D	TAV/*IS/D-RBGS	Tegopen	TEG/PEN
Tawara	TA/WA/RA	Tegretol	TEG/RE/TOL
	TA/WAR/RA	tegument	TEG/YAOUMT
taxa	TAK/SA		TEG/YUMT
-taxia	TAX/YA	tegumental	TEG/YAOUMT/TAL
-taxic	TAX/IK		TEG/YUMT/TAL
Tazicef	TAZ/SEF	tegumentary	TEG/YAOUMT/RI
Tazidime	TAZ/DAOEM		TEG/YUMT/RI
taxis	TAK/SIS	Teichmann	TAOIK/MAN
taxo-	TAX	teichoic	TAOI/KOIK
	TAK/SO		TAOI/KOE/IK
taxology	TAK/SOLG	teichopsia	TAOI/KOPS/YA
	TAX/OLG	tela	TAOE/LA
taxon	TAK/SON	telae	TAOE/LAE
taxonomic	TAX/NOM/IK	telalgia	TEL/AL/JA
taxonomist	TAK/SON/M*IS	telangiectases	TEL/AN/JEKT/SAOEZ
	TAX/ON/M*IS	telangiectasia	TEL/AN/JEK/TAIZ/YA
taxonomy	TAK/SON/M*I	telangiectasis	TEL/AN/JEKT/SIS
	TAX/ON/M*I	telangiectatic	TEL/AN/JEK/TAT/IK
-taxy	TAK/SI	telangiectaticum	TEL/AN/JEK/TAT/KUM
Tay	TAI	telangiectodes	TEL/AN/JEK/TOE/DAOEZ
Tay-Sachs	TAI/H-F/SA*KS	telangiitis	TEL/AN/JAOITS
Tay-Sachs disease	TAI/SAKS/DI/SAOEZ	telangioma	TEL/AN/JOE/MA
	TAI/SA*KS/DI/SAOEZ	telangion	TEL/AN/JON
Taylor	K-P/TAI/LOR	telangiosis	TEL/AN/JOE/SIS
	TA*I/LOR	telar	TAOE/LAR
tazolol	TAIZ/LOL	Teldrin	TEL/DRIN
	TAIZ/LOEL	tele-	TEL
TB	T-RBGS/B*RBGS		TE/LE
T-Cypionate	T-RBGS/SIP/YO/NAIT	telebinocular	TEL/B*I/NOK/LAR
tea	TAE	telecanthus	TEL/KAN/THUS
Teale	TAO*EL	telecardiogram	TEL/KARD/YO/GRAM
	(not TAOEL; see teal)	telecardiography	TEL/KARD/YOG/FI
tear	TAER	telecardiophone	TEL/KARD/YO/FOEN
	TAIR	teleceptive	TEL/SEPT/IV
	(not TAOER; see tier)	teleceptor	TEL/SEP/TOR
tearing	TAER/-G	telecinesia	TEL/SI/NAOEZ/YA
tears	TAER/-S	telecinesis	TEL/SI/NAOE/SIS
Tears Naturale	TAER/-S/NAFP/RAL	telecobalt	TEL/KO/BALT
Tears Plus Lubricant	TAER/-S/PLUS/LAOUB/KANT	telecord	TEL/KORD
teart	TERT	telecurietherapy	TEL/KAOUR/THER/PI
tease	TAOEZ	teledactyl	TEL/DAK/TIL
teaspoon	TAE/SPAON	telediagnosis	TEL/DAOIG/NOE/SIS
teat	TAOET	telediastolic	TEL/DAOI/STOL/IK
tebutate	TEB/TAIT	Tel-E-Dose	TEL/E/DOES
	TEB/YAOU/TAIT	telefluoroscopy	TEL/FLAOU/ROS/KPI
	TEB/YU/TAIT	telegony	TE/LEG/N*I
technetium	TEK/NAOERB/UM	telekinesia	TEL/KI/NAOEZ/YA
	TEK/NAOE/SHUM	telekinesis	TEL/KI/NAOE/SIS
technic	TEK/NIK	telekinetic	TEL/KI/NET/IK
technical	TEK/NI/KAL	telelectrocardiogram	TEL/LEK/TRO/KARD/YO/GRAM
technician	TEK/NIGS	telelectrocardiograph	TEL/LEK/TRO/KARD/YO/GRAF
technique	TEK/NAOEK	telemedicine	TEL/MED/SIN
technocausis	TEK/NO/KAU/SIS	telemeter	TE/LEM/TER
technologist	TEK/NO*LGS	telemetering	TEL/MAOET/ER/-G
technology	TEK/NOLG	telemetry	TE/LEM/TRI
technopsychology	TEK/NO/SAOI/KOLG	telencephalic	TEL/EN/SFAL/IK
teclothiazide	TEK/LO/THAOI/ZAOID	telencephalization	TEL/EN/SEF/LI/ZAIGS
tect(o)-	TEKT		TEL/EN/SEFL/ZAIGS
	TEK/T(O)	telencephalon	TEL/EN/SEF/LON
tecta	TEK/TA	teleneurite	TEL/NAOU/RAOIT
tectal	TEK/TAL	teleneuron	TEL/NAOU/RON
tecti	TEK/TAOI	teleo-	TEL/YO
tectiform	TEKT/FORM		TAOEL/YO
tectocephalic	TEKT/SFAL/IK	teleological	TEL/YO/LOJ/KAL
tectocephaly	TEKT/SEF/LI		TAOEL/YO/LOJ/KAL
tectology	TEK/TOLG	teleology	TEL/YOLG
tectonic	TEK/TON/IK	teleomitosis	TEL/YO/MAOI/TOE/SIS
tectorial	TEK/TOIRL	teleonomic	TEL/YO/NOM/IK
tectorium	TEK/TOIRM	teleonomy	TEL/YON/M*I
tectospinal	TEKT/SPAOINL	teleopsia	TEL/OPS/YA
tectum	TEK/TUM		TEL/YOPS/YA
T-E-Cypionate	T-RBGS/*ERBGS/SIP/YO/NAIT	teleorganic	TEL/OR/GAN/IK
Tedral SA	TED/RAL/S-RBGS/ARBGS		TEL/YOR/GAN/IK
teeth	TAO*ET	teleost	TEL/YO*S
teething	TAO*ET/-G	Telepaque	TEL/PAIK
Teflon	TEF/LON	telepathine	TEL/PA*T/AOEN
teflurane	TEF/LAOU/RAIN	telepath	TEL/PA*T
Tegison Capsules	TEG/SON/KAP/SAOUL/-S	telepathist	TE/LEP/TH*IS
tegmen	TEG/MEN	telepathize	TE/LEP/THAOIZ
tegmenta	TEG/MEN/TA	telepathy	TE/LEP/TH*I
tegmental	TEG/MEN/TAL	teleradiography	TEL/RAID/YOG/FI
tegmenti	TEG/MEN/TAOI	teleradium	TEL/RAID/YUM
tegmentorum	TEG/MEN/TOR/UM	telereceptor	TEL/RE/SEP/TOR
	TEG/MEN/TOER/UM	telergic	TEL/ERJ/IK
tegmentotomy	TEG/MEN/TOT/M*I	telergy	TEL/ERJI
tegmentum	TEG/MEN/TUM	teleroentgenogram	TEL/RENT/GEN/GRAM
tegmina	TEG/MI/NA	teleroentgenography	TEL/RENT/GEN/OG/FI
tegminis	TEG/MI/NIS	teleroentgentherapy	TEL/RENT/GEN/THER/PI

telescope	TEL/SKOEP	temporoparietal	TEFRP/RO/PRAOI/TAL
telescoping	TEL/SKOEP/-G	temporopontile	TEFRP/RO/PON/TAOIL
telesis	TEL/E/SIS	temporopontine	TEFRP/RO/PON/TAOIN
	TE/LAOE/SIS	temporospatial	TEFRP/RO/SPAIRBL
telesthesia	TEL/ES/THAOEZ/YA	temporosphenoid	TEFRP/RO/SFAOE/NOID
telesthetoscope	TEL/ES/THET/SKOEP	temporozygomatic	TEFRP/RO/ZAOIG/MAT/IK
telesystolic	TEL/SIS/TOL/IK	tempostabile	TEFRP/STAI/BAOIL
teletactor	TEL/TAK/TOR		TEFRP/STAI/BIL
teletherapy	TEL/THER/PI		TEM/PO/STAI/BAOIL
telethermometer	TEL/THER/MOM/TER		TEM/PO/STAI/BIL
tellurate	TEL/YAOU/RAIT	tempostable	TEFRP/STAIBL
	TEL/YU/RAIT		TEM/PO/STAIBL
telluric	TE/LAOUR/IK	Tempra	TEM/PRA
	TEL/LAOUR/IK	temps utile	TEFRP/YAOU/TAOEL
tellurism	TEL/YAOU/RIFM	tempus	TEM/PUS
	TEL/YU/RIFM	temulence	TEM/LENS
tellurite	TEL/YAOU/RAOIT		TEM/YAOU/LENS
	TEL/YU/RAOIT		TEM/YU/LENS
tellurium	TE/LAOUR/YUM	ten(o)-	TE/N(O)
	TEL/YAOUR/YUM		TEN
	TEL/LAOUR/YUM		TAOE/N-
telo-	TEL	tenable	TEN/-BL
	TE/LO	tenacious	TE/NAIRBS
telobiosis	TEL/BAO*I/YOE/SIS	tenacity	TE/NAS/TI
telobrachial	TEL/BRAIK/YAL	tenacul-	TE/NAK/L-
telocentric	TEL/SEN/TRIK		TE/NAK/YAOU/L-
telodendron	TEL/DEN/DRON		TE/NAK/YU/L-
telogen	TEL/JEN		TEN/AK/L-
teloglia	TE/LOG/LA		TEN/AK/YAOU/L-
	TEL/OG/LA		TEN/AK/YU/L-
	TE/LOG/LAOE/YA	tenacula	TE/NAK/LA
	TEL/OG/LAOE/YA	tenaculum	TE/NAK/LUM
telognosis	TEL/OG/NOE/SIS	tenalgia	TAOE/NAL/JA
telokinesia	*see* telekinesia		TE/NAL/JA
telolecithal	TEL/LES/THAL	tender	TEND/ER
telolemma	TEL/LEM/MA		TEN/DER
telomere	TEL/MAOER	tenderness	TEND/ER/*NS
telopeptide	TEL/PEP/TAOID		TEN/DER/*NS
telophase	TEL/FAEZ	tendin(o)-	TEND/N(O)
telophragma	TEL/FRAG/MA		TEN/DI/N(O)
telorism	TEL/RIFM	tendineae	TEN/DIN/YAE
telosynapsis	TEL/SNAP/SIS	tendines	TEND/NAOEZ
	TEL/SI/NAP/SIS	tendineum	TEN/DIN/YUM
telotaxis	TEL/TAK/SIS	tendineus	TEN/DIN/YUS
telotism	TEL/TIFM	tendinis	TEND/NIS
Temaril	TEM/RIL	tendinitis	TEND/NAOITS
temazepam	TE/MAZ/PAM	tendinoplasty	TEND/NO/PLAS/TI
Temovate	TEM/VAIT	tendinosus	TEND/NOE/SUS
temper	TEM/PER	tendinosuture	TEND/NO/SAOU/KHUR
	TEFRP/ER	tendinous	TEND/NOUS
temperament	TEFRP/RAMT	tendinum	TEND/NUM
	TEM/PRAMT	tendo	TEN/DOE
temperamental	TEFRP/RAMT/TAL	tendo-	TEND
	TEM/PRAMT/TAL		TEN/DO
temperance	TEFRP/RANS	tendolysis	TEN/DOL/SIS
	TEM/PRANS	tendomucin	TEND/MAOU/SIN
temperantia	TEFRP/RAN/SHA	tendomucoid	TEND/MAOU/KOID
	TEM/PRAN/SHA	tendon	TEN/DON
temperate	TEFRP/RAT	tendonitis	TEN/DO/NAOITS
	TEM/PRAT		(*not* TEND/NAOITS; see tendinitis)
temperature	TEFRP/KHUR	tendophony	TEN/DOF/N*I
	TEFRP/RA/KHUR	tendoplasty	TEND/PLAS/TI
	TEM/PRA/KHUR	tendosynovitis	TEND/SIN/VAOITS
template	TEM/PLAIT	tendotome	TEND/TOEM
	TEM/PLAT	tendotomy	TEN/DOT/M*I
temple	TEFRP/-L	tendovaginal	TEND/VAJ/NAL
	TEM/P-L	tendovaginitis	TEND/VAJ/NAOITS
tempolabile	TEFRP/LAI/BAOIL	tendril	TEN/DRIL
	TEFRP/LAI/BIL	tenectomy	TE/NEKT/M*I
	TEM/PO/LAI/BAOIL		TAOE/NEKT/M*I
	TEM/PO/LAI/BIL	tenella	TE/NEL/LA
tempor(o)-	TEFRP/R(O)	tenesmic	TE/NEZ/MIK
	TEM/PR(O)		TAOE/NEZ/MIK
tempora	TEFRP/RA	tenesmus	TE/NEZ/MUS
temporal	TEFRP/RAL		TAOE/NEZ/MUS
temporales	TEFRP/RAI/LAOEZ	Tenex Tablets	TEN/EX/TAB/LET/-S
temporalis	TEFRP/RAI/LIS	teni(o)-	TAOEN/Y(O)
temporis	TEFRP/RIS	tenia	TAOEN/YA
temporoauricular	TEFRP/RO/AU/RIK/LAR	teniacide	TAOEN/YA/SAO*ID
temporofacial	TEFRP/RO/FAIRBL	teniae	TAOEN/YAE
temporofrontal	TEFRP/RO/FRON/TAL	teniafugal	TAOEN/YA/FAOU/GAL
temporohyoid	TEFRP/RO/HAOI/OID	teniafuge	TAOEN/YA/FAOUJ
temporomalar	TEFRP/RO/MAI/LAR	tenial	TAOEN/YAL
temporomandibular	TEFRP/RO/MAN/DIB/LAR	teniamyotomy	TAOEN/YA/MAOI/OT/M*I
temporomandibulares	TEFRP/RO/MAN/DIB/LAI/RAOEZ	teniasis	TAOE/NAOI/SIS
temporomandibularis	TEFRP/RO/MAN/DIB/LAI/RIS	tenicide	TEN/SAO*ID
temporomaxillaris	TEFRP/RO/MAX/LAI/RIS	teniform	TEN/FORM
temporomaxillary	TEFRP/RO/MAX/LAIR	tenifugal	TE/NIF/GAL
temporo-occipital	TEFRP/RO/OK/SIP/TAL		TE/NIF/YAOU/GAL

	TE/NIF/YU/GAL	tentorium	TEN/TOIRM
tenifuge	TEN/FAOUJ		TEN/TOER/YUM
tenioid	TAOEN/YOID		TEN/TOR/YUM
teniola	TAOE/NAOI/LA	tentum	TEN/TUM
	TAOE/NAOE/LA	Tenuate	TEN/YAIT
Ten-K Tablets	TEN/K-RBGS/TAB/LET/-S		TEN/YAOU/AIT
tennis thumb	TEN/NIS/THUM	tenuicollis	TEN/YAOU/KOL/LIS
teno-	TEN (sometimes)		TEN/YAOU/KLIS
	TE/NO	tenuis	TEN/YIS
	TEN/NO		TEN/YAOU/WIS
tenodesis	TE/NOD/SIS	Tepanil	TEP/NIL
	TEN/DAOE/SIS	tephromalacia	TEF/RO/MA/LAI/SHA
tenodynia	TEN/DIN/YA	tephromyelitis	TEF/RO/MAOI/LAOITS
tenofibril	TEN/NO/FAOI/BRIL	tephrosis	TEF/ROE/SIS
	T*EN/FAOI/BRIL	tephrylometer	TEF/RI/LOM/TER
	(not TEN/FAOI/BRIL; see ten	tepid	TEP/ID
	fibril(s))	tepida	TEP/DA
tenolysis	TE/NOL/SIS	tepidarium	TEP/DAIRM
	TEN/OL/SIS		TEP/DAIR/YUM
tenomyoplasty	TEN/MAOI/PLAS/TI	tepor	TAOE/POR
tenomyotomy	TEN/MAOI/OT/M*I	teprotide	TEP/RO/TAOID
Tenon	TAOE/NON		TAOE/PRO/TAOID
tenonectomy	TEN/NEKT/M*I	teracurie	TER/KAOUR/RAOE
tenoni	TAOEN/NAOI	Teramine	TER/MAOEN
	TEN/NAOI		TER/MIN
tenonitis	TEN/NAOITS	teras	TER/RAS
tenonometer	TEN/NOM/TER	terat(o)-	TER/T(O)
tenonostosis	TEN/ON/OS/TOE/SIS	terata	TER/TA
tenont(o)-	TE/NONT	teratic	TER/AT/IK
	TEN/ONT		TE/RAT/IK
	TE/NON/T(O)	teratism	TER/TIFM
	TEN/ON/T(O)	teratoblastoma	TER/TO/BLAS/TOE/MA
tenontagra	TEN/ON/TAG/RA	teratocarcinogenesis	TER/TO/KARS/NO/JEN/SIS
	TEN/ON/TAI/GRA	teratocarcinoma	TER/TO/KARS/NOE/MA
tenontitis	TEN/ON/TAOITS	teratogen	TER/TO/JEN
tenontodynia	TE/NONT/DIN/YA	teratogenesis	TER/TO/JEN/SIS
tenontography	TEN/NO/TOG/FI	teratogenetic	TER/TO/JE/NET/IK
tenontolemmitis	TE/NONT/LE/MAOITS	teratogenic	TER/TO/JEN/IK
	TE/NONT/LEM/MAOITS	teratogenicity	TER/TO/JE/NIS/TI
tenontology	TEN/NO/TOLG	teratogenous	TER/TOJ/NOUS
tenontomyoplasty	TE/NONT/MAOI/PLAS/TI	teratogeny	TER/TOJ/N*I
tenontomyotomy	TE/NONT/MAOI/OT/M*I	teratoid	TER/TOID
tenontophyma	TE/NONT/FAOI/MA	teratologic	TER/TO/LOJ/IK
tenontoplastic	TE/NONT/PLA*S/IK	teratological	TER/TO/LOJ/KAL
tenontoplasty	TE/NONT/PLAS/TI	teratology	TER/TOLG
tenontothecitis	TE/NONT/THAOE/SAOITS	teratoma	TER/TOE/MA
tenontotomy	TEN/ON/TOT/M*I	teratomata	TER/TOEM/TA
tenophony	TE/NOF/N*I	teratomatous	TER/TOEM/TOUS
tenophyte	TEN/FAOIT	teratophobia	TER/TO/FOEB/YA
tenoplastic	TEN/NO/PLA*S/IK	teratosis	TER/TOE/SIS
	(not TEN/PLA*S/IK; see ten plastic)	teratospermia	TER/TO/SPERM/YA
tenoplasty	TEN/PLAS/TI	Terazol	TER/ZOL
tenoreceptor	TEN/NO/RE/SEP/TOR	terazosin	TE/RAIZ/SIN
	(not TEN/RE/SEP/TOR)	terbium	TERB/YUM
Tenoretic	TEN/RET/IK	terbutaline	TER/BAOUT/LAOEN
Tenormin	TE/NOR/MIN	tere	TAOE/RAOE
tenorrhaphy	TE/NOR/FI		TAOER/RAOE
tenositis	TEN/SAOITS	terebene	TER/BAOEN
tenostosis	BEN/OS/TOE/SIS	terebenthene	TER/BEN/THAOEN
tenosuture	TEN/NO/SAOU/KHUR	terebinth	TER/B*INT
	(not TEN/SAOU/KHUR; see ten	terebinthina	TER/B*INT/NA
	suture(s))	terebinthinate	TER/B*INT/NAIT
tenosynovectomy	TEN/SIN/VEKT/M*I	terebenthine	TER/BIN/THIN
tenosynovial	TEN/SNOEV/YAL		(not TER/BIN/THAOEN; see
tenosynovitis	TEN/SIN/VAOITS		terebenthene)
tenotomize	TE/NOT/MAOIZ	terebinthinism	TER/B*INT/NIFM
tenotomy	TE/NOT/M*I	terebrans	TER/BRANZ
tenovaginitis	TEN/VAJ/NAOITS	terebrant	TER/BRANT
tense	TENS	terebrating	TER/BRAIT/-G
Tensilon	TENS/LON	terebration	TER/BRAIGS
tensio-active	TENS/YO/AKT/IV	teres	TER/RAOEZ
tensiometer	TENS/YOM/TER		TAOE/RAOEZ
tension	TENGS		TAOER/RAOEZ
tensometer	TEN/SOM/TER	terete	TE/RAOET
tensor	TEN/SOR	teretes	TER/TAOEZ
tensores	TEN/SOR/RAOEZ		TAOER/TAOEZ
	TEN/SOE/RAOEZ	teretis	TER/TIS
tensoris	TEN/SOR/RIS		TAOER/TIS
	TEN/SOE/RIS	terfenadine	TER/FEN/DAOEN
tent	TENT	tergal	TER/GAL
tentacle	TENT/K-L	tergum	TER/GUM
tentative	TENT/TIV		TERG/UM
tentoria	TEN/TOER/YA	-terian	TAOERN
	TEN/TOR/YA		TAOER/YAN
tentorial	TEN/TOIRL	ter in die	TER/N-/DAOE
	TEN/TOER/YAL		TER/N-/DAOE/YA
	TEN/TOR/YAL		TER/N-/DAOE/YAI
tentorii	TEN/TOER/YAOI	term	TERM
	TEN/TOR/YAOI	terminad	TERM/NAD

terminal	TERM/NAL	testicularis	TES/TIK/LAI/RIS
terminales	TERM/NAI/LAOEZ	testiculi	TES/TIK/LAOI
terminalis	TERM/NAIL/YA	testiculoma	TES/TIK/LOE/MA
terminalis	TERM/NAI/LIS	testiculus	TES/TIK/LUS
terminate	TERM/NAIT	testis	TES/TIS
terminatio	TERM/NAI/SHOE	testitis	TES/TAOITS
	TERM/NAIRB/YOE	testoid	TES/TOID
termination	TERM/NAIGS		T*ES/OID
terminationes	TERM/NAI/SHOE/NAOEZ	testolactone	T*ES/LAK/TOEN
	TERM/NAIRB/YOE/NAOEZ		TES/TO/LAK/TOEN
terminology	TERM/NOLG	testopathy	TES/TOP/TH*I
termini	TERM/NAOI	testosterone	TES/TO*S/ROEN
terminoterminal	TERM/NO/TERM/NAL	Testred	TES/TRED
terminus	TERM/NUS	tetanal	TET/NAL
termolecular	TER/MOE/LEK/LAR	tetani	TET/NAOI
	TER/MO/LEK/LAR	tetania	TE/TAIN/YA
termone	TER/MOEN	tetanic	TE/TAN/IK
ternary	TER/NAIR	tetaniform	TE/TAN/FORM
	TERN/RI	tetanigenous	TET/NIJ/NOUS
ternitrate	TER/NAOI/TRAIT	tetanilla	TET/NIL/LA
terodiline	TER/DI/LAOEN	tetanism	TET/NIFM
teroxide	TER/OK/SAOID	tetanization	TET/NI/ZAIGS
	TER/OX/AOID	tetanize	TET/NAOIZ
terpene	TER/PAOEN	tetano-	TET/NO
terpenism	TERP/NIFM	tetanode	TET/NOED
	TER/PEN/IFM	tetanoid	TET/NOID
terphenyl	TER/FENL	tetanolysin	TET/NOL/SIN
terpin	TER/PIN	tetanometer	TET/NOM/TER
terpineol	TER/PIN/YOL	tetanomotor	TET/NO/MOE/TOR
terpinol	TERP/NOL	tetanospasmin	TET/NO/SPAZ/MIN
terra	TER/RA	tetanotoxin	TET/NO/TOK/SIN
terrace	TER/RAS	tetanus	TET/NUS
Terra-Cortril	TER/RA/KOR/TRIL	tetany	TET/N*I
	TER/KOR/TRIL	tetarcone	TET/AR/KOEN
terrae	TER/RAE	tetartano-	TET/ART/NO
Terramycin	TER/RA/MAOI/SIN	tetartanope	TET/ART/NOEP
	TER/MAOI/SIN	tetartanopia	TET/ART/NOEP/YA
terrapin	TER/RA/PIN	tetartanopic	TET/ART/NOP/IK
	(*not* TER/PIN; see terpin)		TET/ART/NOEP/IK
terreus	TER/YUS	tetartanopsia	TET/ART/NOPS/YA
Terrey	TER/RAOE	tetarto-	TET/ART
Terrier	TER/YAI		TET/AR/TO
territoriality	TER/TOR/YAL/TI	tetartocone	TET/ART/KOEN
	TER/TOER/YAL/TI	tetartoconid	TET/ART/KO/NID
terror	TER/ROR	tetra-	TET/RA
Terry	TER/RI	tetra-acetic	TET/RA/AI/SET/IK
tersulfide	TER/SUL/FAOID		TET/RA/AI/SAOET/IK
tertia	TER/SHA	tetra-amelia	TET/RA/AI/MAOEL/YA
tertian	TERGS	tetra-amylose	TET/RA/AM/LOES
tertiarism	TER/SHA/RIFM	tetrabasic	TET/RA/BAIS/IK
tertiarismus	TER/SHA/RIZ/MUS	tetrabenazine	TET/RA/BEN/ZAOEN
tertiary	TER/SHAIR	tetrablastic	TET/RA/BLA*S/IK
tertigravida	TER/SHAOE/GRAV/DA	tetraboric	TET/RA/BOR/IK
	TER/SHI/GRAV/DA	tetrabrachius	TET/RA/BRAIK/YUS
tertipara	TER/SHIP/RA	tetrabromophenolphthalein	TET/RA/BROEM/FAOE/NOL/
	TER/TIP/RA		THAL/YIN
tertium	TER/SHUM		TET/RA/BROEM/FAOE/NOL/
tertius	TER/-RBS		THAL/AOEN
tesicam	TES/KAM	tetrabromophthalein	TET/RA/BROEM/THAL/YIN
tesimide	TES/MAOID		TET/RA/BROEM/THAL/AOEN
tesla	TES/LA	tetracaine	TET/RA/KAIN
Tesla	K-P/TES/LA	tetracetate	TET/RAS/TAIT
Teslac	TES/LAK	tetracheirus	*see* tetrachirus
teslaization	TES/LAI/ZAIGS	tetrachirus	TET/RA/KAOI/RUS
tesquorum	TES/KWOR/UM	tetrachlorethane	TET/RA/KLOR/*ET/AIN
	TES/KWOER/UM	tetrachlorethylene	TET/RA/KLOR/*ET/LAOEN
	TES/KWOE/RUM	tetrachloride	TET/RA/KLOR/AOID
Tessalon	TES/LON	tetrachlormethane	TET/RA/KLOR/M*ET/AIN
tessellated	TES/LAIT/-D	tetrachlormethiazide	TET/RA/KLOR/ME/THAOI/ZAOID
test	T*ES	tetrachlorphenoxide	TET/RA/KLOR/FEN/OK/SAOID
test(o)-	TES/T(O)	tetrachromic	TET/RA/KROEM/IK
testa	TES/TA	tetracid	TET/RAS/ID
Testacealobosia	TES/TAI/SHA/LOE/BOEZ/YA	tetracocci	TET/RA/KOK/SAOI
	TES/TAIRB/YA/LOE/BOEZ/YA	tetracoccus	TET/RA/KOK/KUS
testaceous	TES/TAIRBS	tetracosactide	TET/RA/KO/SAK/TAOID
testalgia	TES/TAL/JA		TET/RA/KO/SAK/TID
testane	TES/TAIN	tetracosactin	TET/RA/KO/SAK/TIN
Tes-Tape	TES/TAIP	tetracosanic	TET/RA/KO/SAN/IK
Testaval	TES/TA/VAL	tetracosanoic	TET/RA/KOES/NOIK
	(*not* T*ES/VAL; see test value)		TET/RA/KOES/NOE/IK
test card	T*ES/KARD	tetracrotic	TET/RA/KROT/IK
testectomy	TES/TEKT/M*I	tetracuspid	TET/RA/KUS/PID
testes	TES/TAOEZ	tetracycline	TET/RA/SAOI/KLAOEN
testicle	T*ES/K-L		TET/RA/SAOI/KLIN
testicul(o)-	TES/TIK/L(O)	tetrad	TET/RAD
	TES/TIK/YAOU/L(O)	tetradactyl	TET/RA/DAK/TIL
	TES/TIK/YU/L(O)	tetradactylous	TET/RA/DAKT/LUS
testicular	TES/TIK/LAR	tetradactyly	TET/RA/DAKT/LI
testiculare	TES/TIK/LAI/RAOE	tetradecanoate	TET/RA/DEK/NOE/AIT

tetradecanoic	TET/RA/DEK/NOIK
	TET/RA/DEK/NOE/IK
tetradecanoylphorbol	TET/RA/DEK/NOIL/FOR/BOL
	TET/RA/DEK/NOE/IL/FOR/BOL
tetradic	TE/TRAD/IK
tetraethylammonium	TET/RA/*ET/IL/AI/MOEN/YUM
	TET/RA/*ET/LA/MOEN/YUM
tetraethyllead	TET/RA/*ET/LAED
	TET/RA/*ET/LED
tetraethylmonothionopyrophosphate	
	TET/RA/*ET/IL/MON/THAOI/NO/
	PAOIR/FOS/FAIT
	TET/RA/*ET/IL/MON/THAOI/NO/
	PAOI/RO/FOS/FAIT
tetraethyl pyrophosphate	TET/RA/*ET/IL/PAOI/RO/FOS/
	FAIT
tetraethylthiuram	TET/RA/*ET/IL/THAOI/RAM
	TET/RA/*ET/IL/THAOI/YAOU/
	RAM
	TET/RA/*ET/IL/THAOI/YU/RAM
tetrafilcon	TET/RA/FIL/KON
tetragena	TET/RA/JAOE/NA
tetraglycine	TET/RA/GLAOI/SAOEN
tetragon	TET/RA/GON
tetragonum	TET/RA/GOE/NUM
	TET/RA/GOEN/UM
tetragonus	TET/RA/GOE/NUS
tetrahedron	TET/RA/HAOE/DRON
tetrahydric	TET/RA/HAOI/DRIK
tetrahydrocannabinol	TET/RA/HAOI/DRO/KA/NAB/NOL
tetrahydrofolate	TET/RA/HAOI/DRO/FOE/LAIT
tetrahydrozoline	TET/RA/HAOI/DROZ/LAOEN
Tetrahymena	TET/RA/HAOIM/NA
Tetrahymena pyriformis	TET/RA/HAOIM/NA/PIR/FOR/MIS
tetraiodophenolphthalein	TET/RA/AOI/OED/FAOE/NOL/
	THAL/YIN
	TET/RA/AOI/OED/FAOE/NOL/
	THAL/AOEN
tetraiodophthalein	TET/RA/AOI/OED/THAL/YIN
	TET/RA/AOI/OED/THAL/AOEN
tetraiodothyronine	TET/RA/AOI/OED/THAOIR/
	NAOEN
tetralogy	TET/RALG
	TET/RAL/JI
	TE/TRALG
	TE/TRAL/JI
tetramastia	TET/RA/MA*S/YA
tetramastigote	TET/RA/MA*S/GOET
tetramastous	TET/RA/MA*S/OUS
	TET/RA/MAS/TOUS
tetramazia	TET/RA/MAIZ/YA
tetramelus	TE/TRAM/LUS
Tetrameres	TE/TRAM/RAOEZ
	TET/RAM/RAOEZ
tetrameric	TET/RA/MER/IK
tetramerous	TE/TRAM/ROUS
tetramethylammonium	TET/RA/M*ET/IL/AI/MOEN/YUM
	TET/RA/M*ET/LA/MOEN/YUM
tetramethyldiarsine	TET/RA/M*ET/IL/DI/AR/SAOEN
tetramethylputrescine	TET/RA/M*ET/IL/PAOU/TRES/
	SAOEN
	TET/RA/M*ET/IL/PAOU/TRES/SIN
tetramine	TET/RA/MAOEN
tetramisole	TE/TRAM/SOEL
tetranitrate	TET/RA/NAOI/TRAIT
tetranitrol	TET/RA/NAOI/TROL
tetranophthalmos	TET/RAN/OF/THAL/MOS
tetranopsia	TET/RA/NOPS/YA
	TET/RAN/OPS/YA
tetranucleotide	TET/RA/NAOUK/LO/TAOID
Tetranychus	TET/RAN/KUS
tetraparesis	TET/RA/PAR/SIS
	TET/RA/PA/RAOE/SIS
tetrapeptide	TET/RA/PEP/TAOID
tetraperomelia	TET/RA/PER/MAOEL/YA
tetraphocomelia	TET/RA/FOEK/MAOEL/YA
tetraplegia	TET/RA/PLAOE/JA
tetraplegic	TET/RA/PLAOEJ/IK
tetraploid	TET/RA/PLOID
tetraploidy	TET/RA/PLOI/DI
tetrapodisis	TET/RA/POE/DAOI/SIS
tetrapus	TET/RA/PUS
tetrapyrrole	TET/RA/PIR/ROEL
tetrasaccharide	TET/RA/SAK/RAOID
tetrascelus	TE/TRAS/LUS
	TET/RAS/LUS
tetrasomic	TET/RA/SOEM/IK
tetrasomy	TET/RA/SOE/M*I
tetraster	TET/RA*S/ER

tetrastichiasis	TET/RA/STI/KAOI/SIS
tetraterpene	TET/RA/TER/PAOEN
tetratomic	TET/RA/TOM/IK
Tetratrichomonas	TET/RA/TRI/KOM/NAS
tetravaccine	TET/RA/VAK/SAOEN
tetravalent	TET/RA/VAIL/ENT
	TET/RAV/LENT
tetrazol	TET/RA/ZOL
tetrazole	TET/RA/ZOEL
tetrazolium	TET/RA/ZOEL/YUM
tetrodotoxin	TET/RO/DO/TOK/SIN
tetrodotoxism	TET/RO/DO/TOK/SIFM
	TET/RO/DO/TOX/IFM
tetronal	TET/RO/NAL
tetrophthalmos	TET/ROF/THAL/MOS
tetrophthalmus	TET/ROF/THAL/MUS
tetrose	TET/ROES
tetrotus	TE/TROE/TUS
	TET/ROE/TUS
tetroxide	TE/TROK/SAOID
	TE/TROX/AOID
tetter	TET/ER
Texas	T*X/T*X
	TEK/SAS
	TEX/SAS
texis	TEK/SIS
textiform	TEX/TI/FORM
textoblastic	TEX/TO/BLA*S/IK
textometer	TEX/TO/MAOET/ER
textural	TEX/KHURL
texture	TEX/KHUR
textus	TEX/TUS
thalam(o)-	THAL/M(O)
thalamectomy	THAL/MEKT/M*I
thalamencephalic	THAL/MEN/SFAL/IK
thalamencephalon	THAL/MEN/SEF/LON
thalami	THAL/MAOI
thalamic	THA/LAM/IK
thalamicus	THA/LAM/KUS
thalamocoele	THAL/MO/SAO*EL
thalamocortical	THAL/MO/KORT/KAL
thalamolenticular	THAL/MO/LEN/TIK/LAR
thalamomamillaris	THAL/MO/MAM/LAI/RIS
thalamomamillary	THAL/MO/MAM/LAIR
thalamotegmental	THAL/MO/TEG/MEN/TAL
thalamotomy	THAL/MOT/M*I
thalamus	THAL/MUS
thalass(o)-	THA/LAS
	THAL/S(O)
	THA/LAS/S(O)
thalassanemia	THA/LAS/NAOEM/YA
thalassemia	THAL/SAOEM/YA
thalassophobia	THA/LAS/FOEB/YA
	THAL/SO/FOEB/YA
thalassoposia	THA/LAS/POEZ/YA
	THAL/SO/POEZ/YA
thalassotherapy	THA/LAS/THER/PI
	THAL/SO/THER/PI
thalidomide	THA/LID/MAOID
Thalitone	THAL/TOEN
thallic	THAL/IK
thallium	THAL/YUM
Thallophyta	THA/LOF/TA
	THAL/LOF/TA
thallophyte	THAL/FAOIT
thallospore	THAL/SPOER
thallotoxicosis	THAL/TOX/KOE/SIS
thallous	THAL/OUS
thallus	THAL/LUS
thalmencephalic	THAL/MEN/SFAL/IK
-thalmia	THAL/MA (sometimes)
	THAL/MAOE/YA
-thalmus	THAL/MUS
thalposis	THAL/POE/SIS
thalpotic	THAL/POT/IK
Thamnidium	THAM/NID/YUM
thamuria	THAM/YAOUR/YA
	THA/MAOUR/YA
-thanasia	*T/NAIZ/YA
	THA/NAIZ/YA
thanato-	THAN/TO
thanatobiologic	THAN/TO/BAO*I/LOJ/IK
thanatognomonic	THAN/TO/NOE/MON/IK
thanatography	THAN/TOG/FI
thanatoid	THAN/TOID
thanatology	THAN/TOLG
thanatomania	THAN/TO/MAIN/YA
thanatometer	THAN/TOM/TER
thanatophidia	THAN/TO/FID/YA

thanatophidial	THAN/TO/FID/YAL	thenad	THAOE/NAD
thanatophobia	THAN/TO/FOEB/YA	thenal	THAOENL
thanatophoric	THAN/TO/FOER/IK		THAOE/NAL
thanatopsia	THAN/TOPS/YA	thenaldine	THAOE/NAL/DAOEN
thanatopsy	THAN/TOP/SI	thenar	THAOE/NAR
thanatos	THAN/TOS	thenen	THAOE/NEN
thanatosis	THAN/TOE/SIS		THAOEN/-N
Thane	THA*IN	thenyl	THENL
	(not THAIN; see "that I know")		(not THEN/IL; see then ill)
thaumatropy	THAU/MAT/RO/PI	thenyldiamine	THENL/DAOI/MAOEN
thaumaturgic	THAUM/TURJ/IK		THENL/DI/AM/MAOEN
thea	THAOE/YA		THENL/DI/AM/MIN
theaism	THAOE/IFM	thenylpyramine	THENL/PIR/MAOEN
	THAOE/YIFM	theo-	THAOE
theater	THAOE/TER		THAOE/YO
thebaic	THAOE/BAI/IK	Theo-24	THAOE/YOE/24
thebaine	THAOE/BAIN	Theobid	THAOE/BID
	THAOE/BAI/YIN	Theobroma	THAOE/BROE/MA
	THAOE/BAI/AOEN	theobromine	THAOE/BROE/MAOEN
thebesian	THE/BAOEZ/YAN		THAOE/BROE/MIN
	THE/BAOES/YAN	Theochron	THAOE/KRON
Thebesius	THE/BAOEZ/YUS	Theoclear	THAOE/KLAOER
	THE/BAOES/YUS	Theo-Dur	THAOE/DUR
thec(o)-	THAOEK	Theolair	THAOE/LAIR
	THAOE/K(O)	Theolair-SR	THAOE/LAIR/S-RBGS/R*RBGS
	THAOE/S(O)	theomania	THAOE/MAIN/YA
theca	THAOE/KA	Theon	THAOE/YON
thecae	THAOE/SAE	Theo-Organidin	THAOE/OR/GAN/DIN
thecal	THAOE/KAL	theophobia	THAOE/FOEB/YA
theca-lutein	THAOEK/LAOUT/YIN	theophylline	THAOE/OF/LIN
	THAOE/KA/LAOUT/YIN		THAOE/OF/LAOEN
thecitis	THAOE/SAOITS		THAOE/FLIN
thecocellulare	THAOEK/SEL/YAOU/LAI/RAOE		THAOE/FIL/LIN
thecodont	THAOEK/DONT	theorem	THAOER/EM
thecoma	THAOE/KOE/MA	theory	THAOER/RI
thecomatosis	THAOE/KOEM/TOE/SIS	Theospan	THAOE/SPAN
thecostegnosia	THAOEK/STEG/NOES/YA	Theospan-SR	THAOE/SPAN/S-RBGS/R*RBGS
	THAOEK/STEG/NOEZ/YA	Theostat	THAOE/STAT
thecostegnosis	THAOEK/STEG/NOE/SIS	theotherapy	THAOE/THER/PI
Theden	TAID/-N	theque	T*EK
	TAI/DEN		(not TEK; see tech)
Theile	TAOI/LAOE	Therabid	THER/BID
Theiler	THAOIL/ER	Thera-Flur	THER/FLUR
	THAOI/LER	Thera-Flur-N	THER/FLUR/N-RBGS
theileri	THAOI/RAOI	Thera-Gesic	THER/JAOEZ/IK
	THAOI/LER/RAOI	Theragran	THER/GRAN
Theileria	THAOI/LAOER/YA	Theragran-M	THER/GRAN/M-RBGS
theileriasis	THAOI/RAOI/SIS	therapeusis	THER/PAOU/SIS
thein	see theine	therapeutical	THER/PAOUT/KAL
theine	THAOE/YIN	therapeutics	THER/PAOUT/IK/-S
	TAOE/YIN	therapeutist	THER/PAOU/T*IS
theinism	THAOE/NIFM		THER/PAOUT/*IS
	TAOE/NIFM	therapia	THER/PAOE/YA
theism	THAOE/IFM		THER/PAOI/YA
	TAOE/IFM	therapist	THER/P*IS
thel-	THAOE/L-	therapy	THER/PI
	THAOEL-	therencephalus	THAOER/EN/SEF/LUS
	THEL		THER/EN/SEF/LUS
thelalgia	THAOE/LAL/JA	Therevac Plus	THER/VAK/PLUS
thelarche	THAOE/LAR/KAOE	theriac	THAOER/YAK
Thelazia	THAOE/LAIZ/YA		THER/YAK
thelaziasis	THAOEL/ZAOI/SIS	theriaca	THAOE/RAOI/KA
	THEL/ZAOI/SIS	theriatrics	THAOER/YAT/RIK/-S
	THAOE/LAI/ZAOI/SIS	therio-	THAOER/YO
thele	THAOE/LAOE	theriogenologic	THAOER/YO/JEN/LOJ/IK
theleplasty	THAOEL/PLAS/TI	theriogenological	THAOER/YO/JEN/LOJ/KAL
thelerethism	THAOEL/ER/THIFM	theriogenologist	THAOER/YO/JEN/O*LGS
thelia	THAOEL/YA	theriogenology	THAOER/YO/JE/NOLG
thelioid	THAOEL/YOID		THAOER/YO/JEN/OLG
thelitis	THAOE/LAOITS	theriomorphism	THAOER/YO/MOR/FIFM
thelium	THAOEL/YUM	theriotherapy	THAOER/YO/THER/PI
theloncus	THAOE/LON/KUS	therm	THERM
thelorrhagia	THAOEL/RAI/JA	therm(o)-	THERM
thelothism	THAOEL/THIFM		THER/M(O)
thelotism	THAOEL/TIFM	thermacogenesis	THERM/KO/JEN/SIS
thely-	THEL	thermae	THER/MAE
	THAOEL	thermal	THER/MAL
	THEL/LI	thermalgesia	THER/MAL/JAOEZ/YA
	THAOEL/LI		(not THERM/AL/JAOEZ/YA; see
thelyblast	THEL/BLA*S		thermoalgesia)
thelyblastic	THEL/BLA*S/IK	thermalgia	THER/MAL/JA
thelygenic	THEL/JEN/IK	thermanalgesia	THER/MANL/JAOEZ/YA
	THAOEL/JEN/IK		(not THERM/ANL/JAOEZ/YA; see
thelytocia	THEL/TOE/SHA		thermoanalgesia)
thelytocous	THE/LIT/KOUS	thermanesthesia	THER/MANS/THAOEZ/YA
	THAOE/LIT/KOUS		THER/MAN/ES/THAOEZ/YA
thelytoky	THE/LIT/KI		(not THERM/ANS/THAOEZ/YA, see
	THAOE/LIT/KI		thermoanesthesia)
thematic	THAOE/MAT/IK	thermatology	THERM/TOLG

thermelometer	THERM/LOM/TER
thermesthesia	THER/MES/THAOEZ/YA
	(*not* THERM/ES/THAOEZ/YA; see
	thermoesthesia)
thermesthesiometer	THER/MES/THAOEZ/YOM/TER
	(*not* THERM/ES/THAOEZ/YOM/
	TER; see thermoesthesiometer)
-thermia	THERM/YA
thermic	THERM/IK
thermion	THERM/YON
thermionic	THERM/YON/IK
thermionics	THERM/YON/IK/-S
thermistor	THER/MIS/TOR
thermoalgesia	THERM/AL/JAOEZ/YA
thermoanalgesia	THERM/ANL/JAOEZ/YA
thermoanesthesia	THERM/ANS/THAOEZ/YA
thermocauterectomy	THERM/KAUT/REKT/M*I
thermocautery	THERM/KAUT/RI
thermochemical	THERM/KEM/KAL
thermochemistry	THERM/KEM/STRI
thermochroic	THERM/KROIK
	THERM/KROE/IK
thermochroism	THER/MOK/RO/IFM
thermochrose	THERM/KROES
thermochrosis	THERM/KROE/SIS
thermochrosy	THER/MOK/RO/SI
thermocoagulation	THERM/KO/AG/LAIGS
thermocouple	THERM/KUP/-L
thermocurrent	THERM/KURNT
thermodiffusion	THERM/DI/FAOUGS
	THERM/DIF/FAOUGS
thermodilution	THERM/DI/LAOUGS
thermoduric	THERM/DAOUR/IK
thermodynamics	THERM/DAOI/NAM/IK/-S
thermoelectric	THERM/LEK/TRIK
thermoelectricity	THERM/LEK/TRIS/TI
thermoesthesia	THERM/ES/THAOEZ/YA
thermoesthesiometer	THERM/ES/THAOEZ/YOM/TER
thermoexcitory	THERM/KPAOIT/RI
thermogenesis	THERM/JEN/SIS
thermogenetic	THERM/JE/NET/IK
thermogenic	THERM/JEN/IK
thermogenous	THER/MOJ/NOUS
thermogram	THERM/GRAM
thermograph	THERM/GRAF
thermographic	THERM/GRAFK
thermography	THER/MOG/FI
thermogravimeter	THERM/GRA/VIM/TER
thermohyperalgesia	THERM/HAO*IP/AL/JAOEZ/YA
thermohyperesthesia	THERM/HAO*IP/ES/THAOEZ/YA
thermohypesthesia	THERM/HAOI/PES/THAOEZ/YA
	THERM/HAOIP/ES/THAOEZ/YA
thermohypoesthesia	THERM/HO*IP/ES/THAOEZ/YA
thermoinactivation	THERM/IN/AKT/VAIGS
thermoinhibitory	THERM/IN/HIB/TOIR
thermointegrator	THERM/SPWE/GRAI/TOR
	THERM/INT/GRAI/TOR
thermojunction	THERM/JUNGS
thermokeratoplasty	THERM/KER/TO/PLAS/TI
thermolabile	THERM/LAI/BAOIL
	THERM/LAI/BIL
thermolamp	THERM/LAFRP
thermolaryngoscope	THERM/LARNG/SKOEP
thermology	THER/MOLG
thermoluminescence	THERM/LAOUM/NES/ENS
thermolysis	THER/MOL/SIS
thermolytic	THERM/LIT/IK
thermomassage	THERM/MA/SAJ
	THERM/MAS/SAJ
thermomastography	THERM/MAS/TOG/FI
thermometer	THER/MOM/TER
thermometric	THERM/MET/RIK
thermometry	THER/MOM/TRI
thermoneurosis	THERM/NAOU/ROE/SIS
thermonuclear	THERM/NAOUK/LAR
thermopalpation	THERM/PAL/PAIGS
thermopenetration	THERM/PEN/TRAIGS
thermophil	THERM/FIL
thermophile	THERM/FAOIL
thermophilic	THERM/FIL/IK
thermophobia	THERM/FOEB/YA
thermophore	THERM/FOER
thermyphylic	THERM/FAOIL/IK
thermopile	THERM/PAOIL
thermoplacentography	THERM/PLAS/EN/TOG/FI
	THERM/PLAS/SPWOG/FI
thermoplasma	THERM/PLAZ/MA
Thermoplasma	K-P/THERM/PLAZ/MA
thermoplasmata	THERM/PLAZ/MA/TA
thermoplastic	THERM/PLA*S/IK
thermoplegia	THERM/PLAOE/JA
thermopolypnea	THERM/POL/IP/NAOE/YA
thermopolypneic	THERM/POL/IP/NAOE/IK
	THERM/POL/IP/NIK
thermoprecipitation	THERM/PRE/SIP/TAIGS
thermoprecipitin	THERM/PRE/SIP/TIN
thermoprecipitinogen	THERM/PRE/SIP/TIN/JEN
thermoradiotherapy	THERM/RAID/YO/THER/PI
thermoreceptor	THERM/RE/SEP/TOR
thermoregulation	THERM/REG/LAIGS
thermoregulator	THERM/REG/LAI/TOR
thermoretulatory	THERM/REG/LA/TOIR
thermoresistance	THERM/RE/SIS/TANS
thermoresistant	THERM/RE/SIS/TANT
thermoscope	THERM/SKOEP
thermoset	THERM/SET
thermostabile	THERM/STAI/BAOIL
	THERM/STAI/BIL
thermostability	THERM/STABLT
thermostable	THERM/STAIBL
thermostasis	THERM/STAI/SIS
thermostat	THERM/STAT
thermosteresis	THERM/STE/RAOE/SIS
thermostromuhr	THERM/STROM/YAOUR
	THERM/STROE/MAOUR
thermosystaltic	THERM/SIS/TALT/IK
thermosystaltism	THERM/SIS/TALT/IFM
	THERM/SIS/TAL/TIFM
thermotactic	THERM/TAKT/IK
thermotatic	THERM/TAT/IK
thermotaxic	THERM/TAX/IK
thermotaxis	THERM/TAK/SIS
thermotherapy	THERM/THER/PI
thermotic	THER/MOT/IK
thermotics	THER/MOT/IK/-S
thermotolerant	THERM/TOL/RANT
thermotonometer	THERM/TOE/NOM/TER
thermotracheotomy	THERM/TRAIK/YOT/M*I
thermotropic	THERM/TROEP/IK
thermotropism	THER/MOT/RO/PIFM
-thermy	THER/M*I
theroid	THAOE/ROID
	THAOER/OID
therology	THAOE/ROLG
theromorph	THAOER/MOR/-F
theromorphism	THAOER/MOR/FIFM
thesaurismosis	THAOE/SAU/RIZ/MOE/SIS
	THAOE/SAUR/IZ/MOE/SIS
	THAOE/SAURS/MOE/SIS
thesaurosis	THAOE/SAU/ROE/SIS
theta	THAI/TA
	THET/TA
thia-	THAOI
	THAOI/YA
thiabendazole	THAOI/BEND/ZOEL
thiacetazone	THAOI/SET/ZOEN
Thiacide Tablets	THAOI/SAO*ID/TAB/LET/-S
thialbarbital	THAOI/AL/BARB/TAL
thiambutosine	THAOI/AM/BAOUT/SAOEN
Thiamilate	THAOI/AM/LAIT
thiamin	THAOI/MIN
thiaminase	THAOI/AM/NAIS
thiamine	*see* thiamin
thiamphenicol	THAOI/AM/FEN/KOL
thiamylal	THAOI/AM/LAL
Thiara	THAOI/AR/RA
	THAOI/YAR/RA
thiazide	THAOI/ZAOID
thiazin	THAOI/ZIN
thiazole	THAOI/ZOEL
thiazolsulfone	THAOI/ZOL/SUL/FOEN
thickening	THIK/-NG
thickness	THIK/*NS
Thiele	THAOEL
thiemia	THAOI/AOEM/YA
thienylalanine	THAOI/NIL/AL/NAOEN
Thiersch	TAOER/-RB
thiethylperazine	THAOI/*ET/IL/PER/ZAOEN
thigh	THAOI
thigmesthesia	THIG/MES/THAOEZ/YA
thigmo-	THIG/MO
thigmotactic	THIG/MO/TAKT/IK
thigmotaxis	THIG/MO/TAK/SIS
thigmotropic	THIG/MO/TROP/IK
thigmotropism	THIG/MOT/RO/PIFM
thimble	THIM/-BL
thimerosal	THAOI/MER/SAL
think	THI

436

thinning	THIN/-G	thiosemicarbazide	THAOI/SEM/KARB/ZAOID
thio-	THAOI	thiosemicarbazone	THAOI/SEM/KARB/ZOEN
	THAOI/YO	thiosinamine	THAOI/SIN/MIN
thioacid	THAOI/AS/ID	Thiospira	THAOI/SPAOI/RA
thioalbumose	THAOI/AL/BAOU/MOES	Thiospirillopsis	THAOI/SPAOIR/LOP/SIS
thioalcohol	THAOI/AL/KHOL	Thiospirillum	THAOI/SPAOI/RIL/UM
	THAOI/KHOL	thiosulfate	THAOI/SUL/FAIT
thioallylic	THAOI/AL/LIL/IK	Thiosulfil	THAOI/SUL/FIL
	THAOI/AI/LIL/IK	Thiosulfil Forte	THAOI/SUL/FIL/FOR/TAI
thioamide	THAOI/AM/AOID	thiosulfuric	THAOI/SUL/FAOUR/IK
thioate	THAOI/YO/AIT (required)	thiotepa	THAOI/TAOE/PA
Thiobacillus	THAOI/BA/SIL/LUS		THAOI/TEP/PA
Thiobacteriaceae	THAOI/BAK/TAOER/YAIS/YAE	Thiothece	THAOI/THAOE/SAOE
Thiobacterium	THAOI/BAK/TAOERM	thiothixene	THAOI/THIK/SAOEN
thiobarbital	THAOI/BARB/TAL		THAOI/THIX/AOEN
thiobarbiturate	THAOI/BAR/BIFP/RAT	Thiothrix	THAOI/THRIX
	THAOI/BAR/BIFP/RAIT	thiotransacetylase	THAOI/TRA*NS/AI/SET/LAIS
Thiocapsa	THAOI/KAP/SA	thiouracil	THAOI/YAOUR/SIL
thiocarbamide	THAOI/KARB/MAOID	thiourea	THAOI/YAOU/RAOE/YA
thiocarlide	THAOI/KAR/LAOID	Thiovulum	THAOI/OEV/LUM
thiochrome	THAOI/KROEM		THAOI/OV/LUM
thiocyanate	THAOI/SAOI/NAIT	thioxanthene	THAOI/ZAN/THAOEN
thioctic	THAOI/OKT/IK	thioaxolone	THAOI/OX/LOEN
thiocyanate	THAOI/SAOI/NAIT	thiozine	THAOI/ZAOEN
thiocyanic	THAOI/SAOI/AN/IK		(not THAOI/ZIN; see thiazin)
thiocyanoacetate	THAOI/SAOI/NO/AS/TAIT	thiphenamil	THAOI/FEN/MIL
Thiocystis	THAOI/SIS/TIS	thiram	THAOI/RAM
Thiodictyon	THAOI/DIKT/YON	third intention	THIRD/SPWENGS
thiodiphenylamine	THAOI/DI/FENL/AM/AOEN	thirst	TH*IRS
	THAOI/DI/FENL/AM/MIN	thixo-	THIX
thioethanolamine	THAOI/*ET/NOL/MAOEN		THIK/SO
thioether	THAOI/AO*ET/ER	thixolabile	THIX/LAI/BAOIL
thioethylamine	THAOI/*ET/IL/AM/MIN		THIX/LAI/BIL
thioflavine	THAOI/FLAIVN	thixotropic	THIX/TROP/IK
thiofuran	THAOI/FAOU/RAN	thixotropism	THIK/SOT/RO/PIFM
thiogenic	THAOI/JEN/IK	thixotropy	THIK/SOT/RO/PI
thioglucose	THAOI/GLAOU/KOES	thlipsencephalus	TH-/LIP/SEN/SEF/LUS
thioglucosidase	THAOI/GLAOU/KOES/DAIS		TLIP/SEN/SEF/LUS
	THAOI/GLAOUK/SI/DAIS	Thoma	TOE/MA
thioglycerol	THAOI/GLIS/ROL	Thomas	TOM/MAS
thioglycolic	THAOI/GLAOI/KOL/IK	Thompson	TOFRP/SON
thioglycollamide	THAOI/GLAOI/KOL/MAOID		TOM/-P/SON
thioglycollate	THAOI/GLAOIK/LAIT		(not TOM/SON; see Thomson)
thioguanine	THAOI/GAU/NAOEN	Thomsen	TOM/SEN
	THAOI/GAU/NIN	Thomson	TOM/SON
thiokinase	THAOI/KAOI/NAIS	thomsonianism	TOM/SOEN/YAN/IFM
thiol	THAOI/OL	thonzonium	THON/ZOEN/YUM
	THAOI/YOL	thonzylamine	THON/ZIL/MAOEN
Thiola Tablets	THAOI/LA/TAB/LET/-S		THON/ZIL/MIN
	THAOI/YOE/LA/TAB/LET/-S	thorac(o)-	THOR/K(O)
thiolase	THAOI/LAIS		THOER/K(O)
thiole	THAOI/OEL	thoracal	THOR/KAL
	THAOI/YOEL	thoracales	THOR/KAI/LAOEZ
thiolhistidine	THAOI/OL/H*IS/DAOEN	thoracalgia	THOR/KAL/JA
	THAOI/OL/H*IS/DIN	thoracalis	THOR/KAI/LIS
thiohistidylbetaine	THAOI/H*IS/DIL/BAOET/AOEN	thoracectomy	THOR/SEKT/M*I
	THAOI/H*IS/DIL/BAOE/TAIN	thoracentesis	THOR/SEN/TAOE/SIS
thioltransacetylase	THAOI/OL/TRA*NS/AI/SET/LAIS	thoraces	THRAI/SAOEZ
thiolysis	THAOI/OL/SIS	thoracic(o)-	THRAS/K(O)
thiomalate	THAOI/MAL/AIT		THO/RAS/K(O)
	THAOI/MAI/LAIT		THOE/RAS/K(O)
thiomersal	THAOI/MER/SAL	thoracic	THRAS/IK
thiomersalate	THAOI/MERS/LAIT	thoracica	THRAS/KA
thionase	THAOI/NAIS	thoracicae	THRAS/SAE
thionate	THAOI/NAIT	thoracici	THRAS/SAOI
thioneine	THAOI/NAOEN	thoracicoabdominal	THRAS/KO/AB/DOM/NAL
thionic	THAOI/ON/IK	thoracicoacromial	THRAS/KO/AI/KROEM/YAL
	THAOI/YON/IK	thoracicohumeral	THRAS/KO/HAOUM/RAL
thionine	THAOI/NIN	thoracicolumbar	THRAS/KO/LUM/BAR
thionyl	THAOI/NIL	thoracicus	THRAS/KUS
thiopanic	THAOI/PAN/IK	thoracis	THRAI/SIS
thiopectic	THAOI/PEKT/IK	thoracispinal	THRAS/SPAOINL
thiopental	THAOI/PEN/TAL	thoracoabdominal	THOR/KO/AB/DOM/NAL
Thiopedia	THAOI/PAOED/YA	thoracoacromial	THOR/KO/AI/KROEM/YAL
thiopental	THAOI/PEN/TAL	thoracoacromialis	THOR/KO/AI/KROEM/YAI/LIS
thiopentone	THAOI/PEN/TOEN	thoracobronchotomy	THOR/KO/BRON/KOT/M*I
thiopexic	THAOI/PEX/IK	thoracoceloschisis	THOR/KO/SE/LOS/KI/SIS
thiopexy	THAOI/PEK/SI	thoracocentesis	THOR/KO/SEN/TAOE/SIS
thiophene	THAOI/FAOEN	thoracocyllosis	THOR/KO/SI/LOE/SIS
thiophenicol	THAOI/FEN/KOL		THOR/KO/SIL/LOE/SIS
thiophorase	THAOI/FOR/AIS		THOR/KO/SAOI/LOE/SIS
	THAOI/FOER/AIS	thoracocyrtosis	THOR/KO/SIR/TOE/SIS
Thioploca	THAOI/PLOE/KA	thoracodelphus	THOR/KO/DEL/FUS
Thiopolycoccus	THAOI/POL/KOK/KUS	thoracodidymus	THOR/KO/DID/MUS
thiopropazate	THAOI/PROEP/ZAIT	thoracodynia	THOR/KO/DIN/YA
thioproperazine	THAOI/PRO/PER/ZAOEN	thoracogastrodidymus	THOR/KO/GAS/TRO/DID/MUS
Thiorhodaceae	THAOI/ROE/DAIS/YAE	thoracogastroschisis	THOR/KO/GAS/TROS/KI/SIS
thioridazine	THAOI/RID/ZAOEN	thoracograph	THOR/KO/GRAF
Thiosarcina	THAOI/SAR/SAOI/NA	thoracolaparotomy	THOR/KO/LAP/ROT/M*I

thoracolumbalis	THOR/KO/LUM/BAI/LIS
thoracolumbar	THOR/KO/LUM/BAR
thoracolysis	THOR/KOL/SIS
thoracomelus	THOR/KOM/LUS
thoracometer	THOR/KOM/TER
thoracometry	THOR/KOM/TRI
thoracomyodynia	THOR/KO/MAOI/DIN/YA
thoracopagus	THOR/KOP/GUS
thoracoparacephalus	THOR/KO/PAR/SEF/LUS
thoracopathy	THOR/KO/PTH*I
thoracoplasty	THOR/KO/PLAS/TI
thoracopneumograph	THOR/KO/NAOUM/GRAF
thoracopneumoplasty	THOR/KO/NAOUM/PLAS/TI
thoracoschisis	THOR/KOS/KI/SIS
thoracoscope	THOR/KOS/SKOEP
thoracoscopy	THOR/KOS/KPI
thoracostenosis	THOR/KO/STE/NOE/SIS
thoracostomy	THOR/KO*S/M*I
thoracotomy	THOR/KOT/M*I
thoradelphus	THOR/DEL/FUS
thorax	THOR/AX
Thorazine	THOR/ZAOEN
Thorel	TOER/EL
	TOE/REL
thoriagram	THOR/YA/GRAM
thorium	THOR/YUM
Thormahlen	TORM/LEN
	TOR/MA/LEN
thorn	THORN
Thorn	K-P/THORN
Thornton	THORN/TON
thoroughbred	THOR/ROE/BRED
	THOR/RO/BRED
thoroughfare	THOR/ROE/FAER
	THOR/RO/FAER
thoroughpin	THOR/ROE/PIN
	THOR/RO/PIN
thought	THAUGT
	THAUT
thozalinone	THOE/ZAL/NOEN
thread	THRED
threadworm	THRED/WORM
threaten	THRET/-N
thremmatology	THREM/TOLG
threonic	THRAOE/ON/IK
	THRAOE/YON/IK
threonine	THRAOE/NAOEN
	THRAOE/YO/NIN
	(not THRAOE/NIN; see three anyone)
threose	THRAOE/OES
	THRAOE/YOES
Threostat	THRAOE/YO/STAT
threpsis	THREP/SIS
threpsology	THREP/SOLG
threptic	THREPT/IK
threshold	THRERBLD
	THRERB/OELD
	THRERB/OLD
	THRERB/HOLD
	THRERB/HOELD
thrill	THRIL
thrix	THRIX
-thrix	THRIX
throat	THROET
Throat Discs	THROET/DIS/*KS
throb	THROB
throe	THROE
throes	THROE/-S
thromb(o)-	THROM/B(O)
thrombapheresis	THROM/BA/FER/SIS
thrombase	THROM/BAIS
thrombasthenia	THROM/BAS/THAOEN/YA
thrombectomy	THROM/BEKT/M*I
thrombembolia	THROM/BEM/BOEL/YA
thrombi	THROM/BAOI
thrombin	THROM/BIN
thrombinogen	THROM/BIN/JEN
thrombinogenesis	THROM/BIN/JEN/SIS
	THROM/BI/NO/JEN/SIS
thromboangiitis	THROM/BO/AN/JAOITS
thromboarteritis	THROM/BO/ART/RAOITS
thromboasthenia	THROM/BO/AS/THAOEN/YA
thromboblast	THROM/BO/BLA*S
thromboclasis	THROM/BOK/LA/SIS
thromboclastic	THROM/BO/KLA*S/IK
thrombocyst	THROM/BO/S*IS
thrombocystis	THROM/BO/SIS/TIS
thrombocyt(o)-	THROM/BO/SAOIT

	THROM/BO/SAOI/T(O)
thrombocytapheresis	THROM/BO/SAOIT/FER/SIS
	THROM/BO/SAOI/FRAOE/SIS
thrombocytasthenia	THROM/BO/SAOI/TAS/THAOEN/YA
	THROM/BO/SAOIT/AS/THAOEN/YA
thrombocyte	THROM/BO/SAO*IT
thrombocythemia	THROM/BO/SAOI/THAOEM/YA
thrombocytic	THROM/BO/SIT/IK
thrombocytin	THROM/BO/SAOI/TIN
thrombocytocrit	THROM/BO/SAOIT/KRIT
thrombocytolysis	THROM/BO/SAOI/TOL/SIS
thrombocytopathia	THROM/BO/SAOIT/PA*T/YA
thrombocytopathic	THROM/BO/SAOIT/PA*T/IK
thrombocytopathy	THROM/BO/SAOI/TOP/TH*I
thrombocytopenia	THROM/BO/SAOIT/PAOEN/YA
thrombocytopoiesis	THROM/BO/SAOIT/POI/SIS
thrombocytopoietic	THROM/BO/SAOIT/POIT/IK
thrombocytosis	THROM/BO/SAOI/TOE/SIS
thromboelastogram	THROM/BO/E/LA*S/GRAM
thromboelastograph	THROM/BO/E/LA*S/GRAF
thromboelastography	THROM/BO/E/LAS/TOG/FI
thromboembolectomy	THROM/BO/EM/BLEKT/M*I
	THROM/BO/EM/BO/LEKT/M*I
thromboembolia	THROM/BO/EM/BOEL/YA
thromboembolism	THROM/BO/EM/BLIFM
thromboendarterectomy	THROM/BO/END/ART/REKT/M*I
thromboendarteritis	THROM/BO/END/ART/RAOITS
thromboendocarditis	THROM/BO/*END/KAR/DAOITS
thrombogen	THROM/BO/JEN
thrombogene	THROM/BO/JAOEN
thrombogenesis	THROM/BO/JEN/SIS
thrombogenic	THROM/BO/JEN/IK
thromboid	THROM/BOID
thrombokatilysin	THROM/BO/KAT/LAOI/SIN
thrombokinase	THROM/BO/KAOI/NAIS
thrombokinesis	THROM/BO/KI/NAOE/SIS
thrombokinetics	THROM/BO/KI/NET/IK/-S
thrombolymphangitis	THROM/BO/LIM/FAN/JAOITS
thrombolysis	THROM/BOL/SIS
thrombolytic	THROM/BO/LIT/IK
thrombon	THROM/BON
thrombonecrosis	THROM/BO/NE/KROE/SIS
thrombopathia	THROM/BO/PA*T/YA
thrombopathy	THROM/BOP/TH*I
thrombopenia	THROM/BO/PAOEN/YA
thrombophilia	THROM/BO/FIL/YA
thrombophlebitis	THROM/BO/FLE/BAOITS
thromboplastic	THROM/BO/PLA*S/IK
thromboplastid	THROM/BO/PLAS/TID
thromboplastin	THROM/BO/PLAS/TIN
thromboplastinogen	THROM/BO/PLAS/TIN/JEN
thromboplastinogenase	THROM/BO/PLAS/TIN/JE/NAIS
	THROM/BO/PLA*S/NOJ/NAIS
thromboplastinogenemia	THROM/BO/PLAS/TIN/JEN/AOEM/YA
	THROM/BO/PLAS/TIN/JE/NAOEM/YA
thrombopoiesis	THROM/BO/POI/SIS
thrombopoietic	THROM/BO/POIT/IK
thrombose par effort	THROM/BOES/PAR/E/FOR
	THROM/BOES/PAR/EF/FOR
thrombosed	THROM/BOES/-D
thromboses	THROM/BOE/SAOEZ
thrombosin	THROM/BO/SIN
thrombosinusitis	THROM/BO/SAOIN/SAOITS
thrombosis	THROM/BOE/SIS
thrombostasis	THROM/BO*S/SIS
Thrombostat	THROM/BO/STAT
thrombosthenin	THROM/BO/STHAOE/NIN
thrombotest	THROM/BO/T*ES
thrombotic	THROM/BOT/IK
thrombotonin	THROM/BO/TOE/NIN
thromboxane	THROM/BOK/SAIN
	THROM/BOX/AIN
thrombozyme	THROM/BO/ZAOIM
thrombus	THROM/BUS
throwback	THROU/BA*K
thrush	THRURB
thrust	THR*US
thrypsis	THRIP/SIS
thuja	THAOU/JA
	THAOU/YA
thujol	THAOU/JOL
thujone	THAOU/JOEN
thulium	THAOUL/YUM
thumb	THUM
thumbnail	THUM/NAIL

thumbprint	THUM/PRINT		THAOIR/KOL/OID
thumbprinting	THUM/PRINT/-G	thyrocricotomy	THAOIR/KRAOI/KOT/M*I
thumb-sucking	THUM/SUK/-G	thyrodesmic	THAOIR/DEZ/MIK
thump	THUFRP	thyroepiglottic	THAOIR/EP/GLOT/IK
thus	THUS	thyroesophageus	THAOIR/E/SOF/JAOE/YUS
	THAOUS	thyrofissure	THAOIR/FIRB/SHUR
thylakoid	THAOIL/KOID	thyrogenic	THAOIR/JEN/IK
	THAOI/LA/KOID	thyrogenous	THAOIR/ROJ/NOUS
thylacitis	THAOIL/SAOITS	thyroglobulin	THAOIR/GLOB/LIN
	THAOI/LA/SAOITS	thyroglossal	THAOIR/GLOS/SAL
thyme	TAO*IM	thyroglossus	THAOIR/GLOS/SUS
	(not TAOIM; see time)	thyrohyal	THAOIR/HAOIL
thym(o)-	THAOIM	thyrohyoid	THAOIR/HAOI/OID
	THAOI/M(O)	thyroid	THAOI/ROID
thymectomize	THAOI/MEKT/MAOIZ	thyroid(o)-	THAOI/ROID
thymectomy	THAOI/MEKT/M*I		THAOI/ROI/D(O)
thymelcosis	THAOI/MEL/KOE/SIS	thyroidea	THAOI/ROID/YA
thymi	THAOI/MAOI	thyroideae	THAOI/ROID/YAE
-thymia	THAOIM/YA	thyroidectomize	THAOI/ROI/DEKT/MAOIZ
thymic	THAOIM/IK	thyroidectomy	THAOI/ROI/DEKT/M*I
thymicae	THAOIM/SAE	thyroideus	THAOI/ROID/YUS
thymicolymphatic	THAOIM/KO/LIM/FAT/IK	thyroidism	THAOI/ROI/DIFM
thymic-parathyroid	THAOIM/IK/PAR/THAOI/ROID	thyroiditis	THAOI/ROI/DAOITS
thymidine	THAOIM/DAOEN	thyroidization	THAOI/ROID/ZAIGS
thymidylate	THAOIM/DIL/AIT	thyroidology	THAOI/ROI/DOLG
thymidylic	THAOIM/DIL/IK	thyroidotomy	THAOI/ROI/DOT/M*I
thymin	THAO*I/MIN	Thyrolar	THAOIR/LAR
	(not THAOI/MIN; see thiamin)	thyrolaryngeal	THAOIR/LARN/JAL
thymine	THAOI/MAOEN	thyroliberin	THAOIR/LIB/RIN
thyminic	THAOI/MIN/IK	thyrolingual	THAOIR/LING/WAL
thymion	THIM/YON	thyrolysin	THAOI/ROL/SIN
thymiosis	THIM/YOE/SIS	thyrolytic	THAOIR/LIT/IK
thymitis	THAOI/MAOITS	thyromegaly	THAOIR/MEG/LI
thymocyte	THAOIM/SAO*IT	thyromimetic	THAOIR/MAOI/MET/IK
thymogenic	THAOIM/JEN/IK		THAOIR/MI/MET/IK
thymohydroquinone	THAOIM/HAOI/DRO/KWIN/OEN	thyroneural	THAOIR/NAOURL
thymokesis	THAOIM/KAOE/SIS	thyronine	THAOIR/NAOEN
thymokinetic	THAOIM/KI/NET/IK		THAOIR/NIN
thymol	THAOI/MOL	thyronucleoalbumin	THAOIR/NAOUK/LO/AL/BAOU/
thymoleptic	THAOIM/LEPT/IK		MIN
thymolize	THAOIM/LAOIZ	thyropalatine	THAOIR/PAL/TAOIN
thymolphthalein	THAOI/MOL/THAL/YIN	thyroparathyroidectomy	THAOIR/PAR/THAOI/ROI/DEKT/
thymolysin	THAOI/MOL/SIN		M*I
thymolysis	THAOI/MOL/SIS	thyropathy	THAOI/ROP/TH*I
thymolytic	THAOIM/LIT/IK	thyropenia	THAOIR/PAOEN/YA
thymoma	THAOI/MOE/MA	thyropharyngeal	THAOIR/FRIN/JAL
thymometastasis	THAOIM/ME/TA*S/SIS	thyrophyma	THAOIR/FAOI/MA
thymonuclease	THAOIM/NAOUK/LAIS	thyroprival	THAOIR/PRAOIVL
thymopathic	THAOIM/PA*T/IK	thyroprivia	THAOIR/PRIV/YA
thymopathy	THAOI/MOP/TH*I	thyroprivic	THAOIR/PRIVK
thymopoietin	THAOIM/POI/TIN	thyroprivous	THAOIR/PRIV/OUS
thymopriva	THAOIM/PRAOI/VA		THAOIR/PRAOIV/OUS
thymoprival	THAOIM/PRAOIVL		THAOI/ROP/RI/VOUS
thymoprivic	THAOIM/PRIVK	thyroprotein	THAOIR/PRO/TAOEN
thymoprivous	THAOIM/PRAOIV/OUS	thyroptosis	THAOI/ROP/TOE/SIS
	THAOIM/PRIV/OUS	thyrosis	THAOI/ROE/SIS
	THAOI/MOP/RI/VOUS	thyrotherapy	THAOIR/THER/PI
thymosin	THAOIM/SIN	thyrotome	THAOIR/TOEM
thymotoxic	THAOIM/TOX/IK	thyrotomy	THAOI/ROT/M*I
thymotoxin	THAOIM/TOK/SIN	thyrotoxemia	THAOIR/TOK/SAOEM/YA
thymotrophic	THAOIM/TROFK	thyrotoxia	THAOIR/TOX/YA
	THAOIM/TROEFK	thyrotoxic	THAOIR/TOX/IK
thymoxamine	THAOI/MOX/MAOEN	thyrotoxicosis	THAOIR/TOX/KOE/SIS
thymus	THAOI/MUS	thyrotoxin	THAOIR/TOK/SIN
thymus-dependent	THAOI/MUS/H-F/DPEND/ENT	thyrotrope	THAOIR/TROEP
thymusectomy	THAOIM/SEKT/M*I	thyrotroph	THAOIR/TROEF
	THAOI/MUS/EKT/M*I		THAOIR/TROF
thymus-independent	THAOI/MUS/H-F/IN/DPEND/ENT	thyrotrophic	THAOIR/TROEFK
thypar	THAOI/PAR		THAOIR/TROFK
thyr(o)-	THAOIR	thyrotrophin	THAOIR/TROEFN
	THAOI/R(O)		THAOIR/ROT/RO/FIN
thyremphraxis	THAOI/REM/FRAK/SIS	thyrotropic	THAOIR/TROP/IK
thyre(o)-	THAOIR/Y(O)	thyrotropin	THAOI/ROT/RO/PIN
thyreohyoidei	THAOIR/YO/HAOI/OID/YAOI		THAOIR/TROE/PIN
thyreoidectomica	THAOIR/YOI/DEK/TOM/KA	thyrotropism	THAOI/ROT/RO/PIFM
	THAOIR/YOID/EK/TOM/KA	thyroxine	THAOI/ROK/SAOEN
thyreopriva	THAOIR/YO/PRAOI/VA		THAOI/ROK/SIN
thyroacetic	THAOIR/AI/SAOET/IK	thyroxinemia	THAOI/ROX/NAOEM/YA
thyroactive	THAOIR/AKT/IV	thyroxinic	THAOI/ROK/SIN/IK
thyroadenitis	THAOIR/AD/NAOITS	thyroxinum	THAOI/ROX/NUM
thyroaplasia	THAOIR/AI/PLAIZ/YA	thyrsus	THIR/SUS
thyroarytenoid	THAOIR/AR/TAOE/NOID	Thysanosoma	THIS/NO/SOE/MA
thyrocalcitonin	THAOIR/KALS/TOE/NIN	Thysanosoma actinoides	THIS/NO/SOE/MA/AKT/NOI/
thyrocardiac	THAOIR/KARD/YAK		DAOEZ
thyrocarditis	THAOIR/KAR/DAOITS	tibi(o)-	TIB/Y(O)
thyrocele	THAOIR/SAO*EL	tibia	TIB/YA
thyrocervical	THAOIR/SEFRB/KAL	tibiad	TIB/YAD
thyrochondrotomy	THAOIR/KON/DROT/M*I	tibiae	TIB/YAE
thyrocolloid	THAOIR/KLOID	tibial	TIB/YAL

tibiale	TIB/YAI/LAOE	tingibility	TIN/JIBLT
tibiale posticum	TIB/YAI/LAOE/POS/TAOI/KUM	tingible	TIN/JIBL
tibiales	TIB/YAI/LAOEZ	tingle	TING/-L
tibialgia	TIB/YAL/JA	tingling	TING/-LG
tibialgic	TIB/YAL/JIK	tinidazole	TAOI/NID/ZOEL
tibialis	TIB/YAI/LIS		TI/NID/ZOEL
tibien	TIB/YEN	tinkle	TIN/K-L
tibiocalcanean	TIB/YO/KAL/KAIN/YAN		T*ING/-L
tibiofascialis	TIB/YO/FARB/YAI/LIS		(not TING/-L; see tingle)
	TIB/YO/FAS/YAI/LIS	tinnitus	TI/NAOI/TUS
tibiofemoral	TIB/YO/FEM/RAL		TIN/NAOI/TUS
tibiofibular	TIB/YO/FIB/LAR		(not TIN/NAOITS)
tibiofibularis	TIB/YO/FIB/LAI/RIS	tint	TINT
tibionavicular	TIB/YO/NA/VIK/LAR	tintometer	TIN/TOM/TER
tibionavicularis	TIB/YO/NA/VIK/LAI/RIS	tintometric	TINT/MET/RIK
tibioperoneal	TIB/YO/PER/NAOEL	tintometry	TIN/TOM/TRI
tibioscaphoid	TIB/YO/SKAF/OID	tioconazole	TAOI/KON/ZOEL
tibiotarsal	TIB/YO/TAR/SAL		TAOI/YO/KON/ZOEL
tibolone	TIB/LOEN	tip	TIP
tic	T*IK	tipping	TIP/-G
	(not TIK; see tick)	tipper	TIP/ER
Ticar	TAOI/KAR	tiprenolol	TIP/REN/LOL
ticarcillin	TAOI/KAR/SLIN		TAOI/PREN/LOL
	TAOI/KAR/SIL/LIN	tiqueur	TAOE/KER
tick	TIK		TAOE/KUR
tickle	TIK/-L	tire	TAOIR
tickling	TIK/-LG	tiring	TAOIR/-G
ticlopidine	TAOI/KLOEP/DAOEN	Tiselius	TI/SAIL/YUS
ticrynafen	TAOI/KRIN/FEN		TI/SAOEL/YUS
tictology	TIK/TOLG		TI/SEL/YUS
t.i.d.	T*ID	tissue	TIRB/SHAOU
tidal	TAOI/DAL	tissular	TIRB/LAR
tide	TAOID		TIRB/SHAOU/LAR
Tiedemann	TAOED/MAN		TIRB/YAOU/LAR
Tietze	TAOET/SAOE		TIRB/YU/LAR
	TAOET/ZAOE	titanium	TAOI/TAIN/YUM
Tigan	TAOI/GAN	titer	TAOIT/ER
tiglate	TIG/LAIT	titillate	TIT/LAIT
tiglian	TIG/LAN	titillation	TIT/LAIGS
	TIG/LAOE/YAN	titrant	TAOI/TRANT
tiglic	TIG/LIK	titrate	TAOI/TRAIT
tiglium	TIG/LUM	titration	TAOI/TRAIGS
	TIG/LAOE/UM	titrimetric	TIT/RI/MET/RIK
	TIG/LAOE/YUM		TAOI/TRI/MET/RIK
tigretier	TAOE/GRET/YAI	titrimetry	TAOI/TRIM/TRI
	TI/GRET/YAI	titub-	TIT/B-
tigroid	TAOI/GROID		TIT/YAOU/B-
tigrolysis	TAOI/GROL/SIS		TIT/YU/B-
tiletamine	TAOI/LET/MAOEN	titubant	TIT/BANT
tilidine	TIL/DAOEN	titubation	TIT/BAIGS
Tillaux	TAOE/YOE	Tizzoni	TIZ/ZOE/NAOE
	TAOEL/YOE		TIT/ZOE/NAOE
	TIL/LOE		TID/ZOE/NAOE
tilmus	TIL/MUS	TNM	T-RBGS/N*RBGS/M*RBGS
tiltometer	TIL/TOM/TER	toadskin	TOED/SKIN
timbre	TAM/BER	toadstool	TOED/STAOL
	TIM/BRE	tobacco	TO/BAK/KOE
	T*IM/BER	tobaccoism	TO/BAK/KOE/IFM
	(not TIM/BER; see timber)	tobramycin	TOE/BRA/MAOI/SIN
time	TAOIM	Tobrex	TOE/BREX
Timentin	TAOI/MEN/TIN	toc(o)-	TOEK
timer	TAOIM/ER		TOE/K(O)
Timolide	TIM/LAOID	tocanide	TOE/KAI/NAOID
timolol	TAOIM/LOL		TOE/KAIN/AOID
	TAOIM/LOEL	tocamphyl	TOE/KAM/FIL
Timoptic	TIM/OPT/IK	-tocia	TOE/SHA
tin	TIN		TOERB/YA
tina	TAOE/NA	tocochromanol	TOEK/KROEM/NOL
Tinactin	TIN/AK/TIN	tocodynagraph	TOEK/DAOIN/GRAF
tinctable	TING/TABL		TOK/DAOIN/GRAF
	TINGT/-BL	tocodynamometer	TOEK/DAOIN/MOM/TER
tinction	TINGS		TOK/DAOIN/MOM/TER
tinctorial	TING/TOIRL	tocograph	TOEK/GRAF
tinctura	TING/TAOU/RA		TOK/GRAF
	TING/KHUR/RA	tocography	TOE/KOG/FI
tincturae	TING/TAOU/RAE	tocol	TOE/KOL
	TING/KHUR/RAE	tocology	TOE/KOLG
tincturation	TING/KHU/RAIGS	tocolytic	TOEK/LIT/IK
	TING/KHUR/AIGS	tocometer	TOE/KOM/TER
	TING/KHUR/RAIGS	tocopherol	TOE/KOF/ROL
	TING/TAOU/RAIGS		TOE/KOF/ROEL
tincture	TING/KHUR	tocopherolquinone	TOE/KOF/ROL/KWAOI/NOEN
Tindal	TIN/DAL		TOE/KOF/ROL/KWIN/OEN
tine	TAOIN	tocophobia	TOEK/FOEB/YA
Tine Test	TAOIN/T*ES		TOK/FOEB/YA
	K-P/TAOIN/T*ES	tocoquinone	TOEK/KWAOI/NOEN
tinea	TIN/YA		TOEK/KWIN/OEN
Tinel	TIN/EL	tocotrienol	TOEK/TRAOI/NOL
tinfoil	TIN/FOIL	tocotrienolquinone	TOEK/TRAOI/NOL/KWAOI/NOEN

	TOEK/TRAOI/NOL/KWIN/OEN	tonaphasia	TOEN/FAIZ/YA
tocus	TOE/KUS		TON/FAIZ/YA
Todd	TO*D	tone	TOEN
	(not TOD; see today)	toner	TOEN/ER
toe	TOE	tongs	TONG/-S
toe-crack	TOE/H-F/KRAK	tongue	TUNG
toe-trop	TOE/H-F/DROP	tongue crib	TUNG/KRIB
toenail	TOE/NAIL	tongue-swallowing	TUNG/H-F/SWAL/LOE/-G
tofenacin	TOE/FEN/SIN	tongue thrust	TUNG/THR*US
Tofranil	TOE/FRAI/NIL	tongue-tie	TUNG/TAOI
Tofranil-PM	TOE/FRAI/NIL/P-RBGS/M*RBGS	tongue-tied	TUNG/TAOI/-D
tofu	TOE/FAOU	-tonia	TOEN/YA
Togaviridae	TOEG/VIR/DAE	tonic	TON/IK
	TOE/GA/VIR/DAE	tonicity	TOE/NIS/TI
togavirus	TOEG/VAOI/RUS	tonicize	TON/SAOIZ
	TOE/GA/VAOI/RUS	tonicoclonic	TON/KO/KLON/IK
togoi	TOE/GOI	tonin	TOE/NIN
toilet	TOI/LET	toning	TOEN/-G
	TOIL/ET	tonitrophobia	TOEN/TRO/FOEB/YA
Toison	TWA/SON	Tonocard	TOEN/KARD
	TOI/SON	tonoclonic	TOEN/KLON/IK
token	TOEK/-N		TON/KLON/IK
	TOE/KEN	tonofibril	TOEN/FAOI/BRIL
tolazamide	TOE/LAZ/MAOID		TON/FAOI/BRIL
	TOL/A*Z/MAOID	tonofilament	TOEN/FIL/-MT
tolazoline	TOE/LAZ/LAOEN		TON/FIL/-MT
	TOL/A*Z/LAOEN	tonogram	TOEN/GRAM
tolbutamide	TOL/BAOUT/MAOID		TON/GRAM
tolcyclamide	TOL/SAOI/KLA/MAOID	tonograph	TOEN/GRAF
Tolectin	TOE/LEK/TIN		TON/GRAF
	TOL/EK/TIN	tonography	TOE/NOG/FI
tolerance	TOL/RANS	tonometer	TOE/NOM/TER
tolerant	TOL/RANT	tonometry	TOE/NOM/TRI
tolerata	TOL/RAI/TA	tonophant	TOEN/FANT
toleration	TOL/RAIGS		TON/FANT
Tolerex	TOL/REX	tonoplast	TOEN/PLA*S
tolerogen	TOL/RO/JEN		TON/PLAUS
tolerogenesis	TOL/RO/JEN/SIS	tonoscillograph	TOE/NOS/LO/GRAF
tolerogenic	TOL/RO/JEN/IK	tonoscope	TOE/NOS/SKOEP
Tolfrinic	TOL/FRIN/IK	tonotopic	TOEN/TOP/IK
tolhexamide	TOL/HEX/MAOID	tonotopicity	TOEN/TOE/PIS/TI
Tolinase	TOEL/NAIS	tonotropic	TOEN/TROP/IK
	TOL/NAIS	tonsil	TON/SIL
tolindate	TOE/LIN/DAIT	tonsill(o)-	TONS/L(O)
tolmetin	TOL/ME/TIN		TON/SL(O)
tolnaftate	TOL/NAF/TAIT		TON/SIL
tolonium	TOE/LOEN/YUM	tonsilla	TON/SIL/LA
tolpropamine	TOL/PROEP/MAOEN	tonsillae	TON/SIL/LAE
tolu	TOL/YAOU	tonsillar	TONS/LAR
toluene	TOL/YAOEN	tonsillares	TONS/LAI/RAOEZ
	TOL/YAOU/AOEN	tonsillaris	TONS/LAI/RIS
toluic	TOE/LAOU/IK	tonsillary	TONS/LAIR
	TOL/YAOU/IK	tonsillectome	TONS/LEK/TOEM
	TOL/YIK	tonsillectomy	TONS/LEKT/M*I
toluidine	TOE/LAOU/DAOEN	tonsillith	TONS/L*IT
	TOL/YAOU/DAOEN	tonsillitic	TONS/LIT/IK
	TOE/LAOU/DIN	tonsillitis	TONS/LAOITS
	TOL/YAOU/DIN	tonsilloadenoidectomy	TONS/LO/AD/NOI/DEKT/M*I
toluol	TOL/YOL	tonsillolith	TON/SIL/L*IT
	TOL/YAOU/OL	tonsillomycosis	TONS/LO/MAOI/KOE/SIS
toluric	TOE/LAOUR/IK	tonsillopathy	TONS/LOP/TH*I
	TOL/YAOUR/IK	tonsilloprive	TONS/LO/PRAOIV
toluyl	TOL/YAOU/IL	tonsilloscopy	TONS/LOS/KPI
toluylene	TOL/YAOU/LAOEN	tonsillotome	TON/SIL/TOEM
tolyl	TOL/IL	tonsillotomy	TONS/LOT/M*I
-tome	TOEM	tonus	TOE/NUS
tomentosum	TOE/MEN/TOE/SUM	tooth	TAO*T
	TOE/MEN/TOES/UM	Tooth	K-P/TAO*T
	TOEMT/TOE/SUM	toothache	TAO*T/A*IK
	TOEMT/TOES/UM	tooth-borne	TAO*T/BOERN
tomentum	TOE/MEN/TUM		TAO*T/H-F/BOERN
	TOE/MENT/UM	topagnosia	TOP/AG/NOEZ/YA
	TOEMT/UM	topagnosis	TOP/AG/NOE/SIS
	TOEMT/TUM	topalgia	TOE/PAL/JA
Tomes	TOEMZ	topectomy	TOE/PEKT/M*I
	TOEMS	topesthesia	TOP/ES/THAOEZ/YA
Tommaselli	TOM/SEL/LAOE	Topfer	TEP/FER
tomo-	TOEM-	tophaceous	TOE/FAIRBS
	TOE/MO	tophi	TOE/FAOI
tomogram	TOEM/GRAM	tophic	TOEF/IK
tomograph	TOEM/GRAF	topholipoma	TOF/LI/POE/MA
tomographic	TOEM/GRAFK		TOEF/LI/POE/MA
tomography	TOE/MOG/FI	tophus	TOE/FUS
tomolevel	TOEM/LEVL	topica	TOP/KA
tomomania	TOEM/MAIN/YA	topical	TOP/KAL
-tomy	(O)T/M*I	Topicort Emollient Cream	TOP/KORT/E/MOL/YENT/
ton(o)-	TOEN		KRAOEM
	TON	Topicort Gel	TOP/KORT/JEL
	TOE/N(O)	Topicort LP	TOP/KORT/L-RBGS/P*RBGS

Topicort Ointment	TOP/KORT/OINT/-MT	torticollis	TORT/KOL/LAR
Topinard	TOP/NAIR		TORT/KLIS
	TOP/NAR		TORT/KOL/LIS
	TOP/NARD	tortipelvis	TORT/PEL/VIS
Topisporin	TOP/SPORN	tortoise	TOR/TOS
topistic	TOE/P*IS/IK	tortua	TO*RPBLG/YA
topo-	TOP		TOR/KHAOU/WA
topoanesthesia	TOP/ANS/THAOEZ/YA	tortuous	TOR/KHOUS
topochemistry	TOP/KEM/STRI		TOR/KHAOU/OUS
topodysesthesia	TOP/DIS/ES/THAOEZ/YA	torul-	TOR/L-
topognosia	TOP/OG/NOEZ/YA		TOR/YAOU/L-
topognosis	TOP/OG/NOE/SIS		TOR/YU/L-
topogometer	TOP/GOM/TER	toruli	TOR/LAOI
topographic	TOP/GRAFK	toruloma	TOR/LOE/MA
topographical	TOP/GRAF/KAL	Torulopsis	TOR/LOP/SIS
topography	TOE/POG/FI	torulopsosis	TOR/LOP/SOE/SIS
topology	TOE/POLG	torulus	TOR/LUS
toponarcosis	TOP/NAR/KOE/SIS	torus	TOR/RUS
toponym	TOEP/NIM		TOE/RUS
	TOE/PO/NIM	tosifen	TOES/FEN
	(not TOP/NIM; see top anymore)	tosyl	TOE/SIL
toponymy	TOE/PON/M*I	tosylate	TOES/LAIT
topoparesthesia	TOP/PAR/ES/THAOEZ/YA	totale	TOE/TAI/LAOE
topopathogenesis	TOEP/PA*T/JEN/SIS	totalis	TOE/TAI/LIS
	TOE/PO/PA*T/JEN/SIS	totem	TOET/EM
	TOP/PA*T/JEN/SIS	toti-	TOET
topophobia	TOEP/FOEB/YA		TOE/TI
	TOP/FOEB/YA	totipotence	TOE/TIP/TENS
topophylaxis	TOEP/FLAK/SIS	totipotency	TOET/POE/TEN/SI
	TOP/FLAK/SIS		TOET/POET/EN/SI
toposcope	TOP/SKOEP	totipotent	TOE/TIP/TENT
topothermesthesiometer	TOP/THERM/ES/THAOEZ/YOM/	totipotential	TOET/POE/TEN/-RBL
	TER	totipotentiality	TOET/POE/TEN/SHAL/TI
	TOP/THER/MES/THAOEZ/YOM/		TOET/POE/TEN/-RBL/TI
	TER	touch	TUFP
topovaccinotherapy	TOP/VAX/NO/THER/PI		TOUFP
ToppFast	TO*P/FA*S	tour	TOUR
	(not TOP/FA*S; see top fast)		TAOUR
torcular	TORK/LAR	Tourette	TAOU/RET
torcular herophili	TORK/LAR/HE/ROF/LAOI	tournesol	TOURN/SOL
Torecan	TOR/KAN		TAOURN/SOL
Torek	TOE/REK	tourniquet	TOURN/KET
	TOR/EK		TAOURN/KET
tori	TOR/RAOI	Touton	TAOU/TON
	TOER/RAOI	towelette	TOU/LET
	TOE/RAOI		TOUL/ET
toric	TOR/IK		TOU/EL/ET
	TOE/RIK	tox-	TOX
torment	TORMT		TOK/S(v)
	TOERMT	toxanemia	TOX/NAOEM/YA
tormentor	TORMT/TOR	toxaphene	TOX/FAOEN
	TOERMT/TOR	Toxascaris	TOK/SAS/KRIS
	TOR/MEN/TOR	Toxascaris leonina	TOK/SAS/KRIS/LAOE/NAOI/NA
tormina	TORM/NA	toxemia	TOK/SAOEM/YA
torminal	TORM/NAL	toxemic	TOK/SAOEM/IK
Tornalate	TORN/LAIT	toxenzyme	TOX/EN/ZAOIM
	TOR/NA/LAIT	-toxia	TOX/YA
Tornwaldt	TORN/VALT	toxic	TOX/IK
	TOERN/VALT	toxicant	TOX/KANT
torose	TOE/ROES	toxicaria	TOX/KAIR/YA
	TOR/ROES	toxication	TOX/KAIGS
torous	TOE/ROUS	toxicemia	TOX/SAOEM/YA
	TOR/ROUS	toxicide	TOX/SAO*ID
	TOR/OUS	toxicity	TOK/SIS/TI
torpent	TORP/ENT	toxicodendrol	TOX/KO/DEN/DROL
	TOR/PENT	Toxicodendron	TOX/KO/DEN/DRON
torpid	TORP/ID	toxicoderma	TOX/KO/DER/MA
	TOR/PID	toxicodermatosis	TOX/KO/DERM/TOE/SIS
torpidity	TOR/PID/TI	toxicogenic	TOX/KO/JEN/IK
torpor	TOR/POR	toxicohemia	TOX/KO/HAOEM/YA
torque	TORK	toxicoid	TOX/KOID
torquing	TORK/-G	toxicologic	TOX/KO/LOJ/IK
torr	TOR	toxicologist	TOX/KO*LGS
	(not TOER; see tore)	toxicology	TOX/KOLG
torrefaction	TOR/FA*BGS	toxicomania	TOX/KO/MAIN/YA
torrefy	TOR/FI	toxicomaniac	TOX/KO/MAIN/YAK
torricellian	TOR/KHEL/YAN	toxicopathic	TOX/KO/PA*T/IK
torsade de pointes	TOR/SAUD/DE/POINT	toxicopathy	TOX/KOP/TH*I
	TOR/SAUD/DE/PWAUNT	toxicopectic	TOX/KO/PEKT/IK
torsiometer	TORS/YOM/TER	toxicopexic	TOX/KO/PEX/IK
	TOR/SHOM/TER	toxicopexis	TOX/KO/PEK/SIS
torsion	TORGS	toxicopexy	TOX/KO/PEK/SI
torsional	TORGS/NAL	toxicophobia	TOX/KO/FOEB/YA
torsionometer	TORGS/OM/TER	toxicosis	TOX/KOE/SIS
torsive	TORS/IV	toxicosozin	TOX/KO/SOE/ZIN
torsiversion	TORS/VERGS	toxicum	TOX/KUM
torso	TOR/SOE	toxiferine	TOK/SIF/RAOEN
torsoclusion	TORS/KLAOUGS	toxiferous	TOK/SIF/ROUS
torticollar	TORT/KLAR	toxigenic	TOX/JEN/IK

toxigenicity	TOX/JE/NIS/TI	trachelagra	TRAK/LAG/RA
toxignomic	TOX/IG/NOM/IK		TRAIK/LAG/RA
	TOK/SIG/NOM/IK	trachelalis	TRAK/LAI/LIS
toxilic	TOK/SIL/IK		TRAIK/LAI/LIS
toxin	TOK/SIN	trachelectomy	TRAK/LEKT/M*I
toxin-antitoxin	TOK/SIN/A*ENT/TOK/SIN		TRAIK/LEKT/M*I
toxinic	TOK/SIN/IK	trachelematoma	TRAK/LEM/TOE/MA
toxinogenic	TOX/NO/JEN/IK		TRAIK/LEM/TOE/MA
toxinogenicity	TOX/NO/JE/NIS/TI		TRAK/LAOEM/TOE/MA
toxinoid	TOX/NOID		TRAIK/LAOEM/TOE/MA
toxinology	TOX/NOLG	trachelian	TRA/KAOEL/YAN
toxinosis	TOX/NOE/SIS	trachelism	TRAK/LIFM
toxinum	TOK/SAOIN/UM		TRAIK/LIFM
	TOK/SAOI/NUM	trachelismus	TRAK/LIZ/MUS
	TOX/NUM		TRAIK/LIZ/MUS
toxipathic	TOX/PA*T/IK	trachelitis	TRAK/LAOITS
toxipathy	TOK/SIP/TH*I		TRAIK/LAOITS
toxiphobia	TOX/FOEB/YA	trachelocele	TRAK/LO/SAO*EL
-toxism	TOK/SIFM		TRAIK/LO/SAO*EL
	TOX/IFM	trachelocyrtosis	TRAK/LO/SIR/TOE/SIS
toxisterol	TOK/S*IS/ROL		TRAIK/LO/SIR/TOE/SIS
Toxocara	TOX/KAR/RA	trachelocystitis	TRAK/LO/SIS/TAOITS
	TOX/KAI/RA		TRAIK/LO/SIS/TAOITS
toxocaral	TOX/KAR/RAL	trachelodynia	TRAK/LO/DIN/YA
	TOX/KAI/RAL		TRAIK/LO/DIN/YA
toxocariasis	TOX/KA/RAOI/SIS	trachelokyphosis	TRAK/LO/KAOI/FOE/SIS
toxogen	TOX/JEN		TRAIK/LO/KAOI/FOE/SIS
toxogenin	TOK/SOJ/NIN	trachelologist	TRAK/LO*LGS
	TOX/OJ/NIN		TRAIK/LO*LGS
toxoglobulin	TOX/GLOB/LIN	trachelology	TRAK/LOLG
toxoid	TOK/SOID		TRAIK/LOLG
	TOX/OID	trachelomastoid	TRAK/LO/MAS/TOID
toxoid-antitoxoid	TOK/SOID/A*ENT/TOK/SOID		TRAIK/LO/MAS/TOID
	TOX/OID/A*ENT/TOX/OID	trachelomyitis	TRAK/LO/MAOI/AOITS
toxolecithin	TOX/LES/THIN		TRAIK/LO/MAOI/AOITS
toxon	TOK/SON	trachelo-occipitalis	TRAK/LO/OK/SIP/TAI/LIS
toxone	TOK/SOEN		TRAIK/LO/OK/SIP/TAI/LIS
toxoneme	TOX/NAOEM	trachelopanus	TRAK/LO/PAI/NUS
toxopexic	TOX/PEX/IK		TRAIK/LO/PAI/NUS
toxophil	TOX/FIL	trachelopexia	TRAK/LO/PEX/YA
toxophile	TOX/FAOIL		TRAIK/LO/PEX/YA
toxophilic	TOX/FIL/IK	trachelopexy	TRAK/LO/PEK/SI
toxophilous	TOK/SOF/LUS		TRAIK/LO/PEK/SI
toxophore	TOX/FOER	trachelophyma	TRAK/LO/FAOI/MA
toxophorous	TOK/SOF/ROUS		TRAIK/LO/FAOI/MA
toxophylaxin	TOX/FLAK/SIN	tracheloplasty	TRAK/LO/PLAS/TI
Toxoplasma	TOX/PLAZ/MA		TRAIK/LO/PLAS/TI
Toxoplasma gondii	TOX/PLAZ/MA/GOND/YAOI	trachelorrhaphy	TRAK/LOR/FI
Toxoplasmatidae	TOX/PLAZ/MAT/DAE		TRAIK/LOR/FI
toxoplasmic	TOX/PLAZ/MIK	trachelos	TRAK/LOS
toxoplasmin	TOX/PLAZ/MIN		TRAIK/LOS
toxoplasmosis	TOX/PLAZ/MOE/SIS	tracheloschisis	TRAK/LOS/KI/SIS
toxoprotein	TOX/PRO/TAOEN		TRAIK/LOS/KI/SIS
toxopyrimidine	TOX/PI/RIM/DAOEN	trachelosyringorrhaphy	TRAK/LO/SIRN/GOR/FI
	TOX/PAOI/RIM/DAOEN		TRAIK/LO/SIRN/GOR/FI
-toxy	TOK/SI	trachelotomy	TRAK/LOT/M*I
Toynbee	TOIN/BAOE		TRAIK/LOT/M*I
T-PHYL	T-RBGS/FIL	tacheoaerocele	TRAIK/YO/AER/SAO*EL
trabecul-	TRA/BEK/L-	tracheobiliary	TRAIK/YO/BIL/YAIR
	TRA/BEK/YAOU/L-	tracheobronchial	TRAIK/YO/BRONG/YAL
	TRA/BEK/YU/L-	tracheobronchitis	TRAIK/YO/BRON/KAOITS
trabecula	TRA/BEK/LA	tracheobronchomegaly	TRAIK/YO/BRONG/MEG/LI
trabeculae	TRA/BEK/LAE	tracheobronchoscopy	TRAIK/YO/BRON/KOS/KPI
trabecular	TRA/BEK/LAR	tracheocele	TRAIK/YO/SAO*EL
trabecularism	TRA/BEK/LA/RIFM	tracheoesophageal	TRAIK/YO/E/SOF/JAOEL
	TRA/BEK/LAR/IFM	tracheofissure	TRAIK/YO/FIRB/SHUR
trabeculate	TRA/BEK/LAIT	tracheofistulization	TRAIK/YO/FIS/KHUL/ZAIGS
trabeculation	TRA/BEK/LAIGS	tracheogenic	TRAIK/YO/JEN/IK
trabeculectomy	TRA/BEK/LEKT/M*I	tracheolaryngeal	TRAIK/YO/LARN/JAL
trabeculoplasty	TRA/BEK/LO/PLAS/TI	tracheolaryngotomy	TRAIK/YO/LARN/GOT/M*I
trabeculotomy	TRA/BEK/LOT/M*I	tracheomalacia	TRAIK/YO/MA/LAI/SHA
trabes	TRAI/BAOEZ	tracheopathia	TRAIK/YO/PA*T/YA
trabs	TRABS	tracheopathy	TRAIK/YOP/TH*I
trace	TRAIS	tracheopharyngeal	TRAIK/YO/FRIN/JAL
tracer	TRAIS/ER	tracheophonesis	TRAIK/YO/FOE/NAOE/SIS
trache(o)-	TRAIK/Y(O)	tracheophony	TRAIK/YOF/N*I
trachea	TRAIK/YA	tracheoplasty	TRAIK/YO/PLAS/TI
tracheae	TRAIK/YAE	tracheopyosis	TRAIK/YO/PAOI/YOE/SIS
tracheaectasy	TRAIK/YA/EKT/SI	tracheorrhagia	TRAIK/YO/RAI/JA
tracheal	TRAIK/YAL	tracheorrhaphy	TRAIK/YOR/FI
tracheale	TRAIK/YAI/LAOE	tracheoschisis	TRAIK/YOS/KI/SIS
tracheales	TRAIK/YAI/LAOEZ	tracheoscope	TRAIK/YO/SKOEP
trachealgia	TRAIK/YAL/JA	tracheoscopic	TRAIK/YO/SKOP/IK
trachealia	TRAIK/YAIL/YA	tracheoscopy	TRAIK/YOS/KPI
trachealis	TRAIK/YAI/LIS	tracheostenosis	TRAIK/YO/STE/NOE/SIS
tracheid	TRAIK/YID	tracheostoma	TRAIK/YO*S/MA
tracheitis	TRAIK/YAOITS	tracheostomize	TRAIK/YO*S/MAOIZ
trachel(o)-	TRAK/L(O)	tracheostomy	TRAIK/YO*S/M*I
	TRAIK/L(O)	tracheotome	TRAIK/YO/TOEM

tracheotomize	TRAIK/YOT/MAOIZ	transcalvarial	TRA*NS/KAL/VAIRL
tracheotomy	TRAIK/YOT/M*I		TRA*NS/KAL/VAIR/YAL
trachitis	TRA/KAOITS	transcapsidation	TRA*NS/KAPS/DAIGS
	TRAI/KAOITS		TRA*NS/KAP/SI/DAIGS
trachoma	TRA/KOE/MA	transcarbamoylase	TRA*NS/KARB/MOI/LAIS
trachomata	TRA/KOEM/TA		TRA*NS/KAR/BAM/OI/LAIS
trachomatis	TRA/KOEM/TIS	transcarboxylase	TRA*NS/KAR/BOX/LAIS
trachomatous	TRA/KOEM/TOUS	transcatheter	TRA*NS/KA*T/TER
trachy-	TRAK	transcendental	TRAN/SEN/DEN/TAL
	TRAIK		TRA*NS/SEN/DEN/TAL
trachychromatic	TRAK/KROE/MATIK	transcervical	TRA*NS/SEFRB/KAL
	TRAIK/KROE/MAT/IK	transcobalamin	TRA*NS/KO/BAL/MIN
trachyphonia	TRAK/FOEN/YA	transcolonic	TRA*NS/KO/LON/IK
	TRAIK/FOEN/YA	transcondylar	TRA*NS/KOND/LAR
tracing	TRAIS/-G	transcondyloid	TRA*NS/KOND/LOID
track	TRAK	transcortical	TRA*NS/KORT/KAL
Tracrium	TRAI/KRAOE/UM	transcortin	TRA*NS/KOR/TIN
	TRAI/KRAOE/YUM	transcricothyroid	TRA*NS/KRAOIK/THAOI/ROID
tract	TRAKT	transcriptase	TRAN/SKRIP/TAIS
tractate	TRAK/TAIT		TRA*NS/KRIP/TAIS
tractella	TRAK/TEL/LA	transcription	TRAN/SKRIPGS
tractellum	TRAK/TEL/UM		TRA*NS/KRIPGS
traction	TRA*BGS	transcutaneous	TRA*NS/KAOU/TAIN/YOUS
tractor	TRAK/TOR	transcytosis	TRA*NS/SAOI/TOE/SIS
tractoration	TRAKT/RAIGS	Transderm Scop	TRA*NS/DERM/SKOEP
tractotomy	TRAK/TOT/M*I	Transderm-Nitro	TRA*NS/DERM/NAOI/TROE
tractus	TRAK/TUS	Transderm-NTG	TRA*NS/DERM/N-RBGS/T*RBGS/
tragacanth	TRAG/KA*NT		G*RBGS
tragacantha	TRAG/KAN/THA	transdermic	TRA*NS/DERM/IK
tragal	TRAI/GAL	transduce	TRA*NS/DAOUS
tragi	TRAI/JAOI	transducer	TRA*NS/DAOUS/ER
tragicus	TRAIJ/KUS	transductant	TRA*NS/DUK/TANT
	TRAJ/KUS	transduction	TRA*NS/D*UBGS
tragion	TRAIJ/YON	transdural	TRA*NS/DAOURL
	TRAI/JON	transection	TRAN/S*EBGS
	TRAJ/YON	transepidermal	TRA*NS/EP/DER/MAL
tragomaschalia	TRAG/MAS/KAL/YA	transepithelial	TRA*NS/EP/THAOEL/YAL
tragophonia	TRAG/FOEN/YA	transethmoidal	TRA*NS/*ET/MOI/DAL
tragophony	TRA/GOF/N*I	transfaunation	TRA*NS/FAU/NAIGS
tragopodia	TRAG/POED/YA	transfection	TRA*NS/F*EBGS
tragus	TRAI/GUS	transfer	TRA*NS/FER
train	TRAIN		TR-FR
trainable	TRAIN/-BL	transferable	TRA*NS/FERBL
training	TRAIN/-G		TRA*NS/FER/-BL
trait	TRAIT		TR-FR/-BL
trajector	TRA/JEK/TOR		TR-FRBL
trajectory	TRA/JEKT/RI	transferase	TRA*NS/FRAIS
tramadol	TRAM/DOL		TRA*NS/FER/AIS
tramazoline	TRA/MAZ/LAOEN	transference	TRA*NS/FERNS
tramitis	TRAM/AOITS		TRA*NS/FRENS
	TRA/MAOITS		TR-FR/ENS
trance	TRANS	transferrin	TRA*NS/FER/RIN
Trancopal	TRAN/KO/PAL		TRA*NS/FRIN
Trandate	TRAN/DAIT	transfix	TRA*NS/FIX
tranexamic	TRAN/KPAM/IK	transfixion	TRA*NS/F*IBGS
	TRAN/EX/AM/IK	transform	TRA*NS/FORM
tranquilizer	TRAN/KWIL/AOIZ/ER		TR-FRM
	TRAN/KWI/LAOIZ/ER	transformant	TRA*NS/FOR/MANT
trans	TRANZ	transformation	TRA*NS/FOR/MAIGS
	(not TRANS; see trance)		TR-FRM/MAIGS
trans-	TRA*NS	transformiminase	TRA*NS/FOR/MIM/NAIS
transabdominal	TRA*NS/AB/DOM/NAL	transfructosylase	TRA*NS/FRUKT/SIL/AIS
transacetylase	TRA*NS/AI/SET/LAIS	transfuse	TRA*NS/FAOUZ
	TRA*NS/AS/TIL/AIS	transfusion	TRA*NS/FAOUGS
transacetylation	TRA*NS/AI/SET/LAIGS	transgenation	TRA*NS/JE/NAIGS
	TRA*NS/AS/TIL/AIGS	transglucosylase	TRA*NS/GLAOUK/SIL/AIS
transaction	TRA*NS/A*BGS	transglutaminase	TRA*NS/GLAOU/TAM/NAIS
transactional	TRA*NS/A*BGS/NAL	transglycosidation	TRA*NS/GLAOIK/SI/DAIGS
transacylase	TRA*NS/AS/LAIS	transglycosylase	TRA*NS/GLAOIK/SIL/AIS
transacylation	TRA*NS/AS/LAIGS	transhexosylase	TRA*NS/HEX/SIL/AIS
transaldolase	TRA*NS/ALD/LAIS	transhiatal	TRA*NS/HAOI/AI/TAL
	TRA*NS/AL/DO/LAIS		TRA*NS/HAOI/YAI/TAL
transaldolation	TRA*NS/ALD/LAIGS	transient	TRAN/SHENT
	TRA*NS/AL/DO/LAIGS		TRA*NS/YENT
transamidinase	TRA*NS/AM/DI/NAIS		TRANZ/YENT
	TRA*NS/AM/DIN/AIS	transiliac	TRA*NS/IL/YAK
transamidination	TRA*NS/AM/DI/NAIGS		TRAN/SIL/YAK
transaminase	TRA*NS/AM/NAIS	transilient	TRAN/SIL/YENT
transamination	TRA*NS/AM/NAIGS	transillumination	TRA*NS/LAOUM/NAIGS
transanimation	TRA*NS/AN/MAIGS		TRA*NS/IL/LAOUM/NAIGS
transaortic	TRA*NS/AI/ORT/IK	transinsular	TRA*NS/INS/LAR
transappendageal	TRA*NS/AI/PEND/JAOEL	transischiac	TRA*NS/IS/KAK
transatrial	TRA*NS/AI/TRAL		TRA*NS/IS/KAOE/AK
transaudient	TRA*NS/AUD/YENT	transisthmian	TRA*NS/IS/MAN
transaxial	TRA*NS/AX/YAL		TRA*NS/IS/MAOE/YAN
transbasal	TRA*NS/BAI/SAL	transistor	TRAN/SIS/TOR
transcalent	TRA*NS/KAI/LENT		TRAN/ZIS/TOR
	TRA*NS/KAIL/ENT	transition	TRAN/SIGS
transcalifornium	TRA*NS/KAL/FORN/YUM	transitional	TRAN/SIGS/NAL

transketolase	TRA*NS/KAOET/LAIS	transthoracotomy	TRA*NS/THOR/KOT/M*I
transketolation	TRA*NS/KAOET/LAIGS	transtracheal	TRA*NS/TRAIK/YAL
translateral	TRA*NS/LAT/RAL	transtympanic	TRA*NS/TIM/PAN/IK
translation	TRA*NS/LAIGS	transubstantiation	TRAN/SUB/STAN/SHAIGS
translocation	TRA*NS/LOE/KAIGS	transud-	TRAN/SAOU/D-
translucent	TRA*NS/LAOUS/ENT		TRA*NS/YAOU/D-
translumbar	TRA*NS/LUM/BAR	transudate	TRAN/SAOU/DAIT
transluminal	TRA*NS/LAOUM/NAL	transudation	TRAN/SAOU/DAIGS
transmeatal	TRA*NS/MAOE/AI/TAL	transudative	TRAN/SAOU/DAIT/IV
	TRA*NS/MAOE/YAI/TAL		TRAN/SAOUD/TIV
transmembrane	TRA*NS/MEM/BRAIN	transude	TRAN/SAOUD
transmethylase	TRA*NS/M*ET/LAIS	transuranium	TRA*NS/YAOU/RAIN/YUM
transmethylation	TRA*NS/M*ET/LAIGS	transureteroureteral	TRA*NS/YAOU/RAOET/RO/YAOU/
transmigration	TRA*NS/MAOI/GRAIGS		RAOET/RAL
transmissible	TRA*NS/MIS/-BL	transureteroureterostomy	TRA*NS/YAOU/RAOET/RO/YAOU/
	TRA*NS/MISZ/-BL		RAOET/RO*S/M*I
	TRA*NS/MIS/SIBL	transurethral	TRA*NS/YAOU/RAO*ET/RAL
transmission	TRA*NS/MIGS	transvaginal	TRA*NS/VAJ/NAL
transmitter	TRA*NS/MIT/ER	transvaterian	TRA*NS/VA/TAOERN
transmural	TRA*NS/MAOURL		TRA*NS/VA/TAOER/YAN
transmutation	TRA*NS/MAOU/TAIGS	transvector	TRA*NS/VEK/TOR
transneuronal	TRA*NS/NAOU/RONL	transventricular	TRA*NS/VEN/TRIK/LAR
	TRA*NS/NAOU/ROENL	transversa	TRA*NS/VER/SA
transocular	TRA*NS/OK/LAR	transversae	TRA*NS/VER/SAE
transonance	TRA*NS/NANS	transversal	TRA*NS/VER/SAL
	TRAN/SO/NANS	Trans-Ver-Sal	TRA*NS/H-F/VER/H-F/SAL
transorbital	TRA*NS/ORB/TAL	transversalis	TRA*NS/VER/SAI/LIS
transovarial	TRA*NS/O/VAIRL	transversaria	TRA*NS/VER/SAIR/YA
transovarian	TRA*NS/O/VAIRN	transversarii	TRA*NS/VER/SAIR/YAOI
transoximinase	TRA*NS/OK/SIM/NAIS	transversarium	TRA*NS/VER/SAIRM
transpalatal	TRA*NS/PAL/TAL		TRA*NS/VER/SAIR/YUM
transparent	TRA*NS/PARNT	transverse	TRA*NS/VERS
transparietal	TRA*NS/PRAOI/TAL	transversectomy	TRA*NS/VER/SEKT/M*I
transpentosylase	TRA*NS/PENT/SIL/AIS	transversi	TRA*NS/VER/SAOI
transpeptidase	TRA*NS/PEPT/DAIS	transversion	TRA*NS/VERGS
transpeptidation	TRA*NS/PEPT/DAIGS	transversocostal	TRA*NS/VERS/KOS/TAL
transperitoneal	TRA*NS/PERT/NAOEL		TRA*NS/VER/SO/KOS/TAL
transphosphatase	TRA*NS/FOS/FA/TAIS	transversotomy	TRA*NS/VER/SOT/M*I
transphosphorylase	TRA*NS/FOS/FOR/LAIS	transversourethralis	TRA*NS/VERS/YAOUR/THRAI/LIS
	TRA*NS/FOS/FOER/LAIS		TRA*NS/VER/SO/YAOUR/THRAI/
transphosphorylation	TRA*NS/FOS/FOR/LAIGS		LIS
	TRA*NS/FOS/FOER/LAIGS	transversum	TRA*NS/VER/SUM
transpirable	TRA*NS/PAOIRBL		TRA*NS/VERS/UM
	TRA*NS/PAOIR/-BL	transversus	TRA*NS/VER/SUS
	TRAN/SPAOIRBL	transvesical	TRA*NS/VES/KAL
	TRAN/SPAOIR/-BL	transvestic	TRA*NS/V*ES/IK
transpiration	TRA*NS/PRAIGS	transvestism	TRA*NS/VES/TIFM
	TRA*NS/PI/RAIGS	transvestite	TRA*NS/VES/TAOIT
	TRAN/SPRAIGS	transvestitism	TRA*NS/V*ES/TIFM
	TRAN/SPI/RAIGS	Trantas	TRAN/TAS
transpire	TRA*NS/PAOIR	Tranxene	TRAN/ZAOEN
	TRAN/SPAOIR	Tranxene-SD	TRAN/ZAOEN/S-RBGS/D*RBGS
transplacenta	TRA*NS/PLA/SEN/TA	tranylcypromine	TRANL/SIP/RO/MAOEN
transplacental	TRA*NS/PLA/SEN/TAL		TRAN/IL/SIP/RO/MAOEN
transplant	TRA*NS/PLANT	trapezia	TRA/PAOEZ/YA
transplantar	TRA*NS/PLAN/TAR	trapezial	TRA/PAOEZ/YAL
Trans-Plantar	TRA*NS/H-F/PLAN/TAR	trapeziform	TRA/PAOEZ/FORM
transplantation	TRA*NS/PLAN/TAIGS	trapezii	TRA/PAOIZ/YAOI
transpleural	TRA*NS/PLAOURL	trapeziometacarpal	TRA/PAOEZ/YO/MET/KAR/PAL
transport	TRA*NS/PORT	trapezium	TRA/PAOEZ/YUM
	TR-PT	trapezius	TRA/PAOEZ/YUS
transportation	TRA*NS/POR/TAIGS	trapezoid	TRAP/ZOID
	TR-PGS	trapezoideum	TRAP/ZOID/YUM
transposase	TRA*NS/POEZ/AIS	trapidil	TRAP/DIL
transpose	TRA*NS/POEZ	Trapp	TRA*P
transposition	TRA*NS/POGS		(not TRAP; see trap)
	TRA*NS/PO/SIGS	Traube	TROUB
transposon	TRA*NS/POE/ZON		TRAUB
	TRA*NS/POE/SON	trauma	TRAU/MA
transpubic	TRA*NS/PAOUB/IK	TraumaCal	TRAUM/KAL
transsacral	TRA*NS/SAI/KRAL		TRAU/MA/KAL
transsection	TRA*NS/S*EBGS	traumasthenia	TRAU/MAS/THAOEN/YA
	(not TRAN/S*EBGS; see	traumat(o)-	TRAUM/T(O)
	transection)	traumata	TRAUM/TA
transsegmental	TRA*NS/SEG/MEN/TAL	traumatherapy	TRAUM/THER/PI
transseptal	TRA*NS/SEP/TAL		TRAU/MA/THER/PI
transsexual	TRA*NS/SEX/YAOUL	traumatic	TRAU/MAT/IK
transsexualism	TRA*NS/SEX/YAOUL/IFM	traumatica	TRAU/MAT/KA
transsphenoidal	TRA*NS/SFAOE/NOI/DAL	traumaticum	TRAU/MAT/KUM
transsternal	TRA*NS/STERNL	traumatism	TRAUM/TIFM
transsulfurase	TRA*NS/SUL/FRAIS	traumatize	TRAUM/TAOIZ
	TRA*NS/SUL/FUR/AIS	traumatologist	TRAUM/TO*LGS
transsynaptic	TRA*NS/SNAPT/IK	traumatology	TRAUM/TOLG
	TRA*NS/SI/NAPT/IK	traumatonesis	TRAUM/TO/NAOE/SIS
transtemporal	TRA*NS/TEFRP/RAL		TRAUM/TON/SIS
transtentorial	TRA*NS/TEN/TOIRL	traumatopathy	TRAUM/TOP/TH*I
transthalamic	TRA*NS/THA/LAM/IK	traumatopnea	TRAUM/TOP/NA
transthermia	TRA*NS/THERM/YA		TRAUM/TOP/NAOE/YA
transthoracic	TRA*NS/THRAS/IK	traumatopyra	TRAUM/TO/PAOI/RA

traumatosepsis	TRAUM/TO/SEP/SIS		-tresia	TREP/PE
traumatotherapy	TRAUM/TO/THER/PI		-tresia	TRAOEZ/YA
travail	TRA/VAIL		Tresilian	TRE/SIL/YAN
Travase Ointment	TRAV/AIZ/OINT/-MT			TRAOE/SIL/YAN
	TRAV/AIS/OINT/-MT		tresis	TRAOE/SIS
traveler	TRAV/LER		tretinoin	TRET/NOIN
	TRAVL/ER		Treves	TRAOEVZ
traverse	TRAV/ERS			TRAOEVS
	TRA/VERS		Trexan	TREK/SAN
tray	TRAI		tri-	TR*I
trazodone	TRAIZ/DOEN		Triacet Cream	TRAOI/SET/KRAOEM
	TRAZ/DOEN			TR*I/SET/KRAOEM
treacle	TRAOEK/-L		triacetate	TR*I/AS/TAIT
tread	TRED		triacetic	TR*I/AI/SAOET/IK
treadmill	TRED/MIL		triacetin	TR*I/AS/TIN
treat	TRAOET		triacetylglycerol	TR*I/AS/TIL/GLIS/ROL
treatment	TRAOEMT		triacetyloleandomycin	TR*I/AS/TIL/OEL/YAND/MAOI/
	TRAOET/-MT			SIN
trebenzomine	TRE/BENZ/MAOEN			TR*I/AS/TIL/OEL/YAN/DO/MAOI/
Trecator	TREK/TOR			SIN
Trecator-SC	TREK/TOR/S-RBGS/KR*RBGS		triacid	TR*I/AS/ID
tree	TRAOE		triacylglycerol	TR*I/AS/IL/GRIS/ROL
trehala	TRAOE/HA/LA		triad	TR*I/AD
	TRAOE/HAI/LA		triaditis	TR*I/AD/AOITS
trehalose	TRAOE/HA/LOES			TR*I/DAOITS
	TRAOE/HAI/LOES			TRAOI/DAOITS
Treitz	TRAOITS		triage	TRAOE/AJ
trema	TRAOE/MA			TRAOE/YAJ
Trematoda	TREM/TOE/DA		Triamcinair Cream	TR*I/AM/SI/NAIR/KRAOEM
trematode	TREM/TOED			TR*I/AM/SIN/AIR/KRAOEM
trematoid	TREM/TOID		triamcinolone	TR*I/AM/SIN/LOEN
trematodiasis	TREM/TO/DAOI/SIS		tri-amelia	TR*I/AI/MAOEL/YA
tremble	TREM/-BL		triamine	TR*I/AM/MIN
tremelloid	TREM/LOID			TR*I/AM/AOEN
tremellose	TREM/LOES		Triaminic	TRAOI/MIN/IK
tremens	TRAOE/MENZ			TR*I/MIN/IK
	TREM/ENZ		Triaminic-12	TRAOI/MIN/IK/12
tremogram	TREM/GRAM			TR*I/MIN/IK/12
	TRAOEM/GRAM		Triaminic-DM	TRAOI/MIN/IK/D-RBGS/M*RBGS
tremograph	TREM/GRAF			TR*I/MIN/IK/D-RBGS/M*RBGS
	TRAOEM/GRAF		Triaminic TR	TRAOI/MIN/IK/T-RBGS/R*RBGS
tremolabile	TREM/LAI/BAOIL			TR*I/MIN/IK/T-RBGS/R*RBGS
	TREM/LAI/BIL		Triaminicin	TRAOI/MIN/SIN
	TRAOEM/LAI/BAOIL			TR*I/MIN/SIN
	TRAOEM/LAI/BIL		Triaminicol	TRAOI/MIN/KOL
tremophobia	TREM/FOEB/YA			TR*I/MIN/KOL
	TRAOEM/FOEB/YA		triamterene	TR*I/AM/TRAOEN
tremor	TREM/MOR			TR*I/AM/TE/RAOEN
tremorgram	TREM/MOR/GRAM			TR*I/AM/TER/AOEN
tremostable	TREM/STABL		triamylose	TR*I/AM/LOES
	TRAOEM/STABL		triangle	TR*I/ANG/-L
tremul-	TREM/L-		triangular	TR*I/ANG/LAR
	TREM/YAOU/L-		triangulare	TR*I/ANG/LAI/RAOE
	TREM/YU/L-		triangularis	TR*I/ANG/LAI/RIS
tremulor	TREM/LOR		triantebrachia	TR*I/AENT/BRAIK/YA
tremulous	TREM/LOUS		Triatoma	TRAOI/TOE/MA
trench	TREFRPBLG			TR*I/AT/MA
	TREN/-FP		triatomic	TR*I/AI/TOM/IK
trend	TREND		Triatominae	TRAOI/TOEM/NAE
Trendelenburg	TREN/DEL/EN/BURG		Triavil	TRAOI/VIL
trendscriber	TREND/SKRAOIB/ER			TR*I/VIL
trendscription	TREND/SKRIPGS		triazolam	TR*I/AIZ/LAM
Trental	TREN/TAL			TR*I/A*Z/LAM
trepan	TRE/PAN		triazologuanine	TRAOI/ZOL/GAU/NAOEN
	TRAOE/PAN			TR*I/ZOL/GAU/NAOEN
trepanation	TREP/NAIGS		tribade	TRIB/AID
trephination	TREF/NAIGS		tribadism	TRIB/DIFM
trephine	TRE/FAOIN			TRIB/AID/IFM
	TRE/FAOEN		tribady	TRIB/DI
trephinement	TRE/FAOIN/-MT			TRIB/AI/DI
trephiner	TRE/FAOIN/ER		tribasic	TR*I/BAIS/IK
trephocyte	TREF/SAO*IT		tribasilar	TR*I/BAS/LAR
trepidans	TREP/DANZ		tribe	TRAOIB
trepidant	TREP/DANT		tribology	TRI/BOLG
trepidatio	TREP/DAI/SHOE			TR*I/BOLG
	TREP/DAIRB/YOE		triboluminescence	TRIB/LAOUM/NES/ENS
trepidatio cordis	TREP/DAI/SHOE/KOR/DIS		tribrachia	TR*I/BRAIK/YA
	TREP/DAIRB/YOE/KOR/DIS		tribrachius	TR*I/BRAIK/YUS
trepidation	TREP/DAIGS		tribromaloin	TR*I/BROE/MAL/WIN
treponema	TREP/NAOE/MA			TR*I/BROEM/AL/WIN
Treponema	K-P/TREP/NAOE/MA		tribromide	TR*I/BROE/MAOID
treponemal	TREP/NAOE/MAL		tribromoethanol	TR*I/BROEM/*ET/NOL
Treponemataceae	TREP/NAOEM/TAIS/YAE		tribromoethyl	TR*I/BROEM/*ET/IL
treponematosis	TREP/NAOEM/TOE/SIS		tribromsalan	TR*I/BROM/SA/LAN
treponeme	TREP/NAOEM			TR*I/BROM/SLAN
treponemiasis	TREP/NAOE/MAOI/SIS		tributyrase	TR*I/BAOUT/RAIS
treponemicidal	TREP/NAOEM/SAOI/DAL		tributyrin	TR*I/BAOUT/RIN
trepopnea	TRAOE/POP/NAOE/YA		tributyrinase	TR*I/BAOUT/RIN/NAIS
treppe	TREP/PAOE			TR*I/BAOUT/RIN/AIS

	TR*I/BAOU/TIR/NAIS
tributyrylglycerol	TR*I/BAOUT/RIL/GLIS/ROL
tricalcic	TR*I/KALS/IK
tricalcium	TR*I/KALS/YUM
tricarboxylic	TR*I/KAR/BOK/SIL/IK
tricellular	TR*I/SEL/YAOU/LAR
tricephalus	TR*I/SEF/LUS
triceps	TR*I/SEPS
triceptor	TR*I/SEP/TOR
tricheiria	TR*I/KAOIR/YA
trich(o)-	TRIK
	TRI/K(O)
trichalgia	TRIK/AL/JA
trichangion	TRIK/AN/JON
trichatrophia	TRIK/AI/TROEF/YA
trichauxis	TRIK/AUK/SIS
-trichia	TRIK/YA
trichiasis	TRI/KAOI/SIS
trichilemmal	TRIK/LEM/MAL
trichilemmoma	TRIK/LEM/MOE/MA
	TRIK/LE/MOE/MA
trichina	TRI/KAOI/NA
trichinae	TRI/KAOI/NAE
Trichinella	TRIK/NEL/LA
trichinelliasis	TRIK/NEL/LAOI/SIS
Trichinelloidea	TRIK/NEL/LOID/YA
	TRIK/NEL/OID/YA
trichinellosis	TRIK/NEL/LOE/SIS
trichiniasis	TRIK/NAOI/SIS
trichiniferous	TRIK/NIF/ROUS
trichinization	TRIK/NI/ZAIGS
trichinosis	TRIK/NOE/SIS
trichinous	TRIK/NOUS
trichion	TRIK/YON
trichite	TRIK/AOIT
trichitis	TRI/KAOITS
trichloral	TR*I/KLORL
trichlorfon	TR*I/KLOR/FON
trichloride	TR*I/KLOR/AOID
trichlormethane	TR*I/KLOR/M*ET/AIN
trichlormethiazide	TR*I/KLOR/ME/THAOI/ZAOID
trichlormethine	TR*I/KLOR/M*ET/AOEN
trichloro-	TR*I/KLOR
	TR*I/KLOR/RO
trichloroacetaldehyde	TR*I/KLOR/AS/TALD/HAOID
	TR*I/KLOR/AS/ET/ALD/HAOID
trichloroacetic	TR*I/KLOR/AI/SAOET/IK
trichloroethane	TR*I/KLOR/*ET/AIN
trichloroethanol	TR*I/KLOR/*ET/NOL
trichloroethene	TR*I/KLOR/*ET/AOEN
trichloroethyl	TR*I/KLOR/*ET/IL
trichloroethylene	TR*I/KLOR/*ET/LAOEN
trichlorofluoromethane	TR*I/KLOR/FLAOUR/M*ET/AIN
trichloromethane	TR*I/KLOR/M*ET/AIN
trichloromethylchloroformate	
	TR*I/KLOR/M*ET/IL/KLOR/FOR/ MAIT
trichloromonofluoromethane	
	TR*I/KLOR/MON/FLAOUR/M*ET/ AIN
trichlorophenol	TR*I/KLOR/FAOE/NOL
trichlorotrivinylarsine	TR*I/KLOR/TR*I/VAOINL/AR/SIN
tricho-	TRIK
	TRI/KO
trichoanesthesia	TRIK/ANS/THAOEZ/YA
trichobacteria	TRIK/BAK/TAOER/YA
trichobasalioma	TRIK/BAI/SAL/YOE/MA/
hyalinicum	HAOI/LIN/KUM
trichobezoar	TRIK/BE/ZOER
	TRIK/BAOE/ZOER
trichocardia	TRIK/KARD/YA
trichocephaliasis	TRIK/SEF/LAOI/SIS
trichocephalosis	TRIK/SEF/LOE/SIS
Trichocephalus	TRIK/SEF/LUS
trichoclasia	TRIK/KLAIZ/YA
trichoclasis	TRI/KOK/LA/SIS
	TRIK/OK/LA/SIS
trichocryptosis	TRIK/KRIP/TOE/SIS
trichocyst	TRIK/S*IS
Trichodectes	TRIK/DEK/TAOEZ
Trichoderma	TRIK/DER/MA
trichodiscoma	TRIK/DIS/KOE/MA
trichodynia	TRIK/DIN/YA
trichoepithelioma	TRIK/EP/THAOEL/YOE/MA
trichoesthesia	TRIK/ES/THAOEZ/YA
trichoesthesiometer	TRIK/ES/THAOEZ/YOM/TER
trichofibroacanthoma	TRIK/FAOI/BRO/AK/AN/THOE/MA
trichofibroepithelioma	TRIK/FAOI/BRO/EP/THAOEL/ YOE/MA

trichofolliculoma	TRIK/FLIK/LOE/MA
trichogen	TR*IK/JEN
	TRI/KO/JEN
	(not TRIK/JEN; see trick general(ly))
trichogenous	TRI/KOJ/NOUS
trichoglossia	TRIK/GLOS/YA
trichographism	TRI/KOG/RA/FIFM
trichohyalin	TRIK/HAOI/LIN
trichoid	TRIK/OID
tricholemmome	TRIK/LE/MOE/MA
	TRIK/LEM/MOE/MA
tricholeukocyte	TRIK/LAOUK/SAO*IT
tricholith	TRIK/L*IT
trichologia	TRIK/LOE/JA
trichology	TRI/KOLG
trichoma	TRI/KOE/MA
trichomadesis	TRIK/MA/DAOE/SIS
trichomania	TRIK/MAIN/YA
trichomatose	TRI/KOEM/TOES
trichomatosis	TRI/KOEM/TOE/SIS
trichomatous	TRI/KOEM/TOUS
trichome	TRI/KOEM
	TRIK/KOEM
trichomegaly	TRIK/MEG/LI
trichomonacidal	TRIK/MOEN/SAOI/DAL
trichomonacide	TRIK/MOEN/SAO*ID
trichomonad	TRIK/MOE/NAD
trichomonadicidal	TRIK/MOE/NAD/SAOI/DAL
Trichomonadidae	TRIK/MOE/NAD/DAE
trichomonal	TRIK/MOENL
Trichomonas	TRIK/MOE/NAS
trichomoniasis	TRIK/MOE/NAOI/SIS
	TRIK/MO/NAOI/SIS
Trichomycetes	TRIK/MAOI/SAOE/TAOEZ
trichomycetosis	TRIK/MAOIS/TOE/SIS
trichomycosis	TRIK/MAOI/KOE/SIS
trichonocardiosis	TRIK/NOE/KARD/YOE/SIS
trichonodosis	TRIK/NOE/DOE/SIS
	TRIK/NO/DOE/SIS
trichonosus	TRI/KON/SUS
trichopathic	TRIK/PA*T/IK
trichopathy	TRI/KOP/TH*I
trichophagy	TRI/KOF/JI
trichophobia	TRIK/FOEB/YA
trichophytic	TRIK/FIT/IK
trichophytid	TRI/KOF/TID
	TRIK/FAOI/TID
trichophytin	TRI/KOF/TIN
trichophytobezoar	TRIK/FAOIT/BE/ZOER
	TRIK/FAOIT/BAOE/ZOER
Trichophyton	TRI/KOF/TON
trichophytosis	TRIK/FAOI/TOE/SIS
trichopoliosis	TRIK/POEL/YOE/SIS
Trichoptera	TRI/KOPT/RA
trichoptilosis	TRIK/TI/LOE/SIS
	TRI/KOPT/LOE/SIS
trichorrhea	TRIK/RAOE/YA
trichorrhexis	TRIK/REK/SIS
trichoschisis	TRI/KOS/KI/SIS
	TRIK/OS/KI/SIS
trichoscopy	TRI/KOS/KPI
	TRIK/OS/KPI
trichosiderin	TRIK/SID/RIN
trichosis	TRI/KOE/SIS
Trichosoma	TRIK/SOE/MA
trichosomatous	TRIK/SOEM/TOUS
Trichosporon	TRI/KOS/PRON
	TRIK/SPORN
trichosporosis	TRIK/SPROE/SIS
	TRIK/SPOE/ROE/SIS
trichostasis	TRI/KO*S/SIS
trichostrongyle	TRIK/STRON/JIL
trichostrongyliasis	TRIK/STRONG/LAOI/SIS
Trichostrongylidae	TRIK/STRON/JIL/DAE
trichostrongylosis	TRIK/STRONG/LOE/SIS
Trichostrongylus	TRIK/STRONG/LUS
Trichothecium	TRIK/THAOES/YUM
trichothiodystrophy	TRIK/THAOI/DIS/TRO/FI
trichotillomania	TRIK/TIL/MAIN/YA
trichotomous	TRI/KOT/MOUS
trichotomy	TRI/KOT/M*I
trichotoxin	TRIK/TOK/SIN
trichotrophy	TRI/KOT/RO/FI
trichroic	TR*I/KROIK
	TR*I/KROE/IK
trichroism	TR*I/KROE/IFM
trichromat	TR*I/KROE/MAT
trichromatic	TR*I/KROE/MAT/IK

trichromatism	TR*I/KROEM/TIFM	trigeminal	TR*I/JEM/NAL
trichromatopsia	TR*I/KROEM/TOPS/YA	trigeminale	TR*I/JEM/NAI/LAOE
trichromic	TR*I/KROEM/IK	trigemini	TR*I/JEM/NAOI
trichterbrust	TRIK/TER/BRAO*US	trigeminus	TR*I/JEM/NUS
trichuriasis	TRI/KAOU/RAOI/SIS	trigeminy	TR*I/JEM/N*I
	TRIK/YAOU/RAOI/SIS	trigenic	TR*I/JEN/IK
	TRIK/YU/RAOI/SIS	trigger	TRIG/ER
Trichuris	TRI/KAOU/RIS	triglyceride	TR*I/GLIS/RAOID
	TRIK/YAOU/RIS	trigon(o)-	TR*I/GOEN
	TRIK/YU/RIS		TR*I/GOE/N(O)
Trichuroidea	TRI/KAOU/ROID/YA		TRIG/N-
	TRIK/YAOU/ROID/YA	trigona	TR*I/GOE/NA
	TRIK/YU/ROID/YA	trigonal	TR*I/GOENL
tricipital	TR*I/SIP/TAL	trigone	TR*I/GOEN
tricipitis	TR*I/SIP/TIS	trigonectomy	TR*I/GOEN/EKT/M*I
Tri-Clear Expectorant	TR*I/KLAOER/EX/PEKT/RANT	trigonelline	TRIG/NEL/LIN
	TR*I/KLAOER/KP-PT/RANT	trigonid	TR*I/GOE/NID
Tri-Clear Syrup	TR*I/KLAOER/SIR/RUP		TR*I/GON/ID
triclobisonium	TR*I/KLOEB/SOEN/YUM	trigonitis	TRIG/NAOITS
triclocarban	TR*I/KLOE/KAR/BAN	trigonocephalia	TRIG/NO/SFAIL/YA
triclofenol	TR*I/KLOEF/NOL	trigonocephalic	TRIG/NO/SFAL/IK
triclosan	TR*I/KLOE/SAN	trigonocephalus	TRIG/NO/SEF/LUS
Tricol	TR*I/KOL	trigonocephaly	TRIG/NO/SEF/LI
tricorn	TR*I/KORN		TR*I/GOEN/SEF/LI
tricornute	TR*I/KOR/NAOUT	trigonotome	TR*I/GOEN/TOEM
tricresol	TR*I/KRAOE/SOL	trigonum	TR*I/GOE/NUM
tricrotic	TR*I/KROT/IK		TR*I/GOEN/UM
tricrotism	TR*I/KROE/TIFM	trihexyphenidyl	TR*I/HEX/FEN/DIL
	TR*I/KRO/TIFM	trihybrid	TR*I/HAOI/BRID
tricrotous	TR*I/KROE/TOUS	trihydrate	TR*I/HAOI/DRAIT
	TR*I/KROET/OUS	trihydric	TR*I/HAOI/DRIK
Tricula	TRIK/YAOU/LA	trihydrol	TR*I/HAOI/DROL
	TRIK/YU/LA	trihydroxide	TR*I/HAOI/DROX/AOID
tricuspid	TR*I/KUS/PID		TR*I/HAOI/DROK/SAOID
tricuspidal	TR*I/KUS/PI/DAL	trihydroxyestrin	TR*I/HAOI/DROX/ES/TRIN
tricuspidalis	TR*I/KUS/PI/DAI/LIS	Tri-Immunol	TR*I/IM/YAOU/NOL
tricuspidate	TR*I/KUS/PI/DAIT		TR*I/IM/MAOU/NOL
tricyclamol	TR*I/SAOI/KLA/MOL	triiniodymus	TR*I/IN/YOD/MUS
tricyclic	TR*I/SAOIK/LIK	triiodide	TR*I/AOI/DAOID
tridactylism	TR*I/DAKT/LIFM	triiodomethane	TR*I/AOI/DO/M*ET/AIN
tridactylous	TR*I/DAKT/LOUS	triiodothyronine	TR*I/AOI/OED/THAOIR/NAOEN
trident	TR*I/DENT		TR*I/AOI/DO/THAOIR/NAOEN
tridentate	TR*I/DEN/TAIT	triketohydrindene	TR*I/KAOET/HAOI/DRIN/DAOEN
tridermic	TR*I/DERM/IK	triketopurine	TR*I/KAOET/PAOUR/AOEN
tridermogenesis	TR*I/DERM/JEN/SIS		TR*I/KAOET/PAOUR/RIN
tridermoma	TR*I/DER/MOE/MA	trilabe	TR*I/LAIB
Tridesilon	TR*I/DES/LON	Trilafon	TRIL/FON
tridigitate	TR*I/DIJ/TAIT	trilaminar	TR*I/LAM/NAR
tridihexethyl	TR*I/DI/HEX/*ET/IL	trilateral	TR*I/LAT/RAL
Tridil	TR*I/DIL	Tri-Levlen	TR*I/LEV/LEN
Tridione	TR*I/DI/OEN	Trilisate	TRIL/SAIT
tridymite	TRID/MAOIT	Trillium	TRIL/YUM
tridymus	TRID/MUS	trilobate	TR*I/LOE/BAIT
trielcon	TR*I/EL/KON	trilobectomy	TR*I/LOE/BEKT/M*I
trientine	TR*I/EN/TAOEN	trilobed	TR*I/LOEB/-D
triester	TR*I/ES/TER	trilocular	TR*I/LOK/LAR
	TR*I/*ES/ER	trilogy	TRIL/JI
triethanolamine	TR*I/*ET/NOL/MAOEN		TRILG
triethylamine	TR*I/*ET/IL/AM/MIN	trilostane	TRAOIL/STAIN
triethylene	TR*I/*ET/LAOEN		TR*I/LO/STAIN
triethylenemelamine	TR*I/*ET/LAOEN/MEL/MAOEN	trimanual	TR*I/MAN/YAOUL
triethylenephosphoramide	TR*I/*ET/LAOEN/FOS/FOER/		TR*I/MAN/YUL
	MAOID		TR*I/MAN/YAL
	TR*I/*ET/LAOEN/FOS/FOR/	Trimastigamoeba	TR*I/MAS/TIG/MAOE/BA
	MAOID		TR*I/MA*S/GA/MAOE/BA
triethylenetetramine	TR*I/*ET/LAOEN/TET/RAM/AOEN	trimastigote	TR*I/MA*S/GOET
triethylenethiophosphoramide		trimensual	TR*I/MENS/YAL
	TR*I/*ET/LAOEN/THAOI/FOS/	trimeprazine	TR*I/MEP/RA/ZAOEN
	FOER/MAOID	trimer	TR*I/MER
	TR*I/*ET/LAOEN/THAOI/FOS/	trimercuric	TR*I/MER/KAOUR/IK
	FOR/MAOID	trimeric	TR*I/MER/IK
trifacial	TR*I/FAIRBL	trimester	TR*I/M*ES/ER
trifid	TR*I/FID		TR*I/MES/TER
triflocin	TR*I/FLOE/SIN	trimetaphan	TR*I/MET/FAN
triflumidate	TR*I/FLAOUM/DAIT	trimetaphosphatase	TR*I/MET/FOS/FA/TAIS
trifluoperazine	TR*I/FLAOU/PER/ZAOEN	trimetazidine	TR*I/ME/TAZ/DAOEN
trifluoromethyldeoxyuridine		trimethadione	TR*I/M*ET/DI/OEN
	TR*I/FLAOUR/M*ET/IL/DE/OX/	trimethaphan	TR*I/M*ET/FAN
	YAOUR/DAOEN	trimethidinium	TR*I/M*ET/DIN/YUM
trifluperidol	TR*I/FLAOU/PER/DOL	trimethidium	TR*I/ME/THID/YUM
	TR*I/FLAOU/P*ER/DOL	trimethobenzamide	TR*I/M*ET/BENZ/MAOID
triflupromazine	TR*I/FLAOU/PROEM/ZAOEN	trimethoprim	TR*I/M*ET/PRIM
trifluridine	TR*I/FLAOUR/DAOEN	trimethylacetate	TR*I/M*ET/IL/AS/TAIT
	TR*I/FLAOUR/DIN	trimethylamine	TR*I/M*ET/IL/AM/AOEN
trifocal	TR*I/FOE/KAL		TR*I/M*ET/IL/AM/MIN
trifoliosis	TR*I/FOEL/YOE/SIS	trimethylaminuria	TR*I/M*ET/IL/AM/NAOUR/YA
trifurcation	TR*I/FUR/KAIGS	trimethylcarbinol	TR*I/M*ET/IL/KARB/NOL
trigastric	TR*I/GAS/TRIK	trimethylene	TR*I/M*ET/LAOEN
trigemina	TR*I/JEM/NA	trimethylethylene	TR*I/M*ET/IL/*ET/LAOEN

trimethylglycocoll	TR*I/M*ET/IL/GLAOIK/KOL	triplokoria	TRIP/LO/KOER/YA
trimethylomelamine	TR*I/M*ET/LO/MEL/MAOEN	triplopia	TRIP/LOEP/YA
trimetozine	TR*I/MET/ZAOEN	tripod	TR*I/POD
trimetrexate	TR*I/ME/TREK/SAIT	tripodia	TR*I/POED/YA
	TR*I/ME/TREX/AIT	tripoli	TRIP/LAOE
trimipramine	TR*I/MIP/RA/MAOEN	tripositive	TR*I/POZ/TIV
trimorphic	TR*I/MOR/FIK	triprolidine	TR*I/PROEL/DAOEN
trimorphism	TR*I/MOR/FIFM	triprosopus	TR*I/PRO/SOE/PUS
trimorphous	TR*I/MOR/FOUS	tripsis	TRIP/SIS
Trimox	TR*I/MOX	-tripsy	TRIP/SI
Trimpex	TRIM/PEX	triptokoria	TRIPT/KOER/YA
Trimstat	TRIM/STAT		TRIP/TO/KOER/YA
Trinalin	TRIN/LIN	tripus	TR*I/PUS
Trind	TRIND	triquetra	TR*I/KWAOE/TRA
Trind-DM	TRIND/D-RBGS/M*RBGS		TR*I/KWET/RA
trinegative	TR*I/NEG/TIV	triquetral	TR*I/KWAOE/TRAL
trineural	TR*I/NAOURL		TR*I/KWAOET/RAL
trineuric	TR*I/NAOUR/IK		TR*I/KWET/RAL
trinitrate	TR*I/NAOI/TRAIT	triquetrous	TR*I/KWAOE/TROUS
trinitrin	TR*I/NAOI/TRIN		TR*I/KWAOET/ROUS
trinitrocellulose	TR*I/NAOI/TRO/SEL/YAOU/LOES		TR*I/KWET/ROUS
trinitrocresol	TR*I/NAOI/TRO/KRAOE/SOL	triquetrum	TR*I/KWAOE/TRUM
trinitroglycerin	TR*I/NAOI/TRO/GLIS/RIN		TR*I/KWAOET/RUM
trinitrophenol	TR*I/NAOI/TRO/FAOE/NOL		TR*I/KWET/RUM
trinitrotoluene	TR*I/NAOI/TRO/TOL/YAOEN	triradial	TR*I/RAID/YAL
	TR*I/NAOI/TRO/TOL/YAOU/AOEN	triradiate	TR*I/RAID/YAIT
trinitrotoluol	TR*I/NAO/TRO/TOL/YOL	triradiation	TR*I/RAID/YAIGS
	TR*I/NAOI/TRO/TOL/YAOU/OL	triradius	TR*I/RAID/YUS
trinomial	TR*I/NOEM/YAL	trisaccharidase	TR*I/SAK/RI/DAIS
Tri-Norinyl	TR*I/NOR/NIL	trisaccharide	TR*I/SAK/RAOID
Trinsicon	TRINS/KON	trisimilitubis	TR*I/SIM/LAOI/TAOU/BIS
trinucleate	TR*I/NAOUK/LAIT	triskaidekaphobia	TRIS/KAOI/DEK/FOEB/YA
trinucleotide	TR*I/NAOUK/LO/TAOID	trismic	TRIZ/MIK
trio-	TRAOI	trismoid	TRIZ/MOID
	TR*I	trismus	TRIZ/MUS
	TR*I/YO	trisodium	TR*I/SOED/YUM
Trio-Dophilus	TRAOI/DOF/LUS	trisomia	TR*I/SOEM/YA
triokinase	TRAOI/KAOI/NAIS	trisomic	TR*I/SOEM/IK
triolein	TR*I/OEL/YIN	trisomy	TR*I/SOE/M*I
triolism	TR*I/LIFM	Trisoralen	TR*I/SOR/LEN
	TR*I/YO/LIFM		TR*I/SOER/LEN
trionym	TR*I/NIM	trisplanchnic	TR*I/SPLANG/NIK
	TR*I/YO/NIM	tristearin	TR*I/STAOER/RIN
triophthalmos	TR*I/OF/THAL/MOS	tristichia	TR*I/STIK/YA
triorchid	TR*I/ORK/ID	tristimania	TR*IS/MAIN/YA
	TR*I/OR/KID	trisubstituted	TR*I/SUB/STAOUT/-D
triorchis	TR*I/OR/KIS	Trisulfam	TR*I/SUL/FAM
triorchism	TR*I/OR/KIFM	trisulcant	TR*I/SUL/KANT
triose	TR*I/OES	trisulcate	TR*I/SUL/KAIT
	TR*I/YOES	trisulfapyrimidine	TR*I/SUL/FA/PAOI/RIM/DAOEN
triosekinase	TR*I/OES/KAOI/NAIS	trisulfate	TR*I/SUL/FAIT
	TR*I/YOES/KAOI/NAIS	trisulfide	TR*I/SUL/FAOID
triosephosphate	TR*I/OES/FOS/FAIT	trisymptome	TR*I/SIFRP/TOEM
	TR*I/YOES/FOS/FAIT		TR*I/SIM/TOEM
triotus	TR*I/YOE/TUS	tritanomalopia	TRAOIT/NOM/LOEP/YA
	TR*I/O/TUS		TR*I/TA/NOM/LOEP/YA
trioxide	TR*I/OK/SAOID	tritanomalous	TRAOIT/NOM/LOUS
trioxsalen	TR*I/OX/LEN		TR*I/TA/NOM/LOUS
trioxymethylene	TR*I/OX/M*ET/LAOEN	tritanomaly	TRAOIT/NOM/LI
tripalmitin	TR*I/PAL/MI/TIN		TR*I/TA/NOM/LI
tripara	TRIP/RA	tritanope	TRAOIT/NOEP
triparanol	TR*I/PAR/NOL		TR*I/TA/NOEP
tripartite	TR*I/PAR/TAOIT	tritanopia	TRAOIT/NOEP/YA
tripelennamine	TR*I/PE/LEN/MAOEN		TR*I/TA/NOEP/YA
	TR*I/PE/LEN/MIN	tritanopic	TRAOIT/NOP/IK
tripeptide	TR*I/PEP/TID		TR*I/TA/NOP/IK
triphalangeal	TR*I/FLAN/JAL	tritanopsia	TRAOIT/NOPS/YA
triphalangia	TR*I/FLAN/JA		TR*I/TA/NOPS/YA
triphalangism	TR*I/FAL/AN/JIFM	triterpene	TR*I/TER/PAOEN
	TR*I/FLAN/JIFM	tritiate	TRIT/YAIT
triphasic	TR*I/FAEZ/IK		TRIRB/YAIT
	TR*I/FAIZ/IK	tritiated	TRIT/YAIT/-D
Triphasil	TR*I/FA/SIL		TRIRB/YAIT/-D
Triphasil-21	TR*I/FA/SIL/2/1	triticea	TR*I/TIRB/YA
Triphasil-28	TR*I/FA/SIL/28		TR*I/TIS/YA
triphosphatase	TR*I/FOS/FA/TAIS	triticeal	TR*I/TIRBL
triphosphate	TR*I/FOS/FAIT		TR*I/TIS/YAL
triphosphopyridine	TR*I/FOS/FO/PIR/DAOEN	triticeoglossus	TR*I/TIRB/YO/GLOS/SUS
triphthemia	TRIF/THAOEM/YA	triticeous	TR*I/TIRBS
Tripier	TRAOEP/YAI		TR*I/TIS/YOUS
	TRIP/YAI	triticeum	TR*I/TIRB/UM
triplant	TR*I/PLANT		TR*I/TIRB/YUM
triplegia	TR*I/PLAOE/JA		TR*I/TIS/YUM
triplet	TRIP/LET	tritici	TRIT/SAOI
triplex	TR*I/PLEX	tritium	TRIT/YUM
triplo-	TRIP/LO		TRIRB/UM
triploblastic	TRIP/LO/BLA*S/IK		TRIRB/YUM
triploid	TRIP/LOID	tritocaline	TRIT/KAL/AOEN
triploidy	TRIP/LOI/DI	tritoqualine	TRIT/KWAL/AOEN

Tritrichomonas	TR*I/TRIK/MOE/NAS	trombiculiasis	TROM/BIK/LAOI/SIS
tritubercular	TR*I/TAOU/BERK/LAR	trombiculid	TROM/BIK/LID
tritur-	TRIFP/R-	Trombiculidae	TROM/BIK/LAOI/DAE
	TRIFP/YAOU/R-	Trombidiidae	TROM/BI/DAOI/DAE
	TRIFP/YU/R-	tromethamine	TROE/M*ET/MAOEN
	TRIT/YAOU/R-	Tromner	TROM/NER
	TRIT/YU/R-	tromomania	TROM/MAIN/YA
triturable	TRIFP/RABL	tromophonia	TROM/FOEN/YA
triturate	TRIFP/RAIT	trona	TROE/NA
trituration	TRIFP/RAIGS	Tronolane	TROEN/LAIN
triturator	TRIFP/RAI/TOR		TRON/LAIN
trityl	TR*I/TIL	tropaic	TROE/PAI/IK
trivalence	TR*I/VAIL/ENS	Tropamine	TROEP/MAOEN
	TRIV/LENS	tropane	TROE/PAIN
trivalent	TR*I/VAIL/ENT	tropate	TROE/PAIT
	TRIV/LENT	-trope	TROEP
trivalve	TR*I/VAL/-V	tropeic	TROE/PAOE/IK
trivial	TRIV/YAL	tropeine	TROEP/YIN
Tri-Vi-Flor	TR*I/VAOI/FLOR		TROE/PAOEN
Tri-Vi-Sol	TR*I/VAOI/SOL	tropentane	TROE/PEN/TAIN
trizonal	TR*I/ZOENL	tropeolin	TROE/PAOE/LIN
Trobicin	TROE/BAOI/SIN	tropesis	TROE/PAOE/SIS
trocar	TROE/KAR	-troph	TROEF
trochant-	TROE/KAN/T-		TROF
trochanter	TROE/KANT/ER	troph(o)-	TROF
	TROE/KAN/TER		TROE/F(O)
trochanterian	TROE/KAN/TAOERN	trophectoderm	TROF/EKT/DERM
	TROE/KAN/TAOER/YAN	trophedema	TROF/DAOE/MA
	TROE/KAN/TER/YAN		TROF/E/DAOE/MA
trochanteric	TROE/KAN/TER/IK	trophesial	TROE/FAOEZ/YAL
trochanterica	TROE/KAN/TER/KA	trophesic	TROE/FAOEZ/IK
trochantericae	TROE/KAN/TER/SAE		TROE/FAOES/IK
trochanterplasty	TROE/KANT/ER/PLAS/TI	trophesy	TROF/SI
	TROE/KAN/TER/PLAS/TI	-trophia	TROEF/YA
trochantin	TROE/KAN/TIN	trophic	TROFK
trochantinian	TROE/KAN/TIN/YAN		TROF/IK
troche	TROEK		TROEFK
	TROE/KAOE		TROEF/IK
trochin	TROE/KIN	-trophic	TROFK
trochiscus	TROE/KIS/KUS		TROEFK
trochiter	TROK/TER	trophicity	TROE/FIS/TI
trochiterian	TROK/TAOERN	-trophin	TROEFN
	TROK/TAOER/YAN		TROE/FIN
trochle-	TROK/L-	Troph-Iron Liquid	TROEF/AOIRN/LIK/WID
	TROK/LAOE/Y-	trophism	TROF/IFM
trochlea	TROK/LA		TROEF/IFM
trochleae	TROK/LAE	Trophite	TROE/FAOIT
trochlear	TROK/LAR	trophoblast	TROF/BLA*S
trochleares	TROK/LAI/RAOEZ	trophoblastic	TROF/BLA*S/IK
trochleariform	TROK/LAR/FORM	trophoblastoma	TROF/BLAS/TOE/MA
	TROK/LAIR/FORM	trophochromatin	TROF/KROEM/TIN
trochlearis	TROK/LAI/RIS	trophochrome	TROF/KROEM
trochlearium	TROK/LAIRM	trophochromidia	TROF/KROE/MID/YA
	TROK/LAIR/YUM	trophocyte	TROF/SAO*IT
trochleiform	TROK/LI/FORM	trophoderm	TROF/DERM
	TROK/LAOE/FORM	trophodermatoneurosis	TROF/DERM/TO/NAOU/ROE/SIS
trocho-	TROEK	trophodynamics	TROF/DAOI/NAM/IK/-S
	TROK	tropholecithal	TROF/LES/THAL
	TROE/KO	tropholecithus	TROF/LES/THUS
trochocardia	TROEK/KAR/YA	trophology	TROE/FOLG
	TROK/KARD/YA	trophon	TROF/FON
trochocephalia	TROEK/SFAIL/YA		TROE/FON
trochocephaly	TROEK/SEF/LI	trophoneurosis	TROF/NAOU/ROE/SIS
trochoid	TROE/KOID	trophoneurotic	TROF/NAOU/ROT/IK
	TROEK/OID	trophonosis	TROF/NOE/SIS
trochoidal	TROE/KOI/DAL	trophonucleus	TROF/NAOUK/LUS
trochoidea	TROE/KOID/YA	trophopathia	TROF/PA*T/YA
trochoides	TROE/KOI/DAOEZ	trophopathy	TROE/FOP/TH*I
trochorizocardia	TROEK/RAOIZ/KARD/YA		TROF/OP/TH*I
	TROE/KOR/AOIZ/KARD/YA	trophoplasm	TROF/PLAFM
Trofan	TROE/FAN	trophoplast	TROF/PLA*S
Trofan-DS	TROE/FAN/D-RBGS/S*RBGS	trophospongia	TROF/SPON/JA
Troglotrema	TROG/LO/TRAOE/MA	trophospongium	TROF/SPON/JUM
troilism	TROI/LIFM	trophotaxis	TROF/TAK/SIS
	TROIL/IFM	trophotherapy	TROF/THER/PI
Troisier	TWAUZ/YAI	trophotoxism	TROF/TOK/SIFM
	TROIZ/YAI		TROF/TOX/IFM
	TWAUS/YAI	trophotropic	TROF/TROP/IK
	TROIS/YAI	trophotropism	TROE/FOT/RO/PIFM
trolamine	TROEL/MAOEN	trophozoite	TROF/ZOE/AOIT
troland	TROE/LAND	-trophy	(v)T/RO/FI
Trolard	TROE/LARD		TRO/FI
troleandomycin	TROEL/YAND/MAOI/SIN	tropia	TROEP/YA
trolnitrate	TROL/NAOI/TRAIT	-tropia	TROEP/YA
Troltsch	TREL/-FP	tropic	TROP/IK
trombicul-	TROM/BIK/L-		TROEP/IK
	TROM/BIK/YAOU/L-	tropica	TROP/KA
	TROM/BIK/YU/L-	tropical	TROP/KAL
Trombicula	TROM/BIK/LA	tropicalis	TROP/KAI/LIS

tropicamide	TROE/PIK/MAOID		TRAOI/PAN/SOE/MAOI/SIS
tropicopolitan	TROP/KO/POL/TAN		TR*I/PAN/SOE/MAOI/SIS
tropicum	TROP/KUM	trypanosomic	TRI/PAN/SOEM/IK
tropicus	TROP/KUS		TRIP/NO/SOEM/IK
tropin	TROE/PIN		TRAOI/PAN/SOEM/IK
tropine	TROE/PAOEN		TR*I/PAN/SOEM/IK
tropism	TROEP/IFM	trypanosomicidal	TRI/PAN/SOEM/SAOI/DAL
	TROE/PIFM		TRIP/NO/SOEM/SAOI/DAL
tropo-	TROEP		TRAOI/PAN/SOEM/SAOI/DAL
	TROP		TR*I/PAN/SOEM/SAO/DAL
	TROE/PO	trypanosomicide	TRI/PAN/SOEM/SAO*ID
tropochrome	TROEP/KROEM		TRIP/NO/SOEM/SAO*ID
tropocollagen	TROEP/KOL/JEN		TRAOI/PAN/SOEM/SAO*ID
	TROP/KOL/JEN		TR*I/PAN/SOEM/SAO*ID
tropoelastin	TROEP/E/LAS/TIN	trypanosomid	TRI/PAN/SOE/MID
tropometer	TROE/POM/TER		TRIP/NO/SOE/MID
tropomyosin	TROEP/MAOI/SIN		TRAOI/PAN/SOE/MID
troponin	TROEP/NIN		TR*I/PAN/SOE/MID
trotyl	TROE/TIL	trypanosomosis	TRI/PAN/SOE/MOE/SIS
trough	TROF		TRIP/NO/SOE/MOE/SIS
Trousseau	TRAOU/SOE		TRAOI/PAN/SOE/MOE/SIS
	TRAOUS/SOE		TR*I/PAN/SOE/MOE/SIS
troxerutin	TROX/RAOU/TIN	Trypanozoon	TRAOI/PAN/ZAON
troxidone	TROX/DOEN		TR*I/PAN/ZAON
troy	TROI	tryparsamide	TRAOI/PARS/MAOID
Trudeau	TRAOU/DOE		TR*I/PARS/MAOID
true	TRAOU		TRIP/ARS/MAOID
truncal	TRUN/KAL	trypesis	TRAOI/PAOE/SIS
truncate	TRUN/KAIT		TRI/PAOE/SIS
trunci	TRUN/KAOI		TR*I/PAOE/SIS
	TRUN/SAOI	trypomastigote	TRIP/MA*S/GOET
truncus	TRUN/KUS	trypsin	TRIP/SIN
trunk	TRUN/-K	trypsinize	TRIP/SIN/AOIZ
	TR*UNG		TRIPS/NAOIZ
trusion	TRAOUGS	trypsinogen	TRIP/SIN/JEN
truss	TRUSZ	trypsogen	TRIPS/JEN
try-in	TRAOI/H-F/N-		TRIP/SO/JEN
tryp-	TRIP	Tryptacin	TRIPT/SIN
	TRAOI/P-	tryptamine	TRIPT/MAOEN
trypan blue	TRAOI/PAN/BLU		TRIPT/MIN
trypan(o)-	TRI/PAN	tryptase	TRIP/TAIS
	TRIP/N(O)	tryptic	TRIPT/IK
	TRAOI/PAN	tryptolysis	TRIP/TOL/SIS
	TR*I/PAN	tryptolytic	TRIPT/LIT/IK
trypanid	TRIP/NID	tryptone	TRIP/TOEN
trypanocidal	TRI/PAN/SAOI/DAL	tryptonemia	TRIPT/NAOEM/YA
	TRIP/NO/SAOI/DAL	tryptophan	TRIPT/FAN
	TRAOI/PAN/SAOI/DAL	tryptophanase	TRIPT/FAN/AIS
	TR*I/PAN/SAOI/DAL		TRIPT/FA/NAIS
trypanocide	TRI/PAN/SAO*ID	tryptophane	TRIPT/FAIN
	TRIP/NO/SAO*ID	tryptophanuria	TRIPT/FA/NAOUR/YA
	TRAOI/PAN/SAO*ID		TRIPT/FAN/YAOUR/YA
	TR*I/PAN/SAO*ID	Tryptoplex	TRIPT/PLEX
trypanolysis	TRAOI/PAN/OL/SIS	Trypto-Som	TRIPT/SOM
	TRAOIP/NOL/SIS	Trysul Vaginal Cream	TR*I/SUL/VAJ/NAL/KRAOEM
	TRIP/NOL/SIS		TRAOI/SUL/VAJ/NAL/KRAOEM
	TR*I/PAN/OL/SIS	tsetse	ZET/SAOE
trypanolytic	TRI/PAN/LIT/IK		SET/ZAOE
	TRIP/NO/LIT/IK		SET/SAOE
	TRAOI/PAN/LIT		ZAOET/SAOE
	TR*I/PAN/LIT/IK		SAOET/SAOE
Trypanoplasma	TRI/PAN/PLAZ/MA	T-Stat	T-RBGS/STAT
	TRIP/NO/PLAZ/MA	Tsuga	SAOU/GA
	TRAOI/PAN/PLAZ/MA	tuaminoheptane	TAOU/AM/NO/HEP/TAIN
	TR*I/PAN/PLAZ/MA	tub(o)-	TAOUB
Trypanosoma	TRI/PAN/SOE/MA		TAOU/B(O)
	TRIP/NO/SOE/MA	tuba	TAOU/BA
	TRAOI/PAN/SOE/MA	tubae	TAOU/BAE
	TR*I/PAN/SOE/MA	tubage	TAOUB/AJ
trypanosomal	TRI/PAN/SOE/MAL	tubal	TAOU/BAL
	TRIP/NO/SOE/MAL	tubariae	TAOU/BAIR/YAE
	TRAOI/PAN/SOE/MAL	tubba	TUB/BA
	TR*I/PAN/SOE/MAL	tubbae	TUB/BAE
trypanosomatic	TRAOI/PAN/SOE/MAT/IK	tube	TAOUB
	TR*I/PAN/SOE/MAT/IK	tubectomy	TAOU/BEKT/M*I
tripanosomatid	TRAOI/PAN/SOE/MAT/ID	tuber	TAOUB/ER
	TR*I/PAN/SOE/MAT/ID	tubera	TAOUB/RA
Trypanosomatidae	TRAOI/PAN/SOE/MAT/DAE	tuberale	TAOUB/RAI/LAOE
	TR*I/PAN/SOE/MAT/DAE	tubercle	TAOU/BER/K-L
trypanosomatosis	TRAOI/PAN/SOEM/TOE/SIS		TAOU/BERK/-L
	TR*I/PAN/SOEM/TOE/SIS	tubercul(o)-	TAOU/BERK/L(O)
trypanosomatotropic	TRAOI/PAN/SOEM/TO/TROP/IK		TAOU/BERK/YAOU/L(O)
	TR*I/PAN/SOEM/TO/TROP/IK		TAOU/BERK/YU/L(O)
trypanosome	TRI/PAN/SOEM		TAOU/BER/KAOU/L(O)
	TRIP/NO/SOEM	tubercula	TAOU/BERK/LA
	TRAOI/PAN/SOEM	tubercular	TAOU/BERK/LAR
	TR*I/PAN/SOEM	tuberculate	TAOU/BERK/LAIT
trypanosomiasis	TRI/PAN/SOE/MAOI/SIS	tuberculated	TAOU/BERK/LAIT/-D
	TRIP/NO/SOE/MAOI/SIS	tuberculation	TAOU/BERK/LAIGS

tuberculatum	TAOU/BERK/LAI/TUM	tubulous	TAOUB/LOUS
	TAOU/BERK/LAIT/UM	tubulus	TAOUB/LUS
tuberculi	TAOU/BERK/LAOI	tubus	TAOU/BUS
tuberculid	TAOU/BERK/LID	Tucker	TUK/ER
tuberculigenous	TAOU/BERK/LIJ/NOUS	Tuffier	TAOEF/YAI
tuberculin	TAOU/BERK/LIN		TUF/YAI
tuberculinization	TAOU/BERK/LIN/ZAIGS	Tuffnell	TUF/NEL
tuberculinotherapy	TAOU/BERK/LIN/THER/PI	tuft	TUFT
tuberculinum	TAOU/BERK/LAOIN/UM	tuftsin	TUFT/SIN
	TAOU/BERK/LAOI/NUM	tug	TUG
tuberculitis	TAOU/BERK/LAOITS	tularemia	TAOUL/RAOEM/YA
tuberculization	TAOU/BERK/LIJ/ZAIGS	tularense	TAOUL/REN/SAOE
tuberculocele	TAOU/BERK/LO/SAO*EL	tularensis	TAOUL/REN/SIS
tuberculochemotherapeutic	TAOU/BERK/LO/KAOEM/THER/	tulle gras	TAOUL/GRAU
	PAOUT/IK	Tulpius	TUL/PAOE/YUS
tuberculocidal	TAOU/BERK/LO/SAOI/DAL	tumefacient	TAOUM/FAIRBT
tuberculocide	TAOU/BERK/LO/SAO*ID	tumefaction	TAOUM/FA*BGS
tuberculoderm	TAOU/BERK/LO/DERM	tumefy	TAOUM/FI
tuberculoderma	TAOU/BERK/LO/DER/MA	tumentia	TAOU/MEN/SHA
tuberculofibroid	TAOU/BERK/LO/FAOI/BROID	tumescence	TAOU/MES/ENS
tuberculofibrosis	TAOU/BERK/LO/FAOI/BROE/SIS	tumescent	TAOU/MES/ENT
tuberculoid	TAOU/BERK/LOID	tumid	TAOU/MID
tuberculoma	TAOU/BERK/LOE/MA		TAOUM/ID
tuberculo-opsonic	TAOU/BERK/LO/OP/SON/IK	tumor	TAOU/MOR
tuberculoprotein	TAOU/BERK/LO/PRO/TAOEN	tumoraffin	TAOU/MOR/AFN
tuberculosa	TAOU/BERK/LOE/SA		TAOU/MOR/AF/FIN
tuberculosarium	TAOU/BERK/LOE/SAIRM	tumoral	TAOUM/RAL
	TAOU/BERK/LO/SAIR/YUM		TAOU/MORL
tuberculosilicosis	TAOU/BERK/LO/SIL/KOE/SIS		TAOU/MOR/RAL
tuberculosis	TAOU/BERK/LOE/SIS	tumoricidal	TAOU/MOR/SAOI/DAL
tuberculostat	TAOU/BERK/LO/STAT	tumorigenesis	TAOU/MOR/JEN/SIS
tuberculostatic	TAOU/BERK/LO/STAT/IK	tumorigenic	TAOU/MOR/JEN/IK
tuberculostearic	TAOU/BERK/LO/STAOER/IK	tumorlets	TAOU/MOR/LET/-S
tuberculotic	TAOU/BERK/LOT/IK	tumorous	TAOUM/ROUS
tuberculous	TAOU/BERK/LOUS		TAOU/MOR/OUS
tuberculum	TAOU/BERK/LUM	Tums	TUMZ
tuberiferous	TAOUB/RIF/ROUS		TUMS
tuberoischiadic	TAOUB/RO/IS/KAD/IK	tumultus	TAOU/MUL/TUS
	TAOUB/RO/IS/KAOE/AD/IK	tumultus cordis	TAOU/MUL/TUS/KOR/DIS
tuberosa	TAOUB/ROE/SA	Tunga	TUN/GA
tuberose	TAOUB/ROES	Tunga penetrans	TUN/GA/PEN/TRANZ
tuberosis	TAOUB/ROE/SIS	tungiasis	TUN/GAOI/SIS
tuberositas	TAOUB/ROS/TAS	Tungidae	TUNG/DAE
tuberositates	TAOUB/ROS/TAI/TAOEZ	tungstate	TUNG/STAIT
tuberositatis	TAOUB/ROS/TAI/TIS		TUNGS/TAIT
tuberosity	TAOUB/ROS/TI	tungsten	TUNG/STEN
tuberosum	TAOUB/ROE/SUM		TUNGS/TEN
	TAOUB/ROES/UM	tungstic	TUNG/STIK
tuberous	TAOUB/ROUS		TUNGS/TIK
Tubex	TAOU/BEX	tunic	TAOUN/IK
tubi	TAOU/BAOI	tunica	TAOUN/KA
tubiferous	TAOU/BIF/ROUS	tunicae	TAOUN/KAE
tuboabdominal	TAOUB/AB/DOM/NAL		TAOUN/SAE
tuboadnexopexy	TAOUB/AD/NEX/PEK/SI	tunicary	TAOUN/KAIR
tubocurarine	TAOUB/KAOUR/RIN	tuning fork	TAOUN/-G/FORK
	TAOUB/KAOUR/RAOEN	tunnel	TUN/EL
tuboligamentous	TAOUB/LIG/MEN/TOUS	turanose	TAOUR/NOES
tubo-ovarian	TAOUB/O/VAIRN	Turbatrix	TUR/BAI/TRIX
tubo-ovariectomy	TAOUB/O/VAIR/YEKT/M*I	turbid	TURB/ID
tubo-ovariotomy	TAOUB/O/VAIR/YOT/M*I		TUR/BID
tubo-ovaritis	TAOUB/OEV/RAOITS	turbidimeter	TURB/DIM/TER
tuboperitoneal	TAOUB/PERT/NAOEL	turbidimetric	TURB/ID/MET/RIK
tuboplasty	TAOUB/PLAS/TI		TUR/BID/MET/RIK
tuborrhea	TAOUB/RAOE/YA	turbidimetry	TURB/DIM/TRI
tubotorsion	TAOUB/TORGS	turbidity	TUR/BID/TI
tubotympanal	TAOUB/TIFRP/NAL	turbidometric	TURB/DO/MET/RIK
tubotympanic	TAOUB/TIM/PAN/IK	turbinal	TURB/NAL
tubotympanum	TAOUB/TIFRP/NUM	turbinate	TURB/NAIT
tubouterine	TAOUB/YAOUT/RIN	turbinated	TURB/NAIT/-D
tubovaginal	TAOUB/VAJ/NAL	turbinectomy	TURB/NEKT/M*I
tubul(o)-	TAOUB/L(O)	turbinotome	TURB/NO/TOEM
	TAOUB/YAOU/L(O)		TUR/BIN/TOEM
	TAOU/YU/L(O)	turbinotomy	TURB/NOT/M*I
	TAOU/BAOU/L(O)	Turck	TAO*ERK
tubular	TAOUB/LAR		T*URK
tubulare	TAOUB/LAI/RAOE		(not TAOERK or TURK; see Turk)
tubulature	TAOUB/LA/KHUR	turgescence	TUR/JES/ENS
tubule	TAOUB/YAOUL	turgescent	TUR/JES/ENT
tubuli	TAOUB/LAOI	turgid	TUR/JID
tubuliform	TAOUB/LI/FORM		TURJ/ID
tubulin	TAOUB/LIN	turgidization	TUR/JID/ZAIGS
tubulization	TAOUB/LI/ZAIGS	turgometer	TUR/GOM/TER
tubuloacinar	TAOUB/LO/AS/NAR	turgor	TUR/GOR
tubulocyst	TAOUB/LO/S*IS	turicatae	TUR/KAI/TAE
tubulodermoid	TAOUB/LO/DER/MOID	turista	TAOU/RAOES/TA
tubuloracemose	TAOUB/LO/RAS/MOES		TAOU/RIS/TA
tubulorrhexis	TAOUB/LO/REK/SIS	Turk	TAOERK
tubulosaccular	TAOUB/LO/SAK/LAR		TURK
tubulose	TAOUB/LOES	Turlington	TURL/-G/TON

	TUR/LING/TON
turmeric	TURM/RIK
	TUR/MER/IK
turn	TURN
Turner	TURN/ER
	TUR/NER
turnera	TURN/RA
turnover	TURN/OFR
turpentine	TUR/PEN/TAOIN
	TURP/EN/TAOIN
turps	TURP/-S
turricephaly	TUR/SEF/LI
	TUR/RI/SEF/LI
turunda	TAOU/RUN/DA
turundae	TAOU/RUN/DAE
tush	TURB
Tusibron	TUS/BRON
Tusibron-DM	TUS/BRON/D-RBGS/M*RBGS
tusk	TUS/-K
tuss-	TUS
	TUS/S-
	TUSZ
Tussafed	TUS/FED
tussal	TUS/SAL
Tussar	TUS/SAR
Tussar-2	TUS/SAR/2
Tussar DM	TUS/SAR/D-RBGS/M*RBGS
Tussar SF	TUS/SAR/S-RBGS/F*RBGS
tussicula	TUS/SIK/LA
tussicular	TUS/SIK/LAR
tussiculation	TUS/SIK/LAIGS
tussigenic	TUS/JEN/IK
Tussigon Tablets	TUS/GON/TAB/LET/-S
Tussionex	TUS/YO/NEX
Tussi-Organidin	TUS/OR/GAN/DIN
Tussirex	TUS/REX
tussis	TUS/SIS
tussive	TUS/SIV
	TUSZ/IV
Tuss-Ornade	TUS/OR/NAID
	TUSZ/OR/NAID
tutamen	TAOU/TAI/MEN
	TAOU/TAIM/-N
tutamina	TAOU/TAIM/NA
	TAOU/TAM/NA
Tuttle	TUT/-L
tweed	TWAOED
tweezers	TWAOEZ/ER/-S
twig	TWIG
twilight	TWAOI/LAOIGT
twin	TWIN
twinge	TWIN/-J
twinning	TWIN/-G
twinship	TWIN/SHIP
twitch	TWIFP
TwoCal HN	TWO/KAL/H-RBGS/N*RBGS
Twort	TWORT
tybamate	TAOIB/MAIT
tychastics	TAOI/KA*S/IK/-S
tyle	TAOI/LAOE
tylectomy	TAOI/LEKT/M*I
Tylenol	TAOIL/NOL
	TAOI/LE/NOL
tylia	TIL/YA
	TAOIL/YA
tylion	TIL/YON
	TAOIL/YON
tyloma	TAOI/LOE/MA
tyloses	TAOI/LOE/SAOEZ
tylosis	TAOI/LOE/SIS
tylotic	TAOI/LOT/IK
Tylox	TAOI/LOX
tyloxapol	TAOI/LOX/POL
tymazoline	TAOI/MAZ/LAOEN
Tympagesic	TIFRP/JAOEZ/IK
tympan(o)-	TIFRP/N(O)
	TIM/PA/N(O)
	TIM/PAN
tympana	TIFRP/NA
tympanal	TIFRP/NAL
tympanectomy	TIFRP/NEKT/M*I
tympani	TIFRP/NAOI
tympania	TIM/PAN/YA
tympanic	TIM/PAN/IK
tympanica	TIM/PAN/KA
tympanicae	TIM/PAN/SAE
tympanichord	TIM/PAN/KHORD
tympanichordal	TIM/PAN/KHOR/DAL
tympanici	TIM/PAN/SAOI

tympanicity	TIFRP/NIS/TI
tympanicum	TIM/PAN/KUM
tympanicus	TIM/PAN/KUS
tympanion	TIM/PAN/YON
tympanism	TIFRP/NIFM
tympanites	TIFRP/NAOI/TAOEZ
tympanitic	TIFRP/NIT/IK
tympanitis	TIFRP/NAOITS
tympanoacryloplasty	TIFRP/NO/AI/KRIL/PLAS/TI
	TIFRP/NO/KRIL/PLAS/TI
tympanocentesis	TIFRP/NO/SEN/TAOE/SIS
tympanocervical	TIFRP/NO/SEFRB/KAL
tympanoeustachian	TIFRP/NO/YAOU/STAIK/YAN
	TIFRP/NO/YAOU/STAIGS
tympanogenic	TIFRP/NO/JEN/IK
tympanogram	TIFRP/NO/GRAM
tympanohyal	TIFRP/NO/HAOIL
tympanolabyrinthopexy	TIFRP/NO/LAB/R*INT/PEK/SI
tympanomalleal	TIFRP/NO/MAL/YAL
tympanomandibular	TIFRP/NO/MAN/DIB/LAR
tympanomastoid	TIFRP/NO/MAS/TOID
tympanomastoiditis	TIFRP/NO/MAS/TOI/DAOITS
tympanomeatomastoidectomy	
	TIFRP/NO/MAOE/AIT/MAS/TOI/ DEKT/M*I
	TIFRP/NO/MAOE/YAIT/MAS/TOI/ DEKT/M*I
	TIFRP/NO/MAOE/AI/TO/MAS/TOI/ DEKT/M*I
	TIFRP/NO/MAOE/YAI/TO/MAS/ TOI/DEKT/M*I
tympanometric	TIFRP/NO/MET/RIK
tympanometry	TIFRP/NOM/TRI
tympanophonia	TIFRP/NO/FOEN/YA
tympanophony	TIFRP/NOF/N*I
tympanoplastic	TIFRP/NO/PLA*S/IK
tympanoplasty	TIFRP/NO/PLAS/TI
tympanosclerosis	TIFRP/NO/SKLE/ROE/SIS
tympanosquamosal	TIFRP/NO/SKWAI/MOE/SAL
	TIFRP/NO/SKWA/MOE/SAL
tympanostapedial	TIFRP/NO/STAI/PAOED/YAL
	TIFRP/NO/STA/PAOED/YAL
tympanostomy	TIFRP/NO*S/M*I
tympanosympathectomy	TIFRP/NO/SIFRP/THEKT/M*I
tympanotemporal	TIFRP/NO/TEFRP/RAL
tympanometry	TIFRP/NOM/TRI
tympanotomy	TIFRP/NOT/M*I
tympanous	TIFRP/NOUS
tympanum	TIFRP/NUM
	TIM/PAN/UM
tympany	TIFRP/N*I
Tyndall	T*IN/DAL
	(not TIN/DAL; see Tindal)
tyndallization	TIN/DAL/ZAIGS
type	TAOIP
typhemia	TAOI/FAOEM/YA
typhi	TAOI/FAOI
typhia	TIF/YA
typhic	TAOIF/IK
typhinia	TAOI/FIN/YA
typhl(o)-	TIF/L(O)
typhlectasis	TIF/LEKT/SIS
typhlectomy	TIF/LEKT/M*I
typhlenteritis	TIF/LENT/RAOITS
typhlitis	TIF/LAOITS
typhlocele	TIF/LO/SAO*EL
typhlocolitis	TIF/LO/KO/LAOITS
typhlodicliditis	TIF/LO/DIK/LI/DAOITS
typhloempyema	TIF/LO/EM/PAOI/E/MA
	TIF/LO/EM/PAOI/YAOE/MA
typhloenteritis	TIF/LO/SPWRAOITS
	TIF/LO/SPWER/RAOITS
typhlolithasis	TIF/LO/LI/THAOI/SIS
typhlology	TIF/LOLG
typhlomegaly	TIF/LO/MEG/LI
typhlon	TIF/LON
typhlopexia	TIF/LO/PEX/YA
typhlopexy	TIF/LO/PEK/SI
typhlorrhaphy	TIF/LOR/FI
typhlosis	TIF/LOE/SIS
typhlostenosis	TIF/LO/STE/NOE/SIS
typhlostomy	TIF/LO*S/M*I
typhlotomy	TIF/LOT/M*I
typhloureterostomy	TIF/LO/YAOU/RAOET/RO*S/M*I
typho-	TAOIF
	TAOI/FO
typhoid	TAOI/FOID
typhoidal	TAOI/FOI/DAL
typholysin	TAOI/FOL/SIN

typhomalarial	TAOIF/MA/LAIRL
typhomania	TAOIF/MAIN/YA
typhopaludism	TAOIF/PAL/DIFM
typhopneumonia	TAOIF/NAOU/MOEN/YA
typhosa	TAOI/FOE/SA
typhosepsis	TAOIF/SEP/SIS
typhosum	TAOI/FOES/UM
	TAOI/FOE/SUM
typhosus	TAOI/FOE/SUS
typhous	TAOI/FOUS
	TAOIF/OUS
typhus	TAOI/FUS
typical	TIP/KAL
typing	TAOIP/-G
typodont	TAOIP/DONT
typology	TAOI/POLG
typoscope	TAOIP/SKOEP
typus	TAOI/PUS
tyraminase	TAOIR/MI/NAIS
	TAOIR/MIN/AIS
	TIR/MI/NAIS
	TIR/MIN/AIS
tyramine	TAOIR/MAOEN
	TIR/MAOEN
tyrannism	TIR/NIFM
tyrein	TAOIR/YIN
	TAOI/RAOEN
tyremesis	TAOI/REM/SIS
tyro-	TAOIR
	TAOI/RO
tyrocidin	TAOIR/SAOI/DIN
Tyrode	TAOI/ROED
tyrogenous	TAOI/ROJ/NOUS
Tyroglyphus	TAOI/ROG/LI/FUS
	TAOIR/GLIF/FUS
tyroid	TAOI/ROID
tyroketonuria	TAOIR/KAOET/NAOUR/YA
tyroma	TAOI/ROE/MA
tyromatosis	TAOIR/MA/TOE/SIS
	TAOI/ROEM/TOE/SIS
tyropanoate	TAOIR/PA/NOE/AIT
Tyrophagus	TAOI/ROF/GUS
tyrosinase	TAOIR/SI/NAIS
	TAOIR/SIN/AIS
	TAOI/ROES/NAIS
	TIR/SI/NAIS
	TIR/SIN/AIS
tyrosine	TAOIR/SAOEN
	TAOIR/SIN
tyrosinemia	TAOIR/SI/NAOEM/YA
	TAOI/ROES/NAOEM/YA
	TIR/SI/NAOEM/YA
tyrosinosis	TAOIR/SI/NOE/SIS
	TAOI/ROES/NOE/SIS
tyrosinuria	TAOIR/SI/NAOUR/YA
	TAOI/ROES/NAOUR/YA
tyrosis	TAOI/ROE/SIS
tyrosyluria	TAOIR/SIL/YAOUR/YA
	TAOIR/SI/LAOUR/YA
tyrothricin	TAOIR/THRAOI/SIN
tyrotoxicon	TAOIR/TOX/KON
tyrotoxicosis	TAOIR/TOX/KOE/SIS
tyrotoxism	TAOIR/TOK/SIFM
	TAOIR/TOX/IFM
Tyrrell	TIR/REL
	TIR/EL
Tyson	TAOI/SON
tysonian	TAOI/SOEN/YAN
tysonitis	TAOIS/NAOITS
	TAOI/SON/AOITS
Tyzine	TAOI/ZAOEN
Tyzzeria	TAOI/ZAOER/YA
Tzanck	ZAN/-K (required)

U

U.	UFPLT
uarthritis	YAOU/AR/THRAOITS
uberous	YAOUB/ROUS
uberty	YAOUB/ER/TI
	YAOU/BER/TI
ubihydroquinone	YAOUB/HAOI/DRO/KWAOI/NOEN
ubiquinol	YAOUB/KWIN/OL
	YAOU/BIK/WI/NOL
	YAOUB/KWAOI/NOL
ubiquinone	YAOUB/BIK/WI/NOEN
	YAOUB/KWAOI/NOEN
	YAOUB/KWIN/OEN
ubiquitin	YAOU/BIK/WI/TIN
udder	UD/ER
Uffelmann	AOUF/EL/MAN
	YAOUF/EL/MAN
Uhl	YAO*UL
	(not YAOUL; see yule)
Uhlenhuth	AOUL/EN/HAOUT
	YAOUL/EN/HAOUT
Uhthoff	AOUT/HOF
	YAOUT/HOF
ul(o)-	YAOUL
	YAOU/L(O)
ulaganactesis	YAOU/LAG/AN/AK/TAOE/SIS
ulalgia	YAOU/LAL/JA
ulatrophia	YAOUL/TROEF/YA
ulatrophy	YAOU/LAT/RO/FI
ulcer	ULS/ER
	UL/SER
ulcer(o)-	ULS/R(O)
ulcera	ULS/RA
ulcerate	ULS/RAIT
ulcerated	ULS/RAIT/-D
ulceration	ULS/RAIGS
ulcerativa	ULS/RA/TAOI/VA
ulcerative	ULS/RA/TIV
ulcere	ULS/RAOE
ulcerogangrenous	ULS/RO/GAN/GRE/NOUS
ulcerogenic	ULS/RO/JEN/IK
ulceroglandular	ULS/RO/GLAND/LAR
ulcerogranuloma	ULS/RO/GRAN/LOE/MA
ulceromembranous	ULS/RO/MEM/BRA/NOUS
ulcerosa	ULS/ROE/SA
ulcerous	ULS/ROUS
ulcus	UL/KUS
ulectomy	YAOU/LEKT/M*I
ulegyria	YAOUL/JAOIR/YA
ulemorrhagia	YAOU/LEM/RAI/JA
ulerythema	YAOU/LER/THAOE/MA
uletic	YAOU/LET/IK
uletomy	YAOU/LET/M*I
uliginous	YAOU/LIJ/NOUS
ulitis	YAOU/LAOITS
Ullmann	UL/MAN
Ullrich	UL/RIK
Ulmus	UL/MUS
uln(o)-	UL/N(O)
ulna	UL/NA
ulnad	UL/NAD
ulnae	UL/NAE
ulnar	UL/NAR
ulnare	UL/NAI/RAOE
ulnares	UL/NAI/RAOEZ
ulnaris	UL/NAI/RIS
ulnen	UL/NEN
ulnocarpal	UL/NO/KAR/PAL
ulnoradial	UL/NO/RAID/YAL
ulocace	YAOU/LOK/SAOE
ulocarcinoma	YAOUL/KARS/NOE/MA
ulodermatitis	YAOUL/DERM/TAOITS
uloglossitis	YAOUL/GLOS/SAOITS
uloid	YAOU/LOID
uloncus	YAOU/LON/KUS
ulorrhagia	YAOUL/RAI/JA
ulorrhea	YAOUL/RAOE/YA
ulotomy	YAOU/LOT/M*I
ulotrichous	YAOU/LOT/RI/KOUS
ulotripsis	YAOUL/TRIP/SIS
ultimate	ULT/MAT
ultimisternal	ULT/MI/STERNL
ultimobranchial	ULT/MO/BRANG/YAL
ultimum moriens	ULT/MUM/MOR/YENZ
	ULT/MUM/MOER/YENZ

ultra-	UL/TRA
ultrabrachycephalic	UL/TRA/BRAK/SFAL/IK
Ultracef	UL/TRA/SEF
ultracentrifugation	UL/TRA/SEN/TRIF/GAIGS
ultracentrifuge	UL/TRA/SEN/TRI/FAOUJ
UltraCholine	UL/TRA/KOE/LAOEN
ultracytostome	UL/TRA/SAOIT/STOEM
Ultraderm	UL/TRA/DERM
ultradian	UL/TRAID/YAN
ultradolichocephalic	UL/TRA/DOL/KO/SFAL/IK
ultrafilter	UL/TRA/FILT/ER
ultrafiltrate	UL/TRA/FIL/TRAIT
ultrafiltration	UL/TRA/FIL/TRAIGS
ultragaseous	UL/TRA/GAS/YOUS
Ultralente	UL/TRA/LEN/TAI
Ultralente Insulin	UL/TRA/LEN/TAI/INS/LIN
ultraligation	UL/TRA/LAOI/GAIGS
ultramicrochemistry	UL/TRA/MAOI/KRO/KEM/STRI
ultramicron	UL/TRA/MAOI/KRON
ultramicropipet	UL/TRA/MAOI/KRO/PAOI/PET
ultramicroscope	UL/TRA/MAOI/KRO/SKOEP
ultramicroscopic	UL/TRA/MAOI/KRO/SKOP/IK
ultramicroscopy	UL/TRA/MAOI/KROS/KPI
ultramicrotome	UL/TRA/MAOI/KRO/TOEM
ultramicrotomy	UL/TRA/MAOI/KROT/M*I
Ultra Mide	UL/TRA/MAOID
ultraphagocytosis	UL/TRA/FAG/SAOI/TOE/SIS
ultraprophylaxis	UL/TRA/PROEF/LAK/SIS
ultra-red	UL/TRA/RED
ultrashort	UL/TRA/SHORT
ultrasonic	UL/TRA/SON/IK
ultrasonics	UL/TRA/SON/IK/-S
ultrasonogram	UL/TRA/SON/GRAM
ultrasonograph	UL/TRA/SON/GRAF
ultrasonographer	UL/TRA/SO/NOG/FER
	UL/TRA/SOE/NOG/FER
ultrasonographic	UL/TRA/SON/GRAFK
ultrasonography	UL/TRA/SO/NOG/FI
	UL/TRA/SOE/NOG/FI
ultrasonometry	UL/TRA/SO/NOM/TRI
	UL/TRA/SOE/NOM/TRI
ultrasonosurgery	UL/TRA/SON/SURJ/RI
	UL/TRA/SON/S-RJ
ultrasound	UL/TRA/SOUND
ultraspeed	UL/TRA/SPAOED
ultrastructure	UL/TRA/STRUK/KHUR
ultraterminal	UL/TRA/TERM/NAL
ultratherm	UL/TRA/THERM
ultratoxon	UL/TRA/TOK/SON
ultraviolet	UL/TRA/VAOI/LET
	UL/TRA/VAOIL/ET
ultravirus	UL/TRA/VAOI/RUS
ultravisible	UL/TRA/VIZ/-BL
ultromotivity	UL/TRO/MOE/TIV/TI
ululation	UL/LAIGS
	UL/YAOU/LAIGS
	UL/YU/LAIGS
	YAOU/LAOU/LAIGS
	YAOUL/YAOU/LAIGS
	YAOUL/YU/LAIGS
umbelliferone	UM/BEL/LIF/ROEN
	UM/BE/LIF/ROEN
umber	UM/BER
Umber	K-P/UM/BER
umbilectomy	UM/BI/LEKT/M*I
	UM/BIL/EKT/M*I
umbilical	UM/BIL/KAL
umbilicale	UM/BIL/KAI/LAOE
umbilicales	UM/BIL/KAI/LAOEZ
umbilicalis	UM/BIL/KAI/LIS
umbilicate	UM/BIL/KAIT
umbilicated	UM/BIL/KAIT/-D
umbilication	UM/BIL/KAIGS
umbilici	UM/BIL/KAOI
	UM/BIL/SAOI
umbilicus	UM/BIL/KUS
umbo	UM/BOE
umbonate	UM/BO/NAIT
umbones	UM/BOE/NAOEZ
umbonis	UM/BOE/NIS
umbrascopy	UM/BRAS/KPI
un-	UN
Unasyn	YAOUN/SIN
unazotized	UN/AIZ/TAOIZ/-D
	UN/A*Z/TAOIZ/-D
unbalance	UN/BAL/LANS
unbleached	UN/BLAOEFP/-D
uncal	UN/KAL
uncarthrosis	UN/KAR/THROE/SIS

unci	UN/SAOI	Ungulata	UNG/LAI/TA
unci-	UNS	ungulate	UNG/LAIT
	UN/SI	unguligrade	UNG/LI/GRAID
uncia	UNS/YA	uni-	YAOUN
unciform	UNS/FORM		YAOU/NI
unciforme	UNS/FOR/MAOE	uniarticular	YAOUN/AR/TIK/LAR
uncinal	UNS/NAL	uniaural	YAOUN/AURL
Uncinaria	UNS/NAIR/YA	uniaxial	YAOUN/AX/YAL
uncinariasis	UNS/NA/RAOI/SIS	unibasal	YAOUN/BAI/SAL
	UN/SIN/RAOI/SIS	Uniblue A	YAOUN/BLU/ARBGS
uncinariatic	UNS/NAIR/YAT/IK	unicameral	YAOUN/KAM/RAL
uncinate	UNS/NAIT	unicamerate	YAOUN/KAM/RAIT
uncinatum	UNS/NAI/TUM	Unicap	YAOUN/KAP
	UNS/NAIT/UM	unicellular	YAOUN/SEL/YAOU/LAR
uncipressure	UNS/PRERB/SHUR	unicentral	YAOUN/SEN/TRAL
uncomplemented	UN/KOM/PLEMT/-D		YAOUN/STRAL
unconjugated	UN/KON/JU/GAIT/-D	unicentric	YAON/SEN/TRIK
	UN/KON/JAOU/GAIT/-D	uniceps	YAOUN/SEPS
unconscious	UN/KON/-RBS	uniceptor	YAOUN/SEP/TOR
unconsciousness	UN/KON/-RBS/*NS	unicorn	YAOUN/KORN
unco-ossified	UN/KO/OS/FI/-D	unicornous	YAOUN/KOR/NOUS
	UN/KO/OSZ/FI/-D		YAOUN/KORN/OUS
uncotomy	UN/KOT/M*I	unicuspid	YAOUN/KUS/PID
uncouplers	UN/KUP/LER/-S	unicuspidate	YAOUN/KUS/PI/DAIT
uncovertebral	UN/KO/VERT/BRAL	unidirectional	YAOUN/DR*EBGS/NAL
unction	UNGS		YAOUN/DI/R*EBGS/NAL
unctuous	UNG/-RBS	unifamilial	YAOUN/FA/MIL/YAL
	UNG/KHOUS	Unifiber	YAOUN/FAOIB/ER
uncture	UNG/KHUR		YAOUN/FAOI/BER
uncus	UN/KUS	uniflagellate	YAOUN/FLAJ/LAIT
undecenoic	UN/DES/NOIK	unifocal	YAOUN/FOE/KAL
	UN/DES/NOE/IK	uniforate	YAOUN/FOER/AIT
undecoylium	UN/DEK/IL/YUM		YAOUN/FOR/AIT
undecylenate	UN/DES/LI/NAIT		YAOUN/FOE/RAIT
	UN/DES/LIN/AIT	uniform	YAOUN/FORM
undecylenic	UN/DES/LEN/IK	unigeminal	YAOUN/JEM/NAL
under	URND	unigerminal	YAOUN/JERM/NAL
	UN/DER	uniglandular	YAOUN/GLAND/LAR
under-	UNDZ	unigravida	YAOUN/GRAV/DA
underachievement	UNDZ/AI/KHAOEVMT	unilaminar	YAOUN/LAM/NAR
underachiever	UNDZ/AI/KHAOEVR	unilaminate	YAOUN/LAM/NAIT
underbite	UNDZ/BAOIT	unilateral	YAOUN/LAT/RAL
undercut	UNDZ/KUT	Unilax	YAOUN/LAX
underdrive pacing	UNDZ/DRAOIV/PAIS/-G	unilobar	YAOUN/LOE/BAR
underhorn	UNDZ/HORN	unilobular	YAOUN/LOB/LAR
underhung	UNDZ/HUNG	unilocal	YAOUN/LOE/KAL
undernourished	UNDZ/NOUR/IRB/-D	unilocular	YAOUN/LOK/LAR
	UNDZ/NUR/IRB/-D	unimodal	YAOUN/MOE/DAL
undernutrition	UNDZ/NAOU/TRIGS	unimolecular	YAOUN/MOE/LEK/LAR
undershoot	UNDZ/SHAOT	uninephrectomized	YAOUN/NE/FREKT/MAOIZ/-D
understaffed	UNDZ/STAF/-D	uninhibited	UN/IN/HIBT/-D
understain	UNDZ/STAIN	uninuclear	YAOUN/NAOUK/LAR
undertoe	UNDZ/TOE	uninucleate	YAOUN/NAOUK/LAIT
underventilation	UNDZ/VENT/LAIGS	uninucleated	YAOUN/NAOUK/LAIT/-D
Underwood	UNDZ/WAOD	uniocular	YAOUN/OK/LAR
undifferentiated	UN/DIFRN/SHAIT/-D	union	YAOUN/YON
undifferentiation	UN/DIFRN/SHAIGS	unioval	YAOUN/OEVL
undine	UN/DAOEN	uniovular	YAOUN/OV/LAR
	UN/DAOIN	unipara	YAOU/NIP/RA
undeveloped	UN/DWOP/-D	uniparous	YAOU/NIP/ROUS
	UN/DE/VEL/OP/-D	uniparental	YAOUN/PREN/TAL
undinism	UND/NIFM		YAOUN/PA/REN/TAL
	UN/DI/NIFM	Unipen	YAOUN/PEN
	UN/DIN/IFM	unipennate	YAOUN/PEN/AIT
undiversion	UN/DI/VERGS		YAOUN/PEN/NAIT
undoing	UN/DOING	unipennatus	YAOUN/PEN/AI/TUS
Undritz	UN/DRITS		YAOUN/PEN/NAI/TUS
undulans	UN/DAOU/LANZ	Uniphyl	YAOUN/FIL
undulant	UN/DAOU/LANT	unipolar	YAOUN/POE/LAR
undulate	UN/DAOU/LAIT	uniport	YAOUN/PORT
undulation	UN/DAOU/LAIGS	uniporter	YAOUN/PORT/ER
undulipodia	UN/DAOUL/POED/YA	unipotency	YAOUN/POE/TEN/SI
undulipodium	UN/DAOUL/POED/YUM		YAOUN/POET/EN/SI
ungual	UNG/WAL	unipotent	YAOU/NIP/TENT
unguent	UNG/WENT	unipotential	YAOUN/POE/TEN/-RBL
unguentum	UNG/WEN/TUM	unirritable	UN/IRT/-BL
	UNG/WENT/UM	uniseptate	YAOUN/SEP/TAIT
ungues	UNG/WAOEZ	unisexual	YAOUN/SEX/YAOUL
Unguiculata	UNG/WIK/LAI/TA	Unisom	YAOUN/SOM
unguiculate	UNG/WIK/LAIT	unit	YAOUNT
unguiculus	UNG/WIK/LUS		YAOU/NIT
unguis	UNG/WIS	unitage	YAOUN/TAJ
unguium	UNG/WUM	unitary	YAOUN/TAIR
	UNG/WAOE/UM	United States	YAOITS/FARM/KO/PAOE/YA
	UNG/WAOE/YUM	Pharmacopeia	YAOITS/FARM/KOEP/YA
ungul-	UNG/L-		YAOU/NAOIT/-D/STAIT/-S/FARM/
	UNG/YAOU/L-		KO/PAOE/YA
	UNG/YU/L-		YAOU/NAOIT/-D/STAIT/-S/FARM/
ungula	UNG/LA		KOEP/YA

uniterminal	YAOUN/TERM/NAL	uratemia	YAOUR/TAOEM/YA
univalence	YAOUN/VAIL/ENS	urateribonucleotide	YAOUR/AIT/RAOIB/NAOUK/LO/
	YAOUN/VAI/LENS		TAOID
univalency	YAOUN/VAIL/EN/SI		YAOU/RAIT/RAOIB/NAOUK/LO/
	YAOUN/VAI/LEN/SI		TAOID
univalent	YAOUN/VAIL/ENT	uratic	YAOU/RAT/IK
	YAOUN/VAI/LENT	uratohistechia	YAOUR/TO/HIS/TEK/YA
universal	YAOUN/VER/SAL	uratolysis	YAOUR/TOL/SIS
universalis	YAOUN/VER/SAI/LIS	uratolytic	YAOUR/TO/LIT/IK
univitelline	YAOUN/VAOI/TEL/LIN		YAOU/RAIT/LIT/IK
	YAOUN/VI/TEL/LIN	uratoma	YAOUR/TOE/MA
unmedullated	UN/MED/LAIT/-D	uratosis	YAOUR/TOE/SIS
unmyelinated	UN/MAOI/LI/NAIT/-D	uraturia	YAOUR/TAOUR/YA
Unna	YAOU/NA	Urbach	UR/BAK
	YAOUN/NA	Urban	K-P/UR/BAN
Unna Boot	YAOU/NA/BAOT	urceiform	YAOUR/SAOE/FORM
	YAOUN/NA/BAOT		UR/SAOE/FORM
unofficial	UN/FIRBL	urceolate	YAOUR/SAOE/LAIT
	UN/O/FIRBL		YAOURS/YO/LAIT
unorganized	UN/ORG/-D		YURS/YO/LAIT
	UN/ORG/NAOIZ/-D		UR/SAOE/LAIT
unorientation	UN/OER/YEN/TAIGS		URS/YO/LAIT
	UN/OR/YEN/TAIGS	ur-defense	YAOUR/DE/FENS
unpaired	UN/PAIR/-D		YAOUR/DEFNS
unphysiologic	UN/FIZ/YO/LOJ/IK		UR/DE/FENS
unrest	UN/R*ES		UR/DEFNS
unsanitary	UN/SAN/TAIR	urea	YAOU/RAOE/YA
unsaturated	UN/SAFRP/RAIT/-D	Ureacin	YAOU/RAOE/SIN
unsex	UN/SEX	ureagenesis	YAOU/RAOE/JEN/SIS
unsoundness	UN/SOUND/*NS		YAOU/RAOE/YA/JEN/SIS
unstriated	UN/STRAOI/AIT/-D	ureagenetic	YAOU/RAOE/JE/NET/IK
	UN/STRAOI/YAIT/-D		YAOU/RAOE/YA/JE/NET/IK
unsystematized	UN/S-M/TAOIZ/-D	ureal	YAOU/RAOEL
	UN/SIS/TEM/TAOIZ/-D		YAOU/RAOE/YAL
	UN/S*IS/MA/TAOIZ/-D	urealyticum	YAOU/RAOE/LIT/KUM
unthrifty	UN/THRIF/TI	ureametry	YAOUR/YAM/TRI
Unverricht	AOUN/VER/IKT		YAOUR/AM/TRI
	YAOUN/VER/IKT	Ureaplasma	YAOU/RAOE/PLAZ/MA
	UN/VER/IKT	ureapoiesis	YAOU/RAOE/POI/SIS
upper	UP/ER	urease	YAOUR/YAIS
up-regulation	UP/H-F/REG/LAIGS	urecchysis	YAOU/REK/SIS
upright	UP/RAOIGT	Urecholine	YAOUR/KOE/LIN
upsiloid	UPS/LOID		YAOUR/KOE/LAOEN
	UP/SI/LOID	uredema	YAOUR/DAOE/MA
uptake	UP/TAIK	uredo	YAOU/RAOE/DOE
ur(o)-	YAOUR	ureic	YAOU/RAOE/IK
	YAOU/R(O)	ureide	YAOU/RAOE/YAOID
	YAOUR/R(O)	ureidoisobutyric	YAOU/RAOE/DO/AOIS/BAOU/TIR/
urachal	YAOUR/KAL		IK
urachovesical	YAOUR/KO/VES/KAL	ureidopropionic	YAOU/RAOE/DO/PROEP/YON/IK
urachus	YAOUR/KUS	ureidosuccinic	YAOU/RAOE/DO/SUK/SIN/IK
uracil	YAOUR/SIL	urein	YAOU/RAOE/YIN
uracrasia	YAOUR/KRAIZ/YA	urelcosis	YAOU/REL/KOE/SIS
uracratia	YAOUR/KRAI/SHA		YAOU/EL/KOE/SIS
Uragoga	YAOUR/GOE/GA	uremia	YAOU/RAOEM/YA
uragogue	YAOUR/GOG	uremic	YAOU/RAOEM/IK
uramustine	YAOUR/MUS/TAOEN	uremigenic	YAOU/RAOEM/JEN/IK
uran(o)-	YAOUR/N(O)	ureo-	YAOUR/YO
uranin	YAOUR/NIN	ureolysis	YAOUR/YOL/SIS
uraninite	YAOU/RAN/NAOIT	ureolytic	YAOUR/YO/LIT/IK
uranisc(o)-	YAOUR/NIS/K(O)	ureometry	YAOUR/YOM/TRI
uraniscochasm	YAOUR/NIS/KO/KAFM	ureotelic	YAOUR/YO/TEL/IK
uraniscochasma	YAOUR/NIS/KO/KAZ/MA	uresiesthesia	YAOU/RAOES/YES/THAOEZ/YA
uraniscolalia	YAOUR/NIS/KO/LAIL/YA		YAOU/RAOES/ES/THAOEZ/YA
uranisconitis	YAOUR/NIS/KO/NAOITS	uresiesthesis	YAOU/RAOES/YES/THAOE/SIS
uraniscoplasty	YAOUR/NIS/KO/PLAS/TI		YAOU/RAOES/ES/THAOE/SIS
uraniscorrhaphy	YAOUR/NIS/KOR/FI	uresis	YAOU/RAOE/SIS
uraniscus	YAOUR/NIS/KUS	uret	YAOU/RET
uranism	YAOUR/NIFM	uretal	YAOU/RAOE/TAL
uranium	YAOU/RAIN/YUM	ureter	YAOU/RAOET/ER
uranoplastic	YAOUR/NO/PLA*S/IK	ureter(o)-	YAOU/RAOET/R(O)
uranoplasty	YAOUR/NO/PLAS/TI	ureteral	YAOU/RAOET/RAL
uranoplegia	YAOUR/NO/PLAOE/JA	ureteralgia	YAOU/RAOET/RAL/JA
uranorrhaphy	YAOUR/NOR/FI	ureterectasia	YAOU/RAOET/REK/TAIZ/YA
uranoschisis	YAOUR/NOS/KI/SIS	ureterectasis	YAOU/RAOET/REKT/SIS
uranoschism	YAOU/RAN/SKIFM	ureterectomy	YAOU/RAOET/REKT/M*I
uranostaphyloplasty	YAOUR/NO/STAF/LO/PLAS/TI	ureteric	YAOUR/TER/IK
uranostaphylorrhapy	YAOUR/NO/STAF/LOR/FI	ureteritis	YAOU/RAOET/RAOITS
uranostaphyloschisis	YAOUR/NO/STAF/LOS/KI/SIS	ureterocele	YAOU/RAOET/RO/SAO*EL
uranosteoplasty	YAOUR/NO*S/YO/PLAS/TI	ureterocelectomy	YAOU/RAOET/RO/SE/LEKT/M*I
Uranotaenia	YAOUR/NO/TAOEN/YA	ureterocelorrhaphy	YAOU/RAOET/RO/SE/LOR/FI
uranoveloschisis	YAOUR/NOEV/LOS/KI/SIS	ureterocervical	YAOU/RAOET/RO/SEFRB/KAL
uranyl	YAOUR/NIL	ureterocolostomy	YAOU/RAOET/RO/KO/LO*S/M*I
urapostema	YAOUR/POS/TAOE/MA	ureterocutaneostomy	YAOU/RAOET/RO/KAOU/TAIN/
uraroma	YAOUR/ROE/MA		YO*S/M*I
urarthritis	YAOU/RAR/THRAOITS	ureterocystanastomosis	YAOU/RAOET/RO/S*IS/NA*S/
urate	YAOUR/AIT		MOE/SIS
	YAOU/RAIT	ureterocystoneostomy	YAOU/RAOET/RO/S*IS/NAOE/
	YAOUR/RAIT		O*S/M*I

	YAOU/RAOET/RO/S*IS/NAOE/
	YO*S/M*I
ureterocystoscope	YAOU/RAOET/RO/S*IS/SKOEP
ureterocystostomy	YAOU/RAOET/RO/SIS/TO*S/M*I
ureterodialysis	YAOU/RAOET/RO/DI/AL/SIS
ureteroduodenal	YAOU/RAOET/RO/DAOU/
	DAOENL
	YAOU/RAOET/RO/DWOD/NAL
ureteroenteric	YAOU/RAOET/RO/SPWER/IK
ureteroenteroanastomosis	YAOU/RAOET/RO/SPWER/RO/AI/
	NA*S/MOE/SIS
ureteroenterostomy	YAOU/RAOET/RO/SPWRO*S/M*I
	YAOU/RAOET/RO/SPWER/RO*S/
	M*I
ureterogram	YAOU/RAOET/RO/GRAM
ureterography	YAOU/RAOET/ROG/FI
ureteroheminephrectomy	YAOU/RAOET/RO/HEM/NE/
	FREKT/M*I
ureterohydronephrosis	YAOU/RAOET/RO/HAOI/DRO/
	NEF/ROE/SIS
	YAOU/RAOET/RO/HAOI/DRO/NE/
	FROE/SIS
ureteroileoneocystostomy	YAOU/RAOET/RO/*IL/YO/NAOE/
	SIS/TO*S/M*I
ureteroileocutaneous	YAOU/RAOET/RO/*IL/YO/KAOU/
	TAIN/YOUS
ureteroileostomy	YAOU/RAOET/RO/*IL/YO*S/M*I
ureterointestinal	YAOU/RAOET/RO/SPW*ES/NAL
ureterolith	YAOU/RAOET/RO/L*IT
ureterolithiasis	YAOU/RAOET/RO/LI/THAOI/SIS
ureterolithotomy	YAOU/RAOET/RO/LI/THOT/M*I
ureterolysis	YAOU/RAOET/ROL/SIS
ureteromeatotomy	YAOU/RAOET/RO/MAOE/TOT/M*I
ureteroneocystostomy	YAOU/RAOET/RO/NAOE/SIS/
	TO*S/M*I
ureteroneopyelostomy	YAOU/RAOET/RO/NAOE/PAOI/
	LO*S/M*I
ureteronephrectomy	YAOU/RAOET/RO/NE/FREKT/M*I
ureteropathy	YAOU/RAOET/ROP/TH*I
ureteropelvic	YAOU/RAOET/RO/PEL/VIK
ureteropelvioneostomy	YAOU/RAOET/RO/PEL/VO/NAOE/
	YO*S/M*I
	YAOU/RAOET/RO/PEL/VAOE/YO/
	NAOE/YO*S/M*I
ureteropelvioplasty	YAOU/RAOET/RO/PEL/VO/PLAS/
	TI
	YAOU/RAOET/RO/PEL/VAOE/YO/
	PLAS/TI
ureterophlegma	YAOU/RAOET/RO/FLEG/MA
ureteroplasty	YAOU/RAOET/RO/PLAS/TI
ureteroproctostomy	YAOU/RAOET/RO/PROK/TO*S/
	M*I
ureteropyelitis	YAOU/RAOET/RO/PAOI/LAOITS
ureteropyelography	YAOU/RAOET/RO/PAOI/LOG/FI
ureteropyeloneostomy	YAOU/RAOET/RO/PAOI/LO/
	NAOE/O*S/M*I
	YAOU/RAOET/RO/PAOI/LO/
	NAOE/YO*S/M*I
ureteropyelonephritis	YAOU/RAOET/RO/PAOI/LO/NE/
	FRAOITS
ureteropyelonephrostomy	YAOU/RAOET/RO/PAOI/LO/NE/
	FRO*S/M*I
ureteropyeloplasty	YAOU/RAOET/RO/PAOI/LO/PLAS/
	TI
ureteropyelostomy	YAOU/RAOET/RO/PAOI/LO*S/M*I
ureteropyosis	YAOU/RAOET/RO/PAOI/YOE/SIS
ureterorectal	YAOU/RAOET/RO/REK/TAL
ureterorectoneostomy	YAOU/RAOET/RO/REKT/NAOE/
	O*S/M*I
	YAOU/RAOET/RO/REKT/NAOE/
	YO*S/M*I
ureterorectostomy	YAOU/RAOET/RO/REK/TO*S/M*I
ureterorenoscope	YAOU/RAOET/RO/RAOEN/SKOEP
ureterorenoscopy	YAOU/RAOET/RO/RE/NOS/KPI
ureterorrhagia	YAOU/RAOET/RO/RAI/JA
ureterorrhaphy	YAOU/RAOET/RO/ROR/FI
ureteroscopy	YAOU/RAOET/RO/ROS/KPI
ureterosigmoid	YAOU/RAOET/RO/SIG/MOID
ureterosigmoidostomy	YAOU/RAOET/RO/SIG/MOI/DO*S/
	M*I
ureterostegnosis	YAOU/RAOET/RO/STEG/NOE/SIS
ureterostenoma	YAOU/RAOET/RO/STE/NOE/MA
ureterostenosis	YAOU/RAOET/RO/STE/NOE/SIS
ureterostoma	YAOU/RAOET/RO*S/MA
ureterostomosis	YAOU/RAOET/RO/STOE/MOE/SIS
ureterostomy	YAOU/RAOET/RO*S/M*I
ureterotomy	YAOU/RAOET/ROT/M*I
ureterotrigonal	YAOU/RAOET/RO/TR*I/GOENL
	YAOU/RAOET/RO/TR*I/GOE/NAL

ureterotrigonoenterostomy	YAOU/RAOET/RO/TR*I/GOEN/
	SPWRO*S/M*I
	YAOU/RAOET/RO/TR*I/GOEN/
	SPWER/RO*S/M*I
ureterotrigonosigmoidostomy	
	YAOU/RAOET/RO/TR*I/GOEN/
	SIG/MOI/DO*S/M*I
ureterotubal	YAOU/RAOET/RO/TAOU/BAL
ureteroureteral	YAOU/RAOET/RO/YAOU/RAOET/
	RAL
ureteroureterostomy	YAOU/RAOET/RO/YAOU/RAOET/
	RO*S/M*I
ureterouterine	YAOU/RAOET/RO/YAOUT/RIN
ureterovaginal	YAOU/RAOET/RO/VAJ/NAL
ureterovesical	YAOU/RAOET/RO/VES/KAL
ureterovesicoplasty	YAOU/RAOET/RO/VES/KO/PLAS/
	TI
ureterovesicostomy	YAOU/RAOET/RO/VES/KO*S/M*I
urethan	YAOUR/THAN
urethane	YAOUR/THAIN
urethr(o)-	YAOU/RAO*ET/R(O)
	YAOU/RAOE/THR(O)
	YAOUR/THR-
urethra	YAOU/RAO*ET/RA
urethrae	YAOU/RAO*ET/RAE
urethral	YAOU/RAO*ET/RAL
urethralgia	YAOUR/THRAL/JA
	YAOU/RAO*ET/RAL/JA
urethralis	YAOUR/THRAI/LIS
urethrameter	YAOUR/THRAM/TER
urethrascope	YAOU/RAO*ET/RA/SKOEP
urethratresia	YAOU/RAO*ET/RA/TRAOEZ/YA
urethrectomy	YAOUR/THREKT/M*I
urethremorrhagia	YAOU/RAO*ET/REM/RAI/JA
urethremphraxis	YAOUR/THREM/FRAK/SIS
	YAOU/RAO*ET/REM/FRAK/SIS
urethreurynter	YAOU/RAO*ET/RAOU/RINT/ER
	YAOUR/THRAOU/RINT/ER
urethrism	YAOUR/THRIFM
urethrismus	YAOUR/THRIZ/MUS
urethritica	YAOUR/THRIT/KA
urethritis	YAOUR/THRAOITS
urethrobalanoplasty	YAOU/RAO*ET/RO/BAL/NO/PLAS/
	TI
urethroblennorrhea	YAOU/RAO*ET/RO/BLEN/RAOE/
	YA
urethrobulbar	YAOU/RAO*ET/RO/BUL/BAR
urethrocele	YAOU/RAO*ET/RO/SAO*EL
urethrocystitis	YAOU/RAO*ET/RO/SIS/TAOITS
urethrocystogram	YAOU/RAO*ET/RO/S*IS/GRAM
urethrocystometrography	YAOU/RAO*ET/RO/ME/TROG/FI
	YAOU/RAO*ET/RO/MAOE/TROG/
	FI
urethrocystometry	YAOU/RAO*ET/RO/SIS/TOM/TRI
urethrocystopexy	YAOU/RAO*ET/RO/S*IS/PEK/SI
urethrodynia	YAOU/RAO*ET/RO/DIN/YA
urethrograph	YAOU/RAO*ET/RO/GRAF
urethrography	YAOUR/THROG/FI
urethrometer	YAOUR/THROM/TER
	YAOU/RAO*ET/ROM/TER
urethrometry	YAOUR/THROM/TRI
	YAOU/RAO*ET/ROM/TRI
urethropenile	YAOU/RAO*ET/RO/PAOE/NAOIL
urethroperineal	YAOU/RAO*ET/RO/P*ER/NAOEL
urethroperineoscrotal	YAOU/RAO*ET/RO/P*ER/NAOE/
	SKROE/TAL
urethropexy	YAOU/RAO*ET/RO/PEK/SI
urethrophraxis	YAOU/RAO*ET/RO/FRAK/SIS
urethrophyma	YAOU/RAO*ET/RO/FAOI/MA
urethroplasty	YAOU/RAO*ET/RO/PLAS/TI
urethroprostatic	YAOU/RAO*ET/RO/PROS/TAT/IK
urethrorectal	YAOU/RAO*ET/RO/REK/TAL
urethrorrhagia	YAOU/RAO*ET/RO/RAI/JA
urethrorrhaphy	YAOUR/THROR/FI
	YAOU/RAO*ET/RO/ROR/FI
urethrorrhea	YAOU/RAO*ET/RO/RAOE/YA
urethroscope	YAOU/RAO*ET/RO/SKOEP
urethroscopic	YAOU/RAO*ET/RO/SKOP/IK
urethroscopy	YAOUR/THROS/KPI
	YAOU/RAO*ET/ROS/KPI
urethroscrotal	YAOU/RAO*ET/RO/SKROE/TAL
urethrospasm	YAOU/RAO*ET/RO/SPAFM
urethrostaxis	YAOU/RAO*ET/RO/STAK/SIS
urethrostenosis	YAOU/RAO*ET/RO/STE/NOE/SIS
urethrostomy	YAOUR/THRO*S/M*I
	YAOU/RAO*ET/RO*S/M*I
urethrotome	YAOU/RAO*ET/RO/TOEM
urethrotomy	YAOUR/THROT/M*I
	YAOU/RAO*ET/ROT/M*I

urethrotrigonitis	YAOU/RAO*ET/RO/TRIG/NAOITS
urethrovaginal	YAOU/RAO*ET/RO/VAJ/NAL
urethrovesical	YAOU/RAO*ET/RO/VES/KAL
urethrovesicopexy	YAOU/RAO*ET/RO/VES/KO/PEK/
	SI
uretic	YAOU/RET/IK
Urex	YAOU/REX
urgency	URJ/EN/SI
	UR/JEN/SI
Urginea	UR/JIN/YA
urhidrosis	UR/HID/ROE/SIS
	YAOUR/HI/DROE/SIS
	YAOUR/HID/ROE/SIS
	YAOUR/HAOI/DROE/SIS
-uria	YAOUR/YA
	(c)AOUR/YA
urian	YAOUR/YAN
uric	YAOUR/IK
	YAOURK
uricacidemia	YAOUR/IK/AS/DAOEM/YA
	YAOURK/AS/DAOEM/YA
uricaciduria	YAOUR/IK/AS/DAOUR/YA
	YAOURK/AS/DAOUR/YA
uricase	YAOUR/KAIS
uricemia	YAOUR/SAOEM/YA
uricemic	YAOUR/SAOEM/IK
urico-	YAOUR/KO
uricocholia	YAOUR/KO/KOEL/YA
uricolysis	YAOUR/KOL/SIS
uricolytic	YAOUR/KO/LIT/IK
uricometer	YAOUR/KOM/TER
uricopoiesis	YAOUR/KO/POI/SIS
uricosuria	YAOUR/KO/SAOUR/YA
uricosuric	YAOUR/KO/SAOUR/IK
uricotelic	YAOUR/KO/TEL/IK
uricotelism	YAOUR/KO/TEL/IFM
	YAOUR/KO/TAOE/LIFM
uricoxidase	YAOUR/KOX/DAIS
	YAOURK/OX/DAIS
	YAOUR/IK/OX/DAIS
-uricuria	YAOUR/KAOUR/YA
-uricuric	YAOUR/KAOUR/IK
uridine	YAOUR/DAOEN
	YAOUR/DIN
uridinediphosphogalactose	YAOUR/DAOEN/DI/FOS/FO/
	GLAK/TOES
uridinediphosphoglucose	YAOUR/DAOEN/DI/FOS/FO/
	GLAOU/KOES
uridinediphosphoglucuronic	
	YAOUR/DAOEN/DI/FOS/FO/
	GLAOUK/RON/IK
uridrosis	YAOUR/DROE/SIS
uridylic	YAOUR/DIL/IK
uridyltransferase	YAOUR/DIL/TRA*NS/FRAIS
uriesthesia	YAOUR/ES/THAOEZ/YA
uriesthesis	YAOUR/ES/THAOE/SIS
urina	YAOU/RAOI/NA
urinable	YAOURN/-BL
	YAOUR/RIN/-BL
urinaccelerator	YAOURN/AK/SEL/RAI/TOR
	YAOUR/RIN/AK/SEL/RAI/TOR
urinacidometer	YAOURN/AS/DOM/TER
	YAOUR/RIN/AS/DOM/TER
urinae	YAOU/RAOI/NAE
urinal	YAOURNL
	YAOUR/NAL
urinalysis	YAOUR/NAL/SIS
urinariae	YAOUR/NAIR/YAE
urinary	YAOUR/NAIR
urinate	YAOUR/NAIT
urination	YAOUR/NAIGS
urine	YAOURN
	YAOUR/RIN
urinemia	YAOUR/NAOEM/YA
urine-mucoid	YAOURN/MAOU/KOID
	YAOUR/RIN/MAOU/KOID
urinidrosis	YAOURN/DROE/SIS
uriniferous	YAOUR/NIF/ROUS
urinific	YAOUR/NIFK
	YAOUR/NIF/IK
uriniparous	YAOUR/NIP/ROUS
urinocryoscopy	YAOUR/NO/KRAOI/OS/KPI
urinogenital	YAOUR/NO/JEN/TAL
urinogenous	YAOUR/NOJ/NOUS
urinoglucosometer	YAOUR/NO/GLAOUK/SOM/TER
urinologist	YAOUR/NO*LGS
urinology	YAOUR/NOLG
urinoma	YAOUR/NOE/MA
urinometer	YAOUR/NOM/TER

urinometry	YAOUR/NOM/TRI
urinophilous	YAOUR/NOF/LOUS
urinoscopy	YAOUR/NOS/KPI
urinosexual	YAOUR/NO/SEX/YAOUL
urinous	YAOUR/NOUS
uriposia	YAOUR/POEZ/YA
Urised	YAOUR/SED
Urispas	YAOUR/SPAZ
	YAOUR/SPAS
uritis	YAOU/RAOITS
uro-	YAOUR
	YAOU/RO
	YAOUR/RO
uroacidimeter	YAOUR/AS/DIM/TER
uroammoniac	YAOUR/AI/MOEN/YAK
uroanthelone	YAOUR/A*NT/LOEN
uroazotometer	YAOUR/A*Z/TOM/TER
urobilin	YAOUR/BAOI/LIN
	YAOUR/B*I/LIN
	YAOUR/BIL/LIN
urobilinemia	YAOUR/BIL/NAOEM/YA
urobilinogen	YAOUR/BAOI/LIN/JEN
	YAOUR/B*I/LIN/JEN
	YAOUR/BIL/LIN/JEN
urobilinogenemia	YAOUR/BAOI/LIN/JE/NAOEM/YA
	YAOUR/B*I/LIN/JE/NAOEM/YA
	YAOUR/BIL/LIN/JE/NAOEM/YA
urobilinogenuria	YAOUR/BAOI/LIN/JE/NAOUR/YA
	YAOUR/B*I/LIN/JE/NAOUR/YA
	YAOUR/BIL/LIN/JE/NAOUR/YA
urobilinoid	YAOUR/BIL/NOID
urobilinoiden	YAOUR/BIL/NOI/DEN
urobilinuria	YAOUR/BIL/NAOUR/YA
Urobiotic	YAOUR/BAO*I/OT/IK
Urobiotic-250	YAOUR/BAO*I/OT/IK/250
urocanase	YAOUR/KAN/AIS
urocanate	YAOUR/KAN/AIT
urocanic	YAOUR/KAN/IK
urocanicase	YAOUR/KAN/KAIS
urocele	YAOUR/SAO*EL
urocheras	YAOU/ROK/RAS
urochezia	YAOUR/KAOEZ/YA
urochrome	YAOUR/KROEM
urochromogen	YAOUR/KROEM/JEN
urocinetic	YAOUR/SI/NET/IK
Urocit	YAOUR/SIT
Urocit-K	YAOUR/SIT/K-RBGS
uroclepsia	YAOUR/KLEPS/YA
urocoproporphyria	YAOUR/KOP/RO/POR/FIR/YA
urocrisia	YAOUR/KRIS/YA
	YAOUR/KRIZ/YA
urocrisis	YAOUR/KRAOI/SIS
urocriterion	YAOUR/KRAOI/TAOER/YON
urocyanin	YAOUR/SAOI/NIN
urocyanogen	YAOUR/SAOI/AN/JEN
	YAOUR/SAOI/YAN/JEN
urocyanosis	YAOUR/SAOI/NOE/SIS
urocyst	YAOUR/S*IS
urocystic	YAOUR/S*IS/IK
urocystis	YAOUR/SIS/TIS
urocystitis	YAOUR/SIS/TAOITS
urodeum	YAOUR/DAOE/UM
	YAOUR/DAOE/YUM
urodialysis	YAOUR/DI/AL/SIS
urodochium	YAOUR/DOEK/YUM
urodynamic	YAOUR/DAOI/NAM/IK
urodynamics	YAOUR/DAOI/NAM/IK/-S
urodynia	YAOUR/DIN/YA
urodysfunction	YAOUR/DIS/FUNGS
uroedema	YAOUR/DAOE/MA
	YAOUR/E/DAOE/MA
uroenterone	YAOUR/SPWER/ROEN
	YAOUR/ENT/ROEN
uroerythrin	YAOUR/*ER/THRIN
	YAOUR/ER/THRIN
uroflavin	YAOUR/FLAIVN
	YAOUR/FLAI/VIN
urofollitropin	YAOUR/FOL/TROE/PIN
urofuscin	YAOUR/FUS/SIN
urofuscohematin	YAOUR/FUS/KO/HAOEM/TIN
	YAOUR/FUS/KO/HEM/TIN
urogaster	YAOUR/GA*S/ER
	YAOUR/GAS/TER
urogastrone	YAOUR/GAS/TROEN
urogenital	YAOUR/JEN/TAL
urogenitale	YAOUR/JEN/TAI/LAOE
urogenitalis	YAOUR/JEN/TAI/LIS
urogenous	YAOU/ROJ/NOUS
uroglaucin	YAOUR/GLAU/SIN

urogonadotropin	YAOUR/GOE/NAD/TROE/PIN	uroschesis	YAOU/ROS/KE/SIS
	YAOUR/GON/DO/TROE/PIN	uroscopic	YAOUR/SKOP/IK
urogram	YAOUR/GRAM	uroscopy	YAOU/ROS/KPI
urography	YAOU/ROG/FI	urosemiology	YAOUR/SEM/YOLG
urogravimeter	YAOUR/GRA/VIM/TER		YAOUR/SAOEM/YOLG
urohematin	YAOUR/HAOEM/TIN	urosepsin	YAOUR/SEP/SIN
	YAOUR/HEM/TIN	urosepsis	YAOUR/SEP/SIS
urohematonephrosis	YAOUR/HAOEM/TO/NE/FROE/SIS	uroseptic	YAOUR/SEPT/IK
	YAOUR/HEM/TO/NE/FROE/SIS	urosis	YAOU/ROE/SIS
urohematoporphyrin	YAOUR/HAOEM/TO/POR/FRIN	urospectrin	YAOUR/SPEK/TRIN
	YAOUR/HEM/TO/POR/FRIN	urostalagmometry	YAOUR/STAL/AG/MOM/TRI
urohemolytic	YAOUR/HAOEM/LIT/IK	urostealith	YAOUR/STAOE/L*IT
uroheparin	YAOUR/HEP/RIN	urothelial	YAOUR/THAOEL/YAL
urohypertensin	YAOUR/HAO*IP/TEN/SIN	urothelium	YAOUR/THAOEL/YUM
urokinase	YAOUR/KAOI/NAIS	urothion	YAOUR/THAOI/YON
urokinetic	YAOUR/KI/NET/IK	urothorax	YAOUR/THOR/AX
urokymography	YAOUR/KAOI/MOG/FI	urotoxia	YAOUR/TOX/YA
Uro-KP-Neutral	YAOUR/K-RBGS/P*RBGS/NAOU/	urotoxic	YAOUR/TOX/IK
	TRAL	urotoxicity	YAOUR/TOK/SIS/TI
urolagnia	YAOUR/LAG/NA	urotoxin	YAOUR/TOK/SIN
	YAOUR/LAG/NAOE/YA	urotoxy	YAOUR/TOK/SI
Urolene	YAOUR/LAOEN	uroureter	YAOUR/YAOU/RAOET/ER
Urolene Blue	YAOUR/LAOEN/BLU	uroxanthin	YAOUR/ZAN/THIN
uroleucic	YAOUR/LAOUS/IK	uroxin	YAOU/ROK/SIN
uroleucinic	YAOUR/LAOU/SIN/IK	urtica	UR/TAOI/KA
urolith	YAOUR/L*IT		URT/KA
urolithiasis	YAOUR/LI/THAOI/SIS	urticant	URT/KANT
urolithic	YAOUR/L*IT/IK	urticaria	URT/KAIR/YA
urolithology	YAOUR/LI/THOLG	urticarial	URT/KAIRL
urologic	YAOUR/LOJ/IK		URT/KAIR/YAL
urological	YAOUR/LOJ/KAL	urticariogenic	URT/KAIR/YO/JEN/IK
urologist	YAOU/RO*LGS	urticarioides	URT/KAIR/YOI/DAOEZ
urology	YAOU/ROLG	urticarious	URT/KAIR/YOUS
urolutein	YAOUR/LAOUT/YIN	urticata	URT/KAI/TA
Uro-Mag	YAOUR/MAG	urticate	URT/KAIT
uromancy	YAOUR/MAN/SI	urtication	URT/KAIGS
uromantia	YAOUR/MAN/SHA	urushiol	YAOU/RAOU/SHOL
uromelanin	YAOUR/MEL/NIN		YAOU/RAOURB/YOL
urometer	YAOU/ROM/TER		YAOUR/SHAOE/OL
urometric	YAOUR/MET/RIK		YAOU/RAOU/SHAOE/OL
urometry	YAOU/ROM/TRI	Usher	K-P/URB/ER
uromucoid	YAOUR/MAOU/KOID	usta	US/TA
	YAOUR/MAOUK/OID	Ustilaginales	*US/LAJ/NAI/LAOEZ
uroncus	YAOU/RON/KUS		US/TI/LAJ/NAI/LAOEZ
Uronema caudatum	YAOUR/NAOE/MA/KAU/DAI/TUM	ustilaginism	*US/LAJ/NIFM
	YAOUR/NAOE/MA/KAU/DAIT/UM		US/TI/LAJ/NIFM
uronephrosis	YAOUR/NE/FROE/SIS	Ustilago	*US/LAI/GOE
uronic	YAOU/RON/IK		US/TI/LAI/GOE
uronophile	YAOU/RON/FAOIL	ustion	*US/YON
uropathogen	YAOUR/PA*T/JEN		US/KHON
uropathy	YAOU/ROP/TH*I		US/KHUN
uropenia	YAOUR/PAOEN/YA	ustulation	US/KHU/LAIGS
uropepsin	YAOUR/PEP/SIN		US/TAOU/LAIGS
uropepsinogen	YAOUR/PEP/SIN/JEN		*US/YAOU/LAIGS
urophanic	YAOUR/FAN/IK		*US/YU/LAIGS
urophein	YAOUR/FAOEN	ustum	US/TUM
	YAOUR/FAOE/YIN	ustus	US/TUS
urophilia	YAOUR/FIL/YA	usurpation	YAOU/SUR/PAIGS
urophobia	YAOUR/FOEB/YA	uta	YAOU/TA
Uro-Phosphate	YAOUR/FOS/FAIT	uter(o)-	YAOUT/R(O)
urophosphometer	YAOUR/FOS/FOM/TER	uteralgia	YAOUT/RAL/JA
uroplania	YAOUR/PLAIN/YA	uteri	YAOUT/RAOI
uropoiesis	YAOUR/POI/SIS	uterina	YAOUT/RAOI/NA
uropoietic	YAOUR/POIT/IK	uterinae	YAOUT/RAOI/NAE
uroporphyria	YAOUR/POR/FIR/YA	uterine	YAOUT/RIN
uroporphyrin	YAOUR/POR/FRIN		YAOUT/RAOIN
uroporphyrinogen	YAOUR/POR/FRIN/JEN	uterinus	YAOUT/RAOI/NUS
uropsammus	YAOUR/SAM/MUS	uterismus	YAOUT/RIZ/MUS
uropterin	YAOU/ROPT/RIN	uteritis	YAOUT/RAOITS
uropurpurin	YAOUR/PURP/RIN	uteroabdominal	YAOUT/RO/AB/DOM/NAL
uropyonephrosis	YAOUR/PAOI/NE/FROE/SIS	uterocervical	YAOUT/RO/SEFRB/KAL
uropyoureter	YAOUR/PAOI/YAOU/RAOET/ER	uterocystostomy	YAOUT/RO/SIS/TO*S/M*I
uroradiology	YAOUR/RAID/YOLG	uterodynia	YAOUT/RO/DIN/YA
Uroqid-Acid	YAOUR/KID/AS/ID	uterofixation	YAOUT/RO/FIK/SAIGS
urorectal	YAOUR/REK/TAL	uterogenic	YAOUT/RO/JEN/IK
urorhythmography	YAOUR/R*IT/MOG/FI	uterogestation	YAOUT/RO/JES/TAIGS
urorosein	YAOUR/ROEZ/YIN	uteroglobulin	YAOUT/RO/GLOB/LIN
uroroseinogen	YAOUR/ROEZ/YIN/JEN	uterography	YAOUT/ROG/FI
urorrhagia	YAOUR/RAI/JA	uterolith	YAOUT/RO/L*IT
urorrhea	YAOUR/RAOE/YA	uterometer	YAOUT/ROM/TER
urorrhodin	YAOUR/ROE/DIN	uterometry	YAOUT/ROM/TRI
urorrhodinogen	YAOUR/ROE/DIN/JEN	utero-ovarian	YAOUT/RO/O/VAIRN
urorubin	YAOUR/RAOU/BIN	uteroparietal	YAOUT/RO/PRAOI/TAL
urorubinogen	YAOUR/RAOU/BIN/JEN	uteropelvic	YAOUT/RO/PEL/VIK
urorubrohematin	YAOUR/RAOUB/RO/HAOEM/TIN	uteropexy	YAOUT/RO/PEK/SI
	YAOUR/RAOUB/RO/HEM/TIN	uteroplacental	YAOUT/RO/PLA/SEN/TAL
urosaccharometry	YAOUR/SAK/ROM/TRI	uteroplasty	YAOUT/RO/PLAS/TI
uroscheocele	YAOU/ROS/KO/SAO*EL	uterorectal	YAOUT/RO/REK/TAL
	YAOU/ROS/KAOE/YO/SAO*EL	uterosacral	YAOUT/RO/SAI/KRAL

uterosalpingography	YAOUT/RO/SAL/PIN/GOG/FI
uterosclerosis	YAOUT/RO/SKLE/ROE/SIS
uteroscope	YAOUT/RO/SKOEP
uteroscopy	YAOUT/ROS/KPI
uterothermometry	YAOUT/RO/THER/MOM/TRI
uterotomy	YAOUT/ROT/M*I
uterotonic	YAOUT/RO/TON/IK
uterotropic	YAOUT/RO/TROP/IK
uterotubal	YAOUT/RO/TAOU/BAL
uterotubography	YAOUT/RO/TAOU/BOG/FI
uterovaginal	YAOUT/RO/VAJ/NAL
uteroventral	YAOUT/RO/VEN/TRAL
uteroverdin	YAOUT/RO/VER/DIN
uterovesical	YAOUT/RO/VES/KAL
uterus	YAOUT/RUS
-utia	(c)AOU/SHA
	(c)AOURB/YA
utricle	YAOU/TRI/K-L
	YAOU/TRIK/-L
utricul(o)-	YAOU/TRIK/L(O)
	YAOU/TRIK/YAOU/L(O)
	YAOU/TRIK/YU/L(O)
utricular	YAOU/TRIK/LAR
utricularis	YAOU/TRIK/LAI/RIS
utriculi	YAOU/TRIK/LAOI
utriculitis	YAOU/TRIK/LAOITS
utriculosaccular	YAOU/TRIK/LO/SAK/LAR
utriculosaccularis	YAOU/TRIK/LO/SAK/LAI/RIS
utriculus	YAOU/TRIK/LUS
utriform	YAOU/TRI/FORM
uva	YAOU/VA
uva ursi	YAOU/VA/UR/SAOI
uvaeformis	YAOUV/FOR/MIS
	YAOU/VAOE/FOR/MIS
uve(o)-	YAOUV/Y(O)
uvea	YAOUV/YA
uveae	YAOUV/YAE
uveal	YAOUV/YAL
uveitic	YAOUV/YIT/IK
uveitides	YAOUV/YIT/DAOEZ
uveitis	YAOUV/YAOITS
uveoencephalitis	YAOUV/YO/EN/SEF/LAOITS
uveolabyrinthitis	YAOUV/YO/LAB/RIN/THAOITS
uveomeningitis	YAOUV/YO/MEN/JAOITS
uveoneuraxitis	YAOUV/YO/NAOU/RAK/SAOITS
	YAOUV/YO/NAOUR/AK/SAOITS
uveoparotid	YAOUV/RO/PROT/ID
	YAOUV/RO/PA/ROT/ID
uveoparotidea	YAOUV/YO/PROT/DAOE/YA
	YAOUV/YO/PA/ROT/DAOE/YA
uveoparotitis	YAOUV/YO/PAR/O/TAOITS
	YAOUV/YO/PAR/RO/TAOITS
uveoplasty	YAOUV/YO/PLAS/TI
uveoscleritis	YAOUV/YO/SKLE/RAOITS
	YAOUV/YO/SKLAOE/RAOITS
uviform	YAOUV/FORM
uviofast	YAOUV/YO/FA*S
uviol	YAOUV/YOL
uviolize	YAOUV/YO/LAOIZ
	YAOUV/YOL/AOIZ
uviometer	YAOUV/YOM/TER
uvioresistant	YAOUV/YO/RE/SIS/TANT
uviosensitive	YAOUV/YO/SENS/TIV
uvul(o)-	YAOUV/L(O)
	YAOUV/YAOU/L(O)
	YAOUV/YU/L(O)
	YAOU/VAOU/L(O)
uvula	YAOUV/LA
uvulae	YAOUV/LAE
uvulaptosis	YAOUV/LAP/TOE/SIS
uvular	YAOUV/LAR
uvularis	YAOUV/LAI/RIS
uvulatome	YAOUV/LA/TOEM
uvulectomy	YAOUV/LEKT/M*I
uvuli	YAOUV/LAOI
uvulitis	YAOUV/LAOITS
uvulopalatopharyngoplasty	YAOUV/LO/PAL/TO/FRING/PLAS/TI
uvulopalatoplasty	YAOUV/LO/PAL/TO/PLAS/TI
uvuloptosis	YAOUV/LOP/TOE/SIS
uvulotome	YAOUV/LO/TOEM
uvulotomy	YAOUV/LOT/M*I

V

vaccenic	VAK/SEN/IK
vaccigenous	VAK/SIJ/NOUS
vaccin-	VAX/N-
	VAK/SI/N-
	VAK/SIN
vaccina	VAX/NA
	VAK/SIN/NA
vaccinable	VAK/SIN/-BL
vaccinal	VAX/NAL
vaccinate	VAX/NAIT
vaccination	VAX/NAIGS
vaccinator	VAX/NAI/TOR
vaccinatum	VAX/NAI/TUM
	VAX/NAIT/UM
vaccine	VAK/SAOEN
vaccinia	VAK/SIN/YA
vaccinial	VAK/SIN/YAL
vaccinid	VAX/NID
vaccinifer	VAK/SIN/FER
vacciniform	VAK/SIN/FORM
vaccinist	VAX/N*IS
	VAK/SIN*IS
vaccinization	VAK/SIN/ZAIGS
vaccino-	VAX/NO
	VAK/SI/NO
	VAK/SIN
vaccinogen	VAK/SIN/JEN
vaccinogenous	VAX/NOJ/NOUS
vaccinoid	VAX/NOID
vaccinostyle	VAX/NO/STAOIL
	VAK/SIN/STAOIL
vaccinotherapy	VAX/NO/THER/PI
vaccinum	VAX/NUM
	VAK/SI/NUM
	VAK/SAOIN/UM
	VAK/SAOI/NUM
vacuo-	VAK/YO
	VAK/YAOU
	VAK/WO
vacuolar	VAK/YOE/LAR
vacuolate	VAK/YO/LAIT
vacuolated	VAK/YO/LAIT/-D
vacuolating	VAK/YO/LAIT/-G
vacuolation	VAK/YO/LAIGS
vacuole	VAK/YOEL
vacuolization	VAK/YOEL/ZAIGS
vacuome	VAK/YOEM
vacutome	VAK/YAOU/TOEM
	VAK/TOEM
vacuum	VAK/YAOUM
	VAK/YUM
vadum	VAI/DUM
	VAID/UM
vagal	VAI/GAL
vagectomy	VAI/JEKT/M*I
vagi	VAI/GAOI
	VAI/JAOI
Vagilia	VA/JIL/YA
vagin(o)-	VAJ/N(O)
	VA/JAOIN
	VA/JAOI/N(O)
vagina	VA/JAOI/NA
vaginae	VA/JAOI/NAE
vaginal	VAJ/NAL
vaginale	VAJ/NAI/LAOE
vaginalectomy	VAJ/NA/LEKT/M*I
vaginales	VAJ/NAI/LAOEZ
vaginalia	VAJ/NAIL/YA
vaginalis	VAJ/NAI/LIS
vaginalitis	VAJ/NA/LAOITS
vaginapexy	VA/JAOIN/PEK/SI
	VAJ/NA/PEK/SI
vaginate	VAJ/NAIT
vaginectomy	VAJ/NEKT/M*I
vaginism	VAJ/NIFM
vaginismus	VAJ/NIZ/MUS
vaginitides	VAJ/NAOIT/DAOEZ
	VAJ/NIT/DAOEZ
vaginitis	VAJ/NAOITS
vaginoabdominal	VAJ/NO/AB/DOM/NAL
vaginocele	VAJ/NO/SAO*EL
vaginocutaneous	VAJ/NO/KAOU/TAIN/YOUS
vaginodynia	VAJ/NO/DIN/YA
vaginofixation	VAJ/NO/FIK/SAIGS

vaginogram	VAJ/NO/GRAM
vaginography	VAJ/NOG/FI
vaginohysterectomy	VAJ/NO/H*IS/REKT/M*I
vaginolabial	VAJ/NO/LAIB/YAL
vaginometer	VAJ/NOM/TER
vaginomycosis	VAJ/NO/MAOI/KOE/SIS
vaginopathy	VAJ/NOP/TH*I
vaginoperineal	VAJ/NO/P*ER/NAOEL
vaginoperineoplasty	VAJ/NO/P*ER/NAOE/PLAS/TI
vaginoperineorrhaphy	VAJ/NO/P*ER/NAOE/YOR/FI
vaginoperineotomy	VAJ/NO/P*ER/NAOE/OT/M*I
vaginoperitoneal	VAJ/NO/PERT/NAOEL
vaginopexy	VAJ/NO/PEK/SI
vaginoplasty	VAJ/NO/PLAS/TI
vaginoscope	VAJ/NO/SKOEP
vaginoscopy	VAJ/NOS/KPI
vaginotomy	VAJ/NOT/M*I
vaginovesical	VAJ/NO/VES/KAL
vaginovulvar	VAJ/NO/VUL/VAR
Vagisec	VAJ/SEK
Vagisec Plus	VAJ/SEK/PLUS
Vagistat	VAJ/STAT
vagitus	VA/JAOI/TUS
vagitus uterinus	VA/JAOI/TUS/YAOUT/RAOI/NUS
vagitus vaginalis	VA/JAOI/TUS/VAJ/NAI/LIS
vago-	VAIG
	VAI/GO
vagoaccessorius	VAIG/AK/SES/SOER/YUS
	VAIG/AK/SES/SOR/YUS
vagoglossopharyngeal	VAIG/GLOS/FRIN/JAL
vagogram	VAIG/GRAM
vagolysis	VAI/GOL/SIS
vagolytic	VAIG/LIT/IK
vagomimetic	VAIG/MAOI/MET/IK
	VAIG/MI/MET/IK
vagosplanchnic	VAIG/SPLANG/NIK
vagosympathetic	VAIG/SIFRP/THET/IK
vagotomy	VAI/GOT/M*I
vagotonia	VAIG/TOEN/YA
vagotonic	VAIG/TON/IK
vagotony	VAI/GOT/N*I
vagotropic	VAIG/TROP/IK
vagotropism	VAI/GOT/RO/PIFM
vagovagal	VAIG/VAI/GAL
vagrant	VAI/GRANT
vagus	VAI/GUS
vain	VAIN
valence	VAIL/ENS
	VAI/LENS
valency	VAIL/EN/SI
	VAI/LEN/SI
	VAIL/-N/SI
valent	VAIL/ENT
	VAI/LENT
Valentin	VAL/EN/TIN
	VAL/EN/TAOEN
valeraldehyde	VAL/RALD/HAOID
valerate	VAL/RAIT
	VA/LER/AIT
valerian	VA/LAOERN
	VA/LAOER/YAN
	VA/LER/YAN
valerianate	VA/LAOER/YA/NAIT
	VA/LER/YA/NAIT
valeric	VA/LAOER/IK
	VA/LER/IK
valethamate	VAL/L*ET/MAIT
	VAL/*ET/MAIT
valetudinarian	VAL/TAOUD/NAIRN
	VAL/TAOUD/NAIR/YAN
valetudinarianism	VAL/TAOUD/NAIRN/IFM
	VAL/TAOUD/NAIR/YAN/IFM
valga	VAL/GA
valgoid	VAL/GOID
valgum	VAL/GUM
valgus	VAL/GUS
valid	VAL/ID
validation	VAL/DAIGS
validity	VA/LID/TI
valine	VAL/LIN
valinemia	VAL/NAOEM/YA
Valium	VAL/YUM
valla	VAL/LA
vallate	VAL/AIT
	VAL/LAIT
vallecul-	VA/LEK/L-
	VA/LEK/YAOU/L-
	VA/LEK/YU/L-
	VAL/LEK/L-

	VAL/LEK/YAOU/L-	vanillism	VAN/LIN
	VAL/LEK/YU/L-		VA/NIL/IFM
vallecula	VA/LEK/LAR	vanillylmandelic	VAN/LIL/MAN/DEL/IK
valleculae	VA/LEK/LAE		VA/NIL/IL/MAN/DEL/IK
vallecular	VA/LEK/LAR	Vanoxide	VAN/OK/SAOID
Valleix	VAL/LAIZ		VAN/OX/AOID
valley	VAL/LAOE	Vanoxide-HC	VAN/OK/SAOID/H-RBGS/
vallis	VAL/LIS		KR*RBGS
vallum	VAL/UM		VAN/OX/AOID/H-RBGS/KR*RBGS
	VAL/LUM	Vanquish	VA*N/KWIRB
valmethamide	VAL/M*ET/MAOID		K-P/VAN/KWIRB
Valmid	VAL/MID	Vanseb	VAN/SEB
valnoctamide	VAL/NOKT/MAOID	Vanseb-T	VAN/SEB/T-RBGS
valoid	VAL/OID	Vansil	VAN/SIL
Valpin	VAL/PIN	Van Slyke	VAN/SLAOIK
valproate	VAL/PRO/AIT	van't Hoff	VANT/HOF
	VAL/PROE/AIT	vapo-	VAIP
valproic	VAL/PROIK		VAI/PO
	VAL/PROE/IK	vapocauterization	VAIP/KAUT/RI/ZAIGS
Valrelease	VAL/RE/LAOES		VAIP/KAU/TER/ZAIGS
Valsalva	VAL/SAL/VA	vapor	VAI/POR
Valsalvae	VAL/SAL/VAE	vaporization	VAI/POR/ZAIGS
valsalviana	VAL/SAL/VAI/NA	vaporize	VAIP/RAOIZ
	VAL/SAL/VAOE/YAI/NA	vaporizer	VAIP/RAOIZ/ER
value	VAL	vapors	VAI/POR/-S
	VAL/YAOU	vaporthorax	VAI/POR/THOR/AX
valva	VAL/VA	Vaporub	VAIP/RUB
valvae	VAL/VAE		VAI/PO/RUB
valval	VAL/VAL	vapotherapy	VAIP/THER/PI
valvar	VAL/VAR	Vaquez	VA/KAI
valvate	VAL/VAIT		VA/KEZ
valve	VAL/-V	vara	VAIR/RA
valved	VAL/-VD		VAI/RA
valveless	VAL/-V/LES	variabilis	VAIR/YAB/LIS
valviform	VAL/VI/FORM	variability	VAIRBLT
valvoplasty	VAL/VO/PLAS/TI		VAIR/YABLT
valvotome	VAL/VO/TOEM	variable	VAIRBL
valvotomy	VAL/VOT/M*I		VAIR/YABL
valvul(o)-	VAL/VAOU/L(O)	variance	VAIRNS
	VAL/VAOUL		VAIR/YANS
valvula	VAL/VAOU/LA	variant	VAIRNT
valvulae	VAL/VAOU/LAE		VAIR/YANT
valvular	VAL/VAOU/LAR	variate	VAIR/AIT
valvule	VAL/VAOUL	variation	VAIRGS
valvulitis	VAL/VAOU/LAOITS		VAIR/YAIGS
valvuloplasty	VAL/VAOU/LO/PLAS/TI	varic(o)-	VAIR/K(O)
	VAL/VAOUL/PLAS/TI		VAR/K(O)
valvulotome	VAL/VAOU/LO/TOEM	varication	VAIR/KAIGS
	VAL/VAOUL/TOEM	variceal	VAIR/SAOEL
valvulotomy	VAL/VAOU/LOT/M*I		VAIR/SAOE/YAL
valyl	VAL/IL		VA/RIS/YAL
vampire	VAM/PAOIR	varicella	VAIR/SEL/LA
vanadate	VAN/DAIT	varicellation	VAIR/SE/LAIGS
vanadic	VA/NAD/IK		VAIR/SEL/LAIGS
vanadium	VA/NAID/YUM	varicelliform	VAIR/SEL/FORM
vanadiumism	VA/NAID/YUM/IFM	varicellization	VAIR/SEL/ZAIGS
van Bogaert	VAN/BOE/GART	varicelloid	VAIR/SEL/OID
	VAN/BOE/GAERT	varices	VAIR/SAOEZ
van Buren	VAN/BAOURN	variciform	VAIR/SI/FORM
	VAN/BAOUR/-N		VA/RIS/FORM
	VAN/BAOU/REN		VAIR/IS/FORM
Vancenase	VANS/NAIS		VAR/IS/FORM
Vanceril	VANS/RIL	varicoblepharon	VAIR/KO/BLEF/RON
Vancocin	VAN/KO/SIN	varicocele	VAIR/KO/SAO*EL
Vancoled	VAN/KO/LED	varicocelectomy	VAIR/KO/SE/LEKT/M*I
vancomycin	VAN/KO/MAOI/SIN	varicography	VAIR/KOG/FI
Vancor	VAN/KOR	varicoid	VAIR/KOID
vandal	VAN/DAL	varicole	VAIR/KOEL
van Deen	VAN/DAOEN	varicomphalus	VAIR/KOM/FLUS
Van de Graaff	VAN/DE/GRAF	varicophlebitis	VAIR/KO/FLE/BAOITS
van den Bergh	VAN/DEN/BERG	varicose	VAIR/KOES
van der Velden	VAN/DER/VELD/-N	varicoses	VAIR/KOE/SAOEZ
	VAN/DER/VEL/DEN	varicosis	VAIR/KOE/SIS
Van der Waals	VAN/DER/VAULS	varicosity	VAIR/KOS/TI
	VAN/DER/VALS	varicotomy	VAIR/KOT/M*I
vane	VAEN	varicula	VA/RIK/LA
van Gehuchten	VAN/GAI/HAOUK/TEN	varicule	VAIR/KAOUL
	VAN/GE/HAOUK/TEN	variegatum	VAIR/GAI/TUM
	VAN/GE/HUK/TEN		VAIR/GAIT/UM
van Gieson	VAN/GAOE/SON		VAIR/YE/GAI/TUM
van Helmont	VAN/HEL/MONT		VAIR/YE/GAIT/UM
van Hook	VAN/HAOK	variety	VAIRT
van Hoorne	VAN/HORN		VA/RAOI/TI
	VAN/HAORN	vario-	VAIR/YO
vanilla	VA/NIL/LA		VA/RAOI
vanillate	VA/NIL/AIT	variola	VA/RAOI/LA
	VA/NIL/LAIT	variolar	VA/RAOI/LAR
vanillic	VA/NIL/IK	Variolaria	VAIR/YO/LAIR/YA
vanillin	VA/NIL/LIN	variolate	VAIR/YO/LAIT

variolation	VAIR/YO/LAIGS	vasography	VAI/SOG/FI
variolic	VAIR/YOL/IK		VA/SOG/FI
varioliform	VA/RAOI/LI/FORM		VAS/OG/FI
	VAIR/YOEL/FORM	vasohypertonic	VAIS/HAO*IP/TON/IK
varioliformis	VA/RAOI/LI/FOR/MIS	vasohypotonic	VAIS/HO*IP/TON/IK
	VAIR/YOEL/FOR/MIS	vasoinert	VAIS/IN/ERT
variolization	VA/RAOI/LI/ZAIGS	vasoinhibitor	VAIS/IN/HIB/TOR
	VAIR/YOEL/ZAIGS	vasoinhibitory	VAIS/IN/HIB/TOIR
varioloid	VA/RAOI/LOID	vasolabile	VAIS/LAI/BAOIL
	VAIR/YO/LOID		VAIS/LAI/BIL
variolous	VA/RAOI/LOUS	vasoligation	VAIS/LAOI/GAIGS
variolovaccine	VA/RAOI/LO/VAK/SAOEN		VAIS/LI/GAIGS
varipalpus	VAIR/PAL/PUS	vasoligature	VAIS/LIG/KHUR
varix	VAIR/IX	vasomotion	VAIS/MOEGS
	VAI/RIX	vasomotor	VAIS/MOE/TOR
varnish	VARN/IRB	vasomotoria	VAIS/MOE/TOER/YA
	VAR/NIRB	vasomotorial	VAIS/MOE/TOIRL
varolian	VA/ROEL/YAN		VAIS/MOE/TOER/YAL
Varolius	VA/ROEL/YUS	vasomotoricity	VAIS/MOET/RIS/TI
varus	VAIR/RUS	vasomotorium	VAIS/MOE/TOIRM
	VAI/RUS		VAIS/MOE/TOER/YUM
vas	VAS	vasomotory	VAIS/MOET/RI
vas(o)-	VAIS	vasoneuropathy	VAIS/NAOU/ROP/TH*I
	VAIZ	vasoneurosis	VAIS/NAOU/ROE/SIS
	VAS	vasoneurotic	VAIS/NAOU/ROT/IK
	VA/S(O)	vaso-orchidostomy	VAIS/ORK/DO*S/M*I
	VAI/SO	vasoparalysis	VAIS/PRAL/SIS
	VAI/ZO	vasoparesis	VAIS/PA/RAOE/SIS
vasa	VAI/SA		VAIS/PAR/SIS
vasal	VAI/SAL	vasopermeability	VAIS/PERM/YABLT
vasalgia	VA/SAL/JA	vasopressin	VAIS/PRES/SIN
	VAI/SAL/JA	vasopressor	VAIS/PRES/SOR
vasalium	VA/SAIL/YUM	vasopuncture	VAIS/PUNG/KHUR
vascul(o)-	VAS/KL(O)	vasoreflex	VAIS/RE/FLEX
	VAS/KAOU/L(O)	vasorelaxation	VAIS/RE/LAK/SAIGS
vascula	VAS/KLA		VAIS/RE/LAX/AIGS
vascular	VAS/KLAR	vasoresection	VAIS/RE/S*EBGS
vascularis	VAS/KLAI/RIS	vasorrhaphy	VAI/SOR/FI
vascularity	VAS/KLAIR/TI		VA/SOR/FI
vascularization	VAS/KLAR/ZAIGS		VAS/OR/FI
vascularize	VAS/KLAR/AOIZ	vasorum	VAI/SOER/UM
vasculature	VAS/KLA/KHUR		VAI/SOR/UM
vasculitic	VAS/KLIT/IK		VA/SOER/UM
vasculitis	VAS/KLAOITS		VA/SOR/UM
vasculocardiac	VAS/KLO/KARD/YAK	vasosection	VAIS/S*EBGS
vasculogenesis	VAS/KLO/JEN/SIS	vasosensory	VAIS/SENS/RI
vasculogenic	VAS/KLO/JEN/IK	vasospasm	VAIS/SPAFM
vasculolymphatic	VAS/KLO/LIM/FAT/IK	vasospasmolytic	VAIS/SPAZ/MO/LIT/IK
vasculomotor	VAS/KLO/MOE/TOR	vasospastic	VAIS/SPA*S/IK
vasculomyelinopathy	VAS/KLO/MAOI/LI/NOP/TH*I	vasostimulant	VAIS/STIM/LANT
	VAS/KLO/MAOI/LIN/OP/TH*I	vasostomy	VA/SO*S/M*I
vasculopathy	VAS/KLOP/TH*I		VAS/O*S/M*I
vasculosa	VAS/KLOE/SA		VAI/SO*S/M*I
vasculosi	VAS/KLOE/SAOI	Vasotec	VAIS/TEK
vasculosus	VAS/KLOE/SUS		VAS/TEK
vasculotoxic	VAS/KLO/TOX/IK	vasothrombin	VAIS/THROM/BIN
vasculum	VAS/KLUM	vasotocin	VAIS/TOE/SIN
vas deferens	VAS/DEFRNZ	vasotomy	VAI/SOT/M*I
	VAS/DEF/RENZ		VA/SOT/M*I
vasectomize	VA/SEKT/MAOIZ	vasotonia	VAIS/TOEN/YA
	VAS/EKT/MAOIZ	vasotonic	VAIS/TON/IK
vasectomized	VA/SEKT/MAOIZ/-D	vasotribe	VAIS/TRAOIB
	VAS/EKT/MAOIZ/-D	vasotripsy	VAIS/TRIP/SI
vasectomy	VA/SEKT/M*I	vasotrophic	VAIS/TROFK
	VAS/EKT/M*I	vasotropic	VAIS/TROEP/IK
Vaseretic	VAS/RET/IK		VAIS/TROP/IK
vasifactive	VAS/FAKT/IV	vasovagal	VAIS/VAI/GAL
vasiform	VAS/FORM	vasovasostomy	VAIS/VA/SO*S/M*I
vasis	VAI/SIS		VAIS/VAI/SO*S/M*I
vasitis	VA/SAOITS	vasovesiculectomy	VAIS/VE/SIK/LEKT/M*I
vasoactive	VAIS/AKT/IV	vasovesiculitis	VAIS/VE/SIK/LAOITS
vasoconstriction	VAIS/KON/STR*IBGS	Vasoxyl	VAS/OK/SIL
vasoconstrictive	VAIS/KON/STRIKT/IV		VAS/OX/IL
vasoconstrictor	VAIS/KON/STRIK/TOR	vastus	VAS/TUS
vasocorona	VAIS/KO/ROE/NA	Vater	VAT/ER
vasodentin	VAIS/DEN/TIN		VA/TER
vasodepression	VAIS/DPREGS	vault	VAULT
vasodepressor	VAIS/DPRES/SOR	V-bends	V-RBGS/BENDZ
vasodilatation	VAIS/DIL/TAIGS	vection	V*EBGS
vasodilation	VAIS/DI/LAIGS	vectis	VEK/TIS
vasodilative	VAIS/DI/LAIT/IV	vector	VEK/TOR
vasodilator	VAIS/DI/LAI/TOR	vectorcardiogram	VEK/TOR/KARD/YO/GRAM
vasoepididymography	VAIS/EP/DID/MOG/FI	vectorcardiograph	VEK/TOR/KARD/YO/GRAF
vasoepididymostomy	VAIS/EP/DID/MO*S/M*I	vectorcardiography	VEK/TOR/KARD/YOG/FI
vasofactive	VAIS/FAKT/IV	vectorial	VEK/TOIRL
vasoformation	VAIS/FOR/MAIGS	vectorscope	VEK/TOR/SKOEP
vasoformative	VAIS/FOR/MTIV	vecuronium	VEK/ROEN/YUM
vasoganglion	VAIS/GANG/LON		VEK/YAOU/ROEN/YUM
vasogenic	VAIS/JEN/IK		VEK/YU/ROEN/YUM

Veetids	VAOE/TIDZ		VE/NAOER/YAL
vegan	VEJ/JAN	venereologist	VE/NAOER/YO*LGS
veganism	VEJ/NIFM	venereology	VE/NAOER/YOLG
vegetable	VEJ/TABL	venearophobia	VE/NAOER/YO/FOEB/YA
	VEJT/-BL	venereum	VE/NAOERM
vegetal	VEJ/TAL		VE/NAOER/YUM
vegetality	VEJ/TAL/TI	veneris	VEN/RIS
vegetans	VEJ/TANZ	venerology	VEN/ROLG
vegetarian	VEJ/TAIRN	venery	VEN/RI
	VEJ/TAIR/YAN	Venezuelan	VEN/SWAI/LAN
vegetarianism	VEJ/TAIRN/IFM	venezuelensis	VEN/SWAI/LEN/SIS
	VEJ/TAIR/YAN/IFM	veni-	VEN
vegetation	VEJ/TAIGS	venile	VAOE/NAOIL
vegetative	VEJ/TAIT/IV		VAOE/NIL
vegetoanimal	VEJ/TO/AN/MAL	venin	VEN/NIN
vehicle	VAOEK	veniplex	VEN/PLEX
	VAOE/HIK/-L	venipuncture	VEN/PUNG/KHUR
veil	VA*IL	venisection	VEN/S*EBGS
	(not VAIL; see vail)	venisuture	VEN/SAOU/KHUR
Veillon	VAI/YON	venoatrial	VAOEN/AI/TRAL
	VAI/YAU	venoauricular	VAOEN/AU/RIK/LAR
Veillonella	VAI/NEL/LA	venoclysis	VAOE/NOK/LI/SIS
	VAI/YO/NEL/LA	venofibrosis	VAOEN/FAOI/BROE/SIS
Veillonellaceae	VAI/NEL/LAIS/YAE	Venoglobulin	VAOEN/GLOB/LIN
	VAI/YO/NEL/LAIS/YAE	venogram	VAOEN/GRAM
vein	VA*IN	venography	VAOE/NOG/FI
	(not VAIN; see vain)	venom	VEN/OM
veined	VA*IN/-D	venomization	VEN/MI/ZAIGS
veinlet	VA*IN/LET		VEN/OM/ZAIGS
Vejovis	VAOE/JOE/VIS	venomosalivary	VEN/MO/SAL/VAIR
vela	VAOE/LA	venomotor	VAOEN/MOE/TOR
velamen	VE/LAI/MEN	venomous	VEN/MOUS
	VAOE/LAI/MEN	veno-occlusive	VAOEN/O/KLAOUS/IV
velamenta	VEL/MEN/TA	venoperitoneostomy	VAOEN/PERT/NAOE/O*S/M*I
velamentous	VEL/MEN/TOUS		VAOEN/PERT/NAOE/YO*S/M*I
	VEL/-MT/OUS	venopressor	VAOEN/PRES/SOR
velamentum	VEL/MEN/TUM	venosclerosis	VAOEN/SKLE/ROE/SIS
	VEL/-MT/UM	venose	VAOE/NOES
velamina	VE/LAM/NA	venosi	VAOE/NOE/SAOI
	VAOE/LAM/NA	venosinal	VAOEN/SAOINL
velar	VAOE/LAR	venosity	VAOE/NOS/TI
Velban	VEL/BAN	venostasis	VAOEN/STAI/SIS
veli	VAOE/LAOI		VAOE/NO*S/SIS
veliform	VEL/FORM	venostomy	VAOE/NO*S/M*I
Vella	VEL/LA	venosum	VAOE/NOE/SUM
vellicate	VEL/KAIT		VAOE/NOES/UM
vellication	VEL/KAIGS	venosus	VAOE/NOE/SUS
vellus	VEL/LUS	venotomy	VAOE/NOT/M*I
velocity	VE/LOS/TI	venous	VAOEN/OUS
velogenic	VEL/JEN/IK		VAOE/NOUS
velonoskiascopy	VAOEL/NO/SKAOI/AS/KPI	venovenostomy	VAOEN/VAOE/NO*S/M*I
	VEL/NO/SKAOI/AS/KPI	vent	VENT
velopharyngeal	VAOEL/FRIN/JAL	venter	VENT/ER
	VEL/FRIN/JAL	ventilate	VENT/LAIT
Velosef	VEL/SEF	ventilation	VENT/LAIGS
Velosulin	VEL/SUL/LIN	ventilator	VENT/LAI/TOR
velosynthesis	VAOEL/S*INT/SIS	Ventolin	VENT/LIN
	VEL/S*INT/SIS	ventplant	VENT/PLANT
Velpeau	VEL/POE	ventr(o)-	VEN/TR(O)
velum	VAOE/LUM	ventrad	VEN/TRAD
	VAOEL/UM	ventral	VEN/TRAL
ven(o)-	VAOE/N(O)	ventrale	VEN/TRAI/LAOE
	VAOEN	ventralia	VEN/TRAIL/YA
	VEN	ventralis	VEN/TRAI/LIS
vena	VAOE/NA	ventricle	VEN/TRI/K-L
vena cava	VAOEN/KAI/VA		VEN/TRIK/-L
	VAOEN/KA/VA	ventricornu	VEN/TRI/KOR/NAOU
	VAOE/NA/KAI/VA	ventricornual	VEN/TRI/KOR/NAOUL
	VAOE/NA/KA/VA		VEN/TRI/KORN/YAL
venacavogram	VAOEN/KAIV/GRAM	ventricose	VEN/TRI/KOES
venacavography	VAOEN/KAI/VOG/FI	ventricosus	VEN/TRI/KOE/SUS
venae	VAOE/NAE	ventricul(o)-	VEN/TRIK/L(O)
venae cavae	VAOEN/KAI/VAE		VEN/TRIK/YAOU/L(O)
	VAOE/NAE/KAI/VAE		VEN/TRIK/YU/L(O)
venation	VAOE/NAIGS	ventricular	VEN/TRIK/LAR
venectasia	VAOE/NEK/TAIZ/YA	ventriculare	VEN/TRIK/LAI/RAOE
venectomy	VAOE/NEKT/M*I	ventricularis	VEN/TRIK/LAI/RIS
veneer	VE/NAOER	ventricularization	VEN/TRIK/LAR/ZAIGS
venenata	VEN/NAI/TA	ventriculi	VEN/TRIK/LAOI
venenation	VEN/NAIGS	ventriculilaryngis	VEN/TRIK/LAOI/LARN/JIS
veneniferous	VEN/NIF/ROUS	ventriculitis	VEN/TRIK/LAOITS
venenific	VEN/NIFK	ventriculoatrial	VEN/TRIK/LO/AI/TRAL
venenosalivary	VEN/NO/SAL/VAIR	ventriculoatriostomy	VEN/TRIK/LO/AI/TRO*S/M*I
venenosity	VEN/NOS/TI	ventriculocisternostomy	VEN/TRIK/LO/SIS/TER/NO*S/M*I
venenous	VEN/NOUS		VEN/TRIK/LO/SIS/TERN/O*S/M*I
venenum	VEN/NUM	ventriculocordectomy	VEN/TRIK/LO/KOR/DEKT/M*I
	VE/NAOE/NUM	ventriculogram	VEN/TRIK/LO/GRAM
	VE/NAOEN/UM	ventriculography	VEN/TRIK/LOG/FI
venereal	VE/NAOERL	ventriculomastoidostomy	VEN/TRIK/LO/MAS/TOI/DO*S/M*I

ventriculometry	VEN/TRIK/LOM/TRI	vergency	VERJ/EN/SI
ventriculomyotomy	VEN/TRIK/LO/MAOI/OT/M*I		VER/JEN/SI
ventriculonector	VEN/TRIK/LO/NEK/TOR	Verheyen	VER/HAOI/-N
ventriculophasic	VEN/TRIK/LO/FAEZ/IK		VAOER/HAOI/-N
	VEN/TRIK/LO/FAIZ/IK	Verhoeff	VER/HEF
ventriculoplasty	VEN/TRIK/LO/PLAS/TI	Vermes	VER/MAOEZ
ventriculopuncture	VEN/TRIK/LO/PUNG/KHUR	vermetoid	VERM/TOID
ventriculoscope	VEN/TRIK/LO/SKOEP	vermian	VERM/YAN
ventriculoscopy	VEN/TRIK/LOS/KPI	vermicidal	VERM/SAOI/DAL
ventriculostium	VEN/TRIK/LO*S/YUM	vermicide	VERM/SAO*ID
ventriculostomy	VEN/TRIK/LO*S/M*I	vermicul-	VER/MIK/L-
ventriculosubarachnoid	VEN/TRIK/LO/SUB/AI/RAK/NOID		VER/MIK/YAOU/L-
			VER/MIK/YU/L-
ventriculotomy	VEN/TRIK/LOT/M*I	vermicular	VER/MIK/LAR
ventriculovenostomy	VEN/TRIK/LO/VAOE/N*IS/M*I	vermicularis	VER/MIK/LAI/RIS
ventriculovenous	VEN/TRIK/LO/VAOEN/OUS	vermiculation	VER/MIK/LAIGS
ventriculus	VEN/TRIK/LUS	vermicule	VERM/KAOUL
ventricumbent	VEN/TRI/KUM/BENT	vermiculose	VER/MIK/LOES
ventriduct	VEN/TRI/DUKT	vermiculous	VER/MIK/LOUS
ventriduction	VEN/TRI/D*UBGS	vermiculus	VER/MIK/LUS
ventriflexion	VEN/TRI/FL*EBGS	vermiform	VERM/FORM
ventrimesal	VEN/TRI/MAOE/SAL	vermiformis	VERM/FOR/MIS
ventrimeson	VEN/TRIM/SON	vermifugal	VER/MIF/GAL
	VEN/TRI/MAOE/SON	vermifuge	VERM/FAOUJ
ventro-	VEN/TRO	vermilion	VER/MIL/YON
ventrocystorrhaphy	VEN/TRO/SIS/TOR/FI	vermilionectomy	VER/MIL/YON/EKT/M*I
ventrodorsad	VEN/TRO/DOR/SAD		VER/MIL/YO/NEKT/M*I
ventrodorsal	VEN/TRO/DOR/SAL	vermin	VER/MIN
ventrofixation	VEN/TRO/FIK/SAIGS	verminal	VERM/NAL
ventrohysteropexy	VEN/TRO/H*IS/RO/PEK/SI	vermination	VERM/NAIGS
ventroinguinal	VEN/TRO/ING/WINL	verminosis	VERM/NOE/SIS
ventrolateral	VEN/TRO/LAT/RAL	verminotic	VERM/NOT/IK
ventromedian	VEN/TRO/MAOED/YAN	verminous	VERM/NOUS
ventroposterior	VEN/TRO/POS/TAOER/YOR	vermis	VER/MIS
ventroptosia	VEN/TRO/TOEZ/YA	vermix	VER/MIX
	VEN/TROP/TOEZ/YA	vermography	VER/MOG/FI
ventroptosis	VEN/TRO/TOE/SIS	Vermox	VER/MOX
	VEN/TROP/TOE/SIS	vernal	VERNL
ventroscopy	VEN/TROS/KPI		VER/NAL
ventrose	VEN/TROES	Verner	VERN/ER
ventrosuspension	VEN/TRO/SUS/PENGS	Vernet	VER/NAI
ventrotomy	VEN/TROT/M*I	Verneuil	VER/NAI/YAOE
venul-	VEN/L-	vernier	VERN/YER
	VEN/YAOU/L-	Vernier	VERN/YAI
	VEN/YU/L-		K-P/VERN/YER
venula	VEN/LA	vernix	VERN/IX
venulae	VEN/LAE		VER/NIX
venular	VEN/LAR	vernoestival	VERN/*ES/VAL
venule	VEN/YAOUL		VER/NO/*ES/VAL
venulous	VEN/LOUS	Verocay	VER/KAI
Venus	VAOE/NUS		VER/RO/KAI
venustus	VAOE/NUS/TUS	verole	V-AI/ROEL
VePesid	VEP/SID		VE/ROEL
vera	VAOER/RA	veronal	VE/ROENL
	VAOE/RA		VE/ROE/NAL
verae	VAOER/RAE	Verr-Canth	VER/KA*NT
	VAOE/RAE	Verrex	VER/REX
verapamil	VER/AP/MIL	verruc-	VE/RAOU/K-
	VE/RAP/MIL		VER/RAOU/K-
veratric	VE/RAT/RIK		VE/RAOU/S-
veratrin	VER/TRIN		VER/RAOU/S-
veratrine	VER/TRAOEN	verruca	VE/RAOU/KA
Veratrum	VAOE/RAI/TRUM	verrucae	VE/RAOU/SAE
	VE/RAI/TRUM		VE/RAOU/KAE
verbal	VERBL	verruciform	VE/RAOUS/FORM
	VER/BAL	verruciformis	VE/RAOUS/FOR/MIS
verbalis	VER/BAI/LIS	verrucosa	VER/KOE/SA
verbenol	VER/BAOE/NOL	verrucose	VE/RAOU/KOES
verbenone	VER/BAOE/NOEN		VER/KOES
verbigeration	VER/BIJ/RAIGS	verrucosis	VER/KOE/SIS
verbomania	VERB/MAIN/YA	verrucous	VE/RAOU/KOUS
verdigris	VERD/GRIS		VE/RAOUK/OUS
verdine	VER/DIN		VER/KOUS
	VER/DAOEN	verruga	VE/RAOU/GA
verdo-	VERD		VER/RAOU/GA
	VER/DO	Verrusol	VER/YAOU/SOL
verdoglobin	VERD/GLOE/BIN		VER/YU/SOL
verdohemin	VERD/HAOE/MIN		VER/RAOU/SOL
	VERD/HEM/MIN	Versed	VER/SED
verdohemochrome	VERD/HAOEM/KROEM	versicolor	VERS/KO/LOR
verdohemochromogen	VERD/HAOEM/KROEM/JEN		VER/SIK/LOR
verdohemoglobin	VERD/HAOEM/GLOE/BIN	versicolorata	VERS/KOL/RAI/TA
verdoperoxidase	VERD/PROX/DAIS	version	VERGS
	VERD/PER/OX/DAIS	vertebr(o)-	VERT/BR(O)
Verga	VER/GA	vertebra	VERT/BRA
vergae	VER/GAE	vertebrae	VERT/BRAE
	VER/JAE	vertebral	VERT/BRAL
verge	VERJ	vertebralis	VERT/BRAI/LIS
vergence	VERJ/ENS	vertebrarium	VERT/BRAIRM
	VER/JENS		

466

	VERT/BRAIR/YUM		VES/KO/PUS/TAOU/LAR
vertebrarterial	VERT/BRAR/TAOER/YAL		VES/KO/P*US/LAR
vertebrarum	VERT/BRAIR/UM	vesicopustule	VES/KO/PUS/TAOUL
	VERT/BRAI/RUM		VES/KO/PUS/KHAOUL
	(not VERT/BRAIRM; see	vesicorectal	VES/KO/REK/TAL
	vertebrarium)	vesicorectostomy	VES/KO/REK/TO*S/M*I
Vertebrata	VERT/BRAI/TA	vesicorenal	VES/KO/RAOENL
	VERT/BRA/TA	vesicosigmoid	VES/KO/SIG/MOID
vertebrate	VERT/BRAIT	vesicosigmoidostomy	VES/KO/SIG/MOI/DO*S/M*I
	VERT/BRAT	vesicospinal	VES/KO/SPAOINL
vertebrated	VERT/BRAIT/-D	vesicostomy	VES/KO*S/M*I
vertebrectomy	VERT/BREKT/M*I	vesicotomy	VES/KOT/M*I
vertebroarterial	VERT/BRO/AR/TAOERL	vesicoumbilical	VES/KO/UM/BIL/KAL
vertebrobasilar	VERT/BRO/BAS/LAR	vesicourachal	VES/KO/YAOUR/KAL
vertebrochondral	VERT/BRO/KON/DRAL	vesicoureteral	VES/KO/YAOU/RAOET/RAL
vertebrocostal	VERT/BRO/KOS/TAL	vesicourethral	VES/KO/YAOU/RAO*ET/RAL
vertebrodidymus	VERT/BRO/DID/MUS	vesicouterina	VES/KO/YAOUT/RAOI/NA
vertebrodymus	VERT/BROD/MUS	vesicouterine	VES/KO/YAOUT/RIN
vertebrofemoral	VERT/BRO/FEM/RAL	vesicouterovaginal	VES/KO/YAOUT/RO/VAJ/NAL
vertebrogenic	VERT/BRO/JEN/IK	vesicovaginal	VES/KO/VAJ/NAL
vertebroiliac	VERT/BRO/IL/YAK	vesicovaginorectal	VES/KO/VAJ/NO/REK/TAL
vertebromammary	VERT/BRO/MAM/RI	vesicovisceral	VES/KO/VIS/RAL
vertebrosacral	VERT/BRO/SAI/KRAL	vesicul(o)-	VE/SIK/L(O)
vertebrosternal	VERT/BRO/STERNL		VE/SIK/YAOU/L(O)
vertex	VER/TEX		VE/SIK/YU/L(O)
vertical	VERT/KAL	vesicula	VE/SIK/LA
verticalis	VERT/KAI/LIS	vesiculae	VE/SIK/LAE
vertices	VERT/SAOEZ	vesicular	VE/SIK/LAR
verticil	VERT/SIL	vesiculase	VE/SIK/LAIS
verticillate	VERT/SIL/AIT	vesiculate	VE/SIK/LAIT
	VERT/SIL/LAIT	vesiculated	VE/SIK/LAIT/-D
	VER/TIS/LAIT	vesiculation	VE/SIK/LAIGS
verticillata	VERT/SIL/LAI/TA	vesiculectomy	VE/SIK/LEKT/M*I
	VER/TIS/LAI/TA	vesiculiform	VE/SIK/LI/FORM
Verticillium	VERT/SIL/YUM	vesiculitis	VE/SIK/LAOITS
verticis	VERT/SIS	vesiculobronchial	VE/SIK/LO/BRONG/YAL
verticomental	VERT/KO/MEN/TAL	vesiculocavernous	VE/SIK/LO/KAVR/NOUS
vertiginosa	VER/TIJ/NOE/SA	vesiculogram	VE/SIK/LO/GRAM
	VER/TIG/NOE/SA	vesiculography	VE/SIK/LOG/FI
vertiginous	VER/TIJ/NOUS	vesiculopapular	VE/SIK/LO/PAP/LAR
vertigo	VERT/GOE	vesiculoprostatitis	VE/SIK/LO/PRO*S/TAOITS
vertometer	VER/TOM/TER	vesiculopustular	VE/SIK/LO/P*US/LAR
verum	VAOER/UM		VE/SIK/LO/PUS/TAOU/LAR
	VAOE/RUM		VE/SIK/LO/PUS/KHU/LAR
verumontanitis	VER/MONT/NAOITS	vesiculose	VE/SIK/LOES
	VER/YAOU/MONT/NAOITS	vesiculosi	VE/SIK/LOE/SAOI
verumontanum	VER/MON/TAI/NUM	vesiculosis	VE/SIK/LOE/SIS
	VER/MON/TAIN/UM	vesiculotomy	VE/SIK/LOT/M*I
	VER/YAOU/MON/TAI/NUM	vesiculotubular	VE/SIK/LO/TAOUB/LAR
	VER/YAOU/MON/TAIN/UM	vesiculotympanic	VE/SIK/LO/TIM/PAN/IK
vesalian	VE/SAIL/YAN	vesiculous	VE/SIK/LOUS
	VAOE/SAIL/YAN	Vesiculovirus	VE/SIK/LO/VAOI/RUS
vesalianum	VE/SAIL/YAI/NUM	vesperal	VES/PRAL
	VE/SAIL/YAIN/UM		VES/PERL
	VAOE/SAIL/YAI/NUM		VES/PER/RAL
	VAOE/SAIL/YAIN/UM	vespertilionis	VES/PER/TIL/YOE/NIS
Vesalius	VE/SAIL/YUS	vessel	VES/SEL
	VAOE/SAIL/YUS		VESZ/EL
vesic(o)-	VES/K(O)	vestibul(o)-	VES/TIB/L(O)
vesica	VES/KA		VES/TIB/YAOU/L(O)
	VE/SAOI/KA		VES/TIB/YU/L(O)
vesicae	VES/SAE	vestibula	VES/TIB/LA
	VES/KAE	vestibular	VES/TIB/LAR
	VE/SAOI/SAE	vestibulare	VES/TIB/LAI/RAOE
vesical	VES/KAL	vestibulares	VES/TIB/LAI/RAOEZ
vesicale	VES/KAI/LAOE	vestibularis	VES/TIB/LAI/RIS
vesicales	VES/KAI/LAOEZ	vestibulate	VES/TIB/LAIT
vesicalis	VES/KAI/LIS	vestibule	V*ES/BAOUL
vesicant	VES/KANT	vestibuli	VES/TIB/LAOI
vesicate	VES/KAIT	vestibulocerebellum	VES/TIB/LO/SER/BEL/UM
vesication	VES/KAIGS	vestibulocochlear	VES/TIB/LO/KOK/LAR
vesicatory	VES/KA/TOIR	vestibuloequilibratory	VES/TIB/LO/E/KWI/LIB/TOIR
vesicle	VES/K-L		VES/TIB/LO/E/KWIL/IB/TOIR
vesicoabdominal	VES/KO/AB/DOM/NAL	vestibulogenic	VES/TIB/LO/JEN/IK
vesicobullous	VES/KO/BUL/OUS	vestibulo-ocular	VES/TIB/LO/OK/LAR
vesicocavernous	VES/KO/KAVR/NOUS	vestibuloplasty	VES/TIB/LO/PLAS/TI
vesicocele	VES/KO/SAO*EL	vestibulospinal	VES/TIB/LO/SPAOINL
vesicocervical	VES/KO/SEFRB/KAL	vestibulotomy	VES/TIB/LOT/M*I
vesicoclysis	VES/KOK/LI/SIS	vestibulourethral	VES/TIB/LO/YAOU/RAO*ET/RAL
vesicocolic	VES/KO/KOL/IK	vestibulovaginal	VES/TIB/LO/VAJ/NAL
vesicocolonic	VES/KO/KO/LON/IK	vestibulum	VES/TIB/LUM
vesicoenteric	VES/KO/SPWER/IK	vestige	VES/TIJ
vesicofixation	VES/KO/FIK/SAIGS	vestigia	VES/TIJ/YA
vesicointestinal	VES/KO/SPW*ES/NAL	vestigial	VES/TIJ/YAL
vesicolithiasis	VES/KO/LI/THAOI/SIS		VES/TI/JAL
vesicoperineal	VES/KO/P*ER/NAOEL	vestigium	VES/TIJ/YUM
vesicoprostatic	VES/KO/PROS/TAT/IK		VES/TI/JUM
vesicopubic	VES/KO/PAOUB/IK	vesuvin	VE/SAOUVN
vesicopustular	VES/KO/PUS/KHU/LAR		VE/SAOU/VIN

veterinarian	VET/NAIRN	Victoria	VIK/TOER/YA
	VET/NAIR/YAN		VIK/TOR/YA
	VET/RI/NAIRN	Vidal	VI/DAL
	VET/RI/NAIR/YAN		(*not* VAOE/DAL; see Widal)
veterinary	VET/NAIR	vidarabine	VAOI/DAIR/BAOEN
	VET/RI/NAIR		VAOI/DAR/BAOEN
VF-16	V-RBGS/F*RBGS/H-F/16	Vi-Daylin	VAOI/DAI/LIN
	V-RBGS/F*RBGS/16	videognosis	VID/YOG/NOE/SIS
via	VAOI/YA	vidian	VID/YAN
	VAOE/YA	Vienna	VAOE/YEN/NA
viability	VAOIBLT	Vieussens	VAOE/SANS
viable	VAOIBL		VAOE/SENS
viaduct	VAOI/DUKT		VAOE/YU/SANS
	VAOI/YA/DUKT		VAOE/YU/SENS
viae	VAOI/YAE	view	VAOU
	VAOE/YAE	vigil	VLJ/IL
vial	VAO*IL	vigilambulism	VLJ/LAM/BLIFM
	VAOI/YAL		VLJ/LAM/BAOU/LIFM
	(*not* VAOIL; see vile)	vigilance	VLJ/LANS
vibesate	VAOIB/SAIT	vigintinormal	VAOI/JINT/NOR/MAL
vibex	VAOI/BEX	Vignal	VIN/YAL
vibices	VI/BAOI/SAOEZ		(*not* VAOEN/YAL; see venial)
vibr(o)-	VAOI/BR(O)	vignin	VIG/NIN
	VAOIB/R(O)	vigor	VIG/GOR
Vibramycin	VAOI/BRA/MAOI/SIN		VI/GOR
	VAOIB/RA/MAOI/SIN	vile	VAOIL
Vibra-Tabs	VAOI/BRA/TAB-S	villi	VIL/LAOI
	VAOIB/RA/TAB-S	villiferous	VIL/LIF/ROUS
vibratile	VAOI/BRA/TAOIL		VI/LIF/ROUS
	VAOI/BRA/TIL	villitis	VIL/LAOITS
vibration	VAOI/BRAIGS		VI/LAOITS
vibrative	VAOI/BRA/TIV	villoma	VIL/LOE/MA
	VAOIB/TIV		VI/LOE/MA
vibratode	VAOI/BRA/TOED	villonodular	VIL/NOD/LAR
vibrator	VAOI/BRAI/TOR		VIL/LO/NOD/LAR
vibratory	VAOI/BRA/TOIR	villose	VIL/LOES
	VAOIB/TOIR		VIL/OES
vibrio	VIB/ROE	villositis	VIL/SAOITS
	VIB/RAOE/YOE	villosity	VIL/LOS/TI
Vibrio	K-P/VIB/ROE		VI/LOS/TI
	K-P/VIB/RAOE/YOE	villosum	VIL/LOE/SUM
vibrio-	VIB/RO		VIL/LOES/UM
	VIB/RAOE/YO		VI/LOE/SUM
vibriocidal	VIB/RO/SAOI/DAL		VI/LOES/UM
	VIB/RAOE/YO/SAOI/DAL	villous	VIL/OUS
vibrion	VIB/RON	villus	VIL/LUS
	VIB/RAOE/YON	villusectomy	VIL/SEKT/M*I
vibrion septique	VIB/RON/SEP/TAOEK		VIL/LUS/EKT/M*I
	VIB/RAOE/YON/SEP/TAOEK	viloxazine	VI/LOX/ZAOEN
vibriones	VIB/ROE/NAOEZ	vimentin	VAOI/MEN/TIN
	VIB/RAOE/YOE/NAOEZ	vinaceus	VAOI/NAIRBS
vibrioses	VIB/ROE/SAOEZ	vinbarbital	VIN/BARB/TAL
	VIB/RAOE/YOE/SAOEZ	vinblastine sulfate	VIN/BLAS/TAOEN/SUL/FAIT
vibriosis	VIB/ROE/SIS	Vinca	VIN/KA
	VIB/RAOE/YOE/SIS	Vinca rosea	VIN/KA/ROEZ/YA
vibrissa	VAOI/BRIS/SA	vincaleukoblastine	VIN/KA/LAOUK/BLAS/TAOEN
vibrissae	VAOI/BRIS/SAE	vincamine	VIN/KA/MAOEN
vibrissal	VAOI/BRIS/SAL	Vincent	VIN/SENT
	VIB/RIS/SAL		VINS/ENT
vibrocardiogram	VAOI/BRO/KARD/YO/GRAM	vincentii	VIN/SENT/YAOI
vibrocardiography	VAOI/BRO/KARD/YOG/FI		VIN/SEN/TAOI
vibromasseur	VAOI/BRO/MA/SAOUR	vincristine sulfate	VIN/KRIS/TAOEN/SUL/FAIT
	VAOI/BRO/MAS/SAOUR	vincula	VIN/KLA
vibrophonocardiograph	VAOI/BRO/FOEN/KARD/YO/GRAF		VIN/KAOU/LA
vibrotherapeutics	VAOI/BRO/THER/PAOUT/IK/-S	vinculum	VIN/KLUM
Viburnum	VAOI/BURN/UM		VIN/KAOU/LUM
	VAOI/BUR/NUM	vinegar	VIN/GAR
vicarious	VAOI/KAIR/YOUS	vini	VIN/NAOI
vice	VAOIS		VAOI/NAOI
vicine	VAOI/SAOEN	vinic	VAOIN/IK
vicious	VIRBS		VIN/IK
Vickers	VIK/ERZ	vinometer	VAOI/NOM/TER
	VIK/ERS	vinous	VAOIN/OUS
Vicks	VIX	Vinson	VIN/SON
Vicks Formula 44	VIX/FORM/LA/4/4	vinum	VAOIN/UM
Vicks Nyquil	VIX/NAOI/KWIL		VAOI/NUM
Vicks Vaporub	VIX/VAIP/RUB	vinyl	VAOINL
	VIX/VAI/PO/RUB		VAOI/NIL
Vicodin	VAOIK/DIN	vinylbenzene	VAOINL/BEN/ZAOEN
	VAOI/KO/DIN	vinylene	VAOINL/AOEN
Vicodin ES	VAOIK/DIN/ERBGS/S*RBGS		VAOIN/LAOEN
	VAOI/KO/DIN/ERBGS/S*RBGS	vinylidene	VAOI/NIL/DAOEN
Vicon-C	VAOI/KON/KR-RBGS	vio-	VAOI
Vicon Forte	VAOI/KON/FOR/TAI		VAOI/YO
Vicon Plus	VAOI/KON/PLUS	viocid	VAOI/SID
Vicq d'Azyr	VAOEK/DA/ZAOER	Vioform	VAOI/FORM
	VAOEK/DA/ZIR	Vioform-Hydrocortisone	VAOI/FORM/HAOI/DRO/KORT/
	VIK/DA/ZAOER		SOEN
	VIK/DA/ZIR	Viokase	VAOI/KAIS

468 ©1992 *StenEd* Medical Dictionary

Viola	VAOI/LA	virous	VAOI/ROUS
	VAOI/YOE/LA	virtual	VIR/KHUL
violaceous	VAOI/LAIRBS	virucidal	VAOIR/SAOI/DAL
violescent	VAOI/LES/ENT	virucide	VAOIR/SAO*ID
violet	VAOI/LET	virucopria	VAOIR/KOP/RA
	VAOIL/ET		VAOIR/KOP/RAOE/YA
viomycin	VAOI/MAOI/SIN		VAOI/RU/KOP/RA
viosterol	VAOI/O*S/ROL		VAOI/RU/KOP/RAOE/YA
	VAOI/O*S/ROEL	virulence	VIR/LENS
viper	VAOIP/ER		VIR/YAOU/LENS
Viperidae	VAOI/PER/DAE		VIR/YU/LENS
vipoma	VAOI/POE/MA	virulent	VIR/LENT
viprynium embonate	VIP/RIN/YUM/EM/BO/NAIT		VIR/YAOU/LENT
vir(o)-	VAOI/R(O)		VIR/YU/LENT
	VAOIR	virulicidal	VAOIR/LIS/DAL
	VIR		VAOI/RU/LIS/DAL
Vira-A	VAOI/RA/ARBGS	viruliferous	VAOIR/LIF/ROUS
viraginity	VAOIR/JIN/TI		VAOI/RU/LIF/ROUS
	VAOI/RA/JIN/TI	viruria	VAOI/RAOUR/YA
	VIR/RA/JIN/TI		VAOIR/YAOUR/YA
	(not VIR/JIN/TI; see virginity)	virus	VAOI/RUS
viral	VAOIRL	virusemia	VAOIR/SAOEM/YA
	VAOI/RAL		VAOI/RUS/AOEM/YA
Virales	VAOI/RAI/LAOEZ		VAOI/RU/SAOEM/YA
Viranol	VIR/NOL	virusoid	VAOI/RUS/OID
Virazole	VIR/ZOEL		VAOIR/SOID
Virchow	VIR/KOE	vis	VIS
	VAOER/KOE	viscance	VIS/KANS
viremia	VAOI/RAOEM/YA	viscer(o)-	VIS/R(O)
vires	VAOI/RAOEZ	viscera	VIS/RA
virga	VIR/GA	viscerad	VIS/RAD
virgin	VIR/JIN	visceral	VIS/RAL
virginal	VIRJ/NAL	viscerale	VIS/RAI/LAOE
virginale	VIRJ/NAI/LAOE	visceralgia	VIS/RAL/JA
virginity	VIR/JIN/TI	visceralis	VIS/RAI/LIS
virginium	VIR/JIN/YUM	visceralism	VIS/RAL/IFM
virgophrenia	VIRG/FRAOEN/YA	viscerimotor	VIS/RI/MOE/TOR
	VIR/GO/FRAOEN/YA	viscerocranium	VIS/RO/KRAIN/YUM
viricidal	VAOIR/SAOI/DAL	viscerogenic	VIS/RO/JEN/IK
	VIR/SAOI/DAL	viscerograph	VIS/RO/GRAF
viricide	VAOIR/SAO*ID	viscerography	VIS/ROG/FI
	VIR/SAO*ID	visceroinhibitory	VIS/RO/IN/HIB/TOIR
-viridae	VIR/DAE	visceromegaly	VIS/RO/MEG/LI
viridans	VIR/DANZ	visceromotor	VIS/RO/MOE/TOR
viridis	VIR/DIS	visceroparietal	VIS/RO/PRAOI/TAL
virile	VIRL	visceroperitoneal	VIS/RO/PERT/NAOEL
	VIR/RIL	visceropleural	VIS/RO/PLAOURL
	VIR/RAOIL	visceroptosia	VIS/ROP/TOES/YA
	VIR/IL	visceroptosis	VIS/ROP/TOE/SIS
virilescence	VIR/LES/ENS	viscerosensory	VIS/RO/SENS/RI
virilia	VI/RIL/YA	visceroskeletal	VIS/RO/SKEL/TAL
	VAOI/RIL/YA	visceroskeleton	VIS/RO/SKEL/TON
viriligenic	VIR/LI/JEN/IK	viscerosomatic	VIS/RO/SOE/MAT/IK
	VIRL/JEN/IK		VIS/RO/SMAT/IK
virilis	VIR/LIS	viscerotome	VIS/RO/TOEM
	VI/RIL/LIS	viscerotomy	VIS/ROT/M*I
	VIR/RIL/LIS	viscerotonia	VIS/RO/TOEN/YA
	VI/RAOI/LIS	viscerotrophic	VIS/RO/TROFK
	VIR/RAOI/LIS	viscerotropic	VIS/RO/TROP/IK
virilism	VIR/LIFM	viscerum	VIS/RUM
	VIRL/IFM	viscid	VIS/ID
virility	VI/RIL/TI		VIS/SID
	VIR/RIL/TI	viscidity	VI/SID/TI
	VIRL/TI		VIS/SID/TI
	VAOI/RIL/TI	viscidosis	VIS/DOE/SIS
virilization	VIRL/ZAIGS	visco-	VIS/KO
	VIR/LI/ZAIGS	viscoelasticity	VIS/KO/E/LAS/TIS/TI
virilizing	VIR/LAOIZ/-G	viscogel	VIS/KO/JEL
Virilon	VIR/LON	viscometer	VIS/KOM/TER
virion	VAOIR/YON	viscometry	VIS/KOM/TRI
	VIR/YON	viscosaccharase	VIS/KO/SAK/RAIS
viripotent	VIR/POE/TENT	viscose	VIS/KOES
	VIR/POET/ENT	viscosimeter	VIS/KO/SIM/TER
	VI/RIP/TENT	viscosimetry	VIS/KO/SIM/TRI
	VAOI/RIP/TENT	viscosity	VIS/KOS/TI
virogene	VAOIR/JAOEN	viscous	VIS/KOUS
virogenetic	VAOIR/JE/NET/IK	viscum	VIS/KUM
viroid	VAOI/ROID	viscus	VIS/KUS
virolactia	VAOIR/LAK/SHA	visibility	VIZ/-BLT
virologist	VAOI/RO*LGS	visible	VIZ/-BL
virology	VAOI/ROLG	visile	VIS/IL
viromicrosome	VAOIR/MAOI/KRO/SOEM		VIZ/IL
viropexis	VAOIR/PEK/SIS	Visine	VAOI/ZAOEN
viroplasm	VAOIR/PLAFM		(not VAOI/SAOEN; see vicine)
Viroptic	VAOI/ROPT/IK	vision	VIGS
virosa	VAOI/ROE/SA	Visken	VIS/KEN
virose	VAOI/ROES	visna	VIS/NA
virosis	VAOI/ROE/SIS	Vistaril	V*IS/RIL
virostatic	VAOIR/STAT/IK	visu(o)-	VIRB/Y(O)

	VIRB/W(O)		VIT/RAOE/OL
visual	VIRBL	vitriolated	VIT/RO/LAIT/-D
visualization	VIRBL/ZAIGS		VIT/RAOE/LAIT/-D
visualize	VIRBL/AOIZ	vitulorum	VIT/LOR/UM
visuoauditory	VIRB/YO/AUD/TOIR		VIT/LOER/UM
visuognosis	VIRB/YOG/NOE/SIS		VIT/LOE/RUM
visuolexic	VIRB/YO/LEX/IK	Vivactil	VAOI/VAK/TIL
visuometer	VIRB/YOM/TER	vivaria	VAOI/VAIR/YA
visuomotor	VIRB/YO/MOE/TOR	vivarium	VAOI/VAIRM
visuopsychic	VIRB/YO/SAOIK/IK		VAOI/VAIR/YUM
visuosensory	VIRB/YO/SENS/RI	vivi-	VIV
visuospatial	VIRB/YO/SPAIRBL	vividialysis	VIV/DI/AL/SIS
visuscope	VIZ/YAOU/SKOEP	vividiffusion	VIV/DI/FAOUGS
	VIZ/YU/SKOEP		VIV/DIF/FAOUGS
	VIRB/YAOU/SKOEP	vivification	VIV/FI/KAIGS
	VIRB/YU/SKOEP	viviparity	VIV/PAIR/TI
Vitabese	VAOIT/BAOES	viviparous	VAOI/VIP/ROUS
vitae	VAOI/TAE	vivipation	VIV/PAIGS
Vitafol	VAOIT/FOL	viviperception	VIV/PER/SEPGS
vitagonist	VAOI/TAG/N*IS	vivisect	VIV/SEKT
Vita-Kid	VAOIT/KID	vivisection	VIV/S*EBGS
vital	VAOI/TAL	vivisectionist	VIV/S*EBGS/*IS
Vital High Nitrogen	VAOI/TAL/HAOI/NAOI/TRO/JEN	vivisector	VIV/SEK/TOR
vitalism	VAOIT/LIFM	Vivonex	VAOIV/NEX
vitalist	VAOIT/L*IS	vivosphere	VAOIV/SFAOER
vitalistic	VAOIT/L*IS/IK	Vladimiroff	FLAD/MIR/ROF
vitality	VAOI/TAL/TI		FLAD/MIR/AUF
vitalize	VAOIT/LAOIZ		V-/LAD/MIR/ROF
vitalometer	VAOIT/LOM/TER		V-/LAD/MIR/AUF
vitals	VAOI/TAL/-S	Vlemasque	V-/LAOE/MAS/-K
vitamer	VAOIT/MER	vocal	VOE/KAL
vitameter	VAOI/TAM/TER	vocale	VOE/KAI/LAOE
vitamin	VAOIT/MIN	vocalis	VOE/KAI/LIS
vitaminogenic	VAOI/TAM/NO/JEN/IK	Voegtlin	VEGT/LIN
	VAOIT/MIN/JEN/IK		VEKT/LIN
vitaminoid	VAOIT/MIN/OID	Voges	VOE/JES
	VAOIT/MI/NOID		VOEGS
vitaminology	VAOIT/MIN/OLG	Vogt	VOEGT
vitaminoscope	VAOIT/MIN/SKOEP		VOEKT
vitaminosis	VAOIT/MI/NOE/SIS	voice	VOIS
vitaminotic	VAOIT/MI/NOT/IK	voicebox	VOIS/BOX
vitanition	VAOIT/NIGS	void	VOID
vitellarium	VIT/LAIRM	Voigt	VOIGT
	VIT/LAIR/YUM		VO*IT
vitellary	VIT/LAIR		(not VOIT; see Voit)
vitellicle	VAOI/TEL/K-L	Voit	VOIT
vitelliform	VAOI/TEL/FORM		FOIT
vitellin	VAOI/TEL/LIN	voix	V-/WAU
vitellina	VIT/LAOI/NA		VOI
	VAOIT/LAOI/NA	vola	VOE/LA
vitelline	VAOI/TEL/LAOEN	volar	VOE/LAR
vitello-	VAOI/TEL	volardorsal	VOE/LAR/DOR/SAL
	VAOI/TEL/LO	volares	VOE/LAI/RAOEZ
vitellogenesis	VAOI/TEL/JEN/SIS	volaria	VOE/LAIR/YA
vitellointestinal	VAOI/TEL/SPW*ES/NAL	volaris	VOE/LAI/RIS
vitellolutein	VAOI/TEL/LAOUT/YIN	volatile	VOL/TIL
vitellorubin	VAOI/TEL/RAOU/BIN		VOL/TAOIL
vitellose	VAOI/TEL/OES	volatilization	VOL/TIL/ZAIGS
	VAOI/TEL/LOES	volatilize	VOL/TIL/AOIZ
vitellus	VAOI/TEL/LUS	volatilizer	VOL/TIL/AOIZ/ER
vitiation	VIRB/YAIGS	vole	VOEL
vitiligines	VIT/LIJ/NAOEZ	-volemia	VOE/LAOEM/YA
vitiliginous	VIT/LIJ/NOUS	-volemic	VOE/LAOEM/IK
vitiligo	VIT/LAOI/GOE	Volhard	FOEL/HART
vitiligoidea	VIT/LAOI/GOID/YA		VOEL/HARD
vitium	VIRB/UM	volition	VOE/LIGS
	VIRB/YUM	volitional	VOE/LIGS/NAL
vitochemical	VAOIT/KEM/KAL	Volkmann	VOEK/MAN
	VAOI/TO/KEM/KAL		VOEL/-K/MAN
vitodynamics	VAOIT/DAOI/NAM/IK/-S	volley	VOL/LAOE
	VAOI/TO/DAOI/NAM/IK/-S	volsella	VOL/SEL/LA
vitre(o)-	VIT/R(O)	volt	VOELT
	VIT/RAOE/Y(O)		VOLT
vitrea	VIT/RA	voltage	VOELT/AJ
vitrectomy	VI/TREKT/M*I		VOLT/AJ
vitrein	VIT/RIN		VOEL/TAJ
vitreitis	VIT/RAOITS		VOL/TAJ
vitreocapsulitis	VIT/RO/KAPS/LAOITS	voltaic	VOL/TAI/IK
vitreodentin	VIT/RO/DEN/TIN		VOEL/TAI/IK
vitreoretinal	VIT/RO/RET/NAL	voltaism	VOELT/IFM
vitreoretinopathy	VIT/RO/RET/NOP/TH*I		VOLT/IFM
vitreous	VIT/ROUS		VOEL/TA/IFM
vitreum	VIT/RUM		VOL/TA/IFM
vitrification	VIT/RIF/KAIGS	voltameter	VOEL/TAM/TER
	VIT/RI/FI/KAIGS		VOL/TAM/TER
vitrina	VI/TRAOI/NA	voltammeter	VOELT/AM/MAOET/ER
vitrinal	VI/TRAOINL		VOLT/AM/MAOET/ER
	VIT/RI/NAL	voltampere	VOELT/AM/PAOER
vitriol	VIT/ROL		VOLT/AM/PAOER

Voltaren	VOLT/REN	von Zenker	VON/ZEN/KER
	VOL/TAR/-N	Vontrol	VON/TROEL
voltmeter	VOELT/MAOET/ER		VON/TROL
	VOLT/MAOET/ER	voodoo	VAO/DAO
Voltolini	VOLT/LAOE/NAOE	Voorhees	VAOR/HAOEZ
	VOL/TO/LAOE/NAOE		VAOR/HAOES
volume	VOL/YAOUM	vortex	VOR/TEX
	VOL/YUM	Vorticella	VORT/SEL/LA
volumenometer	VOL/YAOUM/NOM/TER	vortices	VORT/SAOEZ
	VOL/YUM/NOM/TER	vorticosae	VORT/KOE/SAE
	VOL/YAOU/ME/NOM/TER	vorticose	VORT/KOES
	VOL/YU/ME/NOM/TER	VoSol	VOE/SOL
volumetric	VOL/YAOU/MET/RIK	Vossius	VOS/YUS
	VOL/YU/MET/RIK	vox	VOX
volumette	VOL/YAOU/MET	voxel	VOK/SEL
	VOL/YU/MET		VOX/EL
volumination	VOE/LAOUM/NAIGS	voyeur	VOI/YER
	VOL/YAOUM/NAIGS		VOI/YUR
volumometer	VOL/YAOU/MOM/TER		VOI/YAOUR
	VOL/YU/MOM/TER	voyeurism	VOIR/IFM
voluntarily	VOL/TAIR/LI		VOI/YER/IFM
	VOL/UN/TAIR/LI		VOI/YUR/IFM
voluntary	VOL/TAIR		VOI/YAOUR/IFM
	VOL/UN/TAIR	vuerometer	VAOU/ROM/TER
voluntomotory	VOL/UN/TO/MOET/RI		VAOUR/OM/TER
voluptuous	VOE/LUP/KHOUS	vulgaris	VUL/GAI/RIS
	VOE/LUP/-RBS		VUL/GAIR/RIS
volute	VOE/LAOUT	vulgarity	VUL/GAIR/TI
volutin	VOL/YAOU/TIN	vulnerability	VUL/NERBLT
	VOL/YU/TIN		VUL/NER/-BLT
	VOE/LAOU/TIN	vulnerant	VUL/NER/ANT
volution	VOE/LAOUGS	vulnerary	VUL/NER/AIR
Volvox	VOL/VOX		VUL/NE/RAIR
volvulate	VOL/VAOU/LAIT	vulnerate	VUL/NER/AIT
volvulosis	VOL/VAOU/LOE/SIS	vulnus	VUL/NUS
volvulus	VOL/VAOU/LUS	Vulpian	VUL/PAOE/YAN
vomer	VOEM/ER		VUL/PI/YAN
	VOE/MER		VUL/-P/YAN
vomer(o)-	VOEM/R(O)	vulsella	VUL/SEL/LA
vomerine	VOEM/RAOEN	vulsellum	VUL/SEL/UM
	VOEM/RIN		VUL/SEL/LUM
	VOEM/RAOIN	vulv(o)-	VUL/V(O)
vomeris	VOEM/RIS	vulva	VUL/VA
vomerobasilar	VOEM/RO/BAS/LAR	vulvae	VUL/VAE
vomeronasal	VOEM/RO/NAI/ZAL	vulval	VUL/VAL
vomeronasalis	VOEM/RO/NAI/ZAI/LIS	vulvar	VUL/VAR
vomerovaginalis	VOEM/RO/VAJ/NAI/LIS	vulvectomy	VUL/VEKT/M*I
vomica	VOM/KA	vulvismus	VUL/VIZ/MUS
vomicose	VOM/KOES	vulvitis	VUL/VAOITS
vomicus	VOM/KUS	vulvocrural	VUL/VO/KRAOURL
vomit	VOMT	vulvopathy	VUL/VOP/TH*I
	VOM/MIT	vulvorectal	VUL/VO/REK/TAL
vomition	VOE/MIGS	vulvouterine	VUL/VO/YAOUT/RIN
vomitive	VOM/TIV	vulvovaginal	VUL/VO/VAJ/NAL
vomito	VOM/TOE	vulvovaginitis	VUL/VO/VAJ/NAOITS
vomitory	VOM/TOIR	V-Y-plasty	V-RBGS/Y-RBGS/PLAS/TI
vomiturition	VOM/TAOU/RIGS	Vytone	VAOI/TOEN
	VOM/KHU/RIGS		
vomitus	VOM/TUS		
von Behring	VON/BAI/RING		
von Bekhterev	VON/BEKT/REV		
	VON/BEK/TER/YEV		
von Bergmann	VON/BERG/MAN		
von Bezold	VON/BAI/ZOLT		
	VON/BAI/ZOLD		
von Brucke	VON/BRAOE/KAOE		
von Ebner	VON/EB/NER		
von Economo	VON/AI/KON/MOE		
	VON/E/KON/MOE		
von Frisch	VON/FRIRB		
von Gierke	VON/GAOER/KAOE		
von Graefe	VON/GRAI/FAOE		
von Haller	VON/HAL/ER		
von Hippel	VON/HIP/EL		
von Jaksch	VON/YAK/-RB		
von Kossa	VON/KOS/SA		
von Kupffer	VON/KAOUP/FER		
	VON/KUP/FER		
von Langenbeck	VON/LANG/EN/BEK		
von Leyden	VON/LAOID/-N		
	VON/LAOI/DEN		
von Mikulicz	VON/MIK/LIFP		
von Monakow	VON/MOE/NAK/OV		
	VON/MOE/NAK/KOV		
von Pirquet	VON/PIR/KAI		
von Recklinghausen	VON/REK/LING/HOUZ/-N		
	VON/REK/-LG/HOUZ/-N		
von Ruck	VON/RUK		
von Schrotter	VON/SH-/RET/ER		

W

Wachendorf	VAUK/EN/DOR/-F
	VAK/EN/DOR/-F
Wade	K-P/WAID
	WAED
wadding	WAD/-G
waddle	WAD/-L
wafer	WAIFR
Wagner	VAUG/NER
	VAG/NER
	WAG/NER
Wagstaffe	WAG/STAF
waist	WA*IS
wakefulness	WAIK/FL*NS
Walcher	VAL/KER
Waldenburg	VALD/EN/BAOURG
	VAL/DEN/BAOURG
	VALD/EN/BURG
	VAL/DEN/BURG
Waldenstrom	VALD/EN/STREM
	VAL/DEN/STREM
Waldeyer	VAUL/DAOI/ER
	VAUL/DAOI/YER
	VAL/DAOI/ER
	VAL/DAOI/YER
walk	WAUK
walker	WAUK/ER
Walker	K-P/WAUK/ER
walking	WAUK/-G
wall	WAUL
Wallenberg	VAL/EN/BERG
wallerian	WAL/LAOER/YAN
	WAL/LER/YAN
	WAUL/LAOER/YAN
	WAUL/LER/YAN
Wallette Pill Dispenser	WAL/LET/PIL/DIS/PENS/ER
walleye	WAUL/LAOI
	WAL/LAOI
	WAUL/YAOI
	WAL/YAOI
Walter	VAUL/TER
	WAUL/TER
	VAL/TER
	WAL/TER
Walthard	VAUL/TARD
	VAL/TARD
Walther	VA*UL/TER
	VA*L/TER
	(*not* VAL/TER or VAUL/TER; see Walter)
wambles	WAM/-BLS
wander	WAND/ER
wandering	WAND/ER/-G
Wang	WANG
Wangensteen	WANG/EN/STAOEN
Wangiella	WANG/YEL/LA
warble	WARBL
	WARB/-L
	WAR/-BL
Warburg	WAR/BAOURG
	WAR/BURG
ward	WARD
Ward	K-P/WARD
warfarin	WAR/FA/RIN
	WAR/FRIN
Waring	WAIR/-G
warm-blooded	WARM/BLAOD/-D
Warren	WAR/-N
	WAR/REN
	(*not* WARN; see warn)
wart	WART
Wart-Off	WART/H-F/AUF
Wartenberg	WART/EN/BERG/
	WAR/TEN/BERG
wartpox	WART/POX
warty	WAR/TI
	WART/TI
wash	WARB
washout	WARB/O*UT
wasp	WAS/-P
Wassermann	WAS/ER/MAN
	WAS/SER/MAN
Wassermann-fast	WAS/ER/MAN/FA*S
	WAS/SER/MAN/FA*S
waste	WA*ES

	(*not* WA*IS; see waist)
wasting	WA*ES/-G
watch	WAFP
water	WAT/ER
water-borne	WAT/ER/H-F/BOERN
water brash	WAT/ER/BRARB
waterfall	WAT/ER/FAUL
Waterhouse	WAT/ER/HOUS
watermelon	WAT/ER/MEL/LON
waterpox	WAT/ER/POX
waters	WAT/ER/-S
Waters	K-P/WAT/ER/-S
watershed	WAT/ER/SHED
watery	WAT/RI
Watkins	WAT/KINZ
	WAT/KINS
Watson	WAT/SON
watsoni	WAT/SOE/NAOI
Watsonius watsoni	WAT/SOEN/YUS/WAT/SOE/NAOI
watt	WAT
wattage	WAT/AJ
watt-hour	WAT/HOUR
wattmeter	WAT/MAOET/ER
wave	WAEV
	(*not* WAIV; see waive)
wavelength	WAEV/L*ENT
wavenumber	SAEV/NUM/BER
waveshape	WAEV/SHAIP
wax	WAX
waxing	WAX/-G
waxy	WAX/SI
	WAK/SI
WBC	W-RBGS/B*RBGS/KR*RBGS
weak	WAEK
	(*not* WAOEK; see week)
weakness	WAEK/*NS
wean	WAOEN
weanling	WAOEN/-LG
	WAOEN/LING
wear	WAER
	(*not* WAIR; see ware)
weasand	WAOE/ZAND
	WAOE/SAND
web	WEB
webbed	WEB/-D
webbing	WEB/-G
weber	WEB/ER
Weber	K-P/WEB/ER
	VAIB/ER
	VAI/BER
Webster	WEB/STER
Wechsler	WEX/LER
wedge	WEJ
Weeks	WAOEX
weep	WAOEP
Wegner	VEG/NER
Wehless-105	WE/LESZ/10/5
wehnelt	VAI/NELT
Weibel	VAOI/BEL
Weichardt	VAOI/KART
Weichbrodt	VAOIK/BROET
Weichselbaum	VAOIK/SE/BOUM
	VAOIK/SEL/BAUM
Weidel	VAOI/DEL
Weigert	VAOIG/ERT
	VAOI/GERT
weigh	WAIG
weight	WAIGT
weightlessness	WAIGT/LES/*NS
weights and measures	WAIGT/-S/AND/MERB/SHUR/-S
	WAIGT/-S/AND/MERB/SHURS
Weinberg	VAOIN/BERG
	WAOIN/BERG
Weir	WAOER
Weisbach	VAOIS/BAK
	VAOIS/BAUK
	WAOIS/BAK
	WAOIS/BAUK
Weismann	VAOIS/MAN
weismannism	VAOIS/MAN/IFM
Weiss	VAOISZ
	WAOISZ
Weitbrecht	VAOIT/BREKT
Welch	WEL/-FP
welchii	WEL/KHAOI
	WEL/KHAOE/YAOI
Welcker	VEL/KER
well	WEL
Wellbutrin	WEL/BAOU/TRIN

Wellcovorin	WEL/KO/VORN		WIK/MAN
Weller	WEL/ER	Wickham	WIK/KAM
Wells	WELZ		WIK/HAM
	WELS	Widal	VAOE/DAL
welt	WELT		*(not* VI/DAL; see Vidal)
wen	WEN	widow's peak	WID/DOE/AOES/PAEK
Wenckebach	VEN/KE/BAK	width	WID/*T
	VEN/KE/BAUK	Wigand	VAOE/GANT
Wenzell	WEN/ZEL		VAOE/GAND
Werdnig	VERD/NIG	Wigraine	WAOI/GRAIN
Werlhof	VERL/HOF	wild	WAOILD
	WERL/HOF	Wilde	WAO*ILD
Werner	VERN/ER		*(not* WAOILD; see wild)
	VER/NER	Wilder	K-P/WAOILD/ER
Wernicke	VERN/KAOE		WAOIL/DER
	WERN/KAOE		WAO*ILD/ER
Wertheim	VER/TAOIM		*(not* WAOILD/ER; see wilder)
	VERT/HAOIM	Wildermuth	VILD/ER/MAOUT
	WER/TAOIM		VIL/DER/MAOUT
	WERT/HAOIM	wildfire	WAOILD/FAOIR
West	K-P/W*ES	Wilkie	WIL/KAOE
Westberg	V*ES/BERG	Wilkins	WIL/KINZ
	W*ES/BERG		WIL/KINS
Westcort Cream	W*ES/KORT/KRAOEM	Wilkinson	WIL/KIN/SON
Westcort Ointment	W*ES/KORT/OINT/-MT	Willan	WIL/LAN
Westergren	W*ES/ER/GREN	Willett	WIL/ET
	WES/TER/GREN		WIL/LET
westermani	W*ES/ER/MAN/NAOI	Williams	WIL/YAMZ
	WES/TER/MAN/NAOI		WIL/YAMS
Westphal	V*ES/FAL	Williamson	WIL/YAM/SON
	V*ES/FAUL	Willis	WIL/LIS
	W*ES/FAL	willisii	WIL/LIS/YAOI
	W*ES/FAUL		WIL/LIS/SAOI
wet	WET	Williston	WIL/LIS/TON
wet-nurse	WET/NURS	willow	WIL/LOE
wetpox	WET/POX	Wills	WILZ
wetting	WET/-G		WILS
Wetzel	VET/ZEL	Wilms	VIL/-MS
	VET/SEL		WIL/-MS
Wharton	WHAR/TON	Wilson	WIL/SON
whartonitis	WHAR/TON/AOITS	wilt	WILT
	WHART/NAOITS	Winckel	VIN/KEL
wheal	WHAEL		WIN/KEL
	WHAO*EL	wind	WIND
	(not WHAOEL; see wheel)		WAOIND
wheat	WHAOET	windage	WIND/AJ
wheatmeal	WHAOET/MAOEL	windburn	WIND/BURN
Wheatstone	WHAOET/STOEN	windchill	WIND/KHIL
wheel	WHAOEL	windgall	WIND/GAUL
Wheeler	WHAOEL/ER		WIND/GAL
Wheelhouse	WHAOEL/HOUS	windigo	WIND/GOE
wheelchair	WHAOEL/KHAIR	windlass	WIND/LASZ
wheeze	WHAOEZ	window	WIN/DOE
whelp	WHEL/-P	windowing	WIN/DOE/-G
whetstone	WHET/STOEN	windpipe	WIND/PAOIP
whettle	WHET/-L	windpuff	WIND/PUF
whey	WHAI	wind-sucking	WIND/H-F/SUK/-G
whip	WHIP	wine	WAOIN
whiplash	WHIP/LARB	wineglass	WAOIN/GLA*SZ
Whipple	WHIP/-L	wing	WING
whipworm	WHIP/WORM	WinGel	WIN/JEL
whirl	WHIRL	Winiwarter	VIN/VART/ER
whirlbone	WHIRL/BOEN		VIN/VAR/TER
whirlpool	WHIRL/PAOL		WIN/WART/ER
whiskey	WHIS/KAOE		WIN/WAR/TER
whisky	WHIS/KI	wink	WIN/-K
whisper	WHIS/PER		W*ING
whistle	WHIS/-L	Winkelman	VIN/KEL/MAN
white	WHAOIT		WIN/KEL/MAN
White	K-P/WHAOIT	Winkelstein	VIN/KEL/STAOIN
whitehead	WHAOIT/H*ED		WIN/KEL/TAOIN
Whitehead	K-P/WHAOIT/H*ED	Winkler	W*ING/LER
whitepox	WHAOIT/POX		WIN/KLER
whites	WHAOIT/-S		WIN/-K/LER
Whitfield	WHIT/FAOELD		V*ING/LER
whiting	WHAOIT/-G		VIN/KLER
whitlow	WHIT/LOE		VIN/-K/LER
Whitman	WHIT/MAN	Winslow	WINZ/LOE
Whitmore	WHIT/MOR		WINS/LOE
	WHIT/MOER	Winstrol	WIN/STROL
whitmori	WHIT/MOR/RAOI		WIN/STROL
	WHIT/MOER/RAOI	winter	WINT/ER
	WHIT/MOE/RAOI		WIN/TER
Whitten	WHIT/-N	Winterbottom	WINT/ER/BOT/OM
whole	WHOEL		WIN/TER/BOT/OM
whoop	WHAOP	wintergreen	WINT/ER/GRAOEN
whooping cough	WHAOP/-G/KAUF	Winternitz	VINT/ER/NITS
whorl	WHORL		WINT/ER/NITS
Wichmann	VIK/MAN	Wintersteiner	VINT/ER/STAOIN/ER

	WINT/ER/STAOIN/ER	writing	WRAOIT/-G
wire	WAOIR		WRI/-G
wiring	WAOIR/-G	wryneck	WRAOI/NEK
Wirsung	VAOER/SAOUNG		RAOI/NEK
	VIR/SAOUNG	wucher	VAOUK/ER
	VAOER/SUNG		VAOU/KER
	VIR/SUNG	Wuchereria	VAOUK/RER/YA
wiry	WAOIR/RI		VAOUK/RAOER/YA
	WAOI/RI		VAOUK/ER/ER/YA
Wiskott	VIS/KOT		VAOU/KER/ER/YA
	WIS/KOT	wuchereriasis	VAOU/KER/RAOI/SIS
witch hazel	WIFP/HAIZ/EL		VAOUK/ER/RAOI/SIS
withdrawal	WRAUL	Wunderlich	VAOUND/ER/LIK
	W*IT/DRAUL		VAOUN/DER/LIK
withers	W*IT/ER/-S	Wurster	V*URS/ER
within normal limits	W*NL		VURS/TER
	W-N/NOR/MAL/LIMT/-S		VUR/STER
witkop	WIT/KOP		W*URS/ER
Witzel	VIT/SEL		WUR/STER
	VIT/ZEL		WURS/TER
witzelsucht	VIT/SEL/SUKT	Wyamycin	WAOI/MAOI/SIN
	VIT/SEL/SAOUKT		WAOI/YA/MAOI/SIN
	VIT/ZEL/ZUKT	Wyanoids	WAOI/NOIDZ
	VIT/ZEL/ZAOUKT		WAOI/YA/NOIDZ
Wladimiroff	V-/LAD/MIR/AUF	Wyatt	WAOI/YAT
	V-/LAD/MIR/OF	Wyburn	WAOI/BURN
	FLAD/MIR/AUF	Wycillin	WAOI/SLIN
	FLAD/MIR/OF		WAOI/SIL/LIN
wobble	WOB/-L	Wydase	WAOI/DAIS
Wohlfahrtia	VOEL/FART/YA	Wyeomyia	WAOE/MAOI/YA
wohlfahrtiosis	VOEL/FART/YOE/SIS		WAOE/YO/MAOI/YA
Wohlfart	VOEL/FART	Wyeth	WAOI/*ET
wolf	WOL/-F	Wygesic	WAOI/JAOEZ/IK
Wolf	K-P/WOL/-F	Wylie	WAOI/LAOE
Wolfe	WO*L/-F	Wymox	WAOI/MOX
Wolfenden	WOL/FEN/DEN	Wytensin	WAOI/TEN/SIN
Wolff	VOL/-F		
	(not WOL/-F or WO*L/-F)		
Wolffi	VOL/FAOI		
	WOL/FAOI		
wolffian	WOL/FAOE/YAN		
	VOL/FAOE/YAN		
Wolfler	VEL/FLER		
wolfram	WOL/FRAM		
wolframium	WOL/FRAM/YUM		
	WOL/FRAIM/YUM		
Wolfring	VOEL/-F/RING		
	VOEL/FRING		
wolfsbane	WOL/-FS/BAIN		
wolhynica	WOL/HIN/KA		
Wollaston	WOL/LAS/TON		
	WOL/AS/TON		
womb	WAOUM		
	WOM/-B		
Wong	WONG		
Wood	K-P/WAOD		
wooden	WAOD/-N		
wool	WAOL		
Woolner	WAOL/NER		
word salad	WORD/SAL/LAD		
workup	WORK/*UP		
worm	WORM		
Worm	K-P/WORM		
wormian	WORM/YAN		
Wormley	WORM/LAOE		
wormseed	WORM/SAOED		
wormwood	WORM/WAOD		
wort	WORT		
Worth	K-P/WO*RT		
Woulfe	WOUL/-F		
	WUL/-F		
	WAOUL/-F		
	(not WOL/-F, WO*L/-F, or WOL/*F)		
wound	WAOUND		
	WOUND		
woven	WOEVN		
	WOEV/-N		
W-plasty	W-RBGS/PLAS/TI		
wreath	WRAO*ET		
wretch	WREFP		
Wright	WRAOIGT		
Wright's stain	WRAOIGT/AOES/STAIN		
wrinkle	WRIN/K-L		
Wrisberg	WRIS/BERG		
	RIS/BERG		
wrisbergi	WRIS/BER/GAOI		
	RIS/BER/GAOI		
wrist	WR*IS		
wristdrop	WR*IS/DROP		

X

Xanax	ZAN/AX
xanchromatic	ZAN/KROE/MAT/IK
xanoxate	ZA/NOK/SAIT
	ZA/NOX/AIT
xanth(o)-	ZAN/TH(O)
	ZANT (since * is used for Z, can't
	use for th-)
xanthate	ZAN/THAIT
xanthelasma	ZANT/LAZ/MA
	ZAN/THE/LAZ/MA
	ZAN/THEL/AZ/MA
xanthelasmatosis	ZANT/LAZ/MA/TOE/SIS
	ZAN/THE/LAZ/MA/TOE/SIS
	ZAN/THEL/AZ/MA/TOE/SIS
xanthelasmoidea	ZANT/LAZ/MOID/YA
	ZAN/THE/LAZ/MOID/YA
	ZAN/THEL/AZ/MOID/YA
xanthematin	ZAN/THAOEM/TIN
	ZAN/THEM/TIN
xanthemia	ZAN/THAOEM/YA
xanthene	ZAN/THAOEN
xanthic	ZAN/THIK
xanthin	ZAN/TH*IN
	(not ZAN/THIN; see xanthine)
xanthine	ZAN/THIN
	ZAN/THAO*EN
	(not ZAN/THAOEN; see xanthene)
xanthinin	ZAN/THI/NIN
	ZANT/NIN
xanthinol	ZAN/THI/NOL
	ZANT/NOL
xanthinoxidase	ZAN/THIN/OX/DAIS
xanthinuria	ZAN/THI/NAOUR/YA
	ZANT/NAOUR/YA
	ZAN/THIN/YAOUR/YA
xanthinuric	ZAN/THI/NAOUR/IK
	ZANT/NAOUR/IK
	ZAN/THIN/YAOUR/IK
xanthism	ZAN/THIFM
xanthiuria	ZAN/THI/YAOUR/YA
	ZANT/YAOUR/YA
xanthochroia	ZAN/THO/KROI/YA
	ZANT/KROI/YA
xanthochromatic	ZAN/THO/KROE/MATIK
	ZANT/KROE/MAT/IK
xanthochromia	ZAN/THO/KROEM/YA
	ZANT/KROEM/YA
xanthochromic	ZAN/THO/KROEM/IK
	ZANT/KROEM/IK
xanthochroous	ZAN/THOK/ROUS
	ZAN/THOK/RO/OUS
xanthocyanopsia	ZAN/THO/SAOI/NOPS/YA
	ZANT/SAOI/NOPS/YA
xanthocystine	ZAN/THO/SIS/TAOEN
	ZANT/SIS/TAOEN
xanthocyte	ZAN/THO/SAO*IT
	ZANT/SAO*IT
xanthoderma	ZAN/THO/DER/MA
	ZANT/DER/MA
xanthodont	ZAN/THO/DONT
	ZANT/DONT
xanthodontous	ZAN/THO/DON/TOUS
	ZANT/DON/TOUS
xanthoerythrodermia	ZAN/THO/R*IT/RO/DERM/YA
	ZANT/R*IT/RO/DERM/YA
xanthofibroma	ZAN/THO/FAOI/BROE/MA
	ZANT/FAOI/BROE/MA
xanthogranuloma	ZAN/THO/GRAN/LOE/MA
	ZANT/GRAN/LOE/MA
xanthoma	ZAN/THOE/MA
xanthomatosis	ZAN/THOEM/TOE/SIS
xanthomatous	ZAN/THOEM/TOUS
Xanthomonas	ZAN/THO/MOE/NAS
	ZANT/MOE/NAS
xanthone	ZAN/THOEN
xanthopathy	ZAN/THOP/TH*I
xanthophane	ZAN/THO/FAIN
	ZANT/FAIN
xanthophose	ZAN/THO/FOEZ
	ZAN/THO/FOES
	ZANT/FOEZ
	ZANT/FOES
xanthophyll	ZAN/THO/FIL
	ZANT/FIL
xanthopia	ZAN/THOEP/YA
xanthoproteic	ZAN/THO/PRO/TAOE/IK
	ZANT/PRO/TAOE/IK
xanthoprotein	ZAN/THO/PRO/TAOEN
	ZANT/PRO/TAOEN
xanthopsia	ZAN/THOPS/YA
xanthopsin	ZAN/THOP/SIN
xanthopsis	ZAN/THOP/SIS
xanthopsydracia	ZAN/THOPS/DRAIS/YA
	ZAN/THOP/SI/DRAIS/YA
xanthopuccine	ZAN/THO/PUK/SAOEN
	ZAN/THO/PUK/SIN
	ZANT/PUK/SAOEN
	ZANT/PUK/SIN
xanthosarcoma	ZAN/THO/SAR/KOE/MA
	ZANT/SAR/KOE/MA
xanthosine	ZAN/THO/SAOEN
	ZAN/THO/SIN
	ZANT/SAOEN
	ZANT/SIN
xanthosis	ZAN/THOE/SIS
xanthotoxin	ZAN/THO/TOK/SIN
	ZANT/TOK/SIN
xanthous	ZAN/THOUS
xanthurenic	ZAN/THAOU/RAOEN/IK
	ZAN/THAOU/REN/IK
xanthuria	ZAN/THAOUR/YA
xanthyl	ZAN/THIL
xanthylic	ZAN/THIL/IK
xantorubin	ZANT/RAOU/BIN
	ZAN/TO/RAOU/BIN
xenembole	ZEN/EM/BLAOE
	ZEN/EM/BO/LAOE
xenenthesis	ZEN/EN/THAOE/SIS
xenia	ZAOEN/YA
xeno-	ZEN
	ZE/NO
xenobiotic	ZEN/BAO*I/OT/IK
xenocytophilic	ZEN/SAOIT/FIL/IK
xenodiagnosis	ZEN/DAOIG/NOE/SIS
xenodiagnostic	ZEN/DAOIG/NO*S/IK
xenogeneic	ZEN/JE/NAOE/IK
	ZEN/JE/NAI/IK
xenogenesis	ZEN/JEN/SIS
xenogenic	ZEN/JEN/IK
xenogenous	ZE/NOJ/NOUS
	ZEN/OJ/NOUS
xenograft	ZEN/GRAFT
xenology	ZAOE/NOLG
	ZE/NOLG
	ZEN/OLG
xenomenia	ZEN/MAOEN/YA
xenon	ZEN/NON
	ZAOE/NON
xenoparasite	ZEN/PAR/SAOIT
xenophobia	ZEN/FOEB/YA
xenophonia	ZEN/FOEN/YA
xenophthalmia	ZEN/OF/THAL/MA
	ZEN/OF/THAL/MAOE/YA
Xenopsylla	ZEN/OP/SIL/LA
xenorexia	ZEN/REX/YA
xenyl	ZENL
	ZEN/IL
xer(o)-	ZAOER
	ZAOE/R(O)
Xerac	ZAOER/AK
	ZAOE/RAK
xeransis	ZAOE/RAN/SIS
xerantic	ZAOE/RANT/IK
xeraphium	ZAOE/RAF/YUM
xerasia	ZAOE/RAIZ/YA
xerocheilia	ZAOER/KAOIL/YA
xerocollyrium	ZAOER/KLIR/YUM
	ZAOER/KOL/LIR/YUM
xeroderma	ZAOER/DER/MA
xerodermatic	ZAOER/DER/MAT/IK
xerodermia	ZAOER/DERM/YA
xerogel	ZAOER/JEL
xerogram	ZAOER/GRAM
xerography	ZAOER/OG/FI
	ZAOE/ROG/FI
xeroma	ZAOE/ROE/MA
	ZAOER/ROE/MA
xeromammography	ZAOER/MAM/OG/FI
	ZAOER/MA/MOG/FI
xeromenia	ZAOER/MAOEN/YA
xeromycteria	ZAOER/MIK/TAOER/YA
xeronosus	ZAOE/NON/SUS
xerophagia	ZAOER/FAI/JA

xerophagy	ZAOER/OF/JI	xyrospasm	ZAOIR/SPAFM
	ZAOER/ROF/JI		ZAOI/RO/SPAFM
	ZAOE/ROF/JI	xysma	ZIZ/MA
xerophobia	ZAOER/FOEB/YA		ZIS/MA
xeropthalmia	ZAOER/OF/THAL/MA	xyster	ZIS/TER
	ZAOER/OF/THAL/MAOE/YA		(*not* S*IS/ER; see sister)
xerophthalmus	ZAOER/OF/THAL/MUS		
xeradiograph	ZAOER/RAID/YO/GRAF		
xeroradiography	ZAOER/RAID/YOG/FI		
xerose	ZAOE/ROE/SAOE		
	ZE/ROE/SAOE		
	ZAOE/ROES		
	ZAOER/ROES		
xerosialography	ZAOER/SAOI/LOG/FI		
xerosis	ZAOE/ROE/SIS		
	ZAOER/ROE/SIS		
	ZE/ROE/SIS		
xerostomia	ZAOER/STOEM/YA		
xerotes	ZAOE/ROE/TAOEZ		
	ZE/ROE/TAOEZ		
	ZAOER/TAOEZ		
xerotic	ZAOE/ROT/IK		
	ZE/ROT/IK		
xerotica	ZAOE/ROT/KA		
	ZE/ROT/KA		
xerotocia	ZAOER/TOES/YA		
xerotomography	ZAOER/TOE/MOG/FI		
xerotripsis	ZAOER/TRIP/SIS		
X-inactivation	KP-RBGS/IN/AKT/VAIGS		
xipamide	ZIP/MAOID		
xiph(o)-	ZIF		
	ZAOI/F(O)		
	ZI/F(O)		
xiphisternal	ZIF/STERNL		
xiphisternum	ZIF/STER/NUM		
xiphocostal	ZIF/KOS/TAL		
xiphodynia	ZIF/DIN/YA		
xiphoid	ZIF/OID		
	ZAOI/FOID		
xiphoidalgia	ZIF/OI/DAL/JA		
xiphoiditis	ZIF/OI/DAOITS		
xiphopagotomy	ZI/FOP/GOT/M*I		
	ZAOI/FOP/GOT/M*I		
xiphopagus	ZI/FOP/GUS		
	ZAOI/FOP/GUS		
X-linked	KP-RBGS/LIN/-KD		
X-Prep	KP-RBGS/PREP		
x-radiation	KP*/H-F/RAID/YAIGS		
	KPRAID/YAIGS		
x-ray	KPRAI		
	EX/RAI		
	KP*/RAI		
	KP-/RAI		
X-Seb	KP-RBGS/SEB		
X-Seb-T	KP-RBGS/SEB/T-RBGS		
xyl(o)-	ZAOIL		
	ZAOI/L(O)		
xylanthrax	ZAOI/LAN/THRAX		
xylazine	ZAOIL/ZAOEN		
xylem	ZAOIL/EM		
	ZAOI/LEM		
xylene	ZAOI/LAOEN		
xylenol	ZAOIL/NOL		
	ZAOI/LE/NOL		
xylidine	ZAOIL/DAOEN		
	ZAOI/LI/DAOEN		
Xylocaine	ZAOIL/KAIN		
xylogen	ZAOIL/JEN		
xyloidin	ZAOI/LOI/DIN		
xyloketose	ZAOIL/KAOE/TOES		
xyloketosuria	ZAOIL/KAOET/SAOUR/YA		
xylol	ZAOI/LOL		
xyloma	ZAOI/LOE/MA		
xylometazoline	ZAOIL/ME/TAZ/LAOEN		
	ZAOIL/MET/ZOE/LAOEN		
xylopyranose	ZAOIL/PIR/NOES		
xylose	ZAOI/LOES		
xyloside	ZAOIL/SAOID		
xylosuria	ZAOIL/SAOUR/YA		
xylotherapy	ZAOIL/THER/PI		
xylulose	ZAOIL/LOES		
	ZAOI/LAOU/LOES		
	ZAOIL/YAOU/LOES		
	ZAOIL/YU/LOES		
xylulosuria	ZAOIL/LO/SAOUR/YA		
	ZAOI/LAOUL/SAOUR/YA		
	ZAOI/LAOU/LO/SAOUR/YA		
xylyl	ZAOI/LIL		
xylylene	ZAOIL/LAOEN		

Y

yard	YARD
yaw	YAU
yawn	YAUN
yaws	YAUZ
	YAU/-S
yearling	YAOER/-LG
	YAOER/LING
yeast	YAO*ES
Yellen	YEL/-N
yellow	YEL/LOE
yellowish	YEL/LOE/IRB
yerba	YER/BA
yerba santa	YER/BA/SAN/TA
yerbine	YER/BIN
Yerkes	YER/KAOEZ
Yerkes-Bridges	YER/KAOEZ/H-F/K-P/BRIJ/-S
yerli	YER/LAOE
Yersin	YER/SIN
Yersinia	YER/SIN/YA
yersiniosis	YER/SIN/YOE/SIS
yin-yang	YIN/YANG
Yocon	YOE/KON
Yodoxin	YOE/DOK/SIN
yogurt	YOE/GURT
	YOEG/URT
yohimbine	YOE/HIM/BAOEN
Yohimex	YOE/HI/MEX
yoke	YO*EK
	(*not* YOEK; see yolk)
yolk	YOEK
Young	K-P/YUNG
	K-P/YOUNG
yperite	AOIP/RAOIT
ypsiliform	IPS/LI/FORM
	IP/SIL/FORM
ypsiloid	IPS/LOID
	IP/SI/LOID
ytterbium	IT/TERB/YUM
	IT/ERB/YUM
yttrium	IT/RAOE/UM
	IT/RAOE/YUM
	(*not* IT/RUM; see it rum)
yukon	YAOU/KON
Yutopar	YAOUT/PAR
	YAOU/TO/PAR
Yvon	E/VON

Z

zacatilla	ZAK/TAOE/YA
	ZAK/TAOEL/YA
Zaglas	ZAG/LAS
Zahn	ZAUN
	ZAN
Zambusch	ZAM/BAOURB
Zander	ZAND/ER
	ZAN/DER
Zang	ZANG
Zangemeister	ZANG/MAO*IS/ER
	ZANG/MAOIS/TER
Zantac	ZAN/TAK
Zappert	ZAP/ERT
	ZAP/PERT
zaranthan	ZA/RAN/THAN
Zarontin	ZA/RON/TIN
Zaroxolyn	ZA/ROX/LIN
	ZAR/OX/LIN
Zaufal	ZOU/FAL
	ZOU/FAUL
Z-Bec Tablets	STK-RBGS/BEK/TAB/LET/-S
zea	ZAOE/YA
Zea	K-P/ZAOE/YA
zeatin	ZAOE/TIN
	ZAOE/YA/TIN
zebra	ZAOE/BRA
	ZAOEB/RA
Zeeman	ZAOE/MAN
zein	ZAOE/YIN
zeinolysis	ZAOE/NOL/SIS
	ZAOE/YIN/OL/SIS
zeinolytic	ZAOE/NO/LIT/IK
	ZAOE/YIN/LIT/IK
Zeis	ZAOIS
zeiosis	ZAOI/YOE/SIS
zeisian	ZAOIS/YAN
zeism	ZAOE/IFM
zeismus	ZAOE/IZ/MUS
Zeiss	ZAOISZ
zeistic	ZAOE/*IS/IK
Zeitgeist	ZAOIT/GAO*IS
Zeller	ZEL/ER
zelophobia	ZAOEL/FOEB/YA
	ZAOE/LO/FOEB/YA
zelotypia	ZAOEL/TIP/YA
	ZAOE/LO/TIP/YA
Zenate	ZAOE/NAIT
Zenker	ZEN/KER
zenkerism	ZEN/KER/IFM
zenkerize	ZEN/KER/AOIZ
zeo-	ZAOE
	ZAOE/YO
zeolite	ZAOE/YO/LIT
	ZAOE/LAOIT
zeoscope	ZAOE/SKOEP
	ZAOE/YO/SKOEP
Zephiran	ZEF/RAN
Zephrex	ZEF/REX
Zephrex-LA	ZEF/REX/L-RBGS/A*RBGS
zero	ZAOE/ROE
	ZAOER/ROE
Zero family	K-P/ZAOE/ROE/FAM/LI
	K-P/ZAOER/ROE/FAM/LI
zerogravity	ZAOER/GRAV/TI
zestocausis	ZES/TO/KAU/SIS
zestocautery	ZES/TO/KAUT/RI
Zestoretic	ZES/TO/RET/IK
Zestril	ZES/TRIL
zetacrit	ZAIT/KRIT
	ZAI/TA/KRIT
	ZET/KRIT
Zetar	ZAOE/TAR
zeumatography	ZAOUM/TOG/FI
zidovudine	ZAOI/DOEV/DAOEN
	ZAOI/DOE/VAOU/DAOEN
	ZAOI/DOEV/YAOU/DAOEN
Ziegler	ZAOEG/LER
	ZIG/LER
Ziehen	ZAOE/HEN
Ziehl's stain	ZAOEL/AOES/STAIN
(word grouped)	(note: ZAOEL = zeal)
Ziehl-Neelsen	ZAOEL/H-F/NAOEL/SEN
(word grouped)	
Ziemssen	ZAOEM/SEN
Ziffern	ZIFRN
	ZIF/ERN
zigzagplasty	ZIG/ZAG/PLAS/TI
Zimmerlin	ZIM/ER/LIN
	ZIM/MER/LIN
Zimmermann	ZIM/ER/MAN
	ZIM/MER/MAN
Zinacef	ZIN/SEF
zinc	ZIN/-K (required)
zincalism	ZIN/KAL/IFM
zincative	ZIN/KA/TIV
zinciferous	ZIN/KIF/ROUS
zincoid	ZIN/KOID
Zincon Dandruff	ZIN/KON/DAN/DRUF/
Shampoo	SHAM/PAO
zincum	ZIN/KUM
Zincvit	ZIN/-K/VAOIT
	ZIN/-K/VIT
zingiber	ZIN/JI/BER
Zinn	ZIN
Zinni	ZIN/NAOI
zinnii	ZIN/YAOI
Zinsser	ZIN/SER
	ZINS/SER
zinterol	ZINT/ROL
	ZINT/ROEL
zip	ZIP
zipp	ZIP/-P
	(not ZIP; see zip)
zirconium	ZIR/KOEN/YUM
zisp	ZIS/-P
Zittman	ZIT/MAN
zoacanthosis	ZOE/KAN/THOE/SIS
	ZOE/AK/AN/THOE/SIS
zoamylin	ZOE/AM/LIN
zoanthropic	ZOE/AN/THROP/IK
zoanthropy	ZOE/AN/THRO/PI
zoescope	ZOE/SKOEP
zoetic	ZOE/ET/IK
zoetrope	ZOE/TROEP
zoic	ZOIK
	ZOE/IK
zoite	ZOE/AOIT
zolamine	ZOEL/MAOEN
Zolicef	ZOL/SEF
Zollinger	ZOL/IN
Zollner	ZEL/NER
	ZOL/NER
zomepirac	ZOEM/PIR/AK
	ZOEM/PAOER/AK
zometapine	ZOE/MET/PAOEN
zomotherapy	ZOEM/THER/PI
	ZOE/MO/THER/PI
zona	ZOE/NA
zonae	ZOE/NAE
zonal	ZOENL
	ZOE/NAL
zonary	ZOEN/RI
zonate	ZOE/NAIT
	ZOEN/AIT
Zondek	ZON/DEK
zone	ZOEN
Zone-A Cream	ZOEN/ARBGS/KRAOEM
zonesthesia	ZOE/NES/THAOEZ/YA
zonifugal	ZOE/NIF/GAL
zoning	ZOEN/-G
zonipetal	ZOE/NIP/TAL
zonoskeleton	ZOEN/SKEL/TON
	ZOE/NO/SKEL/TON
zonul-	ZOEN/L-
	ZOEN/YAOU/L-
	ZOEN/YU/L-
	ZON/L-
	ZON/YAOU/L-
	ZON/YU/L-
zonula	ZOEN/LA
	ZON/LA
zonulae	ZOEN/LAE
	ZON/LAE
zonular	ZOEN/LAR
	ZON/LAR
zonulares	ZOEN/LAI/RAOEZ
	ZON/LAI/RAOEZ
zonule	ZOEN/YAOUL
	ZON/YAOUL
zonulitis	ZOEN/LAOITS
	ZON/LAOITS
zonulolysis	ZOEN/LOL/SIS
	ZON/LOL/SIS

zonulotomy	ZOEN/LOT/M*I	zoospermia	ZOE/SPERM/YA
	ZON/LOT/M*I	zoosporangia	ZOE/SPRAN/JA
zonulysis	ZOEN/LAOI/SIS	zoosporangium	ZOE/SPRAN/JUM
	ZON/LAOI/SIS	zoospore	ZOE/SPOER
zoo-	ZOE	zoosteroid	ZOE/STAOER/OID
	ZAO	zoosterol	ZOE/STAOER/OL
zooagglutinin	ZOE/AI/GLAOUT/NIN	zootechnics	ZOE/TEK/NIK/-S
zooanaphylactogen	ZOE/AN/FLAKT/JEN	zootic	ZOE/OT/IK
zooanthroponosis	ZOE/AN/THRO/PO/NOE/SIS	zootomist	ZOE/OT/M*IS
zoobiology	ZOE/BAO*I/OLG	zootomy	ZOE/OT/M*I
zoobiotism	ZOE/BAO*I/TIFM	zootoxin	ZOE/TOK/SIN
zooblast	ZOE/BLA*S	zootrophic	ZOE/TROFK
zoochemical	ZOE/KEM/KAL	Zorprin	ZOR/PRIN
zoochemistry	ZOE/KEM/STRI	zoster	ZOS/TER
zoodermic	ZOE/DERM/IK	zosteriform	ZOS/TER/FORM
zoodetritus	ZOE/DE/TRAOI/TUS	zosteroid	ZOS/TER/OID
zoodynamic	ZOE/DAOI/NAM/IK		ZOS/TROID
zoodynamics	ZOE/DAOI/NAM/IK/-S	Zostrix	ZOS/TRIX
zooerastia	ZOE/E/RA*S/YA	Zovirax	ZOE/VAOI/RAX
zoofulvin	ZOE/FUL/VIN	zoxazolamine	ZOX/ZOEL/MAOEN
zoogenesis	ZOE/JEN/SIS		ZOX/ZOL/MAOEN
zoogenous	ZOE/OJ/NOUS	Z-plasty	STK-RBGS/PLAS/TI
zoogeny	ZOE/OJ/N*I	Zsigmondy	ZIG/MON/DI
zoogeography	ZOE/JAOE/OG/FI		SIG/MON/DI
zooglea	ZOE/OG/LA	Zuberella	ZAOUB/REL/LA
	ZOE/GLAOE/YA	zuckergussdarm	ZUK/ER/GUS/DARM
zoogleic	ZOE/GLAOE/IK		ZAOUK/ER/GAOUS/DARM
zoogonous	ZOE/OG/NOUS	zuckergussleber	ZUK/ER/GUS/LAIB/ER
zoogony	ZOE/OG/N*I		ZAOUK/ER/GAOUS/LAIB/ER
zoograft	ZOE/GRAFT	Zuckerkandl	ZUK/ER/KAND/-L
zoografting	ZOE/GRAFT/-G		ZAOUK/ER/KAND/-L
zoohormone	ZOE/HOR/MOEN	zuclomiphene	ZAOU/KLOEM/FAOEN
zooid	ZOE/OID	zurni	ZUR/NAOI
zookinase	ZOE/KAOI/NAIS	zwischenferment	SWIRB/EN/FERMT
zoolagnia	ZOE/LAG/NA	zwischenkorper	SWIRB/EN/KERP/ER
	ZOE/LAG/NAOE/YA	zwischenscheibe	SWIRB/EN/SHAOI/BAOE
zoolite	ZOE/LAOIT		SWIRB/EN/SHAOI/BA
zoolith	ZOE/L*IT	zwitterion	SWIT/ER/AOIN
zoological	ZOE/LOJ/KAL		SWIT/ER/AOI/ON
zoology	ZOE/OLG		SWIT/ER/AOI/YON
zoom	ZAOM	zwitterionic	SWIT/ER/AOIN/IK
zoomania	ZOE/MAIN/YA		SWIT/ER/AOI/ON/IK
Zoomastigina	ZOE/MA*S/JAOI/NA		SWIT/ER/AOI/YON/IK
Zoomastigophora	ZOE/MA*S/GOF/RA	zwolffingerdarm	SWEL/FING/ER/DARM
Zoomastigophorasida	ZOE/MA*S/GO/FOE/RAS/DA	Zydone	ZAOI/DOEN
Zoomastigophorea	ZOE/MA*S/GO/FOER/YA	zygal	ZAOI/GAL
zoomylus	ZOE/OM/LUS	zygapophyseal	see zygapophysial
-zoon	ZAON	zygapophysial	ZAOIG/PO/FIZ/YAL
	ZOE/WON	zygapophyses	ZAOIG/POF/SAOEZ
	(not ZOEN; see zone)	zygapophysis	ZAOIG/POF/SIS
zoonerythrin	ZOE/ON/ER/THRIN	zygia	ZIG/YA
	ZOE/NER/THRIN		ZIJ/YA
zoonite	ZOE/NAOIT	zygion	ZIG/YON
zoonomy	ZOE/ON/M*I		ZIJ/YON
zoonoses	ZOE/NOE/SAOEZ	zygo-	ZAOIG
zoonosis	ZOE/NOE/SIS		ZAOI/GO
zoonosology	ZOE/NOE/SOLG	zygocyte	ZAOIG/SAO*IT
zoonotic	ZOE/NOT/IK	zygodactyly	ZAOIG/DAKT/LI
zooparasite	ZOE/PAR/SAOIT	zygoma	ZAOI/GOE/MA
zooparasitic	ZOE/PAR/SIT/IK	zygomatic	ZAOIG/MAT/IK
zoopathology	ZOE/PA/THOLG	zygomatici	ZAOIG/MAT/SAOI
zooperal	ZOE/OP/RAL	zygomatico-	ZAOIG/MAT/KO
zoopery	ZOE/OP/RI	zygomaticoauricular	ZAOIG/MAT/KO/AU/RIK/LAR
zoophagous	ZOE/OF/GOUS	zygomaticoauricularis	ZAOIG/MAT/KO/AU/RIK/LAI/RIS
zoopharmacology	ZOE/FARM/KOLG	zygomaticofacial	ZAOIG/MAT/KO/FAIRBL
zoopharmacy	ZOE/FARM/SI	zygomaticofrontal	ZAOIG/MAT/KO/FRON/TAL
zoophile	ZOE/FAOIL	zygomaticomaxillary	ZAOIG/MAT/KO/MAX/LAIR
zoophilia	ZOE/FIL/YA	zygomatico-orbital	ZAOIG/MAT/KO/ORB/TAL
zoophilic	ZOE/FIL/IK	zygomaticosphenoid	ZAOIG/MAT/KO/SFAOE/NOID
zoophilism	ZOE/OF/LIFM	zygomaticotemporal	ZAOIG/MAT/KO/TEFRP/RAL
zoophilous	ZOE/OF/LOUS	zygomaticum	ZAOIG/MAT/KUM
zoophobia	ZOE/FOEB/YA	zygomaticus	ZAOIG/MAT/KUS
zoophysiology	ZOE/FIZ/YOLG	zygomaxillare	ZAOIG/MAX/LAI/RAOE
zoophyte	ZOE/FAOIT	zygomaxillary	ZAOIG/MAX/LAIR
zooplankton	ZOE/PLANG/TON	Zygomycetes	ZAOIG/MAOI/SAOE/TAOEZ
zooplasty	ZOE/PLAS/TI	zygon	ZAOI/GON
zooprecipitin	ZOE/PRE/SIP/TIN	zygonema	ZAOIG/NAOE/MA
zooprophylaxis	ZOE/PROEF/LAK/SIS	zygoplast	ZAOIG/PLA*S
zoopsia	ZOE/OPS/YA	zygopodium	ZAOIG/POED/YUM
zoopsychology	ZOE/SAOI/KOLG	zygosis	ZAOI/GOE/SIS
zoosadism	ZOE/SAI/DIFM	zygosity	ZAOI/GOS/TI
	ZOE/SAID/IFM	zygosperm	ZAOIG/SPERM
zooscopy	ZOE/OS/KPI	zygosphere	ZAOIG/SFAOER
zoosensitinogen	ZOE/SENS/TIN/JEN	zygospore	ZAOIG/SPOER
zoosis	ZOE/O/SIS	zygostyle	ZAOIG/STAOIL
	ZOE/YOE/SIS	zygote	ZAOI/GOET
zoosmosis	ZOE/OZ/MOE/SIS	zygotene	ZAOIG/TAOEN
	ZOE/OS/MOE/SIS	zygotic	ZAOI/GOT/IK
zoosperm	ZOE/SPERM	zygoto-	ZAOI/GOET

	ZAOI/GOE/TO
	ZAOIG/TO
zygotoblast	ZAOI/GOET/BLA*S
zygotomere	ZAOI/GOET/MAOER
-zygous	ZAOI/GOUS
	ZAOIG/OUS
Zyloprim	ZAOIL/PRIM
zym(o)-	ZAOIM
	ZAOI/M(O)
zymase	ZAOI/MAIS
zymasis	ZAOIM/SIS
zyme	ZAOIM
zymic	ZAOIM/IK
zymin	ZAOI/MIN
Zymobacterium	ZAOIM/BAK/TAOERM
zymochemistry	ZAOIM/KEM/STRI
zymodeme	ZAOIM/DAOEM
zymoexcitator	ZAOIM/KPAOI/TAI/TOR
zymoexciter	ZAOIM/KPAOIT/ER
zymogen	ZAOIM/JEN
zymogenesis	ZAOIM/JEN/SIS
zymogenic	ZAOIM/JEN/IK
zymogenous	ZAOI/MOJ/NOUS
zymogic	ZAOI/MOJ/IK
zymogram	ZAOIM/GRAM
zymohexase	ZAOIM/HEX/AIS
	ZAOIM/HEK/SAIS
zymohydrolysis	ZAOIM/HAOI/DROL/SIS
zymoid	ZAOIM/OID
	ZAOI/MOID
zymologist	ZAOI/MO*LGS
zymology	ZAOI/MOLG
zymolysis	ZAOI/MOL/SIS
zymolytic	ZAOIM/LIT/IK
Zymonema	ZAOIM/NAOE/MA
zymophore	ZAOIM/FOER
zymophorous	ZAOI/MOF/ROUS
zymophosphate	ZAOIM/FOS/FAIT
zymoprotein	ZAOIM/PRO/TAOEN
zymosan	ZAOIM/SAN
zymoscope	ZAOIM/SKOEP
zymose	ZAOI/MOES
zymosis	ZAOI/MOE/SIS
zymosterol	ZAOI/MO*S/ROL
zymosthenic	ZAOI/MOS/THEN/IK
	ZAOIM/STHEN/IK
zymotic	ZAOI/MOT/IK
zytase	ZAOI/TAIS

APPENDIX 1
MEDICAL ACRONYMS & ABBREVIATIONS

A₂, A₂	second heart sound		AR	atrial regurgitation

A₂, A₂	second heart sound
AAL	anterior axillary line
AAMT	American Association for Medical Transcription
A&W	alive and well
AB, ab.	abortion
Ab	antibody
ABC	aspiration biopsy cytology
abd	abdomen
ABO	three main blood types
ABC	aspiration biopsy cytology
ABGs	arterial blood gases
ABR	auditory brain-stem response; absolute bed rest
AC	air conduction
A.C.	acromioclavicular (joint)
a.c.	before meals
Acc, Accom.	accommodation
ACE	angiotensin-converting enzyme
ACG	angiocardiography
Ach	acetylcholine
ACP	adenocarcinoma of prostate
ACTA	automated computerized transverse axial scanner
ACTH	adrenocorticotropic hormone
AD	right ear
ad lib, ad lib.	as desired
ADEM	acute disseminated encephalomyelitis
adeno-CA	adenocarcinoma
ADH	antidiuretic hormone
ADLs	activities of daily living
AE	above the elbow
AF	atrial fibrillation
AFB	acid-fast bacillus
AFP	alpha-fetoprotein
Ag	antigen
A/G	albumin/globulin ratio
AGN	acute glomerulonephritis
AHF	antihemophilic factor
AI	aortic insufficiency
AIDS	acquired immune deficiency syndrome
AK	above the knee
AKA	above the knee amputation
alk phos	alkaline phosphatase
ALL	acute lymphocytic leukemia
ALP	alkaline phosphatase
ALS	amyotrophic lateral sclerosis
ALT	alanine transaminase
AMA	American Medical Association
AMI	acute myocardial infarction
AML	acute myelocytic leukemia
amp	ampere
ANA	antinuclear antibody
ANS	autonomic nervous system
AP	anteroposterior
A&P	auscultation and percussion; anterior and posterior
APC	atrial premature complex
aq.	water

AR	atrial regurgitation
ara-C	cytosine arabinoside
ARC	abnormal retinal correspondence; AIDS related complex
ARDS	acute respiratory distress syndrome
ARF	acute renal failure; acute respiratory failure
AS	left ear; aortic stenosis; atrial stenosis; arteriosclerosis
ASA	acetylsalicylic acid (aspirin)
ASD	atrial septal defect
ASH	asymmetrical septal hypertrophy
ASHD	arteriosclerotic heart disease
ASO	antistreptolysin-O
AST	aspartate amino transferase
Astigm.	astigmatism
ATN	acute tubular necrosis
Au	gold
ausc.	auscultation
AV	atrioventricular; arteriovenous
AVM	arteriovenous malformation
AVR	aortic valve replacement
AWMI	anterior wall myocardial infarction
B strep	beta streptococcus
BA, B.A.	bachelor of arts degree
Ba	barium
BaE	barium enema
BAEP	brain-stem auditory evoked potential
BAER	brain-stem auditory evoked response
bands	banded neutrophils
basos	basophils
BBB	bundle-branch block
BC	bone conduction
B-cells	B-lymphocytes
BCNU	bischloroethylnitrosourea
BE	barium enema; below the elbow
b/f	black female
b.i.d.	twice a day
b.i.n.	twice a night
b.i.w.	twice a week
BK	below the knee
BKA	below the knee amputation
BM	bowel movement
b/m	black male
BMR	basal metabolic rate
BNO	bladder neck obstruction
BP	blood pressure
BPH	benign prostatic hyperplasia (hyper-trophy)
BRAT	bananas, rice cereal, applesauce, and toast
Broncho	bronchoscopy
BS, B.S.	bachelor of science degree
BSE	breast self-examination
BSP	bromsulphalein
B, S, and U	Bartholin's, Skene's, and urethral glands
BT	bleeding time
BUN	blood urea nitrogen
BUS	Bartholin's, urethral, and Skene's glands
bx	biopsy
C, C.	Celsius, centigrade; cervical vertebra; Clostridium

c̄	with	CZI	crystalline zinc insulin
CA, Ca, ca	cancer, carcinoma	D	diopter (lens strength)
Ca	calcium	d	day
CABG	coronary artery bypass graft	D&C	dilatation (dilation) and curettage
CAD	coronary artery disease	D&E	dilatation (dilation) and evacuation
CAPD	continuous ambulatory peritoneal dialysis	D&V	diarrhea and vomiting
C&S	culture and sensitivity	db, dB	decibel
CAT	computerized axial tomography	D/C, dc	discontinue; discharge
cath	catheter, catheterize	D.C.	Doctor of Chiropractic
CBC	complete blood count	DD	discharge diagnosis
CBD	common bile duct	DDS, D.D.S.	Doctor of Dental Surgery
CBF	cerebral blood flow	DES	diethylstilbestrol
CC	chief complaint; cardiac catheterization	DHL	diffuse histiocytic lymphoma
cc	cubic centimeter	DI	diabetes insipidus; diagnostic imaging
c̄c̄	with correction	DIC	disseminated intravascular coagulation
CCU	coronary care unit; cardiac care unit	DID	dead of intercurrent disease
CEA	carcinoembryonic antigen	DIE	dead in emergency room
CF	cystic fibrosis	diff, diff.	differential
cf.	compare	DIP	distal interphalangeal (joint)
c. gl.	correction with glasses	DJD	degenerative joint disease
CHD	coronary heart disease	DKA	diabetic ketoacidosis
Chem	chemotherapy	dl	deciliter
chem	chemistries	DLE	discoid lupus erythematosus
CHF	congestive heart failure	DM	diabetes mellitus
chr	chronic	DNA	deoxyribonucleic acid
Ci	Curie	DO, D.O.	Doctor of Osteopathy
CIC	clean intermittent catheterization	DOA	dead on arrival
CK	creatine kinase	DOB	date of birth
Cl	chlorine	DOC	died of other causes
CLL	chronic lymphocytic leukemia	D.P.M.	Doctor of Podiatric Medicine
cm	centimeter	DPT	diphtheria-pertussis-tetanus
CMF	Cytoxan, methotrexate, and 5-fluorouracil	DSA	digital subtraction angiography
CMG	cystometrogram	DT	delirium tremens
CML	chronic myelogenous leukemia	DTRs	deep tendon reflexes
CMT	Certified Medical Transcriptionist	DUB	dysfunctional uterine bleeding
CMV	cytomegalovirus	DVP	deep vein thrombosis
CNS	central nervous system	Dx	diagnosis
Co	coccyx; coccygeal; cobalt	EB	Epstein-Barr
CO₂	carbon dioxide	EBNA	Epstein-Barr nuclear antigen
COLD	chronic obstructive lung disease	EBV	Epstein-Barr virus
COP	Cytoxan, Oncovin, and prednisone	ECC	extracorporeal circulation
COPD	chronic obstructive pulmonary disease	ECF	extended-care facility; extracellular fluid
CP	cerebral palsy	ECG	electrocardiogram, electrocardiograph
CPAP	continuous positive airway pressure	ECT	electroconvulsive therapy
CPD	cephalopelvic disproportion	EDC	estimated date of confinement
CPE	chronic pulmonary emphysema	EEG	electroencephalogram, electroencephalograph
CPK	creatinine phosphokinase		
CPR	cardiopulmonary resuscitation	EENT	eyes, ears, nose, and throat
CRF	chronic renal failure	EGD	esophagogastroduodenoscopy
CS, C-section	cesarean section	EKG	electrocardiogram, electrocardiograph
CSF	cerebrospinal fluid	EM	electron microscope
CT	computed tomography	Em	emmetropia
ct.	count	EMG	electromyogram, electromyograph
CV	cardiovascular	ENG	electronystagmography
CVA	cerebrovascular accident; costovertebral angle	ENT	ears, nose, and throat
		EOM	extraocular movement
CVD	cardiovascular disease	eos, eosins	eosinophils
CVP	central venous pressure; Cytoxan, vincristine, and prednisone	epi	epithelial cell; epinephrine
		ER	emergency room; estrogen receptor
CVS	chorionic villus sampling; cardiovascular system	ERV	expiratory reserve volume
		ESR	erythrocyte sedimentation rate
C/W	compare with	ESRD	end-stage renal disease
CWP	childbirth without pain	EST	electroshock therapy
CXR	chest x-ray; chest radiograph	ESWL	extracorporeal shock wave lithotripsy
cysto	cystoscopic examination	ET	esotropia

exc	excision	HNP	herniated nucleus pulposus
F, F.	fahrenheit	h/o	history of
FBS	fasting blood sugar	HP	hemipelvectomy
Fe	iron	hpf	high-power field
FEF	forced expiratory flow	HPI	history of present illness
FEF_{25-75}	forced expiratory flow, 25%-75%	h.s.	at bedtime
FEKG	fetal electrocardiogram	HSG	hysterosalpingography
FEV	forced expiratory volume	h-s megaly	hepatosplenomegaly
FEV_1, FEV-1	forced expiratory volume in 1 second	ht, hct	hematocrit
FH	family history	HVD	hypertensive vascular disease
FHR	fetal heart rate	Hx	history
FHT	fetal heart tone	hypo	hypodermically
FRC	functional residual capacity	Hz	Hertz
FROM	full range of motion	I	iodine
FS	frozen section	IADH	inappropriate antidiuretic hormone
FSH	follicle-stimulating hormone	I&D	incision and drainage; irrigation and drainage
ft.	foot, feet		
FTI	free thyroxine index	I&O	intake and output; in and out
FTND	full-term normal delivery	IBD	inflammatory bowel disease
FTP	full-term pregnancy	IC	inspiratory capacity
F/u	follow-up	ICF	intracellular fluid
FUO	fever of undetermined origin	ICP	intracranial pressure
Fx	fracture	ICSH	interstitial cell-stimulating hormone
G	gravida (pregnant)	ICU	intensive care unit
Ga	gallium	ID	intradermal
GB	gallbladder	IDDM	insulin-dependent diabetes mellitus
GBS	gallbladder series	Ig	immunoglobulin
GC	gonococcus, gonorrhea	IGT	impaired glucose tolerance
GE	gastroesophageal	IH	infectious hepatitis
GER	gastroesophageal reflux	IHSS	idiopathic hypertrophic subaortic stenosis
GFR	glomerular filtration rate		
GGT, GGTP	gamma-glutamyl transpeptidase	IM, I.M.	intramuscular; intramuscularly
GH	growth hormone	in.	inch
GI	gastrointestinal	inf.	inferior; infusion
gm	gram	inj.	injection
gr.	grain	IOL	intraocular lens
Grav. 1	first pregnancy	IOP	intraocular pressure
GTT	glucose tolerance test	IPPA	inspection, palpation, percussion, auscultation
gtt, gtt., Gtt.	drops		
GU	genitourinary	IPPB	intermittent positive-pressure breathing
GYN, Gyn	gynecology	IPPV	intermittent positive-pressure ventilation
H	hydrogen; hypodermic	I.Q.	intelligence quotient
h	hour	IRV	inspiratory reserve volume
H&H	hematocrit and hemoglobin	IS	intercostal space
H&P	history and physical	ITP	idiopathic thrombocytopenic purpura
HAV	hepatitis A virus	IU	international unit
Hb, Hgb	hemoglobin	IUD	intrauterine device
HBV	hepatitis B virus	IV, I.V.	intravenous; intravenously
HCG	human chorionic gonadotropin	IVC	intravenous cholangiogram (cholangiography)
HCl	hydrochloric acid		
HCO_3	bicarbonate	IVCD	intraventricular conduction delay
Hct, HCT, HT	hematocrit	IVP	intravenous pyelogram (pyelography)
HD	hearing distance; hemodialysis; hip disarticulation; Hodgkin's disease	JV	jugular venous
		JVD	jugular venous distention
h.d.	at bedtime	JVP	jugular venous pulse
HDL	high-density lipoprotein	K	potassium
He	helium	KCl	potassium chloride
HEENT	head, eyes, ears, nose, and throat	KD	knee disarticulation
Hg	mercury	kg	kilogram
Hgb, Hb, HGB, hgb	hemoglobin	kilo	kilogram
		KUB	kidney, ureter, bladder
HGH	human growth hormone	L	lumbar vertebra; liter; left; lower
HIV	human immunodeficiency virus	l	liter
HL	hearing level	LA	left atrium; long-acting
HM	hand movements	L&A	light and accommodation
		LAHB	left anterior hemiblock

lap.	laparotomy	MS	mitral stenosis; multiple sclerosis; morphine sulfate; musculoskeletal
LAT, lat.	lateral	MS, M.S.	master of science degree
LB	large bowel	MSH	melanocyte-stimulating hormone
lb.	pound	MSL	midsternal line
LCM	left costal margin	MTP	metatarsophalangeal
LD, LDH	lactic dehydrogenase	MTX	methotrexate
LDL	low-density lipoprotein	multip.	multipara; multiparous
LDL:HDL	low-density to high-density lipoprotein ratio	MVA	motor vehicle accident
LE	lupus erythematosus; lower extremity; left eye	MVP	mitral valve prolapse
		MVR	mitral valve replacement
LFTs	liver function tests	myop.	myopia
LH	luteinizing hormone	N	nitrogen
Lin. ac.	linear accelerator	Na	sodium
LL	left lateral	N&V	nausea and vomiting
LLL	left lower lobe	NB	newborn
LLQ	left lower quadrant	NBS	normal bowel (or breath) sounds
LMN	lower motor neuron	NCV	nerve conduction velocity
LMP	last menstrual period	NED	no evidence of disease
LN	lymph node	neg.	negative
LOC	level of consciousness	NER	no evidence of recurrence
LP	lumbar puncture	NG tube	nasogastric tube
LPN, L.P.N.	Licensed Practical Nurse	NICU	neonatal intensive care unit
LS	lumbosacral	NIDDM	non-insulin-dependent diabetes mellitus
LSK	liver, spleen, and kidneys	NM	neuromuscular
LTH	prolactin (luteotropic hormone)	NMR	nuclear magnetic resonance
LUL	left upper lobe	NOS	not otherwise specified
LUQ	left upper quadrant	NPDL	nodular, poorly differentiated lymphocytes
LV	left ventricle; left ventricular	NPH	neutral protamine Hagedorn insulin
lymphs	lymphocytes	n.p.o.	nothing by mouth
M, m	meter, minim	NRC	normal retinal correspondence
MA, M.A.	master of arts degree	NREM	nonrapid eye movement
MAO	monoamine oxidase	NS	normal saline
MCC	mean corpuscular concentration	NSAID	nonsteroidal anti-inflammatory drug
mcg	microgram	NTP	normal temperature and pressure
MCH	mean corpuscular hemoglobin	O_2	oxygen
MCHC	mean corpuscular hemoglobin concentration	OA	osteoarthritis
mCi	millicurie	OB	obstetrics
MCL	midclavicular line	OB/GYN	obstetrics and gynecology
MCP	metacarpophalangeal	OBS	organic brain syndrome
MCV	mean corpuscular volume	OC	oral contraceptive
MD, M.D.	Doctor of Medicine	OCG	oral cholecystogram
meds	medications	OCP	oral contraceptive pill
MEFR	maximal expiratory flow rate	OD, O.D.	right eye
mEq	milliequivalent	o.d.	once a day; every day
mEq/L	milliequivalent per liter	OHS	open heart surgery
METs, mets	metastases	OPV	oral polio vaccine
MG	myasthenia gravis	OR	operating room
mg	milligram	ORL	otorhinolaryngology
mg/cc	milligram per cubic centimeter	OS, O.S.	left eye
mg/dl	milligram per deciliter	os	mouth
mg/kg	milligram per kilogram	OT	occupational therapy
MH	marital history	OU	each eye; both eyes
MI	myocardial infarction; mitral insufficiency	OV	office visit; both eyes
ml	milliliter	oz.	ounce
mm	millimeter	P	phosphorus; pulse
MMFR	maximum midexpiratory flow rate	P2, P_2	pulmonary valve closure (heart sound)
mmHg	millimeters of mercury	PA	posteroanterior
MMR	measles, mumps, rubella (vaccine)	P.A.	pernicious anemia
monos	monocytes	P&A	percussion and auscultation
MOPP	nitrogen mustard, Oncovin, prednisone, and procarbazine	PAC	premature atrial contractions
		PaO_2	partial pressure of oxygen in arterial blood
MPJ	metacarpophalangeal joint	PAP	pulmonary arterial pressure
MR	mitral regurgitation, reflux	Pap smear	Papanicolaou smear
MRI	magnetic resonance imaging	Para 1	having had one viable birth
mRNA	messenger RNA		

paren.	parenterally	q.a.m.	every morning
PAT	paroxysmal atrial tachycardia	q.d.	every day
PBI	protein-bound iodine	q.h.	every hour
p.c.	after meals	q.h.s.	at bedtime
pCO$_2$	partial pressure of carbon dioxide	q.i.d.	four times a day
PCU	progressive care unit	q.m.	every morning
PCV	packed cell volume	q.n.	every night
PD	peritoneal dialysis	QNS, q.n.s.	quantity not sufficient
PDA	patent ductus arteriosus	q.o.d.	every other day
PDR	Physicians' Desk Reference	q.p.m.	every evening
PE	physical examination	q.#h.	every # hours
PE tube	polyethylene tube	R	right
PEEP	positive end-expiratory pressure	R.	respiration
PEG	pneumoencephalography	RA	rheumatoid arthritis; right atrium
PERRL	pupils equal, round, react to light	Ra	radium
PERRLA	pupils equal, round, react to light and accommodation	rad	radiation absorbed dose
		RAI	radioactive iodine
PET	positron emission tomography	RAIU	radioactive iodine uptake
PFTs	pulmonary function tests	RAM	rapid alternating movement
PGH	pituitary growth hormone	R&R	rate and rhythm
pH	hydrogen ion concentration	RAS	reticular activating system
Ph.D.	Doctor of Philosophy	RAST	radioallergosorbent test
pharm.D.	Doctor of Pharmacology	RATx	radiation therapy
PID	pelvic inflammatory disease	RBC	red blood cell; red blood count
PIH	pregnancy induced hypertension	RBE	relative biological effects
PIP	proximal interphalangeal (joint)	RCM	right costal margin
PKU	phenylketonuria	RD	respiratory disease
plts.	platelets	RDA	recommended daily allowance
PM	post mortem; petit mal; afternoon	RDS	respiratory distress syndrome
PMH	past medical history	RE	right eye
PMI	point of maximal impulse	rehab	rehabilitation
PMN	polymorphonuclear leukocyte (neutrophil)	REM	rapid eye movement
PMP	previous menstrual period	RF	rheumatoid factor
PMS	premenstrual syndrome	Rh	blood factor (Rhesus)
PND	paroxysmal nocturnal dyspnea	RIA	radioimmunoassay
PNS	peripheral nervous system	RL	right lateral
p.o.	by mouth; orally	RLL	right lower lobe
p/o	postoperative	RLQ	right lower quadrant
pO$_2$	oxygen pressure	RML	right middle lobe
polys	polymorphonuclear leukocytes (neutrophils)	RN, R.N.	Registered Nurse
POMP	prednisone, Oncovin, methotrexate, and 6-mercaptopurine	RNA	ribonucleic acid
		R/O	rule out
pos.	positive	ROM	range of motion
postop	postoperative	ROS	review of systems
p.p.	postprandial (after meals)	RP	retrograde pyelogram
PPD	purified protein derivative	RSR	regular sinus rhythm
PPT	partial prothrombin time	RT	radiation therapy
preop	preoperative	RU	routine urinalysis
PRL	prolactin	RUL	right upper lobe
p.r.n.	as needed; as required	RUQ	right upper quadrant
pro time	prothrombin time	RV	residual volume; right ventricle
procto	proctoscopy	Rx	prescription; drug
PSA	prostate specific antigen	S	sacrum; sacral; heart sound
PT	prothrombin time; physical therapy	s̄	without
pt.	patient	SA	sinoatrial
PTA	percutaneous transluminal angioplasty; prior to admission	SBE	subacute bacterial endocarditis
		SBFT	small bowel follow-through
PTCA	percutaneous transluminal coronary angioplasty	s̄c	without correction
		s.c., SC, subcu.	subcutaneous, subcutaneously
PTH	parathyroid hormone	SCD	sudden cardiac death
PTT	partial thromboplastin time	SD	shoulder disarticulation
PTU	propylthiouracil	sed rate	sedimentation rate
PVC	premature ventricular contraction	segs	segmented neutrophils
PZI	protamine zinc insulin	SEP	somatosensory evoked potential
q.	every; each	SG, sp. gr.	specific gravity

s. gl.	without correction; without glasses
SGOT	serum glutamic-oxaloacetic transaminase
SGPT	serum glutamic-pyruvic transaminase
SH	serum hepatitis
SIDS	sudden infant death syndrome
SL	sublingual
SLE	systemic lupus erythematosus
SMA	Sequential Multiple Analyzer
SMAC	Sequential Multiple Analyzer Computer
SMD	senile macular degeneration
SOAP	subjective, objective, assessment, plan
SOB	shortness of breath
sol.	solution
sos	if necessary
S/P	status post
SR	sedimentation rate; sustained release
$\overline{ss}$, ss.	half
SSER	somatosensory evoked responses
ST	speech threshold; esotropia
st.	stage
staph	staphylococcus
stat, STAT	immediately
STD	sexually transmitted disease; skin test dose
STH	somatotropin
strep	streptococcus
subcu., subcu, s.c., SC	subcutaneous, subcutaneously
SVD	spontaneous vaginal delivery
SVT	supraventricular tachycardia
Sx	symptoms
T	thoracic vertebra; temperature
T_3	triiodothyronine
T_4	thyroxine
T&A	tonsillectomy and adenoidectomy
TAH	total abdominal hysterectomy
TB	tuberculosis
TBI	total-body irradiation
T-cells	T-lymphocytes
TDI	toluene diisocyanate
TDT	tone decay test
TED	thromboembolic disease
temp	temperature
TENS	transcutaneous electrical nerve stimulation
TFTs	thyroid function tests
TGV	thoracic gas volume
THA	total hip arthroplasty
THR	total hip replacement
TIA	transient ischemic attack
TIBC	total iron-binding capacity
tic	diverticulum
t.i.d.	three times a day
TKA	total knee arthroplasty
TKR	total knee replacement
TLC	total lung capacity
Tm	maximal transport capacity
TM	tympanic membrane
TMJD	temporomandibular joint dysfunction
TMR	total metabolic rate
TNI	total nodal irradiation
TNM	tumor, nodes, metastases
top.	topically
TORCH	toxoplasmosis, rubella, cytomegalovirus and herpes simplex (test)
TPA	tissue plasminogen activator
TPN	total parenteral nutrition

TPR	temperature, pulse, and respiration
TPUR	transperineal urethral resection
tr., tinct.	tincture
TSH	thyroid-stimulating hormone
TSS	toxic shock syndrome
TT	thrombin time
TTH	thyrotrophic hormone
TTP	thrombotic thrombocytopenic purpura
TTS	temporary threshold shift
TUR	transurethral resection
TURB	transurethral resection of bladder
TURP	transurethral resection of prostate
TV	tidal volume
Tx	treatment, therapy; tumor cannot be assessed
U, U.	unit
UA	urinalysis
UC	uterine contractions
UE	upper extremity
UGI	upper gastrointestinal
UHF	ultrahigh frequency
umb.	umbilicus (navel)
UMN	upper motor neuron
ung.	ointment
UP	ureteropelvic
Ur.	urine
URI	upper respiratory infection
u/s	ultrasound
UTI	urinary tract infection
UTP	uterine term pregnancy
UV	ureterovesical; ultraviolet
VA	visual acuity
VBAC	vaginal birth after cesarean section
VC	vital capacity
VCU	voiding cystourethrogram
VD	venereal disease
VDRL	Venereal Disease Research Laboratory
VEP	visual evoked potential
VER	visual evoked response
VF	visual field
VHD	ventricular heart disease
VLDL	very-low-density lipoprotein
VMO	advancement (vastus medialis obliquus)
VPB	ventricular premature beat
VSD	ventricular septal defect
vWF	von Willebrand's factor
WBC	white blood cell; white blood count
WBC with diff.	white blood count with differential
w/f	white female
w/m	white male
WPW	Wolff-Parkinson-White syndrome
Wt., wt.	weight
w/v	weight by volume
XP	xeroderma pigmentosa
XT	exotropia
XX	female sex chromosomes
XY	male sex chromosomes
y/o	year old

APPENDIX 2
PREFIXES, ROOTS, COMBINING FORMS & SUFFIXES

Word Part	Outline	Meaning	Word Part	Outline	Meaning
a-	AI	negative; not	alveolo-	AL/VAOE/LO	alveolus
ab-	AB	away from	ambi-	AM/BI	both
abdomino-	AB/DOM/NO	abdomen	ambly-	AM/BLI	dullness
-able	-BL	capable of	ambo-	AM/BO	both; both sides
acantho-	AI/KA*NT, AI/KAN/THO, AK/AN/THO	thorny; spiny	amelo-	AI/MEL, AM/LO* (not AM/LO)	enamel
			amido-	AM/DO	amino acid
acaro-	AK/KRO (not AK/RO)	mite	-aminergic	AM/NERJ/IK, AM/NER/JIK	antagonist blockage of receptors
acephalo-	AI/SEF/LO	absence of head			
acervulo-	AI/SEFRB/LO, AI/SEFRB/YAOU/LO, AI/SEFRB/YU/LO, AI/SER/VAOU/LO	aggregation	amino-	AI/MAOEN, AI/MAOE/NO, AM/NO	amino acid
			amnio-	AM/NO, AM/NAOE, AM/NAOE/YO	amnion
acetabulo-	AS/TAB/LO	acetabulum	amphi-	AM/FI	both sides; around, double
aceto-	AI/SAOET, AI/SAOE/TO, AS/TO, AS/ET	acetone; acetyl	ampho-	AM/FO	both
			amygdalo-	AI/MIGD/LO, AI/MIG/DLO, AI/MIG/DA/LO	tonsil; almond shaped
achillo-	AI/KIL/LO, AI/KIL, AK/LO	Achilles tendon			
-acidemia	AS/DAOEM/YA	decreased blood pH	amylo-	AM/LO	starch
acido-	AS/DO, AI/SID	acid	amyo-	AI/MAOI, AI/MAOI/YO	muscular deficiency
acous-	AI/KAOUS	hearing; sound	ana-	AN, AN/NA, AI/NA	up; positive; excessive; back; again
-acousia	AI/KAOUZ/YA, AI/KAOUS/YA	hearing; sound			
			anaero-	AN/RO, AN/NAER, AN/NAER/RO (not AN/AER or AN/AER/RO)	without air
acro-	AK/RO	extremity; limb			
acromio-	AI/KROEM/YO	acromion process			
actino-	AKT/NO	ray; radiation	anaphylacto-	AN/FLAKT, AN/FLAK/TO, AN/FAOI/LAKT, AN/FAOI/LAK/TO	anaphylaxis
acu-	AK, AK/YAOU, AK/YU, AI/KAOU	needle; sharp			
-acusia	AI/KAOUZ/YA, AI/KAOUS/YA	hearing; sound	anatomico-	AN/TOM/KO	anatomy
			ancylo-	AN/SLO, AN/SI/LO, AN/KLO, AN/KI/LO	crooked
-acusis	AI/KAOU/SIS	hearing; sound			
ad-	AD, AI/D-	to; toward	andro-	AN/DRO	man
adeno-	AD/NO	gland	aneurysm-	AN/RIZ/M-, AN/YAOU/RIZ/M-, AN/YU/RIZ/M-	aneurysm
adiadocho-	AI/DAOI/DOEK, AI/DAOI/DOE/KO, AI/DI/AD/KO, AI/DAOI/AD/KO	not succeeding; not repeating			
			angi-	AN/JI	blood vessel
adipo-	AD/PO	fat	angio-	AN/JO, ANG/YO	blood vessel
adnexo-	AD/NEX, AD/NEK/SO	appendages; adjunct parts	aniso-	AN/NAOIS, AN/SO, AN/NAOI/SO (not AN/AOIS)	unequal; uneven; dissimilar
adreno-	AI/DRAOEN, AD/RAOEN, AI/DRAOE/NO, AD/RE/NO, AD/RAOE/NO	adrenal gland			
			ankylo-	AN/KLO, ANG/LO, AN/KI/LO	bent; noose; loop
			annul-	AN/L-, AN/YAOU/L-, AN/YU/L-	ring; ringlike
-ae	(c)AE	plural form	ano-	AI/NO	anus
aero-	AER, AER/RO	air; gas	anomalo-	AI/NOM/LO	anomaly; irregularity
after-	AFR	after; following			
-agra	AG/RA	seizure of acute pain	ante-	AENT	before; in front
albumino-	AL/BAOUM/NO	albumin	antero-	ANT/RO, AENT/RO	anterior; before; front
alge-	AL/JAOE, AL/JE, AL/J-	pain	anthraco-	AN/THRA/KO	carbuncle; coal; carbon dioxide
-algesia	AL/JAOEZ/YA	pain	anthropo-	AN/THRO/PO, AN/THROEP, AN/THROE/PO	human being
algesio-	AL/JAOEZ/YO	pain			
-algia	AL/JA or ALG/YA	pain	anti-	A*ENT, AN/TI	against
algio-	AL/JO	pain	antro-	AN/TRO	antrum (sinus)
algo-	AL/GO	pain	anul-	A*N/L-, A*N/YAOU/L-, A*N/YU/L-	ring; ringlike
alkalo-	AL/KLO, AL/KA/LO	alkali			
allanto-	AI/LANT/TO, AL/LAN/TO	allantois (part of embryo)	aortico-	AI/ORT/KO, AI/YORT/KO	aorta
allelo-	AI/LAOEL, , AI/LAOE/LO, AL/LAOEL, AL/LAOE/LO	allele; other; another	aorto-	AI/ORT, AI/YORT, AI/OR/TO, AI/YOR/TO	aorta
			-aphia	AIF/YA	touch
allergo-	AI/LERG, AL/ERG, AL/LERG, AI/LER/GO, AL/LER/GO	allergy	apo-	AP	from; detached
			append-	AP/EN/D-, AP/PEN/D-	appendix
allo-	AL/LO, AL	not normal; reversal; another	appendico-	AI/PEND/KO, AI/PEND/S(O)	appendix
allotrio-	AI/LOT/RO, AI/LOT/RAOE/YO	strange; foreign	aqua-	AK/WA, AK/KWA	water
alveo-	ALVAOE, AL/VAOE/YO, AL/VO	alveus; alveolus	arachn-	AI/RAK/N-, AR/AK/N-	arachnoid membrane; spider

archeo-	ARK/YO ancient	beginning; original; ancient	-blephary	BLEF/RI	condition of eyelids
archi-	ARK, AR/KI	beginning; original; ancient	-blepsia	BLEPS/YA	vision
			brachio-	BRAIK/YO	arm
argento-	AR/JENT, AR/JEN/TO	silver	brachy-	BRAK, BRA/KI	short
-arial	AIRL, AIR/YAL		brady-	BRAD	slow
arrheno-	AI/RAOEN, AI/RAOE/NO, AR/NO	male	branchio-	BRANG/YO	branchial arches; gills
			brevi-	BREV	short
arseno-	ARS/NO	arsenic	brom-	BROM	bromine
arterio-	AR/TAOER/YO	artery	bromo-	BROEM, BROE/MO	bromine
arteriolo-	AR/TAOER/YOE/LO, ART/RAOE/LO	arteriole	bronchio-	BRONG/YO	bronchiole; bronchus
			bronchiol-	BRONG/YO/L-, BRON/KAOI/L-	bronchiole
arthro-	AR/THRO, A*RT/RO	joint			
articulo-	AR/TIK/LO, AR/TIK/YAOU/LO, AR/TIK/YU/LO	joint; articulation	broncho-	BRONG, BRON/KO	bronchus
			-buccal	BUK/KAL	cheek; buccal surface
			bucco-	BUK, BUK/KO, BUX, BUK/SI	cheek; buccal surface
-ary	AIR, RI				
-ase	AIS	enzyme	bulbo-	BUL/BO	bulb; bulbus
-asthenia	AS/THAOEN/YA	weakness; prostration	burso-	BURS, BUR/SO	bursa
astheno-	AS/THAOEN, AS/THAOE/NO, AS/THE/NO	weakness; asthenia	butyro-	BAOUT/RO, BAOU/TIR	butter; buttery
			caco-	KAK, KA/KO	bad; ill
			calcaneo-	KAL/KAIN/YO	calcaneus (bone of ankle)
astragalo-	AS/TRAG/LO, AI/STRAG/LO	talus (bone of ankle)	calcul-	KAL/KL-, KAL/KAOU/L-	pebble; stone; calculus
astro-	AS/TRO	star; star-shaped; aster	cali-	KAL	calix
atelo-	AT/LO	imperfect; incomplete	calic-	KAL/S-, KAL/K-	calix
athero-	A*T/RO	arterial plaque	campto-	KAFRPT; KAMT, KAFRP/TO, KAM/TO	bent
atlanto-	AT/LANT, AT/LAN/TO	atlas (first cervical vertebra)	canaliculo-	KAN/LIK/LO, KAN/LIK/YAOU/LO, KAN/LIK/YU/LO	canaliculus; small channel
atmo-	AT/MO	steam; vapor			
atreto-	AI/TRAOET, AI/TRAOE/TO	imperforate; closed	cancero-	KANS/RO, KAN/SER/RO, KANS/ER/RO	cancer
atrio-	AI/TRO, AIT/RO, AI/TRAOE/YO	atrium	candid-	KAND/D-, KAN/DI/D-	Candida
audio-	AUD/YO	hearing	cantho-	KA*NT, KAN/THO	canthus
aur-	AUR, AU/R-	ear	-capnia	KAP/NA, KAP/NAOE/YA	level of carbon dioxide
auriculo-	AU/RIK/LO, AU/RIK/YAOU/LO, AU/RIK/YU/LO	ear	capno-	KAP/NO	sooty; smoky
			capsulo-	KAPS/LO, KAP/SLO, KAP/SAOU/LO	capsule
auto-	AUT, AU/TO	self	carbo-	KARB, KAR/BO	carbon; carbon dioxide; charcoal
auxano-	AUX/NO, AUK/SAN	growth			
auxo-	AUX, AUK/SO	growth; stimulation; acceleration	carboxy-	KAR/BOX, KAR/BOK/SI	carbon dioxide; carbon monoxide
			carcino-	KARS/NO, KAR/SIN	cancer; carcinoma
axio-	AX/YO	axis; long axis of tooth	-carcinoma	KARS/NOE/MA	epithelial tumor
axo-	AX, AK/SO	axon	-cardia	KARD/YA	heart
aza-	AIZ, A*Z	nitrogen	cardio-	KARD/YO	heart; cardiac portion of stomach
azo-	A*Z, AI/ZO, AIZ	nitrogen			
bacillo-	BA/SIL, BAS/LO	bacillus	cario-	KAIR/YO	dental caries
bacter-	BAK/TER, BAKT/R-, BAK/TR-	bacterium	carpo-	KARP, KAR/PO	carpus (wrist)
			cata-	KAT, KA/TA	down; negative
-bacter	BAK/TER	bacterium	-caudal	KAU/DAL	toward the tail
bacteri-	BAK/TAOER	bacterium	cavern-	KAVR/N-, KAV/ERN-, KAI/VER/N-	cavity
bacterio-	BAK/TAOER/YO	bacterium			
balano-	BAL/NO, BA/LAN	glans penis	ceco-	SAOEK, SE/KO, SE/SO	cecum
ballisto-	BL*IS, BLIS/TO, BA/L*IS, BA/LIS/TO, BAL/L*IS, BAL/LIS/TO	jerking; twisting; projectile	-cele	SAO*EL	hernia; sac; tumor
			celio-	SAOEL/YO	abdomen
			cello-	SEL, SEL/LO, KREL/LO	cellulose
balneo-	BAL/NO, BAL/NAOE, BAL/NAOE/YO	bath	cellulo-	SEL/YAOU/L-, SEL/YU/L-, KREL/YAOU/LO, KREL/YU/LO	cell; cellulose
bari-	BAIR, BAR	weight; pressure			
baro-	BAR, BAR/RO	weight; pressure			
bary-	BAR/RI (not BAR)	heavy; difficult; thick; dull	celo-	SE/LO, SAOEL	tumor; swelling; cavity
			cemento-	SEMT, SE/MENT, SEMT/TO, SE/MEN/TO, SMENT, SMEN/TO	cementum (connective tissue of tooth)
basi-	BAI/SI (not BAIS)	base; foundation			
-basia	BAIS/YA, BAIZ/YA	walking			
basio-	BAIS/YO	base; foundation	ceno-	SE/NO, SAOEN (sometimes)	new; empty; common feature
baso-	BAI/SO (not BAIS)	basic; base; walking			
batho-	BA*T	deep; depth	cente-	SEN/TAOE	puncture
bathy-	BA*T	deep; depth	-centesis	SEN/TAOE/SIS	perforation; puncture
benzo-	BENZ, BEN/ZO	benzene; benzoic acid	centi-	SENT, SEN/TI	one hundred; one-hundredth
bi-	B*I	two; twice			
bili-	BIL, BIL/LI, BAOI/LI, B*I/LI	bile	centro-	SEN/TRO	center; central
			-cephalia	SFAIL/YA, SE/FAIL/YA	head
bio-	BAO*I, BAOI/YO	life	-cephalism	SEF/LIFM	condition of head
-blast	BLA*S	immature cell	cephalo-	SEF/LO, SEF/AL, SFAL; SE/FAL (not SEFL)	head; toward the head
-blastic	BLA*S/IK	pertaining to immature cell			
blasto-	BLA*S, BLAS/TO	immature cell	-cephaly	SEF/LI	head
blenno-	BLEN, BLEN/NO	mucus	-ceptor	SEP/TOR	that which receives
-blepharia	BLE/FAIR/YA, BLEF/AIR/YA	condition of eyelids	cerato-	SER/TO	cornea; horny tissue
blepharo-	BLEF/RO	eyelid			
-blepharous	BLEF/ROUS	condition of eyelids			

cerco-	SERK, SER/KO	bristlelike	
cerebello-	SER/BEL, SER/BEL/LO	cerebellum	
cerebro-	SER/BRO, SE/RAOEB/RO, SE/RAOE/BRO	cerebrum; brain	
cervico-	SEFRB/KO, SEFRB/SO, SER/VI/KO, SER/VI/SO	neck; cervix uteri	
cesto-	S*ES, SES/TO	cestode	
cheilo-	KAOIL, KAOI/LO	lip	
-cheilia	KAOIL/YA	lip	
-cheiria	KAOIR/YA	hand	
cheiro-	KAOIR, KAOI/RO	hand	
chemo-	KAOEM, KAOE/MO, KEM	chemistry; chemical	
-chiria	KAOIR/YA	hand	
chiro-	KAOIR, KAOI/RO	hand	
-chirurgia	KAOI/RUR/JA, KAOI/RURJ/YA	surgery	
chloro-	KLOR, KLOER, KLOR/RO, KLOER/RO	green; chlorine	
cholangio-	KLAN/JO, KOE/LAN/JO	bile duct	
chole-	KOEL, KOE/LE	bile	
cholecysto-	KOEL/S*IS, KOEL/SIS/TO	gallbladder	
choledocho-	KLED/KO, KOL/KO/K-, KOE/LED/KO	common bile duct	
cholester-	KL*ES/R-, KOE/L*ES/R-, KOE/LES/TR-	cholesterol	
cholo-	KOL	bile	
chondro-	KON/DRO	cartilage	
chordo-	KHORD, KHOR/DO	cord; sinew	
chorio-	KOER/YO, KHOR/YO	chorion; choroid	
choroido-	KOE/ROID, KOE/ROI/DO	choroid	
-chroic	KROIK, KROE/IK	color	
-chroism	KROIFM, KROE/IFM	color	
chroma-	KROEM, KROE/MA	color	
-chromasia	KROE/MAIZ/YA	color	
chromato-	KROEM/TO, KROE/MAT	color; pigment; chromatin; chromosome	
-chromemia	KROE/MAOEM/YA	color of blood	
-chromia	KROEM/YA	color	
chromo-	KROEM, KROE/MO	color; pigment; chromatin; chromosome	
chrono-	KROEN, KRON, KROE/NO	time	
chryso-	KRIS, KRI/SO	gold	
chylo-	KAOIL, KAOI/LO	chyle	
chymo-	KAOIM, KAOI/MO	chyme	
-cidal	SAOI/DAL	that which kills	
-cide	SAO*ID	that which kills	
cilio-	SIL/YO	ciliary body	
-cillin	SLIN, SIL/LIN	penicillin	
cine-	SIN	movement	
-cinesia	SI/NAOEZ/YA, SAOI/NAOEZ/YA	movement	
-cinesis	SI/NAOE/SIS, SAOI/NAOE/SIS	movement	
-cinetic	SI/NET/IK, SAOI/NET/IK	movement	
-cipient	SIP/YENT	that which receives	
circum-	SIR/KUM	around	
cirso-	SIRS, SIR/SO	varix	
clas-	KLAS	break	
-clasia	KLAIZ/YA	break; fracture	
-clasis	(v)K/LA/SIS	break; fracture	
-clast	KLA*S	break; fracture	
clasto-	KLA*S, KLAS/TO	break; fracture	
clavico-	KLAV/KO, KLA/VIK	clavicle (collarbone)	
cleido-	KLAOID, KLAOI/DO	clavicle (collarbone)	
-cleisis	KLAOI/SIS	closure	
clino-	KLAOIN, KLAOI/NO	bent; deviation; bed	
clitor-	KLIT/R-, KLI/TOR, KLAOIT/R-	clitoris	
clitorido-	KLI/TOR/DO, KLAOI/TOR/DO, KLIT/RID	clitoris	
co-	KO	with; together	
coagul-	KO/AG/L-,	clot; clotting	

	KO/AG/YAOU/L-, KO/AG/YU/L-		
-coccemia	KOK/SAOEM/YA	cocci in blood	
cocci-	KOX, KOK/SI	cocci	
coccidio-	KOK/SID/YO	coccidia	
cocco-	KOK, KOK/KO	coccus	
-coccosis	KOK/KOE/SIS	infection with bacteria	
-coccus	KOK/KUS	coccus	
coccy-	KOK, KOK/SI	coccyx (tailbone)	
coccygo-	KOX/GO, KOK/SIJ	coccyx	
-coele	SAO*EL	cavity; space	
cochleo-	KOK/LO, KOK/LAOE/YO	cochlea; spoonful	
cocto-	KOKT, KOK/TO	cooked; heated	
-coele	SAO*EL	cavity; space	
coli-	KOEL, KO/LI, KOL	Escherichia coli; colic	
coll-	KL-, KOL, KOL/L-	with; together; variant of con-	
collageno-	KLAJ/NO, KOL/JE/NO, KOL/JEN	collagen	
colloido-	KLOID, KLOI/DO	colloid	
colo-	KOEL, KO/LO, KOL	colon; large intestine	
colpo-	KOL/PO	vagina	
-colpos	KOL/POS	vagina	
commissuro-	KOM/SAOUR, KMIS/RO, KOM/SAOUR/RO, KOM/SAOU/RO	junction; union of parts	
con-	KON	with; together	
condylo-	KOND/LO, KON/DI/LO	condyle	
-conia	KOEN/YA	fungal spore	
-conid	KO/NID, KON/ID	fungal spore	
conio-	KOEN/YO	dust; small particles	
conjug-	KON/JU/G-, KON/JAOU/G-	union; pairing; blending	
conjunctivo-	KON/JUNG/VO, KON/JUNGT/VO, KON/JUNG/TAOIV, KON/JUNG/TAOI/VO	conjunctivae	
contra-	KON/TRA	against; contrary	
convexo-	KON/VEX, KON/VEK/SO	convex	
copro-	KOP/RO	feces	
coraco-	KOR/KO, KOER/KO	coracoid process	
cordo-	KORD, KOR/DO	cord	
coreo-	KOR/YO, KOER/YO	pupil	
-coria	KOR/YA, KOER/YA	pupil	
corneo-	KORN/YO	cornea	
cort-	KOR/T-, KORT	cortex	
-corticalism	KORT/KAL/IFM, KORT/KLIFM	condition of cortex	
cortico-	KORT/KO	cortex	
costo-	KO*S, KOS/TO	ribs	
counter-	KO*UNT, KOUN/TER	opposition; against; reverse	
coxo-	KOK/SO, KOX	hip	
cranio-	KRAIN/YO	cranium	
-crasia	KRAIZ/YA	temperament; constitution	
crico-	KRAOIK, KRAOI/KO	cricoid cartilage; ring-shaped	
-crinia	KRIN/YA	separate; secretion	
-crotic	KROT/IK	pulse beat	
crymo-	KRAOIM, KRAOI/MO	cold; refrigeration	
cryo-	KRAOI, KRAOI/YO	cold	
crypto-	KRIPT, KRIP/TO	hidden; concealed	
crystallo	KR*IS/LO, KRIS/TAL/LO	crystal	
cubito-	KAOUB/TO	anterior surface of elbow	
culdo-	KUL/DO, KULD	cul-de-sac; cecum; rectouterine excavation	
cuneo-	KAOUN/YO	wedge; cuneus; cuneiform	
cupulo-	KAOUP/LO, KAOUP/YAOU/LO, KAOUP/YU/LO, KAOU/PAOU/LO	small cap over a structure	
cut-	KAOUT, KAOU/T-	skin	
cuticul-	KAOU/TIK/L-, KAOU/TIK/YAOU/L-, KAOU/TIK/YU/L-	cuticle; covering layer	
cyano-	SAOI/NO, SAOI/AN, SAOI/YAN	blue	
cyclo-	SAOI/KLO, SAOIK/LO	round; recurring; cycle	
-cyesis	SAOI/E/SIS	pregnancy	

cylindro-	SLIN/DRO, SI/LIN/DRO, SIL/IN/DRO	cylinder; columnar
cyo-	SAOI, SAOI/YO	fetus; pregnancy
-cyphosis	SAOI/FOE/SIS	kyphosis; hunchback
-cyst	S*IS	cyst
-cystia	S*IS/YA	bladder
cystico-	S*IS/KO	cystic duct
cystido-	S*IS/DO	urinary bladder
cysto-	S*IS, SIS/TO	urinary bladder; cyst
-cystosis	SIS/TOE/SIS	condition of bladder
-cyte	SAO*IT	cell
-cythemia	SAOI/THAOEM/YA	presence of cells in blood
-cytic	SIT/IK	cell
cyto-	SAOIT, SAOI/TO	cell
-cytoma	SAOI/TOE/MA	cell tumor
dacry-	DAK/RI, DAK/RAOE	lacrimal apparatus; tears
dacryo-	DAK/RO, DAK/RI/YO DAK/RAOE/YO,	lacrimal apparatus; tears
-dactylia	DAK/TIL/YA	fingers; toes
-dactylism	DAKT/LIFM	condition of fingers, toes
dactylo-	DAKT/LO, DAK/TIL	fingers; toes
-dactylous	DAKT/LOUS	condition of fingers, toes
-dactyly	DAKT/LI	fingers; toes
de-	DE	down; from; negative
deca-	DEK	ten
deci-	DES	one-tenth; ten
decidu-	DE/SID/Y-, DE/SID/W-	decidua
delta-	DELT, DEL/TA	triangular space
demi-	DEM	half
dendro-	DEN/DRO	treelike; dentrite
dentino-	DENT/NO, DEN/TI/NO	dentin
-dentium	DEN/SHUM	teeth
dento-	DENT, DEN/TO	teeth
denti-	DENT, DEN/TI	teeth
deoxy-	DE/OX	containing one less atom of oxygen
-derma	DER/MA	skin
dermato-	DERM/TO, DERMT	skin
-dermatous	DERM/TOUS	skin
-dermia	DERM/YA	skin
dermo-	DERM, DER/MO	skin
-desia	DAOEZ/YA	suture, surgical fixation
-desis	(v)D/SIS, DAOE/SIS	suture, surgical fixation
desmo-	DEZ/MO, DES/MO	ligament
desoxy-	DES/OX	containing one less atom of oxygen
deutero-	DAOUT/RO	second
deuto-	DAOUT, DAOU/TO	second
dextro-	DEX/TRO	right side
di-	DI	two; apart
dia-	DAOI	through; apart
diadocho-	DI/AD/KO, DAOI/ADKO, DAOI/DOEK, DAOI/DOE/KO	succeeding
diaphragmo-	DAOI/FRAG/MO	diaphragm
diazo-	DI/A*Z, DI/AZ/ZO	diazo compound
dichloro-	DI/KLOR, DI/KLOR/RO	containing two atoms of chlorine
didymo-	DID/MO	testes
dihydro-	DI/HAOI/DRO	containing two hydrogen atoms
dihydroxy-	DI/HAOI/DROX	containing two hydroxyl groups
diplo-	DIP/LO	double; twin; twofold; twice
-dipsia	DIPS/YA	thirst
dipso-	DIPS, DIP/SO	thirst
dis-	DIS	apart; away from
disco-	DIS/KO	intervertebral disk
disto-	D*IS, DIS/TO	distal; distal surface
diverticul-	DI/VER/TIK/L-, DI/VER/TIK/YAOU/L-, DI/VER/TIK/YU/L-	diverticulum
dolicho-	DOL/KO	long
-dont	DONT	teeth
-dontia	DON/SHA	teeth
-dontic	DONT/IK, DON/TIK	teeth
-dontism	DON/TIFM, DONT/IFM	teeth
-dontium	DON/SHUM	teeth
-dontus	DON/TUS	teeth
dorso-	DORS, DOR/SO	dorsal; backside
duodeno-	DAOU/DAOEN, DAOU/DAOE/NO, DWOD/NO,DAOU/DEN, DAOU/DE/N-	duodenum
-dymus	(v)D/MUS	fetus with duplication of parts;conjoined twins
dynamo-	DAOIN/MO, DAOI/NAM	power; strength
-dynia	DIN/YA	pain
dys-	DIS	bad; painful; negative
-dyscrinia	DIS/KRIN/YA	endocrine disorder
-dysplasia	DIS/PLAIZ/YA	abnormal development
e-	E	out; from
ec-	EK	out of
eccentro-	EK/SEN/TRO, KPEN/TRO	away from a center
echino-	E/KAOIN, E/KAOI/NO	spiny; spines
echo-	EK, EK/KO	repetition of a sound; reverberation of sound waves
eco-	E/KO, AOEK	environment
-ectasis	EKT/SIS	dilatation; expansion
ecto-	EKT, EK/TO	outside
-ectomize	EKT/MAOIZ	to excise
-ectomy	EKT/M*I	excision
ectro-	EK/TRO	congenital absence
-edema	DAOE/MA, E/DAOE/MA	swelling
ego-	E/GO, AOEG	self
elasto-	E/LA*S, E/LAS/TO	elastic
electro-	LEK/TRO, E/LEK/TRO	electricity
eleo-	EL/YO	oil
ellipto-	E/LIPT, E/LIP/TO	elliptic
embolo-	EM/BLO, EM/BO/LO, EM/BOL	embolus; clot; insert
embryo-	EM/BRO, EM/BRAOE/YO	embryo
-emesia	MAOEZ/YA, MAOES/YA	vomiting
-emesis	EM/SIS	vomiting
-emia	AOEM/YA	condition of blood
emot-	E/MOE/T-	emotion
emotio-	E/MOE/SHO, E/MOERB/YO	emotion
en-	EN	in; on
enamelo-	E/NAM/LO, EN/AM/LO	enamel
enantio-	E/NANT/YO, EN/ANT/YO	opposite; antagonism
encephalo-	EN/SEF/LO, EN/SFAL	brain
-encephaly	EN/SEF/LI	brain
endo-	*END, EN/DO (not END)	inside
endocardio-	*END/KARD/YO, EN/DO/KARD/YO	endocardium
endocrino-	*END/KRIN, *END/KRI/NO, EN/DOK/RI/NO	endocrine system
endothelio-	*END/THAOEL/YO, EN/DO/THAOEL/YO	endothelium
-ene	AOEN	unsaturated hydrocarbon containing one double bond
entero-	SPWER/RO, SPWR(O)	intestines
-entery	SPWER/RI	intestines
ento-	SPWO, ENT, EN/TO	within; inner
eosino-	E/SIN, E/YO/SIN	eosinophil
ependymo-	EP/END/MO, E/PEND/MO	ependyma
epi-	EP	on; over; in addition
epidermato-	EP/DERM/TO, EP/DERMT	epidermis
epidermo-	EP/DERM, EP/DER/MO	epidermis
epididymo-	EP/DID/MO	epididymis
epilepto-	EP/LEPT, EP/LEP/TO	epilepsy
epiplo-	E/PIP/LO, PIP/LO, EP/PLO	omentum
episio-	E/PIZ/YO, E/PIS/YO	vulva
epithelio-	EP/THAOEL/YO	epithelium
equi-	E/KWI, EK/WI	equal
er-	*ER	
-er	ER	that which does
-ergia	ER/JA, ERJ/YA	work; that which works
ergo-	ERG, *ER/GO	work
eroto-	E/ROT, E/ROET, * ER/TO-	love; sexual desire
eryth-	*ER/TH-	red; reddish

erythro-	R*IT/RO, E/R*IT/RO, *ER/THR(O)	red; erythrocyte (red blood cell)			forehead
			fructo-	FRUKT, FRUK/TO	fructose
erythrocyto-	R*IT/RO/SAOIT, E/R*IT/RO/SAOIT, R*IT/RO/SAOI/TO, E/R*IT/RO/SAOI/TO	erythrocyte (red blood cell)	-fugal	(v)F/GAL, (v)F/YAOU/GAL, (v)F/YU/GAL	banishing; driving away
			-fuge	FAOUJ	that which drives away
-escence	ES/ENS, ES/SENS	process; change; state; condition	fundo-	FUND, FUN/DO	fundus of stomach
			funiculo-	FAOU/NIK/LO, FAOU/NIK/YAOU/LO, FAOU/NIK/YU/LO	spermatic cord
-escent	ES/ENT, ES/SENT	process; change; state; condition			
-esis	(c)AOE/SIS	state; condition	fuso-	FAOUZ, FAOUS, FAOU/ZO, FAOU/SO	spindle-like
eso-	ES, ES/SO	within			
esophago-	E/SOF/GO, E/SOF/JO	esophagus	-galactia	GLAK/SHA, GA/LAK/SHA	milk
-est	*ES	superlative degree (most)	galacto-	GLAKT, GLAK/TO, GA/LAKT, GA/LAK/TO, GAL/AK/TO	milk
-esthesia	ES/THAOEZ/YA	perception; feeling; sensation			
esthesio-	ES/THAOEZ/YO, ES/THAOES/YO	perception; feeling; sensation	galvano-	GAL/VAN, GAL/VA/NO	galvanic electricity; electric current
ethmo-	*ET/MO	ethmoid bone	gameto-	GA/MAOET, GAM/TO, GA/MAOE/TO	gamete
eu-	YAOU	good; well; normal			
eury-	YAOUR, YAOU/RI	wide	gamma-	GAM, GAM/MA	gamma rays; Greek letter G
ex-	EX, KP-	out of			
excito-	KPAOI/TO, EX/SAOI/TO (not KPAOIT)	stimulating; exciting	ganglio-	GANG/LO, GAN/GLO, GAN/GLAOE/YO	ganglion
			-gasia	GAIZ/YA	stimulating activity
exo-	KPO, EK/SO (not EX)	outside; outward	-gastria	GAS/TRA, GAS/TRAOE/YA	stomach
extra-	EX/TRA	outside; beyond			
extro-	EX/TRO	outside; outward	gastro-	GAS/TRO	stomach
-facient	FAIRBT, FAI/SHENT, FAIRB/ENT	that which brings about	-gen-	JEN	produce; originate
			-gen	JEN	productive of
facio-	FAI/SHO, FAIRB/YO, FAIS/YO	face	-geneic	JE/NAOE/IK, JE/NAI/IK	productive of
			-genic	JEN/IK	productive of
fascicul-	FA/SIK/L-, FA/SIK/YU/L-, FA/SIK/YAOU/L- FAS/SIK/L-, FAS/SIK/YU/L- FAS/SIK/YU/L-	fascicle; small bundle or cluster	-genicity	JE/NIS/TI	productive of
			-genin	(v)J/NIN, JEN/NIN, JE/NIN	productive of
			genio-	JAOEN/YO, JE/NAOI	chin
fascio-	FARB/YO, FAS/YO	fascia	genito-	JEN/TO	genitalia
femoro-	FEM/RO	femur; thigh	geno-	J*EN, JEN/NO (not JEN)	reproduction; sex
ferri-	FER/RI	iron			
ferro-	FER, FER/RO	iron	-genous	(v)J/NOUS	productive of
feto-	FAOET, FAOE/TO	fetus	geo-	JAOE, JAOE/YO	earth; soil
fibrilla-	FIB/RI/LA-, FIB/RIL/LA-, FAOI/BRI/LA-, FAOI/BRIL/LA-	fibril; fiber	gero-	JER, JER/RO	old age; the aged
			geronto-	JER/ONT, JE/RONT, JERN/TO, JER/ON/TO, JE/RON/TO	old age; the aged
fibrillo-	FAOI/BRIL	fibril			
fibrino-	FAOI/BRIN, FAOI/BRI/NO	fibrin	geus-	GAOUZ, GAOUS	taste
			-geusia	GAOUZ/YA, GAOUS/YA	taste
fibro-	FAOI/BRO, FAOIB/RO	fiber	giganto-	JAOI/GANT, JAOI/GAN/TO	huge
fibulo-	FIB/LO, FIB/YU/LO FIB/YAOU/LO,	fibula			
			gingivo-	JING/VO, JIN/JI/VO, JIN/JAOI/VO	gingivae (gums)
fimbrio-	FIM/BRO, FIM/BRAOE/YO	fimbria; fringe; border; edge			
			glandul-	GLAND/L-, GLAN/DAOU/L-, GLAND/YAOU/L-, GLAND/YU/L-	gland
fistulo-	F*IS/LO, FIS/KHU/LO, F*IS/YAOU/LO, F*IS/YU/LO, FIS/TAOU/LO, FIS/KHAOU/LO	fistula; abnormal communication			
			gleno-	GLAOEN, GLAOE/NO	pit; socket; glenoid cavity
			glio-	GLAOI, GLAOI/YO	neuroglia; glue
flavo-	FLAIV, FLAI/VO	flavin	globul-	GLOB/L-, GLOB/YAOU/L-, GLOB/YU/L-	globe; globule
flocculo-	FLOK/L-, FLOK/YAOU/L-, FLOK/YU/LO, FLOK/KAOU/LO-	flocculus; small tuft or mass			
			glomerulo-	GLOE/MER/LO, GLOE/MER/YAOU/LO, GLOE/MER/YU/LO	glomerulus
flor-	FLOR, FLOER, FLOE/R-	flower	-glossia	GLOS/YA, GLOSZ/YA	tongue
			glosso-	GLOS, GLOS/SO	tongue
fluoro-	FLAOUR, FLAOU/RO, FLOR, FLOR/RO	fluorine; fluorescent	gluco-	GLAOUK, GLAOU/KO	glucose; sweetness
			gluteo-	GLAOUT/YO	buttocks
folliculo-	FLIK/LO, FLIK/YAOU/LO, FLIK/YU/LO, FOL/LIK/LO, FOL/LIK/YAOU/LO, FOL/LIK/YU/LO, FO/LIK/LO, FO/LIK/YAOU/LO, FO/LIK/YU/LO	follicle	glycero-	GLIS/RO	glycerin; glycerol
			-glycemia	GLAOI/SAOEM/YA	glucose in blood
			glyco-	GLAOIK, GLAOI/KO, GLAOI/S-, GLIS	sugar
			-gnathia	NA*T/YA, NA*IT/YA	jaw; cheek
			-gnathic	NA*T/IK	jaw; cheek
			gnatho-	NA*T, NA/THO	jaw; cheek
			-gnosia	NOEZ/YA, -G/NOEZ/YA	perception; knowledge; recognition
for-	FOR	away; off; utmost; extremely			
			gonado-	GON/DO, GOE/NAD, GOE/NA/D-	gonads
fore-	FOER	before; front; superior			
-form	FORM	characteristic of entity	gonio-	GOEN/YO	angle
fronto-	FRONT, FRON/TO	front; frontal bone;	-gonium	GOEN/YUM	semen; seed

gono-	GON	semen; seed
-gram	GRAM	written/recorded data
granulo-	GRAN/LO, GRAN/YAOU/LO, GRAN/YU/LO	granule
-graph	GRAF	instrument to record data
-graphia	GRAF/YA, GRAIF/YA	writing
grapho-	GRAF, GRA/FO	writing; a record
-graphy	(v)G/FI, (v)G/RA/FI	writing/recording data
gravid-	GRAV/D-	pregnant
gust-	GUS/T-, G*US	taste
gymno-	JIM/NO	nakedness
gynandro-	JI/NAN/DRO, GAOI/NAN/DRO	hermaphroditism
gyneco-	GAOIN/KO, JIN/KO	female
gyno-	GAOIN, GAOI/NO, JIN, JI/NO, JAOIN, JAOI/NO	female
-gyria	JAOIR/YA, JIR/YA	cerebral gyrus
-gyric	JAOIR/IK, JAOI/RIK	cerebral gyrus
gyro-	JAOIR, JAOI/RO	cerebral gyrus
haemo-	HAOEM, HAOE/MO, HEM, HAEM, HAE/MO	blood
hallucin-	HA/LAOUS/N-, HAL/LAOUS/N-	hallucination
halo-	HAL	salt
hamarto-	HAM/ART, HA/MART, HAM/AR/TO, HA/MAR/TO	defect; benign nodule
haph-	HAF	touch
haplo-	HAP/LO	simple; single
hapto-	HAPT, HAP/TO	touch; seizure
hecto-	HEKT, HEK/TO	one hundred
helico-	HEL/KO, HEL/K(O)	coil; snail
helio-	HAOEL/YO	sun
helminth-	HEL/M*INT, HEL/MIN/TH-	parasitic worm
hema-	HAOE/MA, HEM, HAOEM (sometimes)	blood
hemangio-	HE/MAN/JO, HAOE/MAN/JO	blood vessel
hemato-	HEM/TO, HAOEM/TO, HAOE/MAT, HE/MAT	blood
hemi-	HEM	half
-hemia	HAOEM/YA	condition of blood
hemo-	HAOEM, HAOE/MO	blood
-hepatia	HE/PAT/YA, HE/PAI/SHA, HE/PAIRB/YA	liver
hepatico-	HE/PAT/KO	hepatic duct
hepato-	HEPT, HEP/TO, HE/PAT	liver
hepta-	HEPT, HEP/TA	seven
heredo-	HER/DO, HE/RED	hereditary
hetero-	HET/RO	other; another; different
hexa-	HEX	six
hiat-	HAOI/AI/T-, HAOI/AIT, HAOI/YAI/T-, HAOI/YAIT	hiatus; opening; gap; cleft
hidro-	HID/RO, HAOI/DRO	sweat
hiero-	HAOI/RO, HAOIR	sacrum; religion
hippo-	HIP, HIP/PO	horse
histio-	H*IS/YO	tissue
histo-	H*IS, HIS/TO	tissue
holo-	HOL, HOE/LO	whole
homeo-	HOEM/YO	similar; constant
homo-	HOEM, HOE/MO	same; similar
homoio-	HOE/MOI, HOE/MOI/YO	similar; constant
hormono-	HORM/NO, HOR/MOEN, HOR/MOE/NO	hormone
humero-	HAOUM/RO	humerus
hyalo-	HAOI/LO	vitreous body
hydro-	HAOI/DRO	water; hydrogen
hydroxy-	HAOI/DROX	univalent radical OH
hygro-	HAOI/GRO	moisture
hymeno-	HAOIM/NO	hymen
hyo-	HAOI, HAOI/YO	hyoid bone
hyper-	HAO*IP, HAOI/PER	above; beyond; extreme; excess
hypho-	HAOIF, HAOI/FO	web; filament; thread
hypno-	HIP/NO	sleep

hypo-	HO*IP, HAOI/PO	under; below; decreased
hypso-	HIPS, HIP/SO	height
hystero-	H*IS/RO, HIS/TRO, HIS/TER	uterus
-ia	YA	
-iasis	(c)AOI/SIS	morbid process/condition
-iatrics	YAT/RIK/-S	branch of medicine
-iatrist	(c)AOI/TR*IS	specialist
iatro-	AOI/AT/RO, AOI/TRO, AOIT/RO	physician; medicine
-iatry	(c)AOI/TRI	branch of medicine
-ic	IK, (c)IK	
ichthyo-	IK/THO, IK/THAOE, IK/THAOE/YO	fish; fishlike
ictero-	IKT/RO, IK/TRO, IK/TER	jaundice
-id	ID	resembling
-ide	AOID	binary chemical compound
ideo-	AOID/YO	idea; mental impression
idio-	ID/YO	self; separate; distinct
ileo-	*IL/YO (not IL/YO)	ileum
ilio-	IL/YO	ilium
im-	IM	variant of in-
immuno-	IM/NO, IM/MAOU/NO, IM/YAOU/NO, IM/YU/NO	immunity
implanto-	IM/PLANT, IM/PLAN/TO	implant
in-	IN	in; on; not; negative
inciso-	IN/SAOIZ, IN/SAOI/ZO IN/SAOIS, IN/SAOI/SO	incisal surface
inco-	IN/KO	incus (anvil)
incudo-	IN/KAOUD, IN/KAOU/DO	incus (anvil)
infanti-	IN/FANT, IN/FAN/TI, IN/FAN/TAOI	infant
infero-	IN/FRO	below; under; behind; inferior
infra-	IN/FRA	beneath
infundibul-	IN/FUN/DIB/L-, IN/FUN/DIB/YAOU/L-, IN/FUN/DIB/YU/L-	infundibulum
inguino-	ING/WI/NO, ING/WIN	groin
inio-	IN/YO	occiput
ino-	IN, IN/NO	fiber; fibrous material
insul-	INS/L-, IN/SL-, IN/SAOU/L-	insulin
inter-	SPWER	among; between
intero-	SPWER/RO	internal; interior
intra-	SPWRA	inside; within
intro-	SPWRO	into; within
iodo-	AOI/OED, AOI/DO, AOI/YOED	iodine
iono-	AOIN, AOI/NO, AOI/YON	ion
irido-	IR/DO	iris
irrig-	IR/G-, IR/RI/G-	wash out
irrit-	IRT, IR/RIT	tease; irritate
ische-	IS/KAOE	retention; suppression
ischio-	IS/KO, IS/KAOE, IS/KAOE/YO	ischium
-ism	IFM	condition
-ismus	IZ/MUS	condition; variant of -ism
iso-	AOIS, AOIS/SO	equal; alike; same
-ite	(c)AOIT	nature of; resembling; salt; acid; essential portion
-ites	(c)AOI/TAOEZ	denotes adjective; inflammation
-itides	(c)IT/DAOEZ	inflammation; plural of itis
-itis	(c)AOITS, (c)AOI/TIS	inflammation
-ize	AOIZ	subjection to action or treatment
jejuno-	JEJ/NO, JE/JAOUN, JE/JAOU/NO	jejunum
jugul-	JUG/L-, JUG/YAOU/L-, JUG/YU/L-	neck; jugular vein
juxta-	J*UX, JUX/TA	near; next to
-kalemia	KLAOEM/YA	potassium in blood
kao-	KAI, KAI/YO	kaolin
karyo-	KAR/YO	nucleus

-karyosis	KAR/YOE/SIS	state of nucleus	lordo-	LOR/DO	lordosis
-karyote	KAR/YOET	nucleated cell	lumbo-	LUM/BO	lumbar; loins
kerato-	KER/TO	cornea; keratin; horny tissue	luteo-	LAOUT/YO	corpus luteum
keto-	KAOET, KAOE/TO	ketone	lymphadeno-	LIM/FAD/NO	lymph node; lymph gland
kilo-	KIL, KIL/LO, KI/LO	one thousand	lymphangio-	LIM/FAN/JO	lymph vessel
kine-	KIN	movement	lympho-	LIM/FO	lymph; lymph gland; lymphocyte
kinesio-	KI/NAOEZ/YO, KI/NAOES/YO	movement	lymphocyto-	LIM/FO/SAOIT, LIM/FO/SAOI/TO	lymphocyte
kineto-	KI/NAOET, KI/NET, KI/NAOE/TO	moveable; movement	lyo-	LAOI, LAOI/YO	dissolved
kino-	KAOIN, KIN, KAOI/NO	movement	-lysis	(v)L/SIS, LAOI/SIS	destroy; loosen; mobilize
klepto-	KLEPT, KLEP/TO	theft; stealing	lyso-	LAOIS, LAOI/SO	destroy; loosen; mobilize
koilo-	KOIL, KOI/LO	hollow; concave	lysso-	LIS, LIS/SO	rabies
kymo-	KAOIM, KAOI/MO	wave; wavy; movement	macro-	MAK/RO	large
kypho-	KAOIF, KAOI/FO	kyphosis	maculo-	MAK/LO, MAK/YAOU/LO, MAK/YU/LO	macule
-labial	LAIB/YAL	lip; labia; labial surface			
labio-	LAIB/YO	lip; labia; labial surface	magneto-	MAG/NAOET, MAG/NAOE/TO	magnetics; magnetism; magnet
lacrimo-	LAK/RI/MO, LAK/RIM	lacrimal sac; tears	mal-	MAL, MAI/L-	bad; ill; cheek
lacto-	LAKT, LAK/TO	milk	-malacia	MA/LAI/SHA	abnormal softness
-lagnia	LAG/NA, LAG/NAOE/YA	lust	malaco-	MAL/KO	abnormal softness
			malario-	MA/LAIR/YO	malaria
-lalia	LAIL/YA	speech; babble	malleo-	MAL/YO	malleus (hammer)
lalo-	LAL, LA/LO	speech; babble	malto-	MALT, MAL/TO	maltose
lamino-	LAM/NO	lamina	mamill-	MAM/L-, MA/MIL	nipple
laparo-	LAP/RO	abdominal wall; flank	mammo-	MAM, MAM/MO, MA/MO	breast
laryngo-	LARNG, LARN/GO, LA/RING, LA/RIN/GO, LARN/JO	larynx (voicebox)	mandibulo-	MAN/DIB/LO, MAN/DIB/YAOU/LO, MAN/DIB/YU/LO	mandible
latero-	LAT/RO	lateral; to the side	-mania	MAIN/YA	mental aberration
lecitho-	LES/THO	yolk	manno-	MAN, MAN/NO	mannose
leio-	LAOI, LAOI/YO	smooth; smoothness	mascul-	MAS/KL-, MAS/KAOU/L-	male; masculine
-lemma	LEM/MA	sheath; membrane			
lemmo-	LEM, LEM/MO	egg membranes	-mastia	MA*S/YA	breast
lenticulo-	LEN/TIK/LO, LEN/TIK/YAOU/LO, LEN/TIK/YU/LO	lens	masto-	MA*S, MAS/TO	breast; mastoid process
			-matic	MAT/IK	acting
			-matosis	(v)M/TOE/SIS, MA/TOE/SIS	infection; neoplasm
lento-	LEN/TO	lens			
lep-	LEP	flake; scale	-matous	(v)M/TOUS, MA/TOUS	having tumor or neoplasm
lepido-	LEP/DO	flake; scale			
-lepsis	LEP/SIS	seizure	maxillo-	MAK/SIL, MAK/SIL/LO, MAX/LO	maxilla
-lepsy	LEP/SI	seizure			
-leptic	LEPT/IK	seizure	mazo-	MAIZ, MAI/ZO	breast
lepto-	LEPT, LEP/TO	slender; thin; delicate; narrow	meato-	MAOE/YAI/TO, MAOE/AI/TO, MAOE/TO	meatus
leuco-	LAOUK, LAOU/KO	white			
leuko-	LAOUK, LAOU/KO	white; leukocyte (white blood cell)	mechanico-	ME/KAN/KO	machine
			mechano-	MEK/NO	machine
leukocyto-	LAOUK/SAOIT; LAOUK/SAOI/TO	leukocyte (white blood cell)	medico-	MED/KO	medicine
			medio-	MAOED/YO	medial
levo-	LAOEV, LAOE/VO	left; left side	medullo-	ME/DUL, ME/DUL/LO, MED/LO, MED/YAOU/LO, MED/YU/LO, ME/DAOU/LO	medulla; bone marrow
levul-	LEV/L-, LEV/YU/L-, LEV/YAOU/L-,	fructose			
-lexia	LEX/YA	ability to understand words			
			mega-	MEG	one million; large
-lexic	LEX/IK	speech; reading	-megalia	ME/GAIL/YA	enlargement
-lexis	LEK/SIS	speech; reading	megalo-	MEG/LO	great, large
-lexy	LEK/SI	speech; reading	-megaly	MEG/LI	enlargement
lieno-	LAOI/NO, LAOI/AOEN, LAOI/E/NO	spleen	meio-	MAO*I, MAO*I/YO	decrease in size or number; meiosis
lingul-	LING/L-, LING/YAOU/L-, LING/YU/L-, LIN/GAOU/L-	tongue	melano-	MEL/NO	black; melanin
			-melia	MAOEL/YA	limbs
			melo-	MEL, MAOE/LO	cheek; limbs
			-menia	MAOEN/YA	menses
linguo-	LING/WO	tongue; lingual surface	meningo-	ME/NING, ME/NIN/GO, MEN/J(O), MEN/IN/J(O)	meninges
lipo-	LIP, LIP/PO, LAOIP, LAOI/PO	fat; lipid			
-listhesis	LIS/THE/SIS	forward displacement	menisco-	ME/NIS/KO	meniscus; crescent-shaped
-lith	L*IT	stone			
-lithiasis	LI/THAOI/SIS	formation of stone	meno-	MEN, MEN/NO	menstruation
litho-	L*IT, LI/THO	stone	mens-	MEN/S-	menstruation
lobul-	LOB/L-, LOB/YU/L- LOB/YAOU/L-,	lobule; small lobe	mento-	MENT, MEN/TO	chin; mind
			-mer	MER	smallest unit of repeating structure; member of particular group
lochio-	LOEK/YO	discharge following childbirth			
-logia	LOE/JA, LOEJ/YA	study of; collecting; words; speech	mero-	MER, ME/RO, MAOER, MAOE/RO	thigh
			mesio-	MAOEZ/YO, MAOES/YO	mesial (middle) surface
-logic	LOJ/IK	pertaining to study of			
-logist	(O)L/J*IS	specialist	meso-	MES, MEZ	middle
logo-	LOG, LOE/GO	words; speech	meta-	MET, ME/TA	after; next
-logy	(O)LG	body of knowledge			

metacarpo-	MET/KARP, MET/KAR/PO	metacarpus (hand)	necros	NEK/RO	death	
metallo-	ME/TAL, MET/LO, ME/TAL/LO	metal	-necrosis	NE/KROE/SIS	death of tissue	
			nemato-	NEM/TO	nematode; threadlike structure	
metatarso-	MET/TARS, MET/TAR/SO	metatarsus (foot)	neo-	NAOE, NAOE/YO	new; strange	
meteoro-	MAOET/YOR, MAOET/YO/RO	atmosphere; weather	nephelo-	NEF/LO	cloudiness; mistiness	
-meter	(v)M/TER, MAOET/ER	instrument for measuring	nephro-	NEF/RO, NE/FRO	kidney	
			nervi-	NEFRB, NER/VI	nerve	
-metrician	ME/TRIGS	one who measures	nesidio-	NE/SID/YO	islet cell of pancreas	
-metrist	(v)M/TR*IS	one who measures	neuro-	NAOUR, NAOU/RO	nerve	
-metrium	MAOE/TRUM, MAOE/TRAOE/UM, MAOE/TRAOE/YUM	uterus	neuroglio-	NAOU/ROG/LO, NAOU/ROG/LAOE/YO, NAOUR/GLAOI, NAOUR/GLAOI/YO	neuroglia	
metro-	MAOE/TRO, ME/TR-, MET/RO	uterus; measurement	neutro-	NAOU/TRO	neutral; neutrophil	
			nevo-	NAOEV, NAOE/VO	nevus	
-metry	(v)M/TRI	measurement	nitro-	NAOI/TRO	nitrogen; nitrate; nitrite	
micro-	MAOI/KRO	small; extremely small	noci-	NOES, NOE/SI	injury; noxious agent or influence	
microglio-	MAOI/KROG/LO, MAOI/KROG/LAOE/YO	microglia	nodul-	NOD/L-, NOD/YAOU/L-, NOD/YU/L-, NOJ/L-	nodule	
mid-	MID	middle				
milli-	MIL	one-thousandth	non-	NON	not; negative	
-mimesis	MAOI/MAOE/SIS, MI/MAOE/SIS	mimicking; imitation	nona-	NOE/NA (not NOEN)	nine	
			noni-	NOE/NI (not NOEN)	nine	
-mimetic	MAOI/MET/IK, MI/MET/IK	mimicking; imitation	nor-	NOR	denoting two isomeric compounds	
-mimia	MIM/YA	mimicking; imitation	normo-	NORM, NOR/MO	usual; normal	
mini-	MIN	smaller than the usual	noso-	NOS, NOES, NOE/SO	disease	
mio-	MAOI, MAOI/YO	less	noto-	NOET, NOE/TO	back	
mito-	MAOIT, MAOI/TO	threadlike	novo-	NOEV, NOE/VO	new	
-mnesia	-M/NAOEZ/YA, NAOEZ/YA	memory	nucleo-	NAOUK/LO, NAOU/KLO, NAOUK/LAOE/YO, NAOU/KLAOE/YO	cell nucleus	
-mnesis	-M/NAOE/SIS	memory				
mono-	MON, MON/NO, MO/NO	one; only	-nychia	NIK/YA	nails	
-morph	MOR-F	form; shape	nycto-	NIKT, NIK/TO	night; darkness	
-morphia	MOR/FA, MOR/FAOE/YA	form; shape	nympho-	NIM/FO	nymphae (labia minora)	
			ob-	OB	toward; against	
-morphism	MOR/FIFM	form; shape	occipito-	OK/SIPT, OK/SIP/TO	occipital bone; posterior of head	
morpho-	MOR/FO	form; formation	occluso-	O/KLAOUZ, O/KLAOU/ZO, OK/LAOUZ, OK/LAOU/ZO, O/KLAOUZ, O/KLAOU/ZO, OK/KLAOUZ, OK/KLAOU/ZO	occlusion; occlusal surface	
-morphous	MOR/FOUS	form; shape				
mucino-	MAOUS/NO	mucus; mucin				
muco-	MAOUK, MAOU/KO, MAOUS, MAOU/S(O)	mucus				
multi-	MULT	many	octa-	OKT, OK/TA	eight	
musculo-	MUS/KLO, MUS/KAOU/LO	muscle	octi-	OKT, OK/TI	eight	
			oculo-	OK/LO, OK/YAOU/LO, OK/YU/LO	eye	
muta-	MAOUT, MAOU/TA	mutation; change				
myce-	MAOIS, MAOI/SAOE	fungus	-odontia	(c)O/DON/SHA	teeth	
-myces	MAOI/SAOEZ	fungus	odonto-	O/DONT, O/DON/TO	teeth	
-mycete	MAOI/SAOET	fungus	-odynia	(c)O/DIN/YA	pain; distress	
-mycetes	MAOI/SAOE/TAOEZ	fungus	-ogenous	OJ/NOUS	productive of	
-mycetic	MAOI/SET/IK	fungus	-oic	OIK, (c)OE/IK		
myceto-	MAOI/SAOET, MAOIS/TO	fungus	-oid	OID	resembling	
-mycetes	MAOI/SAOE/TAOEZ	fungus	-ol	OL, (c)OL	alcohol; phenol	
-mycin	MAOI/SIN	fungus	oleo-	OEL/YO	oil	
myco-	MAOIK, MAOI/KO	fungus	olfact-	OL/FAK/T-	smell	
-mycosis	MAOI/KOE/SIS	fungus	oligo-	OL/GO	few	
myctero-	MIK/TRO, MIKT/RO	nostrils	-ologist	O*LG, OL/J*IS	one who studies	
myelino-	MAOI/LI/NO, MAOI/LIN	myelin	-ology	OLG	study of	
			-oma	(c)OE/MA, O/MA	tumor; neoplasm	
myelo-	MAOI/LO	spinal cord; bone marrow	-omata	OEM/TA, (c)OE/MA/TA, (c)O/MA/TA	plural of -oma	
myo-	MAOI, MAOI/YO	muscle				
myocardio-	MAOI/KARD/YO	myocardium	omento-	OEMT, OEMT/TO, O/MENT, O/MEN/TO	omentum	
myringo-	MIRNG, MIRN/GO, MI/RING, MI/RIN/GO, MIRN/J(O)	tympanic membrane	omo-	OEM, O/MO	shoulder	
			omphalo-	OM/FLO, OM/FA/LO, OM/FAL	umbilicus (navel)	
myxo-	MIX, MIK/SO	mucus				
nano-	NAN, NAI/NO	small size; one-billionth	onco-	ON/KO	tumor; cancer	
narco-	NARK, NAR/KO	sleep, unconsciousness	-one	(c)OEN, OEN	quintivalent nitrogen; ketone	
naso-	NAIZ, NAI/ZO	nose; nasal bone				
nat-	NAI/T-, NAIT	birth	oneiro-	O/NAOIR, O/NAOI/RO	dream	
-natal	NAI/TAL	birth	-onychia	(c)O/NIK/YA	nails	
-natologist	NAI/TO*LGS, NAI/TOL/J*IS	birth	onycho-	OIN/KO, O/NIK, ON/NI/KO (not ON/KO)	nails	
-natology	NAI/TOLG	birth	oo-	AO	ovum	
navicul-	NA/VIK/L-, NA/VIK/YAOU/L-, NA/VIK/YU/L-	navicular bone	oophoro-	AOF/RO, O/OF/RO, OEF/RO	ovary	
			ophthalmo-	OF/THAL/MO	eye	
nebul-	NEB/L-, NEB/YAOU/L-, NEB/YU/L-	mist; opacity	-opia	OEP/YA	vision	

-opsis	OP/SIS	vision
opsono-	OPS/NO	opsonin
opt-	OPT, OP/T-	vision
optico-	OPT/KO	vision; eyes
opto-	OPT, OP/TO	vision; sight
orbicul-	OR/BIK/L-, OR/BIK/YAOU/L-, OR/BIK/YU/L-	orbiculus; small circle; disk
orbito-	ORB/TO	orbit of eye
-orchidism	ORK/DIFM	testes
orchido-	ORK/DO	testes
orchio-	ORK/YO, OR/K-	testes
-orchism	ORK/IFM, OR/KIFM	testes
-orchium	ORK/YUM	testes
organo-	ORG/NO	organ
-orial	OIRL, OER/YAL, OR/YAL	
oro-	OR/RO, OER/RO, O/RO, O*R/RO	mouth
ortho-	O*RT, OR/THO	straight; normal; correct; isomer
ory-	OIR	
oscheo-	OS/KO, OS/KAOE/YO	scrotum
oscillo-	OS/LO, O/SIL, OS/SIL	oscillation
-ose	OES, (c)OES	sugar; carbohydrate
-oses	(c)OE/SAOEZ	disease process; plural of osis
-osis	(c)OE/SIS, O/SIS	disease process; abnormal increase
-osmia	OZ/MA, OZ/MAOE/YA	smell; odor
osmio-	OZ/MAOE, OZ/MAOE/YO, OS/MAOE, OS/MAOE/YO	osmic acid
osmo-	OZ/MO, OS/MO	smell; odor
osphresio-	OS/FRAOEZ/YO, OS/FRAOES/YO	smell; odor
osseo-	OS/YO, OSZ/YO	bone
ossi-	OS, OS/SI, OSZ	bone
ossicul-	OS/SIK/L-, OS/SIK/YAOU/L-, OS/SIK/YU/L-	ossicle; small bone
osteo-	O*S/YO, OS/TAOE/YO	bone
-ostomy	O*S/M*I	creation of artificial opening
-otia	(c)OE/SHA, (c)OERB/YA	ear
oto-	OET, O/TO	ear
-otomy	OT/M*I	incision; cutting
-ous	(c)OUS, OUS	possessing; full of
out-	O*UT	out
-out	O*UT	out; outside
ovario-	O/VAIR/YO	ovary
over-	OVR	over; above; on; upon; to excess
-over	OFR	over; above; beyond
ovi-	OEV	ovum
ovo-	OEV, O/VO	ovum
ovu-	OV, OV/YAOU, OV/YU	ovum
oxalo-	OX/LO	oxalic acid; oxalate
-oxia	OX/YA	level of oxygen
oxy-	OX, OK/SI	oxygen; sharp; quick; sour
ozo-	OEZ, O/ZO	ozone
pachy-	PAK, PA/KI	thick
-pagia	PAI/JA, PAIJ/YA	attached twins
-pagus	-P/GUS	attached twins
palato-	PAL/TO	palate; palatine bone
paleo-	PAIL/YO	old
pallido-	PAL/DO	globus pallidus (of brain)
palpebr-	PAL/PE/BR-, PAL/PAOE/BR-	eyelid
pan-	PAN	all
pancreatico-	PAN/KRAT/KO, PAN/KRAOE/AT/KO, PAN/KRAOE/YAT/KO	pancreatic duct
pancreato-	PAN/KRA/TO, PAN/KRAOE/TO	pancreas
pancreo-	PAN/KRO, PAN/KRAOE/YO	pancreas
panto-	PANT, PAN/TO	all
papillo-	PAP/LO, PA/PIL	papilla (nipple-shaped projection)
papulo-	PAP/LO, PAP/YAOU/LO, PAP/YU/LO	papule

par-	PAR	bear; give birth
para-	PAR, PA/RA	beside; beyond; different; abnormal
-para	-P/RA	bear; give birth
parathyro-	PAR/THAOIR, PAR/THAOI/RO	parathyroid glands
parenchymo-	PRENG/MO, PA/RENG/MO, PA/REN/KI/MO, PARN/KIM, PAR/EN/KIM	functional elements (not framework) of an organ
parieto-	PRAOI/TO, PA/RAOI/TO	parietal; parietal bone; crown
-parous	-P/ROUS	giving birth
parvo-	PAFRB, PAR/VO	small
patello-	PA/TEL, PA/TEL/LO, PAT/LO	patella (kneecap)
-pathia	PA*T/YA	disease; abnormality
-pathic	PA*T/IK	disease; abnormality
patho-	PA*T, PA/THO	disease; abnormality
-pathy	-P/TH*I	disease; abnormality
pectin-	PEKT/N-, PEK/TI/N-, PEK/TIN	comb-shaped; os pubis
pedi-	PED, PAOED/Y-	foot; child
pedicul-	PE/DIK/L-, PE/DIK/YAOU/L-, PE/DIK/YU/L-	lice
pedo-	PAOE/DO, PAOED	child; foot
pellagr-	PE/LAG/R-, PE/LAI/GR-, PEL/GR-, PEL/LAG/R-, PEL/LAI/GR-	pellagra
pelvi-	PEL/VI, PEL/VAOE	pelvis
pelvio-	PEL/VO, PEL/VAOE/YO, PEL/VI/YO	pelvis
pen-	PAOE/N-, PAOEN, PEN	penis
-penia	PAOEN/YA	deficiency; diminution
penta-	PENT, PEN/TA	five
peps-	PEP/S-, PEPS	digestion; pepsin
-pepsia	PEPS/YA	digestion; pepsin
pept-	PEP/T-, PEPT	digestion; pepsin
per-	PER	through; bear; give birth
peri-	P*ER, PER/RI	around
pericardio-	P*ER/KARD/YO, PER/RI/KARD/YO	pericardium
perineo-	P*ER/NAOE, P*ER/NAOE/YO	perineum
periosteo-	P*ER/O*S/YO	periosteum
periphero-	PRIF/RO, PE/RIF/RO	peripheral; periphery
periton-	PERT/N-, P*ER/TO/N-	peritoneum
peritoneo-	PERT/NAOE, PERT/NAOE/YO, P*ER/TO/NAOE, P*ER/TO/NAOE/YO	peritoneum
pero-	PER, PER/RO, PAOER, PAOE/RO	maimed; deformed
perox-	PER/OX, PROX, PE/ROX	oxide containing more oxygen
-petal	(v)P/TAL	directed or moving toward
petro-	PET/RO	petrous portion, temporal bone
pex-	PEK/S-, PEX	fixation; suturing
-pexia	PEX/YA	fixation; suturing
-pexis	PEK/SIS	fixation; suturing
-pexy	PEK/SI	fixation; suturing
phaco-	FAK, FA/KO	lens
-phage	FALJ	cell/element that lyses
-phagia	FAI/JA, FAIJ/YA	ingestion; perversion of appetite
phago-	FAG, FA/G-, FAJ, FA/J-	ingestion; lysis
-phagy	(v)F/JI	perversion of appetite
-phakia	FAIK/YA	lens
-phalangia	FLAN/JA, FA/LAN/JA	phalanx (finger, toe)
-phalangism	FLAN/JIFM, FA/LAN/JIFM, FAL/AN/JIFM	phalanx (finger, toe)
phalango-	FLANG, FLAN/GO, FA/LANG, FA/LAN/GO, FLAN/JO, FA/LAN/JO	phalanx (finger, toe)
phallo-	FAL, FAL/LO	penis
phanero-	FAN/RO	visible; apparent

pharmaco-	FARM/KO	drug; medicine	-plastia	PLA*S/YA	form; forming
pharyngo-	FRING, FRIN/GO, FARN/GO, FA/RIN/GO, FRIN/JO, FARN/JO	pharynx	plasto-	PLA*S, PLAS/TO	form; forming
			-plasty	PLAS/TI	plastic surgery; surgical formation
-phasia	FAIZ/YA	speech	platy-	PLAT	broad; flat
-phasic	FAIZ/IK	speech	pleio-	PLAOI, PLAOI/YO	more
-phemia	FAOEM/YA	speech	-plegia	PLAOE/JA, PLAOEJ/YA	paralysis; stroke; seizure
phen-	FEN, FE/N-, FAOEN, FAOE/N-	showing; displaying; benzene; phenyl	-plegic	PLAOEJ/IK	paralysis; stroke; seizure
pheno-	FAOEN, FAOE/NO, FE/N(O)	showing; displaying; benzene; phenyl	pleo-	PLAOE, PLAOE/YO	more
			plethysmo-	PLE/THIZ/MO	increase; change in volume
phenyl-	FENL, FEN/IL	phenyl			
pheo-	FAOE, FAOE/YO	brown; dun; dusky	pleuro-	PLAOUR, PLAOU/RO, PLAOUR/RO	pleura
-pheresis	FE/RAOE/SIS, FER/SIS, FRAOE/SIS	withdrawal, separation, return ofblood			
			-plexia	PLEX/YA	paralysis; stroke; seizure
-phil	FIL	affinity for	-plexy	PLEK/SI	paralysis; stroke; seizure
-phile	FAOIL	affinity for	-ploid	PLOID	multiplication of chromosomes
-philia	FIL/YA	affinity for			
-philiac	FIL/YAK	affinity for	-ploidy	PLOI/DI	multiplication of chromosomes
-philic	FIL/IK	affinity for			
phlebo-	FLEB, FLE/BO	vein	pluri-	PLUR, PLAOUR	several; more
phlogo-	FLOEB, FLOE/GO	inflammation	-pnea	-P/NA, -P/NAOE/YA, NAOE/YA	breathing; breath
-phobia	FOEB/YA	fear			
phono-	FOEN, FOE/NO	voice; speech	pneo-	NAOE, NAOE/YO	breath; breathing
-phonia	FOEN/YA	voice; speech	pneumato-	NAOUM/TO, NAOU/MAT	air; gas; respiration
-phore	FOER	carry; bear			
-phoresis	FRAOE/SIS, FOE/RAOE/SIS, FO/RAOE/SIS	transmission	pneumo-	NAOU/MO	lungs; air; respiration
			pneumon-	NAOUM/N-; NAOU/MOEN, NAOU/MOE/N-	lungs; air; respiration
-phoria	FOER/YA	carry; bear; feeling; visual deviation			
			-poiesis	POI/SIS, POI/E/SIS	formation; production; development
-phoric	FOER/IK	carry; bear; feeling; visual deviation			
			-poietic	POIT/IK, POI/ET/IK	formative; productive
phoro-	FOE/RO, FO/RO, FOER, FOER/RO, FOR/RO	carry; bear; feeling; visual deviation	poikilo-	POIK/LO	varied; irregular
			polio-	POEL/YO	poliomyelitis; gray
			poly-	POL	many
phospho-	FOS/FO	phosphate; phosphoric acid	ponto-	PONT, PON/TO	pons
			por-	POR, POER, PO/R-, POE/R-	
photo-	FOET	light			
-phrasia	FRAIZ/YA	speech, especially phrases	porphyro-	POR/FRO, POR/FI/RO, POR/FIR	porphyrin
-phraxis	FRAK/SIS	obstruction	porto-	PORT, POR/TO	portal vein
-phrenia	FRAOEN/YA	mind; phrenic nerve; diaphragm	-posia	POEZ/YA	drinking
			post-	PO*S	after; behind
phrenico-	FREN/KO	phrenic nerve	postero-	PO*S/RO, POS/TRO	posterior; behind
phreno-	FREN, FRE/NO	mind; phrenic nerve; diaphragm	prae-	PRAE	before; in front
			-pragia	PRAI/JA, PRALJ/YA	doing; performance
phyco-	FAOIK, FAOI/KO	seaweed; algae	-praxia	PRAX/YA	doing; performance
-phyllin(e)	FLIN, FIL/LIN	from leaves	pre-	PRE	before; in front
phyllo-	FIL, FIL/LO	leaves	presby-	PRES/BI, PREBS	old; old age
phylo-	FAOIL, FAOI/LO	race; group; humanity	primi-	PRAOIM, PRAOI/MI	first
-phyma	FAOI/MA	growth; swelling; tumor	-prival	PRAOIVL, PRAOI/VAL (v)P/RI/VAL	deprived; to deprive
physico-	FIZ/KO	physics; physical			
physio-	FIZ/YO	nature; physiology; physical	-privic	PRIVK, PRIV/IK, PRAOIVK, PRAOIV/IK	deprived; to deprive
physo-	FAOIS, FAOI/SO	air; gas	pro-	PRO	before; in front
phyto-	FAOIT, FAOI/TO	plants	procto-	PROKT, PROK/TO	rectum; anus
pico-	PAOIK, PAOI/KO	one-trillionth	proprio-	PROEP/RO, PRO/PRAOE/YO	within; wholly
picro-	PIK/RO	bitter			
-piesis	PAOI/E/SIS	pressure	proso-	PROS	forward; anterior
piezo-	PAOI/ZO, PAOI/AOEZ, PAOI/E/ZO	pressure	-prosopia	PRO/SOEP/YA	face
			prosopo-	PROS/PO	face
pigmento-	PIG/MENT, PIG/MEN/TO	pigment	-prosopus	PRO/SOE/PUS, PROS/PUS	face
pilo-	PAOIL, PAOI/LO	hair	prostatico-	PROS/TAT/KO	prostate
pimelo-	PIM/LO	fat	prostato-	PRO*S/TO, PROS/TA/TO, PROS/TAIT, PROS/TAI/TO	prostate
pinealo-	PIN/YA/LO, PIN/YAL	pineal body			
pino-	PIN, PAOIN	drink; pinocytosis			
pio-	PAOI, PAOI/YO	fat	prostho-	PROS/THO	prosthesis
pituit-	PI/TAOU/T-	pituitary gland	proteino-	PRO/TAOEN, PROET/NO, PRO/TAOE/NO	protein
placento-	PLA/SENT, PLA/SEN/TO, PLAS/EN/TO, PLAS/SPWO	placenta			
			proteo-	PROET/YO	protein
			proto-	PROET	first
			proximo-	PROX/MO	proximal; proximal surface
plagio-	PLAI/JO, PLAIJ/YO	oblique			
plano-	PLAIN, PLAI/NO	flat	psammo-	SAM, SAM/MO	sand; sandlike
-plasia	PLAIZ/YA	form; development	pseudo-	SAOUD, SAOU/DO	false; not
-plasm-	PLAZ/M-	plasma	psycho-	SAOIK, SAOI/KO	mind; psyche
-plasm	PLAFM	plasma; formative substance	psychro-	SAOI/KRO	cold
			pterygo-	TER/GO	pterygoid process
plasmo-	PLAZ/MO	plazma; substance of a cell	ptyalo-	TAOI/LO	saliva
			-ptosis	TOE/SIS, -P/TOE/SIS	prolapse; falling
-plast	PLA*S	primitive living cell			

-ptysis	-(v)PT/SIS	expectoration
pubo-	PAOUB, PAOU/BO	pubis; genital region
pulmo-	PUL/MO	lungs
pulpo-	PUL/PO	pulpal surface
pupillo-	PAOUP/LO, PAOU/PIL	pupil
purpur-	PURP/R-, PUR/PAOU/R-, PURP/YAOU/R-, PURP/YU/R-	purple
pustul-	P*US/L-, P*US/YAOU/L-, P*US/YU/L-, PUS/KHU/L-, PUS/TAOU/L-	pustule
pyelo-	PAOI/LO	renal pelvis
pykno-	PIK/NO	thick; compact; frequent
pyle-	PAOIL, PAOI/LAOE, PAOI/LE	portal vein
pylor-	PAOIL/R-, PAOI/LOR, PAOI/LOER	pylorus
pyo-	PAOI, PAOI/YO	pus; purulence
pyr-	PIR, PI/R(O), PAOIR, PAOI/R(O)	fever
pyreto-	PAOI/RET, PAOI/RAOET, PIR/TO, PAOIR/TO	fever
pyro-	PAOIR, PAOI/RO	fever
quadr-	KWAUD/R-, KWAD/R-	four
quinque-	KWIN/KWAOE, KWIN/KWE	five
rachi-	RAIK, RAI/KI, RA/KI	spine
rachio-	RAIK/YO	spine
radiculo-	RA/DIK/LO, RA/DIK/YAOU/LO, RA/DIK/YU/LO	nerve roots
radio-	RAID/YO	radius; radioactivity
re-	RE	back; again
recto-	REKT, REK/TO	rectum
reflexo-	RE/FLEX, RE/FLEK/SO	reflex
reno-	RAOEN, RE/NO	kidney
respir-	RES/PR-, RES/PI/R-, RES/PIR, RES/PAOIR, RE/SPAOIR	respiration
reticulo-	RE/TIK/LO, RE/TIK/YAOU/LO, RE/TIK/YU/LO	protoplasmic network; reticulocyte
retino-	RET/NO	retina
retro-	RET/RO	back; backward
rhabdo-	RABD, RAB/DO	rod
rheo-	RAOE, RAOE/YO, RAOE/O(C)	electric current; flow
rheuma-	RAOUM, RAOU/MA	rheumatism; watery discharge
rhino-	RAOIN, RAOI/NO	nose
rhizo-	RAOIZ, RAOI/ZO	root
rhodo-	ROED, ROE/DO	red
-rhythmia	R*IT/MA, R*IT/MAOE/YA	rhythm; regularly recurring motion
ribo-	RAOIB, RAOI/BO	ribose
roentgeno-	RENT/GEN, RENT/GE/NO	x-rays; roentgen rays
-rrhage	RAJ	profuse flow; hemorrhage
-rrhagia	RAI/JA, RAIJ/YA	profuse flow; hemorrhage
-rrhaphia	RAIF/YA	suture; sew; repair
-rrhaphy	(O)R/FI	suture; sew; repair
-rrhea	RAOE/YA	flow; discharge
-rrheal	RAOEL, RAOE/YAL	flow; discharge
-rrhexis	REK/SIS	rupture; break; burst
rubro-	RAOUB/RO, RAOU/BRO	red nucleus
saccharo-	SAK/RO	sugar
saccul-	SAK/L-, SAK/YAOU/L-, SAK/YU/L-	sacculus
sacro-	SAI/KRO, SAIK/RO	sacrum; sacral
salpingo-	SAL/PING, SAL/PIN/GO, SAL/PIN/J(O)	fallopian tube; eustachian tube
-salpinx	SAL/PINGS	fallopian tube
sangui-	SANG/WI	blood
sanguino-	SANG/WIN, SANG/WI/NO	blood
sanio-	SAIN/YO	sanies; discharge from a wound
sapo-	SAIP, SAP,	soap; soapy; taste

	SAI/PO, SA/PO	
sapro-	SAP/RO, SA/PRO	rotten; putrid; decay
sarco-	SARK, SAR/KO	flesh; sarcoma
-sarcoma	SAR/KOE/MA	connective tissue tumor
scapho-	SKAF, SKA/FO	boat-shaped
scapulo-	SKAP/LO, SKAP/YAOU/LO, SKAP/YU/LO	scapula
scato-	SKAT, SKA/TO	dung; fecal matter
-schesis	(v)S/KE/SIS	retention; suppression
-schisis	(v)S/KI/SIS	split; fissure; cleft
schisto-	SH*IS, SK*IS, SHIS/TO, SKIS/TO	split; cleft
schizo-	SKIZ, SKITS, SKIT/SO	divided; split
schwann-	SWAN/N-, SH-/WAN/N-, SH-/VAN/N-	Schwann cells; sheaths of Schwann
sclero-	SKLAOER, SKLE/R(O), SKLER	sclera; hard
-sclerosis	SKLE/ROE/SIS	hardening; hard
sclerotico-	SKLE/ROT/KO	sclera; hard
scolio-	SKOEL/YO	twisted; crooked; scoliosis
-scope	SKOEP	instrument for examining
-scopic	SKOP/IK	examination
-scopist	-S/KP*IS, -S/KO/P*IS	one who examines
scopo-	SKOEP, SKOE/PO	examine; measure; being seen
scopto-	SKOPT, SKOP/TO	examine; being seen
-scopy	(O)S/KPI, (O)S/KO/PI	act of examining
scoto-	SKOET, SKOE/TO	darkness
se-	SE (not SAOE)	
sebo-	SEB, SE/BO	sebum; sebaceous gland
seco-	SAOEK, SE/KO	cut; cutting
secreto-	SE/KRAOET, SE/KRAOE/TO	secretion
secundi-	SE/KUND, SE/KUN/DI	second
seismo-	SAOIZ/MO, SAOIS/MO	vibration; shock; shaking
self-	SEFL	self
-self	*S (attached to stroke)	self
semi-	SEM	half; part
semino-	SEM/NO, SAOEM/NO	sperm; semen
sensori-	SENS/RI	sensory; sensory nerves
-seps-	SEP/S-	putrefaction; infection
-sepsis	SEP/SIS	putrefaction; infection
-sept-	SEP/T-	putrefaction; infection
septi-	SEP/TI-, SEPT	seven
septico-	SEPT/KO	septic; septicemia
septo-	SEPT, SEP/TO	septum; nasal septum
sero-	SAOER, SAOER/RO, SE/RO	serum; serous membrane
sesqui-	SES/KWI	one and a half
sex-	SEX, SEK/S-	six
sexti-	S*EX, SEX/TI	sixth
-sexual	SEX/YAOUL, SEX/YUL	sexuality
sialo-	SAOI/LO, SAOIL, SAOI/AL	saliva; salivary gland
sidero-	SID/RO	iron
sigmoido-	SIG/MOID, SIG/MOI/DO	sigmoid flexure
silico-	SIL/KO	silica
sinistro-	SIN/STRO, SI/NIS/TRO, SNIS/TRO	left; left side
sino-	SAOIN, SAOI/NO	sinus
sinu-	SIN/YAOU, SIN/Y-, SAOIN/YAOU, SAOIN/Y-	wavy; winding; bending in and out
sinus-	SAOIN/S-	sinus
-sis	SIS	
sitio-	SIT/YO	food
sito-	SAO*IT, SAO*I/TO	food
skia-	SKAOI, SKAOI/YA	shadows of internal structures
socio-	SOES/YO, SOERB/YO	society
-somatia	SOE/MAI/SHA, SOE/MAIRB/YA, SMAI/SHA, SMAIRB/YA	body
somatico-	SOE/MAT/KO, SMAT/KO	body
somato-	SOEM/TO, SOE/MAT, SMAT	body
-some	SOEM (long o); SM- (short o)	body
-somia	SOEM/YA	body

-somiasis	SOE/MAOI/SIS	body		SAOUD/NO	
-somic	SOEM/IK	body	sudo-	SAOUD, SAOU/DO	sweat; sweat glands
somn-	SOM/N-	sleep	sulfa-	SUL/FA	sulfur; sulfate; sulfuric acid
-somnia	SOM/NA, SOM/NAOE/YA	sleep	sulfo-	SUL/FO	sulfur; sulfuric acid
spasmo-	SPAZ/MO	spasm	super-	SAO*UP, SU/PER	superior; above; beyond; excess
spectro-	SPEK/TRO	spectrum	supra-	SU/PRA	above; beyond
sperma-	SPERM, SPER/MA	sperm; semen	-suria	SAOUR/YA	urine
spermato-	SPERM/TO, SPER/MAT	sperm; semen	symbio-	SIM/BO	living together
-spermia	SPERM/YA	sperm; semen		SIM/BAOE/O-,	
spermio-	SPERM/YO	sperm; semen		SIM/BAOE/YO,,	
spermo-	SPERM, SPER/MO	sperm; semen		SIM/BAO*I/O-,	
spheno-	SFAOEN, SFAOE/NO	sphenoid bone		SIM/BAO*I/YO	
sphero-	SFAOER, SFAOE/RO	round; sphere	sympathetico-	SIFRP/THET/KO,	sympathetic nervous
sphinctero-	SFINGT/RO, SFING/TRO	sphincter		SIM/PA/THET/KO	system
sphingo-	SFING, SFIN/GO	sphingosine; sphingolipid	sympathico-	SIM/PA*T/KO	sympathetic nervous system
sphygmo-	SFIG/MO	pulse	sympatho-	SIFRP/THO,	sympathetic nervous
spino-	SPAOIN, SPAOI/NO	spinal cord		SIM/PA/THO	system
spiro-	SPAOIR, SPAOI/RO	breath; breathing	syn-	SIN	with; together; union; association
splanchno-	SPLANG/NO	viscus; splanchnic nerve	synapto-	SI/NAPT,	synapse
spleno-	SPLAOEN,	spleen		SI/NAP/TO, SIN/APT,	
	SPLAOE/NO,			SIN/AP/TO, SNAPT,	
	SPLEN, SPLE/NO			SNAP/TO	
spodo-	SPOD, SPO/DO,	waste materials	syncytio-	SIN/SIRB/YO,	syncytium; placenta
	SPOED, SPOE/DO			SIN/SIT/YO	
spondylo-	SPOND/LO, SPON/DIL	vertebra	syndesmo-	SIN/DEZ/MO,	ligament;
spongio-	SPON/JO	sponge, spongelike		SIN/DES/MO	connective tissue
sporangio-	SPRAN/JO,	encystment	syngenesio-	SIN/JE/NAOEZ/YO,	common source;
	SPOE/RAN/JO,	containing spores		SIN/JE/NAOES/YO	common ancestry
	SPO/RAN/JO		synov-	SIN/V-	synovial fluid; synovial membrane
-sporin	SPORN, SPOR/RIN	spore	synovio-	SNOEV/YO,	synovial fluid;
sporo-	SPOR, SPOER, SPRO,	spores		SI/NOEV/YO	synovial membrane
	SPOR/RO, SPOER/RO,		syphilo-	SIF/LO	syphilis
	SPO/RO, SPOE/RO		syringo-	SIRNG, SIRN/GO,	tube; fistula; syrinx
squamo-	SKWAIM,	squamous portion of		SIN/J-, SI/RIN/GO	
	SKWAI/MO	temporal bone	tabo-	TAIB, TAI/BO	tabes
-stalsis	STAL/SIS	contraction; compression	tac-	TAK	touch
stapedio-	STA/PAOED/YO,	stapes (stirrup)	tachy-	TAK, TA/KI	rapid
	STAI/PAOED/YO		taeni-	TAEN/Y-	tapeworm
staphylo-	STAF/LO	uvula; Staphylococcus	talo-	TAIL, TAI/LO	talus
-stasia	STAIZ/YA	stoppage; diminution	tarso-	TARS, TAR/SO	tarsus (ankle); edge of eyelid
-stasis	(v)*S/SIS, STAI/SIS	stoppage; diminution; equilibrium	tauro-	TAUR, TAU/RO	taurocholic acid; bull-like
-stat	STAT	agent to keep from changing or moving	tauto-	TAUT, TAU/TO	same
			-taxia	TAX/YA	order; regularity
stearo	STAOER,	fat	-taxic	TAX/IK	order; regularity
	STAOER/RO, STAOE/RO		taxo-	TAX, TAK/SO	taxonomy
steato-	STAOE/TO	fat	-taxy	TAK/SI	order; regularity
steno-	STEN, STEN/NO	contracted; narrow	tecto-	TEKT, TEK/TO	roof; membrane
-stenosis	STE/NOE/SIS	narrowing; contraction; constriction	tele-	TEL, TE/LE	end; far away; operating at distance
sterco-	STERK, STER/KO	feces	teleo-	TEL/YO, TAOEL/YO	end result; final value
stereo-	STER/YO,	solid; three	telo-	TEL, TE/LO	end
	STAOER/YO	dimensions; firmly established	temporo-	TEFRP/RO, TEM/PRO	temporal bone
sterno-	STERN, STER/NO	sternum	ten-	TAOE/N-, TEN, TE/N-	tendon
-sterol	*S/ROL, *S/ROEL	certain steroids	tendino-	TEND/NO, TEN/DI/NO	tendon
stetho-	ST*ET, STE/THO	chest	tendo-	TEND, TEN/DO	tendon
stheno-	STHEN, STHE/NO	strength	tenio-	TAOEN/YO	flat band of soft tissue; tapeworm
stomato-	STOEM/TO	mouth; opening	teno-	TEN, TE/NO, TEN/NO	tendon
-stomia	STOEM/YA	mouth; opening	tenonto-	TE/NONT, TEN/ONT,	tendon
-stomiasis	STOE/MAOI/SIS	mouth; opening		TE/NON/TO, TEN/ON/TO	
-stomosis	*S/MOE/SIS	mouth; opening	terato-	TER/TO	malformed fetus
-stomy	*S/M*I	surgical formation of opening	-terian	TAOERN, TAOER/YAN	
strepto-	STREPT, STREP/TO	streptobacillus; Streptococcus; Streptomyces	testiculo-	TES/TIK/LO, TES/TIK/YAOU/LO, TES/TIK/YU/LO	testes
striat-	STRAOI/AI/T-,	striped	testo-	TES/TO	testes
	STRAOI/AIT,		tetano-	TET/NO	tetanus
	STRAOI/YAI/T-,		tetra-	TET/RA	four
	STRAOI/YAIT		thalamo-	THAL/MO	thalamus
strio-	STRAOI, STRAOI/YO	striped	thalasso-	THA/LAS, THAL/SO,	sea; sea water
strongyl-	STRONG/L-,	Strongylus; round		THA/LAS/SO	
	STRON/JI/L-		-thanasia	*T/NAIZ/YA,	death
stropho-	STROF	distorted; twisted		THA/NAIZ/YA	
-strophy	-S/TRO/FI	distorted; twisted	thanato-	THAN/TO	death; dead bodies
stylo-	STAOIL, STAOI/LO	styloid process	theco-	THAOEK, THAOE/KO,	sheath; alveolus
sub-	SUB	under; below		THAOE/S(O)	
succino-	SUX/NO, SUK/SI/NO	succinic acid; amber			
sucro-	SAOU/KRO	sucrose; sugar			
sudano-	SAOU/DAN,	Sudan (a stain)			

thel-	THAOE/L-, THAOEL, THEL	nipple		trocho-	TROEK, TROK, TROE/KO	round; wheel; pulley
-thelia	THAOEL/YA	nipple		-trope	TROEP	nourishment; nutrition
thelo-	THAOEL, THAOE/LO	nipple		-troph	TROEF, TROF	nourishment; nutrition
thely-	THEL, THAOEL, THEL/LI, THAOE/LI	female		-trophia	TROEF/YA	nurture; nourish
				-trophic	TROFK, TROEFK, TROF/IK, TROEF/IK	nourishment; nutrition
theo-	THAOE, THAOE/YO	god; prayer; religion		-trophin	TROEFN, TROE/FIN	nourishment; nutrition
therio-	THAOER/YO	lower animals		tropho-	TROF, TROE/FO	nurture; nourish
-thermia	THERM/YA	heat; temperature		-trophy	(v)T/RO/FI, TRO/FI	nourishment; nutrition
-thermic	THERM/IK	heat; temperature		-tropia	TROEP/YA	strabismus; turning; changing
thermo-	THERM, THER/MO	heat; temperature				
-thermy	THER/M*I	heat; temperature		-tropic	TROP/IK, TROEP/IK	turning; changing
thia-	THAOI, THAOI/YA	sulfur; thiamine		tropo-	TROEP, TROP, TROE/PO	turning; changing; response
thigmo-	THIG/MO	contact; touch				
thio-	THAOI, THAOI/YO	sulfur		trypano-	TRI/PAN, TRIP/NO, TRAOI/PAN, TR*I/PAN	trypanosome; borer
thixo-	THIX, THIK/SO	shaking; stirring				
thoracico-	THRAS/KO, THO/RAS/KO, THOE/RAS/KO	thorax; thoracic		tuberculo-	TAOU/BERK/LO, TAOU/BERK/YU/LO, TAOU/BERK/YAOU/LO, TAOU/BER/KAOU/LO	tubercle; nodule; tuberculosis
thoraco-	THOR/KO, THOER/KO	thorax; thoracic				
-thorax	THOR/AX	thorax				
-thrix	THRIX	hair		tubo-	TAOUB, TAOU/BO	tube; fallopian tube
thrombo-	THROM/BO	thrombus (blood clot)		tubulo-	TAOUB/LO, TAOUB/YAOU/LO, TAOUB/YU/LO, TAOU/BAOU/LO	tubule
thrombocyto-	THROM/BO/SAOIT, THOM/BO/SAOI/TO	thrombocyte (platelet)				
-thymia	THAOIM/YA	mind; emotions; mood; thymus		tuss-	TUS, TUS/S-, TUSZ	cough
				tympano-	TIFRP/NO, TIM/PA/NO, TIM/PAN	tympanic membrane; middle ear
-thymic	THAOIM/IK	mind; emotions; mood; thymus				
				typhlo-	TIF/LO	cecum
thymo-	THAOIM, THAOI/MO	thymus gland; mind; emotions		typho-	TAOIF, TAOI/FO	typhus
				tyro-	TAOIR, TAOI/RO	cheese; caseous
thyreo-	THAOIR/YO	thyroid gland		ulcero-	ULS/RO	ulcer
thyro-	THAOIR, THAOI/RO	thyroid gland		ulno-	UL/NO	ulna
thyroido-	THAOI/ROID, THAOI/ROI/DO	thyroid gland		ulo-	YAOUL, YAOU/LO	scar; gums
				ultra-	UL/TRA	excess; beyond
tibio-	TIB/YO	tibia		un-	UN	not
-tocia	TOE/SHA, TOERB/YA	labor; childbirth		unci-	UNS, UN/SI	hook; hooklike
toco-	TOEK, TOE/KO	labor; childbirth		under-	UNDZ	under; below
-tome	TOEM	instrument for cutting; segment		uni-	YAOUN, YAOU/NI	one
				uranisco-	YAOUR/NIS/KO	palate
tomo-	TOEM, TOE/MO	cutting; designated layer		urano-	YAOUR/NO	palate
-tomy	(v)T/M*I	cutting; incision		-urea	YAOU/RAOE/YA	urea
-tonia	TOEN/YA	tone; tension		ureo-	YAOUR/YO	urea
-tonic	TON/IK	tone; tension		-uresis	YAOU/RAOE/SIS	urine
-tonicity	TOE/NIS/TI	tone; tension		uretero-	YAOU/RAOET/RO	ureter
tono-	TOEN, TON, TOE/NO	tone; tension		-ureter	YAOU/RAOET/ER	ureter
tonsillo-	TONS/LO, TON/SLO, TON/SIL	tonsils		urethro-	YAOU/RAO*ET/RO, YAOU/RAOE/THRO, YAOUR/THR-	urethra
topo-	TOP	place; localized				
torul-	TOR/L-, TOR/YAOU/L-, TOR/YU/L-	swelling; papilla			YAOUT/RO	uterus
				-uria	YAOUR/YA, (c)AOUR/YA	urine
toti-	TOET, TOE/TI	total; all				
-tox-	TOX, TOK/S(v)	toxin; poisoning		-uric	YAOUR/IK, YAOURK	urine
-toxemia	TOK/SAOEM/YA	toxins in blood		urico-	YAOUR/KO	uric acid
toxi-	TOX, TOK/SI	toxin; poison		uro-	YAOUR, YAOU/RO, YAOUR/RO	urine
-toxia	TOX/YA	toxin; poison				
toxico-	TOX/KO	toxin; poison		utero-	YAOUT/RO	uterus
-toxism	TOK/SIFM, TOX/IFM	toxin; poison		utriculo-	YAOU/TRIK/LO, YAOU/TRIK/YU/LO, YAOU/TRIK/YAOU/LO,	utricle (of ear); small sac
toxo-	TOX, TOK/SO	toxin; poison				
-toxy	TOK/SI	toxin; poison		uveo-	YAOUV/YO	uvea
trabecul-	TRA/BEK/L-, TRA/BEK/YAOU/L-, TRA/BEK/YU/L-	connective tissue		uvulo-	YAOUV/LO, YAOUV/YAOU/LO, YAOUV/YU/LO, YAOU/VAOU/LO	uvula
trachelo-	TRAK/LO, TRAIK/LO	neck; necklike structure				
tracheo-	TRAIK/YO	trachea		vaccin-	VAX/N-, VAK/SI/N-, VAK/SIN	vaccine
trachy-	TRAK, TRAIK	rough; deep; strong				
trans-	TRA*NS	across; beyond; through		vacuo-	VAK/YO, VAK/YAOU, VAK/WO	vacuole; small space
transvers-	TRA*NS/VER/S-	transverse process				
-transverse	TRA*NS/VERS	transverse process; transverse		vagino-	VAJ/NO, VA/JAOIN, VA/JAOI/N(O)	vagina
traumato-	TRAUM/TO	trauma; wound; injury		vago-	VAIG, VAI/GO	vagus nerve
-tresia	TRAOEZ/YA	perforation		valvulo-	VAL/VAOU/LO, VAL/VAOUL	valve
tri-	TR*I	three				
-trichia	TRIK/YA	hair		vapo-	VAIP, VAI/PO	vapor
tricho-	TRIK, TRI/KO	hair		varico-	VAIR/KO, VAR/KO	varix
trigono-	TR*I/GOEN, TR*I/GOE/NO, TRIG/N-	trigone		vario-	VAIR/YO, VA/RAOI	smallpox
				vasculo-	VAS/KLO, VAS/KAOU/LO	blood vessel; duct; vessel
trio-	TRAOI, TR*I, TR*I/YO	three				
triplo	TRIP/LO	triple; three		vaso-	VAIS, VAIZ, VAS, VA/SO, VAI/SO, VAI/ZO	blood vessel; duct; vessel
-tripsis	TRIP/SIS	crushing				
-tripsy	TRIP/SI	crushing				
trochle-	TROK/L-, TROK/LAOE/Y-	trochlea; pulley-shaped structure				

veni-	VEN	vein
veno-	VAOEN, VAOE/NO	vein
ventriculo-	VEN/TRIK/LO, VEN/TRIK/YAOU/LO, VEN/TRIK/YU/LO	ventricle
ventro-	VEN/TRO	ventral; front
venul-	VEN/L-, VEN/YAOU/L-, VEN/YU/L-	venule
vertebro-	VERT/BRO	vertebra
vesico-	VES/KO	bladder; vesicle
vesiculo-	VE/SIK/LO, VE/SIK/YAOU/LO, VE/SIK/YU/LO	vesicle; seminal vesicle
vestibulo-	VES/TIB/LO, VES/TIB/YAOU/LO, VES/TIB/YU/LO	vestibule
vibrio-	VIB/RO, VIB/RAOE/YO	Vibrio (a microorganism)
vibro-	VAOI/BRO	vibration
-viridae	VIR/DAE	virus family
viro-	VAOI/RO, VAOIR, VIR	virus
-virus	VAOI/RUS	virus
viscero-	VIS/RO	viscera
visco-	VIS/KO	glutinous; sticky; interior organ
visuo-	VIRB/YO, VIRB/WO	visual
vitello-	VAOI/TEL, VAOI/TEL/LO	yolk; lutein
vitreo-	VIT/RO, VIT/RAOE/YO	vitreous body
vivi-	VIV	life
-volemia	VOE/LAOEM/YA	volume of blood
-volemic	VOE/LAOEM/IK	volume of blood
vomero-	VOEM/RO	vomer
vulvo-	VUL/VO	vulva
xantho-	ZAN/THO, ZANT	yellow
xeno-	ZEN, ZE/NO	strange; foreign material
xero-	ZAOER, ZAOE/RO	dry
xipho-	ZIF, ZAOI/FO, ZI/FO	xiphoid process
xylo-	ZAOIL, ZAOI/LO	wood
zeo-	ZAOE, ZAOE/YO	boiling
zonul-	ZOEL/L-, ZOEN/YAOU/L-, ZOEN/YU/L-, ZON/L-, ZON/YAOU/L-, ZON/YU/L-	zonule; small zone
zoo-	ZOE, ZAO	animal
-zoon	ZAON, ZOE/WON (not ZOEN)	animal
zygo-	ZAOIG, ZAOI/GO	yoked; joined; junction
zygomatico-	ZAOIG/MAT/KO	zygoma; cheekbone
zygoto-	ZAOI/GOET, ZAOI/GOE/TO, ZAOIG/TO	zygote
-zygous	-Z/GOUS, ZAOI/GOUS, ZAOIG/OUS	zygote
zymo-	ZAOIM, ZAOI/MO	enzyme; fermentation

APPENDIX 3
MEDICAL SOUNDALIKE SOLUTIONS

Following is a summary of soundalike solutions following the StenEd theory. Also included are a few words that are not soundalikes but which are so similar many people get them confused. This list contains mainly medical and medical-related words and, thus, is by no means all-inclusive. Appendix IV of StenEd's *Conflict-Free Professional Dictionary* contains a comprehensive list of non-medical soundalike resolutions.

The list is arranged alphabetically. The soundalike words in each group (often spelled quite differently) are also alphabetized.

abduct	AB/DUKT	addisin	AD/DI/SIN	amebic	AI/MAOEB/IK
adduct	AD/DUKT, AI/DUKT	add sin	AD/SIN	amoebic	AI/MAO*EB/IK
		Addison	AD/DI/SON	amelo-	AI/MEL, AM/LO*, AM/ME/LO
aberration	AB/RAIGS	Adson	AD/SON	amylo-	AM/LO
abrasion	AI/BRAIGS				
		adduct	*see abduct*	amelogenesis	AM/LO*/JEN/SIS, AI/MEL/JEN/SIS
ablation	AB/LAIGS			amylogenesis	AM/LO/JEN/SIS
ablution	AB/LAOUGS	ad lib.	AD/L*IB		
		ad lib	AD/LIB	amelogenic	AM/LO*/JEN/IK, AI/MEL/JEN/IK
abrasion	*see aberration*			amylogenic	AM/LO/JEN/IK
		Adrenalin	AI/DREN/L*IN		
absorb	AB/SORB	adrenaline	AI/DREN/LIN	Amicar	A*M/KAR, AM/MI/KAR
adsorb	AD/SORB			am car(rying)	AM/KAR
		Adson	*see Addison*		
acar(o)-	AK/KR(O)	adsorb	*see absorb*	amicine	AM/MI/SIN
acro-	AK/RO			am sin(ning)	AM/SIN
		aerial	AER/YAL		
acarid	AK/KRID, AK/R*ID	-arial	AIRL, AIR/YAL	Amikin	AM/MI/KIN
acrid	AK/RID			am kin	AM/KIN
		affect	AI/FEKT, AFKT, AF/FEKT		
acarophobia	AK/KRO/FOEB/YA	effect	EFKT, E/FEKT	aminolysis	AM/NOL/SIS
acrophobia	AK/RO/FOEB/YA			ammonolysis	AM/MO/NOL/SIS, AI/MOE/NOL/SIS
		afferent	AFRNT, AF/FRENT		
acceptor	AK/SEP/TOR	efferent	EFRNT, EF/FRENT	amnion	AM/NAOE/YON
ceptor	SEP/TOR			am non-	AM/NON
		affusion	AI/FAOUGS		
acetal	AS/TAL	after fusion	AF/FAOUGS	amnios	AM/NAOE/YOS, AM/NAOE/OS
acetyl	AS/TIL			am nos(talgic)	AM/NOS
		after	AF		
acetic	AI/SAOET/IK, AI/SET/IK	apheter	AF/TER	*amoeba*	*see ameba*
ascetic	AS/SET/IK	after-	AFR	*amoebae*	*see amebae*
		-after	AFR	*amoebic*	*see amebic*
acetyl	*see acetal*				
		agmen	AG/M*EN	amorpha	AI/MOR/FA
acheilia	AI/KAOIL/YA	ago men	AG/MEN	amorphia	AI/MOR/FAOE/YA
achylia	AI/KAO*IL/YA				
		aids	AIDZ	ampulla	AM/PUL/LA
acheilous	AI/KAOIL/OUS, AI/KAOI/LOUS	aides	AEDZ	ampullula	AM/PUL/YAOU/LA, AM/PUL/YU/LA
achylous	AI/KAO*IL/OUS, AI/KAO*I/LOUS	AIDS	A*IDZ		
				amyl	AI/MIL, AM/MIL
achylia	*see acheilia*	Albee	AL/BAOE	am ill	AM/IL
achylous	*see acheilous*	Allbee	AUL/BAOE		
acid	*see azide*			amylene	AM/MI/LAOEN
		allegation	AL/GAIGS	am lean	AM/LAOEN
acinesia	AS/NAOEZ/YA	alligation	AL/LI/GAIGS, A*L/GAIGS		
asynesia	AI/SI/NAOEZ/YA, AI/SNAOEZ/YA			*amylo-*	*see amelo-*
		Ambard	AM/BARD	*amylogenesis*	*see amelogenesis*
acneform	AK/NE/FORM	am bar(red)	AM/BAR(/-D)	*amylogenic*	*see amelogenic*
acneiform	AK/NAOE/FORM				
		ameba	AI/MAOE/BA	anacidity	AN/SID/TI, AN/NA/SID/TI
acorea	AI/KO/RAOE/YA	amoeba	AI/MAO*E/BA	an acidity	AN/AI/SID/TI
acoria	AI/KOER/YA				
		amebacidal	AI/MAOE/BA/ SAOI/DAL	Anacin	AN/SIN, AN/NA/SIN
acrid	*see acarid*	amebicidal	AI/MAOEB/SAOI/DAL	anisine	AN/NI/SIN
acro-	*see acaro-*				
acrophobia	*see acarophobia*	amebacide	AI/MAOE/BA/SAO*ID		
		amebicide	AI/MAOEB/SAO*ID		
ad	A*D				
add	AD	amebae	AI/MAOE/BAE		
		amoebae	AI/MAO*E/BAE		

anaero-	AN/RO, AN/NAER, AN/NAER/RO	anode	AN/NOED	aural	AURL, AU/RAL
an aero-	AN/AER, AN/AER/RO	an ode	AN/OED	oral	ORL
anaerobe	AN/ROEB, AN/NAER/ROEB	*anoretic*	*see aneretic*	auricle	AUR/K-L
an aerobe	AN/AER/ROEB	anorganic	A*N/OR/GAN/IK, AN/NOR/GAN/IK	oracle	O*R/K-L, OR/K-L
anaerobic	AN/ROEB/IK, AN/NAER/ROEB/IK	an organic	AN/OR/GAN/IK	*autistic*	*see artistic*
an aerobic	AN/AER/ROEB/IK	anovul-	A*N/OV/L-, etc.	auxiliary	AUK/SIL/RI, AUK/SIL/YAIR
anaerosis	AN/ROE/SIS, AN/NAER/ROE/SIS	an ovul-	AN/OV/L-, etc.	axillary	AX/LAIR
an aerosis	AN/AER/ROE/SIS	*ansate*	*see anisate*	aversion	AI/VERGS
analbuminemia	ANL/BAOUM/NAOEM/YA, AN/NAL/BAOUM/NAOEM/YA	ante-	AENT	eversion	E/VERGS
		anti-	A*ENT, AN/TI	az-	A*Z
an albuminemia	AN/AL/BAOUM/NAOEM/YA	anterior	AN/TAOER/YOR	as	AZ
		interior	SPWAOER/YOR	azide	AZ/SID, AI/ZID, A*Z/ID
anallergic	AN/LERJ/IK	*anul-*	*see annul-*	as id-	AZ/ID
an allergic	AN/AI/LERJ/IK	*anuli*	*see annuli*	acid	AS/ID
analog	AN/LOG, AN/NA/LOG	*anulus*	*see annulus*	azo-	A*Z, AI/ZO, AZ/ZO
analogue	AN/LO*G, AN/NA/LO*G	anuresis	AN/YAOU/RAOE/SIS, AN/YU/RAOE/SIS	as	AZ
anamnestic	AN/NAM/N*ES/IK	enuresis	EN/YAOU/RAOE/SIS, EN/YU/RAOE/SIS	Aztec	A*Z/TEK, AS/TEK
an amnestic	AN/AM/N*ES/IK			as tech-	AZ/TEK
anaphrodisiac	AN/NAF/RO/DAOEZ/YAK, AN/NAF/RO/DIZ/YAK	any	NI	Bailey	BA*I/LAOE, BAI/LAO*E
		-ny	N*I	bailee	BAI/LAOE, BAIL/LAOE
an aphrodisiac	AN/AF/RO/DAOEZ/YAK, AN/AF/RO/DIZ/YAK	anybody	NIB	Band-Aid	BA*ND/H-F/AID, BA*ND/AID
		nib	N*IB	band-aid	BAND/H-F/AID, BAN/DAID
Anaprox	AN/NA/PROX	apatite	A*P/TAOIT, AP/PA/TAOIT	band aid	BAND/AID
an approximate	AN/PROX	appetite	AP/TAOIT	bar, bari-, baro-	BAR
anastral	AN/NAS/TRAL	aphagia	AI/FAI/JA, AI/FAIJ/YA	bary-	BAR/RI
an astral	AN/AS/TRAL	aphasia	AI/FAIZ/YA	barbed	BAR/-BD
anaxon	AN/NAK/SON	*apheter*	*see after*	bashed	BARB/-D
an axon	AN/AK/SON	aphtha	AF/THA*, AP/THA	bare	BAIR
androgenous	AN/DROJ/NOUS	after that	AF/THA	bear	BAER
androgynous	AN/DROJ/NO*US	*appetite*	*see apatite*	Baer	BA*ER
aneretic	AN/E/RET/IK	arborize	AR/BOR/AOIZ, AR/BO/RAOIZ	Bayer	BA*IR, BAI/YER
anoretic	AN/RET/IK	ash rize	ARB/RAOIZ	baring	BAIR/-G
angle	AING/-L, ANG/-L	arc	A*RK	Behring	BAI/RING
ankle	AIN/K-L, AN/K-L	ark	ARK	barn	BARN
anile	AI/NAOIL, AN/NIL	area	AIR/YA, AER/YA	barren	BAIRN, BAIR/-N, BAR/-N, BAR/REN
an ill	AN/IL	aria	AR/YA	base	BAIS
anilide	AN/NI/LID, AN/L*ID	*-arial*	*see aerial*	basi-	BAI/SI
annelid	AN/LID	artefact	AR/TE/FAKT	baso-	BAI/SO
anion	A*N/AOIN	art fact	ART/FAKT	*bashed*	*see barbed*
an ion	AN/AOIN	arthritis	AR/THRAOITS	*Bayer*	*see bare*
anionic	A*N/AOIN/IK	arteritis	ART/RAOITS	*bear*	*see bare*
an ionic	AN/AOIN/IK	artifact	AR/TI/FAKT	*Behring*	*see baring*
anisate	AN/NI/SAIT	art fact	ART/FAKT	bel	B*EL
ansate	AN/SAIT	artistic	AR/T*IS/IK	bell	BEL
anisine	*see Anacin*	autistic	AU/T*IS/IK	benzene	BEN/ZAOEN
aniso-	AN/NAOIS, AN/SO	*ascetic*	*see acetic*	benzin	BEN/ZIN
an iso-	AN/AOIS	assay	AS/SAI	benzine	B*EN/ZAOEN
ankle	*see angle*	essay	ES/SAI	benzoin	BEN/ZOIN
annelid	*see anilide*	asteroid	AS/TROID, A*S/ROID	bi-	B*I
annul-	AN/Y-, etc.	astroid	AS/TRO*ID, A*S/RO*ID	by	BI
anul-	A*N/L-, etc.	asthma	AS/MA, A*Z/MA	buy	BAOI
annuli	AN/LAOI	as ma-	AZ/MA	bye	BAO*I
anuli	A*N/LAOI	*asynesia*	*see acinesia*	bloc	BLO*K
annulus	AN/LUS	athyrea	AI/THAOIR/YA	block	BLOK
anulus	A*N/LUS	athyria	AI/THAO*IR/YA	boar	BOR
				Bohr	BO*R
				boor	BAOR
				bore	BOER
				Boas	BOE/WAZ, BOE/WAS
				bow as	BOE/AZ

brachi- brachy-	BRAIK/Y- BRAK, BRA/KI	carination	KAIR/NAIGS, KAR/RI/NAIGS	cerosin ceresin	SER/RO/SIN SER/SIN
Braun brawn	BRA*UN BRAUN	carnation	KAR/NAIGS	cession session	KREGS SEGS
breach breech	BRAEFP BRAOEFP	cariology karyology	KAIR/YOLG KAR/YOLG	chalasia chalazia	KA/LAIS/YA KA/LAIZ/YA
bread bred	BRAED BRED	carotic -crotic	KA/ROT/IK KROT/IK	chalcosis chalicosis	KA*L/KOE/SIS KAL/KOE/SIS
Bruch Bruck Brucke	BR*UK BRUK BRAOE/KAOE	*carries*	*see caries*	cheilosis chylosis	KAOI/LOE/SIS KAO*I/LOE/SIS
buccal buckle	BUK/KAL BUK/-L	carrion carryon carry-on karyon	KAIR/YON KAIR/RI/O*N KAR/RI/H-F/ON KAR/YON	cheirospasm keirospasm	KAOIR/SPAFM KAO*IR/SPAFM
bur burr	B*UR BUR	caudal caudle coddle	KAU/DAL KAUD/-L KOD/-L	cho- co-	KOE KO
buy *by* *bye*	*see bi-* *see bi-* *see bi-*	*caul*	*see call*	cholecystitis colicystitis	KOEL/SIS/TAOITS KO/LI/SIS/TAOITS
calage collage	KA/LAJ KLAJ	ce- se-	SE SE (unless combined with consonant)	cholerrhagia colorrhagia	KOEL/RAI/JA KO/LO/RAI/JA
calculous	KAL/KLOUS, KAL/KAOU/LOUS	sea see	SAE SAOE	choleuria coliuria	KOEL/YAOUR/YA KO/LI/YAOUR/YA
calculus	KAL/KLUS, KAL/KAOU/LUS	cel cell sell	S*EL, KR*EL KREL SEL	choral coral	KHORL KORL
caliber caliper(s)	KAL/BER KAL/PER	-cele -coele seal	SAO*EL SAO*EL SAOEL	chord cord	KHORD KORD
calices	KAL/SAOEZ, KAL/LI/SAOEZ	cella sella	KREL/LA, S*EL/LA SEL/LA	chordal cordal	KHOR/DAL KOR/DAL
calyces	KAL/SAO*EZ, K*AL/SAOEZ	cellae sellae	KREL/LAE, S*EL/LAE SEL/LAE	chordectomy cordectomy	KHOR/DEKT/M*I KOR/DEKT/M*I
calicine calycine	KAL/SAOEN KAL/SAO*EN	cellar sellar seller	KREL/LAR SEL/LAR SEL/ER	chorditis corditis	KHOR/DAOITS KOR/DAOITS
caliper(s)	*see caliber*	cello- cellul(o)-	SEL/LO SEL/YAOU/L(O), SEL/YU/L(O), KREL/YAOU/L(O), KREL/YU/L(O)	chordo- cordo-	KHORD, KHOR/DO KOERD, KOER/DO
calix	KAI/LIX, KAL/IX			chordotomy cordotomy	KHOR/DOT/M*I KOR/DOT/M*I
calyx	KAI/L*IX, KAL/*IX	cenosite seen site	SE/NO/SAOIT SAOEN/SAOIT	chorea Korea	KOE/RAOE/YA KRAOE/YA, KO/RAOE/YA
call caul	KAUL KA*UL	cenotype seen type	SE/NO/TAOIP SAOEN/TAOIP	-coria	KOER/YA
callosal colossal	KAL/LOE/SAL, KA/LOE/SAL KLOS/SAL, KO/LOS/SAL	censer censor sensor	SENS/ER, SEN/SER KREN/SOR SEN/SOR	choroid corroid	KOER/OID KOR/OID, KOR/ROID
callous callus	KAL/OUS, KAL/LOUS KAL/LUS	cent scent sent	KRENT SKRENT SENT	Chromagen chromogen	KRO*EM/JEN, KROE/MA/JEN KROEM/JEN
calyces *calycine* *calyx*	*see calices* *see calicine* *see calix*	centrifugal centripetal	SEN/TRIF/GAL SEN/TRIP/TAL	chromaphil chromophil	KROE/MA/FIL KROEM/FIL
Caplan Kaplan	KA*P/LAN KAP/LAN	cephal(o)- self-	SEF/L(O), SEF/AL, SFAL, SE/FAL SEFL	chromanol chromenol	KROEM/NOL KROE/MEN/OL
caprillic caprylic	KA/PRIL/IK KAP/RIL/IK	*ceptor*	*see acceptor*	chromhidrosis chromidrosis	KROEM/DROE/SIS KROE/MI/DROE/SIS, KROE/MID/ROE/SIS
caraway car way	KAIR/WAI, KAR/RA/WAI KAR/WAI	cera sera	SE/RA SAOER/RA	*chromogen* *chromophil*	*see Chromagen* *see chromaphil*
carbamide carbimide	KARB/MAOID KAR/BI/MAOID	cerasin ceresin	SER/RA/SIN SER/SIN	chyliform chyle form	KAOI/LI/FORM, KAO*IL/FORM KAOIL/FORM
carbhemoglobin	KARB/HAOEM/ GLOE/BIN	cereal serial	KRAOER/YAL SAOER/YAL	*chylosis*	*see cheilosis*
carbohemoglobin	KAR/BO/HAOEM/ GLOE/BIN	cerium serum	SAOER/YUM, SER/YUM SAOERM, SAOER/UM	-cide side	SAO*ID SAOID
caries carries	KAIR/RAOEZ KAIR/RI/-S	cilium psyllium	SIL/YUM S*IL/YUM		

cimbia	SIM/BAOE/YA	collum	KOL/LUM, KLUM	cristal	KR*IS/TAL
cymba	SIM/BA	column	KOL/UM	crystal	KRIS/TAL
circum-	SIR/KUM	colonic	see clonic	cruise	KRAOUZ
circumstance	SIRK,	colorrhagia	see cholerrhagia	crus	KRAOUS
	SIR/KUM/STANS	colossal	see callosal	Kruse	KRAO*UZ, KRAO*US
		colostrum	see claustrum		
cirrous	SIR/ROUS			cryanesthesia	KRAOI/ANS/
cirrus	SIR/RUS	complement	KOM/PLEMT		THAOEZ/YA
serous	SAOER/OUS	compliment	KOM/PLIMT	cryoanesthesia	KRAOI/YO/ANS/
scirrhous	SKIR/OUS,				THAOEZ/YA
	SKIR/ROUS	con	KON		
		Conn	KO*N	crystal	see cristal
cite	KRAOIT				
-cyte	SAO*IT	contractile	KON/TRAK/TAOIL,	Culp	KUL/-P
sight	SAOIGT		KR-T/TAOIL,	Kulp	K*UL/-P
site	SAOIT		KON/TRAK/TIL		
		contract till	KR-T/TIL	cumidine	see Coumadin
claustrum	KLAUS/TRUM			cure	see coeur
colostrum	KO/LOS/TRUM,	cop	KOP		
	KLOS/TRUM	Kopp	KO*P	curet	KAOU/RET
				curette	KAOU/R*ET,
cline	KLAOIN	coprostanol	KOP/RO*S/NOL		KAO*U/RET
Klein	KLAO*IN	coprostenol	KOP/ROS/TEN/OL		
				cutireaction	KAOU/TI/RE/A*BGS,
clinger	KLING/ER	cor	KO*R		KAO*UT/RE/A*BGS
Klinger	KL*ING/ER	cor-	KOR	cute reaction	KAOUT/RE/A*BGS
		core	KOER		
clip	KLIP	corps	KOERP, KOERPZ	cuvet	KAOU/VET
collip	KOL/IP, KOL/LIP,	corpse	KORPS	cuvette	KAO*U/VET,
	KL*IP				KAOU/V*ET
		coral	see choral		
clonic	KLON/IK	cord	see chord	cyanin	SAOI/NIN
colonic	KO/LON/IK	cordal	see chordal	cyonin	SAOI/YO/NIN
		cordectomy	see chordectomy		
closylate	KLOE/SI/LAIT	corditis	see chorditis	cymba	see cimbia
close late	KLOES/LAIT	cordo-	see chordo-		
		cordotomy	see chordotomy	cystiform	SIS/TI/FORM
co-	see cho-	-coria	see chorea	cyst form	S*IS/FORM
coal	KOEL	corneal	KORN/YAL	cystitome	SIS/TI/TOEM
Cole	KO*EL	cornual	KOR/NAOUL,	cystotome	S*IS/TOEM
			KORN/WAL		
coarse	KAORS			-cyte	see cite
course	KOURS	corner	KORN/ER, KOR/NER		
		coroner	KORN/NER	cyto-	SAOIT, SAOI/TO
coax	KOEX			sito-	SAO*IT, SAO*I/TO
Kocks	KO*EX	cornoid	KORN/OID		
		coronoid	KOR/NOID	cytology	SAOI/TOLG
cob	KOB			sitology	SAO*I/TOLG
Cobb	KO*B	cornual	see corneal		
		coroner	see corner	cytopreparation	SAOI/TO/PREP/RAIGS
coccydynia	KOK/SI/DIN/YA	coronoid	see cornoid	site preparation	SAOIT/PREP/RAIGS
coxodynia	KOX/DIN/YA				
		corporal	KORP/RAL	cytotaxis	SAOIT/TAK/SIS
cochleitis	KOK/LAOE/AOITS	corporeal	KOR/POER/YAL,	sitotaxis	SAO*IT/TAK/SIS
cochlitis	KOK/LAOITS		KOR/POR/YAL,		
			KOR/POIRL	cytotherapy	SAOIT/THER/PI
coddle	see caudal			sitotherapy	SAO*IT/THER/PI
-coele	see -cele	corps	see cor		
		corpse	see cor	cytotoxin	SAOIT/TOK/SIN
coeur	KAO*UR, KOUR	corroid	see choroid	sitotoxin	SAO*IT/TOK/SIN
cure	KAOUR				
		cort-	KOR/T-, KORT	cytotropism	SAOI/TOT/RO/PIFM
coke	KOEK	court	KOURT	sitotropism	SAO*I/TOT/RO/PIFM
Koch	KO*EK				
		Coumadin	KOUM/DIN,	debride	DE/BRAOED,
col	KO*L		KAO*UM/DIN		DAI/BRAOED
col-	KOL			debris	DE/BRAOE,
		cumidine	KAOUM/DIN,		DAI/BRAOE
Cole	see coal		KAOUM/DAOEN		
				deceased	DE/SAOES/-D
colicin	KOL/SIN	course	see coarse	diseased	DI/SAOEZ/-D, D-Z/-D
collacin	KOL/LA/SIN	court	see cort-		
		coxodynia	see coccydynia	decent	DE/SENT, DE/KRENT
colicystitis	see cholecystitis			descent	DES/SENT,
		cream	KRAOEM		DES/KRENT
coliform	KOL/FORM,	creme	KRAO*EM	dissent	DIS/SENT
	KO/LI/FORM				
coal form	KOEL/FORM	creatine	KRAOE/TAOEN,	deem	DAOEM
			KRAOE/YA/TIN	deme	DAEM
coliuria	see choleuria	cretin	KRAOE/TIN		
collage	see calage			defer	DE/FER, DEFR
		creme	see cream	differ	DIFR, DIF/ER
colleague	KLAOEG				
Klieg	KLAO*EG	creosol	KRAO*E/SOL,	deference	DEFRNS, DEF/RENS
			KRAOE/YO/SOL	deferens	DEFRNZ, DEF/RENZ
collip	see clip	cresol	KRAOE/SOL	difference	DIFRNS, DIF/FRENS
		cretin	see creatine		

deferential	DEFRN/-RBL, DEF/REN/-RBL		draft	DRAFT	
differential	DIFRN/-RBL, DIF/FREN/-RBL		draught	DRA*FT, DRAUFT	

deferential DEFRN/-RBL,
DEF/REN/-RBL
differential DIFRN/-RBL,
DIF/FREN/-RBL

defuse DE/FAOUZ
diffuse DIF/FAOUS,
DIF/FAOUZ

delusion DLAOUGS,
DE/LAOUGS
dilution DI/LAOUGS

deme *see deem*

dens DENZ
dense DENS

depravation DEP/RA/VAIGS
deprivation DEP/RI/VAIGS

Descemet DES/SE/MAI
December may DES/MAI

descent *see decent*

di- DI
dia- DAOI
die DAOI
dye DAO*I

diad DI/AD
dyad DAOI/AD, D*I/AD

diarrhea DAOI/RAOE/YA
diurea DI/YAOU/RAOE/YA

diaschisis DI/AS/KI/SIS
diastasis DI/A*S/SIS
diathesis DI/A*T/SIS

die *see di-*

dieretic DI/RET/IK
diuretic DI/YAOU/RET/IK,
DAOI/RET/IK

differ *see defer*
difference *see deference*
differential *see deferential*
diffuse *see defuse*

dilatation DIL/TAIGS
dilation DI/LAIGS

dilution *see delusion*

dine DAOIN
dyne DAO*IN

diseased *see deceased*

disburse DIS/BURS
disperse DIS/PERS

disc DIS/*K
disk DIS/-K

discreet DIS/KRAOET
discrete DIS/KRAET

disillusion DIS/IL/LAOUGS
dissolution DIS/SLAOUGS,
DIS/SO/LAOUGS

disk *see disc*
disperse *see disburse*
dissent *see decent*
diurea *see diarrhea*
diuretic *see dieretic*

dol DO*EL
dole DOEL

done *see dun*

drachm DRA*M
dram DRAM

draft DRAFT
draught DRA*FT, DRAUFT

dun DUN
Dunn D*UN
done DOEN

dural DAOURL
do you recall DAO*URL

durum DAOUR/UM,
DAOU/RUM
do you remember DAOURM

Duval DAOU/VAUL, DU/VAL
due value DAOU/VAL

dyad *see diad*
dye *see di-*
dyne *see dine*

dyseneia DIS/E/NAOE/YA
dyspnea DIS/NAOE/YA

effect *see affect*
efferent *see afferent*

effusion E/FAOUGS,
EF/FAOUGS
infusion IN/FAOUGS

either E/THER
ether E*/THER,
AO*ET/ER

eleven LEVN
levan LEV/VAN
Levin LEV/VIN

elicit E/LIS/SIT
illicit IL/LIS/SIT

Elschnig EL/-RB/NIG,
EL/SH-/NIG
else anything ELS/NIG

elusion E/LAOUGS
elution E/LAO*UGS
illusion IL/LAOUGS

emaciated E/MAIS/YAIT/-D,
E/MAIRB/YAIT/-D
emancipated E/MANS/PAIT/-D

end END
endo- *END, EN/DO

endogenous EN/DOJ/NOUS
indigenous IN/DIJ/NOUS

endoneural *END/NAOURL
endoneurial *END/NAOUR/YAL

enervate EN/ER/VAIT
innervate IN/NER/VAIT

enuresis *see anuresis*

epineural EP/NAOURL
epineurial EP/NAOUR/YAL

er- *ER
-er ER

erupt E/RUPT
irrupt IR/RUPT

essay *see assay*

est- ES/T-
-est *ES

ester ES/TER
-est er- *ES/ER

esterase ES/TRAIS, ES/TER/AIS
-est race *ES/RAIS
Estrace ES/TRA*IS

ether *see either*
eversion *see aversion*

ex- EX, KP-
exo- KPO, EK/SO

exacerbate KPAS/BAIT,
KPAS/ER/BAIT
exaggerate KPAJ/RAIT
exasperate KPAS/PRAIT

executor KPEK/TOR
exsector EX/SEK/TOR

excision KPIGS
incision IN/SIGS

excite KPAOIT
excito- KPAOI/TO, EX/SAOI/TO

expectorate EX/PEK/TRAIT
expect rate EX/PEKT/RAIT,
KP-PT/RAIT

expiration EX/PRAIGS,
EX/PI/RAIGS
extirpation EX/TIR/PAIGS
extrication EX/TRI/KAIGS

exsector *see executor*
extirpation *see expiration*

extorsion EX/TO*RGS
extortion EX/TORGS

extrication *see expiration*

facet FA/SET
facette FA/S*ET

facial FAIRBL
fascial FARBL

failing FAIL/-G
Fehling FAI/LING, FE/LING
felling FEL/-G

fantasy FANT/SI
phantasy FA*NT/SI

farad FA/RAD, FA*R/AD
far ad- FAR/AD
far rad- FAR/RAD

fascial *see facial*

faze FAIZ
phase FAEZ

Fehling *see failing*

fel F*EL
fell FEL
Fell K-P/FEL

felling *see failing*

ferri- FER/RI
ferro- FER, FER/RO

Fiberall FAOIB/RAUL
fiber all FAOI/BER/AUL,
FAOIB/ER/AUL

Fick F*IK
if I can FIK

fila FAOI/LA
phyla FAO*I/LA

filamen FIL/LA/MEN,
F*IL/MEN
fill men FIL/MEN

file FAOIL
phial FAO*IL, FAOI/YAL

filet FI/LAI
fillet FIL/ET, FIL/LAI

filter	FIL/TER, FILT/ER
philter	F*IL/TER, F*ILT/ER
filtrum	FIL/TRUM
philtrum	F*IL/TRUM
filum	FAOI/LUM, FAOIL/UM
phylum	FAO*I/LUM, FAO*IL/UM
finish	FIN/IRB
Finnish	FIN/NIRB
fiscal	FIS/KAL
physical	FIZ/KAL
flagella	FLA/JEL/LA
flagellula	FLA/JEL/YAOU/LA, FLA/JEL/YU/LA
flair	FLAIR
flare	FLAER
flea	FLAE
flee	FLAOE
flecks	FLEK/-S
flex	FLEX
floc	FLO*K
flock	FLOK
flew	FLAOU
flu	FLU
flue	FLAO*U
fluidounce	FLAOUD/O*UNS
fluid ounce	FLAOUD/OUNS
forage	FOR/AJ
forge	FORJ
forcipressure	FOR/SI/PRERB/SHUR
force pressure	FORS/PRERB/SHUR
form	FORM
forme	FO*RM
forum	FOR/UM
formal	FOR/MAL
formyl	FOR/MIL
formication	FORM/KAIGS
fornication	FORN/KAIGS
fraise	FRA*IZ, FRAEZ
phrase	FRAIZ
frenectomy	FRE/NEKT/M*I
phrenectomy	FR*E/NEKT/M*I
frenetic	FRE/NET/IK
phrenetic	FR*E/NET/IK
Friedman	FRAOED/MAN
Friedmann	FRAO*ED/MAN, FRAOED/MA*N
fulgurant	FULG/RANT, FUL/GU/RANT
full grant	FUL/GRANT
fulgurate	FULG/RAIT, FUL/GU/RAIT
full grate	FUL/GRAIT
fungal	FUNG/GAL, F*UN/GAL
fun gal	FUN/GAL
gage	GAEJ
gauge	GAIJ
gait	GAIT
gate	GAET
galactophagous	GAL/AK/TOF/GOUS, GLAK/TOF/GOUS
galactophygous	GAL/AK/TOF/GO*US, GLAK/TOF/GO*US
gangliate	GAN/GLAIT, CANG/LAOE/AIT, GAN/GLAOE/AIT
gang late	GANG/LAIT
gardener	GARD/NER
Gardner	GA*RD/NER, GARD/N*ER
gate	*see gait*
gauge	*see gage*
gel	JEL
jell	J*EL
general	JEN
geno-	J*EN, JEN/NO
genes	JAOEN/-S
jeans	JAEN/-S
Ghon	G*ON
gone	GON
glance	GLANS
glans	GLANZ
glands	GLANDZ
glutaea	GLAOU/TAE/YA
glutea	GLAOUT/YA
glutaeae	GLAOU/TAE/YAE
gluteae	GLAOUT/YAE
glutaei	GLAOU/TAE/YAOI
glutei	GLAOUT/YAOI
gone	*see Ghon*
gray	GRAI
grey	GRA*I
grip	GRIP
grippe	GR*IP
groan	GROEN
grown	GROUN
hafnium	HAF/NAOE/UM, HAF/NAOE/YUM
half numb	HAF/NUM
hale	HA*IL
Hale	K-P/HA*IL
hail	HAIL
heal	HAEL
heel	HAOEL
hallices	HAL/LI/SAOEZ
halluces	HAL/SAOEZ
hapten	HAPT/-N, HA*P/TEN
happen ten	HAP/TEN
Hauch	HO*UK
how can	HOUK
hay	HAI
hey	HA*I
Hey	K-P/HA*I
heal	HAEL
heel	HAOEL
hear	HAER
here	HAOER
heartbeat	HART/BA*ET
heart beat	HART/BAET
heater	HAOET/ER
Hueter	HAOE/TER
heck	HEK
Hueck	H*EK
heel	*see heal*
Heinz	HAOINZ
Heyns	HAO*INZ
Hines	HAOINS
hemarthrosis	HEM/AR/THROE/SIS
hemiarthrosis	H*EM/AR/THROE/SIS, HEM/MI/AR/THROE/SIS
Hemofil	HAO*EM/FIL, HAOEM/F*IL
hemophil	HAOEM/FIL
herbal	HERBL
Heschl	HERB/-L
here	*see hear*
Hering	H*ER/-G
herring	HER/-G
Hermann	H*ER/MAN, HER/MA*N
her man	HER/MAN
heroin	HER/ROIN
heroine	HER/RO*IN
her win	HER/WIN
herring	*see Hering*
Heschl	*see herbal*
heteronomous	HET/RON/MOUS
heteronymous	HET/RO*N/MOUS, HET/RON/MO*US
hey	*see hay*
Hey	*see hay*
Heyns	*see Heinz*
hide	HAOID
Hyde	HAO*ID
hidradenitis	HAOI/DRAD/NAOITS
hydradenitis	HAO*I/DRAD/NAOITS
hidradenoma	HAOI/DRAD/NOE/MA
hydradenoma	HAO*I/DRAD/NOE/MA
hidrorrhea	HID/RO/RAOE/YA, HAO*I/DRO/RAOE/YA
hydrorrhea	HAOI/DRO/RAOE/YA
hila	HAOI/LA
hyla	HAO*I/LA
hilitis	HAOI/LAOITS
hyalitis	HAO*I/LAOITS, HAOI/YA/LAOITS
Hines	*see Heinz*
hoarse	HAORS
horse	HOERS, HORS
Hoffmann	HOF/MA*N
Hofmann	HOF/MAN
hole	HOEL
whole	WHOEL
homogeneous	HOEM/JAOEN/YOUS
homogenous	HOE/MOJ/NOUS
homonomous	HOE/MON/MOUS
homonymous	HOE/MO*N/MOUS, HOE/MON/MO*US
horse	*see hoarse*
Howell	HOU/EL
howl	HOUL
Hueck	*see heck*
Hueter	*see heater*

humeral	HAOUM/RAL	
humoral	HAOU/MORL	
humerus	HAOUM/RUS	
humorous	HAOUM/ROUS	
Hurricaine	H*UR/KAIN, HUR/KA*IN	
hurricane	HUR/KAIN	
Hurthle	HUR/TEL, HURT/EL	
hurtle	HURT/-L	
hyalin	HAOI/LIN	
hyaline	HAOI/LAOIN, HAOI/LAOEN, HAO*I/LIN	
hyalitis	*see hyalitis*	
Hyde	*see hide*	
hydradenitis	*see hidradenitis*	
hydradenoma	*see hidradenoma*	
hydrorrhea	*see hidrorrhea*	
hyla	*see hila*	
hymen	HAOIM/-N, HAO*I/MEN	
high men	HAOI/MEN	
hyper	HAOIP/ER	
hyper-	HAO*IP, HAOI/PER	
hypo-	HO*IP, HAOI/PO	
hypergnosis	HAO*IP/NOE/SIS	
hyperinosis	HAO*IP/IN/NOE/SIS	
hyperthermesthesia	HAO*IP/THER/MES/THAOEZ/YA	
hyperthermoesthesia	HAO*IP/THERM/ES/THAOEZ/YA	
ideo-	AOID/YO	
idio-	ID/YO	
if I can	*see Fick*	
ile(o)-	*IL/Y(O)	
ili(o)-	IL/Y(O)	
ileac	*IL/YAK	
iliac	IL/YAK	
ileocolotomy	*IL/YO/KO/LOT/M*I	
iliocolotomy	IL/YO/KO/LOT/M*I	
ileostomy	*IL/YO*S/M*I	
iliostomy	IL/YO*S/M*I	
ileum	*IL/YUM	
ilium	IL/YUM	
illicit	*see elicit*	
illinition	IL/IN/NIGS, IL/LI/NIGS	
ill in addition	IL/NIGS	
illusion	*see elusion*	
incision	*see excision*	
incite	IN/SAOIT	
inosite	IN/NO/SAOIT	
indigenous	*see endogenous*	
infarction	IN/FA*RBGS	
infraction	IN/FRA*BGS	
infusion	*see effusion*	
innervate	*see enervate*	
inosite	*see incite*	
insolation	IN/SOE/LAIGS	
insulation	INS/LAIGS	
inter-	SPWER	
intra-	SPWRA	
interior	*see anterior*	
intrachondral	SPWRA/KON/DRAL	
intrachondrial	SPWRA/KON/DRAOEL, SPWRA/KON/DRAOE/YAL	
irrupt	*see erupt*	
jeans	*see genes*	
jell	*see gel*	
jewel	JAOUL	
joule	JAO*UL	
Joule	K-P/JAO*UL	
juggler	JUG/LER	
jugular	JUG/LAR, JUG/YAOU/LAR, JUG/YU/LAR	
Jung	YAOUNG, Y*UNG, JUNG	
young	YUNG	
Juneau	JAOU/NOE	
Junod	JAOU/NOED	
Kaplan	*see Caplan*	
karyology	*see cariology*	
karyon	*see carrion*	
keel	KAOEL	
Kiel	KAO*EL	
keirospasm	*see cheirospasm*	
Kilian	K*IL/YAN	
Killian	KIL/YAN	
kill	KIL	
kiln	K*IL, KIL/-N	
Kirk	K*IRK	
can I recollect	KIRK	
Klein	*see cline*	
Klieg	*see colleague*	
Klinger	*see clinger*	
Knapp	NA*P	
nap	NAP	
knead	NAED, NAO*ED	
need	NAOED	
knit	N*IT	
nit	NIT	
knot	NO*T	
not	NOT	
known	NOEN	
nona-	NOE/NA	
Koch	*see coke*	
Kocks	*see coax*	
Kopp	*see cop*	
Korea	*see chorea*	
Kruse	*see cruise*	
Kulp	*see Culp*	
Kwell	KW*EL	
quell	KWEL	
label	LAI/BEL, LAIB/EL	
labial	LAIB/YAL	
labile	LAI/BAOIL, LAI/BIL	
lac	LA*K	
lack	LAK	
lace	LAIS	
lase	LA*IZ, LAEZ	
laze	LAIZ	
lad	LAD	
Ladd	LA*D	
lain	LAIN	
lane	LAEN	
Lane	K-P/LAEN	
lair	LAIR	
layer	LAI/ER, LAI/YER	
lase	*see lace*	
Laurence	LA*URNS, LA*UR/ENS	
Lawrence	LAURNS, LAUR/ENS	
layer	*see lair*	
laze	*see lace*	
leaching	LAEFP/-G	
leeching	LAOEFP/-G	
lead	LAED, LAOED	
led	LED	
leak	LAEK	
leek	LAOEK	
led	*see lead*	
leeching	*see leaching*	
leek	*see leak*	
lema	LAO*E/MA	
Lima	LAOE/MA	
lentiform	LEN/TI/FORM	
lent form	LENT/FORM	
leukotherapy	LAOUK/THER/PI	
lucotherapy	LAO*UK/THER/PI	
levan	*see eleven*	
Levi	LAI/VAOE	
Loewi	LA*I/VAOE	
low	LOE	
Lowe	LO*E, LAI/VE	
Levin	*see eleven*	
Lewis	LAO*U/WIS	
Louis	LAOU/WIS	
lewisite	LAOU/WI/SAOIT, LAO*U/SAOIT	
Lucite	LAOU/SAOIT	
lichen	LAOI/KEN	
liken	LAOIK/-N	
lichenin	LAOI/KEN/NIN, LAOI/KE/NIN	
like anyone	LAOIK/NIN	
licorice	LIK/RIS, LIK/RIRB	
liquorice	L*IK/RIS, L*IK/RIRB	
lie	LAOI	
lye	LAO*I	
lien	LAOI/-N	
line	LAOIN	
lightening	LAOIGT/-NG	
lightning	LAOIGT/NING	
liken	*see lichen*	
Lima	*see lema*	
lime	LAOIM	
Lyme	LAO*IM	
limp	LIFRP	
lymph	LIM/-F	
line	*see lien*	
lion	LAOI/YON	
Lyon	LAO*I/YON	
lipedema	LIP/DAOE/MA	
lipoedema	LIP/E/DAOE/MA	

liquorice	*see licorice*	mandarin	MAND/RIN, MAN/DA/RIN	mil	M*IL
		mandrin	MAN/DRIN	mill	MIL
literal	LIT/RAL				
littoral	LIT/TRAL, LIT/TORL	manikin	MA*N/KIN, MAN/K*IN	Miller	MIL/ER
		mannequin	MAN/KIN	Muller	K-P/MUL/ER, MAOUL/ER
liter	LAOET/ER, LAOE/TER	mannoside	MAN/NO/SAOID		
Littre	LAOET/TER	man side	MAN/SAOID	*mio-*	*see meio-*
				miocardia	MAO*I/KARD/YA
lock	LOK	*Maolate*	*see malate*	myocardia	MAOI/KARD/YA
Locke	LO*K				
		marble	MAR/-BL, MARB/-L	miosis	*see meiosis*
Loeffler	LE*F/LER	marshal	MAR/-RBL	*miotic*	*see meiotic*
Loffler	LEF/LER	Marshall	MA*R/-RBL, MAR/*RBL		
				mistax	MIS/TAX
Loestrin	LO/ES/TRIN	marc	MAR/*K	mystax	M*IS/TAX
low estrin	LOE/ES/TRIN	mark	MARK		
		Mark	MA*RK, K-P/MARK	moaner	MOEN/ER
Loewi	*see Levi*			moner	MOE/NER
Loffler	*see Loeffler*	Marchi	MAR/KAO*E, MA*R/KAOE		
Louis	*see Lewis*	marquee	MAR/KAOE	Moerner	MERN/ER
low	*see Levi*			Morner	M*ERN/ER
Lowe	*see Levi*	Mariotte	MAR/YOT		
		Marriott	MAIR/YOT	mol	MO*L
Luc	L*UK			moll	MOL
luck	LUK	*mark*	*see marc*		
		Mark	*see marc*	mold	MOELD
Lucite	*see lewisite*	*marshal*	*see marble*	mould	MO*ELD, MOULD
lucotherapy	*see leukotherapy*	*Marshall*	*see marble*		
				molt	MOELT
lues	LAOU/WAOEZ	mascot	MAS/KOT	moult	MO*ELT, MOULT
Luys	LAO*U/WAOEZ	massicot	MAS/SI/KOT, MAS/KO*T, MASZ/KOT		
				moner	*see moaner*
lycine	LAO*I/SIN				
lysin	LAOI/SIN	mastoccipital	MAS/TOK/SIP/TAL	moral	MORL
		masto-occipital	MA*S/OK/SIP/TAL	morale	MO/RAL
lye	*see lie*			more al-	MOR/AL/-
Lyme	*see lime*	mater	MAI/TER, MAIT/ER, MAU/TER, MAUT/ER		
lymph	*see limp*			Morison	MOR/SON
Lyon	*see lion*	matter	MAT/ER	Morrison	MOR/RI/SON
lyse	LAOIZ	*maul*	*see mal*	morn	MORN
lyze	LAO*IZ			mourn	MOURN
		maybe	MAIB		
mace	MAIS	may be	MAI/B-	*Morner*	*see Moerner*
maise	MA*IZ			*mould*	*see mold*
maize	MAIZ	*mayer*	*see Maier*	*moult*	*see molt*
maze	MAEZ	*mayor*	*see Maier*		
		maze	*see mace*	Much	MAO*UK
macro-	MAK/RO			muco-	MAOUK
micro-	MAOI/KRO	meio-	MAO*I		
		mio-	MAOI	mucous	MAOU/KOUS, MAOUK/OUS
made	MAED	myo-	MAOI		
maid	MAID			mucus	MAOU/KUS
		meiogenic	MAO*I/JEN/IK		
Magonate	MA*G/NAIT	myogenic	MAOI/JEN/IK	multangular	MUL/TANG/LAR
magnate	MAG/NAIT			multiangular	MULT/ANG/LAR
		meiosis	MAO*I/YOE/SIS		
maid	*see made*	miosis	MAOI/YOE/SIS	multiparity	MULT/PAIR/TI
				multiparty	MULT/PAR/TI
Maier	MA*I/ER	meiotic	MAO*I/OT/IK, MAO*I/YOT/IK		
mayer	MAI/ER			my	MI
mayor	MAI/YOR	miotic	MAOI/OT/IK, MAOI/YOT/IK	-my	M*I
mail	MAIL			myatonia	MAOI/YA/TOEN/YA, MAOI/AI/TOEN/YA
male	MAEL	meletin	MEL/TIN		
		melitin	M*EL/TIN, MEL/LI/TIN	myotonia	MAOI/TOEN/YA
maise	*see mace*				
maize	*see mace*	Menaval	M*EN/VAL	*myo-*	*see meio-*
		men value	MEN/VAL	*myocardia*	*see miocardia*
mal	MA*L			*myogenic*	*see meiogenic*
mal-	MAL	menopause	M*EN/PAUZ, MEN/NO/PAUZ	*myotonia*	*see myatonia*
mall	MAL			*mystax*	*see mixtax*
maul	MAUL	men pause	MEN/PAUZ		
				Naegeli	NAEG/LAOE
malate	MAI/LAIT	menses	M*EN/SAOEZ, MEN/SAO*EZ, MENS/AOEZ	Nagele	NAIG/LAOE
Maolate	MAI/YO/LAIT				
				nap	*see Knapp*
maldevelopment	MA*L/DWOP/-MT, MA*L/DE/VEL/OP/-MT	men seize	MEN/SAOEZ		
				nasal	NAI/ZAL
mall development	MAL/DWOP/-MT, etc.	merit	MER/RIT	NaSal	NAI/SAL
		Merritt	M*ER/RIT		
male	*see mail*			nasion	NAIZ/YON
mall	*see mal*	*micro-*	*see macro-*	nation	NAIGS
mammaplasty	MAM/MA/PLAS/TI			naval	NAIVL, NAI/VAL
mammoplasty	MAM/PLAS/TI			navel	NAI/VEL, NAIV/EL

need	see knead	osmio-	OZ/MAOE, OS/MAOE, OZ/MAOE/YO, OS/MAOE/YO	paracytic	PAR/SAO*IT/IK, PAR/SAOI/TIK, PAR/S*IT/IK
Neisser	NAOI/SER, NAOIS/SER	osmo-	OZ/MO	parasitic	PAR/SIT/IK
nicer	NAOIS/ER	osmol	OZ/MOL	parental	PA/REN/TAL
nervous	NEFRB/OUS, NER/VOUS	osmole	OZ/MOEL	parenteral	PA/RENT/RAL
nervus	NER/VUS	osone	O/SOEN	parity	PAIR/TI, PAR/RI/TI
Neumann	NOI/MAN, NAO*U/MAN	ozone	O/ZOEN	party	PAR/TI
knew man	NAOU/MAN	osteal	O*S/YA*L, OS/TAOE/YAL	*Pasini*	see Pacini
Newcastle	NAOU/KAS/-L, NAOU/KA*S/-L	ostial	O*S/YAL	Pasteur	PAS/TAOUR
new castle	NU/KAS/-L	out	OUT	pastor	PAS/TOR
niacin	NAOI/SIN	out-	O*UT	pasture	PAS/KHUR
nisin	NAO*I/SIN	-out	O*UT	*Paul*	see pal
nib	see anybody	over	OEFR, OEVR	paver	PAIVR
nicer	see Neisser	over-	OVR	pavor	PAI/VOR
nisin	see niacin	-over	OFR	*Payne*	see pain
nit	see knit	*ozone*	see osone	Payr	PAO*IR
nitrile	NAOI/TRIL	Pacini	PA/KHAOE/NAOE	pyre	PAOIR
nitryl	NAOI/TR*IL	Pasini	PA/SAOE/NAOE	pea	PAE
nona-	see known	Palade	PAL/LAID, PA/LAID	pee	PAOE
not	see knot	pal aid	PAL/AID	pis	PAO*E
nucleide	NAOUK/LAOID	pail	PAIL	peace	PAES
nuclide	NAOU/KLAOID	pale	PA*IL	piece	PAOES
nutricius	NAOU/TRIS/YUS	peal	PAEL	peak	PAEK
nutritious	NAOU/TRIRBS	pain	PAIN	peek	PAOEK
oaken	OEK/-N	pane	PAEN	pique	PAO*EK
Oken	O/KEN	Payne	PA*IN	*peal*	see pail
od	O*D	pal	PAL	pedal	PED/DAL
odd	OD	pall	PAUL	peddle	PED/-L
Oken	see oaken	Paul	PA*UL	petal	PET/TAL
onco-	ON/KO	palate	PAL/LAT	*pee*	see pea
onycho-	OIN/KO, O/NIK, ON/NI/KO	palette	PAL/ET	*peek*	see peak
oncolysis	ON/KOL/SIS	pallet	PAL/LET	peer	PAOER
onycholysis	OIN/KOL/SIS	*pale*	see pail	pier	PAO*ER
oncosis	ON/KOE/SIS	palisade	PA*L/SAID, PAL/SAED, PAL/LI/SAID	penal	PAOENL, PAOE/NAL
onychosis	OIN/KOE/SIS	pal said	PAL/SAID	penile	PAOE/NAOIL
oncotomy	ON/KOT/M*I	*pall*	see pal	per	PER
onychotomy	OIN/KOT/M*I	*pallet*	see palate	per-	PER
oracle	see auricle	palpate	PAL/PAIT	peri-	P*ER, PER/RI
oral	see aural	palpitate	PAL/PI/TAIT	pero-	PER, PER/RO
orchic	ORK/IK	*pane*	see pain	per annum	PER/AN/UM
or kick	OR/KIK	pantamorphia	PAN/TA/MOR/FAOE/YA, PAN/TA/MOR/FA	per anum	PER/AI/NUM, PER/AIN/UM
orchid	ORK/ID	pantomorphia	PANT/MOR/FAOE/YA	perineal	P*ER/NAOEL
or kid	OR/KID	pantamorphic	PAN/TA/MOR/FIK	peroneal	PER/NAOEL
orifice	OR/RI/FIS, O*R/FIS	pantomorphic	PANT/MOR/FIK	perineural	P*ER/NAOURL
or fis-	OR/FIS	pantaphobia	PAN/TA/FOEB/YA	perineurial	P*ER/NAOUR/YAL
orificial	OR/RI/FIRBL	pantophobia	PANT/FOEB/YA	perioral	P*ER/ORL
or official	OR/FIRBL	papilla	PA/PIL/LA	peroral	PER/OR/RAL, PER/O*RL
origin	ORJ, O*R/JIN, ORJ/JIN	papillula	PA/PIL/YAOU/LA, PA/PIL/YU/LA	per oral	PER/ORL
or gin	OR/JIN	papillae	PA/PIL/LAE	pernio	PERN/YO*E, P*ERN/YOE
oris	OR/RIS	papillulae	PA/PIL/YAOU/LAE, PA/PIL/YU/LAE	person owe	PERN/YOE
orris	OER/RIS	papilliferous	PAP/LIF/ROUS	*peroneal*	see perineal
Os-Cal	O*S/KAL, OS/H-F/KAL	papuliferous	PAP/YAOU/LIF/ROUS, PAP/YU/LIF/ROUS, PA/P/LIF/ROUS	*peroral*	see perioral
oscheal	OS/KAL			*petal*	see pedal
-oscopy	OS/KPI	papyraceus	PAP/RAIS/YUS	petit	PET/TAOE
-ostomy	O*S/M*I	papyraceous	PAP/RAIRBS	Petit	PE/TAOE
-otomy	OT/M*I			petty	PET/TI
				phantasy	see fantasy
				phase	see faze
				phial	see file

Philips	FIL/IPS	poor	PAOR	retch	REFP
Phillips	FIL/LIPS	por-	POR	wretch	WREFP
		pore	POER		
philter	*see filter*	pour	POUR	retrocolic	RET/RO/KOL/IK
philtrum	*see filtrum*	power	POU/ER	retrocollic	RET/RO/KOL/LIK
phon	FO*EN	Portagen	POR/TA/JEN,	*rile*	*see Reil*
phone	FOEN		PO*RT/JEN		
		port general(ly)	PORT/JEN	Roux	RAO*U
phosphene	FOS/FAOEN			rue	RAOU
phosphine	FOS/FAO*EN,	post	PO*ES		
	FOS/FIN	post-	PO*S	sac	SA*K
				sack	SAK
phosphorous	FOS/FROUS	pot	POT		
phosphorus	FOS/FRUS	Pott	PO*T	Sachs	SA*X
				sax	SAX
phrase	*see fraise*	*pour*	*see poor*		
phrenectomy	*see frenectomy*	*power*	*see poor*	said	SAID
phrenetic	*see frenetic*			sed	SED
phyla	*see fila*	principal	PRINS/PAL		
		principle	PRINS/P-L	salivation	SA*L/VAIGS,
phyloanalysis	FAOI/LO/AI/NAL/SIS,				SAL/VA*IGS
	FAOI/LO/ANL/SIS	prohibit	PRO/HIBT	salvation	SAL/VAIGS
file analysis	FAOIL/ANL/SIS,	ProHIBIT	PRO*/HIBT		
	FAOIL/AI/NAL/SIS			saucer	SAUS/ER
		prostate	PROS/TAIT	saw ser-; saw cer-	SAU/SER
phylum	*see filum*	prostrate	PROS/TRAIT		
physical	*see fiscal*			*sax*	*see Sachs*
		psi	SAO*I		
phytostearin	FAOIT/STAOE/RIN	sigh	SAOI	scene	SAEN
phytosterin	FAOIT/STAOER/RIN			seen	SAOEN
		psilosis	SAO*I/LOE/SIS		
picnic	PIK/NIK	sialosis	SAOI/LOE/SIS	*scent*	*see cent*
pyknic	P*IK/NIK				
		psilotic	SAO*I/LOT/IK	Schafer	SHAIFR, SHAIF/ER
piece	*see peace*	sialotic	SAOI/LOT/IK	Shaeffer	SHAEFR, SHAEF/ER
pier	*see peer*			Shaffer	SHAIF/FER
		psychosis	SAOI/KOE/SIS		
pila	PAOI/LA	sycosis	SAO*I/KOE/SIS	Scheiner	SHAO*IN/ER,
pyla	PAO*I/LA				SHAOI/NER
		psyllium	*see cilium*	shiner	SHAOIN/ER
pilar	PAOI/LAR				
pylar	PAO*I/LAR	ptilosis	TAO*I/LOE/SIS	Schiller	SHIL/ER
		tylosis	TAOI/LOE/SIS	Schuller	SH*IL/ER, SHUL/ER
pillar	PIL/LAR				
pilular	PIL/YAOU/LAR,	pullulate	PUL/YAOU/LAIT,	schilling	SH*IL/-G
	PIL/YU/LAR		PUL/YU/LAIT	Schilling	K-P/SH*IL/-G
		pull late	PUL/LAIT	shilling	SHIL/-G
pique	*see peak*				
		puriform	PAOUR/RI/FORM,	Schneider	SH-/NAOID/ER,
piriform	PIR/FORM		PAOU/RI/FORM		SH-/NAOI/DER
pyriform	P*IR/FORM	pure form	PAOUR/FORM	Snider	SNAOID/ER,
					SNAOI/DER
pis	*see pea*	*pyknic*	*see picnic*	Snyder	SNAO*ID/ER,
		pyla	*see pila*		SNAO*I/DER
plain	PLAIN	*pylar*	*see pilar*		
plane	PLAEN	*pyre*	*see Payr*	*Schuller*	*see Schiller*
		pyriform	*see piriform*		
plait	PLAIT	*quell*	*see Kwell*	Schurmann	SH*UR/MAN
plate	PLAET			Sherman	SHER/MAN
		radical	RAD/KAL	sure man	SHAOUR/MAN,
Planck	PLA*N/-K	radicle	RAD/K-L		SHUR/MAN
plank	PLAN/-K, PLA*NG				
		radices	RAI/DI/SAOEZ,	*scirrhous*	*see cirrous*
plane	*see plain*		RAD/SAOEZ		
		raid seize(d)	RAID/SAOEZ	scission	S*IGS, SIZ/YON
planula	PLAN/YAOU/LA,			situation	SIGS
	PLAN/YU/LA	rasion	RA*IGS, RAIZ/YON		
plan la-	PLAN/LA	ration	RAIGS	*se-*	*see ce-*
				sea	*see ce-*
plasma	PLAZ/MA	Rau	RO*U	*seal*	*see -cele*
plasmia	PLAZ/MAOE/YA	row	ROU		
		raw	RAU	seam	SAEM
plate	*see plait*			seem	SAOEM
		ray	RAI		
pleural	PLAOURL	re	R*E	seamen	SAE/MEN
plural	PLURL	re-	RE	semen	SE/MEN
plumber	PLUM/ER	read	RAED	*sed*	*see said*
Plummer	PL*UM/ER,	red	RED	*see*	*see ce-*
	PLUM/MER	reed	RAOED	*seem*	*see seam*
		Reid	RAO*ED	*seen*	*see scene*
plural	*see pleural*				
		Reil	RAO*IL	Seignette	SAO*IN/YET,
pneusis	NAO*U/SIS	rile	RAOIL		SAOIN/Y*ET
knew sis	NAOU/SIS			sign yet	SAOIN/YET
		renes	RE/NAOEZ		
pollster	POEL/STER	Renese	RE/NAOES	*self-*	*see self*
polster	POL/STER			*sell*	*see cel*

sella	*see cella*	sync	SIN/*K	striker	STRAOIK/ER
sellae	*see cellae*	zinc	S*IN/-K	Stryker	STRAO*IK/ER
sellar	*see cellar*				
seller	*see cellar*	sinister	SIN/STER	*Stuart*	*see Stewart*
semen	*see seamen*	Zinsser	S*IN/SER, S*INS/SER		
sensor	*see censer*			subnasion	SUB/NAIZ/YON,
sent	*see cent*	sister	S*IS/ER		SUB/NAIS/YON
sera	*see cera*	xyster	ZIS/TER	subnation	SUB/NAIGS
serene	SE/RAOEN	*site*	*see cite*	suet	SAOU/ET
serine	SER/AOEN	*sito-*	*see cyto-*	suit	SAOUT
		sitology	*see cytology*		
serial	*see cereal*	*sitotaxis*	*see cytotaxis*	super	SAOUP/ER
		sitotherapy	*see cytotherapy*	super-	SAO*UP, SU/PER
serious	SAOER/YOUS	*sitotoxin*	*see cytotoxin*	supra-	SU/PRA
serous	SAOER/OUS	*sitotropism*	*see cytotropism*		
	(also see cirrous)	*situation*	*see scission*	sura	SAOU/RA
		Snider	*see Schneider*	surra	SAOUR/RA
sero-fast	SAOER/H-F/FA*S,	*Snyder*	*see Schneider*		
	SAOER/RO/FA*S	*so*	*see sew*	*sycosis*	*see psychosis*
sere fast	SAOER/FA*S			*Sylvius*	*see Silvius*
		solanoid	SOE/LA/NOID	*symplex*	*see simplex*
serous	*see cirrous*	solenoid	SOEL/NOID	*Syms*	*see Sims*
serum	*see cerium*			*sync*	*see sing*
session	*see cession*	sole	SOEL		
		soul	SOUL	taedium	TAED/YUM
sew	SOE			tedium	TAOED/YUM
so	SO	*sow*	*see sew*		
sow	SO*E			taeni-	TAEN/Y-
		spay	SPAI	teni-	TAOEN/Y-
Shaeffer	*see Schafer*	Spee	SPA*I		
Shaffer	*see Schafer*			tale	TAEL
		spermatoxin	SPER/MA/TOK/SIN	teal	TAOEL
shear	SHAER	spermotoxin	SPERM/TOK/SIN	Teale	TAO*EL
sheer	SHAOER				
		sphenoccipital	SFAOE/NOK/SIP/TAL	tare	TA*ER
sheath	SHA*ET	spheno-occipital	SFAOEN/OK/SIP/TAL	tear	TAER, TAIR
sheathe	SHAO*ET			tier	TAOER
		sporont	SPOR/RONT		
sheer	*see shear*	spore on the	SPOR/ONT	taught	TAUGT
				taut	TAUT
shellac	SHEL/LAK	stabile	STAI/BAOIL, STAI/BIL		
she lack	SHE/LAK	stable	STAIBL	*teal*	*see tale*
				Teale	*see tale*
Sherman	*see Schurmann*	Stahl	STA*UL	*tear*	*see tare*
shilling	*see schilling*	stall	STAUL		
shiner	*see Scheiner*			tech	TEK
		Stahr	STA*R	theque	T*EK
shrapnel	SHRAP/NEL,	star	STAR		
	SH-/RAP/NEL			*tedium*	*see taedium*
Shrapnell	SHRAP/N*EL,	staff	STAF		
	SHRA*P/NEL,	staph	STA*F	tendinitis	TEND/NAOITS
	SH-/RAP/N*EL,			tendonitis	TEN/DO/NAOITS
	SH-/RA*P/NEL	stair	STAIR		
		stare	STAER	*teni-*	*see taeni-*
sialosis	*see psilosis*				
sialotic	*see psilotic*	*stall*	*see Stahl*	tenofibril	TEN/NO/FAOI/BRIL,
		staph	*see staff*		T*EN/FAOI/BRIL
sic	S*IK	*star*	*see Stahr*	ten fibril(s)	TEN/FAOI/BRIL
sick	SIK				
		steal	STAEL	tenoplastic	TEN/NO/PLA*S/IK
side	*see -cide*	steel	STAOEL	ten plastic	TEN/PLA*S/IK
sigh	*see psi*				
sight	*see cite*	stearic	STAOER/IK	tenosuture	TEN/NO/SAOU/KHUR
		steric	STER/IK	ten suture(s)	TEN/SAOU/KHUR
Silvius	S*IL/VAOE/YUS,				
	S*IL/VUS	*steel*	*see steal*	terebenthene	TER/BIN/THAOEN
Sylvius	SIL/VAOE/YUS,			terebenthine	TER/BIN/THIN
	SIL/VUS	steer	STAOER		
		stere	STAO*ER	terpin	TER/PIN
Similac	S*IM/LAK, SIM/LA*K,			terrapin	TER/RA/PIN
	SIM/MI/LAK	stella	STEL/LA		
similar lack	SIM/LAK	stellula	STEL/YAOU/LA,	Testaval	TES/TA/VAL
			STEL/YU/LA	test value	T*ES/VAL
simplex	SIM/PLEX				
symplex	S*IM/PLEX	stellae	STEL/LAE	Thane	THA*IN
		stellulae	STEL/YAOU/LAE,	that I know	THAIN
Sims	SIMZ, SIMS		STEL/YU/LAE		
Syms	S*IMZ, S*IMS			thenyl	THENL
		stere	*see steer*	then ill	THEN/IL
sinciput	SIN/SI/PUT	*steric*	*see stearic*		
since put(ting)	SINS/PUT			*theque*	*see tech*
		Stewart	STAOU/WART,		
Sine-Off	SAO*IN/AUF		STAO*URT	thermalgesia	THER/MAL/JAOEZ/YA
sign off	SAOIN/AUF	Stuart	STAOU/ART, STAOURT	thermoalgesia	THERM/AL/JAOEZ/YA
sing	SING	stirrup	STIR/RUP		
singe	SIN/-J	stir up	STIR/UP		
sink	SIN/-K				

thermanalgesia	THER/MANL/JAOEZ/YA	trance	TRANS	Walter	VAL/TER, VAUL/TER
thermoanalgesia	THERM/ANL/JAOEZ/YA	trans	TRANZ	Walther	VA*UL/TER, VA*L/TER
		trans-	TRA*NS		
thermanesthesia	THER/MANS/THAOEZ/YA	transection	TRAN/S*EBGS	ware	WAIR
	THER/MAN/ES/THAOEZ/YA	transsection	TRA*NS/S*EBGS	wear	WAER
thermoanesthesia	THERM/ANS/THAOEZ/YA	trap	TRAP	warn	WARN
		Trapp	TRA*P	Warren	WAR/-N, WAR/REN
thermesthesia	THER/MES/THAOEZ/YA	tri-	TR*I	Wart-Off	WART/H-F/AUF
thermoesthesia	THERM/ES/THAOEZ/YA	try	TRAOI	wart off	WART/AUF
		-try	TRI		
thermesthesiometer				waste	see waist
	THER/MES/THAOEZ/YOM/TER	trichogen	TR*IK/JEN, TRI/KO/JEN	wave	see waive
thermoesthesiometer		trick general(ly)	TRIK/JEN	way	WAI
	THERM/ES/THAOEZ/YOM/TER			-way	WA*I
		try	see tri-	weigh	WAIG
thiamin	THAOI/MIN	-try	see tri-		
thymin	THAO*I/MIN			weak	WAEK
thymine	THAOI/MAOEN	Turck	TAO*ERK, T*URK	week	WAOEK
		Turk	TAOERK, TURK		
thiazin	THAOI/ZIN			wear	see ware
thiozine	THAOI/ZAOEN	tylosis	see ptilosis	week	see weak
				weigh	see way
thing	THING	tympanites	TIFRP/NAOI/TAOEZ	weight	see wait
think	THI	tympanitis	TIFRP/NAOITS		
-thy	TH*I			wheal	WHAEL, WHAO*EL
		Tyndall	see Tindal	wheel	WHAOEL
thiozine	see thiozine	Uhl	YAO*UL		
		yule	YAOUL	whole	see hole
Thompson	TOFRP/SON, TOM/-P/SON			Widal	see Vidal
Thomson	TOM/SON	vail	VAIL	wild	WAOILD
		veil	VA*IL	Wilde	WAO*ILD
threonine	THRAOE/NAOEN, THRAOE/YO/NIN	vain	VAIN	wilder	WAOILD/ER
three anyone	THRAOE/NIN	vane	VAEN	Wilder	K-P/WAOILD/ER, WAOIL/DER, WAO*ILD/ER
		vein	VA*IN		
thyme	TAO*IM			wolf	WOL/-F
time	TAOIM	veil	see vail	Wolfe	WO*L/-F
				Wolff	VOL/-F, WOL/*F
thymin	see thiamin	venial	VAOEN/YAL	Woulfe	WOUL/-F, WUL/-F, WAOUL/-F
thymine	see thiamin	Vignal	VIN/YAL		
		venous	VAOEN/OUS, VAOE/NOUS	wretch	see retch
tic	T*IK	Venus	VAOE/NUS	xanthene	ZAN/THAOEN
tick	TIK			xanthin	ZAN/TH*IN
		vertebrarium	VERT/BRAIRM	xanthine	ZAN/THIN, ZAN/THAO*EN
tier	see tare	vertebrarum	VERT/BRAIR/UM, VERT/BRAI/RUM		
				xyster	see sister
tighter	TAOIGT/ER	vial	VAO*IL, VAOI/YAL		
titer	TAOIT/ER	vile	VAOIL	yoke	YO*EK
				yolk	YOEK
timber	TIM/BER	vicine	VAOI/SAOEN		
timbre	TAM/BER, TIM/BRE, T*IM/BER	Visine	VAOI/ZAOEN	young	see Jung
		Vidal	VI/DAL	yttrium	IT/RAOE/UM, IT/RAOE/YUM
time	see thyme	Widal	VAOE/DAL	it rum	IT/RUM
Tindal	TIN/DAL	Vignal	see venial	yule	see Uhl
Tyndall	T*IN/DAL	vile	see vial	zinc	see sing
				Zinsser	see sinister
titer	see tighter	viraginity	VAOIR/JIN/TI, VAOI/RA/JIN/TI, VIR/RA/JIN/TI		
today	TOD	virginity	VIR/JIN/TI	zip	ZIP
Todd	TO*D			zipp	ZIP/-P
		viscous	VIS/KOUS		
tong	TONG	viscus	VIS/KUS	zone	ZOEN
tongue	TUNG			-zoon	ZAON, ZOE/WON
		Visine	see vicine		
toponym	TOEP/NIM, TOE/PO/NIM	Voigt	VOIGT, VO*IT		
top anymore	TOP/NIM	Voit	VOIT		
ToppFast	TO*P/FA*S	waist	WA*IS		
top fast	TOP/FA*S	waste	WA*ES		
tore	TOER	wait	WAIT		
torr	TOR	weight	WAIGT		
		waive	WAIV		
		wave	WAEV		

APPENDIX 4

ALPHABETIC LETTERS & TEXT ENTRY COMMANDS

ALPHABETIC LETTERS FOR ACRONYMS AND INITIALS

TO APPEAR WITHOUT A PERIOD

Lower Case	Standing Alone	Attached to Left	Upper Case	Standing Alone	Attached to Left
a	A*	A*BGZ	A	ARBGS	A*RBGS
b	PW*	PW*BGZ	B	PW-RBGS	PW*RBGS
c	KR*	KR*BGZ	C	KR-RBGS	KR*RBGS
d	TK*	TK*BGZ	D	TK-RBGS	TK*RBGS
e	*E	*EBGZ	E	ERBGS	*ERBGS
f	TP*	TP*BGZ	F	TP-RBGS	TP*RBGS
g	TKPW*	TKPW*BGZ	G	TKPW-RBGS	TKPW*RBGS
h	H*	H*BGZ	H	H-RBGS	H*RBGS
i	*EU	*EUBGZ	I	EURBGS	*EURBGS
j	SKWR*	SKWR*BGZ	J	SKWR-RBGS	SKWR*RBGS
k	K*	K*BGZ	K	K-RBGS	K*RBGS
l	HR*	HR*BGZ	L	HR-RBGS	HR*RBGS
m	PH*	PH*BGZ	M	PH-RBGS	PH*RBGS
n	TPH*	TPH*BGZ	N	TPH-RBGS	TPH*RBGS
o	O*	O*BGZ	O	ORBGS	O*RBGS
p	P*	P*BGZ	P	P-RBGS	P*RBGS
q	KW*	KW*BGZ	Q	KW-RBGS	KW*RBGS
r	R*	R*BGZ	R	R-RBGS	R*RBGS
s	S*	S*BGZ	S	S-RBGS	S*RBGS
t	T*	T*BGZ	T	T-RBGS	T*RBGS
u	*U	*UBGZ	U	U-RBGS	*URBGS
v	SR*	SR*BGZ	V	SR-RBGS	SR*RBGS
w	W*	W*BGZ	W	W-RBGS	W*RBGS
x	KP*	KP*BGZ	X	KP-RBGS	KP*RBGS
y	KWR*	KWR*BGZ	Y	KWR-RBGS	KWR*RBGS
z	STK*	STK*BGZ	Z	STK-RBGS	STK*RBGS

Note: In some text entry systems, you may need to press the space command (SP-S) before spelling out using lower case letters. With these systems, letters with an asterisk (A*, PW*, KR*, etc.) automatically stick together.

TO APPEAR WITH A PERIOD

Lower Case	Standing Alone	Attached to Left	Upper Case	Standing Alone	Attached to Left
a.	A*PD	A*PLD	A.	AFPLT	A*FPLT
b.	PW*PD	PW*PLD	B.	PW-FPLT	PW*FPLT
c.	KR*PD	KR*PLD	C.	KR-FPLT	KR*FPLT
d.	TK*PD	TK*PLD	D.	TK-FPLT	TK*FPLT
e.	*EPD	*EPLD	E.	EFPLT	*EFPLT
f.	TP*PD	TP*PLD	F.	TP-FPLT	TP*FPLT
g.	TKPW*PD	TKPW*PLD	G.	TKPW-FPLT	TKPW*FPLT
h.	H*PD	H*PLD	H.	H-FPLT	H*FPLT
i.	*EUPD	*EUPLD	I.	EUFPLT	*EUFPLT
j.	SKWR*PD	SKWR*PLD	J.	SKWR-FPLT	SKWR*FPLT
k.	K*PD	K*PLD	K.	K-FPLT	K*FPLT
l.	HR*PD	HR*PLD	L.	HR-FPLT	HR*FPLT
m.	PH*PD	PH*PLD	M.	PH-FPLT	PH*FPLT
n.	TPH*PD	TPH*PLD	N.	TPH-FPLT	TPH*FPLT
o.	O*PD	O*PLD	O.	OFPLT	O*FPLT
p.	P*PD	P*PLD	P.	P-FPLT	P*FPLT
q.	KW*PD	KW*PLD	Q.	KW-FPLT	KW*FPLT
r.	R*PD	R*PLD	R.	R-FPLT	R*FPLT
s.	S*PD	S*PLD	S.	S-FPLT	S*FPLT
t.	T*PD	T*PLD	T.	T-FPLT	T*FPLT
u.	*UPD	*UPLD	U.	UFPLT	*UFPLT
v.	SR*PD	SR*PLD	V.	SR-FPLT	SR*FPLT
w.	W*PD	W*PLD	W.	W-FPLT	W*FPLT
x.	KP*PD	KP*PLD	X.	KP-FPLT	KP*FPLT
y.	KWR*PD	KWR*PLD	Y.	KWR-FPLT	KWR*FPLT
z.	STK*PD	STK*PLD	Z.	STK-FPLT	STK*FPLT

TEXT ENTRY COMMANDS

These commands were created for text entry applications (including medical transcription), but many are useful for court reporting as well.

PUNCTUATION AND SYMBOLS

Ampersand	&	M-ND
Apostrophe	'	AOE
Asterisk	*	STR-K
Asterisk, prefix/suffix, to mark WordPerfect files	*	M*RK
At symbol	@	T-T
Backslash	\	BL-RB
Bracket, opening	[	BR-K
Bracket, closing	]	BR-KS
Cent symbol	¢	S-TS
Colon (:), two spaces following and cap	: Cap	-FRPLT
Colon in time	1:11	KL*N
Colon, one space following, no cap	: lower	KL-N
Comma	,	-RBGS
Comma (prefix/suffix, number comma)	1,000	-RBGZ
Dash	—	D-RB
Decimal (period, prefix/suffix, i.e., 2.1)	1.1	P*NT
Decimal (period, prefix only, i.e., .01)	.1	P-NT
Degree symbol	°	D-RG
Division symbol	÷	DW-D
Dollar sign	$	DL-R
Ellipsis, close	...	L-PS
Ellipsis, open	. . .	L-PZ
Equal sign	=	KW-L
Exclamation point	!	STKPWHR-FPLT
Greater than	>	GR-N
Hyphen	-	H-F
Hyphen (space before and after)	-	H-FS
Less than	<	L*N
Minus sign (space before and after)	-	M-NS
Minus sign, prefix	-	M*NS
Multiplication symbol (Times)	x	T-MZ
Number symbol (prefix)	#	N-B
Parenthesis, opening	(	STPH-FPLT
Parenthesis, closing	)	STPH-FPLD
Percent	%	P-KT
Period	.	-FPLT
Plus sign (space before and after)	+	P-LS
Plus sign (suffix)	+	P*LS
Question mark	?	STPH-
Quotation mark, beginning	"	KW-T
Quotation mark, ending	"	KW-TS
Quotation mark, single, beginning	'	SKW-T
Quotation mark, single, ending	'	SKW-TS
Semicolon	;	-FRBGS
Slash	/	SL-RB
Tilde	~	T*LD
Times (Multiplication symbol)	x	T-MZ

MOVEMENT COMMANDS

Beginning of line of code .... STKPWHR-BL
Beginning of line of text .... STKPWHR-BLT
Beginning of text .... STKPWHR-BT
Down arrow (down by line) .... STKPWHR-D
Down by page (Page Down) .... STKPWHR-PD
Down screen .... STKPWHR-DZ
End .... N-ND
End of line .... STKPWHREL
End of text .... STKPWHRET
Go to .... G-T
Home .... H-M
Left arrow (left by character) .... STKPWHR-L
Left by word .... STKPWHR-LD
Left screen .... STKPWHR-LS
Right arrow (right by character) .... STKPWHR-R
Right by word .... STKPWHR-RD
Right screen .... STKPWHR-RS
Tab .... T-B
Up arrow (up by line) .... STKPWHRU
Up by page (Page Up) .... STKPWHRUP
Up screen .... STKPWHRUS

DELETE COMMANDS

Backspace (delete to left by character) .... B-S or DL-BS
Clear screen .... KL-R
Delete (character at cursor) .... DL-
Delete line .... DL-L
Delete previous word (word to left) .... * (asterisk key)
Delete remainder of line from cursor .... DL-RL
Delete remainder of page from cursor .... DL-RP
Delete word to right .... DL-RD

FUNCTION KEYS

	Alone	Shift SH-FT	Alt T-LT	Ctrl KR-RL	Steno Outline
F1	Cancel	Setup	Thesaurus	Shell	1*
F2	→Search	←Search	Replace	Spell	2*
F3	Help	Switch	Reveal Codes	Screen	3*
F4	→Indent	→Indent←	Block	Move	4*
F5	List Files	Date/Outline	Mark Text	Text In/Out	5*
F6	Bold	Center	Flush Right	Tab Align	*6
F7	Exit	Print	Math/Columns	Footnote	*7
F8	Underline	Format	Style	Font	*8
F9	Merge R	Merge Codes	Graphics	Merge/Sort	*9
F10	Save	Retrieve	Macro	Macro Define	10*

COMMANDS USED IN WordPerfect®

Alt	T-LT
Block	BL-K
Bold	B*LD
Cancel/Undelete	1*
Cap (capitalize first character only)	K-P
Cap Lock (capitalize all letters in word; repeat to cancel)	K-PS
Cap or Uncap existing word (toggle the case)	KR-P
Center	SN-R
Control	KR-RL
Enter	SPW-R
Escape	SK-P
Exit (WordPerfect command)	*7
Exit STE program	S-X
Flush Right	FL-RB
Font	F-NT
Format	F-MT
Help Menu (WordPerfect)	3*
Insert/Typeover	N-Z
Join (join two words together; press after first word)	J-N
List Files	L-FLS
Move	M-V
New Page (hard page)	N-P
Print current document	PR-NT
Print Menu (all other print functions)	PR-M
Print Screen	P*Z
Replace	R-PLS
Retrieve	TR-V
Reveal Codes (repeat to cancel)	R-VL
Save	S-V
Screen	SKR-N
Search forward (down to end of document)	SKH-D
Search backward (up to beginning of document)	SKH-U
Shell	SH-L
Shift	SH-FT
Spacebar	SP-S
Spacebar to use with numbers and individual letters	SP-Z
Spell Check	SP-L
Switch	SW-FP
Text In/Out	TO*IX
Thesaurus	TH-RS
Typeover/Insert	N-Z
Undelete/Cancel	1*
Underline	N-RL
Underline cancel	N-RLS